LAROUSSE'S FRENCH-ENGLISH
ENGLISH-FRENCH DICTIONARY
Completely Revised and Updated

Besides offering more entries than ever before, this brand-new edition is edited by the foremost authorities in the field of French-language reference books. Incredibly easy to use, concise and straightforward, with more than 50,000 entries in both languages, it is an indispensable guide if you want the best, most reliable and authentic French-English English-French dictionary at your fingertips.

DICTIONNAIRE LAROUSSE
FRANÇAIS-ANGLAIS ANGLAIS-FRANÇAIS
Entièrement Refondu et Actualisé

Cette toute nouvelle édition, conçue par les meilleurs spécialistes d'ouvrages de référence en langue française, est aussi plus complète que jamais, avec plus de 50000 mots et expressions. Voici, mis à la portée de tous par sa facilité de consultation, sa concision et sa clarté, le dictionnaire français-anglais anglais-français au format poche le plus fiable et le plus authentique à l'heure actuelle.

ALL-NEW EDITION
LAROUSSE'S FRENCH-ENGLISH ENGLISH-FRENCH DICTIONARY

DICTIONNAIRE LAROUSSE FRANÇAIS-ANGLAIS ANGLAIS-FRANÇAIS

POCKET BOOKS

New York   London   Toronto   Sydney

POCKET BOOKS, a division of Simon & Schuster, Inc.
1230 Avenue of the Americas, New York, NY 10020

Copyright © 1996 by Larousse

ISBN -13: 978-1-4391-0103-2
ISBN -10:   1-4391-0103-5

First Pocket Books printing of this revised edition June 1996

10 9 8 7 6 5 4 3

POCKET and colophon are registered trademarks of Simon & Schuster, Inc.

Manufactured in the United States of America

For information regarding special discounts for bulk purchases, please contact Simon & Schuster Special Sales at 1-800-456-6798 or business@simonandschuster.com

PREFACE

Larousse's French-English English-French Dictionary is the natural choice for tourists, students, teachers, business people and all those interested in modern languages.

Over 50,000 vocabulary entries provide a rich source of translations, and a wealth of illustrative examples and idiomatic expressions explain and contextualize difficult phrases. Americanisms and Anglicisms are clearly distinguished. A strong selection of neologisms and colloquialisms enrich the standard vocabulary, and the text features a large number of important and useful abbreviations. Clear typography allows the reader to distinguish headwords, compounds and other derivatives quickly and easily, and the careful use of indicators in square brackets helps to pinpoint exact meanings and contexts, steering the user clear of many of the common pitfalls in translation. Accurate pronunciation is assured through use of the International Phonetic Alphabet throughout.

Supplementary to the main text are verb tables and practical guides to expressing numbers and dates and telling the time. Combined with the above features, they make this dictionary an essential reference work at home or in the office, in schools and colleges, and while traveling abroad on holiday or on business.

PRÉFACE

Le Dictionnaire Larousse Français-Anglais Anglais-Français s'impose tout naturellement comme le compagnon idéal du touriste aussi bien que de l'enseignant, de l'homme d'affaires comme de l'élève ou de l'étudiant.

Tous ceux qui s'intéressent aux langues vivantes y trouveront en effet plus de 50 000 mots et expressions, assortis d'une foule d'exemples et de tournures idiomatiques, qui les guideront vers la traduction appropriée tout en illustrant et éclairant les points les plus délicats. Les variantes américaine et britannique de l'anglais sont signalées sans risque de confusion, et le vocabulaire de base s'enrichit de nombreux néologismes, exemples de langue parlée et abréviations. Grâce à une typographie claire, l'utilisateur distinguera rapidement et aisément les libellés de leurs dérivés - mots composés notamment. Le choix minutieux des indicateurs entre crochets répond au même souci d'efficacité : en délimitant aussi précisément que possible le sens ou contexte désiré, ils permettront d'éviter les pièges classiques de la traduction. La prononciation pouvant elle aussi se révéler problématique, nous avons eu recours tout au long de cet ouvrage à la transcription en alphabet phonétique international. Et, pour être tout à fait complets, nous avons ajouté au corps du texte des tableaux de conjugaison ainsi qu'un guide d'usage portant sur les chiffres, les dates et l'heure.

Au bureau ou chez soi, en contexte scolaire, en vacances ou en voyage d'affaires, toutes ces particularités font de cet ouvrage un outil linguistique indispensable.

abbreviation	*abbr/abr*	abréviation
adjective	*adj*	adjectif
administration, administrative	ADMIN	administration
adverb	*adv*	adverbe
aeronautics, aviation	AERON/AÉRON	aéronautique
agriculture, farming	AGR(IC)	agriculture
American English	*Am*	anglais américain
anatomy	ANAT	anatomie
archaeology	ARCHAEOL/ ARCHÉOL	archéologie
architecture	ARCHIT	architecture
slang	*arg*	argot
article	*art*	article
astrology	ASTROL	astrologie
astronomy	ASTRON	astronomie
automobile, cars	AUT(OM)	automobile
auxiliary	*aux*	auxiliaire
before noun	*avant n*	avant le nom
Belgian French	*Belg*	belgicisme
biology	BIOL	biologie
botany	BOT	botanique
British English	*Br*	anglais britannique
Canadian English/French	*Can*	canadianisme
chemistry	CHEM/CHIM	chimie
cinema, film-making	CIN(EMA)	cinéma
commerce, business	COMM	commerce
compound	*comp*	nom anglais utilisé en apposition
comparative	*compar*	comparatif
computers, computer science	COMPUT	informatique
conjunction	*conj*	conjonction
construction, building trade	CONSTR	construction, bâtiment
continuous	*cont*	progressif
sewing	COUT	couture
culinary, cooking	CULIN	cuisine, art culinaire
definite	*def/déf*	défini
demonstrative	*dem/dém*	démonstratif
ecology	ÉCOL	écologie
economics	ECON/ÉCON	économie
electricity	ELEC/ÉLECTR	électricité
electronics	ELECTRON/ ÉLECTRON	électronique
especially	*esp*	particulièrement
exclamation	*excl*	interjection
feminine	*f*	féminin
informal	*fam*	familier
figurative	*fig*	figuré
finance, financial	FIN	finances
formal	*fml*	soutenu
soccer	FTBL	football

inseparable	*fus*	non séparable
generally, in most cases	*gen/gén*	généralement
geography, geographical	GEOGR/GÉOGR	géographie
geology, geological	GEOL/GÉOL	géologie
geometry	GEOM/GÉOM	géométrie
grammar	GRAM(M)	grammaire
Swiss French	*Helv*	helvétisme
history	HIST	histoire
humorous	*hum*	humoristique
industry	IND	industrie
indefinite	*indef/indéf*	indéfini
informal	*inf*	familier
infinitive	*infin*	infinitif
computers, computer science	INFORM	informatique
exclamation	*interj*	interjection
interrogative	*interr*	interrogatif
invariable	*inv*	invariable
ironic	*iro/iron*	ironique
juridical, legal	JUR	juridique
linguistics	LING	linguistique
literal	*lit/litt*	littéral
phrase(s)	*loc*	locution(s)
adjectival phrase	*loc adj*	locution adjectivale
adverbial phrase	*loc adv*	locution adverbiale
conjunctival phrase	*loc conj*	locution conjonctive
prepositional phrase	*loc prép*	locution prépositionnelle
masculine	*m*	masculin
mathematics	MATH(S)	mathématiques
medicine	MED/MÉD	médecine
weather, meteorology	METEOR/MÉTÉOR	météorologie
military	MIL	domaine militaire
music	MUS	musique
mythology	MYTH	mythologie
noun	*n*	nom
nautical, maritime	NAUT/NAVIG	navigation
numeral	*num*	numéral
oneself	*o.s.*	
pejorative	*pej/péj*	péjoratif
personal	*pers*	personnel
pharmacology, pharmaceutics	PHARM	pharmacologie, pharmacie
philosophy	PHILO	philosophie
photography	PHOT	photographie
phrase(s)	*phr*	locution(s)
physics	PHYS	physique
plural	*pl*	pluriel
politics	POL(IT)	politique
possessive	*poss*	possessif
past participle	*pp*	participe passé
present participle	*ppr*	participe présent

preposition	*prep/prép*	préposition
pronoun	*pron*	pronom
psychology, psychiatry	PSYCH(OL)	psychologie, psychiatrie
past tense	*pt*	passé
	qqch	quelque chose
	qqn	quelqu'un
registered trademark	®	nom déposé
railways	RAIL	rail
relative	*rel*	relatif
religion	RELIG	religion
someone, somebody	*sb*	
school	SCH/SCOL	scolarité
Scottish English	*Scot*	anglais écossais
separable	*sep*	séparable
singular	*sg*	singulier
slang	*sl*	argot
sociology	SOCIOL	sociologie
formal	*sout*	soutenu
stock exchange	ST EX	Bourse
something	*sthg*	
subject	*subj/suj*	sujet
superlative	*superl*	superlatif
technology, technical	TECH(NOL)	domaine technique et technologique
telecommunications	TELEC/ TÉLÉCOM	télécommunications
very informal	*tfam*	très familier
television	TV/TÉLÉ	télévision
printing, typography	TYPO	typographie
uncountable noun	*U*	substantif non comptable
university	UNIV	université
usually	*usu*	habituellement
link verb followed by a predicative adjective or noun	*v attr*	verbe suivi d'un attribut
verb	*vb/v*	verbe
veterinary science	VETER	médecine vétérinaire
intransitive verb	*vi*	verbe intransitif
impersonal verb	*v impers*	verbe impersonnel
very informal	*v inf*	très familier
pronominal verb	*vp*	verbe pronominal
transitive verb	*vt*	verbe transitif
vulgar	*vulg*	vulgaire
zoology	ZOOL	zoologie
cultural equivalent	≃	équivalence culturelle
indicates a new sense division	‖	indique une nouvelle catégorie sémantique
introduces a sub-entry, such as a plural form with its own specific meaning or a set phrase containing the headword (e.g. a phrasal or adverbial phrase)	○	introduit une sous-entrée, par exemple une forme plurielle ayant un sens propre, ou une locution (locution adverbiale, verb verbe pronominal, etc.)

PHONETIC TRANSCRIPTION _____ TRANSCRIPTION PHONÉTIQUE

English Vowels

[ɪ] pit, big, rid
[e] pet, tend
[æ] pat, bag, mad
[ʌ] putt, cut
[ɒ] pot, log
[ʊ] put, full
[ə] mother, suppose
[i:] bean, weed
[ɑ:] barn, car, laugh
[ɔ:] born, lawn
[u:] loop, loose
[ɜ:] burn, learn, bird

English Diphthongs

[eɪ] bay, late, great
[aɪ] buy, light, aisle
[ɔɪ] boy , foil
[əʊ] no, road, blow
[aʊ] now, shout, town
[ɪə] peer, fierce, idea
[eə] pair, bear, share
[ʊə] poor, sure, tour

Semi-vowels

you, spaniel   [j]
wet, why, twin   [w]
                      [ɥ]

Consonants

pop, people   [p]
bottle, bib   [b]
train, tip   [t]
dog, did   [d]
come, kitchen   [k]
gag, great   [g]
chain, wretched   [tʃ]
jig, fridge   [dʒ]
fib, physical   [f]
vine, livid   [v]
think, fifth   [θ]
this, with   [ð]
seal, peace   [s]
zip, his   [z]
sheep, machine   [ʃ]
usual, measure   [ʒ]
how, perhaps   [h]
metal, comb   [m]
night, dinner   [n]
sung, parking   [ŋ]

Voyelles françaises

[i] fille, île
[e] pays, année
[ɛ] bec, aime
[a] lac, papillon
[ɑ] tas, âme
[o] drôle, aube
[ɔ] hotte
[u] outil, goût
[y] usage, lune
[ø] aveu, jeu
[œ] peuple, bœuf
[ə] le, je

Nasales françaises

[ɛ̃] limbe, main
[ɑ̃] champ, ennui
[ɔ̃] ongle, mon
[œ̃] parfum, brun

Semi-voyelles

yeux, lieu
ouest, oui
lui, nuit

Consonnes

prendre, grippe
bateau, rosbif
théâtre, temps
dalle, ronde
coq, quatre
garder, épilogue

physique, fort
voir, rive

cela, savant
fraise, zéro
charrue, schéma
rouge, jabot

mât, drame
nager, trône

	[ɲ]	agneau, peigner
little, help	[l]	halle, lit
right, carry	[r]	arracher, sabre
loch	[x]	

Represents French "h aspiré", e.g. **hachis** [ˈaʃi].	[']	Représente le "h aspiré" français, p. ex. **hachis** [ˈaʃi]
Indicates that the following syllable carries primary stress.	[ˈ]	Indique un accent primaire sur la syllabe suivante.
Indicates that the following syllable carries secondary stress.	[ˌ]	Indique un accent secondaire sur la syllabe suivante.
Indicates that the final "r" is pronounced only when followed by a word beginning with a vowel; nearly always pronounced in American English.	[ʳ]	Indique que le "r" final d'un mot anglais ne se prononce que lorsqu'il forme une liaison avec la voyelle du mot suivant; presque toujours prononcé en anglais américain.

TRADEMARKS

Words considered to be trademarks have been designated in this dictionary by the symbol ®. However, neither the presence nor the absence of such designation should be regarded as affecting the legal status of any trademark.

NOMS DE MARQUE

Les noms de marque sont désignés dans ce dictionnaire par le symbole ®. Néanmoins, ni ce symbole ni son absence éventuelle ne peuvent être considérés comme susceptibles d'avoir une incidence quelconque sur le statut légal d'une marque.

CONJUGAISONS

LÉGENDE: *ppr* = participe présent, *pp* = participe passé, *pr ind* = présent de l'indicatif, *imp* = imparfait, *fut* = futur, *cond* = conditionnel, *pr subj* = présent du subjonctif

acquérir: *pp* acquis, *pr ind* acquiers, acquérons, acquièrent, *imp* acquérais, *fut* acquerrai, *pr subj* acquière

aller: *pp* allé, *pr ind* vais, vas, va, allons, allez, vont, *imp* allais, *fut* irai, *cond* irais, *pr subj* aille

asseoir: *ppr* asseyant, *pp* assis, *pr ind* assieds, asseyons, *imp* asseyais, *fut* assiérai, *pr subj* asseye

atteindre: *ppr* atteignant, *pp* atteint, *pr ind* atteins, atteignons, *imp* atteignais, *pr subj* atteigne

avoir: *ppr* ayant, *pp* eu, *pr ind* ai, as, a, avons, avez, ont, *imp* avais, *fut* aurai, *cond* aurais, *pr subj* aie, aies, ait, ayons, ayez, aient

boire: *ppr* buvant, *pp* bu, *pr ind* bois, buvons, boivent, *imp* buvais, *pr subj* boive

conduire: *ppr* conduisant, *pp* conduit, *pr ind* conduis, conduisons, *imp* conduisais, *pr subj* conduise

connaître: *ppr* connaissant, *pp* connu, *pr ind* connais, connaît, connaissons, *imp* connaissais, *pr subj* connaisse

coudre: *ppr* cousant, *pp* cousu, *pr ind* couds, cousons, *imp* cousais, *pr subj* couse

courir: *pp* couru, *pr ind* cours, courons, *imp* courais, *fut* courrai, *pr subj* coure

couvrir: *pp* couvert, *pr ind* couvre, couvrons, *imp* couvrais, *pr subj* couvre

craindre: *ppr* craignant, *pp* craint, *pr ind* crains, craignons, *imp* craignais, *pr subj* craigne

croire: *ppr* croyant, *pp* cru, *pr ind* crois, croyons, croient, *imp* croyais, *pr subj* croie

cueillir: *pp* cueilli, *pr ind* cueille, cueillons, *imp* cueillais, *fut* cueillerai, *pr subj* cueille

devoir: *pp* dû, due, *pr ind* dois, devons, doivent, *imp* devais, *fut* devrai, *pr subj* doive

dire: *ppr* disant, *pp* dit, *pr ind* dis, disons, dites, disent, *imp* disais, *pr subj* dise

dormir: *pp* dormi, *pr ind* dors, dormons, *imp* dormais, *pr subj* dorme

écrire: *ppr* écrivant, *pp* écrit, *pr ind* écris, écrivons, *imp* écrivais, *pr subj* écrive

essuyer: *pp* essuyé, *pr ind* essuie, essuyons, essuient, *imp* essuyais, *fut* essuierai, *pr subj* essuie

être: *ppr* étant, *pp* été, *pr ind* suis, es, est, sommes, êtes, sont, *imp* étais, *fut* serai, *cond* serais, *pr subj* sois, sois, soit, soyons, soyez, soient

faire: *ppr* faisant, *pp* fait, *pr ind* fais, fais, fait, faisons, faites, font, *imp* faisais, *fut* ferai, *cond* ferais, *pr subj* fasse

falloir: *pp* fallu, *pr ind* faut, *imp* fallait, *fut* faudra, *pr subj* faille

FINIR: *ppr* finissant, *pp* fini, *pr ind* finis, finis, finit, finissons, finissez, finissent, *imp* finissais, finissais, finissait, finissions, finissiez, finissaient, *fut* finirai, finiras, finira, finirons, finirez, finiront, *cond* finirais, finirais, finirait, finirions, finiriez, finiraient, *pr subj* finisse, finisses, finisse, finissions, finissiez, finissent

fuir: *ppr* fuyant, *pp* fui, *pr ind* fuis, fuyons, fuient, *imp* fuyais, *pr subj* fuie

haïr: *ppr* haïssant, *pp* haï, *pr ind* hais, haïssons, *imp* haïssais, *pr subj* haïsse

joindre: *comme* **atteindre**

lire: *ppr* lisant, *pp* lu, *pr ind* lis, lisons, *imp* lisais, *pr subj* lise

mentir: *pp* menti, *pr ind* mens, mentons, *imp* mentais, *pr subj* mente

mettre: *ppr* mettant, *pp* mis, *pr ind* mets, mettons, *imp* mettais, *pr subj* mette

mourir: *pp* mort, *pr ind* meurs, mourons, meurent, *imp* mourais, *fut* mourrai, *pr subj* meure

naître: *ppr* naissant, *pp* né, *pr ind* nais, naît, naissons, *imp* naissais, *pr subj* naisse

offrir: *pp* offert, *pr ind* offre, offrons, *imp* offrais, *pr subj* offre

paraître: *comme* **connaître**

PARLER: *ppr* parlant, *pp* parlé, *pr ind* parle, parles, parle, parlons, parlez, parlent, *imp* parlais, parlais, parlait, parlions, parliez, parlaient, *fut* parlerai, parleras, parlera, parlerons, parlerez, parleront, *cond* parlerais, parlerais, parlerait, parlerions, parleriez, parleraient, *pr subj* parle, parles, parle, parlions, parliez, parlent

partir: *pp* parti, *pr ind* pars, partons, *imp* partais, *pr subj* parte

plaire: *ppr* plaisant, *pp* plu, *pr ind* plais, plaît, plaisons, *imp* plaisais, *pr subj* plaise

pleuvoir: *pp* plu, *pr ind* pleut, *imp* pleuvait, *fut* pleuvra, *pr subj* pleuve

pouvoir: *pp* pu, *pr ind* peux, peux, peut, pouvons, pouvez, peuvent, *imp* pouvais, *fut* pourrai, *pr subj* puisse

prendre: *ppr* prenant, *pp* pris, *pr ind* prends, prenons, prennent, *imp* prenais, *pr subj* prenne

prévoir: *ppr* prévoyant, *pp* prévu, *pr ind* prévois, prévoyons, prévoient, *imp* prévoyais, *fut* prévoirai, *pr subj* prévoie

recevoir: *pp* reçu, *pr ind* reçois, recevons, reçoivent, *imp* recevais, *fut* recevrai, *pr subj* reçoive

RENDRE: *ppr* rendant, *pp* rendu, *pr ind* rends, rends, rend, rendons, rendez, rendent, *imp* rendais, rendais, rendait, rendions, rendiez, rendaient, *fut* rendrai, rendras, rendra, rendrons, rendrez, rendront, *cond* rendrais, rendrais, rendrait, rendrions, rendriez, rendraient, *pr subj* rende, rendes, rende, rendions, rendiez, rendent

résoudre: *ppr* résolvant, *pp* résolu, *pr ind* résous, résolvons, *imp* résolvais, *pr subj* résolve

rire: *ppr* riant, *pp* ri, *pr ind* ris, rions, *imp* riais, *pr subj* rie

savoir: *ppr* sachant, *pp* su, *pr ind* sais, savons, *imp* savais, *fut* saurai, *pr subj* sache

servir: *pp* servi, *pr ind* sers, servons, *imp* servais, *pr subj* serve

sortir: *comme* **partir**

suffire: *ppr* suffisant, *pp* suffi, *pr ind* suffis, suffisons, *imp* suffisais, *pr subj* suffise

suivre: *ppr* suivant, *pp* suivi, *pr ind* suis, suivons, *imp* suivais, *pr subj* suive

taire: *ppr* taisant, *pp* tu, *pr ind* tais, taisons, *imp* taisais, *pr subj* taise

tenir: *pp* tenu, *pr ind* tiens, tenons, tiennent, *imp* tenais, *fut* tiendrai, *pr subj* tienne

vaincre: *ppr* vainquant, *pp* vaincu, *pr ind* vaincs, vainc, vainquons, *imp* vainquais, *pr subj* vainque

valoir: *pp* valu, *pr ind* vaux, valons, *imp* valais, *fut* vaudrai, *pr subj* vaille

venir: *comme* **tenir**

vivre: *ppr* vivant, *pp* vécu, *pr ind* vis, vivons, *imp* vivais, *pr subj* vive

voir: *ppr* voyant, *pp* vu, *pr ind* vois, voyons, voient, *imp* voyais, *fut* verrai, *pr subj* voie

vouloir: *pp* voulu, *pr ind* veux, veux, veut, voulons, voulez, veulent, *imp* voulais, *fut* voudrai, *pr subj* veuille

NUMBERS

Cardinal numbers are used for counting. The most important ones are:

0 zéro	16 seize	80 quatre-vingts
1 un (*f* une)	17 dix-sept	81 quatre-vingt-un (*f* une)
2 deux	18 dix-huit	82 quatre-vingt-deux
3 trois	19 dix-neuf	90 quatre-vingt-dix
4 quatre	20 vingt	91 quatre-vingt-onze
5 cinq	21 vingt et un (*f* une)	92 quatre-vingt-douze
6 six	22 vingt-deux	93 quatre-vingt-treize
7 sept	23 vingt-trois	100 cent
8 huit	30 trente	101 cent un (*f* une)
9 neuf	40 quarante	102 cent deux
10 dix	50 cinquante	110 cent dix
11 onze	60 soixante	120 cent vingt
12 douze	70 soixante-dix	121 cent vingt et un (*f* une)
13 treize	71 soixante et onze	200 deux cents
14 quatorze	72 soixante-douze	300 trois cents
15 quinze	73 soixante-treize	900 neuf cents

1 000 mille	2 000 deux mille
1 001 mille un (*f* une)	3 000 trois mille
1 002 mille deux	1 000 000 un million
1 100 mille cent, onze cents	2 000 000 deux millions
1 200 mille deux cents, douze cents	1 000 000 000 un milliard
1 900 mille neuf cents, dix-neuf cents	

NOTES:

– **mille** never adds an -s in the plural.

– **quatre-vingt** takes an -s when it comes at the end of a number: **quatre-vingts**, **deux cent quatre-vingts**. **Cent** also adds an -s if it refers to two hundred or more and comes at the end of a number: **cinq cents**, **trois mille sept cents**. However, when **cent** and **vingt** do not come at the end of the number, they do not take -s in the plural: **trois cent vingt-cinq**, **quatre-vingt-huit**.

– both **million** and **milliard** are always followed by **de** if they are used with another noun. Unlike their English equivalents, they also add an -s when they are preceded by a plural number: **deux millions de chômeurs**, **trois milliards de francs**.

Ordinal numbers (first, second, third etc.) are used for putting things in order. They are formed by adding -ième to the end of the cardinal number, e.g. **deuxième**, **dixième**. If the cardinal number ends in -e, this is dropped, e.g. **onzième**, **seizième**. There are minor spelling changes with **cinq** and **neuf**: **cinquième**, **neuvième**. The French for first is **premier** (*f* **première**). Twenty-first, thirty-first etc. are translated as **vingt et unième**, **trente et unième** etc.

Contrary to English, French uses a comma to mark the decimal part of a number: **6,5** (**six virgule cinq** = six point five); **8,34** (**huit virgule trente-quatre** = eight point three four). Numbers of four digits and above (**2 000, 10 321**) are normally written with a space before the last three digits.

For more information on numbers, look at the entries for **six** and **sixième** on the French-English side of your dictionary, and at **six** and **sixth** on the English-French side.

DATES

The most usual ways of asking the date are: **quelle date sommes nous?** or **quelle est la date aujourd'hui?** The reply will normally start with **c'est** ... or **nous sommes** ...

Remember that the cardinal numbers are used in dates in French: **le dix janvier, le vingt-cinq février, le premier septembre**.

To say the year in French: 1995 can be pronounced as either mille neuf cent quatre-vingt-cinq or dix-neuf cent quatre-vingt-cinq.

The days of the week are:

Monday	**lundi**
Tuesday	**mardi**
Wednesday	**mercredi**
Thursday	**jeudi**
Friday	**vendredi**
Saturday	**samedi**
Sunday	**dimanche**

The months of the year are:

January	**janvier**
February	**février**
March	**mars**
April	**avril**
May	**mai**
June	**juin**
July	**juillet**
August	**août**
September	**septembre**
October	**octobre**
November	**novembre**
December	**décembre**

Note that the days of the week and the months of the year start with a small letter in French.

For more information on days and months, look at the entries for **samedi** and **septembre** on the French-English side of your dictionary, and at **Saturday** and **September** on the English-French side.

ENGLISH IRREGULAR VERBS

Infinitive	Past Tense	Past Participle	Infinitive	Past Tense	Past Participle
arise	arose	arisen	fly	flew	flown
awake	awoke	awoken	forget	forgot	forgotten
be	was, were	been	forsake	forsook	forsaken
bear	bore	born(e)	freeze	froze	frozen
beat	beat	beaten	get	got	got (*Am* gotten)
befall	befell	befallen	give	gave	given
begin	began	begun	go	went	gone
behold	beheld	beheld	grind	ground	ground
bend	bent	bent	grow	grew	grown
beseech	besought	besought	hang	hung	hung
beset	beset	beset		(hanged)	(hanged)
bet	bet (betted)	bet (betted)	have	had	had
bid	bid (bade)	bid (bidden)	hear	heard	heard
bind	bound	bound	hide	hid	hidden
bite	bit	bitten	hit	hit	hit
bleed	bled	bled	hold	held	held
blow	blew	blown	hurt	hurt	hurt
break	broke	broken	keep	kept	kept
breed	bred	bred	kneel	knelt	knelt
bring	brought	brought		(kneeled)	(kneeled)
build	built	built	know	knew	known
burn	burnt	burnt	lay	laid	laid
	(burned)	(burned)	lead	led	led
burst	burst	burst	lean	leant	leant
buy	bought	bought		(leaned)	(leaned)
can	could	–	leap	leapt	leapt
cast	cast	cast		(leaped)	(leaped)
catch	caught	caught	learn	learnt	learnt
choose	chose	chosen		(learned)	(learned)
cling	clung	clung	leave	left	left
come	came	come	lend	lent	lent
cost	cost	cost	let	let	let
creep	crept	crept	lie	lay	lain
cut	cut	cut	light	lit	lit
deal	dealt	dealt		(lighted)	(lighted)
dig	dug	dug	lose	lost	lost
do	did	done	make	made	made
draw	drew	drawn	may	might	–
dream	dreamed	dreamed	mean	meant	meant
	(dreamt)	(dreamt)	meet	met	met
drink	drank	drunk	mow	mowed	mown
drive	drove	driven			(mowed)
dwell	dwelt	dwelt	pay	paid	paid
eat	ate	eaten	put	put	put
fall	fell	fallen	quit	quit	quit
feed	fed	fed		(quitted)	(quitted)
feel	felt	felt	read	read	read
fight	fought	fought	rend	rent	rent
find	found	found	rid	rid	rid
flee	fled	fled	ride	rode	ridden
fling	flung	flung	ring	rang	rung

Infinitive	Past Tense	Past Participle	Infinitive	Past Tense	Past Participle
rise	rose	risen	spit	spat	spat
run	ran	run	split	split	split
saw	sawed	sawn	spoil	spoiled	spoiled
say	said	said		(spoilt)	(spoilt)
see	saw	seen	spread	spread	spread
seek	sought	sought	spring	sprang	sprung
sell	sold	sold	stand	stood	stood
send	sent	sent	steal	stole	stolen
set	set	set	stick	stuck	stuck
shake	shook	shaken	sting	stung	stung
shall	should	–	stink	stank	stunk
shear	sheared	shorn	stride	strode	stridden
		(sheared)	strike	struck	struck
shed	shed	shed			(stricken)
shine	shone	shone	strive	strove	striven
shoot	shot	shot	swear	swore	sworn
show	showed	shown	sweep	swept	swept
shrink	shrank	shrunk	swell	swelled	swollen
shut	shut	shut			(swelled)
sing	sang	sung	swim	swam	swum
sink	sank	sunk	swing	swung	swung
sit	sat	sat	take	took	taken
slay	slew	slain	teach	taught	taught
sleep	slept	slept	tear	tore	torn
slide	slid	slid	tell	told	told
sling	slung	slung	think	thought	thought
slit	slit	slit	throw	threw	thrown
smell	smelt	smelt	thrust	thrust	thrust
	(smelled)	(smelled)	tread	trod	trodden
sow	sowed	sown	wake	woke	woken
		(sowed)		(waked)	(waked)
speak	spoke	spoken	wear	wore	worn
speed	sped	sped	weave	wove	woven
	(speeded)	(speeded)		(weaved)	(weaved)
spell	spelt	spelt	wed	wedded	wedded
	(spelled)	(spelled)	weep	wept	wept
spend	spent	spent	win	won	won
spill	spilt	spilt	wind	wound	wound
	(spilled)	(spilled)	wring	wrung	wrung
spin	spun	spun	write	wrote	written

THE TIME

The most usual way of asking the time is: **quelle heure est-il?** Here are some possible answers:

il est cinq heures (du matin/du soir)

il est cinq heures cinq

il est cinq heures et quart

il est cinq heures et demie

il est six heures moins vingt-cinq

il est six heures moins le quart

il est midi (= midday)/**il est minuit** (= midnight)

In French you may find times expressed using the twenty-four hour clock: a train departing at **dix-huit heures**, for example, would leave at six o'clock in the evening.

FRANÇAIS–ANGLAIS
FRENCH–ENGLISH

a¹, A [a] *nm inv* a, A; **de A à Z** from beginning to end. ○ **A** (*abr de* **ampère**) A, amp. ‖ (*abr de* **autoroute**) M.

a² → **avoir**.

à [a] *prép (contraction de à + le = au, contraction de à + les = aux)* [introduisant un complément d'objet indirect] to; **donner qqch à qqn** to give sthg to sb, to give sb sthg. ‖ [introduisant un complément de lieu - situation] at, in; [- direction] to; **être à la maison/au bureau** to be at home/at the office; **il habite à Paris/à la campagne** he lives in Paris/in the country; **aller à Paris/à la campagne/au Pérou** to go to Paris/to the country/to Peru. ‖ [introduisant un complément de temps]: **à onze heures** at eleven o'clock; **au mois de février** in the month of February. ‖ [introduisant un complément de manière, de moyen]: **à haute voix** out loud, aloud; **rire aux éclats** to roar with laughter; **à pied/cheval** on foot/horseback. ‖ [indiquant une caractéristique] with; **une fille aux cheveux longs** a girl with long hair. ‖ [introduisant un chiffre]: **ils sont venus à dix** ten of them came; **un livre à 30 francs** a 30-franc book, a book costing 30 francs; **deux à deux** two by two. ‖ [marque l'appartenance]: **c'est à moi/toi/lui/elle** it's mine/yours/his/hers; **ce vélo est à ma sœur** this bike is my sister's *ou* belongs to my sister; **une amie à moi** a friend of mine. ‖ [introduit le but]: **coupe à champagne** champagne goblet; **appartement à vendre/louer** flat for sale/to let.

AB (*abr de* **assez bien**) *fair grade (as assessment of schoolwork).*

abaisser [abese] *vt* [rideau, voile] to lower; [levier, manette] to push *ou* pull down. ‖ [diminuer] to reduce, to lower. ○ **s'abaisser** *vp* [descendre - rideau] to fall, to come down; [- terrain] to fall away. ‖ [s'humilier] to demean o.s.; **s'~ à faire qqch** to lower o.s. to do sthg.

abandon [abɑ̃dɔ̃] *nm* [désertion, délaissement] desertion; **à l'~** [jardin, maison] neglected, in a state of neglect. ‖ [renonciation] abandoning, giving up. ‖ [nonchalance, confiance] abandon.

abandonner [abɑ̃dɔne] *vt* [quitter - femme, enfants] to abandon, to desert; [- voiture, propriété] to abandon. ‖ [renoncer à] to give up, to abandon. ‖ [se retirer de - course, concours] to withdraw from. ‖ [céder]: **~ qqch à qqn** to leave sthg to sb, to leave sb sthg.

abasourdi, -e [abazurdi] *adj* stunned.

abat-jour [abaʒur] *nm inv* lampshade.

abats [aba] *nmpl* [d'animal] offal (*U*); [de volaille] giblets.

abattement [abatmɑ̃] *nm* [faiblesse physique] weakness. ‖ [désespoir] dejection. ‖ [déduction] reduction; **~ fiscal** tax allowance.

abattis [abati] *nmpl* giblets.

abattoir [abatwar] *nm* abattoir, slaughterhouse.

abattre [abatr] *vt* [faire tomber - mur] to knock down; [- arbre] to cut down, to fell; [- avion] to bring down. ‖ [tuer - gén] to kill; [- dans un abattoir] to slaughter. ‖ [épuiser] to wear out; [démoraliser] to demoralize.

abbaye [abei] *nf* abbey.

abbé [abe] *nm* [prêtre] priest.

abc *nm* basics (*pl*).

abcès [apsɛ] *nm* abscess.

abdiquer [abdike] *vi* [roi] to abdicate.

abdomen [abdɔmɛn] *nm* abdomen.

abdominaux [abdɔmino] *nmpl* [muscles] abdominal ou stomach muscles. || [exercices]: **faire des abdominaux** to do exercises for the stomach muscles.

abeille [abɛj] *nf* bee.

aberrant, -e [aberɑ̃, ɑ̃t] *adj* absurd.

abîme [abim] *nm* abyss, gulf.

abîmer [abime] *vt* [détériorer - objet] to damage; [- partie du corps, vue] to ruin. ○ **s'abîmer** *vp* [gén] to be damaged; [- fruits] to go bad.

abject, -e [abʒɛkt] *adj* despicable, contemptible.

aboiement [abwamɑ̃] *nm* bark, barking (*U*).

abolir [abɔlir] *vt* to abolish.

abominable [abɔminabl] *adj* appalling, awful.

abondance [abɔ̃dɑ̃s] *nf* [profusion] abundance. || [opulence] affluence.

abondant, -e [abɔ̃dɑ̃, ɑ̃t] *adj* [gén] plentiful; [végétation, chevelure] luxuriant; [pluie] heavy.

abonder [abɔ̃de] *vi* to abound, to be abundant; **~ en qqch** to be rich in sthg; **~ dans le sens de qqn** to be entirely of sb's opinion.

abonné, -e [abɔne] *nm, f* [à un journal, à une chaîne de télé] subscriber; [à un théâtre] season-ticket holder. || [à un service public] consumer.

abonnement [abɔnmɑ̃] *nm* [à un journal, à une chaîne de télé] subscription; [à un théâtre] season ticket. || [au téléphone] rental; [au gaz, à l'électricité] standing charge.

abonner [abɔne] ○ **s'abonner** *vp*: **s'~ à qqch** [journal, chaîne de télé] to take out a subscription to sthg; [service public] to get connected to sthg; [théâtre] to buy a season ticket for sthg.

abord [abɔr] *nm*: **être d'un ~ facile/difficile** to be very/not very approachable. ○ **abords** *nmpl* [gén] surrounding area (*sg*); [de ville] outskirts. ○ **d'abord** *loc adv* [en premier lieu] first. || [avant tout]: **(tout) d'~** first (of all), in the first place.

abordable [abɔrdabl] *adj* [lieu] accessible; [de prix modéré] affordable.

aborder [abɔrde] **1** *vi* to land. **2** *vt* [personne, lieu] to approach. || [question] to tackle.

aborigène [abɔriʒɛn] *adj* aboriginal. ○ **Aborigène** *nmf* (Australian) aborigine.

aboutir [abutir] *vi* [chemin]: **~ à/dans** to end at/in. || [négociation] to be successful; **~ à qqch** to result in sthg.

aboyer [abwaje] *vi* to bark.

abrasif, -ive [abrazif, iv] *adj* abrasive.

abrégé, -e [abreʒe] *adj* abridged.

abréger [abreʒe] *vt* [visite, réunion] to cut short; [discours] to shorten; [mot] to abbreviate.

abreuvoir [abrœvwar] *nm* [lieu] watering place; [installation] drinking trough.

abréviation [abrevjasjɔ̃] *nf* abbreviation.

abri [abri] *nm* shelter; **à l'~ de** sheltered from; *fig* safe from.

abricot [abriko] *nm & adj inv* apricot.

abriter [abrite] *vt* [protéger]: **~ qqn/qqch (de)** to shelter sb/sthg (from). ○ **s'abriter** *vp*: **s'~ (de)** to shelter (from).

abroger [abrɔʒe] *vt* to repeal.

abrupt, -e [abrypt] *adj* [raide] steep. || [rude] abrupt, brusque.

abruti, -e [abryti] *fam nm, f* moron.

abrutir [abrytir] *vt* [abêtir]: **~ qqn** to deaden sb's mind. || [accabler]: **~ qqn de travail** to work sb silly.

abrutissant, -e [abrytisɑ̃, ɑ̃t] *adj* [bruit, travail] stupefying. || [jeu, feuilleton] moronic.

absence [apsɑ̃s] *nf* [de personne] absence. || [carence] lack.

absent, -e [apsɑ̃, ɑ̃t] **1** *adj* [personne]: **~ (de)** [gén] away (from); [pour maladie] absent (from). || [regard, air] vacant, absent. **2** *nm, f* absentee.

absenter [apsɑ̃te] ○ **s'absenter** *vp*: **s'~ (de la pièce)** to leave (the room).

absinthe [apsɛ̃t] *nf* [boisson] absinth.

absolu, -e [apsɔly] *adj* [gén] absolute; [décision, jugement] uncompromising.

absolument [apsɔlymɑ̃] *adv* absolutely.

absorbant, -e [apsɔrbɑ̃, ɑ̃t] *adj* [matière] absorbent. || [occupation] absorbing.

absorber [apsɔrbe] *vt* [gén] to absorb. || [manger] to take.

abstenir [apstənir] ○ **s'abstenir** *vp* [ne rien faire]: **s'~ (de qqch/de faire qqch)** to refrain (from sthg/from doing sthg). || [ne pas voter] to abstain.

abstention [apstɑ̃sjɔ̃] *nf* abstention.

abstentionnisme [apstɑ̃sjɔnism] *nm* abstaining.

abstinence [apstinɑ̃s] *nf* abstinence.

abstraction [apstraksjɔ̃] *nf* abstraction; **faire** ~ **de** to disregard.

abstrait, -e [apstrɛ, ɛt] *adj* abstract.

absurde [apsyrd] *adj* absurd.

absurdité [apsyrdite] *nf* absurdity; **dire des** ~**s** to talk nonsense (*U*).

abus [aby] *nm* abuse; ~ **de confiance** breach of trust; ~ **de pouvoir** abuse of power.

abuser [abyze] *vi* [dépasser les bornes] to go too far. || [user]: ~ **de** [autorité, pouvoir] to overstep the bounds of; [temps] to take up too much of.

abusif, -ive [abyzif, iv] *adj* [excessif] excessive. || [fautif] improper.

acabit [akabi] *nm*: **du même** ~ *péj* of the same type.

acacia [akasja] *nm* acacia.

académicien, -ienne [akademisjɛ̃, jɛn] *nm, f* academician; [de l'Académie française] member of the French Academy.

académie [akademi] *nf* SCOL & UNIV ≃ school district *Am.* || [institut] academy; **l'Académie française** the French Academy (*learned society of the leading men and women of letters*).

acajou [akaʒu] *nm & adj inv* mahogany.

acariâtre [akarjɑtr] *adj* bad-tempered, cantankerous.

accablant, -e [akablɑ̃, ɑ̃t] *adj* [soleil, chaleur] oppressive. || [preuve, témoignage] overwhelming.

accabler [akable] *vt* [surcharger]: ~ **qqn de** [travail] to overwhelm sb with; ~ **qqn d'injures** to shower sb with abuse.

accalmie [akalmi] *nf litt & fig* lull.

accéder [aksede] ○ **accéder à** *vt* [pénétrer dans] to reach, to get to. || [parvenir à] to attain. || [consentir à] to comply with.

accélérateur [akseleratœr] *nm* accelerator.

accélération [akselerasjɔ̃] *nf* [de voiture, machine] acceleration.

accélérer [akselere] **1** *vt* to accelerate, to speed up. **2** *vi* AUTOM to accelerate.

accent [aksɑ̃] *nm* [gén] accent; ~ **aigu/grave/circonflexe** acute/grave/circumflex (accent). || [intonation] tone; **mettre l'**~ **sur** to stress, to emphasize.

accentuation [aksɑ̃tyasjɔ̃] *nf* [à l'écrit] accenting; [en parlant] stress.

accentuer [aksɑ̃tɥe] *vt* [insister sur, souligner] to emphasize, to accentuate. || [in-

tensifier] to intensify. || [à l'écrit] to put the accents on; [en parlant] to stress. ○ **s'accentuer** *vp* to become more pronounced.

acceptable [akseptabl] *adj* satisfactory, acceptable.

acceptation [akseptasjɔ̃] *nf* acceptance.

accepter [aksepte] *vt* to accept; ~ **de faire qqch** to agree to do sthg; ~ **que** (+ *subjonctif*): ~ **que qqn fasse qqch** to agree to sb doing sthg.

acception [aksepsjɔ̃] *nf* sense.

accès [aksɛ] *nm* [entrée] entry; **avoir/donner** ~ **à** to have/to give access to; «~ **interdit**» "no entry". || [voie d'entrée] entrance. || [crise] bout: ~ **de colère** fit of anger.

accessible [aksesibl] *adj* [lieu, livre] accessible; [prix, équipement] affordable.

accession [aksesjɔ̃] *nf*: ~ **à** [trône, présidence] accession to; [indépendance] attainment of.

accessoire [akseswar] **1** *nm* [gén] accessory. || [de théâtre, cinéma] prop. **2** *adj* secondary.

accident [aksidɑ̃] *nm* accident; **par** ~ by chance, by accident; ~ **de la route/de voiture/du travail** road/car/industrial accident.

accidenté, -e [aksidɑ̃te] **1** *adj* [terrain, surface] uneven. || [voiture] damaged. **2** *nm, f* (*gén pl*): ~ **de la route** accident victim.

accidentel, -elle [aksidɑ̃tɛl] *adj* accidental.

acclamation [aklamasjɔ̃] *nf* (*gén pl*) cheers (*pl*), cheering (*U*).

acclamer [aklame] *vt* to cheer.

acclimatation [aklimatasjɔ̃] *nf* acclimatization.

acclimater [aklimate] *vt* to acclimatize.

accolade [akɔlad] *nf* TYPO brace. || [embrassade] embrace.

accommodant, -e [akɔmɔdɑ̃, ɑ̃t] *adj* obliging.

accommoder [akɔmɔde] *vt* CULIN to prepare.

accompagnateur, -trice [akɔ̃paɲatœr, tris] *nm, f* MUS accompanist. || [guide] guide.

accompagnement [akɔ̃paɲmɑ̃] *nm* MUS accompaniment.

accompagner [akɔ̃paɲe] *vt* [personne] to go with, to accompany. || [agrémenter]: ~ **qqch de** to accompany sthg with. || MUS to accompany.

accompli, -e [akɔpli] *adj* accomplished.

accomplir [akɔplir] *vt* to carry out. ○ **s'accomplir** *vp* to come about.

accomplissement [akɔplismã] *nm* [de travail] fulfilment.

accord [akɔr] *nm* [gén & LING] agreement. ‖ MUS chord. ‖ [acceptation] approval; **donner son ~ à qqch** to approve sthg. ○ **d'accord 1** *loc adv* OK, all right. **2** *loc adj*: **être d'~ (avec)** to agree (with); **tomber** ou **se mettre d'~** to come to an agreement, to agree.

accordéon [akɔrdeɔ̃] *nm* accordion.

accorder [akɔrde] *vt* [donner]: **~ qqch à qqn** to grant sb sthg. ‖ [attribuer]: **~ de l'importance à** to attach importance to sthg. ‖ [harmoniser] to match. ‖ GRAM: **~ qqch avec qqch** to make sthg agree with sthg. ‖ MUS to tune. ○ **s'accorder** *vp* [gén]: **s'~ (pour faire qqch)** to agree (to do sthg); **s'~ à faire qqch** to be unanimous in doing sthg. ‖ [être assorti] to match. ‖ GRAM to agree.

accoster [akɔste] **1** *vt* NAVIG to come alongside. ‖ [personne] to accost. **2** *vi* NAVIG to dock.

accotement [akɔtmã] *nm* [de route] shoulder; **~ non stabilisé** soft verge *Br*, soft shoulder *Am*.

accouchement [akuʃmã] *nm* childbirth; **~ sans douleur** natural childbirth.

accoucher [akuʃe] *vi*: **~ (de)** to give birth (to).

accouder [akude] ○ **s'accouder** *vp*: **s'~ à** to lean one's elbows on.

accoudoir [akudwar] *nm* armrest.

accouplement [akupləmã] *nm* mating, coupling.

accourir [akurir] *vi* to run up, to rush up.

accouru, -e [akury] *pp* → **accourir**.

accoutré, -e [akutre] *adj péj*: **être bizarrement ~** to be oddly got up.

accoutrement [akutrəmã] *nm péj* get-up.

accoutumer [akutyme] *vt*: **~ qqn à qqn/qqch** to get sb used to sthg; **~ qqn à faire qqch** to get sb used to doing sthg. ○ **s'accoutumer** *vp*: **s'~ à qqn/qqch** to get used to sb/sthg; **s'~ à faire qqch** to get used to doing sthg.

accréditer [akredite] *vt* [rumeur] to substantiate.

accro [akro] *fam adj*: **~ à** hooked on.

accroc [akro] *nm* [déchirure] tear. ‖ [incident] hitch.

accrochage [akrɔʃaʒ] *nm* [accident] collision. ‖ *fam* [dispute] row.

accrocher [akrɔʃe] *vt* [suspendre]: **~ qqch (à)** to hang sthg up (on). ‖ [déchirer]: **~ qqch (à)** to catch sthg (on). ‖ [attacher]: **~ qqch (à)** to hitch sthg (to). ○ **s'accrocher** *vp* [s'agripper]: **s'~ (à)** to hang on (to). ‖ *fam* [se disputer] to row, to have a row. ‖ *fam* [persévérer] to stick at it.

accroissement [akrwasmã] *nm* increase, growth.

accroître [akrwatr] *vt* to increase. ○ **s'accroître** *vp* to increase, to grow.

accroupir [akrupir] ○ **s'accroupir** *vp* to squat.

accru, -e [akry] *pp* → **accroître**.

accueil [akœj] *nm* [lieu] reception. ‖ [action] welcome, reception.

accueillant, -e [akœjã, ãt] *adj* welcoming, friendly.

accueillir [akœjir] *vt* [gén] to welcome. ‖ [loger] to accommodate.

accumulateur [akymylatœr] *nm* accumulator, battery.

accumulation [akymylasjɔ̃] *nf* accumulation.

accumuler [akymyle] *vt* to accumulate. ○ **s'accumuler** *vp* to pile up.

accusateur, -trice [akyzatœr, tris] **1** *adj* accusing. **2** *nm, f* accuser.

accusation [akyzasjɔ̃] *nf* [reproche] accusation. ‖ JUR charge; **mettre en ~** to indict; **l'~** the prosecution.

accusé, -e [akyze] *nm, f* accused, defendant. ○ **accusé de réception** *nm* acknowledgement (of receipt).

accuser [akyze] *vt* [porter une accusation contre]: **~ qqn (de qqch)** to accuse sb (of sthg). ‖ JUR: **~ qqn de qqch** to charge sb with sthg.

acerbe [asɛrb] *adj* acerbic.

acéré, -e [asere] *adj* sharp.

acharné, -e [aʃarne] *adj* [combat] fierce; [travail] unremitting.

acharnement [aʃarnəmã] *nm* relentlessness.

acharner [aʃarne] ○ **s'acharner** *vp* [combattre]: **s'~ contre** ou **après** ou **sur qqn** [ennemi, victime] to hound sb; [suj: malheur] to dog sb. ‖ [s'obstiner]: **s'~ (à faire qqch)** to persist (in doing sthg).

achat [aʃa] *nm* purchase; **faire des ~s** to go shopping.

acheminer [aʃmine] *vt* to dispatch. ○ **s'acheminer** *vp*: **s'~ vers** [lieu, désastre] to head for; [solution, paix] to move towards.

acheter [aʃte] *vt litt & fig* to buy; ~ qqch à oı pour qqn to buy sth for sb. to buy sb sthg.

acheteur, -euse [aʃtœr, øz] *nm, f* buyer, purchaser.

achevé, -e [aʃve] *adj sout*: **d'un ridicule** ~ utterly ridiculous.

achèvement [aʃɛvmɑ̃] *nm* completion.

achever [aʃve] *vt* [terminer] to complete, to finish (off). || [tuer, accabler] to finish off. ○ **s'achever** *vp* to end, to come to an end.

achoppement [aʃɔpmɑ̃] → **pierre**.

acide [asid] **1** *adj* [saveur] sour. || [propos] sharp, acid. || CHIM acid. **2** *nm* CHIM acid.

acidité [asidite] *nf* CHIM acidity. || [saveur] sourness. || [de propos] sharpness.

acidulé, -e [asidyle] *adj* slightly acid.

acier [asje] *nm* steel; ~ **inoxydable** stainless steel.

aciérie [asjeri] *nf* steelworks (*sg*).

acné [akne] *nf* acne.

acolyte [akɔlit] *nm péj* henchman.

acompte [akɔ̃t] *nm* deposit.

à-côté [akote] (*pl* **à-côtés**) *nm* [gain d'appoint] extra.

à-coup [aku] (*pl* **à-coups**) *nm* jerk; **par** ~**s** in fits and starts.

acoustique [akustik] *nf* [d'une salle] acoustics (*pl*).

acquéreur [akerœr] *nm* buyer.

acquérir [akerir] *vt* [gén] to acquire.

acquiescer [akjese] *vi* to acquiesce; ~ **à** to agree to.

acquis, -e [aki, iz] **1** *pp* → **acquérir**. **2** *adj* [droit, avantage] established. ○ **acquis** *nmpl* [connaissances] knowledge (*U*).

acquisition [akizisjɔ̃] *nf* acquisition.

acquit [aki] *nm* receipt; **pour** ~ COMM received; **faire qqch par** ~ **de conscience** *fig* to do sthg to set one's mind at rest.

acquittement [akitmɑ̃] *nm* JUR acquittal.

acquitter [akite] *vt* JUR to acquit. || [régler] to pay.

âcre [akr] *adj* [saveur] bitter. || [fumée] acrid.

acrobate [akrɔbat] *nmf* acrobat.

acrobatie [akrɔbasi] *nf* acrobatics (*U*).

acrylique [akrilik] *adj & nm* acrylic.

acte [akt] *nm* [action] act, action; **faire** ~ **de candidature** to submit an application. || THÉÂTRE act. || JUR deed; ~

d'accusation charge; ~ **de naissance/de mariage** birth/marriage certificate; ~ **de vente** bill of sale. || *loc*: **faire** ~ **de présence** to put in an appearance; **prendre** ~ **de** to note, to take note of. ○ **actes** *nmpl* [de colloque] proceedings.

acteur, -trice [aktœr, tris] *nm, f* actor (*f* actress).

actif, -ive [aktif, iv] *adj* [gén] active; **la population active** the working population. ○ **actif** *nm* FIN assets (*pl*). || *loc*: **avoir qqch à son** ~ to have sthg to one's credit.

action [aksjɔ̃] *nf* [gén] action; **sous l'**~ **de** under the effect of. || [acte] action, act; **bonne/mauvaise** ~ good/bad deed. || JUR action, lawsuit. || FIN share.

actionnaire [aksjɔnɛr] *nmf* FIN shareholder.

actionner [aksjɔne] *vt* to work, to activate.

activement [aktivmɑ̃] *adv* actively.

activer [aktive] *vt* to speed up. ○ **s'activer** *vp* to bustle about.

activiste [aktivist] *adj & nmf* activist.

activité [aktivite] *nf* [gén] activity; **en** ~ [volcan] active.

actualiser [aktɥalize] *vt* to bring up to date.

actualité [aktɥalite] *nf* [d'un sujet] topicality. || [événements]: **l'**~ **sportive/ politique/littéraire** the current sports/ political/literary scene. ○ **actualités** *nfpl*: **les** ~**s** the news (*sg*).

actuel, -elle [aktɥɛl] *adj* [contemporain, présent] current, present; **à l'heure** ~**le** at the present time.

actuellement [aktɥɛlmɑ̃] *adv* at present, currently.

acuité [akɥite] *nf* acuteness.

acupuncture, acuponcture [akypɔ̃ktyr] *nf* acupuncture.

adage [adaʒ] *nm* adage, saying.

adaptateur, -trice [adaptatœr, tris] *nm, f* adapter. ○ **adaptateur** *nm* ÉLECTR adapter.

adaptation [adaptasjɔ̃] *nf* adaptation.

adapter [adapte] *vt* [gén] to adapt. || [fixer] to fit. ○ **s'adapter** *vp*: **s'**~ **(à)** to adapt (to).

additif [aditif] *nm* [supplément] rider, additional clause. || [substance] additive.

addition [adisjɔ̃] *nf* [ajout, calcul] addition. || [note] bill *Br*, check *Am*.

additionner [adisjɔne] *vt* [ajouter]: **une poudre d'eau** to add water to a powder. || [calculer] to add up.

adepte [adɛpt] *nmf* follower.

adéquat, -e [adekwa, at] *adj* suitable, appropriate.

adhérence [aderɑ̃s] *nf* [de pneu] grip.

adhérent, -e [aderɑ̃, ɑ̃t] *nm, f*: ~ (de) member (of).

adhérer [adere] *vi* [coller] to stick, to adhere; ~ à [se fixer sur] to stick ou adhere to; [être d'accord avec] *fig* to support, to adhere to. || [être membre]: ~ à to become a member of, to join.

adhésif, -ive [adezif, iv] *adj* sticky, adhesive. ○ **adhésif** *nm* adhesive.

adhésion [adezjɔ̃] *nf* [à idée]: ~ (à) support (for). || [à parti]: ~ (à) membership (of).

adieu [adjø] **1** *interj* goodbye!, farewell! **2** *nm* (*gén pl*) farewell; **faire ses -x à qqn** to say one's farewells to sb.

adjectif [adʒɛktif] *nm* GRAM adjective.

adjoint, -e [adʒwɛ̃, ɛ̃t] **1** *adj* deputy (*avant n*), assistant (*avant n*). **2** *nm, f* deputy, assistant; ~ **au maire** deputy mayor.

adjonction [adʒɔ̃ksjɔ̃] *nf* addition.

adjudant [adʒydɑ̃] *nm* [dans la marine] warrant officer; [dans l'armée] company sergeant major.

adjuger [adʒyʒe] *vt*: ~ **qqch (à qqn)** [aux enchères] to auction sthg (to sb); **adjugé!** sold!

admettre [admɛtr] *vt* [tolérer, accepter] to allow, to accept. || [autoriser] to allow. || [accueillir, reconnaître] to admit.

administrateur, -trice [administratœr, tris] *nm, f* [gérant] administrator.

administratif, -ive [administratif, iv] *adj* administrative.

administration [administrasjɔ̃] *nf* [service public]: **l'Administration** ≃ the Civil Service. || [gestion] administration.

administrer [administre] *vt* [gérer] to manage, to administer. || [médicament, sacrement] to administer.

admirable [admirabl] *adj* [personne, comportement] admirable. || [paysage, spectacle] wonderful.

admiratif, -ive [admiratif, iv] *adj* admiring.

admiration [admirasjɔ̃] *nf* admiration.

admirer [admire] *vt* to admire.

admis, -e [admi, iz] *pp* → **admettre**.

admissible [admisibl] *adj* [attitude] acceptable. || SCOL eligible.

admission [admisjɔ̃] *nf* admission.

ADN (*abr de* **acide désoxyribonucléique**) *nm* DNA.

ado [ado] (*abr de* **adolescent**) *nmf fam* teenager.

adolescence [adɔlesɑ̃s] *nf* adolescence.

adolescent, -e [adɔlesɑ̃, ɑ̃t] *nm, f* adolescent, teenager.

adonner [adɔne] ○ **s'adonner** *vp*: **s'~ à** [sport, activité] to devote o.s. to; [vice] to take to.

adopter [adɔpte] *vt* [gén] to adopt. || [loi] to pass.

adoptif, -ive [adɔptif, iv] *adj* [famille] adoptive; [pays, enfant] adopted.

adoption [adɔpsjɔ̃] *nf* adoption; **d'~** [pays, ville] adopted; [famille] adoptive.

adorable [adɔrabl] *adj* adorable, delightful.

adoration [adɔrasjɔ̃] *nf* [amour] adoration. || RELIG worship.

adorer [adɔre] *vt* [personne, chose] to adore. || RELIG to worship.

adosser [adose] ○ **s'adosser** *vp*: **s'~ à** ou **contre qqch** to lean against sthg.

adoucir [adusir] *vt* [gén] to soften. || [chagrin, peine] to ease, to soothe. ○ **s'adoucir** *vp* [temps] to become ou get milder. || [personne] to mellow.

adoucissant, -e [adusisɑ̃, ɑ̃t] *adj* soothing. ○ **adoucissant** *nm* softener.

adoucisseur [adusisœr] *nm*: ~ **d'eau** water softener.

adresse [adrɛs] *nf* [gén & INFORM] address. || [habileté] skill.

adresser [adrese] *vt* [faire parvenir]: ~ **qqch à qqn** to address sthg to sb. || [envoyer]: ~ **qqn à qqn** to refer sb to sb. ○ **s'adresser** *vp*: **s'~ à** [parler à] to speak to; [être destiné à] to be aimed at, to be intended for.

adroit, -e [adrwa, at] *adj* skilful.

adulte [adylt] *nmf & adj* adult.

adultère [adylter] **1** *nm* [acte] adultery. **2** *adj* adulterous.

advenir [advənir] *v impers* to happen; **qu'est-il advenu de ...?** what has happened to ou become of ...?

advenu [advəny] *pp* → **advenir**.

adverbe [adverb] *nm* adverb.

adversaire [adverser] *nmf* adversary, opponent.

adverse [advers] *adj* [opposé] opposing; → **parti**.

adversité [adversite] *nf* adversity.

aération [aerasjɔ̃] *nf* [circulation d'air] ventilation; [action] airing.

aérer [aere] *vt* [pièce, chose] to air. || *fig* [présentation, mise en page] to lighten.

aérien, -ienne [aerjɛ̃, jɛn] *adj* [câble] overhead (*avant n*). || [transports, attaque] air (*avant n*).

aérobic [aerɔbik] *nm* aerobics (*U*).

aérodrome [aerɔdrom] *nm* aerodrome.

aérodynamique [aerɔdinamik] *adj* streamlined, aerodynamic.

aérogare [aerɔgar] *nf* [aéroport] airport. || [gare] air terminal.

aéroglisseur [aerɔglisœr] *nm* hovercraft.

aéronautique [aerɔnotik] *nf* aeronautics (*U*).

aéronaval, -e, -als [aerɔnaval] *adj* air and sea (*avant n*).

aérophagie [aerɔfaʒi] *nf* abdominal wind.

aéroport [aerɔpɔr] *nm* airport.

aérosol [aerɔsɔl] *nm & adj inv* aerosol.

aérospatial, -e, -iaux [aerɔspasjal, jo] *adj* aerospace (*avant n*). ○ **aérospatiale** *nf* aerospace industry.

affable [afabl] *adj* [personne] affable, agreeable. || [parole] kind.

affaiblir [afeblir] *vt litt & fig* to weaken. ○ **s'affaiblir** *vp litt & fig* to weaken, to become weaker.

affaire [afer] *nf* [question] matter. || [situation, polémique] affair. || [marché] deal; **faire une ~** to get a bargain or a good deal. || [entreprise] business. || [procès] case; || *loc*: **avoir ~ à qqn** to deal with sb; **faire l'~** to do nicely. ○ **affaires** *nfpl* COMM business (*U*). || [objets personnels] things, belongings. || [activités] affairs; **les Affaires étrangères** ≃ the Foreign Office (*sg*).

affairé, -e [afere] *adj* busy.

affairer [afere] ○ **s'affairer** *vp* to bustle about.

affaisser [afese] ○ **s'affaisser** *vp* [se creuser] to subside, to sink. || [tomber] to collapse.

affaler [afale] ○ **s'affaler** *vp* to collapse.

affamé, -e [afame] *adj* starving.

affecter [afɛkte] *vt* [consacrer]: **~ qqch à** to allocate sthg to. || [nommer]: **~ qqn à** to appoint sb to. || [feindre] to feign. || [émouvoir] to affect, to move.

affectif, -ive [afɛktif, iv] *adj* emotional.

affection [afɛksjɔ̃] *nf* [sentiment] affection; **avoir de l'~ pour** to be fond of.

affectionner [afɛksjɔne] *vt* to be fond of.

affectueusement [afɛktɥøzmɑ̃] *adv* affectionately.

affectueux, -euse [afɛktɥø, øz] *adj* affectionate.

affichage [afiʃaʒ] *nm* [d'affiche] putting up, displaying. || ÉLECTRON: **~ à cristaux liquides** LCD, liquid crystal display; **~ numérique** digital display.

affiche [afiʃ] *nf* [gén] poster; [officielle] notice.

afficher [afiʃe] *vt* [liste, affiche] to put up; [vente, réglementation] to put up a notice about. || [laisser transparaître] to display, to exhibit.

affilée [afile] ○ **d'affilée** *loc adv*: **trois jours d'~** three days running.

affiler [afile] *vt* to sharpen.

affiner [afine] *vt litt & fig* to refine.

affinité [afinite] *nf* affinity.

affirmatif, -ive [afirmatif, iv] *adj* [réponse] affirmative. || [personne] positive. ○ **affirmative** *nf*: **dans l'affirmative** if yes, if the answer is yes; **répondre par l'affirmative** to reply in the affirmative.

affirmation [afirmasjɔ̃] *nf* assertion.

affirmer [afirme] *vt* [certifier] to maintain, to claim. || [exprimer] to assert.

affligeant, -e [afliʒɑ̃, ɑ̃t] *adj* [désolant] saddening, distressing. || [lamentable] appalling.

affliger [afliʒe] *vt sout* [attrister] to sadden, to distress. || [de défaut, de maladie]: **être affligé de** to be afflicted with.

affluent [aflyɑ̃] *nm* tributary.

affluer [aflye] *vi* [choses] to pour in, to flood in. || [personnes] to flock. || [sang]: **~ (à)** to rush (to).

afflux [afly] *nm* [de liquide, dons, capitaux] flow. || [de personnes] flood.

affolement [afɔlmɑ̃] *nm* panic.

affoler [afɔle] *vt* [inquiéter] to terrify. ○ **s'affoler** *vp* [paniquer] to panic.

affranchir [afrɑ̃ʃir] *vt* [lettre - avec timbre] to stamp; [- à la machine] to frank.

affreux, -euse [afrø, øz] *adj* [repoussant] horrible. || [effrayant] terrifying. || [détestable] awful, dreadful.

affriolant, -e [afrijɔlɑ̃, ɑ̃t] *adj* enticing.

affront [afrɔ̃] *nm* insult, affront.

affrontement [afrɔ̃tmɑ̃] *nm* confrontation.

affronter [afrɔ̃te] *vt* to confront.

affubler [afyble] *vt péj*: **être affublé de** to be got up in.

affût [afy] *nm*: **être à l'~ (de)** to be lying in wait (for); *fig* to be on the lookout (for).

affûter [afyte] *vt* to sharpen.

Afghanistan [afganistã] *nm*: l'~ Afghanistan.

afin [afɛ̃] ○ **afin de** *loc prép* in order to. ○ **afin que** *loc conj* (+ *subjonctif*) so that.

a fortiori [aforsjori] *adv* all the more.

africain, -e [afrikɛ̃, ɛn] *adj* African. ○ **Africain, -e** *nm, f* African.

Afrique [afrik] *nf*: l'~ Africa; l'~ du Nord North Africa; l'~ du Sud South Africa.

agacer [agase] *vt* to irritate.

âge [aʒ] *nm* age; **quel ~ as-tu?** how old are you?; **prendre de l'~** to age; **l'~ adulte** adulthood; **le troisième ~** [personnes] the over-sixties.

âgé, -e [aʒe] *adj* old, elderly; **être ~ de 20 ans** to be 20 years old ou of age; **un enfant ~ de 3 ans** a 3-year-old child.

agence [aʒɑ̃s] *nf* agency; ~ **immobilière** estate agent's *Br*, real estate agent's *Am*; **Agence nationale pour l'emploi** ≃ job centre; ~ **de publicité** advertising agency; ~ **de voyages** travel agent's travel agency.

agencer [aʒɑ̃se] *vt* to arrange.

agenda [aʒɛ̃da] *nm* diary.

agenouiller [aʒnuje] ○ **s'agenouiller** *vp* to kneel.

agent [aʒɑ̃] *nm* agent; ~ **de change** stockbroker; ~ **de police** police officer; ~ **secret** secret agent.

agglomération [aglɔmerasjɔ̃] *nf* [ville] conurbation.

aggloméré [aglɔmere] *nm* chipboard.

agglomérer [aglɔmere] *vt* to mix together.

agglutiner [aglytine] ○ **s'agglutiner** *vp* [foule] to gather, to congregate.

aggraver [agrave] *vt* to make worse. ○ **s'aggraver** *vp* to get worse, to worsen.

agile [aʒil] *adj* agile, nimble.

agilité [aʒilite] *nf litt & fig* agility.

agios [aʒjo] *nmpl* FIN bank charges.

agir [aʒir] *vi* [faire, être efficace] to act. || [se comporter] to behave. || [influer]: ~ **sur** to have an effect on. ○ **s'agir** *v impers*: **il s'agit de ...** it's a matter of ...; **de quoi s'agit-il?** what's it about?

agissements [aʒismɑ̃] *nmpl péj* schemes, intrigues.

agitateur, -trice [aʒitatœr, tris] *nm, f* POLIT agitator.

agitation [aʒitasjɔ̃] *nf* agitation; [politique, sociale] unrest.

agité, -e [aʒite] *adj* [gén] restless; [enfant, classe] restless, fidgety; [journée, atmosphère] hectic. || [mer] rough.

agiter [aʒite] *vt* [remuer - flacon, objet] to shake; [- drapeau, bras] to wave. ○ **s'agiter** *vp* [personne] to move about, to fidget; [population] to get restless.

agneau [aɲo] *nm* [animal, viande] lamb. || [cuir] lambskin.

agonie [agɔni] *nf* [de personne] mortal agony; *fig* death throes (*pl*).

agoniser [agɔnize] *vi* [personne] to be dying; *fig* to be on its last legs.

agrafe [agraf] *nf* [de bureau] staple. || MÉD clip.

agrafer [agrafe] *vt* [attacher] to fasten.

agrafeuse [agraføz] *nf* stapler.

agraire [agrɛr] *adj* agrarian.

agrandir [agrɑ̃dir] *vt* [élargir - gén & PHOT] to enlarge; [- rue, écart] to widen. || *fig* [développer] to expand. ○ **s'agrandir** *vp* [s'étendre] to grow. || *fig* [se développer] to expand.

agrandissement [agrɑ̃dismɑ̃] *nm* [gén & PHOT] enlargement.

agréable [agreabl] *adj* pleasant, nice.

agréé, -e [agree] *adj* [concessionnaire, appareil] authorized.

agréer [agree] *vt sout* [accepter]: **veuillez ~ mes salutations distinguées** ou **l'expression de mes sentiments distingués** yours faithfully.

agrégation [agregasjɔ̃] *nf* competitive examination for secondary school and university teachers.

agrégé, -e [agreʒe] *nm, f* holder of the *agrégation*.

agrément [agremɑ̃] *nm* [approbation] consent, approval.

agrès [agrɛ] *nmpl* SPORT gym apparatus (U).

agresser [agrese] *vt* [suj: personne] to attack.

agresseur [agresœr] *nm* attacker.

agressif, -ive [agresif, iv] *adj* aggressive.

agression [agresjɔ̃] *nf* attack; MIL & PSYCHOL aggression.

agricole [agrikɔl] *adj* agricultural.

agriculteur, -trice [agrikyltœr, tris] *nm, f* farmer.

agriculture [agrikyltyr] *nf* agriculture, farming.

agripper [agripe] *vt* [personne] to cling ou hang on to. || [objet] to grip, to clutch.

agronomie [agrɔnɔmi] *nf* agronomy.

agrume [agrym] *nm* citrus fruit.

aguets [agɛ] ○ **aux aguets** loc adv: **être/rester aux ~** to be ou keep on the lookout.

ahuri, -e [ayri] adj: **être ~ (par qqch)** to be taken aback (by sthg).

ahurissant, -e [ayrisã, ãt] adj astounding.

ai → avoir.

aide [ɛd] nf [gén] help; **appeler (qqn) à l'~** to call (to sb) for help; **venir en ~ à qqn** to come to sb's aid, to help sb. ‖ [secours financier] aid; **~ sociale** social security Br, welfare Am. ○ **à l'aide de** loc prép with the help ou aid of.

aide-mémoire [ɛdmemwar] nm inv aide-mémoire; [pour examen] revision notes (pl).

aider [ede] vt to help; **~ qqn à faire qqch** to help sb to do sthg. ○ **s'aider** vp [s'assister mutuellement] to help each other. ‖ [avoir recours]: **s'~ de** to use, to make use of.

aide-soignant, -e [ɛdswaɲã, ãt] nm, f nursing auxiliary Br, nurse's aide Am.

aie, aies etc → avoir.

aïe [aj] interj [exprime la douleur] ow!, ouch!

aïeul, -e [ajœl] nm, f sout grandparent, grandfather (f grandmother).

aïeux [ajø] nmpl ancestors.

aigle [ɛgl] nm eagle.

aigre [ɛgr] adj [gén] sour. ‖ [propos] harsh.

aigre-doux, -douce [ɛgrədu, dus] adj CULIN sweet-and-sour.

aigreur [ɛgrœr] nf [d'un aliment] sourness. ‖ [d'un propos] harshness. ○ **aigreurs d'estomac** nfpl heartburn (U).

aigri, -e [egri] adj embittered.

aigu, -uë [egy] adj [son] high-pitched. ‖ [objet, lame] sharp; [angle] acute. ‖ [douleur] sharp, acute. ‖ [intelligence, sens] acute, keen. ○ **aigu** nm high note.

aiguillage [eguijaʒ] nm [RAIL - manœuvre] switching Am; [- dispositif] switch Am.

aiguille [eguij] nf [gén] needle; **~ à tricoter** knitting needle; **~ de pin** pine needle. ‖ [de pendule] hand.

aiguiller [eguije] vt RAIL to switch Am. ‖ [personne, conversation] to steer, to direct.

aiguilleur [eguijœr] nm RAIL switchman Am. ‖ AÉRON: **~ du ciel** air traffic controller.

aiguiser [egize] vt litt & fig to sharpen.

ail [aj] (pl **ails** OU **aulx** [o]) nm garlic (U).

aile [ɛl] nf [gén] wing.

aileron [ɛlrɔ̃] nm [de requin] fin. ‖ [d'avion] aileron.

ailier [elje] nm winger.

aille, ailles etc → aller.

ailleurs [ajœr] adv elsewhere, somewhere else; **nulle part/partout ~** nowhere/everywhere else. ○ **d'ailleurs** loc adv moreover, besides.

aimable [ɛmabl] adj kind, nice.

aimablement [ɛmabləmã] adv kindly.

aimant¹, -e [ɛmã, ãt] adj loving.

aimant² [ɛmã] nm magnet.

aimer [eme] vt [gén] to like; **~ bien qqch/qqn** to like sthg/sb, to be fond of sthg/sb; **~ bien faire qqch** to (really) like doing sthg; **~ (à) faire qqch** to like to do sthg, to like doing sthg; **je n'aime pas que tu rentres seule le soir** I don't like you coming home alone at night; **j'aimerais (bien) que tu viennes avec moi** I'd like you to come with me; **~ mieux qqch** to prefer sthg; **~ mieux faire qqch** to prefer doing ou to do sthg. ‖ [d'amour] to love. ○ **s'aimer** vp (emploi réciproque) to love each other; **s'~ bien** to like each other.

aine [ɛn] nf groin.

aîné, -e [ene] 1 adj [plus âgé] elder, older; [le plus âgé] eldest, oldest. 2 nm, f [plus âgé] older ou elder one; [le plus âgé] oldest, eldest; **elle est mon ~e de deux ans** she is two years older than me.

ainsi [ɛ̃si] adv [manière] in this way, like this. ‖ [valeur conclusive] thus; **et ~ de suite** and so on, and so forth; **pour ~ dire** so to speak. ○ **ainsi que** loc conj [et] as well as.

air [ɛr] nm [gén] air; **en plein ~** (out) in the open air, outside; **en l'~** [projet] (up) in the air; fig [paroles] empty; **~ conditionné** air-conditioning. ‖ [apparence, mine] air, look; **il a l'~ triste** he looks sad; **il a l'~ de faire beau** it looks like being a nice day. ‖ MUS tune.

aire [ɛr] nf [gén] area; **~ d'atterrissage** landing strip; **~ de jeu** playground; **~ de repos** lay-by; **~ de stationnement** parking area.

aisance [ɛzãs] nf [facilité] ease. ‖ [richesse]: **il vit dans l'~** he has an affluent lifestyle.

aise [ɛz] nf: **être à l'~** ou **à son ~** [confortable] to feel comfortable; [financièrement] to be comfortably off; **mettez-vous à l'~** make yourself comfortable; **mettre qqn mal à l'~** to make sb feel ill at ease ou uneasy. ○ **aises** *nfpl*: **aimer ses ~s** to like one's (home) comforts; **prendre ses ~s** to make o.s. comfortable.

aisé, -e [eze] *adj* [facile] easy. ‖ [riche] well-off.

aisselle [ɛsɛl] *nf* armpit.

ajourner [aʒurne] *vt* [reporter - décision etc] to postpone; [- réunion, procès] to adjourn. ‖ [candidat] to refer.

ajout [aʒu] *nm* addition.

ajouter [aʒute] *vt* to add. ○ **s'ajouter** *vp*: **s'~ à qqch** to be in addition to sthg.

ajuster [aʒyste] *vt* [régler] to adjust. ‖ [vêtement] to alter. ‖ [tir, coup] to aim.

alarme [alarm] *nf* alarm; **donner l'~** to give ou raise the alarm.

alarmer [alarme] *vt* to alarm. ○ **s'alarmer** *vp* to get ou become alarmed.

albâtre [albatr] *nm* alabaster.

albatros [albatros] *nm* albatross.

albinos [albinos] *nmf & adj inv* albino.

album [albɔm] *nm* album; **~ (de) photo** photo album.

alcool [alkɔl] *nm* alcohol; **~ à brûler** methylated spirits (*pl*); **~ à 90 degrés** surgical spirit.

alcoolique [alkɔlik] *nmf & adj* alcoholic.

alcoolisé, -e [alkɔlize] *adj* alcoholic.

alcoolisme [alkɔlism] *nm* alcoholism.

Alc(o)otest® [alkɔtɛst] *nm* Breathalyser®.

alcôve [alkov] *nf* recess.

aléatoire [aleatwar] *adj* [avenir] uncertain. ‖ [choix] random.

alentour [alɑ̃tur] *adv* around, round about. ○ **alentours** *nmpl* surroundings; **aux ~s de** [spatial] in the vicinity of; [temporel] around.

alerte [alɛrt] **1** *adj* [personne, esprit] agile, alert. ‖ [style, pas] lively. **2** *nf* alarm, alert; **donner l'~** to sound ou give the alert; **~ à la bombe** bomb scare.

alerter [alɛrte] *vt* to warn, to alert.

algèbre [alʒɛbr] *nf* algebra.

Algérie [alʒeri] *nf*: **l'~** Algeria.

algérien, -ienne [alʒerjɛ̃, jɛn] *adj* Algerian. ○ **Algérien, -ienne** *nm, f* Algerian.

algue [alg] *nf* seaweed (*U*).

alibi [alibi] *nm* alibi.

aliénation [aljenasjɔ̃] *nf* alienation; **~ mentale** insanity.

aliéné, -e [aljene] **1** *adj* MÉD insane. ‖ JUR alienated. **2** *nm, f* MÉD insane person.

aliéner [aljene] *vt* to alienate.

alignement [aliɲmɑ̃] *nm* alignment, lining up.

aligner [aliɲe] *vt* [disposer en ligne] to line up, to align. ‖ [adapter]: **~ qqch sur** to align sthg with, to bring sthg into line with. ○ **s'aligner** *vp* to line up; **s'~ sur** POLIT to align o.s. with.

aliment [alimɑ̃] *nm* [nourriture] food (*U*).

alimentaire [alimɑ̃tɛr] *adj* [gén] food (*avant n*). ‖ JUR maintenance (*avant n*).

alimentation [alimɑ̃tasjɔ̃] *nf* [nourriture] diet; **magasin d'~** food store. ‖ [approvisionnement]: **~ (en)** supply ou supplying (*U*) (of).

alimenter [alimɑ̃te] *vt* [nourrir] to feed. ‖ [approvisionner]: **~ qqch en** to supply sthg with.

alinéa [alinea] *nm* [retrait de ligne] indent. ‖ [dans document officiel] paragraph.

aliter [alite] *vt*: **être alité** to be bedridden. ○ **s'aliter** *vp* to take to one's bed.

allaitement [alɛtmɑ̃] *nm* [d'enfant] breast-feeding; [d'animal] suckling.

allaiter [alɛte] *vt* [enfant] to breast-feed; [animal] to suckle.

alléchant, -e [aleʃɑ̃, ɑ̃t] *adj* mouthwatering, tempting.

allécher [aleʃe] *vt*: **il a été alléché par l'odeur/la perspective** the smell/prospect made his mouth water.

allée [ale] *nf* [dans un jardin] path; [dans une ville] avenue. ‖ [trajet]: **~s et venues** comings and goings.

allégé, -e [aleʒe] *adj* [régime, produit] low-fat.

alléger [aleʒe] *vt* [fardeau] to lighten.

allégorie [alegɔri] *nf* allegory.

allègre [alɛgr] *adj* [ton] cheerful. ‖ [démarche] jaunty.

allégresse [alegrɛs] *nf* elation.

alléguer [alege] *vt*: **~ une excuse** to put forward an excuse; **~ que** to plead (that).

Allemagne [almaɲ] *nf*: **l'~** Germany; **l'(ex-)~ de l'Est** (former) East Germany; **l'(ex-)~ de l'Ouest** (former) West Germany.

allemand, -e [almɑ̃, ɑ̃d] *adj* German. ○ **allemand** *nm* [langue] German. ○ **Allemand, -e** *nm, f* German; **un Allemand de l'Est/l'Ouest** an East/a West German.

aller [ale] **1** *nm* [trajet] outward journey. || [billet] one-way ticket *Am*. **2** *vi* [gén] to go; **allez!** come on!; **vas-y!** go on!; **allons-y!** let's go! || (+ *infinitif*): ~ **faire qqch** to go and do sthg; ~ **travailler/se promener** to go to work/for a walk. || [indiquant un état]: **comment vas-tu?** how are you?; **je vais bien** I'm very well, I'm fine; **comment ça va?** — **ça va** [santé] how are you? — fine ou all right; [situation] how are things? — fine ou all right. || [convenir]: **ce type de clou ne va pas pour ce travail** this kind of nail won't do ou isn't suitable for this job; ~ **avec** to go with; ~ **à qqn** to suit sb; [suj: vêtement, taille] to fit sb; **ces couleurs ne vont pas ensemble** these colours don't go well together. || *loc*: **cela va de soi, cela va sans dire** that goes without saying; **il en va de même pour lui** the same goes for him. **3** *v aux* (+ *infinitif*) [exprime le futur proche] to be going to, will; **je vais arriver en retard** I'm going to arrive late, I'll arrive late. ○ **s'en aller** *vp* [partir] to go, to be off; **allez-vous-en!** go away! || [disparaître] to go away.

allergie [alɛrʒi] *nf* allergy.

allergique [alɛrʒik] *adj*: ~ **(à)** allergic (to).

aller-retour [aleratur] *nm* return (ticket).

alliage [aljaʒ] *nm* alloy.

alliance [aljɑ̃s] *nf* [union - stratégique] alliance; [- par le mariage] union, marriage; **cousin par** ~ cousin by marriage. || [bague] wedding ring.

allié, -e [alje] **1** *adj*: ~ **(à)** allied (to). **2** *nm, f* ally.

allier [alje] *vt* [associer] to combine. ○ **s'allier** *vp* to become allies; **s'** ~ **qqn** to win sb over as an ally; **s'** ~ **à qqn** to ally with sb.

alligator [aligatɔr] *nm* alligator.

allô [alo] *interj* hello!

allocation [alɔkasjɔ̃] *nf* [attribution] allocation. || [aide financière]: ~ **chômage** unemployment benefit (*U*); ~ **logement** housing benefit (*U*); ~**s familiales** child benefit (*U*).

allocution [alɔkysjɔ̃] *nf* short speech.

allongé, -e [alɔ̃ʒe] *adj* [position]: **être** ~ to be lying down ou stretched out. || [forme] elongated.

allonger [alɔ̃ʒe] *vt* [gén] to lengthen, to make longer. || [jambe, bras] to stretch (out). || [personne] to lay down.

○ **s'allonger** *vp* [gén] to get longer. || [se coucher] to lie down.

allumage [alymaʒ] *nm* [de feu] lighting. || [d'appareil électrique] switching ou turning on. || [de moteur] ignition.

allume-cigares [alymsigar] *nm inv* cigar lighter.

allume-gaz [alymgaz] *nm inv* gas lighter.

allumer [alyme] *vt* [lampe, radio, télévision] to turn ou switch on; **allume dans la cuisine** turn the kitchen light on. || [gaz] to light; [cigarette] to light (up). || *fam* [personne] to turn on.

allumette [alymɛt] *nf* match.

allure [alyr] *nf* [vitesse] speed; **à toute** ~ at top ou full speed. || [prestance] presence; **avoir de l'** ~ to have style. || [apparence générale] appearance.

allusion [alyzjɔ̃] *nf* allusion; **faire** ~ **à** to refer ou allude to.

almanach [almana] *nm* almanac.

aloi [alwa] *nm*: **de bon** ~ [mesure] of real worth; **de mauvais** ~ [gaîté] not genuine; [plaisanterie] in bad taste.

alors [alɔr] *adv* [jadis] then, at that time. || [à ce moment-là] then. || [exprimant la conséquence] then, so; **il va se mettre en colère** — **et** ~? he'll be angry — so what? || [emploi expressif] well (then); ~, **qu'est-ce qu'on fait?** well, what are we doing?; **ça** ~! well fancy that! ○ **alors que** *loc conj* [exprimant le temps] while, when. || [exprimant l'opposition] even though; **elle est sortie** ~ **que c'était interdit** she went out even though it was forbidden; **ils aiment le café** ~ **que nous, nous buvons du thé** they like coffee whereas we drink tea.

alouette [alwɛt] *nf* lark.

alourdir [alurdir] *vt* [gén] to weigh down, to make heavy. || *fig* [impôts] to increase.

aloyau [alwajo] *nm* sirloin.

Alpes [alp] *nfpl*: **les** ~ the Alps.

alphabet [alfabɛ] *nm* alphabet.

alphabétique [alfabetik] *adj* alphabetical.

alphabétiser [alfabetize] *vt*: ~ **qqn** to teach sb (how) to read and write.

alpin, -e [alpɛ̃, in] *adj* alpine.

alpinisme [alpinism] *nm* mountaineering.

alter ego [altɛrego] *nm inv* alter ego.

altérer [altere] *vt* [détériorer] to spoil. || [santé] to harm, to affect; [vérité, récit] to distort. ○ **s'altérer** *vp* [matière - métal] to deteriorate; [- aliment] to go off, to spoil. || [santé] to deteriorate.

alternance [altɛrnɑ̃s] *nf* [succession] alternation; **en ~** alternately. || POLIT change of government party.

alternatif, -ive [altɛrnatif, iv] *adj* [périodique] alternating. || [parallèle] alternative. ○ **alternative** *nf* alternative.

alternativement [altɛrnativmɑ̃] *adv* alternately.

alterner [altɛrne] *vi* [se succéder]: **~ (avec)** to alternate (with).

altitude [altityd] *nf* altitude, height; **en ~ at** (high) altitude.

alto [alto] *nm* [MUS - voix] alto; [- instrument] viola.

aluminium [alyminjɔm] *nm* aluminium *Br*, aluminum *Am*.

alvéole [alveɔl] *nf* [cavité] cavity. || [de ruche, poumon] alveolus.

amabilité [amabilite] *nf* kindness; **avoir l'~ de faire qqch** to be so kind as to do sthg.

amadouer [amadwe] *vt* [adoucir] to tame, to pacify; [persuader] to coax.

amaigrir [amegrir] *vt* to make thin or thinner.

amaigrissant, -e [amegrisɑ̃, ɑ̃t] *adj* reducing (*avant n*) *Am*.

amaigrissement [amegrismɑ̃] *nm* loss of weight.

amalgame [amalgam] *nm* TECHNOL amalgam. || [de styles] mixture. || [d'idées, de notions]: **il ne faut pas faire l'~ entre ces deux questions** the two issues must not be confused.

amalgamer [amalgame] *vt* to combine.

amande [amɑ̃d] *nf* almond.

amandier [amɑ̃dje] *nm* almond tree.

amant [amɑ̃] *nm* lover.

amarre [amar] *nf* rope, cable.

amarrer [amare] *vt* NAVIG to moor.

amas [ama] *nm* pile.

amasser [amase] *vt* [objets] to pile up. || [argent] to accumulate.

amateur [amatœr] *nm* [connaisseur - d'art, de bon café]: **~ de** lover of. || [nonprofessionnel] amateur; **faire qqch en ~** to do sthg as a hobby. || *péj* [dilettante] amateur.

amazone [amazon] *nf* horsewoman; **monter en ~** to ride sidesaddle.

Amazonie [amazoni] *nf*: **l'~** the Amazon (Basin).

amazonien, -ienne [amazonjɛ̃, jɛn] *adj* Amazonian; **la forêt ~ne** the Amazon rain forest.

ambassade [ɑ̃basad] *nf* embassy.

ambassadeur, -drice [ɑ̃basadœr, dris] *nm, f* ambassador.

ambiance [ɑ̃bjɑ̃s] *nf* atmosphere.

ambiant, -e [ɑ̃bjɑ̃, ɑ̃t] *adj*: **température ~e** room temperature.

ambidextre [ɑ̃bidɛkstr] *adj* ambidextrous.

ambigu, -uë [ɑ̃bigy] *adj* ambiguous.

ambiguïté [ɑ̃biɡɥite] *nf* ambiguity.

ambitieux, -ieuse [ɑ̃bisjø, jøz] *adj* ambitious.

ambition [ɑ̃bisjɔ̃] *nf* *péj* [arrivisme] ambitiousness. || [désir] ambition; **avoir l'~ de faire qqch** to have an ambition to do sthg.

ambivalent, -e [ɑ̃bivalɑ̃, ɑ̃t] *adj* ambivalent.

ambre [ɑ̃br] *nm* [couleur] amber. || [matière]: **~ (gris)** ambergris.

ambré, -e [ɑ̃bre] *adj* [couleur] amber.

ambulance [ɑ̃bylɑ̃s] *nf* ambulance.

ambulancier, -ière [ɑ̃bylɑ̃sje, jɛr] *nm, f* ambulanceman (*f* ambulancewoman).

ambulant, -e [ɑ̃bylɑ̃, ɑ̃t] *adj* travelling (*avant n*).

âme [ɑm] *nf* [gén] soul; **~ sœur** soulmate. || [caractère] spirit, soul.

amélioration [ameljɔrasjɔ̃] *nf* improvement.

améliorer [ameljɔre] *vt* to improve. ○ **s'améliorer** *vp* to improve.

aménagement [amenaʒmɑ̃] *nm* [de lieu] fitting out.

aménager [amenaʒe] *vt* [pièce] to fit out. || [programme] to plan, to organize.

amende [amɑ̃d] *nf* fine.

amendement [amɑ̃dmɑ̃] *nm* POLIT amendment.

amender [amɑ̃de] *vt* POLIT to amend. || AGRIC to enrich. ○ **s'amender** *vp* to mend one's ways.

amener [amne] *vt* [mener] to bring. || [inciter]: **~ qqn à faire qqch** [suj: circonstances] to lead sb to do sthg; [suj: personne] to get sb to do sthg. || [occasionner, préparer] to bring about.

amenuiser [amənɥize] *vt* [réduire] to diminish, to reduce. ○ **s'amenuiser** *vp* to dwindle, to diminish.

amer, -ère [amer] *adj* bitter.

américain, -e [amerikɛ̃, ɛn] *adj* American. ○ **américain** *nm* [langue] American English. ○ **Américain, -e** *nm, f* American.

américanisme [amerikanism] *nm* Americanism.

Amérique [amerik] *nf*: l'~ America; l'~ **centrale** Central America; l'~ **du Nord** North America; l'~ **du Sud** South America; l'~ **latine** Latin America.

amertume [amɛrtym] *nf* bitterness.

améthyste [ametist] *nf* amethyst.

ameublement [amœbləmɑ̃] *nm* [meubles] furniture; [action de meubler] furnishing.

ami, -e [ami] 1 *adj* friendly. 2 *nm, f* [camarade] friend; **petit ~** boyfriend; **petite ~e** girlfriend.

amiable [amjabl] *adj* [accord] friendly, informal. ○ **à l'amiable** *loc adv & loc adj* out of court.

amiante [amjɑ̃t] *nm* asbestos.

amical, -e, -aux [amikal, o] *adj* friendly. ○ **amicale** *nf* association, club (*for people with a shared interest*).

amicalement [amikalmɑ̃] *adv* [de façon amicale] amicably, in a friendly way. || [dans une lettre] yours (ever), (with) best wishes.

amidon [amidɔ̃] *nm* starch.

amidonner [amidɔne] *vt* to starch.

amincissant, -e [amɛ̃sisɑ̃, ɑ̃t] *adj* slimming.

amiral, -aux [amiral, o] *nm* admiral.

amitié [amitje] *nf* [affection] affection; **prendre qqn en ~** to befriend sb. || [rapports amicaux] friendship; **faire ses ~s à qqn** to give sb one's good ou best wishes.

ammoniac, -iaque [amɔnjak] *adj* CHIM ammoniac. ○ **ammoniac** *nm* ammonia. ○ **ammoniaque** *nf* ammonia (water).

amnésie [amnezi] *nf* amnesia.

amniocentèse [amnjɔsɛtɛz] *nf* amniocentesis.

amnistie [amnisti] *nf* amnesty.

amnistier [amnistje] *vt* to amnesty.

amoindrir [amwɛ̃drir] *vt* to diminish.

amonceler [amɔ̃sle] *vt* to accumulate.

amont [amɔ̃] *nm* upstream (water); **en ~ de** [rivière] upriver ou upstream from; *fig* prior to.

amoral, -e, -aux [amɔral, o] *adj* [qui ignore la morale] amoral.

amorce [amɔrs] *nf* [d'explosif] priming; [de cartouche, d'obus] cap. || PÊCHE bait. || *fig* [commencement] beginnings (*pl*), germ.

amorcer [amɔrse] *vt* [explosif] to prime. || PÊCHE to bait. || *fig* [commencer] to begin, to initiate.

amorphe [amɔrf] *adj* [personne] lifeless.

amortir [amɔrtir] *vt* [atténuer - choc] to absorb; [- bruit] to deaden, to muffle. || [dette] to pay off. || [achat] to write off.

amour [amur] *nm* [gén] love; **faire l'~ à** make love. ○ **amours** *nfpl* [vie sentimentale] love-life.

amoureux, -euse [amurø, øz] 1 *adj* [personne] in love; **être/tomber ~ (de)** to be/fall in love (with). || [regard, geste] loving. 2 *nm, f* [prétendant] suitor.

amour-propre [amurprɔpr] *nm* pride, self-respect.

amovible [amɔvibl] *adj* [déplaçable] detachable, removable.

ampère [ɑ̃pɛr] *nm* amp, ampere.

amphétamine [ɑ̃fetamin] *nf* amphetamine.

amphithéâtre [ɑ̃fiteatr] *nm* HIST amphitheatre. || [d'université] lecture hall ou theatre.

ample [ɑ̃pl] *adj* [vêtement - gén] loose-fitting; [- jupe] full. || [projet] extensive; **pour de plus ~s informations** for further details. || [geste] broad, sweeping.

amplement [ɑ̃pləmɑ̃] *adv* [largement] fully, amply.

ampleur [ɑ̃plœr] *nf* [de vêtement] fullness. || [d'événement, de dégâts] extent.

ampli [ɑ̃pli] *nm* amp.

amplificateur, -trice [ɑ̃plifikatœr, tris] *adj* ÉLECTR amplifying. ○ **amplificateur** *nm* [gén] amplifier.

amplifier [ɑ̃plifje] *vt* [mouvement, son] to amplify; [image] to magnify, to enlarge. || [scandale] to increase; [événement, problème] to highlight.

amplitude [ɑ̃plityd] *nf* [de geste] fullness. || [d'onde] amplitude. || [de température] range.

ampoule [ɑ̃pul] *nf* [de lampe] bulb. || [sur la peau] blister. || [médicament] ampoule, phial.

amputation [ɑ̃pytasjɔ̃] *nf* MÉD amputation.

amputer [ɑ̃pyte] *vt* MÉD to amputate; *fig* [couper] to cut (back ou down).

amulette [amylɛt] *nf* amulet.

amusant, -e [amyzɑ̃, ɑ̃t] *adj* [drôle] funny; [distrayant] amusing; **c'est très ~** it's great fun.

amuse-gueule [amyzgœl] *nm inv fam* cocktail snack, (party) nibble.

amusement [amyzmɑ̃] *nm* amusement (*U*).

amuser [amyze] *vt* to amuse, to entertain. ○ **s'amuser** *vp* to have fun, to have a good time; **s'~ à faire qqch** to amuse o.s. (by) doing sthg.

amygdale [amidal] *nf* tonsil.

an [ɑ̃] *nm* year; **avoir sept ~s** to be seven (years old); **en l'~ 2000** in the year 2000; **le nouvel ~** the New Year.

anachronique [anakrɔnik] *adj* anachronistic.

anagramme [anagram] *nf* anagram.

anal, -e, -aux [anal, o] *adj* anal.

analgésique [analʒezik] *nm & adj* analgesic.

analogie [analɔʒi] *nf* analogy.

analogique [analɔʒik] *adj* analogue.

analogue [analɔg] *adj* analogous, comparable.

analphabète [analfabɛt] *nmf & adj* illiterate.

analyse [analiz] *nf* [étude] analysis. || CHIM & MÉD test, analysis. || [psychanalyse] analysis (*U*).

analyser [analize] *vt* [étudier, psychanalyser] to analyse. || CHIM & MÉD to test, to analyse.

analyste [analist] *nmf* analyst.

analyste-programmeur, -euse [analistprɔgramœr, øz] *nm, f* systems analyst.

analytique [analitik] *adj* analytical.

ananas [anana(s)] *nm* pineapple.

anarchie [anarʃi] *nf* POLIT anarchy. || [désordre] chaos, anarchy.

anarchique [anarʃik] *adj* anarchic.

anarchiste [anarʃist] *nmf & adj* anarchist.

anatomie [anatɔmi] *nf* anatomy.

anatomique [anatɔmik] *adj* anatomical.

ancestral, -e, -aux [ɑ̃sɛstral, o] *adj* ancestral.

ancêtre [ɑ̃sɛtr] *nmf* [aïeul] ancestor; *fig* [forme première] forerunner, ancestor.

anchois [ɑ̃ʃwa] *nm* anchovy.

ancien, -ienne [ɑ̃sjɛ̃, jɛn] *adj* [gén] old. || (*avant n*) [précédent] former, old. || [du passé] ancient.

anciennement [ɑ̃sjɛnmɑ̃] *adv* formerly, previously.

ancienneté [ɑ̃sjɛnte] *nf* [d'une tradition] oldness. || [d'un employé] seniority.

ancre [ɑ̃kr] *nf* NAVIG anchor; **jeter l'~** to drop anchor; **lever l'~** to weigh anchor; *fam* [partir] to make tracks.

ancrer [ɑ̃kre] *vt* [bateau] to anchor; *fig* [idée, habitude] to root.

Andes [ɑ̃d] *nfpl*: **les ~** the Andes.

andouille [ɑ̃duj] *nf* [charcuterie] *type of sausage made of chitterlings (pig's intestines)*. || *fam* [imbécile] prat, twit.

âne [an] *nm* ZOOL ass, donkey. || *fam* [imbécile] ass.

anéantir [aneɑ̃tir] *vt* [détruire] to annihilate; *fig* to ruin, to wreck. || [démoraliser] to crush, to overwhelm.

anecdote [anɛkdɔt] *nf* anecdote.

anecdotique [anɛkdɔtik] *adj* anecdotal.

anémie [anemi] *nf* MÉD anaemia; *fig* enfeeblement.

anémié, -e [anemje] *adj* anaemic.

anémique [anemik] *adj* anaemic.

anémone [anemɔn] *nf* anemone.

ânerie [anri] *nf fam* [parole, acte]: **dire/faire une ~** to say/do something stupid.

ânesse [anɛs] *nf* she-ass, she-donkey.

anesthésie [anɛstezi] *nf* anaesthesia; **~ locale/générale** local/general anaesthetic.

anesthésier [anɛstezje] *vt* to anaesthetize.

anesthésique [anɛstezik] *nm & adj* anaesthetic.

anesthésiste [anɛstezist] *nmf* anaesthetist.

ange [ɑ̃ʒ] *nm* angel; **~ gardien** guardian angel; **être aux ~s** *fig* to be in one's seventh heaven.

angélique [ɑ̃ʒelik] *adj* angelic.

angélus [ɑ̃ʒelys] *nm* [sonnerie] angelus (bell).

angine [ɑ̃ʒin] *nf* [pharyngite] pharyngitis; [amygdalite] tonsillitis.

anglais, -e [ɑ̃glɛ, ɛz] *adj* English. ○ **anglais** *nm* [langue] English. ○ **Anglais, -e** *nm, f* Englishman (*f* Englishwoman); **les Anglais** the English. ○ **anglaises** *nfpl* ringlets.

angle [ɑ̃gl] *nm* [coin] corner. || MATHS angle; **~ droit/aigu/obtus** right/acute/obtuse angle.

Angleterre [ɑ̃glətɛr] *nf*: **l'~** England.

anglican, -e [ɑ̃glikɑ̃, an] *adj & nm, f* Anglican.

anglophone [ɑ̃glɔfɔn] **1** *nmf* English-speaker. **2** *adj* English-speaking, anglophone.

anglo-saxon, -onne [ɑ̃glosaksɔ̃, ɔn] *adj* Anglo-Saxon. ○ **Anglo-Saxon, -onne** *nm, f* Anglo-Saxon.

angoisse [ɑ̃gwas] *nf* anguish.

angoisser [ɑ̃gwase] *vt* [effrayer] to

cause anxiety to. ○ **s'angoisser** *vp* [être anxieux] to be overcome with anxiety.

anguille [ɑ̃gij] *nf* eel.

anguleux, -euse [ɑ̃gylø, øz] *adj* angular.

anicroche [anikrɔʃ] *nf* hitch.

animal, -e, -aux [animal, o] *adj* [propre à l'animal] animal (*avant n*). || [instinctif] instinctive. ○ **animal** *nm* [bête] animal; ~ **sauvage/domestique** wild/domestic animal.

animateur, -trice [animatœr, tris] *nm, f* RADIO & TÉLÉ presenter. || [socioculturel, sportif] activities organizer.

animation [animasjɔ̃] *nf* [de rue] activity, life; [de conversation, visage] animation. || [activités] activities (*pl*). || CIN animation.

animé, -e [anime] *adj* [rue] lively; [conversation, visage] animated; [objet] animate.

animer [anime] *vt* [mettre de l'entrain dans] to animate, to liven up. || [présenter] to present. || [organiser des activités pour] to organize activities for. ○ **s'animer** *vp* [visage] to light up. || [rue] to come to life, to liven up.

animosité [animozite] *nf* animosity.

anis [ani(s)] *nm* BOT anise; CULIN aniseed.

ankylosé, -e [ɑ̃kiloze] *adj* [paralysé] stiff; [engourdi] numb.

annales [anal] *nfpl* [d'examen] past papers.

anneau, -x [ano] *nm* [gén] ring. || [maillon] link.

année [ane] *nf* year; **souhaiter la bonne ~ à qqn** to wish sb a Happy New Year; ~ **bissextile** leap year; **~-lumière** light year; ~ **scolaire** school year.

annexe [anɛks] **1** *nf* [de dossier] appendix, annexe. || [de bâtiment] annexe. **2** *adj* related, associated.

annexer [anekse] *vt* [incorporer]: ~ **qqch (à qqch)** to append ou annex sthg (to sthg). || [pays] to annex.

annexion [anɛksjɔ̃] *nf* annexation.

annihiler [aniile] *vt* [réduire à néant] to destroy, to wreck.

anniversaire [aniverser] *nm* [de mariage, mort, événement] anniversary; [de naissance] birthday; **bon** ou **joyeux ~!** happy birthday!

annonce [anɔ̃s] *nf* [déclaration] announcement; *fig* sign, indication. || [texte] advertisement; **petite ~** classified advertisement, small ad.

annoncer [anɔ̃se] *vt* [faire savoir] to announce. || [prédire] to predict.

annoter [anɔte] *vt* to annotate.

annuaire [anɥɛr] *nm* annual, yearbook; ~ **téléphonique** telephone directory, phone book.

annuel, -elle [anɥɛl] *adj* [tous les ans] annual, yearly. || [d'une année] annual.

annuité [anɥite] *nf* [paiement] annual payment ou instalment. || [année de service] year (of service).

annulaire [anɥlɛr] *nm* ring finger.

annulation [anylasjɔ̃] *nf* [de rendez-vous, réservation] cancellation. || [de mariage] annulment.

annuler [anyle] *vt* [rendez-vous, réservation] to cancel. || [mariage] to annul.

anoblir [anɔblir] *vt* to ennoble.

anodin, -e [anɔdɛ̃, in] *adj* [blessure] minor. || [propos] harmless. || [détail, personne] insignificant.

anomalie [anɔmali] *nf* anomaly.

ânonner [anɔne] *vt & vi* to recite in a drone.

anonymat [anɔnima] *nm* anonymity.

anonyme [anɔnim] *adj* anonymous.

anorak [anɔrak] *nm* anorak.

anorexie [anɔrɛksi] *nf* anorexia.

anormal, -e, -aux [anɔrmal, o] **1** *adj* [inhabituel] abnormal, not normal. || [intolérable, injuste] wrong, not right. || [arriéré] (mentally) subnormal. **2** *nm, f* mental defective.

ANPE (*abr de* **Agence nationale pour l'emploi**) *nf French national employment agency*; ≈ job centre *Br*.

anse [ɑ̃s] *nf* [d'ustensile] handle. || GÉOGR cove.

antagoniste [ɑ̃tagɔnist] *adj* antagonistic.

antarctique [ɑ̃tarktik] *adj* Antarctic; **le cercle polaire ~** the Antarctic Circle. ○ **Antarctique** *nm* [continent]: **l'~** Antarctica. || [océan]: **l'~** the Antarctic (Ocean).

antécédent [ɑ̃tesedɑ̃] *nm* (*gén pl*) [passé] history (*sg*).

antenne [ɑ̃tɛn] *nf* [d'insecte] antenna, feeler. || [de télévision, de radio] aerial *Br*, antenna. || [succursale] branch, office.

antérieur, -e [ɑ̃terjœr] *adj* [dans le temps] earlier, previous; ~ **à** previous ou prior to. || [dans l'espace] front (*avant n*).

antérieurement [ɑ̃terjœrmɑ̃] *adv* earlier, previously; ~ **à** prior to.

anthologie [ɑ̃tɔlɔʒi] *nf* anthology.

anthracite [ɑ̃trasit] 1 *nm* anthracite. 2 *adj inv* charcoal (grey).

anthropologie [ɑ̃trɔpɔlɔʒi] *nf* anthropology.

anthropophage [ɑ̃trɔpɔfaʒ] *nmf* cannibal.

antibiotique [ɑ̃tibjɔtik] *nm & adj* antibiotic.

antibrouillard [ɑ̃tibrujar] *nm & adj inv*: (phare ou feu) ~ fog lamp *Br*, foglight *Am*.

antichambre [ɑ̃tiʃɑ̃br] *nf* antechamber.

anticipation [ɑ̃tisipasjɔ̃] *nf* LITTÉRATURE: roman d'~ science fiction novel.

anticipé, -e [ɑ̃tisipe] *adj* early.

anticiper [ɑ̃tisipe] 1 *vt* to anticipate. 2 *vi*: ~ (sur qqch) to anticipate (sthg).

anticonformiste [ɑ̃tikɔ̃fɔrmist] *adj & nmf* non-conformist.

anticorps [ɑ̃tikɔr] *nm* antibody.

anticyclone [ɑ̃tisiklon] *nm* anticyclone.

antidater [ɑ̃tidate] *vt* to backdate.

antidépresseur [ɑ̃tidepresœr] *nm & adj m* antidepressant.

antidote [ɑ̃tidɔt] *nm* antidote.

antigel [ɑ̃tiʒɛl] *nm inv & adj inv* antifreeze.

antillais, -e [ɑ̃tijɛ, ɛz] *adj* West Indian. ○ **Antillais, -e** *nm, f* West Indian.

Antilles [ɑ̃tij] *nfpl*: les ~ the West Indies.

antilope [ɑ̃tilɔp] *nf* antelope.

antimilitariste [ɑ̃timilitarist] *nmf & adj* antimilitarist.

antimite [ɑ̃timit] *adj inv*: boule ~ mothball.

antipathie [ɑ̃tipati] *nf* antipathy, hostility.

antipathique [ɑ̃tipatik] *adj* unpleasant; elle m'est ~ I dislike her, I don't like her.

antipelliculaire [ɑ̃tipelikyler] *adj*: shampooing ~ anti-dandruff shampoo.

antiphrase [ɑ̃tifraz] *nf* antiphrasis.

antiquaire [ɑ̃tiker] *nmf* antique dealer.

antique [ɑ̃tik] *adj* [de l'antiquité - civilisation] ancient; [- vase, objet] antique. || [vieux] antiquated, ancient.

antiquité [ɑ̃tikite] *nf* [époque]: l'Antiquité antiquity. || [objet] antique.

antirides [ɑ̃tirid] *adj inv* anti-wrinkle.

antirouille [ɑ̃tiruj] *adj inv* [traitement] rust (*avant n*); [revêtement, peinture] rustproof.

antisèche [ɑ̃tisɛʃ] *nm & nf arg scol* crib *Br*, cheat sheet *Am*.

antisémite [ɑ̃tisemit] 1 *nmf* anti-Semite. 2 *adj* anti-Semitic.

antiseptique [ɑ̃tiseptik] *nm & adj* antiseptic.

antisismique [ɑ̃tisismik] *adj* earthquake-proof.

antithèse [ɑ̃titɛz] *nf* antithesis.

antiviral, -aux [ɑ̃tiviral, o] *nm* antivirus.

antivol [ɑ̃tivɔl] *nm inv* anti-theft device.

antre [ɑ̃tr] *nm* den, lair.

anus [anys] *nm* anus.

anxiété [ɑ̃ksjete] *nf* anxiety.

anxieux, -ieuse [ɑ̃ksjø, jøz] 1 *adj* anxious, worried; être ~ de faire qqch to be anxious to do sthg. 2 *nm, f* worrier.

aorte [aɔrt] *nf* aorta.

août [u(t)] *nm* August; *voir aussi* septembre.

apaisement [apɛzmɑ̃] *nm* [moral] comfort. || [de douleur] alleviation. || [de tension, de crise] calming.

apaiser [apeze] *vt* [personne] to calm down, to pacify. || [conscience] to salve; [douleur] to soothe; [soif] to slake, to quench; [faim] to assuage. ○ **s'apaiser** *vp* [personne] to calm down. || [besoin] to be assuaged; [tempête] to subside, to abate; [douleur] to die down.

apanage [apanaʒ] *nm sout* privilege; être l'~ de qqn/qqch to be the prerogative of sb/sthg.

aparté [aparte] *nm* THÉÂTRE aside. || [conversation] private conversation; prendre qqn en ~ to take sb aside.

apartheid [aparted] *nm* apartheid.

apathie [apati] *nf* apathy.

apathique [apatik] *adj* apathetic.

apatride [apatrid] *nmf* stateless person.

apercevoir [apersǝvwar] *vt* [voir] to see, to catch sight of. ○ **s'apercevoir** *vp*: s'~ de qqch to notice sthg; s'~ que to notice (that).

aperçu, -e [apersy] *pp* → apercevoir. ○ **aperçu** *nm* general idea.

apéritif [aperitif] *nm* aperitif; prendre l'~ to have an aperitif, to have drinks (*before a meal*).

apesanteur [apǝzɑ̃tœr] *nf* weightlessness.

à-peu-près [apøprɛ] *nm inv* approximation.

aphone [afɔn] *adj* voiceless.

aphrodisiaque [afrɔdizjak] *nm & adj* aphrodisiac.

aphte [aft] *nm* mouth ulcer.

apitoyer [apitwaje] *vt* to move to pity. ○ **s'apitoyer** *vp* to feel pity; **s'~ sur** to feel sorry for.

ap. J.-C. (*abr de* après Jésus-Christ) AD.

aplanir [aplanir] *vt* [aplatir] to level. || *fig* [difficulté, obstacle] to smooth away, to iron out.

aplatir [aplatir] *vt* [gén] to flatten; [couture] to press flat; [cheveux] to smooth down.

aplomb [aplɔ̃] *nm* [stabilité] balance. || [audace] nerve, cheek. ○ **d'aplomb** *loc adv* steady.

apocalypse [apɔkalips] *nf* apocalypse.

apogée [apɔʒe] *nm* ASTRON apogee; *fig* peak.

apolitique [apɔlitik] *adj* apolitical, unpolitical.

apologie [apɔlɔʒi] *nf* justification, apology.

apoplexie [apɔplɛksi] *nf* apoplexy.

apostrophe [apɔstrɔf] *nf* [signe graphique] apostrophe.

apostropher [apɔstrɔfe] *vt*: **~ qqn** to speak rudely to sb.

apothéose [apɔteoz] *nf* [point culminant - d'un spectacle] grand finale; [- d'une carrière] crowning glory.

apôtre [apotr] *nm* apostle, disciple.

apparaître [aparɛtr] *vi* [gén] to appear. || [se dévoiler] to come to light.

apparat [apara] *nm* pomp; **d'~** [dîner, habit] ceremonial.

appareil [aparɛj] *nm* [gén] device; [électrique] appliance. || [téléphone] phone, telephone; **qui est à l'~?** who's speaking? || [avion] aircraft. ○ **appareil digestif** *nm* digestive system. ○ **appareil photo** *nm* camera.

appareillage [aparɛjaʒ] *nm* [équipement] equipment. || NAVIG getting under way.

appareiller [apareje] **1** *vt* [assortir] to match up. **2** *vi* NAVIG to get under way.

apparemment [aparamɑ̃] *adv* apparently.

apparence [aparɑ̃s] *nf* appearance. ○ **en apparence** *loc adv* seemingly, apparently.

apparent, -e [aparɑ̃, ɑ̃t] *adj* [superficiel, illusoire] apparent. || [visible] visible.

apparenté, -e [aparɑ̃te] *adj*: **~ à** [personne] related to; *fig* [ressemblant] similar to.

apparition [aparisjɔ̃] *nf* [gén] appearance. || [vision - RELIG] vision; [- de fantôme] apparition.

appart [apart] (*abr de* appartement) *nm fam* flat *Br*, apartment *Am*.

appartement [apartəmɑ̃] *nm* flat *Br*, apartment *Am*.

appartenir [apartənir] *vi* [être la propriété de]: **~ à qqn** to belong to sb. || [faire partie de]: **~ à qqch** to belong to sthg, to be a member of sthg.

appartenu [apartəny] *pp inv* → appartenir.

apparu, -e [apary] *pp* → apparaître.

appâter [apate] *vt litt & fig* to lure.

appauvrir [apovrir] *vt* to impoverish. ○ **s'appauvrir** *vp* to grow poorer, to become impoverished.

appel [apɛl] *nm* [gén] call; **faire ~ à qqn** to appeal to sb; **faire ~ à qqch** [avoir recours à] to call on sthg; **~ (téléphonique)** (phone) call. || JUR appeal; **faire ~** JUR to appeal. || [pour vérifier - gén] roll-call; [- SCOL] registration. || COMM: **~ d'offre** invitation to tender. || [signe]: **faire un ~ de phares** to flash one's headlights.

appelé [aple] *nm* conscript.

appeler [aple] *vt* [gén] to call. || [téléphoner] to ring, to call. || [exiger] to call for. ○ **s'appeler** *vp* [se nommer] to be called; **il s'appelle Patrick** his name is Patrick, he's called Patrick. || [se téléphoner]: **on s'appelle demain?** shall we talk tomorrow?

appendice [apɛ̃dis] *nm* appendix.

appendicite [apɛ̃disit] *nf* appendicitis.

appentis [apɑ̃ti] *nm* lean-to.

appesantir [apəzɑ̃tir] ○ **s'appesantir** *vp* [s'alourdir] to become heavy. || [insister]: **s'~ sur qqch** to dwell on sthg.

appétissant, -e [apetisɑ̃, ɑ̃t] *adj* [nourriture] appetizing.

appétit [apeti] *nm* appetite; **bon ~!** enjoy your meal!

applaudir [aplodir] **1** *vt* to applaud. **2** *vi* to clap, to applaud; **~ à qqch** *fig* to applaud sthg; **~ à tout rompre** *fig* to bring the house down.

applaudissements [aplodismɑ̃] *nmpl* applause (*U*), clapping (*U*).

application [aplikasjɔ̃] *nf* [gén & INFORM] application.

applique [aplik] *nf* wall lamp.

appliquer [aplike] *vt* [gén] to apply; [loi] to enforce. ○ **s'appliquer** *vp* [s'étaler, se poser]: **cette peinture s'applique facilement** this paint goes on easily.

|| [se concentrer]: **s'~ (à faire qqch)** to apply o.s. (to doing sthg).

appoint [apwɛ̃] *nm* [monnaie] change; **faire l'~** to give the right money; **d'~** [salaire, chauffage] extra.

appointements [apwɛ̃tmɑ̃] *nmpl* salary (*sg*).

apport [apɔr] *nm* [gén & FIN] contribution. || [de chaleur] input.

apporter [apɔrte] *vt* [gén] to bring. || [raison, preuve] to provide, to give. || [mettre - soin] to exercise; [- attention] to give.

apposer [apoze] *vt* [affiche] to put up. || [signature] to append.

apposition [apozisjɔ̃] *nf* GRAM apposition.

appréciable [apresjabl] *adj* [notable] appreciable. || [précieux]: **un grand jardin, c'est ~!** I/we really appreciate having a big garden.

appréciation [apresjasjɔ̃] *nf* [de valeur] valuation; [de distance, poids] estimation. || [jugement] judgment. || SCOL assessment.

apprécier [apresje] *vt* [gén] to appreciate. || [évaluer] to estimate, to assess.

appréhender [apreɑ̃de] *vt* [arrêter] to arrest. || [craindre]: **~ qqch/de faire qqch** to dread sthg/doing sthg.

appréhension [apreɑ̃sjɔ̃] *nf* apprehension.

apprendre [aprɑ̃dr] *vt* [étudier] to learn; **~ à faire qqch** to learn (how) to do sthg. || [enseigner] to teach; **~ qqch à qqn** to teach sb sthg; **~ à qqn à faire qqch** to teach sb (how) to do sthg. || [nouvelle] to hear of, to learn of; **~ que** to hear that, to learn that; **~ qqch à qqn** to tell sb of sthg.

apprenti, -e [aprɑ̃ti] *nm, f* [élève] apprentice; *fig* beginner.

apprentissage [aprɑ̃tisaʒ] *nm* [de métier] apprenticeship. || [formation] learning.

apprêter [aprete] *vt* to prepare. ○ **s'apprêter** *vp* [être sur le point]: **s'~ à faire qqch** to get ready to do sthg.

appris, -e [apri, iz] *pp* → **apprendre**.

apprivoiser [aprivwaze] *vt* to tame.

approbateur, -trice [aprɔbatœr, tris] *adj* approving.

approbation [aprɔbasjɔ̃] *nf* approval.

approchant, -e [aprɔʃɑ̃, ɑ̃t] *adj* similar.

approche [aprɔʃ] *nf* [arrivée] approach;

à l'~ **des fêtes** as the Christmas holidays draw near.

approcher [aprɔʃe] **1** *vt* [mettre plus près] to move near, to bring near; **~ qqch de qqn/qqch** to move sthg near (to) sb/ sthg. || [aborder] to go up to, to approach. **2** *vi* to approach, to go/come near; **n'approchez pas!** keep or stay away!; **~ de** [moment, fin] to approach. ○ **s'approcher** *vp* to come/go near, to approach; **s'~ de qqn/qqch** to approach sb/sthg.

approfondir [aprɔfɔ̃dir] *vt* [creuser] to make deeper. || [développer] to go further into.

approprié, -e [aprɔprije] *adj*: **~ (à)** appropriate (to).

approprier [aprɔprije] *vt* [adapter] to adapt. || *Belg* to clean. ○ **s'approprier** *vp* [s'adjuger] to appropriate.

approuver [apruve] *vt* [gén] to approve of.

approvisionnement [aprɔvizjɔnmɑ̃] *nm* supplies (*pl*), stocks (*pl*).

approvisionner [aprɔvizjɔne] *vt* [compte en banque] to pay money into. || [magasin, pays] to supply.

approximatif, -ive [aprɔksimatif, iv] *adj* approximate, rough.

approximation [aprɔksimasjɔ̃] *nf* approximation.

approximativement [aprɔksimativmɑ̃] *adv* approximately, roughly.

appt *abr de* **appartement**.

appui [apɥi] *nm* [soutien] support.

appui-tête [apɥitɛt] (*pl* **appuis-tête**) *nm* headrest.

appuyer [apɥije] **1** *vt* [poser]: **~ qqch sur/contre qqch** to lean sthg on/against sthg, to rest sthg on/against sthg. || [presser]: **~ qqch sur/contre** to press sthg on/ against. || *fig* [soutenir] to support. **2** *vi* [reposer]: **~ sur** to lean or rest on. || [presser]: **~ sur** to push; **~ sur** [bouton] to press. || *fig* [insister]: **~ sur** to stress. ○ **s'appuyer** *vp* [se tenir]: **s'~ contre/sur** to lean against/on, to rest against/on. || [se baser]: **s'~ sur** to rely on.

âpre [apr] *adj* [goût, discussion, combat] bitter. || [ton, épreuve, critique] harsh. || [concurrence] fierce.

après [apre] **1** *prép* [gén] after; **~ avoir mangé, ils ...** after having eaten or after they had eaten, they ...; **~ quoi** after which. || [indiquant l'attirance, l'attachement, l'hostilité]: **aboyer ~ qqn** to bark at sb. **2** *adv* [temps] afterwards; **un**

mois ~ one month later; **le mois d'~** the following ou next month. || [lieu, dans un ordre, dans un rang]: **la rue d'~** the next street; **c'est ma sœur qui vient** ~ my sister's next. ○ **après coup** *loc adv* afterwards, after the event. ○ **après que** *loc conj* (+ *indicatif*) after; **je le verrai ~ qu'il aura fini** I'll see him after ou when he's finished. ○ **après tout** *loc adv* after all. ○ **d'après** *loc prép* according to; **d'~ moi** in my opinion. ○ **et après** *loc adv* [questionnement sur la suite] and then what? || [exprime l'indifférence] so what?

après-demain [apʀɛdmɛ̃] *adv* the day after tomorrow.

après-guerre [apʀɛgɛʀ] *nm* post-war years (*pl*); **d'~** post-war.

après-midi [apʀɛmidi] *nm inv ou nf inv* afternoon.

après-rasage [apʀɛʀazaʒ] *nm & adj inv* aftershave.

après-ski [apʀɛski] *nm* [chaussure] snow-boot.

après-soleil [apʀɛsɔlɛj] *adj inv* aftersun (*avant n*).

après-vente [apʀɛvɑ̃t] → **service**.

à-propos [apʀopo] *nm inv* [de remarque] aptness; **faire preuve d'~** to show presence of mind.

apte [apt] *adj*: ~ **à qqch/à faire qqch** capable of doing sthg; ~ **(au service)** MIL fit (for service).

aquarelle [akwaʀɛl] *nf* watercolour.

aquarium [akwaʀjɔm] *nm* aquarium.

aquatique [akwatik] *adj* [plante, animal] aquatic; [milieu, paysage] watery, marshy.

aqueduc [akdyk] *nm* aqueduct.

aqueux, -euse [akø, øz] *adj* watery.

aquilin [akilɛ̃] → **nez**.

arabe [aʀab] **1** *adj* [peuple] Arab. **2** *nm* [langue] Arabic. ○ **Arabe** *nmf* Arab.

arabesque [aʀabɛsk] *nf* [ornement] arabesque. || [ligne sinueuse] flourish.

Arabie [aʀabi] *nf*: **l'~** Arabia; **l'~ Saoudite** Saudi Arabia.

arachide [aʀaʃid] *nf* [plante] groundnut. || [graine] peanut, groundnut.

araignée [aʀɛɲe] *nf* spider. ○ **araignée de mer** *nf* spider crab.

arbalète [aʀbalɛt] *nf* crossbow.

arbitrage [aʀbitʀaʒ] *nm* [SPORT- gén] refereeing; [- au tennis, cricket] umpiring. || JUR arbitration.

arbitraire [aʀbitʀɛʀ] *adj* arbitrary.

arbitre [aʀbitʀ] *nm* [SPORT - gén] referee; [- au tennis, cricket] umpire. || [conciliateur] arbitrator.

arbitrer [aʀbitʀe] *vt* [SPORT - gén] to referee; [- au tennis, cricket] to umpire. || [conflit] to arbitrate.

arbre [aʀbʀ] *nm* BOT & *fig* tree; ~ **fruitier** fruit tree; ~ **généalogique** family tree. || [axe] shaft.

arbuste [aʀbyst] *nm* shrub.

arc [aʀk] *nm* [arme] bow. || [courbe] arc; ~ **de cercle** arc of a circle. || ARCHIT arch.

arcade [aʀkad] *nf* ARCHIT arch; ~**s** arcade (*sg*). || ANAT: ~ **sourcilière** arch of the eyebrows.

arc-bouter [aʀkbute] ○ **s'arc-bouter** *vp* to brace o.s.

arceau, -x [aʀso] *nm* ARCHIT arch. || [objet métallique] hoop.

arc-en-ciel [aʀkɑ̃sjɛl] (*pl* **arcs-en-ciel**) *nm* rainbow.

archaïque [aʀkaik] *adj* archaic.

arche [aʀʃ] *nf* ARCHIT arch.

archéologie [aʀkeɔlɔʒi] *nf* archaeology.

archéologique [aʀkeɔlɔʒik] *adj* archaeological.

archéologue [aʀkeɔlɔg] *nmf* archaeologist.

archet [aʀʃɛ] *nm* MUS bow.

archevêque [aʀʃəvɛk] *nm* archbishop.

archipel [aʀʃipɛl] *nm* archipelago.

architecte [aʀʃitɛkt] *nmf* architect.

architecture [aʀʃitɛktyʀ] *nf* architecture; *fig* structure.

archives [aʀʃiv] *nfpl* [de bureau] records; [de musée] archives.

archiviste [aʀʃivist] *nmf* archivist.

arctique [aʀktik] *adj* Arctic; **le cercle polaire** ~ the Arctic Circle. ○ **Arctique** *nm*: **l'~** the Arctic.

ardemment [aʀdamɑ̃] *adv* fervently, passionately.

ardent, -e [aʀdɑ̃, ɑ̃t] *adj* [soleil] blazing. || [soif, fièvre] raging; [passion] burning.

ardeur [aʀdœʀ] *nf* [vigueur] fervour, enthusiasm. || [chaleur] blazing heat.

ardoise [aʀdwaz] *nf* slate.

ardu, -e [aʀdy] *adj* [travail] arduous; [problème] difficult.

are [aʀ] *nm* 100 square metres.

arène [aʀɛn] *nf* arena. ○ **arènes** *nfpl* [romaines] amphitheatre (*sg*).

arête [aʀɛt] *nf* [de poisson] bone. || [du nez] bridge.

argent [aʀʒɑ̃] *nm* [métal, couleur] silver. || [monnaie] money; ~ **liquide** (ready) cash; ~ **de poche** pocket money.

argenté, -e [arʒɑ̃te] *adj* silvery, silver.

argenterie [arʒɑ̃tri] *nf* silverware.

Argentine [arʒɑ̃tin] *nf*: **l'~** Argentina.

argile [arʒil] *nf* clay.

argileux, -euse [arʒilø, øz] *adj* clayey.

argot [argo] *nm* slang.

argotique [argɔtik] *adj* slang (*avant n*), slangy.

argument [argymɑ̃] *nm* argument.

argumentation [argymɑ̃tasjɔ̃] *nf* argumentation.

argus [argys] *nm*: **coté à l'~** rated in the guide to secondhand car prices.

aride [arid] *adj litt & fig* arid.

aristocrate [aristɔkrat] *nmf* aristocrat.

aristocratie [aristɔkrasi] *nf* aristocracy.

arithmétique [aritmetik] *nf* arithmetic.

armateur [armatœr] *nm* ship owner.

armature [armatyr] *nf* CONSTR & *fig* framework. || [de parapluie] frame; [de soutien-gorge] underwiring.

arme [arm] *nf litt & fig* weapon; **~ blanche** blade; **~ à feu** firearm. ◇ **armes** *nfpl* [blason] coat of arms (*sg*).

armée [arme] *nf* army; **l'~ de l'air** the air force; **l'~ de terre** the army. ◇ **Armée du salut** *nf*: **l'Armée du salut** the Salvation Army.

armement [arməmɑ̃] *nm* [MIL - de personne] arming; [- de pays] armament; [- ensemble d'armes] arms (*pl*); **la course aux ~s** the arms race.

armer [arme] *vt* [pourvoir en armes] to arm; **être armé pour qqch/pour faire qqch** *fig* [préparé] to be equipped for sthg/to do sthg. || [fusil] to cock. || [appareil photo] to wind on. || [navire] to fit out.

armistice [armistis] *nm* armistice.

armoire [armwar] *nf* [gén] closet *Am*; [garde-robe] wardrobe; **c'est une ~ à glace!** *fam fig* he's built like a tank!; **~ à pharmacie** medicine cabinet.

armoiries [armwari] *nfpl* coat of arms (*sg*).

armure [armyr] *nf* armour.

armurier [armyrje] *nm* [d'armes à feu] gunsmith; [d'armes blanches] armourer.

arnaque [arnak] *nf fam* rip-off.

arnaquer [arnake] *vt fam* to do *Br*, to swindle; **se faire ~** to be had.

aromate [arɔmat] *nm* [épice] spice; [fine herbe] herb.

arôme [arom] *nm* [gén] aroma; [de fleur, parfum] fragrance. || [goût] flavour.

arpège [arpɛʒ] *nm* arpeggio.

arpenter [arpɑ̃te] *vt* [marcher] to pace up and down.

arqué, -e [arke] *adj* [jambe] bow (*avant n*), bandy; [sourcil] arched.

arr. *abr de* **arrondissement.**

arrache-pied [araʃpje] ◇ **d'arrache-pied** *loc adv*: **travailler d'~** to work away furiously.

arracher [araʃe] *vt* [extraire - plante] to pull up *ou* out; [- dent] to extract. || [déchirer - page] to tear off *ou* out; [- chemise, bras] to tear off. || [prendre]: **~ qqch à qqn** to snatch sthg from sb. || [soustraire]: **~ qqn à** [milieu, lieu] to drag sb away from; [lit, sommeil] to drag sb from.

arrangeant, -e [arɑ̃ʒɑ̃, ɑ̃t] *adj* obliging.

arrangement [arɑ̃ʒmɑ̃] *nm* [gén] arrangement. || [accord] agreement, arrangement.

arranger [arɑ̃ʒe] *vt* [gén] to arrange. || [convenir à] to suit. || [régler] to settle. || [améliorer] to sort out. || [réparer] to fix. ◇ **s'arranger** *vp* to come to an agreement; **s'~ pour faire qqch** to manage to do sthg; **cela va s'~** things will work out.

arrdt. *abr de* **arrondissement.**

arrestation [arɛstasjɔ̃] *nf* arrest; **être en état d'~** to be under arrest.

arrêt [arɛ] *nm* [d'un mouvement] stopping; **à l'~** [véhicule] stationary; [machine] (switched) off. || [interruption] interruption; **sans ~** [sans interruption] non-stop; [sans relâche] constantly, continually; **être en ~ maladie** to be on sick leave. || [station]: **~ (d'autobus)** (bus) stop. || JUR decision, judgment.

arrêté [arete] *nm* ADMIN order, decree.

arrêter [arete] **1** *vt* [gén] to stop. || [cesser]: **~ de faire qqch** to stop doing sthg; **~ de fumer** to stop smoking. || [voleur] to arrest. **2** *vi* to stop. ◇ **s'arrêter** *vp* to stop; **s'~ de faire** to stop doing.

arrhes [ar] *nfpl* deposit (*sg*).

arrière [arjer] **1** *adj inv* back, rear; **marche ~** reverse gear. **2** *nm* [partie postérieure] back; **à l'~** at the back *Br*, in back *Am*. ◇ **en arrière** *loc adv* [dans la direction opposée] back, backwards. || [derrière, à la traîne] behind; **rester en ~** to lag behind.

arriéré, -e [arjere] *adj* [mentalité, pays] backward. ◇ **arriéré** *nm* arrears (*pl*).

arrière-boutique [arjerbutik] (*pl* **arrière-boutiques**) *nf* back shop.

arrière-garde [arjɛrgard] (*pl* arrière-gardes) *nf* rearguard.

arrière-goût [arjɛrgu] (*pl* arrière-goûts) *nm* aftertaste.

arrière-grand-mère [arjɛrgrɑ̃mɛr] (*pl* arrière-grands-mères) *nf* great-grandmother.

arrière-grand-père [arjɛrgrɑ̃pɛr] (*pl* arrière-grands-pères) *nm* great-grandfather.

arrière-pays [arjɛrpei] *nm inv* hinterland.

arrière-pensée [arjɛrpɑ̃se] (*pl* arrière-pensées) *nf* [raison intéressée] ulterior motive.

arrière-plan [arjɛrplɑ̃] (*pl* arrière-plans) *nm* background.

arrière-saison [arjɛrsezɔ̃] (*pl* arrière-saisons) *nf* late autumn.

arrière-train [arjɛrtrɛ̃] (*pl* arrière-trains) *nm* hindquarters (*pl*).

arrimer [arime] *vt* [attacher] to secure. || NAVIG to stow.

arrivage [arivaʒ] *nm* [de marchandises] consignment, delivery.

arrivée [arive] *nf* [venue] arrival. || TECHNOL inlet.

arriver [arive] 1 *vi* [venir] to arrive; **j'arrive!** (I'm) coming!; **~ à Paris** to arrive in *ou* reach Paris; **l'eau m'arrivait aux genoux** the water came up to my knees. || [parvenir]: **~ à faire qqch** to manage to do sthg, to succeed in doing sthg. 2 *v impers* to happen; **il arrive que** (+ *subjonctif*): **il arrive qu'il soit en retard** he is sometimes late; **il arrive à tout le monde de se tromper** anyone can make a mistake; **il lui arrive d'oublier quel jour on est** he sometimes forgets what day it is; **quoi qu'il arrive** whatever happens.

arrivisme [arivism] *nm péj* ambition.

arrogance [arɔgɑ̃s] *nf* arrogance.

arrogant, -e [arɔgɑ̃, ɑ̃t] *adj* arrogant.

arroger [arɔʒe] ◇ **s'arroger** *vp*: **s'~ le droit de faire qqch** to take it upon o.s. to do sthg.

arrondir [arɔ̃dir] *vt* [forme] to make round. || [chiffre - en haut] to round up; [- en bas] to round down.

arrondissement [arɔ̃dismɑ̃] *nm* ADMIN arrondissement (*administrative division of a département or city*).

arroser [aroze] *vt* [jardin] to water, to spray. || *fam* [célébrer] to celebrate.

arrosoir [arozwar] *nm* watering can.

arsenal, -aux [arsənal, o] *nm* [de navires] naval dockyard. || [d'armes] arsenal.

arsenic [arsənik] *nm* arsenic.

art [ar] *nm* art; **le septième ~** cinema; **~s et métiers** *state-funded institution offering vocational courses by correspondence or evening classes.*

art. *abr de* article.

artère [arter] *nf* ANAT artery. || [rue] arterial road.

artériel, -ielle [arterjɛl] *adj* arterial.

artériosclérose [arterjoskleroz] *nf* arteriosclerosis.

arthrite [artrit] *nf* arthritis.

arthrose [artroz] *nf* osteoarthritis.

artichaut [artiʃo] *nm* artichoke.

article [artikl] *nm* [gén] article. || *loc*: **à l'~ de la mort** at death's door.

articulation [artikylasjɔ̃] *nf* ANAT & TECHNOL joint. || [prononciation] articulation.

articuler [artikyle] *vt* [prononcer] to articulate. || ANAT & TECHNOL to articulate, to joint.

artifice [artifis] *nm* [moyen astucieux] clever device *ou* trick. || [tromperie] trick.

artificiel, -ielle [artifisjɛl] *adj* artificial.

artillerie [artijri] *nf* MIL artillery.

artisan, -e [artizɑ̃, an] *nm, f* craftsman (*f* craftswoman).

artisanal, -e, -aux [artizanal, o] *adj* craft (*avant n*).

artisanat [artizana] *nm* [métier] craft; [classe] craftsmen.

artiste [artist] *nmf* [créateur] artist; **~ peintre** painter. || [interprète] performer.

artistique [artistik] *adj* artistic.

as¹ [a] → **avoir**.

as² [as] *nm* [carte] ace. || [champion] star, ace.

ascendant, -e [asɑ̃dɑ̃, ɑ̃t] *adj* rising. ◇ **ascendant** *nm* [influence] influence, power. || ASTROL ascendant.

ascenseur [asɑ̃sœr] *nm* lift *Br*, elevator *Am*.

ascension [asɑ̃sjɔ̃] *nf* [de montagne] ascent. || [progression] rise. ◇ **Ascension** *nf*: **l'Ascension** Ascension (Day).

ascète [aset] *nmf* ascetic.

asiatique [azjatik] *adj* [de l'Asie en général] Asian. || [d'Extrême-Orient] oriental. ◇ **Asiatique** *nmf* Asian.

Asie [azi] *nf*: **l'~** Asia; **l'~ du Sud-Est** Southeast Asia.

asile [azil] *nm* [refuge] refuge. || POLIT: **demander/accorder l'~ politique** to seek/to grant political asylum. || *vieilli* [psychiatrique] asylum.

asocial, **-e**, **-iaux** [asɔsjal, jo] **1** *adj* antisocial. **2** *nm, f* social misfit.

aspect [aspɛ] *nm* [apparence] appearance; **d'~ agréable** nice-looking. || [angle & LING] aspect.

asperge [aspɛrʒ] *nf* [légume] asparagus.

asperger [aspɛrʒe] *vt*: **~ qqch de qqch** to spray sthg with sthg; **~ qqn de qqch** [arroser] to spray sb with sthg; [éclabousser] to splash sb with sthg.

aspérité [asperite] *nf* [du sol] bump.

asphalte [asfalt] *nm* asphalt.

asphyxier [asfiksje] *vt* MÉD to asphyxiate, to suffocate.

aspic [aspik] *nm* [vipère] asp.

aspirant, **-e** [aspirã, ãt] *adj*: **hotte ~e** cooker hood *Br*, cooker range *Am*; **pompe ~e** suction pump. ○ **aspirant** *nm* [armée] ≃ officer cadet; [marine] ≃ midshipman.

aspirateur [aspiratœr] *nm* Hoover® *Br*, vacuum cleaner; **passer l'~** to do the vacuuming ou hoovering.

aspiration [aspirasjɔ̃] *nf* [souffle] inhalation. || TECHNOL suction. ○ **aspirations** *nfpl* aspirations.

aspirer [aspire] *vt* [air] to inhale; [liquide] to suck up. || TECHNOL to suck up, to draw up. || [désirer]: **~ à qqch/à faire qqch** to aspire to sthg/to do sthg.

aspirine [aspirin] *nf* aspirin.

assagir [asaʒir] *vt* to quieten down. ○ **s'assagir** *vp* to quieten down.

assaillant, **-e** [asajã, ãt] *nm, f* assailant, attacker.

assaillir [asajir] *vt* to attack, to assault; **~ qqn de qqch** *fig* to assail ou bombard sb with sthg.

assainir [asenir] *vt* [logement] to clean up. || ÉCON to rectify, to stabilize.

assaisonnement [asɛzɔnmã] *nm* [sauce] dressing.

assaisonner [asɛzɔne] *vt* [salade] to dress; [viande, plat] to season.

assassin, **-e** [asasɛ̃, in] *adj* provocative. ○ **assassin** *nm* [gén] murderer; POLIT assassin.

assassinat [asasina] *nm* [gén] murder; POLIT assassination.

assassiner [asasine] *vt* [tuer - gén] to murder; [- POLIT] to assassinate.

assaut [aso] *nm* [attaque] assault, attack; **prendre d'~** [lieu] to storm.

assécher [aseʃe] *vt* to drain.

ASSEDIC, **Assedic** [asedik] (*abr de* **Associations pour l'emploi dans l'industrie et le commerce**) *nfpl* French unemployment insurance scheme; **toucher les ~** to get unemployment benefit *Br* ou welfare *Am*.

assemblage [asɑ̃blaʒ] *nm* [gén] assembly.

assemblée [asɑ̃ble] *nf* [réunion] meeting. || [public] gathering. || ADMIN & POLIT assembly; **l'Assemblée nationale** *lower house of the French parliament.*

assembler [asɑ̃ble] *vt* [monter] to put together. || [réunir - objets] to gather (together). || [personnes - gén] to bring together, to assemble. ○ **s'assembler** *vp* to gather.

assener [asəne], **asséner** [asene] *vt*: **~ un coup à qqn** [frapper] to strike sb, to deal sb a blow.

assentiment [asɑ̃timã] *nm* assent.

asseoir [aswar] *vt* [sur un siège] to put; **faire ~ qqn** to seat sb, to ask sb to take a seat. || *fig* [réputation] to establish. ○ **s'asseoir** *vp* to sit (down).

assermenté, **-e** [asɛrmãte] *adj* [fonctionnaire, expert] sworn.

assertion [asɛrsjɔ̃] *nf* assertion.

assez [ase] *adv* [suffisamment] enough; **~ de** enough; **~ de lait/chaises** enough milk/chairs; **en avoir ~ de qqn/qqch** to have had enough of sb/sthg, to be fed up with sb/sthg. || [plutôt] quite, rather.

assidu, **-e** [asidy] *adj* [élève] diligent. || [travail] painstaking. || [empressé]: **~ (auprès de qqn)** attentive (to sb).

assiduité [asidɥite] *nf* [zèle] diligence. || [fréquence]: **avec ~** regularly. ○ **assiduités** *nfpl* péj & sout attentions.

assiéger [asjeʒe] *vt litt & fig* to besiege.

assiette [asjɛt] *nf* [vaisselle] plate; **~ creuse** ou **à soupe** soup plate; **~ à dessert** dessert plate; **~ plate** dinner plate. || [d'impôt] base. || CULIN: **~ anglaise** assorted cold meats (*pl*) *Br*, cold cuts (*pl*) *Am*.

assigner [asiɲe] *vt* JUR: **~ qqn en justice** to issue a writ against sb.

assimiler [asimile] *vt* [aliment, connaissances] to assimilate. || [confondre]: **~ qqch (à qqch)** to liken sthg (to sthg); **~ qqn à qqn** to compare sb to ou with sb.

assis, **-e** [asi, iz] **1** *pp* → **asseoir**. **2** *adj* sitting, seated; **place ~e** seat. ○ **assises** *nfpl* JUR ≃ Circuit court *Am*. || [congrès] conference (*sg*).

assistance [asistãs] *nf* [aide] assistance; **l'Assistance publique** *French authority which manages the social services and state-owned hospitals.* || [auditoire] audience.

assistant, -e [asistã, ãt] *nm, f* [auxiliaire] assistant; **~ sociale** social worker. || UNIV assistant lecturer.

assister [asiste] **1** *vi:* **~ à qqch** to be at sthg, to attend sthg. **2** *vt* to assist.

association [asɔsjasjɔ̃] *nf* [gén] association. || [union] society, association; **sportive** sports club. || COMM partnership.

associé, -e [asɔsje] **1** *adj* associated. **2** *nm, f* [actionnaire] partner.

associer [asɔsje] *vt* [idées] to associate. || [faire participer]: **~ qqn à qqch** [inclure] to bring sb in on sthg. ○ **s'associer** *vp* [prendre part]: **s'~ à qqch** [participer] to join or participate in sthg; [partager] to share sthg. || [collaborer]: **s'~ à** or **avec qqn** to join forces with sb.

assoiffé, -e [aswafe] *adj* thirsty; **~ de pouvoir** *fig* power-hungry.

assombrir [asɔ̃brir] *vt* [plonger dans l'obscurité] to darken. || *fig* [attrister] to cast a shadow over. ○ **s'assombrir** *vp* [devenir sombre] to grow dark. || *fig* [s'attrister] to darken.

assommer [asɔme] *vt* [frapper] to knock out. || [ennuyer] to bore stiff.

Assomption [asɔ̃psjɔ̃] *nf:* **l'~** the Assumption.

assorti, -e [asɔrti] *adj* [accordé]: **bien ~** well-matched; **mal ~** ill-matched; **une cravate ~e au costume** a tie which matches the suit.

assortiment [asɔrtimã] *nm* assortment, selection.

assortir [asɔrtir] *vt* [objets]: **~ qqch à qqch** to match sthg to or with sthg.

assoupi, -e [asupi] *adj* [endormi] dozing.

assoupir [asupir] ○ **s'assoupir** *vp* [s'endormir] to doze off.

assouplir [asuplir] *vt* [corps] to make supple. || [matière] to soften. || [règlement] to relax.

assourdir [asurdir] *vt* [rendre sourd] to deafen. || [amortir] to deaden, to muffle.

assouvir [asuvir] *vt* to satisfy.

assujettir [asyʒetir] *vt* [peuple] to subjugate. || [soumettre]: **~ qqn à qqch** to subject sb to sthg.

assumer [asyme] *vt* [fonction - exercer] to carry out. || [risque, responsabilité] to accept. || [condition] to come to terms with. || [frais] to meet.

assurance [asyrãs] *nf* [gén] assurance. || [contrat] insurance; **~ maladie** health insurance; **~ tous risques** AUTOM comprehensive insurance; **~-vie** life assurance.

assuré, -e [asyre] *nm, f* policy holder.

assurément [asyremã] *adv sout* certainly.

assurer [asyre] *vt* [promettre]: **~ à qqn que** to assure sb (that); **~ qqn de qqch** to assure sb of sthg. || [permanence, liaison] to provide. || [voiture] to insure. ○ **s'assurer** *vp* [vérifier]: **s'~ que** to make sure (that); **s'~ de qqch** to ensure sthg, to make sure of sthg. || COMM: **s'~ (contre qqch)** to insure o.s. (against sthg). || [obtenir]: **s'~ qqch** to secure sthg.

astérisque [asterisk] *nm* asterisk.

asthme [asm] *nm* MÉD asthma.

asticot [astiko] *nm* maggot.

astiquer [astike] *vt* to polish.

astre [astr] *nm* star.

astreignant, -e [astreɲã, ãt] *adj* demanding.

astreindre [astrɛ̃dr] *vt:* **~ qqn à qqch** to subject sb to sthg; **~ qqn à faire qqch** to compel sb to do sthg.

astreint, -e [astrɛ̃, ɛ̃t] *pp* → **astreindre**.

astringent, -e [astrɛ̃ʒã, ãt] *adj* astringent.

astrologie [astrɔlɔʒi] *nf* astrology.

astrologue [astrɔlɔg] *nm* astrologer.

astronaute [astrɔnot] *nmf* astronaut.

astronomie [astrɔnɔmi] *nf* astronomy.

astronomique [astrɔnɔmik] *adj* astronomical.

astuce [astys] *nf* [ruse] (clever) trick. || [ingéniosité] shrewdness (U).

astucieux, -ieuse [astysjø, jøz] *adj* [idée] clever. || [personne] shrewd.

asymétrique [asimetrik] *adj* asymmetric, asymmetrical.

atelier [atəlje] *nm* [d'artisan] workshop. || [de peintre] studio.

athée [ate] *nmf* atheist.

Athènes [atɛn] *n* Athens.

athlète [atlɛt] *nmf* athlete.

athlétisme [atletism] *nm* athletics (U).

atlantique [atlãtik] *adj* Atlantic. ○ **Atlantique** *nm:* **l'Atlantique** the Atlantic (Ocean).

atlas [atlas] *nm* atlas.

atmosphère [atmosfer] *nf* atmosphere.

atome [atom] *nm* atom.

atomique [atɔmik] *adj* [gén] nuclear. ‖ CHIM & PHYS atomic.

atomiseur [atɔmizœr] *nm* spray.

atout [atu] *nm* [carte] trump; **~ cœur/pique/trèfle/carreau** hearts/spades/clubs/diamonds are trumps. ‖ *fig* [ressource] asset, advantage.

atroce [atrɔs] *adj* [crime] atrocious, dreadful. ‖ [souffrance] horrific, atrocious.

atrocité [atrɔsite] *nf* [horreur] atrocity.

atrophier [atrɔfje] ○ **s'atrophier** *vp* to atrophy.

attabler [atable] ○ **s'attabler** *vp* to sit down (at the table).

attachant, -e [ataʃɑ̃, ɑ̃t] *adj* lovable.

attache [ataʃ] *nf* [lien] fastening. ○ **attaches** *nfpl* links, connections.

attaché, -e [ataʃe] *nm, f* attaché; **~ de presse** [diplomatique] press attaché; [d'organisme, d'entreprise] press officer.

attaché-case [ataʃekɛz] (*pl* **attachés-cases**) *nm* attaché case.

attachement [ataʃmɑ̃] *nm* attachment.

attacher [ataʃe] **1** *vt* [lier]: **~ qqch (à)** to fasten or tie sthg (to). ‖ [paquet] to tie up. ‖ [lacet] to do up; [ceinture de sécurité] to fasten. **2** *vi* CULIN: **~ (à)** to stick (to). ○ **s'attacher** *vp* [émotionnellement]: **s'~ à qqn/qqch** to become attached to sb/sthg. ‖ [se fermer] to fasten. ‖ [s'appliquer]: **s'~ à qqch/à faire qqch** to devote o.s. to sthg/to doing sthg, to apply o.s. to sthg/to doing sthg.

attaquant, -e [atakɑ̃, ɑ̃t] *nm, f* attacker.

attaque [atak] *nf* [gén & MÉD] attack; **~ contre qqn/qqch** attack on sb/sthg.

attaquer [atake] *vt* [gén] to attack. ‖ [JUR - personne] to take to court; [- jugement] to contest. ‖ *fam* [plat] to tuck into. ○ **s'attaquer** *vp* [combattre]: **s'~ à qqn** to attack sb. ‖ *fig*: **s'~ à qqch** [tâche] to tackle sthg.

attardé, -e [atarde] *adj* [idées] outdated. ‖ [enfant] backward.

attarder [atarde] ○ **s'attarder** *vp*: **s'~ sur qqch** to dwell on sthg; **s'~ à faire qqch** to stay on to do sthg, to stay behind to do sthg.

atteindre [atɛ̃dr] *vt* [gén] to reach. ‖ [toucher] to hit. ‖ [affecter] to affect.

atteint, -e [atɛ̃, ɛ̃t] **1** *pp* → atteindre. **2** *adj* [malade]: **être ~ de** to be suffering from. ○ **atteinte** *nf* [préjudice]: **porter ~e à** to undermine; **hors d'~e** [hors de portée] out of reach; [inattaquable] beyond reach. ‖ [effet] effect.

attelage [atlaʒ] *nm* [chevaux] team.

atteler [atle] *vt* [animaux, véhicules] to hitch up; [wagons] to couple.

attelle [atɛl] *nf* splint.

attenant, -e [atnɑ̃, ɑ̃t] *adj*: **~ (à qqch)** adjoining (sthg).

attendre [atɑ̃dr] **1** *vt* [gén] to wait for; **~ que** (+ *subjonctif*): **~ que la pluie s'arrête** to wait for the rain to stop; **faire ~ qqn** [personne] to keep sb waiting. ‖ [espérer]: **~ qqch (de qqn/qqch)** to expect sthg (from sb/sthg); [suj: surprise, épreuve] to be in store for. **2** *vi* to wait; **attends!** hang on! ○ **s'attendre** *vp*: **s'~ à** to expect. ○ **en attendant** *loc adv* [pendant ce temps] meanwhile, in the meantime. ‖ [quand même] all the same.

attendrir [atɑ̃drir] *vt* [viande] to tenderize. ‖ [personne] to move. ○ **s'attendrir** *vp*: **s'~ (sur qqn/qqch)** to be moved (by sb/sthg).

attendrissant, -e [atɑ̃drisɑ̃, ɑ̃t] *adj* moving, touching.

attendu, -e [atɑ̃dy] *pp* → attendre. ○ **attendu que** *loc conj* since, considering that.

attentat [atɑ̃ta] *nm* attack; **~ à la bombe** bomb attack, bombing.

attente [atɑ̃t] *nf* [station] wait; **en ~** in abeyance. ‖ [espoir] expectation.

attenter [atɑ̃te] *vi*: **~ à** [liberté, droit] to violate; **~ à ses jours** to attempt suicide.

attentif, -ive [atɑ̃tif, iv] *adj* [auditoire]: **~ (à qqch)** attentive (to sthg).

attention [atɑ̃sjɔ̃] **1** *nf* attention; **à l'~ de** for the attention of; **faire ~ à** [prudence] to be careful of; [concentration] to pay attention to. **2** *interj* watch out!, be careful!

attentionné, -e [atɑ̃sjɔne] *adj* thoughtful.

attentivement [atɑ̃tivmɑ̃] *adv* attentively, carefully.

atténuer [atenye] *vt* [douleur] to ease; [propos, ton] to tone down; [lumière] to dim, to subdue; [bruit] to quieten. ○ **s'atténuer** *vp* [lumière] to dim, to fade; [bruit] to fade; [douleur] to ease.

atterrer [atere] *vt* to stagger.

atterrir [aterir] *vi* to land.

atterrissage [aterisaʒ] *nm* landing.

attestation [atɛstasjɔ̃] *nf* [certificat] certificate.

attester [atɛste] *vt* [confirmer] to vouch for, to testify to. ‖ [certifier] to attest.

attirail [atiraj] *nm fam* [équipement] gear.

attirance [atirãs] *nf* attraction.

attirant, -e [atirã, ãt] *adj* attractive.

attirer [atire] *vt* [gén] to attract. || [amener vers soi]: ~ **qqn à/vers soi** to draw sb to/towards one. || [provoquer]: ~ **des ennuis à qqn** to cause trouble for sb. ○ **s'attirer** *vp*: s'~ **qqch** to bring sthg on o.s.

attiser [atize] *vt* [feu] to poke. || *fig* [haine] to stir up.

attitré, -e [atitre] *adj* [habituel] usual. || [titulaire - fournisseur] by appointment; [- représentant] accredited.

attitude [atityd] *nf* [comportement, approche] attitude. || [posture] posture.

attouchement [atuʃmã] *nm* caress.

attraction [atraksjɔ̃] *nf* [gén] attraction. || [force]: ~ **magnétique** magnetic force. ○ **attractions** *nfpl* [jeux] amusements. || [spectacle] attractions.

attrait [atrɛ] *nm* [séduction] appeal. || [intérêt] attraction.

attrape-nigaud [atrapnigo] (*pl* attrape-nigauds) *nm* con.

attraper [atrape] *vt* [gén] to catch. || *fam* [gronder] to tell off.

attrayant, -e [atrejã, ãt] *adj* attractive.

attribuer [atribɥe] *vt* [tâche, part]: ~ **qqch à qqn** to assign OU allocate sthg to sb, to assign OU allocate sb sthg; [récompense] to award sthg to sb, to award sb sthg. || [faute]: ~ **qqch à qqn** to attribute sthg to sb, to put sthg down to sb. ○ **s'attribuer** *vp* [s'approprier] to appropriate (for o.s.). || [revendiquer] to claim (for o.s.).

attribut [atriby] *nm* [gén] attribute. || GRAM complement.

attribution [atribysjɔ̃] *nf* [de prix] awarding, award. || [de part, tâche] allocation, assignment. || [d'avantage] bestowing. ○ **attributions** *nfpl* [fonctions] duties.

attrister [atriste] *vt* to sadden. ○ **s'attrister** *vp* to be saddened.

attroupement [atrupmã] *nm* crowd.

attrouper [atrupe] ○ **s'attrouper** *vp* to form a crowd, to gather.

au [o] → **à**.

aubade [obad] *nf* dawn serenade.

aubaine [obɛn] *nf* piece of good fortune.

aube [ob] *nf* [aurore] dawn, daybreak; **à l'~** at dawn.

aubépine [obepin] *nf* hawthorn.

auberge [obɛrʒ] *nf* [hôtel] inn; ~ **de jeunesse** youth hostel.

aubergine [obɛrʒin] *nf* BOT aubergine *Br*, eggplant *Am*. || *péj* [contractuelle] traffic warden *Br*, meter maid *Am*.

aubergiste [obɛrʒist] *nmf* innkeeper.

aucun, -e [okœ̃, yn] **1** *adj* [sens négatif]: **ne ... ~** no; **il n'y a ~e voiture dans la rue** there aren't any cars in the street, there are no cars in the street. || [sens positif] any; **il lit plus qu'~ autre enfant** he reads more than any other child. **2** *pron* [sens négatif] none; ~ **des enfants** none of the children; ~ **(des deux)** neither (of them). || [sens positif]: **plus qu'~ de nous** more than any of us.

aucunement [okynmã] *adv* not at all, in no way.

audace [odas] *nf* [hardiesse] daring, boldness. || [insolence] audacity.

audacieux, -ieuse [odasjø, jøz] *adj* [projet] daring, bold. || [personne, geste] bold.

au-dedans [odədã] *loc adv* inside. ○ **au-dedans de** *loc prép* inside.

au-dehors [odəɔr] *loc adv* outside. ○ **au-dehors de** *loc prép* outside.

au-delà [odəla] **1** *loc adv* [plus loin] beyond. || [davantage, plus] more. **2** *nm*: l'~ RELIG the beyond, the afterlife. ○ **au-delà de** *loc prép* beyond.

au-dessous [odəsu] *loc adv* below, underneath. ○ **au-dessous de** *loc prép* below, under.

au-dessus [odəsy] *loc adv* above. ○ **au-dessus de** *loc prép* above, over.

au-devant [odəvã] *loc adv* ahead. ○ **au-devant de** *loc prép*: **aller ~ de** to go to meet; **aller ~ du danger** to court danger.

audible [odibl] *adj* audible.

audience [odjãs] *nf* [public, entretien] audience. || JUR hearing.

Audimat® [odimat] *nm* audience rating.

audionumérique [odjɔnymerik] *adj* digital audio.

audiovisuel, -elle [odjɔvizɥɛl] *adj* audio-visual. ○ **audiovisuel** *nm* TV and radio.

audit [odit] *nm* audit.

auditeur, -trice [oditœr, tris] *nm, f* listener. ○ **auditeur** *nm* UNIV: ~ **libre** *person allowed to attend lectures without being registered*, auditor *Am*. || FIN auditor.

audition [odisjɔ̃] *nf* [fait d'entendre] hearing. || THÉÂTRE audition.

auditionner [odisjɔne] *vt & vi* to audition.

auditoire [oditwar] *nm* [public] audience.

auditorium [oditɔrjɔm] *nm* [de concert] auditorium; [d'enregistrement] studio.

auge [oʒ] *nf* [pour animaux] trough.

augmentation [ogmɑ̃tasjɔ̃] *nf*: ~ (de) increase (in); ~ (de salaire) rise (in salary).

augmenter [ogmɑ̃te] **1** *vt* to increase; [prix, salaire] to raise; [personne] to give a rise *Br* ou raise *Am* to. **2** *vi* to increase, to rise; **la douleur augmente** the pain is getting worse.

augure [ogyr] *nm* [présage] omen; **être de bon/mauvais ~** to be a good/bad sign.

aujourd'hui [oʒurdɥi] *adv* today.

aulx → **ail**.

aumône [omon] *nf*: **faire l'~ à qqn** to give alms to sb.

auparavant [oparavɑ̃] *adv* [tout d'abord] first (of all). || [avant] before, previously.

auprès [opre] ○ **auprès de** *loc prép* [à côté de] beside, next to. || [comparé à] compared with. || [en s'adressant à] to.

auquel [okɛl] → **lequel**.

aurai, auras *etc* → **avoir**.

auréole [oreol] *nf* ASTRON & RELIG halo. || [trace] ring.

auriculaire [orikylɛr] *nm* little finger.

aurore [orɔr] *nf* dawn.

ausculter [oskylte] *vt* MÉD to sound.

auspice [ospis] *nm* (*gén pl*) sign, auspice; **sous les ~s de qqn** under the auspices of sb.

aussi [osi] *adv* [pareillement, en plus] also, too; **moi ~** me too; **j'y vais ~** I'm going too ou as well. || [dans une comparaison]: ~ ... **que** as ... as; **il n'est pas ~ intelligent que son frère** he's not as clever as his brother; **je n'ai jamais rien vu d'~ beau** I've never seen anything so beautiful; ~ **incroyable que cela paraisse** incredible though ou as it may seem. ○ **(tout) aussi bien** *loc adv* just as easily, just as well; **j'aurais pu (tout) ~ bien refuser** I could just as easily have said no.

aussitôt [osito] *adv* immediately. ○ **aussitôt que** *loc conj* as soon as.

austère [oster] *adj* [personne, vie] austere. || [vêtement] severe; [paysage] harsh.

austérité [osterite] *nf* [de personne, vie] austerity. || [de vêtement] severeness; [de paysage] harshness.

austral, -e [ostral] (*pl* **australs** ou **austraux** [ostro]) *adj* southern.

Australie [ostrali] *nf*: l'~ Australia.

australien, -ienne [ostraljɛ̃, jɛn] *adj* Australian. ○ **Australien, -ienne** *nm*, *f* Australian.

autant [otɑ̃] *adv* [comparatif]: ~ **que** as much as; **ce livre coûte ~ que l'autre** this book costs as much as the other one; ~ **de (... que)** [quantité] as much (... as); [nombre] as many (... as); **il a dépensé ~ d'argent que moi** he spent as much money as I did. || [à un tel point, en si grande quantité] so much; [en si grand nombre] so many; **il ne peut pas en dire** ~ he can't say the same; **en faire ~** to do likewise. || [il vaut mieux]: ~ **dire la vérité** we/you *etc* may as well tell the truth. ○ **autant que** *loc conj*: (**pour**) ~ **que je sache** as far as I know. ○ **d'autant** *loc adv* accordingly, in proportion. ○ **d'autant que** *loc conj*: **d'~ (plus) que** all the more so since. ○ **pour autant** *loc adv* for all that.

autel [otɛl] *nm* altar.

auteur [otœr] *nm* [d'œuvre] author. || [responsable] perpetrator.

authentique [otɑ̃tik] *adj* authentic, genuine.

autiste [otist] *adj* autistic.

auto [oto] *nf* car.

autobiographie [otobjɔgrafi] *nf* autobiography.

autobronzant, -e [otobrɔ̃zɑ̃, ɑ̃t] *adj* self-tanning.

autobus [otobys] *nm* bus.

autocar [otokar] *nm* coach.

autochtone [otoktɔn] *nmf & adj* native.

autocollant, -e [otokɔlɑ̃, ɑ̃t] *adj* self-adhesive, sticky. ○ **autocollant** *nm* sticker.

auto-couchettes [otokuʃɛt] *adj inv*: **train ~** ≈ Motorail® train.

autocritique [otokritik] *nf* self-criticism.

autocuiseur [otokɥizœr] *nm* pressure cooker.

autodéfense [otodefɑ̃s] *nf* self-defence.

autodétruire [otodetrɥir] ○ **s'autodétruire** *vp* [machine] to self-destruct.

autodidacte [otodidakt] *nmf* self-taught person.

auto-école [otoekɔl] (*pl* **auto-écoles**) *nf* driving school.

autofinancement [otofinɑ̃smɑ̃] *nm* self-financing.

autofocus [otofɔkys] *nm & adj inv* autofocus.

autographe [otograf] *nm* autograph.

automate [otomat] *nm* [robot] automaton.

automatique [otomatik] **1** *nm* [pistolet] automatic. **2** *adj* automatic.

automatisation [otomatizasjɔ̃] *nf* automation.

automatisme [otomatism] *nm* [réflexe] automatic reaction, automatism.

automne [otɔn] *nm* autumn, fall *Am*; **en ~** in autumn, in the fall *Am*.

automobile [otomɔbil] **1** *nf* car, automobile *Am*. **2** *adj* [industrie, accessoires] car (*avant n*), automobile (*avant n*) *Am*.

automobiliste [otomɔbilist] *nmf* motorist.

autonettoyant, -e [otonɛtwajɑ̃, ɑ̃t] *adj* self-cleaning.

autonome [otonɔm] *adj* [gén] autonomous, independent. ‖ [appareil] self-contained.

autonomie [otonɔmi] *nf* [indépendance] autonomy, independence. ‖ AUTOM & AVIAT range. ‖ POLIT autonomy, self-government.

autonomiste [otonɔmist] *nmf & adj* separatist.

autoportrait [otopɔrtrɛ] *nm* self-portrait.

autopsie [otɔpsi] *nf* post-mortem, autopsy.

autoradio [otoradjo] *nm* car radio.

autorisation [otorizasjɔ̃] *nf* [permission] permission, authorization; **avoir l'~ de faire qqch** to be allowed to do sthg. ‖ [attestation] pass, permit.

autorisé, -e [otorize] *adj* [personne] in authority; **milieux ~s** official circles.

autoriser [otorize] *vt* to authorize, to permit; **~ qqn à faire qqch** [permission] to give sb permission to do sthg; [possibilité] to permit ou allow sb to do sthg.

autoritaire [otoritɛr] *adj* authoritarian.

autorité [otorite] *nf* authority; **faire ~** [ouvrage] to be authoritative; [personne] to be an authority.

autoroute [otorut] *nf* motorway *Br*, highway *Am*, freeway *Am*.

auto-stop [otostɔp] *nm* hitchhiking; **faire de l'~** to hitchhike, to hitch.

auto-stoppeur, -euse [otostɔpœr, øz] *nm, f* hitchhiker, hitcher.

autour [otur] *adv* round, around. ○ **autour de** *loc prép* [sens spatial] round, around. ‖ [sens temporel] about, around.

autre [otr] **1** *adj indéf* [distinct, différent] other, different; **l'un et l'~ projets** both projects; **~ chose** something else. ‖ [supplémentaire] other; **tu veux une ~ tasse de café?** would you like another cup of coffee? ‖ [qui reste] other, remaining; **les ~s passagers ont été rapatriés en autobus** the other ou remaining passengers were bussed home. **2** *pron indéf*: **l'~** the other (one); **un ~** another (one); **d'une semaine à l'~** from one week to the next; **quelqu'un d'~** somebody else, someone else; **rien d'~** nothing else; **l'un et l'~ sont venus** they both came, both of them came; **l'un ou l'~ ira** one or other (of them) will go; **ni l'un ni l'~ n'est venu** neither (of them) came. ○ **entre autres** *loc adv* among other things.

autrefois [otrəfwa] *adv* in the past, formerly.

autrement [otrəmɑ̃] *adv* [différemment] otherwise, differently; **je n'ai pas pu faire ~ que d'y aller** I had no choice but to go; **~ dit** in other words. ‖ [sinon] otherwise.

Autriche [otriʃ] *nf*: **l'~** Austria.

autrichien, -ienne [otriʃjɛ̃, jɛn] *adj* Austrian. ○ **Autrichien, -ienne** *nm, f* Austrian.

autruche [otryʃ] *nf* ostrich.

autrui [otrɥi] *pron* others, other people.

auvent [ovɑ̃] *nm* canopy.

aux [o] → **à**.

auxiliaire [oksiljɛr] **1** *nmf* [assistant] assistant. **2** *nm* GRAM auxiliary (verb). **3** *adj* [secondaire] auxiliary. ‖ ADMIN assistant (*avant n*).

auxquels, auxquelles [okɛl] → **lequel.**

av. *abr de* avenue.

avachi, -e [avaʃi] *adj* [gén] misshapen. ‖ [personne] listless; **il était ~ dans un fauteuil** he was slumped in an armchair.

aval, -als [aval] *nm* backing (*U*), endorsement. ○ **en aval** *loc adv litt & fig* downstream.

avalanche [avalɑ̃ʃ] *nf litt & fig* avalanche.

avaler [avale] *vt* [gén] to swallow. ‖ *fig* [supporter] to take; **dur à ~** difficult to swallow.

avance

avance [avɑ̃s] *nf* [progression, somme d'argent] advance. ‖ [distance, temps] lead; **le train a dix minutes d'~** the train is ten minutes early; **prendre de l'~ (dans qqch)** to get ahead (in sthg). ○ **avances** *nfpl*: **faire des ~s à qqn** to make advances towards sb. ○ **à l'avance** *loc adv* in advance. ○ **d'avance** *loc adv* in advance. ○ **en avance** *loc adv*: **être en ~** to be early; **être en ~ sur qqch** to be ahead of sthg. ○ **par avance** *loc adv* in advance.

avancement [avɑ̃smɑ̃] *nm* [développement] progress. ‖ [promotion] promotion.

avancer [avɑ̃se] **1** *vt* [objet, tête] to move forward; [date, départ] to bring forward; [main] to hold out. ‖ [montre, horloge] to put forward. ‖ [argent]: **~ qqch à qqn** to advance sb sthg. **2** *vi* [approcher] to move forward. ‖ [progresser] to advance. ‖ [faire saillie]: **~ (dans/sur)** to jut out (into/over), to project (into/over). ‖ [montre, horloge]: **ma montre avance de dix minutes** my watch is ten minutes fast. ‖ [servir]: **ça n'avance à rien** that won't get us/you anywhere. ○ **s'avancer** *vp* [s'approcher] to move forward; **s'~ vers qqn/qqch** to move towards sb/sthg. ‖ [s'engager] to commit o.s.

avant [avɑ̃] **1** *prép* before; **tu connais le cinéma? ma maison se situe un peu ~** you know the cinema? my house is just this side of it. **3** *adj inv* front; **les roues ~** the front wheels. **4** *nm* [partie antérieure] front. ‖ SPORT forward. ○ **avant de** *loc prép*: **~ de faire qqch** before doing sthg. ○ **avant que** *loc conj* (+ *subjonctif*): **je dois te parler ~ que tu partes** I must speak to you before you leave. ○ **avant tout** *loc adv* above all; **sa carrière passe ~ tout** his career comes first. ○ **en avant** *loc adv* forward, forwards.

avantage [avɑ̃taʒ] *nm* [gén & TENNIS] advantage; **se montrer à son ~** to look one's best.

avantager [avɑ̃taʒe] *vt* [favoriser] to favour. ‖ [mettre en valeur] to flatter.

avantageux, -euse [avɑ̃taʒø, øz] *adj* [prix] profitable, lucrative.

avant-bras [avɑ̃bra] *nm inv* forearm.

avant-centre [avɑ̃sɑ̃tr] (*pl* avants-centres) *nm* centre forward.

avant-coureur [avɑ̃kurœr] → signe.

avant-dernier, -ière [avɑ̃dɛrnje, jɛr] (*mpl* avant-derniers, *fpl* avant-dernières) *adj* second to last, penultimate.

avant-garde [avɑ̃gard] (*pl* avant-gardes) *nf* MIL. vanguard. ‖ [idées] avant-garde.

avant-goût [avɑ̃gu] (*pl* avant-goûts) *nm* foretaste.

avant-hier [avɑ̃tjɛr] *adv* the day before yesterday.

avant-première [avɑ̃prəmjɛr] (*pl* avant-premières) *nf* preview.

avant-projet [avɑ̃prɔʒɛ] (*pl* avant-projets) *nm* draft.

avant-propos [avɑ̃prɔpo] *nm inv* foreword.

avant-veille [avɑ̃vɛj] (*pl* avant-veilles) *nf*: **l'~** two days earlier.

avare [avar] **1** *nmf* miser. **2** *adj* miserly; **être ~ de qqch** *fig* to be sparing with sthg.

avarice [avaris] *nf* avarice.

avarie [avari] *nf* damage (U).

avarié, -e [avarje] *adj* rotting, bad.

avatar [avatar] *nm* [transformation] metamorphosis. ○ **avatars** *nmpl* [mésaventures] misfortunes.

avec [avɛk] *prép* [gén] with; **~ respect** with respect, respectfully; **et ~ ça?** *fam* [dans un magasin] anything else? ‖ [vis-à-vis de] to, towards.

avenant, -e [avnɑ̃] *adj* pleasant. ○ **avenant** *nm* JUR additional clause. ○ **à l'avenant** *loc adv* in the same vein.

avènement [avɛnmɑ̃] *nm* [d'un roi] accession. ‖ *fig* [début] advent.

avenir [avnir] *nm* future; **avoir de l'~** to have a future; **d'~** [profession, concept] with a future, with prospects. ○ **à l'avenir** *loc adv* in future.

Avent [avɑ̃] *nm*: **l'~** Advent.

aventure [avɑ̃tyr] *nf* [gén] adventure. ‖ [liaison amoureuse] affair.

aventurer [avɑ̃tyre] *vt* [risquer] to risk. ○ **s'aventurer** *vp* to venture (out); **s'~ à faire qqch** *fig* to venture to do sthg.

aventureux, -euse [avɑ̃tyrø, øz] *adj* [personne, vie] adventurous. ‖ [projet] risky.

aventurier, -ière [avɑ̃tyrje, jɛr] *nm, f* adventurer.

avenu [avny] *adj m*: **nul et non ~** JUR null and void.

avenue [avny] *nf* avenue.

avérer [avere] ○ **s'avérer** *vp*: **il s'est**

avéré (être) à la hauteur he proved (to be) up to it.

averse [avɛrs] *nf* downpour.

averti, -e [avɛrti] *adj* [expérimenté] experienced. || [initié]: ~ **(de)** informed or well-informed (about).

avertir [avɛrtir] *vt* [mettre en garde] to warn. || [prévenir] to inform; **avertissez-moi dès que possible** let me know as soon as possible.

avertissement [avɛrtismɑ̃] *nm* [gén] warning. || [avis] notice, notification.

avertisseur [avɛrtisœr] *nm* [Klaxon®] horn. || [d'incendie] alarm.

aveu, -x [avø] *nm* confession.

aveugle [avœgl] 1 *nmf* blind person; **les ~s** the blind. 2 *adj litt & fig* blind.

aveuglement [avœgləmɑ̃] *nm* blindness.

aveuglément [avœglemɑ̃] *adv* blindly.

aveugler [avœgle] *vt litt & fig* [priver de la vue] to blind.

aveuglette [avœglɛt] ○ **à l'aveuglette** *loc adv*: **marcher à l'~** to grope one's way; **avancer à l'~** *fig* to be in the dark.

aviateur, -trice [avjatœr, tris] *nm, f* aviator.

aviation [avjasjɔ̃] *nf* [transport aérien] aviation. || MIL airforce.

avide [avid] *adj* [vorace, cupide] greedy. || [désireux]: ~ **(de qqch/de faire qqch)** eager (for sthg/to do sthg).

avidité [avidite] *nf* [voracité, cupidité] greed. || [passion] eagerness.

avilir [avilir] *vt* [personne] to degrade. ○ **s'avilir** *vp* [personne] to demean o.s.

aviné, -e [avine] *adj* [personne] inebriated. || [haleine] smelling of alcohol.

avion [avjɔ̃] *nm* plane, aeroplane, airplane *Am*; **en ~** by plane, by air; **par ~** [courrier] airmail; ~ **à réaction** jet (plane).

aviron [avirɔ̃] *nm* [rame] oar. || SPORT: **l'~** rowing.

avis [avi] *nm* [opinion] opinion; **changer d'~** to change one's mind; **à mon ~** in my opinion. || [conseil] advice (*U*). || [notification] notification, notice.

avisé, -e [avize] *adj* [sensé] sensible; **être bien/mal ~ de faire qqch** to be well-advised/ill-advised to do sthg.

aviser [avize] 1 *vt* [informer]: ~ **qqn de qqch** to inform sb of sthg. 2 *vi* to reassess the situation. ○ **s'aviser** *vp sout* [s'apercevoir]: **s'~ de qqch** to notice sthg.

|| [oser]: **ne t'avise pas de répondre!** don't you dare answer me back!

av. J.-C. (*abr de* avant Jésus-Christ) BC.

avocat, -e [avɔka, at] *nm, f* JUR lawyer; ~ **de la défense** counsel for the defence *Br*, defense counsel *Am*; ~ **général** ≃ counsel for the prosecution *Br*, prosecuting attorney *Am*. ○ **avocat** *nm* [fruit] avocado.

avoine [avwan] *nf* oats (*pl*).

avoir [avwar] 1 *nm* [biens] assets (*pl*). || [document] credit note. 2 *v aux* to have; **j'ai fini** I have finished; **il a attendu pendant deux heures** he waited for two hours. 3 *vt* [posséder] to have (got). || [être âgé de]: **il a 20 ans** he is 20 (years old); **il a deux ans de plus que son frère** he is two years older than his brother. || [obtenir] to get. || [éprouver] to have; *voir aussi* **faim, peur, soif** *etc*. || *loc*: **se faire ~** *fam* to be had or conned; **j'en ai pour cinq minutes** it'll take me five minutes. ○ **avoir à** *vi* + *prép* [devoir]: ~ **à faire qqch** to have to do sthg; **tu n'avais pas à lui parler sur ce ton** you had no need to speak to him like that; **tu n'avais qu'à me demander** you only had to ask me; **tu n'as qu'à y aller toi-même** just go (there) yourself, why don't you just go (there) yourself? ○ **il y a** *v impers* [présentatif] there is/are; **il y a un problème** there's a problem; **il y a des problèmes** there are (some) problems; **qu'est-ce qu'il y a?** what's the matter?, what is it?; **il n'y a qu'à en finir** we'll/you'll *etc* just have to have done (with it). || [temporel]: **il y a trois ans** three years ago; **il y a longtemps qu'il est parti** he left a long time ago.

avoisinant, -e [avwazinɑ̃, ɑ̃t] *adj* [lieu, maison] neighbouring. || [sens, couleur] similar.

avortement [avɔrtəmɑ̃] *nm* MÉD abortion.

avorter [avɔrte] *vi* MÉD: **(se faire) ~** to have an abortion. || [échouer] to fail.

avorton [avɔrtɔ̃] *nm péj* [nabot] runt.

avouer [avwe] *vt* [confesser] to confess (to). || [reconnaître] to admit.

avril [avril] *nm* April; *voir aussi* **septembre**.

axe [aks] *nm* GÉOM & PHYS axis. || [de roue] axle. || [prolongement]: **dans l'~ de** directly in line with.

axer [akse] *vt*: ~ qqch sur/autour de qqch to centre sthg on/around sthg.

ayant [ɛjɑ̃] *ppr* → **avoir**.

azalée [azale] *nf* azalea.

azimut [azimyt] ○ **tous azimuts** *loc adj* [défense, offensive] all-out.

azote [azɔt] *nm* nitrogen.

azur [azyr] *nm littéraire* [couleur] azure. || [ciel] skies (*pl*).

B

b, B [be] *nm inv* b, B. ○ **B** (*abr de* **bien**), *good grade (as assessment on school-work)*, ≃ B.

BA (*abr de* **bonne action**) *nf fam* good deed.

babines [babin] *nfpl* chops.

bâbord [babɔr] *nm* port; à ~ to port, on the port side.

babouin [babwɛ̃] *nm* baboon.

baby-sitter [bebisitœr] (*pl* **baby-sitters**) *nmf* baby-sitter.

baby-sitting [bebisitiŋ] *nm*: faire du ~ to baby-sit.

bac [bak] *nm* → **baccalauréat**. || [bateau] ferry. || [de réfrigérateur]: ~ à glace ice tray; ~ à légumes vegetable drawer.

baccalauréat [bakalɔrea] *nm* school-leaving examinations leading to university entrance qualification.

bâche [baʃ] *nf* [toile] tarpaulin.

bachelier, -ière [baʃəlje, jɛr] *nm, f* holder of the baccalauréat.

bacille [basil] *nm* bacillus.

bâcler [bakle] *vt* to botch.

bactérie [bakteri] *nf* bacterium.

badaud [bado] *nm* gawper.

badge [badʒ] *nm* badge.

badigeonner [badiʒɔne] *vt* [mur] to whitewash.

badiner [badine] *vi sout* to joke; ne pas ~ avec qqch not to take sthg lightly.

badminton [badmintɔn] *nm* badminton.

baffe [baf] *nf fam* slap.

baffle [bafl] *nm* speaker.

bafouiller [bafuje] *vi & vt* to mumble.

bagage [bagaʒ] *nm* (*gén pl*) [valises, sacs] luggage (*U*), baggage (*U*); faire ses ~s to pack; ~s à main hand luggage. || [connaissances] (fund of) knowledge; ~ intellectuel/culturel intellectual/cultural baggage.

bagagiste [bagaʒist] *nmf* [à l'hôtel etc] porter.

bagarre [bagar] *nf* brawl, fight.

bagarrer [bagare] *vi* to fight. ○ **se bagarrer** *vp* to fight.

bagatelle [bagatɛl] *nf* [objet] trinket. || [somme d'argent]: acheter qqch pour une ~ to buy sthg for next to nothing; la ~ de X francs *iron* a mere X francs. || [chose futile] trifle.

bagnard [baɲar] *nm* convict.

bagne [baɲ] *nm* [prison] labour camp.

bagnole [baɲɔl] *nf fam* car.

bague [bag] *nf* [bijou, anneau] ring; ~ de fiançailles engagement ring. || TECH: ~ de serrage clip.

baguer [bage] *vt* [oiseau, arbre] to ring.

baguette [bagɛt] *nf* [pain] French stick. || [petit bâton] stick; ~ magique magic wand; ~ de tambour drumstick; mener qqn à la ~ to rule sb with a rod of iron. || [pour manger] chopstick. || [de chef d'orchestre] baton.

bahut [bay] *nm* [buffet] sideboard.

baie [bɛ] *nf* [fruit] berry. || GÉOGR bay. || [fenêtre]: ~ vitrée picture window.

baignade [bɛɲad] *nf* [action] bathing (*U*) *Br*, swimming (*U*); «~ interdite» "no bathing/swimming".

baigner [bɛɲe] **1** *vt* [donner un bain à] to bath. || [tremper, remplir] to bathe; baigné de soleil bathed in sunlight. **2** *vi*: ~ dans son sang to lie in a pool of blood; les tomates baignaient dans l'huile the tomatoes were swimming in oil. ○ **se baigner** *vp* [dans la mer] to go swimming, to swim. || [dans une baignoire] to have a bath.

baigneur, -euse [bɛɲœr, øz] *nm, f* bather *Br*, swimmer. ○ **baigneur** *nm* [poupée] baby doll.

baignoire [bɛɲwar] *nf* bath.

bail [baj] (*pl* **baux** [bo]) *nm* JUR lease.

bâillement [bajmɑ̃] *nm* yawning (*U*), yawn.

bâiller [baje] *vi* [personne] to yawn. || [vêtement] to gape.

bailleur, -eresse [bajœr, bajrɛs] *nm, f* lessor; ~ de fonds backer.

bâillon [bajɔ̃] *nm* gag.

bâillonner [bajɔne] *vt* to gag.

bain [bɛ̃] *nm* [gén] bath; **prendre un ~** to have ou take a bath; **~ moussant** foaming bath oil. ‖ [dans mer, piscine] swim; **~ de mer** sea bathing *Br* ou swimming. ‖ *loc*: **prendre un ~ de soleil** to sunbathe.

bain-marie [bɛ̃mari] (*pl* **bains-marie**) *nm*: **au ~** in a bain-marie.

baïonnette [bajɔnɛt] *nf* [arme] bayonet. ‖ ÉLECTR bayonet fitting.

baiser [beze] *nm* kiss.

baisse [bɛs] *nf* [gén]: **~ (de)** drop (in), fall (in); **en ~** falling; **la tendance est à la ~** there is a downward trend.

baisser [bese] **1** *vt* [gén] to lower; [radio] to turn down. **2** *vi* [descendre] to go down; **le jour baisse** it's getting dark. ‖ [santé, vue] to fail. ‖ [prix] to fall. ○ **se baisser** *vp* to bend down.

bajoues [baʒu] *nfpl* jowls.

bal [bal] *nm* ball; **~ masqué/costumé** masked/fancy-dress ball; **~ populaire** ou **musette** *popular old-fashioned dance accompanied by accordion.*

balade [balad] *nf fam* stroll.

balader [balade] *vt fam* [traîner avec soi] to trail around. ‖ [emmener en promenade] to take for a walk. ○ **se balader** *vp fam* [se promener - à pied] to go for a walk; [- en voiture] to go for a drive.

baladeur, -euse [baladœr, øz] *adj* wandering. ○ **baladeur** *nm* personal stereo.

balafre [balafr] *nf* [blessure] gash. ‖ [cicatrice] scar.

balafré, -e [balafre] *adj* scarred.

balai [balɛ] *nm* [de nettoyage] broom, brush. ‖ *fam* [an]: **il a 50 ~s** he's 50 years old.

balai-brosse [balɛbrɔs] *nm* (long-handled) scrubbing brush.

balance [balɑ̃s] *nf* [instrument] scales (*pl*). ‖ COMM & POLIT balance. ○ **Balance** *nf* ASTROL Libra.

balancer [balɑ̃se] *vt* [bouger] to swing. ‖ *fam* [lancer] to chuck. ‖ *fam* [jeter] to chuck out. ○ **se balancer** *vp* [sur une chaise] to rock backwards and forwards. ‖ [sur une balançoire] to swing. ‖ *fam*: **se ~ de qqch** not to give a damn about sthg.

balancier [balɑ̃sje] *nm* [de pendule] pendulum. ‖ [de funambule] pole.

balançoire [balɑ̃swar] *nf* [suspendue] swing; [bascule] see-saw.

balayage [balɛjaʒ] *nm* [gén] sweeping; TECHNOL scanning.

balayer [baleje] *vt* [nettoyer] to sweep. ‖

[chasser] to sweep away. ‖ [suj: radar] to scan; [suj: projecteurs] to sweep (across).

balayette [balɛjɛt] *nf* small brush.

balayeur, -euse [balɛjœr, øz] *nm, f* roadsweeper *Br*, streetsweeper *Am*. ○ **balayeuse** *nf* [machine] roadsweeper.

balbutier [balbysje] **1** *vi* [bafouiller] to stammer. **2** *vt* [bafouiller] to stammer (out).

balcon [balkɔ̃] *nm* [de maison - terrasse] balcony; [- balustrade] parapet. ‖ [de théâtre, de cinéma] circle.

balconnet [balkɔnɛ] *nm*: **soutien-gorge à ~** half-cup bra.

baldaquin [baldakɛ̃] *nm* → **lit**.

baleine [balɛn] *nf* [mammifère] whale. ‖ [de parapluie] rib.

balise [baliz] *nf* NAVIG marker (buoy). ‖ AÉRON runway light. ‖ AUTOM road sign. ‖ INFORM tag.

baliser [balize] *vt* to mark out.

balivernes [balivɛrn] *nfpl* nonsense (*U*).

Balkans [balkɑ̃] *nmpl*: **les ~** the Balkans.

ballade [balad] *nf* ballad.

ballant, -e [balɑ̃, ɑ̃t] *adj*: **les bras ~s** arms dangling.

ballast [balast] *nm* [chemin de fer] ballast. ‖ NAVIG ballast tank.

balle [bal] *nf* [d'arme à feu] bullet; **~ perdue** stray bullet. ‖ [de jeu] ball. ‖ [de marchandises] bale. ‖ *fam* [argent] franc.

ballerine [balrin] *nf* [danseuse] ballerina. ‖ [chaussure] ballet shoe.

ballet [balɛ] *nm* [gén] ballet.

ballon [balɔ̃] *nm* JEU & SPORT ball; **~ de football** football. ‖ [montgolfière, de fête] balloon.

ballonné, -e [balɔne] *adj*: **avoir le ventre ~, être ~** to be bloated.

ballot [balo] *nm* [de marchandises] bundle. ‖ *vieilli* [imbécile] twit.

ballottage [balɔtaʒ] *nm* POLIT second ballot; **en ~** standing for a second ballot.

ballotter [balɔte] **1** *vt* to toss about. **2** *vi* [chose] to roll around.

ball-trap [baltrap] *nm* clay pigeon shooting.

balluchon = **baluchon**.

balnéaire [balneɛr] *adj*: **station ~** seaside resort.

balourd, -e [balur, urd] *adj* clumsy.

balte [balt] *adj* Baltic. ○ **Balte** *nmf* native of the Baltic states.

Baltique [baltik] *nf*: **la ~** the Baltic (Sea).

baluchon, balluchon [balyʃɔ̃] *nm* bundle; **faire son ~** *fam* to pack one's bags (and leave).

balustrade [balystrad] *nf* [de terrasse] balustrade. || [rambarde] guardrail.

bambin [bɑ̃bɛ̃] *nm* kiddie.

bambou [bɑ̃bu] *nm* [plante] bamboo.

ban [bɑ̃] *nm* [de mariage]: **publier** OU **afficher les ~s** to publish OU display the banns.

banal, -e, -als [banal] *adj* commonplace, banal.

banaliser [banalize] *vt*: **voiture banalisée** unmarked police car.

banalité [banalite] *nf* [caractère banal] banality. || [cliché] commonplace.

banane [banan] *nf* [fruit] banana. || [sac] bum-bag. || [coiffure] quiff.

bananier, -ière [bananje, jɛr] *adj* banana (*avant n*). ○ **bananier** *nm* [arbre] banana tree. || [cargo] banana boat.

banc [bɑ̃] *nm* [siège] bench; **le ~ des accusés** JUR the dock; **~ d'essai** test-bed; **~ de sable** sandbank.

bancaire [bɑ̃kɛr] *adj* bank (*avant n*), banking (*avant n*).

bancal, -e, -als [bɑ̃kal] *adj* [meuble] wobbly. || [théorie, idée] unsound.

bandage [bɑ̃daʒ] *nm* [de blessé] bandage.

bande [bɑ̃d] *nf* [de tissu, de papier] strip; **~ dessinée** comic strip. || [bandage] bandage. || [de billard] cushion. || [groupe] band; **en ~** in a group. || [pellicule de film] film. || [d'enregistrement] tape; **~ magnétique** (magnetic) tape; **~ originale** CIN original soundtrack. || [voie]: **~ d'arrêt d'urgence** hard shoulder. || RADIO: **~ de fréquence** waveband. || NAVIG: **donner de la ~** to list.

bande-annonce [bɑ̃dɑnɔ̃s] *nf* trailer.

bandeau [bɑ̃do] *nm* [sur les yeux] blindfold. || [dans les cheveux] headband.

bandelette [bɑ̃dlɛt] *nf* strip (of cloth).

bander [bɑ̃de] **1** *vt* MÉD to bandage; **~ les yeux de qqn** to blindfold sb. || [arc] to draw back. || [muscle] to flex. **2** *vi* *vulg* to have a hard-on.

banderole [bɑ̃drɔl] *nf* streamer.

bande-son [bɑ̃dsɔ̃] (*pl* **bandes-son**) *nf* soundtrack.

bandit [bɑ̃di] *nm* [voleur] bandit.

banditisme [bɑ̃ditism] *nm* serious crime.

bandoulière [bɑ̃duljɛr] *nf* bandolier; **en ~** across the shoulder.

banlieue [bɑ̃ljø] *nf* suburbs (*pl*).

banlieusard, -e [bɑ̃ljøzar, ard] *nm, f* *person living in the suburbs.*

bannière [banjer] *nf* [étendard] banner.

bannir [banir] *vt*: **~ qqn/qqch (de)** to banish sb/sthg (from).

banque [bɑ̃k] *nf* [activité] banking. || [établissement, au jeu] bank. || INFORM: **~ de données** data bank. || MÉD: **~ d'organes/du sang/du sperme** organ/blood/sperm bank.

banqueroute [bɑ̃krut] *nf* bankruptcy; **faire ~** to go bankrupt.

banquet [bɑ̃kɛ] *nm* (celebration) dinner; [de gala] banquet.

banquette [bɑ̃kɛt] *nf* seat.

banquier, -ière [bɑ̃kje, jɛr] *nm, f* banker.

banquise [bɑ̃kiz] *nf* ice field.

baptême [batɛm] *nm* RELIG baptism, christening. || [première fois]: **~ de l'air** maiden flight.

baptiser [batize] *vt* to baptize, to christen.

baquet [bakɛ] *nm* [cuve] tub.

bar [bar] *nm* [café, unité de pression] bar. || [poisson] bass.

baraque [barak] *nf* [cabane] hut. || *fam* [maison] house. || [de forain] stall, stand.

baraqué, -e [barake] *adj* *fam* well-built.

baraquement [barakmɑ̃] *nm* camp (*of huts for refugees, workers etc*).

baratin [baratɛ̃] *nm* *fam* smooth talk; **faire du ~ à qqn** to sweet-talk sb.

baratiner [baratine] *fam* **1** *vt* [femme] to chat up; [client] to give one's sales pitch to. **2** *vi* to be a smooth talker.

barbare [barbar] **1** *nm* barbarian. **2** *adj* *péj* [non civilisé] barbarous. || [cruel] barbaric.

barbe [barb] *nf* beard; **~ à papa** candy floss *Br*, cotton candy *Am*; **quelle** OU **la ~!** *fam* what a drag!

barbelé, -e [barbəle] *adj* barbed. ○ **barbelé** *nm* barbed wire (*U*).

barbiche [barbiʃ] *nf* goatee (beard).

barbiturique [barbityrik] *nm* barbiturate.

barboter [barbɔte] *vi* to paddle.

barboteuse [barbɔtøz] *nf* romper-suit.

barbouillé, -e [barbuje] *adj*: **être ~, avoir l'estomac ~** to feel sick.

barbouiller [barbuje] *vt* [salir]: **~ qqch (de)** to smear sthg (with).

barbu, -e [barby] *adj* bearded. ○ **barbu** *nm* bearded man.

bardé, -e [barde] *adj*: **il est ~ de diplômes** he's got heaps of diplomas.

barder [barde] **1** *vt* CULIN to bard. **2** *vi fam*: **ça va ~** there'll be trouble.

barème [barɛm] *nm* [de référence] table; [de salaires] scale.

baril [baril] *nm* barrel.

bariolé, -e [barjɔle] *adj* multicoloured.

barjo(t) [barʒo] *adj inv fam* nuts.

barmaid [barmɛd] *nf* barmaid.

barman [barman] (*pl* **barmans** OU **barmen** [barmɛn]) *nm* barman.

baromètre [barɔmɛtr] *nm* barometer.

baron, -onne [barɔ̃, ɔn] *nm, f* baron (*f* baroness).

baroque [barɔk] *adj* [style] baroque. || [bizarre] weird.

barque [bark] *nf* small boat.

barquette [barkɛt] *nf* [tartelette] pastry boat. || [récipient - de fruits] punnet; [- de crème glacée] tub.

barrage [baraʒ] *nm* [de rue] roadblock. || CONSTR dam.

barre [bar] *nf* [gén & JUR] bar; **~ d'espacement** [sur machine à écrire] space bar; **~ fixe** GYM high bar; **~ des témoins** JUR witness box *Br* OU stand *Am*. NAVIG helm. || [trait] stroke.

barreau [baro] *nm* bar; **le ~** JUR the Bar.

barrer [bare] *vt* [rue, route] to block. || [mot, phrase] to cross out. || [bateau] to steer. ○ **se barrer** *vp fam* to clear off.

barrette [barɛt] *nf* [pince à cheveux] (hair) slide *Br*, barrette *Am*.

barreur, -euse [barœr, øz] *nm, f* NAVIG helmsman; [à l'aviron] cox.

barricade [barikad] *nf* barricade.

barrière [barjɛr] *nf litt & fig* barrier.

barrique [barik] *nf* barrel.

baryton [baritɔ̃] *nm* baritone.

bas, basse [ba, baz *devant nm commençant par voyelle ou h muet*, bas] *adj* [gén] low. || *péj* [vil] base, low. || MUS bass. ○ **bas 1** *nm* [partie inférieure] bottom, lower part. || [vêtement] stocking. **2** *adv* low; **à ~ ...!** down with ...!; **parler ~** to speak in a low voice, to speak softly; **mettre ~** [animal] to give birth. ○ **en bas** *loc adv* at the bottom; [dans une maison] downstairs. ○ **en bas de** *loc prép* at the bottom of; **attendre qqn en ~ de chez lui** to wait for sb downstairs. ○ **bas de gamme** *adj* downmarket.

basalte [bazalt] *nm* basalt.

basané, -e [bazane] *adj* tanned.

bas-côté [bakote] *nm* [de route] verge.

bascule [baskyl] *nf* [balançoire] seesaw.

basculer [baskyle] **1** *vi* to fall over, to overbalance; [benne] to tip up; **~ dans qqch** *fig* to tip over into sthg. **2** *vt* to tip up, to tilt.

base [baz] *nf* [partie inférieure] base. || [principe fondamental] basis; **de ~** basic; **une boisson à ~ d'orange** an orange-based drink; **sur la ~ de** on the basis of. || INFORM: **~ de données** database.

baser [baze] *vt* to base. ○ **se baser** *vp*: **sur quoi vous basez-vous pour affirmer cela?** what are you basing this statement on?

bas-fond [bafɔ̃] *nm* [de l'océan] shallow. ○ **bas-fonds** *nmpl fig* [de la société] dregs. || [quartiers pauvres] slums.

basilic [bazilik] *nm* [plante] basil.

basilique [bazilik] *nf* basilica.

basique [bazik] *adj* basic.

basket [basket] **1** *nm* = **basket-ball**. **2** *nf* [chaussure] trainer *Br*, sneaker *Am*; **lâche-moi les ~s!** *fam* fig get off my back!

basket-ball [basketbol] *nm* basketball.

basque [bask] **1** *adj* Basque; **le Pays ~** the Basque country. **2** *nm* [langue] Basque. **3** *nf* [vêtement] tail (*of coat*); **être toujours pendu aux ~s de qqn** *fam fig* to be always tagging along after sb. ○ **Basque** *nmf* Basque.

bas-relief [barəljef] *nm* bas-relief.

basse [bas] **1** *adj* → **bas**. **2** *nf* MUS bass.

basse-cour [baskur] *nf* [volaille] poultry. || [partie de ferme] farmyard.

bassement [basmã] *adv* despicably.

basset [basɛ] *nm* basset hound.

bassin [basɛ̃] *nm* [cuvette] bowl. || [pièce d'eau] (ornamental) pond. || [de piscine]: **petit/grand ~** children's/main pool. || ANAT pelvis. || GÉOL basin; **le Bassin parisien** the Paris basin.

bassine [basin] *nf* bowl, basin.

bassiste [basist] *nmf* bass player.

basson [basɔ̃] *nm* [instrument] bassoon; [personne] bassoonist.

bastide [bastid] *nf* traditional farmhouse or country house in southern France; walled town (in south-west France).

bastingage [bastɛ̃gaʒ] *nm* (ship's) rail.

bastion [bastjɔ̃] *nm litt & fig* bastion.

bas-ventre [bavɑ̃tr] *nm* stomach.

bataille [bataj] *nf* MIL battle. || [bagarre] fight. || [jeu de cartes] ≃ beggar-my-neighbour. || *loc*: **en ~** [cheveux] dishevelled.

bataillon [batajɔ̃] *nm* MIL battalion; *fig* horde.

bâtard, -e [batar, ard] **1** *adj* [enfant] illegitimate. || *péj* [style, solution] hybrid. **2** *nm, f* illegitimate child. ○ **bâtard** *nm* [pain] ≃ Vienna loaf. || [chien] mongrel.

batavia [batavja] *nf* Webb lettuce.

bateau [bato] *nm* [embarcation - *gén*] boat; [- plus grand] ship; **~ à voile/ moteur** sailing/motor boat; **~ de pêche** fishing boat; **mener qqn en ~** *fig* to take sb for a ride. || [de trottoir] driveway entrance (*low kerb*). || (*en apposition inv*) [sujet, thème] well-worn.

bâti, -e [bati] *adj* [terrain] developed. || [personne]: **bien ~** well-built.

batifoler [batifɔle] *ri* to frolic.

bâtiment [batimɑ̃] *nm* [édifice] building. || IND: **le ~** the building trade. || NAVIG ship, vessel.

bâtir [batir] *rt* CONSTR to build. || *fig* [réputation, fortune] to build (up); [théorie, phrase] to construct. || COUTURE to tack.

bâtisse [batis] *nf souvent péj* house.

bâton [batɔ̃] *nm* [gén] stick; **~ de ski** ski pole. || *fam fig* 10 000 francs. || *loc:* **mettre des ~s dans les roues à qqn** to put a spoke in sb's wheel; **parler à ~s rompus** to talk of this and that.

bâtonnet [batɔnɛ] *nm* rod.

batracien [batrasjɛ̃] *nm* amphibian.

battage [bataʒ] *nm*: **~ (publicitaire ou médiatique)** (media) hype.

battant, -e [batɑ̃, ɑ̃t] **1** *adj*: **sous une pluie ~e** in the pouring ou driving rain; **le cœur ~** with beating heart. **2** *nm, f* fighter. ○ **battant** *nm* [de porte] door (*of double doors*); [de fenêtre] half (*of double window*). || [de cloche] clapper.

battement [batmɑ̃] *nm* [mouvement - d'ailes] flap, beating (*U*); [- de cœur, pouls] beat, beating (*U*); [- de cils, paupières] flutter, fluttering (*U*). || [intervalle de temps] break; **une heure de ~** an hour free.

batterie [batri] *nf* ÉLECTR & MIL battery; **recharger ses ~s** *fig* to recharge one's batteries. || [attirail]: **~ de cuisine** kitchen utensils (*pl*). || MUS drums (*pl*).

batteur [batœr] *nm* MUS drummer. || CULIN beater, whisk. || [SPORT - de cricket] batsman; [- de base-ball] batter.

battre [batr] **1** *rt* [gén] to beat; **~ en neige** [blancs d'œufs] to beat until stiff. || [cartes] to shuffle. **2** *ri* [gén] to beat; **~ des cils** to blink; **~ des mains** to clap (one's hands). ○ **se battre** *rp* to fight; **se ~ contre qqn** to fight sb.

battu, -e [baty] **1** *pp* → **battre**. **2** *adj* [tassé] hard-packed; **jouer sur terre ~e** TENNIS to play on clay. ○ **battue** *nf* [chasse] beat.

baume [bom] *nm litt & fig* balm; **mettre du ~ au cœur de qqn** to comfort sb.

baux → **bail**.

bavard, -e [bavar, ard] *adj* talkative.

bavardage [bavardaʒ] *nm* [papotage] chattering. || (*gén pl*) [racontar] gossip (*U*).

bavarder [bavarde] *ri* to chatter; *péj* to gossip.

bave [bav] *nf* [salive] dribble. || [d'animal] slaver. || [de limace] slime.

baver [bave] *ri* [personne] to dribble. || [animal] to slaver. || [stylo] to leak. || *loc:* **en ~** *fam* to have a hard ou rough time of it.

bavette [bavɛt] *nf* [bavoir, de tablier] bib. || [viande] flank. || *loc:* **tailler une ~ (avec qqn)** *fam* to have a chinwag (with sb).

baveux, -euse [bavø, øz] *adj* [bébé] dribbling. || [omelette] runny.

bavoir [bavwar] *nm* bib.

bavure [bavyr] *nf* [tache] smudge. || [erreur] blunder.

bayer [baje] *ri*: **~ aux corneilles** to stand gazing into space.

bazar [bazar] *nm* [boutique] general store. || *fam* [désordre] jumble, clutter.

BCBG (*abr de bon chic bon genre*) *nmf & adj* term used to describe an upper-class lifestyle reflected especially in expensive but conservative clothes.

bd *abr de* boulevard.

BD, bédé [bede] (*abr de bande dessinée*) *nf*: **une ~** a comic strip.

béant, -e [beɑ̃, ɑ̃t] *adj* [plaie, gouffre] gaping; [yeux] wide open.

béat, -e [bea, at] *adj* [heureux] blissful.

beau, belle, beaux [bo, bɛl] *adj* (*bel devant voyelle ou h muet*) [joli - femme] beautiful, good-looking; [- homme] handsome, good-looking; [- chose] beautiful. || [temps] fine, good. || (*toujours avant le nom*) [important] fine, excellent; **une belle somme** a tidy sum (of money). || *iron* [mauvais]: **une belle grippe** a nasty dose of the flu; **un beau travail** a fine piece of work. || (*sens intensif*): **un ~ jour** one fine day. ○ **beau 1** *adr:* **il fait ~** the weather is good ou fine; **j'ai ~ essayer** ... however hard I try ... try as I may ... **2** *nm:* **être au ~ fixe** to be set fair; **avoir le moral au ~ fixe** *fig* to have a sunny disposition; **faire le ~** [chien] to sit up and beg. ○ **belle** *nf* [dans un jeu] decider. ○ **de plus belle** *loc adv* more than ever.

beaucoup [boku] **1** *adv* [un grand nombre]: **~ de** a lot of, many. || [une grande quantité]: **~ de** a lot of; **il n'a pas ~ de temps** he hasn't a lot of ou much time. || (*modifiant un verbe*) a lot. **c'est ~ dire** that's saying a lot. || (*modifiant un adjectif comparatif*) much, a lot; **c'est mieux** it's much ou a lot better. **2** *pron inv* many; **nous sommes ~ à penser que ...** many of us think that .... ○ **de beaucoup** *loc adv* by far.

beauf [bof] *nm péj* stereotype of average French man with narrow views. || *fam* [beau-frère] brother-in-law.

beau-fils [bofis] *nm* [gendre] son-in-law. || [de remariage] stepson.

beau-frère [bofʀɛʀ] *nm* brother-in-law.

beau-père [bopɛʀ] *nm* [père du conjoint] father-in-law. || [de remariage] stepfather.

beauté [bote] *nf* beauty; **de toute ~** absolutely beautiful; **en ~** [magnifiquement] in great style.

beaux-arts [bozaʀ] *nmpl* fine art (*sg*). ○ **Beaux-Arts** *nmpl*: **les Beaux-Arts** French national art school.

beaux-parents [bopaʀɑ̃] *nmpl* [de l'homme] husband's parents, in-laws. || [de la femme] wife's parents, in-laws.

bébé [bebe] *nm* baby.

bébé-éprouvette [bebeepʀuvɛt] (*pl* **bébés-éprouvette**) *nm* test-tube baby.

bébête [bebɛt] *adj* silly.

bec [bɛk] *nm* [d'oiseau] beak. || [d'instrument de musique] mouthpiece. || [de casserole etc] lip; **~ de gaz** [réverbère] gaslamp (*in street*); **~ verseur** spout. || *fam* [bouche] mouth; **clouer le ~ à qqn** to shut sb up.

bécane [bekan] *nf fam* [moto, vélo] bike. || [ordinateur etc] machine.

bécasse [bekas] *nf* [oiseau] woodcock. || *fam* [femme sotte] silly goose.

bec-de-lièvre [bɛkdəljɛvʀ] (*pl* **becs-de-lièvre**) *nm* harelip.

bêche [bɛʃ] *nf* spade.

bêcher [beʃe] *vt* to dig.

bécoter [bekɔte] *vt fam* to snog *Br* ou smooch with. ○ **se bécoter** *vp* to snog *Br*, to smooch.

becquée [beke] *nf*: **donner la ~ à** to feed.

becqueter, béqueter [bɛkte] *vt* to peck at.

bedaine [bədɛn] *nf* potbelly.

bédé = **BD**.

bedonnant, -e [bədɔnɑ̃, ɑ̃t] *adj* potbellied.

bée [be] *adj*: **bouche ~** open-mouthed.

bégayer [begeje] **1** *vi* to have a stutter ou stammer. **2** *vt* to stammer (out).

bégonia [begɔnja] *nm* begonia.

bègue [bɛg] **1** *adj*: **être ~** to have a stutter ou stammer. **2** *nmf* stutterer, stammerer.

béguin [begɛ̃] *nm fam*: **avoir le ~ pour qqn** to have a crush on sb.

beige [bɛʒ] *adj & nm* beige.

beignet [bɛɲɛ] *nm* fritter.

bel [bɛl] → **beau**.

bêler [bele] *vi* to bleat.

belette [bəlɛt] *nf* weasel.

belge [bɛlʒ] *adj* Belgian. ○ **Belge** *nmf* Belgian.

Belgique [bɛlʒik] *nf*: **la ~** Belgium.

bélier [belje] *nm* [animal] ram. || [poutre] battering ram. ○ **Bélier** *nm* ASTROL Aries.

belle [bɛl] *adj & nf* → **beau**.

belle-famille [bɛlfamij] *nf* [de l'homme] husband's family, in-laws (*pl*). || [de la femme] wife's family, in-laws (*pl*).

belle-fille [bɛlfij] *nf* [épouse du fils] daughter-in-law. || [de remariage] step-daughter.

belle-mère [bɛlmɛʀ] *nf* [mère du conjoint] mother-in-law. || [de remariage] stepmother.

belle-sœur [bɛlsœʀ] *nf* sister-in-law.

belligérant, -e [beliʒeʀɑ̃, ɑ̃t] *adj & nm*, *f* belligerent.

belliqueux, -euse [belikø, øz] *adj* [peuple] warlike; [humeur, tempérament] aggressive.

belvédère [bɛlvedɛʀ] *nm* [construction] belvedere. || [terrasse] viewpoint.

bémol [bemɔl] *adj & nm* MUS flat.

bénédiction [benediksjɔ̃] *nf* blessing.

bénéfice [benefis] *nm* [avantage] advantage, benefit; **au ~ de** in aid of. || [profit] profit.

bénéficiaire [benefisjɛʀ] **1** *nmf* [gén] beneficiary; [de chèque] payee. **2** *adj* [marge] profit (*avant n*); [résultat, société] profit-making.

bénéficier [benefisje] *vi*: **~ de** [profiter de] to benefit from; [jouir de] to have, to enjoy; [obtenir] to have, to get.

bénéfique [benefik] *adj* beneficial.

Bénélux [benelyks] *nm*: **le ~** Benelux.

bénévole [benevɔl] **1** *adj* voluntary. **2** *nmf* volunteer, voluntary worker.

bénin, -igne [benɛ̃, iɲ] *adj* [maladie, accident] minor; [tumeur] benign.

bénir [benir] *vt* [gén] to bless. || [se réjouir de] to thank God for.

bénitier [benitje] *nm* holy water font.

benjamin, -e [bɛ̃ʒamɛ̃, in] *nm, f* [de famille] youngest child; [de groupe] youngest member.

benne [bɛn] *nf* [de camion] tipper. || [de téléphérique] car. || [pour déchets] skip.

benzine [bɛ̃zin] *nf* benzine.

BEP (*abr de* **brevet d'études professionnelles**) *nm* school-leaver's diploma *(taken at age 18)*.

BEPC, Bepc (*abr de* **brevet d'études du premier cycle**) *nm* former school certificate *(taken at age 16)*.

béquille [bekij] *nf* [pour marcher] crutch. || [d'un deux-roues] stand.

berceau, -x [bɛrso] *nm* cradle.

bercer [bɛrse] *vt* [bébé, bateau] to rock.

berceuse [bɛrsøz] *nf* [chanson] lullaby. || *Can* [fauteuil] rocking chair.

béret [berɛ] *nm* beret.

berge [bɛrʒ] *nf* [bord] bank. || *fam* [an]: **il a plus de 50 ~s** he's over 50.

berger, -ère [bɛrʒe, ɛr] *nm, f* shepherd (*f* shepherdess). ○ **berger allemand** *nm* alsatian *Br*, German shepherd.

bergerie [bɛrʒəri] *nf* sheepfold.

Berlin [bɛrlɛ̃] *n* Berlin.

berline [bɛrlin] *nf* saloon (car) *Br*, sedan *Am*.

berlingot [bɛrlɛ̃go] *nm* [de lait] carton. || [bonbon] boiled sweet.

berlue [bɛrly] *nf*: **j'ai la ~!** I must be seeing things!

bermuda [bɛrmyda] *nm* bermuda shorts (*pl*).

berne [bɛrn] *nf*: **en ~** ≃ at half-mast.

berner [bɛrne] *vt* to fool.

besogne [bəzɔɲ] *nf* job, work (*U*).

besoin [bəzwɛ̃] *nm* need; **avoir ~ de qqch/de faire qqch** to need sthg/to do sthg; **au ~** if necessary, if need ou needs be. ○ **besoins** *nmpl* [exigences] needs. || *loc*: **faire ses ~s** to relieve o.s.

bestial, -e, -iaux [bɛstjal, jo] *adj* bestial, brutish.

bestiole [bɛstjɔl] *nf* (little) creature.

bétail [betaj] *nm* cattle (*pl*).

bête [bɛt] **1** *nf* [animal] animal; [insecte] insect; **~ de somme** beast of burden. **2** *adj* [stupide] stupid.

bêtise [betiz] *nf* [stupidité] stupidity. || [action, remarque] stupid thing; **faire/dire une ~** to do/say something stupid.

béton [betɔ̃] *nm* [matériau] concrete; **~ armé** reinforced concrete.

bétonnière [betɔnjɛr] *nf* cement mixer.

betterave [betrav] *nf* beetroot *Br*, beet *Am*; **~ sucrière** ou **à sucre** sugar beet.

beugler [bøgle] *vi* [bovin] to moo, to low.

beurre [bœr] *nm* [aliment] butter.

beurrer [bœre] *vt* to butter.

beurrier [bœrje] *nm* butter dish.

beuverie [bœvri] *nf* drinking session.

bévue [bevy] *nf* blunder.

biais [bjɛ] *nm* [ligne oblique] slant; **en ~**, **de ~** [de travers] at an angle. || [moyen détourné] expedient; **par le ~ de** by means of.

biaiser [bjeze] *vi fig* to dodge the issue.

bibelot [biblo] *nm* trinket, curio.

biberon [bibrɔ̃] *nm* baby's bottle.

bible [bibl] *nf* bible.

bibliographie [biblijɔgrafi] *nf* bibliography.

bibliophile [biblijɔfil] *nmf* book lover.

bibliothécaire [biblijɔtekɛr] *nmf* librarian.

bibliothèque [biblijɔtɛk] *nf* [meuble] bookcase. || [édifice, collection] library.

biblique [biblik] *adj* biblical.

bicarbonate [bikarbɔnat] *nm*: **~ (de soude)** bicarbonate of soda.

biceps [bisɛps] *nm* biceps.

biche [biʃ] *nf* ZOOL hind, doe.

bicolore [bikɔlɔr] *adj* two-coloured.

bicoque [bikɔk] *nf péj* house.

bicorne [bikɔrn] *nm* cocked hat.

bicyclette [bisiklɛt] *nf* bicycle; **rouler à ~** to cycle.

bide [bid] *nm fam* [ventre] belly. || [échec] flop.

bidet [bidɛ] *nm* [sanitaire] bidet.

bidon [bidɔ̃] *nm* [récipient] can. || *fam* [ventre] belly. || (*en apposition inv*) *fam* [faux] phoney.

bidonville [bidɔ̃vil] *nm* shantytown.

bielle [bjɛl] *nf* connecting rod.

bien [bjɛ̃] (*compar & superl* **mieux**) **1** *adj inv* [satisfaisant] good; **il est ~ comme prof** he's a good teacher. || [en bonne santé] well. || [joli] good-looking; **tu ne trouves pas qu'elle est ~ comme ça?** don't you think she looks good ou nice like that? || [à l'aise] comfortable. || [convenable] respectable. **2** *nm* [sens moral]: **le ~ et le mal** good and evil. || [intérêt] good; **je te dis ça pour ton ~** I'm telling you this for your own good. || [richesse, propriété] property, possession; **~s de consommation** consumer goods. || *loc*: **faire du ~ à qqn** to do sb good; **dire du ~ de qqn/qqch** to speak well of sb/sthg; **mener à ~** to bring to fruition, to complete. **3** *adv* [de manière satisfaisante] well; **tu as ~ fait** you did the right thing; **tu ferais ~ d'y aller** you would be wise to go; **c'est ~ fait!** it serves him/her *etc* right! || [sens intensif] quite, really; **~ souvent** quite often; **j'espère ~ que ...** I DO hope that ...; **on a ~ ri** we had a good laugh; **il y a ~ trois heures que j'attends** I've been waiting for at least three hours. || [renforçant un comparatif]: **il est parti ~ plus tard** he left much later. || [servant à conclure ou à introduire]: **~, je t'écoute** well, I'm listening. || [en effet]: **c'est ~ lui** it really IS him; **c'est ~ ce que je disais** that's just what I said. **4** *interj* **eh ~!** oh well!; **eh ~, qu'en penses-tu?** well, what do you think? ○ **biens** *nmpl* property (*U*). ○ **bien de, bien des** *loc adj*: **~ des gens sont venus** quite a lot of people came; **il a ~ de la chance** he's very or really lucky. ○ **bien entendu** *loc adv* of course. ○ **bien que** *loc conj* (+ *subjonctif*) although, though. ○ **bien sûr** *loc adv* of course, certainly.

bien-aimé, -e [bjɛ̃neme] (*mpl* **bien-aimés,** *fpl* **bien-aimées**) *adj* & *nm, f* beloved.

bien-être [bjɛ̃nɛtr] *nm inv* [physique] wellbeing.

bienfaisance [bjɛ̃fəzɑ̃s] *nf* charity.

bienfaisant, -e [bjɛ̃fəzɑ̃, ɑ̃t] *adj* beneficial.

bienfait [bjɛ̃fɛ] *nm* [effet bénéfique] benefit. || [faveur] kindness.

bienfaiteur, -trice [bjɛ̃fɛtœr, tris] *nm, f* benefactor.

bien-fondé [bjɛ̃fɔ̃de] (*pl* **bien-fondés**) *nm* validity.

bienheureux, -euse [bjɛ̃nœrø, øz] *adj* RELIG blessed. || [heureux] happy.

bientôt [bjɛ̃to] *adv* soon; **à ~!** see you soon!

bienveillance [bjɛ̃vejɑ̃s] *nf* kindness.

bienveillant, -e [bjɛ̃vejɑ̃, ɑ̃t] *adj* kindly.

bienvenu, -e [bjɛ̃vəny] **1** *adj* [qui arrive à propos] welcome. **2** *nm, f*: **être le ~/la ~e** to be welcome; **soyez le ~!** welcome!

○ **bienvenue** *nf* welcome; **souhaiter la ~ à qqn** to welcome sb.

bière [bjɛr] *nf* [boisson] beer; **~ blonde** lager; **~ brune** brown ale; **~ pression** draught beer. || [cercueil] coffin.

bifteck [biftɛk] *nm* steak.

bifurcation [bifyrkasjɔ̃] *nf* [embranchement] fork; *fig* new direction.

bifurquer [bifyrke] *vi* [route, voie ferrée] to fork. || [voiture] to turn off.

bigamie [bigami] *nf* bigamy.

bigoudi [bigudi] *nm* curler.

bijou, -x [biʒu] *nm* [joyau] jewel. || *fig* [chef d'œuvre] gem.

bijouterie [biʒutri] *nf* [magasin] jeweller's (shop).

bijoutier, -ière [biʒutje, jɛr] *nm, f* jeweller.

Bikini® [bikini] *nm vieilli* bikini.

bilan [bilɑ̃] *nm* FIN balance sheet; **déposer son ~** to declare bankruptcy. || [état d'une situation] state of affairs; **faire le ~ (de)** to take stock (of); **~ de santé** check-up.

bilatéral, -e, -aux [bilateral, o] *adj* [stationnement] on both sides (of the road). || [contrat, accord] bilateral.

bile [bil] *nf* bile; **se faire de la ~** *fam* to worry.

biliaire [biljɛr] *adj* biliary; **calcul ~** gallstone; **vésicule ~** gall bladder.

bilingue [bilɛ̃g] *adj* bilingual.

billard [bijar] *nm* [jeu] billiards (*U*). || [table de jeu] billiard table.

bille [bij] *nf* [d'enfant] marble. || [de bois] block of wood.

billet [bijɛ] *nm* [lettre] note. || [argent]: **~ (de banque)** (bank) note; **un ~ de 100 francs** a 100-franc note. || [ticket] ticket.

billetterie [bijetri] *nf* [à l'aéroport] ticket desk; [à la gare] booking office or hall. || BANQUE cash dispenser.

billion [biljɔ̃] *nm* billion *Br*, trillion *Am*.

bimensuel, -elle [bimɑ̃sɥɛl] *adj* twice monthly. ○ **bimensuel** *nm* semi-monthly *Am*.

bimoteur [bimɔtœr] *nm* twin-engined plane.

binaire [binɛr] *adj* binary.

biner [bine] *vt* to hoe.

binocle [binɔkl] *nm* pince-nez. ○ **binocles** *nmpl fam vieilli* specs.

biochimie [bjɔʃimi] *nf* biochemistry.

biodégradable [bjɔdegradabl] *adj* biodegradable.

biographie [bjɔgrafi] *nf* biography.

biologie [bjɔlɔʒi] *nf* biology.

biologique [bjɔlɔʒik] *adj* SCIENCE biological. || [naturel] organic.

biopsie [bjɔpsi] *nf* biopsy.

biréacteur [bireaktœr] *nm* twin-engined jet.

bis¹, -e [bi, biz] *adj* greyish-brown; **pain ~** brown bread.

bis² [bis] *adv* [dans adresse]: 5 ~ 5a. || [à la fin d'un spectacle] encore.

bisannuel, -elle [bizanɥɛl] *adj* biennial.

biscornu, -e [biskɔrny] *adj* [difforme] irregularly shaped. || [bizarre] weird.

biscotte [biskɔt] *nf toasted bread sold in packets and often eaten for breakfast.*

biscuit [biskɥi] *nm* [sec] biscuit *Br*, cookie *Am*; [salé] cracker. || [gâteau] sponge.

bise [biz] *nf* [vent] north wind. || *fam* [baiser] kiss; **grosses ~s** love and kisses.

biseau, -x [bizo] *nm* bevel; **en ~** bevelled.

bison [bizɔ̃] *nm* bison.

bisou [bizu] *nm fam* kiss.

bissextile [bisɛkstil] → **année.**

bistouri [bisturi] *nm* lancet.

bistro(t) [bistro] *nm fam* cafe, bar.

bit [bit] *nm* INFORM bit.

bivouac [bivwak] *nm* bivouac.

bivouaquer [bivwake] *vi* to bivouac.

bizarre [bizar] *adj* strange, odd.

bizutage [bizytaʒ] *nm practical jokes played on new arrivals in a school or college.*

black-out [blakawt] *nm* blackout.

blafard, -e [blafar, ard] *adj* pale.

blague [blag] *nf* [plaisanterie] joke.

blaguer [blage] *fam vi* to joke.

blagueur, -euse [blagœr, øz] *fam* **1** *adj* jokey. **2** *nm, f* joker.

blaireau, -x [blɛro] *nm* [animal] badger. || [de rasage] shaving brush.

blâme [blam] *nm* [désapprobation] disapproval. || [sanction] reprimand.

blâmer [blame] *vt* [désapprouver] to blame. || [sanctionner] to reprimand.

blanc, blanche [blɑ̃, blɑ̃ʃ] *adj* [gén] white. || [non écrit] blank. || [pâle] pale. ○ **blanc** *nm* [couleur] white. || [personne] white (man). || [linge de maison]: **le ~ the** (household) linen. || [sur page] blank (space); **en ~** [chèque] blank. || [de volaille] white meat. || [vin] white (wine). || *loc*: **chauffé à ~** white-hot. ○ **blanche** *nf* [personne] white (woman). || MUS minim. ○ **blanc d'œuf** *nm* egg white.

blancheur [blɑ̃ʃœr] *nf* whiteness.

blanchir [blɑ̃ʃir] **1** *vt* [mur] to whitewash. || [linge, argent] to launder. || [légumes] to blanch. **2** *vi*: ~ **(de)** to go white (with).

blanchissage [blɑ̃ʃisaʒ] *nm* [de linge] laundering.

blanchisserie [blɑ̃ʃisri] *nf* laundry.

blasé, -e [blaze] *adj* blasé.

blason [blazɔ̃] *nm* coat of arms.

blasphème [blasfɛm] *nm* blasphemy.

blasphémer [blasfeme] *vt & vi* to blaspheme.

blatte [blat] *nf* cockroach.

blazer [blazɛr] *nm* blazer.

blé [ble] *nm* [céréale] wheat, corn. || *fam* [argent] dough.

blême [blɛm] *adj*: ~ **(de)** pale (with).

blennorragie [blenɔraʒi] *nf* gonorrhoea.

blessant, -e [blesɑ̃, ɑ̃t] *adj* hurtful.

blessé, -e [blese] *nm, f* wounded ou injured person.

blesser [blese] *vt* [physiquement - accidentellement] to injure, to hurt; [- par arme] to wound. || [moralement] to hurt. ○ **se blesser** *vp* to injure o.s., to hurt o.s.

blessure [blesyr] *nf litt & fig* wound.

bleu, -e [blø] *adj* [couleur] blue. || [viande] very rare. ○ **bleu** *nm* [couleur] blue. || [meurtrissure] bruise. || [fromage] blue cheese. || [vêtement]: ~ **de travail** overalls (*pl*).

bleuet [bløɛ] *nm* cornflower.

bleuir [bløir] *vt & vi* to turn blue.

bleuté, -e [bløte] *adj* bluish.

blindé, -e [blɛ̃de] *adj* [véhicule] armoured; [porte, coffre] armour-plated. ○ **blindé** *nm* armoured car.

blinder [blɛ̃de] *vt* [véhicule] to armour; [porte, coffre] to armour-plate.

blizzard [blizar] *nm* blizzard.

bloc [blɔk] *nm* [gén] block; **en ~** wholesale. || [assemblage] unit; ~ **opératoire** operating theatre.

blocage [blɔkaʒ] *nm* ÉCON freeze, freezing (*U*). || PSYCHOL (mental) block.

blockhaus [blɔkos] *nm* blockhouse.

bloc-notes [blɔknɔt] *nm* notepad.

blocus [blɔkys] *nm* blockade.

blond, -e [blɔ̃, blɔ̃d] **1** *adj* fair, blond. **2** *nm, f* fair-haired ou blond man (*f* fair-haired ou blonde woman). ○ **blond** *nm*: ~ **cendré/vénitien/platine** ash/strawberry/platinum blond. ○ **blonde**

nf [cigarette] Virginia cigarette. || [bière] lager.

blondeur [blɔ̃dœr] *nf* blondness, fairness.

bloquer [blɔke] *vt* [porte, freins] to jam; [roues] to lock. || [route, chemin] to block; [personne]: **être bloqué** to be stuck. || [prix, salaires, crédit] to freeze. ○ **se bloquer** *vp* [se coincer] to jam.

blottir [blɔtir] ○ **se blottir** *vp*: **se ~ (contre)** to snuggle up (to).

blouse [bluz] *nf* [de travail, d'écolier] smock.

blouson [bluzɔ̃] *nm* bomber jacket, blouson.

blue-jean [bludʒin] (*pl* **blue-jeans** [bludʒins]) *nm* jeans (*pl*).

blues [bluz] *nm inv* blues.

bluffer [blœfe] *fam vi & vt* to bluff.

blush [blœʃ] *nm* blusher.

boa [bɔa] *nm* boa.

bobard [bɔbar] *nm fam* fib.

bobine [bɔbin] *nf* [cylindre] reel, spool. || ÉLECTR coil.

bobsleigh [bɔbsleg] *nm* bobsleigh.

bocage [bɔkaʒ] *nm* GÉOGR bocage.

bocal, -aux [bɔkal, o] *nm* jar.

body-building [bɔdibildiŋ] *nm*: **le ~** body building (*U*).

bœuf [bœf, *pl* bø] *nm* [animal] ox. || [viande] beef.

bof [bɔf] *interj fam* [exprime la lassitude] I don't really care.

bohème [bɔɛm] *adj* bohemian.

bohémien, -ienne [bɔemjɛ̃, jɛn] *nm, f* [tsigane] gipsy.

boire [bwar] **1** *vt* [s'abreuver] to drink. || [absorber] to soak up, to absorb. **2** *vi* to drink.

bois [bwa] **1** *nm* wood; **en ~** wooden. **2** *nmpl* MUS woodwind (*U*). || [cornes] antlers.

boisé, -e [bwaze] *adj* wooded.

boiserie [bwazri] *nf* panelling (*U*).

boisson [bwasɔ̃] *nf* [breuvage] drink.

boîte [bwat] *nf* [récipient] box; **en ~** tinned *Br*, canned; **~ de conserve** tin *Br*, can; **~ à gants** glove compartment; **~ aux lettres** [pour la réception] letterbox; [pour l'envoi] postbox *Br*, mailbox *Am*; **~ postale** post office box; **~ de vitesses** gearbox. || [fam] [entreprise] company, firm; [lycée] school. || *fam* [discothèque]: **~ (de nuit)** nightclub, club.

boiter [bwate] *vi* [personne] to limp.

boiteux, -euse [bwatø, øz] *adj* [personne] lame. || [meuble] wobbly. || *fig* [raisonnement] shaky.

boîtier [bwatje] *nm* [boîte] case. || TECHNOL casing.

bol [bɔl] *nm* [récipient] bowl. || [contenu] bowl, bowlful. || *loc*: **prendre un ~ d'air** to get some fresh air.

bolet [bɔle] *nm* boletus.

bolide [bɔlid] *nm* [véhicule] racing car.

Bolivie [bɔlivi] *nf*: **la ~** Bolivia.

bombance [bɔ̃bɑ̃s] *nf*: **faire ~** *fam* to have a feast.

bombardement [bɔ̃bardəmɑ̃] *nm* bombardment, bombing (*U*).

bombarder [bɔ̃barde] *vt* MIL to bomb. || [assaillir]: **~ qqn/qqch de** to bombard sb/sthg with.

bombardier [bɔ̃bardje] *nm* [avion] bomber. || [aviateur] bombardier.

bombe [bɔ̃b] *nf* [projectile] bomb; *fig* bombshell; **~ atomique** atomic bomb; **~ à retardement** time bomb. || [casquette] riding hat. || [atomiseur] spray, aerosol.

bombé, -e [bɔ̃be] *adj* bulging, rounded.

bon, bonne [bɔ̃, bɔn] (*compar & superl* **meilleur**) *adj* [gén] good. || [généreux] good, kind. || [utilisable - billet, carte] valid. || [correct] right. || [dans l'expression d'un souhait]: **bonne année!** Happy New Year!; **bonne chance!** good luck!; **bonnes vacances!** have a nice holiday! || *loc*: **tu es ~ pour une contravention** you'll end up with *ou* you'll get a parking ticket; **~ à** (+ *infinitif*) fit to; **c'est ~ à savoir** that's worth knowing. ○ **bon 1** *adv*: **il fait ~** the weather's fine, it's fine; **sentir ~** to smell good. **2** *interj* [marque de satisfaction] good! || [marque de surprise]: **ah ~!** really? **3** *nm* [constatant un droit] voucher; **~ de commande** order form; **~ du Trésor** FIN Treasury bill *ou* bond. ○ **pour de bon** *loc adv* seriously, really.

bonbon [bɔ̃bɔ̃] *nm* [friandise] piece of candy *Am*. || *Belg* [gâteau] biscuit.

bonbonne [bɔ̃bɔn] *nf* demijohn.

bonbonnière [bɔ̃bɔnjer] *nf* [boîte] sweet-box *Br*, candy box *Am*.

bond [bɔ̃] *nm* [d'animal, de personne] leap, bound; [de balle] bounce; **faire un ~** to leap (forward).

bonde [bɔ̃d] *nf* [d'évier] plug. || [trou] bunghole. || [bouchon] bung.

bondé, -e [bɔ̃de] *adj* packed.

bondir [bɔ̃dir] *vi* [sauter] to leap, to bound; **~ sur qqn/qqch** to pounce on sb/sthg. || [s'élancer] to leap forward.

bonheur [bɔnœr] *nm* [félicité] happiness. || [chance] (good) luck, good fortune; **par ~** happily, fortunately; **porter ~** to be lucky, to bring good luck.

bonhomme [bɔnɔm] (*pl* **bonshommes** [bɔ̃zɔm]) *nm fam péj* [homme] fellow. || [représentation] man; **~ de neige** snowman.

bonification [bɔnifikasjɔ̃] *nf* SPORT bonus points (*pl*).

bonjour [bɔ̃ʒur] *nm* hello; [avant midi] good morning; [après midi] good afternoon.

bonne [bɔn] 1 *nf* maid. 2 *adj* → **bon**.

bonnet [bɔnɛ] *nm* [coiffure] (woolly) hat; **~ de bain** swimming cap. || [de soutien-gorge] cup.

bonneterie [bɔnɛtri] *nf* [commerce] hosiery (business or trade).

bonsoir [bɔ̃swar] *nm* [en arrivant] hello, good evening; [en partant] goodbye, good evening; [en se couchant] good night.

bonté [bɔ̃te] *nf* [qualité] goodness, kindness; **avoir la ~ de faire qqch** *sout* to be so good or kind as to do sthg.

bonus [bɔnys] *nm* [prime d'assurance] no-claims bonus.

bord [bɔr] *nm* [de table, de vêtement] edge; [de verre, de chapeau] rim; **à ras ~** to the brim. || [de rivière] bank; [de lac] edge, shore; **au ~ de la mer** at the seaside. || [de bois, jardin] edge; [de route] edge, side. || [d'un moyen de transport]: **passer par-dessus ~** to fall overboard. ○ **à bord de** *loc prép*: **à ~ de qqch** on board sthg. ○ **au bord de** *loc prép*: **au ~ de qqch** at the edge of; *fig* on the verge of.

bordeaux [bɔrdo] 1 *nm* [vin] Bordeaux. || [couleur] claret. 2 *adj inv* claret.

bordel [bɔrdɛl] *nm vulg* [maison close] brothel. || [désordre] shambles (*sg*).

border [bɔrde] *vt* [vêtement]: **~ qqch de** to edge sthg with. || [être en bordure de] to line. || [couverture, personne] to tuck in.

bordereau, -x [bɔrdəro] *nm* [relevé] slip.

bordure [bɔrdyr] *nf* [bord] edge; **en ~ de** on the edge of. || [de fleurs] border.

borgne [bɔrɲ] *adj* [personne] one-eyed.

borne [bɔrn] *nf* [marque] boundary marker. || *fam* [kilomètre] kilometre. || [limite] limit, bounds (*pl*); **dépasser les ~s** to go too far. || ÉLECTR terminal.

borné, -e [bɔrne] *adj* [personne] narrow-minded; [esprit] narrow.

borner [bɔrne] ○ **se borner** *vp*: **se ~ à qqch/à faire qqch** [suj: personne] to confine o.s. to sthg/to doing sthg.

Bosnie [bɔsni] *nf*: **la ~** Bosnia.

bosniaque [bɔsnjak] *adj* Bosnian. ○ **Bosniaque** *nmf* Bosnian.

bosquet [bɔskɛ] *nm* copse.

bosse [bɔs] *nf* [sur tête, sur route] bump. || [de bossu, chameau] hump.

bosser [bɔse] *vi fam* to work hard.

bossu, -e [bɔsy] 1 *adj* hunchbacked. 2 *nm, f* hunchback.

botanique [bɔtanik] 1 *adj* botanical. 2 *nf*: **la ~** botany.

botte [bɔt] *nf* [chaussure] boot. || [de légumes] bunch. || [en escrime] thrust, lunge.

botter [bɔte] *vt* [chausser]: **être botté de cuir** to be wearing leather boots. || *fam* [donner un coup de pied à] to boot. || *fam vieilli* [plaire à]: **ça me botte !** I dig it.

bottier [bɔtje] *nm* [de bottes] bootmaker; [de chaussures] shoemaker.

Bottin ® [bɔtɛ̃] *nm* phone book.

bottine [bɔtin] *nf* (ankle) boot.

bouc [buk] *nm* [animal] (billy) goat; **~ émissaire** *fig* scapegoat. || [barbe] goatee.

boucan [bukɑ̃] *nm fam* row, racket.

bouche [buʃ] *nf* [gén] mouth; **~ d'incendie** fire hydrant; **~ de métro** metro entrance or exit.

bouché, -e [buʃe] *adj* [en bouteille] bottled. || *fam* [personne] thick *Br*, dumb.

bouche-à-bouche [buʃabuʃ] *nm inv*: **faire du ~ à qqn** to give sb mouth-to-mouth resuscitation.

bouchée [buʃe] *nf* mouthful.

boucher¹ [buʃe] *vt* [fermer - bouteille] to cork; [- trou] to fill (in or up). || [passage, vue] to block.

boucher², -ère [buʃe, ɛr] *nm, f* butcher.

boucherie [buʃri] *nf* [magasin] butcher's (shop). || *fig* [carnage] slaughter.

bouche-trou [buʃtru] (*pl* **bouche-trous**) *nm* [personne]: **servir de ~** to make up (the) numbers. || [objet] stopgap.

bouchon [buʃɔ̃] *nm* [pour obturer - gén] top; [- de réservoir] cap; [- de bouteille] cork. || [de canne à pêche] float. || [embouteillage] traffic jam.

boucle [bukl] *nf* [de ceinture, soulier] buckle. || [bijou]: **~ d'oreille** earring. ||

[de cheveux] curl. || [de fleuve, d'avion & INFORM] loop.

bouclé, -e [bukle] *adj* [cheveux] curly; [personne] curly-haired.

boucler [bukle] *vt* [attacher] to buckle; [ceinture de sécurité] to fasten. || [fermer] to shut. || *fam* [enfermer - voleur] to lock up; [- malade] to shut away. || [encercler] to seal off. || [terminer] to finish.

bouclier [buklije] *nm litt & fig* shield.

bouddhiste [budist] *nmf & adj* Buddhist.

bouder [bude] 1 *vi* to sulk. 2 *vt* [chose] to dislike; [personne] to shun.

boudeur, -euse [budœr, øz] *adj* sulky.

boudin [budɛ̃] *nm* CULIN blood pudding.

boue [bu] *nf* mud.

bouée [bwe] *nf* [balise] buoy. || [pour flotter] rubber ring; ~ de sauvetage lifebelt.

boueux, -euse [buø, øz] *adj* muddy.

bouffe [buf] *nf fam* grub.

bouffée [bufe] *nf* [de fumée] puff; [de parfum] whiff; [d'air] breath.

bouffer [bufe] *vt fam* [manger] to eat.

bouffi, -e [bufi] *adj*: ~ (de) swollen (with).

bouffon, -onne [bufɔ̃, ɔn] *adj* farcical. ○ **bouffon** *nm* HIST jester. || [pitre] clown.

bouge [buʒ] *nm péj* [taudis] hovel. || [café] dive.

bougeoir [buʒwar] *nm* candlestick.

bougeotte [buʒɔt] *nf*: avoir la ~ to have itchy feet.

bouger [buʒe] 1 *vt* [déplacer] to move. 2 *vi* [remuer] to move. || [changer] to change.

bougie [buʒi] *nf* [chandelle] candle. || [de moteur] spark plug, sparking plug.

bougon, -onne [bugɔ̃, ɔn] *adj* grumpy.

bougonner [bugɔne] *vt & vi* to grumble.

bouillant, -e [bujɑ̃, ɑ̃t] *adj* [qui bout] boiling. || [très chaud] boiling hot.

bouillie [buji] *nf* baby's cereal; **réduire en ~** [légumes] to puree; [personne] to reduce to a pulp.

bouillir [bujir] *vi* [aliments] to boil; **faire ~** to boil.

bouilloire [bujwar] *nf* kettle.

bouillon [bujɔ̃] *nm* [soupe] stock. || [bouillonnement] bubble; **faire bouillir à gros ~s** to bring to a rolling boil.

bouillonner [bujɔne] *vi* [liquide] to bubble. || *fig* [personne] to seethe.

bouillotte [bujɔt] *nf* hot-water bottle.

boul. *abr de* **boulevard.**

boulanger, -ère [bulɑ̃ʒe, ɛr] *nm, f* baker.

boulangerie [bulɑ̃ʒri] *nf* [magasin] baker's (shop). || [commerce] bakery trade.

boule [bul] *nf* [gén] ball; [de loto] counter; [de pétanque] bowl; ~ de neige snowball.

bouleau [bulo] *nm* silver birch.

bouledogue [buldɔg] *nm* bulldog.

boulet [bulɛ] *nm* [munition]: ~ de canon cannonball. || [de forçat] ball and chain. || *fig* [fardeau] millstone (round one's neck).

boulette [bulɛt] *nf* [petite boule] pellet. || [de viande] meatball.

boulevard [bulvar] *nm* [rue] boulevard. || THÉÂTRE light comedy (U).

bouleversant, -e [bulvɛrsɑ̃, ɑ̃t] *adj* distressing.

bouleversement [bulvɛrsəmɑ̃] *nm* disruption.

bouleverser [bulvɛrse] *vt* [objets] to turn upside down. || [modifier] to disrupt. || [émouvoir] to distress.

boulier [bulje] *nm* abacus.

boulimie [bulimi] *nf* bulimia.

boulon [bulɔ̃] *nm* bolt.

boulonner [bulɔne] 1 *vt* to bolt. 2 *vi fam* to slog (away).

boulot [bulo] *nm fam* [travail] work. || [emploi] job.

boum [bum] *nf fam vieilli* party.

bouquet [bukɛ] *nm* [de fleurs - gén] bunch (of flowers). || [de vin] bouquet. || [de feu d'artifice] crowning piece.

bouquin [bukɛ̃] *nm fam* book.

bouquiner [bukine] *vi & vt fam* to read.

bouquiniste [bukinist] *nmf* secondhand bookseller.

bourbier [burbje] *nm* [lieu] quagmire, mire; *fig* mess.

bourde [burd] *nf fam* [erreur] blunder.

bourdon [burdɔ̃] *nm* [insecte] bumblebee.

bourdonnement [burdɔnmɑ̃] *nm* [d'insecte, de voix] buzz (U).

bourdonner [burdɔne] *vi* [insecte, machine] to buzz. || [oreille] to ring.

bourgeois, -e [burʒwa, az] 1 *adj* [valeur] middle-class. || [cuisine] plain. || *péj* [personne] bourgeois. 2 *nm, f* bourgeois.

bourgeoisie [burʒwazi] *nf* ≃ middle classes (*pl*).

bourgeon [burʒɔ̃] *nm* bud.

bourgeonner [burʒɔne] *vi* to bud.

Bourgogne [burgɔɲ] *nf*: **la ~** Burgundy.

bourlinguer [burlɛ̃ge] *vi fam* [voyager] to bum around the world.

bourrade [burad] *nf* thump.

bourrage [buraʒ] *nm* [de coussin] stuffing. ○ **bourrage de crâne** *nm* [propagande] brainwashing.

bourrasque [burask] *nf* gust of wind.

bourratif, -ive [buratif, iv] *adj* stodgy.

bourreau, -x [buro] *nm* HIST executioner.

bourrelet [burlɛ] *nm* [de graisse] roll of fat.

bourrer [bure] *vt* [remplir - coussin] to stuff; [- sac, armoire]: **~ qqch (de)** to cram sthg full (with). || *fam* [gaver]: **~ qqn (de)** to stuff sb (with).

bourrique [burik] *nf* [ânesse] she-ass. || *fam* [personne] pigheaded person.

bourru, -e [bury] *adj* [peu aimable] surly.

bourse [burs] *nf* [porte-monnaie] purse. || [d'études] grant. ○ **Bourse** *nf* [lieu] ≃ Wall Street *Am.* || [opérations]: **Bourse des valeurs** stock market, stock exchange; **Bourse de commerce** commodity market.

boursier, -ière [bursje, jɛr] *adj* [élève] on a grant. || FIN stock-market (*avant n*).

boursouflé, -e [bursufle] *adj* [enflé] swollen.

bousculade [buskylad] *nf* [cohue] crush. || [agitation] rush.

bousculer [buskyle] *vt* [faire tomber] to knock over. || [presser] to rush. || [modifier] to overturn.

bouse [buz] *nf*: **~ de vache** cow dung.

bousiller [buzije] *vt fam* [abîmer] to ruin, to knacker *Br.*

boussole [busɔl] *nf* compass.

bout [bu] *nm* [extrémité, fin] end; **au ~ de** [temps] after; [espace] at the end of; **d'un ~ à l'autre** [de ville etc] from one end to the other; [de livre] from beginning to end. || [morceau] bit. || *loc*: **être à ~** to be exhausted; **à ~ portant** at point-blank range; **pousser qqn à ~** to drive sb to distraction; **venir à ~ de** [personne] to get the better of; [difficulté] to overcome.

boutade [butad] *nf* [plaisanterie] jest.

boute-en-train [butɑ̃trɛ̃] *nm inv* live wire; **il était le ~ de la soirée** he was the life and soul of the party.

bouteille [butɛj] *nf* bottle.

boutique [butik] *nf* [gén] shop; [de mode] boutique.

bouton [butɔ̃] *nm* COUTURE button; **~ de manchette** cuff link. || [sur la peau] spot. || [de porte] knob. || [commutateur] switch. || [bourgeon] bud.

bouton-d'or [butɔ̃dɔr] (*pl* **boutons-d'or**) *nm* buttercup.

boutonner [butɔne] *vt* to button (up).

boutonneux, -euse [butɔnø, øz] *adj* spotty.

boutonnière [butɔnjɛr] *nf* [de vêtement] buttonhole.

bouton-pression [butɔ̃presjɔ̃] (*pl* **boutons-pression**) *nm* snap fastener *Am.*

bouture [butyr] *nf* cutting.

bovin, -e [bɔvɛ̃, in] *adj* bovine. ○ **bovins** *nmpl* cattle.

bowling [buliŋ] *nm* [jeu] bowling. || [lieu] bowling alley.

box [bɔks] (*pl* **boxes**) *nm* [d'écurie] loose box. || [compartiment] cubicle; **le ~ des accusés** the dock. || [parking] lock-up garage.

boxe [bɔks] *nf* boxing.

boxer¹ [bɔkse] *vi* to box.

boxer² [bɔksɛr] *nm* [chien] boxer.

boxeur [bɔksœr] *nm* SPORT boxer.

boyau [bwajo] *nm* [chambre à air] inner tube. ○ **boyaux** *nmpl* [intestins] guts.

boycotter [bɔjkɔte] *vt* to boycott.

BP (*abr de* **boîte postale**) *nf* PO Box.

bracelet [braslɛ] *nm* [bijou] bracelet. || [de montre] strap.

bracelet-montre [braslɛmɔ̃tr] *nm* wristwatch.

braconner [brakɔne] *vi* to go poaching, to poach.

braconnier [brakɔnje] *nm* poacher.

brader [brade] *vt* [solder] to sell off; [vendre à bas prix] to sell for next to nothing.

braderie [bradri] *nf* clearance sale.

braguette [bragɛt] *nf* flies (*pl*).

braille [braj] *nm* Braille.

brailler [braje] *vi* to bawl.

braire [brɛr] *vi* [âne] to bray.

braise [brɛz] *nf* embers (*pl*).

bramer [brame] *vi* [cerf] to bell.

brancard [brɑ̃kar] *nm* [civière] stretcher. || [de charrette] shaft.

brancardier, -ière [brɑ̃kardje, jɛr] *nm, f* stretcher-bearer.

branchage [brɑ̃ʃaʒ] *nm* branches (*pl*).

branche [brɑ̃ʃ] *nf* [gén] branch. || [de lunettes] arm.

branché, -e [brɑ̃ʃe] *adj* ÉLECTR plugged in, connected. || *fam* [à la mode] trendy.

branchement [brɑ̃ʃmɑ̃] *nm* [raccordement] connection, plugging in.

brancher [brɑ̃ʃe] *vt* [raccorder & INFORM] to connect; ~ qqch sur ÉLECTR to plug sthg into. || *fam* [orienter] to steer; ~ qqn sur qqch to start sb off on sthg. || *fam* [plaire] to appeal to.

branchies [brɑ̃ʃi] *nfpl* [de poisson] gills.

brandir [brɑ̃dir] *vt* to wave.

branlant, -e [brɑ̃lɑ̃, ɑ̃t] *adj* [escalier, mur] shaky; [meuble, dent] wobbly.

branle-bas [brɑ̃lba] *nm inv* pandemonium (U).

braquer [brake] **1** *vt* [diriger]: ~ qqch sur [arme] to aim sthg at; [regard] to fix sthg on. || *fam* [attaquer] to hold up. **2** *vi* to turn (the wheel). ○ **se braquer** *vp* [personne] to take a stand.

bras [brɑ] *nm* [gén] arm; ~ droit right-hand man ou woman; ~ de fer [jeu] arm wrestling; *fig* trial of strength; **avoir le ~ long** [avoir de l'influence] to have pull. || [de cours d'eau] branch; ~ de mer arm of the sea.

brasier [brazje] *nm* [incendie] blaze, inferno.

bras-le-corps [brɑlkɔr] ○ **à bras-le-corps** *loc adv* bodily.

brassage [brasaʒ] *nm* [de bière] brewing. || *fig* [mélange] mixing.

brassard [brasar] *nm* armband.

brasse [bras] *nf* [nage] breaststroke; ~ papillon butterfly (stroke).

brassée [brase] *nf* armful.

brasser [brase] *vt* [bière] to brew. || [mélanger] to mix. || *fig* [manier] to handle.

brasserie [brasri] *nf* [usine] brewery. || [café-restaurant] brasserie.

brassière [brasjɛr] *nf* [de bébé] (baby's) vest *Br* ou undershirt *Am*. || *Can* [soutien-gorge] bra.

brave [brav] *adj* (*après n*) [courageux] brave. || (*avant n*) [honnête] decent. || [naïf et gentil] nice.

braver [brave] *vt* [parents, règlement] to defy. || [mépriser] to brave.

bravo [bravo] *interj* bravo! ○ **bravos** *nmpl* cheers.

bravoure [bravur] *nf* bravery.

break [brɛk] *nm* [voiture] estate (car) *Br*, station wagon *Am*. || [pause] break.

brebis [brəbi] *nf* ewe; ~ galeuse black sheep.

brèche [brɛʃ] *nf* [de mur] gap. || MIL breach.

bredouiller [brəduje] *vi* to stammer.

bref, brève [brɛf, brɛv] *adj* [gén] short, brief; **soyez ~!** make it brief! || LING short. ○ **bref** *adv* in short, in a word. ○ **brève** *nf* PRESSE brief news item.

brelan [brəlɑ̃] *nm*: **un ~** three of a kind; **un ~ de valets** three jacks.

Brésil [brezil] *nm*: **le ~** Brazil.

Bretagne [brətaɲ] *nf*: **la ~** Brittany.

bretelle [brətɛl] *nf* [d'autoroute] access road. || [de pantalon]: ~s braces *Br*, suspenders *Am*. || [de bustier] strap.

breuvage [brœvaʒ] *nm* [boisson] beverage.

brève → bref.

brevet [brəvɛ] *nm* [certificat] certificate. || [diplôme] diploma. || [d'invention] patent.

breveter [brəvte] *vt* to patent.

bréviaire [brevjɛr] *nm* breviary.

bribe [brib] *nf* [fragment] scrap, bit; *fig* snippet; ~s de conversation snatches of conversation.

bric [brik] ○ **de bric et de broc** *loc adv* any old how.

bric-à-brac [brikabrak] *nm inv* bric-a-brac.

bricolage [brikɔlaʒ] *nm* [travaux] do-it-yourself, DIY. || [réparation provisoire] patching up.

bricole [brikɔl] *nf* [babiole] trinket. || [chose insignifiante] trivial matter.

bricoler [brikɔle] **1** *vi* to do odd jobs (around the house). **2** *vt* [réparer] to fix, to mend. || [fabriquer] to make.

bricoleur, -euse [brikɔlœr, øz] *nm, f* home handyman (*f* handywoman).

bride [brid] *nf* [de cheval] bridle.

bridé [bride] → œil.

brider [bride] *vt* [cheval] to bridle; *fig* to rein (in).

bridge [bridʒ] *nm* bridge.

brièvement [brijɛvmɑ̃] *adv* briefly.

brièveté [brijɛvte] *nf* brevity, briefness.

brigade [brigad] *nf* [d'ouvriers, de soldats] brigade. || [détachement] squad; ~ volante flying squad.

brigand [brigɑ̃] *nm* [bandit] bandit.

brillamment [brijamɑ̃] *adv* [gén] brilliantly; [réussir un examen] with flying colours.

brillant, -e [brijɑ̃, ɑ̃t] *adj* [qui brille - gén] sparkling; [- cheveux] glossy; [- yeux] bright. || [remarquable] brilliant. ○ **brillant** *nm* [diamant] brilliant.

briller [brije] *vi* to shine.

brimer [brime] *vt* to victimize, to bully.

brin [brɛ̃] *nm* [tige] twig; ~ **d'herbe** blade of grass. || [fil] strand. || [petite quantité]: **un ~ (de)** a bit (of).

brindille [brɛ̃dij] *nf* twig.

bringuebaler, **brinquebaler** [brɛ̃gbale] *vi* [voiture] to jolt along.

brio [brijo] *nm* [talent]: **avec ~** brilliantly.

brioche [brijɔʃ] *nf* [pâtisserie] brioche. || *fam* [ventre] paunch.

brioché, **-e** [brijɔʃe] *adj* [pain] brioche-style.

brique [brik] *nf* [pierre] brick. || [emballage] carton. || *fam* [argent] *10,000 francs*.

briquer [brike] *vt* to scrub.

briquet [brikɛ] *nm* (cigarette) lighter.

brisant [brizɑ̃] *nm* [écueil] reef. ○ **brisants** *nmpl* [récif] breakers.

brise [briz] *nf* breeze.

brise-lames [brizlam] *nm inv* breakwater.

briser [brize] *vt* [gén] to break. || *fig* [carrière] to ruin; [espérances] to shatter. ○ **se briser** *vp* [gén] to break. || *fig* [espoir] to be dashed.

bristol [bristɔl] *nm* [papier] Bristol board.

britannique [britanik] *adj* British. ○ **Britannique** *nmf* British person, Briton; **les Britanniques** the British.

broc [bro] *nm* jug.

brocante [brɔkɑ̃t] *nf* [commerce] secondhand trade. || [objets] secondhand goods (*pl*).

brocanteur, **-euse** [brɔkɑ̃tœr, øz] *nm*, *f* dealer in secondhand goods.

broche [brɔʃ] *nf* [bijou] brooch. || CULIN spit; **cuire à la ~** to spit-roast. || ÉLECTR & MÉD pin.

broché, **-e** [brɔʃe] *adj* [tissu] brocade (*avant n*), brocaded. || TYPO: **livre ~** paperback (book).

brochet [brɔʃɛ] *nm* pike.

brochette [brɔʃɛt] *nf* [ustensile] skewer. || [plat] kebab.

brochure [brɔʃyr] *nf* [imprimé] brochure, booklet.

broder [brɔde] *vt & vi* to embroider.

broderie [brɔdri] *nf* [art] embroidery. || [ouvrage] (piece of) embroidery.

bromure [brɔmyr] *nm* bromide.

bronche [brɔ̃ʃ] *nf* bronchus; **j'ai des problèmes de ~s** I've got chest problems.

broncher [brɔ̃ʃe] *vi*: **sans ~** without complaining, uncomplainingly.

bronchite [brɔ̃ʃit] *nf* bronchitis (*U*).

bronzage [brɔ̃zaʒ] *nm* [de peau] tan, suntan.

bronze [brɔ̃z] *nm* bronze.

bronzé, **-e** [brɔ̃ze] *adj* tanned, suntanned.

bronzer [brɔ̃ze] *vi* [peau] to tan; [personne] to get a tan.

brosse [brɔs] *nf* brush; ~ **à cheveux** hairbrush; ~ **à dents** toothbrush; **avoir les cheveux en ~** to have a crew cut.

brosser [brɔse] *vt* [habits, cheveux] to brush. || [paysage, portrait] to paint. ○ **se brosser** *vp*: **se ~ les cheveux/les dents** to brush one's hair/teeth.

brouette [bruɛt] *nf* wheelbarrow.

brouhaha [bruaa] *nm* hubbub.

brouillard [brujar] *nm* [léger] mist; [dense] fog; ~ **givrant** freezing fog.

brouille [bruj] *nf* quarrel.

brouillé, **-e** [bruje] *adj* [fâché]: **être ~ avec qqn** to be on bad terms with sb; **être ~ avec qqch** *fig* to be hopeless or useless at sthg. || [teint] muddy. || → **œuf**.

brouiller [bruje] *vt* [vue] to blur. || RADIO to cause interference to; [- délibérément] to jam. || [rendre confus] to muddle (up). ○ **se brouiller** *vp* [se fâcher] to fall out; **se ~ avec qqn (pour qqch)** to fall out with sb (over sthg). || [se troubler] to become blurred.

brouillon, **-onne** [brujɔ̃, ɔn] *adj* careless, untidy. ○ **brouillon** *nm* rough copy, draft.

broussaille [brusaj] *nf*: **les ~s** the undergrowth; **en ~** *fig* [cheveux] untidy; [sourcils] bushy.

brousse [brus] *nf* GÉOGR scrubland, bush.

brouter [brute] **1** *vt* to graze on. **2** *vi* [animal] to graze. || TECHNOL to judder.

broutille [brutij] *nf* trifle.

broyer [brwaje] *vt* to grind, to crush.

bru [bry] *nf sout* daughter-in-law.

brugnon [brynɔ̃] *nm* nectarine.

bruine [bruin] *nf* drizzle.

bruissement [bruismɑ̃] *nm* [de feuilles, d'étoffe] rustle, rustling (*U*).

bruit [brui] *nm* [son] noise, sound; ~ **de fond** background noise. || [vacarme & TECHNOL] noise; **faire du ~** to make a noise; **sans ~** silently, noiselessly. || [rumeur] rumour. || [retentissement] fuss; **faire du ~** to cause a stir.

bruitage [bruitaʒ] *nm* sound-effects (*pl*).

brûlant, -e [brylɑ̃, ɑ̃t] *adj* [gén] burning (hot); [liquide] boiling (hot); [plat] piping hot.

brûle-pourpoint [brylpurpwɛ̃] O **à brûle-pourpoint** *loc adv* point-blank, straight out.

brûler [bryle] **1** *vt* [gén] to burn; [suj: eau bouillante] to scald; **la fumée me brûle les yeux** the smoke is making my eyes sting. || [feu rouge] to drive through; [étape] to miss out, to skip. **2** *vi* [gén] to burn; [maison, forêt] to be on fire. || [être brûlant] to be burning (hot); ~ **de fièvre** to be running a high temperature. O **se brûler** *vp* to burn o.s.

brûlure [brylyr] *nf* [lésion] burn; ~ **au premier/troisième degré** first-degree/third-degree burn. || [sensation] burning (sensation); **avoir des ~s d'estomac** to have heartburn.

brume [brym] *nf* mist.

brumeux, -euse [brymø, øz] *adj* misty; *fig* hazy.

brun, -e [brœ̃, bryn] **1** *adj* brown; [cheveux] dark. **2** *nm, f* dark-haired man (*f* woman). O **brun** *nm* [couleur] brown. O **brune** *nf* [cigarette] *cigarette made of dark tobacco*. || [bière] brown ale.

brunir [brynir] *vi* [personne] to get a tan; [peau] to tan.

brushing [brœʃiŋ] *nm*: **faire un ~ à qqn** to give sb a blow-dry, to blow-dry sb's hair.

brusque [brysk] *adj* abrupt.

brusquement [bryskəmɑ̃] *adv* abruptly.

brusquer [bryske] *vt* to rush; [élève] to push.

brusquerie [bryskəri] *nf* abruptness.

brut, -e [bryt] *adj* [pierre précieuse, bois] rough; [sucre] unrefined; [métal, soie] raw; [champagne] extra dry; (**pétrole**) crude (oil). || *fig* [fait, idées] crude, raw. || ÉCON gross. O **brute** *nf* brute.

brutal, -e, -aux [brytal, o] *adj* [violent] violent, brutal. || [soudain] sudden. || [manière] blunt.

brutaliser [brytalize] *vt* to mistreat.

brutalité [brytalite] *nf* [violence] violence, brutality. || [caractère soudain] suddenness.

Bruxelles [bry(k)sɛl] *n* Brussels.

bruyamment [brɥijamɑ̃] *adv* noisily.

bruyant, -e [brɥijɑ̃, ɑ̃t] *adj* noisy.

bruyère [brɥijɛr] *nf* [plante] heather.

BT *nm* (*abr de* **brevet de technicien**) *vocational training certificate (taken at age 18)*.

BTS (*abr de* **brevet de technicien supérieur**) *nm advanced vocational training certificate (taken at the end of a 2-year higher education course)*.

bu, -e [by] *pp* → **boire**.

buanderie [bɥɑ̃dri] *nf* laundry.

buccal, -e, -aux [bykal, o] *adj* buccal.

bûche [byʃ] *nf* [bois] log; ~ **de Noël** Yule log.

bûcher¹ [byʃe] *nm* [supplice]: **le ~** the stake. || [funéraire] pyre.

bûcher² [byʃe] **1** *vi* to swot. **2** *vt* to swot up.

bûcheron, -onne [byʃrɔ̃, ɔn] *nm, f* forestry worker.

bûcheur, -euse [byʃœr, øz] **1** *adj* hard-working. **2** *nm, f fam* swot.

bucolique [bykɔlik] *adj* pastoral.

budget [bydʒɛ] *nm* budget.

budgétaire [bydʒeter] *adj* budgetary; **année ~** financial year.

buée [bɥe] *nf* [sur vitre] condensation.

buffet [byfɛ] *nm* [meuble] sideboard. || [repas] buffet. || [café-restaurant]: ~ **de gare** station buffet.

buis [bɥi] *nm* box(wood).

buisson [bɥisɔ̃] *nm* bush.

buissonnière [bɥisɔnjɛr] → **école.**

bulbe [bylb] *nm* bulb.

bulgare [bylgar] *adj* Bulgarian. O **bulgare** *nm* [langue] Bulgarian. O **Bulgare** *nmf* Bulgarian.

Bulgarie [bylgari] *nf*: **la ~** Bulgaria.

bulldozer [byldozer] *nm* bulldozer.

bulle [byl] *nf* [gén] bubble; ~ **de savon** soap bubble. || [de bande dessinée] speech balloon.

bulletin [byltɛ̃] *nm* [communiqué] bulletin; ~ **(de la) météo** weather forecast; ~ **de santé** medical bulletin. || [imprimé] form; ~ **de vote** ballot paper. || SCOL report. || [certificat] certificate; ~ **de salaire** *ou* **de paye** pay slip.

bulletin-réponse [byltɛ̃repɔ̃s] (*pl* **bulletins-réponse**) *nm* reply form.

buraliste [byralist] *nmf* [d'un bureau de tabac] tobacconist.

bureau [byro] *nm* [gén] office; ~ **de change** bureau de change; ~ **d'études** design office; ~ **de poste** post office; ~ **de tabac** tobacconist's; ~ **de vote** polling station. || [meuble] desk.

bureaucrate [byrokrat] *nmf* bureaucrat.

bureaucratie [byrokrasi] *nf* bureaucracy.

bureautique [byrotik] *nf* office automation.

burette [byrɛt] *nf* [de mécanicien] oil-can.

burin [byrɛ̃] *nm* [outil] chisel.

buriné, -e [byrine] *adj* engraved; [visage, traits] lined.

burlesque [byrlɛsk] *adj* [comique] funny. || [ridicule] ludicrous, absurd. || THÉÂTRE burlesque.

bus [bys] *nm* bus.

busqué [byske] → **nez**.

buste [byst] *nm* [torse] chest; [poitrine de femme, sculpture] bust.

bustier [bystje] *nm* [corsage] strapless top; [soutien-gorge] longline bra.

but [byt] *nm* [point visé] target. || [objectif] goal, aim, purpose; **à ~ non lucratif** JUR non-profit-making *Br*, non-profit *Am*; **aller droit au ~** to go straight to the point; **dans le ~ de faire qqch** with the aim ou intention of doing sthg. || SPORT goal. || *loc*: **de ~ en blanc** point-blank, straight out.

butane [bytan] *nm*: **(gaz) ~** butane; [domestique] Calor gas® *Br*, butane.

buté, -e [byte] *adj* stubborn.

buter [byte] **1** *vi* [se heurter]: **~ sur/ contre qqch** to stumble on/over sthg, to trip on/over sthg. **2** *vt tfam* [tuer] to do in, to bump off. ○ **se buter** *vp* to dig one's heels in.

butin [bytɛ̃] *nm* [de guerre] booty; [de vol] loot; [de recherche] finds (*pl*).

butiner [bytine] *vi* to collect nectar.

butte [byt] *nf* [colline] mound, rise; **être en ~ à** *fig* to be exposed to.

buvard [byvar] *nm* [papier] blotting-paper; [sous-main] blotter.

buvette [byvɛt] *nf* [café] refreshment room, buffet.

buveur, -euse [byvœr, øz] *nm, f* drinker.

c¹, C [se] *nm inv* c, C. ○ **C** (*abr de* **celsius, centigrade**) C.

c² *abr de* **centime**.

c' → **ce**.

CA *nm abr de* **chiffre d'affaires**.

ça [sa] *pron dém* [pour désigner] that; [- plus près] this. || [sujet indéterminé] it, that; **~ ira comme ~** that will be fine; **~ y est** that's it; **c'est ~** that's right. || [renforcement expressif]: **où ~?** where?; **qui ~?** who?

çà *adv*: **~ et là** here and there.

caban [kabɑ̃] *nm* reefer (jacket).

cabane [kaban] *nf* [abri] cabin, hut; [remise] shed; **~ à lapins** hutch.

cabanon [kabanɔ̃] *nm* [à la campagne] cottage. || [sur la plage] chalet. || [de rangement] shed.

cabaret [kabarɛ] *nm* cabaret.

cabas [kaba] *nm* shopping-bag.

cabillaud [kabijo] *nm* (fresh) cod.

cabine [kabin] *nf* [de navire, d'avion, de véhicule] cabin. || [compartiment, petit local] cubicle; **~ d'essayage** fitting room; **~ téléphonique** phone box.

cabinet [kabinɛ] *nm* [pièce]: **~ de toilette** ≃ bathroom. || [local professionnel] office; **~ dentaire/médical** dentist's/ doctor's surgery *Br*, dentist's/doctor's office *Am*. || [de ministre] advisers (*pl*). ○ **cabinets** *nmpl* toilet (*sg*).

câble [kabl] *nm* cable; **télévision par ~** cable television.

câblé, -e [kable] *adj* TÉLÉ equipped with cable TV.

cabosser [kabɔse] *vt* to dent.

cabotage [kabɔtaʒ] *nm* coastal navigation.

cabrer [kabre] ○ **se cabrer** *vp* [cheval] to rear (up).

cabri [kabri] *nm* kid.

cabriole [kabrijɔl] *nf* [bond] caper; [pirouette] somersault.

cabriolet [kabrijɔlɛ] *nm* convertible.

CAC, **Cac** [kak] (*abr de* **Compagnie des agents de change**) *nf*: **l'indice ~-40** *the French stock exchange shares index*.

caca [kaka] *nm fam* pooh; **faire ~** to do a pooh; **~ d'oie** greeny-yellow.

cacahouète, **cacahuète** [kakawɛt] *nf* peanut.

cacao [kakao] *nm* [poudre] cocoa (powder). || [boisson] cocoa.

cachalot [kaʃalo] *nm* sperm whale.

cache [kaʃ] **1** *nf* [cachette] hiding place. **2** *nm* [masque] card (*for masking text etc*).

cache-cache [kaʃkaʃ] *nm inv*: **jouer à ~** to play hide and seek.

cachemire [kaʃmir] *nm* [laine] cashmere. || [dessin] paisley.

cache-nez [kaʃne] *nm inv* scarf.

cache-pot [kaʃpo] *nm inv* flowerpot-holder.

cacher [kaʃe] *vt* [gén] to hide; **je ne vous cache pas que ...** to be honest, ... || [vue] to mask. ○ **se cacher** *vp*: **se ~ (de qqn)** to hide (from sb).

cachet [kaʃɛ] *nm* [comprimé] tablet, pill. || [marque] postmark. || [style] style, character. || [rétribution] fee.

cacheter [kaʃte] *vt* to seal.

cachette [kaʃɛt] *nf* hiding place; **en ~** secretly.

cachot [kaʃo] *nm* [cellule] cell.

cachotterie [kaʃɔtri] *nf* little secret; **faire des ~s (à qqn)** to hide things (from sb).

cachottier, -ière [kaʃɔtje, ɛr] *nm, f* secretive person.

cactus [kaktys] *nm* cactus.

cadastre [kadastr] *nm* [registre] ≃ land register; [service] ≃ land office *Am*.

cadavérique [kadaverik] *adj* deathly.

cadavre [kadavr] *nm* corpse, (dead) body.

cadeau, -x [kado] **1** *nm* present, gift; **faire ~ de qqch à qqn** to give sthg to sb (as a present). **2** *adj inv*: **idée ~** gift idea.

cadenas [kadna] *nm* padlock.

cadenasser [kadnase] *vt* to padlock.

cadence [kadɑ̃s] *nf* [rythme musical] rhythm; **en ~** in time. || [de travail] rate.

cadencé, -e [kadɑ̃se] *adj* rhythmical.

cadet, -ette [kadɛ, ɛt] *nm, f* [de deux enfants] younger; [de plusieurs enfants] youngest; **il est mon ~ de deux ans** he's two years younger than me. || SPORT junior.

cadran [kadrɑ̃] *nm* dial; **~ solaire** sundial.

cadre [kadr] *nm* [de tableau, de porte] frame. || [contexte] context. || [décor, milieu] surroundings (*pl*). || [responsable]: **~ moyen/supérieur** middle/senior manager. || [sur formulaire] box.

cadrer [kadre] **1** *vi* to agree, to tally. **2** *vt* CIN, PHOT & TÉLÉ to frame.

caduc, caduque [kadyk] *adj* [feuille] deciduous. || [qui n'est plus valide] obsolete.

cafard [kafar] *nm* [insecte] cockroach. || *fig* [mélancolie]: **avoir le ~** to feel low or down.

café [kafe] *nm* [plante, boisson] coffee; **~ crème** *coffee with frothy milk*; **~ en grains** coffee beans; **~ au lait** white coffee (*with hot milk*); **~ moulu** ground coffee; **~ noir** black coffee; **~ en poudre** or **soluble** instant coffee. || [lieu] bar, cafe.

caféine [kafein] *nf* caffeine.

cafétéria [kafeterja] *nf* cafeteria.

café-théâtre [kafeteatr] *nm* ≃ cabaret.

cafetière [kaftjer] *nf* [récipient] coffee-pot. || [électrique] coffee-maker; [italienne] percolator.

cafouiller [kafuje] *vi fam* [s'embrouiller] to get into a mess. || [moteur] to misfire; TÉLÉ to be on the blink.

cage [kaʒ] *nf* [pour animaux] cage. || [dans une maison]: **~ d'escalier** stairwell. || ANAT: **~ thoracique** rib cage.

cageot [kaʒo] *nm* [caisse] crate.

cagibi [kaʒibi] *nm* storage room *Am*.

cagneux, -euse [kaɲø, øz] *adj*: **avoir les genoux ~** to be knock-kneed.

cagnotte [kaɲɔt] *nf* [caisse commune] kitty. || [économies] savings (*pl*).

cagoule [kagul] *nf* [passe-montagne] balaclava. || [de voleur, de pénitent] hood.

cahier [kaje] *nm* [de notes] exercise book, notebook; **~ de brouillon** rough book; **~ de textes** homework book. || COMM: **~ des charges** specification.

cahin-caha [kaɛ̃kaa] *adv*: **aller ~** to be jogging along.

cahot [kao] *nm* bump, jolt.

cahoter [kaote] *vi* to jolt around.

cahute [kayt] *nf* shack.

caille [kaj] *nf* quail.

caillé, -e [kaje] *adj* [lait] curdled; [sang] clotted.

caillot [kajo] *nm* clot.

caillou, -x [kaju] *nm* [pierre] stone, pebble. || *fam* [crâne] head.

caillouteux, -euse [kajutø, øz] *adj* stony.

caïman [kaimɑ̃] *nm* cayman.

Caire [kɛr] *n*: Le ~ Cairo.

caisse [kɛs] *nf* [boîte] crate, box; ~ **à outils** toolbox. || [guichet] cash desk, till; [de supermarché] checkout, till; ~ **enregistreuse** cash register. || [organisme]: ~ **d'épargne** [fonds] savings fund; [établissement] savings bank; ~ **de retraite** pension fund.

caissier, -ière [kesje, jɛr] *nm, f* cashier.

cajoler [kaʒɔle] *vt* to make a fuss of, to cuddle.

cajou [kaʒu] → **noix**.

cake [kɛk] *nm* fruit-cake.

cal [kal] *nm* callus.

calamar [kalamar], **calmar** [kalmar] *nm* squid.

calamité [kalamite] *nf* disaster.

calandre [kalɑ̃dr] *nf* [de voiture] radiator grille. || [machine] calender.

calanque [kalɑ̃k] *nf* rocky inlet.

calcaire [kalkɛr] **1** *adj* [eau] hard; [sol] chalky; [roche] limestone (*avant n*). **2** *nm* limestone.

calciner [kalsine] *vt* to burn to a cinder.

calcium [kalsjɔm] *nm* calcium.

calcul [kalkyl] *nm* [opération]: le ~ arithmetic; ~ **mental** mental arithmetic. || [compte] calculation. || *fig* [plan] plan. || MÉD: ~ (**rénal**) kidney stone.

calculateur, -trice [kalkylatœr, tris] *adj péj* calculating. ○ **calculateur** *nm* computer. ○ **calculatrice** *nf* calculator.

calculer [kalkyle] **1** *vt* [déterminer] to calculate, to work out. || [prévoir] to plan.

calculette [kalkylɛt] *nf* pocket calculator.

cale [kal] *nf* [de navire] hold; ~ **sèche** dry dock. || [pour immobiliser] wedge.

calé, -e [kale] *adj fam* [personne] clever, brainy; **être ~ en** to be good at.

calèche [kalɛʃ] *nf* (horse-drawn) carriage.

caleçon [kalsɔ̃] *nm* [sous-vêtement masculin] boxer shorts (*pl*), pair of boxer shorts. || [vêtement féminin] leggings (*pl*), pair of leggings.

calembour [kalɑ̃bur] *nm* pun, play on words.

calendrier [kalɑ̃drije] *nm* [système, agenda, d'un festival] calendar. || [emploi du temps] timetable.

cale-pied [kalpje] (*pl* **cale-pieds**) *nm* toe-clip.

calepin [kalpɛ̃] *nm* notebook.

caler [kale] **1** *vt* [avec cale] to wedge. || [stabiliser, appuyer] to prop up. || *fam* [remplir]: ça cale (**l'estomac**) it's filling. **2** *vi* [moteur, véhicule] to stall. || *fam* [personne] to give up.

calfeutrer [kalføtre] *vt* to draughtproof. ○ **se calfeutrer** *vp* to shut o.s. up ou away.

calibre [kalibr] *nm* [de tuyau] diameter, bore; [de fusil] calibre; [de fruit, d'œuf] size. || *fam fig* [envergure] calibre.

Californie [kalifɔrni] *nf*: la ~ California.

californium ○ **à califourchon** [kalifurʃɔ̃] *loc adv* astride; **être** (**assis**) **à ~ sur qqch** to sit astride sthg.

câlin, -e [kalɛ̃, in] *adj* affectionate. ○ **câlin** *nm* cuddle.

câliner [kaline] *vt* to cuddle.

calleux, -euse [kalø, øz] *adj* calloused.

calligraphie [kaligrafi] *nf* calligraphy.

calmant, -e [kalmɑ̃, ɑ̃t] *adj* soothing. ○ **calmant** *nm* [pour la douleur] painkiller; [pour l'anxiété] tranquillizer, sedative.

calmar → **calamar**.

calme [kalm] **1** *adj* quiet, calm. **2** *nm* [gén] calm, calmness. || [absence de bruit] peace (and quiet).

calmer [kalme] *vt* [apaiser] to calm (down). || [réduire - douleur] to soothe; [- inquiétude] to allay. ○ **se calmer** *vp* [s'apaiser - personne, discussion] to calm down; [- tempête] to abate; [- mer] to become calm. || [diminuer - douleur] to ease; [- fièvre, inquiétude, désir] to subside.

calomnie [kalɔmni] *nf* [écrits] libel; [paroles] slander.

calorie [kalɔri] *nf* calorie.

calorique [kalɔrik] *adj* calorific.

calotte [kalɔt] *nf* [bonnet] skullcap. || GÉOGR: ~ **glaciaire** ice cap.

calque [kalk] *nm* [dessin] tracing. || [papier]: (**papier**) ~ tracing paper. || *fig* [imitation] (exact) copy.

calquer [kalke] *vt* [carte] to trace. || [imiter] to copy exactly; ~ **qqch sur qqch** to model sthg on sthg.

calvaire [kalvɛr] *nm* [croix] wayside cross. || *fig* [épreuve] ordeal.

calvitie [kalvisi] *nf* baldness.

camaïeu [kamajø] *nm* monochrome.

camarade [kamarad] *nmf* [compagnon, ami] friend; ~ **de classe** classmate; ~ **d'école** schoolfriend. || POLIT comrade.

camaraderie [kamaradri] *nf* [familiarité, entente] friendship.

caniveau

Cambodge [kãbɔdʒ] *nm*: le ~ Cambodia.

cambouis [kãbwi] *nm* dirty grease.

cambré, -e [kãbre] *adj* arched.

cambriolage [kãbrijolaʒ] *nm* burglary.

cambrioler [kãbrijole] *vt* to burgle *Br*, to burglarize *Am*.

cambrioleur, -euse [kãbrijolœr, øz] *nm, f* burglar.

camée [kame] *nm* cameo.

caméléon [kameleõ] *nm litt & fig* chameleon.

camélia [kamelja] *nm* camellia.

camelote [kamlɔt] *nf* [marchandise de mauvaise qualité] rubbish.

caméra [kamera] *nf* CIN & TÉLÉ camera. || [d'amateur] cinecamera.

cameraman [kameraman] (*pl* **cameramen** [kameramen] OU **cameramans**) *nm* cameraman.

Caméscope® [kameskɔp] *nm* camcorder.

camion [kamjõ] *nm* lorry *Br*, truck *Am*.

camion-citerne [kamjõsitern] *nm* tanker *Br*, tanker truck *Am*.

camionnette [kamjonet] *nf* van.

camionneur [kamjonœr] *nm* [conducteur] truck-driver *Am*. || [entrepreneur] trucker *Am*.

camisole [kamizɔl] ○ **camisole de force** *nf* straitjacket.

camouflage [kamuflaʒ] *nm* [déguisement] camouflage.

camoufler [kamufle] *vt* [déguiser] to camouflage; *fig* [dissimuler] to conceal, to cover up.

camp [kã] *nm* [gén] camp; **~ de concentration** concentration camp. || SPORT half (of the field). || [parti] side.

campagnard, -e [kãpaɲar, ard] *adj* [de la campagne] country (*avant n*). || [rustique] rustic.

campagne [kãpaɲ] *nf* [régions rurales] country; **à la ~** in the country. || MIL, POLIT & PUBLICITÉ campaign; **faire ~ pour/contre** to campaign for/against; **~ électorale** election campaign; **~ de presse** press campaign; **~ publicitaire** advertising campaign.

campement [kãpmã] *nm* camp, encampment.

camper [kãpe] *vi* to camp.

campeur, -euse [kãpœr, øz] *nm, f* camper.

camphre [kãfr] *nm* camphor.

camping [kãpiŋ] *nm* [activité] camping;

faire du ~ to go camping. || [terrain] campsite.

Canada [kanada] *nm*: le ~ Canada.

canadien, -ienne [kanadjɛ̃, jɛn] *adj* Canadian. ○ **canadienne** *nf* [veste] sheepskin jacket. ○ **Canadien, -ienne** *nm, f* Canadian.

canaille [kanaj] *nf* [scélérat] scoundrel.

canal, -aux [kanal, o] *nm* [gén] channel. || [voie d'eau] canal. || ANAT canal, duct. ○ **Canal** *nm*: **Canal+** *French TV pay channel.*

canalisation [kanalizasjõ] *nf* [conduit] pipe.

canaliser [kanalize] *vt* [cours d'eau] to canalize. || *fig* [orienter] to channel.

canapé [kanape] *nm* [siège] sofa.

canapé-lit [kanapeli] *nm* sofa bed.

canard [kanar] *nm* [oiseau] duck. || [fausse note] wrong note. || *fam* [journal] rag.

canari [kanari] *nm* canary.

cancan [kãkã] *nm* [ragot] piece of gossip. || [danse] cancan.

cancer [kãser] *nm* MÉD cancer. ○ **Cancer** *nm* ASTROL Cancer.

cancéreux, -euse [kãserø, øz] **1** *adj* [tumeur] cancerous. **2** *nm, f* [personne] cancer sufferer.

cancérigène [kãseriʒen] *adj* carcinogenic.

cancre [kãkr] *nm fam* dunce.

cancrelat [kãkrəla] *nm* cockroach.

candélabre [kãdelabr] *nm* candelabra.

candeur [kãdœr] *nf* ingenuousness.

candi [kãdi] *adj*: **sucre ~** (sugar) candy.

candidat, -e [kãdida, at] *nm, f*: **~ (à)** candidate (for).

candidature [kãdidatyr] *nf* [à un poste] application; **poser sa ~ pour qqch** to apply for sthg. || [à une élection] candidature.

candide [kãdid] *adj* ingenuous.

cane [kan] *nf* (female) duck.

caneton [kantõ] *nm* (male) duckling.

canette [kanet] *nf* [de fil] spool. || [petite cane] (female) duckling. || [de boisson - bouteille] bottle; [- boîte] can.

canevas [kanva] *nm* COUTURE canvas.

caniche [kaniʃ] *nm* poodle.

canicule [kanikyl] *nf* heatwave.

canif [kanif] *nm* penknife.

canin, -e [kanɛ̃, in] *adj* canine; **exposition ~e** dog show. ○ **canine** *nf* canine (tooth).

caniveau [kanivo] *nm* gutter.

canne [kan] *nf* [bâton] walking stick; ~ à pêche fishing rod. || *fam* [jambe] pin. ○ **canne à sucre** *nf* sugar cane.

cannelle [kanɛl] *nf* [aromate] cinnamon.

cannibale [kanibal] *nmf & adj* cannibal.

canoë [kanɔe] *nm* canoe.

canoë-kayak [kanɔekajak] *nm* kayak.

canon [kanɔ̃] *nm* [arme] gun; HIST cannon. || [tube d'arme] barrel. || MUS: **chanter en ~** to sing in canon.

canot [kano] *nm* dinghy; ~ **pneumatique** inflatable dinghy; ~ **de sauvetage** lifeboat.

cantatrice [kɑ̃tatris] *nf* prima donna.

cantine [kɑ̃tin] *nf* [réfectoire] canteen. || [malle] trunk.

cantique [kɑ̃tik] *nm* hymn.

canton [kɑ̃tɔ̃] *nm* [en France] ≃ district. || [en Suisse] canton.

cantonade [kɑ̃tɔnad] ○ **à la cantonade** *loc adv*: parler à la ~ to speak to everyone (in general).

cantonais, -e [kɑ̃tɔnɛ, ɛz] *adj* Cantonese; **riz ~** egg fried rice. ○ **cantonais** *nm* [langue] Cantonese.

cantonner [kɑ̃tɔne] *vt* MIL to quarter, to billet *Br.* || [maintenir] to confine; ~ **qqn à** ou **dans** to confine sb to.

cantonnier [kɑ̃tɔnje] *nm* roadman.

canular [kanylar] *nm fam* hoax.

caoutchouc [kautʃu] *nm* [substance] rubber. || [plante] rubber plant.

caoutchouteux, -euse [kautʃutø, øz] *adj* rubbery.

cap [kap] *nm* GÉOGR cape; **le ~ de Bonne-Espérance** the Cape of Good Hope; **le ~ Horn** Cape Horn; **passer le ~ de qqch** *fig* to get through sthg. || [direction] course; **changer de ~** to change course; **mettre le ~ sur** to head for. ○ **Cap** *nm*: **Le Cap** Cape Town.

CAP (*abr de* **certificat d'aptitude professionnelle**) *nm vocational training certificate (taken at secondary school)*.

capable [kapabl] *adj* [apte]: ~ **(de qqch/de faire qqch)** capable (of sthg/of doing sthg). || [à même]: ~ **de faire qqch** likely to do sthg.

capacité [kapasite] *nf* [de récipient] capacity. || [de personne] ability.

cape [kap] *nf* [vêtement] cloak; **rire sous ~** *fig* to laugh up one's sleeve.

CAPES, Capes [kapɛs] (*abr de* **certificat d'aptitude au professorat de l'enseignement du second degré**) *nm secondary school teaching certificate*.

capharnaüm [kafarnaɔm] *nm* mess.

capillaire [kapilɛr] *adj* [lotion] hair (*avant n*). || ANAT & BOT capillary.

capitaine [kapitɛn] *nm* captain.

capitainerie [kapitɛnri] *nf* harbour master's office.

capital, -e, -aux [kapital, o] *adj* [décision, événement] major. || JUR capital. ○ **capital** *nm* FIN capital; ~ **social** authorized ou share capital. ○ **capitale** *nf* [ville, lettre] capital. ○ **capitaux** *nmpl* capital (*U*).

capitalisme [kapitalism] *nm* capitalism.

capitaliste [kapitalist] *nmf & adj* capitalist.

capiteux, -euse [kapitø, øz] *adj* [vin] intoxicating; [parfum] heady.

capitonné, -e [kapitɔne] *adj* padded.

capituler [kapityle] *vi* to surrender; ~ **devant qqn/qqch** to surrender to sb/sthg.

caporal, -aux [kapɔral, o] *nm* MIL lance-corporal. || [tabac] caporal.

capot [kapo] *nm* [de voiture] hood *Am.* || [de machine] (protective) cover.

capote [kapɔt] *nf* [de voiture] top *Am.* || *fam* [préservatif]: ~ **(anglaise)** condom.

câpre [kapr] *nf* caper.

caprice [kapris] *nm* whim.

capricieux, -ieuse [kaprisjø, jøz] *adj* [changeant] capricious; [coléreux] temperamental.

capricorne [kaprikɔrn] *nm* ZOOL capricorn beetle. ○ **Capricorne** *nm* ASTROL Capricorn.

capsule [kapsyl] *nf* [de bouteille] cap. || ASTRON, BOT & MÉD capsule.

capter [kapte] *vt* [recevoir sur émetteur] to pick up. || [source, rivière] to harness. || *fig* [attention, confiance] to gain, to win.

captif, -ive [kaptif, iv] **1** *adj* captive. **2** *nm, f* prisoner.

captivant, -e [kaptivɑ̃, ɑ̃t] *adj* [livre, film] enthralling; [personne] captivating.

captiver [kaptive] *vt* to captivate.

captivité [kaptivite] *nf* captivity.

capture [kaptyr] *nf* [action] capture. || [prise] catch.

capturer [kaptyre] *vt* to catch, to capture.

capuche [kapyʃ] *nf* (detachable) hood.

capuchon [kapyʃɔ̃] *nm* [bonnet d'imperméable] hood. || [bouchon] cap, top.

capucine [kapysin] *nf* [fleur] nasturtium.

caquet [kakɛ] *nm péj* [bavardage]: **rabattre le ~ à** ou **de qqn** to shut sb up.

caqueter [kakte] *vi* [poule] to cackle.

car¹ [kar] *nm* coach *Br*, bus *Am*.

car² [kar] *conj* for, because.

carabine [karabin] *nf* rifle.

caractère [karaktɛr] *nm* [gén] character; **avoir du ~** to have character; **avoir mauvais ~** to be bad-tempered; **en petits/gros ~s** in small/large print; **~s d'imprimerie** block capitals.

caractériel, -ielle [karakterjɛl] *adj* [troubles] emotional; [personne] emotionally disturbed.

caractériser [karakterize] *vt* to be characteristic of. ○ **se caractériser** *vp*: **se ~ par qqch** to be characterized by sthg.

caractéristique [karakteristik] **1** *nf* characteristic, feature. **2** *adj*: **~ (de)** characteristic (of).

carafe [karaf] *nf* [pour vin, eau] carafe; [pour alcool] decanter.

Caraïbes [karaib] *nfpl*: **les ~** the Caribbean.

carambolage [karɑ̃bɔlaʒ] *nm* pile-up.

caramel [karamɛl] *nm* CULIN caramel. || [bonbon - dur] toffee, caramel; [- mou] fudge.

carapace [karapas] *nf* shell; *fig* protection, shield.

carapater [karapate] ○ **se carapater** *vp fam* to scarper, to hop it.

carat [kara] *nm* carat; **or à 9 ~s** 9-carat gold.

caravane [karavan] *nf* [de camping, de désert] caravan.

caravaning [karavaniŋ] *nm* caravanning.

carbone [karbɔn] *nm* carbon; **(papier) ~** carbon paper.

carbonique [karbɔnik] *adj*: **gaz ~** carbon dioxide; **neige ~** dry ice.

carboniser [karbɔnize] *vt* to burn to a cinder.

carburant [karbyrɑ̃] *nm* fuel.

carburateur [karbyratœr] *nm* carburettor.

carcan [karkɑ̃] *nm* HIST iron collar; *fig* yoke.

carcasse [karkas] *nf* [d'animal] carcass. || [de bâtiment, navire] framework. || [de véhicule] shell.

cardiaque [kardjak] *adj* cardiac; **être ~** to have a heart condition; **crise ~** heart attack.

cardigan [kardigɑ̃] *nm* cardigan.

cardinal, -e, -aux [kardinal, o] *adj* cardinal. ○ **cardinal** *nm* RELIG cardinal.

cardiologue [kardjɔlɔg] *nmf* heart specialist, cardiologist.

cardio-vasculaire [kardjovaskylɛr] (*pl* **cardio-vasculaires**) *adj* cardiovascular.

Carême [karɛm] *nm*: **le ~** Lent.

carence [karɑ̃s] *nf* [manque]: **~ (en)** deficiency (in).

carène [karɛn] *nf* NAVIG hull.

caressant, -e [karesɑ̃, ɑ̃t] *adj* affectionate.

caresse [karɛs] *nf* caress.

caresser [karese] *vt* [personne] to caress; [animal, objet] to stroke. || *fig* [espoir] to cherish.

cargaison [kargɛzɔ̃] *nf* TRANSPORT cargo.

cargo [kargo] *nm* [navire] freighter. || [avion] cargo plane.

caricature [karikatyr] *nf* [gén] caricature. || *péj* [personne] sight.

carie [kari] *nf* MÉD caries.

carillon [karijɔ̃] *nm* [cloches] bells (*pl*). || [d'horloge, de porte] chime.

carlingue [karlɛ̃g] *nf* [d'avion] cabin.

carnage [karnaʒ] *nm* slaughter, carnage.

carnassier [karnasje] *nm* carnivore.

carnaval [karnaval] *nm* carnival.

carnet [karnɛ] *nm* [petit cahier] notebook; **~ d'adresses** address book; **~ de notes** SCOL report card. || [bloc de feuilles] book; **~ de chèques** cheque book; **~ de tickets** book of tickets.

carnivore [karnivɔr] **1** *adj* carnivorous. **2** *nm* carnivore.

carotte [karɔt] *nf* carrot.

carpe [karp] *nf* carp.

carpette [karpɛt] *nf* [petit tapis] rug. || *fam péj* [personne] doormat.

carquois [karkwa] *nm* quiver.

carré, -e [kare] *adj* [gén] square; **20 mètres ~s** 20 square metres. ○ **carré** *nm* [quadrilatère] square. || CARTES: **un ~ d'as** four aces. || [petit terrain] patch, plot.

carreau [karo] *nm* [carrelage] tile. || [vitre] window pane. || [motif carré] check; **à ~x** [tissu] checked; [papier] squared. || CARTES diamond.

carrefour [karfur] *nm* [de routes, de la vie] crossroads (*sg*).

carrelage [karlaʒ] *nm* [surface] tiles (*pl*).

carrément [karemɑ̃] *adv* [franchement]

bluntly. ‖ [complètement] completely, quite. ‖ [sans hésiter] straight.

carrière [karjɛr] *nf* [profession] career; **faire ~ dans qqch** to make a career (for o.s.) in sthg. ‖ [gisement] quarry.

carriériste [karjerist] *nmf péj* careerist.

carriole [karjɔl] *nf* [petite charrette] cart. ‖ *Can* [traîneau] sleigh.

carrossable [karɔsabl] *adj* suitable for vehicles.

carrosse [karɔs] *nm* (horse-drawn) coach.

carrosserie [karɔsri] *nf* [de voiture] bodywork, body.

carrossier [karɔsje] *nm* coachbuilder.

carrure [karyr] *nf* [de personne] build; *fig* stature.

cartable [kartabl] *nm* schoolbag.

carte [kart] *nf* [gén] card; **~ bancaire** cash card *Br*; **~ de crédit** credit card; **~ d'étudiant** student card; **~ grise** ≃ car registration papers *Am*, ≃ logbook *Br*; **~ d'identité** identity card; **Carte Orange** season ticket (*for use on public transport in Paris*); **~ postale** postcard; **~ à puce** smart card; **~ de séjour** residence permit; **Carte Vermeil** *card entitling senior citizens to reduced rates in cinemas, on public transport etc*; **~ de visite** visiting card *Br*, calling card *Am*; **donner ~ blanche à qqn** *fig* to give sb a free hand. ‖ [de jeu]: **~** (à jouer) (playing) card. ‖ GÉOGR map; **~ routière** road map. ‖ [au restaurant] menu; **à la ~** [menu] à la carte; [horaires] flexible; **~ des vins** wine list.

cartilage [kartilaʒ] *nm* cartilage.

cartomancien, -ienne [kartɔmɑ̃sjɛ̃, jɛn] *nm, f* fortune-teller (*using cards*).

carton [kartɔ̃] *nm* [matière] cardboard. ‖ [emballage] cardboard box; **~ à dessin** portfolio.

cartonné, -e [kartɔne] *adj* [livre] hardback.

carton-pâte [kartɔ̃pat] *nm* pasteboard.

cartouche [kartuʃ] *nf* [gén & INFORM] cartridge. ‖ [de cigarettes] carton.

cas [ka] *nm* case; **au ~ où** in case; **en aucun ~** under no circumstances; **en tout ~** in any case, anyway; **en ~ de** in case of; **en ~ de besoin** if need be; **le ~ échéant** if the need arises, if need be.

casanier, -ière [kazanje, jɛr] *adj & nm, f* stay-at-home.

casaque [kazak] *nf* [veste] overblouse. ‖ HIPPISME blouse.

cascade [kaskad] *nf* [chute d'eau] waterfall; *fig* stream, torrent. ‖ CIN stunt.

cascadeur, -euse [kaskadœr, øz] *nm, f* CIN stuntman (*f* stuntwoman).

cascher = **kas(e)her.**

case [kaz] *nf* [habitation] hut. ‖ [de boîte, tiroir] compartment; [d'échiquier] square; [sur un formulaire] box.

caser [kaze] *vt fam* [trouver un emploi pour] to get a job for. ‖ *fam* [marier] to marry off. ‖ [placer] to put. ○ **se caser** *vp fam* [trouver un emploi] to get (o.s.) a job. ‖ [se marier] to get hitched.

caserne [kazɛrn] *nf* barracks.

cash [kaʃ] *nm* cash; **payer ~** to pay (in) cash.

casier [kazje] *nm* [compartiment] compartment; [pour le courrier] pigeonhole. ‖ [meuble - à bouteilles] rack; [- à courrier] set of pigeonholes. ‖ PÊCHE lobster pot. ○ **casier judiciaire** *nm* police record.

casino [kazino] *nm* casino.

casque [kask] *nm* [de protection] helmet. ‖ [à écouteurs] headphones (*pl*). ○ **Casques bleus** *nmpl*: **les Casques bleus** the UN peace-keeping force.

casquette [kaskɛt] *nf* cap.

cassant, -e [kasɑ̃, ɑ̃t] *adj* [fragile - verre] fragile; [- cheveux] brittle. ‖ [dur] brusque.

cassation [kasasjɔ̃] → **cour.**

casse [kas] **1** *nf fam* [violence] aggro. ‖ [de voitures] scrapyard. **2** *nm fam* [cambriolage] break-in.

casse-cou [kasku] *nmf inv* [personne] daredevil.

casse-croûte [kaskrut] *nm inv* snack.

casse-noisettes [kasnwazɛt], **casse-noix** [kasnwa] *nm inv* nutcrackers (*pl*).

casse-pieds [kaspje] **1** *adj inv fam* annoying. **2** *nmf inv* pain (in the neck).

casser [kase] **1** *vt* [briser] to break. ‖ JUR to quash. ‖ COMM: **~ les prix** to slash prices. **2** *vi* to break. ○ **se casser** *vp* [se briser] to break. ‖ [membre]: **se ~ un bras** to break one's arm.

casserole [kasrɔl] *nf* [ustensile] saucepan.

casse-tête [kastɛt] *nm inv fig* [problème] headache. ‖ [jeu] puzzle.

cassette [kasɛt] *nf* [coffret] casket. ‖ [de musique, vidéo] cassette.

cassis [kasis] *nm* [fruit] blackcurrant; [arbuste] blackcurrant bush; [liqueur] blackcurrant liqueur. ‖ [sur la route] dip.

cassure [kasyr] *nf* break.

caste [kast] *nf* caste.

casting [kastiŋ] *nm* [acteurs] cast; **aller à un ~** to go to an audition.

castor [kastɔr] *nm* beaver.

castrer [kastre] *vt* to castrate; [chat] to neuter; [chatte] to spay.

cataclysme [kataklism] *nm* cataclysm.

catadioptre [katadjɔptr], **Cataphote**® [katafɔt] *nm* [sur la route] cat's eye. ‖ [de véhicule] reflector.

catalogue [katalɔg] *nm* catalogue.

cataloguer [katalɔge] *vt* [classer] to catalogue. ‖ *péj* [juger] to label.

catalytique [katalitik] → **pot**.

catamaran [katamarã] *nm* [voilier] catamaran.

Cataphote® = **catadioptre**.

cataplasme [kataplasm] *nm* poultice.

catapulter [katapylte] *vt* to catapult.

cataracte [katarakt] *nf* cataract.

catastrophe [katastrɔf] *nf* disaster, catastrophe.

catastrophé, -e [katastrɔfe] *adj* shocked, upset.

catastrophique [katastrɔfik] *adj* disastrous, catastrophic.

catch [katʃ] *nm* wrestling.

catéchisme [kateʃism] *nm* catechism.

catégorie [kategɔri] *nf* [gén] category; [de personnel] grade; [de viande, fruits] quality; **~ socio-professionnelle** ÉCON socio-economic group.

catégorique [kategɔrik] *adj* categorical.

cathédrale [katedral] *nf* cathedral.

cathodique [katɔdik] → **tube**.

catholicisme [katɔlisism] *nm* Catholicism.

catholique [katɔlik] *adj* Catholic.

catimini [katimini] ○ **en catimini** *loc adv* secretly.

cauchemar [koʃmar] *nm litt & fig* nightmare.

cauchemardesque [koʃmardɛsk] *adj* nightmarish.

cause [koz] *nf* [gén] cause; **à ~ de** because of; **pour ~ de** on account of, because of. ‖ JUR case. ‖ *loc*: **être en ~** [intérêts] to be at stake; [honnêteté] to be in doubt or in question; **remettre en ~** to challenge, to question.

causer [koze] **1** *vt*: **~ qqch à qqn** to cause sb sthg. **2** *vi* [bavarder]: **~ (de)** to chat (about).

causerie [kozri] *nf* talk.

caustique [kostik] *adj & nm* caustic.

cautériser [koterize] *vt* to cauterize.

caution [kosjɔ̃] *nf* [somme d'argent] guarantee. ‖ [personne] guarantor; **se porter ~ pour qqn** to act as guarantor for sb.

cautionner [kosjɔne] *vt* [se porter garant de] to guarantee. ‖ *fig* [appuyer] to support, to back.

cavalcade [kavalkad] *nf* [de cavaliers] cavalcade. ‖ [d'enfants] stampede.

cavalerie [kavalri] *nf* MIL cavalry.

cavalier, -ière [kavalje, jɛr] *nm, f* [à cheval] rider. ‖ [partenaire] partner. ○ **cavalier** *nm* [aux échecs] knight.

cavalièrement [kavaljɛrmã] *adv* in an offhand manner.

cave [kav] *nf* [sous-sol] cellar. ‖ [de vins] (wine) cellar.

caveau [kavo] *nm* [petite cave] small cellar. ‖ [sépulture] vault.

caverne [kavɛrn] *nf* cave.

caviar [kavjar] *nm* caviar.

cavité [kavite] *nf* cavity.

CCP (*abr de* **compte chèque postal, compte courant postal**) *nm* post office account; ≃ Giro *Br*.

CD *nm* (*abr de* **compact disc**) CD.

CDI *nm* (*abr de* **centre de documentation et d'information**) *school library*.

ce [sə] **1** *adj dém* (**cet** [sɛt] *devant voyelle ou h muet*, *f* **cette** [sɛt], *pl* **ces** [se]) [proche] this, these (*pl*); [éloigné] that, those (*pl*); **cette année**, **cette année-là** that year. **2** *pron dém* (**c'** *devant voyelle*): **c'est** it is, it's; **~ sont they** are, they're; **c'est à Paris** it's in Paris; **qui est~?** who is it?; **~ qui**, **~ que** what; **ils ont eu ~ qui leur revenait** they got what they deserved; **...**, **~ qui est étonnant ...**, which is surprising; **vous savez bien ~ à quoi je pense** you know exactly what I'm thinking about. ○ **n'est-ce pas?** *loc adv* isn't it?/aren't you? *etc*; **~ café est bon**, **n'est~ pas?** this coffee's good, isn't it?; **tu connais Pierre, n'est~ pas?** you know Pierre, don't you?

CE 1 *nm* (*abr de* **cours élémentaire**) **~1** second year of primary school; **~2** third year of primary school. **2** *nf* (*abr de* **Communauté européenne**) EC.

ceci [səsi] *pron dém* this; **à ~ près que** with the exception that, except that.

cécité [sesite] *nf* blindness.

céder [sede] **1** *vt* [donner] to give up. ‖ [revendre] to sell. **2** *vi* [personne]: **~ (à)** to give in (to), to yield (to). ‖ [chaise, plancher] to give way.

CEDEX, Cedex [sedɛks] (*abr de cour-rier d'entreprise à distribution excep-tionnelle*) *nm accelerated postal service for bulk users.*

cédille [sedij] *nf* cedilla.

cèdre [sedr] *nm* cedar.

CEE (*abr de* **Communauté économique européenne**) *nf* EEC.

CEI (*abr de* **Communauté d'États Indé-pendants**) *nf* CIS.

ceinture [sɛtyr] *nf* [gén] belt; ~ **de sé-curité** safety ou seat belt. || ANAT waist.

ceinturon [sɛtyrɔ̃] *nm* belt.

cela [səla] *pron dém* that; ~ **ne vous re-garde pas** it's ou that's none of your busi-ness; **il y a des années de** ~ that was many years ago; **c'est** ~ that's right; ~ **dit ... having said that ....**

célèbre [selɛbr] *adj* famous.

célébrer [selebre] *vt* [gén] to celebrate. || [faire la louange de] to praise.

célébrité [selebrite] *nf* [renommée] fame. || [personne] celebrity.

céleri [sɛlri] *nm* celery.

céleste [selɛst] *adj* heavenly.

célibat [seliba] *nm* celibacy.

célibataire [selibatɛr] **1** *adj* single, un-married. **2** *nmf* single person, single man (*f* woman).

celle → **celui.**

celle-ci → **celui-ci.**

celle-là → **celui-là.**

celles → **celui.**

celles-ci → **celui-ci.**

celles-là → **celui-là.**

cellier [selje] *nm* storeroom.

Cellophane® [selɔfan] *nf* Cellophane®.

cellulaire [selylɛr] *adj* BIOL & TÉLÉCOM cellular.

cellule [selyl] *nf* [gén & INFORM] cell. || [groupe] unit; [réunion] emergency com-mittee meeting.

cellulite [selylit] *nf* cellulite.

celte [sɛlt] *adj* Celtic. ○ **Celte** *nmf* Celt.

celui [səlɥi] (*f* **celle** [sɛl], *mpl* **ceux** [sø], *fpl* **celles** [sɛl]) *pron dém* [suivi d'un complément prépositionnel] the one; **celle de devant** the one in front; **ceux d'entre vous qui ...** those of you who .... || [suivi d'un pronom relatif]: ~ **qui** [objet] the one which ou that; [personne] the one who; **ceux que je connais** those I know.

celui-ci [səlɥisi] (*f* **celle-ci** [sɛlsi], *mpl* **ceux-ci** [søsi], *fpl* **celles-ci** [sɛlsi]) *pron dém* this one, these ones (*pl*).

celui-là [səlɥila] (*f* **celle-là** [sɛlla], *mpl* **ceux-là** [søla], *fpl* **celles-là** [sɛlla]) *pron dém* that one, those ones (*pl*); ~ ... **celui-ci** the former ... the latter.

cendre [sɑ̃dr] *nf* ash.

cendré, -e [sɑ̃dre] *adj* [chevelure]: **blond** ~ ash blond.

cendrier [sɑ̃drije] *nm* [de fumeur] ash-tray. || [de poêle] ashpan.

cène [sɛn] *nf* [Holy] Communion. ○ **Cène** *nf*: **la Cène** the Last Supper.

censé, -e [sɑ̃se] *adj*: **être** ~ **faire qqch** to be supposed to do sthg.

censeur [sɑ̃sœr] *nm* SCOL ≃ vice-principal *Am*. || CIN & PRESSE censor.

censure [sɑ̃syr] *nf* [CIN & PRESSE - contrôle] censorship; [- censeurs] censors (*pl*). || POLIT censure. || PSYCHOL censor.

censurer [sɑ̃syre] *vt* CIN, PRESSE & PSY-CHOL to censor. || [juger] to censure.

cent [sɑ̃] **1** *adj num* one hundred, a hundred. **2** *nm* [nombre] a hundred; *voir aussi* **six.** || [mesure de proportion]: **pour** ~ per cent.

centaine [sɑ̃tɛn] *nf* [cent unités] hun-dred. || [un grand nombre]: **une** ~ **de** about a hundred; **des** ~**s (de)** hundreds (of); **plusieurs** ~**s de** several hundred; **par** ~**s** in hundreds.

centenaire [sɑ̃tnɛr] **1** *adj* hundred-year-old (*avant n*); **être** ~ to be a hun-dred years old. **2** *nmf* centenarian. **3** *nm* [anniversaire] centenary.

centième [sɑ̃tjɛm] *adj num, nm & nmf* hundredth; *voir aussi* **sixième.**

centigrade [sɑ̃tigrad] → **degré.**

centilitre [sɑ̃tilitr] *nm* centilitre.

centime [sɑ̃tim] *nm* centime.

centimètre [sɑ̃timɛtr] *nm* [mesure] centimetre. || [ruban, règle] tape meas-ure.

central, -e, -aux [sɑ̃tral, o] *adj* central. ○ **central** *nm* [de réseau]: ~ **téléphoni-que** telephone exchange. ○ **centrale** *nf* [usine] power plant ou station; ~**e hydro-électrique** hydroelectric power station; ~**e nucléaire** nuclear power plant ou sta-tion. || COMM: ~**e d'achat** buying group.

centraliser [sɑ̃tralize] *vt* to centralize.

centre [sɑ̃tr] *nm* [gén] centre; ~ **aéré** outdoor centre; ~ **commercial** shopping centre; ~ **culturel** arts centre; ~ **de gra-vité** centre of gravity.

centrer [sɑ̃tre] *vt* to centre.

centre-ville [sɑ̃trəvil] *nm* city centre, town centre.

centrifuge [sɑ̃trifyʒ] → **force.**

centrifugeuse [sãtrifyʒøz] *nf* TECHNOL centrifuge. ‖ CULIN juice extractor.

centuple [sãtypl] *nm*: être le ~ de qqch to be a hundred times sthg; au ~ a hundredfold.

cep [sɛp] *nm* stock.

cèpe [sɛp] *nm* cep.

cependant [səpãdã] *conj* however, yet.

céramique [seramik] *nf* [matière, objet] ceramic.

cerceau [sɛrso] *nm* hoop.

cercle [sɛrkl] *nm* circle; ~ vicieux vicious circle.

cercueil [sɛrkœj] *nm* coffin.

céréale [sereal] *nf* cereal.

cérémonial, -als [seremɔnjal] *nm* ceremonial.

cérémonie [seremɔni] *nf* ceremony.

cérémonieux, -ieuse [seremɔnjø, jøz] *adj* ceremonious.

cerf [sɛr] *nm* stag.

cerf-volant [sɛrvɔlã] *nm* [jouet] kite.

cerise [səriz] *nf & adj inv* cherry.

cerisier [sərizje] *nm* [arbre] cherry (tree); [bois] cherry (wood).

cerne [sɛrn] *nm* ring.

cerné [sɛrne] → **œil.**

cerner [sɛrne] *vt* [encercler] to surround. ‖ *fig* [sujet] to define.

certain, -e [sɛrtɛ̃, ɛn] 1 *adj* certain; être ~ de qqch to be certain ou sure of sthg; je suis pourtant ~ d'avoir mis mes clés là but I'm certain ou sure I left my keys there. 2 *adj indéf* (*avant n*) certain; il a un ~ talent he has some talent ou a certain talent; c'est un monsieur d'un ~ âge he's getting on a bit; un ~ M. Lebrun a Mr Lebrun. ○ **certains** (*fpl* certaines) *pron indéf pl* some.

certainement [sɛrtɛnmã] *adv* certainly.

certes [sɛrt] *adv* of course.

certificat [sɛrtifika] *nm* [attestation, diplôme] certificate; ~ médical medical certificate.

certifié, -e [sɛrtifje] *adj*: professeur ~ qualified teacher.

certifier [sɛrtifje] *vt* [assurer]: ~ qqch à qqn to assure sb of sthg. ‖ [authentifier] to certify.

certitude [sɛrtityd] *nf* certainty.

cerveau [sɛrvo] *nm* brain.

cervelle [sɛrvɛl] *nf* ANAT brain. ‖ [facultés mentales, aliment] brains (*pl*).

cervical, -e, -aux [sɛrvikal, o] *adj* cervical.

ces → **ce.**

CES (*abr de* collège d'enseignement secondaire) *nm former secondary school.*

césarienne [sezarjɛn] *nf* caesarean (section).

cesse [sɛs] *nf*: n'avoir de ~ que (+ *subjonctif*) *sout* not to rest until. ○ **sans cesse** *loc adv* continually, constantly.

cesser [sese] 1 *vi* to stop, to cease. 2 *vt* to stop; ~ de faire qqch to stop doing sthg.

cessez-le-feu [seselfø] *nm inv* ceasefire.

cession [sɛsjɔ̃] *nf* transfer.

c'est-à-dire [sɛtadir] *conj* [en d'autres termes]: ~ (que) that is (to say). ‖ [introduit une restriction, précision, réponse]: ~ que well ..., actually ....

cet → **ce.**

cétacé [setase] *nm* cetacean.

cette → **ce.**

ceux → **celui.**

ceux-ci → **celui-ci.**

ceux-là → **celui-là.**

cf. (*abr de* confer) cf.

CFC (*abr de* chlorofluorocarbone) *nm* CFC.

chacun, -e [ʃakœ̃, yn] *pron indéf* each (one); [tout le monde] everyone, everybody; ~ de nous/de vous/d'eux each of us/you/them.

chagrin, -e [ʃagrɛ̃, in] *adj* [caractère, humeur] morose. ○ **chagrin** *nm* grief; avoir du ~ to grieve.

chagriner [ʃagrine] *vt* [peiner] to grieve, to distress. ‖ [contrarier] to upset.

chahut [ʃay] *nm* uproar.

chahuter [ʃayte] 1 *vi* to cause an uproar. 2 *vt* [importuner - professeur] to rag, to tease; [- orateur] to heckle. ‖ [bousculer] to jostle.

chaîne [ʃɛn] *nf* [gén] chain; ~ de montagnes mountain range. ‖ IND: ~ de fabrication/de montage production/assembly line; travail à la ~ production-line work. ‖ TÉLÉ channel. ‖ [appareil] stereo (system); ~ hi-fi hi-fi system.

chaînon [ʃɛnɔ̃] *nm litt & fig* link.

chair [ʃɛr] *nf* flesh; avoir la ~ de poule *fig* to have goosebumps *Am*.

chaire [ʃɛr] *nf* [estrade - de prédicateur] pulpit; [- de professeur] rostrum. ‖ UNIV chair.

chaise [ʃɛz] *nf* chair; ~ longue deckchair.

châle [ʃal] *nm* shawl.

chalet [ʃalɛ] *nm* [de montagne] chalet. ‖ *Can* [maison de campagne] (holiday) cottage.

chaleur [ʃalœr] *nf* heat; [agréable] warmth.

chaleureux, -euse [ʃalœrø, øz] *adj* warm.

challenge [ʃalɑ̃ʒ] *nm* SPORT tournament.

chaloupe [ʃalup] *nf* rowing boat *Br*, rowboat *Am*.

chalumeau [ʃalymo] *nm* TECHNOL blowlamp *Br*, blowtorch *Am*.

chalutier [ʃalytje] *nm* [bateau] trawler.

chamailler [ʃamaje] ○ **se chamailler** *vp fam* to squabble.

chambranle [ʃɑ̃brɑ̃l] *nm* [de porte, fenêtre] frame; [de cheminée] mantelpiece.

chambre [ʃɑ̃br] *nf* [où l'on dort]: ~ (à coucher) bedroom; ~ à un lit, ~ pour une personne single room; ~ pour deux personnes double room; ~ d'amis spare room. ‖ [local] room; ~ froide, ~ froide cold store; ~ noire darkroom. ‖ JUR division; ~ d'accusation court of criminal appeal. ‖ POLIT chamber, house; **Chambre des députés** ≃ House of Commons *Br*, ≃ House of Representatives *Am*. ‖ TECHNOL chamber; ~ à air [de pneu] inner tube.

chambrer [ʃɑ̃bre] *vt* [vin] to bring to room temperature. ‖ *fam* [se moquer]: ~ qqn to pull sb's leg.

chameau, -x [ʃamo] *nm* [mammifère] camel.

chamois [ʃamwa] *nm* chamois; [peau] chamois (leather).

champ [ʃɑ̃] *nm* [gén & INFORM] field; ~ de bataille battlefield; ~ de courses racecourse. ‖ [étendue] area.

champagne [ʃɑ̃paɲ] *nm* champagne.

champêtre [ʃɑ̃pɛtr] *adj* rural.

champignon [ʃɑ̃piɲɔ̃] *nm* BOT & MÉD fungus. ‖ [comestible] mushroom; ~ vénéneux toadstool.

champion, -ionne [ʃɑ̃pjɔ̃, jɔn] **1** *nm, f* champion. **2** *adj fam* brilliant.

championnat [ʃɑ̃pjɔna] *nm* championship.

chance [ʃɑ̃s] *nf* [bonheur] luck (*U*); **avoir de la** ~ to be lucky; **ne pas avoir de** ~ to be unlucky; **porter** ~ to bring good luck. ‖ [probabilité, possibilité] chance, opportunity; **avoir des** ~ **de faire qqch** to have a chance of doing sthg.

chanceler [ʃɑ̃sle] *vi* [personne, gouvernement] to totter; [meuble] to wobble.

chancelier [ʃɑ̃səlje] *nm* [premier ministre] chancellor. ‖ [de consulat, d'ambassade] secretary.

chanceux, -euse [ʃɑ̃sø, øz] *adj* lucky.

chandail [ʃɑ̃daj] *nm* (thick) sweater.

Chandeleur [ʃɑ̃dlœr] *nf* Candlemas.

chandelier [ʃɑ̃dəlje] *nm* [pour une bougie] candlestick; [à plusieurs branches] candelabra.

chandelle [ʃɑ̃dɛl] *nf* [bougie] candle.

change [ʃɑ̃ʒ] *nm* [troc & FIN] exchange. ‖ [couche de bébé] diaper *Am*.

changeant, -e [ʃɑ̃ʒɑ̃, ɑ̃t] *adj* [temps, humeur] changeable.

changement [ʃɑ̃ʒmɑ̃] *nm* change.

changer [ʃɑ̃ʒe] **1** *vt* [gén] to change; ~ **qqn en** to change sb into; ~ **des francs en livres** to change francs into pounds, to exchange francs for pounds. ‖ [modifier] to change, to alter; **ça me/te changera** that will be a (nice) change for me/you. **2** *vi* [gén] to change; ~ **de train** (à) to change trains (at); ~ **d'avis** to change one's mind; **ça changera!** that'll make a change!; ~ **de direction** to change direction; ~ **de place** (avec qqn) to change places (with sb); **pour** ~ for a change.

chanson [ʃɑ̃sɔ̃] *nf* song; **c'est toujours la même** ~ *fig* it's the same old story.

chansonnier, -ière [ʃɑ̃sɔnje, jɛr] *nm, f* cabaret singer-songwriter.

chant [ʃɑ̃] *nm* [chanson] song, singing (*U*); [sacré] hymn. ‖ [art] singing.

chantage [ʃɑ̃taʒ] *nm litt & fig* blackmail; **faire du** ~ **à qqn** to blackmail sb.

chanter [ʃɑ̃te] **1** *vt* [chanson] to sing. ‖ *littéraire* [célébrer] to sing of; **tell of**; ~ **les louanges de qqn** to sing sb's praises. **2** *vi* [gén] to sing. ‖ *loc*: **faire** ~ **qqn** to blackmail sb; **si ça vous chante!** *fam* if you feel like ou fancy it!

chanteur, -euse [ʃɑ̃tœr, øz] *nm, f* singer.

chantier [ʃɑ̃tje] *nm* CONSTR (building) site; [sur la route] roadworks (*pl*); ~ **naval** shipyard, dockyard. ‖ *fig* [désordre] shambles (*sg*), mess.

chantonner [ʃɑ̃tɔne] *vt & vi* to hum.

chaos [kao] *nm* chaos.

chap. (*abr de chapitre*) ch.

chaparder [ʃaparde] *vt* to steal.

chapeau, -x [ʃapo] *nm* [coiffure] hat.

chapeauter [ʃapote] *vt* [service] to head; [personnes] to supervise.

chapelet [ʃaplɛ] *nm* RELIG rosary. ‖ *fig* [d'injures] string, torrent.

chapelle [ʃapɛl] *nf* [petite église] chapel; [partie d'église] choir.

chapelure [ʃaplyr] *nf* (dried) bread-crumbs (*pl*).

chapiteau [ʃapito] *nm* [de cirque] big top.

chapitre [ʃapitr] *nm* [de livre & RELIG] chapter.

chaque [ʃak] *adj indéf* each, every; **j'ai payé ces livres 100 francs ~** I paid 100 francs each for these books.

char [ʃar] *nm* MIL: **~ (d'assaut)** tank. || [de carnaval] float. || *Can* [voiture] car.

charabia [ʃarabja] *nm* gibberish.

charade [ʃarad] *nf* charade.

charbon [ʃarbɔ̃] *nm* [combustible] coal; **~ de bois** charcoal.

charcuter [ʃarkyte] *vt fam péj* to butcher.

charcuterie [ʃarkytri] *nf* [magasin] pork butcher's. || [produits] pork meat products.

charcutier, -ière [ʃarkytje, jɛr] *nm, f* [commerçant] pork butcher.

chardon [ʃardɔ̃] *nm* [plante] thistle.

charge [ʃarʒ] *nf* [fardeau] load. || [fonction] office. || [responsabilité] responsibility; **être à la ~ de** [personne] to be dependent on; **les travaux sont à la ~ du propriétaire** the owner is liable for the cost of the work; **prendre qqch en ~** [s'occuper de] to take charge of sthg. || ÉLECTR, JUR & MIL charge. ○ **charges** *nfpl* [d'appartement] service charge. || ÉCON expenses, costs; **~s sociales** ≃ employer's contributions.

chargé, -e [ʃarʒe] **1** *adj* [véhicule, personne]: **~ (de)** loaded (with). || [responsable]: **~ (de)** responsible (for). || [occupé] full, busy. **2** *nm, f*: **~ d'affaires** chargé d'affaires; **~ de mission** head of mission.

chargement [ʃarʒəmɑ̃] *nm* [action] loading. || [marchandises] load.

charger [ʃarʒe] *vt* [gén & INFORM] to load. || ÉLECTR, JUR & MIL to charge. || [donner une mission à]: **~ qqn de faire qqch** to put sb in charge of doing sthg. ○ **se charger** *vp*: **se ~ de qqn/qqch** to take care of sb/sthg, to take charge of sb/sthg; **se ~ de faire qqch** to undertake to do sthg.

chargeur [ʃarʒœr] *nm* ÉLECTR charger. || [d'arme] magazine.

chariot [ʃarjo] *nm* [charrette] handcart. || [à bagages, dans un hôpital] wagon *Am*. || [de machine à écrire] carriage.

charisme [karism] *nm* charisma.

charitable [ʃaritabl] *adj* charitable.

charité [ʃarite] *nf* [aumône & RELIG] charity. || [bonté] kindness.

charlatan [ʃarlatɑ̃] *nm péj* charlatan.

charmant, -e [ʃarmɑ̃, ɑ̃t] *adj* charming.

charme [ʃarm] *nm* [séduction] charm. || [enchantement] spell. || [arbre] ironwood, hornbeam.

charmer [ʃarme] *vt* to charm; **être charmé de faire qqch** to be delighted to do sthg.

charmeur, -euse [ʃarmœr, øz] *adj* charming.

charnel, -elle [ʃarnɛl] *adj* carnal.

charnier [ʃarnje] *nm* mass grave.

charnière [ʃarnjɛr] **1** *nf* [gond] turning point. **2** *adj* [période] transitional.

charnu, -e [ʃarny] *adj* fleshy.

charogne [ʃarɔɲ] *nf* [d'animal] carrion (*U*).

charpente [ʃarpɑ̃t] *nf* [de bâtiment, de roman] framework. || [ossature] frame.

charpentier [ʃarpɑ̃tje] *nm* carpenter.

charretier, -ière [ʃartje, jɛr] *nm, f* carter.

charrette [ʃarɛt] *nf* cart.

charrier [ʃarje] *vt* to carry. || *fam* [se moquer de]: **~ qqn** to take sb for a ride. **2** *vi fam* [exagérer] to go too far.

charrue [ʃary] *nf* plough, plow *Am*.

charte [ʃart] *nf* charter.

charter [ʃarter] *nm* chartered plane.

chas [ʃa] *nm* eye (*of needle*).

chasse [ʃas] *nf* [action] hunting; **~ à courre** hunting (*on horseback with hounds*). || [période]: **la ~ est ouverte/fermée** it's the open/close season. || [poursuite] chase; **prendre qqn/qqch en ~** to give chase to sb/sthg. || [des cabinets]: **~ (d'eau)** flush; **tirer la ~** to flush the toilet.

chassé-croisé [ʃasekrwaze] *nm* toing and froing.

chasse-neige [ʃasnɛʒ] *nm inv* snow-plough.

chasser [ʃase] *vt* [animal] to hunt. || [faire partir - personne] to drive ou chase away; [- odeur, souci] to dispel.

chasseur, -euse [ʃasœr, øz] *nm, f* hunter. ○ **chasseur** *nm* [d'hôtel] page, messenger. || MIL: **~ alpin** soldier specially trained for operations in mountainous terrain. || [avion] fighter.

châssis [ʃasi] *nm* [de fenêtre, de porte, de machine] frame. || [de véhicule] chassis.

chaste [ʃast] *adj* chaste.

chasteté [ʃastəte] *nf* chastity.

chasuble [ʃazybl] *nf* chasuble.

chat, chatte [ʃa, ʃat] *nm, f* cat.

châtaigne [ʃatɛɲ] *nf* [fruit] chestnut. || *fam* [coup] clout.

châtaignier [ʃateɲe] *nm* [arbre] chestnut (tree); [bois] chestnut.

châtain [ʃatɛ̃] *adj & nm* chestnut, chestnut-brown.

château, -x [ʃato] *nm* [forteresse]: ~ **(fort)** castle. || [résidence - seigneuriale] mansion; [- de monarque, d'évêque] palace; ~ **de sable** sandcastle. || [réservoir]: ~ **d'eau** water tower.

châtiment [ʃatimã] *nm* punishment.

chaton [ʃatɔ̃] *nm* [petit chat] kitten. || BOT catkin.

chatouiller [ʃatuje] *vt* [faire des chatouilles à] to tickle. || *fig* [titiller] to titillate.

chatoyant, -e [ʃatwajã, ãt] *adj* [reflet, étoffe] shimmering; [bijou] sparkling.

châtrer [ʃɑtre] *vt* to castrate; [chat] to neuter; [chatte] to spay.

chatte → **chat**.

chaud, -e [ʃo, ʃod] *adj* [gén] warm; [de température très élevée, sensuel] hot. || *fig* [enthousiaste]: **être ~ pour qqch/pour faire qqch** to be keen on sthg/on doing sthg. ○ **chaud 1** *adv*: **avoir ~** to be warm ou hot; **il fait ~** it's warm ou hot. **2** *nm* heat; **rester au ~** to stay in the warm.

chaudement [ʃodmã] *adv* warmly.

chaudière [ʃodjɛr] *nf* boiler.

chaudron [ʃodrɔ̃] *nm* cauldron.

chauffage [ʃofaʒ] *nm* [appareil] heating (system); ~ **central** central heating.

chauffant, -e [ʃofã, ãt] *adj* heating; **plaque -e** hotplate.

chauffard [ʃofar] *nm péj* reckless driver.

chauffe-eau [ʃofo] *nm inv* water-heater.

chauffer [ʃofe] **1** *vt* [rendre chaud] to heat (up). **2** *vi* [devenir chaud] to heat up. || [moteur] to overheat. || *fam* [barder]: **ça va ~** there's going to be trouble.

chauffeur [ʃofœr] *nm* AUTOM driver.

chaume [ʃom] *nm* [paille] thatch.

chaumière [ʃomjɛr] *nf* cottage.

chaussée [ʃose] *nf* road, roadway; «~ **déformée»** "uneven road surface".

chausse-pied [ʃospje] (*pl* **chausse-pieds**) *nm* shoehorn.

chausser [ʃose] **1** *vt* [chaussures, lunettes, skis] to put on. **2** *vi*: **~ du 39** to take

size 39 (shoes). ○ **se chausser** *vp* to put one's shoes on.

chaussette [ʃosɛt] *nf* sock.

chausson [ʃosɔ̃] *nm* [pantoufle] slipper. || [de danse] ballet shoe. || [de bébé] bootee. || CULIN turnover; ~ **aux pommes** apple turnover.

chaussure [ʃosyr] *nf* [soulier] shoe; ~ **de marche** [de randonnée] hiking ou walking boot; [confortable] walking shoe; ~ **de ski** ski boot. || [industrie] footwear industry.

chauve [ʃov] *adj* [sans cheveux] bald.

chauve-souris [ʃovsuri] *nf* bat.

chauvin, -e [ʃovɛ̃, in] *adj* chauvinistic.

chaux [ʃo] *nf* lime; **blanchi à la ~** white-washed.

chavirer [ʃavire] *vi* [bateau] to capsize. || *fig* [tourner] to spin.

chef [ʃef] *nm* [d'un groupe] head, leader; [au travail] boss; **en ~** in chief; ~ **d'entreprise** company head; ~ **de famille** head of the family; ~ **de gare** stationmaster; ~ **d'orchestre** conductor; ~ **de service** ADMIN departmental manager. || [cuisinier] chef.

chef-d'œuvre [ʃedœvr] (*pl* **chefs-d'œuvre**) *nm* masterpiece.

chef-lieu [ʃefljø] *nm* ≃ county town.

chemin [ʃəmɛ̃] *nm* [voie] path; ~ **de fer** railway; ~ **vicinal** byroad, minor road. || [parcours] way; *fig* road; **en ~** on the way.

cheminée [ʃəmine] *nf* [foyer] fireplace. || [conduit d'usine] chimney. || [encadrement] mantelpiece. || [de paquebot, locomotive] funnel.

cheminement [ʃəminmã] *nm* [progression] advance; *fig* [d'idée] development.

cheminer [ʃəmine] *vi* [avancer] to make one's way; *fig* [idée] to develop.

cheminot [ʃəmino] *nm* railroad man *Am*.

chemise [ʃəmiz] *nf* [d'homme] shirt; ~ **de nuit** [de femme] nightdress. || [dossier] folder.

chemisette [ʃəmizɛt] *nf* [d'homme] short-sleeved shirt; [de femme] short-sleeved blouse.

chemisier [ʃəmizje] *nm* [vêtement] blouse.

chenal, -aux [ʃənal, o] *nm* [canal] channel.

chêne [ʃɛn] *nm* [arbre] oak (tree); [bois] oak.

chenet [ʃənɛ] *nm* firedog.

chenil [ʃənil] *nm* [pour chiens] kennel.

chenille [ʃənij] *nf* [insecte] caterpillar. || [courroie] caterpillar track.

chèque [ʃɛk] *nm* cheque; **faire/toucher un ~** to write/cash a cheque; **~ (bancaire)** (bank) cheque; **~ barré** crossed cheque; **~ postal** post office cheque; **~ sans provision** bad cheque; **~ de voyage** traveller's cheque.

chèque-cadeau [ʃɛkkado] *nm* gift token.

chèque-repas [ʃɛkrəpa] (*pl* **chèques-repas**), **chèque-restaurant** [ʃɛk-rɛstɔrɑ̃] (*pl* **chèques-restaurant**) *nm* luncheon voucher.

chéquier [ʃekje] *nm* chequebook.

cher, chère [ʃɛr] 1 *adj* [aimé] dear (to sb); **Cher Monsieur** [au début d'une lettre] Dear Sir. || [produit, vie, commerçant] expensive. 2 *nm, f hum*: **mon ~** dear. ○ **cher** *adv*: **valoir ~, coûter ~** to be expensive, to cost a lot; **payer ~** to pay a lot.

chercher [ʃɛrʃe] 1 *vt* [gén] to look for. || [prendre]: **aller/venir ~ qqn** [à un rendez-vous] to (go/come and) meet sb; [en voiture] to (go/come and) pick sb up; **aller/venir ~ qqch** to (go/come and) get sthg. 2 *vi*: **~ à faire qqch** to try to do sthg.

chercheur, -euse [ʃɛrʃœr, øz] *nm, f* [scientifique] researcher.

chéri, -e [ʃeri] 1 *adj* dear. 2 *nm, f* darling.

chétif, -ive [ʃetif, iv] *adj* [malingre] sickly, weak.

cheval, -aux [ʃəval, o] *nm* [animal] horse; **être à ~ sur qqch** [être assis] to be sitting astride sthg; *fig* [siècles] to straddle sthg; *fig* [tenir à] to be a stickler for sthg; **~ d'arçons** horse (*in gymnastics*). || [équitation] riding, horse-riding; **faire du ~** to ride. || AUTOM: **~, ~-vapeur** horse-power.

chevalerie [ʃəvalri] *nf* [qualité] chivalry. || HIST knighthood.

chevalet [ʃəvalɛ] *nm* [de peintre] easel.

chevalier [ʃəvalje] *nm* knight.

chevalière [ʃəvaljɛr] *nf* [bague] signet ring.

chevauchée [ʃəvoʃe] *nf* [course] ride, horse-ride.

chevaucher [ʃəvoʃe] *vt* [être assis] to sit ou be astride. ○ **se chevaucher** *vp* to overlap.

chevelu, -e [ʃəvly] *adj* hairy.

chevelure [ʃəvlyr] *nf* [cheveux] hair.

chevet [ʃəvɛ] *nm* head (*of bed*); **être au ~ de qqn** to be at sb's bedside.

cheveu, -x [ʃəvø] *nm* [chevelure] hair;

se faire couper les ~x to have one's hair cut.

cheville [ʃəvij] *nf* ANAT ankle. || [pour fixer une vis] Rawlplug®.

chèvre [ʃɛvr] 1 *nf* [animal] goat. 2 *nm* [fromage] goat's cheese.

chevreau, -x [ʃəvro] *nm* kid.

chèvrefeuille [ʃɛvrəfœj] *nm* honeysuckle.

chevreuil [ʃəvrœj] *nm* [animal] roe deer. || CULIN venison.

chevronné, -e [ʃəvrɔne] *adj* [expérimenté] experienced.

chevrotant, -e [ʃəvrɔtɑ̃, ɑ̃t] *adj* tremulous.

chevrotine [ʃəvrɔtin] *nf* buckshot.

chewing-gum [ʃwiŋɡɔm] (*pl* **chewing-gums**) *nm* chewing gum (*U*).

chez [ʃe] *prép* [dans la maison de]: **il est ~ lui** he's at home; **il rentre ~ lui** he's going home; **aller ~ le médecin/coiffeur** to go to the doctor's/hairdresser's; **il va venir ~ nous** he is going to come to our place ou house. || [en ce qui concerne]: **~ les jeunes** among young people; **~ les Anglais** in England. || [dans les œuvres de]: **~ Proust** in (the works of) Proust. || [dans le caractère de]: **ce que j'apprécie ~ lui, c'est sa gentillesse** what I like about him is his kindness.

chic [ʃik] *adj* (*inv en genre*) [élégant] smart, chic. || *vieilli* [serviable] nice.

chicorée [ʃikɔre] *nf* [salade] endive; [à café] chicory.

chien [ʃjɛ̃] *nm* [animal] dog; **~ de chasse** [d'arrêt] gundog; **~ de garde** guard dog. || [d'arme] hammer. || *loc*: **avoir un mal de ~ à faire qqch** to have a lot of trouble doing sthg; **en ~ de fusil** curled up.

chiendent [ʃjɛ̃dɑ̃] *nm* couch grass.

chien-loup [ʃjɛ̃lu] *nm* Alsatian (dog).

chienne [ʃjɛn] *nf* (female) dog, bitch.

chiffon [ʃifɔ̃] *nm* [linge] rag.

chiffonner [ʃifɔne] *vt* [froisser - faire des plis] to crumple, to crease; [- déformer] to crumple. || *fam fig* [contrarier] to bother.

chiffre [ʃifr] *nm* [caractère] figure, number; **~ arabe/romain** Arabic/Roman numeral. || [montant] sum; **~ d'affaires** COMM turnover *Br*, net revenue *Am*; **~ rond** round number.

chiffrer [ʃifre] *vt* [évaluer] to calculate, to assess. || [coder] to encode.

chignole [ʃiɲɔl] *nf* drill.

chignon [ʃiɲɔ̃] *nm* bun (*in hair*); **se crêper le ~** *fig* to scratch each other's eyes out.

Chili [ʃili] *nm*: **le ~** Chile.

chimie [ʃimi] *nf* chemistry.

chimiothérapie [ʃimjɔterapi] *nf* chemotherapy.

chimique [ʃimik] *adj* chemical.

chimiste [ʃimist] *nmf* chemist.

chimpanzé [ʃɛ̃pɑ̃ze] *nm* chimpanzee.

Chine [ʃin] *nf*: **la ~** China.

chiné, -e [ʃine] *adj* mottled.

chiner [ʃine] *vi* to look for bargains.

chinois, -e [ʃinwa, waz] *adj* Chinese. ○ **chinois** *nm* [langue] Chinese. ‖ [passoire] conical sieve. ○ **Chinois, -e** *nm, f* Chinese person; **les Chinois** the Chinese.

chiot [ʃjo] *nm* puppy.

chipie [ʃipi] *nf* vixen *péj*.

chips [ʃips] *nfpl*: **(pommes) ~** (potato) crisps *Br*, (potato) chips *Am*.

chiquenaude [ʃiknod] *nf* flick.

chiquer [ʃike] **1** *vt* to chew. **2** *vi* to chew tobacco.

chirurgical, -e, -aux [ʃiryrʒikal, o] *adj* surgical.

chirurgie [ʃiryrʒi] *nf* surgery.

chirurgien [ʃiryrʒjɛ̃] *nm* surgeon.

chiure [ʃjyr] *nf*: **~ (de mouche)** flyspecks (*pl*).

chlore [klɔr] *nm* chlorine.

chloroforme [klɔrɔfɔrm] *nm* chloroform.

chlorophylle [klɔrɔfil] *nf* chlorophyll.

choc [ʃɔk] *nm* [heurt, coup] impact. ‖ [conflit] clash. ‖ [émotion] shock. ‖ (*en apposition*): **images--s** shock pictures; **prix--** amazing bargain.

chocolat [ʃɔkɔla] **1** *nm* chocolate; **~ au lait/noir** milk/plain chocolate; **~ à cuire/à croquer** cooking/eating chocolate. **2** *adj inv* chocolate (brown).

chœur [kœr] *nm* [chorale] choir; [d'opéra & *fig*] chorus; **en ~** *fig* all together. ‖ [d'église] choir, chancel.

choisi, -e [ʃwazi] *adj* selected; [termes, langage] carefully chosen.

choisir [ʃwazir] **1** *vt*: **~ (de faire qqch)** to choose (to do sthg). **2** *vi* to choose.

choix [ʃwa] *nm* [gén] choice; **le livre de ton ~** any book you like; **au ~** as you prefer; **avoir le ~** to have the choice. ‖ [qualité]: **de premier ~** grade ou class one; **articles de second ~** seconds.

choléra [kɔlera] *nm* cholera.

cholestérol [kɔlesterɔl] *nm* cholesterol.

chômage [ʃomaʒ] *nm* unemployment; **en ~, au ~** unemployed; **être mis au ~ technique** to be laid off.

chômeur, -euse [ʃomœr, øz] *nm, f*: **les ~s** the unemployed.

chope [ʃɔp] *nf* tankard.

choper [ʃɔpe] *vt fam* [voler, arrêter] to nick *Br*, to pinch. ‖ [attraper] to catch.

choquant, -e [ʃɔkɑ̃, ɑ̃t] *adj* shocking.

choquer [ʃɔke] *vt* [scandaliser] to shock. ‖ [traumatiser] to shake (up).

choral, -e, -als OU **-aux** [kɔral, o] *adj* choral. ○ **chorale** *nf* [groupe] choir.

chorégraphie [kɔregrafi] *nf* choreography.

choriste [kɔrist] *nmf* chorister.

chose [ʃoz] *nf* thing; **c'est (bien) peu de ~** it's nothing really; **c'est la moindre des ~s** it's the least I/we can do; **de deux ~s l'une** (it's got to be) one thing or the other; **parler de ~s et d'autres** to talk of this and that.

chou, -x [ʃu] *nm* [légume] cabbage. ‖ [pâtisserie] choux bun.

chouchou, -oute [ʃuʃu, ut] *nm, f* favourite; [élève] teacher's pet.

choucroute [ʃukrut] *nf* sauerkraut.

chouette [ʃwɛt] **1** *nf* [oiseau] owl. **2** *adj fam vieilli* smashing *Br*, great. **3** *interj*: **~ (alors)!** great!

chou-fleur [ʃuflœr] *nm* cauliflower.

chrétien, -ienne [kretjɛ̃, jɛn] *adj & nm, f* Christian.

Christ [krist] *nm* Christ.

christianisme [kristjanism] *nm* Christianity.

chrome [krom] *nm* CHIM chromium.

chromé, -e [krome] *adj* chrome-plated; **acier ~** chrome steel.

chromosome [krɔmɔzom] *nm* chromosome.

chronique [krɔnik] **1** *nf* [annales] chronicle. ‖ PRESSE: **~ sportive** sports section. **2** *adj* chronic.

chronologie [krɔnɔlɔʒi] *nf* chronology.

chronologique [krɔnɔlɔʒik] *adj* chronological.

chronomètre [krɔnɔmetr] *nm* SPORT stopwatch.

chronométrer [krɔnɔmetre] *vt* to time.

chrysanthème [krizɑ̃tem] *nm* chrysanthemum.

chuchotement [ʃyʃɔtmɑ̃] *nm* whisper.

chuchoter [ʃyʃɔte] *vt & vi* to whisper.

chut [ʃyt] *interj* sh!, hush!

chute [ʃyt] *nf* [gén] fall; ~ **d'eau** waterfall; ~ **de neige** snowfall. ‖ [de tissu] scrap.

ci [si] *adv* (*après n*): **ce livre-~** this book; **ces jours-~** these days.

ci-après [siapʀɛ] *adv* below.

cible [sibl] *nf litt & fig* target.

cicatrice [sikatʀis] *nf* scar.

cicatriser [sikatʀize] *vt litt & fig* to heal.

ci-contre [sikɔ̃tʀ] *adv* opposite.

ci-dessous [sidəsu] *adv* below.

ci-dessus [sidəsy] *adv* above.

cidre [sidʀ] *nm* cider.

Cie (*abr de* **compagnie**) Co.

ciel [sjɛl] (*pl sens 1* **ciels**, *pl sens 2* **cieux**) *nm* [firmament] sky; **à ~ ouvert** open-air. ‖ [paradis, providence] heaven. ⃝ **cieux** *nmpl* heaven (*sg*).

cierge [sjɛʀʒ] *nm* RELIG (votive) candle.

cigale [sigal] *nf* cicada.

cigare [sigaʀ] *nm* cigar.

cigarette [sigaʀɛt] *nf* cigarette.

cigogne [sigɔɲ] *nf* stork.

ci-inclus, -e [siɛ̃kly, yz] *adj* enclosed. ⃝ **ci-inclus** *adv* enclosed.

ci-joint, -e [siʒwɛ̃, ɛ̃t] *adj* enclosed. ⃝ **ci-joint** *adv*: **veuillez trouver ~ ...** please find enclosed ....

cil [sil] *nm* ANAT eyelash, lash.

ciller [sije] *vi* to blink (one's eyes).

cime [sim] *nf* [d'arbre, de montagne] top.

ciment [simɑ̃] *nm* cement.

cimenter [simɑ̃te] *vt* to cement.

cimetière [simtjɛʀ] *nm* cemetery.

ciné [sine] *nm fam* cinema.

cinéaste [sineast] *nmf* film-maker.

ciné-club [sineklœb] (*pl* **ciné-clubs**) *nm* film club.

cinéma [sinema] *nm* [salle, industrie] cinema. ‖ [art] cinema, film.

cinémathèque [sinematɛk] *nf* film archive.

cinématographique [sinematɔgʀafik] *adj* cinematographic.

cinéphile [sinefil] *nmf* film buff.

cinglé, -e [sɛ̃gle] *fam adj* nuts, nutty.

cingler [sɛ̃gle] *vt* to lash.

cinq [sɛ̃k] **1** *adj num* five. **2** *nm* five; *voir aussi* **six**.

cinquantaine [sɛ̃kɑ̃tɛn] *nf* [nombre]: **une ~ de** about fifty. ‖ [âge]: **avoir la ~** to be in one's fifties.

cinquante [sɛ̃kɑ̃t] *adj num & nm* fifty; *voir aussi* **six**.

cinquantième [sɛ̃kɑ̃tjɛm] *adj num, nm & nmf* fiftieth; *voir aussi* **sixième**.

cinquième [sɛ̃kjɛm] **1** *adj num, nm & nmf* fifth. **2** *nf* second year (*of secondary school*); *voir aussi* **sixième**.

cintre [sɛ̃tʀ] *nm* [pour vêtements] coat hanger.

cintré, -e [sɛ̃tʀe] *adj* COUTURE waisted.

cirage [siʀaʒ] *nm* [produit] shoe polish.

circoncision [siʀkɔ̃sizjɔ̃] *nf* circumcision.

circonférence [siʀkɔ̃feʀɑ̃s] *nf* GÉOM circumference. ‖ [pourtour] boundary.

circonflexe [siʀkɔ̃flɛks] → **accent**.

circonscription [siʀkɔ̃skʀipsjɔ̃] *nf* district.

circonscrire [siʀkɔ̃skʀiʀ] *vt* [incendie, épidémie] to contain. ‖ *fig* [sujet] to define.

circonstance [siʀkɔ̃stɑ̃s] *nf* [occasion] occasion. ‖ (*gén pl*) [contexte, conjoncture] circumstance; **~s atténuantes** JUR mitigating circumstances.

circonstancié, -e [siʀkɔ̃stɑ̃sje] *adj* detailed.

circonstanciel, -ielle [siʀkɔ̃stɑ̃sjɛl] *adj* GRAM adverbial.

circuit [siʀkɥi] *nm* [chemin] route. ‖ [parcours touristique] tour. ‖ SPORT & TECHNOL circuit.

circulaire [siʀkylɛʀ] *nf & adj* circular.

circulation [siʀkylasjɔ̃] *nf* [mouvement] circulation; **mettre en ~** to circulate; **~ (du sang)** circulation. ‖ [trafic] traffic.

circuler [siʀkyle] *vi* [sang, air, argent] to circulate; **faire ~ qqch** to circulate sthg. ‖ [aller et venir] to move (along); **on circule mal en ville** the traffic is bad in town. ‖ [train, bus] to run. ‖ *fig* [rumeur, nouvelle] to spread.

cire [siʀ] *nf* [matière] wax. ‖ [encaustique] polish.

ciré, -e [siʀe] *adj* [parquet] polished. ‖ → **toile**. ⃝ **ciré** *nm* oilskin.

cirer [siʀe] *vt* to polish.

cirque [siʀk] *nm* [gén] circus. ‖ GÉOL cirque. ‖ *fam fig* [désordre, chahut] chaos (*U*).

cirrhose [siʀoz] *nf* cirrhosis (*U*).

cisaille [sizaj] *nf* shears (*pl*).

cisailler [sizaje] *vt* [métal] to cut; [branches] to prune.

ciseau, -x [sizo] *nm* chisel. ⃝ **ciseaux** *nmpl* scissors.

ciseler [sizle] *vt* [pierre, métal] to chisel. ‖ [bijou] to engrave.

Cisjordanie [sizʒɔʀdani] *nf*: **la ~** the West Bank.

citadelle [sitadɛl] *nf litt & fig* citadel.

citadin, -e [sitadɛ̃, in] **1** *adj* city (*avant n*), urban. **2** *nm, f* city dweller.

citation [sitasjɔ̃] *nf* JUR summons (*sg*). || [extrait] quote, quotation.

cité [site] *nf* [ville] city. || [lotissement] housing estate; **~ universitaire** halls (*pl*) of residence.

citer [site] *vt* [exemple, propos, auteur] to quote. || JUR [convoquer] to summon.

citerne [sitɛrn] *nf* [d'eau] water tank. || [cuve] tank.

cité U [sitey] *nf fam abr de* **cité universitaire.**

citoyen, -enne [sitwajɛ̃, ɛn] *nm, f* citizen.

citoyenneté [sitwajɛnte] *nf* citizenship.

citron [sitrɔ̃] *nm* lemon; **~ pressé** fresh lemon juice; **~ vert** lime.

citronnade [sitrɔnad] *nf* (still) lemonade.

citronnier [sitrɔnje] *nm* lemon tree.

citrouille [sitruj] *nf* pumpkin.

civet [sivɛ] *nm* stew; **~ de lièvre** jugged hare.

civière [sivjɛr] *nf* stretcher.

civil, -e [sivil] **1** *adj* [gén] civil. || [non militaire] civilian. **2** *nm, f* civilian; **dans le ~** in civilian life; **policier en ~** plain-clothes policeman (*f* policewoman).

civilement [sivilmɑ̃] *adv*: **se marier ~** to get married at a registry office.

civilisation [sivilizasjɔ̃] *nf* civilization.

civilisé, -e [sivilize] *adj* civilized.

civique [sivik] *adj* civic; **instruction ~** civics (*U*).

civisme [sivism] *nm* sense of civic responsibility.

cl (*abr de* **centilitre**) cl.

clair, -e [klɛr] *adj* [gén] clear; **c'est ~ et net** there's no two ways about it. || [lumineux] bright. || [pâle - couleur, teint] light; [- tissu, cheveux] light-coloured. ○ **clair** *nm*: **mettre** OU **tirer qqch au ~** to shed light upon sthg. ○ **clair de lune** (*pl* **clairs de lune**) *nm* moonlight (*U*).

clairement [klɛrmɑ̃] *adv* clearly.

claire-voie [klɛrvwa] ○ **à claire-voie** *loc adv* openwork (*avant n*).

clairière [klɛrjɛr] *nf* clearing.

clairon [klɛrɔ̃] *nm* bugle.

claironner [klɛrɔne] *vt fig* [crier]: **~ qqch** to shout sthg from the rooftops.

clairsemé, -e [klɛrsəme] *adj* [cheveux] thin; [arbres] scattered; [population] sparse.

clairvoyant, -e [klɛrvwajɑ̃, ɑ̃t] *adj* perceptive.

clamer [klame] *vt* to proclaim.

clan [klɑ̃] *nm* clan.

clandestin, -e [klɑ̃dɛstɛ̃, in] **1** *adj* [journal, commerce] clandestine; [activité] covert. **2** *nm, f* [étranger] illegal immigrant OU alien; [voyageur] stowaway.

clapier [klapje] *nm* [à lapins] hutch.

clapoter [klapɔte] *vi* [vagues] to lap.

claquage [klakaʒ] *nm* MÉD strain; **se faire un ~** to pull OU to strain a muscle.

claque [klak] *nf* [gifle] slap.

claquer [klake] **1** *vt* [fermer] to slam. || **faire ~** [langue] to click; [doigts] to snap; [fouet] to crack. || *fam* [dépenser] to blow. **2** *vi* [porte, volet] to bang.

claquettes [klakɛt] *nfpl* [danse] tap dancing (*U*).

clarifier [klarifje] *vt litt & fig* to clarify.

clarinette [klarinɛt] *nf* [instrument] clarinet.

clarté [klarte] *nf* [lumière] brightness. || [netteté] clarity.

classe [klas] *nf* [gén] class; **~ touriste** economy class. || SCOL: **aller en ~** to go to school; **~ de neige** skiing trip (*with school*); **~ verte** field trip (*with school*). || MIL rank. || *loc*: **faire ses ~s** MIL to do one's training.

classé, -e [klase] *adj* [monument] listed.

classement [klasmɑ̃] *nm* [rangement] filing. || [classification] classification. || [rang - SCOL] position; [- SPORT] placing.

classer [klase] *vt* [ranger] to file. || [plantes, animaux] to classify. || [cataloguer]: **~ qqn (parmi)** to label sb (as). || [attribuer un rang à] to rank. ○ **se classer** *vp* to be classed, to rank; **se ~ troisième** to come third.

classeur [klasœr] *nm* [meuble] filing cabinet. || [d'écolier] ring binder.

classification [klasifikasjɔ̃] *nf* classification.

classique [klasik] **1** *nm* [auteur] classical author. || [œuvre] classic. **2** *adj* ART & MUS classical. || [sobre] classic. || [habituel] classic.

clause [kloz] *nf* clause.

claustrophobie [klostrɔfɔbi] *nf* claustrophobia.

clavecin [klavsɛ̃] *nm* harpsichord.

clavicule [klavikyl] *nf* collarbone.

clavier [klavje] *nm* keyboard.

clé, clef [kle] **1** *nf* [gén] key; **mettre qqn/qqch sous ~** to lock sb/sthg up; **~ de contact** AUTOM ignition key. || [outil]: **~**

anglaise ou **à molette** adjustable spanner *Br* ou wrench *Am*, monkey wrench. ‖ MUS [signe] clef; **~ de sol/fa** treble/bass clef. **2** *adj*: **industrie/rôle ~** key industry/role.

clémence [klemɑ̃s] *nf sout* [indulgence] clemency. ‖ *fig* [douceur] mildness.

clément, -e [klemɑ̃, ɑ̃t] *adj* [indulgent] lenient. ‖ *fig* [température] mild.

clémentine [klemɑ̃tin] *nf* clementine.

cleptomane → **kleptomane**.

clerc [klɛr] *nm* [assistant] clerk.

clergé [klɛrʒe] *nm* clergy.

cliché [klife] *nm* PHOT negative. ‖ [banalité] cliché.

client, -e [kliɑ̃, ɑ̃t] *nm, f* [de notaire, d'agence] client; [de médecin] patient. ‖ [acheteur] customer.

clientèle [kliɑ̃tɛl] *nf* [ensemble des clients] customers (*pl*); [de profession libérale] clientele.

cligner [kliɲe] *vi*: **~ de l'œil** to wink; **~ des yeux** to blink.

clignotant, -e [kliɲɔtɑ̃, ɑ̃t] *adj* [lumière] flickering. ○ **clignotant** *nm* AUTOM indicator.

clignoter [kliɲɔte] *vi* [yeux] to blink. ‖ [lumière] to flicker.

climat [klima] *nm litt & fig* climate.

climatisation [klimatizasjɔ̃] *nf* airconditioning.

climatisé, -e [klimatize] *adj* airconditioned.

clin [klɛ̃] ○ **clin d'œil** *nm*: **faire un ~ d'œil (à)** to wink (at); **en un ~ d'œil** in a flash.

clinique [klinik] **1** *nf* clinic. **2** *adj* clinical.

clip [klip] *nm* [vidéo] pop video. ‖ [boucle d'oreilles] clip-on earring.

cliquer [klike] *vi* INFORM to click.

cliqueter [klikte] *vi* [pièces, clés, chaînes] to jingle, to jangle. ‖ [verres] to clink.

clivage [klivaʒ] *nm fig* [division] division.

clochard, -e [klɔʃar, ard] *nm, f* tramp.

cloche [klɔʃ] **1** *nf* [d'église] bell. ‖ *fam* [idiot] idiot. **2** *adj fam*: **ce qu'elle peut être ~, celle-là!** she can be a right idiot!

cloche-pied [klɔʃpje] ○ **à cloche-pied** *loc adv* hopping; **sauter à ~** to hop.

clocher [klɔʃe] *nm* [d'église] church tower.

clochette [klɔʃɛt] *nf* [petite cloche] (little) bell. ‖ [de fleur] bell.

clodo [klɔdo] *nmf fam* tramp.

cloison [klwazɔ̃] *nf* [mur] partition.

cloisonner [klwazɔne] *vt* [pièce, maison] to partition (off); *fig* to compartmentalize.

cloître [klwatr] *nm* cloister.

cloporte [klɔpɔrt] *nm* woodlouse.

cloque [klɔk] *nf* blister.

clore [klɔr] *vt* to close; [négociations] to conclude.

clos, -e [klo, kloz] **1** *pp* → **clore**. **2** *adj* closed.

clôture [klotyr] *nf* [haie] hedge; [de fil de fer] fence. ‖ [fermeture] closing, closure. ‖ [fin] end, conclusion.

clôturer [klotyre] *vt* [terrain] to enclose.

clou [klu] *nm* [pointe] nail; **~ de girofle** CULIN clove. ‖ [attraction] highlight.

clouer [klue] *vt* [fixer - couvercle, planche] to nail (down); [- tableau, caisse] to nail (up); *fig* [immobiliser]: **rester cloué sur place** to be rooted to the spot.

clouté, -e [klute] *adj* [vêtement] studded.

clown [klun] *nm* clown; **faire le ~** to clown around, to act the fool.

club [klœb] *nm* club.

cm (*abr de* **centimètre**) cm.

CM *nm* (*abr de* **cours moyen**): **~1** *fourth year of primary school*; **~2** *fifth year of primary school*.

CNRS (*abr de* **Centre national de la recherche scientifique**) *nm national scientific research organization*.

coaguler [kɔagyle] *vi* [sang] to clot. ‖ [lait] to curdle.

coalition [kɔalisjɔ̃] *nf* coalition.

coasser [kɔase] *vi* [grenouille] to croak.

cobaye [kɔbaj] *nm litt & fig* guinea pig.

cobra [kɔbra] *nm* cobra.

Coca® [kɔka] *nm* [boisson] Coke®.

cocaïne [kɔkain] *nf* cocaine.

cocarde [kɔkard] *nf* [insigne] roundel. ‖ [distinction] rosette.

cocasse [kɔkas] *adj* funny.

coccinelle [kɔksinɛl] *nf* [insecte] ladybird *Br*, ladybug *Am*. ‖ [voiture] Beetle.

coccyx [kɔksis] *nm* coccyx.

cocher¹ [kɔʃe] *nm* coachman.

cocher² [kɔʃe] *vt* to check (off) *Am*.

cochon, -onne [kɔʃɔ̃, ɔn] **1** *adj* dirty, smutty. **2** *nm, f fam péj* pig; **un tour de ~** a dirty trick. ○ **cochon** *nm* pig.

cochonnerie [kɔʃɔnri] *nf fam* [nourriture] muck (*U*). ‖ [chose] rubbish (*U*). ‖ [saleté] mess (*U*). ‖ [obscénité] dirty joke, smut (*U*).

cochonnet [kɔʃɔnɛ] *nm* JEU jack.

cocktail [kɔktɛl] *nm* [réception] cocktail party. || [boisson] cocktail. || *fig* [mélange] mixture.

coco [kɔko] *nm* → **noix**. || *péj* [communiste] commie.

cocon [kɔkɔ̃] *nm* ZOOL & *fig* cocoon.

cocorico [kɔkɔriko] *nm* [du coq] cock-a-doodle-doo.

cocotier [kɔkɔtje] *nm* coconut tree.

cocotte [kɔkɔt] *nf* [marmite] casserole (dish). || [poule] hen. || *péj* [courtisane] tart.

Cocotte-Minute® [kɔkɔtminyt] *nf* pressure cooker.

cocu, -e [kɔky] *nm, f* & *adj fam* cuckold.

code [kɔd] *nm* [gén] code; **~ barres** bar code; **~ pénal** penal code; **~ postal** postcode *Br*, zip code *Am*; **~ de la route** highway code. || [phares] dipped headlights (*pl*).

coder [kɔde] *vt* to code.

coefficient [kɔefisjɑ̃] *nm* coefficient.

coéquipier, -ière [kɔekipje, jɛr] *nm, f* teammate.

cœur [kœr] *nm* heart; **de bon ~** willingly; **de tout son ~** with all one's heart; **apprendre par ~** to learn by heart; **avoir bon ~** to be kind-hearted; **avoir mal au ~** to feel sick; **s'en donner à ~ joie** [prendre beaucoup de plaisir] to have a whale of a time.

coexister [kɔɛgziste] *vi* to coexist.

coffre [kɔfr] *nm* [meuble] chest. || [de voiture] trunk *Am*. || [coffre-fort] safe.

coffre-fort [kɔfrəfɔr] *nm* safe.

coffret [kɔfrɛ] *nm* [petit coffre] casket; **~ à bijoux** jewellery box. || [de disques] boxed set.

cogner [kɔɲe] *vi* [heurter] to bang. || [soleil] to beat down. **○ se cogner** *vp* [se heurter] to bump o.s.; **se ~ à** OU **contre qqch** to bump into sthg; **se ~ la tête/le genou** to hit one's head/knee.

cohabiter [kɔabite] *vi* [habiter ensemble] to live together. || POLIT to cohabit.

cohérence [kɔerɑ̃s] *nf* consistency, coherence.

cohérent, -e [kɔerɑ̃, ɑ̃t] *adj* [logique] consistent, coherent. || [unifié] coherent.

cohésion [kɔezjɔ̃] *nf* cohesion.

cohorte [kɔɔrt] *nf* [groupe] troop.

cohue [kɔy] *nf* [foule] crowd. || [bousculade] crush.

coi, coite [kwa, kwat] *adj*: **rester ~** *sout* to remain silent.

coiffe [kwaf] *nf* headdress.

coiffé, -e [kwafe] *adj*: **être bien/mal ~** to have tidy/untidy hair; **être ~ d'une casquette** to be wearing a cap.

coiffer [kwafe] *vt* [mettre sur la tête]: **~ qqn de qqch** to put sthg on sb's head. || [les cheveux]: **~ qqn** to do sb's hair. **○ se coiffer** *vp* [les cheveux] to do one's hair. || [mettre sur sa tête]: **se ~ de** to wear, to put on.

coiffeur, -euse [kwafœr, øz] *nm, f* hairdresser. **○ coiffeuse** *nf* [meuble] dressing table.

coiffure [kwafyr] *nf* [chapeau] hat. || [cheveux] hairstyle.

coin [kwɛ̃] *nm* [angle] corner; **au ~ du feu** by the fireside. || [parcelle, endroit] place, spot; **dans le ~** in the area; **~ cuisine** kitchen area. || [outil] wedge.

coincer [kwɛ̃se] *vt* [bloquer] to jam. || *fam* [prendre] to nab; *fig* to catch out. || [acculer] to corner, to trap.

coïncidence [kɔɛ̃sidɑ̃s] *nf* coincidence.

coïncider [kɔɛ̃side] *vi* to coincide.

coing [kwɛ̃] *nm* [fruit] quince.

col [kɔl] *nm* [de vêtement] collar; **~ roulé** polo neck *Br*, turtleneck *Am*. || [partie étroite] neck. || ANAT: **~ du fémur** neck of the thighbone OU femur; **~ de l'utérus** cervix, neck of the womb. || GÉOGR pass.

coléoptère [kɔleɔptɛr] *nm* beetle.

colère [kɔlɛr] *nf* [irritation] anger; **être/se mettre en ~** to be/get angry; **piquer une ~** to fly into a rage. || [accès d'humeur] fit of anger OU rage.

coléreux, -euse [kɔlerø, øz], **colérique** [kɔlerik] *adj* [tempérament] fiery; [personne] quick-tempered.

colimaçon [kɔlimasɔ̃] **○ en colimaçon** *loc adv* spiral.

colique [kɔlik] *nf* (*gén pl*) [douleur] colic (*U*). || [diarrhée] diarrhoea.

colis [kɔli] *nm* parcel.

collaborateur, -trice [kɔlabɔratœr, tris] *nm, f* [employé] colleague. || HIST collaborator.

collaboration [kɔlabɔrasjɔ̃] *nf* collaboration.

collaborer [kɔlabɔre] *vi* [coopérer, sous l'Occupation] to collaborate. || [participer]: **~ à** to contribute to.

collant, -e [kɔlɑ̃, ɑ̃t] *adj* [substance] sticky. || *fam* [personne] clinging, clingy. **○ collant** *nm* panty hose (*U*) *Am*.

colle [kɔl] *nf* [substance] glue. || [question] poser. || [SCOL - interrogation] test; [- retenue] detention.

collecte [kɔlɛkt] *nf* collection.

collectif, -ive [kɔlɛktif, iv] *adj* [responsabilité, travail] collective. || [billet, voyage] group (*avant n*).

collection [kɔlɛksjɔ̃] *nf* [d'objets, de livres, de vêtements] collection; **faire la ~ de** to collect. || COMM line.

collectionner [kɔlɛksjɔne] *vt litt & fig* to collect.

collectionneur, -euse [kɔlɛksjɔnœr, øz] *nm, f* collector.

collectivité [kɔlɛktivite] *nf* community; **les ~s locales** ADMIN the local communities.

collège [kɔlɛʒ] *nm* SCOL ≃ secondary school. || [de personnes] college.

collégien, -ienne [kɔleʒjɛ̃, jɛn] *nm, f* schoolboy (*f* schoolgirl).

collègue [kɔlɛg] *nmf* colleague.

coller [kɔle] **1** *vt* (fixer - affiche) to stick (up); [- timbre] to stick. || [appuyer] to press. || *fam* [mettre] to stick, to dump. || SCOL to give (a) detention to, to keep behind. **2** *vi* [adhérer] to stick. || [être adapté]: **~ à qqch** [vêtement] to cling to sthg. ○ **se coller** *vp* [se plaquer]: **se ~ contre qqn/qqch** to press o.s. against sb/sthg.

collerette [kɔlrɛt] *nf* [de vêtement] ruff.

collet [kɔlɛ] *nm* [de vêtement] collar; **être ~ monté** [affecté, guindé] to be strait-laced. || [piège] snare.

collier [kɔlje] *nm* [bijou] necklace. || [d'animal] collar. || [barbe] *fringe of beard along the jawline.*

colline [kɔlin] *nf* hill.

collision [kɔlizjɔ̃] *nf* [choc] collision, crash; **entrer en ~ avec** to collide with.

colloque [kɔlɔk] *nm* colloquium.

colmater [kɔlmate] *vt* [fuite] to plug, to seal off. || [brèche] to fill, to seal.

colombe [kɔlɔ̃b] *nf* dove.

Colombie [kɔlɔ̃bi] *nf*: **la ~** Colombia.

colon [kɔlɔ̃] *nm* settler.

côlon [kɔlɔ̃] *nm* colon.

colonel [kɔlɔnɛl] *nm* colonel.

colonial, -e, -iaux [kɔlɔnjal, jo] *adj* colonial.

colonialisme [kɔlɔnjalism] *nm* colonialism.

colonie [kɔlɔni] *nf* [territoire] colony. || [d'expatriés] community; **~ de vacances** holiday *Br* ou vacation *Am* camp (*for children*).

colonisation [kɔlɔnizasjɔ̃] *nf* colonization.

coloniser [kɔlɔnize] *vt litt & fig* to colonize.

colonne [kɔlɔn] *nf* column. ○ **colonne vertébrale** *nf* spine, spinal column.

colorant, -e [kɔlɔrɑ̃, ɑ̃t] *adj* colouring. ○ **colorant** *nm* colouring.

colorer [kɔlɔre] *vt* [teindre] to colour.

colorier [kɔlɔrje] *vt* to colour in.

coloris [kɔlɔri] *nm* shade.

coloriser [kɔlɔrize] *vt* CIN to colourize.

colossal, -e, -aux [kɔlɔsal, o] *adj* colossal, huge.

colporter [kɔlpɔrte] *vt* [marchandise] to hawk; [information] to spread.

coma [kɔma] *nm* coma; **être dans le ~** to be in a coma.

comateux, -euse [kɔmatø, øz] *adj* comatose.

combat [kɔ̃ba] *nm* [bataille] battle, fight. || *fig* [lutte] struggle. || SPORT fight.

combatif, -ive [kɔ̃batif, iv] *adj* [humeur] fighting (*avant n*).

combattant, -e [kɔ̃batɑ̃, ɑ̃t] *nm, f* [en guerre] combatant; [dans bagarre] fighter; **ancien ~** veteran.

combattre [kɔ̃batr] **1** *vt litt & fig* to fight (against). **2** *vi* to fight.

combattu, -e [kɔ̃baty] *pp* → combattre.

combien [kɔ̃bjɛ̃] **1** *conj* how much; **~ de** [nombre] how many; [quantité] how much; **~ de temps?** how long?; **ça fait ~?** [prix] how much is that?; [longueur, hauteur etc] how long/high etc is it? **2** *adv* how (much). **3** *nm inv*: **le ~ sommes-nous?** what date is it?; **tous les ~?** how often?

combinaison [kɔ̃binɛzɔ̃] *nf* [d'éléments] combination. || [de femme] slip. || [vêtement - de mécanicien] overall *Am*; [- de ski] ski suit. || [de coffre] combination.

combine [kɔ̃bin] *nf fam* trick.

combiné [kɔ̃bine] *nm* receiver.

combiner [kɔ̃bine] *vt* [arranger] to combine. || [organiser] to devise.

comble [kɔ̃bl] **1** *nm* height; **c'est un** ou **le ~!** that beats everything! **2** *adj* packed. ○ **combles** *nmpl* attic (*sg*), loft (*sg*).

combler [kɔ̃ble] *vt* [gâter]: **~ qqn de** to shower sb with. || [boucher] to fill in. || [déficit] to make good; [lacune] to fill.

combustible [kɔ̃bystibl] **1** *nm* fuel. **2** *adj* combustible.

combustion [kɔ̃bystjɔ̃] *nf* combustion.

comédie [kɔmedi] *nf* CIN & THÉÂTRE

comedy; ~ **musicale** musical. || [complication] palaver.

comédien, -ienne [kɔmedjɛ̃, jɛn] *nm, f* [acteur] actor (*f* actress); *fig* & *péj* sham.

comestible [kɔmɛstibl] *adj* edible.

comète [kɔmɛt] *nf* comet.

comique [kɔmik] **1** *nm* THÉÂTRE comic actor. **2** *adj* [style] comic. || [drôle] comical, funny.

comité [kɔmite] *nm* committee; ~ **d'entreprise** works council (*also organizing leisure acrivities*).

commandant [kɔmɑ̃dɑ̃] *nm* commander.

commande [kɔmɑ̃d] *nf* [de marchandises] order; **passer une ~** to place an order; **sur ~** tò order; **disponible sur ~** available on request. || TECHNOL control. || INFORM command.

commander [kɔmɑ̃de] **1** *rt* MIL to command. || [contrôler] to operate, to control. || COMM to order. **2** *vi* to be in charge; **~ à qqn de faire qqch** to order sb to do sthg.

commanditer [kɔmɑ̃dite] *vt* [entreprise] to finance. || [meurtre] to put up the money for.

commando [kɔmɑ̃do] *nm* commando (unit).

comme [kɔm] **1** *conj* [introduisant une comparaison] like. || [exprimant la manière] as; **fais ~ il te plaira** do as you wish; **~ prévu/convenu** as planned/agreed. || [tel que] like, such as. || [en tant que] as. || [ainsi que]: **les filles ~ les garçons iront jouer au foot** both girls and boys will play football. || [introduisant une cause] as, since; **~ il pleuvait nous sommes rentrés** as it was raining we went back. **2** *adv* [marquant l'intensité] how; **~ tu as grandi!** how you've grown!; **~ c'est difficile!** it's so difficult!

commémoration [kɔmemɔrasjɔ̃] *nf* commemoration.

commémorer [kɔmemɔre] *rt* to commemorate.

commencement [kɔmɑ̃smɑ̃] *nm* beginning, start.

commencer [kɔmɑ̃se] **1** *vt* [entreprendre] to begin, to start; [être au début de] to begin. **2** *vi* to start, to begin; **~ à faire qqch** to begin ou start to do sthg. to begin ou start doing sthg; **~ par faire qqch** to begin ou start by doing sthg.

comment [kɔmɑ̃] **1** *adv* how; **~?** what?; **~ ça va?** how are you?; **~ cela?** how come? **2** *nm inr* → **pourquoi**.

commentaire [kɔmɑ̃tɛr] *nm* [explication] commentary. || [observation] comment.

commentateur, -trice [kɔmɑ̃tatœr, tris] *nm, f* RADIO & TÉLÉ commentator.

commenter [kɔmɑ̃te] *rt* to comment on.

commérage [kɔmeraʒ] *nm péj* gossip (*U*).

commerçant, -e [kɔmɛrsɑ̃, ɑ̃t] **1** *adj* [rue] shopping (*avant n*); [quartier] commercial; [personne] business-minded. **2** *nm, f* shopkeeper.

commerce [kɔmɛrs] *nm* [achat et vente] commerce, trade; **~ de gros/détail** wholesale/retail trade; **~ extérieur** foreign trade. || [magasin] business; **le petit ~** small shopkeepers (*pl*).

commercial, -e, -iaux [kɔmɛrsjal, jo] **1** *adj* [entreprise, valeur] commercial; [politique] trade (*avant n*). **2** *nm, f* marketing man (*f* woman).

commercialiser [kɔmɛrsjalize] *vt* to market.

commère [kɔmɛr] *nf péj* gossip.

commettre [kɔmɛtr] *vt* to commit.

commis, -e [kɔmi, iz] *pp* → **commettre**.
○ **commis** *nm* assistant; **~ voyageur** commercial traveller.

commisération [kɔmizerasjɔ̃] *nf sout* commiseration.

commissaire [kɔmiser] *nm* commissioner; **~ de police** (police) captain *Am*.

commissaire-priseur [kɔmiserprizœr] *nm* auctioneer.

commissariat [kɔmisarja] *nm*: **~ de police** police station.

commission [kɔmisjɔ̃] *nf* [délégation] commission, committee. || [message] message. || [rémunération] commission.
○ **commissions** *nfpl* shopping (*U*); **faire les ~s** to do the shopping.

commissure [kɔmisyr] *nf*: **la ~ des lèvres** the corner of the mouth.

commode [kɔmɔd] **1** *nf* chest of drawers. **2** *adj* [pratique - système] convenient; [- outil] handy. || [aimable]: **pas ~** awkward.

commodité [kɔmɔdite] *nf* convenience.

commotion [kɔmosjɔ̃] *nf* MÉD shock; **~ cérébrale** concussion.

commun, -e [kɔmœ̃, yn] *adj* [gén] common; [- décision, effort] joint; [- salle] shared; **avoir qqch en ~** to have sthg in common. || [courant] usual, common.
○ **commune** *nf* town.

communal, -e, -aux [kɔmynal, o] *adj* [école] local; [bâtiments] council (*avant n*).

communauté [kɔmynote] *nf* [groupe] community. ‖ [de sentiments, d'idées] identity. ○ **Communauté européenne** *nf*: **la Communauté européenne** the European Community.

commune → **commun**.

communément [kɔmynemɑ̃] *adv* commonly.

communication [kɔmynikasjɔ̃] *nf* [gén] communication. ‖ TÉLÉCOM: **~ (téléphonique)** (phone) call; **être en ~ avec qqn** to be talking to sb; **obtenir la ~** to get through.

communier [kɔmynje] *vi* RELIG to take communion.

communion [kɔmynjɔ̃] *nf* RELIG communion.

communiqué [kɔmynike] *nm* communiqué; **~ de presse** press release.

communiquer [kɔmynike] *vt*: **~ qqch à** [information, sentiment] to pass on ou communicate sthg to; [chaleur] to transmit sthg to.

communisme [kɔmynism] *nm* communism.

communiste [kɔmynist] *nmf & adj* communist.

commutateur [kɔmytatœr] *nm* switch.

compact, -e [kɔpakt] *adj* [épais, dense] dense. ‖ [petit] compact. ○ **compact** *nm* [disque laser] compact disc, CD.

compagne → **compagnon**.

compagnie [kɔpaɲi] *nf* [gén & COMM] company; **tenir ~ à qqn** to keep sb company; **en ~ de** in the company of. ‖ [assemblée] gathering.

compagnon [kɔpaɲɔ̃], **compagne** [kɔpaɲ] *nm, f* companion.

comparable [kɔparabl] *adj* comparable.

comparaison [kɔparɛzɔ̃] *nf* [parallèle] comparison; **en ~ de, par ~ avec** compared with, in ou by comparison with.

comparaître [kɔparɛtr] *vi* JUR: **~ (devant)** to appear (before).

comparatif, -ive [kɔparatif, iv] *adj* comparative.

comparé, -e [kɔpare] *adj* comparative; [mérites] relative.

comparer [kɔpare] *vt* [confronter]: **~ (avec)** to compare (with). ‖ [assimiler]: **~ qqch à** to compare ou liken sthg to.

compartiment [kɔpartimɑ̃] *nm* compartment.

comparu, -e [kɔpary] *pp* → **comparaître**.

comparution [kɔparysjɔ̃] *nf* JUR appearance.

compas [kɔpa] *nm* [de dessin] pair of compasses, compasses (*pl*). ‖ NAVIG compass.

compassion [kɔpasjɔ̃] *nf* sout compassion.

compatible [kɔpatibl] *adj*: **~ (avec)** compatible (with).

compatir [kɔpatir] *vi*: **~ (à)** to sympathize (with).

compatriote [kɔpatrijɔt] *nmf* compatriot, fellow countryman (*f* countrywoman).

compensation [kɔpɑ̃sasjɔ̃] *nf* [dédommagement] compensation.

compensé, -e [kɔpɑ̃se] *adj* built-up.

compenser [kɔpɑ̃se] *vt* to compensate ou make up for.

compétence [kɔpetɑ̃s] *nf* [qualification] skill, ability. ‖ JUR competence; **cela n'entre pas dans mes ~s** that's outside my scope.

compétent, -e [kɔpetɑ̃, ɑ̃t] *adj* [capable] capable, competent. ‖ ADMIN & JUR competent; **les autorités ~es** the relevant authorities.

compétitif, -ive [kɔpetitif, iv] *adj* competitive.

compétition [kɔpetisjɔ̃] *nf* competition; **faire de la ~** to go in for competitive sport.

complaisant, -e [kɔplɛzɑ̃, ɑ̃t] *adj* [aimable] obliging, kind. ‖ [indulgent] indulgent.

complément [kɔplemɑ̃] *nm* [gén & GRAM] complement. ‖ [reste] remainder.

complémentaire [kɔplemɑ̃tɛr] *adj* [supplémentaire] supplementary. ‖ [caractères, couleurs] complementary.

complet, -ète [kɔplɛ, ɛt] *adj* [gén] complete. ‖ [plein] full. ○ **complet (-veston)** *nm* suit.

complètement [kɔplɛtmɑ̃] *adv* [vraiment] absolutely, totally. ‖ [entièrement] completely.

compléter [kɔplete] *vt* [gén] to complete, to complement; [somme d'argent] to make up.

complexe [kɔplɛks] **1** *nm* PSYCHOL complex; **~ d'infériorité/de supériorité** inferiority/superiority complex. ‖ [ensemble] complex. **2** *adj* complex, complicated.

complexé, -e [kɔ̃plekse] *adj* hung up, mixed up.

complexité [kɔ̃pleksite] *nf* complexity.

complication [kɔ̃plikasjɔ̃] *nf* intricacy, complexity. ○ **complications** *nfpl* complications.

complice [kɔ̃plis] 1 *nmf* accomplice. 2 *adj* [sourire, regard, air] knowing.

complicité [kɔ̃plisite] *nf* complicity.

compliment [kɔ̃plimɑ̃] *nm* compliment.

complimenter [kɔ̃plimɑ̃te] *vt* to compliment.

compliqué, -e [kɔ̃plike] *adj* [problème] complex, complicated; [personne] complicated.

compliquer [kɔ̃plike] *vt* to complicate.

complot [kɔ̃plo] *nm* plot.

comploter [kɔ̃plɔte] *vt & vi litt & fig* to plot.

comportement [kɔ̃pɔrtəmɑ̃] *nm* behaviour.

comporter [kɔ̃pɔrte] *vt* [contenir] to include, to contain. || [être composé de] to consist of, to be made up of. ○ **se comporter** *vp* to behave.

composant [kɔ̃pozɑ̃] *nm* component.

composante [kɔ̃pozɑ̃t] *nf* component.

composé, -e [kɔ̃poze] *adj* compound. ○ **composé** *nm* [mélange] combination. || CHIM & LING compound.

composer [kɔ̃poze] 1 *vt* [constituer] to make up, to form. || [créer - musique] to compose, to write. || [numéro de téléphone] to dial. 2 *vi* to compromise. ○ **se composer** *vp* [être constitué] : **se ~ de** to be composed of, to be made up of.

composite [kɔ̃pozit] *adj* [disparate - mobilier] assorted, of various types; [- foule] heterogeneous. || [matériau] composite.

compositeur, -trice [kɔ̃pozitœr, tris] *nm, f* MUS composer. || TYPO typesetter.

composition [kɔ̃pozisjɔ̃] *nf* [gén] composition; [de roman] writing, composition. || SCOL test. || [caractère] : **être de bonne ~** to be good-natured.

composter [kɔ̃pɔste] *vt* [ticket, billet] to date-stamp.

compote [kɔ̃pɔt] *nf* compote; **~ de pommes** stewed apple.

compréhensible [kɔ̃preɑ̃sibl] *adj* [texte, parole] comprehensible; *fig* [réaction] understandable.

compréhensif, -ive [kɔ̃preɑ̃sif, iv] *adj* understanding.

compréhension [kɔ̃preɑ̃sjɔ̃] *nf* [de texte] comprehension, understanding. || [indulgence] understanding.

comprendre [kɔ̃prɑ̃dr] *vt* [gén] to understand; **je comprends!** I see!; **se faire ~** to make o.s. understood; **mal ~** to misunderstand. || [comporter] to comprise, to consist of. || [inclure] to include.

compresse [kɔ̃pres] *nf* compress.

compresseur [kɔ̃presœr] → **rouleau**.

compression [kɔ̃presjɔ̃] *nf* [de gaz] compression; *fig* cutback, reduction.

comprimé, -e [kɔ̃prime] *adj* compressed. ○ **comprimé** *nm* tablet.

comprimer [kɔ̃prime] *vt* [gaz, vapeur] to compress. || [personnes] : **être comprimés dans** to be packed into.

compris, -e [kɔ̃pri, iz] 1 *pp* → **comprendre**. 2 *adj* [inclus] : **charges (non) ~es** (not) including bills, bills (not) included; **tout ~** all inclusive, all in; **y ~** including.

compromettre [kɔ̃prɔmetr] *vt* to compromise.

compromis, -e [kɔ̃prɔmi, iz] *pp* → **compromettre**. ○ **compromis** *nm* compromise.

compromission [kɔ̃prɔmisjɔ̃] *nf péj* base action.

comptabilité [kɔ̃tabilite] *nf* [comptes] accounts (*pl*); [service] : **la ~** accounts, the accounts department.

comptable [kɔ̃tabl] *nmf* accountant.

comptant [kɔ̃tɑ̃] *adv* : **payer** OU **régler ~** to pay cash. ○ **au comptant** *loc adv* : **payer au ~** to pay cash.

compte [kɔ̃t] *nm* [action] count, counting (*U*); [total] number; **~ à rebours** countdown. || BANQUE, COMM & COMPTABILITÉ account; **~ bancaire** OU **en banque** bank account; **~ courant** current account, checking account *Am*; **~ d'épargne** savings account; **~ postal** post office account. || *loc* : **être/se mettre à son ~** to be/become self-employed; **prendre qqch en ~, tenir ~ de qqch** to take sthg into account; **se rendre ~ de qqch** to realize sthg; **tout ~ fait** all things considered. ○ **comptes** *nmpl* accounts; **faire ses ~s** to do one's accounts.

compte chèques, compte-chèques [kɔ̃tʃɛk] *nm* current account, checking account *Am*.

compte-gouttes [kɔ̃tgut] *nm inv* dropper.

compter [kɔ̃te] 1 *vt* [dénombrer] to count. || [avoir l'intention de] : **~ faire**

qqch to intend to do sthg, to plan to do sthg. **2** *vi* [calculer] to count. ‖ [être important] to count, to matter. ‖ **~ sur** [se fier à] to rely on, count on.

compte rendu, compte-rendu [kɔ̃trɑ̃dy] *nm* report, account.

compteur [kɔ̃tœr] *nm* meter.

comptine [kɔ̃tin] *nf* nursery rhyme.

comptoir [kɔ̃twar] *nm* [de bar] bar; [de magasin] counter. ‖ HIST trading post. ‖ *Helv* [foire] trade fair.

compulser [kɔ̃pylse] *vt* to consult.

comte [kɔ̃t] *nm* count.

comtesse [kɔ̃tɛs] *nf* countess.

con, conne [kɔ̃, kɔn] *tfam* **1** *adj* bloody *Br* ou damned stupid. **2** *nm, f* stupid bastard (*f* bitch).

concave [kɔ̃kav] *adj* concave.

concéder [kɔ̃sede] *vt*: **~ qqch à** [droit, terrain] to grant sthg to; [point, victoire] to concede sthg to; **~ que** to admit (that), to concede (that).

concentration [kɔ̃sɑ̃trasjɔ̃] *nf* concentration.

concentré, -e [kɔ̃sɑ̃tre] *adj* [gén] concentrated. ‖ [personne]: **elle était très -e** she was concentrating hard. ‖ → **lait**. ○ **concentré** *nm* concentrate.

concentrer [kɔ̃sɑ̃tre] *vt* to concentrate. ○ **se concentrer** *vp* [se rassembler] to be concentrated. ‖ [personne] to concentrate.

concentrique [kɔ̃sɑ̃trik] *adj* concentric.

concept [kɔ̃sɛpt] *nm* concept.

conception [kɔ̃sɛpsjɔ̃] *nf* [gén] conception. ‖ [d'un produit, d'une campagne] design, designing (*U*).

concernant [kɔ̃sɛrnɑ̃] *prép* regarding, concerning.

concerner [kɔ̃sɛrne] *vt* to concern; **être/se sentir concerné par qqch** to be/feel concerned by sthg; **en ce qui me concerne** as far as I'm concerned.

concert [kɔ̃sɛr] *nm* MUS concert.

concertation [kɔ̃sɛrtasjɔ̃] *nf* consultation.

concerter [kɔ̃sɛrte] ○ **se concerter** *vp* to consult (each other).

concerto [kɔ̃sɛrto] *nm* concerto.

concession [kɔ̃sesjɔ̃] *nf* [compromis & GRAM] concession. ‖ [autorisation] rights (*pl*), concession.

concessionnaire [kɔ̃sesjɔnɛr] *nmf* [automobile] (car) dealer.

concevable [kɔ̃səvabl] *adj* conceivable.

concevoir [kɔ̃səvwar] *vt* [enfant, projet] to conceive. ‖ [comprendre] to conceive of; **je ne peux pas ~ comment/pourquoi** I cannot conceive how/why.

concierge [kɔ̃sjɛrʒ] *nmf* caretaker, concierge.

conciliation [kɔ̃siljasjɔ̃] *nf* [accord & JUR] conciliation.

concilier [kɔ̃silje] *vt* [mettre d'accord, allier] to reconcile; **~ qqch et** ou **avec qqch** to reconcile sthg with sthg.

concis, -e [kɔ̃si, iz] *adj* [style, discours] concise; [personne] terse.

concision [kɔ̃sizjɔ̃] *nf* conciseness, concision.

concitoyen, -yenne [kɔ̃sitwajɛ̃, jɛn] *nm, f* fellow citizen.

conclu, -e [kɔ̃kly] *pp* → **conclure**.

concluant, -e [kɔ̃klyɑ̃, ɑ̃t] *adj* [convaincant] conclusive.

conclure [kɔ̃klyr] **1** *vt* to conclude; **en ~ que** to deduce (that). **2** *vi*: **les experts ont conclu à la folie** the experts concluded he/she was mad.

conclusion [kɔ̃klyzjɔ̃] *nf* [gén] conclusion. ‖ [partie finale] close.

concombre [kɔ̃kɔ̃br] *nm* cucumber.

concordance [kɔ̃kɔrdɑ̃s] *nf* [conformité] agreement; **~ des temps** GRAM sequence of tenses.

concorder [kɔ̃kɔrde] *vi* [coïncider] to agree, to coincide. ‖ [être en accord]: **~ (avec)** to be in accordance (with).

concourir [kɔ̃kurir] *vi* [contribuer]: **~ à** to work towards. ‖ [participer à un concours] to compete.

concours [kɔ̃kur] *nm* [examen] competitive examination. ‖ [compétition] competition, contest. ‖ [coïncidence]: **~ de circonstances** combination of circumstances.

concret, -ète [kɔ̃krɛ, ɛt] *adj* concrete.

concrétiser [kɔ̃kretize] *vt* [projet] to give shape to; [rêve, espoir] to give solid form to. ○ **se concrétiser** *vp* [projet] to take shape; [rêve, espoir] to materialize.

conçu, -e [kɔ̃sy] *pp* → **concevoir**.

concubinage [kɔ̃kybinaʒ] *nm* living together, cohabitation.

concurrence [kɔ̃kyrɑ̃s] *nf* [rivalité] rivalry. ‖ ÉCON competition.

concurrent, -e [kɔ̃kyrɑ̃, ɑ̃t] **1** *adj* rival, competing. **2** *nm, f* competitor.

concurrentiel, -ielle [kɔ̃kyrɑ̃sjɛl] *adj* competitive.

condamnation [kɔ̃danasjɔ̃] *nf* JUR sentence. ‖ [dénonciation] condemnation.

condamné, -e [kɔ̃dane] *nm, f* convict, prisoner.

condamner [kɔ̃dane] *vt* JUR: ~ **qqn (à)** to sentence sb (to). || *fig* [obliger]: ~ **qqn à qqch** to condemn sb to sthg. || [malade]: **être condamné** to be terminally ill. || [interdire] to forbid. || [blâmer] to condemn. || [fermer] to fill in, to block up.

condensation [kɔ̃dɑ̃sasjɔ̃] *nf* condensation.

condensé [kɔ̃dɑ̃se] **1** *nm* summary. **2** *adj* → **lait**.

condenser [kɔ̃dɑ̃se] *vt* to condense.

condescendant, -e [kɔ̃desɑ̃dɑ̃, ɑ̃t] *adj* condescending.

condiment [kɔ̃dimɑ̃] *nm* condiment.

condisciple [kɔ̃disipl] *nm* fellow student.

condition [kɔ̃disjɔ̃] *nf* [gén] condition; **se mettre en ~** [physiquement] to get into shape. || [place sociale] station. ○ **conditions** *nfpl* [circonstances] conditions; **~s de vie** living conditions. || [de paiement] terms. ○ **à condition de** *loc prép* providing ou provided (that). ○ **à condition que** *loc conj* (+ *subjonctif*) providing ou provided (that).

conditionné, -e [kɔ̃disjɔne] *adj* [emballé]: ~ **sous vide** vacuum-packed. || → **air**.

conditionnel, -elle [kɔ̃disjɔnɛl] *adj* conditional. ○ **conditionnel** *nm* GRAM conditional.

conditionnement [kɔ̃disjɔnmɑ̃] *nm* [action d'emballer] packaging, packing. || [emballage] package. || PSYCHOL & TECHNOL conditioning.

conditionner [kɔ̃disjɔne] *vt* [déterminer] to govern. || PSYCHOL & TECHNOL to condition. || [emballer] to pack.

condoléances [kɔ̃dɔleɑ̃s] *nfpl* condolences.

conducteur, -trice [kɔ̃dyktœr, tris] **1** *adj* conductive. **2** *nm, f* [de véhicule] driver. ○ **conducteur** *nm* ÉLECTR conductor.

conduire [kɔ̃dɥir] **1** *vt* [voiture, personne] to drive. || [transmettre] to conduct. || *fig* [diriger] to manage. || *fig* [à la ruine, au désespoir]: ~ **qqn à qqch** to drive sb to sthg. **2** *vi* AUTOM to drive. || [mener]: ~ **à** to lead to. ○ **se conduire** *vp* to behave.

conduit, -e [kɔ̃dɥi, it] *pp* → **conduire**. ○ **conduit** *nm* [tuyau] conduit, pipe. || ANAT duct, canal. ○ **conduite** *nf* [pilotage d'un véhicule] driving; **~e à droite/**

gauche right-hand/left-hand drive. || [comportement] behaviour (*U*). || [canalisation]: **~e de gaz/d'eau** gas/water main, gas/water pipe.

cône [kon] *nm* GÉOM cone.

confection [kɔ̃fɛksjɔ̃] *nf* [réalisation] making. || [industrie] clothing industry.

confectionner [kɔ̃fɛksjɔne] *vt* to make.

confédération [kɔ̃federasjɔ̃] *nf* [d'états] confederacy. || [d'associations] confederation.

conférence [kɔ̃ferɑ̃s] *nf* [exposé] lecture. || [réunion] conference; **~ de presse** press conference.

conférencier, -ière [kɔ̃ferɑ̃sje, jɛr] *nm, f* lecturer.

conférer [kɔ̃fere] *vt* [accorder]: ~ **qqch à qqn** to confer sthg on sb.

confesser [kɔ̃fese] *vt* [avouer] to confess. ○ **se confesser** *vp* to go to confession.

confession [kɔ̃fesjɔ̃] *nf* confession.

confessionnal, -aux [kɔ̃fesjɔnal, o] *nm* confessional.

confetti [kɔ̃feti] *nm* confetti (*U*).

confiance [kɔ̃fjɑ̃s] *nf* confidence; **avoir ~ en** to have confidence ou faith in; **avoir ~ en soi** to be self-confident; **en toute ~** with complete confidence; **de ~** trustworthy; **faire ~ à qqn/qqch** to trust sb/sthg.

confiant, -e [kɔ̃fjɑ̃, ɑ̃t] *adj* [sans méfiance] trusting.

confidence [kɔ̃fidɑ̃s] *nf* confidence.

confident, -e [kɔ̃fidɑ̃, ɑ̃t] *nm, f* confidant (*f* confidante).

confidentiel, -ielle [kɔ̃fidɑ̃sjɛl] *adj* confidential.

confier [kɔ̃fje] *vt* [donner]: ~ **qqn/qqch à qqn** to entrust sb/sthg to sb. || [dire]: ~ **qqch à qqn** to confide sthg to sb. ○ **se confier** *vp*: **se ~ à qqn** to confide in sb.

confiné, -e [kɔ̃fine] *adj* [air] stale; [atmosphère] enclosed. || [enfermé] shut away.

confins [kɔ̃fɛ̃] ○ **aux confins de** *loc prép* on the borders of.

confirmation [kɔ̃firmasjɔ̃] *nf* confirmation.

confirmer [kɔ̃firme] *vt* [certifier] to confirm. ○ **se confirmer** *vp* to be confirmed.

confiscation [kɔ̃fiskasjɔ̃] *nf* confiscation.

confiserie [kɔ̃fizri] *nf* [magasin] candy

store *Am*, confectioner's. ‖ [sucreries] candy (*U*) *Am*, confectionery (*U*).

confiseur, -euse [kɔ̃fizœr, øz] *nm, f* confectioner.

confisquer [kɔ̃fiske] *vt* to confiscate.

confiture [kɔ̃fityr] *nf* jam.

conflit [kɔ̃fli] *nm* [situation tendue] clash, conflict. ‖ [entre États] conflict.

confondre [kɔ̃fɔ̃dr] *vt* [ne pas distinguer] to confuse. ‖ [accusé] to confound. ‖ [stupéfier] to astound.

confondu, -e [kɔ̃fɔ̃dy] *pp* → **confondre.**

conformation [kɔ̃fɔrmasjɔ̃] *nf* structure.

conforme [kɔ̃fɔrm] *adj*: ~ à in accordance with.

conformément [kɔ̃fɔrmemɑ̃]
○ **conformément à** *loc prép* in accordance with.

conformer [kɔ̃fɔrme] *vt*: ~ qqch à to shape sthg according to. ○ **se conformer** *vp*: se ~ à [s'adapter] to conform to; [obéir] to comply with.

conformiste [kɔ̃fɔrmist] **1** *nmf* conformist. **2** *adj* [traditionaliste] conformist.

conformité [kɔ̃fɔrmite] *nf* [accord]: être en ~ avec to be in accordance with.

confort [kɔ̃fɔr] *nm* comfort; **tout ~** with all modern conveniences *Am*.

confortable [kɔ̃fɔrtabl] *adj* comfortable.

confrère [kɔ̃frɛr], **consœur** [kɔ̃sœr] *nm, f* colleague.

confrontation [kɔ̃frɔ̃tasjɔ̃] *nf* [face à face] confrontation.

confronter [kɔ̃frɔ̃te] *vt* [mettre face à face] to confront; *fig*: être **confronté à** to be confronted or faced with.

confus, -e [kɔ̃fy, yz] *adj* [indistinct, embrouillé] confused. ‖ [gêné] embarrassed.

confusion [kɔ̃fyzjɔ̃] *nf* [gén] confusion. ‖ [embarras] confusion, embarrassment.

congé [kɔ̃ʒe] *nm* [arrêt de travail] leave (*U*); ~ (**de) maladie** sick leave; ~ **de maternité** maternity leave. ‖ [vacances] holiday *Br*, vacation *Am*; **en ~** on holiday; **une journée/semaine de ~** a day/week off. ‖ [renvoi] notice; **donner son ~ à** qqn to give sb his/her notice; **prendre ~ (de** qqn) *sout* to take one's leave (of sb).

congédier [kɔ̃ʒedje] *vt* to dismiss.

congélateur [kɔ̃ʒelatœr] *nm* freezer.

congeler [kɔ̃ʒle] *vt* to freeze.

congénital, -e, -aux [kɔ̃ʒenital, o] *adj* congenital.

congère [kɔ̃ʒɛr] *nf* snowdrift.

congestion [kɔ̃ʒɛstjɔ̃] *nf* congestion; ~ **pulmonaire** pulmonary congestion.

Congo [kɔ̃go] *nm*: **le ~** the Congo.

congratuler [kɔ̃gratyle] *vt* to congratulate.

congrès [kɔ̃grɛ] *nm* [colloque] assembly.

conifère [kɔnifɛr] *nm* conifer.

conjecture [kɔ̃ʒɛktyr] *nf* conjecture.

conjecturer [kɔ̃ʒɛktyre] *vt & vi* to conjecture.

conjoint, -e [kɔ̃ʒwɛ̃, ɛ̃t] **1** *adj* joint. **2** *nm, f* spouse.

conjonction [kɔ̃ʒɔ̃ksjɔ̃] *nf* conjunction.

conjonctivite [kɔ̃ʒɔ̃ktivit] *nf* conjunctivitis (*U*).

conjoncture [kɔ̃ʒɔ̃ktyr] *nf* ÉCON situation, circumstances (*pl*).

conjugaison [kɔ̃ʒygɛzɔ̃] *nf* [union] uniting. ‖ GRAM conjugation.

conjugal, -e, -aux [kɔ̃ʒygal, o] *adj* conjugal.

conjuguer [kɔ̃ʒyge] *vt* [unir] to combine. ‖ GRAM to conjugate.

conjuration [kɔ̃ʒyrasjɔ̃] *nf* [conspiration] conspiracy. ‖ [exorcisme] exorcism.

connaissance [kɔnɛsɑ̃s] *nf* [savoir] knowledge (*U*); **à ma ~** to (the best of) my knowledge; **en ~ de cause** with full knowledge of the facts; **prendre ~ de** qqch to study sthg, to examine sthg. ‖ [personne] acquaintance; **faire ~ (avec** qqn) to become acquainted (with sb); **faire la ~ de** to meet. ‖ [conscience]: **perdre/reprendre ~** to lose/regain consciousness.

connaisseur, -euse [kɔnɛsœr, øz] **1** *adj* expert (*avant n*). **2** *nm, f* connoisseur.

connaître [kɔnɛtr] *vt* [gén] to know; ~ qqn **de nom/de vue** to know sb by name/sight. ‖ [éprouver] to experience. ○ **se connaître** *vp* s'y ~ **en** [être expert] to know about. ‖ [soi-même] to know o.s. ‖ [se rencontrer] to meet (each other).

connecter [kɔnɛkte] *vt* to connect.

connexion [kɔnɛksjɔ̃] *nf* connection.

connu, -e [kɔny] **1** *pp* → **connaître.** **2** *adj* [célèbre] well-known, famous.

conquérant, -e [kɔ̃kerɑ̃, ɑ̃t] **1** *adj* conquering. **2** *nm, f* conqueror.

conquérir [kɔ̃kerir] *vt* to conquer.

conquête [kɔ̃kɛt] *nf* conquest.

conquis, -e [kɔ̃ki, iz] *pp* → **conquérir.**

consacrer [kɔ̃sakre] *vt* RELIG to consecrate. ‖ [employer]: ~ qqch à to devote sthg to. ○ **se consacrer** *vp*: se ~ à to dedicate o.s. to, to devote o.s. to.

conscience [kɔ̃sjɑ̃s] *nf* [connaissance & PSYCHOL] consciousness; **avoir ~ de qqch** to be aware of sthg. || [morale] conscience; **bonne/mauvaise ~** clear/guilty conscience; **~ professionnelle** professional integrity, conscientiousness.

consciencieux, -ieuse [kɔ̃sjɑ̃sjø, jøz] *adj* conscientious.

conscient, -e [kɔ̃sjɑ̃, ɑ̃t] *adj* conscious; **être ~ de qqch** [connaître] to be conscious of sthg.

conscrit [kɔ̃skri] *nm* conscript, recruit, draftee *Am*.

consécration [kɔ̃sekrasjɔ̃] *nf* [reconnaissance] recognition; [de droit, coutume] establishment. || RELIG consecration.

consécutif, -ive [kɔ̃sekytif, iv] *adj* [successif & GRAM] consecutive. || [résultant]: ~ à resulting from.

conseil [kɔ̃sɛj] *nm* [avis] piece of advice, advice (*U*). || [assemblée] council; **~ d'administration** board of directors; **~ de classe** staff meeting.

conseiller¹ [kɔ̃seje] **1** *vt* [recommander] to advise; **~ qqch à qqn** to recommend sthg to sb. || [guider] to advise, to counsel. **2** *vi* [donner un conseil]: **~ à qqn de faire qqch** to advise sb to do sthg.

conseiller², -ère [kɔ̃seje, ɛr] *nm, f* [guide] counsellor. || [d'un conseil] councillor; **~ municipal** town councillor *Br*, city councilman (*f* -woman) *Am*.

consentement [kɔ̃sɑ̃tmɑ̃] *nm* consent.

consentir [kɔ̃sɑ̃tir] *vi*: **~ à qqch** to consent to sthg.

conséquence [kɔ̃sekɑ̃s] *nf* consequence, result; **ne pas tirer à ~** to be of no consequence.

conséquent, -e [kɔ̃sekɑ̃, ɑ̃t] *adj* [cohérent] consistent. || [important] sizeable, considerable. ○ **par conséquent** *loc adv* therefore, consequently.

conservateur, -trice [kɔ̃sɛrvatœr, tris] **1** *adj* conservative. **2** *nm, f* POLIT conservative. || [administrateur] curator. ○ **conservateur** *nm* preservative.

conservation [kɔ̃sɛrvasjɔ̃] *nf* [état, entretien] preservation. || [d'aliment] preserving.

conservatoire [kɔ̃sɛrvatwar] *nm* academy; **~ de musique** music college.

conserve [kɔ̃sɛrv] *nf* tinned *Br* ou canned food; **en ~** [en boîte] tinned, canned; [en bocal] preserved, bottled.

conserver [kɔ̃sɛrve] *vt* [garder, entretenir] to keep.

considérable [kɔ̃siderabl] *adj* considerable.

considération [kɔ̃siderasjɔ̃] *nf* [réflexion, motivation] consideration; **prendre qqch en ~** to take sthg into consideration. || [estime] respect.

considérer [kɔ̃sidere] *vt* to consider; **tout bien considéré** all things considered.

consigne [kɔ̃siɲ] *nf* (*gén pl*) [instruction] instructions (*pl*). || [entrepôt de bagages] checkroom *Am*, baggage room *Am*; **~ automatique** lockers (*pl*).

consigné, -e [kɔ̃siɲe] *adj* returnable.

consistance [kɔ̃sistɑ̃s] *nf* [solidité] consistency; *fig* substance.

consistant, -e [kɔ̃sistɑ̃, ɑ̃t] *adj* [épais] thick. || [nourrissant] substantial.

consister [kɔ̃siste] *vi*: **~ en** to consist of; **~ à faire qqch** to consist in doing sthg.

consœur → **confrère**.

consolation [kɔ̃sɔlasjɔ̃] *nf* consolation.

console [kɔ̃sɔl] *nf* [table] console (table). || INFORM: **~ de visualisation** VDU, visual display unit.

consoler [kɔ̃sɔle] *vt* [réconforter]: **~ qqn (de qqch)** to comfort sb (in sthg).

consolider [kɔ̃sɔlide] *vt litt & fig* to strengthen.

consommateur, -trice [kɔ̃sɔmatœr, tris] *nm, f* [acheteur] consumer; [d'un bar] customer.

consommation [kɔ̃sɔmasjɔ̃] *nf* [utilisation] consumption; **faire une grande** ou **grosse ~ de** to use (up) a lot of. || [boisson] drink.

consommé, -e [kɔ̃sɔme] *adj sout* consummate. ○ **consommé** *nm* consommé.

consommer [kɔ̃sɔme] **1** *vt* [utiliser] to use (up). || [manger] to eat. || [énergie] to consume, to use. **2** *vi* [boire] to drink. || [voiture]: **cette voiture consomme beaucoup** this car uses a lot of fuel.

consonance [kɔ̃sɔnɑ̃s] *nf* consonance.

consonne [kɔ̃sɔn] *nf* consonant.

conspiration [kɔ̃spirasjɔ̃] *nf* conspiracy.

conspirer [kɔ̃spire] *vi* to conspire.

constamment [kɔ̃stamɑ̃] *adv* constantly.

constant, -e [kɔ̃stɑ̃, ɑ̃t] *adj* constant.

constat [kɔ̃sta] *nm* [procès-verbal] report. || [constatation] established fact.

constatation [kɔ̃statasjɔ̃] *nf* [révélation] observation. || [fait retenu] finding.

constater [kɔ̃state] *vt* [se rendre compte de] to see, to note. || [consigner - fait, infraction] to record; [- décès, authenticité] to certify.

constellation [kɔ̃stelasjɔ̃] *nf* ASTRON constellation.

consternation [kɔ̃stɛrnasjɔ̃] *nf* dismay.

consterner [kɔ̃stɛrne] *vt* to dismay.

constipation [kɔ̃stipasjɔ̃] *nf* constipation.

constipé, -e [kɔ̃stipe] *adj* MÉD constipated. || *fam fig* [manière, air] ill at ease.

constituer [kɔ̃stitɥe] *vt* [élaborer] to set up. || [composer] to make up. || [représenter] to constitute.

constitution [kɔ̃stitysjɔ̃] *nf* [création] setting up. || [de pays, de corps] constitution.

constructeur [kɔ̃stryktœr] *nm* [fabricant] manufacturer; [de navire] shipbuilder. || [bâtisseur] builder.

construction [kɔ̃stryksjɔ̃] *nf* IND building, construction; ~ **navale** shipbuilding. || [édifice] structure, building. || GRAM & *fig* construction.

construire [kɔ̃strɥir] *vt* [bâtir, fabriquer] to build. || [théorie, phrase] to construct.

construit, -e [kɔ̃strɥi, it] *pp* → **construire**.

consulat [kɔ̃syla] *nm* [résidence] consulate.

consultation [kɔ̃syltasjɔ̃] *nf* MÉD & POLIT consultation.

consulter [kɔ̃sylte] **1** *vt* [compulser] to consult. || [interroger, demander conseil à] to consult, to ask. || [spécialiste] to consult, to see. **2** *vi* [médecin] to take ou hold surgery; [avocat] to be available for consultation. ○ **se consulter** *vp* to confer.

contact [kɔ̃takt] *nm* [gén] contact; **prendre ~ avec** to make contact with; **rester en ~ (avec)** to stay in touch (with); **au ~ de** on contact with. || AUTOM ignition; **mettre/couper le ~** to switch on/off the ignition.

contacter [kɔ̃takte] *vt* to contact.

contagieux, -ieuse [kɔ̃taʒjø, jøz] *adj* MÉD contagious; *fig* infectious.

contagion [kɔ̃taʒjɔ̃] *nf* MÉD contagion.

contaminer [kɔ̃tamine] *vt* [infecter] to contaminate.

conte [kɔ̃t] *nm* story; ~ **de fées** fairy tale.

contemplation [kɔ̃tɑ̃plasjɔ̃] *nf* contemplation.

contempler [kɔ̃tɑ̃ple] *vt* to contemplate.

contemporain, -e [kɔ̃tɑ̃pɔrɛ̃, ɛn] *nm, f* contemporary.

contenance [kɔ̃tnɑ̃s] *nf* [capacité volumique] capacity. || [attitude]: **se donner une ~** to give an impression of composure; **perdre ~** to lose one's composure.

contenir [kɔ̃tnir] *vt* to contain, to hold, to take. ○ **se contenir** *vp* to contain o.s., to control o.s.

content, -e [kɔ̃tɑ̃, ɑ̃t] *adj* [satisfait]: ~ **(de qqn/qqch)** happy (with sb/sthg), content (with sb/sthg); ~ **de faire qqch** happy to do sthg.

contenter [kɔ̃tɑ̃te] *vt* to satisfy. ○ **se contenter** *vp*: **se ~ de qqch/de faire qqch** to content o.s. with sthg/with doing sthg.

contentieux [kɔ̃tɑ̃sjø] *nm* [litige] dispute; [service] legal department.

contenu, -e [kɔ̃tny] *pp* → **contenir**. ○ **contenu** *nm* [de récipient] contents (*pl*). || [de texte, discours] content.

conter [kɔ̃te] *vt* to tell.

contestable [kɔ̃tɛstabl] *adj* questionable.

contestation [kɔ̃tɛstasjɔ̃] *nf* [protestation] protest, dispute. || POLIT: **la ~** anti-establishment activity.

conteste [kɔ̃tɛst] ○ **sans conteste** *loc adv* unquestionably.

contester [kɔ̃tɛste] **1** *vt* to dispute, to contest. **2** *vi* to protest.

conteur, -euse [kɔ̃tœr, øz] *nm, f* storyteller.

contexte [kɔ̃tɛkst] *nm* context.

contigu, -uë [kɔ̃tigy] *adj*: ~ **(à)** adjacent (to).

continent [kɔ̃tinɑ̃] *nm* continent.

continental, -e, -aux [kɔ̃tinɑ̃tal, o] *adj* continental.

contingent [kɔ̃tɛ̃ʒɑ̃] *nm* MIL draft *Am*. || COMM quota.

continu, -e [kɔ̃tiny] *adj* continuous.

continuation [kɔ̃tinɥasjɔ̃] *nf* continuation.

continuel, -elle [kɔ̃tinɥɛl] *adj* [continu] continuous. || [répété] continual.

continuellement [kɔ̃tinɥɛlmɑ̃] *adv* continually.

continuer [kɔ̃tinɥe] **1** *vt* [poursuivre] to carry on with, to continue (with). **2** *vi* to continue, to go on; ~ **à** ou **de faire qqch** to continue to do ou doing sthg.

continuité [kɔ̃tinɥite] *nf* continuity.

contorsionner [kɔ̃tɔrsjɔne] ○ **se contorsionner** *vp* to contort (o.s.), to writhe.

contour [kɔ̃tur] *nm* [limite] outline. || (*gén pl*) [courbe] bend.

contourner [kɔ̃turne] *vt litt & fig* to bypass, to get round.

contraceptif, -ive [kɔ̃traseptif, iv] *adj* contraceptive. ○ **contraceptif** *nm* contraceptive.

contraception [kɔ̃trasepsjɔ̃] *nf* contraception.

contracter [kɔ̃trakte] *vt* [muscle] to contract, to tense. || [maladie] to contract, to catch. || [engagement] to contract; [assurance] to take out.

contraction [kɔ̃traksjɔ̃] *nf* contraction; [état de muscle] tenseness.

contractuel, -elle [kɔ̃traktɥel] *nm, f* traffic policeman (*f* policewoman) *Am*.

contradiction [kɔ̃tradiksjɔ̃] *nf* contradiction.

contradictoire [kɔ̃tradiktwar] *adj* contradictory; **débat** ~ open debate.

contraignant, -e [kɔ̃treɲɑ̃, ɑ̃t] *adj* restricting.

contraindre [kɔ̃trɛ̃dr] *vt*: ~ **qqn à faire qqch** to compel ou force sb to do sthg; **être contraint de faire qqch** to be compelled ou forced to do sthg.

contraire [kɔ̃trer] **1** *nm*: **le** ~ the opposite; **je n'ai jamais dit le** ~ I have never denied it. **2** *adj* opposite; ~ **à** [non conforme à] contrary to. ○ **au contraire** *loc adv* on the contrary.

contrairement [kɔ̃trermɑ̃] ○ **contrairement à** *loc prép* contrary to.

contrarier [kɔ̃trarje] *vt* [contrecarrer] to thwart, to frustrate. || [irriter] to annoy.

contrariété [kɔ̃trarjete] *nf* annoyance.

contraste [kɔ̃trast] *nm* contrast.

contraster [kɔ̃traste] *vt & vi* to contrast.

contrat [kɔ̃tra] *nm* contract, agreement; ~ **à durée déterminée/indéterminée** fixed-term/permanent contract.

contravention [kɔ̃travɑ̃sjɔ̃] *nf* [amende] fine; ~ **pour stationnement interdit** parking ticket; **dresser une** ~ **à qqn** to fine sb.

contre [kɔ̃tr] *prép* [juxtaposition, opposition] against. || [proportion, comparaison]: **élu à 15 voix** ~ **9** elected by 15 votes

to 9. || [échange] (in exchange) for. ○ **par contre** *loc adv* on the other hand.

contre-attaque [kɔ̃tratak] (*pl* **contre-attaques**) *nf* counterattack.

contrebalancer [kɔ̃trəbalɑ̃se] *vt* to counterbalance, to offset.

contrebande [kɔ̃trəbɑ̃d] *nf* [activité] smuggling; [marchandises] contraband.

contrebandier, -ière [kɔ̃trəbɑ̃dje, jer] *nm, f* smuggler.

contrebas [kɔ̃trəba] ○ **en contrebas** *loc adv* (down) below.

contrebasse [kɔ̃trəbas] *nf* [instrument] (double) bass.

contrecarrer [kɔ̃trəkare] *vt* to thwart, to frustrate.

contrecœur [kɔ̃trəkœr] ○ **à contrecœur** *loc adv* grudgingly.

contrecoup [kɔ̃trəku] *nm* consequence.

contre-courant [kɔ̃trəkurɑ̃] ○ **à contre-courant** *loc adv* against the current.

contredire [kɔ̃trədir] *vt* to contradict. ○ **se contredire** *vp* (*emploi réciproque*) to contradict (each other). || (*emploi réfléchi*) to contradict o.s.

contredit, -e [kɔ̃trədi] *pp* → **contredire**.

contrée [kɔ̃tre] *nf* [pays] land; [région] region.

contre-espionnage [kɔ̃trespjɔnaʒ] *nm* counterespionage.

contre-exemple [kɔ̃trɛgzɑ̃pl] (*pl* **contre-exemples**) *nm* example to the contrary.

contre-expertise [kɔ̃trɛkspertiz] (*pl* **contre-expertises**) *nf* second (expert) opinion.

contrefaçon [kɔ̃trəfasɔ̃] *nf* [activité] counterfeiting; [produit] forgery.

contrefaire [kɔ̃trəfer] *vt* [signature, monnaie] to counterfeit, to forge. || [voix] to disguise.

contrefort [kɔ̃trəfɔr] *nm* [pilier] buttress. || [de chaussure] back. ○ **contreforts** *nmpl* foothills.

contre-indication [kɔ̃trɛ̃dikasjɔ̃] (*pl* **contre-indications**) *nf* contraindication.

contre-jour [kɔ̃trəʒur] ○ **à contre-jour** *loc adv* against the light.

contremaître, -esse [kɔ̃trəmetr, ɛs] *nm, f* foreman (*f* forewoman).

contremarque [kɛ̃trəmark] *nf* [pour sortir d'un spectacle] pass-out ticket.

contre-offensive [kɔ̃trɔfɑ̃siv] (*pl* contre-offensives) *nf* counteroffensive.

contre-ordre = contrordre.

contrepartie [kɔ̃trəparti] *nf* [compensation] compensation. ○ **en contre-partie** *loc adv* in return.

contrepèterie [kɔ̃trəpɛtri] *nf* spoonerism.

contre-pied [kɔ̃trəpje] *nm*: **prendre le ~ de** to do the opposite of.

contreplaqué, contre-plaqué [kɔ̃trəplake] *nm* plywood.

contrepoids [kɔ̃trəpwa] *nm litt & fig* counterbalance, counterweight.

contre-pouvoir [kɔ̃trəpuvwar] (*pl* contre-pouvoirs) *nm* counterbalance.

contrer [kɔ̃tre] *vt* [s'opposer à] to counter. ‖ CARTES to double.

contresens [kɔ̃trəsɑ̃s] *nm* [erreur - de traduction] mistranslation; [- d'interprétation] misinterpretation. ‖ [absurdité] nonsense (*U*). ○ **à contresens** *loc adv litt & fig* the wrong way.

contretemps [kɔ̃trətɑ̃] *nm* hitch, mishap. ○ **à contretemps** *loc adv* MUS out of time; *fig* at the wrong moment.

contribuable [kɔ̃tribɥabl] *nmf* taxpayer.

contribuer [kɔ̃tribɥe] *vi*: ~ **à** to contribute to ou towards.

contribution [kɔ̃tribysjɔ̃] *nf*: ~ (à) contribution (to); **mettre qqn à ~** to call on sb's services. ○ **contributions** *nfpl* taxes.

contrit, -e [kɔ̃tri, it] *adj* contrite.

contrôle [kɔ̃trol] *nm* [vérification - déclaration] check, checking (*U*); [- de documents, billets] inspection; ~ **d'identité** identity check. ‖ [maîtrise, commande] control; **perdre le ~ de qqch** to lose control of sthg. ‖ SCOL test.

contrôler [kɔ̃trole] *vt* [vérifier - documents, billets] to inspect; [- déclaration] to check; [- connaissances] to test. ‖ [maîtriser, diriger] to control. ‖ TECHNOL to monitor, to control.

contrôleur, -euse [kɔ̃trolœr, øz] *nm, f* [de train] ticket inspector; [d'autobus] (bus) conductor (*f* conductress); ~ **aérien** air traffic controller.

contrordre, contre-ordre (*pl* contre-ordres) [kɔ̃trɔrdr] *nm* countermand; **sauf ~** unless otherwise instructed.

controverse [kɔ̃trɔvɛrs] *nf* controversy.

controversé, -e [kɔ̃trɔvɛrse] *adj* [personne, décision] controversial.

contumace [kɔ̃tymas] *nf* JUR: **condamné par ~** sentenced in absentia.

contusion [kɔ̃tyzjɔ̃] *nf* bruise, contusion.

convaincant, -e [kɔ̃vɛ̃kɑ̃, ɑ̃t] *adj* convincing.

convaincre [kɔ̃vɛ̃kr] *vt* [persuader]: ~ **qqn (de qqch)** to convince sb (of sthg); ~ **qqn (de faire qqch)** to persuade sb (to do sthg). ‖ JUR: ~ **qqn de** to find sb guilty of, to convict sb of.

convaincu, -e [kɔ̃vɛ̃ky] **1** *pp* → convaincre. **2** *adj* [partisan] committed; **d'un ton ~, d'un air ~** with conviction.

convainquant [kɔ̃vɛ̃kɑ̃] *ppr* → convaincre.

convalescence [kɔ̃valesɑ̃s] *nf* convalescence; **être en ~** to be convalescing ou recovering.

convalescent, -e [kɔ̃valesɑ̃, ɑ̃t] *adj & nm, f* convalescent.

convenable [kɔ̃vnabl] *adj* [manières, comportement] polite; [tenue, personne] decent, respectable. ‖ [acceptable] adequate, acceptable.

convenance [kɔ̃vnɑ̃s] *nf*: **à ma/votre ~** to my/your convenience. ○ **convenances** *nfpl* proprieties.

convenir [kɔ̃vnir] *vi* [décider]: ~ **de qqch/de faire qqch** to agree on sthg/to do sthg. ‖ [plaire]: ~ **à qqn** to suit sb, to be convenient for sb. ‖ [être approprié]: ~ **à** ou **pour** to be suitable for. ‖ *sout* [admettre]: ~ **de qqch** to admit to sthg; ~ **que** to admit (that).

convention [kɔ̃vɑ̃sjɔ̃] *nf* [règle, assemblée] convention. ‖ [accord] agreement.

conventionnel, -elle [kɔ̃vɑ̃sjɔnɛl] *adj* conventional.

convenu, -e [kɔ̃vny] **1** *pp* → convenir. **2** *adj* [décidé]: **comme ~** as agreed.

convergent, -e [kɔ̃vɛrʒɑ̃, ɑ̃t] *adj* convergent.

converger [kɔ̃vɛrʒe] *vi*: ~ **(vers)** to converge (on).

conversation [kɔ̃vɛrsasjɔ̃] *nf* conversation.

conversion [kɔ̃vɛrsjɔ̃] *nf* [gén]: ~ **(à/en)** conversion (to/into).

convertible [kɔ̃vɛrtibl] *nm* [canapé-lit] sofa-bed.

convertir [kɔ̃vɛrtir] *vt*: ~ **qqn (à)** to convert sb (to); ~ **qqch (en)** to convert sthg (into). ○ **se convertir** *vp*: **se ~ (à)** to be converted (to).

convexe [kɔvɛks] *adj* convex.

conviction [kɔviksjɔ̃] *nf* conviction.

convier [kɔvje] *vt*: ~ **qqn à** to invite sb to.

convive [kɔviv] *nmf* guest (*at a meal*).

convivial, -e, -iaux [kɔvivjal, jo] *adj* [réunion] convivial. || INFORM user-friendly.

convocation [kɔvɔkasjɔ̃] *nf* [avis écrit] summons (*sg*), notification to attend.

convoi [kɔvwa] *nm* [de véhicules] convoy. || [train] train.

convoiter [kɔvwate] *vt* to covet.

convoitise [kɔvwatiz] *nf* covetousness.

convoquer [kɔvɔke] *vt* [assemblée] to convene. || [pour un entretien] to invite. || [subalterne, témoin] to summon. || [à un examen]: ~ **qqn** to ask sb to attend.

convoyer [kɔvwaje] *vt* to escort.

convoyeur, -euse [kɔvwajœr, øz] *nm*, *f* escort; ~ **de fonds** security guard.

convulsion [kɔvylsjɔ̃] *nf* convulsion.

coopération [kɔɔperasjɔ̃] *nf* [collaboration] cooperation. || [aide]: **la** ~ ≃ overseas development.

coopérer [kɔɔpere] *vi*: ~ **(à)** to cooperate (in).

coordination [kɔɔrdinasjɔ̃] *nf* coordination.

coordonnée [kɔɔrdɔne] *nf* MATHS coordinate. ○ **coordonnées** *nfpl* GÉOGR coordinates. || [adresse] address and phone number, details.

coordonner [kɔɔrdɔne] *vt* to coordinate.

copain, -ine [kɔpɛ̃, in] **1** *adj* matey; **être très ~s** to be great pals. **2** *nm*, *f* friend, mate.

copeau, -x [kɔpo] *nm* [de bois] (wood) shaving.

Copenhague [kɔpənag] *n* Copenhagen.

copie [kɔpi] *nf* [double, reproduction] copy. || [SCOL - de devoir] fair copy; [- d'examen] paper, script.

copier [kɔpje] **1** *vt* to copy. **2** *vi*: ~ **sur qqn** to copy from sb.

copieux, -ieuse [kɔpjø, jøz] *adj* copious.

copilote [kɔpilɔt] *nmf* copilot.

copine → copain.

coproduction [kɔprɔdyksjɔ̃] *nf* coproduction.

copropriété [kɔprɔprijete] *nf* co-ownership, joint ownership.

coq [kɔk] *nm* cock, cockerel; **sauter ou passer du ~ à l'âne** to jump from one subject to another.

coque [kɔk] *nf* [de noix] shell. || [de navire] hull.

coquelicot [kɔkliko] *nm* poppy.

coqueluche [kɔklyʃ] *nf* whooping cough.

coquet, -ette [kɔkɛ, ɛt] *adj* [vêtements] smart, stylish; [ville, jeune fille] pretty. || (*avant n*) *hum* [important]: **la ~te somme de 100 livres** the tidy sum of £100. ○ **coquette** *nf* flirt.

coquetier [kɔktje] *nm* eggcup.

coquetterie [kɔketri] *nf* [désir de plaire] coquettishness.

coquillage [kɔkijaʒ] *nm* [mollusque] shellfish. || [coquille] shell.

coquille [kɔkij] *nf* [de mollusque, noix, œuf] shell. || TYPO misprint.

coquillettes [kɔkijɛt] *nfpl* pasta shells.

coquin, -e [kɔkɛ̃, in] **1** *adj* [sous-vêtement] sexy, naughty; [regard, histoire] saucy. **2** *nm*, *f* rascal.

cor [kɔr] *nm* [instrument] horn. || [au pied] corn. ○ **à cor et à cri** *loc adv*: **réclamer qqch à ~ et à cri** to clamour for sthg.

corail, -aux [kɔraj, o] *nm* [gén] coral. || RAIL: **train** ~ ≃ express train.

Coran [kɔrã] *nm*: **le** ~ the Koran.

corbeau, -x [kɔrbo] *nm* [oiseau] crow.

corbeille [kɔrbɛj] *nf* [panier] basket; ~ **à papier** waste paper basket. || THÉÂTRE (dress) circle.

corbillard [kɔrbijar] *nm* hearse.

cordage [kɔrdaʒ] *nm* [de bateau] rigging (*U*). || [de raquette] strings (*pl*).

corde [kɔrd] *nf* [filin] rope; ~ **à linge** washing ou clothes line; ~ **à sauter** skipping rope. || [d'instrument, arc] string. || ANAT: ~ **vocale** vocal cord. || HIPPISME rails (*pl*); ATHLÉTISME inside (lane).

cordial, -e, -iaux [kɔrdjal, jo] *adj* warm, cordial.

cordon [kɔrdɔ̃] *nm* string, cord; ~ **ombilical** umbilical cord; ~ **de police** police cordon.

cordon-bleu [kɔrdɔ̃blø] *nm* cordon bleu cook.

cordonnerie [kɔrdɔnri] *nf* [magasin] shoe repairer's, cobbler's.

cordonnier, -ière [kɔrdɔnje, jɛr] *nm*, *f* shoe repairer, cobbler.

Corée [kɔre] *nf* Korea.

coriace [kɔrjas] *adj litt & fig* tough.

cormoran [kɔrmɔrã] *nm* cormorant.

corne [kɔrn] *nf* [gén] horn; [de cerf] antler. || [callosité] hard skin (*U*), callus.

cornée [kɔrne] *nf* cornea.

côté

corneille [kɔrnɛj] *nf* crow.

cornemuse [kɔrnəmyz] *nf* bagpipes (*pl*).

corner¹ [kɔrne] *vt* [page] to turn down the corner of.

corner² [kɔrnɛr] *nm* FOOTBALL corner (kick).

cornet [kɔrnɛ] *nm* [d'aliment] cornet, cone. || [de jeu] (dice) shaker.

corniche [kɔrniʃ] *nf* [route] cliff road. || [moulure] cornice.

cornichon [kɔrniʃɔ̃] *nm* [condiment] gherkin. || *fam* [imbécile] twit.

Cornouailles [kɔrnwaj] *nf*: la ~ Cornwall.

corolle [kɔrɔl] *nf* corolla.

coron [kɔrɔ̃] *nm* [village] mining village.

corporation [kɔrpɔrasjɔ̃] *nf* corporate body.

corporel, -elle [kɔrpɔrɛl] *adj* [physique - besoin] bodily; [- châtiment] corporal.

corps [kɔr] *nm* [gén] body. || [groupe]: ~ **d'armée** (army) corps; ~ **enseignant** [profession] teaching profession; [d'école] teaching staff.

corpulent, -e [kɔrpylɑ̃, ɑ̃t] *adj* corpulent, stout.

correct, -e [kɔrɛkt] *adj* [exact] correct, right. || [honnête] correct, proper. || [acceptable] decent; [travail] fair.

correcteur, -trice [kɔrɛktœr, tris] *nm, f* [d'examen] examiner, marker *Br*, grader *Am*. || TYPO proofreader.

correction [kɔrɛksjɔ̃] *nf* [d'erreur] correction. || [punition] punishment. || TYPO proofreading. || [notation] marking. || [bienséance] propriety.

corrélation [kɔrelasjɔ̃] *nf* correlation.

correspondance [kɔrɛspɔ̃dɑ̃s] *nf* [gén] correspondence; **cours par** ~ correspondence course. || TRANSPORT connection; **assurer la** ~ **avec** to connect with.

correspondant, -e [kɔrɛspɔ̃dɑ̃, ɑ̃t] **1** *adj* corresponding. **2** *nm, f* [par lettres] penfriend, correspondent. || [par téléphone]: **je vous passe votre** ~ I'll put you through. || PRESSE correspondent.

correspondre [kɔrɛspɔ̃dr] *vi* [être conforme]: ~ **à** to correspond to. || [par lettres]: ~ **avec** to correspond with.

corridor [kɔridɔr] *nm* corridor.

corrigé [kɔriʒe] *nm* correct version.

corriger [kɔriʒe] *vt* TYPO to correct, to proofread. || [noter] to mark. || [modifier] to correct. || [punir] to give sb a good hiding. ○ **se corriger** *vp* [d'un défaut]: se ~ **de** to cure o.s. of.

corroborer [kɔrɔbɔre] *vt* to corroborate.

corroder [kɔrɔde] *vt* [ronger] to corrode; *fig* to erode.

corrompre [kɔrɔ̃pr] *vt* [soudoyer] to bribe. || [dépraver] to corrupt.

corrosion [kɔrozjɔ̃] *nf* corrosion.

corruption [kɔrypsjɔ̃] *nf* [subornation] bribery. || [dépravation] corruption.

corsage [kɔrsaʒ] *nm* [chemisier] blouse. || [de robe] bodice.

corsaire [kɔrsɛr] *nm* [navire, marin] corsair, privateer. || [pantalon] pedal-pushers (*pl*).

corse [kɔrs] **1** *adj* Corsican. **2** *nm* [langue] Corsican. ○ **Corse 1** *nmf* Corsican. **2** *nf*: la **Corse** Corsica.

corsé, -e [kɔrse] *adj* [café] strong; [vin] full-bodied; [plat, histoire] spicy.

corset [kɔrse] *nm* corset.

cortège [kɔrtɛʒ] *nm* procession.

corvée [kɔrve] *nf* MIL fatigue (duty). || [activité pénible] chore.

cosmétique [kɔsmetik] *nm & adj* cosmetic.

cosmique [kɔsmik] *adj* cosmic.

cosmonaute [kɔsmɔnot] *nmf* cosmonaut.

cosmopolite [kɔsmɔpɔlit] *adj* cosmopolitan.

cosmos [kɔsmos] *nm* [univers] cosmos. || [espace] outer space.

cossu, -e [kɔsy] *adj* [maison] opulent.

Costa Rica [kɔstarika] *nm*: le ~ Costa Rica.

costaud (*f* **costaud** OU **-e**) [kɔsto, od] *adj* sturdily built.

costume [kɔstym] *nm* [folklorique, de théâtre] costume. || [vêtement d'homme] suit.

costumé, -e [kɔstyme] *adj* fancy-dress (*avant n*).

costumier, -ière [kɔstymje, jɛr] *nm, f* THÉÂTRE wardrobe master (*f* mistress).

cote [kɔt] *nf* [marque de classement] classification mark; [marque numérale] serial number. || FIN quotation. || [niveau] level; ~ **d'alerte** [de cours d'eau] danger level; *fig* crisis point.

côte [kot] *nf* [ANAT, BOT & de bœuf] rib; [de porc, mouton, agneau] chop; ~ **à** ~ side by side. || [pente] hill. || [littoral] coast.

côté [kote] *nm* [gén] side; **être aux** ~**s de qqn** *fig* to be by sb's side; **d'un** ~ ..., **de l'autre** ~ ... on the one hand ..., on the other hand ... || [endroit, direction] direction, way; **de quel** ~ **est-il parti?** which way did he go?; **de l'autre ~ de** on the other side of; **du ~ de** [près de] near. ○ **à côté** loc adv [lieu - gén] nearby; [- dans la maison adjacente] next door. ○ **à côté de** loc prép [proximité] beside, next to. || [en comparaison avec] beside, compared to. ○ **de côté** loc adv [se placer, marcher] sideways. || [en réserve] aside.

coteau [kɔto] nm [colline] hill. || [versant] slope.

Côte-d'Ivoire [kotdivwar] nf: **la ~** the Ivory Coast.

côtelé, -e [kotle] adj ribbed; **velours ~** corduroy.

côtelette [kotlɛt] nf [de porc, mouton, d'agneau] chop; [de veau] cutlet.

côtier, -ière [kotje, jɛr] adj coastal.

cotisation [kɔtizasjɔ̃] nf [à club, parti] subscription; [à la Sécurité sociale] contribution.

cotiser [kɔtize] vi [à un club, un parti] to subscribe; [à la Sécurité sociale] to contribute. ○ **se cotiser** vp to club together.

coton [kɔtɔ̃] nm cotton; **~ (hydrophile)** cotton wool.

Coton-Tige® [kɔtɔ̃tiʒ] nm cotton bud.

côtoyer [kotwaje] vt fig [fréquenter] to mix with.

cou [ku] nm [de personne, bouteille] neck.

couchant [kuʃɑ̃] 1 adj → **soleil**. 2 nm west.

couche [kuʃ] nf [de peinture, de vernis] coat, layer; [de poussière] film, layer. || [épaisseur] layer; **~ d'ozone** ozone layer. || [de bébé] nappy Br, diaper Am. || [classe sociale] stratum. ○ **fausse couche** nf miscarriage.

couché, -e [kuʃe] adj: **être ~** [étendu] to be lying down; [au lit] to be in bed.

couche-culotte [kuʃkylɔt] nf disposable nappy Br ou diaper Am.

coucher¹ [kuʃe] 1 vt [enfant] to put to bed. || [objet, blessé] to lay down. 2 vi [passer la nuit] to spend the night. || fam [avoir des rapports sexuels]: **~ avec** to sleep with. ○ **se coucher** vp [s'allonger] to lie down. || [se mettre au lit] to go to bed. || [astre] to set.

coucher² [kuʃe] nm [d'astre] setting; **au ~ du soleil** at sunset.

couchette [kuʃɛt] nf [de train] couchette. || [de navire] berth.

coucou [kuku] 1 nm [oiseau] cuckoo. || [pendule] cuckoo clock. || péj [avion] crate. 2 interj peekaboo!

coude [kud] nm [de personne, de vêtement] elbow. || [courbe] bend.

cou-de-pied [kudpje] (pl **cous-de-pied**) nm instep.

coudre [kudr] vt [bouton] to sew on.

couette [kwɛt] nf [édredon] duvet. || [coiffure] bunches (pl).

couffin [kufɛ̃] nm [berceau] Moses basket.

couiner [kwine] vi [animal] to squeal. || [pleurnicher] to whine.

coulée [kule] nf [de matière liquide]: **~ de lave** lava flow; **~ de boue** mudslide. || [de métal] casting.

couler [kule] 1 vi [liquide] to flow. || [beurre, fromage, nez] to run. || [navire, entreprise] to sink. 2 vt [navire] to sink. [métal, bronze] to cast.

couleur [kulœr] 1 nf [teinte, caractère] colour. || [linge] coloureds (pl). || CARTES suit. 2 adj inv [télévision, pellicule] colour (avant n).

couleuvre [kulœvr] nf grass snake.

coulisse [kulis] nf [glissière]: **fenêtre/porte à ~** sliding window/door. ○ **coulisses** nfpl THÉÂTRE wings.

coulisser [kulise] vi to slide.

couloir [kulwar] nm [corridor] corridor. || GÉOGR gully. || SPORT & TRANSPORT lane.

coup [ku] nm [choc - physique, moral] blow; **~ de couteau** stab (with a knife); **un ~ dur** fig a heavy blow; **~ de pied** kick; **~ de poing** punch. || [action nuisible] trick. || [SPORT - au tennis] stroke; [- en boxe] blow, punch; [- au football] kick; **~ franc** free kick. || [d'éponge, chiffon] wipe; **un ~ de crayon** a pencil stroke. || [bruit] noise; **~ de feu** shot, gunshot; **~ de tonnerre** thunderclap. || [action spectaculaire]: **~ d'état** coup (d'état); **~ de théâtre** fig dramatic turn of events. || fam [fois] time. || loc: **boire un ~** to have a drink; **donner un ~ de main à** qqn to give sb a helping hand; **jeter un ~ d'œil à** to glance at; **tenir le ~** to hold out; **valoir le ~** to be well worth it. ○ **coup de fil** nm phone call. ○ **coup de foudre** nm love at first sight. ○ **coup de soleil** nm sunburn (U). ○ **coup de téléphone** nm telephone ou phone call; **donner ou passer un ~ de téléphone à qqn** to telephone ou phone sb. ○ **coup de vent** nm gust of wind; **partir en ~ de vent** to rush off. ○ **coup sûr** loc adv definitely. ○ **après coup** loc adv afterwards. ○ **coup sur coup** loc adv one after the other. ○ **du coup**

loc adr as a result. ○ **tout à coup** *loc adv* suddenly. ○ **sous le coup de** *loc prép* [sous l'effet de] in the grip of.

coupable [kupabl] **1** *adj* [personne, pensée] guilty. || [action, dessein] culpable, reprehensible; [négligence, oubli] sinful. **2** *nmf* guilty person ou party.

coupant, -e [kupã, ãt] *adj* [tranchant] cutting. || *fig* [sec] sharp.

coupe [kup] *nf* [verre] glass. || [à fruits] dish. || SPORT cup. || [de vêtement, aux cartes] cut. || [plan, surface] (cross) section.

coupe-ongles [kupɔ̃gl] *nm inv* nail clippers.

coupe-papier [kuppapje] (*pl inv* OU **coupe-papiers**) *nm* paper knife.

couper [kupe] **1** *vt* [matériau, cheveux, blé] to cut. || [interrompre, trancher] to cut off. || [traverser] to cut across. || [pain, au tennis] to slice; [rôti] to carve. || [mélanger] to dilute. || [CARTES - avec atout] to trump; [- paquet] to cut. || [envie, appétit] to take away. **2** *vi* [gén] to cut. ○ **se couper** *vp* [se blesser] to cut o.s. || [se croiser] to cross. || [s'isoler]: **se ~ de** to cut o.s. off from.

couperet [kuprɛ] *nm* [de boucher] cleaver. || [de guillotine] blade.

couperosé, -e [kuproze] *adj* blotchy.

couple [kupl] *nm* [de personnes] couple.

coupler [kuple] *vt* [objets] to couple.

couplet [kuplɛ] *nm* verse.

coupole [kupɔl] *nf* ARCHIT dome, cupola.

coupon [kupɔ̃] *nm* [d'étoffe] remnant. || [billet] ticket.

coupon-réponse [kupɔ̃repɔ̃s] (*pl* **coupons-réponse**) *nm* reply coupon.

coupure [kupyr] *nf* [gén] cut; [billet de banque]: **petite ~** small denomination note; **~ de courant** ÉLECTR power cut; IN-FORM blackout. || *fig* [rupture] break.

cour [kur] *nf* [espace] courtyard. || [du roi, tribunal] court; *fig & hum* following; **Cour de cassation** Court of Appeal.

courage [kuraʒ] *nm* courage; **bon ~!** good luck!; **je n'ai pas le ~ de faire mes devoirs** I can't bring myself to do my homework.

courageux, -euse [kuraʒø, øz] *adj* [brave] brave. || [audacieux] bold.

couramment [kuramã] *adv* [parler une langue] fluently. || [communément] commonly.

courant, -e [kurã, ãt] *adj* [habituel] everyday (*avant n*). || [en cours] present. ○ **courant** *nm* [marin, atmosphérique, électrique] current; **~ d'air** draught. ||

[d'idées] current. || [laps de temps]: **dans le ~ du mois/de l'année** in the course of the month/the year. ○ **au courant** *loc adv*: **être au ~** to know (about it); **mettre qqn au ~ (de)** to tell sb (about); **tenir qqn au ~ (de)** to keep sb informed (about); **se mettre/se tenir au ~ (de)** to get/keep up to date (with).

courbature [kurbatyr] *nf* ache.

courbaturé, -e [kurbatyre] *adj* aching.

courbe [kurb] **1** *nf* curve; **~ de niveau** [sur une carte] contour (line). **2** *adj* curved.

courber [kurbe] **1** *vt* [tige] to bend. || [tête] to bow. **2** *vi* to bow. ○ **se courber** *vp* [chose] to bend. || [personne] to bow, to bend down.

courbette [kurbɛt] *nf* [révérence] bow; **faire des ~s** *fig* to bow and scrape.

coureur, -euse [kurœr, øz] *nm, f* SPORT runner; **~ cycliste** racing cyclist.

courge [kurʒ] *nf* [légume] marrow *Br*, squash *Am*. || *fam* [imbécile] dimwit.

courgette [kurʒɛt] *nf* zucchini *Am*.

courir [kurir] **1** *vi* [aller rapidement] to run. || SPORT to race. || [se précipiter, rivière] to rush. || [se propager]: **le bruit court que ...** rumour has it that ...; **faire ~ un bruit** to spread a rumour. **2** *vt* SPORT to run in. || [parcourir] to roam (through). || [fréquenter - bals, musées] to do the rounds of.

couronne [kurɔn] *nf* [ornement, autorité] crown. || [de fleurs] wreath.

couronnement [kurɔnmã] *nm* [de monarque] coronation. || *fig* [apogée] crowning achievement.

couronner [kurɔne] *vt* [monarque] to crown. || [récompenser] to give a prize to.

courre [kur] → **chasse**.

courrier [kurje] *nm* mail, letters (*pl*); **~ du cœur** agony column.

courroie [kurwa] *nf* TECHNOL belt; [attache] strap; **~ de transmission** driving belt; **~ de ventilateur** fanbelt.

cours [kur] *nm* [écoulement] flow; **~ d'eau** waterway; **donner** OU **laisser libre ~ à** *fig* to give free rein to. || [déroulement] course; **au ~ de** during, in the course of; **en** [année, dossier] current; [affaires] in hand; **en ~ de route** on the way. || FIN price; **avoir ~** [monnaie] to be legal tender. || [leçon] class, lesson; **donner des ~ (à qqn)** to teach (sb). || [classe]: **~ élémentaire** years two and three of primary school; **~ moyen** last two years *of primary school*; **~ préparatoire** ≃ nursery school *Am*.

course [kurs] *nf* [action] running (*U*); **au pas de ~** at a run. || [compétition] race. || [en taxi] journey. || [commission] errand; **faire des ~s** to go shopping.

coursier, -ière [kursje, jɛr] *nm, f* messenger.

court, -e [kur, kurt] *adj* short. ○ **court** **1** *adv*: **être à ~ d'argent/d'idées/d'arguments** to be short of money/ideas/arguments; **prendre qqn de ~** to catch sb unawares; **tourner ~** to stop suddenly. **2** *nm*: **~ de tennis** tennis court.

court-bouillon [kurbujɔ̃] *nm* court-bouillon.

court-circuit [kursirkɥi] *nm* short circuit.

courtier, -ière [kurtje, jɛr] *nm, f* broker.

courtisan, -e [kurtizɑ̃, an] *nm, f* HIST courtier.

courtiser [kurtize] *vt* [femme] to woo, to court. || *péj* [flatter] to flatter.

court-métrage [kurmetraʒ] *nm* short (film).

courtois, -e [kurtwa, az] *adj* courteous.

courtoisie [kurtwazi] *nf* courtesy.

couru, -e [kury] *pp* → **courir**.

cousin, -e [kuzɛ̃, in] *nm, f* cousin; **~ germain** first cousin.

coussin [kusɛ̃] *nm* [de siège] cushion.

cousu, -e [kuzy] *pp* → **coudre**.

coût [ku] *nm* cost.

couteau, -x [kuto] *nm* [gén] knife; **~ à cran d'arrêt** flick knife.

coûter [kute] **1** *vi* [valoir] to cost; **ça coûte combien?** how much is it?; **~ cher à qqn** to cost sb a lot; *fig* to cost sb dear ou dearly. || *fig* [être pénible] to be difficult. **2** *vt fig* to cost. ○ **coûte que coûte** *adv* at all costs.

coûteux, -euse [kutø, øz] *adj* costly, expensive.

coutume [kutym] *nf* [gén & JUR] custom.

couture [kutyr] *nf* [action] sewing. || [points] seam. || [activité] dressmaking.

couturier, -ière [kutyrje, jɛr] *nm, f* couturier.

couvée [kuve] *nf* [d'œufs] clutch; [de poussins] brood.

couvent [kuvɑ̃] *nm* [de sœurs] convent; [de moines] monastery.

couver [kuve] **1** *vt* [œufs] to sit on. || [dorloter] to mollycoddle. || [maladie] to

be sickening for. **2** *vi* [poule] to brood; *fig* [complot] to hatch.

couvercle [kuvɛrkl] *nm* [de casserole, boîte] lid, cover.

couvert, -e [kuver, ɛrt] **1** *pp* → **couvrir**. **2** *adj* [submergé] covered; **~ de** covered with. || [habillé] dressed; **être bien ~** to be well wrapped up. || [nuageux] overcast. ○ **couvert** *nm* [abri]: **se mettre à ~** to take shelter. || [place à table] place (setting); **mettre ou dresser le ~** to set ou lay the table. ○ **couverts** *nmpl* cutlery (*U*).

couverture [kuvɛrtyr] *nf* [gén] cover. || [de lit] blanket; **~ chauffante** electric blanket. || [toit] roofing (*U*).

couveuse [kuvøz] *nf* [machine] incubator.

couvre-feu [kuvrəfø] (*pl* **couvre-feux**) *nm* curfew.

couvrir [kuvrir] *vt* [gén] to cover; **~ qqn/qqch de** *litt* & *fig* to cover sb/sthg with. || [protéger] to shield. ○ **se couvrir** *vp* [se vêtir] to wrap up. || [se recouvrir]: **se ~ de feuilles/de fleurs** to come into leaf/blossom. || [ciel] to cloud over. || [se protéger] to cover o.s.

CP *nm abr de* **cours préparatoire**.

crabe [krab] *nm* crab.

crachat [kraʃa] *nm* spit (*U*).

cracher [kraʃe] **1** *vi* [personne] to spit. **2** *vt* [sang] to spit (up); [lave, injures] to spit (out).

crachin [kraʃɛ̃] *nm* drizzle.

craie [krɛ] *nf* chalk.

craindre [krɛdr] *vt* [redouter] to fear, to be afraid of; **~ de faire qqch** to be afraid of doing sthg; **je crains d'avoir oublié mes papiers** I'm afraid I've forgotten my papers; **~ que** (+ *subjonctif*) to be afraid (that); **je crains qu'il oublie** ou **n'oublie** I'm afraid he may forget. || [être sensible à] to be susceptible to.

craint, -e [krɛ̃, ɛ̃t] *pp* → **craindre**.

crainte [krɛt] *nf* fear; **de ~ de faire qqch** for fear of doing sthg; **de ~ que** (+ *subjonctif*) for fear that; **il a fui de ~ qu'on ne le voie** he fled for fear that he might be seen ou for fear of being seen.

craintif, -ive [krɛtif, iv] *adj* timid.

cramoisi, -e [kramwazi] *adj* crimson.

crampe [krɑ̃p] *nf* cramp.

crampon [krɑ̃pɔ̃] *nm* [crochet - gén] clamp; [- pour alpinisme] crampon.

cramponner [krɑ̃pone] ○ **se cramponner** *vp* [s'agripper] to hang on; **se ~ à qqn/qqch** *litt* & *fig* to cling to sb/sthg.

cran [krɑ̃] *nm* [entaille, degré] notch, cut. || (*U*) [audace] guts (*pl*).

crâne [krɑn] *nm* skull.

crâner [krane] *vi fam* to show off.

crânien, -ienne [kranjɛ̃, jɛn] *adj*: **boîte ~ne** skull; **traumatisme ~** head injury.

crapaud [krapo] *nm* toad.

crapule [krapyl] *nf* scum (*U*).

craquelure [kraklyr] *nf* crack.

craquement [krakmɑ̃] *nm* crack, cracking (*U*).

craquer [krake] **1** *vi* [produire un bruit] to crack; [plancher, chaussure] to creak. || [se déchirer] to split. || [s'effondrer - personne] to crack up. || [être séduit par]: **pour ~** to fall for. **2** *vt* [allumette] to strike.

crasse [kras] *nf* [saleté] dirt, filth. || *fam* [mauvais tour] dirty trick.

crasseux, -euse [krasø, øz] *adj* filthy.

cratère [krater] *nm* crater.

cravache [kravaʃ] *nf* riding crop.

cravate [kravat] *nf* tie.

crawl [krol] *nm* crawl.

crayon [krejɔ̃] *nm* [gén] pencil; **~ à bille** ballpoint (pen); **~ de couleur** crayon. || TECHNOL pen; **~ optique** light pen.

créancier, -ière [kreɑ̃sje, jer] *nm, f* creditor.

créateur, -trice [kreatœr, tris] **1** *adj* creative. **2** *nm, f* creator.

créatif, -ive [kreatif, iv] *adj* creative.

création [kreasjɔ̃] *nf* creation.

créativité [kreativite] *nf* creativity.

créature [kreatyr] *nf* creature.

crécelle [kresɛl] *nf* rattle.

crèche [krɛʃ] *nf* [de Noël] crib. || [garderie] crèche.

crédible [kredibl] *adj* credible.

crédit [kredi] *nm* [gén] credit; **faire ~ à qqn** to give sb credit; **acheter/vendre qqch à ~** to buy/sell sthg on credit.

crédit-bail [kredibaj] (*pl* **crédits-bails**) *nm* leasing.

créditeur, -trice [kreditœr, tris] **1** *adj* in credit. **2** *nm, f* creditor.

crédule [kredyl] *adj* credulous.

crédulité [kredylite] *nf* credulity.

créer [kree] *vt* [RELIG & inventer] to create. || [fonder] to found, to start up.

crémaillère [kremajer] *nf* [de cheminée] trammel; **pendre la ~** *fig* to have a housewarming (party). || TECHNOL rack.

crémation [kremasjɔ̃] *nf* cremation.

crématoire [krematwar] → **four**.

crème [krɛm] **1** *nf* [gén] cream; **~ fouettée/fraîche/glacée** whipped/fresh/ ice cream; **~ anglaise** custard; **~ hydratante** moisturizer. **2** *adj inv* cream.

crémerie [kremri] *nf* dairy.

crémier, -ière [kremje, jer] *nm, f* dairyman (*f* dairywoman).

créneau, -x [kreno] *nm* [de fortification] crenel. || [pour se garer]: **faire un ~** to reverse into a parking space. || [de marché] niche. || [horaire] window, gap.

créole [kreɔl] *adj* & *nm* creole.

crêpe [krɛp] **1** *nf* CULIN pancake. **2** *nm* [tissu] crepe.

crêperie [krɛpri] *nf* pancake restaurant.

crépi [krepi] *nm* roughcast.

crépir [krepir] *vt* to roughcast.

crépiter [krepite] *vi* [feu, flammes] to crackle; [pluie] to patter.

crépon [krepɔ̃] *adj* → **papier**.

crépu, -e [krepy] *adj* frizzy.

crépuscule [krepyskyl] *nm* [du jour] dusk, twilight; *fig* twilight.

crescendo [kreʃendo, kreʃɛ̃do] **1** *adv* crescendo; **aller ~** *fig* [bruit] to get ou grow louder and louder. **2** *nm inv* MUS & *fig* crescendo.

cresson [kresɔ̃] *nm* watercress.

crête [kret] *nf* [de coq] comb. || [de montagne, vague, oiseau] crest.

crétin, -e [kretɛ̃, in] *fam* **1** *adj* cretinous, idiotic. **2** *nm, f* cretin, idiot.

creuser [krøze] *vt* [trou] to dig. || [objet] to hollow out. || *fig* [approfondir] to go into deeply.

creux, creuse [krø, krøz] *adj* [vide, concave] hollow. || [période - d'activité réduite] slack; [- à tarif réduit] off-peak. || [paroles] empty. ○ **creux** *nm* [concavité] hollow. || [période] lull.

crevaison [krəvɛzɔ̃] *nf* puncture.

crevant, -e [krəvɑ̃, ɑ̃t] *adj fam* [fatigant] exhausting.

crevasse [krəvas] *nf* [de mur] crevice, crack; [de glacier] crevasse.

crevé, -e [krøve] *adj* [pneu] burst, punctured. || *fam* [fatigué] dead, shattered *Br*.

crever [krøve] **1** *vi* [éclater] to burst. || *tfam* [mourir] to die; **~ de** *fig* [jalousie, orgueil] to be bursting with. **2** *vt* [percer] to burst. || *fam* [épuiser] to wear out.

crevette [krəvet] *nf*: **~ (grise)** shrimp; **(rose) prawn**.

cri [kri] *nm* [de personne] cry, shout; [perçant] scream; [d'animal] cry; **pousser un ~** to cry (out), to shout; **pousser un ~**

de douleur to cry out in pain. ‖ [appel] cry; **le dernier ~** *fig* the latest thing.

criant, -e [krijã, ãt] *adj* [injustice] blatant.

criard, -e [krijar, ard] *adj* [voix] strident, piercing. ‖ [couleur] loud.

crible [kribl] *nm* [instrument] sieve; **passer qqch au ~** *fig* to examine sthg closely.

criblé, -e [krible] *adj* riddled; **être ~ de dettes** to be up to one's eyes in debt.

cric [krik] *nm* jack.

cricket [krikɛt] *nm* cricket.

crier [crije] **1** *vi* [pousser un cri] to shout (out), to yell. ‖ [parler fort] to shout. ‖ [protester] : **~ contre** OU **après qqn** to nag sb, to go on at sb. **2** *vt* to shout (out).

crime [krim] *nm* [délit] crime. ‖ [meurtre] murder.

criminalité [kriminalite] *nf* criminality.

criminel, -elle [kriminɛl] **1** *adj* criminal. **2** *nm, f* criminal; **~ de guerre** war criminal.

crin [krɛ̃] *nm* [d'animal] hair.

crinière [krinjɛr] *nf* mane.

crique [krik] *nf* creek.

criquet [krikɛ] *nm* locust; [sauterelle] grasshopper.

crise [kriz] *nf* MÉD attack; **~ cardiaque** heart attack; **~ de foie** bilious attack. ‖ [accès] fit; **~ de nerfs** attack of nerves. ‖ [phase critique] crisis.

crispation [krispasjɔ̃] *nf* [contraction] contraction. ‖ [agacement] irritation.

crispé, -e [krispe] *adj* tense, on edge.

crisper [krispe] *vt* [contracter - visage] to tense; [- poing] to clench. ‖ [agacer] to irritate. ○ **se crisper** *vp* [se contracter] to tense (up). ‖ [s'irriter] to get irritated.

crisser [krise] *vi* [pneu] to screech.

cristal, -aux [kristal, o] *nm* crystal; **~ de roche** quartz.

cristallin, -e [kristalɛ̃, in] *adj* [limpide] crystal clear, crystalline. ‖ [roche] crystalline. ○ **cristallin** *nm* crystalline lens.

critère [kritɛr] *nm* criterion.

critique [kritik] **1** *adj* critical. **2** *nmf* critic. **3** *nf* criticism.

critiquer [kritike] *vt* to criticize.

croasser [krɔase] *vi* to croak, to caw.

croate [krɔat] *adj* Croat, Croatian. ○ **Croate** *nmf* Croat, Croatian.

Croatie [krɔasi] *nf* : **la ~** Croatia.

croc [kro] *nm* [de chien] fang.

croche [krɔʃ] *nf* eighth (note) *Am*.

croche-pied [krɔʃpje] (*pl* **croche-pieds**) *nm* : **faire un ~ à qqn** to trip sb up.

crochet [krɔʃɛ] *nm* [de métal] hook; **vivre aux ~s de qqn** to live off sb. ‖ TRICOT crochet hook. ‖ TYPO square bracket. ‖ BOXE : **~ du gauche/du droit** left/right hook.

crochu, -e [krɔʃy] *adj* [doigts] claw-like; [nez] hooked.

crocodile [krɔkɔdil] *nm* crocodile.

croire [krwar] **1** *vt* [chose, personne] to believe. ‖ [penser] to think; **tu crois?** do you think so?; **il te croyait parti** he thought you'd left; **~ que** to think (that). **2** *vi* : **~ à** to believe in; **~ en** to believe in, to have faith in.

croisade [krwazad] *nf* HIST & *fig* crusade.

croisé, -e [krwaze] *adj* [veste] double-breasted. ○ **croisé** *nm* HIST crusader.

croisement [krwazmã] *nm* [intersection] junction, intersection. ‖ BIOL cross-breeding.

croiser [krwaze] **1** *vt* [jambes] to cross; [bras] to fold. ‖ [passer à côté de] to pass. ‖ [chemin] to cross, to cut across. ‖ [métisser] to interbreed. **2** *vi* NAVIG to cruise. ○ **se croiser** *vp* [chemins] to cross, to intersect; [personnes] to pass; [lettres] to cross; [regards] to meet.

croisière [krwazjɛr] *nf* cruise.

croisillon [krwazijɔ̃] *nm* : **à ~s** lattice (*avant n*).

croissance [krwasãs] *nf* growth, development.

croissant, -e [krwasã, ãt] *adj* increasing, growing. ○ **croissant** *nm* [de lune] crescent. ‖ CULIN croissant.

croître [krwatr] *vi* [grandir] to grow. ‖ [augmenter] to increase.

croix [krwa] *nf* cross; **en ~** in the shape of a cross; **~ gammée** swastika; **la Croix-Rouge** the Red Cross.

croquant, -e [krɔkã, ãt] *adj* crisp, crunchy.

croque-monsieur [krɔkməsjø] *nm inv* toasted cheese and ham sandwich.

croquer [krɔke] **1** *vt* [manger] to crunch. ‖ [dessiner] to sketch. **2** *vi* to be crunchy.

croquette [krɔkɛt] *nf* croquette.

croquis [krɔki] *nm* sketch.

cross [krɔs] *nm* [exercice] cross-country (running); [course] cross-country race.

crotte [krɔt] *nf* [de lapin etc] droppings (*pl*); [de chien] dirt.

crottin [krɔtɛ̃] *nm* [de cheval] (horse) manure.

cumuler

crouler [krule] *vi* to crumble; ~ **sous** *litt* & *fig* to collapse under.

croupe [krup] *nf* rump.

croupier [krupje] *nm* croupier.

croupir [krupir] *vi litt* & *fig* to stagnate.

croustillant, -e [krustijã, ãt] *adj* [croquant - pain] crusty; [- biscuit] crunchy.

croûte [krut] *nf* [du pain, terrestre] crust. || [de fromage] rind. || [de plaie] scab. || *fam péj* [tableau] daub.

croûton [krutɔ̃] *nm* [bout du pain] crust. || [pain frit] crouton.

croyance [krwajãs] *nf* belief.

croyant, -e [krwajã, ãt] **1** *adj*: **être ~** to be a believer. **2** *nm, f* believer.

CRS (*abr de* **Compagnie républicaine de sécurité**) *nm* member of the French riot police.

cru, -e [kry] **1** *pp* → **croire**. **2** *adj* [non cuit] raw. || [violent] harsh. || [direct] blunt. || [grivois] crude.

crû [kry] *pp* → **croître**.

cruauté [kryote] *nf* cruelty.

cruche [kryʃ] *nf* [objet] jug. || *fam péj* [personne niaise] twit.

crucial, -e, -iaux [krysjal, jo] *adj* crucial.

crucifix [krysifi] *nm* crucifix.

crudité [krydite] *nf* crudeness. ○ **crudités** *nfpl* crudités.

crue [kry] *nf* rise in the water level.

cruel, -elle [kryɛl] *adj* cruel.

crustacé [krystase] *nm* shellfish, crustacean; ~**s** shellfish (*U*).

Cuba [kyba] *n* Cuba.

cubain, -aine [kybɛ̃, ɛn] *adj* Cuban. ○ **Cubain, -aine** *nm, f* Cuban.

cube [kyb] *nm* cube.

cueillette [kœjɛt] *nf* picking, harvesting.

cueillir [kœjir] *vt* [fruits, fleurs] to pick.

cuillère, cuiller [kɥijɛr] *nf* spoon; ~ **à café** coffee spoon; CULIN teaspoon; ~ **à dessert** dessertspoon; ~ **à soupe** soup spoon; CULIN tablespoon; **petite ~** teaspoon.

cuillerée [kɥijere] *nf* spoonful; ~ **à café** CULIN teaspoonful; ~ **à soupe** CULIN tablespoonful.

cuir [kɥir] *nm* leather; [non tanné] hide; ~ **chevelu** ANAT scalp.

cuirasse [kɥiras] *nf* [de chevalier] breastplate; *fig* armour.

cuirassé [kɥirase] *nm* battleship.

cuire [kɥir] **1** *vt* [viande, œuf] to cook; [tarte, gâteau] to bake; **faire ~ qqch** to

cook/bake sthg. **2** *vi* [viande, œuf] to cook; [tarte, gâteau] to bake.

cuisine [kɥizin] *nf* [pièce] kitchen. || [art] cooking, cookery; **faire la ~** to do the cooking, to cook.

cuisiné, -e [kɥizine] *adj*: **plat ~** ready-cooked meal.

cuisiner [kɥizine] **1** *vt* [aliment] to cook. || *fam* [personne] to grill. **2** *vi* to cook; **bien/mal ~** to be a good/bad cook.

cuisinier, -ière [kɥizinje, jɛr] *nm, f* cook. ○ **cuisinière** *nf* cooker; **cuisinière électrique/à gaz** electric/gas cooker.

cuisse [kɥis] *nf* ANAT thigh. || CULIN leg.

cuisson [kɥisɔ̃] *nf* cooking.

cuit, -e [kɥi, kɥit] **1** *pp* → **cuire**. **2** *adj*: **bien ~** [steak] well-done.

cuivre [kɥivr] *nm* [métal]: ~ **(rouge)** copper; ~ **jaune** brass. ○ **cuivres** *nmpl*: **les ~s** MUS the brass.

cuivré, -e [kɥivre] *adj* [couleur, reflet] coppery; [teint] bronzed.

cul [ky] *nm tfam* [postérieur] bum. || [de bouteille] bottom.

culbute [kylbyt] *nf* [saut] somersault. || [chute] tumble, fall.

cul-de-sac [kydsak] (*pl* **culs-de-sac**) *nm* dead end.

culinaire [kyliner] *adj* culinary.

culminant [kylminã] → **point**.

culot [kylo] *nm fam* [toupet] cheek, nerve.

culotte [kylɔt] *nf* [sous-vêtement féminin] knickers (*pl*), panties (*pl*), pair of knickers OU panties.

culotté, -e [kylɔte] *adj* [effronté]: **elle est ~e** she's got a nerve.

culpabilité [kylpabilite] *nf* guilt.

culte [kylt] *nm* [vénération, amour] worship. || [religion] religion.

cultivateur, -trice [kyltivatœr, tris] *nm, f* farmer.

cultivé, -e [kyltive] *adj* [personne] educated, cultured.

cultiver [kyltive] *vt* [terre, goût, relation] to cultivate. || [plante] to grow.

culture [kyltyr] *nf* AGRIC cultivation, farming; **les ~s** cultivated land. || [savoir] culture, knowledge; ~ **physique** physical training. || [civilisation] culture.

culturel, -elle [kyltyrɛl] *adj* cultural.

culturisme [kyltyrism] *nm* bodybuilding.

cumin [kymɛ̃] *nm* cumin.

cumuler [kymyle] *vt* [fonctions, titres] to hold simultaneously.

cupide [kypid] *adj* greedy.

cure [kyr] *nf* (course of) treatment; **faire une ~ de fruits** to go on a fruit-based diet; **~ de désintoxication** [d'alcool] drying-out treatment; [de drogue] detoxification treatment; **~ de sommeil** sleep therapy; **faire une ~ thermale** to take the waters.

curé [kyre] *nm* parish priest.

cure-dents [kyrdã] *nm inv* toothpick.

curer [kyre] *vt* to clean out.

curieux, -ieuse [kyrjø, jøz] **1** *adj* [intéressé] curious. || [indiscret] inquisitive. || [étrange] strange, curious. **2** *nm, f* busybody.

curiosité [kyrjozite] *nf* curiosity.

curriculum vitae [kyrikylɔmvite] *nm inv* curriculum vitae.

curry [kyri], **carry** [kari], **cari** [kari] *nm* [épice] curry powder. || [plat] curry.

curseur [kyrsœr] *nm* cursor.

cutané, -e [kytane] *adj* cutaneous, skin (*avant n*).

cuve [kyv] *nf* [citerne] tank. || [à vin] vat.

cuvée [kyve] *nf* [récolte] vintage.

cuvette [kyvɛt] *nf* [récipient] basin, bowl. || [de lavabo] basin; [de W.-C.] bowl. || GÉOGR basin.

CV *nm* (*abr de* **curriculum vitae**) CV. || (*abr de* **cheval-vapeur**) hp; [puissance fiscale] *classification for scaling of car tax.*

cyanure [sjanyr] *nm* cyanide.

cyclable [siklabl] → **piste**.

cycle [sikl] *nm* cycle; **premier ~** UNIV ≃ first and second year; SCOL middle school *Br*, junior high school *Am*; **second ~** UNIV ≃ final year *Br*, ≃ senior year *Am*; SCOL upper school *Br*, high school *Am*; **troisième ~** UNIV ≃ postgraduate year or years.

cyclique [siklik] *adj* cyclic, cyclical.

cyclisme [siklism] *nm* cycling.

cycliste [siklist] *nmf* cyclist.

cyclone [siklon] *nm* cyclone.

cygne [siɲ] *nm* swan.

cylindre [silɛ̃dr] *nm* AUTOM & GÉOM cylinder. || [rouleau] roller.

cymbale [sɛ̃bal] *nf* cymbal.

cynique [sinik] *adj* cynical.

cynisme [sinism] *nm* cynicism.

cyprès [siprɛ] *nm* cypress.

d, D [de] *nm inv* d, D.

d' → **de**.

d'abord [dabɔr] → **abord**.

d'accord [dakɔr] *loc adv*: **~!** all right!, OK!; **être ~ avec** to agree with.

dactylo [daktilo] *nf* [personne] typist; [procédé] typing.

dactylographier [daktilɔgrafje] *vt* to type.

dada [dada] *nm fam* [occupation] hobby. || *fam* [idée] hobbyhorse.

dahlia [dalja] *nm* dahlia.

daigner [deɲe] *vi* to deign.

daim [dɛ̃] *nm* [animal] fallow deer. || [peau] suede.

dallage [dalaʒ] *nm* [action] paving; [dalles] pavement.

dalle [dal] *nf* [de pierre] slab; [de lino] tile.

dalmatien, -ienne [dalmasjɛ̃, jɛn] *nm, f* dalmatian.

daltonien, -ienne [daltɔnjɛ̃, jɛn] *adj* colour-blind.

dame [dam] *nf* [femme] lady. || CARTES & ÉCHECS queen. ○ **dames** *nfpl* checkers *Am*.

damier [damje] *nm* [de jeu] checkerboard *Am*. || [motif]: **à ~** checked.

damné, -e [dane] *adj fam* damned.

dancing [dãsiŋ] *nm* dance hall.

dandiner [dãdine] ○ **se dandiner** *vp* to waddle.

Danemark [danmark] *nm*: **le ~** Denmark.

danger [dãʒe] *nm* danger; **en ~** in danger; **courir un ~** to run a risk.

dangereux, -euse [dãʒrø, øz] *adj* dangerous.

danois, -e [danwa, az] *adj* Danish. ○ **danois** *nm* [langue] Danish. || [chien] Great Dane. ○ **Danois, -e** *nm, f* Dane.

dans [dã] *prép* [dans le temps] in; **je reviens ~ un mois** I'll be back in a month or in a month's time. || [dans l'espace] in. || [avec mouvement] into. || [indiquant

état, manière] in; **vivre ~ la misère** to live in poverty; **il est ~ le commerce** he's in business. || [environ]: **~ les ...** about ....

dansant, -e [dɑ̃sɑ̃, ɑ̃t] *adj litt & fig* dancing; **soirée ~e** dance; **thé ~** tea dance.

danse [dɑ̃s] *nf* [art] dancing. || [musique] dance.

danser [dɑ̃se] **1** *vi* [personne] to dance. **2** *vt* to dance.

danseur, -euse [dɑ̃sœr, øz] *nm, f* dancer.

dard [dar] *nm* [d'animal] sting.

date [dat] *nf* [jour+mois+année] date; **~ de naissance** date of birth. || [moment] event.

dater [date] **1** *vt* to date. **2** *vi* [marquer] to be ou mark a milestone. || *fam* [être démodé] to be dated. ○ **à dater de** *loc prép* as of ou from.

datte [dat] *nf* date.

dattier [datje] *nm* date palm.

dauphin [dofɛ̃] *nm* [mammifère] dolphin. || HIST heir apparent.

daurade, dorade [dɔrad] *nf* sea bream.

davantage [davɑ̃taʒ] *adv* [plus] more; **~ de more**. || [plus longtemps] (any) longer.

de [də] *(contraction de de + le = du* [dy], *de + les = des* [de]*)* **1** *prép* [provenance] from; **revenir ~ Paris** to come back ou return from Paris; **il est sorti ~ la maison** he left the house, he went out of the house. || [avec à]: **~ ... à** from ... to; **~ dix heures à midi** from ten o'clock to ou midday; **il y avait ~ quinze à vingt mille spectateurs** there were between fifteen and twenty thousand spectators. || [appartenance] of; **la porte du salon** the door of the sitting room, the sitting-room door; **le frère ~ Pierre** Pierre's brother. || [indique la détermination, la qualité]: **un verre d'eau** a glass of water; **un peignoir ~ soie** a silk dressing gown; **un bébé ~ trois jours** a three-day-old baby; **le train ~ 9 h 30** the 9.30 train. **2** *article partitif* [dans une phrase affirmative] some; **je voudrais du vin/du lait** I'd like (some) wine/(some) milk; **acheter des légumes** to buy some vegetables. || [dans une interrogation ou une négation] any; **ils n'ont pas d'enfants** they don't have any children, they have no children; **voulez-vous du thé?** would you like some tea?

dé [de] *nm* [à jouer] dice, die. || COUTURE: **~ (à coudre)** thimble.

DEA (*abr de* **diplôme d'études approfondies**) *nm* postgraduate diploma.

dealer[1] [dile] *vt* to deal.

dealer[2] [dilœr] *nm fam* dealer.

déambuler [deɑ̃byle] *vi* to stroll (around).

débâcle [debakl] *nf* [débandade] rout; *fig* collapse.

déballer [debale] *vt* to unpack; *fam fig* to pour out.

débandade [debɑ̃dad] *nf* dispersal.

débarbouiller [debarbuje] *vt*: **~ qqn** to wash sb's face. ○ **se débarbouiller** *vp* to wash one's face.

débarcadère [debarkadɛr] *nm* landing stage.

débardeur [debardœr] *nm* [ouvrier] docker. || [vêtement] slipover.

débarquer [debarke] **1** *vt* [marchandises] to unload; [passagers & MIL] to land. **2** *vi* [d'un bateau] to disembark. || MIL to land. || *fam* [arriver à l'improviste] to turn up; *fig* to know nothing.

débarras [debara] *nm* junk room; **bon ~!** *fig* good riddance!

débarrasser [debarase] *vt* [pièce] to clear up; [table] to clear. || [ôter]: **~ qqn de qqch** to take sthg from sb. ○ **se débarrasser** *vp*: **se ~ de** to get rid of.

débat [deba] *nm* debate.

débattre [debatr] *vt* to debate, to discuss. ○ **se débattre** *vp* to struggle.

débattu, -e [debaty] *pp* > **débattre**.

débauche [deboʃ] *nf* debauchery.

débaucher [deboʃe] *vt* [corrompre] to debauch, to corrupt. || [licencier] to make redundant.

débile [debil] **1** *nmf* [attardé] retarded person; **~ mental** mentally retarded person. || *fam* [idiot] moron. **2** *adj fam* stupid.

débit [debi] *nm* [de liquide] (rate of) flow. || FIN debit; **avoir un ~ de 500 francs** to be 500 francs overdrawn.

débiter [debite] *vt* [arbre] to saw up; [viande] to cut up. || *fam fig* [prononcer] to spout. || FIN to debit.

débiteur, -trice [debitœr, tris] **1** *adj* [personne] debtor (*avant n*). || FIN debit (*avant n*), in the red. **2** *nm, f* debtor.

déblayer [debleje] *vt* [dégager] to clear; **~ le terrain** *fig* to clear the ground.

débloquer [deblɔke] **1** *vt* [machine] to get going again. || [crédit] to release. ||

[compte, salaires, prix] to unfreeze. **2** *vi fam* to talk rubbish.

déboires [debwar] *nmpl* [déceptions] disappointments. || [échecs] setbacks.

déboiser [debwaze] *vt* [région] to deforest; [terrain] to clear (of trees).

déboîter [debwate] **1** *vt* [objet] to dislodge. || [membre] to dislocate. **2** *vi* AUTOM to pull out. ○ **se déboîter** *vp* [se démonter] to come apart. || [membre] to dislocate.

débonnaire [deboner] *adj* good-natured, easy-going.

déborder [deborde] *vi* [fleuve, liquide] to overflow; *fig* to flood; ~ **de** [vie, joie] to be bubbling with.

débouché [debuʃe] *nm* [issue] end. || (*gén pl*) COMM outlet. || [de carrière] prospect, opening.

déboucher [debuʃe] **1** *vt* [bouteille] to open. || [conduite, nez] to unblock. **2** *vi*: ~ **sur** [arriver] to open out into; *fig* to lead to, to achieve.

débourser [deburse] *vt* to pay out.

debout [dəbu] *adv* [gén]: être ~ [sur ses pieds] to be standing (up); [réveillé] to be up; [objet] to be standing up or upright; **mettre qqch** ~ to stand sthg up; **se mettre** ~ to stand up; ~! get up!, on your feet! || *loc*: **tenir** ~ [bâtiment] to remain standing; [argument] to stand up.

déboutonner [debutɔne] *vt* to unbutton, to undo.

débraillé, -e [debraje] *adj* dishevelled.

débrayer [debreje] *vi* AUTOM to disengage the clutch, to declutch.

débris [debri] *nm* piece, fragment.

débrouillard, -e [debrujar, ard] *fam adj* resourceful.

débrouiller [debruje] *vt* [démêler] to untangle. || *fig* [résoudre] to unravel, to solve. ○ **se débrouiller** *vp*: **se** ~ (**pour faire qqch**) to manage (to do sthg); **se** ~ **en anglais/math** to get by in English/maths; **débrouille-toi!** you'll have to sort it out (by) yourself!

débroussailler [debrusaje] *vt* [terrain] to clear; *fig* to do the groundwork for.

début [deby] *nm* beginning, start; **au** ~ **de** at the beginning of; **dès le** ~ (right) from the start.

débutant, -e [debytã, ãt] *nm, f* beginner.

débuter [debyte] *vi* [commencer]: ~ (**par**) to begin (with), to start (with). || [faire ses débuts] to start out.

deçà [dəsa] ○ **en deçà de** *loc prép* [de ce côté-ci de] on this side of. || [en dessous de] short of.

décacheter [dekaʃte] *vt* to open.

décadence [dekadãs] *nf* [déclin] decline. || [débauche] decadence.

décadent, -e [dekadã, ãt] *adj* decadent.

décaféiné, -e [dekafeine] *adj* decaffeinated. ○ **décaféiné** *nm* decaffeinated coffee.

décalage [dekalaʒ] *nm* gap; *fig* gulf, discrepancy; ~ **horaire** [entre zones] time difference; [après un vol] jet lag.

décaler [dekale] *vt* [dans le temps - avancer] to bring forward; [- retarder] to put back. || [dans l'espace] to move, to shift.

décalquer [dekalke] *vt* to trace.

décamper [dekãpe] *vi fam* to clear off.

décapant, -e [dekapã, ãt] *adj* [nettoyant] stripping. ○ **décapant** *nm* (paint) stripper.

décaper [dekape] *vt* to strip, to sand.

décapiter [dekapite] *vt* [personne] to behead; [- accidentellement] to decapitate.

décapotable [dekapɔtabl] *nf & adj* convertible.

décapsuler [dekapsyle] *vt* to take the top off, to open.

décapsuleur [dekapsylœr] *nm* bottle opener.

décédé, -e [desede] *adj* deceased.

décéder [desede] *vi* to die.

déceler [desle] *vt* [repérer] to detect.

décembre [desãbr] *nm* December; *voir aussi* **septembre**.

décemment [desamã] *adv* [convenablement] properly. || [raisonnablement] reasonably.

décence [desãs] *nf* decency.

décennie [deseni] *nf* decade.

décent, -e [desã, ãt] *adj* decent.

décentralisation [desãtralizasjɔ̃] *nf* decentralization.

déception [desɛpsjɔ̃] *nf* disappointment.

décerner [deserne] *vt*: ~ **qqch à** to award sthg to.

décès [desɛ] *nm* death.

décevant, -e [desəvã, ãt] *adj* disappointing.

décevoir [desəvwar] *vt* to disappoint.

déchaîné, -e [deʃene] *adj* [vent, mer] stormy, wild. || [personne] wild.

déchaîner [deʃene] *vt* [passion] to unleash; [rires] to cause an outburst of.

○ **se déchaîner** *vp* [éléments naturels] to erupt. ‖ [personne] to fly into a rage.

déchanter [deʃɑ̃te] *vi* to become disillusioned.

décharge [deʃaʀʒ] *nf* JUR discharge. ‖ ÉLECTR discharge; ~ **électrique** electric shock. ‖ [dépotoir] garbage dump *Am*.

déchargement [deʃaʀʒəmɑ̃] *nm* unloading.

décharger [deʃaʀʒe] *vt* [véhicule, marchandises] to unload. ‖ [arme - tirer] to fire, to discharge; [- enlever la charge] to unload. ‖ [soulager - conscience] to salve; [- colère] to vent. ‖ [libérer]: ~ **qqn de** to release sb from.

décharné, -e [deʃaʀne] *adj* [maigre] emaciated.

déchausser [deʃose] *vt*: ~ **qqn** to take sb's shoes off. ○ **se déchausser** *vp* [personne] to take one's shoes off. ‖ [dent] to come loose.

déchéance [deʃeɑ̃s] *nf* [déclin] degeneration, decline.

déchet [deʃɛ] *nm* [de matériau] scrap. ○ **déchets** *nmpl* refuse (*U*), waste (*U*).

déchiffrer [deʃifʀe] *vt* [inscription, hiéroglyphes] to decipher; [énigme] to unravel. ‖ MUS to sight-read.

déchiqueter [deʃikte] *vt* to tear to shreds.

déchirant, -e [deʃiʀɑ̃, ɑ̃t] *adj* heartrending.

déchirement [deʃiʀmɑ̃] *nm* [souffrance morale] heartbreak, distress.

déchirer [deʃiʀe] *vt* [papier, tissu] to tear up, to rip up. ○ **se déchirer** *vp* [matériau, muscle] to tear.

déchirure [deʃiʀyʀ] *nf* tear; *fig* wrench; ~ **musculaire** MÉD torn muscle.

déchu, -e [deʃy] *adj* [homme, ange] fallen; [souverain] deposed. ‖ JUR: **être ~ de** to be deprived of.

décibel [desibɛl] *nm* decibel.

décidé, -e [deside] *adj* [résolu] determined. ‖ [arrêté] settled.

décidément [desidemɑ̃] *adv* really.

décider [deside] *vt* [prendre une décision]: ~ **(de faire qqch)** to decide (to do sthg). ‖ [convaincre]: ~ **qqn à faire qqch** to persuade sb to do sthg. ○ **se décider** *vp* [personne]: **se ~ (à faire qqch)** to make up one's mind (to do sthg). ‖ [choisir]: **se ~ pour** to decide on, to settle on.

décilitre [desilitʀ] *nm* decilitre.

décimal, -e, -aux [desimal, o] *adj* decimal. ○ **décimale** *nf* decimal.

décimer [desime] *vt* to decimate.

décimètre [desimɛtʀ] *nm* [dixième de mètre] decimetre. ‖ [règle] ruler; **double ~ ≃** foot rule.

décisif, -ive [desizif, iv] *adj* decisive.

décision [desizjɔ̃] *nf* decision.

déclamer [deklame] *vt* to declaim.

déclaration [deklaʀasjɔ̃] *nf* [orale] declaration, announcement. ‖ [écrite] report, declaration; [d'assurance] claim; ~ **d'impôts** tax return; ~ **de revenus** statement of income.

déclarer [deklaʀe] *vt* [annoncer] to declare. ‖ [signaler] to report; **rien à ~** nothing to declare; ~ **une naissance** to register a birth. ○ **se déclarer** *vp* [se prononcer]: **se ~ pour/contre qqch** to come out in favour of/against sthg. ‖ [se manifester] to break out.

déclenchement [deklɑ̃ʃmɑ̃] *nm* [de mécanisme] activating, setting off.

déclencher [deklɑ̃ʃe] *vt* [mécanisme] to activate, to set off; *fig* to launch. ○ **se déclencher** *vp* [mécanisme] to go off, to be activated; *fig* to be triggered off.

déclic [deklik] *nm* [bruit] click.

déclin [deklɛ̃] *nm* [de civilisation, population, santé] decline. ‖ [fin] close.

déclinaison [deklinɛzɔ̃] *nf* GRAM declension.

décliner [dekline] **1** *vi* [santé, population, popularité] to decline. **2** *vt* [offre, honneur] to decline. ‖ GRAM to decline.

décoder [dekɔde] *vt* to decode.

décoiffer [dekwafe] *vt* [cheveux] to mess up.

décoincer [dekwɛ̃se] *vt* [chose] to loosen; [mécanisme] to unjam. ‖ *fam* [personne] to loosen up.

décollage [dekɔlaʒ] *nm* litt & *fig* takeoff.

décoller [dekɔle] **1** *vt* [étiquette, timbre] to unstick; [papier peint] to strip (off). **2** *vi litt* & *fig* to take off.

décolleté, -e [dekɔlte] *adj* [vêtement] low-cut. ○ **décolleté** *nm* [de personne] neck and shoulders (*pl*). ‖ [de vêtement] neckline, neck.

décolonisation [dekɔlɔnizasjɔ̃] *nf* decolonization.

décolorer [dekɔlɔʀe] *vt* [par décolorant] to bleach, to lighten; [par usure] to fade.

décombres [dekɔ̃bʀ] *nmpl* debris (*U*).

décommander [dekɔmɑ̃de] *vt* to cancel.

décomposé, -e [dekɔ̃poze] *adj* [pourri] decomposed. ‖ [visage] haggard; [personne] in shock.

décomposer [dekɔpoze] vt [gén]: ~ (en) to break down (into). ○ **se décomposer** vp [se putréfier] to rot, to decompose. || [se diviser]: **se** ~ **en** to be broken down into.

décomposition [dekɔpozisjɔ̃] nf [putréfaction] decomposition.

décompresser [dekɔprese] **1** vt TECHNOL to decompress. **2** vi to unwind.

décompte [dekɔ̃t] nm [calcul] breakdown (of an amount).

déconcentrer [dekɔ̃sãtre] vt [distraire] to distract. ○ **se déconcentrer** vp to be distracted.

déconcerter [dekɔ̃sɛrte] vt to disconcert.

déconfiture [dekɔ̃fityr] nf collapse, ruin.

décongeler [dekɔ̃ʒle] vt to defrost.

décongestionner [dekɔ̃ʒɛstjɔne] vt to relieve congestion in.

déconnecter [dekɔnɛkte] vt to disconnect.

déconseillé, -e [dekɔ̃seje] adj: **c'est fortement** ~ it's extremely inadvisable.

déconseiller [dekɔ̃seje] vt: ~ **qqch à qqn** to advise sb against sthg; ~ **à qqn de faire qqch** to advise sb against doing sthg.

déconsidérer [dekɔ̃sidere] vt to discredit.

décontaminer [dekɔ̃tamine] vt to decontaminate.

décontenancer [dekɔ̃tnãse] vt to put out.

décontracté, -e [dekɔ̃trakte] adj [détendu] casual, laid-back.

décontracter [dekɔ̃trakte] vt to relax. ○ **se décontracter** vp to relax.

décor [dekɔr] nm [cadre] scenery. || THÉÂTRE scenery (U); CIN sets (pl), décor.

décorateur, -trice [dekɔratœr, tris] nm, f CIN & THÉÂTRE designer; ~ **d'intérieur** interior decorator.

décoratif, -ive [dekɔratif, iv] adj decorative.

décoration [dekɔrasjɔ̃] nf decoration.

décorer [dekɔre] vt to decorate.

décortiquer [dekɔrtike] vt [noix] to shell; [graine] to husk; fig to analyse in minute detail.

découcher [dekuʃe] vi to stay out all night.

découdre [dekudr] vt COUTURE to unpick.

découler [dekule] vi: ~ **de** to follow from.

découpage [dekupaʒ] nm [action] cutting out; [résultat] paper cutout.

découper [dekupe] vt [couper] to cut up. || fig [diviser] to cut out.

découragement [dekuraʒmã] nm discouragement.

décourager [dekuraʒe] vt to discourage; ~ **qqn de qqch** to put sb off sthg; ~ **qqn de faire qqch** to discourage sb from doing sthg. ○ **se décourager** vp to lose heart.

décousu, -e [dekuzy] **1** pp → **découdre**. **2** adj fig [conversation] disjointed.

découvert, -e [dekuver, ert] **1** pp → **découvrir**. **2** adj [tête] bare; [terrain] exposed. ○ **découvert** nm BANQUE overdraft; **être à** ~ **(de 6 000 francs)** to be (6,000 francs) overdrawn. ○ **découverte** nf discovery; **aller à la** ~**e de** to explore.

découvrir [dekuvrir] vt [trouver, surprendre] to discover. || [ôter ce qui couvre, mettre à jour] to uncover.

décrasser [dekrase] vt to scrub.

décret [dekrɛ] nm decree.

décréter [dekrete] vt [décider]: ~ **que** to decide that.

décrire [dekrir] vt to describe.

décrit, -e [dekri, it] pp → **décrire**.

décrocher [dekrɔʃe] **1** vt [enlever] to take down. || [téléphone] to pick up. || fam [obtenir] to land. **2** vi fam [abandonner] to drop out.

décroître [dekrwatr] vi to decrease, to diminish; [jours] to get shorter.

décrypter [dekripte] vt to decipher.

déçu, -e [desy] **1** pp → **décevoir**. **2** adj disappointed.

dédaigner [dedeɲe] vt [mépriser - personne] to despise; [- conseils, injures] to scorn.

dédaigneux, -euse [dedɛɲø, øz] adj disdainful.

dédain [dedɛ̃] nm disdain, contempt.

dédale [dedal] nm litt & fig maze.

dedans [dədã] adv & nm inside. ○ **en dedans** loc adv inside, within. ○ **en dedans de** loc prép inside, within; voir aussi là-dedans.

dédicace [dedikas] nf dedication.

dédicacer [dedikase] vt: ~ **qqch (à qqn)** to sign or autograph sthg (for sb).

dédier [dedje] vt: ~ **qqch (à qqn/à qqch)** to dedicate sthg (to sb/to sthg).

dédire [dedir] ○ **se dédire** vp sout to go back on one's word.

dédommagement [dedɔmaʒmã] *nm* compensation.

dédommager [dedɔmaʒe] *vt* [indemniser] to compensate. || *fig* [remercier] to repay.

dédouaner [dedwane] *vt* [marchandises] to clear through customs.

dédoubler [deduble] *vt* to halve, to split; [fil] to separate.

déduction [dedyksjɔ̃] *nf* deduction.

déduire [dedɥir] *vt*: ~ **qqch** (**de**) [ôter] to deduct sthg (from); [conclure] to deduce sthg (from).

déduit, -e [dedɥi, ɥit] *pp* → déduire.

déesse [dees] *nf* goddess.

défaillance [defajãs] *nf* [incapacité - de machine] failure; [- de personne, organisation] weakness. || [malaise] blackout, fainting fit.

défaillant, e [defajã, ãt] *adj* [faible] failing.

défaillir [defajir] *vi* [s'évanouir] to faint.

défaire [defɛr] *vt* [détacher] to undo; [valise] to unpack; [lit] to strip. ○ **se défaire** *vp* [ne pas tenir] to come undone. || *sout* [se séparer]: **se ~ de** to get rid of.

défait, -e [defɛ, ɛt] 1 *pp* → défaire. 2 *adj fig* [épuisé] haggard. ○ **défaite** *nf* defeat.

défaitiste [defetist] *nmf* & *adj* defeatist.

défaut [defo] *nm* [imperfection] flaw; [- de personne] fault, shortcoming; ~ **de fabrication** manufacturing fault. || [manque] lack; **à ~ de** for lack ou want of; **l'eau fait (cruellement) ~** there is a (serious) water shortage.

défavorable [defavɔrabl] *adj* unfavourable.

défavoriser [defavɔrize] *vt* to handicap, to penalize.

défection [defɛksjɔ̃] *nf* [absence] absence. || [abandon] defection.

défectueux, -euse [defɛktɥø, øz] *adj* faulty, defective.

défendeur, -eresse [defãdœr, rɛs] *nm, f* defendant.

défendre [defãdr] *vt* [personne, opinion, client] to defend. || [interdire] to forbid; ~ **qqch à qqn** to forbid sb sthg; ~ **à qqn de faire qqch** to forbid sb to do sthg; ~ **que qqn fasse qqch** to forbid sb to do sthg. ○ **se défendre** *vp* [se battre, se justifier] to defend o.s. || [nier]: **se ~ de faire qqch** to deny doing sthg. || [thèse] to stand up.

défendu, -e [defãdy] 1 *pp* → défendre.

2 *adj*: «**il est ~ de jouer au ballon**» "no ball games".

défense [defãs] *nf* [d'éléphant] tusk. || [interdiction] prohibition, ban; «**~ de fumer/de stationner/d'entrer**» "no smoking/parking/entry"; «**~ d'afficher**» "stick no bills". || [protection] defence; **prendre la ~ de** to stand up for; **légitime ~** JUR self-defence.

défenseur [defãsœr] *nm* [partisan] champion.

défensif, -ive [defãsif, iv] *adj* defensive. ○ **défensive** *nf*: **être sur la défensive** to be on the defensive.

déférence [deferãs] *nf* deference.

déferlement [defɛrləmã] *nm* [de vagues] breaking; *fig* surge, upsurge.

déferler [defɛrle] *vi* [vagues] to break; *fig* to surge.

défi [defi] *nm* challenge.

défiance [defjãs] *nf* distrust, mistrust.

déficience [defisjãs] *nf* deficiency.

déficit [defisit] *nm* FIN deficit.

déficitaire [defisitɛr] *adj* in deficit.

défier [defje] *vt* [braver]: ~ **qqn de faire qqch** to defy sb to do sthg.

défigurer [defigyre] *vt* [blesser] to disfigure. || [enlaidir] to deface.

défilé [defile] *nm* [parade] parade. || [couloir] defile, narrow pass.

défiler [defile] *vi* [dans une parade] to march past. || [se succéder] to pass. ○ **se défiler** *vp fam* to back out.

défini, -e [defini] *adj* [précis] clear, precise. || GRAM definite.

définir [definir] *vt* to define.

définitif, -ive [definitif, iv] *adj* definitive, final. ○ **en définitive** *loc adv* in the end.

définition [definisjɔ̃] *nf* definition.

définitivement [definitivmã] *adv* for good, permanently.

défoncer [defɔ̃se] *vt* [caisse, porte] to smash in; [route] to break up; [mur] to smash down; [chaise] to break.

déformation [defɔrmasjɔ̃] *nf* [d'objet, de théorie] distortion. || MÉD deformity; ~ **professionnelle** *mental conditioning caused by one's job.*

déformer [defɔrme] *vt* to distort. ○ **se déformer** *vp* [changer de forme] to be distorted, to be deformed; [se courber] to bend.

défouler [defule] *vt fam* to unwind. ○ **se défouler** *vp fam* to let off steam, to unwind.

défricher [defriʃe] *vt* [terrain] to clear; *fig* [question] to do the groundwork for.

défunt, -e [defœ̃, œ̃t] **1** *adj* [décédé] late. **2** *nm, f* deceased.

dégagé, -e [degaʒe] *adj* [ciel, vue] clear; [partie du corps] bare. || [désinvolte] casual, airy. || [libre]: ~ **de** free from.

dégager [degaʒe] **1** *vt* [odeur] to produce, to give off. || [délivrer - blessé] to free, to extricate. || [pièce] to clear. || [libérer]: ~ **qqn de** to release sb from. **2** *vi fam* [partir] to clear off. ○ **se dégager** *vp* [se délivrer]: **se ~ de qqch** to free o.s. from sthg; *fig* to get out of sthg. || [émaner] to be given off. || [émerger] to emerge.

dégarnir [degarnir] *vt* to strip, to clear. ○ **se dégarnir** *vp* [vitrine] to be cleared; [arbre] to lose its leaves; **il se dégarnit** he's going bald.

dégât [dega] *nm litt* & *fig* damage (U); **faire des ~s** to cause damage.

dégel [deʒɛl] *nm* [fonte des glaces] thaw.

dégeler [deʒle] **1** *vt* [produit surgelé] to thaw. **2** *vi* to thaw.

dégénéré, -e [deʒenere] *adj* & *nm, f* degenerate.

dégénérer [deʒenere] *vi* to degenerate; ~ **en** to degenerate into.

dégivrer [deʒivre] *vt* [pare-brise] to de-ice; [réfrigérateur] to defrost.

dégonfler [degɔ̃fle] **1** *vt* to deflate, to let down. **2** *vi* to go down. ○ **se dégonfler** *vp* [objet] to go down. || *fam* [personne] to chicken out.

dégouliner [deguline] *vi* to trickle.

dégourdi, -e [degurdi] *adj* clever.

dégourdir [degurdir] *vt* [membres - ankylosés] to restore the circulation to. || *fig* [déniaiser]: ~ **qqn** to teach sb a thing or two. ○ **se dégourdir** *vp* [membres]: **se ~ les jambes** to stretch one's legs. || *fig* [acquérir de l'aisance] to learn a thing or two.

dégoût [degu] *nm* disgust, distaste.

dégoûtant, -e [degutɑ̃, ɑ̃t] *adj* [sale] filthy, disgusting. || [révoltant, grossier] disgusting.

dégoûter [degute] *vt* to disgust.

dégradé, -e [degrade] *adj* [couleur] shading off. ○ **dégradé** *nm* gradation; **un ~ de bleu** a blue shading. ○ **en dégradé** *loc adv* [cheveux] layered.

dégrader [degrade] *vt* [officier] to degrade. || [abîmer] to damage. || *fig* [avilir] to degrade, to debase. ○ **se dégrader**

vp [bâtiment, santé] to deteriorate. || *fig* [personne] to degrade o.s.

dégrafer [degrafe] *vt* to undo, to unfasten.

degré [dəgre] *nm* [gén] degree; ~**s** centigrades ou **Celsius** degrees centigrade ou Celsius; **prendre qqn/qqch au premier ~** to take sb/sthg at face value.

dégressif, -ive [degresif, iv] *adj*: **tarif ~** decreasing price scale.

dégringoler [degrɛ̃gɔle] *fam vi* [tomber] to tumble; *fig* to crash.

déguerpir [degerpir] *vi* to clear off.

dégueulasse [degœlas] *tfam* **1** *adj* [très sale, grossier] filthy. || [révoltant] dirty, rotten. **2** *nmf* scum (U).

dégueuler [degœle] *vi fam* to throw up.

déguisement [degizmɑ̃] *nm* disguise; [pour bal masqué] fancy dress.

déguiser [degize] *vt* to disguise. ○ **se déguiser** *vp*: **se ~ en** [pour tromper] to disguise o.s. as; [pour s'amuser] to dress up as.

dégustation [degystasjɔ̃] *nf* tasting, sampling; ~ **de vin** wine tasting.

déguster [degyste] **1** *vt* [savourer] to taste, to sample. **2** *vi fam* [subir]: **il va ~!** he'll be for it!

déhancher [deɑ̃ʃe] ○ **se déhancher** *vp* [en marchant] to swing one's hips.

dehors [dəɔr] **1** *adv* outside; **aller ~** to go outside; **dormir ~** to sleep out of doors, to sleep out; **jeter** ou **mettre qqn ~** to throw sb out. **2** *nm* outside. **3** *nmpl*: **les ~** [les apparences] appearances. ○ **en dehors** *loc adv* outside, outwards. ○ **en dehors de** *loc prép* [excepté] apart from.

déjà [deʒa] *adv* [dès cet instant] already. || [précédemment] already, before. || [au fait]: **quel est ton nom ~?** what did you say your name was? || [renforce une affirmation]: **ce n'est ~ pas si mal** that's not bad at all.

déjeuner [deʒœne] **1** *vi* [le matin] to have breakfast. || [à midi] to have lunch. **2** *nm* [repas de midi] lunch. || *Can* [dîner] dinner.

déjouer [deʒwe] *vt* to frustrate; ~ **la surveillance de qqn** to elude sb's surveillance.

delà [dəla] ○ **au-delà de** *loc prép* beyond.

délabré, -e [delabre] *adj* ruined.

délacer [delase] *vt* to unlace, to undo.

délai [delɛ] *nm* [temps accordé] period; **sans ~** immediately, without delay; ~ **de**

livraison delivery time, lead time. ǁ [sursis] extension (of deadline).

délaisser [delese] *vt* [abandonner] to leave. ǁ [négliger] to neglect.

délasser [delase] *vt* to refresh. ○ **se délasser** *vp* to relax.

délation [delasjɔ̃] *nf* informing.

délavé, -e [delave] *adj* faded.

délayer [deleje] *vt* [diluer]: ~ qqch dans qqch to mix sthg with sthg.

délecter [delekte] ○ **se délecter** *vp*: se ~ de qqch/à faire qqch to delight in sthg/in doing sthg.

délégation [delegasjɔ̃] *nf* delegation.

délégué, -e [delege] **1** *adj* [personne] delegated. **2** *nm, f* [représentant]: ~ (à) delegate (to).

déléguer [delege] *vt*: ~ qqn (à qqch) to delegate sb (to sthg).

délester [deleste] *vt* [circulation routière] to set up a diversion on, to divert.

délibération [deliberasjɔ̃] *nf* deliberation.

délibéré, -e [delibere] *adj* [intentionnel] deliberate. ǁ [résolu] determined.

délibérer [delibere] *vi*: ~ (de ou sur) to deliberate (on ou over).

délicat, -e [delika, at] *adj* [gén] delicate. ǁ [exigeant] fussy, difficult.

délicatement [delikatmɑ̃] *adv* delicately.

délicatesse [delikates] *nf* [gén] delicacy. ǁ [tact] delicacy, tact.

délice [delis] *nm* delight.

délicieux, -ieuse [delisjø, jøz] *adj* [savoureux] delicious. ǁ [agréable] delightful.

délié, -e [delje] *adj* [doigts] nimble.

délier [delje] *vt* to untie.

délimiter [delimite] *vt* [frontière] to fix; *fig* [question, domaine] to define, to demarcate.

délinquance [delɛ̃kɑ̃s] *nf* delinquency.

délinquant, -e [delɛ̃kɑ̃, ɑ̃t] *nm, f* delinquent.

délirant, -e [delirɑ̃, ɑ̃t] *adj* MÉD delirious. ǁ [extravagant] frenzied. ǁ *fam* [extraordinaire] crazy.

délire [delir] *nm* MÉD delirium.

délirer [delire] *vi* MÉD to be ou become delirious; *fam fig* to rave.

délit [deli] *nm* crime, offence; **en flagrant ~** red-handed, in the act.

délivrance [delivrɑ̃s] *nf* [soulagement] relief. ǁ [accouchement] delivery.

délivrer [delivre] *vt* [prisonnier] to free, to release. ǁ [pays] to deliver, to free; ~

de to free from; *fig* to relieve from. ǁ [remettre]: ~ qqch (à qqn) to issue sthg (to sb). ǁ [marchandise] to deliver.

déloger [delɔʒe] *vt*: ~ (de) to dislodge (from).

déloyal, -e, -aux [delwajal, o] *adj* [infidèle] disloyal. ǁ [malhonnête] unfair.

delta [delta] *nm* delta.

deltaplane, delta-plane (*pl* deltaplanes) [deltaplan] *nm* hang glider.

déluge [delyʒ] *nm* RELIG: **le Déluge** the Flood. ǁ [pluie] downpour, deluge; **un ~ de** *fig* a flood of.

déluré, -e [delyre] *adj* [malin] quickwitted; *péj* [dévergondé] saucy.

démagogie [demagɔʒi] *nf* pandering to public opinion, demagogy.

demain [dəmɛ̃] **1** *adv* [le jour suivant] tomorrow; ~ **matin** tomorrow morning. ǁ *fig* [plus tard] in the future. **2** *nm* tomorrow; **à ~!** see you tomorrow!

demande [dəmɑ̃d] *nf* [souhait] request. ǁ [démarche] proposal; ~ **en mariage** proposal of marriage. ǁ [candidature] application; ~ **d'emploi** job application; **«~s d'emploi»** "situations wanted". ǁ ÉCON demand.

demandé, -e [dəmɑ̃de] *adj* in demand.

demander [dəmɑ̃de] **1** *vt* [réclamer, s'enquérir] to ask for; ~ **qqch à qqn** to ask sb for sthg. ǁ [appeler] to call; **on vous demande à la réception/au téléphone** you're wanted at reception/on the telephone. ǁ [désirer] to ask, to want. ǁ [exiger] **tu m'en demandes trop** you're asking too much of me. ǁ [nécessiter] to require. **2** *vi* [réclamer]: ~ **à qqn de faire qqch** to ask sb to do sthg; **ne ~ qu'à ...** to be ready to .... ǁ [nécessiter]: **ce projet demande à être étudié** this project requires investigation ou needs investigating. ○ **se demander** *vp*: se ~ (si) to wonder (if ou whether).

demandeur, -euse [dəmɑ̃dœr, øz] *nm, f* [solliciteur]: ~ **d'emploi** job-seeker.

démangeaison [demɑ̃ʒɛzɔ̃] *nf* [irritation] itch, itching (*U*); *fam fig* urge.

démanger [demɑ̃ʒe] *vi* [gratter] to itch; **ça me démange de ...** *fig* I'm itching ou dying to ....

démanteler [demɑ̃tle] *vt* [construction] to demolish; *fig* to break up.

démaquillant, -e [demakijɑ̃, ɑ̃t] *adj* make-up-removing (*avant n*). ○ **démaquillant** *nm* make-up remover.

démaquiller [demakije] *vt* to remove make-up from. ○ **se démaquiller** *vp* to remove one's make-up.

démarche [demarʃ] *nf* [manière de marcher] gait, walk. ‖ [raisonnement] approach, method. ‖ [requête] step; **faire les ~s pour faire qqch** to take the necessary steps to do sthg.

démarcheur, -euse [demarʃœr, øz] *nm, f* [représentant] door-to-door salesman (*f* saleswoman).

démarquer [demarke] *vt* [solder] to mark down. ○ **se démarquer** *vp fig* [se distinguer]: **se ~ (de)** to distinguish o.s. (from).

démarrage [demaraʒ] *nm* starting, start; **~ en côte** hill start.

démarrer [demare] **1** *vi* [véhicule] to start (up); [conducteur] to drive off. ‖ *fig* [affaire, projet] to get off the ground. **2** *vt* [véhicule] to start (up). ‖ *fam fig* [commencer]: **~ qqch** to get sthg going.

démarreur [demarœr] *nm* starter.

démasquer [demaske] *vt* [personne] to unmask. ‖ *fig* [complot, plan] to unveil.

démêlant, -e [demelɑ̃, ɑ̃t] *adj* conditioning (*avant n*). ○ **démêlant** *nm* conditioner.

démêlé [demele] *nm* quarrel; **avoir des ~s avec la justice** to get into trouble with the law.

démêler [demele] *vt* [cheveux, fil] to untangle; *fig* to unravel. ○ **se démêler** *vp*: **se ~ de** *fig* to extricate o.s. from.

déménagement [demenaʒmɑ̃] *nm* removal.

déménager [demenaʒe] **1** *vt* to move. **2** *vi* to move (house).

déménageur [demenaʒœr] *nm* mover *Am*.

démence [demɑ̃s] *nf* MÉD dementia; [bêtise] madness.

démener [demne] ○ **se démener** *vp litt & fig* to struggle.

dément, -e [demɑ̃, ɑ̃t] **1** *adj* MÉD demented; *fam* [extraordinaire, extravagant] crazy. **2** *nm, f* demented person.

démenti [demɑ̃ti] *nm* denial.

démentiel, -ielle [demɑ̃sjɛl] *adj* MÉD demented; *fam* [incroyable] crazy.

démentir [demɑ̃tir] *vt* [réfuter] to deny. ‖ [contredire] to contradict.

démesure [deməzyr] *nf* excess, immoderation.

démettre [demɛtr] *vt* MÉD to put out (of joint). ‖ [congédier]: **~ qqn de** to dismiss sb from. ○ **se démettre** *vp* MÉD: **se ~**

l'épaule to put one's shoulder out (of joint).

demeurant [dəmœrɑ̃] ○ **au demeurant** *loc adv* all things considered.

demeure [dəmœr] *nf sout* [domicile, habitation] residence. ○ **à demeure** *loc adv* permanently.

demeuré, -e [dəmœre] **1** *adj* simple, half-witted. **2** *nm, f* half-wit.

demeurer [dəmœre] *vi* (*aux: avoir*) [habiter] to live. ‖ (*aux: être*) [rester] to remain.

demi, -e [dəmi] *adj* half; **un kilo et ~** one and a half kilos; **il est une heure et ~e** it's half past one; **à ~ half; ouvrir à ~** to half-open; **faire les choses à ~** to do things by halves. ○ **demi** *nm* [bière] beer. ‖ FOOTBALL midfielder.

demi-cercle [dəmiserkl] (*pl* **demi-cercles**) *nm* semicircle.

demi-douzaine [dəmiduzen] (*pl* **demi-douzaines**) *nf* half-dozen; **une ~ (de)** half a dozen.

demi-finale [dəmifinal] (*pl* **demi-finales**) *nf* semifinal.

demi-frère [dəmifrer] (*pl* **demi-frères**) *nm* half-brother.

demi-heure [dəmijœr] (*pl* **demi-heures**) *nf* half an hour, half-hour.

demi-journée [dəmiʒurne] (*pl* **demi-journées**) *nf* half a day, half-day.

demi-litre [dəmilitr] (*pl* **demi-litres**) *nm* half a litre, half-litre.

demi-mot [dəmimo] ○ **à demi-mot** *loc adv*: **comprendre à ~** to understand without things having to be spelled out.

déminer [demine] *vt* to clear of mines.

demi-pension [dəmipɑ̃sjɔ̃] *nf* [d'hôtel] half-board. ‖ [d'école]: **être en ~** to take school dinners (*pl*).

démis, -e [demi, iz] *pp* → **démettre**.

demi-sœur [dəmisœr] (*pl* **demi-sœurs**) *nf* half-sister.

démission [demisjɔ̃] *nf* resignation.

démissionner [demisjɔne] *vi* [d'un emploi] to resign; *fig* to give up.

demi-tarif [dəmitarif] (*pl* **demi-tarifs**) **1** *adj* half-price. **2** *nm* [tarification] half-fare. ‖ [billet] half-price ticket.

demi-tour [dəmitur] (*pl* **demi-tours**) *nm* [gén] half-turn; **faire ~** to turn back.

démocrate [demɔkrat] *nmf* democrat.

démocratie [demɔkrasi] *nf* democracy.

démocratique [demɔkratik] *adj* democratic.

démocratiser [demɔkratize] *vt* to democratize.

démodé, -e [demɔde] *adj* old-fashioned.

démographique [demɔgrafik] *adj* demographic.

demoiselle [dəmwazɛl] *nf* [jeune fille] maid; ~ **d'honneur** bridesmaid.

démolir [demɔlir] *vt* [gén] to demolish.

démolition [demɔlisjɔ̃] *nf* demolition.

démon [demɔ̃] *nm* [diable, personne] devil, demon; **le ~** RELIG the Devil.

démoniaque [demɔnjak] *adj* [diabolique] diabolical.

démonstratif, -ive [demɔ̃stratif, iv] *adj* [personne & GRAM] demonstrative. ○ **démonstratif** *nm* GRAM demonstrative.

démonstration [demɔ̃strasjɔ̃] *nf* [gén] demonstration.

démonter [demɔ̃te] *vt* [appareil] to dismantle, to take apart. || [troubler]: ~ **qqn** to put sb out. ○ **se démonter** *vp fam* to be put out.

démontrer [demɔ̃tre] *vt* [prouver] to prove, to demonstrate. || [témoigner de] to show, to demonstrate.

démoralisant, -e [demɔralizɑ̃, ɑ̃t] *adj* demoralizing.

démoraliser [demɔralize] *vt* to demoralize. ○ **se démoraliser** *vp* to lose heart.

démordre [demɔrdr] *vt*: **ne pas ~ de** to stick to.

démotiver [demɔtive] *vt* to demotivate.

démouler [demule] *vt* to turn out of a mould, to remove from á mould.

démunir [demynir] *vt* to deprive.

dénaturer [denatyre] *vt* [goût] to impair, to mar. || [déformer] to distort.

dénégation [denegasjɔ̃] *nf* denial.

dénicher [denife] *vt fig* [personne] to flush out. || *fam* [objet] to unearth.

dénigrer [denigre] *vt* to denigrate, to run down.

dénivelé [denivle] *nm* difference in level or height.

dénivellation [denivɛlasjɔ̃] *nf* [différence de niveau] difference in height or level. || [pente] slope.

dénombrer [denɔ̃bre] *vt* [compter] to count; [énumérer] to enumerate.

dénominateur [denɔminatœr] *nm* denominator.

dénomination [denɔminasjɔ̃] *nf* name.

dénommé, -e [denɔme] *adj*: **un ~ Robert** someone by the name of Robert.

dénoncer [denɔ̃se] *vt* [gén] to denounce; ~ **qqn à qqn** to denounce sb to sb, to inform on sb. || *fig* [trahir] to betray.

dénonciation [denɔ̃sjasjɔ̃] *nf* denunciation.

dénoter [denɔte] *vt* to show, to indicate.

dénouement [denumɑ̃] *nm* [issue] outcome. || CIN & THÉÂTRE denouement.

dénouer [denwe] *vt* [nœud] to untie, to undo; *fig* to unravel.

dénoyauter [denwajote] *vt* [fruit] to stone.

denrée [dɑ̃re] *nf* [produit] produce (*U*); ~**s alimentaires** foodstuffs.

dense [dɑ̃s] *adj* [gén] dense. || [style] condensed.

densité [dɑ̃site] *nf* density.

dent [dɑ̃] *nf* [de personne, d'objet] tooth; ~ **de lait/de sagesse** milk/wisdom tooth.

dentaire [dɑ̃ter] *adj* dental.

dentelé, -e [dɑ̃tle] *adj* serrated, jagged.

dentelle [dɑ̃tɛl] *nf* lace (*U*).

dentier [dɑ̃tje] *nm* [dents] dentures (*pl*).

dentifrice [dɑ̃tifris] *nm* toothpaste.

dentiste [dɑ̃tist] *nmf* dentist.

dentition [dɑ̃tisjɔ̃] *nf* teeth (*pl*), dentition.

dénuder [denyde] *vt* to leave bare; [fil électrique] to strip.

dénué, -e [denɥe] *adj sout*: ~ **de** devoid of.

dénuement [denymɑ̃] *nm* destitution (*U*).

déodorant, -e [deɔdɔrɑ̃, ɑ̃t] *adj* deodorant. ○ **déodorant** *nm* deodorant.

déontologie [deɔ̃tɔlɔʒi] *nf* professional ethics (*pl*).

dépannage [depanaʒ] *nm* repair.

dépanner [depane] *vt* [réparer] to repair, to fix. || *fam* [aider] to bail out.

dépanneur, -euse [depanœr, øz] *nm, f* repairman　　　(*f*　　　repairwoman). ○ **dépanneuse** *nf* [véhicule] (breakdown) recovery vehicle.

dépareillé, -e [depareje] *adj* [ensemble] non-matching; [paire] odd.

départ [depar] *nm* [de personne] departure, leaving; [de véhicule] departure. || SPORT & *fig* start. ○ **au départ** *loc adv* to start with.

départager [departaʒe] *vt* [concurrents, opinions] to decide between.

département [departəmã] *nm* [territoire] *territorial and administrative division of France.* || [service] department.

départemental, -e, -aux [departəmãtal, o] *adj* of a French département. ○ **départementale** *nf* ≃ secondary road.

dépassé, -e [depase] *adj* [périmé] old-fashioned. || *fam* [déconcerté]: ~ **par** overwhelmed by.

dépassement [depasmã] *nm* [en voiture] overtaking.

dépasser [depase] **1** *vt* [doubler] to overtake. || [être plus grand que] to be taller than. || [excéder] to exceed, to be more than. || [aller au-delà de] to exceed. || [franchir] to pass. **2** *vi*: ~ (**de**) to stick out (from).

dépayser [depeize] *vt* [désorienter] to disorient *Am*. || [changer agréablement] to make a change of scene for.

dépecer [depəse] *vt* [découper] to chop up. || [déchiqueter] to tear apart.

dépêche [depεʃ] *nf* dispatch.

dépêcher [depeʃe] *vt sout* [envoyer] to dispatch. ○ **se dépêcher** *vp* to hurry up; **se ~ de faire qqch** to hurry to do sthg.

dépeindre [depɛ̃dr] *vt* to depict, to describe.

dépeint, -e [depɛ̃, ɛ̃t] *pp* → **dépeindre**.

dépendance [depãdãs] *nf* [de personne] dependence. || [à la drogue] dependency. || [de bâtiment] outbuilding.

dépendre [depãdr] *vt* [être soumis]: ~ **de** to depend on; **ça dépend** it depends. || [appartenir]: ~ **de** to belong to.

dépens [depã] *nmpl* JUR costs; **aux ~ de qqn** at sb's expense; **je l'ai appris à mes ~** I learned that to my cost.

dépense [depãs] *nf* [frais] expense. || FIN & *fig* expenditure (*U*); **les ~s publiques** public spending (*U*).

dépenser [depãse] *vt* [argent] to spend. || *fig* [énergie] to expend. ○ **se dépenser** *vp litt & fig* to exert o.s.

dépensier, -ière [depãsje, jεr] *adj* extravagant.

déperdition [deperdisjɔ̃] *nf* loss.

dépérir [deperir] *vi* [personne] to waste away. || [plante] to wither.

dépeupler [depœple] *vt* [pays] to depopulate. || [étang, rivière, forêt] to drive the wildlife from.

déphasé, -e [defaze] *adj* ÉLECTR out of phase; *fam fig* out of touch.

dépilatoire [depilatwar] *adj*: **crème/lotion ~** depilatory cream/lotion.

dépistage [depistaʒ] *nm* [de maladie] screening; **~ du SIDA** AIDS testing.

dépister [depiste] *vt* [gibier, voleur] to track down. || [maladie] to screen for.

dépit [depi] *nm* pique, spite. ○ **en dépit de** *loc prép* in spite of.

déplacé, -e [deplase] *adj* [propos, attitude, présence] out of place.

déplacement [deplasmã] *nm* [d'objet] moving. || [voyage] travelling (*U*).

déplacer [deplase] *vt* [objet] to move, to shift. || [muter] to transfer. ○ **se déplacer** *vp* [se mouvoir - animal] to move (around); [- personne] to walk. || [voyager] to travel. || MÉD: **se ~ une vertèbre** to slip a disc.

déplaire [deplεr] *vt* [ne pas plaire]: **cela me déplaît** I don't like it.

déplaisant, -e [deplεzã, ãt] *adj sout* unpleasant.

dépliant [deplijã] *nm* leaflet; **~ touristique** tourist brochure.

déplier [deplije] *vt* to unfold.

déploiement [deplwamã] *nm* MIL deployment. || [d'ailes] spreading. || *fig* [d'efforts] display.

déplorer [deplore] *vt* [regretter] to deplore.

déployer [deplwaje] *vt* [déplier - gén] to unfold; [- plan, journal] to open; [ailes] to spread. || MIL to deploy. || [mettre en œuvre] to expend.

déplu [deply] *pp inv* → **déplaire**.

déportation [deportasjɔ̃] *nf* [internement] transportation to a concentration camp.

déporté, -e [deporte] *nm, f* [interné] prisoner (*in a concentration camp*).

déporter [deporte] *vt* [dévier] to carry off course. || [interner] to send to a concentration camp.

déposer [depoze] **1** *vt* [poser] to put down. || [personne, paquet] to drop. || [argent, sédiment] to deposit. || JUR to file; **~ son bilan** FIN to go into liquidation. **2** *vi* JUR to testify, to give evidence. ○ **se déposer** *vp* to settle.

dépositaire [depozitεr] *nmf* COMM agent. || [d'objet] bailee; **~ de** *fig* person entrusted with.

déposition [depozisjɔ̃] *nf* deposition.

déposséder [deposede] *vt*: **~ qqn de** to dispossess sb of.

dépôt [depo] *nm* [d'objet, d'argent, de sédiment] deposit, depositing (*U*); **verser**

un ~ (de garantie) to put down a deposit; ~ d'ordures (rubbish) dump Br, garbage dump Am. ‖ [garage] depot. ‖ [entrepôt] store, warehouse. ‖ [prison] ≃ police cells (pl).

dépotoir [depɔtwar] nm [décharge] garbage dump Am; fam fig dump, tip.

dépouille [depuj] nf [peau] hide, skin. ‖ [humaine] remains (pl).

dépouillement [depujmɑ̃] nm [sobriété] austerity, sobriety.

dépouiller [depuje] vt [priver]: ~ qqn (de) to strip sb (of). ‖ [examiner] to peruse; ~ un scrutin to count the votes.

dépourvu, -e [depurvy] adj: ~ de without, lacking in. ○ **au dépourvu** loc adv: prendre qqn au ~ to catch sb unawares.

dépoussiérer [depusjere] vt to dust (off).

dépravé, -e [deprave] 1 adj depraved. 2 nm, f degenerate.

dépréciation [depresjasjɔ̃] nf depreciation.

déprécier [depresje] vt [marchandise] to reduce the value of. ‖ [œuvre] to disparage. ○ **se déprécier** vp [marchandise] to depreciate. ‖ [personne] to put o.s. down.

dépressif, -ive [depresif, iv] adj depressive.

dépression [depresjɔ̃] nf depression; ~ nerveuse nervous breakdown.

déprimant, -e [deprimɑ̃, ɑ̃t] adj depressing.

déprime [deprim] nf fam: faire une ~ to be (feeling) down.

déprimé, -e [deprime] adj depressed.

déprimer [deprime] 1 vt to depress. 2 vi fam to be (feeling) down.

déprogrammer [deprɔgrame] vt to remove from the schedule; TÉLÉ to take off the air.

depuis [dəpɥi] 1 prép [à partir d'une date ou d'un moment précis] since; il est parti ~ hier he's been away since yesterday; ~ le début jusqu'à la fin from beginning to end. ‖ [exprimant une durée] for; il est malade ~ une semaine he has been ill for a week; ~ 10 ans/longtemps for 10 years/a long time. ‖ [dans l'espace] from; ~ la route, on pouvait voir la mer you could see the sea from the road. 2 adv since (then); ~, nous ne l'avons pas revu we haven't seen him since (then). ○ **depuis que** loc conj since.

député [depyte] nm [au parlement] representative Am.

déraciner [derasine] vt litt & fig to uproot.

déraillement [derajmɑ̃] nm derailment.

dérailler [deraje] vi [train] to leave the rails, to be derailed. ‖ fam fig [personne] to go to pieces.

dérailleur [derajœr] nm [de bicyclette] derailleur.

déraisonnable [derɛzɔnabl] adj unreasonable.

dérangement [derɑ̃ʒmɑ̃] nm trouble; en ~ out of order.

déranger [derɑ̃ʒe] 1 vt [personne] to disturb, to bother; ça vous dérange si je fume? do you mind if I smoke? ‖ [plan] to disrupt. ‖ [maison, pièce] to disarrange, to make untidy. 2 vi to be disturbing. ○ **se déranger** vp [se déplacer] to move. ‖ [se gêner] to put o.s. out.

dérapage [derapaʒ] nm [glissement] skid; fig excess.

déraper [derape] vi [glisser] to skid; fig to get out of hand.

déréglementer [dereɡləmɑ̃te] vt to deregulate.

dérégler [dereɡle] vt [mécanisme] to put out of order; fig to upset. ○ **se dérégler** vp [mécanisme] to go wrong.

dérider [deride] vt fig: ~ qqn to cheer sb up.

dérision [derizjɔ̃] nf derision; **tourner qqch en ~** to hold sthg up to ridicule.

dérisoire [derizwar] adj derisory.

dérivatif, -ive [derivatif, iv] adj derivative. ○ **dérivatif** nm distraction.

dérive [deriv] nf [mouvement] drift, drifting (U); aller ou partir à la ~ fig to fall apart.

dérivé [derive] nm derivative.

dériver [derive] 1 vt [détourner] to divert. 2 vi [aller à la dérive] to drift. ‖ fig [découler]: ~ de to derive from.

dermatologie [dɛrmatɔlɔʒi] nf dermatology.

dermatologue [dɛrmatɔlɔɡ] nmf dermatologist.

dernier, -ière [dɛrnje, jɛr] 1 adj [gén] last; l'année dernière last year. ‖ [ultime] last, final. ‖ [plus récent] latest. 2 nm, f last; ce ~ the latter. ○ **en dernier** loc adv last.

dernièrement [dɛrnjɛrmɑ̃] adv recently, lately.

dernier-né, **dernière-née** [dɛrnjene, dɛrnjerne] nm, f [bébé] youngest (child).

dérobade [derɔbad] nf evasion, shirking (U).

dérobé, **-e** [derobe] adj [caché] hidden. ○ **à la dérobée** loc adv surreptitiously.

dérober [derobe] vt sout to steal. ○ **se dérober** vp [se soustraire]: **se ~ à qqch** to shirk sthg. || [s'effondrer] to give way.

dérogation [derɔgasjɔ̃] nf [action] dispensation; [résultat] exception.

déroulement [derulmɑ̃] nm [de bobine] unwinding. || fig [d'événement] development.

dérouler [derule] vt [fil] to unwind; [papier, tissu] to unroll. ○ **se dérouler** vp to take place.

dérouter [derut] nf MIL rout; fig collapse.

dérouter [derute] vt [déconcerter] to disconcert, to put out. || [dévier] to divert.

derrière [dɛrjɛr] **1** prép & adv behind. **2** nm [partie arrière] back; **la porte de ~** the back door. || [partie du corps] bottom, behind.

des [de] **1** art indéf → **un. 2** prép → **de**.

dès [dɛ] prép from; **~ son arrivée** the minute he arrives/arrived, as soon as he arrives/arrived; **~ l'enfance** since childhood; **~ 1900** as far back as 1900, as early as 1900; **~ maintenant** from now on. ○ **dès que** loc conj as soon as.

désabusé, **-e** [dezabyze] adj disillusioned.

désaccord [dezakɔr] nm disagreement.

désaccordé, **-e** [dezakɔrde] adj out of tune.

désaffecté, **-e** [dezafɛkte] adj disused.

désagréable [dezagreabl] adj unpleasant.

désagréger [dezagreʒe] vt to break up. ○ **se désagréger** vp to break up.

désagrément [dezagremɑ̃] nm annoyance.

désaltérant, **-e** [dezalterɑ̃, ɑ̃t] adj thirst-quenching.

désaltérer [dezaltere] ○ **se désaltérer** vp to quench one's thirst.

désamorcer [dezamɔrse] vt [arme] to remove the primer from; [bombe] to defuse; fig [complot] to nip in the bud.

désappointer [dezapwɛ̃te] vt to disappoint.

désapprobation [dezaprɔbasjɔ̃] nf disapproval.

désapprouver [dezapruve] **1** vt to disapprove of. **2** vi to be disapproving.

désarmement [dezarməmɑ̃] nm disarmament.

désarmer [dezarme] vt to disarm; [fusil] to unload.

désarroi [dezarwa] nm confusion.

désastre [dezastr] nm disaster.

désastreux, **-euse** [dezastrø, øz] adj disastrous.

désavantage [dezavɑ̃taʒ] nm disadvantage.

désavantager [dezavɑ̃taʒe] vt to disadvantage.

désavantageux, **-euse** [dezavɑ̃taʒø, øz] adj unfavourable.

désavouer [dezavwe] vt to disown.

désaxé, **-e** [dezakse] adj [mentalement] disordered, unhinged.

descendance [desɑ̃dɑ̃s] nf [progéniture] descendants (pl).

descendant, **-e** [desɑ̃dɑ̃, ɑ̃t] nm, f [héritier] descendant.

descendre [desɑ̃dr] **1** vt (aux: avoir) [escalier, pente] to go/come down. || [rideau, tableau] to lower. || [apporter] to bring/take down. || fam [personne, avion] to shoot down. **2** vi (aux: être) [gén] to go/come down; [température, niveau] to fall. || [passager] to get off; **~ d'un bus** to get off a bus; **~ d'une voiture** to get out of a car. || [être issu]: **~ de** to be descended from. || [marée] to go out.

descendu, **-e** [desɑ̃dy] pp → **descendre**.

descente [desɑ̃t] nf [action] descent. || [pente] downhill slope ou stretch. || [irruption] raid. || [tapis]: **~ de lit** bedside rug.

descriptif, **-ive** [dɛskriptif, iv] adj descriptive. ○ **descriptif** nm [de lieu] particulars (pl); [d'appareil] specification.

description [dɛskripsjɔ̃] nf description.

désemparé, **-e** [dezɑ̃pare] adj [personne] helpless; [avion, navire] disabled.

désenfler [dezɑ̃fle] vi to go down, to become less swollen.

déséquilibre [dezekilibr] nm imbalance.

déséquilibré, **-e** [dezekilibre] nm, f unbalanced person.

déséquilibrer [dezekilibre] vt [physiquement]: **~ qqn** to throw sb off balance. || [perturber] to unbalance.

désert, **-e** [dezɛr, ɛrt] adj [désertique - île] desert (avant n); [peu fréquenté] deserted. ○ **désert** nm desert.

déserter [dezɛrte] vt & vi to desert.

déserteur [dezɛrtœr] nm MIL deserter.

désertion [dezɛrsjɔ̃] *nf* desertion.

désertique [dezɛrtik] *adj* desert (*avant n*).

désespéré, -e [dezɛspere] *adj* [regard] desperate. || [situation] hopeless.

désespérément [dezɛsperemã] *adv* [avec acharnement] desperately.

désespérer [dezɛspere] **1** *vt* [décourager]: ~ qqn to drive sb to despair. **2** *vi*: ~ (de) to despair (of). ○ **se désespérer** *vp* to despair.

désespoir [dezɛspwar] *nm* despair; en ~ de cause as a last resort.

déshabillé [dezabije] *nm* negligee.

déshabiller [dezabije] *vt* to undress. ○ **se déshabiller** *vp* to undress, to get undressed.

désherbant, -e [dezɛrbã, ãt] *adj* weed-killing. ○ **désherbant** *nm* weed-killer.

déshérité, -e [dezerite] *nm, f* [pauvre] deprived person.

déshériter [dezerite] *vt* to disinherit.

déshonneur [dezɔnœr] *nm* disgrace.

déshonorer [dezɔnɔre] *vt* to disgrace, to bring disgrace on.

déshydrater [dezidrate] *vt* to dehydrate. ○ **se déshydrater** *vp* to become dehydrated.

désigner [dezine] *vt* [choisir] to appoint. || [signaler] to point out. || [nommer] to designate.

désillusion [dezilyzjɔ̃] *nf* disillusion.

désinfectant, -e [dezɛ̃fɛktã, ãt] *adj* disinfectant. ○ **désinfectant** *nm* disinfectant.

désinfecter [dezɛ̃fɛkte] *vt* to disinfect.

désinflation [dezɛ̃flasjɔ̃] *nf* disinflation.

désintégrer [dezɛ̃tegre] *vt* to break up. ○ **se désintégrer** *vp* to disintegrate, to break up.

désintéressé, -e [dezɛ̃terese] *adj* disinterested.

désintéresser [dezɛ̃terese] ○ **se désintéresser** *vp*: se ~ de to lose interest in.

désintoxication [dezɛ̃tɔksikasjɔ̃] *nf* detoxification.

désinvolte [dezɛ̃vɔlt] *adj* [à l'aise] casual. || *péj* [sans-gêne] offhand.

désinvolture [dezɛ̃vɔltyr] *nf* [légèreté] casualness. || *péj* [sans-gêne] offhandedness.

désir [dezir] *nm* [souhait] desire, wish. || [charnel] desire.

désirable [dezirabl] *adj* desirable.

désirer [dezire] *vt sout* [chose]: ~ faire qqch to wish to do sthg; **vous désirez?** [dans un magasin] can I help you?; [dans un café] what can I get you? || [sexuellement] to desire.

désistement [dezistəmã] *nm*: ~ (de) withdrawal (from).

désister [deziste] ○ **se désister** *vp* [se retirer] to withdraw, to stand down.

désobéir [dezɔbeir] *vi*: ~ (à qqn) to disobey (sb).

désobéissant, -e [dezɔbeisã, ãt] *adj* disobedient.

désobligeant, -e [dezɔbliʒã, ãt] *adj sout* offensive.

désodorisant, -e [dezɔdɔrizã, ãt] *adj* deodorant. ○ **désodorisant** *nm* air freshener.

désœuvré, -e [dezœvre] *adj* idle.

désolation [dezɔlasjɔ̃] *nf* [destruction] desolation. || *sout* [affliction] distress.

désolé, -e [dezɔle] *adj* [ravagé] desolate. || [contrarié] very sorry.

désoler [dezɔle] *vt* [affliger] to sadden. || [contrarier] to upset, to make sorry. ○ **se désoler** *vp* [être contrarié] to be upset.

désolidariser [desɔlidarize] ○ **se désolidariser** *vp*: se ~ de to dissociate o.s. from.

désopilant, -e [dezɔpilã, ãt] *adj* hilarious.

désordonné, -e [dezɔrdɔne] *adj* [maison, personne] untidy.

désordre [dezɔrdr] *nm* [fouillis] untidiness; en ~ untidy. || [agitation] disturbances (*pl*), disorder (*U*).

désorganiser [dezɔrganize] *vt* to disrupt.

désorienté, -e [dezɔrjãte] *adj* disoriented, disorientated.

désormais [dezɔrmɛ] *adv* from now on, in future.

désosser [dezɔse] *vt* to bone.

despote [dɛspɔt] *nm* [chef d'État] despot; *fig & péj* tyrant.

despotisme [dɛspɔtism] *nm* [gouvernement] despotism; *fig & péj* tyranny.

desquels, desquelles [dekɛl] → lequel.

DESS (*abr de* diplôme d'études supérieures spécialisées) *nm* postgraduate diploma.

dessécher [deseʃe] *vt* [peau] to dry (out). ○ **se dessécher** *vp* [peau, terre] to dry out; [plante] to wither.

desserrer [desere] *vt* to loosen; [poing, dents] to unclench; [frein] to release.

dessert [desɛr] *nm* dessert.

desserte [desɛrt] *nf* [meuble] sideboard.

desservir [desɛrvir] *vt* TRANSPORT to serve. || [table] to clear. || [désavantager] to do a disservice to.

dessin [desɛ̃] *nm* [graphique] drawing; ~ animé cartoon (*film*); ~ humoristique cartoon (*drawing*). || *fig* [contour] outline.

dessinateur, -trice [desinatœr, tris] *nm, f* artist, draughtsman (*f* draughtswoman).

dessiner [desine] **1** *vt* [représenter] to draw; *fig* to outline. **2** *vi* to draw.

dessous [dəsu] **1** *adv* underneath. **2** *nm* [partie inférieure - gén] underside; [- d'un tissu] wrong side. **3** *nmpl* [sous-vêtements féminins] underwear (*U*). ○ **en dessous** *loc adv* underneath; [plus bas] below.

dessous-de-plat [dəsudpla] *nm inv* tablemat.

dessus [dəsy] **1** *adv* on top; **faites attention à ne pas marcher ~** be careful not to walk on it. **2** *nm* [partie supérieure] top. || [étage supérieur] upstairs; **les voisins du ~** the upstairs neighbours. || *loc*: **avoir le ~** to have the upper hand. ○ **en dessus** *loc adv* on top.

dessus-de-lit [dəsydli] *nm inv* bedspread.

déstabiliser [destabilize] *vt* to destabilize.

destin [destɛ̃] *nm* fate.

destinataire [destinatɛr] *nmf* addressee.

destination [destinasjɔ̃] *nf* [direction] destination; **un avion à ~ de Paris** a plane to or for Paris. || [rôle] purpose.

destinée [destine] *nf* destiny.

destiner [destine] *vt* [consacrer]: ~ **qqch à** to intend sthg for, to mean sthg for. || [vouer]: ~ **qqn à qqch/à faire qqch** [à un métier] to destine sb for sthg/to do sthg.

destituer [destitɥe] *vt* to dismiss.

destructeur, -trice [destryktœr, tris] **1** *adj* destructive. **2** *nm, f* destroyer.

destruction [destryksjɔ̃] *nf* destruction.

désuet, -ète [dezɥɛ, ɛt] *adj* [expression, coutume] obsolete; [style, tableau] outmoded.

désuni, -e [dezyni] *adj* divided.

détachable [detaʃabl] *adj* detachable, removable.

détachant, -e [detaʃɑ̃, ɑ̃t] *adj* stain-removing. ○ **détachant** *nm* stain remover.

détaché, -e [detaʃe] *adj* detached.

détachement [detaʃmɑ̃] *nm* [d'esprit] detachment. || [de fonctionnaire] secondment. || MIL detachment.

détacher [detaʃe] *vt* [enlever]: ~ **qqch (de)** [objet] to detach sthg (from). || [nettoyer] to remove stains from, to clean. || [délier] to undo; [cheveux] to untie. || ADMIN: ~ **qqn auprès de** to second sb to. ○ **se détacher** *vp* [tomber]: **se ~ (de)** to come off. || [se défaire] to come undone. || [ressortir]: **se ~ sur** to stand out on. || [se désintéresser]: **se ~ de qqn** to drift apart from sb.

détail [detaj] *nm* [précision] detail. || COMM: **le ~** retail. ○ **au détail** *loc adj* & *loc adv* retail. ○ **en détail** *loc adv* in detail.

détaillant, -e [detajɑ̃, ɑ̃t] *nm, f* retailer.

détaillé, -e [detaje] *adj* detailed.

détailler [detaje] *vt* [expliquer] to give details of. || [vendre] to retail.

détaler [detale] *vi* [personne] to clear out. || [animal] to bolt.

détartrant, -e [detartrɑ̃, ɑ̃t] *adj* descaling. ○ **détartrant** *nm* descaling agent.

détaxe [detaks] *nf*: ~ **(sur)** [suppression] removal of tax (from); [réduction] reduction in tax (on).

détecter [detɛkte] *vt* to detect.

détecteur, -trice [detɛktœr, tris] *adj* detecting, detector (*avant n*). ○ **détecteur** *nm* detector.

détection [detɛksjɔ̃] *nf* detection.

détective [detɛktiv] *nm* detective; ~ **privé** private detective.

déteindre [detɛ̃dr] *vi* to fade.

déteint, -e [detɛ̃, ɛ̃t] *pp* → **déteindre**.

dételer [detle] *vt* [cheval] to unharness.

détendre [detɑ̃dr] *vt* [corde] to loosen, to slacken. || [personne] to relax. ○ **se détendre** *vp* [se relâcher] to slacken; [atmosphère] to become more relaxed. || [se reposer] to relax.

détendu, -e [detɑ̃dy] **1** *pp* → **détendre**. **2** *adj* [personne] relaxed.

détenir [detnir] *vt* [objet] to have, to hold. || [personne] to detain, to hold.

détente [detɑ̃t] *nf* [de ressort] release. || [d'une arme] trigger. || [repos] relaxation.

détenteur, -trice [detɑ̃tœr, tris] *nm, f* [d'objet, de secret] possessor; [de prix, record] holder.

développer

détention [detãsjɔ̃] *nf* [possession] possession. || [emprisonnement] detention.

détenu, -e [detny] **1** *pp* → **détenir. 2** *adj* detained. **3** *nm, f* prisoner.

détergent, -e [detɛrʒã, ãt] *adj* detergent (*avant n*). ○ **détergent** *nm* detergent.

détérioration [deterjɔrasjɔ̃] *nf* [de bâtiment] deterioration; [de situation] worsening.

détériorer [deterjɔre] *vt* [abîmer] to damage. || [altérer] to ruin. ○ **se détériorer** *vp* [bâtiment] to deteriorate; [situation] to worsen.

déterminant, -e [detɛrminã, ãt] *adj* decisive, determining. ○ **déterminant** *nm* LING determiner.

détermination [detɛrminasjɔ̃] *nf* [résolution] decision.

déterminé, -e [detɛrmine] *adj* [quantité] given (*avant n*). || [expression] determined.

déterminer [detɛrmine] *vt* [préciser] to determine, to specify. || [provoquer] to bring about.

déterrer [detere] *vt* to dig up.

détestable [detɛstabl] *adj* dreadful.

détester [detɛste] *vt* to detest.

détonateur [detɔnatœr] *nm* TECHNOL detonator; *fig* trigger.

détoner [detɔne] *vi* to detonate.

détonner [detɔne] *vi* MUS to be out of tune; [couleur] to clash; [personne] to be out of place.

détour [detur] *nm* [crochet] detour. || [méandre] bend; **sans ~** *fig* directly.

détourné, -e [deturne] *adj* [dévié] indirect; *fig* roundabout (*avant n*).

détournement [deturnəmã] *nm* diversion; **~ d'avion** hijacking; **~ de fonds** embezzlement; **~ de mineur** corruption of a minor.

détourner [deturne] *vt* [dévier - gén] to divert; [- avion] to hijack. || [écarter]: **~ qqn de** to distract sb from, to divert sb from. || [tourner ailleurs] to turn away. || [argent] to embezzle. ○ **se détourner** *vp* to turn away; **se ~ de** *fig* to move away from.

détraquer [detrake] *vt fam* [dérégler] to break; *fig* to upset. ○ **se détraquer** *vp fam* [se dérégler] to go wrong; *fig* to become unsettled.

détresse [detrɛs] *nf* distress.

détriment [detrimã] ○ **au détriment de** *loc prép* to the detriment of.

détritus [detrity(s)] *nm* detritus.

détroit [detrwa] *nm* strait.

détromper [detrɔ̃pe] *vt* to disabuse.

détrôner [detrone] *vt* [souverain] to dethrone; *fig* to oust.

détruire [detrɥir] *vt* [démolir, éliminer] to destroy. || *fig* [anéantir] to ruin.

détruit, -e [detrɥi, ɥit] *pp* → **détruire.**

dette [dɛt] *nf* debt.

DEUG, Deug [dœg] (*abr de* **diplôme d'études universitaires générales**) *nm* university diploma taken after 2 years of arts courses.

deuil [dœj] *nm* [douleur, mort] bereavement; [vêtements, période] mourning (*U*); **porter le ~** to be in ou wear mourning.

deux [dø] **1** *adj num* two; **ses ~ fils** both his sons, his two sons. **2** *nm* two; **les ~** both; **par ~** in pairs; *voir aussi* **six.**

deuxième [døzjɛm] *adj num, nm & nmf* second; *voir aussi* **sixième.**

deux-pièces [døpjɛs] *nm inv* [appartement] two-room flat *Br* ou apartment *Am.* || [bikini] two-piece (swimming costume).

deux-points [døpwɛ̃] *nm inv* colon.

deux-roues [døru] *nm inv* two-wheeled vehicle.

dévaler [devale] *vt* to run down.

dévaliser [devalize] *vt* [cambrioler - maison] to ransack; [- personne] to rob.

dévaloriser [devalɔrize] *vt* [monnaie] to devalue. || [personne] to run ou put down. ○ **se dévaloriser** *vp* [monnaie] to fall in value. || [personne] *fig* to run ou put o.s. down.

dévaluation [devalɥasjɔ̃] *nf* devaluation.

dévaluer [devalɥe] *vt* to devalue. ○ **se dévaluer** *vp* to devalue.

devancer [dəvãse] *vt* [précéder] to arrive before. || [anticiper] to anticipate.

devant [dəvã] **1** *prép* [en face de] in front of. || [en avant de] ahead of, in front of. || [en présence de, face à] in the face of. **2** *adv* [en face] in front. || [en avant] in front, ahead; **prendre les ~s** to make the first move. ○ **de devant** *loc adj* [pattes, roues] front (*avant n*).

devanture [dəvãtyr] *nf* shop window.

dévaster [devaste] *vt* to devastate.

développement [devlɔpmã] *nm* [gén] development. || PHOT developing.

développer [devlɔpe] *vt* to develop; [industrie, commerce] to expand. ○ **se développer** *vp* [s'épanouir] to spread. || ÉCON to grow, to expand.

devenir [dəvnir] *vi* to become; **que devenez-vous?** *fig* how are you doing?

devenu, **-e** [dəvny] *pp* → devenir.

dévergondé, **-e** [devɛrgɔ̃de] **1** *adj* shameless, wild. **2** *nm*, *f* shameless person.

déverser [devɛrse] *rt* [liquide] to pour out. ‖ [ordures] to tip (out).

déviation [devjasjɔ̃] *nf* [gén] deviation. ‖ [d'itinéraire] diversion.

dévier [devje] **1** *vi*: ~ **de** to deviate from. **2** *rt* to divert.

devin, **devineresse** [dəvɛ̃, dəvinrɛs] *nm*, *f*: **je ne suis pas ~!** I'm not psychic!

deviner [dəvine] *rt* to guess.

devinette [dəvinɛt] *nf* riddle.

devis [dəvi] *nm* estimate; **faire un ~** to (give an) estimate.

dévisager [devizaʒe] *rt* to stare at.

devise [dəviz] *nf* [formule] motto. ‖ [monnaie] currency. ○ **devises** *nfpl* [argent] currency (*U*).

dévisser [devise] *rt* to unscrew.

dévoiler [devwale] *rt* to unveil; *fig* to reveal.

devoir [dəvwar] **1** *nm* [obligation] duty. ‖ SCOL homework (*U*); **faire ses ~s** to do one's homework. **2** *rt* [argent, respect]: ~ **qqch (à qqn)** to owe (sb) sthg. ‖ [marque l'obligation]: ~ **faire qqch** to have to do sthg; **je dois partir à l'heure ce soir** I have to ou must leave on time tonight; **tu devrais faire attention** you should be ou ought to be careful. ‖ [marque la probabilité]: **il doit faire chaud là-bas** it must be hot over there. ‖ [marque le futur, l'intention]: ~ **faire qqch** to be (due) to do sthg, to be going to do sthg; **elle doit arriver à 6 heures** she is due to arrive at 6 o'clock; **je dois voir mes parents ce week-end** I'm seeing ou going to see my parents this weekend. ‖ [être destiné à]: **cela devait arriver** it had to happen, it was bound to happen. ○ **se devoir** *vp*: **se ~ de faire qqch** to be duty-bound to do sthg; **comme il se doit** as is proper.

dévolu, **-e** [devɔly] *adj sout*: ~ **à** allotted to. ○ **dévolu** *nm*: **jeter son ~ sur** to set one's sights on.

dévorer [devɔre] *rt* to devour.

dévotion [devɔsjɔ̃] *nf* devotion; **avec ~** [prier] devoutly; [soigner, aimer] devotedly.

dévoué, **-e** [devwe] *adj* devoted.

dévouement [devumɑ̃] *nm* devotion.

dévouer [devwe] ○ **se dévouer** *vp* [se consacrer]: **se ~ à** to devote o.s. to. ‖ *fig*

[se sacrifier]: **se ~ pour qqch/pour faire qqch** to sacrifice o.s. for sthg/to do sthg.

devrai, **devras** *etc* → devoir.

dextérité [dɛksterite] *nf* dexterity, skill.

diabète [djabɛt] *nm* diabetes (*U*).

diabétique [djabetik] *nmf & adj* diabetic.

diable [djabl] *nm* devil.

diabolique [djabɔlik] *adj* diabolical.

diabolo [djabɔlo] *nm* [boisson] fruit cordial and lemonade; ~ **menthe** mint (cordial) and lemonade.

diadème [djadɛm] *nm* diadem.

diagnostic [djagnɔstik] *nm* MÉD & *fig* diagnosis.

diagnostiquer [djagnɔstike] *rt* MÉD & *fig* to diagnose.

diagonale [djagɔnal] *nf* diagonal.

dialecte [djalɛkt] *nm* dialect.

dialogue [djalɔg] *nm* discussion.

dialoguer [djalɔge] *vi* [converser] to converse. ‖ INFORM to interact.

diamant [djamɑ̃] *nm* [pierre] diamond.

diamètre [djamɛtr] *nm* diameter.

diapason [djapazɔ̃] *nm* [instrument] tuning fork.

diapositive [djapozitiv] *nf* slide.

diarrhée [djare] *nf* diarrhoea.

dictateur [diktatœr] *nm* dictator.

dictature [diktatyr] *nf* dictatorship.

dictée [dikte] *nf* dictation.

dicter [dikte] *rt* to dictate.

diction [diksjɔ̃] *nf* diction.

dictionnaire [diksjɔnɛr] *nm* dictionary.

dicton [diktɔ̃] *nm* saying, dictum.

dièse [djɛz] **1** *adj* sharp; **do/fa ~** C/F sharp. **2** *nm* sharp.

diesel [djezɛl] *adj inv* diesel.

diète [djɛt] *nf* diet.

diététicien, **-ienne** [djetetisjɛ̃, jɛn] *nm*, *f* dietician.

diététique [djetetik] **1** *nf* dietetics (*U*). **2** *adj* [produit, magasin] health (*avant n*).

dieu, **-x** [djø] *nm* god. ○ **Dieu** *nm* God; **mon Dieu!** my God!

diffamation [difamasjɔ̃] *nf* [écrite] libel; [orale] slander.

différé, **-e** [difere] *adj* recorded. ○ **différé** *nm*: **en ~** TÉLÉ recorded.

différence [diferɑ̃s] *nf* difference.

différencier [diferɑ̃sje] *rt*: ~ **qqch de qqch** to differentiate sthg from sthg. ○ **se différencier** *vp*: **se ~ de** to be different from.

différend [diferɑ̃] *nm* [désaccord] difference of opinion.

différent, -e [diferɑ̃, ɑ̃t] *adj*: ~ (de) different (from).

différer [difere] 1 *vt* [retarder] to postpone. 2 *vi*: ~ de to differ from, to be different from.

difficile [difisil] *adj* difficult.

difficilement [difisilmɑ̃] *adv* with difficulty.

difficulté [difikylte] *nf* [complexité, peine] difficulty. || [obstacle] problem.

difforme [difɔrm] *adj* deformed.

diffuser [difyze] *vt* [lumière] to diffuse. || [émission] to broadcast. || [livres] to distribute.

diffuseur [difyzœr] *nm* [appareil] diffuser. || [de livres] distributor.

diffusion [difyzjɔ̃] *nf* [d'émission, d'onde] broadcast. || [de livres] distribution.

digérer [diʒere] 1 *vi* to digest. 2 *vt* [repas, connaissance] to digest. || *fam fig* [désagrément] to put up with.

digestif, -ive [diʒestif, iv] *adj* digestive. ○ **digestif** *nm* liqueur.

digestion [diʒestjɔ̃] *nf* digestion.

digital, -e, -aux [diʒital, o] *adj* TECHNOL digital. || → **empreinte**.

digne [diɲ] *adj* [honorable] dignified. || [méritant]: ~ de worthy of.

dignité [diɲite] *nf* dignity.

digression [digresjɔ̃] *nf* digression.

digue [dig] *nf* dike.

dilapider [dilapide] *vt* to squander.

dilater [dilate] *vt* to dilate.

dilemme [dilɛm] *nm* dilemma.

diligence [diliʒɑ̃s] *nf* HIST & *sout* diligence.

diluant [dilyɑ̃] *nm* thinner.

diluer [dilye] *vt* to dilute.

diluvien, -ienne [dilyvjɛ̃, jɛn] *adj* torrential.

dimanche [dimɑ̃ʃ] *nm* Sunday; *voir aussi* **samedi**.

dimension [dimɑ̃sjɔ̃] *nf* [mesure] dimension. || [taille] dimensions (*pl*), size. || *fig* [importance] magnitude.

diminuer [diminɥe] 1 *vt* [réduire] to diminish, to reduce. 2 *vi* [intensité] to diminish, to decrease.

diminutif, -ive [diminytif, iv] *adj* diminutive. ○ **diminutif** *nm* diminutive.

diminution [diminysjɔ̃] *nf* diminution.

dinde [dɛ̃d] *nf* [animal] turkey. || *péj* [femme] stupid woman.

dindon [dɛ̃dɔ̃] *nm* turkey; **être le ~ de la farce** *fig* to be made a fool of.

dîner [dine] 1 *vi* to dine. 2 *nm* dinner.

dingue [dɛ̃g] *fam* 1 *adj* [personne] crazy. || [histoire] incredible. 2 *nmf* loony.

dinosaure [dinozɔr] *nm* dinosaur.

diplomate [diplɔmat] 1 *nmf* [ambassadeur] diplomat. 2 *adj* diplomatic.

diplomatie [diplɔmasi] *nf* diplomacy.

diplomatique [diplɔmatik] *adj* diplomatic.

diplôme [diplom] *nm* diploma.

diplômé, -e [diplome] 1 *adj*: être ~ de/en to be a graduate of/in. 2 *nm, f* graduate.

dire [dir] *vt*: ~ qqch (à qqn) [parole] to say sthg (to sb); [vérité, mensonge, secret] to tell (sb) sthg; ~ à qqn de faire qqch to tell sb to do sthg; **il m'a dit que** ... he told me (that) ...; ~ **du bien/du mal (de)** to speak well/ill (of); **que dirais-tu de ...?** what would you say to ...?; **qu'en dis-tu?** what do you think of (it)?; **on dirait que** ... it looks as if ...; **on dirait de la soie** it looks like silk, you'd think it was silk; **ça ne me dit rien** [pas envie] I don't fancy that; [jamais entendu] I've never heard of it. ○ **se dire** *vp* [penser] to think (to o.s.). || [s'employer]: **ça ne se dit pas** [par décence] you mustn't say that; [par usage] people don't say that, nobody says that. || [se traduire]: «**chat**» **se dit «gato» en espagnol** the Spanish for "cat" is "gato". ○ **cela dit** *loc adv* having said that. ○ **dis donc** *loc adv fam* so; [au fait] by the way; [à qqn qui exagère] look here!

direct, -e [dirɛkt] *adj* direct. ○ **direct** *nm* BOXE jab. || [train] direct train. || RADIO & TÉLÉ: **en ~** live.

directement [dirɛktəmɑ̃] *adv* directly.

directeur, -trice [dirɛktœr, tris] *nm, f* director, manager; ~ **général** general manager, managing director *Br*, chief executive officer *Am*.

direction [dirɛksjɔ̃] *nf* [gestion, ensemble des cadres] management. || [orientation] direction; **en** ou **dans la ~ de** in the direction of. || AUTOM steering.

directive [dirɛktiv] *nf* directive.

directrice → **directeur**.

dirigeable [diriʒabl] *nm*: (**ballon**) ~ airship.

dirigeant, -e [diriʒɑ̃, ɑ̃t] 1 *adj* ruling. 2 *nm, f* [de pays] leader; [d'entreprise] manager.

diriger [diriʒe] *vt* [mener - entreprise] to run, to manage; [- orchestre] to conduct; [- film, acteurs] to direct; [- recherches, projet] to supervise. || [conduire] to steer. || [orienter] : ~ qqch sur/vers to aim sthg at/towards. ○ **se diriger** *vp* : se ~ vers to go ou head towards.

discernement [disɛrnəmɑ̃] *nm* [jugement] discernment.

discerner [disɛrne] *vt* [distinguer] : ~ qqch de to distinguish sthg from. || [deviner] to discern.

disciple [disipl] *nmf* disciple.

disciplinaire [disipliner] *adj* disciplinary.

discipline [disiplin] *nf* discipline.

discipliner [disipline] *vt* [personne] to discipline; [cheveux] to control.

disco [disko] *nm* disco (music).

discontinu, -e [diskɔ̃tiny] *adj* [ligne] broken; [bruit, effort] intermittent.

discordant, -e [diskɔrdɑ̃, ɑ̃t] *adj* discordant.

discorde [diskɔrd] *nf* discord.

discothèque [diskɔtɛk] *nf* [boîte de nuit] discothèque. || [de prêt] record library.

discourir [diskurir] *vi* to talk at length.

discours [diskur] *nm* [allocution] speech.

discréditer [diskredite] *vt* to discredit.

discret, -ète [diskrɛ, ɛt] *adj* [gén] discreet; [réservé] reserved.

discrètement [diskrɛtmɑ̃] *adv* discreetly.

discrétion [diskresjɔ̃] *nf* [réserve, tact, silence] discretion.

discrimination [diskriminasjɔ̃] *nf* discrimination; sans ~ indiscriminately.

discriminatoire [diskriminatwar] *adj* discriminatory.

disculper [diskylpe] *vt* to exonerate. ○ **se disculper** *vp* to exonerate o.s.

discussion [diskysjɔ̃] *nf* [conversation, examen] discussion. || [contestation, altercation] argument.

discutable [diskytabl] *adj* [contestable] questionable.

discuter [diskyte] 1 *vt* [débattre] : ~ (de) qqch to discuss sthg. || [contester] to dispute. 2 *vi* [parlementer] to discuss. || [converser] to talk. || [contester] to argue.

diseur, -euse [dizœr, øz] *nm, f* : ~ de bonne aventure fortune-teller.

disgracieux, -ieuse [disgrasjø, jøz] *adj* [laid] plain.

disjoncteur [disʒɔ̃ktœr] *nm* trip switch, circuit breaker.

disloquer [disləke] *vt* MÉD to dislocate. || [machine, empire] to dismantle. ○ **se disloquer** *vp* [machine] to fall apart ou to pieces; *fig* [empire] to break up.

disparaître [disparɛtr] *vi* [gén] to disappear, to vanish. || [mourir] to die.

disparité [disparite] *nf* [différence - d'éléments] disparity; [- de couleurs] mismatch.

disparition [disparisjɔ̃] *nf* [gén] disappearance; [d'espèce] extinction; en voie de ~ endangered. || [mort] passing.

disparu, -e [dispary] 1 *pp* → disparaître. 2 *nm, f* dead person, deceased.

dispensaire [dispɑ̃sɛr] *nm* community clinic *Br*, free clinic *Am*.

dispense [dispɑ̃s] *nf* [exemption] exemption.

dispenser [dispɑ̃se] *vt* [distribuer] to dispense. || [exempter] : ~ qqn de qqch [corvée] to excuse sb sthg, to let sb off sthg.

disperser [dispɛrse] *vt* to scatter (about ou around); [collection, brume, foule] to break up; *fig* [efforts, forces] to dissipate, to waste. ○ **se disperser** *vp* [feuilles, cendres] to scatter; [brume, foule] to break up, to clear. || [personne] to take on too much at once, to spread o.s. too thin.

disponibilité [disponibilite] *nf* [de choses] availability. || [de fonctionnaire] leave of absence. || [d'esprit] alertness, receptiveness.

disponible [disponibl] *adj* [place, personne] available, free.

disposé, -e [dispoze] *adj* : être ~ à faire qqch to be prepared ou willing to do sthg; être bien ~ envers qqn to be well-disposed towards ou to sb.

disposer [dispoze] 1 *vt* [arranger] to arrange. 2 *vi* : ~ de [moyens, argent] to have available (to one), to have at one's disposal; [chose] to have the use of; [temps] to have free ou available.

dispositif [dispozitif] *nm* [mécanisme] device, mechanism.

disposition [dispozisjɔ̃] *nf* [arrangement] arrangement. || [disponibilité] : à la ~ de at the disposal of, available to. ○ **dispositions** *nfpl* [mesures] arrangements, measures. || [dons] : avoir des ~s pour to have a gift for.

disproportionné, -e [disprɔpɔrsjɔne] *adj* out of proportion.

dispute [dispyt] *nf* argument, quarrel.

disputer [dispyte] *vt* [SPORT - course] to run; [- match] to play. ○ **se disputer** *vp* [se quereller] to quarrel, to fight. || [lutter pour] to fight over ou for.

disquaire [disker] *nm* record dealer.

disqualifier [diskalifje] *vt* to disqualify.

disque [disk] *nm* MUS record; [vidéo] video disc; ~ **compact** ou **laser** compact disc. || ANAT disc. || INFORM disk; ~ **dur** hard disk. || SPORT discus.

disquette [disket] *nf* diskette, floppy disk; ~ **système** system diskette.

dissection [diseksjɔ̃] *nf* dissection.

dissemblable [disɑ̃blabl] *adj* dissimilar.

disséminer [disemine] *vt* [graines, maisons] to scatter; [troupes] to spread (out).

disséquer [diseke] *vt* *litt* & *fig* to dissect.

dissertation [disɛrtasjɔ̃] *nf* essay.

dissident, -e [disidɑ̃, ɑ̃t] *adj* & *nm, f* dissident.

dissimulation [disimylasjɔ̃] *nf* [hypocrisie] duplicity.

dissimuler [disimyle] *vt* to conceal. ○ **se dissimuler** *vp* [se cacher] to conceal o.s., to hide.

dissipation [disipasjɔ̃] *nf* [indiscipline] indiscipline, misbehaviour.

dissiper [disipe] *vt* [chasser] to break up, to clear; *fig* to dispel. || [distraire] to lead astray. ○ **se dissiper** *vp* [brouillard, fumée] to clear. || [élève] to misbehave. || *fig* [malaise, fatigue] to go away; [doute] to be dispelled.

dissocier [disɔsje] *vt* [séparer] to separate, to distinguish.

dissolution [disɔlysjɔ̃] *nf* JUR dissolution. || [mélange] dissolving.

dissolvant, -e [disɔlvɑ̃, ɑ̃t] *adj* solvent. ○ **dissolvant** *nm* [solvant] solvent; [pour vernis à ongles] nail varnish remover.

dissoudre [disudr] *vt*: (**faire**) ~ to dissolve. ○ **se dissoudre** *vp* [substance] to dissolve.

dissous, -oute [disu, ut] *pp* → **dissoudre**.

dissuader [disɥade] *vt* to dissuade.

dissuasion [disɥazjɔ̃] *nf* dissuasion; **force de** ~ deterrent (effect).

distance [distɑ̃s] *nf* [éloignement] distance; **à** ~ at a distance; [télécommander] by remote control; **à une ~ de 300 mètres** 300 metres away. || [intervalle] interval. || [écart] gap.

distancer [distɑ̃se] *vt* to outstrip.

distant, -e [distɑ̃, ɑ̃t] *adj* [éloigné]: **des villes ~es de 10 km** towns 10 km apart. || [froid] distant.

distendre [distɑ̃dr] *vt* [ressort, corde] to stretch. ○ **se distendre** *vp* to distend.

distendu, -e [distɑ̃dy] *pp* → **distendre**.

distiller [distile] *vt* [alcool] to distil; [pétrole] to refine.

distinct, -e [distɛ̃, ɛ̃kt] *adj* distinct.

distinctement [distɛ̃ktəmɑ̃] *adv* distinctly, clearly.

distinctif, -ive [distɛ̃ktif, iv] *adj* distinctive.

distinction [distɛ̃ksjɔ̃] *nf* distinction.

distingué, -e [distɛ̃ge] *adj* distinguished.

distinguer [distɛ̃ge] *vt* [différencier] to tell apart, to distinguish. || [percevoir] to make out, to distinguish. || [rendre différent]: ~ **de** to distinguish from, to set apart from. ○ **se distinguer** *vp* [se différencier]: **se** ~ (**de**) to stand out (from). || [s'illustrer] to distinguish o.s.

distraction [distraksjɔ̃] *nf* [inattention] inattention, absent-mindedness. || [passe-temps] leisure activity.

distraire [distrɛr] *vt* [déranger] to distract. || [divertir] to amuse, to entertain. ○ **se distraire** *vp* to amuse o.s.

distrait, -e [distrɛ, ɛt] **1** *pp* → **distraire. 2** *adj* absent-minded.

distribuer [distribɥe] *vt* to distribute; [courrier] to deliver; [ordres] to give out; [cartes] to deal.

distributeur, -trice [distribytœr, tris] *nm, f* distributor. ○ **distributeur** *nm* AUTOM & COMM distributor. || [machine]: ~ (**automatique**) **de billets** BANQUE cash machine, cash dispenser; TRANSPORT ticket machine; ~ **de boissons** drinks machine.

distribution [distribysjɔ̃] *nf* [répartition, diffusion, disposition] distribution; ~ **des prix** SCOL prize-giving. || CIN & THÉÂTRE cast.

dit, dite [di, dit] **1** *pp* → **dire. 2** *adj* [appelé] known as. || JUR said, above. || [fixé]: **à l'heure ~e** at the appointed time.

divagation [divagasjɔ̃] *nf* wandering.

divaguer [divage] *vi* to ramble.

divan [divɑ̃] *nm* divan (*seat*).

divergence [divɛrʒɑ̃s] *nf* divergence, difference; [d'opinions] difference.

diverger [divɛrʒe] *vi* to diverge; [opinions] to differ.

divers, -e [divɛr, ɛrs] *adj* [différent] different, various. || [disparate] diverse. || (*avant n*) [plusieurs] various, several.

diversifier [divɛrsifje] *vt* to vary, to diversify. ○ **se diversifier** *vp* to diversify.

diversion [divɛrsjɔ̃] *nf* diversion.

diversité [divɛrsite] *nf* diversity.

divertir [divɛrtir] *vt* [distraire] to entertain, to amuse. ○ **se divertir** *vp* to amuse o.s., to entertain o.s.

divertissement [divɛrtismɑ̃] *nm* [passe-temps] form of relaxation.

divin, -e [divɛ̃, in] *adj* divine.

divinité [divinite] *nf* divinity.

diviser [divize] *vt* [gén] to divide, to split up. || MATHS to divide; ~ **8 par 4** to divide 8 by 4.

division [divizjɔ̃] *nf* division.

divorce [divɔrs] *nm* JUR divorce.

divorcé, -e [divɔrse] **1** *adj* divorced. **2** *nm, f* divorcee, divorced person.

divorcer [divɔrse] *vi* to divorce.

divulguer [divylge] *vt* to divulge.

dix [dis] *adj num & nm* ten; *voir aussi* **six**.

dix-huit [dizɥit] *adj num & nm* eighteen; *voir aussi* **six**.

dix-huitième [dizɥitjɛm] *adj num, nm & nmf* eighteenth; *voir aussi* **sixième**.

dixième [dizjɛm] *adj num, nm & nmf* tenth; *voir aussi* **sixième**.

dix-neuf [diznœf] *adj num & nm* nineteen; *voir aussi* **six**.

dix-neuvième [diznœvjɛm] *adj num, nm & nmf* nineteenth; *voir aussi* **sixième**.

dix-sept [disɛt] *adj num & nm* seventeen; *voir aussi* **six**.

dix-septième [disɛtjɛm] *adj num, nm & nmf* seventeenth; *voir aussi* **sixième**.

dizaine [dizɛn] *nf* [environ dix]: **une ~ de** about ten.

do [do] *nm inv* MUS C; [chanté] doh.

doc [dɔk] (*abr de* **documentation**) *nf* literature, brochures (*pl*).

docile [dɔsil] *adj* [obéissant] docile.

dock [dɔk] *nm* [bassin] dock. || [hangar] warehouse.

docker [dɔkɛr] *nm* docker.

docteur [dɔktœr] *nm* [médecin] doctor. || UNIV: ~ **ès lettres/sciences** ≃ PhD.

doctorat [dɔktɔra] *nm* [grade] doctorate.

doctrine [dɔktrin] *nf* doctrine.

document [dɔkymɑ̃] *nm* document.

documentaire [dɔkymɑ̃tɛr] *nm & adj* documentary.

documentaliste [dɔkymɑ̃talist] *nmf* [d'archives] archivist; PRESSE & TÉLÉ researcher.

documentation [dɔkymɑ̃tasjɔ̃] *nf* [travail] research. || [brochures] documentation.

documenter [dɔkymɑ̃te] ○ **se documenter** *vp* to do some research.

dodo [dodo] *nm fam* beddy-byes; **faire ~** to sleep.

dodu, -e [dody] *adj fam* [enfant, joue, bras] chubby; [animal] plump.

dogme [dɔgm] *nm* dogma.

dogue [dɔg] *nm* mastiff.

doigt [dwa] *nm* finger; **un ~ de** (just) a drop OU finger of; **montrer qqch du ~ to** point at sthg; ~ **de pied** toe.

dois → **devoir**.

doive → **devoir**.

dollar [dɔlar] *nm* dollar.

domaine [dɔmɛn] *nm* [propriété] estate. || [secteur, champ d'activité] field, domain.

dôme [dom] *nm* ARCHIT dome.

domestique [dɔmestik] **1** *nmf* [domestic] servant. **2** *adj* family (*avant n*); [travaux] household (*avant n*).

domestiquer [dɔmestike] *vt* [animal] to domesticate.

domicile [dɔmisil] *nm* [gén] (place of) residence; **travailler à ~** to work from OU at home; **ils livrent à ~** they do deliveries.

dominant, -e [dɔminɑ̃, ɑ̃t] *adj* [qui prévaut] dominant.

domination [dɔminasjɔ̃] *nf* [autorité] domination, dominion.

dominer [dɔmine] **1** *vt* [surplomber, avoir de l'autorité sur] to dominate. || [surpasser] to outclass. || [maîtriser] to control, to master. || *fig* [connaître] to master. **2** *vi* [prédominer] to predominate. || [triompher] to be on top, to hold sway. ○ **se dominer** *vp* to control o.s.

Dominique [dɔminik] *nf*: **la ~** Dominica.

domino [dɔmino] *nm* domino.

dommage [dɔmaʒ] *nm* [préjudice] harm (*U*); ~**s et intérêts**, ~**s-intérêts** damages; **c'est ~ que** (+ *subjonctif*) it's a pity OU shame (that). || [dégâts] damage (*U*).

dompter [dɔ̃te] *vt* [animal, fauve] to tame.

dompteur, -euse [dɔ̃tœr, øz] *nm, f* [de fauves] tamer.

DOM-TOM [dɔmtɔm] (*abr de* **départements d'outre-mer/territoires d'outre-**

mer) *nmpl* French overseas *départements and territories.*

don [dɔ̃] *nm* [cadeau] gift. ‖ [aptitude] knack.

donateur, -trice [dɔnatœr, tris] *nm, f* donor.

donation [dɔnasjɔ̃] *nf* settlement.

donc [dɔ̃k] *conj* so; **je disais ~ ...** so as I was saying ...; **allons ~!** come on!; **tais-toi ~!** will you be quiet!

donjon [dɔ̃ʒɔ̃] *nm* keep.

donné, -e [dɔne] *adj* given; **étant ~ que** given that, considering (that). ○ **donnée** *nf* INFORM & MATHS datum, piece of data; **~es numériques** numerical data. ‖ [élément] fact, particular.

donner [dɔne] **1** *vt* [gén] to give; [se débarrasser de] to give away; **~ qqch à qqn** to give sb sthg, to give sthg to sb; **~ sa voiture à réparer** to leave one's car to be repaired; **quel âge lui donnes-tu?** how old do you think he/she is? **2** *vi* [s'ouvrir]: **~ sur** to look out onto. ‖ [produire] to produce, to yield.

donneur, -euse [dɔnœr, øz] *nm, f* MÉD donor. ‖ CARTES dealer.

dont [dɔ̃] *pron rel* [complément de verbe ou d'adjectif]: **la personne ~ tu parles** the person you're speaking about, the person about whom you are speaking; **l'accident ~ il est responsable** the accident for which he is responsible. ‖ [complément de nom ou de pronom - relatif à l'objet] of which, whose; [- relatif à personne] whose; **la boîte ~ le couvercle est jaune** the box whose lid is yellow, the box with the yellow lid; **celui ~ les parents sont divorcés** the one whose parents are divorced. ‖ [indiquant la partie d'un tout]: **plusieurs personnes ont téléphoné, ~ ton frère** several people phoned, one of which was your brother ou among them was your brother.

dopage [dɔpaʒ] *nm* doping.

doper [dɔpe] *vt* to dope. ○ **se doper** *vp* to take stimulants.

dorade [dɔrad] = **daurade.**

doré, -e [dɔre] *adj* [couvert de dorure] gilded, gilt. ‖ [couleur] golden.

dorénavant [dɔrenavɑ̃] *adv* from now on, in future.

dorer [dɔre] *vt* [couvrir d'or] to gild. ‖ [peau] to tan. ‖ CULIN to glaze.

dorloter [dɔrlɔte] *vt* to pamper, to cosset.

dormir [dɔrmir] *vi* [sommeiller] to sleep. ‖ [rester inactif - personne] to slack, to

stand around (doing nothing); [- capitaux] to lie idle.

dortoir [dɔrtwar] *nm* dormitory.

dos [do] *nm* back; **de ~** from behind; **«voir au ~»** "see over"; **~ crawlé** backstroke.

DOS, Dos [dɔs] (*abr de* **Disk Operating System**) *nm* DOS.

dosage [dozaʒ] *nm* [de médicament] dose; [d'ingrédient] amount.

dos-d'âne [dodɑn] *nm* bump.

dose [doz] *nf* [quantité de médicament] dose. ‖ [quantité] share; **forcer la ~** *fam fig* to overdo it.

doser [doze] *vt* [médicament, ingrédient] to measure out; *fig* to weigh up.

dossard [dɔsar] *nm* number (*on competitor's back*).

dossier [dɔsje] *nm* [de fauteuil] back. ‖ [documents] file, dossier. ‖ [classeur] file, folder. ‖ *fig* [question] question.

dot [dɔt] *nf* dowry.

doter [dɔte] *vt* [pourvoir]: **~ de** [talent] to endow with; [machine] to equip with.

douane [dwan] *nf* [service, lieu] customs (*pl*); **passer la ~** to go through customs.

douanier, -ière [dwanje, jɛr] **1** *adj* customs (*avant n*). **2** *nm, f* customs officer.

doublage [dublaʒ] *nm* [renforcement] lining. ‖ [de film] dubbing.

double [dubl] **1** *adj* double. **2** *adv* double. **3** *nm* [quantité]: **le ~** double. ‖ [copie] copy; **en ~** in duplicate. ‖ TENNIS doubles (*pl*).

doublement [dubləmɑ̃] *adv* doubly.

doubler [duble] **1** *vt* [multiplier] to double. ‖ [renforcer]: **~ (de)** to line (with). ‖ [dépasser] to overtake. ‖ [film, acteur] to dub. **2** *vi* [véhicule] to overtake. ‖ [augmenter] to double.

doublure [dublyr] *nf* [renforcement] lining. ‖ CIN stand-in.

douce → **doux.**

doucement [dusmɑ̃] *adv* [descendre] carefully; [frapper] gently. ‖ [parler] softly.

douceur [dusœr] *nf* [de saveur, parfum] sweetness. ‖ [d'éclairage, de peau, de musique] softness. ‖ [de climat] mildness. ‖ [de caractère] gentleness. ○ **douceurs** *nfpl* [friandises] sweets.

douche [duʃ] *nf* [appareil, action] shower. ‖ *fam fig* [déception] letdown.

doucher [duʃe] *vt* [donner une douche à]: **~ qqn** to give sb a shower. ○ **se dou-**

cher *vp* to take or have a shower, to shower.

doué, -e [dwe] *adj* talented; **être ~ pour** to have a gift for.

douillet, -ette [dujɛ, ɛt] *adj* [confortable] snug, cosy. || [sensible] soft.

douloureux, -euse [dulurø, øz] *adj* [physiquement] painful. || [moralement] distressing. || [regard, air] sorrowful.

doute [dut] *nm* doubt. ○ **sans doute** *loc adv* no doubt; **sans aucun ~** without (a) doubt.

douter [dute] **1** *vt* [ne pas croire]: **~ que** (+ *subjonctif*) to doubt (that). **2** *vi* [ne pas avoir confiance]: **~ de qqn/de qqch** to doubt sb/sthg. || **~ de qqn/de qqch** to have doubts about sb/sthg. ○ **se douter** *vp*: **se ~ de qqch** to suspect sthg.

douteux, -euse [dutø, øz] *adj* [incertain] doubtful. || [contestable] questionable. || *péj* [mœurs] dubious; [personne] dubious-looking.

doux, douce [du, dus] *adj* [éclairage, peau, musique] soft. || [saveur, parfum] sweet. || [climat, condiment] mild. || [pente, regard, caractère] gentle.

douzaine [duzɛn] *nf* [douze] dozen. || [environ douze]: **une ~ de** about twelve.

douze [duz] *adj num & nm* twelve; *voir aussi* **six**.

douzième [duzjɛm] *adj num, nm & nmf* twelfth; *voir aussi* **sixième**.

doyen, -enne [dwajɛ̃, ɛn] *nm, f* [le plus ancien] most senior member.

Dr (*abr de* **Docteur**) Dr.

draconien, -ienne [drakɔnjɛ̃, jɛn] *adj* draconian.

dragée [draʒe] *nf* [confiserie] sugared almond. || [comprimé] pill.

dragon [dragɔ̃] *nm* [monstre, personne autoritaire] dragon. || [soldat] dragoon.

draguer [drage] *vt* [nettoyer] to dredge. || *fam* [personne] to chat up, to get off with.

dragueur, -euse [dragœr, øz] *nm, f fam* [homme] womanizer; **quelle dragueuse!** she's always chasing after men!

drainage [drɛnaʒ] *nm* draining.

drainer [drɛne] *vt* [terrain, plaie] to drain. || *fig* [attirer] to drain off.

dramatique [dramatik] **1** *nf* play. **2** *adj* THÉÂTRE dramatic. || [grave] tragic.

dramatiser [dramatize] *vt* [exagérer] to dramatize.

drame [dram] *nm* [catastrophe] tragedy; **faire un ~ de qqch** *fig* to make a drama of sthg. || LITTÉRATURE drama.

drap [dra] *nm* [de lit] sheet. || [tissu] woollen cloth.

drapeau, -x [drapo] *nm* flag; **être sous les ~x** *fig* to be doing military service.

draper [drape] *vt* to drape.

draperie [drapri] *nf* [tenture] drapery.

dresser [drese] *vt* [lever] to raise. || [faire tenir] to put up. || *sout* [construire] to erect. || [acte, liste, carte] to draw up; [procès-verbal] to make out. || [dompter] to train. || *fig* [opposer]: **~ qqn contre qqn** to set sb against sb. ○ **se dresser** *vp* [se lever] to stand up. || [s'élever] to rise (up); *fig* to stand; **se ~ contre qqch** to rise up against sthg.

dresseur, -euse [dresœr, øz] *nm, f* trainer.

dribbler [drible] SPORT *vi* to dribble.

drogue [drɔg] *nf* [stupéfiant & *fig*] drug; **la ~** drugs (*pl*).

drogué, -e [drɔge] **1** *adj* drugged. **2** *nm, f* drug addict.

droguer [drɔge] *vt* [victime] to drug. ○ **se droguer** *vp* [de stupéfiants] to take drugs.

droguerie [drɔgri] *nf* hardware shop.

droit, -e [drwa, drwat] *adj* [du côté droit] right. || [rectiligne, vertical, honnête] straight. ○ **droit 1** *adv* straight; **tout ~** straight ahead. **2** *nm* JUR law. || [prérogative] right; **avoir ~ à** to be entitled to; **avoir le ~ de faire qqch** to be allowed to do sthg; **être en ~ de faire qqch** to have a right to do sthg; **~ de vote** right to vote; **~s de l'homme** human rights. ○ **droite** *nf* [gén] right, right-hand side; **à ~ on** the right; **à ~e de** to the right of. || POLIT: **la ~e** the right (wing); **de ~e** right-wing.

droitier, -ière [drwatje, jɛr] **1** *adj* right-handed. **2** *nm, f* right-handed person, right-hander.

drôle [drol] *adj* [amusant] funny. || **~ de** [bizarre] funny; *fam* [remarquable] amazing.

dromadaire [drɔmadɛr] *nm* dromedary.

dru, -e [dry] *adj* thick.

du → **de**.

dû, due [dy] **1** *pp* → **devoir**. **2** *adj* due, owing. ○ **dû** *nm* due.

Dublin [dyblɛ̃] *n* Dublin.

duc [dyk] *nm* duke.

duchesse [dyʃɛs] *nf* duchess.

duel [dɥɛl] *nm* duel.

dûment [dymɑ̃] *adv* duly.

dune [dyn] *nf* dune.

duo [dɥo] *nm* MUS duet. || [couple] duo.

dupe [dyp] **1** *nf* dupe. **2** *adj* gullible.

duper [dype] *vt sout* to dupe, to take sb in.

duplex [dyplɛks] *nm* [appartement] duplex *Am*. ‖ RADIO & TÉLÉ link-up.

duplicata [dyplikata] *nm inv* duplicate.

dupliquer [dyplike] *vt* [document] to duplicate.

duquel [dykɛl] → **lequel**.

dur, -e [dyr] **1** *adj* [matière, personne, travail] hard; [carton] stiff. ‖ [viande] tough. ‖ [climat, punition, loi] harsh. **2** *nm, f fam*: ~ (à cuire) tough nut. ○ **dur** *adv* hard.

durable [dyrabl] *adj* lasting.

durant [dyrɑ̃] *prép* [pendant] for. ‖ [au cours de] during.

durcir [dyrsir] **1** *vt litt & fig* to harden. **2** *vi* to harden, to become hard.

durée [dyre] *nf* length.

durement [dyrmɑ̃] *adv* [violemment] hard, vigorously. ‖ [péniblement] severely. ‖ [méchamment] harshly.

durer [dyre] *vi* to last.

dureté [dyrte] *nf* [de matériau, de l'eau] hardness. ‖ [d'époque, de climat, de personne] harshness. ‖ [de punition] severity.

dus, dut *etc* → **devoir**.

DUT (*abr de* **diplôme universitaire de technologie**) *nm* university diploma in technology.

duvet [dyvɛ] *nm* [plumes, poils fins] down. ‖ [sac de couchage] sleeping bag.

dynamique [dinamik] *adj* dynamic.

dynamisme [dinamism] *nm* dynamism.

dynamite [dinamit] *nf* dynamite.

dynastie [dinasti] *nf* dynasty.

dyslexique [dislɛksik] *adj* dyslexic.

E

e, E [ə] *nm inv* e, E. ○ **E** (*abr de* **est**) E.

eau, -x [o] *nf* water; ~ douce/salée/de mer fresh/salt/sea water; ~ gazeuse/plate fizzy/still water; ~ courante running water; ~ minérale mineral water; ~ oxygénée hydrogen peroxide; ~ de toilette toilet water; **tomber à l'~** *fig* to fall through.

eau-de-vie [odvi] (*pl* **eaux-de-vie**) *nf* brandy.

ébahi, -e [ebai] *adj* staggered, astounded.

ébauche [eboʃ] *nf* [esquisse] sketch; *fig* outline; **l'~ d'un sourire** the ghost of a smile.

ébaucher [eboʃe] *vt* [esquisser] to rough out. ‖ *fig* [commencer]: ~ un geste to start to make a gesture.

ébène [ebɛn] *nf* ebony.

ébéniste [ebenist] *nm* cabinet-maker.

éberlué, -e [ebɛrlɥe] *adj* flabbergasted.

éblouir [ebluir] *vt* to dazzle.

éblouissement [ebluismɑ̃] *nm* [aveuglement] glare, dazzle. ‖ [vertige] dizziness. ‖ [émerveillement] amazement.

éborgner [ebɔrɲe] *vt*: ~ qqn to put sb's eye out.

éboueur [ebwœr] *nm* garbage collector *Am*.

ébouillanter [ebujɑ̃te] *vt* to scald.

éboulement [ebulmɑ̃] *nm* caving in, fall.

éboulis [ebuli] *nm* mass of fallen rocks.

ébouriffer [eburife] *vt* [cheveux] to ruffle.

ébranler [ebrɑ̃le] *vt* [bâtiment, opinion] to shake. ○ **s'ébranler** *vp* [train] to move off.

ébrécher [ebreʃe] *vt* [assiette, verre] to chip; *fam fig* to break into.

ébriété [ebrijete] *nf* drunkenness.

ébrouer [ebrue] ○ **s'ébrouer** *vp* [animal] to shake o.s.

ébruiter [ebrɥite] *vt* to spread.

ébullition [ebylisjɔ̃] *nf* [de liquide] boiling point. || [effervescence]: **en ~** *fig* in a state of agitation.

écaille [ekaj] *nf* [de poisson, reptile] scale; [de tortue] shell. || [de plâtre, peinture, vernis] flake. || [matière] tortoiseshell; **en ~** [lunettes] horn-rimmed.

écailler [ekaje] *vt* [poisson] to scale. || [huîtres] to open. ○ **s'écailler** *vp* to flake ou peel off.

écarlate [ekarlat] *adj & nf* scarlet.

écarquiller [ekarkije] *vt*: **~ les yeux** to stare wide-eyed.

écart [ekar] *nm* [espace] space. || [temps] gap. || [différence] difference. || [déviation]: **faire un ~** [personne] to step aside; [cheval] to shy; **être à l'~** to be in the background.

écarteler [ekartəle] *vt fig* to tear apart.

écartement [ekartəmɑ̃] *nm*: **~ entre** space between.

écarter [ekarte] *vt* [bras, jambes] to open, to spread; **~ qqch de** to move sthg away from. || [obstacle, danger] to brush aside. || [foule, rideaux] to push aside; [solution] to dismiss; **~ qqn de** to exclude sb from. ○ **s'écarter** *vp* [se séparer] to part. || [se détourner]: **s'~ de** to deviate from.

ecchymose [ekimoz] *nf* bruise.

ecclésiastique [eklezjastik] **1** *nm* clergyman. **2** *adj* ecclesiastical.

écervelé, -e [esɛrvəle] **1** *adj* scatty, scatterbrained. **2** *nm, f* scatterbrain.

échafaud [eʃafo] *nm* scaffold.

échafaudage [eʃafodaʒ] *nm* CONSTR scaffolding. || [amas] pile.

échalote [eʃalɔt] *nf* shallot.

échancrure [eʃɑ̃kryr] *nf* [de robe] low neckline. || [de côte] indentation.

échange [eʃɑ̃ʒ] *nm* [de choses] exchange; **en ~ (de)** in exchange (for).

échanger [eʃɑ̃ʒe] *vt* [troquer] to swap, to exchange. || [marchandise]: **~ qqch (contre)** to change sthg (for). || [communiquer] to exchange.

échantillon [eʃɑ̃tijɔ̃] *nm* [de produit, de population] sample; *fig* example.

échappatoire [eʃapatwar] *nf* way out.

échappement [eʃapmɑ̃] *nm* AUTOM exhaust; → **pot**.

échapper [eʃape] *vi*: **~ à** [personne, situation] to escape from; [danger, mort] to escape; [suj: détail, parole, sens] to escape. || [glisser]: **laisser ~** to let slip. ○ **s'échapper** *vp*: **~ (de)** to escape (from).

écharde [eʃard] *nf* splinter.

écharpe [eʃarp] *nf* scarf; **en ~** in a sling.

écharper [eʃarpe] *vt* to rip to pieces ou shreds.

échasse [eʃas] *nf* [de berger, oiseau] stilt.

échassier [eʃasje] *nm* wader.

échauffement [eʃofmɑ̃] *nm* SPORT warm-up.

échauffer [eʃofe] *vt* [chauffer] to overheat. || [exciter] to excite. || [énerver] to irritate. ○ **s'échauffer** *vp* SPORT to warm up. || *fig* [s'animer] to become heated.

échéance [eʃeɑ̃s] *nf* [délai] expiry; **à longue ~** in the long term. || [date] payment date; **arriver à ~** to fall due.

échéant [eʃeɑ̃] *adj*: **le cas ~** if necessary, if need be.

échec [eʃɛk] *nm* failure; **~ et mat** checkmate. ○ **échecs** *nmpl* chess (*U*).

échelle [eʃɛl] *nf* [objet] ladder. || [ordre de grandeur] scale.

échelon [eʃlɔ̃] *nm* [barreau] rung. || *fig* [niveau] level.

échelonner [eʃlɔne] *vt* [espacer] to spread out.

échevelé, -e [eʃəvle] *adj* [ébouriffé] dishevelled. || [frénétique] wild.

échine [eʃin] *nf* ANAT spine.

échiquier [eʃikje] *nm* JEU chessboard.

écho [eko] *nm* echo.

échographie [ekɔgrafi] *nf* [examen] ultrasound (scan).

échoir [eʃwar] *vi* [être dévolu]: **~ à** to fall to. || [expirer] to fall due.

échouer [eʃwe] *vi* [ne pas réussir] to fail; **~ à un examen** to fail an exam. ○ **s'échouer** *vp* [navire] to run aground.

échu, -e [eʃy] *pp* → **échoir**.

éclabousser [eklabuse] *vt* [suj: liquide] to spatter.

éclair [eklɛr] **1** *nm* [de lumière] flash of lightning. || *fig* [instant]: **~ de** flash of. **2** *adj inv*: **visite ~** flying visit; **guerre ~** blitzkrieg.

éclairage [eklɛraʒ] *nm* [lumière] lighting. || *fig* [point de vue] light.

éclaircie [eklɛrsi] *nf* bright interval, sunny spell.

éclaircir [eklɛrsir] *vt* [rendre plus clair] to lighten. || [rendre moins épais] to thin. || *fig* [clarifier] to clarify. ○ **s'éclaircir** *vp* [devenir plus clair] to clear. || [devenir moins épais] to thin. || [se clarifier] to become clearer.

éclaircissement [eklɛrsismɑ̃] *nm* [explication] explanation.

éclairer [eklere] *vt* [de lumière] to light up. ‖ [expliquer] to clarify. ○ **s'éclairer** *vp* [de lumière] to light one's way. ‖ [regard, visage] to light up. ‖ [rue, ville] to light up.

éclaireur [eklɛrœr] *nm* scout.

éclat [ekla] *nm* [de verre, d'os] splinter; [de pierre] chip. ‖ [de lumière] brilliance. ‖ [de couleur] vividness. ‖ [faste] splendour. ‖ [bruit] burst; ~ **de rire** burst of laughter; ~**s de voix** shouts. ‖ *loc*: **rire aux** ~**s** to roar ou shriek with laughter.

éclater [eklate] *vi* [exploser - pneu] to burst; [- verre] to shatter; [- obus] to explode; **faire** ~ [ballon] to burst; [pétard] to let off. ‖ [incendie, rires] to break out. ‖ *fig* [nouvelles, scandale] to break. ○ **s'éclater** *vp fam* to have a great time.

éclectique [eklɛktik] *adj* eclectic.

éclipse [eklips] *nf* ASTRON eclipse; ~ **de lune/soleil** eclipse of the moon/sun.

éclipser [eklipse] *vt* to eclipse. ○ **s'éclipser** *vp* ASTRON to go into eclipse. ‖ *fam* [s'esquiver] to slip away.

éclopé, -e [eklɔpe] **1** *adj* lame. **2** *nm, f* lame person.

éclore [eklɔr] *vi* [s'ouvrir - fleur] to open out, to blossom; [- œuf] to hatch.

éclos, -e [eklo, oz] *pp* → **éclore**.

écluse [eklyz] *nf* lock.

écœurant, -e [ekœrɑ̃, ɑ̃t] *adj* [gén] disgusting. ‖ [démoralisant] sickening.

écœurer [ekœre] *vt* [dégoûter] to sicken, to disgust. ‖ *fig* [indigner] to sicken. ‖ [décourager] to discourage.

école [ekɔl] *nf* [gén] school; ~ **maternelle** nursery school; ~ **normale** ≈ teacher training college *Br*, ≈ teachers college *Am*; ~ **primaire/secondaire** primary/secondary school *Br*, grade/high school *Am*; **grande** ~ *specialist training establishment, entered by competitive exam and highly prestigious*; **faire l'**~ **buissonnière** to play truant *Br* ou hooky *Am*; **faire** ~ to be accepted. ‖ [éducation] schooling; **l'**~ **privée** private education.

écolier, -ière [ekɔlje, jɛr] *nm, f* [élève] pupil.

écolo [ekɔlɔ] *nmf fam* ecologist; **les** ~**s** the Greens.

écologie [ekɔlɔʒi] *nf* ecology.

écologiste [ekɔlɔʒist] *nmf* ecologist.

éconduire [ekɔ̃dɥir] *vt* [repousser - de-

mande] to dismiss; [- visiteur, soupirant] to show to the door.

économe [ekɔnɔm] **1** *nmf* bursar. **2** *adj* careful, thrifty.

économie [ekɔnɔmi] *nf* [science] economics (*U*). ‖ POLIT economy; ~ **de marché** market economy. ‖ [parcimonie] economy, thrift. ‖ (*gén pl*) [pécule] savings (*pl*); **faire des** ~**s** to save up.

économique [ekɔnɔmik] *adj* ÉCON economic. ‖ [avantageux] economical.

économiser [ekɔnɔmize] *vt litt & fig* to save.

économiste [ekɔnɔmist] *nmf* economist.

écoper [ekɔpe] *vt* NAVIG to bale out. ‖ *fam* [sanction]: ~ (**de**) **qqch** to get sthg.

écorce [ekɔrs] *nf* [d'arbre] bark. ‖ [d'agrume] peel. ‖ GÉOL crust.

écorcher [ekɔrʃe] *vt* [lapin] to skin. ‖ [bras, jambe] to scratch. ‖ *fig* [langue, nom] to mispronounce.

écorchure [ekɔrʃyr] *nf* graze, scratch.

écossais, -e [ekɔsɛ, ɛz] *adj* [de l'Écosse] Scottish; [whisky] Scotch. ‖ [tissu] tartan. ○ **Écossais, -e** *nm, f* Scot, Scotsman (*f* Scotswoman).

Écosse [ekɔs] *nf*: **l'**~ Scotland.

écosser [ekɔse] *vt* to shell.

écouler [ekule] *vt* to sell. ○ **s'écouler** *vp* [eau] to flow. ‖ [temps] to pass.

écourter [ekurte] *vt* to shorten.

écouter [ekute] *vt* to listen to.

écouteur [ekutœr] *nm* [de téléphone] earpiece. ○ **écouteurs** *nmpl* [de radio] headphones.

écoutille [ekutij] *nf* hatchway.

écran [ekrɑ̃] *nm* [de protection] shield. ‖ CIN & INFORM screen; **le petit** ~ television.

écrasant, -e [ekrazɑ̃, ɑ̃t] *adj fig* [accablant] overwhelming.

écraser [ekraze] *vt* [comprimer - cigarette] to stub out; [- pied] to tread on; [- insecte, raisin] to crush. ‖ [vaincre] to crush. ‖ [renverser] to run over. ○ **s'écraser** *vp* [avion, automobile]: **s'**~ (**contre**) to crash (into).

écrémer [ekreme] *vt* [lait] to skim.

écrevisse [ekrəvis] *nf* crayfish.

écrier [ekrije] ○ **s'écrier** *vp* to cry out.

écrin [ekrɛ̃] *nm* case.

écrire [ekrir] *vt* [phrase, livre] to write. ‖ [orthographier] to spell.

écrit, -e [ekri, it] **1** *pp* → **écrire**. **2** *adj* written. ○ **écrit** *nm* [ouvrage] writing. ‖ [examen] written exam. ○ **par écrit** *loc adv* in writing.

écriteau, -x [ekrito] *nm* notice.

écriture [ekrityr] *nf* [gén] writing. || (*gén pl*) COMM [comptes] books (*pl*).

écrivain [ekrivɛ̃] *nm* writer, author.

écrou [ekru] *nm* TECHNOL nut.

écrouer [ekrue] *vt* to imprison.

écrouler [ekrule] ○ **s'écrouler** *vp litt* & *fig* to collapse.

écru, -e [ekry] *adj* [naturel] unbleached.

ECU [eky] (*abr de* **European Currency Unit**) *nm* ECU.

écu [eky] *nm* [bouclier, armoiries] shield. || [monnaie ancienne] crown. || = ECU.

écueil [ekœj] *nm* [rocher] reef. || *fig* [obstacle] stumbling block.

écuelle [ekɥɛl] *nf* [objet] bowl.

éculé, -e [ekyle] *adj* [chaussure] down-at-heel. || *fig* [plaisanterie] hackneyed.

écume [ekym] *nf* [mousse, bave] foam.

écumoire [ekymwar] *nf* skimmer.

écureuil [ekyrœj] *nm* squirrel.

écurie [ekyri] *nf* [pour chevaux & SPORT] stable. || *fig* [local sale] pigsty.

écusson [ekysɔ̃] *nm* [d'armoiries] coat-of-arms. || MIL badge.

écuyer, -ère [ekɥije, jɛr] *nm, f* [de cirque] rider. ○ **écuyer** *nm* [de chevalier] squire.

eczéma [ɛgzema] *nm* eczema.

édenté, -e [edɑ̃te] *adj* toothless.

EDF, Edf (*abr de* **Électricité de France**) *nf French national electricity company.*

édifice [edifis] *nm* [construction] building.

édifier [edifje] *vt* [ville, église] to build. || *fig* [théorie] to construct. || [personne] to edify; *iron* to enlighten.

Édimbourg [edɛ̃bur] *n* Edinburgh.

éditer [edite] *vt* to publish.

éditeur, -trice [editœr, tris] *nm, f* publisher.

édition [edisjɔ̃] *nf* [profession] publishing. || [de journal, livre] edition.

éditorial, -iaux [editɔrjal, jo] *nm* leader, editorial.

édredon [edrədɔ̃] *nm* eiderdown.

éducateur, -trice [edykatœr, tris] *nm, f* teacher; ~ **spécialisé** *teacher of children with special educational needs.*

éducatif, -ive [edykatif, iv] *adj* educational.

éducation [edykasjɔ̃] *nf* [apprentissage] education; **l'Éducation nationale** ≃ the Department of Education *Am*, ≃ the Department for Education *Br*. || [parentale] upbringing. || [savoir-vivre] breeding.

édulcorant [edylkɔrɑ̃] *nm*: ~ **(de synthèse)** (artificial) sweetener.

éduquer [edyke] *vt* to educate.

effacé, -e [efase] *adj* [teinte] faded. || [modeste - rôle] unobtrusive; [- personne] self-effacing.

effacer [efase] *vt* [mot] to erase, to rub out; INFORM to delete. || [souvenir] to erase. ○ **s'effacer** *vp* [s'estomper] to fade (away). || *sout* [s'écarter] to move aside. || *fig* [s'incliner] to give way.

effarant, -e [efarɑ̃, ɑ̃t] *adj* frightening.

effarer [efare] *vt* to frighten, to scare.

effaroucher [efaruʃe] *vt* [effrayer] to scare off. || [intimider] to overawe.

effectif, -ive [efektif, iv] *adj* [aide] positive. ○ **effectif** *nm* MIL strength. || [de groupe] total number.

effectivement [efɛktivmɑ̃] *adv* [réellement] effectively. || [confirmation] in fact.

effectuer [efɛktɥe] *vt* [réaliser - manœuvre] to carry out; [- trajet, paiement] to make.

efféminé, -e [efemine] *adj* effeminate.

effervescent, -e [efɛrvesɑ̃, ɑ̃t] *adj* [boisson] effervescent.

effet [efɛ] *nm* [gén] effect; **sous l'~ de** under the effects of; ~ **de serre** greenhouse effect. || [impression recherchée] impression. || COMM [titre] bill. ○ **en effet** *loc adv* in fact, indeed.

effeuiller [efœje] *vt* [arbre] to remove the leaves from; [fleur] to remove the petals from.

efficace [efikas] *adj* [remède, mesure] effective. || [personne, machine] efficient.

effigie [efiʒi] *nf* effigy.

effiler [efile] *vt* [tissu] to fray. || [lame] to sharpen. || [cheveux] to thin.

effilocher [efilɔʃe] *vt* to fray. ○ **s'effilocher** *vp* to fray.

efflanqué, -e [eflɑ̃ke] *adj* emaciated.

effleurer [eflœre] *vt* [visage, bras] to brush (against). || *fig* [problème, thème] to touch on. || *fig* [suj: pensée, idée]: ~ **qqn** to cross sb's mind.

effluve [eflyv] *nm* exhalation.

effondrement [efɔ̃drəmɑ̃] *nm* collapse.

effondrer [efɔ̃dre] ○ **s'effondrer** *vp litt* & *fig* to collapse.

efforcer [efɔrse] ○ **s'efforcer** *vp*: **s'~ de faire qqch** to make an effort to do sthg.

effort [efɔr] *nm* [de personne] effort.

effraction [efraksjɔ̃] *nf* breaking in; **entrer par ~ dans** to break into.

effrayer [efreje] *vt* to frighten, to scare.

effréné, -e [efrene] *adj* [course] frantic.

effriter [efrite] *vt* to cause to crumble. ○ **s'effriter** *vp* [mur] to crumble.

effroi [efrwa] *nm* fear, dread.

effronté, -e [efrɔ̃te] **1** *adj* insolent. **2** *nm, f* insolent person.

effronterie [efrɔ̃tri] *nf* insolence.

effroyable [efrwajabl] *adj* [catastrophe, misère] appalling. || [laideur] hideous.

effusion [efyzjɔ̃] *nf* [de liquide] effusion. || [de sentiments] effusiveness.

égal, -e, -aux [egal, o] **1** *adj* [équivalent] equal. || [régulier] even. || [indifférent] **ça m'est ~** I don't mind. **2** *nm, f* equal.

également [egalmɑ̃] *adv* [avec égalité] equally. || [aussi] as well, too.

égaler [egale] *vt* MATHS to equal. || [beauté] to match, to compare with.

égaliser [egalize] **1** *vt* [haie, cheveux] to trim. **2** *vi* SPORT to equalize *Br*, to tie *Am*.

égalitaire [egaliter] *adj* egalitarian.

égalité [egalite] *nf* [gén] equality. || [d'humeur] evenness. || SPORT: **être à ~** to be level.

égard [egar] *nm* consideration; **à cet ~** in this respect. ○ **à l'égard de** *loc prép* with regard to, towards.

égarer [egare] *vt* [objet] to mislay, to lose. ○ **s'égarer** *vp* [lettre] to get lost, to go astray; [personne] to get lost, to lose one's way. || *fig & sout* [personne] to stray from the point.

égayer [egeje] *vt* [personne] to cheer up. || [pièce] to brighten up.

égide [eʒid] *nf* protection; **sous l'~ de** *littéraire* under the aegis of.

église [egliz] *nf* church.

égocentrique [egosɑ̃trik] *adj* self-centred, egocentric.

égoïsme [egoism] *nm* selfishness, egoism.

égoïste [egoist] **1** *nmf* selfish person. **2** *adj* selfish, egoistic.

égorger [egɔrʒe] *vt* [animal, personne] to cut the throat of.

égosiller [egozije] ○ **s'égosiller** *vp fam* [crier] to bawl, to shout. || [chanter] to sing one's head off.

égout [egu] *nm* sewer.

égoutter [egute] *vt* [vaisselle] to leave to drain. || [légumes, fromage] to drain. ○ **s'égoutter** *vp* to drip, to drain.

égouttoir [egutwar] *nm* [à légumes] colander, strainer. || [à vaisselle] rack (*for washing-up*).

égratigner [egratiɲe] *vt* to scratch; *fig* to have a go ou dig at. ○ **s'égratigner** *vp*: **s'~ la main** to scratch one's hand.

égratignure [egratiɲyr] *nf* scratch, graze; *fig* dig.

égrener [egrəne] *vt* [détacher les grains de - épi, cosse] to shell; [- grappe] to pick grapes from. || [chapelet] to tell.

égrillard, -e [egrijar, ard] *adj* ribald, bawdy.

Égypte [eʒipt] *nf*: **l'~** Egypt.

égyptien, -ienne [eʒipsjɛ̃, jɛn] *adj* Egyptian. ○ **Égyptien, -ienne** *nm, f* Egyptian.

eh [e] *interj* hey!; **~ bien** well.

éhonté, -e [eɔ̃te] *adj* shameless.

Eiffel [efɛl] *n*: **la tour ~** the Eiffel Tower.

éjaculation [eʒakylasjɔ̃] *nf* ejaculation.

éjectable [eʒɛktabl] *adj*: **siège ~** ejector seat.

éjecter [eʒɛkte] *vt* [douille] to eject. || *fam* [personne] to kick out.

élaboration [elabɔrasjɔ̃] *nf* [de plan, système] working out, development.

élaboré, -e [elabɔre] *adj* elaborate.

élaborer [elabɔre] *vt* [plan, système] to work out, to develop.

élaguer [elage] *vt litt & fig* to prune.

élan [elɑ̃] *nm* ZOOL elk. || SPORT run-up; **prendre son ~** to take a run-up, to gather speed. || *fig* [de joie] outburst.

élancé, -e [elɑ̃se] *adj* slender.

élancer [elɑ̃se] *vi* MÉD to give shooting pains. ○ **s'élancer** *vp* [se précipiter] to rush, to dash. || SPORT to take a run-up.

élargir [elarʒir] *vt* to widen; [vêtement] to let out; *fig* to expand. ○ **s'élargir** *vp* [s'agrandir] to widen; [vêtement] to stretch; *fig* to expand.

élasticité [elastisite] *nf* PHYS elasticity.

élastique [elastik] **1** *nm* [pour attacher] elastic band. || [matière] elastic. **2** *adj* PHYS elastic. || [corps] flexible.

électeur, -trice [elɛktœr, tris] *nm, f* voter, elector.

élection [elɛksjɔ̃] *nf* [vote] election; **~ présidentielle** presidential election; **~s municipales** local elections.

électoral, -e, -aux [elɛktɔral, o] *adj* [campagne, réunion] election (*avant n*).

électricien, -ienne [elɛktrisjɛ̃, jɛn] *nm, f* electrician.

électricité [elɛktrisite] *nf* electricity.

électrifier [elɛktrifje] *vt* to electrify.

électrique [elɛktrik] *adj litt & fig* electric.

électrocardiogramme [elεktrɔkardjɔgram] *nm* electrocardiogram.

électrochoc [elεktrɔʃɔk] *nm* electric shock treatment.

électrocuter [elεktrɔkyte] *vt* to electrocute.

électrode [elεktrɔd] *nf* electrode.

électroencéphalogramme [elεktrɔɑ̃sefalɔgram] *nm* electroencephalogram.

électrogène [elεktrɔʒεn] *adj*: **groupe** ~ generating unit.

électrolyse [elεktrɔliz] *nf* electrolysis.

électromagnétique [elεktrɔmaɲetik] *adj* electromagnetic.

électroménager [elεktrɔmenaʒe] *nm* household electrical appliances (*pl*).

électron [elεktrɔ̃] *nm* electron.

électronicien, -ienne [elεktrɔnisjɛ̃, jεn] *nm, f* electronics specialist.

électronique [elεktrɔnik] **1** *nf* SCIENCE electronics (*U*). **2** *adj* electronic.

électrophone [elεktrɔfɔn] *nm* record player.

élégance [elegɑ̃s] *nf* [de personne, style] elegance.

élégant, -e [elegɑ̃, ɑ̃t] *adj* [personne, style] elegant.

élément [elemɑ̃] *nm* [gén] element; **être dans son** ~ to be in one's element. ‖ [de machine] component.

élémentaire [elemɑ̃tεr] *adj* [gén] elementary. ‖ [installation, besoin] basic.

éléphant [elefɑ̃] *nm* elephant.

élevage [εlvaʒ] *nm* breeding, rearing; [installation] farm.

élevé, -e [εlve] *adj* [haut] high. ‖ [enfant]: **bien/mal** ~ well/badly brought up.

élève [elεv] *nmf* [écolier, disciple] pupil.

élever [εlve] *vt* [gén] to raise. ‖ [statue] to put up, to erect. ‖ [à un rang supérieur] to elevate. ‖ [esprit] to improve. ‖ [enfant] to bring up. ‖ [poulets] to rear, to breed. ○ **s'élever** *vp* [gén] to rise. ‖ [montant]: **s'**~ **à** to add up to. ‖ [protester]: **s'**~ **contre qqn/qqch** to protest against sb/sthg.

éleveur, -euse [εlvœr, øz] *nm, f* breeder.

éligible [eliʒibl] *adj* eligible.

élimé, -e [elime] *adj* threadbare.

élimination [eliminasjɔ̃] *nf* elimination.

éliminatoire [eliminatwar] **1** *nf* (*gén pl*) SPORT qualifying heat *ou* round. **2** *adj* qualifying (*avant n*).

éliminer [elimine] *vt* to eliminate.

élire [elir] *vt* to elect.

élite [elit] *nf* elite; **d'**~ choice, select.

élitiste [elitist] *nmf & adj* elitist.

elle [εl] *pron pers* [sujet - personne] she; [- animal] it, she; [- chose] it. ‖ [complément - personne] her; [- animal] it, her; [- chose] it. ○ **elles** *pron pers pl* [sujet] they. ‖ [complément] them. ○ **elle-même** *pron pers* [personne] herself; [animal] itself, herself; [chose] itself. ○ **elles-mêmes** *pron pers pl* themselves.

ellipse [elips] *nf* GÉOM ellipse. ‖ LING ellipsis.

élocution [elɔkysjɔ̃] *nf* delivery; **défaut d'**~ speech defect.

éloge [elɔʒ] *nm* [louange] praise; **faire l'**~ **de qqn/qqch** [louer] to speak highly of sb/sthg.

élogieux, -ieuse [elɔʒjø, jøz] *adj* laudatory.

éloignement [elwaɲmɑ̃] *nm* [mise à l'écart] removal. ‖ [séparation] absence. ‖ [dans l'espace, le temps] distance.

éloigner [elwaɲe] *vt* [écarter] to move away; ~ **qqch de** to move sthg away from. ‖ [détourner] to turn away. ○ **s'éloigner** *vp* [partir] to move *ou* go away. ‖ *fig* [du sujet] to stray from the point. ‖ [se détacher] to distance o.s.

éloquence [elɔkɑ̃s] *nf* [d'orateur, d'expression] eloquence.

éloquent, -e [elɔkɑ̃, ɑ̃t] *adj* [avocat, silence] eloquent. ‖ [données] significant.

élu, -e [ely] **1** *pp* → **élire**. **2** *adj* POLIT elected. **3** *nm, f* POLIT elected representative.

élucider [elyside] *vt* to clear up.

éluder [elyde] *vt* to evade.

Élysée [elize] *nm*: **l'**~ *the official residence of the French President and, by extension, the President himself.*

émacié, -e [emasje] *adj littéraire* emaciated.

émail, -aux [emaj, emo] *nm* enamel; **en** ~ enamel, enamelled.

émanation [emanasjɔ̃] *nf* emanation; **être l'**~ **de** *fig* to emanate from.

émanciper [emɑ̃sipe] *vt* to emancipate. ○ **s'émanciper** *vp* [se libérer] to become free *ou* liberated.

émaner [emane] *vi*: ~ **de** to emanate from.

émarger [emarʒe] *vt* [signer] to sign.

emballage [ɑ̃balaʒ] *nm* packaging.

emballer [ɑ̃bale] *vt* [objet] to pack (up), to wrap (up). ‖ *fam* [plaire] to thrill. ○ **s'emballer** *vp* [moteur] to race. ‖ [cheval] to bolt. ‖ *fam* [personne -

s'enthousiasmer] to get carried away; [- s'emporter] to lose one's temper.

embarcadère [ɑ̃barkadɛr] *nm* landing stage.

embarcation [ɑ̃barkasjɔ̃] *nf* small boat.

embardée [ɑ̃barde] *nf* swerve; **faire une ~** to swerve.

embargo [ɑ̃bargo] *nm* embargo.

embarquement [ɑ̃barkəmɑ̃] *nm* [de marchandises] loading. || [de passagers] boarding.

embarquer [ɑ̃barke] **1** *vt* [marchandises] to load. || [passagers] to (take on) board. || *fam* [arrêter] to pick up. || *fam fig* [engager]: **~ qqn dans** to involve sb in. || *fam* [emmener] to cart off. **2** *vi*: **~ (pour)** to sail (for). ○ **s'embarquer** *vp* [sur un bateau] to (set) sail. || *fam fig* [s'engager]: **s'~ dans** to get involved in.

embarras [ɑ̃bara] *nm* [incertitude] (state of) uncertainty; **avoir l'~ du choix** to be spoilt for choice. || [situation difficile] predicament; **mettre qqn dans l'~** to place sb in an awkward position. || [gêne] embarrassment.

embarrassé, -e [ɑ̃barase] *adj* [encombré - pièce, bureau] cluttered; **avoir les mains ~es** to have one's hands full. || [gêné] embarrassed. || [confus] confused.

embarrasser [ɑ̃barase] *vt* [encombrer - pièce] to clutter up; [- personne] to hamper. || [gêner] to put in an awkward position. ○ **s'embarrasser** *vp* [se charger]: **s'~ de qqch** to burden o.s. with sthg; *fig* to bother about sthg.

embauche [ɑ̃boʃ] *nf*, **embauchage** [ɑ̃boʃaʒ] *nm* hiring, employment.

embaucher [ɑ̃boʃe] *vt* [employer] to employ, to take on.

embaumer [ɑ̃bome] **1** *vt* [cadavre] to embalm. || [parfumer] to scent. **2** *vi* to be fragrant.

embellir [ɑ̃belir] **1** *vt* [agrémenter] to brighten up. || *fig* [enjoliver] to embellish. **2** *vi* [devenir plus beau] to become more attractive.

embêtant, -e [ɑ̃betɑ̃, ɑ̃t] *adj fam* annoying.

embêtement [ɑ̃betmɑ̃] *nm fam* trouble.

embêter [ɑ̃bete] *vt fam* [contrarier, importuner] to annoy. ○ **s'embêter** *vp fam* [s'ennuyer] to be bored.

emblée [ɑ̃ble] ○ **d'emblée** *loc adv* right away.

emblème [ɑ̃blɛm] *nm* emblem.

emboîter [ɑ̃bwate] *vt*: **~ qqch dans qqch** to fit sthg into sthg. ○ **s'emboîter** *vp* to fit together.

embonpoint [ɑ̃bɔ̃pwɛ̃] *nm* stoutness.

embouchure [ɑ̃buʃyr] *nf* [de fleuve] mouth.

embourber [ɑ̃burbe] ○ **s'embourber** *vp* [s'enliser] to get stuck in the mud; *fig* to get bogged down.

embourgeoiser [ɑ̃burʒwaze] ○ **s'embourgeoiser** *vp* [personne] to adopt middle-class values; [quartier] to become gentrified.

embout [ɑ̃bu] *nm* [protection] tip; [extrémité d'un tube] nozzle.

embouteillage [ɑ̃butejaʒ] *nm* [circulation] traffic jam.

emboutir [ɑ̃butir] *vt fam* [voiture] to crash into. || TECHNOL to stamp.

embranchement [ɑ̃brɑ̃ʃmɑ̃] *nm* [carrefour] junction.

embraser [ɑ̃braze] *vt* [incendier, éclairer] to set ablaze. ○ **s'embraser** *vp* [prendre feu, s'éclairer] to be ablaze.

embrassade [ɑ̃brasad] *nf* embrace.

embrasser [ɑ̃brase] *vt* [donner un baiser à] to kiss. || [étreindre] to embrace. || *fig* [du regard] to take in. ○ **s'embrasser** *vp* to kiss (each other).

embrasure [ɑ̃brazyr] *nf*: **dans l'~ de la fenêtre** in the window.

embrayage [ɑ̃brejaʒ] *nm* [mécanisme] clutch.

embrayer [ɑ̃breje] *vi* AUTOM to engage the clutch.

embrocher [ɑ̃brɔʃe] *vt* to skewer.

embrouillamini [ɑ̃brujamini] *nm fam* muddle.

embrouiller [ɑ̃bruje] *vt* [mélanger] to mix (up), to muddle (up). || *fig* [compliquer] to confuse.

embruns [ɑ̃brœ̃] *nmpl* spray (U).

embryon [ɑ̃brijɔ̃] *nm litt & fig* embryo.

embûche [ɑ̃byʃ] *nf* pitfall.

embuer [ɑ̃bɥe] *vt* [de vapeur] to steam up. || [de larmes] to mist (over).

embuscade [ɑ̃byskad] *nf* ambush.

éméché, -e [emeʃe] *adj fam* tipsy.

émeraude [emrod] *nf* emerald.

émerger [emɛrʒe] *vi* [gén] to emerge. || NAVIG & *fig* to surface.

émeri [emri] *nm*: **papier** OU **toile ~** emery paper.

émerveiller [emɛrveje] *vt* to fill with wonder.

émetteur, **-trice** [emetœr, tris] *adj* transmitting; **poste** ~ transmitter. ○ **émetteur** *nm* [appareil] transmitter.

émettre [emɛtr] *vt* [produire] to emit. || [diffuser] to transmit, to broadcast. || [mettre en circulation] to issue. || [exprimer] to express.

émeute [emœt] *nf* riot.

émietter [emjete] *vt* [du pain] to crumble. || [morceler] to divide up.

émigrant, **-e** [emigrã, ãt] *adj & nm, f* emigrant.

émigré, **-e** [emigre] **1** *adj* migrant. **2** *nm, f* emigrant.

émigrer [emigre] *vi* [personnes] to emigrate. || [animaux] to migrate.

émincé, **-e** [emɛ̃se] *adj* sliced thinly. ○ **émincé** *nm* thin slices of meat served in a sauce.

éminemment [eminamã] *adv* eminently.

éminent, **-e** [eminã, ãt] *adj* eminent, distinguished.

émir [emir] *nm* emir.

émirat [emira] *nm* emirate. ○ **Émirat** *nm* : **les Émirats arabes unis** the United Arab Emirates.

émis, **-e** [emi, iz] *pp* → **émettre**.

émissaire [emisɛr] **1** *nm* [envoyé] emissary, envoy. **2** *adj* → **bouc**.

émission [emisjɔ̃] *nf* [de gaz, de son etc] emission. || [RADIO & TÉLÉ - transmission] transmission, broadcasting; [- programme] programme *Br*, program *Am*. || [mise en circulation] issue.

emmagasiner [ãmagazine] *vt* [stocker] to store. || *fig* [accumuler] to store up.

emmanchure [ãmãʃyr] *nf* armhole.

emmêler [ãmele] *vt* [fils] to tangle up. || *fig* [idées] to muddle up, to confuse. ○ **s'emmêler** *vp* [fils] to get into a tangle. || *fig* [personne] to get mixed up.

emménagement [ãmenaʒmã] *nm* moving in.

emménager [ãmenaʒe] *vi* to move in.

emmener [ãmne] *vt* to take.

emmerder [ãmɛrde] *vt tfam* to piss off. ○ **s'emmerder** *vp tfam* [s'embêter] to be bored stiff.

emmitoufler [ãmitufle] *vt* to wrap up. ○ **s'emmitoufler** *vp* to wrap o.s. up.

émoi [emwa] *nm sout* [émotion] emotion.

émotif, **-ive** [emɔtif, iv] *adj* emotional.

émotion [emosjɔ̃] *nf* [sentiment] emotion. || [peur] fright, shock.

émotionnel, **-elle** [emosjɔnel] *adj* emotional.

émousser [emuse] *vt litt & fig* to blunt.

émouvant, **-e** [emuvã, ãt] *adj* moving.

émouvoir [emuvwar] *vt* [troubler] to disturb, to upset. || [susciter la sympathie de] to move, to touch. ○ **s'émouvoir** *vp* to show emotion, to be upset.

empailler [ãpaje] *vt* [animal] to stuff. || [chaise] to upholster (with straw).

empaqueter [ãpakte] *vt* to pack (up), to wrap (up).

empâter [ãpate] *vt* [visage, traits] to fatten out. ○ **s'empâter** *vp* to put on weight.

empêchement [ãpɛʃmã] *nm* obstacle; **j'ai un** ~ something has come up.

empêcher [ãpeʃe] *vt* to prevent; ~ **qqn/qqch de faire qqch** to prevent sb/sthg from doing sthg; **(il) n'empêche que** nevertheless, all the same.

empereur [ãprœr] *nm* emperor.

empesé, **-e** [ãpəze] *adj* [linge] starched. || *fig* [style] stiff.

empester [ãpɛste] *vi* to stink.

empêtrer [ãpetre] *vt* : **être empêtré dans** to be tangled up in. ○ **s'empêtrer** *vp* : **s'~ (dans)** to get tangled up (in).

emphase [ãfaz] *nf péj* pomposity.

empiéter [ãpjete] *vi* : ~ **sur** to encroach on.

empiffrer [ãpifre] ○ **s'empiffrer** *vp fam* to stuff o.s.

empiler [ãpile] *vt* [entasser] to pile up, to stack up.

empire [ãpir] *nm* HIST & *fig* empire.

empirer [ãpire] *vi & vt* to worsen.

empirique [ãpirik] *adj* empirical.

emplacement [ãplasmã] *nm* site, location.

emplette [ãplɛt] *nf* (*gén pl*) purchase.

emplir [ãplir] *vt sout* : ~ **(de)** to fill (with). ○ **s'emplir** *vp* : **s'~ (de)** to fill (with).

emploi [ãplwa] *nm* [utilisation] use; ~ **du temps** timetable. || [travail] job.

employé, **-e** [ãplwaje] *nm, f* employee; ~ **de bureau** office employee or worker.

employer [ãplwaje] *vt* [utiliser] to use. || [salarier] to employ.

employeur, **-euse** [ãplwajœr, øz] *nm, f* employer.

empocher [ãpɔʃe] *vt fam* to pocket.

empoignade [ãpwaɲad] *nf* row.

empoigner [ãpwaɲe] *vt* [saisir] to

grasp. ○ **s'empoigner** *vp fig* to come to blows.

empoisonnement [ɑ̃pwazɔnmɑ̃] *nm* [intoxication] poisoning.

empoisonner [ɑ̃pwazɔne] *vt* [gén] to poison. || *fam* [ennuyer] to annoy, to bug.

emporté, -e [ɑ̃pɔrte] *adj* short-tempered.

emportement [ɑ̃pɔrtəmɑ̃] *nm* anger.

emporter [ɑ̃pɔrte] *vt* [emmener] to take (away); **à ~** [plats] to take away, to go *Am.* || [entraîner] to carry along. || [arracher] to tear off, to blow off. || [faire mourir] to carry off. || [surpasser]: **l'~ sur** to get the better of. ○ **s'emporter** *vp* to get angry, to lose one's temper.

empoté, -e [ɑ̃pɔte] *fam* **1** *adj* clumsy. **2** *nm, f* clumsy person.

empreinte [ɑ̃prɛ̃t] *nf* [trace] print; *fig* mark, trace; **~s digitales** fingerprints.

empressement [ɑ̃presmɑ̃] *nm* [zèle] attentiveness. || [enthousiasme] eagerness.

empresser [ɑ̃prese] ○ **s'empresser** *vp*: **s'~ de faire qqch** to hurry to do sthg.

emprise [ɑ̃priz] *nf* [ascendant] influence.

emprisonnement [ɑ̃prizɔnmɑ̃] *nm* imprisonment.

emprisonner [ɑ̃prizɔne] *vt* [voleur] to imprison.

emprunt [ɑ̃prœ̃] *nm* FIN loan. || LING & *fig* borrowing.

emprunté, -e [ɑ̃prœ̃te] *adj* awkward, self-conscious.

emprunter [ɑ̃prœ̃te] *vt* [gén] to borrow; **~ qqch à** to borrow sthg from. || [route] to take.

ému, -e [emy] **1** *pp* → **émouvoir**. **2** *adj* [personne] moved, touched; [regard, sourire] emotional.

émulation [emylasjɔ̃] *nf* [concurrence] rivalry. || [imitation] emulation.

émule [emyl] *nmf* [imitateur] emulator.

émulsion [emylsjɔ̃] *nf* emulsion.

en [ɑ̃] **1** *prép* [temps] in; **~ 1994** in 1994; **~ hiver/septembre** in winter/September. || [lieu] in; [direction] to. || [matière] made of; **c'est ~ métal** it's (made of) metal; **une théière ~ argent** a silver teapot. || [état, forme, manière]: **les arbres sont ~ fleurs** the trees are in blossom; **du sucre ~ morceaux** sugar cubes; **je l'ai eu ~ cadeau** I was given it as a present; **dire qqch ~ anglais** to say sthg in English; **~ vacances** on holiday. || [moyen] by; **~ avion/bateau/train** by plane/boat/train. || [mesure] in; **vous l'avez ~ 38?** do you

have it in a 38? || [devant un participe présent]: **~ arrivant à Paris** on arriving in Paris, as he/she *etc* arrived in Paris; **elle répondit ~ souriant** she replied with a smile. **2** *pron adv* [complément de verbe, de nom, d'adjectif]: **il s'~ est souvenu** he remembered it; **nous ~ avons déjà parlé** we've already spoken about it. || [avec un indéfini, exprimant une quantité]: **j'ai du chocolat, tu ~ veux?** I've got some chocolate, do you want some?; **il y ~ a plusieurs** there are several (of them). || [provenance] from there.

ENA, Ena [ena] (*abr de* **École nationale d'administration**) *nf* prestigious *grande école training future government officials.*

encadrement [ɑ̃kadrəmɑ̃] *nm* [de tableau, porte] frame. || [dans une entreprise] managerial staff; [à l'armée] officers (*pl*); [à l'école] staff.

encadrer [ɑ̃kadre] *vt* [photo, visage] to frame. || [employés] to supervise; [soldats] to be in command of; [élèves] to teach.

encaissé, -e [ɑ̃kese] *adj* [vallée] deep and narrow; [rivière] steep-banked.

encaisser [ɑ̃kese] *vt* [argent, coups, insultes] to take. || [chèque] to cash.

encart [ɑ̃kar] *nm* insert.

encastrer [ɑ̃kastre] *vt* to fit. ○ **s'encastrer** *vp* to fit (exactly).

encaustique [ɑ̃kɔstik] *nf* [cire] polish.

enceinte [ɑ̃sɛ̃t] **1** *adj f* pregnant; **~ de 4 mois** 4 months pregnant. **2** *nf* [muraille] wall. || [espace]: **dans l'~ de** within (the confines of). || [baffle]: **~ (acoustique)** speaker.

encens [ɑ̃sɑ̃] *nm* incense.

encenser [ɑ̃sɑ̃se] *vt fig* [louer] to flatter.

encensoir [ɑ̃sɑ̃swar] *nm* censer.

encercler [ɑ̃sɛrkle] *vt* [cerner, environner] to surround; [entourer] to circle.

enchaînement [ɑ̃ʃɛnmɑ̃] *nm* [succession] series. || [liaison] link.

enchaîner [ɑ̃ʃene] **1** *vt* [attacher] to chain up. || [coordonner] to link. **2** *vi*: **~ (sur)** to move on (to). ○ **s'enchaîner** *vp* [se suivre] to follow on from each other.

enchanté, -e [ɑ̃ʃɑ̃te] *adj* [ravi] delighted; **~ de faire votre connaissance** pleased to meet you. || [ensorcelé] enchanted.

enchantement [ɑ̃ʃɑ̃tmɑ̃] *nm* [sortilège] magic spell; **comme par ~** as if by magic. || [merveille] wonder.

enchanter [ɑ̃ʃɑ̃te] *vt* [ensorceler, charmer] to enchant. || [ravir] to delight.

enchâsser [ɑ̃ʃɑse] *vt* [sertir] to set.

enchère [ɑ̃ʃɛr] *nf* bid; **vendre qqch aux ~s** to sell sthg at ot by auction.

enchevêtrer [ɑ̃ʃəvetre] *vt* [emmêler] to tangle up; *fig* to muddle, to confuse.

enclave [ɑ̃klav] *nf* enclave.

enclencher [ɑ̃klɑ̃ʃe] *vt* [mécanisme] to engage. ○ **s'enclencher** *vp* TECHNOL to engage. || *fig* [commencer] to begin.

enclin, -e [ɑ̃klɛ̃, in] *adj*: **~ à qqch/à faire qqch** inclined to sthg/to do sthg.

enclore [ɑ̃klɔr] *vt* to fence in, to enclose.

enclos, -e [ɑ̃klo, oz] *pp* → **enclore**. ○ **enclos** *nm* enclosure.

enclume [ɑ̃klym] *nf* anvil.

encoche [ɑ̃kɔʃ] *nf* notch.

encoignure [ɑ̃kwaɲyr, ɑ̃kɔɲyr] *nf* [coin] corner.

encolure [ɑ̃kɔlyr] *nf* neck.

encombrant, -e [ɑ̃kɔ̃brɑ̃, ɑ̃t] cumbersome; *fig* [personne] undesirable.

encombre [ɑ̃kɔ̃br] ○ **sans encombre** *loc adv* without a hitch.

encombré, -e [ɑ̃kɔ̃bre] *adj* [lieu] busy, congested; *fig* saturated.

encombrement [ɑ̃kɔ̃brəmɑ̃] *nm* [d'une pièce] clutter. || [d'un objet] overall dimensions (*pl*). || [embouteillage] traffic jam. || INFORM footprint.

encombrer [ɑ̃kɔ̃bre] *vt* to clutter (up).

encontre [ɑ̃kɔ̃tr] ○ **à l'encontre de** *loc prép*: **aller à l'~ de** to go against, to oppose.

encore [ɑ̃kɔr] *adv* [toujours] still; **~ un mois** one more month; **pas ~** not yet. || [de nouveau] again; **il m'a ~ menti** he's lied to me again; **l'ascenseur est en panne - ~!** the lift's out of order - not again! || [marque le renforcement] even; **~ mieux/pire** even better/worse. ○ **et encore** *loc adv*: **j'ai eu le temps de prendre un sandwich, et ~!** I had time for a sandwich, but only just!

encouragement [ɑ̃kuraʒmɑ̃] *nm* [parole] (word of) encouragement.

encourager [ɑ̃kuraʒe] *vt* to encourage; **~ qqn à faire qqch** to encourage sb to do sthg.

encourir [ɑ̃kurir] *vt sout* to incur.

encouru, -e [ɑ̃kury] *pp* → **encourir**.

encrasser [ɑ̃krase] *vt* TECHNOL to clog up. ○ **s'encrasser** *vp* TECHNOL to clog up.

encre [ɑ̃kr] *nf* ink.

encrer [ɑ̃kre] *vt* to ink.

encrier [ɑ̃krije] *nm* inkwell.

encroûter [ɑ̃krute] ○ **s'encroûter** *vp* *fam* to get into a rut.

encyclopédie [ɑ̃siklɔpedi] *nf* encyclopedia.

encyclopédique [ɑ̃siklɔpedik] *adj* encyclopedic.

endetter [ɑ̃dete] ○ **s'endetter** *vp* to get into debt.

endeuiller [ɑ̃dœje] *vt* to plunge into mourning.

endiablé, -e [ɑ̃djable] *adj* [frénétique] frantic, frenzied.

endiguer [ɑ̃dige] *vt* [fleuve] to dam. || *fig* [réprimer] to stem.

endimanché, -e [ɑ̃dimɑ̃ʃe] *adj* in one's Sunday best.

endive [ɑ̃div] *nf* chicory (*U*).

endoctriner [ɑ̃dɔktrine] *vt* to indoctrinate.

endommager [ɑ̃dɔmaʒe] *vt* to damage.

endormi, -e [ɑ̃dɔrmi] *adj* [personne] sleeping, asleep. || *fig* [village] sleepy; [jambe] numb; *fam* [apathique] sluggish.

endormir [ɑ̃dɔrmir] *vt* [assoupir, ennuyer] to send to sleep. || [anesthésier- patient] to anaesthetize; [- douleur] to ease. || *fig* [tromper] to allay. ○ **s'endormir** *vp* [s'assoupir] to fall asleep.

endosser [ɑ̃dose] *vt* [vêtement] to put on. || FIN & JUR to endorse. || *fig* [responsabilité] to take on.

endroit [ɑ̃drwa] *nm* [lieu, point] place; **à quel ~?** where? || [passage] part. || [côté] right side; **à l'~** the right way round.

enduire [ɑ̃dɥir] *vt*: **~ qqch (de)** to coat sthg (with).

enduit, -e [ɑ̃dɥi, ɥit] *pp* → **enduire**. ○ **enduit** *nm* coating.

endurance [ɑ̃dyrɑ̃s] *nf* endurance.

endurcir [ɑ̃dyrsir] *vt* to harden. ○ **s'endurcir** *vp*: **s'~ à** to become hardened to.

endurer [ɑ̃dyre] *vt* to endure.

énergétique [enerʒetik] *adj* [aliment] energy-giving.

énergie [enerʒi] *nf* energy.

énergique [enerʒik] *adj* [gén] energetic; [remède] powerful; [mesure] drastic.

énergumène [energymen] *nmf* rowdy character.

énerver [enerve] *vt* to irritate, to annoy. ○ **s'énerver** *vp* to get annoyed.

enfance [ɑ̃fɑ̃s] *nf* [âge] childhood.

enfant [ɑ̃fɑ̃] *nmf* [gén] child; **attendre un ~** to be expecting a baby.

enfanter [ɑ̃fɑ̃te] *rt littéraire* to give birth to.

enfantillage [ɑ̃fɑ̃tijaʒ] *nm* childishness (*U*).

enfantin, -e [ɑ̃fɑ̃tɛ̃, in] *adj* [propre à l'enfance] childlike; *péj* childish; [jeu, chanson] children's (*avant n*). || [facile] childishly simple.

enfer [ɑ̃fɛr] *nm* RELIG & *fig* hell.

enfermer [ɑ̃fɛrme] *rt* [séquestrer, ranger] to shut away. ○ **s'enfermer** *vp* to shut o.s. away or up; **s'~ dans** *fig* to retreat into.

enfilade [ɑ̃filad] *nf* row.

enfiler [ɑ̃file] *vt* [aiguille, sur un fil] to thread. || [vêtements] to slip on.

enfin [ɑ̃fɛ̃] *adv* [en dernier lieu] finally, at last; [dans une liste] lastly. || [introduit une rectification] that is, well. || [introduit une concession] anyway.

enflammer [ɑ̃flame] *rt* [bois] to set fire to. ○ **s'enflammer** *vp* [bois] to catch fire. || *fig* [s'exalter] to flare up.

enflé, -e [ɑ̃fle] *adj* [style] turgid.

enfler [ɑ̃fle] *vi* to swell (up).

enfoncer [ɑ̃fɔ̃se] *rt* [faire pénétrer] to drive in; **~ qqch dans qqch** to drive sthg into sthg. || [enfouir]: **~ ses mains dans ses poches** to thrust one's hands into one's pockets. || [défoncer] to break down. ○ **s'enfoncer** *vp* **s'~ dans** [eau, boue] to sink into; [bois, ville] to disappear into. || [céder] to give way.

enfouir [ɑ̃fwir] *rt* [cacher] to hide. || [ensevelir] to bury.

enfourcher [ɑ̃furʃe] *rt* to mount.

enfourner [ɑ̃furne] *rt* [pain] to put in the oven. || *fam* [avaler] to gobble up.

enfreindre [ɑ̃frɛ̃dr] *rt* to infringe.

enfreint, -e [ɑ̃frɛ̃, ɛ̃t] *pp* → enfreindre.

enfuir [ɑ̃fɥir] ○ **s'enfuir** *vp* [fuir] to run away.

enfumer [ɑ̃fyme] *rt* to fill with smoke.

engagé, -e [ɑ̃ɡaʒe] *adj* [auteur, chanteur] politically committed.

engageant, -e [ɑ̃ɡaʒɑ̃, ɑ̃t] *adj* engaging.

engagement [ɑ̃ɡaʒmɑ̃] *nm* [promesse] commitment. || FOOTBALL & RUGBY kick-off.

engager [ɑ̃ɡaʒe] *rt* [lier] to commit. || [embaucher] to take on, to engage. || [faire entrer]: **~ qqch dans** to insert sthg into. || [commencer] to start. || [impliquer] to involve. || [encourager]: **~ qqn à faire qqch** to urge sb to do sthg. ○ **s'engager** *vp* [promettre]: **s'~ à qqch/à faire qqch** to commit o.s. to sthg/to doing sthg. ||

MIL: **s'~ (dans)** to enlist (in). || [pénétrer]: **s'~ dans** to enter.

engelure [ɑ̃ʒlyr] *nf* chilblain.

engendrer [ɑ̃ʒɑ̃dre] *rt littéraire* to father. || *fig* [produire] to cause, to give rise to; [sentiment] to engender.

engin [ɑ̃ʒɛ̃] *nm* [machine] machine. || MIL missile. || *fam péj* [objet] thing.

englober [ɑ̃ɡlɔbe] *rt* to include.

engloutir [ɑ̃ɡlutir] *rt* [dévorer] to gobble up. || [faire disparaître] to engulf. || *fig* [dilapider] to squander.

engorger [ɑ̃ɡɔrʒe] *rt* [obstruer] to block, to obstruct. || MÉD to engorge. ○ **s'engorger** *vp* to become blocked.

engouement [ɑ̃ɡumɑ̃] *nm* [enthousiasme] infatuation.

engouffrer [ɑ̃ɡufre] *rt fam* [dévorer] to wolf down. ○ **s'engouffrer** *vp*: **s'~ dans** to rush into.

engourdi, -e [ɑ̃ɡurdi] *adj* numb.

engourdir [ɑ̃ɡurdir] *rt* to numb; *fig* to dull. ○ **s'engourdir** *vp* to go numb.

engrais [ɑ̃ɡrɛ] *nm* fertilizer.

engraisser [ɑ̃ɡrese] **1** *rt* [animal] to fatten. || [terre] to fertilize. **2** *ri* to put on weight.

engrenage [ɑ̃ɡrənaʒ] *nm* TECHNOL gears (*pl*). || *fig* [circonstances]: **être pris dans l'~** to be caught up in the system.

engueuler [ɑ̃ɡœle] *rt fam*: **~ qqn** to bawl sb out. ○ **s'engueuler** *vp fam* to have a row.

enhardir [ɑ̃ardir] ○ **s'enhardir** *vp* to pluck up one's courage.

énième [enjɛm] *adj fam*: **la ~ fois** the nth time.

énigmatique [enigmatik] *adj* enigmatic.

énigme [enigm] *nf* [mystère] enigma. || [jeu] riddle.

enivrant, -e [ɑ̃nivrɑ̃, ɑ̃t] *adj litt* & *fig* intoxicating.

enivrer [ɑ̃nivre] *rt litt* to get drunk; *fig* to intoxicate. ○ **s'enivrer** *vp*: **s'~ (de)** to get drunk (on).

enjambée [ɑ̃ʒɑ̃be] *nf* stride.

enjamber [ɑ̃ʒɑ̃be] *rt* [obstacle] to step over. || [cours d'eau] to straddle.

enjeu [ɑ̃ʒø] *nm* [mise] stake.

enjoindre [ɑ̃ʒwɛ̃dr] *rt littéraire*: **~ à qqn de faire qqch** to enjoin sb to do sthg.

enjoint [ɑ̃ʒwɛ̃] *pp inv* → enjoindre.

enjôler [ɑ̃ʒole] *rt* to coax.

enjoliver [ɑ̃ʒɔlive] *rt* to embellish.

enjoliveur [ɑ̃ʒɔlivœr] *nm* [de roue] hub-cap; [de calandre] badge.

enjoué, -e [ɑ̃ʒwe] *adj* cheerful.

enlacer [ɑ̃lase] *vt* [prendre dans ses bras] to embrace, to hug. ○ **s'enlacer** *vp* [s'embrasser] to embrace, to hug.

enlaidir [ɑ̃ledir] **1** *vt* to make ugly. **2** *vi* to become ugly.

enlèvement [ɑ̃lɛvmɑ̃] *nm* [action d'enlever] removal. ‖ [rapt] abduction.

enlever [ɑ̃lve] *vt* [gén] to remove; [vêtement] to take off. ‖ [prendre]: ~ qqch à qqn to take sthg away from sb. ‖ [kidnapper] to abduct.

enliser [ɑ̃lize] ○ **s'enliser** *vp* [s'embourber] to sink, to get stuck. ‖ *fig* [piétiner]: s'~ dans qqch to get bogged down in sthg.

enluminure [ɑ̃lyminyr] *nf* illumination.

enneigé, -e [ɑ̃neʒe] *adj* snow-covered.

ennemi, -e [ɛnmi] **1** *adj* enemy (*avant n*). **2** *nm, f* enemy.

ennui [ɑ̃nɥi] *nm* [lassitude] boredom. ‖ [problème] trouble (*U*).

ennuyer [ɑ̃nɥije] *vt* [agacer, contrarier] to annoy; **cela t'ennuierait de venir me chercher?** would you mind picking me up? ‖ [lasser] to bore. ‖ [inquiéter] to bother. ○ **s'ennuyer** *vp* [se morfondre] to be bored. ‖ [déplorer l'absence]: s'~ de qqn/qqch to miss sb/sthg.

ennuyeux, -euse [ɑ̃nɥijø, øz] *adj* [lassant] boring. ‖ [contrariant] annoying.

énoncé [enɔ̃se] *nm* [libellé] wording.

énoncer [enɔ̃se] *vt* [libeller] to word. ‖ [exposer] to expound.

énorme [enɔrm] *adj litt & fig* [immense] enormous. ‖ *fam fig* [incroyable] far-fetched.

énormément [enɔrmemɑ̃] *adv* enormously; ~ de a great deal of.

enquête [ɑ̃kɛt] *nf* [police, recherches] investigation. ‖ [sondage] survey.

enquêter [ɑ̃kete] *vi* [police, chercheur] to investigate. ‖ [sonder] to conduct a survey.

enragé, -e [ɑ̃raʒe] *adj* [chien] rabid, with rabies. ‖ *fig* [invétéré] keen.

enrager [ɑ̃raʒe] *vi* to be furious; **faire ~ qqn** to infuriate sb.

enrayer [ɑ̃reje] *vt* [épidémie] to check, to stop. ‖ [mécanisme] to jam. ○ **s'enrayer** *vp* [mécanisme] to jam.

enregistrement [ɑ̃rəʒistrəmɑ̃] *nm* [de son, d'images, d'informations] recording. ‖ [inscription] registration. ‖ [à

l'aéroport] check-in; ~ **des bagages** baggage registration.

enregistrer [ɑ̃rəʒistre] *vt* [son, images, informations] to record. ‖ INFORM to store. ‖ [inscrire] to register. ‖ [à l'aéroport] to check in. ‖ *fam* [mémoriser] to make a mental note of.

enrhumé, -e [ɑ̃ryme] *adj*: **je suis ~** I have a cold.

enrhumer [ɑ̃ryme] ○ **s'enrhumer** *vp* to catch (a) cold.

enrichir [ɑ̃riʃir] *vt* [financièrement] to make rich. ‖ [terre & *fig*] to enrich. ○ **s'enrichir** *vp* [financièrement] to grow rich. ‖ [sol & *fig*] to become enriched.

enrobé, -e [ɑ̃rɔbe] *adj* [recouvert]: ~ **de** coated with. ‖ *fam* [grassouillet] plump.

enrober [ɑ̃rɔbe] *vt* [recouvrir]: ~ **qqch de** to coat sthg with. ‖ *fig* [requête, nouvelle] to wrap up.

enrôler [ɑ̃role] *vt* to enrol; MIL to enlist. ○ **s'enrôler** *vp* to enrol; MIL to enlist.

enroué, -e [ɑ̃rwe] *adj* hoarse.

enrouler [ɑ̃rule] *vt* to roll up; ~ **qqch autour de qqch** to wind sthg round sthg. ○ **s'enrouler** *vp* [entourer]: s'~ **sur** OU **autour de qqch** to wind around sthg. ‖ [se pelotonner]: s'~ **dans qqch** to wrap o.s. up in sthg.

ensabler [ɑ̃sable] *vt* to silt up. ○ **s'ensabler** *vp* to silt up.

enseignant, -e [ɑ̃sɛɲɑ̃, ɑ̃t] **1** *adj* teaching (*avant n*). **2** *nm, f* teacher.

enseigne [ɑ̃sɛɲ] *nf* [de commerce] sign.

enseignement [ɑ̃sɛɲmɑ̃] *nm* [gén] teaching; ~ **primaire/secondaire** primary/secondary education.

enseigner [ɑ̃seɲe] *vt litt & fig* to teach: ~ **qqch à qqn** to teach sb sthg, to teach sthg to sb.

ensemble [ɑ̃sɑ̃bl] **1** *adv* together. **2** *nm* [totalité] whole; **idée d'~** general idea; **dans l'~** on the whole. ‖ [harmonie] unity. ‖ [vêtement] outfit. ‖ [série] collection. ‖ MATHS set. ‖ MUS ensemble.

ensemencer [ɑ̃səmɑ̃se] *vt* [terre] to sow. ‖ [rivière] to stock.

enserrer [ɑ̃sere] *vt* [entourer] to encircle; *fig* to imprison.

ensevelir [ɑ̃səvlir] *vt litt & fig* to bury.

ensoleillé, -e [ɑ̃sɔleje] *adj* sunny.

ensoleillement [ɑ̃sɔlejmɑ̃] *nm* sunshine.

ensorceler [ɑ̃sɔrsəle] *vt* to bewitch.

ensuite [ɑ̃sɥit] *adv* [après, plus tard] after, afterwards, later. ‖ [puis] then, next, after that.

ensuivre [ãsyivr] ○ **s'ensuivre** *rp* to follow; **il s'ensuit que** it follows that.

entaille [ãtaj] *nf* cut.

entailler [ãtaje] *vt* to cut.

entamer [ãtame] *vt* [commencer] to start (on); [- bouteille] to start, to open. || [capital] to dip into. || [cuir, réputation] to damage. || [courage] to shake.

entartrer [ãtartre] *vt* to fur up. ○ **s'entartrer** *vp* to fur up.

entasser [ãtase] *vt* [accumuler, multiplier] to pile up. || [serrer] to squeeze. ○ **s'entasser** *vp* [objets] to pile up. || [personnes]: **s'~ dans** to squeeze into.

entendre [ãtãdr] *vt* [percevoir, écouter] to hear; **~ parler de qqch** to hear of ou about sthg. || *sout* [comprendre] to understand; **laisser ~ que** to imply that. || *sout* [vouloir]: **~ faire qqch** to intend to do sthg. || [vouloir dire] to mean. ○ **s'entendre** *vp* [sympathiser]: **s'~ avec qqn** to get on with sb. || [s'accorder] to agree.

entendu, -e [ãtãdy] **1** *pp* → **entendre**. **2** *adj* [compris] agreed, understood. || [complice] knowing.

entente [ãtãt] *nf* [harmonie] understanding. || [accord] agreement.

enterrement [ãtermã] *nm* burial.

enterrer [ãtere] *vt litt & fig* to bury.

en-tête [ãtɛt] *(pl* **en-têtes**) *nm* heading.

entêté, -e [ãtete] *adj* stubborn.

entêter [ãtete] ○ **s'entêter** *vp* to persist; **s'~ à faire qqch** to persist in doing sthg.

enthousiasme [ãtuzjasm] *nm* enthusiasm.

enthousiasmer [ãtuzjasme] *vt* to fill with enthusiasm. ○ **s'enthousiasmer** *vp*: **s'~ pour** to be enthusiastic about.

enticher [ãtife] ○ **s'enticher** *vp*: **s'~ de qqn/qqch** to become obsessed with sb/sthg.

entier, -ière [ãtje, jɛr] *adj* whole, entire. ○ **en entier** *loc adv* in its entirety.

entièrement [ãtjermã] *adv* [complètement] fully. || [pleinement] wholly, entirely.

entité [ãtite] *nf* entity.

entonner [ãtone] *vt* [chant] to strike up.

entonnoir [ãtonwar] *nm* [instrument] funnel. || [cavité] crater.

entorse [ãtors] *nf* MÉD sprain; **se faire une ~ à la cheville/au poignet** to sprain one's ankle/wrist.

entortiller [ãtortije] *vt* [entrelacer] to twist. || [envelopper]: **~ qqch autour de qqch** to wrap sthg round sthg. || *fam fig* [personne] to sweet-talk.

entourage [ãturaʒ] *nm* [milieu] entourage.

entourer [ãture] *vt* [enclore, encercler]: **~ (de)** to surround (with). || *fig* [soutenir] to rally round.

entracte [ãtrakt] *nm* interval; *fig* interlude.

entraide [ãtred] *nf* mutual assistance.

entrailles [ãtraj] *nfpl* [intestins] entrails. || *sout* [profondeurs] depths.

entrain [ãtrɛ̃] *nm* drive.

entraînement [ãtrenmã] *nm* [préparation] practice; SPORT training.

entraîner [ãtrene] *vt* TECHNOL to drive. || [tirer] to pull. || [susciter] to lead to. || SPORT to coach. || [emmener] to take along. ○ **s'entraîner** *vp* to practise; SPORT to train; **s'~ à faire qqch** to practise doing sthg.

entraîneur, -euse [ãtrenœr, øz] *nm, f* trainer, coach.

entrave [ãtrav] *nf* hobble; *fig* obstruction.

entraver [ãtrave] *vt* to hobble; *fig* to hinder.

entre [ãtr] *prép* [gén] between; **~ nous** between you and me, between ourselves. || [parmi] among; **l'un d'~ nous ira** one of us will go; **généralement ils restent ~ eux** they tend to keep themselves to themselves; **ils se battent ~ eux** they're fighting among ou amongst themselves.

entrebâiller [ãtrəbaje] *vt* to open slightly.

entrechoquer [ãtrəʃɔke] *vt* to bang together. ○ **s'entrechoquer** *vp* to bang into each other.

entrecôte [ãtrəkot] *nf* entrecôte.

entrecouper [ãtrəkupe] *vt* to intersperse.

entrecroiser [ãtrəkrwaze] *vt* to interlace. ○ **s'entrecroiser** *vp* to intersect.

entrée [ãtre] *nf* [arrivée, accès] entry, entrance; **«~ interdite»** "no admittance"; **«~ libre»** [dans musée] "admission free"; [dans boutique] "browsers welcome". || [porte] entrance. || [vestibule] (entrance) hall. || [billet] ticket. || [plat] starter, first course.

entrefaites [ãtrəfɛt] *nfpl*: **sur ces ~** just at that moment.

entrefilet [ãtrəfilɛ] *nm* paragraph.

entrejambe, entre-jambes [ãtrəʒãb] *nm* crotch.

entrelacer [ãtrəlase] *vt* to intertwine.

entremêler [ãtrəmele] *vt* to mix; ~ **de** to mix with.

entremets [ãtrəmɛ] *nm* dessert.

entremettre [ãtrəmɛtr] ○ **s'entremettre** *vp*: **s'~ (dans)** to mediate (in).

entremise [ãtrəmiz] *nf* intervention; **par l'~ de** through.

entrepont [ãtrəpɔ̃] *nm* steerage.

entreposer [ãtrəpoze] *vt* to store.

entrepôt [ãtrəpo] *nm* warehouse.

entreprendre [ãtrəprãdr] *vt* to undertake; [commencer] to start; ~ **de faire qqch** to undertake to do sthg.

entrepreneur, -euse [ãtrəprœnœr, øz] *nm, f* [de services & CONSTR] contractor.

entrepris, -e [ãtrəpri, iz] *pp* → entreprendre.

entreprise [ãtrəpriz] *nf* [travail, initiative] enterprise. || [société] company.

entrer [ãtre] **1** *vi* (*aux*: être) [pénétrer] to enter, to go/come in; ~ **dans** [gén] to enter; [pièce] to go/come into; [bain, voiture] to get into; *fig* [sujet] to go into; **faire ~ qqn** to show sb in. || [faire partie]: ~ **dans** to go into, to be part of. || [être admis, devenir membre]: ~ **à** [club, parti] to join; ~ **dans** [les affaires, l'enseignement] to go into; [la police, l'armée] to join; ~ **à l'université** to enter university; ~ **à l'hôpital** to go into hospital. **2** *vt* (*aux*: avoir) [gén] to bring in. || INFORM to enter, to input.

entresol [ãtrəsɔl] *nm* mezzanine.

entre-temps [ãtrətã] *adv* meanwhile.

entretenir [ãtrətnir] *vt* [faire durer] to keep alive. || [cultiver] to maintain. || [soigner] to look after. || [personne, famille] to support. || [parler à]: ~ **qqn de qqch** to speak to sb about sthg. ○ **s'entretenir** *vp* [se parler]: **s'~ (de)** to talk (about).

entretien [ãtrətjɛ̃] *nm* [de voiture, jardin] maintenance, upkeep. || [conversation] discussion; [colloque] debate.

entre-tuer [ãtrətɥe] ○ **s'entre-tuer** *vp* to kill each other.

entrevoir [ãtrəvwar] *vt* [distinguer] to make out. || [voir rapidement] to see briefly. || *fig* [deviner] to glimpse.

entrevu, -e [ãtrəvy] *pp* → entrevoir.

entrevue [ãtrəvy] *nf* meeting.

entrouvert, -e [ãtruvɛr, ɛrt] **1** *pp* → entrouvrir. **2** *adj* half-open.

entrouvrir [ãtruvrir] *vt* to open partly. ○ **s'entrouvrir** *vp* to open partly.

énumération [enymerasjɔ̃] *nf* enumeration.

énumérer [enymere] *vt* to enumerate.

envahir [ãvair] *vt* [gén & MIL.] to invade. || *fig* [suj: sommeil, doute] to overcome. || *fig* [déranger] to intrude on.

envahissant, -e [ãvaisã, ãt] *adj* [herbes] invasive. || [personne] intrusive.

envahisseur [ãvaisœr] *nm* invader.

enveloppe [ãvlɔp] *nf* [de lettre] envelope. || [d'emballage] covering. || [membrane] membrane; [de graine] husk.

envelopper [ãvlɔpe] *vt* [emballer] to wrap (up). || [suj: brouillard] to envelop. || [déguiser] to mask. ○ **s'envelopper** *vp*: **s'~ dans** to wrap o.s. up in.

envenimer [ãvnime] *vt* [blessure] to infect. || *fig* [querelle] to poison. ○ **s'envenimer** *vp* [s'infecter] to become infected. || *fig* [se détériorer] to become poisoned.

envergure [ãvɛrgyr] *nf* [largeur] span; [d'oiseau, d'avion] wingspan. || *fig* [qualité] calibre. || *fig* [importance] scope; **prendre de l'~** to expand.

envers¹ [ãvɛr] *prép* towards.

envers² [ãvɛr] *nm* [de tissu] wrong side; [de feuillet etc] back; [de médaille] reverse. || [face cachée] other side. ○ **à l'envers** *loc adv* [vêtement] inside out; [portrait, feuille] upside down; *fig* the wrong way.

envie [ãvi] *nf* [désir] desire; **avoir ~ de qqch/de faire qqch** to feel like sthg/like doing sthg, to want sthg/to do sthg. || [convoitise] envy; **ce tailleur me fait ~** I covet that suit.

envier [ãvje] *vt* to envy.

envieux, -leuse [ãvjø, jøz] **1** *adj* envious. **2** *nm, f* envious person; **faire des ~** to make other people envious.

environ [ãvirɔ̃] *adv* [à peu près] about.

environnement [ãvirɔnmã] *nm* environment.

environs [ãvirɔ̃] *nmpl* (surrounding) area (*sg*); **aux ~ de** [lieu] near; [époque] round about, around.

envisager [ãvizaʒe] *vt* to consider; ~ **de faire qqch** to be considering doing sthg.

envoi [ãvwa] *nm* [action] sending, dispatch. || [colis] parcel.

envol [ãvɔl] *nm* takeoff.

envolée [ãvɔle] *nf* [d'oiseaux & *fig*] flight. || [augmentation]: **l'~ du dollar** the rapid rise in the value of the dollar.

éponge

envoler [ɑ̃vɔle] ○ **s'envoler** *vp* [oiseau] to fly away. || [avion] to take off. || [disparaître] to disappear into thin air.

envoûter [ɑ̃vute] *vt* to bewitch.

envoyé, -e [ɑ̃vwaje] *nm, f* envoy.

envoyer [ɑ̃vwaje] *vt* to send; ~ qqch à qqn [expédier] to send sb sthg, to send sthg to sb; [jeter] to throw sb sthg, to throw sthg to sb; ~ qqn faire qqch to send sb to do sthg; ~ chercher qqn/qqch to send for sb/sthg.

épagneul [epaɲœl] *nm* spaniel.

épais, -aisse [epɛ, ɛs] *adj* [large, dense] thick. || [grossier] crude.

épaisseur [epɛsœr] *nf* [largeur, densité] thickness. || *fig* [consistance] depth.

épaissir [epesir] *vt & vi* to thicken. ○ **s'épaissir** *vp* [liquide] to thicken. || *fig* [mystère] to deepen.

épanchement [epɑ̃ʃmɑ̃] *nm* [effusion] outpouring. || MÉD effusion.

épancher [epɑ̃ʃe] ○ **s'épancher** *vp* [se confier] to pour one's heart out.

épanoui, -e [epanwi] *adj* [fleur] in full bloom. || [expression] radiant.

épanouir [epanwir] *vt* [personne] to make happy. ○ **s'épanouir** *vp* [fleur] to open. || [visage] to light up. || [corps] to fill out. || [personnalité] to blossom.

épanouissement [epanwismɑ̃] *nm* [de fleur] blooming, opening. || [de personnalité] flowering.

épargnant, -e [eparɲɑ̃, ɑ̃t] *nm, f* saver.

épargne [eparɲ] *nf* [action, vertu] saving. || [somme] savings (*pl*); ~ logement savings account (*to buy property*).

épargner [eparɲe] *vt* [gén] to spare; ~ qqch à qqn to spare sb sthg. || [économiser] to save.

éparpiller [eparpije] *vt* [choses, personnes] to scatter. ○ **s'éparpiller** *vp* [se disperser] to scatter.

épars, -e [epar, ars] *adj sout* [objets] scattered; [végétation, cheveux] sparse.

épatant, -e [epatɑ̃, ɑ̃t] *adj fam* great.

épaté, -e [epate] *adj* [nez] flat. || *fam* [étonné] amazed.

épaule [epol] *nf* shoulder.

épauler [epole] *vt* to support, to back up.

épaulette [epolɛt] *nf* MIL epaulet. || [rembourrage] shoulder pad.

épave [epav] *nf* wreck.

épée [epe] *nf* sword.

épeler [eple] *vt* to spell.

éperdu, -e [eperdy] *adj* [sentiment] passionate; ~ de [personne] overcome with.

éperon [eprɔ̃] *nm* [de cavalier, de montagne] spur; [de navire] ram.

éperonner [eprɔne] *vt* to spur on.

épervier [epervje] *nm* sparrowhawk.

éphémère [efemɛr] **1** *adj* [bref] ephemeral, fleeting. **2** *nm* ZOOL mayfly.

éphéméride [efemerid] *nf* tear-off calendar.

épi [epi] *nm* [de céréale] ear. || [cheveux] tuft.

épice [epis] *nf* spice.

épicéa [episea] *nm* spruce.

épicer [epise] *vt* [plat] to spice.

épicerie [episri] *nf* [magasin] grocer's (shop). || [denrées] groceries (*pl*).

épicier, -ière [episje, jɛr] *nm, f* grocer.

épidémie [epidemi] *nf* epidemic.

épiderme [epiderm] *nm* epidermis.

épier [epje] *vt* [espionner] to spy on. || [observer] to look for.

épilation [epilasjɔ̃] *nf* hair removal.

épilepsie [epilepsi] *nf* epilepsy.

épiler [epile] *vt* [jambes] to remove hair from; [sourcils] to pluck. ○ **s'épiler** *vp*: s'~ les jambes to remove the hair from one's legs; s'~ les sourcils to pluck one's eyebrows.

épilogue [epilɔg] *nm* [de roman] epilogue. || [d'affaire] outcome.

épinards [epinar] *nmpl* spinach (*U*).

épine [epin] *nf* [piquant - de rosier] thorn; [- de hérisson] spine.

épineux, -euse [epinø, øz] *adj* thorny.

épingle [epɛ̃gl] *nf* [instrument] pin.

épingler [epɛ̃gle] *vt* [fixer] to pin (up). || *fam fig* [arrêter] to nab.

épinière [epinjɛr] → moelle.

Épiphanie [epifani] *nf* Epiphany.

épique [epik] *adj* epic.

épisode [epizɔd] *nm* episode.

épisodique [epizɔdik] *adj* [occasionnel] occasional. || [secondaire] minor.

épitaphe [epitaf] *nf* epitaph.

épithète [epitɛt] **1** *nf* GRAM attribute. || [qualificatif] term. **2** *adj* attributive.

éploré, -e [eplɔre] *adj* [personne] in tears; [visage, air] tearful.

épluche-légumes [eplyʃlegym] *nm inv* potato peeler.

éplucher [eplyʃe] *vt* [légumes] to peel. || [textes] to dissect; [comptes] to scrutinize.

épluchure [eplyʃyr] *nf* peelings (*pl*).

éponge [epɔ̃ʒ] *nf* sponge.

éponger [epɔʒe] *vt* [liquide, déficit] to mop up. || [visage] to mop, to wipe.

épopée [epɔpe] *nf* epic.

époque [epɔk] *nf* [de l'année] time. || [de l'histoire] period.

époumoner [epumɔne] ○ **s'époumoner** *vp* to shout o.s. hoarse.

épouse → **époux**.

épouser [epuze] *vt* [personne] to marry. || [forme] to hug. || *fig* [idée, principe] to espouse.

épousseter [epuste] *vt* to dust.

époustouflant, -e [epustuflã, ãt] *adj fam* amazing.

épouvantable [epuvãtabl] *adj* dreadful.

épouvantail [epuvãtaj] *nm* [à moineaux] scarecrow; *fig* bogeyman.

épouvanter [epuvãte] *vt* to terrify.

époux, épouse [epu, epuz] *nm, f* spouse.

éprendre [eprãdr] ○ **s'éprendre** *vp sout*: **s'~ de** to fall in love with.

épreuve [eprœv] *nf* [essai, examen] test; **à l'~ du feu** fireproof; **~ de force** *fig* trial of strength. || [malheur] ordeal. || SPORT event. || TYPO proof. || PHOT print.

épris, -e [epri, iz] **1** *pp* → **éprendre**. **2** *adj sout*: **~ de** in love with.

éprouver [epruve] *vt* [tester] to test. || [ressentir] to feel. || [faire souffrir] to distress. || [difficultés, problèmes] to experience.

éprouvette [epruvɛt] *nf* [tube à essai] test tube. || [échantillon] sample.

EPS (*abr de* **éducation physique et sportive**) *nf* PE.

épuisé, -e [epɥize] *adj* [personne, corps] exhausted. || [marchandise] sold out, out of stock; [livre] out of print.

épuisement [epɥizmã] *nm* exhaustion.

épuiser [epɥize] *vt* to exhaust.

épuisette [epɥizɛt] *nf* landing net.

épurer [epyre] *vt* [eau, huile] to purify. || POLIT to purge.

équarrir [ekarir] *vt* [animal] to cut up. || [poutre] to square.

équateur [ekwatœr] *nm* equator.

Équateur [ekwatœr] *nm*: **l'~** Ecuador.

équation [ekwasjɔ̃] *nf* equation.

équatorial, -e, -iaux [ekwatɔrjal, jo] *adj* equatorial.

équerre [ekɛr] *nf* [instrument] set square; [en T] T-square.

équestre [ekɛstr] *adj* equestrian.

équilatéral, -e, -aux [ekɥilateral, o] *adj* equilateral.

équilibre [ekilibr] *nm* [gén] balance. || [psychique] stability.

équilibré, -e [ekilibre] *adj* [personne] well-balanced. || [vie] stable. || ARCHIT: **aux proportions ~es** well-proportioned.

équilibrer [ekilibre] *vt* to balance. ○ **s'équilibrer** *vp* to balance each other out.

équilibriste [ekilibrist] *nmf* tightrope walker.

équipage [ekipaʒ] *nm* crew.

équipe [ekip] *nf* team.

équipement [ekipmã] *nm* [matériel] equipment. || [aménagement] facilities (*pl*).

équiper [ekipe] *vt* [navire, armée] to equip. || [personne, local] to equip, to fit out; **~ qqn/qqch de** to equip sb/sthg with, to fit sb/sthg out with. ○ **s'équiper** *vp*: **s'~ (de)** to equip o.s. (with).

équipier, -ière [ekipje, jɛr] *nm, f* team member.

équitable [ekitabl] *adj* fair.

équitation [ekitasjɔ̃] *nf* riding, horse-riding.

équité [ekite] *nf* fairness.

équivalent, -e [ekivalã, ãt] *adj* equivalent. ○ **équivalent** *nm* equivalent.

équivaloir [ekivalwar] *vi*: **~ à** to be equivalent to.

équivoque [ekivɔk] **1** *adj* [ambigu] ambiguous. || [mystérieux] dubious. **2** *nf* ambiguity; **sans ~** unequivocal (*adj*), unequivocally (*adv*).

érable [erabl] *nm* maple.

éradiquer [eradike] *vt* to eradicate.

érafler [erafle] *vt* [peau] to scratch. || [mur, voiture] to scrape.

éraflure [eraflyr] *nf* [de peau] scratch. || [de mur, voiture] scrape.

éraillé, -e [eraje] *adj* [voix] hoarse.

ère [ɛr] *nf* era.

érection [erɛksjɔ̃] *nf* erection.

éreintant, -e [erɛ̃tã, ãt] *adj* exhausting.

éreinter [erɛ̃te] *vt* [fatiguer] to exhaust. || [critiquer] to pull to pieces.

ergonomique [ergɔnɔmik] *adj* ergonomic.

ériger [eriʒe] *vt* [monument] to erect. || [tribunal] to set up. || *fig* [transformer]: **~ qqn en** to set sb up as.

ermite [ermit] *nm* hermit.

éroder [erɔde] *vt* to erode.

érogène [erɔʒɛn] *adj* erogenous.

érosion [erozjɔ̃] *nf* erosion.

érotique [erɔtik] *adj* erotic.

érotisme [erɔtism] *nm* eroticism.

errance [erɑ̃s] *nf* wandering.

errer [ere] *vi* to wander.

erreur [erœr] *nf* mistake; **par ~** by mistake.

erroné, -e [erɔne] *adj sout* wrong.

éructer [erykte] *vi* to belch.

érudit, -e [erydi, it] **1** *adj* erudite, learned. **2** *nm, f* learned person.

éruption [erypsjɔ̃] *nf* MÉD rash. || [de volcan] eruption.

es → **être**.

escabeau, -x [ɛskabo] *nm* [échelle] stepladder. || *vieilli* [tabouret] stool.

escadre [ɛskadr] *nf* [navires] fleet. || [avions] wing.

escadrille [ɛskadrij] *nf* [navires] flotilla. || [avions] flight.

escadron [ɛskadrɔ̃] *nm* squadron.

escalade [ɛskalad] *nf* [de montagne, grille] climbing. || [des prix, de violence] escalation.

escalader [ɛskalade] *vt* to climb.

escale [ɛskal] *nf* [lieu - pour navire] port of call; [- pour avion] stopover. || [arrêt - de navire] call; [- d'avion] stopover, stop; **faire ~ à** [navire] to put in at, to call at; [avion] to stop over at.

escalier [ɛskalje] *nm* stairs (*pl*); **descendre/monter l'~** to go downstairs/upstairs; **~ roulant** OU **mécanique** escalator.

escalope [ɛskalɔp] *nf* escalope.

escamotable [ɛskamɔtabl] *adj* [train d'atterrissage] retractable; [antenne] telescopic. || [table] folding.

escamoter [ɛskamɔte] *vt* [faire disparaître] to make disappear. || [voler] to lift. || [rentrer] to retract.

escapade [ɛskapad] *nf* [voyage] outing. || [fugue] escapade.

escargot [ɛskargo] *nm* snail.

escarmouche [ɛskarmuʃ] *nf* skirmish.

escarpé, -e [ɛskarpe] *adj* steep.

escarpement [ɛskarpəmɑ̃] *nm* [de pente] steep slope. || GÉOGR escarpment.

escarpin [ɛskarpɛ̃] *nm* court shoe *Br*.

escarre [ɛskar] *nf* bedsore, pressure sore.

escient [esjɑ̃] *nm*: **à bon ~** advisedly; **à mauvais ~** ill-advisedly.

esclaffer [ɛsklafe] ○ **s'esclaffer** *vp* to burst out laughing.

esclandre [ɛsklɑ̃dr] *nm sout* scene.

esclavage [ɛsklavaʒ] *nm* slavery.

esclave [ɛsklav] **1** *nmf* slave. **2** *adj*: **être ~ de** to be a slave to.

escompte [ɛskɔ̃t] *nm* discount.

escompter [ɛskɔ̃te] *vt* [prévoir] to count on. || FIN to discount.

escorte [ɛskɔrt] *nf* escort.

escorter [ɛskɔrte] *vt* to escort.

escrime [ɛskrim] *nf* fencing.

escrimer [ɛskrime] ○ **s'escrimer** *vp*: **s'~ à faire qqch** to work (away) at doing sthg.

escroc [ɛskro] *nm* swindler.

escroquer [ɛskrɔke] *vt* to swindle; **~ qqch à qqn** to swindle sb out of sthg.

escroquerie [ɛskrɔkri] *nf* swindle, swindling (*U*).

eskimo, Eskimo → **esquimau**.

espace [ɛspas] *nm* space; **~ vert** green space, green area.

espacer [ɛspase] *vt* [dans l'espace] to space out. || [dans le temps - visites] to space out; [- paiements] to spread out.

espadon [ɛspadɔ̃] *nm* [poisson] swordfish.

espadrille [ɛspadrij] *nf* espadrille.

Espagne [ɛspaɲ] *nf*: **l'~** Spain.

espagnol, -e [ɛspaɲɔl] *adj* Spanish. ○ **espagnol** *nm* [langue] Spanish. ○ **Espagnol, -e** *nm, f* Spaniard; **les Espagnols** the Spanish.

espèce [ɛspɛs] *nf* BIOL, BOT & ZOOL species. || [sorte] kind, sort; **~ d'idiot!** you stupid fool! ○ **espèces** *nfpl* cash; **payer en ~s** to pay (in) cash.

espérance [ɛsperɑ̃s] *nf* hope; **~ de vie** life expectancy.

espérer [ɛspere] **1** *vt* to hope for; **~ que** to hope (that); **~ faire qqch** to hope to do sthg. **2** *vi* to hope.

espiègle [ɛspjɛgl] *adj* mischievous.

espion, -ionne [ɛspjɔ̃, jɔn] *nm, f* spy.

espionnage [ɛspjɔnaʒ] *nm* spying; **~ industriel** industrial espionage.

espionner [ɛspjɔne] *vt* to spy on.

esplanade [ɛsplanad] *nf* esplanade.

espoir [ɛspwar] *nm* hope.

esprit [ɛspri] *nm* [entendement, personne, pensée] mind; **reprendre ses ~s** to recover. || [attitude] spirit; **~ de compétition** competitive spirit; **~ critique** critical acumen. || [humour] wit. || [fantôme] spirit, ghost.

esquimau, -aude, -aux, eskimo [ɛskimo, od] *adj* Eskimo. ○ **Esquimau, -aude** *nm, f*, **Eskimo** *nmf* Eskimo.

esquinter [ɛskɛ̃te] *vt fam* [abîmer] to ruin. || [critiquer] to slate *Br*, to pan.

esquiver [ɛskive] *vt* to dodge. ○ **s'esquiver** *vp* to slip away.

essai [ɛsɛ] *nm* [vérification] test, testing (*U*); **à l'~** on trial. || [tentative] attempt. || RUGBY try.

essaim [ɛsɛ̃] *nm litt & fig* swarm.

essayage [esejaʒ] *nm* fitting.

essayer [eseje] *vt* to try; **~ de faire qqch** to try to do sthg.

essence [esɑ̃s] *nf* [fondement, de plante] essence. || [carburant] gas *Am*. || [d'arbre] species.

essentiel, -ielle [esɑ̃sjɛl] *adj* [indispensable] essential. || [fondamental] basic. ○ **essentiel** *nm* [point]: **l'~** [le principal] the essential ou main thing. || [quantité]: **l'~ de** the main ou greater part of.

essentiellement [esɑ̃sjɛlmɑ̃] *adv* [avant tout] above all. || [par essence] essentially.

esseulé, -e [esœle] *adj littéraire* forsaken.

essieu, -x [esjø] *nm* axle.

essor [esɔr] *nm* flight, expansion, boom; **prendre son ~** to take flight; *fig* to take off.

essorer [esɔre] *vt* [à la main, à rouleaux] to wring out; [à la machine] to spin-dry; [salade] to spin, to dry.

essoreuse [esɔrøz] *nf* [à rouleaux] mangle; [électrique] spin-dryer; [à salade] salad spinner.

essouffler [esufle] *vt* to make breathless. ○ **s'essouffler** *vp* to be breathless ou out of breath; *fig* to run out of steam.

essuie-glace [esɥiglas] (*pl* **essuie-glaces**) *nm* windshield wiper *Am*.

essuie-mains [esɥimɛ̃] *nm inv* hand towel.

essuie-tout [esɥitu] *nm inv* kitchen roll.

essuyer [esɥije] *vt* [sécher] to dry. || [nettoyer] to dust. || *fig* [subir] to suffer. ○ **s'essuyer** *vp* to dry o.s.

est¹ [ɛst] **1** *nm* east; **un vent d'~** an easterly wind; **à l'~** in the east; **à l'~ (de)** to the east (of). **2** *adj inv* [gén] east; [province, région] eastern.

est² [ɛ] → **être**.

estafette [ɛstafɛt] *nf* dispatch-rider.

estafilade [ɛstafilad] *nf* slash, gash.

est-allemand, -e [ɛstalmɑ̃, ɑ̃d] *adj* East German.

estampe [ɛstɑ̃p] *nf* print.

est-ce que [ɛskə] *adv interr*: **est-ce qu'il fait beau?** is the weather good?; **~**

vous aimez l'accordéon? do you like the accordion?; **où ~ tu es?** where are you?

esthétique [ɛstetik] *adj* [relatif à la beauté] aesthetic. || [harmonieux] attractive.

estimation [ɛstimasjɔ̃] *nf* estimate, estimation.

estime [ɛstim] *nf* respect, esteem.

estimer [ɛstime] *vt* [expertiser] to value. || [évaluer] to estimate. || [respecter] to respect. || [penser]: **~ que** to feel (that).

estivant, -e [ɛstivɑ̃, ɑ̃t] *nm, f* (summer) holiday-maker *Br* ou vacationer *Am*.

estomac [ɛstɔma] *nm* ANAT stomach.

estomper [ɛstɔ̃pe] *vt* to blur; *fig* [douleur] to lessen. ○ **s'estomper** *vp* to be/become blurred; *fig* [douleur] to lessen.

Estonie [ɛstɔni] *nf*: **l'~** Estonia.

estrade [ɛstrad] *nf* dais.

estragon [ɛstragɔ̃] *nm* tarragon.

estropié, -e [ɛstrɔpje] **1** *adj* crippled. **2** *nm, f* cripple.

estuaire [ɛstɥɛr] *nm* estuary.

esturgeon [ɛstyrʒɔ̃] *nm* sturgeon.

et [e] *conj* [gén] and; **~ moi?** what about me? || [dans les fractions et les nombres composés]: **vingt ~ un** twenty-one; **il y a deux ans ~ demi** two and a half years ago.

ét. (*abr de* étage) fl.

étable [etabl] *nf* cowshed.

établi [etabli] *nm* workbench.

établir [etablir] *vt* [gén] to establish; [record] to set. || [dresser] to draw up. ○ **s'établir** *vp* [s'installer] to settle. || [s'instaurer] to become established.

établissement [etablismɑ̃] *nm* establishment; **~ hospitalier** hospital; **~ scolaire** educational establishment.

étage [etaʒ] *nm* [de bâtiment] storey, floor; **un immeuble à quatre ~s** a fourstorey block of flats; **au premier ~** on the first floor *Br*, on the second floor *Am*. || [de fusée] stage.

étagère [etaʒɛr] *nf* [rayon] shelf. || [meuble] shelves (*pl*), set of shelves.

étain [etɛ̃] *nm* [métal] tin; [alliage] pewter.

étais, était *etc* → **être**.

étal [etal] (*pl* **-s** ou **étaux** [eto]) *nm* [éventaire] stall. || [de boucher] butcher's block.

étalage [etalaʒ] *nm* [action, ensemble d'objets] display; **faire ~ de** *fig* to flaunt. || [devanture] window display.

étalagiste [etalaʒist] *nmf* [décorateur] window-dresser.

étaler [etale] *vt* [exposer] to display. || [étendre] to spread out. || [dans le temps] to stagger. || [mettre une couche de] to spread. || [exhiber] to parade. ○ **s'étaler** *vp* [s'étendre] to spread. || [dans le temps]: **s'~ (sur)** to be spread (over). || *fam* [tomber] to fall flat on one's face.

étalon [etalɔ̃] *nm* [cheval] stallion. || [mesure] standard.

étanche [etɑ̃ʃ] *adj* watertight; [montre] waterproof.

étancher [etɑ̃ʃe] *vt* [sang, larmes] to stem (the flow of). || [assouvir] to quench.

étang [etɑ̃] *nm* pond.

étant *ppr* → être.

étape [etap] *nf* [gén] stage. || [halte] stop; **faire ~ à** to break one's journey at.

état [eta] *nm* [manière d'être] state; **être en ~/hors d'~ de faire qqch** to be in a/in no fit state to do sthg; **en bon/mauvais ~** in good/poor condition; **en ~ de marche** in working order; **~ d'âme** mood; **~ d'esprit** state of mind; **~ de santé** (state of) health; **être dans tous ses ~s** *fig* to be in a state. || [métier, statut] status; **~ civil** ADMIN ≃ marital status. || [inventaire - gén] inventory; [- de dépenses] statement; **~ des lieux** *inventory and inspection of rented property*. ○ **État** *nm* [nation] state.

état-major [etamaʒɔr] *nm* ADMIN & MIL. staff; [de parti] leadership. || [lieu] headquarters (*pl*).

États-Unis [etazyni] *nmpl*: **les ~ (d'Amérique)** the United States (of America).

étau, -x [eto] *nm* vice.

étayer [eteje] *vt* to prop up; *fig* to back up.

etc. (*abr de* et cætera) etc.

été [ete] **1** *pp inv* → être. **2** *nm* summer; **en ~** in (the) summer.

éteindre [etɛ̃dr] *vt* [incendie, bougie, cigarette] to put out; [radio, chauffage, lampe] to turn off, to switch off. ○ **s'éteindre** *vp* [feu, lampe] to go out. || *fig* & *littéraire* [personne] to pass away. || [race] to die out.

étendard [etɑ̃dar] *nm* standard.

étendre [etɑ̃dr] *vt* [déployer] to stretch; [journal, linge] to spread (out). || [coucher] to lay. || [appliquer] to spread. || [accroître] to extend. || [diluer] to dilute. ○ **s'étendre** *vp* [se coucher] to lie down. || [s'étaler au loin]: **s'~ (de/jusqu'à)** to

stretch (from/as far as). || [croître] to spread. || [s'attarder]: **s'~ sur** to elaborate on.

étendu, -e [etɑ̃dy] **1** *pp* → étendre. **2** *adj* [bras, main] outstretched. || [plaine, connaissances] extensive. ○ **étendue** *nf* [surface] area, expanse. || [importance] extent.

éternel, -elle [etɛrnɛl] *adj* eternal; **ce ne sera pas ~** this won't last for ever.

éterniser [etɛrnize] ○ **s'éterniser** *vp* [se prolonger] to drag out. || *fam* [rester] to stay for ever.

éternité [etɛrnite] *nf* eternity.

éternuer [etɛrnɥe] *vi* to sneeze.

êtes → être.

éther [etɛr] *nm* ether.

Éthiopie [etjɔpi] *nf*: **l'~** Ethiopia.

éthique [etik] **1** *nf* ethics (*U or pl*). **2** *adj* ethical.

ethnie [ɛtni] *nf* ethnic group.

ethnique [ɛtnik] *adj* ethnic.

ethnologie [ɛtnɔlɔʒi] *nf* ethnology.

éthylisme [etilism] *nm* alcoholism.

étiez, étions *etc* → être.

étincelant, -e [etɛ̃slɑ̃, ɑ̃t] *adj* sparkling.

étinceler [etɛ̃sle] *vi* to sparkle.

étincelle [etɛ̃sɛl] *nf* spark.

étioler [etjɔle] ○ **s'étioler** *vp* [plante] to wilt; [personne] to weaken.

étiqueter [etikte] *vt litt* & *fig* to label.

étiquette [etiket] *nf* [marque & *fig*] label. || [protocole] etiquette.

étirer [etire] *vt* to stretch. ○ **s'étirer** *vp* to stretch.

étoffe [etɔf] *nf* fabric, material.

étoile [etwal] *nf* star; **~ filante** shooting star; **à la belle ~** *fig* under the stars. ○ **étoile de mer** *nf* starfish.

étoilé, -e [etwale] *adj* [ciel, nuit] starry; **la bannière ~e** the Star-Spangled Banner. || [vitre, pare-brise] shattered.

étole [etɔl] *nf* stole.

étonnant, -e [etɔnɑ̃, ɑ̃t] *adj* astonishing.

étonnement [etɔnmɑ̃] *nm* astonishment, surprise.

étonner [etɔne] *vt* to surprise, to astonish. ○ **s'étonner** *vp*: **s'~ (de)** to be surprised (by); **s'~ que** (+ *subjonctif*) to be surprised (that).

étouffant, -e [etufɑ̃, ɑ̃t] *adj* stifling.

étouffée [etufe] ○ **à l'étouffée** *loc adv* steamed; [viande] braised.

étouffer [etufe] **1** *vt* [gén] to stifle. || [asphyxier] to suffocate. || [feu] to smother. || [scandale, révolte] to suppress. **2** *vi* to suffocate. ○ **s'étouffer** *vp* [s'étrangler] to choke.

étourderie [eturdəri] *nf* [distraction] thoughtlessness. || [bévue] careless mistake; [acte irréfléchi] thoughtless act.

étourdi, -e [eturdi] **1** *adj* scatterbrained. **2** *nm, f* scatterbrain.

étourdir [eturdir] *vt* [assommer] to daze.

étourdissement [eturdismɑ̃] *nm* dizzy spell.

étourneau, -x [eturno] *nm* starling.

étrange [etrɑ̃ʒ] *adj* strange.

étranger, -ère [etrɑ̃ʒe, ɛr] **1** *adj* [gén] foreign. || [différent, isolé] unknown, unfamiliar; **être ~ à qqn** to be unknown to sb. **2** *nm, f* [de nationalité différente] foreigner. || [inconnu] stranger. || [exclu] outsider. ○ **étranger** *nm*: **à l'~** abroad.

étranglement [etrɑ̃gləmɑ̃] *nm* [strangulation] strangulation. || [rétrécissement] constriction.

étrangler [etrɑ̃gle] *vt* [gén] to choke. || [stranguler] to strangle. || [réprimer] to stifle. || [serrer] to constrict. ○ **s'étrangler** *vp* [s'étouffer] to choke.

étrave [etrav] *nf* stem.

être [ɛtr] **1** *nm* being; **les ~s vivants/ humains** living/human beings. **2** *v aux* [pour les temps composés] to have/to be; **il est parti hier** he left yesterday; **il est déjà arrivé** he has already arrived; **il est né en 1952** he was born in 1952. || [pour le passif] to be; **la maison a été vendue** the house has been or was sold. **3** *v attr* [état] to be; **la maison est blanche** the house is white; **il est médecin** he's a doctor. || [possession]: **~ à qqn** to be sb's, to belong to sb; **c'est à vous, cette voiture?** is this your car?, is this car yours? **4** *v impers* [indique le temps]: **quelle heure est-il?** what time is it?, what's the time?; **il est dix heures dix** it's ten past *Br* or after *Am* ten. || [suivi d'un adjectif]: **il est ... it is ...; il est inutile de** it's useless to. **5** *vi* [exister] to be. || [indique une situation, un état] to be; **il est à Paris** he's in Paris; **nous sommes au printemps/en été** it's spring/summer. || [indiquant une origine]: **il est de Paris** he's from Paris. ○ **être à** *v + prép* [indiquant une obligation]: **c'est à vérifier** it needs to be checked.

étreindre [etrɛ̃dr] *vt* [embrasser] to hug, to embrace. ○ **s'étreindre** *vp* to embrace each other.

étreinte [etrɛ̃t] *nf* [enlacement] embrace. || [pression] stranglehold.

étrenner [etrene] *vt* to use for the first time.

étrennes [etren] *nfpl* Christmas box (*sg*).

étrier [etrije] *nm* stirrup.

étriper [etripe] *vt* [animal] to disembowel. || *fam fig* [tuer] to kill. ○ **s'étriper** *vp fam* to tear each other to pieces.

étriqué, -e [etrike] *adj* [vêtement] tight. || [mesquin] narrow.

étroit, -e [etrwa, at] *adj* [gén] narrow. || [intime] close. || [serré] tight. ○ **l'étroit** *loc adj*: **être à l'~** to be cramped.

étroitesse [etrwates] *nf* narrowness.

étude [etyd] *nf* [gén] study; **à l'~** under consideration; **~ de marché** market research (*U*). || [de notaire - local] office; [- charge] practice. || MUS étude. ○ **études** *nfpl* studies; **faire des ~s** to study.

étudiant, -e [etydjɑ̃, ɑ̃t] *nm, f* student.

étudié, -e [etydje] *adj* studied.

étudier [etydje] *vt* to study.

étui [etɥi] *nm* case; **~ à cigarettes/ lunettes** cigarette/glasses case.

étuve [etyv] *nf* [local] steam room; *fig* oven. || [appareil] sterilizer.

étuvée [etyve] ○ **à l'étuvée** *loc adv* braised.

étymologie [etimɔlɔʒi] *nf* etymology.

eu, -e [y] *pp* → avoir.

E-U, E-U A (*abr de* États-Unis (d'Amérique)) *nmpl* US, USA.

eucalyptus [økaliptys] *nm* eucalyptus.

euh [ø] *interj* er.

eunuque [ønyk] *nm* eunuch.

euphémisme [øfemism] *nm* euphemism.

euphorie [øfɔri] *nf* euphoria.

euphorisant, -e [øfɔrizɑ̃, ɑ̃t] *adj* exhilarating. ○ **euphorisant** *nm* antidepressant.

eurent → avoir.

Europe [ørɔp] *nf*: **l'~** Europe.

européen, -enne [ørɔpeɛ̃, ɛn] *adj* European. ○ **Européen, -enne** *nm, f* European.

eus, eut *etc* → avoir.

eût → avoir.

euthanasie [øtanazi] *nf* euthanasia.

eux [ø] *pron pers* [sujet] they; **ce sont ~ qui me l'ont dit** they're the ones who told me. || [complément] them. ○ **euxmêmes** *pron pers* themselves.

évacuer [evakчe] *rt* [gén] to evacuate. || [liquide] to drain.

évadé, -e [evade] *nm, f* escaped prisoner.

évader [evade] ○ **s'évader** *vp*: s'~ (de) to escape (from).

évaluation [evalчasjɔ̃] *nf* [action] valuation; [résultat] estimate.

évaluer [evalчe] *rt* [distance] to estimate; [tableau] to value; [risque] to assess.

évangélique [evɑ̃ʒelik] *adj* evangelical.

évangile [evɑ̃ʒil] *nm* gospel.

évanouir [evanwir] ○ **s'évanouir** *vp* [défaillir] to faint. || [disparaître] to fade.

évanouissement [evanwismɑ̃] *nm* [syncope] fainting fit.

évaporer [evapɔre] ○ **s'évaporer** *vp* to evaporate.

évasé, -e [evaze] *adj* flared.

évasif, -ive [evazif, iv] *adj* evasive.

évasion [evazjɔ̃] *nf* escape.

évêché [eveʃe] *nm* [territoire] diocese.

éveil [evɛj] *nm* awakening; **en ~** on the alert.

éveillé, -e [eveje] *adj* [qui ne dort pas] wide awake. || [vif, alerte] alert.

éveiller [eveje] *vt* to arouse; [intelligence, dormeur] to awaken. ○ **s'éveiller** *vp* [dormeur] to wake, to awaken. || [curiosité] to be aroused. || [esprit, intelligence] to be awakened.

événement [evɛnmɑ̃] *nm* event.

éventail [evɑ̃taj] *nm* [objet] fan; **en ~** fan-shaped. || [choix] range.

éventaire [evɑ̃tɛr] *nm* [étalage] stall, stand. || [corbeille] tray.

éventer [evɑ̃te] *vt* [rafraîchir] to fan. || [divulguer] to give away. ○ **s'éventer** *vp* [se rafraîchir] to fan o.s. || [parfum, vin] to go stale.

éventrer [evɑ̃tre] *vt* [étriper] to disembowel. || [fendre] to rip open.

éventualité [evɑ̃tчalite] *nf* [possibilité] possibility. || [circonstance] eventuality; **dans l'~ de** in the event of.

éventuel, -elle [evɑ̃tчɛl] *adj* possible.

éventuellement [evɑ̃tчɛlmɑ̃] *adv* possibly.

évêque [evɛk] *nm* bishop.

évertuer [evɛrtчe] ○ **s'évertuer** *vp*: s'~ **à faire qqch** to strive to do sthg.

évidemment [evidamɑ̃] *adv* obviously.

évidence [evidɑ̃s] *nf* [caractère] evidence; [fait] obvious fact; **mettre en ~** to emphasize, to highlight.

évident, -e [evidɑ̃, ɑ̃t] *adj* obvious.

évider [evide] *vt* to hollow out.

évier [evje] *nm* sink.

évincer [evɛ̃se] *rt*: ~ **qqn (de)** to oust sb (from).

éviter [evite] *vt* [esquiver] to avoid. || [s'abstenir]: ~ **de faire qqch** to avoid doing sthg. || [épargner]: ~ **qqch à qqn** to save sb sthg.

évocateur, -trice [evɔkatœr, tris] *adj* [geste, regard] meaningful.

évocation [evɔkasjɔ̃] *nf* evocation.

évolué, -e [evɔlчe] *adj* [développé] developed. || [libéral, progressiste] broad-minded.

évoluer [evɔlчe] *vi* [changer] to evolve; [personne] to change. || [se mouvoir] to move about.

évolution [evɔlчsjɔ̃] *nf* [transformation] development. || BIOL evolution. || MÉD progress.

évoquer [evɔke] *vt* [souvenir] to evoke. || [problème] to refer to.

exacerber [ɛgzasɛrbe] *vt* to heighten.

exact, -e [ɛgzakt] *adj* [calcul] correct. || [récit, copie] exact. || [ponctuel] punctual.

exactement [ɛgzaktəmɑ̃] *adv* exactly.

exaction [ɛgzaksjɔ̃] *nf* extortion.

exactitude [ɛgzaktityd] *nf* [de calcul, montre] accuracy. || [ponctualité] punctuality.

ex æquo [ɛgzeko] **1** *adj inv* & *nmf inv* equal. **2** *adv* equal; **troisième ~** third equal.

exagération [ɛgzaʒerasjɔ̃] *nf* exaggeration.

exagéré, -e [ɛgzaʒere] *adj* exaggerated.

exagérer [ɛgzaʒere] *vt* & *vi* to exaggerate.

exalté, -e [ɛgzalte] **1** *adj* [sentiment] elated; [tempérament] over-excited; [imagination] vivid. **2** *nm, f* fanatic.

exalter [ɛgzalte] *vt* to excite. ○ **s'exalter** *vp* to get carried away.

examen [ɛgzamɛ̃] *nm* examination; SCOL exam, examination; ~ **médical** medical (examination).

examinateur, -trice [ɛgzaminatœr, tris] *nm, f* examiner.

examiner [ɛgzamine] *vt* to examine.

exaspération [ɛgzasperasjɔ̃] *nf* exasperation.

exaspérer [ɛgzaspere] *vt* to exasperate.

exaucer [ɛgzose] *vt* to grant.

excédent [ɛksedɑ̃] *nm* surplus; **en ~** surplus (*avant n*).

excéder [ɛksede] *vt* [gén] to exceed. || [exaspérer] to exasperate.

excellence [ɛkselɑ̃s] *nf* excellence; **par ~** par excellence.

excellent, -e [ɛkselɑ̃, ɑ̃t] *adj* excellent.

exceller [ɛksele] *vi*: **~ en** ou **dans qqch** to excel at ou in sthg; **~ à faire qqch** to excel at doing sthg.

excentré, -e [ɛksɑ̃tre] *adj*: **c'est très ~** it's quite a long way out.

excentrique [ɛksɑ̃trik] **1** *nmf* eccentric. **2** *adj* [gén] eccentric. || [quartier] outlying.

excepté, -e [ɛksɛpte] *adj*: **tous sont venus, lui ~** everyone came except (for) him. ○ **excepté** *prép* apart from, except.

exception [ɛksɛpsjɔ̃] *nf* exception; **à l'~ de** except for.

exceptionnel, -elle [ɛksɛpsjɔnɛl] *adj* exceptional.

excès [ɛksɛ] *nm* excess.

excessif, -ive [ɛksesif, iv] *adj* [démesuré] excessive. || [extrême] extreme.

excitant, -e [ɛksitɑ̃, ɑ̃t] *adj* [stimulant, passionnant] exciting. ○ **excitant** *nm* stimulant.

excitation [ɛksitasjɔ̃] *nf* [énervement] excitement. || MÉD stimulation.

excité, -e [ɛksite] **1** *adj* [énervé] excited. **2** *nm, f* hothead.

exciter [ɛksite] *vt* [gén] to excite. || MÉD to stimulate.

exclamation [ɛksklamasjɔ̃] *nf* exclamation.

exclamer [ɛksklame] ○ **s'exclamer** *vp*: **s'~ (devant)** to exclaim (at ou over).

exclu, -e [ɛkskly] **1** *pp* → exclure. **2** *adj* excluded. **3** *nm, f* outsider.

exclure [ɛksklyr] *vt* to exclude; [expulser] to expel.

exclusion [ɛksklyzjɔ̃] *nf* expulsion; **à l'~ de** to the exclusion of.

exclusivement [ɛksklyzivmɑ̃] *adv* [uniquement] exclusively.

exclusivité [ɛksklyzivite] *nf* COMM exclusive rights (*pl*). || CIN sole screening rights (*pl*); **en ~** exclusively. || [de sentiment] exclusiveness.

excrément [ɛkskremɑ̃] *nm* (*gén pl*) excrement (*U*).

excroissance [ɛkskrwasɑ̃s] *nf* excrescence.

excursion [ɛkskyrsjɔ̃] *nf* excursion.

excursionniste [ɛkskyrsjɔnist] *nmf* vacationer *Am*.

excuse [ɛkskyz] *nf* excuse.

excuser [ɛkskyze] *vt* to excuse; **excusez-moi** [pour réparer] I'm sorry; [pour demander] excuse me. ○ **s'excuser** *vp* [demander pardon] to apologize; **s'~ de qqch/de faire qqch** to apologize for sthg/for doing sthg.

exécrable [ɛgzekrabl] *adj* atrocious.

exécutant, -e [ɛgzekytɑ̃, ɑ̃t] *nm, f* [personne] underling. || MUS performer.

exécuter [ɛgzekyte] *vt* [réaliser] to carry out; [tableau] to paint. ○ MUS to play, to perform. || [mettre à mort] to execute. ○ **s'exécuter** *vp* to comply.

exécutif, -ive [ɛgzekytif, iv] *adj* executive. ○ **exécutif** *nm*: **l'~** the executive.

exécution [ɛgzekysjɔ̃] *nf* [réalisation] carrying out; [de tableau] painting. || MUS performance. || [mise à mort] execution.

exemplaire [ɛgzɑ̃plɛr] **1** *nm* copy. **2** *adj* exemplary.

exemple [ɛgzɑ̃pl] *nm* example; **par ~** for example, for instance.

exempté, -e [ɛgzɑ̃te] *adj*: **~ (de)** exempt (from).

exercer [ɛgzɛrse] *vt* [entraîner, mettre en usage] to exercise; [autorité, influence] to exert. || [métier] to carry on; [médecine] to practise. ○ **s'exercer** *vp* [s'entraîner] to practise; **s'~ à qqch/à faire qqch** to practise sthg/doing sthg.

exercice [ɛgzɛrsis] *nm* [gén] exercise. || [de métier, fonction] carrying out.

exhaler [ɛgzale] *vt littéraire* [odeur] to give off. || [plainte, soupir] to utter.

exhaustif, -ive [ɛgzostif, iv] *adj* exhaustive.

exhiber [ɛgzibe] *vt* [présenter] to show; [faire étalage de] to show off. ○ **s'exhiber** *vp* to make an exhibition of o.s.

exhibitionniste [ɛgzibisjɔnist] *nmf* exhibitionist.

exhorter [ɛgzɔrte] *vt*: **~ qqn à qqch/à faire qqch** to urge sb to sthg/to do sthg.

exhumer [ɛgzyme] *vt* to exhume; *fig* to unearth, to dig up.

exigeant, -e [ɛgziʒɑ̃, ɑ̃t] *adj* demanding.

exigence [ɛgziʒɑ̃s] *nf* demand.

exiger [ɛgziʒe] *vt* [demander] to demand; **~ que** (+ *subjonctif*) to demand that; **~ qqch de qqn** to demand sthg from sb. || [nécessiter] to require.

exigible [ɛgziʒibl] *adj* payable.

exigu, -ë [ɛgzigy] *adj* cramped.

exil [ɛgzil] *nm* exile; **en ~** exiled.

exilé, -e [ɛgzile] *nm, f* exile.

exiler [ɛgzile] *vt* to exile. ○ **s'exiler** *vp* POLIT to go into exile.

existence [ɛgzistɑ̃s] *nf* existence.

exister [ɛgziste] *vi* to exist.

exode [ɛgzɔd] *nm* exodus.

exonération [ɛgzɔnerasjɔ̃] *nf* exemption; **~ d'impôts** tax exemption.

exorbitant, -e [ɛgzɔrbitɑ̃, ɑ̃t] *adj* exorbitant.

exorbité, -e [ɛgzɔrbite] → **œil**.

exotique [ɛgzɔtik] *adj* exotic.

exotisme [ɛgzɔtism] *nm* exoticism.

expansif, -ive [ɛkspɑ̃sif, iv] *adj* expansive.

expansion [ɛkspɑ̃sjɔ̃] *nf* expansion.

expansionniste [ɛkspɑ̃sjɔnist] *nmf & adj* expansionist.

expatrié, -e [ɛkspatrije] *adj & nm, f* expatriate.

expatrier [ɛkspatrije] *vt* to expatriate. ○ **s'expatrier** *vp* to leave one's country.

expédier [ɛkspedje] *vt* (lettre, marchandise) to send, to dispatch. || [question] to dispose of. || [travail] to dash off.

expéditeur, -trice [ɛkspeditœr, tris] *nm, f* sender.

expéditif, -ive [ɛkspeditif, iv] *adj* quick, expeditious.

expédition [ɛkspedisjɔ̃] *nf* [envoi] sending. || [voyage, campagne militaire] expedition.

expérience [ɛksperjɑ̃s] *nf* [pratique] experience; **avoir de l'~** to have experience, to be experienced. || [essai] experiment.

expérimental, -e, -aux [ɛksperimɑ̃tal, o] *adj* experimental.

expérimenté, -e [ɛksperimɑ̃te] *adj* experienced.

expert, -e [ɛkspɛr, ɛrt] *adj* expert. ○ **expert** *nm* expert.

expert-comptable [ɛkspɛrkɔ̃tabl] *nm* certified public accountant *Am*.

expertise [ɛkspɛrtiz] *nf* [examen] expert appraisal; [estimation] (expert) valuation. || [compétence] expertise.

expertiser [ɛkspɛrtize] *vt* to value; [dégâts] to assess.

expier [ɛkspje] *vt* to pay for.

expiration [ɛkspirasjɔ̃] *nf* [d'air] exhalation. || [de contrat] expiry.

expirer [ɛkspire] **1** *vt* to breathe out. **2** *vi* [contrat] to expire.

explicatif, -ive [ɛksplikatif, iv] *adj* explanatory.

explication [ɛksplikasjɔ̃] *nf* explanation; **~ de texte** (literary) criticism.

explicite [ɛksplisit] *adj* explicit.

expliciter [ɛksplisite] *vt* to make explicit.

expliquer [ɛksplike] *vt* [gén] to explain. || [texte] to criticize. ○ **s'expliquer** *vp* [se justifier] to explain o.s. || [comprendre] to understand. || [discuter] to have it out. || [devenir compréhensible] to be explained, to become clear.

exploit [ɛksplwa] *nm* exploit, feat.

exploitant, -e [ɛksplwatɑ̃, ɑ̃t] *nm, f* farmer.

exploitation [ɛksplwatasjɔ̃] *nf* [mise en valeur] running; [de mine] working. || [entreprise] operation, concern; **~ agricole** farm. || [d'une personne] exploitation.

exploiter [ɛksplwate] *vt* [gén] to exploit. || [entreprise] to operate, to run.

explorateur, -trice [ɛksplɔratœr, tris] *nm, f* explorer.

explorer [ɛksplɔre] *vt* to explore.

exploser [ɛksploze] *vi* to explode.

explosif, -ive [ɛksplozif, iv] *adj* explosive. ○ **explosif** *nm* explosive.

explosion [ɛksplozjɔ̃] *nf* explosion; [de colère, joie] outburst.

exportateur, -trice [ɛkspɔrtatœr, tris] **1** *adj* exporting. **2** *nm, f* exporter.

exportation [ɛkspɔrtasjɔ̃] *nf* export.

exporter [ɛkspɔrte] *vt* to export.

exposé, -e [ɛkspoze] *adj* [orienté]: **bien ~** facing the sun. || [vulnérable] exposed. ○ **exposé** *nm* account; SCOL talk.

exposer [ɛkspoze] *vt* [orienter, mettre en danger] to expose. || [présenter] to display; [- tableaux] to show, to exhibit. || [expliquer] to explain, to set out. || ○ **s'exposer** *vp*: **s'~ à qqch** to expose o.s. to sthg.

exposition [ɛkspozisjɔ̃] *nf* [présentation] exhibition. || [orientation] aspect.

exprès¹, -esse [ɛkspɛrs] *adj* [formel] formal, express. || (*inv*) [urgent] express.

exprès² [ɛkspre] *adv* on purpose; **faire ~ de faire qqch** to do sthg deliberately ou on purpose.

express [ɛkspres] **1** *nm inv* [train] express. || [café] espresso. **2** *adj inv* express.

expressément [ɛkspresemɑ̃] *adv* expressly.

expressif, -ive [ɛkspresif, iv] *adj* expressive.

expression [ɛkspresjɔ̃] *nf* expression.

exprimer [ɛksprime] *vt* [pensées, sentiments] to express. ○ **s'exprimer** *vp* to express o.s.

expropriation [ɛksprɔprijasjɔ̃] *nf* expropriation.

exproprier [ɛksprɔprije] *vt* to expropriate.

expulser [ɛkspylse] *vt*: ~ (**de**) to expel (from); [locataire] to evict (from).

expulsion [ɛkspylsjɔ̃] *nf* expulsion; [de locataire] eviction.

exquis, -e [ɛkski, iz] *adj* [délicieux] exquisite. || [distingué, agréable] delightful.

extase [ɛkstaz] *nf* ecstasy.

extasier [ɛkstazje] ○ **s'extasier** *vp*: **s'~ devant** to go into ecstasies over.

extensible [ɛkstɑ̃sibl] *adj* stretchable.

extension [ɛkstɑ̃sjɔ̃] *nf* [étirement] stretching. || [élargissement] extension.

exténuer [ɛkstenɥe] *vt* to exhaust.

extérieur, -e [ɛksterjœr] *adj* [au dehors] outside; [étranger] external; [apparent] outward. ○ **extérieur** *nm* [dehors] outside; [de maison] exterior; **à l'~ de qqch** outside sthg.

extérieurement [ɛksterjœrmɑ̃] *adv* [à l'extérieur] on the outside, externally. || [en apparence] outwardly.

extérioriser [ɛksterjɔrize] *vt* to show.

exterminer [ɛkstɛrmine] *vt* to exterminate.

externat [ɛkstɛrna] *nm* SCOL day school.

externe [ɛkstɛrn] **1** *nmf* SCOL day pupil. || MÉD ≃ extern *Am*. **2** *adj* outer, external.

extincteur [ɛkstɛ̃ktœr] *nm* (fire) extinguisher.

extinction [ɛkstɛ̃ksjɔ̃] *nf* [action d'éteindre] putting out, extinguishing. || *fig* [disparition] extinction; ~ **de voix** loss of one's voice.

extirper [ɛkstirpe] *vt*: ~ (**de**) [épine, réponse, secret] to drag (out of).

extorquer [ɛkstɔrke] *vt*: ~ **qqch à qqn** to extort sthg from sb.

extra [ɛkstra] **1** *nm inv* [employé] extra help (*U*). **2** *adj inv* [de qualité] top-quality. || *fam* [génial] great, fantastic.

extraction [ɛkstraksjɔ̃] *nf* extraction.

extrader [ɛkstrade] *vt* to extradite.

extraire [ɛkstrɛr] *vt*: ~ (**de**) to extract (from).

extrait, -e [ɛkstrɛ, ɛt] *pp* → **extraire**. ○ **extrait** *nm* extract; ~ **de naissance** birth certificate.

extraordinaire [ɛkstraɔrdinɛr] *adj* extraordinary.

extrapoler [ɛkstrapɔle] *vt & vi* to extrapolate.

extraterrestre [ɛkstratɛrɛstr] *nmf & adj* extraterrestrial.

extravagance [ɛkstravagɑ̃s] *nf* extravagance.

extravagant, -e [ɛkstravagɑ̃, ɑ̃t] *adj* extravagant; [idée, propos] wild.

extraverti, -e [ɛkstravɛrti] *nm, f & adj* extrovert.

extrême [ɛkstrɛm] **1** *nm* extreme; **d'un ~ à l'autre** from one extreme to the other. **2** *adj* extreme; [limite] furthest.

extrêmement [ɛkstrɛmmɑ̃] *adv* extremely.

Extrême-Orient [ɛkstrɛmɔrjɑ̃] *nm*: **l'~** the Far East.

extrémiste [ɛkstremist] *nmf & adj* extremist.

extrémité [ɛkstremite] *nf* [bout] end. || [situation critique] straights (*pl*).

exubérant, -e [ɛgzyberɑ̃, ɑ̃t] *adj* [personne] exuberant.

exulter [ɛgzylte] *vi* to exult.

f, F [ɛf] *nm inv* f, F; **F3** three-room flat *Br* ot apartment *Am*. ○ **F** (*abr de* **Fahrenheit**) F. || (*abr de franc*) F, Fr.

fa [fa] *nm inv* F; [chanté] fa.

fable [fabl] *nf* fable.

fabricant, -e [fabrikɑ̃, ɑ̃t] *nm, f* manufacturer.

fabrication [fabrikasjɔ̃] *nf* manufacture, manufacturing.

fabrique [fabrik] *nf* [usine] factory.

fabriquer [fabrike] *vt* [confectionner] to manufacture, to make. || *fam* [faire]: **qu'est-ce que tu fabriques?** what are you up to? || [inventer] to fabricate.

fabuleux, -euse [fabylø, øz] *adj* fabulous.

fac [fak] *nf fam* college, uni *Br*.

façade [fasad] *nf litt & fig* facade.

faire

face [fas] *nf* [visage] face. ‖ [côté] side;
faire ~ à qqch [maison] to face sthg, to be
opposite sthg; *fig* [affronter] to face up to
sthg; **de ~** from the front; **en ~ de qqn/
qqch** opposite sb/sthg.

face-à-face [fasafas] *nm inv* debate.

facétie [fasesi] *nf* practical joke.

facette [faset] *nf litt & fig* facet.

fâché, -e [faʃe] *adj* [en colère] angry. ‖
[brouillé] on bad terms.

fâcher [faʃe] *vt* [mettre en colère] to anger, to make angry. ◇ **se fâcher** *vp* [se
mettre en colère]: **se ~ (contre qqn)** to get
angry (with sb). ‖ [se brouiller]: **se ~
(avec qqn)** to fall out (with sb).

fâcheux, -euse [faʃø, øz] *adj* unfortunate.

facile [fasil] *adj* [aisé] easy; **~ à faire/
prononcer** easy to do/pronounce. ‖ [peu
subtil] facile. ‖ [conciliant] easy-going.

facilement [fasilmɑ̃] *adv* easily.

facilité [fasilite] *nf* [de tâche, problème]
easiness. ‖ [capacité] ease. ‖ [dispositions]
aptitude. ‖ COMM: **~s de paiement** easy
(payment) terms.

faciliter [fasilite] *vt* to make easier.

façon [fasɔ̃] *nf* [manière] way. ‖ [imita-
tion]: **~ cuir** imitation leather. ◇ **de façon à** *loc prép* so as to. ◇ **de façon
que** *loc conj* (+ *subjonctif*) so that.
◇ **de toute façon** *loc adv* anyway, in
any case.

fac-similé [faksimile] (*pl* **fac-similés**)
nm facsimile.

facteur, -trice [faktœr, tris] *nm, f* [des
postes] mailman (*f* mailwoman) *Am.*
◇ **facteur** *nm* [élément & MATHS] factor.

factice [faktis] *adj* artificial.

faction [faksjɔ̃] *nf* [groupe] faction.

facture [faktyr] *nf* COMM invoice; [de
gaz, d'électricité] bill. ‖ ART technique.

facturer [faktyre] *vt* COMM to invoice.

facultatif, -ive [fakyltatif, iv] *adj* optional.

faculté [fakylte] *nf* [don & UNIV] faculty;
~ de lettres/de droit/de médecine
Faculty of Arts/Law/Medicine. ‖ [possi-
bilité] freedom. ‖ [pouvoir] power.
◇ **facultés** *nfpl* (mental) faculties.

fade [fad] *adj* [sans saveur] bland. ‖
[sans intérêt] insipid.

fagot [fago] *nm* bundle of sticks.

faible [fɛbl] 1 *adj* [gén] weak; **être ~ en
maths** to be not very good at maths. ‖
[petit - montant, proportion] small;
[- revenu] low. ‖ [lueur, bruit] faint. 2 *nm*
weakness.

faiblement [fɛbləmɑ̃] *adv* [mollement]
weakly, feebly. ‖ [imperceptiblement]
faintly. ‖ [peu] slightly.

faiblesse [fɛbles] *nf* [gén] weakness. ‖
[petitesse] smallness.

faiblir [feblir] *vi* [personne, monnaie] to
weaken. ‖ [forces] to diminish, to fail. ‖
[tempête, vent] to die down.

faïence [fajɑ̃s] *nf* earthenware.

faignant, -e = **fainéant**.

faille [faj] 1 → **faillir**. 2 *nf* GÉOL fault. ‖
[défaut] flaw.

faillir [fajir] *vi* [être sur le point de]: **~
faire qqch** to nearly *ou* almost do sthg.

faillite [fajit] *nf* FIN bankruptcy; **faire ~**
to go bankrupt; **en ~** bankrupt.

faim [fɛ̃] *nf* hunger; **avoir ~** to be hungry.

fainéant, -e [feneɑ̃, ɑ̃t], **feignant, -e,
faignant, -e** [fɛɲɑ̃, ɑ̃t] 1 *adj* lazy, idle. 2
nm, f lazybones.

faire [fɛr] 1 *vt* [fabriquer, préparer] to
make; **~ une tarte/du café/un film** to
make a tart/coffee/a film; **~ qqch de
qqch** [transformer] to make sthg into
sthg. ‖ [s'occuper à, entreprendre] to do;
qu'est-ce qu'il fait dans la vie? what
does he do (for a living)?; **que fais-tu dimanche?** what are you doing on Sunday? ‖ [étudier] to do; **~ de l'anglais/des
maths/du droit** to do English/maths/
law. ‖ [sport, musique] to play; **~ du
football/de la clarinette** to play
football/the clarinet. ‖ [effectuer] to do;
~ la cuisine to cook, to do the cooking. ‖
[occasionner]: **~ de la peine à qqn** to hurt
sb; **~ du bruit** to make a noise; **ça ne fait
rien** it doesn't matter. ‖ [imiter]: **~ le
sourd/l'innocent** to act deaf/(the) innocent. ‖ [calcul, mesure]: **un et un font
deux** one and one *ou* make two; **ça
fait combien (de kilomètres) jusqu'à la
mer?** how far is it to the sea?; **la table
fait 2 mètres de long** the table is 2
metres long. ‖ [dire]: **«tiens», fit-elle**
"really", she said. ‖ **ne ~ que** [faire sans
cesse] to do nothing but; **elle ne fait que
bavarder** she does nothing but gossip,
she's always gossiping; **je ne fais que
passer** I've just popped in. 2 *vi* [agir] to
do, to act; **tu ferais bien d'aller voir ce
qui se passe** you ought to *ou* you'd better
go and see what's happening. 3 *v attr*
[avoir l'air] to look; **~ démodé/joli** to
look old-fashioned/pretty. 4 *v substitut*
to do; **je lui ai dit de prendre une
échelle mais il ne l'a pas fait** I told him

to use a ladder but he didn't. **5** *v impers*
[climat. temps]: **il fait beau/froid** it's
fine/cold; **il fait 20 degrés** it's 20 de-
grees. || [exprime la durée, la distance]: **ça
fait six mois que je ne l'ai pas vu** it's six
months since I last saw him; **ça fait six
mois que je fais du portugais** I've been
going to Portuguese classes for six
months. **6** *v auxiliaire* [à l'actif] to make;
~ démarrer une voiture to start a car; **~
tomber qqch** to make sthg fall; **~ tra-
vailler qqn** to make sb work. || [au pas-
sif]: **~ faire qqch (par qqn)** to have sthg
done (by sb); **~ réparer sa voiture/
nettoyer ses vitres** to have one's car
repaired/one's windows cleaned. ○**se
faire** *vp* [être convenable]: **ça ne se fait
pas (de faire qqch)** it's not done (to do
sthg). || [devenir]: **se ~** (+ *adjectif*) to
get, to become; **il se fait tard** it's getting
late; **se ~ beau** to make o.s. beautiful. ||
[causer] (+ *nom*): **se ~ mal** to hurt o.s.;
se ~ des amis to make friends. || (+ *in-
finitif*): **se ~ écraser** to get run over; **se ~
opérer** to have an operation; **se ~ faire
un costume** to have a suit made (for
o.s.). || *loc*: **comment se fait-il que ...?**
how is it that ...?, how come ...? ○**se
faire à** *vp* + *prép* to get used to.

faire-part [fɛrpar] *nm inv* announcement.

fais, fait *etc* → faire.

faisable [fəzabl] *adj* feasible.

faisan, -e [fəzɑ̃, an] *nm, f* pheasant.

faisandé, -e [fəzɑ̃de] *adj* CULIN high.

faisceau, -x [fɛso] *nm* [rayon] beam.

faisons → faire.

fait, faite [fɛ, fɛt] **1** *pp* → faire. **2** *adj*
[fabriqué] made; **il n'est pas ~ pour me-
ner cette vie** he's not cut out for this kind
of life. || [physique]: **bien ~** well-built. ||
[fromage] ripe. || *loc*: **c'est bien ~ pour
lui** (it) serves him right. ○**fait** *nm* [acte]
act; **mettre qqn devant le ~ accompli** to
present sb with a fait accompli; **prendre
qqn sur le ~** to catch sb in the act; **~s et
gestes** doings, actions. || [événement]
event; **~s divers** news in brief. || [réalité]
fact. ○**au fait** *loc adv* by the way. ○**en
fait** *loc adv* in (actual) fact. ○**en fait
de** *loc prép* by way of.

faîte [fɛt] *nm* [de toit] ridge. || [d'arbre]
top. || *fig* [sommet] pinnacle.

faites → faire.

fait-tout (*pl inv*), **faitout** (*pl fai-
touts*) [fɛtu] *nm* stewpan.

falaise [falɛz] *nf* cliff.

fallacieux, -ieuse [falasjø, jøz] *adj*
[promesse] false. || [argument] fallacious.

falloir [falwar] *v impers*: **il me faut du
temps** I need (some) time; **il faut que tu
partes** you must go ou leave, you'll have
to go ou leave; **il faut faire attention** we/
you *etc* must be careful, we'll/you'll *etc*
have to be careful; **s'il le faut** if necessary. ○**s'en falloir** *v impers*: **il s'en faut
de beaucoup pour qu'il ait l'examen** it'll
take a lot for him to pass the exam; **peu
s'en est fallu qu'il démissionne** he very
nearly resigned, he came close to resign-
ing.

fallu [faly] *pp inv* → falloir.

falot, -e [falo, ɔt] *adj* dull.

falsifier [falsifje] *vt* [document, signature, faits] to falsify.

famé, -e [fame] *adj*: **mal ~** with a (bad)
reputation.

famélique [famelik] *adj* half-starved.

fameux, -euse [famø, øz] *adj* [célèbre]
famous. || *fam* [remarquable] great.

familial, -e, -iaux [familjal, jo] *adj*
family (*avant n*).

familiariser [familjarize] *vt*: **~ qqn
avec** to familiarize sb with.

familiarité [familjarite] *nf* familiarity.
○**familiarités** *nfpl* liberties.

familier, -ière [familje, jɛr] *adj* familiar. ○**familier** *nm* regular (customer).

famille [famij] *nf* family; [ensemble des
parents] relatives, relations.

famine [famin] *nf* famine.

fan [fan] *nm fam* fan.

fanal, -aux [fanal, o] *nm* [de phare] bea-
con. || [lanterne] lantern.

fanatique [fanatik] **1** *nmf* fanatic. **2** *adj*
fanatical.

fanatisme [fanatism] *nm* fanaticism.

faner [fane] **1** *vt* [altérer] to fade. **2** *vi*
[fleur] to wither. || [beauté, couleur] to
fade. ○**se faner** *vp* [fleur] to wither. ||
[beauté, couleur] to fade.

fanfare [fɑ̃far] *nf* [orchestre] brass
band. || [musique] fanfare.

fanfaron, -onne [fɑ̃farɔ̃, ɔn] **1** *adj*
boastful. **2** *nm, f* braggart.

fanion [fanjɔ̃] *nm* pennant.

fantaisie [fɑ̃tezi] **1** *nf* [caprice] whim.
|| (*U*) [goût] fancy. || [imagination] imagi-
nation. **2** *adj inv*: **chapeau ~** fancy hat;
bijoux ~ fake jewellery.

fantaisiste [fɑ̃tezist] **1** *nmf* entertainer.
2 *adj* [bizarre] fanciful.

fantasme [fɑ̃tasm] *nm* fantasy.

faux

fantasque [fɑ̃task] *adj* [personne] whimsical. || [humeur] capricious.

fantassin [fɑ̃tasɛ̃] *nm* infantryman.

fantastique [fɑ̃tastik] **1** *adj* fantastic. **2** *nm*: le ~ the fantastic.

fantoche [fɑ̃tɔʃ] **1** *adj* puppet (*avant n*). **2** *nm* puppet.

fantôme [fɑ̃tom] **1** *nm* ghost. **2** *adj* [inexistant] phantom.

faon [fɑ̃] *nm* fawn.

farandole [farɑ̃dɔl] *nf* farandole.

farce [fars] *nf* CULIN stuffing. || [blague] (practical) joke; ~s et attrapes jokes and novelties.

farceur, -euse [farsœr, øz] *nm, f* (practical) joker.

farcir [farsir] *rt* CULIN to stuff. || [remplir]: ~ qqch de to stuff or cram sthg with.

fard [far] *nm* make-up.

fardeau, -x [fardo] *nm* [poids] load; *fig* burden.

farder [farde] *rt* [maquiller] to make up. ○ **se farder** *rp* to make o.s. up, to put on one's make-up.

farfelu, -e [farfəly] *fam* **1** *adj* weird. **2** *nm, f* weirdo.

farfouiller [farfuje] *ri fam* to rummage.

farine [farin] *nf* flour.

farouche [faruʃ] *adj* [animal] wild, not tame; [personne] shy, withdrawn. || [sentiment] fierce.

fart [far(t)] *nm* (ski) wax.

fascicule [fasikyl] *nm* part, instalment.

fascination [fasinasjɔ̃] *nf* fascination.

fasciner [fasine] *rt* to fascinate.

fascisme [faʃism] *nm* fascism.

fasse, fassions *etc* → **faire**.

faste [fast] **1** *nm* splendour. **2** *adj* [favorable] lucky.

fastidieux, -ieuse [fastidjø, jøz] *adj* boring.

fastueux, -euse [fastɥø, øz] *adj* luxurious.

fatal, -e [fatal] *adj* [mortel, funeste] fatal. || [inévitable] inevitable.

fataliste [fatalist] *adj* fatalistic.

fatalité [fatalite] *nf* [destin] fate. || [inéluctabilité] inevitability.

fatigant, -e [fatigɑ̃, ɑ̃t] *adj* [épuisant] tiring. || [ennuyeux] tiresome.

fatiguant [fatigɑ̃] *ppr* → **fatiguer**.

fatigue [fatig] *nf* tiredness.

fatigué, -e [fatige] *adj* tired; [cœur, yeux] strained.

fatiguer [fatige] **1** *rt* [épuiser, affecter] to tire; [- cœur, yeux] to strain. || [ennuyer] to wear out. **2** *ri* [personne] to grow tired. || [moteur] to strain. ○ **se fatiguer** *rp* to get tired; se ~ de qqch to get tired of sthg; se ~ à faire qqch to wear o.s. out doing sthg.

fatras [fatra] *nm* jumble.

faubourg [fobur] *nm* suburb.

fauché, -e [foʃe] *adj fam* broke, hard-up.

faucher [foʃe] *rt* [couper - herbe, blé] to cut. || *fam* [voler]: ~ qqch à qqn to pinch sthg from sb. || [piéton] to run over.

faucille [fosij] *nf* sickle.

faucon [fokɔ̃] *nm* hawk.

faudra → **falloir**.

faufiler [fofile] *rt* to tack, to baste. ○ **se faufiler** *rp*: se ~ dans to slip into; se ~ entre to thread one's way between.

faune [fon] *nf* [animaux] fauna. || *péj* [personnes]: la ~ qui fréquente ce bar the sort of people who hang round that bar.

faussaire [foser] *nmf* forger.

faussement [fosmɑ̃] *adv* [à tort] wrongly. || [prétendument] falsely.

fausser [fose] *rt* [déformer] to bend. || [rendre faux] to distort.

fausseté [foste] *nf* [hypocrisie] duplicity. || [de jugement, d'idée] falsity.

faut → **falloir**.

faute [fot] *nf* [erreur] mistake, error; ~ de frappe [à la machine à écrire] typing error; [à l'ordinateur] keying error; ~ d'orthographe spelling mistake. || [méfait, infraction] offence; prendre qqn en ~ to catch sb out; ~ professionnelle professional misdemeanour. || TENNIS fault; FOOTBALL foul. || [responsabilité] fault; de ma/ta *etc* ~ my/your *etc* fault; par la ~ de qqn because of sb. ○ **faute de** *loc prép* for want or lack of; ~ de mieux for want or lack of anything better. ○ **sans faute** *loc adv* without fault.

fauteuil [fotœj] *nm* [siège] armchair; ~ roulant wheelchair. || [de théâtre] seat.

fautif, -ive [fotif, iv] **1** *adj* [coupable] guilty. || [défectueux] faulty. **2** *nm, f* guilty party.

fauve [fov] **1** *nm* [animal] big cat. || [couleur] fawn. || ART Fauve. **2** *adj* [animal] wild. || [cuir, cheveux] tawny. || ART Fauvist.

faux, fausse [fo, fos] *adj* [incorrect] wrong. || [postiche, mensonger, hypocrite] false; ~ témoignage JUR perjury. || [monnaie, papiers] forged, fake; [bijou, marbre] imitation, fake. || [injustifié]: **fausse alerte** false alarm. ○ **faux 1** nm [document, tableau] forgery, fake. **2** nf scythe. **3** adv: **chanter/jouer ~** MUS to sing/play out of tune; **sonner ~** fig not to ring true.

faux-filet, **faux filet** [fofilɛ] nm sirloin.

faux-fuyant [fofɥijɑ̃] nm excuse.

faux-monnayeur [fomɔnɛjœr] nm counterfeiter.

faux-sens [fosɑ̃s] nm inv mistranslation.

faveur [favœr] nf favour. ○ **en faveur de** loc prép in favour of.

favorable [favɔrabl] adj: **~ (à)** favourable (to).

favori, -ite [favɔri, it] adj & nm, f favourite.

favoriser [favɔrize] vt [avantager] to favour. || [contribuer à] to promote.

fax [faks] nm [appareil] fax machine; [document] fax.

faxer [fakse] vt to fax.

fayot [fajo] nm fam [personne] creep, crawler.

fébrile [febril] adj feverish.

fécond, -e [fekɔ̃, ɔ̃d] adj [femelle, terre, esprit] fertile. || [écrivain] prolific.

fécondation [fekɔ̃dasjɔ̃] nf fertilization; **~ in vitro** in vitro fertilization.

féconder [fekɔ̃de] vt [ovule] to fertilize. || [femme, femelle] to impregnate.

fécondité [fekɔ̃dite] nf [gén] fertility. || [d'écrivain] productiveness.

fécule [fekyl] nf starch.

féculent, -e [fekylɑ̃, ɑ̃t] adj starchy. ○ **féculent** nm starchy food.

fédéral, -e, -aux [federal, o] adj federal.

fédération [federasjɔ̃] nf federation.

fée [fe] nf fairy.

féerique [fe(e)rik] adj [enchanteur] enchanting.

feignant, -e = **fainéant**.

feindre [fɛ̃dr] **1** vt to feign; **~ de faire qqch** to pretend to do sthg. **2** vi to pretend.

feint, -e [fɛ̃, fɛ̃t] pp → **feindre**.

feinte [fɛ̃t] nf [ruse] ruse. || FOOTBALL dummy; BOXE feint.

fêlé, -e [fele] adj [assiette] cracked. || fam [personne] cracked, loony.

fêler [fele] vt to crack.

félicitations [felisitasjɔ̃] nfpl congratulations.

féliciter [felisite] vt to congratulate. ○ **se féliciter** vp: **se ~ de** to congratulate o.s. on.

félin, -e [felɛ̃, in] adj feline. ○ **félin** nm big cat.

fêlure [felyr] nf crack.

femelle [fəmɛl] nf & adj female.

féminin, -e [feminɛ̃, in] adj [gén] feminine. || [revue, équipe] women's (avant n). ○ **féminin** nm GRAM feminine.

féminisme [feminism] nm feminism.

féminité [feminite] nf femininity.

femme [fam] nf [personne de sexe féminin] woman; **~ de chambre** chambermaid; **~ de ménage** cleaning woman. || [épouse] wife.

fémur [femyr] nm femur.

fendre [fɑ̃dr] vt [bois] to split. || [foule, flots] to cut through. ○ **se fendre** vp [se crevasser] to crack.

fendu, -e [fɑ̃dy] pp → **fendre**.

fenêtre [fənɛtr] nf [gén & INFORM] window.

fenouil [fənuj] nm fennel.

fente [fɑ̃t] nf [fissure] crack. || [interstice, de vêtement] slit.

féodal, -e, -aux [feɔdal, o] adj feudal.

fer [fer] nm iron; **~ à cheval** horseshoe; **~ forgé** wrought iron; **~ à repasser** iron; **~ à souder** soldering iron.

ferai, feras etc → **faire**.

fer-blanc [ferblɑ̃] nm tinplate, tin.

férié, -e [ferje] → **jour**.

férir [ferir] vt: **sans coup ~** without meeting any resistance ou obstacle.

ferme¹ [ferm] nf farm.

ferme² [ferm] **1** adj firm; **être ~ sur ses jambes** to be steady on one's feet. **2** adv [beaucoup] a lot.

fermement [fermǝmɑ̃] adv firmly.

ferment [fermɑ̃] nm [levure] ferment. || fig [germe] seed, seeds (pl).

fermentation [fermɑ̃tasjɔ̃] nf CHIM fermentation; fig ferment.

fermer [ferme] **1** vt [porte, tiroir, yeux] to close, to shut; [rideaux] to close, to draw; [store] to pull down; [enveloppe] to seal. || [bloquer] to close; **~ son esprit à qqch** to close one's mind to sthg. || [gaz, lumière] to turn off. || [vêtement] to do up. || [entreprise] to close down. **2** vi [gén] to shut, to close. || [vêtement] to do up. || [entreprise] to close down. ○ **se fermer** vp [porte] to close, to shut. || [plaie] to close up. || [vêtement] to do up.

fermeté [fermǝte] nf firmness.

fermeture [fermǝtyr] nf [de porte] closing. || [de vêtement, sac] fastening; **~ Éclair®** zip Br, zipper Am. || [d'établissement - temporaire] closing;

[≃ définitive] closure; ~ **hebdomadaire/
annuelle** weekly/annual closing.

fermier, -ière [fɛrmje, jɛr] *nm, f*
farmer.

fermoir [fɛrmwar] *nm* clasp.

féroce [feros] *adj* [animal, appétit] ferocious; [personne, désir] fierce.

ferraille [feraj] *nf* [vieux fer] scrap iron
(*U*). || *fam* [monnaie] loose change.

ferroviaire [fɛrɔvjɛr] *adj* rail (*avant
n*).

ferry-boat [fɛribot] (*pl* ferry-boats)
nm ferry.

fertile [fɛrtil] *adj litt & fig* fertile; ~ **en**
fig filled with, full of.

fertiliser [fɛrtilize] *vt* to fertilize.

fertilité [fɛrtilite] *nf* fertility.

féru, -e [fery] *adj sout* [passionné]: **être
~ de qqch** to have a passion for sthg.

fervent, -e [fɛrvɑ̃, ɑ̃t] *adj* [chrétien] fervent; [amoureux, démocrate] ardent.

ferveur [fɛrvœr] *nf* [dévotion] fervour.

fesse [fɛs] *nf* buttock.

fessée [fese] *nf* spanking, smack (on the
bottom).

festin [fɛstɛ̃] *nm* banquet, feast.

festival, -als [fɛstival] *nm* festival.

festivités [fɛstivite] *nfpl* festivities.

feston [fɛstɔ̃] *nm* COUTURE scallop.

festoyer [fɛstwaje] *vi* to feast.

fêtard, -e [fɛtar, ard] *nm, f* fun-loving
person.

fête [fɛt] *nf* [congé] holiday; **les ~s (de
fin d'année)** the Christmas holidays; ~
nationale national holiday. || [réunion,
réception] celebration. || [kermesse] fair;
~ **foraine** funfair. || [jour de célébration
de personne] saint's day; [~ de saint] feast
(day). || [soirée] party. || *loc:* **faire la ~** to
have a good time.

fêter [fete] *vt* [événement] to celebrate;
[personne] to have a party for.

fétiche [fetiʃ] *nm* [objet de culte] fetish.
|| [mascotte] mascot.

fétichisme [fetiʃism] *nm* [culte, perver-
sion] fetishism.

fétide [fetid] *adj* fetid.

fétu [fety] *nm:* ~ **(de paille)** wisp (of
straw).

feu, -e [fø] *adj:* ~ **M. X** the late Mr X; ~
mon mari my late husband. ○ **feu, -x**
nm [flamme, incendie] fire; **au ~!** fire!; **en
~** *litt & fig* on fire; **avez-vous du ~?** have
you got a light?; **faire ~** MIL to fire; **mettre le ~ à qqch** to set fire to sthg, to set
sthg on fire; **prendre ~** to catch fire; ~ **de
camp** camp fire; ~ **de cheminée** chimney

fire. || [signal] light; ~ **rouge/vert** red/
green light; **~x de croisement** dipped
headlights; **~x de position** sidelights; **~x
de route** headlights on full beam. || CULIN
burner *Am*; **à ~ doux/vif** on a low/high
flame. || CIN & THÉÂTRE light (*U*). ○ **feu
d'artifice** *nm* firework.

feuillage [fœjaʒ] *nm* foliage.

feuille [fœj] *nf* [d'arbre] leaf; ~ **morte**
dead leaf; ~ **de vigne** BOT vine leaf. ||
[page] sheet. || [document] form.

feuillet [fœjɛ] *nm* page.

feuilleter [fœjte] *vt* to flick through.

feuilleton [fœjtɔ̃] *nm* serial.

feutre [føtr] *nm* [étoffe] felt. || [chapeau]
felt hat. || [crayon] felt-tip pen.

feutré, -e [føtre] *adj* [garni de feutre]
trimmed with felt; [qui a l'aspect du feu-
tre] felted. || [bruit, cri] muffled.

feutrine [føtrin] *nf* lightweight felt.

fève [fɛv] *nf* broad bean.

février [fevrije] *nm* February; *voir aussi* **septembre**.

fg *abr de* **faubourg**.

fiable [fjabl] *adj* reliable.

fiacre [fjakr] *nm* hackney carriage.

fiançailles [fjɑ̃saj] *nfpl* engagement
(*sg*).

fiancé, -e [fjɑ̃se] *nm, f* fiancé (*f* fiancée).

fiancer [fjɑ̃se] ○ **se fiancer** *vp:* **se ~
(avec)** to get engaged (to).

fibre [fibr] *nf* ANAT, BIOL & TECHNOL fibre;
~ **de verre** fibreglass, glass fibre.

ficeler [fisle] *vt* [lier] to tie up.

ficelle [fisɛl] *nf* [fil] string. || [pain] *thin
French stick*. || [*gén pl*] [truc] trick.

fiche [fiʃ] *nf* [document] card; ~ **de paie**
pay slip. || ÉLECTR & TECHNOL pin.

ficher [fiʃe] (*pp vt sens 1 & 2* **fiché**, *pp
vt sens 3 & 4* **fichu**) *vt* [enfoncer]: ~ **qqch
dans** to stick sthg into. || [inscrire] to put
on file. || *fam* [faire]: **qu'est-ce qu'il
fiche?** what's he doing? || *fam* [mettre] to
put; ~ **qqch par terre** *fig* to mess ou muck
sthg up. ○ **se ficher** *vp* [s'enfoncer - suj:
clou, pique]: **se ~ dans** to go into. || *fam*
[se moquer]: **se ~ de** to make fun of. ||
fam [ne pas tenir compte]: **se ~ de** not to
give a damn about.

fichier [fiʃje] *nm* file.

fichu, -e [fiʃy] *adj fam* [cassé, fini] done
for. || (*avant n*) [désagréable] nasty. ||
loc: **être mal ~** *fam* [personne] to feel rotten. ○ **fichu** *nm* scarf.

fictif, -ive [fiktif, iv] *adj* [imaginaire]
imaginary. || [faux] false.

fiction [fiksjɔ̃] *nf* LITTÉRATURE fiction. ||
[monde imaginaire] dream world.

fidèle [fidɛl] **1** *nmf* RELIG believer. ||
[adepte] fan. **2** *adj* [loyal, exact, semblable]: ~ (à) faithful (to); ~ **à la réalité**
accurate. || [habitué] regular.

fidélité [fidelite] *nf* faithfulness.

fief [fjɛf] *nm* fief; *fig* stronghold.

fiel [fjɛl] *nm litt & fig* gall.

fier¹, fière [fjɛr] *adj* [gén] proud; ~ **de**
qqn/qqch proud of sb/sthg; ~ **de faire**
qqch proud to be doing sthg. || [noble]
noble.

fier² [fje] ○ **se fier** *vp*: se ~ **à** to trust,
to rely on.

fierté [fjɛrte] *nf* [satisfaction, dignité]
pride. || [arrogance] arrogance.

fièvre [fjɛvr] *nf* MÉD fever; **avoir 40 de** ~
to have a temperature of 105 (degrees).

fiévreux, -euse [fjevrø, øz] *adj litt &*
fig feverish.

fig. *abr de* figure.

figer [fiʒe] *vt* to paralyse. ○ **se figer** *vp*
[s'immobiliser] to freeze. || [se solidifier] to
congeal.

fignoler [fiɲɔle] *vt* to put the finishing
touches to.

figue [fig] *nf* fig.

figuier [figje] *nm* fig-tree.

figurant, -e [figyrã, ãt] *nm, f* extra.

figuratif, -ive [figyratif, iv] *adj* figurative.

figure [figyr] *nf* [gén] figure; **faire ~ de**
to look like. || [visage] face.

figuré, -e [figyre] *adj* [sens] figurative.
○ **figuré** *nm*: **au** ~ in the figurative
sense.

figurer [figyre] **1** *vt* to represent. **2** *vi*: ~
dans/parmi to figure in/among.

figurine [figyrin] *nf* figurine.

fil [fil] *nm* [brin] thread; **perdre le** ~ **(de**
qqch) *fig* to lose the thread (of sthg). ||
[câble] wire; ~ **de fer** wire. || [cours]
course; **au** ~ **de** in the course of. || [tissu]
linen. || [tranchant] edge.

filament [filamã] *nm* ANAT & ÉLECTR filament. || [végétal] fibre. || [de colle, bave]
thread.

filandreux, -euse [filãdrø, øz] *adj*
[viande] stringy.

filature [filatyr] *nf* [usine] mill; [fabrication] spinning. || [poursuite] tailing.

file [fil] *nf* line; **à la** ~ in a line; **se garer**
en double ~ to double-park; ~ **d'attente**
queue *Br*, line *Am*.

filer [file] **1** *vt* [soie, coton] to spin. ○
[personne] to tail. || *fam* [donner]: ~ **qqch**

à qqn to slip sthg to sb, to slip sb sthg. **2**
vi [bas] to run *Am*. || [aller vite - temps,
véhicule] to fly (by). || *fam* [partir] to
dash off. || *loc*: ~ **doux** to behave nicely.

filet [file] *nm* [à mailles] net; ~ **de pêche**
fishing net; ~ **à provisions** string bag. ||
CULIN fillet. || [de liquide] drop, dash; [de
lumière] shaft.

filial, -e, -iaux [filjal, jo] *adj* filial.
○ **filiale** *nf* ÉCON subsidiary.

filiation [filjasjɔ̃] *nf* [lien de parenté]
line.

filière [filjer] *nf* [voie]: **suivre la** ~ **hié-**
rarchique to go through the right channels. || [réseau] network.

filiforme [filiform] *adj* skinny.

filigrane [filigran] *nm* [dessin] watermark; **en** ~ *fig* between the lines.

filin [filɛ̃] *nm* rope.

fille [fij] *nf* [enfant] daughter. || [femme]
girl; **jeune** ~ girl; **vieille** ~ *péj* spinster.

fillette [fijɛt] *nf* little girl.

filleul, -e [fijœl] *nm, f* godchild.

film [film] *nm* [gén] film; ~ **catastrophe**
disaster movie; ~ **d'épouvante** horror
film; ~ **policier** detective film.

filmer [filme] *vt* to film.

filmographie [filmɔgrafi] *nf* filmography, films (*pl*).

filon [filɔ̃] *nm* [de mine] vein. || *fam fig*
[possibilité] cushy number.

fils [fis] *nm* son.

filtrant, -e [filtrã, ãt] *adj* [verre] tinted.

filtre [filtr] *nm* filter; ~ **à café** coffee
filter.

filtrer [filtre] **1** *vt* to filter; *fig* to screen.
2 *vi* to filter; *fig* to filter through.

fin, fine [fɛ̃, fin] **1** *adj* [gén] fine. || [partie du corps] slender; [couche, papier]
thin. || [subtil] shrewd. || [ouïe, vue] keen.
2 *adv* finely; ~ **prêt** quite ready. ○ **fin** *nf*
end; ~ **mars** at the end of March; **mettre**
~ **à** to put a stop oɩ an end to; **prendre** ~
to come to an end; **arriver** oɩ **parvenir à**
ses ~**s** to achieve one's ends oɩ aims.
○ **fin de série** *nf* oddment. ○ **à la fin**
loc adv: **tu vas m'écouter, à la** ~? will
you listen to me? ○ **à la fin de** *loc prép*
at the end of. ○ **sans fin** *loc adj* endless.

final, -e [final] (*pl* **finals** oɩ **finaux**) *adj*
final. ○ **finale** *nf* SPORT final.

finalement [finalmã] *adv* finally.

finaliste [finalist] *nmf & adj* finalist.

finalité [finalite] *nf sout* [fonction] purpose.

finance [finãs] *nf* finance.

financer [finãse] *vt* to finance, to fund.

financier, -ière [finɑ̃sje, jɛr] *adj* financial. O **financier** *nm* financier.

finaud, -e [fino, od] *adj* wily, crafty.

finesse [finɛs] *nf* [gén] fineness. || [minceur] slenderness. || [perspicacité] shrewdness. || [subtilité] subtlety.

fini, -e [fini] *adj péj* [fieffé]: **un crétin ~** a complete idiot. || [limité] finite. O **fini** *nm* [d'objet] finish.

finir [finir] **1** *vt* [gén] to finish, to end. || [vider] to empty. **2** *vi* [gén] to finish, to end; **~ par faire qqch** to do sthg eventually; **mal ~** to end badly. || [arrêter]: **~ de faire qqch** to stop doing sthg; **en ~ (avec)** to finish (with).

finition [finisjɔ̃] *nf* [d'objet] finish.

finlandais, -e [fɛ̃lɑ̃dɛ, ɛz] *adj* Finnish. O **Finlandais, -e** *nm, f* Finn.

Finlande [fɛ̃lɑ̃d] *nf*: **la ~** Finland.

finnois, -e [finwa, az] *adj* Finnish. O **finnois** *nm* [langue] Finnish. O **Finnois, -e** *nm, f* Finn.

fiole [fjɔl] *nf* flask.

fioriture [fjɔrityr] *nf* flourish.

fioul = fuel.

firmament [firmamɑ̃] *nm* firmament.

firme [firm] *nf* firm.

fis, fit *etc* → faire.

fisc [fisk] *nm* ≃ Internal Revenue *Am*.

fiscal, -e, -aux [fiskal, o] *adj* tax (*avant n*), fiscal.

fiscalité [fiskalite] *nf* tax system.

fissure [fisyr] *nf litt & fig* crack.

fissurer [fisyre] *vt* [fendre] to crack; *fig* to split. O **se fissurer** *vp* to crack.

fiston [fistɔ̃] *nm fam* son.

FIV (*abr de* **fécondation in vitro**) *nf* IVF.

fixation [fiksasjɔ̃] *nf* [action de fixer] fixing. || [attache] fastening, fastener; [de ski] binding. || PSYCHOL fixation.

fixe [fiks] *adj* fixed; [encre] permanent. O **fixe** *nm* fixed salary.

fixement [fiksəmɑ̃] *adv* fixedly.

fixer [fikse] *vt* [gén] to fix; [règle] to set; **~ son choix sur** to decide on. || [monter] to hang. || [regarder] to stare at. || [renseigner]: **être fixé sur qqch** to know all about sthg. O **se fixer** *vp* to settle; **se ~ sur** [suj: choix, personne] to settle on; [suj: regard] to rest on.

fjord [fjɔrd] *nm* fjord.

flacon [flakɔ̃] *nm* small bottle.

flageller [flaʒele] *vt* [fouetter] to flagellate.

flageoler [flaʒɔle] *vi* to tremble.

flageolet [flaʒɔlɛ] *nm* [haricot] flageolet bean. || MUS flageolet.

flagrant, -e [flagrɑ̃, ɑ̃t] *adj* flagrant; → délit.

flair [flɛr] *nm* sense of smell; *fig* intuition.

flairer [flɛre] *vt* to sniff, to smell; *fig* to scent.

flamand, -e [flamɑ̃, ɑ̃d] *adj* Flemish.

flamant [flamɑ̃] *nm* flamingo; **~ rose** pink flamingo.

flambeau, -x [flɑ̃bo] *nm* torch; *fig* flame.

flamber [flɑ̃be] **1** *vi* [brûler] to blaze. || *fam* JEU to play for high stakes. **2** *vt* [crêpe] to flambé. || [volaille] to singe.

flamboyant, -e [flɑ̃bwajɑ̃, ɑ̃t] *adj* [ciel, regard] blazing; [couleur] flaming.

flamboyer [flɑ̃bwaje] *vi* to blaze.

flamme [flam] *nf* flame; *fig* fervour, fire.

flan [flɑ̃] *nm* baked custard.

flanc [flɑ̃] *nm* [de personne, navire, montagne] side; [d'animal, d'armée] flank.

flancher [flɑ̃ʃe] *vi fam* to give up.

flanelle [flanɛl] *nf* flannel.

flâner [flane] *vi* [se promener] to stroll.

flanquer [flɑ̃ke] *vt fam* [jeter]: **~ qqch par terre** to fling sthg to the ground; **~ qqn dehors** to chuck ou fling sb out. || *fam* [donner]: **~ une gifle à qqn** to clout sb round the ear; **~ la frousse à qqn** to put the wind up sb. || [accompagner]: **être flanqué de** to be flanked by.

flapi, -e [flapi] *adj fam* dead beat.

flaque [flak] *nf* pool.

flash [flaʃ] *nm* PHOT flash. || RADIO & TÉLÉ: **~ (d'information)** newsflash; **~ publicitaire** commercial.

flash-back [flaʃbak] (*pl inv* OU **flash-backs**) *nm* CIN flashback.

flasher [flaʃe] *vi fam*: **~ sur qqn/qqch** to be turned on by sb/sthg.

flasque [flask] **1** *nf* flask. **2** *adj* flabby, limp.

flatter [flate] *vt* [louer] to flatter. || [caresser] to stroke. O **se flatter** *vp* to flatter o.s.; **je me flatte de le convaincre** I flatter myself that I can convince him.

flatterie [flatri] *nf* flattery.

flatteur, -euse [flatœr, øz] **1** *adj* flattering. **2** *nm, f* flatterer.

fléau, -x [fleo] *nm litt & fig* [calamité] scourge. || [instrument] flail.

flèche [flɛʃ] *nf* [gén] arrow. || [d'église] spire. || *fig* [critique] shaft.

fléchette [fleʃɛt] *nf* dart.

fléchir [fleʃir] 1 *vt* to bend, to flex; *fig* to sway. 2 *vi* to bend; *fig* to weaken.

fléchissement [fleʃismɑ̃] *nm* flexing, bending; *fig* weakening.

flegmatique [flɛgmatik] *adj* phlegmatic.

flegme [flɛgm] *nm* composure.

flemmard, -e [flɛmar, ard] *fam* 1 *adj* lazy. 2 *nm, f* lazybones (*sg*), idler.

flemme [flɛm] *nf fam* laziness; **j'ai la ~ (de sortir)** I can't be bothered (to go out).

flétrir [fletrir] *vt* [fleur, visage] to wither. ○ **se flétrir** *vp* to wither.

fleur [flœr] *nf* BOT & *fig* flower; **en ~, en ~s** [arbre] in flower, in blossom; **à ~s** [motif] flowered.

fleuret [flœrɛ] *nm* foil.

fleuri, -e [flœri] *adj* [jardin, pré] in flower; [tissu] flowered; [table, appartement] decorated with flowers. || *fig* [style] flowery.

fleurir [flœrir] 1 *vi* to blossom; *fig* to flourish. 2 *vt* [maison] to decorate with flowers; [tombe] to lay flowers on.

fleuriste [flœrist] *nmf* florist.

fleuron [flœrɔ̃] *nm fig* jewel.

fleuve [flœv] *nm* [cours d'eau] river. || (*en apposition*) [interminable] lengthy, interminable.

flexible [flɛksibl] *adj* flexible.

flexion [flɛksjɔ̃] *nf* [de genou, de poutre] bending. || LING inflexion.

flic [flik] *nm fam* cop.

flinguer [flɛ̃ge] *vt fam* to gun down. ○ **se flinguer** *vp fam* to blow one's brains out.

flipper [flipœr] *nm* pin-ball machine.

flirter [flœrte] *vi:* **~ (avec qqn)** to flirt (with sb).

flocon [flɔkɔ̃] *nm* flake; **~ de neige** snowflake.

flonflon [flɔ̃flɔ̃] *nm* (*gén pl*) blare.

flop [flɔp] *nm* [échec] flop, failure.

floraison [flɔrɛzɔ̃] *nf litt* & *fig* flowering, blossoming.

floral, -e, -aux [flɔral, o] *adj* floral.

flore [flɔr] *nf* flora.

Floride [flɔrid] *nf:* **la ~** Florida.

florissant, -e [flɔrisɑ̃, ɑ̃t] *adj* [santé] blooming; [économie] flourishing.

flot [flo] *nm* flood, stream; **être à ~** [navire] to be afloat; *fig* to be back to normal. ○ **flots** *nmpl littéraire* waves.

flottaison [flɔtɛzɔ̃] *nf* floating.

flottant, -e [flɔtɑ̃, ɑ̃t] *adj* [gén] floating. || [robe] loose-fitting.

flotte [flɔt] *nf* AÉRON & NAVIG fleet. || *fam* [eau] water. || *fam* [pluie] rain.

flottement [flɔtmɑ̃] *nm* [indécision] hesitation, wavering. || [de monnaie] floating.

flotter [flɔte] 1 *vi* [sur l'eau] to float. || [drapeau] to flap; [brume, odeur] to drift. || [dans un vêtement]: **tu flottes dedans** it's baggy on you. 2 *v impers fam*: **il flotte** it's raining.

flotteur [flɔtœr] *nm* [de ligne de pêche, d'hydravion] float; [de chasse d'eau] ballcock.

flou, -e [flu] *adj* [couleur, coiffure] soft. || [photo] blurred, fuzzy. || [pensée] vague, woolly. ○ **flou** *nm* [de photo] fuzziness; [de décision] vagueness.

flouer [flue] *vt fam* to do, to swindle.

fluctuer [flyktɥe] *vi* to fluctuate.

fluet, -ette [flyɛ, ɛt] *adj* [personne] thin, slender; [voix] thin.

fluide [flɥid] 1 *nm* [matière] fluid. 2 *adj* [matière] fluid; [circulation] flowing freely.

fluidifier [flɥidifje] *vt* [trafic] to improve the flow of.

fluidité [flɥidite] *nf* [gén] fluidity; [de circulation] easy flow.

fluor [flyɔr] *nm* fluorine.

fluorescent, -e [flyɔresɑ̃, ɑ̃t] *adj* fluorescent.

flûte [flyt] 1 *nf* MUS flute. || [verre] flute (glass). 2 *interj fam* bother!

flûtiste [flytist] *nmf* flautist.

fluvial, -e, -iaux [flyvjal, jo] *adj* [eaux, pêche] river (*avant n*); [alluvions] fluvial.

flux [fly] *nm* [écoulement] flow. || [marée] flood tide. || PHYS flux.

FM (*abr de* **frequency modulation**) *nf* FM.

FMI (*abr de* **Fonds monétaire international**) *nm* IMF.

FN (*abr de* **Front national**) *nm extreme right-wing French political party*.

foc [fɔk] *nm* jib.

focal, -e, -aux [fɔkal, o] *adj* focal.

fœtal, -e, -aux [fetal, o] *adj* foetal.

fœtus [fetys] *nm* foetus.

foi [fwa] *nf* RELIG faith. || [confiance] trust; **avoir ~ en qqn/qqch** to trust sb/sthg, to have faith in sb/sthg. || *loc:* **être de bonne/mauvaise ~** to be in good/bad faith.

foie [fwa] *nm* ANAT & CULIN liver.

foin [fwɛ̃] *nm* hay.

foire [fwar] *nf* [fête] funfair. || [exposition, salon] trade fair.

fois [fwa] *nf* time; **une ~** once; **deux ~** twice; **trois/quatre ~** three/four times; **deux ~ plus long** twice as long; **neuf ~ sur dix** nine times out of ten; **deux ~ trois** two times three; **cette ~** this time; **il était une ~ ...** once upon a time there was ...; **une (bonne) ~ pour toutes** once and for all. ○ **à la fois** *loc adv* at the same time, at once. ○ **des fois** *loc adv* [parfois] sometimes. ○ **une fois que** *loc conj* once.

foison [fwazɔ̃] ○ **à foison** *loc adv* in abundance.

foisonner [fwazɔne] *vi* to abound.

folâtre [fɔlatr] *adj* playful.

folâtrer [fɔlatre] *vi* to romp (about).

folie [fɔli] *nf litt & fig* madness.

folklore [fɔlklɔr] *nm* [de pays] folklore.

folklorique [fɔlklɔrik] *adj* [danse] folk. || *fig* [situation, personne] bizarre, quaint.

folle → **fou**.

follement [fɔlmɑ̃] *adv* madly, wildly.

fomenter [fɔmɑ̃te] *vt* to foment.

foncé, -e [fɔ̃se] *adj* dark.

foncer [fɔ̃se] *vi* [teinte] to darken. || [se ruer]: **~ sur** to rush at. || *fam* [se dépêcher] to get a move on.

foncier, -ière [fɔ̃sje, jɛr] *adj* [impôt] land (*avant n*); **propriétaire ~** landowner. || [fondamental] basic, fundamental.

foncièrement [fɔ̃sjɛrmɑ̃] *adv* basically.

fonction [fɔ̃ksjɔ̃] *nf* [gén] function; **faire ~ de** to act as. || [profession] post; **entrer en ~** to take up one's post ou duties. ○ **en fonction de** *loc prép* according to.

fonctionnaire [fɔ̃ksjɔnɛr] *nmf* [de l'État] state employee; [dans l'administration] civil servant.

fonctionnel, -elle [fɔ̃ksjɔnɛl] *adj* functional.

fonctionnement [fɔ̃ksjɔnmɑ̃] *nm* working, functioning.

fonctionner [fɔ̃ksjɔne] *vi* to work, to function.

fond [fɔ̃] *nm* [de récipient, puits, mer] bottom; [de pièce] back; **sans ~** bottomless. || [substance] heart, root; **le ~ de ma pensée** what I really think; **le ~ et la forme** content and form. || [arrière-plan] background. ○ **fond de teint** *nm* foundation. ○ **à fond** *loc adv* [entièrement] thoroughly; **se donner à ~** to give one's all. || [très vite] at top speed. ○ **au fond**,

dans le fond *loc adv* basically. ○ **au fond de** *loc prép*: **au ~ de moi-même/lui-même** *etc* at heart, deep down.

fondamental, -e, -aux [fɔ̃damɑ̃tal, o] *adj* fundamental.

fondant, -e [fɔ̃dɑ̃, ɑ̃t] *adj* [neige, glace] melting; [aliment] which melts in the mouth.

fondateur, -trice [fɔ̃datœr, tris] *nm, f* founder.

fondation [fɔ̃dasjɔ̃] *nf* foundation. ○ **fondations** *nfpl* CONSTR foundations.

fondé, -e [fɔ̃de] *adj* [craintes, reproches] justified, well-founded.

fondement [fɔ̃dmɑ̃] *nm* [base, motif] foundation; **sans ~** groundless, without foundation.

fonder [fɔ̃de] *vt* [créer] to found. || [baser]: **~ qqch sur** to base sthg on. ○ **se fonder** *vp*: **se ~ sur** [suj: personne] to base o.s. on; [suj: argument] to be based on.

fonderie [fɔ̃dri] *nf* [usine] foundry.

fondre [fɔ̃dr] **1** *vt* [beurre, neige] to melt; [sucre, sel] to dissolve; [métal] to melt down. || [mouler] to cast. **2** *vi* [beurre, neige] to melt; [sucre, sel] to dissolve; *fig* to melt away. || [maigrir] to lose weight. || [se ruer]: **~ sur** to swoop down on.

fonds [fɔ̃] **1** *nm* [ressources] fund; **le Fonds monétaire international** the International Monetary Fund. || [bien immobilier]: **~ (de commerce)** business. **2** *nmpl* funds.

fondu, -e [fɔ̃dy] *pp* → **fondre**. ○ **fondue** *nf* fondue.

font → **faire**.

fontaine [fɔ̃tɛn] *nf* [naturelle] spring; [publique] fountain.

fonte [fɔ̃t] *nf* [de glace, beurre] melting; [de métal] melting down. || [alliage] cast iron.

foot [fut] = **football**.

football [futbol] *nm* soccer.

footballeur, -euse [futbolœr, øz] *nm, f* soccer player.

footing [futiŋ] *nm* jogging.

for [fɔr] *nm*: **dans son ~ intérieur** in his/her heart of hearts.

forage [fɔraʒ] *nm* drilling.

forain, -e [fɔrɛ̃, ɛn] *adj* → **fête**. ○ **forain** *nm* stallholder.

forçat [fɔrsa] *nm* convict.

force [fɔrs] *nf* [vigueur] strength. || [violence, puissance, MIL & PHYS] force; **faire qqch à qqn de ~** to force sb to do sthg; **~ centrifuge** PHYS centrifugal force.

○ **forces** *nfpl* [physique] strength (*sg*); **de toutes ses ~s** with all his/her strength.
○ **à force de** *loc prép* by dint of.

forcément [fɔrsemɑ̃] *adv* inevitably.

forcené, -e [fɔrsəne] *nm, f* maniac.

forceps [fɔrsɛps] *nm* forceps (*pl*).

forcer [fɔrse] 1 *vt* [gén] to force; **~ qqn à qqch/à faire qqch** to force sb into sthg/ to do sthg. ‖ [admiration, respect] to compel, to command. ‖ [talent, voix] to strain. 2 *vi*: **ça ne sert à rien de ~, ça ne passe pas** there's no point in forcing it, it won't go through; **~ sur qqch** to overdo sthg. ○ **se forcer** *vp* [s'obliger]: **se ~ à faire qqch** to force o.s. to do sthg.

forcir [fɔrsir] *vi* to put on weight.

forer [fɔre] *vt* to drill.

forestier, -ière [fɔrɛstje, jɛr] *adj* forest (*avant n*).

forêt [fɔrɛ] *nf* forest.

forfait [fɔrfɛ] *nm* [prix fixe] fixed price. ‖ SPORT: **déclarer ~** [abandonner] to withdraw; *fig* to give up. ‖ *littéraire* [crime] heinous crime.

forfaitaire [fɔrfɛtɛr] *adj* inclusive.

forge [fɔrʒ] *nf* forge.

forger [fɔrʒe] *vt* [métal] to forge. ‖ *fig* [caractère] to form.

forgeron [fɔrʒərɔ̃] *nm* blacksmith.

formaliser [fɔrmalize] ○ **se formaliser** *vp*: **se ~ (de)** to take offence (at).

formalisme [fɔrmalism] *nm* formality.

formaliste [fɔrmalist] 1 *nmf* formalist. 2 *adj* [milieu] conventional; [personne]: **être ~** to be a stickler for the rules.

formalité [fɔrmalite] *nf* formality.

format [fɔrma] *nm* [dimension] size.

formatage [fɔrmataʒ] *nm* INFORM formatting.

formater [fɔrmate] *vt* INFORM to format.

formateur, -trice [fɔrmatœr, tris] 1 *adj* formative. 2 *nm, f* trainer.

formation [fɔrmasjɔ̃] *nf* [gén] formation. ‖ [apprentissage] training.

forme [fɔrm] *nf* [aspect] shape, form; **en ~ de** in the shape of. ‖ [état] form; **être en (pleine) ~** to be in (great) shape, to be on (top) form. ○ **formes** *nfpl* figure (*sg*).

formel, -elle [fɔrmɛl] *adj* [définitif, ferme] positive, definite. ‖ [poli] formal.

former [fɔrme] *vt* [gén] to form. ‖ [personnel, élèves] to train. ‖ [goût, sensibilité] to develop. ○ **se former** *vp* [se constituer] to form. ‖ [s'instruire] to train o.s.

Formica® [fɔrmika] *nm inv* Formica®.

formidable [fɔrmidabl] *adj* [épatant] great, tremendous. ‖ [incroyable] incredible.

formol [fɔrmɔl] *nm* formalin.

formulaire [fɔrmylɛr] *nm* form; **remplir un ~** to fill in a form.

formule [fɔrmyl] *nf* [expression] expression; **~ de politesse** [orale] polite phrase; [épistolaire] letter ending. ‖ CHIM & MATHS formula. ‖ [méthode] way, method.

formuler [fɔrmyle] *vt* to formulate, to express.

fort, -e [fɔr, fɔrt] 1 *adj* [gén] strong; **et le plus ~, c'est que ...** and the most amazing thing about it is ...; **c'est plus ~ que moi!** I can't help it. ‖ [corpulent] heavy, big. ‖ [doué] gifted; **être ~ en qqch** to be good at sthg. ‖ [puissant - voix] loud; [- vent, lumière, accent] strong. ‖ [considérable] large; **il y a de ~es chances qu'il gagne** there's a good chance he'll win. 2 *adv* [frapper, battre] hard; [sonner, parler] loud, loudly. ‖ *sout* [très] very. 3 *nm* [château] fort. ‖ [spécialité]: **ce n'est pas mon ~** it's not my forte or strong point.

forteresse [fɔrtərɛs] *nf* fortress.

fortifiant, -e [fɔrtifjɑ̃, ɑ̃t] *adj* fortifying. ○ **fortifiant** *nm* tonic.

fortification [fɔrtifikasjɔ̃] *nf* fortification.

fortifier [fɔrtifje] *vt* [personne, ville] to fortify.

fortuit, -e [fɔrtɥi, it] *adj* chance (*avant n*), fortuitous.

fortune [fɔrtyn] *nf* [richesse] fortune. ‖ [hasard] luck, fortune.

fortuné, -e [fɔrtyne] *adj* [riche] wealthy. ‖ [chanceux] fortunate, lucky.

forum [fɔrɔm] *nm* forum.

fosse [fos] *nf* [trou] pit. ‖ [tombe] grave.

fossé [fose] *nm* ditch; *fig* gap.

fossette [fosɛt] *nf* dimple.

fossile [fosil] *nm* [de plante, d'animal] fossil. ‖ *fig & péj* [personne] fossil, fogy.

fossoyeur, -euse [foswajœr, øz] *nm, f* gravedigger.

fou, folle [fu, fɔl] 1 *adj* (**fol** *devant voyelle ou h muet*) mad, insane; [prodigieux] tremendous. 2 *nm, f* madman (*f* madwoman).

foudre [fudr] *nf* lightning.

foudroyant, -e [fudrwajɑ̃, ɑ̃t] *adj* [progrès, vitesse] lightning (*avant n*); [succès] stunning. ‖ [regard] withering.

foudroyer [fudrwaje] *vt* [suj: foudre] to strike; **l'arbre a été foudroyé** the tree was struck by lightning. || *fig* [abattre] to strike down, to kill; ~ **qqn du regard** to glare at sb.

fouet [fwɛ] *nm* [en cuir] whip. || CULIN whisk.

fouetter [fwete] *vt* [gén] to whip; [suj: pluie] to lash (against).

fougère [fuʒɛr] *nf* fern.

fougue [fug] *nf* ardour.

fougueux, -euse [fugø, øz] *adj* ardent, spirited.

fouille [fuj] *nf* [de personne, maison] search. || [du sol] dig, excavation.

fouiller [fuje] **1** *vt* [gén] to search. || *fig* [approfondir] to examine closely. **2** *vi*: ~ **dans** to go through.

fouillis [fuji] *nm* jumble, muddle.

fouine [fwin] *nf* stone-marten.

fouiner [fwine] *vi* to ferret about.

foulard [fular] *nm* scarf.

foule [ful] *nf* [de gens] crowd.

foulée [fule] *nf* [de coureur] stride.

fouler [fule] *vt* [raisin] to press; [sol] to walk on. ○ **se fouler** *vp* MÉD: **se ~ le poignet/la cheville** to sprain one's wrist/ankle.

foulure [fulyr] *nf* sprain.

four [fur] *nm* [de cuisson] oven; ~ **électrique/à micro-ondes** electric/microwave oven; ~ **crématoire** HIST oven.

fourbe [furb] *adj* treacherous, deceitful.

fourbu, -e [furby] *adj* tired out, exhausted.

fourche [furʃ] *nf* [outil] pitchfork. || [de vélo, route] fork. || *Belg* SCOL free period.

fourchette [furʃet] *nf* [couvert] fork. || [écart] range, bracket.

fourgon [furgɔ̃] *nm* [camionnette] van; ~ **cellulaire** police van *Br*, patrol wagon *Am*. || [ferroviaire]: ~ **à bestiaux** cattle truck; ~ **postal** mail van.

fourgonnette [furgɔnɛt] *nf* small van.

fourmi [furmi] *nf* [insecte] ant.

fourmilière [furmiljɛr] *nf* anthill.

fourmiller [furmije] *vi* [pulluler] to swarm; ~ **de** *fig* to be swarming with.

fournaise [furnɛz] *nf* furnace.

fourneau, -x [furno] *nm* [cuisinière, poêle] stove. || [de fonderie] furnace.

fournée [furne] *nf* batch.

fourni, -e [furni] *adj* [barbe, cheveux] thick.

fournir [furnir] *vt* [procurer]: ~ **qqch à qqn** to supply or provide sb with sthg. || [produire]: ~ **un effort** to make an effort.

|| [approvisionner]: ~ **qqn (en)** to supply sb (with).

fournisseur, -euse [furnisœr, øz] *nm, f* supplier.

fourniture [furnityr] *nf* supply, supplying (*U*). ○ **fournitures** *nfpl*: ~**s de bureau** office supplies; ~**s scolaires** school supplies.

fourrage [furaʒ] *nm* fodder.

fourré [fure] *nm* thicket.

fourreau, -x [furo] *nm* [d'épée] sheath; [de parapluie] cover. || [robe] sheath dress.

fourrer [fure] *vt* CULIN to stuff, to fill. || *fam* [mettre]: ~ **qqch (dans)** to stuff sthg (into). ○ **se fourrer** *vp*: **se ~ une idée dans la tête** to get an idea into one's head; **je ne savais plus où me ~** I didn't know where to put myself.

fourre-tout [furtu] *nm inv* [sac] holdall.

fourreur [furœr] *nm* furrier.

fourrière [furjɛr] *nf* pound.

fourrure [furyr] *nf* fur.

fourvoyer [furvwaje] ○ **se fourvoyer** *vp sout* [se tromper] to go off on the wrong track.

foutre [futr] *vt tfam* [mettre] to shove, to stick; ~ **qqn dehors** or **à la porte** to chuck sb out. || [donner]: ~ **la trouille à qqn** to put the wind up sb; **il lui a foutu une baffe** he thumped him one. || [faire] to do; **j'en ai rien à ~** I don't give a toss. ○ **se foutre** *vp tfam* [se mettre]: **se ~ dans** [situation] to get o.s. into. || [se moquer]: **se ~ de (la gueule de) qqn** to laugh at sb. || [ne pas s'intéresser]: **je m'en fous** I don't give a damn about it.

foyer [fwaje] *nm* [maison] home. || [résidence] home, hostel. || [de lunettes] focus; **verres à double ~** bifocals.

fracas [fraka] *nm* roar.

fracasser [frakase] *vt* to smash, to shatter.

fraction [fraksjɔ̃] *nf* fraction.

fractionner [fraksjɔne] *vt* to divide (up), to split up.

fracture [fraktyr] *nf* MÉD fracture.

fracturer [fraktyre] *vt* MÉD to fracture. || [coffre, serrure] to break open.

fragile [fraʒil] *adj* [gén] fragile; [peau, santé] delicate.

fragiliser [fraʒilize] *vt* to weaken.

fragilité [fraʒilite] *nf* fragility.

fragment [fragmɑ̃] *nm* [morceau] fragment. || [extrait - d'œuvre] extract; [- de conversation] snatch.

fragmenter [fragmãte] *vt* to fragment, to break up.

fraîche → **frais**.

fraîcheur [frɛʃœr] *nf* [d'air, d'accueil] coolness. || [de teint, d'aliment] freshness.

frais, fraîche [frɛ, frɛʃ] *adj* [air, accueil] cool. || [récent - trace] fresh; [- encre] wet. || [teint] fresh, clear. ○ **frais 1** *nm*: **mettre qqch au ~** to put sthg in a cool place. **2** *nmpl* [dépenses] expenses, costs; **faire des ~** to spend a lot of money. **3** *adv*: **il fait ~** it's cool.

fraise [frɛz] *nf* [fruit] strawberry. || [de dentiste] drill; [de menuisier] bit.

fraiseuse [frɛzøz] *nf* milling machine.

fraisier [frɛzje] *nm* [plante] strawberry plant. || [gâteau] strawberry sponge.

framboise [frãbwaz] *nf* [fruit] raspberry. || [liqueur] raspberry liqueur.

franc, franche [frã, frãʃ] *adj* [sincère] frank. || [net] clear, definite. ○ **franc** *nm* franc.

français, -e [frãsɛ, ɛz] *adj* French. ○ **français** *nm* [langue] French. ○ **Français, -e** *nm, f* Frenchman (*f* Frenchwoman); **les Français** the French.

France [frãs] *nf*: **la ~** France; **~ 2, ~ 3** TÉLÉ *French state-owned television channels.*

franche → **franc**.

franchement [frãʃmã] *adv* [sincèrement] frankly. || [nettement] clearly. || [tout à fait] completely, downright.

franchir [frãʃir] *vt* [obstacle] to get over. || [porte] to go through; [seuil] to cross.

franchise [frãʃiz] *nf* [sincérité] frankness. || COMM franchise. || [d'assurance] excess. || [détaxe] exemption.

franc-jeu [frãʒø] *nm*: **jouer ~** to play fair.

franc-maçon, -onne [frãmasɔ̃, ɔn] (*mpl* **francs-maçons**, *fpl* **franc-maçonnes**) *adj* masonic. ○ **franc-maçon** *nm* freemason.

franco [frãko] *adv* COMM: **~ de port** carriage paid.

francophone [frãkɔfɔn] **1** *adj* French-speaking. **2** *nmf* French speaker.

francophonie [frãkɔfɔni] *nf*: **la ~** French-speaking nations (*pl*).

franc-parler [frãparle] *nm*: **avoir son ~** to speak one's mind.

franc-tireur [frãtirœr] *nm* MIL irregular.

frange [frãʒ] *nf* fringe.

frangipane [frãʒipan] *nf* almond paste.

franglais [frãglɛ] *nm* Franglais.

franquette [frãkɛt] ○ **à la bonne franquette** *loc adv* informally, without any ceremony.

frappant, -e [frapã, ãt] *adj* striking.

frapper [frape] **1** *vt* [gén] to strike. || [boisson] to chill. **2** *vi* to knock.

frasques [frask] *nfpl* pranks, escapades.

fraternel, -elle [fratɛrnɛl] *adj* fraternal, brotherly.

fraterniser [fratɛrnize] *vi* to fraternize.

fraternité [fratɛrnite] *nf* brotherhood.

fraude [frod] *nf* fraud.

frauder [frode] *vt & vi* to cheat.

frauduleux, -euse [frodylø, øz] *adj* fraudulent.

frayer [frɛje] ○ **se frayer** *vp*: **se ~ un chemin (à travers une foule)** to force one's way through (a crowd).

frayeur [frɛjœr] *nf* fright, fear.

fredaines [frədɛn] *nfpl* pranks.

fredonner [frədɔne] *vt & vi* to hum.

freezer [frizœr] *nm* freezer compartment.

frégate [fregat] *nf* [bateau] frigate.

frein [frɛ̃] *nm* AUTOM brake. || *fig* [obstacle] brake, check.

freinage [frɛnaʒ] *nm* braking.

freiner [frene] **1** *vt* [mouvement, véhicule] to slow down; [inflation, dépenses] to curb. || [personne] to restrain. **2** *vi* to brake.

frelaté, -e [frəlate] *adj* [vin] adulterated; *fig* corrupt.

frêle [frɛl] *adj* [enfant, voix] frail.

frelon [frəlɔ̃] *nm* hornet.

frémir [fremir] *vi* [corps, personne] to tremble. || [eau] to simmer.

frémissement [fremismã] *nm* [de corps, personne] shiver, trembling (*U*). || [d'eau] simmering.

frêne [frɛn] *nm* ash.

frénésie [frenezi] *nf* frenzy.

frénétique [frenetik] *adj* frenzied.

fréquence [frekãs] *nf* frequency.

fréquent, -e [frekã, ãt] *adj* frequent.

fréquentation [frekãtasjɔ̃] *nf* [d'endroit] frequenting. || [de personne] association. ○ **fréquentations** *nfpl* company (*U*).

fréquenté, -e [frekãte] *adj*: **très ~** busy; **c'est très bien/mal ~** the right/wrong sort of people go there.

fréquenter [frekãte] *vt* [endroit] to frequent. || [personne] to associate with; [petit ami] to go out with, to see.

frère [frɛr] *nm* brother.

fresque [frɛsk] *nf* fresco.

fret [frɛ] *nm* freight.

frétiller [fretije] *vi* [poisson, personne] to wriggle.

fretin [frətɛ̃] *nm*: **le menu ~** the small fry.

friable [frijabl] *adj* crumbly.

friand, -e [frijɑ̃, ɑ̃d] *adj*: **être ~ de** to be partial to.

friandise [frijɑ̃diz] *nf* delicacy.

fric [frik] *nm fam* cash.

friche [friʃ] *nf* fallow land; **en ~** fallow.

friction [friksjɔ̃] *nf* [massage] massage. || *fig* [désaccord] friction.

frictionner [friksjɔne] *vt* to rub.

Frigidaire® [friʒidɛr] *nm* fridge, refrigerator.

frigide [friʒid] *adj* frigid.

frigo [frigo] *nm fam* fridge.

frigorifié, -e [frigɔrifje] *adj fam* frozen.

frileux, -euse [frilø, øz] *adj* [craignant le froid] sensitive to the cold.

frimer [frime] *vi fam* [bluffer] to pretend; [se mettre en valeur] to show off.

frimousse [frimus] *nf fam* dear little face.

fringale [frɛ̃gal] *nf fam*: **avoir la ~** to be starving.

fringant, -e [frɛ̃gɑ̃, ɑ̃t] *adj* high-spirited.

fripe [frip] *nf*: **les ~s** secondhand clothes.

fripon, -onne [fripɔ̃, ɔn] **1** *nm, f fam vieilli* rogue, rascal. **2** *adj* mischievous, cheeky.

fripouille [fripuj] *nf fam* scoundrel.

frire [frir] **1** *vt* to fry. **2** *vi* to fry.

frise [friz] *nf* ARCHIT frieze.

frisé, -e [frize] *adj* [cheveux] curly; [personne] curly-haired.

friser [frize] **1** *vt* [cheveux] to curl. || *fig* [ressembler à] to border on. **2** *vi* to curl.

frisquet [friskɛ] *adj m*: **il fait ~** it's chilly.

frisson [frisɔ̃] *nm* [gén] shiver; [de dégoût] shudder.

frissonner [frisɔne] *vi* [trembler] to shiver; [de dégoût] to shudder.

frit, -e [fri, frit] *pp* → **frire**.

frite [frit] *nf* chip *Br*, (French) fry *Am*.

friteuse [fritøz] *nf* deep fat fryer.

friture [frityr] *nf* [poisson] fried fish. || *fam* RADIO crackle.

frivole [frivɔl] *adj* frivolous.

frivolité [frivɔlite] *nf* frivolity.

froid, froide [frwa, frwad] *adj litt & fig* cold. ○ **froid 1** *nm* [température] cold; **prendre ~** to catch (a) cold. || [tension] coolness. **2** *adv*: **il fait ~** it's cold; **avoir ~** to be cold.

froidement [frwadmɑ̃] *adv* [accueillir] coldly. || [écouter, parler] coolly. || [tuer] cold-bloodedly.

froisser [frwase] *vt* [tissu, papier] to crumple, to crease. || *fig* [offenser] to offend. ○ **se froisser** *vp* [tissu] to crumple, to crease. || MÉD: **se ~ un muscle** to strain a muscle. || [se vexer] to take offence.

frôler [frole] *vt* to brush against; *fig* to have a brush with, to come close to.

fromage [frɔmaʒ] *nm* cheese.

fromagerie [frɔmaʒri] *nf* cheese-dairy.

froment [frɔmɑ̃] *nm* wheat.

froncer [frɔ̃se] *vt* COUTURE to gather. || [plisser]: **~ les sourcils** to frown.

frondaison [frɔ̃dɛzɔ̃] *nf* [phénomène] foliation. || [feuillage] foliage.

fronde [frɔ̃d] *nf* [arme] sling; [jouet] slingshot *Am*. || [révolte] rebellion.

front [frɔ̃] *nm* ANAT forehead. || *fig* [audace] cheek. || [avant] front; **~ de mer** (sea) front. || MÉTÉOR, MIL & POLIT front.

frontal, -e, -aux [frɔ̃tal, o] *adj* ANAT frontal. || [collision, attaque] head-on.

frontalier, -ière [frɔ̃talje, jɛr] **1** *adj* frontier (*avant n*); **travailleur ~** *person who lives on one side of the border and works on the other.* **2** *nm, f* inhabitant of border area.

frontière [frɔ̃tjɛr] **1** *adj* border (*avant n*). **2** *nf* frontier, border; *fig* frontier.

fronton [frɔ̃tɔ̃] *nm* ARCHIT pediment.

frottement [frɔtmɑ̃] *nm* [action] rubbing. || [contact, difficulté] friction.

frotter [frɔte] **1** *vt* to rub; [parquet] to scrub. **2** *vi* to rub, to scrape.

frottis [frɔti] *nm* smear.

fructifier [fryktifje] *vi* [investissement] to give or yield a profit. || [terre] to be productive. || [arbre, idée] to bear fruit.

fructueux, -euse [fryktɥø, øz] *adj* fruitful, profitable.

frugal, -e, -aux [frygal, o] *adj* frugal.

fruit [frɥi] *nm litt & fig* fruit (*U*); **~s de mer** seafood (*U*).

fruité, -e [frɥite] *adj* fruity.

fruitier, -ière [frɥitje, jɛr] **1** *adj* [arbre] fruit (*avant n*). **2** *nm, f* fruiterer.

fruste [fryst] *adj* uncouth.

frustration [frystrasjɔ̃] *nf* frustration.

frustrer [frystre] *vt* [priver]: ~ **qqn de** to deprive sb of. || [décevoir] to frustrate.

fuchsia [fyʃja] *nm* fuchsia.

fuel, fioul [fjul] *nm* [de chauffage] fuel. || [carburant] fuel oil.

fugace [fygas] *adj* fleeting.

fugitif, -ive [fyʒitif, iv] **1** *adj* fleeting. **2** *nm, f* fugitive.

fugue [fyg] *nf* [de personne] flight; **faire une ~** to run away. || MUS fugue.

fui [fɥi] *pp inv* → fuir.

fuir [fɥir] **1** *vi* [détaler] to flee. || [tuyau] to leak. **2** *vt* [éviter] to avoid, to shun.

fuite [fɥit] *nf* [de personne] escape, flight. || [écoulement, d'information] leak.

fulgurant, -e [fylgyrã, ãt] *adj* [découverte] dazzling. || [vitesse] lightning (*avant n*). || [douleur] searing.

fulminer [fylmine] *vi* [personne]: ~ (**contre**) to fulminate (against).

fumé, -e [fyme] *adj* CULIN smoked. || [verres] tinted.

fumée [fyme] *nf* [de combustion] smoke.

fumer [fyme] **1** *vi* [personne, cheminée] to smoke. || [bouilloire, plat] to steam. **2** *vt* [cigarette, aliment] to smoke.

fumeur, -euse [fymœr, øz] *nm, f* smoker.

fumier [fymje] *nm* AGRIC dung, manure.

fumiste [fymist] *nmf péj* shirker.

fumisterie [fymistəri] *nf fam* shirking.

fumoir [fymwar] *nm* [pour aliments] smokehouse. || [pièce] smoking room.

funambule [fynãbyl] *nmf* tightrope walker.

funèbre [fynɛbr] *adj* [de funérailles] funeral (*avant n*). || [lugubre] funereal; [sentiments] dismal.

funérailles [fyneraj] *nfpl* funeral (*sg*).

funéraire [fynerɛr] *adj* funeral (*avant n*).

funeste [fynɛst] *adj* [accident] fatal. || [initiative, erreur] disastrous. || [présage] of doom.

funiculaire [fynikylɛr] *nm* funicular railway.

fur [fyr] ○ **au fur et à mesure** *loc adv* as I/you *etc* go along; **au ~ et à mesure des besoins** as (and when) needed. ○ **au fur et à mesure que** *loc conj* as (and when).

furet [fyrɛ] *nm* [animal] ferret.

fureter [fyrte] *vi* [fouiller] to ferret around.

fureur [fyrœr] *nf* [colère] fury.

furibond, -e [fyribɔ̃, ɔ̃d] *adj* furious.

furie [fyri] *nf* [colère, agitation] fury; **en ~** [personne] infuriated; [éléments] raging. || *fig* [femme] shrew.

furieux, -ieuse [fyrjø, jøz] *adj* [personne] furious. || [énorme] tremendous.

furoncle [fyrɔ̃kl] *nm* boil.

furtif, -ive [fyrtif, iv] *adj* furtive.

fus, fut *etc* → être.

fusain [fyzɛ̃] *nm* [crayon] charcoal. || [dessin] charcoal drawing.

fuseau, -x [fyzo] *nm* [outil] spindle. || [pantalon] ski-pants (*pl*). ○ **fuseau horaire** *nm* time zone.

fusée [fyze] *nf* [pièce d'artifice & AÉRON] rocket.

fuselage [fyzlaʒ] *nm* fuselage.

fuselé, -e [fyzle] *adj* [doigts] tapering; [jambes] slender.

fuser [fyze] *vi* [cri, rire] to burst forth ou out.

fusible [fyzibl] *nm* fuse.

fusil [fyzi] *nm* [arme] gun.

fusillade [fyzijad] *nf* [combat] gunfire (*U*), fusillade.

fusiller [fyzije] *vt* [exécuter] to shoot.

fusion [fyzjɔ̃] *nf* [gén] fusion. || [fonte] smelting. || ÉCON & POLIT merger.

fusionner [fyzjone] *vt & vi* to merge.

fustiger [fystiʒe] *vt* to castigate.

fut → être.

fût [fy] *nm* [d'arbre] trunk. || [tonneau] barrel, cask. || [d'arme] stock.

futile [fytil] *adj* [insignifiant] futile. || [frivole] frivolous.

futur, -e [fytyr] *adj* future (*avant n*). ○ **futur** *nm* future.

futuriste [fytyrist] *adj* futuristic.

fuyant, -e [fɥijã, ãt] *adj* [perspective, front] receding (*avant n*). || [regard] evasive.

fuyard, -e [fɥijar, ard] *nm, f* runaway.

G

g, G [ʒe] *nm inv* g, G.

gabardine [gabardin] *nf* gabardine.

gabarit [gabari] *nm* [dimension] size.

gâcher [gaʃe] *vt* [gaspiller] to waste. ||
[gâter] to spoil. || CONSTR to mix.

gâchette [gaʃɛt] *nf* trigger.

gâchis [gaʃi] *nm* [gaspillage] waste (*U*).

gadget [gadʒɛt] *nm* gadget.

gadoue [gadu] *nf fam* [boue] mud.

gaélique [gaelik] **1** *adj* Gaelic. **2** *nm*
Gaelic.

gaffe [gaf] *nf fam* [maladresse] clanger.
|| [outil] boat hook.

gaffer [gafe] *vi fam* to put one's foot in
it.

gag [gag] *nm* gag.

gage [gaʒ] *nm* [assurance, preuve] proof.
|| [dans jeu] forfeit.

gager [gaʒe] *vt*: ~ **que** to bet (that).

gageure [gaʒyr] *nf* challenge.

gagnant, -e [gaɲɑ̃, ɑ̃t] **1** *adj* winning
(*avant n*). **2** *nm, f* winner.

gagne-pain [gaɲpɛ̃] *nm inv* livelihood.

gagner [gaɲe] **1** *vt* [salaire, argent, repos]
to earn. || [course, prix, affection] to win.
|| [obtenir, économiser] to gain. || [attein-
dre] to reach; [- suj: feu, engourdissement]
to spread to; [- suj: sommeil, froid] to
overcome. **2** *vi* [être vainqueur] to win. ||
[bénéficier] to gain; ~ **à faire qqch** to be
better off doing sthg; **qu'est-ce que j'y
gagne?** what do I get out of it? || [s'a-
méliorer]: ~ **en** to increase in.

gai, -e [gɛ] *adj* [joyeux] cheerful, happy.
|| [vif, plaisant] bright.

gaieté [gete] *nf* [joie] cheerfulness. ||
[vivacité] brightness.

gaillard, -e [gajar, ard] *nm, f* strapping
individual.

gain [gɛ̃] *nm* [profit] gain, profit. || [éco-
nomie] saving. ○ **gains** *nmpl* earnings.

gaine [gɛn] *nf* [étui, enveloppe] sheath. ||
[sous-vêtement] girdle, corset.

gainer [gene] *vt* to sheathe.

gala [gala] *nm* gala, reception.

galant, -e [galɑ̃, ɑ̃t] *adj* [courtois] gal-
lant.

galanterie [galɑ̃tri] *nf* [courtoisie] gal-
lantry, politeness. || [flatterie] compli-
ment.

galaxie [galaksi] *nf* galaxy.

galbe [galb] *nm* curve.

gale [gal] *nf* MÉD scabies (*U*).

galère [galɛr] *nf* NAVIG galley; **quelle ~!**
fig what a hassle!, what a drag!

galérer [galere] *vi fam* to have a hard
time.

galerie [galri] *nf* [gén] gallery. || THÉÂ-
TRE circle. || [porte-bagages] roof rack.

galet [galɛ] *nm* [caillou] pebble.

galette [galɛt] *nf* CULIN pancake.

galipette [galipɛt] *nf fam* somersault.

Galles [gal] → **pays**.

gallicisme [galisism] *nm* [expression]
French idiom; [dans une langue étrangère]
gallicism.

gallois, -e [galwa, az] *adj* Welsh.
○ **gallois** *nm* [langue] Welsh. ○ **Gallois, -e** *nm, f* Welshman (*f* Welshwoman); **les Gallois** the Welsh.

galon [galɔ̃] *nm* COUTURE braid (*U*). ||
MIL stripe.

galop [galo] *nm* [allure] gallop; **au ~
[cheval]** at a gallop; *fig* at the double.

galoper [galɔpe] *vi* [cheval] to gallop. ||
[personne] to run about.

galopin [galɔpɛ̃] *nm fam* brat.

galvaniser [galvanize] *vt litt & fig* to
galvanize.

galvauder [galvode] *vt* [ternir] to tarnish.

gambader [gɑ̃bade] *vi* [sautiller] to leap
about; [agneau] to gambol.

gamelle [gamɛl] *nf* [plat] kit *Am*.

gamin, -e [gamɛ̃, in] **1** *adj* [puéril] childish. **2** *nm, f fam* [enfant] kid.

gamme [gam] *nf* [série] range; ~ **de pro-
duits** product range. || MUS scale.

ganglion [gɑ̃gliʒ̃] *nm* ganglion.

gangrène [gɑ̃grɛn] *nf* gangrene; *fig* corruption, canker.

gangue [gɑ̃g] *nf* [de minerai] gangue. ||
fig [carcan] straitjacket.

gant [gɑ̃] *nm* glove; ~ **de toilette** face
cloth, flannel *Br*.

garage [garaʒ] *nm* garage.

garagiste [garaʒist] *nmf* [propriétaire]
garage owner; [réparateur] garage mechanic.

garant, -e [garɑ̃, ɑ̃t] *nm, f* [responsable]
guarantor; **se porter ~ de** to vouch for.

garantie [garɑ̃ti] *nf* [gén] guarantee.

garantir [garãtir] *vt* [assurer & COMM] to guarantee; ~ **à qqn que** to assure ou guarantee sb that.

garçon [garsɔ̃] *nm* [enfant] boy. || [célibataire]: **vieux ~** confirmed bachelor. || [serveur]: ~ **(de café)** waiter.

garçonnet [garsɔnɛ] *nm* little boy.

garçonnière [garsɔnjɛr] *nf* bachelor flat *Br* ou apartment *Am*.

garde [gard] **1** *nf* [surveillance] protection. || [veille]: **pharmacie de ~** duty chemist. || MIL guard; **monter la ~** to go on guard. || *loc*: **être/se tenir sur ses ~s** to be/stay on one's guard; **mettre qqn en ~ contre qqch** to put sb on their guard about sthg. **2** *nmf* keeper; ~ **du corps** bodyguard.

garde-à-vous [gardavu] *nm inv* attention; **se mettre au ~** to stand to attention.

garde-boue [gardəbu] *nm inv* mudguard *Br*, fender *Am*.

garde-chasse [gardəʃas] (*pl* **gardes-chasse** ou **gardes-chasses**) *nm* gamekeeper.

garde-fou [gardəfu] (*pl* **garde-fous**) *nm* railing, parapet.

garde-malade [gardəmalad] (*pl* **gardes-malades**) *nmf* nurse.

garde-manger [gardəmɑ̃ʒe] *nm inv* [pièce] pantry, larder; [armoire] meat safe *Br*, cooler *Am*.

garde-pêche [gardəpɛʃ] (*pl* **gardes-pêche**) *nm* [personne] fishwarden *Am*.

garder [garde] *vt* [gén] to keep; [vêtement] to keep on. || [surveiller] to mind, to look after; [défendre] to guard. ○ **se garder** *vp* [se conserver] to keep. || [s'abstenir]: **se ~ de faire qqch** to take care not to do sthg.

garderie [gardəri] *nf* crèche *Br*, day nursery *Br*, day-care center *Am*.

garde-robe [gardərɔb] (*pl* **garde-robes**) *nf* wardrobe.

gardien, -ienne [gardjɛ̃, jɛn] *nm, f* [surveillant] guard, keeper; ~ **de but** goalkeeper; ~ **de nuit** night watchman. || *fig* [défenseur] protector, guardian. || [agent]: ~ **de la paix** policeman.

gare [gar] *nf* station; ~ **routière** [de marchandises] road haulage depot; [pour passagers] bus station.

garer [gare] *vt* [ranger] to park. ○ **se garer** *vp* [stationner] to park. || [se ranger] to pull over.

gargariser [gargarize] ○ **se gargariser** *vp* [se rincer] to gargle. || *péj* [se délecter]: **se ~ de** to delight ou revel in.

gargouiller [garguje] *vi* [eau] to gurgle. || [intestins] to rumble.

garnement [garnəmɑ̃] *nm* rascal, pest.

garni [garni] *nm vieilli* furnished accommodation (*U*).

garnir [garnir] *vt* [équiper] to fit out, to furnish. || [remplir] to fill. || [orner]: ~ **qqch de** to decorate sthg with.

garnison [garnizɔ̃] *nf* garrison.

garniture [garnityr] *nf* [ornement] trimming; [de lit] bed linen. || [CULIN - pour accompagner] garnish *Br*, fixings (*pl*) *Am*; [- pour remplir] filling.

garrigue [garig] *nf* scrub.

garrot [garo] *nm* [de cheval] withers (*pl*). || MÉD tourniquet.

gars [ga] *nm fam* [garçon, homme] lad. || [type] guy, bloke *Br*.

gas-oil [gazɔjl, gazwal], **gazole** [gazɔl] *nm* diesel oil.

gaspillage [gaspijaʒ] *nm* waste.

gaspiller [gaspije] *vt* to waste.

gastrique [gastrik] *adj* gastric.

gastro-entérite [gastrɔɑ̃terit] (*pl* **gastro-entérites**) *nf* gastroenteritis (*U*).

gastronome [gastrɔnɔm] *nmf* gourmet.

gastronomie [gastrɔnɔmi] *nf* gastronomy.

gâteau, -x [gato] *nm* cake; ~ **sec** biscuit *Br*, cookie *Am*.

gâter [gate] *vt* [gén] to spoil; [vacances, affaires] to ruin, to spoil. || *iron* [combler] to be too good to. ○ **se gâter** *vp* [temps] to change for the worse. || [situation] to take a turn for the worse.

gâteux, -euse [gato, øz] *adj* senile.

gauche [goʃ] **1** *nf* [côté] left, left-hand side; **à ~ (de)** on the left (of). || POLIT: **la ~** the left (wing); **de ~** left-wing. **2** *adj* [côté] left. || [personne] clumsy.

gaucher, -ère [goʃe, ɛr] **1** *adj* left-handed. **2** *nm, f* left-handed person.

gauchiste [goʃist] *nmf* leftist.

gaufre [gofr] *nf* waffle.

gaufrer [gofre] *vt* to emboss.

gaufrette [gofrɛt] *nf* wafer.

gaule [gol] *nf* [perche] pole. || [canne à pêche] fishing rod.

gauler [gole] *vt* to bring ou shake down.

gaulliste [golist] *nmf & adj* Gaullist.

gaver [gave] *vt* [animal] to force-feed. || [personne]: ~ **qqn de** to feed sb full of.

gay [ge] *adj inv & nm* gay.

gaz [gaz] *nm inv* gas.

gaze [gaz] *nf* gauze.

gazelle [gazɛl] *nf* gazelle.

gazer [gaze] *vt* to gas.

gazette [gazɛt] *nf* newspaper, gazette.

gazeux, -euse [gazø, øz] *adj* CHIM gaseous. || [boisson] fizzy.

gazoduc [gazɔdyk] *nm* gas pipeline.

gazole → **gas-oil**.

gazon [gazɔ̃] *nm* [herbe] grass; [terrain] lawn.

gazouiller [gazuje] *vi* [oiseau] to chirp, to twitter. || [bébé] to gurgle.

GB, G-B (*abr de* **Grande-Bretagne**) *nf* GB.

gd *abr de* **grand**.

GDF, Gdf (*abr de* **Gaz de France**) *French national gas company.*

geai [ʒɛ] *nm* jay.

géant, -e [ʒeɑ̃, ɑ̃t] **1** *adj* gigantic, giant. **2** *nm, f* giant.

geindre [ʒɛ̃dr] *vi* [gémir] to moan. || *fam* [pleurnicher] to whine.

gel [ʒɛl] *nm* MÉTÉOR frost. || [d'eau] freezing. || [cosmétique] gel.

gélatine [ʒelatin] *nf* gelatine.

gelée [ʒəle] *nf* MÉTÉOR frost. || CULIN jelly.

geler [ʒəle] *vt & vi* [gén] to freeze. || [projet] to halt.

gélule [ʒelyl] *nf* capsule.

Gémeaux [ʒemo] *nmpl* ASTROL Gemini.

gémir [ʒemir] *vi* [gén] to moan.

gémissement [ʒemismɑ̃] *nm* [gén] moan; [du vent] moaning (*U*).

gemme [ʒɛm] *nf* gem, precious stone.

gênant, -e [ʒenɑ̃, ɑ̃t] *adj* [encombrant] in the way. || [embarrassant] awkward, embarrassing. || [énervant]: **être ~** to be a nuisance.

gencive [ʒɑ̃siv] *nf* gum.

gendarme [ʒɑ̃darm] *nm* policeman.

gendarmerie [ʒɑ̃darməri] *nf* [corps] police force. || [lieu] police station.

gendre [ʒɑ̃dr] *nm* son-in-law.

gène [ʒɛn] *nm* gene.

gêne [ʒɛn] *nf* [physique] difficulty. || [psychologique] embarrassment. || [financière] difficulty.

généalogie [ʒenealɔʒi] *nf* genealogy.

généalogique [ʒenealɔʒik] *adj* genealogical; **arbre ~** family tree.

gêner [ʒene] *vt* [physiquement - gén] to be too tight for; [- suj: chaussures] to pinch. || [moralement] to embarrass. || [incommoder] to bother. || [encombrer] to hamper.

général, -e, -aux [ʒeneral, o] *adj* general; **en ~** generally, in general; **répétition ~e** dress rehearsal. ○ **général** *nm* MIL general.

généralement [ʒeneralmɑ̃] *adv* generally.

généralisation [ʒeneralizasjɔ̃] *nf* generalization.

généraliser [ʒeneralize] *vt & vi* to generalize. ○ **se généraliser** *vp* to become general ou widespread.

généraliste [ʒeneralist] **1** *nmf* GP *Br*, family doctor. **2** *adj* general.

généralité [ʒeneralite] *nf* [idée] generality.

générateur, -trice [ʒeneratœr, tris] *adj* generating. ○ **générateur** *nm* TECHNOL generator.

génération [ʒenerasjɔ̃] *nf* generation.

générer [ʒenere] *vt* to generate.

généreux, -euse [ʒenerø, øz] *adj* generous; [terre] fertile.

générique [ʒenerik] **1** *adj* generic. **2** *nm* credits (*pl*).

générosité [ʒenerozite] *nf* generosity.

genèse [ʒənɛz] *nf* [création] genesis.

genêt [ʒənɛ] *nm* broom.

génétique [ʒenetik] **1** *adj* genetic. **2** *nf* genetics (*U*).

Genève [ʒənɛv] *n* Geneva.

génial, -e, -iaux [ʒenjal, jo] *adj* [personne] of genius. || [idée, invention] inspired. || *fam* [formidable]: **c'est ~!** that's great!, that's terrific!

génie [ʒeni] *nm* [personne, aptitude] genius. || TECHNOL engineering.

genièvre [ʒənjɛvr] *nm* juniper.

génisse [ʒenis] *nf* heifer.

génital, -e, -aux [ʒenital, o] *adj* genital.

génitif [ʒenitif] *nm* genitive (case).

génocide [ʒenɔsid] *nm* genocide.

genou, -x [ʒənu] *nm* knee; **à ~x** on one's knees, kneeling.

genouillère [ʒənujer] *nf* [bandage] knee bandage. || SPORT kneepad.

genre [ʒɑ̃r] *nm* [type] type, kind. || LITTÉRATURE genre. || [style de personne] style. || GRAM gender.

gens [ʒɑ̃] *nmpl* people.

gentiane [ʒɑ̃sjan] *nf* gentian.

gentil, -ille [ʒɑ̃ti, ij] *adj* [agréable] nice. || [aimable] kind, nice.

gentillesse [ʒɑ̃tijɛs] *nf* kindness.

gentiment [ʒɑ̃timɑ̃] *adv* [sagement] nicely. || [aimablement] kindly, nicely. || *Helv* [tranquillement] calmly, quietly.

génuflexion [ʒenyflɛksjɔ̃] *nf* genuflexion.

géographie [ʒeɔgrafi] *nf* geography.

géologie [ʒeɔlɔʒi] *nf* geology.

géologue [ʒeɔlɔg] *nmf* geologist.

géomètre [ʒeɔmɛtr] *nmf* [spécialiste] geometer, geometrician. || [technicien] surveyor.

géométrie [ʒeɔmetri] *nf* geometry.

gérance [ʒerɑ̃s] *nf* management.

géranium [ʒeranjɔm] *nm* geranium.

gérant, -e [ʒerɑ̃, ɑ̃t] *nm, f* manager.

gerbe [ʒɛrb] *nf* [de blé] sheaf; [de fleurs] spray. || [d'étincelles, d'eau] shower.

gercé, -e [ʒɛrse] *adj* chapped.

gérer [ʒere] *vt* to manage.

germain, -e [ʒɛrmɛ̃, ɛn] → **cousin**.

germanique [ʒɛrmanik] *adj* Germanic.

germe [ʒɛrm] *nm* BOT & MÉD germ; [de pomme de terre] eye. || *fig* [origine] seed, cause.

germer [ʒɛrme] *vi* to germinate.

gésier [ʒezje] *nm* gizzard.

gésir [ʒezir] *vi littéraire* to lie.

gestation [ʒɛstasjɔ̃] *nf* gestation.

geste [ʒɛst] *nm* [mouvement] gesture. || [acte] act, deed.

gesticuler [ʒɛstikyle] *vi* to gesticulate.

gestion [ʒɛstjɔ̃] *nf* management; **~ de fichiers** INFORM file management.

ghetto [geto] *nm litt & fig* ghetto.

gibet [ʒibɛ] *nm* gallows (*sg*), gibbet.

gibier [ʒibje] *nm* game.

giboulée [ʒibule] *nf* sudden shower.

gicler [ʒikle] *vi* to squirt, to spurt.

gifle [ʒifl] *nf* slap.

gifler [ʒifle] *vt* to slap; *fig* [suj: vent, pluie] to whip, to lash.

gigantesque [ʒigɑ̃tɛsk] *adj* gigantic.

gigolo [ʒigɔlo] *nm* gigolo.

gigot [ʒigo] *nm* CULIN leg.

gigoter [ʒigɔte] *vi* to squirm, to wriggle.

gilet [ʒilɛ] *nm* [cardigan] cardigan. || [sans manches] waistcoat *Br*, vest *Am*.

gin [dʒin] *nm* gin.

gingembre [ʒɛ̃ʒɑ̃br] *nm* ginger.

girafe [ʒiraf] *nf* giraffe.

giratoire [ʒiratwar] *adj* gyrating; **sens ~** roundabout *Br*, traffic circle *Am*.

girofle [ʒirɔfl] → **clou**.

girouette [ʒirwɛt] *nf* weathercock.

gisement [ʒizmɑ̃] *nm* deposit.

gît → **gésir**.

gitan, -e [ʒitɑ̃, an] *adj* Gipsy (*avant n*). Ⓞ **Gitan, -e** *nm, f* Gipsy.

gîte [ʒit] *nm* [logement]: **~ (rural)** gîte, self-catering accommodation *in the country*. || [du bœuf] shin *Br*, shank *Am*.

givre [ʒivr] *nm* frost.

glabre [glabr] *adj* hairless.

glace [glas] *nf* [eau congelée] ice. || [crème glacée] ice cream. || [vitre] pane. || [- de voiture] window. || [miroir] mirror.

glacé, -e [glase] *adj* [gelé] frozen. || [très froid] freezing. || *fig* [hostile] cold.

glacer [glase] *vt* [geler, paralyser] to chill. || [étoffe, papier] to glaze. || [gâteau] to ice *Br*, to frost *Am*.

glacial, -e, -iaux [glasjal, jo] *adj litt & fig* icy.

glacier [glasje] *nm* GÉOGR glacier. || [marchand] ice cream seller ou man.

glaçon [glasɔ̃] *nm* [dans boisson] ice cube.

glaïeul [glajœl] *nm* gladiolus.

glaire [glɛr] *nf* MÉD phlegm.

glaise [glɛz] *nf* clay.

gland [glɑ̃] *nm* [de chêne] acorn. || [ornement] tassel. || ANAT glans.

glande [glɑ̃d] *nf* gland.

glaner [glane] *vt* to glean.

glapir [glapir] *vi* to yelp, to yap.

glas [gla] *nm* knell.

glauque [glok] *adj* [couleur] bluey-green. || *fam* [lugubre] gloomy. || *fam* [sordide] sordid.

glissade [glisad] *nf* slip.

glissant, -e [glisɑ̃, ɑ̃t] *adj* slippery.

glissement [glismɑ̃] *nm* [action de glisser] gliding, sliding.

glisser [glise] **1** *vi* [se déplacer]: **~ (sur)** to glide (over), to slide (over). || [déraper]: **~ (sur)** to slip (on). || *fig* [passer rapidement]: **~ sur** to skate over. || [surface] to be slippery. || [progresser] to slip; **~ dans/vers** to slip into/towards, to slide into/towards. **2** *vt* to slip; **~ un regard à qqn** *fig* to give sb a sidelong glance. Ⓞ **se glisser** *vp* to slip; **se ~ dans** [lit] to slip ou slide into; *fig* to slip ou creep into.

glissière [glisjɛr] *nf* runner.

global, -e, -aux [glɔbal, o] *adj* global.

globalement [glɔbalmɑ̃] *adv* on the whole.

globe [glɔb] *nm* [sphère, terre] globe. || [de verre] glass cover.

globule [glɔbyl] *nm* globule; **~ blanc/rouge** white/red corpuscle.

globuleux [glɔbylø] → **œil**.

gloire [glwar] *nf* [renommée] glory; [de vedette] fame, stardom. || [mérite] credit.

glorieux, -ieuse [glɔrjø, jøz] *adj* [mort, combat] glorious; [héros, soldat] renowned.

glossaire [glɔsɛr] *nm* glossary.

glousser [gluse] *vi* [poule] to cluck. || *fam* [personne] to chortle, to chuckle.

glouton, **-onne** [glutɔ̃, ɔn] **1** *adj* greedy. **2** *nm*, *f* glutton.

glu [gly] *nf* [colle] glue.

gluant, **-e** [glyɑ̃, ɑ̃t] *adj* sticky.

glucide [glysid] *nm* glucide.

glycine [glisin] *nf* wisteria.

go [go] ○ **tout de go** *loc adv* straight.

GO (*abr de* **grandes ondes**) *nfpl* LW.

goal [gol] *nm* goalkeeper.

gobelet [gɔblɛ] *nm* beaker, tumbler.

gober [gɔbe] *vt* [avaler] to gulp down. || *fam* [croire] to swallow.

godet [gɔdɛ] *nm* [récipient] jar, pot.

godiller [gɔdije] *vi* [rameur] to scull. || [skieur] to wedeln.

goéland [gɔelɑ̃] *nm* gull, seagull.

goélette [gɔelɛt] *nf* schooner.

goguenard, **-e** [gɔɡnar, ard] *adj* mocking.

goinfre [ɡwɛ̃fr] *nmf fam* pig.

goitre [ɡwatr] *nm* goitre.

golf [ɡɔlf] *nm* [sport] golf; [terrain] golf course.

golfe [ɡɔlf] *nm* gulf, bay; **le ~ de Gascogne** the Bay of Biscay; **le ~ Persique** the (Persian) Gulf.

gomme [ɡɔm] *nf* [substance, bonbon] gum. || [pour effacer] eraser.

gommer [ɡɔme] *vt* to rub out, to erase; *fig* to erase.

gond [ɡɔ̃] *nm* hinge.

gondole [ɡɔ̃dɔl] *nf* gondola.

gondoler [ɡɔ̃dɔle] *vi* [bois] to warp; [carton] to curl.

gonfler [ɡɔ̃fle] **1** *vt* [ballon, pneu] to blow up, to inflate; [rivière, poitrine, yeux] to swell; [joues] to blow out. || *fig* [grossir] to exaggerate. **2** *vi* to swell.

gong [ɡɔ̃ɡ] *nm* gong.

gorge [ɡɔrʒ] *nf* [gosier, cou] throat. || (*gén pl*) [vallée] gorge.

gorgée [ɡɔrʒe] *nf* mouthful.

gorger [ɡɔrʒe] *vt*: **~ qqn de qqch** [gaver] to stuff sb with sthg.

gorille [ɡɔrij] *nm* [animal] gorilla.

gosier [ɡozje] *nm* throat, gullet.

gosse [ɡɔs] *nmf fam* kid.

gothique [ɡɔtik] *adj* ARCHIT Gothic.

gouache [ɡwaʃ] *nf* gouache.

goudron [ɡudrɔ̃] *nm* tar.

goudronner [ɡudrɔne] *vt* to tar.

gouffre [ɡufr] *nm* abyss.

goujat [ɡuʒa] *nm* boor.

goulet [ɡulɛ] *nm* narrows (*pl*).

goulot [ɡulo] *nm* neck.

goulu, **-e** [ɡuly] *adj* greedy, gluttonous.

goupillon [ɡupijɔ̃] *nm* RELIG [holy water] sprinkler. || [à bouteille] bottle brush.

gourd, **-e** [ɡur, ɡurd] *adj* numb.

gourde [ɡurd] **1** *nf* [récipient] flask, waterbottle. || *fam* [personne] idiot. **2** *adj fam* thick.

gourdin [ɡurdɛ̃] *nm* club.

gourmand, **-e** [ɡurmɑ̃, ɑ̃d] **1** *adj* greedy. **2** *nm*, *f* glutton.

gourmandise [ɡurmɑ̃diz] *nf* [caractère] greed, greediness. || [sucrerie] sweet thing.

gourmette [ɡurmɛt] *nf* chain bracelet.

gousse [ɡus] *nf* pod.

goût [ɡu] *nm* taste; **de mauvais ~** tasteless, in bad taste.

goûter [ɡute] **1** *vt* [déguster] to taste. || [savourer] to enjoy. **2** *vi* to have an afternoon snack; **~ à** to taste. **3** *nm* afternoon snack for children, typically consisting of bread, butter, chocolate and a drink.

goutte [ɡut] *nf* [de pluie, d'eau] drop. || MÉD [maladie] gout. ○ **gouttes** *nfpl* MÉD drops.

goutte-à-goutte [ɡutaɡut] *nm inv* (intravenous) drip *Br*, IV *Am*.

gouttelette [ɡutlɛt] *nf* droplet.

gouttière [ɡutjɛr] *nf* [CONSTR - horizontale] gutter; [- verticale] drainpipe. || MÉD splint.

gouvernail [ɡuvɛrnaj] *nm* rudder.

gouvernante [ɡuvɛrnɑ̃t] *nf* [d'enfants] governess. || [de maison] housekeeper.

gouvernement [ɡuvɛrnəmɑ̃] *nm* government.

gouverner [ɡuvɛrne] *vt* to govern.

gouverneur [ɡuvɛrnœr] *nm* governor.

grâce [ɡras] *nf* [charme] grace; **de bonne ~** with good grace, willingly; **de mauvaise ~** with bad grace, reluctantly. || [faveur] favour. || [miséricorde] mercy. ○ **grâce à** *loc prép* thanks to.

gracier [ɡrasje] *vt* to pardon.

gracieusement [ɡrasjøzmɑ̃] *adv* [avec grâce] graciously. || [gratuitement] free (of charge).

gracieux, **-ieuse** [ɡrasjø, jøz] *adj* [charmant] graceful. || [gratuit] free.

gradation [ɡradasjɔ̃] *nf* gradation.

grade [ɡrad] *nm* [échelon] rank; [universitaire] qualification.

gradé, **-e** [ɡrade] **1** *adj* non-commissioned. **2** *nm*, *f* non-commissioned officer, NCO.

gradin [ɡradɛ̃] *nm* [de stade, de théâtre] tier; [de terrain] terrace.

graduation [gradɥasjɔ̃] *nf* graduation.

graduel, -elle [gradɥɛl] *adj* gradual.

graduer [gradɥe] *vt* [récipient, règle] to graduate.

graffiti [grafiti] *nm inv* graffiti (*U*).

grain [grɛ̃] *nm* [gén] grain; [de moutarde] seed; [de café] bean; **~ de raisin** grape. || [point]: **~ de beauté** beauty spot.

graine [grɛn] *nf* BOT seed.

graisse [grɛs] *nf* ANAT & CULIN fat. || [pour lubrifier] grease.

graisser [grese] *vt* [machine] to grease, to lubricate.

grammaire [gramɛr] *nf* grammar.

grammatical, -e, -aux [gramatikal, o] *adj* grammatical.

gramme [gram] *nm* gram, gramme.

grand, -e [grɑ̃, grɑ̃d] **1** *adj* [en hauteur] tall; [en dimensions] big, large; [en quantité, nombre] large, great; **un ~ nombre de** a large ou great number of; **en ~** [dimension] full-size. || [âgé] grown-up; **les ~es personnes** grown-ups; **~ frère** big ou older brother. || [important, remarquable] great; **un ~ homme** a great man. || [intense]: **un ~ buveur/fumeur** a heavy drinker/smoker. **2** *nm, f* (*gén pl*) [personnage] great man (*f* woman). || [enfant] older ou bigger boy (*f* girl).

grand-angle [grɑ̃tɑ̃gl] *nm* wide-angle lens.

grand-chose [grɑ̃ʃoz] ○ **pas grand-chose** *pron indéf* not much.

Grande-Bretagne [grɑ̃dbrətaɲ] *nf*: **la ~** Great Britain.

grandeur [grɑ̃dœr] *nf* [taille] size. || [apogée & *fig*] greatness; **~ d'âme** *fig* magnanimity.

grandir [grɑ̃dir] **1** *vt*: **~ qqn** [suj: chaussures] to make sb look taller; *fig* to increase sb's standing. **2** *vi* [personne, plante] to grow; [obscurité, bruit] to increase, to grow.

grand-mère [grɑ̃mɛr] *nf* grandmother.

grand-père [grɑ̃pɛr] *nm* grandfather.

grands-parents [grɑ̃parɑ̃] *nmpl* grandparents.

grange [grɑ̃ʒ] *nf* barn.

granit(e) [granit] *nm* granite.

granulé, -e [granyle] *adj* [surface] granular. ○ **granulé** *nm* tablet.

granuleux, -euse [granylø, øz] *adj* granular.

graphique [grafik] **1** *nm* diagram; [graphe] graph. **2** *adj* graphic.

graphisme [grafism] *nm* [écriture] handwriting. || ART style of drawing.

graphologie [grafɔlɔʒi] *nf* graphology.

grappe [grap] *nf* [de fruits] bunch; [de fleurs] stem. || *fig* [de gens] knot.

grappiller [grapije] *vt litt* & *fig* to gather, to pick up.

grappin [grapɛ̃] *nm* [ancre] grapnel.

gras, grasse [gra, gras] *adj* [personne, animal] fat. || [plat, aliment] fatty. || [cheveux, mains] greasy. || [crayon] soft. || *fig* [rire] throaty; [toux] phlegmy. ○ **gras 1** *nm* [du jambon] fat. || TYPO bold (type). **2** *adv*: **manger ~** to eat fatty foods.

grassement [grasmɑ̃] *adv* [rire] coarsely. || [payer] a lot.

gratifier [gratifje] *vt* [accorder]: **~ qqn de qqch** to present sb with sthg, to present sthg to sb; *fig* to reward sb with sthg. || [stimuler] to gratify.

gratin [gratɛ̃] *nm* CULIN dish sprinkled *with breadcrumbs or cheese and browned.* || *fam fig* [haute société] upper crust.

gratiné, -e [gratine] *adj* CULIN *sprinkled with breadcrumbs or cheese and browned.* || *fam fig* [ardu] stiff.

gratis [gratis] *adv* free.

gratitude [gratityd] *nf*: **~ (envers)** gratitude (to ou towards).

gratte-ciel [gratsjɛl] *nm inv* skyscraper.

grattement [gratmɑ̃] *nm* scratching.

gratter [grate] **1** *vt* [gén] to scratch; [pour enlever] to scrape off. **2** *vi* [démanger] to itch, to be itchy. || *fam* [écrire] to scribble. ○ **se gratter** *vp* to scratch.

gratuit, -e [gratɥi, it] *adj* [entrée] free. || [violence] gratuitous.

gratuitement [gratɥitmɑ̃] *adv* [sans payer] free, for nothing. || [sans raison] gratuitously.

gravats [grava] *nmpl* rubble (*U*).

grave [grav] *adj* [attitude, faute, maladie] serious, grave; **ce n'est pas ~** [ce n'est rien] don't worry about it. || [voix] deep.

gravement [gravmɑ̃] *adv* gravely, seriously.

graver [grave] *vt* [gén] to engrave. || [bois] to carve. || [disque] to cut.

gravier [gravje] *nm* gravel (*U*).

gravillon [gravijɔ̃] *nm* fine gravel (*U*).

gravir [gravir] *vt* to climb.

gravité [gravite] *nf* [importance] seriousness, gravity. || PHYS gravity.

graviter [gravite] *vi* [astre] to revolve. || *fig* [évoluer] to gravitate.

gravure [gravyr] *nf* [technique]: **~ (sur)**

engraving (on). || [reproduction] print; [dans livre] plate.

gré [gre] *nm* [goût]: **à mon/son ~** for my/his taste. for my/his liking. || [volonté]: **bon ~ mal ~** willy nilly; **de ~ ou de force** *fig* whether you/they *etc* like it or not; **de mon/son plein ~** of my/his own free will.

grec, grecque [grɛk] *adj* Greek. ○ **grec** *nm* [langue] Greek. ○ **Grec, Grecque** *nm, f* Greek.

Grèce [grɛs] *nf*: **la ~** Greece.

gréement [gremɑ̃] *nm* rigging.

greffe [gref] *nf* MÉD transplant; [de peau] graft. || BOT graft.

greffer [grefe] *rt* MÉD to transplant; [peau] to graft; **~ un rein/un cœur à qqn** to give sb a kidney/heart transplant. || BOT to graft.

greffier [grefje] *nm* clerk of the court.

grêle [grɛl] **1** *nf* hail. **2** *adj* [jambes] spindly. || [son] shrill.

grêler [grele] *v impers* to hail; **il grêle** it's hailing.

grêlon [grɛlɔ̃] *nm* hailstone.

grelot [grəlo] *nm* bell.

grelotter [grələte] *ri*: **~ (de)** to shiver (with).

grenade [grənad] *nf* [fruit] pomegranate. || MIL grenade.

grenat [grəna] *adj inv* dark red.

grenier [grənje] *nm* [de maison] attic. || [à foin] loft.

grenouille [grənuj] *nf* frog.

grès [grɛ] *nm* [roche] sandstone. || [poterie] stoneware.

grésiller [grezije] *ri* [friture] to sizzle; [feu] to crackle. || [radio] to crackle.

grève [grɛv] *nf* [arrêt du travail] strike; **faire ~** to strike. to go on strike. || [rivage] shore.

grever [grəve] *rt* to burden; [budget] to put a strain on.

gréviste [grevist] *nmf* striker.

gribouiller [gribuje] *rt & ri* [écrire] to scrawl. || [dessiner] to doodle.

grief [grijef] *nm* grievance; **faire ~ de qqch à qqn** to hold sthg against sb.

grièvement [grijɛvmɑ̃] *adv* seriously.

griffe [grif] *nf* [d'animal] claw. || *Belg* [éraflure] scratch.

griffer [grife] *rt* [suj: chat etc] to claw.

grignoter [griɲɔte] **1** *rt* [manger] to nibble. || *fam fig* [réduire - capital] to eat away (at). **2** *ri* [manger] to nibble. || *fam fig* [prendre]: **~ sur** to nibble away at.

gril [gril] *nm* grill.

grillade [grijad] *nf* CULIN grilled meat.

grillage [grijaʒ] *nm* [de porte, de fenêtre] wire netting. || [clôture] wire fence.

grille [grij] *nf* [portail] gate. || [d'orifice, de guichet] grille; [de fenêtre] bars (*pl*). || [de mots croisés, de loto] grid. || [tableau] table.

grille-pain [grijpɛ̃] *nm inv* toaster.

griller [grije] **1** *rt* [viande] to broil *Am*; [pain] to toast; [café, marrons] to roast. || *fig* [au soleil - personne] to burn; [- végétation] to shrivel. || *fam fig* [dépasser - concurrents] to outstrip; **~ un feu rouge** to jump the lights. || *fig* [compromettre] to ruin. **2** *ri* [ampoule] to blow.

grillon [grijɔ̃] *nm* [insecte] cricket.

grimace [grimas] *nf* grimace.

grimer [grime] *rt* CIN & THÉÂTRE to make up.

grimper [grɛ̃pe] **1** *rt* to climb. **2** *ri* to climb; **~ à un arbre/une échelle** to climb a tree/a ladder.

grincement [grɛ̃smɑ̃] *nm* [de charnière] squeaking; [de porte, plancher] creaking.

grincer [grɛ̃se] *ri* [charnière] to squeak; [porte, plancher] to creak.

grincheux, -euse [grɛ̃ʃø, øz] **1** *adj* grumpy. **2** *nm, f* moaner, grumbler.

grippe [grip] *nf* MÉD flu (*U*).

grippé, -e [gripe] *adj* [malade]: **être ~** to have flu.

gripper [gripe] *ri* [mécanisme] to jam.

gris, -e [gri, griz] *adj* [couleur] grey. || *fig* [morne] dismal. ○ **gris** *nm* [couleur] grey.

grisaille [grizaj] *nf* [de ciel] greyness. || *fig* [de vie] dullness.

grisant, -e [grizɑ̃, ɑ̃t] *adj* intoxicating.

griser [grize] *rt* to intoxicate.

grisonner [grizɔne] *ri* to turn grey.

grisou [grizu] *nm* firedamp.

grive [griv] *nf* thrush.

grivois, -e [grivwa, az] *adj* ribald.

Groenland [grɔɛnlɑ̃d] *nm*: **le ~** Greenland.

grog [grɔg] *nm* (hot) toddy.

grognement [grɔɲmɑ̃] *nm* [son] grunt; [d'ours, de chien] growl.

grogner [grɔɲe] *ri* [émettre un son] to grunt; [ours, chien] to growl.

groin [grwɛ̃] *nm* snout.

grommeler [grɔmle] *rt & ri* to mutter.

grondement [grɔ̃dmɑ̃] *nm* [d'animal] growl; [de tonnerre, de train] rumble; [de torrent] roar.

gronder [grɔ̃de] **1** *ri* [animal] to growl; [tonnerre] to rumble. **2** *rt* to scold.

gros, grosse [gro, gros] *adj* (*gén avant n*) [gén] large, big; *péj* big. || (*avant ou après n*) [corpulent] fat. || [important, grave - ennuis] serious; [- dépense] major. ○ **gros 1** *adv* [beaucoup] a lot. **2** *nm* [partie]: **le (plus) ~ (de qqch)** the main part (of sthg). ○ **en gros** *loc adv & loc adj* COMM wholesale. || [en grands caractères] in large letters. || [grosso modo] roughly.

groseille [grozɛj] *nf* currant.

grosse [gros] *adj* → **gros**.

grossesse [grosɛs] *nf* pregnancy.

grosseur [grosœr] *nf* [dimension, taille] size. || MÉD lump.

grossier, -ière [grosje, jɛr] *adj* [matière] coarse. || [sommaire] rough. || [insolent] rude. || [vulgaire] crude. || [erreur] crass.

grossièrement [grosjɛrmã] *adv* [sommairement] roughly. || [vulgairement] crudely.

grossir [grosir] **1** *vi* [prendre du poids] to put on weight. || [s'intensifier] to increase. **2** *vt* [suj: microscope, verre] to magnify. || [suj: vêtement]: **~ qqn** to make sb look fatter. || [exagérer] to exaggerate.

grossiste [grosist] *nmf* wholesaler.

grosso modo [grosomodo] *adv* roughly.

grotte [grot] *nf* cave.

grouiller [gruje] *vi*: **~ (de)** to swarm (with).

groupe [grup] *nm* group. ○ **groupe sanguin** *nm* blood group.

groupement [grupmã] *nm* [action] grouping. || [groupe] group.

grouper [grupe] *vt* to group. ○ **se grouper** *vp* to come together.

grue [gry] *nf* TECHNOL & ZOOL crane.

grumeau, -x [grymo] *nm* lump.

Guatemala [gwatemala] *nm*: **le ~** Guatemala.

gué [ge] *nm* ford; **traverser à ~** to ford.

guenilles [gənij] *nfpl* rags.

guenon [gənɔ̃] *nf* female monkey.

guépard [gepar] *nm* cheetah.

guêpe [gɛp] *nf* wasp.

guêpier [gepje] *nm* wasp's nest; *fig* hornet's nest.

guère [gɛr] *adv* [peu] hardly; **il ne l'aime ~** he doesn't like him/her very much.

guéridon [geridɔ̃] *nm* pedestal table.

guérilla [gerija] *nf* guerrilla warfare.

guérir [gerir] **1** *vt* to cure. **2** *vi* to recover, to get better.

guérison [gerizɔ̃] *nf* [de malade] recovery. || [de maladie] cure.

guerre [gɛr] *nf* MIL & *fig* war; **faire la ~ à un pays** to make ou wage war on a country; **Première/Seconde Guerre mondiale** First/Second World War.

guerrier, -ière [gɛrje, jɛr] *adj* [de guerre] war (*avant n*). || [peuple] warlike. ○ **guerrier** *nm* warrior.

guet-apens [gɛtapã] *nm* ambush; *fig* trap.

guêtre [gɛtr] *nf* gaiter.

guetter [gete] *vt* [épier] to lie in wait for. || [attendre] to be on the look-out for, to watch for. || [menacer] to threaten.

gueule [gœl] *nf* [d'animal, ouverture] mouth. || *tfam* [bouche de l'homme] yap *Am*. || *fam* [visage] face.

gueuleton [gœltɔ̃] *nm fam* blow-out.

gui [gi] *nm* mistletoe.

guichet [giʃɛ] *nm* counter; [de gare, de théâtre] ticket office.

guide [gid] *nm* [gén] guide. || [livre] guidebook.

guider [gide] *vt* to guide.

guidon [gidɔ̃] *nm* handlebars (*pl*).

guignol [giɲɔl] *nm* [théâtre] ≃ Punch and Judy show.

guillemet [gijmɛ] *nm* inverted comma, quotation mark.

guilleret, -ette [gijrɛ, ɛt] *adj* perky.

guillotine [gijɔtin] *nf* [instrument] guillotine. || [de fenêtre] sash.

guindé, -e [gɛ̃de] *adj* stiff.

guirlande [girlɑ̃d] *nf* [de fleurs] garland. || [de papier] chain; [de Noël] tinsel (*U*).

guise [giz] *nf*: **à ma ~** as I please ou like; **en ~ de** by way of.

guitare [gitar] *nf* guitar.

guitariste [gitarist] *nmf* guitarist.

guttural, -e, -aux [gytyral, o] *adj* guttural.

gymnastique [ʒimnastik] *nf* SPORT & *fig* gymnastics (*U*).

gynécologue [ʒinekɔlɔg] *nmf* gynaecologist.

h¹, H [aʃ] *nm inv* h, H.

h² (*abr de* **heure**) hr.

ha (*abr de* **hectare**) ha.

hab. *abr de* **habitant**.

habile [abil] *adj* skilful; [démarche] clever.

habileté [abilte] *nf* skill.

habiller [abije] *vt* [vêtir] : ~ **qqn (de)** to dress sb (in). || [recouvrir] to cover. ○ **s'habiller** *vp* [se vêtir] to dress, to get dressed. || [se vêtir élégamment] to dress up.

habit [abi] *nm* [costume] suit. || RELIG habit. ○ **habits** *nmpl* [vêtements] clothes.

habitacle [abitakl] *nm* [d'avion] cockpit; [de voiture] passenger compartment.

habitant, -e [abitɑ̃, ɑ̃t] *nm, f* [de pays] inhabitant. || [d'immeuble] occupant. || *Can* [paysan] farmer.

habitation [abitasjɔ̃] *nf* [fait d'habiter] housing. || [résidence] house, home.

habiter [abite] **1** *vt* [résider] to live in. **2** *vi* to live; ~ **à** to live in.

habitude [abityd] *nf* [façon de faire] habit; **avoir l'~ de faire qqch** to be in the habit of doing sthg; **d'~** usually.

habituel, -elle [abityɛl] *adj* [coutumier] usual, customary.

habituer [abitye] *vt* : ~ **qqn à qqch/à faire qqch** to get sb used to sthg/to doing sthg. ○ **s'habituer** *vp* : **s'~ à qqch/à faire qqch** to get used to sthg/to doing sthg.

hache [aʃ] *nf* axe.

hacher [aʃe] *vt* [couper - gén] to chop finely; [- viande] to mince *Br*, to grind *Am*.

hachisch = **haschisch**.

hachoir [aʃwar] *nm* [couteau] chopper. || [appareil] mincer *Br*, grinder *Am*.

hachure [aʃyr] *nf* hatching.

hagard, -e [agar, ard] *adj* haggard.

haie [ɛ] *nf* [d'arbustes] hedge. || [de personnes] row. || SPORT hurdle.

haillons [ajɔ̃] *nmpl* rags.

haine [ɛn] *nf* hatred.

haïr [air] *vt* to hate.

Haïti [aiti] *n* Haiti.

hâle [al] *nm* tan.

hâlé, -e [ale] *adj* tanned.

haleine [alɛn] *nf* breath.

haleter [alte] *vi* to pant.

hall [ol] *nm* [vestibule, entrée] foyer, lobby. || [salle publique] concourse.

halle [al] *nf* covered market.

hallucination [alysinasjɔ̃] *nf* hallucination.

halo [alo] *nm* [cercle lumineux] halo.

halogène [alɔʒɛn] *nm & adj* halogen.

halte [alt] **1** *nf* stop. **2** *interj* stop!

haltère [alter] *nm* dumbbell.

haltérophilie [alterɔfili] *nf* weightlifting.

hamac [amak] *nm* hammock.

hamburger [ɑ̃burgœr] *nm* hamburger.

hameau, -x [amo] *nm* hamlet.

hameçon [amsɔ̃] *nm* fish-hook.

hamster [amster] *nm* hamster.

hanche [ɑ̃ʃ] *nf* hip.

handball [ɑ̃dbal] *nm* handball.

handicap [ɑ̃dikap] *nm* handicap.

handicapé, -e [ɑ̃dikape] **1** *adj* handicapped. **2** *nm, f* handicapped person.

handicaper [ɑ̃dikape] *vt* to handicap.

hangar [ɑ̃gar] *nm* shed; AÉRON hangar.

hanneton [antɔ̃] *nm* cockchafer.

hanter [ɑ̃te] *vt* to haunt.

hantise [ɑ̃tiz] *nf* obsession.

happer [ape] *vt* [attraper] to snap up.

haranguer [arɑ̃ge] *vt* to harangue.

haras [ara] *nm* stud (farm).

harassant, -e [arasɑ̃, ɑ̃t] *adj* exhausting.

harceler [arsəle] *vt* [relancer] to harass. || MIL to harry. || [importuner] : ~ **qqn (de)** to pester sb (with).

hardes [ard] *nfpl* old clothes.

hardi, -e [ardi] *adj* bold, daring.

hareng [arɑ̃] *nm* herring.

hargne [arɲ] *nf* spite (*U*), bad temper.

haricot [ariko] *nm* bean; ~**s verts/blancs/rouges** green/haricot/kidney beans.

harmonica [armɔnika] *nm* harmonica, mouth organ.

harmonie [armɔni] *nf* [gén] harmony.

harmonieux, -ieuse [armɔnjø, jøz] *adj* [gén] harmonious. || [voix] melodious. || [traits, silhouette] regular.

harmoniser [armɔnize] *vt* MUS & *fig* to harmonize; [salaires] to bring into line.

harnacher ['arnaʃe] *vt* [cheval] to harness.

harnais ['arnɛ] *nm* [de cheval, de parachutiste] harness. || TECHNOL train.

harpe ['arp] *nf* harp.

harpon ['arpɔ̃] *nm* harpoon.

harponner ['arpɔne] *vt* [poisson] to harpoon. || *fam* [personne] to waylay.

hasard ['azar] *nm* chance; **au ~** at random; **par ~** by accident, by chance.

hasarder ['azarde] *vt* [tenter] to venture. ○ **se hasarder** *vp*: **se ~ à faire qqch** to risk doing sthg.

haschisch, haschich, hachisch ['aʃiʃ] *nm* hashish.

hâte ['at] *nf* haste.

hâter ['ate] *vt* [avancer] to bring forward. ○ **se hâter** *vp* to hurry.

hausse ['os] *nf* [augmentation] rise, increase.

hausser ['ose] *vt* to raise.

haut, -e [o, ot] *adj* [gén] high; **~ de 20 m** 20 m high. || [classe sociale, pays, région] upper. || [responsable] senior. ○ **haut 1** *adv* [gén] high; [placé] highly. || [fort] loudly. **2** *nm* [hauteur] height; **faire 2 m de ~** to be 2 m high or in height. || [sommet, vêtement] top. || *loc*: **avoir** or **connaître des ~s et des bas** to have one's ups and downs. ○ **de haut en bas** *loc adv* from top to bottom. ○ **du haut de** *loc prép* from the top of. ○ **en haut de** *loc prép* at the top of.

hautain, -e ['otɛ̃, ɛn] *adj* haughty.

hautbois ['obwa] *nm* oboe.

haut de gamme [odgam] *adj* upmarket.

haute-fidélité [otfidelite] *nf* high fidelity, hi-fi.

hauteur ['otœr] *nf* height.

haut-fourneau ['ofurno] *nm* blast furnace.

haut-parleur ['oparlœr] (*pl* **haut-parleurs**) *nm* loudspeaker.

havre ['avr] *nm* [refuge] haven.

Haye ['ɛ] *n*: **La ~** the Hague.

hayon ['ajɔ̃] *nm* hatchback.

hebdomadaire [ɛbdɔmadɛr] *nm & adj* weekly.

héberger [ebɛrʒe] *vt* [loger] to put up. || [suj: hôtel] to take in.

hébété, -e [ebete] *adj* dazed.

hébraïque [ebraik] *adj* Hebrew.

hébreu, -x [ebrø] *adj* Hebrew. ○ **hébreu** *nm* [langue] Hebrew. ○ **Hébreu, -x** *nm* Hebrew.

hécatombe [ekatɔ̃b] *nf litt & fig* slaughter.

hectare [ɛktar] *nm* hectare.

hégémonie [eʒemɔni] *nf* hegemony.

hein ['ɛ̃] *interj fam* eh?, what?; **tu m'en veux, ~?** you're cross with me, aren't you?

hélas [elas] *interj* unfortunately, alas.

héler ['ele] *vt sout* to hail.

hélice [elis] *nf* [d'avion, de bateau] propeller. || MATHS helix.

hélicoptère [elikɔptɛr] *nm* helicopter.

hélium [eljɔm] *nm* helium.

hématome [ematɔm] *nm* MÉD haematoma.

hémicycle [emisikl] *nm* POLIT: **l'~** the Assemblée Nationale.

hémisphère [emisfɛr] *nm* hemisphere.

hémophile [emɔfil] **1** *nmf* haemophiliac. **2** *adj* haemophilic.

hémorragie [emɔraʒi] *nf* MÉD haemorrhage. || *fig* [perte, fuite] loss.

hémorroïdes [emɔrɔid] *nfpl* haemorrhoids, piles.

hennir ['enir] *vi* to neigh, to whinny.

hépatite [epatit] *nf* MÉD hepatitis.

herbe [ɛrb] *nf* BOT grass. || CULIN & MÉD herb. || *fam* [marijuana] grass.

herbicide [ɛrbisid] *nm* weedkiller, herbicide.

héréditaire [ereditɛr] *adj* hereditary.

hérédité [eredite] *nf* [génétique] heredity.

hérésie [erezi] *nf* heresy.

hérisson ['erisɔ̃] *nm* ZOOL hedgehog.

héritage [eritaʒ] *nm* [de biens] inheritance. || [culturel] heritage.

hériter [erite] **1** *vi* to inherit; **~ de qqch** to inherit sthg. **2** *vt*: **~ qqch de qqn** *litt & fig* to inherit sthg from sb.

héritier, -ière [eritje, jɛr] *nm, f* heir (*f* heiress).

hermétique [ɛrmetik] *adj* [étanche] hermetic. || [incompréhensible] inaccessible, impossible to understand. || [impénétrable] impenetrable.

hermine [ɛrmin] *nf* [animal] stoat. || [fourrure] ermine.

hernie ['ɛrni] *nf* hernia.

héroïne [erɔin] *nf* [personne] heroine. || [drogue] heroin.

héroïque [erɔik] *adj* heroic.

héroïsme [erɔism] *nm* heroism.

héron ['erɔ̃] *nm* heron.

héros ['ero] *nm* hero.

hertz ['ɛrts] *nm inv* hertz.

hésitant, -e [ezitɑ̃, ɑ̃t] *adj* hesitant.

hésitation [ezitasjɔ̃] *nf* hesitation.

hésiter [ezite] *vi* to hesitate; ~ **entre/sur** to hesitate between/over; ~ **à faire qqch** to hesitate to do sthg.

hétéroclite [eteɔklit] *adj* motley.

hétérogène [eteɔʒɛn] *adj* heterogeneous.

hétérosexuel, -elle [eteɔsɛksyɛl] *adj & nm, f* heterosexual.

hêtre ['ɛtr] *nm* beech.

heure [œr] *nf* [unité de temps] hour; **250 km à l'~** 250 km per ou an hour; **faire des ~s supplémentaires** to work overtime. || [moment du jour] time; **il est deux ~s** it's two o'clock; **quelle ~ est-il?** what time is it?; **être à l'~** to be on time; ~ **de pointe** rush hour; ~**s de bureau** office hours. || SCOL class, period. || *loc*: **c'est l'~ (de faire qqch)** it's time (to do sthg); **de bonne ~** early.

heureusement [œrøzmɑ̃] *adv* [par chance] luckily, fortunately.

heureux, -euse [œrø, øz] *adj* [gén] happy; [favorable] fortunate.

heurt ['œr] *nm* [choc] collision, impact. || [désaccord] clash.

heurter ['œrte] *vt* [rentrer dans - gén] to hit; [- suj: personne] to bump into. || [offenser - personne, sensibilité] to offend. ○ **se heurter** *vp* [gén]: **se ~ (contre)** to collide (with). || [rencontrer]: **se ~ à qqch** to come up against sthg.

hexagonal, -e, -aux [ɛgzagɔnal, o] *adj* GÉOM hexagonal. || [français] French.

hexagone [ɛgzagɔn] *nm* GÉOM hexagon.

hiatus [jatys] *nm inv* hiatus.

hiberner [ibɛrne] *vi* to hibernate.

hibou, -x ['ibu] *nm* owl.

hideux, -euse ['idø, øz] *adj* hideous.

hier [ijɛr] *adv* yesterday.

hiérarchie ['jerarʃi] *nf* hierarchy.

hiéroglyphe [jerɔglif] *nm* hieroglyph, hieroglyphic.

hilare [ilar] *adj* beaming.

hilarité [ilarite] *nf* hilarity.

Himalaya [imalaja] *nm*: **l'~** the Himalayas (*pl*).

hindou, -e [ɛ̃du] *adj* Hindu. ○ **Hindou, -e** *nm, f* Hindu.

hippie, hippy ['ipi] (*pl* **hippies**) *nmf & adj* hippy.

hippique [ipik] *adj* horse (*avant n*).

hippodrome [ipɔdrom] *nm* racecourse.

hippopotame [ipɔpɔtam] *nm* hippopotamus.

hirondelle [irɔ̃dɛl] *nf* swallow.

hirsute [irsyt] *adj* [chevelure, barbe] shaggy.

hispanique [ispanik] *adj* [gén] Hispanic.

hisser ['ise] *vt* [voile, drapeau] to hoist. || [charge] to heave, to haul. ○ **se hisser** *vp* [grimper]: **se ~ (sur)** to heave ou haul o.s. up (onto).

histoire [istwar] *nf* [science] history. || [récit, mensonge] story. || [aventure] funny ou strange thing. || (*gén pl*) [ennui] trouble (*U*).

historique [istɔrik] *adj* [roman, recherches] historical. || [monument, événement] historic.

hiver [ivɛr] *nm* winter; **en ~** in (the) winter.

HLM (*abr de* **habitation à loyer modéré**) *nm ou nf* low-rent, state-owned housing.

hocher ['ɔʃe] *vt*: ~ **la tête** [affirmativement] to nod (one's head); [négativement] to shake one's head.

hochet ['ɔʃɛ] *nm* rattle.

hockey ['ɔkɛ] *nm* hockey.

holding ['ɔldiŋ] *nm ou nf* holding company.

hold-up ['ɔldœp] *nm inv* hold-up.

hollandais, -e ['ɔlɑ̃dɛ, ɛz] *adj* Dutch. ○ **hollandais** *nm* [langue] Dutch. ○ **Hollandais, -e** *nm, f* Dutchman (*f* Dutchwoman).

Hollande [ɔlɑ̃d] *nf*: **la ~** Holland.

holocauste [ɔlɔkost] *nm* holocaust.

homard ['ɔmar] *nm* lobster.

homéopathie [ɔmeɔpati] *nf* homeopathy.

homicide [ɔmisid] *nm* [meurtre] murder.

hommage [ɔmaʒ] *nm* [témoignage d'estime] tribute; **rendre ~ à qqn/qqch** to pay tribute to sb/sthg.

homme [ɔm] *nm* man; ~ **d'affaires** businessman; ~ **d'État** statesman; ~ **politique** politician.

homogène [ɔmɔʒɛn] *adj* homogeneous.

homologue [ɔmɔlɔg] *nm* counterpart, opposite number.

homonyme [ɔmɔnim] *nm* LING homonym. || [personne, ville] namesake.

homosexualité [ɔmɔsɛksyalite] *nf* homosexuality.

homosexuel, -elle [ɔmɔsɛksyɛl] *adj & nm, f* homosexual.

Honduras ['ɔ̃dyras] *nm*: **le ~** Honduras.

Hongrie ['ɔ̃gri] *nf*: **la ~** Hungary.

hongrois, -e ['ɔ̃grwa, az] *adj* Hungarian. ○ **hongrois** *nm* [langue] Hungarian. ○ **Hongrois, -e** *nm, f* Hungarian.

honnête [ɔnɛt] *adj* [intègre] honest. || [convenable - travail, résultat] reasonable.

honnêtement [ɔnɛtmɑ̃] *adv* [de façon intègre, franchement] honestly.

honnêteté [ɔnɛtte] *nf* honesty.

honneur [ɔnœr] *nm* honour; **faire ~ à qqn/à qqch** to be a credit to sb/to sthg; **faire ~ à un repas** *fig* to do justice to a meal.

honorable [ɔnɔrabl] *adj* [digne] honourable. || [convenable] respectable.

honoraire [ɔnɔrɛr] *adj* honorary. ○ **honoraires** *nmpl* fee (*sg*), fees.

honorer [ɔnɔre] *vt* [faire honneur à] to be a credit to. || [payer] to honour.

honte ['ɔ̃t] *nf* [sentiment] shame; **avoir ~ de qqn/qqch** to be ashamed of sb/sthg; **avoir ~ de faire qqch** to be ashamed of doing sthg.

honteux, -euse ['ɔ̃tø, øz] *adj* shameful; [personne] ashamed.

hôpital, -aux ['ɔpital, o] *nm* hospital.

hoquet ['ɔkɛ] *nm* hiccup.

horaire [ɔrɛr] **1** *nm* [de départ, d'arrivée] timetable. || [de travail] hours (*pl*) (of work). **2** *adj* hourly.

horizon [ɔrizɔ̃] *nm* [ligne, perspective] horizon. || [panorama] view.

horizontal, -e, -aux [ɔrizɔ̃tal, o] *adj* horizontal.

horloge [ɔrlɔʒ] *nf* clock.

hormis ['ɔrmi] *prép* save.

hormone [ɔrmɔn] *nf* hormone.

horodateur [ɔrodatœr] *nm* [à l'usine] clock; [au parking] ticket machine.

horoscope [ɔrɔskɔp] *nm* horoscope.

horreur [ɔrœr] *nf* horror; **avoir ~ de qqn/qqch** to hate sb/sthg; **avoir ~ de faire qqch** to hate doing sthg; **quelle ~!** how dreadful!, how awful!

horrible [ɔribl] *adj* [affreux] horrible. || *fig* [terrible] terrible, dreadful.

horrifier [ɔrifje] *vt* to horrify.

horripiler [ɔripile] *vt* to exasperate.

hors ['ɔr] ○ **hors de** *loc prép* outside.

hors-bord ['ɔrbɔr] *nm inv* speedboat.

hors-d'œuvre ['ɔrdœvr] *nm inv* hors d'oeuvre, starter.

hors-jeu ['ɔrʒø] *nm inv & adj inv* offside.

hors-la-loi ['ɔrlalwa] *nm inv* outlaw.

hors-piste ['ɔrpist] *nm inv* off-piste skiing.

hortensia [ɔrtɑ̃sja] *nm* hydrangea.

horticulture [ɔrtikyltyr] *nf* horticulture.

hospice [ɔspis] *nm* home.

hospitalier, -ière [ɔspitalje, jɛr] *adj* [accueillant] hospitable. || [relatif aux hôpitaux] hospital (*avant n*).

hospitaliser [ɔspitalize] *vt* to hospitalize.

hospitalité [ɔspitalite] *nf* hospitality.

hostie [ɔsti] *nf* host.

hostile [ɔstil] *adj*: **~ (à)** hostile (to).

hostilité [ɔstilite] *nf* hostility.

hôte, hôtesse [ot, otɛs] *nm, f* host (*f* hostess); **hôtesse de l'air** air hostess. ○ **hôte** *nm* [invité] guest.

hôtel [otɛl] *nm* [d'hébergement] hotel. || [établissement public] **~ de ville** town hall.

hotte ['ɔt] *nf* [panier] basket. || [d'aération] hood.

houblon ['ublɔ̃] *nm* BOT hop. || [de la bière] hops (*pl*).

houille ['uj] *nf* coal.

houiller, -ère ['uje, ɛr] *adj* coal (*avant n*). ○ **houillère** *nf* coalmine.

houle ['ul] *nf* swell.

houlette [ulɛt] *nf* *sout*: **sous la ~ de qqn** under the guidance of sb.

houppe ['up] *nf* [à poudre] powder puff. || [de cheveux] tuft.

hourra, hurrah ['ura] *interj* hurrah!

houspiller ['uspije] *vt* to tell off.

housse ['us] *nf* cover.

houx ['u] *nm* holly.

hublot ['yblo] *nm* [de bateau] porthole.

huer ['ye] *vt* [siffler] to boo.

huile [ɥil] *nf* [gén] oil; **~ d'arachide/ d'olive** groundnut/olive oil. || [peinture] oil painting. || *fam* [personnalité] bigwig.

huis [ɥi] *nm littéraire* door; **à ~ clos** JUR in camera.

huissier [ɥisje] *nm* JUR bailiff.

huit [ɥit] **1** *adj num* eight. **2** *nm* eight; **lundi en ~ a** week on *Br* or from *Am* Monday, Monday week *Br*; *voir aussi* **six**.

huitième ['ɥitjɛm] **1** *adj num & nmf* eighth. **2** *nm* eighth. || [championnat]: **le ~ de finale** round before the quarter-final; *voir aussi* **sixième**.

huître [ɥitr] *nf* oyster.

humain, -e [ymɛ̃, ɛn] *adj* [gén] human. || [sensible] humane. ○ **humain** *nm* [être humain] human (being).

humanitaire [ymaniter] *adj* humanitarian.

humanité [ymanite] *nf* humanity.
○ **humanités** *nfpl Belg* humanities.
humble [œbl] *adj* humble.
humecter [ymɛkte] *vt* to moisten.
humer ['yme] *vt* to smell.
humérus [ymerys] *nm* humerus.
humeur [ymœr] *nf* [disposition] mood; **être de bonne/mauvaise ~** to be in a good/bad mood. ‖ [caractère] nature.
humide [ymid] *adj* [air, climat] humid; [terre, herbe, mur] wet, damp; [saison] rainy; [front, yeux] moist.
humidité [ymidite] *nf* [de climat, d'air] humidity; [de terre, mur] dampness.
humiliation [ymiljasjɔ̃] *nf* humiliation.
humilier [ymilje] *vt* to humiliate.
humilité [ymilite] *nf* humility.
humoristique [ymɔristik] *adj* humorous.
humour [ymur] *nm* humour.
humus [ymys] *nm* humus.
huppé, -e ['ype] *adj fam* [société] upper-crust. ‖ [oiseau] crested.
hurlement ['yrləmɑ̃] *nm* howl.
hurler ['yrle] *vi* [gén] to howl.
hurrah = **hourra**.
hutte ['yt] *nf* hut.
hybride [ibrid] *nm & adj* hybrid.
hydratant, -e [idratɑ̃, ɑ̃t] *adj* moisturizing.
hydrater [idrate] *vt* [peau] to moisturize.
hydraulique [idrolik] *adj* hydraulic.
hydravion [idravjɔ̃] *nm* seaplane, hydroplane.
hydrocarbure [idrɔkarbyr] *nm* hydrocarbon.
hydrocution [idrɔkysjɔ̃] *nf* immersion syncope.
hydroélectrique [idrɔelɛktrik] *adj* hydroelectric.
hydrogène [idrɔʒɛn] *nm* hydrogen.
hydroglisseur [idrɔglisœr] *nm* jetfoil, hydroplane.
hydrophile [idrɔfil] *adj* → **coton**.
hyène [jɛn] *nf* hyena.
hygiène [iʒjɛn] *nf* hygiene.
hygiénique [iʒjenik] *adj* [sanitaire] hygienic. ‖ [bon pour la santé] healthy.
hymne [imn] *nm* hymn.
hypermarché [ipɛrmarʃe] *nm* hypermarket.
hypermétrope [ipɛrmetrɔp] **1** *nmf* longsighted person. **2** *adj* longsighted.
hypertension [ipɛrtɑ̃sjɔ̃] *nf* high blood pressure, hypertension.

hypertrophié [ipɛrtrɔfje] *adj* hypertrophic; *fig* exaggerated.
hypnotiser [ipnɔtize] *vt* to hypnotize.
hypocondriaque [ipɔkɔ̃drijak] *nmf & adj* hypochondriac.
hypocrisie [ipɔkrizi] *nf* hypocrisy.
hypocrite [ipɔkrit] **1** *nmf* hypocrite. **2** *adj* hypocritical.
hypoglycémie [ipɔglisemi] *nf* hypoglycaemia.
hypotension [ipɔtɑ̃sjɔ̃] *nf* low blood pressure.
hypothèque [ipɔtɛk] *nf* mortgage.
hypothèse [ipɔtɛz] *nf* hypothesis.
hystérie [isteri] *nf* hysteria.
hystérique [isterik] *adj* hysterical.

i, I [i] *nm inv* i, I; **mettre les points sur les i** to dot the i's and cross the t's.
ibérique [iberik] *adj*: **la péninsule ~** the Iberian Peninsula.
iceberg [ajsbɛrg] *nm* iceberg.
ici [isi] *adv* [lieu] here; **par ~** [direction] this way; [alentour] around here. ‖ [temps] now; **d'~ là** by then.
icône [ikon] *nf* INFORM & RELIG icon.
idéal, -e [ideal] (*pl* **idéals** OU **idéaux** [ideo]) *adj* ideal. ○ **idéal** *nm* ideal.
idéaliste [idealist] **1** *nmf* idealist. **2** *adj* idealistic.
idée [ide] *nf* idea; **à l'~ de/que** at the idea of/that; **se faire des ~s** to imagine things; **cela ne m'est jamais venu à l'~** it never occurred to me.
identification [idɑ̃tifikasjɔ̃] *nf*: **~ (à)** identification (with).
identifier [idɑ̃tifje] *vt* to identify.
○ **s'identifier** *vp*: **s'~ à qqn/qqch** to identify with sb/sthg.
identique [idɑ̃tik] *adj*: **~ (à)** identical (to).
identité [idɑ̃tite] *nf* identity.
idéologie [ideɔlɔʒi] *nf* ideology.
idiomatique [idjɔmatik] *adj* idiomatic.
idiot, -e [idjo, ɔt] **1** *adj* idiotic; MÉD idiot (*avant n*). **2** *nm, f* idiot.

idiotie [idjɔsi] *nf* [stupidité] idiocy. || [action, parole] idiotic thing.

idole [idɔl] *nf* idol.

idylle [idil] *nf* [amour] romance.

idyllique [idilik] *adj* [idéal] idyllic.

igloo, iglou [iglu] *nm* igloo.

ignare [iɲar] *nmf* ignoramus.

ignoble [iɲɔbl] *adj* [abject] base. || [hideux] vile.

ignominie [iɲɔmini] *nf* [état] disgrace. || [action] disgraceful act.

ignorance [iɲɔrɑ̃s] *nf* ignorance.

ignorant, -e [iɲɔrɑ̃, ɑ̃t] **1** *adj* ignorant. **2** *nm, f* ignoramus.

ignorer [iɲɔre] *vt* [ne pas savoir] not to know, to be unaware of. || [ne pas tenir compte de] to ignore.

il [il] *pron pers* [sujet - personne] he; [- animal] it, he; [- chose] it. || [sujet d'un verbe impersonnel] it; **~ pleut** it's raining. ○ **ils** *pron pers pl* they.

île [il] *nf* island; **les ~s Anglo-Normandes** the Channel Islands; **les ~s Baléares** the Balearic Islands; **les ~s Britanniques** the British Isles; **les ~s Canaries** the Canary Islands; **les ~s Malouines** the Falkland Islands.

illégal, -e, -aux [ilegal, o] *adj* illegal.

illégitime [ileʒitim] *adj* [enfant] illegitimate; [union] unlawful. || [non justifié] unwarranted.

illettré, -e [iletre] *adj & nm, f* illiterate.

illicite [ilisit] *adj* illicit.

illimité, -e [ilimite] *adj* [sans limites] unlimited. || [indéterminé] indefinite.

illisible [ilizibl] *adj* [indéchiffrable] illegible. || [incompréhensible & INFORM] unreadable.

illogique [ilɔʒik] *adj* illogical.

illumination [ilyminasjɔ̃] *nf* [éclairage] lighting. || [idée soudaine] inspiration.

illuminer [ilymine] *vt* to light up; [bâtiment, rue] to illuminate.

illusion [ilyzjɔ̃] *nf* illusion.

illustration [ilystrasjɔ̃] *nf* illustration.

illustre [ilystr] *adj* illustrious.

illustré, -e [ilystre] *adj* illustrated. ○ **illustré** *nm* illustrated magazine.

illustrer [ilystre] *vt* [gén] to illustrate. ○ **s'illustrer** *vp* to distinguish o.s.

îlot [ilo] *nm* [île] small island, islet. || *fig* [de résistance] pocket.

ils → il.

image [imaʒ] *nf* [vision mentale, comparaison, ressemblance] image. || [dessin] picture.

imaginaire [imaʒinɛr] *adj* imaginary.

imagination [imaʒinasjɔ̃] *nf* imagination; **avoir de l'~** to be imaginative.

imaginer [imaʒine] *vt* [supposer, croire] to imagine. || [trouver] to think of. ○ **s'imaginer** *vp* [se voir] to see o.s. || [croire] to imagine.

imbattable [ɛ̃batabl] *adj* unbeatable.

imbécile [ɛ̃besil] *nmf* imbecile.

imberbe [ɛ̃bɛrb] *adj* beardless.

imbiber [ɛ̃bibe] *vt*: **~ qqch de qqch** to soak sthg with OU in sthg.

imbriqué, -e [ɛ̃brike] *adj* overlapping.

imbroglio [ɛ̃brɔljo] *nm* imbroglio.

imbu, -e [ɛ̃by] *adj*: **être ~ de** to be full of.

imbuvable [ɛ̃byvabl] *adj* [eau] undrinkable. || *fam* [personne] unbearable.

imitateur, -trice [imitatœr, tris] *nm, f* [comique] impersonator. || *péj* [copieur] imitator.

imitation [imitasjɔ̃] *nf* imitation.

imiter [imite] *vt* [s'inspirer de, contrefaire] to imitate. || [reproduire l'aspect de] to look (just) like.

immaculé, -e [imakyle] *adj* immaculate.

immangeable [ɛ̃mɑ̃ʒabl] *adj* inedible.

immanquable [ɛ̃mɑ̃kabl] *adj* impossible to miss; [sort, échec] inevitable.

immatriculation [imatrikylasjɔ̃] *nf* registration.

immédiat, -e [imedja, at] *adj* immediate.

immédiatement [imedjatmɑ̃] *adv* immediately.

immense [imɑ̃s] *adj* immense.

immerger [imɛrʒe] *vt* to submerge. ○ **s'immerger** *vp* to submerge o.s.

immeuble [imœbl] *nm* building.

immigration [imigrasjɔ̃] *nf* immigration.

immigré, -e [imigre] *adj & nm, f* immigrant.

immigrer [imigre] *vi* to immigrate.

imminent, -e [iminɑ̃, ɑ̃t] *adj* imminent.

immiscer [imise] ○ **s'immiscer** *vp*: **s'~ dans** to interfere in OU with.

immobile [imɔbil] *adj* [personne, visage] motionless. || [mécanisme] fixed, stationary. || *fig* [figé] immovable.

immobilier, -ière [imɔbilje, jɛr] *adj*: **biens ~s** property *Br*, real estate (*U*) *Am*.

immobiliser [imɔbilize] *vt* to immobilize. ○ **s'immobiliser** *vp* to stop.

immobilité [imɔbilite] *nf* immobility.

immodéré, -e [imɔdere] *adj* inordinate.

immonde [imɔ̃d] *adj* [sale] foul. || [abject] vile.

immondices [imɔ̃dis] *nfpl* waste (U), refuse (U).

immoral, -e, -aux [imɔral, o] *adj* immoral.

immortaliser [imɔrtalize] *vt* to immortalize.

immortel, -elle [imɔrtɛl] *adj* immortal.

immuable [imɥabl] *adj* [éternel - loi] immutable. || [constant] unchanging.

immuniser [imynize] *vt* [vacciner] to immunize. || *fig* [garantir]: ~ qqn contre qqch to make sb immune to sthg.

immunité [imynite] *nf* immunity.

impact [ɛ̃pakt] *nm* impact; avoir de l'~ sur to have an impact on.

impair, -e [ɛ̃pɛr] *adj* odd. ○ **impair** *nm* [faux-pas] gaffe.

imparable [ɛ̃parabl] *adj* [coup] unstoppable. || [argument] unanswerable.

impardonnable [ɛ̃pardɔnabl] *adj* unforgivable.

imparfait, -e [ɛ̃parfɛ, ɛt] *adj* [défectueux] imperfect. || [inachevé] incomplete. ○ **imparfait** *nm* GRAM imperfect (tense).

impartial, -e, -iaux [ɛ̃parsjal, jo] *adj* impartial.

impasse [ɛ̃pas] *nf* [rue] dead end. || *fig* [difficulté] impasse, deadlock.

impassible [ɛ̃pasibl] *adj* impassive.

impatience [ɛ̃pasjɑ̃s] *nf* impatience.

impatient, -e [ɛ̃pasjɑ̃, ɑ̃t] *adj* impatient.

impatienter [ɛ̃pasjɑ̃te] *vt* to annoy. ○ **s'impatienter** *vp*: s'~ (de/contre) to get impatient (at/with).

impayé, -e [ɛ̃peje] *adj* unpaid, outstanding. ○ **impayé** *nm* outstanding payment.

impeccable [ɛ̃pekabl] *adj* [parfait] impeccable, faultless. || [propre] spotless, immaculate.

impénétrable [ɛ̃penetrabl] *adj* impenetrable.

impénitent, -e [ɛ̃penitɑ̃, ɑ̃t] *adj* unrepentant.

impensable [ɛ̃pɑ̃sabl] *adj* unthinkable.

impératif, -ive [ɛ̃peratif, iv] *adj* [ton, air] imperious. || [besoin] imperative, essential. ○ **impératif** *nm* GRAM imperative.

impératrice [ɛ̃peratris] *nf* empress.

imperceptible [ɛ̃pɛrsɛptibl] *adj* imperceptible.

imperfection [ɛ̃pɛrfɛksjɔ̃] *nf* imperfection.

impérialisme [ɛ̃perjalism] *nm* POLIT imperialism; *fig* dominance.

impérieux, -ieuse [ɛ̃perjø, jøz] *adj* [ton, air] imperious. || [nécessité] urgent.

impérissable [ɛ̃perisabl] *adj* undying.

imperméabiliser [ɛ̃permeabilize] *vt* to waterproof.

imperméable [ɛ̃permeabl] **1** *adj* waterproof. **2** *nm* raincoat.

impersonnel, -elle [ɛ̃pɛrsɔnɛl] *adj* impersonal.

impertinence [ɛ̃pɛrtinɑ̃s] *nf* impertinence (U).

impertinent, -e [ɛ̃pɛrtinɑ̃, ɑ̃t] **1** *adj* impertinent. **2** *nm, f* impertinent person.

imperturbable [ɛ̃pɛrtyrbabl] *adj* imperturbable.

impétueux, -euse [ɛ̃petɥø, øz] *adj* [personne, caractère] impetuous.

impitoyable [ɛ̃pitwajabl] *adj* merciless, pitiless.

implacable [ɛ̃plakabl] *adj* implacable.

implanter [ɛ̃plɑ̃te] *vt* [entreprise, système] to establish. || *fig* [préjugé] to implant. ○ **s'implanter** *vp* [entreprise] to set up; [coutume] to become established.

implication [ɛ̃plikasjɔ̃] *nf* [participation]: ~ (dans) involvement (in). || (*gén pl*) [conséquence] implication.

implicite [ɛ̃plisit] *adj* implicit.

impliquer [ɛ̃plike] *vt* [compromettre]: ~ qqn dans to implicate sb in. || [requérir, entraîner] to imply. ○ **s'impliquer** *vp*: s'~ dans to become involved in.

implorer [ɛ̃plɔre] *vt* to beseech.

implosion [ɛ̃plozjɔ̃] *nf* implosion.

impoli, -e [ɛ̃pɔli] *adj* rude, impolite.

impopulaire [ɛ̃pɔpylɛr] *adj* unpopular.

importance [ɛ̃pɔrtɑ̃s] *nf* [gén] importance; [de problème, montant] magnitude. || [de dommages] extent. || [de ville] size.

important, -e [ɛ̃pɔrtɑ̃, ɑ̃t] *adj* [gén] important. || [considérable] considerable, sizeable; [- dommages] extensive.

importation [ɛ̃pɔrtasjɔ̃] *nf* COMM & *fig* import.

importer [ɛ̃pɔrte] **1** *vt* to import. **2** *v impers*: ~ (à) to matter (to); **il importe de/que** it is important to/that; **qu'importe!, peu importe!** it doesn't matter!; **n'importe qui** anyone (at all); **n'importe quoi** anything (at all); **n'importe où** anywhere (at all); **n'importe quand** at any time (at all).

import-export [ɛpɔrɛkspɔr] *nm* import-export.

importuner [ɛpɔrtyne] *vt* to irk.

imposable [ɛpozabl] *adj* taxable.

imposant, -e [ɛpozɑ̃, ɑ̃t] *adj* imposing.

imposer [ɛpoze] *vt* [gén]: ~ **qqch/qqn à qqn** to impose sthg/sb on sb. || [impressionner]: **en ~ à qqn** to impress sb. || [taxer] to tax. ○ **s'imposer** *vp* [être nécessaire] to be essential *ou* imperative. || [forcer le respect] to stand out.

impossibilité [ɛpɔsibilite] *nf* impossibility; **être dans l'~ de faire qqch** to find it impossible *ou* to be unable to do sthg.

impossible [ɛpɔsibl] **1** *adj* impossible. **2** *nm*: **tenter l'~** to attempt the impossible.

imposteur [ɛpɔstœr] *nm* impostor.

impôt [ɛpo] *nm* tax; **~s locaux** council tax *Br*, local tax *Am*; **~ sur le revenu** income tax.

impotent, -e [ɛpɔtɑ̃, ɑ̃t] *adj* disabled.

impraticable [ɛpratikabl] *adj* [inaccessible] impassable.

imprécis, -e [ɛpresi, iz] *adj* imprecise.

imprégner [ɛpreɲe] *vt* [imbiber]: **~ qqch de qqch** to soak sthg in sthg. ○ **s'imprégner** *vp*: **s'~ de qqch** [s'imbiber] to soak sthg up; *fig* to soak sthg up, to steep o.s. in sthg.

imprenable [ɛprənabl] *adj* [forteresse] impregnable. || [vue] unimpeded.

imprésario, impresario [ɛpresarjo] *nm* impresario.

impression [ɛpresjɔ̃] *nf* [gén] impression; **avoir l'~ que** to have the impression *ou* feeling that. || [de livre, tissu] printing. || PHOT print.

impressionner [ɛpresjɔne] *vt* [frapper] to impress. || [choquer] to shock, to upset. || [intimider] to frighten. || PHOT to expose.

impressionniste [ɛpresjɔnist] *nmf & adj* impressionist.

imprévisible [ɛprevizibl] *adj* unforeseeable.

imprévu, -e [ɛprevy] *adj* unforeseen. ○ **imprévu** *nm* unforeseen situation.

imprimante [ɛprimɑ̃t] *nf* printer.

imprimé, -e [ɛprime] *adj* printed. ○ **imprimé** *nm* POSTES printed matter (*U*). || [formulaire] printed form. || [sur tissu] print.

imprimer [ɛprime] *vt* [texte, tissu] to print. || [mouvement] to impart.

imprimerie [ɛprimri] *nf* [technique] printing. || [usine] printing works (*sg*).

improbable [ɛprɔbabl] *adj* improbable.

improductif, -ive [ɛprɔdyktif, iv] *adj* unproductive.

impromptu, -e [ɛprɔ̃pty] *adj* impromptu.

impropre [ɛprɔpr] *adj* GRAM incorrect. || [inadapté]: **~ à** unfit for.

improviser [ɛprɔvize] *vt* to improvise. ○ **s'improviser** *vp* [devenir]: **s'~ metteur en scène** to act as director.

improviste [ɛprɔvist] ○ **à l'improviste** *loc adv* unexpectedly, without warning.

imprudence [ɛprydɑ̃s] *nf* [de personne, d'acte] rashness. || [acte] rash act.

imprudent, -e [ɛprydɑ̃, ɑ̃t] **1** *adj* rash. **2** *nm, f* rash person.

impudent, -e [ɛpydɑ̃, ɑ̃t] **1** *adj* impudent. **2** *nm, f* impudent person.

impudique [ɛpydik] *adj* shameless.

impuissant, -e [ɛpɥisɑ̃, ɑ̃t] *adj* [incapable]: **~ à faire qqch** powerless to do sthg. || [homme, fureur] impotent.

impulsif, -ive [ɛpylsif, iv] **1** *adj* impulsive. **2** *nm, f* impulsive person.

impulsion [ɛpylsjɔ̃] *nf* [poussée, essor] impetus. || [instinct] impulse, instinct. || *fig*: **sous l'~ de qqn** [influence] at the prompting *ou* instigation of sb; **sous l'~ de qqch** [effet] impelled by sthg.

impunément [ɛpynemɑ̃] *adv* with impunity.

impunité [ɛpynite] *nf* impunity; **en toute ~** with impunity.

impur, -e [ɛpyr] *adj* impure.

impureté [ɛpyrte] *nf* impurity.

imputer [ɛpyte] *vt*: **~ qqch à qqn/à qqch** to attribute sthg to sb/to sthg; **~ qqch à qqch** FIN to charge sthg to sthg.

imputrescible [ɛpytresibl] *adj* [bois] rotproof; [déchets] non-degradable.

inabordable [inabɔrdabl] *adj* [prix] prohibitive. || [personne] unapproachable.

inacceptable [inakseptabl] *adj* unacceptable.

inaccessible [inaksesibl] *adj* [destination, domaine, personne] inaccessible; [objectif, poste] unattainable.

inaccoutumé, -e [inakutyme] *adj* unaccustomed.

inachevé, -e [inaʃve] *adj* unfinished, uncompleted.

inactif, -ive [inaktif, iv] *adj* [sans occupation, non utilisé] idle. || [sans emploi] non-working.

inaction [inaksjɔ̃] *nf* inaction.

inadapté, -e [inadapte] *adj* [non adapté]: ~ (à) unsuitable (for), unsuited (to). || [asocial] maladjusted.

inadmissible [inadmisibl] *adj* [conduite] unacceptable.

inadvertance [inadvɛrtɑ̃s] *nf littéraire* oversight; **par ~** inadvertently.

inaltérable [inalterabl] *adj* [matériau] stable. || [sentiment] unfailing.

inamovible [inamɔvibl] *adj* fixed.

inanimé, -e [inanime] *adj* [sans vie] inanimate. || [inerte, évanoui] senseless.

inanition [inanisjɔ̃] *nf*: **tomber/mourir d'~** to faint with/die of hunger.

inaperçu, -e [inapɛrsy] *adj* unnoticed.

inappréciable [inapresjabl] *adj* [précieux] invaluable.

inapprochable [inaprɔʃabl] *adj*: **il est vraiment ~ en ce moment** you can't say anything to him at the moment.

inapte [inapt] *adj* [incapable]: ~ **à qqch/à faire qqch** incapable of sthg/of doing sthg. || MIL unfit.

inattaquable [inatakabl] *adj* [irréprochable] irreproachable, beyond reproach. || [irréfutable] irrefutable.

inattendu, -e [inatɑ̃dy] *adj* unexpected.

inattention [inatɑ̃sjɔ̃] *nf* inattention; **faute d'~** careless mistake.

inaudible [inodibl] *adj* [impossible à entendre] inaudible.

inauguration [inogyrasjɔ̃] *nf* [cérémonie] inauguration, opening (ceremony).

inaugurer [inogyre] *vt* [monument] to unveil; [installation, route] to open; [procédé, édifice] to inaugurate.

inavouable [inavwabl] *adj* unmentionable.

incalculable [ɛ̃kalkylabl] *adj* incalculable.

incandescence [ɛ̃kɑ̃desɑ̃s] *nf* incandescence.

incantation [ɛ̃kɑ̃tasjɔ̃] *nf* incantation.

incapable [ɛ̃kapabl] **1** *nmf* [raté] incompetent. **2** *adj*: ~ **de faire qqch** [inapte à] incapable of doing sthg; [dans l'impossibilité de] unable to do sthg.

incapacité [ɛ̃kapasite] *nf* [impossibilité]: ~ **à** OU **de faire qqch** inability to do sthg. || [invalidité] disability.

incarcération [ɛ̃karserasjɔ̃] *nf* incarceration.

incarner [ɛ̃karne] *vt* [personnifier] to be the incarnation of. || CIN & THÉÂTRE to play.

incassable [ɛ̃kasabl] *adj* unbreakable.

incendie [ɛ̃sɑ̃di] *nm* fire; *fig* flames (*pl*).

incendier [ɛ̃sɑ̃dje] *vt* [mettre le feu à] to set alight, to set fire to.

incertain, -e [ɛ̃sɛrtɛ̃, ɛn] *adj* [gén] uncertain; [temps] unsettled.

incertitude [ɛ̃sɛrtityd] *nf* uncertainty.

incessamment [ɛ̃sesamɑ̃] *adv* at any moment, any moment now.

incessant, -e [ɛ̃sesɑ̃, ɑ̃t] *adj* incessant.

inceste [ɛ̃sɛst] *nm* incest.

inchangé, -e [ɛ̃ʃɑ̃ʒe] *adj* unchanged.

incidence [ɛ̃sidɑ̃s] *nf* [conséquence] effect, impact (*U*).

incident, -e [ɛ̃sidɑ̃, ɑ̃t] *adj* [accessoire] incidental. ○ **incident** *nm* [gén] incident; [ennui] hitch.

incinérer [ɛ̃sinere] *vt* [corps] to cremate. || [ordures] to incinerate.

inciser [ɛ̃size] *vt* to incise, to make an incision in.

incisif, -ive [ɛ̃sizif, iv] *adj* incisive. ○ **incisive** *nf* incisor.

inciter [ɛ̃site] *vt* [provoquer]: ~ **qqn à qqch/à faire qqch** to incite sb to sthg/to do sthg. || [encourager]: ~ **qqn à faire qqch** to encourage sb to do sthg.

inclassable [ɛ̃klasabl] *adj* unclassifiable.

inclinable [ɛ̃klinabl] *adj* reclinable, reclining.

inclinaison [ɛ̃klinɛzɔ̃] *nf* [pente] incline. || [de tête, chapeau] angle, tilt.

incliner [ɛ̃kline] *vt* [pencher] to tilt, to lean. ○ **s'incliner** *vp* [se pencher] to tilt, to lean. || [céder]: **s'~ (devant)** to give in (to), to yield (to).

inclure [ɛ̃klyr] *vt* [mettre dedans]: ~ **qqch dans qqch** to include sthg in sthg; [joindre] to enclose sthg with sthg.

inclus, -e [ɛ̃kly, yz] **1** *pp* → **inclure**. **2** *adj* [compris - taxe, frais] included; [joint - lettre] enclosed; [y compris]: **jusqu'à la page 10 ~e** up to and including page 10.

incognito [ɛ̃kɔɲito] *adv* incognito.

incohérent, -e [ɛ̃kɔerɑ̃, ɑ̃t] *adj* [paroles] incoherent; [actes] inconsistent.

incollable [ɛ̃kɔlabl] *adj* [riz] nonstick. || *fam* [imbattable] unbeatable.

incolore [ɛ̃kɔlɔr] *adj* colourless.

incomber [ɛ̃kɔ̃be] *vi*: ~ **à qqn** to be sb's responsibility; **il incombe à qqn de faire qqch** (*emploi impersonnel*) it falls to sb OU it is incumbent on sb to do sthg.

incommoder [ɛ̃kɔmɔde] *vt sout* to trouble.

incomparable [ɛ̃kɔ̃parabl] *adj* [sans pareil] incomparable.

incompatible [ɛ̃kɔ̃patibl] *adj* incompatible.

incompétent, -e [ɛ̃kɔ̃petɑ̃, ɑ̃t] *adj* [incapable] incompetent.

incomplet, -ète [ɛ̃kɔ̃plɛ, ɛt] *adj* incomplete.

incompréhensible [ɛ̃kɔ̃preɑ̃sibl] *adj* incomprehensible.

incompris, -e [ɛ̃kɔ̃pri, iz] *nm, f* misunderstood person.

inconcevable [ɛ̃kɔ̃svabl] *adj* unimaginable.

inconciliable [ɛ̃kɔ̃siljabl] *adj* irreconcilable.

inconditionnel, -elle [ɛ̃kɔ̃disjɔnɛl] 1 *adj* [total] unconditional. || [fervent] ardent. 2 *nm, f* ardent supporter ou admirer.

inconfortable [ɛ̃kɔ̃fɔrtabl] *adj* uncomfortable.

incongru, -e [ɛ̃kɔ̃gry] *adj* [malséant] unseemly, inappropriate. || [bizarre] incongruous.

inconnu, -e [ɛ̃kɔny] 1 *adj* unknown. 2 *nm, f* stranger.

inconsciemment [ɛ̃kɔ̃sjamɑ̃] *adv* [sans en avoir conscience] unconsciously, unwittingly. || [à la légère] thoughtlessly.

inconscient, -e [ɛ̃kɔ̃sjɑ̃, ɑ̃t] *adj* [évanoui, machinal] unconscious. || [irresponsable] thoughtless. ○ **inconscient** *nm*: l'~ the unconscious.

inconsidéré, -e [ɛ̃kɔ̃sidere] *adj* ill-considered, thoughtless.

inconsistant, -e [ɛ̃kɔ̃sistɑ̃, ɑ̃t] *adj* [caractère] frivolous.

inconsolable [ɛ̃kɔ̃sɔlabl] *adj* inconsolable.

incontestable [ɛ̃kɔ̃tɛstabl] *adj* unquestionable, indisputable.

incontinent, -e [ɛ̃kɔ̃tinɑ̃, ɑ̃t] *adj* MÉD incontinent.

incontournable [ɛ̃kɔ̃turnabl] *adj* unavoidable.

inconvenant, -e [ɛ̃kɔ̃vnɑ̃, ɑ̃t] *adj* improper, unseemly.

inconvénient [ɛ̃kɔ̃venjɑ̃] *nm* [obstacle] problem. || [désavantage] disadvantage, drawback. || [risque] risk.

incorporé, -e [ɛ̃kɔrpore] *adj* [intégré] built-in.

incorporer [ɛ̃kɔrpore] *vt* [gén] to incorporate; ~ **qqch dans** to incorporate sthg into; ~ **qqch à** CULIN to mix ou blend sthg into. || MIL to enlist.

incorrect, -e [ɛ̃kɔrɛkt] *adj* [faux] incorrect. || [inconvenant] inappropriate; [impoli] rude. || [déloyal] unfair.

incorrection [ɛ̃kɔrɛksjɔ̃] *nf* [impolitesse] impropriety. || [de langage] grammatical mistake.

incorrigible [ɛ̃kɔriʒibl] *adj* incorrigible.

incorruptible [ɛ̃kɔryptibl] *adj* incorruptible.

incrédule [ɛ̃kredyl] *adj* [sceptique] incredulous, sceptical. || RELIG unbelieving.

increvable [ɛ̃krəvabl] *adj* [ballon, pneu] puncture-proof. || *fam fig* [personne] tireless; [machine] that will withstand rough treatment.

incriminer [ɛ̃krimine] *vt* [personne] to incriminate. || [conduite] to condemn.

incroyable [ɛ̃krwajabl] *adj* incredible, unbelievable.

incroyant, -e [ɛ̃krwajɑ̃, ɑ̃t] *nm, f* unbeliever.

incruster [ɛ̃kryste] *vt* [insérer]: ~ **qqch dans qqch** to inlay sthg into sthg. || [décorer]: ~ **qqch de qqch** to inlay sthg with sthg. ○ **s'incruster** *vp* [s'insérer]: **s'~ dans qqch** to become embedded in sthg.

incubation [ɛ̃kybasjɔ̃] *nf* [d'œuf, de maladie] incubation; [fig] hatching.

inculpation [ɛ̃kylpasjɔ̃] *nf* charge.

inculper [ɛ̃kylpe] *vt* to charge; ~ **qqn de** to charge sb with.

inculquer [ɛ̃kylke] *vt*: ~ **qqch à qqn** to instil sthg in sb.

inculte [ɛ̃kylt] *adj* [terre] uncultivated. || *péj* [personne] uneducated.

incurable [ɛ̃kyrabl] *adj* incurable.

incursion [ɛ̃kyrsjɔ̃] *nf* incursion, foray.

Inde [ɛ̃d] *nf*: l'~ India.

indécent, -e [ɛ̃desɑ̃, ɑ̃t] *adj* [impudique] indecent. || [immoral] scandalous.

indéchiffrable [ɛ̃deʃifrabl] *adj* [texte, écriture] indecipherable. || *fig* [regard] inscrutable, impenetrable.

indécis, -e [ɛ̃desi, iz] *adj* [personne - sur le moment] undecided; [- de nature] indecisive. || [sourire] vague.

indécision [ɛ̃desizjɔ̃] *nf* indecision; [perpétuelle] indecisiveness.

indécrottable [ɛ̃dekrɔtabl] *adj* *fam* [incorrigible] hopeless.

indéfendable [ɛ̃defɑ̃dabl] *adj* indefensible.

indéfini, -e [ɛ̃defini] *adj* [quantité, pronom] indefinite.

indéfinissable [ɛ̃definisabl] *adj* indefinable.

indéformable [ɛdefɔrmabl] *adj* that retains its shape.

indélébile [ɛdelebil] *adj* indelible.

indélicat, -e [ɛdelika, at] *adj* [mufle] indelicate. || [malhonnête] dishonest.

indemne [ɛdɛmn] *adj* unscathed, unharmed.

indemniser [ɛdɛmnize] *vt*: ~ qqn de qqch [perte, préjudice] to compensate sb for sthg.

indemnité [ɛdɛmnite] *nf* [de perte, préjudice] compensation. || [de frais] allowance.

indémodable [ɛdemɔdabl] *adj*: **ce style est** ~ this style doesn't date.

indéniable [ɛdenjabl] *adj* undeniable.

indépendance [ɛdepɑ̃dɑ̃s] *nf* independence.

indépendant, -e [ɛdepɑ̃dɑ̃, ɑ̃t] *adj* [gén] independent; [entrée] separate; ~ de ma volonté beyond my control. || [travailleur] self-employed.

indéracinable [ɛderasinabl] *adj* [arbre] impossible to uproot; *fig* ineradicable.

indescriptible [ɛdɛskriptibl] *adj* indescribable.

indestructible [ɛdɛstryktibl] *adj* indestructible.

indéterminé, -e [ɛdetermine] *adj* [indéfini] indeterminate, indefinite.

index [ɛdɛks] *nm* [doigt] index finger. || [registre] index.

indexer [ɛdɛkse] *vt* ÉCON: ~ qqch sur qqch to index sthg to sthg. || [livre] to index.

indicateur, -trice [ɛdikatœr, tris] *adj*: **poteau** ~ signpost; **panneau** ~ road sign. ○ **indicateur** *nm* [guide] directory, guide; ~ **des chemins de fer** railway timetable. || TECHNOL gauge. || ÉCON indicator. || [de police] informer.

indicatif, -ive [ɛdikatif, iv] *adj* indicative. ○ **indicatif** *nm* RADIO & TÉLÉ signature tune. || [code]: ~ **(téléphonique)** dialling code *Br*, dial code *Am*. || GRAM: **l'**~ the indicative.

indication [ɛdikasjɔ̃] *nf* [mention] indication. || [renseignement] information (*U*). || [directive] instruction; **sauf** ~ **contraire** unless otherwise instructed.

indice [ɛdis] *nm* [signe] sign. || [dans une enquête] clue. || [taux] rating; ~ **du coût de la vie** ÉCON cost-of-living index. || MATHS index.

indicible [ɛdisibl] *adj* inexpressible.

indien, -ienne [ɛdjɛ̃, jɛn] *adj* [d'Inde] Indian. || [d'Amérique] American Indian,

Native American. ○ **Indien, -ienne** *nm*, *f* [d'Inde] Indian. || [d'Amérique] American Indian, Native American.

indifféremment [ɛdiferamɑ̃] *adv* indifferently.

indifférent, -e [ɛdiferɑ̃, ɑ̃t] *adj* [gén]: ~ à indifferent to.

indigène [ɛdiʒɛn] **1** *nmf* native. **2** *adj* [peuple] native; [faune, flore] indigenous.

indigent, -e [ɛdiʒɑ̃, ɑ̃t] *adj* [pauvre] destitute, poverty-stricken; *fig* [intellectuellement] impoverished.

indigeste [ɛdiʒɛst] *adj* indigestible.

indigestion [ɛdiʒɛstjɔ̃] *nf* [alimentaire] indigestion. || *fig* [saturation] surfeit.

indignation [ɛdiɲasjɔ̃] *nf* indignation.

indigné, -e [ɛdiɲe] *adj* indignant.

indigner [ɛdiɲe] *vt* to make indignant. ○ **s'indigner** *vp*: **s'**~ **de** OU **contre qqch** to get indignant about sthg.

indigo [ɛdigo] **1** *nm* indigo. **2** *adj inv* indigo (blue).

indiquer [ɛdike] *vt* [désigner] to indicate, to point out. || [afficher, montrer - suj: carte, pendule, aiguille] to show, to indicate. || [recommander]: ~ **qqn/qqch à qqn** to tell sb of sb/sthg, to suggest sb/sthg to sb. || [dire, renseigner sur] to tell. || [fixer - heure, date, lieu] to name, to indicate.

indirect, -e [ɛdirɛkt] *adj* [gén] indirect; [itinéraire] roundabout.

indiscipliné, -e [ɛdisipline] *adj* [écolier, esprit] undisciplined, unruly. || *fig* [mèches de cheveux] unmanageable.

indiscret, -ète [ɛdiskrɛ, ɛt] **1** *adj* indiscreet; [curieux] inquisitive. **2** *nm*, *f* indiscreet person.

indiscrétion [ɛdiskresjɔ̃] *nf* indiscretion; [curiosité] curiosity.

indiscutable [ɛdiskytabl] *adj* unquestionable, indisputable.

indispensable [ɛdispɑ̃sabl] *adj* indispensable, essential; ~ **à** indispensable to, essential to; **il est** ~ **de faire qqch** it is essential OU vital to do sthg.

indisposer [ɛdispoze] *vt* sout [rendre malade] to indispose.

indistinct, -e [ɛdistɛ̃(kt), ɛkt] *adj* indistinct; [souvenir] hazy.

individu [ɛdividy] *nm* individual.

individuel, -elle [ɛdividɥɛl] *adj* individual.

indivisible [ɛdivizibl] *adj* indivisible.

Indochine [ɛdɔʃin] *nf*: **l'**~ Indochina.

indolent, -e [ɛdɔlɑ̃, ɑ̃t] *adj* [personne] indolent, lethargic.

indolore [ɛdɔlɔr] *adj* painless.

indomptable [ɛdɔ̃tabl] *adj* [animal] untamable. || [personne] indomitable.

Indonésie [ɛdɔnezi] *nf:* l'~ Indonesia.

indu, -e [ɛdy] *adj* [heure] ungodly, unearthly.

indubitable [ɛdybitabl] *adj* indubitable, undoubted; **il est ~ que** it is indisputable ou beyond doubt that.

induire [ɛdɥir] *vt* to induce; **~ qqn à faire qqch** to induce sb to do sthg; **~ qqn en erreur** to mislead sb.

indulgence [ɛdylʒɑ̃s] *nf* [de juge] leniency; [de parent] indulgence.

indulgent, -e [ɛdylʒɑ̃, ɑ̃t] *adj* [juge] lenient; [parent] indulgent.

indûment [ɛdymɑ̃] *adv* unduly.

industrialiser [ɛdystrijalize] *vt* to industrialize. ○ **s'industrialiser** *vp* to become industrialized.

industrie [ɛdystri] *nf* industry.

industriel, -ielle [ɛdystrijɛl] *adj* industrial. ○ **industriel** *nm* industrialist.

inébranlable [inebrɑ̃labl] *adj fig* [conviction] unshakeable.

inédit, -e [inedi, it] *adj* [texte] unpublished. || [trouvaille] novel, original.

ineffaçable [inefasabl] *adj* indelible.

inefficace [inefikas] *adj* [personne, machine] inefficient. || [solution, remède, mesure] ineffective.

inefficacité [inefikasite] *nf* [de personne, machine] inefficiency. || [de solution, remède, mesure] ineffectiveness.

inégal, -e, -aux [inegal, o] *adj* [différent, disproportionné] unequal. || [irrégulier] uneven.

inégalé, -e [inegale] *adj* unequalled.

inégalité [inegalite] *nf* [injustice, disproportion] inequality. || [différence] difference, disparity. || [irrégularité] unevenness. || [d'humeur] changeability.

inélégant, -e [inelegɑ̃, ɑ̃t] *adj* [dans l'habillement] inelegant. || *fig* [indélicat] discourteous.

inéligible [ineliʒibl] *adj* ineligible.

inéluctable [inelyktabl] *adj* inescapable.

inepte [inɛpt] *adj* inept.

ineptie [inɛpsi] *nf* [bêtise] ineptitude. || [chose idiote] nonsense (*U*).

inépuisable [inepɥizabl] *adj* inexhaustible.

inerte [inɛrt] *adj* [corps, membre] lifeless. || [personne] passive, inert.

inertie [inɛrsi] *nf* [manque de réaction] apathy, inertia.

inespéré, -e [inɛspere] *adj* unexpected, unhoped-for.

inestimable [inɛstimabl] *adj:* **d'une valeur ~** priceless; *fig* invaluable.

inévitable [inevitabl] *adj* [obstacle] unavoidable; [conséquence] inevitable.

inexact, -e [inɛgza(kt), akt] *adj* [faux, incomplet] inaccurate, inexact. || [en retard] unpunctual.

inexactitude [inɛgzaktityd] *nf* [erreur, imprécision] inaccuracy.

inexcusable [inɛkskyzabl] *adj* unforgivable, inexcusable.

inexistant, -e [inɛgzistɑ̃, ɑ̃t] *adj* nonexistent.

inexorable [inɛgzɔrabl] *adj* inexorable.

inexpérience [inɛksperjɑ̃s] *nf* lack of experience, inexperience.

inexplicable [inɛksplikabl] *adj* inexplicable, unexplainable.

inexpliqué, -e [inɛksplike] *adj* unexplained.

inexpressif, -ive [inɛkspresif, iv] *adj* inexpressive.

inexprimable [inɛksprimabl] *adj* inexpressible.

in extremis [inɛkstremis] *adv* at the last minute.

inextricable [inɛkstrikabl] *adj* [fouillis] inextricable. || *fig* [affaire, mystère] that cannot be unravelled.

infaillible [ɛ̃fajibl] *adj* [personne, méthode] infallible; [instinct] unerring.

infâme [ɛ̃fam] *adj* [ignoble] despicable. || *hum ou littéraire* [dégoûtant] vile.

infanterie [ɛ̃fɑ̃tri] *nf* infantry.

infanticide [ɛ̃fɑ̃tisid] **1** *nmf* infanticide, child-killer. **2** *adj* infanticidal.

infantile [ɛ̃fɑ̃til] *adj* [maladie] childhood (*avant n*). || [médecine] for children. || [comportement] infantile.

infarctus [ɛ̃farktys] *nm* infarction, infarct; **~ du myocarde** coronary thrombosis, myocardial infarction.

infatigable [ɛ̃fatigabl] *adj* [personne] tireless. || [attitude] untiring.

infect, -e [ɛ̃fɛkt] *adj* [dégoûtant] vile.

infecter [ɛ̃fɛkte] *vt* [plaie] to infect. ○ **s'infecter** *vp* to become infected, to turn septic.

infectieux, -ieuse [ɛ̃fɛksjø, jøz] *adj* infectious.

infection [ɛ̃fɛksjɔ̃] *nf* MÉD infection. || *fig & péj* [puanteur] stench.

inférieur, -e [ɛ̃ferjœr] **1** *adj* [qui est en bas] lower. || [dans une hiérarchie] inferior; ~ à [qualité] inferior to; [quantité] less than. **2** *nm, f* inferior.

infériorité [ɛ̃ferjɔrite] *nf* inferiority.

infernal, -e, -aux [ɛ̃fɛrnal, o] *adj* [enfant] unbearable. || *fig* [bruit, chaleur, rythme] infernal.

infester [ɛ̃fɛste] *vt* to infest; **être infesté de** [rats, moustiques] to be infested with.

infidèle [ɛ̃fidɛl] *adj* [mari, femme, ami]: ~ (à) unfaithful (to).

infidélité [ɛ̃fidelite] *nf* [trahison] infidelity.

infiltration [ɛ̃filtrasjɔ̃] *nf* infiltration.

infiltrer [ɛ̃filtre] *vt* to infiltrate. ○ **s'infiltrer** *vp* [pluie, lumière]: **s'~ par/dans** to filter through/into.

infime [ɛ̃fim] *adj* minute, infinitesimal.

infini, -e [ɛ̃fini] *adj* [sans bornes] infinite, boundless. || *fig* [interminable] endless, interminable. ○ **infini** *nm* infinity.

infiniment [ɛ̃finimɑ̃] *adv* extremely, immensely.

infinité [ɛ̃finite] *nf* infinity, infinite number.

infinitif, -ive [ɛ̃finitif, iv] *adj* infinitive. ○ **infinitif** *nm* infinitive.

infirme [ɛ̃firm] **1** *adj* [handicapé] disabled; [avec l'âge] infirm. **2** *nmf* disabled person.

infirmerie [ɛ̃firməri] *nf* infirmary.

infirmier, -ière [ɛ̃firmje, jɛr] *nm, f* nurse.

infirmité [ɛ̃firmite] *nf* [handicap] disability; [de vieillesse] infirmity.

inflammable [ɛ̃flamabl] *adj* inflammable, flammable.

inflammation [ɛ̃flamasjɔ̃] *nf* inflammation.

inflation [ɛ̃flasjɔ̃] *nf* ÉCON inflation.

inflationniste [ɛ̃flasjɔnist] *adj & nmf* inflationist.

infléchir [ɛ̃fleʃir] *vt fig* [politique] to modify.

inflexible [ɛ̃flɛksibl] *adj* inflexible.

inflexion [ɛ̃flɛksjɔ̃] *nf* [de tête] nod. || [de voix] inflection.

infliger [ɛ̃fliʒe] *vt*: ~ **qqch à qqn** to inflict sthg on sb; [amende] to impose sthg on sb.

influençable [ɛ̃flyɑ̃sabl] *adj* easily influenced.

influence [ɛ̃flyɑ̃s] *nf* influence.

influencer [ɛ̃flyɑ̃se] *vt* to influence.

influer [ɛ̃flye] *vi*: ~ **sur qqch** to influence sthg, to have an effect on sthg.

informaticien, -ienne [ɛ̃fɔrmatisjɛ̃, jɛn] *nm, f* computer scientist.

information [ɛ̃fɔrmasjɔ̃] *nf* [renseignement] piece of information. || [renseignements & INFORM] information (U). || [nouvelle] piece of news. ○ **informations** *nfpl* MÉDIA news (sg).

informatique [ɛ̃fɔrmatik] **1** *nf* [technique] data-processing. || [science] computer science. **2** *adj* data-processing (avant n), computer (avant n).

informatiser [ɛ̃fɔrmatize] *vt* to computerize.

informe [ɛ̃fɔrm] *adj* [masse, vêtement, silhouette] shapeless.

informel, -elle [ɛ̃fɔrmɛl] *adj* informal.

informer [ɛ̃fɔrme] *vt* to inform; ~ **qqn sur** ou **de qqch** to inform sb about sthg. ○ **s'informer** *vp* to inform o.s.; **s'~ sur qqch** to find out about sthg.

infortune [ɛ̃fɔrtyn] *nf* misfortune.

infos [ɛ̃fo] (abr de **informations**) *nfpl fam*: **les ~** the news (sg).

infraction [ɛ̃fraksjɔ̃] *nf*: **être en ~** to be in breach of the law.

infranchissable [ɛ̃frɑ̃ʃisabl] *adj* insurmountable.

infrarouge [ɛ̃fraruʒ] *nm & adj* infrared.

infrastructure [ɛ̃frastryktyr] *nf* infrastructure.

infroissable [ɛ̃frwasabl] *adj* crease-resistant.

infructueux, -euse [ɛ̃fryktɥø, øz] *adj* fruitless.

infuser [ɛ̃fyze] *vi* [tisane] to infuse; [thé] to brew.

infusion [ɛ̃fyzjɔ̃] *nf* infusion.

ingénier [ɛ̃ʒenje] ○ **s'ingénier** *vp*: **s'~ à faire qqch** to try hard to do sthg.

ingénieur [ɛ̃ʒenjœr] *nm* engineer.

ingénieux, -ieuse [ɛ̃ʒenjø, jøz] *adj* ingenious.

ingéniosité [ɛ̃ʒenjozite] *nf* ingenuity.

ingénu, -e [ɛ̃ʒeny] *adj hum & péj* [trop candide] naïve.

ingérable [ɛ̃ʒerabl] *adj* unmanageable.

ingérer [ɛ̃ʒere] *vt* to ingest. ○ **s'ingérer** *vp*: **s'~ dans** to interfere in.

ingrat, -e [ɛ̃gra, at] **1** *adj* [personne] ungrateful. || [métier] thankless, unrewarding. || [sol] barren. || [physique] unattractive. **2** *nm, f* ungrateful wretch.

ingratitude [ɛ̃gratityd] *nf* ingratitude.

ingrédient [ɛ̃gredjɑ̃] *nm* ingredient.

inguérissable [ɛ̃gerisabl] *adj* incurable.

ingurgiter [ɛ̃gyrʒite] *vt* [avaler] to swallow. || *fig* [connaissances] to absorb.

inhabitable [inabitabl] *adj* uninhabitable.

inhabité, -e [inabite] *adj* uninhabited.

inhabituel, -elle [inabityɛl] *adj* unusual.

inhalateur, -trice [inalatœr, tris] *adj*: **appareil ~** inhaler. ○ **inhalateur** *nm* inhaler.

inhalation [inalasjɔ̃] *nf* inhalation.

inhérent, -e [inerɑ̃, ɑ̃t] *adj*: **~ à** inherent in.

inhibition [inibisjɔ̃] *nf* inhibition.

inhospitalier, -ière [inɔspitalje, jɛr] *adj* inhospitable.

inhumain, -e [inymɛ̃, ɛn] *adj* inhuman.

inhumation [inymasjɔ̃] *nf* burial.

inhumer [inyme] *vt* to bury.

inimaginable [inimaʒinabl] *adj* incredible, unimaginable.

inimitable [inimitabl] *adj* inimitable.

ininflammable [inɛ̃flamabl] *adj* nonflammable.

inintelligible [inɛ̃teliʒibl] *adj* unintelligible.

inintéressant, -e [inɛ̃teresɑ̃, ɑ̃t] *adj* uninteresting.

ininterrompu, -e [inɛ̃terɔ̃py] *adj* [file, vacarme] uninterrupted; [ligne, suite] unbroken; [travail, effort] continuous.

initial, -e, -iaux [inisjal, jo] *adj* [lettre] initial. ○ **initiale** *nf* initial.

initiateur, -trice [inisjatœr, tris] *nm, f* [précurseur] innovator.

initiation [inisjasjɔ̃] *nf*: **~ (à)** [discipline] introduction (to); [rituel] initiation (into).

initiative [inisjativ] *nf* initiative; **prendre l'~ de qqch/de faire qqch** to take the initiative for sthg/in doing sthg.

initié, -e [inisje] *nm, f* initiate.

initier [inisje] *vt*: **~ qqn à** to initiate sb into.

injecté, -e [ɛ̃ʒɛkte] *adj*: **yeux ~s de sang** bloodshot eyes.

injecter [ɛ̃ʒɛkte] *vt* to inject.

injection [ɛ̃ʒɛksjɔ̃] *nf* injection.

injoignable [ɛ̃ʒwaɲabl] *adj*: **j'ai essayé de lui téléphoner mais il est ~** I tried to phone him but I couldn't get through to him/I couldn't reach him/I couldn't get hold of him.

injonction [ɛ̃ʒɔ̃ksjɔ̃] *nf* injunction.

injure [ɛ̃ʒyr] *nf* insult.

injurier [ɛ̃ʒyrje] *vt* to insult.

injurieux, -ieuse [ɛ̃ʒyrjø, jøz] *adj* abusive, insulting.

injuste [ɛ̃ʒyst] *adj* unjust, unfair.

injustice [ɛ̃ʒystis] *nf* injustice.

inlassable [ɛ̃lasabl] *adj* tireless.

inlassablement [ɛ̃lasabləmɑ̃] *adv* tirelessly.

inné, -e [ine] *adj* innate.

innocence [inɔsɑ̃s] *nf* innocence.

innocent, -e [inɔsɑ̃, ɑ̃t] **1** *adj* innocent. **2** *nm, f* JUR innocent person. || [inoffensif, candide] innocent. || *vieilli* [idiot] simpleton.

innocenter [inɔsɑ̃te] *vt* JUR to clear.

innombrable [inɔ̃brabl] *adj* innumerable; [foule] vast.

innover [inɔve] *vi* to innovate.

inoccupé, -e [inɔkype] *adj* [lieu] empty, unoccupied.

inoculer [inɔkyle] *vt* MÉD: **~ qqch à qqn** [volontairement] to inoculate sb with sthg.

inodore [inɔdɔr] *adj* odourless.

inoffensif, -ive [inɔfɑ̃sif, iv] *adj* harmless.

inondation [inɔ̃dasjɔ̃] *nf* [action] flooding. || [résultat] flood.

inonder [inɔ̃de] *vt* to flood; **~ de** *fig* to flood with.

inopérable [inɔperabl] *adj* inoperable.

inopérant, -e [inɔperɑ̃, ɑ̃t] *adj* ineffective.

inopiné, -e [inɔpine] *adj* unexpected.

inopportun, -e [inɔpɔrtœ̃, yn] *adj* inopportune.

inoubliable [inublijabl] *adj* unforgettable.

inouï, -e [inwi] *adj* incredible, extraordinary.

Inox® [inɔks] *nm inv* & *adj inv* stainless steel.

inoxydable [inɔksidabl] *adj* stainless; [casserole] stainless steel (*avant n*).

inqualifiable [ɛ̃kalifjabl] *adj* unspeakable.

inquiet, -iète [ɛ̃kjɛ, jɛt] *adj* [gén] anxious. || [tourmenté] feverish.

inquiéter [ɛ̃kjete] *vt* [donner du souci à] to worry. ○ **s'inquiéter** *vp* [s'alarmer] to be worried. || [se préoccuper]: **s'~ de** [s'enquérir de] to enquire about; [se soucier de] to worry about.

inquiétude [ɛ̃kjetyd] *nf* anxiety, worry.

insaisissable [ɛ̃sezisabl] *adj* [personne] elusive. || *fig* [nuance] imperceptible.

insalubre [ɛ̃salybr] *adj* unhealthy.

insatiable [ɛ̃sasjabl] *adj* insatiable.

insatisfait, -e [ɛ̃satisfɛ, ɛt] **1** *adj* [personne] dissatisfied. **2** *nm, f* malcontent.

inscription [ɛ̃skripsjɔ̃] *nf* [action, écrit] inscription. || [enregistrement] enrolment, registration.

inscrire [ɛ̃skrir] *vt* [écrire] to write down; [- sur la pierre, le métal] to inscribe. || [personne]: ~ qqn à qqch to enrol ou register sb for sthg; ~ qqn sur qqch to put sb's name down on sthg. ○ **s'inscrire** *vp* [personne]: s'~ à qqch to enrol ou register for sthg; s'~ sur qqch to put one's name down on sthg.

inscrit, -e [ɛ̃skri, it] **1** *pp* → inscrire. **2** *adj* [sur liste] registered; être ~ sur une liste to have one's name on a list.

insecte [ɛ̃sɛkt] *nm* insect.

insecticide [ɛ̃sɛktisid] *nm & adj* insecticide.

insécurité [ɛ̃sekyrite] *nf* insecurity.

insémination [ɛ̃seminasjɔ̃] *nf* insemination; ~ artificielle artificial insemination.

insensé, -e [ɛ̃sɑ̃se] *adj* [déraisonnable] insane. || [incroyable, excentrique] extraordinary.

insensibiliser [ɛ̃sɑ̃sibilize] *vt* to anaesthetize.

insensible [ɛ̃sɑ̃sibl] *adj* [gén]: ~ (à) insensitive (to). || [imperceptible] imperceptible.

insensiblement [ɛ̃sɑ̃sibləmɑ̃] *adv* imperceptibly.

inséparable [ɛ̃separabl] *adj*: ~ (de) inseparable (from).

insérer [ɛ̃sere] *vt* to insert; ~ une annonce dans un journal to put an advertisement in a newspaper. ○ **s'insérer** *vp* [s'intégrer]: s'~ dans to fit into.

insidieux, -ieuse [ɛ̃sidjø, jøz] *adj* insidious.

insigne [ɛ̃siɲ] **1** *nm* badge. **2** *adj* littéraire [honneur] distinguished. || *hum* [maladresse] remarkable.

insignifiant, -e [ɛ̃siɲifjɑ̃, ɑ̃t] *adj* insignificant.

insinuation [ɛ̃sinɥasjɔ̃] *nf* insinuation, innuendo.

insinuer [ɛ̃sinɥe] *vt* to insinuate, to imply. ○ **s'insinuer** *vp*: s'~ dans [eau, humidité, odeur] to seep into; *fig* [personne] to insinuate o.s. into.

insipide [ɛ̃sipid] *adj* [aliment] insipid, tasteless; *fig* insipid.

insistance [ɛ̃sistɑ̃s] *nf* insistence.

insister [ɛ̃siste] *vi* to insist; ~ sur to insist on; ~ pour faire qqch to insist on doing sthg.

insolation [ɛ̃sɔlasjɔ̃] *nf* [malaise] sunstroke (*U*).

insolence [ɛ̃sɔlɑ̃s] *nf* insolence (*U*).

insolent, -e [ɛ̃sɔlɑ̃, ɑ̃t] **1** *adj* [personne, acte] insolent. **2** *nm, f* insolent person.

insolite [ɛ̃sɔlit] *adj* unusual.

insoluble [ɛ̃sɔlybl] *adj* insoluble.

insolvable [ɛ̃sɔlvabl] *adj* insolvent.

insomnie [ɛ̃sɔmni] *nf* insomnia (*U*).

insondable [ɛ̃sɔ̃dabl] *adj* [gouffre, mystère] unfathomable; [bêtise] abysmal.

insonoriser [ɛ̃sɔnɔrize] *vt* to soundproof.

insouciance [ɛ̃susjɑ̃s] *nf* [légèreté] carefree attitude.

insouciant, -e [ɛ̃susjɑ̃, ɑ̃t] *adj* [sanssouci] carefree.

insoumis, -e [ɛ̃sumi, iz] *adj* [caractère] rebellious. || [soldat] deserting.

insoupçonné, -e [ɛ̃supsɔne] *adj* unsuspected.

insoutenable [ɛ̃sutnabl] *adj* [rythme] unsustainable. || [scène, violence] unbearable. || [théorie] untenable.

inspecter [ɛ̃spɛkte] *vt* to inspect.

inspecteur, -trice [ɛ̃spɛktœr, tris] *nm, f* inspector.

inspection [ɛ̃spɛksjɔ̃] *nf* [contrôle] inspection. || [fonction] inspectorate.

inspiration [ɛ̃spirasjɔ̃] *nf* [gén] inspiration; [idée] bright idea, brainwave; avoir de l'~ to be inspired. || [d'air] breathing in.

inspirer [ɛ̃spire] *vt* [gén] to inspire; ~ qqch à qqn to inspire sb with sthg. || [air] to breathe in, to inhale. ○ **s'inspirer** *vp* [prendre modèle sur]: s'~ de qqn/qqch to be inspired by sb/sthg.

instable [ɛ̃stabl] *adj* [gén] unstable. || [vie, temps] unsettled.

installation [ɛ̃stalasjɔ̃] *nf* [de gaz, eau, électricité] installation. || [de personne - comme médecin, artisan] setting up; [- dans appartement] settling in. || (*gén pl*) [équipement] installations (*pl*), fittings (*pl*); [industrielle] plant (*U*); [de loisirs] facilities (*pl*); ~ électrique wiring.

installer [ɛ̃stale] *vt* [gaz, eau, électricité] to install, to put in. || [rideaux, étagères] to put up; [meubles] to put in. || [personne]: ~ qqn to get sb settled, to install sb. ○ **s'installer** *vp* [comme médecin, artisan etc] to set (o.s.) up. || [emménager] to settle in; s'~ chez qqn to move in with sb. || [dans fauteuil] to settle down. || *fig* [maladie, routine] to set in.

instamment [ɛ̃stamɑ̃] *adv* insistently.

instance [ɛ̃stɑ̃s] *nf* [autorité] authority. || JUR proceedings (*pl*). ○ **en instance** *loc adj* pending. ○ **en instance de** *loc adv* on the point of.

instant [ɛ̃stɑ̃] *nm* instant; **à l'~** [il y a peu de temps] a moment ago; [immédiatement] this minute; **à tout ~** [en permanence] at all times; **pour l'~** for the moment.

instantané, -e [ɛ̃stɑ̃tane] *adj* [immédiat] instantaneous. || [soluble] instant. ○ **instantané** *nm* snapshot.

instar [ɛ̃star] ○ **à l'instar de** *loc prép* following the example of.

instaurer [ɛ̃stɔre] *vt* [instituer] to establish; *fig* [peur, confiance] to instil.

instigateur, -trice [ɛ̃stigatœr, tris] *nm, f* instigator.

instigation [ɛ̃stigasjɔ̃] *nf* ○ **à l'instigation de, sur l'instigation de** *loc prép* at the instigation of.

instinct [ɛ̃stɛ̃] *nm* instinct.

instinctif, -ive [ɛ̃stɛ̃ktif, iv] **1** *adj* instinctive. **2** *nm, f* instinctive person.

instituer [ɛ̃stitɥe] *vt* [pratique] to institute. || JUR [personne] to appoint.

institut [ɛ̃stity] *nm* [gén] institute. || [de soins] : **~ de beauté** beauty salon.

instituteur, -trice [ɛ̃stitytœr, tris] *nm, f* primary *Br* ou grade *Am* school teacher.

institution [ɛ̃stitysjɔ̃] *nf* [gén] institution. || [école privée] private school. ○ **institutions** *nfpl* POLIT institutions.

instructif, -ive [ɛ̃stryktif, iv] *adj* instructive, educational.

instruction [ɛ̃stryksjɔ̃] *nf* [enseignement, savoir] education. || [directive] order. || JUR (pre-trial) investigation. ○ **instructions** *nfpl* instructions.

instruit, -e [ɛ̃strɥi, ɥit] *adj* educated.

instrument [ɛ̃strymɑ̃] *nm* instrument; **~ de musique** musical instrument.

insu [ɛ̃sy] ○ **à l'insu de** *loc prép* : **à l'~ de qqn** without sb knowing; **ils ont tout organisé à mon ~** they organized it all without my knowing.

insubmersible [ɛ̃sybmɛrsibl] *adj* unsinkable.

insubordination [ɛ̃sybɔrdinasjɔ̃] *nf* insubordination.

insuccès [ɛ̃syksɛ] *nm* failure.

insuffisance [ɛ̃syfizɑ̃s] *nf* [manque] in-sufficiency. || MÉD deficiency. ○ **insuffisances** *nfpl* [faiblesses] shortcomings.

insuffisant, -e [ɛ̃syfizɑ̃, ɑ̃t] *adj* [en quantité] insufficient. || [en qualité] inadequate, unsatisfactory.

insulaire [ɛ̃sylɛr] **1** *nmf* islander. **2** *adj* GÉOGR island (*avant n*).

insuline [ɛ̃sylin] *nf* insulin.

insulte [ɛ̃sylt] *nf* insult.

insulter [ɛ̃sylte] *vt* to insult.

insupportable [ɛ̃sypɔrtabl] *adj* unbearable.

insurgé, -e [ɛ̃syrʒe] *adj & nm, f* insurgent, rebel.

insurger [ɛ̃syrʒe] ○ **s'insurger** *vp* to rebel, to revolt; **s'~ contre qqch** to be outraged by sthg.

insurmontable [ɛ̃syrmɔ̃tabl] *adj* [difficulté] insurmountable; [dégoût] uncontrollable.

insurrection [ɛ̃syrɛksjɔ̃] *nf* insurrection.

intact, -e [ɛ̃takt] *adj* intact.

intarissable [ɛ̃tarisabl] *adj* inexhaustible; **il est ~** he could go on talking for ever.

intégral, -e, -aux [ɛ̃tegral, o] *adj* [paiement] in full; [texte] unabridged, complete. || MATHS : **calcul ~** integral calculus.

intégralement [ɛ̃tegralmɑ̃] *adv* fully, in full.

intégrant, -e [ɛ̃tegrɑ̃, ɑ̃t] → **parti**.

intègre [ɛ̃tegr] *adj* honest, of integrity.

intégré, -e [ɛ̃tegre] *adj* [élément] built-in.

intégrer [ɛ̃tegre] *vt* [assimiler] : **~ (à ou dans)** to integrate (into). ○ **s'intégrer** *vp* [s'incorporer] : **s'~ dans** ou **à** to fit into. || [s'adapter] to integrate.

intégrisme [ɛ̃tegrism] *nm* fundamentalism.

intégrité [ɛ̃tegrite] *nf* [totalité] entirety. || [honnêteté] integrity.

intellectuel, -elle [ɛ̃telɛktɥel] *adj & nm, f* intellectual.

intelligence [ɛ̃teliʒɑ̃s] *nf* [facultés mentales] intelligence; **~ artificielle** artificial intelligence.

intelligent, -e [ɛ̃teliʒɑ̃, ɑ̃t] *adj* intelligent.

intelligible [ɛ̃teliʒibl] *adj* [voix] clear. || [concept, texte] intelligible.

intello [ɛ̃telo] *adj inv & nmf péj* highbrow.

intempéries [ɛ̃tɑ̃peri] *nfpl* bad weather (U).

intempestif, -ive [ɛ̃tɑ̃pɛstif, iv] *adj* untimely.

intenable [ɛ̃tənabl] *adj* [chaleur, personne] unbearable. ‖ [position] untenable, indefensible.

intendance [ɛ̃tɑ̃dɑ̃s] *nf* MIL commissariat; SCOL & UNIV bursar's office.

intendant, -e [ɛ̃tɑ̃dɑ̃, ɑ̃t] *nm, f* SCOL & UNIV bursar.

intense [ɛ̃tɑ̃s] *adj* [gén] intense.

intensif, -ive [ɛ̃tɑ̃sif, iv] *adj* intensive.

intensité [ɛ̃tɑ̃site] *nf* intensity.

intenter [ɛ̃tɑ̃te] *vt* JUR: ~ qqch contre ou à qqn to bring sthg against sb.

intention [ɛ̃tɑ̃sjɔ̃] *nf* intention; **avoir l'~ de faire qqch** to intend to do sthg. ○ **à l'intention de** *loc prép* for.

intentionné, -e [ɛ̃tɑ̃sjɔne] *adj*: **bien ~** well-meaning; **mal ~** ill-disposed.

intentionnel, -elle [ɛ̃tɑ̃sjɔnɛl] *adj* intentional.

interactif, -ive [ɛ̃tɛraktif, iv] *adj* interactive.

intercalaire [ɛ̃tɛrkaler] **1** *nm* insert. **2** *adj*: **feuillet ~** insert.

intercaler [ɛ̃tɛrkale] *vt*: ~ **qqch dans qqch** [feuillet, citation] to insert sthg in sthg; [dans le temps] to fit sthg into sthg.

intercéder [ɛ̃tɛrsede] *vi*: ~ **pour** ou **en faveur de qqn auprès de qqn** to intercede with sb on behalf of sb.

intercepter [ɛ̃tɛrsɛpte] *vt* [lettre, ballon] to intercept. ‖ [chaleur] to block.

interchangeable [ɛ̃tɛrʃɑ̃ʒabl] *adj* interchangeable.

interclasse [ɛ̃tɛrklas] *nm* break.

interdiction [ɛ̃tɛrdiksjɔ̃] *nf* [défense]: «**~ de stationner**» "strictly no parking". ‖ [prohibition, suspension]: ~ **(de)** ban (on), banning (of); ~ **de séjour** *order banning released prisoner from living in certain areas.*

interdire [ɛ̃tɛrdir] *vt* [prohiber]: ~ **qqch à qqn** to forbid sb sthg; ~ **à qqn de faire qqch** to forbid sb to do sthg. ‖ [empêcher] to prevent; ~ **à qqn de faire qqch** to prevent sb from doing sthg. ‖ [bloquer] to block.

interdit, -e [ɛ̃tɛrdi, it] **1** *pp* → **interdire**. **2** *adj* [défendu] forbidden; **il est ~ de fumer** you're not allowed to smoke. ‖ [ébahi]: **rester ~** to be stunned.

intéressant, -e [ɛ̃teresɑ̃, ɑ̃t] *adj* [captivant] interesting. ‖ [avantageux] advantageous, good.

intéressé, -e [ɛ̃terese] *adj* [concerné]

concerned, involved; *péj* [motivé] self-interested.

intéresser [ɛ̃terese] *vt* [captiver] to interest. ‖ COMM [faire participer]: ~ **les employés (aux bénéfices)** to give one's employees a share in the profits. ‖ [concerner] to concern. ○ **s'intéresser** *vp*: s'~ **à qqn/qqch** to take an interest in sb/sthg, to be interested in sb/sthg.

intérêt [ɛ̃terɛ] *nm* [gén] interest; ~ **pour** interest in; **tu as ~ à réserver** you would be well advised to book. ‖ [importance] significance. ○ **intérêts** *nmpl* FIN interest (*sg*). ‖ COMM: **avoir des ~s dans** to have a stake in.

interface [ɛ̃tɛrfas] *nf* INFORM interface; ~ **graphique** graphic interface.

interférer [ɛ̃tɛrfere] *vi* PHYS to interfere. ‖ *fig* [s'immiscer]: ~ **dans qqch** to interfere in sthg.

intérieur, -e [ɛ̃terjœr] *adj* [gén] inner. ‖ [de pays] domestic. ○ **intérieur** *nm* [gén] inside; **à l'~ (de qqch)** inside (sthg). ‖ [de pays] interior.

intérim [ɛ̃terim] *nm* [période] interim period; **par ~** acting. ‖ [travail temporaire] temporary ou casual work; [dans bureau] temping.

intérimaire [ɛ̃terimɛr] **1** *adj* [ministre, directeur] acting (*avant n*). ‖ [employé, fonctions] temporary. **2** *nmf* [employé] temp.

intérioriser [ɛ̃terjɔrize] *vt* to internalize.

interjection [ɛ̃tɛrʒɛksjɔ̃] *nf* LING interjection.

interligne [ɛ̃tɛrliɲ] *nm* (line) spacing.

interlocuteur, -trice [ɛ̃tɛrlɔkytœr, tris] *nm, f* [dans conversation] speaker; **mon ~** the person to whom I am/was speaking. ‖ [dans négociation] negotiator.

interloquer [ɛ̃tɛrlɔke] *vt* to disconcert.

interlude [ɛ̃tɛrlyd] *nm* interlude.

intermède [ɛ̃tɛrmɛd] *nm* interlude.

intermédiaire [ɛ̃tɛrmedjɛr] **1** *nm* intermediary, go-between; **par l'~ de qqn/qqch** through sb/sthg. **2** *adj* intermediate.

interminable [ɛ̃tɛrminabl] *adj* never-ending, interminable.

intermittence [ɛ̃tɛrmitɑ̃s] *nf* [discontinuité]: **par ~** intermittently, off and on.

intermittent, -e [ɛ̃tɛrmitɑ̃, ɑ̃t] *adj* intermittent.

internat [ɛ̃tɛrna] *nm* [SCOL - établissement] boarding school; [- système] boarding.

international, -e, -aux [ɛ̃tɛrnasjɔnal, o] *adj* international.

interne [ɛ̃tɛrn] **1** *nmf* [élève] boarder. ‖ MÉD & UNIV intern *Am*. **2** *adj* ANAT internal; [oreille] inner. ‖ [du pays] domestic.

interner [ɛ̃tɛrne] *vt* POLIT to intern. ‖ MÉD to confine (*to psychiatric hospital*).

interpeller [ɛ̃tɛrpəle] *vt* [apostropher] to call oι shout out to. ‖ [interroger] to take in for questioning.

Interphone® [ɛ̃tɛrfɔn] *nm* intercom; [d'un immeuble] entry phone.

interposer [ɛ̃tɛrpoze] ○ **s'interposer** *vp*: **s'~ entre qqn et qqn** to intervene oι come between sb and sb.

interprète [ɛ̃tɛrprɛt] *nmf* [gén] interpreter. ‖ CIN, MUS & THÉÂTRE performer.

interpréter [ɛ̃tɛrprete] *vt* to interpret.

interrogateur, -trice [ɛ̃tɛrɔgatœr, tris] *adj* inquiring (*avant n*).

interrogatif, -ive [ɛ̃tɛrɔgatif, iv] *adj* GRAM interrogative.

interrogation [ɛ̃tɛrɔgasjɔ̃] *nf* [de prisonnier] interrogation; [de témoin] questioning. ‖ [question] question. ‖ SCOL test.

interrogatoire [ɛ̃tɛrɔgatwar] *nm* [de police, juge] questioning.

interrogeable [ɛ̃tɛrɔʒabl] *adj*: **répondeur ~ à distance** answerphone with remote playback facility.

interroger [ɛ̃tɛrɔʒe] *vt* [questionner] to question; [accusé, base de données] to interrogate; **~ qqn (sur qqch)** to question sb (about sthg). ○ **s'interroger** *vp*: **s'~ sur** to wonder about.

interrompre [ɛ̃tɛrɔ̃pr] *vt* to interrupt. ○ **s'interrompre** *vp* to stop.

interrompu, -e [ɛ̃tɛrɔ̃py] *pp* → **interrompre**.

interrupteur [ɛ̃teryptœr] *nm* switch.

interruption [ɛ̃terypsjɔ̃] *nf* [arrêt] break. ‖ [action] interruption.

intersection [ɛ̃tɛrsɛksjɔ̃] *nf* intersection.

interstice [ɛ̃tɛrstis] *nm* chink, crack.

interurbain, -e [ɛ̃teryrbɛ̃, ɛn] *adj* long-distance.

intervalle [ɛ̃tɛrval] *nm* [spatial] space, gap. ‖ [temporel] interval, period (of time); **à 6 jours d'~** after 6 days. ‖ MUS interval.

intervenant, -e [ɛ̃tɛrvənɑ̃, ɑ̃t] *nm, f* [orateur] speaker.

intervenir [ɛ̃tɛrvənir] *vi* [personne] to intervene; **~ auprès de qqn** to intervene with sb; **faire ~ qqn** to bring oι call in sb. ‖ [événement] to take place.

intervention [ɛ̃tɛrvɑ̃sjɔ̃] *nf* [gén] intervention. ‖ MÉD operation; **subir une ~ chirurgicale** to have an operation, to have surgery. ‖ [discours] speech.

intervenu, -e [ɛ̃tɛrvəny] *pp* → **intervenir**.

intervertir [ɛ̃tɛrvɛrtir] *vt* to reverse, to invert.

interview [ɛ̃tɛrvju] *nf* interview.

interviewer [ɛ̃tɛrvjuve] *vt* to interview.

intestin [ɛ̃tɛstɛ̃] *nm* intestine.

intestinal, -e, -aux [ɛ̃tɛstinal, o] *adj* intestinal.

intime [ɛ̃tim] **1** *nmf* close friend. **2** *adj* [gén] intimate; [vie, journal] private.

intimider [ɛ̃timide] *vt* to intimidate.

intimité [ɛ̃timite] *nf* [familiarité, confort] intimacy. ‖ [vie privée] privacy.

intitulé [ɛ̃tityle] *nm* [titre] title; [de paragraphe] heading.

intituler [ɛ̃tityle] *vt* to call, to entitle. ○ **s'intituler** *vp* [ouvrage] to be called oι entitled.

intolérable [ɛ̃tɔlerabl] *adj* intolerable.

intolérance [ɛ̃tɔlerɑ̃s] *nf* [religieuse, politique] intolerance.

intolérant, -e [ɛ̃tɔlerɑ̃, ɑ̃t] *adj* intolerant.

intonation [ɛ̃tɔnasjɔ̃] *nf* intonation.

intouchable [ɛ̃tuʃabl] *nmf* & *adj* untouchable.

intoxication [ɛ̃tɔksikasjɔ̃] *nf* [empoisonnement] poisoning.

intoxiquer [ɛ̃tɔksike] *vt*: **~ qqn par** [empoisonner] to poison sb with.

intraduisible [ɛ̃tradɥizibl] *adj* [texte] untranslatable.

intraitable [ɛ̃trɛtabl] *adj*: **~ (sur)** inflexible (about).

intransigeant, -e [ɛ̃trɑ̃ziʒɑ̃, ɑ̃t] *adj* intransigent.

intransitif, -ive [ɛ̃trɑ̃zitif, iv] *adj* intransitive.

intransportable [ɛ̃trɑ̃spɔrtabl] *adj*: **il est ~** he/it cannot be moved.

intraveineux, -euse [ɛ̃travenø, øz] *adj* intravenous.

intrépide [ɛ̃trepid] *adj* bold, intrepid.

intrigue [ɛ̃trig] *nf* [manœuvre] intrigue. ‖ CIN, LITTÉRATURE & THÉÂTRE plot.

intriguer [ɛ̃trige] **1** *vt* to intrigue. **2** *vi* to scheme, to intrigue.

introduction [ɛ̃trɔdyksjɔ̃] *nf* [gén]: **~ (à)** introduction (to). ‖ [insertion] insertion.

introduire [ɛ̃trɔdɥir] *vt* [gén] to introduce. || [faire entrer] to show in. || [insérer] to insert. ○ **s'introduire** *vp* [pénétrer] to enter.

introduit, -e [ɛ̃trɔdɥi, it] *pp* → **introduire**.

introspection [ɛ̃trɔspɛksjɔ̃] *nf* introspection.

introuvable [ɛ̃truvabl] *adj* nowhere to be found.

introverti, -e [ɛ̃trɔvɛrti] 1 *adj* introverted. 2 *nm, f* introvert.

intrus, -e [ɛ̃try, yz] *nm, f* intruder.

intrusion [ɛ̃tryzjɔ̃] *nf* [gén & GÉOL] intrusion. || [ingérence] interference.

intuitif, -ive [ɛ̃tɥitif, iv] *adj* intuitive.

intuition [ɛ̃tɥisjɔ̃] *nf* intuition.

inusable [inyzabl] *adj* hardwearing.

inusité, -e [inyzite] *adj* unusual, uncommon.

inutile [inytil] *adj* [objet, personne] useless; [effort, démarche] pointless.

inutilisable [inytilizabl] *adj* unusable.

inutilité [inytilite] *nf* [de personne, d'objet] uselessness; [de démarche, d'effort] pointlessness.

invaincu, -e [ɛ̃vɛ̃ky] *adj* SPORT unbeaten.

invalide [ɛ̃valid] 1 *nmf* disabled person. 2 *adj* disabled.

invalidité [ɛ̃validite] *nf* MÉD disability.

invariable [ɛ̃varjabl] *adj* [immuable] unchanging. || GRAM invariable.

invasion [ɛ̃vazjɔ̃] *nf* invasion.

invendable [ɛ̃vɑ̃dabl] *adj* unsaleable, unsellable.

invendu, -e [ɛ̃vɑ̃dy] *adj* unsold. ○ **invendu** *nm* (*gén pl*) remainder.

inventaire [ɛ̃vɑ̃tɛr] *nm* [gén] inventory. || [COMM - activité] stocktaking *Br*, inventory *Am*; [- liste] list.

inventer [ɛ̃vɑ̃te] *vt* to invent.

inventeur [ɛ̃vɑ̃tœr] *nm* [de machine] inventor.

invention [ɛ̃vɑ̃sjɔ̃] *nf* [découverte, mensonge] invention. || [imagination] inventiveness.

inventorier [ɛ̃vɑ̃tɔrje] *vt* to make an inventory of.

inverse [ɛ̃vɛrs] 1 *nm* opposite, reverse. 2 *adj* [sens] opposite; [ordre] reverse; **en sens ~ (de)** in the opposite direction (to).

inversement [ɛ̃vɛrsəmɑ̃] *adv* MATHS inversely. || [au contraire] on the other hand. || [vice versa] vice versa.

inverser [ɛ̃vɛrse] *vt* to reverse.

investigation [ɛ̃vɛstigasjɔ̃] *nf* investigation.

investir [ɛ̃vɛstir] *vt* to invest.

investissement [ɛ̃vɛstismɑ̃] *nm* investment.

investisseur, -euse [ɛ̃vɛstisœr, øz] *nm, f* investor.

investiture [ɛ̃vɛstityr] *nf* investiture.

invétéré, -e [ɛ̃vetere] *adj péj* inveterate.

invincible [ɛ̃vɛ̃sibl] *adj* [gén] invincible.

inviolable [ɛ̃vjɔlabl] *adj* JUR inviolable. || [coffre] impregnable.

invisible [ɛ̃vizibl] *adj* invisible.

invitation [ɛ̃vitasjɔ̃] *nf*: ~ (à) invitation (to); **sur** ~ by invitation.

invité, -e [ɛ̃vite] *nm, f* guest.

inviter [ɛ̃vite] *vt* to invite; ~ **qqn à faire qqch** to invite sb to do sthg.

in vitro [invitro] → **fécondation**.

invivable [ɛ̃vivabl] *adj* unbearable.

involontaire [ɛ̃vɔlɔ̃tɛr] *adj* [acte] involuntary.

invoquer [ɛ̃vɔke] *vt* [alléguer] to put forward. || [citer, appeler à l'aide] to invoke; [paix] to call for.

invraisemblable [ɛ̃vrɛsɑ̃blabl] *adj* [incroyable] unlikely, improbable. || [extravagant] incredible.

invulnérable [ɛ̃vylnerabl] *adj* invulnerable.

iode [jɔd] *nm* iodine.

ion [jɔ̃] *nm* ion.

IRA [ira] (*abr de* Irish Republican Army) *nf* IRA.

irai, iras *etc* → **aller**.

Irak, Iraq [irak] *nm*: l'~ Iraq.

irakien, -ienne, iraqien, -ienne [irakjɛ̃, jɛn] *adj* Iraqi. ○ **Irakien, -ienne, Iraqien, -ienne** *nm, f* Iraqi.

Iran [irɑ̃] *nm*: l'~ Iran.

iranien, -ienne [iranjɛ̃, jɛn] *adj* Iranian. ○ **iranien** *nm* [langue] Iranian. ○ **Iranien, -ienne** *nm, f* Iranian.

Iraq = **Irak**.

iraqien = **irakien**.

irascible [irasibl] *adj* irascible.

iris [iris] *nm* ANAT & BOT iris.

irisé, -e [irize] *adj* iridescent.

irlandais, -e [irlɑ̃dɛ, ɛz] *adj* Irish. ○ **irlandais** *nm* [langue] Irish. ○ **Irlandais, -e** *nm, f* Irishman (*f* Irishwoman).

Irlande [irlɑ̃d] *nf*: l'~ Ireland; l'~ **du Nord/Sud** Northern/Southern Ireland.

ironie [irɔni] *nf* irony.

ironique [irɔnik] *adj* ironic.

ironiser [irɔnize] *vi* to speak ironically.

irradier [iradje] **1** *vi* to radiate. **2** *vt* to irradiate.

irraisonné, -e [irɛzɔne] *adj* irrational.

irrationnel, -elle [irasjɔnɛl] *adj* irrational.

irréalisable [irealizabl] *adj* unrealizable.

irrécupérable [irekyperabl] *adj* [irréparable] beyond repair. || *fam* [personne] beyond hope.

irréductible [iredyktibl] **1** *nmf* diehard. **2** *adj* CHIM, MATHS & MÉD irreducible. || *fig* [volonté] indomitable; [personne] implacable; [communiste] diehard (*avant n*).

irréel, -elle [ireɛl] *adj* unreal.

irréfléchi, -e [irefleʃi] *adj* unthinking.

irréfutable [irefytabl] *adj* irrefutable.

irrégularité [iregylarite] *nf* [gén] irregularity. || [de terrain, performance] unevenness.

irrégulier, -ière [iregylje, jɛr] *adj* [gén] irregular. || [terrain, surface] uneven, irregular. || [employé, athlète] erratic.

irrémédiable [iremedjabl] *adj* [irréparable] irreparable.

irremplaçable [irɑ̃plasabl] *adj* irreplaceable.

irréparable [ireparabl] *adj* [objet] beyond repair. || *fig* [perte, erreur] irreparable.

irrépressible [irepresibl] *adj* irrepressible.

irréprochable [ireprɔʃabl] *adj* irreproachable.

irrésistible [irezistibl] *adj* [tentation, femme] irresistible. || [amusant] entertaining.

irrésolu, -e [irezɔly] *adj* [indécis] irresolute. || [sans solution] unresolved.

irrespirable [irespirabl] *adj* [air] unbreathable. || *fig* [oppressant] oppressive.

irresponsable [irɛspɔ̃sabl] **1** *nmf* irresponsible person. **2** *adj* irresponsible.

irréversible [ireversibl] *adj* irreversible.

irrévocable [irevɔkabl] *adj* irrevocable.

irrigation [irigasjɔ̃] *nf* irrigation.

irriguer [irige] *vt* to irrigate.

irritable [iritabl] *adj* irritable.

irritation [iritasjɔ̃] *nf* irritation.

irriter [irite] *vt* [exaspérer] to irritate, to annoy. || MÉD to irritate. ○ **s'irriter** *vp*

to get irritated; **s'~ contre qqn/de qqch** to get irritated with sb/at sthg.

irruption [irypsjɔ̃] *nf* [invasion] invasion. || [entrée brusque] irruption.

islam [islam] *nm* Islam.

islamique [islamik] *adj* Islamic.

islandais, -e [islɑ̃dɛ, ɛz] *adj* Icelandic.

Islande [islɑ̃d] *nf*: l'~ Iceland.

isolant, -e [izɔlɑ̃, ɑ̃t] *adj* insulating. ○ **isolant** *nm* insulator, insulating material.

isolation [izɔlasjɔ̃] *nf* insulation.

isolé, -e [izɔle] *adj* isolated.

isoler [izɔle] *vt* [séparer] to isolate. || CONSTR & ÉLECTR to insulate; **~ qqch du froid** to insulate sthg (against the cold); **~ qqch du bruit** to soundproof sthg. ○ **s'isoler** *vp*: **s'~ (de)** to isolate o.s. (from).

isoloir [izɔlwar] *nm* polling booth.

isotherme [izɔtɛrm] *adj* isothermal.

Israël [israɛl] *n* Israel.

israélien, -ienne [israeljɛ̃, jɛn] *adj* Israeli. ○ **Israélien, -ienne** *nm, f* Israeli.

israélite [israelit] *adj* Jewish. ○ **Israélite** *nmf* Jew.

issu, -e [isy] *adj*: **~ de** [résultant de] emerging ou stemming from. ○ **issue** *nf* [sortie] exit; **~e de secours** emergency exit. || *fig* [solution] way out, solution. || [terme] outcome.

isthme [ism] *nm* isthmus.

Italie [itali] *nf*: l'~ Italy.

italien, -ienne [italjɛ̃, jɛn] *adj* Italian. ○ **italien** *nm* [langue] Italian. ○ **Italien, -ienne** *nm, f* Italian.

italique [italik] *nm* TYPO italics (*pl*).

itinéraire [itinerɛr] *nm* itinerary, route.

itinérant, -e [itinerɑ̃, ɑ̃t] *adj* [spectacle, troupe] itinerant.

IUT (*abr de* **institut universitaire de technologie**) *nm* ≃ technical college.

IVG (*abr de* **interruption volontaire de grossesse**) *nf* abortion.

ivoire [ivwar] *nm* ivory.

ivre [ivr] *adj* drunk.

ivresse [ivrɛs] *nf* drunkenness.

ivrogne [ivrɔɲ] *nmf* drunkard.

J, J [ʒi] *nm inv* j, J.

j' → je.

jabot [ʒabo] *nm* [d'oiseau] crop. || [de chemise] frill.

jacasser [ʒakase] *vi péj* to chatter, to jabber.

jacinthe [ʒasɛ̃t] *nf* hyacinth.

Jacuzzi® [ʒakuzi] *nm* Jacuzzi®.

jade [ʒad] *nm* jade.

jadis [ʒadis] *adv* formerly, in former times.

jaguar [ʒagwar] *nm* jaguar.

jaillir [ʒajir] *vi* [liquide] to gush; [flammes] to leap. || [cri] to ring out. || [personne] to spring out.

jais [ʒɛ] *nm* jet.

jalon [ʒalɔ̃] *nm* marker pole.

jalonner [ʒalɔne] *vt* to mark (out).

jalousie [ʒaluzi] *nf* [envie] jealousy. || [store] blind.

jaloux, -ouse [ʒalu, uz] *adj*: ~ (de) jealous (of).

Jamaïque [ʒamaik] *nf*: la ~ Jamaica.

jamais [ʒamɛ] *adv* [sens négatif] never; **je ne reviendrai ~, ~ je ne reviendrai** I'll never come back; **je ne viendrai ~ plus, plus ~ je ne viendrai** I'll never come here again. || [sens positif]: **plus que ~** more than ever; **il est plus triste que ~** he's sadder than ever; **si ~ tu le vois** if you should happen to see him, should you happen to see him. ○ **à jamais** *loc adv* for ever.

jambe [ʒɑ̃b] *nf* leg.

jambières [ʒɑ̃bjɛr] *nfpl* [de football] shin pads; [de cricket] pads.

jambon [ʒɑ̃bɔ̃] *nm* ham.

jante [ʒɑ̃t] *nf* (wheel) rim.

janvier [ʒɑ̃vje] *nm* January; *voir aussi* septembre.

Japon [ʒapɔ̃] *nm*: le ~ Japan.

japonais, -e [ʒapɔnɛ, ɛz] *adj* Japanese. ○ **japonais** *nm* [langue] Japanese. ○ **Japonais, -e** *nm, f* Japanese (person); **les Japonais** the Japanese.

japper [ʒape] *vi* to yap.

jaquette [ʒakɛt] *nf* [vêtement] jacket. || [de livre] (dust) jacket.

jardin [ʒardɛ̃] *nm* garden; ~ **public** park.

jardinage [ʒardinaʒ] *nm* gardening.

jardinier, -ière [ʒardinje, jɛr] *nm, f* gardener. ○ **jardinière** *nf* [bac à fleurs] window box.

jargon [ʒargɔ̃] *nm* [langage spécialisé] jargon. || *fam* [charabia] gibberish.

jarret [ʒarɛ] *nm* ANAT back of the knee. || CULIN knuckle of veal.

jarretelle [ʒartɛl] *nf* garter *Am*.

jarretière [ʒartjɛr] *nf* garter.

jaser [ʒaze] *vi* [bavarder] to gossip.

jasmin [ʒasmɛ̃] *nm* jasmine.

jatte [ʒat] *nf* bowl.

jauge [ʒoʒ] *nf* [instrument] gauge.

jauger [ʒoʒe] *vt* to gauge.

jaunâtre [ʒonatr] *adj* yellowish.

jaune [ʒon] **1** *nm* [couleur] yellow. **2** *adj* yellow. ○ **jaune d'œuf** *nm* (egg) yolk.

jaunir [ʒonir] *vt & vi* to turn yellow.

jaunisse [ʒonis] *nf* MÉD jaundice.

java [ʒava] *nf* type of popular dance.

Javel [ʒavɛl] *nf*: (eau de) ~ bleach.

javelot [ʒavlo] *nm* javelin.

jazz [dʒaz] *nm* jazz.

J.-C. (*abr de* Jésus-Christ) J.C.

je [ʒə], **j'** (*devant voyelle et h muet*) *pron pers* I.

jean [dʒin], **jeans** [dʒins] *nm* jeans (*pl*), pair of jeans.

Jeep® [dʒip] *nf* Jeep®.

jerrycan, jerricane [ʒerikan] *nm* jerry can.

jersey [ʒɛrzɛ] *nm* jersey.

jésuite [ʒezɥit] *nm* Jesuit.

Jésus-Christ [ʒezykri] *nm* Jesus Christ.

jet¹ [ʒɛ] *nm* [action de jeter] throw. || [de liquide] jet.

jet² [dʒɛt] *nm* [avion] jet.

jetable [ʒətabl] *adj* disposable.

jetée [ʒəte] *nf* jetty.

jeter [ʒəte] *vt* to throw; [se débarrasser de] to throw away; ~ **qqch à qqn** to throw sthg to sb, to throw sb sthg; [pour faire mal] to throw sthg at sb. ○ **se jeter** *vp*: **se ~ sur** to pounce on; **se ~ dans** [suj: rivière] to flow into.

jeton [ʒətɔ̃] *nm* [de jeu] counter; [de téléphone] token.

jeu, -x [ʒø] *nm* [divertissement] play (*U*), playing (*U*); ~ **de mots** play on words, pun. || [régi par des règles] game; ~ **de société** parlour game. || [d'argent]: **le ~**

gambling. || [d'échecs, de clés] set; ~ **de cartes** pack of cards. || [manière de jouer - MUS] playing; [- THÉÂTRE] acting; [- SPORT] game. || [TECHNOL] play. || *loc:* **cacher son ~** to play one's cards close to one's chest. ○ **Jeux Olympiques** *nmpl:* **les Jeux Olympiques** the Olympic Games.

jeudi [ʒødi] *nm* Thursday; *voir aussi* **samedi**.

jeun [ʒœ̃] ○ **à jeun** *loc adv* on an empty stomach.

jeune [ʒœn] **1** *adj* young; [style, apparence] youthful; ~ **homme/femme** young man/woman. **2** *nm* young person; **les ~s** young people.

jeûne [ʒøn] *nm* fast.

jeunesse [ʒœnɛs] *nf* [âge] youth; [de style, apparence] youthfulness. || [jeunes gens] young people (*pl*).

JO *nmpl* (*abr de* **Jeux Olympiques**) Olympic Games.

joaillier, -ière [ʒɔaje, jɛr] *nm, f* jeweller.

job [dʒɔb] *nm fam* job.

jockey [ʒɔkɛ] *nm* jockey.

jogging [dʒɔgiŋ] *nm* [activité] jogging. || [vêtement] tracksuit, jogging suit.

joie [ʒwa] *nf* joy.

joindre [ʒwɛ̃dr] *vt* [rapprocher] to join; [mains] to put together. || [ajouter]: ~ **qqch (à)** to attach sthg (to); [adjoindre] to enclose sthg (with). || [par téléphone] to contact, to reach. ○ **se joindre** *vp:* **se ~ à qqn** to join sb; **se ~ à qqch** to join in sthg.

joint, -e [ʒwɛ̃, ɛ̃t] *pp* → **joindre**. ○ **joint** *nm* [d'étanchéité] seal. || *fam* [drogue] joint.

joli, -e [ʒɔli] *adj* [femme, chose] pretty, attractive. || [somme, situation] nice.

joliment [ʒɔlimɑ̃] *adv* [bien] prettily, attractively; *iron* nicely. || *fam* [beaucoup] really.

jonc [ʒɔ̃] *nm* rush, bulrush.

joncher [ʒɔ̃ʃe] *vt* to strew; **être jonché de** to be strewn with.

jonction [ʒɔ̃ksjɔ̃] *nf* [de routes] junction.

jongler [ʒɔ̃gle] *vi* to juggle.

jongleur, -euse [ʒɔ̃glœr, øz] *nm, f* juggler.

jonquille [ʒɔ̃kij] *nf* daffodil.

Jordanie [ʒɔrdani] *nf:* **la ~** Jordan.

joue [ʒu] *nf* cheek; **tenir** OU **mettre qqn en ~** *fig* to take aim at sb.

jouer [ʒwe] **1** *vi* [gén] to play; ~ **à qqch** [jeu, sport] to play sthg; ~ **de** MUS to play. || CIN & THÉÂTRE to act. || [parier] to gamble. **2** *vt* [carte, partie] to play. || [somme d'argent] to bet, to wager; *fig* to gamble with. || [THÉÂTRE - personnage, rôle] to play; [- pièce] to put on, to perform. || CIN to show. || MUS to perform, to play.

jouet [ʒwe] *nm* toy.

joueur, -euse [ʒwœr, øz] *nm, f* SPORT player; ~ **de football** footballer, football player. || [au casino] gambler.

joufflu, -e [ʒufly] *adj* [personne] chubby-cheeked.

joug [ʒu] *nm* yoke.

jouir [ʒwir] *vi* [profiter]: ~ **de** to enjoy. || [sexuellement] to have an orgasm.

jouissance [ʒwisɑ̃s] *nf* JUR [d'un bien] use. || [sexuelle] orgasm.

joujou, -x [ʒuʒu] *nm* toy.

jour [ʒur] *nm* [unité de temps] day; **huit ~s** a week; **quinze ~s** a fortnight *Br*, two weeks; **de ~ en ~** day by day; **au ~ le ~** from day to day; **le ~ de l'an** New Year's Day; ~ **de congé** day off; ~ **férié** public holiday; ~ **ouvrable** working day. || [lumière] daylight; **de ~** in the daytime, by day. || *loc:* **mettre qqch à ~** to update sthg, to bring sthg up to date; **de nos ~s** these days, nowadays.

journal, -aux [ʒurnal, o] *nm* [publication] newspaper, paper. || TÉLÉ: ~ **télévisé** television news. || [écrit]: ~ **(intime)** diary, journal.

journalier, -ière [ʒurnalje, jɛr] *adj* daily.

journalisme [ʒurnalism] *nm* journalism.

journaliste [ʒurnalist] *nmf* journalist, reporter.

journée [ʒurne] *nf* day.

joute [ʒut] *nf* joust; *fig* duel.

jovial, -e, -iaux [ʒɔvjal, jo] *adj* jovial, jolly.

joyau, -x [ʒwajo] *nm* jewel.

joyeux, -euse [ʒwajø, øz] *adj* joyful, happy; ~ **Noël!** Merry Christmas!

jubiler [ʒybile] *vi fam* to be jubilant.

jucher [ʒyʃe] *vt:* ~ **qqn sur qqch** to perch sb on sthg.

judaïque [ʒydaik] *adj* [loi] Judaic; [tradition, religion] Jewish.

judaïsme [ʒydaism] *nm* Judaism.

judas [ʒyda] *nm* [ouverture] peephole.

judiciaire [ʒydisjɛr] *adj* judicial.

judicieux, -ieuse [ʒydisjø, jøz] *adj* judicious.

judo [ʒydo] *nm* judo.

juge [ʒyʒ] *nm* judge; ~ **d'instruction** examining magistrate.

jugé [ʒyʒe] ○ **au jugé** *loc adv* by guesswork; **tirer au ~ to** fire blind.

jugement [ʒyʒmɑ̃] *nm* judgment.

jugeote [ʒyʒɔt] *nf fam* common sense.

juger [ʒyʒe] **1** *vt* to judge; [accusé] to try; ~ **que** to judge (that), to consider (that); ~ **qqn/qqch inutile** to consider sb/sthg useless. **2** *vi* to judge; ~ **de qqch** to judge sthg; **si j'en juge d'après mon expérience** judging from my experience.

juif, -ive [ʒɥif, iv] *adj* Jewish. ○ **Juif, -ive** *nm, f* Jew.

juillet [ʒɥije] *nm* July; **la fête du 14 Juillet** *national holiday to mark the anniversary of the storming of the Bastille*; *voir aussi* **septembre**.

juin [ʒɥɛ̃] *nm* June; *voir aussi* **septembre**.

juke-box [dʒukbɔks] *nm inv* jukebox.

jumeau, -elle, -x [ʒymo, ɛl, o] **1** *adj* twin (*avant n*). **2** *nm, f* twin. ○ **jumelles** *nfpl* OPTIQUE binoculars.

jumelé, -e [ʒymle] *adj* [villes] twinned; [maisons] semidetached.

jumeler [ʒymle] *vt* to twin.

jumelle → **jumeau**.

jument [ʒymɑ̃] *nf* mare.

jungle [ʒœ̃gl] *nf* jungle.

junior [ʒynjɔr] *adj & nmf* SPORT junior.

junte [ʒœ̃t] *nf* junta.

jupe [ʒyp] *nf* skirt.

jupe-culotte [ʒypkylɔt] *nf* culottes (*pl*).

jupon [ʒypɔ̃] *nm* petticoat, slip.

juré [ʒyre] *nm* JUR juror.

jurer [ʒyre] **1** *vt*: ~ **qqch à qqn** to swear OU pledge sthg to sb; ~ (**à qqn**) **que ...** to swear (to sb) that ...; ~ **de faire qqch** to swear OU vow to do sthg. **2** *vi* [blasphémer] to swear, to curse. || [ne pas aller ensemble]: ~ (**avec**) to clash (with).

juridiction [ʒyridiksjɔ̃] *nf* jurisdiction.

juridique [ʒyridik] *adj* legal.

jurisprudence [ʒyrisprydɑ̃s] *nf* jurisprudence.

juriste [ʒyrist] *nmf* lawyer.

juron [ʒyrɔ̃] *nm* swearword, oath.

jury [ʒyri] *nm* JUR jury. || [SCOL - d'examen] examining board; [- de concours] admissions board.

jus [ʒy] *nm* [de fruits, légumes] juice. || [de viande] gravy.

jusque, jusqu' [ʒysk(ə)] ○ **jusqu'à** *loc prép* [sens temporel] until, till; **jusqu'à** présent up until now, so far. || [sens spatial] as far as; **jusqu'au bout** to the end. || [même] even. ○ **jusqu'à ce que** *loc conj* until, till. ○ **jusqu'en** *loc prép* up until. ○ **jusqu'ici** *loc adv* [lieu] up to here; [temps] up until now, so far. ○ **jusque-là** *loc adv* [lieu] up to there; [temps] up until then.

justaucorps [ʒystokɔr] *nm* [maillot] leotard.

juste [ʒyst] **1** *adj* [équitable] fair. || [exact] right, correct. || [trop petit] tight. **2** *adv* [bien] correctly, right. || [exactement, seulement] just.

justement [ʒystəmɑ̃] *adv* [avec raison] rightly. || [précisément] exactly, precisely.

justesse [ʒystɛs] *nf* [de remarque] aptness; [de raisonnement] soundness. ○ **de justesse** *loc adv* only just.

justice [ʒystis] *nf* JUR justice; **passer en** ~ to stand trial. || [équité] fairness.

justicier, -ère [ʒystisje, jɛr] *nm, f* righter of wrongs.

justifiable [ʒystifjabl] *adj* justifiable.

justificatif, -ive [ʒystifikatif, iv] *adj* supporting. ○ **justificatif** *nm* written proof (*U*).

justification [ʒystifikasjɔ̃] *nf* justification.

justifier [ʒystifje] *vt* [gén] to justify. ○ **se justifier** *vp* to justify o.s.

jute [ʒyt] *nm* jute.

juteux, -euse [ʒytø, øz] *adj* juicy.

juvénile [ʒyvenil] *adj* youthful.

juxtaposer [ʒykstapoze] *vt* to juxtapose.

k, K [ka] *nm inv* k, K.

K7 [kasɛt] (*abr de* **cassette**) *nf* cassette.

kaki [kaki] **1** *nm* [couleur] khaki. || [fruit] persimmon. **2** *adj inv* khaki.

kaléidoscope [kaleidɔskɔp] *nm* kaleidoscope.

kamikaze [kamikaz] *nm* kamikaze pilot.

kangourou [kãguru] *nm* kangaroo.

karaoké [karaɔke] *nm* karaoke.

karaté [karate] *nm* karate.

karting [kartiŋ] *nm* go-karting.

kas(c)her, cascher [kaʃɛr] *adj inv* kosher.

kayak [kajak] *nm* kayak.

Kenya [kenja] *nm*: le ~ Kenya.

képi [kepi] *nm* kepi.

kermesse [kɛrmɛs] *nf* [foire] fair. || [fête de bienfaisance] fête.

kérosène [kerɔzɛn] *nm* kerosene.

ketchup [kɛtʃœp] *nm* ketchup.

kg (*abr de* **kilogramme**) kg.

kibboutz [kibutz] *nm inv* kibbutz.

kidnapper [kidnape] *vt* to kidnap.

kidnappeur, -euse [kidnapœr, øz] *nm, f* kidnapper.

kilo [kilo] *nm* kilo.

kilogramme [kilɔgram] *nm* kilogram.

kilométrage [kilɔmetraʒ] *nm* [de voiture] ≃ mileage. || [distance] distance.

kilomètre [kilɔmɛtr] *nm* kilometre.

kilo-octet [kilɔɔktɛ] *nm* INFORM kilobyte.

kilowatt [kilɔwat] *nm* kilowatt.

kilt [kilt] *nm* kilt.

kimono [kimɔno] *nm* kimono.

kinésithérapeute [kineziterapøt] *nmf* physiotherapist.

kiosque [kjɔsk] *nm* [de vente] kiosk. || [pavillon] pavilion.

kirsch [kirʃ] *nm* cherry brandy.

kitchenette [kitʃɔnɛt] *nf* kitchenette.

kitsch [kitʃ] *adj inv* kitsch.

kiwi [kiwi] *nm* [oiseau] kiwi. || [fruit] kiwi, kiwi fruit (*U*).

Klaxon® [klaksɔ̃] *nm* horn.

klaxonner [klaksɔne] *vi* to hoot.

kleptomane, cleptomane [klɛptɔman] *nmf* kleptomaniac.

km (*abr de* **kilomètre**) km.

km/h (*abr de* **kilomètre par heure**) kph.

Ko (*abr de* **kilo-octet**) K.

K.-O. [kao] *nm*: mettre qqn ~ to knock sb out.

Koweït [kɔwɛt] *nm*: le ~ Kuwait.

krach [krak] *nm* crash; ~ **boursier** stock market crash.

kurde [kyrd] **1** *adj* Kurdish. **2** *nm* [langue] Kurdish. ○ **Kurde** *nmf* Kurd.

kyrielle [kirjɛl] *nf fam* stream.

kyste [kist] *nm* cyst.

l, L [ɛl] **1** *nm inv* l, L. **2** (*abr de* **litre**) l.

la¹ [la] *art déf & pron déf*→ **le**.

la² [la] *nm inv* MUS A; [chanté] la.

là [la] *adv* [lieu] there; **passe par ~** go that way; **c'est ~ que je travaille** that's where I work; **je suis ~** I'm here. || [temps] then; **à quelques jours de ~** a few days later, a few days after that. || [avec une proposition relative]: **~ où** [lieu] where; [temps] when; *voir aussi* **ce, là-bas, là-dedans** *etc.*

là-bas [laba] *adv* (over) there.

label [label] *nm* [étiquette]: ~ **de qualité** label guaranteeing quality. || [commerce] label, brand name.

labeur [labœr] *nm sout* labour.

labo [labo] (*abr de* **laboratoire**) *nm fam* lab.

laborantin, -e [labɔrãtɛ̃, in] *nm, f* laboratory assistant.

laboratoire [labɔratwar] *nm* laboratory.

laborieux, -ieuse [labɔrjø, jøz] *adj* [difficile] laborious.

labourer [labure] *vt* AGRIC to plough.

laboureur [laburœr] *nm* ploughman.

labyrinthe [labirɛ̃t] *nm* labyrinth.

lac [lak] *nm* lake; **les Grands Lacs** the Great Lakes; **le ~ Léman** Lake Geneva.

lacer [lase] *vt* to tie.

lacérer [lasere] *vt* [déchirer] to shred. || [blesser, griffer] to slash.

lacet [lase] *nm* [cordon] lace. || [de route] bend. || [piège] snare.

lâche [laʃ] **1** *nmf* coward. **2** *adj* [nœud] loose. || [personne, comportement] cowardly.

lâcher [laʃe] **1** *vt* [libérer - bras, objet] to let go of; [- animal] to let go, to release; *fig* [- mot] to let slip. || [laisser tomber]: ~ qqch to drop sthg. **2** *vi* to give way.

lâcheté [laʃte] *nf* [couardise] cowardice.

laconique [lakɔnik] *adj* laconic.

lacrymogène [lakrimɔʒɛn] *adj* tear (*avant n*).

lacune [lakyn] *nf* [manque] gap.

là-dedans [ladədɑ̃] *adv* inside, in there; **il y a quelque chose qui m'intrigue ~** there's something in that which intrigues me.

là-dessous [ladsu] *adv* underneath, under there; *fig* behind that.

là-dessus [ladsy] *adv* on that; **~, il partit** at that point ou with that, he left; **je suis d'accord ~** I agree about that.

lagon [lagɔ̃] *nm*, **lagune** [lagyn] *nf* lagoon.

là-haut [lao] *adv* up there.

laïc (*f* **laïque**), **laïque** [laik] *adj* lay (*avant n*); [école] state (*avant n*).

laid, -e [lɛ, lɛd] *adj* [esthétiquement] ugly. || [moralement] wicked.

laideron [lɛdrɔ̃] *nm* ugly woman.

laideur [lɛdœr] *nf* [physique] ugliness.

lainage [lɛnaʒ] *nm* [étoffe] woollen material; [vêtement] woolly ou woollen garment.

laine [lɛn] *nf* wool.

laineux, -euse [lɛnø, øz] *adj* woolly.

laïque → **laïc**.

laisse [lɛs] *nf* [corde] lead, leash; **tenir en ~** [chien] to keep on a lead ou leash.

laisser [lese] **1** *v aux* (*+infinitif*): **~ qqn faire qqch** to let sb do sthg; **laisse-le faire** leave him alone, don't interfere; **~ tomber qqch** *litt & fig* to drop sthg. **2** *vt* [gén] to leave. || [céder]: **~ qqch à qqn** to let sb have sthg. **○ se laisser** *vp*: **se ~ faire** to let o.s. be persuaded; **se ~ aller** to relax; [dans son apparence] to let o.s. go.

laisser-aller [leseale] *nm inv* carelessness.

laissez-passer [lesepase] *nm inv* pass.

lait [lɛ] *nm* [gén] milk; **~ entier/écrémé** whole/skimmed milk; **~ concentré** ou **condensé** [sucré] condensed milk; [non sucré] evaporated milk. || [cosmétique]: **~ démaquillant** cleansing milk ou lotion.

laitage [lɛtaʒ] *nm* milk product.

laiterie [lɛtri] *nf* dairy.

laitier, -ière [letje, jɛr] **1** *adj* dairy (*avant n*). **2** *nm, f* milkman (*f* milkwoman).

laiton [lɛtɔ̃] *nm* brass.

laitue [lety] *nf* lettuce.

laïus [lajys] *nm* long speech.

lambeau, -x [lɑ̃bo] *nm* [morceau] shred.

lambris [lɑ̃bri] *nm* panelling.

lame [lam] *nf* [fer] blade; **~ de rasoir** razor blade. || [lamelle] strip. || [vague] wave.

lamé, -e [lame] *adj* lamé. **○ lamé** *nm* lamé.

lamelle [lamɛl] *nf* [de champignon] gill. || [tranche] thin slice. || [de verre] slide.

lamentable [lamɑ̃tabl] *adj* [résultats, sort] appalling. || [ton] plaintive.

lamentation [lamɑ̃tasjɔ̃] *nf* [plainte] lamentation. || (*gén pl*) [jérémiade] moaning (*U*).

lamenter [lamɑ̃te] **○ se lamenter** *vp* to complain.

laminer [lamine] *vt* IND to laminate; *fig* [personne, revenus] to eat away at.

lampadaire [lɑ̃padɛr] *nm* [dans maison] standard lamp *Br*, floor lamp *Am*; [de rue] street lamp ou light.

lampe [lɑ̃p] *nf* lamp, light; **~ de chevet** bedside lamp; **~ halogène** halogen light; **~ de poche** torch *Br*, flashlight *Am*.

lampion [lɑ̃pjɔ̃] *nm* Chinese lantern.

lance [lɑ̃s] *nf* [arme] spear. || [de tuyau] nozzle; **~ d'incendie** fire hose.

lance-flammes [lɑ̃sflam] *nm inv* flame-thrower.

lancement [lɑ̃smɑ̃] *nm* [d'entreprise, produit, navire] launching.

lance-pierres [lɑ̃spjɛr] *nm inv* catapult.

lancer [lɑ̃se] **1** *vt* [pierre, javelot] to throw; **~ qqch sur qqn** to throw sthg at sb. || [fusée, produit, style] to launch. || [cri] to let out; [injures] to hurl. || [moteur] to start up. || [INFORM - programme] to start; [- système] to boot (up). || *fig* [sur un sujet]: **~ qqn sur qqch** to get sb started on sthg. **2** *nm* PÊCHE casting. || SPORT throwing; **~ du poids** shotput. **○ se lancer** *vp* [s'engager]: **se ~ dans** [dépenses, explication, lecture] to embark on.

lancinant, -e [lãsinã, ãt] *adj* [douleur] shooting. || *fig* [obsédant] haunting.

landau [lãdo] *nm* [d'enfant] pram.

lande [lãd] *nf* moor.

langage [lãgaʒ] *nm* language.

lange [lãʒ] *nm* nappy *Br*, diaper *Am*.

langer [lãʒe] *vt* to change.

langoureux, -euse [lãgurø, øz] *adj* languorous.

langouste [lãgust] *nf* crayfish.

langoustine [lãgustin] *nf* langoustine.

langue [lãg] *nf* ANAT & *fig* tongue. || LING language; ~ **maternelle** mother tongue; ~ **morte/vivante** dead/modern language.

languette [lãgɛt] *nf* tongue.

langueur [lãgœr] *nf* [apathie] apathy.

languir [lãgir] *vi sout* [attendre] to wait; **faire ~ qqn** to keep sb waiting.

lanière [lanjɛr] *nf* strip.

lanterne [lãtɛrn] *nf* [éclairage] lantern. || [phare] light.

laper [lape] *vt & vi* to lap.

lapider [lapide] *vt* [tuer] to stone.

lapin, -e [lapɛ̃, in] *nm, f* CULIN & ZOOL rabbit. || [fourrure] rabbit fur.

laps [laps] *nm*: **(dans) un ~ de temps** (in) a while.

lapsus [lapsys] *nm* slip (of the tongue/pen).

laque [lak] *nf* [vernis, peinture] lacquer. || [pour cheveux] hair spray, lacquer.

laqué, -e [lake] *adj* lacquered.

laquelle → **lequel**.

larcin [larsɛ̃] *nm* [vol] larceny, theft.

lard [lar] *nm* [graisse de porc] lard. || [viande] bacon.

lardon [lardɔ̃] *nm* CULIN *cube or strip of bacon*. || *fam* [enfant] kid.

large [larʒ] **1** *adj* [étendu, grand] wide; ~ **de 5 mètres** 5 metres wide. || [important, considérable] large, big. || [esprit, sourire] broad. || [généreux - personne] generous. **2** *nm* [largeur]: **5 mètres de ~** 5 metres wide. || [mer]: **le ~** the open sea; **au ~ de la côte française** off the French coast.

largement [larʒəmã] *adv* [diffuser, répandre] widely. || [dépasser] considerably; [récompenser] amply; **avoir ~ le temps** to have plenty of time. || [au moins] easily.

largeur [larʒœr] *nf* [d'avenue, de cercle] width. || *fig* [d'idées, d'esprit] breadth.

larguer [large] *vt* [voile] to unfurl. || [bombe, parachutiste] to drop. || *fam fig* [abandonner] to chuck.

larme [larm] *nf* [pleur] tear; **être en ~s** to be in tears.

larmoyant, -e [larmwajã, ãt] *adj* [yeux, personne] tearful. || *péj* [histoire] tearjerking.

larve [larv] *nf* ZOOL larva. || *péj* [personne] wimp.

laryngite [larɛ̃ʒit] *nf* laryngitis (*U*).

larynx [larɛ̃ks] *nm* larynx.

las, lasse [la, las] *adj littéraire* [fatigué] weary.

lascif, -ive [lasif, iv] *adj* lascivious.

laser [lazɛr] **1** *nm* laser. **2** *adj inv* laser (*avant n*).

lasser [lase] *vt sout* [personne] to weary. ○ **se lasser** *vp* to weary.

lassitude [lasityd] *nf* lassitude.

lasso [laso] *nm* lasso.

latent, -e [latã, ãt] *adj* latent.

latéral, -e, -aux [lateral, o] *adj* lateral.

latex [latɛks] *nm inv* latex.

latin, -e [latɛ̃, in] *adj* Latin. ○ **latin** *nm* [langue] Latin.

latiniste [latinist] *nmf* [spécialiste] Latinist; [étudiant] Latin student.

latino-américain, -e [latinoamerikɛ̃, ɛn] (*mpl* **latino-américains**, *fpl* **latino-américaines**) *adj* Latin-American, Hispanic.

latitude [latityd] *nf litt* & *fig* latitude.

latrines [latrin] *nfpl* latrines.

latte [lat] *nf* lath, slat.

lauréat, -e [lɔrea, at] *nm, f* prize-winner, winner.

laurier [lɔrje] *nm* BOT laurel.

lavable [lavabl] *adj* washable.

lavabo [lavabo] *nm* [cuvette] basin. || (*gén pl*) [local] toilet.

lavage [lavaʒ] *nm* washing.

lavande [lavãd] *nf* BOT lavender.

lave [lav] *nf* lava.

lave-glace [lavglas] (*pl* **lave-glaces**) *nm* windshield washer *Am*.

lave-linge [lavlɛ̃ʒ] *nm inv* washing machine.

laver [lave] *vt* [nettoyer] to wash. || *fig* [disculper]: ~ **qqn de qqch** to clear sb of sthg. ○ **se laver** *vp* [se nettoyer] to wash o.s., to have a wash; **se ~ les mains/les cheveux** to wash one's hands/hair.

laverie [lavri] *nf* [commerce] laundry; ~ **automatique** launderette.

lavette [lavɛt] *nf* [en tissu] dishcloth. || *fam* [homme] drip.

laveur, -euse [lavœr, øz] *nm, f* washer; ~ **de carreaux** window cleaner (*person*).

lave-vaisselle [lavvɛsɛl] *nm inv* dishwasher.

lavoir [lavwar] *nm* [lieu] laundry.

laxatif, -ive [laksatif, iv] *adj* laxative. ○ **laxatif** *nm* laxative.

laxisme [laksism] *nm* laxity.

laxiste [laksist] *adj* lax.

layette [lεjεt] *nf* layette.

le [lə], **l'** *(devant voyelle ou h muet)* (*f* **la** [la], *pl* **les** [lε]) **1** *art déf* [gén] the. || [devant les noms abstraits]: **l'amour** love; **la liberté** freedom. || [temps]: **~ 15 janvier 1993** 15th January 1993; **je suis arrivé ~ 15 janvier 1993** I arrived on the 15th of January 1993; **~ lundi** [habituellement] on Mondays; [jour précis] on (the) Monday. || [possession]: **se laver les mains to** wash one's hands; **avoir les cheveux blonds** to have fair hair. || [distributif] per, a; **10 francs ~ mètre** 10 francs per ou a metre. **2** *pron pers* [personne] him (*f* her), (*pl*) them; [chose] it, (*pl*) them; [animal] it, him (*f* her), (*pl*) them; **tu dois avoir la clé, donne-la moi** you must have the key, give it to me. || [représente une proposition]: **je ~ sais bien** I know, I'm well aware (of it).

LEA (*abr de* **langues étrangères appliquées**) *nfpl* applied modern languages.

leader [lidœr] *nm* [de parti, course] leader.

lécher [leʃe] *vt* [passer la langue sur, effleurer] to lick; [suj: vague] to wash against. || *fam* [fignoler] to polish (up).

lèche-vitrines [lεʃvitrin] *nm inv* window-shopping; **faire du ~** to go window-shopping.

leçon [ləsɔ̃] *nf* [gén] lesson; **~s de conduite** driving lessons; **~s particulières** private lessons ou classes. || [conseil] advice (*U*); **faire la ~ à qqn** to lecture sb.

lecteur, -trice [lεktœr, tris] *nm, f* [de livres] reader. || UNIV foreign language assistant. ○ **lecteur** *nm* [gén] head; **~ de cassettes/CD** cassette/CD player. || INFORM reader.

lecture [lεktyr] *nf* reading.

légal, -e, -aux [legal, o] *adj* legal.

légalement [legalmɑ̃] *adv* legally.

légaliser [legalize] *vt* [rendre légal] to legalize.

légalité [legalite] *nf* [de contrat, d'acte] legality, lawfulness. || [loi] law.

légataire [legater] *nmf* legatee.

légendaire [leʒɑ̃dεr] *adj* legendary.

légende [leʒɑ̃d] *nf* [fable] legend. || [de carte, de schéma] key; [de photo] caption.

léger, -ère [leʒe, εr] *adj* [objet, étoffe, repas] light. || [bruit, différence, odeur] slight. || [alcool, tabac] low-strength. ||

[insouciant - ton] light-hearted; [- conduite] thoughtless. ○ **à la légère** *loc adv* lightly, thoughtlessly.

légèrement [leʒεrmɑ̃] *adv* [s'habiller, poser] lightly. || [agir] thoughtlessly. || [blesser, remuer] slightly.

légèreté [leʒεrte] *nf* [d'objet, de repas, de punition] lightness. || [de style] gracefulness. || [de conduite] thoughtlessness.

légiférer [leʒifere] *vi* to legislate.

légion [leʒjɔ̃] *nf* MIL legion.

légionnaire [leʒjɔnεr] *nm* legionary.

législatif, -ive [leʒislatif, iv] *adj* legislative. ○ **législatives** *nfpl*: **les législatives** the legislative elections.

législation [leʒislasjɔ̃] *nf* legislation.

légiste [leʒist] *adj* [juriste] jurist. || → **médecin**.

légitime [leʒitim] *adj* legitimate.

légitimer [leʒitime] *vt* [reconnaître] to recognize; [enfant] to legitimize. || [justifier] to justify.

legs [lεg] *nm* legacy.

léguer [lege] *vt*: **~ qqch à qqn** JUR to bequeath sthg to sb; *fig* to pass sthg on to sb.

légume [legym] *nm* vegetable.

leitmotiv [lajtmɔtif, lεtmɔtif] *nm* leitmotif.

Léman [lemɑ̃] → **lac**.

lendemain [lɑ̃dmε̃] *nm* [jour] day after; **le ~ matin** the next morning; **au ~ de** after, in the days following.

lent, -e [lɑ̃, lɑ̃t] *adj* slow.

lente [lɑ̃t] *nf* nit.

lentement [lɑ̃tmɑ̃] *adv* slowly.

lenteur [lɑ̃tœr] *nf* slowness (*U*).

lentille [lɑ̃tij] *nf* BOT & CULIN lentil. || [d'optique] lens; **~s de contact** contact lenses.

léopard [leɔpar] *nm* leopard.

LEP, Lep (*abr de* **lycée d'enseignement professionnel**) *nm* former secondary school for vocational training.

lèpre [lεpr] *nf* MÉD leprosy.

lequel [ləkεl] (*f* **laquelle** [lakεl], *mpl* **lesquels** [lekεl], *fpl* **lesquelles** [lekεl]) (*contraction de* **à** + **lequel** = **auquel, de** + **lequel** = **duquel, à** + **lesquels/ lesquelles** = **auxquels/auxquelles, de** + **lesquels/lesquelles** = **desquels/desquelles**) **1** *pron rel* [complément - personne] whom; [- chose] which. || [sujet - personne] who; [- chose] which. **2** *pron interr*: **~?** which (one)?

les → **le**.

lesbienne [lεsbjεn] *nf* lesbian.

léser [leze] *vt* [frustrer] to wrong.

lésiner [lezine] *vi* to skimp; **ne pas ~ sur** not to skimp on.

lésion [lezjɔ̃] *nf* lesion.

lesquels, lesquelles → lequel.

lessive [lesiv] *nf* [nettoyage, linge] washing. || [produit] washing powder.

lest [lest] *nm* ballast.

leste [lest] *adj* [agile] nimble, agile. || [licencieux] crude.

lester [leste] *vt* [garnir de lest] to ballast.

léthargie [letaʒi] *nf litt & fig* lethargy.

Lettonie [lɛtɔni] *nf* : **la ~** Latvia.

lettre [lɛtr] *nf* [gén] letter; **en toutes ~s** in words, in full. || [sens des mots]: **à la ~** to the letter. ○ **lettres** *nfpl* [culture littéraire] letters. || UNIV arts; **~s classiques** classics; **~s modernes** French language and literature.

leucémie [løsemi] *nf* leukemia.

leur [lœr] *pron pers inv* (to) them; **je voudrais ~ parler** I'd like to speak to them; **je ~ ai donné la lettre** I gave them the letter, I gave the letter to them. ○ **leur** (*pl* **leurs**) *adj poss* their. ○ **le leur** (*f* **la leur,** *pl* **les leurs**) *pron poss* theirs.

leurrer [lœre] *vt* to deceive. ○ **se leurrer** *vp* to deceive o.s.

levain [ləvɛ̃] *nm* CULIN: **pain au ~/sans ~** leavened/unleavened bread.

levant [ləvɑ̃] **1** *nm* east. **2** *adj* → soleil.

lever [ləve] **1** *vt* [objet, blocus, interdiction] to lift. || [main, tête, armée] to raise. || [séance] to close, to end. || [enfant, malade]: **~ qqn** to get sb up. **2** *vi* [pâte] to rise. **3** *nm* [d'astre] rising, rise; **~ du jour** daybreak; **~ du soleil** sunrise. || [de personne]: **il est toujours de mauvaise humeur au ~** he's always in a bad mood when he gets up. ○ **se lever** *vp* [personne] to get up, to rise; [vent] to get up. || [soleil, lune] to rise; [jour] to break. || [temps] to clear.

lève-tard [lɛvtar] *nmf inv* late riser.

lève-tôt [lɛvto] *nmf inv* early riser.

levier [ləvje] *nm litt & fig* lever; **~ de vitesses** gear lever *Br*, gear shift *Am*.

lévitation [levitasjɔ̃] *nf* levitation.

lèvre [lɛvr] *nf* ANAT lip; [de vulve] labium.

lévrier, levrette [levrije, ləvrɛt] *nm, f* greyhound.

levure [ləvyr] *nf* yeast; **~ chimique** baking powder.

lexique [lɛksik] *nm* [dictionnaire] glossary. || [vocabulaire] vocabulary.

lézard [lezar] *nm* [animal] lizard.

lézarder [lezarde] **1** *vt* to crack. **2** *vi fam* [paresser] to bask. ○ **se lézarder** *vp* to crack.

liaison [ljezɔ̃] *nf* [jonction, enchaînement] connection. || CULIN & LING liaison. || [contact, relation] contact; **avoir une ~** to have an affair. || TRANSPORT link.

liane [ljan] *nf* creeper.

liant, -e [ljɑ̃, ɑ̃t] *adj* sociable. ○ **liant** *nm* [substance] binder.

liasse [ljas] *nf* bundle; [de billets de banque] wad.

Liban [libɑ̃] *nm* : **le ~** Lebanon.

libanais, -e [libanɛ, ɛz] *adj* Lebanese. ○ **Libanais, -e** *nm, f* Lebanese (person); **les Libanais** the Lebanese.

libeller [libele] *vt* [chèque] to make out. || [lettre] to word.

libellule [libelyl] *nf* dragonfly.

libéral, -e, -aux [liberal, o] **1** *adj* [attitude, idée, parti] liberal. **2** *nm, f* POLIT liberal.

libéraliser [liberalize] *vt* to liberalize.

libéralisme [liberalism] *nm* liberalism.

libération [liberasjɔ̃] *nf* [de prisonnier] release, freeing. || [de pays, de la femme] liberation. || [d'énergie] release.

libérer [libere] *vt* [prisonnier, fonds] to release, to free. || [pays, la femme] to liberate; **~ qqn de qqch** to free sb from sthg. || [passage] to clear. || [énergie] to release. ○ **se libérer** *vp* [se rendre disponible] to get away. || [se dégager]: **se ~ de** [lien] to free o.s. from; [engagement] to get out of.

liberté [liberte] *nf* [gén] freedom; **en ~** free; **parler en toute ~** to speak freely; **~ d'expression** freedom of expression; **~ d'opinion** freedom of thought. || JUR release. || [loisir] free time.

libertin, -e [libertɛ̃, in] *nm, f* libertine.

libidineux, -euse [libidinø, øz] *adj* lecherous.

libido [libido] *nf* libido.

libraire [librɛr] *nmf* bookseller.

librairie [libreri] *nf* [magasin] bookshop.

libre [libr] *adj* [gén] free; **~ de qqch** free from sthg; **être ~ de faire qqch** to be free to do sthg. || [école, secteur] private. || [passage] clear.

libre-échange [libreʃɑ̃ʒ] *nm* free trade (*U*).

librement [librəmɑ̃] *adv* freely.

libre-service [librəsɛrvis] *nm* [maga-

limpide

sin] self-service store ou shop; [restaurant] self-service restaurant.

Libye [libi] *nf*: la ~ Libya.

libyen, -yenne [libjɛ̃, jɛn] *adj* Libyan. ○ **Libyen, -yenne** *nm, f* Libyan.

licence [lisɑ̃s] *nf* [permis] permit; COMM licence. || UNIV (first) degree; ~ **ès lettres/en droit** ≃ Bachelor of Arts/Law degree. || *littéraire* [liberté] licence.

licencié, -e [lisɑ̃sje] **1** *adj* UNIV graduate (*avant n*). **2** *nm, f* UNIV graduate.

licenciement [lisɑ̃simɑ̃] *nm* dismissal; [économique] layoff.

licencier [lisɑ̃sje] *vt* to dismiss; [pour cause économique] to lay off.

lichen [likɛn] *nm* lichen.

licite [lisit] *adj* lawful, legal.

licorne [likɔrn] *nf* unicorn.

lie [li] *nf* [dépôt] dregs (*pl*), sediment. ○ **lie-de-vin** *adj inv* burgundy, wine-coloured.

lié, -e [lje] *adj* [mains] bound. || [amis]: **être très ~ avec** to be great friends with.

liège [ljɛʒ] *nm* cork.

lien [ljɛ̃] *nm* [sangle] bond. || [relation, affinité] bond, tie; **avoir des ~s de parenté avec** to be related to. || *fig* [enchaînement] connection, link.

lier [lje] *vt* [attacher] to tie (up); ~ **qqn/qqch à** to tie sb/sthg to. || [suj: contrat, promesse] to bind. || [relier par la logique] to link, to connect; ~ **qqch à** to link sthg to, to connect sthg with. || [commencer]: ~ **connaissance/conversation avec** to strike up an acquaintance/a conversation with. || [suj: sentiment, intérêt] to unite. || CULIN to thicken. ○ **se lier** *vp* [s'attacher]: **se ~ (d'amitié) avec qqn** to make friends with sb.

lierre [ljɛr] *nm* ivy.

liesse [ljɛs] *nf* jubilation.

lieu, -x [ljø] *nm* [endroit] place; **en ~ sûr** in a safe place; ~ **de naissance** birthplace. || *loc*: **avoir ~** to take place. ○ **lieux** *nmpl* [scène] scene (*sg*), spot (*sg*); **sur les ~x (d'un crime/d'un accident)** at the scene (of a crime/an accident). || [domicile] premises. ○ **lieu commun** *nm* commonplace. ○ **lieu-dit** *nm* locality, place. ○ **au lieu de** *loc prép*: **au ~ de qqch/de faire qqch** instead of sthg/of doing sthg. ○ **en dernier lieu** *loc adv* lastly. ○ **en premier lieu** *loc adv* in the first place.

lieue [ljø] *nf* league.

lieutenant [ljøtnɑ̃] *nm* lieutenant.

lièvre [ljɛvr] *nm* hare.

lifter [lifte] *vt* TENNIS to spin, to put a spin on.

lifting [liftiŋ] *nm* face-lift.

ligament [ligamɑ̃] *nm* ligament.

ligaturer [ligatyre] *vt* MÉD to ligature, to ligate.

ligne [liɲ] *nf* [gén] line; **à la** ~ new line ou paragraph; **en** ~ [personnes] in a line; ~ **de départ/d'arrivée** starting/finishing line; ~ **aérienne** airline. || [forme - de voiture, meuble] lines (*pl*). || [silhouette]: **garder la** ~ to keep one's figure; **surveiller sa** ~ to watch one's waistline. || [de pêche] fishing line; **pêcher à la** ~ to go angling. || *loc*: **dans les grandes ~s** in outline; **entrer en ~ de compte** to be taken into account.

lignée [liɲe] *nf* [famille] descendants (*pl*); **dans la** ~ **de** *fig* [d'écrivains, d'artistes] in the tradition of.

ligoter [ligɔte] *vt* [attacher] to tie up; ~ **qqn à qqch** to tie sb to sthg.

ligue [lig] *nf* league.

liguer [lige] ○ **se liguer** *vp* to form a league; **se ~ contre** to conspire against.

lilas [lila] *nm & adj inv* lilac.

limace [limas] *nf* ZOOL slug.

limaille [limaj] *nf* filings (*pl*).

limande [limɑ̃d] *nf* dab.

lime [lim] *nf* [outil] file; ~ **à ongles** nail file. || BOT lime.

limer [lime] *vt* [ongles] to file; [aspérités] to file down; [barreau] to file through.

limier [limje] *nm* [chien] bloodhound. || [détective] sleuth.

limitation [limitasjɔ̃] *nf* limitation; [de naissances] control; ~ **de vitesse** speed limit.

limite [limit] **1** *nf* [gén] limit; **à la** ~ [au pire] at worst. || [terme, échéance] deadline; ~ **d'âge** age limit. **2** *adj* [extrême] maximum (*avant n*); **cas** ~ borderline case; **date** ~ deadline; **date** ~ **de vente/consommation** sell-by/use-by date.

limiter [limite] *vt* [borner] to border, to bound. || [restreindre] to limit. ○ **se limiter** *vp* [se restreindre]: **se ~ à qqch/à faire qqch** to limit o.s. to sthg/to doing sthg. || [se borner]: **se ~ à** to be limited to.

limitrophe [limitrɔf] *adj* [frontalier] border (*avant n*). || [voisin] adjacent.

limoger [limɔʒe] *vt* to dismiss.

limon [limɔ̃] *nm* GÉOL alluvium, silt.

limonade [limɔnad] *nf* lemonade.

limpide [lɛ̃pid] *adj* [eau] limpid. || [ciel, regard] clear. || [explication, style] clear, lucid.

lin [lɛ̃] *nm* BOT flax. || [tissu] linen.

linceul [lɛ̃sœl] *nm* shroud.

linéaire [lineɛr] *adj* [mesure, perspective] linear.

linge [lɛ̃ʒ] *nm* [lessive] washing. || [de lit, de table] linen. || [sous-vêtements] underwear. || [morceau de tissu] cloth.

lingerie [lɛ̃ʒri] *nf* [local] linen room. || [sous-vêtements] lingerie.

lingot [lɛ̃go] *nm* ingot.

linguistique [lɛ̃gɥistik] **1** *nf* linguistics (*U*). **2** *adj* linguistic.

linoléum [linɔleɔm] *nm* lino, linoleum.

lion, lionne [ljɔ̃, ljɔn] *nm, f* lion (*f* lioness). ○ **Lion** *nm* ASTROL Leo.

lionceau, -x [ljɔ̃so] *nm* lion cub.

lipide [lipid] *nm* lipid.

liquéfier [likefje] *vt* to liquefy. ○ **se liquéfier** *vp* [matière] to liquefy. || *fig* [personne] to turn to jelly.

liqueur [likœr] *nf* liqueur.

liquidation [likidasjɔ̃] *nf* [de compte & BOURSE] settlement. || [de société, stock] liquidation.

liquide [likid] **1** *nm* [substance] liquid. || [argent] cash; **en ~ in** cash. **2** *adj* [corps & LING] liquid.

liquider [likide] *vt* [compte & BOURSE] to settle. || [société, stock] to liquidate. || *arg crime* [témoin] to liquidate, to eliminate; *fig* [problème] to eliminate, to get rid of.

lire[1] [lir] *vt* to read.

lire[2] [lir] *nf* lira.

lis, lys [lis] *nm* lily.

Lisbonne [lizbɔn] *n* Lisbon.

liseré [lizre], **liséré** [lizere] *nm* [ruban] binding. || [bande] border, edging.

liseron [lizrɔ̃] *nm* bindweed.

liseuse [lizøz] *nf* [vêtement] bedjacket. || [lampe] reading light.

lisible [lizibl] *adj* [écriture] legible.

lisière [lizjɛr] *nf* [limite] edge.

lisse [lis] *adj* [surface, peau] smooth.

lisser [lise] *vt* [papier, vêtements] to smooth (out). || [moustache, cheveux] to smooth (down). || [plumes] to preen.

liste [list] *nf* list; **~ d'attente** waiting list; **~ électorale** electoral roll; **~ de mariage** wedding present list; **être sur la ~ rouge** to be ex-directory.

lister [liste] *vt* to list.

listing [listiŋ] *nm* listing.

lit [li] *nm* [gén] bed; **faire son ~** to make one's bed; **garder le ~** to stay in bed; **se mettre au ~** to go to bed; **~ à baldaquin** four-poster bed; **~ de camp** camp bed.

litanie [litani] *nf* litany.

literie [litri] *nf* bedding.

lithographie [litɔgrafi] *nf* [procédé] lithography. || [image] lithograph.

litière [litjɛr] *nf* litter.

litige [litiʒ] *nm* JUR lawsuit. || [désaccord] dispute.

litigieux, -ieuse [litiʒjø, jøz] *adj* JUR litigious. || [douteux] disputed.

litre [litr] *nm* [mesure, quantité] litre. || [récipient] litre bottle.

littéraire [literɛr] *adj* literary.

littéral, -e, -aux [literal, o] *adj* [gén] literal. || [écrit] written.

littérature [literatyr] *nf* [gén] literature.

littoral, -e, -aux [litɔral, o] *adj* coastal. ○ **littoral** *nm* coast, coastline.

Lituanie [lituani] *nf*: **la ~** Lithuania.

liturgie [lityrʒi] *nf* liturgy.

livide [livid] *adj* [blême] pallid.

livraison [livrɛzɔ̃] *nf* [de marchandise] delivery; **~ à domicile** home delivery.

livre [livr] **1** *nm* [gén] book; **~ de cuisine** cookery book; **~ de poche** paperback. **2** *nf* pound; **~ sterling** pound sterling.

livrée [livre] *nf* [uniforme] livery.

livrer [livre] *vt* COMM to deliver. || [coupable, complice]: **~ qqn à qqn** to hand sb over to sb. || [abandonner]: **~ qqn à lui-même** to leave sb to his own devices. ○ **se livrer** *vp* [se rendre]: **se ~ à** [police, ennemi] to give o.s. up to. || [se confier]: **se ~ à** [ami] to open up to, to confide in. || [se consacrer]: **se ~ à** [occupation] to devote o.s. to; [excès] to indulge in.

livret [livre] *nm* [carnet] booklet; **~ de caisse d'épargne** passbook, bankbook; **~ de famille** *official family record book, given by registrar to newlyweds*; **~ scolaire** ≃ school report.

livreur, -euse [livrœr, øz] *nm, f* delivery man (*f* woman).

lobby [lɔbi] (*pl* **lobbies**) *nm* lobby.

lobe [lɔb] *nm* ANAT & BOT lobe.

lober [lɔbe] *vt* to lob.

local, -e, -aux [lɔkal, o] *adj* local; [douleur] localized. ○ **local** *nm* room, premises (*pl*). ○ **locaux** *nmpl* premises, offices.

localiser [lɔkalize] *vt* [avion, bruit] to locate. || [épidémie, conflit] to localize.

localité [lɔkalite] *nf* (small) town.

locataire [lɔkatɛr] *nmf* tenant.

location [lɔkasjɔ̃] *nf* [de propriété - par propriétaire] letting *Br*, renting *Am*; [- par locataire] renting; [de machine] leasing. || [bail] lease. || [maison, appartement] rented property.

location-vente [lɔkasjɔ̃vɑ̃t] *nf* ≃ hire purchase *Br*, ≃ installment plan *Am*.

locomotion [lɔkɔmɔsjɔ̃] *nf* locomotion.

locomotive [lɔkɔmɔtiv] *nf* [machine] locomotive. || *fig* [leader] moving force.

locution [lɔkysjɔ̃] *nf* expression, phrase.

loft [lɔft] *nm* (converted) loft.

logarithme [lɔgaritm] *nm* logarithm.

loge [lɔʒ] *nf* [de concierge, de francs-maçons] lodge. || [d'acteur] dressing room.

logement [lɔʒmɑ̃] *nm* [hébergement] accommodation. || [appartement] flat *Br*, apartment *Am*; ~ **de fonction** company flat *Br* ou apartment *Am*.

loger [lɔʒe] 1 *vi* [habiter] to live. 2 *vt* [amis, invités] to put up. || [suj: hôtel, maison] to accommodate, to take. ○ **se loger** *vp* [trouver un logement] to find accommodation. || [se placer - ballon, balle]: **se ~ dans** to lodge in, to stick in.

logiciel [lɔʒisjɛl] *nm* software (*U*); ~ **intégré** integrated software.

logique [lɔʒik] 1 *nf* logic. 2 *adj* logical.

logiquement [lɔʒikmɑ̃] *adv* logically.

logis [lɔʒi] *nm* abode.

logistique [lɔʒistik] *nf* logistics (*pl*).

logo [logo] *nm* logo.

loi [lwa] *nf* [gén] law.

loin [lwɛ̃] *adv* [dans l'espace] far; **plus ~** further. || [dans le temps - passé] a long time ago; [- futur] a long way off. ○ **au loin** *loc adv* in the distance, far off. ○ **de loin** *loc adv* [depuis une grande distance] from a distance. ○ **loin de** *loc prép* [gén] far from; ~ **de là!** *fig* far from it! || [dans le temps]: **il n'est pas ~ de 9 h** it's nearly 9 o'clock, it's not far off 9 o'clock.

lointain, -e [lwɛ̃tɛ̃, ɛn] *adj* [pays, avenir, parent] distant.

loir [lwar] *nm* dormouse.

loisir [lwazir] *nm* [temps libre] leisure. || (*gén pl*) [distractions] leisure activities (*pl*).

londonien, -ienne [lɔ̃dɔnjɛ̃, jɛn] *adj* London (*avant n*). ○ **Londonien, -ienne** *nm, f* Londoner.

Londres [lɔ̃dr] *n* London.

long, longue [lɔ̃, lɔ̃g] *adj* [gén] long. || [lent] slow; **être ~ à faire qqch** to take a long time doing sth. ○ **long 1** *nm* [longueur]: **4 mètres de ~** 4 metres long ou in length; **de ~ en large** up and down, to

and fro; **en ~ et en large** in great detail; **(tout) le ~ de** [espace] all along; **tout au ~ de** [année, carrière] throughout. **2** *adv* [beaucoup]: **en savoir ~ sur qqch** to know a lot about sth. ○ **à la longue** *loc adv* in the end.

longe [lɔ̃ʒ] *nf* [courroie] halter.

longer [lɔ̃ʒe] *vt* [border] to go along ou alongside. || [marcher le long de] to walk along; [raser] to stay close to, to hug.

longévité [lɔ̃ʒevite] *nf* longevity.

longiligne [lɔ̃ʒiliɲ] *adj* long-limbed.

longitude [lɔ̃ʒityd] *nf* longitude.

longtemps [lɔ̃tɑ̃] *adv* (for) a long time; **depuis ~** (for) a long time; **il y a ~ qu'il est là** he's been here a long time; **mettre ~ à faire qqch** to take a long time to do sth.

longue → **long**.

longuement [lɔ̃gmɑ̃] *adv* [longtemps] for a long time. || [en détail] at length.

longueur [lɔ̃gœr] *nf* length; **faire 5 mètres de ~** to be 5 metres long; **à ~ de journée/temps** the entire day/time. ○ **longueurs** *nfpl* [de film, de livre] boring parts.

longue-vue [lɔ̃gvy] *nf* telescope.

look [luk] *nm* look.

looping [lupiŋ] *nm* loop the loop.

lopin [lɔpɛ̃] *nm*: ~ **(de terre)** patch ou plot of land.

loquace [lɔkas] *adj* loquacious.

loque [lɔk] *nf* [lambeau] rag. || *fig* [personne] wreck.

loquet [lɔkɛ] *nm* latch.

lorgner [lɔrɲe] *vt fam* [observer] to eye. || [guigner] to have one's eye on.

lors [lɔr] *adv*: **depuis ~** since that time; ~ **de** at the time of.

lorsque [lɔrsk(ə)] *conj* when.

losange [lɔzɑ̃ʒ] *nm* lozenge.

lot [lo] *nm* [part] share; [de terre] plot. || [stock] batch. || [prix] prize. || *fig* [destin] fate, lot.

loterie [lɔtri] *nf* lottery.

loti, -e [lɔti] *adj*: **être bien/mal ~** to be well/badly off.

lotion [lɔsjɔ̃] *nf* lotion.

lotir [lɔtir] *vt* to divide up.

lotissement [lɔtismɑ̃] *nm* [terrain] plot.

loto [lɔto] *nm* [jeu de société] lotto. || [loterie] *popular national lottery*.

lotte [lɔt] *nf* monkfish.

lotus [lɔtys] *nm* lotus.

louange [lwɑ̃ʒ] *nf* praise.

louche¹ [luʃ] *nf* ladle.

louche² [luʃ] *adj fam* [personne, histoire] suspicious.

loucher [luʃe] *vi* [être atteint de strabisme] to squint. || *fam fig* [lorgner]: ~ **sur** to have one's eye on.

louer [lwe] *vt* [glorifier] to praise. || [donner en location] to rent (out); **à ~ for** rent. || [prendre en location] to rent. || [réserver] to book. ○ **se louer** *vp sout* [se féliciter]: **se ~ de qqch/de faire qqch** to be very pleased about sthg/about doing sthg.

loufoque [lufɔk] *fam adj* nuts, crazy.

loup [lu] *nm* [carnassier] wolf. || [poisson] bass. || [masque] mask.

loupe [lup] *nf* [optique] magnifying glass.

louper [lupe] *vt fam* [travail] to make a mess of; [train] to miss.

loup-garou [lugaru] (*pl* **loups-garous**) *nm* werewolf.

lourd, -e [lur, lurd] *adj* [gén] heavy; ~ **de** *fig* full of. || [tâche] difficult; [faute] serious. || MÉTÉOR close. ○ **lourd** *adv*: **peser ~** to be heavy, to weigh a lot; **il n'en fait pas ~** *fam* he doesn't do much.

loutre [lutr] *nf* otter.

louve [luv] *nf* she-wolf.

louveteau, -x [luvto] *nm* ZOOL wolf cub. || [scout] cub.

louvoyer [luvwaje] *vi* NAVIG to tack. || *fig* [tergiverser] to beat about the bush.

Louvre [luvr] *n*: **le ~** the Louvre (museum).

lover [lɔve] ○ **se lover** *vp* [serpent] to coil up.

loyal, -e, -aux [lwajal, o] *adj* [fidèle] loyal. || [honnête] fair.

loyauté [lwajote] *nf* [fidélité] loyalty. || [honnêteté] fairness.

loyer [lwaje] *nm* rent.

LP (*abr de* **lycée professionnel**) *nm* secondary school for vocational training.

lu, -e [ly] *pp* → **lire**.

lubie [lybi] *nf fam* whim.

lubrifier [lybrifje] *vt* to lubricate.

lubrique [lybrik] *adj* lewd.

lucarne [lykarn] *nf* [fenêtre] skylight. || FOOTBALL top corner of the net.

lucide [lysid] *adj* lucid.

lucidité [lysidite] *nf* lucidity.

lucratif, -ive [lykratif, iv] *adj* lucrative.

ludique [lydik] *adj* play (*avant n*).

ludothèque [lydɔtɛk] *nf* toy library.

lueur [lɥœr] *nf* [de bougie, d'étoile] light; **à la ~ de** by the light of. || *fig* [de colère]

gleam; [de raison] spark; ~ **d'espoir** glimmer of hope.

luge [lyʒ] *nf* toboggan.

lugubre [lygybr] *adj* lugubrious.

lui¹ [lɥi] *pp inv* → **luire**.

lui² [lɥi] *pron pers* [complément d'objet indirect - homme] (to) him; [- femme] (to) her; [- animal, chose] (to) it; **je ~ ai parlé** I've spoken to him/to her; **il ~ a serré la main** he shook his/her hand. || [sujet, en renforcement de «il»] he. || [objet, après préposition, comparatif - personne] him; [- animal, chose] it; **elle est plus jeune que ~** she's younger than him OU than he is. || [remplaçant «soi» en fonction de pronom réfléchi - personne] himself; [- animal, chose] itself; **il est content de ~** he's pleased with himself. ○ **lui-même** *pron pers* [personne] himself; [animal, chose] itself.

luire [lɥir] *vi* [soleil, métal] to shine; *fig* [espoir] to glow, to glimmer.

luisant, -e [lɥizɑ̃, ɑ̃t] *adj* gleaming.

lumière [lymjɛr] *nf* [éclairage & *fig*] light.

lumineux, -euse [lyminø, øz] *adj* [couleur, cadran] luminous. || *fig* [visage] radiant; [idée] brilliant. || [explication] clear.

luminosité [lyminozite] *nf* [du regard, ciel] radiance. || PHYS & SCIENCE luminosity.

lump [lœp] *nm*: **œufs de ~** lumpfish roe.

lunaire [lynɛr] *adj* ASTRON lunar. || *fig* [visage] moon (*avant n*); [paysage] lunar.

lunatique [lynatik] *adj* temperamental.

lunch [lœʃ] *nm* buffet lunch.

lundi [lœdi] *nm* Monday; *voir aussi* **samedi**.

lune [lyn] *nf* ASTRON moon; **pleine ~** full moon; ~ **de miel** *fig* honeymoon.

lunette [lynɛt] *nf* ASTRON telescope. ○ **lunettes** *nfpl* glasses; ~s **de soleil** sunglasses.

lurette [lyrɛt] *nf*: **il y a belle ~ que ...** *fam* it's been ages since ....

lustre [lystr] *nm* [luminaire] chandelier. || [éclat] sheen, shine; *fig* reputation.

lustrer [lystre] *vt* [faire briller] to make shine. || [user] to wear.

luth [lyt] *nm* lute.

lutte [lyt] *nf* [combat] fight, struggle; **la ~ des classes** the class struggle. || SPORT wrestling.

lutter [lyte] *vi* to fight, to struggle; ~ **contre** to fight (against).

lutteur, -euse [lytœr, øz] nm, f SPORT wrestler; fig fighter.

luxation [lyksɑsjɔ̃] nf dislocation.

luxe [lyks] nm luxury; **de ~** luxury.

Luxembourg [lyksɑ̃bur] nm [pays]: **le ~** Luxembourg.

luxueux, -euse [lyksɥø, øz] adj luxurious.

luzerne [lyzɛrn] nf lucerne, alfalfa.

lycée [lise] nm ≃ high school Am; **~ technique/professionnel** ≃ technical/training college.

lycéen, -enne [liseɛ̃, ɛn] nm, f high school pupil Am.

lymphatique [lɛ̃fatik] adj MÉD lymphatic. || fig [apathique] sluggish.

lyncher [lɛ̃ʃe] vt to lynch.

lynx [lɛ̃ks] nm lynx.

Lyon [ljɔ̃] n Lyons.

lyre [lir] nf lyre.

lyrique [lirik] adj [poésie & fig] lyrical; [drame, chanteur, poète] lyric.

lys = **lis**.

m, M [ɛm] 1 nm inv m, M. 2 (abr de mètre) m. ○ **M** (abr de **Monsieur**) Mr. || (abr de **million**) M.

ma → **mon**.

macabre [makabr] adj macabre.

macadam [makadam] nm [revêtement] macadam; [route] road.

macaron [makarɔ̃] nm [pâtisserie] macaroon. || [autocollant] sticker.

macaronis [makarɔni] nmpl CULIN macaroni (U).

macédoine [masedwan] nf CULIN: **~ de fruits** fruit salad.

macérer [masere] 1 vt to steep. 2 vi [mariner] to steep; **faire ~** to steep. || fig & péj [personne] to wallow.

mâche [mɑʃ] nf lamb's lettuce.

mâcher [mɑʃe] vt [mastiquer] to chew.

machiavélique [makjavelik] adj Machiavellian.

machin [maʃɛ̃] nm [chose] thing, thingamajig.

Machin, -e [maʃɛ̃, in] nm, f fam what's his name (f what's her name).

machinal, -e, -aux [maʃinal, o] adj mechanical.

machination [maʃinɑsjɔ̃] nf machination.

machine [maʃin] nf TECHNOL machine; **~ à coudre** sewing machine; **~ à écrire** typewriter; **~ à laver** washing machine. || NAVIG engine.

machine-outil [maʃinuti] nf machine tool.

machiniste [maʃinist] nm CIN & THÉÂTRE scene shifter. || TRANSPORT driver.

macho [matʃo] péj nm macho man.

mâchoire [mɑʃwar] nf jaw.

mâchonner [maʃɔne] vt [mâcher, mordiller] to chew.

maçon [masɔ̃] nm mason.

maçonnerie [masɔnri] nf [travaux] building; [construction] masonry; [franc-maçonnerie] freemasonry.

macramé [makrame] nm macramé.

maculer [makyle] vt to stain.

madame [madam] (pl mesdames [medam]) nf [titre]: **~ X** Mrs X; **bonjour ~!** good morning!; [dans hôtel, restaurant] good morning, madam!; **bonjour mesdames!** good morning (ladies)!; **Madame le Ministre n'est pas là** the Minister is out.

mademoiselle [madmwazɛl] (pl mesdemoiselles [medmwazɛl]) nf [titre]: **~ X** Miss X; **bonjour ~!** good morning!; [à l'école, dans hôtel] good morning, miss!; **bonjour mesdemoiselles!** good morning (ladies)!

madone [madɔn] nf ART & RELIG Madonna.

Madrid [madrid] n Madrid.

madrier [madrije] nm beam.

maf(f)ia [mafja] nf Mafia.

magasin [magazɛ̃] nm [boutique] store Am; **grand ~** department store; **faire les ~s** fig to go round the shops Br ou stores Am. || [d'arme, d'appareil photo] magazine.

magazine [magazin] nm magazine.

mage [maʒ] nm: **les trois Rois ~s** the Three Wise Men.

maghrébin, -e [magrebɛ̃, in] adj North African. ○ **Maghrébin, -e** nm, f North African.

magicien, -ienne [maʒisjɛ̃, jɛn] nm, f magician.

magie [maʒi] nf magic.

magique [maʒik] *adj* [occulte] magic. ||
[merveilleux] magical.

magistral, -e, -aux [maʒistral, o] *adj*
[œuvre, habileté] masterly. || [dispute, fes-
sée] enormous. || [attitude, ton] authori-
tative.

magistrat [maʒistra] *nm* magistrate.

magistrature [maʒistratyr] *nf* magis-
tracy, magistrature.

magma [magma] *nm* GÉOL magma. || *fig*
[mélange] muddle.

magnanime [maɲanim] *adj* magnanimous.

magnat [maɲa] *nm* magnate, tycoon.

magnésium [maɲezjɔm] *nm* magnesium.

magnétique [maɲetik] *adj* magnetic.

magnétisme [maɲetism] *nm* [PHYS &
fascination] magnetism.

magnéto(phone) [maɲetɔ(fɔn)] *nm*
tape recorder.

magnétoscope [maɲetɔskɔp] *nm*
videorecorder.

magnifique [maɲifik] *adj* magnificent.

magnum [magnɔm] *nm* magnum.

magot [mago] *nm fam* tidy sum, packet.

mai [mɛ] *nm* May; **le premier ~** May
Day; *voir aussi* **septembre.**

maigre [mɛgr] *adj* [très mince] thin. ||
[aliment] low-fat; [viande] lean. || [peu
important] meagre; [végétation] sparse.

maigreur [mɛgrœr] *nf* thinness.

maigrir [mɛgrir] *vi* to lose weight.

maille [maj] *nf* [de tricot] stitch. || [de
filet] mesh.

maillet [majɛ] *nm* mallet.

maillon [majɔ̃] *nm* link.

maillot [majo] *nm* [de sport] shirt, jersey; **~ de bain** swimsuit; **~ de corps** vest
Br, undershirt *Am.*

main [mɛ̃] *nf* hand; **à la ~** by hand; **attaque à ~ armée** armed attack; **donner
la ~ à qqn** to take sb's hand; **haut les ~s!**
hands up!

main-d'œuvre [mɛ̃dœvr] *nf* labour,
workforce.

mainmise [mɛ̃miz] *nf* seizure.

maint, -e [mɛ̃, mɛ̃t] *adj littéraire* many
a; **~s** many; **~es fois** time and time again.

maintenance [mɛ̃tnɑ̃s] *nf* maintenance.

maintenant [mɛ̃tnɑ̃] *adv* now.
○ **maintenant que** *loc prép* now that.

maintenir [mɛ̃tnir] *vt* [soutenir] to sup-
port; **~qqn à distance** to keep sb away. ||
[garder, conserver] to maintain. || [affir-
mer]: **~ que** to maintain (that). ○ **se**

maintenir *vp* [durer] to last. || [rester]
to remain.

maintenu, -e [mɛ̃tny] *pp* → **maintenir.**

maintien [mɛ̃tjɛ̃] *nm* [conservation]
maintenance; [de tradition] upholding. ||
[tenue] posture.

maire [mɛr] *nm* mayor.

mairie [meri] *nf* [bâtiment] city hall *Am.*
|| [administration] city hall *Am.*

mais [mɛ] **1** *conj* but; **~ non!** of course
not! **2** *adv* but; **vous êtes prêts? - ~ bien
sûr!** are you ready? - but of course! **3**
nm: **il n'y a pas de ~** (there are) no buts.

maïs [mais] *nm* maize *Br*, corn *Am.*

maison [mɛzɔ̃] *nf* [habitation, lignée &
ASTROL] house; **~ individuelle** detached
house. || [foyer] home; [famille] family; **à
la ~** [au domicile] at home. || COMM com-
pany. || [institut]: **~ d'arrêt** prison; **~ de
la culture** arts centre; **~ de retraite** old
people's home. || (*en apposition*) [artisa-
nal] homemade; [dans restaurant - vin]
house (*avant n*).

Maison-Blanche [mɛzɔ̃blɑ̃ʃ] *nf*: **la ~**
the White House.

maisonnée [mɛzɔne] *nf* household.

maisonnette [mɛzɔnɛt] *nf* small house.

maître, -esse [mɛtr, mɛtrɛs] *nm, f* [pro-
fesseur] teacher; **~ d'école** schoolteacher;
~ nageur swimming instructor. || [mo-
dèle, artiste & *fig*] master. || [dirigeant]
ruler; [d'animal] master (*f* mistress); **~
d'hôtel** head waiter; **être ~ de soi** to be in
control of oneself, to have self-control. ||
(*en apposition*) [principal] main, principal. ○ **maîtresse** *nf* mistress.

maître-assistant, -e [mɛtrasistɑ̃, ɑ̃t]
nm, f ≈ assistant professor *Am.*

maîtresse → **maître.**

maîtrise [mɛtriz] *nf* [sang-froid, domi-
nation] control. || [connaissance] mastery,
command. || UNIV ≈ master's degree.

maîtriser [mɛtrize] *vt* [animal, forcené]
to subdue. || [émotion, réaction] to con-
trol, to master. || [incendie] to bring un-
der control. ○ **se maîtriser** *vp* to control o.s.

majesté [maʒɛste] *nf* majesty. ○ **Majesté** *nf*: **Sa Majesté** His/Her Majesty.

majestueux, -euse [maʒɛstɥø, øz] *adj*
majestic.

majeur, -e [maʒœr] *adj* [gén] major. ||
[personne] of age. ○ **majeur** *nm* middle
finger.

major [maʒɔr] *nm* MIL ≈ adjutant.

majordome [maʒɔrdɔm] *nm* major-
domo.

malus

majorer [maʒɔre] *vt* to increase.

majorette [maʒɔrɛt] *nf* majorette.

majoritaire [maʒɔritɛr] *adj* majority (*avant n*); **être ~** to be in the majority.

majorité [maʒɔrite] *nf* majority; **en (grande) ~** in the majority; **~ absolue/relative** POLIT absolute/relative majority.

majuscule [maʒyskyl] 1 *nf* capital (letter). 2 *adj* capital (*avant n*).

mal, maux [mal, mo] *nm* [ce qui est contraire à la morale] evil. ‖ [souffrance physique] pain; **avoir ~ au cœur** to feel sick; **avoir ~ au dos** to have backache; **avoir ~ à la gorge** to have a sore throat; **avoir le ~ de mer** to be seasick; **avoir ~ aux dents/à la tête** to have toothache/a headache; **faire ~ à qqn** to hurt sb; **ça fait ~** it hurts; **se faire ~** to hurt o.s. ‖ [difficulté] difficulty. ‖ [douleur morale] pain, suffering (*U*); **faire du ~ (à qqn)** to hurt (sb). ○ **mal** *adv* [malade] ill; **aller ~** not to be well; **se sentir ~** to feel ill. ‖ [respirer] with difficulty. ‖ [informé, se conduire] badly; **~ prendre qqch** to take sthg badly; **~ tourner** to go wrong. ‖ *loc*: **pas ~** not bad (*adj*), not badly (*adv*); **pas ~ de** quite a lot of.

malade [malad] 1 *nmf* invalid, sick person; **~ mental** mentally ill person. 2 *adj* [souffrant - personne] ill, sick; [- organe] bad; **tomber ~** to fall ill ou sick. ‖ *fam* [fou] crazy.

maladie [maladi] *nf* MÉD illness. ‖ [passion, manie] mania.

maladresse [maladrɛs] *nf* [inhabileté] clumsiness. ‖ [bévue] blunder.

maladroit, -e [maladrwa, at] *adj* clumsy.

malaise [malɛz] *nm* [indisposition] discomfort. ‖ [trouble] unease (*U*).

Malaisie [malɛzi] *nf*: **la ~** Malaya.

malaria [malarja] *nf* malaria.

malaxer [malakse] *vt* to knead.

malchance [malʃɑ̃s] *nf* bad luck (*U*).

malchanceux, -euse [malʃɑ̃sø, øz] 1 *adj* unlucky. 2 *nm, f* unlucky person.

mâle [mal] 1 *adj* [enfant, animal, hormone] male. ‖ [voix, assurance] manly. ‖ ÉLECTR male. 2 *nm* male.

malédiction [malediksjɔ̃] *nf* curse.

maléfique [malefik] *adj* sout evil.

malencontreux, -euse [malɑ̃kɔ̃trø, øz] *adj* [hasard, rencontre] unfortunate.

malentendant, -e [malɑ̃tɑ̃dɑ̃, ɑ̃t] *nm, f* person who is hard of hearing.

malentendu [malɑ̃tɑ̃dy] *nm* misunderstanding.

malfaçon [malfasɔ̃] *nf* defect.

malfaiteur [malfɛtœr] *nm* criminal.

malfamé, -e, mal famé, -e [malfame] *adj* disreputable.

malformation [malfɔrmasjɔ̃] *nf* malformation.

malfrat [malfra] *nm* fam crook.

malgré [malgre] *prép* in spite of; **~ tout** [quoi qu'il arrive] in spite of everything; [pourtant] even so, yet.

malhabile [malabil] *adj* clumsy.

malheur [malœr] *nm* misfortune; **par ~** unfortunately; **porter ~ à qqn** to bring sb bad luck.

malheureusement [malœrøzmɑ̃] *adv* unfortunately.

malheureux, -euse [malœrø, øz] 1 *adj* [triste] unhappy. ‖ [désastreux, regrettable] unfortunate. ‖ [malchanceux] unlucky. ‖ (*avant n*) [sans valeur] pathetic, miserable. 2 *nm, f* [infortuné] poor soul.

malhonnête [malɔnɛt] 1 *nmf* dishonest person. 2 *adj* [personne, affaire] dishonest. ‖ *hum* [proposition, propos] indecent.

malhonnêteté [malɔnɛtte] *nf* [de personne] dishonesty.

malice [malis] *nf* mischief.

malicieux, -leuse [malisjø, jøz] *adj* mischievous.

malin, -igne [malɛ̃, iɲ] 1 *adj* [rusé] crafty, cunning. ‖ [méchant] malicious, spiteful. ‖ MÉD malignant. 2 *nm, f* cunning ou crafty person.

malingre [malɛ̃gr] *adj* sickly.

malle [mal] *nf* [coffre] trunk; [de voiture] boot *Br*, trunk *Am*.

malléable [maleabl] *adj* malleable.

mallette [malɛt] *nf* briefcase.

mal-logé, -e [malɔʒe] (*mpl* **mal-logés**, *fpl* **mal-logées**) *nm, f* person living in poor accommodation.

malmener [malməne] *vt* [brutaliser] to handle roughly, to ill-treat.

malnutrition [malnytrisjɔ̃] *nf* malnutrition.

malodorant, -e [malɔdɔrɑ̃, ɑ̃t] *adj* smelly.

malotru, -e [malɔtry] *nm, f* lout.

malpoli, -e [malpɔli] *nm, f* rude person.

malpropre [malprɔpr] *adj* [sale] dirty.

malsain, -e [malsɛ̃, ɛn] *adj* unhealthy.

malt [malt] *nm* [whisky] malt (whisky).

maltraiter [maltrete] *vt* to ill-treat; [en paroles] to attack, to run down.

malus [malys] *nm* increase in car insur-

ance charges, due to loss of no-claims bonus.

malveillant, -e [malvɛjɑ̃, ɑ̃t] *adj* spiteful.

malversation [malvɛrsasjɔ̃] *nf* embezzlement.

malvoyant, -e [malvwajɑ̃, ɑ̃t] *nm, f* person who is partially sighted.

maman [mamɑ̃] *nf* mummy.

mamelle [mamɛl] *nf* teat; [de vache] udder.

mamelon [mamlɔ̃] *nm* [du sein] nipple.

mamie, mamy [mami] *nf* granny, grandma.

mammifère [mamifɛr] *nm* mammal.

mammouth [mamut] *nm* mammoth.

mamy = mamie.

manager [manadʒɛr] *nm* manager.

manche [mɑ̃ʃ] **1** *nf* [de vêtement] sleeve; **~s courtes/longues** short/long sleeves. || [de jeu] round, game; TENNIS set. **2** *nm* [d'outil] handle; **~ à balai** broomstick. || MUS neck.

Manche [mɑ̃ʃ] *nf* [mer]: **la ~** the English Channel.

manchette [mɑ̃ʃɛt] *nf* [de chemise] cuff. || [de journal] headline.

manchon [mɑ̃ʃɔ̃] *nm* [en fourrure] muff.

manchot, -ote [mɑ̃ʃo, ɔt] **1** *adj* one-armed. **2** *nm, f* one-armed person. ○ **manchot** *nm* penguin.

mandarine [mɑ̃darin] *nf* mandarin (orange).

mandat [mɑ̃da] *nm* [pouvoir, fonction] mandate. || JUR warrant; **~ de perquisition** search warrant. || [titre postal] money order.

mandataire [mɑ̃datɛr] *nmf* proxy, representative.

mandibule [mɑ̃dibyl] *nf* mandible.

mandoline [mɑ̃dɔlin] *nf* mandolin.

manège [manɛʒ] *nm* [attraction] carousel *Am*. || [de chevaux - lieu] riding school. || [manœuvre] scheme, game.

manette [manɛt] *nf* lever.

mangeable [mɑ̃ʒabl] *adj* edible.

mangeoire [mɑ̃ʒwar] *nf* manger.

manger [mɑ̃ʒe] **1** *vt* [nourriture] to eat. || [fortune] to get through, to squander. **2** *vi* to eat.

mangue [mɑ̃g] *nf* mango.

maniable [manjabl] *adj* [instrument] manageable.

maniaque [manjak] **1** *nmf* [méticuleux] fusspot. || [fou] maniac. **2** *adj* [méticuleux] fussy. || [fou] maniacal.

manie [mani] *nf* [habitude] funny habit; **avoir la ~ de qqch/de faire qqch** to have a mania for sthg/for doing sthg. || [obsession] mania.

maniement [manimɑ̃] *nm* handling.

manier [manje] *vt* [manipuler, utiliser] to handle; *fig* [ironie, mots] to handle skilfully.

manière [manjɛr] *nf* [méthode] manner, way; **de toute ~** at any rate; **d'une ~ générale** generally speaking. ○ **manières** *nfpl* manners. ○ **de manière à (ce que)** *loc conj* (+ *subjonctif*) so that. ○ **de manière que** *loc conj* (+ *subjonctif*) in such a way that.

maniéré, -e [manjere] *adj* affected.

manif [manif] *nf fam* demo.

manifestant, -e [manifɛstɑ̃, ɑ̃t] *nm, f* demonstrator.

manifestation [manifɛstasjɔ̃] *nf* [témoignage] expression. || [mouvement collectif] demonstration. || [apparition - de maladie] appearance.

manifester [manifɛste] **1** *vt* to show, to express. **2** *vi* to demonstrate. ○ **se manifester** *vp* [apparaître] to show or manifest itself. || [se montrer] to turn up, to appear.

manigancer [manigɑ̃se] *vt fam* to plot.

manioc [manjɔk] *nm* manioc.

manipuler [manipyle] *vt* [colis, appareil] to handle. || [statistiques, résultats] to falsify, to rig. || *péj* [personne] to manipulate.

manivelle [manivɛl] *nf* crank.

mannequin [mankɛ̃] *nm* [forme humaine] dummy. || [personne] model.

manœuvre [manœvr] **1** *nf* [d'appareil, de véhicule] driving, handling. || MIL manoeuvre, exercise. || [machination] ploy, scheme. **2** *nm* labourer.

manœuvrer [manœvre] **1** *vi* to manoeuvre. **2** *vt* [faire fonctionner] to operate, to work; [voiture] to manoeuvre. || [influencer] to manipulate.

manoir [manwar] *nm* manor, country house.

manquant, -e [mɑ̃kɑ̃, ɑ̃t] *adj* missing.

manque [mɑ̃k] *nm* [pénurie] lack, shortage; **par ~ de** for want of. || [de toxicomane] withdrawal symptoms (*pl*). || [lacune] gap.

manqué, -e [mɑ̃ke] *adj* [raté] failed; [rendez-vous] missed.

manquer [mɑ̃ke] **1** *vi* [faire défaut] to be lacking, to be missing; **l'argent/le temps me manque** I don't have enough money/time; **tu me manques** I miss you. || [être absent]: **~ (à)** to be absent (from), to be missing (from). || [échouer] to fail. || [ne pas avoir assez]: **~ de qqch** to lack sthg, to be short of sthg. || [faillir]: **il a manqué de se noyer** he nearly ou almost drowned; **je n'y manquerai pas** I certainly will, I'll definitely do it. || [ne pas respecter]: **~ à** [devoir] to fail in; **~ à sa parole** to break one's word. **2** *vt* [gén] to miss. || [échouer à] to bungle, to botch. **3** *v impers*: **il manque quelqu'un** somebody is missing; **il me manque 20 francs** I'm 20 francs short.

mansarde [mɑ̃sard] *nf* attic.

mansardé, -e [mɑ̃sarde] *adj* attic (*avant n*).

manteau, -x [mɑ̃to] *nm* [vêtement] coat.

manucure [manykyr] *nmf* manicurist.

manuel, -elle [manɥɛl] *adj* manual. ○ **manuel** *nm* manual.

manufacture [manyfaktyr] *nf* [fabrique] factory.

manuscrit, -e [manyskri, it] *adj* handwritten. ○ **manuscrit** *nm* manuscript.

manutention [manytɑ̃sjɔ̃] *nf* handling.

manutentionnaire [manytɑ̃sjɔnɛr] *nmf* packer.

mappemonde [mapmɔ̃d] *nf* [carte] map of the world. || [sphère] globe.

maquereau, -elle, -x [makro, ɛl, o] *nm, f fam* pimp (*f* madam). ○ **maquereau** *nm* mackerel.

maquette [makɛt] *nf* [ébauche] pasteup. || [modèle réduit] model.

maquillage [makijaʒ] *nm* [action, produits] make-up.

maquiller [makije] *vt* [farder] to make up. || [fausser] to disguise; [- passeport] to falsify; [- chiffres] to doctor. ○ **se maquiller** *vp* to make up, to put on one's make-up.

maquis [maki] *nm* [végétation] scrub, brush. || HIST Maquis.

maraîcher, -ère [mareʃe, ɛr] **1** *adj* truck farming (*avant n*) *Am*. **2** *nm, f* truck farmer *Am*.

marais [marɛ] *nm* [marécage] marsh, swamp; **~ salant** saltpan.

marasme [marasm] *nm* [récession] stagnation.

marathon [maratɔ̃] *nm* marathon.

marâtre [maratr] *nf* [mauvaise mère] bad mother. || [belle-mère] stepmother.

maraude [marod] *nf*, **maraudage** [marodaʒ] *nm* pilfering.

marbre [marbr] *nm* [roche, objet] marble.

marc [mar] *nm* [eau-de-vie] *spirit distilled from grape residue*. || [de fruits] residue; [de thé] leaves; **~ de café** grounds (*pl*).

marcassin [markasɛ̃] *nm* young wild boar.

marchand, -e [marʃɑ̃, ɑ̃d] **1** *adj* [valeur] market (*avant n*). **2** *nm, f* [commerçant] merchant; [détaillant] storekeeper *Am*; **~ de journaux** newsagent.

marchander [marʃɑ̃de] *vi* to bargain, to haggle.

marchandise [marʃɑ̃diz] *nf* merchandise (*U*), goods (*pl*).

marche [marʃ] *nf* [d'escalier] step. || [de personne] walking; [promenade] walk; **~ à pied** walking; **~ à suivre** *fig* correct procedure. || MUS march. || [déplacement - du temps, d'astre] course; **en ~ arrière** in reverse; **faire ~ arrière** to reverse; *fig* to backpedal, to backtrack. || [fonctionnement] running, working; **en ~** running; **se mettre en ~** to start (up).

marché [marʃe] *nm* [gén] market; **~ noir** black market; **~ aux puces** flea market. || [contrat] bargain, deal; **(à) bon ~** cheap. ○ **Marché commun** *nm*: **le Marché commun** the Common Market.

marchepied [marʃəpje] *nm* [de train] step.

marcher [marʃe] *vi* [aller à pied] to walk. || [poser le pied] to step. || [fonctionner, tourner] to work; **son affaire marche bien** his business is doing well. || *fam* [accepter] to agree. || *loc*: **faire ~ qqn** *fam* to take sb for a ride.

mardi [mardi] *nm* Tuesday; **~ gras** Shrove Tuesday; *voir aussi* **samedi**.

mare [mar] *nf* pool.

marécage [marekaʒ] *nm* marsh, bog.

marécageux, -euse [marekaʒø, øz] *adj* [terrain] marshy, boggy.

maréchal, -aux [mareʃal, o] *nm* marshal.

marée [mare] *nf* [de la mer] tide; **(à) haute/basse** (at) high/low tide. || *fig* [de personnes] wave, surge. ○ **marée noire** *nf* oil slick.

marelle [marɛl] *nf* hopscotch.

margarine [margarin] *nf* margarine.

marge [marʒ] *nf* [espace] margin; **vivre en ~ de la société** *fig* to live on the fringes of society. || [latitude] leeway; **~ d'erreur** margin of error. || COMM margin.

margelle [marʒɛl] *nf* coping.

marginal, -e, -aux [marʒinal, o] **1** adj [gén] marginal. ‖ [groupe] dropout (avant n). **2** nm, f dropout.

marguerite [margərit] nf BOT daisy.

mari [mari] nm husband.

mariage [marjaʒ] nm [union, institution] marriage; ~ **civil/religieux** civil/church wedding. ‖ [cérémonie] wedding. ‖ fig [de choses] blend.

Marianne [marian] n personification of the French Republic.

marié, -e [marje] **1** adj married. **2** nm, f groom, bridegroom (f bride).

marier [marje] vt [personne] to marry. ‖ fig [couleurs] to blend. ○ **se marier** vp [personnes] to get married; **se ~ avec qqn** to marry sb. ‖ fig [couleurs] to blend.

marihuana [marirwana], **marijuana** [mariʒwana] nf marijuana.

marin, -e [marɛ̃, in] adj [de la mer] sea (avant n); [faune, biologie] marine. ‖ NAVIG [carte, mille] nautical. ○ **marin** nm [matelot] sailor; ~ **pêcheur** deep-sea fisherman. ○ **marine 1** nf [navires] navy; **~e marchande** merchant navy; **~e nationale** navy. **2** nm MIL marine. ‖ [couleur] navy (blue). **3** adj inv navy.

mariner [marine] vi [aliment] to marinate; **faire ~ qqch** to marinate sthg. ‖ fam fig [attendre] to hang around; **faire ~ qqn** to let sb stew.

marionnette [marjɔnɛt] nf puppet.

marital, -e, -aux [marital, o] adj: **autorisation ~e** husband's permission.

maritime [maritim] adj [navigation] maritime; [ville] coastal.

mark [mark] nm [monnaie] mark.

marketing [marketiŋ] nm marketing; ~ **téléphonique** telemarketing.

marmaille [marmaj] nf fam brood (of kids).

marmelade [marməlad] nf stewed fruit.

marmite [marmit] nf [casserole] pot.

marmonner [marmɔne] vt & vi to mutter, to mumble.

marmot [marmo] nm fam kid.

marmotte [marmɔt] nf marmot.

Maroc [marɔk] nm: **le ~** Morocco.

marocain, -e [marɔkɛ̃, ɛn] adj Moroccan. ○ **Marocain, -e** nm, f Moroccan.

maroquinerie [marɔkinri] nf [magasin] leather-goods shop Br ou store Am.

marotte [marɔt] nf [dada] craze.

marquant, -e [markɑ̃, ɑ̃t] adj outstanding.

marque [mark] nf [signe, trace] mark; fig stamp, mark. ‖ [label, fabricant]

make, brand; **de ~** designer (avant n); fig important; **~ déposée** registered trademark. ‖ SPORT score; **à vos ~s, prêts, partez!** on your marks, get set, go! ‖ [témoignage] sign, token.

marqué, -e [marke] adj [net] marked, pronounced. ‖ [personne, visage] marked.

marquer [marke] **1** vt [gén] to mark. ‖ fam [écrire] to write down, to note down. ‖ [indiquer, manifester] to show. ‖ SPORT - but, point] to score; [- joueur] to mark. **2** vi SPORT to score.

marqueur [markœr] nm [crayon] marker (pen).

marquis, -e [marki, iz] nm, f marquis (f marchioness).

marraine [marɛn] nf [de filleul] godmother. ‖ [de navire] christener.

marrant, -e [marɑ̃, ɑ̃t] adj fam funny.

marre [mar] adv: **en avoir ~ (de)** fam to be fed up (with).

marrer [mare] ○ **se marrer** vp fam to split one's sides.

marron, -onne [marɔ̃, ɔn] adj péj [médecin] quack (avant n); [avocat] crooked. ○ **marron 1** nm [fruit] chestnut. ‖ [couleur] brown. **2** adj inv brown.

marronnier [marɔnje] nm chestnut tree.

mars [mars] nm March; voir aussi **septembre**.

Marseille [marsɛj] n Marseilles.

marteau, -x [marto] nm [gén] hammer; ~ **piqueur**, ~ **pneumatique** pneumatic drill. ‖ [heurtoir] knocker. ○ **marteau** adj fam barmy.

marteler [martəle] vt [pieu] to hammer; [table, porte] to hammer on, to pound. ‖ [phrase] to rap out.

martial, -e, -iaux [marsjal, jo] adj martial.

martinet [martinɛ] nm ZOOL swift. ‖ [fouet] whip.

martingale [martɛ̃gal] nf [de vêtement] half-belt. ‖ JEU winning system.

martini [martini] nm martini.

martyr, -e [martir] **1** adj martyred. **2** nm, f martyr. ○ **martyre** nm martyrdom.

martyriser [martirize] vt to torment.

marxisme [marksism] nm Marxism.

mascarade [maskarad] nf [mise en scène] masquerade.

mascotte [maskɔt] nf mascot.

masculin, -e [maskylɛ̃, in] adj [apparence & GRAM] masculine; [métier, popula-

tion, sexe] male. ○ **masculin** *nm* GRAM masculine.

maso [mazo] *fam* 1 *nm* masochist. 2 *adj* masochistic.

masochisme [mazɔʃism] *nm* masochism.

masque [mask] *nm* [gén] mask; ~ à gaz gas mask. || *fig* [façade] front, façade.

masquer [maske] *vt* [vérité, crime, problème] to conceal. || [maison, visage] to conceal, to hide.

massacre [masakr] *nm* *litt* & *fig* massacre.

massacrer [masakre] *vt* to massacre.

massage [masaʒ] *nm* massage.

masse [mas] *nf* [de pierre] block; [d'eau] volume. || [grande quantité]: **une ~ de** masses (*pl*) OU loads (*pl*) of. || PHYS mass. || ÉLECTR earth *Br*, ground *Am*. || [maillet] sledgehammer. ○ **en masse** *loc adv* [venir] en masse, all together.

masser [mase] *vt* [assembler] to assemble. || [frotter] to massage. ○ **se masser** *vp* [s'assembler] to assemble, to gather. || [se frotter]: **se ~ le bras** to massage one's arm.

masseur, -euse [masœr, øz] *nm, f* [personne] masseur (*f* masseuse).

massif, -ive [masif, iv] *adj* [monument, personne, dose] massive. || [or, chêne] solid. ○ **massif** *nm* [de plantes] clump. || [de montagnes] massif.

massue [masy] *nf* club.

mastic [mastik] *nm* mastic, putty.

mastiquer [mastike] *vt* [mâcher] to chew.

masturber [mastyrbe] ○ **se masturber** *vp* to masturbate.

masure [mazyr] *nf* hovel.

mat, -e [mat] *adj* [peinture, surface] matt. || [peau, personne] dusky. || [bruit, son] dull. || [aux échecs] checkmated. ○ **mat** *nm* checkmate.

mât [ma] *nm* NAVIG mast. || [poteau] pole, post.

match [matʃ] (*pl* matches OU matchs) *nm* match; (faire) ~ nul (to) draw.

matelas [matla] *nm inv* [de lit] mattress; ~ pneumatique airbed.

matelot [matlo] *nm* sailor.

mater [mate] *vt* [soumettre, neutraliser] to subdue. || *fam* [regarder] to eye up.

matérialiser [materjalize] ○ **se matérialiser** *vp* [aspirations] to be realized.

matérialiste [materjalist] 1 *nmf* materialist. 2 *adj* materialistic.

matériau, -x [materjo] *nm* material. ○ **matériaux** *nmpl* CONSTR material (*U*), materials.

matériel, -ielle [materjel] *adj* [être, substance] material, physical; [confort, avantage, aide] material. || [considération] practical. ○ **matériel** *nm* [gén] equipment (*U*). || INFORM hardware (*U*).

maternel, -elle [maternel] *adj* maternal; [langue] mother (*avant n*). ○ **maternelle** *nf* nursery school.

maternité [maternite] *nf* [qualité] maternity, motherhood. || [hôpital] maternity hospital.

mathématicien, -ienne [matematisjɛ̃, jen] *nm, f* mathematician.

mathématique [matematik] *adj* mathematical. ○ **mathématiques** *nfpl* mathematics (*U*).

maths [mat] *nfpl* *fam* math *Am*.

matière [matjer] *nf* [substance] matter; ~s grasses fats. || [matériau] material; ~s premières raw materials. || [discipline, sujet] subject; **en ~ de sport/littérature** as far as sport/literature is concerned.

matin [matɛ̃] *nm* morning; **le ~** in the morning; **ce ~** this morning; **à trois heures du ~** at 3 o'clock in the morning.

matinal, -e, -aux [matinal, o] *adj* [gymnastique, émission] morning (*avant n*). || [personne]: **être ~** to be an early riser.

matinée [matine] *nf* [matin] morning; **faire la grasse ~** *fig* to have a lie in. || [spectacle] matinée, afternoon performance.

matraque [matrak] *nf* truncheon.

matraquer [matrake] *vt* [frapper] to beat, to club.

matrice [matris] *nf* [moule] mould. || MATHS matrix. || ANAT womb.

matricule [matrikyl] *nm*: (numéro) ~ number.

matrimonial, -e, -iaux [matrimɔnjal, jo] *adj* matrimonial.

matrone [matrɔn] *nf* *péj* old bag.

mature [matyr] *adj* mature.

mâture [matyr] *nf* masts (*pl*).

maturité [matyrite] *nf* maturity; [de fruit] ripeness.

maudire [modir] *vt* to curse.

maudit, -e [modi, it] 1 *pp* → maudire. 2 *adj* [réprouvé] accursed. || (*avant n*) [exécrable] damned.

maugréer [mogree] 1 *vt* to mutter. 2 *vi*: ~ (contre) to grumble (about).

mausolée [mozɔle] *nm* mausoleum.

maussade [mosad] *adj* [personne, air] sullen. || [temps] gloomy.

mauvais, -e [movε, εz] *adj* [gén] bad. || [moment, numéro, réponse] wrong. || [mer] rough. || [personne, regard] nasty. ○ **mauvais** *adv*: **il fait ~** the weather is bad; **sentir ~** to smell bad.

mauve [mov] *nm & adj* mauve.

maux → **mal**.

max [maks] (*abr de* **maximum**) *nm fam*: **un ~ de fric** loads of money.

max. (*abr de* **maximum**) max.

maxillaire [maksilεr] *nm* jawbone.

maxime [maksim] *nf* maxim.

maximum [maksimɔm] (*pl* **maxima** [maksima]) 1 *nm* maximum; **le ~ de personnes** the greatest (possible) number of people; **au ~** at the most. 2 *adj* maximum.

mayonnaise [majɔnεz] *nf* mayonnaise.

mazout [mazut] *nm* fuel oil.

me [mə], **m'** (*devant voyelle ou h muet*) *pron pers* [complément d'objet direct] me. || [complément d'objet indirect] (to) me. || [réfléchi] myself. || [avec un présentatif]: **~ voici** I am.

méandre [meɑ̃dr] *nm* [de rivière] meander, bend.

mec [mεk] *nm fam* guy, bloke.

mécanicien, -ienne [mekanisjɛ̃, jɛn] *nm, f* [de garage] mechanic. || [conducteur de train] train driver *Br*, engineer *Am*.

mécanique [mekanik] 1 *nf* TECHNOL mechanical engineering. || [mécanisme] mechanism. 2 *adj* mechanical.

mécanisme [mekanism] *nm* mechanism.

mécène [mesεn] *nm* patron.

méchamment [meʃamɑ̃] *adv* [cruellement] nastily.

méchanceté [meʃɑ̃ste] *nf* [attitude] nastiness. || *fam* [rosserie] nasty thing.

méchant, -e [meʃɑ̃, ɑ̃t] *adj* [malveillant, cruel] nasty, wicked; [animal] vicious. || [désobéissant] naughty.

mèche [mεʃ] *nf* [de bougie] wick. || [de cheveux] lock. || [de bombe] fuse.

méchoui [meʃwi] *nm whole roast sheep*.

méconnaissable [mekɔnεsabl] *adj* unrecognizable.

méconnu, -e [mekɔny] *adj* unrecognized.

mécontent, -e [mekɔ̃tɑ̃, ɑ̃t] 1 *adj* unhappy. 2 *nm, f* malcontent.

mécontenter [mekɔ̃tɑ̃te] *vt* to displease.

Mecque [mεk] *n*: **La ~** Mecca.

mécréant, -e [mekreɑ̃, ɑ̃t] *nm, f* non-believer.

médaille [medaj] *nf* [pièce, décoration] medal. || [bijou] medallion. || [de chien] identification disc, tag.

médaillon [medajɔ̃] *nm* [bijou] locket. || ART & CULIN medallion.

médecin [medsɛ̃] *nm* doctor; **~ de famille** family doctor, GP *Br*; **~ de garde** doctor on duty, duty doctor; **~ légiste** forensic scientist *Br*, medical examiner *Am*; **~ traitant** consulting physician.

médecine [medsin] *nf* medicine.

média [medja] *nm*: **les ~s** the (mass) media.

médian, -e [medjɑ̃, an] *adj* median. ○ **médiane** *nf* median.

médiateur, -trice [medjatœr, tris] *nm, f* mediator; [dans conflit de travail] arbitrator. ○ **médiateur** *nm* ADMIN ombudsman. ○ **médiatrice** *nf* median.

médiathèque [medjatεk] *nf* media library.

médiatique [medjatik] *adj* media (*avant n*).

médical, -e, -aux [medikal, o] *adj* medical.

médicament [medikamɑ̃] *nm* medicine, drug.

médicinal, -e, -aux [medisinal, o] *adj* medicinal.

médiéval, -e, -aux [medjeval, o] *adj* medieval.

médiocre [medjɔkr] *adj* mediocre.

médiocrité [medjɔkrite] *nf* mediocrity.

médire [medir] *vi* to gossip; **~ de qqn** to speak ill of sb.

médisant, -e [medizɑ̃, ɑ̃t] *adj* slanderous.

méditation [meditasjɔ̃] *nf* meditation.

méditer [medite] 1 *vt* [projeter] to plan; **~ de faire qqch** to plan to do sthg. 2 *vi*: **~ (sur)** to meditate (on).

Méditerranée [mediterane] *nf*: **la ~** the Mediterranean (Sea).

méditerranéen, -enne [mediteraneɛ̃, εn] *adj* Mediterranean. ○ **Méditerranéen, -enne** *nm, f* person from the Mediterranean.

médium [medjɔm] *nm* [personne] medium.

médius [medjys] *nm* middle finger.

méduse [medyz] *nf* jellyfish.

méduser [medyze] *vt* to dumbfound.

ménager

meeting [mitiŋ] *nm* meeting.

méfait [mefɛ] *nm* misdemeanour, misdeed. ○ **méfaits** *nmpl* [du temps] ravages.

méfiance [mefjɑ̃s] *nf* suspicion, distrust.

méfiant, -e [mefjɑ̃, ɑ̃t] *adj* suspicious, distrustful.

méfier [mefje] ○ **se méfier** *vp* to be wary ou careful; **se ~ de qqn/qqch** to distrust sb/sthg.

mégalo [megalo] *nmf & adj fam* megalomaniac.

mégalomane [megaloman] *nmf & adj* megalomaniac.

mégalomanie [megalomani] *nf* megalomania.

mega-octet [megaɔktɛ] *nm* megabyte.

mégapole [megapɔl] *nf* megalopolis, megacity.

mégarde [megard] ○ **par mégarde** *loc adv* by mistake.

mégère [meʒɛr] *nf péj* shrew.

mégot [mego] *nm fam* butt *Am*.

meilleur, -e [mejœr] **1** *adj* (*compar*) better; (*superl*) best. **2** *nm, f* best. ○ **meilleur** *adv* better.

mélancolie [melɑ̃kɔli] *nf* melancholy.

mélancolique [melɑ̃kɔlik] *adj* melancholy.

mélange [melɑ̃ʒ] *nm* [action] mixing. || [mixture] mixture.

mélanger [melɑ̃ʒe] *vt* [mettre ensemble] to mix. || [déranger] to mix up, to muddle up. ○ **se mélanger** *vp* [se mêler] to mix. || [se brouiller] to get mixed up.

mêlée [mele] *nf* RUGBY scrum.

mêler [mele] *vt* [mélanger] to mix. || [déranger] to muddle up, to mix up. || [impliquer]: **~ qqn à qqch** to involve sb in sthg. ○ **se mêler** *vp* [se joindre]: **se ~ à** [groupe] to join. || [s'ingérer]: **se ~ de qqch** to get mixed up in sthg; **mêlez-vous de ce qui vous regarde!** mind your own business!

mélèze [melɛz] *nm* larch.

mélo [melo] *nm fam* melodrama.

mélodie [melɔdi] *nf* melody.

mélodieux, -ieuse [melɔdjø, jøz] *adj* melodious, tuneful.

mélodrame [melɔdram] *nm* melodrama.

mélomane [melɔman] **1** *nmf* music lover. **2** *adj* music-loving.

melon [məlɔ̃] *nm* [fruit] melon. || [chapeau] bowler (hat).

membrane [mɑ̃bran] *nf* membrane.

membre [mɑ̃br] **1** *nm* [du corps] limb. || [personne, pays, partie] member. **2** *adj* member (*avant n*).

mémé = **mémère**.

même [mɛm] **1** *adj indéf* [indique une identité ou une ressemblance] same; **il a le ~ âge que moi** he's the same age as me. || [sert à souligner]: **ce sont ses paroles ~s** those are his very words; **elle est la bonté ~** she's kindness itself. **2** *pron indéf*: **le/la ~** the same one; **ce sont toujours les ~s qui gagnent** it's always the same people who win. **3** *adv* even. ○ **de même** *loc adv* similarly, likewise; **il en va de ~ pour lui** the same goes for him. ○ **de même que** *loc conj* just as. ○ **tout de même** *loc adv* all the same. ○ **à même** *loc prép*: **s'asseoir à ~ le sol** to sit on the bare ground. ○ **à même de** *loc prép*: **être à ~ de faire qqch** to be able to do sthg, to be in a position to do sthg. ○ **même si** *loc conj* even if.

mémento [memɛ̃to] *nm* [agenda] pocket diary.

mémère [memɛr], **mémé** [meme] *nf fam* [grand-mère] granny. || *péj* [vieille femme] old biddy.

mémoire [memwar] **1** *nf* [gén & INFORM] memory; **de ~** from memory; **avoir bonne/mauvaise ~** to have a good/bad memory; **mettre en ~** INFORM to store; **~ vive** INFORM random access memory; **à la ~ de** in memory of. **2** *nm* UNIV dissertation, paper. ○ **mémoires** *nmpl* memoirs.

mémorable [memɔrabl] *adj* memorable.

mémorial, -iaux [memɔrjal, jo] *nm* [monument] memorial.

menaçant, -e [mənasɑ̃, ɑ̃t] *adj* threatening.

menace [mənas] *nf*: **~ (pour)** threat (to).

menacer [mənase] **1** *vt* to threaten; **~ de faire qqch** to threaten to do sthg; **~ qqn de qqch** to threaten sb with sthg. **2** *vi*: **la pluie menace** it looks like rain.

ménage [menaʒ] *nm* [nettoyage] housework (*U*); **faire le ~** to do the housework. || [couple] couple. || ÉCON household.

ménagement [menaʒmɑ̃] *nm* [égards] consideration; **sans ~** brutally.

ménager¹, -ère [menaʒe, ɛr] *adj* household (*avant n*), domestic. ○ **ménagère** *nf* [femme] housewife. || [de couverts] canteen.

ménager² [menaʒe] *vt* [bien traiter] to treat gently. || [économiser - sucre, réserves] to use sparingly; ~ **ses forces** to conserve one's strength. || [pratiquer - espace] to make. ○ **se ménager** *vp* to take care of o.s., to look after o.s.

ménagerie [menaʒri] *nf* menagerie.

mendiant, -e [mɑ̃djɑ̃, ɑ̃t] *nm, f* beggar.

mendier [mɑ̃dje] **1** *vt* [argent] to beg for. **2** *vi* to beg.

mener [məne] **1** *vt* [emmener] to take. || [diriger - débat, enquête] to conduct; [- affaires] to manage, to run; ~ **qqch à bonne fin** ou **à bien** to see sthg through, to bring sthg to a successful conclusion. || [être en tête de] to lead. **2** *vi* to lead.

meneur, -euse [mənœr, øz] *nm, f* [chef] ringleader; ~ **d'hommes** born leader.

menhir [menir] *nm* standing stone.

méningite [menɛ̃ʒit] *nf* meningitis (*U*).

ménisque [menisk] *nm* meniscus.

ménopause [menopoz] *nf* menopause.

menotte [mənɔt] *nf* [main] little hand. ○ **menottes** *nfpl* handcuffs; **passer les ~s à qqn** to handcuff sb.

mensonge [mɑ̃sɔ̃ʒ] *nm* [propos] lie.

mensonger, -ère [mɑ̃sɔ̃ʒe, ɛr] *adj* false.

menstruel, -elle [mɑ̃stryɛl] *adj* menstrual.

mensualiser [mɑ̃sɥalize] *vt* to pay monthly.

mensualité [mɑ̃sɥalite] *nf* [traite] monthly instalment.

mensuel, -elle [mɑ̃sɥel] *adj* monthly. ○ **mensuel** *nm* monthly (magazine).

mensuration [mɑ̃syrasjɔ̃] *nf* measuring. ○ **mensurations** *nfpl* measurements.

mental, -e, -aux [mɑ̃tal, o] *adj* mental.

mentalité [mɑ̃talite] *nf* mentality.

menteur, -euse [mɑ̃tœr, øz] *nm, f* liar.

menthe [mɑ̃t] *nf* mint.

mention [mɑ̃sjɔ̃] *nf* [citation] mention. || [note] note; «**rayer la ~ inutile**» "delete as appropriate". || UNIV: **avec ~** with distinction.

mentionner [mɑ̃sjɔne] *vt* to mention.

mentir [mɑ̃tir] *vi*: ~ **(à)** to lie (to).

menton [mɑ̃tɔ̃] *nm* chin.

menu, -e [məny] *adj* [très petit] tiny; [mince] thin. ○ **menu** *nm* [gén & INFORM] menu; [repas à prix fixe] set menu; ~ **gastronomique/touristique** gourmet/tourist menu.

menuiserie [mənɥizri] *nf* [métier] join-ery, carpentry. || [atelier] joinery (work-shop).

menuisier [mənɥizje] *nm* joiner, carpenter.

méprendre [meprɑ̃dr] ○ **se méprendre** *vp littéraire*: **se ~ sur** to be mistaken about.

mépris, -e [mepri, iz] *pp* → **méprendre.** ○ **mépris** *nm* [dédain]: ~ **(pour)** contempt (for), scorn (for). || [indifférence]: ~ **de** disregard for. ○ **au mépris de** *loc prép* regardless of.

méprisable [meprizabl] *adj* contemptible, despicable.

méprisant, -e [meprizɑ̃, ɑ̃t] *adj* contemptuous, scornful.

mépriser [meprize] *vt* to despise; [danger, offre] to scorn.

mer [mɛr] *nf* sea; **en ~** at sea; **prendre la ~** to put to sea; **haute** ou **pleine ~** open sea; **la ~ d'Irlande** the Irish Sea; **la ~ Morte** the Dead Sea; **la ~ Noire** the Black Sea; **la ~ du Nord** the North Sea.

mercantile [mɛrkɑ̃til] *adj péj* mercenary.

mercenaire [mɛrsənɛr] *nm & adj* mercenary.

mercerie [mɛrsəri] *nf* [articles] notions (*pl*) *Am*. || [boutique] notions store *Am*.

merci [mɛrsi] **1** *interj* thank you!, thanks!; ~ **beaucoup!** thank you very much! **2** *nm*: ~ **(de** ou **pour)** thank you (for). **3** *nf* mercy; **être à la ~ de** to be at the mercy of.

mercier, -ière [mɛrsje, jɛr] *nm, f* notions dealer *Am*.

mercredi [mɛrkrədi] *nm* Wednesday; *voir aussi* **samedi.**

mercure [mɛrkyr] *nm* mercury.

merde [mɛrd] *tfam nf* shit.

mère [mɛr] *nf* mother; ~ **de famille** mother.

merguez [mɛrgɛz] *nf inv* North African spiced sausage.

méridien, -ienne [meridjɛ̃, jɛn] *adj* [ligne] meridian. ○ **méridien** *nm* meridian.

méridional, -e, -aux [meridjɔnal, o] *adj* southern; [du sud de la France] Southern (French).

meringue [mərɛ̃g] *nf* meringue.

merisier [mərizje] *nm* [arbre] wild cherry (tree). || [bois] cherry.

mérite [merit] *nm* merit; **avoir du ~** [personne] to have talent.

mériter [merite] *vt* [être digne de, encourir] to deserve. || [valoir] tò be worth, to merit.

merlan [mɛrlɑ̃] *nm* whiting.

merle [mɛrl] *nm* blackbird.

merveille [mɛrvɛj] *nf* marvel, wonder; **à ~** marvellously, wonderfully.

merveilleux, -euse [mɛrvɛjø, øz] *adj* [remarquable, prodigieux] marvellous, wonderful. || [magique] magic, magical.

mes → mon.

mésange [mezɑ̃ʒ] *nf* ZOOL tit.

mésaventure [mezavɑ̃tyr] *nf* misfortune.

mesdames → madame.

mesdemoiselles → mademoiselle.

mésentente [mezɑ̃tɑ̃t] *nf* disagreement.

mesquin, -e [mɛskɛ̃, in] *adj* mean, petty.

mesquinerie [mɛskinri] *nf* [étroitesse d'esprit] meanness, pettiness.

mess [mɛs] *nm* mess.

message [mesaʒ] *nm* message; **laisser un ~ à qqn** to leave a message for sb.

messager, -ère [mesaʒe, ɛr] *nm, f* messenger.

messagerie [mesaʒri] *nf* (*gén pl*) [transport de marchandises] freight (*U*). || INFORM: ~ **électronique** electronic mail.

messe [mɛs] *nf* mass.

messie [mesi] *nm* Messiah; *fig* saviour.

messieurs → monsieur.

mesure [məzyr] *nf* [disposition, acte] measure, step. || [évaluation, dimension] measurement; **prendre les ~s de qqn/qqch** to measure sb/sthg. || [étalon, récipient] measure. || MUS time, tempo. || [modération] moderation. || *loc*: **dans la ~ du possible** as far as possible; **être en ~ de** to be in a position to. ○ **à mesure que** *loc conj* as. ○ **outre mesure** *loc adv* excessively. ○ **sur mesure** *loc adj* custom-made; [costume] made-to-measure.

mesurer [məzyre] *vt* [gén] to measure; **elle mesure 1,50 m** she's 5 feet tall; **la table mesure 1,50 m** the table is 5 feet long. || [risques, portée, ampleur] to weigh up. ○ **se mesurer** *vp*: **se ~ avec** OU **à qqn** to pit o.s. against sb.

métabolisme [metabɔlism] *nm* metabolism.

métal, -aux [metal, o] *nm* metal.

métallique [metalik] *adj* [en métal] metal (*avant n*). || [éclat, son] metallic.

métallurgie [metalyrʒi] *nf* [industrie] metallurgical industry.

métamorphose [metamɔrfoz] *nf* metamorphosis.

métaphore [metafɔr] *nf* metaphor.

métaphysique [metafizik] **1** *nf* metaphysics (*U*). **2** *adj* metaphysical.

métayer, -ère [meteje, metɛjɛr] *nm, f* tenant farmer.

météo [meteo] *nf* [bulletin] weather forecast. || [service] ≃ Met Office *Br*, ≃ National Weather Service *Am*.

météore [meteɔr] *nm* meteor.

météorite [meteɔrit] *nm ou nf* meteorite.

météorologie [meteɔrɔlɔʒi] *nf* SCIENCE meteorology.

météorologique [meteɔrɔlɔʒik] *adj* meteorological, weather (*avant n*).

méthane [metan] *nm* methane.

méthode [metɔd] *nf* [gén] method. || [ouvrage - gén] manual; [- de lecture, de langue] primer.

méthodologie [metɔdɔlɔʒi] *nf* methodology.

méticuleux, -euse [metikylø, øz] *adj* meticulous.

métier [metje] *nm* [profession - manuelle] occupation, trade; [- intellectuelle] occupation, profession.

métis, -isse [metis] *nm, f* half-caste, half-breed. ○ **métis** *nm* [tissu] cotton-linen mix.

métrage [metraʒ] *nm* [mesure] measurement, measuring. || [COUTURE - coupon] length. || CIN footage; **long ~** feature film; **court ~** short (film).

mètre [mɛtr] *nm* LITTÉRATURE & MATHS metre; **~ carré/cube** square/cubic metre. || [instrument] rule.

métro [metro] *nm* subway *Am*.

métronome [metrɔnɔm] *nm* metronome.

métropole [metrɔpɔl] *nf* [ville] metropolis. || [pays] home country.

métropolitain, -e [metrɔpɔlitɛ̃, ɛn] *adj* metropolitan.

mets [mɛ] *nm* CULIN dish.

metteur [metœr] *nm*: **~ en scène** THÉÂTRE producer; CIN director.

mettre [mɛtr] *vt* [placer] to put; **~ de l'eau à bouillir** to put some water on to boil. || [revêtir] to put on; **mets ta robe noire** put your black dress on; **je ne mets plus ma robe noire** I don't wear my black dress any more. || [consacrer - temps] to take; [- argent] to spend. || [allumer - radio, chauffage] to put on, to switch on. || [installer] to put in; **faire ~**

de la moquette to have a carpet put down ou fitted. || [inscrire] to put (down).
O **se mettre** *vp* [se placer]: **où est-ce que ça se met?** where does this go?; **se ~ au lit** to get into bed; **se ~ à côté de qqn** to sit/stand near to sb. || [devenir]: **se ~ en colère** to get angry. || [commencer]: **se ~ à qqch/à faire qqch** to start sthg/doing sthg. || [revêtir] to put on; **je n'ai rien à me ~** I haven't got a thing to wear.

meuble [mœbl] *nm* piece of furniture; **~s** furniture (*U*).

meublé, -e [mœble] *adj* furnished.
O **meublé** *nm* furnished apartment *Am*.

meubler [mœble] *vt* [pièce, maison] to furnish. || *fig* [occuper]: **~ qqch (de)** to fill sthg (with).

meugler [møgle] *vi* to moo.

meule [møl] *nf* [à moudre] millstone. || [à aiguiser] grindstone. || [de fromage] round. || AGRIC stack; **~ de foin** haystack.

meunier, -ière [mønje, jɛr] *nm, f* miller (*f* miller's wife).

meurtre [mœrtr] *nm* murder.

meurtrier, -ière [mœrtrije, jɛr] **1** *adj* [épidémie, arme] deadly; [fureur] murderous; [combat] bloody. **2** *nm, f* murderer.

meurtrir [mœrtrir] *vt* [contusionner] to bruise. || *fig* [blesser] to wound.

meurtrissure [mœrtrisyr] *nf* [marque] bruise.

meute [møt] *nf* pack.

mexicain, -e [mɛksikɛ̃, ɛn] *adj* Mexican. O **Mexicain, -e** *nm, f* Mexican.

Mexique [mɛksik] *nm*: **le ~** Mexico.

mezzanine [mɛdzanin] *nf* mezzanine.

mi [mi] *nm inv* E; [chanté] mi.

mi- [mi] **1** *adj inv* half; **à la ~juin** in mid-June. **2** *adv* half-.

miasme [mjasm] *nm* (*gén pl*) putrid ou foul smell.

miaulement [mjolmɑ̃] *nm* miaowing.

miauler [mjole] *vi* to miaow.

mi-bas [miba] *nm inv* knee-sock.

mi-carême [mikarɛm] *nf* feast day on third Thursday in Lent.

mi-chemin [miʃmɛ̃] O **à mi-chemin** *loc adv* halfway (there).

mi-clos, -e [miklo, oz] *adj* half-closed.

micro [mikro] *nm* [microphone] mike. || [micro-ordinateur] micro.

microbe [mikrɔb] *nm* MÉD microbe, germ. || *péj* [avorton] (little) runt.

microclimat [mikrɔklima] *nm* microclimate.

microcosme [mikrɔksm] *nm* microcosm.

microfiche [mikrɔfiʃ] *nf* microfiche.

microfilm [mikrɔfilm] *nm* microfilm.

micro-ondes [mikrɔɔ̃d] *nfpl* microwaves; **four à ~** microwave (oven).

micro-ordinateur [mikrɔɔrdinatœr] (*pl* **micro-ordinateurs**) *nm* micro, microcomputer.

microphone [mikrɔfɔn] *nm* microphone.

microprocesseur [mikrɔprɔsesœr] *nm* microprocessor.

microscope [mikrɔskɔp] *nm* microscope.

midi [midi] *nm* [période du déjeuner] lunchtime. || [heure] midday, noon. O **Midi** *nm*: **le Midi** the South of France.

mie [mi] *nf* [de pain] soft part, inside.

miel [mjɛl] *nm* honey.

mielleux, -euse [mjelø, øz] *adj* [personne] unctuous; [paroles, air] honeyed.

mien [mjɛ̃] O **le mien** (*f* **la mienne** [lamjɛn], *mpl* **les miens** [lemjɛ̃], *fpl* **les miennes** [lemjɛn]) *pron poss* mine.

miette [mjɛt] *nf* [de pain] crumb, breadcrumb. || (*gén pl*) [débris] shreds (*pl*).

mieux [mjø] **1** *adv* [comparatif]: **~ (que)** better (than); **il pourrait ~ faire** he could do better; **il va ~** he's better; **vous feriez ~ de vous taire** you would do better to keep quiet, you would be well-advised to keep quiet. || [superlatif] best; **il est le ~ payé du service** he's the best ou highest paid member of the department; **le ~ qu'il peut** as best he can. **2** *adj* better. **3** *nm* (*sans déterminant*): **j'espérais ~** I was hoping for something better. || (*avec déterminant*) best; **il y a un** ou **du ~** there's been an improvement; **faire de son ~** to do one's best. O **au mieux** *loc adv* at best. O **de mieux en mieux** *loc adv* better and better.

mièvre [mjɛvr] *adj* insipid.

mignon, -onne [miɲɔ̃, ɔn] *adj* [charmant] sweet, cute. || [gentil] nice.

migraine [migrɛn] *nf* headache; MÉD migraine.

migrant, -e [migrɑ̃, ɑ̃t] *nm, f* migrant.

migrateur, -trice [migratœr, tris] *adj* migratory.

migration [migrasjɔ̃] *nf* migration.

mijoter [miʒɔte] **1** *vt fam* [tramer] to cook up. **2** *vi* CULIN to simmer.

mi-journée [miʒurne] *nf*: **les informations de la ~** the lunchtime news.

milan [milɑ̃] *nm* kite (*bird*).

milice [milis] *nf* militia.

milicien, -ienne [milisjɛ̃, jɛn] *nm, f* militiaman (*f* militiawoman).

milieu, -x [miljø] *nm* [centre] middle; **au ~ de** [au centre de] in the middle of; [parmi] among, surrounded by. ‖ [stade intermédiaire] middle course. ‖ BIOL & SOCIOL environment; **~ familial** family background. ‖ [pègre]: **le ~** the underworld. ‖ FOOTBALL: **~ de terrain** midfielder, midfield player.

militaire [militer] **1** *nm* soldier; **~ de carrière** professional soldier. **2** *adj* military.

militant, -e [militɑ̃, ɑ̃t] *adj & nm, f* militant.

militer [milite] *vi* to be active; **~ pour/contre** to militate in favour of/against.

mille [mil] **1** *nm inv* [unité] a *ou* one thousand. ‖ [de cible]: **dans le ~** on target. ‖ NAVIG: **~ marin** nautical mile. ‖ *Can* [distance] mile. **2** *adj inv* thousand; **je lui ai dit ~ fois** I've told him/her a thousand times.

mille-feuille [milfœj] (*pl* **mille-feuilles**) *nm* ≃ napoleon *Am*.

millénaire [milener] **1** *nm* millennium, thousand years (*pl*). **2** *adj* thousand-year-old (*avant n*).

mille-pattes [milpat] *nm inv* centipede, millipede.

millésime [milezim] *nm* [de pièce] date. ‖ [de vin] vintage, year.

millésimé, -e [milezime] *adj* [vin] vintage (*avant n*).

millet [mijɛ] *nm* millet.

milliard [miljar] *nm* billion *Am*.

milliardaire [miljarder] *nmf* billionaire *Am*.

millier [milje] *nm* thousand; **un ~ de francs/personnes** about a thousand francs/people; **par ~s** in (their) thousands.

milligramme [miligram] *nm* milligram, milligramme.

millilitre [mililitr] *nm* millilitre.

millimètre [milimɛtr] *nm* millimetre.

million [miljɔ̃] *nm* million; **un ~ de francs** a million francs.

millionnaire [miljɔner] *nmf* millionaire.

mime [mim] *nm* mime.

mimer [mime] *vt* [exprimer sans parler] to mime. ‖ [imiter] to mimic.

mimétisme [mimetism] *nm* mimicry.

mimique [mimik] *nf* [grimace] face.

mimosa [mimɔza] *nm* mimosa.

min. (*abr de* minimum) min.

minable [minabl] *adj fam* [misérable] seedy, shabby. ‖ [médiocre] pathetic.

minaret [minarɛ] *nm* minaret.

minauder [minode] *vi* to simper.

mince [mɛ̃s] *adj* [maigre - gén] thin; [- personne, taille] slender, slim. ‖ *fig* [faible] small, meagre.

minceur [mɛ̃sœr] *nf* [gén] thinness; [de personne] slenderness, slimness. ‖ *fig* [insuffisance] meagreness.

mincir [mɛ̃sir] *vi* to get thinner *ou* slimmer.

mine [min] *nf* [expression] look; **avoir bonne/mauvaise ~** to look well/ill. ‖ [apparence] appearance. ‖ [gisement & *fig*] mine; **~ de charbon** coalmine. ‖ [explosif] mine. ‖ [de crayon] lead.

miner [mine] *vt* MIL to mine. ‖ [ronger] to undermine, to wear away; *fig* to wear down.

minerai [minrɛ] *nm* ore.

minéral, -e, -aux [mineral, o] *adj* CHIM inorganic. ‖ [eau, source] mineral (*avant n*). ○ **minéral** *nm* mineral.

minéralogie [mineralɔʒi] *nf* mineralogy.

minéralogique [mineralɔʒik] *adj* AUTOM → **plaque.** ‖ GÉOL mineralogical.

minet, -ette [minɛ, ɛt] *nm, f fam* [chat] pussycat, pussy. ‖ [personne] trendy.

mineur, -e [minœr] **1** *adj* minor. **2** *nm, f* JUR minor. ○ **mineur** *nm* [ouvrier] miner; **~ de fond** face worker.

miniature [minjatyr] **1** *nf* miniature. **2** *adj* miniature.

miniaturiser [minjatyrize] *vt* to miniaturize.

minibus [minibys] *nm* minibus.

minichaîne [miniʃɛn] *nf* portable hi-fi.

minier, -ière [minje, jɛr] *adj* mining (*avant n*).

minijupe [miniʒyp] *nf* miniskirt.

minimal, -e, -aux [minimal, o] *adj* minimum.

minimalisme [minimalism] *nm* minimalism.

minime [minim] **1** *nmf* SPORT ≃ junior. **2** *adj* minimal.

minimiser [minimize] *vt* to minimize.

minimum [minimɔm] (*pl* **minimums** *ou* **minima** [minima]) **1** *nm* [gén & MATHS] minimum; **au ~** at least; **le strict ~** the bare minimum. **2** *adj* minimum.

ministère [minister] *nm* [département] department. ‖ [cabinet] government.

ministériel, -ielle [ministerjɛl] *adj* [du ministère] ministerial *Br*, departmental.

ministre [ministr] *nm* minister *Br*, secretary; **~ d'État** secretary of state, cabinet minister *Br*; **premier ~** prime minister.

Minitel® [minitɛl] *nm* teletext system run by the French national telephone company, *providing an information and communication network*.

minois [minwa] *nm* sweet (little) face.

minoritaire [minɔritɛr] *adj* minority (*avant n*); **être ~** to be in the minority.

minorité [minɔrite] *nf* minority; **en ~** in the minority.

minuit [minɥi] *nm* midnight.

minuscule [minyskyl] **1** *nf* [lettre] small letter. **2** *adj* [lettre] small. || [très petit] tiny, minuscule.

minute [minyt] **1** *nf* minute; **dans une ~** in a minute; **d'une ~ à l'autre** in next to no time. **2** *interj fam* hang on (a minute)!

minuter [minyte] *vt* [chronométrer] to time (precisely).

minuterie [minytri] *nf* [d'éclairage] time switch, timer.

minuteur [minytœr] *nm* timer.

minutie [minysi] *nf* [soin] meticulousness; [précision] attention to detail; **avec ~** [avec soin] meticulously; [dans le détail] in minute detail.

minutieux, -ieuse [minysjø, jøz] *adj* [méticuleux] meticulous; [détaillé] minutely detailed.

mioche [mjɔʃ] *nmf fam* kiddy.

mirabelle [mirabɛl] *nf* [fruit] mirabelle (plum). || [alcool] plum brandy.

miracle [mirakl] *nm* miracle; **par ~** by some *ou* a miracle, miraculously.

miraculeux, -euse [mirakylø, øz] *adj* miraculous.

mirador [miradɔr] *nm* MIL watchtower.

mirage [miraʒ] *nm* mirage.

mire [mir] *nf* TÉLÉ test card. || [visée]: **ligne de ~** line of sight.

mirifique [mirifik] *adj* fabulous.

mirobolant, -e [mirɔbɔlɑ̃, ɑ̃t] *adj* fabulous, fantastic.

miroir [mirwar] *nm* mirror.

miroiter [mirwate] *vi* to sparkle, to gleam; **faire ~ qqch à qqn** to hold out the prospect of sthg to sb.

mis, mise [mi, miz] *pp* → mettre.

misanthrope [mizɑ̃trɔp] **1** *nmf* misanthropist, misanthrope. **2** *adj* misanthropic.

mise [miz] *nf* [action] putting; **~ à jour** updating; **~ au point** PHOT focusing; *fig* clarification; **~ en scène** production. || [d'argent] stake.

miser [mize] **1** *vt* to bet. **2** *vi*: **~ sur** to bet on; *fig* to count on.

misérable [mizerabl] *adj* [pauvre] poor, wretched. || [sans valeur] paltry, miserable.

misère [mizɛr] *nf* [indigence] poverty. || [infortune] misery. || *fig* [bagatelle] trifle.

miséricorde [mizerikɔrd] *nf* [clémence] mercy.

misogyne [mizɔʒin] *adj* misogynous.

missel [misɛl] *nm* missal.

missile [misil] *nm* missile.

mission [misjɔ̃] *nf* mission; **en ~** on a mission.

missionnaire [misjɔnɛr] *nmf* missionary.

missive [misiv] *nf* letter.

mitaine [mitɛn] *nf* fingerless glove.

mite [mit] *nf* (clothes) moth.

mité, -e [mite] *adj* moth-eaten.

mi-temps [mitɑ̃] *nf inv* [SPORT - période] half; [- pause] half-time. **○ à mi-temps** *loc adj & loc adv* part-time.

miteux, -euse [mitø, øz] *fam adj* seedy, dingy.

mitigé, -e [mitiʒe] *adj* [tempéré] lukewarm. || *fam* [mélangé] mixed.

mitonner [mitɔne] *vt* [préparer avec soin] to prepare lovingly.

mitoyen, -enne [mitwajɛ̃, ɛn] *adj* party (*avant n*), common.

mitrailler [mitraje] *vt* MIL to machinegun. || *fam* [photographier] to click away at.

mitraillette [mitrajɛt] *nf* submachine gun.

mitrailleuse [mitrajøz] *nf* machinegun.

mi-voix [mivwa] **○ à mi-voix** *loc adv* in a low voice.

mixage [miksaʒ] *nm* CIN & RADIO (sound) mixing.

mixer[1], mixeur [miksœr] *nm* (food) mixer.

mixer[2] [mikse] *vt* to mix.

mixte [mikst] *adj* mixed.

mixture [mikstyr] *nf* CHIM & CULIN mixture. || *péj* [mélange] concoction.

MJC (*abr de* maison des jeunes et de la culture) *nf* youth and cultural centre.

ml (*abr de* millilitre) ml.

Mlle (*abr de* Mademoiselle) Miss.

mm (*abr de* millimètre) mm.

MM (*abr de* Messieurs) Messrs.

Mme (*abr de* **Madame**) Mrs.

Mo (*abr de* **méga-octet**) MB.

mobile [mɔbil] **1** *nm* [objet] mobile. ||
[motivation] motive. **2** *adj* [gén] movable,
mobile; [partie, pièce] moving. || [popula-
tion, main-d'œuvre] mobile.

mobilier, -ière [mɔbilje, jɛr] *adj* JUR
movable. ○ **mobilier** *nm* furniture.

mobilisation [mɔbilizasjɔ̃] *nf* mobiliza-
tion.

mobiliser [mɔbilize] *vt* [gén] to mobi-
lize. || [moralement] to rally. ○ **se mobi-
liser** *vp* to mobilize, to rally.

mobilité [mɔbilite] *nf* mobility.

Mobylette® [mɔbilɛt] *nf* moped.

mocassin [mɔkasɛ̃] *nm* moccasin.

moche [mɔʃ] *adj fam* [laid] ugly. ||
[triste, méprisable] lousy, rotten.

modalité [mɔdalite] *nf* [convention]
form; **~s de paiement** methods of payment.

mode [mɔd] **1** *nf* [gén] fashion; **à la ~** in
fashion, fashionable. || [coutume] cus-
tom, style; **à la ~ de** in the style of. **2** *nm*
[manière] mode, form; **~ de vie** way of
life. || [méthode] method; **~ d'emploi** in-
structions (for use). || GRAM mood. || MUS
mode.

modèle [mɔdɛl] *nm* [gén] model; **~ dé-
posé** registered design. || (*en apposi-
tion*) [exemplaire] model (*avant n*).

modeler [mɔdle] *vt* to shape; **~ qqch
sur qqch** *fig* to model sthg on sthg.

modélisme [mɔdelism] *nm* modelling
(*of scale models*).

modération [mɔderasjɔ̃] *nf* moderation.

modéré, -e [mɔdere] *adj & nm, f* moderate.

modérer [mɔdere] *vt* to moderate. ○ **se
modérer** *vp* to restrain o.s., to control
o.s.

moderne [mɔdɛrn] *adj* modern.

moderniser [mɔdɛrnize] *vt* to modernize. ○ **se moderniser** *vp* to become
(more) modern.

modeste [mɔdɛst] *adj* modest; [origine]
humble.

modestie [mɔdɛsti] *nf* modesty; **fausse
~** false modesty.

modification [mɔdifikasjɔ̃] *nf* alteration, modification.

modifier [mɔdifje] *vt* to alter, to
modify. ○ **se modifier** *vp* to alter.

modique [mɔdik] *adj* modest.

modiste [mɔdist] *nf* milliner.

modulation [mɔdylasjɔ̃] *nf* modulation.

module [mɔdyl] *nm* module.

moduler [mɔdyle] *vt* [air] to warble. ||
[structure] to adjust.

moelle [mwal] *nf* ANAT marrow.
○ **moelle épinière** *nf* spinal cord.

moelleux, -euse [mwalø, øz] *adj* [ca-
napé, tapis] soft. || [fromage, vin] mellow.

moellon [mwalɔ̃] *nm* rubble stone.

mœurs [mœr(s)] *nfpl* [morale] morals. ||
[coutumes] customs, habits. || ZOOL be-
haviour (*U*).

mohair [mɔɛr] *nm* mohair.

moi [mwa] *pron pers* [objet, après préposition, comparatif] me; **aide-~** help me;
plus âgé que ~ older than me ou than I
(*am*). || [sujet] I; **~ non plus, je n'en sais
rien** I don't know anything about it
either; **qui est là? - (c'est) ~** who's there?
- it's me. ○ **moi-même** *pron pers* myself.

moignon [mwaɲɔ̃] *nm* stump.

moindre [mwɛ̃dr] **1** *adj superl*: **le/la ~**
the least; (*avec négation*) the least ou
slightest; **les ~s détails** the smallest details; **sans la ~ difficulté** without the
slightest problem; **c'est la ~ des choses**
it's the least I/you *etc* could do. **2** *adj
compar* less; [prix] lower.

moine [mwan] *nm* monk.

moineau, -x [mwano] *nm* sparrow.

moins [mwɛ̃] **1** *adv* [quantité] less; **~ de**
less (than); **~ de lait** less milk; **~ de gens**
fewer people; **~ de dix** less than ten. ||
[comparatif]: **~ (que)** less (than); **bien ~
grand que** much smaller than; **~ il
mange, ~ il travaille** the less he eats, the
less he works. || [superlatif]: **le ~** (the)
least; **le ~ riche des hommes** the poorest
man; **c'est lui qui travaille le ~** he works
(the) least; **le ~ possible** as little as possible. **2** *prép* [gén] minus; **dix ~ huit font
deux** ten minus eight is two, ten take
away eight is two; **il fait ~ vingt** it's
twenty below, it's minus twenty. || [ser-
vant à indiquer l'heure]: **il est 3 heures ~
le quart** it's quarter to 3; **il est ~ dix** it's
ten to. **3** *nm loc*: **le ~ qu'on puisse dire,
c'est que ...** it's an understatement to say
.... ○ **à moins de** *loc prép* unless; **à ~ de
battre le record** unless I/you own beat the
record. ○ **à moins que** *loc adv* (+ *subjonctif*) unless. ○ **au moins** *loc adv* at
least. ○ **de moins en moins** *loc adv*
less and less. ○ **du moins** *loc adv* at
least. ○ **en moins** *adv*: **il a une dent en**

~ he's missing ou minus a tooth. ○ **pour le moins** *loc adv* at (the very) least. ○ **tout au moins** *loc adv* at (the very) least.

moiré, -e [mware] *adj* [tissu] watered.

mois [mwa] *nm* [laps de temps] month.

moisi, -e [mwazi] *adj* mouldy. ○ **moisi** *nm* mould.

moisir [mwazir] *vi* [pourrir] to go mouldy. || *fig* [personne] to rot.

moisissure [mwazisyr] *nf* mould.

moisson [mwasɔ̃] *nf* [récolte] harvest; **faire la ~** ou **les ~s** to harvest, to bring in the harvest. || *fig* [d'idées, de projets] wealth.

moissonner [mwasɔne] *vt* to harvest, to gather (in); *fig* to collect, to gather.

moissonneuse-batteuse [mwasɔnøzbatøz] *nf* combine (harvester).

moite [mwat] *adj* [peau, mains] moist, sweaty; [atmosphère] muggy.

moiteur [mwatœr] *nf* [de peau, mains] moistness; [d'atmosphère] mugginess.

moitié [mwatje] *nf* [gén] half; **à ~ vide** half-empty; **faire qqch à ~** to half-do sthg; **la ~ du temps** half the time; **à la ~ de qqch** halfway through sthg.

moka [mɔka] *nm* [café] mocha (coffee). || [gâteau] coffee cake.

mol → **mou**.

molaire [mɔlɛr] *nf* molar.

molécule [mɔlekyl] *nf* molecule.

molester [mɔlɛste] *vt* to manhandle.

molle → **mou**.

mollement [mɔlmɑ̃] *adv* [faiblement] weakly, feebly.

mollesse [mɔlɛs] *nf* [de chose] softness. || [de personne] lethargy.

mollet [mɔlɛ] **1** *nm* calf. **2** *adj* → **œuf**.

mollir [mɔlir] *vi* [physiquement, moralement] to give way. || [vent] to drop, to die down.

mollusque [mɔlysk] *nm* ZOOL mollusc.

molosse [mɔlɔs] *nm* [chien] large ferocious dog. || *fig & péj* [personne] hulking great brute ou fellow.

môme [mom] *fam nmf* [enfant] kid, youngster.

moment [mɔmɑ̃] *nm* [gén] moment; **au ~ de l'accident** at the time of the accident, when the accident happened; **au ~ de partir** just as we/you *etc* were leaving; **au ~ où** just as; **dans un ~** in a moment; **d'un ~ à l'autre, à tout ~** (at) any moment, any moment now; **par ~s** at times, now and then; **en ce ~** at the moment; **pour le ~** for the moment. || [du-rée] (short) time; **passer un mauvais ~** to have a bad time. || [occasion] time; **n'est pas le ~ (de faire qqch)** this is not the time (to do sthg). ○ **du moment que** *loc prép* since, as.

momentané, -e [mɔmɑ̃tane] *adj* temporary.

momie [mɔmi] *nf* mummy.

mon [mɔ̃] (*f* **ma** [ma], *pl* **mes** [me]) *adj poss* my.

Monaco [mɔnako] *n*: **(la principauté de)** ~ (the principality of) Monaco.

monarchie [mɔnarʃi] *nf* monarchy; **~ absolue/constitutionnelle** absolute/constitutional monarchy.

monarque [mɔnark] *nm* monarch.

monastère [mɔnastɛr] *nm* monastery.

monceau, -x [mɔ̃so] *nm* [tas] heap.

mondain, -e [mɔ̃dɛ̃, ɛn] *adj* [chronique, journaliste] society (*avant n*). || *péj* [futile] frivolous, superficial.

mondanités [mɔ̃danite] *nfpl* [événements] society life (*U*). || [paroles] small talk (*U*); [comportements] formalities.

monde [mɔ̃d] *nm* [gén] world; **le/la plus ... au ~, le/la plus ... du ~** the most ... in the world; **pour rien au ~** not for the world, not for all the tea in China; **mettre un enfant au ~** to bring a child into the world. || [gens] people (*pl*); **beaucoup/peu de ~** a lot of/not many people; **tout le ~** everyone, everybody. || *loc*: **c'est un ~!** that's really the limit!; **se faire un ~ de qqch** to make too much of sthg; **noir de ~** packed with people.

mondial, -e, -iaux [mɔ̃djal, jo] *adj* world (*avant n*).

mondialement [mɔ̃djalmɑ̃] *adv* throughout ou all over the world.

monétaire [mɔnetɛr] *adj* monetary.

Mongolie [mɔ̃gɔli] *nf*: **la ~** Mongolia.

mongolien, -ienne [mɔ̃gɔljɛ̃, jɛn] *vieilli nm, f* mongol.

moniteur, -trice [mɔnitœr, tris] *nm, f* [enseignant] instructor, coach; **~ d'auto-école** driving instructor. || [de colonie de vacances] supervisor, leader. ○ **moniteur** *nm* [appareil & INFORM] monitor.

monnaie [mɔnɛ] *nf* [moyen de paiement] money. || [de pays] currency. || [pièces] change; **faire (de) la ~** to get (some) change.

monnayer [mɔneje] *vt* [biens] to convert into cash. || *fig* [silence] to buy.

monochrome [mɔnɔkrom] *adj* monochrome, monochromatic.

monocle [mɔnɔkl] *nm* monocle.

monocoque [mɔnɔkɔk] *nm* & *adj* [bateau] monohull.

monocorde [mɔnɔkɔrd] *adj* [monotone] monotonous.

monogramme [mɔnɔgram] *nm* monogram.

monolingue [mɔnɔlɛ̃g] *adj* monolingual.

monologue [mɔnɔlɔg] *nm* THÉÂTRE soliloquy. || [discours individuel] monologue.

monologuer [mɔnɔlɔge] *vi* THÉÂTRE to soliloquize. || *fig* & *péj* [parler] to talk away.

monoplace [mɔnɔplas] *adj* single-seater (*avant n*).

monopole [mɔnɔpɔl] *nm* monopoly; **avoir le ~ de qqch** *litt* & *fig* to have a monopoly of *ou* on sthg.

monopoliser [mɔnɔpɔlize] *vt* to monopolize.

monoski [mɔnɔski] *nm* [objet] monoski. || [sport] monoskiing.

monosyllabe [mɔnɔsilab] **1** *nm* monosyllable. **2** *adj* monosyllabic.

monotone [mɔnɔtɔn] *adj* monotonous.

monotonie [mɔnɔtɔni] *nf* monotony.

monseigneur [mɔ̃sɛɲœr] (*pl* **messeigneurs** [mesɛɲœr]) *nm* [titre - d'évêque, de duc] His Grace; [- de cardinal] His Eminence; [- de prince] His (Royal) Highness.

monsieur [məsjø] (*pl* **messieurs** [mesjø]) *nm* [titre]: **~ X** Mr X; **bonjour ~** good morning; [dans hôtel, restaurant] good morning, sir; **bonjour messieurs** good morning (gentlemen); **Monsieur le Ministre n'est pas là** the Minister is out. || [homme quelconque] gentleman.

monstre [mɔ̃str] *nm* [gén] monster. || (*en apposition*) *fam* [énorme] colossal.

monstrueux, -euse [mɔ̃stryø, øz] *adj* [gén] monstrous. || *fig* [erreur] terrible.

monstruosité [mɔ̃stryozite] *nf* monstrosity.

mont [mɔ̃] *nm* GÉOGR Mount; **le ~ Blanc** Mont Blanc; **le ~ Cervin** the Matterhorn.

montage [mɔ̃taʒ] *nm* [assemblage] assembly; [de bijou] setting. || PHOT photomontage. || CIN editing.

montagnard, -e [mɔ̃taɲar, ard] *nm, f* mountain dweller.

montagne [mɔ̃taɲ] *nf* [gén] mountain; **les ~s Rocheuses** the Rocky Mountains. || [région]: **la ~** the mountains (*pl*); **à la ~** in the mountains; **en haute ~** at high altitudes. ○ **montagnes russes** *nfpl* big dipper (*sg*), roller coaster (*sg*).

montant, -e [mɔ̃tɑ̃, ɑ̃t] *adj* [mouvement] rising. ○ **montant** *nm* [pièce verticale] upright. || [somme] total (amount).

mont-de-piété [mɔ̃dpjete] (*pl* **monts-de-piété**) *nm* pawnshop.

monte-charge [mɔ̃tʃarʒ] *nm inv* goods lift *Br*, service elevator *Am*.

montée [mɔ̃te] *nf* [de montagne] climb, ascent. || [de prix] rise. || [relief] slope, gradient.

monte-plats [mɔ̃tpla] *nm inv* dumbwaiter.

monter [mɔ̃te] **1** *vi* (*aux: être*) [personne] to come/go up; [température, niveau] to rise; [route, avion] to climb; **~ sur qqch** to climb onto sthg. || [passager] to get on; **~ dans un bus** to get on a bus; **~ dans une voiture** to get into a car. || [cavalier] to ride; **~ à cheval** to ride. || [marée] to go/come in. **2** *vt* (*aux: avoir*) [escalier, côte] to climb, to come/go up. || [chauffage, son] to turn up. || [valise] to take/bring up. || [meuble] to assemble; COUTURE to assemble, to put *ou* sew together; [tente] to put up. || [cheval] to mount. || THÉÂTRE to put on. || [société, club] to set up. || CULIN to beat, to whisk (up). ○ **se monter** *vp* [atteindre]: **se ~ à** to amount to, to add up to.

monteur, -euse [mɔ̃tœr, øz] *nm, f* TECHNOL fitter. || CIN editor.

monticule [mɔ̃tikyl] *nm* mound.

montre [mɔ̃tr] *nf* watch; **~ à quartz** quartz watch; **~ en main** to the minute, exactly; **contre la ~** [sport] time-trialling; [épreuve] time trial.

montre-bracelet [mɔ̃trəbrasle] *nf* wristwatch.

montrer [mɔ̃tre] *vt* [gén] to show; **~ qqch à qqn** to show sb sthg, to show sthg to sb. || [désigner] to show, to point out. ○ **se montrer** *vp* [se faire voir] to appear. || *fig* [se présenter] to show o.s. || *fig* [se révéler] to prove (to be).

monture [mɔ̃tyr] *nf* [animal] mount. || [de lunettes] frame.

monument [mɔnymɑ̃] *nm* [gén]: **~ (à)** monument (to); **~ aux morts** war memorial.

monumental, -e, -aux [mɔnymɑ̃tal, o] *adj* monumental.

moquer [mɔke] ○ **se moquer** *vp*: **se ~ de** [plaisanter sur] to make fun of, to laugh at; [ne pas se soucier de] not to give a damn about.

moquerie [mɔkri] *nf* mockery (*U*), jibe.

moquette [mɔkɛt] *nf* (fitted) carpet.

moqueur, -euse [mɔkœr, øz] *adj* mocking.

moral, -e, -aux [mɔral, o] *adj* moral. ○ **moral** *nm* [état d'esprit] morale, spirits (*pl*); **avoir/ne pas avoir le ~** to be in good/bad spirits; **remonter le ~ à qqn** to cheer sb up. ○ **morale** *nf* [science] moral philosophy, morals (*pl*). || [mœurs] morals (*pl*). || [leçon] moral; **faire la ~e à qqn** to preach at or lecture sb.

moralisateur, -trice [mɔralizatœr, tris] 1 *adj* moralizing. 2 *nm, f* moralizer.

moraliste [mɔralist] *nmf* moralist.

moralité [mɔralite] *nf* [gén] morality. || [enseignement] morals.

moratoire [mɔratwar] *nm* moratorium.

morbide [mɔrbid] *adj* morbid.

morceau, -x [mɔrso] *nm* [gén] piece. || [de poème, de musique] passage.

morceler [mɔrsəle] *vt* to break up, to split up.

mordant, -e [mɔrdã, ãt] *adj* biting. ○ **mordant** *nm* [vivacité] keenness, bite.

mordiller [mɔrdije] *vt* to nibble.

mordoré, -e [mɔrdɔre] *adj* bronze.

mordre [mɔrdr] 1 *vt* [blesser] to bite. 2 *vi* [saisir avec les dents]: **~ à** to bite. || [croquer]: **~ dans qqch** to bite into sthg. || SPORT: **~ sur la ligne** to step over the line.

mordu, -e [mɔrdy] 1 *pp* → **mordre**. 2 *adj* [amoureux] hooked. 3 *nm, f*: **~ de foot/ski** *etc* football/ski *etc* addict.

morfondre [mɔrfɔ̃dr] ○ **se morfondre** *vp* to mope.

morgue [mɔrg] *nf* [attitude] pride. || [lieu] morgue.

moribond, -e [mɔribɔ̃, ɔ̃d] 1 *adj* dying. 2 *nm, f* dying person.

morille [mɔrij] *nf* morel.

morne [mɔrn] *adj* [personne, visage] gloomy; [paysage, temps, ville] dismal, dreary.

morose [mɔroz] *adj* gloomy.

morphine [mɔrfin] *nf* morphine.

morphologie [mɔrfɔlɔʒi] *nf* morphology.

mors [mɔr] *nm* bit.

morse [mɔrs] *nm* ZOOL walrus. || [code] Morse (code).

morsure [mɔrsyr] *nf* bite.

mort, -e [mɔr, mɔrt] 1 *pp* → **mourir**. 2 *adj* dead; **~ de fatigue** *fig* dead tired; **~**

de peur *fig* frightened to death. 3 *nm, f* [cadavre] corpse, dead body. || [défunt] dead person. ○ **mort** 1 *nm* [victime] fatality. 2 *nf litt & fig* death; **se donner la ~** to take one's own life, to commit suicide.

mortadelle [mɔrtadɛl] *nf* mortadella.

mortalité [mɔrtalite] *nf* mortality, death rate.

mort-aux-rats [mɔrora] *nf inv* rat poison.

mortel, -elle [mɔrtɛl] 1 *adj* [humain] mortal. || [accident, maladie] fatal. || *fig* [ennuyeux] deadly (dull). 2 *nm, f* mortal.

morte-saison [mɔrtsɛzɔ̃] *nf* slack season, off-season.

mortier [mɔrtje] *nm* mortar.

mortification [mɔrtifikasjɔ̃] *nf* mortification.

mort-né, -e [mɔrne] (*mpl* **mort-nés**, *fpl* **mort-nées**) *adj* [enfant] still-born.

mortuaire [mɔrtɥɛr] *adj* funeral (*avant n*).

morue [mɔry] *nf* ZOOL cod.

mosaïque [mɔzaik] *nf litt & fig* mosaic.

Moscou [mɔsku] *n* Moscow.

mosquée [mɔske] *nf* mosque.

mot [mo] *nm* [gén] word; **gros ~** swear-word; **~ de passe** password; **~s croisés** crossword (puzzle) (*sg*). || [message] note, message.

motard [mɔtar] *nm* [motocycliste] motorcyclist. || [policier] motorcycle policeman.

motel [mɔtɛl] *nm* motel.

moteur, -trice [mɔtœr, tris] *adj* [force, énergie] driving (*avant n*); **à quatre roues motrices** AUTOM with four-wheel drive. ○ **moteur** *nm* TECHNOL motor, engine; *fig* driving force.

motif [mɔtif] *nm* [raison] motive, grounds (*pl*). || [dessin, impression] motif.

motion [mɔsjɔ̃] *nf* POLIT motion; **~ de censure** motion of censure.

motiver [mɔtive] *vt* [stimuler] to motivate. || [justifier] to justify.

moto [mɔto] *nf* motorbike.

motocross [mɔtɔkrɔs] *nm* motocross.

motoculteur [mɔtɔkyltœr] *nm* ≃ Rotavator®.

motocyclette [mɔtɔsiklɛt] *nf* motorcycle, motorbike.

motocycliste [mɔtɔsiklist] *nmf* motorcyclist.

motorisé, -e [mɔtɔrize] *adj* motorized; **être ~** *fam* to have a car, to have wheels.

motrice → **moteur**.

motte [mɔt] *nf*: ~ **(de terre)** clod, lump of earth; ~ **de beurre** slab of butter.

mou, molle [mu, mɔl] *adj* (**mol** *devant voyelle ou h muet*) [gén] soft. || [faible] weak. || [résistance, protestation] half-hearted. || *fam* [de caractère] wet, wimpy.

mouchard, -e [muʃar, ard] *nm, f fam* [personne] sneak. ○ **mouchard** *nm fam* [dans camion, train] spy in the cab.

mouche [muʃ] *nf* ZOOL fly. || [accessoire féminin] beauty spot.

moucher [muʃe] *vt* [nez] to wipe; ~ **un enfant** to wipe a child's nose. || [chandelle] to snuff out. || *fam fig* [personne]: ~ **qqn** to put sb in his/her place. ○ **se moucher** *vp* to blow ou wipe one's nose.

moucheron [muʃrɔ̃] *nm* [insecte] gnat.

moucheté, -e [muʃte] *adj* [laine] flecked. || [animal] spotted, speckled.

mouchoir [muʃwar] *nm* handkerchief.

moudre [mudr] *vt* to grind.

moue [mu] *nf* pout; **faire la ~** to pull a face.

mouette [mwɛt] *nf* seagull.

moufle [mufl] *nf* mitten.

mouillage [muja3] *nm* [NAVIG - emplacement] anchorage, moorings (*pl*).

mouillé, -e [muje] *adj* wet.

mouiller [muje] *vt* [personne, objet] to wet. || NAVIG: ~ **l'ancre** to drop anchor. || *fam fig* [compromettre] to involve. ○ **se mouiller** *vp* [se tremper] to get wet. || *fam fig* [prendre des risques] to stick one's neck out.

moulage [mula3] *nm* [action] moulding, casting. || [objet] cast.

moule [mul] 1 *nm* mould; ~ **à gâteau** cake tin; ~ **à tarte** flan dish. 2 *nf* ZOOL mussel.

mouler [mule] *vt* [objet] to mould. || [forme] to make a cast of.

moulin [mulɛ̃] *nm* mill; ~ **à café** coffee mill; ~ **à paroles** *fig* chatterbox.

moulinet [mulinɛ] *nm* PÊCHE reel. || [mouvement]: **faire des ~s** to whirl one's arms around.

Moulinette® [mulinɛt] *nf* food mill.

moulu, -e [muly] *adj* [en poudre] ground.

moulure [mulyr] *nf* moulding.

mourant, -e [murɑ̃, ɑ̃t] 1 *adj* [moribond] dying. || *fig* [voix] faint. 2 *nm, f* dying person.

mourir [murir] *vi* [personne] to die; **s'ennuyer à ~** to be bored to death.

mousquetaire [muskətɛr] *nm* musketeer.

moussant, -e [musɑ̃, ɑ̃t] *adj* foaming.

mousse [mus] 1 *nf* BOT moss. || [substance] foam; ~ **à raser** shaving foam. || CULIN mousse. || [matière plastique] foam rubber. 2 *nm* NAVIG cabin boy.

mousseline [muslin] *nf* muslin.

mousser [muse] *vi* to foam, to lather.

mousseux, -euse [musø, øz] *adj* [shampooing] foaming, frothy. || [vin, cidre] sparkling. ○ **mousseux** *nm* sparkling wine.

mousson [musɔ̃] *nf* monsoon.

moustache [mustaʃ] *nf* moustache. ○ **moustaches** *nfpl* [d'animal] whiskers.

moustachu, -e [mustaʃy] *adj* with a moustache.

moustiquaire [mustikɛr] *nf* mosquito net.

moustique [mustik] *nm* mosquito.

moutarde [mutard] *nf* mustard.

mouton [mutɔ̃] *nm* ZOOL & *fig* sheep. || [viande] mutton. || *fam* [poussière] piece of fluff, fluff (*U*).

mouture [mutyr] *nf* [de céréales, de café] grinding. || [de thème, d'œuvre] rehash.

mouvant, -e [muvɑ̃, ɑ̃t] *adj* [terrain] unstable. || [situation] uncertain.

mouvement [muvmɑ̃] *nm* [gén] movement; **en ~** on the move. || [de colère, d'indignation] burst, fit.

mouvementé, -e [muvmɑ̃te] *adj* [terrain] rough. || [réunion, soirée] eventful.

mouvoir [muvwar] *vt* to move. ○ **se mouvoir** *vp* to move.

moyen, -enne [mwajɛ̃, ɛn] *adj* [intermédiaire] medium. || [médiocre, courant] average. ○ **moyen** *nm* means (*sg*); way; ~ **de communication** means of communication; ~ **de locomotion** ou **transport** means of transport. ○ **moyenne** *nf* average; **en moyenne** on average. ○ **moyens** *nmpl* [ressources] means; **avoir les ~s** to be comfortably off. || [capacités] powers, ability; **faire qqch par ses propres ~s** to do sthg on one's own. ○ **au moyen de** *loc prép* by means of.

Moyen Âge [mwajɛna3] *nm*: **le ~** the Middle Ages (*pl*).

Moyen-Orient [mwajɛnɔrjɑ̃] *nm*: **le ~** the Middle East.

mû, mue [my] *pp* → **mouvoir**.

mue [my] *nf* [de pelage] moulting. || [de serpent] skin, slough. || [de voix] breaking.

muer [mɥe] *vi* [mammifère] to moult. ‖ [serpent] to slough its skin. ‖ [voix] to break.

muet, muette [mɥe, ɛt] **1** *adj* MÉD dumb. ‖ [silencieux] silent; **~ d'admiration/d'étonnement** speechless with admiration/surprise. ‖ LING silent, mute. **2** *nm, f* mute, dumb person. ○ **muet** *nm:* **le ~** CIN silent films (*pl*).

mufle [myfl] *nm* [d'animal] muzzle, snout. ‖ *fig* [goujat] lout.

mugir [myʒir] *vi* [vache] to moo. ‖ [vent, sirène] to howl.

muguet [mygɛ] *nm* [fleur] lily of the valley. ‖ MÉD thrush.

mule [myl] *nf* mule.

mulet [mylɛ] *nm* [âne] mule. ‖ [poisson] mullet.

mulot [mylo] *nm* field mouse.

multicolore [myltikɔlɔr] *adj* multicoloured.

multifonction [myltifɔ̃ksjɔ̃] *adj inv* multifunction.

multilatéral, -e, -aux [myltilateral, o] *adj* multilateral.

multinational, -e, -aux [myltinasjɔnal, o] *adj* multinational. ○ **multinationale** *nf* multinational (company).

multiple [myltipl] **1** *nm* multiple. **2** *adj* [nombreux] multiple, numerous. ‖ [divers] many, various.

multiplication [myltiplikasjɔ̃] *nf* multiplication.

multiplier [myltiplije] *vt* [accroître] to increase. ‖ MATHS to multiply; **X multiplié par Y égale Z** X multiplied by ou times Y equals Z. ○ **se multiplier** *vp* to multiply.

multiracial, -e, -iaux [myltirasjal, jo] *adj* multiracial.

multirisque [myltirisk] *adj* comprehensive.

multitude [myltityd] *nf:* **~ (de)** multitude (of).

municipal, -e, -aux [mynisipal, o] *adj* municipal. ○ **municipales** *nfpl:* **les ~es** the local government elections.

municipalité [mynisipalite] *nf* [commune] municipality. ‖ [conseil] town council.

munir [mynir] *vt:* **~ qqn/qqch de** to equip sb/sthg with. ○ **se munir** *vp:* **se ~ de** to equip o.s. with.

munitions [mynisjɔ̃] *nfpl* ammunition (*U*), munitions.

muqueuse [mykøz] *nf* mucous membrane.

mur [myr] *nm* [gén] wall. ‖ *fig* [obstacle] barrier, brick wall; **~ du son** AÉRON sound barrier.

mûr, mûre [myr] *adj* ripe; [personne] mature. ○ **mûre** *nf* [de mûrier] mulberry. ‖ [de ronce] blackberry, bramble.

muraille [myraj] *nf* wall.

murène [myrɛn] *nf* moray eel.

murer [myre] *vt* [boucher] to wall up, to block up. ‖ [enfermer] to wall in. ○ **se murer** *vp* to shut o.s. up ou away.

muret [myrɛ] *nm* low wall.

mûrier [myrje] *nm* [arbre] mulberry tree. ‖ [ronce] blackberry bush, bramble bush.

mûrir [myrir] *vi* [fruits, légumes] to ripen. ‖ *fig* [idée, projet] to develop. ‖ [personne] to mature.

murmure [myrmyr] *nm* murmur.

murmurer [myrmyre] *vt & vi* to murmur.

musaraigne [myzarɛɲ] *nf* shrew.

musarder [myzarde] *vi fam* to dawdle.

muscade [myskad] *nf* nutmeg.

muscat [myska] *nm* [raisin] muscat grape. ‖ [vin] *sweet wine.*

muscle [myskl] *nm* muscle.

musclé, -e [myskle] *adj* [personne] muscular. ‖ *fig* [mesure, décision] forceful.

muscler [myskle] *vt:* **~ son corps** to build up one's muscles. ○ **se muscler** *vp* to build up one's muscles.

musculation [myskylasjɔ̃] *nf:* **faire de la ~** to do muscle-building exercises.

muse [myz] *nf* muse.

museau [myzo] *nm* [d'animal] muzzle, snout. ‖ *fam* [de personne] face.

musée [myze] *nm* museum; [d'art] art gallery.

museler [myzle] *vt litt & fig* to muzzle.

muselière [myzəljɛr] *nf* muzzle.

musette [myzɛt] *nf* haversack.

musical, -e, -aux [myzikal, o] *adj* [son] musical. ‖ [émission, critique] music (*avant n*).

music-hall [myzikol] (*pl* music-halls) *nm* music-hall.

musicien, -ienne [myzisjɛ̃, jɛn] **1** *adj* musical. **2** *nm, f* musician.

musique [myzik] *nf* music; **~ de chambre** chamber music; **~ de film** film *Br* ou movie *Am* score.

musulman, -e [myzylmɑ̃, an] *adj & nm, f* Muslim.

mutant, -e [mytɑ̃, ɑ̃t] *adj* mutant.
○ **mutant** *nm* mutant.
mutation [mytasjɔ̃] *nf* BIOL mutation. ||
fig [changement] transformation. || [de
fonctionnaire] transfer.
muter [myte] *vt* to transfer.
mutilation [mytilasjɔ̃] *nf* mutilation.
mutilé, -e [mytile] *nm, f* disabled person.
mutiler [mytile] *vt* to mutilate.
mutinerie [mytinri] *nf* rebellion; MIL &
NAVIG mutiny.
mutisme [mytism] *nm* silence.
mutualité [mytɥalite] *nf* [assurance]
mutual insurance.
mutuel, -elle [mytɥɛl] *adj* mutual.
○ **mutuelle** *nf* mutual insurance company.
mycose [mikoz] *nf* mycosis, fungal infection.
myocarde [mjɔkard] *nm* myocardium.
myopathie [mjɔpati] *nf* myopathy.
myope [mjɔp] **1** *nmf* shortsighted person. **2** *adj* shortsighted, myopic.
myopie [mjɔpi] *nf* shortsightedness,
myopia.
myosotis [mjɔzɔtis] *nm* forget-me-not.
myrtille [mirtij] *nf* blueberry *Am*.
mystère [mister] *nm* [gén] mystery.
mystérieux, -ieuse [misterjø, jøz] *adj*
mysterious.
mysticisme [mistisism] *nm* mysticism.
mystification [mistifikasjɔ̃] *nf* [tromperie] hoax, practical joke.
mystifier [mistifje] *vt* [duper] to take
in.
mystique [mistik] **1** *nmf* mystic. **2** *adj*
mystic, mystical.
mythe [mit] *nm* myth.
mythique [mitik] *adj* mythical.
mythologie [mitɔlɔʒi] *nf* mythology.
mythomane [mitɔman] *nmf* pathological liar.

n, N [ɛn] *nm inv* [lettre] n, N. ○ **N** (*abr
de nord*) N.
nacelle [nasɛl] *nf* [de montgolfière] basket.
nacre [nakr] *nf* mother-of-pearl.
nage [naʒ] *nf* [natation] swimming; **traverser à la ~** to swim across. || *loc*: **en ~**
bathed in sweat.
nageoire [naʒwar] *nf* fin.
nager [naʒe] *vi* [se baigner] to swim. ||
[flotter] to float. || *fig* [dans vêtement]: **~
dans** to be lost in.
nageur, -euse [naʒœr, øz] *nm, f* swimmer.
naguère [nagɛr] *adv littéraire* a short
time ago.
naïf, naïve [naif, iv] *adj* [ingénu, art]
naive. || *péj* [crédule] gullible.
nain, -e [nɛ̃, nɛn] **1** *adj* dwarf (*avant
n*). **2** *nm, f* dwarf.
naissance [nɛsɑ̃s] *nf* [de personne]
birth; **donner ~ à** to give birth to. || [endroit] source; [du cou] nape. || *fig* [de
science, nation] birth; **donner ~ à** to give
rise to.
naissant, -e [nɛsɑ̃, ɑ̃t] *adj* [brise] rising;
[jour] dawning. || [barbe] incipient.
naître [nɛtr] *vi* [enfant] to be born; **elle
est née en 1965** she was born in 1965. ||
[espoir] to spring up; **~ de** to arise from;
faire ~ qqch to give rise to sthg.
naïveté [naivte] *nf* [candeur] innocence.
|| *péj* [crédulité] gullibility.
nana [nana] *nf fam* [jeune fille] girl.
nanti, -e [nɑ̃ti] *nm, f* wealthy person.
nappe [nap] *nf* [de table] tablecloth,
cloth. || *fig* [étendue - gén] sheet; [- de
brouillard] blanket. || [couche] layer.
napper [nape] *vt* CULIN to coat.
napperon [naprɔ̃] *nm* tablemat.
narcisse [narsis] *nm* BOT narcissus.
narcissisme [narsisism] *nm* narcissism.
narcotique [narkɔtik] *nm & adj* narcotic.

narguer [narge] *vt* [danger] to flout; [personne] to scorn, to scoff at.

narine [narin] *nf* nostril.

narquois, -e [narkwa, az] *adj* sardonic.

narrateur, -trice [naratœr, tris] *nm, f* narrator.

narrer [nare] *vt littéraire* to narrate.

nasal, -e, -aux [nazal, o] *adj* nasal.

naseau, -x [nazo] *nm* nostril.

nasillard, -e [nazijar, ard] *adj* nasal.

nasse [nas] *nf* keep net.

natal, -e, -als [natal] *adj* [d'origine] native.

natalité [natalite] *nf* birth rate.

natation [natasjɔ̃] *nf* swimming; **faire de la ~** to swim.

natif, -ive [natif, iv] **1** *adj* [originaire]: **~ de** native of. **2** *nm, f* native.

nation [nasjɔ̃] *nf* nation. ○ **Nations unies** *nfpl*: **les Nations unies** the United Nations.

national, -e, -aux [nasjonal, o] *adj* national. ○ **nationale** *nf*: (route) **~e** ≃ A road *Br*, ≃ state highway *Am*.

nationaliser [nasjonalize] *vt* to nationalize.

nationalisme [nasjonalism] *nm* nationalism.

nationalité [nasjonalite] *nf* nationality; **de ~ française** of French nationality.

natte [nat] *nf* [tresse] plait. ‖ [tapis] mat.

naturaliser [natyralize] *vt* [personne, plante] to naturalize. ‖ [empailler] to stuff.

nature [natyr] **1** *nf* nature. **2** *adj inv* [simple] plain. ‖ *fam* [spontané] natural.

naturel, -elle [natyrɛl] *adj* natural. ○ **naturel** *nm* [tempérament] nature; **être d'un ~ affable/sensible** *etc* to be affable/sensitive *etc* by nature. ‖ [aisance, spontanéité] naturalness.

naturellement [natyrɛlmɑ̃] *adv* [gén] naturally. ‖ [logiquement] rationally.

naturiste [natyrist] *nmf* naturist.

naufrage [nofraʒ] *nm* [navire] shipwreck; **faire ~** to be wrecked. ‖ *fig* [effondrement] collapse.

naufragé, -e [nofraʒe] **1** *adj* shipwrecked. **2** *nm, f* shipwrecked person.

nauséabond, -e [nozeabɔ̃, ɔ̃d] *adj* nauseating.

nausée [noze] *nf MÉD* nausea; **avoir la ~** to feel nauseous *ou* sick.

nautique [notik] *adj* nautical; [ski, sport] water (*avant n*).

naval, -e, -als [naval] *adj* naval.

navet [navɛ] *nm BOT* turnip. ‖ *fam péj* [œuvre] load of rubbish.

navette [navɛt] *nf* shuttle; **~ spatiale** *AÉRON* space shuttle; **faire la ~** to shuttle.

navigable [navigabl] *adj* navigable.

navigateur, -trice [navigatœr, tris] *nm, f* navigator.

navigation [navigasjɔ̃] *nf* navigation; *COMM* shipping.

naviguer [navige] *vi* [voguer] to sail. ‖ [piloter] to navigate.

navire [navir] *nm* ship.

navrant, -e [navrɑ̃, ɑ̃t] *adj* [triste] upsetting, distressing. ‖ [regrettable, mauvais] unfortunate.

navrer [navre] *vt* to upset; **être navré de qqch/de faire qqch** to be sorry about sthg/to do sthg.

nazi, -e [nazi] *nm, f* Nazi.

nazisme [nazism] *nm* Nazism.

NB (*abr de* Nota Bene) NB.

NDLR (*abr de* note de la rédaction) editor's note.

NDT (*abr de* note du traducteur) translator's note.

ne, n' (*devant voyelle ou h muet*) *adv* [négation] → **pas, plus, rien** *etc*. ‖ [négation implicite]: **il se porte mieux que je ~ (le) croyais** he's in better health than I thought (he would be). ‖ [avec verbes ou expressions marquant le doute, la crainte etc]: **je crains qu'il n'oublie** I'm afraid he'll forget.

né, -e [ne] *adj* born; **~ en 1965** born in 1965; **Mme X, ~e Y** Mrs X née Y.

néanmoins [neɑ̃mwɛ̃] *adv* nevertheless.

néant [neɑ̃] *nm* [absence d'existence] nothingness; **réduire à ~** to reduce to nothing.

nébuleux, -euse [nebylø, øz] *adj* [ciel] cloudy. ‖ [idée, projet] nebulous. ○ **nébuleuse** *nf ASTRON* nebula.

nécessaire [nesesɛr] **1** *adj* necessary; **~ à** necessary for; **il est ~ de faire qqch** it is necessary to do sthg; **il est ~ que** (+ *subjonctif*): **il est ~ qu'elle vienne** she must come. **2** *nm* [biens] necessities (*pl*); **le strict ~** the bare essentials (*pl*). ‖ [mesures]: **faire le ~** to do the necessary. ‖ [trousse] bag.

nécessité [nesesite] *nf* [obligation, situation] necessity.

nécessiter [nesesite] *vt* to necessitate.

nécrologique [nekrɔlɔʒik] *adj* obituary (*avant n*).

nectar [nɛktar] *nm* nectar.

nectarine [nɛktarin] *nf* nectarine.

néerlandais, -e [neerlɑ̃dɛ, ɛz] adj Dutch. ○ **néerlandais** nm [langue] Dutch. ○ **Néerlandais, -e** nm, f Dutchman (f Dutchwoman); les **Néerlandais** the Dutch.

nef [nɛf] nf [d'église] nave.

néfaste [nefast] adj [jour, événement] fateful. || [influence] harmful.

négatif, -ive [negatif, iv] adj negative. ○ **négatif** nm PHOT negative. ○ **négative** nf: répondre par la négative to reply in the negative.

négation [negasjɔ̃] nf [rejet] denial. || GRAM negative.

négligé, -e [negliʒe] adj [travail, tenue] untidy. || [ami, jardin] neglected.

négligeable [negliʒabl] adj negligible.

négligemment [negliʒamɑ̃] adv [avec indifférence] casually.

négligence [negliʒɑ̃s] nf [laisser-aller] carelessness. || [omission] negligence.

négligent, e [negliʒɑ̃, ɑ̃t] adj [sans soin] careless. || [indifférent] casual.

négliger [negliʒe] vt [ami, jardin] to neglect; ~ de faire qqch to fail to do sthg. || [avertissement] to ignore. ○ **se négliger** vp to neglect o.s.

négoce [negɔs] nm business.

négociant, -e [negɔsjɑ̃, ɑ̃t] nm, f dealer.

négociateur, -trice [negɔsjatœr, tris] nm, f negotiator.

négociation [negɔsjasjɔ̃] nf negotiation; ~s de paix peace negotiations.

négocier [negɔsje] vt to negotiate.

nègre, négresse [nɛgr, negrɛs] nm, f negro (f negress) (beware: the terms 'nègre' and 'négresse' are considered racist). ○ **nègre** nm fam ghost writer.

neige [nɛʒ] nf [flocons] snow.

neiger [neʒe] v impers: il neige it is snowing.

neigeux, -euse [nɛʒø, øz] adj snowy.

nénuphar [nenyfar] nm water-lily.

néologisme [neɔlɔʒism] nm neologism.

néon [neɔ̃] nm [gaz] neon. || [enseigne] neon light.

néophyte [neɔfit] nmf novice.

néo-zélandais, -e [neɔzelɑ̃dɛ, ɛz] (mpl inv, fpl néo-zélandaises) adj New Zealand (avant n). ○ **Néo-Zélandais, -e** nm, f New Zealander.

Népal [nepal] nm: le ~ Nepal.

nerf [nɛr] nm ANAT nerve. || fig [vigueur] spirit.

nerveux, -euse [nɛrvø, øz] adj [gén] nervous. || [voiture] nippy.

nervosité [nɛrvozite] nf nervousness.

nervure [nɛrvyr] nf [de feuille, d'aile] vein.

n'est-ce pas [nɛspa] adv: vous me croyez, ~? you believe me, don't you?

net, nette [nɛt] adj [écriture, image, idée] clear. || [propre, rangé] clean, neat. || COMM & FIN net; ~ d'impôt tax-free. ○ **net** adv [sur le coup] on the spot; s'arrêter ~ to stop dead; se casser ~ to break clean off.

nettement [nɛtmɑ̃] adv [clairement] clearly. || [incontestablement] definitely; ~ plus/moins much more/less.

netteté [nɛtte] nf clearness.

nettoyage [netwajaʒ] nm [de vêtement] cleaning; ~ à sec dry cleaning.

nettoyer [netwaje] vt [gén] to clean. || [grenier] to clear out.

neuf¹, neuve [nœf, nœv] adj new. ○ **neuf** nm: quoi de ~? what's new?

neuf² [nœf] adj num & nm nine; voir aussi six.

neurasthénique [nørastenik] nmf & adj depressive.

neurologie [nørɔlɔʒi] nf neurology.

neutraliser [nøtralize] vt to neutralize.

neutralité [nøtralite] nf neutrality.

neutre [nøtr] 1 nm LING neuter. 2 adj [gén] neutral. || LING neuter.

neutron [nøtrɔ̃] nm neutron.

neuve → neuf.

neuvième [nœvjɛm] adj num, nm & nmf ninth; voir aussi sixième.

névé [neve] nm snowbank.

neveu, -x [nəvø] nm nephew.

névralgie [nevralʒi] nf MÉD neuralgia.

névrose [nevroz] nf neurosis.

névrosé, -e [nevroze] adj & nm, f neurotic.

nez [ne] nm nose; saigner du ~ to have a nosebleed; ~ aquilin aquiline nose; ~ busqué hooked nose; ~ à ~ face to face.

ni [ni] conj: sans pull ~ écharpe without a sweater or a scarf. ○ **ni ... ni** loc corrélative neither ... nor; ~ lui ~ moi neither of us; je ne les aime ~ l'un ~ l'autre I don't like either of them.

niais, e [njɛ, njɛz] 1 adj silly, foolish. 2 nm, f fool.

Nicaragua [nikaragwa] nm: le ~ Nicaragua.

niche [niʃ] nf [de chien] kennel. || [de statue] niche.

nicher [niʃe] vi [oiseaux] to rest.

nickel [nikɛl] **1** *nm* nickel. **2** *adj inv fam* spotless, spick and span.

nicotine [nikɔtin] *nf* nicotine.

nid [ni] *nm* nest.

nièce [njɛs] *nf* niece.

nier [nje] *vt* to deny.

nigaud, -e [nigo, od] *nm, f* simpleton.

Niger [niʒɛr] *nm* [fleuve]: **le ~** the River Niger. || [État]: **le ~** Niger.

Nigeria [niʒerja] *nm*: **le ~** Nigeria.

Nil [nil] *nm*: **le ~** the Nile.

n'importe → **importer**.

nippon, -one [nipɔ̃, ɔn] *adj* Japanese. ○ **Nippon, -one** *nm, f* Japanese (person); **les Nippons** the Japanese.

nitrate [nitrat] *nm* nitrate.

nitroglycérine [nitrɔgliserin] *nf* nitroglycerine.

niveau, -x [nivo] *nm* [gén] level; **le ~ de la mer** sea level; **~ de vie** standard of living; **au ~ de** at the level of; *fig* [en ce qui concerne] as regards.

niveler [nivle] *vt* to level; *fig* to level out.

n° (*abr de* **numéro**) no.

noble [nɔbl] **1** *nmf* nobleman (*f* noblewoman). **2** *adj* noble.

noblesse [nɔbles] *nf* nobility.

noce [nɔs] *nf* [mariage] wedding. ○ **noces** *nfpl* wedding (*sg*); **~s d'or/d'argent** golden/silver wedding (anniversary).

nocif, -ive [nɔsif, iv] *adj* [produit, gaz] noxious.

noctambule [nɔktɑ̃byl] *nmf* night bird.

nocturne [nɔktyrn] **1** *nm ou nf* [d'un magasin] late opening. **2** *adj* [émission, attaque] night (*avant n*). || [animal] nocturnal.

Noël [nɔɛl] *nm* Christmas; **joyeux ~!** happy ou merry Christmas!

nœud [nø] *nm* [de fil, de bois] knot; **double ~** double knot. || NAVIG knot. || [de l'action, du problème] crux. || [ornement] bow; **~ de cravate** knot (*in one's tie*); **~ papillon** bow tie. || ANAT, ASTRON, ÉLECTR & RAIL node.

noir, -e [nwar] *adj* [gén] black; **~ de** [poussière, suie] black with. || [pièce, couloir] dark. ○ **Noir, -e** *nm, f* black. ○ **noir** *nm* [couleur] black; **~ sur blanc** *fig* in black and white. || [obscurité] dark. || *loc*: **travail au ~** moonlighting. ○ **noire** *nf* quarter note *Am*.

noirâtre [nwaratr] *adj* blackish.

noirceur [nwarsœr] *nf fig* [méchanceté] wickedness.

noircir [nwarsir] **1** *vi* to darken. **2** *vt litt & fig* to blacken.

noisetier [nwaztje] *nm* hazel tree.

noisette [nwazet] *nf* [fruit] hazelnut.

noix [nwa] *nf* [fruit] walnut; **~ de cajou** cashew (nut); **~ de coco** coconut; **~ de muscade** nutmeg. || *loc*: **à la ~** *fam* dreadful.

nom [nɔ̃] *nm* [gén] name; **au ~ de** in the name of; **~ déposé** trade name; **~ de famille** surname; **~ de jeune fille** maiden name. || [prénom] (first) name. || GRAM noun; **~ propre/commun** proper/common noun.

nomade [nɔmad] **1** *nmf* nomad. **2** *adj* nomadic.

nombre [nɔ̃br] *nm* number; **~ pair/impair** even/odd number.

nombreux, -euse [nɔ̃brø, øz] *adj* [famille, foule] large. || [erreurs, occasions] numerous; **peu ~** few.

nombril [nɔ̃bril] *nm* navel; **il se prend pour le ~ du monde** he thinks the world revolves around him.

nominal, -e, -aux [nɔminal, o] *adj* [liste] of names. || [valeur, autorité] nominal. || GRAM noun (*avant n*).

nomination [nɔminasjɔ̃] *nf* nomination, appointment.

nommé, -e [nɔme] *adj* [désigné] named. || [choisi] appointed.

nommément [nɔmemɑ̃] *adv* [citer] by name.

nommer [nɔme] *vt* [appeler] to name, to call. || [qualifier] to call. || [promouvoir] to appoint, to nominate. || [dénoncer, mentionner] to name. ○ **se nommer** *vp* [s'appeler] to be called.

non [nɔ̃] **1** *adv* [réponse négative] no. || [se rapportant à une phrase précédente] not; **moi ~** not me; **moi ~ plus** (and) neither am/do *etc* I. || [sert à demander une confirmation]: **c'est une bonne idée, ~?** it's a good idea, isn't it? || [modifie un adjectif ou un adverbe] not; **~ loin d'ici** not far from here. **2** *nm inv* no. ○ **non (pas) que ...** *loc corrélative* not that ... but. ○ **non seulement ... mais (encore)** *loc corrélative* not only ... but also.

nonagénaire [nɔnaʒenɛr] *nmf & adj* nonagenarian.

non-agression [nɔnagresjɔ̃] *nf* non-aggression.

nonante [nɔnɑ̃t] *adj num Belg & Helv* ninety.

nonchalance [nɔ̃ʃalɑ̃s] *nf* nonchalance, casualness.

non-fumeur, -euse [nɔ̃fymœr, øz] *nm, f* non-smoker.

non-lieu [nɔ̃ljø] (*pl* **non-lieux**) *nm* JUR dismissal through lack of evidence.

nonne [nɔn] *nf* nun.

non-sens [nɔ̃sɑ̃s] *nm inv* [absurdité] nonsense. || [contresens] meaningless word.

non-violence [nɔ̃vjɔlɑ̃s] *nf* non-violence.

non-voyant, -e [nɔ̃vwajɑ̃, ɑ̃t] *nm, f* visually handicapped.

nord [nɔr] **1** *nm* north; **un vent du ~ a** northerly wind; **au ~** in the north; **au ~ (de)** to the north (of); **le grand Nord** the frozen North. **2** *adj inv* north; [province, région] northern.

nord-africain, -e [nɔrafrikɛ̃, ɛn] (*mpl* **nord-africains,** *fpl* **nord-africaines**) *adj* North African. ○ **Nord-Africain, -e** *nm, f* North African.

nord-américain, -e [nɔramerikɛ̃, ɛn] (*mpl* **nord-américains,** *fpl* **nord-américaines**) *adj* North American. ○ **Nord-Américain, -e** *nm, f* North American.

nord-est [nɔrɛst] *nm & adj inv* north-east.

nordique [nɔrdik] *adj* Nordic, Scandinavian. ○ **Nordique** *nmf* [Scandinave] Scandinavian. || *Can* North Canadian.

nord-ouest [nɔrwɛst] *nm & adj inv* north-west.

normal, -e, -aux [nɔrmal, o] *adj* normal. ○ **normale** *nf*: **la ~e** the norm.

normalement [nɔrmalmɑ̃] *adv* normally, usually; **~ il devrait déjà être arrivé** he should have arrived by now.

normaliser [nɔrmalize] *vt* [situation] to normalize. || [produit] to standardize.

normand, -e [nɔrmɑ̃, ɑ̃d] *adj* Norman. ○ **Normand, -e** *nm, f* Norman.

Normandie [nɔrmɑ̃di] *nf*: **la ~** Normandy.

norme [nɔrm] *nf* [gén] standard, norm.

Norvège [nɔrvɛʒ] *nf*: **la ~** Norway.

norvégien, -ienne [nɔrveʒjɛ̃, jɛn] *adj* Norwegian. ○ **norvégien** *nm* [langue] Norwegian. ○ **Norvégien, -ienne** *nm, f* Norwegian.

nos → **notre**.

nostalgie [nɔstalʒi] *nf* nostalgia.

nostalgique [nɔstalʒik] *adj* nostalgic.

notable [nɔtabl] **1** *adj* noteworthy, notable. **2** *nm* notable.

notaire [nɔtɛr] *nm* ≃ lawyer.

notamment [nɔtamɑ̃] *adv* in particular.

note [nɔt] *nf* [gén & MUS] note; **prendre des ~s** to take notes. || SCOL & UNIV mark, grade *Am.* || [facture] bill.

noter [nɔte] *vt* [écrire] to note down. || [constater] to note, to notice. || SCOL & UNIV to mark, to grade *Am.*

notice [nɔtis] *nf* instructions (*pl*).

notifier [nɔtifje] *vt*: **~ qqch à qqn** to notify sb of sthg.

notion [nɔsjɔ̃] *nf* [conscience, concept] notion, concept. || (*gén pl*) [rudiment] smattering (*U*).

notoire [nɔtwar] *adj* [fait] well-known; [criminel] notorious.

notre [nɔtr] (*pl* **nos** [no]) *adj poss* our.

nôtre [notr] ○ **le nôtre** (*f* **la nôtre,** *pl* **les nôtres**) *pron poss* ours.

nouer [nwe] *vt* [corde, lacet] to tie; [bouquet] to tie up. ○ **se nouer** *vp* [gorge] to tighten up. || [intrigue] to start.

noueux, -euse [nwø, øz] *adj* [bois] knotty; [mains] gnarled.

nougat [nuga] *nm* nougat.

nouille [nuj] *nf fam péj* idiot. ○ **nouilles** *nfpl* [pâtes] pasta (*U*), noodles (*pl*).

nourrice [nuris] *nf* [garde d'enfants] nanny, child-minder; [qui allaite] wet nurse.

nourrir [nurir] *vt* [gén] to feed. || [sentiment, projet] to nurture. ○ **se nourrir** *vp* to eat; **se ~ de qqch** *litt & fig* to live on sthg.

nourrissant, -e [nurisɑ̃, ɑ̃t] *adj* nutritious, nourishing.

nourrisson [nurisɔ̃] *nm* infant.

nourriture [nurityr] *nf* food.

nous [nu] *pron pers* [sujet] we. || [objet] us. ○ **nous-mêmes** *pron pers* ourselves.

nouveau, -elle, -x [nuvo, ɛl, o] (**nouvel** *devant voyelle et h muet*) **1** *adj* new; **~x mariés** newlyweds. **2** *nm, f* new boy (*f* new girl). ○ **nouveau** *nm*: **il y a du ~** there's something new. ○ **nouvelle** *nf* [information] (piece of) news (*U*). || [court récit] short story. ○ **nouvelles** *nfpl* news; **les nouvelles** MÉDIA the news (*sg*); **il a donné de ses nouvelles** I/we *etc* have heard from him. ○ **à nouveau** *loc adv* [encore] again. ○ **de nouveau** *loc adv* again.

nouveau-né, -e [nuvone] (*mpl*

nouveau-nés, *fpl* **nouveau-nées**) *nm, f* newborn baby.

nouveauté [nuvote] *nf* [actualité] novelty. || [innovation] something new. || [ouvrage] new book/film etc.

nouvel, nouvelle → **nouveau.**

Nouvelle-Calédonie [nuvɛlkaledɔni] *nf*: **la** ~ New Caledonia.

Nouvelle-Zélande [nuvɛlzelãd] *nf*: **la** ~ New Zealand.

novateur, -trice [nɔvatœr, tris] **1** *adj* innovative. **2** *nm, f* innovator.

novembre [nɔvãbr] *nm* November; *voir aussi* **septembre.**

novice [nɔvis] **1** *nmf* novice. **2** *adj* inexperienced.

noyade [nwajad] *nf* drowning.

noyau, -x [nwajo] *nm* [de fruit] stone, pit. || ASTRON, BIOL & PHYS nucleus. || *fig* [d'amis] group, circle; [d'opposants, de résistants] cell; ~ **dur** hard core. || *fig* [centre] core.

noyé, -e [nwaje] **1** *adj* [inondé] flooded; **yeux ~s de larmes** eyes swimming with tears. **2** *nm, f* drowned person.

noyer [nwaje] *vt* [animal, personne] to drown. || [terre, moteur] to flood. || [estomper, diluer] to swamp; [contours] to blur. ○ **se noyer** *vp* [personne] to drown. || *fig* [se perdre]: **se** ~ **dans** to become bogged down in.

N/Réf (*abr de* **Notre référence**) O/Ref.

nu, -e [ny] *adj* [personne] naked. || [paysage, fil électrique] bare. || [style, vérité] plain. ○ **nu** *nm* nude; **à** ~ stripped, bare; **mettre à** ~ to strip bare.

nuage [nɥaʒ] *nm* [gén] cloud. || [petite quantité]: **un** ~ **de lait** a drop of milk.

nuageux, -euse [nɥaʒø, øz] *adj* [temps, ciel] cloudy. || *fig* [esprit] hazy.

nuance [nɥãs] *nf* [de couleur] shade; [de son, de sens] nuance.

nubile [nybil] *adj* nubile.

nucléaire [nykleer] **1** *nm* nuclear energy. **2** *adj* nuclear.

nudisme [nydism] *nm* nudism, naturism.

nudité [nydite] *nf* [de personne] nudity, nakedness. || [de lieu, style] bareness.

nuée [nɥe] *nf* [multitude]: **une** ~ **de** a horde of. || *littéraire* [nuage] cloud.

nues [ny] *nfpl*: **tomber des** ~ to be completely taken aback.

nui [nɥi] *pp inv* → **nuire.**

nuire [nɥir] *vi*: ~ **à** to harm, to injure.

nuisance [nɥizãs] *nf* nuisance (*U*), harm (*U*).

nuisible [nɥizibl] *adj* harmful.

nuit [nɥi] *nf* [laps de temps] night; **cette** ~ [la nuit dernière] last night; [la nuit prochaine] tonight; **de** ~ at night; **bateau/vol de** ~ night ferry/flight; ~ **blanche** sleepless night. || [obscurité] darkness, night; **il fait** ~ it's dark.

nuitée [nɥite] *nf* overnight stay.

nul, nulle [nyl] **1** *adj indéf* (*avant n*) *littéraire* no. **2** *adj* (*après n*) [égal à zéro] nil. || [sans valeur] useless, hopeless; **être** ~ **en maths** to be hopeless ou useless at maths. **3** *nm, f péj* nonentity. **4** *pron indéf sout* no one, nobody. ○ **nulle part** *adv* nowhere.

nullement [nylmã] *adv* by no means.

nullité [nylite] *nf* [médiocrité] incompetence. || JUR invalidity, nullity.

numéraire [nymerer] *nm* cash.

numérique [nymerik] *adj* [gén] numerical. || INFORM digital.

numéro [nymero] *nm* [gén] number; **faire un faux** ~ to dial a wrong number; ~ **minéralogique** ou **d'immatriculation** registration *Br* ou license *Am* number; ~ **de téléphone** telephone number; ~ **vert** ≃ freefone number. || [de spectacle] act, turn. || *fam* [personne]: **quel** ~! what a character!

numéroter [nymerɔte] *vt* to number.

nu-pieds [nypje] *nm inv* [sandale] sandal.

nuptial, -e, -iaux [nypsjal, jo] *adj* nuptial.

nuque [nyk] *nf* nape.

nurse [nœrs] *nf* children's nurse, nanny.

nutritif, -ive [nytritif, iv] *adj* nutritious.

nutritionniste [nytrisjɔnist] *nmf* nutritionist, dietician.

Nylon® [nilɔ̃] *nm* nylon.

nymphomane [nɛ̃fɔman] *nf & adj* nymphomaniac.

o, O [o] *nm inv* [lettre] o, O. ○○ (*abr de Ouest*) W.

oasis [ɔazis] *nf* [dans désert] oasis.

obéir [ɔbeir] *vi* [personne]: ~ à qqn/ qqch to obey sb/sthg. || [freins] to respond.

obéissant, -e [ɔbeisɑ̃, ɑ̃t] *adj* obedient.

obélisque [ɔbelisk] *nm* obelisk.

obèse [ɔbɛz] *adj* obese.

obésité [ɔbezite] *nf* obesity.

objecteur [ɔbʒɛktœr] *nm* objector; ~ de conscience conscientious objector.

objectif, -ive [ɔbʒɛktif, iv] *adj* objective. ○ **objectif** *nm* PHOT lens. || [but, cible] objective, target.

objection [ɔbʒɛksjɔ̃] *nf* objection.

objectivité [ɔbʒɛktivite] *nf* objectivity.

objet [ɔbʒɛ] *nm* [chose] object; ~ d'art objet d'art; ~ de valeur valuable; ~s trouvés lost property office *Br*, lost and found (office) *Am*. || [sujet] subject.

obligation [ɔbligasjɔ̃] *nf* [gén] obligation; être dans l'~ de faire qqch to be obliged to do sthg. || FIN bond, debenture.

obligatoire [ɔbligatwar] *adj* [imposé] compulsory, obligatory. || *fam* [inéluctable] inevitable.

obligeance [ɔbliʒɑ̃s] *nf sout* obligingness; avoir l'~ de faire qqch to be good ou kind enough to do sthg.

obliger [ɔbliʒe] *vt* [forcer]: ~ qqn à qqch to impose sthg on sb; ~ qqn à faire qqch to force sb to do sthg; être obligé de faire qqch to be obliged to do sthg. || [rendre service à] to oblige. ○ **s'obliger** *vp*: s'~ à qqch to impose sthg on o.s.; s'~ à faire qqch to force o.s. to do sthg.

oblique [ɔblik] *adj* oblique.

obliquer [ɔblike] *vi* to turn off.

oblitérer [ɔblitere] *vt* [tamponner] to cancel. || MÉD to obstruct. || [effacer] to obliterate.

obnubiler [ɔbnybile] *vt* to obsess; être obnubilé par to be obsessed with ou by.

obole [ɔbɔl] *nf* small contribution.

obscène [ɔpsɛn] *adj* obscene.

obscénité [ɔpsenite] *nf* obscenity.

obscur, -e [ɔpskyr] *adj* [sombre] dark. || [inconnu, douteux] obscure.

obscurantisme [ɔpskyrɑ̃tism] *nm* obscurantism.

obscurcir [ɔpskyrsir] *vt* [assombrir] to darken. || [embrouiller] to confuse. ○ **s'obscurcir** *vp* [s'assombrir] to grow dark. || [s'embrouiller] to become confused.

obscurité [ɔpskyrite] *nf* [nuit] darkness.

obsédé, -e [ɔpsede] 1 *adj* obsessed. 2 *nm, f* obsessive.

obséder [ɔpsede] *vt* to obsess, to haunt.

obsèques [ɔpsɛk] *nfpl* funeral (*sg*).

obséquieux, -ieuse [ɔpsekjø, jøz] *adj* obsequious.

observateur, -trice [ɔpsɛrvatœr, tris] 1 *adj* observant. 2 *nm, f* observer.

observation [ɔpsɛrvasjɔ̃] *nf* [gén] observation; être en ~ MÉD to be under observation. || [critique] remark.

observatoire [ɔpsɛrvatwar] *nm* ASTRON observatory.

observer [ɔpsɛrve] *vt* [regarder, remarquer, respecter] to observe. || [épier] to watch. || [constater]: faire ~ qqch à qqn to point sthg out to sb.

obsession [ɔpsesjɔ̃] *nf* obsession.

obsolète [ɔpsɔlɛt] *adj* obsolete.

obstacle [ɔpstakl] *nm* [entrave] obstacle. || *fig* [difficulté] hindrance; faire ~ à qqch/qqn to hinder sthg/sb.

obstination [ɔpstinasjɔ̃] *nf* stubbornness, obstinacy.

obstiné, -e [ɔpstine] *adj* [entêté] stubborn, obstinate. || [acharné] dogged.

obstiner [ɔpstine] ○ **s'obstiner** *vp* to insist; s'~ à faire qqch to persist stubbornly in doing sthg; s'~ dans qqch to cling stubbornly to sthg.

obstruction [ɔpstryksjɔ̃] *nf* MÉD obstruction, blockage. || POLIT & SPORT obstruction.

obstruer [ɔpstrye] *vt* to block, to obstruct. ○ **s'obstruer** *vp* to become blocked.

obtempérer [ɔptɑ̃pere] *vi*: ~ à to comply with.

obtenir [ɔptənir] *vt* to get, to obtain; ~ qqch de qqn to get sthg from sb.

obtention [ɔptɑ̃sjɔ̃] *nf* obtaining.

obtenu, -e [ɔptəny] *pp* → obtenir.

obturer [ɔptyre] vt to close, to seal; [dent] to fill.

obtus, -e [ɔpty, yz] adj obtuse.

obus [ɔby] nm shell.

OC (abr de **ondes courtes**) SW.

occasion [ɔkazjɔ̃] nf [possibilité, chance] opportunity, chance; **saisir l'~ (de faire qqch)** to seize or grab the chance (to do sthg); **à l'~** some time; [de temps en temps] sometimes, on occasion; **à la première ~** at the first opportunity. || [circonstance] occasion; **à l'~ de** on the occasion of. || [bonne affaire] bargain. ○ **d'occasion** loc adv & loc adj second-hand.

occasionnel, -elle [ɔkazjɔnɛl] adj [irrégulier - visite, problème] occasional; [- travail] casual.

occasionner [ɔkazjɔne] vt to cause.

occident [ɔksidɑ̃] nm west. ○ **Occident** nm: **l'Occident** the West.

occidental, -e, -aux [ɔksidɑtal, o] adj western. ○ **Occidental, -e, -aux** nm, f Westerner.

occlusion [ɔklyzjɔ̃] nf MÉD blockage, obstruction. || LING & CHIM occlusion.

occulte [ɔkylt] adj occult.

occulter [ɔkylte] vt [sentiments] to conceal.

occupation [ɔkypasjɔ̃] nf [activité] occupation, job. || MIL occupation.

occupé, -e [ɔkype] adj [personne] busy. || [appartement, zone] occupied. || [place] taken; [toilettes] engaged; **c'est ~** [téléphone] it's engaged Br ou busy Am.

occuper [ɔkype] vt [gén] to occupy. || [espace] to take up. || [fonction, poste] to hold. ○ **s'occuper** vp [s'activer] to keep o.s. busy; **s'~ à qqch/à faire qqch** to be busy with sthg/doing sthg. || **s'~ de qqch** [se charger de] to take care of sthg, to deal with sthg; [s'intéresser à] to take an interest in, to be interested in; **occupez-vous de vos affaires!** mind your own business! || [prendre soin]: **s'~ de qqn** to take care of sb, to look after sb.

occurrence [ɔkyrɑ̃s] nf [circonstance]: **en l'~** in this case. || LING occurrence.

OCDE (abr de **Organisation de coopération et de développement économique**) nf OECD.

océan [ɔseɑ̃] nm ocean; **l'~ Antarctique** the Antarctic Ocean; **l'~ Arctique** the Arctic Ocean; **l'~ Atlantique** the Atlantic Ocean; **l'~ Indien** the Indian Ocean; **l'~ Pacifique** the Pacific Ocean.

Océanie [ɔseani] nf: **l'~** Oceania.

océanique [ɔseanik] adj ocean (avant n).

ocre [ɔkr] adj inv & nf ochre.

octante [ɔktɑ̃t] adj num Belg & Helv eighty.

octave [ɔktav] nf octave.

octet [ɔktɛ] nm INFORM byte.

octobre [ɔktɔbr] nm October; voir aussi **septembre**.

octogénaire [ɔktɔʒenɛr] nmf & adj octogenarian.

octroyer [ɔktrwaje] vt: **~ qqch à qqn** to grant sb sthg, to grant sthg to sb. ○ **s'octroyer** vp to grant o.s., to treat o.s. to.

oculaire [ɔkylɛr] adj ocular, eye (avant n).

oculiste [ɔkylist] nmf ophthalmologist.

ode [ɔd] nf ode.

odeur [ɔdœr] nf smell.

odieux, -ieuse [ɔdjø, jøz] adj [crime] odious, abominable. || [personne, attitude] unbearable, obnoxious.

odorant, -e [ɔdɔrɑ̃, ɑ̃t] adj sweet-smelling, fragrant.

odorat [ɔdɔra] nm (sense of) smell.

œdème [edɛm] nm oedema.

œil [œj] (pl **yeux** [jø]) nm [gén] eye; **yeux bridés/exorbités/globuleux** slanting/bulging/protruding eyes; **avoir les yeux cernés** to have bags under one's eyes. || loc: **avoir qqch/qqn à l'~** to have one's eye on sthg/sb; **n'avoir pas froid aux yeux** not to be afraid of anything, to have plenty of nerve; **mon ~!** fam like hell; **cela saute aux yeux** it's obvious.

œillade [œjad] nf wink; **lancer une ~ à qqn** to wink at sb.

œillère [œjɛr] nf eyebath. ○ **œillères** nfpl blinkers Br, blinders Am.

œillet [œjɛ] nm [fleur] carnation. || [de chaussure] eyelet.

œnologue [enɔlɔg] nmf wine expert.

œsophage [ezɔfaʒ] nm oesophagus.

œstrogène [estrɔʒɛn] nm œstrogen.

œuf [œf] nm egg; **~ à la coque/au plat/poché** boiled/fried/poached egg; **~ mollet/dur** soft-boiled/hard-boiled egg; **~s brouillés** scrambled eggs.

œuvre [œvr] nf [travail] work; **se mettre à l'~** to get down to work; **mettre qqch en ~** to make use of sthg; [loi, accord, projet] to implement sthg. || [d'artiste] work; [- ensemble de sa production] works (pl); **~ d'art** work of art. || [organisation] charity; **~ de bienfaisance** charity, charitable organization.

offense [ɔfɑ̃s] *nf* [insulte] insult.

offenser [ɔfɑ̃se] *vt* [personne] to offend. || [bon goût] to offend against. ○ **s'offenser** *vp* : **s'~ de** to take offence at, to be offended by.

offensif, -ive [ɔfɑ̃sif, iv] *adj* offensive. ○ **offensive** *nf* MIL offensive; **passer à l'offensive** to go on the offensive; **prendre l'offensive** to take the offensive.

offert, -e [ɔfɛr, ɛrt] *pp* → **offrir**.

office [ɔfis] *nm* [bureau] office, agency; **~ du tourisme** tourist office. || [fonction]: **faire ~ de** to act as; **remplir son ~** to do its job, to fulfil its function. || RELIG service. ○ **d'office** *loc adv* automatically, as a matter of course; **commis d'~** officially appointed.

officialiser [ɔfisjalize] *vt* to make official.

officiel, -ielle [ɔfisjɛl] *adj & nm, f* official.

officier¹ [ɔfisje] *vi* to officiate.

officier² [ɔfisje] *nm* officer.

officieux, -ieuse [ɔfisjø, jøz] *adj* unofficial.

offrande [ɔfrɑ̃d] *nf* [don] offering. || RELIG offertory.

offre [ɔfr] *nf* [proposition] offer; [aux enchères] bid; [pour contrat] tender; **«~s d'emploi»** "situations vacant", "vacancies"; **~ d'essai** trial offer; **~ de lancement** introductory offer; **~ publique d'achat** takeover bid. || ÉCON supply.

offrir [ɔfrir] *vt* [faire cadeau]: **~ qqch à qqn** to give sb sthg, to give sthg to sb. || [proposer]: **~ (qqch à qqn)** to offer (sb sthg ou sthg to sb). || [présenter] to offer, to present. ○ **s'offrir** *vp* [croisière, livre] to treat o.s. to. || [se présenter] to present itself. || [se proposer] to offer one's services, to offer o.s.

offusquer [ɔfyske] *vt* to offend. ○ **s'offusquer** *vp* : **s'~ (de)** to take offence (at).

ogive [ɔʒiv] *nf* ARCHIT ogive. || [MIL - d'obus] head; [- de fusée] nosecone; **~ nucléaire** nuclear warhead.

ogre, ogresse [ɔgr, ɔgrɛs] *nm, f* ogre (*f* ogress).

oh [o] *interj* oh!; **~ la la!** dear oh dear!

ohé [ɔe] *interj* hey!

oie [wa] *nf* goose.

oignon [ɔɲɔ̃] *nm* [plante] onion. || [bulbe] bulb. || MÉD bunion.

oiseau, -x [wazo] *nm* ZOOL bird; **~ de proie** bird of prey.

oisif, -ive [wazif, iv] **1** *adj* idle. **2** *nm, f* man of leisure (*f* woman of leisure).

oisillon [wazijɔ̃] *nm* fledgling.

oisiveté [wazivte] *nf* idleness.

O.K. [ɔke] *interj fam* okay.

oléoduc [ɔleɔdyk] *nm* (oil) pipeline.

olfactif, -ive [ɔlfaktif, iv] *adj* olfactory.

olive [ɔliv] *nf* olive.

olivier [ɔlivje] *nm* [arbre] olive tree; [bois] olive wood.

OLP (*abr de* **Organisation de libération de la Palestine**) *nf* PLO.

olympique [ɔlɛ̃pik] *adj* Olympic (*avant n*).

ombilical, -e, -aux [ɔbilikal, o] *adj* umbilical.

ombrage [ɔbraʒ] *nm* shade.

ombragé, -e [ɔbraʒe] *adj* shady.

ombrageux, -euse [ɔbraʒø, øz] *adj* [personne] touchy, prickly. || [cheval] nervous, skittish.

ombre [ɔbr] *nf* [zone sombre] shade; **à l'~ de** [arbre] in the shade of; **laisser qqch dans l'~** *fig* to deliberately ignore sthg. || [forme, fantôme] shadow. || [trace] hint.

ombrelle [ɔbrɛl] *nf* parasol.

omelette [ɔmlɛt] *nf* omelette.

omettre [ɔmɛtr] *vt* to omit; **~ de faire qqch** to omit to do sthg.

omis, -e [ɔmi, iz] *pp* → **omettre**.

omission [ɔmisjɔ̃] *nf* omission; **par ~** by omission.

omnibus [ɔmnibys] *nm* stopping ou local train.

omniprésent, -e [ɔmniprezɑ̃, ɑ̃t] *adj* omnipresent.

omnivore [ɔmnivɔr] **1** *nm* omnivore. **2** *adj* omnivorous.

omoplate [ɔmɔplat] *nf* [os] shoulder blade; [épaule] shoulder.

OMS (*abr de* **Organisation mondiale de la santé**) *nf* WHO.

on [ɔ̃] *pron pers indéf* [indéterminé] you, one; **~ n'a pas le droit de fumer ici** you're not allowed ou one isn't allowed to smoke here, smoking isn't allowed here. || [les gens, l'espèce humaine] they, people. || [quelqu'un] someone; **~ vous a appelé au téléphone ce matin** there was a telephone call for you this morning. || *fam* [nous] we.

oncle [ɔ̃kl] *nm* uncle.

onctueux, -euse [ɔ̃ktɥø, øz] *adj* smooth.

onde [ɔ̃d] *nf* PHYS wave. ○ **ondes** *nfpl* [radio] air (*sg*).

ondée [ɔ̃de] *nf* shower (of rain).

ondulation [ɔ̃dylasjɔ̃] *nf* [mouvement] rippling; [de sol, terrain] undulation. ‖ [de coiffure] wave.

onduler [ɔ̃dyle] *vi* [drapeau] to ripple, to wave; [cheveux] to be wavy; [route] to undulate.

onéreux, -euse [ɔnerø, øz] *adj* costly.

ongle [ɔ̃gl] *nm* [de personne] fingernail, nail. ‖ [d'animal] claw.

onglet [ɔ̃glɛ] *nm* [de lame] thumbnail groove. ‖ CULIN top skirt.

onguent [ɔ̃gɑ̃] *nm* ointment.

onomatopée [ɔnɔmatɔpe] *nf* onomatopoeia.

ont → **avoir**.

ONU, Onu [ɔny] (*abr de* **Organisation des Nations unies**) *nf* UN, UNO.

onyx [ɔniks] *nm* onyx.

onze [ɔ̃z] *adj num* & *nm* eleven; *voir aussi* **six**.

onzième [ɔ̃zjɛm] *adj num, nm* & *nmf* eleventh; *voir aussi* **sixième**.

OPA (*abr de* **offre publique d'achat**) *nf* take-over bid.

opale [ɔpal] *nf* & *adj inv* opal.

opaline [ɔpalin] *nf* opaline.

opaque [ɔpak] *adj*: ~ (à) opaque (to).

OPEP, Opep (*abr de* **Organisation des pays exportateurs de pétrole**) *nf* OPEC.

opéra [ɔpera] *nm* MUS opera. ‖ [théâtre] opera house.

opéra-comique [ɔperakɔmik] *nm* light opera.

opérateur, -trice [ɔperatœr, tris] *nm, f* operator.

opération [ɔperasjɔ̃] *nf* [gén] operation. ‖ COMM deal, transaction.

opérationnel, -elle [ɔperasjɔnɛl] *adj* operational.

opérer [ɔpere] **1** *vt* MÉD to operate on. ‖ [exécuter] to carry out, to implement; [choix, tri] to make. **2** *vi* [agir] to take effect; [personne] to operate, to proceed. ○ **s'opérer** *vp* to come about, to take place.

opérette [ɔperɛt] *nf* operetta.

ophtalmologiste [ɔftalmɔlɔʒist] *nmf* ophthalmologist.

opiniâtre [ɔpinjatr] *adj* [caractère, personne] stubborn, obstinate. ‖ [effort] dogged; [travail] unrelenting; [fièvre, toux] persistent.

opinion [ɔpinjɔ̃] *nf* opinion; **l'~ publique** public opinion.

opium [ɔpjɔm] *nm* opium.

opportun, -e [ɔpɔrtœ̃, yn] *adj* opportune, timely.

opportuniste [ɔpɔrtynist] **1** *nmf* opportunist. **2** *adj* opportunistic.

opportunité [ɔpɔrtynite] *nf* [à-propos] opportuneness, timeliness. ‖ [occasion] opportunity.

opposant, -e [ɔpozɑ̃, ɑ̃t] **1** *adj* opposing. **2** *nm, f*: ~ (à) opponent (of).

opposé, -e [ɔpoze] *adj* [direction, côté, angle] opposite. ‖ [intérêts, opinions] conflicting; [forces] opposing. ‖ [hostile]: ~ à opposed to. ○ **opposé** *nm*: **l'~** the opposite; **à l'~ de** in the opposite direction from; *fig* unlike, contrary to.

opposer [ɔpoze] *vt* [mettre en opposition - choses, notions]: ~ **qqch** (à) to contrast sthg (with). ‖ [mettre en présence - personnes, armées] to oppose; ~ **deux équipes** to bring two teams together; ~ **qqn à qqn** to pit ou set sb against sb. ‖ [refus, protestation, objection] to put forward. ‖ [diviser] to divide. ○ **s'opposer** *vp* [contraster] to contrast. ‖ [entrer en conflit] to clash. ‖ **s'~ à** [se dresser contre] to oppose, to be opposed to; **s'~ à ce que qqn fasse qqch** to be opposed to sb's doing sthg.

opposition [ɔpozisjɔ̃] *nf* [gén] opposition; **faire ~ à** [décision, mariage] to oppose; [chèque] to stop; **entrer en ~ avec** to come into conflict with. ‖ JUR: ~ (à) objection (to). ‖ [contraste] contrast; **par ~ à** in contrast with, as opposed to.

oppresser [ɔprese] *vt* [étouffer] to suffocate, to stifle. ‖ *fig* [tourmenter] to oppress.

oppresseur [ɔprɛsœr] *nm* oppressor.

oppressif, -ive [ɔprɛsif, iv] *adj* oppressive.

oppression [ɔprɛsjɔ̃] *nf* [asservissement] oppression. ‖ [malaise] tightness of the chest.

opprimé, -e [ɔprime] **1** *adj* oppressed. **2** *nm, f* oppressed person.

opprimer [ɔprime] *vt* [asservir] to oppress. ‖ [étouffer] to stifle.

opter [ɔpte] *vi*: ~ **pour** to opt for.

opticien, -ienne [ɔptisjɛ̃, jɛn] *nm, f* optician.

optimal, -e, -aux [ɔptimal, o] *adj* optimal.

optimiste [ɔptimist] **1** *nmf* optimist. **2** *adj* optimistic.

option [ɔpsjɔ̃] *nf* [gén] option; **prendre une ~ sur** FIN to take (out) an option on. ‖ [accessoire] optional extra.

optionnel, -elle [ɔpsjɔnɛl] *adj* optional.

optique [ɔptik] **1** *nf* [science, technique] optics (*U*). || [perspective] viewpoint. **2** *adj* [nerf] optic; [verre] optical.

opulence [ɔpylɑ̃s] *nf* [richesse] opulence. || [ampleur] fullness, ampleness.

opulent, -e [ɔpylɑ̃, ɑ̃t] *adj* [riche] rich. || [gros] ample.

or¹ [ɔr] *nm* [métal, couleur] gold; **en ~** [objet] gold (*avant n*); **une occasion en ~** a golden opportunity; **une affaire en ~** [achat] an excellent bargain. || [dorure] gilding.

or² [ɔr] *conj* [pour introduire un contraste] well, but.

oracle [ɔrakl] *nm* oracle.

orage [ɔraʒ] *nm* [tempête] storm.

orageux, -euse [ɔraʒø, øz] *adj* stormy.

oraison [ɔrɛzɔ̃] *nf* prayer; **~ funèbre** funeral oration.

oral, -e, -aux [ɔral, o] *adj* oral. O **oral** *nm* oral (examination).

oralement [ɔralmɑ̃] *adv* orally.

orange [ɔrɑ̃ʒ] **1** *nf* orange. **2** *nm* & *adj inv* [couleur] orange.

orangé, -e [ɔrɑ̃ʒe] *adj* orangey.

orangeade [ɔrɑ̃ʒad] *nf* orange squash.

oranger [ɔrɑ̃ʒe] *nm* orange tree.

orang-outan, orang-outang [ɔrɑ̃utɑ̃] *nm* orangutang.

orateur, -trice [ɔratœr, tris] *nm, f* [conférencier] speaker. || [personne éloquente] orator.

orbital, -e, -aux [ɔrbital, o] *adj* [mouvement] orbital; [station] orbiting.

orbite [ɔrbit] *nf* ANAT (eye) socket. || ASTRON & *fig* orbit; **mettre sur ~** AÉRON to put into orbit; *fig* to launch.

orchestre [ɔrkɛstr] *nm* MUS orchestra. || CIN & THÉÂTRE stalls (*pl*) *Br*, orchestra *Am*; **fauteuil d'~** seat in the stalls *Br*, orchestra seat *Am*.

orchestrer [ɔrkɛstre] *vt litt* & *fig* to orchestrate.

orchidée [ɔrkide] *nf* orchid.

ordinaire [ɔrdinɛr] *adj* [usuel, standard] ordinary, normal. || *péj* [commun] ordinary, common. O **d'ordinaire** *loc adv* normally, usually.

ordinal, -e, -aux [ɔrdinal, o] *adj* ordinal. O **ordinal, -aux** *nm* ordinal (number).

ordinateur [ɔrdinatœr] *nm* computer; **~ individuel** personal computer, PC.

ordonnance [ɔrdɔnɑ̃s] **1** *nf* MÉD prescription. || [de gouvernement, juge] order. **2** *nm ou nf* MIL orderly.

ordonné, -e [ɔrdɔne] *adj* [maison, élève] tidy.

ordonner [ɔrdɔne] *vt* [ranger] to organize, to put in order. || [enjoindre] to order, to tell; **~ à qqn de faire qqch** to order sb to do sthg.

ordre [ɔrdr] *nm* [gén, MIL & RELIG] order; **par ~ alphabétique/chronologique/décroissant** in alphabetical/chronological/descending order; **donner un ~ à qqn** to give sb an order; **être aux ~s de qqn** to be at sb's disposal; **jusqu'à nouvel ~** until further notice; **l'~ public** law and order. || [bonne organisation] tidiness, orderliness; **en ~** orderly, tidy; **mettre en ~** to put in order, to tidy (up). || [catégorie]: **de premier/second ~** first-/second-rate; **d'~ privé/pratique** of a private/practical nature; **pouvez-vous me donner un ~ de grandeur?** can you give me some idea of the size/amount *etc*? || [corporation] professional association; **l'Ordre des médecins** ≃ the American Medical Association *Am*. || FIN: **à l'~ de** payable to. O **ordre du jour** *nm* [de réunion] agenda; **à l'~ du jour** [de réunion] on the agenda.

ordure [ɔrdyr] *nf fig* [grossièreté] filth (*U*). || *péj* [personne] scum (*U*), bastard. O **ordures** *nfpl* [déchets] rubbish (*U*) *Br*, garbage (*U*) *Am*.

ordurier, -ière [ɔrdyrje, jɛr] *adj* filthy, obscene.

orée [ɔre] *nf* edge.

oreille [ɔrɛj] *nf* ANAT ear. || [ouïe] hearing. || [de fauteuil, écrou] wing; [de marmite, tasse] handle.

oreiller [ɔreje] *nm* pillow.

oreillette [ɔrɛjɛt] *nf* [du cœur] auricle. || [de casquette] earflap.

oreillons [ɔrɛjɔ̃] *nmpl* mumps (*sg*).

ores [ɔr] O **d'ores et déjà** *loc adv* from now on.

orfèvre [ɔrfɛvr] *nm* goldsmith; [d'argent] silversmith.

orfèvrerie [ɔrfɛvrəri] *nf* [art] goldsmith's art; [d'argent] silversmith's art.

organe [ɔrgan] *nm* ANAT organ. || [institution] organ, body. || *fig* [porte-parole] representative.

organigramme [ɔrganigram] *nm* [hiérarchie] organization chart. || INFORM flow chart.

organique [ɔrganik] *adj* organic.

organisateur, -trice [ɔrganizatœr, tris] 1 *adj* organizing (*avant n*). 2 *nm, f* organizer.

organisation [ɔrganizasjɔ̃] *nf* organization.

organisé, -e [ɔrganize] *adj* organized.

organiser [ɔrganize] *vt* to organize. ○ **s'organiser** *vp* [personne] to be ou get organized. || [prendre forme] to take shape.

organisme [ɔrganism] *nm* BIOL & ZOOL organism. || [institution] body, organization.

organiste [ɔrganist] *nmf* organist.

orgasme [ɔrgasm] *nm* orgasm.

orge [ɔrʒ] *nf* barley.

orgie [ɔrʒi] *nf* orgy.

orgue [ɔrg] *nm* organ.

orgueil [ɔrgœj] *nm* pride.

orgueilleux, -euse [ɔrgœjø, øz] 1 *adj* proud. 2 *nm, f* proud person.

orient [ɔrjɑ̃] *nm* east. ○ **Orient** *nm*: **l'Orient** the Orient, the East.

oriental, -e, -aux [ɔrjɑ̃tal, o] *adj* [région, frontière] eastern; [d'Extrême-Orient] oriental.

orientation [ɔrjɑ̃tasjɔ̃] *nf* [direction] orientation; **avoir le sens de l'~** to have a good sense of direction. || SCOL career. || [de maison] aspect. || *fig* [de politique, recherche] direction, trend.

orienter [ɔrjɑ̃te] *vt* [disposer] to position. || [voyageur, élève, recherches] to guide, to direct. ○ **s'orienter** *vp* [se repérer] to find ou get one's bearings. || *fig* [se diriger]: **s'~ vers** to move towards.

orifice [ɔrifis] *nm* orifice.

originaire [ɔriʒiner] *adj* [natif]: **être ~ de** [personne] to be a native of.

original, -e, -aux [ɔriʒinal, o] 1 *adj* [premier, inédit] original. || [singulier] eccentric. 2 *nm, f* [personne] (outlandish) character. ○ **original, -aux** *nm* [œuvre, document] original.

originalité [ɔriʒinalite] *nf* [nouveauté] originality. || [excentricité] eccentricity.

origine [ɔriʒin] *nf* [gén] origin; **d'~** [originel] original; [de départ] of origin; **pays d'~** country of origin; **d'~ anglaise** of English origin; **à l'~** originally. || [souche] origins (*pl*). || [provenance] source.

ORL *nmf* (*abr de* **oto-rhino-laryngologiste**) ENT specialist.

orme [ɔrm] *nm* elm.

ornement [ɔrnəmɑ̃] *nm* [gén & MUS] ornament; **d'~** [plante, arbre] ornamental.

orner [ɔrne] *vt* [décorer]: **~ (de)** to decorate (with). || [agrémenter] to adorn.

ornière [ɔrnjer] *nf* rut.

ornithologie [ɔrnitɔlɔʒi] *nf* ornithology.

orphelin, -e [ɔrfəlɛ̃, in] 1 *adj* orphan (*avant n*), orphaned. 2 *nm, f* orphan.

orphelinat [ɔrfəlina] *nm* orphanage.

orteil [ɔrtej] *nm* toe.

orthodontiste [ɔrtɔdɔ̃tist] *nmf* orthodontist.

orthodoxe [ɔrtɔdɔks] 1 *adj* RELIG Orthodox. || [conformiste] orthodox. 2 *nmf* RELIG Orthodox Christian.

orthographe [ɔrtɔgraf] *nf* spelling.

orthopédiste [ɔrtɔpedist] *nmf* orthopaedist.

orthophoniste [ɔrtɔfɔnist] *nmf* speech therapist.

ortie [ɔrti] *nf* nettle.

os [ɔs, *pl* o] *nm* [gén] bone; **~ à moelle** marrowbone. || *fam fig* [difficulté] snag, hitch.

oscillation [ɔsilasjɔ̃] *nf* oscillation; [de navire] rocking.

osciller [ɔsile] *vi* [se balancer] to swing; [navire] to rock.

osé, -e [oze] *adj* daring, audacious.

oseille [ozej] *nf* BOT sorrel.

oser [oze] *vt* to dare; **~ faire qqch** to dare (to) do sthg.

osier [ozje] *nm* BOT osier. || [fibre] wicker.

ossature [ɔsatyr] *nf* ANAT skeleton. || *fig* [structure] framework.

ossements [ɔsmɑ̃] *nmpl* bones.

osseux, -euse [ɔsø, øz] *adj* ANAT & MÉD bone (*avant n*). || [maigre] bony.

ossuaire [ɔsyer] *nm* ossuary.

ostensible [ɔstɑ̃sibl] *adj* conspicuous.

ostentation [ɔstɑ̃tasjɔ̃] *nf* ostentation.

ostéopathe [ɔsteɔpat] *nmf* osteopath.

otage [ɔtaʒ] *nm* hostage; **prendre qqn en ~** to take sb hostage.

OTAN, Otan [ɔtɑ̃] (*abr de* **Organisation du traité de l'Atlantique Nord**) *nf* NATO.

otarie [ɔtari] *nf* sea lion.

ôter [ote] *vt* [enlever] to take off. || [soustraire] to take away. || [retirer, prendre]: **~ qqch à qqn** to take sthg away from sb.

otite [ɔtit] *nf* ear infection.

oto-rhino-laryngologie [ɔtɔrinɔlarɛ̃gɔlɔʒi] *nf* ear, nose and throat medicine, ENT.

ou [u] *conj* [indique une alternative, une approximation] or. || [sinon] ~ (**bien**) or (else). ○ **ou** (**bien**) ... **ou** (**bien**) *loc corrélative* either ... or; ~ **c'est elle, ~ c'est moi!** it's either her or me!

où [u] 1 *pron rel* [spatial] where; **le village ~ j'habite** the village where I live, the village I live in; **partout ~ vous irez** wherever you go. || [temporel] that; **le jour ~ je suis venu** the day (that) I came. 2 *adv* where; **je vais ~ je veux** I go where I please; **~ que vous alliez** wherever you go. 3 *adv interr* where? ○ **d'où** *loc adv* [conséquence] hence.

ouaté, -e [wate] *adj* [garni d'ouate] cotton (*avant n*) *Am*; [vêtement] quilted. || *fig* [feutré] muffled.

oubli [ubli] *nm* [acte d'oublier] forgetting. || [négligence] omission; [étourderie] oversight. || [général] oblivion; **tomber dans l'~** to sink into oblivion.

oublier [ublije] *vt* to forget; **~ de faire qqch** to forget to do sthg.

oubliettes [ublijet] *nfpl* dungeon (*sg*).

ouest [west] 1 *nm* west; **un vent d'~** a westerly wind; **à l'~** in the west; **à l'~** (**de**) to the west (of). 2 *adj inv* [gén] west; [province, région] western.

ouest-allemand, -e [westalmã, ãd] *adj* West German.

ouf [uf] *interj* phew!

oui [wi] 1 *adv* yes; **tu viens, ~ ou non?** are you coming or not?, are you coming or aren't you?; **je crois que ~** I think so. 2 *nm inv* yes; **pour un ~ pour un non** for no apparent reason.

ouï-dire [widir] *nm inv*: **par ~** by ou from hearsay.

ouïe [wi] *nf* hearing; **avoir l'~ fine** to have excellent hearing. ○ **ouïes** *nfpl* [de poisson] gills.

ouragan [uragã] *nm* MÉTÉOR hurricane.

ourlet [urlε] *nm* COUTURE hem.

ours [urs] *nm* bear; **~** (**en peluche**) teddy (bear); **~ polaire** polar bear.

ourse [urs] *nf* she-bear.

oursin [ursε̃] *nm* sea urchin.

ourson [ursõ] *nm* bear cub.

outil [uti] *nm* tool.

outillage [utijaʒ] *nm* [équipement] tools (*pl*), equipment.

outrage [utraʒ] *nm* JUR: **~ à la pudeur** indecent behaviour (*U*).

outrager [utraʒe] *vt* [offenser] to insult.

outrance [utrãs] *nf* excess; **à ~** excessively.

outrancier, -ière [utrãsje, jεr] *adj* extravagant.

outre¹ [utr] *nf* wineskin.

outre² [utr] 1 *prép* besides, as well as. 2 *adv*: **passer ~** to go on, to proceed further. ○ **en outre** *loc adv* moreover, besides.

outre-Atlantique [utratlãtik] *loc adv* across the Atlantic.

outre-Manche [utrəmãʃ] *loc adv* across the Channel.

outremer [utrəmεr] *adj inv* ultramarine.

outre-mer [utrəmεr] *loc adv* overseas.

outrepasser [utrəpase] *vt* to exceed.

outrer [utre] *vt* [personne] to outrage.

outre-Rhin [utrərε̃] *loc adv* across the Rhine.

ouvert, -e [uvεr, εrt] 1 *pp* → **ouvrir**. 2 *adj* [gén] open; **grand ~** wide open. || [robinet] on, running.

ouvertement [uvεrtəmã] *adv* openly.

ouverture [uvεrtyr] *nf* [gén] opening; [d'hostilités] outbreak; **~ d'esprit** open-mindedness. || MUS overture. || PHOT aperture. ○ **ouvertures** *nfpl* [propositions] overtures.

ouvrable [uvrabl] *adj* working.

ouvrage [uvraʒ] *nm* [travail] work (*U*), task; **se mettre à l'~** to start work. || [objet produit] (piece of) work; COUTURE work (*U*). || [livre, écrit] work.

ouvré, -e [uvre] *adj*: **jour ~** working day.

ouvre-boîtes [uvrəbwat] *nm inv* tin opener *Br*, can opener.

ouvre-bouteilles [uvrəbutεj] *nm inv* bottle opener.

ouvreuse [uvrøz] *nf* usherette.

ouvrier, -ière [uvrije, jεr] 1 *adj* [quartier, enfance] working-class; [questions, statut] labour (*avant n*); **classe ouvrière** working class. 2 *nm, f* worker; **~ agricole** farm worker; **~ qualifié** skilled worker; **~ spécialisé** semi-skilled worker.

ouvrir [uvrir] 1 *vt* [gén] to open. || [chemin, voie] to open up. || [gaz] to turn on. 2 *vi* to open; **~ sur qqch** to open onto sthg. ○ **s'ouvrir** *vp* [porte, fleur] to open. || [route, perspectives] to open up. || [personne]: **s'~** (**à qqn**) to confide (in sb), to open up (to sb). || [se blesser]: **s'~ le genou** to cut one's knee open; **s'~ les veines** to slash ou cut one's wrists.

ovaire [ɔvεr] *nm* ovary.

ovale [ɔval] *adj & nm* oval.

ovation [ɔvasjɔ̃] nf ovation; **faire une ~ à qqn** to give sb an ovation.

overdose [ɔvœrdoz] nf overdose.

ovin, -e [ɔvɛ̃, in] adj ovine. ○ **ovin** nm sheep.

OVNI, Ovni [ɔvni] (abr de objet volant non identifié) nm UFO.

oxydation [ɔksidasjɔ̃] nf oxidation, oxidization.

oxyde [ɔksid] nm oxide.

oxyder [ɔkside] vt to oxidize.

oxygène [ɔksiʒɛn] nm oxygen.

oxygéné, -e [ɔksiʒene] adj CHIM oxygenated; → **eau.**

ozone [ozon] nm ozone.

p¹, P [pe] nm inv p, P.

p² (abr de page) p. || abr de pièce.

pachyderme [paʃidɛrm] nm elephant.

pacifier [pasifje] vt to pacify.

pacifique [pasifik] adj peaceful.

Pacifique [pasifik] nm: **le ~** the Pacific (Ocean).

pacifiste [pasifist] nmf & adj pacifist.

pack [pak] nm pack.

pacotille [pakɔtij] nf shoddy goods (pl), rubbish; **de ~** cheap.

pacte [pakt] nm pact.

pactiser [paktize] vi: **~ avec** [faire un pacte avec] to make a pact with; [transiger avec] to come to terms with.

pactole [paktɔl] nm gold mine fig.

pagaie [pagɛ] nf paddle.

pagaille, pagaye, pagaïe [pagaj] nf fam mess.

pagayer [pageje] vi to paddle.

page [paʒ] **1** nf [feuillet] page; **~ blanche** blank page; **mettre en ~s** TYPO to make up (into pages). || loc: **être à la ~** to be up-to-date. **2** nm page (boy).

pagne [paɲ] nm loincloth.

pagode [pagɔd] nf pagoda.

pale, paye [pɛ] nf pay (U), wages (pl).

paiement, payement [pɛmɑ̃] nm payment.

païen, -ïenne [pajɛ̃, jɛn] adj & nm, f pagan, heathen.

paillard, -e [pajar, ard] adj bawdy.

paillasse [pajas] nf [matelas] straw mattress. || [d'évier] draining board.

paillasson [pajasɔ̃] nm [tapis] doormat.

paille [paj] nf BOT straw. || [pour boire] straw. ○ **paille de fer** nf steel wool.

pailleté, -e [pajte] adj sequined.

paillette [pajɛt] nf (gén pl) [sur vêtements] sequin, spangle. || [de lessive, savon] flake; **savon en ~s** soap flakes (pl).

pain [pɛ̃] nm [aliment] bread; **un ~ a** loaf; **petit ~** (bread) roll; **~ complet** wholemeal bread; **~ d'épice** ≃ gingerbread; **~ de mie** sandwich loaf. || [de savon, cire] bar.

pair, -e [pɛr] adj even. ○ **pair** nm peer. ○ **paire** nf pair; **une ~e de** [lunettes, ciseaux, chaussures] a pair of. ○ **au pair** loc adv for board and lodging, for one's keep; **jeune fille au ~** au pair (girl). ○ **de pair** loc adv: **aller de ~ avec** to go hand in hand with.

paisible [pɛzibl] adj peaceful.

paître [pɛtr] vi to graze.

paix [pɛ] nf peace; **avoir la ~** to have peace and quiet.

Pakistan [pakistɑ̃] nm: **le ~** Pakistan.

palace [palas] nm luxury hotel.

palais [palɛ] nm [château] palace. || [grand édifice] centre; **~ de justice** JUR law courts (pl). || ANAT palate.

palan [palɑ̃] nm block and tackle, hoist.

pale [pal] nf [de rame, d'hélice] blade.

pâle [pal] adj pale.

Palestine [palɛstin] nf: **la ~** Palestine.

palet [palɛ] nm HOCKEY puck.

palette [palɛt] nf [de peintre] palette.

pâleur [palœr] nf [de visage] pallor.

palier [palje] nm [d'escalier] landing. || [étape] level. || TECHNOL bearing.

pâlir [palir] vi [couleur, lumière] to fade; [personne] to turn ou go pale.

palissade [palisad] nf [clôture] fence.

palliatif, -ive [paljatif, iv] adj palliative. ○ **palliatif** nm MÉD palliative. || fig stopgap measure.

pallier [palje] vt to make up for.

palmarès [palmarɛs] nm [de lauréats] list of (medal) winners; SCOL list of prizewinners. || [de succès] record (of achievements).

palme [palm] nf [de palmier] palm-leaf. || [de nageur] flipper.

palmé, -e [palme] adj BOT palmate. || ZOOL web-footed; [patte] webbed.

palmier [palmje] *nm* BOT palm tree.

palmipède [palmiped] *nm* web-footed bird.

palombe [palɔ̃b] *nf* woodpigeon.

pâlot, -otte [palo, ɔt] *adj* pale, sickly-looking.

palourde [palurd] *nf* clam.

palper [palpe] *vt* [toucher] to feel, to finger; MÉD to palpate.

palpitant, -e [palpitɑ̃, ɑ̃t] *adj* exciting, thrilling.

palpitation [palpitasjɔ̃] *nf* palpitation.

palpiter [palpite] *vi* [paupières] to flutter; [cœur] to pound.

paludisme [palydism] *nm* malaria.

pamphlet [pɑ̃flɛ] *nm* satirical tract.

pamplemousse [pɑ̃pləmus] *nm* grapefruit.

pan [pɑ̃] **1** *nm* [de vêtement] tail. || [d'affiche] piece, bit; ~ **de mur** section of wall. **2** *interj* bang!

panache [panaʃ] *nm* [de plumes, fumée] plume. || [éclat] panache.

panaché, -e [panaʃe] *adj* [de plusieurs couleurs] multicoloured. || [mélangé] mixed. ○ **panaché** *nm* shandy.

Panama [panama] *nm* [pays]: **le ~** Panama.

panaris [panari] *nm* whitlow.

pancarte [pɑ̃kart] *nf* [de manifestant] placard. || [de signalisation] sign.

pancréas [pɑ̃kreas] *nm* pancreas.

pané, -e [pane] *adj* breaded, in breadcrumbs.

panier [panje] *nm* basket; ~ **à provisions** shopping basket.

panique [panik] **1** *nf* panic. **2** *adj* panicky; **être pris d'une peur ~** to be panic-stricken.

paniquer [panike] *vt & vi* to panic.

panne [pan] *nf* [arrêt] breakdown; **tomber en ~** to break down; ~ **de courant** ou **d'électricité** power failure.

panneau, -x [pano] *nm* [pancarte] sign; ~ **indicateur** signpost; ~ **publicitaire** (advertising) hoarding *Br*, billboard *Am*; ~ **de signalisation** road sign. || [élément] panel.

panoplie [panɔpli] *nf* [jouet] outfit. || *fig* [de mesures] package.

panorama [panɔrama] *nm* [vue] view, panorama; *fig* overview.

panse [pɑ̃s] *nf* [d'estomac] first stomach, rumen. || *fam* [gros ventre] belly, paunch.

pansement [pɑ̃smɑ̃] *nm* dressing, bandage; ~ **(adhésif)** (sticking) plaster *Br*, Bandaid® *Am*.

panser [pɑ̃se] *vt* [plaie] to dress, to bandage; [jambe] to put a dressing on, to bandage; [avec pansement adhésif] to put a plaster *Br* ou Bandaid® *Am* on. || [cheval] to groom.

pantalon [pɑ̃talɔ̃] *nm* pants (*pl*) *Am*.

pantelant, -e [pɑ̃tlɑ̃, ɑ̃t] *adj* panting, gasping.

panthère [pɑ̃tɛr] *nf* panther.

pantin [pɑ̃tɛ̃] *nm* [jouet] jumping jack. || *péj* [personne] puppet.

pantomime [pɑ̃tɔmim] *nf* [art, pièce] mime.

pantoufle [pɑ̃tufl] *nf* slipper.

PAO (*abr de* **publication assistée par ordinateur**) *nf* DTP.

paon [pɑ̃] *nm* peacock.

papa [papa] *nm* dad, daddy.

pape [pap] *nm* RELIG pope.

paperasse [papras] *nf péj* [papier sans importance] bumf (*U*) *Br*, papers (*pl*). || [papiers administratifs] paperwork (*U*).

papeterie [papetri] *nf* [magasin] stationer's; [fabrique] paper mill.

papetier, -ière [paptje, jɛr] *nm, f* [commerçant] stationer; [fabricant] paper manufacturer.

papier [papje] *nm* [matière, écrit] paper; ~ **alu** ou **aluminium** aluminium *Br* ou aluminum *Am* foil, tinfoil; ~ **carbone** carbon paper; ~ **crépon** crêpe paper; ~ **d'emballage** wrapping paper; ~ **à en-tête** headed notepaper; ~ **hygiénique** toilet paper; ~ **à lettres** writing paper, notepaper; ~ **peint** wallpaper; ~ **de verre** glasspaper, sandpaper. ○ **papiers** *nmpl*: ~**s (d'identité)** (identity) papers.

papier-calque [papjekalk] (*pl* **papiers-calque**) *nm* tracing paper.

papillon [papijɔ̃] *nm* ZOOL butterfly. || [nage] butterfly (stroke).

papillonner [papijɔne] *vi* to flit about ou around.

papillote [papijɔt] *nf* [de bonbon] candy paper *Am*. || [de cheveux] curl paper.

papilloter [papijɔte] *vi* [lumière] to twinkle; [yeux] to blink.

papoter [papɔte] *vi fam* to chatter.

paprika [paprika] *nm* paprika.

paquebot [pakbo] *nm* liner.

pâquerette [pakrɛt] *nf* daisy.

Pâques [pak] *nfpl* Easter (*sg*).

paquet [pakɛ] *nm* [colis] parcel. || [emballage] packet; ~**-cadeau** gift-wrapped parcel.

paquetage [paktaʒ] *nm* MIL kit.

par [par] *prép* [spatial] through, by (way of); **passer ~ la Suède et le Danemark** to go via Sweden and Denmark; **regarder ~ la fenêtre** to look out of the window; **~ endroits** in places; **~ ici/là** this/that way; **mon cousin habite ~ ici** my cousin lives round here. || [temporel] on; **~ un beau jour d'été** on a lovely summer's day; **~ le passé** in the past. || [moyen, manière, cause] by; **~ bateau/train/avion** by boat/train/plane; **~ pitié** out of ou from pity; **~ accident** by accident, by chance. || [introduit le complément d'agent] by; **faire faire qqch ~ qqn** to have sthg done by sb. || [sens distributif] per, a; **une heure ~ jour** one hour a ou per day; **deux ~ deux** two at a time. ○ **par-ci par-là** *loc adv* here and there.

para [para] (*abr de* **parachutiste**) *nm* para.

parabole [parabɔl] *nf* [récit] parable. || MATHS parabola.

parabolique [parabɔlik] *adj* parabolic; **antenne ~** dish ou parabolic aerial.

parachever [paraʃve] *vt* to put the finishing touches to.

parachute [paraʃyt] *nm* parachute; **~ ascensionnel** parachute (*for parascending*).

parachutiste [paraʃytist] *nmf* parachutist; MIL paratrooper.

parade [parad] *nf* [spectacle] parade. || [défense] parry; *fig* riposte.

paradis [paradi] *nm* paradise.

paradoxal, -e, -aux [paradɔksal, o] *adj* paradoxical.

paradoxe [paradɔks] *nm* paradox.

parafer, parapher [parafe] *vt* to initial.

paraffine [parafin] *nf* paraffin *Br*, kerosene *Am*; [solide] paraffin wax.

parages [paraʒ] *nmpl*: **être** ou **se trouver dans les ~** *fig* to be in the area ou vicinity.

paragraphe [paragraf] *nm* paragraph.

Paraguay [paragwe] *nm*: **le ~** Paraguay.

paraître [parɛtr] **1** *v attr* to look, to seem, to appear. **2** *vi* [se montrer] to appear. || [être publié] to come out, to be published. **3** *v impers*: **il paraît/paraîtrait que** it appears/would appear that.

parallèle [paralɛl] **1** *nm* parallel; **établir un ~ entre** *fig* to draw a parallel between. **2** *nf* parallel (line). **3** *adj* [action, en maths] parallel. || [marché] unofficial; [médecine, énergie] alternative.

parallélisme [paralelism] *nm* parallelism; [de roues] alignment.

paralyser [paralize] *vt* to paralyse.

paralysie [paralizi] *nf* paralysis.

paramédical, -e, -aux [paramedikal, o] *adj* paramedical.

paramètre [parametr] *nm* parameter.

paranoïa [paranɔja] *nf* paranoia.

paranoïaque [paranɔjak] **1** *adj* paranoid. **2** *nmf* paranoiac.

parapente [parapãt] *nm* paragliding.

parapet [parapɛ] *nm* parapet.

paraphe = **parafe**.

parapher = **parafer**.

paraphrase [parafraz] *nf* paraphrase.

paraplégique [parapleʒik] *nmf* & *adj* paraplegic.

parapluie [paraplɥi] *nm* umbrella.

parasite [parazit] **1** *nm* parasite. **2** *adj* parasitic. ○ **parasites** *nmpl* RADIO & TÉLÉ interference (*U*).

parasol [parasɔl] *nm* parasol, sunshade.

paratonnerre [paratɔner] *nm* lightning conductor.

paravent [paravã] *nm* screen.

parc [park] *nm* [jardin] park; [de château] grounds (*pl*); **~ d'attractions** amusement park; **~ national** national park. || [pour l'élevage] pen. || [de bébé] playpen.

parcelle [parsɛl] *nf* [petite partie] fragment, particle. || [terrain] parcel of land.

parce que [parsk(ə)] *loc conj* because.

parchemin [parʃəmɛ̃] *nm* parchment.

parcimonieux, -ieuse [parsimɔnjø, jøz] *adj* parsimonious.

parcmètre [parkmɛtr] *nm* parking meter.

parcourir [parkurir] *vt* [région, route] to cover. || [journal, dossier] to skim ou glance through, to scan.

parcours [parkur] *nm* [trajet, voyage] journey; [itinéraire] route. || GOLF [terrain] course; [trajet] round.

parcouru, -e [parkury] *pp* → **parcourir**.

par-delà [pardəla] *prép* beyond.

par-derrière [pardɛrjɛr] *adv* [par le côté arrière] round the back. || [en cachette] behind one's back.

par-dessous [pardəsu] *prép* & *adv* under, underneath.

pardessus [pardəsy] *nm inv* overcoat.

par-dessus [pardəsy] *prép* over, over the top of; **~ tout** above all.

par-devant [pardəvã] **1** *prép* in front of. **2** *adv* in front.

pardi [pardi] *interj fam* of course!

pardon [pardɔ̃] **1** nm forgiveness; demander ~ to say (one is) sorry. **2** interj [excuses] (I'm) sorry!; [pour attirer l'attention] excuse me!; ~? (I beg your) pardon? Br, pardon me? Am.

pardonner [pardɔne] **1** vt to forgive; ~ qqch à qqn to forgive sb for sthg; ~ à qqn d'avoir fait qqch to forgive sb for doing sthg. **2** vi: ce genre d'erreur ne pardonne pas this kind of mistake is fatal.

paré, -e [pare] adj [prêt] ready.

pare-balles [parbal] adj inv bulletproof.

pare-brise [parbriz] nm inv windscreen Br, windshield Am.

pare-chocs [parʃɔk] nm inv bumper.

pareil, -eille [parɛj] adj [semblable]: ~ (à) similar (to). || [tel] such; un ~ film such a film, a film like this. ○ **pareil** adv fam the same (way).

parent, -e [parɑ̃, ɑ̃t] **1** adj: ~ (de) related (to). **2** nm, f relative, relation. ○ **parents** nmpl [père et mère] parents, mother and father.

parenté [parɑ̃te] nf [lien, affinité] relationship.

parenthèse [parɑ̃tɛz] nf [digression] digression, parenthesis. || TYPO bracket, parenthesis; **entre ~s** in brackets; fig incidentally, by the way.

parer [pare] **1** vt sout [orner] to adorn. || [vêtir]: ~ qqn de qqch to dress sb up in sthg, to deck sb out in sthg; fig to attribute sthg to sb. || [contrer] to ward off, to parry. **2** vi: ~ à [faire face à] to deal with; [pourvoir à] to prepare for; ~ **au plus pressé** to see to what is most urgent.

pare-soleil [parsɔlɛj] nm inv sun visor.

paresse [parɛs] nf [fainéantise] laziness, idleness. || MÉD sluggishness.

paresser [parɛse] vi to laze about or around.

paresseux, -euse [parɛsø, øz] **1** adj [fainéant] lazy. || MÉD sluggish. **2** nm, f [personne] lazy ou idle person.

parfaire [parfɛr] vt to complete, to perfect.

parfait, -e [parfɛ, ɛt] adj perfect. ○ **parfait** nm GRAM perfect (tense).

parfaitement [parfɛtmɑ̃] adv [admirablement, très] perfectly. || [marque l'assentiment] absolutely.

parfois [parfwa] adv sometimes.

parfum [parfœ̃] nm [de fleur] scent, fragrance. || [à base d'essences] perfume, scent. || [de glace] flavour.

parfumé, -e [parfyme] adj [fleur] fragrant. || [mouchoir] perfumed. || [femme]: **elle est trop ~e** she's wearing too much perfume.

parfumer [parfyme] vt [suj: fleurs] to perfume. || [mouchoir] to perfume, to scent. || CULIN to flavour. ○ **se parfumer** vp to put perfume on.

parfumerie [parfymri] nf perfumery.

pari [pari] nm [entre personnes] bet.

paria [parja] nm pariah.

parier [parje] vt: ~ (sur) to bet (on).

parieur [parjœr] nm punter.

Paris [pari] n Paris.

parisien, -ienne [parizjɛ̃, jɛn] adj [vie, société] Parisian; [métro, banlieue, région] Paris (avant n). ○ **Parisien, -ienne** nm, f Parisian.

parité [parite] nf parity.

parjure [parʒyr] **1** nmf [personne] perjurer. **2** nm [faux serment] perjury.

parjurer [parʒyre] ○ **se parjurer** vp to perjure o.s.

parka [parka] nm ou nf parka.

parking [parkiŋ] nm [parc] car park Br, parking lot Am.

parlant, -e [parlɑ̃, ɑ̃t] adj [qui parle]: **le cinéma** ~ talking pictures; **l'horloge** ~e TÉLÉCOM the speaking clock. || fig [chiffres, données] eloquent; [portrait] vivid.

parlement [parləmɑ̃] nm parliament; **le Parlement européen** the European Parliament.

parlementaire [parləmɑ̃tɛr] **1** nmf [député] member of parliament; [négociateur] negotiator. **2** adj parliamentary.

parlementer [parləmɑ̃te] vi [négocier] to negotiate, to parley.

parler [parle] **1** vi [gén] to talk, to speak; ~ **à/avec qqn** to speak to/with sb, to talk to/with sb; ~ **de qqch à qqn** to speak ou talk to sb about sthg; ~ **de qqn/qqch** to talk about sb/sthg; ~ **de faire qqch** to talk about doing sthg; ~ **en français** to speak in French; **sans** ~ **de** apart from, not to mention; **à propre-ment** ~ strictly speaking; **tu parles!** fam you can say that again!; **n'en parlons plus** we'll say no more about it. || [avouer] to talk. **2** vt [langue] to speak; ~ **(le) français** to speak French.

parloir [parlwar] nm parlour.

parmi [parmi] prép among.

parodie [parɔdi] nf parody.

parodier [parɔdje] vt to parody.

paroi [parwa] nf [mur] wall; [cloison]

partition; ~ **rocheuse** rock face. ‖ [de ré-cipient] inner side.

paroisse [parwas] *nf* parish.

paroissial, -e, -iaux [parwasjal, jo] *adj* parish (*avant n*).

paroissien, -ienne [parwasjɛ̃, jɛn] *nm, f* parishioner.

parole [parɔl] *nf* [faculté de parler]: **la ~** speech. ‖ [propos, discours]: **adresser la ~ à qqn** to speak to sb; **couper la ~ à qqn** to cut sb off; **prendre la ~** to speak. ‖ [promesse, mot] word; **tenir ~** to keep one's word; **donner sa ~ (d'honneur)** to give one's word (of honour). ○ **paroles** *nfpl* MUS words, lyrics.

paroxysme [parɔksism] *nm* height.

parquer [parke] *vt* [animaux] to pen in ou up. ‖ [prisonniers] to shut up ou in.

parquet [parke] *nm* [plancher] parquet floor. ‖ JUR ≃ District Attorney's Office *Am*.

parqueter [parkəte] *vt* to lay a parquet floor in.

parrain [parɛ̃] *nm* [d'enfant] godfather. ‖ [de festival, sportif] sponsor.

parrainer [parɛne] *vt* to sponsor, to back.

parsemer [parsəme] *vt*: **~ (de)** to strew (with).

part [par] *nf* [de gâteau] portion; [de bonheur, héritage] share; [partie] part. ‖ [participation]: **prendre ~ à qqch** to take part in sthg. ‖ *loc*: **c'est de la ~ de qui?** [au téléphone] who's speaking ou call-ing?; **dites-lui de ma ~ que ...** tell him from me that ...; **ce serait bien aimable de votre ~** it would be very kind of you; **pour ma ~** as far as I'm concerned; **faire ~ à qqn de qqch** to inform sb of sthg. ○ **à part 1** *loc adv* aside, separately. **2** *loc adj* exceptional. **3** *loc prép* apart from. ○ **autre part** *loc adv* somewhere else. ○ **d'autre part** *loc adv* besides, moreover. ○ **d'une part ..., d'autre part** *loc corrélative* on the one hand ..., on the other hand. ○ **nulle part** *loc adv* nowhere. ○ **quelque part** *loc adv* somewhere.

part. *abr de* **particulier.**

partage [partaʒ] *nm* [action] sharing (out).

partager [partaʒe] *vt* [morceler] to di-vide (up). ‖ [mettre en commun]: **~ qqch avec qqn** to share sthg with sb. ○ **se partager** *vp* [se diviser] to be divided. ‖ [partager son temps] to divide one's time.

‖ [se répartir]: **se ~ qqch** to share sthg be-tween themselves/ourselves *etc.*

partance [partɑ̃s] *nf*: **en ~** outward bound; **en ~ pour** bound for.

partant, -e [partɑ̃, ɑ̃t] *adj*: **être ~ pour** to be ready for. ○ **partant** *nm* starter.

partenaire [partənɛr] *nmf* partner.

partenariat [partənarja] *nm* partner-ship.

parterre [partɛr] *nm* [de fleurs] (flower) bed. ‖ THÉÂTRE orchestra *Am*.

parti, -e [parti] **1** *pp* → **partir. 2** *adj* *fam* [ivre] tipsy. ○ **parti** *nm* POLIT party. ‖ [choix, décision] course of action; **pren-dre ~** to make up one's mind; **en prendre son ~** to be resigned; **être de ~ pris** to be prejudiced ou biased; **tirer ~ de** to make (good) use of. ‖ [personne à marier] match. ○ **partie** *nf* [élément, portion] part; **en grande ~e** largely; **en majeure ~e** for the most part; **faire ~e (inté-grante) de qqch** to be (an integral) part of sthg. ‖ SPORT game. ‖ JUR party; **la ~ adverse** the opposing party. ‖ *loc*: **pren-dre qqn à ~e** to attack sb. ○ **en partie** *loc adv* partly, in part.

partial, -e, -iaux [parsjal, jo] *adj* biased.

partialité [parsjalite] *nf* partiality, bias.

participant, -e [partisipɑ̃, ɑ̃t] *nm, f* [à réunion] participant. ‖ SPORT competitor. ‖ [à concours] entrant.

participation [partisipasjɔ̃] *nf* [colla-boration] participation. ‖ ÉCON interest; **~ aux bénéfices** profit-sharing.

participe [partisip] *nm* participle; **~ passé/présent** past/present participle.

participer [partisipe] *vi*: **~ à** [réunion, concours] to take part in; [frais] to con-tribute to; [bénéfices] to share in.

particularité [partikylarite] *nf* distinc-tive feature.

particule [partikyl] *nf* [gén & LING] par-ticle. ‖ [nobiliaire] nobiliary particle.

particulier, -ière [partikylje, jɛr] *adj* [personnel, privé] private. ‖ [spécial] par-ticular, special; [propre] peculiar, chara-cteristic; **~ à** peculiar to, characteristic of. ‖ [remarquable] unusual, exceptional; **cas ~** special case. ‖ [assez bizarre] pecu-liar.

particulièrement [partikyljermɑ̃] *adv* particularly; **tout ~** especially.

partie → **parti.**

partiel, -ielle [parsjɛl] *adj* partial. ○ **partiel** *nm* UNIV ≃ end-of-term exam.

partir [partir] *vi* [personne] to go, to leave; ~ à to go to; ~ **pour** to leave for; ~ **de** [bureau] to leave; [aéroport, gare] to leave from; [hypothèse, route] to start from; [date] to run from. ‖ [voiture] to start. ‖ [coup de feu] to go off; [bouchon] to pop. ‖ [tache] to come out, to go. ○ **à partir de** *loc prép* from.

partisan, -e [partizã, an] *adj* [partial] partisan; être ~ **de** to be in favour of. ○ **partisan** *nm* [adepte] supporter, advocate.

partition [partisjɔ̃] *nf* [séparation] partition. ‖ MUS score.

partout [partu] *adv* everywhere.

paru, -e [pary] *pp* → **paraître**.

parure [paryr] *nf* (matching) set.

parution [parysjɔ̃] *nf* publication.

parvenir [parvənir] *vi*: ~ **à faire qqch** to manage to do sthg; **faire** ~ **qqch à qqn** to send sthg to sb.

parvenu, -e [parvəny] **1** *pp* → **parvenir**. **2** *nm, f péj* parvenu, upstart.

pas¹ [pa] *nm* [gén] step; **allonger le** ~ to quicken one's pace; **revenir sur ses** ~ to retrace one's steps; ~ **à** ~ step by step; **à** ~ **de loup** *fig* stealthily. ‖ TECHNOL thread. ‖ *loc*: **c'est à deux** ~ **(d'ici)** it's very near (here); **faire les cent** ~ to pace up and down; **faire un faux** ~ to slip; *fig* to make a faux pas; **faire le premier** ~ to make the first move; **(rouler) au** ~ (to move) at a snail's pace; **sur le** ~ **de la porte** on the doorstep.

pas² [pa] *adv* [avec ne] not; **elle n'a** ~ **mangé** she hasn't eaten; **je ne le connais** ~ I don't know him; **il n'y a** ~ **de vin** there's no wine, there isn't any wine; **je préférerais ne** ~ **le rencontrer** I would prefer not to meet him, I would rather not meet him. ‖ [sans ne] not; **l'as-tu vu ou** ~? have you seen him or not?; **il est très satisfait, moi** ~ he's very pleased, but I'm not; ~ **encore** not yet. ‖ [avec pron indéf]: ~ **un** [aucun] none, not one.

pascal, -e [paskal] (*pl* **pascals** OU **pascaux** [pasko]) *adj* Easter (*avant n*).

passable [pasabl] *adj* passable, fair.

passage [pasaʒ] *nm* [action - de passer] going past; [- de traverser] crossing; **être de** ~ to be passing through. ‖ [endroit] passage, way; «~ **interdit**» "no entry"; ~ **clouté** OU **pour piétons** pedestrian crossing; ~ **à niveau** level crossing *Br*, grade crossing *Am*; ~ **souterrain** underpass *Br*, subway *Am*. ‖ [extrait] passage.

passager, -ère [pasaʒe, εr] **1** *adj* [bonheur] fleeting, short-lived. **2** *nm, f* passenger.

passant, -e [pasã, ãt] **1** *adj* busy. **2** *nm, f* passer-by. ○ **passant** *nm* [de ceinture] (belt) loop.

passe [pas] **1** *nm* passkey. **2** *nf* [au sport] pass. ‖ NAVIG channel.

passé, -e [pase] *adj* [qui n'est plus] past; [précédent]: **la semaine** ~ last week; **au cours de la semaine** ~**e** in the last week; **il est trois heures** ~**es** it's gone three *Br*, it's after three. ‖ [fané] faded. ○ **passé 1** *nm* past; ~ **composé** perfect tense; ~ **simple** past historic. **2** *prép* after.

passe-droit [pasdrwa] (*pl* **passe-droits**) *nm* privilege.

passe-montagne [pasmɔ̃taɲ] (*pl* **passe-montagnes**) *nm* Balaclava (helmet).

passe-partout [paspartu] *nm inv* [clé] passkey. ‖ (*en apposition*) [tenue] all-purpose; [phrase] stock (*avant n*).

passeport [paspɔr] *nm* passport.

passer [pase] **1** *vi* [se frayer un chemin] to pass, to get past. ‖ [défiler] to go by OU past. ‖ [aller] to go; ~ **chez qqn** to call on sb, to drop in on sb; ~ **devant** [bâtiment] to pass; [juge] to come before; **en passant** in passing. ‖ [venir - facteur] to come, to call. ‖ SCOL to pass, to be admitted; ~ **dans la classe supérieure** to move up, to be moved up (a class). ‖ [être accepté] to be accepted. ‖ [fermer les yeux]: ~ **sur qqch** to pass over sthg. ‖ [temps] to pass, to go by. ‖ [disparaître - souvenir, couleur] to fade; [- douleur] to pass, to go away. ‖ CIN, TÉLÉ & THÉÂTRE to be on; ~ **à la radio/télévision** to be on the radio/television. ‖ CARTES to pass. ‖ *loc*: ~ **inaperçu** to pass OU go unnoticed; **passons ...** let's move on ...; ~ **pour** to be regarded as; **se faire** ~ **pour qqn** to pass o.s. off as sb. **2** *vt* [franchir - frontière, rivière] to cross; [- douane] to go through. ‖ [soirée, vacances] to spend. ‖ [sauter - ligne, tour] to miss. ‖ [faire aller - bras] to pass, to put. ‖ [filtrer - huile] to strain; [- café] to filter. ‖ [film, disque] to put on. ‖ [vêtement] to slip on. ‖ [vitesses] to change; ~ **la** OU **en troisième** to change into third (gear). ‖ [donner]: ~ **qqch à qqn** to pass sb sthg; MÉD to give sb sthg. ‖ [accord]: ~ **un contrat avec qqn** to have an agreement with sb. ‖ SCOL & UNIV [examen] to sit, to take. ‖ [au téléphone]: **je vous passe Mme Ledoux** [transmettre]

I'll put you through to Mme Ledoux; [donner l'écouteur à] I'll hand you Mme Ledoux. ○ **se passer** *vp* [événement] to happen, to take place; **comment ça s'est passé?** how did it go? ‖ [s'abstenir]: **se ~ de qqch/de faire qqch** to do without sthg/doing sthg.

passerelle [pasʀɛl] *nf* [pont] footbridge. ‖ [passage mobile] gangway.

passe-temps [pastɑ̃] *nm inv* pastime.

passif, -ive [pasif, iv] *adj* passive. ○ **passif** *nm* GRAM passive. ‖ FIN liabilities (*pl*).

passion [pasjɔ̃] *nf* passion; **avoir la ~ de qqch** to have a passion for sthg.

passionnant, -e [pasjɔnɑ̃, ɑ̃t] *adj* exciting, fascinating.

passionné, -e [pasjɔne] **1** *adj* [personne] passionate. ‖ [récit, débat] impassioned. **2** *nm, f* passionate person; **~ de ski/d'échecs** *etc* skiing/chess *etc* fanatic.

passionnel, -elle [pasjɔnɛl] *adj* [crime] of passion.

passionner [pasjɔne] *vt* [personne] to grip, to fascinate. ○ **se passionner** *vp*: **se ~ pour** to have a passion for.

passivité [pasivite] *nf* passivity.

passoire [paswaʀ] *nf* [à liquide] sieve; [à légumes] colander.

pastel [pastɛl] **1** *nm* pastel. **2** *adj inv* [couleur] pastel (*avant n*).

pastèque [pastɛk] *nf* watermelon.

pasteur [pastœʀ] *nm littéraire* [berger] shepherd. ‖ RELIG pastor, minister.

pasteuriser [pastœʀize] *vt* to pasteurize.

pastille [pastij] *nf* [bonbon] pastille, lozenge.

pastis [pastis] *nm aniseed-flavoured aperitif.*

patate [patat] *nf fam* [pomme de terre] spud. ‖ *fam* [imbécile] fathead.

patauger [patoʒe] *vi* [barboter] to splash about.

pâte [pat] *nf* [à tarte] pastry; [à pain] dough; **~ brisée** shortcrust pastry; **~ feuilletée** puff *ou* flaky pastry; **~ à frire** batter. ‖ [mélange] paste; **~ d'amandes** almond paste; **~ de fruits** *jelly made from fruit paste;* **~ à modeler** modelling clay. ○ **pâtes** *nfpl* pasta (*sg*).

pâté [pate] *nm* CULIN pâté; **~ de campagne** farmhouse pâté; **~ en croûte** pâté *baked in a pastry case;* **~ de foie** liver pâté. ‖ [tache] ink blot. ‖ [bloc]: **~ de maisons** block (of houses).

patelin [patlɛ̃] *nm fam* village, place.

patente [patɑ̃t] *nf* licence fee (*for traders and professionals*).

patère [patɛʀ] *nf* [portemanteau] coat hook.

paternalisme [patɛʀnalism] *nm* paternalism.

paternel, -elle [patɛʀnɛl] *adj* [devoir, autorité] paternal; [amour, ton] fatherly.

paternité [patɛʀnite] *nf* paternity, fatherhood; *fig* authorship, paternity.

pâteux, -euse [patø, øz] *adj* [aliment] doughy; [encre] thick.

pathétique [patetik] *adj* moving, pathetic.

pathologie [patɔlɔʒi] *nf* pathology.

patibulaire [patibylɛʀ] *adj péj* sinister.

patience [pasjɑ̃s] *nf* [gén] patience. ‖ [jeu de cartes] patience *Br*, solitaire *Am*.

patient, -e [pasjɑ̃, ɑ̃t] **1** *adj* patient. **2** *nm, f* MÉD patient.

patienter [pasjɑ̃te] *vi* to wait.

patin [patɛ̃] *nm* SPORT skate; **~ à glace/à roulettes** ice/roller skate; **faire du ~ à glace/à roulettes** to go ice-/roller-skating.

patinage [patinaʒ] *nm* SPORT skating; **~ artistique/de vitesse** figure/speed skating.

patiner [patine] *vi* SPORT to skate. ‖ [véhicule] to skid. ○ **se patiner** *vp* to take on a patina.

patineur, -euse [patinœʀ, øz] *nm, f* skater.

patinoire [patinwaʀ] *nf* ice *ou* skating rink.

pâtisserie [patisʀi] *nf* [gâteau] pastry. ‖ [commerce] ≃ cake shop.

pâtissier, -ière [patisje, jɛʀ] **1** *adj*: **crème pâtissière** confectioner's custard. **2** *nm, f* pastrycook.

patois [patwa] *nm* patois.

patriarche [patrijarʃ] *nm* patriarch.

patrie [patri] *nf* country, homeland.

patrimoine [patrimwan] *nm* [familial] inheritance; [collectif] heritage.

patriote [patrijɔt] *nmf* patriot.

patriotique [patrijɔtik] *adj* patriotic.

patron, -onne [patrɔ̃, ɔn] *nm, f* [d'entreprise] head. ‖ [chef] boss. ‖ RELIG patron saint. ○ **patron** *nm* [modèle] pattern.

patronage [patrɔnaʒ] *nm* [protection] patronage; [de saint] protection.

patronal, -e, -aux [patrɔnal, o] *adj* [organisation, intérêts] employers' (*avant n*).

patronat [patrɔna] *nm* employers.

patronyme [patrɔnim] *nm* patronymic.

patrouille [patruj] *nf* patrol.

patte [pat] *nf* [d'animal] paw; [d'oiseau] foot. || *fam* [jambe] leg; [pied] foot; [main] hand, paw. || [favori] sideburn.

pâturage [patyraʒ] *nm* [lieu] pasture land.

pâture [patyr] *nf* [nourriture] food, fodder; *fig* intellectual nourishment.

paume [pom] *nf* [de main] palm.

paumé, -e [pome] *fam* 1 *adj* lost. 2 *nm, f* down and out.

paumer [pome] *fam vt* to lose. ○ **se paumer** *vp* to get lost.

paupière [popjɛr] *nf* eyelid.

pause [poz] *nf* [arrêt] break; **~-café** coffee-break. || MUS pause.

pauvre [povr] 1 *nmf* poor person. 2 *adj* poor; **~ en** low in.

pauvreté [povrəte] *nf* poverty.

pavaner [pavane] ○ **se pavaner** *vp* to strut.

pavé, -e [pave] *adj* cobbled. ○ **pavé** *nm* [de pierre] cobblestone, paving stone. || *fam* [livre] tome. || INFORM: **~ numérique** keypad.

pavillon [pavijɔ̃] *nm* [bâtiment] detached house. || [drapeau] flag.

pavot [pavo] *nm* poppy.

payant, -e [pɛjɑ̃, ɑ̃t] *adj* [hôte] paying (*avant n*). || [spectacle] with an admission charge. || *fam* [affaire] profitable.

paye = **paie**.

payement = **paiement**.

payer [peje] 1 *vt* [gén] to pay; [achat] to pay for; **~ qqch à qqn** to buy sthg for sb, to buy sb sthg, to treat sb to sthg. || [expier - crime, faute] to pay for. 2 *vi*: **~ (pour)** to pay (for).

pays [pei] *nm* [gén] country. || [région, province] region. ○ **pays de Galles** *nm*: **le ~ de Galles** Wales.

paysage [peizaʒ] *nm* [site, vue] landscape, scenery. || [tableau] landscape.

paysagiste [peizaʒist] *nmf* [peintre] landscape artist. || [concepteur de parcs] landscape gardener.

paysan, -anne [peizɑ̃, an] 1 *adj* [vie, coutume] country (*avant n*), rural; [organisation, revendication] farmers' (*avant n*); *péj* peasant (*avant n*). 2 *nm, f* [agriculteur] (small) farmer. || *péj* [rustre] peasant.

Pays-Bas [peiba] *nmpl*: **les ~** the Netherlands.

PC *nm* (*abr de* **Parti communiste**) Communist Party. || (*abr de* **personal computer**) PC.

PCV (*abr de* **à percevoir**) *nm* reverse charge call.

P-DG (*abr de* **président-directeur général**) *nm* Chairman and President *Am*.

péage [peaʒ] *nm* toll.

peau [po] *nf* [gén] skin. || [cuir] hide, leather (*U*).

péché [peʃe] *nm* sin.

pêche [pɛʃ] *nf* [fruit] peach. || [activité] fishing; [poissons] catch; **aller à la ~** to go fishing.

pécher [peʃe] *vi* to sin.

pêcher¹ [peʃe] *vt* [poisson] to catch. || *fam* [trouver] to dig up.

pêcher² [peʃe] *nm* peach tree.

pécheur, -eresse [peʃœr, peʃrɛs] 1 *adj* sinful. 2 *nm, f* sinner.

pêcheur, -euse [peʃœr, øz] *nm, f* fisherman (*f* fisherwoman).

pectoral, -e, -aux [pɛktɔral, o] *adj* [sirop] cough (*avant n*). ○ **pectoraux** *nmpl* pectorals.

pécuniaire [pekynjɛr] *adj* financial.

pédagogie [pedagɔʒi] *nf* [science] education, pedagogy. || [qualité] teaching ability.

pédagogue [pedagɔg] 1 *nmf* teacher. 2 *adj*: **être ~** to be a good teacher.

pédale [pedal] *nf* [gén] pedal.

pédaler [pedale] *vi* [à bicyclette] to pedal.

pédalo [pedalo] *nm* pedal boat.

pédant, -e [pedɑ̃, ɑ̃t] *adj* pedantic.

pédéraste [pederast] *nm* homosexual, pederast.

pédiatre [pedjatr] *nmf* pediatrician.

pédicure [pedikyr] *nmf* chiropodist.

peigne [pɛɲ] *nm* [démêloir, barrette] comb.

peigner [peɲe] *vt* [cheveux] to comb. ○ **se peigner** *vp* to comb one's hair.

peignoir [peɲwar] *nm* dressing gown *Br*, robe *Am*, bathrobe *Am*.

peindre [pɛ̃dr] *vt* to paint; *fig* [décrire] to depict.

peine [pɛn] *nf* [châtiment] punishment, penalty; JUR sentence; **sous ~ de qqch** on pain of sthg; **~ capitale** OU **de mort** capital punishment, death sentence. || [chagrin] sorrow, sadness (*U*); **faire de la ~ à qqn** to upset sb, to distress sb. || [effort] trouble; **ça ne vaut pas** OU **ce n'est pas la ~** it's not worth it. || [difficulté] difficulty; **avoir de la ~ à faire qqch** to have difficulty or trouble doing sthg; **à grand-~** with great difficulty. ○ **à peine** *loc adv* scarcely, hardly; **à ~ ... que** hardly ... than.

peint, -e [pɛ̃, pɛ̃t] *pp* → peindre.

peintre [pɛ̃tr] *nm* painter.

peinture [pɛ̃tyr] *nf* [gén] painting. || [produit] paint; «~ **fraîche**» "wet paint".

péjoratif, -ive [peʒɔratif, iv] *adj* pejorative.

Pékin [pekɛ̃] *n* Peking, Beijing.

pelage [pəlaʒ] *nm* coat, fur.

pêle-mêle [pɛlmɛl] *adv* pell-mell.

peler [pəle] *vt & vi* to peel.

pèlerin [pɛlrɛ̃] *nm* pilgrim.

pèlerinage [pɛlrinaʒ] *nm* [voyage] pilgrimage. || [lieu] place of pilgrimage.

pélican [pelikɑ̃] *nm* pelican.

pelle [pɛl] *nf* [instrument] shovel. || [machine] digger.

pellicule [pelikyl] *nf* film. ○ **pellicules** *nfpl* dandruff (*U*).

pelote [pəlɔt] *nf* [de laine, ficelle] ball.

peloter [pəlɔte] *vt fam* to paw.

peloton [pəlɔtɔ̃] *nm* [de soldats] squad; ~ **d'exécution** firing squad. || [de concurrents] pack.

pelotonner [pəlɔtɔne] ○ **se pelotonner** *vp* to curl up.

pelouse [pəluz] *nf* [de jardin] lawn.

peluche [pəlyʃ] *nf* [jouet] soft toy. || [d'étoffe] piece of fluff.

pelure [pəlyr] *nf* [fruit] peel.

pénal, -e, -aux [penal, o] *adj* penal.

pénaliser [penalize] *vt* to penalize.

penalty [penalti] (*pl* **penaltys** OU **penalties**) *nm* penalty.

penaud, -e [pəno, od] *adj* sheepish.

penchant [pɑ̃ʃɑ̃] *nm* [inclination] tendency. || [sympathie]: ~ **pour** liking or fondness for.

pencher [pɑ̃ʃe] **1** *vi* to lean; ~ **vers/pour** *fig* to incline towards/in favour of. **2** *vt* to bend. ○ **se pencher** *vp* [s'incliner] to lean over; [se baisser] to bend down.

pendaison [pɑ̃dɛzɔ̃] *nf* hanging.

pendant¹, -e [pɑ̃dɑ̃, ɑ̃t] *adj* [bras] hanging, dangling. ○ **pendant** *nm* [bijou]: ~ **d'oreilles** (drop) earring. || [de paire] counterpart.

pendant² [pɑ̃dɑ̃] *prép* during. ○ **pendant que** *loc conj* while, whilst; ~ **que j'y suis,** ... while I'm at it, ...

pendentif [pɑ̃dɑ̃tif] *nm* pendant.

penderie [pɑ̃dri] *nf* wardrobe.

pendre [pɑ̃dr] **1** *vi* [être fixé en haut]: ~ (**à**) to hang (from). || [descendre trop bas]

to hang down. **2** *vt* [rideaux, tableau] to hang (up), to put up. || [personne] to hang. ○ **se pendre** *vp* [se suicider] to hang o.s.

pendule [pɑ̃dyl] **1** *nm* pendulum. **2** *nf* clock.

pénétrer [penetre] **1** *vi* to enter. **2** *vt* [mur, vêtement] to penetrate.

pénible [penibl] *adj* [travail] laborious. || [nouvelle, maladie] painful. || *fam* [personne] tiresome.

péniche [peniʃ] *nf* barge.

pénicilline [penisilin] *nf* penicillin.

péninsule [penɛ̃syl] *nf* peninsula.

pénis [penis] *nm* penis.

pénitence [penitɑ̃s] *nf* [repentir] penitence. || [peine, punition] penance.

pénitencier [penitɑ̃sje] *nm* prison, penitentiary *Am*.

pénombre [penɔ̃br] *nf* half-light.

pense-bête [pɑ̃sbɛt] (*pl* **pense-bêtes**) *nm* reminder.

pensée [pɑ̃se] *nf* [idée, faculté] thought. || [esprit] mind, thoughts (*pl*). || [doctrine] thought, thinking. || BOT pansy.

penser [pɑ̃se] **1** *vi* to think; ~ **à qqn/qqch** [avoir à l'esprit] to think of sb/sthg, to think about sb/sthg; [se rappeler] to remember sb/sthg; ~ **à faire qqch** [se rappeler] to remember to do sthg; **qu'est-ce que tu en penses?** what do you think (of it)? **2** *vt* to think; **je pense que oui** I think so; **je pense que non** I don't think so; ~ **faire qqch** to be planning to do sthg.

pensif, -ive [pɑ̃sif, iv] *adj* pensive, thoughtful.

pension [pɑ̃sjɔ̃] *nf* [allocation] pension; ~ **alimentaire** [dans un divorce] alimony. || [hébergement] board and lodgings; ~ **complète** full board; **demi-~** half board. || [hôtel] guesthouse; ~ **de famille** guesthouse, boarding house. || [internat] boarding school.

pensionnaire [pɑ̃sjɔnɛr] *nmf* [élève] boarder. || [hôte payant] lodger.

pensionnat [pɑ̃sjɔna] *nm* [internat] boarding school.

pentagone [pɛ̃tagɔn] *nm* pentagon.

pente [pɑ̃t] *nf* slope; **en ~** sloping, inclined.

pentecôte [pɑ̃tkot] *nf* [juive] Pentecost; [chrétienne] Whitsun.

pénurie [penyri] *nf* shortage.

pépin [pepɛ̃] *nm* [graine] pip. || *fam* [ennui] hitch.

pépinière [pepinjɛr] *nf* tree nursery.

pépite [pepit] *nf* nugget.

perçant, -e [pɛrsɑ̃, ɑ̃t] *adj* [regard, son] piercing. || [froid] bitter, biting.

percepteur [pɛrsɛptœr] *nm* tax collector.

perception [pɛrsɛpsjɔ̃] *nf* [bureau] tax office. || [sensation] perception.

percer [pɛrse] **1** *vt* [mur, roche] to make a hole in; [coffre-fort] to crack. || [trou] to make; [avec perceuse] to drill. || [silence, oreille] to pierce. || *fig* [mystère] to penetrate. **2** *vi* [soleil] to break through. || [abcès] to burst; **avoir une dent qui perce** to be cutting a tooth. || [réussir] to make a name for o.s., to break through.

perceuse [pɛrsøz] *nf* drill.

percevoir [pɛrsəvwar] *vt* [intention, nuance] to perceive. || [retraite, indemnité] to receive. || [impôts] to collect.

perche [pɛrʃ] *nf* [poisson] perch. || [de bois, métal] pole.

percher [pɛrʃe] **1** *vi* [oiseau] to perch. **2** *vt* to perch. ○ **se percher** *vp* to perch.

perchoir [pɛrʃwar] *nm* perch.

percolateur [pɛrkɔlatœr] *nm* percolator.

perçu, -e [pɛrsy] *pp* → **percevoir.**

percussion [pɛrkysjɔ̃] *nf* percussion.

percutant, -e [pɛrkytɑ̃, ɑ̃t] *adj* [obus] explosive. || *fig* [argument] forceful.

percuter [pɛrkyte] **1** *vt* to strike, to smash into. **2** *vi* to explode.

perdant, -e [pɛrdɑ̃, ɑ̃t] **1** *adj* losing. **2** *nm, f* loser.

perdre [pɛrdr] **1** *vt* [gén] to lose. || [temps] to waste; [occasion] to miss, to waste. || [suj: bonté, propos] to be the ruin of. **2** *vi* to lose. ○ **se perdre** *vp* [coutume] to die out, to become lost. || [personne] to get lost, to lose one's way.

perdrix [pɛrdri] *nf* partridge.

perdu, -e [pɛrdy] **1** *pp* → **perdre. 2** *adj* [égaré] lost. || [endroit] out-of-the-way. || [balle] stray. || [temps, occasion] wasted. || [récolte, robe] spoilt, ruined.

père [pɛr] *nm* [gén] father; ~ **de famille** father. ○ **père Noël** *nm*: **le** ~ Noël Father Christmas, Santa Claus.

péremptoire [perɑ̃ptwar] *adj* peremptory.

perfection [pɛrfɛksjɔ̃] *nf* [qualité] perfection.

perfectionner [pɛrfɛksjɔne] *vt* to perfect. ○ **se perfectionner** *vp* to improve.

perfide [pɛrfid] *adj* perfidious.

perforer [pɛrfɔre] *vt* to perforate.

performance [pɛrfɔrmɑ̃s] *nf* performance.

performant, -e [pɛrfɔrmɑ̃, ɑ̃t] *adj* [personne] efficient. || [machine] high-performance (*avant n*).

perfusion [pɛrfyzjɔ̃] *nf* perfusion.

péridurale [peridyral] *nf* epidural.

péril [peril] *nm* peril.

périlleux, -euse [perijø, øz] *adj* perilous, dangerous.

périmé, -e [perime] *adj* out-of-date; *fig* [idées] outdated.

périmètre [perimɛtr] *nm* [contour] perimeter. || [contenu] area.

période [perjɔd] *nf* period.

périodique [perjɔdik] **1** *nm* periodical. **2** *adj* periodic.

péripétie [peripesi] *nf* event.

périphérie [periferi] *nf* [de ville] outskirts (*pl*). || [bord] periphery; [de cercle] circumference.

périphérique [periferik] **1** *nm* [route] ring road *Br*, beltway *Am.* || INFORM peripheral device. **2** *adj* peripheral.

périphrase [perifraz] *nf* periphrasis.

périple [peripl] *nm* [voyage] trip.

périr [perir] *vi* to perish.

périssable [perisabl] *adj* [denrée] perishable. || [sentiment] transient.

perle [pɛrl] *nf* [de nacre] pearl. || [de bois, verre] bead. || [personne] gem.

permanence [pɛrmanɑ̃s] *nf* [continuité] permanence; en ~ constantly. || [service]: **être** ~ to be on duty. || SCOL: **(salle de)** ~ study room.

permanent, -e [pɛrmanɑ̃, ɑ̃t] *adj* permanent; [cinéma] with continuous showings. ○ **permanente** *nf* perm.

permettre [pɛrmɛtr] *vt* to permit, to allow; ~ **à qqn de faire qqch** to permit ou allow sb to do sthg. ○ **se permettre** *vp*: **se** ~ **qqch** to allow o.s. sthg; [avoir les moyens de] to be able to afford sthg; **se** ~ **de faire qqch** to take the liberty of doing sthg.

permis, -e [pɛrmi, iz] *pp* → **permettre.** ○ **permis** *nm* licence, permit; ~ **de conduire** driving licence *Br*, driver's license *Am*; ~ **de construire** planning permission *Br*, building permit *Am*.

permission [pɛrmisjɔ̃] *nf* [autorisation] permission. || MIL leave.

permuter [pɛrmyte] **1** *vt* to change round; [mots, figures] to transpose. **2** *vi* to change, to switch.

pérorer [perɔre] *vi péj* to hold forth.

Pérou [peru] *nm*: **le** ~ Peru.

perpendiculaire [pɛrpɑ̃dikylɛr] **1** *nf* perpendicular. **2** *adj*: ~ (à) perpendicular (to).

perpétrer [pɛrpetre] *vt* to perpetrate.

perpétuel, -elle [pɛrpetɥɛl] *adj* [fréquent, continu] perpetual.

perpétuer [pɛrpetɥe] *vt* to perpetuate. ○ **se perpétuer** *vp* to continue; [espèce] to perpetuate itself.

perpétuité [pɛrpetɥite] *nf* perpetuity; **à ~ for life**; **être condamné à ~** to be sentenced to life imprisonment.

perplexe [pɛrplɛks] *adj* perplexed.

perquisition [pɛrkizisjɔ̃] *nf* search.

perron [pɛrɔ̃] *nm* steps (*pl*).

perroquet [pɛrɔkɛ] *nm* [animal] parrot.

perruche [pɛryʃ] *nf* budgerigar.

perruque [pɛryk] *nf* wig.

persan, -e [pɛrsɑ̃, an] *adj* Persian.

persécuter [pɛrsekyte] *vt* [martyriser] to persecute. || [harceler] to harass.

persécution [pɛrsekysjɔ̃] *nf* persecution.

persévérant, -e [pɛrseverɑ̃, ɑ̃t] *adj* persevering.

persévérer [pɛrsevere] *vi*: ~ (dans) to persevere (in).

persienne [pɛrsjɛn] *nf* shutter.

persil [pɛrsi] *nm* parsley.

Persique [pɛrsik] → **golfe**.

persistant, -e [pɛrsistɑ̃, ɑ̃t] *adj* persistent; **arbre à feuillage ~** evergreen (tree).

persister [pɛrsiste] *vi* to persist; ~ **à faire qqch** to persist in doing sthg.

personnage [pɛrsɔnaʒ] *nm* THÉÂTRE character; ART figure.

personnalité [pɛrsɔnalite] *nf* [gén] personality. || JUR status.

personne [pɛrsɔn] **1** *nf* person; ~**s** people; **en ~** in person, personally; ~ **âgée** elderly person. **2** *pron indéf* [quelqu'un] anybody, anyone. || [aucune personne] nobody, no one; ~ **ne viendra** nobody will come; **il n'y a jamais ~** there's never anybody there.

personnel, -elle [pɛrsɔnɛl] *adj* [gén] personal. || [égoïste] self-centred. ○ **personnel** *nm* staff, personnel.

personnellement [pɛrsɔnɛlmɑ̃] *adv* personally.

personnifier [pɛrsɔnifje] *vt* to personify.

perspective [pɛrspɛktiv] *nf* [ART & point de vue] perspective. || [panorama] view. || [éventualité] prospect.

perspicace [pɛrspikas] *adj* perspicacious.

persuader [pɛrsɥade] *vt*: ~ **qqn de qqch/de faire qqch** to persuade sb of sthg/to do sthg, to convince sb of sthg/to do sthg.

persuasif, -ive [pɛrsɥazif, iv] *adj* persuasive.

persuasion [pɛrsɥazjɔ̃] *nf* persuasion.

perte [pɛrt] *nf* [gén] loss. || [gaspillage - de temps] waste. ○ **pertes** *nfpl* [morts] losses. ○ **à perte de vue** *loc adv* as far as the eye can see.

pertinent, -e [pɛrtinɑ̃, ɑ̃t] *adj* pertinent, relevant.

perturber [pɛrtyrbe] *vt* [gén] to disrupt; ~ **l'ordre public** to disturb the peace. || PSYCHOL to disturb.

pervenche [pɛrvɑ̃ʃ] *nf* BOT periwinkle. || *fam* [contractuelle] meter maid *Am*.

pervers, -e [pɛrvɛr, ɛrs] **1** *adj* [vicieux] perverted. || [effet] unwanted. **2** *nm*, *f* pervert.

perversion [pɛrvɛrsjɔ̃] *nf* perversion.

perversité [pɛrvɛrsite] *nf* perversity.

pervertir [pɛrvɛrtir] *vt* to pervert.

pesamment [pəzamɑ̃] *adv* heavily.

pesant, -e [pəzɑ̃, ɑ̃t] *adj* [lourd] heavy. || [style, architecture] ponderous.

pesanteur [pəzɑ̃tœr] *nf* PHYS gravity.

pesée [pəze] *nf* [opération] weighing.

pèse-personne [pɛzpɛrsɔn] (*pl inv* OU **pèse-personnes**) *nm* scales (*pl*).

peser [pəze] **1** *vt* to weigh. **2** *vi* [avoir un certain poids] to weigh. || [être lourd] to be heavy. || [appuyer]: ~ **sur qqch** to press (down) on sthg.

peseta [pezeta] *nf* peseta.

pessimisme [pesimism] *nm* pessimism.

pessimiste [pesimist] **1** *nmf* pessimist. **2** *adj* pessimistic.

peste [pɛst] *nf* MÉD plague.

pestilentiel, -ielle [pɛstilɑ̃sjɛl] *adj* pestilential.

pet [pɛ] *nm fam* fart.

pétale [petal] *nm* petal.

pétanque [petɑ̃k] *nf* ≈ bowls (*U*).

pétarader [petarade] *vi* to backfire.

pétard [petar] *nm* [petit explosif] banger *Br*, firecracker. || *fam* [revolver] gun. || *fam* [haschisch] joint.

péter [pete] **1** *vi tfam* [personne] to fart. || *fam* [câble, élastique] to snap. **2** *vt fam* to bust.

pétiller [petije] *vi* [vin, eau] to sparkle, to bubble. || *fig* [yeux] to sparkle.

philanthropie

petit, -e [pəti, it] 1 *adj* [de taille, jeune] small, little; ~ **frère** little ou younger brother. || [voyage, visite] short, little. || [faible, infime - somme d'argent] small; [- bruit] faint, slight. || [de peu d'importance, de peu de valeur] minor. || [médiocre, mesquin] petty. || [de rang modeste - commerçant, propriétaire, pays] small; [- fonctionnaire] minor. 2 *nm, f* [enfant] little one, child; **pauvre** ~! poor little thing!; **la classe des** ~**s** SCOL the infant class. 3 *nm* [jeune animal] young (*U*); **faire des** ~**s** to have puppies/kittens *etc*. ○ **petit à petit** *loc adv* little by little, gradually.

petit déjeuner [p(ə)tidezøne] *nm* breakfast.

petite-fille [p(ə)titfij] *nf* granddaughter.

petit-fils [p(ə)tifis] *nm* grandson.

petit-four [p(ə)tifur] *nm* petit-four.

pétition [petisjɔ̃] *nf* petition.

petit-lait [p(ə)tile] *nm* whey.

petit-nègre [p(ə)tinɛgr] *nm inv fam* pidgin French.

petits-enfants [p(ə)tizɑ̃fɑ̃] *nmpl* grandchildren.

petit-suisse [p(ə)tisɥis] *nm fresh soft cheese, eaten with sugar.*

pétrifier [petrifje] *vt litt & fig* to petrify.

pétrin [petrɛ̃] *nm* [de boulanger] kneading machine. || *fam* [embarras] pickle; **se fourrer/être dans le** ~ to get into/to be in a pickle.

pétrir [petrir] *vt* [pâte, muscle] to knead.

pétrole [petrɔl] *nm* oil, petroleum.

pétrolier, -ère [petrɔlje, jɛr] *adj* oil (*avant n*), petroleum (*avant n*). ○ **pétrolier** *nm* [navire] oil tanker.

pétrolifère [petrɔlifɛr] *adj* oil-bearing.

pétulant, -e [petylɑ̃, ɑ̃t] *adj* exuberant.

peu [pø] 1 *adv* (*avec verbe, adjectif, adverbe*): **il a** ~ **dormi** he didn't sleep much, he slept little; ~ **souvent** not very often, rarely. || ~ **de** (+ *nom sg*) little, not much; (+ *nom pl*) few, not many; ~ **de gens le connaissent** few ou not many know him. 2 *nm*: **un** ~ a little, a bit; **un (tout) petit** ~ a little bit; **elle est un** ~ **sotte** she's a bit stupid; **un** ~ **de** a little; **un** ~ **de vin/patience** a little wine/patience. ○ **avant peu** *loc adv* soon, before long. ○ **depuis peu** *loc adv* recently. ○ **peu à peu** *loc adv* gradually, little by little. ○ **pour peu que** *loc conj* (+ *subjonctif*) if ever, if only. ○ **pour**

un peu *loc adv* nearly, almost. ○ **sous peu** *loc adv* soon, shortly.

peuplade [pœplad] *nf* tribe.

peuple [pœpl] *nm* [gén] people; **le** ~ the (common) people. || *fam* [multitude]: **quel** ~! what a crowd!

peuplement [pœpləmɑ̃] *nm* [action] populating. || [population] population.

peupler [pœple] *vt* [pourvoir d'habitants - région] to populate; [- bois, étang] to stock. || [habiter, occuper] to inhabit. || *fig* [remplir] to fill. ○ **se peupler** *vp* [région] to become populated. || [rue, salle] to be filled.

peuplier [pœplije] *nm* poplar.

peur [pœr] *nf* fear; **avoir** ~ **de qqn/qqch** to be afraid of sb/sthg; **avoir** ~ **de faire qqch** to be afraid of doing sthg; **j'ai** ~ **qu'il ne vienne pas** I'm afraid he won't come; **faire** ~ **à qqn** to frighten sb; **par** ou **de** ~ **de qqch** for fear of sthg; **par** ou **de** ~ **de faire qqch** for fear of doing sthg.

peureux, -euse [pœrø, øz] 1 *adj* fearful, timid. 2 *nm, f* fearful ou timid person.

peut → **pouvoir**.

peut-être [pøtɛtr] *adv* perhaps, maybe; ~ **qu'ils ne viendront pas, ils ne viendront** ~ **pas** perhaps ou maybe they won't come.

peux → **pouvoir**.

phalange [falɑ̃ʒ] *nf* ANAT phalanx.

phallocrate [falɔkrat] *nm* male chauvinist.

phallus [falys] *nm* phallus.

pharaon [faraɔ̃] *nm* pharaoh.

phare [far] 1 *nm* [tour] lighthouse. || AUTOM headlight; ~ **antibrouillard** fog lamp.

pharmaceutique [farmasøtik] *adj* pharmaceutical.

pharmacie [farmasi] *nf* [science] pharmacology. || [magasin] chemist's Br, drugstore Am. || [meuble]: (**armoire à**) ~ medicine cupboard.

pharmacien, -ienne [farmasjɛ̃, jɛn] *nm, f* chemist Br, druggist Am.

pharynx [farɛ̃ks] *nm* pharynx.

phase [faz] *nf* phase.

phénoménal, -e, -aux [fenɔmenal, o] *adj* phenomenal.

phénomène [fenɔmɛn] *nm* [fait] phenomenon. || [être anormal] freak. || *fam* [excentrique] character.

philanthropie [filɑ̃trɔpi] *nf* philanthropy.

philatélie [filateli] *nf* philately, stamp-collecting.

philharmonique [filarmɔnik] *adj* philharmonic.

Philippines [filipin] *nfpl*: **les ~** the Philippines.

philosophe [filɔzɔf] **1** *nmf* philosopher. **2** *adj* philosophical.

philosophie [filɔzɔfi] *nf* philosophy.

phobie [fɔbi] *nf* phobia.

phonétique [fɔnetik] **1** *nf* phonetics (*U*). **2** *adj* phonetic.

phonographe [fɔnɔgraf] *nm vieilli* gramophone *Br*, phonograph *Am*.

phoque [fɔk] *nm* seal.

phosphate [fɔsfat] *nm* phosphate.

phosphore [fɔsfɔr] *nm* phosphorus.

phosphorescent, -e [fɔsfɔresɑ̃, ɑ̃t] *adj* phosphorescent.

photo [fɔto] *nf* [technique] photography. || [image] photo, picture; **prendre qqn en ~** to take a photo of sb; **~ d'identité** passport photo.

photocopie [fɔtɔkɔpi] *nf* [procédé] photocopying. || [document] photocopy.

photocopier [fɔtɔkɔpje] *vt* to photocopy.

photocopieur [fɔtɔkɔpjœr] *nm*, **photocopieuse** [fɔtɔkɔpjøz] *nf* photocopier.

photoélectrique [fɔtɔelektrik] *adj* photoelectric.

photogénique [fɔtɔʒenik] *adj* photogenic.

photographe [fɔtɔgraf] *nmf* [artiste, technicien] photographer. || [commerçant] camera dealer.

photographie [fɔtɔgrafi] *nf* [technique] photography. || [cliché] photograph.

photographier [fɔtɔgrafje] *vt* to photograph.

Photomaton® [fɔtɔmatɔ̃] *nm* photo booth.

phrase [fraz] *nf* LING sentence; **~ toute faite** stock phrase. || MUS phrase.

physicien, -ienne [fizisjɛ̃, jɛn] *nm, f* physicist.

physiologie [fizjɔlɔʒi] *nf* physiology.

physiologique [fizjɔlɔʒik] *adj* physiological.

physionomie [fizjɔnɔmi] *nf* [faciès] face. || [apparence] physiognomy.

physionomiste [fizjɔnɔmist] *adj*: **être ~** to have a good memory for faces.

physique [fizik] **1** *adj* physical. **2** *nf* SCIENCE physics (*U*). **3** *nm* [constitution] physical well-being. || [apparence] physique.

physiquement [fizikmɑ̃] *adv* physically.

piaffer [pjafe] *vi* [cheval] to paw the ground. || [personne] to fidget.

piailler [pjaje] *vi* [oiseaux] to cheep. || [enfant] to squawk.

pianiste [pjanist] *nmf* pianist.

piano [pjano] *nm* piano.

pianoter [pjanɔte] *vi* [jouer du piano] to plunk away (on the piano). || [sur table] to drum one's fingers.

piaule [pjol] *nf fam* [hébergement] place; [chambre] room.

pic [pik] *nm* [outil] pick, pickaxe. || [montagne] peak. ○ **à pic** *loc adv* [verticalement] vertically; **couler à ~** to sink like a stone. || *fam fig* [à point nommé] just at the right moment.

pichenette [piʃnɛt] *nf* flick (of the finger).

pichet [piʃɛ] *nm* jug.

pickpocket [pikpɔkɛt] *nm* pickpocket.

picorer [pikɔre] *vi & vt* to peck.

picotement [pikɔtmɑ̃] *nm* prickling (*U*), prickle.

pie [pi] **1** *nf* [oiseau] magpie. || *fig & péj* [bavard] chatterbox. **2** *adj inv* [cheval] piebald.

pièce [pjɛs] *nf* [élément] piece; [de moteur] part; **~ de collection** collector's item; **~ détachée** spare part. || [unité]: **quinze francs ~** fifteen francs each ou apiece; **acheter/vendre qqch à la ~** to buy/sell sthg singly, to buy/sell sthg separately; **travailler à la ~** to do piece work. || [document] document, paper; **~ d'identité** identification papers (*pl*); **~ justificative** written proof (*U*), supporting document. || [œuvre littéraire ou musicale] piece; **~ (de théâtre)** play. || [argent]: **~ (de monnaie)** coin. || [de maison] room. || COUTURE patch.

pied [pje] *nm* [gén] foot; **à ~** on foot; **avoir ~** to be able to touch the bottom; **perdre ~** *litt & fig* to be out of one's depth; **être/marcher ~s nus** ou **nu-~s** to be/to go barefoot. || [base - de montagne, table] foot; [- de verre] stem; [- de lampe] base. || [plant - de tomate] stalk; [- de vigne] stock. || *loc*: **être sur ~** to be (back) on one's feet, to be up and about; **faire du ~ à** to play footsie with; **mettre qqch sur ~** to get sthg on its feet, to get sthg off the ground; **je n'ai jamais mis les ~s**

chez lui I've never set foot in his house; **au ~ de la lettre** literally, to the letter.

pied-de-biche [pjedbiʃ] (*pl* **pieds-de-biche**) *nm* [outil] nail claw.

piédestal, -aux [pjedɛstal, o] *nm* pedestal.

pied-noir [pjenwar] *nmf* French settler in Algeria.

piège [pjɛʒ] *nm litt & fig* trap.

piéger [pjeʒe] *vt* [animal, personne] to trap. || [colis, véhicule] to boobytrap.

pierraille [pjɛraj] *nf* loose stones (*pl*).

pierre [pjɛr] *nf* stone; **~ d'achoppement** *fig* stumbling block; **~ précieuse** precious stone.

pierreries [pjɛrri] *nfpl* precious stones, jewels.

piété [pjete] *nf* piety.

piétiner [pjetine] **1** *vi* [trépigner] to stamp (one's feet). || *fig* [ne pas avancer] to make no progress, to be at a standstill. **2** *vt* [personne, parterre] to trample.

piéton, -onne [pjetɔ̃, ɔn] **1** *nm, f* pedestrian. **2** *adj* pedestrian (*avant n*).

piétonnier, -ière [pjetɔnje, jɛr] *adj* pedestrian (*avant n*).

piètre [pjɛtr] *adj* poor.

pieu, -x [pjø] *nm* [poteau] post, stake. || *fam* [lit] pit *Br*, sack *Am*.

pieuvre [pjœvr] *nf* octopus.

pieux, pieuse [pjø, pjøz] *adj* [personne, livre] pious.

pif [pif] *nm fam* conk; **au ~** *fig* by guesswork.

pigeon [piʒɔ̃] *nm* [oiseau] pigeon. || *fam péj* [personne] sucker.

pigeonnier [piʒɔnje] *nm* [pour pigeons] pigeon loft, dovecote.

pigment [pigmɑ̃] *nm* pigment.

pignon [piɲɔ̃] *nm* [de mur] gable. || [d'engrenage] gearwheel. || [de pomme de pin] pine kernel.

pile [pil] **1** *nf* [de livres, journaux] pile. || ÉLECTR battery. || [de pièce]: **~ ou face** heads or tails. **2** *adv fam* on the dot; **tomber/arriver ~** to come/to arrive at just the right time.

piler [pile] **1** *vt* [amandes] to crush, to grind. **2** *vi fam* AUTOM to jam on the brakes.

pilier [pilje] *nm* [de construction] pillar. || *fig* [soutien] mainstay, pillar. || RUGBY prop (forward).

pillard, -e [pijar, ard] *nm, f* looter.

piller [pije] *vt* [ville, biens] to loot.

pilon [pilɔ̃] *nm* [instrument] pestle. || [de poulet] drumstick.

pilonner [pilɔne] *vt* to pound.

pilori [pilɔri] *nm* pillory; **mettre** or **clouer qqn au ~** *fig* to pillory sb.

pilotage [pilɔtaʒ] *nm* piloting.

pilote [pilɔt] **1** *nm* [d'avion] pilot; [de voiture] driver; **~ automatique** autopilot; **~ de chasse** fighter pilot; **~ de course** racing driver; **~ d'essai** test pilot; **~ de ligne** airline pilot. **2** *adj* pilot (*avant n*), experimental.

piloter [pilɔte] *vt* [avion] to pilot; [voiture] to drive. || [personne] to show around.

pilotis [pilɔti] *nm* pile.

pilule [pilyl] *nf* pill; **prendre la ~** to be on the pill.

piment [pimɑ̃] *nm* [plante] pepper, capsicum; **~ rouge** chilli pepper, hot red pepper. || *fig* [piquant] spice.

pimpant, -e [pɛ̃pɑ̃, ɑ̃t] *adj* smart.

pin [pɛ̃] *nm* pine; **~ parasol** umbrella pine; **~ sylvestre** Scots pine.

pince [pɛ̃s] *nf* [grande] pliers (*pl*). || [petite]: **~ (à épiler)** tweezers (*pl*); **~ à linge** clothes peg. || [de crabe] pincer. || COUTURE dart.

pinceau, -x [pɛ̃so] *nm* [pour peindre] brush.

pincée [pɛ̃se] *nf* pinch.

pincer [pɛ̃se] **1** *vt* [serrer] to pinch; MUS to pluck; [lèvres] to purse. || *fam fig* [arrêter] to catch.

pincettes [pɛ̃sɛt] *nfpl* [ustensile] tongs.

pingouin [pɛ̃gwɛ̃] *nm* penguin.

ping-pong [piŋpɔ̃g] *nm* ping pong, table tennis.

pinson [pɛ̃sɔ̃] *nm* chaffinch.

pintade [pɛ̃tad] *nf* guinea fowl.

pin-up [pinœp] *nf inv* pinup (girl).

pioche [pjɔʃ] *nf* [outil] pick. || JEU pile.

piocher [pjɔʃe] **1** *vt* [terre] to dig. || JEU to take. || *fig* [choisir] to pick at random. **2** *vi* [creuser] to dig. || JEU to pick up; **~ dans** [tas] to delve into.

pion, pionne [pjɔ̃, pjɔn] *nm, f fam* SCOL supervisor (often a student who does this as a part-time job). ○ **pion** *nm* [aux échecs] pawn; [aux dames] piece.

pionnier, -ière [pjɔnje, jɛr] *nm, f* pioneer.

pipe [pip] *nf* pipe.

pipeline, pipe-line [pajplajn, piplin] (*pl* **pipe-lines**) *nm* pipeline.

pipi [pipi] *nm fam* wee; **faire ~** to have a wee.

piquant, -e [pikɑ̃, ɑ̃t] *adj* [barbe, feuille] prickly. || [sauce] spicy, hot. ○ **piquant**

nm [d'animal] spine; [de végétal] thorn, prickle. ‖ *fig* [d'histoire] spice.

pique [pik] 1 *nf* [arme] pike. ‖ *fig* [mot blessant] barbed comment. 2 *nm* [aux cartes] spade.

pique-assiette [pikasjɛt] (*pl inv* OU pique-assiettes) *nmf péj* sponger.

pique-nique [piknik] (*pl* pique-niques) *nm* picnic.

piquer [pike] 1 *vt* [suj: guêpe, méduse] to sting; [suj: serpent, moustique] to bite. ‖ [avec pointe] to prick. ‖ [animal] to put down. ‖ [fleur]: ~ qqch dans to stick sthg into. ‖ [suj: tissu, barbe] to prickle. ‖ [suj: fumée, froid] to sting. ‖ COUTURE to sew, to machine. ‖ *fam* [voler] to pinch. ‖ *fam* [voleur, escroc] to catch. 2 *vi* [ronce] to prick; [ortie] to sting. ‖ [guêpe, méduse] to sting; [serpent, moustique] to bite. ‖ [épice] to burn. ‖ [avion] to dive.

piquet [pike] *nm* [pieu] peg, stake. ○ **piquet de grève** *nm* picket.

piqûre [pikyr] *nf* [de guêpe, méduse] sting; [de serpent, moustique] bite. ‖ [d'ortie] sting. ‖ [injection] jab *Br*, shot.

piratage [pirataʒ] *nm* piracy; INFORM hacking.

pirate [pirat] 1 *nm* [corsaire] pirate; ~ de l'air hijacker, skyjacker. 2 *adj* pirate (*avant n*).

pire [pir] 1 *adj* [comparatif relatif] worse. ‖ [superlatif]: le/la ~ the worst. 2 *nm*: le ~ (de) the worst (of).

pirogue [pirɔg] *nf* dugout canoe.

pirouette [pirwɛt] *nf* [saut] pirouette. ‖ *fig* [faux-fuyant] prevarication, evasive answer.

pis [pi] 1 *adv* worse; de mal en ~ from bad to worse. 2 *nm* udder.

pis-aller [pizale] *nm inv* last resort.

pisciculture [pisikyltyr] *nf* fish farming.

piscine [pisin] *nf* swimming pool; couverte/découverte indoor/open-air swimming pool.

pissenlit [pisɑ̃li] *nm* dandelion.

pisser [pise] *fam* 1 *vt* [suj: plaie]: son genou pissait le sang blood was gushing from his knee. 2 *vi* to pee, to piss.

pissotière [pisɔtjɛr] *nf fam* public urinal.

pistache [pistaʃ] *nf* [fruit] pistachio (nut).

piste [pist] *nf* [trace] trail. ‖ [zone aménagée]: ~ d'atterrissage runway; ~ cyclable cycle track; ~ de danse dance floor; ~ de ski ski run. ‖ [chemin] path, track. ‖ [d'enregistrement] track.

pistil [pistil] *nm* pistil.

pistolet [pistɔlɛ] *nm* [arme] pistol, gun. ‖ [à peinture] spray gun.

piston [pistɔ̃] *nm* [de moteur] piston. ‖ *fig* [appui] string-pulling.

pistonner [pistɔne] *vt* to pull strings for; se faire ~ to have strings pulled for one.

pitance [pitɑ̃s] *nf péj & vieilli* sustenance.

piteux, -euse [pitø, øz] *adj* piteous.

pitié [pitje] *nf* pity; avoir ~ de qqn to have pity on sb, to pity sb.

piton [pitɔ̃] *nm* [clou] piton. ‖ [pic] peak.

pitoyable [pitwajabl] *adj* pitiful.

pitre [pitr] *nm* clown.

pitrerie [pitrəri] *nf* tomfoolery.

pittoresque [pitɔrɛsk] *adj* [région] picturesque. ‖ [détail] colourful, vivid.

pivot [pivo] *nm* [de machine, au basket] pivot. ‖ [de dent] post. ‖ [centre] *fig* mainspring.

pivoter [pivɔte] *vi* to pivot; [porte] to revolve.

pizza [pidza] *nf* pizza.

Pl., pl. *abr de* place.

placard [plakar] *nm* [armoire] cupboard. ‖ [affiche] poster, notice.

placarder [plakarde] *vt* [affiche] to put up, to stick up; [mur] to placard, to stick a notice on.

place [plas] *nf* [espace] space, room; prendre de la ~ to take up (a lot of) space. ‖ [emplacement, position] position; changer qqch de ~ to put sthg in a different place, to move sthg; prendre la ~ de qqn to take sb's place; à la ~ de qqn instead of sb, in sb's place. ‖ [siège] seat; ~ assise seat. ‖ [rang] place. ‖ [de ville] square. ‖ [emploi] position, job. ‖ MIL [garnison] garrison (town); ~ forte fortified town.

placement [plasmɑ̃] *nm* [d'argent] investment. ‖ [d'employé] placing.

placenta [plasɛ̃ta] *nm* ANAT placenta.

placer [plase] *vt* [gén] to put, to place; [invités, spectateurs] to seat. ‖ [mot, anecdote] to put in, to get in. ‖ [argent] to invest. ○ **se placer** *vp* [prendre place - debout] to stand; [- assis] to sit (down). ‖ *fig* [dans situation] to put o.s. ‖ [se classer] to come, to be.

placide [plasid] *adj* placid.

plafond [plafɔ̃] *nm litt & fig* ceiling; **faux ~** false ceiling.

plafonner [plafɔne] *vi* [prix, élève] to peak; [avion] to reach its ceiling.

plage [plaʒ] *nf* [de sable] beach. || [d'ombre, de prix] band; *fig* [de temps] slot. || [de disque] track. || [dans voiture]: **~ arrière** back shelf.

plagiat [plaʒja] *nm* plagiarism.

plagier [plaʒje] *vt* to plagiarize.

plaider [plede] JUR **1** *vt* to plead. **2** *vi* to plead; **~ pour qqn** JUR to plead for sb; [justifier] to plead sb's cause.

plaidoirie [pledwari] *nf*, **plaidoyer** [pledwaje] *nm* JUR speech for the defence; *fig* plea.

plaie [plɛ] *nf litt & fig* [blessure] wound. || *fam* [personne] pest.

▶ **plaindre** [plɛ̃dr] *vt* to pity. ○ **se plaindre** *vp* to complain.

plaine [plɛn] *nf* plain.

plain-pied [plɛ̃pje] ○ **de plain-pied** *loc adv* [pièce] on one floor; **de ~ avec** *litt & fig* on a level with. || *fig* [directement] straight.

plaint, -e [plɛ̃, plɛ̃t] *pp* → plaindre.

plainte [plɛ̃t] *nf* [gémissement] moan, groan; *fig & litt* [du vent] moan. || [doléance & JUR] complaint; **porter ~** to lodge a complaint.

plaintif, -ive [plɛ̃tif, iv] *adj* plaintive.

plaire [plɛr] *vi* to be liked; **il me plaît** I like him; **ça te plairait d'aller au cinéma?** would you like to go to the cinema?; **s'il vous/te plaît** please.

plaisance [plɛzɑ̃s] ○ **de plaisance** *loc adj* sailing (*avant n*); **navigation de ~** sailing; **port de ~** marina.

plaisant, -e [plɛzɑ̃, ɑ̃t] *adj* pleasant.

plaisanter [plɛzɑ̃te] *vi* to joke; **tu plaisantes?** you must be joking!

plaisanterie [plɛzɑ̃tri] *nf* joke; **c'est une ~?** *iron* you must be joking!

plaisantin [plɛzɑ̃tɛ̃] *nm* joker.

plaisir [plezir] *nm* pleasure; **avoir du/prendre ~ à faire qqch** to have/to take pleasure in doing sthg; **faire ~ à qqn** to please sb; **avec ~** with pleasure; **j'ai le ~ de vous annoncer que ~** I have the (great) pleasure of announcing that ....

plan¹, -e [plɑ̃, plan] *adj* level, flat.

plan² [plɑ̃] *nm* [dessin - de ville] map; [- de maison] plan. || [projet] plan; **faire des ~s** to make plans. || [domaine]: **sur tous les ~s** in all respects; **sur le ~ familial** as far as the family is concerned. || [surface]: **~ d'eau** lake; **~ de travail** work surface, worktop. || GÉOM plane. || CIN take; **gros ~** close-up. ○ **au premier plan** *loc adv* [dans l'espace] in the foreground. ○ **en plan** *loc adv*: **laisser qqn en ~** to leave sb stranded, to abandon sb; **il a tout laissé en ~** he dropped everything.

planche [plɑ̃ʃ] *nf* [en bois] plank; **~ à dessin** drawing board; **~ à repasser** ironing board; **~ à voile** [planche] sailboard; [sport] windsurfing; **faire la ~** *fig* to float. || [d'illustration] plate.

plancher [plɑ̃ʃe] *nm* [de maison, de voiture] floor. || *fig* [limite] floor, lower limit.

plancton [plɑ̃ktɔ̃] *nm* plankton.

planer [plane] *vi* [avion, oiseau] to glide. || [nuage, fumée, brouillard] to float. || *fig* [danger]: **~ sur qqn** to hang over sb. || *fam fig* [personne] to be out of touch with reality, to have one's head in the clouds.

planétaire [planeter] *adj* ASTRON planetary. || [mondial] world (*avant n*).

planétarium [planetarjɔm] *nm* planetarium.

planète [planɛt] *nf* planet.

planeur [planœr] *nm* glider.

planification [planifikasjɔ̃] *nf* ÉCON planning.

planisphère [planisfɛr] *nm* map of the world, planisphere.

planning [planiŋ] *nm* [de fabrication] workflow schedule. || [agenda personnel] schedule; **~ familial** [organisme] family planning centre.

planque [plɑ̃k] *nf fam* [cachette] hideout. || *fig* [situation, travail] cushy number.

plant [plɑ̃] *nm* [plante] seedling.

plantaire [plɑ̃tɛr] *adj* plantar.

plantation [plɑ̃tasjɔ̃] *nf* [exploitation - d'arbres, de coton, de café] plantation; [- de légumes] patch. || [action] planting.

plante [plɑ̃t] *nf* BOT plant; **~ verte** OU **d'appartement** OU **d'intérieur** house OU pot plant. || ANAT sole.

planter [plɑ̃te] *vt* [arbre, terrain] to plant. || [clou] to hammer in, to drive in; [pieu] to drive in; [couteau, griffes] to stick in. || [tente] to pitch. || *fam fig* [laisser tomber] to dump.

plantureux, -euse [plɑ̃tyrø, øz] *adj* [repas] lavish. || [femme] buxom.

plaque [plak] *nf* [de métal, de verre, de verglas] sheet; [de marbre] slab; **~ chauffante** OU **de cuisson** hotplate; **~ de chocolat** bar of chocolate. || [gravée] plaque; **~ d'immatriculation** OU **minéralogique**

number plate *Br*, license plate *Am*. || [insigne] badge. || [sur la peau] patch.

plaqué, -e [plake] *adj* [métal] plated; ~ or/argent gold-/silver-plated. ○ **plaqué** *nm* [métal]: du ~ or/argent gold/silver plate.

plaquer [plake] *vt* [bois] to veneer. || [aplatir] to flatten; ~ **qqn contre qqch** to pin sb against sthg. || RUGBY to tackle. || MUS [accord] to play. || *fam* [travail, personne] to chuck.

plaquette [plaket] *nf* [de métal] plaque; [de marbre] tablet. || [de chocolat] bar; [de beurre] pat. || [de comprimés] packet, strip. || AUTOM: ~ **de frein** brake pad.

plasma [plasma] *nm* plasma.

plastique [plastik] *adj* & *nm* plastic.

plat, -e [pla, plat] *adj* [gén] flat. || [eau] still. ○ **plat** *nm* [partie plate] flat. || [récipient] dish. || [mets] course; ~ **cuisiné** ready-cooked meal ou dish; ~ **du jour** today's special; ~ **de résistance** main course. || [plongeon] belly-flop. ○ **à plat** *loc adv* [horizontalement, dégonflé] flat. || *fam* [épuisé] exhausted.

platane [platan] *nm* plane tree.

plateau, -x [plato] *nm* [de cuisine] tray; ~ **de/à fromages** cheese board. || [de balance] pan. || GÉOGR & *fig* plateau. || THÉÂTRE stage; CIN & TÉLÉ set. || [de vélo] chain wheel.

plateau-repas [platorəpa] *nm* tray (of food).

plate-bande [platbɑ̃d] *nf* flower bed.

plate-forme [platfɔrm] *nf* [gén] platform; ~ **de forage** drilling platform.

platine [platin] *1 adj inv* platinum. *2 nm* [métal] platinum. *3 nf* [de tourne-disque] deck; ~ **laser** compact disc player.

platonique [platɔnik] *adj* [amour, amitié] platonic.

plâtras [platra] *nm* [gravats] rubble.

plâtre [platr] *nm* CONSTR & MÉD plaster. || [sculpture] plaster cast.

plâtrer [platre] *vt* [mur] to plaster. || MÉD to put in plaster.

plausible [plozibl] *adj* plausible.

play-back [plebak] *nm inv* miming; **chanter en** ~ to mime.

play-boy [plebɔj] (*pl* play-boys) *nm* playboy.

plébiscite [plebisit] *nm* plebiscite.

plein, -e [plɛ̃, plɛn] *adj* [rempli, complet] full; **en** ~**e nuit** in the middle of the night; **en** ~ **air** in the open air. || [non creux] solid. || [femelle] pregnant.

○ **plein** *1 adv fam*: **il a de l'encre** ~ **les doigts** he has ink all over his fingers; **en** ~ **dans/sur qqch** right in/on sthg. *2 nm* [de réservoir] full tank; **le** ~, **s'il vous plaît** fill her up please; **faire le** ~ to fill up.

plein-temps [plɛ̃tɑ̃] *nm* full-time work (U). ○ **à plein temps** *loc adj* & *loc adv* full-time.

plénitude [plenityd] *nf* fullness.

pléonasme [pleonasm] *nm* pleonasm.

pleurer [plœre] *1 vi* [larmoyer] to cry; ~ **de joie** to weep for joy, to cry with joy. || *péj* [se plaindre] to whinge. || [se lamenter]: ~ **sur** to lament. *2 vt* to mourn.

pleurnicher [plœrniʃe] *vi* to whine, to whinge.

pleurs [plœr] *nmpl*: **être en** ~ to be in tears.

pleuvoir [pløvwar] *v impers litt* & *fig* to rain; **il pleut** it is raining.

Plexiglas® [pleksiglas] *nm* Plexiglass®.

plexus [pleksys] *nm* plexus; ~ **solaire** solar plexus.

pli [pli] *nm* [de tissu] pleat; [de pantalon] crease; **faux** ~ crease. || [du front] line; [du cou] fold. || [lettre] letter; [enveloppe] envelope; **sous** ~ **séparé** under separate cover. || CARTES trick. || GÉOL fold.

pliant, -e [plijɑ̃, ɑ̃t] *adj* folding (*avant n*).

plier [plije] *1 vt* [papier, tissu] to fold. || [vêtement, vélo] to fold (up). || [branche, bras] to bend. *2 vi* [arbre] to bend. || *fig* [céder] to bow. ○ **se plier** *vp* [être pliable] to fold (up). || *fig* [se soumettre]: **se** ~ **à qqch** to bow to sthg.

plinthe [plɛ̃t] *nf* plinth.

plissé, -e [plise] *adj* [jupe] pleated. || [peau] wrinkled.

plissement [plismɑ̃] *nm* [de front] creasing; [d'yeux] screwing up.

plisser [plise] *1 vt* COUTURE to pleat. || [front] to crease; [lèvres] to pucker; [yeux] to screw up. *2 vi* [étoffe] to crease.

plomb [plɔ̃] *nm* [métal, de vitrail] lead. || [de chasse] shot. || ÉLECTR fuse; **les** ~**s ont sauté** a fuse has blown ou gone. || [de pêche] sinker.

plombage [plɔ̃baʒ] *nm* [de dent] filling.

plomber [plɔ̃be] *vt* [ligne] to weight (with lead). || [dent] to fill.

plombier [plɔ̃bje] *nm* plumber.

plonge [plɔ̃ʒ] *nf* dishwashing; **faire la** ~ to wash dishes.

plongeant, -e [plɔ̃ʒɑ̃, ɑ̃t] *adj* [vue] from above. || [décolleté] plunging.

poète

plongeoir [plɔʒwar] *nm* diving board.

plongeon [plɔʒɔ̃] *nm* [dans l'eau, au football] dive.

plonger [plɔʒe] **1** *vt* [immerger, enfoncer] to plunge; **~ la tête sous l'eau** to put one's head under the water. || *fig* [précipiter]: **~ qqn dans qqch** to throw sb into sthg. **2** *vi* [dans l'eau, gardien de but] to dive. ○ **se plonger** *vp* [s'immerger] to submerge. || *fig* [s'absorber]: **se ~ dans qqch** to immerse o.s. in sthg.

plongeur, -euse [plɔʒœr, øz] *nm, f* [dans l'eau] diver. || [dans restaurant] dishwasher.

ployer [plwaje] *vt & vi litt & fig* to bend.

plu [ply] **1** *pp inv* → **plaire**. **2** *pp inv* → **pleuvoir**.

pluie [plɥi] *nf* [averse] rain (*U*); **sous la ~ in the rain.** || *fig* [grande quantité]: **une ~ de** a shower of.

plume [plym] *nf* [d'oiseau] feather. || [pour écrire - d'oiseau] quill pen; [- de stylo] nib.

plumeau, -x [plymo] *nm* feather duster.

plumer [plyme] *vt* [volaille] to pluck. || *fam fig & péj* [personne] to fleece.

plumier [plymje] *nm* pencil box.

plupart [plypar] *nf*: **la ~ de** most of, the majority of; **pour la ~** mostly, for the most part.

pluriel, -ielle [plyrjɛl] *adj* GRAM plural. || [société] pluralist. ○ **pluriel** *nm* plural; **au ~** in the plural.

plus [ply(s)] **1** *adv* [quantité] more; **beaucoup ~ de** (+ *n sg*) a lot more, much more; (+ *n pl*) a lot more, many more; **un peu ~ de** (+ *n sg*) a little more; (+ *n pl*) a few more; **~ j'y pense, ~ je me dis que ...** the more I think about it, the more I'm sure .... || [comparaison] more; **c'est ~ court par là** it's shorter that way; **viens ~ souvent** come more often; **c'est ~ simple qu'on ne le croit** it's simpler than you think. || [superlatif]: **le ~ the most**; **le ~ souvent** the most often; **le ~ loin** the furthest; **le ~ vite possible** as quickly as possible. || [négation] no more; **~ un mot!** not another word!; **ne ... ~** no longer, no more; **il ne vient ~ me voir** he doesn't come to see me any more, he no longer comes to see me. **2** *nm* [signe] plus (sign). || *fig* [atout] plus. **3** *prép* plus; **trois ~ trois font six** three plus three is six, three and three are six. || MATH plus *adv* de at the most; **tout au ~** at the very most. ○ **de plus** *loc adv* [en supplément, en

trop] more; **elle a cinq ans de ~ que moi** she's five years older than me. || [en outre] furthermore, what's more. ○ **de plus en plus** *loc adv* more and more. ○ **de plus en plus de** *loc prép* more and more. ○ **en plus** *loc adv* [en supplément] extra. || [d'ailleurs] moreover, what's more. ○ **en plus de** *loc prép* in addition to. ○ **ni plus ni moins** *loc adv* no more no less. ○ **plus ou moins** *loc adv* more or less. ○ **sans plus** *loc adv*: **elle est gentille, sans ~** she's nice, but no more than that.

plusieurs [plyzjœr] *adj indéf pl & pron indéf mfpl* several.

plus-que-parfait [plyskəparfɛ] *nm* GRAM pluperfect.

plus-value [plyvaly] *nf* [d'investissement] appreciation.

plutôt [plyto] *adv* rather; **~ que de faire qqch** instead of doing sthg, rather than doing sthg.

pluvieux, -ieuse [plyvjø, jøz] *adj* rainy.

PME (*abr de* **petite et moyenne entreprise**) *nf* SME.

PMU (*abr de* **Pari mutuel urbain**) *nm system for betting on horses.*

PNB (*abr de* **produit national brut**) *nm* GNP.

pneu, -x [pnø] *nm* [de véhicule] tyre.

pneumatique [pnømatik] **1** *nf* PHYS pneumatics (*U*). **2** *adj* [fonctionnant à l'air] pneumatic. || [gonflé à l'air] inflatable.

pneumonie [pnømɔni] *nf* pneumonia.

PO (*abr de* **petites ondes**) MW.

poche [pɔʃ] *nf* [de vêtement, de sac, d'air] pocket; **de ~** pocket (*avant n*). || [sac, sous les yeux] bag; **faire des ~s** [vêtement] to bag.

pocher [pɔʃe] *vt* CULIN to poach. || [blesser]: **~ l'œil à qqn** to give sb a black eye.

pochette [pɔʃɛt] *nf* [enveloppe] envelope; [d'allumettes] book; [de photos] packet. || [de disque] sleeve. || [mouchoir] (pocket) handkerchief.

pochoir [pɔʃwar] *nm* stencil.

podium [pɔdjɔm] *nm* podium.

poêle [pwal] **1** *nf* pan; **~ à frire** frying pan. **2** *nm* stove.

poème [pɔɛm] *nm* poem.

poésie [pɔezi] *nf* [genre littéraire] poetry. || [pièce écrite] poem.

poète [pɔɛt] *nm* [écrivain] poet. || *fig & hum* [rêveur] dreamer.

poids [pwa] *nm* [gén] weight; **quel ~ fait-il?** how heavy is it/he?; **vendre au ~** to sell by weight; **~ lourd** [camion] heavy goods vehicle; **de ~** [argument] weighty. || SPORT [lancer] shot.

poignant, -e [pwaɲɑ̃, ɑ̃t] *adj* poignant.

poignard [pwaɲar] *nm* dagger.

poignée [pwaɲe] *nf* [quantité, petit nombre] handful. || [manche] handle. ○ **poignée de main** *nf* handshake.

poignet [pwaɲɛ] *nm* ANAT wrist. || [de vêtement] cuff.

poil [pwal] *nm* [du corps] hair. || [d'animal] hair, coat. || [de pinceau] bristle; [de tapis] strand. || *fam* [peu]: **il s'en est fallu d'un ~ que je réussisse** I came within a hair's breadth of succeeding.

poilu, -e [pwaly] *adj* hairy.

poinçon [pwɛ̃sɔ̃] *nm* [outil] awl. || [marque] hallmark.

poinçonner [pwɛ̃sɔne] *vt* [bijou] to hallmark. || [billet, tôle] to punch.

poing [pwɛ̃] *nm* fist.

point [pwɛ̃] **1** *nm* COUTURE & TRICOT stitch; **~s de suture** MÉD stitches. || [de ponctuation]: **~ (final)** full stop *Br*, period *Am*; **~ d'interrogation/d'exclamation** question/exclamation mark; **~s de suspension** suspension points. || [petite tache] dot; **~ noir** [sur la peau] blackhead; *fig* [problème] problem. || [endroit] spot, point; *fig* point; **~ culminant** [en montagne] summit; *fig* climax; **~ de repère** [temporel] reference point; [spatial] landmark; **~ de vente** point of sale, sale outlet; **~ de vue** [panorama] viewpoint; *fig* [opinion, aspect] point of view; **avoir un ~ commun avec qqn** to have something in common with sb. || [degré] point; **au ~ que, à tel ~ que** to such an extent that; **je ne pensais pas que cela le vexerait à ce ~** I didn't think it would make him so cross; **être ... au ~ de faire qqch** to be so ... as to do sthg. || *fig* [position] position. || [réglage]: **mettre au ~** [machine] to adjust; [idée, projet] to finalize; **à ~** [cuisson] just right; **à ~ (nommé)** just in time. || [question, détail] point, detail; **~ faible** weak point. || [score] point. || [douleur] pain; **~ de côté** stitch. || [début]: **être sur le ~ de faire qqch** to be on the point of doing sthg, to be about to do sthg. || AUTOM: **au ~ mort** in neutral. || GÉOGR: **~s cardinaux** points of the compass. **2** *adv vieilli*: **ne ~** not (at all).

pointe [pwɛ̃t] *nf* [extrémité] point; [de nez] tip; **se hausser sur la ~ des pieds** to stand on tiptoe; **~ d'asperge** asparagus tip. || [clou] tack. || [sommet] peak, summit; **à la ~ de la technique** at the forefront ou leading edge of technology. || *fig* [trait d'esprit] witticism. || *fig* [petite quantité]: **une ~ de** a touch of. ○ **pointes** *nfpl* DANSE points; **faire des ou ~s** to dance on one's points. ○ **de pointe** *loc adj* [vitesse] maximum, top. || [industrie, secteur] leading; [technique] latest.

pointer [pwɛ̃te] **1** *vt* [cocher] to tick (off). || [employés - à l'entrée] to check in; [- à la sortie] to check out. || [diriger]: **~ qqch vers/sur** to point sthg towards/at. **2** *vi* [à l'usine - à l'entrée] to clock in; [- à la sortie] to clock out.

pointillé [pwɛ̃tije] *nm* [ligne] dotted line; **en ~** [ligne] dotted. || [perforations] perforations (*pl*).

pointilleux, -euse [pwɛ̃tijø, øz] *adj*: **~ (sur)** particular (about).

pointu, -e [pwɛ̃ty] *adj* [objet] pointed. || [étude, formation] specialized.

pointure [pwɛ̃tyr] *nf* size.

point-virgule [pwɛ̃virgyl] *nm* semicolon.

poire [pwar] *nf* [fruit] pear. || *fam* [visage] face. || *fam* [naïf] dope.

poireau, -x [pwaro] *nm* leek.

poirier [pwarje] *nm* pear tree.

pois [pwa] *nm* BOT pea; **~ chiche** chickpea; **petits ~** garden peas, petits pois; **~ de senteur** sweet pea. || *fig* [motif] dot, spot; **à ~** spotted, polka-dot.

poison [pwazɔ̃] **1** *nm* [substance] poison. **2** *nmf fam fig* [personne] drag, pain.

poisse [pwas] *nf fam* bad luck; **porter la ~** to be bad luck.

poisseux, -euse [pwasø, øz] *adj* sticky.

poisson [pwasɔ̃] *nm* fish; **~ d'avril** [farce] April fool; [en papier] *paper fish pinned to someone's back as a prank on April Fools' Day*; **~ rouge** goldfish. ○ **Poissons** *nmpl* ASTROL Pisces (*sg*).

poissonnerie [pwasɔnri] *nf* [boutique] fish shop, fishmonger's (shop).

poissonnier, -ière [pwasɔnje, jɛr] *nm, f* fishmonger.

poitrine [pwatrin] *nf* [thorax] chest; [de femme] chest, bust.

poivre [pwavr] *nm* pepper; **~ blanc** white pepper; **~ gris, ~ noir** black pepper.

poivrier [pwavrije] *nm*, **poivrière** [pwavrijɛr] *nf* pepper pot.

pondéré

poivron [pwavrɔ̃] *nm* pepper, capsicum; ~ **rouge/vert** red/green pepper.

poker [pokɛr] *nm* poker.

polaire [polɛr] *adj* polar.

polar [polar] *nm fam* thriller, whodunnit.

Polaroïd® [polaroid] *nm* Polaroid®.

pôle [pol] *nm* pole; ~ **Nord/Sud** North/South Pole.

polémique [polemik] *nf* controversy.

poli, -e [poli] *adj* [personne] polite. || [surface] polished.

police [polis] *nf* [force de l'ordre] police; ~ **secours** emergency service provided by the police. || [contrat] policy; ~ **d'assurance** insurance policy.

polichinelle [poliʃinɛl] *nm* [personnage] Punch; **secret de** ~ *fig* open secret.

policier, -ière [polisje, jɛr] *adj* [de la police] police (*avant n*). || [film, roman] detective (*avant n*). ○ **policier** *nm* police officer.

poliomyélite [poljomjelit] *nf* poliomyelitis.

polir [polir] *vt* to polish.

polisson, -onne [polisɔ̃, ɔn] **1** *adj* [chanson, propos] lewd, suggestive. || [enfant] naughty. **2** *nm, f* [enfant] naughty child.

politesse [polites] *nf* [courtoisie] politeness. || [action] polite action.

politicien, -ienne [politisjɛ̃, jɛn] **1** *adj péj* politiking, politically unscrupulous. **2** *nm, f* politician, politico.

politique [politik] **1** *nf* [de gouvernement, de personne] policy. || [affaires publiques] politics (*U*). **2** *adj* [pouvoir, théorie] political.

politiser [politize] *vt* to politicize.

pollen [polɛn] *nm* pollen.

polluer [polɥe] *vt* to pollute.

pollution [polysjɔ̃] *nf* pollution.

polo [polo] *nm* [sport] polo. || [chemise] polo shirt.

Pologne [polɔɲ] *nf*: **la** ~ Poland.

polonais, -e [polonɛ, ɛz] *adj* Polish. ○ **polonais** *nm* [langue] Polish. ○ **Polonais, -e** *nm, f* Pole.

poltron, -onne [poltrɔ̃, ɔn] **1** *nm, f* coward. **2** *adj* cowardly.

polychrome [polikrom] *adj* polychrome, polychromatic.

polyclinique [poliklinik] *nf* general hospital.

polycopié, -e [polikopje] *adj* duplicate (*avant n*). ○ **polycopié** *nm* duplicated lecture notes.

polyester [poliɛstɛr] *nm* polyester.

polygame [poligam] *adj* polygamous.

polyglotte [poliglɔt] *nmf & adj* polyglot.

polygone [poligon] *nm* MATHS polygon.

Polynésie [polinezi] *nf*: **la** ~ Polynesia.

polystyrène [polistirɛn] *nm* polystyrene.

polytechnicien, -ienne [politɛknisjɛ̃, jɛn] *nm, f* student or ex-student of the École Polytechnique.

Polytechnique [politɛknik] *n*: **l'École** ~ *prestigious engineering college.*

polyvalent, -e [polivalɑ̃, ɑ̃t] *adj* [salle] multi-purpose. || [personne] versatile.

pommade [pomad] *nf* [médicament] ointment.

pomme [pom] *nf* [fruit] apple; ~ **de pin** pine ou fir cone. || [pomme de terre]: ~**s frites** chips *Br*, (French) fries *Am*; ~**s vapeur** steamed potatoes. ○ **pomme d'Adam** *nf* Adam's apple.

pomme de terre [pomdətɛr] *nf* potato.

pommette [pomɛt] *nf* cheekbone.

pommier [pomje] *nm* apple tree.

pompe [pɔ̃p] *nf* [appareil] pump; ~ **à essence** petrol pump *Br*, gas pump *Am*. || [magnificence] pomp, ceremony. || *fam* [chaussure] shoe. ○ **pompes funèbres** *nfpl* undertaker's (*sg*), mortician's (*sg*) *Am*.

pomper [pɔ̃pe] *vt* [eau, air] to pump.

pompeux, -euse [pɔ̃pø, øz] *adj* pompous.

pompier [pɔ̃pje] *nm* fire fighter *Am*.

pompiste [pɔ̃pist] *nmf* petrol *Br* ou gas *Am* pump attendant.

pompon [pɔ̃pɔ̃] *nm* pompom.

pomponner [pɔ̃pɔne] ○ **se pomponner** *vp* to get dressed up.

ponce [pɔ̃s] *adj*: **pierre** ~ pumice (stone).

poncer [pɔ̃se] *vt* [bois] to sand (down).

ponceuse [pɔ̃søz] *nf* sander, sanding machine.

ponction [pɔ̃ksjɔ̃] *nf* [MÉD - lombaire] puncture; [- pulmonaire] tapping.

ponctualité [pɔ̃ktɥalite] *nf* punctuality.

ponctuation [pɔ̃ktɥasjɔ̃] *nf* punctuation.

ponctuel, -elle [pɔ̃ktɥɛl] *adj* [action] specific, selective. || [personne] punctual.

ponctuer [pɔ̃ktɥe] *vt* to punctuate.

pondéré, -e [pɔ̃dere] *adj* [personne] level-headed. || ÉCON weighted.

pondre [pɔ̃dr] *vt* [œufs] to lay. || *fam fig* [projet, texte] to produce.

pondu, -e [pɔ̃dy] *pp* → **pondre**.

poney [pɔnɛ] *nm* pony.

pont [pɔ̃] *nm* CONSTR bridge; ~**s et chaussées** ADMIN ≃ highways department. || [lien] link, connection; ~ **aérien** airlift. || [congé] day off granted by an employer to fill the gap between a national holiday and a weekend. || [de navire] deck.

ponte [pɔ̃t] **1** *nf* [action] laying; [œufs] clutch. **2** *nm fam* [autorité] big shot.

pont-levis [pɔ̃ləvi] *nm* drawbridge.

ponton [pɔ̃tɔ̃] *nm* [plate-forme] pontoon.

pop [pɔp] **1** *nm* pop. **2** *adj* pop (*avant n*).

pop-corn [pɔpkɔrn] *nm inv* popcorn (*U*).

populace [pɔpylas] *nf péj* mob.

populaire [pɔpylɛr] *adj* [du peuple - volonté] popular, of the people; [- quartier] working-class; [- art, chanson] folk. || [personne] popular.

populariser [pɔpylarize] *vt* to popularize.

popularité [pɔpylarite] *nf* popularity.

population [pɔpylasjɔ̃] *nf* population; ~ **active** working population.

porc [pɔr] *nm* [animal] pig, hog *Am*. || *fig & péj* [personne] pig, swine. || [viande] pork. || [peau] pigskin.

porcelaine [pɔrsəlɛn] *nf* [matière] china, porcelain. || [objet] piece of china ou porcelain.

porc-épic [pɔrkepik] *nm* porcupine.

porche [pɔrʃ] *nm* porch.

porcherie [pɔrʃəri] *nf litt & fig* pigsty.

porcin, -e [pɔrsɛ̃, in] *adj* [élevage] pig (*avant n*). || *fig & péj* [yeux] piggy.

pore [pɔr] *nm* pore.

poreux, -euse [pɔrø, øz] *adj* porous.

pornographie [pɔrnɔgrafi] *nf* pornography.

port [pɔr] *nm* [lieu] port; ~ **de commerce/pêche** commercial/fishing port. || [fait de porter sur soi - d'objet] carrying; [- de vêtement, décoration] wearing; ~ **d'armes** carrying of weapons. || [transport] carriage.

portable [pɔrtabl] **1** *nm* [TV] portable; INFORM laptop, portable. **2** *adj* [vêtement] wearable. || [ordinateur, machine à écrire] portable, laptop.

portail [pɔrtaj] *nm* portal.

portant, -e [pɔrtɑ̃, ɑ̃t] *adj*: **être bien/mal ~** to be in good/poor health.

portatif, -ive [pɔrtatif, iv] *adj* portable.

porte [pɔrt] *nf* [de maison, voiture] door; **mettre qqn à la ~** to throw sb out; ~ **d'entrée** front door. || [AÉRON, SKI & de ville] gate.

porte-à-faux [pɔrtafo] *nm inv* [roche] overhang; CONSTR cantilever; **en ~** overhanging; CONSTR cantilevered; *fig* in a delicate situation.

porte-à-porte [pɔrtapɔrt] *nm inv*: **faire du ~** to sell from door to door.

porte-avions [pɔrtavjɔ̃] *nm inv* aircraft carrier.

porte-bagages [pɔrtbagaʒ] *nm inv* luggage rack; [de voiture] roof rack.

porte-bonheur [pɔrtbɔnœr] *nm inv* lucky charm.

porte-clefs, porte-clés [pɔrtəkle] *nm inv* keyring.

porte-documents [pɔrtdɔkymɑ̃] *nm inv* attaché ou document case.

portée [pɔrte] *nf* [de missile] range; **à ~ de main** within reach; **à ~ de voix** within earshot; **à ~ de vue** in sight; **à la ~ de qqn** *fig* within sb's reach. || [d'événement] impact, significance. || MUS stave, staff. || [de femelle] litter.

porte-fenêtre [pɔrtfənɛtr] *nf* French window ou door *Am*.

portefeuille [pɔrtəfœj] *nm* [pour billets] wallet. || FIN & POLIT portfolio.

porte-jarretelles [pɔrtʒartɛl] *nm inv* suspender belt *Br*, garter belt *Am*.

portemanteau, -x [pɔrtmɑ̃to] *nm* [au mur] coat-rack; [sur pied] coat stand.

porte-monnaie [pɔrtmɔnɛ] *nm inv* purse.

porte-parole [pɔrtparɔl] *nm inv* spokesman (*f* spokeswoman).

porter [pɔrte] **1** *vt* [gén] to carry. || [vêtement, lunettes, montre] to wear; [barbe] to have. || [nom, date, inscription] to bear. **2** *vi* [remarque] to strike home. || [voix, tir] to carry. ○ **se porter 1** *vp* [se sentir]: **se ~ bien/mal** to be well/unwell. **2** *v attr*: **se ~ garant de qqch** to guarantee sthg, to vouch for sthg; **se ~ candidat à** to stand for election to *Br*, to run for *Am*.

porte-savon [pɔrtsavɔ̃] (*pl inv* ou **porte-savons**) *nm* soap dish.

porte-serviettes [pɔrtsɛrvjɛt] *nm inv* towel rail.

porteur, -euse [pɔrtœr, øz] **1** *nm, f* [de message, nouvelle] bringer, bearer. || [de bagages] porter. || [détenteur - de papiers, d'actions] holder; [- de chèque] bearer. || [de maladie] carrier.

portier [pɔrtje] nm commissionaire.

portière [pɔrtjɛr] nf [de voiture, train] door.

portillon [pɔrtijɔ̃] nm barrier, gate.

portion [pɔrsjɔ̃] nf [de gâteau] portion, helping.

portique [pɔrtik] nm ARCHIT portico. || SPORT crossbeam (for hanging apparatus).

porto [pɔrto] nm port.

Porto Rico [pɔrtoriko], **Puerto Rico** [pwɛrtoriko] n Puerto Rico.

portrait [pɔrtrɛ] nm portrait; PHOT photograph; **faire le ~ de qqn** fig to describe sb.

portraitiste [pɔrtretist] nmf portrait painter.

portrait-robot [pɔrtrerobo] nm Photofit® picture, Identikit® picture.

portuaire [pɔrtɥɛr] adj port (avant n), harbour (avant n).

portugais, -e [pɔrtyɡɛ, ɛz] adj Portuguese. ○ **portugais** nm [langue] Portuguese. ○ **Portugais, -e** nm, f Portuguese (person); **les Portugais** the Portuguese.

Portugal [pɔrtyɡal] nm: **le ~** Portugal.

pose [poz] nf [de pierre, moquette] laying; [de papier peint, rideaux] hanging. || [position] pose. || PHOT exposure.

posé, -e [poze] adj sober, steady.

poser [poze] **1** vt [mettre] to put down; **~ qqch sur qqch** to put sthg on sthg. || [installer - rideaux, papier peint] to hang; [- étagère] to put up; [- moquette, carrelage] to lay. || [donner à résoudre - problème, difficulté] to pose; **~ une question** to ask a question; **~ sa candidature** to apply; POLIT to stand for election. **2** vi to pose. ○ **se poser** vp [oiseau, avion] to land. || [question, problème] to arise, to come up.

positif, -ive [pozitif, iv] adj positive.

position [pozisjɔ̃] nf position; **prendre ~** fig to take up a position, to take a stand.

posologie [pozɔlɔʒi] nf dosage.

posséder [posede] vt [détenir - voiture, maison] to possess, to own; [- diplôme] to have; [- capacités, connaissances] to possess, to have. || [langue, art] to have mastered. || fam [personne] to have.

possesseur [posesœr] nm [de bien] pos-

sessor, owner. || [de secret, diplôme] holder.

possessif, -ive [posesif, iv] adj possessive. ○ **possessif** nm GRAM possessive.

possession [posesjɔ̃] nf [gén] possession; **être en ma/ta** etc **~** to be in my/your etc possession.

possibilité [posibilite] nf [gén] possibility. || [moyen] chance, opportunity.

possible [posibl] **1** adj possible; **dès que** OU **aussitôt que ~** as soon as possible. **2** nm: **faire tout son ~** to do one's utmost, to do everything possible; **dans la mesure du ~** as far as possible.

postal, -e, -aux [pɔstal, o] adj postal.

poste [pɔst] **1** nf [service] post Br, mail Am. || [bureau] post office; **~ restante** poste restante Br, general delivery Am. **2** nm [emplacement] post; **~ de police** police station. || [emploi] position, post. || [appareil]: **~ de radio** radio; **~ de télévision** television (set). || TÉLÉCOM extension.

poster¹ [pɔstɛr] nm poster.

poster² [pɔste] vt [lettre] to post Br, to mail Am. || [sentinelle] to post. ○ **se poster** vp to position o.s., to station o.s.

postérieur, -e [pɔsterjœr] adj [date] later, subsequent. || [membre] hind (avant n), back (avant n). ○ **postérieur** nm posterior.

posteriori [pɔsterjɔri] ○ **a posteriori** loc adv a posteriori.

postérité [pɔsterite] nf [générations à venir] posterity.

posthume [pɔstym] adj posthumous.

postiche [pɔstiʃ] adj false.

postier, -ière [pɔstje, jɛr] nm, f post-office worker.

postillonner [pɔstijɔne] vi to splutter.

post-scriptum [pɔstskriptɔm] nm inv postscript.

postulant, -e [pɔstylɑ̃, ɑ̃t] nm, f [pour emploi] applicant.

postuler [pɔstyle] vt [emploi] to apply for. || PHILO to postulate.

posture [pɔstyr] nf posture; **être** OU **se trouver en mauvaise ~** fig to be in a difficult position.

pot [po] nm [récipient] pot, jar; [à eau, à lait] jug; **~ de chambre** chamber pot; **~ de fleurs** flowerpot. || AUTOM: **~ catalytique** catalytic convertor; **~ d'échappement** exhaust (pipe). || fam [boisson] drink.

potable [pɔtabl] adj [liquide] drinkable; **eau ~** drinking water. || *fam* [travail] acceptable.

potage [pɔtaʒ] *nm* soup.

potager, -ère [pɔtaʒe, ɛr] *adj*: **jardin ~** vegetable garden; **plante potagère** vegetable. ❍ **potager** *nm* kitchen ou vegetable garden.

potassium [pɔtasjɔm] *nm* potassium.

pot-au-feu [pɔtofø] *nm inv* [plat] *boiled beef with vegetables.*

pot-de-vin [podvɛ̃] (*pl* **pots-de-vin**) *nm* bribe.

pote [pɔt] *nm fam* mate *Br*, buddy *Am*.

poteau, -x [pɔto] *nm* post; **~ de but** goalpost; **~ indicateur** signpost; **~ télégraphique** telegraph pole.

potelé, -e [pɔtle] *adj* plump, chubby.

potence [pɔtɑ̃s] *nf* CONSTR bracket. || [de pendaison] gallows (*sg*).

potentiel, -ielle [pɔtɑ̃sjɛl] *adj* potential. ❍ **potentiel** *nm* potential.

poterie [pɔtri] *nf* [art] pottery. || [objet] piece of pottery.

potiche [pɔtiʃ] *nf* [vase] vase.

potier, -ière [pɔtje, jɛr] *nm, f* potter.

potin [pɔtɛ̃] *nm fam* [bruit] din. ❍ **potins** *nmpl fam* [ragots] gossip (*U*).

potion [posjɔ̃] *nf* potion.

potiron [pɔtirɔ̃] *nm* pumpkin.

pot-pourri [popuri] *nm* potpourri.

pou, -x [pu] *nm* louse.

poubelle [pubɛl] *nf* trashcan *Am*.

pouce [pus] *nm* [de main] thumb; [de pied] big toe. || [mesure] inch.

poudre [pudr] *nf* powder.

poudreux, -euse [pudrø, øz] *adj* powdery. ❍ **poudreuse** *nf* powder (snow).

poudrier [pudrije] *nm* [boîte] powder compact.

poudrière [pudrijɛr] *nf* powder magazine; *fig* powder keg.

pouf [puf] **1** *nm* pouffe. **2** *interj* thud!

pouffer [pufe] *vi*: **~ (de rire)** to snigger.

pouilleux, -euse [pujø, øz] *adj* [personne, animal] flea-ridden. || [endroit] squalid.

poulailler [pulaje] *nm* [de ferme] henhouse. || *fam* THÉÂTRE gods (*sg*).

poulain [pulɛ̃] *nm* foal; *fig* protégé.

poule [pul] *nf* ZOOL hen. || *fam péj* [femme] broad *Am*. || SPORT [compétition] round robin; RUGBY [groupe] pool.

poulet [pulɛ] *nm* ZOOL chicken. || *fam* [policier] cop.

pouliche [puliʃ] *nf* filly.

poulie [puli] *nf* pulley.

poulpe [pulp] *nm* octopus.

pouls [pu] *nm* pulse.

poumon [pumɔ̃] *nm* lung.

poupe [pup] *nf* stern.

poupée [pupe] *nf* [jouet] doll.

poupon [pupɔ̃] *nm* [jouet] baby doll.

pouponnière [pupɔnjɛr] *nf* nursery.

pour [pur] **1** *prép* [gén] for. || (+ *infinitif*): **~ faire** in order to do, (so as) to do; **~ m'avoir aidé** for having helped me, for helping me. || [indique un rapport] for; **avancé ~ son âge** advanced for his/her age; **~ moi** for my part, as far as I'm concerned; **~ ce qui est de** as regards, with regard to. **2** *adv*: **je suis ~** I'm (all) for it. **3** *nm*: **le ~ et le contre** the pros and cons (*pl*). ❍ **pour que** *loc conj* (+ *subjonctif*) so that, in order that.

pourboire [purbwar] *nm* tip.

pourcentage [pursɑ̃taʒ] *nm* percentage.

pourparlers [purparle] *nmpl* talks.

pourpre [purpr] *nm & adj* crimson.

pourquoi [purkwa] **1** *adv* why; **~ pas?** why not?; **c'est ~ ...** that's why .... **2** *nm inv*: **le ~ (de)** the reason (for).

pourri, -e [puri] *adj* [fruit] rotten. || [personne, milieu] corrupt. || [enfant] spoiled rotten, ruined.

pourrir [purir] **1** *vt* [matière, aliment] to rot, to spoil. || [enfant] to ruin, to spoil rotten. **2** *vi* [matière] to rot; [fruit, aliment] to go rotten ou bad.

pourriture [purityr] *nf* [d'aliment] rot. || *fig* [de personne, de milieu] corruption.

poursuite [pursɥit] *nf* [de personne] chase. || [d'argent, de vérité] pursuit. || [de négociations] continuation. ❍ **poursuites** *nfpl* JUR (legal) proceedings.

poursuivi, -e [pursɥivi] *pp* → poursuivre.

poursuivre [pursɥivr] **1** *vt* [voleur] to pursue, to chase; [gibier] to hunt. || [enquête, travail] to carry on with, to continue. || JUR [criminel] to prosecute; [voisin] to sue. **2** *vi* to go on, to carry on.

pourtant [purtɑ̃] *adv* nevertheless, even so.

pourtour [purtur] *nm* perimeter.

pourvoir [purvwar] **1** *vt*: **~ qqn de** to provide sb with; **~ qqch de** to equip ou fit sthg with. **2** *vi*: **~ à** to provide for.

pourvu, -e [purvy] *pp* → pourvoir. ❍ **pourvu que** *loc conj* (+ *subjonctif*) [condition] providing, provided (that). || [souhait] let's hope (that).

pousse [pus] *nf* [croissance] growth. || [bourgeon] shoot.

poussé, -e [puse] *adj* [travail] meticulous. || [moteur] souped-up.

pousse-café [puskafe] *nm inv fam* liqueur.

poussée [puse] *nf* [pression] pressure. || [coup] push. || [de fièvre, inflation] rise.

pousse-pousse [puspus] *nm inv* [voiture] rickshaw. || *Helv* [poussette] pushchair.

pousser [puse] 1 *vt* [personne, objet] to push. || [moteur, voiture] to drive hard. || [cri, soupir] to give. || [inciter]: ~ qqn à faire qqch to urge sb to do sthg. || [au crime, au suicide]: ~ qqn à to drive sb to. 2 *vi* [exercer une pression] to push. || [croître] to grow. || *fam* [exagérer] to overdo it. ○ **se pousser** *vp* to move up.

poussette [puset] *nf* pushchair.

poussière [pusjɛr] *nf* [gén] dust.

poussiéreux, -euse [pusjerø, øz] *adj* [meuble] dusty.

poussif, -ive [pusif, iv] *adj fam* wheezy.

poussin [pusɛ̃] *nm* ZOOL chick. || SPORT under-11.

poutre [putr] *nf* beam.

poutrelle [putrɛl] *nf* girder.

pouvoir [puvwar] 1 *nm* [gén] power; ~ d'achat purchasing power; les ~s publics the authorities. 2 *vt* [avoir la possibilité de, parvenir à]: ~ faire qqch to be able to do sthg; je ne peux pas venir ce soir I can't come tonight; je n'en peux plus [exaspéré] I'm at the end of my tether; [fatigué] I'm exhausted; je/tu n'y peux rien there's nothing I/you can do about it. || [avoir la permission de]: je peux prendre la voiture? can I borrow the car?; aucun élève ne peut partir no pupil may leave. || [indiquant l'éventualité]: vous pourriez rater votre train you could ou might miss your train. ○ **se pouvoir** *v impers*: il se peut que je me trompe I may be mistaken; cela se peut/pourrait bien that's quite possible.

pragmatique [pragmatik] *adj* pragmatic.

Prague [prag] *n* Prague.

prairie [preri] *nf* meadow; [aux États-Unis] prairie.

praline [pralin] *nf* [amande] sugared almond. || *Belg* [chocolat] chocolate.

praticable [pratikabl] *adj* [route] passable. || [plan] feasible, practicable.

praticien, -ienne [pratisjɛ̃, jɛn] *nm, f* practitioner; MÉD medical practitioner.

pratiquant, -e [pratikɑ̃, ɑ̃t] *adj* practising.

pratique [pratik] 1 *nf* [expérience] practical experience. || [usage] practice; mettre qqch en ~ to put sthg into practice. 2 *adj* practical; [gadget, outil] handy.

pratiquement [pratikmɑ̃] *adv* [en fait] in practice. || [quasiment] practically.

pratiquer [pratike] 1 *vt* [métier] to practice *Am*; [méthode] to apply. || [ouverture] to make. 2 *vi* RELIG to be a practising Christian/Jew/Muslim *etc*.

pré [pre] *nm* meadow.

préalable [prealabl] 1 *adj* prior, previous. 2 *nm* precondition. ○ **au préalable** *loc adv* first, beforehand.

préambule [preɑ̃byl] *nm* [introduction, propos] preamble; sans ~ immediately.

préau, -x [preo] *nm* [d'école] (covered) play area.

préavis [preavi] *nm inv* advance notice ou warning.

précaire [prekɛr] *adj* [incertain] precarious.

précaution [prekosjɔ̃] *nf* [prévoyance] precaution; prendre des ~s to take precautions. || [prudence] caution.

précédent, -e [presedɑ̃, ɑ̃t] *adj* previous. ○ **précédent** *nm* precedent; sans ~ unprecedented.

précéder [presede] *vt* [dans le temps - gén] to precede; [- suj: personne] to arrive before. || [marcher devant] to go in front of. || *fig* [devancer] to get ahead of.

précepte [presɛpt] *nm* precept.

précepteur, -trice [preseptœr, tris] *nm, f* (private) tutor.

prêcher [preʃe] *vt & vi* to preach.

précieux, -ieuse [presjø, jøz] *adj* [pierre, métal] precious; [objet] valuable; [collaborateur] invaluable, valued. || *péj* [style] precious, affected.

précipice [presipis] *nm* precipice.

précipitation [presipitasjɔ̃] *nf* [hâte] haste. ○ **précipitations** *nfpl* MÉTÉOR precipitation (*U*).

précipiter [presipite] *vt* [objet, personne] to throw, to hurl; ~ qqn/qqch du haut de to throw sb/sthg off, to hurl sb/sthg off. || [départ] to hasten. ○ **se précipiter** *vp* [se jeter] to throw o.s., to hurl o.s. || [s'élancer]: se ~ (vers qqn) to rush ou hurry (towards sb). || [s'accélérer - gén] to speed up; [- choses, événements] to move faster.

précis, -e [presi, iz] *adj* [exact] precise,

accurate. || [fixé] definite, precise. ○ **précis** nm handbook.

précisément [presizemɑ̃] adv precisely, exactly.

préciser [presize] vt [heure, lieu] to specify. || [pensée] to clarify. ○ **se préciser** vp to become clear.

précision [presizjɔ̃] nf [de style, d'explication] precision. || [détail] detail.

précoce [prekɔs] adj [plante, fruit] early. || [enfant] precocious.

préconçu, -e [prekɔ̃sy] adj preconceived.

préconiser [prekɔnize] vt to recommend.

précurseur [prekyrsœr] 1 nm precursor, forerunner. 2 adj precursory.

prédécesseur [predesesœr] nm predecessor.

prédestiner [predɛstine] vt to predestine.

prédicateur, -trice [predikatœr, tris] nm, f preacher.

prédiction [prediksjɔ̃] nf prediction.

prédilection [predilɛksjɔ̃] nf partiality, liking.

prédire [predir] vt to predict.

prédit, -e [predi, it] pp → **prédire**.

prédominer [predɔmine] vt to predominate.

préfabriqué, -e [prefabrike] adj [maison] prefabricated. ○ **préfabriqué** nm prefabricated material.

préface [prefas] nf preface.

préfecture [prefɛktyr] nf prefecture.

préférable [preferabl] adj preferable.

préféré, -e [prefere] adj & nm, f favourite.

préférence [preferɑ̃s] nf preference; de ~ preferably.

préférentiel, -ielle [preferɑ̃sjɛl] adj preferential.

préférer [prefere] vt: ~ qqn/qqch (à) to prefer sb/sthg (to); je **préfère rentrer** I would rather go home, I would prefer to go home.

préfet [prefɛ] nm prefect.

préfixe [prefiks] nm prefix.

préhistoire [preistwar] nf prehistory.

préjudice [preʒydis] nm harm (U), detriment (U); porter ~ à qqn to harm sb.

préjugé [preʒyʒe] nm: ~ (contre) prejudice (against).

prélasser [prelase] ○ **se prélasser** vp to lounge.

prélavage [prelavaʒ] nm pre-wash.

prélèvement [prelɛvmɑ̃] nm MÉD removal; [de sang] sample. || FIN deduction; ~ **automatique** direct debit; ~ **mensuel** monthly standing order; ~s **obligatoires** tax and social security contributions.

prélever [prelɛve] vt FIN: ~ **de l'argent (sur)** to deduct money (from). || MÉD to remove; ~ **du sang** to take a blood sample.

préliminaire [preliminɛr] adj preliminary. ○ **préliminaires** nmpl [de paix] preliminary talks. || [de discours] preliminaries.

prématuré, -e [prematyre] 1 adj premature. 2 nm, f premature baby.

préméditation [premeditasjɔ̃] nf premeditation; avec ~ [meurtre] premeditated; [agir] with premeditation.

premier, -ière [prəmje, jɛr] 1 adj [gén] first; [étage] first Br, second Am. || [qualité] top. || [état] original. 2 nm, f first. ○ **première** nf CIN première; THÉÂTRE première, first night. || [exploit] feat. || [première classe] first class. || SCOL ≃ eleventh grade Am. || AUTOM first (gear). ○ **premier de l'an** nm: le ~ **de l'an** New Year's Day. ○ **en premier** loc adv first, firstly.

premièrement [prəmjɛrmɑ̃] adv first, firstly.

prémonition [premɔnisjɔ̃] nf premonition.

prémunir [premynir] vt: ~ qqn (contre) to protect sb (against). ○ **se prémunir** vp to protect o.s.; **se ~ contre qqch** to guard against sthg.

prénatal, -e [prenatal] (pl **prénatals** OU **prénataux** [prenato]) adj antenatal.

prendre [prɑ̃dr] 1 vt [gén] to take. || [enlever] to take (away); ~ **qqch à qqn** to take sthg from sb. || [aller chercher - objet] to get, to fetch; [- personne] to pick up. || [repas, boisson] to have; **vous prendrez quelque chose?** would you like something to eat/drink? || [voleur] to catch; **se faire ~** to get caught. || [responsabilité] to take (on). || [aborder - personne] to handle; [- problème] to tackle. || [poids] to gain, to put on. 2 vi [ciment, sauce] to set. || [plante, greffe] to take; [mode] to catch on. || [feu] to catch. || [se diriger]: ~ **à droite** to turn right. ○ **se prendre** vp [se considérer]: **pour qui se prend-il?** who does he think he is? || loc: **s'en ~ à qqn** [physiquement] to set about sb; [verbalement] to take it out on sb; **je**

sais comment m'y ~ I know how to do it ou go about it.

prénom [prenɔ̃] *nm* first name.

prénommer [prenɔme] *vt* to name, to call. ○ **se prénommer** *vp* to be called.

prénuptial, -e, -iaux [prenypsjal, jo] *adj* premarital.

préoccupation [preɔkypasjɔ̃] *nf* preoccupation.

préoccuper [preɔkype] *vt* to preoccupy. ○ **se préoccuper** *vp*: se ~ de qqch to be worried about sthg.

préparatifs [preparatif] *nmpl* preparations.

préparation [preparasjɔ̃] *nf* preparation.

préparer [prepare] *vt* [gén] to prepare; [plat, repas] to cook, to prepare; ~ qqn à qqch to prepare sb for sthg. || [réserver]: ~ qqch à qqn to have sthg in store for sb. || [congrès] to organize. ○ **se préparer** *vp* [personne]: se ~ à qqch/à faire qqch to prepare for sthg/to do sthg.

prépondérant, -e [prepɔ̃derɑ̃, ɑ̃t] *adj* dominating.

préposé, -e [prepoze] *nm, f* (minor) official; [de vestiaire] attendant; [facteur] mailman (*f* mailwoman) *Am*; ~ à qqch person in charge of sthg.

préposition [prepozisjɔ̃] *nf* preposition.

préretraite [preʀətʀɛt] *nf* early retirement.

prérogative [preʀɔgativ] *nf* prerogative.

près [pʀɛ] *adv* near, close. ○ **de près** *loc adv* closely. ○ **près de** *loc prép* [dans l'espace] near, close to. || [dans le temps] close to. || [presque] nearly, almost. ○ **à peu près** *loc adv* more or less, just about. ○ **à ceci près que, à cela près que** *loc conj* except that, apart from the fact that. ○ **à ... près** *loc adv*: à dix centimètres ~ to within ten centimetres; il n'en est pas à un ou deux jours ~ a day or two more or less won't make any difference.

présage [preza3] *nm* omen.

présager [preza3e] *vt* [annoncer] to portend. || [prévoir] to predict.

presbytère [pʀɛsbitɛʀ] *nm* presbytery.

presbytie [pʀɛsbisi] *nf* longsightedness *Br*, farsightedness *Am*.

prescription [pʀɛskʀipsjɔ̃] *nf* MÉD prescription. || JUR limitation.

prescrire [pʀɛskʀiʀ] *vt* [mesures, condi-

tions] to lay down, to stipulate. || MÉD to prescribe.

prescrit, e [pʀɛskʀi, it] *pp* → **prescrire**.

préséance [preseɑ̃s] *nf* precedence.

présence [prezɑ̃s] *nf* [gén] presence; **en ~** face to face; **en ~ de** in the presence of. || [compagnie] company (*U*). || [assiduité] attendance. ○ **présence d'esprit** *nf* presence of mind.

présent, -e [prezɑ̃, ɑ̃t] *adj* [gén] present; **le ~ ouvrage** this work; **avoir qqch ~ à l'esprit** to remember sthg. ○ **présent** *nm* [gén] present; **à ~** at present; **à ~ que** now that; **jusqu'à ~** up to now, so far. || GRAM: **le ~** the present tense.

présentable [prezɑ̃tabl] *adj* [d'aspect] presentable.

présentateur, -trice [prezɑ̃tatœʀ, tʀis] *nm, f* presenter.

présentation [prezɑ̃tasjɔ̃] *nf* [de personne] introduction; **faire les ~s** to make the introductions. || [aspect extérieur] appearance. || [de papiers, de produit, de film] presentation. || [de magazine] layout.

présenter [prezɑ̃te] *vt* [gén] to present; [projet] to present, to submit. || [invité] to introduce. || [condoléances, félicitations, avantages] to offer; [hommages] to pay; ~ qqch à qqn to offer sb sthg. ○ **se présenter** *vp* [se faire connaître]: se ~ (à) to introduce o.s. (to). || [être candidat]: se ~ à [élection] to stand in *Br*, to run in *Am*; [examen] to sit *Br*, to take. || [occasion, situation] to arise, to present itself. || [affaire, contrat]: se ~ bien/mal to look good/bad.

présentoir [prezɑ̃twaʀ] *nm* display stand.

préservatif [prezɛʀvatif] *nm* condom.

préserver [prezɛʀve] *vt* to preserve. ○ **se préserver** *vp*: se ~ de to protect o.s. from.

présidence [prezidɑ̃s] *nf* [de groupe] chairmanship. || [d'État] presidency.

président, -e [prezidɑ̃, ɑ̃t] *nm, f* [d'assemblée] chairman (*f* chairwoman). || [d'État] president; ~ de la République President (of the Republic) of France. || JUR [de tribunal] presiding judge; [de jury] foreman (*f* forewoman).

présider [prezide] *vt* [réunion] to chair. || [banquet, dîner] to preside over.

présomption [prezɔ̃psjɔ̃] *nf* [hypothèse] presumption. || JUR presumption.

présomptueux, -euse [prezɔ̃ptɥø, øz] *adj* presumptuous.

presque [prɛsk] *adv* almost, nearly; ~ **rien** next to nothing, scarcely anything; ~ **jamais** hardly ever.

presqu'île [prɛskil] *nf* peninsula.

pressant, -e [prɛsɑ̃, ɑ̃t] *adj* pressing.

presse [prɛs] *nf* press.

pressé, -e [prese] *adj* [travail] urgent. || [personne]: **être ~** to be in a hurry. || [citron, orange] freshly squeezed.

pressentiment [presɑ̃timɑ̃] *nm* premonition.

pressentir [presɑ̃tir] *vt* [événement] to have a premonition of.

presse-papiers [prɛspapje] *nm inv* paperweight.

presser [prese] *vt* [écraser - olives] to press; [- citron, orange] to squeeze. || [bouton] to press, to push. || [accélérer] to speed up; ~ **le pas** to speed up, to walk faster. ○ **se presser** *vp* [se dépêcher] to hurry (up). || [s'agglutiner]: **se ~ (autour de)** to crowd (around). || [se serrer] to huddle.

pressing [presiŋ] *nm* [établissement] dry cleaner's.

pression [presjɔ̃] *nf* [gén] pressure; **exercer une ~ sur qqch** to exert pressure on sthg; **sous ~** [liquide & *fig*] under pressure. || [sur vêtement] snap fastener *Am*. || [bière] draught beer.

pressoir [preswar] *nm* [machine] press.

prestance [prɛstɑ̃s] *nf* bearing; **avoir de la ~** to have presence.

prestataire [prɛstatɛr] *nmf* [bénéficiaire] person in receipt of benefit, claimant. || [fournisseur] provider; ~ **de service** service provider.

prestation [prɛstasjɔ̃] *nf* [allocation] benefit; ~ **en nature** payment in kind. || [de comédien] performance.

preste [prɛst] *adj littéraire* nimble.

prestidigitateur, -trice [prɛstidiʒitatœr, tris] *nm, f* conjurer.

prestige [prɛstiʒ] *nm* prestige.

prestigieux, -ieuse [prɛstiʒjø, jøz] *adj* [réputé] prestigious.

présumer [prezyme] **1** *vt* to presume, to assume; **être présumé coupable/innocent** to be presumed guilty/innocent. **2** *vi*: ~ **de qqch** to overestimate sthg.

prêt, -e [prɛ, prɛt] *adj* ready; ~ **à qqch/à faire qqch** ready for sthg/to do sthg; ~**s? partez!** SPORT get set, go! ○ **prêt** *nm* [action] lending (*U*); [somme] loan.

prêt-à-porter [prɛtaporte] *nm* ready-to-wear clothing (*U*).

prétendant [pretɑ̃dɑ̃] *nm* [au trône] pretender. || [amoureux] suitor.

prétendre [pretɑ̃dr] *vt* [affecter]: ~ **faire qqch** to claim to do sthg. || [affirmer]: ~ **que** to claim (that), to maintain (that).

prétendu, -e [pretɑ̃dy] **1** *pp* → **prétendre**. **2** *adj* (*avant n*) so-called.

prête-nom [prɛtnɔ̃] (*pl* **prête-noms**) *nm* front man.

prétentieux, -ieuse [pretɑ̃sjø, jøz] *adj* pretentious.

prétention [pretɑ̃sjɔ̃] *nf* [suffisance] pretentiousness. || [ambition] pretension, ambition; **avoir la ~ de faire qqch** to claim ou pretend to do sthg.

prêter [prete] *vt* [fournir]: ~ **qqch (à qqn)** [objet, argent] to lend (sb) sthg; *fig* [concours, appui] to lend (sb) sthg, to give (sb) sthg. || [attribuer]: ~ **qqch à qqn** to attribute sthg to sb. ○ **se prêter** *vp*: **se ~ à** [convenir à] to fit, to suit.

prétérit [preterit] *nm* preterite.

prêteur, -euse [pretœr, øz] *nm, f*: ~ **sur gages** pawnbroker.

prétexte [pretɛkst] *nm* pretext, excuse; **sous ~ de faire qqch/que** on the pretext of doing sthg/that, under the pretext of doing sthg/that; **sous aucun ~** on no account.

prétexter [pretɛkste] *vt* to give as an excuse.

prêtre [prɛtr] *nm* priest.

preuve [prœv] *nf* [gén] proof. || JUR evidence. || [témoignage] sign, token; **faire ~ de qqch** to show sthg; **faire ses ~s** to prove o.s./itself.

prévaloir [prevalwar] *vi* [dominer]: ~ **(sur)** to prevail (over). ○ **se prévaloir** *vp*: **se ~ de** to boast about.

prévalu [prevaly] *pp inv* → **prévaloir**.

prévenance [prevnɑ̃s] *nf* [attitude] thoughtfulness, consideration.

prévenant, -e [prevnɑ̃, ɑ̃t] *adj* considerate, attentive.

prévenir [prevnir] *vt* [employé, élève]: ~ **qqn (de)** to warn sb (about). || [police] to inform. || [désirs] to anticipate. || [maladie] to prevent.

préventif, -ive [prevɑ̃tif, iv] *adj* [mesure, médecine] preventive.

prévention [prevɑ̃sjɔ̃] *nf* [protection]: ~ **(contre)** prevention (of); ~ **routière** road safety (measures). || JUR remand.

prévenu, -e [prevny] **1** pp → prévenir. **2** nm, f accused, defendant.

prévision [previzjɔ̃] nf forecast (U), prediction; [de coûts] estimate; ÉCON forecast; **les ~s météorologiques** the weather forecast. ○ **en prévision de** loc prép in anticipation of.

prévoir [prevwar] vt [s'attendre à] to expect. || [prédire] to predict. || [anticiper] to foresee, to anticipate. || [programmer] to plan; **comme prévu** as planned, according to plan.

prévoyant, -e [prevwajɑ̃, ɑ̃t] adj provident.

prévu, e [prevy] pp → prévoir.

prier [prije] **1** vt RELIG to pray to. || [implorer] to beg; **(ne pas) se faire** (pour faire qqch) (not) to need to be persuaded (to do sthg); **je vous en prie** [de grâce] please, I beg you; [de rien] don't mention it, not at all. || sout [demander]: ~ **qqn de faire qqch** to request sb to do sthg. **2** vi RELIG to pray.

prière [prijer] nf [RELIG - recueillement] prayer (U), praying (U); [- formule] prayer. || littéraire [demande] entreaty; ~ **de frapper avant d'entrer** please knock before entering.

primaire [primer] adj [premier]: **études ~s** primary education (U). || péj [primitif] limited.

prime [prim] nf [d'employé] bonus. || [allocation - de déménagement, de transport] allowance; [- à l'exportation] incentive. || [d'assurance] premium.

primer [prime] **1** vi to take precedence, to come first. **2** vt [être supérieur à] to take precedence over. || [récompenser] to award a prize to.

primeur [primœr] nf immediacy; **avoir la ~ de qqch** to be the first to hear sthg. ○ **primeurs** nfpl early produce (U).

primevère [primver] nf primrose.

primitif, -ive [primitif, iv] adj [gén] primitive. || [aspect] original.

primordial, -e, -iaux [primɔrdjal, jo] adj essential.

prince [prɛ̃s] nm prince.

princesse [prɛ̃ses] nf princess.

princier, -ière [prɛ̃sje, jer] adj princely.

principal, -e, -aux [prɛ̃sipal, o] **1** adj [gén] main, principal. **2** nm, f [important]: **le ~** the main thing. || SCOL principal Am.

principalement [prɛ̃sipalmɑ̃] adv mainly, principally.

principauté [prɛ̃sipote] nf principality.

principe [prɛ̃sip] nm principle; **par ~** on principle. ○ **en principe** loc adv theoretically, in principle.

printanier, -ière [prɛ̃tanje, jer] adj [temps] spring-like.

printemps [prɛ̃tɑ̃] nm [saison] spring.

priori [priɔri] ○ **a priori 1** loc adv in principle. **2** nm inv initial reaction.

prioritaire [prijɔriter] adj [industrie, mesure] priority (avant n). || AUTOM with right of way.

priorité [prijɔrite] nf [importance primordiale] priority; **en ~** first. || AUTOM right of way; ~ **à droite** give way to the right.

pris, -e [pri, priz] **1** pp → prendre. **2** adj [place] taken; [personne] busy; [mains] full. || [nez] blocked; [gorge] sore. ○ **prise** nf [sur barre, sur branche] grip, hold; **lâcher ~e** to let go; fig to give up. || [action de prendre - de ville] seizure, capture; ~**e de sang** blood test; ~**e de vue** shot. || [à la pêche] haul. || ÉLECTR: ~**e (de courant)** [mâle] plug; [femelle] socket. || [de judo] hold.

prisme [prism] nm prism.

prison [prizɔ̃] nf [établissement] prison. || [réclusion] imprisonment.

prisonnier, -ière [prizɔnje, jer] **1** nm, f prisoner; **faire qqn ~** to take sb prisoner, to capture sb. **2** adj imprisoned; fig trapped.

privation [privasjɔ̃] nf deprivation. ○ **privations** nfpl privations, hardships.

privatisation [privatizasjɔ̃] nf privatization.

privatiser [privatize] vt to privatize.

privé, -e [prive] adj private. ○ **privé** nm ÉCON private sector. || [détective] private eye. || [intimité]: **en ~** in private; **dans le ~** in private life.

priver [prive] vt: ~ **qqn (de)** to deprive sb (of).

privilège [privileʒ] nm privilege.

privilégié, -e [privileʒje] **1** adj [personne] privileged. || [climat, site] favoured. **2** nm, f privileged person.

prix [pri] nm [coût] price; ~ **d'achat** purchase price; **à ~ fixe** set-price (avant n); **hors de ~** too expensive; **à tout ~** at all costs; ~ **de revient** cost price; **y mettre le ~** to pay a lot. || [importance] value. || [récompense] prize.

probabilité [prɔbabilite] nf [chance] probability. || [vraisemblance] probability, likelihood; **selon toute ~** in all probability.

probable [prɔbabl] *adj* probable, likely.

probant, -e [prɔbɑ̃, ɑ̃t] *adj* convincing, conclusive.

probité [prɔbite] *nf* integrity.

problème [prɔblɛm] *nm* problem; **(il n'y a) pas de ~!** *fam* no problem!

procédé [prɔsede] *nm* [méthode] process. || [conduite] behaviour (*U*).

procéder [prɔsede] *vi* [agir] to proceed. || [exécuter]: **~ à qqch** to set about sthg.

procédure [prɔsedyr] *nf* procedure; [démarche] proceedings (*pl*).

procès [prɔsɛ] *nm* JUR trial; **intenter un ~ à qqn** to sue sb.

processeur [prɔsesœr] *nm* processor.

procession [prɔsesjɔ̃] *nf* procession.

processus [prɔsesys] *nm* process.

procès-verbal [prɔsɛvɛrbal] *nm* [contravention - gén] ticket; [- pour stationnement interdit] parking ticket. || [compte-rendu] minutes.

prochain, -e [prɔʃɛ̃, ɛn] *adj* [suivant] next; **à la ~e!** *fam* see you! || [imminent] impending. ○ **prochain** *nm littéraire* [semblable] fellow man.

prochainement [prɔʃɛnmɑ̃] *adv* soon, shortly.

proche [prɔʃ] *adj* [dans l'espace] near; **~ de** near, close to; [semblable à] very similar to, closely related to. || [dans le temps] imminent, near; **dans un ~ avenir** in the immediate future. || [ami, parent] close. ○ **proches** *nmpl*: **les ~s** the close family (*sg*).

Proche-Orient [prɔʃɔrjɑ̃] *nm*: **le ~** the Near East.

proclamation [prɔklamasjɔ̃] *nf* proclamation.

proclamer [prɔklame] *vt* to proclaim, to declare.

procréer [prɔkree] *vt littéraire* to procreate.

procuration [prɔkyrasjɔ̃] *nf* proxy; **par ~** by proxy.

procurer [prɔkyre] *vt*: **~ qqch à qqn** [suj: personne] to obtain sthg for sb; [suj: chose] to give ou bring sb sthg. ○ **se procurer** *vp*: **se ~ qqch** to obtain sthg.

procureur [prɔkyrœr] *nm*: **Procureur de la République** ≃ Attorney General.

prodige [prɔdiʒ] *nm* [miracle] miracle. || [tour de force] marvel, wonder. || [génie] prodigy.

prodigieux, -ieuse [prɔdiʒjø, jøz] *adj* fantastic, incredible.

prodigue [prɔdig] *adj* [dépensier] extravagant.

prodiguer [prɔdige] *vt littéraire* [soins, amitié]: **~ qqch (à)** to lavish sthg (on).

producteur, -trice [prɔdyktœr, tris] **1** *nm, f* [gén] producer. || AGRIC producer, grower. **2** *adj*: **~ de pétrole** oil-producing (*avant n*).

productif, -ive [prɔdyktif, iv] *adj* productive.

production [prɔdyksjɔ̃] *nf* [gén] production; **la ~ littéraire d'un pays** the literature of a country.

productivité [prɔdyktivite] *nf* productivity.

produire [prɔdɥir] *vt* [gén] to produce. || [provoquer] to cause. ○ **se produire** *vp* [arriver] to occur, to take place. || [acteur, chanteur] to appear.

produit, -e [prɔdɥi, ɥit] *pp* → **produire**. ○ **produit** *nm* [gén] product; **~ de beauté** cosmetic, beauty product; **~s d'entretien** cleaning products.

proéminent, -e [prɔeminɑ̃, ɑ̃t] *adj* prominent.

profane [prɔfan] *adj* [laïc] secular. || [ignorant] ignorant.

profaner [prɔfane] *vt* [église] to desecrate. || *fig* [mémoire] to defile.

proférer [prɔfere] *vt* to utter.

professeur [prɔfesœr] *nm* [enseignant] teacher. || [titre] professor.

profession [prɔfesjɔ̃] *nf* [métier] occupation; **sans ~** unemployed; **~ libérale** profession. || [corps de métier - libéral] profession; [- manuel] trade.

professionnel, -elle [prɔfesjɔnɛl] **1** *adj* [gén] professional. || [école] technical. **2** *nm, f* professional.

professorat [prɔfesɔra] *nm* teaching.

profil [prɔfil] *nm* [de personne, d'emploi] profile; [de bâtiment] outline; **de ~** [visage, corps] in profile.

profiler [prɔfile] *vt* to shape. ○ **se profiler** *vp* [bâtiment, arbre] to stand out. || [solution] to emerge.

profit [prɔfi] *nm* [avantage] benefit; **au ~ de** in aid of; **tirer ~ de** to profit from, to benefit from. || [gain] profit.

profitable [prɔfitabl] *adj* profitable; **être ~ à qqn** to benefit sb, to be beneficial to sb.

profiter [prɔfite] *vi* [tirer avantage]: **~ de** [vacances] to benefit from; [personne] to take advantage of; **~ de qqch pour**

faire qqch to take advantage of sthg to do sthg; **en ~** to make the most of it.

profond, -e [prɔfɔ̃, ɔ̃d] *adj* [gén] deep. || [pensée] deep, profound.

profondément [prɔfɔ̃demɑ̃] *adv* [enfoui] deep. || [intensément - aimer, intéresser] deeply; [- dormir] soundly; **être ~ endormi** to be fast asleep. || [extrêmement - convaincu, ému] deeply, profoundly; [- différent] profoundly.

profondeur [prɔfɔ̃dœr] *nf* depth; **en ~** in depth.

profusion [prɔfyzjɔ̃] *nf*: **à ~** in abundance, in profusion.

progéniture [prɔʒenityr] *nf* offspring.

programmable [prɔgramabl] *adj* programmable.

programmateur, -trice [prɔgramatœr, tris] *nm, f* programme planner. ○ **programmateur** *nm* automatic control unit.

programmation [prɔgramasjɔ̃] *nf* INFORM programming. || RADIO & TÉLÉ programme planning.

programme [prɔgram] *nm* [gén] program *Am*. || INFORM program. || [planning] schedule. || SCOL syllabus.

programmer [prɔgrame] *vt* [organiser] to plan. || RADIO & TÉLÉ to schedule. || INFORM to program.

programmeur, -euse [prɔgramœr, øz] *nm, f* INFORM (computer) programmer.

progrès [prɔgrɛ] *nm* progress (*U*); **faire des ~** to make progress.

progresser [prɔgrese] *vi* [avancer] to progress, to advance. || [maladie] to spread. || [élève] to make progress.

progressif, -ive [prɔgresif, iv] *adj* progressive; [difficulté] increasing.

progression [prɔgresjɔ̃] *nf* [avancée] advance. || [de maladie, du nationalisme] spread.

prohiber [prɔibe] *vt* to ban, to prohibit.

proie [prwa] *nf* prey; **être la ~ de qqch** *fig* to be the victim of sthg; **être en ~ à** [sentiment] to be prey to.

projecteur [prɔʒɛktœr] *nm* [de lumière] floodlight; THÉÂTRE spotlight. || [d'images] projector.

projectile [prɔʒɛktil] *nm* missile.

projection [prɔʒɛksjɔ̃] *nf* [gén] projection. || [jet] throwing.

projectionniste [prɔʒɛksjɔnist] *nmf* projectionist.

projet [prɔʒɛ] *nm* [perspective] plan. || [étude, ébauche] draft; **~ de loi** bill.

projeter [prɔʃte] *vt* [envisager] to plan; **~ de faire qqch** to plan to do sthg. || [missile, pierre] to throw. || [film, diapositives] to show.

prolétaire [prɔletɛr] *nmf* & *adj* proletarian.

prolétariat [prɔletarja] *nm* proletariat.

proliférer [prɔlifere] *vi* to proliferate.

prolifique [prɔlifik] *adj* prolific.

prologue [prɔlɔg] *nm* prologue.

prolongation [prɔlɔ̃gasjɔ̃] *nf* [extension] extension, prolongation. ○ **prolongations** *nfpl* SPORT extra time (*U*).

prolongement [prɔlɔ̃ʒmɑ̃] *nm* [de mur, quai] extension; **être dans le ~ de** to be a continuation of.

prolonger [prɔlɔ̃ʒe] *vt* [dans le temps]: **~ qqch (de)** to prolong sthg (by). || [dans l'espace]: **~ qqch (de)** to extend sthg (by).

promenade [prɔmnad] *nf* [balade] walk, stroll; *fig* trip, excursion; **~ en voiture** drive; **~ à vélo** bike) ride; **faire une ~** to go for a walk. || [lieu] promenade.

promener [prɔmne] *vt* [personne] to take out (for a walk); [en voiture] to take for a drive. || *fig* [regard, doigts]: **~ qqch sur** to run sthg over. ○ **se promener** *vp* to go for a walk.

promesse [prɔmɛs] *nf* [serment] promise; **tenir sa ~** to keep one's promise. || *fig* [espérance]: **être plein de ~s** to be very promising.

prometteur, -euse [prɔmetœr, øz] *adj* promising.

promettre [prɔmɛtr] **1** *vt* to promise; **~ qqch à qqn** to promise sb sthg; **~ de faire qqch** to promise to do sthg; **~ à qqn que** to promise sb that. **2** *vi* to be promising; **ça promet!** *iron* that bodes well!

promis, -e [prɔmi, iz] **1** *pp* → **promettre**. **2** *adj* promised. **3** *nm, f hum* intended.

promiscuité [prɔmiskɥite] *nf* overcrowding.

promontoire [prɔmɔ̃twar] *nm* promontory.

promoteur, -trice [prɔmɔtœr, tris] *nm, f* [novateur] instigator. || [constructeur] property developer.

promotion [prɔmɔsjɔ̃] *nf* [gén] promotion; **en ~** [produit] on special offer. || MIL & SCOL year.

promouvoir [prɔmuvwar] *vt* to promote.

prompt, -e [prɔ̃, prɔ̃t] *adj sout*: **~ (à faire qqch)** swift (to do sthg).

promu, -e [prɔmy] *pp* → **promouvoir**.

promulguer [promylge] *vt* to promulgate.

prôner [prone] *vt sout* to advocate.

pronom [prɔnɔ̃] *nm* pronoun.

pronominal, -e, -aux [prɔnɔminal, o] *adj* pronominal.

prononcé, -e [prɔnɔ̃se] *adj* marked.

prononcer [prɔnɔ̃se] *vt* JUR & LING to pronounce. || [dire] to utter. ○ **se prononcer** *vp* [se dire] to be pronounced. || [trancher - assemblée] to decide, to reach a decision; [- magistrat] to deliver a verdict; **se ~ sur** to give one's opinion of.

prononciation [prɔnɔ̃sjasjɔ̃] *nf* LING pronunciation. || JUR pronouncement.

pronostic [prɔnɔstik] *nm* (*gén pl*) [prévision] forecast. || MÉD prognosis.

propagande [prɔpagɑ̃d] *nf* [endoctrinement] propaganda.

propager [prɔpaʒe] *vt* to spread. ○ **se propager** *vp* to spread; BIOL to be propagated; PHYS to propagate.

propane [prɔpan] *nm* propane.

prophète [prɔfɛt], **prophétesse** [prɔfetɛs] *nm, f* prophet (*f* prophetess).

prophétie [prɔfesi] *nf* prophecy.

propice [prɔpis] *adj* favourable.

proportion [prɔpɔrsjɔ̃] *nf* proportion; **toutes ~s gardées** relatively speaking.

proportionné, -e [prɔpɔrsjɔne] *adj*: **bien/mal ~** well-/badly-proportioned.

proportionnel, -elle [prɔpɔrsjɔnɛl] *adj*: **~ (à)** proportional (to). ○ **proportionnelle** *nf*: **la ~le** proportional representation.

propos [prɔpo] **1** *nm* [discours] talk. || [but] intention; **c'est à quel ~?** what is it about?; **hors de ~** at the wrong time. **2** *nmpl* [paroles] talk (*U*), words. ○ **à propos** *loc adv* [opportunément] at (just) the right time. || [au fait] by the way. ○ **à propos de** *loc prép* about.

proposer [prɔpoze] *vt* [offrir] to offer, to propose; **~ qqch à qqn** to offer sb sthg, to offer sthg to sb; || [suggérer] to suggest, to propose; **~ de faire qqch** to suggest ou propose doing sthg.

proposition [prɔpozisjɔ̃] *nf* [offre] offer, proposal. || [suggestion] suggestion, proposal. || GRAM clause.

propre [prɔpr] **1** *adj* [nettoyé] clean. || [soigné] neat, tidy. || [personnel] own. || [particulier]: **~ à** peculiar to. **2** *nm* [propreté] cleanness, cleanliness; **recopier qqch au ~** to make a fair copy of sthg, to copy sthg up.

proprement [prɔprəmɑ̃] *adv* [convenablement - habillé] neatly, tidily; [- se tenir] correctly. || [véritablement] completely; **à ~ parler** strictly ou properly speaking; **l'événement ~ dit** the event itself, the actual event.

propreté [prɔprəte] *nf* cleanness, cleanliness.

propriétaire [prɔprijeter] *nmf* [possesseur] owner; **~ terrien** landowner. || [dans l'immobilier] landlord.

propriété [prɔprijete] *nf* [gén] property; **~ privée** private property. || [droit] ownership. || [terres] property (*U*).

propulser [prɔpylse] *vt litt & fig* to propel; *fig* to fling. ○ **se propulser** *vp* to move forward, to propel o.s. forward ou along; *fig* to shoot.

prorata [prɔrata] ○ **au prorata de** *loc prép* in proportion to.

prosaïque [prozaik] *adj* prosaic, mundane.

proscrit, -e [prɔskri, it] *adj* [interdit] banned, prohibited.

prose [proz] *nf* prose; **en ~** in prose.

prospecter [prɔspɛkte] *vt* [pays, région] to prospect. || COMM to canvass.

prospection [prɔspɛksjɔ̃] *nf* [de ressources] prospecting. || COMM canvassing

prospectus [prɔspɛktys] *nm* (advertising) leaflet.

prospérer [prɔspere] *vi* to prosper, to thrive; [plante, insecte] to thrive.

prospérité [prɔsperite] *nf* [richesse] prosperity. || [bien-être] well-being.

prostate [prɔstat] *nf* prostate (gland).

prosterner [prɔsterne] ○ **se prosterner** *vp* to bow down.

prostituée [prɔstitɥe] *nf* prostitute.

prostituer [prɔstitɥe] ○ **se prostituer** *vp* to prostitute o.s.

prostitution [prɔstitysjɔ̃] *nf* prostitution.

prostré, -e [prɔstre] *adj* prostrate.

protagoniste [prɔtagɔnist] *nmf* protagonist, hero (*f* heroine).

protecteur, -trice [prɔtɛktœr, tris] **1** *adj* protective. **2** *nm, f* [défenseur] protector. || [des arts] patron.

protection [prɔtɛksjɔ̃] *nf* [défense] protection; **prendre qqn sous sa ~** to take sb under one's wing. || [des arts] patronage.

protectionnisme [prɔtɛksjɔnism] *nm* protectionism.

protégé, -e [prɔteʒe] **1** *adj* protected. **2** *nm, f* protégé.

protège-cahier [prɔtɛʒkaje] (*pl* **protège-cahiers**) *nm* exercise book cover.

protéger [prɔteʒe] *vt* [gén] to protect.

protéine [prɔtein] *nf* protein.

protestant, -e [prɔtɛstɑ̃, ɑ̃t] *adj & nm, f* Protestant.

protestation [prɔtɛstasjɔ̃] *nf* [contestation] protest.

protester . [prɔtɛste] *vi* to protest; ~ **contre qqch** to protest against sthg, to protest sthg *Am*.

prothèse [prɔtɛz] *nf* prosthesis; ~ **dentaire** dentures (*pl*), false teeth (*pl*).

protide [prɔtid] *nm* protein.

protocolaire [prɔtɔkɔlɛr] *adj* [question] of protocol.

protocole [prɔtɔkɔl] *nm* protocol.

proton [prɔtɔ̃] *nm* proton.

prototype [prɔtɔtip] *nm* prototype.

protubérance [prɔtyberɑ̃s] *nf* bulge, protuberance.

proue [pru] *nf* bows (*pl*), prow.

prouesse [prues] *nf* feat.

prouver [pruve] *vt* [établir] to prove. || [montrer] to demonstrate, to show.

provenance [prɔvnɑ̃s] *nf* origin; **en ~ de** from.

provenir [prɔvnir] *vi*: ~ **de** to come from; *fig* to be due to, to be caused by.

proverbe [prɔvɛrb] *nm* proverb.

proverbial, -e, -iaux [prɔvɛrbjal, jo] *adj* proverbial.

providence [prɔvidɑ̃s] *nf* providence.

providentiel, -ielle [prɔvidɑ̃sjɛl] *adj* providential.

province [prɔvɛ̃s] *nf* [gén] province. || [campagne] provinces (*pl*).

provincial, -e, -iaux [prɔvɛ̃sjal, jo] *adj & nm, f* provincial.

proviseur [prɔvizœr] *nm* ≈ principal *Am*.

provision [prɔvizjɔ̃] *nf* [réserve] stock, supply. || FIN retainer; → **chèque**. ○ **provisions** *nfpl* provisions.

provisoire [prɔvizwar] 1 *adj* temporary; JUR provisional. 2 *nm*: **ce n'est que du ~** it's only a temporary arrangement.

provocant, -e [prɔvɔkɑ̃, ɑ̃t] *adj* provocative.

provocation [prɔvɔkasjɔ̃] *nf* provocation.

provoquer [prɔvɔke] *vt* [entraîner] to cause. || [personne] to provoke.

proxénète [prɔksenɛt] *nm* pimp.

proximité [prɔksimite] *nf* [de lieu] proximity, nearness; **à ~ de** near.

prude [pryd] *adj* prudish.

prudence [prydɑ̃s] *nf* care, caution.

prudent, -e [prydɑ̃, ɑ̃t] *adj* careful, cautious.

prune [pryn] *nf* plum.

pruneau, -x [pryno] *nm* [fruit] prune.

prunelle [prynɛl] *nf* ANAT pupil.

prunier [prynje] *nm* plum tree.

PS¹ (*abr de* **Parti socialiste**) *nm* French socialist party.

PS², P-S (*abr de* **post-scriptum**) *nm* PS.

psaume [psom] *nm* psalm.

pseudonyme [psødɔnim] *nm* pseudonym.

psy [psi] *fam nmf* (*abr de* **psychiatre**) psychiatrist, shrink *fam*.

psychanalyse [psikanaliz] *nf* psychoanalysis.

psychanalyste [psikanalist] *nmf* psychoanalyst, analyst.

psychédélique [psikedelik] *adj* psychedelic.

psychiatre [psikjatr] *nmf* psychiatrist.

psychiatrie [psikjatri] *nf* psychiatry.

psychique [psifik] *adj* psychic; [maladie] psychosomatic.

psychologie [psikɔlɔʒi] *nf* psychology.

psychologique [psikɔlɔʒik] *adj* psychological.

psychologue [psikɔlɔg] 1 *nmf* psychologist. 2 *adj* psychological.

psychose [psikoz] *nf* MÉD psychosis. || [crainte] obsessive fear.

psychosomatique [psikɔsɔmatik] *adj* psychosomatic.

psychothérapie [psikɔterapi] *nf* psychotherapy.

PTT (*abr de* **Postes, télécommunications et télédiffusion**) *nfpl former French post office and telecommunications network*.

pu [py] *pp* → **pouvoir**.

puant, -e [pɥɑ̃, ɑ̃t] *adj* [fétide] smelly, stinking. || *fam fig* [personne] bumptious, full of oneself.

puanteur [pɥɑ̃tœr] *nf* stink, stench.

pub¹ [pyb] *nf fam* ad, advert *Br*; [métier] advertising.

pub² [pœb] *nm* pub.

pubère [pybɛr] *adj* pubescent.

puberté [pybɛrte] *nf* puberty.

pubis [pybis] *nm* [zone] pubis.

public, -ique [pyblik] *adj* public. ○ **public** *nm* [auditoire] audience; **en ~** in public. || [population] public.

publication [pyblikasjɔ̃] *nf* publication.

publicitaire [pyblisiter] *adj* [campagne] advertising (*avant n*); [vente, film] promotional.

publicité [pyblisite] *nf* [domaine] advertising; ~ **comparative** comparative advertising; ~ **mensongère** misleading advertising, deceptive advertising. || [réclame] advertisement, advert. || [autour d'une affaire] publicity (*U*).

publier [pyblije] *vt* [livre] to publish; [communiqué] to issue, to release.

puce [pys] *nf* [insecte] flea. || INFORM (silicon) chip.

pudeur [pydœr] *nf* [physique] modesty, decency. || [morale] restraint.

pudibond, -e [pydibɔ̃, ɔ̃d] *adj* prudish, prim and proper.

pudique [pydik] *adj* [physiquement] modest, decent. || [moralement] restrained.

puer [pɥe] **1** *vi* to stink; **ça pue ici!** it stinks in here! **2** *vt* to reek of, to stink of.

puéricultrice [pɥerikyltris] *nf* nursery nurse.

puériculture [pɥerikyltyr] *nf* childcare.

puéril, -e [pɥeril] *adj* childish.

Puerto Rico = **Porto Rico**.

pugilat [pyʒila] *nm* fight.

puis [pɥi] *adv* then; **et ~** [d'ailleurs] and moreover ou besides.

puiser [pɥize] *vt* [liquide] to draw; ~ **qqch dans qqch** *fig* to draw ou take sthg from sthg.

puisque [pɥiskə] *conj* [gén] since.

puissance [pɥisɑ̃s] *nf* power. ○ **en puissance** *loc adj* potential.

puissant, -e [pɥisɑ̃, ɑ̃t] *adj* powerful.

puisse, puisses *etc* → **pouvoir**.

puits [pɥi] *nm* [d'eau] well. || [de gisement] shaft; ~ **de pétrole** oil well.

pull [pyl], **pull-over** [pylɔvɛr] (*pl* **pull-overs**) *nm* jumper *Br*, sweater.

pulluler [pylyle] *vi* to swarm.

pulmonaire [pylmɔnɛr] *adj* lung (*avant n*), pulmonary.

pulpe [pylp] *nf* pulp.

pulsation [pylsasjɔ̃] *nf* beat, beating (*U*).

pulsion [pylsjɔ̃] *nf* impulse.

pulvériser [pylverize] *vt* [projeter] to spray. || [détruire] to pulverize; *fig* to smash.

puma [pyma] *nm* puma.

punaise [pynɛz] *nf* [insecte] bug. || [clou] drawing pin *Br*, thumbtack *Am*.

punch [pɔ̃ʃ] *nm* punch.

puni, -e [pyni] *adj* punished.

punir [pynir] *vt*: ~ **qqn (de)** to punish sb (with).

punition [pynisjɔ̃] *nf* punishment.

pupille [pypij] **1** *nf* ANAT pupil. **2** *nmf* [orphelin] ward; ~ **de l'État** ≃ child in care.

pupitre [pypitr] *nm* [d'orateur] lectern; MUS stand. || TECHNOL console. || [d'écolier] desk.

pur, -e [pyr] *adj* [gén] pure. || *fig* [absolu] pure, sheer; ~ **et simple** pure and simple. || *fig & littéraire* [intention] honourable. || [lignes] pure, clean.

purée [pyre] *nf* purée; ~ **de pommes de terre** mashed potatoes.

purement [pyrmɑ̃] *adv* purely; ~ **et simplement** purely and simply.

pureté [pyrte] *nf* [gén] purity. || [de sculpture, de diamant] perfection. || [d'intention] honourableness.

purgatoire [pyrgatwar] *nm* purgatory.

purge [pyrʒ] *nf* MÉD & POLIT purge.

purger [pyrʒe] *vt* MÉD & POLIT to purge. || [radiateur] to bleed. || [peine] to serve.

purifier [pyrifje] *vt* to purify.

purin [pyrɛ̃] *nm* slurry.

puritain, -e [pyritɛ̃, ɛn] **1** *adj* [pudibond] puritanical. **2** *nm, f* [prude] puritan. || RELIG Puritan.

puritanisme [pyritanism] *nm* puritanism; RELIG Puritanism.

pur-sang [pyrsɑ̃] *nm inv* thoroughbred.

purulent, -e [pyrylɑ̃, ɑ̃t] *adj* purulent.

pus [py] *nm* pus.

putréfier [pytrefje] ○ **se putréfier** *vp* to putrefy, to rot.

putsch [putʃ] *nm* uprising, coup.

puzzle [pœzl] *nm* jigsaw (puzzle).

P-V *nm abr de* **procès-verbal**.

pyjama [piʒama] *nm* pyjamas (*pl*).

pylône [pilon] *nm* pylon.

pyramide [piramid] *nf* pyramid.

Pyrénées [pirene] *nfpl*: **les ~** the Pyrenees.

Pyrex® [pirɛks] *nm* Pyrex®.

pyromane [piroman] *nmf* arsonist; MÉD pyromaniac.

python [pitɔ̃] *nm* python.

q, Q [ky] *nm inv* [lettre] q, Q.

QCM (*abr de* **questionnaire à choix multiple**) *nm* multiple choice questionnaire.

QG (*abr de* **quartier général**) *nm* HQ.

QI (*abr de* **quotient intellectuel**) *nm* IQ.

qqch (*abr de* **quelque chose**) sthg.

qqn (*abr de* **quelqu'un**) s.o., sb.

quadragénaire [kwadraʒenɛr] *nmf* forty year old.

quadrilatère [kwadrilatɛr] *nm* quadrilateral.

quadrillage [kadrijaʒ] *nm* [de papier, de tissu] criss-cross pattern. ‖ [policier] combing.

quadriller [kadrije] *vt* [papier] to mark with squares. ‖ [ville - suj: rues] to criss-cross; [- suj: police] to comb.

quadrimoteur [kwadrimɔtœr] *nm* four-engined plane.

quadrupède [k(w)adrypɛd] *nm & adj* quadruped.

quadruplés, -ées [k(w)adryple] *nm, f pl* quadruplets, quads.

quai [kɛ] *nm* [de gare] platform. ‖ [de port] quay, wharf. ‖ [de rivière] embankment.

qualificatif, -ive [kalifikatif, iv] *adj* qualifying. ○ **qualificatif** *nm* term.

qualification [kalifikasjɔ̃] *nf* [gén] qualification.

qualifier [kalifje] *vt* [gén] to qualify; être qualifié pour qqch/pour faire qqch to be qualified for sthg/to do sthg. ‖ [caractériser]: ~ qqn/qqch de qqch to describe sb/sthg as sthg, to call sb/sthg sthg. ○ **se qualifier** *vp* to qualify.

qualitatif, -ive [kalitatif, iv] *adj* qualitative.

qualité [kalite] *nf* [gén] quality; **de bonne/mauvaise ~** of good/poor quality. ‖ [condition] position, capacity.

quand [kɑ̃] **1** *conj* [lorsque, alors que] when; **~ tu le verras, demande-lui de me téléphoner** when you see him, ask him

to phone me. **2** *adv interr* when; **~ arriveras-tu?** when will you arrive?; **jusqu'à ~ restez-vous?** how long are you staying for? ○ **quand même 1** *loc adv* all the same. **2** *interj*: **~ même, à son âge!** really, at his/her age! ○ **quand bien même** *loc conj sout* even though, even if.

quant [kɑ̃] ○ **quant à** *loc prép* as for.

quantifier [kɑ̃tifje] *vt* to quantify.

quantitatif, -ive [kɑ̃titatif, iv] *adj* quantitative.

quantité [kɑ̃tite] *nf* [mesure] quantity, amount. ‖ [abondance]: **(une) ~ de** a great many, a lot of; **en ~** in large numbers.

quarantaine [karɑ̃tɛn] *nf* [nombre]: **une ~ de** about forty. ‖ [âge]: **avoir la ~** to be in one's forties. ‖ [isolement] quarantine.

quarante [karɑ̃t] *adj num & nm* forty; *voir aussi* **six**.

quarantième [karɑ̃tjɛm] *adj num, nm & nmf* fortieth; *voir aussi* **sixième**.

quart [kar] *nm* [fraction] quarter; **deux heures moins le ~** (a) quarter to two, (a) quarter of two *Am*; **deux heures et ~** (a) quarter past two, (a) quarter after two *Am*; **il est moins le ~** it's (a) quarter to; **un ~ d'heure** a quarter of an hour. ‖ NAVIG watch. ‖ **~ de finale** quarter final.

quartier [kartje] *nm* [de ville] area, district. ‖ [de fruit] piece; [de viande] quarter. ‖ [héraldique, de lune] quarter. ‖ (*gén pl*) MIL quarters (*pl*); **~ général** headquarters (*pl*).

quartz [kwarts] *nm* quartz; **montre à ~** quartz watch.

quasi [kazi] *adv* almost, nearly.

quasi- [kazi] *préfixe* near.

quasiment [kazimɑ̃] *adv fam* almost, nearly.

quatorze [katɔrz] *adj num & nm* fourteen; *voir aussi* **six**.

quatorzième [katɔrzjɛm] *adj num, nm & nmf* fourteenth; *voir aussi* **sixième**.

quatrain [katrɛ̃] *nm* quatrain.

quatre [katr] **1** *adj num* four; **monter l'escalier ~ à ~** to take the stairs four at a time; **se mettre en ~ pour qqn** to bend over backwards for sb. **2** *nm* four; *voir aussi* **six**.

quatre-vingt = **quatre-vingts**.

quatre-vingt-dix [katrəvɛ̃dis] *adj num & nm* ninety; *voir aussi* **six**.

quatre-vingt-dixième [katrə-

vɛ̃dizjɛm] *adj num, nm & nmf* ninetieth;
voir aussi **sixième**.

quatre-vingtième [katrəvɛ̃tjɛm] *adj
num, nm & nmf* eightieth; *voir aussi*
sixième.

quatre-vingts, quatre-vingt [katrə-
vɛ̃] *adj num & nm* eighty; *voir aussi* **six**.

quatrième [katrijɛm] 1 *adj num, nm &
nmf* fourth; *voir aussi* **sixième**. 2 *nf* SCOL
≃ ninth grade *Am*.

quatuor [kwatɥɔr] *nm* quartet.

que [k(ə)] 1 *conj* [introduit une subordon-
née] that; **il a dit qu'il viendrait** he said
(that) he'd come. || [introduit une hypo-
thèse] whether; **~ vous le vouliez ou non**
whether you like it or not. || [reprend une
autre conjonction]: **s'il fait beau et ~ nous
avons le temps ...** if the weather is good
and we have time .... || [indique un ordre,
un souhait]: **qu'il entre!** let him come in!
|| [après un présentatif]: **voilà/voici ~ ça
recommence!** here we go again! || [-
comparatif - après moins, plus] than; [-
après autant, aussi, même] as; **plus jeune
~ moi** younger than I (am) ou than me. ||
[seulement]: **ne ... ~** only; **je n'ai qu'une
sœur** I've only got one sister. 2 *pron rel*
[chose, animal] which, that; [personne]
whom, that; **le livre qu'il m'a prêté** the
book (which ou that) he lent me. 3 *pron
interr* what; **~ savez-vous au juste?** what
exactly do you know?; **je me demande ~
faire** I wonder what I should do. 4 *adv
excl*: **qu'elle est belle!** how beautiful she
is!; **~ de monde!** what a lot of people!
○ **c'est que** *loc conj* it's because; **si je
vais me coucher, c'est ~ j'ai sommeil** if
I'm going to bed, it's because I'm tired.
○ **qu'est-ce que** *pron interr* what;
qu'est-ce ~ tu veux encore? what else do
you want? ○ **qu'est-ce qui** *pron interr*
what; **qu'est-ce qui se passe?** what's
going on?

Québec [kebɛk] *nm* [province]: **le ~**
Quebec.

québécois, -e [kebekwa, az] *adj* Quebec (*avant n*). ○ **québécois** *nm* [lan-
gue] Quebec French. ○ **Québécois, -e**
nm, f Quebecker, Quebecois.

quel [kɛl] (*f* **quelle**, *mpl* **quels**, *fpl* **quelles**) 1 *adj interr* [personne] which;
[chose] what, which; **~ livre voulez-
vous?** what ou which book do you want?;
je ne sais ~s sont ses projets I don't
know what his plans are; **quelle heure
est-il?** what time is it?, what's the time?
2 *adj excl*: **~ idiot!** what an idiot!; **quelle**

honte! the shame of it! 3 *adj indéf*: **~ que**
(+ *subjonctif*) [chose, animal] whatever;
[personne] whoever; **il se baigne, ~ que
soit le temps** he goes swimming whatever the weather. 4 *pron interr* which
(one); **de vous trois, ~ est le plus jeune?**
which (one) of you three is the youngest?

quelconque [kɛlkɔ̃k] *adj* [n'importe le-
quel] any; **donner un prétexte ~** to give
any old excuse; **si pour une raison ~ ...** if
for any reason ...; **une ~ observation**
some remark or other. || (*après n*) *péj*
[banal] ordinary, mediocre.

quelque [kɛlk(ə)] 1 *adj indéf* some; **à ~
distance de là** some way away (from
there); **j'ai ~s lettres à écrire** I have some
ou a few letters to write; **les ~s fois où
j'étais absent** the few times I wasn't
there; **les ~s 200 francs qu'il m'a prêtés**
the 200 francs or so (that) he lent me; **~
route que je prenne** whatever route I
take; **~ peu** somewhat, rather. 2 *adv* [en-
viron] about; **200 francs et ~** some ou
about 200 francs; **il est midi et ~** *fam* it's
just after midday.

quelque chose [kɛlkəʃoz] *pron indéf*
something; **~ de différent** something different; **~ d'autre** something else; **tu veux
boire ~?** do you want something ou anything to drink?; **apporter un petit ~ à
qqn** to give sb a little something; **c'est ~!**
[ton admiratif] it's really something!;
cela m'a fait ~ I really felt it.

quelquefois [kɛlkəfwa] *adv* sometimes,
occasionally.

quelque part [kɛlkəpar] *adv* somewhere; **l'as-tu vu ~?** did you see him anywhere?, have you seen him anywhere?

quelques-uns, quelques-unes [kɛl-
kəzœ̃, yn] *pron indéf* some, a few.

quelqu'un [kɛlkœ̃] *pron indéf m* someone, somebody; **c'est ~ d'ouvert/
d'intelligent** he's/she's a frank/an intelligent person.

quémander [kemɑ̃de] *vt* to beg for; **~
qqch à qqn** to beg sb for sthg.

qu'en-dira-t-on [kɑ̃diratɔ̃] *nm inv fam*
tittle-tattle.

quenelle [kənɛl] *nf* very finely chopped
mixture of fish or chicken cooked in
stock.

querelle [kərɛl] *nf* quarrel.

quereller [kərele] ○ **se quereller** *vp*:
se ~ (**avec**) to quarrel (with).

querelleur, -euse [kərɛlœr, øz] *adj*
quarrelsome.

qu'est-ce que [kɛskə] → **que.**

qu'est-ce qui [kɛski] → **que.**

question [kɛstjɔ̃] nf question; **poser une ~ à qqn** to ask sb a question; **il est ~ de faire qqch** it's a question or matter of doing sthg; **il n'en est pas ~** there is no question of it; **remettre qqn/qqch en ~** to question sb/sthg, to challenge sb/ sthg; **~ subsidiaire** tiebreaker.

questionnaire [kɛstjɔnɛr] nm questionnaire.

questionner [kɛstjɔne] vt to question.

quête [kɛt] nf sout [d'objet, de personne] quest; **se mettre en ~ de** to go in search of. || [d'aumône]: **faire la ~** to take a collection.

quêter [kete] **1** vi to collect. **2** vt fig to seek, to look for.

queue [kø] nf [d'animal] tail; **faire une ~ de poisson à qqn** fig & AUTOM to cut sb up. || [de fruit] stalk. || [de poêle] handle. || [de liste, de classe] bottom; [de file, peloton] rear. || [file] queue Br, line Am; **faire la ~** to queue Br, to stand in line Am; **à la ~ leu leu** in single file.

queue-de-cheval [kødʃəval] (pl **queues-de-cheval**) nf ponytail.

queue-de-pie [kødpi] (pl **queues-de-pie**) nf fam tails (pl).

qui [ki] **1** pron rel (sujet) [personne] who; [chose] which, that; **l'homme ~ parle** the man who's talking; **~ plus est** (and) what's more. || (complément d'objet direct) who; **tu vois ~ je veux dire** you see who I mean; **invite ~ tu veux** invite whoever or anyone you like. || (après une préposition) who, whom; **la personne à ~ je parle** the person I'm talking to, the person to whom I'm talking. || (indéfini): **~ que tu sois** whoever you are. **2** pron interr (sujet) who; **~ es-tu?** who are you? || (complément d'objet, après une préposition) who, whom; **dites-moi ~ vous demandez** tell me who you want to see; **à ~ vas-tu le donner?** who are you going to give it to?, to whom are you going to give it? ○ **qui est-ce qui** pron interr who. ○ **qui est-ce que** pron interr who, whom.

quiche [kiʃ] nf quiche.

quiconque [kikɔ̃k] **1** pron indéf anyone, anybody. **2** pron rel indéf sout anyone who, whoever.

quiétude [kjetyd] nf tranquillity.

quignon [kiɲɔ̃] nm fam hunk.

quille [kij] nf [de bateau] keel.

○ **quilles** nfpl [jeu]: **(jeu de) ~s** skittles (U).

quincaillerie [kɛ̃kajri] nf [magasin] ironmonger's (shop) Br, hardware shop.

quinconce [kɛ̃kɔ̃s] nm: **en ~** in a staggered arrangement.

quinine [kinin] nf quinine.

quinquagénaire [kɛ̃kaʒenɛr] nmf fifty year old.

quinquennal, -e, -aux [kɛ̃kenal, o] adj [plan] five-year (avant n); [élection] five-yearly.

quintal, -aux [kɛ̃tal, o] nm quintal.

quinte [kɛ̃t] nf MUS fifth. ○ **quinte de toux** nf coughing fit.

quintuple [kɛ̃typl] nm & adj quintuple.

quinzaine [kɛ̃zɛn] nf [nombre] fifteen (or so); **une ~ de** about fifteen. || [deux semaines] fortnight Br, two weeks (pl).

quinze [kɛ̃z] **1** adj num fifteen; **dans ~ jours** in a fortnight Br, in two weeks. **2** nm [chiffre] fifteen; voir aussi **six.**

quinzième [kɛ̃zjɛm] adj num, nm & nmf fifteenth; voir aussi **sixième.**

quiproquo [kiprɔko] nm misunderstanding.

quittance [kitɑ̃s] nf receipt.

quitte [kit] adj quits; **en être ~ pour qqch/pour faire qqch** to get off with sthg/doing sthg; **~ à faire qqch** even if it means doing sthg.

quitter [kite] vt [gén] to leave; **ne quittez pas!** [au téléphone] hold the line, please! || [fonctions] to give up. ○ **se quitter** vp to part.

qui-vive [kiviv] nm inv: **être sur le ~** to be on the alert.

quoi [kwa] **1** pron rel (après prép): **ce à ~ je me suis intéressé** what I was interested in; **après ~** after which; **avoir de ~ vivre** to have enough to live on; **avez-vous de ~ écrire?** have you got something to write with?; **merci — il n'y a pas de ~** thank you — don't mention it. **2** pron interr what; **à ~ penses-tu?** what are you thinking about?; **je ne sais pas ~ dire** I don't know what to say; **décide-toi, ~!** fam make your mind up, will you? ○ **quoi que** loc conj (+ subjonctif) whatever; **~ qu'il arrive** whatever happens; **~ qu'il dise** whatever he says; **~ qu'il en soit** be that as it may.

quoique [kwakə] conj although, though.

quolibet [kɔlibɛ] nm sout jeer, taunt.

quota [k(w)ɔta] nm quota.

quotidien, -ienne [kɔtidjɛ̃, jɛn] *adj*
daily. ○ **quotidien** *nm* [routine] daily
life; **au ~** on a day-to-day basis. || [jour-
nal] daily (newspaper).

quotient [kɔsjɑ̃] *nm* quotient; **~ intellectuel** intelligence quotient.

r¹, R [ɛr] *nm inv* [lettre] r, R.

r² *abr de* **rue.**

rabâcher [rabaʃe] **1** *vi fam* to harp on. **2**
vt to go over (and over).

rabais [rabɛ] *nm* reduction, discount.

rabaisser [rabese] *vt* [réduire] to re-
duce; [orgueil] to humble. || [personne] to
belittle. ○ **se rabaisser** *vp* [se déprécier]
to belittle o.s. || [s'humilier]: **se ~ à faire
qqch** to demean o.s. by doing sthg.

rabat [raba] *nm* [partie rabattue] flap.

rabat-joie [rabaʒwa] **1** *nm inv* killjoy. **2**
adj inv: **être ~** to be a killjoy.

rabattre [rabatr] *vt* [col] to turn down.
|| [siège] to tilt back; [couvercle] to shut. ||
[gibier] to drive. ○ **se rabattre** *vp*
[siège] to tilt back; [couvercle] to shut. ||
[voiture, coureur] to cut in. || [se conten-
ter]: **se ~ sur** to fall back on.

rabattu, -e [rabaty] *pp* → **rabattre.**

rabbin [rabɛ̃] *nm* rabbi.

râblé, -e [rable] *adj* stocky.

rabot [rabo] *nm* plane.

raboter [rabɔte] *vt* to plane.

rabougri, -e [rabugri] *adj* [plante]
stunted. || [personne] shrivelled, wizened.

rabrouer [rabrue] *vt* to snub.

raccommodage [rakɔmɔdaʒ] *nm*
mending.

raccommoder [rakɔmɔde] *vt* [vête-
ment] to mend. || *fam fig* [personnes] to
reconcile, to get back together.

raccompagner [rakɔ̃paɲe] *vt* to see
home, to take home.

raccord [rakɔr] *nm* [liaison] join. ||
[pièce] connector, coupling. || CIN link.

raccordement [rakɔrdəmɑ̃] *nm* connection, linking.

raccorder [rakɔrde] *vt*: **~ qqch (à)** to
connect sthg (to), to join sthg (to). ○ **se
raccorder** *vp*: **se ~ à** to be connected to.

raccourci [rakursi] *nm* shortcut.

raccourcir [rakursir] **1** *vt* to shorten. **2**
vi to grow shorter.

raccrocher [rakrɔʃe] **1** *vt* to hang back
up. **2** *vi* [au téléphone]: **~ (au nez de qqn)**
to hang up (on sb), to put the phone
down (on sb). ○ **se raccrocher** *vp*: **se ~
à** to cling to, to hang on to.

race [ras] *nf* [humaine] race; [animale]
breed; **de ~** pedigree; [cheval]
thoroughbred.

racé, -e [rase] *adj* [animal] purebred. ||
[voiture] of distinction.

rachat [raʃa] *nm* [transaction] re-
purchase. || *fig* [de péchés] atonement.

racheter [raʃte] *vt* [acheter en plus-
gén] to buy another; [- pain, lait] to buy
some more. || [acheter après avoir vendu]
to buy back. || *fig* [péché, faute] to atone
for; [défaut, lapsus] to make up for. ||
COMM [société] to buy out. ○ **se racheter** *vp fig* to redeem o.s.

rachitique [raʃitik] *adj* suffering from
rickets.

racial, -e, -iaux [rasjal, jo] *adj* racial.

racine [rasin] *nf* root; [de nez] base; **~
carrée/cubique** MATHS square/cube root.

racisme [rasism] *nm* racism.

raciste [rasist] *nmf & adj* racist.

racketter [rakɛte] *vt*: **~ qqn** to subject
sb to a protection racket.

raclée [rakle] *nf* hiding, thrashing.

racler [rakle] *vt* to scrape. ○ **se racler**
vp: **se ~ la gorge** to clear one's throat.

racoler [rakɔle] *vt fam péj* [suj: prosti-
tuée] to solicit.

racoleur, -euse [rakɔlœr, øz] *adj fam
péj* [air, sourire] come-hither; [publicité]
strident.

racontar [rakɔ̃tar] *nm fam péj* piece of
gossip. ○ **racontars** *nmpl fam péj*
tittle-tattle (*U*).

raconter [rakɔ̃te] *vt* [histoire] to tell, to
relate; [événement] to relate, to tell
about; **~ qqch à qqn** to tell sb sthg, to re-
late sthg to sb. || [ragot, mensonge] to tell.

radar [radar] *nm* radar.

rade [rad] *nf* (natural) harbour.

radeau, -x [rado] *nm* [embarcation]
raft.

radiateur [radjatœr] *nm* radiator.

radiation [radjasjɔ̃] *nf* PHYS radiation.

radical, -e, -aux [radikal, o] *adj* radical. ○ **radical** *nm* [gén] radical. || LING stem.

radier [radje] *vt* to strike off.

radieux, -ieuse [radjø, jøz] *adj* radiant; [soleil] dazzling.

radin, -e [radɛ̃, in] *fam péj* **1** *adj* stingy. **2** *nm, f* skinflint.

radio [radjo] *nf* [station, poste] radio; **à la ~** on the radio. || MÉD: **passer une ~** to have an X-ray, to be X-rayed.

radioactif, -ive [radjoaktif, iv] *adj* radioactive.

radioactivité [radjoaktivite] *nf* radioactivity.

radiodiffuser [radjodifyze] *vt* to broadcast.

radiographie [radjografi] *nf* [technique] radiography. || [image] X-ray.

radiologue [radjolog], **radiologiste** [radjolɔʒist] *nmf* radiologist.

radioréveil, radio-réveil [radjorevej] *nm* radio alarm, clock radio.

radiotélévisé, -e [radjotelevize] *adj* broadcast on both radio and television.

radis [radi] *nm* radish.

radoter [radote] *vi* to ramble.

radoucir [radusir] *vt* to soften. ○ **se radoucir** *vp* [temps] to become milder; [personne] to calm down.

radoucissement [radusismɑ̃] *nm* [d'attitude] softening. || [de température] rise; **un ~ du temps** a spell of milder weather.

rafale [rafal] *nf* [de vent] gust. || [de coups de feu, d'applaudissements] burst.

raffermir [rafɛrmir] *vt* [muscle] to firm up. || *fig* [pouvoir] to strengthen.

raffinage [rafinaʒ] *nm* refining.

raffiné, -e [rafine] *adj* refined.

raffinement [rafinmɑ̃] *nm* refinement.

raffiner [rafine] *vt* to refine.

raffinerie [rafinri] *nf* refinery.

raffoler [rafɔle] *vi*: **~ de qqn/qqch** to adore sb/sthg.

raffut [rafy] *nm fam* row, racket.

rafistoler [rafistɔle] *vt fam* to patch up.

rafle [rafl] *nf* raid.

rafler [rafle] *vt* to swipe.

rafraîchir [rafreʃir] *vt* [nourriture, vin] to chill, to cool; [air] to cool. || [vêtement, appartement] to smarten up; *fig* [mémoire, idées] to refresh. ○ **se rafraîchir** *vp* [se refroidir] to cool (down). || *fam* [personne] to have a drink.

rafraîchissant, -e [rafreʃisɑ̃, ɑ̃t] *adj* refreshing.

rafraîchissement [rafreʃismɑ̃] *nm* [de climat] cooling. || [boisson] cold drink.

raft(ing) [raft(iŋ)] *nm* whitewater rafting.

ragaillardir [ragajardir] *vt fam* to buck up, to perk up.

rage [raʒ] *nf* [fureur] rage; **faire ~** [tempête] to rage. || [maladie] rabies (*U*). ○ **rage de dents** *nf* (raging) toothache.

rager [raʒe] *vi fam* to fume.

rageur, -euse [raʒœr, øz] *adj* bad-tempered.

ragot [rago] *nm* (*gén pl*) *fam* (malicious) rumour, tittle-tattle (*U*).

ragoût [ragu] *nm* stew.

rai [rɛ] *nm littéraire* [de soleil] ray.

raid [rɛd] *nm* AÉRON, BOURSE & MIL raid.

raide [rɛd] **1** *adj* [cheveux] straight. || [tendu - corde] taut; [- membre] stiff. || [pente] steep. || *fam* [histoire] hard to swallow, far-fetched. **2** *adv* [abruptement] steeply. || *loc*: **tomber ~ mort** to fall down dead.

raideur [rɛdœr] *nf* [de membre] stiffness.

raidir [rɛdir] *vt* [muscle] to tense; [corde] to tighten, to tauten. ○ **se raidir** *vp* [se contracter] to grow stiff, to stiffen.

raie [rɛ] *nf* [rayure] stripe. || [dans les cheveux] parting *Br*, part *Am*. || [des fesses] crack. || [poisson] skate.

rail [raj] *nm* rail.

raillerie [rajri] *nf sout* mockery (*U*).

railleur, -euse [rajœr, øz] *sout* **1** *adj* mocking. **2** *nm, f* scoffer.

rainure [rɛnyr] *nf* [longue] groove, channel; [courte] slot.

raisin [rɛzɛ̃] *nm* [fruit] grapes.

raison [rɛzɔ̃] *nf* [gén] reason; **à plus forte ~** all the more (so); **se faire une ~** to resign o.s.; **~ de plus pour faire qqch** all the more reason to do sthg. || [justesse, équité]: **avoir ~** to be right; **donner ~ à qqn** to prove sb right. ○ **à raison de** *loc prép* at (the rate of). ○ **en raison de** *loc prép* owing to, because of.

raisonnable [rɛzɔnabl] *adj* reasonable.

raisonnement [rɛzɔnmɑ̃] *nm* [faculté] reason, power of reasoning. || [argumentation] reasoning, argument.

raisonner [rɛzɔne] **1** *vt* [personne] to reason with. **2** *vi* [penser] to reason. || [discuter]: **~ avec** to reason with.

rajeunir [raʒœnir] **1** *vt* [suj: couleur, vêtement]: **~ qqn** to make sb look younger. || [suj: personne]: **~ qqn de trois ans** to take three years off sb's age. || [vêtement, canapé] to renovate, to do up; [meubles] to modernize. **2** *vi* [personne] to look younger; [se sentir plus jeune] to feel younger ou rejuvenated.

rajouter [raʒute] *vt* to add; **en ~** *fam* to exaggerate.

rajuster [raʒyste], **réajuster** [reaʒyste] *vt* to adjust; [cravate] to straighten. ○ **se rajuster** *vp* to straighten one's clothes.

râle [ral] *nm* moan; [de mort] death rattle.

ralenti, -e [ralãti] *adj* slow. ○ **ralenti** *nm* AUTOM idling speed; **tourner au ~** AUTOM to idle. || CIN slow motion.

ralentir [ralãtir] **1** *vt* [allure, expansion] to slow (down). || [rythme] to slacken. **2** *vi* to slow down ou up.

ralentissement [ralãtismã] *nm* [d'allure, d'expansion] slowing (down). || [de rythme] slackening. || [embouteillage] hold-up. || PHYS deceleration.

râler [rale] *vi* [malade] to breathe with difficulty. || *fam* [grogner] to moan.

ralliement [ralimã] *nm* rallying.

rallier [ralje] *vt* [poste, parti] to join. || [suffrages] to win. || [troupes] to rally. ○ **se rallier** *vp* to rally; **se ~ à** [parti] to join; [cause] to rally to; [avis] to come round to.

rallonge [ralɔ̃ʒ] *nf* [de table] leaf, extension. || [électrique] extension (lead).

rallonger [ralɔ̃ʒe] *vt* to lengthen.

rallumer [ralyme] *vt* [feu, cigarette] to relight; *fig* [querelle] to revive. || [appareil, lumière électrique] to switch (back) on again.

rallye [rali] *nm* rally.

ramadan [ramadã] *nm* Ramadan.

ramassage [ramasaʒ] *nm* collection; **~ scolaire** [service] school bus.

ramasser [ramase] *vt* [récolter, réunir] to gather, to collect. || [prendre] to pick up. || *fam* [claque, rhume] to get. ○ **se ramasser** *vp* [se replier] to crouch.

rambarde [rãbard] *nf* (guard) rail.

rame [ram] *nf* [aviron] oar. || RAIL train. || [de papier] ream.

rameau, -x [ramo] *nm* branch.

ramener [ramne] *vt* [remmener] to take back. || [rapporter, restaurer] to bring back. || [réduire]: **~ qqch à qqch** to reduce sthg to sthg, to bring sthg down to sthg.

ramer [rame] *vi* [rameur] to row.

rameur, -euse [ramœr, øz] *nm, f* rower.

ramification [ramifikasjɔ̃] *nf* [division] branch.

ramolli, -e [ramɔli] *adj* soft; *fig* soft (in the head).

ramollir [ramɔlir] *vt* [beurre] to soften. ○ **se ramollir** *vp* [beurre] to go soft, to soften.

ramoner [ramɔne] *vt* to sweep.

ramoneur [ramɔnœr] *nm* (chimney) sweep.

rampant, -e [rãpã, ãt] *adj* [animal] crawling. || [plante] creeping.

rampe [rãp] *nf* [d'escalier] banister, handrail. || [d'accès] ramp; **~ de lancement** launch pad. || THÉÂTRE: **la ~** the footlights (*pl*).

ramper [rãpe] *vi* [animal, soldat, enfant] to crawl. || [plante] to creep.

rance [rãs] *adj* [beurre] rancid.

rancir [rãsir] *vi* to go rancid.

rancœur [rãkœr] *nf* rancour, resentment.

rançon [rãsɔ̃] *nf* ransom; *fig* price.

rancune [rãkyn] *nf* rancour, spite; **garder** ou **tenir ~ à qqn de qqch** to hold a grudge against sb for sthg; **sans ~!** no hard feelings!

rancunier, -ière [rãkynje, jɛr] *adj* vindictive, spiteful.

randonnée [rãdɔne] *nf* [à pied] walk. || [à bicyclette] ride; [en voiture] drive.

randonneur, -euse [rãdɔnœr, øz] *nm, f* walker, rambler.

rang [rã] *nm* [d'objets, de personnes] row; **se mettre en ~ par deux** to line up in twos. || MIL rank. || [position sociale] station. || *Can* [peuplement rural] rural district. || *Can* [chemin] country road.

rangé, -e [rãʒe] *adj* [sérieux] well-ordered, well-behaved.

rangée [rãʒe] *nf* row.

rangement [rãʒmã] *nm* tidying up.

ranger [rãʒe] *vt* [chambre] to tidy. || [objets] to arrange. || [voiture] to park. ○ **se ranger** *vp* [élèves, soldats] to line up. || [voiture] to pull in. || [piéton] to step aside. || [s'assagir] to settle down.

ranimer [ranime] *vt* [personne] to revive, to bring round. || [feu] to rekindle. || *fig* [sentiment] to reawaken.

rapace [rapas] **1** *nm* bird of prey. **2** *adj* [cupide] rapacious, grasping.

rapatrier [rapatrije] *vt* to repatriate.

râpe [rap] *nf* [de cuisine] grater.

râpé, -e [rape] *adj* CULIN grated. || [manteau] threadbare. || *fam* [raté]: **c'est ~!** we've had it!

râper [rape] *vt* CULIN to grate.

râpeux, -euse [rapø, øz] *adj* [tissu] rough. || [vin] harsh.

rapide [rapid] **1** *adj* [gén] rapid. || [train, coureur] fast. || [musique, intelligence] lively, quick. **2** *nm* [train] express (train). || [de fleuve] rapid.

rapidement [rapidmɑ̃] *adv* rapidly.

rapidité [rapidite] *nf* rapidity.

rapiécer [rapjese] *vt* to patch.

rappel [rapɛl] *nm* [de réservistes, d'ambassadeur] recall. || [souvenir] reminder; ~ **à l'ordre** call to order. || [de paiement] back pay. || [de vaccination] booster. || [au spectacle] curtain call, encore. || SPORT abseiling; **descendre en ~ to abseil** (down).

rappeler [raple] *vt* [gén] to call back; ~ **qqn à qqch** *fig* to bring sb back to sthg. || [faire penser à]: ~ **qqch à qqn** to remind sb of sthg. ○ **se rappeler** *vp* to remember.

rapport [rapɔr] *nm* [corrélation] link, connection. || [compte-rendu] report. || [profit] return, yield. || MATHS ratio. ○ **rapports** *nmpl* [relations] relations. || [sexuels]: ~**s** (**sexuels**) intercourse (*sg*). ○ **par rapport à** *loc prép* in comparison to, compared with.

rapporter [rapɔrte] *vt* to bring back. ○ **se rapporter** *vp*: **se ~ à** to refer ou relate to.

rapporteur, -euse [rapɔrtœr, øz] *nm, f* sneak, telltale. ○ **rapporteur** *nm* [de commission] rapporteur. || GÉOM protractor.

rapprochement [raprɔʃmɑ̃] *nm* [d'objets, de personnes] bringing together. || *fig* [entre événements] link, connection. || *fig* [de pays, de parti] rapprochement.

rapprocher [raprɔʃe] *vt* [mettre plus près]: ~ **qqn/qqch de qqch** to bring sb/ sthg nearer to sthg, to bring sb/sthg closer to sthg. || *fig* [personnes] to bring together. || *fig* [idée, texte]: ~ **qqch (de)** to compare sthg (with). ○ **se rapprocher** *vp* [approcher]: **se ~ (de qqn/qqch)** to approach (sb/sthg). || [se ressembler] [se ~ **de qqch** to be similar to sthg. || [se réconcilier]: **se ~ de qqn** to become closer to sb.

rapt [rapt] *nm* abduction.

raquette [rakɛt] *nf* [de tennis, de squash] racket; [de ping-pong] bat. || [à neige] snowshoe.

rare [rar] *adj* [peu commun, peu fréquent] rare; **ses ~s amis** his few friends.

raréfier [rarefje] *vt* to rarefy. ○ **se raréfier** *vp* to become rarefied.

rarement [rarmɑ̃] *adv* rarely.

rareté [rarte] *nf* [de denrées, de nouvelles] scarcity. || [de visites, de lettres] infrequency. || [objet précieux] rarity.

ras, -e [ra, raz] *adj* [herbe, poil] short. || [mesure] full. ○ **ras** *adv* short; **à ~ de** level with; **en avoir ~ le bol** *fam* to be fed up.

rasade [razad] *nf* glassful.

rasage [razaʒ] *nm* shaving.

rasant, -e [razɑ̃, ɑ̃t] *adj* [lumière] low-angled. || *fam* [film, discours] boring.

raser [raze] *vt* [barbe, cheveux] to shave off. || [mur, sol] to hug. || [village] to raze. || *fam* [personne] to bore. ○ **se raser** *vp* [avec rasoir] to shave.

ras-le-bol [ralbɔl] *nm inv fam* discontent.

rasoir [razwar] **1** *nm* razor; ~ **électrique** electric shaver. **2** *adj inv fam* boring.

rassasier [rasazje] *vt* to satisfy.

rassemblement [rasɑ̃bləmɑ̃] *nm* [foule] crowd, gathering. || [union, parti] union. || MIL parade; ~! fall in!

rassembler [rasɑ̃ble] *vt* [personnes, documents] to collect, to gather. || [courage] to summon up; [idées] to collect. ○ **se rassembler** *vp* [manifestants] to assemble. || [famille] to get together.

rasseoir [raswar] ○ **se rasseoir** *vp* to sit down again.

rassis, -e [rasi, iz] *adj* [pain] stale.

rassurant, -e [rasyrɑ̃, ɑ̃t] *adj* reassuring.

rassuré, -e [rasyre] *adj* confident, at ease.

rassurer [rasyre] *vt* to reassure.

rat [ra] *nm* rat.

ratatiné, -e [ratatine] *adj* [fruit, personne] shrivelled.

rate [rat] *nf* [animal] female rat. || [organe] spleen.

raté, -e [rate] *nm, f* [personne] failure. ○ **raté** *nm* (*gén pl*) AUTOM misfiring (*U*); **faire des ~s** to misfire.

râteau, -x [rato] *nm* rake.

rater [rate] **1** *vt* [train, occasion] to miss. || [plat, affaire] to make a mess of; [examen] to fail. **2** *vi* to go wrong.

ratification [ratifikasjɔ̃] *nf* ratification.

ratifier [ratifje] *vt* to ratify.

ration [rasjɔ̃] *nf* [quantité] portion; *fig* share.

rationaliser [rasjɔnalize] *vt* to rationalize.

rationnel, -elle [rasjɔnɛl] *adj* rational.

rationnement [rasjɔnmɑ̃] *nm* rationing.

rationner [rasjɔne] *vt* to ration.

ratissage [ratisaʒ] *nm* [de jardin] raking. || [de quartier] search.

ratisser [ratise] *vt* [jardin] to rake. || [quartier] to search, to comb.

raton [ratɔ̃] *nm* ZOOL young rat. ○ **raton laveur** *nm* racoon.

RATP (*abr de* Régie autonome des transports parisiens) *nf* Paris transport authority.

rattacher [rataʃe] *vt* [attacher de nouveau] to do up, to fasten again. || [relier]: ~ qqch à to join sthg to; *fig* to link sthg with. || [unir]: ~ qqn à to bind sb to. ○ **se rattacher** *vp*: se ~ à to be linked to.

rattrapage [ratrapaʒ] *nm* SCOL: **cours de ~** remedial class.

rattraper [ratrape] *vt* [animal, prisonnier] to recapture. || [temps]: **le temps perdu** to make up for lost time. || [rejoindre] to catch up with. || [erreur] to correct. || [personne qui tombe] to catch. ○ **se rattraper** *vp* [se retenir]: **se ~ à qqn/qqch** to catch hold of sb/sthg. || [se faire pardonner] to make amends.

rature [ratyr] *nf* alteration.

rauque [rok] *adj* hoarse, husky.

ravagé, -e [ravaʒe] *adj fam* [fou]: **être ~** to be off one's head.

ravager [ravaʒe] *vt* [gén] to devastate, to ravage.

ravages [ravaʒ] *nmpl* [de troupes, d'inondation] devastation (*sg*).

ravaler [ravale] *vt* [façade] to clean, to restore. || [personne]: ~ **qqn au rang de to** lower sb to the level of. || *fig* [larmes, colère] to stifle, to hold back.

ravauder [ravode] *vt* to mend, to repair.

ravi, -e [ravi] *adj*: ~ **(de)** delighted (with); ~ **de vous connaître** pleased to meet you.

ravin [ravɛ̃] *nm* ravine, gully.

raviolis [ravjɔli] *nmpl* ravioli (*U*).

ravir [ravir] *vt* [charmer] to delight; **à ~** beautifully.

raviser [ravize] ○ **se raviser** *vp* to change one's mind.

ravissant, -e [ravisɑ̃, ɑ̃t] *adj* delightful, beautiful.

ravisseur, -euse [ravisœr, øz] *nm, f* abductor.

ravitaillement [ravitajmɑ̃] *nm* [en denrées] resupplying; [en carburant] refuelling.

ravitailler [ravitaje] *vt* [en denrées] to resupply; [en carburant] to refuel.

raviver [ravive] *vt* [feu] to rekindle. || [couleurs] to brighten up. || *fig* [douleur] to revive. || [plaie] to reopen.

rayer [reje] *vt* [disque, vitre] to scratch. || [nom, mot] to cross out.

rayon [rejɔ̃] *nm* [de lumière] beam, ray. || (*gén pl*) [radiation] radiation (*U*); ~ **laser** laser beam; **~s X** X-rays. || [de roue] spoke. || GÉOM radius; **dans un ~ de** *fig* within a radius of. || [étagère] shelf. || [dans un magasin] department.

rayonnant, -e [rejɔnɑ̃, ɑ̃t] *adj litt & fig* radiant.

rayonnement [rejɔnmɑ̃] *nm* [gén] radiance. || PHYS radiation.

rayonner [rejɔne] *vi* [soleil] to shine; ~ **de joie** *fig* to radiate happiness. || [touriste] to tour around (*from a base*).

rayure [rejyr] *nf* [sur étoffe] stripe. || [sur disque, sur meuble] scratch.

raz [ra] ○ **raz de marée** *nm* tidal wave; POLIT & *fig* landslide.

razzia [razja] *nf fam* raid.

RDA (*abr de* République démocratique allemande) *nf* GDR.

RdC *abr de* rez-de-chaussée.

ré [re] *nm inv* MUS D; [chanté] re.

réacteur [reaktœr] *nm* [d'avion] jet engine; ~ **nucléaire** nuclear reactor.

réaction [reaksjɔ̃] *nf*: ~ **(à/contre)** reaction (to/against).

réactionnaire [reaksjɔnɛr] *nmf & adj péj* reactionary.

réactiver [reaktive] *vt* to reactivate.

réactualiser [reaktɥalize] *vt* [moderniser] to update, to bring up to date.

réadapter [readapte] *vt* to readapt.

réagir [reaʒir] *vi*: ~ **(à/contre)** to react (to/against); ~ **sur** to affect.

réajuster = **rajuster**.

réalisable [realizabl] *adj* [projet] feasible. || FIN realizable.

réalisateur, -trice [realizatœr, tris] *nm, f* CIN & TÉLÉ director.

réaliser [realize] *vt* [projet] to carry out; [ambitions, rêves] to achieve, to realize. || CIN & TÉLÉ to produce. || [s'apercevoir de] to realize. ○ **se réaliser** *vp* [ambition] to be realized; [rêve] to come true.

réaliste [realist] **1** *nmf* realist. **2** *adj* [personne, objectif] realistic. || ART & LITTÉRATURE realist.

réalité [realite] *nf* reality; **en ~** in reality.

réaménagement [reamena3mɑ̃] *nm* [de projet] restructuring.

réamorcer [reamɔrse] *vt* to start up again.

réanimation [reanimasjɔ̃] *nf* resuscitation; **en ~** in intensive care.

réanimer [reanime] *vt* to resuscitate.

réapparaître [reaparɛtr] *vi* to reappear.

rébarbatif, -ive [rebarbatif, iv] *adj* [travail] daunting.

rebâtir [rɑbatir] *vt* to rebuild.

rebattu, -e [rɑbaty] *adj* overworked, hackneyed.

rebelle [rɑbɛl] *adj* [personne] rebellious; [troupes] rebel (*avant n*). || [mèche, boucle] unruly.

rebeller [rɑbele] ○ **se rebeller** *vp*: **se ~ (contre)** to rebel (against).

rébellion [rebeljɔ̃] *nf* rebellion.

rebiffer [rɑbife] ○ **se rebiffer** *vp fam*: **se ~ (contre)** to rebel (against).

reboiser [rɑbwaze] *vt* to reafforest.

rebond [rɑbɔ̃] *nm* bounce.

rebondir [rɑbɔ̃dir] *vi* [objet] to bounce; [contre mur] to rebound. || *fig* [affaire] to come to life (again).

rebondissement [rɑbɔ̃dismɑ̃] *nm* [d'affaire] new development.

rebord [rɑbɔr] *nm* [de table] edge; [de fenêtre] sill, ledge.

reboucher [rɑbuʃe] *vt* [bouteille] to put the cork back in, to recork; [trou] to fill in.

rebours [rɑbur] ○ **à rebours** *loc adv* the wrong way.

rebrousse-poil [rɑbruspwal] ○ **à rebrousse-poil** *loc adv* the wrong way; **prendre qqn à ~** *fig* to rub sb up the wrong way.

rebrousser [rɑbruse] *vt* to brush back; **~ chemin** *fig* to retrace one's steps.

rébus [rebys] *nm* rebus.

rebut [rɑby] *nm* scrap; **mettre qqch au ~** to get rid of sthg, to scrap sthg.

rebuter [rɑbyte] *vt* [suj: travail] to dishearten.

récalcitrant, -e [rekalsitrɑ̃, ɑ̃t] *adj* recalcitrant, stubborn.

recaler [rɑkale] *vt fam* to fail.

récapitulatif, -ive [rekapitylatif, iv] *adj* summary (*avant n*). ○ **récapitulatif** *nm* summary.

récapituler [rekapityle] *vt* to recapitulate, to recap.

recel [rɑsɛl] *nm* [délit] possession of stolen goods.

receleur, -euse [rɑsɑlœr, øz] *nm, f* receiver (*of stolen goods*).

récemment [resamɑ̃] *adv* recently.

recensement [rɑsɑ̃smɑ̃] *nm* [de population] census. || [d'objets] inventory.

recenser [rɑsɑ̃se] *vt* [population] to take a census of. || [objets] to take an inventory of.

récent, -e [resɑ̃, ɑ̃t] *adj* recent.

recentrer [rɑsɑ̃tre] *vt* to refocus.

récépissé [resepise] *nm* receipt.

récepteur, -trice [reseptœr, tris] *adj* receiving. ○ **récepteur** *nm* receiver.

réception [resepsjɔ̃] *nf* [gén] reception. || [de marchandises] receipt. || [bureau] reception (desk). || SPORT [de sauteur, skieur] landing.

réceptionner [resepsjone] *vt* [marchandises] to take delivery of.

réceptionniste [resepsjonist] *nmf* receptionist.

récession [resesjɔ̃] *nf* recession.

recette [rɑsɛt] *nf* COMM takings (*pl*). || CULIN recipe.

recevable [rɑsɑvabl] *adj* [excuse, offre] acceptable. || JUR admissible.

receveur, -euse [rɑsɑvœr, øz] *nm, f* ADMIN: **~ des impôts** tax collector; **~ des postes** postmaster (*f* postmistress).

recevoir [rɑsɑvwar] *vt* [gén] to receive. || [coup] to get, to receive. || [invités] to entertain; [client] to see. || SCOL & UNIV: **être reçu à un examen** to pass an exam. ○ **se recevoir** *vp* SPORT to land.

rechange [rɑʃɑ̃ʒ] ○ **de rechange** *loc adj* spare; *fig* alternative.

réchapper [reʃape] *vi*: **~ de** to survive.

recharge [rɑʃarʒ] *nf* [cartouche] refill.

rechargeable [rɑʃarʒabl] *adj* [batterie] rechargeable; [briquet] refillable.

réchaud [reʃo] *nm* (portable) stove.

réchauffé, -e [reʃofe] *adj* [plat] reheated; *fig* rehashed.

réchauffement [reʃofmɑ̃] *nm* warming (up).

réchauffer [reʃofe] *vt* [nourriture] to reheat. || [personne] to warm up. ○ **se réchauffer** *vp* to warm up.

rêche [rɛʃ] *adj* rough.

recherche [rɑʃɛrʃ] *nf* [quête & INFORM] search; **être à la ~ de** to be in search of; **faire OU effectuer des ~s** to make inquiries. || SCIENCE research; **faire de la ~** to do research. || [raffinement] elegance.

recherché, -e [rəʃɛrʃe] *adj* [ouvrage] sought-after. || [raffiné - vocabulaire] refined; [- mets] exquisite.

rechercher [rəʃɛrʃe] *vt* [objet, personne] to search for, to hunt for.

rechigner [rəʃiɲe] *vi*: ~ à to balk at.

rechute [rəʃyt] *nf* relapse.

récidiver [residive] *vi* JUR to commit another offence. || MÉD to recur.

récidiviste [residivist] *nmf* repeat ou persistent offender.

récif [resif] *nm* reef.

récipient [resipjā] *nm* container.

réciproque [resiprɔk] **1** *adj* reciprocal. **2** *nf*: **la ~** the reverse.

réciproquement [resiprɔkmā] *adv* mutually; **et ~** and vice versa.

récit [resi] *nm* story.

récital, -als [resital] *nm* recital.

récitation [resitasjɔ̃] *nf* recitation.

réciter [resite] *vt* to recite.

réclamation [reklamasjɔ̃] *nf* complaint; **faire/déposer une ~** to make/lodge a complaint.

réclame [reklam] *nf* [annonce] advert, advertisement. || [promotion]: **en ~** on special offer.

réclamer [reklame] *vt* [demander] to ask for, to request; [avec insistance] to demand. || [nécessiter] to require, to demand.

reclasser [rəklase] *vt* [dossiers] to refile. || ADMIN to regrade.

réclusion [reklyzjɔ̃] *nf* imprisonment; ~ **à perpétuité** life imprisonment.

recoiffer [rəkwafe] ◯ **se recoiffer** *vp* to do one's hair again.

recoin [rəkwɛ̃] *nm* nook.

recoller [rəkɔle] *vt* [objet brisé] to stick back together.

récolte [rekɔlt] *nf* [AGRIC - action] harvesting (*U*), gathering (*U*); [- produit] harvest, crop. || *fig* collection.

récolter [rekɔlte] *vt* to harvest; *fig* to collect.

recommandable [rəkɔmādabl] *adj* commendable; **peu ~** undesirable.

recommandation [rəkɔmādasjɔ̃] *nf* recommendation.

recommandé, -e [rəkɔmāde] *adj* [envoi] registered; **envoyer qqch en ~** to send sthg by registered post *Br* ou mail *Am*. || [conseillé] advisable.

recommander [rəkɔmāde] *vt* to recommend; ~ **à qqn de faire qqch** to advise sb to do sthg.

recommencer [rəkɔmāse] **1** *vt* [travail] to start ou begin again; ~ **à faire qqch** to start ou begin doing sthg again. **2** *vi* to start ou begin again; **ne recommence pas!** don't do that again!

récompense [rekɔ̃pɑ̃s] *nf* reward.

récompenser [rekɔ̃pɑ̃se] *vt* to reward.

recompter [rəkɔ̃te] *vt* to recount.

réconciliation [rekɔ̃siljasjɔ̃] *nf* reconciliation.

réconcilier [rekɔ̃silje] *vt* to reconcile.

reconduire [rəkɔ̃dɥir] *vt* [personne] to accompany, to take. || [politique, bail] to renew.

reconduit, -e [rəkɔ̃dɥi, ɥit] *pp* → **reconduire**.

réconfort [rekɔ̃fɔr] *nm* comfort.

réconfortant, -e [rekɔ̃fɔrtā, āt] *adj* comforting.

réconforter [rekɔ̃fɔrte] *vt* to comfort.

reconnaissable [rəkɔnɛsabl] *adj* recognizable.

reconnaissance [rəkɔnɛsɑ̃s] *nf* [gén] recognition. || MIL reconnaissance; **aller/partir en ~** to go out on reconnaissance. || [gratitude] gratitude.

reconnaissant, -e [rəkɔnɛsā, āt] *adj* grateful.

reconnaître [rəkɔnɛtr] *vt* [gén] to recognize. || [erreur] to admit, to acknowledge. || MIL to reconnoitre.

reconnu, -e [rəkɔny] **1** *pp* → **reconnaître**. **2** *adj* well-known.

reconquérir [rəkɔ̃kerir] *vt* to reconquer.

reconquis, -e [rəkɔ̃ki, iz] *pp* → **reconquérir**.

reconsidérer [rəkɔ̃sidere] *vt* to reconsider.

reconstituant, -e [rəkɔ̃stitɥā, āt] *adj* invigorating. ◯ **reconstituant** *nm* tonic.

reconstituer [rəkɔ̃stitɥe] *vt* [puzzle] to put together. || [crime, délit] to reconstruct.

reconstitution [rəkɔ̃stitysjɔ̃] *nf* [de puzzle] putting together. || [de crime, délit] reconstruction.

reconstruction [rəkɔ̃stryksjɔ̃] *nf* reconstruction, rebuilding.

reconstruire [rəkɔ̃strɥir] *vt* to reconstruct, to rebuild.

reconstruit, -e [rəkɔ̃strɥi, ɥit] *pp* → **reconstruire**.

reconversion [rəkɔ̃versjɔ̃] *nf* [d'employé] redeployment. || [d'usine, de société] conversion.

reconvertir [rəkɔ̃vɛrtir] *vt* [employé] to redeploy. ○ **se reconvertir** *vp*: se ~ dans to move into.

recopier [rəkɔpje] *vt* to copy out.

record [rəkɔr] **1** *nm* record; détenir/améliorer/battre un ~ to hold/improve/beat a record. **2** *adj inv* record (*avant n*).

recoucher [rəkuʃe] ○ **se recoucher** *vp* to go back to bed.

recoudre [rəkudr] *vt* to sew (up) again.

recoupement [rəkupmɑ̃] *nm* cross-check; par ~ by cross-checking.

recouper [rəkupe] ○ **se recouper** *vp* [lignes] to intersect. ‖ [témoignages] to match up.

recourir [rəkurir] *vi*: ~ à [médecin, agence] to turn to; [force, mensonge] to resort to.

recours [rəkur] *nm* [emploi]: **avoir** ~ à [médecin, agence] to turn to; [force, mensonge] to resort to, to have recourse to. ‖ [solution] solution, way out; **en dernier** ~ as a last resort. ‖ JUR action.

recouvert, -e [rəkuver, ɛrt] *pp* → recouvrir.

recouvrir [rəkuvrir] *vt* [gén] to cover. ○ **se recouvrir** *vp* [surface]: se ~ (de) to be covered (with).

recracher [rəkraʃe] *vt* to spit out.

récréatif, -ive [rekreatif, iv] *adj* entertaining.

récréation [rekreasjɔ̃] *nf* [détente] relaxation, recreation. ‖ SCOL break.

recréer [rəkree] *vt* to recreate.

récrimination [rekriminasjɔ̃] *nf* complaint.

récrire [rekrir], **réécrire** [reekrir] *vt* to rewrite.

recroqueviller [rəkrɔkvije] ○ **se recroqueviller** *vp* to curl up.

recru, -e [rəkry] *adj*: ~ de fatigue *littéraire* exhausted. ○ **recrue** *nf* recruit.

recrudescence [rəkrydesɑ̃s] *nf* renewed outbreak.

recrutement [rəkrytmɑ̃] *nm* recruitment.

recruter [rəkryte] *vt* to recruit.

rectal, -e, -aux [rɛktal, o] *adj* rectal.

rectangle [rɛktɑ̃gl] *nm* rectangle.

rectangulaire [rɛktɑ̃gyler] *adj* rectangular.

recteur [rɛktœr] *nm* SCOL *chief administrative officer of an education authority.*

rectificatif, -ive [rɛktifikatif, iv] *adj* correcting. ○ **rectificatif** *nm* correction.

rectification [rɛktifikasjɔ̃] *nf* [correction] correction. ‖ [de tir] adjustment.

rectifier [rɛktifje] *vt* [tir] to adjust. ‖ [erreur] to rectify, to correct.

rectiligne [rɛktiliɲ] *adj* rectilinear.

recto [rɛkto] *nm* right side; ~ verso on both sides.

rectorat [rɛktɔra] *nm* SCOL *offices of the education authority.*

reçu, -e [rəsy] *pp* → recevoir. ○ **reçu** *nm* receipt.

recueil [rəkœj] *nm* collection.

recueillement [rəkœjmɑ̃] *nm* meditation.

recueillir [rəkœjir] *vt* [fonds] to collect. ‖ [suffrages] to win. ‖ [enfant] to take in. ○ **se recueillir** *vp* to meditate.

recul [rəkyl] *nm* [mouvement arrière] step backwards; MIL retreat. ‖ [d'arme à feu] recoil. ‖ [d'inflation, de chômage]: ~ (de) downturn (in). ‖ *fig* [retrait]: **avec du** ~ with hindsight.

reculé, -e [rəkyle] *adj* distant.

reculer [rəkyle] **1** *vt* [voiture] to back up. ‖ [date] to put back, to postpone. **2** *vi* [aller en arrière] to move backwards; [voiture] to reverse. ‖ [maladie, pauvreté] to be brought under control.

reculons [rəkylɔ̃] ○ **à reculons** *adv* backwards.

récupération [rekyperasjɔ̃] *nf* salvage.

récupérer [rekypere] **1** *vt* [objet] to get back. ‖ [déchets] to salvage. ‖ [journée] to make up. **2** *vi* to recover.

récurer [rekyre] *vt* to scour.

récuser [rekyze] *vt* JUR to challenge. ‖ *sout* [refuser] to reject.

recyclage [rəsiklaʒ] *nm* [d'employé] retraining. ‖ [de déchets] recycling.

recycler [rəsikle] *vt* [employé] to retrain. ‖ [déchets] to recycle. ○ **se recycler** *vp* [employé] to retrain.

rédacteur, -trice [redaktœr, tris] *nm, f* [de journal] subeditor; [d'ouvrage de référence] editor; ~ **en chef** editor-in-chief.

rédaction [redaksjɔ̃] *nf* [de texte] editing. ‖ SCOL essay. ‖ [personnel] editorial staff.

redécouvrir [rədekuvrir] *vt* to rediscover.

redéfinir [rədefinir] *vt* to redefine.

redemander [rədəmɑ̃de] *vt* to ask again for.

rédemption [redɑ̃psjɔ̃] *nf* redemption.

redescendre [rədəsãdr] **1** *vt* (*aux:* *avoir*) [escalier] to go/come down again. || [objet - d'une étagère] to take down again. **2** *vi* (*aux: être*) to go/come down again.

redevable [rədəvabl] *adj*: être ~ à qqn de qqch [service] to be indebted to sb for sthg.

redevance [rədəvãs] *nf* [de radio, télévision] licence fee; [téléphonique] rental (fee).

rédhibitoire [redibitwar] *adj* [défaut] crippling; [prix] prohibitive.

rediffusion [rədifyzjɔ̃] *nf* repeat.

rédiger [rediʒe] *vt* to write.

redire [rədir] *vt* to repeat; avoir ou trouver à ~ à qqch *fig* to find fault with sthg.

redistribuer [rədistribɥe] *vt* to redistribute.

redit, -e [rədi, it] *pp* → redire.

redite [rədit] *nf* repetition.

redonner [rədɔne] *vt* to give back; [confiance, forces] to restore.

redoublant, -e [rədublã, ãt] *nm, f* pupil who is repeating a year.

redoubler [rəduble] **1** *vt* SCOL to repeat. **2** *vi* to intensify.

redoutable [rədutabl] *adj* formidable.

redouter [rədute] *vt* to fear.

redressement [rədrɛsmã] *nm* [de pays, d'économie] recovery. || JUR: ~ fiscal payment of back taxes.

redresser [rədrɛse] **1** *vt* [poteau, arbre] to put ou set upright; ~ la tête to raise one's head. || [situation] to set right. **2** *vi* AUTOM to straighten up. ○ se redresser *vp* [personne] to stand ou sit straight. || [pays] to recover.

réducteur, -trice [redyktœr, tris] *adj* [limitatif] simplistic.

réduction [redyksjɔ̃] *nf* [gén] reduction. || MÉD setting.

réduire [redɥir] **1** *vt* [gén] to reduce; ~ en to reduce to. || MÉD to set. || Helv [ranger] to put away. **2** *vi* CULIN to reduce.

réduit, -e [redɥi, ɥit] **1** *pp* → réduire. **2** *adj* reduced. ○ réduit *nm* [local] small room.

rééchelonner [reeʃlɔne] *vt* to reschedule.

réécrire = récrire.

réédition [reedisjɔ̃] *nf* new edition.

rééducation [reedykasjɔ̃] *nf* [de délinquant, malade] rehabilitation.

réel, -elle [reɛl] *adj* real.

réélection [reelɛksjɔ̃] *nf* re-election.

réellement [reɛlmã] *adv* really.

rééquilibrer [reekilibre] *vt* to balance (again).

réévaluer [reevalɥe] *vt* to revalue.

réexpédier [reɛkspedje] *vt* to send back.

réf. (*abr de référence*). ref.

refaire [rəfɛr] *vt* [faire de nouveau - travail, devoir] to do again; [- voyage] to make again. || [mur, toit] to repair.

refait, -e [rəfɛ, ɛt] *pp* → refaire.

réfection [refɛksjɔ̃] *nf* repair.

réfectoire [refɛktwar] *nm* refectory.

référence [referãs] *nf* reference; faire ~ à to refer to.

référendum [referɛ̃dɔm] *nm* referendum.

référer [refere] *vi*: en ~ à qqn to refer the matter to sb.

refermer [rəfɛrme] *vt* to close ou shut again.

réfléchi, -e [refleʃi] *adj* [action] considered. || [personne] thoughtful. || GRAM reflexive.

réfléchir [refleʃir] **1** *vt* [refléter] to reflect. **2** *vi* to think, to reflect; ~ à ou sur qqch to think about sthg.

reflet [rəflɛ] *nm* [image] reflection. || [de lumière] glint.

refléter [rəflete] *vt* to reflect. ○ se refléter *vp* [se réfléchir] to be reflected. || [transparaître] to be mirrored.

refleurir [rəflœrir] *vi* [fleurir à nouveau] to flower again.

réflexe [reflɛks] *nm* reflex.

réflexion [reflɛksjɔ̃] *nf* [de lumière, d'ondes] reflection. || [pensée] reflection, thought. || [remarque] remark.

refluer [rəflɥe] *vi* [liquide] to flow back. || [foule] to flow back.

reflux [rəfly] *nm* [d'eau] ebb.

refonte [rəfɔ̃t] *nf* [de métal] remelting. || [d'ouvrage] recasting. || [d'institution, de système] overhaul, reshaping.

reforestation [rəfɔrɛstasjɔ̃] *nf* reforestation.

réformateur, -trice [reformatœr, tris] **1** *adj* reforming. **2** *nm, f* [personne] reformer. || RELIG Reformer.

réforme [reform] *nf* reform.

reformer [rəfɔrme] *vt* to re-form.

réformer [reforme] *vt* [améliorer] to reform, to improve. || MIL to invalid out.

réformiste [reformist] *adj & nmf* reformist.

refoulé, -e [rəfule] **1** *adj* repressed, frustrated. **2** *nm, f* repressed person.

refouler [rəfule] vt [personnes] to repel, to repulse. ‖ PSYCHOL to repress.

réfractaire [refraktεr] **1** adj [rebelle] insubordinate; ~ à resistant to. ‖ [matière] refractory. **2** nmf insubordinate.

refrain [rəfrɛ̃] nm MUS refrain, chorus.

refréner [rəfrene] vt to check, to hold back.

réfrigérant, -e [refriʒerɑ̃, ɑ̃t] adj [liquide] refrigerating, refrigerant.

réfrigérateur [refriʒeratœr] nm refrigerator.

refroidir [rəfrwadir] **1** vt [plat] to cool. ‖ [décourager] to discourage. **2** vi to cool.

refroidissement [rəfrwadismɑ̃] nm [de température] drop, cooling. ‖ [grippe] chill.

refuge [rəfyʒ] nm [abri] refuge. ‖ [de montagne] hut.

réfugié, -e [refyʒje] nm, f refugee.

réfugier [refyʒje] ○ **se réfugier** vp to take refuge.

refus [rəfy] nm inv refusal; **ce n'est pas de ~** fam I wouldn't say no.

refuser [rəfyze] vt [repousser] to refuse; ~ **de faire qqch** to refuse to do sthg. ‖ [contester]: ~ **qqch à qqn** to deny sb sthg. ‖ [clients, spectateurs] to turn away. ‖ [candidat]: **être refusé** to fail. ○ **se refuser** vp: **se ~ à faire qqch** to refuse to do sthg.

réfuter [refyte] vt to refute.

regagner [rəgaɲe] vt [reprendre] to regain, to win back. ‖ [revenir à] to get back to.

regain [rəgɛ̃] nm [retour]: **un ~** de a revival of, a renewal of.

régal, -als [regal] nm treat, delight.

régaler [regale] vt to treat; **c'est moi qui régale!** it's my treat! ○ **se régaler** vp: **je me régale** [nourriture] I'm thoroughly enjoying it; [activité] I'm having the time of my life.

regard [rəgar] nm look.

regardant, -e [rəgardɑ̃, ɑ̃t] adj fam [minutieux]: **être très/peu ~ sur qqch** to be very/not very particular about sthg.

regarder [rəgarde] **1** vt [observer, examiner, consulter] to look at; [télévision, spectacle] to watch; ~ **qqn faire qqch** to watch sb doing sthg; ~ **les trains passer** to watch the trains go by. ‖ [concerner] to concern; **cela ne te regarde pas** it's none of your business. **2** vi [observer, examiner] to look. ‖ [faire attention]: **sans ~ à la dépense** regardless of the expense; **y ~ à deux fois** to think twice about it.

régate [regat] nf (gén pl) regatta.

régénérer [reʒenere] vt to regenerate. ○ **se régénérer** vp to regenerate.

régent, -e [reʒɑ̃, ɑ̃t] nm, f regent.

régenter [reʒɑ̃te] vt: **vouloir tout ~** péj to want to be the boss.

reggae [rege] nm & adj inv reggae.

régie [reʒi] nf [entreprise] state-controlled company. ‖ RADIO & TÉLÉ [pièce] control room.

regimber [rəʒɛ̃be] vi to balk.

régime [reʒim] nm [politique] regime. ‖ [alimentaire] diet; **se mettre au/suivre un ~** to go on/to be on a diet. ‖ [de moteur] speed. ‖ [de fleuve, des pluies] cycle. ‖ [de bananes, dattes] bunch.

régiment [reʒimɑ̃] nm MIL regiment.

région [reʒjɔ̃] nf region.

régional, -e, -aux [reʒjɔnal, o] adj regional.

régir [reʒir] vt to govern.

régisseur [reʒisœr] nm [intendant] steward. ‖ [de théâtre] stage manager.

registre [rəʒistr] nm [gén] register; ~ **de comptabilité** ledger.

réglable [reglabl] adj [adaptable] adjustable. ‖ [payable] payable.

réglage [reglaʒ] nm adjustment, setting.

règle [rεgl] nf [instrument] ruler. ‖ [principe, loi] rule; **je suis en ~** my papers are in order. ○ **en règle générale** loc adv as a general rule. ○ **règles** nfpl [menstruation] period (sg).

réglé, -e [regle] adj [organisé] regular, well-ordered.

règlement [rεgləmɑ̃] nm [résolution] settling; ~ **de comptes** fig settling of scores. ‖ [règle] regulation. ‖ [paiement] settlement.

réglementaire [rεgləmɑ̃tεr] adj [régulier] statutory. ‖ [imposé] regulation (avant n).

réglementation [rεgləmɑ̃tasjɔ̃] nf [action] regulation. ‖ [ensemble de règles] regulations (pl), rules (pl).

régler [regle] vt [affaire, conflit] to settle, to sort out. ‖ [appareil] to adjust. ‖ [payer - note] to settle, to pay; [- commerçant] to pay.

réglisse [reglis] nf liquorice.

règne [rεɲ] nm [de souverain] reign; **sous le ~ de** in the reign of. ‖ [pouvoir] rule. ‖ BIOL kingdom.

régner [reɲe] vi [souverain] to rule, to reign. ‖ [silence] to reign.

regorger [rəgɔrʒe] vi: ~ **de** to be abundant in.

régresser [regrese] *vi* [sentiment, douleur] to diminish. || [personne] to regress.

régression [regresjɔ̃] *nf* [recul] decline. || PSYCHOL regression.

regret [rəgrɛ] *nm*: ~ **(de)** regret (for); **à** ~ with regret; **sans** ~ with no regrets.

regrettable [rəgrɛtabl] *adj* regrettable.

regretter [rəgrete] **1** *vt* [époque] to miss, to regret; [personne] to miss. || [faute] to regret; ~ **d'avoir fait qqch** to regret having done sthg. || [déplorer]: ~ **que** (+ *subjonctif*) to be sorry or to regret that. **2** *vi* to be sorry.

regrouper [rəgrupe] *vt* [réunir] to group together. ◯ **se regrouper** *vp* to gather, to assemble.

régulariser [regylarize] *vt* [documents] to sort out, to put in order; [situation] to straighten out.

régularité [regylarite] *nf* [gén] regularity. || [de travail, résultats] consistency.

régulation [regylasjɔ̃] *nf* [contrôle] control, regulation.

régulier, -ière [regylje, jɛr] *adj* [gén] regular. || [uniforme, constant] steady, regular. || [travail, résultats] consistent. || [légal] legal; **être en situation régulière** to have all the legally required documents.

régulièrement [regyljɛrmɑ̃] *adv* [gén] regularly. || [uniformément] steadily, regularly; [étalé, façonné] evenly.

réhabilitation [reabilitasjɔ̃] *nf* rehabilitation.

réhabiliter [reabilite] *vt* [accusé] to rehabilitate, to clear; *fig* [racheter] to restore to favour. || [rénover] to restore.

rehausser [rəose] *vt* [surélever] to heighten. || *fig* [mettre en valeur] to enhance.

rein [rɛ̃] *nm* kidney. ◯ **reins** *nmpl* small of the back (*sg*); **avoir mal aux ~s** to have backache.

réincarnation [reɛ̃karnasjɔ̃] *nf* reincarnation.

reine [rɛn] *nf* queen.

réinsertion [reɛ̃sɛrsjɔ̃] *nf* [de délinquant] reintegration.

réintégrer [reɛ̃tegre] *vt* [rejoindre] to return to. || JUR to reinstate.

rejaillir [rəʒajir] *vi* to splash up; ~ **sur qqn** *fig* to rebound on sb.

rejet [rəʒɛ] *nm* [gén] rejection. || [pousse] shoot.

rejeter [rəʒte] *vt* [offre, personne] to reject. || [partie du corps]: ~ **la tête/les bras en arrière** to throw back one's head/

one's arms. || [imputer]: ~ **la responsabilité de qqch sur qqn** to lay the responsibility for sthg at sb's door.

rejeton [rəʒtɔ̃] *nm* offspring (*U*).

rejoindre [rəʒwɛ̃dr] *vt* [retrouver] to join. || [regagner] to return to. || [rattraper] to catch up with. ◯ **se rejoindre** *vp* [personnes, routes] to meet.

rejoint, -e [rəʒwɛ̃, ɛt] *pp* → **rejoindre**.

réjoui, -e [reʒwi] *adj* joyful.

réjouir [reʒwir] *vt* to delight. ◯ **se réjouir** *vp* to be delighted; **se ~ de qqch** to be delighted at or about sthg.

réjouissance [reʒwisɑ̃s] *nf* rejoicing. ◯ **réjouissances** *nfpl* festivities.

relâche [rəlɑʃ] *nf* [pause]: **sans** ~ without respite or a break. || THÉÂTRE: **faire** ~ to be closed.

relâchement [rəlɑʃmɑ̃] *nm* relaxation.

relâcher [rəlɑʃe] *vt* [étreinte, cordes] to loosen. || [discipline, effort] to relax, to slacken. || [prisonnier] to release. ◯ **se relâcher** *vp* [se desserrer] to loosen. || [faiblir - discipline] to become lax; [- attention] to flag. || [se laisser aller] to slacken off.

relais [rəlɛ] *nm* [auberge] post house. || SPORT & TÉLÉ: **prendre/passer le** ~ to take/hand over.

relance [rəlɑ̃s] *nf* [économique] revival, boost; [de projet] relaunch.

relancer [rəlɑ̃se] *vt* [renvoyer] to throw back. || [faire reprendre - économie] to boost; [- projet] to relaunch; [- moteur, machine] to restart.

relater [rəlate] *vt littéraire* to relate.

relatif, -ive [rəlatif, iv] *adj* relative; ~ **à** relating to; **tout est** ~ it's all relative.

relation [rəlasjɔ̃] *nf* relationship; **mettre qqn en ~ avec qqn** to put sb in touch with sb. ◯ **relations** *nfpl* [rapport] relationship (*sg*); **~s sexuelles** sexual relations, intercourse (*U*). || [connaissance] acquaintance; **avoir des ~s** to have connections.

relative → **relatif**.

relativement [rəlativmɑ̃] *adv* relatively.

relativiser [rəlativize] *vt* to relativize.

relativité [rəlativite] *nf* relativity.

relax, relaxe [rəlaks] *adj fam* relaxed.

relaxation [rəlaksasjɔ̃] *nf* relaxation.

réflaxe = **relax**.

relaxer [rəlakse] *vt* [reposer] to relax. || JUR to discharge. ◯ **se relaxer** *vp* to relax.

relayer [rǝlɛje] *vt* to relieve. ○ **se re-layer** *vp* to take over from one another.

relecture [rǝlɛktyr] *nf* second reading, rereading.

reléguer [rǝlege] *vt* to relegate.

relent [rǝlɑ̃] *nm* [odeur] stink, stench.

relevé, -e [rǝlve] *adj* CULIN spicy. ○ **relevé** *nm* reading; **faire le ~ de qqch** to read sthg; **~ de compte** bank statement; **~ d'identité bancaire** bank account number.

relève [rǝlɛv] *nf* relief; **prendre la ~** to take over.

relever [rǝlve] **1** *vt* [redresser - personne] to help up; [- pays, économie] to rebuild; [- moral, niveau] to raise. || [ramasser] to collect. || [tête, col, store] to raise; [manches] to push up. || [CULIN - mettre en valeur] to bring out; [- pimenter] to season. || [compteur] to read. || [relayer] to take over from, to relieve. || [erreur] to note. **2** *vi* [être du domaine] : **~ de** to come under. ○ **se relever** *vp* [se mettre debout] to stand up; [sortir du lit] to get up.

relief [rǝljɛf] *nm* relief; **en ~** in relief, raised; **une carte en ~** relief map; **mettre en ~** *fig* to enhance, to bring out.

relier [rǝlje] *vt* [livre] to bind. || [joindre] to connect. || *fig* [associer] to link up.

religieux, -ieuse [rǝliʒjø, jøz] *adj* [vie, chant] religious; [mariage] religious, church (*avant n*). || [respectueux] reverent. ○ **religieux** *nm* monk. ○ **religieuse** *nf* RELIG nun.

religion [rǝliʒjɔ̃] *nf* [culte] religion. || [croyance] religion, faith.

relique [rǝlik] *nf* relic.

relire [rǝlir] *vt* [lire] to reread. || [vérifier] to read over.

reliure [rǝljyr] *nf* binding.

reloger [rǝlɔʒe] *vt* to rehouse.

relu, -e [rǝly] *pp* → **relire**.

reluire [rǝlɥir] *vi* to shine, to gleam.

reluisant, -e [rǝlɥizɑ̃, ɑ̃t] *adj* shining, gleaming; **peu** OU **pas très ~** *fig* [avenir, situation] not all that marvellous.

remaniement [rǝmanimɑ̃] *nm* restructuring; **~ ministériel** cabinet reshuffle.

remarier [rǝmarje] ○ **se remarier** *vp* to remarry.

remarquable [rǝmarkabl] *adj* remarkable.

remarque [rǝmark] *nf* [observation] remark; [critique] critical remark. || [annotation] note.

remarquer [rǝmarke] **1** *vt* [apercevoir] to notice; **faire ~ qqch (à qqn)** to point

sthg out (to sb); **se faire ~** *péj* to draw attention to o.s. || [noter] to remark, to comment. **2** *vi*: **ce n'est pas l'idéal, remarque!** it's not ideal, mind you!

remblai [rɑ̃blɛ] *nm* embankment.

rembobiner [rɑ̃bɔbine] *vt* to rewind.

rembourrer [rɑ̃bure] *vt* to stuff, to pad.

remboursement [rɑ̃bursǝmɑ̃] *nm* refund, repayment.

rembourser [rɑ̃burse] *vt* [dette] to pay back, to repay. || [personne] to pay back; **~ qqn de qqch** to reimburse sb for sthg.

remède [rǝmɛd] *nm litt* & *fig* remedy, cure.

remédier [rǝmedje] *vi*: **~ à qqch** to put sthg right, to remedy sthg.

remembrement [rǝmɑ̃brǝmɑ̃] *nm* land regrouping.

remerciement [rǝmɛrsimɑ̃] *nm* thanks (*pl*); **une lettre de ~** a thank-you letter.

remercier [rǝmɛrsje] *vt* [dire merci à] to thank; **~ qqn de** OU **pour qqch** to thank sb for sthg; **non, je vous remercie** no, thank you. || [congédier] to dismiss.

remettre [rǝmɛtr] *vt* [replacer] to put back; **~ en question** to call into question; **~ qqn à sa place** to put sb in his place. || [enfiler de nouveau] to put back on. || [rétablir - lumière, son] to put back on; **~ qqch en marche** to restart sthg; **~ une montre à l'heure** to put a watch right. || [donner] : **~ qqch à qqn** to hand sthg over to sb; [médaille, prix] to present sthg to sb. || [ajourner] : **~ qqch (à)** to put sthg off (until). ○ **se remettre** *vp* [recommencer] : **se ~ à qqch** to take up sthg again; **se ~ à fumer** to start smoking again. || [se rétablir] to get better; **se ~ de qqch** to get over sthg. || [redevenir] : **se ~ debout** to stand up again.

réminiscence [reminisɑ̃s] *nf* reminiscence.

remis, -e [rǝmi, iz] *pp* → **remettre**.

remise [rǝmiz] *nf* [action] : **~ en jeu** throw-in; **~ en question** OU **cause** calling into question. || [de message, colis] handing over; [de médaille, prix] presentation. || [réduction] discount; **~ de peine** JUR remission. || [hangar] shed.

rémission [remisjɔ̃] *nf* remission.

remodeler [rǝmɔdle] *vt* [forme] to remodel. || [remanier] to restructure.

remontant, -e [rǝmɔ̃tɑ̃, ɑ̃t] *adj* [tonique] invigorating. ○ **remontant** *nm* tonic.

remonte-pente [rəmɔ̃tpɑ̃t] (*pl* **remonte-pentes**) *nm* ski-tow.

remonter [rəmɔ̃te] **1** *vt* (*aux: avoir*) [escalier, pente] to go/come back up. ‖ [assembler] to put together again. ‖ [manches] to turn up. ‖ [horloge, montre] to wind up. ‖ [ragaillardir] to put new life into, to cheer up. **2** *vi* (*aux: être*) [monter à nouveau - personne] to go/come back up; [- baromètre] to rise again; [- prix, température] to go up again, to rise; [- sur vélo] to get back on; **~ dans une voiture** to get back into a car. ‖ [dater]: **~ à** to date *ou* go back to.

remontoir [rəmɔ̃twar] *nm* winder.

remontrer [rəmɔ̃tre] *vt* to show again; **vouloir en ~ à qqn** to try to show sb up.

remords [rəmɔr] *nm* remorse.

remorque [rəmɔrk] *nf* trailer; **être en ~** to be on tow.

remorquer [rəmɔrke] *vt* [voiture, bateau] to tow.

remorqueur [rəmɔrkœr] *nm* tug, tugboat.

remous [rəmu] **1** *nm* [de bateau] wash, backwash; [de rivière] eddy. **2** *nmpl fig* stir, upheaval.

rempailler [rɑ̃paje] *vt* to re-cane.

rempart [rɑ̃par] *nm* (*gén pl*) rampart.

remplaçant, -e [rɑ̃plasɑ̃, ɑ̃t] *nm, f* [suppléant] stand-in; SPORT substitute.

remplacement [rɑ̃plasmɑ̃] *nm* [changement] replacing, replacement. ‖ [intérim] substitution; **faire des ~s** to stand in; [docteur] to act as a locum.

remplacer [rɑ̃plase] *vt* [gén] to replace. ‖ [prendre la place de] to stand in for; SPORT to substitute.

remplir [rɑ̃plir] *vt* [gén] to fill; **~ de** to fill with; **~ qqn de joie/d'orgueil** to fill sb with happiness/pride. ‖ [questionnaire] to fill in *ou* out. ‖ [mission, fonction] to complete, to fulfil.

remplissage [rɑ̃plisaʒ] *nm* [de récipient] filling up. ‖ *fig & péj* [de texte] padding out.

remporter [rɑ̃pɔrte] *vt* [repartir avec] to take away again. ‖ [gagner] to win.

remuant, -e [rəmɥɑ̃, ɑ̃t] *adj* restless, overactive.

remue-ménage [rəmymenaʒ] *nm inv* commotion, confusion.

remuer [rəmɥe] **1** *vt* [bouger, émouvoir] to move. ‖ [café, thé] to stir; [salade] to toss. **2** *vi* to move, to stir; **arrête de ~ comme ça** stop being so restless. ○ **se**

remuer *vp* [se mouvoir] to move. ‖ *fig* [réagir] to make an effort.

rémunération [remyneʀasjɔ̃] *nf* remuneration.

rémunérer [remynere] *vt* [personne] to remunerate, to pay. ‖ [activité] to pay for.

renâcler [rənakle] *vi fam* to make a fuss; **~ devant** *ou* **à qqch** to balk at sthg.

renaissance [rənɛsɑ̃s] *nf* rebirth.

renaître [rənɛtr] *vi* [ressusciter] to come back to life, to come to life again; **faire ~** [passé, tradition] to revive. ‖ [revenir - sentiment, printemps] to return; [- économie] to revive, to recover.

renard [rənar] *nm* fox.

renchérir [rɑ̃ʃerir] *vi* [augmenter] to become more expensive; [prix] to go up. ‖ [surenchérir]: **~ sur** to add to.

rencontre [rɑ̃kɔ̃tr] *nf* [gén] meeting; **faire une mauvaise ~** to meet an unpleasant person; **aller/venir à la ~ de qqn** to go/come to meet sb.

rencontrer [rɑ̃kɔ̃tre] *vt* [gén] to meet. ‖ [heurter] to strike. ○ **se rencontrer** *vp* [gén] to meet. ‖ [opinions] to agree.

rendement [rɑ̃dmɑ̃] *nm* [de machine, travailleur] output; [de terre, placement] yield.

rendez-vous [rɑ̃devu] *nm inv* [rencontre] appointment; [amoureux] date; **on a tous ~ au café** we're all meeting at the café; **prendre ~ avec qqn** to make an appointment with sb; **donner ~ à qqn** to arrange to meet sb. ‖ [lieu] meeting place.

rendormir [rɑ̃dɔrmir] ○ **se rendormir** *vp* to go back to sleep.

rendre [rɑ̃dr] **1** *vt* [restituer]: **~ qqch à qqn** to give sthg back to sb, to return sthg to sb. ‖ [donner en retour - invitation, coup] to return. ‖ [JUR - jugement] to pronounce. ‖ [vomir] to vomit, to cough up. ‖ (+ *adj*) [faire devenir] to make; **~ qqn fou** to drive sb mad. ‖ [exprimer] to render. **2** *vi* [produire - champ] to yield. ‖ [vomir] to be sick. ○ **se rendre** *vp* [céder, capituler] to give in; **j'ai dû me ~ à l'évidence** I had to face facts. ‖ [aller]: **se ~ à** to go to. ‖ (+ *adj*) [se faire tel]: **se ~ utile/malade** to make o.s. useful/ill.

rêne [rɛn] *nf* rein.

renégat, -e [rənega, at] *nm, f sout* renegade.

renfermé, -e [rɑ̃fɛrme] *adj* introverted,

withdrawn. ○ **renfermé** *nm*: ça sent le ~ it smells stuffy in here.

renfermer [rɑ̃fɛrme] *vt* [contenir] to contain. ○ **se renfermer** *vp* to withdraw.

renflé, -e [rɑ̃fle] *adj* bulging.

renflouer [rɑ̃flue] *vt* [bateau] to refloat. || *fig* [entreprise, personne] to bail out.

renfoncement [rɑ̃fɔ̃smɑ̃] *nm* recess.

renforcer [rɑ̃fɔrse] *vt* to reinforce, to strengthen.

renfort [rɑ̃fɔr] *nm* reinforcement; **venir en ~** to come as reinforcements.

renfrogné, -e [rɑ̃frɔɲe] *adj* scowling.

renfrogner [rɑ̃frɔɲe] ○ **se renfrogner** *vp* to scowl, to pull a face.

rengaine [rɑ̃gɛn] *nf* [formule répétée] (old) story. || [chanson] (old) song.

rengorger [rɑ̃gɔrʒe] ○ **se rengorger** *vp fig* to puff o.s. up.

renier [rɑ̃je] *vt* [famille, ami] to disown. || [foi, opinion] to renounce, to repudiate.

renifler [rɑ̃nifle] **1** *vi* to sniff. **2** *vt* to sniff.

renne [rɛn] *nm* reindeer (*inv*).

renom [rɑ̃nɔ̃] *nm* renown, fame.

renommé, -e [rɑ̃nɔme] *adj* renowned, famous. ○ **renommée** *nf* renown, fame; **de ~e internationale** world-famous, internationally renowned.

renoncement [rɑ̃nɔ̃smɑ̃] *nm*: ~ (à) renunciation (of).

renoncer [rɑ̃nɔ̃se] *vi*: **~ à** to give up; **~ à comprendre qqch** to give up trying to understand sthg.

renouer [rɑ̃nwe] **1** *vt* [lacet, corde] to re-tie, to tie up again. || [contact, conversation] to resume. **2** *vi*: **~ avec qqn** to take up with sb again.

renouveau, -x [rɑ̃nuvo] *nm* [transformation] revival.

renouvelable [rɑ̃nuvlabl] *adj* renewable; [expérience] repeatable.

renouveler [rɑ̃nuvle] *vt* [gén] to renew. ○ **se renouveler** *vp* [être remplacé] to be renewed. || [se répéter] to be repeated, to recur.

renouvellement [rɑ̃nuvɛlmɑ̃] *nm* renewal.

rénovation [renovasjɔ̃] *nf* renovation, restoration.

rénover [renove] *vt* [immeuble] to renovate, to restore.

renseignement [rɑ̃sɛɲmɑ̃] *nm* information (*U*); **un ~** a piece of information; **prendre des ~s (sur)** to make enquiries

(about). ○ **renseignements** *nmpl* [service d'information] enquiries, information.

renseigner [rɑ̃sɛɲe] *vt*: **~ qqn (sur)** to give sb information (about), to inform sb (about). ○ **se renseigner** *vp* [s'enquérir] to make enquiries, to ask for information. || [s'informer] to find out.

rentabiliser [rɑ̃tabilize] *vt* to make profitable.

rentabilité [rɑ̃tabilite] *nf* profitability.

rentable [rɑ̃tabl] *adj* COMM profitable.

rente [rɑ̃t] *nf* [d'un capital] revenue, income. || [pension] pension, annuity.

rentier, -ière [rɑ̃tje, jɛr] *nm, f* person of independent means.

rentrée [rɑ̃tre] *nf* [fait de rentrer] return. || [reprise des activités]: **la ~ parlementaire** the reopening of parliament; **la ~ des classes** the start of the new school year. || [recette] income.

rentrer [rɑ̃tre] **1** *vi* (*aux*: être) [entrer de nouveau] to go/come back in; **tout a fini par ~ dans l'ordre** everything returned to normal. || [entrer] to go/come in. || [revenir chez soi] to go/come back, to go/come home. || [recouvrer, récupérer]: **~ dans ses frais** to cover one's costs, to break even. || [se jeter avec violence]: **~ dans** to crash into. || [s'emboîter] to go in, to fit. || [être perçu - fonds] to come in. **2** *vt* (*aux*: avoir) [mettre ou remettre à l'intérieur] to bring in. || [ventre] to pull in; [griffes] to retract, to draw in; [chemise] to tuck in. || *fig* [rage, larmes] to hold back.

renversant, -e [rɑ̃vɛrsɑ̃, ɑ̃t] *adj* staggering, astounding.

renverse [rɑ̃vɛrs] *nf*: **tomber à la ~** to fall over backwards.

renversement [rɑ̃vɛrsəmɑ̃] *nm* [de situation] reversal.

renverser [rɑ̃vɛrse] *vt* [mettre à l'envers] to turn upside down. || [faire tomber] to knock over; [- piéton] to run over; [- liquide] to spill. || *fig* [régime] to overthrow; [ministre] to throw out of office. || [tête, buste] to tilt back. ○ **se renverser** *vp* [incliner le corps en arrière] to lean back. || [tomber] to overturn.

renvoi [rɑ̃vwa] *nm* [licenciement] dismissal. || [de colis, lettre] return, sending back. || [ajournement] postponement. || [référence] cross-reference. || JUR referral. || [éructation] belch.

renvoyer [rãvwaje] *vt* [faire retourner] to send back. || [congédier] to dismiss. || [colis, lettre] to send back, to return. || [balle] to throw back. || [réfléchir - lumière] to reflect; [- son] to echo. || [référer] : ~ qqn à to refer sb to. || [différer] to postpone, to put off.

réorganisation [reɔrganizasjɔ̃] *nf* reorganization.

réorganiser [reɔrganize] *vt* to reorganize.

réouverture [reuvertyr] *nf* reopening.

repaire [rəper] *nm* den.

répandre [repɑ̃dr] *vt* [verser, renverser] to spill. || [diffuser, dégager] to give off. || *fig* [effroi, terreur, nouvelle] to spread.

répandu, -e [repɑ̃dy] **1** *pp* → répandre. **2** *adj* [opinion, maladie] widespread.

réparable [reparabl] *adj* [objet] repairable. || [erreur] that can be put right.

réparateur, -trice [reparatœr, tris] **1** *adj* [sommeil] refreshing. **2** *nm, f* repairer.

réparation [reparasjɔ̃] *nf* [d'objet - action] repairing; [- résultat] repair; **en ~** under repair. || [de faute] : ~ (de) atonement (for). || [indemnité] reparation, compensation.

réparer [repare] *vt* [objet] to repair. || [faute, oubli] to make up for.

reparler [rəparle] *vi* : ~ de qqn/qqch to talk about sb/sthg again.

repartie [rəparti] *nf* retort; **avoir de la ~** to be good at repartee.

repartir [rəpartir] *vi* [retourner] to go back, to return. || [partir de nouveau] to set off again. || [recommencer] to start again.

répartir [repartir] *vt* [partager] to share out, to divide up. || [dans l'espace] to spread out, to distribute. || [classer] to divide ou split up. **○ se répartir** *vp* to divide up.

répartition [repartisjɔ̃] *nf* [partage] sharing out; [de tâches] allocation. || [dans l'espace] distribution.

repas [rəpa] *nm* meal; **prendre son ~** to eat.

repassage [rəpasaʒ] *nm* ironing.

repasser [rəpase] **1** *vi* (*aux: être*) [passer à nouveau] to go/come back; [film] to be on again. **2** *vt* (*aux: avoir*) [frontière, montagne] to cross again, to recross. || [examen] to resit. || [film] to show again. || [linge] to iron.

repêcher [rəpeʃe] *vt* [noyé, voiture] to fish out. || *fam* [candidat] to let through.

repeindre [rəpɛ̃dr] *vt* to repaint.

repeint, -e [rəpɛ̃, ɛt] *pp* → repeindre.

repentir [rəpɑ̃tir] *nm* repentance. **○ se repentir** *vp* to repent; **se ~ de qqch/d'avoir fait qqch** to be sorry for sthg/for having done sthg.

répercussion [reperkysjɔ̃] *nf* repercussion.

répercuter [reperkyte] *vt* [lumière] to reflect; [son] to throw back. || [ordre, augmentation] to pass on. **○ se répercuter** *vp* [lumière] to be reflected; [son] to echo. || [influer] : **se ~ sur** to have repercussions on.

repère [rəper] *nm* [marque] mark; [objet concret] landmark.

repérer [rəpere] *vt* [situer] to locate, to pinpoint. || *fam* [remarquer] to spot.

répertoire [repertwar] *nm* [agenda] thumb-indexed notebook. || [de théâtre, d'artiste] repertoire. || INFORM directory.

répertorier [repertɔrje] *vt* to make a list of.

répéter [repete] **1** *vt* [gén] to repeat. || [leçon] to go over, to learn; [rôle] to rehearse. **2** *vi* to rehearse. **○ se répéter** *vp* [radoter] to repeat o.s. || [se reproduire] to be repeated.

répétitif, -ive [repetitif, iv] *adj* repetitive.

répétition [repetisjɔ̃] *nf* [réitération] repetition. || MUS & THÉÂTRE rehearsal.

repeupler [rəpœple] *vt* [région, ville] to repopulate. || [forêt] to replant; [étang] to restock.

repiquer [rəpike] *vt* [replanter] to plant out. || [disque, cassette] to re-record.

répit [repi] *nm* respite.

replacer [rəplase] *vt* [remettre] to replace, to put back. || [situer] to place, to put.

replanter [rəplɑ̃te] *vt* to replant.

replet, -ète [rəplɛ, ɛt] *adj* chubby.

repli [rəpli] *nm* [de tissu] fold; [de rivière] bend. || [de troupes] withdrawal.

replier [rəplije] *vt* [plier de nouveau] to fold up again. || [ramener en pliant] to fold back. || [armée] to withdraw. **○ se replier** *vp* [armée] to withdraw. || [personne] : **se ~ sur soi-même** to withdraw into o.s. || [journal, carte] to fold.

réplique [replik] *nf* [riposte] reply. || [d'acteur] line; **donner la ~ à qqn** to play opposite sb. || [copie] replica.

répliquer [replike] **1** *vt* : ~ à qqn que to reply to sb that. **2** *vi* [répondre] to reply;

[avec impertinence] to answer back. || *fig* [riposter] to retaliate.

replonger [rəplɔ̃ʒe] **1** *vt* to plunge back. **2** *vi* to dive back. ○ **se replonger** *vp*: se ~ dans qqch to immerse o.s. in sthg again.

répondeur [repɔ̃dœr] *nm*: ~ (téléphonique ou automatique ou -enregistreur) answering machine.

répondre [repɔ̃dr] **1** *vi*: ~ à qqn [faire connaître sa pensée] to answer sb, to reply to sb; [riposter] to answer sb back; ~ à qqch [en se défendant] to respond to sthg; ~ au téléphone to answer the telephone. **2** *vt* to answer, to reply. ○ **répondre à** *vt* [correspondre à - besoin] to answer; [- conditions] to meet. || [ressembler à - description] to match. ○ **répondre de** *vt* to answer for.

réponse [repɔ̃s] *nf* [action de répondre] answer, reply; en ~ à votre lettre ... in reply ou in answer ou in response to your letter .... || [solution] answer. || [réaction] response.

report [rəpɔr] *nm* [de réunion, rendez-vous] postponement.

reportage [rəpɔrtaʒ] *nm* [article, enquête] report.

reporter[1] [rəpɔrter] *nm* reporter.

reporter[2] [rəpɔrte] *vt* [rapporter] to take back. || [différer]: ~ qqch à to postpone sthg till, to put sthg off till. || [transférer]: ~ sur to transfer to. ○ **se reporter** *vp*: se ~ à [se référer à] to refer to.

repos [rəpo] *nm* [gén] rest; prendre un jour de ~ to take a day off. || [tranquillité] peace and quiet.

reposé, -e [rəpoze] *adj* rested; à tête ~e with a clear head.

reposer [rəpoze] **1** *vt* [poser à nouveau] to put down again, to put back down. || [remettre] to put back. || [poser de nouveau - question] to ask again. || [appuyer] to rest. || [délasser] to rest, to relax. **2** *vi* [pâte] to sit, to stand; [vin] to stand. || [théorie]: ~ sur to rest on. ○ **se reposer** *vp* [se délasser] to rest. || [faire confiance]: se ~ sur qqn to rely on sb.

repoussant, -e [rəpusɑ̃, ɑ̃t] *adj* repulsive.

repousser [rəpuse] **1** *vi* to grow again, to grow back. **2** *vt* [écarter] to push away, to push back; [l'ennemi] to repel, to drive back. || [éconduire] to reject. || [proposition] to reject, to turn down. || [différer] to put back, to postpone.

répréhensible [repreɑ̃sibl] *adj* reprehensible.

reprendre [rəprɑ̃dr] **1** *vt* [prendre de nouveau] to take again; ~ haleine to get one's breath back. || [récupérer - objet prêté] to take back; [- prisonnier, ville] to recapture. || COMM [entreprise, affaire] to take over. || [se resservir]: ~ un gâteau/de la viande to take another cake/some more meat. || [recommencer] to resume. || [corriger] to correct. **2** *vi* [affaires, plante] to pick up. || [recommencer] to start again.

représailles [rəprezaj] *nfpl* reprisals.

représentant, -e [rəprezɑ̃tɑ̃, ɑ̃t] *nm, f* representative.

représentatif, -ive [rəprezɑ̃tatif, iv] *adj* representative.

représentation [rəprezɑ̃tasjɔ̃] *nf* [gén] representation. || [spectacle] performance.

représentativité [rəprezɑ̃tativite] *nf* representativeness.

représenter [rəprezɑ̃te] *vt* to represent. ○ **se représenter** *vp* [s'imaginer]: se ~ qqch to visualize sthg. || [se présenter à nouveau]: se ~ à [aux élections] to stand again at; [à un examen] to resit, to represent.

répression [represjɔ̃] *nf* [de révolte] repression. || [de criminalité, d'injustices] suppression.

réprimande [reprimɑ̃d] *nf* reprimand.

réprimander [reprimɑ̃de] *vt* to reprimand.

réprimer [reprime] *vt* [émotion, rire] to repress, to check. || [révolte, crimes] to put down, to suppress.

repris, -e [rəpri, iz] *pp* → reprendre. ○ **repris** *nm*: ~ de justice habitual criminal.

reprise [rəpriz] *nf* [recommencement - des hostilités] resumption, renewal; [- des affaires] revival, recovery; [- de pièce] revival; à plusieurs ~s on several occasions, several times. || BOXE round. || [raccommodage] mending.

repriser [rəprize] *vt* to mend.

réprobateur, -trice [reprɔbatœr, tris] *adj* reproachful.

réprobation [reprɔbasjɔ̃] *nf* disapproval.

reproche [rəprɔʃ] *nm* reproach; faire des ~s à qqn to reproach sb.

reprocher [rəprɔʃe] *vt*: ~ qqch à qqn to reproach sb for sthg. ○ **se reprocher** *vp*: se ~ (qqch) to blame o.s. (for sthg).

reproducteur, -trice [rəprɔdyktœr, tris] *adj* reproductive.

reproduction [rəprɔdyksjɔ̃] *nf* reproduction.

reproduire [rəprɔdɥir] *vt* to reproduce. ○ **se reproduire** *vp* BIOL to reproduce, to breed. ‖ [se répéter] to recur.

reproduit, -e [rəprɔdɥi, ɥit] *pp* → **reproduire**.

réprouver [repruve] *vt* [blâmer] to reprove.

reptile [rɛptil] *nm* reptile.

repu, -e [rəpy] *adj* full, sated.

républicain, -e [repyblikɛ̃, ɛn] *adj & nm, f* republican.

république [repyblik] *nf* republic.

répudier [repydje] *vt* [femme] to repudiate.

répugnance [repyɲɑ̃s] *nf* [horreur] repugnance. ‖ [réticence] reluctance; **avoir** ou **éprouver de la ~ à faire qqch** to be reluctant to do sthg.

répugnant, -e [repyɲɑ̃, ɑ̃t] *adj* repugnant.

répugner [repyɲe] *vi*: **~ à qqn** to disgust sb, to fill sb with repugnance; **~ à faire qqch** to be reluctant to do sthg, to be loath to do sthg.

répulsion [repylsjɔ̃] *nf* repulsion.

réputation [repytasjɔ̃] *nf* reputation; **avoir bonne/mauvaise ~** to have a good/bad reputation.

réputé, -e [repyte] *adj* famous, wellknown.

requérir [rəkerir] *vt* [nécessiter] to require, to call for. ‖ [solliciter] to solicit.

requête [rəkɛt] *nf* [prière] petition. ‖ JUR appeal.

requiem [rekɥijɛm] *nm inv* requiem.

requin [rəkɛ̃] *nm* shark.

requis, -e [rəki, iz] **1** *pp* → **requérir**. **2** *adj* required, requisite.

réquisition [rekizisjɔ̃] *nf* MIL requisition.

réquisitionner [rekizisjɔne] *vt* to requisition.

réquisitoire [rekizitwar] *nm* JUR closing speech for the prosecution.

RER (*abr de* réseau express régional) *nm train service linking central Paris with its suburbs and airports.*

rescapé, -e [rɛskape] *nm, f* survivor.

rescousse [rɛskus] ○ **à la rescousse** *loc adv*: **venir à la ~ de qqn** to come to sb's rescue; **appeler qqn à la ~** to call on sb for help.

réseau, -x [rezo] *nm* network.

réservation [rezɛrvasjɔ̃] *nf* reservation.

réserve [rezɛrv] *nf* [gén] reserve; **en ~** in reserve. ‖ [restriction] reservation; **faire des ~s (sur)** to have reservations (about); **sous ~ de** subject to; **sans ~** unreservedly. ‖ [territoire] reserve; [- d'Indiens] reservation; **~ naturelle** nature reserve. ‖ [local] storeroom.

réservé, -e [rezɛrve] *adj* reserved.

réserver [rezɛrve] *vt* [destiner]: **~ qqch (à qqn)** [chambre, place] to reserve ou book sthg (for sb); *fig* [surprise, désagrément] to have sthg in store (for sb). ‖ [mettre de côté, garder]: **~ qqch (pour)** to put sthg on one side (for), to keep sthg (for). ○ **se réserver** *vp* [s'accorder]: **se ~ qqch** to keep sthg for o.s. ‖ [se ménager] to save o.s.

réservoir [rezɛrvwar] *nm* [cuve] tank. ‖ [bassin] reservoir.

résidence [rezidɑ̃s] *nf* [habitation] residence; **~ principale** main residence ou home; **~ secondaire** second home; **~ universitaire** hall of residence. ‖ [immeuble] luxury apartment block *Am.*

résident, -e [rezidɑ̃, ɑ̃t] *nm, f* [de pays]: **les ~s français en Écosse** French nationals resident in Scotland. ‖ [habitant d'une résidence] resident.

résidentiel, -ielle [rezidɑ̃sjɛl] *adj* residential.

résider [rezide] *vi* [habiter]: **~ à/dans/en** to reside in. ‖ [consister]: **~ dans** to lie in.

résidu [rezidy] *nm* [reste] residue; [déchet] waste.

résignation [reziɲasjɔ̃] *nf* resignation.

résigné, -e [reziɲe] *adj* resigned.

résigner [reziɲe] ○ **se résigner** *vp*: **se ~ (à)** to resign o.s. (to).

résilier [rezilje] *vt* to cancel, to terminate.

résille [rezij] *nf* [pour cheveux] hairnet. ‖ **bas ~** fishnet stockings.

résine [rezin] *nf* resin.

résistance [rezistɑ̃s] *nf* [gén, ÉLECTR & PHYS] resistance; **manquer de ~** to lack stamina; **opposer une ~** to put up resistance. ‖ [de radiateur, chaudière] element.

résistant, -e [rezistɑ̃, ɑ̃t] **1** *adj* [personne] tough; [tissu] hard-wearing, tough; **être ~ au froid/aux infections** to be resistant to the cold/to infection. **2** *nm, f* [gén] resistance fighter; [de la Résistance] member of the Resistance.

résister [reziste] *vi* to resist; ~ à [attaque, désir] to resist; [tempête, fatigue] to withstand; [personne] to stand up to, to oppose.

résolu, -e [rezɔly] 1 *pp* → résoudre. 2 *adj* resolute; **être bien ~ à faire qqch** to be determined to do sthg.

résolument [rezɔlymɑ̃] *adv* resolutely.

résolution [rezɔlysjɔ̃] *nf* [décision] resolution; **prendre la ~ de faire qqch** to make a resolution to do sthg. || [détermination] resolve, determination. || [solution] solving.

résonance [rezɔnɑ̃s] *nf* ÉLECTR & PHYS resonance. || *fig* [écho] echo.

résonner [rezɔne] *vi* [retentir] to resound; [renvoyer le son] to echo.

résorber [rezɔrbe] *vt* [déficit] to absorb. || MÉD to resorb. ○ **se résorber** *vp* [déficit] to be absorbed. || MÉD to be resorbed.

résoudre [rezudr] *vt* [problème] to solve, to resolve. ○ **se résoudre** *vp*: **se ~ à faire qqch** to make up one's mind to do sthg, to decide to resolve to do sthg.

respect [rɛspɛ] *nm* respect.

respectable [rɛspɛktabl] *adj* respectable.

respecter [rɛspɛkte] *vt* to respect; **faire ~ la loi** to enforce the law.

respectif, -ive [rɛspɛktif, iv] *adj* respective.

respectivement [rɛspɛktivmɑ̃] *adv* respectively.

respectueux, -euse [rɛspɛktɥø, øz] *adj* respectful; **être ~ de** to have respect for.

respiration [rɛspirasjɔ̃] *nf* breathing (U); **retenir sa ~** to hold one's breath.

respiratoire [rɛspiratwar] *adj* respiratory.

respirer [rɛspire] 1 *vi* [inspirer-expirer] to breathe. || *fig* [être soulagé] to be able to breathe again. 2 *vt* [aspirer] to breathe in. || *fig* [exprimer] to exude.

resplendissant, -e [rɛsplɑ̃disɑ̃, ɑ̃t] *adj* radiant.

responsabilité [rɛspɔ̃sabilite] *nf* [morale] responsibility; **avoir la ~ de** to be responsible for, to have the responsibility of. || JUR liability.

responsable [rɛspɔ̃sabl] 1 *adj* [gén] : ~ **(de)** responsible (for); [légalement] liable (for); [chargé de] in charge (of), responsible (for). || [sérieux] responsible. 2 *nmf* [auteur, coupable] person responsible. || [dirigeant] official. || [personne compétente] person in charge.

resquiller [rɛskije] *vi* [au théâtre etc] to sneak in without paying. || [dans autobus etc] to dodge paying the fare.

resquilleur, -euse [rɛskijœr, øz] *nm, f* [au théâtre etc] person who sneaks in without paying. || [dans autobus etc] fare-dodger.

ressac [rəsak] *nm* undertow.

ressaisir [rəsezir] ○ **se ressaisir** *vp* to pull o.s. together.

ressasser [rəsase] *vt* [répéter] to keep churning out.

ressemblance [rəsɑ̃blɑ̃s] *nf* [gén] resemblance, likeness; [trait] resemblance.

ressemblant, -e [rəsɑ̃blɑ̃, ɑ̃t] *adj* lifelike.

ressembler [rəsɑ̃ble] *vi*: ~ **à** [physiquement] to resemble, to look like; [moralement] to be like, to resemble; **cela ne lui ressemble pas** that's not like him. ○ **se ressembler** *vp* to look alike, to resemble each other.

ressemeler [rəsəmle] *vt* to resole.

ressentiment [rəsɑ̃timɑ̃] *nm* resentment.

ressentir [rəsɑ̃tir] *vt* to feel.

resserrer [rəsere] *vt* [ceinture, boulon] to tighten. || *fig* [lien] to strengthen. ○ **se resserrer** *vp* [route] to (become) narrow. || [nœud, étreinte] to tighten. || *fig* [relations] to grow stronger, to strengthen.

resservir [rəservir] 1 *vt* [personne] to give another helping to. 2 *vi* to be used again. ○ **se resservir** *vp*: **se ~ de qqch** [plat] to take another helping of sthg.

ressort [rəsɔr] *nm* [mécanisme] spring. || *fig* [énergie] spirit. || *fig* [compétence] : **être du ~ de qqn** to be sb's area of responsibility, to come under sb's jurisdiction. ○ **en dernier ressort** *loc adv* in the last resort, as a last resort.

ressortir [rəsɔrtir] 1 *vi* (*aux: être*) [personne] to go out again. || *fig* [couleur] : ~ **(sur)** to stand out (against); **faire ~** to highlight. || *fig* [résulter de] : ~ **de** to emerge from. 2 *vt* (*aux: avoir*) to take ou get ou bring out again.

ressortissant, -e [rəsɔrtisɑ̃, ɑ̃t] *nm, f* national.

ressource [rəsurs] *nf* resort. ○ **ressources** *nfpl* [financières] means. || [énergétiques, de langue] resources; **~s naturelles** natural resources.

ressurgir [rəsyrʒir] *vi* to reappear.

ressusciter [resysite] *vi* to rise (from the dead); *fig* to revive.

restant, -e [rɛstɑ̃, ɑ̃t] *adj* remaining, left. ○ **restant** *nm* rest, remainder.

restaurant [rɛstɔrɑ̃] *nm* restaurant; **manger au ~** to eat out; **~ d'entreprise** staff canteen.

restaurateur, -trice [rɛstɔratœr, tris] *nm, f* CULIN restaurant owner. || ART restorer.

restauration [rɛstɔrasjɔ̃] *nf* CULIN restaurant business; **~ rapide** fast food. || ART & POLIT restoration.

restaurer [rɛstɔre] *vt* to restore. ○ **se restaurer** *vp* to have something to eat.

reste [rɛst] *nm* [de lait, temps]: **le ~ (de)** the rest (of). || MATHS remainder. ○ **restes** *nmpl* [de repas] leftovers. ○ **au reste, du reste** *loc adv* besides.

rester [rɛste] **1** *vi* [dans lieu, état] to stay, to remain. || [subsister] to remain, to be left; **le seul bien qui me reste** the only thing I have left. || [s'arrêter]: **en ~ à qqch** to stop at sthg; **en ~ là** to finish there. || *loc*: **y ~** *fam* [mourir] to pop one's clogs. **2** *v impers*: **il en reste un peu** there's still a little left; **il te reste de l'argent?** do you still have some money left?

restituer [rɛstitɥe] *vt* [argent, objet volé] to return, to restore. || [énergie] to release. || [son] to reproduce.

resto [rɛsto] *nm fam* restaurant; **les ~s du cœur** *charity food distribution centres*; **~U** UNIV refectory.

restreindre [rɛstrɛ̃dr] *vt* to restrict. ○ **se restreindre** *vp* [domaine, champ] to narrow. || [personne] to cut back.

restreint, -e [rɛstrɛ̃, ɛ̃t] *pp* → **restreindre**.

restrictif, -ive [rɛstriktif, iv] *adj* restrictive.

restriction [rɛstriksjɔ̃] *nf* [condition] condition; **sans ~** unconditionally. || [limitation] restriction.

restructurer [rɛstryktyre] *vt* to restructure.

résultat [rezylta] *nm* result; [d'action] outcome.

résulter [rezylte] **1** *vi*: **~ de** to be the result of, to result from. **2** *v impers*: **il en résulte que ...** as a result, ...

résumé [rezyme] *nm* summary, résumé; **en ~** [pour conclure] to sum up.

résumer [rezyme] *vt* to summarize. ○ **se résumer** *vp* [se réduire]: **se ~ à qqch/à faire qqch** to come down to sthg/to doing sthg.

résurgence [rezyrʒɑ̃s] *nf* resurgence.

résurrection [rezyrɛksjɔ̃] *nf* resurrection.

rétablir [retablir] *vt* [gén] to restore. || [communications, contact] to re-establish. ○ **se rétablir** *vp* [silence] to return, to be restored. || [malade] to recover. || GYM to pull o.s. up.

rétablissement [retablismɑ̃] *nm* [d'ordre] restoration. || [de communications] re-establishment. || [de malade] recovery. || GYM pull-up.

retard [rətar] *nm* [délai] delay; **être en ~** [sur heure] to be late; [sur échéance] to be behind; **avoir du ~** to be late ou delayed. || [de pays, peuple, personne] backwardness.

retardataire [rətardatɛr] *nmf* [en retard] latecomer.

retardement [rətardəmɑ̃] *nm*: **à ~** belatedly; *voir aussi* **bombe**.

retarder [rətarde] **1** *vt* [personne, train] to delay; [sur échéance] to put back. || [ajourner - rendez-vous] to put back ou off; [- départ] to put back ou off, to delay. **2** *vi* [horloge] to be slow. || *fam* [ne pas être au courant] to be behind the times.

retenir [rətnir] *vt* [physiquement - objet, personne, cri] to hold back; [- souffle] to hold. || [retarder] to keep, to detain. || [chambre] to reserve. || [leçon, cours] to remember. || [projet] to accept, to adopt. || [eau, chaleur] to retain. || MATHS to carry. || [intérêt, attention] to hold. ○ **se retenir** *vp* [s'accrocher]: **se ~ à** to hold onto. || [se contenir] to hold on; **se ~ de faire qqch** to refrain from doing sthg.

rétention [retɑ̃sjɔ̃] *nf* MÉD retention.

retentir [rətɑ̃tir] *vi* [son] to ring (out). || *fig* [fatigue, blessure]: **~ sur** to have an effect on.

retentissant, -e [rətɑ̃tisɑ̃, ɑ̃t] *adj* resounding.

retentissement [rətɑ̃tismɑ̃] *nm* [de mesure] repercussions (*pl*).

retenu, -e [rətny] *pp* → **retenir**.

retenue [rətny] *nf* [prélèvement] deduction. || MATHS amount carried. || SCOL detention. || *fig* [de personne - dans relations] reticence; [- dans comportement] restraint; **sans ~** without restraint.

réticence [retisɑ̃s] *nf* [hésitation] hesitation, reluctance; **avec ~** hesitantly.

réticent, -e [retisɑ̃, ɑ̃t] *adj* hesitant, reluctant.

rétine [retin] *nf* retina.

retiré, -e [rətire] *adj* [lieu] remote, isolated; [vie] quiet.

retirer [rǝtire] *vt* [vêtement, emballage] to take off, to remove; [permis, jouet] to take away; ~ **qqch à qqn** to take sthg away from sb. ‖ [plainte] to withdraw, to take back. ‖ [avantages, bénéfices]: ~ **qqch de qqch** to get ou derive sthg from sthg. ‖ [bagages, billet] to collect; [argent] to withdraw. ○ **se retirer** *vp* [s'isoler] to withdraw, to retreat. ‖ [refluer] to recede.

retombées [rǝtɔ̃be] *nfpl* repercussions, fallout (*sg*).

retomber [rǝtɔ̃be] *vi* [gymnaste, chat] to land. ‖ [redevenir]: ~ **malade** to relapse. ‖ [cheveux] to hang down. ‖ *fig* [responsabilité]: ~ **sur** to fall on.

rétorquer [retɔrke] *vt* to retort; ~ **à qqn que ...** to retort to sb that ....

retors, -e [rǝtɔr, ɔrs] *adj* wily.

rétorsion [retɔrsjɔ̃] *nf* retaliation; **mesures de** ~ reprisals.

retouche [rǝtuʃ] *nf* [de texte, vêtement] alteration. ‖ ART & PHOT touching up.

retoucher [rǝtuʃe] *vt* [texte, vêtement] to alter. ‖ ART & PHOT to touch up.

retour [rǝtur] *nm* [gén] return; **à mon/ ton** ~ when I/you get back, on my/your return; **être de** ~ **(de)** to be back (from). ‖ [trajet] journey back, return journey.

retourner [rǝturne] 1 *vt* (*aux: avoir*) [carte, matelas] to turn over; [terre] to turn over. ‖ [compliment, objet prêté]: ~ **qqch (à qqn)** to return sthg (to sb). ‖ [lettre, colis] to send back, to return. 2 *vi* (*aux: être*) to come/go back; ~ **en arrière** ou **sur ses pas** to retrace one's steps. ○ **se retourner** *vp* [basculer] to turn over. ‖ [pivoter] to turn round. ‖ *fig* [s'opposer]: **se** ~ **contre** to turn against.

retracer [rǝtrase] *vt* [ligne] to redraw. ‖ [événement] to relate.

rétracter [retrakte] *vt* to retract. ○ **se rétracter** *vp* [se contracter] to retract. ‖ [se dédire] to back down.

retrait [rǝtrɛ] *nm* [gén] withdrawal. ‖ [de bagages] collection. ‖ [des eaux] ebbing. ○ **en retrait** *loc adj* & *loc adv* [maison] set back from the road; **rester en** ~ *fig* to hang back. ‖ [texte] indented.

retraite [rǝtrɛt] *nf* [gén] retreat. ‖ [cessation d'activité] retirement; **être à la** ~ to be retired. ‖ [revenu] (retirement) pension.

retraité, -e [rǝtrete] 1 *adj* [personne] retired. 2 *nm, f* retired person, pensioner.

retrancher [rǝtrɑ̃ʃe] *vt* [montant]: ~ **qqch (de)** to take sthg away (from), to deduct sthg (from). ○ **se retrancher** *vp* to entrench o.s.; **se** ~ **derrière/dans** *fig* to take refuge behind/in.

retransmettre [rǝtrɑ̃smɛtr] *vt* to broadcast.

retransmis, -e [rǝtrɑ̃smi, iz] *pp* → **retransmettre**.

retransmission [rǝtrɑ̃smisjɔ̃] *nf* broadcast.

retravailler [rǝtravaje] 1 *vt*: ~ **qqch** to work on sthg again. 2 *vi* to start work again.

rétrécir [retresir] *vi* [tissu] to shrink.

rétrécissement [retresismɑ̃] *nm* [de vêtement] shrinkage. ‖ MÉD stricture.

rétribution [retribysjɔ̃] *nf* remuneration.

rétro [retro] 1 *nm fam* [rétroviseur] rear-view mirror. 2 *adj inv* old-style.

rétroactif, -ive [retrɔaktif, iv] *adj* retrospective.

rétrograde [retrɔgrad] *adj péj* reactionary.

rétrograder [retrɔgrade] 1 *vt* to demote. 2 *vi* AUTOM to change down.

rétroprojecteur [retrɔprɔʒɛktœr] *nm* overhead projector.

rétrospectif, -ive [retrɔspɛktif, iv] *adj* retrospective. ○ **rétrospective** *nf* retrospective.

rétrospectivement [retrɔspɛktivmɑ̃] *adv* retrospectively.

retrousser [rǝtruse] *vt* [manches, pantalon] to roll up. ‖ [lèvres] to curl.

retrouvailles [rǝtruvaj] *nfpl* reunion (*sg*).

retrouver [rǝtruve] *vt* [gén] to find; [appétit] to recover, to regain. ‖ [ami] to meet, to see. ○ **se retrouver** *vp* [entre amis] to meet (up) again; **on se retrouve au café?** shall we meet up ou see each other at the café? ‖ [être de nouveau] to find o.s. again. ‖ [s'orienter] to find one's way; **ne pas s'y** ~ [dans papiers] to be completely lost.

rétroviseur [retrɔvizœr] *nm* rear-view mirror.

réunification [reynifikasjɔ̃] *nf* reunification.

réunion [reynjɔ̃] *nf* [séance] meeting. ‖ [jonction] union, merging. ‖ [d'amis, de famille] reunion.

réunir [reynir] *vt* [fonds] to collect. ‖ [qualités] to combine. ‖ [personnes] to bring together; [- après séparation] to reunite. ○ **se réunir** *vp* [personnes] to meet. ‖ [fleuves, rues] to converge.

réussi, -e [reysi] *adj* successful.

réussir [reysir] **1** *vi* [personne, affaire] to succeed, to be a success; ~ **à faire qqch** to succeed in doing sthg. || [climat]: ~ **à** to agree with. **2** *vt* [portrait, plat] to make a success of. || [examen] to pass.

réussite [reysit] *nf* [succès] success. || [jeu de cartes] patience *Br*, solitaire *Am*.

réutiliser [reytilize] *vt* to reuse.

revaloriser [rəvalɔrize] *vt* [monnaie] to revalue; [salaires] to raise.

revanche [rəvɑ̃ʃ] *nf* [vengeance] revenge; **prendre sa** ~ to take one's revenge. || SPORT return (match). || **en revanche** *loc adv* [par contre] on the other hand.

rêvasser [revase] *vi* to daydream.

rêve [rɛv] *nm* dream.

rêvé, -e [reve] *adj* ideal.

revêche [rəvɛʃ] *adj* surly.

réveil [revɛj] *nm* [de personne] waking (up). || [pendule] alarm clock.

réveiller [reveje] *vt* [personne] to wake up. || [courage] to revive. ○ **se réveiller** *vp* [personne] to wake (up).

réveillon [revɛjɔ̃] *nm* [jour - de Noël] Christmas Eve; [- de nouvel an] New Year's Eve.

réveillonner [revɛjɔne] *vi* to have a Christmas Eve/New Year's Eve meal.

révélateur, -trice [revelatœr, tris] *adj* revealing.

révélation [revelasjɔ̃] *nf* [gén] revelation. || [artiste] discovery.

révéler [revele] *vt* [gén] to reveal. || [artiste] to discover. ○ **se révéler** *vp* [s'avérer] to prove to be.

revenant [rəvnɑ̃] *nm* [fantôme] spirit, ghost. || *fam* [personne] stranger.

revendeur, -euse [rəvɑ̃dœr, øz] *nm, f* retailer.

revendication [rəvɑ̃dikasjɔ̃] *nf* claim, demand.

revendiquer [rəvɑ̃dike] *vt* [dû, responsabilité] to claim; [avec force] to demand.

revendre [rəvɑ̃dr] *vt* [après utilisation] to resell.

revendu, -e [rəvɑ̃dy] *pp* → **revendre**.

revenir [rəvnir] *vi* [gén] to come back, to return; ~ **sur** [sujet] to go over again; [décision] to go back on; ~ **à soi** to come to. || [mot, sujet] to crop up. || [à l'esprit]: ~ **à** to come back to. || [impliquer]: **cela revient au même/à dire que** ... it amounts to the same thing/to saying (that) .... || [coûter]: ~ **à** to come to, to amount to; ~ **cher** to be expensive. ||

[honneur, tâche]: ~ **à** to fall to. || CULIN: **faire** ~ to brown. || *loc*: **sa tête ne me revient pas** I don't like the look of him/her; **il n'en revenait pas** he couldn't get over it.

revente [rəvɑ̃t] *nf* resale.

revenu, -e [rəvny] *pp* → **revenir**. ○ **revenu** *nm* [de pays] revenue; [de personne] income.

rêver [reve] **1** *vi* to dream; [rêvasser] to daydream; ~ **de/à** to dream of/about. **2** *vt* to dream; ~ **que** to dream (that).

réverbération [reverberasjɔ̃] *nf* reverberation.

réverbère [reverber] *nm* street lamp ou light.

révérence [reverɑ̃s] *nf* [salut] bow.

révérend, -e [reverɑ̃, ɑ̃d] *adj* reverend. ○ **révérend** *nm* reverend.

rêverie [revri] *nf* reverie.

revers [rəver] *nm* [de main] back; [de pièce] reverse. || [de veste] lapel; [de pantalon] turn-up *Br*, cuff *Am*. || TENNIS backhand. || *fig* [de fortune] reversal.

réversible [reversibl] *adj* reversible.

revêtement [rəvɛtmɑ̃] *nm* surface.

revêtir [rəvɛtir] *vt* [mur, surface]: ~ **(de)** to cover (with). || [aspect] to take on, to assume. || [vêtement] to put on.

revêtu, -e [rəvɛty] *pp* → **revêtir**.

rêveur, -euse [revœr, øz] **1** *adj* dreamy. **2** *nm, f* dreamer.

revient [rəvjɛ̃] → **prix**.

revigorer [rəvigɔre] *vt* to invigorate.

revirement [rəvirmɑ̃] *nm* change.

réviser [revize] *vt* [réexamine, modifier] to revise, to review. || SCOL to revise. || [machine] to check.

révision [revizjɔ̃] *nf* [réexamen, modification] revision, review. || SCOL revision. || [de machine] checkup.

revisser [rəvise] *vt* to screw back again.

revivre [rəvivr] **1** *vi* [personne] to come back to life, to revive; *fig* [espoir] to be revived, to revive; **faire** ~ to revive. **2** *vt* to relive; **faire** ~ **qqch à qqn** to bring sthg back to sb.

revoici [rəvwasi] *prép*: **me** ~! it's me again!, I'm back!

revoir [rəvwar] *vt* [renouer avec] to see again. || [corriger, étudier] to review *Am*. ○ **se revoir** *vp* [amis] to see each other again. ○ **au revoir** *interj & nm* goodbye.

révoltant, -e [revɔltɑ̃, ɑ̃t] *adj* revolting.

révolte [revɔlt] *nf* revolt.

ring

révolter [revolte] *vt* to disgust. ○ **se révolter** *vp*: se ~ (contre) to revolt (against).

révolu, -e [revɔly] *adj* past; **avoir 15 ans ~s** ADMIN to be over 15.

révolution [revɔlysjɔ̃] *nf* [gén] revolution. || *fam* [effervescence] uproar.

révolutionnaire [revɔlysjɔnɛr] *nmf & adj* revolutionary.

révolutionner [revɔlysjɔne] *vt* [transformer] to revolutionize. || [mettre en émoi] to stir up.

revolver [revɔlvɛr] *nm* revolver.

révoquer [revɔke] *vt* [fonctionnaire] to dismiss. || [loi] to revoke.

revue [rəvy] *nf* [gén] review; ~ **de presse** press review; **passer en ~** *fig* to review. || [défilé] march-past. || [magazine] magazine. || [spectacle] revue.

rez-de-chaussée [redʃose] *nm inv* ground floor *Br*, first floor *Am*.

RFA (*abr de* **République fédérale d'Allemagne**) *nf* FRG.

rhabiller [rabije] *vt* to dress again. ○ **se rhabiller** *vp* to get dressed again.

rhésus [rezys] *nm* rhesus (factor); ~ **positif/négatif** rhesus positive/negative.

rhétorique [retɔrik] *nf* rhetoric.

Rhin [rɛ̃] *nm*: le ~ the Rhine.

rhinocéros [rinɔserɔs] *nm* rhinoceros.

rhino-pharyngite [rinofarɛ̃ʒit] (*pl* **rhino-pharyngites**) *nf* throat infection.

rhododendron [rɔdɔdɛdrɔ̃] *nm* rhododendron.

Rhône [ron] *nm*: le ~ the (River) Rhone.

rhubarbe [rybarb] *nf* rhubarb.

rhum [rɔm] *nm* rum.

rhumatisme [rymatism] *nm* rheumatism.

rhume [rym] *nm* cold; **attraper un ~** to catch a cold; ~ **des foins** hay fever.

ri [ri] *pp inv* → **rire**.

riant, -e [rijɑ̃, ɑ̃t] *adj* smiling; *fig* cheerful.

RIB, Rib [rib] (*abr de* **relevé d'identité bancaire**) *nm bank account identification slip*.

ribambelle [ribɑ̃bɛl] *nf*: ~ **de** string of.

ricaner [rikane] *vi* to snigger.

riche [riʃ] **1** *adj* [gén] rich; [personne, pays] rich, wealthy; ~ **en** OU **de** rich in. **2** *nmf* rich person; **les ~s** the rich.

richesse [riʃɛs] *nf* [de personne, pays] wealth (*U*). || [de faune, flore] abundance. ○ **richesses** *nfpl* [gén] wealth (*U*).

ricochet [rikɔʃɛ] *nm litt & fig* rebound; [de balle d'arme] ricochet.

rictus [riktys] *nm* rictus.

ride [rid] *nf* wrinkle; [de surface d'eau] ripple.

rideau, -x [rido] *nm* curtain; ~ **de fer** [frontière] Iron Curtain.

rider [ride] *vt* [peau] to wrinkle. || [surface] to ruffle. ○ **se rider** *vp* to become wrinkled.

ridicule [ridikyl] **1** *adj* ridiculous. **2** *nm*: **se couvrir de ~** to make o.s. look ridiculous; **tourner qqn/qqch en ~** to ridicule sb/sthg.

ridiculiser [ridikylize] *vt* to ridicule. ○ **se ridiculiser** *vp* to make o.s. look ridiculous.

rien [rjɛ̃] **1** *pron indéf* [en contexte négatif]: **ne ... rien** nothing, not ... anything; **je n'ai ~ fait** I've done nothing, I haven't done anything. || [aucune chose] nothing; **que fais-tu? — —** what are you doing? — nothing; ~ **de nouveau** nothing new; ~ **du tout** nothing at all; ~ **à faire** it's no good; **de ~!** don't mention it!, not at all!; **pour ~** for nothing. || [quelque chose] anything; **sans ~ dire** without saying anything. **2** *nm*: **pour un ~** [se fâcher, pleurer] for nothing, at the slightest thing; **en un ~ de temps** in no time at all. ○ **rien que** *loc adv* only, just; **la vérité, ~ que la vérité** the truth and nothing but the truth.

rieur, rieuse [rijœr, rijøz] *adj* cheerful.

rigide [riʒid] *adj* rigid; [muscle] tense.

rigidité [riʒidite] *nf* rigidity; [de principes, mœurs] strictness.

rigole [rigɔl] *nf* channel.

rigoler [rigɔle] *vi fam* [rire] to laugh. || [plaisanter]: ~ **(de)** to joke (about).

rigolo, -ote [rigɔlo, ɔt] *fam* **1** *adj* funny. **2** *nm, f péj* phoney.

rigoureux, -euse [rigurø, øz] *adj* [discipline, hiver] harsh. || [analyse] rigorous.

rigueur [rigœr] *nf* [de punition] severity, harshness. || [de climat] harshness. || [d'analyse] rigour, exactness. ○ **à la rigueur** *loc adv* if necessary, if need be.

rime [rim] *nf* rhyme.

rimer [rime] *vi*: ~ **(avec)** to rhyme (with).

rinçage [rɛ̃saʒ] *nm* rinsing.

rincer [rɛ̃se] *vt* [bouteille] to rinse out; [cheveux, linge] to rinse.

ring [riŋ] *nm* BOXE ring. || *Belg* [route] bypass.

riposte [ripɔst] *nf* [réponse] retort, riposte. || [contre-attaque] counterattack.

riposter [ripɔste] 1 *vt* : ~ que to retort or riposte that. 2 *vi* [répondre] to riposte. || [contre-attaquer] to counter, to retaliate.

rire [rir] 1 *nm* laugh; **éclater de ~** to burst out laughing. 2 *vi* [gén] to laugh. || [plaisanter]: **pour ~** *fam* as a joke, for a laugh.

risée [rize] *nf* ridicule; **être la ~ de** to be the laughing stock of.

risible [rizibl] *adj* [ridicule] ridiculous.

risque [risk] *nm* risk; **à tes/vos ~s et périls** at your own risk.

risqué, -e [riske] *adj* [entreprise] risky, dangerous.

risquer [riske] *vt* [vie, prison] to risk; ~ **de faire qqch** to be likely to do sthg; **je risque de perdre tout ce que j'ai** I'm running the risk of losing everything I have. || [tenter] to venture. ○ **se risquer** *vp* to venture; **se ~ à faire qqch** to dare to do sthg.

rissoler [risɔle] *vi* to brown.

rite [rit] *nm* RELIG rite. || [cérémonial & *fig*] ritual.

rituel, -elle [ritɥɛl] *adj* ritual. ○ **rituel** *nm* ritual.

rivage [rivaʒ] *nm* shore.

rival, -e, -aux [rival, o] 1 *adj* rival (*avant n*). 2 *nm, f* rival.

rivaliser [rivalize] *vi* : ~ **avec** to compete with.

rivalité [rivalite] *nf* rivalry.

rive [riv] *nf* [de rivière] bank.

river [rive] *vt* [fixer] : ~ **qqch à qqch** to rivet sthg to sthg. || [clou] to clinch; **être rivé à** *fig* to be riveted or glued to.

riverain, -e [rivrɛ̃, ɛn] *nm, f* resident.

rivet [rivɛ] *nm* rivet.

rivière [rivjɛr] *nf* river.

rixe [riks] *nf* fight, brawl.

riz [ri] *nm* rice.

rizière [rizjɛr] *nf* paddy (field).

RMI (*abr de* **revenu minimum d'insertion**) *nm minimum guaranteed income (for people with no other source of income).*

robe [rɔb] *nf* [de femme] dress; ~ **de mariée** wedding dress. || [peignoir] : ~ **de chambre** dressing gown. || [de cheval] coat. || [de vin] colour.

robinet [rɔbinɛ] *nm* tap.

robinetterie [rɔbinɛtri] *nf* [installations] taps (*pl*).

robot [rɔbo] *nm* [gén] robot. || [ménager] food processor.

robotique [rɔbɔtik] *nf* robotics (*U*).

robuste [rɔbyst] *adj* [personne, santé] robust. || [plante] hardy. || [voiture] sturdy.

roc [rɔk] *nm* rock.

rocade [rɔkad] *nf* bypass.

rocaille [rɔkaj] *nf* [cailloux] loose stones (*pl*). || [dans jardin] rock garden, rockery.

rocailleux, -euse [rɔkajø, øz] *adj* [terrain] rocky. || *fig* [voix] harsh.

rocambolesque [rɔkãbɔlɛsk] *adj* fantastic.

roche [rɔʃ] *nf* rock.

rocher [rɔʃe] *nm* rock.

rocheux, -euse [rɔʃø, øz] *adj* rocky. ○ **Rocheuses** *nfpl* : **les Rocheuses** the Rockies.

rock [rɔk] *nm* rock ('n' roll).

rodage [rɔdaʒ] *nm* [de véhicule] running-in; «**en ~**» "running in".

rodéo [rɔdeo] *nm* rodeo.

roder [rɔde] *vt* [véhicule] to run in. || *fam* [méthode] to run in, to debug; [personne] to break in.

rôdeur, -euse [rodœr, øz] *nm, f* prowler.

rogne [rɔɲ] *nf fam* bad temper; **être/se mettre en ~** to be in/to get into a bad mood, to be in/to get into a temper.

rogner [rɔɲe] 1 *vt* [ongles] to trim. || [revenus] to eat into. 2 *vi* : ~ **sur qqch** to cut down on sthg.

roi [rwa] *nm* king; **tirer les ~s** to celebrate Epiphany.

rôle [rol] *nm* role, part.

romain, -e [rɔmɛ̃, ɛn] *adj* Roman. ○ **Romain, -e** *nm, f* Roman.

roman, -e [rɔmã, an] *adj* [langue] Romance. || ARCHIT Romanesque. ○ **roman** *nm* LITTÉRATURE novel.

romance [rɔmãs] *nf* [chanson] love song.

romancier, -ière [rɔmãsje, jɛr] *nm, f* novelist.

romanesque [rɔmanɛsk] *adj* LITTÉRATURE novelistic. || [aventure] fabulous, storybook (*avant n*).

roman-feuilleton [rɔmãfœjtɔ̃] *nm* serial; *fig* soap opera.

roman-photo [rɔmãfɔto] *nm* story told in photographs.

romantique [rɔmãtik] *nmf & adj* romantic.

romantisme [rɔmãtism] *nm* ART Romantic movement. || [sensibilité] romanticism.

rouler

romarin [rɔmarɛ̃] *nm* rosemary.

rompre [rɔ̃pr] **1** *vt sout* [objet] to break. || [charme, marché] to break; [fiançailles, relations] to break off. **2** *vi* to break; ~ avec qqn *fig* to break up with sb. ○ **se rompre** *vp* to break; se ~ le cou/les reins to break one's neck/back.

ronce [rɔ̃s] *nf* [arbuste] bramble.

ronchonner [rɔ̃ʃɔne] *vi fam*: ~ (après) to grumble (at).

rond, -e [rɔ̃, rɔ̃d] *adj* [forme, chiffre] round. || [joue, ventre] chubby, plump. || *fam* [ivre] tight. ○ **rond** *nm* [cercle] circle; **en** ~ in a circle ou ring; **tourner en** ~ *fig* to go round in circles. || [anneau] ring. || *fam* [argent]: **je n'ai pas un** ~ I haven't got a penny ou bean.

ronde [rɔ̃d] *nf* [de surveillance] rounds (*pl*); [de policier] beat. || [danse] round. || MUS semibreve *Br*, whole note *Am.* ○ **à la ronde** *loc adv*: **à des kilomètres à la** ~ for miles around.

rondelle [rɔ̃dɛl] *nf* [de saucisson] slice. || [de métal] washer.

rondeur [rɔ̃dœr] *nf* [forme] roundness. || [partie charnue] curve.

rond-point [rɔ̃pwɛ̃] *nm* roundabout *Br*, traffic circle *Am.*

ronflant, -e [rɔ̃flɑ̃, ɑ̃t] *adj péj* grandiose.

ronflement [rɔ̃fləmɑ̃] *nm* [de dormeur] snore. || [de poêle, moteur] hum, purr.

ronfler [rɔ̃fle] *vi* [dormeur] to snore. || [poêle, moteur] to hum, to purr.

ronger [rɔ̃ʒe] *vt* [bois, os] to gnaw; [métal, falaise] to eat away at. ○ **se ronger** *vp* [grignoter]: se ~ **les ongles** to bite one's nails. || *fig* [se tourmenter] to worry, to torture o.s.

rongeur, -euse [rɔ̃ʒœr, øz] *adj* gnawing, rodent (*avant n*). ○ **rongeur** *nm* rodent.

ronronner [rɔ̃rɔne] *vi* [chat] to purr; [moteur] to purr, to hum.

rosace [rozas] *nf* [vitrail] rose window. || [figure géométrique] rosette.

rosbif [rɔzbif] *nm* [viande] roast beef.

rose [roz] **1** *nf* rose. **2** *nm* pink. **3** *adj* pink.

rosé, -e [roze] *adj* [teinte] rosy. ○ **rosé** *nm* rosé. ○ **rosée** *nf* dew.

roseau, -x [rozo] *nm* reed.

rosier [rozje] *nm* rose bush.

rosir [rozir] *vt & vi* to turn pink.

rosser [rɔse] *vt* to thrash.

rossignol [rɔsiɲɔl] *nm* [oiseau] nightingale.

rot [ro] *nm* burp.

rotatif, -ive [rɔtatif, iv] *adj* rotary.

rotation [rɔtasjɔ̃] *nf* rotation.

roter [rɔte] *vi fam* to burp.

rôti, -e [roti] *adj* roast. ○ **rôti** *nm* roast, joint.

rotin [rɔtɛ̃] *nm* rattan.

rôtir [rotir] *vt* to roast.

rôtisserie [rotisri] *nf* [magasin] *shop selling roast meat.*

rotonde [rɔtɔ̃d] *nf* [bâtiment] rotunda.

rotule [rɔtyl] *nf* kneecap.

rouage [rwaʒ] *nm* cog, gearwheel; **les** ~**s de l'État** *fig* the wheels of State.

rouble [rubl] *nm* rouble.

roucouler [rukule] *vi* to coo.

roue [ru] *nf* [gén] wheel; ~ **de secours** spare wheel. || [de paon]: **faire la** ~ to display. || GYM cartwheel.

rouer [rwe] *vt*: ~ **qqn de coups** to thrash sb, to beat sb up.

rouge [ruʒ] **1** *nm* [couleur] red. || *fam* [vin] red (wine). || [fard] rouge, blusher; ~ **à lèvres** lipstick. || AUTOM: **passer au** ~ to turn red; [conducteur] to go through a red light. **2** *adj* [gén] red. || [fer, tison] red-hot.

rouge-gorge [ruʒgɔrʒ] *nm* robin.

rougeole [ruʒɔl] *nf* measles (*sg*).

rougeoyer [ruʒwaje] *vi* to turn red.

rougeur [ruʒœr] *nf* [sur peau] red spot ou blotch.

rougir [ruʒir] **1** *vt* [colorer] to turn red. || [chauffer] to make red-hot. **2** *vi* [devenir rouge] to turn red. || [d'émotion]: ~ (**de**) [de plaisir, colère] to flush (with); [de gêne] to blush (with). || *fig* [avoir honte]: ~ **de qqch** to be ashamed of sthg.

rouille [ruj] **1** *nf* [oxyde] rust. || CULIN *spicy garlic sauce for fish soup.* **2** *adj inv* rust.

rouiller [ruje] **1** *vt* to rust, to make rusty. **2** *vi* to rust.

roulade [rulad] *nf* [galipette] roll.

rouleau, -x [rulo] *nm* [gén & TECHNOL] roller; ~ **compresseur** steamroller. || [de papier] roll. || [à pâtisserie] rolling pin.

roulement [rulmɑ̃] *nm* [de personnel] rotation. || [de tambour, tonnerre] roll. || TECHNOL rolling bearing.

rouler [rule] **1** *vt* [déplacer] to wheel. || [enrouler - tapis] to roll up; [- cigarette] to roll. || LING to roll. || *fam fig* [duper] to swindle, to do. **2** *vi* [ballon, bateau] to roll. || [véhicule] to go, to run; [suj: personne] to drive. ○ **se rouler** *vp* to roll about; **se ~ en boule** to roll o.s. into a ball.

roulette [rulɛt] *nf* [petite roue] castor. || [de dentiste] drill. || JEU roulette.

roulis [ruli] *nm* roll.

roulotte [rulɔt] *nf* [de gitan] caravan; [de tourisme] caravan *Br*, trailer *Am*.

roumain, -e [rumɛ̃, ɛn] *adj* Romanian. ○ **roumain** *nm* [langue] Romanian. ○ **Roumain, -e** *nm, f* Romanian.

Roumanie [rumani] *nf*: **la ~** Romania.

rouquin, -e [rukɛ̃, in] *fam* 1 *adj* red-headed. 2 *nm, f* redhead.

rouspéter [ruspete] *vi fam* to grumble, to moan.

rousse → roux.

rousseur → tache.

roussir [rusir] 1 *vt* [rendre roux] to turn brown. || [brûler légèrement] to singe. 2 *vi* to turn brown; CULIN to brown.

route [rut] *nf* [gén] road; **en ~** on the way; **en ~!** let's go!; **mettre en ~** [démarrer] to start up; *fig* to get under way. || [itinéraire] route.

routier, -ière [rutje, jɛr] *adj* road (*avant n*). ○ **routier** *nm* [chauffeur] long-distance lorry driver *Br* ou trucker *Am*. || [restaurant] ≃ truck stop *Am*.

routine [rutin] *nf* routine.

rouvert, -e [ruvɛr, ɛrt] *pp* → rouvrir.

rouvrir [ruvrir] *vt* to reopen, to open again. ○ **se rouvrir** *vp* to reopen, to open again.

roux, rousse [ru, rus] 1 *adj* [cheveux] red. || [sucre] brown. 2 *nm, f* [personne] redhead.

royal, -e, -aux [rwajal, o] *adj* [de roi] royal. || [magnifique] princely.

royaliste [rwajalist] *nmf & adj* royalist.

royaume [rwajom] *nm* kingdom.

Royaume-Uni [rwajomyni] *nm*: **le ~** the United Kingdom.

royauté [rwajote] *nf* [fonction] kingship. || [régime] monarchy.

RPR (*abr de* **Rassemblement pour la République**) *nm French political party to the right of the political spectrum*.

rte *abr de* route.

ruade [rɥad] *nf* kick.

ruban [rybɑ̃] *nm* ribbon; **~ adhésif** adhesive tape.

rubéole [rybeɔl] *nf* German measles (*sg*), rubella.

rubis [rybi] *nm* [pierre précieuse] ruby.

rubrique [rybrik] *nf* [chronique] column. || [dans classement] heading.

ruche [ryʃ] *nf* [abri] hive, beehive.

rude [ryd] *adj* [surface] rough. || [voix] harsh. || [personne, manières] rough, uncouth. || [hiver, épreuve] harsh, severe; [tâche, adversaire] tough.

rudement [rydmɑ̃] *adv* [brutalement - tomber] hard; [- répondre] harshly. || *fam* [très] damn.

rudesse [rydɛs] *nf* harshness, severity.

rudimentaire [rydimɑ̃tɛr] *adj* rudimentary.

rudoyer [rydwaje] *vt* to treat harshly.

rue [ry] *nf* street.

ruée [rɥe] *nf* rush.

ruelle [rɥɛl] *nf* [rue] alley, lane.

ruer [rɥe] *vi* to kick. ○ **se ruer** *vp*: **se ~ sur** to pounce on.

rugby [rygbi] *nm* rugby.

rugir [ryʒir] *vi* to roar; [vent] to howl.

rugissement [ryʒismɑ̃] *nm* roar, roaring (*U*); [de vent] howling.

rugosité [rygozite] *nf* [de surface] roughness. || [aspérité] rough patch.

rugueux, -euse [rygø, øz] *adj* rough.

ruine [rɥin] *nf* [gén] ruin. || [effondrement] ruin, downfall. || [humaine] wreck.

ruiner [rɥine] *vt* to ruin. ○ **se ruiner** *vp* to ruin o.s., to bankrupt o.s.

ruineux, -euse [rɥinø, øz] *adj* ruinous.

ruisseau, -x [rɥiso] *nm* [cours d'eau] stream. || *fig & péj* [caniveau] gutter.

ruisseler [rɥisle] *vi*: **~ (de)** to stream (with).

rumeur [rymœr] *nf* [bruit] murmur. || [nouvelle] rumour.

ruminer [rymine] *vt* to ruminate; *fig* to mull over.

rupture [ryptyr] *nf* [cassure] breaking. || *fig* [changement] abrupt change. || [de négociations, fiançailles] breaking off; [de contrat] breach. || [amoureuse] breakup.

rural, -e, -aux [ryral, o] *adj* country (*avant n*), rural.

ruse [ryz] *nf* [habileté] cunning, craftiness. || [subterfuge] ruse.

rusé, -e [ryze] *adj* cunning, crafty.

russe [rys] 1 *adj* Russian. 2 *nm* [langue] Russian. ○ **Russe** *nmf* Russian.

Russie [rysi] *nf*: **la ~** Russia.

rustine [rystin] *nf* small rubber patch for repairing bicycle tyres.

rustique [rystik] *adj* rustic.

rustre [rystr] *péj nmf* lout.

rutilant, -e [rytilɑ̃, ɑ̃t] *adj* [brillant] gleaming.

rythme [ritm] *nm* MUS rhythm. || [de travail, production] pace, rate.

rythmique [ritmik] *adj* rhythmical.

sain

S

s, S [ɛs] *nm inv* [lettre] s, S. || [forme] zig-zag. ○ **S** (*abr de* **Sud**) S.

s' → **se**.

s/ *abr de* **sur**.

sa → **son**.

SA (*abr de* **société anonyme**) *nf* ≃ Ltd *Br*, ≃ Inc. *Am*.

sabbatique [sabatik] *adj* RELIG Sabbath (*avant n*). || [congé] sabbatical.

sable [sabl] *nm*; **~s mouvants** quicksand (*sg*), quicksands.

sablé, -e [sable] *adj* [route] sandy. ○ **sablé** *nm* ≃ shortbread (*U*).

sabler [sable] *vt* [route] to sand. || [boire]: **~ le champagne** to crack a bottle of champagne.

sablier [sablije] *nm* hourglass.

sablonneux, -euse [sablɔnø, øz] *adj* sandy.

saborder [sabɔrde] *vt* [navire] to scuttle; *fig* [entreprise] to wind up.

sabot [sabo] *nm* [chaussure] clog. || [de cheval] hoof. || AUTOM: **~ de Denver** wheel clamp, Denver boot.

sabotage [sabɔtaʒ] *nm* [volontaire] sabotage. || [bâclage] bungling.

saboter [sabɔte] *vt* [volontairement] to sabotage. || [bâcler] to bungle.

saboteur, -euse [sabɔtœr, øz] *nm, f* MIL & POLIT saboteur.

sabre [sabr] *nm* sabre.

sac [sak] *nm* [gén] bag; [pour grains] sack; **~ de couchage** sleeping bag; **~ à dos** rucksack; **~ à main** handbag. || *fam* [10 francs] 10 francs.

saccade [sakad] *nf* jerk.

saccadé, -e [sakade] *adj* jerky.

saccage [sakaʒ] *nm* havoc.

saccager [sakaʒe] *vt* [piller] to sack. || [dévaster] to destroy.

sachant *ppr* → **savoir**.

sache, saches *etc* → **savoir**.

sachet [saʃɛ] *nm* [de bonbons] bag; [de shampooing] sachet; **~ de thé** tea-bag.

sacoche [sakɔʃ] *nf* [de médecin, d'écolier] bag. || [de cycliste] pannier.

sac-poubelle [sakpubɛl] (*pl* **sacs-poubelle**) *nm* [petit] dustbin liner.

sacre [sakr] *nm* [de roi] coronation.

sacré, -e [sakre] *adj* [gén] sacred. || RELIG [ordres, écritures] holy. || (*avant n*) *fam* [maudit] goddam (*avant n*) *Am*.

sacrement [sakrəmɑ̃] *nm* sacrament.

sacrément [sakremɑ̃] *adv* *fam vieilli* dashed.

sacrer [sakre] *vt* [roi] to crown. || *fig* [déclarer] to hail.

sacrifice [sakrifis] *nm* sacrifice.

sacrifier [sakrifje] *vt* [gén] to sacrifice; **~ qqn/qqch à** to sacrifice sb/sthg to. ○ **se sacrifier** *vp*: **se ~ à/pour** to sacrifice o.s. to/for.

sacrilège [sakrilɛʒ] **1** *nm* sacrilege. **2** *adj* sacrilegious.

sacristain [sakristɛ̃] *nm* sacristan.

sacristie [sakristi] *nf* sacristy.

sadique [sadik] **1** *nmf* sadist. **2** *adj* sadistic.

sadisme [sadism] *nm* sadism.

safari [safari] *nm* safari.

safran [safrɑ̃] *nm* [épice] saffron.

saga [saga] *nf* saga.

sage [saʒ] **1** *adj* [personne, conseil] wise, sensible. || [enfant, chien] good. **2** *nm* wise man, sage.

sage-femme [saʒfam] *nf* midwife.

sagement [saʒmɑ̃] *adv* [avec bon sens] wisely, sensibly. || [docilement] like a good girl/boy.

sagesse [saʒɛs] *nf* [bon sens] wisdom, good sense. || [docilité] good behaviour.

Sagittaire [saʒitɛr] *nm* ASTROL Sagittarius.

Sahara [saara] *nm*: **le ~** the Sahara.

saignant, -e [sɛɲɑ̃, ɑ̃t] *adj* [blessure] bleeding. || [viande] rare, underdone.

saignement [sɛɲmɑ̃] *nm* bleeding.

saigner [sɛɲe] **1** *vt* [malade, animal] to bleed. || [financièrement]: **~ qqn (à blanc)** to bleed sb (white). **2** *vi* to bleed; **je saigne du nez** my nose is bleeding, I've got a nosebleed.

saillant, -e [sajɑ̃, ɑ̃t] *adj* [proéminent] projecting, protruding; [muscles] bulging; [pommettes] prominent.

saillie [saji] *nf* [avancée] projection; **en ~** projecting.

saillir [sajir] *vi* [muscles] to bulge.

sain, -e [sɛ̃, sɛn] *adj* [gén] healthy; **~ et sauf** safe and sound. || [lecture] wholesome. || [fruit] fit to eat.

saint, -e [sɛ̃, sɛ̃t] **1** adj [sacré] holy. **2** nm, f saint.

saint-bernard [sɛ̃bɛrnar] nm inv [chien] St Bernard.

saintement [sɛ̃tmɑ̃] adv: **vivre ~ to** lead a saintly life.

sainte-nitouche [sɛ̃tnituʃ] nf péj: **c'est une ~** butter wouldn't melt in her mouth.

sainteté [sɛ̃tte] nf holiness.

sais, sait etc → **savoir**.

saisie [sezi] nf FISC & JUR distraint, seizure. || INFORM input; **~ de données** data capture.

saisir [sezir] vt [empoigner] to take hold of; [avec force] to seize. || FIN & JUR to seize, to distrain. || INFORM to capture. || [comprendre] to grasp. || [suj: sensation, émotion] to grip, to seize. || [surprendre]: **être saisi par** to be struck by. || CULIN to seal. ○ **se saisir** vp: **se ~ de qqn/qqch** to seize sb/sthg, to grab sb/sthg.

saisissant, -e [sezisɑ̃, ɑ̃t] adj [spectacle] gripping; [ressemblance] striking.

saison [sɛzɔ̃] nf season; **en/hors ~** in/out of season; **la haute/basse/morte ~** the high/low/off season.

saisonnier, -ière [sɛzɔnje, jɛr] **1** adj seasonal. **2** nm, f seasonal worker.

salace [salas] adj salacious.

salade [salad] nf [plante] lettuce. || [plat] (green) salad.

saladier [saladje] nm salad bowl.

salaire [salɛr] nm [rémunération] salary, wage. || fig [récompense] reward.

salant [salɑ̃] → **marais**.

salarial, -e, -iaux [salarjal, jo] adj wage (avant n).

salarié, -e [salarje] **1** adj [personne] wage-earning. || [travail] paid. **2** nm, f salaried employee.

salaud [salo] vulg **1** nm bastard. **2** adj m shitty.

sale [sal] adj [linge, mains] dirty; [couleur] dirty, dingy. || (avant n) [type, gueule, coup] nasty; [tour, histoire] dirty; [bête, temps] filthy.

salé, -e [sale] adj [eau, saveur] salty; [beurre] salted; [viande, poisson] salt (avant n), salted. || fig [histoire] spicy. || fam fig [addition, facture] steep.

saler [sale] vt [gén] to salt.

saleté [salte] nf [malpropreté] dirtiness, filthiness. || [crasse] dirt (U), filth (U). || **faire des ~s** to make a mess. || fam [maladie] bug. || [obscénité] dirty thing, obscenity; **il m'a dit des ~s** he used obscenities to me. || [action] disgusting thing; **faire une ~ à qqn** to play a dirty trick on sb.

salière [saljɛr] nf saltcellar.

salir [salir] vt [linge, mains] to (make) dirty, to soil. || fig [réputation, personne] to sully.

salissant, -e [salisɑ̃, ɑ̃t] adj [tissu] easily soiled. || [travail] dirty, messy.

salive [saliv] nf saliva.

saliver [salive] vi to salivate.

salle [sal] nf [pièce] room; **~ d'attente** waiting room; **~ de bains** bathroom; **~ de classe** classroom; **~ d'embarquement** departure lounge; **~ à manger** dining room; **~ d'opération** operating theatre; **~ de séjour** living room; **~ de spectacle** theatre; **~ des ventes** saleroom. || [de spectacle] auditorium.

salon [salɔ̃] nm [de maison] lounge Br, living room. || [commerce]: **~ de coiffure** hairdressing salon, hairdresser's; **~ de thé** tearoom. || [foire-exposition] show.

salope [salɔp] nf vulg bitch.

saloperie [salɔpri] nf fam [pacotille] rubbish (U). || [maladie] bug. || [saleté] junk (U), rubbish (U). || [action] dirty trick; **faire des ~s à qqn** to play dirty tricks on sb. || [propos] dirty comment.

salopette [salɔpɛt] nf [d'ouvrier] overalls (pl); [à bretelles] dungarees (pl).

saltimbanque [saltɛ̃bɑ̃k] nmf acrobat.

salubrité [salybrite] nf healthiness.

saluer [salɥe] vt [accueillir] to greet. || [dire au revoir à] to take one's leave of. || MIL & fig to salute. ○ **se saluer** vp to say hello/goodbye (to one another).

salut [saly] **1** nm [de la main] wave; [de la tête] nod; [propos] greeting. || MIL salute. || RELIG salvation. **2** interj fam [bonjour] hi!; [au revoir] bye!, see you!

salutaire [salytɛr] adj [conseil, expérience] salutary. || [remède, repos] beneficial.

salutation [salytasjɔ̃] nf littéraire salutation, greeting. ○ **salutations** nfpl: **veuillez agréer, Monsieur, mes distinguées** ou **mes sincères ~s** sout yours faithfully, yours sincerely.

salve [salv] nf salvo.

samedi [samdi] nm Saturday; **nous sommes partis ~** we left on Saturday; **~ 13 septembre** Saturday 13th September; **~ dernier/prochain** last/next Saturday; **le ~** on Saturdays.

SAMU, Samu [samy] (abr de Service

d'aide médicale d'urgence) *nm French ambulance and emergency service.*

sanatorium [sanatɔrjɔm] *nm* sanatorium.

sanction [sɑ̃ksjɔ̃] *nf* sanction; *fig* [conséquence] penalty, price; **prendre des ~s contre** to impose sanctions on.

sanctionner [sɑ̃ksjɔne] *vt* to sanction.

sanctuaire [sɑ̃ktɥɛr] *nm* [d'église] sanctuary. || [lieu saint] shrine.

sandale [sɑ̃dal] *nf* sandal.

sandalette [sɑ̃dalɛt] *nf* sandal.

sandwich [sɑ̃dwitʃ] (*pl* **sandwiches** OU **sandwichs**) *nm* sandwich.

sang [sɑ̃] *nm* blood.

sang-froid [sɑ̃frwa] *nm inv* calm; **de ~** in cold blood; **perdre/garder son ~** to lose/to keep one's head.

sanglant, -e [sɑ̃glɑ̃, ɑ̃t] *adj* bloody.

sangle [sɑ̃gl] *nf* strap; [de selle] girth.

sangler [sɑ̃gle] *vt* [attacher] to strap; [cheval] to girth.

sanglier [sɑ̃glije] *nm* boar.

sanglot [sɑ̃glo] *nm* sob; **éclater en ~s** to burst into sobs.

sangloter [sɑ̃glɔte] *vi* to sob.

sangsue [sɑ̃sy] *nf* leech; *fig* [personne] bloodsucker.

sanguin, -e [sɑ̃gɛ̃, in] *adj* ANAT blood (*avant n*). || [rouge - visage] ruddy; [- orange] blood (*avant n*).

sanguinaire [sɑ̃giner] *adj* [tyran] bloodthirsty. || [lutte] bloody.

Sanisette® [sanizɛt] *nf automatic public toilet.*

sanitaire [saniter] *adj* [service, mesure] health (*avant n*). || [installation, appareil] bathroom (*avant n*). ○ **sanitaires** *nmpl* toilets and showers.

sans [sɑ̃] **1** *prép* without; **~ argent** without any money; **~ faire un effort** without making an effort. **2** *adv*: **passe-moi mon manteau, je ne veux pas sortir ~** pass me my coat, I don't want to go out without it. ○ **sans que** *loc conj*: **~ que vous le sachiez** without your knowing.

sans-abri [sɑ̃zabri] *nmf inv* homeless person.

sans-emploi [sɑ̃zɑ̃plwa] *nmf inv* unemployed person.

sans-gêne [sɑ̃ʒɛn] **1** *nm inv* [qualité] rudeness, lack of consideration. **2** *adj inv* rude, inconsiderate.

santé [sɑ̃te] *nf* health; **à ta/votre ~!** cheers!, good health!

santon [sɑ̃tɔ̃] *nm figure placed in Christmas crib.*

saoul = **soûl**.

saouler = **soûler**.

sapeur-pompier [sapœrpɔ̃pje] *nm* fireman, fire fighter.

saphir [safir] *nm* sapphire.

sapin [sapɛ̃] *nm* [arbre] fir, firtree; **~ de Noël** Christmas tree. || [bois] fir, deal *Br*.

sarcasme [sarkasm] *nm* sarcasm.

sarcastique [sarkastik] *adj* sarcastic.

sarcler [sarkle] *vt* to weed.

sarcophage [sarkɔfaʒ] *nm* sarcophagus.

Sardaigne [sardɛɲ] *nf*: **la ~** Sardinia.

sardine [sardin] *nf* sardine.

SARL, Sarl (*abr de* **société à responsabilité limitée**) *nf* limited liability company; **Leduc, ~** ≃ Leduc Ltd.

sarment [sarmɑ̃] *nm* [de vigne] shoot.

sas [sas] *nm* AÉRON & NAVIG airlock. || [d'écluse] lock. || [tamis] sieve.

satanique [satanik] *adj* satanic.

satellite [satelit] *nm* satellite.

satiété [sasjete] *nf*: **à ~** [boire, manger] one's fill; [répéter] ad nauseam.

satin [satɛ̃] *nm* satin.

satiné, -e [satine] *adj* satin (*avant n*); [peau] satiny-smooth.

satire [satir] *nf* satire.

satirique [satirik] *adj* satirical.

satisfaction [satisfaksjɔ̃] *nf* satisfaction.

satisfaire [satisfer] *vt* to satisfy. ○ **se satisfaire** *vp*: **se ~ de** to be satisfied with.

satisfaisant, -e [satisfəzɑ̃, ɑ̃t] *adj* [travail] satisfactory. || [expérience] satisfying.

satisfait, -e [satisfe, ɛt] **1** *pp* → **satisfaire**. **2** *adj* satisfied; **être ~ de** to be satisfied with.

saturation [satyrasjɔ̃] *nf* saturation.

saturé, -e [satyre] *adj*: **~ (de)** saturated (with).

saturne [satyrn] *nm vieilli* lead. ○ **Saturne** *nf* ASTRON Saturn.

satyre [satir] *nm* satyr; *fig* sex maniac.

sauce [sos] *nf* CULIN sauce.

saucière [sosjer] *nf* sauceboat.

saucisse [sosis] *nf* CULIN sausage.

saucisson [sosisɔ̃] *nm* slicing sausage.

sauf¹, sauve [sof, sov] *adj* [personne] safe, unharmed; *fig* [honneur] saved, intact.

sauf² [sof] *prép* [à l'exclusion de] except, apart from. || [sous réserve de] barring; **~ que** except (that).

sauf-conduit [sofkɔ̃dɥi] (*pl* **sauf-conduits**) *nm* safe-conduct.

sauge [soʒ] *nf* CULIN sage.

saugrenu, -e [sogrəny] *adj* ridiculous, nonsensical.

saule [sol] *nm* willow; ~ **pleureur** weeping willow.

saumon [somɔ̃] *nm* salmon.

saumoné, -e [somɔne] *adj* salmon (*avant n*).

saumure [somyr] *nf* brine.

sauna [sona] *nm* sauna.

saupoudrer [sopudre] *vt*: ~ **qqch de** to sprinkle sthg with.

saurai, sauras *etc* → **savoir**.

saut [so] *nm* [bond] leap, jump; ~ **en hauteur** SPORT high jump; ~ **en longueur** SPORT long jump, broad jump *Am*; **faire un ~ chez qqn** *fig* to pop in and see sb.

sauté, -e [sote] *adj* sautéed.

saute-mouton [sotmutɔ̃] *nm inv*: **jouer à** ~ to play leapfrog.

sauter [sote] **1** *vi* [bondir] to jump, to leap; ~ **à la corde** to skip; ~ **d'un sujet à l'autre** *fig* to jump from one subject to another; ~ **au cou de qqn** *fig* to throw one's arms around sb. || [exploser] to blow up; [fusible] to blow. || [partir - bouchon] to fly out; [- serrure] to burst off; [- bouton] to fly off; [- chaîne de vélo] to come off. **2** *vt* [fossé, obstacle] to jump ou leap over. || *fig* [page, repas] to skip.

sauterelle [sotrɛl] *nf* ZOOL grasshopper.

sautiller [sotije] *vi* to hop.

sautoir [sotwar] *nm* [bijou] chain.

sauvage [sovaʒ] **1** *adj* [plante, animal] wild. || [farouche - animal familier] shy, timid; [- personne] unsociable. || [conduite, haine] savage. **2** *nmf* [solitaire] recluse. || *péj* [brute, indigène] savage.

sauvagerie [sovaʒri] *nf* [férocité] brutality, savagery. || [insociabilité] unsociableness.

sauve → **sauf**.

sauvegarde [sovgard] *nf* [protection] safeguard. || INFORM saving.

sauvegarder [sovgarde] *vt* [protéger] to safeguard. || INFORM to save; [copier] to back up.

sauve-qui-peut [sovkipø] **1** *nm inv* [débandade] stampede. **2** *interj* every man for himself!

sauver [sove] *vt* [gén] to save; ~ **qqn/qqch de** to save sb/sthg from, to rescue sb/sthg from. || [navire, biens] to salvage. ○ **se sauver** *vp*: **se** ~ **(de)** to run away (from); [prisonnier] to escape (from).

sauvetage [sovtaʒ] *nm* [de personne] rescue. || [de navire, biens] salvage.

sauveteur [sovtœr] *nm* rescuer.

sauvette [sovet] ○ **à la sauvette** *loc adv* hurriedly, at great speed.

savamment [savamɑ̃] *adv* [avec habileté] skilfully, cleverly.

savane [savan] *nf* savanna.

savant, -e [savɑ̃, ɑ̃t] *adj* [érudit] scholarly. || [animal] performing (*avant n*). ○ **savant** *nm* scientist.

saveur [savœr] *nf* flavour; *fig* savour.

savoir [savwar] **1** *vt* [gén] to know; **faire** ~ **qqch à qqn** to tell sb sthg, to inform sb of sthg; **sans le** ~ unconsciously, without being aware of it; **tu (ne) peux pas** ~ *fam* you have no idea; **pas que je sache** not as far as I know. || [être capable de] to know how to; **sais-tu conduire?** can you drive? **2** *nm* learning. ○ **à savoir** *loc conj* namely, that is.

savoir-faire [savwarfer] *nm inv* know-how, expertise.

savoir-vivre [savwarvivr] *nm inv* good manners (*pl*).

savon [savɔ̃] *nm* [matière] soap; [pain] cake ou bar of soap. || *fam* [réprimande] telling-off.

savonner [savɔne] *vt* [linge] to soap.

savonnette [savɔnet] *nf* guest soap.

savourer [savure] *vt* to savour.

savoureux, -euse [savurø, øz] *adj* [mets] tasty. || *fig* [anecdote] juicy.

saxophone [saksɔfɔn] *nm* saxophone.

scabreux, -euse [skabrø, øz] *adj* [propos] shocking, indecent.

scalpel [skalpɛl] *nm* scalpel.

scalper [skalpe] *vt* to scalp.

scandale [skɑ̃dal] *nm* [fait choquant] scandal. || [indignation] uproar. || [tapage] scene; **faire du** ou **un** ~ to make a scene.

scandaleux, -euse [skɑ̃dalø, øz] *adj* scandalous, outrageous.

scandaliser [skɑ̃dalize] *vt* to shock, to scandalize.

scander [skɑ̃de] *vt* [vers] to scan. || [slogan] to chant.

scandinave [skɑ̃dinav] *adj* Scandinavian. ○ **Scandinave** *nmf* Scandinavian.

Scandinavie [skɑ̃dinavi] *nf*: **la** ~ Scandinavia.

scanner¹ [skane] *vt* to scan.

scanner² [skaner] *nm* scanner.

scaphandre [skafɑ̃dr] *nm* [de plongeur] diving suit. || [d'astronaute] spacesuit.

scarabée [skarabe] *nm* beetle, scarab.

scatologique [skatɔlɔʒik] *adj* scatological.

sceau, -x [so] *nm* seal; *fig* stamp, hallmark.

scélérat, -e [selera, at] *nm, f* villain.

sceller [sele] *vt* [gén] to seal. ‖ CONSTR [fixer] to embed.

scénario [senarjo] *nm* CIN, LITTÉRATURE & THÉÂTRE [canevas] scenario. ‖ CIN & TÉLÉ [découpage, synopsis] screenplay, script. ‖ *fig* [rituel] pattern.

scénariste [senarist] *nmf* scriptwriter.

scène [sɛn] *nf* [gén] scene. ‖ [estrade] stage; **mettre en ~** THÉÂTRE to stage; CIN to direct.

scepticisme [sɛptisism] *nm* scepticism.

sceptique [sɛptik] **1** *nmf* sceptic. **2** *adj* [incrédule] sceptical. ‖ PHILO sceptic.

sceptre [sɛptr] *nm* sceptre.

schéma [ʃema] *nm* [diagramme] diagram.

schématique [ʃematik] *adj* [dessin] diagrammatic. ‖ [interprétation, exposé] simplified.

schématiser [ʃematize] *vt péj* [généraliser] to oversimplify.

schisme [ʃism] *nm* RELIG schism. ‖ [d'opinion] split.

schizophrène [skizɔfrɛn] *nmf* & *adj* schizophrenic.

schizophrénie [skizɔfreni] *nf* schizophrenia.

sciatique [sjatik] **1** *nf* sciatica. **2** *adj* sciatic.

scie [si] *nf* [outil] saw.

sciemment [sjamã] *adv* knowingly.

science [sjãs] *nf* [connaissances scientifiques] science; **~s humaines** ou **sociales** UNIV social sciences. ‖ [érudition] knowledge. ‖ [art] art.

science-fiction [sjãsfiksjɔ̃] *nf* science fiction.

scientifique [sjãtifik] **1** *nmf* scientist. **2** *adj* scientific.

scier [sje] *vt* [branche] to saw.

scierie [siri] *nf* sawmill.

scinder [sɛ̃de] *vt*: **~ (en)** to split (into), to divide (into). ○ **se scinder** *vp*: **se ~ (en)** to split (into), to divide (into).

scintiller [sɛ̃tije] *vi* to sparkle.

scission [sisjɔ̃] *nf* split.

sciure [sjyr] *nf* sawdust.

sclérose [skleroz] *nf* sclerosis; *fig* ossification; **~ en plaques** multiple sclerosis.

sclérosé, -e [skleroze] *adj* sclerotic; *fig* ossified.

scolaire [skɔlɛr] *adj* school (*avant n*); *péj* bookish.

scolarité [skɔlarite] *nf* schooling; **frais de ~** SCOL school fees; UNIV tuition fees.

scooter [skutœr] *nm* scooter.

scorbut [skɔrbyt] *nm* scurvy.

score [skɔr] *nm* SPORT score.

scorpion [skɔrpjɔ̃] *nm* scorpion. ○ **Scorpion** *nm* ASTROL Scorpio.

scotch [skɔtʃ] *nm* [alcool] whisky, Scotch.

Scotch® [skɔtʃ] *nm* [adhésif] ≃ Scotch tape® *Am*.

scotcher [skɔtʃe] *vt* to scotch-tape *Am*.

scout, -e [skut] *adj* scout (*avant n*). ○ **scout** *nm* scout.

scribe [skrib] *nm* HIST scribe.

script [skript] *nm* CIN & TÉLÉ script.

scripte [skript] *nmf* CIN & TÉLÉ continuity person.

scrupule [skrypyl] *nm* scruple; **sans ~s** [être] unscrupulous; [agir] unscrupulously.

scrupuleux, -euse [skrypylø, øz] *adj* scrupulous.

scrutateur, -trice [skrytatœr, tris] *adj* searching.

scruter [skryte] *vt* to scrutinize.

scrutin [skrytɛ̃] *nm* [vote] ballot. ‖ [système] voting system; **~ majoritaire** first-past-the-post system; **~ proportionnel** proportional representation system.

sculpter [skylte] *vt* to sculpt.

sculpteur [skyltœr] *nm* sculptor.

sculpture [skyltyr] *nf* sculpture.

SDF (*abr de* **sans domicile fixe**) *nmf*: **les ~** the homeless.

se [sə], **s'** (*devant voyelle ou h muet*) *pron pers* (*réfléchi*) [personne] oneself, himself (*f* herself), (*pl*) themselves; [chose, animal] itself, (*pl*) themselves; **elle ~ regarde dans le miroir** she looks at herself in the mirror. ‖ (*réciproque*) each other, one another; **ils ~ sont rencontrés hier** they met yesterday. ‖ (*passif*): **ce produit ~ vend bien/partout** this product is selling well/is sold everywhere. ‖ [remplace l'adjectif possessif]: **~ laver les mains** to wash one's hands.

séance [seãs] *nf* [réunion] meeting, sitting, session. ‖ [période] session; [de pose] sitting. ‖ CIN & THÉÂTRE performance. ‖ *loc*: **~ tenante** right away, forthwith.

seau, -x [so] *nm* [récipient] bucket. ‖ [contenu] bucketful.

sec, sèche [sɛk, sɛʃ] *adj* [gén] dry. ‖ [fruits] dried. ‖ [personne - maigre] lean; [- austère] austere. ‖ *fig* [cœur] hard; [voix, ton] sharp. ○ **sec 1** *adv* [beaucoup]: **boire ~** to drink heavily. **2** *nm*: **tenir au ~** to keep in a dry place.

sécable [sekabl] *adj* divisible.

sécateur [sekatœr] *nm* secateurs (*pl*).

sécession [sesesjɔ̃] *nf* secession; **faire ~ (de)** to secede (from).

sèche-cheveux [sɛʃʃəvø] *nm inv* hairdryer.

sécher [seʃe] **1** *vt* [linge] to dry. ‖ *arg scol* [cours] to skip. **2** *vi* [linge] to dry. ‖ [peau] to dry out. ‖ *arg scol* [ne pas savoir répondre] to dry up.

sécheresse [seʃrɛs] *nf* [de terre, climat, style] dryness. ‖ [absence de pluie] drought. ‖ [de réponse] curtness.

séchoir [seʃwar] *nm* [tringle] airer, clotheshorse. ‖ [électrique] dryer; **~ à cheveux** hairdryer.

second, -e [səgɔ̃, ɔ̃d] **1** *adj num* second; **dans un état ~** dazed. **2** *nm, f* second; *voir aussi* **sixième**. ○ **seconde** *nf* [unité de temps & MUS] second. ‖ SCOL ≃ tenth grade *Am*. ‖ TRANSPORT second class.

secondaire [səgɔ̃dɛr] *adj* [gén & SCOL] secondary; **effets ~s** MÉD side effects.

seconder [səgɔ̃de] *vt* to assist.

secouer [səkwe] *vt* [gén] to shake. ○ **se secouer** *vp fam* to snap out of it.

secourable [səkurabl] *adj* helpful.

secourir [səkurir] *vt* [blessé, miséreux] to help; [personne en danger] to rescue.

secouriste [səkurist] *nmf* first-aid worker.

secours [səkur] *nm* [aide] help; **appeler au ~** to call for help; **au ~!** help! ‖ [dons] aid, relief. ‖ [soins] aid; **les premiers ~** first aid (*U*). ○ **de secours** *loc adj* [trousse, poste] first-aid (*avant n*). ‖ [éclairage, issue] emergency (*avant n*). ‖ [roue] spare.

secouru, -e [səkury] *pp* → **secourir**.

secousse [səkus] *nf* [mouvement] jerk, jolt. ‖ *fig* [psychologique] shock. ‖ [tremblement de terre] tremor.

secret, -ète [səkrɛ, ɛt] *adj* [gén] secret. ‖ [personne] reticent. ○ **secret** *nm* [gén] secret. ‖ [discrétion] secrecy.

secrétaire [səkretɛr] **1** *nmf* [personne] secretary; **~ de direction** executive secretary. **2** *nm* [meuble] writing desk, secretaire.

secrétariat [səkretarja] *nm* [bureau] secretary's office; [d'organisation internationale] secretariat. ‖ [métier] secretarial work.

sécréter [sekrete] *vt* to secrete.

sécrétion [sekresjɔ̃] *nf* secretion.

sectaire [sɛktɛr] *nmf & adj* sectarian.

secte [sɛkt] *nf* sect.

secteur [sɛktœr] *nm* [zone] area; **se trouver dans le ~** *fam* to be somewhere around. ‖ ADMIN district. ‖ ÉCON, GÉOM & MIL sector. ‖ ÉLECTR mains; **sur ~** off ou from the mains.

section [sɛksjɔ̃] *nf* [gén] section; [de parti] branch. ‖ MIL platoon.

sectionner [sɛksjɔne] *vt fig* [diviser] to divide into sections. ‖ [trancher] to sever.

Sécu [seky] *fam abr de* **Sécurité sociale**.

séculaire [sekylɛr] *adj* [ancien] age-old.

sécurisant, -e [sekyrizɑ̃, ɑ̃t] *adj* [milieu] secure; [attitude] reassuring.

sécurité [sekyrite] *nf* [d'esprit] security. ‖ [absence de danger] safety; **la ~ routière** road safety. ‖ [dispositif] safety catch. ‖ [organisme]: **la Sécurité sociale** ≃ the Social Security *Am*.

sédatif, -ive [sedatif, iv] *adj* sedative. ○ **sédatif** *nm* sedative.

sédentaire [sedɑ̃tɛr] *adj* [personne, métier] sedentary; [casanier] stay-at-home.

sédentariser [sedɑ̃tarize] ○ **se sédentariser** *vp* [tribu] to settle, to become settled.

sédiment [sedimɑ̃] *nm* sediment.

sédition [sedisjɔ̃] *nf* sedition.

séducteur, -trice [sedyktœr, tris] **1** *adj* seductive. **2** *nm, f* seducer (*f* seductress).

séduire [sedɥir] *vt* [plaire à] to attract, to appeal to. ‖ [abuser de] to seduce.

séduisant, -e [sedɥizɑ̃, ɑ̃t] *adj* attractive.

séduit, -e [sedɥi, ɥit] *pp* → **séduire**.

segment [sɛgmɑ̃] *nm* GÉOM segment.

segmenter [sɛgmɑ̃te] *vt* to segment.

ségrégation [segregasjɔ̃] *nf* segregation.

seigle [sɛgl] *nm* rye.

seigneur [sɛɲœr] *nm* lord. ○ **Seigneur** *nm*: **le Seigneur** the Lord.

sein [sɛ̃] *nm* breast; *fig* bosom; **donner le ~ (à un bébé)** to breast-feed (a baby). ○ **au sein de** *loc prép* within.

Seine [sɛn] *nf*: **la ~** the (River) Seine.

séisme [seism] *nm* earthquake.

seize [sɛz] *adj num & nm* sixteen; *voir aussi* **six**.

seizième [sɛzjɛm] *adj num, nm & nmf* sixteenth; *voir aussi* **sixième**.

séparatiste

séjour [seʒur] *nm* [durée] stay; **interdit de ~** ≃ banned; **~ linguistique** stay abroad (*to develop language skills*). || [pièce] living room.

séjourner [seʒurne] *vi* to stay.

sel [sɛl] *nm* salt; *fig* piquancy.

sélection [selɛksjɔ̃] *nf* selection.

sélectionner [selɛksjɔne] *vt* to select, to pick.

self-service [sɛlfsɛrvis] (*pl* self-services) *nm* self-service cafeteria.

selle [sɛl] *nf* [gén] saddle.

seller [sele] *vt* to saddle.

selon [səlɔ̃] *prép* [conformément à] in accordance with. || [d'après] according to. ○ **selon que** *loc conj* depending on whether.

semaine [səmɛn] *nf* [période] week.

sémantique [semãtik] *adj* semantic.

semblable [sãblabl] **1** *nm* [prochain] fellow man. **2** *adj* [analogue] similar; **~ à** like, similar to. || (*avant n*) [tel] such.

semblant [sãblɑ̃] *nm*: **un ~ de** a semblance of; **faire ~ (de faire qqch)** to pretend (to do sthg).

sembler [sãble] **1** *vi* to seem. **2** *v impers*: **il (me/te) semble que** it seems (to me/you) that.

semelle [səmɛl] *nf* [de chaussure - dessous] sole; [- à l'intérieur] insole.

semence [səmãs] *nf* [graine] seed. || [sperme] semen (*U*).

semer [səme] *vt* [planter & *fig*] to sow. || [répandre] to scatter. || *fam* [se débarrasser de] to shake off.

semestre [səmɛstr] *nm* half year, six-month period; SCOL semester.

semestriel, -ielle [səmɛstrijɛl] *adj* [qui a lieu tous les six mois] half-yearly, six-monthly.

séminaire [seminɛr] *nm* RELIG seminary. || [UNIV & colloque] seminar.

séminariste [seminarist] *nm* seminarist.

semi-remorque [səmirəmɔrk] (*pl* semi-remorques) *nm* semitrailer *Am*.

semis [səmi] *nm* [méthode] sowing broadcast. || [plant] seedling.

semoule [səmul] *nf* semolina.

sempiternel, -elle [sãpitɛrnɛl] *adj* eternal.

sénat [sena] *nm* senate; **le Sénat** upper house of the French parliament.

sénateur [senatœr] *nm* senator.

Sénégal [senegal] *nm*: **le ~** Senegal.

sénile [senil] *adj* senile.

sénilité [senilite] *nf* senility.

sens [sãs] *nm* [fonction, instinct, raison] sense; **avoir le ~ de l'humour** to have a sense of humour; **bon ~** good sense. || [direction] direction; **dans le ~ de la longueur** lengthways; **dans le ~ des aiguilles d'une montre** clockwise; **dans le ~ contraire des aiguilles d'une montre** anticlockwise; **~ dessus dessous** upside down; **~ interdit** *ou* **unique** one-way street. || [signification] meaning; **~ propre/figuré** literal/figurative sense.

sensation [sãsasjɔ̃] *nf* [perception] sensation, feeling. || [impression] feeling.

sensationnel, -elle [sãsasjɔnɛl] *adj* sensational.

sensé, -e [sãse] *adj* sensible.

sensibiliser [sãsibilize] *vt fig* [public]: **~ (à)** to make aware (of).

sensibilité [sãsibilite] *nf*: **~ (à)** sensitivity (to).

sensible [sãsibl] *adj* [gén]: **~ (à)** sensitive (to). || [notable] considerable, appreciable.

sensiblement [sãsibləmã] *adv* [à peu près] more or less. || [notablement] appreciably, considerably.

sensoriel, -ielle [sãsɔrjɛl] *adj* sensory.

sensualité [sãsɥalite] *nf* [lascivité] sensuousness; [charnelle] sensuality.

sensuel, -elle [sãsɥɛl] *adj* [charnel] sensual. || [lascif] sensuous.

sentence [sãtãs] *nf* [jugement] sentence. || [maxime] adage.

sentencieux, -ieuse [sãtãsjø, jøz] *adj péj* sententious.

senteur [sãtœr] *nf littéraire* perfume.

sentier [sãtje] *nm* path.

sentiment [sãtimã] *nm* feeling; **veuillez agréer, Monsieur, l'expression de mes ~s distingués/cordiaux/les meilleurs** yours faithfully/sincerely/truly.

sentimental, -e, -aux [sãtimãtal, o] *adj* [amoureux] love (*avant n*). || [sensible, romanesque] sentimental.

sentinelle [sãtinɛl] *nf* sentry.

sentir [sãtir] **1** *vt* [percevoir - par l'odorat] to smell; [- par le goût] to taste; [- par le toucher] to feel. || [exhaler - odeur] to smell of. || [danger] to sense, to be aware of. **2** *vi*: **~ bon/mauvais** to smell good/bad. ○ **se sentir 1** *v attr*: **se ~ bien/fatigué** to feel well/tired. **2** *vp* [être perceptible]: **ça se sent!** you can really tell!

séparation [separasjɔ̃] *nf* separation.

séparatiste [separatist] *nmf* separatist.

séparé, -e [separe] *adj* [intérêts] separate. || [couple] separated.

séparer [separe] *vt* [gén]: ~ (de) to separate (from). || [suj: divergence] to divide. ○ **se séparer** *vp* [se défaire]: se ~ de to part with. || [conjoints] to separate, to split up; se ~ de to separate from, to split up with. || [route]: se ~ (en) to split (into), to divide (into).

sept [set] *adj num & nm* seven; *voir aussi* **six.**

septembre [septãbr] *nm* September; **en ~, au mois de ~** in September; **début ~, au début du mois de ~** at the beginning of September; **fin ~, à la fin du mois de ~** at the end of September; **d'ici ~** by September; **(à la) mi-~** (in) mid-September; **le premier/deux/dix ~** the first/second/tenth of September.

septennat [septena] *nm* seven-year term (of office).

septicémie [septisemi] *nf* septicaemia, blood poisoning.

septième [setjɛm] *adj num, nm & nmf* seventh; *voir aussi* **sixième.**

sépulcre [sepylkr] *nm* sepulchre.

sépulture [sepyltyr] *nf* [lieu] burial place. || [inhumation] burial.

séquelle [sekel] *nf* (*gén pl*) aftermath; MÉD aftereffect.

séquence [sekãs] *nf* sequence.

séquestrer [sekestre] *vt* [personne] to confine. || [biens] to impound.

serai, seras *etc* → **être.**

serbe [serb] *adj* Serbian. ○ **Serbe** *nmf* Serb.

Serbie [serbi] *nf:* **la ~** Serbia.

serein, -e [sərɛ̃, ɛn] *adj* [calme] serene.

sérénade [serenad] *nf* MUS serenade.

sérénité [serenite] *nf* serenity.

serf, serve [serf, serv] *nm, f* serf.

sergent [serʒã] *nm* sergeant.

série [seri] *nf* [gén] series (*sg*). || SPORT rank; [au tennis] seeding.

sérieusement [serjøzmã] *adv* seriously.

sérieux, -ieuse [serjø, jøz] *adj* [grave] serious. || [digne de confiance] reliable; [client, offre] genuine. || [consciencieux] responsible; **ce n'est pas ~** it's irresponsible. || [considérable] considerable. ○ **sérieux** *nm* [application] sense of responsibility. || [gravité] seriousness; **garder son ~** to keep a straight face; **prendre qqn/qqch au ~** to take sb/sthg seriously.

serin, -e [sərɛ̃, in] *nm, f* [oiseau] canary.

seringue [sərɛ̃g] *nf* syringe.

serment [sermã] *nm* [affirmation solennelle] oath; **sous ~** on OU under oath. || [promesse] vow, pledge.

sermon [sermɔ̃] *nm litt & fig* sermon.

séronégatif, -ive [seronegatif, iv] *adj* HIV-negative.

séropositif, -ive [seropozitif, iv] *adj* HIV-positive.

serpe [serp] *nf* billhook.

serpent [serpã] *nm* ZOOL snake.

serpenter [serpãte] *vi* to wind.

serpillière [serpijer] *nf* floor cloth.

serre [ser] *nf* [bâtiment] greenhouse, glasshouse. ○ **serres** *nfpl* ZOOL talons, claws.

serré, -e [sere] *adj* [écriture] cramped; [rangs] serried. || [vêtement, chaussure] tight. || [match] close-fought. || [poing, dents] clenched; **la gorge ~e** with a lump in one's throat. || [café] strong.

serrer [sere] **1** *vt* [saisir] to grip, to hold tight; ~ **la main à qqn** to shake sb's hand; ~ **qqn dans ses bras** to hug sb. || *fig* [rapprocher] to bring together; ~ **les rangs** to close ranks. || [poing, dents] to clench; [lèvres] to purse; *fig* [cœur] to wring. || [suj: vêtement, chaussure] to be too tight for. || [vis, ceinture] to tighten. **2** *vi* AUTOM: ~ **à droite/gauche** to keep right/left. ○ **se serrer** *vp* [se blottir]: se ~ **contre** to huddle up to OU against. || [se rapprocher] to squeeze up.

serre-tête [sertet] *nm inv* headband.

serrure [seryr] *nf* lock.

serrurier [seryrje] *nm* locksmith.

sertir [sertir] *vt* [pierre précieuse] to set. || TECHNOL [assujettir] to crimp.

sérum [serɔm] *nm* serum.

servante [servãt] *nf* [domestique] maidservant.

serveur, -euse [servœr, øz] *nm, f* [de restaurant] waiter (*f* waitress); [de bar] barman (*f* barmaid). ○ **serveur** *nm* INFORM server.

serviable [servjabl] *adj* helpful, obliging.

service [servis] *nm* [gén] service; **être en ~** to be in use, to be set up; **hors ~** out of order. || [travail] duty; **pendant le ~** while on duty. || [département] department; ~ **d'ordre** police and stewards (*at a demonstration*). || MIL: ~ **(militaire)** military OU national service. || [aide, assistance] favour; **rendre un ~ à qqn** to do sb a favour; **rendre ~** to be helpful; ~ **après-vente** after-sales service. || [à table]: **premier/deuxième ~** first/second sitting. || [pourboire] service (charge); **~ compris/non compris** service included/not included. || [assortiment - de porcelaine] service, set; [- de linge] set.

serviette [sɛrvjɛt] *nf* [de table] serviette, napkin. || [de toilette] towel. || [porte-documents] briefcase. ○ **serviette hygiénique** *nf* sanitary napkin *Am*.

serviette-éponge [sɛrvjɛtepɔ̃ʒ] *nf* terry towel.

servile [sɛrvil] *adj* [gén] servile. || [traduction, imitation] slavish.

servir [sɛrvir] 1 *vt* [gén] to serve; **~ qqch à qqn** to serve sb sthg, to help sb to sthg. || [avantager] to serve (well), to help. 2 *vi* [avoir un usage] to be useful or of use. || [être utile]: **~ à qqch/à faire qqch** to be used for sthg/for doing sthg; **ça ne sert à rien** it's pointless. || [tenir lieu]: **~ de** [personne] to act as; [chose] to serve as. || MIL & SPORT to serve. || CARTES to deal. ○ **servir** *vp* [prendre]: **se ~ (de)** to help o.s. (to). || [utiliser]: **se ~ de qqn/qqch** to use sb/sthg.

serviteur [sɛrvitœr] *nm* servant.

servitude [sɛrvityd] *nf* [esclavage] servitude. || (*gén pl*) [contrainte] constraint.

ses → **son**.

session [sesjɔ̃] *nf* [d'assemblée] session, sitting. || UNIV exam session. || INFORM: **fermer** or **clore une ~** to log out or off.

set [sɛt] *nm* TENNIS set. || [napperon]: **~ (de table)** set of table or place mats.

seuil [sœj] *nm litt & fig* threshold.

seul, -e [sœl] 1 *adj* [isolé] alone; **~ à ~** alone (together), privately. || [unique]: **le ~ ...** the only ...; **un ~ ...** a single ...; **pas un ~** not one, not a single. || [esseulé] lonely. 2 *nm, f*: **le ~** the only one; **un ~ a** single one, only one. ○ **seul** *adv* [sans compagnie] alone, by o.s.; **parler tout ~** to talk to o.s. || [sans aide] on one's own, by o.s.

seulement [sœlmɑ̃] *adv* [gén] only.

sève [sɛv] *nf* BOT sap.

sévère [sevɛr] *adj* severe.

sévérité [severite] *nf* severity.

sévices [sevis] *nmpl sout* ill treatment (*U*).

sévir [sevir] *vi* [épidémie, guerre] to rage. || [punir] to give out a punishment.

sevrer [səvre] *vt* to wean.

sexe [sɛks] *nm* [gén] sex. || [organe] genitals (*pl*).

sexiste [sɛksist] *nmf & adj* sexist.

sexologue [sɛksɔlɔg] *nmf* sexologist.

sex-shop [sɛksʃɔp] (*pl* **sex-shops**) *nm* sex shop.

sextant [sɛkstɑ̃] *nm* sextant.

sexualité [sɛksɥalite] *nf* sexuality.

sexuel, -elle [sɛksɥɛl] *adj* sexual.

sexy [sɛksi] *adj inv fam* sexy.

seyant, -e [sejɑ̃, ɑ̃t] *adj* becoming.

shampooing [ʃɑ̃pwɛ̃] *nm* shampoo.

shérif [ʃerif] *nm* sheriff.

shopping [ʃɔpiŋ] *nm* shopping; **faire du ~** to go (out) shopping.

short [ʃɔrt] *nm* shorts (*pl*), pair of shorts.

show-business [ʃobiznɛs] *nm inv* show business.

si[1] [si] *nm inv* MUS B; [chanté] ti.

si[2] [si] 1 *adv* [tellement] so; **il roulait ~ vite qu'il a eu un accident** he was driving so fast (that) he had an accident; **ce n'est pas ~ facile que ça** it's not as easy as that; **~ vieux qu'il soit** however old he may be, old as he is. || [oui] yes. 2 *conj* [gén] if; **~ tu veux, on y va** we'll go if you want; **~ seulement** if only. || [dans une question indirecte] if, whether. ○ **si bien que** *loc conj* so that, with the result that.

SI *nm* (*abr de* **syndicat d'initiative**) tourist office.

siamois, -e [sjamwa, az] *adj*: **frères ~, sœurs ~es** MÉD Siamese twins.

Sibérie [siberi] *nf*: **la ~** Siberia.

sibyllin, -e [sibilɛ̃, in] *adj* enigmatic.

SICAV, Sicav [sikav] (*abr de* **société d'investissement à capital variable**) *nf* [société] unit trust, mutual fund. || [action] share in a unit trust.

Sicile [sisil] *nf*: **la ~** Sicily.

SIDA, Sida [sida] (*abr de* **syndrome immuno-déficitaire acquis**) *nm* AIDS.

side-car [sidkar] (*pl* **side-cars**) *nm* sidecar.

sidérer [sidere] *vt fam* to stagger.

sidérurgie [sideryrʒi] *nf* [industrie] iron and steel industry.

siècle [sjɛkl] *nm* [cent ans] century. || (*gén pl*) *fam* [longue durée] ages (*pl*).

siège [sjɛʒ] *nm* [meuble & POLIT] seat. || MIL siege. || [d'organisme] headquarters, head office; **~ social** registered office. || MÉD: **se présenter par le ~** to be in the breech position.

siéger [sjeʒe] *vi* [juge, assemblée] to sit.

sien [sjɛ̃] ○ **le sien** (*f* **la sienne** [lasjɛn], *mpl* **les siens** [lesjɛ̃], *fpl* **les siennes** [lesjɛn]) *pron poss* [d'homme] his; [de femme] hers; [de chose, d'animal] its.

sieste [sjɛst] *nf* siesta.

sifflement [siflǝmã] *nm* [son] whistling; [de serpent] hissing.

siffler [sifle] **1** *vi* to whistle; [serpent] to hiss. **2** *vt* [air de musique] to whistle. || [femme] to whistle at. || [chien] to whistle (for). || [acteur] to boo, to hiss. || *fam* [verre] to knock back.

sifflet [sifle] *nm* whistle. ○ **sifflets** *nmpl* hissing (*U*), boos.

siffloter [siflɔte] *vi* & *vt* to whistle.

sigle [sigl] *nm* acronym, (set of) initials.

signal, -aux [siɲal, o] *nm* [geste, son] signal; **~ d'alarme** alarm (signal); **donner le ~ (de)** to give the signal (for). || [panneau] sign.

signalement [siɲalmã] *nm* description.

signaler [siɲale] *vt* [fait] to point out; **rien à ~** nothing to report. || [à la police] to denounce.

signalisation [siɲalizasjɔ̃] *nf* [signaux] signs (*pl*); NAVIG signals (*pl*).

signataire [siɲatɛr] *nmf* signatory.

signature [siɲatyr] *nf* [nom, marque] signature. || [acte] signing.

signe [siɲ] *nm* [gén] sign; **être ~ de** to be a sign of; **~ avant-coureur** advance indication. || [trait] mark; **~ particulier** distinguishing mark.

signer [siɲe] *vt* to sign. ○ **se signer** *vp* to cross o.s.

signet [siɲɛ] *nm* bookmark (*attached to spine of book*).

significatif, -ive [siɲifikatif, iv] *adj* significant.

signification [siɲifikasjɔ̃] *nf* [sens] meaning.

signifier [siɲifje] *vt* [vouloir dire] to mean. || [faire connaître] to make known. || JUR to serve notice of.

silence [silɑ̃s] *nm* [gén] silence; **garder le ~ (sur)** to remain silent (about). || MUS rest.

silencieux, -ieuse [silɑ̃sjø, jøz] *adj* [lieu, appareil] quiet; [personne - taciturne] quiet; [- muet] silent. ○ **silencieux** *nm* silencer.

silex [silɛks] *nm* flint.

silhouette [silwet] *nf* [de personne] silhouette; [de femme] figure; [d'objet] outline. || ART silhouette.

silicium [silisjɔm] *nm* silicon.

silicone [silikɔn] *nf* silicone.

sillage [sijaʒ] *nm* wake.

sillon [sijɔ̃] *nm* [tranchée, ride] furrow. || [de disque] groove.

sillonner [sijɔne] *vt* [champ] to furrow. || [ciel] to crisscross.

silo [silo] *nm* silo.

simagrées [simagre] *nfpl péj*: **faire des ~** to make a fuss.

similaire [similɛr] *adj* similar.

similicuir [similikɥir] *nm* imitation leather.

similitude [similityd] *nf* similarity.

simple [sɛ̃pl] **1** *adj* [gén] simple. || [ordinaire] ordinary. || [billet]: **un aller ~** a single ticket. **2** *nm* TENNIS singles (*sg*).

simplicité [sɛ̃plisite] *nf* simplicity.

simplifier [sɛ̃plifje] *vt* to simplify.

simpliste [sɛ̃plist] *adj péj* simplistic.

simulacre [simylakr] *nm* [semblant]: **un ~ de** a pretence of, a sham. || [action simulée] enactment.

simulateur, -trice [simylatœr, tris] *nm, f* pretender; [de maladie] malingerer. ○ **simulateur** *nm* TECHNOL simulator.

simulation [simylasjɔ̃] *nf* [gén] simulation. || [comédie] shamming, feigning.

simuler [simyle] *vt* [gén] to simulate. || [feindre] to feign, to sham.

simultané, -e [simyltane] *adj* simultaneous.

sincère [sɛ̃sɛr] *adj* sincere.

sincèrement [sɛ̃sɛrmã] *adv* [franchement] honestly, sincerely. || [vraiment] really, truly.

sincérité [sɛ̃serite] *nf* sincerity.

sine qua non [sinekwanɔn] *adj*: **condition ~** prerequisite.

Singapour [sɛ̃gapur] *n* Singapore.

singe [sɛ̃ʒ] *nm* ZOOL monkey; [de grande taille] ape.

singer [sɛ̃ʒe] *vt* [personne] to mimic, to ape. || [sentiment] to feign.

singerie [sɛ̃ʒri] *nf* [grimace] face.

singulariser [sɛ̃gylarize] ○ **se singulariser** *vp* to draw ou call attention to o.s.

singularité [sɛ̃gylarite] *nf littéraire* [particularité] peculiarity.

singulier, -ière [sɛ̃gylje, jɛr] *adj sout* [bizarre] strange; [spécial] uncommon. || GRAM singular. || [d'homme à homme]: **combat ~** single combat. ○ **singulier** *nm* GRAM singular.

singulièrement [sɛ̃gyljɛrmã] *adv littéraire* [bizarrement] strangely. || [beaucoup, très] particularly.

sinistre [sinistr] **1** *nm* [catastrophe] disaster. || JUR damage (*U*). **2** *adj* [personne, regard] sinister; [maison, ambiance] gloomy.

sinistré, -e [sinistre] **1** *adj* [région] disaster (*avant n*), disaster-stricken; [fa-

mille] disaster-stricken. **2** *nm, f* disaster victim.

sinon [sinɔ̃] *conj* [autrement] or else, otherwise. || [si ce n'est] if not.

sinueux, -euse [sinɥø, øz] *adj* winding.

sinus [sinys] *nm* ANAT sinus. || MATHS sine.

sinusite [sinyzit] *nf* sinusitis (*U*).

sionisme [sjɔnism] *nm* Zionism.

siphon [sifɔ̃] *nm* [tube] siphon. || [bouteille] soda siphon.

siphonner [sifɔne] *vt* to siphon.

sirène [siren] *nf* siren.

sirop [siro] *nm* syrup; ~ **d'érable** maple syrup; ~ **de menthe** mint cordial.

siroter [sirɔte] *vt fam* to sip.

sis, -e [si, siz] *adj* JUR located.

sismique [sismik] *adj* seismic.

site [sit] *nm* [emplacement] site; ~ **archéologique/historique** archaeological/historic site. || [paysage] beauty spot.

sitôt [sito] *adv*: **pas de** ~ not for some time, not for a while; ~ **dit,** ~ **fait** no sooner said than done. **O sitôt que** *loc conj* as soon as.

situation [sitɥasjɔ̃] *nf* [position, emplacement] position, location. || [contexte, circonstance] situation; ~ **de famille** marital status. || [emploi] job, position. || FIN financial statement.

situer [sitɥe] *vt* [maison] to site, to situate; **bien/mal situé** well/badly situated. || [sur carte] to locate. **O se situer** *vp* [scène] to be set; [dans classement] to be.

six [sis *en fin de phrase, si devant consonne ou h aspiré*, siz *devant voyelle ou h muet*] **1** *adj num* six; **il a** ~ **ans** he is six (years old); **il est** ~ **heures** it's six (o'clock); **le** ~ **janvier** (on) the sixth of January; **daté du** ~ **septembre** dated the sixth of September; **Charles Six** Charles the Sixth; **page** ~ page six. **2** *nm inv* [gén] six; ~ **de pique** six of spades. || [adresse] (number) six. **3** *pron* six; **ils étaient** ~ there were six of them; ~ **par** ~ six at a time.

sixième [sizjɛm] **1** *adj num* sixth. **2** *nmf* sixth; **arriver/se classer** ~ to come (in)/ to be placed sixth. **3** *nf* SCOL ≃ sixth grade *Am*; **être en** ~ to be in sixth grade *Am*. **4** *nm* [part]: **le/un** ~ **de** one/a sixth of; **cinq ~s** five sixths. || [arrondissement] sixth arrondissement. || [étage] seventh floor *Am*.

skateboard [skɛtbɔrd] *nm* skateboard.

sketch [skɛtʃ] (*pl* **sketches**) *nm* sketch (*in a revue etc*).

ski [ski] *nm* [objet] ski. || [sport] skiing; **faire du** ~ to ski; ~ **acrobatique/alpin/ de fond** freestyle/alpine/cross-country skiing; ~ **nautique** water-skiing.

skier [skje] *vi* to ski.

skieur, -ieuse [skjœr, jøz] *nm, f* skier.

skipper [skipœr] *nm* [capitaine] skipper. || [barreur] helmsman.

slalom [slalɔm] *nm* SKI slalom.

slave [slav] *adj* Slavonic. **O Slave** *nmf* Slav.

slip [slip] *nm* briefs (*pl*); ~ **de bain** [d'homme] swimming trunks (*pl*).

slogan [slɔgɑ̃] *nm* slogan.

Slovaquie [slɔvaki] *nf*: **la** ~ Slovakia.

Slovénie [slɔveni] *nf*: **la** ~ Slovenia.

slow [slo] *nm* slow dance.

smasher [smaʃe] *vi* TENNIS to smash (the ball).

SME (*abr de Système monétaire européen*) *nm* EMS.

SMIC, Smic [smik] (*abr de salaire minimum interprofessionnel de croissance*) *nm* index-linked guaranteed minimum wage.

smoking [smɔkiŋ] *nm* tuxedo *Am*.

SNCF (*abr de Société nationale des chemins de fer français*) *nf* French railways board.

snob [snɔb] **1** *nmf* snob. **2** *adj* snobbish.

snober [snɔbe] *vt* to snub, to cold-shoulder.

snobisme [snɔbism] *nm* snobbery, snobbishness.

sobre [sɔbr] *adj* [personne] temperate. || [style] sober; [décor, repas] simple.

sobriété [sɔbrijete] *nf* sobriety.

sobriquet [sɔbrikɛ] *nm* nickname.

soc [sɔk] *nm* ploughshare.

sociable [sɔsjabl] *adj* sociable.

social, -e, -iaux [sɔsjal, jo] *adj* [rapports, classe, service] social. || COMM: **raison ~e** company name.

socialisme [sɔsjalism] *nm* socialism.

socialiste [sɔsjalist] *nmf & adj* socialist.

sociétaire [sɔsjeter] *nmf* member.

société [sɔsjete] *nf* [communauté, classe sociale, groupe] society; **en** ~ in society. || [présence] company, society. || COMM company, firm.

sociologie [sɔsjɔlɔʒi] *nf* sociology.

sociologue [sɔsjɔlɔg] *nmf* sociologist.

socioprofessionnel, -elle [sɔsjo-prɔfesjɔnɛl] *adj* socioprofessional.

socle [sɔkl] *nm* [de statue] plinth, pedestal. || [de lampe] base.

socquette [sɔkεt] *nf* ankle ou short sock.

soda [sɔda] *nm* fizzy drink.

sodium [sɔdjɔm] *nm* sodium.

sodomiser [sɔdɔmize] *vt* to sodomize.

sœur [sœr] *nf* [gén] sister; **grande/petite ~** big/little sister. || RELIG nun, sister.

sofa [sɔfa] *nm* sofa.

software [sɔftwεr] *nm* software.

soi [swa] *pron pers* oneself. ○ **soi-même** *pron pers* oneself.

soi-disant [swadizɑ̃] **1** *adj inv (avant n)* so-called. **2** *adv fam* supposedly.

soie [swa] *nf* [textile] silk. || [poil] bristle.

soierie [swari] *nf (gén pl)* [textile] silk.

soif [swaf] *nf* thirst; **~ (de)** *fig* thirst (for), craving (for); **avoir ~** to be thirsty.

soigné, -e [swaɲe] *adj* [travail] meticulous. || [personne] well-groomed; [jardin, mains] well-cared-for.

soigner [swaɲe] *vt* [suj: médecin] to treat; [suj: infirmière, parent] to nurse. || [invités, jardin, mains] to look after. || [travail, présentation] to take care over. ○ **se soigner** *vp* to take care of o.s., to look after o.s.

soigneusement [swaɲøzmɑ̃] *adv* carefully.

soigneux, -euse [swaɲø, øz] *adj* [personne] tidy, neat. || [travail] careful.

soin [swɛ̃] *nm* [attention] care; **avoir** ou **prendre ~ de faire qqch** to be sure to do sthg; **avec ~** carefully; **sans ~** [procéder] carelessly; [travail] careless. ○ **soins** *nmpl* care (*U*); **les premiers ~s** first aid (*sg*).

soir [swar] *nm* evening; **demain ~** tomorrow evening ou night; **le ~** in the evening; **à ce ~!** see you tonight!

soirée [sware] *nf* [soir] evening. || [réception] party.

sois → **être**.

soit¹ [swat] *adv* so be it.

soit² [swa] **1** *vb* → **être**. **2** *conj* [c'est-à-dire] in other words, that is to say. || MATHS [étant donné]: **~ une droite AB** given a straight line AB. ○ **soit ... soit** *loc corrélative* either ... or.

soixante [swasɑ̃t] **1** *adj num* sixty. **2** *nm* sixty; *voir aussi* **six**.

soixante-dix [swasɑ̃tdis] **1** *adj num* seventy. **2** *nm* seventy; *voir aussi* **six**.

soixante-dixième [swasɑ̃tdizjεm] *adj num, nm & nmf* seventieth; *voir aussi* **sixième**.

soixantième [swasɑ̃tjεm] *adj num, nm & nmf* sixtieth; *voir aussi* **sixième**.

soja [sɔʒa] *nm* soya.

sol [sɔl] *nm* [terre] ground. || [de maison] floor. || [territoire] soil. || MUS G; [chanté] so.

solaire [sɔlεr] *adj* [énergie, four] solar. || [crème] sun (*avant n*).

solarium [sɔlarjɔm] *nm* solarium.

soldat [sɔlda] *nm* MIL soldier; [grade] private. || [jouet] (toy) soldier.

solde [sɔld] **1** *nm* [de compte, facture] balance; **~ créditeur/débiteur** credit/debit balance. || [rabais]: **en ~** [acheter] in a sale. **2** *nf* MIL pay. ○ **soldes** *nmpl* sales.

solder [sɔlde] *vt* [compte] to close. || [marchandises] to sell off. ○ **se solder** *vp*: **se ~ par** *fig* [aboutir] to end in.

sole [sɔl] *nf* sole.

soleil [sɔlεj] *nm* [astre, motif] sun; **~ couchant/levant** setting/rising sun. || [lumière, chaleur] sun, sunlight; **au ~** in the sun; **en plein ~** right in the sun.

solennel, -elle [sɔlanεl] *adj* [cérémonieux] ceremonial. || [grave] solemn.

solennité [sɔlanite] *nf* [gravité] solemnity. || [raideur] stiffness, formality.

solfège [sɔlfεʒ] *nm*: **apprendre le ~** to learn the rudiments of music.

solidaire [sɔlidεr] *adj* [lié]: **être ~ de qqn** to be behind sb, to show solidarity with sb. || [relié] interdependent, integral.

solidarité [sɔlidarite] *nf* [entraide] solidarity; **par ~** [se mettre en grève] in sympathy.

solide [sɔlid] **1** *adj* [état, corps] solid. || [construction] solid, sturdy. || [personne] sturdy, robust. || [argument] solid, sound. || [relation] stable, strong. **2** *nm* solid.

solidifier [sɔlidifje] *vt* [ciment, eau] to solidify. || [structure] to reinforce. ○ **se solidifier** *vp* to solidify.

solidité [sɔlidite] *nf* [de matière, construction] solidity. || [de mariage] stability, strength. || [de raisonnement, d'argument] soundness.

soliste [sɔlist] *nmf* soloist.

solitaire [sɔlitεr] **1** *adj* [de caractère] solitary. || [esseulé, retiré] lonely. **2** *nmf* [personne] loner, recluse. **3** *nm* [jeu, diamant] solitaire.

solitude [sɔlityd] *nf* [isolement] loneliness. || [retraite] solitude.

sollicitation [sɔlisitasjɔ̃] *nf (gén pl)* entreaty.

solliciter [sɔlisite] *vt* [demander - entretien, audience] to request; [- attention, intérêt] to seek. || [s'intéresser à]: **être sollicité** to be in demand. || [faire appel à]: **~ qqn pour faire qqch** to appeal to sb to do sthg.

sollicitude [sɔlisityd] *nf* solicitude, concern.

solo [solo] *nm* solo; **en ~** solo.

solstice [sɔlstis] *nm*: **~ d'été/d'hiver** summer/winter solstice.

soluble [sɔlybl] *adj* [matière] soluble; [café] instant. || *fig* [problème] solvable.

solution [sɔlysjɔ̃] *nf* [résolution] solution, answer. || [liquide] solution.

solvable [sɔlvabl] *adj* solvent, creditworthy.

solvant [sɔlvɑ̃] *nm* solvent.

Somalie [sɔmali] *nf*: **la ~** Somalia.

sombre [sɔ̃br] *adj* [couleur, costume, pièce] dark. || *fig* [pensées, avenir] dark, gloomy.

sombrer [sɔ̃bre] *vi* to sink.

sommaire [sɔmɛr] **1** *adj* [explication] brief. || [exécution] summary. || [installation] basic. **2** *nm* summary.

sommation [sɔmasjɔ̃] *nf* [assignation] summons (*sg*). || [ordre - de payer] demand; [- de se rendre] warning.

somme [sɔm] **1** *nf* [addition] total, sum. || [d'argent] sum, amount. || [ouvrage] overview. **2** *nm* nap. ○ **en somme** *loc adv* in short. ○ **somme toute** *loc adv* when all's said and done.

sommeil [sɔmɛj] *nm* sleep; **avoir ~** to be sleepy.

sommeiller [sɔmeje] *vi* [personne] to doze. || *fig* [qualité] to be dormant.

sommelier, -ière [sɔmɔlje, jɛr] *nm, f* wine waiter (*f* wine waitress).

sommes → être.

sommet [sɔmɛ] *nm* [de montagne] summit, top. || *fig* [de hiérarchie] top; [de perfection] height. || GÉOM apex.

sommier [sɔmje] *nm* base, bed base.

sommité [sɔmite] *nf* [personne] leading light.

somnambule [sɔmnɑ̃byl] **1** *nmf* sleepwalker. **2** *adj*: **être ~** to be a sleepwalker.

somnifère [sɔmnifer] *nm* sleeping pill.

somnolent, -e [sɔmnɔlɑ̃, ɑ̃t] *adj* [personne] sleepy, drowsy.

somnoler [sɔmnɔle] *vi* to doze.

somptueux, -euse [sɔ̃ptɥø, øz] *adj* sumptuous, lavish.

somptuosité [sɔ̃ptɥozite] *nf* lavishness.

son¹ [sɔ̃] *nm* [bruit] sound; **~ et lumière** son et lumière. || [céréale] bran.

son² [sɔ̃] (*f* **sa** [sa], *pl* **ses** [se]) *adj poss* [possesseur défini - homme] his; [- femme] her; [- chose, animal] its. || [possesseur indéfini] one's; [- après «chacun», «tout le monde» etc] his/her, their.

sonate [sɔnat] *nf* sonata.

sondage [sɔ̃daʒ] *nm* [enquête] poll, survey; **~ d'opinion** opinion poll. || TECHNOL drilling. || MÉD probing.

sonde [sɔ̃d] *nf* MÉTÉOR sonde; [spatiale] probe. || MÉD probe. || NAVIG sounding line. || TECHNOL drill.

sonder [sɔ̃de] *vt* MÉD & NAVIG to sound. || [terrain] to drill. || *fig* [opinion, personne] to sound out.

songe [sɔ̃ʒ] *nm littéraire* dream.

songer [sɔ̃ʒe] **1** *vt*: **~ que** to consider that. **2** *vi*: **~ à** to think about.

songeur, -euse [sɔ̃ʒœr, øz] *adj* pensive, thoughtful.

sonnant, -e [sɔnɑ̃, ɑ̃t] *adj*: **à six heures ~es** at six o'clock sharp.

sonné, -e [sɔne] *adj* [passé]: **il est trois heures ~es** it's gone three o'clock; **il a quarante ans bien ~s** *fam* he's the wrong side of forty. || *fig* [étourdi] groggy.

sonner [sɔne] **1** *vt* [cloche] to ring. || [retraite, alarme] to sound. || [domestique] to ring for. **2** *vi* [gén] to ring; **~ chez qqn** to ring sb's bell.

sonnerie [sɔnri] *nf* [bruit] ringing. || [mécanisme] striking mechanism. || [signal] call.

sonnet [sɔnɛ] *nm* sonnet.

sonnette [sɔnɛt] *nf* bell.

sono [sɔno] *nf fam* [de salle] P.A. (system); [de discothèque] sound system.

sonore [sɔnɔr] *adj* CIN & PHYS sound (*avant n*). || [voix, rire] ringing, resonant. || [salle] resonant.

sonorisation [sɔnɔrizasjɔ̃] *nf* [action - de film] addition of the soundtrack; [- de salle] wiring for sound.

sonoriser [sɔnɔrize] *vt* [film] to add the soundtrack to. || [salle] to wire for sound.

sonorité [sɔnɔrite] *nf* [de piano, voix] tone. || [de salle] acoustics (*pl*).

sont → être.

sophistiqué, -e [sɔfistike] *adj* sophisticated.

soporifique [sɔpɔrifik] *adj* soporific.

soprano [sɔprano] (*pl* **sopranos** OU **soprani** [sɔprani]) *nm* & *nmf* soprano.

sorbet [sɔrbɛ] *nm* sorbet.

sorcellerie [sɔrselri] *nf* witchcraft, sorcery.

sorcier, -ière [sɔrsje, jɛr] *nm, f* sorcerer (*f* witch).

sordide [sɔrdid] *adj* squalid; *fig* sordid.

sornettes [sɔrnɛt] *nfpl* nonsense (*U*).

sort [sɔr] *nm* [maléfice] spell; **jeter un ~ (à qqn)** to cast a spell (on sb). || [destinée] fate. || [condition] lot. || [hasard]: **le ~** fate; **tirer au ~** to draw lots.

sortant, -e [sɔrtɑ̃, ɑ̃t] *adj* [numéro] winning. || [président, directeur] outgoing (*avant n*).

sorte [sɔrt] *nf* sort, kind; **une ~ de** a sort of, a kind of; **toutes ~s de** all kinds of, all sorts of.

sortie [sɔrti] *nf* [issue] exit, way out; [d'eau, d'air] outlet; **~ de secours** emergency exit. || [départ]: **à la ~ du travail** when work finishes, after work. || [de produit] launch, launching; [de disque] release; [de livre] publication. || (*gén pl*) [dépense] outgoings (*pl*), expenditure (*U*). || [excursion] outing. || MIL sortie. || INFORM: **~ imprimante** printout.

sortilège [sɔrtilɛʒ] *nm* spell.

sortir [sɔrtir] 1 *vi* (*aux: être*) [de la maison, du bureau etc] to leave, to go/come out; **~ de** to go/come out of, to leave. || [pour se distraire] to go out. || *fig* [de maladie]: **~ de** to get over, to recover from; [coma] to come out of. || [film, livre, produit] to come out; [disque] to be released. || [au jeu - carte, numéro] to come up. || [s'écarter de]: **~ de** [sujet] to get away from. || *loc*: **~ de l'ordinaire** to be out of the ordinary; **d'où il sort, celui-là?** where did HE spring from? 2 *vt* (*aux: avoir*) [gén]: **~ qqch (de)** to take sthg out (of). || [de situation difficile] to get out, to extract. || [produit] to launch; [disque] to bring out, to release; [livre] to bring out, to publish. ○ **se sortir** *vp fig* [de pétrin] to get out; **s'en ~** [en réchapper] to come out of it; [y arriver] to get through it.

SOS *nm* SOS; **lancer un ~** to send out an SOS.

sosie [sɔzi] *nm* double.

sot, sotte [so, sɔt] 1 *adj* silly, foolish. 2 *nm, f* fool.

sottise [sɔtiz] *nf* stupidity (*U*), foolishness (*U*); **dire/faire une ~** to say/do something stupid.

sou [su] *nm*: **être sans le ~** to be penniless. ○ **sous** *nmpl fam* money (*U*).

soubassement [subasmɑ̃] *nm* base.

soubresaut [subrəso] *nm* [de voiture] jolt. || [de personne] start.

souche [suʃ] *nf* [d'arbre] stump. || [de carnet] counterfoil, stub.

souci [susi] *nm* [tracas] worry; **se faire du ~** to worry. || [préoccupation] concern.

soucier [susje] ○ **se soucier** *vp*: **se ~ de** to care about.

soucieux, -ieuse [susjø, jøz] *adj* [préoccupé] worried, concerned. || [concerné]: **être ~ de qqch/de faire qqch** to be concerned about sthg/about doing sthg.

soucoupe [sukup] *nf* [assiette] saucer. || [vaisseau]: **~ volante** flying saucer.

soudain, -e [sudɛ̃, ɛn] *adj* sudden. ○ **soudain** *adv* suddenly, all of a sudden.

soude [sud] *nf* soda.

souder [sude] *vt* TECHNOL to weld, to solder. || MÉD to knit. || *fig* [unir] to bind together.

soudoyer [sudwaje] *vt* to bribe.

soudure [sudyr] *nf* TECHNOL welding; [résultat] weld.

souffert, -e [sufɛr, ɛrt] *pp* → **souffrir**.

souffle [sufl] *nm* [respiration] breathing; **un ~ d'air** *fig* a breath of air, a puff of wind. || [d'explosion] blast. || MÉD: **~ au cœur** heart murmur. || *loc*: **avoir le ~ coupé** to have one's breath taken away.

souffler [sufle] 1 *vt* [bougie] to blow out. || [vitre] to blow out, to shatter. || [chuchoter]: **~ qqch à qqn** to whisper sthg to sb. 2 *vi* [gén] to blow. || [respirer] to puff, to pant.

soufflet [suflɛ] *nm* [instrument] bellows (*sg*). || [de train] connecting corridor, concertina vestibule. || COUTURE gusset.

souffleur, -euse [suflœr, øz] *nm, f* THÉÂTRE prompt. ○ **souffleur** *nm* [de verre] blower.

souffrance [sufrɑ̃s] *nf* suffering.

souffrant, -e [sufrɑ̃, ɑ̃t] *adj* poorly.

souffre-douleur [sufrədulœr] *nm inv* whipping boy.

souffrir [sufrir] 1 *vi* to suffer; **~ de** to suffer from; **~ du dos/cœur** to have back/heart problems. 2 *vt littéraire* [supporter] to stand, to bear.

soufre [sufr] *nm* sulphur.

souhait [swɛ] *nm* wish; **à tes/vos ~s!** bless you!

souhaiter [swete] *vt*: **~ faire qqch** to hope to do sthg; **~ qqch à qqn** to wish sb sthg; **~ à qqn de faire qqch** to hope that sb does sthg; **souhaiter que ...** (+ *subjonctif*) to hope that ....

souiller [suje] *vt littéraire* [salir] to soil; *fig & sout* to sully.

soûl, -e, saoul, -e [su, sul] *adj* drunk.

soulagement [sulaʒmɑ̃] *nm* relief.

soulager [sulaʒe] *vt* [gén] to relieve.

soûler, saouler [sule] *vt fam* [enivrer]: ~ **qqn** to get sb drunk; *fig* to intoxicate sb. || *fig & péj* [de plaintes]: ~ **qqn** to bore sb silly. ○ **se soûler** *vp fam* to get drunk.

soulèvement [sulɛvmɑ̃] *nm* uprising.

soulever [sulve] *vt* [fardeau, poids] to lift; [rideau] to raise. || *fig* [question] to raise, to bring up. || *fig* [enthousiasme] to generate, to arouse; [tollé] to stir up. ○ **se soulever** *vp* [s'élever] to raise o.s., to lift o.s. || [se révolter] to rise up.

soulier [sulje] *nm* shoe.

souligner [suliɲe] *vt* [par un trait] to underline. || *fig* [insister sur] to underline, to emphasize. || [mettre en valeur] to emphasize.

soumettre [sumɛtr] *vt* [astreindre]: ~ **qqn à** to subject sb to. || [ennemi, peuple] to subjugate. || [projet, problème]: ~ **qqch (à)** to submit sthg (to). ○ **se soumettre** *vp*: se ~ (à) to submit (to).

soumis, -e [sumi, iz] 1 *pp* → soumettre. 2 *adj* submissive.

soumission [sumisjɔ̃] *nf* submission.

soupape [supap] *nf* valve.

soupçon [supsɔ̃] *nm* [suspicion, intuition] suspicion.

soupçonner [supsɔne] *vt* [suspecter] to suspect; ~ **qqn de qqch/de faire qqch** to suspect sb of sthg/of doing sthg.

soupçonneux, -euse [supsɔnø, øz] *adj* suspicious.

soupe [sup] *nf* CULIN soup; ~ **populaire** soup kitchen.

souper [supe] 1 *nm* supper. 2 *vi* to have supper.

soupeser [supəze] *vt* [poids] to feel the weight of. || *fig* [évaluer] to weigh up.

soupière [supjɛr] *nf* tureen.

soupir [supir] *nm* [souffle] sigh; **pousser un** ~ to let out ou give a sigh. || MUS crotchet rest *Br*, quarter-note rest *Am*.

soupirail, -aux [supiraj, o] *nm* barred basement window.

soupirant [supirɑ̃] *nm* suitor.

soupirer [supire] *vi* [souffler] to sigh.

souple [supl] *adj* [gymnaste] supple. || [paquet, col] soft. || [tissu, cheveux] flowing. || [tuyau, horaire, caractère] flexible.

souplesse [suples] *nf* [de gymnaste] suppleness. || [flexibilité - de tuyau] pliability, flexibility; [- de matière] suppleness. || [de personne] flexibility.

source [surs] *nf* [gén] source. || [d'eau] spring; **prendre sa** ~ à to rise in.

sourcil [sursi] *nm* eyebrow.

sourcilière [sursiljɛr] → arcade.

sourciller [sursije] *vi*: sans ~ without batting an eyelid.

sourcilleux, -euse [sursijø, øz] *adj* fussy, finicky.

sourd, -e [sur, surd] 1 *adj* [personne] deaf. || [bruit, voix] muffled. || [douleur] dull. || [lutte, hostilité] silent. 2 *nm, f* deaf person.

sourdine [surdin] *nf* mute; **en** ~ [sans bruit] softly; [secrètement] in secret.

sourd-muet, sourde-muette [surmɥɛ, surdmɥɛt] *nm, f* deaf-mute, deaf and dumb person.

souriant, -e [surjɑ̃, ɑ̃t] *adj* smiling, cheerful.

souricière [surisjɛr] *nf* mousetrap; *fig* trap.

sourire [surir] 1 *vi* to smile; ~ **à qqn** to smile at sb; *fig* [destin, chance] to smile on sb. 2 *nm* smile.

souris [suri] *nf* INFORM & ZOOL mouse.

sournois, -e [surnwa, az] 1 *adj* [personne] underhand. || *fig* [maladie, phénomène] unpredictable.

sous [su] *prép* [gén] under; **nager** ~ **l'eau** to swim underwater; ~ **la pluie** in the rain; ~ **cet aspect** ou **angle** from that point of view. || [dans un délai de] within.

sous-alimenté, -e [suzalimɑ̃te] *adj* malnourished, underfed.

sous-bois [subwa] *nm inv* undergrowth.

souscription [suskripsjɔ̃] *nf* subscription.

souscrire [suskrir] *vi*: ~ **à** to subscribe to.

sous-développé, -e [sudevlɔpe] *adj* ÉCON underdeveloped; *fig & péj* backward.

sous-directeur, -trice [sudirɛktœr, tris] *nm, f* assistant manager (*f* assistant manageress).

sous-ensemble [suzɑ̃sɑ̃bl] *nm* subset.

sous-entendu [suzɑ̃tɑ̃dy] *nm* insinuation.

sous-estimer [suzɛstime] *vt* to underestimate, to underrate.

sous-évaluer [suzevalɥe] *vt* to underestimate.

sous-jacent, -e [suʒasɑ̃, ɑ̃t] *adj* underlying.

sous-louer [sulwe] *vt* to sublet.

sous-marin, -e [sumarɛ̃, in] *adj* underwater (*avant n*). ○ **sous-marin** *nm* submarine.

sous-officier [suzɔfisje] *nm* non-commissioned officer.

sous-préfecture [suprefɛktyr] *nf* sub-prefecture.

sous-préfet [suprefɛ] *nm* sub-prefect.

sous-produit [suprɔdɥi] *nm* [objet] by-product.

soussigné, -e [susiɲe] **1** *adj*: **je ~** I the undersigned. **2** *nm, f* undersigned.

sous-sol [susɔl] *nm* [de bâtiment] basement. || [naturel] subsoil.

sous-tasse [sutas] *nf* saucer.

sous-titre [sutitr] *nm* subtitle.

soustraction [sustraksjɔ̃] *nf* MATHS subtraction.

soustraire [sustrɛr] *vt* [retrancher]: **~ qqch de** to subtract sthg from. || *sout* [voler]: **~ qqch à qqn** to take sthg away from sb. ○ **se soustraire** *vp*: **se ~ à** to escape from.

sous-traitant, -e [sutretɑ̃, ɑ̃t] *adj* subcontracting. ○ **sous-traitant** *nm* subcontractor.

sous-verre [suvɛr] *nm inv* picture or document framed between a sheet of glass and a rigid backing.

sous-vêtement [suvetmɑ̃] *nm* undergarment; **~s** underwear (*U*), underclothes.

soutane [sutan] *nf* cassock.

soute [sut] *nf* hold.

soutenance [sutnɑ̃s] *nf* viva.

souteneur [sutnœr] *nm* procurer.

soutenir [sutnir] *vt* [immeuble, personne] to support, to hold up. || [encourager] to support; POLIT to back, to support. || [affirmer]: **~ que** to maintain (that).

soutenu, -e [sutny] *adj* [style, langage] elevated. || [attention, rythme] sustained. || [couleur] vivid.

souterrain, -e [suterɛ̃, ɛn] *adj* underground. ○ **souterrain** *nm* underground passage.

soutien [sutjɛ̃] *nm* support.

soutien-gorge [sutjɛ̃gɔrʒ] (*pl* soutiens-gorge) *nm* bra.

soutirer [sutire] *vt fig* [tirer]: **~ qqch à qqn** to extract sthg from sb.

souvenir [suvnir] *nm* [réminiscence, mémoire] memory. || [objet] souvenir. ○ **se souvenir** *vp* [ne pas oublier]: **se ~ de qqch/de qqn** to remember sthg/sb.

souvent [suvɑ̃] *adv* often.

souvenu, -e [suvny] *pp* → **souvenir**.

souverain, -e [suvrɛ̃, ɛn] **1** *adj* [remède, état] sovereign. || [indifférence] supreme. **2** *nm, f* [monarque] sovereign, monarch.

souveraineté [suvrɛnte] *nf* sovereignty.

soviétique [sɔvjetik] *adj* Soviet. ○ **Soviétique** *nmf* Soviet (citizen).

soyeux, -euse [swajø, øz] *adj* silky.

soyez → **être**.

SPA (*abr de* Société protectrice des animaux) *nf* French society for the protection of animals, ≃ SPCA *Am*.

spacieux, -ieuse [spasjø, jøz] *adj* spacious.

spaghettis [spaɡeti] *nmpl* spaghetti (*U*).

sparadrap [sparadra] *nm* sticking plaster.

spasme [spasm] *nm* spasm.

spasmodique [spasmɔdik] *adj* spasmodic.

spatial, -e, -iaux [spasjal, jo] *adj* space (*avant n*).

spatule [spatyl] *nf* [ustensile] spatula. || [de ski] tip.

speaker, speakerine [spikœr, spikrin] *nm, f* announcer.

spécial, -e, -iaux [spesjal, jo] *adj* [particulier] special. || *fam* [bizarre] peculiar.

spécialiser [spesjalize] *vt* to specialize. ○ **se spécialiser** *vp*: **se ~ (dans)** to specialize (in).

spécialiste [spesjalist] *nmf* specialist.

spécialité [spesjalite] *nf* speciality.

spécifier [spesifje] *vt* to specify.

spécifique [spesifik] *adj* specific.

spécimen [spesimɛn] *nm* [représentant] specimen. || [exemplaire] sample.

spectacle [spɛktakl] *nm* [représentation] show. || [domaine] show business, entertainment. || [tableau] spectacle, sight.

spectaculaire [spɛktakylɛr] *adj* spectacular.

spectateur, -trice [spɛktatœr, tris] *nm, f* [témoin] witness. || [de spectacle] spectator.

spectre [spɛktr] *nm* [fantôme] spectre. || PHYS spectrum.

spéculateur, -trice [spekylatœr, tris] *nm, f* speculator.

spéculation [spekylasjɔ̃] *nf* speculation.

spéculer [spekyle] *vi*: **~ sur** FIN to speculate in; *fig* [miser] to count on.

spéléologie [speleɔlɔʒi] *nf* [exploration] potholing; [science] speleology.

spermatozoïde [spɛrmatɔzɔid] *nm* sperm, spermatozoon.

sperme [spɛrm] *nm* sperm, semen.

sphère [sfɛr] *nf* sphere.

sphérique [sferik] *adj* spherical.

spirale [spiral] *nf* spiral.

spirituel, -elle [spirityɛl] *adj* [de l'âme, moral] spiritual. || [vivant, drôle] witty.

splendeur [splɑ̃dœr] *nf* [beauté, prospérité] splendour. || [merveille]: **c'est une ~!** it's magnificent!

splendide [splɑ̃did] *adj* magnificent, splendid.

spongieux, -ieuse [spɔ̃ʒjø, jøz] *adj* spongy.

sponsor [spɔ̃sɔr] *nm* sponsor.

sponsoriser [spɔ̃sɔrize] *vt* to sponsor.

spontané, -e [spɔ̃tane] *adj* spontaneous.

spontanéité [spɔ̃taneite] *nf* spontaneity.

sporadique [spɔradik] *adj* sporadic.

sport [spɔr] *nm* sport; **~s d'hiver** winter sports.

sportif, -ive [spɔrtif, iv] **1** *adj* [association, résultats] sports (*avant n*). || [personne, physique] sporty, athletic. **2** *nm, f* sportsman (*f* sportswoman).

spot [spɔt] *nm* [lampe] spot, spotlight. || [publicité]: **~ (publicitaire)** commercial, advert.

sprint [sprint] *nm* [SPORT - accélération] spurt; [- course] sprint.

square [skwar] *nm* small public garden.

squash [skwaʃ] *nm* squash.

squelette [skəlɛt] *nm* skeleton.

squelettique [skəletik] *adj* [corps] emaciated.

St (*abr de* **saint**) St.

stabiliser [stabilize] *vt* [gén] to stabilize; [meuble] to steady. ○ **se stabiliser** *vp* [véhicule, prix, situation] to stabilize. || [personne] to settle down.

stabilité [stabilite] *nf* stability.

stable [stabl] *adj* [gén] stable. || [meuble] steady, stable.

stade [stad] *nm* [terrain] stadium. || [étape & MÉD] stage.

stage [staʒ] *nm* COMM work placement; [sur le temps de travail] in-service training; **faire un ~** [cours] to go on a training course; [expérience professionnelle] to go on a work placement.

stagiaire [staʒjɛr] *nmf* trainee.

stagnant, -e [stagnɑ̃, ɑ̃t] *adj* stagnant.

stagner [stagne] *vi* to stagnate.

stalactite [stalaktit] *nf* stalactite.

stalagmite [stalagmit] *nf* stalagmite.

stand [stɑ̃d] *nm* [d'exposition] stand. || [de fête] stall.

standard [stɑ̃dar] **1** *adj inv* standard. **2** *nm* [norme] standard. || [téléphonique] switchboard.

standardiste [stɑ̃dardist] *nmf* switchboard operator.

standing [stɑ̃diŋ] *nm* standing; **quartier de grand ~** select district.

star [star] *nf* CIN star.

starter [starter] *nm* AUTOM choke; **mettre le ~** to pull the choke out.

starting-block [startiŋblɔk] (*pl* **starting-blocks**) *nm* starting-block.

station [stasjɔ̃] *nf* [arrêt - de bus] stop; [- de métro] station; **~ de taxis** taxi rank. || [installations] station; **~ d'épuration** sewage treatment plant. || [ville] resort; **~ balnéaire** seaside resort; **~ de ski/de sports d'hiver** ski/winter sports resort; **~ thermale** spa (town). || INFORM: **~ de travail** work station.

stationnaire [stasjɔner] *adj* stationary.

stationnement [stasjɔnmɑ̃] *nm* parking; **«~ interdit»** "no parking".

stationner [stasjɔne] *vi* to park.

station-service [stasjɔ̃sɛrvis] (*pl* **stations-service**) *nf* gas station *Am*.

statique [statik] *adj* static.

statisticien, -ienne [statistisjɛ̃, jɛn] *nm, f* statistician.

statistique [statistik] **1** *adj* statistical. **2** *nf* [donnée] statistic.

statue [staty] *nf* statue.

statuer [statɥe] *vi*: **~ sur** to give a decision on.

statuette [statɥɛt] *nf* statuette.

statu quo [statykwo] *nm inv* status quo.

stature [statyr] *nf* stature.

statut [staty] *nm* status. ○ **statuts** *nmpl* statutes.

Ste (*abr de* **sainte**) St.

Sté (*abr de* **société**) Co.

steak [stɛk] *nm* steak; **~ haché** mince.

stèle [stɛl] *nf* stele.

sténo [steno] *nf* shorthand.

sténodactylo [stenɔdaktilo] *nmf* shorthand typist.

sténodactylographie [stenɔdaktilografi] *nf* shorthand typing.

steppe [stɛp] *nf* steppe.

stéréo [stereo] **1** *adj inv* stereo. **2** *nf* stereo; **en ~** in stereo.

stéréotype [stereɔtip] *nm* stereotype.

stérile [steril] *adj* [personne] sterile, infertile; [terre] barren. || *fig* [inutile - discussion] sterile; [- efforts] futile. || MÉD sterile.

stérilet [sterilɛ] *nm* IUD, intra-uterine device.

stériliser [sterilize] *vt* to sterilize.

stérilité [sterilite] *nf litt & fig* sterility.

sternum [stɛrnɔm] *nm* breastbone, sternum.

stéthoscope [stetɔskɔp] *nm* stethoscope.

steward [stiwart] *nm* steward.

stigmate [stigmat] *nm* (*gén pl*) mark, scar.

stimulant, -e [stimylã, ãt] *adj* stimulating. ○ **stimulant** *nm* [remontant] stimulant.

stimulation [stimylasjɔ̃] *nf* stimulation.

stimuler [stimyle] *vt* to stimulate.

stipuler [stipyle] *vt*: ~ que to stipulate (that).

stock [stɔk] *nm* stock; **en ~** in stock.

stocker [stɔke] *vt* [marchandises] to stock. || INFORM to store.

stoïque [stɔik] *adj* stoical.

stop [stɔp] **1** *interj* stop! **2** *nm* [panneau] stop sign. || [auto-stop] hitch-hiking, hitching.

stopper [stɔpe] **1** *vt* [arrêter] to stop, to halt. **2** *vi* to stop.

store [stɔr] *nm* [de fenêtre] blind. || [de magasin] awning.

strabisme [strabism] *nm* squint.

strangulation [strãgylasjɔ̃] *nf* strangulation.

strapontin [strapɔ̃tɛ̃] *nm* [siège] pull-down seat.

strass [stras] *nm* paste.

stratagème [strataʒɛm] *nm* stratagem.

stratégie [strateʒi] *nf* strategy.

stratégique [strateʒik] *adj* strategic.

stress [strɛs] *nm* stress.

stressant, -e [stresã, ãt] *adj* stressful.

strict, -e [strikt] *adj* [personne, règlement] strict. || [sobre] plain. || [absolu - minimum] bare, absolute; [- vérité] absolute; **dans la plus ~e intimité** strictly in private.

strident, -e [stridã, ãt] *adj* strident, shrill.

strié, -e [strije] *adj* [rayé] striped.

strip-tease [striptiz] (*pl* **strip-teases**) *nm* striptease.

strophe [strɔf] *nf* verse.

structure [stryktyr] *nf* structure.

structurer [stryktyre] *vt* to structure.

studieux, -ieuse [stydjø, jøz] *adj* [personne] studious.

studio [stydjo] *nm* CIN, PHOT & TÉLÉ studio. || [appartement] studio apartment *Am*.

stupéfaction [stypefaksjɔ̃] *nf* astonishment, stupefaction.

stupéfait, -e [stypefɛ, ɛt] *adj* astounded, stupefied.

stupéfiant, -e [stypefjã, ãt] *adj* astounding, stunning. ○ **stupéfiant** *nm* narcotic, drug.

stupeur [stypœr] *nf* [stupéfaction] astonishment. || MÉD stupor.

stupide [stypid] *adj péj* [abruti] stupid. || [insensé - mort] senseless; [- accident] stupid.

stupidité [stypidite] *nf* stupidity.

style [stil] *nm* [gén] style. || GRAM: ~ direct/indirect direct/indirect speech.

styliste [stilist] *nmf* COUTURE designer.

stylo [stilo] *nm* pen; ~ plume fountain pen.

stylo-feutre [stiloføtr] *nm* felt-tip pen.

su, -e [sy] *pp* → savoir.

suave [sɥav] *adj* [voix] smooth.

subalterne [sybaltɛrn] **1** *nmf* subordinate, junior. **2** *adj* [rôle] subordinate; [employé] junior.

subconscient, -e [sybkɔ̃sjã, ãt] *adj* subconscious. ○ **subconscient** *nm* subconscious.

subdiviser [sybdivize] *vt* to subdivide.

subir [sybir] *vt* [conséquences, colère] to suffer; [personne] to put up with. || [opération, épreuve, examen] to undergo. || [dommages, pertes] to sustain, to suffer.

subit, -e [sybi, it] *adj* sudden.

subitement [sybitmã] *adv* suddenly.

subjectif, -ive [sybʒɛktif, iv] *adj* [personnel, partial] subjective.

subjonctif [sybʒɔ̃ktif] *nm* subjunctive.

subjuguer [sybʒyge] *vt* to captivate.

sublime [syblim] *adj* sublime.

submerger [sybmɛrʒe] *vt* [inonder] to flood. || [déborder] to overwhelm; **être submergé de travail** to be swamped with work.

subordonné, -e [sybɔrdɔne] **1** *adj* GRAM subordinate, dependent. **2** *nm, f* subordinate.

subornation [sybɔrnasjɔ̃] *nf* bribing, subornation.

subrepticement [sybrɛptismã] *adv* surreptitiously.

subsidiaire [sybzidjɛr] *adj* subsidiary.

subsistance [sybzistɑ̃s] *nf* subsistence.

subsister [sybziste] *vi* [chose] to remain. || [personne] to live, to subsist.

substance [sypstɑ̃s] *nf* [matière] substance. || [essence] gist.

substantiel, -ielle [sypstɑ̃sjɛl] *adj* substantial.

substantif [sypstɑ̃tif] *nm* noun.

substituer [sypstitɥe] *vt*: ~ qqch à qqch to substitute sthg for sthg. ○ **se substituer** *vp*: se ~ à [personne] to stand in for, to substitute for; [chose] to take the place of.

substitut [sypstity] *nm* [remplacement] substitute.

substitution [sypstitysjɔ̃] *nf* substitution.

subterfuge [sypterfyʒ] *nm* subterfuge.

subtil, -e [syptil] *adj* subtle.

subtiliser [syptilize] *vt* to steal.

subtilité [syptilite] *nf* subtlety.

subvenir [sybvənir] *vi*: ~ à to meet, to cover.

subvention [sybvɑ̃sjɔ̃] *nf* grant, subsidy.

subventionner [sybvɑ̃sjɔne] *vt* to give a grant to, to subsidize.

subversif, -ive [sybversif, iv] *adj* subversive.

succédané [syksedane] *nm* substitute.

succéder [syksede] *vt*: ~ à [suivre] to follow; [remplacer] to succeed, to take over from. ○ **se succéder** *vp* to follow one another.

succès [syksɛ] *nm* [gén] success; **avoir du ~** to be very successful; **sans ~** [essayer] unsuccessfully. || [chanson, pièce] hit.

successeur [syksesœr] *nm* [gén] successor. || JUR successor, heir.

successif, -ive [syksesif, iv] *adj* successive.

succession [syksesjɔ̃] *nf* [gén] succession; **prendre la ~ de qqn** to take over from sb, to succeed sb. || JUR succession, inheritance; **droits de ~** death duties.

succinct, -e [syksɛ̃, ɛ̃t] *adj* [résumé] succinct. || [repas] frugal.

succion [sysjɔ̃] *nf* suction, sucking.

succomber [sykɔ̃be] *vi*: ~ (à) to succumb (to).

succulent, -e [sykylɑ̃, ɑ̃t] *adj* delicious.

succursale [sykyrsal] *nf* branch.

sucer [syse] *vt* to suck.

sucette [sysɛt] *nf* [friandise] lollipop.

sucre [sykr] *nm* sugar; ~ **en morceaux** lump sugar; ~ **en poudre**, ~ **semoule** caster sugar.

sucré, -e [sykre] *adj* [goût] sweet.

sucrer [sykre] *vt* [café, thé] to sweeten, to sugar.

sucrerie [sykrəri] *nf* [usine] sugar refinery. || [friandise] sweet *Br*, candy *Am*.

sucrette [sykrɛt] *nf* sweetener.

sucrier [sykrije] *nm* sugar bowl.

sud [syd] **1** *nm* south; **un vent du ~ a** southerly wind; **au ~** in the south; **au ~ (de)** to the south (of). **2** *adj inv* [gén] south; [province, région] southern.

sud-africain, -e [sydafrikɛ̃, ɛn] (*mpl* **sud-africains,** *fpl* **sud-africaines**) *adj* South African. ○ **Sud-Africain, -e** *nm,* *f* South African.

sud-américain, -e [sydamerikɛ̃, ɛn] (*mpl* **sud-américains,** *fpl* **sud-américaines**) *adj* South American. ○ **Sud-Américain, -e** *nm,* *f* South American.

sud-est [sydɛst] *nm & adj inv* southeast.

sud-ouest [sydwɛst] *nm & adj inv* southwest.

Suède [sɥɛd] *nf*: **la ~** Sweden.

suédois, -e [sɥedwa, az] *adj* Swedish. ○ **suédois** *nm* [langue] Swedish. ○ **Suédois, -e** *nm, f* Swede.

suer [sɥe] *vi* [personne] to sweat.

sueur [sɥœr] *nf* sweat; **avoir des ~s froides** *fig* to be in a cold sweat.

Suez [sɥɛz] *n*: **le canal de ~** the Suez Canal.

suffi [syfi] *pp inv* → **suffire**.

suffire [syfir] **1** *vi* [être assez]: ~ **pour qqch/pour faire qqch** to be enough for sthg/to do sthg, to be sufficient for sthg/to do sthg; **ça suffit!** that's enough! || [satisfaire]: ~ **à** to be enough for. **2** *v impers*: **il suffit de ...** all that is necessary is ..., all that you have to do is ...; **il suffit que vous lui écriviez** all (that) you need do is write to him. ○ **se suffire** *vp*: se ~ **à soi-même** to be self-sufficient.

suffisamment [syfizamɑ̃] *adv* sufficiently.

suffisant, -e [syfizɑ̃, ɑ̃t] *adj* [satisfaisant] sufficient. || [vaniteux] self-important.

suffixe [syfiks] *nm* suffix.

suffoquer [syfɔke] **1** *vt* [suj: chaleur, fumée] to suffocate, to choke; *fig* [suj: colère] to choke; [suj: nouvelle, révélation] to astonish, to stun. **2** *vi* to choke.

suffrage [syfraʒ] *nm* vote.

suggérer [sygʒere] *vt* [proposer] to suggest; ~ à qqn de faire qqch to suggest that sb (should) do sthg. ‖ [faire penser à] to evoke.

suggestif, -ive [sygʒestif, iv] *adj* [pose, photo] suggestive.

suggestion [sygʒestjɔ̃] *nf* suggestion.

suicidaire [sɥisider] *adj* suicidal.

suicide [sɥisid] *nm* suicide.

suicider [sɥiside] ○ **se suicider** *vp* to commit suicide, to kill o.s.

suie [sɥi] *nf* soot.

suinter [sɥɛ̃te] *vi* [eau, sang] to ooze, to seep. ‖ [surface, mur] to sweat; [plaie] to weep.

suis → être.

suisse [sɥis] *adj* Swiss. ○ **Suisse 1** *nf* [pays]: la ~ Switzerland; la ~ allemande/italienne/romande German-/Italian-/French-speaking Switzerland. 2 *nmf* [personne] Swiss (person); les Suisses the Swiss.

suite [sɥit] *nf* [de liste, feuilleton] continuation. ‖ [série - de maisons, de succès] series; [- d'événements] sequence. ‖ [succession]: **prendre la ~ de** [personne] to succeed, to take over from. à la ~ one after the other; à la ~ de *fig* following. ‖ [escorte] retinue. ‖ [appartement] suite. ○ **suites** *nfpl* consequences. ○ **par suite de** *loc prép* owing to, because of.

suivant, -e [sɥivɑ̃, ɑ̃t] 1 *adj* next, following. 2 *nm, f* next *ou* following one; au ~! next!

suivi, -e [sɥivi] 1 *pp* → **suivre**. 2 *adj* [visites] regular; [travail] sustained; [qualité] consistent. ○ **suivi** *nm* follow-up.

suivre [sɥivr] 1 *vt* [gén] to follow; «faire ~» "please forward"; à ~ to be continued. ‖ [suj: médecin] to treat. 2 *vi* SCOL to keep up. ‖ [venir après] to follow. ○ **se suivre** *vp* to follow one another.

sujet, -ette [syʒɛ, ɛt] 1 *adj*: être ~ à qqch to be subject *ou* prone to sthg. 2 *nm, f* [de souverain] subject. ○ **sujet** *nm* [gén] subject; **c'est à quel ~?** what is it about?; **au ~ de** about, concerning.

sulfate [sylfat] *nm* sulphate.

sulfurique [sylfyrik] *adj* sulphuric.

super [syper] *fam* 1 *adj inv* super, great. 2 *nm* premium *Am.*

superbe [syperb] *adj* superb; [enfant, femme] beautiful.

supercherie [syperʃəri] *nf* deception.

superficie [syperfisi] *nf* [surface] area. ‖ *fig* [aspect superficiel] surface.

superficiel, -ielle [syperfisjel] *adj* superficial.

superflu, -e [syperfly] *adj* superfluous.

supérieur, -e [syperjœr] 1 *adj* [étage] upper. ‖ [intelligence, qualité] superior; ~ à superior to; [température] higher than, above. ‖ [dominant - équipe] superior; [- cadre] senior. ‖ SCOL - classe] upper, senior; [- enseignement] higher. ‖ *péj* [air] superior. 2 *nm, f* superior.

supériorité [syperjɔrite] *nf* superiority.

superlatif [syperlatif] *nm* superlative.

supermarché [sypermarʃe] *nm* supermarket.

superposer [syperpoze] *vt* to stack. ○ **se superposer** *vp* to be stacked.

superproduction [syperprɔdyksjɔ̃] *nf* spectacular.

superpuissance [syperpɥisɑ̃s] *nf* superpower.

supersonique [sypersɔnik] *adj* supersonic.

superstitieux, -ieuse [syperstisjø, jøz] *adj* superstitious.

superstition [syperstisjɔ̃] *nf* [croyance] superstition.

superviser [sypervize] *vt* to supervise.

supplanter [syplɑ̃te] *vt* to supplant.

suppléant, -e [sypleɑ̃, ɑ̃t] 1 *adj* acting (*avant n*), temporary. 2 *nm, f* substitute, deputy.

suppléer [syplee] *vt littéraire* [carence] to compensate for. ‖ [personne] to stand in for.

supplément [syplemɑ̃] *nm* [surplus]: **un ~ de détails** additional details, extra details. ‖ PRESSE supplement. ‖ [de billet] extra charge.

supplémentaire [syplemɑ̃ter] *adj* extra, additional.

supplication [syplikasjɔ̃] *nf* plea.

supplice [syplis] *nm* torture; *fig* [souffrance] torture, agony.

supplier [syplije] *vt*: ~ qqn de faire qqch to beg *ou* implore sb to do sthg.

support [sypɔr] *nm* [socle] support, base. ‖ *fig* [de communication] medium; ~ publicitaire advertising medium.

supportable [sypɔrtabl] *adj* [douleur] bearable.

supporter¹ [sypɔrte] *vt* [soutenir, encourager] to support. ‖ [endurer] to bear, to stand; ~ que (+ *subjonctif*): **il ne supporte pas qu'on le contredise** he cannot bear being contradicted. ‖ [résister à] to withstand.

supporter² [sypɔrtɛr] *nm* supporter.

supposer [sypoze] *vt* [imaginer] to suppose, to assure; **en supposant que** (+ *subjonctif*), **à ~ que** (+ *subjonctif*) supposing (that). || [impliquer] to imply, to presuppose.

supposition [sypozisjɔ̃] *nf* supposition, assumption.

suppositoire [sypozitwar] *nm* suppository.

suppression [sypresjɔ̃] *nf* [de mot, passage] deletion. || [de loi, poste] abolition.

supprimer [syprime] *vt* [obstacle, difficulté] to remove. || [mot, passage] to delete. || [loi, poste] to abolish. || [témoin] to do away with, to eliminate. || [permis de conduire, revenus]: ~ **qqch à qqn** to take sthg away from sb. || [douleur] to take away, to suppress.

suprématie [sypremasi] *nf* supremacy.

suprême [syprɛm] *adj* [gén] supreme.

sur [syr] *prép* [position - dessus] on; [- au-dessus de] above, over; ~ **la table** on the table. || [direction] towards; ~ **la droite/gauche** on the right/left, to the right/left. || [distance]: **travaux ~ 10 kilomètres** roadworks for 10 kilometres. || [au sujet de] on, about. || [proportion] out of; [mesure] by; **9 ~ 10** 9 out of 10; **un mètre ~ deux** one metre by two; **un jour ~ deux** every other day. ○ **sur ce** *loc adv* whereupon.

sûr, -e [syr] *adj* [sans danger] safe. || [digne de confiance - personne] reliable, trustworthy; [- goût] reliable, sound; [- investissement] sound. || [certain] sure, certain; ~ **de** sure of; ~ **de soi** self-confident.

surabondance [syrabɔ̃dɑ̃s] *nf* over-abundance.

suraigu, -ë [syregy] *adj* high-pitched, shrill.

suranné, -e [syrane] *adj littéraire* old-fashioned, outdated.

surcharge [syrʃarʒ] *nf* [excès de poids] excess load; [- de bagages] excess weight. || *fig* [surcroît]: **une ~ de travail** extra work. || [de document] alteration.

surcharger [syrʃarʒe] *vt* [véhicule, personne]: ~ **(de)** to overload (with).

surcroît [syrkrwa] *nm*: **un ~ de travail/d'inquiétude** additional work/anxiety.

surdité [syrdite] *nf* deafness.

surdoué, -e [syrdwe] *adj* exceptionally ou highly gifted.

sureffectif [syrefɛktif] *nm* overmanning, overstaffing.

surélever [syrɛlve] *vt* to raise, to heighten.

sûrement [syrmɑ̃] *adv* [certainement] certainly; ~ **pas!** *fam* no way!, definitely not! || [sans doute] certainly, surely.

surenchère [syrɑ̃ʃɛr] *nf* higher bid; *fig* overstatement, exaggeration.

surenchérir [syrɑ̃ʃerir] *vi* to bid higher; *fig* to try to go one better.

surendetté, -e [syrɑ̃dɛte] *adj* overindebted.

surestimer [syrɛstime] *vt* [exagérer] to overestimate. || [surévaluer] to overvalue. ○ **se surestimer** *vp* to overestimate o.s.

sûreté [syrte] *nf* [sécurité] safety; **en ~** safe; **de ~** safety (*avant n*). || [fiabilité] reliability. || JUR surety.

surexposer [syrɛkspoze] *vt* to overexpose.

surf [sœrf] *nm* surfing.

surface [syrfas] *nf* [extérieur, apparence] surface. || [superficie] surface area. ○ **grande surface** *nf* hypermarket.

surfait, -e [syrfɛ, ɛt] *adj* overrated.

surfer [sœrfe] *vi* to go surfing.

surgelé, -e [syrʒəle] *adj* frozen. ○ **surgelé** *nm* frozen food.

surgir [syrʒir] *vi* to appear suddenly; *fig* [difficulté] to arise, to come up.

surhumain, -e [syrymɛ̃, ɛn] *adj* super-human.

surimpression [syrɛ̃presjɔ̃] *nf* double exposure.

sur-le-champ [syrləʃɑ̃] *loc adv* immediately, straightaway.

surlendemain [syrlɑ̃dmɛ̃] *nm*: **le ~** two days later; **le ~ de mon départ** two days after I left.

surligner [syrliɲe] *vt* to highlight.

surligneur [syrliɲœr] *nm* highlighter (pen).

surmenage [syrmənaʒ] *nm* overwork.

surmener [syrməne] *vt* to overwork. ○ **se surmener** *vp* to overwork.

surmonter [syrmɔ̃te] *vt* [obstacle, peur] to overcome, to surmount. || [suj: statue, croix] to surmount, to top.

surnager [syrnaʒe] *vi* [flotter] to float (on the surface).

surnaturel, -elle [syrnatyrɛl] *adj* supernatural. ○ **surnaturel** *nm*: **le ~** the supernatural.

surnom [syrnɔ̃] *nm* nickname.

surpasser [syrpase] *vt* to surpass, to outdo. ○ **se surpasser** *vp* to surpass ou excel o.s.

surpeuplé, -e [syrpœple] *adj* over-populated.

surplomb [syrplɔ̃] ○ **en surplomb** *loc adj* overhanging.

surplomber [syrplɔ̃be] **1** *vt* to overhang. **2** *vi* to be out of plumb.

surplus [syrply] *nm* [excédent] surplus.

surprenant, -e [syrprənɑ̃, ɑ̃t] *adj* surprising, amazing.

surprendre [syrprɑ̃dr] *vt* [voleur] to catch (in the act). ‖ [prendre à l'improviste] to surprise, to catch unawares. ‖ [étonner] to surprise, to amaze.

surpris, -e [syrpri, iz] *pp* → **surprendre.**

surprise [syrpriz] *nf* surprise; **par ~** by surprise; **faire une ~ à qqn** to give sb a surprise.

surproduction [syrprɔdyksjɔ̃] *nf* overproduction.

surréalisme [syrrealism] *nm* surrealism.

sursaut [syrso] *nm* [de personne] jump, start; **en ~** with a start.

sursauter [syrsote] *vi* to start, to give a start.

sursis [syrsi] *nm* JUR & *fig* reprieve; **six mois avec ~** six months' suspended sentence.

surtaxe [syrtaks] *nf* surcharge.

surtout [syrtu] *adv* [avant tout] above all. ‖ [spécialement] especially, particularly; **~ pas** certainly not. ○ **surtout que** *loc conj fam* especially as.

survécu, -e [syrveky] *pp* → **survivre.**

surveillance [syrvɛjɑ̃s] *nf* supervision.

surveillant, -e [syrvɛjɑ̃, ɑ̃t] *nm, f* supervisor; [de prison] warder *Br*, guard.

surveiller [syrveje] *vt* [enfant] to watch, to keep an eye on. ‖ [travaux] to supervise; [examen] to invigilate. ‖ [ligne, langage] to watch. ○ **se surveiller** *vp* to watch o.s.

survenir [syrvənir] *vi* [incident] to occur.

survenu, -e [syrvəny] *pp* → **survenir.**

survêtement [syrvɛtmɑ̃] *nm* tracksuit.

survie [syrvi] *nf* [de personne] survival.

survivant, -e [syrvivɑ̃, ɑ̃t] **1** *nm, f* survivor. **2** *adj* surviving.

survivre [syrvivr] *vi* to survive; **~ à** [personne] to outlive, to survive; [accident, malheur] to survive.

survoler [syrvɔle] *vt* [territoire] to fly over. ‖ [texte] to skim (through).

sus [sy(s)] ○ **en sus** *loc adv* moreover,

in addition; **en ~ de** over and above, in addition to.

susceptibilité [sysɛptibilite] *nf* touchiness, sensitivity.

susceptible [sysɛptibl] *adj* [ombrageux] touchy, sensitive. ‖ [en mesure de]: **~ de faire qqch** liable *ou* likely to do sthg.

susciter [sysite] *vt* [admiration, curiosité] to arouse.

suspect, -e [syspɛ, ɛkt] **1** *adj* [personne] suspicious. ‖ [douteux] suspect. **2** *nm, f* suspect.

suspecter [syspɛkte] *vt* to suspect, to have one's suspicions about; **~ qqn de qqch/de faire qqch** to suspect sb of sthg/of doing sthg.

suspendre [syspɑ̃dr] *vt* [lustre, tableau] to hang (up). ‖ [pourparlers] to suspend; [séance] to adjourn. ‖ [fonctionnaire, constitution] to suspend. ‖ [jugement] to postpone, to defer.

suspendu, -e [syspɑ̃dy] **1** *pp* → **suspendre. 2** *adj* [fonctionnaire] suspended. ‖ [séance] adjourned. ‖ [lustre, tableau]: **~ au plafond/au mur** hanging from the ceiling/on the wall.

suspens [syspɑ̃] ○ **en suspens** *loc adv* in abeyance.

suspense [syspɛns] *nm* suspense.

suspension [syspɑ̃sjɔ̃] *nf* [gén] suspension. ‖ [de combat] halt; [d'audience] adjournment. ‖ [lustre] light fitting.

suspicion [syspisjɔ̃] *nf* suspicion.

susurrer [sysyre] *vt & vi* to murmur.

suture [sytyr] *nf* suture.

svelte [zvɛlt] *adj* slender.

SVP *abr de* **s'il vous plaît.**

sweat-shirt [switʃœrt] (*pl* **sweat-shirts**) *nm* sweatshirt.

syllabe [silab] *nf* syllable.

symbole [sɛ̃bɔl] *nm* symbol.

symbolique [sɛ̃bɔlik] *adj* [figure] symbolic. ‖ [geste, contribution] token (*avant n*). ‖ [rémunération] nominal.

symboliser [sɛ̃bɔlize] *vt* to symbolize.

symétrie [simetri] *nf* symmetry.

symétrique [simetrik] *adj* symmetrical.

sympa [sɛ̃pa] *adj fam* [personne] likeable, nice; [soirée, maison] pleasant, nice; [ambiance] friendly.

sympathie [sɛ̃pati] *nf* [pour personne, projet] liking. ‖ [condoléances] sympathy.

sympathique [sɛ̃patik] *adj* [personne] likeable, nice; [soirée, maison] pleasant, nice; [ambiance] friendly. ‖ ANAT & MÉD sympathetic.

sympathiser [sɛ̃patize] *vi* to get on well; ~ **avec qqn** to get on well with sb.

symphonie [sɛ̃fɔni] *nf* symphony.

symphonique [sɛ̃fɔnik] *adj* [musique] symphonic; [concert, orchestre] symphony (*avant n*).

symptomatique [sɛ̃ptɔmatik] *adj* symptomatic.

symptôme [sɛ̃ptom] *nm* symptom.

synagogue [sinagɔg] *nf* synagogue.

synchroniser [sɛ̃krɔnize] *vt* to synchronize.

syncope [sɛ̃kɔp] *nf* [évanouissement] blackout. ‖ MUS syncopation.

syndic [sɛ̃dik] *nm* [de copropriété] representative.

syndicaliste [sɛ̃dikalist] **1** *nmf* trade unionist. **2** *adj* (trade) union (*avant n*).

syndicat [sɛ̃dika] *nm* [d'employés, d'agriculteurs] (trade) union; [d'employeurs, de propriétaires] association. ○ **syndicat d'initiative** *nm* tourist office.

syndiqué, -e [sɛ̃dike] *adj* unionized.

syndrome [sɛ̃drom] *nm* syndrome.

synonyme [sinɔnim] **1** *nm* synonym. **2** *adj* synonymous.

syntaxe [sɛ̃taks] *nf* syntax.

synthèse [sɛ̃tɛz] *nf* [opération & CHIM] synthesis. ‖ [exposé] overview.

synthétique [sɛ̃tetik] *adj* [vue] overall. ‖ [produit] synthetic.

synthétiseur [sɛ̃tetizœr] *nm* synthesizer.

syphilis [sifilis] *nf* syphilis.

Syrie [siri] *nf*: **la ~** Syria.

syrien, -ienne [sirjɛ̃, jɛn] *adj* Syrian. ○ **Syrien, -ienne** *nm, f* Syrian.

systématique [sistematik] *adj* systematic.

systématiser [sistematize] *vt* to systematize.

système [sistɛm] *nm* system; ~ **expert** INFORM expert system; ~ **d'exploitation** INFORM operating system; ~ **nerveux** nervous system; ~ **solaire** solar system.

t, T [te] *nm inv* t, T.

ta → **ton**.

tabac [taba] *nm* [plante, produit] tobacco; ~ **blond** mild ou Virginia tobacco; ~ **brun** dark tobacco; ~ **à priser** snuff. ‖ [magasin] tobacconist's.

tabagisme [tabaʒism] *nm* [intoxication] nicotine addiction. ‖ [habitude] smoking.

table [tabl] *nf* [meuble] table; **à ~!** lunch/dinner *etc* is ready!; **se mettre à ~** to sit down to eat; **dresser** ou **mettre la ~** to lay the table; ~ **de chevet** ou **de nuit** bedside table. ○ **table des matières** *nf* contents (*pl*), table of contents. ○ **table de multiplication** *nf* (multiplication) table.

tableau, -x [tablo] *nm* [peinture] painting, picture; *fig* [description] picture. ‖ [panneau] board; ~ **d'affichage** notice board *Br*, bulletin board *Am*; ~ **de bord** AÉRON instrument panel; AUTOM dashboard; ~ **noir** blackboard. ‖ [de données] table.

tabler [table] *vi*: ~ **sur** to count ou bank on.

tablette [tablɛt] *nf* [planchette] shelf. ‖ [de chewing-gum] stick; [de chocolat] bar.

tableur [tablœr] *nm* INFORM spreadsheet.

tablier [tablije] *nm* [de cuisinière] apron; [d'écolier] smock. ‖ [de pont] roadway, deck.

tabloïd(e) [tablɔid] *nm* tabloid.

tabou, -e [tabu] *adj* taboo. ○ **tabou** *nm* taboo.

tabouret [taburɛ] *nm* stool.

tabulateur [tabylatœr] *nm* tabulator, tab.

tac [tak] *nm*: **du ~ au ~** tit for tat.

tache [taʃ] *nf* [de pelage] marking; [de peau] mark; ~ **de rousseur** ou **de son** freckle. ‖ [de couleur, lumière] spot, patch. ‖ [sur nappe, vêtement] stain.

tâche [taʃ] *nf* task.

tacher [taʃe] *vt* [nappe, vêtement] to stain, to mark.

tâcher [taʃe] *vi*: ~ **de faire qqch** to try to do sthg.

tacheter [taʃte] *vt* to spot, to speckle.

tacite [tasit] *adj* tacit.

taciturne [tasityrn] *adj* taciturn.

tact [takt] *nm* [délicatesse] tact; **manquer de ~** to be tactless.

tactique [taktik] **1** *adj* tactical. **2** *nf* tactics (*pl*).

tag [tag] *nm* identifying name written with a spray can on walls, the sides of trains etc.

taie [tɛ] *nf* [enveloppe]: ~ **(d'oreiller)** pillowcase, pillow slip.

taille [taj] *nf* [action - de pierre, diamant] cutting; [- d'arbre, haie] pruning. || [stature] height. || [mesure, dimensions] size; **vous faites quelle ~?** what size are you?, what size do you take?; **de ~** sizeable, considerable. || [milieu du corps] waist.

taille-crayon [tajkrɛjɔ̃] (*pl* **taille-crayons**) *nm* pencil sharpener.

tailler [taje] *vt* [couper - chair, pierre, diamant] to cut; [- arbre, haie] to prune; [- crayon] to sharpen; [- bois] to carve. || [vêtement] to cut out.

tailleur [tajœr] *nm* [couturier] tailor. || [vêtement] (lady's) suit. || [de diamants, pierre] cutter.

taillis [taji] *nm* coppice, copse.

tain [tɛ̃] *nm* silvering; **miroir sans ~** two-way mirror.

taire [tɛr] *vt* to conceal. ○ **se taire** *vp* [rester silencieux] to be silent ou quiet. || [cesser de s'exprimer] to fall silent; **tais-toi!** shut up!

Taiwan [tajwan] *n* Taiwan.

talc [talk] *nm* talcum powder.

talent [talɑ̃] *nm* talent; **avoir du ~** to be talented, to have talent.

talentueux, -euse [talɑ̃tɥø, øz] *adj* talented.

talisman [talismɑ̃] *nm* talisman.

talkie-walkie [tɔkiwɔki] *nm* walkie-talkie.

talon [talɔ̃] *nm* [gén] heel; **~s aiguilles/hauts** stiletto/high heels; **~s plats** low ou flat heels. || [de chèque] counterfoil, stub. || CARTES stock.

talonner [talɔne] *vt* [suj: poursuivant] to be hard on the heels of.

talonnette [talɔnɛt] *nf* [de chaussure] heel cushion, heel-pad.

talquer [talke] *vt* to put talcum powder on.

talus [taly] *nm* embankment.

tambour [tɑ̃bur] *nm* [instrument, cylindre] drum. || [musicien] drummer. || [porte à tourniquet] revolving door.

tambourin [tɑ̃burɛ̃] *nm* [à grelots] tambourine. || [tambour] tambourin.

tambouriner [tɑ̃burine] *vi*: ~ **sur** ou **à** to drum on; ~ **contre** to drum against.

tamis [tami] *nm* [crible] sieve.

Tamise [tamiz] *nf*: **la ~** the Thames.

tamisé, -e [tamize] *adj* [éclairage] subdued.

tamiser [tamize] *vt* [farine] to sieve. || [lumière] to filter.

tampon [tɑ̃pɔ̃] *nm* [bouchon] stopper, plug. || [éponge] pad; ~ **à récurer** scourer. || [de coton, d'ouate] pad; ~ **hygiénique** ou **périodique** tampon. || [cachet] stamp. || *litt* & *fig* [amortisseur] buffer.

tamponner [tɑ̃pɔne] *vt* [document] to stamp. || [plaie] to dab.

tam-tam [tamtam] (*pl* **tam-tams**) *nm* tom-tom.

tandem [tɑ̃dɛm] *nm* [vélo] tandem. || [duo] pair; **en ~** together, in tandem.

tandis [tɑ̃di] ○ **tandis que** *loc conj* [pendant que] while. || [alors que] while, whereas.

tangage [tɑ̃gaʒ] *nm* pitching, pitch.

tangent, -e [tɑ̃ʒɑ̃, ɑ̃t] *adj*: **c'était ~** *fig* it was close, it was touch and go. ○ **tangente** *nf* tangent.

tangible [tɑ̃ʒibl] *adj* tangible.

tango [tɑ̃go] *nm* tango.

tanguer [tɑ̃ge] *vi* to pitch.

tanière [tanjɛr] *nf* den, lair.

tank [tɑ̃k] *nm* tank.

tanner [tane] *vt* [peau] to tan.

tant [tɑ̃] *adv* [quantité]: ~ **de travail** so much work. || [nombre]: ~ **de livres/d'élèves** so many books/pupils. || [tellement] such a lot, so much. || [quantité indéfinie] so much; **ça coûte ~** it costs so much. || [comparatif]: ~ **que** as much as. || [valeur temporelle]: ~ **que** (aussi longtemps que) as long as; [pendant que] while. ○ **en tant que** *loc conj* as. ○ **tant bien que mal** *loc adv* after a fashion, somehow or other. ○ **tant mieux** *loc adv* so much the better; ~ **mieux pour lui** good for him. ○ **tant pis** *loc adv* too bad.

tante [tɑ̃t] *nf* [parente] aunt.

tantinet [tɑ̃tinɛ] *nm*: **un ~ exagéré/trop long** a bit exaggerated/too long.

tantôt [tɑ̃to] *adv* [parfois] sometimes.

te

tapage [tapaʒ] *nm* [bruit] row. || *fig* [battage] fuss (U).

tapageur, -euse [tapaʒœr, øz] *adj* [style] flashy. || [liaison, publicité] blatant.

tape [tap] *nf* slap.

tape-à-l'œil [tapalœj] *adj inv* flashy.

taper [tape] **1** *vt* [personne, cuisse] to slap; ~ (un coup) à la porte to knock at the door. || [à la machine] to type. **2** *vi* [frapper] to hit; ~ du poing sur to bang one's fist on. || [à la machine] to type. || *fam* [soleil] to beat down.

tapis [tapi] *nm* carpet; [de gymnase] mat; ~ roulant [pour bagages] conveyor belt; [pour personnes] travolator.

tapisser [tapise] *vt*: ~ (de) to cover (with).

tapisserie [tapisri] *nf* tapestry.

tapissier, -ière [tapisje, jɛr] *nm, f* [décorateur] (interior) decorator. || [commerçant] upholsterer.

tapoter [tapɔte] **1** *vt* to tap; [joue] to pat. **2** *vi*: ~ sur to tap on.

taquin, -e [takɛ̃, in] *adj* teasing.

taquiner [takine] *vt* [suj: personne] to tease. || [suj: douleur] to worry.

tarabuster [tarabyste] *vt* [suj: personne] to badger. || [suj: idée] to niggle at.

tard [tar] *adv* late; plus ~ later; au plus ~ at the latest.

tarder [tarde] **1** *vi*: ~ à faire qqch [être lent à] to take a long time to do sthg; elle ne devrait plus ~ maintenant she should be here any time now. **2** *v impers*: il me tarde de te revoir/qu'il vienne I am longing to see you again/for him to come.

tardif, -ive [tardif, iv] *adj* [heure] late.

tare [tar] *nf* [défaut] defect. || [de balance] tare.

tarif [tarif] *nm* [prix - de restaurant, café] price; [- de service] rate, price; [douanier] tariff; demi-~ half rate or price; ~ réduit reduced price; [au cinéma, théâtre] concession. || [tableau] price list.

tarir [tarir] *vi* to dry up; elle ne tarit pas d'éloges sur son professeur she never stops praising her teacher. ○ se tarir *vp* to dry up.

tarot [taro] *nm* tarot. ○ tarots *nmpl* tarot cards.

tartare [tartar] *adj* Tartar; (steak) ~ steak tartare.

tarte [tart] **1** *nf* [gâteau] tart. || *fam fig* [gifle] slap. **2** *adj* (avec ou sans accord) *fam* [idiot] stupid.

tartine [tartin] *nf* [de pain] piece of bread and butter.

tartiner [tartine] *vt* [pain] to spread; chocolat/fromage à ~ chocolate/cheese spread. || *fam fig* [pages] to cover.

tartre [tartr] *nm* [de dents, vin] tartar. || [de chaudière] fur, scale.

tas [ta] *nm* heap; un ~ de a lot of.

tasse [tas] *nf* cup; ~ à café/à thé coffee/tea cup.

tasser [tase] *vt* [neige] to compress, to pack down. || [vêtements, personnes]: ~ qqn/qqch dans to stuff sb/sthg into. ○ se tasser *vp* [fondations] to settle. || *fig* [vieillard] to shrink. || [personnes] to squeeze up. || *fam fig* [situation] to settle down.

tâter [tate] *vt* to feel; *fig* to sound out. ○ se tâter *vp fam fig* [hésiter] to be in two minds.

tatillon, -onne [tatijɔ̃, ɔn] *adj* finicky.

tâtonner [tatɔne] *vi* to grope around.

tâtons [tatɔ̃] ○ à tâtons *loc adv*: marcher/procéder à ~ to feel one's way.

tatouage [tatwaʒ] *nm* [dessin] tattoo.

tatouer [tatwe] *vt* to tattoo.

taudis [todi] *nm* slum.

taupe [top] *nf litt & fig* mole.

taureau, -x [tɔro] *nm* [animal] bull. ○ Taureau *nm* ASTROL Taurus.

tauromachie [tɔrɔmaʃi] *nf* bullfighting.

taux [to] *nm* rate; [de cholestérol, d'alcool] level; ~ de change exchange rate; ~ d'intérêt interest rate.

taverne [tavɛrn] *nf* tavern.

taxe [taks] *nf* tax; hors ~ COMM exclusive of tax, before tax; toutes ~s comprises inclusive of tax; ~ sur la valeur ajoutée value added tax.

taxer [takse] *vt* [imposer] to tax.

taxi [taksi] *nm* [voiture] taxi. || [chauffeur] taxi driver.

TB, tb (*abr de* très bien) VG.

tchécoslovaque [tʃekɔslɔvak] *adj* Czechoslovakian. ○ Tchécoslovaque *nmf* Czechoslovak.

Tchécoslovaquie [tʃekɔslɔvaki] *nf*: la ~ Czechoslovakia.

tchèque [tʃɛk] **1** *adj* Czech. **2** *nm* [langue] Czech. ○ Tchèque *nmf* Czech.

TD (*abr de* travaux dirigés) *nmpl* supervised practical work.

te [tə], **t'** *pron pers* [complément d'objet direct] you. || [complément d'objet indirect] (to) you. || [réfléchi] yourself.

technicien, -ienne [tɛknisjɛ̃, jɛn] *nm, f* [professionnel] technician.

technico-commercial, -e [tɛkniko-kɔmɛrsjal] (*mpl* **technico-commerciaux**, *fpl* **technico-commerciales**) *nm, f* sales engineer.

technique [tɛknik] **1** *adj* technical. **2** *nf* technique.

technocrate [tɛknɔkrat] *nmf* technocrat.

technologie [tɛknɔlɔʒi] *nf* technology.

technologique [tɛknɔlɔʒik] *adj* technological.

teckel [tekɛl] *nm* dachshund.

tee-shirt (*pl* tee-shirts), **T-shirt** (*pl* T-shirts) [tiʃœrt] *nm* T-shirt.

teigne [tɛɲ] *nf* [mite] moth. || MÉD ringworm. || *fam fig & péj* [femme] cow; [homme] bastard.

teindre [tɛ̃dr] *vt* to dye.

teint, -e [tɛ̃, tɛ̃t] **1** *pp* → teindre. **2** *adj* dyed. ○ **teint** *nm* [carnation] complexion. ○ **teinte** *nf* colour.

teinté, -e [tɛ̃te] *adj* tinted.

teinter [tɛ̃te] *vt* to stain.

teinture [tɛ̃tyr] *nf* [action] dyeing. || [produit] dye. ○ **teinture d'iode** *nf* tincture of iodine.

teinturerie [tɛ̃tyrri] *nf* [pressing] dry cleaner's. || [métier] dyeing.

teinturier, -ière [tɛ̃tyrje, jɛr] *nm, f* [de pressing] dry cleaner.

tel [tɛl] (*f* **telle**, *mpl* **tels**, *fpl* **telles**) *adj* [valeur indéterminée] such-and-such a. || [semblable] such; **un ~ homme** such a man; **je n'ai rien dit de ~** I never said anything of the sort. || [valeur emphatique ou intensive] such; **un ~ génie** such a genius. || [introduit un exemple ou une énumération]: **~ (que)** such as, like. || [introduit une comparaison] like; **il est ~ que je l'avais toujours rêvé** he's just like I always dreamt he would be; **~ quel** as it is/was *etc.* ○ **de telle sorte que** *loc conj* with the result that, so that.

tél. (*abr de* **téléphone**) tel.

télé [tele] *nf fam* TV, telly *Br.*

téléachat [teleaʃa] *nm* teleshopping.

télécommande [telekɔmãd] *nf* remote control.

télécommunication [telekɔmynikasjɔ̃] *nf* telecommunications (*pl*).

télécopie [telekɔpi] *nf* fax.

télécopieur [telekɔpjœr] *nm* fax (machine).

téléfilm [telefilm] *nm* film made for television.

télégramme [telegram] *nm* telegram.

télégraphe [telegraf] *nm* telegraph.

télégraphier [telegrafje] *vt* to telegraph.

téléguider [telegide] *vt* to operate by remote control; *fig* to mastermind.

télématique [telematik] *nf* telematics (U).

téléobjectif [teleɔbʒɛktif] *nm* telephoto lens (*sg*).

télépathie [telepati] *nf* telepathy.

téléphérique [teleferik] *nm* cableway.

téléphone [telefɔn] *nm* telephone; **~ sans fil** cordless telephone.

téléphoner [telefɔne] *vi* to telephone, to phone; **~ à qqn** to telephone sb, to phone sb (up).

téléphonique [telefɔnik] *adj* telephone (*avant n*), phone (*avant n*).

télescope [teleskɔp] *nm* telescope.

télescoper [teleskɔpe] *vt* [véhicule] to crash into. ○ **se télescoper** *vp* [véhicules] to concertina.

télescopique [teleskɔpik] *adj* [antenne] telescopic.

téléscripteur [teleskriptœr] *nm* teleprinter *Br*, teletypewriter *Am*.

télésiège [telesjɛʒ] *nm* chairlift.

téléski [teleski] *nm* ski tow.

téléspectateur, -trice [telespɛktatœr, tris] *nm, f* (television) viewer.

téléviseur [televizœr] *nm* television (set).

télévision [televizjɔ̃] *nf* television; **à la ~** on television.

télex [telɛks] *nm inv* telex.

tellement [tɛlmã] *adv* [si, à ce point] so; (+ *comparatif*) so much; **~ plus jeune que** so much younger than; **pas ~ not** especially, not particularly. || [autant]: **~ de** [personnes, objets] so many; [gentillesse, travail] so much. || [tant] so much; **elle a ~ changé** she's changed so much; **je ne comprends rien ~ il parle vite** he talks so quickly that I can't understand a word.

téméraire [temerɛr] **1** *adj* [audacieux] bold. || [imprudent] rash. **2** *nmf* hothead.

témérité [temerite] *nf* [audace] boldness. || [imprudence] rashness.

témoignage [temwaɲaʒ] *nm* JUR testimony, evidence (U); **faux ~** perjury. || [gage] token, expression; **en ~ de** as a token of. || [récit] account.

témoigner [temwaɲe] **1** *vt* [manifester] to show, to display. **2** *vi* JUR to testify; **~ contre** to testify against.

témoin [temwɛ̃] **1** *nm* [gén] witness; être ~ de qqch to be a witness to sthg, to witness sthg; ~ **oculaire** eyewitness. || SPORT baton. **2** *adj* [appartement] show (*avant n*).

tempe [tɑ̃p] *nf* temple.

tempérament [tɑ̃peramɑ̃] *nm* temperament; **avoir du** ~ to be hot-blooded.

température [tɑ̃peratyr] *nf* temperature; **avoir de la** ~ to have a temperature.

tempéré, -e [tɑ̃pere] *adj* [climat] temperate.

tempérer [tɑ̃pere] *vt* [adoucir] to temper; *fig* [enthousiasme, ardeur] to moderate.

tempête [tɑ̃pɛt] *nf* storm.

temple [tɑ̃pl] *nm* HIST temple. || [protestant] church.

tempo [tempo] *nm* tempo.

temporaire [tɑ̃pɔrɛr] *adj* temporary.

temporairement [tɑ̃pɔrɛrmɑ̃] *adv* temporarily.

temporel, -elle [tɑ̃pɔrɛl] *adj* [défini dans le temps] time (*avant n*).

temps [tɑ̃] *nm* [gén] time; **à plein** ~ full-time; **à mi-~, à** ~ **partiel** part-time; **au** ou **du** ~ **où** [dans les days] when; **de mon** ~ in my day; **ces** ~ **-ci, ces derniers** ~ these days; **pendant ce** ~ meanwhile; **en** ~ **de guerre/paix** in wartime/ peacetime; **il était** ~! *iron* and about time too!; **avoir le** ~ **de faire qqch** to have time to do sthg; ~ **libre** free time; **à** ~ in time; **de** ~ **à autre** now and then ou again; **de** ~ **en** ~ from time to time; **en même** ~ at the same time; **tout le** ~ all the time, the whole time; || MUS beat. || GRAM tense. || MÉTÉOR weather.

tenable [tənabl] *adj* bearable.

tenace [tənas] *adj* [gén] stubborn. || *fig* [odeur, rhume] lingering.

ténacité [tenasite] *nf* [de préjugé, personne] stubbornness.

tenailler [tənaje] *vt* to torment.

tenailles [tənaj] *nfpl* pincers.

tenancier, -ière [tənɑ̃sje, jɛr] *nm, f* manager (*f* manageress).

tendance [tɑ̃dɑ̃s] *nf* [disposition] tendency; **avoir** ~ **à qqch/à faire qqch** to have a tendency to sthg/to do sthg, to be inclined to sthg/to do sthg. || [économique, de mode] trend.

tendancieux, -ieuse [tɑ̃dɑ̃sjø, jøz] *adj* tendentious.

tendeur [tɑ̃dœr] *nm* [sangle] elastic strap (*for fastening luggage etc*).

tendinite [tɑ̃dinit] *nf* tendinitis.

tendon [tɑ̃dɔ̃] *nm* tendon.

tendre¹ [tɑ̃dr] *adj* [gén] tender. || [matériau] soft. || [couleur] delicate.

tendre² [tɑ̃dr] *vt* [corde] to tighten. || [muscle] to tense. || [objet, main]: ~ **qqch à qqn** to hold out sthg to sb. || [bâche] to hang. || [piège] to set (up). ○ **se tendre** *vp* to tighten; *fig* [relations] to become strained.

tendresse [tɑ̃drɛs] *nf* [affection] tenderness. || [indulgence] sympathy.

tendu, -e [tɑ̃dy] **1** *pp* → **tendre**. **2** *adj* [fil, corde] taut. || [personne] tense. || [atmosphère, rapports] strained. || [main] outstretched.

ténèbres [tenɛbr] *nfpl* darkness (*sg*).

ténébreux, -euse [tenebrø, øz] *adj fig* [dessein, affaire] mysterious. || [personne] serious, solemn.

teneur [tənœr] *nf* content; [de traité] terms (*pl*); ~ **en alcool/cuivre** alcohol/ copper content.

tenir [tənir] **1** *vt* [objet, personne, solution] to hold. || [garder, conserver, respecter] to keep. || [gérer - boutique] to keep, to run. || [apprendre]: ~ **qqch de qqn** to have sthg from sb. || [considérer]: ~ **qqn pour** to regard sb as. **2** *vi* [être solide] to stay up, to hold together. || [durer] to last. || [pouvoir être contenu] to fit. || [être attaché]: ~ **à** [personne] to care about; [privilèges] to value. || [vouloir absolument]: ~ **à faire qqch** to insist on doing sthg. || [ressembler]: ~ **de** to take after. || [relever de]: ~ **de** to have something of. || *loc*: ~ **bon** to stand firm; **tiens!** [en donnant] here!; [surprise] well, well!; [pour attirer attention] look! ○ **se tenir** *vp* [réunion] to be held. || [personnes] to hold one another; **se** ~ **par la main** to hold hands. || [être présent] to be. || [être cohérent] to make sense. || [se conduire] to behave (o.s.). || [se retenir]: **se** ~ **(à)** to hold on (to). || [se borner]: **s'en** ~ **à** to stick to.

tennis [tenis] **1** *nm* [sport] tennis. **2** *nmpl* tennis shoes.

ténor [tenɔr] *nm* [chanteur] tenor.

tension [tɑ̃sjɔ̃] *nf* [contraction, désaccord] tension. || MÉD pressure; **avoir de la** ~ to have high blood pressure. || ÉLECTR voltage; **haute/basse** ~ high/low voltage.

tentant, -e [tɑ̃tɑ̃, ɑ̃t] *adj* tempting.

tentation [tɑ̃tasjɔ̃] *nf* temptation.

tentative [tɑ̃tativ] *nf* attempt.

tente [tɑ̃t] *nf* tent.

tenter [tɑ̃te] *vt* [entreprendre]: ~ **qqch/**

de faire qqch to attempt sthg/to do sthg. || [plaire] to tempt.

tenture [tɑ̃tyr] *nf* hanging.

tenu, -e [təny] 1 *pp* → **tenir**. 2 *adj* [obligé]: **être ~ de faire qqch** to be required ou obliged to do sthg. || [en ordre]: **bien/mal ~** [maison] well/badly kept.

ténu, -e [teny] *adj* [fil] fine; *fig* [distinction] tenuous. || [voix] thin.

tenue [təny] *nf* [entretien] running. || [manières] good manners (*pl*). || [costume] dress; **être en petite ~** to be scantily dressed. O **tenue de route** *nf* roadholding.

ter [tɛr] 1 *adv* MUS three times. 2 *adj*: 12 ~ 12B.

Tergal® [tɛrgal] *nm* ≃ Terylene®.

tergiverser [tɛrʒivɛrse] *vi* to shilly-shally.

terme [tɛrm] *nm* [fin] end; **mettre un ~ à** to put an end ou a stop to. || [de grossesse] term; **avant ~** prematurely. || [échéance] time limit; [de loyer] rent day; **à court/moyen/long ~** [calculer] in the short/medium/long term; [projet] short-/medium-/long-term. || [mot, élément] term. O **termes** *nmpl* [expressions] words. || [de contrat] terms.

terminaison [tɛrminɛzɔ̃] *nf* GRAM ending.

terminal, -e, -aux [tɛrminal, o] *adj* [au bout] final. || MÉD [phase] terminal. O **terminal, -aux** *nm* terminal. O **terminale** *nf* SCOL ≃ senior year *Am*.

terminer [tɛrmine] *vt* to end, to finish; [travail, repas] to finish. O **se terminer** *vp* to end, to finish.

terminologie [tɛrminɔlɔʒi] *nf* terminology.

terminus [tɛrminys] *nm* terminus.

termite [tɛrmit] *nm* termite.

terne [tɛrn] *adj* dull.

ternir [tɛrnir] *vt* to dirty; [métal, réputation] to tarnish.

terrain [tɛrɛ̃] *nm* [sol] soil; **vélo tout ~** mountain bike. || [surface] piece of land. || [emplacement - de football, rugby] pitch; [- de golf] course; **~ d'aviation** airfield; **~ de camping** campsite. || *fig* [domaine] ground.

terrasse [tɛras] *nf* terrace.

terrassement [tɛrasmɑ̃] *nm* [action] excavation.

terrasser [tɛrase] *vt* [suj: personne] to bring down; [suj: émotion] to overwhelm; [suj: maladie] to conquer.

terre [tɛr] *nf* [monde] world. || [sol] ground; **par ~** on the ground; **~ à ~** *fig* down-to-earth. || [matière] earth, soil. || [propriété] land (*U*). || [territoire, continent] land. || ÉLECTR earth *Br*, ground *Am*. O **Terre** *nf*: **la Terre** Earth.

terreau [tɛro] *nm* compost.

terre-plein [tɛrplɛ̃] (*pl* **terre-pleins**) *nm* platform.

terrer [tɛre] O **se terrer** *vp* to go to earth.

terrestre [tɛrɛstr] *adj* [croûte, atmosphère] of the earth. || [animal, transport] land (*avant n*).

terreur [tɛrœr] *nf* terror.

terrible [tɛribl] *adj* [gén] terrible. || [appétit, soif] terrific, enormous. || *fam* [excellent] brilliant.

terriblement [tɛribləmɑ̃] *adv* terribly.

terrien, -ienne [tɛrjɛ̃, jɛn] 1 *adj* [foncier]: **propriétaire ~** landowner. 2 *nm, f* [habitant de la Terre] earthling.

terrier [tɛrje] *nm* [tanière] burrow. || [chien] terrier.

terrifier [tɛrifje] *vt* to terrify.

terrine [tɛrin] *nf* terrine.

territoire [tɛritwar] *nm* [pays, zone] territory. O **territoire d'outre-mer** *nm* (French) overseas territory.

territorial, -e, -iaux [tɛritɔrjal, jo] *adj* territorial.

terroir [tɛrwar] *nm* [sol] soil. || [région rurale] country.

terroriser [tɛrɔrize] *vt* to terrorize.

terrorisme [tɛrɔrism] *nm* terrorism.

terroriste [tɛrɔrist] *nmf* terrorist.

tertiaire [tɛrsjɛr] *adj* tertiary.

tes → **ton**.

tesson [tɛsɔ̃] *nm* piece of broken glass.

test [tɛst] *nm* test.

testament [tɛstamɑ̃] *nm* will.

tester [tɛste] *vt* to test.

testicule [tɛstikyl] *nm* testicle.

tétaniser [tetanize] *vt* to cause to go into spasm; *fig* to paralyse.

tétanos [tetanos] *nm* tetanus.

têtard [tɛtar] *nm* tadpole.

tête [tɛt] *nf* [gén] head; **de la ~ aux pieds** from head to foot ou toe; **la ~ la première** head first; **calculer qqch de ~** to calculate sthg in one's head; **~ de lecture** INFORM read head; **~ de liste** POLIT main candidate; **être ~ en l'air** to have one's head in the clouds; **faire la ~** to sulk; **tenir ~ à qqn** to stand up to sb. || [visage] face. || [devant - de cortège, peloton] head, front; **en ~** SPORT in the lead.

tête-à-queue [tɛtakø] *nm inv* spin.

tête-à-tête [tɛtatɛt] *nm inv* tête-à-tête.

tête-bêche [tɛtbɛʃ] *loc adv* head to tail.

tétée [tete] *nf* feed.

tétine [tetin] *nf* [de biberon, mamelle] teat. || [sucette] dummy *Br*, pacifier *Am*.

têtu, -e [tety] *adj* stubborn.

texte [tɛkst] *nm* [écrit] wording. || [imprimé] text. || [extrait] passage.

textile [tɛkstil] **1** *adj* textile (*avant n*). **2** *nm* [matière] textile. || [industrie]: **le ~ textiles** (*pl*), the textile industry.

textuel, -elle [tɛkstɥɛl] *adj* [analyse] textual; [citation] exact. || [traduction] literal.

texture [tɛkstyr] *nf* texture.

TF1 (*abr de* Télévision Française 1) *nf* French independent television company.

TGV (*abr de* train à grande vitesse) *nm* French high-speed train linking major cities.

thaïlandais, -e [tajlɑ̃dɛ, ɛz] *adj* Thai. ○ **Thaïlandais, -e** *nm, f* Thai.

Thaïlande [tajlɑ̃d] *nf*: **la ~** Thailand.

thalasso(thérapie) [talaso(terapi)] *nf* seawater therapy.

thé [te] *nm* tea.

théâtral, -e, -aux [teatral, o] *adj* [ton] theatrical.

théâtre [teatr] *nm* [bâtiment, représentation] theatre. || [art]: **faire du ~** to be on the stage; **adapté pour le ~** adapted for the stage. || [lieu] scene; **~ d'opérations** MIL theatre of operations.

théière [tejɛr] *nf* teapot.

thématique [tematik] *adj* thematic.

thème [tɛm] *nm* [sujet & MUS] theme. || SCOL prose.

théologie [teɔlɔʒi] *nf* theology.

théorème [teɔrɛm] *nm* theorem.

théorie [teɔri] *nf* theory; **en ~** in theory.

théorique [teɔrik] *adj* theoretical.

thérapeute [terapøt] *nmf* therapist.

thérapie [terapi] *nf* therapy.

thermal, -e, -aux [tɛrmal, o] *adj* thermal.

thermes [tɛrm] *nmpl* thermal baths.

thermique [tɛrmik] *adj* thermal.

thermomètre [tɛrmɔmɛtr] *nm* [instrument] thermometer.

Thermos® [tɛrmos] *nm ou nf* Thermos® (flask).

thermostat [tɛrmɔsta] *nm* thermostat.

thèse [tɛz] *nf* [opinion] argument. || PHI-LO & UNIV thesis; **~ de doctorat** doctorate. || [théorie] theory.

thon [tɔ̃] *nm* tuna.

thorax [tɔraks] *nm* thorax.

thym [tɛ̃] *nm* thyme.

thyroïde [tiroid] *nf* thyroid (gland).

Tibet [tibɛ] *nm*: **le ~** Tibet.

tibia [tibja] *nm* tibia.

tic [tik] *nm* tic.

ticket [tikɛ] *nm* ticket; **~ de caisse** (till) receipt; **~-repas** ≃ luncheon voucher.

tic-tac [tiktak] *nm inv* tick-tock.

tiède [tjɛd] *adj* [boisson, eau] tepid, lukewarm. || [vent] mild.

tiédir [tjedir] **1** *vt* to warm. **2** *vi* to become warm; **faire ~ qqch** to warm sthg.

tien [tjɛ̃] (*f* **la tienne** [latjɛn], *mpl* **les tiens** [letjɛ̃], *fpl* **les tiennes** [letjɛn]) *pron poss* yours; **à la tienne!** cheers!

tierce [tjɛrs] **1** *nf* MUS third. || CARTES & ESCRIME tierce. **2** *adj* → **tiers**.

tiercé [tjɛrse] *nm* system of betting involving the first three horses in a race.

tiers, tierce [tjɛr, tjɛrs] *adj*: **une tierce personne** a third party. ○ **tiers** *nm* [tierce personne] third party. || [de fraction]: **le ~ de** one-third of.

tiers-monde [tjɛrmɔ̃d] *nm*: **le ~** the Third World.

tige [tiʒ] *nf* [de plante] stem, stalk. || [de bois, métal] rod.

tignasse [tiɲas] *nf fam* mop (of hair).

tigre [tigr] *nm* tiger.

tigresse [tigrɛs] *nf* tigress.

tilleul [tijœl] *nm* lime (tree).

timbale [tɛ̃bal] *nf* [gobelet] (metal) cup. || MUS kettledrum.

timbre [tɛ̃br] *nm* [gén] stamp. || [de voix] timbre. || [de bicyclette] bell.

timbrer [tɛ̃bre] *vt* to stamp.

timide [timid] *adj* [personne] shy. || [protestation, essai] timid.

timoré, -e [timɔre] *adj* fearful, timorous.

tintamarre [tɛ̃tamar] *nm fam* racket.

tintement [tɛ̃tmɑ̃] *nm* [de cloche, d'horloge] chiming; [de pièces] jingling.

tinter [tɛ̃te] *vi* [cloche, horloge] to chime. || [pièces] to jingle.

tir [tir] *nm* [SPORT - activité] shooting; [- lieu]: **(centre de) ~** shooting range. || [trajectoire] shot. || [salve] fire (*U*).

tirage [tiraʒ] *nm* [de journal] circulation; [de livre] print run; **à grand ~** mass circulation. || [du loto] draw; **~ au sort** drawing lots. || [de cheminée] draught.

tiraillement [tirajmɑ̃] *nm* (*gén pl*) [crampe] cramp. || *fig* [conflit] conflict.

tirailler [tiraje] 1 *vt* [tirer sur] to tug (at). || *fig* [écarteler]: **être tiraillé par/entre qqch** to be torn by/between sthg. 2 *vi* to fire wildly.

tiré, -e [tire] *adj* [fatigué]: **avoir les traits ~s** ou **le visage ~** to look drawn.

tire-bouchon [tirbuʃɔ̃] (*pl* tire-bouchons) *nm* corkscrew. ○ **en tire-bouchon** *loc adv* corkscrew (*avant n*).

tirelire [tirlir] *nf* moneybox.

tirer [tire] 1 *vt* [gén] to pull; [rideaux] to draw. || [tracer - trait] to draw. || [revue, livre] to print. || [avec arme] to fire. || [faire sortir - vin] to draw off; **~ qqn** *de litt* & *fig* to help ou get sb out of; **~ un revolver/un mouchoir de sa poche** to pull a gun/a handkerchief out of one's pocket; **~ la langue** to stick out one's tongue. || [aux cartes, au loto] to draw. || [plaisir, profit] to derive. || [déduire - conclusion] to draw; **~ leçon** to learn. 2 *vi* [tendre]: **~ sur** to pull on ou at. || [couleur]: **bleu tirant sur le vert** greenish blue. || [cheminée] to draw. || [avec arme] to fire, to shoot. || SPORT to shoot. ○ **se tirer** *vp fam* [s'en aller] to push off. || [se sortir]: **se ~ de** to get o.s. out of; **s'en ~** *fam* to escape.

tiret [tire] *nm* dash.

tireur, -euse [tirœr, øz] *nm, f* [avec arme] gunman.

tiroir [tirwar] *nm* drawer.

tiroir-caisse [tirwarkɛs] *nm* till.

tisane [tizan] *nf* herb tea.

tisonnier [tizɔnje] *nm* poker.

tissage [tisaʒ] *nm* weaving.

tisser [tise] *vt litt* & *fig* to weave; [suj: araignée] to spin.

tissu [tisy] *nm* [étoffe] cloth, material. || BIOL tissue.

titiller [titije] *vt* to titillate.

titre [titr] *nm* [gén] title. || [de presse] headline; **gros ~** headline. || [universitaire] diploma, qualification. || FIN security, bond. ○ **titre de transport** *nm* ticket. ○ **à titre de** *loc prép*: **à ~ d'exemple** by way of example; **à ~ d'information** for information.

tituber [titybe] *vi* to totter.

titulaire [titylɛr] 1 *adj* [employé] permanent; UNIV with tenure. 2 *nmf* [de passeport, permis] holder; [de poste, chaire] occupant.

titulariser [titylarize] *vt* to give tenure to.

toast [tost] *nm* [pain grillé] toast (*U*). || [discours] toast; **porter un ~ à** to drink a toast to.

toboggan [tɔbɔgɑ̃] *nm* [de terrain de jeu] slide; [de piscine] chute.

toc [tɔk] 1 *interj*: **et ~!** so there! 2 *nm fam*: **en ~** fake (*avant n*).

toi [twa] *pron pers* you. ○ **toi-même** *pron pers* yourself.

toile [twal] *nf* [étoffe] cloth; [de lin] linen; **~ cirée** oilcloth. || [tableau] canvas, picture. ○ **toile d'araignée** *nf* spider's web.

toilette [twalɛt] *nf* [de personne, d'animal] washing; **faire sa ~** to (have a) wash. || [parure, vêtements] outfit. ○ **toilettes** *nfpl* toilet (*sg*), toilets.

toise [twaz] *nf* height gauge.

toison [twazɔ̃] *nf* [pelage] fleece. || [chevelure] mop (of hair).

toit [twa] *nm* roof; **~ ouvrant** sunroof.

toiture [twatyr] *nf* roof, roofing.

tôle [tol] *nf* [de métal] sheet metal; **~ ondulée** corrugated iron.

tolérance [tɔlerɑ̃s] *nf* [gén] tolerance. || [liberté] concession.

tolérant, -e [tɔlerɑ̃, ɑ̃t] *adj* [large d'esprit] tolerant. || [indulgent] liberal.

tolérer [tɔlere] *vt* to tolerate.

tollé [tɔle] *nm* protest.

tomate [tɔmat] *nf* tomato.

tombal, -e, -aux [tɔ̃bal, o] *adj*: **pierre ~e** gravestone.

tombant, -e [tɔ̃bɑ̃, ɑ̃t] *adj* [moustaches] drooping; [épaules] sloping.

tombe [tɔ̃b] *nf* [fosse] grave, tomb.

tombeau, -x [tɔ̃bo] *nm* tomb.

tombée [tɔ̃be] *nf* fall; **à la ~ du jour** ou **de la nuit** at nightfall.

tomber [tɔ̃be] *vi* [gén] to fall; **faire ~ qqn** to knock sb over ou down; **~ bien** [robe] to hang well; *fig* [visite, personne] to come at a good time. || [cheveux] to fall out. || [diminuer - prix] to drop, to fall; [- fièvre, vent] to drop; [- jour] to come to an end; [- colère] to die down. || [devenir brusquement]: **~ malade** to fall ill; **~ amoureux** to fall in love; **être bien/mal tombé** to be lucky/unlucky. || [trouver]: **~ sur** to come across. || [date, événement] to fall on.

tombola [tɔ̃bɔla] *nf* raffle.

tome [tɔm] *nm* volume.

ton¹ [tɔ̃] *nm* [de voix] tone; **hausser/baisser le ~** to raise/lower one's voice. || MUS key; **donner le ~** to give an "A"; *fig* to set the tone.

ton² [tɔ̃] (*f* ta [ta], *pl* tes [te]) *adj poss* your.

tonalité [tɔnalite] *nf* MUS tonality. || [au téléphone] dialling tone.

tondeuse [tɔ̃døz] *nf* [à cheveux] clippers (*pl*); ~ (à gazon) mower, lawn-mower.

tondre [tɔ̃dr] *vt* [gazon] to mow; [mouton] to shear; [caniche, cheveux] to clip.

tondu, -e [tɔ̃dy] *adj* [caniche, cheveux] clipped; [pelouse] mown.

tonifier [tɔnifje] *vt* [peau] to tone; [esprit] to stimulate.

tonique [tɔnik] *adj* [boisson] tonic (*avant n*); [froid] bracing; [lotion] toning. || LING & MUS tonic.

tonitruant, -e [tɔnitryɑ̃, ɑ̃t] *adj* booming.

tonnage [tɔnaʒ] *nm* tonnage.

tonne [tɔn] *nf* [1000 kg] tonne.

tonneau, -x [tɔno] *nm* [baril] barrel, cask. || [de voiture] roll. || NAVIG ton.

tonnelle [tɔnɛl] *nf* bower, arbour.

tonner [tɔne] *vi* to thunder.

tonnerre [tɔnɛr] *nm* thunder; **coup de** ~ thunderclap; *fig* bombshell.

tonte [tɔ̃t] *nf* [de mouton] shearing; [de gazon] mowing; [de caniche, cheveux] clipping.

tonus [tɔnys] *nm* [dynamisme] energy. || [de muscle] tone.

top [tɔp] *nm* [signal] beep.

topographie [tɔpɔgrafi] *nf* topography.

toque [tɔk] *nf* [de juge, de jockey] cap; [de cuisinier] hat.

torche [tɔrʃ] *nf* torch.

torcher [tɔrʃe] *vt fam* [assiette, fesses] to wipe. || [travail] to dash off.

torchon [tɔrʃɔ̃] *nm* [serviette] cloth. || *fam* [travail] mess.

tordre [tɔrdr] *vt* [gén] to twist. ○ **se tordre** *vp*: **se** ~ **la cheville** to twist one's ankle; **se** ~ **de rire** *fam fig* to double up with laughter.

tordu, -e [tɔrdy] **1** *pp* → **tordre**. **2** *adj fam* [bizarre, fou] crazy; [esprit] warped.

tornade [tɔrnad] *nf* tornado.

torpeur [tɔrpœr] *nf* torpor.

torpille [tɔrpij] *nf* MIL torpedo.

torréfaction [tɔrefaksjɔ̃] *nf* roasting.

torrent [tɔrɑ̃] *nm* torrent; **un** ~ **de** *fig* [injures] a stream of.

torrentiel, -ielle [tɔrɑ̃sjɛl] *adj* torrential.

torride [tɔrid] *adj* torrid.

torse [tɔrs] *nm* chest.

torsade [tɔrsad] *nf* [de cheveux] twist, coil. || [de pull] cable.

torsion [tɔrsjɔ̃] *nf* twisting; PHYS torsion.

tort [tɔr] *nm* [erreur] fault; **avoir** ~ to be wrong; **être dans son** OU **en** ~ to be in the wrong; **à** ~ wrongly. || [préjudice] wrong.

torticolis [tɔrtikɔli] *nm* stiff neck.

tortiller [tɔrtije] *vt* [enrouler] to twist. ○ **se tortiller** *vp* to writhe, to wriggle.

tortionnaire [tɔrsjɔnɛr] *nmf* torturer.

tortue [tɔrty] *nf* tortoise; *fig* slowcoach *Br*, slowpoke *Am*.

tortueux, -euse [tɔrtɥø, øz] *adj* winding, twisting; *fig* tortuous.

torture [tɔrtyr] *nf* torture.

torturer [tɔrtyre] *vt* to torture.

tôt [to] *adv* [de bonne heure] early. || [vite] soon, early. ○ **au plus tôt** *loc adv* at the earliest.

total, -e, -aux [tɔtal, o] *adj* total. ○ **total** *nm* total.

totalement [tɔtalmɑ̃] *adv* totally.

totaliser [tɔtalize] *vt* [additionner] to add up, to total. || [réunir] to have a total of.

totalitaire [tɔtalitɛr] *adj* totalitarian.

totalitarisme [tɔtalitarism] *nm* totalitarianism.

totalité [tɔtalite] *nf* whole; **en** ~ entirely.

toubib [tubib] *nmf fam* doc.

touchant, -e [tuʃɑ̃, ɑ̃t] *adj* touching.

touche [tuʃ] *nf* [de clavier] key; ~ **de fonction** function key. || [de peinture] stroke. || *fig* [note]: **une** ~ **de** a touch of. || PÊCHE bite. || [FOOTBALL - ligne] touch line; [- remise en jeu] throw-in; [RUGBY - ligne] touch (line); [- remise en jeu] line-out. || ESCRIME hit.

toucher [tuʃe] **1** *nm*: **le** ~ the (sense of) touch; **au** ~ to the touch. **2** *vt* [palper, émouvoir] to touch. || [cible] to hit. || [salaire] to get, to be paid; [chèque] to cash. || [concerner] to affect, to concern. **3** *vi*: **à** to touch; [problème] to touch on; ~ **à sa fin** to draw to a close. ○ **se toucher** *vp* [maisons] to be adjacent (to each other), to adjoin (each other).

touffe [tuf] *nf* tuft.

touffu, -e [tufy] *adj* [forêt] dense; [barbe] bushy.

toujours [tuʒur] *adv* [continuité, répétition] always; **ils s'aimeront** ~ they will always love one another, they will love one another forever; ~ **plus** more and more. || [encore] still. || [de toute façon] anyway, anyhow. ○ **pour toujours** *loc adv* forever, for good. ○ **toujours est-il que** *loc conj* the fact remains that.

toupet [tupɛ] *nm* [de cheveux] quiff *Br*, tuft of hair. || *fam fig* [aplomb] cheek; **avoir du ~, ne pas manquer de ~** *fam* to have a cheek.

toupie [tupi] *nf* (spinning) top.

tour [tur] **1** *nm* [périmètre] circumference; **faire le ~ de** to go round; **faire un ~** to go for a walk/drive *etc*; **~ d'horizon** survey; **~ de piste** SPORT lap; **~ de taille** waist measurement. || [rotation] turn; **fermer à double ~** to double-lock. || [plaisanterie] trick. || [succession] turn; **à ~ de rôle** in turn; **~ à ~** alternately, in turn. || [de potier] wheel. **2** *nf* [monument, de château] tower; [immeuble] high-rise *Am*. || ÉCHECS rook, castle. ○ **tour de contrôle** *nf* control tower.

tourbe [turb] *nf* peat.

tourbillon [turbijɔ̃] *nm* [de vent] whirlwind. || [de poussière, fumée] swirl. || [d'eau] whirlpool.

tourbillonner [turbijɔne] *vi* to whirl, to swirl; *fig* to whirl (round).

tourelle [turɛl] *nf* turret.

tourisme [turism] *nm* tourism.

touriste [turist] *nmf* tourist.

touristique [turistik] *adj* tourist (*avant n*).

tourment [turmɑ̃] *nm sout* torment.

tourmente [turmɑ̃t] *nf littéraire* [tempête] storm, tempest. || *fig* turmoil.

tourmenter [turmɑ̃te] *vt* to torment. ○ **se tourmenter** *vp* to worry o.s., to fret.

tournage [turnaʒ] *nm* CIN shooting.

tournant, -e [turnɑ̃, ɑ̃t] *adj* [porte] revolving; [fauteuil] swivel (*avant n*); [pont] swing (*avant n*). ○ **tournant** *nm* bend; *fig* turning point.

tourne-disque [turnədisk] (*pl* **tourne-disques**) *nm* record player.

tournée [turne] *nf* [voyage] tour. || *fam* [consommations] round.

tourner [turne] **1** *vt* [gén] to turn. || CIN to shoot. **2** *vi* [gén] to turn; [moteur] to turn over; [planète] to revolve; **~ autour de qqn** *fig* to hang around sb; **~ autour du pot** OU **du sujet** *fig* to beat about the bush. || *fam* [entreprise] to tick over. || [lait] to go off. ○ **se tourner** *vp* to turn (right) round; **se ~ vers** to turn towards.

tournesol [turnəsɔl] *nm* [plante] sunflower.

tournevis [turnəvis] *nm* screwdriver.

tourniquet [turnikɛ] *nm* [entrée] turnstile. || MÉD tourniquet.

tournis [turni] *nm fam*: **avoir le ~** to feel dizzy OU giddy.

tournoi [turnwa] *nm* tournament.

tournoyer [turnwaje] *vi* to wheel, to whirl.

tournure [turnyr] *nf* [apparence] turn. || [formulation] form; **~ de phrase** turn of phrase.

tourteau, -x [turto] *nm* [crabe] crab.

tourterelle [turtərɛl] *nf* turtledove.

tous → **tout**.

Toussaint [tusɛ̃] *nf*: **la ~** All Saints' Day.

tousser [tuse] *vi* to cough.

toussoter [tusɔte] *vi* to cough.

tout [tu] (*f* **toute** [tut], *mpl* **tous** [tus], *fpl* **toutes** [tut]) **1** *adj qualificatif* (*avec substantif singulier déterminé*) all; **~ le vin** all the wine; **~ un gâteau** a whole cake; **toute la journée/la nuit** all day/night, the whole day/night. || (*avec pronom démonstratif*): **~ ceci/cela** all this/that; **~ ce que je sais** all I know. **2** *adj indéf* [exprime la totalité] all; **tous les gâteaux** all the cakes; **tous les deux** both of us/them *etc*; **tous les trois** all three of us/them *etc*. || [chaque] every; **tous les deux ans** every two years. || [n'importe quel] any. **3** *pron indéf* everything, all; **je t'ai ~ dit** I've told you everything; **ils voulaient tous la voir** they all wanted to see her. ○ **tout 1** *adv* [entièrement, tout à fait] very, quite; **~ jeune/près** very young/near; **~ en haut** right at the top. || [avec un gérondif]: **~ en marchant** while walking. **2** *nm*: **le ~ est de ...** the main thing is to .... ○ **pas du tout** *loc adv* not at all. ○ **tout à fait** *loc adv* [complètement] quite, entirely. || [exactement] exactly. ○ **tout à l'heure** *loc adv* [futur] in a little while, shortly; **à ~ à l'heure!** see you later! || [passé] a little while ago. ○ **tout de suite** *loc adv* immediately, at once.

tout-à-l'égout [tutalegu] *nm inv* mains drainage.

toutefois [tutfwa] *adv* however.

tout-petit [tup(ə)ti] (*pl* **tout-petits**) *nm* toddler, tot.

tout-puissant, toute-puissante [tupɥisɑ̃, tutpɥisɑ̃t] (*mpl* **tout-puissants**, *fpl* **toutes-puissantes**) *adj* omnipotent, all-powerful.

toux [tu] *nf* cough.

toxicomane [tɔksikɔman] *nmf* drug addict.

toxine [tɔksin] *nf* toxin.

toxique [tɔksik] *adj* toxic.

trac [trak] *nm* nerves (*pl*); THÉÂTRE stage fright; **avoir le ~** to get nervous; THÉÂTRE to get stage fright.

tracas [traka] *nm* worry.

tracasser [trakase] *vt* to worry, to bother. ○ **se tracasser** *vp* to worry.

tracasserie [trakasri] *nf* annoyance.

trace [tras] *nf* [d'animal] track. || [de brûlure, fatigue] mark. || (*gén pl*) [vestige] trace. || [très petite quantité]: **une ~** de a trace of.

tracé [trase] *nm* [lignes] plan, drawing; [de parcours] line.

tracer [trase] *vt* [dessiner, dépeindre] to draw. || [route, piste] to mark out.

trachéite [trakeit] *nf* throat infection.

tract [trakt] *nm* leaflet.

tractations [traktasjɔ̃] *nfpl* negotiations, dealings.

tracter [trakte] *vt* to tow.

tracteur [traktœr] *nm* tractor.

traction [traksjɔ̃] *nf* [action de tirer] towing, pulling; **~ avant/arrière** front-/rear-wheel drive. || [SPORT - au sol] push-up *Am*; [- à la barre] pull-up.

tradition [tradisjɔ̃] *nf* tradition.

traditionnel, -elle [tradisjɔnɛl] *adj* [de tradition] traditional. || [habituel] usual.

traducteur, -trice [tradyktœr, tris] *nm, f* translator.

traduction [tradyksjɔ̃] *nf* [gén] translation.

traduire [traduir] *vt* [texte] to translate; **~ qqch en français/anglais** to translate sthg into French/English. || [révéler - crise] to reveal, to betray; [- sentiments, pensée] to render, to express. || JUR: **~ qqn en justice** to bring sb before the courts.

trafic [trafik] *nm* [de marchandises] traffic, trafficking. || [circulation] traffic.

trafiquant, -e [trafikɑ̃, ɑ̃t] *nm, f* trafficker, dealer.

trafiquer [trafike] **1** *vt* [falsifier] to tamper with. || *fam* [manigancer]: **qu'est-ce que tu trafiques?** what are you up to? **2** *vi* to be involved in trafficking.

tragédie [traʒedi] *nf* tragedy.

tragique [traʒik] *adj* tragic.

tragiquement [traʒikmɑ̃] *adv* tragically.

trahir [trair] *vt* [gén] to betray. || [suj: moteur] to let down; [suj: forces] to fail. ○ **se trahir** *vp* to give o.s. away.

trahison [traizɔ̃] *nf* [gén] betrayal. || JUR treason.

train [trɛ̃] *nm* TRANSPORT train. || [allure] pace. ○ **train de vie** *nm* lifestyle. ○ **en train de** *loc prép*: **être en ~ de lire/travailler** to be reading/working.

traînant, -e [trɛnɑ̃, ɑ̃t] *adj* [voix] drawling; [démarche] dragging.

traîne [trɛn] *nf* [de robe] train. || *loc*: **être à la ~** to lag behind.

traîneau, -x [trɛno] *nm* sleigh, sledge.

traînée [trene] *nf* [trace] trail. || *tfam péj* [prostituée] tart, whore.

traîner [trene] **1** *vt* [tirer, emmener] to drag. || [trimbaler] to lug around, to cart around. **2** *vi* [personne] to dawdle. || [maladie, affaire] to drag on; **~ en longueur** to drag. || [vêtements, livres] to lie around ou about. ○ **se traîner** *vp* [personne] to drag o.s. along.

train-train [trɛ̃trɛ̃] *nm fam* routine, daily grind.

traire [trer] *vt* [vache] to milk.

trait [trɛ] *nm* [ligne] line, stroke; **~ d'union** hyphen. || (*gén pl*) [de visage] feature. || [caractéristique] trait, feature. || *loc*: **avoir ~ à** to be to do with, to concern. ○ **d'un trait** *loc adv* [boire, lire] in one go.

traitant, -e [trɛtɑ̃, ɑ̃t] *adj* [shampooing, crème] medicated; → **médecin**.

traite [trɛt] *nf* [de vache] milking. || COMM bill, draft. ○ **d'une seule traite** *loc adv* without stopping, in one go.

traité [trete] *nm* [ouvrage] treatise. || POLIT treaty.

traitement [trɛtmɑ̃] *nm* [gén & MÉD] treatment; **mauvais ~** ill-treatment. || [rémunération] wage. || IND & INFORM processing; **~ de texte** word processing. || [de problème] handling.

traiter [trete] **1** *vt* [gén & MÉD] to treat. || [qualifier]: **~ qqn d'imbécile/de lâche** *etc* to call sb an imbecile/a coward *etc*. || [question, thème] to deal with. || IND & INFORM to process. **2** *vi* [négocier] to negotiate. || [livre]: **~ de** to deal with.

traiteur [trɛtœr] *nm* caterer.

traître, -esse [trɛtr, ɛs] **1** *adj* treacherous. **2** *nm, f* traitor.

traîtrise [trɛtriz] *nf* [déloyauté] treachery. || [acte] act of treachery.

trajectoire [traʒɛktwar] *nf* trajectory, path; *fig* framework.

trajet [traʒɛ] *nm* [distance] distance. || [itinéraire] route. || [voyage] journey.

trame [tram] *nf* weft; *fig* framework.

tramer [trame] *vt sout* to plot. ○ **se tramer** 1 *vp* to be plotted. 2 *v impers*: **il se trame quelque chose** there's something afoot.

trampoline [trɑ̃pɔlin] *nm* trampoline.

tram(way) [tram(wɛ)] *nm* tram *Br*, streetcar *Am*.

tranchant, -e [trɑ̃ʃɑ̃, ɑ̃t] *adj* [instrument] sharp. ‖ [personne] assertive. ‖ [ton] curt. ○ **tranchant** *nm* edge.

tranche [trɑ̃ʃ] *nf* [de gâteau, jambon] slice; ~ **d'âge** *fig* age bracket. ‖ [de livre, pièce] edge. ‖ [de revenus] portion; [de paiement] instalment; [fiscale] bracket.

trancher [trɑ̃ʃe] 1 *vt* [couper] to cut; [pain, jambon] to slice; ~ **la question** *fig* to settle the question. 2 *vi fig* [décider] to decide. ‖ [contraster]: ~ **avec** ou **sur** to contrast with.

tranquille [trɑ̃kil] *adj* [endroit, vie] quiet; **laisser qqn/qqch** ~ to leave sb/sthg alone. ‖ [rassuré] at ease, easy; **soyez** ~ don't worry.

tranquillement [trɑ̃kilmɑ̃] *adv* [sans s'agiter] quietly.

tranquillisant, -e [trɑ̃kilizɑ̃, ɑ̃t] *adj* [médicament] tranquillizing. ○ **tranquillisant** *nm* tranquillizer.

tranquilliser [trɑ̃kilize] *vt* to reassure.

tranquillité [trɑ̃kilite] *nf* [calme] peacefulness, quietness. ‖ [sérénité] peace, tranquillity.

transaction [trɑ̃zaksjɔ̃] *nf* transaction.

transat [trɑ̃zat] *nm* deckchair.

transatlantique [trɑ̃zatlɑ̃tik] 1 *adj* transatlantic. 2 *nm* transatlantic liner. 3 *nf* transatlantic race.

transcription [trɑ̃skripsjɔ̃] *nf* [de document & MUS] transcription; [dans un autre alphabet] transliteration.

transcrire [trɑ̃skrir] *vt* [document & MUS] to transcribe; [dans un autre alphabet] to transliterate.

transcrit, -e [trɑ̃skri, it] *pp* → transcrire.

transe [trɑ̃s] *nf*: **être en** ~ *fig* to be beside o.s.

transférer [trɑ̃sfere] *vt* to transfer.

transfert [trɑ̃sfɛr] *nm* transfer.

transfigurer [trɑ̃sfigyre] *vt* to transfigure.

transformateur, -trice [trɑ̃sfɔrmatœr, tris] *adj* IND processing (*avant n*). ○ **transformateur** *nm* transformer.

transformation [trɑ̃sfɔrmasjɔ̃] *nf* [de pays, personne] transformation. ‖ IND processing. ‖ RUGBY conversion.

transformer [trɑ̃sfɔrme] *vt* [gén] to transform; [magasin] to convert; ~ **qqch en** to turn sthg into. ‖ IND & RUGBY to convert. ○ **se transformer** *vp*: **se ~ en monstre/papillon** to turn into a monster/butterfly.

transfuge [trɑ̃sfyʒ] *nmf* renegade.

transfuser [trɑ̃sfyze] *vt* [sang] to transfuse.

transfusion [trɑ̃sfyzjɔ̃] *nf*: ~ **(sanguine)** (blood) transfusion.

transgresser [trɑ̃sgrese] *vt* [loi] to infringe; [ordre] to disobey.

transhumance [trɑ̃zymɑ̃s] *nf* transhumance.

transi, -e [trɑ̃zi] *adj*: **être** ~ **de froid** to be chilled to the bone.

transiger [trɑ̃ziʒe] *vi*: ~ **(sur)** to compromise (on).

transistor [trɑ̃zistɔr] *nm* transistor.

transit [trɑ̃zit] *nm* transit.

transiter [trɑ̃zite] *vi* to pass in transit.

transitif, -ive [trɑ̃sitif, iv] *adj* transitive.

transition [trɑ̃zisjɔ̃] *nf* transition; **sans** ~ with no transition, abruptly.

transitoire [trɑ̃zitwar] *adj* [passager] transitory.

translucide [trɑ̃slysid] *adj* translucent.

transmettre [trɑ̃smɛtr] *vt* [message, salutations]: ~ **qqch (à)** to pass sthg on (to). ‖ [tradition, propriété]: ~ **qqch (à)** to hand sthg down (to). ‖ [fonction, pouvoir]: ~ **qqch (à)** to hand sthg over (to). ‖ [maladie]: ~ **qqch (à)** to transmit sthg (to), to pass sthg on (to). ‖ [concert, émission] to broadcast. ○ **se transmettre** *vp* [maladie] to be passed on, to be transmitted. ‖ [courant, onde] to be transmitted. ‖ [tradition] to be handed down.

transmis, -e [trɑ̃smi, iz] *pp* → transmettre.

transmissible [trɑ̃smisibl] *adj* [maladie] transmissible.

transmission [trɑ̃smisjɔ̃] *nf* [de biens] transfer. ‖ [de maladie] transmission. ‖ [de message] passing on. ‖ [de tradition] handing down.

transparaître [trɑ̃sparɛtr] *vi* to show.

transparence [trɑ̃sparɑ̃s] *nf* transparency.

transparent, -e [trɑ̃sparɑ̃, ɑ̃t] *adj* transparent. ○ **transparent** *nm* transparency.

transpercer [trɑ̃spɛrse] *vt* to pierce; *fig* [suj: froid, pluie] to go right through.

transpiration [trãspirasjɔ̃] *nf* [sueur] perspiration.

transpirer [trãspire] *vi* [suer] to perspire.

transplanter [trãsplɑ̃te] *vt* to transplant.

transport [trãspɔr] *nm* transport (*U*); ~s en commun public transport (*sg*).

transportable [trãspɔrtabl] *adj* [marchandise] transportable; [blessé] fit to be moved.

transporter [trãspɔrte] *vt* [marchandises, personnes] to transport.

transporteur [trãspɔrtœr] *nm* [personne] carrier; ~ routier road haulier.

transposer [trãspoze] *vt* [déplacer] to transpose. || [adapter]: ~ qqch (à) to adapt sthg (for).

transposition [trãspozisjɔ̃] *nf* [déplacement] transposition. || [adaptation]: ~ (à) adaptation (for).

transsexuel, -elle [trãsseksyel] *adj* & *nm, f* transsexual.

transvaser [trãsvaze] *vt* to decant.

transversal, -e, -aux [trãsversal, o] *adj* [coupe] cross (*avant n*). || [chemin] cross (*avant n*) *Am*.

trapèze [trapez] *nm* GÉOM trapezium. || GYM trapeze.

trapéziste [trapezist] *nmf* trapeze artist.

trappe [trap] *nf* [ouverture] trapdoor. || [piège] trap.

trapu, -e [trapy] *adj* [personne] stocky, solidly built. || [édifice] squat.

traquenard [traknar] *nm* trap.

traquer [trake] *vt* [animal] to track; [personne, faute] to track ou hunt down.

traumatiser [tromatize] *vt* to traumatize.

traumatisme [tromatism] *nm* traumatism.

travail [travaj] *nm* [gén] work (*U*); se mettre au ~ to get down to work. || [tâche, emploi] job. || [du métal, du bois] working. || [phénomène - du bois] warping; [- du temps, fermentation] action. || MÉD: être/entrer en ~ to be in/go into labour. ○ **travaux** *nmpl* [d'aménagement] work (*U*); [routiers] roadworks; **travaux publics** civil engineering (*sg*). || SCOL: **travaux dirigés** class work; **travaux manuels** arts and crafts; **travaux pratiques** practical work (*U*).

travaillé, -e [travaje] *adj* [matériau] wrought, worked. || [style] laboured.

travailler [travaje] **1** *vi* [gén] to work; ~ à qqch to work on sthg. || [métal, bois] to warp. **2** *vt* [étudier] to work at ou on; [piano] to practise. || [suj: idée, remords] to torment. || [matière] to work, to fashion.

travailleur, -euse [travajœr, øz] **1** *adj* hard-working. **2** *nm, f* worker.

travelling [travliŋ] *nm* [mouvement] travelling shot.

travers [traver] *nm* failing, fault. ○ **à travers** *loc adv* & *loc prép* through. ○ **au travers** *loc adv* through. ○ **au travers de** *loc prép* through. ○ **de travers** *loc adv* [nez, escalier] crooked. || [obliquement] sideways. || [mal] wrong; comprendre qqch de ~ to misunderstand sthg. ○ **en travers** *loc adv* crosswise. ○ **en travers de** *loc prép* across.

traverse [travers] *nf* [de chemin de fer] sleeper, tie *Am*. || [chemin] short cut.

traversée [traverse] *nf* crossing.

traverser [traverse] *vt* [rue, mer, montagne] to cross; [ville] to go through. || [peau, mur] to go through, to pierce. || [crise, période] to go through.

traversin [traversɛ̃] *nm* bolster.

travestir [travestir] *vt* [déguiser] to dress up. || *fig* [vérité, idée] to distort. ○ **se travestir** *vp* [pour bal] to wear fancy dress. || [en femme] to put on drag.

trébucher [trebyʃe] *vi*: ~ (sur/contre) to stumble (over/against).

trèfle [trefl] *nm* [plante] clover. || [carte] club; [famille] clubs (*pl*).

treille [trej] *nf* [vigne] climbing vine. || [tonnelle] trellised vines (*pl*).

treillis [treji] *nm* [clôture] trellis (fencing). || MIL combat uniform.

treize [trez] *adj num* & *nm* thirteen; *voir aussi* **six**.

treizième [trezjem] *adj num, nm* & *nmf* thirteenth; *voir aussi* **sixième**.

trekking [trekiŋ] *nm* trek.

tréma [trema] *nm* diaeresis.

tremblant, -e [trãblã, ãt] *adj* [personne - de froid] shivering; [- d'émotion] trembling, shaking. || [voix] quavering.

tremblement [trãbləmã] *nm* [de corps] trembling. || [de voix] quavering. || [de feuilles] fluttering. ○ **tremblement de terre** *nm* earthquake.

trembler [trãble] *vi* [personne - de froid] to shiver; [- d'émotion] to tremble, to shake. || [voix] to quaver. || [lumière] to flicker. || [terre] to shake.

trembloter [trɑ̃blɔte] vi [personne] to tremble. || [voix] to quaver.

trémousser [tremuse] ○ **se trémousser** vp to jig up and down.

trempe [trɑ̃p] nf [envergure] calibre; **de sa ~** of his/her calibre. || fam [coups] thrashing.

tremper [trɑ̃pe] **1** vt [mouiller] to soak. || [plonger]: **~ qqch dans** to dip sthg into. || [métal] to harden, to quench. **2** vi [linge] to soak.

tremplin [trɑ̃plɛ̃] nm litt & fig springboard; SKI ski jump.

trentaine [trɑ̃tɛn] nf [nombre]: **une ~ de** about thirty. || [âge]: **avoir la ~** to be in one's thirties.

trente [trɑ̃t] **1** adj num thirty. **2** nm thirty; voir aussi **six**.

trentième [trɑ̃tjɛm] adj num, nm & nmf thirtieth; voir aussi **sixième**.

trépidant, -e [trepidɑ̃, ɑ̃t] adj [vie] hectic.

trépied [trepje] nm [support] tripod.

trépigner [trepiɲe] vi to stamp one's feet.

très [trɛ] adv very; **~ bien** very well; **être ~ aimé** to be much or greatly liked; **j'ai ~ envie de ...** I'd very much like to ....

trésor [trezɔr] nm treasure. ○ **Trésor** nm: **le Trésor public** the public revenue department.

trésorerie [trezɔrri] nf [service] accounts department. || [gestion] accounts (pl). || [fonds] finances (pl), funds (pl).

trésorier, -ière [trezɔrje, jɛr] nm, f treasurer.

tressaillement [tresajmɑ̃] nm [de joie] thrill; [de douleur] wince.

tressaillir [tresajir] vi [de joie] to thrill; [de douleur] to wince. || [sursauter] to start, to jump.

tressauter [tresote] vi [sursauter] to jump, to start; [dans véhicule] to be tossed about.

tresse [trɛs] nf [de cheveux] plait. || [de rubans] braid.

tresser [trese] vt [cheveux] to plait. || [osier] to braid. || [panier, guirlande] to weave.

tréteau, -x [treto] nm trestle.

treuil [trœj] nm winch, windlass.

trêve [trɛv] nf [cessez-le-feu] truce. || fig [répit] rest, respite; **~ de plaisanteries/de sottises** that's enough joking/nonsense.

tri [tri] nm [de lettres] sorting; [de candidats] selection.

triage [trijaʒ] nm [de lettres] sorting.

triangle [trijɑ̃gl] nm triangle.

triangulaire [trijɑ̃gylɛr] adj triangular.

triathlon [trijatlɔ̃] nm triathlon.

tribal, -e, -aux [tribal, o] adj tribal.

tribord [tribɔr] nm starboard; **à ~** on the starboard side, to starboard.

tribu [triby] nf tribe.

tribulations [tribylasjɔ̃] nfpl tribulations, trials.

tribunal, -aux [tribynal, o] nm JUR court; **~ correctionnel** ≃ Magistrates' Court; **~ de grande instance** ≃ Crown Court.

tribune [tribyn] nf [d'orateur] platform. || (gén pl) [de stade] stand.

tribut [triby] nm littéraire tribute.

tributaire [tribytɛr] adj: **être ~ de** to depend on or be dependent on.

tricher [triʃe] vi [au jeu, à examen] to cheat. || [mentir]: **~ sur** to lie about.

tricherie [triʃri] nf cheating.

tricheur, -euse [triʃœr, øz] nm, f cheat.

tricolore [trikɔlɔr] adj [à trois couleurs] three-coloured. || [français] French.

tricot [triko] nm [vêtement] jumper Br, sweater. || [ouvrage] knitting; **faire du ~** to knit. || [étoffe] knitted fabric, jersey.

tricoter [trikɔte] vi & vt to knit.

tricycle [trisikl] nm tricycle.

trier [trije] vt [classer] to sort out. || [sélectionner] to select.

trilingue [trilɛ̃g] adj trilingual.

trimestre [trimɛstr] nm [période] term.

trimestriel, -ielle [trimɛstrijɛl] adj [loyer, magazine] quarterly; SCOL end-of-term (avant n).

tringle [trɛ̃gl] nf rod.

trinquer [trɛ̃ke] vi [boire] to toast, to clink glasses; **~ à** to drink to.

trio [trijo] nm trio.

triomphal, -e, -aux [trijɔ̃fal, o] adj [succès] triumphal; [accueil] triumphant.

triomphant, -e [trijɔ̃fɑ̃, ɑ̃t] adj [équipe] winning; [air] triumphant.

triomphe [trijɔ̃f] nm triumph.

triompher [trijɔ̃fe] vi [gén] to triumph; **~ de** to triumph over.

tripes [trip] nfpl [d'animal, de personne] guts. || CULIN tripe (sg).

triple [tripl] **1** adj triple. **2** nm: **le ~ (de)** three times as much (as).

triplé [triple] nm [au turf] bet on three horses winning in three different races. ○ **triplés, -ées** nm, f pl triplets.

trouver

triste [trist] adj [personne, nouvelle] sad; **être ~ de qqch/de faire qqch** to be sad about sthg/about doing sthg. ‖ [paysage, temps] gloomy; [couleur] dull. ‖ (avant n) [lamentable] sorry.

tristesse [tristes] nf [de personne, nouvelle] sadness. ‖ [de paysage, temps] gloominess.

triturer [trityre] vt fam [mouchoir] to knead. **○ se triturer** vp fam: **se ~ l'esprit** ou **les méninges** to rack one's brains.

trivial, -e, -iaux [trivjal, jo] adj [banal] trivial. ‖ péj [vulgaire] crude, coarse.

troc [trɔk] nm [échange] exchange. ‖ [système économique] barter.

trois [trwa] 1 nm three. 2 adj num three; voir aussi **six**.

troisième [trwazjɛm] 1 adj num & nmf third. 2 nm third; [étage] third floor Br, fourth floor Am. 3 nf SCOL fourth year. ‖ [vitesse] third (gear); voir aussi **sixième**.

trombe [trɔ̃b] nf water spout.

trombone [trɔ̃bɔn] nm [agrafe] paper clip. ‖ [instrument] trombone.

trompe [trɔ̃p] nf [instrument] trumpet. ‖ [d'éléphant] trunk. ‖ [d'insecte] proboscis. ‖ ANAT tube.

trompe-l'œil [trɔ̃plœj] nm inv [peinture] trompe-l'oeil.

tromper [trɔ̃pe] vt [personne] to deceive. ‖ [vigilance] to elude. **○ se tromper** vp to make a mistake, to be mistaken; **se ~ de jour/maison** to get the wrong day/house.

tromperie [trɔ̃pri] nf deception.

trompette [trɔ̃pɛt] nf trumpet.

trompettiste [trɔ̃petist] nmf trumpeter.

trompeur, -euse [trɔ̃pœr, øz] adj [calme, apparence] deceptive.

tronc [trɔ̃] nm [d'arbre, de personne] trunk. ‖ [d'église] collection box. **○ tronc commun** nm SCOL core syllabus.

tronçon [trɔ̃sɔ̃] nm [morceau] piece, length. ‖ [de route, de chemin de fer] section.

tronçonneuse [trɔ̃sɔnøz] nf chain saw.

trône [tron] nm throne.

trôner [trone] vi [personne] to sit enthroned; [objet] to have pride of place.

trop [tro] adv (devant adj, adv) too; **avoir ~ chaud/froid/peur** to be too hot/cold/frightened. ‖ (avec verbe) too much; **je n'aime pas ~ le chocolat** I don't like chocolate very much. ‖ (avec complément): **~ de** [quantité] too much; [nombre] too many. **○ en trop, de trop** loc adv too much/many; **10 francs de** ou **en ~ 10** francs too much; **être de ~** [personne] to be in the way, to be unwelcome.

trophée [trɔfe] nm trophy.

tropical, -e, -aux [trɔpikal, o] adj tropical.

tropique [trɔpik] nm tropic.

trop-plein [trɔplɛ̃] (pl trop-pleins) nm [excès] excess; fig excess, surplus.

troquer [trɔke] vt: **~ qqch (contre)** to barter sthg (for); fig to swap sthg (for).

trot [tro] nm trot; **au ~** at a trot.

trotter [trɔte] vi [cheval] to trot. ‖ [personne] to run around.

trotteur, -euse [trɔtœr, øz] nm, f trotter. **○ trotteuse** nf second hand.

trottiner [trɔtine] vi to trot.

trottoir [trɔtwar] nm sidewalk Am.

trou [tru] nm [gén] hole; **~ d'air** air pocket. ‖ [manque, espace vide] gap; **~ de mémoire** memory lapse.

troublant, -e [trublɑ̃, ɑ̃t] adj disturbing.

trouble [trubl] 1 adj [eau] cloudy. ‖ [image, vue] blurred. 2 nm [désordre] trouble, discord. ‖ [gêne] confusion. ‖ (gén pl) [dérèglement] disorder. **○ troubles** nmpl unrest (U).

trouble-fête [trubləfɛt] nmf inv spoilsport.

troubler [truble] vt [eau] to cloud, to make cloudy. ‖ [image, vue] to blur. ‖ [inquiéter, émouvoir] to disturb. ‖ [rendre perplexe] to trouble. **○ se troubler** vp [eau] to become cloudy. ‖ [personne] to become flustered.

trouée [true] nf gap; MIL breach.

trouer [true] vt [chaussette] to make a hole in. ‖ fig [silence] to disturb.

trouille [truj] nf fam fear, terror.

troupe [trup] nf MIL troop. ‖ [d'amis] group, band. ‖ THÉÂTRE theatre group.

troupeau, -x [trupo] nm [de vaches, d'éléphants] herd; [de moutons, d'oies] flock; péj [de personnes] herd.

trousse [trus] nf case, bag; **~ de secours** first-aid kit; **~ de toilette** toilet bag.

trousseau, -x [truso] nm [de mariée] trousseau. ‖ [de clefs] bunch.

trouvaille [truvaj] nf [découverte] find, discovery. ‖ [invention] new idea.

trouver [truve] 1 vt to find; **~ que** to feel (that); **~ bon/mauvais que ...** to think (that) it is right/wrong that .... 2 v *impers*: **il se trouve que ...** the fact is that .... ○ **se trouver** *vp* [dans un endroit] to be. || [dans un état] to find o.s. || [se sentir] to feel; **se ~ mal** [s'évanouir] to faint.

truand [tryɑ̃] *nm* crook.

truc [tryk] *nm* [combine] trick. || *fam* [chose] thing, thingamajig.

trucage = **truquage**.

truculent, -e [trykylɑ̃, ɑ̃t] *adj* colourful.

truelle [tryɛl] *nf* trowel.

truffe [tryf] *nf* [champignon] truffle. || [museau] muzzle.

truffer [tryfe] *vt* [volaille] to garnish with truffles. || *fig* [discours]: **~ de** to stuff with.

truie [trɥi] *nf* sow.

truite [trɥit] *nf* trout.

truquage, trucage [trykaʒ] *nm* CIN (special) effect.

truquer [tryke] *vt* [élections] to rig.

trust [trœst] *nm* [groupement] trust. || [entreprise] corporation.

tsar, tzar [tzar] *nm* tsar.

tsigane = **tzigane**.

TSVP (*abr de* **tournez s'il vous plaît**) PTO.

tt conf. *abr de* **tout confort**.

TTX (*abr de* **traitement de texte**) WP.

tu¹, -e [ty] *pp* → **taire**.

tu² [ty] *pron* pers you.

tuba [tyba] *nm* MUS tuba. || [de plongée] snorkel.

tube [tyb] *nm* [gén] tube; **~ cathodique** cathode ray tube. || *fam* [chanson] hit. ○ **tube digestif** *nm* digestive tract.

tubercule [tybɛrkyl] *nm* BOT tuber.

tuberculose [tybɛrkyloz] *nf* tuberculosis.

tuer [tɥe] *vt* to kill. ○ **se tuer** *vp* [se suicider] to kill o.s. || [par accident] to die.

tuerie [tyri] *nf* slaughter.

tue-tête [tytɛt] ○ **à tue-tête** *loc adv* at the top of one's voice.

tueur, -euse [tɥœr, øz] *nm, f* [meurtrier] killer.

tuile [tɥil] *nf* [de toit] tile. || *fam* [désagrément] blow.

tulipe [tylip] *nf* tulip.

tulle [tyl] *nm* tulle.

tuméfié, -e [tymefje] *adj* swollen.

tumeur [tymœr] *nf* tumour.

tumulte [tymylt] *nm* [désordre] hubbub. || *littéraire* [trouble] tumult.

tunique [tynik] *nf* tunic.

Tunisie [tynizi] *nf*: **la ~** Tunisia.

tunisien, -ienne [tynizjɛ̃, jɛn] *adj* Tunisian. ○ **Tunisien, -ienne** *nm, f* Tunisian.

tunnel [tynɛl] *nm* tunnel.

turban [tyrbɑ̃] *nm* turban.

turbine [tyrbin] *nf* turbine.

turbo [tyrbo] *nm & nf* turbo.

turbulence [tyrbylɑ̃s] *nf* MÉTÉOR turbulence.

turbulent, -e [tyrbylɑ̃, ɑ̃t] *adj* boisterous.

turc, turque [tyrk] *adj* Turkish. ○ **turc** *nm* [langue] Turkish. ○ **Turc, Turque** *nm, f* Turk.

turf [tœrf] *nm* [activité]: **le ~** racing.

turque → **turc**.

Turquie [tyrki] *nf*: **la ~** Turkey.

turquoise [tyrkwaz] *nf & adj inv* turquoise.

tutelle [tytɛl] *nf* JUR guardianship. || [dépendance] supervision.

tuteur, -trice [tytœr, tris] *nm, f* guardian. ○ **tuteur** *nm* [pour plante] stake.

tutoyer [tytwaje] *vt*: **~ qqn** to use the "tu" form to sb.

tuyau, -x [tɥijo] *nm* [conduit] pipe; **~ d'arrosage** hosepipe. || *fam* [renseignement] tip.

tuyauterie [tɥijotri] *nf* piping (*U*), pipes (*pl*).

TV (*abr de* **télévision**) *nf* TV.

TVA (*abr de* **taxe à la valeur ajoutée**) *nf* ≈ VAT.

tweed [twid] *nm* tweed.

tympan [tɛ̃pɑ̃] *nm* ANAT eardrum.

type [tip] **1** *nm* [genre] type. || *fam* [individu] guy, bloke. **2** *adj inv* [caractéristique] typical.

typhoïde [tifɔid] *nf* typhoid.

typhon [tifɔ̃] *nm* typhoon.

typhus [tifys] *nm* typhus.

typique [tipik] *adj* typical.

typographie [tipɔgrafi] *nf* typography.

tyran [tirɑ̃] *nm* tyrant.

tyrannique [tiranik] *adj* tyrannical.

tyranniser [tiranize] *vt* to tyrannize.

tzar = **tsar**.

tzigane, tsigane [tsigan] *nmf* gipsy.

u, U [y] *nm inv* u, U.

UDF (*abr de* **Union pour la démocratie française**) *nf* French political party to the right of the political spectrum.

Ukraine [ykrɛn] *nf*: **l'~** the Ukraine.

ulcère [ylsɛr] *nm* ulcer.

ULM (*abr de* **ultra léger motorisé**) *nm* microlight.

ultérieur, -e [ylterjœr] *adj* later, subsequent.

ultimatum [yltimatɔm] *nm* ultimatum.

ultime [yltim] *adj* ultimate, final.

ultramoderne [yltramɔdɛrn] *adj* ultramodern.

ultrasensible [yltrasɑ̃sibl] *adj* [pellicule] high-speed.

ultrason [yltrasɔ̃] *nm* ultrasound (*U*).

ultraviolet, -ette [yltravjɔlɛ, ɛt] *adj* ultraviolet. ○ **ultraviolet** *nm* ultraviolet.

un [œ̃] (*f* **une** [yn]) **1** *art indéf* a, an (*devant voyelle*); **une pomme** an apple. **2** *pron indéf* one; **l'~ de mes amis** one of my friends; **l'~ l'autre** each other; **les ~s les autres** one another; **les ~s ..., les autres** some ..., others. **3** *adj num* one. **4** *nm* one; *voir aussi* **six**. ○ **une** *nf*: **faire la/être à la une** PRESSE to make the/to be on the front page.

unanime [ynanim] *adj* unanimous.

unanimité [ynanimite] *nf* unanimity; **faire l'~** to be unanimously approved; **à l'~** unanimously.

UNESCO, Unesco [ynɛsko] (*abr de* **United Nations Educational, Scientific and Cultural Organization**) *nf* UNESCO.

uni, -e [yni] *adj* [joint, réuni] united. || [famille, couple] close. || [surface, mer] smooth; [route] even. || [étoffe, robe] self-coloured.

UNICEF, Unicef [ynisɛf] (*abr de* **United Nations International Children's Emergency Fund**) *nm* UNICEF.

unifier [ynifje] *vt* [régions, parti] to unify. || [programmes] to standardize.

uniforme [ynifɔrm] **1** *adj* uniform; [régulier] regular. **2** *nm* uniform.

uniformiser [ynifɔrmize] *vt* [couleur] to make uniform. || [programmes, lois] to standardize.

unilatéral, -e, -aux [ynilateral, o] *adj* unilateral; **stationnement ~** parking on only one side of the street.

union [ynjɔ̃] *nf* [mariage] union; **~ libre** cohabitation. || [de pays] union; [de syndicats] confederation. || [entente] unity. ○ **Union soviétique** *nf*: **l'(ex-)Union soviétique** the (former) Soviet Union.

unique [ynik] *adj* [seul - enfant, veston] only; [- préoccupation] sole. || [principe, prix] single. || [exceptionnel] unique.

uniquement [ynikmɑ̃] *adv* [exclusivement] only, solely. || [seulement] only, just.

unir [ynir] *vt* [assembler - mots, qualités] to put together, to combine; [- pays] to unite; **~ qqch à** [pays] to unite sthg with; [mot, qualité] to combine sthg with. || [marier] to unite, to join in marriage. ○ **s'unir** *vp* [s'associer] to unite, to join together. || [se marier] to be joined in marriage.

unitaire [yniter] *adj* [à l'unité]: **prix ~** unit price.

unité [ynite] *nf* [cohésion] unity. || COMM, MATHS & MIL unit. ○ **unité centrale** *nf* INFORM central processing unit.

univers [yniver] *nm* universe; *fig* world.

universel, -elle [yniversɛl] *adj* universal.

universitaire [yniversiter] **1** *adj* university (*avant n*). **2** *nmf* academic.

université [yniversite] *nf* university.

uranium [yranjɔm] *nm* uranium.

urbain, -e [yrbɛ̃, ɛn] *adj* [de la ville] urban. || *littéraire* [affable] urbane.

urbaniser [yrbanize] *vt* to urbanize.

urbanisme [yrbanism] *nm* town planning.

urgence [yrʒɑ̃s] *nf* [de mission] urgency. || MÉD emergency; **les ~s** the casualty department (*sg*). ○ **d'urgence** *loc adv* immediately.

urgent, -e [yrʒɑ̃, ɑ̃t] *adj* urgent.

urine [yrin] *nf* urine.

uriner [yrine] *vi* to urinate.

urinoir [yrinwar] *nm* urinal.

urne [yrn] *nf* [vase] urn. || [de vote] ballot box.

URSS (*abr de* **Union des républiques socialistes soviétiques**) *nf*: l'(ex-)~ the (former) USSR.

urticaire [yrtiker] *nf* urticaria, hives (*pl*).

Uruguay [yrygwɛ] *nm*: l'~ Uruguay.

USA (*abr de* **United States of America**) *nmpl* USA.

usage [yzaʒ] *nm* [gén] use; à ~ **externe/ interne** for external/internal use; **hors d'~** out of action. || [coutume] custom.

usagé, -e [yzaʒe] *adj* worn, old.

usager [yzaʒe] *nm* user.

usé, -e [yze] *adj* [détérioré] worn; **eaux ~es** waste water (*sg*). || [plaisanterie] hackneyed, well-worn.

user [yze] *vt* [consommer] to use. || [vêtement] to wear out. [santé] to ruin; [personne] to wear out. ○ **s'user** *vp* [chaussure] to wear out.

usine [yzin] *nf* factory.

usité, -e [yzite] *adj* in common use.

ustensile [ystãsil] *nm* implement, tool.

usuel, -elle [yzɥɛl] *adj* common, usual.

usure [yzyr] *nf* [de vêtement, meuble] wear. || [intérêt] usury.

usurier, -ière [yzyrje, jɛr] *nm, f* usurer.

usurpateur, -trice [yzyrpatœr, tris] *nm, f* usurper.

usurper [yzyrpe] *vt* to usurp.

ut [yt] *nm inv* C.

utérus [yterys] *nm* uterus, womb.

utile [ytil] *adj* useful; **être ~ à qqn** to be useful ou of help to sb, to help sb.

utilisateur, -trice [ytilizatœr, tris] *nm, f* user.

utiliser [ytilize] *vt* to use.

utilitaire [ytiliter] **1** *adj* [pratique] utilitarian; [véhicule] commercial. **2** *nm* IN-FORM utility (program).

utilité [ytilite] *nf* [usage] usefulness. || JUR: **organisme d'~ publique** registered charity.

utopie [ytɔpi] *nf* [idéal] utopia. || [projet irréalisable] unrealistic idea.

utopiste [ytɔpist] *nmf* utopian.

UV 1 *nf* (*abr de* **unité de valeur**) ≃ credit *Am*. **2** (*abr de* **ultraviolet**) UV.

v, V [ve] *nm inv* v, V.

v. || (*abr de* **vers**) [environ] approx.

va [va] *interj*: **courage, ~!** come on, cheer up!; **~ pour 50 francs/demain** OK, let's say 50 francs/tomorrow.

vacance [vakãs] *nf* vacancy. ○ **vacances** *nfpl* vacation (*sg*) *Am*; **être/partir en ~s** to be/go on holiday; **les grandes ~s** the summer holidays.

vacancier, -ière [vakãsje, jer] *nm, f* vacationer *Am*.

vacant, -e [vakã, ãt] *adj* [poste] vacant; [logement] vacant, unoccupied.

vacarme [vakarm] *nm* racket, din.

vacataire [vakater] **1** *adj* [employé] temporary. **2** *nmf* temporary worker.

vacation [vakasjɔ̃] *nf* [d'expert] session.

vaccin [vaksɛ̃] *nm* vaccine.

vaccination [vaksinasjɔ̃] *nf* vaccination.

vacciner [vaksine] *vt*: **~ qqn (contre)** MÉD to vaccinate sb (against).

vache [vaʃ] **1** *nf* ZOOL cow. || [cuir] cowhide. || *fam péj* [femme] cow; [homme] pig. **2** *adj fam* rotten.

vachement [vaʃmã] *adv fam* real *Am*.

vaciller [vasije] *vi* [jambes, fondations] to shake; [lumière] to flicker. || [mémoire, santé] to fail.

va-et-vient [vaevjɛ̃] *nm inv* [de personnes] comings and goings (*pl*), toing and froing. || [de balancier] to-and-fro movement. || ÉLECTR two-way switch.

vagabond, -e [vagabɔ̃, ɔ̃d] *nm, f* [rôdeur] vagrant, tramp.

vagabondage [vagabɔ̃daʒ] *nm* [délit] vagrancy; [errance] wandering, roaming.

vagin [vaʒɛ̃] *nm* vagina.

vagissement [vaʒismã] *nm* cry, wail.

vague [vag] **1** *adj* [idée, promesse] vague. || [vêtement] loose-fitting. **2** *nf* wave; **une ~ de froid** a cold spell; **~ de chaleur** heatwave.

vaguement [vagmã] *adv* vaguely.

vaillant, -e [vajɑ̃, ɑ̃t] *adj* [enfant, vieillard] hale and hearty. || *littéraire* [héros] vaillant.

vain, -e [vɛ̃, vɛn] *adj* [inutile] vain, useless; **en ~** in vain, to no avail. || *littéraire* [vaniteux] vain.

vaincre [vɛ̃kr] *vt* [ennemi] to defeat. || [obstacle, peur] to overcome.

vaincu, -e [vɛ̃ky] 1 *pp* → vaincre. 2 *adj* defeated. 3 *nm, f* defeated person.

vainement [vɛnmɑ̃] *adv* vainly.

vainqueur [vɛ̃kœr] 1 *nm* [de combat] conqueror, victor. || SPORT winner. 2 *adj m* victorious, conquering.

vais → aller.

vaisseau, -x [vɛso] *nm* NAVIG vessel, ship; **~ spatial** AÉRON spaceship. || ANAT vessel.

vaisselle [vɛsɛl] *nf* crockery; **faire** ou **laver la ~** to do the dishes, to wash up.

valable [valabl] *adj* [passeport] valid. || [raison, excuse] valid, legitimate.

valet [valɛ] *nm* [serviteur] servant. || CARTES jack, knave.

valeur [valœr] *nf* [gén & MUS] value; **avoir de la ~** to be valuable; **mettre en ~** [talents] to bring out; **~ ajoutée** ÉCON added value; **de (grande) ~** [chose] (very) valuable. || (*gén pl*) BOURSE stocks and shares (*pl*), securities (*pl*). || [mérite] worth, merit. || *fig* [importance] value, importance.

valide [valid] *adj* [personne] spry. || [contrat] valid.

valider [valide] *vt* to validate, to authenticate.

validité [validite] *nf* validity.

valise [valiz] *nf* case, suitcase; **faire sa ~/ses ~s** to pack one's case/cases; *fam fig* [partir] to pack one's bags.

vallée [vale] *nf* valley.

vallon [valɔ̃] *nm* small valley.

vallonné, -e [valone] *adj* undulating.

valoir [valwar] 1 *vi* [gén] to be worth; **ça vaut combien?** how much is it?; **ne rien ~** not to be any good, to be worthless; **ça vaut mieux** *fam* that's best; **faire ~** [vues] to assert; [talent] to show. || [règle]: **~ pour** to apply to, to hold good for. 2 *vt* [médaille, gloire] to bring, to earn. 3 *v impers*: **il vaudrait mieux que nous partions** it would be better if we left, we'd better leave. ○ **se valoir** *vp* to be equally good/bad.

valoriser [valorize] *vt* [immeuble, région] to develop; [individu, société] to improve the image of.

valse [vals] *nf* waltz.

valser [valse] *vi* to waltz; **envoyer ~ qqch** *fam fig* to send sthg flying.

valu [valy] *pp inv* → valoir.

valve [valv] *nf* valve.

vampire [vɑ̃pir] *nm* [fantôme] vampire. || ZOOL vampire bat.

vandalisme [vɑ̃dalism] *nm* vandalism.

vanille [vanij] *nf* vanilla.

vanité [vanite] *nf* vanity.

vaniteux, -euse [vanitø, øz] *adj* vain, conceited.

vanne [van] *nf* [d'écluse] lockgate. || *fam* [remarque] gibe.

vannerie [vanri] *nf* basketwork, wickerwork.

vantard, -e [vɑ̃tar, ard] 1 *adj* bragging, boastful. 2 *nm, f* boaster.

vanter [vɑ̃te] *vt* to vaunt. ○ **se vanter** *vp* to boast, to brag; **se ~ de faire qqch** to boast ou brag about doing sthg.

va-nu-pieds [vanypje] *nmf inv fam* beggar.

vapeur [vapœr] *nf* [d'eau] steam; **à la ~** steamed. || [émanation] vapour.

vapocuiseur [vapokɥizœr] *nm* pressure cooker.

vaporisateur [vaporizatœr] *nm* [atomiseur] spray, atomizer. || IND vaporizer.

vaporiser [vaporize] *vt* [parfum, déodorant] to spray. || PHYS to vaporize.

vaquer [vake] *vi*: **~ à** to see to, to attend to.

varappe [varap] *nf* rock climbing.

variable [varjabl] 1 *adj* [temps] changeable. || [distance, résultats] varied, varying. || [température] variable. 2 *nf* variable.

variante [varjɑ̃t] *nf* variant.

variateur [varjatœr] *nm* ÉLECTR dimmer switch.

variation [varjasjɔ̃] *nf* variation.

varice [varis] *nf* varicose vein.

varicelle [varisɛl] *nf* chickenpox.

varié, -e [varje] *adj* [divers] various. || [non monotone] varied, varying.

varier [varje] *vt & vi* to vary.

variété [varjete] *nf* variety. ○ **variétés** *nfpl* variety show (*sg*).

variole [varjol] *nf* smallpox.

Varsovie [varsovi] *n* Warsaw.

vase [vaz] 1 *nm* vase. 2 *nf* mud, silt.

vaste [vast] *adj* vast, immense.

Vatican [vatikɑ̃] *nm*: **le ~** the Vatican.

vaudrait → valoir.

vaut → valoir.

vautour [votur] *nm* vulture.

vd *abr de* vend.

veau, -x [vo] *nm* [animal] calf. ‖ [viande] veal. ‖ [peau] calfskin.

vecteur [vɛktœr] *nm* GÉOM vector.

vécu, -e [veky] **1** *pp* → vivre. **2** *adj* real.

vedette [vədɛt] *nf* NAVIG patrol boat. ‖ [star] star.

végétal, -e, -aux [veʒetal, o] *adj* [huile] vegetable (*avant n*); [cellule, fibre] plant (*avant n*).

végétalien, -ienne [veʒetaljɛ̃, jɛn] *adj & nm, f* vegan.

végétarien, -ienne [veʒetarjɛ̃, jɛn] *adj & nm, f* vegetarian.

végétation [veʒetasjɔ̃] *nf* vegetation. ○ **végétations** *nfpl* adenoids.

végéter [veʒete] *vi* to vegetate.

véhémence [veemɑ̃s] *nf* vehemence.

véhicule [veikyl] *nm* vehicle.

veille [vɛj] *nf* [jour précédent] day before, eve; **la ~ de mon anniversaire** the day before my birthday; **la ~ de Noël** Christmas Eve.

veillée [veje] *nf* [soirée] evening. ‖ [de mort] watch.

veiller [veje] **1** *vi* [rester éveillé] to stay up. ‖ [rester vigilant]: **~ à qqch** to look after sthg; **~ à faire qqch** to see that sthg is done; **~ sur** to watch over. **2** *vt* to sit up with.

veilleur [vejœr] *nm*: **~ de nuit** night watchman.

veilleuse [vejøz] *nf* [lampe] nightlight. ‖ AUTOM sidelight. ‖ [de chauffe-eau] pilot light.

veinard, -e [vɛnar, ard] *fam* **1** *adj* lucky. **2** *nm, f* lucky devil.

veine [vɛn] *nf* [gén] vein. ‖ [de bois] grain. ‖ *fam* [chance] luck.

veineux, -euse [vɛnø, øz] *adj* ANAT venous. ‖ [marbre] veined; [bois] grainy.

véliplanchiste [veliplɑ̃ʃist] *nmf* windsurfer.

velléité [veleite] *nf* whim.

vélo [velo] *nm fam* bike; **faire du ~** to go cycling.

vélodrome [velodrom] *nm* velodrome.

vélomoteur [velomotœr] *nm* light motorcycle.

velours [vəlur] *nm* velvet.

velouté, -e [vəlute] *adj* velvety. ○ **velouté** *nm* [potage] cream soup.

velu, -e [vəly] *adj* hairy.

vénal, -e, -aux [venal, o] *adj* venal.

vendange [vɑ̃dɑ̃ʒ] *nf* [récolte] grape harvest, wine harvest. ‖ [période]: **les ~s** (grape) harvest time (*sg*).

vendanger [vɑ̃dɑ̃ʒe] *vi* to harvest the grapes.

vendeur, -euse [vɑ̃dœr, øz] *nm, f* salesman (*f* saleswoman).

vendre [vɑ̃dr] *vt* to sell.

vendredi [vɑ̃drədi] *nm* Friday; **Vendredi Saint** Good Friday; *voir aussi* samedi.

vendu, -e [vɑ̃dy] **1** *pp* → vendre. **2** *nm, f* traitor.

vénéneux, -euse [venenø, øz] *adj* poisonous.

vénérable [venerabl] *adj* venerable.

vénération [venerasjɔ̃] *nf* veneration, reverence.

vénérer [venere] *vt* to venerate, to revere.

vénérien, -ienne [venerjɛ̃, jɛn] *adj* venereal.

Venezuela [venezɥela] *nm*: **le ~** Venezuela.

vengeance [vɑ̃ʒɑ̃s] *nf* vengeance.

venger [vɑ̃ʒe] *vt* to avenge. ○ **se venger** *vp* to get one's revenge; **se ~ de qqn** to take revenge on sb; **se ~ de qqch** to take revenge for sthg; **se ~ sur** to take it out on.

vengeur, vengeresse [vɑ̃ʒœr, vɑ̃ʒrɛs] **1** *adj* vengeful. **2** *nm, f* avenger.

venimeux, -euse [vənimø, øz] *adj* venomous.

venin [vənɛ̃] *nm* venom.

venir [vənir] *vi* to come; **~ de** [personne, mot] to come from; [échec] to be due to; **je viens de la voir** I've just seen her; **où veux-tu en ~?** what are you getting at?

vent [vɑ̃] *nm* wind.

vente [vɑ̃t] *nf* [cession, transaction] sale; **en ~** on sale; **en ~ libre** available over the counter; **~ par correspondance** mail order. ‖ [technique] selling.

venteux, -euse [vɑ̃tø, øz] *adj* windy.

ventilateur [vɑ̃tilatœr] *nm* fan.

ventilation [vɑ̃tilasjɔ̃] *nf* [de pièce] ventilation. ‖ FIN breakdown.

ventouse [vɑ̃tuz] *nf* [de caoutchouc] suction pad; [d'animal] sucker. ‖ MÉD cupping glass. ‖ TECHNOL air vent.

ventre [vɑ̃tr] *nm* [de personne] stomach; **avoir/prendre du ~** to have/be getting (a bit of) a paunch; **à plat ~** flat on one's stomach.

ventriloque [vɑ̃trilɔk] *nmf* ventriloquist.

venu, -e [vəny] **1** *pp* → venir. **2** *adj*: **il serait mal ~ de faire cela** it would be improper to do that. **3** *nm, f*: **nouveau ~** newcomer. ○ **venue** *nf* coming, arrival.

vêpres [vɛpr] *nfpl* vespers.

ver [vɛr] *nm* worm.

véracité [verasite] *nf* truthfulness.

véranda [verɑ̃da] *nf* veranda.

verbal, -e, -aux [verbal, o] *adj* [promesse, violence] verbal. ‖ GRAM verb (*avant n*).

verbaliser [verbalize] **1** *vt* to verbalize. **2** *vi* to make out a report.

verbe [verb] *nm* GRAM verb.

verdeur [verdœr] *nf* [de personne] vigour, vitality. ‖ [de langage] crudeness.

verdict [verdikt] *nm* verdict.

verdir [verdir] *vt & vi* to turn green.

verdoyant, -e [verdwajɑ̃, ɑ̃t] *adj* green.

verdure [verdyr] *nf* [végétation] greenery.

véreux, -euse [verø, øz] *adj* worm-eaten, maggoty; *fig* shady.

verge [vɛrʒ] *nf* ANAT penis. ‖ *littéraire* [baguette] rod, stick.

verger [verʒe] *nm* orchard.

vergeture [verʒətyr] *nf* stretchmark.

verglas [vergla] *nm* (black) ice.

véridique [veridik] *adj* truthful.

vérification [verifikasjɔ̃] *nf* [contrôle] check, checking.

vérifier [verifje] *vt* [contrôler] to check. ‖ [confirmer] to prove, to confirm.

véritable [veritabl] *adj* real; [ami] true.

vérité [verite] *nf* [chose vraie, réalité, principe] truth (*U*).

vermeil, -eille [vermɛj] *adj* scarlet. ○ **vermeil** *nm* silver-gilt.

vermicelle [vermisɛl] *nm* vermicelli (*U*).

vermine [vermin] *nf* [parasites] vermin.

vermoulu, -e [vermuly] *adj* riddled with woodworm; *fig* moth-eaten.

verni, -e [verni] *adj* [bois] varnished. ‖ [souliers] **chaussures ~es** patent-leather shoes. ‖ *fam* [chanceux] lucky.

vernir [vernir] *vt* to varnish.

vernis [verni] *nm* varnish; *fig* veneer; **~ à ongles** nail polish OU varnish.

vernissage [vernisaʒ] *nm* [d'exposition] private viewing.

verre [vɛr] *nm* [matière, récipient] glass; [quantité] glassful, glass. ‖ [optique] lens; **~s de contact** contact lenses. ‖ [boisson] drink; **boire un ~** to have a drink.

verrière [verjɛr] *nf* [toit] glass roof.

verrou [veru] *nm* bolt.

verrouillage [verujaʒ] *nm* AUTOM: **~ central** central locking.

verrouiller [veruje] *vt* [porte] to bolt.

verrue [very] *nf* wart; **~ plantaire** verruca.

vers¹ [ver] **1** *nm* line. **2** *nmpl*: **en ~** in verse; **faire des ~** to write poetry.

vers² [ver] *prép* [dans la direction de] towards. ‖ [aux environs de - temporel] around, about; [- spatial] near; **~ la fin du mois** towards the end of the month.

versant [versɑ̃] *nm* side.

versatile [versatil] *adj* changeable, fickle.

verse [vers] ○ **à verse** *loc adv*: **pleuvoir à ~** to pour down.

Verseau [verso] *nm* ASTROL Aquarius.

versement [versəmɑ̃] *nm* payment.

verser [verse] *vt* [eau] to pour; [larmes, sang] to shed. ‖ [argent] to pay.

verset [verse] *nm* verse.

version [versjɔ̃] *nf* [gén] version. ‖ [traduction] translation (*into mother tongue*).

verso [verso] *nm* back.

vert, -e [ver, vert] *adj* [couleur, fruit, légume, bois] green. ‖ *fig* [vieillard] sprightly. ○ **vert** *nm* [couleur] green. ○ **Verts** *nmpl*: **les Verts** POLIT the Greens.

vertébral, -e, -aux [vertebral, o] *adj* vertebral.

vertèbre [vertɛbr] *nf* vertebra.

vertement [vertəmɑ̃] *adv* sharply.

vertical, -e, -aux [vertikal, o] *adj* vertical. ○ **verticale** *nf* vertical; **à la ~e** [descente] vertical; [descendre] vertically.

vertige [vertiʒ] *nm* [peur du vide] vertigo. ‖ [étourdissement] dizziness; **avoir des ~s** to suffer from OU have dizzy spells.

vertigineux, -euse [vertiʒinø, øz] *adj* *fig* [vue, vitesse] breathtaking. ‖ [hauteur] dizzy.

vertu [verty] *nf* [morale, chasteté] virtue. ‖ [pouvoir] properties (*pl*), power.

vertueux, -euse [vertyø, øz] *adj* virtuous.

verve [verv] *nf* eloquence.

vésicule [vezikyl] *nf* vesicle.

vessie [vesi] *nf* bladder.

veste [vest] *nf* [vêtement] jacket; **~ croisée/droite** double-/single-breasted jacket.

vestiaire [vestjɛr] *nm* [au théâtre] cloakroom. ‖ (*gén pl*) SPORT changing-room, locker-room.

vestibule [vestibyl] *nm* [pièce] hall, vestibule.

vestige [vestiʒ] *nm* (*gén pl*) [de ville]

remains (*pl*); *fig* [de civilisation, grandeur] vestiges (*pl*), relic.

vestimentaire [vɛstimɑ̃tɛr] *adj* [industrie] clothing (*avant n*); [dépense] on clothes; **détail** ~ accessory.

veston [vɛstɔ̃] *nm* jacket.

vêtement [vɛtmɑ̃] *nm* garment, article of clothing; ~s clothing (*U*), clothes.

vétéran [veterɑ̃] *nm* veteran.

vétérinaire [veteriner] *nmf* vet, veterinary surgeon.

vêtir [vetir] *vt* to dress. ○ **se vêtir** *vp* to dress, to get dressed.

veto [veto] *nm inv* veto; **mettre son** ~ **à qqch** to veto sthg.

vêtu, -e [vety] 1 *pp* → **vêtir**. 2 *adj*: ~ **(de)** dressed (in).

vétuste [vetyst] *adj* dilapidated.

veuf, veuve [vœf, vœv] *nm, f* widower (*f* widow).

veuille *etc* → **vouloir**.

veuve → **veuf**.

vexation [vɛksasjɔ̃] *nf* [humiliation] insult.

vexer [vɛkse] *vt* to offend. ○ **se vexer** *vp* to take offence.

VF (*abr de* **version française**) *nf indicates that a film has been dubbed into French.*

via [vja] *prép* via.

viable [vjabl] *adj* viable.

viaduc [vjadyk] *nm* viaduct.

viager, -ère [vjaʒe, ɛr] *adj* life (*avant n*). ○ **viager** *nm* life annuity.

viande [vjɑ̃d] *nf* meat.

vibration [vibrasjɔ̃] *nf* vibration.

vibrer [vibre] *vi* [trembler] to vibrate.

vice [vis] *nm* [de personne] vice. || [d'objet] fault, defect.

vice-président, -e [visprezidɑ̃, ɑ̃t] (*mpl* **vice-présidents**, *fpl* **vice-présidentes**) *nm, f* POLIT vice-president; [de société] vice-chairman.

vice versa [visversa] *loc adv* vice versa.

vicié, -e [visje] *adj* [air] polluted.

vicieux, -euse [visjø, jøz] *adj* [personne, conduite] perverted, depraved. || [animal] restive. || [attaque] underhand.

victime [viktim] *nf* victim; [blessé] casualty.

victoire [viktwar] *nf* MIL victory; POLIT & SPORT win, victory.

victorieux, -euse [viktorjø, jøz] *adj* MIL victorious; POLIT & SPORT winning (*avant n*), victorious. || [air] triumphant.

victuailles [viktɥaj] *nfpl* provisions.

vidange [vidɑ̃ʒ] *nf* [action] emptying, draining. || AUTOM oil change. || [mécanisme] waste outlet.

vidanger [vidɑ̃ʒe] *vt* to empty, to drain.

vide [vid] 1 *nm* [espace] void; *fig* [néant, manque] emptiness. || [absence d'air] vacuum; **conditionné sous** ~ vacuum-packed. || [ouverture] gap, space. 2 *adj* empty.

vidéo [video] 1 *nf* video. 2 *adj inv* video (*avant n*).

vidéocassette [videokasɛt] *nf* video cassette.

vidéodisque [videodisk] *nm* videodisc.

vide-ordures [vidordyr] *nm inv* rubbish chute.

vidéothèque [videotɛk] *nf* video library.

vide-poches [vidpɔʃ] *nm inv* [de voiture] glove compartment.

vider [vide] *vt* [rendre vide] to empty. || [évacuer]: ~ **les lieux** to vacate the premises. || [poulet] to clean. || *fam* [personne - épuiser] to drain; [- expulser] to chuck out. ○ **se vider** *vp* [baignoire, salle] to empty.

videur [vidœr] *nm* bouncer.

vie [vi] *nf* [gén] life; **sauver la** ~ **à qqn** to save sb's life; **être en** ~ to be alive; **à** ~ for life. || [subsistance] cost of living; **gagner sa** ~ to earn one's living.

vieil → **vieux**.

vieillard [vjejar] *nm* old man.

vieille → **vieux**.

vieillerie [vjɛjri] *nf* [objet] old thing.

vieillesse [vjɛjɛs] *nf* [fin de la vie] old age.

vieillir [vjejir] 1 *vi* [personne] to grow old, to age. || CULIN to mature, to age. || [tradition, idée] to become dated *ou* outdated. 2 *vt* [suj: coiffure, vêtement]: ~ **qqn** to make sb look older.

vieillissement [vjejismɑ̃] *nm* [de personne] ageing.

Vienne [vjɛn] *n* [en Autriche] Vienna.

vierge [vjɛrʒ] 1 *nf* virgin; **la (Sainte) Vierge** the Virgin (Mary). 2 *adj* [personne] virgin. || [terre] virgin; [page] blank; [casier judiciaire] clean. ○ **Vierge** *nf* ASTROL Virgo.

Việt-nam [vjɛtnam] *nm*: **le** ~ Vietnam.

vieux, vieille [vjø, vjɛj] 1 *adj* (*vieil devant voyelle ou h muet*) old; ~ **jeu** old-fashioned. 2 *nm, f* [personne âgée] old man (*f* woman); **les** ~ **the old**. || *fam* [ami]: **mon** ~ old chap *ou* boy *Br*, old buddy *Am*; **ma vieille** old girl.

visée

vif, **vive** [vif, viv] *adj* [preste - enfant]
lively; [- imagination] vivid. || [couleur,
œil] bright. || [reproche] sharp; [discus-
sion] bitter. || [douleur, déception] acute;
[intérêt] keen. ○ **à vif** *loc adj* [plaie]
open; **j'ai les nerfs à ~** *fig* my nerves are
frayed.

vigie [viʒi] *nf* [NAVIG - personne] lookout; [- poste] crow's nest.

vigilant, -e [viʒilɑ̃, ɑ̃t] *adj* vigilant,
watchful.

vigile [viʒil] *nm* watchman.

vigne [viɲ] *nf* [plante] vine, grapevine. ||
[plantation] vineyard.

vigneron, -onne [viɲrɔ̃, ɔn] *nm, f* wine
grower.

vignette [viɲɛt] *nf* [timbre] label; [de
médicament] price sticker (*for reim-
bursement by the social security ser-
vices*); AUTOM tax disc. || [motif] vignette.

vignoble [viɲɔbl] *nm* [plantation] vine-
yard. || [vignes] vineyards (*pl*).

vigoureux, -euse [vigurø, øz] *adj*
[corps, personne] vigorous.

vigueur [vigœr] *nf* vigour. ○ **en vigueur** *loc adj* in force.

vilain, -e [vilɛ̃, ɛn] *adj* [gén] nasty. ||
[laid] ugly.

vilebrequin [vilbrəkɛ̃] *nm* [outil] brace
and bit. || AUTOM crankshaft.

villa [vila] *nf* villa.

village [vilaʒ] *nm* village.

villageois, -e [vilaʒwa, az] *nm, f* villager.

ville [vil] *nf* [petite, moyenne] town; [im-
portante] city.

villégiature [vileʒjatyr] *nf* holiday.

vin [vɛ̃] *nm* wine; ~ **blanc/rosé/rouge**
white/rosé/red wine. ○ **vin d'honneur**
nm reception.

vinaigre [vinɛgr] *nm* vinegar.

vinaigrette [vinɛgrɛt] *nf* oil and vinegar dressing.

vindicatif, -ive [vɛ̃dikatif, iv] *adj* vindictive.

vingt [vɛ̃] *adj num & nm* twenty; *voir
aussi* **six**.

vingtaine [vɛ̃tɛn] *nf*: **une ~ de** about
twenty.

vingtième [vɛ̃tjɛm] *adj num, nm & nmf*
twentieth; *voir aussi* **sixième**.

vinicole [vinikɔl] *adj* wine-growing,
wine-producing.

viol [vjɔl] *nm* [de femme] rape. || [de sé-
pulture] desecration.

violation [vjɔlasjɔ̃] *nf* violation,
breach.

violence [vjɔlɑ̃s] *nf* violence; **se faire ~**
to force o.s.

violent, -e [vjɔlɑ̃, ɑ̃t] *adj* [personne,
tempête] violent. || *fig* [douleur, angoisse,
chagrin] acute; [haine, passion] violent.

violer [vjɔle] *vt* [femme] to rape. || [loi,
traité] to break. || [sépulture] to des-
ecrate; [sanctuaire] to violate.

violet, -ette [vjɔlɛ, ɛt] *adj* purple;
[pâle] violet. ○ **violet** *nm* purple.

violette [vjɔlɛt] *nf* violet.

violeur [vjɔlœr] *nm* rapist.

violon [vjɔlɔ̃] *nm* [instrument] violin.

violoncelle [vjɔlɔ̃sɛl] *nm* [instrument]
cello.

violoniste [vjɔlɔnist] *nmf* violinist.

vipère [vipɛr] *nf* viper.

virage [viraʒ] *nm* [sur route] bend.

viral, -e, -aux [viral, o] *adj* viral.

virement [virmɑ̃] *nm* FIN transfer; ~
bancaire/postal bank/giro transfer.

virer [vire] **1** *vi* [tourner]: ~ **à droite/à
gauche** to turn right/left. || [étoffe] to
change colour; ~ **au blanc/jaune** to go
white/yellow. **2** *vt* FIN to transfer. || *fam*
[renvoyer] to kick out.

virevolter [virvɔlte] *vi* [tourner] to
twirl or spin round.

virginité [virʒinite] *nf* [de personne] vir-
ginity. || [de sentiment] purity.

virgule [virgyl] *nf* [entre mots] comma;
[entre chiffres] (decimal) point.

viril, -e [viril] *adj* virile.

virilité [virilite] *nf* virility.

virtuel, -elle [virtɥɛl] *adj* potential.

virtuose [virtɥoz] *nmf* virtuoso.

virulence [virylɑ̃s] *nf* virulence.

virulent, -e [virylɑ̃, ɑ̃t] *adj* virulent.

virus [virys] *nm* INFORM & MÉD virus.

vis [vis] *nf* screw.

visa [viza] *nm* visa.

visage [vizaʒ] *nm* face.

vis-à-vis [vizavi] *nm* [personne] person
sitting opposite. || [immeuble]: **avoir un ~**
to have a building opposite. ○ **vis-à-vis
de** *loc prép* [en face de] opposite. || [à
l'égard de] towards.

viscéral, -e, -aux [viseral, o] *adj* ANAT
visceral. || *fam* [réaction] gut (*avant n*);
[haine, peur] deep-seated.

viscère [visɛr] *nm* (*gén pl*) innards
(*pl*).

viscose [viskoz] *nf* viscose.

visé, -e [vize] *adj* [concerné] concerned.

visée [vize] *nf* [avec arme] aiming. ||
(*gén pl*) *fig* [intention, dessein] aim.

viser [vize] **1** *vt* [cible] to aim at. || *fig* [poste] to aspire to, to aim for; [personne] to be directed or aimed at. || [document] to check, to stamp. **2** *vi* to aim, to take aim; **~ à faire qqch** to aim to do sthg, to be intended to do sthg.

viseur [vizœr] *nm* [d'arme] sights (*pl*). || PHOT viewfinder.

visibilité [vizibilite] *nf* visibility.

visible [vizibl] *adj* [gén] visible. || [personne]: **il n'est pas ~** he's not seeing visitors.

visiblement [vizibləmɑ̃] *adv* visibly.

visière [vizjɛr] *nf* [de casque] visor. || [de casquette] peak. || [de protection] eyeshade.

vision [vizjɔ̃] *nf* [faculté] eyesight, vision. || [représentation] view, vision. || [mirage] vision.

visionnaire [vizjɔnɛr] *nmf & adj* visionary.

visionner [vizjɔne] *vt* to view.

visite [vizit] *nf* [chez ami, officielle] visit; **rendre ~ à qqn** to pay sb a visit. || [MÉD - à l'extérieur] call, visit; [- dans hôpital] rounds (*pl*); **passer une ~ médicale** to have a medical. || [de monument] tour.

visiter [vizite] *vt* [en touriste] to tour. || [malade, prisonnier] to visit.

visiteur, -euse [vizitœr, øz] *nm, f* visitor.

vison [vizɔ̃] *nm* mink.

visqueux, -euse [viskø, øz] *adj* [liquide] viscous. || [surface] sticky.

visser [vise] *vt* [planches] to screw together. || [couvercle] to screw down. || [bouchon] to screw in; [écrou] to screw on.

visualiser [vizɥalize] *vt* [gén] to visualize. || INFORM to display.

visuel, -elle [vizɥɛl] *adj* visual.

vital, -e, -aux [vital, o] *adj* vital.

vitalité [vitalite] *nf* vitality.

vitamine [vitamin] *nf* vitamin.

vitaminé, -e [vitamine] *adj* with added vitamins, vitamin-enriched.

vite [vit] *adv* [rapidement] quickly, fast; **fais ~!** hurry up! || [tôt] soon.

vitesse [vitɛs] *nf* [gén] speed; **à toute ~** at top speed. || AUTOM gear.

viticole [vitikɔl] *adj* wine-growing.

viticulteur, -trice [vitikyltœr, tris] *nm, f* wine-grower.

vitrail, -aux [vitraj, o] *nm* stained-glass window.

vitre [vitr] *nf* [de fenêtre] pane of glass,

window pane. || [de voiture, train] window.

vitré, -e [vitre] *adj* glass (*avant n*).

vitreux, -euse [vitrø, øz] *adj* [roche] vitreous. || [œil, regard] glassy, glazed.

vitrine [vitrin] *nf* [de boutique] (shop) window. || [meuble] display cabinet.

vivable [vivabl] *adj* [appartement] livable-in; [situation] bearable, tolerable; [personne]: **il n'est pas ~** he's impossible to live with.

vivace [vivas] *adj* [plante] perennial; [arbre] hardy. || *fig* [haine, ressentiment] deep-rooted, entrenched; [souvenir] enduring.

vivacité [vivasite] *nf* [promptitude - de personne] liveliness, vivacity; **~ d'esprit** quick-wittedness. || [de propos] sharpness.

vivant, -e [vivɑ̃, ɑ̃t] *adj* [en vie] alive, living. || [enfant, quartier] lively. || [souvenir] still fresh. ○ **vivant** *nm* [personne]: **les ~s** the living.

vive [viv] *interj* three cheers for; **~ le roi!** long live the King!

vivement [vivmɑ̃] **1** *adv* [agir] quickly. || [répondre] sharply. **2** *interj*: **~ les vacances!** roll on the holidays!; **~ que l'été arrive** I'll be glad when summer comes, summer can't come quick enough.

vivifiant, -e [vivifjɑ̃, ɑ̃t] *adj* invigorating, bracing.

vivisection [vivisɛksjɔ̃] *nf* vivisection.

vivre [vivr] **1** *vi* to live; [être en vie] to be alive; **~ de** to live on; **faire ~ sa famille** to support one's family; **être difficile/facile à ~** to be hard/easy to get on with. **2** *vt* [passer] to spend. || [éprouver] to experience. ○ **vivres** *nmpl* provisions.

VO (*abr de* version originale) *nf* indicates that a film has not been dubbed.

vocable [vɔkabl] *nm* term.

vocabulaire [vɔkabylɛr] *nm* [gén] vocabulary. || [livre] lexicon, glossary.

vocal, -e, -aux [vɔkal, o] *adj*: **ensemble ~** choir; **→ corde**.

vocation [vɔkasjɔ̃] *nf* [gén] vocation. || [d'organisation] mission.

vociférer [vɔsifere] *vt* to shout, to scream.

vodka [vɔdka] *nf* vodka.

vœu, -x [vø] *nm* [RELIG & résolution] vow; **faire ~ de silence** to take a vow of silence. || [souhait, requête] wish. ○ **vœux** *nmpl* greetings.

vogue [vɔg] *nf* vogue, fashion; **en ~** fashionable, in vogue.

voguer [vɔge] *vi littéraire* to sail.

voici [vwasi] *prép* [pour désigner, introduire] here is/are; **le ~** here he/it is; **les ~** here they are; **~ ce qui s'est passé** this is what happened. ‖ [il y a]: **~ trois mois** three months ago; **~ quelques années que je ne l'ai pas vu** I haven't seen him for some years (now), it's been some years since I last saw him.

voie [vwa] *nf* [route] road; **route à deux ~s** two-lane road; **la ~ publique** the public highway. ‖ RAIL track, line; **~ ferrée** railway line *Br*, railroad line *Am*. ‖ [mode de transport] route. ‖ ANAT passage, tract; **par ~ buccale** ou **orale** orally, by mouth; **~ respiratoire** respiratory tract. ‖ *fig* [chemin] way. ‖ [filière, moyen] means (*pl*). ○ **Voie lactée** *nf*: la Voie lactée the Milky Way. ○ **en voie de** *loc prép* on the way to; **en ~ de développement** developing.

voilà [vwala] *prép* [pour désigner] there is/are; **le ~** there he/it is; **les ~** there they are; **nous ~ arrivés** we've arrived. ‖ [reprend ce dont on a parlé] that is; [introduit ce dont on va parler] this is; **~ ce que j'en pense** this is/that is what I think; **~ tout** that's all; **et ~!** there we are! ‖ [il y a]: **~ dix jours** ten days ago; **~ dix ans que je le connais** I've known him for ten years (now).

voile [vwal] **1** *nf* [de bateau] sail. ‖ [activité] sailing. **2** *nm* [textile] voile. ‖ [coiffure] veil. ‖ [de brume] mist.

voilé, -e [vwale] *adj* [visage, allusion] veiled. ‖ [ciel, regard] dull. ‖ [roue] buckled. ‖ [son, voix] muffled.

voiler [vwale] *vt* [visage] to veil. ‖ [suj: brouillard, nuages] to cover. ○ **se voiler** *vp* [femme] to wear a veil. ‖ [ciel] to cloud over. ‖ [roue] to buckle.

voilier [vwalje] *nm* [bateau] sailing boat, sailboat *Am*.

voilure [vwalyr] *nf* [de bateau] sails (*pl*).

voir [vwar] **1** *vt* [gén] to see; **je l'ai vu tomber** I saw him fall; **faire ~ qqch à qqn** to show sb sthg; **ne rien avoir à ~ avec** *fig* to have nothing to do with; **voyons, ...** [en réfléchissant] let's see, ... **2** *vi* to see. ○ **se voir** *vp* [se rencontrer] to see one another ou each other. ‖ [se remarquer] to be obvious, to show.

voire [vwar] *adv* even.

voirie [vwari] *nf* ADMIN ≃ Department of Transport.

voisin, -e [vwazɛ̃, in] **1** *adj* [pays, ville] neighbouring; [maison] next-door. ‖ [idée] similar. **2** *nm, f* neighbour.

voisinage [vwazinaʒ] *nm* [quartier] neighbourhood. ‖ [environs] vicinity.

voiture [vwatyr] *nf* [automobile] car; **~ de fonction** company car; **~ de location** hire car; **~ d'occasion/de sport** second-hand/sports car. ‖ [de train] carriage.

voix [vwa] *nf* [gén] voice; **à mi-~** in an undertone; **à ~ basse** in a low voice, quietly; **à ~ haute** [parler] in a loud voice; [lire] aloud; **de vive ~** in person. ‖ [suffrage] vote.

vol [vɔl] *nm* [d'oiseau, avion] flight; **à ~ d'oiseau** as the crow flies. ‖ [groupe d'oiseaux] flight, flock. ‖ [délit] theft.

vol. (*abr de* volume) vol.

volage [vɔlaʒ] *adj littéraire* fickle.

volaille [vɔlaj] *nf*: **la ~** poultry, (domestic) fowl.

volant, -e [vɔlɑ̃, ɑ̃t] *adj* [qui vole] flying. ‖ [mobile]: **feuille ~e** loose sheet. ○ **volant** *nm* [de voiture] steering wheel. ‖ [de robe] flounce. ‖ [de badminton] shuttlecock.

volatiliser [vɔlatilize] ○ **se volatiliser** *vp fig* to vanish into thin air.

volcan [vɔlkɑ̃] *nm* volcano; *fig* spitfire.

volcanique [vɔlkanik] *adj* volcanic; *fig* [tempérament] fiery.

volée [vɔle] *nf* [de flèches] volley; **une ~ de coups** a hail of blows. ‖ FOOTBALL & TENNIS volley.

voler [vɔle] **1** *vi* to fly. **2** *vt* [personne] to rob; [chose] to steal.

volet [vɔle] *nm* [de maison] shutter. ‖ [de dépliant] leaf; [d'émission] part.

voleur, -euse [vɔlœr, øz] *nm, f* thief.

volière [vɔljer] *nf* aviary.

volley-ball [vɔlebol] (*pl* volley-balls) *nm* volleyball.

volontaire [vɔlɔ̃ter] **1** *nmf* volunteer. **2** *adj* [omission] deliberate; [activité] voluntary. ‖ [enfant] strong-willed.

volonté [vɔlɔ̃te] *nf* [vouloir] will; **à ~** unlimited, as much as you like. ‖ [disposition]: **bonne ~** willingness, good will; **mauvaise ~** unwillingness. ‖ [détermination] willpower.

volontiers [vɔlɔ̃tje] *adv* [avec plaisir] with pleasure, gladly, willingly.

volt [vɔlt] *nm* volt.

voltage [vɔltaʒ] *nm* voltage.

volte-face [vɔltəfas] *nf inv* about-face *Am*.

voltige

voltige [vɔltiʒ] *nf* [au trapèze] trapeze work; **haute ~** flying trapeze act; *fam fig* mental gymnastics (*U*). ‖ [à cheval] circus riding. ‖ [en avion] aerobatics (*U*).

voltiger [vɔltiʒe] *vi* [insecte, oiseau] to flit ou flutter about. ‖ [feuilles] to flutter about.

volubile [vɔlybil] *adj* voluble.

volume [vɔlym] *nm* volume.

volumineux, -euse [vɔlyminø, øz] *adj* voluminous, bulky.

volupté [vɔlypte] *nf* [sensuelle] sensual ou voluptuous pleasure.

voluptueux, -euse [vɔlyptɥø, øz] *adj* voluptuous.

volute [vɔlyt] *nf* [de fumée] wreath. ‖ ARCHIT volute, helix.

vomi [vɔmi] *nm fam* vomit.

vomir [vɔmir] *vt* [aliments] to bring up. ‖ [injures] to spit out.

vorace [vɔras] *adj* voracious.

voracité [vɔrasite] *nf* voracity.

vos → votre.

vote [vɔt] *nm* vote.

voter [vɔte] **1** *vi* to vote. **2** *vt* POLIT to vote for; [crédits] to vote; [loi] to pass.

votre [vɔtr] (*pl* **vos** [vo]) *adj poss* your.

vôtre [votr] ○ **le vôtre** (*f* **la vôtre**, *pl* **les vôtres**) *pron poss* yours; **à la ~!** your good health!

vouer [vwe] *vt* [promettre, jurer]: **~ qqch à qqn** to swear ou vow sthg to sb. ‖ [consacrer] to devote. ‖ [condamner]: **être voué à** to be doomed to.

vouloir [vulwar] **1** *vt* [gén] to want; **je voudrais savoir** I would like to know; **~ que** (+ *subjonctif*): **je veux qu'il parte** I want him to leave; **combien voulez-vous de votre maison?** how much do you want for your house?; **ne pas ~ de qqn/qqch** not to want sb/sthg; **je veux bien** I don't mind; **veuillez vous asseoir** please take a seat; **sans le ~** without meaning ou wishing to, unintentionally. ‖ [suj: coutume] to demand. ‖ *loc*: **~ dire** to mean; **si on veut** more or less, if you like; **en ~ à qqn** to have a grudge against sb. **2** *nm*: **le bon ~ de qqn** sb's good will. ○ **se vouloir** *vp*: **elle se veut différente** she thinks she's different; **s'en ~ de faire qqch** to be cross with o.s. for doing sthg.

voulu, -e [vuly] **1** *pp* → vouloir. **2** *adj* [requis] requisite. ‖ [délibéré] intentional.

vous [vu] *pron pers* [sujet, objet direct] you. ‖ [objet indirect] (to) you. ‖ [après préposition, comparatif] you. ‖ [réfléchi] yourself, (*pl*) yourselves. ○ **vous-**

même *pron pers* yourself. ○ **vous-mêmes** *pron pers* yourselves.

voûte [vut] *nf* ARCHIT vault; *fig* arch. ‖ ANAT: **~ du palais** roof of the mouth; **~ plantaire** arch (of the foot).

voûter [vute] ○ **se voûter** *vp* to be ou become stooped.

vouvoyer [vuvwaje] *vt*: **~ qqn** to use the "vous" form to sb.

voyage [vwajaʒ] *nm* journey, trip; **les ~s** travel (*sg*), travelling (*U*); **partir en ~** to go away, to go on a trip; **~ d'affaires** business trip; **~ organisé** package tour; **~ de noces** honeymoon.

voyager [vwajaʒe] *vi* to travel.

voyageur, -euse [vwajaʒœr, øz] *nm, f* traveller.

voyant, -e [vwajã, ãt] **1** *adj* loud, gaudy. **2** *nm, f* [devin] seer. ○ **voyant** *nm* [lampe] light; AUTOM indicator (light); **~ d'essence/d'huile** petrol/oil warning light.

voyelle [vwajɛl] *nf* vowel.

voyeur, -euse [vwajœr, øz] *nm, f* voyeur, Peeping Tom.

voyou [vwaju] *nm* [garnement] urchin. ‖ [loubard] lout.

vrac [vrak] ○ **en vrac** *loc adv* [sans emballage] loose. ‖ [en désordre] higgledy-piggledy. ‖ [au poids] in bulk.

vrai, -e [vrɛ] *adj* [histoire] true. ‖ [or, perle, nom] real. ‖ [personne] natural. ‖ [ami, raison] real, true. ○ **vrai** *nm*: **à ~ dire, à dire ~** to tell the truth.

vraiment [vrɛmã] *adv* really.

vraisemblable [vrɛsãblabl] *adj* likely, probable; [excuse] plausible.

vraisemblance [vrɛsãblãs] *nf* likelihood, probability; [d'excuse] plausibility.

V/Réf (*abr de* **Votre référence**) your ref.

vrille [vrij] *nf* BOT tendril. ‖ [outil] gimlet. ‖ [spirale] spiral.

vrombir [vrɔbir] *vi* to hum.

VTT (*abr de* **vélo tout terrain**) *nm* mountain bike.

vu, -e [vy] **1** *pp* → voir. **2** *adj* [perçu]: **être bien/mal ~** to be acceptable/unacceptable. ‖ [compris] clear. ○ **vu** *prép* given, in view of. ○ **vue** *nf* [sens, vision] sight, eyesight. ‖ [regard] gaze; **à première ~** at first sight; **de ~** by sight; **perdre qqn de ~** to lose touch with sb. ‖ [panorama, idée] view. ‖ CIN → **prise**. ○ **en vue de** *loc prép* with a view to. ○ **vu que** *loc conj* given that, seeing that.

vulgaire [vylgɛr] *adj* [grossier] vulgar, coarse. ‖ (*avant n*) *péj* [quelconque] common.
vulgarisation [vylgarizasjɔ̃] *nf* popularization.
vulgarité [vylgarite] *nf* vulgarity, coarseness.
vulnérable [vylnerabl] *adj* vulnerable.
vulve [vylv] *nf* vulva.

w, W [dublǝve] *nm inv* w, W.
wagon [vagɔ̃] *nm* carriage.
wagon-lit [vagɔ̃li] *nm* sleeping car, sleeper.
wagon-restaurant [vagɔ̃rɛstɔrɑ̃] *nm* restaurant ou dining car.
Walkman® [wɔkman] *nm* personal stereo, Walkman®.
wallon, -onne [walɔ̃, ɔn] *adj* Walloon.
○ **wallon** *nm* [langue] Walloon.
○ **Wallon, -onne** *nm, f* Walloon.
Washington [waʃiŋtɔn] *n* [ville] Washington D.C. ‖ [État] Washington State.
water-polo [watɛrpolo] *nm* water polo.
watt [wat] *nm* watt.
W.-C. [vese] (*abr de* water closet) *nmpl* WC (*sg*), toilets.
week-end [wikɛnd] (*pl* week-ends) *nm* weekend.
western [wɛstɛrn] *nm* western.
whisky [wiski] (*pl* whiskies) *nm* whisky.
white-spirit [wajtspirit] (*pl* white-spirits) *nm* white spirit.

x, X [iks] *nm inv* x, X.
xénophobie [gzenɔfɔbi] *nf* xenophobia.
xérès [gzerɛs, kserɛs] *nm* sherry.
xylophone [ksilɔfɔn] *nm* xylophone.

y¹, Y [igrɛk] *nm inv* y, Y.
y² [i] **1** *adv* [lieu] there; **j'y vais demain** I'm going there tomorrow; **mets-y du sel** put some salt in it. **2** *pron* (*la traduction varie selon la préposition utilisée avec le verbe*): **pensez-y** think about it; **n'y comptez pas** don't count on it; **j'y suis!** I've got it!; *voir aussi* aller, avoir *etc*.
yacht [jot] *nm* yacht.
yaourt [jaurt], **yogourt, yoghourt** [jɔgurt] *nm* yoghurt.
yen [jɛn] *nm* yen.
yeux → œil.
yiddish [jidiʃ] *nm inv & adj inv* Yiddish.
yoga [jɔga] *nm* yoga.
yoghourt = yaourt.
yogourt = yaourt.
yougoslave [jugɔslav] *adj* Yugoslav, Yugoslavian. ○ **Yougoslave** *nmf* Yugoslav, Yugoslavian.
Yougoslavie [jugɔslavi] *nf*: **la ~** Yugoslavia.

z, Z [zɛd] *nm inv* z, Z.

zapper [zape] *vi* to zap, to channel-hop.

zapping [zapiŋ] *nm* zapping, channel-hopping.

zèbre [zɛbr] *nm* zebra; **un drôle de ~** *fam fig* an oddball.

zébrure [zebryr] *nf* [de pelage] stripe. ‖ [marque] weal.

zèle [zɛl] *nm* zeal; **faire du ~** *péj* to be over-zealous.

zélé, -e [zele] *adj* zealous.

zénith [zenit] *nm* zenith.

zéro [zero] **1** *nm* [chiffre] zero, nought; [dans numéro de téléphone] O *Br*, zero *Am*. ‖ [nombre] nought, nothing. ‖ [de graduation] freezing point, zero; **au-dessus/au-dessous de ~** above/below (zero); **avoir le moral à ~** *fig* to be ou feel down. **2** *adj*: **~ faute** no mistakes.

zeste [zɛst] *nm* peel, zest.

zézayer [zezeje] *vi* to lisp.

zigzag [zigzag] *nm* zigzag; **en ~** winding.

zigzaguer [zigzage] *vi* to zigzag (along).

zinc [zɛ̃g] *nm* [matière] zinc.

zizi [zizi] *nm fam* willy *Br*, peter *Am*.

zodiaque [zɔdjak] *nm* zodiac.

zone [zon] *nf* [région] zone, area; **~ bleue** restricted parking zone; **~ industrielle** industrial estate; **~ piétonne** ou **piétonnière** pedestrian precinct *Br* ou zone *Am*. ‖ *fam* [faubourg]: **la ~** the slum belt.

zoo [zo(o)] *nm* zoo.

zoologie [zɔɔlɔʒi] *nf* zoology.

zoom [zum] *nm* [objectif] zoom (lens). ‖ [gros plan] zoom.

zut [zyt] *interj fam* damn!

a¹ (*pl* a's OR as), **A** (*pl* A's OR As) [eɪ] *n* [letter] a *m inv*, A *m inv*; **to get from A to B** aller d'un point à un autre. ○ **A** *n* MUS la *m inv*. || SCH [mark] A *m inv*.

a² [*stressed* eɪ, *unstressed* ə] (*before vowel or silent 'h'* **an** [*stressed* æn, *unstressed* ən]) *indef art* [gen] un (une); **a boy** un garçon; **a table** une table; **an orange** une orange. || [referring to occupation]: **to be a doctor/lawyer/plumber** être médecin/avocat/plombier. || [instead of the number one] un (une); **a hundred/thousand pounds** cent/mille livres. || [to express prices, ratios etc]: **20p a kilo** 20p le kilo; **£10 a person** 10 livres par personne; **twice a week/month** deux fois par semaine/mois; **50 km an hour** 50 km à l'heure.

AA *n* (*abbr of* **Automobile Association**) automobile club britannique, ≃ ACF *m*, ≃ TCF *m*.

AAA *n* (*abbr of* **American Automobile Association**) automobile club américain, ≃ ACF *m*, ≃ TCF *m*.

AB *n Am abbr of* **Bachelor of Arts**.

aback [ə'bæk] *adv*: **to be taken a** être décontenancé(e).

abandon [ə'bændən] **1** *vt* abandonner. **2** *n*: **with a** avec abandon.

abate [ə'beɪt] *vi* [storm, fear] se calmer.

abattoir ['æbətwɑːr] *n* abattoir *m*.

abbey ['æbɪ] *n* abbaye *f*.

abbot ['æbət] *n* abbé *m*.

abbreviate [ə'briːvɪeɪt] *vt* abréger.

abbreviation [ə,briːvɪ'eɪʃn] *n* abréviation *f*.

ABC *n* [alphabet] alphabet *m*.

abdicate ['æbdɪkeɪt] *vt & vi* abdiquer.

abdomen ['æbdəmən] *n* abdomen *m*.

abduct [əb'dʌkt] *vt* enlever.

aberration [,æbə'reɪʃn] *n* aberration *f*.

abet [ə'bet] *vt* → **aid**.

abide [ə'baɪd] *vt* supporter, souffrir. ○ **abide by** *vt fus* respecter, se soumettre à.

ability [ə'bɪlətɪ] *n* [capacity, capability] aptitude *f*. || [skill] talent *m*.

abject ['æbdʒekt] *adj* [poverty] noir(e). || [person] pitoyable; [apology] servile.

ablaze [ə'bleɪz] *adj* [on fire] en feu.

able ['eɪbl] *adj* [capable]: **to be a to do sthg** pouvoir faire qqch. || [accomplished] compétent(e).

abnormal [æb'nɔːml] *adj* anormal(e).

aboard [ə'bɔːd] **1** *adv* à bord. **2** *prep* [ship, plane] à bord; [bus, train] dans.

abode [ə'bəʊd] *n fml*: **of no fixed a** sans domicile fixe.

abolish [ə'bɒlɪʃ] *vt* abolir.

abolition [,æbə'lɪʃn] *n* abolition *f*.

aborigine [,æbə'rɪdʒənɪ] *n* aborigène *mf* d'Australie.

abort [ə'bɔːt] *vt fig* [plan, project] abandonner, faire avorter. || COMPUT abandonner.

abortion [ə'bɔːʃn] *n* avortement *m*, interruption *f* (volontaire) de grossesse; **to have an a** se faire avorter.

abortive [ə'bɔːtɪv] *adj* manqué(e).

abound [ə'baʊnd] *vi* [be plentiful] abonder. || [be full]: **to a with** OR **in** abonder en.

about [ə'baʊt] **1** *adv* [approximately] environ, à peu près; **a fifty/a hundred/a thousand** environ cinquante/cent/mille; **at a five o'clock** vers cinq heures; **I'm just a ready** je suis presque prêt. || [referring to place]: **to run ~** courir çà et là; **to leave things lying ~** laisser traîner des affaires; **to walk ~** aller et venir, se promener. || [on the point of]: **to be ~ to do sthg** être sur le point de faire qqch. **2** *prep* [relating to, concerning] au sujet de; **a film ~ Paris** un film sur Paris; **what is it ~?** de quoi s'agit-il?; **to talk ~ sthg** parler de qqch. || [referring to place]: **his belongings were scattered ~ the room** ses affaires étaient éparpillées dans toute la pièce; **to wander ~ the streets** errer de par les rues.

about-turn, **about-face** *n* MIL demitour *m*; *fig* volte-face *f inv*.

above [ə'bʌv] **1** *adv* [on top, higher up] au-dessus. || [in text] ci-dessus, plus haut. || [more, over] plus; **children aged 5 and ~** les enfants âgés de 5 ans et plus OR de plus de 5 ans. **2** *prep* [on top of, higher up than] au-dessus de. || [more than] plus de. ○ **above all** *adv* avant tout.

aboveboard [ə,bʌv'bɔ:d] *adj* honnête.

abrasive [ə'breisiv] *adj* [substance] abrasif(ive); *fig* caustique, acerbe.

abreast [ə'brest] *adv* de front. ○ **abreast of** *prep*: **to keep ~ of** se tenir au courant de.

abridged [ə'bridʒd] *adj* abrégé(e).

abroad [ə'brɔ:d] *adv* à l'étranger.

abrupt [ə'brʌpt] *adj* [sudden] soudain(e), brusque. || [brusque] abrupt(e).

abscess ['æbsis] *n* abcès *m*.

abscond [əb'skɒnd] *vi* s'enfuir.

abseil ['æbseil] *vi* descendre en rappel.

absence ['æbsəns] *n* absence *f*.

absent ['æbsənt] *adj*: **~ (from)** absent(e) (de).

absentee [,æbsən'ti:] *n* absent *m*, -e *f*.

absent-minded [-'maindid] *adj* distrait(e).

absolute ['æbsəlu:t] *adj* [complete - fool, disgrace] complet(ète). || [totalitarian - ruler, power] absolu(e).

absolutely ['æbsəlu:tli] *adv* absolument.

absolve [əb'zɒlv] *vt*: **to ~ sb (from)** absoudre qqn (de).

absorb [əb'sɔ:b] *vt* absorber; [information] retenir, assimiler; **to be ~ed in sthg** être absorbé dans qqch.

absorbent [əb'sɔ:bənt] *adj* absorbant(e).

absorption [əb'sɔ:pʃn] *n* absorption *f*.

abstain [əb'stein] *vi*: **to ~ (from)** s'abstenir (de).

abstention [əb'stenʃn] *n* abstention *f*.

abstract ['æbstrækt] **1** *adj* abstrait(e). **2** *n* [summary] résumé *m*, abrégé *m*.

absurd [əb'sɜ:d] *adj* absurde.

abundant [ə'bʌndənt] *adj* abondant(e).

abuse [*n* ə'bju:s, *vb* ə'bju:z] **1** *n* (*U*) [offensive remarks] insultes *fpl*, injures *fpl*. || [maltreatment] mauvais traitement *m*; **child ~** mauvais traitements infligés aux enfants. || [of power, drugs etc] abus *m*. **2** *vt* [insult] insulter, injurier. || [maltreat] maltraiter. || [power, drugs etc] abuser de.

abusive [ə'bju:siv] *adj* grossier(ière), injurieux(ieuse).

abysmal [ə'bizml] *adj* épouvantable, abominable.

abyss [ə'bis] *n* abîme *m*, gouffre *m*.

a/c (*abbr of* **account (current)**) cc.

AC *n* (*abbr of* **alternating current**) courant *m* alternatif.

academic [,ækə'demik] **1** *adj* [of college, university] universitaire. || [person] intellectuel(elle). || [question, discussion] théorique. **2** *n* universitaire *mf*.

academy [ə'kædəmi] *n* [school, college] école *f*; **~ of music** conservatoire *m*. || [institution, society] académie *f*.

accede [æk'si:d] *vi* [agree]: **to ~ to** agréer, donner suite à. || [monarch]: **to ~ to the throne** monter sur le trône.

accelerate [ək'seləreit] *vi* [car, driver] accélérer. || [inflation, growth] s'accélérer.

accelerator [ək'seləreitər] *n* accélérateur *m*.

accent ['æksent] *n* accent *m*.

accept [ək'sept] *vt* [gen] accepter; [for job, as member of club] recevoir, admettre. || [agree]: **to ~ that ...** admettre que ....

acceptable [ək'septəbl] *adj* acceptable.

acceptance [ək'septəns] *n* [gen] acceptation *f*. || [for job, as member of club] admission *f*.

access ['ækses] *n* [entry, way in] accès *m*. || [opportunity to use, see]: **to have ~ to sthg** avoir qqch à sa disposition, disposer de qqch.

accessible [ək'sesəbl] *adj* [reachable - place] accessible. || [available] disponible.

accessory [ək'sesəri] *n* [of car, vacuum cleaner] accessoire *m*. || JUR complice *mf*.

accident ['æksidənt] *n* accident *m*; **by ~** par hasard, par accident.

accidental [,æksi'dentl] *adj* accidentel(elle).

accidentally [,æksi'dentəli] *adv* [drop, break] par mégarde. || [meet] par hasard.

accident-prone adj prédisposé(e) aux accidents.

acclaim [ə'kleɪm] n (U) éloges mpl.

acclimatize, -ise [ə'klaɪmətaɪz], **acclimate** Am ['æklǝmeɪt] vi: **to ~ (to)** s'acclimater (à).

accommodate [ə'kɒmǝdeɪt] vt [provide room for] loger. || [oblige - person, wishes] satisfaire.

accommodation Br [ǝ,kɒmǝ'deɪʃn] n, **accommodations** Am [ǝ,kɒmǝ'deɪʃnz] npl logement m.

accompany [ə'kʌmpǝnɪ] vt [gen] accompagner.

accomplice [ə'kʌmplɪs] n complice mf.

accomplish [ə'kʌmplɪʃ] vt accomplir.

accomplishment [ə'kʌmplɪʃmǝnt] n [action] accomplissement m. || [achievement] réussite f. ○ **accomplishments** npl talents mpl.

accord [ə'kɔːd] n: **to do sthg of one's own ~** faire qqch de son propre chef OR de soi-même.

accordance [ə'kɔːdǝns] n: **in ~ with** conformément à.

according [ə'kɔːdɪŋ] ○ **according to** prep [as stated or shown by] d'après; **to go ~ to plan** se passer comme prévu. || [with regard to] suivant, en fonction de.

accordingly [ə'kɔːdɪŋlɪ] adv [appropriately] en conséquence. || [consequently] par conséquent.

accordion [ə'kɔːdjǝn] n accordéon m.

accost [ə'kɒst] vt accoster.

account [ə'kaʊnt] n [with bank, shop, company] compte m. || [report] compterendu m. || phr: **to take ~ of sthg, to take sthg into ~** prendre qqch en compte; **on no ~** sous aucun prétexte, en aucun cas. ○ **accounts** npl [of business] comptabilité f, comptes mpl. ○ **by all accounts** adv d'après ce que l'on dit, au dire de tous. ○ **on account of** prep à cause de. ○ **account for** vt fus [explain] justifier, expliquer. || [represent] représenter.

accountable [ə'kaʊntǝbl] adj [responsible]: **~ (for)** responsable (de).

accountant [ə'kaʊntǝnt] n comptable mf.

accumulate [ə'kjuːmjʊleɪt] **1** vt accumuler, amasser. **2** vi s'accumuler.

accuracy ['ækjʊrǝsɪ] n [of description, report] exactitude f. || [of weapon, typist, figures] précision f.

accurate ['ækjʊrǝt] adj [description, re-

port] exact(e). || [weapon, typist, figures] précis(e).

accurately ['ækjʊrǝtlɪ] adv [truthfully - describe, report] fidèlement. || [precisely - aim] avec précision; [- type] sans faute.

accusation [,ækjuː'zeɪʃn] n accusation f.

accuse [ə'kjuːz] vt: **to ~ sb of sthg/of doing sthg** accuser qqn de qqch/de faire qqch.

accused [ə'kjuːzd] (pl inv) n JUR: **the ~** l'accusé m, -e f.

accustomed [ə'kʌstǝmd] adj: **to be ~ to sthg/to doing sthg** avoir l'habitude de qqch/de faire qqch.

ace [eɪs] n as m.

ache [eɪk] **1** n douleur f. **2** vi [back, limb] faire mal; **my head ~s** j'ai mal à la tête.

achieve [ə'tʃiːv] vt [success, victory] obtenir, remporter; [goal] atteindre; [ambition] réaliser; [fame] parvenir à.

achievement [ə'tʃiːvmǝnt] n [success] réussite f.

Achilles' tendon [ə'kɪliːz-] n tendon m d'Achille.

acid ['æsɪd] **1** adj lit & fig acide. **2** n acide m.

acid rain n (U) pluies fpl acides.

acknowledge [ǝk'nɒlɪdʒ] vt [fact, situation, person] reconnaître. || [letter]: **to ~ (receipt of)** accuser réception de.

acknowledg(e)ment [ǝk'nɒlɪdʒmǝnt] n [gen] reconnaissance f. || [letter] accusé m de réception. ○ **acknowledg(e)ments** npl [in book] remerciements mpl.

acne ['æknɪ] n acné f.

acorn ['eɪkɔːn] n gland m.

acoustic [ǝ'kuːstɪk] adj acoustique. ○ **acoustics** npl [of room] acoustique f.

acquaint [ə'kweɪnt] vt: **to ~ sb with sthg** mettre qqn au courant de qqch; **to be ~ed with sb** connaître qqn.

acquaintance [ə'kweɪntǝns] n [person] connaissance f.

acquire [ə'kwaɪǝr] vt acquérir.

acquit [ə'kwɪt] vt JUR acquitter. || [perform]: **to ~ o.s. well/badly** bien/mal se comporter.

acquittal [ə'kwɪtl] n acquittement m.

acre ['eɪkǝr] n = 4046,9 m², ≃ demi-hectare m.

acrid ['ækrɪd] adj [taste, smell] âcre.

acrobat ['ækrǝbæt] n acrobate mf.

across [ə'krɒs] **1** adv [from one side to the other] en travers. || [in measurements]: **the river is 2 km ~** la rivière mesure 2 km de large. || [in crossword]: **21 ~ 21** horizontalement. **2** *prep* [from one side to the other] d'un côté à l'autre de, en travers de; **to walk ~ the road** traverser la route. || [on the other side of] de l'autre côté de; **the house ~ the road** la maison d'en face. ○ **across from** *prep* en face de.

acrylic [ə'krılık] **1** *adj* acrylique. **2** *n* acrylique *m*.

act [ækt] **1** *n* [action, deed] acte *m*; **to catch sb in the ~ of doing sthg** surprendre qqn en train de faire qqch. || JUR loi *f*. || [of play, opera] acte *m*; [in cabaret etc] numéro *m*; *fig* [pretence]: **to put on an ~** jouer la comédie. || *phr*: **to get one's ~ together** se reprendre en main. **2** *vi* [gen] agir. || [behave] se comporter; **to ~ as if** se conduire comme si, se comporter comme si; **to ~ like** se conduire comme, se comporter comme. || [in play, film] jouer; *fig* [pretend] jouer la comédie. || [function]: **to ~ as** [person] être; [object] servir de. **3** *vt* [part] jouer.

ACT (*abbr of* **American College Test**) *n* examen américain de fin d'études secondaires.

acting ['æktıŋ] **1** *adj* par intérim, provisoire. **2** *n* [in play, film] interprétation *f*.

action ['ækʃn] *n* [gen] action *f*; **to take ~** agir, prendre des mesures; **to put sthg into ~** mettre qqch à exécution; **in ~** [person] en action; [machine] en marche; **out of ~** [person] hors de combat; [machine] hors service, hors d'usage. || JUR procès *m*, action *f*.

action replay *n* répétition *f* immédiate (au ralenti).

activate ['æktıveıt] *vt* mettre en marche.

active ['æktıv] *adj* [gen] actif(ive); [encouragement] vif (vive). || [volcano] en activité.

actively ['æktıvlı] *adv* activement.

activity [æk'tıvətı] *n* activité *f*.

actor ['æktər] *n* acteur *m*.

actress ['æktrıs] *n* actrice *f*.

actual ['æktʃʊəl] *adj* réel(elle).

actually ['æktʃʊəlı] *adv* [really, in truth] vraiment. || [by the way] au fait.

acumen ['ækjʊmen] *n* flair *m*.

acupuncture ['ækjʊpʌŋktʃər] *n* acuponcture *f*.

acute [ə'kjuːt] *adj* [severe - pain, illness] aigu(ë); [- danger] sérieux(ieuse), grave. || [perceptive - person, mind] perspicace. || [keen - eyesight] perçant(e); [- hearing] fin(e); [- sense of smell] développé(e). ||

MATH: **~ angle** angle *m* aigu. || LING: **e ~ e** accent aigu.

ad [æd] (*abbr of* **advertisement**) *n inf* [in newspaper] annonce *f*; [on TV] pub *f*.

AD (*abbr of* **Anno Domini**) ap. J.-C.

adamant ['ædəmənt] *adj*: **to be ~** être inflexible.

Adam's apple ['ædəmz-] *n* pomme *f* d'Adam.

adapt [ə'dæpt] **1** *vt* adapter. **2** *vi*: **to ~ (to)** s'adapter (à).

adaptable [ə'dæptəbl] *adj* [person] souple.

adapter, adaptor [ə'dæptər] *n* [ELEC - for several devices] prise *f* multiple; [- for foreign plug] adaptateur *m*.

add [æd] *vt* [gen]: **to ~ sthg (to)** ajouter qqch (à). || [numbers] additionner. ○ **add on** *vt sep*: **to ~ sthg on (to)** ajouter qqch (à); [charge, tax] rajouter qqch (à). ○ **add to** *vt fus* ajouter à, augmenter. ○ **add up** *vt sep* additionner. ○ **add up to** *vt fus* se monter à.

adder ['ædər] *n* vipère *f*.

addict ['ædıkt] *n lit & fig* drogué *m*, -e *f*; **drug ~** drogué.

addicted [ə'dıktıd] *adj*: **~ (to)** drogué(e) (à); *fig* passionné(e) (de).

addictive [ə'dıktıv] *adj* qui rend dépendant(e).

addition [ə'dıʃn] *n* addition *f*; **in ~ (to)** en plus (de).

additional [ə'dıʃənl] *adj* supplémentaire.

additive ['ædıtıv] *n* additif *m*.

address [ə'dres] **1** *n* [place] adresse *f*. || [speech] discours *m*. **2** *vt* [gen] adresser. || [meeting, conference] prendre la parole à. || [problem, issue] aborder, examiner.

address book *n* carnet *m* d'adresses.

adept ['ædept] *adj*: **~ (at)** doué(e) (pour).

adequate ['ædıkwət] *adj* adéquat(e).

adhere [əd'hıər] *vi* [stick]: **to ~ (to)** adhérer (à). || [observe]: **to ~ to** obéir à. || [keep]: **to ~ to** adhérer à.

adhesive [əd'hiːsıv] *n* adhésif *m*.

adhesive tape *n* ruban *m* adhésif.

adjacent [ə'dʒeısənt] *adj*: **~ (to)** adjacent(e) (à), contigu(ë) (à).

adjective ['ædʒıktıv] *n* adjectif *m*.

adjoining [ə'dʒɔınıŋ] **1** *adj* voisin(e). **2** *prep* attenant à.

adjourn [ə'dʒɜːn] **1** *vt* ajourner. **2** *vi* suspendre la séance.

adjust [ə'dʒʌst] **1** *vt* ajuster, régler. **2** *vi*: **to ~ (to)** s'adapter (à).

adjustable [ə'dʒʌstəbl] *adj* réglable.

adjustment [ə'dʒʌstmənt] *n* [modification] ajustement *m*; TECH réglage *m*. || [change in attitude]: ~ **(to)** adaptation *f* (à).

ad lib [ˌæd'lɪb] *adv* à volonté. ○ **ad-lib** *vi* improviser.

administer [əd'mɪnɪstəʳ] *vt* [company, business] administrer, gérer. || [justice, punishment] dispenser. || [drug, medication] administrer.

administration [əd,mɪnɪ'streɪʃn] *n* administration *f*.

administrative [əd'mɪnɪstrətɪv] *adj* administratif(ive).

admiral ['ædmərəl] *n* amiral *m*.

admiration [ˌædmə'reɪʃn] *n* admiration *f*.

admire [əd'maɪəʳ] *vt* admirer.

admirer [əd'maɪərəʳ] *n* admirateur *m*, -trice *f*.

admission [əd'mɪʃn] *n* [permission to enter] admission *f*. || [to museum etc] entrée *f*. || [confession] confession *f*, aveu *m*.

admit [əd'mɪt] **1** *vt* [confess] reconnaître; **to ~ (that)** ... reconnaître que ...; **to ~ doing sthg** reconnaître avoir fait qqch; **to ~ defeat** *fig* s'avouer vaincu(e). || [allow to enter, join] admettre; **to be admitted to hospital** *Br* OR **to the hospital** *Am* être admis(e) à l'hôpital. **2** *vi*: **to ~ to** admettre, reconnaître.

admittance [əd'mɪtəns] *n* admission *f*; "**no ~**" «entrée interdite».

admittedly [əd'mɪtɪdlɪ] *adv* de l'aveu général.

ad nauseam [ˌæd'nɔːzɪæm] *adv* [talk] à n'en plus finir.

ado [ə'duː] *n*: **without further** OR **more ~** sans plus de cérémonie.

adolescence [ˌædə'lesns] *n* adolescence *f*.

adolescent [ˌædə'lesnt] **1** *adj* adolescent(e); *pej* puéril(e). **2** *n* adolescent *m*, -e *f*.

adopt [ə'dɒpt] *vt* adopter.

adoption [ə'dɒpʃn] *n* adoption *f*.

adore [ə'dɔːʳ] *vt* adorer.

adorn [ə'dɔːn] *vt* orner.

adrenalin [ə'drenəlɪn] *n* adrénaline *f*.

Adriatic [ˌeɪdrɪ'ætɪk] *n*: **the ~ (Sea)** l'Adriatique *f*, la mer Adriatique.

adrift [ə'drɪft] **1** *adj* à la dérive. **2** *adv*: **to go ~** *fig* aller à la dérive.

adult ['ædʌlt] **1** *adj* [gen] adulte. || [films, literature] pour adultes. **2** *n* adulte *mf*.

adultery [ə'dʌltərɪ] *n* adultère *m*.

advance [əd'vɑːns] **1** *n* [gen] avance *f*. || [progress] progrès *m*. **2** *comp* à l'avance. **3** *vt* [gen] avancer. || [improve] faire progresser OR avancer. **4** *vi* [gen] avancer. || [improve] progresser. ○ **advances** *npl*: **to make ~s to sb** [sexual] faire des avances à qqn; [business] faire des propositions à qqn. ○ **in advance** *adv* à l'avance.

advanced [əd'vɑːnst] *adj* avancé(e).

advantage [əd'vɑːntɪdʒ] *n*: ~ **(over)** avantage *m* (sur); **to be to one's ~** être à son avantage; **to take ~ of sthg** profiter de qqch; **to take ~ of sb** exploiter qqn.

advent ['ædvənt] *n* avènement *m*. ○ **Advent** *n* RELIG Avent *m*.

adventure [əd'ventʃəʳ] *n* aventure *f*.

adventure playground *n* terrain *m* d'aventures.

adventurous [əd'ventʃərəs] *adj* aventureux(euse).

adverb ['ædvɜːb] *n* adverbe *m*.

adverse ['ædvɜːs] *adj* défavorable.

advert ['ædvɜːt] *Br* = **advertisement**.

advertise ['ædvətaɪz] **1** *vt* COMM faire de la publicité pour; [event] annoncer. **2** *vi* faire de la publicité; **to ~ for sb/sthg** chercher qqn/qqch par voie d'annonce.

advertisement [əd'vɜːtɪsmənt] *n* [in newspaper] annonce *f*; COMM & *fig* publicité *f*.

advertiser ['ædvətaɪzəʳ] *n* annonceur *m*.

advertising ['ædvətaɪzɪŋ] *n* (*U*) publicité *f*.

advice [əd'vaɪs] *n* (*U*) conseils *mpl*; **a piece of ~** un conseil; **to take sb's ~** suivre les conseils de qqn.

advisable [əd'vaɪzəbl] *adj* conseillé(e), recommandé(e).

advise [əd'vaɪz] **1** *vt* [give advice to]: **to ~ sb to do sthg** conseiller à qqn de faire qqch; **to ~ sb against sthg** déconseiller qqch à qqn. || [professionally]: **to ~ sb on sthg** conseiller qqn sur qqch. || [inform]: **to ~ sb (of sthg)** aviser qqn (de qqch). **2** *vi* [give advice]: **to ~ against sthg/against doing sthg** déconseiller qqch/de faire qqch. || [professionally]: **to ~ on sthg** conseiller sur qqch.

adviser *Br*, **advisor** *Am* [əd'vaɪzəʳ] *n* conseiller *m*, -ère *f*.

advisory [əd'vaɪzərɪ] *adj* consultatif(ive).

advocate [*n* 'ædvəkət, *vb* 'ædvəkeɪt] **1**

n JUR avocat *m*, -e *f.* ‖ [supporter] partisan *m.* **2** *vt* préconiser, recommander.

Aegean [i:'dʒi:ən] *n*: the ~ (Sea) la mer Égée.

aerial ['eərɪəl] **1** *adj* aérien(ne). **2** *n Br* antenne *f.*

aerobics [eə'rəubɪks] *n* (U) aérobic *m.*

aerodynamic [,eərəudaɪ'næmɪk] *adj* aérodynamique.

aerosol ['eərəsɒl] *n* aérosol *m.*

aesthetic, esthetic *Am* [i:s'θetɪk] *adj* esthétique.

afar [ə'fɑ:r] *adv*: from ~ de loin.

affable ['æfəbl] *adj* affable.

affair [ə'feər] *n* [gen] affaire *f.* ‖ [extramarital relationship] liaison *f.*

affect [ə'fekt] *vt* [influence] avoir un effet OR des conséquences sur. ‖ [emotionally] affecter, émouvoir.

affection [ə'fekʃn] *n* affection *f.*

affectionate [ə'fekʃnət] *adj* affectueux(euse).

affirm [ə'fɜ:m] *vt* [declare] affirmer. ‖ [confirm] confirmer.

affix [ə'fɪks] *vt* [stamp] coller.

afflict [ə'flɪkt] *vt* affliger; **to be ~ed with** souffrir de.

affluence ['æfluəns] *n* prospérité *f.*

affluent ['æfluənt] *adj* riche.

afford [ə'fɔ:d] *vt* [buy, pay for]: **to be able to ~ sthg** avoir les moyens d'acheter qqch. ‖ [spare]: **to be able to ~ the time (to do sthg)** avoir le temps (de faire qqch). ‖ [harmful, embarrassing thing]: **to be able to ~ sthg** pouvoir se permettre qqch. ‖ [provide, give] procurer.

Afghanistan [æf'gænɪstæn] *n* Afghanistan *m.*

afield [ə'fi:ld] *adv*: **far ~** loin.

afloat [ə'fləʊt] *adj lit & fig* à flot.

afoot [ə'fʊt] *adj* en préparation.

afraid [ə'freɪd] *adj* [frightened]: **to be ~ (of)** avoir peur (de); **to be ~ of doing** OR **to do sthg** avoir peur de faire qqch. ‖ [reluctant, apprehensive]: **to be ~ of doing** craindre. ‖ [in apologies]: **to be ~ (that) ...** regretter que ...; **I'm ~ so/not** j'ai bien peur que oui/non.

afresh [ə'freʃ] *adv* de nouveau.

Africa ['æfrɪkə] *n* Afrique *f.*

African ['æfrɪkən] **1** *adj* africain(e). **2** *n* Africain *m*, -e *f.*

aft [ɑ:ft] *adv* sur OR à l'arrière.

after ['ɑ:ftər] **1** *prep* [gen] après; **~ you!** après vous!; **to be ~ sb/sthg** *inf* [in search of] chercher qqn/qqch. ‖ *Am* [telling the time]: **it's twenty ~ three** il est trois heu-

res vingt. **2** *adv* après. **3** *conj* après que. ○ **after all** *adv* après tout.

aftereffects ['ɑ:ftərɪ,fekts] *npl* suites *fpl*, répercussions *fpl.*

aftermath ['ɑ:ftəmæθ] *n* conséquences *fpl*, suites *fpl.*

afternoon [,ɑ:ftə'nu:n] *n* après-midi *m inv*; **in the ~** l'après-midi; **good ~** bonjour.

aftershave ['ɑ:ftəʃeɪv] *n* après-rasage *m.*

aftertaste ['ɑ:ftəteɪst] *n lit & fig* arrière-goût *m.*

afterthought ['ɑ:ftəθɔ:t] *n* pensée *f* OR réflexion *f* après coup.

afterward(s) ['ɑ:ftəwəd(z)] *adv* après.

again [ə'gen] *adv* encore une fois, de nouveau; **to do ~** refaire; **to say ~** répéter; **to start ~** recommencer; **~ and ~** à plusieurs reprises; **all over ~** une fois de plus; **time and ~** maintes et maintes fois; **half as much ~** à moitié autant; **(twice) as much ~** deux fois autant; **then** OR **there ~** d'autre part.

against [ə'genst] *prep & adv* contre; **(as) ~** contre.

age [eɪdʒ] (*cont* **ageing** OR **aging**) **1** *n* [gen] âge *m*; **she's 20 years of ~** elle a 20 ans; **what ~ are you?** quel âge avez-vous?; **to be under ~** être mineur; **to come of ~** atteindre sa majorité. ‖ [old age] vieillesse *f.* ‖ [in history] époque *f.* **2** *vt & vi* vieillir. ○ **ages** *npl*: **~s ago** il y a une éternité; **I haven't seen him for ~s** je ne l'ai pas vu depuis une éternité.

aged [*adj sense 1* eɪdʒd, *adj sense 2 & npl* 'eɪdʒɪd] **1** *adj* [of stated age]: **~ 15** âgé(e) de 15 ans. ‖ [very old] âgé(e), vieux (vieille). **2** *npl*: **the ~** les personnes *fpl* âgées.

age group *n* tranche *f* d'âge.

agency ['eɪdʒənsɪ] *n* [business] agence *f.* ‖ [organization] organisme *m.*

agenda [ə'dʒendə] (*pl* -**s**) *n* ordre *m* du jour.

agent ['eɪdʒənt] *n* agent *m.*

aggravate ['ægrəveɪt] *vt* [make worse] aggraver. ‖ [annoy] agacer.

aggregate ['ægrɪgət] **1** *adj* total(e). **2** *n* [total] total *m.*

aggressive [ə'gresɪv] *adj* agressif(ive).

aghast [ə'gɑ:st] *adj*: **~ (at sthg)** atterré(e) (par qqch).

agile [*Br* 'ædʒaɪl, *Am* 'ædʒəl] *adj* agile.

agitate ['ædʒɪteɪt] *vt* [disturb] inquiéter.

AGM (*abbr of* **annual general meeting**) *n Br* AGA *f*.

agnostic [æg'nɒstɪk] **1** *adj* agnostique. **2** *n* agnostique *mf*.

ago [ə'gəʊ] *adv*: **a long time ~** il y a longtemps; **three days ~** il y a trois jours.

agonizing ['ægənaɪzɪŋ] *adj* déchirant(e).

agony ['ægənɪ] *n* [physical pain] douleur *f* atroce; **to be in ~** souffrir le martyre. || [mental pain] angoisse *f*; **to be in ~** être angoissé.

agony aunt *n Br inf* personne qui tient la rubrique du courrier du cœur.

agree [ə'griː] **1** *vi* [concur]: **to ~ (with/about)** être d'accord (avec/au sujet de); **to ~ on** [price, terms] convenir de. || [consent]: **to ~ (to sthg)** donner son consentement (à qqch). || [be consistent] concorder. || [food]: **to ~ with** être bon (bonne) pour, réussir à. || GRAMM: **to ~ (with)** s'accorder (avec). **2** *vt* [price, conditions] accepter, convenir de. || [concur, concede]: **to ~ (that)** ... admettre que .... || [arrange]: **to ~ to do sthg** se mettre d'accord pour faire qqch.

agreeable [ə'griːəbl] *adj* [pleasant] agréable. || [willing]: **to be ~ to** consentir à.

agreed [ə'griːd] *adj*: **to be ~ (on sthg)** être d'accord (à propos de qqch).

agreement [ə'griːmənt] *n* [gen] accord *m*; **to be in ~ (with)** être d'accord (avec). || [consistency] concordance *f*.

agricultural [ˌægrɪ'kʌltʃərəl] *adj* agricole.

agriculture ['ægrɪkʌltʃər] *n* agriculture *f*.

aground [ə'graʊnd] *adv*: **to run ~** s'échouer.

ahead [ə'hed] *adv* [in front] devant, en avant; **right ~, straight ~** droit devant. || [in better position] en avance; **Scotland are ~ by two goals to one** l'Écosse mène par deux à un; **to get ~** [be successful] réussir. || [in time] à l'avance; **the months ~** les mois à venir. ○ **ahead of** *prep* [in front of] devant. || [in time] avant; **~ of schedule** [work] en avance sur le planning.

aid [eɪd] **1** *n* aide *f*; **with the ~ of** [person] avec l'aide de; [thing] à l'aide de; **in ~ of** au profit de. **2** *vt* [help] aider. || JUR: **to ~ and abet** être complice de.

AIDS, Aids [eɪdz] (*abbr of* **acquired immune deficiency syndrome**) *n* SIDA *m*, Sida *m*.

ailing ['eɪlɪŋ] *adj* [ill] souffrant(e). || *fig* [economy, industry] dans une mauvaise passe.

ailment ['eɪlmənt] *n* maladie *f*.

aim [eɪm] **1** *n* [objective] but *m*, objectif *m*. || [in firing gun, arrow]: **to take ~ at** viser. **2** *vt* [gun, camera]: **to ~ sthg at** braquer qqch sur. || *fig*: **to be ~ed at** [plan, campaign etc] être destiné(e) à, viser; [criticism] être dirigé(e) contre. **3** *vi*: **to ~ (at)** viser; **to ~ at** OR **for** *fig* viser; **to ~ to do sthg** viser à faire qqch.

aimless ['eɪmlɪs] *adj* [person] désœuvré(e); [life] sans but.

ain't [eɪnt] *inf* = **am not, are not, is not, have not, has not**.

air [eər] **1** *n* [gen] air *m*; **to throw sthg into the ~** jeter qqch en l'air; **by ~** [travel] par avion; **to be (up) in the ~** *fig* [plans] être vague. || RADIO & TV: **on the ~** à l'antenne. **2** *comp* [transport] aérien(ienne). **3** *vt* [gen] aérer. || [make publicly known] faire connaître OR communiquer. **4** *vi* sécher.

airbag ['eəbæg] *n* AUT coussin *m* pneumatique (de sécurité).

airbase ['eəbeɪs] *n* base *f* aérienne.

airbed ['eəbed] *n Br* matelas *m* pneumatique.

airborne ['eəbɔːn] *adj* [plane] qui a décollé.

air-conditioned [-kən'dɪʃnd] *adj* climatisé(e), à air conditionné.

air-conditioning [-kən'dɪʃnɪŋ] *n* climatisation *f*.

aircraft ['eəkrɑːft] (*pl inv*) *n* avion *m*.

aircraft carrier *n* porte-avions *m inv*.

airfield ['eəfiːld] *n* terrain *m* d'aviation.

airforce ['eəfɔːs] *n* armée *f* de l'air.

airgun ['eəgʌn] *n* carabine *f* OR fusil *m* à air comprimé.

airhostess ['eəˌhəʊstɪs] *n* hôtesse *f* de l'air.

airlift ['eəlɪft] **1** *n* pont *m* aérien. **2** *vt* transporter par pont aérien.

airline ['eəlaɪn] *n* compagnie *f* aérienne.

airliner ['eəlaɪnər] *n* [short-distance] (avion *m*) moyen-courrier *m*; [long-distance] (avion) long-courrier *m*.

airlock ['eəlɒk] *n* [in tube, pipe] poche *f* d'air. || [airtight chamber] sas *m*.

airmail ['eəmeɪl] *n* poste *f* aérienne; **by ~** par avion.

airplane ['eəpleɪn] *n Am* avion *m*.

airport ['eəpɔːt] *n* aéroport *m*.

air raid *n* attaque *f* aérienne.

air rifle n carabine f à air comprimé.

airsick ['eəsɪk] adj: **to be ~** avoir le mal de l'air.

airspace ['eəspeɪs] n espace m aérien.

air steward n steward m.

airstrip ['eəstrɪp] n piste f.

air terminal n aérogare f.

airtight ['eətaɪt] adj hermétique.

air-traffic controller n aiguilleur m (du ciel).

airy ['eərɪ] adj [room] aéré(e). || [notions, promises] chimérique, vain(e). || [nonchalant] nonchalant(e).

aisle [aɪl] n allée f. || [in plane] couloir m.

ajar [ə'dʒɑːʳ] adj entrouvert(e).

aka (abbr of **also known as**) alias.

alarm [ə'lɑːm] 1 n [fear] alarme f, inquiétude f. || [device] alarme f; **to raise** OR **sound the ~** donner OR sonner l'alarme. 2 vt alarmer, alerter.

alarm clock n réveil m, réveille-matin m inv.

alarming [ə'lɑːmɪŋ] adj alarmant(e), inquiétant(e).

alas [ə'læs] excl hélas!

albeit [ɔːl'biːɪt] conj bien que (+ subjunctive).

albino [æl'biːnəʊ] (pl -s) n albinos mf.

album ['ælbəm] n album m.

alcohol ['ælkəhɒl] n alcool m.

alcoholic [,ælkə'hɒlɪk] 1 adj [drink] alcoolisé(e). 2 n alcoolique mf.

alcove ['ælkəʊv] n alcôve f.

alderman ['ɔːldəmən] (pl -men [-mən]) n conseiller m municipal.

ale [eɪl] n bière f.

alert [ə'lɜːt] 1 adj [vigilant] vigilant(e). || [perceptive] vif (vive), éveillé(e). || [aware]: **to be ~** être conscient(e) de. 2 n [warning] alerte f; **on the ~** [watchful] sur le qui-vive; MIL en état d'alerte. 3 vt alerter; **to ~ sb to sthg** avertir qqn de qqch.

A-level (abbr of **Advanced level**) n ≃ baccalauréat m.

algebra ['ældʒɪbrə] n algèbre f.

Algeria [æl'dʒɪərɪə] n Algérie f.

alias ['eɪlɪəs] (pl -es) 1 adv alias. 2 n faux nom m, nom d'emprunt.

alibi ['ælɪbaɪ] n alibi m.

alien ['eɪljən] 1 adj [gen] étranger(ère). || [from outer space] extraterrestre. 2 n [from outer space] extraterrestre mf. || JUR [foreigner] étranger m, -ère f.

alienate ['eɪljəneɪt] vt aliéner.

alight [ə'laɪt] 1 adj allumé(e), en feu. 2 vi [bird etc] se poser. || [from bus, train]: **to ~ from** descendre de.

align [ə'laɪn] vt [line up] aligner.

alike [ə'laɪk] 1 adj semblable. 2 adv de la même façon; **to look ~** se ressembler.

alimony ['ælɪmənɪ] n pension f alimentaire.

alive [ə'laɪv] adj [living] vivant(e), en vie. || [practice, tradition] vivace; **to keep ~** préserver. || [lively] plein(e) de vitalité; **to come ~** [story, description] prendre vie; [person, place] s'animer.

alkali ['ælkəlaɪ] (pl -s OR -es) n alcali m.

all [ɔːl] 1 adj (with sg noun) tout (toute). **~ day/night/evening** toute la journée/la nuit/la soirée; **~ the drink** toute la boisson; **~ the time** tout le temps. || (with pl noun) tous (toutes); **~ the boxes** toutes les boîtes; **~ men** tous les hommes; **~ three died** ils sont morts tous les trois, tous les trois sont morts. 2 pron (sg) [the whole amount] tout m; **drank it ~, she drank ~ of it** elle a tout bu. || (pl) [everybody, everything] tous (toutes); **~ of them came, they ~ came** ils sont tous venus. || (with superl): **... of ~** de tous (toutes); **I like this one best of ~** je préfère celui-ci entre tous. || **above ~** → above; **after ~** → after; **at ~** → at. 3 adv [entirely] complètement; **~ alone** tout seul (toute seule). || [in sport, competitions]: **the score is five ~** le score est cinq partout. || (with compar): **to run ~ the faster** courir d'autant plus vite; **~ the better** d'autant mieux. O **all but** adv presque, pratiquement. O **all in all** adv dans l'ensemble. O **in all** adv en tout.

Allah ['ælə] n Allah m.

all-around Am = **all-round**.

allay [ə'leɪ] vt [fears, anger] apaiser, calmer; [doubts] dissiper.

all clear n signal m de fin d'alerte; fig feu m vert.

allegation [,ælɪ'geɪʃn] n allégation f.

allege [ə'ledʒ] vt prétendre, alléguer; **she is ~d to have done it** on prétend qu'elle l'a fait.

allegedly [ə'ledʒɪdlɪ] adv prétendument.

allegiance [ə'liːdʒəns] n allégeance f.

allergic [ə'lɜːdʒɪk] adj: **~ (to)** allergique (à).

allergy ['ælədʒɪ] n allergie f; **to have an ~ to sthg** être allergique à qqch.

alleviate [ə'liːvɪeɪt] vt apaiser, soulager.

alley(way) ['ælɪ(weɪ)] n [street] ruelle f.

alliance [ə'laɪəns] n alliance f.

allied ['ælaɪd] adj MIL allié(e). ‖ [related] connexe.

alligator ['ælɪgeɪtər] (pl inv OR -s) n alligator m.

all-important adj capital(e), crucial(e).

all-night adj [party etc] qui dure toute la nuit; [bar etc] ouvert(e) toute la nuit.

allocate ['æləkeɪt] vt [money, resources]: **to ~ sthg (to sb)** attribuer qqch (à qqn).

allot [ə'lɒt] vt [job] assigner; [money, resources] attribuer; [time] allouer.

all-out adj [effort] maximum (inv); [war] total(e).

allow [ə'laʊ] vt [permit - activity, behaviour] autoriser, permettre; **to ~ sb to do sthg** permettre à qqn de faire qqch, autoriser qqn à faire qqch. ‖ [set aside - money, time] prévoir. ‖ [officially accept] accepter. ‖ [concede]: **to ~ that ...** admettre que .... ○ **allow for** vt fus tenir compte de.

allowance [ə'laʊəns] n [money received] indemnité f. ‖ Am [pocket money] argent m de poche. ‖ [excuse]: **to make ~s for sb** faire preuve d'indulgence envers qqn; **to make ~s for sthg** prendre qqch en considération.

alloy ['ælɔɪ] n alliage m.

all right 1 adv bien; [in answer - yes] d'accord. **2** adj [healthy] en bonne santé; [unharmed] sain et sauf (saine et sauve). ‖ inf [acceptable, satisfactory]: **it was ~** c'était pas mal; **that's ~** [never mind] ce n'est pas grave.

all-round Br, **all-around** Am adj [multi-skilled] doué(e) dans tous les domaines.

all-time adj [record] sans précédent.

allude [ə'lu:d] vi: **to ~ to** faire allusion à.

alluring [ə'ljʊərɪŋ] adj séduisant(e).

allusion [ə'lu:ʒn] n allusion f.

ally [n 'ælaɪ, vb ə'laɪ] **1** n allié m, -e f. **2** vt: **to ~ o.s. with** s'allier à.

almond ['ɑ:mənd] n [nut] amande f.

almost ['ɔ:lməʊst] adv presque; **I ~ missed the bus** j'ai failli rater le bus.

aloft [ə'lɒft] adv [in the air] en l'air.

alone [ə'ləʊn] **1** adj seul(e). **2** adv seul; **to leave sthg ~** ne pas toucher à qqch; **leave me ~!** laisse-moi tranquille! ○ **let alone** conj encore moins.

along [ə'lɒŋ] **1** adv: **to walk ~** se promener; **to move ~** avancer; **can I come ~ (with you)?** est-ce que je peux venir

(avec vous)? **2** prep le long de; **to run/ walk ~ the street** courir/marcher le long de la rue. ○ **all along** adv depuis le début. ○ **along with** prep ainsi que.

alongside [ə,lɒŋ'saɪd] **1** prep le long de, à côté de; [person] à côté de. **2** adv bord à bord.

aloof [ə'lu:f] **1** adj distant(e). **2** adv: **to remain ~ (from)** garder ses distances (vis-à-vis de).

aloud [ə'laʊd] adv à voix haute, tout haut.

alphabet ['ælfəbet] n alphabet m.

alphabetical [,ælfə'betɪkl] adj alphabétique.

Alps [ælps] npl: **the ~** les Alpes fpl.

already [ɔ:l'redɪ] adv déjà.

alright [,ɔ:l'raɪt] = all right.

Alsatian [æl'seɪʃn] n [dog] berger m allemand.

also ['ɔ:lsəʊ] adv aussi.

altar ['ɔ:ltər] n autel m.

alter ['ɔ:ltər] **1** vt changer, modifier. **2** vi changer.

alteration [,ɔ:ltə'reɪʃn] n modification f, changement m.

alternate [adj Br ɔ:l'tɜ:nət, Am 'ɔ:ltərnət, vb 'ɔ:ltərneɪt] **1** adj alterné(e), alternatif(ive); **~ days** tous les deux jours, un jour sur deux. **2** vt faire alterner. **3** vi: **to ~ (with)** alterner (avec); **to ~ between sthg and sthg** passer de qqch à qqch.

alternately [ɔ:l'tɜ:nətlɪ] adv alternativement.

alternating current ['ɔ:ltəneɪtɪŋ-] n courant m alternatif.

alternative [ɔ:l'tɜ:nətɪv] **1** adj [different] autre. ‖ [non-traditional - society] parallèle; [- art, energy] alternatif(ive). **2** n [between two solutions] alternative f. ‖ [other possibility]: **~ (to)** solution f de remplacement (à); **to have no ~ but to do sthg** ne pas avoir d'autre choix que de faire qqch.

alternatively [ɔ:l'tɜ:nətɪvlɪ] adv ou bien.

alternative medicine n médecine f parallèle OR douce.

alternator ['ɔ:ltəneɪtər] n ELEC alternateur m.

although [ɔ:l'ðəʊ] conj bien que (+ subjunctive).

altitude ['æltɪtju:d] n altitude f.

alto ['æltəʊ] (pl -s) n [male voice] haute-contre f. ‖ [female voice] contralto m.

altogether [ˌɔːltəˈgeðəʳ] *adv* [completely] entièrement, tout à fait. ‖ [considering all things] tout compte fait. ‖ [in all] en tout.

aluminium *Br* [ˌæljʊˈmɪnɪəm], **aluminum** *Am* [əˈluːmɪnəm] *n* aluminium *m*.

always [ˈɔːlweɪz] *adv* toujours.

am [æm] → be.

a.m. (*abbr of* ante meridiem): at 3 ~ à 3h (du matin).

AM (*abbr of* amplitude modulation) *n* AM *f*.

amalgamate [əˈmælgəmeɪt] *vt & vi* [unite] fusionner.

amass [əˈmæs] *vt* amasser.

amateur [ˈæmətəʳ] **1** *adj* amateur (*inv*); *pej* d'amateur. **2** *n* amateur *m*.

amaze [əˈmeɪz] *vt* étonner, stupéfier.

amazed [əˈmeɪzd] *adj* stupéfait(e).

amazement [əˈmeɪzmənt] *n* stupéfaction *f*.

amazing [əˈmeɪzɪŋ] *adj* [surprising] étonnant(e), ahurissant(e). ‖ [wonderful] excellent(e).

Amazon [ˈæməzn] *n* [river]: **the ~** l'Amazone *f*. ‖ [region]: **the ~ (Basin)** l'Amazonie *f*; **the ~ rainforest** la forêt amazonienne.

ambassador [æmˈbæsədəʳ] *n* ambassadeur *m*, -drice *f*.

amber [ˈæmbəʳ] **1** *adj* [amber-coloured] ambré(e). ‖ *Br* [traffic light] orange (*inv*). **2** *n* [substance] ambre *m*.

ambiguous [æmˈbɪgjʊəs] *adj* ambigu(ë).

ambition [æmˈbɪʃn] *n* ambition *f*.

ambitious [æmˈbɪʃəs] *adj* ambitieux(ieuse).

amble [ˈæmbl] *vi* déambuler.

ambulance [ˈæmbjʊləns] *n* ambulance *f*.

ambush [ˈæmbʊʃ] **1** *n* embuscade *f*. **2** *vt* tendre une embuscade à.

amenable [əˈmiːnəbl] *adj*: ~ **(to)** ouvert(e) (à).

amend [əˈmend] *vt* modifier; [law] amender. ○ **amends** *npl*: **to make ~s (for)** se racheter (pour).

amendment [əˈmendmənt] *n* modification *f*; [to law] amendement *m*.

amenities [əˈmiːnətɪz] *npl* aménagements *mpl*, équipements *mpl*.

America [əˈmerɪkə] *n* Amérique *f*; **in ~** en Amérique.

American [əˈmerɪkn] **1** *adj* américain(e). **2** *n* Américain *m*, -e *f*.

American Indian *n* Indien *m*, -ienne *f* d'Amérique, Amérindien *m*, -ienne *f*.

amicable [ˈæmɪkəbl] *adj* amical(e).

amid(st) [əˈmɪd(st)] *prep* au milieu de, parmi.

ammonia [əˈməʊnjə] *n* [liquid] ammoniaque *f*.

ammunition [ˌæmjʊˈnɪʃn] *n* (*U*) MIL munitions *fpl*. ‖ *fig* [argument] argument *m*.

amnesia [æmˈniːzjə] *n* amnésie *f*.

amnesty [ˈæmnəstɪ] *n* amnistie *f*.

among(st) [əˈmʌŋ(st)] *prep* parmi, entre; ~ **other things** entre autres (choses).

amoral [ˌeɪˈmɒrəl] *adj* amoral(e).

amorous [ˈæmərəs] *adj* amoureux (euse).

amount [əˈmaʊnt] *n* [quantity] quantité *f*; **a great ~ of** beaucoup de. ‖ [sum of money] somme *f*, montant *m*. ○ **amount to** *vt fus* [total] se monter à, s'élever à. ‖ [be equivalent to] revenir à, équivaloir à.

amp [æmp] *n abbr of* ampere.

ampere [ˈæmpeəʳ] *n* ampère *m*.

amphibious [æmˈfɪbɪəs] *adj* amphibie.

ample [ˈæmpl] *adj* [enough] suffisamment de, assez de. ‖ [large] ample.

amplifier [ˈæmplɪfaɪəʳ] *n* amplificateur *m*.

amputate [ˈæmpjʊteɪt] *vt & vi* amputer.

Amsterdam [ˌæmstəˈdæm] *n* Amsterdam.

Amtrak [ˈæmtræk] *n* société nationale de chemins de fer aux États-Unis.

amuse [əˈmjuːz] *vt* [make laugh] amuser, faire rire. ‖ [entertain] divertir, distraire; **to ~ o.s. (by doing sthg)** s'occuper (à faire qqch).

amused [əˈmjuːzd] *adj* [laughing] amusé(e); **to be ~ at** OR **by sthg** trouver qqch amusant. ‖ [entertained]: **to keep o.s. ~** s'occuper.

amusement [əˈmjuːzmənt] *n* [laughter] amusement *m*. ‖ [diversion, game] distraction *f*.

amusement arcade *n* galerie *f* de jeux.

amusement park *n* parc *m* d'attractions.

amusing [əˈmjuːzɪŋ] *adj* amusant(e).

an [stressed æn, unstressed ən] → a.

anabolic steroid [ˌænəˈbɒlɪk-] *n* (stéroïde *m*) anabolisant *m*.

anaemic *Br*, **anemic** *Am* [ə'niːmɪk] *adj* anémique; *fig* & *pej* fade, plat(e).

anaesthetic *Br*, **anesthetic** *Am* [ˌænɪs'θetɪk] *n* anesthésique *m*; **under ~** sous anesthésie; **local/general ~** anesthésie *f* locale/générale.

analogy [ə'nælədʒɪ] *n* analogie *f*.

analyse *Br*, **analyze** *Am* ['ænəlaɪz] *vt* analyser.

analysis [ə'næləsɪs] (*pl* **analyses** [ə'næləsiːz]) *n* analyse *f*.

analyst ['ænəlɪst] *n* analyste *mf*.

analytic(al) [ˌænə'lɪtɪk(l)] *adj* analytique.

analyze *Am* = **analyse**.

anarchist ['ænəkɪst] *n* anarchiste *mf*.

anarchy ['ænəkɪ] *n* anarchie *f*.

anathema [ə'næθəmə] *n* anathème *m*.

anatomy [ə'nætəmɪ] *n* anatomie *f*.

ANC (*abbr of* **African National Congress**) *n* ANC *m*.

ancestor ['ænsestə'] *n* *lit* & *fig* ancêtre *m*.

anchor ['æŋkə'] **1** *n* ancre *f*; **to drop/weigh ~** jeter/lever l'ancre. **2** *vt* [secure] ancrer. ‖ TV présenter. **3** *vi* NAUT jeter l'ancre.

anchovy ['æntʃəvɪ] (*pl inv* OR **-ies**) *n* anchois *m*.

ancient ['eɪnʃənt] *adj* [monument etc] historique; [custom] ancien(ienne). ‖ *hum* [car etc] antique; [person] vieux (vieille).

ancillary [æn'sɪlərɪ] *adj* auxiliaire.

and [*strong form* ænd, *weak form* ənd, ən] *conj* [as well as, plus] et. ‖ [in numbers]: **one hundred ~ eighty** cent quatre-vingts; **six ~ a half** six et demi. ‖ [to]: **come ~ see!** venez voir!; **try ~ come** essayez de venir; **wait ~ see** vous verrez bien. ○ **and so on, and so forth** *adv* et ainsi de suite.

Andes ['ændiːz] *npl*: **the ~** les Andes *fpl*.

Andorra [æn'dɔːrə] *n* Andorre *f*.

anecdote ['ænɪkdəʊt] *n* anecdote *f*.

anemic *Am* = **anaemic**.

anesthetic *etc Am* = **anaesthetic** *etc*.

anew [ə'njuː] *adv*: **to start ~** recommencer (à zéro).

angel ['eɪndʒəl] *n* ange *m*.

anger ['æŋgə'] **1** *n* colère *f*. **2** *vt* fâcher, irriter.

angina [æn'dʒaɪnə] *n* angine *f* de poitrine.

angle ['æŋgl] *n* [gen] angle *m*; **at an ~ de** travers, en biais. ‖ [point of view] point *m* de vue, angle *m*.

angler ['æŋglə'] *n* pêcheur *m* (à la ligne).

Anglican ['æŋglɪkən] *adj* anglican(e).

angling ['æŋglɪŋ] *n* pêche *f* à la ligne.

angry ['æŋgrɪ] *adj* [person] en colère, fâché(e); [words, quarrel] violent(e); **to be ~ with** OR **at sb** être en colère OR fâché contre qqn; **to get ~** se mettre en colère, se fâcher.

anguish ['æŋgwɪʃ] *n* angoisse *f*.

animal ['ænɪml] *n* animal *m*; *pej* brute *f*.

animate ['ænɪmət] *adj* animé(e), vivant(e).

animated ['ænɪmeɪtɪd] *adj* animé(e).

aniseed ['ænɪsiːd] *n* anis *m*.

ankle ['æŋkl] **1** *n* cheville *f*. **2** *comp*: **~ socks** socquettes *fpl*; **~ boots** bottines *fpl*.

annex(e) ['æneks] **1** *n* [building] annexe *f*. **2** *vt* annexer.

annihilate [ə'naɪəleɪt] *vt* anéantir, annihiler.

anniversary [ˌænɪ'vɜːsərɪ] *n* anniversaire *m*.

announce [ə'naʊns] *vt* annoncer.

announcement [ə'naʊnsmənt] *n* [statement] déclaration *f*; [in newspaper] avis *m*. ‖ (*U*) [act of stating] annonce *f*.

announcer [ə'naʊnsə'] *n* RADIO & TV speaker *m*, speakerine *f*.

annoy [ə'nɔɪ] *vt* agacer, contrarier.

annoyance [ə'nɔɪəns] *n* contrariété *f*.

annoyed [ə'nɔɪd] *adj* mécontent(e), agacé(e); **to get ~** se fâcher; **to be ~ at** **sthg** être contrarié par qqch; **to be ~ with** **sb** être fâché contre qqn.

annoying [ə'nɔɪɪŋ] *adj* agaçant(e).

annual ['ænjʊəl] **1** *adj* annuel(elle). **2** *n* [plant] plante *f* annuelle. ‖ [book - gen] publication *f* annuelle; [- for children] album *m*.

annual general meeting *n* assemblée *f* générale annuelle.

annul [ə'nʌl] *vt* annuler; [law] abroger.

annum ['ænəm] → **per annum**.

anomaly [ə'nɒmǝlɪ] *n* anomalie *f*.

anonymous [ə'nɒnɪməs] *adj* anonyme.

anorak ['ænəræk] *n* anorak *m*.

anorexia (nervosa) [ˌænə'reksɪə(nɜː'vəʊsə)] *n* anorexie *f* mentale.

anorexic [ˌænə'reksɪk] *adj* anorexique.

another [ə'nʌðə'] **1** *adj* [additional]: **~ apple** encore une pomme, une pomme de plus, une autre pomme; **(would you** **like) ~ drink?** encore un verre? ‖ [different]: **~ job** un autre travail. **2** *pron* [additional one] un autre (une autre), encore un (encore une); **one after ~** l'un après l'autre (l'une après l'autre). || [different one] un autre (une autre); **one ~** l'un l'autre (l'une l'autre).

answer ['ɑːnsər] **1** n [gen] réponse f; **in ~ to** en réponse à. || [to problem] solution f. **2** vt répondre à; **to ~ the door** aller ouvrir la porte; **to ~ the phone** répondre au téléphone. **3** vi [reply] répondre. ○ **answer back** vi répondre. ○ **answer for** vt fus être responsable de, répondre de.

answerable ['ɑːnsərəbl] adj: **~ to sb/for sthg** responsable devant qqn/de qqch.

answering machine ['ɑːnsərɪŋ-] n répondeur m.

ant [ænt] n fourmi f.

antagonism [æn'tæɡənɪzm] n antagonisme m, hostilité f.

antagonize, -ise [æn'tæɡənaɪz] vt éveiller l'hostilité de.

Antarctic [æn'tɑːktɪk] **1** n: **the ~** l'Antarctique m. **2** adj antarctique.

antelope ['æntɪləup] (pl inv OR -s) n antilope f.

antenatal [,æntɪ'neɪtl] adj prénatal(e).

antenatal clinic n service m de consultation prénatale.

antenna [æn'tenə] (pl sense 1 -nae [-niː], pl sense 2 -s) n [of insect] antenne f. || Am [for TV, radio] antenne f.

anthem ['ænθəm] n hymne m.

anthology [æn'θɒlədʒɪ] n anthologie f.

antibiotic [,æntɪbaɪ'ɒtɪk] n antibiotique m.

antibody ['æntɪ,bɒdɪ] n anticorps m.

anticipate [æn'tɪsɪpeɪt] vt [expect] s'attendre à, prévoir. || [request, movement] anticiper; [competitor] prendre de l'avance sur. || [look forward to] savourer à l'avance.

anticipation [æn,tɪsɪ'peɪʃn] n [expectation] attente f; [eagerness] impatience f; **in ~ of** en prévision de.

anticlimax [,æntɪ'klaɪmæks] n déception f.

anticlockwise [,æntɪ'klɒkwaɪz] adj & adv Br dans le sens inverse des aiguilles d'une montre.

antics ['æntɪks] npl [of children, animals] gambades fpl. || pej [of politicians etc] bouffonneries fpl.

anticyclone [,æntɪ'saɪkləun] n anticyclone m.

antidepressant [,æntɪdɪ'presnt] n antidépresseur m.

antidote ['æntɪdəut] n lit & fig: **~ (to)** antidote m (contre).

antifreeze ['æntɪfriːz] n antigel m.

antihistamine [,æntɪ'hɪstəmɪn] n antihistaminique m.

antiperspirant [,æntɪ'pɜːspərənt] n déodorant m.

antiquated ['æntɪkweɪtɪd] adj dépassé(e).

antique [æn'tiːk] **1** adj ancien(ienne). **2** n [object] objet m ancien; [piece of furniture] meuble m ancien.

antique shop n magasin m d'antiquités.

anti-Semitism [,æntɪ'semɪtɪzm] n antisémitisme m.

antiseptic [,æntɪ'septɪk] n désinfectant m.

antisocial [,æntɪ'səuʃl] adj [against society] antisocial(e). || [unsociable] peu sociable, sauvage.

antlers [,æntləz] npl bois mpl.

anus ['eɪnəs] n anus m.

anvil ['ænvɪl] n enclume f.

anxiety [æŋ'zaɪətɪ] n [worry] anxiété f. || [cause of worry] souci m.

anxious ['æŋkʃəs] adj [worried] anxieux(ieuse), très inquiet(iète); **to be ~ about** se faire du souci au sujet de. || [keen: **to be ~ to do sthg** tenir à faire qqch; **to be ~ that** tenir à ce que (+ subjunctive).

any ['enɪ] **1** adj (with negative) de, d'; I haven't got **~ money/tickets** je n'ai pas d'argent/de billets; **he never does ~ work** il ne travaille jamais. || [some - with sg noun] du, de l', de la; [- with pl noun] des; **have you got ~ money/milk/cousins?** est-ce que vous avez de l'argent/du lait/des cousins? || [no matter which] n'importe quel (n'importe quelle); **~ box will do** n'importe quelle boîte fera l'affaire; see also **case, day, moment, rate. 2** pron (with negative) en; I didn't buy **~** (of them) je n'en ai pas acheté; I didn't know **~ of the guests** je ne les connaissais aucun des invités. || [some] en; **do you have ~?** est-ce que vous en avez? || [no matter which one or ones] n'importe lequel (n'importe laquelle); **take ~ you like** prenez n'importe lequel/laquelle, prenez celui/celle que vous voulez. **3** adv (with negative): I can't stand it **~ longer** je ne peux plus le supporter. || [some, a little] un peu; **do you want ~ more potatoes?** voulez-vous encore des pommes de terre?; **is that ~ better/different?** est-ce que c'est mieux/différent comme ça?

anybody ['enɪ,bɒdɪ] = anyone.

anyhow ['enɪhaʊ] *adv* [in spite of that] quand même, néanmoins. || [carelessly] n'importe comment. || [in any case] de toute façon.

anyone ['enɪwʌn] *pron* (*in negative sentences*): **I didn't see ~** je n'ai vu personne. || (*in questions*) quelqu'un. || [any person] n'importe qui.

anyplace *Am* = **anywhere**.

anything ['enɪθɪŋ] *pron* (*in negative sentences*): **I didn't see ~** je n'ai rien vu. || (*in questions*) quelque chose. || [any object, event] n'importe quoi; **if ~ happens** ... s'il arrive quoi que ce soit ....

anyway ['enɪweɪ] *adv* [in any case] de toute façon.

anywhere ['enɪweər], **anyplace** *Am* ['enɪpleɪs] *adv* (*in negative sentences*): **I haven't seen him ~** je ne l'ai vu nulle part. || (*in questions*) quelque part. || [any place] n'importe où.

apart [ə'pɑːt] *adv* [separated] séparé(e), éloigné(e). || [to one side] à l'écart. || [aside]: **joking ~** sans plaisanter, plaisanterie à part. ◯ **apart from** *prep* [except for] à part, sauf. || [as well as] en plus de, outre.

apartheid [ə'pɑːtheɪt] *n* apartheid *m*.

apartment [ə'pɑːtmənt] *n* appartement *m*.

apartment building *n Am* immeuble *m* (*d'habitation*).

apathy ['æpəθɪ] *n* apathie *f*.

ape [eɪp] **1** *n* singe *m*. **2** *vt* singer.

aperitif [əperə'tiːf] *n* apéritif *m*.

aperture ['æpə,tjʊər] *n* [hole, opening] orifice *m*, ouverture *f*. || PHOT ouverture *f*.

apex ['eɪpeks] (*pl* **-es** OR **apices**) *n* sommet *m*.

apices ['eɪpɪsiːz] *pl* → **apex**.

apiece [ə'piːs] *adv* [for each person] chacun(e), par personne; [for each thing] chacun(e), pièce (*inv*).

apologetic [ə,pɒlə'dʒetɪk] *adj* [letter etc] d'excuse; **to be ~ about sthg** s'excuser de qqch.

apologize, **-ise** [ə'pɒlədʒaɪz] *vi* s'excuser; **to ~ to sb (for sthg)** faire des excuses à qqn (pour qqch).

apology [ə'pɒlədʒɪ] *n* excuses *fpl*.

apostle [ə'pɒsl] *n* RELIG apôtre *m*.

apostrophe [ə'pɒstrəfɪ] *n* apostrophe *f*.

appal *Br*, **appall** *Am* [ə'pɔːl] *vt* horrifier.

appalling [ə'pɔːlɪŋ] *adj* épouvantable.

apparatus [,æpə'reɪtəs] (*pl inv* OR **-es**)

n [device] appareil *m*, dispositif *m*. || (*U*) [in gym] agrès *mpl*.

apparel [ə'pærəl] *n Am* habillement *m*.

apparent [ə'pærənt] *adj* [evident] évident(e). || [seeming] apparent(e).

apparently [ə'pærəntlɪ] *adv* [it seems] à ce qu'il paraît. || [seemingly] apparemment, en apparence.

appeal [ə'piːl] **1** *vi* [request]: **to ~ (to sb for sthg)** lancer un appel (à qqn pour obtenir qqch). || [make a plea]: **to ~** faire appel à. || JUR: **to ~ (against)** faire appel (de). || [attract, interest]: **to ~ to sb** plaire à qqn. **2** *n* [request] appel *m*. || JUR appel *m*. || [charm, interest] intérêt *m*, attrait *m*.

appealing [ə'piːlɪŋ] *adj* [attractive] attirant(e), sympathique.

appear [ə'pɪər] *vi* [gen] apparaître; [book] sortir, paraître. || [seem] sembler, paraître; **to ~ to be/do** sembler être/faire; **it would ~ (that)** ... il semblerait que .... || [in play, film etc] jouer. || JUR comparaître.

appearance [ə'pɪərəns] *n* [gen] apparition *f*; **to make an ~** se montrer. || [look] apparence *f*, aspect *m*.

appease [ə'piːz] *vt* apaiser.

append [ə'pend] *vt* ajouter; [signature] apposer.

appendices [ə'pendɪsiːz] *pl* → **appendix**.

appendicitis [ə,pendɪ'saɪtɪs] *n* (*U*) appendicite *f*.

appendix [ə'pendɪks] (*pl* **-dixes** OR **-dices**) *n* appendice *m*; **to have one's ~ out** OR **removed** se faire opérer de l'appendicite.

appetite ['æpɪtaɪt] *n* [for food]: **~ (for)** appétit *m* (pour). || *fig* [enthusiasm]: **~ (for)** goût *m* (de OR pour).

appetizer, **-iser** ['æpɪtaɪzər] *n* [food] amuse-gueule *m inv*; [drink] apéritif *m*.

appetizing, **-ising** ['æpɪtaɪzɪŋ] *adj* [food] appétissant(e).

applaud [ə'plɔːd] **1** *vt* [clap] applaudir. || [approve] approuver, applaudir à. **2** *vi* applaudir.

applause [ə'plɔːz] *n* (*U*) applaudissements *mpl*.

apple ['æpl] *n* pomme *f*.

apple tree *n* pommier *m*.

appliance [ə'plaɪəns] *n* [device] appareil *m*.

applicable [ə'plɪkəbl] *adj*: **~ (to)** applicable (à).

applicant ['æplɪkənt] *n*: **~ (for)** [job]

candidat *m*, -e *f* (à); [state benefit] demandeur *m*, -euse *f* (de).

application [,æplɪ'keɪʃn] *n* [gen] application *f*. ‖ [for job etc]: ~ **(for)** demande *f* (de).

application form *n* formulaire *m* de demande.

apply [ə'plaɪ] **1** *vt* appliquer. **2** *vi* [for work, grant]: **to ~ (for)** faire une demande (de); **to ~ for a job** faire une demande d'emploi; **to ~ to sb (for sthg)** s'adresser à qqn (pour obtenir qqch). ‖ [be relevant]: **to ~ (to)** s'appliquer (à), concerner.

appoint [ə'pɔɪnt] *vt* [to job, position]: **to ~ sb (as sthg)** nommer qqn (qqch); **to ~ sb to sthg** nommer qqn à qqch. ‖ [time, place] fixer.

appointment [ə'pɔɪntmənt] *n* [to job, position] nomination *f*, désignation *f*. ‖ [job, position] poste *m*, emploi *m*. ‖ [arrangement to meet] rendez-vous *m*; **to make an ~** prendre un rendez-vous.

appraisal [ə'preɪzl] *n* évaluation *f*.

appreciable [ə'priːʃəbl] *adj* [difference] sensible; [amount] appréciable.

appreciate [ə'priːʃɪeɪt] **1** *vt* [value, like] apprécier, aimer. ‖ [recognize, understand] comprendre, se rendre compte de. ‖ [be grateful for] être reconnaissant(e) de. **2** *vi* FIN prendre de la valeur.

appreciation [ə,priːʃɪ'eɪʃn] *n* [liking] contentement *m*. ‖ [understanding] compréhension *f*. ‖ [gratitude] reconnaissance *f*.

apprehensive [,æprɪ'hensɪv] *adj* inquiet(iète); **to be ~ about sthg** appréhender OR craindre qqch.

apprentice [ə'prentɪs] *n* apprenti *m*, -e *f*.

apprenticeship [ə'prentɪsʃɪp] *n* apprentissage *m*.

approach [ə'prəʊtʃ] **1** *n* [gen] approche *f*. ‖ [method] démarche *f*, approche *f*. ‖ [to person]: **to make an ~ to sb** faire une proposition à qqn. **2** *vt* [come near to - place, person, thing] s'approcher de. ‖ [ask]: **to ~ sb about sthg** aborder qqch avec qqn; COMM entrer en contact avec qqn au sujet de qqch. ‖ [tackle - problem] aborder. **3** *vi* s'approcher.

approachable [ə'prəʊtʃəbl] *adj* accessible.

appropriate [ə'prəʊprɪət] *adj* [clothing] convenable; [action] approprié(e); [moment] opportun(e).

approval [ə'pruːvl] *n* approbation *f*; **on ~** COMM à condition, à l'essai.

approve [ə'pruːv] **1** *vi*: **to ~ (of sthg)** approuver (qqch). **2** *vt* [ratify] approuver, ratifier.

approx. [ə'prɒks] *(abbr of* **approximately)** approx., env.

approximate [ə'prɒksɪmət] *adj* approximatif(ive).

approximately [ə'prɒksɪmətlɪ] *adv* à peu près, environ.

apricot ['eɪprɪkɒt] *n* abricot *m*.

April ['eɪprəl] *n* avril *m*; *see also* **September.**

April Fools' Day *n* le premier avril.

apron ['eɪprən] *n* [clothing] tablier *m*.

apt [æpt] *adj* [pertinent] pertinent(e), approprié(e). ‖ [likely]: **to be ~ to do sthg** avoir tendance à faire qqch.

aptitude ['æptɪtjuːd] *n* aptitude *f*, disposition *f*; **to have an ~ for** avoir des dispositions pour.

aptly ['æptlɪ] *adv* avec justesse, à propos.

aqualung ['ækwəlʌŋ] *n* scaphandre *m* autonome.

aquarium [ə'kweərɪəm] *(pl* -riums OR -ria [-rɪə]*) n* aquarium *m*.

Aquarius [ə'kweərɪəs] *n* Verseau *m*.

aqueduct ['ækwɪdʌkt] *n* aqueduc *m*.

Arab ['ærəb] **1** *adj* arabe. **2** *n* [person] Arabe *mf*.

Arabian [ə'reɪbjən] *adj* d'Arabie, arabe.

Arabic ['ærəbɪk] **1** *adj* arabe. **2** *n* arabe *m*.

Arabic numeral *n* chiffre *m* arabe.

arable ['ærəbl] *adj* arable.

arbitrary ['ɑːbɪtrərɪ] *adj* arbitraire.

arbitration [,ɑːbɪ'treɪʃn] *n* arbitrage *m*; **to go to ~** recourir à l'arbitrage.

arcade [ɑː'keɪd] *n* [for shopping] galerie *f* marchande. ‖ [covered passage] arcades *fpl.*

arch [ɑːtʃ] **1** *adj* malicieux(ieuse), espiègle. **2** *n* ARCHIT arc *m*, voûte *f*. ‖ [of foot] voûte *f* plantaire, cambrure *f*. **3** *vt* cambrer, arquer.

archaeologist [,ɑːkɪ'ɒlədʒɪst] *n* archéologue *mf*.

archaeology [,ɑːkɪ'ɒlədʒɪ] *n* archéologie *f*.

archaic [ɑː'keɪɪk] *adj* archaïque.

archbishop [,ɑːtʃ'bɪʃəp] *n* archevêque *m*.

archenemy [,ɑːtʃ'enɪmɪ] *n* ennemi *m* numéro un.

archeology etc [ˌɑːkɪˈɒlədʒɪ] = archaeology etc.

archer [ˈɑːtʃər] n archer m.

archery [ˈɑːtʃərɪ] n tir m à l'arc.

archetypal [ˌɑːkɪˈtaɪpl] adj typique.

architect [ˈɑːkɪtekt] n lit & fig architecte m.

architecture [ˈɑːkɪtektʃər] n [gen & COMPUT] architecture f.

archives [ˈɑːkaɪvz] npl archives fpl.

archway [ˈɑːtʃweɪ] n passage m voûté.

Arctic [ˈɑːktɪk] 1 adj GEOGR arctique. || inf [very cold] glacial(e). 2 n: the ~ l'Arctique m.

ardent [ˈɑːdənt] adj fervent(e), passionné(e).

arduous [ˈɑːdjʊəs] adj ardu(e).

are [weak form ər, strong form ɑːr] → be.

area [ˈeərɪə] n [region] région f; **parking ~** aire de stationnement; **in the ~ of** [approximately] environ, à peu près. || [surface size] aire f, superficie f. || [of knowledge, interest etc] domaine m.

area code n indicatif m de zone.

aren't [ɑːnt] = are not.

Argentina [ˌɑːdʒənˈtiːnə] n Argentine f.

Argentine [ˈɑːdʒəntaɪn], **Argentinian** [ˌɑːdʒənˈtɪnɪən] 1 adj argentin(ine). 2 n Argentin m, -ine f.

argue [ˈɑːgjuː] 1 vi [quarrel]: **to ~ (with sb about sthg)** se disputer (avec qqn à propos de qqch). || [reason]: **to ~ (for/against)** argumenter (pour/contre). 2 vt débattre de, discuter de; **to ~ that** soutenir OR maintenir que.

argument [ˈɑːgjʊmənt] n [quarrel] dispute f; **to have an ~ (with sb)** se disputer (avec qqn). || [reason] argument m.

argumentative [ˌɑːgjʊˈmentətɪv] adj querelleur(euse), batailleur(euse).

arid [ˈærɪd] adj lit & fig aride.

Aries [ˈeəriːz] n Bélier m.

arise [əˈraɪz] (pt arose, pp arisen [əˈrɪzn]) vi [appear] surgir, survenir; **to ~ from** résulter de, provenir de; **if the need ~s** si le besoin se fait sentir.

aristocrat [Br ˈærɪstəkræt, Am əˈrɪstəkræt] n aristocrate mf.

arithmetic [əˈrɪθmətɪk] n arithmétique f.

ark [ɑːk] n arche f.

arm [ɑːm] 1 n [of person, chair] bras m; ~ **in ~** bras dessus bras dessous; **to twist sb's ~** fig forcer la main à qqn. || [of garment] manche f. 2 vt armer. ○ **arms** npl armes fpl; **to be up in ~s about sthg** s'élever contre qqch.

armaments [ˈɑːməmənts] npl [weapons] matériel m de guerre, armements mpl.

armchair [ˈɑːmtʃeər] n fauteuil m.

armed [ɑːmd] adj lit & fig: ~ **(with)** armé(e) (de).

armed forces npl forces fpl armées.

armhole [ˈɑːmhəʊl] n emmanchure f.

armour Br, **armor** Am [ˈɑːmər] n [for person] armure f.

armoured car [ˌɑːməd-] n voiture f blindée.

armpit [ˈɑːmpɪt] n aisselle f.

armrest [ˈɑːmrest] n accoudoir m.

arms control [ˈɑːmz-] n contrôle m des armements.

army [ˈɑːmɪ] n lit & fig armée f.

A road n Br route f nationale.

aroma [əˈrəʊmə] n arôme m.

arose [əˈrəʊz] pt → arise.

around [əˈraʊnd] 1 adv [about, round]: **to walk ~** marcher par-ci par-là, errer; **to lie ~** [clothes etc] traîner. || [on all sides] (tout) autour. || [near] dans les parages. || [in circular movement]: **to turn ~** se retourner. || phr: **he has been ~** inf il n'est pas né d'hier, il a de l'expérience. 2 prep [gen] autour de; **to walk ~ a garden/town** faire le tour d'un jardin/d'une ville; **all ~ the country** dans tout le pays. || [near]: ~ **here** par ici. || [approximately] environ, à peu près.

arouse [əˈraʊz] vt [excite - feeling] éveiller, susciter; [- person] exciter.

arrange [əˈreɪndʒ] vt [flowers, books, furniture] arranger, disposer. || [event, meeting etc] organiser, fixer; **to ~ to do sthg** convenir de faire qqch. || MUS arranger.

arrangement [əˈreɪndʒmənt] n [agreement] accord m, arrangement m; **to come to an ~** s'entendre, s'arranger. || [of furniture, books] arrangement m. || MUS arrangement m. ○ **arrangements** npl dispositions fpl, préparatifs mpl.

array [əˈreɪ] n [of objects] étalage m.

arrears [əˈrɪəz] npl [money owed] arriéré m; **to be in ~** [late] être en retard; [owing money] avoir des arriérés.

arrest [əˈrest] 1 n [by police] arrestation f; **under ~** en état d'arrestation. 2 vt [gen] arrêter.

arrival [əˈraɪvl] n [gen] arrivée f; **late ~** [of train etc] retard m. || [person - at airport, hotel] arrivant m, -e f; **new ~** [person] nouveau venu m, nouvelle venue f; [baby] nouveau-né m, nouveau-née f.

arrive [əˈraɪv] *vi* arriver; [baby] être né(e); **to ~ at** [conclusion, decision] arriver à.

arrogant [ˈærəgənt] *adj* arrogant(e).

arrow [ˈærəʊ] *n* flèche *f*.

arse *Br* [ɑːs], **ass** *Am* [æs] *n v inf* cul *m*.

arsenic [ˈɑːsnɪk] *n* arsenic *m*.

arson [ˈɑːsn] *n* incendie *m* criminel OR volontaire.

art [ɑːt] **1** *n* art *m*. **2** *comp* [exhibition] d'art; [college] des beaux-arts; **~ student** étudiant *m*, -e *f* d'une école des beaux-arts. ○ **arts** *npl* SCH & UNIV lettres *fpl*. ∥ [fine arts]: **the ~s** les arts *mpl*.

artefact [ˈɑːtɪfækt] = **artifact**.

artery [ˈɑːtərɪ] *n* artère *f*.

art gallery *n* [public] musée *m* d'art; [for selling paintings] galerie *f* d'art.

arthritis [ɑːˈθraɪtɪs] *n* arthrite *f*.

artichoke [ˈɑːtɪtʃəʊk] *n* artichaut *m*.

article [ˈɑːtɪkl] *n* article *m*.

articulate [ɑːˈtɪkjʊlət] *adj* [person] qui sait s'exprimer; [speech] net (nette), distinct(e).

articulated lorry [ɑːˈtɪkjʊleɪtɪd-] *n Br* semi-remorque *m*.

artifact [ˈɑːtɪfækt] *n* objet *m* fabriqué.

artificial [ˌɑːtɪˈfɪʃl] *adj* [not natural] artificiel(ielle). ∥ [insincere] affecté(e).

artillery [ɑːˈtɪlərɪ] *n* artillerie *f*.

artist [ˈɑːtɪst] *n* artiste *mf*.

artiste [ɑːˈtiːst] *n* artiste *mf*.

artistic [ɑːˈtɪstɪk] *adj* [person] artiste; [style etc] artistique.

as [*unstressed* əz, *stressed* æz] **1** *conj* [referring to time] comme, alors que; **she rang (just) ~ I was leaving** elle m'a téléphoné au moment même où OR juste comme je partais; **~ time goes by** à mesure que le temps passe, avec le temps. ∥ [referring to manner, way] comme; **do ~ I say** fais ce que je (te) dis. ∥ [introducing a statement] comme; **~ you know, ...** comme tu le sais, ... ∥ [because] comme. **2** *prep* [referring to function, characteristic] en, comme, en tant que; **I'm speaking ~ your friend** je te parle en ami; **she works ~ a nurse** elle est infirmière. ∥ [referring to attitude, reaction]: **it came ~ a shock** cela nous a fait un choc. **3** *adv* (*in comparisons*): **~ rich ~** aussi riche que; **~ red ~ a tomato** rouge comme une tomate; **he's ~ tall ~ I am** il est aussi grand que moi; **twice ~ big ~** deux fois plus gros que; **~ much/many ~** autant que; **much wine/many chocolates ~** autant de vin/de chocolats que. ○ **as for** *prep*

quant à. ○ **as from, as of** *prep* dès, à partir de. ○ **as if, as though** *conj* comme si; **it looks ~ though it will rain** on dirait qu'il va pleuvoir.

a.s.a.p. (*abbr of* **as soon as possible**) d'urgence, dans les meilleurs délais.

asbestos [æsˈbestəs] *n* asbeste *m*, amiante *m*.

ascend [əˈsend] *vt & vi* monter.

ascent [əˈsent] *n lit & fig* ascension *f*.

ascertain [ˌæsəˈteɪn] *vt* établir.

ascribe [əˈskraɪb] *vt*: **to ~ sthg to** attribuer qqch à; [blame] imputer qqch à.

ash [æʃ] *n* [from cigarette, fire] cendre *f*. ∥ [tree] frêne *m*.

ashamed [əˈʃeɪmd] *adj* honteux(euse), confus(e); **to be ~ of** avoir honte de; **to be ~ to do sthg** avoir honte de faire qqch.

ashore [əˈʃɔːr] *adv* à terre.

ashtray [ˈæʃtreɪ] *n* cendrier *m*.

Ash Wednesday *n* le mercredi des Cendres.

Asia [*Br* ˈeɪʃə, *Am* ˈeɪʒə] *n* Asie *f*.

Asian [*Br* ˈeɪʃn, *Am* ˈeɪʒn] **1** *adj* asiatique. **2** *n* [person] Asiatique *mf*.

aside [əˈsaɪd] **1** *adv* [to one side] de côté; **to move ~** s'écarter; **to take sb ~** prendre qqn à part. ∥ [apart] à part; **~ from** à l'exception de. **2** *n* [in play] aparté *m*. ∥ [remark] réflexion *f*, commentaire *m*.

ask [ɑːsk] **1** *vt* [gen] demander; **to ~ sb sthg** demander qqch à qqn; **he ~ed me my name** il m'a demandé mon nom; **to ~ sb for sthg** demander qqch à qqn; **to ~ sb to do sthg** demander à qqn de faire qqch. ∥ [put - question] poser. ∥ [invite] inviter. **2** *vi* demander. ○ **ask after** *vt fus* demander des nouvelles de. ○ **ask for** *vt fus* [person] demander à voir. ∥ [thing] demander.

askew [əˈskjuː] *adj* [not straight] de travers.

asking price [ˈɑːskɪŋ-] *n* prix *m* demandé.

asleep [əˈsliːp] *adj* endormi(e); **to fall ~** s'endormir.

asparagus [əˈspærəgəs] *n* (*U*) asperges *fpl*.

aspect [ˈæspekt] *n* [gen] aspect *m*. ∥ [of building] orientation *f*.

aspersions [əˈspɜːʃnz] *npl*: **to cast ~ on** jeter le discrédit sur.

asphalt [ˈæsfælt] *n* asphalte *m*.

asphyxiate [əsˈfɪksɪeɪt] *vt* asphyxier.

aspiration [ˌæspəˈreɪʃn] *n* aspiration *f*.

aspire [əˈspaɪər] *vi*: **to ~ to sthg/to do sthg** aspirer à qqch/à faire qqch.

at

aspirin ['æsprɪn] n aspirine f.

ass [æs] n [donkey] âne m. ‖ Br inf [idiot] imbécile mf, idiot m, -e f. ‖ Am v inf = arse.

assailant [ə'seɪlənt] n assaillant m, -e f.

assassin [ə'sæsɪn] n assassin m.

assassinate [ə'sæsɪneɪt] vt assassiner.

assassination [ə,sæsɪ'neɪʃn] n assassinat m.

assault [ə'sɔːlt] 1 n MIL: ~ (on) assaut m (de), attaque f (de). ‖ [physical attack]: ~ (on sb) agression f (contre qqn). 2 vt [attack - physically] agresser; [- sexually] violenter.

assemble [ə'sembl] 1 vt [gather] réunir. ‖ [fit together] assembler, monter. 2 vi se réunir, s'assembler.

assembly [ə'semblɪ] n [gen] assemblée f. ‖ [fitting together] assemblage m.

assembly line n chaîne f de montage.

assent [ə'sent] 1 n consentement m, assentiment m. 2 vi: to ~ (to) donner son consentement OR assentiment (à).

assert [ə'sɜːt] vt [fact, belief] affirmer, soutenir. ‖ [authority] imposer.

assertive [ə'sɜːtɪv] adj assuré(e).

assess [ə'ses] vt évaluer, estimer.

assessment [ə'sesmənt] n [opinion] opinion f. ‖ [calculation] évaluation f, estimation f.

assessor [ə'sesər] n [of tax] contrôleur m (des impôts).

asset ['æset] n avantage m, atout m. ○ **assets** npl COMM actif m.

assign [ə'saɪn] vt [allot]: to ~ sthg (to) assigner qqch (à). ‖ [give task to]: to ~ sb (to sthg/to do sthg) nommer qqn (à qqch/pour faire qqch).

assignment [ə'saɪnmənt] n [task] mission f, SCH devoir m. ‖ [act of assigning] attribution f.

assimilate [ə'sɪmɪleɪt] vt assimiler.

assist [ə'sɪst] vt: to ~ sb (with sthg/in doing sthg) aider qqn (dans qqch/à faire qqch); [professionally] assister qqn (dans qqch/pour faire qqch).

assistance [ə'sɪstəns] n aide f; to be of ~ (to) être utile (à).

assistant [ə'sɪstənt] 1 n assistant m, -e f; (shop) ~ vendeur m, -euse f. 2 comp: ~ editor rédacteur en chef adjoint m, rédactrice en chef adjointe f; ~ manager sous-directeur m, -trice f.

associate [adj & n ə'səʊʃɪət, vb ə'səʊʃɪeɪt] 1 adj associé(e). 2 n associé m, -e f. 3 vt: to ~ sb/sthg (with) associer qqn/qqch (à); to be ~d with être associé(e) à. 4 vi: to ~ with sb fréquenter qqn.

association [ə,səʊsɪ'eɪʃn] n association f; in ~ with avec la collaboration de.

assorted [ə'sɔːtɪd] adj varié(e).

assortment [ə'sɔːtmənt] n mélange m.

assume [ə'sjuːm] vt [suppose] supposer, présumer. ‖ [power, responsibility] assumer. ‖ [appearance, attitude] adopter.

assumed name [ə'sjuːmd-] n nom m d'emprunt.

assuming [ə'sjuːmɪŋ] conj en supposant que.

assumption [ə'sʌmpʃn] n [supposition] supposition f.

assurance [ə'ʃʊərəns] n [gen] assurance f. ‖ [promise] garantie f, promesse f.

assure [ə'ʃʊər] vt: to ~ sb (of) assurer qqn (de).

asterisk ['æstərɪsk] n astérisque m.

asthma ['æsmə] n asthme m.

astonish [ə'stɒnɪʃ] vt étonner.

astonishment [ə'stɒnɪʃmənt] n étonnement m.

astound [ə'staʊnd] vt stupéfier.

astray [ə'streɪ] adv: to go ~ [become lost] s'égarer; to lead sb ~ détourner qqn du droit chemin.

astride [ə'straɪd] prep à cheval OR califourchon sur.

astrology [ə'strɒlədʒɪ] n astrologie f.

astronaut ['æstrənɔːt] n astronaute mf.

astronomical [,æstrə'nɒmɪkl] adj astronomique.

astronomy [ə'strɒnəmɪ] n astronomie f.

astute [ə'stjuːt] adj malin(igne).

asylum [ə'saɪləm] n asile m.

at [unstressed ət, stressed æt] prep [indicating place, position] à; ~ my father's chez mon père; ~ home à la maison, chez soi; ~ school à l'école; ~ work au travail. ‖ [indicating direction] vers; to look ~ sb regarder qqn; to smile ~ sb sourire à qqn. ‖ [indicating a particular time] à; ~ midnight/noon/eleven o'clock à minuit/midi/onze heures; ~ night la nuit. ‖ [indicating age, speed, rate] à; ~ 52 (years of age) à 52 ans; ~ 100 mph à 160 km/h. ‖ [indicating price]: ~ £50 a pair 50 livres la paire. ‖ [indicating particular state, condition] en; ~ peace/war en paix/guerre; to be ~ lunch/dinner être en train de déjeuner/dîner. ‖ (after adjectives): amused/appalled/puzzled ~ sthg diverti/effaré/intrigué par qqch; delighted ~ sthg ravi de qqch; to be bad/good ~ sthg être mauvais/bon en qqch. ○ **at all** adv (with *negative*): **not ~ all** [when thanked] je vous en prie; [when answering a question] pas du tout; **she's not ~ all happy** elle n'est pas du tout contente. ‖ [in the slightest]: **anything ~ all** will do n'importe quoi fera l'affaire; **do you know her ~ all?** est-ce que vous la connaissez?

ate [*Br* et, *Am* eɪt] *pt* → eat.

atheist ['eɪθɪɪst] *n* athée *mf*.

Athens ['æθɪnz] *n* Athènes.

athlete ['æθliːt] *n* athlète *mf*.

athletic [æθ'letɪk] *adj* athlétique. ○ **athletics** *npl* athlétisme *m*.

Atlantic [ət'læntɪk] *n*: **the ~ (Ocean)** l'océan *m* Atlantique, l'Atlantique *m*.

atlas ['ætləs] *n* atlas *m*.

atmosphere ['ætmə,sfɪər] *n* atmosphère *f*.

atmospheric [,ætməs'ferɪk] *adj* [pressure, pollution etc] atmosphérique. ‖ [film, music etc] d'ambiance.

atom ['ætəm] *n* TECH atome *m*.

atom bomb *n* bombe *f* atomique.

atomic [ə'tɒmɪk] *adj* atomique.

atomic bomb = atom bomb.

atomizer, -iser ['ætəmaɪzər] *n* atomiseur *m*, vaporisateur *m*.

atone [ə'təʊn] *vi*: **to ~ for** racheter.

A to Z *n* plan *m* de ville.

atrocious [ə'trəʊʃəs] *adj* [very bad] atroce, affreux(euse).

atrocity [ə'trɒsətɪ] *n* [terrible act] atrocité *f*.

attach [ə'tætʃ] *vt* [gen]: **to ~ sthg (to)** attacher qqch (à). ‖ [letter etc] joindre.

attaché case [ə'tæʃeɪ-] *n* attaché-case *m*.

attached [ə'tætʃt] *adj* [fond]: **~ to** attaché(e) à.

attachment [ə'tætʃmənt] *n* [device] accessoire *m*. ‖ [fondness]: **~ (to)** attachement *m* (à).

attack [ə'tæk] **1** *n* [physical, verbal]: **~ (on)** attaque *f* (contre). ‖ [of illness] crise *f*. **2** *vt* [gen] attaquer. ‖ [job, problem] s'attaquer à. **3** *vi* attaquer.

attacker [ə'tækər] *n* [assailant] agresseur *m*. ‖ SPORT attaquant *m*, -e *f*.

attain [ə'teɪn] *vt* atteindre, parvenir à.

attempt [ə'tempt] **1** *n*: **~ (at)** tentative *f* (de); **~ on sb's life** tentative d'assassinat. **2** *vt* tenter, essayer; **to ~ to do sthg** essayer OR tenter de faire qqch.

attend [ə'tend] **1** *vt* [meeting, party] assister à. ‖ [school, church] aller à. **2** *vi* [be present] être présent(e). ‖ [pay attention]: **to ~ (to)** prêter attention (à). ○ **attend**

to *vt fus* [deal with] s'occuper de, régler. ‖ [look after - customer] s'occuper de; [- patient] soigner.

attendance [ə'tendəns] *n* [number present] assistance *f*, public *m*. ‖ [presence] présence *f*.

attendant [ə'tendənt] *n* [at museum, car park] gardien *m*, -ienne *f*; [at petrol station] pompiste *mf*.

attention [ə'tenʃn] **1** *n* (*U*) [gen] attention *f*; **to bring sthg to sb's ~, to draw sb's ~ to sthg** attirer l'attention de qqn sur qqch; **to attract** OR **catch sb's ~** attirer l'attention de qqn; **to pay ~ to** prêter attention à; **for the ~ of** COMM à l'attention de. ‖ [care] soins *mpl*, attentions *fpl*. **2** *excl* MIL garde-à-vous!

attentive [ə'tentɪv] *adj* attentif(ive).

attic ['ætɪk] *n* grenier *m*.

attitude ['ætɪtjuːd] *n* [gen]: **~ (to** OR **towards)** attitude *f* (envers). ‖ [posture] pose *f*.

attn. (*abbr of* **for the attention of**) à l'attention de.

attorney [ə'tɜːnɪ] *n Am* avocat *m*, -e *f*.

attorney general (*pl* **attorneys general**) *n* ministre *m* de la Justice.

attract [ə'trækt] *vt* attirer.

attraction [ə'trækʃn] *n* [gen] attraction *f*; **~ to sb** attirance *f* envers qqn. ‖ [of thing] attrait *m*.

attractive [ə'træktɪv] *adj* [person] attirant(e), séduisant(e); [thing, idea] attrayant(e), séduisant.

attribute [*vb* ə'trɪbjuːt, *n* 'ætrɪbjuːt] **1** *vt*: **to ~ sthg to** attribuer qqch à. **2** *n* attribut *m*.

auburn ['ɔːbən] *adj* auburn (*inv*).

auction ['ɔːkʃn] **1** *n* vente *f* aux enchères; **at** OR **by ~** aux enchères. **2** *vt* vendre aux enchères. ○ **auction off** *vt sep* vendre aux enchères.

auctioneer [,ɔːkʃə'nɪər] *n* commissaire-priseur *m*.

audacious [ɔː'deɪʃəs] *adj* audacieux(ieuse).

audible ['ɔːdəbl] *adj* audible.

audience ['ɔːdjəns] *n* [of play, film] public *m*, spectateurs *mpl*; [of TV programme] téléspectateurs *mpl*. ‖ [formal meeting] audience *f*.

audio-visual [,ɔːdɪəʊ-] *adj* audiovisuel(elle).

audit ['ɔːdɪt] **1** *n* audit *m*, vérification *f* des comptes. **2** *vt* vérifier, apurer.

audition [ɔː'dɪʃn] *n* THEATRE audition *f*; CINEMA bout *m* d'essai.

auditor [ˈɔːdɪtər] *n* auditeur *m*, -trice *f*.

auditorium [ˌɔːdɪˈtɔːrɪəm] (*pl* **-riums** OR **-ria** [-rɪə]) *n* salle *f*.

augur [ˈɔːgər] *vi*: **to ~ well/badly** être de bon/mauvais augure.

August [ˈɔːgəst] *n* août *m*; *see also* **September**.

Auld Lang Syne [ˌɔːldlæŋˈsaɪn] *n* chant traditionnel britannique correspondant à «*ce n'est qu'un au revoir, mes frères*».

aunt [ɑːnt] *n* tante *f*.

auntie, aunty [ˈɑːntɪ] *n inf* tata *f*, tantine *f*.

au pair [ˌəʊˈpeər] *n* jeune fille *f* au pair.

aura [ˈɔːrə] *n* atmosphère *f*.

aural [ˈɔːrəl] *adj* auditif(ive).

auspices [ˈɔːspɪsɪz] *npl*: **under the ~ of** sous les auspices de.

auspicious [ɔːˈspɪʃəs] *adj* prometteur(euse).

austere [ɒˈstɪər] *adj* austère.

austerity [ɒˈsterətɪ] *n* austérité *f*.

Australia [ɒˈstreɪljə] *n* Australie *f*.

Australian [ɒˈstreɪljən] **1** *adj* australien(ienne). **2** *n* Australien *m*, -ienne *f*.

Austria [ˈɒstrɪə] *n* Autriche *f*.

Austrian [ˈɒstrɪən] **1** *adj* autrichien(ienne). **2** *n* Autrichien *m*, -ienne *f*.

authentic [ɔːˈθentɪk] *adj* authentique.

author [ˈɔːθər] *n* auteur *m*.

authoritarian [ɔːˌθɒrɪˈteərɪən] *adj* autoritaire.

authoritative [ɔːˈθɒrɪtətɪv] *adj* [person, voice] autoritaire. || [study] qui fait autorité.

authority [ɔːˈθɒrətɪ] *n* [organization, power] autorité *f*; **to be in ~** être la responsable. || [permission] autorisation *f*. || [expert]: **~ (on sthg)** expert *m*, -e *f* (en qqch). ○ **authorities** *npl*: **the authorities** les autorités *fpl*.

authorize, -ise [ˈɔːθəraɪz] *vt*: **to ~ sb (to do sthg)** autoriser qqn (à faire qqch).

autistic [ɔːˈtɪstɪk] *adj* [child] autiste; [behaviour] autistique.

auto [ˈɔːtəʊ] (*pl* **-s**) *n Am* auto *f*, voiture *f*.

autobiography [ˌɔːtəbaɪˈɒgrəfɪ] *n* autobiographie *f*.

autograph [ˈɔːtəgrɑːf] **1** *n* autographe *m*. **2** *vt* signer.

automatic [ˌɔːtəˈmætɪk] **1** *adj* [gen] automatique. **2** *n* [car] voiture *f* à transmission automatique. || [gun] automatique *m*. || [washing machine] lave-linge *m* automatique.

automatically [ˌɔːtəˈmætɪklɪ] *adv* [gen] automatiquement.

automation [ˌɔːtəˈmeɪʃn] *n* automatisation *f*, automation *f*.

automobile [ˈɔːtəməbiːl] *n Am* automobile *f*.

autonomy [ɔːˈtɒnəmɪ] *n* autonomie *f*.

autopsy [ˈɔːtɒpsɪ] *n* autopsie *f*.

autumn [ˈɔːtəm] *n* automne *m*.

auxiliary [ɔːgˈzɪljərɪ] **1** *adj* auxiliaire. **2** *n* auxiliaire *mf*.

Av. (*abbr of* **avenue**) av.

available [əˈveɪləbl] *adj* disponible.

avalanche [ˈævəlɑːnʃ] *n lit* & *fig* avalanche *f*.

avarice [ˈævərɪs] *n* avarice *f*.

Ave. (*abbr of* **avenue**) av.

avenge [əˈvendʒ] *vt* venger.

avenue [ˈævənjuː] *n* avenue *f*.

average [ˈævərɪdʒ] **1** *adj* moyen(enne). **2** *n* moyenne *f*; **on ~** en moyenne. **3** *vt*: **the cars were averaging 90 mph** les voitures roulaient en moyenne à 150 km/h.

aversion [əˈvɜːʃn] *n*: **~ (to)** aversion *f* (pour).

avert [əˈvɜːt] *vt* [avoid] écarter; [accident] empêcher. || [eyes, glance] détourner.

avid [ˈævɪd] *adj*: **~ (for)** avide (de).

avocado [ˌævəˈkɑːdəʊ] (*pl* **-s** OR **-es**) *n*: **~ (pear)** avocat *m*.

avoid [əˈvɔɪd] *vt* éviter; **to ~ doing sthg** éviter de faire qqch.

avoidance [əˈvɔɪdəns] *n* → **tax avoidance**.

await [əˈweɪt] *vt* attendre.

awake [əˈweɪk] (*pt* **awoke** OR **awaked**, *pp* **awoken**) **1** *adj* [not sleeping] réveillé(e); **are you ~?** tu dors? **2** *vt* [wake up] réveiller. || *fig* [feeling] éveiller. **3** *vi* [wake up] se réveiller. || *fig* [feeling] s'éveiller.

awakening [əˈweɪknɪŋ] *n* [from sleep] réveil *m*. || *fig* [of feeling] éveil *m*.

award [əˈwɔːd] **1** *n* [prize] prix *m*. **2** *vt*: **to ~ sb sthg, to ~ sthg to sb** [prize] décerner qqch à qqn; [compensation, free kick] accorder qqch à qqn.

aware [əˈweər] *adj*: **to be ~ of sthg** se rendre compte de qqch, être conscient(e) de qqch; **to be ~ that** se rendre compte que, être conscient que.

awareness [əˈweənɪs] *n* (*U*) conscience *f*.

away [əˈweɪ] **1** *adv* [in opposite direction]: **to move** OR **walk ~ (from)** s'éloigner (de); **to look ~** détourner le regard; **to turn ~** se détourner. || [in distance]: **we**

live 4 miles ~ (**from here**) nous habitons à 6 kilomètres (d'ici). ‖ [in time]: **the elections are a month ~** les élections se dérouleront dans un mois. ‖ [absent] absent(e); **she's ~ on holiday** elle est partie en vacances. ‖ [in safe place]: **to put sthg ~ ranger** qqch. ‖ [so as to be gone or used up]: **to fade ~** disparaître; **to give sthg ~** donner qqch, faire don de qqch; **to take sthg ~** emporter qqch. ‖ [continuously]: **to be working ~** travailler sans arrêt. **2** *adj* SPORT [team, fans] de l'équipe des visiteurs; **~ game** match *m* à l'extérieur.

awe [ɔː] *n* respect *m* mêlé de crainte; **to be in ~ of sb** être impressionné par qqn.

awesome ['ɔːsəm] *adj* impressionnant(e).

awful ['ɔːful] *adj* [terrible] affreux (euse). ‖ *inf* [very great]: **an ~ lot (of)** énormément (de).

awfully ['ɔːflɪ] *adv inf* [bad, difficult] affreusement; [nice, good] extrêmement.

awkward ['ɔːkwəd] *adj* [clumsy] gauche, maladroit(e). ‖ [embarrassed] mal à l'aise, gêné(e). ‖ [difficult - person, problem, task] difficile. ‖ [inconvenient] incommode. ‖ [embarrassing] embarrassant(e), gênant(e).

awning ['ɔːnɪŋ] *n* [of tent] auvent *m*. ‖ [of shop] banne *f*.

awoke [ə'wəuk] *pt* → awake.

awoken [ə'wəukn] *pp* → awake.

axe *Br*, **ax** *Am* [æks] **1** *n* hache *f*. **2** *vt* [project] abandonner; [jobs] supprimer.

axes ['æksiːz] *pl* → axis.

axis ['æksɪs] (*pl* axes) *n* axe *m*.

axle ['æksl] *n* essieu *m*.

B

b (*pl* **b's** OR **bs**), **B** (*pl* **B's** OR **Bs**) [biː] *n* [letter] b *m inv*, B *m inv*. ○ **B** *n* MUS si *m*. ‖ SCH [mark] B *m inv*.

BA *n abbr of* **Bachelor of Arts**.

babble ['bæbl] **1** *n* [of voices] murmure *m*, rumeur *f*. **2** *vi* [person] babiller.

baboon [bə'buːn] *n* babouin *m*.

baby ['beɪbɪ] *n* [child] bébé *m*. ‖ *inf* [darling] chéri *m*, -e *f*.

baby buggy *n Br* [foldable pushchair] poussette *f*. ‖ *Am* = **baby carriage**.

baby carriage *n Am* landau *m*.

baby-sit *vi* faire du baby-sitting.

baby-sitter [-,sɪtə] *n* baby-sitter *mf*.

bachelor ['bætʃələ] *n* célibataire *m*.

Bachelor of Arts *n* licencié *m*, -e *f* en OR ès Lettres.

Bachelor of Science *n* licencié *m*, -e *f* en OR ès Sciences.

back [bæk] **1** *adv* [backwards] en arrière; **to step/move ~** reculer; **to push ~** repousser. ‖ [to former position or state]: **I'd like my money ~** [in shop] je voudrais me faire rembourser; **to go ~** retourner; **to come ~** revenir, rentrer; **to go ~ to sleep** se rendormir; **to be ~ (in fashion)** revenir à la mode. ‖ [in time]: **to think ~ (to)** se souvenir (de). ‖ [in return]: **to phone** OR **call ~** rappeler. **2** *n* [of person, animal] dos *m*; **behind sb's ~** *fig* derrière le dos de qqn. ‖ [of door, book, hand] dos *m*; [of head] derrière *m*; [of envelope, cheque] revers *m*; [of page] verso *m*; [of chair] dossier *m*. ‖ [of room, fridge] fond *m*; [of car] arrière *m*. ‖ SPORT arrière *m*. **3** *adj* (*in compounds*) [at the back] de derrière; [seat, wheel] arrière (*inv*); [page] dernier(ière). ‖ [overdue]: **~ rent** arriéré *m* de loyer. **4** *vt* [reverse] reculer. ‖ [support] appuyer, soutenir. ‖ [bet on] parier sur, miser sur. **5** *vi* reculer. ○ **back to back** *adv* [stand] dos à dos. ‖ [happen] l'un après l'autre. ○ **back to front** *adv* à l'envers. ○ **back down** *vi* céder. ○ **back out** *vi* [of promise etc] se dédire.

bail

○ **back up 1** *vt sep* [support - claim] appuyer, soutenir; [- person] épauler, soutenir. ‖ [reverse] reculer. ‖ COMPUT sauvegarder, faire une copie de sauvegarde de. **2** *vi* [reverse] reculer.

backache ['bækeɪk] *n*: **to have ~** avoir mal aux reins OR au dos.

backbone ['bækbəʊn] *n* épine *f* dorsale, colonne *f* vertébrale; *fig* [main support] pivot *m*.

backdate [,bæk'deɪt] *vt* antidater.

back door *n* porte *f* de derrière.

backdrop ['bækdrɒp] *n lit & fig* toile *f* de fond.

backfire [,bæk'faɪə*r*] *vi* AUT pétarader. ‖ [plan]: **to ~ (on sb)** se retourner (contre qqn).

backgammon ['bæk,gæmən] *n* backgammon *m*, ≃ jacquet *m*.

background ['bækgraʊnd] *n* [in picture, view] arrière-plan *m*; **in the ~** dans le fond, à l'arrière-plan; *fig* [main support] plan. ‖ [of event, situation] contexte *m*. ‖ [upbringing] milieu *m*.

backhand ['bækhænd] *n* revers *m*.

backing ['bækɪŋ] *n* [support] soutien *m*. ‖ [lining] doublage *m*.

backlash ['bæklæʃ] *n* contrecoup *m*, choc *m* en retour.

backlog ['bæklɒg] *n*: **~ (of work)** arriéré *m* de travail, travail *m* en retard.

back number *n* vieux numéro *m*.

backpack ['bækpæk] *n* sac *m* à dos.

back pay *n* rappel *m* de salaire.

back seat *n* [in car] siège *m* OR banquette *f* arrière; **to take a ~** *fig* jouer un rôle secondaire.

backside [,bæk'saɪd] *n inf* postérieur *m*, derrière *m*.

backstage [,bæk'steɪdʒ] *adv* dans les coulisses.

back street *n* petite rue *f*.

backstroke ['bækstrəʊk] *n* dos *m* crawlé.

backup ['bækʌp] **1** *adj* [plan, team] de secours, de remplacement. **2** *n* [gen] aide *f*, soutien *m*. ‖ COMPUT (copie *f* de) sauvegarde *f*.

backward ['bækwəd] **1** *adj* [movement, look] en arrière. ‖ [country] arriéré(e); [person] arriéré, attardé(e). **2** *adv Am* = **backwards.**

backwards ['bækwədz], **backward** *Am adv* [move, go] en arrière, à reculons; [read list] à rebours, à l'envers; **~ and forwards** [movement] de va-et-vient,

d'avant en arrière et d'arrière en avant; **to walk ~ and forwards** aller et venir.

backwater ['bæk,wɔːtə*r*] *n fig* désert *m*.

backyard [,bæk'jɑːd] *n Br* [yard] arrière-cour *f*. ‖ *Am* [garden] jardin *m* de derrière.

bacon ['beɪkən] *n* bacon *m*.

bacteria [bæk'tɪərɪə] *npl* bactéries *fpl*.

bad [bæd] (*compar* **worse**, *superl* **worst**) **1** *adj* [not good] mauvais(e); **to be ~ at sthg** être mauvais en qqch; **too ~!** dommage!; **not ~** pas mal. ‖ [unhealthy] malade; **smoking is ~ for you** fumer est mauvais pour la santé; **I'm feeling ~** je ne suis pas dans mon assiette. ‖ [serious]: **a ~ cold** un gros rhume. ‖ [rotten] pourri(e), gâté(e); **to go ~** se gâter, s'avarier. ‖ [guilty]: **to feel ~ about sthg** se sentir coupable de qqch. ‖ [naughty] méchant(e). **2** *adv Am* = **badly.**

badge [bædʒ] *n* [metal, plastic] badge *m*. ‖ [sewn-on] écusson *m*.

badger ['bædʒə*r*] **1** *n* blaireau *m*. **2** *vt*: **to ~ sb (to do sthg)** harceler qqn (pour qu'il fasse qqch).

badly ['bædlɪ] (*compar* **worse**, *superl* **worst**) *adv* [not well] mal. ‖ [seriously - wounded] grièvement; [- affected] gravement, sérieusement; **to be ~ in need of sthg** avoir vraiment OR absolument besoin de qqch.

badly-off *adj* [poor] pauvre, dans le besoin.

bad-mannered [-'mænəd] *adj* [child] mal élevé(e); [shop assistant] impoli(e).

badminton ['bædmɪntən] *n* badminton *m*.

bad-tempered [-'tempəd] *adj* [by nature] qui a un mauvais caractère. ‖ [in a bad mood] de mauvaise humeur.

baffle ['bæfl] *vt* déconcerter, confondre.

bag [bæg] *n* [gen] sac *m*; **to pack one's ~s** *fig* plier bagage. ‖ [handbag] sac *m* à main. ○ **bags** *npl* [under eyes] poches *fpl*. ‖ *inf* [lots]: **~s of** plein OR beaucoup de.

bagel ['beɪgəl] *n petit pain en couronne.*

baggage ['bægɪdʒ] *n* (U) bagages *mpl*.

baggage reclaim *n* retrait *m* des bagages.

baggy ['bægɪ] *adj* ample.

bagpipes ['bægpaɪps] *npl* cornemuse *f*.

Bahamas [bə'hɑːməz] *npl*: **the ~** les Bahamas *fpl*.

bail [beɪl] *n* (U) caution *f*; **on ~** sous caution. ○ **bail out 1** *vt sep* [pay bail for] se porter garant de. ‖ *fig* [rescue] tirer d'affaire. **2** *vi* [from plane] sauter (en parachute).

bailiff ['beɪlɪf] *n* huissier *m*.

bait [beɪt] **1** *n* appât *m*. **2** *vt* [put bait on] appâter. ‖ [tease] tourmenter.

bake [beɪk] **1** *vt* CULIN faire cuire au four. ‖ [clay, bricks] cuire. **2** *vi* [food] cuire au four.

baked beans [beɪkt-] *npl* haricots *mpl* blancs à la tomate.

baked potato [beɪkt-] *n* pomme *f* de terre in robe de chambre.

baker ['beɪkər] *n* boulanger *m*, -ère *f*; **~'s (shop)** boulangerie *f*.

bakery ['beɪkərɪ] *n* boulangerie *f*.

baking ['beɪkɪŋ] *n* cuisson *f*.

balance ['bæləns] **1** *n* [equilibrium] équilibre *m*; **to keep/lose one's ~** garder/perdre l'équilibre; **off-** déséquilibré(e). ‖ *fig* [counterweight] contrepoids *m*; [of evidence] poids *m*, force *f*. ‖ FIN solde *m*. **2** *vt* [keep in balance] maintenir en équilibre. ‖ [compare]: **to ~ sthg against sthg** mettre qqch et qqch en balance. ‖ [in accounting]: **to ~ a budget** équilibrer un budget; **to ~ the books** clôturer les comptes, dresser le bilan. **3** *vi* [maintain equilibrium] se tenir en équilibre. ‖ [budget, accounts] s'équilibrer. ○ **on balance** *adv* tout bien considéré.

balance of payments *n* balance *f* des paiements.

balance of trade *n* balance *f* commerciale.

balance sheet *n* bilan *m*.

balcony ['bælkənɪ] *n* balcon *m*.

bald [bɔːld] *adj* [head, man] chauve. ‖ [tyre] lisse. ‖ *fig* [blunt] direct(e).

bale [beɪl] *n* balle *f*. ○ **bale out** *Br* **1** *vt sep* [boat] écoper, vider. **2** *vi* [from plane] sauter en parachute.

Balearic Islands [,bælɪ'ærɪk-], **Balearics** [,bælɪ'ærɪks] *npl*: **the ~** les Baléares *fpl*.

balk [bɔːk] *vi*: **to ~ (at)** hésiter OR reculer (devant).

Balkans ['bɔːlkənz], **Balkan States** ['bɔːlkən-] *npl*: **the ~** les Balkans *mpl*, les États *mpl* balkaniques.

ball [bɔːl] *n* [round shape] boule *f*; [in game] balle *f*; [football] ballon *m*; **to be on the ~** *fig* connaître son affaire, s'y connaître. ‖ [of foot] plante *f*. ‖ [dance] bal *m*. ○ **balls** *v inf* **1** *npl* [testicles] couilles *fpl*. **2** *n* (*U*) [nonsense] conneries *fpl*.

ballad ['bæləd] *n* ballade *f*.

ballast ['bæləst] *n* lest *m*.

ball bearing *n* roulement *m* à billes.

ball boy *n* ramasseur *m* de balles.

ballerina [,bælə'riːnə] *n* ballerine *f*.

ballet ['bæleɪ] *n* (*U*) [art of dance] danse *f*. ‖ [work] ballet *m*.

ballet dancer *n* danseur *m*, -euse *f* de ballet.

ball game *n Am* [baseball match] match *m* de base-ball. ‖ *inf* [situation]: **it's a whole new ~** c'est une autre paire de manches.

balloon [bə'luːn] *n* [gen] ballon *m*. ‖ [in cartoon] bulle *f*.

ballot ['bælət] **1** *n* [voting paper] bulletin *m* de vote. ‖ [voting process] scrutin *m*. **2** *vt* appeler à voter.

ballot box *n* [container] urne *f*. ‖ [voting process] scrutin *m*.

ballot paper *n* bulletin *m* de vote.

ball park *n Am* terrain *m* de base-ball.

ballpoint (pen) ['bɔːlpɔɪnt-] *n* stylo *m* à bille.

ballroom ['bɔːlrum] *n* salle *f* de bal.

ballroom dancing *n* (*U*) danse *f* de salon.

balmy ['bɑːmɪ] *adj* doux (douce).

balsa(wood) ['bɒlsə(wud)] *n* balsa *m*.

Baltic ['bɔːltɪk] **1** *adj* [port, coast] de la Baltique. **2** *n*: **the ~ (Sea)** la Baltique.

Baltic Republic *n*: **the ~s** les républiques *fpl* baltes.

bamboo [bæm'buː] *n* bambou *m*.

bamboozle [bæm'buːzl] *vt inf* embobiner.

ban [bæn] **1** *n* interdiction *f*. **2** *vt* interdire; **to ~ sb from doing sthg** interdire à qqn de faire qqch.

banal [bə'nɑːl] *adj pej* banal(e), ordinaire.

banana [bə'nɑːnə] *n* banane *f*.

band [bænd] *n* [MUS - rock] groupe *m*; [- military] fanfare *f*; [- jazz] orchestre *m*. ‖ [group, strip] bande *f*. ‖ [stripe] rayure *f*. ‖ [range] tranche *f*. ○ **band together** *vi* s'unir.

bandage ['bændɪdʒ] **1** *n* bandage *m*, bande *f*. **2** *vt* mettre un pansement OR un bandage sur.

Band-Aid® *n* pansement *m* adhésif.

b and b, B and B *n abbr of* bed and breakfast.

bandit ['bændɪt] *n* bandit *m*.

bandstand ['bændstænd] *n* kiosque *m* à musique.

bandwagon ['bændwægən] *n*: **to jump on the ~** suivre le mouvement.

bandy ['bændɪ] *adj* qui a les jambes arquées. ○ **bandy about**, **bandy around** *vt sep* répandre, faire circuler.

bandy-legged [-,legd] *adj* = **bandy**.

bang [bæŋ] **1** *adv* [exactly]: ~ **in the middle** en plein milieu; **to be ~ on time** être pile à l'heure. **2** *n* [blow] coup *m* violent. ‖ [of gun etc] détonation *f*; [of door] claquement *m*. **3** *vt* frapper violemment; [door] claquer; **to ~ one's head/knee** se cogner la tête/le genou. **4** *vi* [knock]: **to ~ on** frapper à. ‖ [make a loud noise - gun etc] détoner; [- door] claquer. ‖ [crash]: **to ~ into** se cogner contre. **5** *excl* boum! ○ **bangs** *npl Am* frange *f*.

bangle ['bæŋgl] *n* bracelet *m*.

banish ['bænɪʃ] *vt* bannir.

banister ['bænɪstər] *n*, **banisters** ['bænɪstəz] *npl* rampe *f*.

bank [bæŋk] **1** *n* FIN & *fig* banque *f*. ‖ [of river, lake] rive *f*, bord *m*. ‖ [of earth] talus *m*. **2** *vt* FIN mettre OR déposer à la banque. **3** *vi* FIN: **to ~ with** avoir un compte à. ‖ [plane] tourner. ○ **bank on** *vt fus* compter sur.

bank account *n* compte *m* en banque.

bank balance *n* solde *m* bancaire.

bank charges *npl* frais *mpl* bancaires.

bank draft *n* traite *f* bancaire.

banker ['bæŋkər] *n* banquier *m*.

bank holiday *n* Br jour *m* férié.

bank manager *n* directeur *m* de banque.

bank note *n* billet *m* de banque.

bank rate *n* taux *m* d'escompte.

bankrupt ['bæŋkrʌpt] *adj* failli(e); **to go ~** faire faillite.

bankruptcy ['bæŋkrəptsɪ] *n* [gen] faillite *f*.

bank statement *n* relevé *m* de compte.

banner ['bænər] *n* banderole *f*.

bannister(s) ['bænɪstə(z)] = **banister(s)**.

banquet ['bæŋkwɪt] *n* banquet *m*.

banter ['bæntər] *n* (*U*) plaisanterie *f*, badinage *m*.

baptism ['bæptɪzm] *n* baptême *m*.

Baptist ['bæptɪst] *n* baptiste *mf*.

baptize, **-ise** [Br bæp'taɪz, Am 'bæptaɪz] *vt* baptiser.

bar [bɑːr] **1** *n* [piece - of gold] lingot *m*; [- of chocolate] tablette *f*; **a ~ of soap** une savonnette. ‖ [length of wood, metal] barre *f*; **to be behind ~s** être derrière les barreaux OR sous les verrous. ‖ *fig* [obstacle] obstacle *m*. ‖ [pub] bar *m*. ‖ [counter

of pub] comptoir *m*, zinc *m*. ‖ MUS mesure *f*. **2** *vt* [door, road] barrer; [window] mettre des barreaux à; **to ~ sb's way** barrer la route OR le passage à qqn. ‖ [ban] interdire, défendre; **to ~ sb (from)** interdire à qqn (de). **3** *prep* sauf, excepté; **~ none** sans exception. ○ **Bar** *n* JUR: **the Bar** Br le barreau; Am les avocats *mpl*.

barbaric [bɑːˈbærɪk] *adj* barbare.

barbecue ['bɑːbɪkjuː] *n* barbecue *m*.

barbed wire [bɑːbd-] *n* (*U*) fil *m* de fer barbelé.

barber ['bɑːbər] *n* coiffeur *m* (pour hommes); **~'s (shop)** salon *m* de coiffure (pour hommes); **to go to the ~'s** aller chez le coiffeur.

barbiturate [bɑːˈbɪtjʊrət] *n* barbiturique *m*.

bar code *n* code *m* (à) barres.

bare [beər] **1** *adj* [feet, arms etc] nu(e); [trees, hills etc] dénudé(e). ‖ [absolute, minimum]: **the ~ facts** les simples faits; **the ~ minimum** le strict minimum. ‖ [empty] vide. **2** *vt* découvrir; **to ~ one's teeth** montrer les dents.

bareback ['beəbæk] *adv* à cru, à nu.

barefoot(ed) [,beə'fʊt(ɪd)] **1** *adj* aux pieds nus. **2** *adv* nu-pieds, pieds nus.

barely ['beəlɪ] *adv* [scarcely] à peine, tout juste.

bargain ['bɑːgɪn] **1** *n* [agreement] marché *m*; **into the ~** en plus, par-dessus le marché. ‖ [good buy] affaire *f*, occasion *f*. **2** *vi* négocier; **to ~ with sb for sthg** négocier qqch avec qqn. ○ **bargain for**, **bargain on** *vt fus* compter sur, prévoir.

barge [bɑːdʒ] **1** *n* péniche *f*. **2** *vi inf*: **to ~ past sb** bousculer qqn. ○ **barge in** *vi inf*: **to ~ in (on)** interrompre.

baritone ['bærɪtəʊn] *n* baryton *m*.

bark [bɑːk] **1** *n* [of dog] aboiement *m*. ‖ [on tree] écorce *f*. **2** *vi* [dog]: **to ~ (at)** aboyer (après).

barley ['bɑːlɪ] *n* orge *f*.

barmaid ['bɑːmeɪd] *n* barmaid *f*, serveuse *f* de bar.

barman ['bɑːmən] (*pl* **-men** [-mən]) *n* barman *m*, serveur *m* de bar.

barn [bɑːn] *n* grange *f*.

barometer [bəˈrɒmɪtər] *n* lit & *fig* baromètre *m*.

baron ['bærən] *n* baron *m*.

baroness ['bærənɪs] *n* baronne *f*.

barrack ['bærək] *vt* Br huer, conspuer. ○ **barracks** *npl* caserne *f*.

barrage ['bærɑːʒ] *n* [of firing] barrage

m. || [of questions etc] avalanche *f*, déluge *m*.

barrel ['bærəl] *n* [for beer, wine] tonneau *m*, fût *m*. || [for oil] baril *m*. || [of gun] canon *m*.

barren ['bærən] *adj* stérile.

barricade [,bærɪ'keɪd] *n* barricade *f*.

barrier ['bærɪər] *n lit & fig* barrière *f*.

barring ['bɑːrɪŋ] *prep* sauf.

barrister ['bærɪstər] *n Br* avocat *m*, -e *f*.

barrow ['bærəʊ] *n* brouette *f*.

bartender ['bɑːtendər] *n Am* barman *m*.

barter ['bɑːtər] **1** *n* troc *m*. **2** *vt*: to ~ sthg (for) troquer OR échanger qqch (contre). **3** *vi* faire du troc.

base [beɪs] **1** *n* base *f*. **2** *vt* baser; to ~ sthg on OR upon baser OR fonder qqch sur. **3** *adj* indigne, ignoble.

baseball ['beɪsbɔːl] *n* base-ball *m*.

baseball cap *n* casquette *f* de base-ball.

basement ['beɪsmənt] *n* sous-sol *m*.

base rate *n* taux *m* de base.

bases ['beɪsiːz] *pl* → basis.

bash [bæʃ] *inf* **1** *n* [painful blow] coup *m*. || [attempt]: to have a ~ tenter le coup. **2** *vt* [hit - gen] frapper, cogner; [- car] percuter.

bashful ['bæʃfʊl] *adj* timide.

basic ['beɪsɪk] *adj* fondamental(e); [vocabulary, salary] de base. ○ **basics** *npl* [rudiments] éléments *mpl*, bases *fpl*.

BASIC ['beɪsɪk] (*abbr of* Beginner's All-purpose Symbolic Instruction Code) *n* basic *m*.

basically ['beɪsɪklɪ] *adv* [essentially] au fond, fondamentalement. || [really] en fait.

basil ['bæzl] *n* basilic *m*.

basin ['beɪsn] *n Br* [bowl - for cooking] terrine *f*; [- for washing] cuvette *f*. || [in bathroom] lavabo *m*. || GEOGR bassin *m*.

basis ['beɪsɪs] (*pl* -ses) *n* base *f*; on the ~ of sur la base de; on a regular ~ de façon régulière.

bask [bɑːsk] *vi*: to ~ in the sun se chauffer au soleil.

basket ['bɑːskɪt] *n Br* corbeille *f*; [with handle] panier *m*.

basketball ['bɑːskɪtbɔːl] *n* basket-ball *m*, basket *m*.

bass [beɪs] **1** *adj* bas (basse). **2** *n* [singer] basse *f*. || [double bass] contrebasse *f*. || = bass guitar.

bass drum [beɪs-] *n* grosse caisse *f*.

bass guitar [beɪs-] *n* basse *f*.

bassoon [bə'suːn] *n* basson *m*.

bastard ['bɑːstəd] *n* [illegitimate child] bâtard *m*, -e *f*, enfant naturel *m*, enfant naturelle *f*. || *v inf* [unpleasant person] salaud *m*, saligaud *m*.

bat [bæt] *n* [animal] chauve-souris *f*. || [for cricket, baseball] batte *f*; [for table-tennis] raquette *f*. || *phr*: to do sthg off one's own ~ faire qqch de son propre chef.

batch [bætʃ] *n* [of papers] tas *m*, liasse *f*; [of letters, applicants] série *f*. || [of products] lot *m*.

bath [bɑːθ] **1** *n* [bathtub] baignoire *f*. || [act of washing] bain *m*; to have OR take a bath prendre un bain. **2** *vt* baigner, donner un bain à. ○ **baths** *npl Br* piscine *f*.

bathe [beɪð] **1** *vt* [wound] laver. || [subj: light, sunshine]: to be ~d in OR with être baigné(e) de. **2** *vi* [swim] se baigner. || *Am* [take a bath] prendre un bain.

bathing ['beɪðɪŋ] *n* (*U*) baignade *f*.

bathing cap *n* bonnet *m* de bain.

bathing costume, bathing suit *n* maillot *m* de bain.

bathrobe ['bɑːθrəʊb] *n* [made of towelling] sortie *f* de bain; [dressing gown] peignoir *m*.

bathroom ['bɑːθrʊm] *n Br* [room with bath] salle *f* de bains. || *Am* [toilet] toilettes *fpl*.

bath towel *n* serviette *f* de bain.

bathtub ['bɑːθtʌb] *n* baignoire *f*.

baton ['bætən] *n* [of conductor] baguette *f*. || [in relay race] témoin *m*.

batsman ['bætsmən] (*pl* -men [-mən]) *n* batteur *m*.

battalion [bə'tæljən] *n* bataillon *m*.

batten ['bætn] *n* planche *f*, latte *f*.

batter ['bætər] **1** *n* (*U*) pâte *f*. **2** *vt* battre.

battered ['bætəd] *adj* [child, woman] battu(e). || [car, hat] cabossé(e).

battery ['bætərɪ] *n* batterie *f*; [of calculator, toy] pile *f*.

battle ['bætl] **1** *n* [in war] bataille *f*. || [struggle]: ~ (for/against/with) lutte *f* (pour/contre/avec), combat *m* (pour/contre/avec). **2** *vi*: to ~ (for/against/with) se battre (pour/contre/avec), lutter (pour/contre/avec).

battlefield ['bætlfiːld], **battleground** ['bætlgraʊnd] *n* MIL champ *m* de bataille.

battlements ['bætlmənts] *npl* remparts *mpl*.

battleship ['bætlʃɪp] *n* cuirassé *m*.

bauble ['bɔːbl] *n* babiole *f*, colifichet *m*.

baulk [bɔːk] = balk.

beating

bawdy ['bɔːdɪ] *adj* grivois(e), salé(e).

bawl [bɔːl] *vt & vi* brailler.

bay [beɪ] *n* GEOGR baie *f*. || [for loading] aire *f* (de chargement). || [for parking] place *f* (de stationnement). || *phr*: **to keep sb/sthg at ~** tenir qqn/qqch à distance, tenir qqn/qqch en échec.

bay leaf *n* feuille *f* de laurier.

bay window *n* fenêtre *f* en saillie.

bazaar [bə'zɑːr] *n* [market] bazar *m*.

B & B *n abbr of* **bed and breakfast**.

BBC (*abbr of* **British Broadcasting Corporation**) *n office national britannique de radiodiffusion*.

BC (*abbr of* **before Christ**) av. J.-C.

be [biː] (*pt* **was** OR **were**, *pp* **been**) 1 *aux vb* (*in combination with pp: to form cont tense*): **what is he doing?** qu'est-ce qu'il fait?; **it's snowing** il neige. || (*in combination with pp: to form passive*) être; **to ~ loved** être aimé(e); **there was no one to ~ seen** il n'y avait personne. || (*in question tags*): **she's pretty, isn't she?** elle est jolie, n'est-ce pas?; **the meal was delicious, wasn't it?** le repas était délicieux, non? OR vous n'avez pas trouvé? || (*followed by* "to" + *infin*): **the firm is to ~ sold** on va vendre la société; **you're not to tell anyone** ne le dis à personne. 2 *copulative vb* (*with adj, n*) être; **to ~ a doctor/lawyer/plumber** être médecin/avocat/plombier; **she's intelligent/attractive** elle est intelligente/jolie; **I'm hot/cold** j'ai chaud/froid; **1 and 1 are 2** 1 et 1 font 2. || [referring to health] aller, se porter; **to ~ seriously ill** être gravement malade; **she's better now** elle va mieux maintenant; **how are you?** comment allez-vous? || [referring to age]: **how old are you?** quel âge avez-vous?; **I'm 20 (years old)** j'ai 20 ans. || [cost] coûter, faire; **how much was it?** combien cela a-t-il coûté?, combien ça faisait? 3 *vi* [exist] être, exister; **~ that as it may** quoi qu'il en soit. || [referring to place] être; **Toulouse is in France** Toulouse se trouve OR est en France; **he will ~ here tomorrow** il sera là demain. || [referring to movement] aller, être; **I've been to the cinema** j'ai été or je suis allé au cinéma. 4 *v impers* [referring to time, dates, distance] être; **it's two o'clock** il est deux heures; **it's 3 km to the next town** la ville voisine est à 3 km. || [referring to the weather] faire; **it's hot/cold** il fait chaud/froid. || [for emphasis]: **it's me/**Paul/the milkman c'est moi/Paul/le laitier.

beach [biːtʃ] 1 *n* plage *f*. 2 *vt* échouer.

beacon ['biːkən] *n* [warning fire] feu *m*, fanal *m*. || [lighthouse] phare *m*. || [radio beacon] radiophare *m*.

bead [biːd] *n* [of wood, glass] perle *f*. || [of sweat] goutte *f*.

beagle ['biːgl] *n* beagle *m*.

beak [biːk] *n* bec *m*.

beaker ['biːkər] *n* gobelet *m*.

beam [biːm] 1 *n* [of wood, concrete] poutre *f*. || [of light] rayon *m*. 2 *vt* [signal, news] transmettre. 3 *vi* [smile] faire un sourire radieux.

bean [biːn] *n* [gen] haricot *m*; [of coffee] grain *m*; **to be full of ~s** *inf* péter le feu; **to spill the ~s** *inf* manger le morceau.

beanbag ['biːnbæg] *n* [chair] sacco *m*.

beanshoot ['biːnʃuːt], **beansprout** ['biːnspraut] *n* germe *m* OR pousse *f* de soja.

bear [beər] (*pt* **bore**, *pp* **borne**) 1 *n* [animal] ours *m*. 2 *vt* [carry] porter. || [support, tolerate] supporter. || [feeling]: **to ~ sb a grudge** garder rancune à qqn. 3 *vi*: **to ~ left/right** se diriger vers la gauche/la droite; **to bring pressure/influence to ~ on sb** exercer une pression/une influence sur qqn. ○ **bear down** *vi*: **to ~ down on sb/sthg** s'approcher de qqn/qqch de façon menaçante. ○ **bear out** *vt sep* confirmer, corroborer. ○ **bear up** *vi* tenir le coup. ○ **bear with** *vt fus* être patient(e) avec.

beard [bɪəd] *n* barbe *f*.

bearer ['beərər] *n* [gen] porteur *m*, -euse *f*. || [of passport] titulaire *mf*.

bearing ['beərɪŋ] *n* [connection]: **~ (on)** rapport *m* (avec). || [deportment] allure *f*, maintien *m*. || TECH [for shaft] palier *m*. || [on compass] orientation *f*; **to get one's ~s** s'orienter, se repérer.

beast [biːst] *n* [animal] bête *f*. || *inf pej* [person] brute *f*.

beat [biːt] (*pt* **beat**, *pp* **beaten** ['biːtn]) 1 *n* [of heart, drum, wings] battement *m*. || MUS [rhythm] mesure *f*, temps *m*. || [of policeman] ronde *f*. 2 *vt* [gen] battre; **it ~s me** *inf* ça me dépasse. || [be better than] être bien mieux que, valoir mieux que. || *phr*: **~ it!** *inf* décampe!, fiche le camp! 3 *vi* battre. ○ **beat off** *vt sep* [resist] repousser. ○ **beat up** *vt sep inf* tabasser.

beating ['biːtɪŋ] *n* [blows] raclée *f*, rossée *f*. || [defeat] défaite *f*.

beautiful ['bju:tɪfʊl] *adj* [gen] beau (belle). || *inf* [very good] joli(e).

beautifully ['bju:təflɪ] *adv* [attractively - dressed] élégamment; [- decorated] avec goût. || *inf* [very well] parfaitement, à la perfection.

beauty ['bju:tɪ] *n* [gen] beauté *f*.

beauty parlour *n* institut *m* de beauté.

beauty salon = beauty parlour.

beauty spot *n* [picturesque place] site *m* pittoresque. || [on skin] grain *m* de beauté.

beaver ['bi:vər] *n* castor *m*.

became [bɪ'keɪm] *pt* → become.

because [bɪ'kɒz] *conj* parce que. ○ **because of** *prep* à cause de.

beck [bek] *n*: **to be at sb's ~ and call** être aux ordres OR à la disposition de qqn.

beckon ['bekən] 1 *vt* [signal to] faire signe à. 2 *vi* [signal]: **to ~ to sb** faire signe à qqn.

become [bɪ'kʌm] (*pt* **became**, *pp* **become**) *vi* devenir; **to ~ quieter** se calmer; **to ~ irritated** s'énerver.

bed [bed] *n* [to sleep on] lit *m*; **to go to ~** se coucher; **to go to ~ with sb** *euphemism* coucher avec qqn. || [flowerbed] parterre *m*. || [of sea, river] lit *m*, fond *m*.

bed and breakfast *n* ≃ chambre *f* d'hôte.

bedclothes ['bedkləʊðz] *npl* draps *mpl* et couvertures *fpl*.

bedlam ['bedləm] *n* pagaille *f*.

bed linen *n* (U) draps *mpl* et taies *fpl*.

bedraggled [bɪ'drægld] *adj* [person] débraillé(e); [hair] embroussaillé(e).

bedridden ['bed,rɪdn] *adj* grabataire.

bedroom ['bedrʊm] *n* chambre *f* (à coucher).

bedside ['bedsaɪd] *n* chevet *m*.

bedsore ['bedsɔːr] *n* escarre *f*.

bedspread ['bedspred] *n* couvre-lit *m*, dessus-de-lit *m inv*.

bedtime ['bedtaɪm] *n* heure *f* du coucher.

bee [bi:] *n* abeille *f*.

beech [bi:tʃ] *n* hêtre *m*.

beef [bi:f] *n* bœuf *m*.

beefburger ['bi:f,bɜːgər] *n* hamburger *m*.

beefsteak ['bi:f,steɪk] *n* bifteck *m*.

beehive ['bi:haɪv] *n* [for bees] ruche *f*.

beeline ['bi:laɪn] *n*: **to make a ~ for** *inf* aller tout droit OR directement vers.

been [bi:n] *pp* → be.

beer [bɪər] *n* bière *f*.

beet [bi:t] *n* betterave *f*.

beetle ['bi:tl] *n* scarabée *m*.

beetroot ['bi:tru:t] *n* betterave *f*.

before [bɪ'fɔːr] 1 *adv* auparavant, avant; **I've never been there ~** je n'y suis jamais allé; **I've seen it ~** je l'ai déjà vu; **the year ~** l'année d'avant OR précédente. 2 *prep* [in time] avant. || [in space] devant. 3 *conj* avant de (+ *infin*), avant que (+ *subjunctive*); **~ leaving** avant de partir; **~ you leave** avant que vous ne partiez.

beforehand [bɪ'fɔːhænd] *adv* à l'avance.

befriend [bɪ'frend] *vt* prendre en amitié.

beg [beg] 1 *vt* [money, food] mendier. || [favour] solliciter, quémander; [forgiveness] demander; **to ~ sb to do sthg** prier OR supplier qqn de faire qqch. 2 *vi* [for money, food]: **to ~ (for sthg)** mendier (qqch). || [plead] supplier; **to ~ for** [forgiveness etc] demander.

began [bɪ'gæn] *pt* → begin.

beggar ['begər] *n* mendiant *m*, -e *f*.

begin [bɪ'gɪn] (*pt* **began**, *pp* **begun**) 1 *vt* commencer; **to ~ doing** OR **to do sthg** commencer OR se mettre à faire qqch. 2 *vi* commencer; **to ~ with** pour commencer, premièrement.

beginner [bɪ'gɪnər] *n* débutant *m*, -e *f*.

beginning [bɪ'gɪnɪŋ] *n* début *m*, commencement *m*.

begrudge [bɪ'grʌdʒ] *vt* [envy]: **to ~ sb sthg** envier qqch à qqn. || [do unwillingly]: **to ~ doing sthg** rechigner à faire qqch.

begun [bɪ'gʌn] *pp* → begin.

behalf [bɪ'hɑːf] *n*: **on ~ of** Br, **in ~ of** Am de la part de, au nom de.

behave [bɪ'heɪv] 1 *vt*: **to ~ o.s.** se conduire OR se comporter bien. 2 *vi* [in a particular way] se conduire, se comporter. || [acceptably] se tenir bien.

behaviour Br, **behavior** Am [bɪ'heɪvjər] *n* conduite *f*, comportement *m*.

behead [bɪ'hed] *vt* décapiter.

behind [bɪ'haɪnd] 1 *prep* [gen] derrière. || [in time] en retard sur. 2 *adv* [gen] derrière. || [in time] en retard; **to leave sthg ~** oublier qqch; **to stay ~** rester; **to be ~ with sthg** être en retard dans qqch. 3 *n inf* derrière *m*, postérieur *m*.

beige [beɪʒ] 1 *adj* beige. 2 *n* beige *m*.

Beijing [,beɪ'dʒɪŋ] *n* Beijing.

being ['bi:ɪŋ] *n* [creature] être *m*. || [existence]: **in ~** existant(e); **to come into ~** voir le jour, prendre naissance.

Beirut [,beɪ'ruːt] *n* Beyrouth.

belch [beltʃ] **1** *n* renvoi *m*, rot *m*. **2** *vt* [smoke, fire] vomir, cracher. **3** *vi* [person] éructer, roter.

Belgian ['beldʒən] **1** *adj* belge. **2** *n* Belge *mf*.

Belgium ['beldʒəm] *n* Belgique *f*; **in ~** en Belgique.

Belgrade [,bel'greɪd] *n* Belgrade.

belie [bɪ'laɪ] (*cont* **belying**) *vt* [disprove] démentir. || [give false idea of] donner une fausse idée de.

belief [bɪ'liːf] *n* [faith, certainty]: **~ (in)** croyance *f* (en). || [principle, opinion] opinion *f*, conviction *f*.

believe [bɪ'liːv] **1** *vt* croire; **~ it or not** tu ne me croiras peut-être pas. **2** *vi* croire; **to ~ in sb** croire en qqn; **to ~ in sthg** croire à qqch.

believer [bɪ'liːvər] *n* RELIG croyant *m*, -e *f*. || [in idea, action]: **~ in** partisan *m*, -e *f* de.

belittle [bɪ'lɪtl] *vt* dénigrer, rabaisser.

bell [bel] *n* [of church] cloche *f*; [handbell] clochette *f*; [on door] sonnette *f*; [on bike] timbre *m*.

bellow ['beləʊ] *vi* [person] brailler, beugler. || [bull] beugler.

bellows ['beləʊz] *npl* soufflet *m*.

belly ['belɪ] *n* [of person] ventre *m*; [of animal] panse *f*.

bellyache ['belɪeɪk] *n* mal *m* de ventre.

belly button *n inf* nombril *m*.

belong [bɪ'lɒŋ] *vi* [be property]: **to ~ to sb** appartenir OR être à qqn. || [be member]: **to ~ to sthg** être membre de qqch. || [be in right place] être à sa place; **that chair ~s here** ce fauteuil va ici.

belongings [bɪ'lɒŋɪŋz] *npl* affaires *fpl*.

beloved [bɪ'lʌvd] *adj* bien-aimé(e).

below [bɪ'ləʊ] **1** *adv* [lower] en dessous, en bas. || [in text] ci-dessous. || NAUT en bas. **2** *prep* sous, au-dessous de.

belt [belt] **1** *n* [for clothing] ceinture *f*. || TECH courroie *f*. **2** *vt inf* flanquer une raclée à.

beltway ['belt,weɪ] *n Am* route *f* périphérique.

bemused [bɪ'mjuːzd] *adj* perplexe.

bench [bentʃ] *n* [gen & POL] banc *m*. || [in lab, workshop] établi *m*.

bend [bend] (*pt & pp* **bent**) **1** *n* [in road] courbe *f*, virage *m*. || [in pipe, river] coude *m*. || *phr*: **round the ~** *inf* dingue, fou (folle). **2** *vt* [arm, leg] plier. || [wire,

fork etc] tordre, courber. **3** *vi* [person] se baisser, se courber; [tree, rod] plier; **to ~ over backwards for sb** se mettre en quatre pour qqn.

beneath [bɪ'niːθ] **1** *adv* dessous, en bas. **2** *prep* [under] sous. || [unworthy of] indigne de.

benefactor ['benɪfæktər] *n* bienfaiteur *m*.

beneficial [,benɪ'fɪʃl] *adj*: **~ (to sb)** salutaire (à qqn); **~ (to sthg)** utile (à qqch).

beneficiary [,benɪ'fɪʃərɪ] *n* bénéficiaire *mf*.

benefit ['benɪfɪt] **1** *n* [advantage] avantage *m*; **for the ~ of** dans l'intérêt de; **to be to sb's ~, to be of ~ to sb** être dans l'intérêt de qqn. || ADMIN [allowance of money] allocation *f*, prestation *f*. **2** *vt* profiter à. **3** *vi*: **to ~ from** tirer avantage de, profiter de.

Benelux ['benɪlʌks] *n* Bénélux *m*.

benevolent [bɪ'nevələnt] *adj* bienveillant(e).

benign [bɪ'naɪn] *adj* [person] gentil(ille), bienveillant(e). || MED bénin(igne).

bent [bent] **1** *pt & pp* → **bend**. **2** *adj* [wire, bar] tordu(e). || [person, body] courbé(e), voûté(e). || [determined]: **to be ~ on doing sthg** vouloir absolument faire qqch, être décidé(e) à faire qqch. **3** *n*: **~ (for)** penchant *m* (pour).

bequeath [bɪ'kwiːð] *vt lit & fig* léguer.

bequest [bɪ'kwest] *n* legs *m*.

bereaved [bɪ'riːvd] (*pl inv*) **1** *adj* endeuillé(e), affligé(e). **2** *n*: **the ~** la famille du défunt.

beret ['bereɪ] *n* béret *m*.

Berlin [bɜː'lɪn] *n* Berlin.

berm [bɜːm] *n Am* bas-côté *m*.

Bermuda [bə'mjuːdə] *n* Bermudes *fpl*.

Bern [bɜːn] *n* Berne.

berry ['berɪ] *n* baie *f*.

berserk [bə'zɜːk] *adj*: **to go ~** devenir fou furieux (folle furieuse).

berth [bɜːθ] **1** *n* [in harbour] poste *m* d'amarrage, mouillage *m*. || [in ship, train] couchette *f*. **2** *vi* [ship] accoster, se ranger à quai.

beset [bɪ'set] (*pt & pp* **beset**) **1** *adj*: **~ with** OR **by** [doubts etc] assailli(e) de. **2** *vt* assaillir.

beside [bɪ'saɪd] *prep* [next to] à côté de, auprès de. || [compared with] comparé(e) à, à côté de. || *phr*: **to be ~ o.s. with anger** être hors de soi; **to be ~ o.s. with joy** être fou (folle) de joie.

besides [bɪ'saɪdz] **1** *adv* en outre, en plus. **2** *prep* en plus de.

besiege [bɪ'siːdʒ] *vt* [town, fortress] assiéger.

besotted [bɪ'sɒtɪd] *adj*: ~ (with sb) entiché(e) (de qqn).

best [best] **1** *adj* le meilleur (la meilleure). **2** *adv* le mieux. **3** *n* le meilleur; **to do one's** ~ faire de son mieux; **all the** ~! meilleurs souhaits!; **to be for the** ~ être pour le mieux; **to make the** ~ **of sthg** s'accommoder de qqch, prendre son parti de qqch. ○ **at best** *adv* au mieux.

best man *n* garçon *m* d'honneur.

bestow [bɪ'stəʊ] *vt fml*: **to** ~ **sthg on sb** conférer qqch à qqn.

best-seller *n* [book] best-seller *m*.

bet [bet] (*pt & pp* **bet** OR **-ted**) **1** *n* pari *m*. **2** *vt* parier. **3** *vi* parier; **I wouldn't** ~ **on it** *fig* je n'en suis pas si sûr.

betray [bɪ'treɪ] *vt* trahir.

betrayal [bɪ'treɪəl] *n* [of person] trahison *f*.

better ['betər] **1** *adj (compar of good)* meilleur(e); **to get** ~ s'améliorer; [after illness] se remettre, se rétablir. **2** *adv (compar of well)* mieux; **I'd** ~ **leave** il faut que je parte, je dois partir. **3** *n* meilleur *m*, -e *f*; **to get the** ~ **of sb** avoir raison de qqn. **4** *vt* améliorer; **to** ~ **o.s.** s'élever.

better off *adj* [financially] plus à son aise. || [in better situation] mieux.

betting ['betɪŋ] *n (U)* paris *mpl*.

between [bɪ'twiːn] **1** *prep* entre. **2** *adv*: **(in)** ~ [in space] au milieu; [in time] dans l'intervalle.

beverage ['bevərɪdʒ] *n fml* boisson *f*.

beware [bɪ'weər] *vi*: **to** ~ **(of)** prendre garde (à), se méfier (de); ~ **of** ... attention à ....

bewildered [bɪ'wɪldəd] *adj* déconcerté(e), perplexe.

beyond [bɪ'jɒnd] **1** *prep* [in space] au-delà de. || [in time] après, plus tard que. || [exceeding] au-dessus de; **it's** ~ **my control** je n'y peux rien; **it's** ~ **my responsibility** cela n'entre pas dans le cadre de mes responsabilités. **2** *adv* au-delà.

bias ['baɪəs] *n* [prejudice] préjugé *m*, parti *m* pris. || [tendency] tendance *f*.

biased ['baɪəst] *adj* partial(e); **to be** ~ **towards sb/sthg** favoriser qqn/qqch; **to be** ~ **against sb/sthg** défavoriser qqn/qqch.

bib [bɪb] *n* [for baby] bavoir *m*, bavette *f*.

Bible ['baɪbl] *n*: **the** ~ la Bible.

bicarbonate of soda [baɪ'kɑːbənət-] *n* bicarbonate *m* de soude.

biceps ['baɪseps] (*pl inv*) *n* biceps *m*.

bicker ['bɪkər] *vi* se chamailler.

bicycle ['baɪsɪkl] **1** *n* bicyclette *f*, vélo *m*. **2** *vi* aller en bicyclette OR vélo.

bicycle path *n* piste *f* cyclable.

bicycle pump *n* pompe *f* à vélo.

bid [bɪd] (*pt & pp* **bid**) **1** *n* [attempt] tentative *f*. || [at auction] enchère *f*. || COMM offre *f*. **2** *vt* [at auction] faire une enchère de. **3** *vi* [at auction]: **to** ~ **(for)** faire une enchère (pour). || [attempt]: **to** ~ **for sthg** briguer.

bidder ['bɪdər] *n* enchérisseur *m*, -euse *f*.

bidding ['bɪdɪŋ] *n (U)* enchères *fpl*.

bide [baɪd] *vt*: **to** ~ **one's time** attendre son heure OR le bon moment.

bifocals [,baɪ'fəʊklz] *npl* lunettes *fpl* bifocales.

big [bɪg] *adj* [gen] grand(e). || [in amount, bulk - box, problem, book] gros (grosse).

bigamy ['bɪgəmɪ] *n* bigamie *f*.

big deal *inf* **1** *n*: **it's no** ~ ce n'est pas dramatique; **what's the** ~? où est le problème? **2** *excl* tu parles!, et alors?

Big Dipper [-'dɪpər] *n Am* ASTRON: **the** ~ la Grande Ourse.

bigheaded [,bɪg'hedɪd] *adj inf* crâneur(euse).

bigot ['bɪgət] *n* sectaire *mf*.

bigoted ['bɪgətɪd] *adj* sectaire.

big toe *n* gros orteil *m*.

big top *n* chapiteau *m*.

bike [baɪk] *n inf* [bicycle] vélo *m*. || [motorcycle] bécane *f*, moto *f*.

bikeway ['baɪkweɪ] *n Am* piste *f* cyclable.

bikini [bɪ'kiːnɪ] *n* Bikini® *m*.

bile [baɪl] *n* [fluid] bile *f*. || [anger] mauvaise humeur *f*.

bilingual [baɪ'lɪŋgwəl] *adj* bilingue.

bill [bɪl] **1** *n* [statement of cost]: ~ **(for)** note *f* OR facture *f* (de); [in restaurant] addition *f* (de). || [in parliament] projet *m* de loi. || [of show, concert] programme *m*. || *Am* [banknote] billet *m* de banque. || [poster]: **"post** OR **stick no** ~**s"** «défense d'afficher». || [beak] bec *m*. **2** *vt* [invoice]: **to** ~ **sb (for)** envoyer une facture à qqn (pour).

billboard ['bɪlbɔːd] *n* panneau *m* d'affichage.

billet ['bɪlɪt] *n* logement *m* (chez l'habitant).

billfold ['bɪlfəʊld] *n Am* portefeuille *m*.

billiards ['bɪljədz] *n* billard *m*.

billion ['bɪljən] *num Am* [thousand million] milliard *m*. ‖ *Br* [million million] billion *m*.

Bill of Rights *n*: the ~ *les dix premiers amendements à la Constitution américaine*.

bin [bɪn] *n Br* [for rubbish] poubelle *f*. ‖ [for grain, coal] coffre *m*.

bind [baɪnd] (*pt & pp* bound) *vt* [tie up] attacher, lier. ‖ [unite - people] lier. ‖ [bandage] panser. ‖ [book] relier. ‖ [constrain] contraindre, forcer.

binder ['baɪndə*r*] *n* [cover] classeur *m*.

binding ['baɪndɪŋ] **1** *adj* qui lie OR engage; [agreement] irrévocable. **2** *n* [on book] reliure *f*.

binge [bɪndʒ] *inf* **1** *n*: to go on a ~ prendre une cuite. **2** *vi*: to ~ on sthg se gaver OR se bourrer de qqch.

bingo ['bɪŋɡəʊ] *n* bingo *m*, ≈ loto *m*.

binoculars [bɪ'nɒkjʊləz] *npl* jumelles *fpl*.

biochemistry [,baɪəʊ'kemɪstrɪ] *n* biochimie *f*.

biodegradable [,baɪəʊdɪ'ɡreɪdəbl] *adj* biodégradable.

biography [baɪ'ɒɡrəfɪ] *n* biographie *f*.

biological [,baɪə'lɒdʒɪkl] *adj* biologique; [washing powder] aux enzymes.

biology [baɪ'ɒlədʒɪ] *n* biologie *f*.

birch [bɜːtʃ] *n* [tree] bouleau *m*.

bird [bɜːd] *n* [creature] oiseau *m*. ‖ *inf* [woman] gonzesse *f*.

birdie ['bɜːdɪ] *n* GOLF birdie *m*.

bird's-eye view *n* vue *f* aérienne.

bird-watcher [-,wɒtʃə*r*] *n* observateur *m*, -trice *f* d'oiseaux.

Biro® ['baɪərəʊ] *n* stylo *m* à bille.

birth [bɜːθ] *n lit & fig* naissance *f*; to give ~ (to) donner naissance (à).

birth certificate *n* acte *m* OR extrait *m* de naissance.

birth control *n* (*U*) régulation *f* OR contrôle *m* des naissances.

birthday ['bɜːθdeɪ] *n* anniversaire *m*.

birthmark ['bɜːθmɑːk] *n* tache *f* de vin.

birthrate ['bɜːθreɪt] *n* (taux *m* de) natalité *f*.

Biscay ['bɪskeɪ] *n*: the Bay of ~ le golfe de Gascogne.

biscuit ['bɪskɪt] *n Am* scone *m*.

bisect [baɪ'sekt] *vt* couper OR diviser en deux.

bishop ['bɪʃəp] *n* RELIG évêque *m*. ‖ [in chess] fou *m*.

bison ['baɪsn] (*pl inv* OR -s) *n* bison *m*.

bit [bɪt] **1** *pt* → **bite**. **2** *n* [small piece - of paper, cheese etc] morceau *m*, bout *m*; [- of book, film] passage *m*; to take sthg to ~s démonter qqch. ‖ [amount]: a ~ of un peu de; a ~ of shopping quelques courses; it's a ~ of a nuisance c'est un peu embêtant; a ~ of trouble un petit problème; quite a ~ of pas mal de, beaucoup de. ‖ [short time]: for a ~ pendant quelque temps. ‖ [of drill] mèche *f*. ‖ [of bridle] mors *m*. ‖ COMPUT bit *m*. ○ **a bit** *adv* un peu. ○ **bit by bit** *adv* petit à petit.

bitch [bɪtʃ] *n* [female dog] chienne *f*. ‖ *v inf pej* [woman] salope *f*, garce *f*.

bitchy [bɪtʃɪ] *adj inf* vache, rosse.

bite [baɪt] (*pt* bit, *pp* bitten) **1** *n* [act of biting] morsure *f*, coup *m* de dent. ‖ *inf* [food]: to have a ~ (to eat) manger un morceau. ‖ [wound] piqûre *f*. **2** *vt* [subj: person, animal] mordre. ‖ [subj: insect, snake] piquer, mordre. **3** *vi* [animal, person]: to ~ (into) mordre (dans); to ~ off sthg arracher qqch d'un coup de dents. ‖ [insect, snake] mordre, piquer.

biting ['baɪtɪŋ] *adj* [very cold] cinglant(e), piquant(e). ‖ [humour, comment] mordant(e), caustique.

bitten ['bɪtn] *pp* → **bite**.

bitter ['bɪtə*r*] *adj* [gen] amer(ère). ‖ [icy] glacial(e). ‖ [argument] violent(e).

bitter lemon *n* Schweppes® *m* au citron.

bitterness ['bɪtənɪs] *n* [gen] amertume *f*. ‖ [of wind, weather] âpreté *f*.

bizarre [bɪ'zɑːr] *adj* bizarre.

blab [blæb] *vi inf* lâcher le morceau.

black [blæk] **1** *adj* [colour] noir *m*. ‖ [person] noir *m*, -e *f*. ‖ *phr*: ~ and white [in writing] noir sur blanc, par écrit; in the ~ [financially solvent] solvable, sans dettes. ○ **black out** *vi* [faint] s'évanouir.

blackberry ['blækbərɪ] *n* mûre *f*.

blackbird ['blækbɜːd] *n* merle *m*.

blackboard ['blækbɔːd] *n* tableau *m* (noir).

blackcurrant [,blæk'kʌrənt] *n* cassis *m*.

blacken ['blækn] **1** *vt* [make dark] noircir. **2** *vi* s'assombrir.

black eye *n* œil *m* poché OR au beurre noir.

blackhead ['blækhed] *n* point *m* noir.

black ice *n* verglas *m*.

blackleg ['blækleɡ] *n pej* jaune *m*.

blacklist ['blæklɪst] **1** n liste f noire. **2** vt mettre sur la liste noire.

blackmail ['blækmeɪl] **1** n lit & fig chantage m. **2** vt [for money] faire chanter. || fig [emotionally] faire du chantage à.

black market n marché m noir.

blackout ['blækaʊt] n MIL & PRESS black-out m. || [power cut] panne f d'électricité. || [fainting fit] évanouissement m.

Black Sea n: the ~ la mer Noire.

black sheep n brebis f galeuse.

blacksmith ['blæksmɪθ] n forgeron m; [for horses] maréchal-ferrant m.

black spot n AUT point m noir.

bladder ['blædə'] n vessie f.

blade [bleɪd] n [of knife, saw] lame f. || [of propeller] pale f. || [of grass] brin m.

blame [bleɪm] **1** n responsabilité f, faute f; to take the ~ for sthg endosser la responsabilité de qqch. **2** vt blâmer, condamner; to ~ sthg on rejeter la responsabilité de qqch sur, imputer qqch à; to ~ sb/sthg for sthg reprocher qqch à qqn/qqch; to be to ~ for sthg être responsable de qqch.

bland [blænd] adj [person] terne. || [food] fade, insipide. || [music, style] insipide.

blank [blæŋk] **1** adj [sheet of paper] blanc (blanche); [wall] nu(e). || fig [look] vide, sans expression. **2** n [empty space] blanc m. || [cartridge] cartouche f à blanc.

blank cheque n chèque m en blanc.

blanket ['blæŋkɪt] n [for bed] couverture f. || [of snow] couche f, manteau m; [of fog] nappe f.

blare [bleə'] vi hurler; [radio] beugler.

blasphemy ['blæsfəmɪ] n blasphème m.

blast [blɑːst] **1** n [explosion] explosion f. || [of air, from bomb] souffle m. **2** vt [hole, tunnel] creuser à la dynamite. ○ **(at) full blast** adv [play music etc] à pleins gaz OR tubes.

blasted ['blɑːstɪd] adj inf fichu(e), maudit(e).

blast-off n SPACE lancement m.

blatant ['bleɪtənt] adj criant(e), flagrant(e).

blaze [bleɪz] **1** n [fire] incendie m. || fig [of colour, light] éclat m, flamboiement m. **2** vi [fire] flamber. || fig [with colour] flamboyer.

blazer ['bleɪzə'] n blazer m.

bleach [bliːtʃ] **1** n eau f de Javel. **2** vt [hair] décolorer; [clothes] blanchir.

bleached [bliːtʃt] adj décoloré(e).

bleachers ['bliːtʃəz] npl Am SPORT gradins mpl.

bleak [bliːk] adj [future] sombre. || [place, weather, face] lugubre, triste.

bleary-eyed [,blɪərɪ'aɪd] adj aux yeux troubles OR voilés.

bleat [bliːt] **1** n bêlement m. **2** vi bêler.

bleed [bliːd] (pt & pp **bled** [bled]) **1** vt [radiator etc] purger. **2** vi saigner.

bleeper ['bliːpə'] n bip m, bip-bip m.

blemish ['blemɪʃ] n lit & fig défaut m.

blend [blend] **1** n mélange m. **2** vt: to ~ sthg (with) mélanger qqch (avec OR à). **3** vi: to ~ (with) se mêler (à OR avec).

blender ['blendə'] n mixer m.

bless [bles] (pt & pp **-ed** OR **blest**) vt bénir; ~ you! [after sneezing] à vos souhaits!; [thank you] merci mille fois!

blessing ['blesɪŋ] n lit & fig bénédiction f.

blest [blest] pt & pp → bless.

blew [bluː] pt → blow.

blind [blaɪnd] **1** adj lit & fig aveugle; to be ~ to sthg ne pas voir qqch. **2** n [for window] store m. **3** npl: the ~ les aveugles mpl. **4** vt aveugler; to ~ sb to sthg fig cacher qqch à qqn.

blind alley n lit & fig impasse f.

blind corner n virage m sans visibilité.

blind date n rendez-vous avec quelqu'un qu'on ne connaît pas.

blinders ['blaɪndəz] npl Am œillères fpl.

blindfold ['blaɪndfəʊld] **1** adv les yeux bandés. **2** n bandeau m. **3** vt bander les yeux à.

blindly ['blaɪndlɪ] adv lit & fig à l'aveuglette, aveuglément.

blindness ['blaɪndnɪs] n cécité f; ~ (to) fig aveuglement m (devant).

blind spot n AUT angle m mort. || fig [inability to understand] blocage m.

blink [blɪŋk] **1** n phr: on the ~ [machine] détraqué(e). **2** vt [eyes] cligner. **3** vi [person] cligner des yeux. || [light] clignoter.

blinkered ['blɪŋkəd] adj: to be ~ lit & fig avoir des œillères.

bliss [blɪs] n bonheur m suprême, félicité f.

blissful ['blɪsfʊl] adj [day, silence] merveilleux(euse); [ignorance] total(e).

blister ['blɪstə'] **1** n [on skin] ampoule f, cloque f. **2** vi [skin] se couvrir d'ampoules. || [paint] cloquer, se boursoufler.

blur

blithely [ˈblaɪðlɪ] adv gaiement, joyeusement.

blitz [blɪts] n MIL bombardement m aérien.

blizzard [ˈblɪzəd] n tempête f de neige.

bloated [ˈbləʊtɪd] adj [face] bouffi(e). ‖ [with food] ballonné(e).

blob [blɒb] n [drop] goutte f. ‖ [indistinct shape] forme f; a ~ of colour une tache de couleur.

block [blɒk] 1 n [building]: office ~ immeuble m de bureaux. ‖ Am [of buildings] pâté m de maisons. ‖ [of stone, ice] bloc m. ‖ [obstruction] blocage m. 2 vt [road, pipe, view] boucher. ‖ [prevent] bloquer, empêcher.

blockade [blɒˈkeɪd] 1 n blocus m. 2 vt faire le blocus de.

blockage [ˈblɒkɪdʒ] n obstruction f.

blockbuster [ˈblɒkbʌstə‍ʳ] n inf [book] best-seller m; [film] film m à succès.

block capitals npl majuscules fpl d'imprimerie.

block letters npl majuscules fpl d'imprimerie.

blond [blɒnd] adj blond(e).

blonde [blɒnd] 1 adj blond(e). 2 n [woman] blonde f.

blood [blʌd] n sang m; in cold ~ de sang-froid.

blood cell n globule m.

blood donor n donneur m, -euse f de sang.

blood group n groupe m sanguin.

bloodhound [ˈblʌdhaʊnd] n limier m.

blood poisoning n septicémie f.

blood pressure n tension f artérielle; to have high ~ faire de l'hypertension.

bloodshed [ˈblʌdʃed] n carnage m.

bloodstream [ˈblʌdstriːm] n sang m.

blood test n prise f de sang.

bloodthirsty [ˈblʌdˌθɜːstɪ] adj sanguinaire.

blood transfusion n transfusion f sanguine.

bloody [ˈblʌdɪ] adj [gen] sanglant(e).

bloom [bluːm] 1 n fleur f. 2 vi fleurir.

blossom [ˈblɒsəm] 1 n [of tree] fleurs fpl; in ~ en fleur OR fleurs. 2 vi [tree] fleurir. ‖ fig [person] s'épanouir.

blot [blɒt] 1 n lit & fig tache f. 2 vt [paper] faire des pâtés sur. ‖ [ink] sécher. ○ **blot out** vt sep voiler, cacher; [memories] effacer.

blotchy [ˈblɒtʃɪ] adj couvert(e) de marbrures OR taches.

blotting paper [ˈblɒtɪŋ-] n (U) (papier m) buvard m.

blouse [blaʊz] n chemisier m.

blow [bləʊ] (pt blew, pp blown) 1 vi [gen] souffler. ‖ [in wind]: to ~ off s'envoler. ‖ [fuse] sauter. 2 vt [subj: wind] faire voler, chasser. ‖ [clear]: to ~ one's nose se moucher. ‖ [trumpet] jouer de, souffler dans; to ~ a whistle donner un coup de sifflet, siffler. 3 n [hit] coup m. ○ **blow out** 1 vt sep souffler. 2 vi [candle] s'éteindre. ‖ [tyre] éclater. ○ **blow over** vi se calmer. ○ **blow up** 1 vt sep [inflate] gonfler. ‖ [with bomb] faire sauter. ‖ [photograph] agrandir. 2 vi exploser.

blow-dry 1 n brushing m. 2 vt faire un brushing à.

blowlamp Br [ˈbləʊlæmp], **blowtorch** [ˈbləʊtɔːtʃ] n chalumeau m, lampe f à souder.

blown [bləʊn] pp → blow.

blowout [ˈbləʊaʊt] n [of tyre] éclatement m.

blowtorch = blowlamp.

blubber [ˈblʌbə‍ʳ] 1 n graisse f de baleine. 2 vi pej chialer.

blue [bluː] 1 adj [colour] bleu(e). ‖ inf [sad] triste, cafardeux(euse). ‖ [pornographic] porno (inv). 2 n bleu m; out of the ~ [happen] subitement; [arrive] à l'improviste. ○ **blues** npl: the ~s MUS le blues; inf [sad feeling] le blues, le cafard.

bluebell [ˈbluːbel] n jacinthe f des bois.

blueberry [ˈbluːbərɪ] n myrtille f.

bluebottle [ˈbluːˌbɒtl] n mouche f bleue, mouche de la viande.

blue cheese n (fromage m) bleu m.

blue-collar adj manuel(elle).

blue jeans npl Am blue-jean m, jean m.

blueprint [ˈbluːprɪnt] n photocalque m; fig plan m, projet m.

bluff [blʌf] 1 adj franc (franche). 2 n [deception] bluff m; to call sb's ~ prendre qqn au mot. 3 vt bluffer, donner le change à. 4 vi faire du bluff, bluffer.

blunder [ˈblʌndə‍ʳ] 1 n gaffe f, bévue f. 2 vi [make mistake] faire une gaffe, commettre une bévue.

blunt [blʌnt] 1 adj [knife] émoussé(e); [pencil] épointé(e); [object, instrument] contondant(e). ‖ [person, manner] direct(e), carré(e). 2 vt lit & fig émousser.

blur [blɜː‍ʳ] 1 n forme f confuse, tache f floue. 2 vt [vision] troubler, brouiller.

blurb [blɜ:b] *n* texte *m* publicitaire.

blurt [blɜ:t] ○ **blurt out** *vt sep* laisser échapper.

blush [blʌʃ] **1** *n* rougeur *f*. **2** *vi* rougir.

blusher ['blʌʃə'] *n* fard *m* à joues, blush *m*.

blustery ['blʌstərɪ] *adj* venteux(euse).

BMX (*abbr of* **bicycle motorcross**) *n* bicross *m*.

BO *abbr of* **body odour**.

boar [bɔ:'] *n* [male pig] verrat *m*. || [wild pig] sanglier *m*.

board [bɔ:d] **1** *n* [plank] planche *f*. || [for notices] panneau *m* d'affichage. || [for games - gen] tableau *m*; [- for chess] échiquier *m*. || [blackboard] tableau *m* (noir). || [of company]: ~ **(of directors)** conseil *m* d'administration. || [committee] comité *m*, conseil *m*. || **on** ~ [on ship, plane, bus, train] à bord. || *phr*: **to take sthg on** ~ [knowledge] assimiler qqch; [advice] accepter qqch; **above** ~ régulier(ière), dans les règles. **2** *vt* [ship, aeroplane] monter à bord de; [train, bus] monter dans.

boarder ['bɔ:də'] *n* [lodger] pensionnaire *mf*. || [at school] interne *mf*, pensionnaire *mf*.

boarding card ['bɔ:dɪŋ-] *n* carte *f* d'embarquement.

boardinghouse ['bɔ:dɪŋhaus, *pl* -hauzɪz] *n* pension *f* de famille.

boarding school ['bɔ:dɪŋ-] *n* pensionnat *m*, internat *m*.

boardroom ['bɔ:drum] *n* salle *f* du conseil (d'administration).

boast [bəust] **1** *n* vantardise *f*, fanfaronnade *f*. **2** *vi*: **to** ~ **(about)** se vanter (de).

boastful ['bəustful] *adj* vantard(e), fanfaron(onne).

boat [bəut] *n* [large] bateau *m*; [small] canot *m*, embarcation *f*; **by** ~ en bateau.

boater ['bəutə'] *n* [hat] canotier *m*.

boatswain ['bəusn] *n* maître *m* d'équipage.

bob [bɒb] **1** *n* [hairstyle] coupe *f* au carré. || *Br inf dated* [shilling] shilling *m*. || = **bobsleigh**. **2** *vi* [boat, ship] tanguer.

bobbin ['bɒbɪn] *n* bobine *f*.

bobsleigh ['bɒbsleɪ] *n* bobsleigh *m*.

bode [bəud] *vi literary*: **to** ~ **ill/well (for)** être de mauvais/bon augure (pour).

bodily ['bɒdɪlɪ] **1** *adj* [needs] matériel(ielle). **2** *adv* [lift, move] à bras-lecorps.

body ['bɒdɪ] *n* [of person] corps *m*. || [corpse] corps *m*, cadavre *m*. || [organization] organisme *m*, organisation *f*. || [of car] carrosserie *f*; [of plane] fuselage *m*. || (*U*) [of wine] corps *m*. || (*U*) [of hair] volume *m*. || [garment] body *m*.

body building *n* culturisme *m*.

bodyguard ['bɒdɪgɑ:d] *n* garde *m* du corps.

body odour *n* odeur *f* corporelle.

bodywork ['bɒdɪwɜ:k] *n* carrosserie *f*.

bog [bɒg] *n* [marsh] marécage *m*.

bogged down [,bɒgd-] *adj fig* [in work]: ~ **(in)** submergé(e) (de). || [car etc]: ~ **(in)** enlisé(e) (dans).

boggle ['bɒgl] *vi*: **the mind** ~**s!** ce n'est pas croyable!, on croit rêver!

bogus ['bəugəs] *adj* faux (fausse), bidon (*inv*).

boil [bɔɪl] **1** *n* MED furoncle *m*. || [boiling point]: **to bring sthg to the** ~ porter qqch à ébullition; **to come to the** ~ venir à ébullition. **2** *vt* [water, food] faire bouillir. || [kettle] mettre sur le feu. **3** *vi* [water] bouillir. ○ **boil down to** *vt fus fig* revenir à, se résumer à. ○ **boil over** *vi* [liquid] déborder. || *fig* [feelings] exploser.

boiled ['bɔɪld] *adj*: ~ **egg** œuf *m* à la coque; ~ **sweet** *Br* bonbon *m* (dur).

boiler ['bɔɪlə'] *n* chaudière *f*.

boiling ['bɔɪlɪŋ] *adj* [liquid] bouillant(e). || *inf* [weather] très chaud(e), torride; [person]: **I'm** ~ **(hot)!** je crève de chaleur!

boiling point *n* point *m* d'ébullition.

boisterous ['bɔɪstərəs] *adj* turbulent(e), remuant(e).

bold [bəuld] *adj* [confident] hardi(e), audacieux(ieuse). || [lines, design] hardi(e); [colour] vif (vive), éclatant(e). || TYPO: **type** OR **print** caractères *mpl* gras.

bollard ['bɒlɑ:d] *n* [on road] borne *f*.

bolster ['bəulstə'] **1** *n* [pillow] traversin *m*. **2** *vt* renforcer, affirmer. ○ **bolster up** *vt fus* soutenir, appuyer.

bolt [bəult] **1** *n* [on door, window] verrou *m*. || [type of screw] boulon *m*. **2** *adv*: ~ **upright** droit(e) comme un piquet. **3** *vt* [fasten together] boulonner. || [close - door, window] verrouiller. || [food] engouffrer, engloutir. **4** *vi* [run] détaler.

bomb [bɒm] **1** *n* bombe *f*. **2** *vt* bombarder.

bombard [bɒm'bɑ:d] *vt* MIL & *fig*: **to** ~ **(with)** bombarder (de).

bombastic [bɒm'bæstɪk] *adj* pompeux(euse).

bomb disposal squad *n* équipe *f* de déminage.

bomber ['bɒmər] n [plane] bombardier m. || [person] plastiqueur m.

bombing ['bɒmɪŋ] n bombardement m.

bombshell ['bɒmʃel] n fig bombe f.

bona fide [,bəʊnə'faɪdɪ] adj véritable, authentique; [offer] sérieux(ieuse).

bond [bɒnd] **1** n [between people] lien m. || [promise] engagement m. || FIN bon m, titre m. **2** vt [glue]: **to ~ sthg to sthg** coller qqch sur qqch. || fig [people] unir.

bondage ['bɒndɪdʒ] n servitude f, esclavage m.

bone [bəʊn] **1** n os m; [of fish] arête f. **2** vt [meat] désosser; [fish] enlever les arêtes de.

bone-dry adj tout à fait sec (sèche).

bone-idle adj paresseux(euse) comme une couleuvre OR un lézard.

bonfire ['bɒn,faɪər] n [for fun] feu m de joie; [to burn rubbish] feu.

Bonn [bɒn] n Bonn.

bonnet ['bɒnɪt] n [hat] bonnet m.

bonus ['bəʊnəs] (pl **-es**) n [extra money] prime f, gratification f. || fig [added advantage] plus m.

bony ['bəʊnɪ] adj [person, hand, face] maigre, osseux(euse). || [meat] plein(e) d'os; [fish] plein d'arêtes.

boo [buː] (pl **-s**) **1** excl hou! **2** n huée f. **3** vt & vi huer.

boob [buːb] n inf [mistake] gaffe f, bourde f. ○ **boobs** npl Br v inf nichons mpl.

booby trap ['buːbɪ-] n [bomb] objet m piégé. || [practical joke] farce f.

book [bʊk] **1** n [for reading] livre m. || [of stamps, tickets, cheques] carnet m; [of matches] pochette f. **2** vt [reserve - gen] réserver; [- performer] engager; **to be fully ~ed** être complet. || inf [subj: police] coller un PV à. **3** vi réserver. ○ **books** npl COMM livres mpl de comptes. ○ **book up** vt sep réserver, retenir.

bookcase ['bʊkkeɪs] n bibliothèque f.

bookie ['bʊkɪ] n inf bookmaker m.

booking ['bʊkɪŋ] n [reservation] réservation f.

booking office n bureau m de réservation OR location.

bookkeeping ['bʊk,kiːpɪŋ] n comptabilité f.

booklet ['bʊklɪt] n brochure f.

bookmaker ['bʊk,meɪkər] n bookmaker m.

bookmark ['bʊkmɑːk] n signet m.

bookseller ['bʊk,selər] n libraire mf.

bookshelf ['bʊkʃelf] (pl **-shelves** [-ʃelvz]) n rayon m OR étagère f à livres.

bookshop Br ['bʊkʃɒp], **bookstore** Am ['bʊkstɔːr] n librairie f.

book token n chèque-livre m.

boom [buːm] **1** n [loud noise] grondement m. || [in business, trade] boom m. || NAUT bôme f. || [for TV camera, microphone] girafe f, perche f. **2** vi [make noise] gronder. || [business, trade] être en plein essor OR en hausse.

boon [buːn] n avantage m, bénédiction f.

boost [buːst] **1** n [to production, sales] augmentation f; [to economy] croissance f. **2** vt [production, sales] stimuler. || [popularity] accroître, renforcer.

booster ['buːstər] n MED rappel m.

boot [buːt] **1** n [for walking, sport] chaussure f. || [fashion item] botte f. || Br [of car] coffre m. **2** vt inf flanquer des coups de pied à. ○ **to boot** adv par-dessus le marché, en plus.

booth [buːð] n [at fair] baraque f foraine. || [telephone booth] cabine f. || [voting booth] isoloir m.

booty ['buːtɪ] n butin m.

booze [buːz] inf **1** n (U) alcool m, boisson f alcoolisée. **2** vi picoler.

bop [bɒp] inf **1** n [hit] coup m. || [disco, dance] boum f. **2** vi [dance] danser.

border ['bɔːdər] **1** n [between countries] frontière f. || [edge] bord m. || [in garden] bordure f. **2** vt [country] border, être limitrophe de. || [edge] border. ○ **border on** vt fus friser, être voisin(e) de.

borderline ['bɔːdəlaɪn] **1** adj: ~ **case** cas m limite. **2** n fig limite f, ligne f de démarcation.

bore [bɔːr] **1** pt → **bear**. **2** n [person] raseur m, -euse f; [situation, event] corvée f. || [of gun] calibre m. **3** vt [person] ennuyer, raser; **to ~ sb stiff** OR **to tears** OR **to death** ennuyer qqn à mourir. || [drill] forer, percer.

bored [bɔːd] adj [person] qui s'ennuie; [look] d'ennui; **to be ~ with** en avoir assez de.

boredom ['bɔːdəm] n (U) ennui m.

boring ['bɔːrɪŋ] adj ennuyeux(euse).

born [bɔːn] adj né(e); **to be ~** naître; **I was ~ in 1965** je suis né en 1965; **when were you ~?** quelle est ta date de naissance?

borne [bɔːn] pp → **bear**.

borough ['bʌrə] n municipalité f.

borrow ['bɒrəʊ] *vt* emprunter; **to ~ sthg (from sb)** emprunter qqch (à qqn).

Bosnia ['bɒznɪə] *n* Bosnie *f*.

Bosnia-Herzegovina [-,hɜːtsəgə-'viːnə] *n* Bosnie-Herzégovine *f*.

Bosnian ['bɒznɪən] **1** *adj* bosniaque. **2** *n* Bosniaque *mf*.

bosom ['buzəm] *n* poitrine *f*, seins *mpl*; *fig* sein *m*; **~ friend** ami *m* intime.

boss [bɒs] *n* patron *m*, -onne *f*, chef *m*. ○ **boss about**, **boss around** *vt sep pej* donner des ordres à, régenter.

bossy ['bɒsɪ] *adj* autoritaire.

bosun ['bəʊsn] = **boatswain**.

botany ['bɒtənɪ] *n* botanique *f*.

botch [bɒtʃ] ○ **botch up** *vt sep inf* bousiller, saboter.

both [bəʊθ] **1** *adj* les deux. **2** *pron*: **~ (of them)** (tous) les deux ((toutes) les deux); **~ of us are coming** on vient tous les deux. **3** *adv*: **she is ~ intelligent and amusing** elle est à la fois intelligente et drôle.

bother ['bɒðər] **1** *vt* [worry] ennuyer, inquiéter; **to ~ o.s. (about)** se tracasser (au sujet de); **I can't be ~ed to do it** je n'ai vraiment pas envie de le faire. || [pester, annoy] embêter; **I'm sorry to ~ you** excusez-moi de vous déranger. **2** *vi*: **to ~ about sthg** s'inquiéter de qqch; **don't ~ (to do it)** ce n'est pas la peine (de le faire). **3** *n* (*U*) embêtement *m*; **it's no ~ at all** cela ne me dérange OR m'ennuie pas du tout.

bothered ['bɒðəd] *adj* inquiet(iète).

bottle ['bɒtl] **1** *n* [gen] bouteille *f*; [for medicine, perfume] flacon *m*; [for baby] biberon *m*. **2** *vt* [wine etc] mettre en bouteilles; [fruit] mettre en bocal. ○ **bottle up** *vt sep* [feelings] refouler, contenir.

bottle bank *n* container *m* pour verre usagé.

bottleneck ['bɒtlnek] *n* [in traffic] bouchon *m*, embouteillage *m*. || [in production] goulet *m* d'étranglement.

bottle-opener *n* ouvre-bouteilles *m inv*, décapsuleur *m*.

bottom ['bɒtəm] **1** *adj* [lowest] du bas. || [in class] dernier(ière). **2** *n* [of bottle, lake, garden] fond *m*; [of page, ladder, street] bas *m*; [of hill] pied *m*. || [of scale] bas *m*; [of class] dernier *m*, -ière *f*. || [buttocks] derrière *m*. || [cause]: **to get to the ~ of sthg** aller au fond de qqch, découvrir la cause de qqch. ○ **bottom out** *vi* atteindre son niveau le plus bas.

bottom line *n fig*: **the ~** l'essentiel *m*.

bought [bɔːt] *pt & pp* → **buy**.

boulder ['bəʊldər] *n* rocher *m*.

bounce [baʊns] **1** *vi* [ball] rebondir; [person] sauter. || *inf* [cheque] être sans provision. **2** *vt* [ball] faire rebondir. **3** *n* rebond *m*.

bouncer ['baʊnsər] *n inf* videur *m*.

bound [baʊnd] **1** *pt & pp* → **bind**. **2** *adj* [certain]: **it's ~ to win** il va sûrement gagner; **she's ~ to see it** elle ne peut pas manquer de le voir. || [obliged]: **to be ~ to do sthg** être obligé(e) OR tenu(e) de faire qqch; **I'm ~ to say/admit** je dois dire/reconnaître. || [for place]: **to be ~ for** [subj: person] être en route pour; [subj: plane, train] être à destination de. **3** *n* [leap] bond *m*, saut *m*. **4** *vt*: **to be ~ed by** [subj: field] être limité(e) OR délimité(e) par; [subj: country] être limitrophe de. ○ **bounds** *npl* limites *fpl*; **out of ~s** interdit, défendu.

boundary ['baʊndərɪ] *n* [gen] frontière *f*; [of property, land] borne *f*.

bourbon ['bɜːbən] *n* bourbon *m*.

bout [baʊt] *n* [of illness] accès *m*; **a ~ of flu** une grippe. || [session] période *f*. || [boxing match] combat *m*.

bow[1] [baʊ] **1** *n* [in greeting] révérence *f*. || [of ship] proue *f*, avant *m*. **2** *vt* [head] baisser, incliner. **3** *vi* [make a bow] saluer. || [defer]: **to ~ to** s'incliner devant.

bow[2] [bəʊ] *n* [weapon] arc *m*. || MUS archet *m*. || [knot] nœud *m*.

bowels ['baʊəlz] *npl* intestins *mpl*; *fig* entrailles *fpl*.

bowl [bəʊl] *n* [container - gen] jatte *f*, saladier *m*; [- small] bol *m*; [- for washing up] cuvette *f*. || [of toilet, sink] cuvette *f*; [of pipe] fourneau *m*. ○ **bowls** *n* (*U*) boules *fpl* (*sur herbe*). ○ **bowl over** *vt sep lit & fig* renverser.

bow-legged [,bəʊ'legɪd] *adj* aux jambes arquées.

bowler ['bəʊlər] *n*: **~ (hat)** chapeau *m* melon.

bowling ['bəʊlɪŋ] *n* (*U*) bowling *m*.

bowling alley *n* [building] bowling *m*; [alley] piste *f* de bowling.

bowling green *n* terrain *m* de boules (*sur herbe*).

bow tie [bəʊ-] *n* nœud *m* papillon.

box [bɒks] **1** *n* [gen] boîte *f*. || THEATRE loge *f*. **2** *vi* boxer, faire de la boxe.

boxer ['bɒksər] *n* [fighter] boxeur *m*. || [dog] boxer *m*.

boxer shorts *npl* caleçon *m*.

boxing ['bɒksɪŋ] *n* boxe *f*.

Boxing Day *n jour des étrennes en Grande-Bretagne (le 26 décembre).*

boxing glove *n* gant *m* de boxe.

box office *n* bureau *m* de location.

boy [bɔɪ] **1** *n* [male child] garçon *m*. **2** *excl inf*: **(oh) ~!** ben, mon vieux!, ben, dis-donc!

boycott ['bɔɪkɒt] **1** *n* boycott *m*, boycottage *m*. **2** *vt* boycotter.

boyfriend ['bɔɪfrend] *n* copain *m*, petit ami *m*.

boyish ['bɔɪɪʃ] *adj* [appearance - of man] gamin(e); [- of woman] de garçon; [behaviour] garçonnier(ière).

BR (*abbr of* **British Rail**) *n* ≃ SNCF *f*.

bra [brɑː] *n* soutien-gorge *m*.

brace [breɪs] **1** *n* [on teeth] appareil *m* (dentaire). || [on leg] appareil *m* orthopédique. **2** *vt* [steady] soutenir, consolider; **to ~ o.s.** s'accrocher, se cramponner. || *fig* [prepare]: **to ~ o.s. (for sthg)** se préparer (à qqch). **O braces** *npl Br* bretelles *fpl*.

bracelet ['breɪslɪt] *n* bracelet *m*.

bracing ['breɪsɪŋ] *adj* vivifiant(e).

bracken ['brækn] *n* fougère *f*.

bracket ['brækɪt] *n* [support] support *m*. || [parenthesis - round] parenthèse *f*; [- square] crochet *m*; **in ~s** entre parenthèses/crochets. || [group]: **age/income ~** tranche *f* d'âge/de revenus.

brag [bræg] *vi* se vanter.

braid [breɪd] **1** *n* [on uniform] galon *m*. || [of hair] tresse *f*, natte *f*. **2** *vt* [hair] tresser, natter.

brain [breɪn] *n* cerveau *m*. **O brains** *npl* [intelligence] intelligence *f*.

brainchild ['breɪntʃaɪld] *n inf* idée *f* personnelle, invention *f* personnelle.

brainwash ['breɪnwɒʃ] *vt* faire un lavage de cerveau à.

brainwave ['breɪnweɪv] *n* idée *f* géniale OR de génie.

brainy ['breɪnɪ] *adj inf* intelligent(e).

brake [breɪk] **1** *n lit* & *fig* frein *m*. **2** *vi* freiner.

brake light *n* stop *m*, feu *m* arrière.

bramble ['bræmbl] *n* [bush] ronce *f*; [fruit] mûre *f*.

bran [bræn] *n* son *m*.

branch [brɑːntʃ] **1** *n* [of tree, subject] branche *f*. || [of railway] bifurcation *f*, embranchement *m*. || [of company] filiale *f*, succursale *f*; [of bank] agence *f*. **2** *vi* bifurquer. **O branch out** *vi* [person, company] étendre ses activités, se diversifier.

brand [brænd] **1** *n* COMM marque *f*. || *fig* [type, style] type *m*, genre *m*. **2** *vt* [cattle] marquer au fer rouge. || *fig* [classify]: **to ~ sb (as) sthg** étiqueter qqn comme qqch, coller à qqn l'étiquette de qqch.

brandish ['brændɪʃ] *vt* brandir.

brand name *n* marque *f*.

brand-new *adj* flambant neuf (flambant neuve), tout neuf (toute neuve).

brandy ['brændɪ] *n* cognac *m*.

brash [bræʃ] *adj* effronté(e).

brass [brɑːs] *n* [metal] laiton *m*, cuivre *m* jaune. || MUS: **the ~** les cuivres *mpl*.

brass band *n* fanfare *f*.

brassiere [*Br* 'bræsɪər, *Am* brə'zɪr] *n* soutien-gorge *m*.

brat [bræt] *n inf pej* sale gosse *m*.

bravado [brə'vɑːdəʊ] *n* bravade *f*.

brave [breɪv] **1** *adj* courageux(euse), brave. **2** *n* guerrier *m* indien, brave *m*. **3** *vt* braver, affronter.

bravery ['breɪvərɪ] *n* courage *m*, bravoure *f*.

brawl [brɔːl] *n* bagarre *f*, rixe *f*.

brawn [brɔːn] *n* (*U*) [muscle] muscle *m*.

brazen ['breɪzn] *adj* [person] effronté(e), impudent(e); [lie] éhonté(e). **O brazen out** *vt sep*: **to ~ it out** crâner.

brazier ['breɪzjər] *n* brasero *m*.

Brazil [brə'zɪl] *n* Brésil *m*.

Brazilian [brə'zɪljən] **1** *adj* brésilien(ienne). **2** *n* Brésilien *m*, -ienne *f*.

brazil nut *n* noix *f* du Brésil.

breach [briːtʃ] **1** *n* [of law, agreement] infraction *f*, violation *f*; [of promise] rupture *f*; **to be in ~ of sthg** enfreindre OR violer qqch; **~ of contract** rupture *f* de contrat. || [opening, gap] trou *m*, brèche *f*. **2** *vt* [agreement, contract] rompre. || [make hole in] faire une brèche dans.

breach of the peace *n* atteinte *f* à l'ordre public.

bread [bred] *n* pain *m*; **~ and butter** tartine *f* beurrée, pain beurré; *fig* gagnepain *m*.

bread bin *Br*, **bread box** *Am n* boîte *f* à pain.

breadcrumbs ['bredkrʌmz] *npl* chapelure *f*.

breadline ['bredlaɪn] *n*: **to be on the ~** être sans ressources OR sans le sou.

breadth [bretθ] *n* [width] largeur *f*. || *fig* [scope] ampleur *f*, étendue *f*.

breadwinner ['bred,wɪnər] *n* soutien *m* de famille.

break [breɪk] (*pt* **broke**, *pp* **broken**) **1** *n* [gap]: **~ (in)** trouée *f* (dans). || [fracture]

fracture *f*. ‖ [pause - gen] pause *f*; [- at school] récréation *f*; **to take a ~** [short] faire une pause; [longer] prendre des jours de congé; **without a ~** sans interruption. ‖ *inf* [luck]: **(lucky) ~** chance *f*, veine *f*. **2** *vt* [gen] casser, briser; **to ~ one's arm/leg** se casser le bras/la jambe; **to ~ a record** battre un record. ‖ [interrupt - journey] interrompre; [- contact, silence] rompre. ‖ [not keep - law, rule] enfreindre, violer; [- promise] manquer à. ‖ [tell]: **to ~ the news (of sthg to sb)** annoncer la nouvelle (de qqch à qqn). **3** *vi* [gen] se casser, se briser; **to ~ loose** OR **free** se dégager, s'échapper. ‖ [pause] s'arrêter, faire une pause. ‖ [weather] se gâter. ‖ [voice - with emotion] se briser; [- at puberty] muer. ‖ [news] se répandre, éclater. ‖ *phr*: **to ~ even** rentrer dans ses frais. ❍ **break down 1** *vt sep* [destroy - barrier] démolir; [- door] enfoncer. ‖ [analyse] analyser. **2** *vi* [car, machine] tomber en panne; [resistance] céder; [negotiations] échouer. ‖ [emotionally] fondre en larmes, éclater en sanglots. ❍ **break in 1** *vi* [burglar] entrer par effraction. ‖ [interrupt]: **to ~ in (on sb/sthg)** interrompre (qqn/qqch). **2** *vt sep* [horse] dresser; [person] rompre, accoutumer. ❍ **break into** *vt fus* [subj: burglar] entrer par effraction dans. ‖ [begin]: **to ~ into song/applause** se mettre à chanter/applaudir. ❍ **break off 1** *vt sep* [detach] détacher. ‖ [talks, relationship] rompre; [holiday] interrompre. **2** *vi* [become detached] se casser, se détacher. ‖ [stop talking] s'interrompre, se taire. ❍ **break out** *vi* [begin - fire] se déclarer; [- fighting] éclater. ‖ [escape]: **to ~ out (of)** s'échapper (de), s'évader (de). ❍ **break up 1** *vt sep* [into smaller pieces] mettre en morceaux. ‖ [end - marriage, relationship] détruire; [- fight, party] mettre fin à. **2** *vi* [into smaller pieces - gen] se casser en morceaux; [- ship] se briser. ‖ [end - marriage, relationship] se briser; [- talks, party] prendre fin; [- school] finir, fermer; **to ~ up (with sb)** rompre (avec qqn). ‖ [crowd] se disperser.

breakage ['breɪkɪdʒ] *n* bris *m*.

breakdown ['breɪkdaʊn] *n* [of vehicle, machine] panne *f*; [of negotiations] échec *m*; [in communications] rupture *f*. ‖ [analysis] détail *m*.

breakfast ['brekfəst] *n* petit déjeuner *m*.

break-in *n* cambriolage *m*.

breaking ['breɪkɪŋ] *n*: **~ and entering** JUR entrée *f* par effraction.

breakthrough ['breɪkθruː] *n* percée *f*.

breakup ['breɪkʌp] *n* [of marriage, relationship] rupture *f*.

breast [brest] *n* [of woman] sein *m*; [of man] poitrine *f*. ‖ [meat of bird] blanc *m*.

breast-feed *vt* & *vi* allaiter.

breaststroke ['breststrəʊk] *n* brasse *f*.

breath [breθ] *n* souffle *m*, haleine *f*; **out of ~** hors d'haleine, à bout de souffle; **to get one's ~ back** reprendre haleine OR son souffle.

breathalyse *Br*, **-yze** *Am* ['breθəlaɪz] *vt* ≃ faire subir l'Alcootest® à.

breathe [briːð] **1** *vi* respirer. **2** *vt* [inhale] respirer. ‖ [exhale - smell] souffler des relents de. ❍ **breathe in 1** *vi* inspirer. **2** *vt sep* aspirer. ❍ **breathe out** *vi* expirer.

breather ['briːðə'] *n inf* moment *m* de repos OR répit.

breathing ['briːðɪŋ] *n* respiration *f*.

breathless ['breθlɪs] *adj* [out of breath] hors d'haleine, essoufflé(e). ‖ [with excitement] fébrile, fiévreux(euse).

breathtaking ['breθ,teɪkɪŋ] *adj* à vous couper le souffle.

breed [briːd] (*pt* & *pp* **bred** [bred]) **1** *n lit* & *fig* race *f*, espèce *f*. **2** *vt* [animals, plants] élever. ‖ *fig* [suspicion, contempt] faire naître, engendrer. **3** *vi* se reproduire.

breeding ['briːdɪŋ] *n* (*U*) [of animals, plants] élevage *m*. ‖ [manners] bonnes manières *fpl*, savoir-vivre *m*.

breeze [briːz] *n* brise *f*.

breezy ['briːzɪ] *adj* [windy] venteux(euse). ‖ [cheerful] jovial(e), enjoué(e).

brevity ['brevɪtɪ] *n* brièveté *f*.

brew [bruː] **1** *vt* [beer] brasser; [tea] faire infuser; [coffee] préparer, faire. **2** *vi* [tea] infuser; [coffee] se faire. ‖ *fig* [trouble, storm] se préparer, couver.

brewery ['brʊərɪ] *n* brasserie *f*.

bribe [braɪb] **1** *n* pot-de-vin *m*. **2** *vt*: **to ~ sb (to do sthg)** soudoyer qqn (pour qu'il fasse qqch).

bribery ['braɪbərɪ] *n* corruption *f*.

brick [brɪk] *n* brique *f*.

bricklayer ['brɪk,leɪə'] *n* maçon *m*.

bridal ['braɪdl] *adj* [dress] de mariée; [suite etc] nuptial(e).

bride [braɪd] *n* mariée *f*.

bridegroom ['braɪdgrʊm] *n* marié *m*.

bridesmaid ['braɪdzmeɪd] *n* demoiselle *f* d'honneur.

bridge [brɪdʒ] **1** *n* [gen] pont *m*. || [on ship] passerelle *f*. || [of nose] arête *f*. || [card game, for teeth] bridge *m*. **2** *vt fig* [gap] réduire.

bridle ['braɪdl] *n* bride *f*.

bridle path *n* piste *f* cavalière.

brief [briːf] **1** *adj* [short] bref (brève), court(e); **in ~** en bref, en deux mots. || [revealing] très court(e). **2** *n* JUR affaire *f*, dossier *m*. **3** *vt*: **to ~ sb (on)** [bring up to date] mettre qqn au courant (de); [instruct] briefer qqn (sur). ○ **briefs** *npl* slip *m*.

briefcase ['briːfkeɪs] *n* serviette *f*.

briefing ['briːfɪŋ] *n* instructions *fpl*, briefing *m*.

briefly ['briːflɪ] *adv* [for a short time] un instant. || [concisely] brièvement.

brigade [brɪ'geɪd] *n* brigade *f*.

brigadier [,brɪgə'dɪər] *n* général *m* de brigade.

bright [braɪt] *adj* [room] clair(e); [light, colour] vif (vive); [sunlight] éclatant(e); [eyes, future] brillant(e). || [intelligent] intelligent(e).

brighten ['braɪtn] *vi* [become lighter] s'éclaircir. ○ **brighten up 1** *vt sep* égayer. **2** *vi* [person] s'égayer, s'animer. || [weather] se dégager, s'éclaircir.

brilliance ['brɪljəns] *n* [cleverness] intelligence *f*. || [of colour, light] éclat *m*.

brilliant ['brɪljənt] *adj* [gen] brillant(e). || [colour] éclatant(e). || *inf* [wonderful] super (*inv*), génial(e).

Brillo pad® ['brɪləʊ-] *n* ≃ tampon *m* Jex®.

brim [brɪm] **1** *n* bord *m*. **2** *vi*: **to ~ with** *lit* & *fig* être plein(e) de.

brine [braɪn] *n* saumure *f*.

bring [brɪŋ] (*pt* & *pp* **brought**) *vt* [person] amener; [object] apporter. || [cause - happiness, shame] entraîner, causer; **to ~ sthg to an end** mettre fin à qqch. ○ **bring about** *vt sep* causer, provoquer. ○ **bring around** *vt sep* [make conscious] ranimer. ○ **bring back** *vt sep* [object] rapporter; [person] ramener. || [memories] rappeler. || [reinstate] rétablir. ○ **bring down** *vt sep* [plane] abattre; [government] renverser. || [prices] faire baisser. ○ **bring forward** *vt sep* [gen] avancer. || [in bookkeeping] reporter. ○ **bring in** *vt sep* [law] introduire. || [money - subj: person] gagner; [- subj: deal] rapporter. ○ **bring off** *vt sep* [plan] réaliser, réussir; [deal] conclure,

mener à bien. ○ **bring out** *vt sep* [product] lancer; [book] publier, faire paraître. || [cause to appear] faire ressortir. ○ **bring round, bring to** = **bring around.** ○ **bring up** *vt sep* [raise - children] élever. || [mention] mentionner. || [vomit] rendre, vomir.

brink [brɪŋk] *n*: **on the ~ of** au bord de, à la veille de.

brisk [brɪsk] *adj* [quick] vif (vive), rapide. || [manner, tone] déterminé(e).

bristle ['brɪsl] **1** *n* poil *m*. **2** *vi lit* & *fig* se hérisser.

Britain ['brɪtn] *n* Grande-Bretagne *f*; **in ~** en Grande-Bretagne.

British ['brɪtɪʃ] **1** *adj* britannique. **2** *npl*: **the ~** les Britanniques *mpl*.

British Isles *npl*: **the ~** les îles *fpl* Britanniques.

Briton ['brɪtn] *n* Britannique *mf*.

Brittany ['brɪtənɪ] *n* Bretagne *f*.

brittle ['brɪtl] *adj* fragile.

broach [brəʊtʃ] *vt* [subject] aborder.

broad [brɔːd] *adj* [wide] large; [- range, interests] divers(e), varié(e). || [description] général(e). || [hint] transparent(e); [accent] prononcé(e). ○ **in broad daylight** *adv* en plein jour.

broad bean *n* fève *f*.

broadcast ['brɔːdkɑːst] (*pt* & *pp* **broadcast**) **1** *n* RADIO & TV émission *f*. **2** *vt* RADIO radiodiffuser; TV téléviser.

broaden ['brɔːdn] **1** *vt* élargir. **2** *vi* s'élargir.

broadly ['brɔːdlɪ] *adv* [generally] généralement.

broadminded [,brɔːd'maɪndɪd] *adj* large d'esprit.

broccoli ['brɒkəlɪ] *n* brocoli *m*.

brochure ['brəʊʃər] *n* brochure *f*, prospectus *m*.

broil [brɔɪl] *vt Am* griller.

broke [brəʊk] **1** *pt* → **break. 2** *adj inf* fauché(e).

broken ['brəʊkn] **1** *pp* → **break. 2** *adj* [gen] cassé(e); **to have a ~ leg** avoir la jambe cassée. || [interrupted - journey, sleep] interrompu(e); [- line] brisé(e). || [marriage] brisé(e), détruit(e); [home] désuni(e). || [hesitant]: **to speak in ~ English** parler un anglais hésitant.

broker ['brəʊkər] *n* courtier *m*; **(insurance)** ~ assureur *m*, courtier *m* d'assurances.

bronchitis [brɒŋ'kaɪtɪs] *n* (*U*) bronchite *f*.

bronze [brɒnz] **1** adj [colour] (couleur) bronze (inv). **2** n [gen] bronze m.

brooch [brəʊtʃ] n broche f.

brood [bru:d] vi: **to ~ (over** OR **about** sthg) ressasser (qqch), remâcher (qqch).

brook [brʊk] n ruisseau m.

broom [bru:m] n balai m.

broomstick ['bru:mstɪk] n manche m à balai.

Bros, bros (abbr of **brothers**) Frères.

broth [brɒθ] n bouillon m.

brothel ['brɒθl] n bordel m.

brother ['brʌðər] n frère m.

brother-in-law (pl **brothers-in-law**) n beau-frère m.

brought [brɔ:t] pt & pp → **bring**.

brow [braʊ] n [forehead] front m. || [eyebrow] sourcil m. || [of hill] sommet m.

brown [braʊn] **1** adj [colour] brun(e), marron (inv); **~ bread** pain m bis. || [tanned] bronzé(e), hâlé(e). **2** n [colour] marron m, brun m. **3** vt [food] faire dorer.

Brownie (Guide) ['braʊnɪ-] n ≃ jeannette f.

Brownie point ['braʊnɪ-] n bon point m.

brown paper n papier m d'emballage, papier kraft.

brown rice n riz m complet.

brown sugar n sucre m roux.

browse [braʊz] vi [look]: **I'm just browsing** (in shop] je ne fais que regarder; **to ~ through** [magazines etc] feuilleter. || [animal] brouter.

bruise [bru:z] **1** n bleu m. **2** vt [skin, arm] se faire un bleu à; [fruit] taler.

brunch [brʌntʃ] n brunch m.

brunette [bru:'net] n brunette f.

brunt [brʌnt] n: **to bear** OR **take the ~ of** subir le plus gros de.

brush [brʌʃ] **1** n [gen] brosse f; [of painter] pinceau m. || [encounter]: **to have a ~ with the police** avoir des ennuis avec la police. **2** vt [clean with brush] brosser. || [touch lightly] effleurer. ○ **brush aside** vt sep fig écarter, repousser. ○ **brush off** vt sep [dismiss] envoyer promener. ○ **brush up** vi: **to ~ up on sthg** réviser qqch.

brush-off n inf: **to give sb the ~** envoyer promener qqn.

brusque [bru:sk] adj brusque.

Brussels ['brʌslz] n Bruxelles.

brussels sprout n chou m de Bruxelles.

brutal ['bru:tl] adj brutal(e).

brute [bru:t] **1** adj [force] brutal(e). **2** n brute f.

BSc (abbr of **Bachelor of Science**) n (titulaire d'une) licence de sciences.

bubble ['bʌbl] **1** n bulle f. **2** vi [liquid] faire des bulles, bouillonner.

bubble bath n bain m moussant.

bubble gum n bubble-gum m.

bubblejet printer ['bʌbldʒet-] n imprimante f à bulle d'encre.

Bucharest [,bju:kə'rest] n Bucarest.

buck [bʌk] n [male animal] mâle m. || inf [dollar] dollar m. || inf [responsibility]: **to pass the ~** refiler la responsabilité. **2** vi [horse] ruer. ○ **buck up** inf vi [hurry up] se remuer, se dépêcher. || [cheer up] ne pas se laisser abattre.

bucket ['bʌkɪt] n [gen] seau m.

Buckingham Palace ['bʌkɪŋəm-] n le palais de Buckingham (résidence officielle du souverain britannique).

buckle ['bʌkl] **1** n boucle f. **2** vt [fasten] boucler. || [bend] voiler. **3** vi [wheel] voiler; [knees, legs] se plier.

bud [bʌd] **1** n bourgeon m. **2** vi bourgeonner.

Budapest [,bju:də'pest] n Budapest.

Buddha ['bʊdə] n Bouddha m.

Buddhism ['bʊdɪzm] n bouddhisme m.

buddy ['bʌdɪ] n inf pote m.

budge [bʌdʒ] **1** vt faire bouger. **2** vi bouger.

budgerigar ['bʌdʒərɪgɑ:r] n perruche f.

budget ['bʌdʒɪt] **1** adj [holiday, price] pour petits budgets. **2** n budget m. ○ **budget for** vt fus prévoir.

budgie ['bʌdʒɪ] n inf perruche f.

buff [bʌf] **1** adj [brown] chamois (inv). **2** n inf [expert] mordu m, -e f.

buffalo ['bʌfələʊ] (pl inv OR **-es** OR **-s**) n buffle m.

buffer ['bʌfər] n [gen] tampon m. || COMPUT mémoire f tampon.

buffet [Br 'bʊfeɪ, Am bə'feɪ] n [food, cafeteria] buffet m.

buffet car ['bʊfeɪ-] n wagon-restaurant m.

bug [bʌg] **1** n [insect] punaise f. || inf [germ] microbe m. || inf [listening device] micro m. || COMPUT défaut m, bug m. **2** vt inf [telephone] mettre sur table d'écoute; [room] cacher des micros dans. || inf [annoy] embêter.

buggy ['bʌgɪ] n [carriage] boghei m. || [pushchair] poussette f; Am [pram] landau m.

bugle ['bju:gl] *n* clairon *m*.

build [bɪld] (*pt & pp* **built**) **1** *vt lit & fig* construire, bâtir. **2** *n* carrure *f*. ○ **build on, build upon 1** *vt fus* [success] tirer avantage de. **2** *vt sep* [base on] baser sur. ○ **build up 1** *vt sep* [business] développer; [reputation] bâtir. **2** *vi* [clouds] s'amonceler; [traffic] augmenter.

builder ['bɪldər] *n* entrepreneur *m*.

building ['bɪldɪŋ] *n* bâtiment *m*.

building and loan association *n Am* *société d'épargne et de financement immobilier.*

building site *n* chantier *m*.

building society *n Br* ≃ société *f* d'épargne et de financement immobilier.

buildup ['bɪldʌp] *n* [increase] accroissement *m*.

built [bɪlt] *pt & pp* → **build**.

built-in *adj* CONSTR encastré(e). || [inherent] inné(e).

built-up *adj*: ~ **area** agglomération *f*.

bulb [bʌlb] *n* ELEC ampoule *f*. || BOT oignon *m*.

Bulgaria [bʌl'geərɪə] *n* Bulgarie *f*.

Bulgarian [bʌl'geərɪən] **1** *adj* bulgare. **2** *n* [person] Bulgare *mf*. || [language] bulgare *m*.

bulge [bʌldʒ] **1** *n* [lump] bosse *f*. **2** *vi*: **to** ~ **(with)** être gonflé (de).

bulk [bʌlk] **1** *n* [mass] volume *m*. || [of person] corpulence *f*. || COMM: **in** ~ **en** gros. || [majority]: **the** ~ **of** le plus gros de. **2** *adj* en gros.

bulky ['bʌlkɪ] *adj* volumineux(euse).

bull [bul] *n* [male cow] taureau *m*; [male elephant, seal] mâle *m*.

bulldog ['buldɒg] *n* bouledogue *m*.

bulldozer ['buldəʊzər] *n* bulldozer *m*.

bullet ['bulɪt] *n* [for gun] balle *f*.

bulletin ['bulətɪn] *n* bulletin *m*.

bullet-proof *adj* pare-balles (*inv*).

bullfight ['bulfaɪt] *n* corrida *f*.

bullfighter ['bul,faɪtər] *n* toréador *m*.

bullfighting ['bul,faɪtɪŋ] *n* (*U*) courses *fpl* de taureaux; [art] tauromachie *f*.

bullion ['buljən] *n* (*U*): **gold** ~ or *m* en barres.

bullock ['bulək] *n* bœuf *m*.

bullring ['bulrɪŋ] *n* arène *f*.

bull's-eye *n* centre *m*.

bully ['bulɪ] **1** *n* tyran *m*. **2** *vt* tyranniser, brutaliser.

bum [bʌm] *n v inf* [bottom] derrière *m*. || *inf pej* [tramp] clochard *m*.

bumblebee ['bʌmblbi:] *n* bourdon *m*.

bump [bʌmp] **1** *n* [lump] bosse *f*. || [knock, blow] choc *m*. || [noise] bruit *m* sourd. **2** *vt* [head etc] cogner; [car] heurter. ○ **bump into** *vt fus* [meet by chance] rencontrer par hasard.

bumper ['bʌmpər] **1** *adj* [harvest, edition] exceptionnel(elle). **2** *n* AUT parechocs *m inv*. || *Am* RAIL tampon *m*.

bumpy ['bʌmpɪ] *adj* [surface] défoncé(e). || [ride] cahoteux(euse); [sea crossing] agité(e).

bun [bʌn] *n* [cake] petit pain *m* aux raisins; [bread roll] petit pain au lait. || [hairstyle] chignon *m*.

bunch [bʌntʃ] *n* [of people] groupe *m*; [of flowers] bouquet *m*; [of grapes] grappe *f*; [of bananas] régime *m*; [of keys] trousseau *m*. ○ **bunches** *npl* [hairstyle] couettes *fpl*.

bundle ['bʌndl] **1** *n* [of clothes] paquet *m*; [of notes, newspapers] liasse *f*; [of wood] fagot *m*. **2** *vt* [put roughly - person] entasser; [- clothes] fourrer, entasser.

bungalow ['bʌŋgələʊ] *n* bungalow *m*.

bungle ['bʌŋgl] *vt* gâcher, bâcler.

bunion ['bʌnjən] *n* oignon *m*.

bunk [bʌŋk] *n* [bed] couchette *f*.

bunk bed *n* lit *m* superposé.

bunker ['bʌŋkər] *n* GOLF & MIL bunker *m*. || [for coal] coffre *m*.

bunny ['bʌnɪ] *n*: ~ **(rabbit)** lapin *m*.

bunting ['bʌntɪŋ] *n* (*U*) guirlandes *fpl* (de drapeaux).

buoy [*Br* bɔɪ, *Am* 'bu:ɪ] *n* bouée *f*.

buoyant ['bɔɪənt] *adj* [able to float] qui flotte. || *fig* [person] enjoué(e); [economy] florissant(e); [market] ferme.

burden ['bɜ:dn] **1** *n lit & fig*: ~ **(on)** charge *f* (pour), fardeau *m* (pour). **2** *vt*: **to** ~ **sb with** [responsibilities, worries] accabler qqn de.

bureau ['bjuərəʊ] (*pl* -**x**) *n Br* [desk] bureau *m*; *Am* [chest of drawers] commode *f*. || [office] bureau *m*.

bureaucracy [bjuə'rɒkrəsɪ] *n* bureaucratie *f*.

bureaux ['bjuərəʊz] *pl* → **bureau**.

burger ['bɜ:gər] *n* hamburger *m*.

burglar ['bɜ:glər] *n* cambrioleur *m*, -euse *f*.

burglar alarm *n* système *m* d'alarme.

burglarize *Am* = **burgle**.

burglary ['bɜ:glərɪ] *n* cambriolage *m*.

burgle ['bɜ:gl], **burglarize** *Am* ['bɜ:gləraɪz] *vt* cambrioler.

Burgundy ['bɜ:gəndɪ] *n* Bourgogne *f*.

burial ['berɪəl] *n* enterrement *m*.

Burma ['bɜːmə] n Birmanie f.

burn [bɜːn] (pt & pp burnt OR -ed) 1 vt brûler. 2 vi brûler. 3 n brûlure f. ○ **burn down** 1 vt sep [building, town] incendier. 2 vi [building] brûler complètement.

burner ['bɜːnər] n brûleur m.

burnt [bɜːnt] pt & pp → burn.

burp [bɜːp] inf 1 n rot m. 2 vi roter.

burrow ['bʌrəu] 1 n terrier m. 2 vi [dig] creuser un terrier. || fig [search] fouiller.

bursar ['bɜːsər] n intendant m, -e f.

burst [bɜːst] (pt & pp burst) 1 vi [gen] éclater. 2 vt faire éclater. 3 n [of gunfire] rafale f. || [of enthusiasm] élan m. ○ **burst into** vt fus [room] faire irruption dans. || [begin suddenly]: to ~ into tears fondre en larmes; to ~ into flames prendre feu. ○ **burst out** vt fus [say suddenly] s'exclamer; to ~ out laughing éclater de rire.

bury ['berɪ] vt [in ground] enterrer. || [hide] cacher, enfouir.

bus [bʌs] n autobus m, bus m; [long-distance] car m; by ~ en autobus/car.

bush [buʃ] n [plant] buisson m. || [open country]: the ~ la brousse. || phr: she doesn't beat about the ~ elle n'y va pas par quatre chemins.

bushy ['buʃɪ] adj touffu(e).

business ['bɪznɪs] n (U) [commerce] affaires fpl; on ~ pour affaires; to mean ~ inf ne pas plaisanter; to go out of ~ fermer, faire faillite. || [company, shop] affaire f; mind your own ~! inf occupe-toi de tes oignons! || [affair, matter] histoire f, affaire f.

business class n classe f affaires.

businesslike ['bɪznɪslaɪk] adj efficace.

businessman ['bɪznɪsmæn] (pl -men [-men]) n homme m d'affaires.

business trip n voyage m d'affaires.

businesswoman ['bɪznɪs,wumən] (pl -women [-,wɪmɪn]) n femme f d'affaires.

bus shelter n Abribus® m.

bus station n gare f routière.

bus stop n arrêt m de bus.

bust [bʌst] (pt & pp bust OR -ed) 1 adj inf [broken] foutu(e). || [bankrupt]: to go ~ faire faillite. 2 n [bosom] poitrine f. || [statue] buste m. 3 vt inf [break] péter.

bustle ['bʌsl] 1 n (U) [activity] remue-ménage m. 2 vi s'affairer.

busy ['bɪzɪ] adj [gen] occupé(e); to be ~ doing sthg être occupé à faire qqch. || [life, week] chargé(e); [town, office] animé(e).

busybody ['bɪzɪ,bɒdɪ] n pej mouche f du coche.

busy signal n Am TELEC tonalité f «occupé».

but [bʌt] 1 conj mais. 2 prep sauf, excepté; he has no one ~ himself to blame il ne peut s'en prendre qu'à lui-même. 3 adv fml seulement, ne ... que; we can ~ try on peut toujours essayer. ○ **but for** prep sans.

butcher ['butʃər] 1 n boucher m; ~'s (shop) boucherie f. 2 vt fig [massacre] massacrer.

butler ['bʌtlər] n maître m d'hôtel (chez un particulier).

butt [bʌt] 1 n [of cigarette, cigar] mégot m. || [of rifle] crosse f. || [for water] tonneau m. || [of joke, criticism] cible f. 2 vt donner un coup de tête à. ○ **butt in** vi [interrupt]: to ~ in on sb interrompre qqn; to ~ in on sthg s'immiscer OR s'imposer dans qqch.

butter ['bʌtər] 1 n beurre m. 2 vt beurrer.

buttercup ['bʌtəkʌp] n bouton m d'or.

butter dish n beurrier m.

butterfly ['bʌtəflaɪ] n SWIMMING & ZOOL papillon m.

buttocks ['bʌtəks] npl fesses fpl.

button ['bʌtn] 1 n [gen] bouton m. || Am [badge] badge m. 2 vt = button up. ○ **button up** vt sep boutonner.

button mushroom n champignon m de Paris.

buttress ['bʌtrɪs] n contrefort m.

buy [baɪ] (pt & pp bought) 1 vt acheter; to ~ sthg from sb acheter qqch à qqn. 2 n: a good ~ une bonne affaire. ○ **buy up** vt sep acheter en masse.

buyer ['baɪər] n acheteur m, -euse f.

buyout ['baɪaut] n rachat m.

buzz [bʌz] 1 n [of insect] bourdonnement m. || inf [telephone call]: to give sb a ~ passer un coup de fil à qqn. 2 vi: to ~ (with) bourdonner (de). 3 vt [on intercom] appeler.

buzzer ['bʌzər] n sonnerie f.

buzzword ['bʌzwɜːd] n inf mot m à la mode.

by [baɪ] 1 prep [indicating cause, agent] par. || [indicating means, method, manner]: to pay ~ cheque payer par chèque; to travel ~ bus/train/plane/ship voyager en bus/par le train/en avion/en bateau; he's a lawyer ~ profession il est avocat de son métier; ~ doing sthg en faisant qqch. || [beside, close to]: ~ the ~ the sea au bord de la mer; I sat ~ her bed j'étais assis à son chevet. || [past]: to pass

~ **sb/sthg** passer devant qqn/qqch. || [via, through] par. || [at or before a particular time] avant, pas plus tard que; **I'll be there** ~ **eight** j'y serai avant huit heures; ~ **now** déjà. || [during]: ~ **day** le OR de jour; ~ **night** la OR de nuit. || [according to] selon, suivant; ~ **law** conformément à la loi. || [in arithmetic] par; **divide/multiply 20** ~ **2** divisez/multipliez 20 par 2. || [in measurements]: **2 metres** ~ **4 2** mètres sur 4. || [in quantities, amounts] à; ~ **the yard** au mètre; ~ **the thousand** par milliers; **paid** ~ **the day/week/month** payé à la journée/à la semaine/au mois; **to cut prices** ~ **50%** réduire les prix de 50%. || [indicating gradual change]: **day** ~ **day** jour après jour, de jour en jour; **one** ~ **one** un à un, un par un. || **phr**: **(all)** ~ **oneself** (tout) seul ((toute) seule). **2** *adv* → **go, pass** *etc.*

bye(-bye) [baɪ(baɪ)] *excl inf* au revoir!, salut!

bye-election = **by-election**.

byelaw ['baɪlɔ:] = **bylaw**.

by-election *n* élection *f* partielle.

bylaw ['baɪlɔ:] *n* arrêté *m*.

bypass ['baɪpɑ:s] **1** *n* [road] route *f* de contournement. || MED: ~ **(operation)** pontage *m*. **2** *vt* [town, difficulty] contourner; [subject] éviter.

by-product *n* [product] dérivé *m*.

bystander ['baɪˌstændər] *n* spectateur *m*, -trice *f*.

byte [baɪt] *n* COMPUT octet *m*.

byword ['baɪwɜ:d] *n* [symbol]: **to be a** ~ **for** être synonyme de.

C

c (*pl* **c's** OR **cs**), **C** (*pl* **C's** OR **Cs**) [si:] *n* [letter] c *m inv*, C *m inv*. ○ **C** *n* MUS do *m*. || SCH [mark] C *m inv*. || (*abbr of* **Celsius, centigrade**) C.

c., ca. *abbr of* **circa**.

cab [kæb] *n* [taxi] taxi *m*. || [of lorry] cabine *f*.

cabaret ['kæbəreɪ] *n* cabaret *m*.

cabbage ['kæbɪdʒ] *n* [vegetable] chou *m*.

cabin ['kæbɪn] *n* [on ship, plane] cabine *f*. || [house] cabane *f*.

cabin class *n* seconde classe *f*.

cabinet ['kæbɪnɪt] *n* [cupboard] meuble *m*. || POL cabinet *m*.

cable ['keɪbl] **1** *n* câble *m*. **2** *vt* [news] câbler; [person] câbler à.

cable car *n* téléphérique *m*.

cable television, cable TV *n* télévision *f* par câble.

cackle ['kækl] *vi* [hen] caqueter. || [person] jacasser.

cactus ['kæktəs] (*pl* **-tuses** OR **-ti** [-taɪ]) *n* cactus *m*.

cadet [kə'det] *n* élève *m* officier.

caesarean (section) *Br*, **cesarean (section)** *Am* [sɪ'zeərɪən-] *n* césarienne *f*.

cafe, café ['kæfeɪ] *n* café *m*.

cafeteria [ˌkæfɪ'tɪərɪə] *n* cafétéria *f*.

caffeine ['kæfi:n] *n* caféine *f*.

cage [keɪdʒ] *n* [for animal] cage *f*.

cajole [kə'dʒəʊl] *vt*: **to** ~ **sb (into doing sthg)** enjôler qqn (pour qu'il fasse qqch).

cake [keɪk] *n* CULIN gâteau *m*; [of fish, potato] croquette *f*; **it's a piece of** ~ *inf fig* c'est du gâteau. || [of soap] pain *m*.

calcium ['kælsɪəm] *n* calcium *m*.

calculate ['kælkjʊleɪt] *vt* [result, number] calculer; [consequences] évaluer. || [plan]: **to be** ~**d to do sthg** être calculé(e) pour faire qqch.

calculating ['kælkjʊleɪtɪŋ] *adj pej* calculateur(trice).

calculation [ˌkælkjʊ'leɪʃn] *n* calcul *m*.

calculator ['kælkjʊleɪtər] *n* calculatrice *f*.

calendar ['kælɪndər] *n* calendrier *m*.

calendar year *n* année *f* civile.

calf [kɑːf] (*pl* **calves**) *n* [of cow, leather] veau *m*; [of elephant] éléphanteau *m*; [of seal] bébé *m* phoque. ‖ ANAT mollet *m*.

calibre, **caliber** *Am* ['kælɪbər] *n* calibre *m*.

California [,kælɪ'fɔːnjə] *n* Californie *f*.

calipers *Am* = **callipers**.

call [kɔːl] **1** *n* [cry] appel *m*, cri *m*. ‖ TELEC appel *m* (téléphonique). ‖ [summons, invitation] appel *m*; **to be on ~** [doctor etc] être de garde. ‖ [visit] visite *f*; **to pay a ~ on sb** rendre visite à qqn. ‖ [demand]: **~ (for)** demande *f* (de). **2** *vt* [name, summon, phone] appeler; **she's ~ed Joan** elle s'appelle Joan; **let's ~ it £10** disons 10 livres. ‖ [label]: **he ~ed me a liar** il m'a traité de menteur. ‖ [shout] appeler, crier. ‖ [announce - meeting] convoquer; [- strike] lancer; [- flight] appeler; [- election] annoncer. **3** *vi* [shout - person] crier; [- animal, bird] pousser un cri/des cris. ‖ TELEC appeler; **who's ~ing?** qui est à l'appareil? ‖ [visit] passer. ○ **call back 1** *vt sep* rappeler. **2** *vi* TELEC rappeler. ‖ [visit again] repasser. ○ **call for** *vt fus* [collect - person] passer prendre; [- package, goods] passer chercher. ‖ [demand] demander. ○ **call in 1** *vt sep* [expert, police etc] faire venir. **2** *vi* passer. ○ **call off** *vt sep* [cancel] annuler. ‖ [dog] rappeler. ○ **call on** *vt fus* [visit] passer voir. ‖ [ask]: **to ~ on sb to do sthg** demander à qqn de faire qqch. ○ **call out 1** *vt sep* [police, doctor] appeler. ‖ [cry out] crier. **2** *vi* [cry out] crier. ○ **call round** *vi* passer. ○ **call up** *vt sep* MIL & TELEC appeler. ‖ COMPUT rappeler.

caller ['kɔːlər] *n* [visitor] visiteur *m*, -euse *f*. ‖ TELEC demandeur *m*.

call-in *n Am* RADIO & TV programme *m* à ligne ouverte.

calling ['kɔːlɪŋ] *n* [profession] métier *m*. ‖ [vocation] vocation *f*.

calling card *n Am* carte *f* de visite.

callipers *Br*, **calipers** *Am* ['kælɪpəz] *npl* MATH compas *m*. ‖ MED appareil *m* orthopédique.

callous ['kæləs] *adj* dur(e).

callus ['kæləs] (*pl* -es) *n* cal *m*, durillon *m*.

calm [kɑːm] **1** *adj* calme. **2** *n* calme *m*. **3** *vt* calmer. ○ **calm down 1** *vt sep* calmer. **2** *vi* se calmer.

calorie ['kælərɪ] *n* calorie *f*.

calves [kɑːvz] *pl* → **calf**.

camber ['kæmbər] *n* [of road] bombement *m*.

Cambodia [kæm'bəʊdjə] *n* Cambodge *m*.

camcorder ['kæm,kɔːdər] *n* Caméscope® *m*.

came [keɪm] *pt* → **come**.

camel ['kæml] *n* chameau *m*.

cameo ['kæmɪəʊ] (*pl* -s) *n* [jewellery] camée *m*. ‖ CINEMA & THEATRE courte apparition *f* (d'une grande vedette).

camera ['kæmərə] *n* PHOT appareil-photo *m*; CINEMA & TV caméra *f*.

cameraman ['kæmərəmæn] (*pl* -men [-men]) *n* cameraman *m*.

Cameroon [,kæmə'ruːn] *n* Cameroun *m*.

camouflage ['kæməflɑːʒ] **1** *n* camouflage *m*. **2** *vt* camoufler.

camp [kæmp] **1** *n* camp *m*. **2** *vi* camper. ○ **camp out** *vi* camper.

campaign [kæm'peɪn] **1** *n* campagne *f*. **2** *vi*: **to ~ (for/against)** mener une campagne (pour/contre).

camp bed *n* lit *m* de camp.

camper ['kæmpər] *n* [person] campeur *m*, -euse *f*. ‖ [vehicle]: **~ (van)** camping-car *m*.

campground ['kæmpgraʊnd] *n Am* terrain *m* de camping.

camping ['kæmpɪŋ] *n* camping *m*; **to go ~** faire du camping.

camping site, **campsite** ['kæmpsaɪt] *n* (terrain *m* de) camping *m*.

campus ['kæmpəs] (*pl* -es) *n* campus *m*.

can¹ [kæn] (*pt* & *pp* -ned, *cont* -ning) **1** *n* [of drink, food] boîte *f*; [of oil] bidon *m*; [of paint] pot *m*. **2** *vt* mettre en boîte.

can² [*weak form* kən, *strong form* kæn] (*pt* & *conditional* **could**, *negative* **cannot** OR **can't**) *modal vb* [be able to] pouvoir; **~ you come to lunch?** tu peux venir déjeuner?; **~ you see/hear/smell something?** tu vois/entends/sens quelque chose? ‖ [know how to] savoir; **~ you drive/cook?** tu sais conduire/cuisiner?; **I ~ speak French** je parle le français. ‖ [indicating permission, in polite requests] pouvoir; **~ I speak to John, please?** est-ce que je pourrais parler à John, s'il vous plaît? ‖ [indicating disbelief, puzzlement] pouvoir; **what ~ she have done with it?** qu'est-ce qu'elle a bien pu en faire? ‖ [indicating possibility]: **I could see**

you tomorrow je pourrais vous voir demain; **the train could have been cancelled** peut-être que le train a été annulé.

Canada ['kænədə] *n* Canada *m*; **in ~** au Canada.

Canadian [kə'neɪdjən] **1** *adj* canadien(ienne). **2** *n* Canadien *m*, -ienne *f*.

canal [kə'næl] *n* canal *m*.

Canaries [kə'neərɪz] *npl*: **the ~** les Canaries *fpl*.

canary [kə'neərɪ] *n* canari *m*.

cancel ['kænsl] *vt* [gen] annuler; [appointment, delivery] décommander. || [stamp] oblitérer; [cheque] faire opposition à. **○ cancel out** *vt sep* annuler; **to ~ each other out** s'annuler.

cancellation [,kænsə'leɪʃn] *n* annulation *f*.

cancer ['kænsə'] *n* cancer *m*. **○ Cancer** *n* Cancer *m*.

candid ['kændɪd] *adj* franc (franche).

candidate ['kændɪdət] *n*: **~ (for)** candidat *m*, -e *f* (pour).

candle ['kændl] *n* bougie *f*, chandelle *f*.

candlelight ['kændllaɪt] *n* lueur *f* d'une bougie *OR* d'une chandelle.

candlelit ['kændllɪt] *adj* aux chandelles.

candlestick ['kændlstɪk] *n* bougeoir *m*.

candour *Br*, **candor** *Am* ['kændə'] *n* franchise *f*.

candy ['kændɪ] *n* (*U*) [confectionery] confiserie *f*. || [sweet] bonbon *m*.

cane [keɪn] **1** *n* (*U*) [for furniture] rotin *m*. || [walking stick] canne *f*. || [for punishment]: **the ~** la verge. || [for supporting plant] tuteur *m*. **2** *vt* fouetter.

canine ['keɪnaɪn] **1** *adj* canin(e). **2** *n*: **~ (tooth)** canine *f*.

canister ['kænɪstə'] *n* [for film, tea] boîte *f*; [for gas, smoke] bombe *f*.

cannabis ['kænəbɪs] *n* cannabis *m*.

canned [kænd] *adj* [food, drink] en boîte.

cannibal ['kænɪbl] *n* cannibale *mf*.

cannon ['kænən] (*pl inv OR* **-s**) *n* canon *m*.

cannonball ['kænənbɔːl] *n* boulet *m* de canon.

cannot ['kænɒt] *fml* → **can²**.

canoe [kə'nuː] *n* canoë *m*, kayak *m*.

canoeing [kə'nuːɪŋ] *n* (*U*) canoë-kayak *m*.

canon ['kænən] *n* canon *m*.

can opener *n* ouvre-boîtes *m inv*.

canopy ['kænəpɪ] *n* [over bed] balda-

quin *m*; [over seat] dais *m*. || [of trees, branches] voûte *f*.

can't [kɑːnt] = **cannot**.

cantankerous [kæn'tæŋkərəs] *adj* hargneux(euse).

canteen [kæn'tiːn] *n* [restaurant] cantine *f*. || [box of cutlery] ménagère *f*.

canter ['kæntə'] **1** *n* petit galop *m*. **2** *vi* aller au petit galop.

cantilever ['kæntɪliːvə'] *n* cantilever *m*.

canvas ['kænvəs] *n* toile *f*.

canvass ['kænvəs] *vt POL* [person] solliciter la voix de. || [opinion] sonder.

canyon ['kænjən] *n* cañon *m*.

cap [kæp] **1** *n* [hat - gen] casquette *f*. || [of pen] capuchon *m*; [of bottle] capsule *f*; [of lipstick] bouchon *m*. **2** *vt* [top]: **to be capped with** être coiffé(e) de. || [outdo]: **to ~ it all** pour couronner le tout.

capability [,keɪpə'bɪlətɪ] *n* capacité *f*.

capable ['keɪpəbl] *adj*: **~ (of)** capable (de).

capacity [kə'pæsɪtɪ] *n* (*U*) [limit] capacité *f*, contenance *f*. || [ability]: **~ (for)** aptitude *f* (à). || [role] qualité *f*; **in an advisory ~** en tant que conseiller.

cape [keɪp] *n GEOGR* cap *m*. || [cloak] cape *f*.

caper ['keɪpə'] *n CULIN* câpre *f*. || *inf* [dishonest activity] coup *m*, combine *f*.

capita → **per capita**.

capital ['kæpɪtl] **1** *adj* [letter] majuscule. || [offence] capital(e). **2** *n* [of country]: **~ (city)** capitale *f*. || *TYPO*: **~ (letter)** majuscule *f*. || (*U*) [money] capital *m*.

capital expenditure *n* (*U*) dépenses *fpl* d'investissement.

capital gains tax *n* impôt *m* sur les plus-values.

capital goods *npl* biens *mpl* d'équipement.

capitalism ['kæpɪtəlɪzm] *n* capitalisme *m*.

capitalist ['kæpɪtəlɪst] **1** *adj* capitaliste. **2** *n* capitaliste *mf*.

capitalize, **-ise** ['kæpɪtəlaɪz] *vi*: **to ~ on** tirer parti de.

capital punishment *n* peine *f* capitale *OR* de mort.

Capitol Hill ['kæpɪtl-] *n siège du Congrès à Washington.*

capitulate [kə'pɪtjuleɪt] *vi* capituler.

Capricorn ['kæprɪkɔːn] *n* Capricorne *m*.

capsize [kæp'saɪz] **1** *vt* faire chavirer. **2** *vi* chavirer.

capsule ['kæpsju:l] *n* [gen] capsule *f.* || MED gélule *f.*

captain ['kæptɪn] *n* capitaine *m.*

caption ['kæpʃn] *n* légende *f.*

captive ['kæptɪv] **1** *adj* captif(ive). **2** *n* captif *m*, -ive *f.*

captor ['kæptə^r] *n* ravisseur *m*, -euse *f.*

capture ['kæptʃə^r] **1** *vt* [person, animal] capturer; [city] prendre. || [attention, imagination] captiver. || COMPUT saisir. **2** *n* [of person, animal] capture *f*; [of city] prise *f.*

car [kɑ:^r] **1** *n* AUT voiture *f.* || RAIL wagon *m*, voiture *f.* **2** *comp* [door, accident] de voiture; [industry] automobile.

carafe [kə'ræf] *n* carafe *f.*

caramel ['kærəmel] *n* caramel *m.*

caravan ['kærəvæn] *n* [gen] caravane *f*; [towed by horse] roulotte *f.*

carbohydrate [,kɑ:bəʊ'haɪdreɪt] *n* CHEM hydrate *m* de carbone. ○ **carbohydrates** *npl* [in food] glucides *mpl.*

carbon ['kɑ:bən] *n* [element] carbone *m.*

carbonated ['kɑ:bəneɪtɪd] *adj* [mineral water] gazeux(euse).

carbon copy *n* [document] carbone *m.* || *fig* [exact copy] réplique *f.*

carbon dioxide [-daɪ'ɒksaɪd] *n* gaz *m* carbonique.

carbon monoxide [-mɒ'nɒksaɪd] *n* oxyde *m* de carbone.

carbon paper *n* (*U*) (papier *m*) carbone *m.*

carburettor *Br*, **carburetor** *Am* [,kɑ:bə'retə^r] *n* carburateur *m.*

carcass ['kɑ:kəs] *n* [of animal] carcasse *f.*

card [kɑ:d] *n* [gen] carte *f.* || (*U*) [cardboard] carton *m.* ○ **cards** *npl*: **to play ~s** jouer aux cartes.

cardboard ['kɑ:dbɔ:d] *n* (*U*) carton *m.*

cardboard box *n* boîte *f* en carton.

cardiac ['kɑ:dɪæk] *adj* cardiaque.

cardigan ['kɑ:dɪgən] *n* cardigan *m.*

cardinal ['kɑ:dɪnl] **1** *adj* cardinal(e). **2** *n* RELIG cardinal *m.*

care [keə^r] **1** *n* (*U*) [protection, attention] soin *m*, attention *f*; **to take ~ of** [look after] s'occuper de; **to take ~ (to do sthg)** prendre soin (de faire qqch); **take ~!** faites bien attention à vous! || [cause of worry] souci *m.* **2** *vi* [be concerned]: **to ~ about** se soucier de. || [mind]: **I don't ~ ça** m'est égal; **who ~s?** qu'est-ce que ça peut faire? ○ **care of** *prep* chez.

career [kə'rɪə^r] *n* carrière *f.*

careers adviser [kə'rɪəz-] *n* conseiller *m*, -ère *f* d'orientation.

carefree ['keəfri:] *adj* insouciant(e).

careful ['keəful] *adj* [cautious] prudent(e); **to be ~ to do sthg** prendre soin de faire qqch, faire attention à faire qqch; **be ~!** fais attention!; **to be ~ with one's money** regarder à la dépense. || [work] soigné(e); [worker] consciencieux(ieuse).

carefully ['keəflɪ] *adv* [cautiously] prudemment. || [thoroughly] soigneusement.

careless ['keəlɪs] *adj* [work] peu soigné(e); [driver] négligent(e). || [unconcerned] insouciant(e).

caress [kə'res] **1** *n* caresse *f.* **2** *vt* caresser.

caretaker ['keə,teɪkə^r] *n* *Br* gardien *m*, -ienne *f.*

car ferry *n* ferry *m.*

cargo ['kɑ:gəʊ] (*pl* **-es** OR **-s**) *n* cargaison *f.*

car hire *n* *Br* location *f* de voitures.

Caribbean [*Br* kærɪ'bɪən, *Am* kə'rɪbɪən] *n*: **the ~ (Sea)** la mer des Caraïbes OR des Antilles.

caring ['keərɪŋ] *adj* bienveillant(e).

carnage ['kɑ:nɪdʒ] *n* carnage *m.*

carnation [kɑ:'neɪʃn] *n* œillet *m.*

carnival ['kɑ:nɪvl] *n* carnaval *m.*

carnivorous [kɑ:'nɪvərəs] *adj* carnivore.

carol ['kærəl] *n*: **(Christmas) ~** chant *m* de Noël.

carousel [,kærə'sel] *n* [at fair] manège *m.* || [at airport] carrousel *m.*

carp [kɑ:p] (*pl inv* OR **-s**) **1** *n* carpe *f.* **2** *vi*: **to ~ (about sthg)** critiquer (qqch).

carpenter ['kɑ:pəntə^r] *n* [on building site, in shipyard] charpentier *m*; [furniture-maker] menuisier *m.*

carpentry ['kɑ:pəntrɪ] *n* [on building site, in shipyard] charpenterie *f*; [furniture-making] menuiserie *f.*

carpet ['kɑ:pɪt] *n* lit & fig tapis *m*; (fitted) ~ moquette *f.*

carpet sweeper [-,swi:pə^r] *n* balai *m* mécanique.

car phone *n* téléphone *m* pour automobile.

car rental *n* *Am* location *f* de voitures.

carriage ['kærɪdʒ] *n* [of train, horse-drawn] voiture *f.* || (*U*) [transport of goods] transport *m*; **~ paid** OR **free** *Br* franco de port.

carriage return *n* retour *m* chariot.

carrier ['kærɪə'] n COMM transporteur m. || [of disease] porteur m, -euse f. || = **carrier bag**.

carrier bag n sac m (en plastique).

carrot ['kærət] n carotte f.

carry ['kærɪ] 1 vt [subj: person, wind, water] porter; [- subj: vehicle] transporter. || [disease] transmettre. || [responsibility] impliquer; [consequences] entraîner. || [motion, proposal] voter. || [baby] attendre. || MATH retenir. 2 vi [sound] porter. ○ **carry away** vt fus: **to get carried away** s'enthousiasmer. ○ **carry forward** vt sep FIN reporter. ○ **carry off** vt sep [plan] mener à bien. || [prize] remporter. ○ **carry on 1** vt fus continuer; **to ~ on doing sthg** continuer à OR de faire qqch. 2 vi [continue] continuer; **to ~ on with sthg** continuer qqch. ○ **carry out** vt fus [task] remplir; [plan, order] exécuter; [experiment] effectuer; [investigation] mener. ○ **carry through** vt sep [accomplish] réaliser.

carryall ['kærɪɔːl] n Am fourre-tout m inv.

carrycot ['kærɪkɒt] n couffin m.

carry-out n plat m à emporter.

carsick ['kɑːˌsɪk] adj: **to be ~** être malade en voiture.

cart [kɑːt] 1 n charrette f. 2 vt inf traîner.

carton ['kɑːtn] n [box] boîte f en carton. || [of cream, yoghurt] pot m; [of milk] carton m.

cartoon [kɑːˈtuːn] n [satirical drawing] dessin m humoristique. || [comic strip] bande f dessinée. || [film] dessin m animé.

cartridge ['kɑːtrɪdʒ] n [for gun, pen] cartouche f. || [for camera] chargeur m.

cartwheel ['kɑːtwiːl] n [movement] roue f.

carve [kɑːv] 1 vt [wood, stone] sculpter; [design, name] graver. || [slice - meat] découper. 2 vi découper. ○ **carve out** vt sep fig se tailler. ○ **carve up** vt sep fig diviser.

carving ['kɑːvɪŋ] n [of wood] sculpture f, [of stone] ciselure f.

carving knife n couteau m à découper.

car wash n [process] lavage m de voitures; [place] station f de lavage de voitures.

case [keɪs] n [gen] cas m; **to be the ~** être le cas; **in ~ of** en cas de; **in that ~** dans ce cas; **in which ~** auquel cas; **as OR whatever the ~ may be** selon le cas. || [argu-

ment]: **~ (for/against)** arguments mpl (pour/contre). || JUR affaire f, procès m. || [container - gen] caisse f; [- for glasses etc] étui m. ○ **in any case** adv quoi qu'il en soit, de toute façon. ○ **in case 1** conj au cas où. 2 adv: (just) **in ~** à tout hasard.

cash [kæʃ] 1 n (U) [notes and coins] liquide m; **to pay (in) ~** payer comptant OR en espèces. || inf [money] sous mpl, fric m. || [payment]: **~ in advance** paiement m à l'avance; **~ on delivery** paiement à la livraison. 2 vt encaisser.

cash and carry n libre-service m de gros, cash-and-carry m.

cashbook ['kæʃbʊk] n livre m de caisse.

cash box n caisse f.

cash card n carte f de retrait.

cash dispenser [-dɪˌspensə'] n distributeur m automatique de billets.

cashew (nut) ['kæʃuː-] n noix f de cajou.

cashier [kæˈʃɪə'] n caissier m, -ière f.

cash machine n distributeur m de billets.

cashmere [kæʃˈmɪə'] n cachemire m.

cash register n caisse f enregistreuse.

casing ['keɪsɪŋ] n revêtement m; TECH boîtier m.

casino [kəˈsiːnəʊ] (pl -s) n casino m.

cask [kɑːsk] n tonneau m.

casket ['kɑːskɪt] n [for jewels] coffret m. || Am [coffin] cercueil m.

casserole ['kæsərəʊl] n [stew] ragoût m. || [pan] cocotte f.

cassette [kæˈset] n [of magnetic tape] cassette f; PHOT recharge f.

cassette player n lecteur m de cassettes.

cassette recorder n magnétophone m à cassettes.

cast [kɑːst] (pt & pp cast) 1 n [CINEMA & THEATRE - actors] acteurs mpl; [- list of actors] distribution f. 2 vt [throw] jeter; **to ~ doubt on sthg** jeter le doute sur qqch. || CINEMA & THEATRE donner un rôle à. || [vote]: **to ~ one's vote** voter. || [metal] couler; [statue] mouler. ○ **cast aside** vt sep fig écarter, rejeter. ○ **cast off** vi NAUT larguer les amarres.

castaway ['kɑːstəweɪ] n naufragé m, -e f.

caster ['kɑːstə'] n [wheel] roulette f.

casting vote ['kɑːstɪŋ-] n voix f prépondérante.

cast iron n fonte f.

castle ['kɑːsl] n [building] château m. || CHESS tour f.

castor ['kɑːstər] = caster.

castor oil n huile f de ricin.

castor sugar = caster sugar.

castrate [kæ'streɪt] vt châtrer.

casual ['kæʒʊəl] adj [relaxed, indifferent] désinvolte. || [offhand] sans-gêne. || [chance] fortuit(e). || [clothes] décontracté(e), sport (inv). || [work, worker] temporaire.

casually ['kæʒʊəlɪ] adv [in a relaxed manner] avec désinvolture; ~ **dressed** habillé simplement.

casualty ['kæʒjʊəltɪ] n [dead person] mort m, -e f, victime f; [injured person] blessé m, -e f; [of road accident] accidenté m, -e f. || = **casualty department**.

casualty department n service m des urgences.

cat [kæt] n [domestic] chat m. || [wild] fauve m.

catalogue Br, **catalog** Am ['kætəlɒg] 1 n [gen] catalogue m; [in library] fichier m. 2 vt cataloguer.

catalyst ['kætəlɪst] n lit & fig catalyseur m.

catalytic convertor [,kætə'lɪtɪk-kən'vɜːtər] n pot m catalytique.

cataract ['kætərækt] n cataracte f.

catarrh [kə'tɑːr] n catarrhe m.

catastrophe [kə'tæstrəfɪ] n catastrophe f.

catch [kætʃ] (pt & pp **caught**) 1 vt [gen] attraper; **to ~ sight OR a glimpse of** apercevoir; **to ~ sb's attention** attirer l'attention de qqn. || [discover, surprise] prendre, surprendre; **to ~ sb doing sthg** surprendre qqn à faire qqch. || [hear clearly] saisir, comprendre. || [trap]: **I caught my finger in the door** je me suis pris le doigt dans la porte. || [strike] frapper. 2 vi [become hooked, get stuck] se prendre. || [fire] prendre, partir. 3 n [of ball, thing caught] prise f. || [fastener - of box] fermoir m; [- of window] loqueteau m; [- of door] loquet m. || [snag] hic m, entourloupette f. ○ **catch on** vi [become popular] prendre. || inf [understand]: **to ~ on (to sthg)** piger (qqch). ○ **catch out** vt sep [trick] prendre en défaut, coincer. ○ **catch up** 1 vt sep rattraper. 2 vi: **to ~ up on sthg** rattraper qqch. ○ **catch up with** vt fus rattraper.

catching ['kætʃɪŋ] adj contagieux (ieuse).

catchphrase ['kætʃfreɪz] n rengaine f, scie f.

catchy ['kætʃɪ] adj facile à retenir, entraînant(e).

categorically [,kætə'gɒrɪklɪ] adv catégoriquement.

category ['kætəgərɪ] n catégorie f.

cater ['keɪtər] vi [provide food] s'occuper de la nourriture, prévoir les repas.

caterer ['keɪtərər] n traiteur m.

catering ['keɪtərɪŋ] n [trade] restauration f.

caterpillar ['kætəpɪlər] n chenille f.

caterpillar tracks npl chenille f.

cathedral [kə'θiːdrəl] n cathédrale f.

Catholic ['kæθlɪk] 1 adj catholique. 2 n catholique mf.

cattle ['kætl] npl bétail m.

catwalk ['kætwɔːk] n passerelle f.

caucus ['kɔːkəs] n Am POL comité m électoral (d'un parti).

caught [kɔːt] pt & pp → catch.

cauliflower ['kɒlɪ,flaʊər] n chou-fleur m.

cause [kɔːz] 1 n cause f; **to have ~ to do sthg** avoir lieu OR des raisons de faire qqch. 2 vt causer; **to ~ sb to do sthg** faire qqch à qqn; **to ~ sthg to be done** faire faire qqch.

caustic ['kɔːstɪk] adj caustique.

caution ['kɔːʃn] 1 n (U) [care] précaution f, prudence f. || [warning] avertissement m. 2 vt [warn]: **to ~ sb against doing sthg** déconseiller à qqn de faire qqch.

cautious ['kɔːʃəs] adj prudent(e).

cavalry ['kævlrɪ] n cavalerie f.

cave [keɪv] n caverne f, grotte f. ○ **cave in** vi [roof, ceiling] s'affaisser.

caveman ['keɪvmæn] (pl -men [-men]) n homme m des cavernes.

cavernous ['kævənəs] adj [room, building] immense.

caviar(e) ['kævɪɑːr] n caviar m.

cavity ['kævətɪ] n cavité f.

cavort [kə'vɔːt] vi gambader.

CB n (abbr of citizens' band) CB f.

cc 1 n (abbr of cubic centimetre) cm³. 2 (abbr of carbon copy) pcc.

CD n (abbr of compact disc) CD m.

CD player n lecteur m de CD.

CD-ROM [,siːdiː'rɒm] (abbr of compact disc read only memory) n CD-ROM m, CD-Rom m.

cease [siːs] fml 1 vt cesser; **to ~ doing OR to do sthg** cesser de faire qqch. 2 vi cesser.

chain-smoke

cease-fire *n* cessez-le-feu *m inv*.

cedar (tree) ['si:dər-] *n* cèdre *m*.

cedilla [sɪ'dɪlə] *n* cédille *f*.

ceiling ['si:lɪŋ] *n lit & fig* plafond *m*.

celebrate ['selɪbreɪt] **1** *rt* [gen] célébrer, fêter. **2** *vi* faire la fête.

celebrated ['selɪbreɪtɪd] *adj* célèbre.

celebration [,selɪ'breɪʃn] *n* (*U*) [activity, feeling] fête *f*, festivités *fpl*. ‖ [event] festivités *fpl*.

celebrity [sɪ'lebrətɪ] *n* célébrité *f*.

celery ['selərɪ] *n* céleri *m* (en branches).

celibate ['selɪbət] *adj* célibataire.

cell [sel] *n* [gen & COMPUT] cellule *f*.

cellar ['selər] *n* cave *f*.

cello ['tʃeləʊ] (*pl* -s) *n* violoncelle *m*.

Cellophane® ['seləfeɪn] *n* Cellophane® *f*.

Celsius ['selsɪəs] *adj* Celsius (*inv*).

Celt [kelt] *n* Celte *mf*.

Celtic ['keltɪk] **1** *adj* celte. **2** *n* [language] celte *m*.

cement [sɪ'ment] **1** *n* ciment *m*. **2** *vt lit & fig* cimenter.

cement mixer *n* bétonnière *f*.

cemetery ['semɪtrɪ] *n* cimetière *m*.

censor ['sensər] **1** *n* censeur *m*. **2** *vt* censurer.

censorship ['sensəʃɪp] *n* censure *f*.

censure ['senʃər] **1** *n* blâme *m*, critique *f*. **2** *vt* blâmer, critiquer.

census ['sensəs] (*pl* censuses) *n* recensement *m*.

cent [sent] *n* cent *m*.

centenary *Br* [sen'ti:nərɪ], **centennial** *Am* [sen'tenjəl] *n* centenaire *m*.

center *Am* = centre.

centigrade ['sentɪgreɪd] *adj* centigrade.

centilitre *Br*, **centiliter** *Am* ['sentɪ,li:tər] *n* centilitre *m*.

centimetre *Br*, **centimeter** *Am* ['sentɪ,mi:tər] *n* centimètre *m*.

centipede ['sentɪpi:d] *n* mille-pattes *m inv*.

central ['sentrəl] *adj* central(e).

Central America *n* Amérique *f* centrale.

central heating *n* chauffage *m* central.

centralize, -ise ['sentrəlaɪz] *vt* centraliser.

central locking [-'lɒkɪŋ] *n* AUT verrouillage *m* centralisé.

centre *Br*, **center** *Am* ['sentər] **1** *n* centre *m*. **2** *adj* [middle] central(e); **a ~ parting** une raie au milieu. ‖ POL du centre, centriste. **3** *vt* centrer.

centre back *n* FTBL arrière *m* central.

centre forward *n* FTBL avant-centre *m inv*.

centre half *n* FTBL arrière *m* central.

century ['sentʃʊrɪ] *n* siècle *m*.

ceramic [sɪ'ræmɪk] *adj* en céramique. ○ **ceramics** *npl* [objects] objets *mpl* en céramique.

cereal ['sɪərɪəl] *n* céréale *f*.

ceremonial [,serɪ'məʊnjəl] **1** *adj* [dress] de cérémonie; [duties] honorifique. **2** *n* cérémonial *m*.

ceremony ['serɪmənɪ] *n* [event] cérémonie *f*. ‖ (*U*) [pomp, formality] cérémonies *fpl*; **to stand on ~** faire des cérémonies.

certain ['sɜ:tn] *adj* [gen] certain(e); **he is ~ to be late** il est certain qu'il sera en retard, il sera certainement en retard; **to be ~ of sthg/of doing sthg** être assuré de qqch/de faire qqch, être sûr de qqch/de faire qqch; **to make ~** vérifier; **to make ~ of** s'assurer de; **to a ~ extent** jusqu'à un certain point, dans une certaine mesure.

certainly ['sɜ:tnlɪ] *adv* certainement.

certainty ['sɜ:tntɪ] *n* certitude *f*.

certificate [sə'tɪfɪkət] *n* certificat *m*.

certified ['sɜ:tɪfaɪd] *adj* [teacher] diplômé(e); [document] certifié(e).

certified mail *n Am* envoi *m* recommandé.

certified public accountant *n Am* expert-comptable *m*.

certify ['sɜ:tɪfaɪ] *vt* [declare true]: **to ~ (that)** certifier OR attester que. ‖ [declare insane] déclarer mentalement aliéné(e).

cervical smear [sə'vaɪkl] *n* frottis *m* vaginal.

cervix ['sɜ:vɪks] (*pl* -ices [-ɪsi:z]) *n* col *m* de l'utérus.

cesarean (section) = caesarean (section).

cesspit ['sespɪt], **cesspool** ['sespu:l] *n* fosse *f* d'aisance.

cf. (*abbr of* confer) cf.

CFC (*abbr of* chlorofluorocarbon) *n* CFC *m*.

ch. (*abbr of* chapter) chap.

chafe [tʃeɪf] *vt* [rub] irriter.

chaffinch ['tʃæfɪntʃ] *n* pinson *m*.

chain [tʃeɪn] **1** *n* chaîne *f*; **~ of events** suite *f* OR série *f* d'événements. **2** *vt* [person, animal] enchaîner; [object] attacher avec une chaîne.

chain reaction *n* réaction *f* en chaîne.

chain saw *n* tronçonneuse *f*.

chain-smoke *vi* fumer cigarette sur cigarette.

chain store n grand magasin m (à suc-cursales multiples).

chair [tʃeəʳ] **1** n [gen] chaise f; [arm-chair] fauteuil m. || [university post] chaire f. || [of meeting] présidence f. **2** vt [meeting] présider; [discussion] diriger.

chair lift n télésiège m.

chairman ['tʃeəmən] (pl -men [-mən]) n président m.

chairperson ['tʃeə,pɜːsn] (pl -s) n président m, -e f.

chalet ['ʃæleɪ] n chalet m.

chalk [tʃɔːk] n craie f.

chalkboard ['tʃɔːkbɔːd] n Am tableau m (noir).

challenge ['tʃælɪndʒ] **1** n défi m. **2** vt [to fight, competition]: **she ~d me to a race/a game of chess** elle m'a défié à la course/aux échecs; **to ~ sb to do sthg** défier qqn de faire qqch. || [question] mettre en question OR en doute.

challenging ['tʃælɪndʒɪŋ] adj [task, job] stimulant(e). || [look, tone of voice] pro-vocateur(trice).

chambermaid ['tʃeɪmbəmeɪd] n femme f de chambre.

chamber music n musique f de cham-bre.

chamber of commerce n chambre f de commerce.

chameleon [kə'miːljən] n caméléon m.

champagne [,ʃæm'peɪn] n champagne m.

champion ['tʃæmpjən] n champion m, -ionne f.

championship ['tʃæmpjənʃɪp] n cham-pionnat m.

chance [tʃɑːns] **1** n (U) [luck] hasard m; **by ~** par hasard. || [likelihood] chance f; **she didn't stand a ~ (of doing sthg)** elle n'avait aucune chance (de faire qqch); **on the off ~** à tout hasard. || [opportunity] occasion f. || [risk] risque m; **to take a ~** risquer le coup. **2** adj fortuit(e), acciden-tel(elle). **3** vt [risk] risquer; **to ~ it** tenter sa chance.

chancellor ['tʃɑːnsələʳ] n [chief minis-ter] chancelier m. || UNIV président m, -e f honoraire.

Chancellor of the Exchequer n Br Chancelier m de l'Échiquier, ≃ ministre m des Finances.

chandelier [,ʃændə'lɪəʳ] n lustre m.

change [tʃeɪndʒ] **1** n [gen]: **~ (in sb/in sthg)** changement m (en qqn/de qqch); **for a ~** pour changer (un peu). || [money] monnaie f. **2** vt [gen] changer; **to ~ sthg**

into sthg changer OR transformer qqch en qqch; **to ~ one's mind** changer d'avis. || [jobs, trains, sides] changer de. || [money - into smaller units] faire la monnaie de; [- into different currency] changer. **3** vi [gen] changer. || [change clothes] se chan-ger. || [be transformed]: **to ~ into** se chan-ger en. ○ **change over** vi [convert]: **to ~ over from/to** passer de/à.

changeable ['tʃeɪndʒəbl] adj [mood] changeable; [weather] variable.

change machine n distributeur m de monnaie.

changeover ['tʃeɪndʒ,əʊvəʳ] n: **~ (to)** passage m (à), changement m (pour).

changing ['tʃeɪndʒɪŋ] adj changeant(e).

changing room n SPORT vestiaire m; [in shop] cabine f d'essayage.

channel ['tʃænl] **1** n TV chaîne f; RADIO station f. || [for irrigation] canal m; [duct] conduit m. || [on river, sea] chenal m. **2** vt lit & fig canaliser. ○ **Channel** n: **the (English) Channel** la Manche. ○ **channels** npl: **to go through the proper ~s** suivre OR passer la filière.

Channel Islands npl: **the ~** les îles fpl Anglo-Normandes.

Channel tunnel n: **the ~** le tunnel sous la Manche.

chant [tʃɑːnt] **1** n chant m. **2** vt RELIG chanter. || [words, slogan] scander.

chaos ['keɪɒs] n chaos m.

chaotic [keɪ'ɒtɪk] adj chaotique.

chapel ['tʃæpl] n chapelle f.

chaplain ['tʃæplɪn] n aumônier m.

chapped [tʃæpt] adj [skin, lips] ger-cé(e).

chapter ['tʃæptəʳ] n chapitre m.

char [tʃɑːʳ] vt [burn] calciner.

character ['kærəktəʳ] n [gen] caractère m. || [in film, book, play] personnage m. || inf [eccentric] phénomène m, original m.

characteristic [,kærəktə'rɪstɪk] **1** adj caractéristique. **2** n caractéristique f.

characterize, -ise ['kærəktəraɪz] vt ca-ractériser.

charade [ʃə'rɑːd] n farce f.

charcoal ['tʃɑːkəʊl] n [for drawing] charbon m; [for burning] charbon m de bois.

charge [tʃɑːdʒ] **1** n [cost] prix m; **free of ~** gratuit. || JUR accusation f, inculpation f. || [responsibility]: **to take ~ of** se char-ger de; **to be in ~ of, to have ~ of** être res-ponsable de, s'occuper de; **in ~** respon-sable. || ELEC & MIL charge f. **2** vt [cus-tomer, sum] faire payer; **how much do**

you ~? vous prenez combien?; **to ~ sthg to sb** mettre qqch sur le compte de qqn. || [suspect, criminal]: **to ~ sb (with)** accuser qqn (de). || ELEC & MIL charger. **3** *vi* [rush] se précipiter, foncer.

charge card *n* carte *f* de compte crédit (*auprès d'un magasin*).

charger ['tʃɑːdʒər] *n* [for batteries] chargeur *m*.

charisma [kə'rɪzmə] *n* charisme *m*.

charity ['tʃærətɪ] *n* charité *f*.

charm [tʃɑːm] **1** *n* charme *m*. **2** *vt* charmer.

charming ['tʃɑːmɪŋ] *adj* charmant(e).

chart [tʃɑːt] **1** *n* [diagram] graphique *m*, diagramme *m*. || [map] carte *f*. **2** *vt* [plot, map] porter sur une carte. || *fig* [record] retracer. ○ **charts** *npl*: **the ~s** le hit-parade.

charter ['tʃɑːtər] **1** *n* [document] charte *f*. **2** *vt* [plane, boat] affréter.

charter flight *n* vol *m* charter.

chase [tʃeɪs] **1** *n* [pursuit] poursuite *f*, chasse *f*. **2** *vt* [pursue] poursuivre. || [drive away] chasser. **3** *vi*: **to ~ after sb/ sthg** courir après qqn/qqch.

chassis ['ʃæsɪ] (*pl inv*) *n* châssis *m*.

chat [tʃæt] **1** *n* causerie *f*, bavardage *m*; **to have a ~** causer, bavarder. **2** *vi* causer, bavarder.

chatter ['tʃætər] **1** *n* [of person] bavardage *m*. || [of animal, bird] caquetage *m*. **2** *vi* [person] bavarder. || [animal, bird] jacasser, caqueter. || [teeth]: **his teeth were ~ing** il claquait des dents.

chatterbox ['tʃætəbɒks] *n inf* moulin *m* à paroles.

chauffeur ['ʃəʊfər] *n* chauffeur *m*.

chauvinist ['ʃəʊvɪnɪst] *n* [sexist] macho *m*. || [nationalist] chauvin *m*, -e *f*.

cheap [tʃiːp] **1** *adj* [inexpensive] pas cher (chère), bon marché (*inv*). || [at a reduced price - fare, rate] réduit(e); [- ticket] à prix réduit. || [low-quality] de mauvaise qualité. || [joke, comment] facile. **2** *adv* (à) bon marché.

cheapen ['tʃiːpn] *vt* [degrade] rabaisser.

cheaply ['tʃiːplɪ] *adv* à bon marché, pour pas cher.

cheat [tʃiːt] **1** *n* tricheur *m*, -euse *f*. **2** *vt* tromper; **to ~ sb out of sthg** escroquer qqch à qqn. **3** *vi* [in game, exam] tricher. || *inf* [be unfaithful]: **to ~ on sb** tromper qqn.

check [tʃek] **1** *n* [inspection, test]: **~ (on)** contrôle *m* (de). || [restraint]: **~ (on)** frein *m* (à), restriction *f* (sur). || *Am* [bill] note

f. || [pattern] carreaux *mpl*. || *Am* = **cheque**. **2** *vt* [test, verify] vérifier; [passport, ticket] contrôler. || [restrain, stop] enrayer, arrêter. **3** *vi*: **to ~ (for sthg)** vérifier (qqch); **to ~ on sthg** vérifier OR contrôler qqch. ○ **check in 1** *vt sep* [luggage, coat] enregistrer. **2** *vi* [at hotel] signer le registre. || [at airport] se présenter à l'enregistrement. ○ **check out 1** *vt sep* [luggage, coat] retirer. || [investigate] vérifier. **2** *vi* [from hotel] régler sa note. ○ **check up** *vi*: **to ~ up on sb** prendre des renseignements sur qqn; **to ~ up (on sthg)** vérifier (qqch).

checkbook *Am* = **chequebook**.

checked [tʃekt] *adj* à carreaux.

checkered *Am* = **chequered**.

checkers ['tʃekəz] *n* (*U*) *Am* jeu *m* de dames.

check-in *n* enregistrement *m*.

checking account ['tʃekɪŋ-] *n Am* compte *m* courant.

checkmate ['tʃekmeɪt] *n* échec et mat *m*.

checkout ['tʃekaʊt] *n* [in supermarket] caisse *f*.

checkpoint ['tʃekpɔɪnt] *n* [place] (poste *m* de) contrôle *m*.

checkup ['tʃekʌp] *n* MED bilan *m* de santé, check-up *m*.

Cheddar (cheese) ['tʃedər-] *n* (fromage *m* de) cheddar *m*.

cheek [tʃiːk] *n* [of face] joue *f*. || *inf* [impudence] culot *m*.

cheekbone ['tʃiːkbəʊn] *n* pommette *f*.

cheeky ['tʃiːkɪ] *adj* insolent(e), effronté(e).

cheer [tʃɪər] **1** *n* [shout] acclamation *f*. **2** *vt* [shout for] acclamer. || [gladden] réjouir. **3** *vi* applaudir. ○ **cheers** *excl* [said before drinking] santé! || *inf* [goodbye] salut!, ciao!, tchao! || *inf* [thank you] merci. ○ **cheer up** *vt sep* remonter le moral à. **2** *vi* s'égayer.

cheerful ['tʃɪəfʊl] *adj* joyeux(euse), gai(e).

cheerio [,tʃɪərɪ'əʊ] *excl inf* au revoir!, salut!

cheese [tʃiːz] *n* fromage *m*.

cheeseboard ['tʃiːzbɔːd] *n* plateau *m* à fromage.

cheeseburger ['tʃiːz,bɜːgər] *n* cheeseburger *m*, hamburger *m* au fromage.

cheesecake ['tʃiːzkeɪk] *n* CULIN gâteau *m* au fromage blanc, cheesecake *m*.

cheetah ['tʃiːtə] *n* guépard *m*.

chef [ʃef] *n* chef *m*.

chemical ['kemɪkl] 1 adj chimique. 2 n produit m chimique.

chemist ['kemɪst] n [scientist] chimiste mf.

chemistry ['kemɪstrɪ] n chimie f.

cheque Br, **check** Am [tʃek] n chèque m.

chequebook Br, **checkbook** Am ['tʃekbuk] n chéquier m, carnet m de chèques.

cheque card n Br carte f bancaire.

cherish ['tʃerɪʃ] vt chérir; [hope] nourrir, caresser.

cherry ['tʃerɪ] n [fruit] cerise f; ~ (tree) cerisier m.

chess [tʃes] n échecs mpl.

chessboard ['tʃesbɔːd] n échiquier m.

chessman ['tʃesmæn] (pl -men [-men]) n pièce f.

chest [tʃest] n ANAT poitrine f. || [box] coffre m.

chestnut ['tʃesnʌt] 1 adj [colour] châtain (inv). 2 n [nut] châtaigne f; ~ (tree) châtaignier m.

chest of drawers (pl **chests of drawers**) n commode f.

chew [tʃuː] 1 n [sweet] bonbon m (à mâcher). 2 vt mâcher. ○ **chew up** vt sep mâchouiller.

chewing gum ['tʃuːɪŋ-] n chewing-gum m.

chic [ʃiːk] adj chic (inv).

chick [tʃɪk] n [baby bird] oisillon m.

chicken ['tʃɪkɪn] n [bird, food] poulet m. || inf [coward] froussard m, -e f. ○ **chicken out** vi inf se dégonfler.

chickenpox ['tʃɪkɪnpɒks] n (U) varicelle f.

chickpea ['tʃɪkpiː] n pois m chiche.

chicory ['tʃɪkərɪ] n [vegetable] endive f.

chief [tʃiːf] 1 adj [main - aim, problem] principal(e). || [head] en chef. 2 n chef m.

chief executive n directeur général m, directrice générale f.

chiefly ['tʃiːflɪ] adv [mainly] principalement. || [above all] surtout.

chiffon ['ʃɪfɒn] n mousseline f.

chilblain ['tʃɪlbleɪn] n engelure f.

child [tʃaɪld] (pl **children**) n enfant mf.

childbirth ['tʃaɪldbɜːθ] n (U) accouchement m.

childhood ['tʃaɪldhʊd] n enfance f.

childish ['tʃaɪldɪʃ] adj pej puéril(e), enfantin(e).

children ['tʃɪldrən] pl → child.

children's home n maison f d'enfants.

Chile ['tʃɪlɪ] n Chili m.

Chilean ['tʃɪlɪən] 1 adj chilien(ienne). 2 n Chilien m, -ienne f.

chili ['tʃɪlɪ] = chilli.

chill [tʃɪl] 1 adj frais (fraîche). 2 n [illness] coup m de froid. || [in temperature]: there's a ~ in the air le fond de l'air est frais. || [feeling of fear] frisson m. 3 vt [drink, food] mettre au frais. || [person] faire frissonner. 4 vi [drink, food] rafraîchir.

chilli ['tʃɪlɪ] (pl -ies) n [vegetable] piment m.

chilling ['tʃɪlɪŋ] adj [very cold] glacial(e). || [frightening] qui glace le sang.

chilly ['tʃɪlɪ] adj froid(e); to feel ~ avoir froid; it's ~ il fait froid.

chime [tʃaɪm] 1 n [of bell, clock] carillon m. 2 vt [time] sonner. 3 vi [bell, clock] carillonner.

chimney ['tʃɪmnɪ] n cheminée f.

chimneypot ['tʃɪmnɪpɒt] n mitre f de cheminée.

chimneysweep ['tʃɪmnɪswiːp] n ramoneur m.

chimp(anzee) [tʃɪmp(ənˈziː)] n chimpanzé m.

chin [tʃɪn] n menton m.

china ['tʃaɪnə] n porcelaine f.

China ['tʃaɪnə] n Chine f.

Chinese [ˌtʃaɪˈniːz] 1 adj chinois(e). 2 n [language] chinois m. 3 npl: the ~ les Chinois mpl.

Chinese cabbage n chou m chinois.

chink [tʃɪŋk] n [narrow opening] fente f. || [sound] tintement m.

chip [tʃɪp] 1 n Br [fried potato] frite f; Am [potato crisp] chip m. || [of glass, metal] éclat m; [of wood] copeau m. || [flaw] ébréchure f. || [microchip] puce f. || [for gambling] jeton m. 2 vt [cup, glass] ébrécher. ○ **chip in** vi inf [contribute] contribuer. || [interrupt] mettre son grain de sel. ○ **chip off** vt sep enlever petit morceau par petit morceau.

chipboard ['tʃɪpbɔːd] n aggloméré m.

chiropodist [kɪˈrɒpədɪst] n pédicure mf.

chirp [tʃɜːp] vi [bird] pépier; [cricket] chanter.

chirpy ['tʃɜːpɪ] adj gai(e).

chisel ['tʃɪzl] 1 n [for wood] ciseau m; [for metal, rock] burin m. 2 vt ciseler.

chit [tʃɪt] n [note] note f, reçu m.

chitchat ['tʃɪttʃæt] n (U) inf bavardage m.

chivalry ['ʃɪvlrɪ] n (U) literary [of

knights] chevalerie f. || [good manners] galanterie f.

chives [tʃaɪvz] npl ciboulette f.

chlorine ['klɔːriːn] n chlore m.

chock [tʃɒk] n cale f.

chock-a-block, chock-full adj inf: ~ (with) plein(e) à craquer (de).

chocolate ['tʃɒkələt] **1** n chocolat m. **2** comp au chocolat.

choice [tʃɔɪs] **1** n choix m. **2** adj de choix.

choir ['kwaɪər] n chœur m.

choirboy ['kwaɪəbɔɪ] n jeune choriste m.

choke [tʃəʊk] **1** n AUT starter m. **2** vt [strangle] étrangler, étouffer. || [block] obstruer, boucher. **3** vi s'étrangler.

cholera ['kɒlərə] n choléra m.

choose [tʃuːz] (pt chose, pp chosen) **1** vt [select] choisir. || [decide]: **to ~ to do sthg** décider OR choisir de faire qqch. **2** vi [select]: **to ~ (from)** choisir (parmi OR entre).

choos(e)y ['tʃuːzɪ] (compar -ier, superl -iest) adj difficile.

chop [tʃɒp] **1** n CULIN côtelette f. **2** vt [wood] couper; [vegetables] hacher. || inf fig [funding, budget] réduire. O **chop down** vt sep [tree] abattre. O **chop up** vt sep couper en morceaux.

chopper ['tʃɒpər] n [axe] couperet m. || inf [helicopter] hélico m.

choppy ['tʃɒpɪ] adj [sea] agité(e).

chopsticks ['tʃɒpstɪks] npl baguettes fpl.

chord [kɔːd] n MUS accord m.

chore [tʃɔːr] n corvée f; **household ~s** travaux mpl ménagers.

chortle ['tʃɔːtl] vi glousser.

chorus ['kɔːrəs] n [part of song] refrain m. || [singers] chœur m. || fig [of praise, complaints] concert m.

chose [tʃəʊz] pt → choose.

chosen ['tʃəʊzn] pp → choose.

Christ [kraɪst] **1** n Christ m. **2** excl Seigneur!, bon Dieu!

christen ['krɪsn] vt [baby] baptiser. || [name] nommer.

christening ['krɪsnɪŋ] n baptême m.

Christian ['krɪstʃən] **1** adj RELIG chrétien(ienne). **2** n chrétien m, -ienne f.

Christianity [ˌkrɪstɪ'ænətɪ] n christianisme m.

Christian name n prénom m.

Christmas ['krɪsməs] n Noël m; **happy OR merry ~!** joyeux Noël!

Christmas card n carte f de Noël.

Christmas Day n jour m de Noël.

Christmas Eve n veille f de Noël.

Christmas tree n arbre m de Noël.

chrome [krəʊm], **chromium** ['krəʊmɪəm] **1** n chrome m. **2** comp chromé(e).

chronic ['krɒnɪk] adj [illness, unemployment] chronique; [liar, alcoholic] invétéré(e).

chronicle ['krɒnɪkl] n chronique f.

chronological [ˌkrɒnə'lɒdʒɪkl] adj chronologique.

chrysanthemum [krɪ'sænθəməm] (pl -s) n chrysanthème m.

chubby ['tʃʌbɪ] adj [cheeks, face] joufflu(e); [person, hands] potelé(e).

chuck [tʃʌk] vt inf [throw] lancer, envoyer. || [job, boyfriend] laisser tomber. O **chuck away, chuck out** vt sep inf jeter, balancer.

chuckle ['tʃʌkl] vi glousser.

chug [tʃʌg] vi [train] faire teuf-teuf.

chum [tʃʌm] n inf copain m, copine f.

chunk [tʃʌŋk] n gros morceau m.

church [tʃɜːtʃ] n [building] église f; **to go to ~** aller à l'église; [Catholics] aller à la messe.

Church of England n: **the ~** l'Église d'Angleterre.

churchyard ['tʃɜːtʃjɑːd] n cimetière m.

churn [tʃɜːn] **1** n [for making butter] baratte f. || [for milk] bidon m. **2** vt [stir up] battre. O **churn out** vt sep inf produire en série.

chute [ʃuːt] n glissière f; **rubbish ~** vide-ordures m inv.

chutney ['tʃʌtnɪ] n chutney m.

CIA (abbr of **Central Intelligence Agency**) n CIA f.

cider ['saɪdər] n cidre m.

cigar [sɪ'gɑːr] n cigare m.

cigarette [ˌsɪgə'ret] n cigarette f.

cinder ['sɪndər] n cendre f.

Cinderella [ˌsɪndə'relə] n Cendrillon f.

cine-camera ['sɪnɪ-] n caméra f.

cine-film ['sɪnɪ-] n film m.

cinema ['sɪnəmə] n cinéma m.

cinnamon ['sɪnəmən] n cannelle f.

circa ['sɜːkə] prep environ.

circle ['sɜːkl] **1** n [gen] cercle m; **to go round in ~s** fig tourner en rond. || [in theatre, cinema] balcon m. **2** vt [draw a circle round] entourer (d'un cercle). || [move round] faire le tour de. **3** vi [plane] tourner en rond.

circuit ['sɜːkɪt] n [gen & ELEC] circuit m.

|| [lap] tour *m*; [movement round] révolution *f*.

circular ['sɜːkjʊləʳ] **1** *adj* [gen] circulaire. **2** *n* [letter] circulaire *f*; [advertisement] prospectus *m*.

circulate ['sɜːkjʊleɪt] **1** *vi* [gen] circuler. || [socialize] se mêler aux invités. **2** *vt* [rumour] propager; [document] faire circuler.

circulation [,sɜːkjʊ'leɪʃn] *n* [gen] circulation *f*. || PRESS tirage *m*.

circumcision [,sɜːkəm'sɪʒn] *n* circoncision *f*.

circumference [sə'kʌmfərəns] *n* circonférence *f*.

circumflex ['sɜːkəmfleks] *n*: ~ (**accent**) accent *m* circonflexe.

circumspect ['sɜːkəmspekt] *adj* circonspect(e).

circumstances ['sɜːkəmstənsɪz] *npl* circonstances *fpl*; **under** OR **in no** ~ en aucun cas; **under** OR **in the** ~ en de telles circonstances.

circumvent [,sɜːkəm'vent] *vt fml* [law, rule] tourner.

circus ['sɜːkəs] *n* cirque *m*.

CIS (*abbr of* **Commonwealth of Independent States**) *n* CEI *f*.

cistern ['sɪstən] *n* [in toilet] réservoir *m* de chasse d'eau.

cite [saɪt] *vt* citer.

citizen ['sɪtɪzn] *n* [of country] citoyen *m*, -enne *f*. || [of town] habitant *m*, -e *f*.

Citizens' Band *n* fréquence radio réservée au public, citizen band *f*.

citizenship ['sɪtɪznʃɪp] *n* citoyenneté *f*.

citrus fruit ['sɪtrəs-] *n* agrume *m*.

city ['sɪtɪ] *n* ville *f*, cité *f*. ○ **City** *n* Br: **the City** la City (*quartier financier de Londres*).

city centre *n* centre-ville *m*.

city hall *n* Am ≃ mairie *f*, ≃ hôtel *m* de ville.

civic ['sɪvɪk] *adj* [leader, event] municipal(e); [duty, pride] civique.

civil ['sɪvl] *adj* [public] civil(e). || [polite] courtois(e), poli(e).

civil engineering *n* génie *m* civil.

civilian [sɪ'vɪljən] **1** *n* civil *m*, -e *f*. **2** *comp* civil(e).

civilization [,sɪvɪlaɪ'zeɪʃn] *n* civilisation *f*.

civilized ['sɪvɪlaɪzd] *adj* civilisé(e).

civil law *n* droit *m* civil.

civil liberties *npl* libertés *fpl* civiques.

civil rights *npl* droits *mpl* civils.

civil servant *n* fonctionnaire *mf*.

civil service *n* fonction *f* publique.

civil war *n* guerre *f* civile.

cl (*abbr of* **centilitre**) cl.

claim [kleɪm] **1** *n* [for pay etc] revendication *f*; [for expenses, insurance] demande *f*. || [right] droit *m*; **to lay ~ to sthg** revendiquer qqch. || [assertion] affirmation *f*. **2** *vt* [ask for] réclamer. || [responsibility, credit] revendiquer. || [maintain] prétendre. **3** *vi*: **to ~ for sthg** faire une demande d'indemnité pour qqch; **to ~ (on one's insurance)** faire une déclaration de sinistre.

claimant ['kleɪmənt] *n* [to throne] prétendant *m*, -e *f*; [of state benefit] demandeur *m*, -eresse *f*, requérant *m*, -e *f*.

clairvoyant [kleə'vɔɪənt] *n* voyant *m*, -e *f*.

clam [klæm] *n* palourde *f*.

clamber ['klæmbəʳ] *vi* grimper.

clamp [klæmp] **1** *n* [gen] pince *f*, agrafe *f*; [for carpentry] serre-joint *m*; MED clamp *m*. **2** *vt* [gen] serrer. || AUT poser un sabot de Denver à. ○ **clamp down** *vi*: **to ~ down (on)** sévir (contre).

clan [klæn] *n* clan *m*.

clandestine [klæn'destɪn] *adj* clandestin(e).

clang [klæŋ] *n* bruit *m* métallique.

clap [klæp] **1** *vt* [hands]: **to ~ one's hands** applaudir, taper des mains. **2** *vi* applaudir, taper des mains.

clapping ['klæpɪŋ] *n* (*U*) applaudissements *mpl*.

claret ['klærət] *n* [wine] bordeaux *m* rouge. || [colour] bordeaux *m inv*.

clarify ['klærɪfaɪ] *vt* [explain] éclaircir, clarifier.

clarinet [,klærə'net] *n* clarinette *f*.

clarity ['klærətɪ] *n* clarté *f*.

clash [klæʃ] **1** *n* [of interests, personalities] conflit *m*. || [fight, disagreement] heurt *m*, affrontement *m*. || [noise] fracas *m*. **2** *vi* [fight, disagree] se heurter. || [differ, conflict] entrer en conflit. || [coincide]: **to ~ (with sthg)** tomber en même temps (que qqch). || [colours] jurer.

clasp [klɑːsp] **1** *n* [on necklace etc] fermoir *m*; [on belt] boucle *f*. **2** *vt* [hold tight] serrer.

class [klɑːs] **1** *n* [gen] classe *f*. || [lesson] cours *m*, classe *f*. || [category] catégorie *f*. **2** *vt* classer.

classic ['klæsɪk] **1** *adj* classique. **2** *n* classique *m*.

classical ['klæsɪkl] *adj* classique.

classified ['klæsıfaıd] adj [information, document] classé secret (classée secrète).

classified ad n petite annonce f.

classify ['klæsıfaı] vt classifier, classer.

classmate ['klɑ:smeıt] n camarade mf de classe.

classroom ['klɑ:srʊm] n (salle f de) classe f.

clatter ['klætər] n cliquetis m; [louder] fracas m.

clause [klɔ:z] n [in document] clause f. || GRAMM proposition f.

claw [klɔ:] 1 n [of cat, bird] griffe f. || [of crab, lobster] pince f. 2 vt griffer. 3 vi [person]: **to ~ at** s'agripper à.

clay [kleı] n argile f.

clean [kli:n] 1 adj [not dirty] propre. || [sheet of paper, driving licence] vierge; [reputation] sans tache. || [joke] de bon goût. || [smooth] net (nette). 2 vt nettoyer; **to ~ one's teeth** se brosser OR laver les dents. 3 vi faire le ménage. ○ **clean out** vt sep [room, drawer] nettoyer à fond. ○ **clean up** vt sep [clear up] nettoyer.

cleaner ['kli:nər] n [person] personne f qui fait le ménage. || [substance] produit m d'entretien.

cleaning ['kli:nıŋ] n nettoyage m.

cleanliness ['klenlınıs] n propreté f.

cleanse [klenz] vt [skin, wound] nettoyer. || fig [make pure] purifier.

cleanser ['klenzər] n [detergent] détergent m; [for skin] démaquillant m.

clean-shaven [-'ʃeıvn] adj rasé(e) de près.

clear [klıər] 1 adj [gen] clair(e); [glass, plastic] transparent(e); [difference] net (nette); **to make sthg ~ (to sb)** expliquer qqch clairement (à qqn); **to make it ~ that** préciser que; **to make o.s. ~** bien se faire comprendre. || [voice, sound] qui s'entend nettement. || [road, space] libre, dégagé(e). 2 adv: **to stand ~** s'écarter; **to stay ~ of sb/sthg, to steer ~ of sb/sthg** éviter qqn/qqch. 3 vt [road, path] dégager; [table] débarrasser. || [obstacle, fallen tree] enlever. || [jump] sauter, franchir. || [debt] s'acquitter de. || [authorize] donner le feu vert à. || JUR innocenter. 4 vi [fog, smoke] se dissiper; [weather, sky] s'éclaircir. ○ **clear away** vt sep [plates] débarrasser; [books] enlever. ○ **clear out** 1 vt sep [cupboard] vider; [room] ranger. 2 vi inf [leave] dégager. ○ **clear up** 1 vt sep [tidy] ranger. || [mystery, mis-understanding] éclaircir. 2 vi [weather] s'éclaircir. || [tidy up] tout ranger.

clearance ['klıərəns] n [of rubbish] enlèvement m; [of land] déblaiement m. || [permission] autorisation f.

clear-cut adj net (nette).

clearing ['klıərıŋ] n [in wood] clairière f.

clearly ['klıəlı] adv [distinctly, lucidly] clairement. || [obviously] manifestement.

cleavage ['kli:vıdʒ] n [between breasts] décolleté m.

cleaver ['kli:vər] n couperet m.

clef [klef] n clef f.

cleft [kleft] n fente f.

clench [klentʃ] vt serrer.

clergy ['klɜ:dʒı] npl: **the ~** le clergé.

clergyman ['klɜ:dʒımən] (pl -men [-mən]) n membre m du clergé.

clerical ['klerıkl] adj ADMIN de bureau. || RELIG clérical(e).

clerk [Br klɑ:k, Am klɜ:rk] n [in office] employé m, -e f de bureau. || JUR clerc m. || Am [shop assistant] vendeur m, -euse f.

clever ['klevər] adj [intelligent - person] intelligent(e); [- idea] ingénieux(ieuse). || [skilful] habile, adroit(e).

click [klık] 1 n [of lock] déclic m; [of tongue, heels] claquement m. 2 vt faire claquer. 3 vi [heels] claquer; [camera] faire un déclic.

client ['klaıənt] n client m, -e f.

cliff [klıf] n falaise f.

climate ['klaımıt] n climat m.

climax ['klaımæks] n [culmination] apogée m.

climb [klaım] 1 n ascension f, montée f. 2 vt [tree, rope] monter à; [stairs] monter; [wall, hill] escalader. 3 vi [person] monter, grimper. || [plant] grimper; [road] monter; [plane] prendre de l'altitude. || [increase] augmenter.

climb-down n reculade f.

climber ['klaımər] n [person] alpiniste mf, grimpeur m, -euse f.

climbing ['klaımıŋ] n [rock climbing] varappe f; [mountain climbing] alpinisme m.

cling [klıŋ] (pt & pp **clung**) vi [hold tightly]: **to ~ (to)** s'accrocher (à), se cramponner (à). || [clothes]: **to ~ (to)** coller (à).

clinic ['klınık] n [building] centre m médical, clinique f.

clinical ['klınıkl] adj MED clinique. || fig [attitude] froid(e).

clink [klıŋk] vi tinter.

clip [klɪp] **1** *n* [for paper] trombone *m*; [for hair] pince *f*; [of earring] clip *m*; TECH collier *m*. ‖ [excerpt] extrait *m*. **2** *vt* [fasten] attacher. ‖ [nails] couper; [hedge] tailler; [newspaper cutting] découper.

clipboard ['klɪpbɔːd] *n* écritoire *f* à pince, clipboard *m*.

clippers ['klɪpəz] *npl* [for hair] tondeuse *f*; [for nails] pince *f* à ongles; [for hedge] cisaille *f* à haie; [for pruning] sécateur *m*.

clipping ['klɪpɪŋ] *n* [from newspaper] coupure *f*.

cloak [kləʊk] *n* [garment] cape *f*.

cloakroom ['kləʊkrʊm] *n* [for clothes] vestiaire *m*. ‖ *Br* [toilets] toilettes *fpl*.

clock [klɒk] *n* [large] horloge *f*; [small] pendule *f*; **round the ~** [work, be open] 24 heures sur 24. ‖ AUT [mileometer] compteur *m*.

clockwise ['klɒkwaɪz] *adj & adv* dans le sens des aiguilles d'une montre.

clockwork ['klɒkwɜːk] **1** *n*: **to go like ~** *fig* aller OR marcher comme sur des roulettes. **2** *comp* [toy] mécanique.

clog [klɒg] *vt* boucher. ○ **clogs** *npl* sabots *mpl*. ○ **clog up 1** *vt sep* boucher. **2** *vi* se boucher.

close[1] [kləʊs] **1** *adj* [near]: **~ (to)** proche (de), près (de); **a ~ friend** un ami intime (une amie intime); **~ up, ~ to** de près; **~ by, ~ at hand** tout près; **that was a ~ shave** OR **thing** OR **call** on l'a échappé belle. ‖ [link, resemblance] fort(e); [cooperation, connection] étroit(e). ‖ [questioning] serré(e); [examination] minutieux(ieuse); **to keep a ~ watch on sb/ sthg** surveiller qqn/qqch de près; **to pay ~ attention** faire très attention. ‖ [weather] lourd(e); [air in room] renfermé(e). ‖ [result, contest, race] serré(e). **2** *adv*: **~ (to)** près (de); **to come ~r (together)** se rapprocher. ○ **close on, close to** *prep* [almost] près de.

close[2] [kləʊz] **1** *vt* [gen] fermer. ‖ [end] clore. **2** *vi* [shop, bank] fermer; [door, lid] (se) fermer. ‖ [end] se terminer, finir. **3** *n* fin *f*. ○ **close down** *vt sep & vi* fermer.

closed [kləʊzd] *adj* fermé(e).

close-knit [,kləʊs-] *adj* (très) uni(e).

closely ['kləʊslɪ] *adv* [listen, examine, watch] de près; [resemble] beaucoup; **to be ~ related to** OR **with** être proche parent de.

closet ['klɒzɪt] **1** *n Am* [cupboard] placard *m*. **2** *adj inf* non avoué(e).

close-up ['kləʊs-] *n* gros plan *m*.

closing time ['kləʊzɪŋ-] *n* heure *f* de fermeture.

closure ['kləʊʒər] *n* fermeture *f*.

clot [klɒt] **1** *n* [of blood, milk] caillot *m*. **2** *vi* [blood] coaguler.

cloth [klɒθ] *n* (*U*) [fabric] tissu *m*. ‖ [duster] chiffon *m*; [for drying] torchon *m*.

clothes [kləʊðz] *npl* vêtements *mpl*, habits *mpl*; **to put one's ~ on** s'habiller; **to take one's ~ off** se déshabiller.

clothes brush *n* brosse *f* à habits.

clothesline ['kləʊðzlaɪn] *n* corde *f* à linge.

clothes peg *Br*, **clothespin** *Am* ['kləʊðzpɪn] *n* pince *f* à linge.

clothing ['kləʊðɪŋ] *n* (*U*) vêtements *mpl*, habits *mpl*.

cloud [klaʊd] *n* nuage *m*. ○ **cloud over** *vi* [sky] se couvrir.

cloudy ['klaʊdɪ] *adj* [sky, day] nuageux(euse). ‖ [liquid] trouble.

clove [kləʊv] *n*: **a ~ of garlic** une gousse d'ail. ○ **cloves** *npl* [spice] clous *mpl* de girofle.

clover ['kləʊvər] *n* trèfle *m*.

clown [klaʊn] **1** *n* [performer] clown *m*. ‖ [fool] pitre *m*. **2** *vi* faire le pitre.

cloying ['klɔɪɪŋ] *adj* [smell] écœurant(e). ‖ [sentimentality] à l'eau de rose.

club [klʌb] **1** *n* [organization, place] club *m*. ‖ [weapon] massue *f*. ‖ (**golf**) **~ club** *m*. **2** *vt* matraquer. ○ **clubs** *npl* CARDS trèfle *m*. ○ **club together** *vi* se cotiser.

club car *n Am* RAIL wagon-restaurant *m*.

clubhouse ['klʌbhaʊs, *pl* -haʊzɪz] *n* club *m*, pavillon *m*.

cluck [klʌk] *vi* glousser.

clue [kluː] *n* [in crime] indice *m*; **I haven't (got) a ~ (about)** je n'ai aucune idée (sur). ‖ [in crossword] définition *f*.

clump [klʌmp] *n* [of trees, bushes] massif *m*, bouquet *m*.

clumsy ['klʌmzɪ] *adj* [ungraceful] gauche, maladroit(e). ‖ [tactless] sans tact.

clung [klʌŋ] *pt & pp* → **cling**.

cluster ['klʌstər] **1** *n* [group] groupe *m*. **2** *vi* [people] se rassembler; [buildings etc] être regroupé(e).

clutch [klʌtʃ] **1** *n* AUT embrayage *m*. **2** *vt* agripper. **3** *vi*: **to ~ at** s'agripper à.

clutter ['klʌtər] **1** *n* désordre *m*. **2** *vt* mettre en désordre.

cm (*abbr of* **centimetre**) *n* cm.

CND (*abbr of* **Campaign for Nuclear**

Disarmament) *n mouvement pour le désarmement nucléaire.*

c/o (*abbr of* **care of**) a/s.

Co. (*abbr of* **Company**) Cie. || *abbr of* **County**.

coach [kəʊtʃ] **1** *n* [bus] car *m*, autocar *m*. || RAIL voiture *f*. || [horsedrawn] carrosse *m*. || SPORT entraîneur *m*. || [tutor] répétiteur *m*, -trice *f*. **2** *vt* SPORT entraîner. || [tutor] donner des leçons (particulières) à.

coal [kəʊl] *n* charbon *m*.

coalfield ['kəʊlfiːld] *n* bassin *m* houiller.

coalition [,kəʊə'lɪʃn] *n* coalition *f*.

coalmine ['kəʊlmaɪn] *n* mine *f* de charbon.

coarse [kɔːs] *adj* [rough - cloth] grossier(ière); [- hair] épais(aisse); [- skin] granuleux(euse). || [vulgar] grossier(ière).

coast [kəʊst] **1** *n* côte *f*. **2** *vi* [in car, on bike] avancer en roue libre.

coastal ['kəʊstl] *adj* côtier(ière).

coaster ['kəʊstər] *n* [small mat] dessous *m* de verre.

coastguard ['kəʊstgɑːd] *n* [person] garde-côte *m*. || [organization]: **the ~** la gendarmerie maritime.

coastline ['kəʊstlaɪn] *n* côte *f*.

coat [kəʊt] **1** *n* [garment] manteau *m*. || [of animal] pelage *m*. || [layer] couche *f*. **2** *vt*: **to ~ sthg (with)** recouvrir qqch (de); [with paint etc] enduire qqch (de).

coat hanger *n* cintre *m*.

coating ['kəʊtɪŋ] *n* couche *f*; CULIN glaçage *m*.

coat of arms (*pl* **coats of arms**) *n* blason *m*.

coax [kəʊks] *vt*: **to ~ sb (to do OR into doing sthg)** persuader qqn (de faire qqch) à force de cajoleries.

cob [kɒb] *n* → **corn**.

cobbled ['kɒbld] *adj* pavé(e).

cobbler ['kɒblər] *n* cordonnier *m*.

cobbles ['kɒblz], **cobblestones** ['kɒblstəʊnz] *npl* pavés *mpl*.

cobweb ['kɒbweb] *n* toile *f* d'araignée.

Coca-Cola® [,kəʊkə'kəʊlə] *n* Coca-Cola® *m*.

cocaine [kəʊ'keɪn] *n* cocaïne *f*.

cock [kɒk] **1** *n* [male chicken] coq *m*. || [male bird] mâle *m*. **2** *vt* [gun] armer. || [head] incliner.

cockerel ['kɒkrəl] *n* jeune coq *m*.

cockle ['kɒkl] *n* [shellfish] coque *f*.

cockpit ['kɒkpɪt] *n* [in plane] cockpit *m*.

cockroach ['kɒkrəʊtʃ] *n* cafard *m*.

cocksure [,kɒk'ʃɔːr] *adj* trop sûr(e) de soi.

cocktail ['kɒkteɪl] *n* cocktail *m*.

cocky ['kɒkɪ] *adj inf* suffisant(e).

cocoa ['kəʊkəʊ] *n* cacao *m*.

coconut ['kəʊkənʌt] *n* noix *f* de coco.

cod [kɒd] (*pl inv*) *n* morue *f*.

COD *abbr of* **cash on delivery**.

code [kəʊd] **1** *n* code *m*. **2** *vt* coder.

cod-liver oil *n* huile *f* de foie de morue.

coerce [kəʊ'ɜːs] *vt*: **to ~ sb (into doing sthg)** contraindre qqn (à faire qqch).

C of E *abbr of* **Church of England**.

coffee ['kɒfɪ] *n* café *m*.

coffee break *n* pause-café *f*.

coffeepot ['kɒfɪpɒt] *n* cafetière *f*.

coffee shop *n* *Br* [shop] café *m*. || *Am* [restaurant] ≃ café-restaurant *m*.

coffee table *n* table *f* basse.

coffin ['kɒfɪn] *n* cercueil *m*.

cog [kɒg] *n* [tooth on wheel] dent *f*; [wheel] roue *f* dentée.

coherent [kəʊ'hɪərənt] *adj* cohérent(e).

coil [kɔɪl] **1** *n* [of rope etc] rouleau *m*; [one loop] boucle *f*. || ELEC bobine *f*. **2** *vt* enrouler. **3** *vi* s'enrouler. ○ **coil up** *vt sep* enrouler.

coin [kɔɪn] *n* pièce *f* (de monnaie).

coinage ['kɔɪnɪdʒ] *n* (*U*) [currency] monnaie *f*.

coincide [,kəʊɪn'saɪd] *vi* coïncider.

coincidence [kəʊ'ɪnsɪdəns] *n* coïncidence *f*.

coincidental [kəʊ,ɪnsɪ'dentl] *adj* de coïncidence.

coke [kəʊk] *n* [fuel] coke *m*. || *drugs sl* coco *f*.

Coke® [kəʊk] *n* Coca® *m*.

cola ['kəʊlə] *n* cola *m*.

colander ['kʌləndər] *n* passoire *f*.

cold [kəʊld] **1** *adj* froid(e); **it's ~** il fait froid; **to be ~** avoir froid; **to get ~** [person] avoir froid; [hot food] refroidir. **2** *n* [illness] rhume *m*; **to catch (a) ~** attraper un rhume, s'enrhumer. || [low temperature] froid *m*.

cold-blooded [-'blʌdɪd] *adj fig* [killer] sans pitié; [murder] de sang-froid.

cold sore *n* bouton *m* de fièvre.

cold war *n*: **the ~** la guerre froide.

coleslaw ['kəʊlslɔː] *n* chou *m* cru mayonnaise.

colic ['kɒlɪk] *n* colique *f*.

collaborate [kə'læbəreɪt] *vi* collaborer.

collapse [kə'læps] **1** *n* [gen] écroulement *m*, effondrement *m*; [of marriage] échec *m.* **2** *vi* [building, person] s'effondrer, s'écrouler; [marriage] échouer. || [fold up] être pliant(e).

collapsible [kə'læpsəbl] *adj* pliant(e).

collar ['kɒlə'] *n* [on clothes] col *m.* || [for dog] collier *m.*

collarbone ['kɒləbəʊn] *n* clavicule *f.*

collate [kə'leɪt] *vt* collationner.

collateral [kɒ'lætərəl] *n* (*U*) nantissement *m.*

colleague ['kɒli:g] *n* collègue *mf.*

collect [kə'lekt] **1** *vt* [gather together - gen] rassembler, recueillir; [- wood etc] ramasser; **to ~ o.s.** se reprendre. || [as a hobby] collectionner. || [go to get] aller chercher, passer prendre. || [money] recueillir; [taxes] percevoir. **2** *vi* [crowd, people] se rassembler. || [dust, leaves, dirt] s'amasser, s'accumuler. || [for charity, gift] faire la quête. **3** *adv Am* TELEC: **to call (sb) ~** téléphoner (à qqn) en PCV.

collection [kə'lek∫n] *n* [of objects] collection *f.* || LITERATURE recueil *m.* || [of money] quête *f.* || [of mail] levée *f.*

collective [kə'lektɪv] **1** *adj* collectif(ive). **2** *n* coopérative *f.*

collector [kə'lektə'] *n* [as a hobby] collectionneur *m*, -euse *f.* || [of debts, rent] encaisseur *m*; **~ of taxes** percepteur *m.*

college ['kɒlɪdʒ] *n* [gen] ≃ école *f* d'enseignement (technique) supérieur. || [of university] maison communautaire d'étudiants sur un campus universitaire.

college of education *n* ≃ institut *m* de formation de maîtres.

collide [kə'laɪd] *vi*: **to ~ (with)** entrer en collision (avec).

collie ['kɒlɪ] *n* colley *m.*

colliery ['kɒljərɪ] *n* mine *f.*

collision [kə'lɪʒn] *n* [crash]: **~ (with/ between)** collision *f* (avec/entre); **to be on a ~ course (with)** *fig* aller au-devant de l'affrontement (avec).

colloquial [kə'ləʊkwɪəl] *adj* familier(ière).

collude [kə'lu:d] *vi*: **to ~ with sb** comploter avec qqn.

Colombia [kə'lɒmbɪə] *n* Colombie *f.*

colon ['kəʊlən] *n* ANAT côlon *m.* || [punctuation mark] deux-points *m inv.*

colonel ['k3:nl] *n* colonel *m.*

colonial [kə'ləʊnjəl] *adj* colonial(e).

colonize, -ise ['kɒlənaɪz] *vt* coloniser.

colony ['kɒlənɪ] *n* colonie *f.*

color *etc Am* = **colour** *etc.*

colour *Br*, **color** *Am* ['kʌlə'] **1** *n* couleur *f*; **in ~** en couleur. **2** *adj* en couleur. **3**

vt [food, liquid etc] colorer; [with pen, crayon] colorier. || [dye] teindre. || *fig* [judgment] fausser. **4** *vi* rougir.

colour bar *n* discrimination *f* raciale.

colour-blind *adj* daltonien(ienne).

coloured *Br*, **colored** *Am* ['kʌləd] *adj* de couleur; **brightly ~** de couleur vive.

colourful *Br*, **colorful** *Am* ['kʌləfʊl] *adj* [gen] coloré(e). || [person, area] haut(e) en couleur (*inv*).

colouring *Br*, **coloring** *Am* ['kʌlərɪŋ] *n* [dye] colorant *m.* || (*U*) [complexion] teint *m.*

colour scheme *n* combinaison *f* de couleurs.

colt [kəʊlt] *n* [young horse] poulain *m.*

column ['kɒləm] *n* [gen] colonne *f.* || PRESS [article] rubrique *f.*

columnist ['kɒləmnɪst] *n* chroniqueur *m.*

coma ['kəʊmə] *n* coma *m.*

comb [kəʊm] **1** *n* [for hair] peigne *m.* **2** *vt* [hair] peigner. || [search] ratisser.

combat ['kɒmbæt] **1** *n* combat *m.* **2** *vt* combattre.

combination [,kɒmbɪ'neɪ∫n] *n* combinaison *f.*

combine [kəm'baɪn] **1** *vt* [gen] rassembler; [pieces] combiner; **to ~ sthg with sthg** [two substances] mélanger qqch avec OR à qqch; *fig* allier qqch à qqch. **2** *vi* COMM & POL: **to ~ (with)** fusionner (avec).

combine harvester [-'hɑːvɪstə'] *n* moissonneuse-batteuse *f.*

come [kʌm] (*pt* **came**, *pp* **come**) *vi* [move] venir; [arrive] arriver, venir; **coming!** j'arrive! || [reach]: **to ~ up to** arriver à, monter jusqu'à; **to ~ down to** descendre OR tomber jusqu'à. || [happen] arriver, se produire; **what may ~** quoi qu'il arrive. || [become]: **to ~ true** se réaliser; **to ~ undone** se défaire. || [begin gradually]: **to ~ to do sthg** en arriver à OR en venir à faire qqch. || [be placed in order]: venir, être placé(e); **she came second in the exam** elle était deuxième à l'examen. || *phr*: **~ to think of it** maintenant que j'y pense, réflexion faite. ○ **to come** *adv* à venir. ○ **come about** *vi* [happen] arriver, se produire. ○ **come across** *vt fus* tomber sur, trouver par hasard. ○ **come along** *vi* [arrive by chance] arriver. || [improve - work] avancer; [- student] faire des progrès. ○ **come apart** *vi* [fall to pieces] tomber en morceaux. || [come off] se détacher.

○ **come back** *vi* [in talk, writing]: to ~ back to sthg revenir à qqch. || [memory]: to ~ (to sb) revenir (à qqn). ○ **come down** *vi* [decrease] baisser. || [descend] descendre. ○ **come down to** *vt fus* se résumer à, se réduire à. ○ **come down with** *vt fus* [cold, flu] attraper. ○ **come forward** *vi* se présenter. ○ **come from** *vt fus* venir de. ○ **come in** *vi* [enter] entrer. ○ **come in for** *vt fus* [criticism] être l'objet de. ○ **come into** *vt fus* [inherit] hériter de. || [begin to be]: to ~ into being prendre naissance, voir le jour. ○ **come off** *vi* [button, label] se détacher; [stain] s'enlever. || [joke, attempt] réussir. || *phr*: ~ off it! *inf* et puis quoi encore!, non mais sans blague! ○ **come on** *vi* [start] commencer, apparaître. || [start working - light, heating] s'allumer. || [progress, improve] avancer, faire des progrès. || *phr*: ~ on! [expressing encouragement] allez!; [hurry up] allez, dépêche-toi!; [expressing disbelief] allons donc! ○ **come out** *vi* [become known] être découvert(e). || [appear - product, book, film] sortir, paraître; [- sun, moon, stars] paraître. || [go on strike] faire grève. || [declare publicly]: to ~ out for/against sthg se déclarer pour/contre qqch. ○ **come round** *vi* [regain consciousness] reprendre connaissance, revenir à soi. ○ **come through** *vt fus* survivre à. ○ **come to** *vt fus* [reach]: to ~ to an end se terminer, prendre fin; to ~ to a decision arriver à une décision. || [amount to] s'élever à. 2 *vi* [regain consciousness] revenir à soi, reprendre connaissance. ○ **come under** *vt fus* [be governed by] être soumis(e) à. || [suffer]: to ~ under attack (from) être en butte aux attaques (de). ○ **come up** *vi* [be mentioned] survenir. || [be imminent] approcher. || [happen unexpectedly] se présenter. || [sun, moon] se lever. ○ **come up against** *vt fus* se heurter à. ○ **come up to** *vt fus* [approach - in space] s'approcher de. ○ **come up with** *vt fus* [answer, idea] proposer.

comeback ['kʌmbæk] *n* come-back *m*; to make a ~ [actor etc] revenir à la scène.

comedian [kə'mi:djən] *n* [comic] comique *m*; THEATRE comédien *m*.

comedown ['kʌmdaun] *n inf*: it was a ~ for her elle est tombée bien bas pour faire ça.

comedy ['kɒmədɪ] *n* comédie *f*.

comet ['kɒmɪt] *n* comète *f*.

come-uppance [,kʌm'ʌpəns] *n*: to get one's ~ *inf* recevoir ce qu'on mérite.

comfort ['kʌmfət] 1 *n* (U) [ease] confort *m*. || [luxury] commodité *f*. || [solace] réconfort *m*, consolation *f*. 2 *vt* réconforter, consoler.

comfortable ['kʌmftəbl] *adj* [gen] confortable. || *fig* [person - at ease, financially] à l'aise. || [after operation, accident]: he's ~ son état est stationnaire.

comfortably ['kʌmftəblɪ] *adv* [sit, sleep] confortablement. || [without financial difficulty] à l'aise. || [win] aisément.

comfort station *n Am* toilettes *fpl* publiques.

comic ['kɒmɪk] 1 *adj* comique, amusant(e). 2 *n* [comedian] comique *m*, actrice *f* comique. || [magazine] bande *f* dessinée.

comical ['kɒmɪkl] *adj* comique, drôle.

comic strip *n* bande *f* dessinée.

coming ['kʌmɪŋ] 1 *adj* [future] à venir, futur(e). 2 *n*: ~s and goings allées et venues *fpl*.

comma ['kɒmə] *n* virgule *f*.

command [kə'mɑ:nd] 1 *n* [order] ordre *m*. || (U) [control] commandement *m*. || [of language, subject] maîtrise *f*; to have at one's ~ [language] maîtriser; [resources] avoir à sa disposition. || COMPUT commande *f*. 2 *vt* [order]: to ~ sb to do sthg ordonner OR commander à qqn de faire qqch. || MIL [control] commander. || [deserve - respect] inspirer; [- attention, high price] mériter.

commandeer [,kɒmən'dɪə[r]] *vt* réquisitionner.

commander [kə'mɑ:ndə[r]] *n* [in army] commandant *m*. || [in navy] capitaine *m* de frégate.

commando [kə'mɑ:ndəu] (*pl* -s OR -es) *n* commando *m*.

commemorate [kə'meməreɪt] *vt* commémorer.

commemoration [kə,memə'reɪʃn] *n* commémoration *f*.

commence [kə'mens] *fml* 1 *vt* commencer, entamer; to ~ doing sthg commencer à faire qqch. 2 *vi* commencer.

commend [kə'mend] *vt* [praise]: to ~ sb (on OR for) féliciter qqn (de). || [recommend]: to ~ sthg (to sb) recommander qqch (à qqn).

comment ['kɒment] 1 *n* commentaire *m*, remarque *f*; no ~! sans commentaire! 2 *vt*: to ~ that remarquer que. 3 *vi*: to ~

(on) faire des commentaires OR remarques (sur).

commentary ['kɒməntrɪ] *n* commentaire *m*.

commentator ['kɒmənteɪtər] *n* commentateur *m*, -trice *f*.

commerce ['kɒmɜːs] *n* (*U*) commerce *m*, affaires *fpl*.

commercial [kə'mɜːʃl] **1** *adj* commercial(e). **2** *n* publicité *f*, spot *m* publicitaire.

commercial break *n* publicités *fpl*.

commission [kə'mɪʃn] **1** *n* [money, investigative body] commission *f*. ‖ [order for work] commande *f*. **2** *vt* [work] commander; **to ~ sb to do sthg** charger qqn de faire qqch.

commissioner [kə'mɪʃnər] *n* [in police] commissaire *m*.

commit [kə'mɪt] *vt* [crime, sin etc] commettre; **to ~ suicide** se suicider. ‖ [promise - money, resources] allouer; **to ~ o.s. (to sthg/to doing sthg)** s'engager (à qqch/à faire qqch). ‖ [consign]: **to ~ sb to prison** faire incarcérer qqn; **to ~ sthg to memory** apprendre qqch par cœur.

commitment [kə'mɪtmənt] *n* (*U*) [dedication] engagement *m*. ‖ [responsibility] obligation *f*.

committee [kə'mɪtɪ] *n* commission *f*, comité *m*.

commodity [kə'mɒdətɪ] *n* marchandise *f*.

common ['kɒmən] **1** *adj* [frequent] courant(e). ‖ [shared]: **~ (to)** commun(e) (à). ‖ [ordinary] banal(e). **2** *n* [land] terrain *m* communal. ○ **in common** *adv* en commun.

common law *n* droit *m* coutumier. ○ **common-law** *adj*: **common-law wife** concubine *f*.

commonly ['kɒmənlɪ] *adv* [generally] d'une manière générale, généralement.

Common Market *n*: **the ~** le Marché commun.

commonplace ['kɒmənpleɪs] *adj* banal(e), ordinaire.

common room *n* [staffroom] salle *f* des professeurs; [for students] salle commune.

Commons ['kɒmənz] *npl Br*: **the ~** les Communes *fpl*, la Chambre des Communes.

common sense *n* (*U*) bon sens *m*.

Commonwealth ['kɒmənwelθ] *n*: **the ~** le Commonwealth.

Commonwealth of Independent States *n*: **the ~** la Communauté des États Indépendants.

commotion [kə'məʊʃn] *n* remue-ménage *m*.

communal ['kɒmjʊnl] *adj* [kitchen, garden] commun(e); [life etc] communautaire, collectif(ive).

commune [*n* 'kɒmjuːn, *vb* kə'mjuːn] **1** *n* communauté *f*. **2** *vi*: **to ~ with** communier avec.

communicate [kə'mjuːnɪkeɪt] *vt & vi* communiquer.

communication [kə,mjuːnɪ'keɪʃn] *n* contact *m*; TELEC communication *f*.

communion [kə'mjuːnjən] *n* communion *f*.

Communism ['kɒmjʊnɪzm] *n* communisme *m*.

Communist ['kɒmjʊnɪst] **1** *adj* communiste. **2** *n* communiste *mf*.

community [kə'mjuːnətɪ] *n* communauté *f*.

community centre *n* foyer *m* municipal.

commutation ticket *n Am* carte *f* de transport.

commute [kə'mjuːt] **1** *vt* JUR commuer. **2** *vi* [to work] faire la navette pour se rendre à son travail.

commuter [kə'mjuːtər] *n personne qui fait tous les jours la navette de banlieue en ville pour se rendre à son travail.*

compact [*adj & vb* kəm'pækt, *n* 'kɒmpækt] **1** *adj* compact(e). **2** *n* [for face powder] poudrier *m*. ‖ *Am* AUT: **~ (car)** petite voiture *f*.

compact disc *n* compact *m* (disc *m*), disque *m* compact.

compact disc player *n* lecteur *m* de disques compacts.

companion [kəm'pænjən] *n* [person] camarade *mf*.

companionship [kəm'pænjənʃɪp] *n* compagnie *f*.

company ['kʌmpənɪ] *n* [COMM - gen] société *f*; [- insurance, airline, shipping company] compagnie *f*. ‖ [companionship] compagnie *f*; **to keep sb ~** tenir compagnie à qqn. ‖ [of actors] troupe *f*.

company secretary *n* secrétaire général *m*, secrétaire générale *f*.

comparable ['kɒmprəbl] *adj*: **~ (to OR with)** comparable (à).

comparative [kəm'pærətɪv] *adj* [relative] relatif(ive). ‖ [study, in grammar] comparatif(ive).

comparatively [kəm'pærətıvlı] *adv* [relatively] relativement.

compare [kəm'peə^r] **1** *vt*: to ~ sb/sthg (with), to ~ sb/sthg (to) comparer qqn/qqch (avec), comparer qqn/qqch (à); ~d with OR to par rapport à. **2** *vi*: to ~ (with) être comparable (à).

comparison [kəm'pærısn] *n* comparaison *f*; in ~ with OR to en comparaison de, par rapport à.

compartment [kəm'pɑːtmənt] *n* compartiment *m*.

compass ['kʌmpəs] *n* [magnetic] boussole *f*. ○ **compasses** *npl*: (a pair of) ~es un compas.

compassion [kəm'pæʃn] *n* compassion *f*.

compassionate [kəm'pæʃənət] *adj* compatissant(e).

compatible [kəm'pætəbl] *adj* [gen & COMPUT]: ~ (with) compatible (avec).

compel [kəm'pel] *vt* [force]: to ~ sb (to do sthg) contraindre OR obliger qqn (à faire qqch).

compelling [kəm'pelıŋ] *adj* [forceful] irrésistible.

compensate ['kɒmpenseıt] **1** *vt*: to ~ sb for sthg [financially] dédommager OR indemniser qqn de qqch. **2** *vi*: to ~ for sthg compenser qqch.

compensation [ˌkɒmpen'seıʃn] *n* [money]: ~ (for) dédommagement *m* (pour). || [way of compensating]: ~ (for) compensation *f* (pour).

compete [kəm'piːt] *vi* [vie - people]: to ~ with sb for sthg disputer qqch à qqn; to ~ for sthg se disputer qqch. || COMM: to ~ (with) être en concurrence (avec); to ~ for sthg se faire concurrence pour qqch. || [take part] être en compétition.

competence ['kɒmpıtəns] *n* (*U*) [proficiency] compétence *f*, capacité *f*.

competent ['kɒmpıtənt] *adj* compétent(e).

competition [ˌkɒmpı'tıʃn] *n* (*U*) [rivalry] rivalité *f*, concurrence *f*. || (*U*) COMM concurrence *f*. || [race, contest] concours *m*, compétition *f*.

competitive [kəm'petətıv] *adj* [person] qui a l'esprit de compétition; [match, sport] de compétition. || [COMM - goods] compétitif(ive); [- manufacturer] concurrentiel(ielle).

competitor [kəm'petıtə^r] *n* concurrent *m*, -e *f*.

compile [kəm'paıl] *vt* rédiger.

complacency [kəm'pleısnsı] *n* autosatisfaction *f*.

complain [kəm'pleın] *vi* [moan]: to ~ (about) se plaindre (de). || MED: to ~ of se plaindre de.

complaint [kəm'pleınt] *n* [gen] plainte *f*; [in shop] réclamation *f*. || MED affection *f*, maladie *f*.

complement [*n* 'kɒmplımənt, *vb* 'kɒmplıˌment] **1** *n* [accompaniment] accompagnement *m*. || [number] effectif *m*. || GRAMM complément *m*. **2** *vt* aller bien avec.

complementary [ˌkɒmplı'mentərı] *adj* complémentaire.

complete [kəm'pliːt] **1** *adj* [gen] complet(ète); ~ with doté(e) de, muni(e) de. || [finished] achevé(e). **2** *vt* [make whole] compléter. || [finish] achever, terminer. || [questionnaire, form] remplir.

completely [kəm'pliːtlı] *adv* complètement.

completion [kəm'pliːʃn] *n* achèvement *m*.

complex ['kɒmpleks] **1** *adj* complexe. **2** *n* [mental, of buildings] complexe *m*.

complexion [kəm'plekʃn] *n* teint *m*.

complicate ['kɒmplıkeıt] *vt* compliquer.

complicated ['kɒmplıkeıtıd] *adj* compliqué(e).

complication [ˌkɒmplı'keıʃn] *n* complication *f*.

compliment [*n* 'kɒmplımənt, *vb* 'kɒmplıment] **1** *n* compliment *m*. **2** *vt*: to ~ sb (on) féliciter qqn (de).

complimentary [ˌkɒmplı'mentərı] *adj* [admiring] flatteur(euse). || [free] gratuit(e).

comply [kəm'plaı] *vi*: to ~ with se conformer à.

component [kəm'pəʊnənt] *n* composant *m*.

compose [kəm'pəʊz] *vt* [gen] composer; to be ~d of se composer de, être composé de. || [calm]: to ~ o.s. se calmer.

composed [kəm'pəʊzd] *adj* [calm] calme.

composer [kəm'pəʊzə^r] *n* compositeur *m*, -trice *f*.

composition [ˌkɒmpə'zıʃn] *n* composition *f*.

compost [*Br* 'kɒmpɒst, *Am* 'kɒmpəʊst] *n* compost *m*.

composure [kəm'pəʊʒə^r] *n* sang-froid *m*, calme *m*.

compound ['kɒmpaʊnd] *n* CHEM & LING composé *m*. ‖ [enclosed area] enceinte *f*.

comprehend [ˌkɒmprɪ'hend] *vt* [understand] comprendre.

comprehension [ˌkɒmprɪ'henʃn] *n* compréhension *f*.

comprehensive [ˌkɒmprɪ'hensɪv] *adj* [account, report] exhaustif(ive), détaillé(e). ‖ [insurance] tous-risques (*inv*).

compress [kəm'pres] *vt* [squeeze, press] comprimer. ‖ [shorten - text] condenser.

comprise [kəm'praɪz] *vt* comprendre; **to be ~d of** consister en, comprendre.

compromise ['kɒmprəmaɪz] **1** *n* compromis *m*. **2** *vt* compromettre. **3** *vi* transiger.

compulsive [kəm'pʌlsɪv] *adj* [smoker, liar etc] invétéré(e). ‖ [book, TV programme] captivant(e).

compulsory [kəm'pʌlsərɪ] *adj* obligatoire.

computer [kəm'pjuːtər] **1** *n* ordinateur *m*. **2** *comp*: **~ graphics** infographie *f*; **~ program** programme *m* informatique.

computer game *n* jeu *m* électronique.

computing [kəm'pjuːtɪŋ], **computer science** *n* informatique *f*.

comrade ['kɒmreɪd] *n* camarade *mf*.

con [kɒn] *inf* **1** *n* [trick] escroquerie *f*. **2** *vt* [trick]: **to ~ sb (out of)** escroquer qqn (de).

concave [ˌkɒn'keɪv] *adj* concave.

conceal [kən'siːl] *vt* cacher, dissimuler; **to ~ sthg from sb** cacher qqch à qqn.

concede [kən'siːd] **1** *vt* concéder. **2** *vi* céder.

conceit [kən'siːt] *n* [arrogance] vanité *f*.

conceited [kən'siːtɪd] *adj* vaniteux(euse).

conceive [kən'siːv] *vi* MED concevoir. ‖ [imagine]: **to ~ of** concevoir.

concentrate ['kɒnsəntreɪt] **1** *vt* concentrer. **2** *vi*: **to ~ (on)** se concentrer (sur).

concentration [ˌkɒnsən'treɪʃn] *n* concentration *f*.

concentration camp *n* camp *m* de concentration.

concept ['kɒnsept] *n* concept *m*.

concern [kən'sɜːn] **1** *n* [worry, anxiety] souci *m*, inquiétude *f*. ‖ COMM [company] affaire *f*. **2** *vt* [worry] inquiéter; **to be ~ed (about)** s'inquiéter (de). ‖ [involve] concerner, intéresser; **as far as I'm ~ed** en ce qui me concerne; **to be ~ed with** [subj: person] s'intéresser à. ‖ [subj: book, film] traiter de.

concerning [kən'sɜːnɪŋ] *prep* en ce qui concerne.

concert ['kɒnsət] *n* concert *m*.

concerted [kən'sɜːtɪd] *adj* [effort] concerté(e).

concert hall *n* salle *f* de concert.

concertina [ˌkɒnsə'tiːnə] *n* concertina *m*.

concerto [kən'tʃeətəʊ] (*pl* **-s**) *n* concerto *m*.

concession [kən'seʃn] *n* [gen] concession *f*. ‖ [special price] réduction *f*.

conciliatory [kən'sɪlɪətrɪ] *adj* conciliant(e).

concise [kən'saɪs] *adj* concis(e).

conclude [kən'kluːd] **1** *vt* conclure. **2** *vi* [meeting] prendre fin; [speaker] conclure.

conclusion [kən'kluːʒn] *n* conclusion *f*.

conclusive [kən'kluːsɪv] *adj* concluant(e).

concoct [kən'kɒkt] *vt* préparer; *fig* concocter.

concourse ['kɒnkɔːs] *n* [hall] hall *m*.

concrete ['kɒnkriːt] **1** *adj* [definite] concret(ète). **2** *n* (*U*) béton *m*.

concur [kən'kɜːr] *vi* [agree]: **to ~ (with)** être d'accord (avec).

concurrently [kən'kʌrəntlɪ] *adv* simultanément.

concussion [kən'kʌʃn] *n* commotion *f*.

condemn [kən'dem] *vt* condamner.

condensation [ˌkɒnden'seɪʃn] *n* condensation *f*.

condense [kən'dens] **1** *vt* condenser. **2** *vi* se condenser.

condensed milk [kən'denst-] *n* lait *m* condensé.

condescending [ˌkɒndɪ'sendɪŋ] *adj* condescendant(e).

condition [kən'dɪʃn] **1** *n* [gen] condition *f*; **in (a) good/bad ~** en bon/mauvais état; **out of ~** pas en forme. ‖ MED maladie *f*. **2** *vt* [gen] conditionner.

conditional [kən'dɪʃənl] *adj* conditionnel(elle).

conditioner [kən'dɪʃnər] *n* [for hair] après-shampooing *m*. ‖ [for clothes] assouplissant *m*.

condolences [kən'dəʊlənsɪz] *npl* condoléances *fpl*.

condom ['kɒndəm] *n* préservatif *m*.

condominium [ˌkɒndə'mɪnɪəm] *n* *Am* [apartment] appartement *m* dans un immeuble en copropriété. ‖ [apartment block] immeuble *m* en copropriété.

condone [kən'dəʊn] *vt* excuser.

conducive [kən'dju:sɪv] *adj*: to be ~ to sthg/to doing sthg inciter à qqch/à faire qqch.

conduct [*n* 'kɒndʌkt, *vb* kən'dʌkt] **1** *n* conduite *f*. **2** *vt* [carry out, transmit] conduire. ‖ MUS diriger.

conducted tour [kən'dʌktɪd-] *n* visite *f* guidée.

conductor [kən'dʌktə*r*] *n* MUS chef *m* d'orchestre. ‖ [on bus] receveur *m*. ‖ *Am* [on train] chef *m* de train.

conductress [kən'dʌktrɪs] *n* [on bus] receveuse *f*.

cone [kəʊn] *n* [shape] cône *m*. ‖ [for ice cream] cornet *m*. ‖ [from tree] pomme *f* de pin.

confectioner [kən'fekʃnə*r*] *n* confiseur *m*; ~'s (shop) confiserie *f*.

confectionery [kən'fekʃnərɪ] *n* confiserie *f*.

confederation [kən,fedə'reɪʃn] *n* confédération *f*.

confer [kən'fɜ:*r*] **1** *vt*: to ~ sthg (on sb) conférer qqch (à qqn). **2** *vi*: to ~ (with sb on OR about sthg) s'entretenir (avec qqn de qqch).

conference ['kɒnfərəns] *n* conférence *f*.

confess [kən'fes] **1** *vt* [admit] avouer, confesser. ‖ RELIG confesser. **2** *vi*: to ~ (to sthg) avouer (qqch).

confession [kən'feʃn] *n* confession *f*.

confetti [kən'fetɪ] *n* (*U*) confettis *mpl*.

confide [kən'faɪd] *vi*: to ~ in sb se confier à qqn.

confidence ['kɒnfɪdəns] *n* [self-assurance] confiance *f* en soi, assurance *f*. ‖ [trust] confiance *f*; to have ~ in avoir confiance en. ‖ [secrecy]: in ~ en confidence. ‖ [secret] confidence *f*.

confidence trick *n* abus *m* de confiance.

confident ['kɒnfɪdənt] *adj* [self-assured]: to be ~ avoir confiance en soi. ‖ [sure] sûr(e).

confidential [,kɒnfɪ'denʃl] *adj* confidentiel(ielle).

confine [kən'faɪn] *vt* [limit] limiter; to ~ o.s. to se limiter à. ‖ [shut up] enfermer, confiner.

confined [kən'faɪnd] *adj* [space, area] restreint(e).

confinement [kən'faɪnmənt] *n* [imprisonment] emprisonnement *m*.

confirm [kən'fɜ:m] *vt* confirmer.

confirmation [,kɒnfə'meɪʃn] *n* confirmation *f*.

confirmed [kən'fɜ:md] *adj* [habitual] invétéré(e); [bachelor, spinster] endurci(e).

confiscate ['kɒnfɪskeɪt] *vt* confisquer.

conflict [*n* 'kɒnflɪkt, *vb* kən'flɪkt] **1** *n* conflit *m*. **2** *vi*: to ~ (with) s'opposer (à), être en conflit (avec).

conflicting [kən'flɪktɪŋ] *adj* contradictoire.

conform [kən'fɔ:m] *vi*: to ~ (to OR with) se conformer (à).

confront [kən'frʌnt] *vt* [problem, enemy] affronter. ‖ [challenge]: to ~ sb (with) confronter qqn (avec).

confrontation [,kɒnfrʌn'teɪʃn] *n* affrontement *m*.

confuse [kən'fju:z] *vt* [disconcert] troubler. ‖ [mix up] confondre.

confused [kən'fju:zd] *adj* [not clear] compliqué(e). ‖ [disconcerted] troublé(e), désorienté(e); I'm ~ je n'y comprends rien.

confusing [kən'fju:zɪŋ] *adj* pas clair(e).

confusion [kən'fju:ʒn] *n* confusion *f*.

congeal [kən'dʒi:l] *vi* [blood] se coaguler.

congested [kən'dʒestɪd] *adj* [street, area] encombré(e). ‖ MED congestionné(e).

congestion [kən'dʒestʃn] *n* [of traffic] encombrement *m*. ‖ MED congestion *f*.

conglomerate [,kən'glɒmərət] *n* COMM conglomérat *m*.

congratulate [kən'grætʃʊleɪt] *vt*: to ~ sb (on sthg/on doing sthg) féliciter qqn (de qqch/d'avoir fait qqch).

congratulations [kən,grætʃʊ'leɪʃənz] *npl* félicitations *fpl*.

congregate ['kɒŋgrɪgeɪt] *vi* se rassembler.

congregation [,kɒŋgrɪ'geɪʃn] *n* assemblée *f* des fidèles.

congress ['kɒŋgres] *n* [meeting] congrès *m*. ○ **Congress** *n Am* POL le Congrès.

congressman ['kɒŋgresmən] (*pl* -men [-mən]) *n Am* POL membre *m* du Congrès.

conifer ['kɒnɪfə*r*] *n* conifère *m*.

conjugation [,kɒndʒʊ'geɪʃn] *n* GRAMM conjugaison *f*.

conjunction [kən'dʒʌŋkʃn] *n* GRAMM conjonction *f*.

conjunctivitis [kən,dʒʌŋktɪ'vaɪtɪs] *n* conjonctivite *f*.

conjure ['kʌndʒə*r*] *vi* [by magic] faire des tours de prestidigitation. ○ **conjure up** *vt sep* évoquer.

conjurer ['kʌndʒərər] n prestidigitateur m, -trice f.

conjuror ['kʌndʒərər] = conjurer.

conman ['kɒnmæn] (pl -men [-men]) n escroc m.

connect [kə'nekt] 1 vt [join]: **to ~ sthg (to)** relier qqch (à). || [on telephone] mettre en communication. || [associate] associer; **to ~ sb/sthg to, to ~ sb/sthg with** associer qqn/qqch à. || ELEC [to power supply]: **to ~ sthg to** brancher qqch à. 2 vi [train, plane, bus]: **to ~ (with)** assurer la correspondance (avec).

connected [kə'nektɪd] adj [related]: **to be ~ with** avoir un rapport avec.

connection [kə'nekʃn] n [relationship]: **~ (between/with)** rapport m (entre/avec); **in ~ with** à propos de. || ELEC branchement m, connexion f. || [on telephone] communication f. || [plane, train, bus] correspondance f. || [professional acquaintance] relation f.

connive [kə'naɪv] vi [plot] comploter. || [allow to happen]: **to ~ at sthg** fermer les yeux sur qqch.

connoisseur [,kɒnə'sɜːr] n connaisseur m, -euse f.

conquer ['kɒŋkər] vt [country, people etc] conquérir. || [fears, inflation etc] vaincre.

conqueror ['kɒŋkərər] n conquérant m, -e f.

conquest ['kɒŋkwest] n conquête f.

conscience ['kɒnʃəns] n conscience f.

conscientious [,kɒnʃɪ'enʃəs] adj consciencieux(ieuse).

conscious ['kɒnʃəs] adj [not unconscious] conscient(e). || [aware]: **~ of sthg** conscient(e) de qqch. || [intentional - insult] délibéré(e), intentionnel(elle); [- effort] conscient(e).

consciousness ['kɒnʃəsnɪs] n conscience f.

conscript ['kɒnskrɪpt] MIL n conscrit m.

conscription [kən'skrɪpʃn] n conscription f.

consecutive [kən'sekjʊtɪv] adj consécutif(ive).

consent [kən'sent] 1 n (U) [permission] consentement m. || [agreement] accord m. 2 vi: **to ~ (to)** consentir (à).

consequence ['kɒnsɪkwəns] n [result] conséquence f; **in ~** par conséquent. || [importance] importance f.

consequently ['kɒnsɪkwəntlɪ] adv par conséquent.

conservation [,kɒnsə'veɪʃn] n [of nature] protection f; [of buildings] conservation f; [of energy, water] économie f.

conservative [kən'sɜːvətɪv] 1 adj [not modern] traditionnel(elle). || [cautious] prudent(e). 2 n traditionaliste mf. ○ **Conservative** POL 1 adj conservateur(trice). 2 n conservateur m, -trice f.

conservatory [kən'sɜːvətrɪ] n [of house] véranda f.

conserve [n 'kɒnsɜːv, vb kən'sɜːv] 1 n confiture f. 2 vt [energy, supplies] économiser; [nature, wildlife] protéger.

consider [kən'sɪdər] vt [think about] examiner. || [take into account] prendre en compte; **all things ~ed** tout compte fait. || [judge] considérer.

considerable [kən'sɪdərəbl] adj considérable.

considerably [kən'sɪdərəblɪ] adv considérablement.

considerate [kən'sɪdərət] adj prévenant(e).

consideration [kən,sɪdə'reɪʃn] n (U) [careful thought] réflexion f; **to take sthg into ~** tenir compte de qqch, prendre qqch en considération; **under ~** à l'étude. || (U) [care] attention f. || [factor] facteur m.

considering [kən'sɪdərɪŋ] 1 prep étant donné. 2 conj étant donné que.

consign [kən'saɪn] vt: **to ~ sb/sthg to** reléguer qqn/qqch à.

consignment [,kən'saɪnmənt] n [load] expédition f.

consist [kən'sɪst] ○ **consist of** vt fus consister en.

consistency [kən'sɪstənsɪ] n [coherence] cohérence f. || [texture] consistance f.

consistent [kən'sɪstənt] adj [regular - behaviour] conséquent(e); [- improvement] régulier(ière); [- supporter] constant(e). || [coherent] cohérent(e); **to be ~ with** [with one's position] être compatible avec; [with the facts] correspondre avec.

consolation [,kɒnsə'leɪʃn] n réconfort m.

console [n 'kɒnsəʊl, vt kən'səʊl] 1 n tableau m de commande. 2 vt consoler.

consonant ['kɒnsənənt] n consonne f.

consortium [kən'sɔːtjəm] (pl -tiums OR -tia [-tjə]) n consortium m.

conspicuous [kən'spɪkjʊəs] adj voyant(e), qui se remarque.

conspiracy [kən'spɪrəsɪ] n conspiration f, complot m.

conspire [kən'spaɪəʳ] vt: **to ~ to do sthg** comploter de faire qqch; [subj: events] contribuer à faire qqch.

constabulary [kən'stæbjʊlərɪ] n police f.

constant ['kɒnstənt] adj [unvarying] constant(e). ‖ [recurring] continuel(elle).

constantly ['kɒnstəntlɪ] adv constamment.

consternation [ˌkɒnstə'neɪʃn] n consternation f.

constipated ['kɒnstɪpeɪtɪd] adj constipé(e).

constipation [ˌkɒnstɪ'peɪʃn] n constipation f.

constituency [kən'stɪtjʊənsɪ] n [area] circonscription f électorale.

constituent [kən'stɪtjʊənt] n [voter] électeur m, -trice f. ‖ [element] composant m.

constitute ['kɒnstɪtjuːt] vt [form, represent] représenter, constituer. ‖ [establish, set up] constituer.

constitution [ˌkɒnstɪ'tjuːʃn] n constitution f.

constraint [kən'streɪnt] n [restriction]: **~ (on)** limitation f (à). ‖ (U) [self-control] retenue f, réserve f. ‖ [coercion] contrainte f.

construct [kən'strʌkt] vt construire.

construction [kən'strʌkʃn] n construction f.

constructive [kən'strʌktɪv] adj constructif(ive).

construe [kən'struː] vt fml [interpret]: **to ~ sthg as** interpréter qqch comme.

consul ['kɒnsəl] n consul m.

consulate ['kɒnsjʊlət] n consulat m.

consult [kən'sʌlt] 1 vt consulter. 2 vi: **to ~ with sb** s'entretenir avec qqn.

consultant [kən'sʌltənt] n [expert] expert-conseil m.

consultation [ˌkɒnsəl'teɪʃn] n [meeting, discussion] entretien m.

consulting room [kən'sʌltɪŋ-] n cabinet m de consultation.

consume [kən'sjuːm] vt [food, fuel etc] consommer.

consumer [kən'sjuːməʳ] n consommateur m, -trice f.

consumer goods npl biens mpl de consommation.

consummate ['kɒnsəmeɪt] vt consommer.

consumption [kən'sʌmpʃn] n [use] consommation f.

cont. abbr of **continued**.

contact ['kɒntækt] 1 n (U) [touch, communication] contact m; **in ~ (with sb)** en rapport OR contact (avec qqn); **to lose ~ with sb** perdre le contact avec qqn; **to make ~ with sb** prendre contact OR entrer en contact avec qqn. ‖ [person] relation f, contact m. 2 vt contacter, prendre contact avec; [by phone] joindre, contacter.

contact lens n verre m de contact, lentille f (cornéenne).

contagious [kən'teɪdʒəs] adj contagieux(ieuse).

contain [kən'teɪn] vt [hold, include] contenir, renfermer.

container [kən'teɪnəʳ] n [box, bottle etc] récipient m. ‖ [for transporting goods] conteneur m, container m.

contaminate [kən'tæmɪneɪt] vt contaminer.

cont'd abbr of **continued**.

contemplate ['kɒntəmpleɪt] 1 vt [consider] envisager. ‖ fml [look at] contempler. 2 vi [consider] méditer.

contemporary [kən'tempərərɪ] 1 adj contemporain(e). 2 n contemporain m, -e f.

contempt [kən'tempt] n [scorn]: **~ (for)** mépris m (pour). ‖ JUR: **~ (of court)** outrage m à la cour.

contemptuous [kən'temptʃʊəs] adj méprisant(e).

contend [kən'tend] 1 vi [deal]: **to ~ with sthg** faire face à qqch. ‖ [compete]: **to ~ for** [subj: several people] se disputer; [subj: one person] se battre pour; **to ~ against** lutter contre. 2 vt fml [claim]: **to ~ that ...** soutenir OR prétendre que ....

contender [kən'tendəʳ] n [in election] candidat m, -e f; [in competition] concurrent m, -e f; [in boxing etc] prétendant m, -e f.

content [n 'kɒntent, adj & vb kən'tent] 1 adj: **~ (with)** satisfait(e) (de), content(e) (de); **to be ~ to do sthg** ne pas demander mieux que de faire qqch. 2 n [amount] teneur f. ‖ [subject matter] contenu m. 3 vt: **to ~ o.s. with/with doing sthg** se contenter de qqch/de faire qqch. ○ **contents** npl [of container, document] contenu m. ‖ [at front of book] table f des matières.

contented [kən'tentɪd] adj satisfait(e).

contention [kən'tenʃn] n fml [argument, assertion] assertion f, affirmation f. ‖ (U) [disagreement] dispute f, contestation f.

contest [*n* 'kɒntest, *vb* kən'test] **1** *n* [competition] concours *m*. || [for power, control] combat *m*, lutte *f*. **2** *vt* [compete for] disputer. || [dispute] contester.

contestant [kən'testənt] *n* concurrent *m*, -e *f*.

context ['kɒntekst] *n* contexte *m*.

continent ['kɒntɪnənt] *n* continent *m*.

continental [,kɒntɪ'nentl] *adj* GEOGR continental(e).

continental breakfast *n* petit déjeuner *m* (*par opposition à 'English breakfast'*).

contingency [kən'tɪndʒənsɪ] *n* éventualité *f*.

contingency plan *n* plan *m* d'urgence.

continual [kən'tɪnjʊəl] *adj* continuel(elle).

continually [kən'tɪnjʊəlɪ] *adv* continuellement.

continuation [kən,tɪnjʊ'eɪʃn] *n* (*U*) [act] continuation *f*. || [sequel] suite *f*.

continue [kən'tɪnjuː] **1** *vt* [carry on] continuer, poursuivre; **to ~ doing OR to do sthg** continuer à OR de faire qqch. || [after an interruption] reprendre. **2** *vi* [carry on] continuer; **to ~ with sthg** poursuivre qqch, continuer qqch. || [after an interruption] reprendre, se poursuivre.

continuous [kən'tɪnjʊəs] *adj* continu(e).

continuously [kən'tɪnjʊəslɪ] *adv* sans arrêt, continuellement.

contort [kən'tɔːt] *vt* tordre.

contortion [kən'tɔːʃn] *n* (*U*) [twisting] torsion *f*. || [position] contorsion *f*.

contour ['kɒn,tʊəʳ] *n* [outline] contour *m*. || [on map] courbe *f* de niveau.

contraband ['kɒntrəbænd] **1** *adj* de contrebande. **2** *n* contrebande *f*.

contraception [,kɒntrə'sepʃn] *n* contraception *f*.

contraceptive [,kɒntrə'septɪv] *n* contraceptif *m*.

contract [*n* 'kɒntrækt, *vb* kən'trækt] **1** *n* contrat *m*. **2** *vt* [gen] contracter. || COMM: **to ~ sb (to do sthg)** passer un contrat avec qqn (pour faire qqch); **to ~ to do sthg** s'engager par contrat à faire qqch. **3** *vi* [decrease in size, length] se contracter.

contraction [kən'trækʃn] *n* contraction *f*.

contractor [kən'træktəʳ] *n* entrepreneur *m*.

contradict [,kɒntrə'dɪkt] *vt* contredire.

contradiction [,kɒntrə'dɪkʃn] *n* contradiction *f*.

contraflow ['kɒntrəfləʊ] *n* circulation *f* à contre-sens.

contraption [kən'træpʃn] *n* machin *m*, truc *m*.

contrary ['kɒntrərɪ, *adj sense 2* kən'treərɪ] **1** *adj* [opposite]: **~ (to)** contraire (à), opposé(e) (à). || [awkward] contrariant(e). **2** *n* contraire *m*; **on the ~** au contraire. ○ **contrary to** *prep* contrairement à.

contrast [*n* 'kɒntrɑːst, *vb* kən'trɑːst] **1** *n* contraste *m*; **by** OR **in ~** par contraste. **2** *vt* contraster. **3** *vi*: **to ~ (with)** faire contraste (avec).

contravene [,kɒntrə'viːn] *vt* enfreindre, transgresser.

contribute [kən'trɪbjuːt] **1** *vt* [money] apporter; [help, advice, ideas] donner, apporter. **2** *vi* [gen]: **to ~ (to)** contribuer (à). || [write material]: **to ~ to** collaborer à.

contribution [,kɒntrɪ'bjuːʃn] *n* [of money]: **~ (to)** cotisation *f* (à), contribution *f* (à). || [article] article *m*.

contributor [kən'trɪbjʊtəʳ] *n* [of money] donateur *m*, -trice *f*. || [to magazine, newspaper] collaborateur *m*, -trice *f*.

contrive [kən'traɪv] *vt fml* [engineer] combiner. || [manage]: **to ~ to do sthg** se débrouiller pour faire qqch, trouver moyen de faire qqch.

contrived [kən'traɪvd] *adj* tiré(e) par les cheveux.

control [kən'trəʊl] **1** *n* [gen] contrôle *m*; [of traffic] régulation *f*; **to get sb/sthg under ~** maîtriser qqn/qqch; **to be in ~ of sthg** [subj: boss, government] diriger qqch; [subj: army] avoir le contrôle de qqch; [of emotions, situation] maîtriser qqch; **to lose ~** [of emotions] perdre le contrôle. **2** *vt* [company, country] être à la tête de, diriger. || [operate] commander, faire fonctionner. || [restrict, restrain - disease] enrayer, juguler; [- inflation] mettre un frein à, contenir; [- children] tenir; [- crowd] contenir; [- emotions] maîtriser, contenir; **to ~ o.s.** se maîtriser, se contrôler. ○ **controls** *npl* [of machine, vehicle] commandes *fpl*.

controller [kən'trəʊləʳ] *n* [person] contrôleur *m*.

control panel *n* tableau *m* de bord.

control tower *n* tour *f* de contrôle.

controversial [,kɒntrə'vɜːʃl] *adj* [writer, theory etc] controversé(e); **to be ~** donner matière à controverse.

controversy ['kɒntrəvɜːsɪ, *Br* kən-'trɒvəsɪ] *n* controverse *f*, polémique *f*.

convalesce [ˌkɒnvə'les] *vi* se remettre d'une maladie, relever de maladie.

convene [kən'viːn] **1** *vt* convoquer, réunir. **2** *vi* se réunir, s'assembler.

convenience [kən'viːnjəns] *n* [usefulness] commodité *f*. ‖ [personal comfort, advantage] agrément *m*, confort *m*; **at your earliest ~** *fml* dès que possible.

convenience store *n Am* petit supermarché de quartier.

convenient [kən'viːnjənt] *adj* [suitable] qui convient. ‖ [handy] pratique, commode.

convent ['kɒnvənt] *n* couvent *m*.

convention [kən'venʃn] *n* [agreement, assembly] convention *f*. ‖ [practice] usage *m*, convention *f*.

conventional [kən'venʃənl] *adj* conventionnel(elle).

converge [kən'vɜːdʒ] *vi*: **to ~ (on)** converger (sur).

conversation [ˌkɒnvə'seɪʃn] *n* conversation *f*.

converse [*n & adj* 'kɒnvɜːs, *vb* kən'vɜːs] **1** *n* [opposite]: **the ~** le contraire, l'inverse *m*. **2** *vi fml* converser.

conversely [kən'vɜːslɪ] *adv fml* inversement.

conversion [kən'vɜːʃn] *n* [changing, in religious beliefs] conversion *f*. ‖ [in building] aménagement *m*, transformation *f*. ‖ RUGBY transformation *f*.

convert [*vb* kən'vɜːt, *n* 'kɒnvɜːt] **1** *vt* [change]: **to ~ sthg to** OR **into** convertir qqch en; **to ~ sb (to)** RELIG convertir qqn (à). ‖ [building, ship]: **to ~ sthg to** OR **into** transformer qqch en, aménager qqch en. **2** *vi*: **to ~ from sthg to sthg** passer de qqch à qqch. **3** *n* converti *m*, -e *f*.

convertible [kən'vɜːtəbl] *n* (voiture) décapotable *f*.

convex [kɒn'veks] *adj* convexe.

convey [kən'veɪ] *vt* [express]: **to ~ sthg (to sb)** communiquer qqch (à qqn).

conveyer belt [kən'veɪər-] *n* convoyeur *m*, tapis *m* roulant.

convict [*n* 'kɒnvɪkt, *vb* kən'vɪkt] **1** *n* détenu *m*. **2** *vt*: **to ~ sb of sthg** reconnaître qqn coupable de qqch.

conviction [kən'vɪkʃn] *n* [belief, fervour] conviction *f*. ‖ JUR [of criminal] condamnation *f*.

convince [kən'vɪns] *vt* convaincre, persuader; **to ~ sb of sthg/to do sthg** convaincre qqn de qqch/de faire qqch, persuader qqn de qqch/de faire qqch.

convincing [kən'vɪnsɪŋ] *adj* [persuasive] convaincant(e).

convoluted ['kɒnvəluːtɪd] *adj* [tortuous] compliqué(e).

convoy ['kɒnvɔɪ] *n* convoi *m*.

convulsion [kən'vʌlʃn] *n* MED convulsion *f*.

coo [kuː] *vi* roucouler.

cook [kʊk] **1** *n* cuisinier *m*, -ière *f*. **2** *vt* [food] faire cuire; [meal] préparer. **3** *vi* [person] cuisiner, faire la cuisine; [food] cuire.

cookbook ['kʊk,bʊk] = **cookery book.**

cooker ['kʊkər] *n* [stove] cuisinière *f*.

cookery ['kʊkərɪ] *n* cuisine *f*.

cookery book *n* livre *m* de cuisine.

cookie ['kʊkɪ] *n Am* [biscuit] biscuit *m*, gâteau *m* sec.

cooking ['kʊkɪŋ] *n* cuisine *f*.

cool [kuːl] **1** *adj* [not warm] frais (fraîche); [dress] léger(ère). ‖ [calm] calme. ‖ [unfriendly] froid(e). ‖ *inf* [excellent] génial(e); [trendy] branché(e). **2** *vt* faire refroidir. **3** *vi* [become less warm] refroidir. **4** *n* [calm]: **to keep/lose one's ~** garder/perdre son sang-froid, garder/perdre son calme. ○ **cool down** *vi* [become less warm - food, engine] refroidir; [- person] se rafraîchir.

cool box *n* glacière *f*.

coop [kuːp] *n* poulailler *m*. ○ **coop up** *vt sep inf* confiner.

Co-op ['kəʊ,ɒp] (*abbr of* co-operative society) *n* Coop *f*.

cooperate [kəʊ'ɒpəreɪt] *vi*: **to ~ (with sb/sthg)** coopérer (avec qqn/à qqch), collaborer (avec qqn/à qqch).

cooperation [kəʊ,ɒpə'reɪʃn] *n* (*U*) [collaboration] coopération *f*, collaboration *f*. ‖ [assistance] aide *f*, concours *m*.

cooperative [kəʊ'ɒpərətɪv] **1** *adj* coopératif(ive). **2** *n* coopérative *f*.

coordinate [*n* kəʊ'ɔːdɪnət, *vt* kəʊ'ɔːdɪneɪt] **1** *n* [on map, graph] coordonnée *f*. **2** *vt* coordonner. ○ **coordinates** *npl* [clothes] coordonnés *mpl*.

coordination [kəʊ,ɔːdɪ'neɪʃn] *n* coordination *f*.

cop [kɒp] *n inf* flic *m*.

cope [kəʊp] *vi* se débrouiller; **to ~ with** faire face à.

Copenhagen [ˌkəʊpən'heɪgən] *n* Copenhague *f*.

copier ['kɒpɪəʳ] n copieur m, photocopieur m.

copper ['kɒpəʳ] n [metal] cuivre m.

copy ['kɒpɪ] **1** n [imitation] copie f, reproduction f. || [duplicate] copie f. || [of book] exemplaire m; [of magazine] numéro m. **2** vt [imitate] copier, imiter. || [photocopy] photocopier.

copyright ['kɒpɪraɪt] n copyright m, droit m d'auteur.

coral ['kɒrəl] n corail m.

cord [kɔːd] n [string] ficelle f; [rope] corde f. || [electric] fil m, cordon m. || [fabric] velours m côtelé. ○ **cords** npl pantalon m en velours côtelé.

cordial ['kɔːdjəl] **1** adj cordial(e), chaleureux(euse). **2** n cordial m.

cordon ['kɔːdn] n cordon m. ○ **cordon off** vt sep barrer (par un cordon de police).

corduroy ['kɔːdərɔɪ] n velours m côtelé.

core [kɔːʳ] **1** n [of apple etc] trognon m, cœur m. || [of cable, Earth] noyau m; [of nuclear reactor] cœur m. || fig [of people] noyau m; [of problem, policy] essentiel m. **2** vt enlever le cœur de.

corgi ['kɔːgɪ] (pl -s) n corgi m.

coriander [,kɒrɪ'ændəʳ] n coriandre f.

cork [kɔːk] n [material] liège m. || [stopper] bouchon m.

corkscrew ['kɔːkskruː] n tire-bouchon m.

corn [kɔːn] n Am [maize] maïs m; ~ **on the cob** épi m de maïs cuit. || [on foot] cor m.

cornea ['kɔːnɪə] (pl -s) n cornée f.

corned beef [kɔːnd-] n corned-beef m inv.

corner ['kɔːnəʳ] **1** n [angle] coin m, angle m; **to cut ~s** fig brûler les étapes. || [bend in road] virage m, tournant m. **2** vt [person, animal] acculer.

corner shop n magasin m du coin OR du quartier.

cornet ['kɔːnɪt] n [instrument] cornet m à pistons.

cornflakes ['kɔːnfleɪks] npl corn-flakes mpl.

cornflour Br ['kɔːnflaʊəʳ], **cornstarch** Am ['kɔːnstɑːtʃ] n ≃ Maïzena® f, fécule f de maïs.

Cornwall ['kɔːnwɔːl] n Cornouailles f.

corny ['kɔːnɪ] adj inf [joke] peu original(e); [story, film] à l'eau de rose.

coronary ['kɒrənrɪ], **coronary**

thrombosis [-θrɒm'bəʊsɪs] n infarctus m du myocarde.

coronation [,kɒrə'neɪʃn] n couronnement m.

coroner ['kɒrənəʳ] n coroner m.

corporal ['kɔːpərəl] n [gen] caporal m; [in artillery] brigadier m.

corporal punishment n châtiment m corporel.

corporate ['kɔːpərət] adj [business] corporatif(ive), de société. || [collective] collectif(ive).

corporation [,kɔːpə'reɪʃn] n [town council] conseil m municipal. || [large company] compagnie f, société f enregistrée.

corps [kɔːʳ] (pl inv) n corps m.

corpse [kɔːps] n cadavre m.

correct [kə'rekt] **1** adj [accurate] correct(e), exact(e); **you're quite ~** tu as parfaitement raison. || [proper, socially acceptable] correct(e), convenable. **2** vt corriger.

correction [kə'rekʃn] n correction f.

correspond [,kɒrɪ'spɒnd] vi [gen]: **to ~ (with** OR **to)** correspondre (à). || [write letters]: **to ~ (with sb)** correspondre (avec qqn).

correspondence [,kɒrɪ'spɒndəns] n: ~ **(with)** correspondance f (avec).

correspondence course n cours m par correspondance.

correspondent [,kɒrɪ'spɒndənt] n correspondant m, -e f.

corridor ['kɒrɪdɔːʳ] n [in building] couloir m, corridor m.

corrode [kə'rəʊd] **1** vt corroder, attaquer. **2** vi se corroder.

corrosion [kə'rəʊʒn] n corrosion f.

corrugated ['kɒrəgeɪtɪd] adj ondulé(e).

corrugated iron n tôle f ondulée.

corrupt [kə'rʌpt] **1** adj [gen & COMPUT] corrompu(e). **2** vt corrompre, dépraver.

corruption [kə'rʌpʃn] n corruption f.

corset ['kɔːsɪt] n corset m.

Corsica ['kɔːsɪkə] n Corse f.

cosh [kɒʃ] n matraque f, gourdin m.

cosmetic [kɒz'metɪk] **1** n cosmétique m, produit m de beauté. **2** adj fig superficiel(ielle).

cosmopolitan [kɒzmə'pɒlɪtn] adj cosmopolite.

cost [kɒst] (pt & pp cost OR -ed) **1** n lit & fig coût m; **at all ~s** à tout prix, coûte que coûte. **2** vt lit & fig coûter. || COMM [estimate] évaluer le coût de. **3** vi coûter;

how much does it ~? combien ça coûte?, combien cela coûte-t-il? ○ **costs** *npl* JUR dépens *mpl*.

co-star ['kəʊ-] *n* partenaire *mf*.

Costa Rica [,kɒstə'riːkə] *n* Costa Rica *m*.

cost-effective *adj* rentable.

costing ['kɒstɪŋ] *n* évaluation *f* du coût.

costly ['kɒstlɪ] *adj lit* & *fig* coûteux(euse).

cost of living *n*: **the ~** le coût de la vie.

cost price *n* prix *m* coûtant.

costume ['kɒstjuːm] *n* [gen] costume *m*. ‖ [swimming costume] maillot *m* (de bain).

costume jewellery *n* (U) bijoux *mpl* fantaisie.

cosy *Br*, **cozy** *Am* ['kəʊzɪ] *adj* [house, room] douillet(ette); [atmosphere] chaleureux(euse).

cot [kɒt] *n Am* [folding bed] lit *m* de camp.

cottage ['kɒtɪdʒ] *n* cottage *m*, petite maison *f* (de campagne).

cottage cheese *n* fromage *m* blanc.

cotton ['kɒtn] *n* [gen] coton *m*.

cotton candy *n Am* barbe *f* à papa.

cotton wool *n* ouate *f*, coton *m* hydrophile.

couch [kaʊtʃ] *n* [sofa] canapé *m*. ‖ [in doctor's surgery] lit *m*.

cough [kɒf] **1** *n* toux *f*. **2** *vi* tousser.

could [kʊd] *pt* → **can²**.

couldn't ['kʊdnt] = could not.

could've ['kʊdəv] = could have.

council ['kaʊnsl] *n* conseil *m* municipal.

council estate *n* quartier *m* de logements sociaux.

councillor ['kaʊnsələr] *n* conseiller municipal *m*, conseillère municipale *f*.

counsel ['kaʊnsəl] *n* (U) *fml* [advice] conseil *m*. ‖ [lawyer] avocat *m*, -e *f*.

counsellor *Br*, **counselor** *Am* ['kaʊnsələr] *n* [gen] conseiller *m*, -ère *f*. ‖ *Am* [lawyer] avocat *m*.

count [kaʊnt] **1** *n* [total] total *m*; **to keep ~ of** tenir le compte de; **to lose ~ of sthg** ne plus savoir qqch, ne pas se rappeler qqch. ‖ [aristocrat] comte *m*. **2** *vt* [gen] compter. ‖ [consider]: **to ~ sb as sthg** considérer qqn comme qqch. **3** *vi* [gen] compter. ○ **count against** *vt fus* jouer contre. ○ **count (up)on** *vt fus* [rely on] compter sur. ‖ [expect] s'attendre à, prévoir. ○ **count up** *vt fus* compter.

countdown ['kaʊntdaʊn] *n* compte *m* à rebours.

counter ['kaʊntər] **1** *n* [in shop, bank] comptoir *m*. ‖ [in board game] pion *m*. **2** *vt*: **to ~ sthg (with)** [criticism etc] riposter à qqch (par). **3** *vi*: **to ~ with sthg/by doing sthg** riposter par qqch/en faisant qqch. ○ **counter to** *adv* contrairement à; **to run ~ to** aller à l'encontre de.

counteract [,kaʊntə'rækt] *vt* contrebalancer, compenser.

counterattack [,kaʊntərə'tæk] *vt* & *vi* contre-attaquer.

counterclockwise [,kaʊntə'klɒkwaɪz] *adj* & *adv Am* dans le sens inverse des aiguilles d'une montre.

counterfeit ['kaʊntəfɪt] **1** *adj* faux (fausse). **2** *vt* contrefaire.

counterfoil ['kaʊntəfɔɪl] *n* talon *m*, souche *f*.

counterpart ['kaʊntəpɑːt] *n* [person] homologue *mf*; [thing] équivalent *m*, -e *f*.

counterproductive [,kaʊntəprə'dʌktɪv] *adj* qui a l'effet inverse.

countess ['kaʊntɪs] *n* comtesse *f*.

countless ['kaʊntlɪs] *adj* innombrable.

country ['kʌntrɪ] *n* [nation] pays *m*. ‖ [countryside]: **the ~** la campagne; **in the ~** à la campagne.

country dancing *n* (U) danse *f* folklorique.

country house *n* manoir *m*.

countryman ['kʌntrɪmən] (*pl* **-men** [-mən]) *n* [from same country] compatriote *m*.

countryside ['kʌntrɪsaɪd] *n* campagne *f*.

county ['kaʊntɪ] *n* comté *m*.

coup [kuː] *n* [rebellion]: **~ (d'état)** coup *m* d'État. ‖ [success] coup *m* (de maître), beau coup *m*.

couple ['kʌpl] **1** *n* [in relationship] couple *m*. ‖ [small number]: **a ~ (of)** [two] deux; [a few] quelques, deux ou trois. **2** *vt* [join]: **to ~ sthg (to)** atteler qqch (à).

coupon ['kuːpɒn] *n* [voucher] bon *m*. ‖ [form] coupon *m*.

courage ['kʌrɪdʒ] *n* courage *m*.

courier ['kʊrɪər] *n* [on holiday] guide *m*, accompagnateur *m*, -trice *f*. ‖ [to deliver letters, packages] courrier *m*, messager *m*.

course [kɔːs] *n* [gen & SCH] cours *m*; **~ of action** ligne *f* de conduite; **in the ~ of** au cours de. ‖ MED [of injections] série *f*; **~ of treatment** traitement *m*. ‖ [of ship, plane] route *f*; **to be on ~** suivre le cap fixé; *fig* [on target] être dans la bonne voie; **to be off ~** faire fausse route. ‖ [of meal] plat

m. || SPORT terrain *m.* ○ **of course** *adv*
[inevitably, not surprisingly] évidemment,
naturellement. || [certainly] bien sûr; **of ~
not** bien sûr que non.

coursebook ['kɔːsbʊk] *n* livre *m* de
cours.

coursework ['kɔːswɜːk] *n* (U) travail
m personnel.

court [kɔːt] *n* [JUR - building, room] cour
f, tribunal *m*; [- judge, jury etc]: **the ~** la
justice; **to take sb to ~** faire un procès à
qqn. || [SPORT - gen] court *m*; [- for
basketball, volleyball] terrain *m.* || [court-
yard, of monarch] cour *f.*

courtesy ['kɜːtɪsɪ] *n* courtoisie *f*, politesse *f.* ○ **(by) courtesy of** *prep* avec
la permission de.

courthouse ['kɔːthaʊs, *pl* -haʊzɪz] *n*
Am palais *m* de justice, tribunal *m.*

courtier ['kɔːtjər] *n* courtisan *m.*

court-martial (*pl* **court-martials** OR
courts-martial) *n* cour *f* martiale.

courtroom ['kɔːtrʊm] *n* salle *f* de tribunal.

courtyard ['kɔːtjɑːd] *n* cour *f.*

cousin ['kʌzn] *n* cousin *m*, -e *f.*

cove [kəʊv] *n* [bay] crique *f.*

covenant ['kʌvənənt] *n* [of money] engagement *m* contractuel.

cover ['kʌvər] **1** *n* [covering - of furni-
ture] housse *f*; [- of pan] couvercle *m*;
[- of book, magazine] couverture *f.* ||
[blanket] couverture *f.* || [protection, shel-
ter] abri *m*; **to take ~** s'abriter, se mettre
à l'abri; **under ~** à l'abri, à couvert. ||
[concealment] couverture *f.* || [insurance]
couverture *f*, garantie *f.* **2** *vt* [gen]: **to ~
sthg (with)** couvrir qqch (de). || [insure]:
to ~ sb against couvrir qqn en cas de. ||
[include] englober, comprendre.
○ **cover up** *vt sep fig* [scandal etc] dissimuler, cacher.

coverage ['kʌvərɪdʒ] *n* [of news] reportage *m.*

cover charge *n* couvert *m.*

covering ['kʌvərɪŋ] *n* [of floor etc] revêtement *m*; [of snow, dust] couche *f.*

covering letter *Br*, **cover letter** *Am*
n lettre *f* explicative OR d'accompagnement.

cover-up *n* étouffement *m.*

covet ['kʌvɪt] *vt* convoiter.

cow [kaʊ] **1** *n* [female type of cattle] vache
f. || [female elephant etc] femelle *f.* **2**
vt intimider, effrayer.

coward ['kaʊəd] *n* lâche *mf.*

cowardly ['kaʊədlɪ] *adj* lâche.

cowboy ['kaʊbɔɪ] *n* [cattlehand] cowboy *m.*

cower ['kaʊər] *vi* se recroqueviller.

cox [kɒks], **coxswain** ['kɒksən] *n* barreur *m.*

coy [kɔɪ] *adj* qui fait le/la timide.

cozy *Am* = **cosy.**

CPA *n abbr of* **certified public accountant.**

crab [kræb] *n* crabe *m.*

crab apple *n* pomme *f* sauvage.

crack [kræk] **1** *n* [in glass, pottery] fêlure
f; [in wall, wood, ground] fissure *f*; [in
skin] gerçure *f.* || [gap - in door] entre-
bâillement *m*; [- in curtains] interstice *m.*
|| [noise - of whip] claquement *m*; [- of
twigs] craquement *m.* || *inf* [attempt]: **to
have a ~ at sthg** tenter qqch, essayer de
faire qqch. || *drugs sl* crack *m.* **2** *vt* [glass,
plate] fêler; [wood, wall] fissurer. || [egg,
nut] casser. || [whip] faire claquer. ||
[bang, hit sharply]: **to ~ one's head** se co-
gner la tête. || [solve - problem] résoudre;
[- code] déchiffrer. **3** *vi* [glass, pottery] se
fêler; [ground, wood, wall] se fissurer;
[skin] se crevasser, se gercer. || [break
down - person] craquer, s'effondrer; [- re-
sistance] se briser. ○ **crack down** *vi*: **to
~ down (on)** sévir (contre). ○ **crack up**
vi craquer.

cracker ['krækər] *n* [biscuit] cracker *m*,
craquelin *m.*

crackle ['krækl] *vi* [frying food] grésiller;
[fire] crépiter; [radio etc] crachoter.

cradle ['kreɪdl] **1** *n* berceau *m.* **2** *vt* [baby]
bercer; [object] tenir délicatement.

craft [krɑːft] (*pl sense 2 inv*) *n* [trade,
skill] métier *m.* || [boat] embarcation *f.*

craftsman ['krɑːftsmən] (*pl* **-men**
[-mən]) *n* artisan *m*, homme *m* de métier.

craftsmanship ['krɑːftsmənʃɪp] *n* (U)
[skill] dextérité *f*, art *m.* || [skilled work]
travail *m*, exécution *f.*

craftsmen *pl* → **craftsman.**

crafty ['krɑːftɪ] *adj* rusé(e).

crag [kræg] *n* rocher *m* escarpé.

cram [kræm] **1** *vt* [stuff] fourrer. ||
[overfill]: **to ~ sthg with** bourrer qqch de.
2 *vi* bachoter.

cramp [kræmp] *n* crampe *f.*

cranberry ['krænbərɪ] *n* canneberge *f.*

crane [kreɪn] *n* grue *f.*

crank [kræŋk] **1** *n* TECH manivelle *f.* || *inf*
[person] excentrique *mf.* **2** *vt* [wind -

handle] tourner; [- mechanism] remonter (à la manivelle).

crankshaft ['kræŋkʃɑːft] n vilebrequin m.

cranny ['krænɪ] n → nook.

crap [kræp] n (U) v inf merde f; **it's a load of ~** tout ça, c'est des conneries.

crash [kræʃ] **1** n [accident] accident m. || [noise] fracas m. **2** vt: **I -ed the car** j'ai eu un accident avec la voiture. **3** vi [cars, trains] se percuter, se rentrer dedans; [car, train] avoir un accident; [plane] s'écraser; **to ~ into** [wall] rentrer dans, emboutir. || [FIN - business, company] faire faillite; [- stock market] s'effondrer.

crash course n cours m intensif.

crash helmet n casque m de protection.

crash-land vi atterrir en catastrophe.

crass [kræs] adj grossier(ière).

crate [kreɪt] n cageot m, caisse f.

crater ['kreɪtər] n cratère m.

cravat [krəˈvæt] n cravate f.

crave [kreɪv] **1** vt [affection, luxury] avoir soif de; [cigarette, chocolate] avoir un besoin fou OR maladif de. **2** vi: **to ~ for** [affection, luxury] avoir soif de; [cigarette, chocolate] avoir un besoin fou OR maladif de.

crawl [krɔːl] **1** vi [baby] marcher à quatre pattes; [person] se traîner. || [insect] ramper. || [vehicle, traffic] avancer au pas. || inf [place, floor]: **to be ~ing with** grouiller de. **2** n [swimming stroke]: **the ~** le crawl.

crayfish ['kreɪfɪʃ] (pl inv OR -es) n écrevisse f.

crayon ['kreɪɒn] n crayon m de couleur.

craze [kreɪz] n engouement m.

crazy ['kreɪzɪ] adj inf [mad] fou (folle). || [enthusiastic]: **to be ~ about sb/sthg** être fou (folle) de qqn/qqch.

creak [kriːk] vi [door, handle] craquer; [floorboard, bed] grincer.

cream [kriːm] **1** adj [in colour] crème (inv). **2** n [gen] crème f.

cream cheese n fromage m frais.

crease [kriːs] **1** n [in fabric - deliberate] pli m; [- accidental] (faux) pli. **2** vt froisser. **3** vi [fabric] se froisser.

create [kriːˈeɪt] vt créer.

creation [kriːˈeɪʃn] n création f.

creative [kriːˈeɪtɪv] adj créatif(ive).

creature ['kriːtʃər] n créature f.

credentials [krɪˈdenʃlz] npl [papers] pièce f d'identité; fig [qualifications] capacités fpl. || [references] références fpl.

credibility [ˌkredəˈbɪlətɪ] n crédibilité f.

credit ['kredɪt] **1** n FIN crédit m; **to be in ~** [person] avoir un compte approvisionné; [account] être approvisionné; **on ~** à crédit. || (U) [praise] honneur m, mérite m; **to give sb ~ for sthg** reconnaître que qqn a fait qqch. || UNIV unité f de valeur. **2** vt FIN: **to ~ £10 to an account, to ~ an account with £10** créditer un compte de 10 livres. || inf [believe] croire. || [give the credit to]: **to ~ sb with sthg** accorder OR attribuer qqch à qqn. **○ credits** npl CINEMA générique m.

credit card n carte f de crédit.

credit note n avoir m; FIN note f de crédit.

creditor ['kredɪtər] n créancier m, -ière f.

creed [kriːd] n RELIG croyance f.

creek [kriːk] n [inlet] crique f. || Am [stream] ruisseau m.

creep [kriːp] (pt & pp crept) **1** vi [insect] ramper; [traffic] avancer au pas. || [move stealthily] se glisser. **2** n inf [nasty person] sale type m. **○ creeps** npl: **to give sb the ~s** inf donner la chair de poule à qqn.

creeper ['kriːpər] n [plant] plante f grimpante.

creepy ['kriːpɪ] adj inf qui donne la chair de poule.

cremate [krɪˈmeɪt] vt incinérer.

cremation [krɪˈmeɪʃn] n incinération f.

crematorium Br [ˌkreməˈtɔːrɪəm] (pl -riums OR -ria [-rɪə]), **crematory** Am ['kremətrɪ] n crématorium m.

crepe [kreɪp] n [cloth, rubber] crêpe m. || [pancake] crêpe f.

crepe paper n (U) papier m crépon.

crept [krept] pt & pp → creep.

crescent ['kresnt] n [shape] croissant. || [street] rue f en demi-cercle.

cress [kres] n cresson m.

crest [krest] n [of bird, hill] crête f. || [on coat of arms] timbre m.

crevice ['krevɪs] n fissure f.

crew [kruː] n [of ship, plane] équipage m. || [team] équipe f.

crew cut n coupe f en brosse.

crew-neck(ed) [-nek(t)] adj ras du cou.

crib [krɪb] **1** n [cot] lit m d'enfant. **2** vt inf [copy]: **to ~ sthg off OR from sb** copier qqch sur qqn.

crick [krɪk] n [in neck] torticolis m.

cricket ['krɪkɪt] n [game] cricket m. || [insect] grillon m.

crime [kraɪm] *n* crime *m*.

criminal ['krɪmɪnl] **1** *adj* criminel(elle). **2** *n* criminel *m*, -elle *f*.

crimson ['krɪmzn] **1** *adj* [in colour] rouge foncé (*inv*); [with embarrassment] cramoisi(e). **2** *n* cramoisi *m*.

cringe [krɪndʒ] *vi* [in fear] avoir un mouvement de recul (par peur). || *inf* [with embarrassment]: **to ~ (at sthg)** ne plus savoir où se mettre (devant qqch).

cripple ['krɪpl] **1** *n dated & offensive* infirme *mf*. **2** *vt* MED [disable] estropier. || [country] paralyser; [ship, plane] endommager.

crisis ['kraɪsɪs] (*pl* **crises** ['kraɪsi:z]) *n* crise *f*.

crisp [krɪsp] *adj* [pastry] croustillant(e); [apple, vegetables] croquant(e). || [weather, manner] vif (vive).

crisscross ['krɪskrɒs] **1** *adj* entrecroisé(e). **2** *vt* entrecroiser.

criterion [kraɪ'tɪərɪən] (*pl* **-rions** OR **-ria** [-rɪə]) *n* critère *m*.

critic ['krɪtɪk] *n* [reviewer] critique *m*. || [detractor] détracteur *m*, -trice *f*.

critical ['krɪtɪkl] *adj* critique; **to be ~ of sb/sthg** critiquer qqn/qqch.

critically ['krɪtɪklɪ] *adv* [ill] gravement; **~ important** d'une importance capitale. || [analytically] de façon critique.

criticism ['krɪtɪsɪzm] *n* critique *f*.

criticize, -ise ['krɪtɪsaɪz] *vt & vi* critiquer.

croak [krəʊk] *vi* [frog] coasser; [raven] croasser. || [person] parler d'une voix rauque.

Croat ['krəʊæt], **Croatian** [krəʊ'eɪʃn] **1** *adj* croate. **2** *n* [person] Croate *mf*. || [language] croate *m*.

Croatia [krəʊ'eɪʃə] *n* Croatie *f*.

Croatian = **Croat**.

crochet ['krəʊʃeɪ] *n* crochet *m*.

crockery ['krɒkərɪ] *n* vaisselle *f*.

crocodile ['krɒkədaɪl] (*pl inv* OR **-s**) *n* crocodile *m*.

crocus ['krəʊkəs] (*pl* **-cuses**) *n* crocus *m*.

crook [krʊk] *n* [criminal] escroc *m*. || [of arm, elbow] pliure *f*. || [shepherd's staff] houlette *f*.

crooked ['krʊkɪd] *adj* [bent] courbé(e). || [teeth, tie] de travers. || *inf* [dishonest] malhonnête.

crop [krɒp] *n* [kind of plant] culture *f*. || [harvested produce] récolte *f*. || [whip] cravache *f*. ○ **crop up** *vi* survenir.

croquette [krɒ'ket] *n* croquette *f*.

cross [krɒs] **1** *adj* [person] fâché(e); [look] méchant(e); **to get ~ (with sb)** se fâcher (contre qqn). **2** *n* [gen] croix *f*. || [hybrid] croisement *m*. **3** *vt* [gen] traverser. || [arms, legs] croiser. || *Br* [cheque] barrer. **4** *vi* [intersect] se croiser. ○ **cross off, cross out** *vt sep* rayer.

crossbar ['krɒsbɑ:r] *n* SPORT barre *f* transversale. || [on bicycle] barre *f*.

cross-Channel *adj* transmanche.

cross-country **1** *adj*: **~ running** cross *m*; **~ skiing** ski *m* de fond. **2** *n* cross-country *m*, cross *m*.

cross-examine *vt* JUR faire subir un contre-interrogatoire à; *fig* questionner de près.

cross-eyed [-aɪd] *adj* qui louche.

crossfire ['krɒs,faɪər] *n* (*U*) feu *m* croisé.

crossing ['krɒsɪŋ] *n* [on road] passage *m* clouté; [on railway line] passage à niveau. || [sea journey] traversée *f*.

cross-legged [-legd] *adv* en tailleur.

cross-purposes *npl*: **to talk at ~** ne pas parler de la même chose; **to be at ~** ne pas être sur la même longueur d'ondes.

cross-reference *n* renvoi *m*.

crossroads ['krɒsrəʊdz] (*pl inv*) *n* croisement *m*.

cross-section *n* [drawing] coupe *f* transversale. || [sample] échantillon *m*.

crosswalk ['krɒswɔ:k] *n Am* passage *m* clouté, passage pour piétons.

crossways ['krɒsweɪz] = **crosswise**.

crosswind ['krɒswɪnd] *n* vent *m* de travers.

crosswise ['krɒswaɪz] *adv* en travers.

crossword (puzzle) ['krɒswɜ:d-] *n* mots croisés *mpl*.

crotch [krɒtʃ] *n* entrejambe *m*.

crotchety ['krɒtʃɪtɪ] *adj Br inf* grognon(onne).

crouch [kraʊtʃ] *vi* s'accroupir.

crow [krəʊ] **1** *n* corbeau *m*; **as the ~ flies** à vol d'oiseau. **2** *vi* [cock] chanter. || *inf* [person] frimer.

crowbar ['krəʊbɑ:r] *n* pied-de-biche *m*.

crowd [kraʊd] **1** *n* [mass of people] foule *f*. **2** *vi* s'amasser. **3** *vt* [streets, town] remplir. || [force into small space] entasser.

crowded ['kraʊdɪd] *adj*: **~ (with)** bondé(e) (de), plein(e) (de).

crown [kraʊn] **1** *n* [of king, on tooth] couronne *f*. || [of head, hill] sommet *m*; [of hat] fond *m*. **2** *vt* couronner. ○ **Crown** *n*: **the Crown** [monarchy] la Couronne.

crown jewels *npl* joyaux *mpl* de la Couronne.

crown prince *n* prince *m* héritier.

crow's feet *npl* pattes *fpl* d'oie.

crucial ['kru:ʃl] *adj* crucial(e).

crucifix ['kru:sɪfɪks] *n* crucifix *m*.

Crucifixion [,kru:sɪ'fɪkʃn] *n*: the ~ la Crucifixion.

crude [kru:d] *adj* [material] brut(e). || [joke, drawing] grossier(ière).

crude oil *n* (*U*) brut *m*.

cruel [kruəl] *adj* cruel(elle).

cruelty ['kruəltɪ] *n* (*U*) cruauté *f*.

cruet ['kru:ɪt] *n* service *m* à condiments.

cruise [kru:z] **1** *n* croisière *f*. **2** *vi* [sail] croiser. || [car] rouler; [plane] voler.

cruiser ['kru:zər] *n* [warship] croiseur *m*. || [cabin cruiser] yacht *m* de croisière.

crumb [krʌm] *n* [of food] miette *f*.

crumble ['krʌmbl] **1** *n* crumble *m* (aux fruits). **2** *vt* émietter. **3** *vi* [bread, cheese] s'émietter; [building, wall] s'écrouler; [cliff] s'ébouler; [plaster] s'effriter. || *fig* [society, relationship] s'effondrer.

crumbly ['krʌmblɪ] *adj* friable.

crumpet ['krʌmpɪt] *n* CULIN petite crêpe *f* épaisse.

crumple ['krʌmpl] *vt* [crease] froisser.

crunch [krʌntʃ] **1** *n* crissement *m*; **if it comes to the ~** *inf* s'il le faut. **2** *vt* [with teeth] croquer. || [underfoot] crisser.

crunchy ['krʌntʃɪ] *adj* [food] croquant(e).

crusade [kru:'seɪd] *n lit & fig* croisade *f*.

crush [krʌʃ] **1** *n* [crowd] foule *f*. || *inf* [infatuation]: **to have a ~ on sb** avoir le béguin pour qqn. **2** *vt* [gen] écraser; [ice] piler. || *fig* [hopes] anéantir.

crust [krʌst] *n* croûte *f*.

crutch [krʌtʃ] *n* [stick] béquille *f*.

crux [krʌks] *n* nœud *m*.

cry [kraɪ] **1** *n* [of person, bird] cri *m*. **2** *vi* [weep] pleurer. || [shout] crier. ○ **cry off** *vi* se dédire. ○ **cry out** **1** *vt* crier. **2** *vi* crier; [in pain, dismay] pousser un cri.

cryptic ['krɪptɪk] *adj* mystérieux(ieuse), énigmatique.

crystal ['krɪstl] *n* cristal *m*.

crystal clear *adj* [obvious] clair(e) comme de l'eau de roche.

cub [kʌb] *n* [young animal] petit *m*. || [boy scout] louveteau *m*.

Cuba ['kju:bə] *n* Cuba.

Cuban ['kju:bən] **1** *adj* cubain(e). **2** *n* Cubain *m*, -e *f*.

cubbyhole ['kʌbɪhəʊl] *n* cagibi *m*.

cube [kju:b] **1** *n* cube *m*. **2** *vt* MATH élever au cube.

cubic ['kju:bɪk] *adj* cubique.

cubicle ['kju:bɪkl] *n* cabine *f*.

Cub Scout *n* louveteau *m*.

cuckoo ['kuku:] *n* coucou *m*.

cuckoo clock *n* coucou *m*.

cucumber ['kju:kʌmbər] *n* concombre *m*.

cuddle ['kʌdl] **1** *n* caresse *f*, câlin *m*. **2** *vt* caresser, câliner. **3** *vi* s'enlacer.

cuddly toy ['kʌdlɪ-] *n* jouet *m* en peluche.

cue [kju:] *n* RADIO, THEATRE & TV signal *m*; **on ~** au bon moment. || [in snooker, pool] queue *f* (de billard).

cuff [kʌf] *n* [of sleeve] poignet *m*; **off the ~** au pied levé. || *Am* [of trousers] revers *m inv*. || [blow] gifle *f*.

cuff link *n* bouton *m* de manchette.

cul-de-sac ['kʌldəsæk] *n* cul-de-sac *m*.

cull [kʌl] **1** *n* massacre *m*. **2** *vt* [kill] massacrer. || [gather] recueillir.

culminate ['kʌlmɪneɪt] *vi*: **to ~ in sthg** se terminer par qqch, aboutir à qqch.

culmination [,kʌlmɪ'neɪʃn] *n* apogée *m*.

culottes [kju:'lɒts] *npl* jupe-culotte *f*.

culprit ['kʌlprɪt] *n* coupable *mf*.

cult [kʌlt] **1** *n* culte *m*. **2** *comp* culte.

cultivate ['kʌltɪveɪt] *vt* cultiver.

cultivation [,kʌltɪ'veɪʃn] *n* (*U*) [farming] culture *f*.

cultural ['kʌltʃərəl] *adj* culturel(elle).

culture ['kʌltʃər] *n* culture *f*.

cultured ['kʌltʃəd] *adj* [educated] cultivé(e).

cumbersome ['kʌmbəsəm] *adj* [object] encombrant(e).

cunning ['kʌnɪŋ] *adj* [person] rusé(e); [plan, method, device] astucieux(ieuse).

cup [kʌp] *n* [container, unit of measurement] tasse *f*. || [prize, competition] coupe *f*. || [of bra] bonnet *m*.

cupboard ['kʌbəd] *n* placard *m*.

curate ['kjʊərət] *n* vicaire *m*.

curator [,kjʊə'reɪtər] *n* conservateur *m*.

curb [kɜ:b] **1** *n* [control]: ~ **(on)** frein *m* (à). || *Am* [of road] bord *m* du trottoir. **2** *vt* mettre un frein à.

curdle ['kɜ:dl] *vi* cailler.

cure [kjʊər] **1** *n*: ~ **(for)** MED remède *m* (contre); *fig* remède (à). **2** *vt* MED guérir. || [solve - problem] éliminer. || **to ~ sb of sthg** guérir qqn de qqch, faire perdre l'habitude de qqch à qqn. || [preserve - by smoking] fumer; [- by salting] saler.

curfew ['kɜ:fju:] *n* couvre-feu *m*.

curiosity [,kjuəri'Dsəti] n curiosité f.

curious ['kjuəriəs] adj: ~ (about) curieux(ieuse) (à propos de).

curl [k3:l] **1** n [of hair] boucle f. **2** vt [hair] boucler. ‖ [roll up] enrouler. **3** vi [hair] boucler. ‖ [roll up] s'enrouler. ○ **curl up** vi [person, animal] se mettre en boule, se pelotonner.

curler ['k3:lər] n bigoudi m.

curling tongs ['k3:lɪŋ] npl fer m à friser.

curly ['k3:lɪ] adj [hair] bouclé(e).

currant ['kʌrənt] n [dried grape] raisin m de Corinthe, raisin sec.

currency ['kʌrənsɪ] n [type of money] monnaie f. ‖ (U) [money] devise f. ‖ fml [acceptability]: **to gain ~** s'accréditer.

current ['kʌrənt] **1** adj [price, method] actuel(elle); [year, week] en cours; [boyfriend, girlfriend] du moment; **~ issue** dernier numéro. **2** n [of water, air, electricity] courant m.

current affairs npl actualité f, questions fpl d'actualité.

currently ['kʌrəntlɪ] adv actuellement.

curriculum [kə'rɪkjələm] (pl **-lums** OR **-la** [-lə]) n programme m d'études.

curriculum vitae [-'vi:taɪ] (pl **curricula vitae**) n curriculum vitae m.

curry ['kʌrɪ] n curry m.

curse [k3:s] **1** n [evil spell] malédiction f; fig fléau m. ‖ [swearword] juron m. **2** vt maudire. **3** vi jurer.

cursor ['k3:sər] n COMPUT curseur m.

curt [k3:t] adj brusque.

curtain ['k3:tn] n rideau m.

curts(e)y ['k3:tsɪ] (pt & pp **curtsied**) **1** n révérence f. **2** vi faire une révérence.

curve [k3:v] **1** n courbe f. **2** vi faire une courbe.

cushion ['kuʃn] **1** n coussin m. **2** vt [fall, blow, effects] amortir.

custard ['kʌstəd] n crème f anglaise.

custodian [kʌ'stəʊdjən] n [of building] gardien m, -ienne f; [of museum] conservateur m.

custody ['kʌstədɪ] n [of child] garde f. ‖ JUR: **in ~** en garde à vue.

custom ['kʌstəm] n [tradition, habit] coutume f. ‖ COMM clientèle f. ○ **customs** n [place] douane f.

customary ['kʌstəmrɪ] adj [behaviour] coutumier(ière); [way, time] habituel(elle).

customer ['kʌstəmər] n [client] client m, -e f. ‖ inf [person] type m.

customize, -ise ['kʌstəmaɪz] vt [make] fabriquer OR assembler sur commande; [modify] modifier sur commande.

customs duty n droit m de douane.

customs officer n douanier m, -ière f.

cut [kʌt] (pt & pp **cut**) **1** n [in wood etc] entaille f; [in skin] coupure f. ‖ [of meat] morceau m. ‖ [reduction]: **~ (in)** [taxes, salary, personnel] réduction f (de); [film, article] coupure f (dans). ‖ [of suit, hair] coupe f. **2** vt [gen] couper; [taxes, costs, workforce] réduire; **to ~ one's finger** se couper le doigt. **3** vi [gen] couper. ‖ [intersect] se couper. ○ **cut back 1** vt sep [prune] tailler. ‖ [reduce] réduire. **2** vi: **to ~ back on** réduire, diminuer. ○ **cut down 1** vt sep [chop down] couper. ‖ [reduce] réduire, diminuer. **2** vi: **to ~ down on smoking/eating/spending** fumer/manger/dépenser moins. ○ **cut in** vi [interrupt]: **to ~ in (on sb)** interrompre (qqn). ‖ AUT & SPORT se rabattre. ○ **cut off** vt sep [piece, crust] couper; [finger, leg - subj: surgeon] amputer. ‖ [power, telephone, funding] couper. ‖ [separate]: **to be ~ off (from)** [person] être coupé(e) (de); [village] être isolé(e) (de). ○ **cut out** vt sep [photo, article] découper; [sewing pattern] couper; [dress] tailler. ‖ [stop]: **to ~ out smoking/chocolates** arrêter de fumer/de manger des chocolats; **~ it out!** inf ça suffit! ‖ [exclude] exclure. ○ **cut up** vt sep [chop up] couper, hacher.

cutback ['kʌtbæk] n: **~ (in)** réduction f (de).

cute [kju:t] adj [appealing] mignon(onne).

cuticle ['kju:tɪkl] n envie f.

cutlery ['kʌtlərɪ] n (U) couverts mpl.

cutlet ['kʌtlɪt] n côtelette f.

cutout ['kʌtaʊt] n [on machine] disjoncteur m. ‖ [shape] découpage m.

cut-price, cut-rate Am adj à prix réduit.

cutthroat ['kʌtθrəʊt] adj [ruthless] acharné(e).

cutting ['kʌtɪŋ] **1** adj [sarcastic - remark] cinglant(e); [- wit] acerbe. **2** n [of plant] bouture f. ‖ [from newspaper] coupure f. ‖ Br [for road, railway] tranchée f.

CV (abbr of **curriculum vitae**) n CV m.

cwt. abbr of **hundredweight**.

cyanide ['saɪənaɪd] n cyanure m.

cycle ['saɪkl] **1** n [of events, songs] cycle m. ‖ [bicycle] bicyclette f. **2** comp [path, track] cyclable; [race] cycliste; [shop] de cycles. **3** *vi* faire de la bicyclette.

cycling ['saɪklɪŋ] *n* cyclisme *m*.

cyclist ['saɪklɪst] *n* cycliste *mf*.

cygnet ['sɪgnɪt] *n* jeune cygne *m*.

cylinder ['sɪlɪndər] *n* cylindre *m*.

cymbals ['sɪmblz] *npl* cymbales *fpl*.

cynic ['sɪnɪk] *n* cynique *mf*.

cynical ['sɪnɪkl] *adj* cynique.

cynicism ['sɪnɪsɪzm] *n* cynisme *m*.

cypress ['saɪprəs] *n* cyprès *m*.

Cyprus ['saɪprəs] *n* Chypre *f*.

cyst [sɪst] *n* kyste *m*.

cystitis [sɪs'taɪtɪs] *n* cystite *f*.

czar [zɑːr] *n* tsar *m*.

Czech [tʃek] **1** *adj* tchèque. **2** *n* [person] Tchèque *mf*. || [language] tchèque *m*.

Czechoslovak [ˌtʃekə'sləʊvæk] = Czechoslovakian.

Czechoslovakia [ˌtʃekəslə'vækɪə] *n* Tchécoslovaquie *f*.

Czechoslovakian [ˌtʃekəslə'vækɪən] **1** *adj* tchécoslovaque. **2** *n* Tchécoslovaque *mf*.

d (*pl* **d's** OR **ds**), **D** (*pl* **D's** OR **Ds**) [diː] *n* [letter] d *m inv*, D *m inv*. ○ **D** *n* MUS ré *m*. || SCH [mark] D *m inv*.

DA *abbr of* **district attorney**.

dab [dæb] **1** *n* [of cream, powder, ointment] petit peu *m*; [of paint] touche *f*. **2** *vt* [skin, wound] tamponner. || [apply - cream, ointment]: **to ~ sthg on** OR **onto** appliquer qqch sur.

dabble ['dæbl] *vi*: **to ~ in** toucher un peu à.

dachshund ['dækshʊnd] *n* teckel *m*.

dad [dæd], **daddy** ['dædɪ] *n inf* papa *m*.

daddy longlegs [-'lɒŋlegz] (*pl inv*) *n* faucheur *m*.

daffodil ['dæfədɪl] *n* jonquille *f*.

daft [dɑːft] *adj inf* stupide, idiot(e).

dagger ['dægər] *n* poignard *m*.

daily ['deɪlɪ] **1** *adj* [newspaper, occurrence] quotidien(ienne). || [rate, output] journalier(ière). **2** *adv* [happen, write]

quotidiennement; **twice ~** deux fois par jour. **3** *n* [newspaper] quotidien *m*.

dainty ['deɪntɪ] *adj* délicat(e).

dairy ['deərɪ] *n* [on farm] laiterie *f*. || [shop] crémerie *f*.

dairy products *npl* produits *mpl* laitiers.

dais ['deɪɪs] *n* estrade *f*.

daisy ['deɪzɪ] *n* [weed] pâquerette *f*; [cultivated] marguerite *f*.

daisy-wheel printer *n* imprimante *f* à marguerite.

dam [dæm] **1** *n* [across river] barrage *m*. **2** *vt* construire un barrage sur.

damage ['dæmɪdʒ] **1** *n* [physical harm] dommage *m*, dégât *m*. || [harmful effect] tort *m*. **2** *vt* [harm physically] endommager, abîmer. || [have harmful effect on] nuire à. ○ **damages** *npl* JUR dommages et intérêts *mpl*.

damn [dæm] **1** *adj inf* fichu(e), sacré(e). **2** *adv* sacrément. **3** *n inf*: **not to give** OR **care a ~ (about sthg)** se ficher pas mal (de qqch). **4** *vt* RELIG [condemn] damner. **5** *excl inf* zut!

damned [dæmd] *inf adj* fichu(e), sacré(e); **well I'll be** OR **I'm ~!** c'est trop fort!, elle est bien bonne celle-là!

damp [dæmp] **1** *adj* humide. **2** *n* humidité *f*. **3** *vt* [make wet] humecter.

dampen ['dæmpən] *vt* [make wet] humecter. || *fig* [emotion] abattre.

damson ['dæmzn] *n* prune *f* de Damas.

dance [dɑːns] **1** *n* [gen] danse *f*. || [social event] bal *m*. **2** *vi* danser.

dancer ['dɑːnsər] *n* danseur *m*, -euse *f*.

dancing ['dɑːnsɪŋ] *n* (*U*) danse *f*.

dandelion ['dændɪlaɪən] *n* pissenlit *m*.

dandruff ['dændrʌf] *n* (*U*) pellicules *fpl*.

Dane [deɪn] *n* Danois *m*, -e *f*.

danger ['deɪndʒər] *n* (*U*) [possibility of harm] danger *m*; **in ~** en danger; **out of ~** hors de danger. || [hazard, risk]: **~ (to)** risque *m* (pour); **to be in ~ of doing sthg** risquer de faire qqch.

dangerous ['deɪndʒərəs] *adj* dangereux(euse).

dangle ['dæŋgl] **1** *vt* laisser pendre. **2** *vi* pendre.

Danish ['deɪnɪʃ] **1** *adj* danois(e). **2** *n* [language] danois *m*. || *Am* = **Danish pastry. 3** *npl*: **the ~** les Danois *mpl*.

Danish pastry *n* gâteau feuilleté fourré aux fruits.

dapper ['dæpər] *adj* pimpant(e).

dappled ['dæpld] adj [light] tacheté(e).
|| [horse] pommelé(e).

dare [deəʳ] 1 vt [be brave enough]: to ~ to
do sthg oser faire qqch. || [challenge]: to
~ sb to do sthg défier qqn de faire qqch.
|| phr: I ~ say je suppose, sans doute. 2 vi
oser; how ~ you! comment osez-vous! 3
n défi m.

daredevil ['deə,devl] n casse-cou mf
inv.

daring ['deərɪŋ] 1 adj audacieux(ieuse).
2 n audace f.

dark [dɑːk] 1 adj [room, night] sombre;
it's getting ~ il commence à faire nuit. ||
[in colour] foncé(e). || [dark-haired]
brun(e); [dark-skinned] basané(e). 2 n
[darkness]: **the ~** l'obscurité f; **to be in
the ~ about sthg** ignorer tout de qqch. ||
[night]: **before/after ~** avant/après la
tombée de la nuit.

darken ['dɑːkn] 1 vt assombrir. 2 vi
s'assombrir.

dark glasses npl lunettes fpl noires.

darkness ['dɑːknɪs] n obscurité f.

darkroom ['dɑːkrum] n chambre f
noire.

darling ['dɑːlɪŋ] n [loved person, term of
address] chéri m, -e f. || [idol] chouchou
m, idole f.

darn [dɑːn] 1 vt repriser. 2 adj inf sa-
cré(e), satané(e). 3 adv inf sacrément.

dart [dɑːt] 1 n [arrow] fléchette f. 2 vi se
précipiter. **O darts** n [game] jeu m de
fléchettes.

dartboard ['dɑːtbɔːd] n cible f de jeu
de fléchettes.

dash [dæʃ] 1 n [of milk, wine] goutte f;
[of cream] soupçon m; [of salt] pincée f;
[of colour, paint] touche f. || [in punctua-
tion] tiret m. || [rush]: **to make a ~ for** se
ruer vers. 2 vt [throw] jeter avec violence.
|| [hopes] anéantir. 3 vi se précipiter.

dashboard ['dæʃbɔːd] n tableau m de
bord.

dashing ['dæʃɪŋ] adj fringant(e).

data ['deɪtə] n (U) données fpl.

database ['deɪtəbeɪs] n base f de données.

data processing n traitement m de
données.

date [deɪt] 1 n [in time] date f; **to ~** à ce
jour. || [appointment] rendez-vous m. ||
[person] petit ami m, petite amie f. ||
[fruit] datte f. 2 vt [gen] dater. || [go out
with] sortir avec. 3 vi [go out of fashion]
dater.

dated ['deɪtɪd] adj qui date.

date of birth n date f de naissance.

daub [dɔːb] vt: **to ~ sthg with sthg** barbouiller qqch de qqch.

daughter ['dɔːtəʳ] n fille f.

daughter-in-law (pl **daughters-in-
law**) n belle-fille f.

daunting ['dɔːntɪŋ] adj intimidant(e).

dawdle ['dɔːdl] vi flâner.

dawn [dɔːn] 1 n lit & fig aube f. 2 vi
[day] poindre. **O dawn (up)on** vt fus
venir à l'esprit de.

day [deɪ] n jour m; [duration] journée f;
the ~ before la veille; **the ~ after** le lendemain; **the ~ before yesterday** avant-hier;
the ~ after tomorrow après-demain; **any
~ now** d'un jour à l'autre; **one ~, some ~,
one of these ~s** un jour (ou l'autre), un
de ces jours; **in my ~** de mon temps; **to
make sb's ~** réchauffer le cœur de qqn.
O days adv le jour.

daybreak ['deɪbreɪk] n aube f; **at ~** à
l'aube.

daydream ['deɪdriːm] vi rêvasser.

daylight ['deɪlaɪt] n [light] lumière f du
jour. || [dawn] aube f.

day off (pl **days off**) n jour m de congé.

daytime ['deɪtaɪm] 1 n jour m, journée
f. 2 comp [television] pendant la journée;
[job, flight] de jour.

day-to-day adj [routine, life] journa-
lier(ière); **on a ~ basis** au jour le jour.

day trip n excursion f d'une journée.

daze [deɪz] 1 n: **in a ~** hébété(e), ahu-
ri(e). 2 vt [subj: blow] étourdir. || fig
[subj: shock, event] abasourdir, sidérer.

dazzle ['dæzl] vt éblouir.

DC (abbr of **direct current**) courant m
continu.

D-day ['diːdeɪ] n le jour J.

DEA (abbr of **Drug Enforcement Administration**) n agence américaine de
lutte contre la drogue.

deacon ['diːkn] n diacre m.

deactivate [,diːˈæktɪveɪt] vt désamorcer.

dead [ded] 1 adj [not alive, not lively]
mort(e). || [numb] engourdi(e). || [not
operating - battery] à plat. || [complete -
silence] de mort. 2 adv [directly, pre-
cisely]: **~ ahead** droit devant soi; **~ on
time** pile à l'heure. || inf [completely] tout
à fait. || [suddenly]: **to stop ~** s'arrêter
net. 3 npl: **the ~** les morts mpl.

deaden ['dedn] vt [sound] assourdir;
[pain] calmer.

dead end n impasse f.

dead heat n arrivée f ex-aequo.

deception

deadline ['dedlaɪn] n dernière limite f.

deadlock ['dedlɒk] n impasse f.

dead loss n inf: **to be a ~** [person] être bon (bonne) à rien; [object] ne rien valoir.

deadly ['dedlɪ] 1 adj [poison, enemy] mortel(elle). || [accuracy] imparable. 2 adv [boring, serious] tout à fait.

deadpan ['dedpæn] 1 adj pince-sans-rire (inv). 2 adv impassiblement.

deaf [def] 1 adj sourd(e); **to be ~ to sthg** être sourd à qqch. 2 npl: **the ~** les sourds mpl.

deaf-and-dumb adj sourd-muet (sourde-muette).

deafen ['defn] vt assourdir.

deaf-mute 1 adj sourd-muet (sourde-muette). 2 n sourd-muet m, sourde-muette f.

deafness ['defnɪs] n surdité f.

deal [di:l] (pt & pp dealt) 1 n [quantity: **a good** OR **great ~**] beaucoup; **a good** OR **great ~ of** beaucoup de, bien de/des. || [business agreement] marché m, affaire f; **to do** OR **strike a ~ with sb** conclure un marché avec qqn. || inf [treatment]: **to get a bad ~** ne pas faire une affaire. 2 vt [strike]: **to ~ sb/sthg a blow, to ~ a blow to sb/sthg** porter un coup à qqn/qqch. || [cards] donner, distribuer. 3 vi [at cards] donner, distribuer. || [in drugs] faire le trafic (de drogues). O **deal in** vt fus COMM faire le commerce de. O **deal out** vt sep distribuer. O **deal with** vt fus [handle] s'occuper de. || [be about] traiter de. || [be faced with] avoir affaire à.

dealer ['di:lər] n [trader] négociant m; [in drugs] trafiquant m. || [cards] donneur m.

dealing ['di:lɪŋ] n commerce m. O **dealings** npl relations fpl, rapports mpl.

dealt [delt] pt & pp → deal.

dean [di:n] n doyen m.

dear [dɪər] 1 adj: **~ (to)** cher (chère) (à); **Dear Sir** [in letter] Cher Monsieur; **Dear Madam** Chère Madame. 2 n chéri m, -e f. 3 excl: **oh ~!** mon Dieu!

dearly ['dɪəlɪ] adv [love, wish] de tout son cœur.

death [deθ] n mort f; **to frighten sb to ~** faire une peur bleue à qqn; **to be sick to ~ of sthg/of doing sthg** en avoir marre de qqch/de faire qqch.

death certificate n acte m de décès.

death duty Br, **death tax** Am n droits mpl de succession.

death penalty n peine f de mort.

death rate n taux m de mortalité.

death tax Am = death duty.

death trap n inf véhicule m/bâtiment m dangereux.

debar [di:'bɑːr] vt: **to ~ sb (from)** [place] exclure qqn (de); **to ~ sb from doing sthg** interdire à qqn de faire qqch.

debate [dɪ'beɪt] 1 n débat m; **open to ~** discutable. 2 vt débattre, discuter; **to ~ whether** s'interroger pour savoir si.

debating society [dɪ'beɪtɪŋ-] n club m de débats.

debauchery [dɪ'bɔːtʃərɪ] n débauche f.

debit ['debɪt] 1 n débit m. 2 vt débiter.

debit note n note f de débit.

debris ['deɪbriː] n (U) débris mpl.

debt [det] n dette f; **to be in ~** avoir des dettes, être endetté(e); **to be in sb's ~** être redevable à qqn.

debt collector n agent m de recouvrement.

debtor ['detər] n débiteur m, -trice f.

debug [,di:'bʌg] vt COMPUT [program] mettre au point, déboguer.

debut ['deɪbjuː] n débuts mpl.

decade ['dekeɪd] n décennie f.

decadence ['dekədəns] n décadence f.

decadent ['dekədənt] adj décadent(e).

decaffeinated [dɪ'kæfɪneɪtɪd] adj décaféiné(e).

decanter [dɪ'kæntər] n carafe f.

decathlon [dɪ'kæθlɒn] n décathlon m.

decay [dɪ'keɪ] 1 n [of body, plant] pourriture f, putréfaction f; [of tooth] carie f. || fig [of building] délabrement m; [of society] décadence f. 2 vi [rot] pourrir; [tooth] se carier.

deceased [dɪ'siːst] (pl inv) 1 adj décédé(e). 2 n: **the ~** le défunt, la défunte.

deceit [dɪ'siːt] n tromperie f, supercherie f.

deceitful [dɪ'siːtful] adj trompeur(euse).

deceive [dɪ'siːv] vt [person] tromper, duper; [subj: memory, eyes] jouer des tours à; **to ~ o.s.** se leurrer, s'abuser.

December [dɪ'sembər] n décembre m; see also **September**.

decency ['diːsnsɪ] n décence f, bienséance f.

decent ['diːsnt] adj [behaviour, dress] décent(e). || [wage, meal] correct(e), décent(e). || [person] gentil(ille), brave.

deception [dɪ'sepʃn] n [lie, pretence] tromperie f, duperie f. || (U) [act of lying] supercherie f.

deceptive [dɪ'septɪv] *adj* trompeur(euse).

decide [dɪ'saɪd] 1 *vt* décider; **to ~ to do sthg** décider de faire qqch. 2 *vi* se décider. ○ **decide (up)on** *vt fus* se décider pour, choisir.

decided [dɪ'saɪdɪd] *adj* [definite] certain(e), incontestable. || [resolute] décidé(e), résolu(e).

decidedly [dɪ'saɪdɪdlɪ] *adv* [clearly] manifestement, incontestablement. || [resolutely] résolument.

deciduous [dɪ'sɪdjʊəs] *adj* à feuilles caduques.

decimal ['desɪml] 1 *adj* décimal(e). 2 *n* décimale *f*.

decimal point *n* virgule *f*.

decipher [dɪ'saɪfə*r*] *vt* déchiffrer.

decision [dɪ'sɪʒn] *n* décision *f*.

decisive [dɪ'saɪsɪv] *adj* [person] déterminé(e), résolu(e). || [factor, event] décisif(ive).

deck [dek] *n* [of ship] pont *m*. || [of bus] impériale *f*. || [of cards] jeu *m*. || *Am* [of house] véranda *f*.

deckchair ['dektʃeə*r*] *n* chaise longue *f*, transat *m*.

declaration [,deklə'reɪʃn] *n* déclaration *f*.

Declaration of Independence *n*: **the ~** la *Déclaration d'Indépendance des États-Unis d'Amérique (1776)*.

declare [dɪ'kleə*r*] *vt* déclarer.

decline [dɪ'klaɪn] 1 *n* déclin *m*; **to be in ~** être en déclin; **on the ~** en baisse. 2 *vt* décliner; **to ~ to do sthg** refuser de faire qqch. 3 *vi* [deteriorate] décliner. || [refuse] refuser.

decode [,di:'kəʊd] *vt* décoder.

decompose [,di:kəm'pəʊz] *vi* se décomposer.

decongestant [,di:kən'dʒestənt] *n* décongestionnant *m*.

decorate ['dekəreɪt] *vt* décorer.

decoration [,dekə'reɪʃn] *n* décoration *f*.

decorator ['dekəreɪtə*r*] *n* décorateur *m*, -trice *f*.

decoy [*n* 'di:kɔɪ, *vt* dɪ'kɔɪ] 1 *n* [for hunting] appât *m*, leurre *m*; [person] compère *m*. 2 *vt* attirer dans un piège.

decrease [*n* 'di:kri:s, *vb* dɪ'kri:s] 1 *n*: **~ (in)** diminution *f* (de), baisse *f* (de). 2 *vt* diminuer, réduire. 3 *vi* diminuer, décroître.

decree [dɪ'kri:] 1 *n* [order, decision] décret *m*. || *Am* JUR arrêt *m*, jugement *m*. 2 *vt* décréter, ordonner.

decrepit [dɪ'krepɪt] *adj* [person] décrépit(e); [house] délabré(e).

dedicate ['dedɪkeɪt] *vt* [book etc] dédier. || [life, career] consacrer.

dedication [,dedɪ'keɪʃn] *n* [commitment] dévouement *m*. || [in book] dédicace *f*.

deduce [dɪ'dju:s] *vt* déduire, conclure.

deduct [dɪ'dʌkt] *vt* déduire, retrancher.

deduction [dɪ'dʌkʃn] *n* déduction *f*.

deed [di:d] *n* [action] action *f*, acte *m*. || JUR acte *m* notarié.

deem [di:m] *vt* juger, considérer; **to ~ it wise to do sthg** juger prudent de faire qqch.

deep [di:p] 1 *adj* profond(e). 2 *adv* profondément; **~ down** [fundamentally] au fond.

deepen ['di:pn] *vi* [river, sea] devenir profond(e). || [crisis, recession, feeling] s'aggraver.

deep freeze *n* congélateur *m*.

deep fry *vt* faire frire.

deeply ['di:plɪ] *adv* profondément.

deep-sea *adj*: **~ diving** plongée *f* sous-marine; **~ fishing** pêche *f* hauturière.

deer [dɪə*r*] (*pl inv*) *n* cerf *m*.

deface [dɪ'feɪs] *vt* barbouiller.

default [dɪ'fɔ:lt] 1 *n* [failure] défaillance *f*; **by ~** par défaut. || COMPUT valeur *f* par défaut. 2 *vi* manquer à ses engagements.

defeat [dɪ'fi:t] 1 *n* défaite *f*; **to admit ~** s'avouer battu(e) OR vaincu(e). 2 *vt* [team, opponent] vaincre, battre. || [motion, proposal] rejeter.

defeatist [dɪ'fi:tɪst] *adj* défaitiste.

defect [*n* 'di:fekt, *vi* dɪ'fekt] 1 *n* défaut *m*. 2 *vi*: **to ~ to** passer à.

defective [dɪ'fektɪv] *adj* défectueux(euse).

defence *Br*, **defense** *Am* [dɪ'fens] *n* [gen] défense *f*. || [protective device, system] protection *f*. || JUR: **the ~** la défense.

defenceless *Br*, **defenseless** *Am* [dɪ'fenslɪs] *adj* sans défense.

defend [dɪ'fend] *vt* défendre.

defendant [dɪ'fendənt] *n* défendeur *m*, -eresse *f*.

defender [dɪ'fendə*r*] *n* défenseur *m*.

defense *Am* = **defence**.

defenseless *Am* = **defenceless**.

defensive [dɪ'fensɪv] 1 *adj* défensif(ive). 2 *n*: **on the ~** sur la défensive.

defer [dɪ'fɜ:*r*] 1 *vt* différer. 2 *vi*: **to ~ to sb** s'en remettre à (l'opinion de) qqn.

defiance [dɪˈfaɪəns] n défi m; **in ~ of** au mépris de.

defiant [dɪˈfaɪənt] adj [person] intraitable, intransigeant(e); [action] de défi.

deficiency [dɪˈfɪʃnsɪ] n [lack] manque m; [of vitamins etc] carence f. || [inadequacy] imperfection f.

deficient [dɪˈfɪʃnt] adj [lacking]: **to be ~ in** manquer de. || [inadequate] insuffisant(e), médiocre.

deficit [ˈdefɪsɪt] n déficit m.

defile [dɪˈfaɪl] vt souiller, salir.

define [dɪˈfaɪn] vt définir.

definite [ˈdefɪnɪt] adj [plan] bien déterminé(e); [date] certain(e). || [improvement, difference] net (nette), marqué(e). || [answer] précis(e), catégorique.

definitely [ˈdefɪnɪtlɪ] adv [without doubt] sans aucun doute, certainement. || [for emphasis] catégoriquement.

definition [ˌdefɪˈnɪʃn] n [gen] définition f. || [clarity] clarté f, précision f.

deflate [dɪˈfleɪt] **1** vt [balloon, tyre] dégonfler. **2** vi [balloon, tyre] se dégonfler.

deflation [dɪˈfleɪʃn] n ECON déflation f.

deflect [dɪˈflekt] vt [ball, bullet] dévier; [criticism] détourner.

defogger [ˌdiːˈfɒgər] n Am AUT dispositif m antibuée.

deformed [dɪˈfɔːmd] adj difforme.

defraud [dɪˈfrɔːd] vt [person] escroquer; [Inland Revenue etc] frauder.

defrost [ˌdiːˈfrɒst] **1** vt [fridge] dégivrer; [frozen food] décongeler. || Am [AUT - de-ice] dégivrer; [- demist] désembuer. **2** vi [fridge] dégivrer; [frozen food] se décongeler.

deft [deft] adj adroit(e).

defunct [dɪˈfʌŋkt] adj qui n'existe plus.

defy [dɪˈfaɪ] vt [gen] défier; **to ~ sb to do sthg** mettre qqn au défi de faire qqch. || [efforts] résister à, faire échouer.

degenerate [adj & n dɪˈdʒenərət, vb dɪˈdʒenəreɪt] **1** adj dégénéré(e). **2** vi: **to ~ (into)** dégénérer (en).

degrading [dɪˈgreɪdɪŋ] adj dégradant(e), avilissant(e).

degree [dɪˈgriː] n [measurement] degré m. || UNIV diplôme m universitaire; **to have/take a ~ (in)** avoir/faire une licence (de). || [amount]: **to a certain ~** jusqu'à un certain point, dans une certaine mesure; **a ~ of truth** une certaine part de vérité; **by ~s** progressivement, petit à petit.

dehydrated [ˌdiːhaɪˈdreɪtɪd] adj déshydraté(e).

de-ice [ˌdiːˈaɪs] vt dégivrer.

deign [deɪn] vt: **to ~ to do sthg** daigner faire qqch.

deity [ˈdiːɪtɪ] n dieu m, déesse f, divinité f.

dejected [dɪˈdʒektɪd] adj abattu(e), découragé(e).

delay [dɪˈleɪ] **1** n retard m, délai m. **2** vt [cause to be late] retarder. || [defer] différer; **to ~ doing sthg** tarder à faire qqch. **3** vi: **to ~ (in doing sthg)** tarder (à faire qqch).

delayed [dɪˈleɪd] adj: **to be ~** [person, train] être retardé(e).

delegate [n ˈdelɪgət, vb ˈdelɪgeɪt] **1** n délégué m, -e f. **2** vt déléguer; **to ~ sb to do sthg** déléguer qqn pour faire qqch; **to ~ sthg to sb** déléguer qqch à qqn.

delegation [ˌdelɪˈgeɪʃn] n délégation f.

delete [dɪˈliːt] vt supprimer, effacer.

deli [ˈdelɪ] n inf abbr of delicatessen.

deliberate [adj dɪˈlɪbərət, vb dɪˈlɪbərət] **1** adj [intentional] voulu(e), délibéré(e). || [slow] lent(e), sans hâte. **2** vi délibérer.

deliberately [dɪˈlɪbərətlɪ] adv [on purpose] exprès, à dessein.

delicacy [ˈdelɪkəsɪ] n [gen] délicatesse f. || [food] mets m délicat.

delicate [ˈdelɪkət] adj délicat(e); [movement] gracieux(ieuse).

delicatessen [ˌdelɪkəˈtesn] n épicerie f fine.

delicious [dɪˈlɪʃəs] adj délicieux(ieuse).

delight [dɪˈlaɪt] **1** n [great pleasure] délice m; **to take ~ in doing sthg** prendre grand plaisir à faire qqch. **2** vt enchanter, charmer. **3** vi: **to ~ in sthg/in doing sthg** prendre grand plaisir à qqch/à faire qqch.

delighted [dɪˈlaɪtɪd] adj: **~ (by OR with)** enchanté(e) (de), ravi(e) (de); **to be ~ to do sthg** être enchanté OR ravi de faire qqch.

delightful [dɪˈlaɪtfʊl] adj ravissant(e), charmant(e); [meal] délicieux(ieuse).

delinquent [dɪˈlɪŋkwənt] **1** adj délinquant(e). **2** n délinquant m, -e f.

delirious [dɪˈlɪrɪəs] adj lit & fig délirant(e).

deliver [dɪˈlɪvər] vt [distribute]: **to ~ sthg (to sb)** [mail, newspaper] distribuer qqch (à qqn); COMM livrer qqch (à qqn). || [speech] faire; [message] remettre; [blow, kick] donner, porter. || [baby] mettre au monde. || Am POL [votes] obtenir.

delivery [dɪˈlɪvərɪ] n COMM livraison f. ||

[way of speaking] élocution *f*. || [birth] accouchement *m*.

delude [dɪˈluːd] *vt* tromper, induire en erreur; **to ~ o.s.** se faire des illusions.

delusion [dɪˈluːʒn] *n* illusion *f*.

delve [delv] *vi*: **to ~ into** [past] fouiller; [bag etc] fouiller dans.

demand [dɪˈmɑːnd] **1** *n* [claim, firm request] revendication *f*, exigence *f*; **on ~** sur demande. || [need]: **~ (for)** demande *f* (de); **in ~** demandé(e), recherché(e). **2** *vt* [ask for - justice, money] réclamer; [- explanation, apology] exiger; **to ~ to do sthg** exiger de faire qqch. || [require] demander, exiger.

demanding [dɪˈmɑːndɪŋ] *adj* [exhausting] astreignant(e). || [not easily satisfied] exigeant(e).

demean [dɪˈmiːn] *vt*: **to ~ o.s.** s'abaisser.

demeaning [dɪˈmiːnɪŋ] *adj* avilissant(e), dégradant(e).

demented [dɪˈmentɪd] *adj* fou (folle), dément(e).

demise [dɪˈmaɪz] *n* (U) décès *m*; *fig* mort *f*, fin *f*.

demo [ˈdeməʊ] (*abbr of* **demonstration**) *n inf* manif *f*.

democracy [dɪˈmɒkrəsɪ] *n* démocratie *f*.

democrat [ˈdeməkræt] *n* démocrate *mf*. ○ **Democrat** *n Am* démocrate *mf*.

democratic [ˌdeməˈkrætɪk] *adj* démocratique. ○ **Democratic** *adj Am* démocrate.

Democratic Party *n Am*: **the ~** le Parti démocrate.

demolish [dɪˈmɒlɪʃ] *vt* [destroy] démolir.

demonstrate [ˈdemənstreɪt] **1** *vt* [prove] démontrer, prouver. || [machine, computer] faire une démonstration de. **2** *vi*: **to ~ (for/against)** manifester (pour/contre).

demonstration [ˌdemənˈstreɪʃn] *n* [of machine, emotions] démonstration *f*. || [public meeting] manifestation *f*.

demonstrator [ˈdemənstreɪtər] *n* [in march] manifestant *m*, -e *f*. || [of machine, product] démonstrateur *m*, -trice *f*.

demoralized [dɪˈmɒrəlaɪzd] *adj* démoralisé(e).

demote [ˌdiːˈməʊt] *vt* rétrograder.

den [den] *n* [of animal] antre *m*, tanière *f*.

denial [dɪˈnaɪəl] *n* [of rights, facts, truth] dénégation *f*; [of accusation] démenti *m*.

denier [ˈdenɪə] *n* denier *m*.

denim [ˈdenɪm] *n* jean *m*. ○ **denims** *npl*: **a pair of ~s** un jean.

Denmark [ˈdenmɑːk] *n* Danemark *m*.

denomination [dɪˌnɒmɪˈneɪʃn] *n* RELIG confession *f*. || [money] valeur *f*.

denounce [dɪˈnaʊns] *vt* dénoncer.

dense [dens] *adj* [crowd, forest] dense; [fog] dense, épais(aisse). || *inf* [stupid] bouché(e).

density [ˈdensətɪ] *n* densité *f*.

dent [dent] **1** *n* bosse *f*. **2** *vt* cabosser.

dental [ˈdentl] *adj* dentaire; **~ appointment** rendez-vous *m* chez le dentiste.

dental floss *n* fil *m* dentaire.

dental surgeon *n* chirurgien-dentiste *m*.

dentist [ˈdentɪst] *n* dentiste *mf*.

dentures [ˈdentʃəz] *npl* dentier *m*.

deny [dɪˈnaɪ] *vt* [refute] nier. || *fml* [refuse] nier, refuser; **to ~ sb sthg** refuser qqch à qqn.

deodorant [diːˈəʊdərənt] *n* déodorant *m*.

depart [dɪˈpɑːt] *vi fml* [leave]: **to ~ (from)** partir de. || [differ]: **to ~ from sthg** s'écarter de qqch.

department [dɪˈpɑːtmənt] *n* [in organization] service *m*. || [in shop] rayon *m*. || SCH & UNIV département *m*. || [in government] département *m*, ministère *m*.

department store *n* grand magasin *m*.

departure [dɪˈpɑːtʃər] *n* [leaving] départ *m*. || [change] nouveau départ *m*.

departure lounge *n* salle *f* d'embarquement.

depend [dɪˈpend] *vi*: **to ~ on** [be dependent on] dépendre de; [rely on] compter sur; [emotionally] se reposer sur; **it ~s** cela dépend; **~ing on** selon.

dependable [dɪˈpendəbl] *adj* [person] sur qui on peut compter; [car] fiable.

dependant [dɪˈpendənt] *n* personne *f* à charge.

dependent [dɪˈpendənt] *adj* [reliant]: **~ (on)** dépendant(e) (de); **to be ~ on sb/sthg** dépendre de qqn/qqch. || [addicted] dépendant(e), accro. || [contingent]: **to be ~ on** dépendre de.

depict [dɪˈpɪkt] *vt* [show in picture] représenter. || [describe]: **to ~ sb/sthg as** dépeindre qqn/qqch comme.

deplete [dɪˈpliːt] *vt* épuiser.

deplorable [dɪˈplɔːrəbl] *adj* déplorable.

deplore [dɪˈplɔːr] *vt* déplorer.

deploy [dɪˈplɔɪ] *vt* déployer.

depopulation [diː,pɒpjuˈleɪʃn] n dépeuplement m.

deport [dɪˈpɔːt] vt expulser.

depose [dɪˈpəʊz] vt déposer.

deposit [dɪˈpɒzɪt] 1 n [gen] dépôt m; **to make a ~** [into bank account] déposer de l'argent. || [payment - as guarantee] caution f; [- as instalment] acompte m; [- on bottle] consigne f. 2 vt déposer.

depot ['depəʊ] n [gen] dépôt m. || Am [station] gare.

depreciate [dɪˈpriːʃɪeɪt] vi se déprécier.

depress [dɪˈpres] vt [sadden, discourage] déprimer. || [weaken - economy] affaiblir; [- prices] faire baisser.

depressed [dɪˈprest] adj [sad] déprimé(e). || [run-down - area] en déclin.

depressing [dɪˈpresɪŋ] adj déprimant(e).

depression [dɪˈpreʃn] n [gen] dépression f. || [sadness] tristesse f.

deprivation [,deprɪˈveɪʃn] n privation f.

deprive [dɪˈpraɪv] vt: **to ~ sb of sthg** priver qqn de qqch.

depth [depθ] n profondeur f; **in ~** [study, analyse] en profondeur; **to be out of one's ~** [in water] ne pas avoir pied; fig avoir perdu pied, être dépassé. ○ **depths** npl: **in the ~s of winter** au cœur de l'hiver; **to be in the ~s of despair** toucher le fond du désespoir.

deputation [,depjuˈteɪʃn] n délégation f.

deputize, -ise ['depjutaɪz] vi: **to ~ for sb** assurer les fonctions de qqn, remplacer qqn.

deputy ['depjutɪ] 1 adj adjoint(e); **~ chairman** vice-président m; **~ head** SCH directeur m adjoint; **~ leader** POL vice-président m. 2 n [second-in-command] adjoint m, -e f. || Am [deputy sheriff] shérif m adjoint.

derail [dɪˈreɪl] vt [train] faire dérailler.

derby [Br 'dɑːbɪ, Am 'dɜːbɪ] n SPORT derby m. || Am [hat] chapeau m melon.

derelict ['derəlɪkt] adj en ruines.

deride [dɪˈraɪd] vt railler.

derivative [dɪˈrɪvətɪv] n dérivé m.

derive [dɪˈraɪv] 1 vt [draw, gain]: **to ~ sthg from sthg** tirer qqch de qqch. || [originate]: **to be ~d from** venir de. 2 vi: **to ~ from** venir de.

derogatory [dɪˈrɒgətrɪ] adj désobligeant(e).

descend [dɪˈsend] 1 vt fml [go down] descendre. 2 vi fml [go down] descendre.

|| [fall]: **to ~ (on)** [enemy] s'abattre (sur); [subj: silence, gloom] tomber (sur). || [stoop]: **to ~ to sthg/to doing sthg** s'abaisser à qqch/à faire qqch.

descendant [dɪˈsendənt] n descendant m, -e f.

descended [dɪˈsendɪd] adj: **to be ~ from sb** descendre de qqn.

descent [dɪˈsent] n [downwards movement] descente f. || (U) [origin] origine f.

describe [dɪˈskraɪb] vt décrire.

description [dɪˈskrɪpʃn] n [account] description f. || [type] sorte f, genre m.

desecrate ['desɪkreɪt] vt profaner.

desert [n 'dezət, vb & npl dɪˈzɜːt] 1 n désert m. 2 vt [place] déserter. || [person, group] déserter, abandonner. 3 vi MIL déserter. ○ **deserts** npl: **to get one's just ~s** recevoir ce que l'on mérite.

deserted [dɪˈzɜːtɪd] adj désert(e).

deserter [dɪˈzɜːtər] n déserteur m.

desert island ['dezət-] n île f déserte.

deserve [dɪˈzɜːv] vt mériter; **to ~ to do sthg** mériter de faire qqch.

design [dɪˈzaɪn] 1 n [plan, drawing] plan m, étude f. || (U) [art] design m. || [pattern] motif m, dessin m. || [shape] ligne f; [of dress] style m. || [intention] dessein m; **by ~** à dessein. 2 vt [draw plans for - building, car] faire les plans de, dessiner; [- dress] créer. || [plan] concevoir, mettre au point; **to be ~ed for sthg/to do sthg** être conçu pour qqch/pour faire qqch.

designate [adj 'dezɪgnət, vb 'dezɪgneɪt] 1 adj désigné(e). 2 vt désigner.

designer [dɪˈzaɪnər] 1 adj de marque. 2 n INDUSTRY concepteur m, -trice f, ARCHIT dessinateur m, -trice f; [of dresses etc] styliste mf; THEATRE décorateur m, -trice f.

desirable [dɪˈzaɪərəbl] adj [enviable, attractive] désirable. || fml [appropriate] désirable, souhaitable.

desire [dɪˈzaɪər] 1 n désir m; **~ for sthg/to do sthg** désir de qqch/de faire qqch. 2 vt désirer.

desist [dɪˈzɪst] vi fml: **to ~ (from doing sthg)** cesser (de faire qqch).

desk [desk] n bureau m; **reception ~** réception f; **information ~** bureau m de renseignements.

desktop publishing ['desk,tɒp-] n publication f assistée par ordinateur, PAO f.

desolate ['desələt] adj [place] abandonné(e). || [person] désespéré(e), désolé(e).

despair [dɪ'speər] **1** n (U) désespoir m. **2** vi désespérer; **to ~ of** désespérer de.

despatch [dɪ'spætʃ] = dispatch.

desperate ['despərət] adj désespéré(e); **to be ~ for sthg** avoir absolument besoin de qqch.

desperately ['despərətlɪ] adv désespérément; **~ ill** gravement malade.

desperation [,despə'reɪʃn] n désespoir m; **in ~** de désespoir.

despicable [dɪ'spɪkəbl] adj ignoble.

despise [dɪ'spaɪz] vt [person] mépriser; [racism] exécrer.

despite [dɪ'spaɪt] prep malgré.

despondent [dɪ'spɒndənt] adj découragé(e).

dessert [dɪ'zɜːt] n dessert m.

dessertspoon [dɪ'zɜːtspuːn] n [spoon] cuillère f à dessert.

destination [,destɪ'neɪʃn] n destination f.

destined ['destɪnd] adj [intended]: **~ for** destiné(e) à; **~ to do sthg** destiné à faire qqch. || [bound]: **~ for** à destination de.

destiny ['destɪnɪ] n destinée f.

destroy [dɪ'strɔɪ] vt [ruin] détruire.

destruction [dɪ'strʌkʃn] n destruction f.

detach [dɪ'tætʃ] vt [pull off] détacher; **to ~ sthg from sthg** détacher qqch de qqch. || [dissociate]: **to ~ o.s. from sthg** [from reality] se détacher de qqch; [from proceedings, discussions] s'écarter de qqch.

detached house n maison f individuelle.

detachment [dɪ'tætʃmənt] n détachement m.

detail ['diːteɪl] **1** n [small point] détail m; **in ~** en détail. **2** vt [list] détailler. ○ **details** npl [personal information] coordonnées fpl.

detailed ['diːteɪld] adj détaillé(e).

detain [dɪ'teɪn] vt [in police station] détenir. || [delay] retenir.

detect [dɪ'tekt] vt [subj: person] déceler. || [subj: machine] détecter.

detection [dɪ'tekʃn] n (U) [of crime] dépistage m. || [of aircraft, submarine] détection f.

detective [dɪ'tektɪv] n détective m.

detective novel n roman m policier.

detention [dɪ'tenʃn] n [of suspect, criminal] détention f. || SCH retenue f.

deter [dɪ'tɜːr] vt dissuader; **to ~ sb from doing sthg** dissuader qqn de faire qqch.

detergent [dɪ'tɜːdʒənt] n détergent m.

deteriorate [dɪ'tɪərɪəreɪt] vi se détériorer.

determination [dɪ,tɜːmɪ'neɪʃn] n détermination f.

determine [dɪ'tɜːmɪn] vt [establish, control] déterminer. || [fml [decide]: **to ~ to do sthg** décider de faire qqch.

determined [dɪ'tɜːmɪnd] adj [person] déterminé(e); **~ to do sthg** déterminé à faire qqch. || [effort] obstiné(e).

deterrent [dɪ'terənt] n moyen m de dissuasion.

detest [dɪ'test] vt détester.

detonate ['detəneɪt] vt faire détoner.

detour ['diː,tʊər] n détour m.

detract [dɪ'trækt] vi: **to ~ from** diminuer.

detriment ['detrɪmənt] n: **to the ~ of** au détriment de.

detrimental [,detrɪ'mentl] adj préjudiciable.

deuce [djuːs] n TENNIS égalité f.

devaluation [,diːvæljʊ'eɪʃn] n dévaluation f.

devastated ['devəsteɪtɪd] adj [area, city] dévasté(e). || fig [person] accablé(e).

devastating ['devəsteɪtɪŋ] adj [hurricane, remark] dévastateur(trice). || [upsetting] accablant(e).

develop [dɪ'veləp] **1** vt [gen] développer. || [land, area] aménager, développer. || [illness, fault, habit] contracter. || [resources] développer, exploiter. **2** vi [grow, advance] se développer. || [appear - problem, trouble] se déclarer.

developing country [dɪ'veləpɪŋ-] n pays m en voie de développement.

development [dɪ'veləpmənt] n [gen] développement m. || (U) [of land, area] exploitation f. || [land being developed] zone f d'aménagement; [developed area] zone aménagée. || (U) [of illness, fault] évolution f.

deviate ['diːvɪeɪt] vi: **to ~ (from)** dévier (de), s'écarter (de).

device [dɪ'vaɪs] n [apparatus] appareil m, dispositif m. || [plan, method] moyen m.

devil ['devl] n [evil spirit] diable m. || inf [person] type m; **poor ~!** pauvre diable! || [for emphasis]: **who/where/why the ~ ...?** qui/où/pourquoi diable ...? ○ **Devil** n [Satan]: **the Devil** le Diable.

devious ['diːvjəs] adj [dishonest - person] retors(e), à l'esprit tortueux; [- scheme, means] détourné(e). || [tortuous] tortueux(euse).

dike

devise [dɪ'vaɪz] *vt* concevoir.

devolution [ˌdiːvə'luːʃn] *n* POL décentralisation *f*.

devote [dɪ'vəʊt] *vt*: to ~ sthg to sthg consacrer qqch à qqch.

devoted [dɪ'vəʊtɪd] *adj* dévoué(e).

devotee [ˌdevə'tiː] *n* [fan] passionné *m*, -e *f*.

devotion [dɪ'vəʊʃn] *n* [commitment]: ~ (to) dévouement *m* (à).

devour [dɪ'vaʊər] *vt lit & fig* dévorer.

devout [dɪ'vaʊt] *adj* dévot(e).

dew [djuː] *n* rosée *f*.

diabetes [ˌdaɪə'biːtiːz] *n* diabète *m*.

diabetic [ˌdaɪə'betɪk] 1 *adj* [person] diabétique. 2 *n* diabétique *mf*.

diabolic(al) [ˌdaɪə'bɒlɪk(l)] *adj* [evil] diabolique. || *inf* [very bad] atroce.

diagnose ['daɪəgnəʊz] *vt* diagnostiquer.

diagnosis [ˌdaɪəg'nəʊsɪs] (*pl* -oses [-əʊsiːz]) *n* diagnostic *m*.

diagonal [daɪ'ægənl] 1 *adj* [line] diagonal(e). 2 *n* diagonale *f*.

diagram ['daɪəgræm] *n* diagramme *m*.

dial ['daɪəl] 1 *n* cadran *m*; [of radio] cadran de fréquences. 2 *vt* [number] composer.

dialect ['daɪəlekt] *n* dialecte *m*.

dialling tone *Br* ['daɪəlɪŋ-], **dial tone** *Am n* tonalité *f*.

dialogue *Br*, **dialog** *Am* ['daɪəlɒg] *n* dialogue *m*.

dial tone *Am* = dialling tone.

dialysis [daɪ'ælɪsɪs] *n* dialyse *f*.

diameter [daɪ'æmɪtər] *n* diamètre *m*.

diamond ['daɪəmənd] *n* [gem] diamant *m*. || [shape] losange *m*. ○ **diamonds** *npl* carreau *m*.

diaper ['daɪpər] *n Am* couche *f*.

diaphragm ['daɪəfræm] *n* diaphragme *m*.

diarrh(o)ea [ˌdaɪə'rɪə] *n* diarrhée *f*.

diary ['daɪərɪ] *n* [appointment book] agenda *m*. || [journal] journal *m*.

dice [daɪs] (*pl inv*) 1 *n* [for games] dé *m*. 2 *vt* couper en dés.

dictate [*vb* dɪk'teɪt, *n* 'dɪkteɪt] 1 *vt* dicter. 2 *n* ordre *m*.

dictation [dɪk'teɪʃn] *n* dictée *f*.

dictator [dɪk'teɪtər] *n* dictateur *m*.

dictatorship [dɪk'teɪtəʃɪp] *n* dictature *f*.

dictionary ['dɪkʃənrɪ] *n* dictionnaire *m*.

did [dɪd] *pt* → do.

didn't ['dɪdnt] = did not.

die [daɪ] (*pl* dice, *pt & pp* died, *cont* dying) 1 *vi* mourir; to be dying se mou-

rir; to be dying to do sthg mourir d'envie de faire qqch. 2 *n* [dice] dé *m*. ○ **die away** *vi* [sound] s'éteindre; [wind] tomber. ○ **die down** *vi* [sound] s'affaiblir; [wind] tomber; [fire] baisser. ○ **die out** *vi* s'éteindre, disparaître.

diehard ['daɪhɑːd] *n*: to be a ~ être coriace; [reactionary] être réactionnaire.

diesel ['diːzl] *n* diesel *m*.

diesel engine *n* AUT moteur *m* diesel; RAIL locomotive *f* diesel.

diesel fuel, diesel oil *n* diesel *m*.

diet ['daɪət] 1 *n* [eating pattern] alimentation *f*. || [to lose weight] régime *m*; to be on a ~ être au régime, faire un régime. 2 *comp* [low-calorie] de régime. 3 *vi* suivre un régime.

differ ['dɪfər] *vi* [be different] être différent(e), différer; [people] être différent; to ~ from être différent de. || [disagree]: to ~ with sb (about sthg) ne pas être d'accord avec qqn (à propos de qqch).

difference ['dɪfrəns] *n* différence *f*.

different ['dɪfrənt] *adj*: ~ (from) différent(e) (de).

differentiate [ˌdɪfə'renʃɪeɪt] *vi*: to ~ (between) faire la différence (entre).

difficult ['dɪfɪkəlt] *adj* difficile.

difficulty ['dɪfɪkltɪ] *n* difficulté *f*; to have ~ in doing sthg avoir de la difficulté OR du mal à faire qqch.

diffident ['dɪfɪdənt] *adj* [person] qui manque d'assurance; [manner, voice, approach] hésitant(e).

diffuse [dɪ'fjuːz] *vt* diffuser, répandre.

dig [dɪg] (*pt & pp* dug) 1 *vi* [in ground] creuser. || [subj: belt, strap]: to ~ into sb couper qqn. 2 *n fig* [unkind remark] pique *f*. || ARCHEOL fouilles *fpl*. 3 *vt* [hole] creuser. || [garden] bêcher. ○ **dig out** *vt sep inf* [find] dénicher. ○ **dig up** *vt sep* [from ground] déterrer; [potatoes] arracher. || *inf* [information] dénicher.

digest [*n* 'daɪdʒest, *vb* dɪ'dʒest] 1 *n* résumé *m*, digest *m*. 2 *vt lit & fig* digérer.

digestion [dɪ'dʒestʃn] *n* digestion *f*.

digit ['dɪdʒɪt] *n* [figure] chiffre *m*. || [finger] doigt *m*; [toe] orteil *m*.

digital ['dɪdʒɪtl] *adj* numérique, digital(e).

dignified ['dɪgnɪfaɪd] *adj* digne, plein(e) de dignité.

dignity ['dɪgnətɪ] *n* dignité *f*.

digress [daɪ'gres] *vi*: to ~ (from) s'écarter (de).

dike [daɪk] *n* [wall, bank] digue *f*. || *inf pej* [lesbian] gouine *f*.

dilapidated [dɪ'læpɪdeɪtɪd] *adj* déla-bré(e).

dilate [daɪ'leɪt] *vi* se dilater.

dilemma [dɪ'lemə] *n* dilemme *m*.

diligent ['dɪlɪdʒənt] *adj* appliqué(e).

dilute [daɪ'luːt] **1** *adj* dilué(e). **2** *vt*: to ~ sthg (with) diluer qqch (avec).

dim [dɪm] **1** *adj* [dark - light] faible; [- room] sombre. || [indistinct - memory, outline] vague. || [weak - eyesight] faible. || *inf* [stupid] borné(e). **2** *vt & vi* baisser.

dime [daɪm] *n Am* (pièce *f* de) dix cents *mpl*.

dimension [dɪ'menʃn] *n* dimension *f*.

diminish [dɪ'mɪnɪʃ] *vt & vi* diminuer.

diminutive [dɪ'mɪnjotɪv] *fml* **1** *adj* minuscule. **2** *n* GRAMM diminutif *m*.

dimmers ['dɪməz] *npl Am* [dipped headlights] phares *mpl* code (*inv*); [parking lights] feux *mpl* de position.

dimmer (switch) ['dɪmər-] *n* variateur *m* de lumière.

dimple ['dɪmpl] *n* fossette *f*.

din [dɪn] *n inf* barouf *m*.

dine [daɪn] *vi fml* dîner.

diner ['daɪnə'] *n* [person] dîneur *m*, -euse *f*. || *Am* [café] ≃ resto *m* routier.

dinghy ['dɪŋgɪ] *n* [for sailing] dériveur *m*; [for rowing] (petit) canot *m*.

dingy ['dɪndʒɪ] *adj* miteux(euse), crasseux(euse).

dining car ['daɪnɪŋ-] *n* wagon-restaurant *m*.

dining room ['daɪnɪŋ-] *n* [in house] salle *f* à manger. || [in hotel] restaurant *m*.

dinner ['dɪnə'] *n* dîner *m*.

dinner jacket *n* smoking *m*.

dinner party *n* dîner *m*.

dinnertime ['dɪnətaɪm] *n* heure *f* du dîner.

dinosaur ['daɪnəsɔːr] *n* dinosaure *m*.

dint [dɪnt] *n fml*: by ~ of à force de.

dip [dɪp] **1** *n* [in road, ground] déclivité *f*. || [sauce] sauce *f*, dip *m*. || [swim] baignade *f* (rapide); to go for a ~ aller se baigner en vitesse, aller faire trempette. **2** *vt* [into liquid]: to ~ sthg in OR into tremper OR plonger qqch dans. **3** *vi* [sun] baisser, descendre à l'horizon; [wing] plonger. || [road, ground] descendre.

diploma [dɪ'pləʊmə] (*pl* -s) *n* diplôme *m*.

diplomacy [dɪ'pləʊməsɪ] *n* diplomatie *f*.

diplomat ['dɪpləmæt] *n* diplomate *m*.

diplomatic [,dɪplə'mætɪk] *adj* [service, corps] diplomatique. || [tactful] diplomate.

dipstick ['dɪpstɪk] *n* AUT jauge *f* (*de niveau d'huile*).

dire ['daɪə'] *adj* [need, consequences] extrême; [warning] funeste.

direct [dɪ'rekt] **1** *adj* direct(e); [challenge] manifeste. **2** *vt* [gen] diriger. || [aim]: to ~ sthg at sb [question, remark] adresser qqch à qqn; the campaign is ~ed at teenagers cette campagne vise les adolescents. || [order]: to ~ sb to do sthg ordonner à qqn de faire qqch. **3** *adv* directement.

direct current *n* courant *m* continu.

direction [dɪ'rekʃn] *n* direction *f*. ○ **directions** *npl* [to find a place] indications *fpl*. || [for use] instructions *fpl*.

directly [dɪ'rektlɪ] *adv* [in straight line] directement. || [honestly, clearly] sans détours. || [exactly - behind, above] exactement. || [immediately] immédiatement. || [very soon] tout de suite.

director [dɪ'rektə'] *n* [of company] directeur *m*, -trice *f*. || THEATRE metteur *m* en scène; CINEMA & TV réalisateur *m*, -trice *f*.

directory [dɪ'rektərɪ] *n* [annual publication] annuaire *m*. || COMPUT répertoire *m*.

dire straits *npl*: in ~ dans une situation désespérée.

dirt [dɜːt] *n* (U) [mud, dust] saleté *f*. || [earth] terre *f*.

dirt cheap *inf* **1** *adj* très bon marché, donné(e). **2** *adv* pour trois fois rien.

dirty ['dɜːtɪ] **1** *adj* [not clean, not fair] sale. || [smutty - language, person] grossier(ière); [- book, joke] cochon(onne). **2** *vt* salir.

disability [,dɪsə'bɪlətɪ] *n* infirmité *f*.

disabled [dɪs'eɪbld] **1** *adj* [person] handicapé(e), infirme. **2** *npl*: the ~ les handicapés, les infirmes.

disadvantage [,dɪsəd'vɑːntɪdʒ] *n* désavantage *m*, inconvénient *m*.

disagree [,dɪsə'griː] *vi* [have different opinions]: to ~ (with) ne pas être d'accord (avec). || [differ] ne pas concorder. || [subj: food, drink]: to ~ with sb ne pas réussir à qqn.

disagreeable [,dɪsə'griːəbl] *adj* désagréable.

disagreement [,dɪsə'griːmənt] *n* [in opinion] désaccord *m*. || [argument] différend *m*.

disappear [,dɪsə'pɪə'] *vi* disparaître.

disappearance [,dɪsə'pɪərəns] *n* disparition *f*.

disappoint [,dɪsə'pɔɪnt] *vt* décevoir.

disappointed [,dɪsə'pɔɪntɪd] *adj*: ~ (in OR with) déçu(e) (par).

disappointing [,dɪsə'pɔɪntɪŋ] *adj* décevant(e).

disappointment [,dɪsə'pɔɪntmənt] *n* déception *f*.

disapproval [,dɪsə'pru:vl] *n* désapprobation *f*.

disapprove [,dɪsə'pru:v] *vi*: **to ~ of sb/ sthg** désapprouver qqn/qqch; **do you ~?** est-ce que tu as quelque chose contre?

disarm [dɪs'ɑ:m] *vt & vi lit & fig* désarmer.

disarmament [dɪs'ɑ:məmənt] *n* désarmement *m*.

disarray [,dɪsə'reɪ] *n*: **in ~** en désordre; [government] en pleine confusion.

disaster [dɪ'zɑ:stər] *n* [damaging event] catastrophe *f*. || (*U*) [misfortune] échec *m*, désastre *m*. || *inf* [failure] désastre *m*.

disastrous [dɪ'zɑ:strəs] *adj* désastreux(euse).

disband [dɪs'bænd] 1 *vt* dissoudre. 2 *vi* se dissoudre.

disbelief [,dɪsbɪ'li:f] *n*: **in** OR **with ~** avec incrédulité.

disc *Br*, **disk** *Am* [dɪsk] *n* disque *m*.

discard [dɪs'kɑ:d] *vt* mettre au rebut.

discern [dɪ'sɜ:n] *vt* discerner, distinguer.

discerning [dɪ'sɜ:nɪŋ] *adj* judicieux(ieuse).

discharge [*n* 'dɪstʃɑ:dʒ, *vt* dɪs'tʃɑ:dʒ] 1 *n* [of patient] autorisation *f* de sortie, décharge *f*; JUR relaxe *f*; **to get one's ~** MIL être rendu à la vie civile. || [emission - of smoke] émission *f*; [- of sewage] déversement *m*; MED écoulement *m*. 2 *vt* [allow to leave - patient] signer la décharge de; [- prisoner, defendant] relaxer; [- soldier] rendre à la vie civile. || [emit - smoke] émettre; [- sewage, chemicals] déverser.

disciple [dɪ'saɪpl] *n* disciple *m*.

discipline ['dɪsɪplɪn] 1 *n* discipline *f*. 2 *vt* [control] discipliner. || [punish] punir.

disc jockey *n* disc-jockey *m*.

disclaim [dɪs'kleɪm] *vt fml* nier.

disclose [dɪs'kləʊz] *vt* révéler, divulguer.

disclosure [dɪs'kləʊʒər] *n* révélation *f*, divulgation *f*.

disco ['dɪskəʊ] (*pl* **-s**) (*abbr of* **discotheque**) *n* discothèque *f*.

discomfort [dɪs'kʌmfət] *n* (*U*) [physical pain] douleur *f*. || (*U*) [anxiety, embarrassment] malaise *m*.

disconcert [,dɪskən'sɜ:t] *vt* déconcerter.

disconnect [,dɪskə'nekt] *vt* [detach] détacher. || [from gas, electricity - appliance] débrancher; [- house] couper. || TELEC couper.

discontent [,dɪskən'tent] *n*: **~ (with)** mécontentement *m* (à propos de).

discontented [,dɪskən'tentɪd] *adj* mécontent(e).

discontinue [,dɪskən'tɪnju:] *vt* cesser, interrompre.

discord ['dɪskɔ:d] *n* (*U*) [disagreement] discorde *f*, désaccord *m*. || MUS dissonance *f*.

discotheque ['dɪskəʊtek] *n* discothèque *f*.

discount [*n* 'dɪskaʊnt, *vb Br* dɪs'kaʊnt, *Am* 'dɪskaʊnt] 1 *n* remise *f*. 2 *vt* [report, claim] ne pas tenir compte de.

discourage [dɪs'kʌrɪdʒ] *vt* décourager; **to ~ sb from doing sthg** dissuader qqn de faire qqch.

discover [dɪ'skʌvər] *vt* découvrir.

discovery [dɪ'skʌvərɪ] *n* découverte *f*.

discredit [dɪs'kredɪt] 1 *n* discrédit *m*. 2 *vt* discréditer.

discreet [dɪ'skri:t] *adj* discret(ète).

discrepancy [dɪ'skrepənsɪ] *n*: **~ (in/ between)** divergence *f* (entre).

discretion [dɪ'skreʃn] *n* (*U*) [tact] discrétion *f*. || [judgment] jugement *m*, discernement *m*; **at the ~ of** avec l'autorisation de.

discriminate [dɪ'skrɪmɪneɪt] *vi* [distinguish] différencier, distinguer; **to ~ between** faire la distinction entre. || [be prejudiced]: **to ~ against sb** faire de la discrimination envers qqn.

discrimination [dɪ,skrɪmɪ'neɪʃn] *n* [prejudice] discrimination *f*. || [judgment] discernement *m*, jugement *m*.

discus ['dɪskəs] (*pl* **-es**) *n* disque *m*.

discuss [dɪ'skʌs] *vt* discuter (de); **to ~ sthg with sb** discuter de qqch avec qqn.

discussion [dɪ'skʌʃn] *n* discussion *f*; **under ~** en discussion.

disdain [dɪs'deɪn] *n*: **~ (for)** dédain *m* (pour).

disease [dɪ'zi:z] *n* [illness] maladie *f*.

disembark [,dɪsɪm'bɑ:k] *vi* débarquer.

disenchanted [,dɪsɪn'tʃɑ:ntɪd] *adj*: **~ (with)** désenchanté(e) (de).

disengage [,dɪsɪn'geɪdʒ] *vt* [release]: **to ~ sthg (from)** libérer OR dégager qqch (de). || TECH déclencher; **to ~ the gears** débrayer.

disfavour *Br*, **disfavor** *Am* [dɪs'feɪvəʳ] *n* [dislike, disapproval] désapprobation *f*.

disfigure [dɪs'fɪgəʳ] *vt* défigurer.

disgrace [dɪs'greɪs] **1** *n* [shame] honte *f*; **in ~** en défaveur. || [cause of shame - thing] honte *f*, scandale *m*; [- person] honte *f*. **2** *vt* faire honte à; **to ~ o.s.** se couvrir de honte.

disgraceful [dɪs'greɪsfʊl] *adj* honteux(euse), scandaleux(euse).

disgruntled [dɪs'grʌntld] *adj* mécontent(e).

disguise [dɪs'gaɪz] **1** *n* déguisement *m*; **in ~** déguisé(e). **2** *vt* [person, voice] déguiser. || [hide - fact, feelings] dissimuler.

disgust [dɪs'gʌst] **1** *n*: **~ (at)** [behaviour, violence etc] dégoût *m* (pour); [decision] dégoût (devant). **2** *vt* dégoûter, écœurer.

disgusting [dɪs'gʌstɪŋ] *adj* dégoûtant(e).

dish [dɪʃ] *n* plat *m*; *Am* [plate] assiette *f*. ○ **dishes** *npl* vaisselle *f*; **to do** OR **wash the ~es** faire la vaisselle.

dish aerial *Br*, **dish antenna** *Am n* antenne *f* parabolique.

dishcloth ['dɪʃklɒθ] *n* lavette *f*.

disheartened [dɪs'hɑːtnd] *adj* découragé(e).

dishevelled *Br*, **disheveled** *Am* [dɪ'ʃevəld] *adj* [person] échevelé(e); [hair] en désordre.

dishonest [dɪs'ɒnɪst] *adj* malhonnête.

dishonor *etc Am* = **dishonour** *etc*.

dishonour *Br*, **dishonor** *Am* [dɪs'ɒnəʳ] **1** *n* déshonneur *m*. **2** *vt* déshonorer.

dishonourable *Br*, **dishonorable** *Am* [dɪs'ɒnərəbl] *adj* [person] peu honorable; [behaviour] déshonorant(e).

dish soap *n Am* liquide *m* pour la vaisselle.

dish towel *n Am* torchon *m*.

dishwasher ['dɪʃˌwɒʃəʳ] *n* [machine] lave-vaisselle *m inv*.

disillusioned [ˌdɪsɪ'luːʒnd] *adj* désillusionné(e), désenchanté(e); **to be ~ with** ne plus avoir d'illusions sur.

disinclined [ˌdɪsɪn'klaɪnd] *adj*: **to be ~ to do sthg** être peu disposé(e) à faire qqch.

disinfect [ˌdɪsɪn'fekt] *vt* désinfecter.

disinfectant [ˌdɪsɪn'fektənt] *n* désinfectant *m*.

disintegrate [dɪs'ɪntɪgreɪt] *vi* [object] se désintégrer, se désagréger.

disinterested [ˌdɪs'ɪntrəstɪd] *adj* [objective] désintéressé(e). || *inf* [uninterested]: **~ (in)** indifférent(e) (à).

disjointed [dɪs'dʒɔɪntɪd] *adj* décousu(e).

disk [dɪsk] *n* COMPUT disque *m*, disquette *f*. || *Am* = **disc**.

disk drive *Br*, **diskette drive** *Am n* COMPUT lecteur *m* de disques OR de disquettes.

diskette [dɪsk'et] *n* COMPUT disquette *f*.

diskette drive *n Am* = **disk drive**.

dislike [dɪs'laɪk] **1** *n*: **~ (of)** aversion *f* (pour); **to take a ~ to sb/sthg** prendre qqn/qqch en grippe. **2** *vt* ne pas aimer.

dislocate ['dɪsləkeɪt] *vt* MED se démettre. || [disrupt] désorganiser.

dislodge [dɪs'lɒdʒ] *vt*: **to ~ sthg (from)** déplacer qqch (de); [free] décoincer qqch (de).

disloyal [ˌdɪs'lɔɪəl] *adj*: **~ (to)** déloyal(e) (envers).

dismal ['dɪzml] *adj* [gloomy, depressing] lugubre. || [unsuccessful - attempt] infructueux(euse); [- failure] lamentable.

dismantle [dɪs'mæntl] *vt* démanteler.

dismay [dɪs'meɪ] **1** *n* consternation *f*. **2** *vt* consterner.

dismiss [dɪs'mɪs] *vt* [from job]: **to ~ sb (from)** congédier qqn (de). || [refuse to take seriously - idea, person] écarter; [- plan, challenge] rejeter. || [allow to leave - class] laisser sortir; [- troops] faire rompre les rangs à.

dismissal [dɪs'mɪsl] *n* [from job] licenciement *m*, renvoi *m*.

dismount [ˌdɪs'maʊnt] *vi*: **to ~ (from)** descendre (de).

disobedience [ˌdɪsə'biːdjəns] *n* désobéissance *f*.

disobedient [ˌdɪsə'biːdjənt] *adj* désobéissant(e).

disobey [ˌdɪsə'beɪ] *vt* désobéir à.

disorder [dɪs'ɔːdəʳ] *n* [disarray]: **in ~** en désordre. || (U) [rioting] troubles *mpl*. || MED trouble *m*.

disorganized, -ised [dɪs'ɔːgənaɪzd] *adj* [person] désordonné(e), brouillon(onne); [system] mal conçu(e).

disorientated *Br* [dɪs'ɔːrɪənteɪtɪd], **disoriented** *Am* [dɪs'ɔːrɪəntɪd] *adj* désorienté(e).

disown [dɪs'əʊn] *vt* désavouer.

disparaging [dɪ'spærɪdʒɪŋ] *adj* désobligeant(e).

dispatch [dɪ'spætʃ] **1** *n* [message] dépêche *f*. **2** *vt* [send] envoyer, expédier.

dispel [dɪ'spel] *vt* [feeling] dissiper, chasser.

dispensary [dɪ'spensərɪ] *n* officine *f.*

dispense [dɪ'spens] *vt* [justice, medicine] administrer. ○ **dispense with** *vt fus* [do without] se passer de. || [make unnecessary] rendre superflu(e).

dispensing chemist *Br*, **dispensing pharmacist** *Am* [dɪ'spensɪŋ-] *n* pharmacien *m*, -ienne *f.*

disperse [dɪ'spɜːs] **1** *vt* [crowd] disperser. || [knowledge, news] répandre, propager. **2** *vi* se disperser.

dispirited [dɪ'spɪrɪtɪd] *adj* découragé(e), abattu(e).

displace [dɪs'pleɪs] *vt* [cause to move] déplacer. || [supplant] supplanter.

display [dɪ'spleɪ] **1** *n* [arrangement] exposition *f.* || [demonstration] manifestation *f.* || [public event] spectacle *m.* || [COMPUT - device] écran *m*; [- information displayed] affichage *m*, visualisation *f.* **2** *vt* [arrange] exposer. || [show] faire preuve de, montrer.

displease [dɪs'pliːz] *vt* déplaire à, mécontenter; **to be ~d with** être mécontent(e) de.

displeasure [dɪs'pleʒəʳ] *n* mécontentement *m.*

disposable [dɪ'spəʊzəbl] *adj* [throw away] jetable. || [income] disponible.

disposal [dɪ'spəʊzl] *n* [removal] enlèvement *m.* || [availability]: **at sb's ~** à la disposition de qqn.

dispose [dɪ'spəʊz] ○ **dispose of** *vt fus* [get rid of] se débarrasser de; [problem] résoudre.

disposed [dɪ'spəʊzd] *adj* [willing]: **to be ~ to do sthg** être disposé(e) à faire qqch. || [friendly]: **to be well ~ to** OR **towards sb** être bien disposé(e) envers qqn.

disposition [,dɪspə'zɪʃn] *n* [temperament] caractère *m*, tempérament *m.* || [tendency]: **~ to do sthg** tendance *f* à faire qqch.

disprove [,dɪs'pruːv] *vt* réfuter.

dispute [dɪ'spjuːt] **1** *n* [quarrel] dispute *f.* || (*U*) [disagreement] désaccord *m.* || INDUSTRY conflit *m.* **2** *vt* contester.

disqualify [,dɪs'kwɒlɪfaɪ] *vt* [subj: authority]: **to ~ sb (from doing sthg)** interdire à qqn (de faire qqch). || SPORT disqualifier.

disquiet [dɪs'kwaɪət] *n* inquiétude *f.*

disregard [,dɪsrɪ'gɑːd] **1** *n* (*U*): **~ (for)** [money, danger] mépris *m* (pour); [feelings] indifférence *f* (à). **2** *vt* [fact] igno-

rer; [danger] mépriser; [warning] ne pas tenir compte de.

disrepair [,dɪsrɪ'peəʳ] *n* délabrement *m*; **to fall into ~** tomber en ruines.

disreputable [dɪs'repjʊtəbl] *adj* peu respectable.

disrepute [,dɪsrɪ'pjuːt] *n*: **to bring sthg into ~** discréditer qqch; **to fall into ~** acquérir une mauvaise réputation.

disrupt [dɪs'rʌpt] *vt* perturber.

dissatisfaction ['dɪs,sætɪs'fækʃn] *n* mécontentement *m.*

dissatisfied [,dɪs'sætɪsfaɪd] *adj*: **~ (with)** mécontent(e) (de), pas satisfait(e) (de).

dissect [dɪ'sekt] *vt lit & fig* disséquer.

dissent [dɪ'sent] *n* dissentiment *m.*

dissertation [,dɪsə'teɪʃn] *n* dissertation *f.*

disservice [,dɪs'sɜːvɪs] *n*: **to do sb a ~** rendre un mauvais service à qqn.

dissimilar [,dɪ'sɪmɪləʳ] *adj*: **~ (to)** différent(e) (de).

dissociate [dɪ'səʊʃɪeɪt] *vt* dissocier; **to ~ o.s. from** se désolidariser de.

dissolve [dɪ'zɒlv] **1** *vt* dissoudre. **2** *vi* [substance] se dissoudre.

dissuade [dɪ'sweɪd] *vt*: **to ~ sb (from)** dissuader qqn (de).

distance ['dɪstəns] *n* distance *f*; **at a ~** assez loin; **from a ~** de loin; **in the ~** au loin.

distant ['dɪstənt] *adj* [gen]: **~ (from)** éloigné(e) (de). || [reserved - person, manner] distant(e).

distaste [dɪs'teɪst] *n*: **~ (for)** dégoût *m* (pour).

distasteful [dɪs'teɪstfʊl] *adj* répugnant(e), déplaisant(e).

distil *Br*, **distill** *Am* [dɪ'stɪl] *vt* [liquid] distiller. || *fig* [information] tirer.

distillery [dɪ'stɪlərɪ] *n* distillerie *f.*

distinct [dɪ'stɪŋkt] *adj* [different]: **~ (from)** distinct(e) (de), différent(e) (de); **as ~ from** par opposition à. || [definite - improvement] net (nette).

distinction [dɪ'stɪŋkʃn] *n* [difference] distinction *f*, différence *f*; **to draw** OR **make a ~ between** faire une distinction entre. || (*U*) [excellence] distinction *f.* || [exam result] mention *f* très bien.

distinctive [dɪ'stɪŋktɪv] *adj* caractéristique.

distinguish [dɪ'stɪŋgwɪʃ] *vt* [tell apart]: **to ~ sthg from sthg** distinguer qqch de qqch, faire la différence entre qqch et qqch. || [perceive] distinguer. || [characterize] caractériser.

distinguished [dɪ'stɪŋgwɪʃt] *adj* distingué(e).

distinguishing [dɪ'stɪŋgwɪʃɪŋ] *adj* [feature, mark] caractéristique.

distort [dɪ'stɔːt] *vt* déformer.

distract [dɪ'strækt] *vt*: **to ~ sb (from)** distraire qqn (de).

distracted [dɪ'stræktɪd] *adj* [preoccupied] soucieux(ieuse).

distraction [dɪ'strækʃn] *n* [interruption, diversion] distraction *f*.

distraught [dɪ'strɔːt] *adj* éperdu(e).

distress [dɪ'stres] **1** *n* [anxiety] détresse *f*. **2** *vt* affliger.

distressing [dɪ'stresɪŋ] *adj* [news, image] pénible.

distribute [dɪ'strɪbjuːt] *vt* [gen] distribuer. || [spread out] répartir.

distribution [ˌdɪstrɪ'bjuːʃn] *n* [gen] distribution *f*. || [spreading out] répartition *f*.

distributor [dɪ'strɪbjutər] *n* AUT & COMM distributeur *m*.

district ['dɪstrɪkt] *n* [area - of country] région *f*; [- of town] quartier *m*. || ADMIN district *m*.

district attorney *n Am* ≃ procureur *m* de la République.

distrust [dɪs'trʌst] **1** *n* méfiance *f*. **2** *vt* se méfier de.

disturb [dɪ'stɜːb] *vt* [interrupt] déranger. || [upset, worry] inquiéter. || [sleep, surface] troubler.

disturbance [dɪ'stɜːbəns] *n* POL troubles *mpl*; [fight] tapage *m*. || [interruption] dérangement *m*. || [of mind, emotions] trouble *m*.

disturbed [dɪ'stɜːbd] *adj* [emotionally, mentally] perturbé(e). || [worried] inquiet(iète).

disturbing [dɪ'stɜːbɪŋ] *adj* [image] bouleversant(e); [news] inquiétant(e).

disuse [ˌdɪs'juːs] *n*: **to fall into ~** [factory] être à l'abandon; [regulation] tomber en désuétude.

disused [ˌdɪs'juːzd] *adj* désaffecté(e).

ditch [dɪtʃ] *n* fossé *m*.

dither ['dɪðər] *vi* hésiter.

ditto ['dɪtəʊ] *adv* idem.

dive [daɪv] (*Br pt & pp* **-d**, *Am pt & pp* **-d** OR **dove**) **1** *vi* plonger; [bird, plane] piquer. **2** *n* [gen] plongeon *m*. || [of plane] piqué *m*.

diver ['daɪvər] *n* plongeur *m*, -euse *f*.

diverge [daɪ'vɜːdʒ] *vi*: **to ~ (from)** diverger (de).

diversify [daɪ'vɜːsɪfaɪ] **1** *vt* diversifier. **2** *vi* se diversifier.

diversion [daɪ'vɜːʃn] *n* [amusement] distraction *f*; [tactical] diversion *f*. || [of traffic] déviation *f*. || [of river, funds] détournement *m*.

diversity [daɪ'vɜːsəti] *n* diversité *f*.

divert [daɪ'vɜːt] *vt* [traffic] dévier. || [river, funds] détourner. || [person - amuse] distraire; [- tactically] détourner.

divide [dɪ'vaɪd] **1** *vt* [separate] séparer. || [share out] diviser, partager. || [split up]: **to ~ sthg (into)** diviser qqch (en). || MATH: **89 ~d by 3** 89 divisé par 3. || [people - in disagreement] diviser. **2** *vi* se diviser.

dividend ['dɪvɪdend] *n* dividende *m*.

divine [dɪ'vaɪn] *adj* divin(e).

diving ['daɪvɪŋ] *n* (*U*) plongeon *m*; [with breathing apparatus] plongée *f* (sous-marine).

divingboard ['daɪvɪŋbɔːd] *n* plongeoir *m*.

divinity [dɪ'vɪnəti] *n* [godliness, god] divinité *f*. || [study] théologie *f*.

division [dɪ'vɪʒn] *n* [gen] division *f*. || [separation] séparation *f*.

divorce [dɪ'vɔːs] **1** *n* divorce *m*. **2** *vt* [husband, wife] divorcer.

divorced [dɪ'vɔːst] *adj* divorcé(e).

divorcee [dɪvɔː'siː] *n* divorcé *m*, -e *f*.

divulge [daɪ'vʌldʒ] *vt* divulguer.

dizzy ['dɪzɪ] *adj* [giddy]: **to feel ~** avoir la tête qui tourne.

DJ *n* (*abbr of* disc jockey) disc-jockey *m*.

DNA (*abbr of* deoxyribonucleic acid) *n* ADN *m*.

do [duː] (*pt* **did**, *pp* **done**, *pl* **dos** OR **do's**) **1** *aux vb* (*in negatives*): **don't leave it there** ne le laisse pas là. || (*in questions*): **what did he want?** qu'est-ce qu'il voulait? || **~ you think she'll come?** tu crois qu'elle viendra? || (*referring back to previous verb*): **she reads more than I ~** elle lit plus que moi; **I like reading — so ~ I** j'aime lire — moi aussi. || (*in question tags*): **so you think you can dance, ~ you?** alors tu t'imagines que tu sais danser, c'est ça? || [for emphasis]: **I did tell you but you've forgotten** je te l'avais bien dit, mais tu l'as oublié; **~ come in** entrez donc. **2** *vt* [perform an activity, a service] faire; **to ~ aerobics/gymnastics** faire de l'aérobic/de la gymnastique; **to ~ one's hair** se coiffer. ||

[take action] faire; **to ~ something about sthg** trouver une solution pour qqch. || [referring to job]: **what do you ~?** qu'est-ce que vous faites dans la vie? || [study] faire; **I did physics at school** j'ai fait de la physique à l'école. || [travel at a particular speed] faire, rouler; **the car can ~ 110 mph** ≃ la voiture peut faire du 180 à l'heure. **3** vi [act] faire; **~ as I tell you** fais comme je te dis. || [perform in a particular way]: **they're ~ing really well** leurs affaires marchent bien; **he could ~ better** il pourrait mieux faire. || [be good enough, be sufficient] suffire, aller; **that will ~** ça suffit. **4** n [party] fête f, soirée f. ○ **dos** npl: **~s and don'ts** ce qu'il faut faire et ne pas faire. ○ **do away with** vt fus supprimer. ○ **do out of** vt sep inf: **to ~ sb out of sthg** escroquer OR carotter qqch à qqn. ○ **do up** vt sep [fasten - shoelaces, shoes] attacher; [- buttons, coat] boutonner. || [decorate - room, house] refaire. || [wrap up] emballer. ○ **do with** vt fus [need] avoir besoin de. || [have connection with]: **that has nothing to ~ with it** ça n'a rien à voir, ça n'a aucun rapport. ○ **do without 1** vt fus se passer de. **2** vi s'en passer.

docile [Br 'dəʊsaɪl, Am 'dɒsəl] adj docile.

dock [dɒk] **1** n [in harbour] docks mpl. || JUR banc m des accusés. **2** vi [ship] arriver à quai.

docker ['dɒkər] n docker m.

dockworker ['dɒkwɜːkər] = **docker**.

dockyard ['dɒkjɑːd] n chantier m naval.

doctor ['dɒktər] **1** n MED docteur m, médecin m; **to go to the ~'s** aller chez le docteur. || UNIV docteur m. **2** vt [results, report] falsifier; [text, food] altérer.

doctorate ['dɒktərət], **doctor's degree** n doctorat m.

doctrine ['dɒktrɪn] n doctrine f.

document ['dɒkjʊmənt] n document m.

documentary [,dɒkjʊ'mentərɪ] **1** adj documentaire. **2** n documentaire m.

dodge [dɒdʒ] vt éviter, esquiver.

doe [dəʊ] n [deer] biche f.

does [weak form dəz, strong form dʌz] → **do**.

doesn't ['dʌznt] = **does not**.

dog [dɒg] **1** n [animal] chien m, chienne f. **2** vt [subj: person - follow] suivre de près. || [subj: problems, bad luck] poursuivre.

dog collar n [of dog] collier m de chien. || [of priest] col m d'ecclésiastique.

dog-eared [-ɪəd] adj écorné(e).

dog food n nourriture f pour chiens.

dogged ['dɒgɪd] adj opiniâtre.

doing ['duːɪŋ] n: **is this your ~?** c'est toi qui es cause de tout cela?

do-it-yourself n (U) bricolage m.

doldrums ['dɒldrəmz] npl: **to be in the ~** fig être dans le marasme.

dole [dəʊl] ○ **dole out** vt sep [food, money] distribuer au compte-gouttes.

doll [dɒl] n poupée f.

dollar ['dɒlər] n dollar m.

dollop ['dɒləp] n inf bonne cuillerée f.

dolphin ['dɒlfɪn] n dauphin m.

domain [də'meɪn] n lit & fig domaine m.

dome [dəʊm] n dôme m.

domestic [də'mestɪk] **1** adj [policy, politics, flight] intérieur(e). || [chores, animal] domestique. **2** n domestique mf.

domestic appliance n appareil m ménager.

dominant ['dɒmɪnənt] adj dominant(e); [personality, group] dominateur(trice).

dominate ['dɒmɪneɪt] vt dominer.

domineering [,dɒmɪ'nɪərɪŋ] adj autoritaire.

dominion [də'mɪnjən] n (U) [power] domination f. || [land] territoire m.

domino ['dɒmɪnəʊ] (pl -es) n domino m. ○ **dominoes** npl dominos mpl.

donate [də'neɪt] vt faire don de.

done [dʌn] **1** pp → **do**. **2** adj [job, work] achevé(e). || [cooked] cuit(e). **3** excl [to conclude deal] tope!

donkey ['dɒŋkɪ] (pl donkeys) n âne m, ânesse f.

donor ['dəʊnər] n MED donneur m, -euse f. || [to charity] donateur m, -trice f.

donor card n carte f de donneur.

don't [dəʊnt] = **do not**.

doodle ['duːdl] **1** n griffonnage m. **2** vi griffonner.

doom [duːm] n [fate] destin m.

doomed [duːmd] adj condamné(e); **the plan was ~ to failure** le plan était voué à l'échec.

door [dɔːr] n porte f; [of vehicle] portière f.

doorbell ['dɔːbel] n sonnette f.

doorknob ['dɔːnɒb] n bouton m de porte.

doorman ['dɔːmən] (pl -men [-mən]) n portier m.

doormat ['dɔːmæt] *n lit & fig* paillasson *m*.

doorstep ['dɔːstep] *n* pas *m* de la porte.

doorway ['dɔːweɪ] *n* embrasure *f* de la porte.

dope [dəʊp] **1** *n inf drugs sl* dope *f*. || [for athlete, horse] dopant *m*. || *inf* [fool] imbécile *mf*. **2** *vt* [horse] doper.

dormant ['dɔːmənt] *adj* [volcano] endormi(e). || [law] inappliqué(e).

dormitory ['dɔːmətrɪ] *n* [gen] dortoir *m*. || *Am* [in university] ≃ cité *f* universitaire.

DOS [dɒs] (*abbr of* **disk operating system**) *n* DOS *m*.

dose [dəʊs] *n* MED dose *f*. || *fig* [amount]: **a ~ of the measles** la rougeole.

dot [dɒt] **1** *n* point *m*; **on the ~** à l'heure pile. **2** *vt*: **dotted with** parsemé(e) de.

dote [dəʊt] ○ **dote (up)on** *vt fus* adorer.

dot-matrix printer *n* imprimante *f* matricielle.

dotted line ['dɒtɪd-] *n* ligne *f* pointillée.

double ['dʌbl] **1** *adj* double. **2** *adv* [twice]: **~ the amount** deux fois plus; **to see ~** voir double. || [in two] en deux; **to bend ~** se plier en deux. **3** *n* [twice as much]: **I earn ~ what I used to** je gagne le double de ce que je gagnais auparavant. || [drink, look-alike] double *m*. || CINEMA doublure *f*. **4** *vt* doubler. **5** *vi* [increase twofold] doubler. ○ **doubles** *npl* TENNIS double *m*.

double-barrelled *Br*, **double-barreled** *Am* [-'bærəld] *adj* [shotgun] à deux coups. || [name] à rallonge.

double bass [-beɪs] *n* contrebasse *f*.

double bed *n* lit *m* pour deux personnes, grand lit.

double-breasted [-'brestɪd] *adj* [jacket] croisé(e).

double-check *vt & vi* revérifier.

double chin *n* double menton *m*.

double-cross *vt* trahir.

double-decker [-'dekər] *n* [bus] autobus *m* à impériale.

double-glazing [-'gleɪzɪŋ] *n* double vitrage *m*.

double room *n* chambre *f* pour deux personnes.

double vision *n* vue *f* double.

doubly ['dʌblɪ] *adv* doublement.

doubt [daʊt] **1** *n* doute *m*; **there is no ~ that** il n'y a aucun doute que; **without (a) ~** sans aucun doute; **to be in ~** [outcome] être incertain(e); **no ~** sans aucun doute.
2 *vt* douter; **to ~ whether** OR **if** douter que.

doubtful ['daʊtfʊl] *adj* [decision, future] incertain(e). || [person, value] douteux(euse).

doubtless ['daʊtlɪs] *adv* sans aucun doute.

dough [dəʊ] *n* (*U*) CULIN pâte *f*.

doughnut ['dəʊnʌt] *n* beignet *m*.

douse [daʊs] *vt* [fire, flames] éteindre. || [drench] tremper.

dove¹ [dʌv] *n* [bird] colombe *f*.

dove² [dəʊv] *Am pt* → **dive**.

Dover ['dəʊvər] *n* Douvres.

dovetail ['dʌvteɪl] *fig vi* coïncider.

dowdy ['daʊdɪ] *adj* peu chic.

down [daʊn] **1** *adv* [downwards] en bas, vers le bas; **to bend ~** se pencher; **to climb ~** descendre; **to fall ~** tomber (par terre). || [along]: **we went ~ to have a look** on est allé jeter un coup d'œil; **I'm going ~ to the shop** je vais au magasin. || [southwards]: **we travelled ~ to London** on est descendu à Londres. || [lower in amount]: **prices are coming ~** les prix baissent; **~ to the last detail** jusqu'au moindre détail. **2** *prep* [downwards]: **they ran ~ the hill/stairs** ils ont descendu la colline/l'escalier en courant. || [along]: **to walk ~ the street** descendre la rue. **3** *adj inf* [depressed]: **to feel ~** avoir le cafard. || [computer, telephones] en panne. **4** *n* (*U*) duvet *m*.

down-and-out 1 *adj* indigent(e). **2** *n* personne dans le besoin.

down-at-heel *adj* déguenillé(e).

downbeat ['daʊnbiːt] *adj inf* pessimiste.

downcast ['daʊnkɑːst] *adj* [sad] démoralisé(e).

downfall ['daʊnfɔːl] *n* (*U*) ruine *f*.

downhearted [,daʊn'hɑːtɪd] *adj* découragé(e).

downhill [,daʊn'hɪl] **1** *adj* [downward] en pente. **2** *n* SKIING [race] descente *f*. **3** *adv*: **to walk ~** descendre la côte; **her career is going ~** *fig* sa carrière est sur le déclin.

down payment *n* acompte *m*.

downpour ['daʊnpɔːr] *n* pluie *f* torrentielle.

downright ['daʊnraɪt] **1** *adj* franc (franche); [lie] effronté(e). **2** *adv* franchement.

downstairs [,daʊn'steəz] **1** *adj* du bas; [on floor below] à l'étage en-dessous. **2**

drawn

adv en bas; [on floor below] à l'étage en-dessous; **to come** OR **go** ~ descendre.

downstream [ˌdaʊn'striːm] *adv* en aval.

down-to-earth *adj* pragmatique, terre-à-terre (*inv*).

downtown [ˌdaʊn'taʊn] **1** *adj*: ~ **New York** le centre de New York. **2** *adv* en ville.

downturn ['daʊntɜːn] *n*: ~ **(in)** baisse *f* (de).

down under *adv* en Australie/ Nouvelle-Zélande.

downward ['daʊnwəd] **1** *adj* [towards ground] vers le bas. || [trend] à la baisse. **2** *adv Am* = **downwards**.

downwards ['daʊnwədz] *adv* [look, move] vers le bas.

dowry ['daʊərɪ] *n* dot *f*.

doz. (*abbr of* **dozen**) douz.

doze [dəʊz] **1** *n* somme *m*. **2** *vi* sommeil-ler. **O doze off** *vi* s'assoupir.

dozen ['dʌzn] **1** *num adj*: **a** ~ **eggs** une douzaine d'œufs. **2** *n* douzaine *f*; **-s of** *inf* des centaines de.

Dr. (*abbr of* **Drive**) av. || (*abbr of* **Doctor**) Dr.

drab [dræb] *adj* terne.

draft [drɑːft] **1** *n* [early version] premier jet *m*, ébauche *f*; [of letter] brouillon *m*. || [money order] traite *f*. || *Am* MIL: **the** ~ la conscription *f*. || *Am* = **draught**. **2** *vt* [speech] ébaucher, faire le plan de; [letter] faire le brouillon de. || *Am* MIL appeler; [staff] muter.

draftsman *Am* = **draughtsman**.

drafty *Am* = **draughty**.

drag [dræg] **1** *vt* [gen] traîner. || [lake, river] draguer. **2** *vi* [dress, coat] traîner. || *fig* [time, action] traîner en longueur. **3** *n inf* [bore] plaie *f*. || *inf* [on cigarette] bouf-fée *f*. || [cross-dressing]: **in** ~ en travesti. **O drag on** *vi* [meeting, time] s'éterniser, traîner en longueur.

dragon ['drægən] *n lit & fig* dragon *m*.

dragonfly ['drægnflaɪ] *n* libellule *f*.

drain [dreɪn] **1** *n* [pipe] égout *m*. || [de-pletion - of resources, funds]: ~ **on** épuise-ment *m* de. **2** *vt* [vegetables] égoutter; [land] assécher, drainer. || [strength, re-sources] épuiser. || [drink, glass] boire. **3** *vi* [dishes] égoutter.

drainage ['dreɪnɪdʒ] *n* [pipes, ditches] (système *m* du) tout-à-l'égout *m*. || [draining - of land] drainage *m*.

draining board *Br* ['dreɪnɪŋ-], **drain-board** *Am* ['dreɪnbɔːd] *n* égouttoir *m*.

drainpipe ['dreɪnpaɪp] *n* tuyau *m* d'écoulement.

drama ['drɑːmə] *n* [play, excitement] drame *m*. || (*U*) [art] théâtre *m*.

dramatic [drə'mætɪk] *adj* [gen] drama-tique. || [sudden, noticeable] spectacu-laire.

dramatist ['dræmətɪst] *n* dramaturge *mf*.

dramatize, -ise ['dræmətaɪz] *vt* [re-write as play, film] adapter pour la télévision/la scène/l'écran. || *pej* [make exciting] dramatiser.

drank [dræŋk] *pt* → **drink**.

drape [dreɪp] *vt* draper; **to be ~d with** OR **in** être drapé(e) de. **O drapes** *npl Am* rideaux *mpl*.

drastic ['dræstɪk] *adj* [measures] dras-tique, radical(e). || [improvement, de-cline] spectaculaire.

draught *Br*, **draft** *Am* [drɑːft] *n* [air current] courant *m* d'air. || [from barrel]: **on** ~ [beer] à la pression.

draughtsman *Br* (*pl* **-men** [-mən]), **draftsman** *Am* (*pl* **-men** [-mən]) ['drɑːftsmən] *n* dessinateur *m*, -trice *f*.

draughty *Br*, **drafty** *Am* ['drɑːftɪ] *adj* plein(e) de courants d'air.

draw [drɔː] (*pt* **drew**, *pp* **drawn**) **1** *vt* [gen] tirer. || [sketch] dessiner. || [com-parison, distinction] établir, faire. || [at-tract] attirer, entraîner; **to** ~ **sb's atten-tion to** attirer l'attention de qqn sur. **2** *vi* [sketch] dessiner. || [move]: **to** ~ **near** [person] s'approcher; [time] approcher; **to** ~ **away** reculer. || SPORT faire match nul; **to be ~ing** être à égalité. **3** *n* SPORT [result] match *m* nul. || [lottery] tirage *m*. || [attraction] attraction *f*. **O draw out** *vt sep* [encourage - person] faire sortir de sa coquille. || [prolong] prolonger. || [money] faire un retrait de, retirer. **O draw up** **1** *vt sep* [contract, plan] éta-blir, dresser. **2** *vi* [vehicle] s'arrêter.

drawback ['drɔːbæk] *n* inconvénient *m*, désavantage *m*.

drawbridge ['drɔːbrɪdʒ] *n* pont-levis *m*.

drawer ['drɔːr] *n* [in desk, chest] tiroir *m*.

drawing ['drɔːɪŋ] *n* dessin *m*.

drawing board *n* planche *f* à dessin.

drawing room *n* salon *m*.

drawl [drɔːl] *n* voix *f* traînante.

drawn [drɔːn] *pp* → **draw**.

dread [dred] **1** n (U) épouvante f. **2** vt appréhender; **to ~ doing sthg** appréhender de faire qqch.

dreadful ['dredful] adj affreux(euse), épouvantable.

dreadfully ['dredfuli] adv [badly] terriblement. || [extremely] extrêmement; **I'm ~ sorry** je regrette infiniment.

dream [driːm] (pt & pp **-ed** OR **dreamt**) **1** n rêve m. **2** adj de rêve. **3** vt: **to ~ (that)** ... rêver que .... **4** vi: **to ~ (of** OR **about)** rêver (de); **I wouldn't ~ of it** cela ne me viendrait même pas à l'idée. ○ **dream up** vt sep inventer.

dreamt [dremt] pp → dream.

dreamy ['driːmi] adj [distracted] rêveur(euse). || [dreamlike] de rêve.

dreary ['drɪəri] adj [weather] morne. || [dull, boring] ennuyeux(euse).

dredge [dredʒ] vt draguer. ○ **dredge up** vt sep [with dredger] draguer. || fig [from past] déterrer.

dregs [dregz] npl lit & fig lie f.

drench [drentʃ] vt tremper; **to be ~ed in** OR **with** être inondé(e) de.

dress [dres] **1** n [woman's garment] robe f. || (U) [clothing] costume m, tenue f. **2** vt [clothe] habiller; **to be ~ed** être habillé(e); **to be ~ed in** être vêtu(e) de; **to get ~ed** s'habiller. || [bandage] panser. || CU-LIN [salad] assaisonner. **3** vi s'habiller. ○ **dress up** vi [in costume] se déguiser. || [in best clothes] s'habiller (élégamment).

dresser ['dresər] n [for dishes] vaisselier m. || Am [chest of drawers] commode f.

dressing ['dresɪŋ] n [bandage] pansement m. || [for salad] assaisonnement m. || Am [for turkey etc] farce f.

dressing gown n robe f de chambre.

dressing room n THEATRE loge f. || SPORT vestiaire m.

dressing table n coiffeuse f.

dressmaker ['dres,meɪkər] n couturier m, -ière f.

dressmaking ['dres,meɪkɪŋ] n couture f.

dress rehearsal n générale f.

drew [druː] pt → draw.

dribble ['drɪbl] **1** n [saliva] bave f. || [trickle] traînée f. **2** vt SPORT dribbler. **3** vi [drool] baver. || [liquid] tomber goutte à goutte, couler.

dried [draɪd] adj [milk, eggs] en poudre; [fruit] sec (sèche); [flowers] séché(e).

drier ['draɪər] = dryer.

drift [drɪft] **1** n [movement] mouvement m; [direction] direction f, sens m. ||

[meaning] sens m général. || [of snow] congère f; [of sand, leaves] amoncellement m, entassement m. **2** vi [boat] dériver. || [snow, sand, leaves] s'amasser, s'amonceler.

driftwood ['drɪftwʊd] n bois m flottant.

drill [drɪl] **1** n [tool] perceuse f; [dentist's] fraise f; [in mine etc] perforatrice f. || [exercise, training] exercice m. **2** vt [wood, hole] percer; [tooth] fraiser; [well] forer. || [soldiers] entraîner. **3** vi [excavate]: **to ~ for oil** forer à la recherche de pétrole.

drink [drɪŋk] (pt **drank**, pp **drunk**) **1** n [gen] boisson f; **to have a ~** boire un verre. || (U) [alcohol] alcool m. **2** vt boire. **3** vi boire.

drink-driving Br, **drunk-driving** Am n conduite f en état d'ivresse.

drinker ['drɪŋkər] n buveur m, -euse f.

drinking water ['drɪŋkɪŋ-] n eau f potable.

drip [drɪp] **1** n [drop] goutte f. || MED goutte-à-goutte m inv. **2** vi [gen] goutter, tomber goutte à goutte.

drip-dry adj qui ne se repasse pas.

drive [draɪv] (pt **drove**, pp **driven**) **1** n [in car] trajet m (en voiture); **to go for a ~** faire une promenade (en voiture). || [urge] désir m, besoin m. || [campaign] campagne f. || (U) [energy] dynamisme m, énergie f. || [road to house] allée f. || SPORT drive m. **2** vt [vehicle, passenger] conduire. || TECH entraîner, actionner. || [animals, people] pousser. || [motivate] pousser. || [force]: **to ~ sb to sthg/to do sthg** pousser qqn à qqch/à faire qqch, conduire qqn à qqch/à faire qqch; **to ~ sb mad** OR **crazy** rendre qqn fou. || [nail, stake] enfoncer. **3** vi [driver] conduire; [travel by car] aller en voiture.

drivel ['drɪvl] n (U) inf foutaises fpl, idioties fpl.

driven ['drɪvn] pp → drive.

driver ['draɪvər] n [of vehicle - gen] conducteur m, -trice f; [- of taxi] chauffeur m.

driver's license Am = driving licence.

drive shaft n arbre m de transmission.

driveway ['draɪvweɪ] n allée f.

driving ['draɪvɪŋ] n (U) conduite f.

driving instructor n moniteur m, -trice f d'auto-école.

driving lesson n leçon f de conduite.

driving licence Br, **driver's license** Am n permis m de conduire.

driving mirror n rétroviseur m.

due

driving school n auto-école f.

driving test n (examen m du) permis m de conduire.

drizzle ['drɪzl] 1 n bruine f. 2 v impers bruiner.

droll [drəʊl] adj drôle.

drone [drəʊn] n [of traffic, voices] ronronnement m; [of insect] bourdonnement m.

drool [dru:l] vi baver; **to ~ over** fig baver (d'admiration) devant.

droop [dru:p] vi [head] pencher; [shoulders, eyelids] tomber.

drop [drɒp] 1 n [of liquid] goutte f. || [sweet] pastille f. || [decrease]: **~ (in)** baisse f (de). || [distance down] dénivellation f; **sheer ~** à-pic m inv. 2 vt [let fall] laisser tomber. || [voice, speed, price] baisser. || [abandon] abandonner; [player] exclure. || [let out of car] déposer. || [write]: **to ~ sb a note** OR **line** écrire un petit mot à qqn. 3 vi [fall] tomber. || [temperature, demand] baisser; [voice, wind] tomber. ○ **drops** npl MED gouttes fpl. ○ **drop in** vi inf: **to ~ in (on sb)** passer (chez qqn). ○ **drop off** 1 vt sep déposer. 2 vi [fall asleep] s'endormir. || [interest, sales] baisser. ○ **drop out** vi: **to ~ out (of** OR **from sthg)** abandonner (qqch); **to ~ out of society** vivre en marge de la société.

dropout ['drɒpaʊt] n [from society] marginal m, -e f; [from college] étudiant m, -e f qui abandonne ses études.

droppings ['drɒpɪŋz] npl [of bird] fiente f; [of animal] crottes fpl.

drought [draʊt] n sécheresse f.

drove [drəʊv] pt → drive.

drown [draʊn] 1 vt [in water] noyer. 2 vi se noyer.

drowsy ['draʊzɪ] adj assoupi(e), somnolent(e).

drug [drʌg] 1 n [medicine] médicament m. || [narcotic] drogue f. 2 vt droguer.

drug abuse n usage m de stupéfiants.

drug addict n drogué m, -e f.

druggist ['drʌgɪst] n Am pharmacien m, -ienne f.

drugstore ['drʌgstɔ:r] n Am drugstore m.

drum [drʌm] 1 n MUS tambour m. || [container] bidon m. 2 vt & vi tambouriner. ○ **drums** npl batterie f. ○ **drum up** vt sep [support, business] rechercher, solliciter.

drummer ['drʌmər] n [gen] (joueur m,

-euse f de) tambour m; [in pop group] batteur m, -euse f.

drumstick ['drʌmstɪk] n [for drum] baguette f de tambour. || [of chicken] pilon m.

drunk [drʌŋk] 1 pp → drink. 2 adj [on alcohol] ivre, soûl(e); **to get ~** se soûler, s'enivrer. 3 n soûlard m, -e f.

drunkard ['drʌŋkəd] n alcoolique mf.

drunk-driving Am = drink-driving.

drunken ['drʌŋkn] adj [person] ivre; [quarrel] d'ivrognes.

drunken driving = drink-driving.

dry [draɪ] 1 adj [gen] sec (sèche); [day] sans pluie. || [river, earth] asséché(e). || [wry] pince-sans-rire (inv). 2 vt [gen] sécher; [with cloth] essuyer. 3 vi sécher. ○ **dry up** 1 vt sep [dishes] essuyer. 2 vi [river, lake] s'assécher; [supply] se tarir.

dry cleaner n: **~'s** pressing m.

dryer ['draɪər] n [for clothes] séchoir m.

dry land n terre f ferme.

dry rot n pourriture f sèche.

dry ski slope n piste f de ski artificielle.

DTP (abbr of desktop publishing) n PAO f.

dual ['dju:əl] adj double.

dubbed [dʌbd] adj CINEMA doublé(e). || [nicknamed] surnommé(e).

dubious ['dju:bjəs] adj [suspect] douteux(euse). || [uncertain] hésitant(e), incertain(e); **to be ~ about doing sthg** hésiter à faire qqch.

Dublin ['dʌblɪn] n Dublin.

duchess ['dʌtʃɪs] n duchesse f.

duck [dʌk] 1 n canard m. 2 vt [head] baisser. || [responsibility] esquiver, se dérober à. 3 vi [lower head] se baisser.

duckling ['dʌklɪŋ] n caneton m.

duct [dʌkt] n [pipe] canalisation f. || ANAT canal m.

dud [dʌd] 1 adj [bomb] non éclaté(e); [cheque] sans provision, en bois. 2 n obus m non éclaté.

dude [dju:d] n Am inf [man] gars m, type m.

due [dju:] 1 adj [expected]: **she's ~ back shortly** elle devrait rentrer sous peu; **when is the train ~?** à quelle heure le train doit-il arriver? || [appropriate] dû (due), qui convient; **in ~ course** [at the appropriate time] en temps voulu; [eventually] à la longue. || [owed, owing] dû (due). 2 adv: **~ west** droit vers l'ouest. 3 n dû m. ○ **dues** npl cotisation f. ○ **due to** prep [owing to] dû à; [because of] provoqué par, à cause de.

duel ['dju:əl] **1** n duel m. **2** vi se battre en duel.

duet [dju:'et] n duo m.

duffel bag ['dʌfl-] n sac m marin.

duffel coat ['dʌfl-] n duffel-coat m.

duffle bag ['dʌfl-] = duffel bag.

duffle coat ['dʌfl-] = duffel coat.

dug [dʌg] pt & pp → dig.

duke [dju:k] n duc m.

dull [dʌl] **1** adj [boring - book, conversation] ennuyeux(euse); [- person] terne. || [colour, light] terne. || [weather] maussade. || [sound, ache] sourd(e). **2** vt [pain] atténuer; [senses] émousser. || [make less bright] ternir.

duly ['dju:lɪ] adv [properly] dûment. || [as expected] comme prévu.

dumb [dʌm] adj [unable to speak] muet(ette). || inf [stupid] idiot(e).

dumbfound [dʌm'faund] vt stupéfier, abasourdir; **to be ~ed** ne pas en revenir.

dummy ['dʌmɪ] **1** adj faux (fausse). **2** n [of tailor] mannequin m. || [copy] maquette f. || SPORT feinte f.

dump [dʌmp] **1** n [for rubbish] décharge f. || MIL dépôt m. **2** vt [put down] déposer. || [dispose of] jeter. || inf [boyfriend, girlfriend] laisser tomber, plaquer.

dumper (truck) Br ['dʌmpər-], **dump truck** Am n tombereau m, dumper m.

dumping ['dʌmpɪŋ] n décharge f; "no ~" «décharge interdite».

dumpling ['dʌmplɪŋ] n boulette f de pâte.

dump truck Am = dumper (truck).

dumpy ['dʌmpɪ] adj inf boulot(otte).

dunce [dʌns] n cancre m.

dune [dju:n] n dune f.

dung [dʌŋ] n fumier m.

dungarees [,dʌŋgə'ri:z] npl Br [for work] bleu m de travail; [fashion garment] salopette f.

dungeon ['dʌndʒən] n cachot m.

Dunkirk [dʌn'kɜ:k] n Dunkerque.

duo ['dju:əu] n duo m.

duplex ['dju:pleks] n Am [apartment] duplex m. || [house] maison f jumelée.

duplicate [adj & n 'dju:plɪkət, vb 'dju:plɪkeɪt] **1** adj [key, document] en double. **2** n double m; **in ~** en double. **3** vt [copy - gen] faire un double de; [- on photocopier] photocopier.

durable ['djuərəbl] adj solide, résistant(e).

duration [djuˈreɪʃn] n durée f; **for the ~ of** jusqu'à la fin de.

duress [dju'res] n: **under ~** sous la contrainte.

Durex® ['djuəreks] n préservatif m.

during ['djuərɪŋ] prep pendant, au cours de.

dusk [dʌsk] n crépuscule m.

dust [dʌst] **1** n (U) poussière f. **2** vt [clean] épousseter. || [cover with powder]: **to ~ sthg (with)** saupoudrer qqch (de).

duster ['dʌstər] n [cloth] chiffon m (à poussière).

dust jacket n [on book] jaquette f.

dustpan ['dʌstpæn] n pelle f à poussière.

dusty ['dʌstɪ] adj poussiéreux(euse).

Dutch [dʌtʃ] **1** adj néerlandais(e), hollandais(e). **2** n [language] néerlandais m, hollandais m. **3** npl: **the ~** les Néerlandais, les Hollandais. **4** adv: **to go ~** partager les frais.

dutiful ['dju:tɪful] adj obéissant(e).

duty ['dju:tɪ] n (U) [responsibility] devoir m; **to do one's ~** faire son devoir. || [work]: **to be on/off ~** être/ne pas être de service. || [tax] droit m. ○ **duties** npl fonctions fpl.

duty-free adj hors taxe.

dwarf [dwɔ:f] (pl -s OR **dwarves** [dwɔ:vz]) **1** n nain m, -e f. **2** vt [tower over] écraser.

dwell [dwel] (pt & pp **dwelt** OR -**ed**) vi literary habiter. ○ **dwell on** vt fus s'étendre sur.

dwelt [dwelt] pt & pp → dwell.

dwindle ['dwɪndl] vi diminuer.

dye [daɪ] **1** n teinture f. **2** vt teindre.

dying ['daɪɪŋ] **1** cont → die. **2** adj [person] mourant(e), moribond(e); [plant, language, industry] moribond.

dyke [daɪk] = dike.

dynamic [daɪ'næmɪk] adj dynamique.

dynamite ['daɪnəmaɪt] n (U) lit & fig dynamite f.

dynamo ['daɪnəməu] (pl -s) n dynamo f.

dynasty [Br 'dɪnəstɪ, Am 'daɪnəstɪ] n dynastie f.

dyslexia [dɪs'leksɪə] n dyslexie f.

dyslexic [dɪs'leksɪk] adj dyslexique.

e (*pl* e's OR es), **E** (*pl* E's OR Es) [iː] *n* [letter] e *m inv*, E *m inv*. ○ **E** *n* MUS mi *m*. ‖ (*abbr of* east) E.

each [iːtʃ] **1** *adj* chaque. **2** *pron* chacun(e); **the books cost £10.99 ~** les livres coûtent 10.99 livres (la) pièce; **~ other** l'un l'autre (l'une l'autre), les uns les autres (les unes les autres); **they love ~ other** ils s'aiment.

eager ['iːgər] *adj* passionné(e), avide; **to be ~ for** être avide de; **to be ~ to do sthg** être impatient de faire qqch.

eagle ['iːgl] *n* [bird] aigle *m*.

ear [ɪər] *n* [gen] oreille *f*. ‖ [of corn] épi *m*.

earache ['ɪəreɪk] *n*: **to have ~** avoir mal à l'oreille.

eardrum ['ɪədrʌm] *n* tympan *m*.

earl [ɜːl] *n* comte *m*.

earlier ['ɜːlɪər] **1** *adj* [previous] précédent(e); [more early] plus tôt. **2** *adv* plus tôt; **~ on** plus tôt.

earliest ['ɜːlɪəst] **1** *adj* [first] premier(ière); [most early] le plus tôt. **2** *n*: **at the ~** au plus tôt.

earlobe ['ɪələub] *n* lobe *m* de l'oreille.

early ['ɜːlɪ] **1** *adj* [before expected time] en avance. ‖ [in day] de bonne heure; **the ~ train** le premier train; **to make an ~ start** partir de bonne heure. ‖ [at beginning]: **in the ~ sixties** au début des années soixante. **2** *adv* [before expected time] en avance; **I was ten minutes ~** j'étais en avance de dix minutes. ‖ [in day] tôt, de bonne heure; **as ~ as** dès; **~ on** tôt. ‖ [at beginning]: **~ in her life** dans sa jeunesse.

early retirement *n* retraite *f* anticipée.

earmark ['ɪəmɑːk] *vt*: **to be ~ed for** être réservé(e) à.

earn [ɜːn] *vt* [as salary] gagner. ‖ COMM rapporter. ‖ *fig* [respect, praise] gagner, mériter.

earnest ['ɜːnɪst] *adj* sérieux(ieuse). ○ **in earnest 1** *adj* sérieux(ieuse). **2** *adv* pour de bon, sérieusement.

earnings ['ɜːnɪŋz] *npl* [of person] salaire *m*, gains *mpl*; [of company] bénéfices *mpl*.

earphones ['ɪəfəʊnz] *npl* casque *m*.

earplugs ['ɪəplʌgz] *npl* boules *fpl* Quiès®.

earring ['ɪərɪŋ] *n* boucle *f* d'oreille.

earshot ['ɪəʃɒt] *n*: **within ~** à portée de voix; **out of ~** hors de portée de voix.

earth [ɜːθ] *n* [gen & ELEC] terre *f*; **how/what/where/why on ~ ...?** mais comment/que/où/pourquoi donc ...?

earthquake ['ɜːθkweɪk] *n* tremblement *m* de terre.

earthworm ['ɜːθwɜːm] *n* ver *m* de terre.

earthy ['ɜːθɪ] *adj fig* [humour, person] truculent(e). ‖ [taste, smell] de terre, terreux(euse).

earwig ['ɪəwɪg] *n* perce-oreille *m*.

ease [iːz] **1** *n* (*U*) [lack of difficulty] facilité *f*; **to do sthg with ~** faire qqch sans difficulté OR facilement. ‖ [comfort]: **at ~** à l'aise; **ill at ~** mal à l'aise. **2** *vt* [pain] calmer; [restrictions] modérer. ‖ [move carefully]: **to ~ sthg in/out** faire entrer/sortir qqch délicatement. ○ **ease off** *vi* [pain] s'atténuer; [rain] diminuer. ○ **ease up** *vi* [rain] diminuer. ‖ [relax] se détendre.

easel ['iːzl] *n* chevalet *m*.

easily ['iːzɪlɪ] *adv* [without difficulty] facilement. ‖ [without doubt] de loin. ‖ [in a relaxed manner] tranquillement.

east [iːst] **1** *n* [direction] est *m*. ‖ [region]: **the ~** l'est *m*. **2** *adj* est (*inv*); [wind] d'est. **3** *adv* à l'est, vers l'est; **~ of** à l'est de. ○ **East** *n*: **the East** [gen & POL] l'Est *m*; [Asia] l'Orient *m*.

Easter ['iːstər] *n* Pâques *m*.

Easter egg *n* œuf *m* de Pâques.

easterly ['iːstəlɪ] *adj* à l'est, de l'est; [wind] de l'est.

eastern ['iːstən] *adj* de l'est. ○ **Eastern** *adj* [gen & POL] de l'Est; [from Asia] oriental(e).

East German 1 *adj* d'Allemagne de l'Est. **2** *n* Allemand *m*, -e *f* de l'Est.

East Germany *n*: (former) **~** (l'ex-) Allemagne *f* de l'Est.

eastward ['iːstwəd] **1** *adj* à l'est, vers l'est. **2** *adv* = **eastwards**.

eastwards ['iːstwədz] *adv* vers l'est.

easy ['i:zɪ] **1** *adj* [not difficult, comfortable] facile. || [relaxed - manner] naturel(elle). **2** *adv*: **to take it** OR **things ~** *inf* ne pas se fatiguer.

easy chair *n* fauteuil *m*.

easygoing ['i:zɪ'gəʊɪŋ] *adj* [person] facile à vivre; [manner] complaisant(e).

eat [i:t] (*pt* **ate**, *pp* **eaten**) *vt & vi* manger. ○ **eat away, eat into** *vt fus* [subj: acid, rust] ronger. || [deplete] grignoter.

eaten ['i:tn] *pp* → **eat**.

eaves ['i:vz] *npl* avant-toit *m*.

eavesdrop ['i:vzdrɒp] *vi*: **to ~ (on sb)** écouter (qqn) de façon indiscrète.

ebb [eb] **1** *n* reflux *m*. **2** *vi* [tide, sea] se retirer, refluer.

ebony ['ebənɪ] **1** *adj* [colour] noir(e) d'ébène. **2** *n* ébène *f*.

EC (*abbr of* **European Community**) *n* CE *f*.

eccentric [ɪk'sentrɪk] **1** *adj* [odd] excentrique, bizarre. **2** *n* [person] excentrique *mf*.

echo ['ekəʊ] (*pl* **-es**) **1** *n lit & fig* écho *m*. **2** *vt* [words] répéter; [opinion] faire écho à. **3** *vi* retentir, résonner.

eclipse [ɪ'klɪps] **1** *n lit & fig* éclipse *f*. **2** *vt fig* éclipser.

ecological [ˌi:kə'lɒdʒɪkl] *adj* écologique.

ecology [ɪ'kɒlədʒɪ] *n* écologie *f*.

economic [ˌi:kə'nɒmɪk] *adj* ECON économique. || [profitable] rentable.

economical [ˌi:kə'nɒmɪkl] *adj* [cheap] économique. || [person] économe.

economics [ˌi:kə'nɒmɪks] **1** *n* (*U*) économie *f* politique, économie *f*. **2** *npl* [of plan, business] aspect *m* financier.

economize, -ise [ɪ'kɒnəmaɪz] *vi* économiser.

economy [ɪ'kɒnəmɪ] *n* économie *f*.

economy class *n* classe *f* touriste.

ecstasy ['ekstəsɪ] *n* extase *f*, ravissement *m*.

ecstatic [ek'stætɪk] *adj* [person] en extase; [feeling] extatique.

ECU, Ecu ['ekju:] (*abbr of* **European Currency Unit**) *n* ECU *m*, écu *m*.

eczema ['eksɪmə] *n* eczéma *m*.

Eden ['i:dn] *n*: **(the Garden of) ~** le jardin *m* d'Éden, l'Éden *m*.

edge [edʒ] **1** *n* [gen] bord *m*; [of coin, book] tranche *f*; [of knife] tranchant *m*; **to be on the ~ of** *fig* être à deux doigts de. || [advantage]: **to have an ~ over** OR **the ~ on** avoir un léger avantage sur. **2** *vi*: **to ~**

forward avancer tout doucement. ○ **on edge** *adj* contracté(e), tendu(e).

edgeways ['edʒweɪz], **edgewise** ['edʒwaɪz] *adv* latéralement, de côté.

edgy ['edʒɪ] *adj* contracté(e), tendu(e).

edible ['edɪbl] *adj* [safe to eat] comestible.

edict ['i:dɪkt] *n* décret *m*.

Edinburgh ['edɪnbrə] *n* Édimbourg.

edit ['edɪt] *vt* [correct - text] corriger. || CINEMA monter; RADIO & TV réaliser. || [magazine] diriger; [newspaper] être le rédacteur en chef de.

edition [ɪ'dɪʃn] *n* édition *f*.

editor ['edɪtə*r*] *n* [of magazine] directeur *m*, -trice *f*; [of newspaper] rédacteur *m*, -trice *f* en chef. || [of text] correcteur *m*, -trice *f*. || CINEMA monteur *m*, -euse *f*; RADIO & TV réalisateur *m*, -trice *f*.

editorial [ˌedɪ'tɔ:rɪəl] **1** *adj* [department, staff] de la rédaction; [style, policy] éditorial(e). **2** *n* éditorial *m*.

educate ['edʒʊkeɪt] *vt* SCH & UNIV instruire. || [inform] informer, éduquer.

education [ˌedʒʊ'keɪʃn] *n* [gen] éducation *f*. || [teaching] enseignement *m*, instruction *f*.

educational [ˌedʒʊ'keɪʃənl] *adj* [establishment, policy] pédagogique. || [toy, experience] éducatif(ive).

EEC (*abbr of* **European Economic Community**) *n* ancien nom de la Communauté Européenne.

eel [i:l] *n* anguille *f*.

eerie ['ɪərɪ] *adj* inquiétant(e), sinistre.

efface [ɪ'feɪs] *vt* effacer.

effect [ɪ'fekt] **1** *n* [gen] effet *m*; **to have an ~ on** avoir OR produire un effet sur; **to take ~** [law] prendre effet, entrer en vigueur; **to put sthg into ~** [policy, law] mettre qqch en application. **2** *vt* [repairs, change] effectuer; [reconciliation] amener. ○ **effects** *npl*: **(special) ~s** effets *mpl* spéciaux.

effective [ɪ'fektɪv] *adj* [successful] efficace. || [actual, real] effectif(ive).

effectively [ɪ'fektɪvlɪ] *adv* [successfully] efficacement. || [in fact] effectivement.

effectiveness [ɪ'fektɪvnɪs] *n* efficacité *f*.

efficiency [ɪ'fɪʃənsɪ] *n* [of person, method] efficacité *f*; [of factory, system] rendement *m*.

efficient [ɪ'fɪʃənt] *adj* efficace.

effluent ['efluənt] *n* effluent *m*.

effort ['efət] n effort m; **to be worth the ~** valoir la peine; **with ~** avec peine; **to make an/no ~ to do sthg** faire un effort/ne faire aucun effort pour faire qqch.

effortless ['efətlɪs] adj [easy] facile; [natural] aisé(e).

e.g. (abbr of **exempli gratia**) adv par exemple.

egg [eg] n œuf m. ○ **egg on** vt sep pousser, inciter.

eggcup ['egkʌp] n coquetier m.

eggplant ['egplɑːnt] n Am aubergine f.

eggshell ['egʃel] n coquille f d'œuf.

egg white n blanc m d'œuf.

egg yolk [-jəuk] n jaune m d'œuf.

ego ['iːgəu] (pl -s) n moi m.

egotistic(al) [,iːgə'tɪstɪk(l)] adj égotiste.

Egypt ['iːdʒɪpt] n Égypte f.

Egyptian [ɪ'dʒɪpʃn] 1 adj égyptien(ienne). 2 n Égyptien m, -ienne f.

eiderdown ['aɪdədaun] n [bed cover] édredon m.

eight [eɪt] num huit; see also **six**.

eighteen [,eɪ'tiːn] num dix-huit; see also **six**.

eighth [eɪtθ] num huitième; see also **sixth**.

eighty ['eɪtɪ] num quatre-vingts; see also **sixty**.

Eire ['eərə] n République f d'Irlande.

either ['aɪðər, 'iːðər] 1 adj [one or the other] l'un ou l'autre (l'une ou l'autre) (des deux); **she couldn't find ~ jumper** elle ne trouva ni l'un ni l'autre des pulls; **~ way** de toute façon. ‖ [each] chaque; **on ~ side** de chaque côté. 2 pron: **~ (of them)** l'un ou l'autre m (l'une ou l'autre f); **I don't like ~ (of them)** je n'aime aucun des deux, je n'aime ni l'un ni l'autre. 3 adv (in negatives) non plus; **I don't ~** moi non plus. 4 conj: **~ ... or** soit ... soit, ou ... ou; **I'm not fond of ~ him or his wife** je ne les aime ni lui ni sa femme.

eject [ɪ'dʒekt] vt [object] éjecter, émettre. ‖ [person] éjecter, expulser.

eke [iːk] ○ **eke out** vt sep [money, food] économiser, faire durer.

elaborate [adj ɪ'læbrət, vb ɪ'læbəreɪt] 1 adj [ceremony, procedure] complexe; [explanation, plan] détaillé(e), minutieux(ieuse). 2 vi: **to ~ (on)** donner des précisions (sur).

elapse [ɪ'læps] vi s'écouler.

elastic [ɪ'læstɪk] 1 adj lit & fig élastique. 2 n (U) élastique m.

elasticated [ɪ'læstɪkeɪtɪd] adj élastique.

elbow ['elbəu] n coude m.

elder ['eldər] 1 adj aîné(e). 2 n [older person] aîné m, -e f. ‖ [of tribe, church] ancien m. ‖ **~ (tree)** sureau m.

elderly ['eldəlɪ] 1 adj âgé(e). 2 npl: **the ~** les personnes fpl âgées.

eldest ['eldɪst] adj aîné(e).

elect [ɪ'lekt] 1 adj élu(e). 2 vt [by voting] élire.

election [ɪ'lekʃn] n élection f; **to have** OR **hold an ~** procéder à une élection.

elector [ɪ'lektər] n électeur m, -trice f.

electorate [ɪ'lektərət] n: **the ~** l'électorat m.

electric [ɪ'lektrɪk] adj lit & fig électrique.

electrical [ɪ'lektrɪkl] adj électrique.

electrical shock Am = electric shock.

electric blanket n couverture f chauffante.

electric cooker n cuisinière f électrique.

electric fire n radiateur m électrique.

electrician [,ɪlek'trɪʃn] n électricien m, -ienne f.

electricity [,ɪlek'trɪsətɪ] n électricité f.

electric shock Br, **electrical shock** Am n décharge f électrique.

electrify [ɪ'lektrɪfaɪ] vt TECH électrifier. ‖ fig [excite] galvaniser, électriser.

electrocute [ɪ'lektrəkjuːt] vt électrocuter.

electrolysis [,ɪlek'trɒləsɪs] n électrolyse f.

electron [ɪ'lektrɒn] n électron m.

electronic [,ɪlek'trɒnɪk] adj électronique. ○ **electronics 1** n (U) [technology, science] électronique f. **2** npl [equipment] (équipement m) électronique f.

electronic data processing n traitement m électronique de données.

electronic mail n courrier m électronique.

elegant ['elɪgənt] adj élégant(e).

element ['elɪmənt] n [gen] élément m; **an ~ of truth** une part de vérité. ‖ [in heater, kettle] résistance f. ○ **elements** npl [basics] rudiments mpl. ‖ [weather]: **the ~s** les éléments mpl.

elementary [,elɪ'mentərɪ] adj élémentaire.

elementary school n Am école f primaire.

elephant ['elɪfənt] (pl inv OR -s) n éléphant m.

elevate ['elɪveɪt] *vt* [give importance to]: **to ~ sb/sthg (to)** élever qqn/qqch (à). || [raise] soulever.

elevator ['elɪveɪtər] *n Am* ascenseur *m*.

eleven [ɪ'levn] *num* onze; *see also* **six**.

eleventh [ɪ'levnθ] *num* onzième; *see also* **sixth**.

elicit [ɪ'lɪsɪt] *vt fml*: **to ~ sthg (from sb)** arracher qqch (à qqn).

eligible ['elɪdʒəbl] *adj* [suitable, qualified] admissible; **to be ~ for sthg** avoir droit à qqch.

eliminate [ɪ'lɪmɪneɪt] *vt*: **to ~ sb/sthg (from)** éliminer qqn/qqch (de).

elite [ɪ'liːt] **1** *adj* d'élite. **2** *n* élite *f*.

elitist [ɪ'liːtɪst] **1** *adj* élitiste. **2** *n* élitiste *mf*.

elk [elk] (*pl inv* OR **-s**) *n* élan *m*.

elm [elm] *n*: **~ (tree)** orme *m*.

elocution [,elə'kjuːʃn] *n* élocution *f*, diction *f*.

elongated ['iːlɒŋgeɪtɪd] *adj* allongé(e); [fingers] long (longue).

elope [ɪ'ləʊp] *vi*: **to ~ (with)** s'enfuir (avec).

eloquent ['eləkwənt] *adj* éloquent(e).

El Salvador [,el'sælvədɔːr] *n* Salvador *m*.

else [els] *adv*: **anything ~** n'importe quoi d'autre; **anything ~?** [in shop] et avec ça?, il vous faudra autre chose?; **everyone ~** tous les autres; **nothing ~** rien d'autre; **someone ~** quelqu'un d'autre; **something ~** quelque chose d'autre; **somewhere ~** autre part; **who/what ~?** qui/quoi d'autre?; **where ~?** (à) quel autre endroit? ○ **or else** *conj* [or if not] sinon, sans quoi.

elsewhere [els'weər] *adv* ailleurs, autre part.

elude [ɪ'luːd] *vt* échapper à.

elusive [ɪ'luːsɪv] *adj* insaisissable; [success] qui échappe.

emaciated [ɪ'meɪʃieɪtɪd] *adj* [face] émacié(e); [person, limb] décharné(e).

E-mail (*abbr of* **electronic mail**) *n* BAL *f*.

emancipate [ɪ'mænsɪpeɪt] *vt*: **to ~ sb (from)** affranchir OR émanciper qqn (de).

embankment [ɪm'bæŋkmənt] *n* [of river] berge *f*; [of railway] remblai *m*; [of road] banquette *f*.

embark [ɪm'bɑːk] *vi* [board ship]: **to ~ (on)** embarquer (sur). || [start]: **to ~ on** OR **upon sthg** s'embarquer dans qqch.

embarkation [,embɑː'keɪʃn] *n* embarquement *m*.

embarrass [ɪm'bærəs] *vt* embarrasser.

embarrassed [ɪm'bærəst] *adj* embarrassé(e).

embarrassing [ɪm'bærəsɪŋ] *adj* embarrassant(e).

embarrassment [ɪm'bærəsmənt] *n* embarras *m*.

embassy ['embəsɪ] *n* ambassade *f*.

embedded [ɪm'bedɪd] *adj* [buried]: **~ in** [in rock, wood] incrusté(e) dans; [in mud] noyé(e) dans. || [ingrained] enraciné(e).

embellish [ɪm'belɪʃ] *vt* [decorate]: **to ~ sthg (with)** [room, house] décorer qqch (de). || [story] enjoliver.

embers ['embəz] *npl* braises *fpl*.

embezzle [ɪm'bezl] *vt* détourner.

emblem ['embləm] *n* emblème *m*.

embody [ɪm'bɒdɪ] *vt* incarner; **to be embodied in sthg** être exprimé dans qqch.

embossed [ɪm'bɒst] *adj* [heading, design]: **~ (on)** inscrit(e) (sur), gravé(e) en relief (sur). || [wallpaper] gaufré(e); [leather] frappé(e).

embrace [ɪm'breɪs] **1** *n* étreinte *f*. **2** *vt* embrasser. **3** *vi* s'embrasser, s'étreindre.

embroider [ɪm'brɔɪdər] **1** *vt* SEWING broder. || *pej* [embellish] enjoliver. **2** *vi* SEWING broder.

embroidery [ɪm'brɔɪdərɪ] *n* (*U*) broderie *f*.

embroil [ɪm'brɔɪl] *vt*: **to be ~ed (in)** être mêlé(e) (à).

embryo ['embrɪəʊ] (*pl* **-s**) *n* embryon *m*.

emerald ['emərəld] **1** *adj* [colour] émeraude (*inv*). **2** *n* [stone] émeraude *f*.

emerge [ɪ'mɜːdʒ] **1** *vi* [come out]: **to ~ (from)** émerger (de). || [from experience, situation]: **to ~ from** sortir de. || [become known] apparaître. **2** *vt*: **it ~s that ...** il ressort OR il apparaît que ....

emergence [ɪ'mɜːdʒəns] *n* émergence *f*.

emergency [ɪ'mɜːdʒənsɪ] **1** *adj* d'urgence. **2** *n* urgence *f*; **in an ~,** **in emergencies** en cas d'urgence.

emergency exit *n* sortie *f* de secours.

emergency landing *n* atterrissage *m* forcé.

emergency services *npl* ≃ police-secours *f*.

emery board ['emərɪ-] *n* lime *f* à ongles.

emigrant ['emɪgrənt] *n* émigré *m*, -e *f*.

emigrate ['emɪgreɪt] *vi*: **to ~ (to)** émigrer (en/à).

eminent ['emɪnənt] *adj* éminent(e).

emission [ɪ'mɪʃn] *n* émission *f.*

emit [ɪ'mɪt] *vt* émettre.

emotion [ɪ'məʊʃn] *n* (U) [strength of feeling] émotion *f.* || [particular feeling] sentiment *m.*

emotional [ɪ'məʊʃənl] *adj* [sensitive, demonstrative] émotif(ive). || [moving] émouvant(e). || [psychological] émotionnel(elle).

emperor ['empərər] *n* empereur *m.*

emphasis ['emfəsɪs] (*pl* -ases [-əsi:z]) *n*: ~ (on) accent *m* (sur); **to lay** OR **place ~ on sthg** insister sur OR souligner qqch.

emphasize, -ise ['emfəsaɪz] *vt* insister sur.

emphatic [ɪm'fætɪk] *adj* [forceful] catégorique.

emphatically [ɪm'fætɪklɪ] *adv* [with emphasis] catégoriquement. || [certainly] absolument.

empire ['empaɪər] *n* empire *m.*

employ [ɪm'plɔɪ] *vt* employer; **to be ~ed as** être employé comme.

employee [ɪm'plɔɪi:] *n* employé *m*, -e *f.*

employer [ɪm'plɔɪər] *n* employeur *m*, -euse *f.*

employment [ɪm'plɔɪmənt] *n* emploi *m*, travail *m.*

employment agency *n* bureau *m* OR agence *f* de placement.

empress ['emprɪs] *n* impératrice *f.*

empty ['emptɪ] **1** *adj* [containing nothing] vide. || *pej* [meaningless] vain(e). **2** *vt* vider; **to ~ sthg into/out of** vider qqch dans/de. **3** *vi* se vider.

empty-handed [-'hændɪd] *adv* les mains vides.

EMS (*abbr of* **European Monetary System**) *n* SME *m.*

emulate ['emjʊleɪt] *vt* imiter.

emulsion [ɪ'mʌlʃn] *n*: ~ (**paint**) peinture *f* mate OR à émulsion.

enable [ɪ'neɪbl] *vt*: **to ~ sb to do sthg** permettre à qqn de faire qqch.

enact [ɪ'nækt] *vt* JUR promulguer.

enamel [ɪ'næml] *n* [material] émail *m.* || [paint] peinture *f* laquée.

encampment [ɪn'kæmpmənt] *n* campement *m.*

encase [ɪn'keɪs] *vt*: **to be ~d in** [armour] être enfermé(e) dans; [leather] être bardé(e) de.

enchanted [ɪn'tʃɑːntɪd] *adj*: ~ (**by/with**) enchanté(e) (par/de).

enchanting [ɪn'tʃɑːntɪŋ] *adj* enchanteur(eresse).

encircle [ɪn'sɜːkl] *vt* entourer; [subj: troops] encercler.

enclose [ɪn'kləʊz] *vt* [surround, contain] entourer. || [put in envelope] joindre; **please find ~d ...** veuillez trouver ci-joint ....

enclosure [ɪn'kləʊʒər] *n* [place] enceinte *f.* || [in letter] pièce *f* jointe.

encompass [ɪn'kʌmpəs] *vt fml* [include] contenir. || [surround] entourer; [subj: troops] encercler.

encore ['ɒŋkɔːr] **1** *n* rappel *m.* **2** *excl* bis!

encounter [ɪn'kaʊntər] **1** *n* rencontre *f.* **2** *vt fml* rencontrer.

encourage [ɪn'kʌrɪdʒ] *vt* [give confidence to]: **to ~ sb (to do sthg)** encourager qqn (à faire qqch). || [promote] encourager, favoriser.

encouragement [ɪn'kʌrɪdʒmənt] *n* encouragement *m.*

encroach [ɪn'krəʊtʃ] *vi*: **to ~ on** OR **upon** empiéter sur.

encyclop(a)edia [ɪn,saɪklə'pi:djə] *n* encyclopédie *f.*

end [end] **1** *n* [gen] fin *f*; **at an ~** terminé, fini; **to come to an ~** se terminer, s'arrêter; **to put an ~ to sthg** mettre fin à qqch; **at the ~ of the day** *fig* en fin de compte; **in the ~** [finally] finalement. || [of rope, path, garden, table etc] bout *m*, extrémité *f*; [of box] côté *m.* || [leftover part - of cigarette] mégot *m*; [- of pencil] bout *m.* **2** *vt* mettre fin à; [day] finir; **to ~ sthg with** terminer OR finir qqch par. **3** *vi* se terminer; **to ~ in** se terminer par; **to ~ with** se terminer par OR avec. ○ **on end** *adv* [upright] debout. || [continuously] d'affilée. ○ **end up** *vi* finir; **to ~ up doing sthg** finir par faire qqch.

endanger [ɪn'deɪndʒər] *vt* mettre en danger.

endearing [ɪn'dɪərɪŋ] *adj* engageant(e).

endeavour *Br*, **endeavor** *Am* [ɪn'devər] *fml* **1** *n* effort *m*, tentative *f.* **2** *vt*: **to ~ to do sthg** s'efforcer OR tenter de faire qqch.

ending ['endɪŋ] *n* fin *f*, dénouement *m.*

endive ['endaɪv] *n* [salad vegetable] endive *f.* || [chicory] chicorée *f.*

endless ['endlɪs] *adj* [unending] interminable; [patience, possibilities] infini(e); [resources] inépuisable. || [vast] infini(e).

endorse [ɪn'dɔːs] *vt* [approve] approuver. || [cheque] endosser.

endorsement [ɪn'dɔːsmənt] *n* [approval] approbation *f.*

endow [ɪn'daʊ] *vt* [equip]: **to be ~ed with sthg** être doté(e) de qqch. || [donate money to] faire des dons à.

endurance [ɪn'djʊərəns] *n* endurance *f*.

endure [ɪn'djʊə] **1** *vt* supporter, endurer. **2** *vi* perdurer.

endways *Br* ['endweɪz], **endwise** *Am* ['endwaɪz] *adv* [not sideways] en long. || [with ends touching] bout à bout.

enemy ['enɪmɪ] *n* ennemi *m*, -e *f*.

energetic [,enə'dʒetɪk] *adj* énergique; [person] plein(e) d'entrain.

energy ['enədʒɪ] *n* énergie *f*.

enforce [ɪn'fɔːs] *vt* appliquer, faire respecter.

enforced [ɪn'fɔːst] *adj* forcé(e).

engage [ɪn'ɡeɪdʒ] **1** *vt* [attention, interest] susciter, éveiller. || TECH engager. || *fml* [employ] engager; **to be ~d in OR on sthg** prendre part à qqch. **2** *vi* [be involved]: **to ~ in** s'occuper de.

engaged [ɪn'ɡeɪdʒd] *adj* [to be married]: **~ (to sb)** fiancé(e) (à qqn); **to get ~** se fiancer. || [busy] occupé(e); **~ in sthg** engagé dans qqch. || [telephone, toilet] occupé(e).

engagement [ɪn'ɡeɪdʒmənt] *n* [to be married] fiançailles *fpl*. || [appointment] rendez-vous *m inv*.

engagement ring *n* bague *f* de fiançailles.

engaging [ɪn'ɡeɪdʒɪŋ] *adj* engageant(e); [personality] attirant(e).

engine ['endʒɪn] *n* [of vehicle] moteur *m*. || RAIL locomotive *f*.

engineer [,endʒɪ'nɪə] *n* [of roads] ingénieur *m*; [of machinery, on ship] mécanicien *m*; [of electrical equipment] technicien *m*. || *Am* [engine driver] mécanicien *m*.

engineering [,endʒɪ'nɪərɪŋ] *n* ingénierie *f*.

England ['ɪŋɡlənd] *n* Angleterre *f*; **in ~** en Angleterre.

English ['ɪŋɡlɪʃ] **1** *adj* anglais(e). **2** *n* [language] anglais *m*. **3** *npl*: **the ~** les Anglais.

English breakfast *n* petit déjeuner anglais traditionnel.

English Channel *n*: **the ~** la Manche.

Englishman ['ɪŋɡlɪʃmən] (*pl* -men [-mən]) *n* Anglais *m*.

Englishwoman ['ɪŋɡlɪʃ,wʊmən] (*pl* -women [-wɪmɪn]) *n* Anglaise *f*.

engrave [ɪn'ɡreɪv] *vt*: **to ~ sthg (on stone/in one's memory)** graver qqch (sur la pierre/dans sa mémoire).

engraving [ɪn'ɡreɪvɪŋ] *n* gravure *f*.

engrossed [ɪn'ɡrəʊst] *adj*: **to be ~ (in sthg)** être absorbé(e) (par qqch).

engulf [ɪn'ɡʌlf] *vt* engloutir.

enhance [ɪn'hɑːns] *vt* accroître.

enjoy [ɪn'dʒɔɪ] *vt* [like] aimer; **to ~ doing sthg** avoir plaisir à OR aimer faire qqch; **to ~ o.s.** s'amuser. || *fml* [possess] jouir de.

enjoyable [ɪn'dʒɔɪəbl] *adj* agréable.

enjoyment [ɪn'dʒɔɪmənt] *n* [gen] plaisir *m*.

enlarge [ɪn'lɑːdʒ] *vt* agrandir. ○ **enlarge (up)on** *vt fus* développer.

enlargement [ɪn'lɑːdʒmənt] *n* [expansion] extension *f*. || PHOT agrandissement *m*.

enlighten [ɪn'laɪtn] *vt* éclairer.

enlightened [ɪn'laɪtnd] *adj* éclairé(e).

enlist [ɪn'lɪst] **1** *vt* MIL enrôler. || [recruit] recruter. || [obtain] s'assurer. **2** *vi* MIL: **to ~ (in)** s'enrôler (dans).

enmity ['enmɪtɪ] *n* hostilité *f*.

enormity [ɪ'nɔːmətɪ] *n* [extent] étendue *f*.

enormous [ɪ'nɔːməs] *adj* énorme; [patience, success] immense.

enough [ɪ'nʌf] **1** *adj* assez de; **~ money/time** assez d'argent/de temps. **2** *pron* assez; **more than ~** largement assez; **to have had ~ (of sthg)** en avoir assez (de qqch). **3** *adv* [sufficiently] assez; **to be good ~ to do sthg** *fml* être assez gentil pour OR de faire qqch, être assez aimable pour OR de faire qqch. || [rather] plutôt; **strangely ~** bizarrement, c'est bizarre.

enquire [ɪn'kwaɪə] **1** *vt*: **to ~ when/whether/how ...** demander quand/si/comment .... **2** *vi*: **to ~ (about)** se renseigner (sur).

enquiry [ɪn'kwaɪərɪ] *n* [question] demande *f* de renseignements; **"Enquiries"** «renseignements». || [investigation] enquête *f*.

enraged [ɪn'reɪdʒd] *adj* déchaîné(e); [animal] enragé(e).

enrol, enroll *Am* [ɪn'rəʊl] **1** *vt* inscrire. **2** *vi*: **to ~ (in)** s'inscrire (à).

ensue [ɪn'sjuː] *vi* s'ensuivre.

ensure [ɪn'ʃʊə] *vt* assurer; **to ~ (that) ...** s'assurer que ....

ENT (*abbr of* **Ear, Nose & Throat**) *n* ORL *f*.

entail [ɪn'teɪl] *vt* entraîner; **what does the work ~?** en quoi consiste le travail?

enter ['entə^r] **1** vt [room, vehicle] entrer dans. || [university, army] entrer à; [school] s'inscrire à, s'inscrire dans. || [competition, race] s'inscrire à; [politics] se lancer dans. || [register]: **to ~ sb/sthg for sthg** inscrire qqn/qqch à qqch. || [write down] inscrire. || COMPUT entrer. **2** vi [come or go in] entrer. || [register]: **to ~ (for)** s'inscrire (à). ○ **enter into** vt fus [negotiations, correspondence] entamer.

enter key n COMPUT (touche f) entrée f.

enterprise ['entəpraiz] n entreprise f.

enterprising ['entəpraizɪŋ] adj qui fait preuve d'initiative.

entertain [,entə'teɪn] vt [amuse] divertir. || [invite - guests] recevoir. || fml [thought, proposal] considérer.

entertainer [,entə'teɪnə^r] n fantaisiste mf.

entertaining [,entə'teɪnɪŋ] adj divertissant(e).

entertainment [,entə'teɪnmənt] n (U) [amusement] divertissement m. || [show] spectacle m.

enthral, enthrall Am [ɪn'θrɔːl] vt captiver.

enthusiasm [ɪn'θjuːzɪæzm] n [passion, eagerness]: **~ (for)** enthousiasme m (pour). || [interest] passion f.

enthusiast [ɪn'θjuːzɪæst] n amateur m, -trice f.

enthusiastic [ɪn,θjuːzɪ'æstɪk] adj enthousiaste.

entice [ɪn'taɪs] vt entraîner.

entire [ɪn'taɪə^r] adj entier(ière).

entirely [ɪn'taɪəlɪ] adv totalement.

entirety [ɪn'taɪrətɪ] n: **in its ~** en entier.

entitle [ɪn'taɪtl] vt [allow]: **to ~ sb to sthg** donner droit à qqch à qqn; **to ~ sb to do sthg** autoriser qqn à faire qqch.

entitled [ɪn'taɪtld] adj [allowed] autorisé(e); **to be ~ to sthg** avoir droit à qqch; **to be ~ to do sthg** avoir le droit de faire qqch. || [called] intitulé(e).

entrance [n 'entrəns, vt ɪn'trɑːns] **1** n [way in]: **~ (to)** entrée f (de). || [arrival] entrée f. || [entry]: **to gain ~ to** [building] obtenir l'accès à. **2** vt ravir, enivrer.

entrance examination n examen m d'entrée.

entrance fee n [to cinema, museum] droit m d'entrée. || [for club] droit m d'inscription.

entrant ['entrənt] n [in race, competition] concurrent m, -e f.

entreat [ɪn'triːt] vt: **to ~ sb (to do sthg)** supplier qqn (de faire qqch).

entrepreneur [,ɒntrəprə'nɜː^r] n entrepreneur m.

entrust [ɪn'trʌst] vt: **to ~ sthg to sb, to ~ sb with sthg** confier qqch à qqn.

entry ['entrɪ] n [gen] entrée f; **to gain ~ to** avoir accès à; **"no ~"** «défense d'entrer»; AUT «sens interdit». || [in competition] inscription f. || [in dictionary] entrée f; [in diary, ledger] inscription f.

entry form n formulaire m OR feuille f d'inscription.

entry phone n portier m électronique.

envelop [ɪn'veləp] vt envelopper.

envelope ['envələup] n enveloppe f.

envious ['envɪəs] adj envieux(ieuse).

environment [ɪn'vaɪərənmənt] n [surroundings] milieu m, cadre m. || [natural world]: **the ~** l'environnement m.

environmental [ɪn,vaɪərən'mentl] adj [pollution, awareness] de l'environnement; [impact] sur l'environnement.

environmentally [ɪn,vaɪərən'mentəlɪ] adv [damaging] pour l'environnement; **~ friendly** qui préserve l'environnement.

envisage [ɪn'vɪzɪdʒ], **envision** Am [ɪn'vɪʒn] vt envisager.

envoy ['envɔɪ] n émissaire m.

envy ['envɪ] **1** n envie f, jalousie f. **2** vt envier; **to ~ sb sthg** envier qqch à qqn.

epic ['epɪk] **1** adj épique. **2** n épopée f.

epidemic [,epɪ'demɪk] n épidémie f.

epileptic [,epɪ'leptɪk] **1** adj épileptique. **2** n épileptique mf.

episode ['epɪsəud] n épisode m.

epistle [ɪ'pɪsl] n épître f.

epitaph ['epɪtɑːf] n épitaphe f.

epitome [ɪ'pɪtəmɪ] n: **the ~ of** le modèle de.

epitomize, -ise [ɪ'pɪtəmaɪz] vt incarner.

epoch ['iːpɒk] n époque f.

equal ['iːkwəl] **1** adj [gen]: **~ (to)** égal(e) (à). || [capable]: **~ to sthg** à la hauteur de qqch. **2** n égal m, -e f. **3** vt égaler.

equality [iː'kwɒlətɪ] n égalité f.

equalize, -ise ['iːkwəlaɪz] **1** vt niveler. **2** vi SPORT égaliser.

equalizer ['iːkwəlaɪzə^r] n SPORT but m égalisateur.

equally ['iːkwəlɪ] adv [important, stupid etc] tout aussi. || [in amount] en parts égales. || [also] en même temps.

equal opportunities npl égalité f des chances.

equate [ɪ'kweɪt] vt: **to ~ sthg with** assimiler qqch à.

equation [ɪ'kweɪʒn] n équation f.

equator [ɪ'kweɪtər] n: **the ~** l'équateur m.

equilibrium [,i:kwɪ'lɪbrɪəm] n équilibre m.

equip [ɪ'kwɪp] vt équiper; **to ~ sb/sthg with** équiper qqn/qqch de, munir qqn/ qqch de; **he's well equipped for the job** il est bien préparé pour ce travail.

equipment [ɪ'kwɪpmənt] n (U) équipement m, matériel m.

equities ['ekwətɪz] npl ST EX actions fpl ordinaires.

equivalent [ɪ'kwɪvələnt] **1** adj équivalent(e); **to be ~ to** être équivalent à, équivaloir à. **2** n équivalent m.

er [ɜːr] excl euh!

era ['ɪərə] (pl -s) n ère f, période f.

eradicate [ɪ'rædɪkeɪt] vt éradiquer.

erase [ɪ'reɪz] vt [rub out] gommer. || fig [memory] effacer; [hunger, poverty] éliminer.

eraser [ɪ'reɪzər] n gomme f.

erect [ɪ'rekt] **1** adj [person, posture] droit(e). || [penis] en érection. **2** vt [statue] ériger; [building] construire. || [tent] dresser.

erection [ɪ'rekʃn] n (U) [of statue] érection f; [of building] construction f. || [erect penis] érection f.

ERM (abbr of **Exchange Rate Mechanism**) n mécanisme m des changes (du SME).

erode [ɪ'rəʊd] **1** vt [rock, soil] éroder. || fig [confidence, rights] réduire. **2** vi [rock, soil] s'éroder. || fig [confidence] diminuer; [rights] se réduire.

erosion [ɪ'rəʊʒn] n [of rock, soil] érosion f. || fig [of confidence] baisse f; [of rights] diminution f.

erotic [ɪ'rɒtɪk] adj érotique.

err [ɜːr] vi se tromper.

errand ['erənd] n course f, commission f; **to go on** OR **run an ~** faire une course.

erratic [ɪ'rætɪk] adj irrégulier(ière).

error ['erər] n erreur f; **a spelling/ typing ~** une faute d'orthographe/de frappe.

erupt [ɪ'rʌpt] vi [volcano] entrer en éruption.

eruption [ɪ'rʌpʃn] n [of volcano] éruption f.

escalate ['eskəleɪt] vi [conflict] s'intensifier. || [costs] monter en flèche.

escalator ['eskəleɪtər] n escalier m roulant.

escapade [,eskə'peɪd] n aventure f, exploit m.

escape [ɪ'skeɪp] **1** n [gen] fuite f, évasion f; **to make one's ~** s'échapper; **to have a lucky ~** l'échapper belle. || [leakage - of gas, water] fuite f. **2** vt échapper à. **3** vi [gen] s'échapper, fuir; [from prison] s'évader; **to ~ from** [place] s'échapper de; [danger, person] échapper à. || [survive] s'en tirer.

escapism [ɪ'skeɪpɪzm] n (U) évasion f (de la réalité).

escort [n 'eskɔːt, vb ɪ'skɔːt] **1** n [guard] escorte f; **under ~** sous escorte. || [companion - male] cavalier m; [- female] hôtesse f. **2** vt escorter, accompagner.

Eskimo ['eskɪməʊ] (pl -s) n [person] Esquimau m, -aude f.

espadrille [,espə'drɪl] n espadrille f.

especially [ɪ'speʃəlɪ] adv [in particular] surtout. || [more than usually] particulièrement. || [specifically] spécialement.

espionage ['espɪə,nɑːʒ] n espionnage m.

esplanade [,esplə'neɪd] n esplanade f.

Esquire [ɪ'skwaɪər] n: **G. Curry ~** Monsieur G. Curry.

essay ['eseɪ] n SCH & UNIV dissertation f. || LITERATURE essai m.

essence ['esns] n [nature] essence f, nature f; **in ~** par essence. || CULIN extrait m.

essential [ɪ'senʃl] adj [absolutely necessary]: **~ (to** OR **for)** indispensable (à). || [basic] essentiel(ielle), de base. ○ **essentials** npl [basic commodities] produits mpl de première nécessité. || [most important elements] essentiel m.

essentially [ɪ'senʃəlɪ] adv fondamentalement, avant tout.

establish [ɪ'stæblɪʃ] vt [gen] établir. || [organization, business] fonder, créer.

establishment [ɪ'stæblɪʃmənt] n [gen] établissement m. || [of organization, business] fondation f, création f. ○ **Establishment** n [status quo]: **the Establishment** l'ordre m établi, l'Establishment m.

estate [ɪ'steɪt] n [land, property] propriété f, domaine m. || **(housing) ~** lotissement m. || **(industrial) ~** zone f industrielle. || JUR [inheritance] biens mpl.

esteem [ɪ'stiːm] **1** n estime f. **2** vt estimer.

esthetic etc Am = **aesthetic** etc.

estimate [n 'estɪmət, vb 'estɪmeɪt] **1** n [calculation, judgment] estimation f, évaluation f. || COMM devis m. **2** vt estimer, évaluer.

estimation [ˌestɪˈmeɪʃn] *n* [opinion] opinion *f*. || [calculation] estimation *f*, évaluation *f*.

Estonia [eˈstəʊnɪə] *n* Estonie *f*.

estranged [ɪˈstreɪndʒd] *adj* [couple] séparé(e); [husband, wife] dont on s'est séparé.

estuary [ˈestjʊərɪ] *n* estuaire *m*.

etc. (*abbr of* **et cetera**) etc.

etching [ˈetʃɪŋ] *n* gravure *f* à l'eau forte.

eternal [ɪˈtɜːnl] *adj* [life] éternel(elle). || *fig* [complaints, whining] sempiternel(elle). || [truth, value] immuable.

eternity [ɪˈtɜːnətɪ] *n* éternité *f*.

ethic [ˈeθɪk] *n* éthique *f*, morale *f*. ○ **ethics** 1 *n* (*U*) [study] éthique *f*, morale *f*. 2 *npl* [morals] morale *f*.

ethical [ˈeθɪkl] *adj* moral(e).

Ethiopia [ˌiːθɪˈəʊpɪə] *n* Éthiopie *f*.

ethnic [ˈeθnɪk] *adj* [traditions, groups] ethnique. || [clothes] folklorique.

etiquette [ˈetɪket] *n* convenances *fpl*, étiquette *f*.

eulogy [ˈjuːlədʒɪ] *n* panégyrique *m*.

euphemism [ˈjuːfəmɪzm] *n* euphémisme *m*.

euphoria [juːˈfɔːrɪə] *n* euphorie *f*.

Euro MP *n* député *m* européen.

Europe [ˈjʊərəp] *n* Europe *f*.

European [ˌjʊərəˈpiːən] 1 *adj* européen(enne). 2 *n* Européen *m*, -enne *f*.

European Community *n*: the ~ la Communauté européenne.

European Monetary System *n*: the ~ le Système monétaire européen.

European Parliament *n*: the ~ le Parlement européen.

euthanasia [ˌjuːθəˈneɪzjə] *n* euthanasie *f*.

evacuate [ɪˈvækjʊeɪt] *vt* évacuer.

evade [ɪˈveɪd] *vt* [gen] échapper à. || [issue, question] esquiver, éluder.

evaluate [ɪˈvæljʊeɪt] *vt* évaluer.

evaporate [ɪˈvæpəreɪt] *vi* [liquid] s'évaporer. || *fig* [hopes, fears] s'envoler; [confidence] disparaître.

evaporated milk [ɪˈvæpəreɪtɪd-] *n* lait *m* condensé (non sucré).

evasion [ɪˈveɪʒn] *n* [of responsibility] dérobade *f*. || [lie] faux-fuyant *m*.

evasive [ɪˈveɪsɪv] *adj* évasif(ive); **to take ~ action** faire une manœuvre d'évitement.

eve [iːv] *n* veille *f*.

even [ˈiːvn] 1 *adj* [speed, rate] régulier(ière); [temperature, temperament] égal(e). || [flat, level] plat(e), régu-

lier(ière). || [equal - contest] équilibré(e); [- teams, players] de la même force; [- scores] à égalité; **to get ~ with sb** se venger de qqn. || [not odd - number] pair(e). 2 *adv* [gen] même; **~ now** encore maintenant; **~ then** même alors. || [in comparisons]: **~ bigger/better/more stupid** encore plus grand/mieux/plus bête. ○ **even if** *conj* même si. ○ **even so** *adv* quand même. ○ **even though** *conj* bien que (+ *subjunctive*). ○ **even out** 1 *vt sep* égaliser. 2 *vi* s'égaliser.

evening [ˈiːvnɪŋ] *n* soir *m*; [duration, entertainment] soirée *f*; **in the ~** le soir. ○ **evenings** *adv Am* le soir.

evening class *n* cours *m* du soir.

evening dress *n* [worn by man] habit *m* de soirée; [worn by woman] robe *f* du soir.

event [ɪˈvent] *n* [happening] événement *m*. || SPORT épreuve *f*. || [case]: **in the ~ of** en cas de; **in the ~ that** au cas où. ○ **in any event** *adv* en tout cas, de toute façon.

eventful [ɪˈventfʊl] *adj* mouvementé(e).

eventual [ɪˈventʃʊəl] *adj* final(e).

eventuality [ɪˌventʃʊˈælətɪ] *n* éventualité *f*.

eventually [ɪˈventʃʊəlɪ] *adv* finalement, en fin de compte.

ever [ˈevə[r]] *adv* [at any time] jamais; **have you ~ been to Paris?** êtes-vous déjà allé à Paris? **I hardly ~ see him** je ne le vois presque jamais. || [all the time] toujours; **as ~** comme toujours; **for ~** pour toujours. || [for emphasis]: **~ so** tellement; **~ such** vraiment; **why/how ~ ?** pourquoi/comment donc? ○ **ever since** 1 *adv* depuis (ce moment-là). 2 *conj* depuis que. 3 *prep* depuis.

evergreen [ˈevəgriːn] *n* arbre *m* à feuilles persistantes.

everlasting [ˌevəˈlɑːstɪŋ] *adj* éternel(elle).

every [ˈevrɪ] *adj* chaque; **~ morning** chaque matin, tous les matins. ○ **every now and then, every so often** *adv* de temps en temps, de temps à autre. ○ **every other** *adj*: **~ other day** tous les deux jours, un jour sur deux; **~ other street** une rue sur deux. ○ **every which way** *adv Am* partout, de tous côtés.

everybody [ˈevrɪˌbɒdɪ] = **everyone**.

everyday [ˈevrɪdeɪ] *adj* quotidien(ienne).

everyone [ˈevrɪwʌn] *pron* chacun, tout le monde.

everyplace *Am* = everywhere.

everything ['evrɪθɪŋ] *pron* tout.

everywhere ['evrɪweəʳ], **everyplace** *Am* ['evrɪ,pleɪs] *adv* partout.

evict [ɪ'vɪkt] *vt* expulser.

evidence ['evɪdəns] *n* (U) [proof] preuve *f*. || JUR [of witness] témoignage *m*; **to give** ~ témoigner.

evident ['evɪdənt] *adj* évident(e), manifeste.

evidently ['evɪdəntlɪ] *adv* [seemingly] apparemment. || [obviously] de toute évidence, manifestement.

evil ['i:vl] 1 *adj* [person] mauvais(e), malveillant(e). 2 *n* mal *m*.

evoke [ɪ'vəʊk] *vt* [memory] évoquer; [emotion, response] susciter.

evolution [,i:və'lu:ʃn] *n* évolution *f*.

evolve [ɪ'vɒlv] *vi*: **to** ~ **(into/from)** se développer (en/à partir de).

ewe [ju:] *n* brebis *f*.

ex- [eks] *prefix* ex-.

exacerbate [ɪg'zæsəbeɪt] *vt* [feeling] exacerber; [problems] aggraver.

exact [ɪg'zækt] 1 *adj* exact(e), précis(e). 2 *vt*: **to** ~ **sthg (from)** exiger qqch (de).

exacting [ɪg'zæktɪŋ] *adj* [job, standards] astreignant(e); [person] exigeant(e).

exactly [ɪg'zæktlɪ] 1 *adv* exactement. 2 *excl* exactement!, parfaitement!

exaggerate [ɪg'zædʒəreɪt] *vt & vi* exagérer.

exaggeration [ɪg,zædʒə'reɪʃn] *n* exagération *f*.

exam [ɪg'zæm] *n* examen *m*; **to take** OR **sit an** ~ passer un examen.

examination [ɪg,zæmɪ'neɪʃn] *n* examen *m*.

examine [ɪg'zæmɪn] *vt* [gen] examiner; [passport] contrôler. || JUR, SCH & UNIV interroger.

examiner [ɪg'zæmɪnəʳ] *n* examinateur *m*, -trice *f*.

example [ɪg'zɑ:mpl] *n* exemple *m*; **for** ~ par exemple.

exasperate [ɪg'zæspəreɪt] *vt* exaspérer.

exasperation [ɪg,zæspə'reɪʃn] *n* exaspération *f*.

excavate ['ekskəveɪt] *vt* [land] creuser. || [object] déterrer.

exceed [ɪk'si:d] *vt* [amount, number] excéder. || [limit, expectations] dépasser.

exceedingly [ɪk'si:dɪŋlɪ] *adv* extrêmement.

excel [ɪk'sel] *vi*: **to** ~ **(in** OR **at)** exceller (dans); **to** ~ **o.s.** *Br* se surpasser.

excellence ['eksələns] *n* excellence *f*, supériorité *f*.

excellent ['eksələnt] *adj* excellent(e).

except [ɪk'sept] 1 *prep & conj*: ~ **(for)** à part, sauf. 2 *vt*: **to** ~ **sb (from)** exclure qqn (de).

excepting [ɪk'septɪŋ] *prep & conj* = except.

exception [ɪk'sepʃn] *n* [exclusion]: ~ **(to)** exception *f* (à); **with the** ~ **of** à l'exception de. || [offence]: **to take** ~ **to** s'offenser de, se froisser de.

exceptional [ɪk'sepʃənl] *adj* exceptionnel(elle).

excerpt ['eksɜ:pt] *n*: ~ **(from)** extrait *m* (de), passage *m* (de).

excess [ɪk'ses, *before nouns* 'ekses] 1 *adj* excédentaire. 2 *n* excès *m*.

excess baggage *n* excédent *m* de bagages.

excessive [ɪk'sesɪv] *adj* excessif(ive).

exchange [ɪks'tʃeɪndʒ] 1 *n* [gen] échange *m*; **in** ~ **(for)** en échange (de). || TELEC: **(telephone)** ~ central *m* (téléphonique). 2 *vt* [swap] échanger; **to** ~ **sthg for sthg** échanger qqch contre qqch.

exchange rate *n* FIN taux *m* de change.

excise ['eksaɪz] *n* (U) contributions *fpl* indirectes.

excite [ɪk'saɪt] *vt* exciter.

excited [ɪk'saɪtɪd] *adj* excité(e).

excitement [ɪk'saɪtmənt] *n* [state] excitation *f*.

exciting [ɪk'saɪtɪŋ] *adj* passionnant(e); [prospect] excitant(e).

exclaim [ɪk'skleɪm] 1 *vt* s'écrier. 2 *vi* s'exclamer.

exclamation [,eksklə'meɪʃn] *n* exclamation *f*.

exclamation mark *Br*, **exclamation point** *Am n* point *m* d'exclamation.

exclude [ɪk'sklu:d] *vt*: **to** ~ **sb/sthg (from)** exclure qqn/qqch (de).

excluding [ɪk'sklu:dɪŋ] *prep* sans compter, à l'exclusion de.

exclusive [ɪk'sklu:sɪv] 1 *adj* [high-class] fermé(e). || [unique - use, news story] exclusif(ive). 2 *n* PRESS exclusivité *f*. ○ **exclusive of** *prep*: ~ **of interest** intérêts non compris.

excrement ['ekskrɪmənt] *n* excrément *m*.

excruciating [ɪk'skru:ʃɪeɪtɪŋ] *adj* atroce.

excursion [ɪk'skɜːʃn] *n* [trip] excursion *f.*

excuse [*n* ɪk'skjuːs, *vb* ɪk'skjuːz] 1 *n* excuse *f.* 2 *vt* [gen] excuser; **to ~ sb for sthg/for doing sthg** excuser qqn de qqch/de faire qqch; **~ me** [to attract attention] excusez-moi; [forgive me] pardon, excusez-moi; *Am* [sorry] pardon. || [let off]: **to ~ sb (from)** dispenser qqn (de).

execute ['eksɪkjuːt] *vt* exécuter.

execution [,eksɪ'kjuːʃn] *n* exécution *f.*

executioner [,eksɪ'kjuːʃnər] *n* bourreau *m.*

executive [ɪg'zekjʊtɪv] 1 *adj* [power, board] exécutif(ive). 2 *n* COMM cadre *m.* || [of government] exécutif *m.*

executive director *n* cadre *m* supérieur.

executor [ɪg'zekjʊtər] *n* exécuteur *m* testamentaire.

exemplify [ɪg'zemplɪfaɪ] *vt* [typify] exemplifier. || [give example of] exemplifier, illustrer.

exempt [ɪg'zempt] 1 *adj*: **~ (from)** exempt(e) (de). 2 *vt*: **to ~ sb (from)** exempter qqn (de).

exercise ['eksəsaɪz] 1 *n* exercice *m.* 2 *vt* [gen] exercer. 3 *vi* prendre de l'exercice.

exercise book *n* [notebook] cahier *m* d'exercices; [published book] livre *m* d'exercices.

exert [ɪg'zɜːt] *vt* exercer; [strength] employer; **to ~ o.s.** se donner du mal.

exertion [ɪg'zɜːʃn] *n* effort *m.*

exhale [eks'heɪl] *vi* expirer.

exhaust [ɪg'zɔːst] 1 *n* (*U*) [fumes] gaz *mpl* d'échappement. || **~ (pipe)** pot *m* d'échappement. 2 *vt* épuiser.

exhausted [ɪg'zɔːstɪd] *adj* épuisé(e).

exhausting [ɪg'zɔːstɪŋ] *adj* épuisant(e).

exhaustion [ɪg'zɔːstʃn] *n* épuisement *m.*

exhaustive [ɪg'zɔːstɪv] *adj* complet(ète), exhaustif(ive).

exhibit [ɪg'zɪbɪt] 1 *n* ART objet *m* exposé. || JUR pièce *f* à conviction. 2 *vt* [demonstrate - feeling] montrer; [- skill] faire preuve de. || ART exposer.

exhibition [,eksɪ'bɪʃn] *n* ART exposition *f.* || [of feeling] démonstration *f.*

exhilarating [ɪg'zɪləreɪtɪŋ] *adj* [experience] grisant(e); [walk] vivifiant(e).

exile ['eksaɪl] 1 *n* [condition] exil *m*; **in ~** en exil. || [person] exilé *m*, -e *f.* 2 *vt*: **to ~ sb (from/to)** exiler qqn (de/vers).

exist [ɪg'zɪst] *vi* exister.

existence [ɪg'zɪstəns] *n* existence *f*; **in ~** qui existe, existant(e); **to come into ~** naître.

existing [ɪg'zɪstɪŋ] *adj* existant(e).

exit ['eksɪt] 1 *n* sortie *f.* 2 *vi* sortir.

exodus ['eksədəs] *n* exode *m.*

exonerate [ɪg'zɒnəreɪt] *vt*: **to ~ sb (from)** disculper qqn (de).

exorbitant [ɪg'zɔːbɪtənt] *adj* exorbitant(e).

exotic [ɪg'zɒtɪk] *adj* exotique.

expand [ɪk'spænd] 1 *vt* [production, influence] accroître; [business, department, area] développer. 2 *vi* [population, influence] s'accroître; [business, department, market] se développer; [metal] se dilater. ○ **expand (up)on** *vt fus* développer.

expanse [ɪk'spæns] *n* étendue *f.*

expansion [ɪk'spænʃn] *n* [of production, population] accroissement *m*; [of business, department, area] développement *m*; [of metal] dilatation *f.*

expect [ɪk'spekt] 1 *vt* [anticipate] s'attendre à; [event, letter, baby] attendre; **to ~ sb to do sthg** s'attendre à ce que qqn fasse qqch. || [count on] compter sur. || [demand] exiger, demander; **to ~ sb to do sthg** attendre de qqn qu'il fasse qqch. || [suppose] supposer; **I ~ so** je crois que oui. 2 *vi* [anticipate]: **to ~ to do sthg** compter faire qqch. || [be pregnant]: **to be ~ing** être enceinte, attendre un bébé.

expectant [ɪk'spektənt] *adj* qui est dans l'expectative.

expectant mother *n* femme *f* enceinte.

expectation [,ekspek'teɪʃn] *n* [hope] espoir *m*, attente *f.* || [belief]: **it's my ~ that ...** à mon avis, ...; **against all ~** OR **~s, contrary to all ~** OR **~s** contre toute attente.

expedient [ɪk'spiːdjənt] *fml* 1 *adj* indiqué(e). 2 *n* expédient *m.*

expedition [,ekspɪ'dɪʃn] *n* expédition *f.*

expel [ɪk'spel] *vt* [gen] expulser. || SCH renvoyer.

expend [ɪk'spend] *vt*: **to ~ time/money (on)** consacrer du temps/de l'argent (à).

expendable [ɪk'spendəbl] *adj* dont on peut se passer, qui n'est pas indispensable.

expenditure [ɪk'spendɪtʃər] *n* (*U*) dépense *f.*

expense [ɪk'spens] *n* [amount spent] dépense *f.* || (*U*) [cost] frais *mpl*; **at the ~ of**

au prix de; **at sb's ~** [financial] aux frais de qqn; *fig* aux dépens de qqn. ○ **expenses** *npl* COMM frais *mpl*.

expense account *n* frais *mpl* de représentation.

expensive [ɪk'spensɪv] *adj* [financially - gen] cher (chère), coûteux(euse); [- tastes] dispendieux(ieuse). || [mistake] qui coûte cher.

experience [ɪk'spɪərɪəns] **1** *n* expérience *f*. **2** *vt* [difficulty] connaître; [loss, change] subir.

experienced [ɪk'spɪərɪənst] *adj* expérimenté(e).

experiment [ɪk'sperɪmənt] **1** *n* expérience *f*. **2** *vi*: **to ~ (with sthg)** expérimenter (qqch).

expert ['ekspɜːt] **1** *adj* expert(e); [advice] d'expert. **2** *n* expert *m*, -e *f*.

expertise [ˌekspɜː'tiːz] *n* (*U*) compétence *f*.

expire [ɪk'spaɪər] *vi* expirer.

expiry [ɪk'spaɪərɪ] *n* expiration *f*.

explain [ɪk'spleɪn] **1** *vt* expliquer; **to ~ sthg to sb** expliquer qqch à qqn. **2** *vi* s'expliquer; **to ~ to sb (about sthg)** expliquer (qqch) à qqn.

explanation [ˌeksplə'neɪʃn] *n*: **~ (for)** explication *f* (de).

explicit [ɪk'splɪsɪt] *adj* explicite.

explode [ɪk'spləʊd] **1** *vt* [bomb] faire exploser. **2** *vi* lit & fig exploser.

exploit [*n* 'eksplɔɪt, *vb* ɪk'splɔɪt] **1** *n* exploit *m*. **2** *vt* exploiter.

exploitation [ˌeksplɔɪ'teɪʃn] *n* (*U*) exploitation *f*.

exploration [ˌeksplə'reɪʃn] *n* exploration *f*.

explore [ɪk'splɔːr] *vt & vi* explorer.

explorer [ɪk'splɔːrər] *n* explorateur *m*, -trice *f*.

explosion [ɪk'spləʊʒn] *n* explosion *f*.

explosive [ɪk'spləʊsɪv] **1** *adj* lit & fig explosif(ive). **2** *n* explosif *m*.

exponent [ɪk'spəʊnənt] *n* [of theory] défenseur *m*.

export [*n & comp* 'ekspɔːt, *vb* ɪk'spɔːt] **1** *n* exportation *f*. **2** *vt* exporter.

exporter [ek'spɔːtər] *n* exportateur *m*, -trice *f*.

expose [ɪk'spəʊz] *vt* [uncover] exposer, découvrir; **to be ~d to sthg** être exposé à qqch. || [unmask - corruption] révéler; [- person] démasquer.

exposed [ɪk'spəʊzd] *adj* [land, house, position] exposé(e).

exposure [ɪk'spəʊʒər] *n* [to light, radiation] exposition *f*. || MED: **to die of ~** mourir de froid. || [PHOT - time] temps *m* de pose; [- photograph] pose *f*. || (*U*) [publicity] publicité *f*; [coverage] couverture *f*.

exposure meter *n* posemètre *m*.

express [ɪk'spres] **1** *adj* [train, coach] express (*inv*). || *fml* [specific] exprès(esse). **2** *n* [train] rapide *m*, express *m*. **3** *vt* exprimer.

expression [ɪk'spreʃn] *n* expression *f*.

expressive [ɪk'spresɪv] *adj* expressif(ive).

expressly [ɪk'spreslɪ] *adv* expressément.

expressway [ɪk'spresweɪ] *n* Am voie *f* express.

exquisite [ɪk'skwɪzɪt] *adj* exquis(e).

ext., extn. (*abbr of* extension): **~ 4174** p. 4174.

extend [ɪk'stend] **1** *vt* [enlarge - building] agrandir. || [make longer - gen] prolonger; [- visa] proroger; [- deadline] repousser. || [expand - rules, law] étendre (la portée de); [- power] accroître. || [offer - help] apporter, offrir; [- credit] accorder. **2** *vi* [stretch - in space] s'étendre; [- in time] continuer.

extension [ɪk'stenʃn] *n* [to building] agrandissement *m*. || [lengthening - gen] prolongement *m*; [- of visit] prolongation *f*; [- of visa] prorogation *f*; [- of deadline] report *m*. || [of power] accroissement *m*; [of law] élargissement *m*. || TELEC poste *m*. || ELEC prolongateur *m*.

extension cable *n* rallonge *f*.

extensive [ɪk'stensɪv] *adj* [in amount] considérable. || [in area] vaste. || [in range - discussions] approfondi(e); [- changes, use] considérable.

extensively [ɪk'stensɪvlɪ] *adv* [in amount] considérablement. || [in range] abondamment, largement.

extent [ɪk'stent] *n* [of land, area] étendue *f*, superficie *f*; [of problem, damage] étendue. || [degree]: **to what ~ ...?** dans quelle mesure ...?; **to the ~ that** [in so far as] dans la mesure où; [to the point where] au point que; **to a large** OR **great ~** en grande partie; **to some ~** en partie.

extenuating circumstances [ɪk'stenjʊeɪtɪŋ-] *npl* circonstances *fpl* atténuantes.

exterior [ɪk'stɪərɪər] **1** *adj* extérieur(e). **2** *n* [of house, car] extérieur *m*.

exterminate [ɪk'stɜːmɪneɪt] *vt* exterminer.

external [ɪk'stɜ:nl] *adj* externe.

extinct [ɪk'stɪŋkt] *adj* [species] disparu(e). || [volcano] éteint(e).

extinguish [ɪk'stɪŋgwɪʃ] *vt* [fire, cigarette] éteindre.

extinguisher [ɪk'stɪŋgwɪʃər] *n* extincteur *m*.

extn. = ext.

extol, extoll *Am* [ɪk'stəʊl] *vt* louer.

extort [ɪk'stɔ:t] *vt*: **to ~ sthg from sb** extorquer qqch à qqn.

extortionate [ɪk'stɔ:ʃnət] *adj* exorbitant(e).

extra ['ekstrə] **1** *adj* supplémentaire. **2** *n* [addition] supplément *m*; **optional ~** option *f*. || CINEMA & THEATRE figurant *m*, -e *f*. **3** *adv* [hard, big etc] extra; [pay, charge etc] en plus.

extra- ['ekstrə] *prefix* extra-.

extract [*n* 'ekstrækt, *vb* ɪk'strækt] **1** *n* extrait *m*. **2** *vt* [take out - tooth] arracher; **to ~ sthg from** tirer qqch de. || [confession, information]: **to ~ sthg (from sb)** arracher qqch (à qqn), tirer qqch (de qqn). || [coal, oil] extraire.

extradite ['ekstrədaɪt] *vt*: **to ~ sb (from/to)** extrader qqn (de/vers).

extramarital [ˌekstrə'mærɪtl] *adj* extraconjugal(e).

extramural [ˌekstrə'mjʊərəl] *adj* UNIV hors faculté.

extraordinary [ɪk'strɔ:dnrɪ] *adj* extraordinaire.

extravagance [ɪk'strævəgəns] *n* (*U*) [excessive spending] gaspillage *m*, prodigalités *fpl*. || [luxury] extravagance *f*, folie *f*.

extravagant [ɪk'strævəgənt] *adj* [wasteful - person] dépensier(ière); [- use, tastes] dispendieux(ieuse). || [elaborate, exaggerated] extravagant(e).

extreme [ɪk'stri:m] **1** *adj* extrême. **2** *n* extrême *m*.

extremely [ɪk'stri:mlɪ] *adv* extrêmement.

extremist [ɪk'stri:mɪst] *n* extrémiste *mf*.

extricate ['ekstrɪkeɪt] *vt*: **to ~ sthg (from)** dégager qqch (de); **to ~ o.s. (from)** [from seat belt etc] s'extirper (de); [from difficult situation] se tirer (de).

extrovert ['ekstrəvɜ:t] **1** *adj* extraverti(e). **2** *n* extraverti *m*, -e *f*.

exuberance [ɪg'zju:bərəns] *n* exubérance *f*.

eye [aɪ] (*cont* eyeing OR eying) **1** *n* [gen] œil *m*; **to catch sb's ~** attirer l'attention de qqn; **to have one's ~ on sb** avoir qqn à l'œil; **to have one's ~ on sthg** avoir repéré qqch; **to keep one's ~s open for sthg** [try to find] essayer de repérer qqch; **to keep an ~ on sthg** surveiller qqch, garder l'œil sur qqch. || [of needle] chas *m*. **2** *vt* regarder, reluquer.

eyeball ['aɪbɔ:l] *n* globe *m* oculaire.

eyebrow ['aɪbraʊ] *n* sourcil *m*.

eyebrow pencil *n* crayon *m* à sourcils.

eyedrops ['aɪdrɒps] *npl* gouttes *fpl* pour les yeux.

eyelash ['aɪlæʃ] *n* cil *m*.

eyelid ['aɪlɪd] *n* paupière *f*.

eyeliner ['aɪ,laɪnər] *n* eye-liner *m*.

eye-opener *n inf* révélation *f*.

eye shadow *n* fard *m* à paupières.

eyesight ['aɪsaɪt] *n* vue *f*.

eyesore ['aɪsɔ:r] *n* horreur *f*.

eyestrain ['aɪstreɪn] *n* fatigue *f* des yeux.

eyewitness [ˌaɪ'wɪtnɪs] *n* témoin *m* oculaire.

f (*pl* **f's** OR **fs**), **F** (*pl* **F's** OR **Fs**) [ef] *n* [letter] f *m inv*, F *m inv*. ○ **F** *n* MUS fa *m*. || (*abbr of* **Fahrenheit**) F.

fable ['feɪbl] *n* fable *f*.

fabric ['fæbrɪk] *n* [cloth] tissu *m*. || [of building, society] structure *f*.

fabrication [ˌfæbrɪ'keɪʃn] *n* [lie, lying] fabrication *f*, invention *f*.

fabulous ['fæbjʊləs] *adj* [gen] fabuleux(euse). || *inf* [excellent] sensationnel(elle), fabuleux(euse).

facade [fə'sɑ:d] *n* façade *f*.

face [feɪs] **1** *n* [of person] visage *m*, figure *f*; **~ to ~** face à face. || [expression] visage *m*, mine *f*; **to make** OR **pull a ~** faire la grimace. || [of cliff, mountain] face *f*, paroi *f*; [of clock, watch] cadran *m*; [of coin, shape] face. || [surface - of planet] surface *f*; **on the ~ of it** à première vue. || [respect]: **to save/lose ~** sauver/perdre la face. **2** *vt* [look towards - subj: person] faire face à; **the house ~s the sea/south**

la maison donne sur la mer/est orientée vers le sud. || [decision, crisis] être confronté(e) à; [problem, danger] faire face à. || [facts, truth] faire face à, admettre. || *inf* [cope with] affronter. ○ **face down** *adv* [person] face contre terre; [object] à l'envers; [card] face en dessous. ○ **face up** *adv* [person] sur le dos; [object] à l'endroit; [card] face en dessus. ○ **in the face of** *prep* devant. ○ **face up to** *vt fus* faire face à.

face cream *n* crème *f* pour le visage.

face-lift *n* lifting *m*; *fig* restauration *f*, rénovation *f*.

face powder *n* poudre *f* de riz, poudre pour le visage.

face-saving [-ˌseɪvɪŋ] *adj* qui sauve la face.

facet ['fæsɪt] *n* facette *f*.

facetious [fəˈsiːʃəs] *adj* facétieux(ieuse).

face value *n* [of coin, stamp] valeur *f* nominale; **to take sthg at ~** prendre qqch au pied de la lettre.

facility [fəˈsɪlətɪ] *n* [feature] fonction *f*. ○ **facilities** *npl* [amenities] équipement *m*, aménagement *m*.

facing ['feɪsɪŋ] *adj* d'en face; [sides] opposé(e).

facsimile [fækˈsɪmɪlɪ] *n* [fax] télécopie *f*, fax *m*. || [copy] fac-similé *m*.

fact [fækt] *n* [true piece of information] fait *m*. || (*U*) [truth] faits *mpl*, réalité *f*. ○ **in fact 1** *adv* de fait, effectivement. **2** *conj* en fait.

fact of life *n* fait *m*, réalité *f*; **the facts of life** *euphemism* les choses *fpl* de la vie.

factor ['fæktər] *n* facteur *m*.

factory ['fæktərɪ] *n* fabrique *f*, usine *f*.

factual ['fæktʃʊəl] *adj* factuel(elle), basé(e) sur les faits.

faculty ['fækltɪ] *n* [gen] faculté *f*. || *Am* [in college]: **the ~** le corps enseignant.

fad [fæd] *n* engouement *m*, mode *f*; [personal] marotte *f*.

fade [feɪd] **1** *vt* [jeans, curtains, paint] décolorer. **2** *vi* [jeans, curtains, paint] se décolorer; [colour] passer; [flower] se flétrir. || [light] baisser, diminuer. || [sound] diminuer, s'affaiblir. || [memory] s'effacer; [feeling, interest] diminuer.

faeces *Br*, **feces** *Am* ['fiːsiːz] *npl* fèces *fpl*.

fag [fæg] *n inf Am pej* [homosexual] pédé *m*.

Fahrenheit ['færənhaɪt] *adj* Fahrenheit (*inv*).

fail [feɪl] **1** *vt* [exam, test] rater, échouer à. || [not succeed]: **to ~ to do sthg** ne pas arriver à faire qqch. || [neglect]: **to ~ to do sthg** manquer OR omettre de faire qqch. || [candidate] refuser. **2** *vi* [not succeed] ne pas réussir OR y arriver. || [not pass exam] échouer. || [stop functioning] lâcher. || [weaken - health, daylight] décliner; [- eyesight] baisser.

failing ['feɪlɪŋ] **1** *n* [weakness] défaut *m*, point *m* faible. **2** *prep* à moins de; **~ that** à défaut.

failure ['feɪljər] *n* [lack of success, unsuccessful thing] échec *m*. || [person] raté *m*, -e *f*. || [of engine, brake etc] défaillance *f*.

faint [feɪnt] **1** *adj* [smell] léger(ère); [memory] vague; [sound, hope] faible. || [slight - chance] petit(e), faible. || [dizzy]: **I'm feeling a bit ~** je ne me sens pas bien. **2** *vi* s'évanouir.

fair [feər] **1** *adj* [just] juste, équitable. || [quite large] grand(e), important(e). || [quite good] assez bon (assez bonne). || [hair] blond(e). || [skin, complexion] clair(e). || [weather] beau (belle). **2** *n* [trade fair] foire *f*. **3** *adv* [fairly] loyalement.

fair-haired [-ˈheəd] *adj* [person] blond(e).

fairly ['feəlɪ] *adv* [rather] assez; **~ certain** presque sûr. || [justly] équitablement; [describe] avec impartialité; [fight, play] loyalement.

fairness ['feənɪs] *n* [justness] équité *f*.

fairy ['feərɪ] *n* [imaginary creature] fée *f*.

fairy tale *n* conte *m* de fées.

faith [feɪθ] *n* [belief] foi *f*, confiance *f*. || RELIG foi *f*.

faithful ['feɪθfʊl] *adj* fidèle.

faithfully ['feɪθfʊlɪ] *adv* [loyally] fidèlement.

fake [feɪk] **1** *adj* faux (fausse). **2** *n* [object, painting] faux *m*. || [person] imposteur *m*. **3** *vt* [results] falsifier; [signature] imiter. || [illness, emotions] simuler. **4** *vi* [pretend] simuler, faire semblant.

falcon ['fɔːlkən] *n* faucon *m*.

Falkland Islands ['fɔːklənd-], **Falklands** ['fɔːkləndz] *npl*: **the ~** les îles *fpl* Falkland, les Malouines *fpl*.

fall [fɔːl] (*pt* fell, *pp* fallen) **1** *vi* [gen] tomber; **to ~ flat** [joke] tomber à plat. || [decrease] baisser. || [become]: **to ~ asleep** s'endormir; **to ~ in love** tomber amoureux(euse). **2** *n* [gen]: **~ (in)** chute (de). || *Am* [autumn] automne *m*. ○ **falls** *npl* chutes *fpl*. ○ **fall apart** *vi* [disintegrate - book, chair] tomber en morceaux. || *fig* [country] tomber en ruine; [person] s'effondrer. ❍ **fall back on** *vt fus* [resort to] se rabattre sur. ❍ **fall behind** *vi* [in race] se faire distancer. || [with rent] être en retard; **to ~ behind with one's work** avoir du retard dans son travail. ❍ **fall for** *vt fus inf* [fall in love with] tomber amoureux(euse) de. || [trick, lie] se laisser prendre à. ❍ **fall in** *vi* [roof, ceiling] s'écrouler, s'affaisser. ❍ **fall off** *vi* [branch, handle] se détacher, tomber. || [demand, numbers] baisser, diminuer. ❍ **fall out** *vi* [hair, tooth] tomber. || [friends] se brouiller. ❍ **fall over** 1 *vt fus*: **to ~ over sthg** trébucher sur qqch et tomber. 2 *vi* [person, chair etc] tomber. ❍ **fall through** *vi* [plan, deal] échouer.

fallacy ['fæləsɪ] *n* erreur *f*, idée *f* fausse.

fallen ['fɔːln] *pp* → **fall**.

fallible ['fæləbl] *adj* faillible.

fallout ['fɔːlaʊt] *n* (*U*) [radiation] retombées *fpl*.

fallout shelter *n* abri *m* antiatomique.

fallow ['fæləʊ] *adj*: **to lie ~** être en jachère.

false [fɔːls] *adj* faux (fausse).

false alarm *n* fausse alerte *f*.

falsely ['fɔːlslɪ] *adv* à tort; [smile, laugh] faussement.

false teeth *npl* dentier *m*.

falsify ['fɔːlsɪfaɪ] *vt* falsifier.

falter ['fɔːltə*] *vi* [move unsteadily] chanceler. || [steps, voice] devenir hésitant(e). || [hesitate, lose confidence] hésiter.

fame [feɪm] *n* gloire *f*, renommée *f*.

familiar [fə'mɪljə*] *adj* familier(ière); **~ with sthg** familiarisé(e) avec qqch.

familiarity [fə,mɪlɪ'ærətɪ] *n* (*U*) [knowledge]: **~ with sthg** connaissance *f* de qqch, familiarité *f* avec qqch.

familiarize, -ise [fə'mɪljəraɪz] *vt*: **to ~ o.s. with sthg** se familiariser avec qqch.

family ['fæmlɪ] *n* famille *f*.

family doctor *n* médecin *m* de famille.

family planning *n* planning *m* familial; **~ clinic** centre *m* de planning familial.

famine ['fæmɪn] *n* famine *f*.

famished ['fæmɪʃt] *adj inf* [very hungry] affamé(e); **I'm ~!** je meurs de faim!

famous ['feɪməs] *adj*: **~ (for)** célèbre (pour).

famously ['feɪməslɪ] *adv dated*: **to get on** OR **along ~** s'entendre comme larrons en foire.

fan [fæn] 1 *n* [of paper, silk] éventail *m*. || [electric or mechanical] ventilateur *m*. || [enthusiast] fan *mf*. 2 *vt* [face] éventer. ❍ **fan out** *vi* se déployer.

fanatic [fə'nætɪk] *n* fanatique *mf*.

fan belt *n* courroie *f* de ventilateur.

fancy ['fænsɪ] 1 *adj* [elaborate - hat, clothes] extravagant(e); [- food, cakes] raffiné(e). || [expensive - restaurant, hotel] de luxe; [- prices] fantaisiste. 2 *n* [desire, liking] envie *f*, lubie *f*; **to take a ~ to sthg** prendre d'affection pour qqn; **to take a ~ to sthg** se mettre à aimer qqch; **to take sb's ~** faire envie à qqn, plaire à qqn. 3 *vt.inf* [want] avoir envie de; **to ~ doing sthg** avoir envie de faire qqch. || *inf* [like]: **I ~ her** elle me plaît. || [imagine]: **~ that!** ça alors!

fancy dress *n* (*U*) déguisement *m*.

fancy-dress party *n* bal *m* costumé.

fanfare ['fænfeə*] *n* fanfare *f*.

fang [fæŋ] *n* [of wolf] croc *m*; [of snake] crochet *m*.

fan heater *n* radiateur *m* soufflant.

fanny ['fænɪ] *n* Am inf [buttocks] fesses *fpl*.

fantasize, -ise ['fæntəsaɪz] *vi*: **to ~ (about sthg/about doing sthg)** fantasmer (sur qqch/sur le fait de faire qqch).

fantastic [fæn'tæstɪk] *adj inf* [wonderful] fantastique, formidable. || [incredible] extraordinaire, incroyable.

fantasy ['fæntəsɪ] *n* [dream, imaginary event] rêve *m*, fantasme *m*. || (*U*) [fiction] fiction *f*. || [imagination] fantaisie *f*.

fao (*abbr of* **for the attention of**) à l'attention de.

far [fɑː*] (*compar* **farther** OR **further**, *superl* **farthest** OR **furthest**) 1 *adv* [in distance] loin; **how ~ is it?** c'est à quelle distance?, (est-ce que) c'est loin?; **~ away** OR **off** loin; **as ~ as** jusqu'à. || [in time]: **~ away** OR **off** loin; **so ~** jusqu'à maintenant, jusqu'ici. || [in degree or extent] bien; **as ~ as** autant que; **as ~ as I'm concerned** en ce qui me concerne; **as ~ as possible** autant que possible, dans la mesure du possible; **~ and away, by ~** de loin; **~ from it** loin de là, au contraire. 2 *adj* [extreme]: **the ~ end of the street** l'autre bout de la rue; **the ~ right of the party** l'extrême droite du parti.

faraway ['fɑːrəweɪ] *adj* lointain(e).

farce [fɑːs] *n* THEATRE farce *f*. || *fig* [disaster] pagaille *f*, vaste rigolade *f*.

farcical ['fɑːsɪkl] *adj* grotesque.

fare

fare [feə^r] *n* [payment] prix *m*, tarif *m*. || *dated* [food] nourriture *f*.

Far East *n*: the ~ l'Extrême-Orient *m*.

farewell [ˌfeə'wel] **1** *n* adieu *m*. **2** *excl literary* adieu!

farm [fɑːm] **1** *n* ferme *f*. **2** *vt* cultiver.

farmer ['fɑːmə^r] *n* fermier *m*.

farmhand ['fɑːmhænd] *n* ouvrier *m*, -ière *f* agricole.

farmhouse ['fɑːmhaus, *pl* -hauzɪz] *n* ferme *f*.

farming ['fɑːmɪŋ] *n* (*U*) agriculture *f*; [of animals] élevage *m*.

farm labourer = farmhand.

farmland ['fɑːmlænd] *n* (*U*) terres *fpl* cultivées OR arables.

farmstead ['fɑːmsted] *n Am* ferme *f*.

farm worker = farmhand.

farmyard ['fɑːmjɑːd] *n* cour *f* de ferme.

far-reaching [-'riːtʃɪŋ] *adj* d'une grande portée.

farsighted [ˌfɑː'saɪtɪd] *adj* [person] prévoyant(e); [plan] élaboré(e) avec clairvoyance. || *Am* [longsighted] hypermétrope.

fart [fɑːt] *v inf* **1** *n* [air] pet *m*. **2** *vi* péter.

farther ['fɑːðə^r] *compar* → far.

farthest ['fɑːðəst] *superl* → far.

fascinate ['fæsɪneɪt] *vt* fasciner.

fascinating ['fæsɪneɪtɪŋ] *adj* [person, country] fascinant(e); [job] passionnant(e); [idea, thought] très intéressant(e).

fascination [ˌfæsɪ'neɪʃn] *n* fascination *f*.

fascism ['fæʃɪzm] *n* fascisme *m*.

fashion ['fæʃn] *n* [clothing, style] mode *f*; **to be in/out of ~** être/ne plus être à la mode. || [manner] manière *f*.

fashionable ['fæʃnəbl] *adj* à la mode.

fashion show *n* défilé *m* de mode.

fast [fɑːst] **1** *adj* [rapid] rapide. || [clock, watch] qui avance. **2** *adv* [rapidly] vite. || [firmly] solidement; **to hold ~ to sthg** *lit* & *fig* s'accrocher à qqch; **~ asleep** profondément endormi. **3** *n* jeûne *m*. **4** *vi* jeûner.

fasten ['fɑːsn] **1** *vt* [jacket, bag] fermer; [seat belt] attacher; **to ~ sthg to sthg** attacher qqch à qqch. **2** *vi*: **to ~ on to sb/sthg** se cramponner à qqn/qqch.

fastener ['fɑːsnə^r] *n* [of bag, necklace] fermoir *m*; [of dress] fermeture *f*.

fastening ['fɑːsnɪŋ] *n* fermeture *f*.

fast food *n* fast food *m*.

fat [fæt] **1** *adj* [overweight] gros (grosse), gras (grasse); **to get ~** grossir. || [not lean]

- meat] gras (grasse). **2** *n* [flesh, on meat, in food] graisse *f*. || (*U*) [for cooking] matière *f* grasse.

fatal ['feɪtl] *adj* [serious - mistake] fatal(e); [- decision, words] fatidique. || [accident, illness] mortel(elle).

fatality [fə'tælətɪ] *n* [accident victim] mort *m*.

fate [feɪt] *n* [destiny] destin *m*; **to tempt ~** tenter le diable. || [result, end] sort *m*.

fateful ['feɪtful] *adj* fatidique.

father ['fɑːðə^r] *n* père *m*.

father-in-law (*pl* **father-in-laws** OR **fathers-in-law**) *n* beau-père *m*.

fatherly ['fɑːðəlɪ] *adj* paternel(elle).

fathom ['fæðəm] **1** *n* brasse *f*. **2** *vt*: **to ~ sb/sthg (out)** comprendre qqn/qqch.

fatigue [fə'tiːg] *n* [exhaustion] épuisement *m*. || [in metal] fatigue *f*.

fatten ['fætn] *vt* engraisser.

fattening ['fætnɪŋ] *adj* qui fait grossir.

fatty ['fætɪ] **1** *adj* gras (grasse). **2** *n inf pej* gros *m*, grosse *f*.

faucet ['fɔːsɪt] *n Am* robinet *m*.

fault ['fɔːlt] **1** *n* [responsibility, in tennis] faute *f*; **it's my ~** c'est de ma faute. || [mistake, imperfection] défaut *m*; **to find ~ with sb/sthg** critiquer qqn/qqch; **at ~** fautif(ive). || GEOL faille *f*. **2** *vt*: **to ~ sb (on sthg)** prendre qqn en défaut (sur qqch).

faultless ['fɔːltlɪs] *adj* impeccable.

faulty ['fɔːltɪ] *adj* défectueux(euse).

fauna ['fɔːnə] *n* faune *f*.

favour *Br*, **favor** *Am* ['feɪvə^r] **1** *n* [approval] faveur *f*, approbation *f*; **in sb's ~** en faveur de qqn; **to be in/out of ~ with sb** avoir/ne pas avoir les faveurs de qqn, avoir/ne pas avoir la cote avec qqn. || [kind act] service *m*; **to do sb a ~** rendre (un) service à qqn. **2** *vt* [prefer] préférer, privilégier. || [treat better, help] favoriser. O **in favour** *adv* [in agreement] pour, d'accord. O **in favour of** *prep* [in preference to] au profit de. || [in agreement with]: **to be in ~ of sthg/of doing sthg** être partisan(e) de qqch/de faire qqch.

favourable *Br*, **favorable** *Am* ['feɪvrəbl] *adj* [positive] favorable.

favourite *Br*, **favorite** *Am* ['feɪvrɪt] **1** *adj* favori(ite). **2** *n* favori *m*, -ite *f*.

favouritism *Br*, **favoritism** *Am* ['feɪvrɪtɪzm] *n* favoritisme *m*.

fawn [fɔːn] **1** *adj* fauve (*inv*). **2** *n* [animal] faon *m*.

fax [fæks] **1** *n* fax *m*, télécopie *f*. **2** *vt* [person] envoyer un fax à. || [document] envoyer en fax.

fax machine n fax m, télécopieur m.

FBI (abbr of **Federal Bureau of Investigation**) n FBI m.

fear [fɪəʳ] **1** n (U) [feeling] peur f. || [object of fear] crainte f. || [risk] risque m; **for ~ of** de peur de (+ infin), de peur que (+ subjunctive). **2** vt [be afraid of] craindre, avoir peur de. || [anticipate] craindre; **to ~ (that) ...** craindre que ..., avoir peur que ....

fearful ['fɪəful] adj fml [frightened] peureux(euse); **to be ~ of sthg** avoir peur de qqch. || [frightening] effrayant(e).

fearless ['fɪəlɪs] adj intrépide.

feasible ['fiːzəbl] adj faisable, possible.

feast [fiːst] **1** n [meal] festin m, banquet m. **2** vi: **to ~ on** OR **off sthg** se régaler de qqch.

feat [fiːt] n exploit m, prouesse f.

feather ['feðəʳ] n plume f.

feature ['fiːtʃəʳ] **1** n [characteristic] caractéristique f. || GEOGR particularité f. || [article] article m de fond. || RADIO & TV émission f spéciale, spécial m. || CINEMA long métrage m. **2** vt [subj: film, exhibition] mettre en vedette. || [comprise] présenter, comporter. **3** vi: **to ~ (in)** figurer en vedette (dans). ○ **features** npl [of face] traits mpl.

feature film n long métrage m.

February ['februərɪ] n février m; see also **September**.

feces Am = **faeces**.

fed [fed] pt & pp → **feed**.

federal ['fedrəl] adj fédéral(e).

federation [ˌfedə'reɪʃn] n fédération f.

fed up adj: **to be ~ (with)** en avoir marre (de).

fee [fiː] n [of school] frais mpl; [of doctor] honoraires mpl; [for membership] cotisation f; [for entrance] tarif m, prix m.

feeble ['fiːbl] adj faible.

feed [fiːd] (pt & pp **fed**) **1** vt [give food to] nourrir. || [fire, fears etc] alimenter. || [put, insert]: **to ~ sthg into sthg** mettre OR insérer qqch dans qqch. **2** vi [take food]: **to ~ (on** OR **off)** se nourrir (de). **3** n [for baby] repas m. || [animal food] nourriture f.

feedback ['fiːdbæk] n (U) [reaction] réactions fpl.

feel [fiːl] (pt & pp **felt**) **1** vt [touch] toucher. || [sense, experience, notice] sentir; [emotion] ressentir; **to ~ o.s. doing sthg** se sentir faire qqch. || [believe]: **to ~ (that) ...** croire que ..., penser que .... **2** vi [have sensation]: **to ~ cold/hot/sleepy** avoir

froid/chaud/sommeil; **to ~ like sthg/like doing sthg** [be in mood for] avoir envie de qqch/de faire qqch. || [have emotion] se sentir; **to ~ angry** être en colère. || [seem] sembler; **it ~s strange** ça fait drôle. || [by touch]: **to ~ for sthg** chercher qqch. **3** n [sensation, touch] toucher m, sensation f. || [atmosphere] atmosphère f.

feeler ['fiːləʳ] n antenne f.

feeling ['fiːlɪŋ] n [emotion] sentiment m. || [physical sensation] sensation f. || [intuition, sense] sentiment m, impression f. || [understanding] sensibilité f. ○ **feelings** npl sentiments mpl; **to hurt sb's ~s** blesser (la sensibilité de) qqn.

feet [fiːt] pl → **foot**.

fell [fel] **1** pt → **fall**. **2** vt [tree, person] abattre. ○ **fells** npl GEOGR lande f.

fellow ['feləʊ] **1** n dated [man] homme m. || [comrade, peer] camarade m, compagnon m. || [of society, college] membre m, associé m. **2** adj: **one's ~ men** ses semblables; **~ student** camarade mf (d'études).

fellowship ['feləʊʃɪp] n [comradeship] amitié f, camaraderie f. || [society] association f, corporation f. || [of society, college] titre m de membre OR d'associé.

felony ['felənɪ] n JUR crime m, forfait m.

felt [felt] **1** pt & pp → **feel**. **2** n (U) feutre m.

felt-tip pen n stylo-feutre m.

female ['fiːmeɪl] **1** adj [person] de sexe féminin; [animal, plant] femelle; [sex, figure] féminin(e); **~ student** étudiante f. **2** n femelle f.

feminine ['femɪnɪn] **1** adj féminin(e). **2** n GRAMM féminin m.

feminist ['femɪnɪst] n féministe mf.

fence [fens] **1** n [barrier] clôture f. **2** vt clôturer, entourer d'une clôture.

fencing ['fensɪŋ] n SPORT escrime f.

fend [fend] vi: **to ~ for o.s.** se débrouiller tout seul. ○ **fend off** vt sep [blows] parer; [questions, reporters] écarter.

fender ['fendəʳ] n [round fireplace] pare-feu m inv.; || Am [on car] aile f.

ferment [n 'fɜːment, vb fə'ment] **1** n (U) [unrest] agitation f, effervescence f. **2** vi [wine, beer] fermenter.

fern [fɜːn] n fougère f.

ferocious [fə'rəʊʃəs] adj féroce.

ferret ['ferɪt] n furet m. ○ **ferret about, ferret around** vi inf fureter un peu partout.

ferris wheel ['ferɪs-] n grande roue f.

ferry ['ferɪ] **1** n ferry m, ferry-boat m; [smaller] bac m. **2** vt transporter.

ferryboat ['ferɪbəʊt] n = ferry.

fertile ['fɜːtaɪl] adj [land, imagination] fertile, fécond(e). || [woman] féconde.

fertilizer ['fɜːtɪlaɪzər] n engrais m.

fervent ['fɜːvənt] adj fervent(e).

fester ['festər] vi [wound, sore] suppurer.

festival ['festəvl] n [event, celebration] festival m. || [holiday] fête f.

festive ['festɪv] adj de fête.

festive season n: **the ~** la période des fêtes.

festivities [fes'tɪvətɪz] npl réjouissances fpl.

fetch [fetʃ] vt [go and get] aller chercher. || [raise - money] rapporter.

fete, fête [feɪt] n fête f, kermesse f.

fetish ['fetɪʃ] n [sexual obsession] objet m de fétichisme. || [mania] manie f, obsession f.

fetus ['fiːtəs] = foetus.

feud [fjuːd] **1** n querelle f. **2** vi se quereller.

feudal ['fjuːdl] adj féodal(e).

fever ['fiːvər] n fièvre f.

feverish ['fiːvərɪʃ] adj fiévreux(euse).

few [fjuː] **1** adj peu de; **the first ~ pages** les toutes premières pages; **quite a ~, a good ~** pas mal de, un bon nombre de. **2** pron peu; **a ~** quelques-uns mpl, quelques-unes fpl.

fewer ['fjuːər] **1** adj moins (de). **2** pron moins.

fewest ['fjuːəst] adj le moins (de).

fiancé [fɪ'ɒnseɪ] n fiancé m.

fiancée [fɪ'ɒnseɪ] n fiancée f.

fiasco [fɪ'æskəʊ] (Br pl -s, Am pl -es) n fiasco m.

fib [fɪb] inf **1** n bobard m, blague f. **2** vi raconter des bobards OR des blagues.

fibre Br, **fiber** Am ['faɪbər] n fibre f.

fibreglass Br, **fiberglass** Am ['faɪbəglɑːs] n (U) fibre f de verre.

fickle ['fɪkl] adj versatile.

fiction ['fɪkʃn] n fiction f.

fictional ['fɪkʃənl] adj fictif(ive).

fictitious [fɪk'tɪʃəs] adj [false] fictif(ive).

fiddle ['fɪdl] **1** vi [play around]: **to ~ with sthg** tripoter qqch. **2** n [violin] violon m.

fidget ['fɪdʒɪt] vi remuer.

field [fiːld] n [gen & COMPUT] champ m. || [for sports] terrain m. || [of knowledge] domaine m.

field day n: **to have a ~** s'en donner à cœur joie.

field glasses npl jumelles fpl.

field marshal n ≃ maréchal m (de France).

field trip n voyage m d'étude.

fieldwork ['fiːldwɜːk] n (U) recherches fpl sur le terrain.

fiend [fiːnd] n [cruel person] monstre m. || inf [fanatic] fou m, folle f, mordu m, -e f.

fierce [fɪəs] adj féroce; [heat] torride; [storm, temper] violent(e).

fiery ['faɪərɪ] adj [burning] ardent(e). || [volatile - speech] enflammé(e); [- temper, person] fougueux(euse).

fifteen [fɪf'tiːn] num quinze; see also six.

fifth [fɪfθ] num cinquième; see also sixth.

fifty ['fɪftɪ] num cinquante; see also sixty.

fifty-fifty **1** adj moitié-moitié, fifty-fifty; **to have a ~ chance** avoir cinquante pour cent de chances. **2** adv moitié-moitié, fifty-fifty.

fig [fɪg] n figue f.

fight [faɪt] (pt & pp fought) **1** n [physical] bagarre f; **to have a ~ (with sb)** se battre (avec qqn), se bagarrer (avec qqn). || fig [battle, struggle] lutte f, combat m. || [argument] dispute f; **to have a ~ (with sb)** se disputer (avec qqn). **2** vt [physically] se battre contre OR avec. || [conduct - war] mener. || [enemy, racism] combattre. **3** vi [in war, punch-up] se battre. || fig [struggle]: **to ~ for/against sthg** lutter pour/contre qqch. || [argue]: **to ~ (about OR over)** se battre OR se disputer (à propos de). ○ **fight back 1** vt fus refouler. **2** vi riposter.

fighter ['faɪtər] n [plane] avion m de chasse, chasseur m. || [soldier] combattant m.

fighting ['faɪtɪŋ] n (U) [punch-up] bagarres fpl; [in war] conflits mpl.

figment ['fɪgmənt] n: **a ~ of sb's imagination** le fruit de l'imagination de qqn.

figurative ['fɪgərətɪv] adj [meaning] figuré(e).

figure [Br 'fɪgər, Am 'fɪgjər] **1** n [statistic, number] chiffre m. || [human shape, outline] silhouette f, forme f. || [personality, diagram] figure f. || [shape of body] ligne f. **2** vt [suppose] penser, supposer. **3** vi [feature] figurer, apparaître. ○ **figure**

out *vt sep* [understand] comprendre; [find] trouver.

figurehead ['fɪgəhed] *n* [on ship] figure *f* de proue. || *fig & pej* [leader] homme *m* de paille.

figure of speech *n* figure *f* de rhétorique.

file [faɪl] **1** *n* [folder, report] dossier *m*. || COMPUT fichier *m*. || [tool] lime *f*. || [line]: **in single** ∼ en file indienne. **2** *vt* [document] classer. || JUR - accusation, complaint] porter, déposer; [- lawsuit] intenter. || [fingernails, wood] limer. **3** *vi* [walk in single file] marcher en file indienne. || JUR: **to** ∼ **for divorce** demander le divorce.

filet *Am* = fillet.

filing cabinet ['faɪlɪŋ-] *n* classeur *m*, fichier *m*.

Filipino [ˌfɪlɪ'piːnəʊ] (*pl* -s) **1** *adj* philippin(e). **2** *n* Philippin *m*, -e *f*.

fill [fɪl] **1** *vt* [gen] remplir; **to** ∼ **sthg with sthg** remplir qqch de qqch. || [gap, hole] boucher. || [vacancy - subj: employer] pourvoir à; [- subj: employee] prendre. **2** *n*: **to eat one's** ∼ manger à sa faim. ○ **fill in 1** *vt sep* [form] remplir. || [inform]: **to** ∼ **sb in (on)** mettre qqn au courant (de). **2** *vi* [substitute]: **to** ∼ **in for sb** remplacer qqn. ○ **fill out 1** *vt sep* [form] remplir. **2** *vi* [get fatter] prendre de l'embonpoint. ○ **fill up 1** *vt sep* remplir. **2** *vi* se remplir.

fillet *Br*, **filet** *Am* ['fɪlɪt] *n* filet *m*.

fillet steak *n* filet *m* de bœuf.

filling ['fɪlɪŋ] **1** *adj* qui rassasie, très nourrissant(e). **2** *n* [in tooth] plombage *m*. || [in cake, sandwich] garniture *f*.

filling station *n* station-service *f*.

film [fɪlm] **1** *n* [movie] film *m*. || [layer, for camera] pellicule *f*. || [footage] images *fpl*. **2** *vt & vi* filmer.

film star *n* vedette *f* de cinéma.

filter ['fɪltər] **1** *n* filtre *m*. **2** *vt* [coffee] passer; [water, oil, air] filtrer.

filter coffee *n* café *m* filtre.

filter-tipped [-'tɪpt] *adj* à bout filtre.

filth [fɪlθ] *n* (*U*) [dirt] saleté *f*, crasse *f*. || [obscenity] obscénités *fpl*.

filthy ['fɪlθɪ] *adj* [very dirty] dégoûtant(e), répugnant(e). || [obscene] obscène.

fin [fɪn] *n* [of fish] nageoire *f*.

final ['faɪnl] **1** *adj* [last] dernier(ière). || [at end] final(e). || [definitive] définitif(ive). **2** *n* finale *f*. ○ **finals** *npl* UNIV examens *mpl* de dernière année.

finale [fɪ'nɑːlɪ] *n* finale *m*.

finalize, -ise ['faɪnəlaɪz] *vt* mettre au point.

finally ['faɪnəlɪ] *adv* enfin.

finance [*n* 'faɪnæns, *vb* faɪ'næns] **1** *n* (*U*) finance *f*. **2** *vt* financer. ○ **finances** *npl* finances *fpl*.

financial [fɪ'nænʃl] *adj* financier(ière).

find [faɪnd] (*pt & pp* found) **1** *vt* [gen] trouver. || [realize]: **to** ∼ **(that)** ... s'apercevoir que .... || [be found guilty/not guilty (of)] être déclaré(e) coupable/non coupable (de). **2** *n* trouvaille *f*. ○ **find out 1** *vi* se renseigner. **2** *vt fus* [information] se renseigner sur. || [truth] découvrir, apprendre. **3** *vt sep* démasquer.

findings ['faɪndɪŋz] *npl* conclusions *fpl*.

fine [faɪn] **1** *adj* [good - work] excellent(e); [- building, weather] beau (belle). || [perfectly satisfactory] très bien; **I'm** ∼ ça va bien. || [thin, smooth] fin(e). || [minute - detail, distinction] subtil(e); [- adjustment, tuning] délicat(e). **2** *adv* [very well] très bien. **3** *n* amende *f*. **4** *vt* condamner à une amende.

fine arts *npl* beaux-arts *mpl*.

fine-tune *vt* [mechanism] régler au quart de tour; *fig* régler minutieusement.

finger ['fɪŋgər] **1** *n* doigt *m*. **2** *vt* [feel] palper.

fingernail ['fɪŋgəneɪl] *n* ongle *m* (*de la main*).

fingerprint ['fɪŋgəprɪnt] *n* empreinte *f* (digitale).

fingertip ['fɪŋgətɪp] *n* bout *m* du doigt; **at one's** ∼**s** sur le bout des doigts.

finish ['fɪnɪʃ] **1** *n* [end] fin *f*; [of race] arrivée *f*. || [texture] finition *f*. **2** *vt* finir, terminer; **to** ∼ **doing sthg** finir OR terminer de faire qqch. **3** *vi* finir, terminer; [school, film] se terminer. ○ **finish off** *vt sep* finir, terminer. ○ **finish up** *vi* finir.

finishing line ['fɪnɪʃɪŋ-] *n* ligne *f* d'arrivée.

finishing school ['fɪnɪʃɪŋ-] *n* école privée pour jeunes filles surtout axée sur l'enseignement de bonnes manières.

finite ['faɪnaɪt] *adj* fini(e).

Finland ['fɪnlənd] *n* Finlande *f*.

Finn [fɪn] *n* Finlandais *m*, -e *f*.

Finnish ['fɪnɪʃ] **1** *adj* finlandais(e), finnois(e). **2** *n* [language] finnois *m*.

fir [fɜːr] *n* sapin *m*.

fire ['faɪər] **1** *n* [gen] feu *m*; **on** ∼ en feu; **to catch** ∼ prendre feu; **to set** ∼ **to sthg** mettre le feu à qqch. || [out of control] incendie *m*. || (*U*) [shooting] coups *mpl* de

feu; **to open ~ (on)** ouvrir le feu (sur). **2**
vt [shoot] tirer. ‖ [dismiss] renvoyer. **3** *vi*:
to ~ (on OR **at)** faire feu (sur), tirer (sur).

fire alarm *n* avertisseur *m* d'incendie.

firearm ['faɪrɑːm] *n* arme *f* à feu.

firebomb ['faɪəbɒm] **1** *n* bombe *f* incendiaire. **2** *vt* lancer des bombes incendiaires à.

fire brigade *Br*, **fire department**
Am n sapeurs-pompiers *mpl*.

fire door *n* porte *f* coupe-feu.

fire engine *n* voiture *f* de pompiers.

fire escape *n* escalier *m* de secours.

fire extinguisher *n* extincteur *m*
d'incendie.

fireguard ['faɪəgɑːd] *n* garde-feu *m inv*.

firelighter ['faɪəlaɪtər] *n* allume-feu *m*
inv.

fireman ['faɪəmən] (*pl* **-men** [-mən]) *n*
pompier *m*.

fireplace ['faɪəpleɪs] *n* cheminée *f*.

fireproof ['faɪəpruːf] *adj* ignifugé(e).

fireside ['faɪəsaɪd] *n*: **by the ~** au coin
du feu.

fire station *n* caserne *f* des pompiers.

firewood ['faɪəwʊd] *n* bois *m* de chauffage.

firework ['faɪəwɜːk] *n* fusée *f* de feu
d'artifice.

firing ['faɪərɪŋ] *n* (*U*) MIL tir *m*, fusillade
f.

firing squad *n* peloton *m* d'exécution.

firm [fɜːm] **1** *adj* [gen] ferme; **to stand ~**
tenir bon. ‖ [support, structure] solide. ‖
[evidence, news] certain(e). **2** *n* firme *f*,
société *f*.

first [fɜːst] **1** *adj* premier(ière); **for the
~ time** pour la première fois; **~ thing in
the morning** tôt le matin. **2** *adv* [before
anyone else] en premier. ‖ [before anything else] d'abord; **~ of all** tout d'abord.
‖ [for the first time] (pour) la première
fois. **3** *n* [person] premier *m*, -ière *f*. ‖
[unprecedented event] première *f*. ○ **at
first** *adv* d'abord. ○ **at first hand** *adv*
de première main.

first aid *n* (*U*) premiers secours *mpl*.

first-aid kit *n* trousse *f* de premiers secours.

first-class *adj* [excellent] excellent(e). ‖
[ticket, compartment] de première classe;
[stamp, letter] tarif normal.

first floor *n Br* premier étage *m*; *Am*
rez-de-chaussée *m*.

firsthand [fɜːst'hænd] *adj & adv* de
première main.

first lady *n* première dame *f* du pays.

firstly ['fɜːstlɪ] *adv* premièrement.

first name *n* prénom *m*.

first-rate *adj* excellent(e).

firtree ['fɜːtriː] = **fir**.

fish [fɪʃ] (*pl inv*) **1** *n* poisson *m*. **2** *vi*
[fisherman]: **to ~ (for sthg)** pêcher
(qqch).

fishbowl ['fɪʃbəʊl] *n* bocal *m* (à poissons).

fishcake ['fɪʃkeɪk] *n* croquette *f* de poisson.

fisherman ['fɪʃəmən] (*pl* **-men** [-mən])
n pêcheur *m*.

fish fingers *Br*, **fish sticks** *Am npl* bâtonnets *mpl* de poisson panés.

fishing ['fɪʃɪŋ] *n* pêche *f*; **to go ~** aller à
la pêche.

fishing boat *n* bateau *m* de pêche.

fishing line *n* ligne *f*.

fishing rod *n* canne *f* à pêche.

fishmonger ['fɪʃ,mʌŋgər] *n* poissonnier
m, -ière *f*; **~'s (shop)** poissonnerie *f*.

fish sticks *Am* = **fish fingers**.

fishy ['fɪʃɪ] *adj* [smell, taste] de poisson.
‖ [suspicious] louche.

fist [fɪst] *n* poing *m*.

fit [fɪt] **1** *adj* [suitable] convenable; **to be
~ for sthg** être bon (bonne) à qqch. ‖
[healthy] en forme; **to keep ~** se maintenir en forme. **2** *n* [of clothes, shoes etc]
ajustement *m*; **it's a tight ~** c'est un peu
juste; **it's a good ~** c'est la bonne taille. ‖
[epileptic seizure] crise *f*; **to have a ~** avoir
une crise; *fig* piquer une crise. ‖ [bout - of
crying] crise *f*; [- of rage] accès *m*; [- in
sneezing] suite *f*; **in ~s and starts** par à-coups. **3** *vt* [be correct size for] aller à.
[place]: **to ~ sthg into sthg** insérer qqch
dans qqch. ‖ [provide]: **to ~ sthg with
sthg** équiper qqch OR munir qqch de qqch.
[be suitable for] correspondre à. **4** *vi* [be
correct size, go] aller; [into container] entrer. ○ **fit in 1** *vt sep* [accommodate]
prendre. **2** *vi* s'intégrer; **to ~ in with sthg**
correspondre à qqch; **to ~ in with sb**
s'accorder à qqm.

fitful ['fɪtfʊl] *adj* [sleep] agité(e); [wind,
showers] intermittent(e).

fitness ['fɪtnɪs] *n* (*U*) [health] forme *f*. ‖
[suitability]: **~ (for)** aptitude *f* (pour).

fitted carpet [,fɪtəd-] *n* moquette *f*.

fitter ['fɪtər] *n* [mechanic] monteur *m*.

fitting ['fɪtɪŋ] **1** *adj fml* approprié(e). **2**
n [part] appareil *m*. ‖ [for clothing] essayage *m*. ○ **fittings** *npl* installations
fpl.

fitting room *n* cabine *f* d'essayage.

five [faɪv] *num* cinq; *see also* **six.**

fiver ['faɪvər] *n inf Am* [amount] cinq dollars *mpl*; [note] billet *m* de cinq dollars.

fix [fɪks] **1** *vt* [gen] fixer; **to ~ sthg to sthg** fixer qqch à qqch. || [in memory] graver. || [repair] réparer. || *inf* [rig] truquer. || [food, drink] préparer. **2** *n inf* [difficult situation]: **to be in a ~** être dans le pétrin. || [drugs *sl*] piqûre *f.* ○ **fix up** *vt sep* [provide]: **to ~ sb up with sthg** obtenir qqch pour qqn. || [arrange] arranger.

fixation [fɪk'seɪʃn] *n*: ~ **(on** OR **about)** obsession *f* (de).

fixed [fɪkst] *adj* [attached] fixé(e). || [set, unchanging] fixe; [smile] figé(e).

fixture ['fɪkstʃər] *n* [furniture] installation *f.* || [permanent feature] tradition *f* bien établie. || SPORT rencontre *f* (sportive).

fizz [fɪz] *vi* [lemonade, champagne] pétiller; [fireworks] crépiter.

fizzle ['fɪzl] ○ **fizzle out** *vi* [fire] s'éteindre; [firework] se terminer; [interest, enthusiasm] se dissiper.

fizzy ['fɪzɪ] *adj* pétillant(e).

flabbergasted ['flæbəgɑːstɪd] *adj* sidéré(e).

flabby ['flæbɪ] *adj* mou (molle).

flag [flæg] **1** *n* drapeau *m*. **2** *vi* [person, enthusiasm, energy] faiblir; [conversation] traîner. ○ **flag down** *vt sep* [taxi] héler; **to ~ sb down** faire signe à qqn de s'arrêter.

flagpole ['flægpəʊl] *n* mât *m*.

flagrant ['fleɪgrənt] *adj* flagrant(e).

flagstone ['flægstəʊn] *n* dalle *f.*

flair [fleər] *n* [talent] don *m*. || (*U*) [stylishness] style *m*.

flak [flæk] *n* (*U*) [gunfire] tir *m* antiaérien. || *inf* [criticism] critiques *fpl* sévères.

flake [fleɪk] **1** *n* [of paint, plaster] écaille *f*; [of snow] flocon *m*. **2** *vi* [paint, plaster] s'écailler; [skin] peler.

flamboyant [flæm'bɔɪənt] *adj* [showy, confident] extravagant(e). || [brightly coloured] flamboyant(e).

flame [fleɪm] *n* flamme *f*; **in ~s** en flammes; **to burst into ~s** s'enflammer.

flamingo [flə'mɪŋgəʊ] (*pl* -s OR -es) *n* flamant *m* rose.

flammable ['flæməbl] *adj* inflammable.

flan [flæn] *n* tarte *f.*

flank [flæŋk] **1** *n* flanc *m*. **2** *vt*: **to be ~ed by** être flanqué(e) de.

flannel ['flænl] *n* [fabric] flanelle *f.*

flap [flæp] **1** *n* [of envelope, pocket] rabat *m*; [of skin] lambeau *m*. || *inf* [panic]: **in a ~** paniqué(e). **2** *vt & vi* battre.

flapjack ['flæpdʒæk] *n Am* [pancake] crêpe *f* épaisse.

flare [fleər] **1** *n* [distress signal] fusée *f* éclairante. **2** *vi* [burn brightly]: **to ~ (up)** s'embraser. || [intensify]: **to ~ (up)** [war, revolution] s'intensifier soudainement; [person] s'emporter. || [widen - trousers, skirt] s'évaser; [- nostrils] se dilater.

flash [flæʃ] **1** *n* [of light, colour] éclat *m*; ~ **of lightning** éclair *m*. || PHOT flash *m*. || [sudden moment] éclair *m*; **in a ~** en un rien de temps. **2** *vt* [shine] projeter; **to ~ one's headlights** faire un appel de phares. || [send out - signal, smile] envoyer; [- look] jeter. || [show] montrer. **3** *vi* [torch] briller. || [light - on and off] clignoter; [eyes] jeter des éclairs. || [rush]: **to ~ by** OR **past** passer comme un éclair.

flashback ['flæʃbæk] *n* flashback *m*, retour *m* en arrière.

flashbulb ['flæʃbʌlb] *n* ampoule *f* de flash.

flashgun ['flæʃgʌn] *n* flash *m*.

flashlight ['flæʃlaɪt] *n* [torch] lampe *f* électrique.

flashy ['flæʃɪ] *adj inf* tape-à-l'œil (*inv*).

flask [flɑːsk] *n* [thermos flask] thermos® *m* or *f.*

flat [flæt] **1** *adj* [gen] plat(e). || [tyre] crevé(e). || [refusal, denial] catégorique. || [dull - voice, tone] monotone; [- performance, writing] terne. || [MUS - person] qui chante trop grave; [- note] bémol. || [fare, price] fixe. || [beer, lemonade] éventé(e). || [battery] à plat. **2** *adv* [level] à plat. || [exactly]: **two hours ~** deux heures pile. **3** *n* MUS bémol *m.* ○ **flat out** *adv* [work] d'arrache-pied; [travel - subj: vehicle] le plus vite possible.

flatly ['flætlɪ] *adv* [absolutely] catégoriquement. || [dully - say] avec monotonie; [- perform] de façon terne.

flat rate *n* tarif *m* forfaitaire.

flatten ['flætn] *vt* [make flat - steel, paper] aplatir; [- wrinkles, bumps] aplanir. || [destroy] raser. ○ **flatten out 1** *vi* s'aplanir. **2** *vt sep* aplanir.

flatter ['flætər] *vt* flatter.

flattering ['flætərɪŋ] *adj* [complimentary] flatteur(euse). || [clothes] seyant(e).

flattery ['flætərɪ] *n* flatterie *f.*

flaunt [flɔːnt] *vt* faire étalage de.

flavour *Br*, **flavor** *Am* ['fleɪvər] **1** *n* [of food] goût *m*; [of ice cream, yoghurt] parfum *m*. ‖ *fig* [atmosphere] atmosphère *f*. 2 *vt* parfumer.

flavouring *Br*, **flavoring** *Am* ['fleɪvərɪŋ] *n* (*U*) parfum *m*.

flaw [flɔː] *n* [in material, character] défaut *m*; [in plan, argument] faille *f*.

flawless ['flɔːlɪs] *adj* parfait(e).

flea [fliː] *n* puce *f*.

flea market *n* marché *m* aux puces.

fleck [flek] 1 *n* moucheture *f*, petite tache *f*. 2 *vt*: **~ed with** moucheté(e) de.

fled [fled] *pt* & *pp* → **flee**.

flee [fliː] (*pt* & *pp* **fled**) *vt* & *vi* fuir.

fleece [fliːs] 1 *n* toison *f*. 2 *vt inf* escroquer.

fleet [fliːt] *n* [of ships] flotte *f*. ‖ [of cars, buses] parc *m*.

fleeting ['fliːtɪŋ] *adj* [moment] bref (brève); [look] fugitif(ive); [visit] éclair (*inv*).

Flemish ['flemɪʃ] 1 *adj* flamand(e). 2 *n* [language] flamand *m*. 3 *npl*: **the ~** les Flamands *mpl*.

flesh [fleʃ] *n* chair *f*; **his/her ~ and blood** [family] les siens.

flew [fluː] *pt* → **fly**.

flex [fleks] 1 *n* ELEC fil *m*. 2 *vt* [bend] fléchir.

flexible ['fleksəbl] *adj* flexible.

flexitime ['fleksɪtaɪm] *n* (*U*) horaire *m* à la carte OR flexible.

flick [flɪk] 1 *n* [of whip, towel] petit coup *m*. ‖ [with finger] chiquenaude *f*. 2 *vt* [switch] appuyer sur. ○ **flick through** *vt fus* feuilleter.

flicker ['flɪkər] *vi* [candle, light] vaciller. ‖ [shadow] trembler; [eyelids] ciller.

flight [flaɪt] *n* [gen] vol *m*. ‖ [of steps, stairs] volée *f*. ‖ [escape] fuite *f*.

flight attendant *n* steward *m*, hôtesse *f* de l'air.

flight crew *n* équipage *m*.

flight deck *n* [of aircraft carrier] pont *m* d'envol. ‖ [of plane] cabine *f* de pilotage.

flight recorder *n* enregistreur *m* de vol.

flimsy ['flɪmzɪ] *adj* [dress, material] léger(ère); [building, bookcase] peu solide.

flinch [flɪntʃ] *vi* tressaillir; **to ~ from sthg/from doing sthg** reculer devant qqch/à l'idée de faire qqch.

fling [flɪŋ] (*pt* & *pp* **flung**) 1 *n* [affair] aventure *f*, affaire *f*. 2 *vt* lancer.

flint [flɪnt] *n* [in lighter] pierre *f*.

flip [flɪp] 1 *vt* [turn - pancake] faire sauter; [- record] tourner. ‖ [switch] appuyer sur. 2 *vi inf* [become angry] piquer une

colère. 3 *n* [flick] chiquenaude *f*. ‖ [somersault] saut *m* périlleux. ○ **flip through** *vt fus* feuilleter.

flip-flop *n* [shoe] tong *f*.

flippant ['flɪpənt] *adj* désinvolte.

flipper ['flɪpər] *n* [of animal] nageoire *f*. ‖ [for swimmer, diver] palme *f*.

flirt [flɜːt] 1 *n* flirt *m*. 2 *vi* [with person]: **to ~ (with sb)** flirter (avec qqn).

flirtatious [flɜːˈteɪʃəs] *adj* flirteur(euse).

flit [flɪt] *vi* [bird] voleter.

float [fləʊt] 1 *n* [for buoyancy] flotteur *m*. ‖ [in procession] char *m*. ‖ [money] petite caisse *f*. 2 *vt* [on water] faire flotter. 3 *vi* [on water] flotter; [through air] glisser.

flock [flɒk] *n* [of birds] vol *m*; [of sheep] troupeau *m*. ‖ *fig* [of people] foule *f*.

flog [flɒg] *vt* [whip] flageller.

flood [flʌd] 1 *n* [of water] inondation *f*. ‖ [great amount] déluge *m*, avalanche *f*. 2 *vt* [with water, light] inonder. ‖ [overwhelm]: **to ~ sthg (with)** inonder qqch (de).

flooding ['flʌdɪŋ] *n* (*U*) inondations *fpl*.

floodlight ['flʌdlaɪt] *n* projecteur *m*.

floor [flɔːr] 1 *n* [of room] sol *m*; [of club, disco] piste *f*. ‖ [of valley, sea, forest] fond *m*. ‖ [storey] étage *m*. 2 *vt* [knock down] terrasser. ‖ [baffle] dérouter.

floorboard ['flɔːbɔːd] *n* plancher *m*.

floor show *n* spectacle *m* de cabaret.

flop [flɒp] *inf n* [failure] fiasco *m*.

floppy ['flɒpɪ] *adj* [flower] flasque; [collar] lâche.

floppy (disk) *n* disquette *f*, disque *m* souple.

flora ['flɔːrə] *n* flore *f*.

florid ['flɒrɪd] *adj* [red] rougeaud(e). ‖ [extravagant] fleuri(e).

florist ['flɒrɪst] *n* fleuriste *mf*; **~'s (shop)** magasin *m* de fleuriste.

flotsam ['flɒtsəm] *n* (*U*): **~ and jetsam** débris *mpl*; *fig* épaves *fpl*.

flounder ['flaʊndər] *vi* [in water, mud, snow] patauger. ‖ [in conversation] bredouiller.

flour ['flaʊər] *n* farine *f*.

flourish ['flʌrɪʃ] 1 *vi* [plant, flower] bien pousser; [company, business] prospérer; [arts] s'épanouir. 2 *vt* brandir. 3 *n* grand geste *m*.

flout [flaʊt] *vt* bafouer.

flow [fləʊ] 1 *n* [movement - of water, information] circulation *f*; [- of funds] mouvement *m*; [- of words] flot *m*. ‖ [of tide]

flux m. 2 vi [gen] couler. || [traffic, days, weeks] s'écouler. || [hair, clothes] flotter.

flow chart, flow diagram n organigramme m.

flower ['flauər] 1 n fleur f. 2 vi [bloom] fleurir.

flowerbed ['flauəbed] n parterre m.

flowerpot ['flauəpɒt] n pot m de fleurs.

flowery ['flauərɪ] adj [dress, material] à fleurs. || pej [style] fleuri(e).

flown [fləʊn] pp → fly.

flu [fluː] n (U) grippe f.

fluctuate ['flʌktʃueɪt] vi fluctuer.

fluency ['fluːənsɪ] n aisance f.

fluent ['fluːənt] adj [in foreign language]: **to speak ~ French** parler couramment le français.

fluff [flʌf] n (U) [down] duvet m. || [dust] moutons mpl.

fluffy ['flʌfɪ] adj duveteux(euse); [toy] en peluche.

fluid ['fluːɪd] 1 n fluide m; [in diet, for cleaning] liquide m. 2 adj [flowing] fluide.

fluid ounce n = 0,03 litre.

fluke [fluːk] n inf [chance] coup m de bol.

flung [flʌŋ] pt & pp → fling.

flunk [flʌŋk] inf vt [exam, test] rater. || [student] recaler.

fluorescent [fluə'resnt] adj fluorescent(e).

fluoride ['fluəraɪd] n fluorure m.

flurry ['flʌrɪ] n [of rain, snow] rafale f. || [of activity, excitement] débordement m.

flush [flʌʃ] 1 adj [level]: **~ with** de niveau avec. 2 n [in lavatory] chasse f d'eau. || [blush] rougeur f. || [sudden feeling] accès m. 3 vt [toilet]: **to ~ the toilet** tirer la chasse d'eau. 4 vi [blush] rougir.

flushed [flʌʃt] adj [red-faced] rouge. || [excited]: **~ with** exalté(e) par.

flustered ['flʌstəd] adj troublé(e).

flute [fluːt] n MUS flûte f.

flutter ['flʌtər] 1 n [of wings] battement m. || inf [of excitement] émoi m. 2 vi [bird, insect] voleter; [wings] battre. || [flag, dress] flotter.

flux [flʌks] n [change]: **to be in a state of ~** être en proie à des changements permanents.

fly [flaɪ] (pt **flew**, pp **flown**) 1 n [insect] mouche f. || [of trousers] braguette f. 2 vt [kite, plane] faire voler. || [passengers, supplies] transporter par avion. || [flag] faire flotter. 3 vi [bird, insect, plane] voler. || [pilot] faire voler un avion. || [passenger] voyager en avion. || [move fast,

pass quickly] filer. || [flag] flotter. **○ fly away** vi s'envoler.

flying ['flaɪɪŋ] n: **to like ~** aimer prendre l'avion.

flying colours npl: **to pass (sthg) with ~** réussir (qqch) haut la main.

flying picket n piquet m de grève volant.

flying saucer n soucoupe f volante.

flying start n: **to get off to a ~** prendre un départ sur les chapeaux de roue.

flying visit n visite f éclair.

flysheet ['flaɪʃiːt] n auvent m.

fly spray n insecticide m.

FM (abbr of frequency modulation) n FM f.

foal [fəʊl] n poulain m.

foam [fəʊm] 1 n (U) [bubbles] mousse f. || **~ (rubber)** caoutchouc m mousse. 2 vi [water, champagne] mousser.

fob [fɒb] **○ fob off** vt sep repousser; **to ~ sthg off on sb** refiler qqch à qqn; **to ~ sb off with sthg** se débarrasser de qqn à l'aide de qqch.

focal point ['fəʊkl-] n foyer m; fig point m central.

focus ['fəʊkəs] (pl **-cuses** OR **-ci** [-kaɪ]) 1 n PHOT mise f au point; **in ~** net; **out of ~** flou. || [centre - of rays] foyer m; [- of earthquake] centre m. 2 vt [lens, camera] mettre au point. 3 vi [with camera, lens] se fixer; [eyes] accommoder; **to ~ on sthg** [with camera, lens] se fixer sur qqch; [with eyes] fixer qqch. || [attention]: **to ~ on sthg** se concentrer sur qqch.

fodder ['fɒdər] n (U) fourrage m.

foe [fəʊ] n literary ennemi m.

foetus ['fiːtəs] n fœtus m.

fog [fɒg] n (U) brouillard m.

foggy ['fɒgɪ] adj [misty] brumeux(euse).

foghorn ['fɒghɔːn] n sirène f de brume.

fog lamp n feu m de brouillard.

foible ['fɔɪbl] n marotte f.

foil [fɔɪl] 1 n (U) [metal sheet - of tin, silver] feuille f; [- CULIN] papier m d'aluminium. 2 vt déjouer.

fold [fəʊld] 1 vt [bend, close up] plier; **to ~ one's arms** croiser les bras. || [wrap] envelopper. 2 vi [close up - table, chair] se plier; [- petals, leaves] se refermer. || inf [company, project] échouer; THEATRE quitter l'affiche. 3 n [in material, paper] pli m. || [for animals] parc m. || fig [spiritual home]: **the ~** le bercail. **○ fold up** 1 vt sep plier. 2 vi [close up - table, map] se plier; [- petals, leaves] se refermer. || [company, project] échouer.

folder ['fəʊldər] n [for papers - wallet] chemise f; [- binder] classeur m.

folding ['fəʊldɪŋ] adj [table, umbrella] pliant(e).

foliage ['fəʊlɪɪdʒ] n feuillage m.

folk [fəʊk] **1** adj [art, dancing] folklorique; [medicine] populaire. **2** npl [people] gens mpl. ○ **folks** npl inf [relatives] famille f.

folklore ['fəʊklɔːr] n folklore m.

folk music n musique f folk.

folk song n chanson f folk.

follow ['fɒləʊ] **1** vt suivre. **2** vi [gen] suivre. || [be logical] tenir debout; **it ~s that ... il s'ensuit que ....** ○ **follow up** vt sep [pursue - idea, suggestion] prendre en considération; [- advertisement] donner suite à. || [complete]: **to ~ sthg up with** faire suivre qqch de.

follower ['fɒləʊər] n [believer] disciple mf.

following ['fɒləʊɪŋ] **1** adj suivant(e). **2** n groupe m d'admirateurs. **3** prep après.

folly ['fɒlɪ] n (U) [foolishness] folie f.

fond [fɒnd] adj [affectionate] affectueux(euse); **to be ~ of** aimer beaucoup.

fondle ['fɒndl] vt caresser.

font [fɒnt] n [in church] fonts mpl baptismaux. || COMPUT & TYPO police f (de caractères).

food [fuːd] n nourriture f.

food mixer n mixer m.

food poisoning [-,pɔɪznɪŋ] n intoxication f alimentaire.

food processor [-,prəʊsesər] n robot m ménager.

foodstuffs ['fuːdstʌfs] npl denrées fpl alimentaires.

fool [fuːl] **1** n [idiot] idiot m, -e f. **2** vt duper; **to ~ sb into doing sthg** amener qqn à faire qqch en le dupant. ○ **fool about**, **fool around** vi [behave foolishly] faire l'imbécile. || [be unfaithful] être infidèle.

foolhardy ['fuːl,hɑːdɪ] adj téméraire.

foolish ['fuːlɪʃ] adj idiot(e), stupide.

foolproof ['fuːlpruːf] adj infaillible.

foot [fʊt] (pl sense 1 **feet**, pl sense 2 inv OR **feet**) **1** n [gen] pied m; [of animal] patte f; [of page, stairs] bas m; **to get to one's feet** se mettre debout, se lever; **on ~** à pied; **to put one's ~ in it** mettre les pieds dans le plat; **to put one's feet up** se reposer. || [unit of measurement] = 30,48 cm, ≃ pied m. **2** vt inf: **to ~ the bill** payer la note.

footage ['fʊtɪdʒ] n (U) séquences fpl.

football ['fʊtbɔːl] n [game - soccer] football m, foot m; [- American football] football américain. || [ball] ballon m de football OR foot.

footbrake ['fʊtbreɪk] n frein m (à pied).

footbridge ['fʊtbrɪdʒ] n passerelle f.

foothills ['fʊthɪlz] npl contreforts mpl.

foothold ['fʊthəʊld] n prise f (de pied).

footing ['fʊtɪŋ] n [foothold] prise f; **to lose one's ~** trébucher. || fig [basis] position f.

footlights ['fʊtlaɪts] npl rampe f.

footnote ['fʊtnəʊt] n note f en bas de page.

footpath ['fʊtpɑːθ, pl -pɑːðz] n sentier m.

footprint ['fʊtprɪnt] n empreinte f (de pied), trace f (de pas).

footstep ['fʊtstep] n [sound] bruit m de pas. || [footprint] empreinte f (de pied).

footwear ['fʊtweər] n (U) chaussures fpl.

for [fɔːr] **1** prep [referring to intention, destination, purpose] pour; **this is ~ you** c'est pour vous; **the plane ~ Paris** l'avion à destination de Paris; **what's it ~?** ça sert à quoi? || [representing, on behalf of] pour; **the MP ~ Barnsley** le député de Barnsley; **let me do that ~ you** laissez-moi faire, je vais vous le faire. || [because of] pour, en raison de; **~ various reasons** pour plusieurs raisons; **a prize ~ swimming** un prix de natation. || [with regard to] pour; **to be ready ~ sthg** être prêt pour qqch; **it's not ~ me to say** ce n'est pas à moi à le dire; **to feel sorry ~ sb** plaindre qqn. || [indicating amount of time, space]: **there's no time ~ that now** on n'a pas le temps de faire cela OR de s'occuper de cela maintenant; **there's room ~ another person** il y a de la place pour encore une personne. || [indicating period of time]: **she'll be away ~ a month** elle sera absente (pendant) un mois; **I've lived here ~ 3 years** j'habite ici depuis 3 ans, cela fait 3 ans que j'habite ici; **I can do it for you ~ tomorrow** je peux vous le faire pour demain. || [indicating distance] pendant, sur; **I walked ~ miles** j'ai marché (pendant) des kilomètres. || [indicating particular occasion] pour; **~ Christmas** pour Noël. || [indicating amount of money, price]: **they're 50p ~ ten** cela coûte 50p les dix; **I bought/sold it ~ £10** je l'ai acheté/vendu 10 livres. || [in favour of, in support of] pour; **to be all ~ sthg** être tout à fait pour OR en faveur de qqch. ‖ [in ratios] pour. ‖ [indicating meaning]: **P ~ Peter** P comme Peter; **what's the Greek ~ "mother"?** comment dit-on «mère» en grec? **2** *conj fml* [as, since] car. ○ **for all 1** *prep* malgré. **2** *conj* bien que (+ *subjunctive*); **~ all I know** pour ce que j'en sais.

foray ['foreɪ] *n*: **~ (into)** *lit & fig* incursion *f* (dans).

forbad [fə'bæd], **forbade** [fə'beɪd] *pt* → forbid.

forbid [fə'bɪd] (*pt* -**bade** OR -**bad**, *pp* **forbid** OR -**bidden**) *vt* interdire, défendre; **to ~ sb to do sthg** interdire OR défendre à qqn de faire qqch.

forbidden [fə'bɪdn] **1** *pp* → forbid. **2** *adj* interdit(e), défendu(e).

forbidding [fə'bɪdɪŋ] *adj* [severe, unfriendly] austère; [threatening] sinistre.

force [fɔːs] **1** *n* [gen] force *f*; **by ~ de force**. ‖ [effect]: **to be in/to come into ~** être/entrer en vigueur. **2** *vt* [gen] forcer; **to ~ sb to do sthg** forcer qqn à faire qqch. ‖ [press]: **to ~ sthg on sb** imposer qqch à qqn. ○ **forces** *npl*: **the ~s** les forces *fpl* armées; **to join ~s** joindre ses efforts.

force-feed *vt* nourrir de force.

forceful ['fɔːsful] *adj* [person] énergique; [speech] vigoureux(euse).

forceps ['fɔːseps] *npl* forceps *m*.

forcibly ['fɔːsəblɪ] *adv* [using physical force] de force. ‖ [powerfully] avec vigueur.

ford [fɔːd] *n* gué *m*.

fore [fɔːr] **1** *adj* NAUT à l'avant. **2** *n*: **to come to the ~** s'imposer.

forearm ['fɔːrɑːm] *n* avant-bras *m inv*.

foreboding [fɔː'bəʊdɪŋ] *n* pressentiment *m*.

forecast ['fɔːkɑːst] (*pt & pp* **forecast** OR -**ed**) **1** *n* prévision *f*; **(weather) ~** prévisions météorologiques. **2** *vt* prévoir.

foreclose [fɔː'kləʊz] **1** *vt* saisir. **2** *vi*: **to ~ on sb** saisir qqn.

forecourt ['fɔːkɔːt] *n* [of petrol station] devant *m*; [of building] avant-cour *f*.

forefinger ['fɔː,fɪŋɡər] *n* index *m*.

forefront ['fɔːfrʌnt] *n*: **in** OR **at the ~ of** au premier plan de.

forego [fɔː'ɡəʊ] = forgo.

foregone conclusion ['fɔːɡɒn-] *n*: **it's a ~** c'est couru.

foreground ['fɔːɡraʊnd] *n* premier plan *m*.

forehand ['fɔːhænd] *n* TENNIS coup *m* droit.

forehead ['fɔːhed] *n* front *m*.

foreign ['fɒrən] *adj* [gen] étranger(ère); [correspondent] à l'étranger. ‖ [policy, trade] extérieur(e).

foreign affairs *npl* affaires *fpl* étrangères.

foreign currency *n* (U) devises *fpl* étrangères.

foreigner ['fɒrənər] *n* étranger *m*, -ère *f*.

foreign minister *n* ministre *m* des Affaires étrangères.

Foreign Office *n Br*: **the ~** ≃ le ministère des Affaires étrangères.

Foreign Secretary *n Br* ≃ ministre *m* des Affaires étrangères.

foreleg ['fɔːleg] *n* [of horse] membre *m* antérieur; [of other animals] patte *f* de devant.

foreman ['fɔːmən] (*pl* -**men** [-mən]) *n* [of workers] contremaître *m*.

foremost ['fɔːməʊst] **1** *adj* principal(e). **2** *adv*: **first and ~** tout d'abord.

forensic medicine, forensic science *n* médecine *f* légale.

forerunner ['fɔː,rʌnər] *n* précurseur *m*.

foresee [fɔː'siː] (*pt* -**saw** [-'sɔː], *pp* -**seen**) *vt* prévoir.

foreseeable [fɔː'siːəbl] *adj* prévisible; **for the ~ future** pour tous les jours/mois *etc* à venir.

foreseen [fɔː'siːn] *pp* → foresee.

foreshadow [fɔː'ʃædəʊ] *vt* présager.

foresight ['fɔːsaɪt] *n* (U) prévoyance *f*.

forest ['fɒrɪst] *n* forêt *f*.

forestall [fɔː'stɔːl] *vt* [attempt, discussion] prévenir; [person] devancer.

forestry ['fɒrɪstrɪ] *n* sylviculture *f*.

foretaste ['fɔːteɪst] *n* avant-goût *m*.

foretell [fɔː'tel] (*pt & pp* -**told**) *vt* prédire.

foretold [fɔː'təʊld] *pt & pp* → foretell.

forever [fə'revər] *adv* [eternally] (pour) toujours.

forewarn [fɔː'wɔːn] *vt* avertir.

foreword ['fɔːwɜːd] *n* avant-propos *m inv*.

forfeit ['fɔːfɪt] **1** *n* amende *f*; [in game] gage *m*. **2** *vt* perdre.

forgave [fə'ɡeɪv] *pt* → forgive.

forge [fɔːdʒ] **1** *n* forge *f*. **2** *vt* INDUSTRY & *fig* forger. ‖ [signature, money] contrefaire; [passport] falsifier. ○ **forge ahead** *vi* prendre de l'avance.

forger ['fɔːdʒər] *n* faussaire *mf*.

forgery ['fɔːdʒərɪ] *n* (*U*) [crime] contre-façon *f*. || [forged article] faux *m*.

forget [fə'get] (*pt* -got, *pp* -gotten) 1 *vt* oublier; **to ~ to do sthg** oublier de faire qqch; **~ it!** laisse tomber! 2 *vi*: **to ~ (about sthg)** oublier (qqch).

forgetful [fə'getful] *adj* distrait(e), étourdi(e).

forget-me-not *n* myosotis *m*.

forgive [fə'gɪv] (*pt* -gave, *pp* -given [-'gɪvən]) *vt* pardonner; **to ~ sb for sthg/for doing sthg** pardonner qqch à qqn/à qqn d'avoir fait qqch.

forgiveness [fə'gɪvnɪs] *n* (*U*) pardon *m*.

forgo [fɔː'gəʊ] (*pt* -went, *pp* -gone [-'gɒn]) *vt* renoncer à.

forgot [fə'gɒt] *pt* → forget.

forgotten [fə'gɒtn] *pp* → forget.

fork [fɔːk] 1 *n* [for eating] fourchette *f*. || [for gardening] fourche *f*. || [in road] bifurcation *f*; [of river] embranchement *m*. 2 *vi* bifurquer. ○ **fork out** *inf* 1 *vt fus* allonger, débourser. 2 *vi*: **to ~ out (for)** casquer (pour).

forklift truck ['fɔːklɪft-] *n* chariot *m* élévateur.

forlorn [fə'lɔːn] *adj* [person, face] malheureux(euse), triste. || [place, landscape] désolé(e). || [hope, attempt] désespéré(e).

form [fɔːm] 1 *n* [shape, fitness, type] forme *f*; **on ~** *Br*, **in ~** *Am* en forme; **off ~** pas en forme; **in the ~ of** sous forme de. || [questionnaire] formulaire *m*. 2 *vt* former. 3 *vi* se former.

formal ['fɔːml] *adj* [person] formaliste; [language] soutenu(e). || [dinner party, announcement] officiel(ielle); [dress] de cérémonie.

formality [fɔː'mælətɪ] *n* formalité *f*.

format ['fɔːmæt] 1 *n* [gen & COMPUT] format *m*. 2 *vt* COMPUT formater.

formation [fɔː'meɪʃn] *n* [gen] formation *f*. || [of idea, plan] élaboration *f*.

former ['fɔːmər] 1 *adj* [previous] ancien(ienne); **~ husband** ex-mari *m*; **~ pupil** ancien élève *m*, ancienne élève *f*. || [first of two] premier(ière). 2 *n*: **the ~** le premier (la première), celui-là (celle-là).

formerly ['fɔːməlɪ] *adv* autrefois.

formidable ['fɔːmɪdəbl] *adj* impressionnant(e).

formula ['fɔːmjʊlə] (*pl* -as OR -ae [-iː]) *n* formule *f*.

formulate ['fɔːmjʊleɪt] *vt* formuler.

forsaken [fə'seɪkn] *adj* abandonné(e).

fort [fɔːt] *n* fort *m*.

forte ['fɔːtɪ] *n* point *m* fort.

forthcoming [fɔː'θkʌmɪŋ] *adj* [imminent] à venir. || [helpful] communicatif(ive).

forthright ['fɔːθraɪt] *adj* franc (franche), direct(e).

fortified wine ['fɔːtɪfaɪd-] *n* vin *m* de liqueur.

fortify ['fɔːtɪfaɪ] *vt* MIL fortifier. || *fig* [resolve etc] renforcer.

fortnight ['fɔːtnaɪt] *n Br* quinze jours *mpl*, quinzaine *f*.

fortnightly ['fɔːt,naɪtlɪ] *Br* 1 *adj* bimensuel(elle). 2 *adv* tous les quinze jours.

fortress ['fɔːtrɪs] *n* forteresse *f*.

fortunate ['fɔːtʃnət] *adj* heureux(euse); **to be ~** avoir de la chance.

fortunately ['fɔːtʃnətlɪ] *adv* heureusement.

fortune ['fɔːtʃuːn] *n* [wealth] fortune *f*. || [luck] fortune *f*, chance *f*. || [future]: **to tell sb's ~** dire la bonne aventure à qqn.

fortune-teller [-,telər] *n* diseuse *f* de bonne aventure.

forty ['fɔːtɪ] *num* quarante; *see also* **sixty**.

forward ['fɔːwəd] 1 *adj* [movement] en avant. || [planning] à long terme. || [impudent] effronté(e). 2 *adv* [ahead] en avant; **to go OR move ~** avancer. || [in time]: **to bring a meeting ~** avancer la date d'une réunion. 3 *n* SPORT avant *m*. 4 *vt* [letter] faire suivre; [goods] expédier.

forwarding address ['fɔːwədɪŋ-] *n* adresse *f* où faire suivre le courrier.

forwards ['fɔːwədz] *adv* = forward.

forwent [fɔː'went] *pt* → forgo.

fossil ['fɒsl] *n* fossile *m*.

foster ['fɒstər] 1 *adj* [family] d'accueil. 2 *vt* [child] accueillir. || *fig* [nurture] nourrir, entretenir.

foster child *n* enfant *m* placé en famille d'accueil.

foster parent *n* parent *m* nourricier.

fought [fɔːt] *pt* & *pp* → fight.

foul [faʊl] 1 *adj* [gen] infect(e); [water] croupi(e). || [language] ordurier(ière). 2 *n* SPORT faute *f*. 3 *vt* [make dirty] souiller, salir. || SPORT commettre une faute contre.

found [faʊnd] 1 *pt* & *pp* → find. 2 *vt* [hospital, town] fonder. || [base]: **to ~ sthg on** fonder OR baser qqch sur.

foundation [faʊn'deɪʃn] *n* [creation, organization] fondation *f*. || [basis] fondement *m*, base *f*. || **~ (cream)** fond *m* de teint. ○ **foundations** *npl* CONSTR fondations *fpl*.

founder ['faʊndə^r] **1** *n* fondateur *m*, -trice *f*. **2** *vi* [ship] sombrer.

foundry ['faʊndrɪ] *n* fonderie *f*.

fountain ['faʊntɪn] *n* fontaine *f*.

fountain pen *n* stylo *m* à encre.

four [fɔ:^r] *num* quatre; **on all ~s** à quatre pattes; *see also* **six**.

four-letter word *n* mot *m* grossier.

four-poster (bed) *n* lit *m* à baldaquin.

foursome ['fɔ:səm] *n* groupe *m* de quatre.

fourteen [,fɔ:'ti:n] *num* quatorze; *see also* **six**.

fourth [fɔ:θ] *num* quatrième; *see also* **sixth**.

Fourth of July *n*: **the ~** Fête de l'Indépendance américaine.

four-wheel drive *n*: **with ~** à quatre roues motrices.

fowl [faʊl] (*pl inv* OR **-s**) *n* volaille *f*.

fox [fɒks] **1** *n* renard *m*. **2** *vt* laisser perplexe.

foxglove ['fɒksglʌv] *n* digitale *f*.

foyer ['fɔɪeɪ] *n* [of hotel, theatre] foyer *m*. || *Am* [of house] hall *m* d'entrée.

fracas ['fræka:, *Am* 'freɪkəs] (*Br pl inv*, *Am pl* **-cases**) *n* bagarre *f*.

fraction ['frækʃn] *n* fraction *f*.

fractionally ['frækʃnəlɪ] *adv* un tout petit peu.

fracture ['fræktʃə^r] **1** *n* fracture *f*. **2** *vt* fracturer.

fragile ['frædʒaɪl] *adj* fragile.

fragment ['frægmənt] *n* fragment *m*.

fragrance ['freɪgrəns] *n* parfum *m*.

fragrant ['freɪgrənt] *adj* parfumé(e).

frail [freɪl] *adj* fragile.

frame [freɪm] **1** *n* [gen] cadre *m*; [of glasses] monture *f*; [of door, window] encadrement *m*. || [physique] charpente *f*. **2** *vt* [gen] encadrer. || [express] formuler. || *inf* [set up] monter un coup contre.

frame of mind *n* état *m* d'esprit.

framework ['freɪmwɜ:k] *n* [structure] armature *f*, carcasse *f*. || *fig* [basis] structure *f*, cadre *m*.

France [fra:ns] *n* France *f*; **in ~** en France.

franchise ['fræntʃaɪz] *n* POL droit *m* de vote. || COMM franchise *f*.

frank [fræŋk] **1** *adj* franc (franche). **2** *vt* affranchir.

frankly ['fræŋklɪ] *adv* franchement.

frantic ['fræntɪk] *adj* frénétique.

fraternity [frə'tɜ:nətɪ] *n* [community] confrérie *f*. || (U) [friendship] fraternité *f*. || *Am* [of students] club *m* d'étudiants.

fraternize, -ise ['frætənaɪz] *vi* fraterniser.

fraud [frɔ:d] *n* (U) [crime] fraude *f*. || *pej* [impostor] imposteur *m*.

fraught [frɔ:t] *adj* [full]: **~ with** plein(e) de. || *Br* [person] tendu(e); [time, situation] difficile.

fray [freɪ] **1** *vt fig*: **my nerves were ~ed** j'étais extrêmement tendu(e), j'étais à bout de nerfs. **2** *vi* [material, sleeves] s'user; **tempers ~ed** *fig* l'atmosphère était tendue OR électrique.

frayed [freɪd] *adj* [jeans, collar] élimé(e).

freak [fri:k] **1** *adj* bizarre, insolite. **2** *n* [strange creature] monstre *m*, phénomène *m*. || [unusual event] accident *m* bizarre. || *inf* [fanatic] fana *mf*.

freckle ['frekl] *n* tache *f* de rousseur.

free [fri:] (*compar* **freer**, *superl* **freest**, *pt & pp* **freed**) **1** *adj* [gen] libre; **to be ~ to do sthg** être libre de faire qqch; **feel ~!** je t'en prie!; **to set ~** libérer. || [not paid for] gratuit(e); **~ of charge** gratuitement. **2** *adv* [without payment] gratuitement; **for ~** gratuitement. || [run, live] librement. **3** *vt* [gen] libérer. || [trapped person, object] dégager.

freedom ['fri:dəm] *n* [gen] liberté *f*; **~ of speech** liberté d'expression. || [exception]: **~ (from)** exemption *f* (de).

free-for-all *n* mêlée *f* générale.

free gift *n* prime *f*.

freehand ['fri:hænd] *adj & adv* à main levée.

freehold ['fri:həʊld] *n* propriété *f* foncière inaliénable.

free kick *n* coup *m* franc.

freelance ['fri:lɑ:ns] **1** *adj* indépendant(e), free-lance (*inv*). **2** *n* indépendant *m*, -e *f*, free-lance *mf*.

freely ['fri:lɪ] *adv* [gen] librement. || [generously] sans compter.

Freemason ['fri:,meɪsn] *n* franc-maçon *m*.

freepost ['fri:pəʊst] *n* port *m* payé.

free-range *adj* de ferme.

freestyle ['fri:staɪl] *n* SWIMMING nage *f* libre.

free trade *n* (U) libre-échange *m*.

freeway ['fri:weɪ] *n Am* autoroute *f*.

freewheel [,fri:'wi:l] *vi* [on bicycle] rouler en roue libre; [in car] rouler au point mort.

free will n (U) libre arbitre m; **to do sthg of one's own ~** faire qqch de son propre gré.

freeze [fri:z] (pt **froze**, pp **frozen**) 1 vt [gen] geler; [food] congeler. || [wages, prices] bloquer. 2 vi [gen] geler. || [stop moving] s'arrêter. 3 n [cold weather] gel m. || [of wages, prices] blocage m.

freeze-dried [-'draɪd] adj lyophilisé(e).

freezer ['fri:zər] n congélateur m.

freezing ['fri:zɪŋ] 1 adj glacé(e); **I'm ~** je gèle. 2 n = **freezing point**.

freezing point n point m de congélation.

freight [freɪt] n [goods] fret m.

freight train n train m de marchandises.

French [frentʃ] 1 adj français(e). 2 n [language] français m. 3 npl: **the ~** les Français mpl.

French bean n haricot m vert.

French bread n (U) baguette f.

French Canadian 1 adj canadien français (canadienne française). 2 n Canadien français m, Canadienne française f.

French doors = **French windows**.

French dressing n [in UK] vinaigrette f; [in US] sauce-salade à base de mayonnaise et de ketchup.

French fries npl frites fpl.

Frenchman ['frentʃmən] (pl **-men** [-mən]) n Français m.

French windows npl porte-fenêtre f.

Frenchwoman ['frentʃ,wʊmən] (pl **-women** [-,wɪmɪn]) n Française f.

frenetic [frə'netɪk] adj frénétique.

frenzy ['frenzɪ] n frénésie f.

frequency ['fri:kwənsɪ] n fréquence f.

frequent [adj 'fri:kwənt, vb frɪ'kwent] 1 adj fréquent(e). 2 vt fréquenter.

frequently ['fri:kwəntlɪ] adv fréquemment.

fresh [freʃ] adj [gen] frais (fraîche). || [not salty] doux (douce). || [new - drink, piece of paper] autre; [- look, approach] nouveau(elle).

freshen ['freʃn] vt rafraîchir. ○ **freshen up** vi faire un brin de toilette.

freshly ['freʃlɪ] adv [squeezed, ironed] fraîchement.

freshman ['freʃmən] (pl **-men** [-mən]) n étudiant m, -e f de première année.

freshness ['freʃnɪs] n (U) [gen] fraîcheur f. || [originality] nouveauté f.

freshwater ['freʃ,wɔːtər] adj d'eau douce.

fret [fret] vi [worry] s'inquiéter.

friar ['fraɪər] n frère m.

friction ['frɪkʃn] n (U) friction f.

Friday ['fraɪdɪ] n vendredi m; see also **Saturday**.

fridge [frɪdʒ] n frigo m.

fried [fraɪd] adj frit(e); **~ egg** œuf m au plat.

friend [frend] n ami m, -e f; **to be ~ with sb** être ami avec qqn; **to make ~s (with sb)** se lier d'amitié (avec qqn).

friendly ['frendlɪ] adj [person, manner, match] amical(e); [nation] ami(e); **to be ~ with sb** être ami avec qqn.

friendship ['frendʃɪp] n amitié f.

fries [fraɪz] = **French fries**.

frieze [fri:z] n frise f.

fright [fraɪt] n peur f; **to give sb a ~** faire peur à qqn; **to take ~** prendre peur.

frighten ['fraɪtn] vt faire peur à, effrayer.

frightened ['fraɪtnd] adj apeuré(e); **to be ~ of sthg/of doing sthg** avoir peur de qqch/de faire qqch.

frightening ['fraɪtnɪŋ] adj effrayant(e).

frigid ['frɪdʒɪd] adj [sexually] frigide.

frill [frɪl] n [decoration] volant m. || inf [extra] supplément m.

fringe [frɪndʒ] n [gen] frange f. || [edge - of village] bordure f; [- of wood, forest] lisière f.

fringe benefit n avantage m extrasalarial.

frisk [frɪsk] vt fouiller.

frisky ['frɪskɪ] adj inf vif (vive).

fritter ['frɪtər] n beignet m. ○ **fritter away** vt sep gaspiller.

frivolous ['frɪvələs] adj frivole.

frizzy ['frɪzɪ] adj crépu(e).

fro [frəʊ] → **to**.

frock [frɒk] n dated robe f.

frog [frɒg] n [animal] grenouille f; **to have a ~ in one's throat** avoir un chat dans la gorge.

frogman ['frɒgmən] (pl **-men**) n homme-grenouille m.

frogmen ['frɒgmən] pl → **frogman**.

frolic ['frɒlɪk] (pt & pp **-ked**, cont **-king**) vi folâtrer.

from [weak form frəm, strong form frɒm] prep [indicating source, origin, removal] de; **where are you ~?** d'où venez-vous?, d'où êtes-vous?; **a flight ~ Paris** un vol en provenance de Paris; **to translate ~ Spanish into English** traduire d'espagnol en anglais; **to take sthg (away) ~ sb** prendre qqch à qqn. || [indicating a deduction] de; **to deduct sthg ~ sthg** retrancher qqch de qqch. || [indicating escape, separation] de; **he ran away ~ home** il a fait une fugue, il s'est sauvé de chez lui. || [indicating position] de; **seen ~ above/below** vu d'en haut/d'en bas. || [indicating distance] de; **it's 60 km ~ here** c'est à 60 km d'ici. || [indicating material object is made out of] en; **it's made ~ wood/plastic** c'est en bois/plastique. || [starting at a particular time] de; **~ 2 pm to** OR **till 6 pm** de 14 h à 18 h. || [indicating difference] de; **to be different ~ sb/sthg** être différent de qqn/qqch. || [indicating change]: **~ ... to ... à; the price went up ~ £100 to £150** le prix est passé OR monté de 100 livres à 150 livres. || [because of, as a result of] de; **to suffer ~ cold/hunger** souffrir du froid/de la faim. || [on the evidence of] d'après, à. || [indicating lowest amount] depuis, à partir de; **prices start ~ £50** le premier prix est de 50 livres.

front [frʌnt] **1** *n* [most forward part - gen] avant *m*; [- of dress, envelope, house] devant *m*; [- of class] premier rang *m*. || METEOR & MIL front *m*. || **(sea) ~** front *m* de mer. || [outward appearance - of person] contenance *f*, *pej* [- of business] façade *f*. **2** *adj* [tooth, garden] de devant; [row, page] premier(ière). ○ **in front** *adv* [further forward - walk, push] devant; [- people] à l'avant; [- winning] **to be in ~** mener. ○ **in front of** *prep* devant.

front door *n* porte *f* d'entrée.

frontier ['frʌn,tɪər, *Am* frʌn'tɪər] *n* [border] frontière *f*, *fig* limite *f*.

front man *n* [of company, organization] porte-parole *m inv*. || TV présentateur *m*.

front room *n* salon *m*.

front-runner *n* favori *m*, -ite *f*.

front-wheel drive *n* traction *f* avant.

frost [frɒst] *n* gel *m*.

frostbite ['frɒstbaɪt] *n* (*U*) gelure *f*.

frosted ['frɒstɪd] *adj* [glass] dépoli(e). || *Am* CULIN glacé(e).

frosty ['frɒstɪ] *adj* [weather, welcome] glacial(e). || [field, window] gelé(e).

froth [frɒθ] *n* [on beer] mousse *f*; [on sea] écume *f*.

frown [fraʊn] *vi* froncer les sourcils. ○ **frown (up)on** *vt fus* désapprouver.

froze [frəʊz] *pt* → freeze.

frozen ['frəʊzn] **1** *pp* → freeze. **2** *adj* gelé(e); [food] congelé(e).

frugal ['fruːgl] *adj* [meal] frugal(e). || [person, life] économe.

fruit [fruːt] (*pl inv* OR **fruits**) *n* fruit *m*.

fruitcake ['fruːtkeɪk] *n* cake *m*.

fruitful ['fruːtfʊl] *adj* [successful] fructueux(euse).

fruition [fruː'ɪʃn] *n*: **to come to ~** se réaliser.

fruit juice *n* jus *m* de fruits.

fruitless ['fruːtlɪs] *adj* vain(e).

fruit salad *n* salade *f* de fruits.

frumpy ['frʌmpɪ] *adj* mal attifé(e), mal fagoté(e).

frustrate [frʌ'streɪt] *vt* [annoy, disappoint] frustrer. || [prevent] faire échouer.

frustrated [frʌ'streɪtɪd] *adj* [person, artist] frustré(e). || [effort, love] vain(e).

frustration [frʌ'streɪʃn] *n* frustration *f*.

fry [fraɪ] (*pt* & *pp* -ied) *vt* & *vi* frire.

frying pan ['fraɪŋ-] *n* poêle *f* à frire.

ft. *abbr of* **foot, feet.**

fuck [fʌk] *vulg vt* & *vi* baiser. ○ **fuck off** *vi vulg*: fous le camp!

fudge [fʌdʒ] *n* (*U*) [sweet] caramel *m* (mou).

fuel ['fjʊəl] **1** *n* combustible *m*; [for engine] carburant *m*. **2** *vt* [supply with fuel] alimenter (en combustible/carburant). || *fig* [speculation] nourrir.

fuel pump *n* pompe *f* d'alimentation.

fuel tank *n* réservoir *m* à carburant.

fugitive ['fjuːdʒətɪv] *n* fugitif *m*, -ive *f*.

fulfil, fulfill *Am* [fʊl'fɪl] *vt* [duty, role] remplir; [hope] répondre à; [ambition, prophecy] réaliser. || [satisfy - need] satisfaire.

fulfilment, fulfillment *Am* [fʊl'fɪlmənt] *n* (*U*) [satisfaction] grande satisfaction *f*. || [of ambition, dream] réalisation *f*; [of role, promise] exécution *f*; [of need] satisfaction *f*.

full [fʊl] **1** *adj* [gen] plein(e); [bus, car park] complet(ète); [with food] gavé(e), repu(e). || [complete - recovery, control] total(e); [- explanation, day] entier(ère); [- volume] maximum. || [busy - life] rempli(e); [- timetable, day] chargé(e). || [flavour] riche. || [plump - figure] rondelet(ette); [- mouth] charnu(e). || [skirt, sleeve] ample. **2** *adv* [very]: **you know ~ well that** tu sais très bien que .... **3** *n*: **in ~** complètement, entièrement.

full board *n* pension *f* complète.

full-fledged *Am* = fully-fledged.

full moon *n* pleine lune *f*.

full-scale *adj* [life-size] grandeur na-

ture (*inv*). || [complete] de grande enver-
gure.

full stop *n* point *m*.

full time *n Br* SPORT fin *f* de match.
○ **full-time** *adj & adv* [work, worker] à
temps plein.

full up *adj* [bus, train] complet(ète);
[with food] gavé(e), repu(e).

fully ['fuli] *adv* [understand, satisfy] tout
à fait; [trained, describe] entièrement.

fully-fledged *Br*, **full-fledged** *Am*
[-'fledʒd] *adj* diplômé(e).

fumble ['fʌmbl] *vi* fouiller, tâtonner; **to
~ for** fouiller pour trouver.

fume [fju:m] *vi* [with anger] rager.
○ **fumes** *npl* [from paint] émanations
fpl; [from smoke] fumées *fpl*; [from car]
gaz *mpl* d'échappement.

fumigate ['fju:mɪgeɪt] *vt* fumiger.

fun [fʌn] *n* (*U*) [pleasure, amusement]: **to
have ~** s'amuser. || [playfulness]: **to be
full of ~** être plein(e) d'entrain. || [ri-
dicule]: **to make ~ of** OR **poke ~ at sb** se
moquer de qqn.

function ['fʌŋkʃn] **1** *n* [gen] fonction *f*.
|| [formal social event] réception *f* offi-
cielle. **2** *vi* fonctionner; **to ~ as** servir de.

functional ['fʌŋkʃnəl] *adj* [practical]
fonctionnel(elle). || [operational] en état
de marche.

fund [fʌnd] **1** *n* fonds *m*. **2** *vt* financer.
○ **funds** *npl* fonds *mpl*.

fundamental [,fʌndə'mentl] *adj*: **~ (to)**
fondamental(e) (à).

funding ['fʌndɪŋ] *n* (*U*) financement *m*.

funeral ['fju:nərəl] *n* obsèques *fpl*.

funeral parlour *n* entreprise *f* de pompes funèbres.

funfair ['fʌnfeəʳ] *n* fête *f* foraine.

fungus ['fʌŋgəs] (*pl* **-gi** [-gaɪ] OR
-guses) *n* champignon *m*.

funnel ['fʌnl] *n* [tube] entonnoir *m*. || [of
ship] cheminée *f*.

funny ['fʌnɪ] *adj* [amusing, odd] drôle. ||
[ill] tout drôle (toute drôle).

fur [fɜ:ʳ] *n* fourrure *f*.

fur coat *n* (manteau *m* de) fourrure *f*.

furious ['fjʊərɪəs] *adj* [very angry] fu-
rieux(ieuse).

furlong ['fɜ:lɒŋ] *n* = 201,17 mètres.

furnace ['fɜ:nɪs] *n* [fire] fournaise *f*.

furnish ['fɜ:nɪʃ] *vt* [fit out] meubler. ||
fml [provide] fournir; **to ~ sb with sthg**
fournir qqch à qqn.

furnished ['fɜ:nɪʃt] *adj* meublé(e).

furnishings ['fɜ:nɪʃɪŋz] *npl* mobilier *m*.

furniture ['fɜ:nɪtʃəʳ] *n* (*U*) meubles
mpl; **a piece of ~** un meuble.

furry ['fɜ:rɪ] *adj* [animal] à fourrure. ||
[material] recouvert(e) de fourrure.

further ['fɜ:ðəʳ] **1** *compar* → **far**. **2** *adv*
[gen] plus loin; **how much ~ is it?**
combien de kilomètres y a-t-il? **~ on**
plus loin. || [more - complicate, develop]
davantage; [- enquire] plus avant. || [in
addition] de plus. **3** *adj* nouveau(elle),
supplémentaire; **until ~ notice** jusqu'à
nouvel ordre. **4** *vt* [career, aims] faire
avancer; [cause] encourager.

furthermore [,fɜ:ðə'mɔ:ʳ] *adv* de plus.

furthest ['fɜ:ðɪst] **1** *superl* → **far**. **2** *adj*
le plus éloigné (la plus éloignée). **3** *adv* le
plus loin.

furtive ['fɜ:tɪv] *adj* [person] sour-
nois(e); [glance] furtif(ive).

fury ['fjʊərɪ] *n* fureur *f*.

fuse *esp Br*, **fuze** *Am* [fju:z] **1** *n* ELEC fu-
sible *m*, plomb *m*. || [of bomb] détonateur
m. **2** *vt* [join by heat] réunir par la fusion.
|| [combine] fusionner. **3** *vi* ELEC: **the
lights have ~d** les plombs ont sauté. ||
[join by heat] fondre. || [combine] fusion-
ner.

fuse-box *n* boîte *f* à fusibles.

fused [fju:zd] *adj* [plug] avec fusible incorporé.

fuss [fʌs] **1** *n* [excitement, anxiety] agita-
tion *f*; **to make a ~** faire des histoires. ||
(*U*) [complaints] protestations *fpl*. **2** *vi*
faire des histoires.

fussy ['fʌsɪ] *adj* [fastidious - person] ta-
tillon(onne); [- eater] difficile. || [over-
decorated] tarabiscoté(e).

futile ['fju:taɪl] *adj* vain(e).

futon ['fu:tɒn] *n* futon *m*.

future ['fju:tʃəʳ] **1** *n* [gen] avenir *m*; **in
~** à l'avenir; **in the ~** dans le futur, à
l'avenir. || GRAMM: **~ (tense)** futur *m*. **2** *adj*
futur(e).

fuze *Am* = **fuse**.

fuzzy ['fʌzɪ] *adj* [photo, image] flou(e).

G

g¹ (*pl* **g's** OR **gs**), **G** (*pl* **G's** OR **Gs**) [dʒiː] *n* [letter] g *m inv*, G *m inv*. ○ **G** *n* MUS sol *m*. || (*abbr of* **good**) B.

g² (*abbr of* **gram**) g.

gabble ['gæbl] *vt* & *vi* baragouiner.

gable ['geɪbl] *n* pignon *m*.

gadget ['gædʒɪt] *n* gadget *m*.

Gaelic ['geɪlɪk] **1** *adj* gaélique. **2** *n* gaélique *m*.

gag [gæg] **1** *n* [for mouth] bâillon *m*. || *inf* [joke] blague *f*, gag *m*. **2** *vt* [put gag on] bâillonner.

gage *Am* = **gauge**.

gaiety ['geɪətɪ] *n* gaieté *f*.

gaily ['geɪlɪ] *adv* [cheerfully] gaiement. || [thoughtlessly] allègrement.

gain [geɪn] **1** *n* [gen] profit *m*. || [improvement] augmentation *f*. **2** *vt* [acquire] gagner. || [increase in - speed, weight] prendre; [- confidence] gagner en. **3** *vi* [advance]: **to ~ in sthg** gagner en qqch. || [benefit]: **to ~ from** OR **by sthg** tirer un avantage de qqch. || [watch, clock] avancer. ○ **gain on** *vt fus* rattraper.

gal. *abbr of* **gallon**.

gala ['gɑːlə] *n* [celebration] gala *m*.

galaxy ['gæləksɪ] *n* galaxie *f*.

gale [geɪl] *n* [wind] grand vent *m*.

gall [gɔːl] *n* [nerve]: **to have the ~ to do sthg** avoir le toupet de faire qqch.

gallant [sense 1 'gælənt, sense 2 gə'lænt, 'gælənt] *adj* [courageous] courageux(euse). || [polite to women] galant.

gall bladder *n* vésicule *f* biliaire.

gallery ['gælərɪ] *n* [gen] galerie *f*. || [for displaying art] musée *m*.

galley ['gælɪ] (*pl* **galleys**) *n* [ship] galère *f*. || [kitchen] cuisine *f*.

Gallic ['gælɪk] *adj* français(e).

galling ['gɔːlɪŋ] *adj* humiliant(e).

gallon ['gælən] *n* = 4,546 *litres*, gallon *m*.

gallop ['gæləp] **1** *n* galop *m*. **2** *vi* galoper.

gallows ['gæləʊz] (*pl inv*) *n* gibet *m*.

gallstone ['gɔːlstəʊn] *n* calcul *m* biliaire.

galore [gə'lɔːʳ] *adj* en abondance.

galvanize, -ise ['gælvənaɪz] *vt* [impel]: **to ~ sb into action** pousser qqn à agir.

gambit ['gæmbɪt] *n* entrée *f* en matière.

gamble ['gæmbl] **1** *n* [calculated risk] risque *m*. **2** *vi* [bet] jouer; **to ~ on** jouer de l'argent sur. || [take risk]: **to ~ on** miser sur.

gambler ['gæmbləʳ] *n* joueur *m*, -euse *f*.

gambling ['gæmblɪŋ] *n* (U) jeu *m*.

game [geɪm] **1** *n* [gen] jeu *m*. || [match] match *m*. || (U) [hunted animals] gibier *m*. **2** *adj* [brave] courageux(euse). || [willing]: **~ (for sthg/to do sthg)** partant(e) (pour qqch/pour faire qqch). ○ **games** **1** *n* SCH éducation *f* physique. **2** *npl* [sporting contest] jeux *mpl*.

gamekeeper ['geɪmˌkiːpəʳ] *n* garde-chasse *m*.

game reserve *n* réserve *f* (de chasse).

gammon ['gæmən] *n* jambon *m* fumé.

gamut ['gæmət] *n* gamme *f*.

gang [gæŋ] *n* [of criminals] gang *m*. || [of young people] bande *f*. ○ **gang up** *vi inf*: **to ~ up (on)** se liguer (contre).

gangland ['gæŋlænd] *n* (U) milieu *m*.

gangrene ['gæŋgriːn] *n* gangrène *f*.

gangster ['gæŋstəʳ] *n* gangster *m*.

gantry ['gæntrɪ] *n* portique *m*.

gap [gæp] *n* [empty space] trou *m*; [in text] blanc *m*; *fig* [in knowledge, report] lacune *f*. || [interval of time] période *f*. || *fig* [great difference] fossé *m*.

gape [geɪp] *vi* [person] rester bouche bée. || [hole, shirt] bâiller.

gaping ['geɪpɪŋ] *adj* [open-mouthed] bouche bée (*inv*). || [wide-open] béant(e).

garage [*Br* 'gærɑːʒ, 'gærɪdʒ, *Am* gə'rɑːʒ] *n* [gen] garage *m*.

garbage ['gɑːbɪdʒ] *n* (U) [refuse] détritus *mpl*. || *inf* [nonsense] idioties *fpl*.

garbage can *n Am* poubelle *f*.

garbage truck *n Am* camion-poubelle *m*.

garbled ['gɑːbld] *adj* confus(e).

garden ['gɑːdn] **1** *n* jardin *m*. **2** *vi* jardiner.

garden centre *n* jardinerie *f*, garden centre *m*.

gardener ['gɑːdnəʳ] *n* [professional] jardinier *m*, -ière *f*.

gardening ['gɑːdnɪŋ] *n* jardinage *m*.

gargle ['gɑːgl] *vi* se gargariser.

gargoyle ['gɑːgɔɪl] *n* gargouille *f*.

garish ['geərɪʃ] *adj* criard(e).

garland ['gɑːlənd] *n* guirlande *f* de fleurs.

garlic ['gɑːlɪk] *n* ail *m*.

garlic bread *n* pain *m* à l'ail.

garment ['gɑːmənt] *n* vêtement *m*.

garnish ['gɑːnɪʃ] **1** *n* garniture *f*. **2** *vt* garnir.

garrison ['gærɪsn] *n* [soldiers] garnison *f*.

garrulous ['gærələs] *adj* volubile.

garter ['gɑːtər] *n* [for socks] support-chaussette *m*; [for stockings] jarretière *f*. ‖ *Am* [suspender] jarretelle *f*.

gas [gæs] (*pl* **-es** OR **-ses**) **1** *n* [gen] gaz *m inv*. ‖ *Am* [for vehicle] essence *f*. **2** *vt* gazer.

gas cylinder *n* bouteille *f* de gaz.

gas gauge *n Am* jauge *f* d'essence.

gash [gæʃ] **1** *n* entaille *f*. **2** *vt* entailler.

gasket ['gæskɪt] *n* joint *m* d'étanchéité.

gasman ['gæsmæn] (*pl* **-men** [-men]) *n* [who reads meter] employé *m* du gaz; [for repairs] installateur *m* de gaz.

gas mask *n* masque *m* à gaz.

gas meter *n* compteur *m* à gaz.

gasoline ['gæsəliːn] *n Am* essence *f*.

gasp [gɑːsp] **1** *n* halètement *m*. **2** *vi* [breathe quickly] haleter. ‖ [in shock, surprise] avoir le souffle coupé.

gas pedal *n Am* accélérateur *m*.

gas station *n Am* station-service *f*.

gas tank *n Am* réservoir *m*.

gas tap *n* [for mains supply] robinet *m* de gaz; [on gas fire] prise *f* de gaz.

gastroenteritis ['gæstrəʊˌentəˈraɪtɪs] *n* gastro-entérite *f*.

gastronomy [gæsˈtrɒnəmɪ] *n* gastronomie *f*.

gasworks ['gæswɜːks] (*pl inv*) *n* usine *f* à gaz.

gate [geɪt] *n* [of garden, farm] barrière *f*; [of town, at airport] porte *f*; [of park] grille *f*.

gatecrash ['geɪtkræʃ] *vt & vi inf* prendre part à une réunion, une réception sans y avoir été convié.

gateway ['geɪtweɪ] *n* [entrance] entrée *f*. ‖ [means of access]: **~** porte *f* de.

gather ['gæðər] **1** *vt* [collect] ramasser; [flowers] cueillir; [information] recueillir; [courage, strength] rassembler; **to ~ together** rassembler. ‖ [increase - speed, force] prendre. ‖ [understand]: **to ~ (that)** ... croire comprendre que .... ‖ [cloth - into folds] plisser. **2** *vi* [come together] se rassembler; [clouds] s'amonceler.

gathering ['gæðərɪŋ] *n* [meeting] rassemblement *m*.

gaudy ['gɔːdɪ] *adj* voyant(e).

gauge, gage *Am* [geɪdʒ] **1** *n* [for rain] pluviomètre *m*; [for fuel] jauge *f* (d'essence); [for tyre pressure] manomètre *m*. ‖ [of gun, wire] calibre *m*. ‖ RAIL écartement *m*. **2** *vt* [measure] mesurer. ‖ [evaluate] jauger.

Gaul [gɔːl] *n* [country] Gaule *f*. ‖ [person] Gaulois *m*, -e *f*.

gaunt [gɔːnt] *adj* [thin] hâve. ‖ [bare, grim] désolé(e).

gauntlet ['gɔːntlɪt] *n* gant *m* (de protection); **to run the ~ of sthg** endurer qqch; **to throw down the ~ (to sb)** jeter le gant (à qqn).

gauze [gɔːz] *n* gaze *f*.

gave [geɪv] *pt* → **give**.

gawky ['gɔːkɪ] *adj* [person] dégingandé(e); [movement] désordonné(e).

gawp [gɔːp] *vi*: **to ~ (at)** rester bouche bée (devant).

gay [geɪ] **1** *adj* [gen] gai(e). ‖ [homosexual] homo (*inv*), gay (*inv*). **2** *n* homo *mf*, gay *mf*.

gaze [geɪz] **1** *n* regard *m* (fixe). **2** *vi*: **to ~ at sb/sthg** regarder qqn/qqch (fixement).

gazelle [gəˈzel] (*pl inv* OR **-s**) *n* gazelle *f*.

gazetteer [ˌgæzɪˈtɪər] *n* index *m* géographique.

GB (*abbr of* **Great Britain**) *n* G-B *f*.

GDP (*abbr of* **gross domestic product**) *n* PIB *m*.

gear [gɪər] **1** *n* TECH [mechanism] embrayage *m*. ‖ [speed - of car, bicycle] vitesse *f*; **to be in/out of ~** être en prise/au point mort. ‖ (*U*) [equipment, clothes] équipement *m*. **2** *vt*: **to ~ sthg to sb/sthg** destiner qqch à qqn/qqch. ○ **gear up** *vi*: **to ~ up for sthg/to do sthg** se préparer pour qqch/à faire qqch.

gearbox ['gɪəbɒks] *n* boîte *f* de vitesses.

gear lever, gear stick *Br*, **gear shift** *Am* *n* levier *m* de changement de vitesse.

gear wheel *n* pignon *m*, roue *f* d'engrenage.

geese [giːs] *pl* → **goose**.

gel [dʒel] **1** *n* [for hair] gel *m*. **2** *vi* [thicken] prendre. ‖ *fig* [take shape] prendre tournure.

gelatin ['dʒelətɪn], **gelatine** [ˌdʒeləˈtiːn] *n* gélatine *f*.

gelignite ['dʒelɪgnaɪt] *n* gélignite *f*.

gem [dʒem] *n* [jewel] pierre *f* précieuse, gemme *f*. ‖ *fig* [person, thing] perle *f*.

Gemini ['dʒemɪnaɪ] *n* Gémeaux *mpl*.

gender ['dʒendər] *n* [sex] sexe *m*. ‖ GRAMM genre *m*.

gene [dʒiːn] *n* gène *m*.

general ['dʒenərəl] **1** *adj* général(e). **2** *n* général *m*. ○ **in general** *adv* en général.

general anaesthetic *n* anesthésie *f* générale.

general delivery *n* Am poste *f* restante.

general election *n* élection *f* générale.

generalization [,dʒenərəlaɪ'zeɪʃn] *n* généralisation *f*.

general knowledge *n* culture *f* générale.

generally ['dʒenərəlɪ] *adv* [usually, in most cases] généralement. ‖ [unspecifically] en général; [describe] en gros.

general practitioner *n* (médecin *m*) généraliste *m*.

general public *n*: **the ~** le grand public.

general strike *n* grève *f* générale.

generate ['dʒenəreɪt] *vt* [energy, jobs] générer; [electricity, heat] produire; [interest, excitement] susciter.

generation [,dʒenə'reɪʃn] *n* [gen] génération *f*. ‖ [creation - of jobs] création *f*; [- of interest, excitement] induction *f*; [- of electricity] production *f*.

generator ['dʒenəreɪtər] *n* générateur *m*; ELEC génératrice *f*, générateur.

generosity [,dʒenə'rɒsətɪ] *n* générosité *f*.

generous ['dʒenərəs] *adj* généreux (euse).

genetic [dʒɪ'netɪk] *adj* génétique. ○ **genetics** *n* (U) génétique *f*.

Geneva [dʒɪ'niːvə] *n* Genève.

genial ['dʒiːnjəl] *adj* affable.

genitals ['dʒenɪtlz] *npl* organes *mpl* génitaux.

genius ['dʒiːnjəs] (*pl* -es) *n* génie *m*.

genteel [dʒen'tiːl] *adj* raffiné(e).

gentle ['dʒentl] *adj* doux (douce); [hint] discret(ète); [telling-off] léger(ère).

gentleman ['dʒentlmən] (*pl* -men [-mən]) *n* [well-behaved man] gentleman *m*. ‖ [man] monsieur *m*.

gently ['dʒentlɪ] *adv* [gen] doucement; [speak, smile] avec douceur.

gentry ['dʒentrɪ] *n* petite noblesse *f*.

genuine ['dʒenjuɪn] *adj* authentique; [interest, customer] sérieux(ieuse); [person, concern] sincère.

geography [dʒɪ'ɒgrəfɪ] *n* géographie *f*.

geology [dʒɪ'ɒlədʒɪ] *n* géologie *f*.

geometric(al) [,dʒɪə'metrɪk(l)] *adj* géométrique.

geometry [dʒɪ'ɒmətrɪ] *n* géométrie *f*.

geranium [dʒɪ'reɪnjəm] (*pl* -s) *n* géranium *m*.

gerbil ['dʒɜːbɪl] *n* gerbille *f*.

geriatric [,dʒerɪ'ætrɪk] *adj* MED gériatrique.

germ [dʒɜːm] *n* [bacterium] germe *m*.

German ['dʒɜːmən] **1** *adj* allemand(e). **2** *n* [person] Allemand *m*, -e *f*. ‖ [language] allemand *m*.

German measles *n* (U) rubéole *f*.

Germany ['dʒɜːmənɪ] *n* Allemagne *f*.

germinate ['dʒɜːmɪneɪt] *vi* lit & fig germer.

gerund ['dʒerənd] *n* gérondif *m*.

gesticulate [dʒes'tɪkjuleɪt] *vi* gesticuler.

gesture ['dʒestʃər] **1** *n* geste *m*. **2** *vi*: **to ~ to** OR **towards sb** faire signe à qqn.

get [get] (*Br pt* & *pp* got, *Am pt* got, *pp* gotten) **1** *vt* [cause to do]: **to ~ sb to do sthg** faire faire qqch à qqn; **I'll ~ my sister to help** je vais demander à ma sœur de nous aider. ‖ [cause to be done]: **to ~ sthg done** faire faire qqch. ‖ [cause to become]: **to ~ sb pregnant** rendre qqn enceinte; **I can't ~ the car started** je n'arrive pas à mettre la voiture en marche. ‖ [cause to move]: **to ~ sb/sthg through sthg** faire passer qqn/qqch par qqch; **to ~ sb/sthg out of sthg** faire sortir qqn/qqch de qqch. ‖ [bring, fetch] aller chercher; **can I ~ you something to eat/ drink?** est-ce que je peux vous offrir quelque chose à manger/boire? ‖ [obtain - gen] obtenir; [- job, house] trouver. ‖ [receive] recevoir, avoir; **she ~s a good salary** elle touche un bon traitement. ‖ [experience a sensation] avoir; **do you ~ the feeling he doesn't like us?** tu n'as pas l'impression qu'il ne nous aime pas? ‖ [be infected with, suffer from] avoir, attraper; **to ~ a cold** attraper un rhume. ‖ [understand] comprendre, saisir. ‖ [catch - bus, train, plane] prendre. ‖ [capture] prendre, attraper. ‖ [find]: **you ~ a lot of artists here** on trouve OR il y a beaucoup d'artistes ici; *see also* have. **2** *vi* [become] devenir; **to ~ suspicious** devenir méfiant; **I'm getting cold/bored** je commence à avoir froid/à m'ennuyer; **it's getting late** il se fait tard. ‖ [arrive] arriver; **I only got back yesterday** je suis rentré hier seulement. || [eventually succeed in]: **to ~ to do sthg** parvenir à OR finir par faire qqch; **did you ~ to see him?** est-ce que tu as réussi à le voir? || [progress]: **how far have you got?** où en es-tu?; **now we're getting somewhere** enfin on avance. **3** *aux vb*: **to ~ excited** s'exciter; **to ~ hurt** se faire mal; **to ~ beaten up** se faire tabasser; **let's ~ going** OR **moving** allons-y; *see also* have. ○ **get about**, **get around** *vi* [move from place to place] se déplacer. || [circulate - news, rumour] circuler, se répandre; *see also* get around. ○ **get along** *vi* [manage] se débrouiller. || [progress] avancer, faire des progrès. || [have a good relationship] s'entendre. ○ **get around**, **get round** **1** *vt fus* [overcome] venir à bout de, surmonter. **2** *vi* [circulate] circuler, se répandre. || [eventually do]: **to ~ around to (doing) sthg** trouver le temps de faire qqch; *see also* get about. ○ **get at** *vt fus* [reach] parvenir à. || [imply] vouloir dire; **what are you getting at?** où veux-tu en venir? || *inf* [criticize] critiquer, dénigrer. ○ **get away** *vi* [leave] partir, s'en aller. || [go on holiday] partir en vacances. || [escape] s'échapper, s'évader. ○ **get away with** *vt fus*: **to let sb ~ away with sthg** passer qqch à qqn. ○ **get back 1** *vt sep* [recover, regain] retrouver, récupérer. **2** *vi* [move away] s'écarter. ○ **get back to** *vt fus* [return to previous state, activity] revenir à; **to ~ back to sleep** se rendormir; **to ~ back to work** [after pause] se remettre au travail; [after illness] reprendre son travail. || *inf* [phone back] rappeler. ○ **get down** *vt sep* [depress] déprimer. || [fetch from higher level] descendre. ○ **get down to** *vt fus*: **to ~ down to doing sthg** se mettre à faire qqch. ○ **get in** *vi* [enter - gen] entrer; [- referring to vehicle] monter. || [arrive] arriver; [arrive home] rentrer. ○ **get into** *vt fus* [car] monter dans. || [become involved in] se lancer dans; **to ~ into an argument with sb** se disputer avec qqn. || [enter into a particular situation, state]: **to ~ into a panic** s'affoler; **to ~ into trouble** s'attirer des ennuis. ○ **get off 1** *vt sep* [remove] enlever. **2** *vt fus* [go away from] partir de. || [train, bus etc] descendre de. **3** *vi* [leave bus, train] descendre. || [escape punishment] s'en tirer. || [depart] partir. ○ **get on 1** *vt fus* [bus, train, plane] monter dans. || [horse] monter sur. **2** *vi* [enter bus, train] monter. || [have good relation-

ship] s'entendre, s'accorder. || [progress] avancer, progresser; **how are you getting on?** comment ça va? || [proceed]: **to ~ on (with sthg)** continuer (qqch), poursuivre (qqch). || [be successful professionally] réussir. ○ **get out 1** *vt sep* [take out] sortir. || [remove] enlever. **2** *vi* [from car, bus, train] descendre. || [news] s'ébruiter. ○ **get out of** *vt fus* [car etc] descendre de. || [escape from] s'évader de, s'échapper de. || [avoid] éviter, se dérober à; **to ~ out of doing sthg** se dispenser de faire qqch. ○ **get over** *vt fus* [recover from] se remettre de. || [overcome] surmonter, venir à bout de. || [communicate] communiquer. ○ **get round = get around.** ○ **get through 1** *vt fus* [job, task] arriver au bout de. || [exam] réussir à. || [food, drink] consommer. || [unpleasant situation] endurer, supporter. **2** *vi* [make o.s. understood]: **to ~ through (to sb)** se faire comprendre (de qqn). || TELEC obtenir la communication. ○ **get together 1** *vt sep* [organize - team, belongings] rassembler; [- project, report] préparer. **2** *vi* se réunir. ○ **get up 1** *vi* se lever. **2** *vt fus* [petition, demonstration] organiser. ○ **get up to** *vt fus inf* faire.

getaway ['getəweı] *n* fuite *f*.

get-together *n inf* réunion *f*.

geyser ['giːzə^r] *n* [hot spring] geyser *m*.

ghastly ['gɑːstlı] *adj inf* [very bad, unpleasant] épouvantable. || [horrifying, macabre] effroyable.

gherkin ['gɜːkın] *n* cornichon *m*.

ghetto ['getəʊ] *n* (*pl* -s OR -es) *n* ghetto *m*.

ghetto blaster [-ˌblɑːstə^r] *n inf* grand radiocassette *m* portatif.

ghost [gəʊst] *n* [spirit] spectre *m*.

giant ['dʒaıənt] **1** *adj* géant(e). **2** *n* géant *m*.

gibberish ['dʒıbərıʃ] *n* (*U*) charabia *m*, inepties *fpl*.

gibe [dʒaıb] *n* insulte *f*.

giblets ['dʒıblıts] *npl* abats *mpl*.

Gibraltar [dʒıˈbrɔːltə^r] *n* Gibraltar *m*.

giddy ['gıdı] *adj* [dizzy]: **to feel ~** avoir la tête qui tourne.

gift [gıft] *n* [present] cadeau *m*. || [talent] don *m*.

gifted ['gıftıd] *adj* doué(e).

gig [gıg] *n inf* [concert] concert *m*.

gigabyte ['gaıgəbaıt] *n* COMPUT gigaoctet *m*.

gigantic [dʒaıˈgæntık] *adj* énorme, gigantesque.

glassware

giggle ['gɪgl] 1 *n* [laugh] gloussement *m*. 2 *vi* [laugh] glousser.

gilded ['gɪldɪd] *adj* = gilt.

gill [dʒɪl] *n* [unit of measurement] = *0,142 litre*, quart *m* de pinte.

gills [gɪlz] *npl* [of fish] branchies *fpl*.

gilt [gɪlt] 1 *adj* [covered in gold] doré(e). 2 *n* (U) [gold layer] dorure *f*.

gimmick ['gɪmɪk] *n pej* artifice *m*.

gin [dʒɪn] *n* gin *m*; ~ **and tonic** gin tonic.

ginger ["dʒɪndʒər] *n* [root] gingembre *m*. || [powder] gingembre *m* en poudre.

ginger ale *n* boisson gazeuse au gingembre.

ginger beer *n* boisson non-alcoolisée au gingembre.

gingerbread ['dʒɪndʒəbred] *n* pain *m* d'épice.

ginger-haired [-'heəd] *adj* roux (rousse).

gingerly ['dʒɪndʒəlɪ] *adv* avec précaution.

gipsy ['dʒɪpsɪ] 1 *adj* gitan(e). 2 *n* gitan *m*, -e *f*; *Br pej* bohémien *m*, -ienne *f*.

giraffe [dʒɪ'rɑːf] (*pl inv* OR -**s**) *n* girafe *f*.

girder ['gɜːdər] *n* poutrelle *f*.

girdle ['gɜːdl] *n* [corset] gaine *f*.

girl [gɜːl] *n* [gen] fille *f*. || [girlfriend] petite amie *f*.

girlfriend ['gɜːlfrend] *n* [female lover] petite amie *f*. || [female friend] amie *f*.

girl guide *Br*, **girl scout** *Am n* éclaireuse *f*, guide *f*.

girth [gɜːθ] *n* [circumference - of tree] circonférence *f*; [- of person] tour *m* de taille. || [of horse] sangle *f*.

gist [dʒɪst] *n* substance *f*; **to get the ~ of sthg** comprendre OR saisir l'essentiel de qqch.

give [gɪv] (*pt* **gave**, *pp* **given**) 1 *vt* [gen] donner; [message] transmettre; [attention, time] consacrer; **to ~ sb/sthg sthg** donner qqch à qqn/qqch; **to ~ sb pleasure/a fright/a smile** faire plaisir/peur/un sourire à qqn. || [as present]: **to ~ sb sthg, to ~ sthg to sb** donner qqch à qqn, offrir qqch à qqn. 2 *vi* [collapse, break] céder, s'affaisser. 3 *n* [elasticity] élasticité *f*, souplesse *f*. **◇ give or take** *prep*: ~ **or take a day/£10** à un jour/10 livres près. **◇ give away** *vt sep* [get rid of] donner. || [reveal] révéler. **◇ give back** *vt sep* [return] rendre. **◇ give in** *vi* [admit defeat] abandonner, se rendre. || [agree unwillingly]: **to ~ in to sthg** céder à qqch. **◇ give off** *vt fus* [smell] exhaler; [smoke] faire; [heat] produire. **◇ give out** 1 *vt sep* [distribute] distribuer. 2 *vi* [supplies] s'épuiser; [car] lâcher. **◇ give up** 1 *vt sep* [stop] renoncer à; **to ~ up drinking/smoking** arrêter de boire/de fumer. || [surrender]: **to ~ o.s. up (to sb)** se rendre (à qqn). 2 *vi* abandonner, se rendre.

given ['gɪvn] 1 *adj* [set, fixed] convenu(e), fixé(e). || [prone]: **to be ~ to sthg/ to doing sthg** être enclin(e) à qqch/à faire qqch. 2 *prep* étant donné; ~ **that** étant donné que.

given name *n Am* prénom *m*.

glacier ['glæsjər] *n* glacier *m*.

glad [glæd] *adj* [happy, pleased] content(e); **to be ~ about sthg** être content de qqch. || [willing]: **to be ~ to do sthg** faire qqch volontiers OR avec plaisir. || [grateful]: **to be ~ of sthg** être content(e) de qqch.

gladly ['glædlɪ] *adv* [happily, eagerly] avec joie. || [willingly] avec plaisir.

glamor *Am* = glamour.

glamorous ['glæmərəs] *adj* [person] séduisant(e); [appearance] élégant(e); [job, place] prestigieux(ieuse).

glamour *Br*, **glamor** *Am* ['glæmər] *n* [of person] charme *m*; [of appearance] élégance *f*, chic *m*; [of job, place] prestige *m*.

glance [glɑːns] 1 *n* [quick look] regard *m*, coup d'œil *m*; **at a ~** d'un coup d'œil; **at first ~** au premier coup d'œil. 2 *vi* [look quickly]: **to ~ at sb/sthg** jeter un coup d'œil à qqn/qqch. **◇ glance off** *vt fus* [subj: ball, bullet] ricocher sur.

gland [glænd] *n* glande *f*.

glandular fever [,glændjulər-] *n* mononucléose *f* infectieuse.

glare [gleər] 1 *n* [scowl] regard *m* mauvais. || (U) [of headlights, publicity] lumière *f* aveuglante. 2 *vi* [scowl]: **to ~ at sb/sthg** regarder qqn/qqch d'un œil mauvais. || [sun, lamp] briller d'une lumière éblouissante.

glaring ['gleərɪŋ] *adj* [very obvious] flagrant(e). || [blazing, dazzling] aveuglant(e).

glasnost ['glæznɒst] *n* glasnost *f*, transparence *f*.

glass [glɑːs] 1 *n* [gen] verre *m*. || (U) [glassware] verrerie *f*. 2 *comp* [bottle, jar] en OR de verre; [door, partition] vitré(e). **◇ glasses** *npl* [spectacles] lunettes *fpl*.

glassware ['glɑːsweər] *n* (U) verrerie *f*.

glassy ['glɑ:sɪ] *adj* [smooth, shiny] lisse comme un miroir. ‖ [blank, lifeless] vitreux(euse).

glaze [gleɪz] **1** *n* [on pottery] vernis *m*; [on pastry, flan] glaçage *m*. **2** *vt* [pottery, tiles, bricks] vernisser; [pastry, flan] glacer.

glazier ['gleɪzjər] *n* vitrier *m*.

gleam [gli:m] **1** *n* [of gold] reflet *m*; [of fire, sunset, disapproval] lueur *f*. **2** *vi* [surface, object] luire. ‖ [light, eyes] briller.

gleaming ['gli:mɪŋ] *adj* brillant(e).

glee [gli:] *n* (*U*) [joy] joie *f*, jubilation *f*.

glib [glɪb] *adj pej* [salesman, politician] qui a du bagout; [promise, excuse] facile.

glide [glaɪd] *vi* [move smoothly - dancer, boat] glisser sans effort; [- person] se mouvoir sans effort. ‖ [fly] planer.

glider ['glaɪdər] *n* [plane] planeur *m*.

gliding ['glaɪdɪŋ] *n* [sport] vol *m* à voile.

glimmer ['glɪmər] *n* [faint light] faible lueur *f*; *fig* signe *m*, lueur.

glimpse [glɪmps] **1** *n* [look, sight] aperçu *m*. ‖ [idea, perception] idée *f*. **2** *vt* [catch sight of] apercevoir, entrevoir. ‖ [perceive] pressentir.

glint [glɪnt] **1** *n* [flash] reflet *m*. ‖ [in eyes] éclair *m*. **2** *vi* étinceler.

glisten ['glɪsn] *vi* briller.

glitter ['glɪtər] **1** *n* (*U*) scintillement *m*. **2** *vi* [object, light] scintiller. ‖ [eyes] briller.

gloat [gləʊt] *vi*: **to ~ (over sthg)** se réjouir (de qqch).

global ['gləʊbl] *adj* [worldwide] mondial(e).

global warming [-'wɔ:mɪŋ] *n* réchauffement *m* de la planète.

globe [gləʊb] *n* [Earth]: **the ~** la terre. ‖ [spherical map] globe *m* terrestre. ‖ [spherical object] globe *m*.

gloom [glu:m] *n* (*U*) [darkness] obscurité *f*. ‖ [unhappiness] tristesse *f*.

gloomy ['glu:mɪ] *adj* [room, sky, prospects] sombre. ‖ [person, atmosphere, mood] triste, lugubre.

glorious ['glɔ:rɪəs] *adj* [beautiful, splendid] splendide. ‖ [very enjoyable] formidable. ‖ [successful, impressive] magnifique.

glory ['glɔ:rɪ] *n* (*U*) [fame, admiration] gloire *f*. ‖ (*U*) [beauty] splendeur *f*. ○ **glory in** *vt fus* [relish] savourer.

gloss [glɒs] *n* [shine] brillant *m*, lustre *m*. ‖ **~ (paint)** peinture *f* brillante. ○ **gloss over** *vt fus* passer sur.

glossary ['glɒsərɪ] *n* glossaire *m*.

glossy ['glɒsɪ] *adj* [hair, surface] brillant(e). ‖ [book, photo] sur papier glacé.

glove [glʌv] *n* gant *m*.

glove compartment *n* boîte *f* à gants.

glow [gləʊ] **1** *n* (*U*) [of fire, light, sunset] lueur *f*. **2** *vi* [shine out - fire] rougeoyer; [light, stars, eyes] flamboyer. ‖ [shine in light] briller.

glower ['glaʊər] *vi*: **to ~ (at)** lancer des regards noirs (à).

glucose ['glu:kəʊs] *n* glucose *m*.

glue [glu:] (*cont* **glueing** OR **gluing**) **1** *n* (*U*) colle *f*. **2** *vt* [stick with glue] coller; **to ~ sthg to sthg** coller qqch à OR avec qqch.

glum [glʌm] *adj* [unhappy] morne.

glut [glʌt] *n* surplus *m*.

glutton ['glʌtn] *n* [greedy person] glouton *m*, -onne *f*; **to be a ~ for punishment** être maso, être masochiste.

gnarled [nɑ:ld] *adj* [tree, hands] noueux(euse).

gnat [næt] *n* moucheron *m*.

gnaw [nɔ:] **1** *vt* [chew] ronger. **2** *vi* [worry]: **to ~ (away) at sb** ronger qqn.

gnome [nəʊm] *n* gnome *m*, lutin *m*.

GNP (*abbr of* **gross national product**) *n* PNB *m*.

go [gəʊ] (*pt* **went**, *pp* **gone**, *pl* **goes**) **1** *vi* [move, travel] aller; **he's gone to Portugal** il est allé au Portugal; **where does this path ~?** où mène ce chemin?; **to ~ and do sthg** aller faire qqch; **to ~ for a walk** aller se promener, faire une promenade. ‖ [depart] partir, s'en aller; **what time does the bus ~?** à quelle heure part le bus?; **let's ~!** allons-y! ‖ [become] devenir; **to ~ grey** grisonner, devenir gris. ‖ [pass - time] passer. ‖ [progress] marcher, se dérouler; **to ~ well/badly** aller bien/mal; **how's it ~ing?** *inf* comment ça va? ‖ [function, work] marcher; **the car won't ~** la voiture ne veut pas démarrer. ‖ [indicating intention, expectation]: **to be ~ing to do sthg** aller faire qqch; **we're ~ing (to ~) to America in June** on va (aller) en Amérique en juin; **she's ~ing to have a baby** elle attend un bébé. ‖ [bell, alarm] sonner. ‖ [stop working, break - light bulb, fuse] sauter. ‖ [deteriorate - hearing, sight etc] baisser. ‖ [match, be compatible]: **to ~ (with)** aller (avec); **those colours don't really ~** ces couleurs ne vont pas bien ensemble. ‖ [fit] aller. ‖ [belong] aller, se mettre. ‖ [in division]: **three into two won't ~** deux divisé par trois n'y va pas. ‖ *inf* [expressing irritation, surprise]: **now**

what's he gone and done? qu'est-ce qu'il a fait encore? 2 *n* [turn] tour *m*; **it's my ~** c'est à moi (de jouer). || *inf* [attempt]: **to have a ~ (at sthg)** essayer (de faire qqch). || *phr*: **to be on the ~** *inf* être sur la brèche. ○ **to go** *adv* [remaining]: **there are only three days to ~** il ne reste que trois jours. ○ **go about 1** *vt fus* [perform]: **to ~ about one's business** vaquer à ses occupations. **2** *vi* = **go around.** ○ **go ahead** *vi* [proceed]: **to ~ ahead with sthg** mettre qqch à exécution; **~ ahead!** allez-y! || [take place] avoir lieu. ○ **go along** *vi* [proceed] avancer; **as you ~ along** au fur et à mesure. ○ **go along with** *vt fus* [suggestion, idea] appuyer, soutenir; [person] suivre. ○ **go around** *vi* [frequent]: **to ~ around with sb** fréquenter qqn. || [spread] circuler, courir. ○ **go back on** *vt fus* [one's word, promise] revenir sur. ○ **go back to** *vt fus* [return to activity] reprendre, se remettre à; **to ~ back to sleep** se rendormir. || [date from] remonter à, dater de. ○ **go by 1** *vi* [time] s'écouler, passer. **2** *vt fus* [be guided by] suivre. || [judge from] juger d'après. ○ **go down 1** *vi* [get lower - prices etc] baisser. || [be accepted]: **to ~ down well/badly** être bien/mal accueilli. || [sun] se coucher. || [tyre, balloon] se dégonfler. **2** *vt fus* descendre. ○ **go for** *vt fus* [choose] choisir. || [be attracted to] être attiré(e) par. || [attack] tomber sur, attaquer. || [try to obtain - job, record] essayer d'obtenir. ○ **go in** *vi* entrer. ○ **go in for** *vt fus* [competition] prendre part à; [exam] se présenter à. || [activity - enjoy] aimer; [- participate in] faire, s'adonner à. ○ **go into** *vt fus* [investigate] étudier, examiner. || [take up as a profession] entrer dans. ○ **go off 1** *vi* [explode] exploser. || [alarm] sonner. || [go bad - food] se gâter. || [lights, heating] s'éteindre. **2** *vt fus* [lose interest in] ne plus aimer. ○ **go on 1** *vi* [take place, happen] se passer. || [heating etc] se mettre en marche. || [continue]: **to ~ on (doing)** continuer (à faire). || [proceed to further activity]: **to ~ on to sthg** passer à qqch; **to ~ on to do sthg** faire qqch après. || [talk for too long] parler à n'en plus finir; **to ~ on about sthg** ne pas arrêter de parler de qqch. **2** *vt fus* [be guided by] se fonder sur. ○ **go out** *vi* [leave] sortir. ○ **go out** for amusement: **to ~ out (with sb)** sortir (avec qqn). || [light, fire, cigarette] s'éteindre. ○ **go over** *vt fus* [examine] examiner, vérifier. || [repeat, review] re-

passer. ○ **go round** *vi* [revolve] tourner; *see also* **go around.** ○ **go through** *vt fus* [experience] subir, souffrir. || [study, search through] examiner; **she went through his pockets** elle lui a fait les poches, elle a fouillé dans ses poches. ○ **go through with** *vt fus* [action, threat] aller jusqu'au bout de. ○ **go towards** *vt fus* contribuer à. ○ **go under** *vi lit & fig* couler. ○ **go up 1** *vi* [gen] monter. || [prices] augmenter. **2** *vt fus* monter. ○ **go without 1** *vt fus* se passer de. **2** *vi* s'en passer.

goad [gəʊd] *vt* [provoke] talonner.

go-ahead 1 *adj* [dynamic] dynamique. **2** *n* (*U*) [permission] feu *m* vert.

goal [gəʊl] *n* but *m*.

goalkeeper ['gəʊl,kiːpə'] *n* gardien *m* de but.

goalmouth ['gəʊlmaʊθ, *pl* -maʊðz] *n* but *m*.

goalpost ['gəʊlpəʊst] *n* poteau *m* de but.

goat [gəʊt] *n* chèvre *f*.

gobble ['gɒbl] *vt* engloutir. ○ **gobble down, gobble up** *vt sep* engloutir.

go-between *n* intermédiaire *mf*.

go-cart = **go-kart.**

god [gɒd] *n* dieu *m*, divinité *f*. ○ **God 1** *n* Dieu *m*; **God knows** Dieu seul le sait; **for God's sake** pour l'amour de Dieu; **thank God** Dieu merci. **2** *excl*: **(my) God!** mon Dieu!

godchild ['gɒdtʃaɪld] (*pl* **-children** [-,tʃɪldrən]) *n* filleul *m*, -e *f*.

goddaughter ['gɒd,dɔːtə'] *n* filleule *f*.

goddess ['gɒdɪs] *n* déesse *f*.

godfather ['gɒd,faːðə'] *n* parrain *m*.

godforsaken ['gɒdfə,seɪkn] *adj* morne, désolé(e).

godmother ['gɒd,mʌðə'] *n* marraine *f*.

godsend ['gɒdsend] *n* aubaine *f*.

godson ['gɒdsʌn] *n* filleul *m*.

goes [gəʊz] → **go.**

goggles ['gɒglz] *npl* lunettes *fpl*.

going ['gəʊɪŋ] *n* (*U*) [rate of advance] allure *f*. || [travel conditions] conditions *fpl*.

go-kart [-,kaːt] *n* kart *m*.

gold [gəʊld] **1** *n* (*U*) [metal, jewellery] or *m*. **2** *comp* [made of gold] en or. **3** *adj* [gold-coloured] doré(e).

golden ['gəʊldən] *adj* [made of gold] en or. || [gold-coloured] doré(e).

goldfish ['gəʊldfɪʃ] (*pl inv*) *n* poisson *m* rouge.

gold leaf *n* (*U*) feuille *f* d'or.

gold medal *n* médaille *f* d'or.

goldmine ['gəʊldmaɪn] *n lit & fig* mine *f* d'or.

gold-plated [-'pleɪtɪd] *adj* plaqué(e) or.

goldsmith ['gəʊldsmɪθ] *n* orfèvre *m*.

golf [gɒlf] *n* golf *m*.

golf ball *n* [for golf] balle *f* de golf. || [for typewriter] boule *f*.

golf club *n* [stick, place] club *m* de golf.

golf course *n* terrain *m* de golf.

golfer ['gɒlfər] *n* golfeur *m*, -euse *f*.

gone [gɒn] **1** *pp* → go. **2** *adj* [no longer here] parti(e). **3** *prep*: it's ~ ten (o'clock) il est dix heures passées.

gong [gɒŋ] *n* gong *m*.

good [gʊd] (*compar* better, *superl* best) **1** *adj* [gen] bon (bonne); it's ~ to see you again ça fait plaisir de te revoir; to be ~ at sthg être bon en qqch; it's ~ for you c'est bon pour toi OR pour la santé; to feel ~ [person] se sentir bien; it's ~ that ... c'est bien que ...; ~! très bien! || [kind - person] gentil(ille); to be ~ to sb être très attentionné envers qqn; to be ~ enough to do sthg avoir l'amabilité de faire qqch. || [well-behaved - child] sage; [- behaviour] correct(e); be ~! sois sage!, tiens-toi tranquille! **2** *n* (U) [benefit] bien *m*; it will do him ~ ça lui fera du bien. || [use] utilité *f*; what's the ~ of doing that? à quoi bon faire ça?; it's no ~ ça ne sert à rien. || (U) [morally correct behaviour] bien *m*; to be up to no ~ préparer un sale coup. ○ **goods** *npl* [merchandise] marchandises *fpl*, articles *mpl*. ○ **as good as** *adv* pratiquement, pour ainsi dire. ○ **for good** *adv* [forever] pour de bon, définitivement. ○ **good afternoon** *excl* bonjour! ○ **good evening** *excl* bonsoir! ○ **good morning** *excl* bonjour! ○ **good night** *excl* bonsoir!; [at bedtime] bonne nuit!

goodbye [,gʊd'baɪ] **1** *excl* au revoir! **2** *n* au revoir *m*.

Good Friday *n* Vendredi *m* saint.

good-humoured [-'hjuːməd] *adj* [person] de bonne humeur; [smile, remark, rivalry] bon enfant.

good-looking [-'lʊkɪŋ] *adj* [person] beau (belle).

good-natured [-'neɪtʃəd] *adj* [person] d'un naturel aimable; [rivalry, argument] bon enfant.

goodness ['gʊdnɪs] **1** *n* (U) [kindness] bonté *f*. || [nutritive quality] valeur *f* nutritive. **2** *excl*: (my) ~! mon Dieu!, Sei-

gneur!; **for ~' sake!** par pitié!, pour l'amour de Dieu!; **thank ~!** grâce à Dieu!

goodwill [,gʊd'wɪl] *n* bienveillance *f*.

goody ['gʊdɪ] *inf* **1** *n* [person] bon *m*. **2** *excl* chouette! ○ **goodies** *npl inf* [delicious food] friandises *fpl*. || [desirable objects] merveilles *fpl*, trésors *mpl*.

goose [guːs] (*pl* geese) *n* [bird] oie *f*.

gooseberry ['gʊzbəri] *n* [fruit] groseille *f* à maquereau.

gooseflesh ['guːsfleʃ] *n*, **goose pimples** *Br*, **goosebumps** *Am* ['guːsbʌmps] *npl* chair *f* de poule.

gore [gɔːr] **1** *n* (U) *literary* [blood] sang *m*. **2** *vt* encorner.

gorge [gɔːdʒ] **1** *n* gorge *f*, défilé *m*. **2** *vt*: to ~ o.s. on OR with sthg se bourrer OR se goinfrer de qqch.

gorgeous ['gɔːdʒəs] *adj* divin(e); *inf* [good-looking] magnifique, splendide.

gorilla [gə'rɪlə] *n* gorille *m*.

gorse [gɔːs] *n* (U) ajonc *m*.

gory ['gɔːrɪ] *adj* sanglant(e).

gosh [gɒʃ] *excl inf* ça alors!

gospel ['gɒspl] *n* [doctrine] évangile *m*. ○ **Gospel** *n* Évangile *m*.

gossip ['gɒsɪp] **1** *n* [conversation] bavardage *m*; *pej* commérage *m*. || [person] commère *f*. **2** *vi* [talk] bavarder, papoter; *pej* cancaner.

gossip column *n* échos *mpl*.

got [gɒt] *pt & pp* → get.

gotten ['gɒtn] *Am pp* → get.

goulash ['guːlæʃ] *n* goulache *m*.

gourmet ['gʊəmeɪ] **1** *n* gourmet *m*. **2** *comp* [food, restaurant] gastronomique; [cook] gastronome.

gout [gaʊt] *n* (U) goutte *f*.

govern ['gʌvən] **1** *vt* [gen] gouverner. || [control] régir. **2** *vi* POL gouverner.

governess ['gʌvənɪs] *n* gouvernante *f*.

government ['gʌvnmənt] *n* gouvernement *m*.

governor ['gʌvənər] *n* POL gouverneur *m*. || [of school] ≃ membre *m* du conseil d'établissement; [of bank] gouverneur *m*. || [of prison] directeur *m*.

gown [gaʊn] *n* [for woman] robe *f*. || [for surgeon] blouse *f*; [for judge, academic] robe *f*, toge *f*.

GP *n abbr of* general practitioner.

grab [græb] **1** *vt* [seize] saisir. || *inf* [sandwich] avaler en vitesse; **to ~ a few hours' sleep** dormir quelques heures. || *inf* [appeal to] emballer. **2** *vi*: to ~ at sthg faire un geste pour attraper qqch.

grasp

grace [greɪs] **1** n [elegance] grâce f. ‖ (U) [extra time] répit m. ‖ [prayer] grâces fpl.

graceful ['greɪsfʊl] adj gracieux(ieuse), élégant(e).

gracious ['greɪʃəs] **1** adj [polite] courtois(e). **2** excl: (good) ~! juste ciel!

grade [greɪd] **1** n [quality - of worker] catégorie f; [- of wool, paper] qualité f; [- of petrol] type m; [- of eggs] calibre m. ‖ Am [class] classe f. ‖ [mark] note f. **2** vt [classify] classer. ‖ [mark, assess] noter.

grade crossing n Am passage m à niveau.

grade school n Am école f primaire.

gradient ['greɪdjənt] n pente f, inclinaison f.

gradual ['grædʒʊəl] adj graduel(elle), progressif(ive).

gradually ['grædʒʊəlɪ] adv graduellement, petit à petit.

graduate [n 'grædʒʊət, vb 'grædʒʊeɪt] **1** n [from university] diplômé m, -e f. ‖ Am [of high school] ≃ titulaire mf du baccalauréat. **2** vi [from university]: **to ~ (from)** ≃ obtenir son diplôme (à). ‖ Am [from high school]: **to ~ (from)** ≃ obtenir son baccalauréat (à).

graduation [ˌgrædʒʊ'eɪʃn] n (U) [ceremony] remise f des diplômes.

graffiti [grə'fi:tɪ] n (U) graffiti mpl.

graft [grɑ:ft] **1** n [from plant] greffe f, greffon m. ‖ MED greffe f. ‖ Am inf [corruption] graissage m de patte. **2** vt [plant, skin] greffer.

grain [greɪn] n [gen] grain m. ‖ (U) [crops] céréales fpl. ‖ (U) [pattern - in wood] fil m; [- in material] grain m; [- in stone, marble] veines fpl.

gram [græm] n gramme m.

grammar ['græmər] n grammaire f.

grammar school n [in UK] ≃ lycée m; [in US] école f primaire.

grammatical [grə'mætɪkl] adj grammatical(e).

grand [grænd] **1** adj [impressive] grandiose, imposant(e). ‖ [ambitious] grand(e). ‖ [important] important(e); [socially] distingué(e). ‖ inf dated [excellent] sensationnel(elle), formidable. **2** inf [thousand dollars] mille dollars mpl.

grandad ['grændæd] n inf papi m, pépé m.

grandchild ['græntʃaɪld] (pl -children [-ˌtʃɪldrən]) n [boy] petit-fils m; [girl] petite-fille f. O **grandchildren** npl petits-enfants mpl.

granddad = grandad.

granddaughter ['grænˌdɔ:tər] n petite-fille f.

grandeur ['grændʒər] n [splendour] splendeur f, magnificence f.

grandfather ['grændˌfɑ:ðər] n grand-père m.

grandma ['grænmɑ:] n inf mamie f, mémé f.

grandmother ['grænˌmʌðər] n grand-mère f.

grandpa ['grænpɑ:] n inf papi m, pépé m.

grandparents ['grænˌpeərənts] npl grands-parents mpl.

grand piano n piano m à queue.

grand slam n SPORT grand chelem m.

grandson ['grænsʌn] n petit-fils m.

grandstand ['grændstænd] n tribune f.

grand total n somme f globale, total m général.

granite ['grænɪt] n granit m.

granny ['grænɪ] n inf mamie f, mémé f.

grant [grɑ:nt] **1** n subvention f; [for study] bourse f. **2** vt [wish, appeal] accorder; [request] accéder à. ‖ [admit] admettre, reconnaître. ‖ [give] accorder; **to take sb for ~ed** [not appreciate sb's help] penser que tout ce que qqn fait va de soi; [not value sb's presence] penser que qqn fait partie des meubles; **to take sthg for ~ed** [result, sb's agreement] considérer qqch comme acquis.

granulated sugar ['grænjʊleɪtɪd-] n sucre m cristallisé.

granule ['grænju:l] n granule m; [of sugar] grain m.

grape [greɪp] n (grain m de) raisin m; **a bunch of ~s** une grappe de raisin.

grapefruit ['greɪpfru:t] (pl inv OR -s) n pamplemousse m.

grapevine ['greɪpvaɪn] n vigne f; **on the ~** fig par le téléphone arabe.

graph [grɑ:f] n graphique m.

graphic ['græfɪk] adj [vivid] vivant(e). ART graphique. O **graphics** npl graphique f.

graph paper n (U) papier m millimétré.

grapple ['græpl] O **grapple with** vt fus [person, animal] lutter avec. ‖ [problem] se débattre avec, se colleter avec.

grasp [grɑ:sp] **1** n [grip] prise f. ‖ [understanding] compréhension f; **to have a good ~ of sthg** avoir une bonne connaissance de qqch. **2** vt [grip, seize] saisir, empoigner. ‖ [understand] saisir, comprendre. ‖ [opportunity] saisir.

grass [grɑːs] n BOT & drugs sl herbe f.

grasshopper ['grɑːsˌhɒpər] n sauterelle f.

grass roots 1 npl fig base f. 2 comp du peuple.

grass snake n couleuvre f.

grate [greɪt] 1 n grille f de foyer. 2 vt râper. 3 vi grincer, crisser.

grateful ['greɪtfʊl] adj: **to be ~ to sb (for sthg)** être reconnaissant(e) à qqn (de qqch).

grater ['greɪtər] n râpe f.

gratify ['grætɪfaɪ] vt [please - person]: **to be gratified** être content(e), être satisfait(e). ‖ [satisfy - wish] satisfaire, assouvir.

grating ['greɪtɪŋ] 1 adj grinçant(e); [voix] de crécelle. 2 n [grille] grille f.

gratitude ['grætɪtjuːd] n (U): **~ (to sb for sthg)** gratitude f OR reconnaissance f (envers qqn de qqch).

gratuitous [grə'tjuːɪtəs] adj fml gratuit(e).

grave[1] [greɪv] 1 adj grave; [concern] sérieux(ieuse). 2 n tombe f.

grave[2] [grɑːv] adj LING: **e ~ e** m accent grave.

gravel ['grævl] n (U) gravier m.

gravestone ['greɪvstəʊn] n pierre f tombale.

graveyard ['greɪvjɑːd] n cimetière m.

gravity ['grævətɪ] n [force] gravité f, pesanteur f. ‖ [seriousness] gravité f.

gravy ['greɪvɪ] n (U) [meat juice] jus m de viande.

gray Am = grey.

graze [greɪz] 1 vt [subj: cows, sheep] brouter, paître. ‖ [subj: farmer] faire paître. ‖ [skin] écorcher, égratigner. ‖ [touch lightly] frôler, effleurer. 2 vi brouter, paître. 3 n écorchure f, égratignure f.

grease [griːs] 1 n graisse f. 2 vt graisser.

greasy ['griːzɪ] adj [covered in grease] graisseux(euse); [clothes] taché(e) de graisse. ‖ [food, skin, hair] gras (grasse).

great [greɪt] adj [gen] grand(e); **~ big** énorme. ‖ inf [splendid] génial(e), formidable; **to feel ~** se sentir en pleine forme; **~!** super!, génial!

Great Britain n Grande-Bretagne f; **in ~** en Grande-Bretagne.

greatcoat ['greɪtkəʊt] n pardessus m.

Great Dane n danois m.

great-grandchild n [boy] arrière-petit-fils m; [girl] arrière-petite-fille f.

○ **great-grandchildren** npl arrière-petits-enfants mpl.

great-grandfather n arrière-grand-père m.

great-grandmother n arrière-grand-mère f.

greatly ['greɪtlɪ] adv beaucoup; [different] très.

greatness ['greɪtnɪs] n grandeur f.

Greece [griːs] n Grèce f.

greed [griːd] n (U) [for food] gloutonnerie f. ‖ fig [for money, power]: **~ (for)** avidité f (de).

greedy ['griːdɪ] adj [for food] glouton(onne). ‖ [for money, power]: **~ for sthg** avide de qqch.

Greek [griːk] 1 adj grec (grecque). 2 n [person] Grec m, Grecque f. ‖ [language] grec m.

green [griːn] 1 adj [in colour, unripe] vert(e). ‖ [ecological - issue, politics] écologique; [- person] vert(e). ‖ inf [inexperienced] inexpérimenté(e), jeune. 2 n [colour] vert m. ‖ GOLF vert m. ‖ [village] pelouse f communale. ○ **Green** n POL vert m, -e f, écologiste mf; **the Greens** les Verts, les Écologistes. ○ **greens** npl [vegetables] légumes mpl verts.

greenback ['griːnbæk] n Am inf billet m vert.

green card n Am [residence permit] carte f de séjour.

greenery ['griːnərɪ] n verdure f.

greenfly ['griːnflaɪ] (pl inv OR **-ies**) n puceron m.

greengage ['griːngeɪdʒ] n reine-claude f.

greengrocer ['griːnˌgrəʊsər] n marchand m, -e f de légumes; **~'s (shop)** magasin m de fruits et légumes.

greenhouse ['griːnhaʊs] (pl **-hauziz**) n serre f.

greenhouse effect n: **the ~** l'effet m de serre.

Greenland ['griːnlənd] n Groenland m.

green salad n salade f verte.

greet [griːt] vt [say hello to] saluer. ‖ [receive] accueillir.

greeting ['griːtɪŋ] n salutation f, salut m. ○ **greetings** npl: **Christmas/birthday ~s** vœux mpl de Noël/d'anniversaire.

greetings card Br, **greeting card** Am n carte f de vœux.

grenade [grə'neɪd] n: **(hand) ~** grenade f (à main).

grew [gruː] pt → grow.

grey *Br*, **gray** *Am* [greɪ] **1** *adj* [in colour] gris(e). || [grey-haired]: **to go ~** grisonner. || [dull, gloomy] morne, triste. **2** *n* gris *m*.

grey-haired [-'heəd] *adj* aux cheveux gris.

greyhound ['greɪhaʊnd] *n* lévrier *m*.

grid [grɪd] *n* [grating] grille *f*. || [system of squares] quadrillage *m*.

griddle ['grɪdl] *n* plaque *f* à cuire.

gridlock ['grɪdlɒk] *n Am* embouteillage *m*.

grief [gri:f] *n* (*U*) [sorrow] chagrin *m*, peine *f*. || *inf* [trouble] ennuis *mpl*. || *phr*: **to come to ~** échouer; **good ~!** Dieu du ciel!, mon Dieu!

grievance ['gri:vns] *n* grief *m*, doléance *f*.

grieve [gri:v] *vi* [at death] être en deuil; **to ~ for sb/sthg** pleurer qqn/qqch.

grievous bodily harm *n* (*U*) coups *mpl* et blessures *fpl*.

grill [grɪl] **1** *n* [on cooker, fire] gril *m*. **2** *rt* [cook on grill] griller, faire griller. || *inf* [interrogate] cuisiner.

grille [grɪl] *n* grille *f*.

grim [grɪm] *adj* [stern - face, expression] sévère; [- determination] inflexible. || [cheerless - truth, news] sinistre; [- room, walls] lugubre; [- day] morne, triste.

grimace [grɪ'meɪs] **1** *n* grimace *f*. **2** *vi* grimacer, faire la grimace.

grime [graɪm] *n* (*U*) crasse *f*, saleté *f*.

grimy ['graɪmɪ] *adj* sale, encrassé(e).

grin [grɪn] **1** *n* (large) sourire *m*. **2** *vi*: **to ~ (at sb/sthg)** adresser un large sourire (à qqn/qqch).

grind [graɪnd] (*pt & pp* **ground**) **1** *rt* [crush] moudre. **2** *vi* [scrape] grincer. **3** *n* [hard, boring work] corvée *f*. ○ **grind down** *vt sep* [oppress] opprimer. ○ **grind up** *vt sep* pulvériser.

grinder ['graɪndər] *n* moulin *m*.

grip [grɪp] **1** *n* [grasp, hold] prise *f*. || [control] contrôle *m*; **he's got a good ~ on the situation** il a la situation bien en main; **to get to ~s with sthg** s'attaquer à qqch; **to get a ~ on o.s.** se ressaisir. || [adhesion] adhérence *f*. || [handle] poignée *f*. **2** *rt* [grasp] saisir; [subj: tyres] adhérer à. || *fig* [imagination, country] captiver.

gripping ['grɪpɪŋ] *adj* passionnant(e).

grisly ['grɪzlɪ] *adj* [horrible, macabre] macabre.

gristle ['grɪsl] *n* (*U*) nerfs *mpl*.

grit [grɪt] **1** *n* (*U*) [stones] gravillon *m*; [in eye] poussière *f*. **2** *rt* sabler.

gritty ['grɪtɪ] *adj* [stony] couvert(e) de gravillon.

groan [grəʊn] **1** *n* gémissement *m*. **2** *vi* [moan] gémir. || [creak] grincer, gémir.

grocer ['grəʊsər] *n* épicier *m*, -ière *f*; **~'s (shop)** épicerie *f*.

groceries ['grəʊsərɪz] *npl* [foods] provisions *fpl*.

grocery ['grəʊsərɪ] *n* [shop] épicerie *f*.

groggy ['grɒgɪ] *adj* groggy (*inv*).

groin [grɔɪn] *n* aine *f*.

groom [gru:m] **1** *n* [of horses] palefrenier *m*, garçon *m* d'écurie. || [bridegroom] marié *m*. **2** *rt* [brush] panser. || *fig* [prepare]: **to ~ sb (for sthg)** préparer OR former qqn (pour qqch).

groove [gru:v] *n* [in metal, wood] rainure *f*; [in record] sillon *m*.

grope [grəʊp] *vi*: **to ~ (about) for sthg** chercher qqch à tâtons.

gross [grəʊs] (*pl inv* OR **-es**) **1** *adj* [total] brut(e). || *fml* [serious - negligence] coupable; [- misconduct] choquant(e); [- inequality] flagrant(e). || [coarse, vulgar] grossier(ière). || *inf* [obese] obèse, énorme. **2** *n* grosse *f*, douze douzaines *fpl*.

grossly ['grəʊslɪ] *adv* [seriously] extrêmement, énormément.

grotesque [grəʊ'tesk] *adj* grotesque.

grotto ['grɒtəʊ] (*pl* **-es** OR **-s**) *n* grotte *f*.

ground [graʊnd] **1** *pt & pp* → **grind**. **2** *n* (*U*) [surface of earth] sol *m*, terre *f*; **above ~ en surface**; **below ~** sous terre; **on the ~** par terre, au sol. || (*U*) [area of land] terrain *m*. || [for sport etc] terrain *m*. || [advantage]: **to gain/lose ~** gagner/perdre du terrain. **3** *rt* [base]: **to be ~ed on OR in sthg** être fondé(e) sur qqch. || [aircraft, pilot] interdire de vol. || *inf* [child] priver de sortie. || *Am* ELEC: **to be ~ed** être à la masse. ○ **grounds** *npl* [reason] motif *m*, raison *f*; **~s for sthg** motifs de qqch. || [land round building] parc *m*. || [of coffee] marc *m*.

ground crew *n* personnel *m* au sol.

ground floor *n* rez-de-chaussée *m*.

grounding ['graʊndɪŋ] *n*: **~ (in)** connaissances *fpl* de base (en).

groundless ['graʊndlɪs] *adj* sans fondement.

groundsheet ['graʊndʃi:t] *n* tapis *m* de sol.

ground staff *n* [at sports ground] personnel *m* d'entretien (*d'un terrain de sport*). || *Br* = **ground crew**.

groundwork ['graʊndwɜːk] *n* (*U*) travail *m* préparatoire.

group [gruːp] **1** *n* groupe *m*. **2** *vt* grouper, réunir. **3** *vi*: **to ~ (together)** se grouper.

groupie ['gruːpɪ] *n inf* groupie *f*.

grouse [graʊs] (*pl inv* OR **-s**) *n* [bird] grouse *f*, coq *m* de bruyère.

grove [grəʊv] *n* [group of trees] bosquet *m*.

grovel ['grɒvl] *vi*: **to ~ (to sb)** ramper (devant qqn).

grow [grəʊ] (*pt* **grew**, *pp* **grown**) **1** *vi* [gen] pousser; [person, animal] grandir; [company, city] s'agrandir; [fears, influence, traffic] augmenter, s'accroître; [problem, idea, plan] prendre de l'ampleur; [economy] se développer. || [become] devenir; **to ~ old** vieillir; **to ~ tired of sthg** se fatiguer de qqch. **2** *vt* [plants] faire pousser. || [hair, beard] laisser pousser. ○ **grow on** *vt fus inf*: **it'll ~ on you** cela finira par te plaire. ○ **grow out of** *vt fus* [clothes, shoes] devenir trop grand pour. || [habit] perdre. ○ **grow up** *vi* [become adult] grandir, devenir adulte; **~ up!** ne fais pas l'enfant! || [develop] se développer.

grower ['grəʊər] *n* cultivateur *m*, -trice *f*.

growl [graʊl] *vi* [animal] grogner, gronder; [person] grogner.

grown [grəʊn] **1** *pp* → **grow**. **2** *adj* adulte.

grown-up 1 *adj* [fully grown] adulte, grand(e). || [mature] mûr(e). **2** *n* adulte *mf*, grande personne *f*.

growth [grəʊθ] *n* [increase - gen] croissance *f*; [- of opposition, company] développement *m*; [- of population] augmentation *f*, accroissement *m*. || MED [lump] tumeur *f*, excroissance *f*.

grub [grʌb] *n* [insect] larve *f*. || *inf* [food] bouffe *f*.

grubby ['grʌbɪ] *adj* sale, malpropre.

grudge [grʌdʒ] **1** *n* rancune *f*; **to bear sb a ~, to bear a ~ against sb** garder rancune à qqn. **2** *vt*: **to ~ sb sthg** donner qqch à qqn à contrecœur; [success] en vouloir à qqn à cause de qqch.

gruelling *Br*, **grueling** *Am* ['grʊəlɪŋ] *adj* épuisant(e), exténuant(e).

gruesome ['gruːsəm] *adj* horrible.

gruff [grʌf] *adj* [hoarse] gros (grosse). || [rough, unfriendly] brusque, bourru(e).

grumble ['grʌmbl] *vi* [complain]: **to ~**

about sthg rouspéter OR grommeler contre qqch.

grumpy ['grʌmpɪ] *adj inf* renfrogné(e).

grunt [grʌnt] **1** *n* grognement *m*. **2** *vi* grogner.

guarantee [,gærən'tiː] **1** *n* garantie *f*. **2** *vt* garantir.

guard [gɑːd] **1** *n* [person] garde *m*; [in prison] gardien *m*. || [group of guards] garde *f*. || [defensive operation] garde *f*; **to be on ~** être de garde OR de faction; **to catch sb off ~** prendre qqn au dépourvu. || [protective device - for body] protection *f*; [- for fire] garde-feu *m inv*. **2** *vt* [protect - building] protéger, garder; [- person] protéger. || [prisoner] garder, surveiller. || [hide - secret] garder.

guard dog *n* chien *m* de garde.

guarded ['gɑːdɪd] *adj* prudent(e).

guardian ['gɑːdjən] *n* [of child] tuteur *m*, -trice *f*. || [protector] gardien *m*, -ienne *f*, protecteur *m*, -trice *f*.

guardrail ['gɑːdreɪl] *n Am* [on road] barrière *f* de sécurité.

guerilla [gə'rɪlə] = **guerrilla**.

guerrilla [gə'rɪlə] *n* guérillero *m*.

guerrilla warfare *n* (*U*) guérilla *f*.

guess [ges] **1** *n* conjecture *f*. **2** *vt* deviner; **~ what?** tu sais quoi? **3** *vi* [conjecture] deviner; **to ~ at sthg** deviner qqch. || [suppose]: **I ~ (so)** je suppose (que oui).

guesswork ['gesw3ːk] *n* (*U*) conjectures *fpl*, hypothèses *fpl*.

guest [gest] *n* [gen] invité *m*, -e *f*. || [at hotel] client *m*, -e *f*.

guesthouse ['gesthaʊs, *pl* -haʊzɪz] *n* pension *f* de famille.

guestroom ['gestrʊm] *n* chambre *f* d'amis.

guffaw [gʌ'fɔː] **1** *n* gros rire *m*. **2** *vi* rire bruyamment.

guidance ['gaɪdəns] *n* (*U*) [help] conseils *mpl*. || [leadership] direction *f*.

guide [gaɪd] **1** *n* [person, book] guide *m*. || [indication] indication *f*. **2** *vt* [show by leading] guider. || [control] diriger. || [influence]: **to be ~d by sb/sthg** se laisser guider par qqn/qqch. ○ **Guide** *n* = **girl guide**.

guide book *n* guide *m*.

guide dog *n* chien *m* d'aveugle.

guidelines ['gaɪdlaɪnz] *npl* directives *fpl*, lignes *fpl* directrices.

guild [gɪld] *n* [association] association *f*.

guillotine ['gɪlə,tiːn] **1** *n* [for executions] guillotine *f*. || [for paper] massicot *m*. **2** *vt* [execute] guillotiner.

guilt [gɪlt] n culpabilité f.

guilty ['gɪltɪ] adj coupable; **to be ~ of** sthg être coupable de qqch; **to be found ~/not ~** JUR être reconnu coupable/non coupable.

guinea pig ['gɪnɪ-] n cobaye m.

guitar [gɪ'tɑːr] n guitare f.

guitarist [gɪ'tɑːrɪst] n guitariste mf.

gulf [gʌlf] n [sea] golfe m. || [breach, chasm]: ~ **(between)** abîme m (entre). ○ **Gulf** n: **the Gulf** le Golfe.

gull [gʌl] n mouette f.

gullet ['gʌlɪt] n œsophage m; [of bird] gosier m.

gullible ['gʌləbl] adj crédule.

gully ['gʌlɪ] n [valley] ravine f. || [ditch] rigole f.

gulp [gʌlp] 1 n [of drink] grande gorgée f; [of food] grosse bouchée f. 2 vt avaler. 3 vi avoir la gorge nouée. ○ **gulp down** vt sep avaler.

gum [gʌm] 1 n [chewing gum] chewing-gum m. || [adhesive] colle f, gomme f. || ANAT gencive f. 2 vt coller.

gun [gʌn] n [weapon - small] revolver m; [- rifle] fusil m; [- large] canon m. || [starting pistol] pistolet m. || [tool] pistolet m; [for staples] agrafeuse f. ○ **gun down** vt sep abattre.

gunboat ['gʌnbəʊt] n canonnière f.

gunfire ['gʌnfaɪər] n (U) coups mpl de feu.

gunman ['gʌnmən] (pl **-men** [-mən]) n personne f armée.

gunpoint ['gʌnpɔɪnt] n: **at ~** sous la menace d'un fusil OR pistolet.

gunpowder ['gʌn,paʊdər] n poudre f à canon.

gunshot ['gʌnʃɒt] n [firing of gun] coup m de feu.

gunsmith ['gʌnsmɪθ] n armurier m.

gurgle ['gɜːgl] vi [water] glouglouter. || [baby] gazouiller.

guru ['gʊruː] n gourou m, guru m.

gush [gʌʃ] 1 n jaillissement m. 2 vi [flow out] jaillir. || pej [enthuse] s'exprimer de façon exubérante.

gusset ['gʌsɪt] n gousset m.

gust [gʌst] n rafale f, coup m de vent.

gusto ['gʌstəʊ] n: **with ~** avec enthousiasme.

gut [gʌt] 1 n MED intestin m. 2 vt [remove organs from] vider. || [destroy] réduire à rien. ○ **guts** npl inf [intestines] intestins mpl; **to hate sb's ~s** ne pas pouvoir piffer qqn, ne pas pouvoir voir qqn en peinture. || [courage] cran m.

gutter ['gʌtər] n [ditch] rigole f. || [on roof] gouttière f.

gutter press n presse f à sensation.

guy [gaɪ] n inf [man] type m. || [person] copain m, copine f.

guy rope n corde f de tente.

guzzle ['gʌzl] 1 vt bâfrer; [drink] lamper. 2 vi s'empiffrer.

gym [dʒɪm] n inf [gymnasium] gymnase m. || [exercises] gym f.

gymnasium [dʒɪm'neɪzjəm] (pl **-iums** OR **-ia** [-jə]) n gymnase m.

gymnast ['dʒɪmnæst] n gymnaste mf.

gymnastics [dʒɪm'næstɪks] n (U) gymnastique f.

gym shoes npl (chaussures fpl de) tennis mpl.

gynaecologist Br, **gynecologist** Am [,gaɪnə'kɒlədʒɪst] n gynécologue mf.

gynaecology Br, **gynecology** Am [,gaɪnə'kɒlədʒɪ] n gynécologie f.

gypsy ['dʒɪpsɪ] = gipsy.

gyrate [dʒaɪ'reɪt] vi tournoyer.

h (pl **h's** OR **hs**), **H** (pl **H's** OR **Hs**) [eɪtʃ] n [letter] h m inv, H m inv.

haberdashery ['hæbədæʃərɪ] n mercerie f.

habit ['hæbɪt] n [customary practice] habitude f; **out of ~** par habitude; **to make a ~ of doing sthg** avoir l'habitude de faire qqch. || [garment] habit m.

habitat ['hæbɪtæt] n habitat m.

habitual [hə'bɪtjʊəl] adj [usual, characteristic] habituel(elle). || [regular] invétéré(e).

hack [hæk] 1 n [writer] écrivailleur m, -euse f. 2 vt [cut] tailler. ○ **hack into** vt fus COMPUT pirater.

hacker ['hækər] n: **(computer) ~** pirate m informatique.

hackneyed ['hæknɪd] adj rebattu(e).

hacksaw ['hæksɔː] n scie f à métaux.

had [weak form həd, strong form hæd] pt & pp → have.

haddock ['hædək] (*pl inv*) *n* églefin *m*, aiglefin *m*.

hadn't ['hædnt] = had not.

haemophiliac [ˌhiːməˈfɪlɪˌæk] = hemophiliac.

haemorrhage ['hemərɪdʒ] = hemorrhage.

haemorrhoids ['hemərɔɪdz] = hemorrhoids.

haggard ['hægəd] *adj* [face] défait(e); [person] abattu(e).

haggle ['hægl] *vi* marchander; **to ~ over** OR **about sthg** marchander qqch.

Hague [heɪg] *n*: **The ~** La Haye.

hail [heɪl] **1** *n* grêle *f*; *fig* pluie *f*. **2** *vt* [call] héler. || [acclaim]: **to ~ sb/sthg as sthg** acclamer qqn/qqch comme qqch. **3** *v impers* grêler.

hailstone ['heɪlstəʊn] *n* grêlon *m*.

hair [heəʳ] *n* (*U*) [on human head] cheveux *mpl*; **to do one's ~** se coiffer. || (*U*) [on animal, human skin] poils *mpl*. || [individual hair - on head] cheveu *m*; [- on skin] poil *m*.

hairbrush ['heəbrʌʃ] *n* brosse *f* à cheveux.

haircut ['heəkʌt] *n* coupe *f* de cheveux.

hairdresser ['heəˌdresəʳ] *n* coiffeur *m*, -euse *f*; **~'s (salon)** salon *m* de coiffure.

hairdryer ['heəˌdraɪəʳ] *n* [handheld] sèche-cheveux *m inv*; [with hood] casque *m*.

hair gel *n* gel *m* coiffant.

hairpin ['heəpɪn] *n* épingle *f* à cheveux.

hairpin bend *n* virage *m* en épingle à cheveux.

hair-raising [-ˌreɪzɪŋ] *adj* à faire dresser les cheveux sur la tête; [journey] effrayant(e).

hair remover [-rɪˌmuːvəʳ] *n* (crème *f*) dépilatoire *m*.

hairspray ['heəspreɪ] *n* laque *f*.

hairstyle ['heəstaɪl] *n* coiffure *f*.

hairy ['heərɪ] *adj* [covered in hair] velu(e), poilu(e). || *inf* [dangerous] à faire dresser les cheveux sur la tête.

Haiti ['heɪtɪ] *n* Haïti *m*.

hake [heɪk] (*pl inv* OR **-s**) *n* colin *m*, merluche *f*.

half [*Br* hɑːf, *Am* hæf] (*pl senses 1 and 2* **halves**, *pl senses 3, 4 and 5* **halves** OR **halfs**) **1** *adj* demi(e); **~ a dozen** une demi-douzaine; **~ an hour** une demi-heure; **~ a pound** une demi-livre; **~ English** à moitié anglais. **2** *adv* [gen] à moitié; **~-and-~** moitié-moitié. || [by half] de moitié. || [in telling the time]: **~ past ten**

Br, **~ after ten** *Am* dix heures et demie; **it's ~ past** il est la demie. **3** *n* [gen] moitié *f*; **in ~** en deux; **to go halves (with sb)** partager (avec qqn). || SPORT [of match] mi-temps *f*. || SPORT [halfback] demi *m*. || [of beer] demi *m*. || [child's ticket] demi-tarif *m*, tarif *m* enfant. **4** *pron* la moitié; **~ of them** la moitié d'entre eux.

halfback ['hɑːfbæk] *n* demi *m*.

half board *n* demi-pension *f*.

half-breed 1 *adj* métis(isse). **2** *n* métis *m*, -isse *f* (*attention: le terme 'half-breed' est considéré raciste*).

half-caste [-kɑːst] **1** *adj* métis(isse). **2** *n* métis *m*, -isse *f* (*attention: le terme 'half-caste' est considéré raciste*).

half-hearted [-'hɑːtɪd] *adj* sans enthousiasme.

half hour *n* demi-heure *f*.

half-mast *n*: **at ~** [flag] en berne.

half moon *n* demi-lune *f*.

half note *n Am* MUS blanche *f*.

half-price *adj* à moitié prix.

half time *n* (*U*) mi-temps *f*.

halfway [hɑːf'weɪ] **1** *adj* à mi-chemin. **2** *adv* [in space] à mi-chemin. || [in time] à la moitié.

halibut ['hælɪbət] (*pl inv* OR **-s**) *n* flétan *m*.

hall [hɔːl] *n* [in house] vestibule *m*, entrée *f*. || [meeting room, building] salle *f*. || [country house] manoir *m*.

hallmark ['hɔːlmɑːk] *n* [typical feature] marque *f*. || [on metal] poinçon *m*.

hallo [hə'ləʊ] = hello.

Hallowe'en [ˌhæləʊ'iːn] *n* Halloween *f* (*fête des sorcières et des fantômes*).

hallucinate [hə'luːsɪneɪt] *vi* avoir des hallucinations.

hallway ['hɔːlweɪ] *n* vestibule *m*.

halo ['heɪləʊ] (*pl* **-es** OR **-s**) *n* nimbe *m*; ASTRON halo *m*.

halt [hɔːlt] **1** *n* [stop]: **to come to a ~** [vehicle] s'arrêter, s'immobiliser; [activity] s'interrompre; **to call a ~ to sthg** mettre fin à qqch. **2** *vt* arrêter. **3** *vi* s'arrêter.

halterneck ['hɔːltənek] *adj* dos nu (*inv*).

halve [*Br* hɑːv, *Am* hæv] *vt* [reduce by half] réduire de moitié. || [divide] couper en deux.

halves [*Br* hɑːvz, *Am* hævz] *pl* → **half**.

ham [hæm] **1** *n* [meat] jambon *m*. **2** *comp* au jambon.

hamburger ['hæmbɜːgəʳ] *n* [burger] hamburger *m*. || (*U*) *Am* [mince] viande *f* hachée.

hamlet ['hæmlɪt] n hameau m.

hammer ['hæmə'] 1 n marteau m. 2 vt [with tool] marteler; [nail] enfoncer à coups de marteau. || [with fist] marteler du poing. || fig [fact]: **to ~ sthg into sb** faire entrer qqch dans la tête de qqn. || inf [defeat] battre à plates coutures. 3 vi [with fist]: **to ~ (on)** cogner du poing (à). ○ **hammer out** vt fus [agreement, solution] parvenir finalement à.

hammock ['hæmək] n hamac m.

hamper ['hæmpə'] 1 n [for food] panier m d'osier. || Am [for laundry] coffre m à linge. 2 vt gêner.

hamster ['hæmstə'] n hamster m.

hamstring ['hæmstrɪŋ] n tendon m du jarret.

hand [hænd] 1 n [part of body] main f; **to hold ~s** se tenir la main; **by ~** à la main; **to get out of ~** échapper à tout contrôle; **to have one's ~s full** avoir du pain sur la planche; **to try one's ~ at sthg** s'essayer à qqch. || [help] coup m de main; **to give** OR **lend sb a ~ (with sthg)** donner un coup de main à qqn (pour faire qqch). || [worker] ouvrier m, -ière f. || [of clock, watch] aiguille f. || [handwriting] écriture f. || [of cards] jeu m, main f. 2 vt: **to ~ sthg to sb, to ~ sb sthg** passer qqch à qqn. ○ **(close) at hand** adv proche. ○ **on hand** adv disponible. ○ **on the other hand** conj d'autre part. ○ **out of hand** adv [completely] d'emblée. ○ **to hand** adv à portée de la main, sous la main. ○ **hand down** vt sep transmettre. ○ **hand in** vt sep remettre. ○ **hand out** vt sep distribuer. ○ **hand over** 1 vt sep [baton, money] remettre. || [responsibility, power] transmettre. 2 vi: **to ~ over (to)** passer le relais (à).

handbag ['hændbæg] n sac m à main.

handbook ['hændbʊk] n manuel m; [for tourist] guide m.

handbrake ['hændbreɪk] n frein m à main.

handcuffs ['hændkʌfs] npl menottes fpl.

handful ['hændfʊl] n [of sand, grass, people] poignée f.

handgun ['hændgʌn] n revolver m, pistolet m.

handicap ['hændɪkæp] 1 n handicap m. 2 vt handicaper; [progress, work] entraver.

handicapped ['hændɪkæpt] 1 adj handicapé(e). 2 npl: **the ~** les handicapés mpl.

handicraft ['hændɪkrɑːft] n activité f artisanale.

handiwork ['hændɪwɜːk] n (U) ouvrage m.

handkerchief ['hæŋkətʃɪf] (pl -chiefs OR -chieves [-tʃiːvz]) n mouchoir m.

handle ['hændl] 1 n poignée f; [of jug, cup] anse f; [of knife, pan] manche m. 2 vt [with hands] manipuler; [without permission] toucher à. || [deal with, be responsible for] s'occuper de; [difficult situation] faire face à. || [treat] traiter, s'y prendre avec.

handlebars ['hændlbɑːz] npl guidon m.

handler ['hændlə'] n [of dog] maître-chien m. || [at airport]: **(baggage) ~** bagagiste m.

handmade [,hænd'meɪd] adj fait(e) (à la) main.

handout ['hændaʊt] n [gift] don m. || [leaflet] prospectus m.

handrail ['hændreɪl] n rampe f.

handset ['hændset] n combiné m.

handshake ['hændʃeɪk] n serrement m OR poignée f de main.

handsome ['hænsəm] adj [good-looking] beau (belle). || [reward, profit] beau (belle); [gift] généreux(euse).

handstand ['hændstænd] n équilibre m (sur les mains).

handwriting ['hænd,raɪtɪŋ] n écriture f.

handy ['hændɪ] adj inf [useful] pratique; **to come in ~** être utile. || [skilful] adroit(e). || [near] tout près, à deux pas.

handyman ['hændɪmæn] (pl -men [-men]) n bricoleur m.

hang [hæŋ] (pt & pp sense 1 hung, pt & pp sense 2 hung OR hanged) 1 vt [fasten] suspendre. || [execute] pendre. 2 vi [be fastened] pendre, être accroché(e). || [be executed] être pendu(e). 3 n: **to get the ~ of sthg** inf saisir le truc OR attraper le coup pour faire qqch. ○ **hang about**, **hang around** vi traîner. ○ **hang on** vi [keep hold]: **to ~ on (to)** s'accrocher OR se cramponner (à). || inf [continue waiting] attendre. || [persevere] tenir bon. ○ **hang out** vi inf [spend time] traîner. ○ **hang round** = hang about. ○ **hang up** 1 vt sep pendre. 2 vi [on telephone] raccrocher. ○ **hang up on** vt fus TELEC raccrocher au nez de.

hangar ['hæŋə'] n hangar m.

hanger ['hæŋə'] n cintre m.

hanger-on (pl hangers-on) n parasite m.

hang gliding n deltaplane m, vol m libre.

hangover ['hæŋ,əʊvəʳ] n [from drinking] gueule f de bois.

hang-up n inf complexe m.

hanker ['hæŋkəʳ] ○ **hanker after**, **hanker for** vt fus convoiter.

hankie, hanky ['hæŋkɪ] (abbr of handkerchief) n inf mouchoir m.

haphazard [,hæp'hæzəd] adj fait(e) au hasard.

happen ['hæpən] vi [occur] arriver, se passer; **to ~ to sb** arriver à qqn. || [chance]: **I just ~ed to meet him** je l'ai rencontré par hasard; **as it ~s** en fait.

happening ['hæpənɪŋ] n événement m.

happily ['hæpɪlɪ] adv [with pleasure] de bon cœur. || [contentedly]: **to be ~ doing sthg** être bien tranquillement en train de faire qqch. || [fortunately] heureusement.

happiness ['hæpɪnɪs] n bonheur m.

happy ['hæpɪ] adj [gen] heureux(euse); **to be ~ to do sthg** être heureux de faire qqch; **~ Christmas/birthday!** joyeux Noël/anniversaire!; **~ New Year!** bonne année! || [satisfied] heureux(euse), content(e); **to be ~ with** OR **about sthg** être heureux de qqch.

happy-go-lucky adj décontracté(e).

happy medium n juste milieu m.

harangue [hə'ræŋ] 1 n harangue f. 2 vt haranguer.

harass ['hærəs] vt harceler.

harbour Br, **harbor** Am ['hɑ:bəʳ] 1 n port m. 2 vt [feeling] entretenir; [doubt, grudge] garder. || [person] héberger.

hard [hɑ:d] 1 adj [gen] dur(e); **to be ~ on sb/sthg** être dur avec qqn/pour qqch. || [winter, frost] rude. || [water] calcaire. || [fact] concret(ète); [news] sûr(e), vérifié(e). 2 adv [strenuously - work] dur; [- listen, concentrate] avec effort; **to try ~ (to do sthg)** faire de son mieux (pour faire qqch). || [forcefully] fort. || [heavily - rain] à verse; [- snow] dru. || phr: **to be ~ pushed** OR **put** OR **pressed to do sthg** avoir bien de la peine à faire qqch.

hardback ['hɑ:dbæk] n livre m relié.

hardboard ['hɑ:dbɔ:d] n panneau m de fibres.

hard-boiled adj CULIN: **~ egg** œuf m dur.

hard cash n (U) espèces fpl.

hard copy n COMPUT sortie f papier.

hard disk n COMPUT disque m dur.

harden ['hɑ:dn] 1 vt durcir; [steel] trem-

per. 2 vi [glue, concrete] durcir. || [attitude, opposition] se durcir.

hard-headed [-'hedɪd] adj [decision] pragmatique; **to be ~** [person] avoir la tête froide.

hard-hearted [-'hɑ:tɪd] adj insensible, impitoyable.

hard labour n (U) travaux mpl forcés.

hard-liner n partisan m de la manière forte.

hardly ['hɑ:dlɪ] adv [scarcely] à peine, ne ... guère; **~ ever/anything** presque jamais/rien. || [only just] à peine.

hardness ['hɑ:dnɪs] n [firmness] dureté f. || [difficulty] difficulté f.

hardship ['hɑ:dʃɪp] n (U) [difficult conditions] épreuves fpl. || [difficult circumstance] épreuve f.

hard up adj inf fauché(e); **~ for sthg** à court de qqch.

hardware ['hɑ:dweəʳ] n (U) [tools, equipment] quincaillerie f. || COMPUT hardware m, matériel m.

hardware shop n quincaillerie f.

hardworking [,hɑ:d'wɜ:kɪŋ] adj travailleur(euse).

hardy ['hɑ:dɪ] adj [person, animal] vigoureux(euse), robuste. || [plant] résistant(e), vivace.

hare [heəʳ] n lièvre m.

harebrained ['heə,breɪnd] adj inf [person] écervelé(e); [scheme, idea] insensé(e).

harelip [,heə'lɪp] n bec-de-lièvre m.

haricot (bean) ['hærɪkəʊ-] n haricot m blanc.

harm [hɑ:m] 1 n [injury] mal m. || [damage - to clothes, plant] dommage m; [- to reputation] tort m; **to do ~ to sb, to do sb ~** faire du tort à qqn; **to do ~ to sthg, to do sthg ~** endommager qqch; **to be out of ~'s way** [person] être en sûreté OR lieu sûr; [thing] être en lieu sûr. 2 vt [injure] faire du mal à. || [damage - clothes, plant] endommager; [- reputation] faire du tort à.

harmful ['hɑ:mfʊl] adj nuisible, nocif(ive).

harmless ['hɑ:mlɪs] adj [not dangerous] inoffensif(ive). || [inoffensive] innocent(e).

harmonica [hɑ:'mɒnɪkə] n harmonica m.

harmonize, -ise ['hɑ:mənaɪz] 1 vt harmoniser. 2 vi s'harmoniser.

harmony ['hɑ:mənɪ] n harmonie f.

Hawaii

harness ['hɑːnɪs] 1 n [for horse, child] harnais m. 2 vt [horse] harnacher. ‖ [energy, resources] exploiter.

harp [hɑːp] n harpe f. ○ **harp on** vi: to ~ on (about sthg) rabâcher (qqch).

harpoon [hɑː'puːn] n harpon m.

harrowing ['hærəʊɪŋ] adj [experience] éprouvant(e); [report, film] déchirant(e).

harsh [hɑːʃ] adj [life, conditions] rude; [criticism, treatment] sévère. ‖ [to senses - sound] discordant(e); [- light, voice] criard(e).

harvest ['hɑːvɪst] 1 n [of cereal crops] moisson f; [of fruit] récolte f; [of grapes] vendange f, vendanges fpl. 2 vt [cereals] moissonner; [fruit] récolter; [grapes] vendanger.

has [weak form həz, strong form hæz] → have.

has-been n inf pej ringard m, -e f.

hash [hæʃ] n [meat] hachis m. ‖ inf [mess]: to make a ~ of sthg faire un beau gâchis de qqch.

hashish ['hæʃiːʃ] n haschich m.

hasn't ['hæznt] = has not.

hassle ['hæsl] inf 1 n [annoyance] tracas m, embêtement m. 2 vt tracasser.

haste [heɪst] n hâte f; to do sthg in ~ faire qqch à la hâte.

hasten ['heɪsn] fml 1 vt hâter, accélérer. 2 vi se hâter, se dépêcher; to ~ to do sthg s'empresser de faire qqch.

hastily ['heɪstɪlɪ] adv [quickly] à la hâte. ‖ [rashly] sans réfléchir.

hasty ['heɪstɪ] adj [quick] hâtif(ive). ‖ [rash] irréfléchi(e).

hat [hæt] n chapeau m.

hatch [hætʃ] 1 vt [chick] faire éclore; [egg] couver. ‖ fig [scheme, plot] tramer. 2 vi [chick, egg] éclore. 3 n [for serving food] passe-plats m inv.

hatchback ['hætʃ,bæk] n voiture f avec hayon.

hatchet ['hætʃɪt] n hachette f.

hatchway ['hætʃ,weɪ] n passe-plats m inv, guichet m.

hate [heɪt] 1 n (U) haine f. 2 vt [detest] haïr. ‖ [dislike] détester; to ~ doing sthg avoir horreur de faire qqch.

hateful ['heɪtfʊl] adj odieux(ieuse).

hatred ['heɪtrɪd] n (U) haine f.

hat trick n SPORT: to score a ~ marquer trois buts.

haughty ['hɔːtɪ] adj hautain(e).

haul [hɔːl] 1 n [of drugs, stolen goods] prise f, butin m. ‖ [distance]: long ~ long

voyage m OR trajet m. 2 vt [pull] traîner, tirer.

haulage ['hɔːlɪdʒ] n transport m routier, camionnage m.

haulier Br ['hɔːlɪər], **hauler** Am ['hɔːlər] n entrepreneur m de transports routiers.

haunch [hɔːntʃ] n [of person] hanche f; [of animal] derrière m, arrière-train m.

haunt [hɔːnt] 1 n repaire m. 2 vt hanter.

have [hæv] (pt & pp had) 1 aux vb (to form perfect tenses - gen) avoir; (- with many intransitive verbs) être; to ~ eaten avoir mangé; to ~ left être parti(e); she hasn't gone yet, has she? elle n'est pas encore partie, si?; I was out of breath, having run all the way j'étais essoufflé d'avoir couru tout le long du chemin. 2 vt [possess, receive]: to ~ (got) avoir; I ~ no money, I haven't got any money je n'ai pas d'argent. ‖ [experience illness] avoir; to ~ flu avoir la grippe. ‖ (referring to an action, instead of another verb): to ~ a read lire; to ~ a bath/shower prendre un bain/une douche; to ~ a meeting tenir une réunion. ‖ [give birth to]: to ~ a baby avoir un bébé. ‖ [cause to be done]: to ~ sb do sthg faire faire qqch à qqn; to ~ sthg done faire faire qqch; to ~ one's hair cut se faire couper les cheveux. ‖ [be treated in a certain way]: I had my car stolen je me suis fait voler ma voiture, on m'a volé ma voiture. ‖ inf [cheat]: to be had se faire avoir. ‖ phr: to ~ it in for sb en avoir après qqn, en vouloir à qqn; to ~ had it [car, machine, clothes] avoir fait son temps. 3 modal vb [be obliged]: to ~ (got) to do sthg devoir faire qqch, être obligé(e) de faire qqch; do you ~ to go?, you got to go? est-ce que tu dois partir?, est-ce que tu es obligé de partir?; I've got to go to work il faut que j'aille travailler. ○ **have on** vt sep [be wearing] porter. ‖ [tease] faire marcher. ○ **have out** vt sep [have removed]: to ~ one's appendix/tonsils out se faire opérer de l'appendicite/des amygdales. ‖ [discuss frankly]: to ~ it out with sb s'expliquer avec qqn.

haven ['heɪvn] n havre m.

haven't ['hævnt] = have not.

haversack ['hævəsæk] n sac m à dos.

havoc ['hævək] n (U) dégâts mpl; to play ~ with [gen] abîmer; [with health] détraquer; [with plans] ruiner.

Hawaii [hə'waiɪ] n Hawaii m.

hawk [hɔːk] *n* faucon *m*.

hawker ['hɔːkər] *n* colporteur *m*.

hay [heɪ] *n* foin *m*.

hay fever *n* (*U*) rhume *m* des foins.

haystack ['heɪˌstæk] *n* meule *f* de foin.

haywire ['heɪˌwaɪər] *adj inf*: **to go ~** [person] perdre la tête; [machine] se détraquer.

hazard ['hæzəd] *n* hasard *m*.

hazardous ['hæzədəs] *adj* hasardeux(euse).

haze [heɪz] *n* brume *f*.

hazel ['heɪzl] *adj* noisette (*inv*).

hazelnut ['heɪzl,nʌt] *n* noisette *f*.

hazy ['heɪzɪ] *adj* [misty] brumeux(euse). || [memory, ideas] flou(e), vague.

he [hiː] *pers pron* (*unstressed*) il; **~'s tall** il est grand; **there ~ is** le voilà. || (*stressed*) lui; **HE can't do it** lui ne peut pas le faire.

head [hed] **1** *n* [of person, animal] tête *f*; **a** OR **per ~** par tête, par personne; **to be off one's ~** *Br*, **to be out of one's ~** *Am* être dingue; **to be soft in the ~** être débile; **to go to one's ~** [alcohol, praise] monter à la tête; **to keep one's ~** garder son sang-froid; **to lose one's ~** perdre la tête. || [of table, bed, hammer] tête *f*; [of stairs, page] haut *m*. || [of flower] tête *f*; [of cabbage] pomme *f*. || [leader] chef *m*. || [head teacher] directeur *m*, -trice *f*. **2** *vt* [procession, list] être en tête de. || [be in charge of] être à la tête de. **3** *vi*: **where are you ~ing?** où allez-vous? ○ **heads** *npl* [on coin] face *f*; **~s or tails?** pile ou face? ○ **head for** *vt fus* [place] se diriger vers. || *fig* [trouble, disaster] aller au-devant de.

headache ['hedeɪk] *n* mal *m* de tête; **to have a ~** avoir mal à la tête.

headband ['hedbænd] *n* bandeau *m*.

headdress ['hed,dres] *n* coiffe *f*.

headfirst [,hed'fɜːst] *adv* (la) tête la première.

heading ['hedɪŋ] *n* titre *m*, intitulé *m*.

headland ['hedlənd] *n* cap *m*.

headlight ['hedlaɪt] *n* phare *m*.

headline ['hedlaɪn] *n* [in newspaper] gros titre *m*; TV & RADIO grand titre *m*.

headlong ['hedlɒŋ] *adv* [quickly] à toute allure. || [unthinkingly] tête baissée. || [headfirst] (la) tête la première.

headmaster [,hed'mɑːstər] *n* directeur *m* (d'une école).

headmistress [,hed'mɪstrɪs] *n* directrice *f* (d'une école).

head office *n* siège *m* social.

head-on **1** *adj* [collision] de plein fouet; [confrontation] de front. **2** *adv* de plein fouet.

headphones ['hedfəʊnz] *npl* casque *m*.

headquarters [,hed'kwɔːtəz] *npl* [of business, organization] siège *m*; [of armed forces] quartier *m* général.

headrest ['hedrest] *n* appui-tête *m*.

headroom ['hedrʊm] *n* (*U*) hauteur *f*.

headscarf ['hedskɑːf] (*pl* **-scarves** [-skɑːvz]) OR **-scarfs**) *n* foulard *m*.

headset ['hedset] *n* casque *m*.

head start *n* avantage *m* au départ; **~ on** OR **over** avantage sur.

headstrong ['hedstrɒŋ] *adj* volontaire, têtu(e).

head waiter *n* maître *m* d'hôtel.

headway ['hedweɪ] *n*: **to make ~** faire des progrès.

heady ['hedɪ] *adj* [exciting] grisant(e). || [causing giddiness] capiteux(euse).

heal [hiːl] **1** *vt* [cure] guérir. || *fig* [troubles, discord] apaiser. **2** *vi* se guérir.

healing ['hiːlɪŋ] **1** *adj* curatif(ive). **2** (*U*) guérison *f*.

health [helθ] *n* santé *f*.

health centre *n* ≃ centre *m* médico-social.

health food *n* produits *mpl* diététiques.

health food shop *n* magasin *m* de produits diététiques.

health service *n* ≃ sécurité *f* sociale.

healthy ['helθɪ] *adj* [gen] sain(e). || [well] en bonne santé, bien portant(e). || *fig* [economy, company] qui se porte bien. || [profit] bon (bonne).

heap [hiːp] **1** *n* tas *m*. **2** *vt* [pile up] entasser. ○ **heaps** *npl inf*: **~s of** [people, objects] des tas de; [time, money] énormément de.

hear [hɪər] (*pt* & *pp* **heard** [hɜːd]) **1** *vt* [gen & JUR] entendre. || [learn of] apprendre; **to ~ (that)** ... apprendre que .... **2** *vi* [perceive sound] entendre. || [know]: **to ~ about** entendre parler de. || [receive news]: **to ~ about** avoir des nouvelles de; **to ~ from sb** recevoir des nouvelles de qqn. || *phr*: **to have heard of** avoir entendu parler de; **I won't ~ of it!** je ne veux pas en entendre parler!

hearing ['hɪərɪŋ] *n* [sense] ouïe *f*; **hard of ~** dur(e) d'oreille. || [trial] audience *f*.

hearing aid *n* audiophone *m*.

hearsay ['hɪəseɪ] *n* ouï-dire *m*.

hearse [hɜːs] *n* corbillard *m*.

heart [hɑːt] *n lit & fig* cœur *m*; **to lose ~** perdre courage; **to break sb's ~** briser le cœur à qqn. ○ **hearts** *npl* cœur *m*. ○ **at heart** *adv* au fond (de soi). ○ **by heart** *adv* par cœur.

heartache ['hɑːteɪk] *n* peine *f* de cœur.

heart attack *n* crise *f* cardiaque.

heartbeat ['hɑːtbiːt] *n* battement *m* de cœur.

heartbroken ['hɑːt,brəʊkn] *adj* qui a le cœur brisé.

heartburn ['hɑːtbɜːn] *n* (U) brûlures *fpl* d'estomac.

heart failure *n* arrêt *m* cardiaque.

heartfelt ['hɑːtfelt] *adj* sincère.

hearth [hɑːθ] *n* foyer *m*.

heartless ['hɑːtlɪs] *adj* sans cœur.

heartwarming ['hɑːt,wɔːmɪŋ] *adj* réconfortant(e).

hearty ['hɑːtɪ] *adj* [greeting, person] cordial(e). ‖ [substantial - meal] copieux(ieuse); [- appetite] gros (grosse).

heat [hiːt] **1** *n* (U) [warmth] chaleur *f*. ‖ (U) *fig* [pressure] pression *f*. ‖ [eliminating round] éliminatoire *f*. ‖ ZOOL: **on** *Br* OR **in ~** en chaleur. **2** *vt* chauffer. ○ **heat up 1** *vt sep* réchauffer. **2** *vi* chauffer.

heated ['hiːtɪd] *adj* [argument, discussion, person] animé(e); [issue] chaud(e).

heater ['hiːtər] *n* appareil *m* de chauffage.

heath [hiːθ] *n* lande *f*.

heathen ['hiːðn] **1** *adj* païen(enne). **2** *n* païen *m*, -enne *f*.

heather ['heðər] *n* bruyère *f*.

heating ['hiːtɪŋ] *n* chauffage *m*.

heatstroke ['hiːtstrəʊk] *n* (U) coup *m* de chaleur.

heat wave *n* canicule *f*, vague *f* de chaleur.

heave [hiːv] **1** *vt* [pull] tirer (avec effort); [push] pousser (avec effort). **2** *vi* [pull] tirer. ‖ [rise and fall] se soulever. ‖ [retch] avoir des haut-le-cœur.

heaven ['hevn] *n* paradis *m*. ○ **heavens 1** *npl*: **the ~s** *literary* les cieux *mpl*. **2** *excl*: **(good) ~s!** juste ciel!

heavenly ['hevnlɪ] *adj inf* [delightful] délicieux(ieuse), merveilleux(euse).

heavily ['hevɪlɪ] *adv* [booked, in debt] lourdement; [rain, smoke, drink] énormément. ‖ [solidly - built] solidement. ‖ [breathe, sigh] péniblement, bruyamment. ‖ [fall, sit down] lourdement.

heavy ['hevɪ] *adj* [gen] lourd(e); **how ~ is it?** ça pèse combien? ‖ [traffic] dense; [rain] battant(e); [fighting] acharné(e); [casualties, corrections] nombreux(euses) [smoker, drinker] gros (grosse). ‖ [noisy - breathing] bruyant(e). ‖ [schedule] chargé(e). ‖ [physically exacting - work, job] pénible.

heavy cream *n Am* crème *f* fraîche épaisse.

heavyweight ['hevɪweɪt] SPORT **1** *adj* poids lourd. **2** *n* poids lourd *m*.

Hebrew ['hiːbruː] **1** *adj* hébreu, hébraïque. **2** *n* [person] Hébreu *m*, Israélite *mf*. ‖ [language] hébreu *m*.

heck [hek] *excl inf*: **what/where/why the ~ ...?** que/où/pourquoi diable ...?; **a ~ of a nice guy** un type vachement sympa; **a ~ of a lot of people** un tas de gens.

heckle ['hekl] *vi* interrompre bruyamment.

hectic ['hektɪk] *adj* [meeting, day] agité(e), mouvementé(e).

he'd [hiːd] = **he had, he would**.

hedge [hedʒ] **1** *n* haie *f*. **2** *vi* [prevaricate] répondre de façon détournée.

hedgehog ['hedʒhɒg] *n* hérisson *m*.

heed [hiːd] **1** *n*: **to take ~ of sthg** tenir compte de qqch. **2** *vt fml* tenir compte de.

heedless ['hiːdlɪs] *adj*: **~ of sthg** qui ne tient pas compte de qqch.

heel [hiːl] *n* talon *m*.

hefty ['heftɪ] *adj* [well-built] costaud(e). ‖ [large] gros (grosse).

heifer ['hefər] *n* génisse *f*.

height [haɪt] *n* [of building, mountain] hauteur *f*; [of person] taille *f*; **5 metres in ~** 5 mètres de haut; **what ~ is it?** ça fait quelle hauteur?; **what ~ are you?** combien mesurez-vous? ‖ [above ground - of aircraft] altitude *f*. ‖ [zenith]: **at the ~ of the summer/season** au cœur de l'été/de la saison; **at the ~ of his fame** au sommet de sa gloire.

heighten ['haɪtn] *vt & vi* augmenter.

heir [eər] *n* héritier *m*.

heiress ['eərɪs] *n* héritière *f*.

heirloom ['eəluːm] *n* meuble *m*/bijou *m* de famille.

heist [haɪst] *n inf* casse *m*.

held [held] *pt & pp* → **hold**.

helicopter ['helɪkɒptər] *n* hélicoptère *m*.

helium ['hiːlɪəm] *n* hélium *m*.

hell [hel] **1** *n lit & fig* enfer *m*. ‖ *inf* [for emphasis]: **he's a ~ of a nice guy** c'est un type vachement sympa; **what/where/why the ~ ...?** que/où/pourquoi ..., bon sang? || *phr*: **to do sthg for the ~ of it** *inf* faire qqch pour le plaisir, faire qqch juste comme ça; **go to ~!** *v inf* va te faire foutre! 2 *excl inf* merde!, zut!

he'll [hi:l] = **he will**.

hello [hə'ləʊ] *excl* [as greeting] bonjour!; [on phone] allô! || [to attract attention] hé!

helm [helm] *n lit & fig* barre *f*.

helmet ['helmɪt] *n* casque *m*.

help [help] 1 *n* (*U*) [assistance] aide *f*; **he gave me a lot of ~** il m'a beaucoup aidé; **with the ~ of sthg** à l'aide de qqch; **with sb's ~** avec l'aide de qqn; **to be of ~** rendre service. || (*U*) [emergency aid] secours *m*. || [useful person or object]: **to be a ~** aider, rendre service. 2 *vi* aider. 3 *vt* [assist] aider; **to ~ sb (to) do sthg** aider qqn à faire qqch; **to ~ sb with sthg** aider qqn à faire qqch. || [avoid]: **I can't ~ it** je n'y peux rien; **I couldn't ~ laughing** je ne pouvais pas m'empêcher de rire. || *phr*: **to ~ o.s. (to sthg)** se servir (de qqch). 4 *excl* au secours!, à l'aide! ○ **help out** *vt sep & vi* aider.

helper ['helpə'] *n* [gen] aide *mf*. || *Am* [to do housework] femme *f* de ménage.

helpful ['helpfʊl] *adj* [person] serviable. || [advice, suggestion] utile.

helping ['helpɪŋ] *n* portion *f*; [of cake, tart] part *f*.

helpless ['helplɪs] *adj* impuissant(e); [look, gesture] d'impuissance.

helpline ['helplaɪn] *n* ligne *f* d'assistance téléphonique.

hem [hem] 1 *n* ourlet *m*. 2 *vt* ourler. ○ **hem in** *vt sep* encercler.

hemisphere ['hemɪ,sfɪə'] *n* hémisphère *m*.

hemline ['hemlaɪn] *n* ourlet *m*.

hemophiliac [,hi:mə'fɪlɪæk] *n* hémophile *mf*.

hemorrhage ['hemərɪdʒ] *n* hémorragie *f*.

hemorrhoids ['hemərɔɪdz] *npl* hémorroïdes *fpl*.

hen [hen] *n* [female chicken] poule *f*.

hence [hens] *adv fml* [therefore] d'où. || [from now] d'ici.

henceforth [,hens'fɔːθ] *adv fml* dorénavant.

henchman ['hentʃmən] (*pl* -**men** [-mən]) *n pej* acolyte *m*.

henna ['henə] *n* henné *m*.

henpecked ['henpekt] *adj pej* dominé par sa femme.

her [hɜː'] 1 *pers pron* (*direct* - *unstressed*) la, l' (+ *vowel or silent 'h'*);

(- *stressed*) elle; **I know/like ~** je la connais/l'aime; **it's ~** c'est elle. || (*referring to animal, car, ship etc*) *follow the gender of your translation*. || (*indirect*) lui; **we spoke to ~** nous lui avons parlé; **he sent ~ a letter** il lui a envoyé une lettre. || (*after prep, in comparisons etc*) elle; **I'm shorter than ~** je suis plus petit qu'elle. 2 *poss adj* son (sa), ses (*pl*); **~ coat** son manteau; **~ bedroom** sa chambre; **~ children** ses enfants; **it was HER fault** c'était de sa faute à elle.

herald ['herəld] 1 *vt fml* annoncer. 2 *n* [messenger] héraut *m*.

herb [hɜːb] *n* herbe *f*.

herd [hɜːd] 1 *n* troupeau *m*. 2 *vt* [cattle, sheep] mener. || *fig* [people] conduire, mener; [into confined space] parquer.

here [hɪə'] *adv* [in this place] ici; **~ he is/they are** le/les voici; **~ is/are** voici; **~ and there** çà et là. || [present] là.

hereabouts *Br* [,hɪərə'baʊts], **hereabout** *Am* [,hɪərə'baʊt] *adv* par ici.

hereafter [,hɪər'ɑːftə'] 1 *adv fml* ciaprès. 2 *n*: **the ~** l'au-delà *m*.

hereby [,hɪə'baɪ] *adv fml* par la présente.

hereditary [hɪ'redɪtrɪ] *adj* héréditaire.

heresy ['herəsɪ] *n* hérésie *f*.

herewith [,hɪə'wɪð] *adv fml* [with letter] ci-joint, ci-inclus.

heritage ['herɪtɪdʒ] *n* héritage *m*, patrimoine *m*.

hermetically [hɜː'metɪklɪ] *adv*: **~ sealed** fermé(e) hermétiquement.

hermit ['hɜːmɪt] *n* ermite *m*.

hernia ['hɜːnjə] *n* hernie *f*.

hero ['hɪərəʊ] (*pl* -**es**) *n* héros *m*.

heroic [hɪ'rəʊɪk] *adj* héroïque.

heroin ['herəʊɪn] *n* héroïne *f*.

heroine ['herəʊɪn] *n* héroïne *f*.

heron ['herən] (*pl inv* OR -**s**) *n* héron *m*.

herring ['herɪŋ] (*pl inv* OR -**s**) *n* hareng *m*.

hers [hɜːz] *poss pron* le sien (la sienne), les siens (les siennes) (*pl*); **that money is ~** cet argent est à elle OR est le sien; **a friend of ~** un ami à elle, un de ses amis.

herself [hɜː'self] *pron* (*reflexive*) se; (*after prep*) elle. || (*for emphasis*) elle-même.

he's [hi:z] = **he is**, **he has**.

hesitant ['hezɪtənt] *adj* hésitant(e).

hesitate ['hezɪteɪt] *vi* hésiter; **to ~ to do sthg** hésiter à faire qqch.

hesitation [,hezɪ'teɪʃn] *n* hésitation *f*.

heterosexual [,hetərəʊ'seksʊəl] **1** *adj* hétérosexuel(elle). **2** *n* hétérosexuel *m*, -elle *f*.

het up [het-] *adj inf* excité(e), énervé(e).

hexagon ['heksəgən] *n* hexagone *m*.

hey [heɪ] *excl* hé!

heyday ['heɪdeɪ] *n* âge *m* d'or.

hi [haɪ] *excl inf* salut!

hiatus [haɪ'eɪtəs] (*pl* -es) *n fml* pause *f*.

hibernate ['haɪbəneɪt] *vi* hiberner.

hiccough, hiccup ['hɪkʌp] **1** *n* hoquet *m*; *fig* [difficulty] accroc *m*; **to have ~s** avoir le hoquet. **2** *vi* hoqueter.

hid [hɪd] *pt* → hide.

hidden ['hɪdn] **1** *pp* → hide. **2** *adj* caché(e).

hide [haɪd] (*pt* hid, *pp* hidden) **1** *vt*: **to ~ sthg (from sb)** cacher qqch (à qqn); [information] taire qqch (à qqn). **2** *vi* se cacher. **3** *n* [animal skin] peau *f*. || [for watching birds, animals] cachette *f*.

hide-and-seek *n* cache-cache *m*.

hideaway ['haɪdəweɪ] *n* cachette *f*.

hideous ['hɪdɪəs] *adj* hideux(euse).

hiding ['haɪdɪŋ] *n* [concealment]: **to be in ~** se tenir caché(e). || *inf* [beating]: **to give sb a (good) ~** donner une (bonne) raclée OR correction à qqn.

hiding place *n* cachette *f*.

hierarchy ['haɪərɑːkɪ] *n* hiérarchie *f*.

hi-fi ['haɪfaɪ] *n* hi-fi *f inv*.

high [haɪ] **1** *adj* [gen] haut(e); **it's 3 feet/6 metres ~** cela fait 3 pieds/6 mètres de haut; **how ~ is it?** cela fait combien de haut? || [speed, figure, altitude, office] élevé(e). || [high-pitched] aigu(uë). || *drugs sl* qui plane, défoncé(e). **2** *adv* haut. **3** *n* [highest point] maximum *m*.

highbrow ['haɪbraʊ] *adj* intellectuel(elle).

high chair *n* chaise *f* haute (*d'enfant*).

high-class *adj* de premier ordre; [hotel, restaurant] de grande classe.

higher ['haɪər] *adj* [exam, qualification] supérieur(e).

higher education *n* (*U*) études *fpl* supérieures.

high-handed [-'hændɪd] *adj* despotique.

high jump *n* saut *m* en hauteur.

Highland Games ['haɪlənd-] *npl* jeux *mpl* écossais.

Highlands ['haɪləndz] *npl*: **the ~** les Highlands *fpl* (*région montagneuse du nord de l'Écosse*).

highlight ['haɪlaɪt] **1** *n* [of event, occasion] moment *m* OR point *m* fort. **2** *vt* souligner; [with highlighter] surligner. ○ **highlights** *npl* [in hair] reflets *mpl*, mèches *fpl*.

highlighter (pen) ['haɪlaɪtər-] *n* surligneur *m*.

highly ['haɪlɪ] *adv* [very] extrêmement, très. || [in important position]: **~ placed** haut placé(e). || [favourably]: **to think ~ of sb/sthg** penser du bien de qqn/qqch.

highly-strung *adj* nerveux(euse).

Highness ['haɪnɪs] *n*: **His/Her/Your (Royal) ~** Son/Votre Altesse (Royale); **their (Royal) ~es** leurs Altesses (Royales).

high-pitched [-'pɪtʃt] *adj* aigu(uë).

high point *n* [of occasion] point *m* fort.

high-powered [-'paʊəd] *adj* [powerful] de forte puissance. || [prestigious - activity, place] de haut niveau; [- job, person] important(e).

high-ranking [-'ræŋkɪŋ] *adj* de haut rang.

high-rise *adj*: **~ block of flats** tour *f*.

high school *n Br* lycée *m*; *Am* établissement *m* d'enseignement supérieur.

high season *n* haute saison *f*.

high spot *n* point *m* fort.

high-tech [-'tek] *adj* [method, industry] de pointe.

high tide *n* marée *f* haute.

highway ['haɪweɪ] *n Am* [motorway] autoroute *f*. || [main road] grande route *f*.

hijack ['haɪdʒæk] **1** *n* détournement *m*. **2** *vt* détourner.

hijacker ['haɪdʒækər] *n* [of aircraft] pirate *m* de l'air; [of vehicle] pirate *m* de la route.

hike [haɪk] **1** *n* [long walk] randonnée *f*. **2** *vi* faire une randonnée.

hiker ['haɪkər] *n* randonneur *m*, -euse *f*.

hiking ['haɪkɪŋ] *n* marche *f*.

hilarious [hɪ'leərɪəs] *adj* hilarant(e).

hill [hɪl] *n* [mound] colline *f*. || [slope] côte *f*.

hillside ['hɪlsaɪd] *n* coteau *m*.

hilly ['hɪlɪ] *adj* vallonné(e).

hilt [hɪlt] *n* garde *f*; **to support/defend sb to the ~** soutenir/défendre qqn à fond.

him [hɪm] *pers pron* (*direct - unstressed*) le, l' (+ *vowel or silent 'h'*); (- *stressed*) lui; **I know/like ~** je le connais/l'aime; **it's ~** c'est lui. || (*indirect*) lui; **we spoke to ~** nous lui avons parlé; **she sent ~ a letter** elle lui a envoyé une lettre. || (*after prep, in comparisons*) lui; **I'm shorter than** ~ je suis plus petit que lui.

Himalayas [,hɪmə'leɪəz] *npl*: **the** ~ l'Himalaya *m*.

himself [hɪm'self] *pron* (*reflexive*) se; (*after prep*) lui. || (*for emphasis*) lui-même.

hind [haɪnd] (*pl inv* OR **-s**) **1** *adj* de derrière. **2** *n* biche *f*.

hinder ['hɪndər] *vt* gêner, entraver.

Hindi ['hɪndɪ] *n* hindi *m*.

hindrance ['hɪndrəns] *n* obstacle *m*.

hindsight ['haɪndsaɪt] *n*: **with the benefit of** ~ avec du recul.

Hindu ['hɪnduː] (*pl* **-s**) **1** *adj* hindou(e). **2** *n* Hindou *m*, **-e** *f*.

hinge [hɪndʒ] **1** *n* [whole fitting] charnière *f*; [pin] gond *m*. ○ **hinge (up)on** *vt fus* [depend on] dépendre de.

hint [hɪnt] **1** *n* [indication] allusion *f*; **to drop a** ~ faire une allusion. || [piece of advice] conseil *m*, indication *f*. || [small amount] soupçon *m*. **2** *vi*: **to** ~ **at sthg** faire allusion à qqch. **3** *vt*: **to** ~ **that** ... insinuer que ....

hip [hɪp] *n* hanche *f*.

hippie ['hɪpɪ] = **hippy**.

hippo ['hɪpəʊ] (*pl* **-s**) *n* hippopotame *m*.

hippopotamus [,hɪpə'pɒtəməs] (*pl* **-muses** OR **-mi** [-maɪ]) *n* hippopotame *m*.

hippy ['hɪpɪ] *n* hippie *mf*.

hire ['haɪər] **1** *n* (*U*) [of car, equipment] location *f*; **for** ~ [bicycles etc] à louer; [taxi] libre. **2** *vt* [rent] louer. || [employ] employer les services de. ○ **hire out** *vt sep* louer.

his [hɪz] **1** *poss adj* son (sa), ses (*pl*); ~ **house** sa maison; ~ **money** son argent; ~ **children** ses enfants; ~ **name is** Joe il s'appelle Joe. **2** *poss pron* le sien (la sienne), les siens (les siennes) (*pl*); **that money is** ~ cet argent est à lui OR est le sien; **it wasn't her fault, it was** HIS ce n'était pas de sa faute à elle, c'était de sa faute à lui; **a friend of** ~ un ami à lui, un de ses amis.

hiss [hɪs] **1** *n* [of animal, gas etc] sifflement *m*; [of crowd] sifflet *m*. **2** *vi* [animal, gas etc] siffler.

historic [hɪ'stɒrɪk] *adj* historique.

historical [hɪ'stɒrɪkəl] *adj* historique.

history ['hɪstərɪ] *n* [gen] histoire *f*. || [past record] antécédents *mpl*; **medical** ~ passé *m* médical.

hit [hɪt] (*pt & pp* **hit**) **1** *n* [blow] coup *m*. || [successful strike] coup *m* OR tir *m* réussi; [in fencing] touche *f*. || [success] succès *m*; **to be a** ~ **with** plaire à. **2** *comp* à succès. **3** *vt* [strike] frapper; [nail] taper sur. || [crash into] heurter, percuter. || [reach] atteindre. || [affect badly] toucher, affecter. || *phr*: **to** ~ **it off** (**with sb**) bien s'entendre (avec qqn).

hit-and-miss = **hit-or-miss**.

hit-and-run *adj* [accident] avec délit de fuite; ~ **driver** chauffard *m* (*qui a commis un délit de fuite*).

hitch [hɪtʃ] **1** *n* [problem, snag] ennui *m*. **2** *vt* [catch]: **to** ~ **a lift** faire du stop. || [fasten]: **to** ~ **sthg on** OR **onto** accrocher qqch à. **3** *vi* [hitchhike] faire du stop. ○ **hitch up** *vt sep* [pull up] remonter.

hitchhike ['hɪtʃhaɪk] *vi* faire de l'auto-stop.

hitchhiker ['hɪtʃhaɪkər] *n* auto-stoppeur *m*, -euse *f*.

hi-tech [,haɪ'tek] = **high-tech**.

hit-or-miss *adj* aléatoire.

HIV (*abbr of* **human immunodeficiency virus**) *n* VIH, HIV *m*; **to be** ~-**positive** être séropositif.

hive [haɪv] *n* ruche *f*; **a** ~ **of activity** une véritable ruche. ○ **hive off** *vt sep* [assets] séparer.

hoard [hɔːd] **1** *n* [store] réserves *fpl*; [of useless items] tas *m*. **2** *vt* amasser; [food, petrol] faire des provisions de.

hoarse [hɔːs] *adj* [person, voice] enroué(e); [shout, whisper] rauque.

hoax [həʊks] *n* canular *m*.

hobble ['hɒbl] *vi* [limp] boitiller.

hobby ['hɒbɪ] *n* passe-temps *m inv*, hobby *m*.

hobbyhorse ['hɒbɪhɔːs] *n* [toy] cheval *m* à bascule. || *fig* [favourite topic] dada *m*.

hobo ['həʊbəʊ] (*pl* **-es** OR **-s**) *n* Am clochard *m*, **-e** *f*.

hockey ['hɒkɪ] *n* [on grass] hockey *m*. || Am [ice hockey] hockey *m* sur glace.

hoe [həʊ] **1** *n* houe *f*. **2** *vt* biner.

hog [hɒg] **1** *n* Am [pig] cochon *m*. || *inf* [greedy person] goinfre *m*. || *phr*: **to go the whole** ~ aller jusqu'au bout. **2** *vt inf* [monopolize] accaparer, monopoliser.

hoist [hɔɪst] **1** *n* [device] treuil *m*. **2** *vt* hisser.

hold [həʊld] (*pt & pp* **held**) **1** *vt* [gen] tenir. || [keep in position] maintenir. || [as prisoner] détenir; **to** ~ **sb prisoner/**

hostage détenir qqn prisonnier/comme otage. ‖ [have, possess] avoir. ‖ *fml* [consider] considérer, estimer; **to ~ sb responsible for sthg** rendre qqn responsable de qqch, tenir qqn pour responsable de qqch. ‖ [on telephone]: **please ~ the line** ne quittez pas, je vous prie. ‖ [keep, maintain] retenir. ‖ [sustain, support] supporter. ‖ [contain] contenir. ‖ *phr*: **~ it!**, **~ everything!** attendez!, arrêtez!; **to ~ one's own** se défendre. **2** *vi* [remain unchanged - gen] tenir; [- luck] persister; [- weather] se maintenir; **to ~ still** OR **steady** ne pas bouger, rester tranquille. ‖ [on phone] attendre. **3** *n* [grasp, grip] prise *f*, étreinte *f*; **to take** OR **lay ~ of sthg** saisir qqch; **to get ~ of sthg** [obtain] se procurer qqch; **to get ~ of sb** [find] joindre. ‖ [of ship, aircraft] cale *f*. ‖ [control, influence] prise *f*. ○ **hold back** *vt sep* [restrain, prevent] retenir; [anger] réprimer. ‖ [keep secret] cacher. ○ **hold down** *vt sep* [job] garder. ○ **hold off** *vt sep* [fend off] tenir à distance. ○ **hold on** *vi* [wait] attendre; [on phone] ne pas quitter. ‖ [grip]: **to ~ on (to sthg)** se tenir (à qqch). ○ **hold out 1** *vt sep* [hand, arms] tendre. **2** *vi* [last] durer. ‖ [resist]: **to ~ out (against sb/sthg)** résister (à qqn/qqch). ○ **hold up** *vt sep* [raise] lever. ‖ [delay] retarder.

holder ['həʊldər] *n* [for cigarette] porte-cigarettes *m inv*. ‖ [owner] détenteur *m*, -trice *f*; [of position, title] titulaire *mf*.

holding ['həʊldɪŋ] *n* [investment] effets *mpl* en portefeuille. ‖ [farm] ferme *f*.

holdup ['həʊldʌp] *n* [robbery] hold-up *m*. ‖ [delay] retard *m*.

hole [həʊl] *n* [gen] trou *m*. ‖ *inf* [predicament] pétrin *m*.

holiday ['hɒlɪdeɪ] *n* [vacation] vacances *fpl*; **to be/go on ~** être/partir en vacances. ‖ [public holiday] jour *m* férié.

holistic [həʊ'lɪstɪk] *adj* holistique.

Holland ['hɒlənd] *n* Hollande *f*.

holler ['hɒlər] *vi* & *vt inf* gueuler, brailler.

hollow ['hɒləʊ] **1** *adj* creux (creuse); [eyes] cave; [promise, victory] faux (fausse); [laugh] qui sonne faux. **2** *n* creux *m*. ○ **hollow out** *vt sep* creuser, évider.

holly ['hɒlɪ] *n* houx *m*.

holocaust ['hɒləkɔːst] *n* [destruction] destruction *f*, holocauste *m*. ○ **Holocaust** *n*: **the Holocaust** l'holocauste *m*.

holster ['həʊlstər] *n* étui *m*.

holy ['həʊlɪ] *adj* saint(e); [ground] sacré(e).

Holy Ghost *n*: **the ~** le Saint-Esprit.

Holy Land *n*: **the ~** la Terre sainte.

Holy Spirit *n*: **the ~** le Saint-Esprit.

home [həʊm] **1** *n* [house, institution] maison *f*; **to make one's ~** s'établir, s'installer. ‖ [own country] patrie *f*; [city] ville *f* natale. ‖ [one's family] foyer *m*; **to leave ~** quitter la maison. ‖ *fig* [place of origin] berceau *m*. **2** *adj* [not foreign] intérieur(e); [- product] national(e). ‖ [in one's own home - cooking] familial(e); [- life] de famille; [- improvements] domestique. ‖ [SPORT - game] sur son propre terrain; [- team] qui reçoit. **3** *adv* [to or at one's house] chez soi, à la maison. ○ **at home** *adv* [in one's house, flat] chez soi, à la maison. ‖ [comfortable] à l'aise; **at ~ with sthg** à l'aise dans qqch; **to make o.s. at ~** faire comme chez soi. ‖ [in one's own country] chez nous.

home address *n* adresse *f* du domicile.

home brew *n* (*U*) [beer] bière *f* faite à la maison.

home computer *n* ordinateur *m* domestique.

home economics *n* (*U*) économie *f* domestique.

homeland ['həʊmlænd] *n* [country of birth] patrie *f*. ‖ [in South Africa] homeland *m*, bantoustan *m*.

homeless ['həʊmlɪs] **1** *adj* sans abri. **2** *npl*: **the ~** les sans-abri *mpl*.

homely ['həʊmlɪ] *adj* [simple] simple. ‖ [unattractive] ordinaire.

homemade [,həʊm'meɪd] *adj* fait(e) (à la) maison.

Home Office *n Br*: **the ~** ≃ le ministère de l'Intérieur.

homeopathy [,həʊmɪ'ɒpəθɪ] *n* homéopathie *f*.

Home Secretary *n Br* ≃ ministre *m* de l'Intérieur.

homesick ['həʊmsɪk] *adj* qui a le mal du pays.

hometown ['həʊmtaʊn] *n* ville *f* natale.

homeward ['həʊmwəd] **1** *adj* de retour. **2** *adv* = **homewards**.

homewards ['həʊmwədz] *adv* vers la maison.

homework ['həʊmwɜːk] *n* (*U*) SCH devoirs *mpl*. ‖ *inf* [preparation] boulot *m*.

homey, homy ['həʊmɪ] *adj Am* confortable, agréable.

homicide ['hɒmɪsaɪd] *n* homicide *m*.

homoeopathy *etc* [ˌhəʊmɪˈɒpəθɪ] = **homeopathy** *etc.*

homosexual [ˌhɒməˈsekʃʊəl] **1** *adj* homosexuel(elle). **2** *n* homosexuel *m*, -elle *f*.

homy = **homey**.

hone [həʊn] *vt* aiguiser.

honest [ˈɒnɪst] **1** *adj* [trustworthy] honnête, probe. || [frank] franc (franche), sincère; **to be ~, ...** pour dire la vérité, ..., à dire vrai, ... || [legal] légitime. **2** *adv inf* = **honestly** 2.

honestly [ˈɒnɪstlɪ] **1** *adv* [truthfully] honnêtement. || [expressing sincerity] je vous assure. **2** *excl* [expressing impatience, disapproval] franchement!

honesty [ˈɒnɪstɪ] *n* honnêteté *f*, probité *f*.

honey [ˈhʌnɪ] *n* [food] miel *m*. || [dear] chéri *m*, -e *f*.

honeycomb [ˈhʌnɪkəʊm] *n* gâteau *m* de miel.

honeymoon [ˈhʌnɪmuːn] *n lit & fig* lune *f* de miel.

honeysuckle [ˈhʌnɪˌsʌkl] *n* chèvrefeuille *m*.

Hong Kong [ˌhɒŋˈkɒŋ] *n* Hong Kong, Hongkong.

honk [hɒŋk] **1** *vi* [motorist] klaxonner. || [goose] cacarder. **2** *vt*: **to ~ the horn** klaxonner.

honor *etc Am* = **honour** *etc.*

honorary [*Br* ˈɒnərərɪ, *Am* ɒnəˈreərɪ] *adj* honoraire.

honour *Br*, **honor** *Am* [ˈɒnər] **1** *n* honneur *m*; **in ~ of sb/sthg** en l'honneur de qqn/qqch. **2** *vt* honorer. ○ **honours** *npl* [tokens of respect] honneurs *mpl*. || [of university degree] ≃ licence *f*.

honourable *Br*, **honorable** *Am* [ˈɒnrəbl] *adj* honorable.

hood [hʊd] *n* [on cloak, jacket] capuchon *m*. || [of cooker] hotte *f*. || [of pram, convertible car] capote *f*. || *Am* [car bonnet] capot *m*.

hoodlum [ˈhuːdləm] *n Am inf* gangster *m*, truand *m*.

hoof [huːf, hʊf] (*pl* -s OR **hooves**) *n* sabot *m*.

hook [hʊk] **1** *n* [for hanging things on] crochet *m*. || [for catching fish] hameçon *m*. || [fastener] agrafe *f*. || [of telephone]: **off the ~** décroché. **2** *vt* [attach with hook] accrocher. || [catch with hook] prendre. ○ **hook up** *vt sep*: **to ~ sthg up to sthg** connecter qqch à qqch.

hooked [hʊkt] *adj* [shaped like a hook] crochu(e). || *inf* [addicted]: **to be ~ (on)** être accro (à); [music, art] être mordu(e) (de).

hook(e)y [ˈhʊkɪ] *n Am inf*: **to play ~** faire l'école buissonnière.

hooligan [ˈhuːlɪgən] *n* hooligan *m*, vandale *m*.

hoop [huːp] *n* [circular band] cercle *m*. || [toy] cerceau *m*.

hooray [hʊˈreɪ] = **hurray**.

hoot [huːt] **1** *n* [of owl] hululement *m*. || [of horn] coup *m* de Klaxon®. **2** *vi* [owl] hululer. || [horn] klaxonner. **3** *vt*: **to ~ the horn** klaxonner.

hooter [ˈhuːtər] *n* [horn] Klaxon® *m*.

hooves [huːvz] *pl* → **hoof**.

hop [hɒp] **1** *n* saut *m*; [on one leg] saut à cloche-pied. **2** *vi* sauter; [on one leg] sauter à cloche-pied; [bird] sautiller. ○ **hops** *npl* houblon *m*.

hope [həʊp] **1** *vi* espérer; **to ~ for sthg** espérer qqch; **I ~ so** j'espère bien; **I ~ not** j'espère bien que non. **2** *vt*: **to ~ (that)** espérer que; **to ~ to do sthg** espérer faire qqch. **3** *n* espoir *m*; **in the ~ of** dans l'espoir de.

hopeful [ˈhəʊpfʊl] *adj* [optimistic] plein(e) d'espoir; **to be ~ of doing sthg** avoir l'espoir de faire qqch; **to be ~ of sthg** espérer qqch. || [promising] encourageant(e), qui promet.

hopefully [ˈhəʊpfəlɪ] *adv* [in a hopeful way] avec bon espoir, avec optimisme. || [with luck]: **~, ...** espérons que ....

hopeless [ˈhəʊplɪs] *adj* [gen] désespéré(e); [tears] de désespoir. || *inf* [useless] nul (nulle).

hopelessly [ˈhəʊplɪslɪ] *adv* [despairingly] avec désespoir. || [completely] complètement.

horizon [həˈraɪzn] *n* horizon *m*.

horizontal [ˌhɒrɪˈzɒntl] **1** *adj* horizontal(e). **2** *n*: **the ~** l'horizontale *f*.

hormone [ˈhɔːməʊn] *n* hormone *f*.

horn [hɔːn] *n* [of animal] corne *f*. || MUS [instrument] cor *m*. || [on car] Klaxon® *m*; [on ship] sirène *f*.

hornet [ˈhɔːnɪt] *n* frelon *m*.

horny [ˈhɔːnɪ] *adj* [hard] corné(e); [hand] calleux(euse). || *v inf* [sexually excited] excité(e) (sexuellement).

horoscope [ˈhɒrəskəʊp] *n* horoscope *m*.

horrendous [hɒˈrendəs] *adj* horrible.

horrible [ˈhɒrəbl] *adj* horrible.

horrid ['hɒrɪd] *adj* [unpleasant] horrible.

horrific [hɒ'rɪfɪk] *adj* horrible.

horrify ['hɒrɪfaɪ] *vt* horrifier.

horror ['hɒrər] *n* horreur *f*.

horror film *n* film *m* d'épouvante.

horse [hɔːs] *n* [animal] cheval *m*.

horseback ['hɔːsbæk] **1** *adj* à cheval; ~ **riding** *Am* équitation *f*. **2** *n*: **on** ~ à cheval.

horse chestnut *n* [nut] marron *m* d'Inde; ~ (**tree**) marronnier *m* d'Inde.

horseman ['hɔːsmən] (*pl* -**men** [-mən]) *n* cavalier *m*.

horsepower ['hɔːs,paʊər] *n* puissance *f* en chevaux.

horse racing *n* (*U*) courses *fpl* de chevaux.

horseradish ['hɔːs,rædɪʃ] *n* [plant] raifort *m*.

horse riding *n* équitation *f*.

horseshoe ['hɔːsʃuː] *n* fer *m* à cheval.

horsewoman ['hɔːs,wʊmən] (*pl* -**women** [-,wɪmɪn]) *n* cavalière *f*.

horticulture ['hɔːtɪkʌltʃər] *n* horticulture *f*.

hose [həʊz] **1** *n* [hosepipe] tuyau *m*. **2** *vt* arroser au jet.

hosepipe ['həʊzpaɪp] *n* = **hose**.

hosiery ['həʊzɪərɪ] *n* bonneterie *f*.

hospitable [hɒ'spɪtəbl] *adj* hospitalier(ière), accueillant(e).

hospital ['hɒspɪtl] *n* hôpital *m*.

hospitality [,hɒspɪ'tælətɪ] *n* hospitalité *f*.

host [həʊst] **1** *n* [gen] hôte *m*. || [compere] animateur *m*, -trice *f*. || [large number]: **a** ~ **of** une foule de. **2** *vt* présenter, animer.

hostage ['hɒstɪdʒ] *n* otage *m*.

hostel ['hɒstl] *n* [basic accommodation] foyer *m*. || [youth hostel] auberge *f* de jeunesse.

hostess ['həʊstes] *n* hôtesse *f*.

hostile [*Br* 'hɒstaɪl, *Am* 'hɒstl] *adj*: ~ (**to**) hostile (à).

hostility [hɒ'stɪlətɪ] *n* [antagonism, unfriendliness] hostilité *f*. ○ **hostilities** *npl* hostilités *fpl*.

hot [hɒt] *adj* [gen] chaud(e); **I'm** ~ j'ai chaud; **it's** ~ il fait chaud. || [spicy] épicé(e). || *inf* [expert] fort(e), calé(e); **to be** ~ **on** OR **at sthg** être fort OR calé en qqch. || [recent] de dernière heure OR minute. || [temper] colérique.

hot-air balloon *n* montgolfière *f*.

hotbed ['hɒtbed] *n* foyer *m*.

hot-cross bun *n* petit pain sucré que l'on mange le vendredi saint.

hot dog *n* hot dog *m*.

hotel [həʊ'tel] *n* hôtel *m*.

hot flush *Br*, **hot flash** *Am* *n* bouffée *f* de chaleur.

hotfoot ['hɒt,fʊt] *adv* à toute vitesse.

hotheaded [,hɒt'hedɪd] *adj* impulsif(ive).

hothouse ['hɒthaʊs, *pl* -hauzɪz] *n* [greenhouse] serre *f*.

hot line *n* [between government heads] téléphone *m* rouge. || [special line] *ligne ouverte 24 heures sur 24*.

hotly ['hɒtlɪ] *adv* [passionately] avec véhémence. || [closely] de près.

hotplate ['hɒtpleɪt] *n* plaque *f* chauffante.

hot-tempered [-'tempəd] *adj* colérique.

hot-water bottle *n* bouillotte *f*.

hound [haʊnd] **1** *n* [dog] chien *m*. **2** *vt* [persecute] poursuivre, pourchasser. || [drive]: **to** ~ **sb out (of)** chasser qqn (de).

hour ['aʊər] *n* heure *f*; **half an** ~ une demi-heure; **70 miles per** OR **an** ~ 110 km à l'heure; **on the** ~ à l'heure juste. ○ **hours** *npl* [of business] heures *fpl* d'ouverture.

hourly ['aʊəlɪ] **1** *adj* [happening every hour] toutes les heures. || [per hour] à l'heure. **2** *adv* [every hour] toutes les heures. || [per hour] à l'heure.

house [*n* & *adj* haʊs, *pl* 'haʊzɪz, *vb* haʊz] **1** *n* [gen] maison *f*; **on the** ~ aux frais de la maison. || POL chambre *f*. || [in debates] assistance *f*. || THEATRE [audience] auditoire *m*, salle *f*; **to bring the house down** *inf* faire crouler la salle sous les applaudissements. **2** *vt* [accommodate] loger, héberger; [department, store] abriter. **3** *adj* [within business] d'entreprise. || [wine] maison (*inv*).

house arrest *n*: **under** ~ en résidence surveillée.

houseboat ['haʊsbəʊt] *n* péniche *f* aménagée.

housebreaking ['haʊs,breɪkɪŋ] *n* (*U*) cambriolage *m*.

housecoat ['haʊskəʊt] *n* peignoir *m*.

household ['haʊshəʊld] **1** *adj* [domestic] ménager(ère). || [word, name] connu(e) de tous. **2** *n* maison *f*, ménage *m*.

housekeeper ['haʊs,kiːpər] *n* gouvernante *f*.

housekeeping ['haʊs,ki:pɪŋ] *n* (*U*) [work] ménage *m*. ‖ ~ (**money**) argent *m* du ménage.

house music *n* house music *f*.

House of Representatives *n Am*: the ~ la Chambre des représentants.

houseplant ['haʊsplɑ:nt] *n* plante *f* d'appartement.

Houses of Parliament *npl*: the ~ le Parlement britannique (*où se réunissent la Chambre des communes et la Chambre des lords*).

housewarming (party) ['haʊs-,wɔ:mɪŋ-] *n* pendaison *f* de crémaillère.

housewife ['haʊswaɪf] (*pl* -**wives** [-waɪvz]) *n* femme *f* au foyer.

housework ['haʊswɜ:k] *n* (*U*) ménage *m*.

housing ['haʊzɪŋ] *n* (*U*) [accommodation] logement *m*.

housing estate *Br*, **housing project** *Am n* cité *f*.

hovel ['hɒvl] *n* masure *f*, taudis *m*.

hover ['hɒvər] *vi* [fly] planer.

hovercraft ['hɒvəkrɑ:ft] (*pl inv* OR -**s**) *n* aéroglisseur *m*, hovercraft *m*.

how [haʊ] *adv* [gen] comment; ~ **are you?** comment allez-vous?; ~ **do you do?** enchanté(e) (de faire votre connaissance). ‖ [referring to degree, amount]: ~ **high is it?** combien cela fait-il de haut?, quelle en est la hauteur?; ~ **long have you been waiting?** cela fait combien de temps que vous attendez?; ~ **many people came?** combien de personnes sont venues?; ~ **old are you?** quel âge as-tu? ‖ [in exclamations]: ~ **nice!** que c'est bien!; ~ **awful!** quelle horreur! ○ **how about** *adv*: ~ **about a drink?** si on prenait un verre?; ~ **about you?** et toi? ○ **how much 1** *pron* combien; ~ **much does it cost?** combien ça coûte? **2** *adj* combien de; ~ **much bread?** combien de pain?

however [haʊ'evər] **1** *adv* [nevertheless] cependant, toutefois. ‖ [no matter how] quelque ... que (+ *subjunctive*), si ... que (+ *subjunctive*); ~ **many/much** peu importe la quantité de. ‖ [how] comment. **2** *conj* [in whatever way] de quelque manière que (+ *subjunctive*).

howl [haʊl] **1** *n* hurlement *m*; [of laughter] éclat *m*. **2** *vi* hurler; [with laughter] rire aux éclats.

hp (*abbr of* **horsepower**) *n* CV *m*.

HQ (*abbr of* **headquarters**) *n* QG *m*.

hr (*abbr of* **hour**) h.

hub [hʌb] *n* [of wheel] moyeu *m*. ‖ [of activity] centre *m*.

hubbub ['hʌbʌb] *n* vacarme *m*, brouhaha *m*.

hubcap ['hʌbkæp] *n* enjoliveur *m*.

huddle ['hʌdl] **1** *vi* se blottir. **2** *n* petit groupe *m*.

hue [hju:] *n* [colour] teinte *f*, nuance *f*.

huff [hʌf] *n*: **in a** ~ froissé(e).

hug [hʌg] **1** *n* étreinte *f*; **to give sb a** ~ serrer qqn dans ses bras. **2** *vt* [embrace] étreindre, serrer dans ses bras. ‖ [hold] tenir. ‖ [stay close to] serrer.

huge [hju:dʒ] *adj* énorme; [subject] vaste; [success] fou (folle).

hulk [hʌlk] *n* [of ship] carcasse *f*. ‖ [person] malabar *m*, mastodonte *m*.

hull [hʌl] *n* coque *f*.

hullo [hə'ləʊ] *excl* = **hello**.

hum [hʌm] **1** *vi* [buzz] bourdonner; [machine] vrombir, ronfler. ‖ [sing] fredonner, chantonner. ‖ [be busy] être en pleine activité. **2** *vt* fredonner, chantonner.

human ['hju:mən] **1** *adj* humain(e). **2** *n*: ~ (**being**) être *m* humain.

humane [hju:'meɪn] *adj* humain(e).

humanitarian [hju:,mænɪ'teərɪən] *adj* humanitaire.

humanity [hju:'mænətɪ] *n* humanité *f*. ○ **humanities** *npl*: the **humanities** les humanités *fpl*, les sciences *fpl* humaines.

human race *n*: the ~ la race humaine.

human rights *npl* droits *mpl* de l'homme.

humble ['hʌmbl] **1** *adj* humble; [origins, employee] modeste. **2** *vt* humilier.

humbug ['hʌmbʌg] *n dated* [hypocrisy] hypocrisie *f*.

humdrum ['hʌmdrʌm] *adj* monotone.

humid ['hju:mɪd] *adj* humide.

humidity [hju:'mɪdətɪ] *n* humidité *f*.

humiliate [hju:'mɪlɪeɪt] *vt* humilier.

humiliation [hju:,mɪlɪ'eɪʃn] *n* humiliation *f*.

humility [hju:'mɪlətɪ] *n* humilité *f*.

humor *Am* = **humour**.

humorous ['hju:mərəs] *adj* humoristique; [person] plein(e) d'humour.

humour *Br*, **humor** *Am* ['hju:mər] **1** *n* [sense of fun] humour *m*. ‖ [of situation, remark] côté *m* comique. **2** *vt* se montrer conciliant(e) envers.

hump [hʌmp] *n* bosse *f*.

humpbacked bridge ['hʌmpbækt-] *n* pont *m* en dos d'âne.

hunch [hʌntʃ] *n inf* pressentiment *m*, intuition *f*.

hunchback ['hʌntʃbæk] *n* bossu *m*, -e *f*.

hunched ['hʌntʃt] *adj* voûté(e).

hundred ['hʌndrəd] *num* cent; **a** OR **one ~** cent; *see also* **six**. ○ **hundreds** *npl* des centaines.

hundredth ['hʌndrətθ] *num* centième; *see also* **sixth**.

hundredweight ['hʌndrədweɪt] *n* [in US] poids *m* de 100 livres, = *45,3 kg*.

hung [hʌŋ] *pt & pp* → **hang**.

Hungarian [hʌŋ'geərɪən] **1** *adj* hongrois(e). **2** *n* [person] Hongrois *m*, -e *f*. ‖ [language] hongrois *m*.

Hungary ['hʌŋgərɪ] *n* Hongrie *f*.

hunger ['hʌŋgər] *n* [gen] faim *f*. ‖ [strong desire] soif *f*.

hunger strike *n* grève *f* de la faim.

hung over *adj inf*: **to be ~** avoir la gueule de bois.

hungry ['hʌŋgrɪ] *adj* [for food]: **to be ~** avoir faim; [starving] être affamé(e). ‖ [eager]: **to be ~ for** être avide de.

hung up *adj inf*: **to be ~ (on** OR **about)** être obsédé(e) (par).

hunk [hʌŋk] *n* [large piece] gros morceau *m*. ‖ *inf* [man] beau mec *m*.

hunt [hʌnt] **1** *n* chasse *f*; [for missing person] recherches *fpl*. **2** *vi* [chase animals, birds] chasser. ‖ [search]: **to ~ (for sthg)** chercher partout (qqch). **3** *vt* [animals, birds] chasser. ‖ [person] poursuivre, pourchasser.

hunter ['hʌntər] *n* [of animals, birds] chasseur *m*.

hunting ['hʌntɪŋ] *n* [of animals] chasse *f*.

hurdle ['hɜ:dl] *n* [in race] haie *f*. ‖ [obstacle] obstacle *m*.

hurl [hɜ:l] *vt* [throw] lancer avec violence. ‖ [shout] lancer.

hurray [hʊ'reɪ] *excl* hourra!

hurricane ['hʌrɪkən] *n* ouragan *m*.

hurried ['hʌrɪd] *adj* [hasty] précipité(e).

hurriedly ['hʌrɪdlɪ] *adv* précipitamment; [eat, write] vite, en toute hâte.

hurry ['hʌrɪ] **1** *vt* [person] faire se dépêcher; [process] hâter; **to ~ to do sthg** se dépêcher OR se presser de faire qqch. **2** *vi* se dépêcher, se presser. **3** *n* hâte *f*, précipitation *f*; **to be in a ~** être pressé; **to do sthg in a ~** faire qqch à la hâte. ○ **hurry up** *vi* se dépêcher.

hurt [hɜ:t] (*pt & pp* **hurt**) **1** *vt* [physically, emotionally] blesser; [one's leg, arm]

se faire mal à; **to ~ o.s.** se faire mal. ‖ *fig* [harm] faire du mal à. **2** *vi* [gen] faire mal; **my leg ~s** ma jambe me fait mal. ‖ *fig* [do harm] faire du mal. **3** *adj* blessé(e); [voice] offensé(e).

hurtful ['hɜ:tful] *adj* blessant(e).

hurtle ['hɜ:tl] *vi* aller à toute allure.

husband ['hʌzbənd] *n* mari *m*.

hush [hʌʃ] *excl* silence!, chut!

husk [hʌsk] *n* [of seed, grain] enveloppe *f*.

husky ['hʌskɪ] **1** *adj* [hoarse] rauque. **2** *n* chien *m* esquimau.

hustle ['hʌsl] **1** *vt* [hurry] pousser, bousculer. **2** *n* agitation *f*.

hut [hʌt] *n* [rough house] hutte *f*. ‖ [shed] cabane *f*.

hutch [hʌtʃ] *n* clapier *m*.

hyacinth ['haɪəsɪnθ] *n* jacinthe *f*.

hydrant ['haɪdrənt] *n* bouche *f* d'incendie.

hydraulic [haɪ'drɔ:lɪk] *adj* hydraulique.

hydroelectric [ˌhaɪdrəʊɪ'lektrɪk] *adj* hydro-électrique.

hydrofoil ['haɪdrəfɔɪl] *n* hydrofoil *m*.

hydrogen ['haɪdrədʒən] *n* hydrogène *m*.

hyena [haɪ'i:nə] *n* hyène *f*.

hygiene ['haɪdʒi:n] *n* hygiène *f*.

hygienic [haɪ'dʒi:nɪk] *adj* hygiénique.

hymn [hɪm] *n* hymne *m*, cantique *m*.

hype [haɪp] *inf* **1** *n* (*U*) battage *m* publicitaire. **2** *vt* faire un battage publicitaire autour de.

hyperactive [ˌhaɪpər'æktɪv] *adj* hyperactif(ive).

hypermarket ['haɪpəˌmɑ:kɪt] *n* hypermarché *m*.

hyphen ['haɪfn] *n* trait *m* d'union.

hypnosis [hɪp'nəʊsɪs] *n* hypnose *f*.

hypnotic [hɪp'nɒtɪk] *adj* hypnotique.

hypnotize, -ise ['hɪpnətaɪz] *vt* hypnotiser.

hypocrisy [hɪ'pɒkrəsɪ] *n* hypocrisie *f*.

hypocrite ['hɪpəkrɪt] *n* hypocrite *mf*.

hypocritical [ˌhɪpə'krɪtɪkl] *adj* hypocrite.

hypothesis [haɪ'pɒθɪsɪs] (*pl* **-theses** [-θɪsi:z]) *n* hypothèse *f*.

hypothetical [ˌhaɪpə'θetɪkl] *adj* hypothétique.

hysteria [hɪs'tɪərɪə] *n* hystérie *f*.

hysterical [hɪs'terɪkl] *adj* [gen] hystérique. ‖ *inf* [very funny] désopilant(e).

hysterics [hɪs'terɪks] *npl* [panic, excitement] crise *f* de nerfs. ‖ *inf* [laughter] fou rire *m*.

I (*pl* **i's** OR **is**), **I** (*pl* **I's** OR **Is**) [aɪ] *n* [letter] i *m inv*, I *m inv*.

I [aɪ] *pers pron* (*unstressed*) je, j' (*before vowel or silent 'h'*); **he and I are leaving for Paris** lui et moi (nous) partons pour Paris. || (*stressed*) moi; **I can't do it** moi je ne peux pas le faire.

ice [aɪs] *n* [frozen water, ice cream] glace *f*. || [on road] verglas *m*. || (*U*) [ice cubes] glaçons *mpl*. ○ **ice over, ice up** *vi* [lake, pond] geler; [window, windscreen] givrer; [road] se couvrir de verglas.

iceberg [ˈaɪsbɜːg] *n* iceberg *m*.

icebox [ˈaɪsbɒks] *n* Am [refrigerator] réfrigérateur *m*.

ice cream *n* glace *f*.

ice cube *n* glaçon *m*.

ice hockey *n* hockey *m* sur glace.

Iceland [ˈaɪslənd] *n* Islande *f*.

ice pick *n* pic *m* à glace.

ice rink *n* patinoire *f*.

ice skate *n* patin *m* à glace. ○ **ice-skate** *vi* faire du patin (à glace).

ice-skating *n* patinage *m* (sur glace).

icicle [ˈaɪsɪkl] *n* glaçon *m* (naturel).

icing [ˈaɪsɪŋ] *n* (*U*) glaçage *m*, glace *f*.

icon [ˈaɪkɒn] *n* [gen & COMPUT] icône *f*.

icy [ˈaɪsɪ] *adj* [weather, manner] glacial(e). || [covered in ice] verglacé(e).

I'd [aɪd] = I would, I had.

ID *n* (*abbr of* **identification**) (*U*) papiers *mpl*.

idea [aɪˈdɪə] *n* idée *f*; [intention] intention *f*; **to have an ~ (that)** ... avoir idée que ...; **to have no ~** n'avoir aucune idée; **to get the ~** *inf* piger.

ideal [aɪˈdɪəl] **1** *adj* idéal(e). **2** *n* idéal *m*.

ideally [aɪˈdɪəlɪ] *adv* idéalement; [suited] parfaitement.

identical [aɪˈdentɪkl] *adj* identique.

identification [aɪˌdentɪfɪˈkeɪʃn] *n* (*U*) [gen]: **~ (with)** identification *f* (à). || [documentation] pièce *f* d'identité.

identify [aɪˈdentɪfaɪ] **1** *vt* [recognize] identifier. || [subj: document, card] permettre de reconnaître. || [associate]: **to ~ sb with sthg** associer qqn à qqch. **2** *vi* [empathize]: **to ~ with** s'identifier à.

identikit picture® [aɪˈdentɪkɪt-] *n* portrait-robot *m*.

identity [aɪˈdentətɪ] *n* identité *f*.

identity card *n* carte *f* d'identité.

identity parade *n* séance d'identification d'un suspect dans un échantillon de plusieurs personnes.

idiom [ˈɪdɪəm] *n* [phrase] expression *f* idiomatique. || *fml* [style] langue *f*.

idiomatic [ˌɪdɪəˈmætɪk] *adj* idiomatique.

idiosyncrasy [ˌɪdɪəˈsɪŋkrəsɪ] *n* particularité *f*, caractéristique *f*.

idiot [ˈɪdɪət] *n* idiot *m*, -e *f*, imbécile *mf*.

idiotic [ˌɪdɪˈɒtɪk] *adj* idiot(e).

idle [ˈaɪdl] **1** *adj* [lazy] oisif(ive), désœuvré(e). || [not working - machine, factory] arrêté(e); [- worker] qui chôme, en chômage. || [threat] vain(e). || [curiosity] simple, pur(e). **2** *vi* tourner au ralenti. ○ **idle away** *vt sep* [time] perdre à ne rien faire.

idol [ˈaɪdl] *n* idole *f*.

idolize, -ise [ˈaɪdəlaɪz] *vt* idolâtrer, adorer.

idyllic [ɪˈdɪlɪk] *adj* idyllique.

i.e. (*abbr of* **id est**) c-à-d.

if [ɪf] *conj* [gen] si; **~ I were you** à ta place, si j'étais toi. || [though] bien que. || [that] que. ○ **if not** *conj* sinon. ○ **if only** *conj* [naming a reason] ne serait-ce que. || [expressing regret] si seulement.

igloo [ˈɪgluː] (*pl* **-s**) *n* igloo *m*, iglou *m*.

ignite [ɪgˈnaɪt] *vi* prendre feu, s'enflammer.

ignition [ɪgˈnɪʃn] *n* [act of igniting] ignition *f*. || AUT allumage *m*; **to switch on the ~** mettre le contact.

ignition key *n* clef *f* de contact.

ignorance [ˈɪgnərəns] *n* ignorance *f*.

ignorant [ˈɪgnərənt] *adj* [uneducated, unaware] ignorant(e); **to be ~ of sthg** être ignorant de qqch. || [rude] mal élevé(e).

ignore [ɪgˈnɔːr] *vt* [advice, facts] ne pas tenir compte de; [person] faire semblant de ne pas voir.

ill [ɪl] **1** *adj* [unwell] malade; **to feel ~** se sentir malade OR souffrant; **to be taken ~, to fall ~** tomber malade. || [bad] mauvais(e); **~ luck** malchance *f*. **2** *adv* mal; **to speak/think ~ of sb** dire/penser du mal de qqn.

I'll [aɪl] = I will, I shall.

ill-advised [-əd'vaɪdz] *adj* [remark, action] peu judicieux(ieuse); [person] malavisé(e).

ill at ease *adj* mal à l'aise.

illegal [ɪ'li:gl] *adj* illégal(e); [immigrant] en situation irrégulière.

illegible [ɪ'ledʒəbl] *adj* illisible.

illegitimate [ˌɪlɪ'dʒɪtɪmət] *adj* illégitime.

ill-equipped [-ɪ'kwɪpt] *adj*: **to be ~ to do sthg** être mal placé(e) pour faire qqch.

ill-fated [-'feɪtɪd] *adj* fatal(e), funeste.

ill feeling *n* animosité *f*.

ill health *n* mauvaise santé *f*.

illicit [ɪ'lɪsɪt] *adj* illicite.

illiteracy [ɪ'lɪtərəsɪ] *n* analphabétisme *m*, illettrisme *m*.

illiterate [ɪ'lɪtərət] *adj* analphabète, illettré(e).

illness ['ɪlnɪs] *n* maladie *f*.

illogical [ɪ'lɒdʒɪkl] *adj* illogique.

ill-suited *adj* mal assorti(e); **to be ~ for sthg** être inapte à qqch.

ill-timed [-'taɪmd] *adj* déplacé(e), mal à propos.

ill-treat *vt* maltraiter.

illuminate [ɪ'lu:mɪneɪt] *vt* éclairer.

illumination [ɪˌlu:mɪ'neɪʃn] *n* [lighting] éclairage *m*.

illusion [ɪ'lu:ʒn] *n* illusion *f*; **to have no ~s about** ne se faire OR n'avoir aucune illusion sur; **to be under the ~ that** croire OR s'imaginer que, avoir l'illusion que.

illustrate ['ɪləstreɪt] *vt* illustrer.

illustration [ˌɪlə'streɪʃn] *n* illustration *f*.

illustrious [ɪ'lʌstrɪəs] *adj* illustre, célèbre.

ill will *n* animosité *f*.

I'm [aɪm] = **I am**.

image ['ɪmɪdʒ] *n* [gen] image *f*. ‖ [of company, politician] image *f* de marque.

imagery ['ɪmɪdʒrɪ] *n* (*U*) images *fpl*.

imaginary [ɪ'mædʒɪnrɪ] *adj* imaginaire.

imagination [ɪˌmædʒɪ'neɪʃn] *n* [ability] imagination *f*. ‖ [fantasy] invention *f*.

imaginative [ɪ'mædʒɪnətɪv] *adj* imaginatif(ive); [solution] plein(e) d'imagination.

imagine [ɪ'mædʒɪn] *vt* imaginer; **to ~ doing sthg** s'imaginer OR se voir faisant qqch; **~ (that)!** tu t'imagines!

imbalance [ˌɪm'bæləns] *n* déséquilibre *m*.

imbecile ['ɪmbɪsi:l] *n* imbécile *mf*, idiot *m*, -e *f*.

IMF (*abbr of* **International Monetary Fund**) *n* FMI *m*.

imitate ['ɪmɪteɪt] *vt* imiter.

imitation [ˌɪmɪ'teɪʃn] **1** *n* imitation *f*. **2** *adj* [leather] imitation (*before n*); [jewellery] en toc.

immaculate [ɪ'mækjʊlət] *adj* impeccable.

immaterial [ˌɪmə'tɪərɪəl] *adj* [unimportant] sans importance.

immature [ˌɪmə'tjʊəʳ] *adj* [lacking judgment] qui manque de maturité. ‖ [not fully grown] jeune, immature.

immediate [ɪ'mi:djət] *adj* [urgent] immédiat(e); [problem, meeting] urgent(e). ‖ [very near] immédiat(e); [family] le plus proche.

immediately [ɪ'mi:djətlɪ] **1** *adv* [at once] immédiatement. ‖ [directly] directement. **2** *conj* dès que.

immense [ɪ'mens] *adj* immense; [improvement, change] énorme.

immerse [ɪ'mɜ:s] *vt*: **to ~ sthg in sthg** immerger OR plonger qqch dans qqch; **to ~ o.s. in sthg** *fig* se plonger dans qqch.

immersion heater [ɪ'mɜ:ʃn-] *n* chauffe-eau *m inv* électrique.

immigrant ['ɪmɪgrənt] *n* immigré *m*, -e *f*.

immigration [ˌɪmɪ'greɪʃn] *n* immigration *f*.

imminent ['ɪmɪnənt] *adj* imminent(e).

immobilize, -ise [ɪ'məʊbɪlaɪz] *vt* immobiliser.

immoral [ɪ'mɒrəl] *adj* immoral(e).

immortal [ɪ'mɔ:tl] **1** *adj* immortel(elle). **2** *n* immortel *m*, -elle *f*.

immune [ɪ'mju:n] *adj* MED: **~ (to)** immunisé(e) (contre).

immunity [ɪ'mju:nətɪ] *n* MED: **~ (to)** immunité *f* (contre).

immunize, -ise ['ɪmju:naɪz] *vt*: **to ~ sb (against)** immuniser qqn (contre).

imp [ɪmp] *n* [creature] lutin *m*. ‖ [naughty child] petit diable *m*, coquin *m*, -e *f*.

impact ['ɪmpækt] *n* impact *m*; **to make an ~ on** OR **upon sb** faire une forte impression sur qqn; **to make an ~ on** OR **upon sthg** avoir un impact sur qqch.

impair [ɪm'peəʳ] *vt* affaiblir, abîmer; [efficiency] réduire.

impart [ɪm'pɑ:t] *vt fml* [information]: **to ~ sthg (to sb)** communiquer OR transmettre qqch (à qqn). ‖ [feeling, quality]: **to ~ sthg (to)** donner qqch (à).

impartial [ɪm'pɑ:ʃl] *adj* impartial(e).

impassive [ɪm'pæsɪv] *adj* impassible.

impatience [ɪmˈpeɪʃns] n [gen] impatience f. || [irritability] irritation f.

impatient [ɪmˈpeɪʃnt] adj [gen] impatient(e); **to be ~ to do sthg** être impatient de faire qqch; **to be ~ for sthg** attendre qqch avec impatience. || [irritable]: **to become** OR **get ~** s'impatienter.

impeccable [ɪmˈpekəbl] adj impeccable.

impede [ɪmˈpiːd] vt entraver, empêcher; [person] gêner.

impediment [ɪmˈpedɪmənt] n [obstacle] obstacle m. || [disability] défaut m.

impel [ɪmˈpel] vt: **to ~ sb to do sthg** inciter qqn à faire qqch.

impending [ɪmˈpendɪŋ] adj imminent(e).

imperative [ɪmˈperətɪv] 1 adj [essential] impératif(ive), essentiel(ielle). 2 n impératif m.

imperfect [ɪmˈpɜːfɪkt] 1 adj imparfait(e). 2 n GRAMM: ~ **(tense)** imparfait m.

imperial [ɪmˈpɪərɪəl] adj [of empire] impérial(e).

impersonal [ɪmˈpɜːsnl] adj impersonnel(elle).

impersonate [ɪmˈpɜːsəneɪt] vt se faire passer pour.

impersonation [ɪmˌpɜːsəˈneɪʃn] n usurpation f d'identité; [by mimic] imitation f.

impertinent [ɪmˈpɜːtɪnənt] adj impertinent(e).

impervious [ɪmˈpɜːvjəs] adj [not influenced]: **~ to** indifférent(e) à.

impetuous [ɪmˈpetʃʊəs] adj impétueux(euse).

impetus [ˈɪmpɪtəs] n (U) [momentum] élan m. || [stimulus] impulsion f.

impinge [ɪmˈpɪndʒ] vi: **to ~ on sb/sthg** affecter qqn/qqch.

implant [n ˈɪmplɑːnt, vb ɪmˈplɑːnt] 1 n implant m. 2 vt: **to ~ sthg in** OR **into sb** implanter qqch dans qqn.

implausible [ɪmˈplɔːzəbl] adj peu plausible.

implement [n ˈɪmplɪmənt, vb ˈɪmplɪment] 1 n outil m, instrument m. 2 vt exécuter, appliquer.

implication [ˌɪmplɪˈkeɪʃn] n implication f; **by ~** par voie de conséquence.

implicit [ɪmˈplɪsɪt] adj [inferred] implicite. || [belief, faith] absolu(e).

implore [ɪmˈplɔː] vt: **to ~ sb (to do sthg)** implorer qqn (de faire qqch).

imply [ɪmˈplaɪ] vt [suggest] sous-

entendre, laisser supposer OR entendre. || [involve] impliquer.

impolite [ˌɪmpəˈlaɪt] adj impoli(e).

import [n ˈɪmpɔːt, vb ɪmˈpɔːt] 1 n [product, action] importation f. 2 vt [gen & COMPUT] importer.

importance [ɪmˈpɔːtns] n importance f.

important [ɪmˈpɔːtnt] adj important(e); **to be ~ to sb** importer à qqn.

importer [ɪmˈpɔːtə] n importateur m, -trice f.

impose [ɪmˈpəʊz] 1 vt [force]: **to ~ sthg (on)** imposer qqch (à). 2 vi [cause trouble]: **to ~ (on sb)** abuser (de la gentillesse de qqn).

imposing [ɪmˈpəʊzɪŋ] adj imposant(e).

imposition [ˌɪmpəˈzɪʃn] n [of tax, limitations etc] imposition f. || [cause of trouble]: **it's an ~** c'est abuser de ma/notre gentillesse.

impossible [ɪmˈpɒsəbl] adj impossible.

impostor, imposter Am [ɪmˈpɒstə] n imposteur m.

impotent [ˈɪmpətənt] adj impuissant(e).

impound [ɪmˈpaʊnd] vt confisquer.

impoverished [ɪmˈpɒvərɪʃt] adj appauvri(e).

impractical [ɪmˈpræktɪkl] adj pas pratique.

impregnable [ɪmˈpregnəbl] adj [fortress, defences] imprenable.

impregnate [ˈɪmpregneɪt] vt [introduce substance into]: **to ~ sthg with** imprégner qqch de. || fml [fertilize] féconder.

impress [ɪmˈpres] vt [person] impressionner. || [stress]: **to ~ sthg on sb** faire bien comprendre qqch à qqn.

impression [ɪmˈpreʃn] n [gen] impression f; **to be under the ~ (that)** ... avoir l'impression que ...; **to make an ~** faire impression. || [by mimic] imitation f.

impressive [ɪmˈpresɪv] adj impressionnant(e).

imprint [ˈɪmprɪnt] n [mark] empreinte f.

imprison [ɪmˈprɪzn] vt emprisonner.

improbable [ɪmˈprɒbəbl] adj [story, excuse] improbable.

impromptu [ɪmˈprɒmptjuː] adj impromptu(e).

improper [ɪmˈprɒpə] adj [unsuitable] impropre. || [incorrect, illegal] incorrect(e). || [rude] indécent(e).

improve [ɪmˈpruːv] 1 vi s'améliorer; [patient] aller mieux; **to ~ on** OR **upon sthg** améliorer qqch. 2 vt améliorer.

improvement [ɪm'pruːvmənt] *n*: ~ **(in/on)** amélioration *f* (de/par rapport à).

improvise ['ɪmprəvaɪz] *vt & vi* improviser.

impudent ['ɪmpjʊdənt] *adj* impudent(e).

impulse ['ɪmpʌls] *n* impulsion *f*; **on ~** par impulsion.

impulsive [ɪm'pʌlsɪv] *adj* impulsif(ive).

impunity [ɪm'pjuːnətɪ] *n*: **with ~** avec impunité.

impurity [ɪm'pjʊərətɪ] *n* impureté *f*.

in [ɪn] **1** *prep* [indicating place, position] dans; ~ **Paris** à Paris; ~ **Belgium** en Belgique; ~ **the United States** aux États-Unis; ~ **the country** à la campagne; ~ **here** ici; ~ **there** là. || [wearing] en; **dressed ~ a suit** vêtu d'un costume. || [at a particular time, season]: ~ **1994** en 1994; ~ **April** en avril; ~ **(the) spring** au printemps; ~ **(the) winter** en hiver. || [period of time - within] en; [- after] dans; **he learned to type ~ two weeks** il a appris à taper à la machine en deux semaines; **I'll be ready ~ five minutes** je serai prêt dans 5 minutes. || [during]: **it's my first decent meal ~ weeks** c'est mon premier repas correct depuis des semaines. || [indicating situation, circumstances]: ~ **the sun** au soleil; ~ **the rain** sous la pluie; ~ **danger/difficulty** en danger/difficulté. || [indicating manner, condition]: ~ **a loud/soft voice** d'une voix forte/douce; **to write ~ pencil/ink** écrire au crayon/à l'encre; **to speak ~ English/French** parler (en) anglais/français. || [indicating emotional state]: ~ **anger** sous le coup de la colère; ~ **joy/delight** avec joie/plaisir. || [specifying area of activity] dans; **he's ~ computers** il est dans l'informatique. || [referring to quantity, numbers, age]: ~ **large/small quantities** en grande/petite quantité; **she's ~ her sixties** elle a la soixantaine. || [describing arrangement]: ~ **twos** par deux; ~ **a line/row/circle** en ligne/rang/cercle. || [as regards]: **to be three metres ~ length/width** faire trois mètres de long/large; **a change ~ direction** un changement de direction. || [in ratios]: **one ~ ten** un sur dix. || (*after superl*) de; **the longest river ~ the world** le fleuve le plus long du monde. || (+ *present participle*): ~ **doing sthg** en faisant qqch. **2** *adv* [inside] dedans, à l'intérieur. || [at home, work] là; **I'm staying ~ tonight** je

reste à la maison OR chez moi ce soir; **is Judith ~?** est-ce que Judith est là? || [of train, boat, plane]: **to be ~** être arrivé(e). || [of tide]: **the tide's ~** c'est la marée haute. || *phr*: **you're ~ for a shock** tu vas avoir un choc. **3** *adj inf* à la mode. ○ **ins** *npl*: **the ~s and outs** les tenants et les aboutissants *mpl*.

in. *abbr of* **inch.**

inability [ˌɪnə'bɪlətɪ] *n*: ~ **(to do sthg)** incapacité *f* (à faire qqch).

inaccessible [ˌɪnək'sesəbl] *adj* inaccessible.

inaccurate [ɪn'ækjʊrət] *adj* inexact(e).

inadequate [ɪn'ædɪkwət] *adj* insuffisant(e).

inadvertently [ˌɪnəd'vɜːtəntlɪ] *adv* par inadvertance.

inadvisable [ˌɪnəd'vaɪzəbl] *adj* déconseillé(e).

inane [ɪ'neɪn] *adj* inepte; [person] stupide.

inanimate [ɪn'ænɪmət] *adj* inanimé(e).

inappropriate [ˌɪnə'prəʊprɪət] *adj* inopportun(e); [expression, word] impropre; [clothing] peu approprié(e).

inarticulate [ˌɪnɑː'tɪkjʊlət] *adj* inarticulé(e), indistinct(e); [person] qui s'exprime avec difficulté; [explanation] mal exprimé(e).

inasmuch [ˌɪnəz'mʌtʃ] ○ **inasmuch as** *conj fml* attendu que.

inaudible [ɪ'nɔːdɪbl] *adj* inaudible.

inaugural [ɪ'nɔːgjʊrəl] *adj* inaugural(e):

inauguration [ɪˌnɔːgjʊ'reɪʃn] *n* [of leader, president] investiture *f*; [of building, system] inauguration *f*.

in-between *adj* intermédiaire.

inborn [ˌɪn'bɔːn] *adj* inné(e).

inbound ['ɪnbaʊnd] *adj Am* qui arrive.

inbred [ˌɪn'bred] *adj* [closely related] consanguin(e); [animal] croisé(e). || [inborn] inné(e).

inbuilt [ˌɪn'bɪlt] *adj* [inborn] inné(e).

inc. (*abbr of* **inclusive**): **12-15 April ~** du 12 au 15 avril inclus.

Inc. [ɪŋk] (*abbr of* **incorporated**) ≃ SARL.

incapable [ɪn'keɪpəbl] *adj* incapable; **to be ~ of sthg/of doing sthg** être incapable de qqch/de faire qqch.

incapacitated [ˌɪnkə'pæsɪteɪtɪd] *adj* inapte physiquement.

incarcerate [ɪn'kɑːsəreɪt] *vt* incarcérer.

incendiary device [ɪn'sendɪərɪ-] *n* dispositif *m* incendiaire.

incense [*n* 'ɪnsens, *vb* ɪn'sens] **1** *n* encens *m*. **2** *vt* [anger] mettre en colère.

incentive [ɪn'sentɪv] *n* [encouragement] motivation *f*. || COMM récompense *f*, prime *f*.

incentive scheme *n* programme *m* d'encouragement.

inception [ɪn'sepʃn] *n fml* commencement *m*.

incessant [ɪn'sesnt] *adj* incessant(e).

incessantly [ɪn'sesntlɪ] *adv* sans cesse.

incest ['ɪnsest] *n* inceste *m*.

inch [ɪntʃ] **1** *n* = 2,5 cm, ≃ pouce *m*. **2** *vi*: **to ~ forward** avancer petit à petit.

incidence ['ɪnsɪdəns] *n* [of disease, theft] fréquence *f*.

incident ['ɪnsɪdənt] *n* incident *m*.

incidental [,ɪnsɪ'dentl] *adj* accessoire.

incidentally [,ɪnsɪ'dentəlɪ] *adv* à propos.

incinerate [ɪn'sɪnəreɪt] *vt* incinérer.

incisive [ɪn'saɪsɪv] *adj* incisif(ive).

incite [ɪn'saɪt] *vt* inciter; **to ~ sb to do sthg** inciter qqn à faire qqch.

inclination [,ɪnklɪ'neɪʃn] *n* (*U*) [liking, preference] inclination *f*, goût *m*. || [tendency]: **~ to do sthg** inclination *f* à faire qqch.

incline [*n* 'ɪnklaɪn, *vb* ɪn'klaɪn] **1** *n* inclinaison *f*. **2** *vt* [head] incliner.

inclined [ɪn'klaɪnd] *adj* [tending]: **to be ~ to sthg/to do sthg** avoir tendance à qqch/à faire qqch. || [wanting]: **to be ~ to do sthg** être enclin(e) à faire qqch.

include [ɪn'kluːd] *vt* inclure.

included [ɪn'kluːdɪd] *adj* inclus(e).

including [ɪn'kluːdɪŋ] *prep* y compris.

inclusive [ɪn'kluːsɪv] *adj* inclus(e); [including all costs] tout compris; **~ of VAT** TVA incluse ou comprise.

incoherent [,ɪnkəʊ'hɪərənt] *adj* incohérent(e).

income ['ɪŋkʌm] *n* revenu *m*.

income tax *n* impôt *m* sur le revenu.

incompatible [,ɪnkəm'pætɪbl] *adj*: **~ (with)** incompatible (avec).

incompetent [ɪn'kɒmpɪtənt] *adj* incompétent(e).

incomplete [,ɪnkəm'pliːt] *adj* incomplet(ète).

incomprehensible [ɪn,kɒmprɪ'hensəbl] *adj* incompréhensible.

inconceivable [,ɪnkən'siːvəbl] *adj* inconcevable.

inconclusive [,ɪnkən'kluːsɪv] *adj* peu concluant(e).

incongruous [ɪn'kɒngruəs] *adj* incongru(e).

inconsiderable [,ɪnkən'sɪdərəbl] *adj*: **not ~** non négligeable.

inconsiderate [,ɪnkən'sɪdərət] *adj* inconsidéré(e); [person] qui manque de considération.

inconsistency [,ɪnkən'sɪstənsɪ] *n* inconsistance *f*.

inconsistent [,ɪnkən'sɪstənt] *adj* [not agreeing, contradictory] contradictoire; [person] inconséquent(e); **~ with sthg** en contradiction avec qqch. || [erratic] inconsistant(e).

inconspicuous [,ɪnkən'spɪkjuəs] *adj* qui passe inaperçu(e).

inconvenience [,ɪnkən'viːnjəns] **1** *n* désagrément *m*. **2** *vt* déranger.

inconvenient [,ɪnkən'viːnjənt] *adj* inopportun(e).

incorporate [ɪn'kɔːpəreɪt] *vt* [integrate]: **to ~ sb/sthg (into)** incorporer qqn/qqch (dans). || [comprise] contenir, comprendre.

incorporated [ɪn'kɔːpəreɪtɪd] *adj* COMM constitué(e) en société commerciale.

incorrect [,ɪnkə'rekt] *adj* incorrect(e).

increase [*n* 'ɪnkriːs, *vb* ɪn'kriːs] **1** *n*: **~ (in)** augmentation *f* (de); **to be on the ~** aller en augmentant. **2** *vt* & *vi* augmenter.

increasing [ɪn'kriːsɪŋ] *adj* croissant(e).

increasingly [ɪn'kriːsɪŋlɪ] *adv* de plus en plus.

incredible [ɪn'kredəbl] *adj* incroyable.

increment ['ɪnkrɪmənt] *n* augmentation *f*.

incriminating [ɪn'krɪmɪneɪtɪŋ] *adj* compromettant(e).

incubator ['ɪnkjʊbeɪtər] *n* [for baby] incubateur *m*, couveuse *f*.

incumbent [ɪn'kʌmbənt] *fml n* [of post] titulaire *m*.

incur [ɪn'kɜːr] *vt* encourir.

indebted [ɪn'detɪd] *adj* [grateful]: **~ to sb** redevable à qqn.

indecent [ɪn'diːsnt] *adj* [improper] indécent(e). || [unreasonable] malséant(e).

indecent assault *n* attentat *m* à la pudeur.

indecent exposure *n* outrage *m* public à la pudeur.

indecisive [,ɪndɪ'saɪsɪv] *adj* indécis(e).

indeed [ɪn'diːd] *adv* [certainly, to express surprise] vraiment; **~ I am, yes ~** certainement. || [in fact] en effet. || [for emphasis]: **very big/bad** ~ extrêmement grand/mauvais, vraiment grand/mauvais.

indefinite [ɪn'defɪnɪt] *adj* [not fixed] indéfini(e). || [imprecise] vague.

indefinitely [ɪn'defɪnətlɪ] *adv* [for unfixed period] indéfiniment. || [imprecisely] vaguement.

indemnity [ɪn'demnətɪ] *n* indemnité *f.*

indent [ɪn'dent] *vt* [dent] entailler. || [text] mettre en retrait.

independence [,ɪndɪ'pendəns] *n* indépendance *f.*

Independence Day *n* fête de l'indépendance américaine, le 4 juillet.

independent [,ɪndɪ'pendənt] *adj*: ~ (**of**) indépendant(e) (de).

in-depth *adj* approfondi(e).

indescribable [,ɪndɪ'skraɪbəbl] *adj* indescriptible.

indestructible [,ɪndɪ'strʌktəbl] *adj* indestructible.

index ['ɪndeks] (*pl senses 1 and 2* -es, *sense 3* -es OR **indices**) *n* [of book] index *m.* || [in library] répertoire *m*, fichier *m.* || ECON indice *m.*

index card *n* fiche *f.*

index finger *n* index *m.*

index-linked [-lɪŋkt] *adj* indexé(e).

India ['ɪndjə] *n* Inde *f.*

Indian ['ɪndjən] **1** *adj* indien(ienne). **2** *n* Indien *m*, -ienne *f.*

Indian Ocean *n*: **the** ~ l'océan *m* Indien.

indicate ['ɪndɪkeɪt] **1** *vt* indiquer. **2** *vi* AUT mettre son clignotant.

indication [,ɪndɪ'keɪʃn] *n* [suggestion] indication *f.* || [sign] signe *m.*

indicative [ɪn'dɪkətɪv] **1** *adj*: ~ **of** indicatif(ive) de. **2** *n* GRAMM indicatif *m.*

indicator ['ɪndɪkeɪtər] *n* [sign] indicateur *m.* || AUT clignotant *m.*

indices ['ɪndɪsiːz] *pl* → **index**.

indict [ɪn'daɪt] *vt*: **to** ~ **sb** (**for**) accuser qqn (de).

indictment [ɪn'daɪtmənt] *n* JUR acte *m* d'accusation. || [criticism] mise *f* en accusation.

indifference [ɪn'dɪfrəns] *n* indifférence *f.*

indifferent [ɪn'dɪfrənt] *adj* [uninterested]: ~ (**to**) indifférent(e) (à). || [mediocre] médiocre.

indigenous [ɪn'dɪdʒɪnəs] *adj* indigène.

indigestion [,ɪndɪ'dʒestʃn] *n* (*U*) indigestion *f.*

indignant [ɪn'dɪgnənt] *adj*: ~ (**at**) indigné(e) (de).

indignity [ɪn'dɪgnətɪ] *n* indignité *f.*

indigo ['ɪndɪgəʊ] *adj* indigo (*inv*).

indirect [,ɪndɪ'rekt] *adj* indirect(e).

indiscreet [,ɪndɪ'skriːt] *adj* indiscret(ète).

indiscriminate [,ɪndɪ'skrɪmɪnət] *adj* [person] qui manque de discernement; [treatment] sans distinction; [killing] commis au hasard.

indispensable [,ɪndɪ'spensəbl] *adj* indispensable.

indisputable [,ɪndɪ'spjuːtəbl] *adj* indiscutable.

indistinguishable [,ɪndɪ'stɪŋgwɪʃəbl] *adj*: ~ (**from**) que l'on ne peut distinguer (de).

individual [,ɪndɪ'vɪdʒʊəl] **1** *adj* [separate, for one person] individuel(elle). || [distinctive] personnel(elle). **2** *n* individu *m.*

individually [,ɪndɪ'vɪdʒʊəlɪ] *adv* individuellement.

indoctrination [ɪn,dɒktrɪ'neɪʃn] *n* endoctrinement *m.*

Indonesia [,ɪndə'niːzjə] *n* Indonésie *f.*

indoor ['ɪndɔːr] *adj* d'intérieur; [swimming pool] couvert(e); [sports] en salle.

indoors [,ɪn'dɔːz] *adv* à l'intérieur.

induce [ɪn'djuːs] *vt* [persuade]: **to** ~ **sb to do sthg** inciter OR pousser qqn à faire qqch. || [bring about] provoquer.

inducement [ɪn'djuːsmənt] *n* [incentive] incitation *f*, encouragement *m.*

induction [ɪn'dʌkʃn] *n* [into official position]: ~ (**into**) installation *f* (à).

induction course *n* stage *m* d'initiation.

indulge [ɪn'dʌldʒ] **1** *vt* [whim, passion] céder à. || [child, person] gâter. **2** *vi*: **to** ~ **in sthg** se permettre qqch.

indulgence [ɪn'dʌldʒəns] *n* [act of indulging] indulgence *f.* || [special treat] gâterie *f.*

indulgent [ɪn'dʌldʒənt] *adj* indulgent(e).

industrial [ɪn'dʌstrɪəl] *adj* industriel(ielle).

industrial action *n*: **to take** ~ se mettre en grève.

industrial estate *Br*, **industrial park** *Am n* zone *f* industrielle.

industrialist [ɪn'dʌstrɪəlɪst] *n* industriel *m.*

industrial park *Am* = **industrial estate**.

industrial relations npl relations fpl patronat-syndicats.

industrial revolution n révolution f industrielle.

industrious [ɪn'dʌstrɪəs] adj industrieux(ieuse).

industry ['ɪndəstrɪ] n [gen] industrie f.

inebriated [ɪ'ni:brɪeɪtɪd] adj fml ivre.

inedible [ɪn'edɪbl] adj [meal, food] immangeable. || [plant, mushroom] non comestible.

ineffective [,ɪnɪ'fektɪv] adj inefficace.

ineffectual [,ɪnɪ'fektʃʊəl] adj inefficace; [person] incapable, incompétent(e).

inefficiency [,ɪnɪ'fɪʃnsɪ] n inefficacité f; [of person] incapacité f, incompétence f.

inefficient [,ɪnɪ'fɪʃnt] adj inefficace; [person] incapable, incompétent(e).

ineligible [ɪn'elɪdʒəbl] adj inéligible; **to be ~ for** sthg ne pas avoir droit à qqch.

inept [ɪ'nept] adj inepte; [person] stupide.

inequality [,ɪnɪ'kwɒlətɪ] n inégalité f.

inert [ɪ'nɜ:t] adj inerte.

inertia [ɪ'nɜ:ʃə] n inertie f.

inescapable [,ɪnɪ'skeɪpəbl] adj inéluctable.

inevitable [ɪn'evɪtəbl] adj inévitable.

inevitably [ɪn'evɪtəblɪ] adv inévitablement.

inexcusable [,ɪnɪk'skju:zəbl] adj inexcusable, impardonnable.

inexpensive [,ɪnɪk'spensɪv] adj bon marché (inv), pas cher (chère).

inexperienced [,ɪnɪk'spɪərɪənst] adj inexpérimenté(e), qui manque d'expérience.

inexplicable [,ɪnɪk'splɪkəbl] adj inexplicable.

infallible [ɪn'fæləbl] adj infaillible.

infamous ['ɪnfəməs] adj infâme.

infancy ['ɪnfənsɪ] n petite enfance f.

infant ['ɪnfənt] n [baby] nouveau-né m, nouveau-née f, nourrisson m. || [young child] enfant mf en bas âge.

infantry ['ɪnfəntrɪ] n infanterie f.

infatuated [ɪn'fætjʊeɪtɪd] adj: ~ (with) entiché(e) (de).

infatuation [ɪn,fætjʊ'eɪʃn] n: ~ (with) béguin m (pour).

infect [ɪn'fekt] vt MED infecter.

infection [ɪn'fekʃn] n infection f.

infectious [ɪn'fekʃəs] adj [disease] infectieux(ieuse). || fig [feeling, laugh] contagieux(ieuse).

infer [ɪn'fɜ:r] vt [deduce]: **to ~** sthg **(from)** déduire qqch (de).

inferior [ɪn'fɪərɪər] **1** adj [in status] inférieur(e). || [product] de qualité inférieure; [work] médiocre. **2** n [in status] subalterne mf.

inferiority [ɪn,fɪərɪ'ɒrətɪ] n infériorité f.

inferiority complex n complexe m d'infériorité.

inferno [ɪn'fɜ:nəʊ] (pl -s) n brasier m.

infertile [ɪn'fɜ:taɪl] adj [woman] stérile. || [soil] infertile.

infested [ɪn'festɪd] adj: ~ **with** infesté(e) de.

infighting ['ɪn,faɪtɪŋ] n (U) querelles fpl intestines.

infiltrate ['ɪnfɪltreɪt] vt infiltrer.

infinite ['ɪnfɪnət] adj infini(e).

infinitive [ɪn'fɪnɪtɪv] n infinitif m.

infinity [ɪn'fɪnətɪ] n infini m.

infirm [ɪn'fɜ:m] adj infirme.

infirmary [ɪn'fɜ:mərɪ] n [hospital] hôpital m.

inflamed [ɪn'fleɪmd] adj MED enflammé(e).

inflammable [ɪn'flæməbl] adj inflammable.

inflammation [,ɪnflə'meɪʃn] n MED inflammation f.

inflatable [ɪn'fleɪtəbl] adj gonflable.

inflate [ɪn'fleɪt] vt [tyre, life jacket etc] gonfler.

inflation [ɪn'fleɪʃn] n ECON inflation f.

inflationary [ɪn'fleɪʃnrɪ] adj ECON inflationniste.

inflict [ɪn'flɪkt] vt: **to ~** sthg **on** sb infliger qqch à qqn.

influence ['ɪnflʊəns] **1** n influence f; **under the ~ of** [person, group] sous l'influence de; [alcohol, drugs] sous l'effet OR l'empire de. **2** vt influencer.

influential [,ɪnflʊ'enʃl] adj influent(e).

influenza [,ɪnflʊ'enzə] n (U) grippe f.

influx ['ɪnflʌks] n afflux m.

inform [ɪn'fɔ:m] vt: **to ~** sb **(of)** informer qqn (de); **to ~** sb **about** renseigner qqn sur. ○ **inform on** vt fus dénoncer.

informal [ɪn'fɔ:ml] adj [party, person] simple; [clothes] de tous les jours. || [negotiations, visit] officieux(ieuse); [meeting] informel(elle).

informant [ɪn'fɔ:mənt] n informateur m, -trice f.

information [,ɪnfə'meɪʃn] n (U): ~ **(on** OR **about)** renseignements mpl OR informations fpl (sur); **a piece of ~** un renseignement; **for your** ~ *fml* à titre d'information.

information desk *n* bureau *m* de renseignements.

information technology *n* informatique *f*.

informative [ɪn'fɔːmətɪv] *adj* informatif(ive).

informer [ɪn'fɔːmər] *n* indicateur *m*, -trice *f*.

infrared [ˌɪnfrə'red] *adj* infrarouge.

infrastructure ['ɪnfrəˌstrʌktʃər] *n* infrastructure *f*.

infringe [ɪn'frɪndʒ] 1 *vt* [right] empiéter sur. || [law, agreement] enfreindre. 2 *vi* [on right]: **to ~ on** empiéter sur. || [on law, agreement]: **to ~ on** enfreindre.

infringement [ɪn'frɪndʒmənt] *n* [of right]: ~ **(of)** atteinte *f* (à). || [of law, agreement] transgression *f*.

infuriating [ɪn'fjʊərieɪtɪŋ] *adj* exaspérant(e).

ingenious [ɪn'dʒiːnjəs] *adj* ingénieux(ieuse).

ingenuity [ˌɪndʒɪ'njuːətɪ] *n* ingéniosité *f*.

ingot ['ɪŋgət] *n* lingot *m*.

ingrained [ˌɪn'greɪnd] *adj* [dirt] incrusté(e). || *fig* [belief, hatred] enraciné(e).

ingratiating [ɪn'greɪʃieɪtɪŋ] *adj* doucereux(euse), mielleux(euse).

ingredient [ɪn'griːdjənt] *n* ingrédient *m*; *fig* élément *m*.

inhabit [ɪn'hæbɪt] *vt* habiter.

inhabitant [ɪn'hæbɪtənt] *n* habitant *m*, -e *f*.

inhale [ɪn'heɪl] 1 *vt* inhaler, respirer. 2 *vi* [breathe in] respirer.

inhaler [ɪn'heɪlər] *n* MED inhalateur *m*.

inherent [ɪn'hɪərənt, ɪn'herənt] *adj*: ~ **(in)** inhérent(e) (à).

inherit [ɪn'herɪt] 1 *vt*: **to ~ sthg (from sb)** hériter qqch (de qqn). 2 *vi* hériter.

inheritance [ɪn'herɪtəns] *n* héritage *m*.

inhibit [ɪn'hɪbɪt] *vt* [prevent] empêcher. || PSYCH inhiber.

inhibition [ˌɪnhɪ'bɪʃn] *n* inhibition *f*.

inhospitable [ˌɪnhɒ'spɪtəbl] *adj* inhospitalier(ière).

in-house 1 *adj* interne; [staff] de la maison. 2 *adv* [produce, work] sur place.

inhuman [ɪn'hjuːmən] *adj* inhumain(e).

initial [ɪ'nɪʃl] 1 *adj* initial(e), premier(ière); ~ **letter** initiale *f*. 2 *vt* parapher. ○ **initials** *npl* initiales *fpl*.

initially [ɪ'nɪʃəlɪ] *adv* initialement, au début.

initiate [ɪ'nɪʃieɪt] *vt* [talks] engager; [scheme] ébaucher, inaugurer. || [teach]: **to ~ sb into sthg** initier qqn à qqch.

initiative [ɪ'nɪʃətɪv] *n* [gen] initiative *f*. || [advantage]: **to have the ~** avoir l'avantage *m*.

inject [ɪn'dʒekt] *vt* MED: **to ~ sb with sthg, to ~ sthg into sb** injecter qqch à qqn. || *fig* [excitement] insuffler; [money] injecter.

injection [ɪn'dʒekʃn] *n* *lit* & *fig* injection *f*.

injure ['ɪndʒər] *vt* [limb, person] blesser. || *fig* [reputation, chances] compromettre.

injured ['ɪndʒəd] 1 *adj* [limb, person] blessé(e). 2 *npl*: **the ~** les blessés *mpl*.

injury ['ɪndʒərɪ] *n* [to limb, person] blessure *f*; **to do o.s. an ~** se blesser. || *fig* [to reputation] coup *m*, atteinte *f*.

injury time *n* (U) arrêts *mpl* de jeu.

injustice [ɪn'dʒʌstɪs] *n* injustice *f*.

ink [ɪŋk] *n* encre *f*.

ink-jet printer *n* COMPUT imprimante *f* à jet d'encre.

inkling ['ɪŋklɪŋ] *n*: **to have an ~ of** avoir une petite idée de.

inlaid [ˌɪn'leɪd] *adj*: ~ **(with)** incrusté(e) (de).

inland [*adj* 'ɪnlənd, *adv* ɪn'lænd] 1 *adj* intérieur(e). 2 *adv* à l'intérieur.

inlet ['ɪnlet] *n* [of lake, sea] avancée *f*. || TECH arrivée *f*.

inmate ['ɪnmeɪt] *n* [of prison] détenu *m*, -e *f*; [of mental hospital] interné *m*, -e *f*.

inn [ɪn] *n* auberge *f*.

innate [ˌɪ'neɪt] *adj* inné(e).

inner ['ɪnər] *adj* [on inside] interne, intérieur(e). || [feelings] intime.

inner city *n*: **the ~** les quartiers *mpl* pauvres.

inner tube *n* chambre *f* à air.

innocence ['ɪnəsəns] *n* innocence *f*.

innocent ['ɪnəsənt] *adj* innocent(e); ~ **of** [crime] non coupable de.

innocuous [ɪ'nɒkjʊəs] *adj* inoffensif(ive).

innovation [ˌɪnə'veɪʃn] *n* innovation *f*.

innovative ['ɪnəvətɪv] *adj* [idea, design] innovateur(trice). || [person, company] novateur(trice).

innuendo [ˌɪnjuː'endəʊ] (*pl* **-es** OR **-s**) *n* insinuation *f*.

innumerable [ɪ'njuːmərəbl] *adj* innombrable.

inoculate [ɪ'nɒkjʊleɪt] *vt*: **to ~ sb (with sthg)** inoculer (qqch à) qqn.

in-patient n malade hospitalisé m, malade hospitalisée f.

input ['ɪnpʊt] (pt & pp **input** OR **-ted**) 1 n [contribution] contribution f, concours m. || COMPUT & ELEC entrée f. 2 vt COMPUT entrer.

inquest ['ɪnkwest] n enquête f.

inquire [ɪn'kwaɪər] vt: **to ~ when/whether/how ...** demander quand/si/comment .... 2 vi: **to ~ (about)** se renseigner (sur). ○ **inquire after** vt fus s'enquérir de. ○ **inquire into** vt fus enquêter sur.

inquiry [ɪn'kwaɪərɪ] n [question] demande f de renseignements; **"Inquiries"** «renseignements». || [investigation] enquête f.

inquiry desk n bureau m de renseignements.

inquisitive [ɪn'kwɪzətɪv] adj inquisiteur(trice).

inroads ['ɪnrəʊdz] npl: **to make ~ into** [savings] entamer.

insane [ɪn'seɪn] adj fou (folle).

insanity [ɪn'sænətɪ] n folie f.

insatiable [ɪn'seɪʃəbl] adj insatiable.

inscription [ɪn'skrɪpʃn] n [engraved] inscription f. || [written] dédicace f.

inscrutable [ɪn'skruːtəbl] adj impénétrable.

insect ['ɪnsekt] n insecte m.

insecticide [ɪn'sektɪsaɪd] n insecticide m.

insect repellent n crème f anti-insectes.

insecure [,ɪnsɪ'kjʊər] adj [person] anxieux(ieuse). || [job, investment] incertain(e).

insensitive [ɪn'sensətɪv] adj: **~ (to)** insensible (à).

inseparable [ɪn'seprəbl] adj inséparable.

insert [vb ɪn'sɜːt, n 'ɪnsɜːt] 1 vt: **to ~ sthg (in** OR **into)** insérer qqch (dans). 2 n [in newspaper] encart m.

insertion [ɪn'sɜːʃn] n insertion f.

inshore [adj 'ɪnʃɔːr, adv ɪn'ʃɔːr] 1 adj côtier(ière). 2 adv [be situated] près de la côte; [move] vers la côte.

inside [ɪn'saɪd] 1 prep [building, object] à l'intérieur de, dans; [group, organization] au sein de. || [time]: **~ three weeks** en moins de trois semaines. 2 adv [gen] dedans, à l'intérieur; **to go ~** entrer. || prison sl en taule. 3 adj intérieur(e). 4 n [interior]: **the ~** l'intérieur m; **~ out** [clothes] à l'envers; **to know sthg ~ out**

connaître qqch à fond. || AUT: **the ~** [in Europe, US etc] la droite. ○ **inside of** prep Am [building, object] à l'intérieur de, dans.

inside lane n AUT [in Europe, US etc] voie f de droite.

insight ['ɪnsaɪt] n [wisdom] sagacité f, perspicacité f. || [glimpse]: **~ (into)** aperçu m (de).

insignificant [,ɪnsɪg'nɪfɪkənt] adj insignifiant(e).

insincere [,ɪnsɪn'sɪər] adj pas sincère.

insinuate [ɪn'sɪnjʊeɪt] vt insinuer, laisser entendre.

insipid [ɪn'sɪpɪd] adj insipide.

insist [ɪn'sɪst] 1 vt [claim]: **to ~ (that)** ... insister sur le fait que .... || [demand]: **to ~ (that)** ... insister pour que (+ subjunctive) .... 2 vi: **to ~ (on sthg)** exiger (qqch); **to ~ on doing sthg** tenir à faire qqch, vouloir absolument faire qqch.

insistent [ɪn'sɪstənt] adj [determined] insistant(e); **to be ~ on** insister sur. || [continual] incessant(e).

insole ['ɪnsəʊl] n semelle f intérieure.

insolent ['ɪnsələnt] adj insolent(e).

insolvent [ɪn'sɒlvənt] adj insolvable.

insomnia [ɪn'sɒmnɪə] n insomnie f.

inspect [ɪn'spekt] vt [letter, person] examiner. || [factory, troops etc] inspecter.

inspection [ɪn'spekʃn] n [investigation] examen m. || [official check] inspection f.

inspector [ɪn'spektər] n inspecteur m, -trice f.

inspiration [,ɪnspə'reɪʃn] n inspiration f.

inspire [ɪn'spaɪər] vt: **to ~ sb to do sthg** pousser OR encourager qqn à faire qqch; **to ~ sb with sthg, to ~ sthg in sb** inspirer qqch à qqn.

install Br, **instal** Am [ɪn'stɔːl] vt [fit] installer.

installation [,ɪnstə'leɪʃn] n installation f.

instalment Br, **installment** Am [ɪn'stɔːlmənt] n [payment] acompte m; **in ~s** par acomptes. || [episode] épisode m.

instance ['ɪnstəns] n exemple m; **for ~** par exemple.

instant ['ɪnstənt] 1 adj [immediate] instantané(e), immédiat(e). || [coffee] soluble; [food] à préparation rapide. 2 n instant m; **this ~** tout de suite, immédiatement.

instantly ['ɪnstəntlɪ] adv immédiatement.

instead [ɪn'sted] *adv* au lieu de cela.
○ **instead of** *prep* au lieu de; ~ **of him** à sa place.

instep ['ɪnstep] *n* cou-de-pied *m*.

instigate ['ɪnstɪgeɪt] *vt* être à l'origine de, entreprendre.

instil *Br*, **instill** *Am* [ɪn'stɪl] *vt*: **to ~ sthg in** OR **into sb** instiller qqch à qqn.

instinct ['ɪnstɪŋkt] *n* [intuition] instinct *m*. || [impulse] réaction *f*, mouvement *m*.

instinctive [ɪn'stɪŋktɪv] *adj* instinctif(ive).

institute ['ɪnstɪtjuːt] **1** *n* institut *m*. **2** *vt* instituer.

institution [,ɪnstɪ'tjuːʃn] *n* institution *f*.

instruct [ɪn'strʌkt] *vt* [tell, order]: **to ~ sb to do sthg** charger qqn de faire qqch. || [teach] instruire; **to ~ sb in sthg** enseigner qqch à qqn.

instruction [ɪn'strʌkʃn] *n* instruction *f*.
○ **instructions** *npl* mode *m* d'emploi, instructions *fpl*.

instructor [ɪn'strʌktər] *n* [gen] instructeur *m*, -trice *f*, moniteur *m*, -trice *f*. || *Am* SCH enseignant *m*, -e *f*.

instrument ['ɪnstrʊmənt] *n* *lit* & *fig* instrument *m*.

instrumental [,ɪnstrʊ'mentl] *adj* [important, helpful]: **to be ~ in** contribuer à.

instrument panel *n* tableau *m* de bord.

insubstantial [,ɪnsəb'stænʃl] *adj* [structure] peu solide.

insufficient [,ɪnsə'fɪʃnt] *adj fml* insuffisant(e).

insular ['ɪnsjʊlər] *adj* [outlook] borné(e); [person] à l'esprit étroit.

insulate ['ɪnsjʊleɪt] *vt* [loft, cable] isoler; [hot water tank] calorifuger.

insulation [,ɪnsjʊ'leɪʃn] *n* isolation *f*.

insulin ['ɪnsjʊlɪn] *n* insuline *f*.

insult [*vt* ɪn'sʌlt, *n* 'ɪnsʌlt] **1** *vt* insulter, injurier. **2** *n* insulte *f*, injure *f*.

insuperable [ɪn'suːprəbl] *adj fml* insurmontable.

insurance [ɪn'ʃʊərəns] *n* [against fire, accident, theft] assurance *f*. || *fig* [safeguard, protection] protection *f*, garantie *f*.

insurance policy *n* police *f* d'assurance.

insure [ɪn'ʃʊər] **1** *vt* [against fire, accident, theft]: **to ~ sb/sthg against sthg** assurer qqn/qqch contre qqch. || *Am* [make certain] s'assurer. **2** *vi* [prevent]: **to ~ against** se protéger de.

insurer [ɪn'ʃʊərər] *n* assureur *m*.

insurmountable [,ɪnsə'maʊntəbl] *adj fml* insurmontable.

intact [ɪn'tækt] *adj* intact(e).

intake ['ɪnteɪk] *n* [amount consumed] consommation *f*. || [people recruited] admission *f*. || [inlet] prise *f*, arrivée *f*.

integral ['ɪntɪgrəl] *adj* intégral(e); **to be ~ to sthg** faire partie intégrante de qqch.

integrate ['ɪntɪgreɪt] **1** *vi* s'intégrer. **2** *vt* intégrer.

integrity [ɪn'tegrəti] *n* [honour] intégrité *f*, honnêteté *f*.

intellect ['ɪntəlekt] *n* [ability to think] intellect *m*. || [cleverness] intelligence *f*.

intellectual [,ɪntə'lektjʊəl] **1** *adj* intellectuel(elle). **2** *n* intellectuel *m*, -elle *f*.

intelligence [ɪn'telɪdʒəns] *n* (*U*) [ability to think] intelligence *f*. || [information service] service *m* de renseignements.

intelligent [ɪn'telɪdʒənt] *adj* intelligent(e).

intelligent card *n* carte *f* à puce OR à mémoire.

intend [ɪn'tend] *vt* [mean] avoir l'intention de; **to be ~ed for** être destiné à; **to ~ doing** OR **to do sthg** avoir l'intention de faire qqch.

intended [ɪn'tendɪd] *adj* [result] voulu(e); [victim] visé(e).

intense [ɪn'tens] *adj* [gen] intense. || [serious - person] sérieux(ieuse).

intensely [ɪn'tensli] *adv* [irritating, boring] extrêmement; [suffer] énormément. || [look] intensément.

intensify [ɪn'tensɪfaɪ] **1** *vt* intensifier, augmenter. **2** *vi* s'intensifier.

intensity [ɪn'tensətɪ] *n* intensité *f*.

intensive [ɪn'tensɪv] *adj* intensif(ive).

intensive care *n* réanimation *f*.

intent [ɪn'tent] **1** *adj* [absorbed] absorbé(e). || [determined]: **to be ~ on** OR **upon doing sthg** être résolu(e) OR décidé(e) à faire qqch. **2** *n fml* intention *f*, dessein *m*; **to all ~s and purposes** pratiquement, virtuellement.

intention [ɪn'tenʃn] *n* intention *f*.

intentional [ɪn'tenʃənl] *adj* intentionnel(elle), voulu(e).

intently [ɪn'tentli] *adv* avec attention, attentivement.

interact [,ɪntər'ækt] *vi* [communicate, work together]: **to ~ (with sb)** communiquer (avec qqn). || [react]: **to ~ (with sthg)** interagir (avec qqch).

intercede [,ɪntə'siːd] *vi fml*: **to ~ (with sb)** intercéder (auprès de qqn).

intercept [,ɪntə'sept] *vt* intercepter.

interchange [n ˈɪntətʃeɪndʒ, vb ˌɪntəˈtʃeɪndʒ] **1** n [exchange] échange m. || [road junction] échangeur m. **2** vt échanger.

interchangeable [ˌɪntəˈtʃeɪndʒəbl] adj: ~ (with) interchangeable (avec).

intercom [ˈɪntəkɒm] n Interphone® m.

intercourse [ˈɪntəkɔːs] n (U) [sexual] rapports mpl (sexuels).

interest [ˈɪntrəst] **1** n [gen] intérêt m; to lose ~ se désintéresser. || [hobby] centre m d'intérêt. || (U) FIN intérêt m, intérêts mpl. **2** vt intéresser.

interested [ˈɪntrəstɪd] adj intéressé(e); to be ~ in s'intéresser à; I'm not ~ in that cela ne m'intéresse pas; to be ~ in doing sthg avoir envie de faire qqch.

interesting [ˈɪntrəstɪŋ] adj intéressant(e).

interest rate n taux m d'intérêt.

interface [ˈɪntəfeɪs] n COMPUT interface f. || fig [junction] rapports mpl, relations fpl.

interfere [ˌɪntəˈfɪər] vi [meddle]: to ~ in sthg s'immiscer dans qqch, se mêler de qqch. || [damage]: to ~ with sthg gêner OR contrarier qqch; [routine] déranger qqch.

interference [ˌɪntəˈfɪərəns] n (U) [meddling]: ~ (with OR in) ingérence f (dans), intrusion f (dans). || TELEC parasites mpl.

interim [ˈɪntərɪm] **1** adj provisoire. **2** n: in the ~ dans l'intérim, entre-temps.

interior [ɪnˈtɪərɪər] **1** adj [inner] intérieur(e). || POL de l'Intérieur. **2** n intérieur m.

interlock [ˌɪntəˈlɒk] vi [gears] s'enclencher, s'engrener; [fingers] s'entrelacer.

interloper [ˈɪntələupər] n intrus m, -e f.

interlude [ˈɪntəluːd] n [pause] intervalle m. || [interval] interlude m.

intermediary [ˌɪntəˈmiːdjərɪ] n intermédiaire mf.

intermediate [ˌɪntəˈmiːdjət] adj [transitional] intermédiaire. || [post-beginner - level] moyen(enne); [- student, group] de niveau moyen.

interminable [ɪnˈtɜːmɪnəbl] adj interminable, sans fin.

intermission [ˌɪntəˈmɪʃn] n entracte m.

intermittent [ˌɪntəˈmɪtənt] adj intermittent(e).

intern [vb ɪnˈtɜːn, n ˈɪntɜːn] **1** vt interner. **2** n Am [gen] stagiaire mf; MED interne mf.

internal [ɪnˈtɜːnl] adj [gen] interne. || [within country] intérieur(e).

internally [ɪnˈtɜːnəlɪ] adv [within the body]: to bleed ~ faire une hémorragie interne. || [within country] à l'intérieur. || [within organization] intérieurement.

Internal Revenue n Am: the ~ ≃ le fisc.

international [ˌɪntəˈnæʃənl] adj international(e).

interpret [ɪnˈtɜːprɪt] **1** vt: to ~ sthg (as) interpréter qqch (comme). **2** vi [translate] faire l'interprète.

interpreter [ɪnˈtɜːprɪtər] n interprète mf.

interracial [ˌɪntəˈreɪʃl] adj entre des races différentes, racial(e).

interrelate [ˌɪntərɪˈleɪt] vi: to ~ (with) être lié(e) (à), être en corrélation (avec).

interrogate [ɪnˈterəgeɪt] vt interroger.

interrogation [ɪnˌterəˈgeɪʃn] n interrogatoire m.

interrogation mark n Am point m d'interrogation.

interrogative [ˌɪntəˈrɒgətɪv] GRAMM **1** adj interrogatif(ive). **2** n interrogatif m.

interrupt [ˌɪntəˈrʌpt] **1** vt interrompre; [calm] rompre. **2** vi interrompre.

interruption [ˌɪntəˈrʌpʃn] n interruption f.

intersect [ˌɪntəˈsekt] **1** vi s'entrecroiser, s'entrecouper. **2** vt croiser, couper.

intersection [ˌɪntəˈsekʃn] n [in road] croisement m, carrefour m.

intersperse [ˌɪntəˈspɜːs] vt: to be ~d with être émaillé(e) de, être entremêlé(e) de.

interstate (highway) [ˈɪntəsteɪt-] n Am autoroute f.

interval [ˈɪntəvl] n [gen] intervalle m; at ~s par intervalles; at monthly/yearly ~s tous les mois/ans.

intervene [ˌɪntəˈviːn] vi [person, police]: to ~ (in) intervenir (dans), s'interposer (dans). || [event, war, strike] survenir. || [time] s'écouler.

intervention [ˌɪntəˈvenʃn] n intervention f.

interview [ˈɪntəvjuː] **1** n [for job] entrevue f, entretien m. || PRESS interview f. **2** vt [for job] faire passer une entrevue OR un entretien à. || PRESS interviewer.

intestine [ɪnˈtestɪn] n intestin m.

intimacy [ˈɪntɪməsɪ] n [closeness]: ~ (between/with) intimité f (entre/avec).

intimate [adj & n ˈɪntɪmət, vb ˈɪntɪmeɪt] **1** adj [gen] intime. || [detailed -

knowledge] approfondi(e). **2** *vt fml* faire savoir, faire connaître.

intimately ['ɪntɪmətlɪ] *adv* [very closely] étroitement. || [as close friends] intimement. || [in detail] à fond.

intimidate [ɪn'tɪmɪdeɪt] *vt* intimider.

into ['ɪntu] *prep* [inside] dans. || [against]: **to bump ~ sthg** se cogner contre qqch; **to crash ~ sthg** rentrer dans qqch. || [referring to change in state] en; **to translate sthg ~ Spanish** traduire qqch en espagnol. || [concerning]: **research/investigation ~** recherche/enquête sur. || MATH: 3 ~ 2 2 divisé par 3. || *inf* [interested in]: **to be ~ sthg** être passionné(e) par qqch.

intolerable [ɪn'tɒlrəbl] *adj* intolérable, insupportable.

intolerance [ɪn'tɒlərəns] *n* intolérance *f*.

intolerant [ɪn'tɒlərənt] *adj* intolérant(e).

intoxicated [ɪn'tɒksɪkeɪtɪd] *adj* [drunk] ivre. || *fig* [excited]: **to be ~ by** OR **with sthg** être grisé(e) OR enivré(e) par qqch.

intransitive [ɪn'trænzətɪv] *adj* intransitif(ive).

intravenous [ˌɪntrə'viːnəs] *adj* intraveineux(euse).

in-tray *n* casier *m* des affaires à traiter.

intricate ['ɪntrɪkət] *adj* compliqué(e).

intrigue [ɪn'triːg] **1** *n* intrigue *f*. **2** *vt* intriguer, exciter la curiosité de.

intriguing [ɪn'triːgɪŋ] *adj* fascinant(e).

intrinsic [ɪn'trɪnsɪk] *adj* intrinsèque.

introduce [ˌɪntrə'djuːs] *vt* [present] présenter; **to ~ sb to sb** présenter qqn à qqn. || [bring in]: **to ~ sthg (to** OR **into)** introduire qqch (dans). || [allow to experience]: **to ~ sb to sthg** initier qqn à qqch, faire découvrir qqch à qqn. || [signal beginning of] annoncer.

introduction [ˌɪntrə'dʌkʃn] *n* [in book, of new method etc] introduction *f*. || [of people]: **~ (to sb)** présentation *f* (à qqn).

introductory [ˌɪntrə'dʌktrɪ] *adj* d'introduction, préliminaire.

introvert ['ɪntrəvɜːt] *n* introverti *m*, -e *f*.

introverted ['ɪntrəvɜːtɪd] *adj* introverti(e).

intrude [ɪn'truːd] *vi* faire intrusion; **to ~ on sb** déranger qqn.

intruder [ɪn'truːdər] *n* intrus *m*, -e *f*.

intrusive [ɪn'truːsɪv] *adj* gênant(e), importun(e).

intuition [ˌɪntjuː'ɪʃn] *n* intuition *f*.

inundate ['ɪnʌndeɪt] *vt* [overwhelm]: **to be ~d with** être submergé(e) de.

invade [ɪn'veɪd] *vt* MIL. & *fig* envahir. || [disturb - privacy etc] violer.

invalid [*adj* ɪn'vælɪd, *n* & *vb* 'ɪnvəlɪd] **1** *adj* [illegal, unacceptable] non valide, non valable. || [not reasonable] non valable. **2** *n* invalide *mf*.

invaluable [ɪn'væljʊəbl] *adj*: **~ (to)** [help, advice, person] précieux(ieuse) (pour); [experience, information] inestimable (pour).

invariably [ɪn'veərɪəblɪ] *adv* invariablement, toujours.

invasion [ɪn'veɪʒn] *n lit & fig* invasion *f*.

invent [ɪn'vent] *vt* inventer.

invention [ɪn'venʃn] *n* invention *f*.

inventive [ɪn'ventɪv] *adj* inventif(ive).

inventor [ɪn'ventər] *n* inventeur *m*, -trice *f*.

inventory ['ɪnventrɪ] *n* [list] inventaire *m*. || *Am* [goods] stock *m*.

invert [ɪn'vɜːt] *vt* retourner.

invest [ɪn'vest] **1** *vt* [money]: **to ~ sthg (in)** investir qqch (dans). || [time, energy]: **to ~ sthg in sthg/in doing sthg** consacrer qqch à qqch/à faire qqch, employer qqch à qqch/à faire qqch. **2** *vi* FIN: **to ~ (in sthg)** investir (dans qqch). || *fig* [buy]: **to ~ in sthg** se payer qqch, s'acheter qqch.

investigate [ɪn'vestɪgeɪt] *vt* enquêter sur, faire une enquête sur; [subj: scientist] faire des recherches sur.

investigation [ɪnˌvestɪ'geɪʃn] *n* [enquiry]: **~ (into)** enquête *f* (sur); [scientific] recherches *fpl* (sur). || (*U*) [investigating] investigation *f*.

investment [ɪn'vestmənt] *n* FIN investissement *m*, placement *m*.

investor [ɪn'vestər] *n* investisseur *m*.

inveterate [ɪn'vetərət] *adj* invétéré(e).

invigorating [ɪn'vɪgəreɪtɪŋ] *adj* tonifiant(e), vivifiant(e).

invincible [ɪn'vɪnsɪbl] *adj* [army, champion] invincible; [record] imbattable.

invisible [ɪn'vɪzɪbl] *adj* invisible.

invitation [ˌɪnvɪ'teɪʃn] *n* [request] invitation *f*.

invite [ɪn'vaɪt] *vt* [ask to come]: **to ~ sb (to)** inviter qqn (à). || [ask politely]: **to ~ sb to do sthg** inviter qqn à faire qqch. || [encourage]: **to ~ trouble** aller au devant des ennuis; **to ~ gossip** faire causer.

inviting [ɪn'vaɪtɪŋ] *adj* attrayant(e), agréable; [food] appétissant(e).

invoice [ˈɪnvɔɪs] **1** *n* facture *f*. **2** *vt* [client] envoyer la facture à. || [goods] facturer.

invoke [ɪnˈvəʊk] *vt fml* [law, act] invoquer. || [help] demander, implorer.

involuntary [ɪnˈvɒləntrɪ] *adj* involontaire.

involve [ɪnˈvɒlv] *vt* [entail] nécessiter; **what's ~d?** de quoi s'agit-il?; **to ~ doing sthg** nécessiter de faire qqch. || [concern, affect] toucher. || [person]: **to ~ sb in sthg** impliquer qqn dans qqch.

involved [ɪnˈvɒlvd] *adj* [complex] complexe, compliqué(e). || [participating]: **to be ~ in sthg** participer OR prendre part à qqch. || [in relationship]: **to be ~ with sb** avoir des relations intimes avec qqn.

involvement [ɪnˈvɒlvmənt] *n* [participation]: **~ (in)** participation *f* (à). || [concern, enthusiasm]: **~ (in)** engagement *m* (dans).

inward [ˈɪnwəd] **1** *adj* [inner] intérieur(e). || [towards the inside] vers l'intérieur. **2** *adv Am* = **inwards**.

inwards [ˈɪnwədz] *adv* vers l'intérieur.

iodine [*Am* ˈaɪədaɪn] *n* iode *m*.

iota [aɪˈəʊtə] *n* brin *m*, grain *m*.

IOU (*abbr of* **I owe you**) *n* reconnaissance *f* de dette.

IQ (*abbr of* **intelligence quotient**) *n* QI *m*.

IRA *n* (*abbr of* **Irish Republican Army**) IRA *f*.

Iran [ɪˈrɑːn] *n* Iran *m*.

Iranian [ɪˈreɪnjən] **1** *adj* iranien(ienne). **2** *n* Iranien *m*, -ienne *f*.

Iraq [ɪˈrɑːk] *n* Iraq *m*, Irak *m*.

Iraqi [ɪˈrɑːkɪ] **1** *adj* iraquien(ienne), irakien(ienne). **2** *n* Iraquien *m*, -ienne *f*, Irakien *m*, -ienne *f*.

irate [aɪˈreɪt] *adj* furieux(ieuse).

Ireland [ˈaɪələnd] *n* Irlande *f*.

iris [ˈaɪərɪs] (*pl* -es) *n* iris *m*.

Irish [ˈaɪrɪʃ] **1** *adj* irlandais(e). **2** *n* [language] irlandais *m*. **3** *npl*: **the ~** les Irlandais.

Irishman [ˈaɪrɪʃmən] (*pl* -men [-mən]) *n* Irlandais *m*.

Irish Sea *n*: **the ~** la mer d'Irlande.

Irishwoman [ˈaɪrɪʃˌwʊmən] (*pl* -women [-ˌwɪmɪn]) *n* Irlandaise *f*.

irksome [ˈɜːksəm] *adj* ennuyeux(euse), assommant(e).

iron [ˈaɪən] **1** *adj* [made of iron] de OR en fer. || *fig* [very strict] de fer. **2** *n* [metal, golf club] fer *m*. || [for clothes] fer *m* à re-

passer. **3** *vt* repasser. ○ **iron out** *vt sep fig* [difficulties] aplanir; [problems] résoudre.

Iron Curtain *n*: **the ~** le rideau de fer.

ironic(al) [aɪˈrɒnɪk(l)] *adj* ironique.

ironing [ˈaɪənɪŋ] *n* repassage *m*.

ironing board *n* planche *f* OR table *f* à repasser.

irony [ˈaɪrənɪ] *n* ironie *f*.

irrational [ɪˈræʃənl] *adj* irrationnel(elle), déraisonnable; [person] non rationnel(elle).

irreconcilable [ɪˌrekənˈsaɪləbl] *adj* inconciliable.

irregular [ɪˈregjʊləʳ] *adj* irrégulier(ière).

irrelevant [ɪˈreləvənt] *adj* sans rapport.

irreparable [ɪˈrepərəbl] *adj* irréparable.

irreplaceable [ˌɪrɪˈpleɪsəbl] *adj* irremplaçable.

irrepressible [ˌɪrɪˈpresəbl] *adj* [enthusiasm] que rien ne peut entamer; **he's ~** il est d'une bonne humeur à toute épreuve.

irresistible [ˌɪrɪˈzɪstəbl] *adj* irrésistible.

irrespective [ˌɪrɪˈspektɪv] ○ **irrespective of** *prep* sans tenir compte de.

irresponsible [ˌɪrɪˈspɒnsəbl] *adj* irresponsable.

irrigate [ˈɪrɪgeɪt] *vt* irriguer.

irrigation [ˌɪrɪˈgeɪʃn] *n* irrigation *f*.

irritable [ˈɪrɪtəbl] *adj* irritable.

irritate [ˈɪrɪteɪt] *vt* irriter.

irritating [ˈɪrɪteɪtɪŋ] *adj* irritant(e).

irritation [ˌɪrɪˈteɪʃn] *n* [anger, soreness] irritation *f*. || [cause of anger] source *f* d'irritation.

IRS (*abbr of* **Internal Revenue Service**) *n Am*: **the ~** ≃ le fisc.

is [ɪz] → **be**.

Islam [ˈɪzlɑːm] *n* islam *m*.

island [ˈaɪlənd] *n* [isle] île *f*. || AUT refuge *m* pour piétons.

islander [ˈaɪləndəʳ] *n* habitant *m*, -e *f* d'une île.

isle [aɪl] *n* île *f*.

isn't [ˈɪznt] = **is not**.

isobar [ˈaɪsəbɑːʳ] *n* isobare *f*.

isolate [ˈaɪsəleɪt] *vt*: **to ~ sb/sthg (from)** isoler qqn/qqch (de).

isolated [ˈaɪsəleɪtɪd] *adj* isolé(e).

Israel [ˈɪzreɪəl] *n* Israël *m*.

Israeli [ɪzˈreɪlɪ] **1** *adj* israélien(ienne). **2** *n* Israélien *m*, -ienne *f*.

issue [ˈɪʃuː] **1** *n* [important subject] question *f*, problème *m*; **to make an ~ of sthg**

faire toute une affaire de qqch; **at ~ en**
question, en cause. || [edition] numéro *m*.
|| [bringing out - of banknotes, shares]
émission *f*. **2** *vt* [make public - decree,
statement] faire; [- warning] lancer. ||
[bring out - banknotes, shares] émettre; [-
book] publier. || [passport etc] délivrer.

isthmus ['ısməs] *n* isthme *m*.

it [ıt] *pron* [referring to specific person or
thing - subj] il (elle); [- direct object] le
(la), l' (+ *vowel or silent 'h'*); [- indirect
object] lui; **did you find ~?** tu l'as trou-
vé(e)?; **give ~ to me at once** donne-moi
ça tout de suite. || [with prepositions]:
in/to/at ~ y; **on ~** dessus; **about ~** en; **under ~** dessous; **beside ~** à côté; **from/of ~**
en; **he's very proud of ~** il en est très fier.
|| [impersonal use] il, ce; **~ is cold today** il
fait froid aujourd'hui; **~'s two o'clock** il
est deux heures; **who is ~? — ~'s Mary/
me** qui est-ce? — c'est Mary/moi.

IT *n abbr of* **information technology.**

Italian [ı'tæljən] **1** *adj* italien(ienne). **2**
n [person] Italien *m*, -ienne *f*. || [lan-
guage] italien *m*.

italic [ı'tælık] *adj* italique. ○ **italics** *npl*
italiques *fpl*.

Italy ['ıtəlı] *n* Italie *f*.

itch [ıtʃ] **1** *n* démangeaison *f*. **2** *vi* [be
itchy]: **my arm ~es** mon bras me dé-
mange. || *fig* [be impatient]: **to be ~ing to
do sthg** mourir d'envie de faire qqch.

it'd ['ıtəd] = **it would, it had.**

item ['aıtəm] *n* [gen] chose *f*, article *m*;
[on agenda] question *f*, point *m*. || PRESS
article *m*.

itemize, -ise ['aıtəmaız] *vt* détailler.

itinerary [aı'tınərərı] *n* itinéraire *m*.

it'll [ıtl] = **it will.**

its [ıts] *poss adj* son (sa), ses (*pl*).

it's [ıts] = **it is, it has.**

itself [ıt'self] *pron* (*reflexive*) se; (*after
prep*) soi. || (*for emphasis*) lui-même
(elle-même); **in ~** en soi.

I've [aıv] = **I have.**

ivory ['aıvərı] *n* ivoire *m*.

ivy ['aıvı] *n* lierre *m*.

Ivy League *n Am* les huit grandes uni-
versités de l'est des États-Unis.

j (*pl* **j's** OR **js**), **J** (*pl* **J's** OR **Js**) [dʒeı] *n*
[letter] j *m inv*, J *m inv*.

jab [dʒæb] *vt*: **to ~ sthg into** planter OR
enfoncer qqch dans.

jabber ['dʒæbə'] *vt & vi* baragouiner.

jack [dʒæk] *n* [device] cric *m*. || [playing
card] valet *m*. ○ **jack up** *vt sep* [car]
soulever avec un cric. || *fig* [prices] faire
grimper.

jackal ['dʒækəl] *n* chacal *m*.

jackdaw ['dʒækdɔː] *n* choucas *m*.

jacket ['dʒækıt] *n* [garment] veste *f*. ||
[of potato] peau *f*, pelure *f*. || [of book] ja-
quette *f*. || *Am* [of record] pochette *f*.

jacket potato *n* pomme de terre *f* en
robe de chambre.

jackhammer ['dʒæk,hæmə'] *n Am*
marteau-piqueur *m*.

jack knife *n* canif *m*. ○ **jack-knife** *vi*
[lorry] se mettre en travers de la route.

jack plug *n* jack *m*.

jackpot ['dʒækpɒt] *n* gros lot *m*.

jaded ['dʒeıdıd] *adj* blasé(e).

jagged ['dʒægıd] *adj* déchiqueté(e),
dentelé(e).

jail [dʒeıl] **1** *n* prison *f*. **2** *vt* emprisonner,
mettre en prison.

jailer ['dʒeılə'] *n* geôlier *m*, -ière *f*.

jam [dʒæm] **1** *n* [preserve] confiture *f*. ||
[of traffic] embouteillage *m*, bouchon *m*.
|| *inf* [difficult situation]: **to get into/be in
a ~** se mettre/être dans le pétrin. **2** *vt*
[mechanism, door] bloquer, coincer. ||
[push tightly]: **to ~ sthg into** entasser OR
tasser qqch dans; **to ~ sthg onto** enfoncer
qqch sur. || [block - streets] embouteiller;
[- switchboard] surcharger. || RADIO
brouiller. **3** *vi* [lever, door] se coincer;
[brakes] se bloquer.

Jamaica [dʒə'meıkə] *n* la Jamaïque.

jam-packed [-'pækt] *adj inf* plein(e) à
craquer.

jangle ['dʒæŋgl] **1** *vt* [keys] faire cliqueter; [bells] faire retentir. **2** *vi* [keys] cliqueter; [bells] retentir.

janitor ['dʒænɪtə^r] n Am & Scot concierge mf.

January ['dʒænjʊərɪ] n janvier m; see also **September**.

Japan [dʒə'pæn] n Japon m.

Japanese [,dʒæpə'niːz] (pl inv) 1 adj japonais(e). 2 n [language] japonais m. 3 npl [people]: the ~ les Japonais mpl.

jar [dʒɑː^r] 1 n pot m. 2 vt [shake] secouer. 3 vi [noise, voice]: to ~ (on sb) irriter (qqn), agacer (qqn). || [colours] jurer.

jargon ['dʒɑːgən] n jargon m.

jaundice ['dʒɔːndɪs] n jaunisse f.

jaunt [dʒɔːnt] n balade f.

jaunty ['dʒɔːntɪ] adj désinvolte, insouciant(e).

javelin ['dʒævlɪn] n javelot m.

jaw [dʒɔː] n mâchoire f.

jay [dʒeɪ] n geai m.

jaywalker ['dʒeɪwɔːkə^r] n piéton m qui traverse en dehors des clous.

jazz [dʒæz] n MUS jazz m.

jazzy ['dʒæzɪ] adj [bright] voyant(e).

jealous ['dʒeləs] adj jaloux(ouse).

jealousy ['dʒeləsɪ] n jalousie f.

jeans [dʒiːnz] npl jean m, blue-jean m.

Jeep® [dʒiːp] n Jeep® f.

jeer [dʒɪə^r] 1 vt huer, conspuer. 2 vi: to ~ (at sb) huer (qqn), conspuer (qqn).

Jehovah's Witness [dʒɪ,həʊvəz-] n témoin m de Jéhovah.

Jello® ['dʒeləʊ] n Am gelée f.

jelly ['dʒelɪ] n gelée f.

jellyfish ['dʒelɪfɪʃ] (pl inv OR -es) n méduse f.

jeopardize, -ise ['dʒepədaɪz] vt compromettre, mettre en danger.

jerk [dʒɜːk] 1 n [movement] secousse f, saccade f. || v inf [fool] abruti m, -e f. 2 vi [person] sursauter; [vehicle] cahoter.

jersey ['dʒɜːzɪ] (pl jerseys) n [sweater] pull m. || [cloth] jersey m.

jest [dʒest] n plaisanterie f; in ~ pour rire.

Jesus (Christ) ['dʒiːzəs-] n Jésus m, Jésus-Christ m.

jet [dʒet] n [plane] jet m, avion m à réaction. || [of fluid] jet m. || [nozzle, outlet] ajutage m.

jet-black adj noir(e) comme (du) jais.

jet engine n moteur m à réaction.

jetfoil ['dʒetfɔɪl] n hydroglisseur m.

jet lag n fatigue f due au décalage horaire.

jetsam ['dʒetsəm] → **flotsam**.

jettison ['dʒetɪsən] vt [cargo] jeter, larguer.

jetty ['dʒetɪ] n jetée f.

Jew [dʒuː] n Juif m, -ive f.

jewel ['dʒuːəl] n bijou m.

jeweller Br, **jeweler** Am ['dʒuːələ^r] n bijoutier m; ~'s (shop) bijouterie f.

jewellery Br, **jewelry** Am ['dʒuːəlrɪ] n (U) bijoux mpl.

Jewess ['dʒuːɪs] n juive f.

Jewish ['dʒuːɪʃ] adj juif(ive).

jib [dʒɪb] n [of crane] flèche f. || [sail] foc m.

jibe [dʒaɪb] n sarcasme m, moquerie f.

jiffy ['dʒɪfɪ] n inf: in a ~ en un clin d'œil.

Jiffy bag® n enveloppe f matelassée.

jig [dʒɪg] n gigue f.

jigsaw (puzzle) ['dʒɪgsɔː-] n puzzle m.

jilt [dʒɪlt] vt laisser tomber.

jingle ['dʒɪŋgl] 1 n [sound] cliquetis m. || [song] jingle m, indicatif m. 2 vi [bell] tinter; [coins, bracelets] cliqueter.

jinx [dʒɪŋks] n poisse f.

jitters ['dʒɪtəz] npl inf: the ~ le trac.

job [dʒɒb] n [employment] emploi m, boulot m inf. || [task] travail m, tâche f. || [difficult task]: to have a ~ doing sthg avoir du mal à faire qqch.

jobless ['dʒɒblɪs] adj au chômage.

jobsharing ['dʒɒbʃeərɪŋ] n partage m de l'emploi.

jockey ['dʒɒkɪ] (pl jockeys) 1 n jockey m. 2 vi: to ~ for position manœuvrer pour devancer ses concurrents.

jocular ['dʒɒkjʊlə^r] adj [cheerful] enjoué(e), jovial(e). || [funny] amusant(e).

jodhpurs ['dʒɒdpəz] npl jodhpurs mpl, culotte f de cheval.

jog [dʒɒg] 1 n: to go for a ~ faire du jogging. 2 vt pousser; to ~ sb's memory rafraîchir la mémoire de qqn. 3 vi faire du jogging, jogger.

jogging ['dʒɒgɪŋ] n jogging m.

john [dʒɒn] n Am inf petit coin m, cabinets mpl.

join [dʒɔɪn] 1 n raccord m, joint m. 2 vt [connect - gen] unir, joindre; [- towns etc] relier. || [get together with] rejoindre, retrouver. || [political party] devenir membre de; [club] s'inscrire à; to ~ a queue Br, to ~ a line Am prendre la queue. 3 vi [connect] se joindre. || [become a member - gen] devenir membre; [- of club] s'inscrire. ○ **join in** vt fus prendre part à, participer à. 2 vi participer. ○ **join up** vi MIL s'engager dans l'armée.

joiner ['dʒɔɪnə^r] n menuisier m.

joinery ['dʒɔɪnərɪ] n menuiserie f.

joint [dʒɔɪnt] **1** adj [effort] conjugué(e); [responsibility] collectif(ive). **2** n [gen & TECH] joint m. || ANAT articulation f. || inf [place] bouge m. || drugs sl joint m.

joint account n compte m joint.

jointly ['dʒɔɪntlɪ] adv conjointement.

joke [dʒəʊk] **1** n blague f, plaisanterie f; **to play a ~ on sb** faire une blague à qqn, jouer un tour à qqn. **2** vi plaisanter, blaguer; **to ~ about sthg** plaisanter sur qqch, se moquer de qqch.

joker ['dʒəʊkər] n [person] blagueur m, -euse f. || [playing card] joker m.

jolly ['dʒɒlɪ] adj [person] jovial(e), enjoué(e); [time, party] agréable.

jolt [dʒəʊlt] **1** n [jerk] secousse f, soubresaut m. || [shock] choc m. **2** vt secouer.

Jordan ['dʒɔːdn] n Jordanie f.

jostle ['dʒɒsl] **1** vt bousculer. **2** vi se bousculer.

jot [dʒɒt] n [of truth] grain m, brin m.
○ **jot down** vt sep noter, prendre note de.

jotter ['dʒɒtər] n [notepad] bloc-notes m.

journal ['dʒɜːnl] n [magazine] revue f. || [diary] journal m.

journalism ['dʒɜːnəlɪzm] n journalisme m.

journalist ['dʒɜːnəlɪst] n journaliste mf.

journey ['dʒɜːnɪ] (pl **journeys**) n voyage m.

jovial ['dʒəʊvjəl] adj jovial(e).

joy [dʒɔɪ] n joie f.

joyful ['dʒɔɪfʊl] adj joyeux(euse).

joyride ['dʒɔɪraɪd] (pt **-rode**, pp **-ridden**) vi faire une virée dans une voiture volée.

joystick ['dʒɔɪstɪk] n AERON manche m (à balai); COMPUT manette f.

Jr. (abbr of **Junior**) Jr.

jubilant ['dʒuːbɪlənt] adj [person] débordant(e) de joie, qui jubile.

jubilee ['dʒuːbɪliː] n jubilé m.

judge [dʒʌdʒ] **1** n juge m. **2** vt [gen] juger. || [estimate] évaluer, juger. **3** vi juger; **to ~ from** OR **by, judging from** OR **by** à en juger par.

judg(e)ment ['dʒʌdʒmənt] n jugement m.

judicial [dʒuː'dɪʃl] adj judiciaire.

judiciary [dʒuː'dɪʃərɪ] n: **the ~** la magistrature.

judicious [dʒuː'dɪʃəs] adj judicieux(ieuse).

judo ['dʒuːdəʊ] n judo m.

jug [dʒʌg] n pot m, pichet m.

juggernaut ['dʒʌgənɔːt] n poids m lourd.

juggle ['dʒʌgl] **1** vt lit & fig jongler avec. **2** vi jongler.

juggler ['dʒʌglər] n jongleur m, -euse f.

juice [dʒuːs] n jus m.

juicy ['dʒuːsɪ] adj [fruit] juteux(euse).

jukebox ['dʒuːkbɒks] n juke-box m.

July [dʒuː'laɪ] n juillet m; see also **September**.

jumble ['dʒʌmbl] **1** n [mixture] mélange m, fatras m. **2** vt: **to ~ (up)** mélanger, embrouiller.

jumbo jet ['dʒʌmbəʊ-] n jumbo-jet m.

jumbo-sized [-saɪzd] adj géant(e).

jump [dʒʌmp] **1** n [leap] saut m, bond m. || [rapid increase] flambée f, hausse f brutale. **2** vt [fence, stream etc] sauter, franchir d'un bond. || inf [attack] sauter sur, tomber sur. **3** vi [gen] sauter, bondir; [in surprise] sursauter. || [increase rapidly] grimper en flèche, faire un bond. ○ **jump at** vt fus fig sauter sur.

jumper ['dʒʌmpər] n Am [dress] robe f chasuble.

jump leads npl câbles mpl de démarrage.

jump-start vt: **to ~ a car** faire démarrer une voiture en la poussant.

jumpy ['dʒʌmpɪ] adj nerveux(euse).

Jun. = **Junr**.

junction ['dʒʌŋkʃn] n [of roads] carrefour m; RAIL embranchement m.

June [dʒuːn] n juin m; see also **September**.

jungle ['dʒʌŋgl] n lit & fig jungle f.

junior ['dʒuːnjər] **1** adj [gen] jeune. || Am [after name] junior. **2** n [in rank] subalterne mf. || [in age] cadet m, -ette f. || Am SCH ≃ élève m f de première; UNIV ≃ étudiant m, -e f de deuxième année.

junior high school n Am ≃ collège m d'enseignement secondaire.

junk [dʒʌŋk] n [unwanted objects] bric-à-brac m.

junk food n (U) pej cochonneries fpl.

junkie ['dʒʌŋkɪ] n drugs sl drogué m, -e f.

junk mail n (U) pej prospectus mpl publicitaires envoyés par la poste.

junk shop n boutique f de brocanteur.

Junr (abbr of **Junior**) Jr.

Jupiter ['dʒuːpɪtər] n [planet] Jupiter f.

jurisdiction [,dʒʊərɪs'dɪkʃn] n juridiction f.

juror ['dʒʊərər] n juré m, -e f.

jury ['dʒʊərɪ] n jury m.

just [dʒʌst] **1** *adv* [recently]: he's ~ left il vient de partir. ‖ [at that moment]: **I was ~ about to go** j'allais juste partir, j'étais sur le point de partir; **I'm ~ going to do it now** je vais le faire tout de suite OR à l'instant; **she arrived ~ as I was leaving** elle est arrivée au moment même où je partais OR juste comme je partais. ‖ [only, simply]: **it's ~ a rumour** ce n'est qu'une rumeur; **~ add water** vous n'avez plus qu'à ajouter de l'eau; **~ a minute** OR **moment** OR **second!** un (petit) instant! ‖ [almost not] tout juste, à peine; **I only ~ missed the train** j'ai manqué le train de peu; **we have ~ enough time** on a juste assez de temps. ‖ [for emphasis]: **~ look at this mess!** non, mais regarde un peu ce désordre! ‖ [exactly, precisely] tout à fait, exactement. ‖ [in requests]: **could you ~ move over please?** pourriez-vous vous pousser un peu s'il vous plaît? **2** *adj* juste, équitable. ○ **just about** *adv* à peu près, plus ou moins. ○ **just as** *adv* [in comparison] tout aussi. ○ **just now** *adv* [a short time ago] tout à l'heure. ‖ [at this moment] en ce moment.
justice ['dʒʌstɪs] *n* [gen] justice *f.* ‖ [of claim, cause] bien-fondé *m.*
justify ['dʒʌstɪfaɪ] *vt* [give reasons for] justifier.
jut [dʒʌt] *vi*: **to ~ (out)** faire saillie, avancer.
juvenile ['dʒuːvənaɪl] **1** *adj* JUR mineur(e), juvénile. ‖ [childish] puéril(e). **2** *n* JUR mineur *m*, -e *f.*
juxtapose [,dʒʌkstə'pəʊz] *vt* juxtaposer.

k (*pl* **k's** OR **ks**), **K** (*pl* **K's** OR **Ks**) [keɪ] *n* [letter] k *m inv*, K *m. inv.* ○ **K** (*abbr of* **kilobyte**) Ko. ‖ (*abbr of* **thousand**) K.
kaleidoscope [kə'laɪdəskəʊp] *n* kaléidoscope *m.*
kangaroo [,kæŋgə'ruː] *n* kangourou *m.*
karat ['kærət] *n Am* carat *m.*
karate [kə'rɑːtɪ] *n* karaté *m.*
kayak ['kaɪæk] *n* kayak *m.*
KB (*abbr of* **kilobyte(s)**) *n* COMPUT Ko *m.*
kcal (*abbr of* **kilocalorie**) Kcal.
kebab [kɪ'bæb] *n* brochette *f.*
keel [kiːl] *n* quille *f*; **on an even ~** stable. ○ **keel over** *vi* [ship] chavirer; [person] tomber dans les pommes.
keen [kiːn] *adj* [enthusiastic] enthousiaste, passionné(e); **to be ~ on sthg** avoir la passion de qqch; **he's ~ on her** elle lui plaît; **to be ~ on doing sthg** tenir à faire qqch. ‖ [interest, desire, mind] vif (vive); [competition] âpre, acharné(e). ‖ [sense of smell] fin(e); [eyesight] perçant(e).
keep [kiːp] (*pt & pp* **kept**) **1** *vt* [retain, store] garder; **to ~ sthg warm** garder OR tenir qqch au chaud. ‖ [prevent]: **to keep sb/sthg from doing sthg** empêcher qqn/ qqch de faire qqch. ‖ [detain] retenir; [prisoner] détenir; **to ~ sb waiting** faire attendre qqn. ‖ [promise] tenir; [appointment] aller à; [vow] être fidèle à. ‖ [not disclose]: **to ~ sthg from sb** cacher qqch à qqn; **to ~ sthg to o.s.** garder qqch pour soi. ‖ [diary, record, notes] tenir. ‖ [own - sheep, pigs etc] élever; [- shop] tenir. **2** *vi* [remain]: **to ~ warm** se tenir au chaud; **to ~ quiet** garder le silence. ‖ [continue]: **he ~s interrupting me** il n'arrête pas de m'interrompre; **to ~ talking/walking** continuer à parler/à marcher. ‖ [continue moving]: **to ~ left/right** garder sa gauche/sa droite. ‖ [food] se conserver. **3** *n*: **to earn one's ~** gagner sa vie. ○ **keeps** *n*: **for ~s** pour toujours. ○ **keep back** *vt sep* [information] ca-

kindly

cher, ne pas divulguer; [money] retenir. ○ **keep off** *vt fus*: "~ **off the grass**" «(il est) interdit de marcher sur la pelouse». ○ **keep on** *vi* [continue]: **to ~ on (doing sthg)** [without stopping] continuer (de OR à faire qqch); [repeatedly] ne pas arrêter (de faire qqch). || [talk incessantly]: **to ~ on (about sthg)** ne pas arrêter de parler (de qqch). ○ **keep out** *vt sep* empêcher d'entrer. 2 *vi*: "~ **out**" «défense d'entrer». ○ **keep to** *vt fus* [rules, deadline] respecter, observer. ○ **keep up** *vt sep* [continue to] continuer; [maintain] maintenir. 2 *vi* [maintain pace, level etc]: **to ~ up (with sb)** aller aussi vite (que qqn).

keeper ['ki:pər] *n* gardien *m*, -ienne *f*.

keeping ['ki:pɪŋ] *n* [care] garde *f*. || [conformity, harmony]: **to be in/out of ~ with** [rules etc] être/ne pas être conforme à; [subj: clothes, furniture] aller/ne pas aller avec.

keepsake ['ki:pseɪk] *n* souvenir *m*.

keg [keg] *n* tonnelet *m*, baril *m*.

kennel ['kenl] *n* [shelter for dog] niche *f*. || *Am* = **kennels**. ○ **kennels** *npl Br* chenil *m*.

Kenya ['kenjə] *n* Kenya *m*.

kept [kept] *pt & pp* → **keep**.

kernel ['kɜ:nl] *n* amande *f*.

kerosene ['kerəsi:n] *n* kérosène *m*.

ketchup ['ketʃəp] *n* ketchup *m*.

kettle ['ketl] *n* bouilloire *f*.

key [ki:] 1 *n* [gen & MUS] clef *f*, clé *f*; **the ~ (to sthg)** *fig* la clé (de qqch). || [of typewriter, computer, piano] touche *f*. || [of map] légende *f*. 2 *adj* clé (*after n*).

keyboard ['ki:bɔ:d] *n* [gen & COMPUT] clavier *m*.

keyed up [,ki:d-] *adj* tendu(e), énervé(e).

keyhole ['ki:həʊl] *n* trou *m* de serrure.

keynote ['ki:nəʊt] 1 *n* note *f* dominante. 2 *comp*: ~ **speech** discours-programme *m*.

keypad ['ki:pæd] *n* COMPUT pavé *m* numérique.

key ring *n* porte-clés *m inv*.

kg (*abbr of* **kilogram**) kg.

khaki ['kɑ:kɪ] 1 *adj* kaki (*inv*). 2 *n* [colour] kaki *m*.

kick [kɪk] 1 *n* [with foot] coup *m* de pied. || *inf* [excitement]: **to get a ~ from sthg** trouver qqch excitant. 2 *vt* [with foot] donner un coup de pied à; **to ~ o.s.** *fig* se donner des gifles OR des claques. || *inf* [give up]: **to ~ the habit** arrêter. 3 *vi* [per-

son - repeatedly] donner des coups de pied; [- once] donner un coup de pied; [baby] gigoter; [animal] ruer. ○ **kick out** *vt sep inf* vider, jeter dehors.

kid [kɪd] 1 *n inf* [child] gosse *mf*, gamin *m*, -e *f*. || *inf* [young person] petit jeune *m*, petite jeune *f*. || [goat, leather] chevreau *m*. 2 *comp inf* [brother, sister] petit(e). 3 *vt inf* [tease] faire marcher. || [delude]: **to ~ o.s.** se faire des illusions. 4 *vi inf*: **to be kidding** plaisanter.

kidnap ['kɪdnæp] *vt* kidnapper, enlever.

kidnapper *Br*, **kidnaper** *Am* ['kɪdnæpər] *n* kidnappeur *m*, -euse *f*, ravisseur *m*, -euse *f*.

kidnapping *Br*, **kidnaping** *Am* ['kɪdnæpɪŋ] *n* enlèvement *m*.

kidney ['kɪdnɪ] (*pl* **kidneys**) *n* ANAT rein *m*. || CULIN rognon *m*.

kidney bean *n* haricot *m* rouge.

kill [kɪl] 1 *vt* [cause death of] tuer. || *fig* [hope, chances] mettre fin à; [pain] supprimer. 2 *vi* tuer. 3 *n* mise *f* à mort.

killer ['kɪlər] *n* [person] meurtrier *m*, -ière *f*; [animal] tueur *m*, -euse *f*.

killing ['kɪlɪŋ] *n* meurtre *m*.

killjoy ['kɪldʒɔɪ] *n* rabat-joie *m inv*.

kiln [kɪln] *n* four *m*.

kilo ['ki:ləʊ] (*pl* -**s**) (*abbr of* **kilogram**) *n* kilo *m*.

kilobyte ['kɪləbaɪt] *n* COMPUT kilo-octet *m*.

kilogram(me) ['kɪləgræm] *n* kilogramme *m*.

kilohertz ['kɪləhɜ:tz] (*pl inv*) *n* kilohertz *m*.

kilometre *Br* ['kɪlə,mi:tər], **kilometer** *Am* [kɪ'lɒmɪtər] *n* kilomètre *m*.

kilowatt ['kɪləwɒt] *n* kilowatt *m*.

kilt [kɪlt] *n* kilt *m*.

kin [kɪn] *n* → **kith**.

kind [kaɪnd] 1 *adj* gentil(ille), aimable. 2 *n* genre *m*, sorte *f*; **they're two of a ~** ils se ressemblent; **in ~** [payment] en nature; **a ~ of** une espèce de, une sorte de; **~ of** *Am inf* un peu.

kindergarten ['kɪndə,gɑ:tn] *n* jardin *m* d'enfants.

kind-hearted [-'hɑ:tɪd] *adj* qui a bon cœur, bon (bonne).

kindle ['kɪndl] *vt* [fire] allumer. || *fig* [feeling] susciter.

kindly ['kaɪndlɪ] 1 *adj* [person] plein(e) de bonté, bienveillant(e). || [gesture] plein(e) de gentillesse. 2 *adv* [speak, smile etc] avec gentillesse. || [please]: ~ **leave the room!** veuillez sortir, s'il vous plaît!; **will you ~ ...?** veuillez .... je vous prie de ....

kindness ['kaɪndnɪs] *n* gentillesse *f*.

kindred ['kɪndrɪd] *adj* [similar] semblable, similaire; **~ spirit** âme *f* sœur.

king [kɪŋ] *n* roi *m*.

kingdom ['kɪŋdəm] *n* [country] royaume *m*. || [of animals, plants] règne *m*.

kingfisher ['kɪŋˌfɪʃə'] *n* martin-pêcheur *m*.

king-size(d) [-saɪz(d)] *adj* [cigarette] long (longue); [pack] géant(e); **a ~ bed** un grand lit (*de 195 cm*).

kinky ['kɪŋkɪ] *adj inf* vicieux(ieuse).

kiosk ['ki:ɒsk] *n* [small shop] kiosque *m*.

kipper ['kɪpə'] *n* hareng *m* fumé OR saur.

kiss [kɪs] **1** *n* baiser *m*; **to give sb a ~** embrasser qqn, donner un baiser à qqn. **2** *vt* embrasser. **3** *vi* s'embrasser.

kiss of life *n*: **the ~** le bouche-à-bouche.

kit [kɪt] *n* [set] trousse *f*. || [to be assembled] kit *m*.

kit bag *n* sac *m* de marin.

kitchen ['kɪtʃɪn] *n* cuisine *f*.

kitchen sink *n* évier *m*.

kitchen unit *n* élément *m* de cuisine.

kite [kaɪt] *n* [toy] cerf-volant *m*.

kith [kɪθ] *n*: **~ and kin** parents et amis *mpl*.

kitten ['kɪtn] *n* chaton *m*.

kitty ['kɪtɪ] *n* [shared fund] cagnotte *f*.

kiwi ['ki:wi:] *n* [bird] kiwi *m*, aptéryx *m*.

kiwi fruit *n* kiwi *m*.

km (*abbr of* **kilometre**) km.

km/h (*abbr of* **kilometres per hour**) km/h.

knack [næk] *n*: **to have a** OR **the ~ (for doing sthg)** avoir le coup (pour faire qqch).

knapsack ['næpsæk] *n* sac *m* à dos.

knead [ni:d] *vt* pétrir.

knee [ni:] *n* genou *m*.

kneecap ['ni:kæp] *n* rotule *f*.

kneel [ni:l] (*Br pt & pp* **knelt**, *Am pt & pp* **knelt** OR **-ed**) *vi* se mettre à genoux, s'agenouiller. O **kneel down** *vi* se mettre à genoux, s'agenouiller.

knelt [nelt] *pt & pp* → **kneel**.

knew [nju:] *pt* → **know**.

knickers ['nɪkəz] *npl Am* [knickerbockers] pantalon *m* de golf.

knick-knack ['nɪknæk] *n* babiole *f*, bibelot *m*.

knife [naɪf] (*pl* **knives**) **1** *n* couteau *m*. **2** *vt* donner un coup de couteau à, poignarder.

knight [naɪt] **1** *n* [in history, member of nobility] chevalier *m*. || [in chess] cavalier *m*. **2** *vt* faire chevalier.

knighthood ['naɪthʊd] *n* titre *m* de chevalier.

knit [nɪt] (*pt & pp* **knit** OR **-ted**) **1** *adj*: **closely** OR **tightly ~** *-fig* très uni(e). **2** *vt* tricoter. **3** *vi* [with wool] tricoter. || [broken bones] se souder.

knitting ['nɪtɪŋ] *n* (U) tricot *m*.

knitting needle *n* aiguille *f* à tricoter.

knitwear ['nɪtweə'] *n* (U) tricots *mpl*.

knives [naɪvz] *pl* → **knife**.

knob [nɒb] *n* [on door] poignée *f*, bouton *m*; [on drawer] poignée; [on bedstead] pomme *f*. || [on TV, radio etc] bouton *m*.

knock [nɒk] **1** *n* [hit] coup *m*. || *inf* [piece of bad luck] coup *m* dur. **2** *vt* [hit] frapper, cogner; **to ~ sb/sthg over** renverser qqn/qqch. || *inf* [criticize] critiquer, dire du mal de. **3** *vi* [on door]: **to ~ (at** OR **on)** frapper (à). || [car engine] cogner, avoir des ratés. O **knock down** *vt sep* [subj: car, driver] renverser. || [building] démolir. O **knock off** *vi inf* [stop working] finir son travail OR sa journée. O **knock out** *vt sep* [make unconscious] assommer. || [from competition] éliminer.

knocker ['nɒkə'] *n* [on door] heurtoir *m*.

knock-kneed [-'ni:d] *adj* cagneux (euse), qui a les genoux cagneux.

knockout ['nɒkaʊt] *n* knock-out *m*, K.-O. *m*.

knot [nɒt] **1** *n* [gen] nœud *m*; **to tie/ untie a ~** faire/défaire un nœud. **2** *vt* nouer, faire un nœud à.

knotty ['nɒtɪ] *adj fig* épineux(euse).

know [nəʊ] (*pt* **knew**, *pp* **known**) **1** *vt* [gen] savoir; [language] savoir parler; **to ~ (that)** ... savoir que ...; **to let sb ~ (about sthg)** faire savoir (qqch) à qqn, informer qqn (de qqch); **to ~ how to do sthg** savoir faire qqch; **to get to ~ sthg** apprendre qqch. || [person, place] connaître; **to get to ~ sb** apprendre à mieux connaître qqn. **2** *vi* savoir; **to ~ of sthg** connaître qqch; **to ~ about** [be aware of] être au courant de; [be expert in] s'y connaître en. **3** *n*: **to be in the ~** être au courant.

know-how *n* savoir-faire *m*, technique *f*.

knowing ['nəʊɪŋ] *adj* [smile, look] entendu(e).

knowingly ['nəʊɪŋlɪ] *adv* [smile, look] d'un air entendu. || [intentionally] sciemment.

knowledge ['nɒlɪdʒ] *n* (U) [gen] connaissance *f*; **without my ~** à mon insu; **to the best of my ~** à ma connaissance, autant que je sache. || [learning, understanding] savoir *m*, connaissances *fpl*.

knowledgeable ['nɒlɪdʒəbl] *adj* bien informé(e).

known [nəʊn] *pp* → **know**.

knuckle ['nʌkl] *n* ANAT articulation *f* OR jointure *f* du doigt. || [of meat] jarret *m*.

knuckle-duster *n* coup-de-poing *m* américain.

koala (bear) [kəʊ'ɑːlə-] *n* koala *m*.

Koran [kɒ'rɑːn] *n*: **the ~** le Coran.

Korea [kə'rɪə] *n* Corée *f*.

Korean [kə'rɪən] **1** *adj* coréen(enne). **2** *n* [person] Coréen *m*, -enne *f*. || [language] coréen *m*.

kosher ['kəʊʃər] *adj* [meat] kasher (*inv*).

Koweit = Kuwait.

kung fu [ˌkʌŋ'fuː] *n* kung-fu *m*.

Kurd [kɜːd] *n* Kurde *mf*.

Kuwait [ku'weɪt], **Koweit** [kəʊ'weɪt] *n* [country] Koweït *m*. || [city] Koweït City.

l[1] (*pl* **l's** OR **ls**), **L** (*pl* **L's** OR **Ls**) [el] *n* [letter] l *m inv*, L *m inv*.

l[2] (*abbr of* **litre**) l.

lab [læb] *n inf* labo *m*.

label ['leɪbl] **1** *n* [identification] étiquette *f*. || [of record] label *m*, maison *f* de disques. **2** *vt* [fix label to] étiqueter. || [describe]: **to ~ sb (as)** cataloguer OR étiqueter qqn (comme).

labor *etc Am* = **labour** *etc.*

laboratory [*Br* lə'bɒrətrɪ, *Am* 'læbrə,tɔːrɪ] *n* laboratoire *m*.

laborious [lə'bɔːrɪəs] *adj* laborieux (ieuse).

labor union *n Am* syndicat *m*.

labour *Br*, **labor** *Am* ['leɪbər] **1** *n* [gen & MED] travail *m*. || [workers, work carried out] main d'œuvre *f*. **2** *vi* travailler dur; **to ~ at** OR **over** peiner sur.

laboured *Br*, **labored** *Am* ['leɪbəd] *adj* [breathing] pénible; [style] lourd(e), laborieux(ieuse).

labourer *Br*, **laborer** *Am* ['leɪbərər] *n* travailleur manuel *m*, travailleuse manuelle *f*; [agricultural] ouvrier agricole *m*, ouvrière agricole *f*.

Labrador ['læbrədɔːr] *n* [dog] labrador *m*.

labyrinth ['læbərɪnθ] *n* labyrinthe *m*.

lace [leɪs] **1** *n* [fabric] dentelle *f*. || [of shoe etc] lacet *m*. **2** *vt* [shoe etc] lacer. || [drink] verser de l'alcool dans. ○ **lace up** *vt sep* lacer.

lack [læk] **1** *n* manque *m*; **for** OR **through ~ of** par manque de; **no ~ of** bien assez de. **2** *vt* manquer de. **3** *vi*: **to be ~ing in** sthg manquer de qqch; **to be ~ing** manquer, faire défaut.

lackadaisical [ˌlækə'deɪzɪkl] *adj pej* nonchalant(e).

lacklustre *Br*, **lackluster** *Am* ['læk,lʌstər] *adj* terne.

laconic [lə'kɒnɪk] *adj* laconique.

lacquer ['lækər] **1** *n* [for wood] vernis *m*, laque *f*; [for hair] laque *f*. **2** *vt* laquer.

lad [læd] *n inf* [boy] garçon *m*, gars *m*.

ladder ['lædər] *n* [for climbing] échelle *f*.

laden ['leɪdn] *adj*: **~ (with)** chargé(e) (de).

ladies *Br* ['leɪdɪz], **ladies' room** *Am n* toilettes *fpl* (pour dames).

ladle ['leɪdl] **1** *n* louche *f*. **2** *vt* servir (à la louche).

lady ['leɪdɪ] **1** *n* [gen] dame *f*. **2** *comp*: **a ~ doctor** une femme docteur. ○ **Lady** *n* Lady *f*.

ladybird *Br* ['leɪdɪbɜːd], **ladybug** *Am* ['leɪdɪbʌg] *n* coccinelle *f*.

lady-in-waiting [-'weɪtɪŋ] (*pl* **ladies-in-waiting**) *n* dame *f* d'honneur.

ladylike ['leɪdɪlaɪk] *adj* distingué(e).

Ladyship ['leɪdɪʃɪp] *n*: **her/your ~** Madame la baronne/la duchesse *etc*.

lag [læg] **1** *vi*: **to ~ (behind)** [person, runner] traîner; [economy, development] être en retard, avoir du retard. **2** *vt* [roof, pipe] calorifuger. **3** *n* [timelag] décalage *m*.

lager ['lɑːgər] *n* (bière *f*) blonde *f*.

lagoon [lə'guːn] *n* lagune *f*.

laid [leɪd] *pt & pp* → **lay**.

laid-back *adj inf* relaxe, décontracté(e).

lain [leɪn] *pp* → **lie**.

lair [leər] *n* repaire *m*, antre *m*.

lake [leɪk] *n* lac *m*.

Lake Geneva n le lac Léman OR de Genève.

lamb [læm] n agneau m.

lambswool ['læmzwʊl] **1** n lambswool m. **2** comp en lambswool, en laine d'agneau.

lame [leɪm] adj lit & fig boiteux(euse).

lament [lə'ment] **1** n lamentation f. **2** vt [lack, loss, fate] se lamenter sur.

lamentable ['læməntəbl] adj lamentable.

laminated ['læmɪneɪtɪd] adj [wood] stratifié(e); [glass] feuilleté(e); [steel] laminé(e).

lamp [læmp] n lampe f.

lampoon [læm'puːn] **1** n satire f. **2** vt faire la satire de.

lamppost ['læmppəʊst] n réverbère m.

lampshade ['læmpʃeɪd] n abat-jour m inv.

lance [lɑːns] **1** n lance f. **2** vt [boil] percer.

land [lænd] **1** n [solid ground] terre f (ferme); [farming ground] terre, terrain m. ‖ [property] terres fpl, propriété f. ‖ [nation] pays m. **2** vt [from ship, plane] débarquer. ‖ [catch - fish] prendre. ‖ [plane] atterrir. ‖ inf [obtain] décrocher. ‖ inf [place]: **to ~ sb in trouble** attirer des ennuis à qqn; **to be ~ed with sthg** se coltiner qqch. **3** vi [plane] atterrir. ‖ [fall] tomber. ○ **land up** vi inf atterrir.

landing ['lændɪŋ] n [of stairs] palier m. ‖ AERON atterrissage m. ‖ [of goods from ship] débarquement m.

landing card n carte f de débarquement.

landing gear n (U) train m d'atterrissage.

landing stage n débarcadère m.

landing strip n piste f d'atterrissage.

landlady ['lænd,leɪdɪ] n [living in] logeuse f; [owner] propriétaire f.

landlord ['lændlɔːd] n [of rented property] propriétaire m. ‖ [of pub] patron m.

landmark ['lændmɑːk] n point m de repère; fig événement m marquant.

landowner ['lænd,əʊnə'] n propriétaire foncier m, propriétaire foncière f.

landscape ['lændskeɪp] n paysage m.

landslide ['lændslaɪd] n [of earth] glissement m de terrain; [of rocks] éboulement m. ‖ fig [election victory] victoire f écrasante.

lane [leɪn] n [in country] petite route f, chemin m. ‖ [in town] ruelle f. ‖ [for

traffic] voie f; **"keep in ~"** «ne changez pas de file». ‖ AERON & SPORT couloir m.

language ['læŋgwɪdʒ] n [of people, country] langue f. ‖ [terminology, ability to speak] langage m.

language laboratory n laboratoire m de langues.

languish ['læŋgwɪʃ] vi languir.

lank [læŋk] adj terne.

lanky ['læŋkɪ] adj dégingandé(e).

lantern ['læntən] n lanterne f.

lap [læp] **1** n [of person]: **on sb's ~** sur les genoux de qqn. ‖ [of race] tour m de piste. **2** vt [subj: animal] laper. ‖ [in race] prendre un tour d'avance sur. **3** vi [water, waves] clapoter.

lapel [lə'pel] n revers m.

lapse [læps] **1** n [failing] défaillance f. ‖ [in behaviour] écart m de conduite. ‖ [of time] intervalle m, laps m de temps. **2** vi [passport] être périmé(e); [membership] prendre fin; [tradition] se perdre. ‖ [person]: **to ~ into bad habits** prendre de mauvaises habitudes.

lap-top (computer) n (ordinateur m) portable m.

larceny ['lɑːsənɪ] n (U) vol m (simple).

lard [lɑːd] n saindoux m.

larder ['lɑːdə'] n garde-manger m inv.

large [lɑːdʒ] adj grand(e); [person, animal, book] gros (grosse). ○ **at large** adv [as a whole] dans son ensemble. ‖ [prisoner, animal] en liberté. ○ **by and large** adv dans l'ensemble.

largely ['lɑːdʒlɪ] adv en grande partie.

lark [lɑːk] n [bird] alouette f. ‖ inf [joke] blague f. ○ **lark about** vi s'amuser.

laryngitis [,lærɪn'dʒaɪtɪs] n (U) laryngite f.

larynx ['lærɪŋks] n larynx m.

lasagna, lasagne [lə'zænjə] n (U) lasagnes fpl.

laser ['leɪzə'] n laser m.

laser printer n imprimante f (à) laser.

lash [læʃ] **1** n [eyelash] cil m. ‖ [with whip] coup m de fouet. **2** vt [gen] fouetter. ‖ [tie] attacher. ○ **lash out** vi [physically]: **to ~ out (at** OR **against)** envoyer un coup (à).

lass [læs] n jeune fille f.

lasso [læ'suː] (pl **-s**) **1** n lasso m. **2** vt attraper au lasso.

last [lɑːst] **1** adj dernier(ière); **~ night** hier soir; **~ but one** avant-dernier (avant-dernière). **2** adv [most recently] la dernière fois. ‖ [finally] en dernier, le dernier (la dernière). **3** pron: **the Satur-**

day before ~ pas samedi dernier, mais le samedi d'avant: **the year before** ~ il y a deux ans; **the** ~ **but one** l'avant-dernier *m*, l'avant-dernière *f*; **to leave sthg till** ~ faire qqch en dernier. **4** *n*: **the** ~ **I saw of him** la dernière fois que je l'ai vu. **5** *vi* durer; [food] se garder, se conserver; [feeling] persister. ○ **at (long) last** *adv* enfin.

lasting ['lɑːstɪŋ] *adj* durable.

lastly ['lɑːstlɪ] *adv* pour terminer, finalement.

last-minute *adj* de dernière minute.

last name *n* nom *m* de famille.

latch [lætʃ] *n* loquet *m*.

late [leɪt] **1** *adj* [not on time]: **to be** ~ **(for sthg)** être en retard (pour qqch). ‖ [near end of]: **in** ~ **December** vers la fin décembre. ‖ [later than normal] tardif(ive). ‖ [former] ancien(ienne). ‖ [dead] feu(e). **2** *adv* [not on time] en retard; **to arrive 20 minutes** ~ arriver avec 20 minutes de retard. ‖ [later than normal] tard. ○ **of late** *adv* récemment, dernièrement.

latecomer ['leɪt,kʌmər] *n* retardataire *mf*.

lately ['leɪtlɪ] *adv* ces derniers temps, dernièrement.

latent ['leɪtənt] *adj* latent(e).

later ['leɪtər] **1** *adj* [date] ultérieur(e); [edition] postérieur(e). **2** *adv*: ~ **(on)** plus tard.

lateral ['lætərəl] *adj* latéral(e).

latest ['leɪtɪst] **1** *adj* dernier(ière). **2** *n*: **at the** ~ au plus tard.

lathe [leɪð] *n* tour *m*.

lather ['lɑːðər] **1** *n* mousse *f* (de savon). **2** *vt* savonner.

Latin ['lætɪn] **1** *adj* latin(e). **2** *n* [language] latin *m*.

Latin America *n* Amérique *f* latine.

Latin American 1 *adj* latino-américain(e). **2** *n* [person] Latino-Américain *m*, -e *f*.

latitude ['lætɪtjuːd] *n* latitude *f*.

latter ['lætər] **1** *adj* [later] dernier(ière). ‖ [second] deuxième. **2** *n*: **the** ~ celui-ci (celle-ci), ce dernier (cette dernière).

lattice ['lætɪs] *n* treillis *m*, treillage *m*.

Latvia ['lætvɪə] *n* Lettonie *f*.

laudable ['lɔːdəbl] *adj* louable.

laugh [lɑːf] **1** *n* rire *m*; **we had a good** ~ *inf* on a bien rigolé, on s'est bien amusé. **2** *vi* rire. ○ **laugh at** *vt fus* [mock] se moquer de, rire de. ○ **laugh off** *vt sep* tourner en plaisanterie.

laughable ['lɑːfəbl] *adj* ridicule, risible.

laughingstock ['lɑːfɪŋstɒk] *n* risée *f*.

laughter ['lɑːftər] *n* (*U*) rire *m*, rires *mpl*.

launch [lɔːntʃ] **1** *n* [gen] lancement *m*. ‖ [boat] chaloupe *f*. **2** *vt* lancer.

launch(ing) pad ['lɔːntʃ(ɪŋ)-] *n* pas *m* de tir.

launder ['lɔːndər] *vt lit & fig* blanchir.

laund(e)rette [lɔːn'dret], **Laundromat**® *Am* ['lɔːndrəmæt] *n* laverie *f* automatique.

laundry ['lɔːndrɪ] *n* (*U*) [clothes] lessive *f*. ‖ [business] blanchisserie *f*.

laurel ['lɒrəl] *n* laurier *m*.

lava ['lɑːvə] *n* lave *f*.

lavatory ['lævətrɪ] *n* toilettes *fpl*.

lavender ['lævəndər] *n* [plant] lavande *f*.

lavish ['lævɪʃ] **1** *adj* [generous] généreux(euse); **to be** ~ **with** être prodigue de. ‖ [sumptuous] somptueux(euse). **2** *vt*: **to** ~ **sthg on sb** prodiguer qqch à qqn.

law [lɔː] *n* [gen] loi *f*; **against the** ~ contraire à la loi, illégal(e); **to break the** ~ enfreindre OR transgresser la loi; ~ **and order** ordre *m* public. ‖ JUR droit *m*.

law-abiding [-ə,baɪdɪŋ] *adj* respectueux(euse) des lois.

law court *n* tribunal *m*, cour *f* de justice.

lawful ['lɔːfʊl] *adj* légal(e), licite.

lawn [lɔːn] *n* pelouse *f*, gazon *m*.

lawnmower ['lɔːn,məʊər] *n* tondeuse *f* à gazon.

lawn tennis *n* tennis *m*.

law school *n* faculté *f* de droit.

lawsuit ['lɔːsuːt] *n* procès *m*.

lawyer ['lɔːjər] *n* [in court] avocat *m*; [for company] conseiller *m* juridique; [for wills, sales] notaire *m*.

lax [læks] *adj* relâché(e).

laxative ['læksətɪv] *n* laxatif *m*.

lay [leɪ] (*pt & pp* **laid**) **1** *pt* → **lie**. **2** *vt* [gen] poser, mettre; *fig*: **to** ~ **the blame for sthg on sb** rejeter la responsabilité de qqch sur qqn. ‖ [trap, snare] tendre; dresser; [plans] faire; **to** ~ **the table** mettre la table OR le couvert. ‖ [egg] pondre. **3** *adj* RELIG laïque. ‖ [untrained] profane. ○ **lay aside** *vt sep* mettre de côté. ○ **lay down** *vt sep* [guidelines, rules] imposer, stipuler. ‖ [put down] déposer. ○ **lay off 1** *vt sep* [make redundant] licencier. **2** *vt fus inf* [leave alone] ficher la paix à. ‖ [give up] arrêter. ○ **lay out** *vt sep* [arrange] arranger, disposer. ‖ [design] concevoir.

layer ['leɪə'] n couche f, fig [level] niveau m.

layman ['leɪmən] (pl **-men** [-mən]) n [untrained person] profane m. || RELIG laïc m.

layout ['leɪaʊt] n [of office, building] agencement m; [of garden] plan m; [of page] mise f en page.

laze [leɪz] vi: to ~ (about OR around) paresser.

lazy ['leɪzɪ] adj [person] paresseux(euse), fainéant(e); [action] nonchalant(e).

lazybones ['leɪzɪbəʊnz] (pl inv) n paresseux m, -euse f, fainéant m, -e f.

lb (abbr of **pound**) livre (unité de poids).

LCD (abbr of **liquid crystal display**) n affichage à cristaux liquides.

lead[1] [liːd] (pt & pp led) 1 n [winning position]: **to be in** OR **have the ~** mener, être en tête. || [amount ahead]: **to have a ~ of ...** devancer de .... || [initiative, example] initiative f, exemple m; **to take the ~** montrer l'exemple. || THEATRE: **the ~** le rôle principal. || [clue] indice m. || [for dog] laisse f. || [wire, cable] câble m, fil m. 2 adj [role etc] principal(e). 3 vt [be at front of] mener, être à la tête de. || [guide] guider, conduire. || [be in charge of] être à la tête de, diriger. || [organize - protest etc] mener, organiser. || [life] mener. || [cause]: **to ~ sb to do sthg** inciter OR pousser qqn à faire qqch. 4 vi [path, cable etc] mener, conduire. || [give access]: **to ~ to/into** donner sur, donner accès à. || [in race, match] mener. || [result in]: **to ~ to sthg** aboutir à qqch, causer qqch. ○ **lead up to** vt fus [precede] conduire à, amener à. || [build up to] amener.

lead[2] [led] 1 n plomb m; [in pencil] mine f. 2 comp en OR de plomb.

leaded ['ledɪd] adj [petrol] au plomb.

leader ['liːdə'] n [head, chief] chef m; POL leader m. || [in race, competition] premier m, -ière f. || Br PRESS éditorial m.

leadership ['liːdəʃɪp] n [people in charge]: **the ~** les dirigeants mpl. || [position of leader] direction f. || [qualities of leader] qualités fpl de chef.

lead-free [led-] adj sans plomb.

leading ['liːdɪŋ] adj [most important] principal(e). || [at front] de tête.

leaf [liːf] (pl **leaves**) n [of tree, plant] feuille f. || [of table - hinged] abattant m; [- pull-out] rallonge f. || [of book] feuille f, page f. ○ **leaf through** vt fus [magazine etc] parcourir, feuilleter.

leaflet ['liːflɪt] n prospectus m.

league [liːg] n ligue f; SPORT championnat m; **to be in ~ with** être de connivence avec.

leak [liːk] 1 n lit & fig fuite f. 2 vt fig [secret, information] divulguer. 3 vi fuir. ○ **leak out** vi [liquid] fuir. || fig [secret, information] transpirer, être divulgué(e).

lean [liːn] (pt & pp **leant** OR **-ed**) 1 adj [slim] mince. || [meat] maigre. || fig [month, time] mauvais(e). 2 vt [rest]: **to ~ sthg against** appuyer qqch contre, adosser qqch à. 3 vi [bend, slope] se pencher. || [rest]: **to ~ on/against** s'appuyer sur/contre.

leaning ['liːnɪŋ] n: ~ **(towards)** penchant m (pour).

leant [lent] pt & pp → **lean**.

lean-to (pl **lean-tos**) n appentis m.

leap [liːp] (pt & pp **leapt** OR **-ed**) 1 n lit & fig bond m. 2 vi [gen] bondir. || fig [increase] faire un bond.

leapfrog ['liːpfrɒg] 1 n saute-mouton m. 2 vi: **to ~ over** sauter par-dessus.

leapt [lept] pt & pp → **leap**.

leap year n année f bissextile.

learn [lɜːn] (pt & pp **-ed** OR **learnt**) 1 vt: **to ~ (that) ...** apprendre que ...; **to ~ (how) to do sthg** apprendre à faire qqch. 2 vi: **to ~ (of** OR **about sthg)** apprendre (qqch).

learned ['lɜːnɪd] adj savant(e).

learner ['lɜːnə'] n débutant m, -e f.

learner (driver) n conducteur débutant m, conductrice débutante f (qui n'a pas encore son permis).

learning ['lɜːnɪŋ] n savoir m, érudition f.

learnt [lɜːnt] pt & pp → **learn**.

lease [liːs] 1 n bail m. 2 vt louer; **to ~ sthg from sb** louer qqch à qqn; **to ~ sthg to sb** louer qqch à qqn.

leasehold ['liːshəʊld] 1 adj loué(e) à bail, tenu(e) à bail. 2 adv à bail.

leash [liːʃ] n laisse f.

least [liːst] (superl of **little**) 1 adj: **the ~** le moindre (la moindre), le plus petit (la plus petite). 2 pron [smallest amount]: **the ~** le moins; **it's the ~ (that) he can do** c'est la moindre des choses qu'il puisse faire; **not in the ~** pas du tout, pas le moins du monde; **to say the ~** c'est le moins qu'on puisse dire. 3 adv: **(the) ~** moins (la moins). ○ **at least** adv au moins; [to correct] du moins. ○ **least of all** adv surtout pas, encore moins. ○ **not least** adv fml notamment.

leather ['leðər] n cuir m.

leave [li:v] (pt & pp **left**) **1** rt [gen] laisser. || [go away from] quitter; **to ~ sb alone** laisser qqn tranquille. || [bequeath]: **to ~ sb sthg, to ~ sthg to sb** léguer or laisser qqch à qqn; see also **left**. **2** ri partir. **3** n congé m; **to be on ~** [from work] être en congé; [from army] être en permission. ○ **leave behind** rt sep [abandon] abandonner, laisser. || [forget] oublier, laisser. ○ **leave out** rt sep ômettre, exclure.

leave of absence n congé m.

leaves [li:vz] pl → **leaf**.

Lebanon ['lebənən] n Liban m.

lecherous ['letʃərəs] adj lubrique, libidineux(euse).

lecture ['lektʃər] **1** n [talk - gen] conférence f; [- UNIV] cours m magistral. || [scolding]: **to give sb a ~** réprimander qqn, sermonner qqn. **2** rt [scold] réprimander, sermonner. **3** ri: **to ~ on sthg** faire un cours sur qqch; **to ~ in sthg** être professeur de qqch.

lecturer ['lektʃərər] n [speaker] conférencier m, -ière f; UNIV maître assistant m.

led [led] pt & pp → **lead**[1].

ledge [ledʒ] n [of window] rebord m. || [of mountain] corniche f.

ledger ['ledʒər] n grand livre m.

leech [li:tʃ] n lit & fig sangsue f.

leek [li:k] n poireau m.

leer [liər] **1** ri: **to ~ at** reluquer.

leeway ['li:wei] n [room to manoeuvre] marge f de manœuvre.

left [left] **1** pt & pp → **leave**. **2** adj [remaining]: **to be ~** rester; **have you any money ~?** il te reste de l'argent? || [not right] gauche. **3** adr à gauche. **4** n: **on** or **to the ~** à gauche. ○ **Left** n POL: **the Left** la Gauche.

left-hand adj de gauche; **~ side** gauche f, côté m gauche.

left-hand drive adj [car] avec la conduite à gauche.

left-handed [-'hændid] adj [person] gaucher(ère). || [implement] pour gaucher.

leftover ['leftəʊvər] adj qui reste, en surplus. ○ **leftovers** npl restes mpl.

left wing POL n gauche f. ○ **left-wing** adj de gauche.

leg [leg] n [of person, trousers] jambe f; [of animal] patte f; **to pull sb's ~** faire marcher qqn. || CULIN [of lamb] gigot m;

[of pork, chicken] cuisse f. || [of furniture] pied m. || [of journey, match] étape f.

legacy ['legəsi] n lit & fig legs m, héritage m.

legal ['li:gl] adj [concerning the law] juridique. || [lawful] légal(e).

legalize, -ise ['li:gəlaiz] rt légaliser, rendre légal.

legal tender n monnaie f légale.

legend ['ledʒənd] n lit & fig légende f.

leggings ['leginz] npl jambières fpl, leggings mpl or fpl.

legible ['ledʒəbl] adj lisible.

legislation [,ledʒis'leiʃn] n législation f.

legislature ['ledʒisleitʃər] n corps m législatif.

legitimate [li'dʒitimət] adj légitime.

legroom ['legrum] n (U) place f pour les jambes.

leg-warmers [-,wɔ:məz] npl jambières fpl.

leisure [Br 'leʒər, Am 'li:ʒər] n loisir m, temps m libre.

leisure centre n centre m de loisirs.

leisurely [Br 'leʒəli, Am 'li:ʒərli] adj [pace] lent(e), tranquille.

leisure time n (U) temps m libre, loisirs mpl.

lemon ['lemən] n [fruit] citron m.

lemonade [,lemə'neid] n [still] citronnade f.

lemon juice n jus m de citron.

lemon squeezer [-'skwi:zər] n presse-citron m inr.

lemon tea n thé m (au) citron.

lend [lend] (pt & pp **lent**) rt [loan] prêter; **to ~ sb sthg, to ~ sthg to sb** prêter qqch à qqn. || [offer]: **to ~ support (to sb)** offrir son soutien (à qqn); **to ~ assistance (to sb)** prêter assistance (à qqn). || [add]: **to ~ sthg to sthg** [quality etc] ajouter qqch à qqch.

lending rate ['lendiŋ-] n taux m de crédit.

length [leŋθ] n [gen] longueur f; **what ~ is it?** ça fait quelle longueur? || [piece - of string, wood] morceau m, bout m; [- of cloth] coupon m. || [duration] durée f. || phr: **to go to great ~s to do sthg** tout faire pour faire qqch. ○ **at length** adr [eventually] enfin. || [in detail] à fond.

lengthen ['leŋθən] **1** rt [dress etc] rallonger; [life] prolonger. **2** ri allonger.

lengthways ['leŋθweiz] adr dans le sens de la longueur.

lengthy ['leŋθi] adj très long (longue).

lenient ['li:njənt] *adj* [person] indulgent(e); [laws] clément(e).

lens [lenz] *n* [of camera] objectif *m*; [of glasses] verre *m*. || [contact lens] verre *m* de contact, lentille *f* (cornéenne).

lent [lent] *pt & pp* → **lend**.

Lent [lent] *n* Carême *m*.

lentil ['lentıl] *n* lentille *f*.

Leo ['li:əu] *n* le Lion.

leopard ['lepəd] *n* léopard *m*.

leotard ['li:əta:d] *n* collant *m*.

leper ['lepər] *n* lépreux *m*, -euse *f*.

leprosy ['leprəsı] *n* lèpre *f*.

lesbian ['lezbıən] *n* lesbienne *f*.

less [les] (*compar of* **little**) **1** *adj* moins de; ~ **money/time than me** moins d'argent/de temps que moi. **2** *pron* moins; **it costs** ~ **than you think** ça coûte moins cher que tu ne le crois; **no** ~ **than** £50 pas moins de 50 livres; **the** ~ ... **the** ~ ... moins ... moins .... **3** *adv* moins; ~ **than five** moins de cinq; ~ **and** ~ de moins en moins. **4** *prep* [minus] moins.

lessen ['lesn] **1** *vt* [risk, chance] diminuer, réduire; [pain] atténuer. **2** *vi* [gen] diminuer; [pain] s'atténuer.

lesser ['lesər] *adj* moindre; **to a** ~ **extent** OR **degree** à un degré moindre.

lesson ['lesn] *n* leçon *f*, cours *m*; **to teach sb a** ~ *fig* donner une (bonne) leçon à qqn.

let [let] (*pt & pp* **let**) *vt* [allow]: **to** ~ **sb do sthg** laisser qqn faire qqch; **to** ~ **sb know sthg** dire qqch à qqn; **to** ~ **go of sb/sthg** lâcher qqn/qqch; **to** ~ **sb go** [gen] laisser (partir) qqn; [prisoner] libérer qqn. || [in verb forms]: ~ **them wait** qu'ils attendent; ~'s **go!** allons-y! || [rent out] louer; **"to** ~**"** «à louer». O **let alone** *adv* encore moins, sans parler de. O **let down** *vt sep* [deflate] dégonfler. || [disappoint] décevoir. O **let in** *vt sep* [admit] laisser OR faire entrer. O **let off** *vt sep* [excuse]: **to** ~ **sb off sthg** dispenser qqn de qqch. || [not punish] ne pas punir. || [bomb] faire éclater; [gun, firework] faire partir. O **let on** *vi*: **don't** ~ **on!** ne dis rien (à personne)! O **let out** *vt sep* [allow to go out] laisser sortir; [air, water] faire sortir; [sound] émettre. O **air out of sthg** dégonfler qqch. O **let up** *vi* [rain] diminuer. || [person] s'arrêter.

letdown ['letdaun] *n inf* déception *f*.

lethal ['li:θl] *adj* mortel(elle), fatal(e).

lethargic [lə'θɑ:dʒık] *adj* léthargique.

let's [lets] = **let us**.

letter ['letər] *n* lettre *f*.

letter bomb *n* lettre *f* piégée.

letter of credit *n* lettre *f* de crédit.

lettuce ['letıs] *n* laitue *f*, salade *f*.

letup ['letʌp] *n* [in fighting] répit *m*; [in work] relâchement *m*.

leuk(a)emia [lu:'ki:mıə] *n* leucémie *f*.

level ['levl] **1** *adj* [equal in height] à la même hauteur; [horizontal] horizontal(e); **to be** ~ **with** être au niveau de. || [equal in standard] à égalité. || [flat] plat(e), plan(e). **2** *n* [gen] niveau *m*. || *Am* [spirit level] niveau *m* à bulle. **3** *vt* [make flat] niveler, aplanir. || [demolish] raser. O **level off**, **level out** *vi* [inflation etc] se stabiliser. || [aeroplane] se mettre en palier. O **level with** *vt fus inf* être franc (franche) OR honnête avec.

level-headed [-'hedıd] *adj* raisonnable.

lever [*Br* 'li:vər, *Am* 'levər] *n* levier *m*.

levy ['levı] **1** *n* prélèvement *m*, impôt *m*. **2** *vt* prélever, percevoir.

lewd [lju:d] *adj* obscène.

liability [,laıə'bılətı] *n* responsabilité *f*; *fig* [person] danger *m* public. O **liabilities** *npl* FIN dettes *fpl*, passif *m*.

liable ['laıəbl] *adj* [likely]: **to be** ~ **to do sthg** risquer de faire qqch, être susceptible de faire qqch. || [prone]: **to be** ~ **to sthg** être sujet(ette) à qqch. || JUR: **to be** ~ **(for)** être responsable (de).

liaise [lı'eız] *vi*: **to** ~ **with** assurer la liaison avec.

liar ['laıər] *n* menteur *m*, -euse *f*.

libel ['laıbl] **1** *n* diffamation *f*. **2** *vt* diffamer.

liberal ['lıbərəl] **1** *adj* [tolerant] libéral(e). || [generous] généreux(euse). **2** *n* libéral *m*, -e *f*. O **Liberal** POL **1** *adj* libéral(e). **2** *n* libéral *m*, -e *f*.

liberate ['lıbəreıt] *vt* libérer.

liberation [,lıbə'reıʃn] *n* libération *f*.

liberty ['lıbətı] *n* liberté *f*; **at** ~ en liberté; **to be at** ~ **to do sthg** être libre de faire qqch; **to take liberties (with sb)** prendre des libertés (avec qqn).

Libra ['li:brə] *n* Balance *f*.

librarian [laı'breərıən] *n* bibliothécaire *mf*.

library ['laıbrərı] *n* bibliothèque *f*.

library book *n* livre *m* de bibliothèque.

libretto [lı'bretəu] (*pl* -**s**) *n* livret *m*.

Libya ['lıbıə] *n* Libye *f*.

lice [laıs] *pl* → **louse**.

licence ['laısəns] **1** *n* [gen] permis *m*, autorisation *f*; **driving** ~ permis *m* de

conduire; TV ~ redevance *f* télé. || COMM
licence *f.* 2 *vt Am* = license.

license ['laɪsəns] 1 *vt* autoriser. 2 *n Am*
= licence.

licensed ['laɪsənst] *adj* [person]: to be ~
to do sthg avoir un permis pour OR
l'autorisation de faire qqch.

license plate *n Am* plaque *f* d'immatriculation.

lick [lɪk] *vt* [gen] lécher. || *inf* [defeat]
écraser.

licorice ['lɪkərɪs] = liquorice.

lid [lɪd] *n* [cover] couvercle *m.* || [eyelid]
paupière *f.*

lie [laɪ] (*pt sense 1* lied, *pt senses 2-6*
lay, *pp sense 1* lied, *pp senses 2-6* lain,
cont all senses lying) 1 *n* mensonge *m*; to
tell ~s mentir, dire des mensonges. 2 *vi*
[tell lie]: to ~ (to sb) mentir (à qqn). || [be
horizontal] être allongé(e), être cou-
ché(e). || [lie down] s'allonger, se cou-
cher. || [be situated] se trouver, être. ||
[difficulty, solution etc] résider. || *phr*: to ~
low se planquer, se tapir. ○ **lie about**,
lie around *vi* traîner. ○ **lie down** *vi*
s'allonger, se coucher.

lieutenant [*Br* lef'tenənt, *Am* lu:-
'tenənt] *n* lieutenant *m.*

life [laɪf] (*pl* lives) *n* [gen] vie *f*; that's ~!
c'est la vie!; for ~ à vie; to come to ~
s'éveiller, s'animer; to scare the ~ out of
sb faire une peur bleue à qqn. || (*U*) *inf*
[life imprisonment] emprisonnement *m*
perpétuel.

life assurance = life insurance.

life belt *n* bouée *f* de sauvetage.

lifeboat ['laɪfbəʊt] *n* canot *m* de sauvetage.

life buoy *n* bouée *f* de sauvetage.

life expectancy [-ɪk'spektənsɪ] *n* espérance *f* de vie.

lifeguard ['laɪfgɑːd] *n* [at swimming
pool] maître-nageur sauveteur *m*; [at
beach] gardien *m* de plage.

life imprisonment [-ɪm'prɪznmənt] *n*
emprisonnement *m* à perpétuité.

life insurance *n* assurance-vie *f.*

life jacket *n* gilet *m* de sauvetage.

lifeless ['laɪflɪs] *adj* [dead] sans vie, ina-
nimé(e). || [listless - performance] qui
manque de vie; [- voice] monotone.

lifelike ['laɪflaɪk] *adj* [statue, doll] qui
semble vivant(e). || [portrait] ressem-
blant(e).

lifeline ['laɪflaɪn] *n* corde *f* (de sauvetage); *fig* lien *m* vital (avec l'extérieur).

lifelong ['laɪflɒŋ] *adj* de toujours.

life preserver [-prɪˌzɜːvəʳ] *n Am* [life
belt] bouée *f* de sauvetage; [life jacket] gilet *m* de sauvetage.

life raft *n* canot *m* pneumatique (de
sauvetage).

lifesaver ['laɪfˌseɪvəʳ] *n* [person]
maître-nageur sauveteur *m.*

life sentence *n* condamnation *f* à perpétuité.

life-size(d) [-saɪz(d)] *adj* grandeur nature (*inv*).

lifespan ['laɪfspæn] *n* [of person, animal]
espérance *f* de vie.

lifestyle ['laɪfstaɪl] *n* style *m* de vie.

life-support system *n* respirateur *m*
artificiel.

lifetime ['laɪftaɪm] *n* vie *f*; in my ~ de
mon vivant.

lift [lɪft] 1 *n* [in car]: to give sb a ~ emmener OR prendre qqn en voiture. 2 *vt*
[gen] lever; [weight] soulever. || [plagia-
rize] plagier. || *inf* [steal] voler. 3 *vi* [lid
etc] s'ouvrir. || [fog etc] se lever.

lift-off *n* décollage *m.*

light [laɪt] (*pt & pp* lit OR -ed) 1 *adj*
[not dark] clair(e). || [not heavy] lé-
ger(ère). || [traffic] fluide; [corrections]
peu nombreux(euses). || [work] facile. 2
n (*U*) [brightness] lumière *f.* || [device]
lampe *f*; [AUT - gen] feu *m*; [- headlamp]
phare *m.* || [for cigarette etc] feu *m*; have
you got a ~? vous avez du feu?; to set ~
to sthg mettre le feu à qqch. || [perspec-
tive]: in the ~ of *Br*, in ~ of *Am* à la lu-
mière de. || *phr*: to come to ~ être décou-
vert(e) OR dévoilé(e). 3 *vt* [fire, cigarette]
allumer. || [room, stage] éclairer. 4 *adv*:
to travel ~ voyager léger. ○ **light up** 1 *vi*
sep [illuminate] éclairer. || [cigarette etc]
allumer. 2 *vi* [face] s'éclairer. || *inf* [start
smoking] allumer une cigarette.

light bulb *n* ampoule *f.*

lighten ['laɪtn] 1 *vt* [in colour] éclaircir.
|| [make less heavy] alléger. 2 *vi* [brighten]
s'éclaircir.

lighter ['laɪtəʳ] *n* [cigarette lighter] briquet *m.*

light-headed [-'hedɪd] *adj*: to feel ~
avoir la tête qui tourne.

light-hearted [-'hɑːtɪd] *adj* [cheerful]
joyeux(euse), gai(e). || [amusing] amu-
sant(e).

lighthouse ['laɪthaʊs, *pl* -haʊzɪz] *n*
phare *m.*

lighting ['laɪtɪŋ] *n* éclairage *m.*

light meter *n* posemètre *m*, cellule *f*
photoélectrique.

lightning ['laɪtnɪŋ] *n* (*U*) éclair *m*, foudre *f*.

lightweight ['laɪtweɪt] **1** *adj* [object] léger(ère). **2** *n* [boxer] poids *m* léger.

likable ['laɪkəbl] *adj* sympathique.

like [laɪk] **1** *prep* [gen] comme; **to look ~ sb/sthg** ressembler à qqn/qqch; **to taste ~ sthg** avoir un goût de qqch; **~ this/that** comme ci/ça. ‖ [such as] tel que, comme. **2** *vt* [gen] aimer; **I ~ her** elle me plaît; **to ~ doing** OR **to do sthg** aimer faire qqch. ‖ [expressing a wish]: **would you ~ some more cake?** vous prendrez encore du gâteau?; **I'd ~ to go** je voudrais bien OR j'aimerais y aller; **I'd ~ you to come** je voudrais bien OR j'aimerais que vous veniez; **if you ~** si vous voulez. **3** *n*: **the ~** une chose pareille. ○ **likes** *npl*: **~s and dislikes** goûts *mpl*.

likeable ['laɪkəbl] = likable.

likelihood ['laɪklɪhʊd] *n* (*U*) chances *fpl*, probabilité *f*.

likely ['laɪklɪ] *adj* [probable] probable; **he's ~ to get angry** il risque de se fâcher; **a ~ story!** *iro* à d'autres! ‖ [candidate] prometteur(euse).

liken ['laɪkn] *vt*: **to ~ sb/sthg to** assimiler qqn/qqch à.

likewise ['laɪkwaɪz] *adv* [similarly] de même; **to do ~** faire pareil OR de même.

liking ['laɪkɪŋ] *n* [for person] affection *f*, sympathie *f*; [for food, music] goût *m*, penchant *m*; **to be to sb's ~** être du goût de qqn, plaire à qqn.

lilac ['laɪlək] **1** *adj* [colour] lilas (*inv*). **2** *n* lilas *m*.

lily ['lɪlɪ] *n* lis *m*.

lily of the valley (*pl* **lilies of the valley**) *n* muguet *m*.

limb [lɪm] *n* [of body] membre *m*.

limber ['lɪmbə'] ○ **limber up** *vi* s'échauffer.

limbo ['lɪmbəʊ] (*pl* -s) *n* (*U*) [uncertain state]: **to be in ~** être dans les limbes.

lime [laɪm] *n* [fruit] citron *m* vert. ‖ [drink]: **~ (juice)** jus *m* de citron vert. ‖ [linden tree] tilleul *m*. ‖ [substance] chaux *f*.

limelight ['laɪmlaɪt] *n*: **to be in the ~** être au premier plan.

limerick ['lɪmərɪk] *n* poème humoristique en cinq vers.

limestone ['laɪmstəʊn] *n* (*U*) pierre *f* à chaux, calcaire *m*.

limey ['laɪmɪ] (*pl* **limeys**) *n* Am inf terme péjoratif désignant un Anglais.

limit ['lɪmɪt] **1** *n* limite *f*; **off ~s** d'accès interdit; **within ~s** [to an extent] dans une certaine mesure. **2** *vt* limiter, restreindre.

limitation [,lɪmɪ'teɪʃn] *n* limitation *f*, restriction *f*.

limited ['lɪmɪtɪd] *adj* limité(e), restreint(e).

limited (liability) company *n* société *f* anonyme.

limousine ['lɪməzi:n] *n* limousine *f*.

limp [lɪmp] **1** *adj* mou (molle). **2** *n*: **to have a ~** boiter. **3** *vi* boiter.

limpet ['lɪmpɪt] *n* patelle *f*, bernique *f*.

line [laɪn] **1** *n* [gen] ligne *f*. ‖ [row] rangée *f*. ‖ [queue] file *f*, queue *f*; **to stand** OR **wait in ~** faire la queue. ‖ [RAIL - track] voie *f*; [- route] ligne *f*. ‖ [of poem, song] vers *m*. ‖ [wrinkle] ride *f*. ‖ [string, wire etc] corde *f*; **a fishing ~** une ligne. ‖ TELEC ligne *f*; **hold the ~!** ne quittez pas! ‖ *inf* [short letter]: **to drop sb a ~** écrire un (petit) mot à qqn. ‖ [borderline] frontière *f*. ‖ COMM gamme *f*. ‖ *phr*: **to draw the ~ at sthg** refuser de faire qqch OR d'aller jusqu'à faire qqch; **to step out of ~** faire cavalier seul. **2** *vt* [drawer, box] tapisser; [clothes] doubler. ○ **out of line** *adj* [remark, behaviour] déplacé(e). ○ **line up** *vt sep* [in rows] aligner. ‖ [organize] prévoir. **2** *vi* [in row] s'aligner; [in queue] faire la queue.

lined [laɪnd] *adj* [paper] réglé(e). ‖ [wrinkled] ridé(e).

linen ['lɪnɪn] *n* (*U*) [cloth] lin *m*. ‖ [tablecloths, sheets] linge *m* (de maison).

liner ['laɪnə'] *n* [ship] paquebot *m*.

linesman ['laɪnzmən] (*pl* -men [-mən]) *n* TENNIS juge *m* de ligne.

lineup ['laɪnʌp] *n* SPORT équipe *f*. ‖ *Am* [identification parade] rangée *f* de suspects (*pour identification par un témoin*).

linger ['lɪŋgə'] *vi* [person] s'attarder. ‖ [doubt, pain] persister.

linguist ['lɪŋgwɪst] *n* linguiste *mf*.

linguistics [lɪŋ'gwɪstɪks] *n* (*U*) linguistique *f*.

lining ['laɪnɪŋ] *n* [of coat, curtains, box] doublure *f*. ‖ [of stomach] muqueuse *f*. ‖ AUT [of brakes] garniture *f*.

link [lɪŋk] **1** *n* [of chain] maillon *m*. ‖ [connection]: **~ (between/with)** lien *m* (entre/avec). **2** *vt* [cities, parts] relier; [events etc] lier; **to ~ arms** se donner le bras. ○ **link up** *vt sep* relier; **to ~ sthg up with sthg** relier qqch avec OR à qqch.

loaded

links [lɪŋks] (pl inv) n terrain m de golf (au bord de la mer).

lino ['laɪnəʊ], **linoleum** [lɪ'nəʊlɪəm] n lino m, linoléum m.

lion ['laɪən] n lion m.

lioness ['laɪənes] n lionne f.

lip [lɪp] n [of mouth] lèvre f. ‖ [of container] bord m.

lip-read vi lire sur les lèvres.

lip service n: to pay ~ to sthg approuver qqch pour la forme.

lipstick ['lɪpstɪk] n rouge m à lèvres.

liqueur [lɪ'kjʊər] n liqueur f.

liquid ['lɪkwɪd] 1 adj liquide. 2 n liquide m.

liquidation [,lɪkwɪ'deɪʃn] n liquidation f.

liquor ['lɪkər] n (U) alcool m, spiritueux mpl.

liquorice ['lɪkərɪs, 'lɪkərɪʃ] n réglisse f.

liquor store n Am magasin m de vins et d'alcools.

Lisbon ['lɪzbən] n Lisbonne.

lisp [lɪsp] 1 n zézaiement m. 2 vi zézayer.

list [lɪst] 1 n liste f. 2 vt [in writing] faire la liste de; [in speech] énumérer.

listen ['lɪsn] vi: to ~ to (sb/sthg) écouter (qqn/qqch); to ~ for sthg guetter qqch.

listener ['lɪsnər] n auditeur m, -trice f.

listless ['lɪstlɪs] adj apathique, mou (molle).

lit [lɪt] pt & pp → **light**.

liter Am = **litre**.

literacy ['lɪtərəsɪ] n fait m de savoir lire et écrire.

literal ['lɪtərəl] adj littéral(e).

literally ['lɪtərəlɪ] adv littéralement; **to take sthg** ~ prendre qqch au pied de la lettre.

literary ['lɪtərərɪ] adj littéraire.

literate ['lɪtərət] adj [able to read and write] qui sait lire et écrire. ‖ [well-read] cultivé(e).

literature ['lɪtrətʃər] n littérature f; [printed information] documentation f.

lithe [laɪð] adj souple, agile.

Lithuania [,lɪθjʊ'eɪnɪə] n Lituanie f.

litigation [,lɪtɪ'geɪʃn] n litige m; **to go to** ~ aller en justice.

litre Br, **liter** Am ['li:tər] n litre m.

litter ['lɪtər] 1 n (U) [rubbish] ordures fpl, détritus mpl. ‖ [of animals] portée f. 2 vt: to be ~ed with être couvert(e) de.

little ['lɪtl] (compar sense 2 **less**, superl sense 2 **least**) 1 adj [not big] petit(e); **a ~ while** un petit moment. ‖ [not much] peu de; ~ **money** peu d'argent; **a ~ money** un

peu d'argent. 2 pron: ~ **of the money was left** il ne restait pas beaucoup d'argent, il restait peu d'argent; **a ~** un peu. 3 adv peu, pas beaucoup; **by ~** peu à peu.

little finger n petit doigt m, auriculaire m.

live[1] [lɪv] 1 vi [gen] vivre. ‖ [have one's home] habiter, vivre; **to ~ in Paris** habiter (à) Paris. 2 vt: **to ~ a quiet life** mener une vie tranquille; **to ~ it up** inf faire la noce. ○ **live down** vt sep faire oublier. ○ **live off** vt fus [savings, the land] vivre de; [family] vivre aux dépens de. ○ **live on** 1 vt fus vivre de. 2 vi [memory, feeling] rester, survivre. ○ **live together** vi vivre ensemble. ○ **live up to** vt fus: **to ~ up to sb's expectations** répondre à l'attente de qqn; **to ~ up to one's reputation** faire honneur à sa réputation. ○ **live with** vt fus [cohabit with] vivre avec. ‖ inf [accept] se faire à, accepter.

live[2] [laɪv] adj [living] vivant(e). ‖ [coal] ardent(e). ‖ [bullet, bomb] non explosé(e). ‖ ELEC sous tension. ‖ RADIO & TV en direct; [performance] en public.

livelihood ['laɪvlɪhʊd] n gagne-pain m.

lively ['laɪvlɪ] adj [person] plein(e) d'entrain. ‖ [debate, meeting] animé(e).

liven ['laɪvn] ○ **liven up** 1 vt sep [person] égayer; [place] animer. 2 vi s'animer.

liver ['lɪvər] n foie m.

livery ['lɪvərɪ] n livrée f.

lives [laɪvz] pl → **life**.

livestock ['laɪvstɒk] n (U) bétail m.

livid ['lɪvɪd] adj [angry] furieux (ieuse).

living ['lɪvɪŋ] 1 adj vivant(e), en vie. 2 n: **to earn** OR **make a** ~ gagner sa vie; **what do you do for a** ~? qu'est-ce que vous faites dans la vie?

living conditions npl conditions fpl de vie.

living room n salle f de séjour, living m.

living standards npl niveau m de vie.

living wage n minimum m vital.

lizard ['lɪzəd] n lézard m.

llama ['lɑ:mə] (pl inv OR **-s**) n lama m.

load [ləʊd] 1 n [something carried] chargement m, charge f. ‖ [large amount]: ~**s of**, **a ~ of** inf des tas de, plein de; **a ~ of rubbish** inf de la foutaise. 2 vt [gen & COMPUT] charger; [video recorder] mettre une vidéo-cassette dans; **to ~ sb/sthg with** charger qqn/qqch de. ○ **load up** vt sep & vi charger.

loaded ['ləʊdɪd] adj [question] insidieux(ieuse). ‖ inf [rich] plein(e) aux as.

loading bay ['ləʊdɪŋ-] *n* aire *f* de chargement.

loaf [ləʊf] (*pl* **loaves**) *n*: **a ~ (of bread)** un pain.

loafer ['ləʊfər] *n* [shoe] mocassin *m*.

loan [ləʊn] **1** *n* prêt *m*; **on ~** prêté(e). **2** *rt* prêter; **to ~ sthg to sb, to ~ sb sthg** prêter qqch à qqn.

loath [ləʊθ] *adj*: **to be ~ to do sthg** ne pas vouloir faire qqch, hésiter à faire qqch.

loathe [ləʊð] *rt* détester; **to ~ doing sthg** avoir horreur de OR détester faire qqch.

loaves [ləʊvz] *pl* → **loaf**.

lob [lɒb] **1** *n* TENNIS lob *m*. **2** *rt* [throw] lancer. || TENNIS: **to ~ a ball** lober, faire un lob.

lobby ['lɒbɪ] **1** *n* [of hotel] hall *m*. || [pressure group] lobby *m*, groupe *m* de pression. **2** *rt* faire pression sur.

lobe [ləʊb] *n* lobe *m*.

lobster ['lɒbstər] *n* homard *m*.

local ['ləʊkl] **1** *adj* local(e). **2** *n inf* [person]: **the ~s** les gens *mpl* du coin OR du pays.

local call *n* communication *f* urbaine.

local government *n* administration *f* municipale.

locality [ləʊ'kælətɪ] *n* endroit *m*.

locally ['ləʊkəlɪ] *adr* [on local basis] localement. || [nearby] dans les environs, à proximité.

locate [*Br* ləʊ'keɪt, *Am* 'ləʊkeɪt] *rt* [find - position] trouver, repérer; [- source, problem] localiser. || [situate - business, factory] implanter, établir; **to be ~d** être situé.

location [ləʊ'keɪʃn] *n* [place] emplacement *m*. || CINEMA: **on ~** en extérieur.

lock [lɒk] **1** *n* [of door etc] serrure *f*. || [on canal] écluse *f*. || [of hair] mèche *f*. **2** *rt* [door, car, drawer] fermer à clef; [bicycle] cadenasser. || [immobilize] bloquer. **3** *ri* [door, suitcase] fermer à clef. || [become immobilized] se bloquer. ○ **lock in** *rt sep* enfermer (à clef). ○ **lock out** *rt sep* [accidentally] enfermer dehors, laisser dehors; **to ~ o.s. out** s'enfermer dehors. || [deliberately] empêcher d'entrer, mettre à la porte. ○ **lock up** *rt sep* [person - in prison] mettre en prison OR sous les verrous; [- in asylum] enfermer; [house] fermer à clef; [valuables] enfermer, mettre sous clef.

locker ['lɒkər] *n* casier *m*.

locker room *n Am* vestiaire *m*.

locket ['lɒkɪt] *n* médaillon *m*.

locksmith ['lɒksmɪθ] *n* serrurier *m*.

locomotive [,ləʊkə'məʊtɪv] *n* locomotive *f*.

locust ['ləʊkəst] *n* sauterelle *f*, locuste *f*.

lodge [lɒdʒ] **1** *n* [of caretaker, freemasons] loge *f*. || [of manor house] pavillon *m* (de gardien). || [for hunting] pavillon *m* de chasse. **2** *ri* [stay]: **to ~ with sb** loger chez qqn. || [become stuck] se loger, se coincer. || *fig* [in mind] s'enraciner, s'ancrer. **3** *rt* [complaint] déposer; **to ~ an appeal** interjeter OR faire appel.

lodger ['lɒdʒər] *n* locataire *mf*.

lodgings *npl* chambre *f* meublée.

loft [lɒft] *n* grenier *m*.

log [lɒg] **1** *n* [of wood] bûche *f*. || [of ship] journal *m* de bord; [of plane] carnet *m* de vol. **2** *rt* consigner, enregistrer.

logbook ['lɒgbʊk] *n* [of ship] journal *m* de bord; [of plane] carnet *m* de vol. || [of car] ≃ carte *f* grise.

loggerheads ['lɒgəhedz] *n*: **at ~** en désaccord.

logic ['lɒdʒɪk] *n* logique *f*.

logical ['lɒdʒɪkl] *adj* logique.

logistics [lə'dʒɪstɪks] **1** *n* (*U*) MIL logistique *f*. **2** *npl fig* organisation *f*.

logo ['ləʊgəʊ] (*pl* **-s**) *n* logo *m*.

loin [lɔɪn] *n* filet *m*.

loiter ['lɔɪtər] *ri* traîner.

loll [lɒl] *ri* [sit, lie about] se prélasser. || [hang down - head, tongue] pendre.

lollipop ['lɒlɪpɒp] *n* sucette *f*.

lolly ['lɒlɪ] *n inf* [lollipop] sucette *f*.

London ['lʌndən] *n* Londres.

Londoner ['lʌndənər] *n* Londonien *m*, -ienne *f*.

lone [ləʊn] *adj* solitaire.

loneliness ['ləʊnlɪnɪs] *n* [of person] solitude *f*; [of place] isolement *m*.

lonely ['ləʊnlɪ] *adj* [person] solitaire, seul(e). || [childhood] solitaire. || [place] isolé(e).

loner ['ləʊnər] *n* solitaire *mf*.

lonesome ['ləʊnsəm] *adj Am inf* [person] solitaire, seul(e). || [place] isolé(e).

long [lɒŋ] **1** *adj* long (longue); **two days/years ~** de deux jours/ans, qui dure deux jours/ans; **10 metres/miles ~** long de 10 mètres/miles, de 10 mètres/miles (de long). **2** *adr* longtemps; **how ~ will it take?** combien de temps cela va-t-il prendre?; **how ~ will you be?** tu en as pour combien de temps?; **I can't wait any ~er** je ne peux pas attendre plus longtemps; **so ~!** *inf* au revoir!, salut!;

before ~ sous peu. 3 *vt*: to ~ to do sthg avoir très envie de faire qqch. ○ **as long as, so long as** *conj* tant que. ○ **long for** *vt fus* [peace and quiet] désirer ardemment; [holidays] attendre avec impatience.

long-distance call *n* communication *f* interurbaine.

longhand ['lɒŋhænd] *n* écriture *f* normale.

long-haul *adj* long-courrier.

longing ['lɒŋɪŋ] *n* [desire] envie *f*, convoitise *f*; **a ~ for** un grand désir ᴏʀ une grande envie de. || [nostalgia] nostalgie *f*, regret *m*.

longitude ['lɒndʒɪtjuːd] *n* longitude *f*.

long jump *n* saut *m* en longueur.

long-life *adj* [milk] longue conservation (*inv*); [battery] longue durée (*inv*).

long-range *adj* [missile, bomber] à longue portée. || [plan, forecast] à long terme.

long shot *n* [guess] coup *m* à tenter (*sans grand espoir de succès*).

longsighted [,lɒŋ'saɪtɪd] *adj* presbyte.

long-standing *adj* de longue date.

longsuffering [,lɒŋ'sʌfərɪŋ] *adj* [person] à la patience infinie.

long term *n*: **in the ~** à long terme.

long wave *n* (*U*) grandes ondes *fpl*.

longwinded [,lɒŋ'wɪndɪd] *adj* [person] prolixe, verbeux(euse); [speech] interminable, qui n'en finit pas.

look [lʊk] 1 *n* [with eyes] regard *m*; **to take** ᴏʀ **have a ~ (at sthg)** regarder (qqch), jeter un coup d'œil (à qqch); **to give sb a ~** jeter un regard à qqn, regarder qqn de travers. || [search]: **to have a ~ (for sthg)** chercher (qqch). || [appearance] aspect *m*, air *m*; **by the ~ ᴏʀ ~s of it, by the ~ ᴏʀ ~s of things** vraisemblablement, selon toute probabilité. 2 *vi* [with eyes] regarder. || [search] chercher. || [building, window]: **to ~ (out) onto** donner sur. || [seem] avoir l'air, sembler; **it ~s like rain ᴏʀ as if it will rain** on dirait qu'il va pleuvoir; **she ~s like her mother** elle ressemble à sa mère. ○ **looks** *npl* [attractiveness] beauté *f*. ○ **look after** *vt fus* s'occuper de. ○ **look at** *vt fus* [see, glance at] regarder; [examine] examiner. || [judge] considérer. ○ **look down on** *vt fus* [condescend to] mépriser. ○ **look for** *vt fus* chercher. ○ **look forward to** *vt fus* attendre avec impatience. ○ **look into** *vt fus* examiner, étudier. ○ **look out** *vi* prendre garde, faire attention; **~ out!** attention! ○ **look out for** *vt fus* [person] guetter; [new book] être à l'affût de, essayer de repérer. ○ **look round** 1 *vt fus* [house, shop, town] faire le tour de. 2 *vi* [turn] se retourner. || [browse] regarder. ○ **look up** 1 *vt sep* [in book] chercher. || [visit - person] aller ᴏʀ passer voir. 2 *vi* [improve - business] reprendre; **things are ~ing up** ça va mieux, la situation s'améliore. ○ **look up to** *vt fus* admirer.

lookout ['lʊkaʊt] *n* [place] poste *m* de guet. || [person] guetteur *m*. || [search]: **to be on the ~ for** être à la recherche de.

loom [luːm] 1 *n* métier *m* à tisser. 2 *vi* [building, person] se dresser; *fig* [date, threat] être imminent(e). ○ **loom up** *vi* surgir.

loony ['luːni] *inf* 1 *adj* cinglé(e), timbré(e). 2 *n* cinglé *m*, -e *f*, fou *m*, folle *f*.

loop [luːp] *n* [gen & ᴄᴏᴍᴘᴜᴛ] boucle *f*. || [contraceptive] stérilet *m*.

loophole ['luːphəʊl] *n* faille *f*, échappatoire *f*.

loose [luːs] *adj* [not firm - joint] desserré(e); [- handle, post] branlant(e); [- tooth] qui bouge ᴏʀ branle; [- knot] défait(e). || [unpackaged - sweets, nails] en vrac, au poids. || [clothes] ample, large. || [not restrained - hair] dénoué(e); [- animal] en liberté, détaché(e). || *pej & dated* [woman] facile; [living] dissolu(e). || [inexact - translation] approximatif(ive).

loose change *n* petite ᴏʀ menue monnaie *f*.

loose end *n*: **to be at a ~** *Br*, **to be at ~s** *Am* être désœuvré, n'avoir rien à faire.

loosely ['luːslɪ] *adv* [not firmly] sans serrer. || [inexactly] approximativement.

loosen ['luːsn] *vt* desserrer, défaire. ○ **loosen up** *vi* [before game, race] s'échauffer. || *inf* [relax] se détendre.

loot [luːt] 1 *n* butin *m*. 2 *vt* piller.

looting ['luːtɪŋ] *n* pillage *m*.

lop [lɒp] *vt* élaguer, émonder. ○ **lop off** *vt sep* couper.

lop-sided [-'saɪdɪd] *adj* [table] bancal(e), boiteux(euse); [picture] de travers.

lord [lɔːd] *n* seigneur *m*. ○ **Lord** *n* ʀᴇ-ʟɪɢ: **the Lord** [God] le Seigneur. || [in titles] Lord *m*; [as form of address]: **my Lord** Monsieur le duc/comte *etc*.

Lordship ['lɔːdʃɪp] *n*: **your/his ~** Monsieur le duc/comte *etc*.

lore [lɔːr] *n* (*U*) traditions *fpl*.

lose [luːz] (*pt & pp* lost) **1** *vt* [gen] perdre; **to ~ sight of** *lit & fig* perdre de vue; **to ~ one's way** se perdre, perdre son chemin. || [subj: clock, watch] retarder de; **to ~ time** retarder. || [pursuers] semer. **2** *vi* perdre. ○ **lose out** *vi* être perdant(e).

loser [luːzər] *n* [gen] perdant *m*, -e *f*. || *inf pej* [unsuccessful person] raté *m*, -e *f*.

loss [lɒs] *n* [gen] perte *f*. || *phr*: **to be at a ~** être perplexe, être embarrassé(e).

lost [lɒst] **1** *pt & pp* → **lose**. **2** *adj* [gen] perdu(e); **to get ~** se perdre; **get ~!** *inf* fous/foutez le camp!

lost-and-found office *n Am* bureau *m* des objets trouvés.

lot [lɒt] *n* [large amount]: **a ~ (of)**, **~s (of)** beaucoup (de); [entire amount]: **the ~** le tout. || [at auction] lot *m*. || [destiny] sort *m*. || *Am* [of land] terrain *m*; [car park] parking *m*. || *phr*: **to draw ~s** tirer au sort. ○ **a lot** *adv* beaucoup.

lotion [ləʊʃn] *n* lotion *f*.

lottery [lɒtəri] *n lit & fig* loterie *f*.

loud [laʊd] **1** *adj* [not quiet, noisy - gen] fort(e); [- person] bruyant(e). || [colour, clothes] voyant(e). **2** *adv* fort; **out ~** tout haut.

loudly [laʊdli] *adv* [noisily] fort. || [gaudily] de façon voyante.

loudspeaker [ˌlaʊdˈspiːkər] *n* haut-parleur *m*.

lounge [laʊndʒ] **1** *n* [in house] salon *m*. || [in airport] hall *m*, salle *f*. **2** *vi* se prélasser.

louse [laʊs] (*pl sense 1* lice, *pl sense 2* -s) *n* [insect] pou *m*. || *inf pej* [person] salaud *m*.

lousy [laʊzi] *adj inf* minable, nul(le); [weather] pourri(e).

lout [laʊt] *n* rustre *m*.

louvre *Br*, **louver** *Am* [luːvər] *n* persienne *f*.

lovable [lʌvəbl] *adj* adorable.

love [lʌv] **1** *n* [gen] amour *m*; **to be in ~** être amoureux(euse); **to fall in ~** tomber amoureux(euse); **to make ~** faire l'amour; **give her my ~** embrasse-la pour moi; **~ from** [at end of letter] affectueusement, grosses bises. || *inf* [form of address] mon chéri (ma chérie). || TENNIS zéro *m*. **2** *vt* aimer; **to ~ to do sthg OR doing sthg** aimer OR adorer faire qqch.

love affair *n* liaison *f*.

love life *n* vie *f* amoureuse.

lovely [lʌvli] *adj* [beautiful] très joli(e). || [pleasant] très agréable, excellent(e).

lover [lʌvər] *n* [sexual partner] amant *m*, -e *f*. || [enthusiast] passionné *m*, -e *f*, amoureux *m*, -euse *f*.

loving [lʌvɪŋ] *adj* [person, relationship] affectueux(euse); [care] tendre.

low [ləʊ] **1** *adj* [not high - gen] bas (basse); [- wall, building] peu élevé(e); [- standard, quality] mauvais(e); [- intelligence] faible; [- neckline] décolleté(e); [little remaining] presque épuisé(e). || [not loud - voice] bas (basse); [- whisper, moan] faible. || [depressed] déprimé(e). **2** *adv* [not high] bas. || [not loudly - speak] à voix basse; [- whisper] faiblement. **3** *n* [low point] niveau *m* OR point *m* bas. || METEOR dépression *f*.

low-calorie *adj* à basses calories.

low-cut *adj* décolleté(e).

lower [ləʊər] **1** *adj* inférieur(e). **2** *vt* [gen] baisser; [flag] abaisser. || [reduce - price, level] baisser; [- age of consent] abaisser; [- resistance] diminuer.

low-fat *adj* [yoghurt, crisps] allégé(e); [milk] demi-écrémé(e).

low-key *adj* discret(ète).

lowly [ləʊli] *adj* modeste, humble.

low-lying *adj* bas (basse).

loyal [lɔɪəl] *adj* loyal(e).

loyalty [lɔɪəlti] *n* loyauté *f*.

lozenge [lɒzɪndʒ] *n* [tablet] pastille *f*. || [shape] losange *m*.

LP (*abbr of* **long-playing record**) *n* 33 tours *m*.

Ltd, **ltd** (*abbr of* **limited**) ≃ SARL; **Smith and Sons, ~** ≃ Smith & Fils, SARL.

lubricant [luːbrɪkənt] *n* lubrifiant *m*.

lubricate [luːbrɪkeɪt] *vt* lubrifier.

lucid [luːsɪd] *adj* lucide.

luck [lʌk] *n* chance *f*; **good ~ chance**; **good ~!** bonne chance!; **bad ~** malchance *f*; **bad OR hard ~!** pas de chance!; **to be in ~** avoir de la chance; **with (any) ~** avec un peu de chance.

luckily [lʌkɪli] *adv* heureusement.

lucky [lʌki] *adj* [fortunate - person] qui a de la chance; [- event] heureux(euse). || [bringing good luck] porte-bonheur (*inv*).

lucrative [luːkrətɪv] *adj* lucratif(ive).

ludicrous [luːdɪkrəs] *adj* ridicule.

lug [lʌg] *vt inf* traîner.

lukewarm [luːkwɔːm] *adj lit & fig* tiède.

lull [lʌl] **1** *n*: **~ (in)** [storm] accalmie *f* (de); [fighting, conversation] arrêt *m* (de). **2** *vt*: **to ~ sb to sleep** endormir qqn en le berçant; **to ~ sb into a false sense of security** endormir les soupçons de qqn.

lullaby ['lʌləbaɪ] *n* berceuse *f*.

lumber ['lʌmbər] *n* (*U*) *Am* [timber] bois *m* de charpente.

lumberjack ['lʌmbədʒæk] *n* bûcheron *m*, -onne *f*.

luminous ['lu:mɪnəs] *adj* [dial] lumineux(euse); [paint, armband] phosphorescent(e).

lump [lʌmp] **1** *n* [gen] morceau *m*; [of earth, clay] motte *f*; [in sauce] grumeau *m*. ‖ [on body] grosseur *f*. **2** *vt*: **to ~ sthg together** réunir qqch; **to ~ it** *inf* faire avec, s'en accommoder.

lump sum *n* somme *f* globale.

lunacy ['lu:nəsɪ] *n* folie *f*.

lunar ['lu:nər] *adj* lunaire.

lunatic ['lu:nətɪk] **1** *adj pej* dément(e), démentiel(ielle). **2** *n pej* [fool] fou *m*, folle *f*. ‖ [insane person] fou *m*, folle *f*, aliéné *m*, -e *f*.

lunch [lʌntʃ] **1** *n* déjeuner *m*. **2** *vi* déjeuner.

luncheon meat *n* sorte de saucisson.

lunch hour *n* pause *f* de midi.

lunchtime ['lʌntʃtaɪm] *n* heure *f* du déjeuner.

lung [lʌŋ] *n* poumon *m*.

lunge [lʌndʒ] *vi* faire un brusque mouvement (du bras) en avant; **to ~ at sb** s'élancer sur qqn.

lurch [lɜːtʃ] **1** *n* [of person] écart *m* brusque; [of car] embardée *f*; **to leave sb in the ~** laisser qqn dans le pétrin. **2** *vi* [person] tituber; [car] faire une embardée.

lure [ljʊər] **1** *n* charme *m* trompeur. **2** *vt* attirer OR persuader par la ruse.

lurid ['ljʊərɪd] *adj* [outfit] aux couleurs criardes. ‖ [story, details] affreux(euse).

lurk [lɜːk] *vi* [person] se cacher, se dissimuler. ‖ [memory, danger, fear] subsister.

luscious ['lʌʃəs] *adj* [delicious] succulent(e). ‖ *fig* [woman] appétissant(e).

lush [lʌʃ] *adj* [luxuriant] luxuriant(e). ‖ [rich] luxueux(euse).

lust [lʌst] *n* [sexual desire] désir *m*. ‖ *fig*: **~ for sthg** soif *f* de qqch. ○ **lust after**, **lust for** *vt fus* [wealth, power etc] être assoiffé(e) de. ‖ [person] désirer.

Luxembourg ['lʌksəmbɜːg] *n* [country] Luxembourg *m*. ‖ [city] Luxembourg.

luxurious [lʌg'ʒʊərɪəs] *adj* [expensive] luxueux(euse). ‖ [pleasurable] voluptueux(euse).

luxury ['lʌkʃərɪ] **1** *n* luxe *m*. **2** *comp* de luxe.

LW (*abbr of* **long wave**) GO.

Lycra® ['laɪkrə] *n* Lycra® *m*.

lying ['laɪɪŋ] **1** *adj* [person] menteur(euse). **2** *n* (*U*) mensonges *mpl*.

lynch [lɪntʃ] *vt* lyncher.

lyrical ['lɪrɪkl] *adj* lyrique.

lyrics ['lɪrɪks] *npl* paroles *fpl*.

m¹ (*pl* **m's** OR **ms**), **M** (*pl* **M's** OR **Ms**) [em] *n* [letter] m *m inv*, M *m inv*.

m² (*abbr of* **metre**) m. ‖ (*abbr of* **million**) M. ‖ *abbr of* **mile**.

MA *n abbr of* **Master of Arts**.

macaroni [,mækə'rəʊnɪ] *n* (*U*) macaronis *mpl*.

mace [meɪs] *n* [ornamental rod] masse *f*. ‖ [spice] macis *m*.

machine [mə'ʃiːn] **1** *n* lit & fig machine *f*. **2** *vt* SEWING coudre à la machine. ‖ TECH usiner.

machinegun [mə'ʃiːngʌn] *n* mitrailleuse *f*.

machine language *n* COMPUT langage *m* machine.

machinery [mə'ʃiːnərɪ] *n* (*U*) machines *fpl*; *fig* mécanisme *m*.

macho ['mætʃəʊ] *adj* macho (*inv*).

mackerel ['mækrəl] (*pl inv* OR **-s**) *n* maquereau *m*.

mad [mæd] *adj* [insane] fou (folle); **to go ~** devenir fou. ‖ [foolish] insensé(e). ‖ [furious] furieux(ieuse). ‖ [hectic - rush, pace] fou (folle). ‖ [very enthusiastic]: **to be ~ about sb/sthg** être fou (folle) de qqn/qqch.

Madagascar [,mædə'gæskər] *n* Madagascar *m*.

madam ['mædəm] *n* madame *f*.

madcap ['mædkæp] *adj* risqué(e), insensé(e).

madden ['mædn] *vt* exaspérer.

made [meɪd] *pt* & *pp* → **make**.

made-to-measure *adj* fait(e) sur mesure.

made-up *adj* [with make-up] maquillé(e). || [invented] fabriqué(e).

madly ['mædlɪ] *adv* [frantically] comme un fou; ~ **in love** follement amoureux.

madman ['mædmən] (*pl* -**men** [-mən]) *n* fou *m*.

madness ['mædnɪs] *n lit & fig* folie *f*, démence *f*.

Madrid [mə'drɪd] *n* Madrid.

Mafia ['mæfɪə] *n*: **the** ~ la Mafia.

magazine [,mægə'ziːn] *n* PRESS revue *f*, magazine *m*; RADIO & TV magazine. || [of gun] magasin *m*.

maggot ['mægət] *n* ver *m*, asticot *m*.

magic ['mædʒɪk] **1** *adj* magique. **2** *n* magie *f*.

magical ['mædʒɪkl] *adj* magique.

magician [mə'dʒɪʃn] *n* magicien *m*.

magistrate ['mædʒɪstreɪt] *n* magistrat *m*, juge *m*.

magnanimous [mæg'nænɪməs] *adj* magnanime.

magnate ['mægneɪt] *n* magnat *m*.

magnesium [mæg'niːzɪəm] *n* magnésium *m*.

magnet ['mægnɪt] *n* aimant *m*.

magnetic [mæg'netɪk] *adj lit & fig* magnétique.

magnetic tape *n* bande *f* magnétique.

magnificent [mæg'nɪfɪsənt] *adj* magnifique, superbe.

magnify ['mægnɪfaɪ] *vt* [in vision] grossir; [sound] amplifier; *fig* exagérer.

magnifying glass ['mægnɪfaɪɪŋ-] *n* loupe *f*.

magnitude ['mægnɪtjuːd] *n* envergure *f*, ampleur *f*.

magpie ['mægpaɪ] *n* pie *f*.

mahogany [mə'hɒgənɪ] *n* acajou *m*.

maid [meɪd] *n* [servant] domestique *f*.

maiden ['meɪdn] **1** *adj* [flight, voyage] premier(ère). **2** *n literary* jeune fille *f*.

maiden aunt *n* tante *f* célibataire.

maiden name *n* nom *m* de jeune fille.

mail [meɪl] **1** *n* [letters, parcels] courrier *m*. || [system] poste *f*. **2** *vt* poster.

mailbox ['meɪlbɒks] *n Am* boîte *f* à OR aux lettres.

mailing list ['meɪlɪŋ-] *n* liste *f* d'adresses.

mailman ['meɪlmən] (*pl* -**men** [-mən]) *n Am* facteur *m*.

mail order *n* vente *f* par correspondance.

mailshot ['meɪlʃɒt] *n* publipostage *m*.

maim [meɪm] *vt* estropier.

main [meɪn] **1** *adj* principal(e). **2** *n* [pipe] conduite *f*. ○ **mains** *npl*: **the** ~**s** secteur. ○ **in the main** *adv* dans l'ensemble.

main course *n* plat *m* principal.

mainframe (computer) ['meɪnfreɪm-] *n* ordinateur *m* central.

mainland ['meɪnlənd] **1** *adj* continental(e). **2** *n*: **the** ~ le continent.

mainly ['meɪnlɪ] *adv* principalement.

main road *n* route *f* à grande circulation.

mainstay ['meɪnsteɪ] *n* pilier *m*, élément *m* principal.

mainstream ['meɪnstriːm] **1** *adj* dominant(e). **2** *n*: **the** ~ la tendance générale.

maintain [meɪn'teɪn] *vt* [preserve, keep constant] maintenir. || [provide for, look after] entretenir. || [assert]: **to** ~ **(that)** ... maintenir que ..., soutenir que ....

maintenance ['meɪntənəns] *n* [of public order] maintien *m*. || [care] entretien *m*, maintenance *f*. || JUR pension *f* alimentaire.

maize [meɪz] *n* maïs *m*.

majestic [mə'dʒestɪk] *adj* majestueux(euse).

majesty ['mædʒəstɪ] *n* [grandeur] majesté *f*. ○ **Majesty** *n*: **His/Her Majesty** Sa Majesté le roi/la reine.

major ['meɪdʒər] **1** *adj* [important] majeur(e). || [main] principal(e). || MUS majeur(e). **2** *n* [in army] ≃ chef *m* de bataillon; [in air force] commandant *m*. || UNIV [subject] matière *f*.

Majorca [mə'dʒɔːkə, mə'jɔːkə] *n* Majorque *f*.

majority [mə'dʒɒrətɪ] *n* majorité *f*; **in a** OR **the** ~ dans la majorité.

make [meɪk] (*pt & pp* **made**) **1** *vt* [gen-produce] faire; [- manufacture] faire, fabriquer; **to** ~ **a meal** préparer un repas; **to** ~ **a film** tourner OR réaliser un film. || [perform an action] faire; **to** ~ **a decision** prendre une décision; **to** ~ **a mistake** faire une erreur, se tromper. || [cause to be] rendre; **to** ~ **sb happy/sad** rendre qqn heureux/triste. || [force, cause to do]: **to** ~ **sb do sthg** faire faire qqch à qqn, obliger qqn à faire qqch; **to** ~ **sb laugh** faire rire qqn. || [be constructed]: **to be made of** être en. || [add up to] faire; **2 and 2** ~ **4** 2 et 2 font 4. || [calculate]: **I** ~ **it 50** d'après moi il y en a 50, j'en ai compté 50; **what time do you** ~ **it?** quelle heure as-tu? || [earn] gagner, se faire; **to** ~ **a profit** faire des bénéfices; **to** ~ **a loss** essuyer des pertes. ‖ [reach] arriver à. ‖ [gain - friend, enemy] se faire; **to ~ friends (with sb)** se lier d'amitié (avec qqn). ‖ *phr*: **to ~ it** [reach in time] arriver à temps; [be a success] réussir, arriver; [be able to attend] se libérer, pouvoir venir; **to ~ do with** se contenter de. 2 *n* [brand] marque *f*. ○ **make for** *vt fus* [move towards] se diriger vers. ‖ [contribute to, be conducive to] rendre probable, favoriser. ○ **make of** *vt sep* [understand] comprendre. ‖ [have opinion of] penser de. ○ **make out** 1 *vt sep* [see, hear] discerner; [understand] comprendre. ‖ [fill out - cheque] libeller; [- bill, receipt] faire. 2 *vt fus* [pretend, claim]: **to ~ out (that) ...** prétendre que .... ○ **make up** 1 *vt sep* [compose, constitute] composer, constituer. ‖ [story, excuse] inventer. ‖ [apply cosmetics to] maquiller. ‖ [prepare - gen] faire; [- prescription] préparer, exécuter. ‖ [make complete] compléter. 2 *vi* [become friends again] se réconcilier. ○ **make up for** *vt fus* compenser. ○ **make up to** *vt sep*: **to ~ it up to sb (for sthg)** se racheter auprès de qqn (pour qqch).

make-believe *n*: it's all ~ c'est (de la) pure fantaisie.

maker ['meɪkə'] *n* [of product] fabricant *m*, -e *f*; [of film] réalisateur *m*, -trice *f*.

makeshift ['meɪkʃɪft] *adj* de fortune.

make-up *n* [cosmetics] maquillage *m*; ~ **remover** démaquillant *m*. ‖ [person's character] caractère *m*. ‖ [of team, group, object] constitution *f*.

making ['meɪkɪŋ] *n* fabrication *f*; **his problems are of his own ~** ses problèmes sont de sa faute; **in the ~** en formation; **to have the ~s of** avoir l'étoffe de.

malaria [mə'leərɪə] *n* malaria *f*.

Malaysia [mə'leɪzɪə] *n* Malaysia *f*.

male [meɪl] 1 *adj* [gen] mâle; [sex] masculin(e). 2 *n* mâle *m*.

male nurse *n* infirmier *m*.

malevolent [mə'levələnt] *adj* malveillant(e).

malfunction [mæl'fʌŋkʃn] 1 *n* mauvais fonctionnement *m*. 2 *vi* mal fonctionner.

malice ['mælɪs] *n* méchanceté *f*.

malicious [mə'lɪʃəs] *adj* malveillant(e).

malign [mə'laɪn] 1 *adj* pernicieux (ieuse). 2 *vt* calomnier.

malignant [mə'lɪgnənt] *adj* MED malin(igne).

mall [mɔːl] *n*: **(shopping) ~** centre *m* commercial.

mallet ['mælɪt] *n* maillet *m*.

malnutrition [,mælnju:'trɪʃn] *n* malnutrition *f*.

malpractice [,mæl'præktɪs] *n* (*U*) JUR faute *f* professionnelle.

malt [mɔːlt] *n* malt *m*.

mammal ['mæml] *n* mammifère *m*.

mammoth ['mæməθ] 1 *adj* gigantesque. 2 *n* mammouth *m*.

man [mæn] (*pl* **men** [men]) 1 *n* homme *m*; **the ~ in the street** l'homme de la rue. ‖ [as form of address] mon vieux. 2 *vt* [ship, spaceship] fournir du personnel pour; [telephone] répondre au; [switchboard] assurer le service de.

manage ['mænɪdʒ] 1 *vi* [cope] se débrouiller, y arriver. ‖ [survive, get by] s'en sortir. 2 *vt* [succeed]: **to ~ to do sthg** arriver à faire qqch. ‖ [be responsible for, control] gérer.

manageable ['mænɪdʒəbl] *adj* maniable.

management ['mænɪdʒmənt] *n* [control, running] gestion *f*. ‖ [people in control] direction *f*.

manager ['mænɪdʒə'] *n* [of organization] directeur *m*, -trice *f*; [of shop, restaurant, hotel] gérant *m*, -e *f*; [of football team, pop star] manager *m*.

managerial [,mænɪ'dʒɪərɪəl] *adj* directorial(e).

managing director ['mænɪdʒɪŋ-] *n* directeur général *m*, directrice générale *f*.

mandarin ['mændərɪn] *n* [fruit] mandarine *f*.

mandate ['mændeɪt] *n* mandat *m*.

mandatory ['mændətrɪ] *adj* obligatoire.

mane [meɪn] *n* crinière *f*.

maneuver *Am* = manoeuvre.

manfully ['mænfʊlɪ] *adv* courageusement, vaillamment.

mangle ['mæŋgl] *vt* mutiler, déchirer.

mango ['mæŋgəʊ] (*pl* **-es** OR **-s**) *n* mangue *f*.

mangy ['meɪndʒɪ] *adj* galeux(euse).

manhandle ['mæn,hændl] *vt* malmener.

manhole ['mænhəʊl] *n* regard *m*, trou *m* d'homme.

manhood ['mænhʊd] *n*: **to reach ~** devenir un homme.

mania ['meɪnjə] *n*: ~ **(for)** manie *f* (de).

maniac ['meɪnɪæk] *n* fou *m*, folle *f*; **a sex ~** un obsédé sexuel (une obsédée sexuelle).

manic ['mænɪk] *adj fig* [person] surexcité(e); [behaviour] de fou.

manicure ['mænɪˌkjʊəʳ] *n* manucure *f*.

manifesto [ˌmænɪ'festəʊ] (*pl* -**s** OR -**es**) *n* manifeste *m*.

manipulate [mə'nɪpjʊleɪt] *rt lit* & *fig* manipuler.

manipulative [mə'nɪpjʊlətɪv] *adj* [person] rusé(e); [behaviour] habile, subtil(e).

mankind [mæn'kaɪnd] *n* humanité *f*, genre *m* humain.

manly ['mænlɪ] *adj* viril(e).

man-made *adj* [fabric, fibre] synthétique; [environment] artificiel(ielle); [problem] causé (causée) par l'homme.

manner ['mænəʳ] *n* [method] manière *f*, façon *f*. ‖ [attitude] attitude *f*, comportement *m*. ○ **manners** *npl* manières *fpl*.

mannerism ['mænərɪzm] *n* tic *m*, manie *f*.

manoeuvre *Br*, **maneuver** *Am* [mə'nuːvəʳ] **1** *n* manœuvre *f*. **2** *rt* & *ri* manœuvrer.

manor ['mænəʳ] *n* manoir *m*.

manpower ['mænˌpaʊəʳ] *n* main-d'œuvre *f*.

mansion ['mænʃn] *n* château *m*.

manslaughter ['mænˌslɔːtəʳ] *n* homicide *m* involontaire.

mantelpiece ['mæntlpiːs] *n* (dessus *m* de) cheminée *f*.

manual ['mænjʊəl] **1** *adj* manuel(elle). **2** *n* manuel *m*.

manual worker *n* travailleur manuel *m*, travailleuse manuelle *f*.

manufacture [ˌmænjʊ'fæktʃəʳ] **1** *n* fabrication *f*; [of cars] construction *f*. **2** *rt* fabriquer; [cars] construire.

manufacturer [ˌmænjʊ'fæktʃərəʳ] *n* fabricant *m*; [of cars] constructeur *m*.

manure [mə'njʊəʳ] *n* fumier *m*.

manuscript ['mænjʊskrɪpt] *n* manuscrit *m*.

many ['menɪ] (*compar* **more**, *superl* **most**) **1** *adj* beaucoup de; **how ~** ...? combien de ...?; **too ~** trop de; **as ~ ... as** autant de ... que; **so ~** autant de; **a good** OR **great ~** un grand nombre de. **2** *pron* [a lot, plenty] beaucoup.

map [mæp] *n* carte *f*. ○ **map out** *rt sep* [plan] élaborer; [timetable] établir; [task] définir.

maple ['meɪpl] *n* érable *m*.

mar [mɑːʳ] *rt* gâter, gâcher.

marathon ['mærəθn] *n* marathon *m*.

marble ['mɑːbl] *n* [stone] marbre *m*. ‖ [for game] bille *f*.

march [mɑːtʃ] **1** *n* marche *f*. **2** *vi* [soldiers etc] marcher au pas. ‖ [demonstrators] manifester, faire une marche de protestation. ‖ [quickly]: **to ~ up to sb** s'approcher de qqn d'un pas décidé.

March [mɑːtʃ] *n* mars *m*; *see also* **September**.

marcher ['mɑːtʃəʳ] *n* [protester] marcheur *m*, -euse *f*.

mare [meəʳ] *n* jument *f*.

margarine [ˌmɑːdʒə'riːn] *n* margarine *f*.

margin ['mɑːdʒɪn] *n* [gen] marge *f*; **to win by a narrow ~** gagner de peu OR de justesse. ‖ [edge - of an area] bord *m*.

marginal ['mɑːdʒɪnl] *adj* [unimportant] marginal(e), secondaire.

marginally ['mɑːdʒɪnəlɪ] *adv* très peu.

marigold ['mærɪgəʊld] *n* souci *m*.

marihuana, marijuana [ˌmærɪ'wɑːnə] *n* marihuana *f*.

marine [mə'riːn] **1** *adj* marin(e). **2** *n* marine *m*.

marital ['mærɪtl] *adj* [sex, happiness] conjugal(e); [problems] matrimonial(e).

marital status *n* situation *f* de famille.

maritime ['mærɪtaɪm] *adj* maritime.

mark [mɑːk] **1** *n* [stain] tache *f*, marque *f*. ‖ [sign, written symbol] marque *f*. ‖ [in exam] note *f*, point *m*. ‖ [stage, level] barre *f*. ‖ [currency] mark *m*. **2** *rt* [gen] marquer. ‖ [stain] marquer, tacher. ‖ [exam, essay] noter, corriger. ○ **mark off** *rt sep* [cross off] cocher.

marked [mɑːkt] *adj* [change, difference] marqué(e); [improvement, deterioration] sensible.

marker ['mɑːkəʳ] *n* [sign] repère *m*.

marker pen *n* marqueur *m*.

market ['mɑːkɪt] **1** *n* marché *m*. **2** *rt* commercialiser.

market garden *n* jardin *m* maraîcher.

marketing ['mɑːkɪtɪŋ] *n* marketing *m*.

marketplace ['mɑːkɪtpleɪs] *n* [in a town] place *f* du marché. ‖ COMM marché *m*.

market research *n* étude *f* de marché.

market value *n* valeur *f* marchande.

marking ['mɑːkɪŋ] *n* SCH correction *f*. ○ **markings** *npl* [on animal, flower] taches *fpl*, marques *fpl*; [on road] signalisation *f* horizontale.

marksman ['mɑːksmən] (*pl* -**men** [-mən]) *n* tireur *m* d'élite.

marmalade ['mɑːməleɪd] *n* confiture *f* d'oranges amères.

maroon [mə'ruːn] *adj* bordeaux (*inv*).

marooned [mə'ru:nd] *adj* abandonné(e).

marquee [mɑː'kiː] *n* grande tente *f.*

marriage ['mærɪdʒ] *n* mariage *m.*

marriage certificate *n* acte *m* de mariage.

marriage guidance *n* conseil *m* conjugal.

married ['mærɪd] *adj* [person] marié(e); **to get ~** se marier. || [life] conjugal(e).

marrow ['mærəʊ] *n* [in bones] moelle *f.*

marry ['mærɪ] 1 *vt* [become spouse of] épouser, se marier avec. || [subj: priest, registrar] marier. 2 *vi* se marier.

Mars [mɑːz] *n* [planet] Mars *f.*

marsh [mɑːʃ] *n* marais *m*, marécage *m.*

marshal ['mɑːʃl] 1 *n* MIL maréchal *m.* || [steward] membre *m* du service d'ordre. || *Am* [law officer] officier *m* de police fédérale. 2 *vt lit & fig* rassembler.

martial arts [,mɑːʃl-] *npl* arts *mpl* martiaux.

martial law [,mɑːʃl-] *n* loi *f* martiale.

martyr ['mɑːtə*r*] *n* martyr *m*, -e *f.*

martyrdom ['mɑːtədəm] *n* martyre *m.*

marvel ['mɑːvl] 1 *n* merveille *f.* 2 *vi*: **to ~ (at)** s'émerveiller (de), s'étonner (de).

marvellous *Br*, **marvelous** *Am* ['mɑːvələs] *adj* merveilleux(euse).

Marxism ['mɑːksɪzm] *n* marxisme *m.*

Marxist ['mɑːksɪst] 1 *adj* marxiste. 2 *n* marxiste *mf.*

marzipan ['mɑːzɪpæn] *n* (*U*) pâte *f* d'amandes.

mascara [mæs'kɑːrə] *n* mascara *m.*

masculine ['mæskjʊlɪn] *adj* masculin(e).

mash [mæʃ] *vt* faire une purée de.

mashed potatoes [mæʃt-] *npl* purée *f* de pommes de terre.

mask [mɑːsk] *lit & fig* 1 *n* masque *m.* 2 *vt* masquer.

masochist ['mæsəkɪst] *n* masochiste *mf.*

mason ['meɪsn] *n* [stonemason] maçon *m.* || [freemason] franc-maçon *m.*

masonry ['meɪsnrɪ] *n* [stones] maçonnerie *f.*

masquerade [,mæskə'reɪd] *vi*: **to ~ as** se faire passer pour.

mass [mæs] 1 *n* [gen & PHYSICS] masse *f.* 2 *adj* [protest, meeting] en masse, en nombre; [unemployment, support] massif(ive). 3 *vi* se masser. ○ **Mass** *n* RELIG messe *f.* ○ **masses** *npl inf* [lots]: **~es (of)** des masses (de); [food] des tonnes (de). || [workers]: **the ~es** les masses *fpl.*

massacre ['mæsəkə*r*] 1 *n* massacre *m.* 2 *vt* massacrer.

massage [*Br* 'mæsɑːʒ, *Am* mə'sɑːʒ] 1 *n* massage *m.* 2 *vt* masser.

massive ['mæsɪv] *adj* massif(ive), énorme.

mass media *n* *or npl*: **the ~** les (mass) media *mpl.*

mast [mɑːst] *n* [on boat] mât *m.* || RADIO & TV pylône *m.*

master ['mɑːstə*r*] 1 *n* [gen] maître *m.* 2 *adj* maître. 3 *vt* maîtriser; [difficulty] surmonter, vaincre; [situation] se rendre maître de.

master key *n* passe *m*, passe-partout *m* *inv.*

masterly ['mɑːstəlɪ] *adj* magistral(e).

mastermind ['mɑːstəmaɪnd] 1 *n* cerveau *m.* 2 *vt* organiser, diriger.

Master of Arts (*pl* **Masters of Arts**) *n* [degree] maîtrise *f* ès lettres. || [person] titulaire *mf* d'une maîtrise ès lettres.

Master of Science (*pl* **Masters of Science**) *n* [degree] maîtrise *f* ès sciences. || [person] titulaire *mf* d'une maîtrise ès sciences.

masterpiece ['mɑːstəpiːs] *n* chef-d'œuvre *m.*

master's degree *n* ≃ maîtrise *f.*

mastery ['mɑːstərɪ] *n* maîtrise *f.*

mat [mæt] *n* [on floor] petit tapis *m*; [at door] paillasson *m.* || [on table] set *m* de table; [coaster] dessous *m* de verre.

match [mætʃ] 1 *n* [game] match *m.* || [for lighting] allumette *f.* || [equal]: **to be no ~ for sb** ne pas être de taille à lutter contre qqn. 2 *vt* [be the same as] correspondre à, s'accorder avec. || [pair off] faire correspondre. || [be equal with] égaler, rivaliser avec. 3 *vi* [be the same] correspondre. || [go together well] être assorti(e).

matchbox ['mætʃbɒks] *n* boîte *f* à allumettes.

matching ['mætʃɪŋ] *adj* assorti(e).

mate [meɪt] 1 *n inf* [friend] copain *m*, copine *f*, pote *m.* || [of female animal] mâle *m*; [of male animal] femelle *f.* || NAUT: (**first**) **~** second *m.* 2 *vi* s'accoupler.

material [mə'tɪərɪəl] 1 *adj* [goods, benefits, world] matériel(ielle). || [important] important(e), essentiel(ielle). 2 *n* [substance] matière *f*, substance *f*; [type of substance] matériau *m*, matière *f.* || [fabric] tissu *m*, étoffe *f*; [type of fabric] tissu. || (*U*) [information - for book, article etc] matériaux *mpl.* ○ **materials** *npl* matériaux *mpl.*

materialistic [mə,tɪərɪə'lɪstɪk] *adj* matérialiste.

materialize, -ise [mə'tɪərɪəlaɪz] *vi* [offer, threat] se concrétiser, se réaliser. || [person, object] apparaître.

maternal [mə'tɜːnl] *adj* maternel(elle).

maternity [mə'tɜːnətɪ] *n* maternité *f.*

maternity hospital *n* maternité *f.*

math *Am* = **maths.**

mathematical [,mæθə'mætɪkl] *adj* mathématique.

mathematics [,mæθə'mætɪks] *n* (*U*) mathématiques *fpl.*

maths *Br* [mæθs], **math** *Am* [mæθ] (*abbr of* **mathematics**) *inf n* (*U*) maths *fpl.*

matinée ['mætɪneɪ] *n* matinée *f.*

mating season ['meɪtɪŋ-] *n* saison *f* des amours.

matrices ['meɪtrɪsiːz] *pl* → **matrix.**

matriculation [mə,trɪkju'leɪʃn] *n* inscription *f.*

matrimony ['mætrɪmənɪ] *n* (*U*) mariage *m.*

matrix ['meɪtrɪks] (*pl* **matrices** OR **-es**) *n* [context, framework] contexte *m*, structure *f.* || MATH & TECH matrice *f.*

matron ['meɪtrən] *n* [in school] infirmière *f.*

matt *Br*, **matte** *Am* [mæt] *adj* mat(e).

matted ['mætɪd] *adj* emmêlé(e).

matter ['mætər] **1** *n* [question, situation] question *f*, affaire *f*; **that's another** OR **a different ~** c'est tout autre chose. c'est une autre histoire; **as a ~ of course** automatiquement; **to make ~s worse** aggraver la situation; **and to make ~s worse ...** pour tout arranger ...; **that's a ~ of opinion** c'est (une) affaire OR question d'opinion. || [trouble, cause of pain]: **there's something the ~ with my radio** il y a quelque chose qui cloche OR ne va pas dans ma radio; **what's the ~?** qu'est-ce qu'il y a?; **what's the ~ with him?** qu'est-ce qu'il a? || PHYSICS matière *f.* || (*U*) [material] matière *f*; **reading ~** choses *fpl* à lire. **2** *vi* [be important] importer, avoir de l'importance; **it doesn't ~** cela n'a pas d'importance. ○ **as a matter of fact** en fait, à vrai dire. ○ **for that matter** *adv* d'ailleurs. ○ **no matter** *adv*: **no ~ what** coûte que coûte. à tout prix; **no ~ how hard I try to explain ...** j'ai beau essayer de lui expliquer ....

Matterhorn ['mætəhɔːn] *n*: **the ~** le mont Cervin.

matter-of-fact *adj* terre-à-terre, neutre.

mattress ['mætrɪs] *n* matelas *m.*

mature [mə'tjʊər] **1** *adj* [person, attitude] mûr(e). || [cheese] fait(e); [wine] arrivé(e) à maturité. **2** *vi* [person] mûrir. || [cheese, wine] se faire.

maul [mɔːl] *vt* mutiler.

mauve [məʊv] **1** *adj* mauve. **2** *n* mauve *m.*

max. [mæks] (*abbr of* **maximum**) max.

maxim ['mæksɪm] (*pl* **-s**) *n* maxime *f.*

maximum ['mæksɪməm] (*pl* **maxima** ['mæksɪmə] OR **-s**) **1** *adj* maximum (*inr*). **2** *n* maximum *m.*

may [meɪ] *modal vb* [expressing possibility]: **it ~ rain** il se peut qu'il pleuve. il va peut-être pleuvoir; **be that as it ~** quoi qu'il en soit. || [can] pouvoir; **on a clear day the coast ~ be seen** on peut voir la côte par temps clair. || [asking permission]: **~ I come in?** puis-je entrer? || [as contrast]: **it ~ be expensive, but ...** c'est peut-être cher, mais .... || *fml* [expressing wish, hope]: **~ they be happy!** qu'ils soient heureux!; *see also* **might.**

May [meɪ] *n* mai *m*; *see also* **September.**

maybe ['meɪbiː] *adv* peut-être.

May Day *n* le Premier mai.

mayhem ['meɪhem] *n* pagaille *f.*

mayonnaise [,meɪə'neɪz] *n* mayonnaise *f.*

mayor [meər] *n* maire *m.*

mayoress ['meərɪs] *n* [female mayor] femme *f* maire. || [mayor's wife] femme *f* du maire.

maze [meɪz] *n* lit & fig labyrinthe *m*, dédale *m.*

MB (*abbr of* **megabyte**) Mo.

MD *n abbr of* **managing director.**

me [miː] *pers pron* [direct, indirect] me, m' (+ *vowel or silent* "*h*"); **can you see/hear ~?** tu me vois/m'entends?; **it's ~** c'est moi; **they spoke to ~** ils m'ont parlé; **she gave it to ~** elle me l'a donné. || [stressed, after prep, in comparisons etc] moi; **you can't expect ME to do it** tu ne peux pas exiger que ce soit moi qui le fasse; **she's shorter than ~** elle est plus petite que moi.

meadow ['medəʊ] *n* prairie *f*, pré *m.*

meagre *Br*, **meager** *Am* ['miːgər] *adj* maigre.

meal [miːl] *n* repas *m.*

mealtime ['mi:ltaɪm] *n* heure *f* du repas.

mean [mi:n] (*pt & pp* **meant**) **1** *rt* [signify] signifier, vouloir dire; **money ~s nothing to him** l'argent ne compte pas pour lui. || [intend]: **to ~ to do sthg** vouloir faire qqch, avoir l'intention de faire qqch; **I didn't ~ to drop it** je n'ai pas fait exprès de le laisser tomber; **to be meant for sb/sthg** être destiné(e) à qqn/qqch; **to be meant to do sthg** être censé(e) faire qqch; **to ~ well** agir dans une bonne intention. || [be serious about]: **I ~ it** je suis sérieux(ieuse). || [entail] occasionner, entraîner. || *phr*: **I ~** [as explanation] c'est vrai; [as correction] je veux dire. **2** *adj* [miserly] radin(e), chiche; **to be ~ with sthg** être avare de qqch. || [unkind] mesquin(e), méchant(e); **to be ~ to sb** être mesquin envers qqn. || [average] moyen(enne). **3** *n* [average] moyenne *f*; *see also* **means**.

meander [mɪ'ændə'] *ri* [river, road] serpenter; [person] errer.

meaning ['mi:nɪŋ] *n* sens *m*, signification *f*.

meaningful ['mi:nɪŋfʊl] *adj* [look] significatif(ive); [relationship, discussion] important(e).

meaningless ['mi:nɪŋlɪs] *adj* [gesture, word] dénué(e) OR vide de sens; [proposal, discussion] sans importance.

means [mi:nz] **1** *n* [method, way] moyen *m*; **by ~ of** au moyen de. **2** *npl* [money] moyens *mpl*, ressources *fpl*. ○ **by all means** *adv* mais certainement, bien sûr. ○ **by no means** *adv fml* nullement, en aucune façon.

meant [ment] *pt & pp* → **mean**.

meantime ['mi:n,taɪm] *n*: **in the ~** en attendant.

meanwhile ['mi:n,waɪl] *adv* [at the same time] pendant ce temps. || [between two events] en attendant.

measles ['mi:zlz] *n*: **(the) ~** la rougeole.

measly ['mi:zlɪ] *adj inf* misérable, minable.

measure ['meʒə'] **1** *n* [gen] mesure *f*. || [indication]: **it is a ~ of her success that ...** la preuve de son succès, c'est que ... **2** *rt & vi* mesurer.

measurement ['meʒəmənt] *n* mesure *f*.

meat [mi:t] *n* viande *f*.

meatball ['mi:tbɔ:l] *n* boulette *f* de viande.

meaty ['mi:tɪ] *adj fig* important(e).

Mecca ['mekə] *n* La Mecque.

mechanic [mɪ'kænɪk] *n* mécanicien *m*, -ienne *f*.

mechanical [mɪ'kænɪkl] *adj* [device] mécanique. || [routine, automatic] machinal(e).

mechanism ['mekənɪzm] *n lit & fig* mécanisme *m*.

medal ['medl] *n* médaille *f*.

medallion [mɪ'dæljən] *n* médaillon *m*.

meddle ['medl] *ri*: **to ~ in** se mêler de.

media ['mi:djə] **1** *pl* → **medium**. **2** *n or npl*: **the ~** les médias *mpl*.

mediaeval [,medɪ'i:vl] = **medieval**.

median ['mi:djən] *n Am* [of road] bande *f* médiane (*qui sépare les deux côtés d'une grande route*).

mediate ['mi:dɪeɪt] *ri*: **to ~ (for/between)** servir de médiateur (pour/entre).

mediator ['mi:dɪeɪtə'] *n* médiateur *m*, -trice *f*.

Medicaid ['medɪkeɪd] *n Am assistance médicale aux personnes sans ressources.*

medical ['medɪkl] **1** *adj* médical(e). **2** *n* examen *m* médical.

Medicare ['medɪkeə'] *n Am programme fédéral d'assistance médicale pour personnes âgées.*

medicated ['medɪkeɪtɪd] *adj* traitant(e).

medicine ['medsɪn] *n* [subject, treatment] médecine *f*. || [substance] médicament *m*.

medieval [,medɪ'i:vl] *adj* médiéval(e).

mediocre [,mi:dɪ'əʊkə'] *adj* médiocre.

meditate ['medɪteɪt] *ri*: **to ~ (on OR upon)** méditer (sur).

Mediterranean [,medɪtə'reɪnjən] **1** *n* [sea]: **the ~ (Sea)** la (mer) Méditerranée. **2** *adj* méditerranéen(enne).

medium ['mi:djəm] (*pl sense 1* **media**, *pl sense 2* **mediums**) **1** *adj* moyen (enne). **2** *n* [way of communicating] moyen *m*. || [spiritualist] médium *m*.

medium-size(d) [-saɪz(d)] *adj* de taille moyenne.

medium wave *n* ondes *f* moyenne.

medley ['medlɪ] (*pl* **medleys**) *n* [mixture] mélange *m*. || MUS pot-pourri *m*.

meek [mi:k] *adj* docile.

meet [mi:t] (*pt & pp* **met**) **1** *rt* [gen] rencontrer; [by arrangement] retrouver. || [go to meet - person] aller/venir attendre, aller/venir chercher; [- train, plane] aller attendre. || [need, requirement] satisfaire, répondre à. || [problem] résoudre; [challenge] répondre à. || [costs] payer. || [join]

rejoindre. **2** *vi* [gen] se rencontrer; [by arrangement] se retrouver; [for a purpose] se réunir. || [join] se joindre. **3** *n Am* [meeting] meeting *m*. ○ **meet up** *vi* se retrouver; **to ~ up with sb** rencontrer qqn, retrouver qqn. ○ **meet with** *vt fus* [encounter - disapproval] être accueilli(e) par; [- success] remporter; [- failure] essuyer. || *Am* [by arrangement] retrouver.

meeting ['miːtɪŋ] *n* [for discussions, business] réunion *f*. || [by chance] rencontre *f*; [by arrangement] entrevue *f*.

megabyte ['megəbaɪt] *n* COMPUT mégaoctet *m*.

megaphone ['megəfəʊn] *n* mégaphone *m*, porte-voix *m inv*.

melancholy ['melənkəlɪ] **1** *adj* [person] mélancolique; [news, facts] triste. **2** *n* mélancolie *f*.

mellow ['meləʊ] **1** *adj* [light, voice] doux (douce); [taste, wine] moelleux(euse). **2** *vi* s'adoucir.

melody ['melədɪ] *n* mélodie *f*.

melon ['melən] *n* melon *m*.

melt [melt] **1** *vt* faire fondre. **2** *vi* [become liquid] fondre. || *fig*: **his heart ~ed at the sight** il fut tout attendri devant ce spectacle. ○ **melt down** *vt sep* fondre.

melting pot ['meltɪŋ-] *n fig* creuset *m*.

member ['membər] *n* membre *m*; [of club] adhérent *m*, -e *f*.

Member of Congress (*pl* **Members of Congress**) *n Am* membre *m* du Congrès.

Member of Parliament (*pl* **Members of Parliament**) *n Br* ≃ député *m*.

membership ['membəʃɪp] *n* [of organization] adhésion *f*. || [number of members] nombre *m* d'adhérents. || [members]: **the ~ les membres** *mpl*.

membership card *n* carte *f* d'adhésion.

memento [mɪ'mentəʊ] (*pl* -**s**) *n* souvenir *m*.

memo ['meməʊ] (*pl* -**s**) *n* note *f* de service.

memoirs ['memwɑːz] *npl* mémoires *mpl*.

memorial [mɪ'mɔːrɪəl] **1** *adj* commémoratif(ive). **2** *n* monument *m*.

memorize, -ise ['meməraɪz] *vt* [phone number, list] retenir; [poem] apprendre par cœur.

memory ['memərɪ] *n* [gen & COMPUT] mémoire *f*; **from ~** de mémoire. || [event, experience] souvenir *m*.

men [men] *pl* → **man**.

menace ['menəs] **1** *n* [gen] menace *f*. || *inf* [nuisance] plaie *f*. **2** *vt* menacer.

menacing ['menəsɪŋ] *adj* menaçant(e).

mend [mend] *vt* réparer; [clothes] raccommoder; [sock, pullover] repriser.

menial ['miːnjəl] *adj* avilissant(e).

meningitis [ˌmenɪn'dʒaɪtɪs] *n* (*U*) méningite *f*.

menopause ['menəpɔːz] *n*: **the ~** la ménopause.

men's room *n Am*: **the ~** les toilettes *fpl* pour hommes.

menstruation [ˌmenstrʊ'eɪʃn] *n* menstruation *f*.

menswear ['menzweər] *n* (*U*) vêtements *mpl* pour hommes.

mental ['mentl] *adj* mental(e); [image, picture] dans la tête.

mental hospital *n* hôpital *m* psychiatrique.

mentality [men'tælətɪ] *n* mentalité *f*.

mentally handicapped ['mentəlɪ-] *npl*: **the ~** les handicapés *mpl* mentaux.

mention ['menʃn] **1** *vt* mentionner, signaler; **not to ~** sans parler de; **don't ~ it!** je vous en prie! **2** *n* mention *f*.

menu ['menjuː] *n* [gen & COMPUT] menu *m*.

meow *Am* = **miaow**.

MEP (*abbr of* **Member of the European Parliament**) *n* parlementaire *m* européen.

mercenary ['mɜːsɪnrɪ] **1** *adj* mercenaire. **2** *n* mercenaire *m*.

merchandise ['mɜːtʃəndaɪz] *n* (*U*) marchandises *fpl*.

merchant ['mɜːtʃənt] *n* marchand *m*, -e *f*, commerçant *m*, -e *f*.

merchant navy *Br*, **merchant marine** *Am n* marine *f* marchande.

merciful ['mɜːsɪfʊl] *adj* [person] clément(e). || [death, release] qui est une délivrance.

merciless ['mɜːsɪlɪs] *adj* impitoyable.

mercury ['mɜːkjʊrɪ] *n* mercure *m*.

Mercury ['mɜːkjʊrɪ] *n* [planet] Mercure *f*.

mercy ['mɜːsɪ] *n* [kindness, pity] pitié *f*; **at the ~ of** *fig* à la merci de.

mere [mɪər] *adj* seul(e); **she's a ~ child** ce n'est qu'une enfant.

merely ['mɪəlɪ] *adv* seulement, simplement.

merge [mɜːdʒ] **1** *vt* COMM & COMPUT fusionner. **2** *vi* COMM: **to ~ (with)** fusionner (avec). || [roads, lines]: **to ~ (with)** se joindre (à). || [colours] se fondre.

merger ['mɜːdʒəʳ] *n* fusion *f.*

meringue [mə'ræŋ] *n* meringue *f.*

merit ['merɪt] **1** *n* [value] mérite *m*, valeur *f.* **2** *vt* mériter. ○ **merits** *npl* [advantages] qualités *fpl.*

mermaid ['mɜːmeɪd] *n* sirène *f.*

merry ['merɪ] *adj literary* [happy] joyeux(euse); **Merry Christmas!** joyeux Noël! ‖ *inf* [tipsy] gai(e), éméché(e).

merry-go-round *n* manège *m.*

mesh [meʃ] **1** *n* maille *f* (du filet); **wire ~** grillage *m.* **2** *vi* [gears] s'engrener.

mesmerize, -ise ['mezməraɪz] *vt*: to be ~d by être fasciné(e) par.

mess [mes] *n* [untidy state] désordre *m*; *fig* gâchis *m.* ‖ MIL mess *m.* ○ **mess about, mess around** *inf* **1** *vt sep*: to ~ sb about traiter qqn par-dessus OR par-dessous la jambe. **2** *vi* [fool around] perdre OR gaspiller son temps. ‖ [interfere]: to ~ about with sthg s'immiscer dans qqch. ○ **mess up** *vt sep inf* [room] mettre en désordre; [clothes] salir. ‖ *fig* [spoil] gâcher.

message ['mesɪdʒ] *n* message *m.*

messenger ['mesɪndʒəʳ] *n* messager *m*, -ère *f.*

messy ['mesɪ] *adj* [dirty] sale; [untidy] désordonné(e); **a ~ job** un travail salissant. ‖ *inf* [divorce] difficile; [situation] embrouillé(e).

met [met] *pt* & *pp* → **meet.**

metal ['metl] *n* métal *m.*

metallic [mɪ'tælɪk] *adj* [sound, ore] métallique. ‖ [paint, finish] métallisé(e).

metalwork ['metlwɜːk] *n* [craft] ferronnerie *f.*

metaphor ['metəfəʳ] *n* métaphore *f.*

mete [miːt] ○ **mete out** *vt sep* [punishment] infliger.

meteor ['miːtɪəʳ] *n* météore *m.*

meteorology [miːtjə'rɒlədʒɪ] *n* météorologie *f.*

meter ['miːtəʳ] **1** *n* [device] compteur *m.* ‖ *Am* = metre. **2** *vt* [gas, electricity] établir la consommation de.

method ['meθəd] *n* méthode *f.*

methodical [mɪ'θɒdɪkl] *adj* méthodique.

Methodist ['meθədɪst] **1** *adj* méthodiste. **2** *n* méthodiste *mf.*

methylated spirits ['meθɪleɪtɪd-] *n* alcool *m* à brûler.

meticulous [mɪ'tɪkjʊləs] *adj* méticuleux(euse).

metre *Br*, **meter** *Am* ['miːtəʳ] *n* mètre *m.*

metric ['metrɪk] *adj* métrique.

metronome ['metrənəʊm] *n* métronome *m.*

metropolitan [metrə'pɒlɪtn] *adj* métropolitain(e).

mettle ['metl] *n*: to be on one's ~ être d'attaque; to show OR prove one's ~ montrer ce dont on est capable.

mew [mjuː] = miaow.

Mexican ['meksɪkn] **1** *adj* mexicain(e). **2** *n* Mexicain *m*, -e *f.*

Mexico ['meksɪkəʊ] *n* Mexique *m.*

miaow *Br* [miːˈaʊ], **meow** *Am* [mɪˈaʊ] **1** *n* miaulement *m*, miaou *m.* **2** *vi* miauler.

mice [maɪs] *pl* → mouse.

microchip ['maɪkrəʊtʃɪp] *n* COMPUT puce *f.*

microcomputer [maɪkrəʊkəm'pjuːtəʳ] *n* micro-ordinateur *m.*

microfilm ['maɪkrəfɪlm] *n* microfilm *m.*

microphone ['maɪkrəfəʊn] *n* microphone *m*, micro *m.*

microscope ['maɪkrəskəʊp] *n* microscope *m.*

microscopic [maɪkrə'skɒpɪk] *adj* microscopique.

microwave (oven) ['maɪkrəweɪv-] *n* (four *m* à) micro-ondes *m.*

mid- [mɪd] *prefix*: ~height mi-hauteur; ~morning milieu de la matinée; ~winter plein hiver.

midair [mɪd'eəʳ] **1** *adj* en plein ciel. **2** *n*: in ~ en plein ciel.

midday [mɪd'deɪ] *n* midi *m.*

middle ['mɪdl] **1** *adj* [centre] du milieu, du centre. **2** *n* [centre] milieu *m*, centre *m*; in the ~ (of) au milieu (de). ‖ [in time] milieu *m*; to be in the ~ of doing sthg être en train de faire qqch; to be in the ~ of a meeting être en pleine réunion; in the ~ of the night au milieu de la nuit, en pleine nuit. ‖ [waist] taille *f.*

middle-aged *adj* d'une cinquantaine d'années.

Middle Ages *npl*: the ~ le Moyen Âge.

middle-class *adj* bourgeois(e).

middle classes *npl*: the ~ la bourgeoisie.

Middle East *n*: the ~ le Moyen-Orient.

middleman ['mɪdlmæn] (*pl* -men [-mən]) *n* intermédiaire *mf.*

middle name *n* second prénom *m.*

middling ['mɪdlɪŋ] *adj* moyen(enne).

Mideast [mɪd'iːst] *n Am*: the ~ le Moyen-Orient.

midge [mɪdʒ] *n* moucheron *m.*

midget ['mɪdʒɪt] n nain m, -e f.

midi system ['mɪdɪ-] n chaîne f midi.

midnight ['mɪdnaɪt] n minuit m.

midriff ['mɪdrɪf] n diaphragme m.

midst [mɪdst] n [in space]: **in the ~ of** au milieu de. || [in time]: **to be in the ~ of doing sthg** être en train de faire qqch.

midsummer ['mɪd,sʌmər] n cœur m de l'été.

Midsummer Day n la Saint-Jean.

midway [,mɪd'weɪ] adv [in space]: ~ (between) à mi-chemin (entre). || [in time]: ~ through the meeting en pleine réunion.

midweek [adj 'mɪdwiːk, adv mɪd'wiːk] 1 adj du milieu de la semaine. 2 adv en milieu de semaine.

midwife ['mɪdwaɪf] (pl -wives [-waɪvz]) n sage-femme f.

might [maɪt] 1 modal vb [expressing possibility]: **the criminal ~ be armed** il est possible que le criminel soit armé. || [expressing suggestion]: **it ~ be better to wait** il vaut peut-être mieux attendre. || fml [asking permission]: **he asked if he ~ leave the room** il demanda s'il pouvait sortir de la pièce. || [expressing concession]: **you ~ well be right** vous avez peut-être raison. || phr: **I ~ have known** OR **guessed** j'aurais dû m'en douter. 2 n (U) force f.

mighty ['maɪtɪ] 1 adj [powerful] puissant(e). 2 adv Am inf drôlement, vachement.

migraine ['miːgreɪn, 'maɪgreɪn] n migraine f.

migrant ['maɪgrənt] 1 adj [bird, animal] migrateur(trice). || [workers] émigré(e). 2 n [bird, animal] migrateur m. || [person] émigré m, -e f.

migrate [Br maɪ'greɪt, Am 'maɪgreɪt] vi [bird, animal] migrer. || [person] émigrer.

mike [maɪk] (abbr of **microphone**) n inf micro m.

mild [maɪld] adj [disinfectant, reproach] léger(ère). || [tone, weather] doux (douce). || [illness] bénin(igne).

mildew ['mɪldjuː] n (U) moisissure f.

mildly ['maɪldlɪ] adv [gently] doucement; **to put it ~** le moins qu'on puisse dire. || [not strongly] légèrement. || [slightly] un peu.

mile [maɪl] n mile m; NAUT mille m; **to be ~s away** fig être très loin.

mileage ['maɪlɪdʒ] n distance f en miles, ≃ kilométrage m.

mileometer [maɪ'lɒmɪtər] n compteur m de miles, ≃ compteur kilométrique.

milestone ['maɪlstəʊn] n [marker stone] borne f, fig événement m marquant OR important.

militant ['mɪlɪtənt] 1 adj militant(e). 2 n militant m, -e f.

military ['mɪlɪtrɪ] 1 adj militaire. 2 n: **the ~** les militaires mpl, l'armée f.

militia [mɪ'lɪʃə] n milice f.

milk [mɪlk] 1 n lait m. 2 vt [cow] traire.

milk chocolate n chocolat m au lait.

milkman ['mɪlkmən] (pl -men [-mən]) n laitier m.

milk shake n milk-shake m.

milky ['mɪlkɪ] adj [pale white] laiteux(euse).

Milky Way n: **the ~** la Voie lactée.

mill [mɪl] 1 n [flour-mill, grinder] moulin m. || [factory] usine f. 2 vt moudre. ○ **mill about, mill around** vi grouiller.

millennium [mɪ'lenɪəm] (pl -nnia [-nɪə]) n millénaire m.

miller ['mɪlər] n meunier m.

milligram(me) ['mɪlɪgræm] n milligramme m.

millimetre Br, **millimeter** Am ['mɪlɪ,miːtər] n millimètre m.

millinery ['mɪlɪnrɪ] n chapellerie f féminine.

million ['mɪljən] n million m; **a ~, ~s of** fig des milliers de, un million de.

millionaire [,mɪljə'neər] n millionnaire mf.

millstone ['mɪlstəʊn] n meule f.

milometer [maɪ'lɒmɪtər] = **mileometer**.

mime [maɪm] 1 n mime m. 2 vt & vi mimer.

mimic ['mɪmɪk] (pt & pp -ked, cont -king) 1 n imitateur m, -trice f. 2 vt imiter.

mimicry ['mɪmɪkrɪ] n imitation f.

min. [mɪn] (abbr of **minute**) mn, min. || (abbr of **minimum**) min.

mince [mɪns] 1 vt [meat] hacher. 2 vi marcher à petits pas maniérés.

mincemeat ['mɪnsmiːt] n [fruit] mélange de pommes, raisins secs et épices utilisé en pâtisserie. || Am [meat] viande f hachée.

mince pie n tartelette f de Noël.

mincer ['mɪnsər] n hachoir m.

mind [maɪnd] 1 n [gen] esprit m; **to bear sthg in ~** ne pas oublier qqch; **to come into/cross sb's ~** venir à/traverser l'esprit de qqn; **to have sthg on one's ~** avoir l'esprit préoccupé, être préoccupé par qqch; **to keep an open ~** réserver son jugement; **to have a ~ to do sthg** avoir bien envie de faire qqch; **to have sthg in ~** avoir qqch dans l'idée; **to make one's ~ up** se décider. ‖ [attention]: **to put one's ~ to sthg** s'appliquer à qqch; **to keep one's ~ on sthg** se concentrer sur qqch. ‖ [opinion]: **to change one's ~** changer d'avis; **to my ~** à mon avis; **to speak one's ~** parler franchement; **to be in two ~s (about sthg)** se tâter OR être indécis (à propos de qqch). ‖ [person] cerveau *m*. 2 *vi* [be bothered]: **I don't ~** ça m'est égal; **I hope you don't ~** j'espère que vous n'y voyez pas d'inconvénient; **never ~** [don't worry] ne t'en fais pas; [it's not important] ça ne fait rien. 3 *vt* [be bothered about, dislike]: **I don't ~ waiting** ça ne me gêne OR dérange pas d'attendre; **do you ~ if ...?** cela ne vous ennuie pas si ...?; **I wouldn't ~ a beer** je prendrais bien une bière. ‖ [pay attention to] faire attention à, prendre garde à. ‖ [take care of - luggage] garder, surveiller; [- shop] tenir. ○ **mind you** *adv* remarquez.

mindful ['maɪndful] *adj*: **~ of** [risks] attentif(ive) à; [responsibility] soucieux (ieuse) de.

mindless ['maɪndlɪs] *adj* stupide, idiot(e).

mine¹ [maɪn] *poss pron* le mien (la mienne), les miens (les miennes) (*pl*); **that money is ~** cet argent est à moi; **it wasn't your fault, it was MINE** ce n'était pas de votre faute, c'était de la mienne OR de ma faute à moi; **a friend of ~** un ami à moi, un de mes amis.

mine² [maɪn] 1 *n* mine *f*. 2 *vt* [coal, gold] extraire. ‖ [road, beach, sea] miner.

minefield ['maɪnfiːld] *n* champ *m* de mines; *fig* situation *f* explosive.

miner ['maɪnər] *n* mineur *m*.

mineral ['mɪnərəl] 1 *adj* minéral(e). 2 *n* minéral *m*.

mineral water *n* eau *f* minérale.

mingle ['mɪŋgl] *vi*: **to ~ (with)** [sounds, fragrances] se mélanger (à); [people] se mêler (à).

miniature ['mɪnətʃər] 1 *adj* miniature. 2 *n* [painting] miniature *f*. ‖ [of alcohol] bouteille *f* miniature. ‖ [small scale]: **in ~** en miniature.

minibus ['mɪnɪbʌs] (*pl* **-es**) *n* minibus *m*.

minima ['mɪnɪmə] *pl* → **minimum**.

minimal ['mɪnɪml] *adj* [cost] insignifiant(e); [damage] minime.

minimum ['mɪnɪməm] (*pl* **-mums** OR **-ma**) 1 *adj* minimum (*inv*). 2 *n* minimum *m*.

mining ['maɪnɪŋ] 1 *n* exploitation *f* minière. 2 *adj* minier(ière).

miniskirt ['mɪnɪskɜːt] *n* minijupe *f*.

minister ['mɪnɪstər] *n* POL ministre *m*. ‖ RELIG pasteur *m*.

ministerial [,mɪnɪ'stɪərɪəl] *adj* ministériel(ielle).

minister of state *n* secrétaire *mf* d'État.

ministry ['mɪnɪstrɪ] *n* POL ministère *m*. ‖ RELIG: **the ~** le saint ministère.

mink [mɪŋk] (*pl inv*) *n* vison *m*.

minor ['maɪnər] 1 *adj* [gen & MUS] mineur(e); [detail] petit(e); [role] secondaire. 2 *n* mineur *m*, -e *f*.

minority [maɪ'nɒrətɪ] *n* minorité *f*.

mint [mɪnt] 1 *n* [herb] menthe *f*. ‖ [sweet] bonbon *m* à la menthe. ‖ [for coins]: **the Mint** l'hôtel de la Monnaie; **in ~ condition** en parfait état. 2 *vt* [coins] battre.

minus ['maɪnəs] (*pl* **-es**) 1 *prep* moins. 2 *adj* [answer, quantity] négatif(ive). 3 *n* [disadvantage] handicap *m*.

minus sign *n* signe *m* moins.

minute¹ ['mɪnɪt] *n* minute *f*; **at any ~** à tout moment, d'une minute à l'autre; **stop that this ~!** arrête tout de suite OR immédiatement! ○ **minutes** *npl* procès-verbal *m*, compte *m* rendu.

minute² [maɪ'njuːt] *adj* minuscule.

miracle ['mɪrəkl] *n* miracle *m*.

miraculous [mɪ'rækjʊləs] *adj* miraculeux(euse).

mirage [mɪ'rɑːʒ] *n lit & fig* mirage *m*.

mirror ['mɪrər] 1 *n* miroir *m*, glace *f*. 2 *vt* refléter.

mirth [mɜːθ] *n* hilarité *f*, gaieté *f*.

misadventure [,mɪsəd'ventʃər] *n*: **death by ~** JUR mort *f* accidentelle.

misapprehension ['mɪs,æprɪ'henʃn] *n* idée *f* fausse.

misappropriation ['mɪsə,prəʊprɪ'eɪʃn] *n* détournement *m*.

misbehave [,mɪsbɪ'heɪv] *vi* se conduire mal.

miscalculate [,mɪs'kælkjʊleɪt] 1 *vt* mal calculer. 2 *vi* se tromper.

miscarriage [,mɪs'kærɪdʒ] *n* MED fausse couche *f*; **to have a ~** faire une fausse couche.

miscellaneous [,mɪsə'leɪnjəs] *adj* varié(e), divers(e).

mischief ['mɪstʃɪf] *n* (*U*) [playfulness] malice *f*, espièglerie *f*. ‖ [naughty behaviour] sottises *fpl*, bêtises *fpl*. ‖ [harm] dégât *m*.

mischievous ['mɪstʃɪvəs] *adj* [playful] malicieux(ieuse). ‖ [naughty] espiègle, coquin(e).

misconduct [,mɪs'kɒndʌkt] *n* inconduite *f*.

misconstrue [,mɪskən'struː] *vt fml* mal interpréter.

miscount [,mɪs'kaunt] *vt* & *vi* mal compter.

misdeed [,mɪs'diːd] *n* méfait *m*.

misdemeanour *Br*, **misdemeanor** *Am* [,mɪsdɪ'miːnər] *n* JUR délit *m*.

miser ['maɪzər] *n* avare *mf*.

miserable ['mɪzrəbl] *adj* [person] malheureux(euse), triste. ‖ [conditions, life] misérable; [pay] dérisoire; [weather] maussade. ‖ [failure] pitoyable, lamentable.

miserly ['maɪzəlɪ] *adj* avare.

misery ['mɪzərɪ] *n* [of person] tristesse *f*. ‖ [of conditions, life] misère *f*.

misfire [,mɪs'faɪər] *vi* [gun, plan] rater.

misfit ['mɪsfɪt] *n* inadapté *m*, -e *f*.

misfortune [mɪs'fɔːtʃuːn] *n* [bad luck] malchance *f*. ‖ [piece of bad luck] malheur *m*.

misgivings [mɪs'gɪvɪŋz] *npl* craintes *fpl*, doutes *mpl*.

misguided [,mɪs'gaɪdɪd] *adj* [person] malavisé(e); [attempt] malencontreux(euse); [opinion] peu judicieux(ieuse).

mishandle [,mɪs'hændl] *vt* [person, animal] manier sans précaution. ‖ [negotiations] mal mener; [business] mal gérer.

mishap ['mɪshæp] *n* mésaventure *f*.

misinterpret [,mɪsɪn'tɜːprɪt] *vt* mal interpréter.

misjudge [,mɪs'dʒʌdʒ] *vt* [distance, time] mal évaluer. ‖ [person, mood] méjuger, se méprendre sur.

mislay [,mɪs'leɪ] (*pt* & *pp* **-laid** [-'leɪd]) *vt* égarer.

mislead [,mɪs'liːd] (*pt* & *pp* **-led**) *vt* induire en erreur.

misleading [,mɪs'liːdɪŋ] *adj* trompeur(euse).

misled [,mɪs'led] *pt* & *pp* → **mislead**.

misnomer [,mɪs'nəumər] *n* nom *m* mal approprié.

misplace [,mɪs'pleɪs] *vt* égarer.

misprint ['mɪsprɪnt] *n* faute *f* d'impression.

miss [mɪs] **1** *vt* [gen] rater, manquer. ‖ [home, person]: **I ~ my family/her** ma famille/elle me manque. ‖ [avoid, escape] échapper à; **I just ~ed being run over** j'ai failli me faire écraser. **2** *vi* rater. **3** *n*: **to give sthg a ~** *inf* ne pas aller à qqch. **○ miss out 1** *vt sep* [omit - by accident] oublier; [- deliberately] omettre. **2** *vi*: **to ~ out on sthg** ne pas pouvoir profiter de qqch.

Miss [mɪs] *n* Mademoiselle *f*.

misshapen [,mɪs'ʃeɪpn] *adj* difforme.

missile [*Br* 'mɪsaɪl, *Am* 'mɪsəl] *n* [weapon] missile *m*.

missing ['mɪsɪŋ] *adj* [lost] perdu(e), égaré(e). ‖ [not present] manquant(e), qui manque.

mission ['mɪʃn] *n* mission *f*.

missionary ['mɪʃənrɪ] *n* missionnaire *mf*.

mist [mɪst] *n* brume *f*. **○ mist over, mist up** *vi* s'embuer.

mistake [mɪ'steɪk] (*pt* **-took**, *pp* **-taken**) **1** *n* erreur *f*; **by ~** par erreur; **to make a ~** faire une erreur, se tromper. **2** *vt* [misunderstand - meaning] mal comprendre; [- intention] se méprendre sur. ‖ [fail to recognize]: **to ~ sb/sthg for** prendre qqn/qqch pour, confondre qqn/qqch avec.

mistaken [mɪ'steɪkn] **1** *pp* → **mistake**. **2** *adj* [person]: **to be ~ (about)** se tromper (en ce qui concerne *or* sur). ‖ [belief, idea] erroné(e), faux (fausse).

mister ['mɪstər] *n inf* monsieur *m*. **○ Mister** *n* Monsieur *m*.

mistletoe ['mɪsltəu] *n* gui *m*.

mistook [mɪ'stuk] *pt* → **mistake**.

mistreat [,mɪs'triːt] *vt* maltraiter.

mistress ['mɪstrɪs] *n* maîtresse *f*.

mistrust [,mɪs'trʌst] **1** *n* méfiance *f*. **2** *vt* se méfier de.

misty ['mɪstɪ] *adj* brumeux(euse).

misunderstand [,mɪsʌndə'stænd] (*pt* & *pp* **-stood**) *vt* & *vi* mal comprendre.

misunderstanding [,mɪsʌndə'stændɪŋ] *n* malentendu *m*.

misunderstood [,mɪsʌndə'stud] *pt* & *pp* → **misunderstand**.

misuse [*n* ,mɪs'juːs, *vb* ,mɪs'juːz] **1** *n* [of one's time, resources] mauvais emploi *m*. ‖ [of power] abus *m*; [of funds] détournement *m*. **2** *vt* [one's time, resources] mal employer. ‖ [power] abuser de; [funds] détourner.

moneybox

miter *Am* = mitre.

mitigate ['mɪtɪgeɪt] *vt* atténuer, mitiger.

mitre *Br*, **miter** *Am* ['maɪtər] *n* [hat] mitre *f*. || [joint] onglet *m*.

mitt [mɪt] *n* = **mitten**. || [in baseball] gant *m*.

mitten ['mɪtn] *n* moufle *f*.

mix [mɪks] **1** *vt* [gen] mélanger. || [activities]: **to ~ sthg with sthg** combiner OR associer qqch et qqch. || [drink] préparer. **2** *vi* [gen] se mélanger. || [socially]: **to ~ with** fréquenter. **3** *n* [gen] mélange *m*.
○ **mix up** *vt sep* [confuse] confondre. || [disorganize] mélanger.

mixed [mɪkst] *adj* [assorted] assortis(ies). || [education] mixte.

mixed grill *n* assortiment *m* de grillades.

mixed up *adj* [confused - person] qui ne sait plus où il en est, paumé(e); [- mind] embrouillé(e). || [involved]: **to be ~ in sthg** être mêlé(e) à qqch.

mixer ['mɪksər] *n* [for food] mixer *m*.

mixture ['mɪkstʃər] *n* [gen] mélange *m*. || MED préparation *f*.

mix-up *n inf* confusion *f*.

mm (*abbr of* millimetre) mm.

moan [məʊn] **1** *n* [of pain, sadness] gémissement *m*. **2** *vi* [in pain, sadness] gémir. || *inf* [complain]: **to ~ (about)** rouspéter OR râler (à propos de).

moat [məʊt] *n* douves *fpl*.

mob [mɒb] **1** *n* foule *f*. **2** *vt* assaillir.

mobile ['məʊbaɪl] **1** *adj* [gen] mobile. || [able to travel] motorisé(e). **2** *n* mobile *m*.

mobile home *n* auto-caravane *f*.

mobile phone *n* téléphone *m* portatif.

mobilize, -ise ['məʊbɪlaɪz] *vt & vi* mobiliser.

mock [mɒk] **1** *adj* faux (fausse); **~ exam** examen blanc. **2** *vt* se moquer de.

mockery ['mɒkərɪ] *n* moquerie *f*.

mode [məʊd] *n* mode *m*.

model ['mɒdl] **1** *n* [gen] modèle *m*. || [fashion model] mannequin *m*. **2** *adj* [perfect] modèle. || [reduced-scale] (en) modèle réduit. **3** *vt* [clay] modeler. || [clothes]: **to ~ a dress** présenter un modèle de robe. || [copy]: **to ~ o.s. on sb** prendre modèle OR exemple sur qqn, se modeler sur qqn. **4** *vi* être mannequin.

modem ['məʊdem] *n* COMPUT modem *m*.

moderate [*adj* & *n* 'mɒdərət, *vb* 'mɒdəreɪt] **1** *adj* modéré(e). **2** *vt* modérer.

moderation [,mɒdə'reɪʃn] *n* modération *f*; **in ~** avec modération.

modern ['mɒdən] *adj* moderne.

modernize, -ise ['mɒdənaɪz] **1** *vt* moderniser. **2** *vi* se moderniser.

modern languages *npl* langues *fpl* vivantes.

modest ['mɒdɪst] *adj* modeste.

modesty ['mɒdɪstɪ] *n* modestie *f*.

modify ['mɒdɪfaɪ] *vt* modifier.

module ['mɒdjuːl] *n* module *m*.

mogul ['məʊgl] *n fig* magnat *m*.

mohair ['məʊheər] *n* mohair *m*.

moist [mɔɪst] *adj* [soil, climate] humide; [cake] moelleux(euse).

moisten ['mɔɪsn] *vt* humecter.

moisture ['mɔɪstʃər] *n* humidité *f*.

moisturizer ['mɔɪstʃəraɪzər] *n* crème *f* hydratante, lait *m* hydratant.

molar ['məʊlər] *n* molaire *f*.

molasses [mə'læsɪz] *n* (*U*) mélasse *f*.

mold *etc Am* = **mould**.

mole [məʊl] *n* [animal, spy] taupe *f*. || [on skin] grain *m* de beauté.

molecule ['mɒlɪkjuːl] *n* molécule *f*.

molest [mə'lest] *vt* [attack sexually] attenter à la pudeur de. || [attack] molester.

molt *Am* = **moult**.

molten ['məʊltn] *adj* en fusion.

mom [mɒm] *n Am inf* maman *f*.

moment ['məʊmənt] *n* moment *m*, instant *m*; **at any ~** d'un moment à l'autre; **at the ~** en ce moment; **for the ~** pour le moment.

momentarily ['məʊməntərɪlɪ] *adv* [for a short time] momentanément. || *Am* [soon] très bientôt.

momentary ['məʊməntrɪ] *adj* momentané(e), passager(ère).

momentous [mə'mentəs] *adj* capital(e), très important(e).

momentum [mə'mentəm] *n* (*U*) PHYSICS moment *m*. || *fig* [speed, force] vitesse *f*; **to gather ~** prendre de la vitesse.

momma ['mɒmə], **mommy** ['mɒmɪ] *n Am* maman *f*.

Monaco ['mɒnəkəʊ] *n* Monaco.

monarch ['mɒnək] *n* monarque *m*.

monarchy ['mɒnəkɪ] *n* monarchie *f*.

monastery ['mɒnəstrɪ] *n* monastère *m*.

Monday ['mʌndɪ] *n* lundi *m*; *see also* **Saturday**.

monetary ['mʌnɪtrɪ] *adj* monétaire.

money ['mʌnɪ] *n* argent *m*; **to make ~** gagner de l'argent.

moneybox ['mʌnɪbɒks] *n* tirelire *f*.

moneylender ['mʌnɪ,lendər] n prêteur m, -euse f sur gages.

money order n mandat m postal.

money-spinner [-,spɪnər] n inf mine f d'or.

Mongolia [mɒŋ'gəʊlɪə] n Mongolie f.

mongrel ['mʌŋgrəl] n [dog] bâtard m.

monitor ['mɒnɪtər] 1 n COMPUT, MED & TV moniteur m. 2 vt [check] contrôler, suivre de près. || [broadcasts, messages] être à l'écoute de.

monk [mʌŋk] n moine m.

monkey ['mʌŋkɪ] (pl **monkeys**) n singe m.

monkey wrench n clef f à molette.

mono ['mɒnəʊ] 1 adj mono (inv). 2 n [sound] monophonie f.

monochrome ['mɒnəkrəʊm] adj monochrome.

monocle ['mɒnəkl] n monocle m.

monologue, monolog Am ['mɒnəlɒg] n monologue m.

monopolize, -ise [mə'nɒpəlaɪz] vt monopoliser.

monopoly [mə'nɒpəlɪ] n: ~ (on OR of) monopole m (de).

monotone ['mɒnətəʊn] n ton m monocorde.

monotonous [mə'nɒtənəs] adj monotone.

monotony [mə'nɒtənɪ] n monotonie f.

monsoon [mɒn'suːn] n mousson f.

monster ['mɒnstər] n [creature, cruel person] monstre m. || [huge thing, person] colosse m.

monstrosity [mɒn'strɒsətɪ] n monstruosité f.

monstrous ['mɒnstrəs] adj monstrueux(euse).

Mont Blanc [,mɔ̃'blɑ̃] n le mont Blanc.

month [mʌnθ] n mois m.

monthly ['mʌnθlɪ] 1 adj mensuel(elle). 2 adv mensuellement. 3 n [publication] mensuel m.

Montreal [,mɒntrɪ'ɔːl] n Montréal m.

monument ['mɒnjʊmənt] n monument m.

monumental [,mɒnjʊ'mentl] adj monumental(e).

moo [muː] (pl -s) 1 n meuglement m, beuglement m. 2 vi meugler, beugler.

mood [muːd] n humeur f; **in a (bad) ~** de mauvaise humeur; **in a good ~** de bonne humeur.

moody ['muːdɪ] adj pej [changeable] lunatique. || [bad-tempered] de mauvaise humeur, mal luné(e).

moon [muːn] n lune f.

moonlight ['muːnlaɪt] (pt & pp -ed) 1 n clair m de lune. 2 vi travailler au noir.

moonlighting ['muːnlaɪtɪŋ] n (U) travail m (au) noir.

moonlit ['muːnlɪt] adj [countryside] éclairé(e) par la lune; [night] de lune.

moor [mɔːr] 1 n lande f. 2 vt amarrer. 3 vi mouiller.

moorland ['mɔːlənd] n lande f.

moose [muːs] (pl inv) n [North American] orignal m.

mop [mɒp] 1 n [for cleaning] balai m à laver. || inf [hair] tignasse f. 2 vt [floor] laver. || [sweat] essuyer; **to ~ one's face** s'essuyer le visage. ○ **mop up** vt sep [clean up] éponger.

mope [məʊp] vi broyer du noir.

moped ['məʊped] n vélomoteur m.

moral ['mɒrəl] 1 adj moral(e). 2 n [lesson] morale f. ○ **morals** npl moralité f.

morale [mə'rɑːl] n (U) moral m.

morality [mə'rælətɪ] n moralité f.

morbid ['mɔːbɪd] adj morbide.

more [mɔːr] 1 adv (with adjectives and adverbs) plus; **~ often/quickly (than)** plus souvent/rapidement (que). || [to a greater degree] plus, davantage. || [another time]: **once/twice ~** une fois/deux fois de plus, encore une fois/deux fois. 2 adj [larger number, amount of] plus de, davantage de; **there are ~ trains in the morning** il y a plus de trains le matin; **~ than 70 people died** plus de 70 personnes ont péri. || [an extra amount of] encore (de); **I finished two ~ chapters today** j'ai fini deux autres OR encore deux chapitres aujourd'hui; **we need ~ money/time** il nous faut plus d'argent/de temps, il nous faut davantage d'argent/de temps. 3 pron plus, davantage; **~ than five** plus de cinq; **he's got ~ than I have** il en a plus que moi; **there's no ~ (left)** il n'y en a plus, il n'en reste plus; **(and) what's ~** de plus, qui plus est. ○ **any more** adv: **not ... any ~** ne ... plus. ○ **more and more** 1 adv & pron de plus en plus. 2 adj de plus en plus de. ○ **more or less** adv [almost] plus ou moins. || [approximately] environ, à peu près.

moreover [mɔː'rəʊvər] adv de plus.

morgue [mɔːg] n morgue f.

Mormon ['mɔːmən] n mormon m, -e f.

morning ['mɔːnɪŋ] n matin m; [duration] matinée f; **I'll do it tomorrow ~** OR in the ~ je le ferai demain. ○ **mornings** *adv Am* le matin.

Moroccan [mə'rɒkən] **1** *adj* marocain(e). **2** *n* Marocain *m*, -e *f*.

Morocco [mə'rɒkəʊ] *n* Maroc *m*.

moron ['mɔːrɒn] *n inf* idiot *m*, -e *f*, crétin *m*, -e *f*.

morphine ['mɔːfiːn] *n* morphine *f*.

Morse (code) [mɔːs-] *n* morse *m*.

morsel ['mɔːsl] *n* bout *m*, morceau *m*.

mortal ['mɔːtl] **1** *adj* mortel(elle). **2** *n* mortel *m*, -elle *f*.

mortality [mɔː'tælətɪ] *n* mortalité *f*.

mortar ['mɔːtər] *n* mortier *m*.

mortgage ['mɔːgɪdʒ] **1** *n* emprunt-logement *m*. **2** *rt* hypothéquer.

mortified ['mɔːtɪfaɪd] *adj* mortifié(e).

mortuary ['mɔːtʃʊərɪ] *n* morgue *f*.

mosaic [mə'zeɪɪk] *n* mosaïque *f*.

Moscow ['mɒskəʊ] *n* Moscou.

Moslem ['mɒzləm] = **Muslim.**

mosque [mɒsk] *n* mosquée *f*.

mosquito [mə'skiːtəʊ] (*pl* -es OR -s) *n* moustique *m*.

moss [mɒs] *n* mousse *f*.

most [məʊst] (*superl of* many) **1** *adj* [the majority of] la plupart de; ~ **tourists here are German** la plupart des touristes ici sont allemands. || [largest amount of]: (the) ~ le plus de; **she's got (the) ~ money/sweets** c'est elle qui a le plus d'argent/de bonbons. **2** *pron* [the majority] la plupart; ~ **of the tourists here are German** la plupart des touristes ici sont allemands; ~ **of them** la plupart d'entre eux. || [largest amount]: (the) ~ le plus; **at** ~ **au maximum, tout au plus.** || *phr*: **to make the** ~ **of sthg** profiter de qqch au maximum. **3** *adv* [to greatest extent]: (the) ~ le plus. || *Am* [almost] presque.

mostly ['məʊstlɪ] *adv* principalement, surtout.

motel [məʊ'tel] *n* motel *m*.

moth [mɒθ] *n* papillon *m* de nuit; [in clothes] mite *f*.

mothball ['mɒθbɔːl] *n* boule *f* de naphtaline.

mother ['mʌðər] **1** *n* mère *f*. **2** *vt* [child] materner, dorloter.

motherhood ['mʌðəhʊd] *n* maternité *f*.

mother-in-law (*pl* mothers-in-law OR mother-in-laws) *n* belle-mère *f*.

motherly ['mʌðəlɪ] *adj* maternel(elle).

mother-of-pearl *n* nacre *f*.

mother-to-be (*pl* mothers-to-be) *n* future maman *f*.

mother tongue *n* langue *f* maternelle.

motif [məʊ'tiːf] *n* motif *m*.

motion ['məʊʃn] **1** *n* [gen] mouvement *m*; **to set sthg in** ~ mettre qqch en branle. || [in debate] motion *f*. **2** *vt*: **to** ~ **sb to do sthg** faire signe à qqn de faire qqch. **3** *vi*: **to** ~ **to sb** faire signe à qqn.

motionless ['məʊʃənlɪs] *adj* immobile.

motion picture *n Am* film *m*.

motivated ['məʊtɪveɪtɪd] *adj* motivé(e).

motivation [,məʊtɪ'veɪʃn] *n* motivation *f*.

motive ['məʊtɪv] *n* motif *m*.

motor ['məʊtər] *n* [engine] moteur *m*.

motorbike ['məʊtəbaɪk] *n inf* moto *f*.

motorboat ['məʊtəbəʊt] *n* canot *m* automobile.

motorcycle ['məʊtə,saɪkl] *n* moto *f*.

motorcyclist ['məʊtə,saɪklɪst] *n* motocycliste *mf*.

motoring ['məʊtərɪŋ] *n* tourisme *m* automobile.

motorist ['məʊtərɪst] *n* automobiliste *mf*.

motor racing *n* (U) course *f* automobile.

motor scooter *n* scooter *m*.

motor vehicle *n* véhicule *m* automobile.

mottled ['mɒtld] *adj* [leaf] tacheté(e); [skin] marbré(e).

motto ['mɒtəʊ] (*pl* -s OR -es) *n* devise *f*.

mould, mold *Am* [məʊld] **1** *n* [growth] moisissure *f*. || [shape] moule *m*. **2** *vt* [shape] mouler, modeler. || *fig* [influence] former, façonner.

moulding, molding *Am* ['məʊldɪŋ] *n* [decoration] moulure *f*.

mouldy, moldy *Am* ['məʊldɪ] *adj* moisi(e).

moult, molt *Am* [məʊlt] *vi* muer.

mound [maʊnd] *n* [small hill] tertre *m*, butte *f*. || [pile] tas *m*, monceau *m*.

mount [maʊnt] **1** *n* [support - for jewel] monture *f*; [- for photograph] carton *m* de montage; [- for machine] support *m*. || [horse] monture *f*. || [mountain] mont *m*. **2** *vt* monter; **to** ~ **a horse** monter sur un cheval; **to** ~ **a bike** monter sur OR enfourcher un vélo. **3** *vi* [increase] monter, augmenter. || [climb on horse] se mettre en selle.

mountain ['maʊntɪn] *n lit & fig* montagne *f*.

mountain bike *n* VTT *m*.

mountaineer [,maʊntɪ'nɪəʳ] *n* alpiniste *mf*.

mountaineering [,maʊntɪ'nɪərɪŋ] *n* alpinisme *m*.

mountainous ['maʊntɪnəs] *adj* [region] montagneux(euse).

mourn [mɔːn] **1** *vt* pleurer. **2** *vi*: **to ~ (for sb)** pleurer (qqn).

mourner ['mɔːnəʳ] *n* [related] parent *m* du défunt; [unrelated] ami *m*, -e *f* du défunt.

mournful ['mɔːnfʊl] *adj* [face] triste; [sound] lugubre.

mourning ['mɔːnɪŋ] *n* deuil *m*; **in ~** en deuil.

mouse [maʊs] (*pl* **mice**) *n* COMPUT & ZOOL souris *f*.

mousetrap ['maʊstræp] *n* souricière *f*.

mousse [muːs] *n* mousse *f*.

moustache *Br* [mə'stɑːʃ], **mustache** *Am* ['mʌstæʃ] *n* moustache *f*.

mouth [maʊθ] *n* [of person, animal] bouche *f*; [of dog, cat, lion] gueule *f*. || [of cave] entrée *f*; [of river] embouchure *f*.

mouthful ['maʊθfʊl] *n* [of food] bouchée *f*; [of drink] gorgée *f*.

mouthorgan ['maʊθ,ɔːgən] *n* harmonica *m*.

mouthpiece ['maʊθpiːs] *n* [of telephone] microphone *m*; [of musical instrument] bec *m*. || [spokesperson] porte-parole *m inv*.

mouthwash ['maʊθwɒʃ] *n* eau *f* dentifrice.

mouth-watering [-,wɔːtərɪŋ] *adj* alléchant(e).

movable ['muːvəbl] *adj* mobile.

move [muːv] **1** *n* [movement] mouvement *m*; **to get a ~ on** *inf* se remuer, se grouiller. || [change - of house] déménagement *m*; [- of job] changement *m* d'emploi. || [in game - action] coup *m*; [- turn to play] tour *m*; *fig* démarche *f*. **2** *vt* [shift] déplacer, bouger. || [change - job, office] changer de; **to ~ house** déménager. || [cause]: **to ~ sb to do sthg** inciter qqn à faire qqch. || [emotionally] émouvoir. || [propose]: **to ~ sthg/that ...** proposer qqch/que .... **3** *vi* [shift] bouger. || [act] agir. || [to new house] déménager; [to new job] changer d'emploi. ○ **move about** *vi* [fidget] remuer. || [travel] voyager. ○ **move along** *vi* se déplacer; **the police asked him to ~ along** la police lui a demandé de circuler. ○ **move around** = move about. ○ **move away** *vi* [leave] partir. ○ **move in** *vi* [to house]

emménager. ○ **move on** *vi* [after stopping] se remettre en route. || [in discussion] changer de sujet. ○ **move out** *vi* [from house] déménager. ○ **move over** *vi* s'écarter, se pousser. ○ **move up** *vi* [on bench etc] se déplacer.

moveable ['muːvəbl] = movable.

movement ['muːvmənt] *n* mouvement *m*.

movie ['muːvɪ] *n* film *m*.

movie camera *n* caméra *f*.

moving ['muːvɪŋ] *adj* [emotionally] émouvant(e), touchant(e). || [not fixed] mobile.

mow [maʊ] (*pt* **-ed**, *pp* **-ed** OR **mown**) *vt* faucher; [lawn] tondre. ○ **mow down** *vt sep* faucher.

mower ['maʊəʳ] *n* tondeuse *f* à gazon.

mown [maʊn] *pp* → mow.

MP *n* (*abbr of* **Military Police**) PM. || *Br* (*abbr of* **Member of Parliament**) ≃ député *m*.

mpg (*abbr of* **miles per gallon**) *n* miles au gallon.

mph (*abbr of* **miles per hour**) *n* miles à l'heure.

Mr ['mɪstəʳ] *n* Monsieur *m*; [on letter] M.

Mrs ['mɪsɪz] *n* Madame *f*; [on letter] Mme.

Ms [mɪz] *n* titre que les femmes peuvent utiliser au lieu de madame ou mademoiselle pour éviter la distinction entre les femmes mariées et les célibataires.

MS *n* (*abbr of* **multiple sclerosis**) SEP *f*.

MSc (*abbr of* **Master of Science**) *n* (*titulaire d'une*) maîtrise de sciences.

much [mʌtʃ] (*compar* **more**, *superl* **most**) **1** *adj* beaucoup de; **there isn't ~ rice left** il ne reste pas beaucoup de riz; **as ~ money as ...** autant d'argent que ...; **too ~** trop de; **how ~ ...?** combien de ...? **2** *pron* beaucoup; **I don't think ~ of his new house** sa nouvelle maison ne me plaît pas trop; **as ~ as** autant que; **too ~** trop; **how ~?** combien?; **I'm not ~ of a cook** je suis un piètre cuisinier; **so ~ for all my hard work** tout ce travail pour rien; **I thought as ~** c'est bien ce que je pensais. **3** *adv* beaucoup; **as ~ as** autant que; **thank you very ~** merci beaucoup; **without so ~ as ...** sans même .... ○ **much as** *conj* bien que (+ *subjunctive*).

muck [mʌk] *n* (*U*) *inf* [dirt] saletés *fpl*. || [manure] fumier *m*.

mucky ['mʌkɪ] *adj* sale.

mucus ['mjuːkəs] *n* mucus *m*.

mud [mʌd] *n* boue *f*.

muddle ['mʌdl] **1** *n* désordre *m*, fouillis *m*. **2** *vt* [papers] mélanger. || [person] embrouiller. ○ **muddle through** *vi* se tirer d'affaire, s'en sortir tant bien que mal. ○ **muddle up** *vt sep* mélanger.

muddy ['mʌdɪ] **1** *adj* boueux(euse). **2** *vt fig* embrouiller.

mudguard ['mʌdgɑːd] *n* garde-boue *m inv*.

mudslinging ['mʌd,slɪŋɪŋ] *n* (*U*) *fig* attaques *fpl*.

muff [mʌf] **1** *n* manchon *m*. **2** *vt inf* louper.

muffin ['mʌfɪn] *n* muffin *m*.

muffle ['mʌfl] *vt* étouffer.

muffler ['mʌflər] *n Am* [for car] silencieux *m*.

mug [mʌg] **1** *n* [cup] (grande) tasse *f*. || *inf* [fool] andouille *f*. **2** *vt* [attack] agresser.

mugging ['mʌgɪŋ] *n* agression *f*.

muggy ['mʌgɪ] *adj* lourd(e), moite.

mule [mjuːl] *n* mule *f*.

mull [mʌl] ○ **mull over** *vt sep* ruminer, réfléchir à.

mulled [mʌld] *adj*: ~ wine vin *m* chaud.

multicoloured *Br*, **multicolored** *Am* ['mʌltɪ,kʌləd] *adj* multicolore.

multilateral [,mʌltɪ'lætərəl] *adj* multilatéral(e).

multinational [,mʌltɪ'næʃənl] *n* multinationale *f*.

multiple ['mʌltɪpl] **1** *adj* multiple. **2** *n* multiple *m*.

multiple sclerosis [-sklɪ'rəʊsɪs] *n* sclérose *f* en plaques.

multiplex cinema ['mʌltɪpleks-] *n* grand cinéma *m* à plusieurs salles.

multiplication [,mʌltɪplɪ'keɪʃn] *n* multiplication *f*.

multiply ['mʌltɪplaɪ] **1** *vt* multiplier. **2** *vi* se multiplier.

multistorey *Br*, **multistory** *Am* [,mʌltɪ'stɔːrɪ] *adj* à étages.

multitude ['mʌltɪtjuːd] *n* multitude *f*.

mumble ['mʌmbl] *vt & vi* marmotter.

mummy ['mʌmɪ] *n* [preserved body] momie *f*.

mumps [mʌmps] *n* (*U*) oreillons *mpl*.

munch [mʌntʃ] *vt & vi* croquer.

mundane [mʌn'deɪn] *adj* banal(e), ordinaire.

municipal [mjuː'nɪsɪpl] *adj* municipal(e).

municipality [mjuː,nɪsɪ'pælətɪ] *n* municipalité *f*.

mural ['mjuːərəl] *n* peinture *f* murale.

murder ['mɜːdər] **1** *n* meurtre *m*. **2** *vt* assassiner.

murderer ['mɜːdərər] *n* meurtrier *m*, assassin *m*.

murky ['mɜːkɪ] *adj* [place] sombre. || [water, past] trouble.

murmur ['mɜːmər] **1** *n* murmure *m*; MED souffle *m* au cœur. **2** *vt & vi* murmurer.

muscle ['mʌsl] *n* muscle *m*. ○ **muscle in** *vi* intervenir, s'immiscer.

muscular ['mʌskjʊlər] *adj* [spasm, pain] musculaire. || [person] musclé(e).

muse [mjuːz] **1** *n* muse *f*. **2** *vi* méditer, réfléchir.

museum [mjuː'zɪːəm] *n* musée *m*.

mushroom ['mʌʃrʊm] **1** *n* champignon *m*. **2** *vi* [organization, party] se développer, grandir; [houses] proliférer.

music ['mjuːzɪk] *n* musique *f*.

musical ['mjuːzɪkl] **1** *adj* [event, voice] musical(e). || [child] doué(e) pour la musique, musicien(ienne). **2** *n* comédie *f* musicale.

musical instrument *n* instrument *m* de musique.

music centre *n* chaîne *f* compacte.

musician [mjuː'zɪʃn] *n* musicien *m*, -ienne *f*.

Muslim ['mʊzlɪm] **1** *adj* musulman(e). **2** *n* musulman *m*, -e *f*.

muslin ['mʌzlɪn] *n* mousseline *f*.

mussel ['mʌsl] *n* moule *f*.

must [mʌst] **1** *modal vb* [expressing obligation] devoir; I ~ go il faut que je m'en aille, je dois partir. || [expressing likelihood]: they ~ have known ils devaient le savoir. **2** *n inf*: **a** ~ un must, un impératif.

mustache *Am* = **moustache**.

mustard ['mʌstəd] *n* moutarde *f*.

muster ['mʌstər] *vt* rassembler.

mustn't [mʌsnt] = **must not**.

must've [mʌstəv] = **must have**.

musty ['mʌstɪ] *adj* [smell] de moisi; [room] qui sent le renfermé OR le moisi.

mute [mjuːt] **1** *adj* muet(ette). **2** *n* muet *m*, -ette *f*.

muted ['mjuːtɪd] *adj* [colour] sourd(e). || [reaction] peu marqué(e); [protest] voilé(e).

mutilate ['mjuːtɪleɪt] *vt* mutiler.

mutiny ['mjuːtɪnɪ] **1** *n* mutinerie *f*. **2** *vi* se mutiner.

mutter ['mʌtər] **1** *vt* [threat, curse] marmonner. **2** *vi* marmotter, marmonner.

mutton ['mʌtn] *n* mouton *m*.

mutual ['mjuːtʃʊəl] *adj* [feeling, help] réciproque, mutuel(elle). ‖ [friend, interest] commun(e).

mutually ['mjuːtʃʊəlɪ] *adv* mutuellement, réciproquement.

muzzle ['mʌzl] **1** *n* [of dog - mouth] museau *m*; [- guard] muselière *f*. ‖ [of gun] gueule *f*. **2** *vt lit & fig* museler.

MW (*abbr of* **medium wave**) PO.

my [maɪ] *poss adj* [referring to oneself] mon (ma), mes (*pl*); ~ **dog** mon chien; ~ **house** ma maison; ~ **children** mes enfants; ~ **name is Joe/Sarah** je m'appelle Joe/Sarah; **it wasn't MY fault** ce n'était pas de ma faute à moi. ‖ [in titles]: **yes, ~ Lord** oui, monsieur le comte/duc *etc*.

myself [maɪ'self] *pron* (*reflexive*) me; (*after prep*) moi. ‖ (*for emphasis*) moi-même; **I did it ~** je l'ai fait tout seul.

mysterious [mɪ'stɪərɪəs] *adj* mystérieux(ieuse).

mystery ['mɪstərɪ] *n* mystère *m*.

mystical ['mɪstɪkl] *adj* mystique.

mystified ['mɪstɪfaɪd] *adj* perplexe.

mystifying ['mɪstɪfaɪɪŋ] *adj* inexplicable, déconcertant(e).

mystique [mɪ'stiːk] *n* mystique *f*.

myth [mɪθ] *n* mythe *m*.

mythical ['mɪθɪkl] *adj* mythique.

mythology [mɪ'θɒlədʒɪ] *n* mythologie *f*.

n (*pl* **n's** OR **ns**), **N** (*pl* **N's** OR **Ns**) [en] *n* [letter] *n m inv*, N *m inv*. ○ **N** (*abbr of* **north**) N.

n/a, N/A (*abbr of* **not applicable**) s.o.

nab [næb] *vt inf* [arrest] pincer. ‖ [get quickly] attraper, accaparer.

nag [næg] **1** *vt* harceler. **2** *n inf* [horse] canasson *m*.

nagging ['nægɪŋ] *adj* [doubt] persistant(e), tenace. ‖ [husband, wife] enquiquineur(euse).

nail [neɪl] **1** *n* [for fastening] clou *m*. ‖ [of finger, toe] ongle *m*. **2** *vt* clouer. ○ **nail down** *vt sep* [lid] clouer. ‖ *fig* [person]:

to ~ sb down to sthg faire préciser qqch à qqn.

nailbrush ['neɪlbrʌʃ] *n* brosse *f* à ongles.

nail file *n* lime *f* à ongles.

nail polish *n* vernis *m* à ongles.

nail scissors *npl* ciseaux *mpl* à ongles.

nail varnish *n* vernis *m* à ongles.

nail varnish remover [-rɪ'muːvər] *n* dissolvant *m*.

naive, naïve [naɪ'iːv] *adj* naïf(ïve).

naked ['neɪkɪd] *adj* [body, flame] nu(e); **with the ~ eye** à l'œil nu. ‖ [emotions] manifeste, évident(e); [aggression] non déguisé(e).

name [neɪm] **1** *n* [identification] nom *m*; **what's your ~?** comment vous appelez-vous?; **in my/his ~** à mon/son nom; **in the ~ of peace** au nom de la paix; **to call sb ~s** traiter qqn de tous les noms, injurier qqn. ‖ [reputation] réputation *f*. ‖ [famous person] grand nom *m*, célébrité *f*. **2** *vt* [gen] nommer; **to ~ sb/sthg after** *Br*, **to ~ sb/sthg for** *Am* donner à qqn/à qqch le nom de. ‖ [date, price] fixer.

nameless ['neɪmlɪs] *adj* inconnu(e), sans nom; [author] anonyme.

namely ['neɪmlɪ] *adv* à savoir, c'est-à-dire.

namesake ['neɪmseɪk] *n* homonyme *m*.

nanny ['nænɪ] *n* nurse *f*, bonne *f* d'enfants.

nap [næp] *n*: **to have** OR **take a ~** faire un petit somme.

nape [neɪp] *n* nuque *f*.

napkin ['næpkɪn] *n* serviette *f*.

narcotic [nɑː'kɒtɪk] *n* stupéfiant *m*.

narrative ['nærətɪv] **1** *adj* narratif(ive). **2** *n* [story] récit *m*, narration *f*. ‖ [skill] art *m* de la narration.

narrator [*Br* nə'reɪtər, *Am* 'næreɪtər] *n* narrateur *m*, -trice *f*.

narrow ['nærəʊ] **1** *adj* [gen] étroit(e); **to have a ~ escape** l'échapper belle. ‖ [victory, majority] de justesse. **2** *vt* [reduce] réduire, limiter. ‖ [eyes] fermer à demi, plisser. **3** *vi lit & fig* se rétrécir. ○ **narrow down** *vt sep* réduire, limiter.

narrowly ['nærəʊlɪ] *adv* [win, lose] de justesse. ‖ [miss] de peu.

narrow-minded [-'maɪndɪd] *adj* [person] à l'esprit étroit, borné(e); [attitude] étroit(e), borné(e).

nasal ['neɪzl] *adj* nasal(e).

nasty ['nɑːstɪ] *adj* [unpleasant - smell, feeling] mauvais(e); [- weather] vilain(e), mauvais(e). ‖ [unkind] méchant(e). ‖

[problem] difficile, délicat(e). || [injury] vilain(e); [accident] grave; [fall] mauvais(e).

nation ['neɪʃn] n nation f.

national ['næʃənl] 1 adj national(e); [campaign, strike] à l'échelon national; [custom] du pays, de la nation. 2 n ressortissant m, -e f.

national anthem n hymne m national.

national dress n costume m national.

nationalism ['næʃnəlɪzm] n nationalisme m.

nationalist ['næʃnəlɪst] 1 adj nationaliste. 2 n nationaliste mf.

nationality [,næʃə'nælətɪ] n nationalité f.

nationalize, -ise ['næʃnəlaɪz] vt nationaliser.

national park n parc m national.

nationwide ['neɪʃənwaɪd] 1 adj dans tout le pays; [campaign, strike] à l'échelon national. 2 adv à travers tout le pays.

native ['neɪtɪv] 1 adj [country, area] natal(e). || [language] maternel(elle); **an English ~ speaker** une personne de langue maternelle anglaise. || [plant, animal] indigène; **~ to** originaire de. 2 n autochtone mf; [of colony] indigène mf.

Native American n Indien m, -ienne f d'Amérique, Amérindien m, -ienne f.

Nativity [nə'tɪvətɪ] n: **the ~** la Nativité.

NATO ['neɪtəu] (abbr of **North Atlantic Treaty Organization**) n OTAN f.

natural ['nætʃrəl] adj [gen] naturel(elle). || [instinct, talent] inné(e). || [footballer, musician] né(e).

natural gas n gaz m naturel.

naturalize, -ise ['nætʃrəlaɪz] vt naturaliser; **to be ~d** se faire naturaliser.

naturally ['nætʃrəlɪ] adv [gen] naturellement. || [unaffected] sans affectation, avec naturel.

natural wastage n (U) départs mpl volontaires.

nature ['neɪtʃər] n nature f; **by ~** [basically] par essence; [by disposition] de nature, naturellement.

nature reserve n réserve f naturelle.

naughty ['nɔːtɪ] adj [badly behaved] vilain(e), méchant(e). || [rude] grivois(e).

nausea ['nɔːsjə] n nausée f.

nauseam ['nɔːzɪæm] → **ad nauseam**.

nauseating ['nɔːsɪeɪtɪŋ] adj lit & fig écœurant(e).

nautical ['nɔːtɪkl] adj nautique.

naval ['neɪvl] adj naval(e).

nave [neɪv] n nef f.

navel ['neɪvl] n nombril m.

navigate ['nævɪgeɪt] 1 vt [plane] piloter; [ship] gouverner. || [seas, river] naviguer sur. 2 vi AERON & NAUT naviguer; AUT lire la carte.

navigation [,nævɪ'geɪʃn] n navigation f.

navigator ['nævɪgeɪtər] n navigateur m.

navy ['neɪvɪ] 1 n marine f. 2 adj [colour] bleu marine (inv).

navy blue 1 adj bleu marine (inv). 2 n bleu m marine.

Nazareth ['næzərɪθ] n Nazareth.

Nazi ['nɑːtsɪ] (pl -s) 1 adj nazi(e). 2 n Nazi m, -e f.

NB (abbr of **nota bene**) NB.

near [nɪər] 1 adj proche; **a ~ disaster** une catastrophe évitée de justesse OR de peu; **in the ~ future** dans un proche avenir, dans un avenir prochain; **it was a ~ thing** il était moins cinq. 2 adv [close] près. || [almost]: **~ impossible** presque impossible; **nowhere ~ ready/enough** loin d'être prêt/assez. 3 prep: **~ (to)** [in space] près de; [in time] près de, vers; **~ to tears** au bord des larmes; **~ (to) death** sur le point de mourir; **~ (to) the truth** proche de la vérité. 4 vt approcher de. 5 vi approcher.

nearby [nɪə'baɪ] 1 adj proche. 2 adv tout près, à proximité.

nearly ['nɪəlɪ] adv presque; **I ~ fell** j'ai failli tomber; **not ~ enough/as good** loin d'être suffisant/aussi bon.

near miss n SPORT coup m qui a raté de peu. || [between planes, vehicles] quasi-collision f.

nearside ['nɪəsaɪd] n [right-hand drive] côté m gauche; [left-hand drive] côté droit.

nearsighted [,nɪə'saɪtɪd] adj Am myope.

neat [niːt] adj [room, house] bien tenu(e), en ordre; [work] soigné(e); [handwriting] net (nette); [appearance] soigné(e), net (nette). || [solution, manoeuvre] habile, ingénieux(ieuse). || [alcohol] pur(e), sans eau. || Am inf [very good] chouette, super (inv).

neatly ['niːtlɪ] adv [arrange] avec ordre; [write] soigneusement; [dress] avec soin. || [skilfully] habilement, adroitement.

necessarily [Br 'nesəsrəlɪ, ,nesə'serɪlɪ] adv forcément, nécessairement.

necessary ['nesəsrı] *adj* [required] nécessaire, indispensable; **to make the ~
arrangements** faire le nécessaire. ‖ [in-
evitable] inévitable, inéluctable.

necessity [nı'sesətı] *n* nécessité *f*.

neck [nek] **1** *n* ANAT cou *m*. ‖ [of shirt,
dress] encolure *f*. ‖ [of bottle] col *m*, goulot *m*. **2** *vi inf* se bécoter.

necklace ['neklıs] *n* collier *m*.

neckline ['neklaın] *n* encolure *f*.

necktie ['nektaı] *n Am* cravate *f*.

nectarine ['nektərın] *n* brugnon *m*,
nectarine *f*.

need [ni:d] **1** *n* besoin *m*; **~ for sthg/to
do sthg** besoin de qqch/de faire qqch; **to
be in OR have ~ of sthg** avoir besoin de
qqch; **if ~ be** si besoin est, si nécessaire;
in ~ dans le besoin; **there's no ~ to get up**
ce n'est pas la peine de te lever. **2** *vt* [re-
quire]: **to ~ sthg/to do sthg** avoir besoin
de qqch/de faire qqch; **I ~ to go to the
doctor** il faut que j'aille chez le médecin.
‖ [be obliged]: **to ~ to do sthg** être obli-
gé(e) de faire qqch. **3** *modal vb*: **~ we go?**
faut-il qu'on y aille? **it ~ not happen**
cela ne doit pas forcément se produire.

needle ['ni:dl] **1** *n* [gen] aiguille *f*. ‖ [sty-
lus] saphir *m*. **2** *vt inf* [annoy] asticoter,
lancer des piques à.

needless ['ni:dlıs] *adj* [risk, waste] inutile; [remark] déplacé(e); **~ to say ...** bien
entendu ...

needlework ['ni:dlwɜ:k] *n* [embroi-
dery] travail *m* d'aiguille. ‖ (*U*) [activity]
couture *f*.

needn't ['ni:dnt] = **need not**.

needy ['ni:dı] *adj* nécessiteux(euse), in-
digent(e).

negative ['negǝtıv] **1** *adj* négatif(ive). **2**
n PHOT négatif *m*. ‖ LING négation *f*.

neglect [nı'glekt] **1** *n* [of garden] mauvais entretien *m*; [of children] manque *m*
de soins; [of duty] manquement *m*. **2** *vt*
négliger; [garden] laisser à l'abandon; **to
~ to do sthg** négliger OR omettre de faire
qqch.

negligee ['neglıʒeı] *n* déshabillé *m*, né-
gligé *m*.

negligence ['neglıdʒəns] *n* négligence *f*.

negligible ['neglıdʒǝbl] *adj* négligeable.

negotiate [nı'gǝʊʃıeıt] **1** *vt* COMM & POL
négocier. ‖ [obstacle] franchir; [bend]
prendre, négocier. **2** *vi* négocier; **to ~
with sb (for sthg)** engager des négocia-
tions avec qqn (pour obtenir qqch).

negotiation [nı,gǝʊʃı'eıʃn] *n* négociation *f*.

Negress ['ni:grıs] *n* négresse *f*.

Negro ['ni:grǝʊ] (*pl* -es) **1** *adj* noir(e).
2 *n* Noir *m*.

neigh [neı] *vi* [horse] hennir.

neighbour *Br*, **neighbor** *Am* ['neıbǝr]
n voisin *m*, -e *f*.

neighbourhood *Br*, **neighborhood**
Am ['neıbǝhʊd] *n* [of town] voisinage *m*,
quartier *m*. ‖ [approximate figure]: **in the
~ of £300** environ 300 livres, dans les
300 livres.

neighbouring *Br*, **neighboring** *Am*
['neıbǝrıŋ] *adj* avoisinant(e).

neighbourly *Br*, **neighborly** *Am*
['neıbǝlı] *adj* bon voisin (bonne voisine).

neither ['naıðǝr, 'ni:ðǝr] **1** *adv*: **~ good
nor bad** ni bon ni mauvais; **that's ~ here
nor there** cela n'a rien à voir. **2** *pron* &
adj ni l'un ni l'autre (ni l'une ni l'autre).
3 *conj*: **~ do I** moi non plus.

neon ['ni:ɒn] *n* néon *m*.

neon light *n* néon *m*, lumière *f* au néon.

nephew ['nefju:] *n* neveu *m*.

Neptune ['neptju:n] *n* [planet] Neptune
f.

nerve [nɜ:v] *n* ANAT nerf *m*. ‖ [courage]
courage *m*, sang-froid *m*; **to lose one's ~**
se dégonfler, flancher. ‖ [cheek] culot *m*,
toupet *m*. ○ **nerves** *npl* nerfs *mpl*; **to get
on sb's ~s** taper sur les nerfs OR le système de qqn.

nerve-racking [-,rækıŋ] *adj* angois-
sant(e), éprouvant(e).

nervous ['nɜ:vǝs] *adj* [gen] ner-
veux(euse). ‖ [apprehensive - smile, person etc] inquiet(iète); [- performer] qui a
le trac; **to be ~ about sthg** appréhender
qqch.

nervous breakdown *n* dépression *f*
nerveuse.

nest [nest] **1** *n* nid *m*; **~ of tables** table *f*
gigogne. **2** *vi* [bird] faire son nid, nicher.

nest egg *n* pécule *m*, bas *m* de laine.

nestle ['nesl] *vi* se blottir.

net [net] **1** *adj* net (nette); **~ result** résultat final. **2** *n* [gen] filet *m*. ‖ [fabric]
voile *m*, tulle *m*. **3** *vt* [fish] prendre au
filet. ‖ [money - subj: person] toucher net,
gagner net; [- subj: deal] rapporter net.

netball ['netbɔ:l] *n* netball *m*.

net curtains *npl* voilage *m*.

Netherlands ['neðǝlǝndz] *npl*: **the ~** les
Pays-Bas *mpl*.

net profit *n* bénéfice *m* net.

net revenue *n Am* chiffre *m* d'affaires.

nett [net] *adj* = **net**.

netting ['netɪŋ] *n* [metal, plastic] grillage *m*. || [fabric] voile *m*, tulle *m*.

nettle ['netl] *n* ortie *f*.

network ['netwɜːk] *n* réseau *m*.

neurosis [ˌnjʊə'rəʊsɪs] (*pl* -ses) *n* névrose *f*.

neurotic [ˌnjʊə'rɒtɪk] *adj* névrosé(e).

neuter ['njuːtər] **1** *adj* neutre. **2** *vt* [cat] châtrer.

neutral ['njuːtrəl] **1** *adj* [gen] neutre. **2** *n* AUT point *m* mort.

neutrality [njuː'trælətɪ] *n* neutralité *f*.

neutralize, -ise ['njuːtrəlaɪz] *vt* neutraliser.

never ['nevər] *adv* jamais ... ne, ne ... jamais; **~ ever** jamais, au grand jamais; **well I ~!** ça par exemple!

never-ending *adj* interminable.

nevertheless [ˌnevəðə'les] *adv* néanmoins, pourtant.

new [adj sing *n* njuː] *adj* [gen] nouveau(elle). || [not used] neuf (neuve); **as good as ~** comme neuf. ⚬ **news** *n* (*U*) [information] nouvelle *f*; **a piece of ~s** une nouvelle. || RADIO informations *fpl*. || TV journal *m* télévisé, actualités *fpl*.

newborn ['njuːbɔːn] *adj* nouveau-né(e).

newcomer ['njuːˌkʌmər] *n*: **~ (to sthg)** nouveau-venu *m*, nouvelle-venue *f* (dans qqch).

newfangled [ˌnjuː'fæŋgld] *adj inf pej* ultramoderne, trop moderne.

new-found *adj* récent(e), de fraîche date.

newly ['njuːlɪ] *adv* récemment, fraîchement.

newlyweds ['njuːlɪwedz] *npl* nouveaux OR jeunes mariés *mpl*.

new moon *n* nouvelle lune *f*.

news agency *n* agence *f* de presse.

newsagent *Br* ['njuːzeɪdʒənt], **newsdealer** *Am* ['njuːzdiːlər] *n* marchand *m* de journaux.

newscaster ['njuːzˌkɑːstər] *n* présentateur *m*, -trice *f*.

newsdealer *Am* = newsagent.

newsflash ['njuːzflæʃ] *n* flash *m* d'information.

newsletter ['njuːzˌletər] *n* bulletin *m*.

newspaper ['njuːzˌpeɪpər] *n* journal *m*.

newsprint ['njuːzprɪnt] *n* papier *m* journal.

newsreader ['njuːzˌriːdər] *n* présentateur *m*, -trice *f*.

newsreel ['njuːzriːl] *n* actualités *fpl* filmées.

newsstand ['njuːzstænd] *n* kiosque *m* à journaux.

newt [njuːt] *n* triton *m*.

New Year *n* nouvel an *m*, nouvelle année *f*; **Happy ~!** bonne année!

New Year's Day *n* jour *m* de l'an, premier *m* de l'an.

New Year's Eve *n* la Saint-Sylvestre.

New York [-'jɔːk] *n* [city]: **~ (City)** New York. || [state]: **~ (State)** l'État *m* de New York.

New Zealand [-'ziːlənd] *n* Nouvelle-Zélande *f*.

New Zealander [-'ziːləndər] *n* Néo-Zélandais *m*, -e *f*.

next [nekst] **1** *adj* prochain(e); [room] d'à côté; [page] suivant(e); **~ Tuesday** mardi prochain; **~ time** la prochaine fois; **~ week** la semaine prochaine; **the ~ week** la semaine suivante OR d'après; **~ year** l'année prochaine; **~, please!** au suivant!; **the day after ~** le surlendemain; **the week after ~** dans deux semaines. **2** *adv* [afterwards] ensuite, après. || [again] la prochaine fois. || (*with superlatives*): **he's the ~ biggest after Dan** c'est le plus grand après OR à part Dan. **3** *prep* **~ to** *prep* à côté de. ⚬ **next to** *prep* à côté de; **it cost ~ to nothing** cela a coûté une bagatelle OR trois fois rien; **I know ~ to nothing** je ne sais presque OR pratiquement rien.

next door *adv* à côté. ⚬ **next-door** *adj*: **next-door neighbour** voisin *m*, -e *f* d'à côté.

next of kin *n* plus proche parent *m*.

nib [nɪb] *n* plume *f*.

nibble ['nɪbl] *vt* grignoter, mordiller.

Nicaragua [ˌnɪkə'rægjʊə] *n* Nicaragua *m*.

nice [naɪs] *adj* [holiday, food] bon (bonne); [day, picture] beau (belle); [dress] joli(e). || [person] gentil(ille), sympathique; **to be ~ to sb** être gentil OR aimable avec qqn.

nice-looking [-'lʊkɪŋ] *adj* joli(e), beau (belle).

nicely ['naɪslɪ] *adv* [made, manage etc] bien; [dressed] joliment; **that will do ~** cela fera très bien l'affaire. || [politely - ask] poliment, gentiment; [- behave] bien.

niche [niːʃ] *n* [in wall] niche *f*; *fig* bonne situation *f*, voie *f*.

nick [nɪk] **1** *n* [cut] entaille *f*, coupure *f*. || *phr*: **in the ~ of time** juste à temps. **2** *vt* [cut] couper, entailler.

nickel ['nɪkl] *n* [metal] nickel *m*. || *Am* [coin] pièce *f* de cinq cents.

nickname ['nɪkneɪm] **1** *n* sobriquet *m*, surnom *m*. **2** *vt* surnommer.

nicotine ['nɪkəti:n] *n* nicotine *f*.

niece [ni:s] *n* nièce *f*.

Nigeria [naɪ'dʒɪərɪə] *n* Nigeria *m*.

Nigerian [naɪ'dʒɪərɪən] **1** *adj* nigérian(e). **2** *n* Nigérian *m*, -e *f*.

night [naɪt] *n* [not day] nuit *f*; **at ~** la nuit. || [evening] soir *m*; **at ~** le soir. ||, *phr*: **to have an early ~** se coucher de bonne heure; **to have a late ~** veiller, se coucher tard. ○ **nights** *adv Am* [at night] la nuit.

nightcap ['naɪtkæp] *n* [drink] *boisson alcoolisée prise avant de se coucher*.

nightclub ['naɪtklʌb] *n* boîte *f* de nuit, night-club *m*.

nightdress ['naɪtdres] *n* chemise *f* de nuit.

nightfall ['naɪtfɔ:l] *n* tombée *f* de la nuit OR du jour.

nightgown ['naɪtgaʊn] *n* chemise *f* de nuit.

nightie ['naɪtɪ] *n inf* chemise *f* de nuit.

nightingale ['naɪtɪŋgeɪl] *n* rossignol *m*.

nightlife ['naɪtlaɪf] *n* vie *f* nocturne, activités *fpl* nocturnes.

nightly ['naɪtlɪ] **1** *adj* (de) toutes les nuits OR tous les soirs. **2** *adv* toutes les nuits, tous les soirs.

nightmare ['naɪtmeəʳ] *n lit & fig* cauchemar *m*.

night porter *n* veilleur *m* de nuit.

night school *n* (*U*) cours *mpl* du soir.

night shift *n* [period] poste *m* de nuit.

nightshirt ['naɪtʃɜ:t] *n* chemise *f* de nuit d'homme.

nighttime ['naɪttaɪm] *n* nuit *f*.

nil [nɪl] *n* néant *m*; *Br* SPORT zéro *m*.

Nile [naɪl] *n*: **the ~** le Nil.

nimble ['nɪmbl] *adj* agile, leste; *fig* [mind] vif (vive).

nine [naɪn] *num* neuf; *see also* **six**.

nineteen [,naɪn'ti:n] *num* dix-neuf; *see also* **six**.

ninety ['naɪntɪ] *num* quatre-vingt-dix; *see also* **sixty**.

ninth [naɪnθ] *num* neuvième; *see also* **sixth**.

nip [nɪp] **1** *n* [pinch] pinçon *m*; [bite] morsure *f*. || [of drink] goutte *f*, doigt *m*. **2** *vt* [pinch] pincer; [bite] mordre.

nipple ['nɪpl] *n* ANAT bout *m* de sein, mamelon *m*. || [of bottle] tétine *f*.

nit [nɪt] *n* [in hair] lente *f*.

nitpicking ['nɪtpɪkɪŋ] *n inf* ergotage *m*, pinaillage *m*.

nitrogen ['naɪtrədʒən] *n* azote *m*.

nitty-gritty [,nɪtɪ'grɪtɪ] *n inf*: **to get down to the ~** en venir à l'essentiel OR aux choses sérieuses.

no [nəʊ] (*pl* **-es**) **1** *adv* [gen] non; [expressing disagreement] mais non. || [not any]: **~ bigger/smaller** pas plus grand/petit; **~ better** pas mieux. **2** *adj* aucun(e), pas de; **there's ~ telling what will happen** impossible de dire ce qui va se passer; **he's ~ friend of mine** je ne le compte pas parmi mes amis. **3** *n* non *m*; **she won't take ~ for an answer** elle n'accepte pas de refus OR qu'on lui dise non.

No., no. (*abbr of* **number**) No, no.

nobility [nə'bɪlətɪ] *n* noblesse *f*.

noble ['nəʊbl] **1** *adj* noble. **2** *n* noble *m*.

nobody ['nəʊbədɪ] **1** *pron* personne, aucun(e). **2** *n pej* rien-du-tout *mf*, moins que rien *m*.

nocturnal [nɒk'tɜ:nl] *adj* nocturne.

nod [nɒd] **1** *vt*: **to ~ one's head** incliner la tête, faire un signe de tête. **2** *vi* [in agreement] faire un signe de tête affirmatif, faire signe que oui. || [to indicate sthg] faire un signe de tête. || [as greeting]: **to ~ to sb** saluer qqn d'un signe de tête. ○ **nod off** *vi* somnoler, s'assoupir.

noise [nɔɪz] *n* bruit *m*.

noisy ['nɔɪzɪ] *adj* bruyant(e).

no-man's-land *n* no man's land *m*.

nominal ['nɒmɪnl] *adj* [in name only] de nom seulement, nominal(e). || [very small] nominal(e), insignifiant(e).

nominate ['nɒmɪneɪt] *vt* [propose]: **to ~ sb (for/as sthg)** proposer qqn (pour/comme qqch). || [appoint]: **to ~ sb (as sthg)** nommer qqn (qqch).

nominee [,nɒmɪ'ni:] *n* personne *f* nommée OR désignée.

nonalcoholic [,nɒnælkə'hɒlɪk] *adj* non-alcoolisé(e).

nonchalant [*Br* 'nɒnʃələnt, *Am* ,nɒnʃə'lɑ:nt] *adj* nonchalant(e).

noncommittal [,nɒnkə'mɪtl] *adj* évasif(ive).

nonconformist [,nɒnkən'fɔ:mɪst] *adj* non-conformiste.

nondescript [*Br* 'nɒndɪskrɪpt, *Am* ,nɒndɪ'skrɪpt] *adj* quelconque, terne.

none [nʌn] **1** *pron* [gen] aucun(e); **there was ~ left** il n'y en avait plus, il n'en restait plus. || [nobody] personne, nul (nulle). **2** *adv*: **~ the worse/wiser** pas plus mal/avancé; **~ the better** pas mieux. ○ **none too** *adv* pas tellement OR trop.

nonentity [nɒ'nentətɪ] *n* nullité *f*, zéro *m*.

nonetheless [ˌnʌnðə'les] *adv* néanmoins, pourtant.

nonexistent [ˌnɒnɪg'zɪstənt] *adj* inexistant(e).

nonfiction [ˌnɒn'fɪkʃn] *n* (*U*) ouvrages *mpl* généraux.

no-nonsense *adj* direct(e), sérieux(ieuse).

nonpayment [nɒn'peɪmənt] *n* nonpaiement *m*.

nonplussed, **nonplused** *Am* [ˌnɒn'plʌst] *adj* déconcerté(e), perplexe.

nonreturnable [ˌnɒnrɪ'tɜːnəbl] *adj* [bottle] non consigné(e).

nonsense ['nɒnsəns] **1** *n* (*U*) [meaningless words] charabia *m*. ‖ [foolish idea] **it was ~ to suggest** .... il était absurde de suggérer .... ‖ [foolish behaviour] bêtises *fpl*, idioties *fpl*; **to make (a) ~ of sthg** gâcher OR saboter qqch. **2** *excl* quelles bêtises OR foutaises!

nonsmoker [ˌnɒn'sməʊkəʳ] *n* nonfumeur *m*, -euse *f*, personne *f* qui ne fume pas.

nonstick [ˌnɒn'stɪk] *adj* qui n'attache pas, téflonisé(e).

nonstop [ˌnɒn'stɒp] **1** *adj* [flight] direct(e), sans escale; [activity] continu(e); [rain] continuel(elle). **2** *adv* [talk, work] sans arrêt; [rain] sans discontinuer.

noodles ['nuːdlz] *npl* nouilles *fpl*.

nook [nʊk] *n* [of room] coin *m*, recoin *m*; **every ~ and cranny** tous les coins, les coins et les recoins.

noon [nuːn] *n* midi *m*.

no one *pron* = **nobody**.

noose [nuːs] *n* nœud *m* coulant.

no-place *Am* = **nowhere**.

nor [nɔːʳ] *conj* **~ do I** moi non plus; → **neither**.

norm [nɔːm] *n* norme *f*.

normal ['nɔːml] *adj* normal(e).

normality [nɔː'mælɪtɪ], **normalcy** *Am* ['nɔːmlsɪ] *n* normalité *f*.

normally ['nɔːməlɪ] *adv* normalement.

Normandy ['nɔːməndɪ] *n* Normandie *f*.

north [nɔːθ] **1** *n* [direction] nord *m*. ‖ [region]: **the ~** le nord. **2** *adj* nord (*inv*); [wind] du nord. **3** *adv* au nord, vers le nord; **~ of** au nord de.

North Africa *n* Afrique *f* du Nord.

North America *n* Amérique *f* du Nord.

North American 1 *adj* nord-américain(aine). **2** *n* Nord-Américain *m*, -aine *f*.

northeast [ˌnɔːθ'iːst] **1** *n* [direction] nord-est *m*. ‖ [region]: **the ~** le nord-est. **2** *adj* nord-est (*inv*); [wind] du nord-est. **3** *adv* au nord-est, vers le nord-est; **~ of** au nord-est de.

northerly ['nɔːðəlɪ] *adj* du nord; **in a ~ direction** vers le nord, en direction du nord.

northern ['nɔːðən] *adj* du nord, nord (*inv*).

Northern Ireland *n* Irlande *f* du Nord.

northernmost ['nɔːðənməʊst] *adj* le plus au nord (la plus au nord), à l'extrême nord.

North Korea *n* Corée *f* du Nord.

North Pole *n*: **the ~** le pôle Nord.

North Sea *n*: **the ~** la mer du Nord.

northward ['nɔːθwəd] **1** *adj* au nord. **2** *adv* = **northwards**.

northwards ['nɔːθwədz] *adv* au nord, vers le nord.

northwest [ˌnɔːθ'west] **1** *n* [direction] nord-ouest *m*. ‖ [region]: **the ~** le nord-ouest. **2** *adj* nord-ouest (*inv*); [wind] du nord-ouest. **3** *adv* au nord-ouest, vers le nord-ouest; **~ of** au nord-ouest de.

Norway ['nɔːweɪ] *n* Norvège *f*.

Norwegian [nɔː'wiːdʒən] **1** *adj* norvégien(ienne). **2** *n* [person] Norvégien *m*, -ienne *f*. ‖ [language] norvégien *m*.

nose [nəʊz] *n* nez *m*; **to look down one's ~ at sb** *fig* traiter qqn de haut (en bas); **to poke** OR **stick one's ~ into sthg** mettre OR fourrer son nez dans qqch; **to turn up one's ~ at sthg** dédaigner qqch. ○ **nose about**, **nose around** *vi* fouiner, fureter.

nosebleed ['nəʊzbliːd] *n*: **to have a ~** saigner du nez.

nosedive ['nəʊzdaɪv] **1** *n* [of plane] piqué *m*. **2** *vi* [plane] descendre en piqué, piquer du nez. ‖ *fig* [prices] dégringoler; [hopes] s'écrouler.

nosey ['nəʊzɪ] = **nosy**.

nostalgia [nɒ'stældʒə] *n*: **~ (for sthg)** nostalgie *f* (de qqch).

nostril ['nɒstrəl] *n* narine *f*.

nosy ['nəʊzɪ] *adj* curieux(ieuse), fouinard(e).

not [nɒt] *adv* ne pas, pas; **I think ~** je ne crois pas; **I'm afraid ~** je crains que non; **~ always** pas toujours; **~ that ...** ce n'est pas que .... non pas que ...; **~ at all** [no] pas du tout; [to acknowledge thanks] de rien, je vous en prie.

notable ['nəʊtəbl] *adj* notable, remarquable; **to be ~ for sthg** être célèbre pour qqch.

notably ['nəʊtəblɪ] *adv* [in particular] notamment, particulièrement. || [noticeably] sensiblement, nettement.

notary ['nəʊtərɪ] *n*: ~ **(public)** notaire *m*.

notch [nɒtʃ] *n* [cut] entaille *f*, encoche *f*. || *fig* [on scale] cran *m*.

note [nəʊt] **1** *n* [gen & MUS] note *f*; [short letter] mot *m*; **to take ~ of sthg** prendre note de qqch. || [money] billet *m* (de banque). **2** *vt* [notice] remarquer, constater. ○ **notes** *npl* [in book] notes *fpl*. ○ **note down** *vt sep* noter, inscrire.

notebook ['nəʊtbʊk] *n* [for notes] carnet *m*, calepin *m*. || COMPUT ordinateur *m* portable compact.

noted ['nəʊtɪd] *adj* célèbre, éminent(e).

notepad ['nəʊtpæd] *n* bloc-notes *m*.

notepaper ['nəʊtpeɪpər] *n* papier *m* à lettres.

noteworthy ['nəʊt,wɜːðɪ] *adj* remarquable, notable.

nothing ['nʌθɪŋ] **1** *pron* rien; **I've got ~ to do** je n'ai rien à faire; **~ but** ne ... que, rien que. **2** *adv*: **you're ~ like your brother** tu ne ressembles pas du tout OR en rien à ton frère; **I'm ~ like finished** je suis loin d'avoir fini.

notice ['nəʊtɪs] **1** *n* [written announcement] affiche *f*, placard *m*. || [attention]: **to take ~ (of sb/sthg)** faire OR prêter attention (à qqn/qqch). || [warning] avis *m*, avertissement *m*; **at short ~** dans un bref délai; **until further ~** jusqu'à nouvel ordre. || [at work]: **to be given one's ~** recevoir son congé, être renvoyé(e); **to hand in one's ~** donner sa démission, demander son congé. **2** *vt* remarquer, s'apercevoir de.

noticeable ['nəʊtɪsəbl] *adj* sensible, perceptible.

notice board *n* panneau *m* d'affichage.

notify ['nəʊtɪfaɪ] *vt*: **to ~ sb (of sthg)** avertir OR aviser qqn (de qqch).

notion ['nəʊʃn] *n* idée *f*, notion *f*. ○ **notions** *npl Am* mercerie *f*.

notorious [nəʊ'tɔːrɪəs] *adj* [criminal] notoire; [place] mal famé(e).

nought [nɔːt] *num* zéro *m*; **~s and crosses** morpion *m*.

noun [naʊn] *n* nom *m*.

nourish ['nʌrɪʃ] *vt* nourrir.

nourishing ['nʌrɪʃɪŋ] *adj* nourrissant(e).

nourishment ['nʌrɪʃmənt] *n* (*U*) nourriture *f*, aliments *mpl*.

novel ['nɒvl] **1** *adj* nouveau(nouvelle), original(e). **2** *n* roman *m*.

novelist ['nɒvəlɪst] *n* romancier *m*, -ière *f*.

novelty ['nɒvltɪ] *n* [gen] nouveauté *f*. || [cheap object] gadget *m*.

November [nə'vembər] *n* novembre *m*; *see also* **September**.

novice ['nɒvɪs] *n* novice *mf*.

now [naʊ] **1** *adv* [at this time, at once] maintenant; **any day/time ~** d'un jour/moment à l'autre; **~ and then** OR **again** de temps en temps, de temps à autre. || [in past] à ce moment-là, alors. || [to introduce statement]: **~ let's just calm down** bon, on se calme maintenant. **2** *conj*: **~ (that)** maintenant que. **3** *n*: **for ~** pour le présent; **from ~ on** à partir de maintenant, désormais; **up until ~** jusqu'à présent; **by ~** déjà.

nowadays ['naʊədeɪz] *adv* actuellement, aujourd'hui.

nowhere *Br* ['nəʊweər], **no-place** *Am adv* nulle part; **~ near** loin de; **we're getting ~** on n'avance pas, on n'arrive à rien.

nozzle ['nɒzl] *n* ajutage *m*, buse *f*.

nuance ['njuːɑːns] *n* nuance *f*.

nuclear bomb *n* bombe *f* nucléaire.

nuclear disarmament *n* désarmement *m* nucléaire.

nuclear energy *n* énergie *f* nucléaire.

nuclear power *n* énergie *f* nucléaire.

nuclear reactor *n* réacteur *m* nucléaire.

nucleus ['njuːklɪəs] (*pl* **-lei** [-lɪaɪ]) *n lit & fig* noyau *m*.

nude [njuːd] **1** *adj* nu(e). **2** *n* nu *m*; **in the ~** nu(e).

nudge [nʌdʒ] *vt* pousser du coude.

nudist ['njuːdɪst] **1** *adj* nudiste. **2** *n* nudiste *mf*.

nugget ['nʌgɪt] *n* pépite *f*.

nuisance ['njuːsns] *n* ennui *m*, embêtement *m*; **to make a ~ of o.s.** embêter le monde; **what a ~!** quelle plaie!

null [nʌl] *adj*: **~ and void** nul et non avenu.

numb [nʌm] **1** *adj* engourdi(e); **to be ~ with** [fear] être paralysé par; [cold] être transi de. **2** *vt* engourdir.

number ['nʌmbər] **1** *n* [numeral] chiffre *m*. ‖ [of telephone, house, car] numéro *m*. ‖ [quantity] nombre *m*; **a ~ of** un certain nombre de, plusieurs; **any ~ of** un grand nombre de, bon nombre de. ‖ [song] chanson *f*. **2** *vt* [amount to, include] compter. ‖ [give number to] numéroter.

number one 1 *adj* premier(ière), principal(e). **2** *n inf* [oneself] soi, sa pomme.

numberplate ['nʌmbəpleɪt] *n* plaque *f* d'immatriculation.

numeral ['nju:mərəl] *n* chiffre *m*.

numerical [nju:'merɪkl] *adj* numérique.

numerous ['nju:mərəs] *adj* nombreux(euse).

nun [nʌn] *n* religieuse *f*, sœur *f*.

nurse [nɜ:s] **1** *n* infirmière *f*; **(male) ~** infirmier *m*. **2** *vt* [patient, cold] soigner. ‖ *fig* [desires, hopes] nourrir. ‖ [subj: mother] allaiter.

nursery ['nɜ:səri] *n* [for children] garderie *f*. ‖ [for plants] pépinière *f*.

nursery rhyme *n* comptine *f*.

nursery school *n* (école *f*) maternelle *f*.

nursery slopes *npl* pistes *fpl* pour débutants.

nursing ['nɜ:sɪŋ] *n* métier *m* d'infirmière.

nursing home *n* [for old people] maison *f* de retraite privée; [for childbirth] maternité *f* privée.

nurture ['nɜ:tʃər] *vt* [children] élever; [plants] soigner. ‖ *fig* [hopes etc] nourrir.

nut [nʌt] *n* [to eat] *terme générique désignant les fruits tels que les noix, noisettes etc.* ‖ [of metal] écrou *m*. ‖ *inf* [mad person] cinglé *m*, -e *f*. ○ **nuts 1** *adj inf*: **to be ~s** être dingue. **2** *excl Am inf* zut!

nutcrackers ['nʌt,krækəz] *npl* casse-noix *m inr*, casse-noisettes *m inr*.

nutmeg ['nʌtmeg] *n* noix *f* (de) muscade.

nutritious [nju:'trɪʃəs] *adj* nourrissant(e).

nutshell ['nʌtʃel] *n*: **in a ~** en un mot.

nuzzle ['nʌzl] *vi*: **to ~ (up) against** se frotter contre, frotter son nez contre.

nylon ['naɪlɒn] **1** *n* Nylon® *m*. **2** *comp* en Nylon®.

o (*pl* **o's** OR **os**), **O** (*pl* **O's** OR **Os**) [əʊ] *n* [letter] o *m inr*, O *m inr*. ‖ [zero] 'zéro *m*.

oak [əʊk] *n* chêne *m*.

oar [ɔ:r] *n* rame *f*, aviron *m*.

oasis [əʊ'eɪsɪs] (*pl* **oases** [əʊ'eɪsi:z]) *n* oasis *f*.

oath [əʊθ] *n* [promise] serment *m*; **on** OR **under ~** sous serment. ‖ [swearword] juron *m*.

oatmeal ['əʊtmi:l] *n* (*U*) flocons *mpl* d'avoine.

oats [əʊts] *npl* [grain] avoine *f*.

obedience [ə'bi:djəns] *n* obéissance *f*.

obedient [ə'bi:djənt] *adj* obéissant(e), docile.

obese [əʊ'bi:s] *adj fml* obèse.

obey [ə'beɪ] **1** *vt* obéir à. **2** *vi* obéir.

obituary [ə'bɪtʃʊəri] *n* nécrologie *f*.

object [*n* 'ɒbdʒɪkt, *vb* əb'dʒekt] **1** *n* [gen] objet *m*. ‖ [aim] objectif *m*, but *m*. ‖ GRAMM complément *m* d'objet. **2** *vt* objecter. **3** *vi* protester; **to ~ to sthg** faire objection à qqch, s'opposer à qqch; **to ~ to doing sthg** se refuser à faire qqch.

objection [əb'dʒekʃn] *n* objection *f*; **to have no ~ to sthg/to doing sthg** ne voir aucune objection à qqch/à faire qqch.

objectionable [əb'dʒekʃənəbl] *adj* [person, behaviour] désagréable.

objective [əb'dʒektɪv] **1** *adj* objectif(ive). **2** *n* objectif *m*.

obligation [,ɒblɪ'geɪʃn] *n* obligation *f*.

obligatory [ə'blɪgətrɪ] *adj* obligatoire.

oblige [ə'blaɪdʒ] *vt* [force]: **to ~ sb to do sthg** forcer OR obliger qqn à faire qqch.

obliging [ə'blaɪdʒɪŋ] *adj* obligeant(e).

oblique [ə'bli:k] **1** *adj* oblique; [reference, hint] indirect(e). **2** *n* TYPO barre *f* oblique.

obliterate [ə'blɪtəreɪt] *vt* [destroy] détruire, raser.

oblivion [ə'blɪvɪən] *n* oubli *m*.

oblivious [ə'blɪvɪəs] *adj*: **to be ~ to** OR **of** être inconscient(e) de.

oblong ['ɒblɒŋ] **1** *adj* rectangulaire. **2** *n* rectangle *m*.

obnoxious [əb'nɒkʃəs] *adj* [person] odieux(ieuse); [comment] désobligeant(e).

oboe ['əʊbəʊ] *n* hautbois *m*.

obscene [əb'si:n] *adj* obscène.

obscure [əb'skjʊə'] **1** *adj* obscur(e). **2** *vt* [gen] obscurcir. || [view] masquer.

observance [əb'zɜ:vəns] *n* observation *f*.

observant [əb'zɜ:vnt] *adj* observateur(trice).

observation [ˌɒbzə'veɪʃn] *n* observation *f*.

observatory [əb'zɜ:vətrɪ] *n* observatoire *m*.

observe [əb'zɜ:v] *vt* [gen] observer. || [remark] remarquer, faire observer.

observer [əb'zɜ:və'] *n* observateur *m*, -trice *f*.

obsess [əb'ses] *vt*: **to be ~ed by** OR **with sb/sthg** être obsédé par qqn/qqch.

obsessive [əb'sesɪv] *adj* [person] obsessionnel(elle).

obsolescent [ˌɒbsə'lesnt] *adj* [system] qui tombe en désuétude; [machine] obsolescent(e).

obsolete ['ɒbsəli:t] *adj* obsolète.

obstacle ['ɒbstəkl] *n* obstacle *m*.

obstetrics [ɒb'stetrɪks] *n* obstétrique *f*.

obstinate ['ɒbstənət] *adj* [stubborn] obstiné(e). || [cough] persistant(e); [stain, resistance] tenace.

obstruct [əb'strʌkt] *vt* [block] obstruer. || [hinder] entraver, gêner.

obstruction [əb'strʌkʃn] *n* [in road] encombrement *m*; [in pipe] engorgement *m*. || SPORT obstruction *f*.

obtain [əb'teɪn] *vt* obtenir.

obtainable [əb'teɪnəbl] *adj* que l'on peut obtenir.

obtrusive [əb'tru:sɪv] *adj* [behaviour] qui attire l'attention; [smell] fort(e).

obtuse [əb'tju:s] *adj* obtus(e).

obvious ['ɒbvɪəs] *adj* évident(e).

obviously ['ɒbvɪəslɪ] *adv* [of course] bien sûr. || [clearly] manifestement.

occasion [ə'keɪʒn] *n* [gen] occasion *f*. || [important event] événement *m*; **to rise to the ~** se montrer à la hauteur de la situation.

occasional [ə'keɪʒənl] *adj* [showers] passager(ère); [visit] occasionnel(elle); **I have the ~ drink/cigarette** je bois un verre/je fume une cigarette de temps à autre.

occasionally [ə'keɪʒnəlɪ] *adv* de temps en temps, quelquefois.

occult [ɒ'kʌlt] *adj* occulte.

occupant ['ɒkjʊpənt] *n* occupant *m*, -e *f*; [of vehicle] passager *m*.

occupation [ˌɒkjʊ'peɪʃn] *n* [job] profession *f*. || [pastime, by army] occupation *f*.

occupational hazard [ɒkjʊˌpeɪʃənl-] *n* risque *m* du métier.

occupational therapy [ɒkjʊˌpeɪʃənl-] *n* thérapeutique *f* occupationnelle, ergothérapie *f*.

occupier ['ɒkjʊpaɪə'] *n* occupant *m*, -e *f*.

occupy ['ɒkjʊpaɪ] *vt* occuper; **to ~ o.s.** s'occuper.

occur [ə'kɜ:'] *vi* [happen - gen] avoir lieu, se produire; [- difficulty] se présenter. || [be present] se trouver, être présent(e). || [thought, idea]: **to ~ to sb** venir à l'esprit de qqn.

occurrence [ə'kʌrəns] *n* [event] événement *m*, circonstance *f*.

ocean ['əʊʃn] *n* océan *m*; *Am* [sea] mer *f*.

oceangoing ['əʊʃnˌgəʊɪŋ] *adj* au long cours.

o'clock [ə'klɒk] *adv*: **two ~** deux heures.

octave ['ɒktɪv] *n* octave *f*.

October [ɒk'təʊbə'] *n* octobre *m*; *see also* **September.**

octopus ['ɒktəpəs] (*pl* **-puses** OR **-pi** [-paɪ]) *n* pieuvre *f*.

OD *abbr of* **overdose.** || *abbr of* **overdrawn.**

odd [ɒd] *adj* [strange] bizarre, étrange. || [leftover] qui reste. || [occasional]: **I play the ~ game of tennis** je joue au tennis de temps en temps. || [not part of pair] dépareillé(e). || [number] impair(e). || *phr*: **twenty ~ years** une vingtaine d'années. ○ **odds** *npl*: **the ~s** les chances *fpl*; **the ~s are that ...** il y a des chances pour que ...; (+ *subjunctive*), il est probable que ...; **against the ~s** envers et contre tout; **~s and ends** petites choses *fpl*, petits bouts *mpl*.

oddity ['ɒdɪtɪ] (*pl* **-ies**) *n* [person] personne *f* bizarre; [thing] chose *f* bizarre.

odd jobs *npl* petits travaux *mpl*.

oddly ['ɒdlɪ] *adv* curieusement; **~ enough** chose curieuse.

oddments ['ɒdmənts] *npl* fins *fpl* de série.

odds-on ['ɒdz-] *adj* *inf*: **~ favourite** grand favori.

odour *Br*, **odor** *Am* ['əʊdə'] *n* odeur *f*.

of [*unstressed* əv, *stressed* ɒv] *prep* [gen] de; **the cover ~ a book** la couverture d'un livre; **to die ~ cancer** mourir d'un cancer. ‖ [expressing quantity, amount, age etc] de; **thousands ~ people** des milliers de gens; **a piece ~ cake** un morceau de gâteau. ‖ [made from] en. ‖ [with dates, periods of time]: **the 12th ~ February** le 12 février.

off [ɒf] **1** *adv* [at a distance, away]: **10 miles ~** à 16 kilomètres; **two days ~** dans deux jours; **far ~** au loin; **to be ~** partir, s'en aller. ‖ [so as to remove]: **to take ~** enlever; **to cut sthg ~** couper qqch. ‖ [so as to complete]: **to finish ~** terminer; **to kill ~** achever. ‖ [not at work etc]: **a day/week ~** un jour/une semaine de congé. ‖ [discounted]: **£10 ~** 10 livres de remise OR réduction. **2** *prep* [at a distance from, away from] de; **to get ~ a bus** descendre d'un bus; **to take a book ~ a shelf** prendre un livre sur une étagère; **~ the coast** près de la côte. ‖ [not attending]: **to be ~ work** ne pas travailler; **~ school** absent de l'école. ‖ [no longer liking]: **she's ~ her food** elle n'a pas d'appétit. ‖ [deducted from] sur. ‖ *inf* [from]: **to buy sthg ~ sb** acheter qqch à qqn. **3** *adj* [food] avarié(e), gâté(e); [milk] tourné(e). ‖ [TV, light] éteint(e); [engine] coupé(e). ‖ [cancelled] annulé(e). ‖ [not at work etc] absent(e). ‖ *inf* [offhand]: **he was a bit ~ with me** il n'a pas été sympa avec moi.

offal [ɒfl] *n* (*U*) abats *mpl*.

off-chance *n*: **on the ~ that ...** au cas où ....

off colour *adj* [ill] patraque.

off duty *adj* qui n'est pas de service; [doctor, nurse] qui n'est pas de garde.

offence *Br*, **offense** *Am* [ə'fens] *n* [crime] délit *m*. ‖ [upset]: **to cause sb ~** vexer qqn; **to take ~** se vexer.

offend [ə'fend] *vt* offenser.

offender [ə'fendər] *n* [criminal] criminel *m*, -elle *f*. ‖ [culprit] coupable *mf*.

offense [*sense 2* ɒfens] *n Am* = **offence**. ‖ SPORT attaque *f*.

offensive [ə'fensɪv] **1** *adj* [behaviour, comment] blessant(e). ‖ [weapon, action] offensif(ive). **2** *n* offensive *f*.

offer ['ɒfər] **1** *n* [gen] offre *f*, proposition *f*. ‖ [price, bid] offre *f*. ‖ [in shop] promotion *f*; **on ~** [available] en vente; [at a special price] en réclame, en promotion. **2** *vt* [gen] offrir; **to ~ sthg to sb, to ~ sb sthg** offrir qqch à qqn; **to ~ to do sthg** proposer OR offrir de faire qqch. ‖ [provide -

services etc] proposer; [- hope] donner. **3** *vi* s'offrir.

offering ['ɒfərɪŋ] *n* RELIG offrande *f*.

off-guard *adj* au dépourvu.

offhand [,ɒf'hænd] **1** *adj* cavalier(ière). **2** *adv* tout de suite.

office ['ɒfɪs] *n* [place, staff] bureau *m*. ‖ [department] département *m*, service *m*. ‖ [position] fonction *f*, poste *m*; **in ~** en fonction; **to take ~** entrer en fonction.

office block *n* immeuble *m* de bureaux.

office hours *npl* heures *fpl* de bureau.

officer ['ɒfɪsər] *n* [in armed forces] officier *m*. ‖ [in organization] agent *m*, fonctionnaire *mf*. ‖ [in police force] officier *m* (de police).

office worker *n* employé *m*, -e *f* de bureau.

official [ə'fɪʃl] **1** *adj* officiel(ielle). **2** *n* fonctionnaire *mf*.

offing ['ɒfɪŋ] *n*: **in the ~** en vue, en perspective.

off-line *adj* COMPUT non connecté(e).

off-peak *adj* [electricity] utilisé(e) aux heures creuses; [fare] réduit(e) aux heures creuses.

off-putting [-,pʊtɪŋ] *adj* désagréable, rébarbatif(ive).

off season *n*: **the ~** la morte-saison.

offset ['ɒfset] (*pt* & *pp* **offset**) *vt* [losses] compenser.

offshoot ['ɒfʃuːt] *n*: **to be an ~ of sthg** être né(e) OR provenir de qqch.

offshore ['ɒfʃɔːr] **1** *adj* [oil rig] offshore (*inv*); [island] proche de la côte; [fishing] côtier(ière). **2** *adv* au large.

offside [*adj* & *adv* ,ɒf'saɪd, *n* 'ɒfsaɪd] **1** *adj* [right-hand drive] de droite; [left-hand drive] de gauche. ‖ SPORT hors-jeu (*inv*). **2** *adv* SPORT hors-jeu. **3** *n* [right-hand drive] côté *m* droit; [left-hand drive] côté gauche.

offspring ['ɒfsprɪŋ] (*pl inv*) *n* rejeton *m*.

offstage [,ɒf'steɪdʒ] *adj* & *adv* dans les coulisses.

off-the-cuff **1** *adj* impromptu(e). **2** *adv* impromptu.

off-the-record *adv* confidentiellement.

off-white *adj* blanc cassé (*inv*).

often ['ɒfn, 'ɒftn] *adv* souvent, fréquemment; **how ~ do you visit her?** vous la voyez tous les combien?; **as ~ as not** assez souvent; **every so ~** de temps en temps; **more ~ than not** le plus souvent, la plupart du temps.

ogle ['əʊgl] *vt* reluquer.

oh [əʊ] *excl* oh!; [expressing hesitation] euh!

oil [ɔɪl] **1** *n* [gen] huile *f*. || [for heating] mazout *m*. || [petroleum] pétrole *m*. **2** *vt* graisser, lubrifier.

oilcan ['ɔɪlkæn] *n* burette *f* d'huile.

oilfield ['ɔɪlfiːld] *n* gisement *m* pétrolifère.

oil filter *n* filtre *m* à huile.

oil-fired [-,faɪəd] *adj* au mazout.

oil painting *n* peinture *f* à l'huile.

oilrig ['ɔɪlrɪg] *n* [at sea] plate-forme *f* de forage OR pétrolière; [on land] derrick *m*.

oilskins ['ɔɪlskɪnz] *npl* ciré *m*.

oil slick *n* marée *f* noire.

oil tanker *n* [ship] pétrolier *m*, tanker *m*. || [lorry] camion-citerne *m*.

oil well *n* puits *m* de pétrole.

oily ['ɔɪlɪ] *adj* [rag etc] graisseux(euse); [food] gras (grasse).

ointment ['ɔɪntmənt] *n* pommade *f*.

OK (*pt & pp* **OKed**, *cont* **OKing**), **okay** [,əʊ'keɪ] *inf* **1** *adj*: **is it ~ with** OR **by you?** ça vous va?, vous êtes d'accord?; **are you ~?** ça va? **2** *excl* [expressing agreement] d'accord, O.K. || [to introduce new topic]: **~, can we start now?** bon, on commence? **3** *vt* approuver, donner le feu vert à.

old [əʊld] **1** *adj* [gen] vieux (vieille), âgé(e); **I'm 20 years ~** j'ai 20 ans; **how ~ are you?** quel âge as-tu? || [former] ancien(ienne). || *inf* [as intensifier]: **any ~** n'importe quel (n'importe quelle). **2** *npl*: **the ~** les personnes *fpl* âgées.

old age *n* vieillesse *f*.

old-fashioned [-'fæʃnd] *adj* [outmoded] démodé(e), passé(e) de mode. || [traditional] vieux jeu (*inv*).

old people's home *n* hospice *m* de vieillards.

olive ['ɒlɪv] **1** *adj* olive (*inv*). **2** *n* olive *f*.

olive green *adj* vert olive (*inv*).

olive oil *n* huile *f* d'olive.

Olympic [ə'lɪmpɪk] *adj* olympique.

Olympic Games *npl*: **the ~** les Jeux *mpl* Olympiques.

ombudsman ['ɒmbʊdzmən] (*pl* -men [-mən]) *n* ombudsman *m*.

omelet(te) ['ɒmlɪt] *n* omelette *f*.

omen ['əʊmən] *n* augure *m*, présage *m*.

ominous ['ɒmɪnəs] *adj* [event, situation] de mauvais augure; [sign] inquiétant(e); [look, silence] menaçant(e).

omission [ə'mɪʃn] *n* omission *f*.

omit [ə'mɪt] *vt* omettre; **to ~ to do sthg** oublier de faire qqch.

on [ɒn] **1** *prep* [indicating position, location] sur; **~ a chair/the wall** sur une chaise/le mur; **~ the ceiling** au plafond; **~ the left/right** à gauche/droite. || [indicating means]: **the car runs ~ petrol** la voiture marche à l'essence; **~ the radio** à la radio; **~ the telephone** au téléphone; **to hurt o.s. ~ sthg** se faire mal avec qqch. || [indicating mode of transport]: **to travel ~ a bus/train/ship** voyager en bus/par le train/en bateau; **I was ~ the bus** j'étais dans le bus; **~ foot** à pied. || [concerning] sur; **a book ~ astronomy** un livre sur l'astronomie. || [indicating time, activity]: **~ Thursday** jeudi; **~ the 10th of February** le 10 février; **~ my return, ~ returning** à mon retour; **~ holiday** en vacances. || [indicating influence] sur; **the impact ~ the environment** l'impact sur l'environnement. || [using, supported by]: **he's ~ tranquillizers** il prend des tranquillisants; **to be ~ drugs** se droguer. || [earning]: **to be ~ £25,000 a year** gagner 25 000 livres par an; **to be ~ a low income** avoir un faible revenu. || [referring to musical instrument]: **to play sthg ~ the violin/flute/guitar** jouer qqch au violon/à la flûte/à la guitare. || *inf* [paid by]: **the drinks are ~ me** c'est moi qui régale, c'est ma tournée. **2** *adv* [indicating covering, clothing]: **put the lid ~** mettez le couvercle; **to put a sweater ~** mettre un pull; **what did she have ~?** qu'est-ce qu'elle portait?; **he had nothing ~** il était tout nu. || [being shown]: **what's ~ at the Ritz?** qu'est-ce qu'on joue OR donne au Ritz? || [working - radio, TV, light] allumé(e); [- machine] en marche; [- tap] ouvert(e); **turn ~ the power** mets le courant. || [indicating continuing action]: **to work ~** continuer à travailler; **he kept ~ walking** il continua à marcher. || [forward]: **send my mail ~ (to me)** faites suivre mon courrier; **later ~** plus tard; **earlier ~** plus tôt. || *inf* [referring to behaviour]: **it's just not ~!** cela ne se fait pas! ○ **from ... on** *adv*: **from now ~** dorénavant, désormais; **from then ~** à partir de ce moment-là. ○ **on and off** *adv* de temps en temps. ○ **on to, onto** *prep* (*only written as* **onto** *for senses 4 and 5*) [to a position on top of] sur; **she jumped ~ to the chair** elle a sauté sur la chaise. || [to a position on a vehicle] dans; **she got ~**

to the bus elle est montée dans le bus. ||
[to a position attached to]: **stick the photo
~ to the page with glue** colle la photo sur
la page. || [aware of wrongdoing]: **to be
onto sb** être sur la piste de qqn. || [into
contact with]: **get onto the factory**
contactez l'usine.

once [wʌns] **1** adv [on one occasion] une
fois; **~ a day** une fois par jour; **~ again** OR
more encore une fois; **~ and for all** une
fois pour toutes; **~ in a while** de temps en
temps; **~ or twice** une ou deux fois; **for ~**
pour une fois. || [previously] autrefois, ja-
dis; **~ upon a time** il était une fois. **2** conj
dès que. ○**at once** adv [immediately]
immédiatement. || [at the same time] en
même temps; **all at ~** tout d'un coup.

one [wʌn] **1** num [the number 1] un
(une); **~ of my friends** l'un de mes amis,
un ami à moi; **~ fifth** un cinquième. **2**
adj [only] seul(e), unique; **it's her ~
ambition/love** c'est son unique am-
bition/son seul amour. || [indefinite]: **~ of
these days** un de ces jours. **3** pron [refer-
ring to a particular thing or person]: **which
~ do you want?** lequel voulez-vous?; **this
~** celui-ci; **that ~** celui-là; **she's the ~ I
told you about** c'est celle dont je vous ai
parlé. || fml [you, anyone] on; **to do ~'s
duty** faire son devoir. ○**for one** adv: **I
for ~ remain unconvinced** pour ma part
je ne suis pas convaincu.

one-armed bandit n machine f à sous.

one-man adj [business] dirigé(e) par un
seul homme.

one-man band n [musician] homme-
orchestre m.

one-off inf adj [offer, event, product]
unique.

one-on-one Am = **one-to-one**.

one-parent family n famille f mono-
parentale.

oneself [wʌn'self] pron (reflexive) se;
(after prep) soi. || (emphatic) soi-
même.

one-sided [-'saɪdɪd] adj [unequal] iné-
gal(e). || [biased] partial(e).

one-to-one Br, **one-on-one** Am adj
[discussion] en tête-à-tête; **~ tuition**
cours mpl particuliers.

one-upmanship [,wʌn'ʌpmənʃɪp] n art
m de faire toujours mieux que les autres.

one-way adj [street] à sens unique. ||
[ticket] simple.

ongoing ['ɒn,gəʊɪŋ] adj en cours, conti-
nu(e).

onion ['ʌnjən] n oignon m.

online ['ɒnlaɪn] adj & adv COMPUT en ligne, connecté(e).

onlooker ['ɒn,lʊkər] n spectateur m,
-trice f.

only ['əʊnlɪ] **1** adj seul(e), unique; **an ~
child** un enfant unique. **2** adv [gen] ne ...
que, seulement; **he ~ reads science
fiction** il ne lit que de la science fiction;
it's ~ a scratch c'est juste une égratignure; **he left ~ a few minutes ago** il est
parti il n'y a pas deux minutes. || [for em-
phasis]: **I ~ wish I could** je voudrais bien;
it's ~ natural (that) ... c'est tout à fait
normal que ...; **not ~ ... but also** non seulement ... mais encore; **I ~ just caught
the train** j'ai eu le train de justesse. **3**
conj seulement, mais.

onset ['ɒnset] n début m, commencement m.

onshore ['ɒnʃɔːr] adj & adv [from sea]
du large; [on land] à terre.

onslaught ['ɒnslɔːt] n attaque f.

onto [unstressed before consonant
'ɒntə, unstressed before vowel 'ɒntʊ,
stressed 'ɒntuː] = **on to.**

onus ['əʊnəs] n responsabilité f, charge
f.

onward ['ɒnwəd] adj & adv en avant.

onwards ['ɒnwədz] adv en avant; **from
now ~** dorénavant, désormais; **from then
~** à partir de ce moment-là.

ooze [uːz] **1** vt fig [charm, confidence]
respirer. **2** vi: **to ~ from** OR **out of sthg**
suinter de qqch.

opaque [əʊ'peɪk] adj opaque.

OPEC ['əʊpek] (abbr of **Organization
of Petroleum Exporting Countries**) n
OPEP f.

open ['əʊpn] **1** adj [gen] ouvert(e). || [re-
ceptive]: **to be ~ (to)** être réceptif(ive) (à).
|| [view, road, space] dégagé(e). || [uncov-
ered - car] découvert(e). || [meeting] pu-
blic(ique); [competition] ouvert(e) à
tous. || [disbelief, honesty] manifeste, évi-
dent(e). || [unresolved] non résolu(e). **2**
n: **in the ~** [sleep] à la belle étoile; [eat]
au grand air; **to bring sthg out into the ~**
divulguer qqch, exposer qqch au grand
jour. **3** vt [gen] ouvrir. || [inaugurate]
inaugurer. **4** vi [door, flower] s'ouvrir. ||
[shop, library etc] ouvrir. || [meeting, play
etc] commencer. ○**open on to** vt fus
[subj: room, door] donner sur. ○**open
up 1** vt sep [develop] exploiter, développer. **2** vi [possibilities etc] s'offrir, se pré-
senter. || [unlock door] ouvrir.

opener ['əʊpnər] n [for cans] ouvre-boîtes m inv; [for bottles] ouvre-bouteilles m inv, décapsuleur m.

opening ['əʊpnɪŋ] 1 adj [first] premier(ière); [remarks] préliminaire. 2 n [beginning] commencement m, début m. || [in fence] trou m, percée f; [in clouds] trouée f, déchirure f. || [opportunity - gen] occasion f; [- COMM] débouché m. || [job vacancy] poste m.

opening hours npl heures fpl d'ouverture.

openly ['əʊpənlɪ] adv ouvertement, franchement.

open-minded [-'maɪndɪd] adj [person] qui a l'esprit large; [attitude] large.

open-plan adj non cloisonné(e).

opera ['ɒpərə] n opéra m.

opera house n opéra m.

operate ['ɒpəreɪt] 1 vt [machine] faire marcher, faire fonctionner. 2 vi [rule, law, system] jouer, être appliqué(e); [machine] fonctionner, marcher. || COMM opérer, travailler. || MED opérer; **to ~ on sb/sthg** opérer qqn/qqch.

operating theatre Br, **operating room** Am ['ɒpəreɪtɪŋ-] n salle f d'opération.

operation [,ɒpə'reɪʃn] n [gen & MED] opération f; **to have an ~ (for)** se faire opérer (de). || [of machine] marche f, fonctionnement m; **to be in ~** [machine] être en marche OR en service; [law, system] être en vigueur. || [COMM - company] exploitation f; [- management] administration f, gestion f.

operational [,ɒpə'reɪʃənl] adj [machine] en état de marche.

operative ['ɒprətɪv] 1 adj en vigueur. 2 n ouvrier m, -ière f.

operator ['ɒpəreɪtər] n TELEC standardiste mf. || [of machine] opérateur m, -trice f. || COMM directeur m, -trice f.

opinion [ə'pɪnjən] n opinion f, avis m; **in my ~** à mon avis.

opinionated [ə'pɪnjəneɪtɪd] adj pej dogmatique.

opinion poll n sondage m d'opinion.

opponent [ə'pəʊnənt] n adversaire mf.

opportune ['ɒpətjuːn] adj opportun(e).

opportunist [,ɒpə'tjuːnɪst] n opportuniste mf.

opportunity [,ɒpə'tjuːnətɪ] n occasion f; **to take the ~ to do** OR **of doing sthg** profiter de l'occasion pour faire qqch.

oppose [ə'pəʊz] vt s'opposer à.

opposed [ə'pəʊzd] adj: **to be ~ to** être contre, être opposé à; **as ~ to** par opposition à.

opposing [ə'pəʊzɪŋ] adj opposé(e).

opposite ['ɒpəzɪt] 1 adj opposé(e); [house] d'en face. 2 adv en face. 3 prep en face de. 4 n contraire m.

opposite number n homologue mf.

opposition [,ɒpə'zɪʃn] n [gen] opposition f. || [opposing team] adversaire mf.

oppress [ə'pres] vt [persecute] opprimer. || [depress] oppresser.

oppressive [ə'presɪv] adj [unjust] oppressif(ive). || [weather, heat] étouffant(e), lourd(e). || [silence] oppressant(e).

opt [ɒpt] 1 vt: **to ~ to do sthg** choisir de faire qqch. 2 vi: **to ~ for** opter pour. ○ **opt out** vi: **to ~ out (of)** [gen] choisir de ne pas participer (à); [of responsibility] se dérober (à).

optical ['ɒptɪkl] adj optique.

optician [ɒp'tɪʃn] n [who sells glasses] opticien m, -ienne f. || [ophthalmologist] ophtalmologiste mf.

optimist ['ɒptɪmɪst] n optimiste mf.

optimistic [,ɒptɪ'mɪstɪk] adj optimiste.

optimum ['ɒptɪməm] adj optimum.

option ['ɒpʃn] n option f, choix m.

optional ['ɒpʃənl] adj facultatif(ive); **an ~ extra** un accessoire.

or [ɔːr] conj [gen] ou. || [after negative]: **he can't read ~ write** il ne sait ni lire ni écrire. || [otherwise] sinon. || [as correction] ou plutôt.

oral ['ɔːrəl] 1 adj [spoken] oral(e). 2 n oral m, épreuve f orale.

orally ['ɔːrəlɪ] adv [in spoken form] oralement. || MED par voie orale.

orange ['ɒrɪndʒ] 1 adj orange (inv). 2 n [fruit] orange f. || [colour] orange m.

orbit ['ɔːbɪt] 1 n orbite f. 2 vt décrire une orbite autour de.

orchard ['ɔːtʃəd] n verger m.

orchestra ['ɔːkɪstrə] n orchestre m.

orchestral [ɔː'kestrəl] adj orchestral(e).

orchid ['ɔːkɪd] n orchidée f.

ordain [ɔː'deɪn] vt [decree] ordonner, décréter. || RELIG: **to be ~ed** être ordonné prêtre.

ordeal [ɔː'diːl] n épreuve f.

order ['ɔːdər] 1 n [gen] ordre m; **to be under ~s to do sthg** avoir (reçu) l'ordre de faire qqch. || COMM commande f; **to place an ~ with sb for sthg** passer une commande de qqch à qqn; **to ~** sur commande. ‖ [sequence] ordre *m*; **in ~** dans l'ordre. ‖ [fitness for use]: **in working ~** en état de marche; **out of ~** [machine] en panne; [behaviour] déplacé(e); **in ~** [correct] en ordre. ‖ (*U*) [discipline - gen] ordre *m*; [- in classroom] discipline *f*. ‖ *Am* [portion] part *f*. **2** *vt* [command] ordonner; **to ~ sb to do sthg** ordonner à qqn de faire qqch. ‖ COMM commander. ○ **in the order of** *Br*, ○ **in the order of** *Am* *prep* environ, de l'ordre de. ○ **in order that** *conj* pour que, afin que. ○ **in order to** *conj* pour, afin de. ○ **order about**, **order around** *vt sep* commander.

order form *n* bulletin *m* de commande.

orderly ['ɔːdəlɪ] **1** *adj* [person] ordonné(e); [crowd] discipliné(e). **2** *n* [in hospital] garçon *m* de salle.

ordinarily ['ɔːdənrəlɪ] *adv* d'habitude, d'ordinaire.

ordinary ['ɔːdənrɪ] **1** *adj* [normal] ordinaire. ‖ *pej* [unexceptional] ordinaire, quelconque. **2** *n*: **out of the ~** qui sort de l'ordinaire, exceptionnel(elle).

ordnance ['ɔːdnəns] *n* (*U*) [supplies] matériel *m* militaire. ‖ [artillery] artillerie *f*.

ore [ɔːʳ] *n* minerai *m*.

oregano [ˌɒrɪ'gɑːnəʊ] *n* origan *m*.

organ ['ɔːgən] *n* [gen] organe *m*. ‖ MUS orgue *m*.

organic [ɔː'gænɪk] *adj* [of animals, plants] organique. ‖ [farming, food] biologique.

organization [ˌɔːgənaɪ'zeɪʃn] *n* organisation *f*.

organize, -ise ['ɔːgənaɪz] *vt* organiser.

organizer ['ɔːgənaɪzəʳ] *n* organisateur *m*, -trice *f*.

orgasm ['ɔːgæzm] *n* orgasme *m*.

orgy ['ɔːdʒɪ] *n* *lit & fig* orgie *f*.

Orient ['ɔːrɪənt] *n*: **the ~** l'Orient *m*.

oriental [ˌɔːrɪ'entl] *adj* oriental(e).

orienteering [ˌɔːrɪən'tɪərɪŋ] *n* (*U*) course *f* d'orientation.

origami [ˌɒrɪ'gɑːmɪ] *n* origami *m*.

origin ['ɒrɪdʒɪn] *n* [of river] source *f*; [of word, conflict] origine *f*. ‖ [birth]: **country of ~** pays *m* d'origine.

original [ə'rɪdʒənl] **1** *adj* original(e); [owner] premier(ière). **2** *n* original *m*.

originally [ə'rɪdʒənəlɪ] *adv* à l'origine, au départ.

originate [ə'rɪdʒəneɪt] *vi* [belief, custom]: **to ~ (in)** prendre naissance (dans); **to ~ from** provenir de.

ornament ['ɔːnəmənt] *n* [object] bibelot *m*. ‖ (*U*) [decoration] ornement *m*.

ornamental [ˌɔːnə'mentl] *adj* [garden, pond] d'agrément; [design] décoratif (ive).

ornate [ɔː'neɪt] *adj* orné(e).

ornithology [ˌɔːnɪ'θɒlədʒɪ] *n* ornithologie *f*.

orphan ['ɔːfn] **1** *n* orphelin *m*, -e *f*. **2** *vt*: **to be ~ed** devenir orphelin(e).

orphanage ['ɔːfənɪdʒ] *n* orphelinat *m*.

orthodox ['ɔːθədɒks] *adj* [conventional] orthodoxe. ‖ RELIG [traditional] traditionaliste.

orthopaedic [ˌɔːθə'piːdɪk] *adj* orthopédique.

orthopedic *etc* [ˌɔːθə'piːdɪk] = **orthopaedic** *etc*.

oscillate ['ɒsɪleɪt] *vi* *lit & fig* osciller.

ostensible [ɒ'stensəbl] *adj* prétendu(e).

ostentatious [ˌɒsten'teɪʃəs] *adj* ostentatoire.

osteopath ['ɒstɪəpæθ] *n* ostéopathe *mf*.

ostracize, -ise ['ɒstrəsaɪz] *vt* frapper d'ostracisme, mettre au ban.

ostrich ['ɒstrɪtʃ] *n* autruche *f*.

other ['ʌðəʳ] **1** *adj* autre; **the ~ one** l'autre; **the ~ day/week** l'autre jour/semaine. **2** *adv*: **there was nothing to do ~ than confess** il ne pouvait faire autrement que d'avouer; **~ than John** John à part. **3** *pron*: **~s** d'autres; **the ~** l'autre; **the ~s** les autres; **one after the ~** l'un après l'autre (l'une après l'autre); **one or ~ of you** l'un (l'une) de vous deux; **none ~ than** nul (nulle) autre que. ○ **something or other** *pron* quelque chose, je ne sais quoi. ○ **somehow or other** *adv* d'une manière ou d'une autre.

otherwise ['ʌðəwaɪz] **1** *adv* autrement; **or ~** [or not] ou non. **2** *conj* sinon.

otter ['ɒtəʳ] *n* loutre *f*.

ouch [aʊtʃ] *excl* aïe!, ouïe!

ought [ɔːt] *aux vb* [sensibly]: **I really ~ to go** il faut absolument que je m'en aille; **you ~ to see a doctor** tu devrais aller chez le docteur. ‖ [morally]: **you ~ not to have done that** tu n'aurais pas dû faire cela. ‖ [expressing probability]: **she ~ to pass her exam** elle devrait réussir à son examen.

ounce [aʊns] *n* = 28,35 g, once *f*.

our ['auər] *poss adj* notre, nos (*pl*); ~ money/house notre argent/maison; ~ children nos enfants; it wasn't OUR fault ce n'était pas de notre faute à nous.

ours ['auəz] *poss pron* le nôtre (la nôtre), les nôtres (*pl*); that money is ~ cet argent est à nous OR est le nôtre; it wasn't their fault, it was OURS ce n'était pas de leur faute, c'était de notre faute à nous OR de la nôtre; a friend of ~ un ami à nous, un de nos amis.

ourselves [auə'selvz] *pron pl* (*reflexive*) nous. || (*for emphasis*) nous-mêmes; we did it by ~ nous l'avons fait tout seuls.

oust [aust] *vt*: to ~ sb (from) évincer qqn (de).

out [aut] *adv* [not inside, out of doors] dehors; I'm going ~ for a walk je sors me promener; to run ~ sortir en courant; ~ here ici; ~ there là-bas. || [away from home, office, published] sorti(e); John's ~ at the moment John est sorti, John n'est pas là en ce moment. || [extinguished] éteint(e); the lights went ~ les lumières se sont éteintes. || [of tides]: the tide is ~ la marée est basse. || [out of fashion] démodé(e), passé(e) de mode. || [in flower] en fleur. || *inf* [on strike] en grève. || [determined]: to be ~ to do sthg être résolu(e) OR décidé(e) à faire qqch. ○ **out of** *prep* [outside] en dehors de; to go ~ of the room sortir de la pièce; to be ~ of the country être à l'étranger. || [indicating cause] par; ~ of spite/love/boredom par dépit/amour/ennui. || [indicating origin, source] de, dans; a page ~ of a book une page d'un livre; it's made ~ of plastic c'est en plastique. || [without] sans; ~ of petrol/money à court d'essence/d'argent. || [sheltered from] à l'abri de. || [to indicate proportion] sur; one ~ of ten people une personne sur dix; ten ~ of ten dix sur dix.

out-and-out *adj* [liar] fieffé(e); [disgrace] complet(ète).

outboard (motor) ['autbɔːd-] *n* (moteur *m*) hors-bord *m inv*.

outbreak ['autbreɪk] *n* [of war, crime] début *m*, déclenchement *m*; [of spots etc] éruption *f*.

outburst ['autbɜːst] *n* explosion *f*.

outcast ['autkɑːst] *n* paria *m*.

outcome ['autkʌm] *n* issue *f*, résultat *m*.

outcrop ['autkrɒp] *n* affleurement *m*.

outcry ['autkraɪ] *n* tollé *m*.

outdated [,aut'deɪtɪd] *adj* démodé(e), vieilli(e).

outdid [,aut'dɪd] *pt* → outdo.

outdo [,aut'duː] (*pt* -did, *pp* -done [-'dʌn]) *vt* surpasser.

outdoor ['autdɔːr] *adj* [life, swimming pool] en plein air; [activities] de plein air.

outdoors [aut'dɔːz] *adv* dehors.

outer ['autər] *adj* extérieur(e).

outer space *n* cosmos *m*.

outfit ['autfɪt] *n* [clothes] tenue *f*.

outgoing ['aut,gəuɪŋ] *adj* [chairman etc] sortant(e); [mail] à expédier; [train] en partance. || [friendly, sociable] ouvert(e).

outgrow [,aut'grəu] (*pt* -grew, *pp* -grown) *vt* [clothes] devenir trop grand(e) pour. || [habit] se défaire de.

outhouse ['authaus, *pl* -hauzɪz] *n* appentis *m*.

outing ['autɪŋ] *n* [trip] sortie *f*.

outlandish [aut'lændɪʃ] *adj* bizarre.

outlaw ['autlɔː] **1** *n* hors-la-loi *m inv*. **2** *vt* [practice] proscrire.

outlay ['autleɪ] *n* dépenses *fpl*.

outlet ['autlet] *n* [for emotion] exutoire *m*. || [hole, pipe] sortie *f*. || [shop]: retail ~ point *m* de vente. || *Am* ELEC prise *f* (de courant).

outline ['autlaɪn] **1** *n* [brief description] grandes lignes *fpl*; in ~ en gros. || [silhouette] silhouette *f*. **2** *vt* [describe briefly] exposer les grandes lignes de.

outlive [,aut'lɪv] *vt* [subj: person] survivre à.

outlook ['autluk] *n* [disposition] attitude *f*, conception *f*. || [prospect] perspective *f*.

outlying ['aut,laɪɪŋ] *adj* [village] reculé(e); [suburbs] écarté(e).

outnumber [,aut'nʌmbər] *vt* surpasser en nombre.

out-of-date *adj* [passport] périmé(e); [clothes] démodé(e); [belief] dépassé(e).

out of doors *adv* dehors.

outpatient ['aut,peɪʃnt] *n* malade *mf* en consultation externe.

outpost ['autpəust] *n* avant-poste *m*.

output ['autput] *n* [production] production *f*. || COMPUT sortie *f*.

outrage ['autreɪdʒ] **1** *n* [emotion] indignation *f*. || [act] atrocité *f*. **2** *vt* outrager.

outrageous [aut'reɪdʒəs] *adj* [offensive, shocking] scandaleux(euse), monstrueux(euse). || [very unusual] choquant(e).

outright [*adj* 'aʊtraɪt, *adv* ˌaʊt'raɪt] **1** *adj* absolu(e), total(e). **2** *adv* [deny] carrément, franchement. || [win, fail] complètement, totalement.

outset ['aʊtset] *n*: **at the ~** au commencement, au début.

outside [*n* ˌaʊt'saɪd, *adj, prep & n* 'aʊtsaɪd] **1** *adj* [gen] extérieur(e); **an ~ opinion** une opinion indépendante. || [unlikely - chance, possibility] faible. **2** *adv* à l'extérieur; **to go/run/look ~** aller/courir/regarder dehors. **3** *prep* [not inside] à l'extérieur de, en dehors de. || [beyond]: **~ office hours** en dehors des heures de bureau. **4** *n* extérieur *m*. ○ **outside of** *prep* Am [apart from] à part.

outside lane *n* AUT [in Europe, US] voie *f* de gauche.

outside line *n* TELEC ligne *f* extérieure.

outsider [ˌaʊt'saɪdər] *n* [in race] outsider *m*. || [from society] étranger *m*, -ère *f*.

outsize ['aʊtsaɪz] *adj* [bigger than usual] énorme, colossal(e). || [clothes] grande taille (*inv*).

outskirts ['aʊtskɜːts] *npl*: **the ~** la banlieue.

outspoken [ˌaʊt'spəʊkn] *adj* franc (franche).

outstanding [ˌaʊt'stændɪŋ] *adj* [excellent] exceptionnel(elle), remarquable. || [example] marquant(e). || [not paid] impayé(e). || [unfinished - work, problem] en suspens.

outstretched [ˌaʊt'stretʃt] *adj* [arms, hands] tendu(e); [wings] déployé(e).

outstrip [ˌaʊt'strɪp] *vt* devancer.

out-tray *n* corbeille *f* pour le courrier à expédier.

outward ['aʊtwəd] **1** *adj* [going away]: **~ journey** aller *m*. || [apparent, visible] extérieur(e). **2** *adv* Am = **outwards**.

outwardly ['aʊtwədlɪ] *adv* [apparently] en apparence.

outwards Br ['aʊtwədz], **outward** Am *adv* vers l'extérieur.

outweigh [ˌaʊt'weɪ] *vt fig* primer sur.

outwit [ˌaʊt'wɪt] *vt* se montrer plus malin(igne) que.

oval ['əʊvl] **1** *adj* ovale. **2** *n* ovale *m*.

Oval Office *n*: **the ~** bureau du président des États-Unis à la Maison-Blanche.

ovary ['əʊvərɪ] *n* ovaire *m*.

ovation [əʊ'veɪʃn] *n* ovation *f*; **the audience gave her a standing ~** le public l'a ovationnée.

oven ['ʌvn] *n* [for cooking] four *m*.

ovenproof ['ʌvnpruːf] *adj* qui va au four.

over ['əʊvər] **1** *prep* [above] au-dessus de. || [on top of] sur. || [on other side of] de l'autre côté de; **they live ~ the road** ils habitent en face. || [to other side of] par-dessus; **to go ~ the border** franchir la frontière. || [more than] plus de; **~ and above** en plus de. || [concerning] à propos de, au sujet de. || [during] pendant. **2** *adv* [distance away]: **~ here** ici; **~ there** là-bas. || [across]: **they flew ~ to America** ils se sont envolés pour les États-Unis; **we invited them ~** nous les avons invités chez nous. || [more] plus. || [remaining]: **there's nothing (left) ~** il ne reste rien. || RADIO: **~ and out!** à vous! || [involving repetitions]: **(all) ~ again** (tout) au début; **~ and ~ again** à maintes reprises, maintes fois. **3** *adj* [finished] fini(e), terminé(e). ○ **all over 1** *prep* [throughout] partout, dans tout; **all ~ the world** dans le monde entier. **2** *adv* [everywhere] partout. **3** *adj* [finished] fini(e).

overall [*adj & n* 'əʊvərɔːl, *adv* ˌəʊvər'ɔːl] **1** *adj* [general] d'ensemble. **2** *adv* en général. **3** *n* [gen] tablier *m*. || Am [for work] bleu *m* de travail. ○ **overalls** *npl* Am [dungarees] salopette *f*.

overawe [ˌəʊvər'ɔː] *vt* impressionner.

overbalance [ˌəʊvə'bæləns] *vi* basculer.

overbearing [ˌəʊvə'beərɪŋ] *adj* autoritaire.

overboard ['əʊvəbɔːd] *adv*: **to fall ~** tomber par-dessus bord.

overbook [ˌəʊvə'bʊk] *vi* surréserver.

overcame [ˌəʊvə'keɪm] *pt* → **overcome**.

overcast [ˌəʊvə'kɑːst] *adj* couvert(e).

overcharge [ˌəʊvə'tʃɑːdʒ] *vt*: **to ~ sb (for sthg)** faire payer (qqch) trop cher à qqn.

overcoat ['əʊvəkəʊt] *n* pardessus *m*.

overcome [ˌəʊvə'kʌm] (*pt* -came, *pp* -come) *vt* [fears, difficulties] surmonter. || [overwhelm]: **to be ~ (by OR with)** [emotion] être submergé(e) (de); [grief] être accablé(e) (de).

overcrowded [ˌəʊvə'kraʊdɪd] *adj* bondé(e).

overcrowding [ˌəʊvə'kraʊdɪŋ] *n* surpeuplement *m*.

overdo [ˌəʊvə'duː] (*pt* -did [-'dɪd], *pp* -done) *vt* [exaggerate] exagérer. || [do too much] trop faire; **to ~ it** se surmener. || [overcook] trop cuire.

overdone [,əʊvə'dʌn] **1** *pp* → **overdo. 2** *adj* [food] trop cuit(e).

overdose ['əʊvədəʊs] *n* overdose *f.*

overdraft ['əʊvədrɑːft] *n* découvert *m.*

overdrawn [,əʊvə'drɔːn] *adj* à découvert.

overdue [,əʊvə'djuː] *adj* [late]: **~ (for)** en retard (pour). || [change, reform]: **(long)** ~ attendu(e) (depuis longtemps). || [unpaid] arriéré(e), impayé(e).

overestimate [,əʊvər'estɪmeɪt] *vt* surestimer.

overflow [*vb* ,əʊvə'fləʊ, *n* 'əʊvəfləʊ] **1** *vi* [gen] déborder. **2** *n* [pipe, hole] trop-plein *m.*

overgrown [,əʊvə'grəʊn] *adj* [garden] envahi(e) par les mauvaises herbes.

overhaul [*n* 'əʊvəhɔːl, *vb* ,əʊvə'hɔːl] **1** *n* [of car, machine] révision *f.* || *fig* [of system] refonte *f*, remaniement *m.* **2** *vt* [car, machine] réviser. || *fig* [system] refondre, remanier.

overhead [*adv* ,əʊvə'hed, *adj & n* 'əʊvəhed] **1** *adj* aérien(ienne). **2** *adv* au-dessus. **3** *n* *Am* (*U*) frais *mpl* généraux.

overhead projector *n* rétroprojecteur *m.*

overhear [,əʊvə'hɪər] (*pt & pp* **-heard** [-'hɜːd]) *vt* entendre par hasard.

overheat [,əʊvə'hiːt] **1** *vt* surchauffer. **2** *vi* [engine] chauffer.

overjoyed [,əʊvə'dʒɔɪd] *adj*: **~ (at)** transporté(e) de joie (à).

overladen [,əʊvə'leɪdn] **1** *pp* → **overload. 2** *adj* surchargé(e).

overland ['əʊvəlænd] *adj & adv* par voie de terre.

overlap [,əʊvə'læp] *vi* lit & fig se chevaucher.

overleaf [,əʊvə'liːf] *adv* au verso, au dos.

overload [,əʊvə'ləʊd] (*pp* **-loaded** OR **-laden**) *vt* surcharger.

overlook [,əʊvə'lʊk] *vt* [subj: building, room] donner sur. || [disregard, miss] oublier, négliger. || [excuse] passer sur, fermer les yeux sur.

overnight [*adj* 'əʊvənaɪt, *adv* ,əʊvə'naɪt] **1** *adj* [journey, parking] de nuit; [stay] d'une nuit. || *fig* [sudden]: **~ success** succès *m* immédiat. **2** *adv* [stay, leave] la nuit. || [suddenly] du jour au lendemain.

overpass ['əʊvəpɑːs] *n* *Am* ≃ Toboggan® *m.*

overpower [,əʊvə'paʊər] *vt* [in fight] vaincre. || *fig* [overwhelm] accabler, terrasser.

overpowering [,əʊvə'paʊərɪŋ] *adj* [desire] irrésistible; [smell] entêtant(e).

overran [,əʊvə'ræn] *pt* → **overrun.**

overrated [,əʊvə'reɪtɪd] *adj* surfait(e).

override [,əʊvə'raɪd] (*pt* **-rode,** *pp* **-ridden**) *vt* [be more important than] l'emporter sur, prévaloir sur. || [overrule - decision] annuler.

overriding [,əʊvə'raɪdɪŋ] *adj* [need, importance] primordial(e).

overrode [,əʊvə'rəʊd] *pt* → **override.**

overrule [,əʊvə'ruːl] *vt* [person] prévaloir contre; [decision] annuler; [objection] rejeter.

overrun [,əʊvə'rʌn] (*pt* **-ran,** *pp* **-run**) **1** *vt* *fig* [cover, fill]: **to be ~ with** [weeds] être envahi(e) de; [rats] être infesté(e) de. **2** *vi* dépasser (le temps alloué).

oversaw [,əʊvə'sɔː] *pt* → **oversee.**

overseas [*adj* 'əʊvəsiːz, *adv* ,əʊvə'siːz] **1** *adj* [sales, company] à l'étranger; [market] extérieur(e); [visitor, student] étranger(ère); **~ aid** aide *f* aux pays étrangers. **2** *adv* à l'étranger.

oversee [,əʊvə'siː] (*pt* **-saw,** *pp* **-seen** [-'siːn]) *vt* surveiller.

overseer ['əʊvə,siːər] *n* contremaître *m.*

overshadow [,əʊvə'ʃædəʊ] *vt* [subj: building, tree] dominer; *fig* éclipser.

overshoot [,əʊvə'ʃuːt] (*pt & pp* **-shot**) *vt* dépasser, rater.

oversight ['əʊvəsaɪt] *n* oubli *m.*

oversleep [,əʊvə'sliːp] (*pt & pp* **-slept** [-'slept]) *vi* ne pas se réveiller à temps.

overspill ['əʊvəspɪl] *n* [of population] excédent *m.*

overstep [,əʊvə'step] *vt* dépasser; **to ~ the mark** dépasser la mesure.

overt ['əʊvɜːt] *adj* déclaré(e), non déguisé(e).

overtake [,əʊvə'teɪk] (*pt* **-took,** *pp* **-taken** [-'teɪkn]) **1** *vt* AUT doubler, dépasser. **2** *vi* AUT doubler.

overthrow [*n* 'əʊvəθrəʊ, *vb* ,əʊvə'θrəʊ] (*pt* **-threw** [-'θruː], *pp* **-thrown** [-'θrəʊn]) **1** *n* [of government] coup *m* d'État. **2** *vt* [government] renverser.

overtime ['əʊvətaɪm] **1** *n* (*U*) [extra work] heures *fpl* supplémentaires. || *Am* SPORT prolongations *fpl.* **2** *adv*: **to work ~** faire des heures supplémentaires.

overtones ['əʊvətəʊnz] *npl* notes *fpl*, accents *mpl.*

overtook [,əʊvə'tʊk] *pt* → **overtake.**

overture ['əʊvə,tjʊər] *n* MUS ouverture *f*.

overturn [,əʊvə'tɜːn] 1 *vt* [gen] renverser. || [decision] annuler. 2 *vi* [vehicle] se renverser; [boat] chavirer.

overweight [,əʊvə'weɪt] *adj* trop gros (grosse).

overwhelm [,əʊvə'welm] *vt* [subj: grief, despair] accabler; **to be ~ed with joy** être au comble de la joie. || MIL [gain control of] écraser.

overwhelming [,əʊvə'welmɪŋ] *adj* [overpowering] irrésistible, irrépressible. || [defeat, majority] écrasant(e).

overwork [,əʊvə'wɜːk] 1 *n* surmenage *m*. 2 *vt* [person, staff] surmener.

overwrought [,əʊvə'rɔːt] *adj* excédé(e), à bout.

owe [əʊ] *vt*: **to ~ sthg to sb, to ~ sb sthg** devoir qqch à qqn.

owing ['əʊɪŋ] *adj* dû (due). ○ **owing to** *prep* à cause de, en raison de.

owl [aʊl] *n* hibou *m*.

own [əʊn] 1 *adj* propre; **she has her ~ style** elle a son style à elle. 2 *pron*: **I've got my ~** j'ai le mien; **he has a house of his ~** il a une maison à lui, il a sa propre maison; **on one's ~** tout seul (toute seule); **to get one's ~ back** *inf* prendre sa revanche. 3 *vt* posséder. ○ **own up** *vi*: **to ~ up (to sthg)** avouer OR confesser (qqch).

owner ['əʊnər] *n* propriétaire *mf*.

ownership ['əʊnəʃɪp] *n* propriété *f*.

ox [ɒks] (*pl* **oxen**) *n* bœuf *m*.

oxen ['ɒksn] *pl* → **ox**.

oxtail soup ['ɒksteɪl-] *n* soupe *f* à la queue de bœuf.

oxygen ['ɒksɪdʒən] *n* oxygène *m*.

oxygen mask *n* masque *m* à oxygène.

oxygen tent *n* tente *f* à oxygène.

oyster ['ɔɪstər] *n* huître *f*.

oz. *abbr of* **ounce**.

ozone-friendly *adj* qui préserve la couche d'ozone.

ozone layer *n* couche *f* d'ozone.

p¹ (*pl* **p's** OR **ps**), **P** (*pl* **P's** OR **Ps**) [piː] *n* [letter] p *m inv*, P *m inv*.

p² (*abbr of* **page**) p.

pa [pɑː] *n inf* papa *m*.

p.a. (*abbr of* **per annum**) p.a.

PA *n* (*abbr of* **public address system**) sono *f*.

pace [peɪs] 1 *n* [speed, rate] vitesse *f*, allure *f*; **to keep ~ (with sthg)** se maintenir au même niveau (que qqch). || [step] pas *m*. 2 *vi*: **to ~ (up and down)** faire les cent pas.

pacemaker ['peɪs,meɪkər] *n* MED stimulateur *m* cardiaque, pacemaker *m*.

Pacific [pə'sɪfɪk] 1 *adj* du Pacifique. 2 *n*: **the ~ (Ocean)** l'océan *m* Pacifique, le Pacifique.

pacifier ['pæsɪfaɪər] *n Am* [for child] tétine *f*, sucette *f*.

pacifist ['pæsɪfɪst] *n* pacifiste *mf*.

pacify ['pæsɪfaɪ] *vt* [person, baby] apaiser. || [country] pacifier.

pack [pæk] 1 *n* [bag] sac *m*. || [packet] paquet *m*. || [of cards] jeu *m*. || [of dogs] meute *f*; [of wolves, thieves] bande *f*. 2 *vt* [clothes, belongings] emballer; **to ~ one's bags** faire ses bagages. || [fill] remplir; **to be ~ed into** être entassé dans. 3 *vi* [for journey] faire ses bagages OR sa valise. ○ **pack off** *vt sep inf* [send away] expédier.

package ['pækɪdʒ] 1 *n* [of books, goods] paquet *m*. || COMPUT progiciel *m*. 2 *vt* [wrap up] conditionner.

package deal *n* contrat *m* global.

package tour *n* vacances *fpl* organisées.

packaging ['pækɪdʒɪŋ] *n* conditionnement *m*.

packed [pækt] *adj*: **~ (with)** bourré(e) (de).

packet ['pækɪt] *n* [gen] paquet *m*.

packing ['pækɪŋ] *n* [material] emballage *m*.

packing case *n* caisse *f* d'emballage.

pact [pækt] *n* pacte *m*.

pad [pæd] **1** *n* [of cotton wool etc] morceau *m*. ‖ [of paper] bloc *m*. ‖ [of cat, dog] coussinet *m*. **2** *rt* [furniture. jacket] rembourrer; [wound] tamponner. **3** *ri* [walk softly] marcher à pas feutrés.

padding ['pædɪŋ] *n* [material] rembourrage *m*. ‖ *fig* [in speech. letter] délayage *m*.

paddle ['pædl] **1** *n* [for canoe etc] pagaie *f*. ‖ [in sea]: **to have a ~** faire trempette. **2** *ri* [in canoe etc] avancer en pagayant. ‖ [in sea] faire trempette.

paddle boat, paddle steamer *n* bateau *m* à aubes.

paddock ['pædək] *n* [small field] enclos *m*. ‖ [at racecourse] paddock *m*.

paddy field ['pædɪ-] *n* rizière *f*.

padlock ['pædlɒk] **1** *n* cadenas *m*. **2** *rt* cadenasser.

paediatrics [,piːdɪ'ætrɪks] = **pediatrics**.

pagan ['peɪgən] **1** *adj* païen(ïenne). **2** *n* païen *m*, -ïenne *f*.

page [peɪdʒ] **1** *n* [of book] page *f*. ‖ [sheet of paper] feuille *f*. **2** *rt* [in airport] appeler au micro.

pageant ['pædʒənt] *n* [show] spectacle *m* historique.

pageantry ['pædʒəntrɪ] *n* apparat *m*.

paid [peɪd] **1** *pt* & *pp* → **pay**. **2** *adj* [work. holiday, staff] rémunéré(e), payé(e).

pail [peɪl] *n* seau *m*.

pain [peɪn] *n* [hurt] douleur *f*; **to be in ~** souffrir. ‖ *inf* [annoyance]: **it's/he is such a ~** c'est/il est vraiment assommant. ○ **pains** *npl* [effort, care]: **to be at ~s to do sthg** vouloir absolument faire qqch; **to take ~s to do sthg** se donner beaucoup de mal OR peine pour faire qqch.

pained [peɪnd] *adj* peiné(e).

painful ['peɪnfʊl] *adj* [physically] douloureux(euse). ‖ [emotionally] pénible.

painfully ['peɪnfʊlɪ] *adv* [fall, hit] douloureusement. ‖ [remember, feel] péniblement.

painkiller ['peɪn,kɪlər] *n* calmant *m*, analgésique *m*.

painless ['peɪnlɪs] *adj* [without hurt] indolore, sans douleur. ‖ *fig* [changeover] sans heurt.

painstaking ['peɪnz,teɪkɪŋ] *adj* [worker] assidu(e); [detail, work] soigné(e).

paint [peɪnt] **1** *n* peinture *f*. **2** *rt* [gen] peindre.

paintbrush ['peɪntbrʌʃ] *n* pinceau *m*.

painter ['peɪntər] *n* peintre *m*.

painting ['peɪntɪŋ] *n* (U) [gen] peinture *f*. ‖ [picture] toile *f*, tableau *m*.

paint stripper *n* décapant *m*.

paintwork ['peɪntwɜːk] *n* (U) surfaces *fpl* peintes.

pair [peər] *n*. [of shoes. wings etc] paire *f*; **a ~ of trousers** un pantalon. ‖ [couple] couple *m*.

pajamas [pə'dʒɑːməz] = **pyjamas**.

Pakistan [*Br* ,pɑːkɪ'stɑːn, *Am* ,pækɪ-'stæn] *n* Pakistan *m*.

Pakistani [*Br* ,pɑːkɪ'stɑːnɪ, *Am* ,pækɪ'stænɪ] **1** *adj* pakistanais(e). **2** *n* Pakistanais *m*, -e *f*.

pal [pæl] *n inf* [friend] copain *m*, copine *f*. ‖ [as term of address] mon vieux *m*.

palace ['pælɪs] *n* palais *m*.

palatable ['pælətəbl] *adj* [food] agréable au goût.

palate ['pælət] *n* palais *m*.

palaver [pə'lɑːvər] *n* (U) *inf* [talk] palabres *fpl*. ‖ [fuss] histoire *f*, affaire *f*.

pale [peɪl] *adj* pâle.

Palestine ['pælə,staɪn] *n* Palestine *f*.

Palestinian [,pælə'stɪnɪən] **1** *adj* palestinien(ienne). **2** *n* Palestinien *m*, -ienne *f*.

palette ['pælət] *n* palette *f*.

pall [pɔːl] **1** *n* [of smoke] voile *m*. ‖ *Am* [coffin] cercueil *m*. **2** *ri* perdre de son charme.

pallet ['pælɪt] *n* palette *f*.

pallor ['pælər] *n literary* pâleur *f*.

palm [pɑːm] *n* [tree] palmier *m*. ‖ [of hand] paume *f*. ○ **palm off** *rt sep inf*: **to ~ sthg off on sb** refiler qqch à qqn; **to ~ sb off with sthg** se débarrasser de qqn avec qqch.

Palm Sunday *n* dimanche *m* des Rameaux.

palm tree *n* palmier *m*.

palpable ['pælpəbl] *adj* évident(e), manifeste.

paltry ['pɔːltrɪ] *adj* dérisoire.

pamper ['pæmpər] *rt* choyer, dorloter.

pamphlet ['pæmflɪt] *n* brochure *f*.

pan [pæn] **1** *n* [gen] casserole *f*. ‖ *Am* [for bread. cakes etc] moule *m*. **2** *rt inf* [criticize] démolir. **3** *ri* CINEMA faire un panoramique.

panacea [,pænə'sɪə] *n* panacée *f*.

Panama [,pænə'mɑː] *n* Panama *m*.

Panama Cánal *n*: **the ~** le canal de Panama.

pancake ['pænkeɪk] *n* crêpe *f*.

Pancake Tuesday *n* mardi gras *m*.

panda ['pændə] (*pl inv* OR **-s**) *n* panda *m*.

pandemonium [,pændɪ'məʊnjəm] *n* tohu-bohu *m inv*.

pander ['pændər] *vi*: **to ~ to sb** se prêter aux exigences de qqn; **to ~ to sthg** se plier à qqch.

pane [peɪn] *n* vitre *f*, carreau *m*.

panel ['pænl] *n* TV & RADIO invités *mpl*; [of experts] comité *m*. || [of wood] panneau *m*. || [of machine] tableau *m* de bord.

panelling *Br*, **paneling** *Am* ['pænəlɪŋ] *n* (*U*) lambris *m*.

pang [pæŋ] *n* tiraillement *m*.

panic ['pænɪk] (*pt* & *pp* **-ked**, *cont* **-king**) **1** *n* panique *f*. **2** *vi* paniquer.

panicky ['pænɪkɪ] *adj* [person] paniqué(e); [feeling] de panique.

panic-stricken *adj* affolé(e), pris(e) de panique.

panorama [,pænə'rɑːmə] *n* panorama *m*.

pansy ['pænzɪ] *n* [flower] pensée *f*.

pant [pænt] *vi* haleter.

panther ['pænθər] (*pl inv* OR **-s**) *n* panthère *f*.

panties ['pæntɪz] *npl inf* culotte *f*.

pantihose ['pæntɪhəʊz] = **panty hose**.

pantry ['pæntrɪ] *n* garde-manger *m inv*.

pants [pænts] *npl Am* [trousers] pantalon *m*.

panty hose ['pæntɪhəʊz] *npl Am* collant *m*.

papa [*Br* pə'pɑː, *Am* 'pæpə] *n* papa *m*.

paper ['peɪpər] **1** *n* (*U*) [for writing on] papier *m*; **a piece of ~** [sheet] une feuille de papier; [scrap] un bout de papier. || [newspaper] journal *m*. || [in exam - test] épreuve *f*; [- answers] copie *f*. || [essay: - (on)] essai *m* (sur). **2** *adj* [hat, bag etc] en papier. **3** *vt* tapisser. ○ **papers** *npl* [official documents] papiers *mpl*.

paperback ['peɪpəbæk] *n*: **~ (book)** livre *m* de poche.

paper clip *n* trombone *m*.

paper handkerchief *n* mouchoir *m* en papier.

paper knife *n* coupe-papier *m inv*.

paperweight ['peɪpəweɪt] *n* presse-papiers *m inv*.

paperwork ['peɪpəwɜːk] *n* paperasserie *f*.

paprika ['pæprɪkə] *n* paprika *m*.

par [pɑːr] *n* [parity]: **on a ~ with** à égalité avec. || GOLF par *m*. || [good health]: **below** OR **under ~** pas en forme.

parable ['pærəbl] *n* parabole *f*.

parachute ['pærəʃuːt] **1** *n* parachute *m*. **2** *vi* sauter en parachute.

parade [pə'reɪd] **1** *n* [celebratory] parade *f*, revue *f*. || MIL défilé *m*. **2** *vt* [people] faire défiler. || [object] montrer. || *fig* [flaunt] afficher. **3** *vi* défiler.

paradise ['pærədaɪs] *n* paradis *m*.

paradox ['pærədɒks] *n* paradoxe *m*.

paraffin ['pærəfɪn] *n* paraffine *f*.

paragon ['pærəgən] *n* modèle *m*, parangon *m*.

paragraph ['pærəgrɑːf] *n* paragraphe *m*.

Paraguay ['pærəgwaɪ] *n* Paraguay *m*.

parallel ['pærəlel] **1** *adj lit* & *fig*: **~ (to** OR **with)** parallèle (à). **2** *n* GEOM parallèle *f*. || [similarity & GEOGR] parallèle *m*. || *fig* [similar person, object] équivalent *m*.

paralyse *Br*, **-yze** *Am* ['pærəlaɪz] *vt lit* & *fig* paralyser.

paralysis [pə'rælɪsɪs] (*pl* **-lyses** [-lɪsiːz]) *n* paralysie *f*.

paramedic [,pærə'medɪk] *n* auxiliaire médical *m*, auxiliaire médicale *f*.

parameter [pə'ræmɪtər] *n* paramètre *m*.

paramount ['pærəmaʊnt] *adj* primordial(e); **of ~ importance** d'une importance suprême.

paranoid ['pærənɔɪd] *adj* paranoïaque.

paraphernalia [,pærəfə'neɪljə] *n* (*U*) attirail *m*, bazar *m*.

parasite ['pærəsaɪt] *n lit* & *fig* parasite *m*.

parasol ['pærəsɒl] *n* [above table] parasol *m*; [hand-held] ombrelle *f*.

paratrooper ['pærətruːpər] *n* parachutiste *mf*.

parcel ['pɑːsl] *n* paquet *m*. ○ **parcel up** *vt sep* empaqueter.

parched [pɑːtʃt] *adj* [gen] desséché(e). || *inf* [very thirsty] assoiffé(e), mort(e) de soif.

parchment ['pɑːtʃmənt] *n* parchemin *m*.

pardon ['pɑːdn] **1** *n* JUR grâce *f*. || (*U*) [forgiveness] pardon *m*; **I beg your ~?** [showing surprise, asking for repetition] comment?, pardon?; **I beg your ~!** [to apologize] je vous demande pardon! **2** *vt* [forgive] pardonner; **to ~ sb for sthg** pardonner qqch à qqn; **~ me!** pardon!, excusez-moi! || JUR gracier. **3** *excl* comment?

parent ['peərənt] *n* père *m*, mère *f*. ○ **parents** *npl* parents *mpl*.

parental [pə'rentl] *adj* parental(e).

Paris ['pærɪs] *n* Paris.

parish ['pærɪʃ] *n* RELIG paroisse *f.*

Parisian [pə'rɪzjən] **1** *adj* parisien (ienne). **2** *n* Parisien *m*, -ienne *f.*

parity ['pærətɪ] *n* égalité *f.*

park [pɑːk] **1** *n* parc *m*, jardin *m* public. **2** *vt* garer. **3** *vi* se garer, stationner.

parking ['pɑːkɪŋ] *n* stationnement *m*; "no ~" «défense de stationner», «stationnement interdit».

parking lot *n Am* parking *m.*

parking meter *n* parcmètre *m.*

parking ticket *n* contravention *f*, PV *m.*

parlance ['pɑːləns] *n*: in common/legal *etc* ~ en langage courant/juridique *etc.*

parliament ['pɑːləmənt] *n* parlement *m.*

parliamentary [,pɑːlə'mentərɪ] *adj* parlementaire.

parochial [pə'rəʊkjəl] *adj pej* de clocher.

parody ['pærədɪ] **1** *n* parodie *f.* **2** *vt* parodier.

parole [pə'rəʊl] *n* (*U*) parole *f*; on ~ en liberté conditionnelle.

parrot ['pærət] *n* perroquet *m.*

parry ['pærɪ] *vt* [blow] parer. || [question] éluder.

parsley ['pɑːslɪ] *n* persil *m.*

parsnip ['pɑːsnɪp] *n* panais *m.*

parson ['pɑːsn] *n* pasteur *m.*

part [pɑːt] **1** *n* [gen] partie *f*; for the most ~ dans l'ensemble. || [of TV serial *etc*] épisode *m.* || [component] pièce *f.* || [in proportions] mesure *f.* || THEATRE rôle *m.* || [involvement]: ~ in participation *f* à; to play an important ~ in jouer un rôle important dans; to take ~ in participer à; for my ~ en ce qui me concerne. || *Am* [hair parting] raie *f.* **2** *adv* en partie. **3** *vt* to ~ one's hair se faire une raie. **4** *vi* [couple] se séparer. || [curtains] s'écarter, s'ouvrir. ◯ **parts** *npl*: in these ~s dans cette région. ◯ **part with** *vt fus* [money] débourser; [possession] se défaire de.

part exchange *n* reprise *f*; in ~ comme reprise en compte.

partial ['pɑːʃl] *adj* [incomplete] partiel(ielle). || [biased] partial(e). || [fond]: to be ~ to avoir un penchant pour.

participant [pɑː'tɪsɪpənt] *n* participant *m*, -e *f.*

participate [pɑː'tɪsɪpeɪt] *vi*: to ~ (in) participer (à).

participation [pɑː,tɪsɪ'peɪʃn] *n* participation *f.*

participle ['pɑːtɪsɪpl] *n* participe *m.*

particle ['pɑːtɪkl] *n* particule *f.*

particular [pə'tɪkjʊləʳ] *adj* [gen] particulier(ière). || [fussy] pointilleux(euse); ~ about exigeant(e) à propos de. ◯ **particulars** *npl* renseignements *mpl.* ◯ **in particular** *adv* en particulier.

particularly [pə'tɪkjʊləlɪ] *adv* particulièrement.

parting ['pɑːtɪŋ] *n* [separation] séparation *f.* || *Br* [in hair] raie *f.*

partisan [,pɑːtɪ'zæn] *n* partisan *m*, -e *f.*

partition [pɑː'tɪʃn] **1** *n* [wall, screen] cloison *f.* **2** *vt* [room] cloisonner. || [country] partager.

partly ['pɑːtlɪ] *adv* partiellement, en partie.

partner ['pɑːtnəʳ] **1** *n* [gen] partenaire *mf.* || [in a business, crime] associé *m*, -e *f.* **2** *vt* être le partenaire de.

partnership ['pɑːtnəʃɪp] *n* association *f.*

partridge ['pɑːtrɪdʒ] *n* perdrix *f.*

part-time *adj & adv* à temps partiel.

party ['pɑːtɪ] *n* POL parti *m.* || [social gathering] fête *f*, réception *f.* || [group] groupe *m.* || JUR partie *f.*

party line *n* POL ligne *f* du parti. || TELEC ligne *f* commune à deux abonnés.

pass [pɑːs] **1** *n* SPORT passe *f.* || [document - for security] laissez-passer *m inv*; [- for travel] carte *f* d'abonnement. || [between mountains] col *m.* || *phr*: to make a ~ at sb faire du plat à qqn. **2** *vt* [object, time] passer; to ~ sthg to sb, to ~ sb sthg passer qqch à qqn. || [person in street *etc*] croiser. || [place] passer devant. || *AUT* dépasser, doubler. || [exceed] dépasser. || [exam] réussir (à); [driving test] passer. || [law, motion] voter. || [judgment] rendre, prononcer. **3** *vi* [gen] passer. || *AUT* doubler, dépasser. || SPORT faire une passe. || [in exam] réussir, être reçu(e). ◯ **pass as** *vt fus* passer pour. ◯ **pass away** *vi* s'éteindre. ◯ **pass by 1** *vt sep*: the news ~ed him by la nouvelle ne l'a pas affecté. **2** *vi* passer à côté. ◯ **pass for** = pass as. ◯ **pass on 1** *vt sep*: to ~ sthg on (to) [object] faire passer qqch (à); [tradition, information] transmettre qqch (à). **2** *vi* [move on] continuer son chemin. || = pass away. ◯ **pass out** *vi* [faint] s'évanouir. ◯ **pass over** *vt fus* [problem, topic] passer sous silence. ◯ **pass up** *vt* *sep* [opportunity, invitation] laisser passer.

passable ['pɑːsəbl] *adj* [satisfactory] passable. || [road] praticable; [river] franchissable.

passage ['pæsɪdʒ] *n* [gen] passage *m*. || [between rooms] couloir *m*. || [sea journey] traversée *f*.

passageway ['pæsɪdʒweɪ] *n* [between houses] passage *m*; [between rooms] couloir *m*.

passbook ['pɑːsbʊk] *n* livret *m* de banque.

passenger ['pæsɪndʒər] *n* passager *m*, -ère *f*.

passerby [,pɑːsə'baɪ] (*pl* **passersby** [,pɑːsəz'baɪ]) *n* passant *m*, -e *f*.

passing ['pɑːsɪŋ] *adj* [remark] en passant; [trend] passager(ère). ○ **in passing** *adv* en passant.

passion ['pæʃn] *n* passion *f*.

passionate ['pæʃənət] *adj* passionné(e).

passive ['pæsɪv] *adj* passif(ive).

Passover ['pɑːs,əʊvər] *n*: (the) ~ la Pâque juive.

passport ['pɑːspɔːt] *n* [document] passeport *m*.

passport control *n* contrôle *m* des passeports.

password ['pɑːswɜːd] *n* mot *m* de passe.

past [pɑːst] **1** *adj* [former] passé(e); **for the ~ five years** ces cinq dernières années; **the ~ week** la semaine passée OR dernière. || [finished] fini(e). **2** *adv* [in times]: **it's ten ~** il est dix. || [in front]: **to drive ~** passer (devant) en voiture; **to run ~** passer (devant) en courant. **3** *n* passé *m*; **in the ~** dans le temps. **4** *prep* [in times]: **it's half ~ eight** il est huit heures et demie; **it's five ~ nine** il est neuf heures cinq. || [in front of] devant; **we drove ~ them** nous les avons dépassés en voiture. || [beyond] après, au-delà de.

pasta ['pæstə] *n* (U) pâtes *fpl*.

paste [peɪst] **1** *n* [gen] pâte *f*. CULIN pâté *m*. || (U) [glue] colle *f*. **2** *vt* coller.

pastel ['pæstl] *adj* pastel (*inv*).

pasteurize, -ise ['pɑːstʃəraɪz] *vt* pasteuriser.

pastille ['pæstɪl] *n* pastille *f*.

pastime ['pɑːstaɪm] *n* passe-temps *m inv*.

pastor ['pɑːstər] *n* pasteur *m*.

past participle *n* participe *m* passé.

pastry ['peɪstrɪ] *n* [mixture] pâte *f*. || [cake] pâtisserie *f*.

past tense *n* passé *m*.

pasture ['pɑːstʃər] *n* pâturage *m*, pré *m*.

pasty ['peɪstɪ] *adj* blafard(e), terreux(euse).

pat [pæt] **1** *n* [light stroke] petite tape *f*; [to animal] caresse *f*. || [of butter] noix *f*, noisette *f*. **2** *vt* [person] tapoter, donner une tape à; [animal] caresser.

patch [pætʃ] **1** *n* [piece of material] pièce *f*; [to cover eye] bandeau *m*. || [small area - of snow, ice] plaque *f*. || [of land] parcelle *f*, lopin *m*. || [period of time]: **a difficult ~** une mauvaise passe. **2** *vt* rapiécer. ○ **patch up** *vt sep* [mend] rafistoler, bricoler. || *fig* [quarrel] régler, arranger.

patchwork ['pætʃwɜːk] *n* patchwork *m*.

patchy ['pætʃɪ] *adj* [gen] inégal(e); [knowledge] insuffisant(e), imparfait(e).

pâté ['pæteɪ] *n* pâté *m*.

patent [*Br* 'peɪtənt, *Am* 'pætənt] **1** *n* brevet *m* (d'invention). **2** *vt* faire breveter.

patent leather *n* cuir *m* verni.

paternal [pə'tɜːnl] *adj* paternel(elle).

path [pɑːθ, *pl* pɑːðz] *n* [track] chemin *m*, sentier *m*. || [way ahead, course of action] voie *f*, chemin *m*. || [trajectory] trajectoire *f*.

pathetic [pə'θetɪk] *adj* [causing pity] pitoyable, attendrissant(e). || [useless - efforts, person] pitoyable, minable.

pathology [pə'θɒlədʒɪ] *n* pathologie *f*.

pathos ['peɪθɒs] *n* pathétique *m*.

pathway ['pɑːθweɪ] *n* chemin *m*, sentier *m*.

patience ['peɪʃns] *n* [of person] patience *f*. || [card game] réussite *f*.

patient ['peɪʃnt] **1** *adj* patient(e). **2** *n* [in hospital] patient *m*, -e *f*, malade *mf*; [of doctor] patient.

patio ['pætɪəʊ] (*pl* -s) *n* patio *m*.

patriotic [*Br* ,pætrɪ'ɒtɪk, *Am* ,peɪtrɪ'ɒtɪk] *adj* [gen] patriotique; [person] patriote.

patrol [pə'trəʊl] **1** *n* patrouille *f*. **2** *vt* patrouiller dans, faire une patrouille dans.

patrol car *n* voiture *f* de police.

patrolman [pə'trəʊlmən] (*pl* -men [-mən]) *n Am* agent *m* de police.

patron ['peɪtrən] *n* [of arts] mécène *m*, protecteur *m*, -trice *f*. || *fml* [customer] client *m*, -e *f*.

patronize, -ise ['pætrənaɪz] *vt* [talk down to] traiter avec condescendance. || *fml* [back financially] patronner, protéger.

patronizing ['pætrənaɪzɪŋ] *adj* condescendant(e).

patter ['pætər] **1** *n* [sound - of rain] crépitement *m*. || [talk] baratin *m*, bavardage *m*. **2** *vi* [feet, paws] trottiner; [rain] frapper, fouetter.

pattern ['pætən] *n* [design] motif *m*, dessin *m*. || [of distribution, population] schéma *m*; [of life, behaviour] mode *m*. || [diagram]: **(sewing) ~** patron *m*. || [model] modèle *m*.

paunch [pɔːntʃ] *n* bedaine *f*.

pauper ['pɔːpər] *n* indigent *m*, -e *f*, nécessiteux *m*, -euse *f*.

pause [pɔːz] **1** *n* [short silence] pause *f*, silence *m*. || [break] pause *f*, arrêt *m*. **2** *vi* [stop speaking] marquer un temps. || [stop moving, doing] faire une pause, s'arrêter.

pave [peɪv] *vt* paver; **to ~ the way for sb/sthg** ouvrir la voie à qqn/qqch.

pavement ['peɪvmənt] *n Am* [roadway] chaussée *f*.

pavilion [pə'vɪljən] *n* pavillon *m*.

paving ['peɪvɪŋ] *n* (*U*) pavé *m*.

paving stone *n* pavé *m*.

paw [pɔː] *n* patte *f*.

pawn [pɔːn] **1** *n lit* & *fig* pion *m*. **2** *vt* mettre en gage.

pawnbroker ['pɔːn,brəʊkər] *n* prêteur *m*, -euse *f* sur gages.

pawnshop ['pɔːnʃɒp] *n* mont-de-piété *m*.

pay [peɪ] (*pt* & *pp* **paid**) **1** *vt* [gen] payer; **to ~ sb for sthg** payer qqn pour qqch, payer qqch à qqn; **to ~ a cheque into an account** déposer un chèque sur un compte. || [be profitable to] rapporter à. || [give, make]: **to ~ attention (to sb/sthg)** prêter attention (à qqn/qqch); **to ~ sb a compliment** faire un compliment à qqn; **to ~ sb a visit** rendre visite à qqn. **2** *vi* payer; **to ~ dearly for sthg** *fig* payer qqch cher. **3** *n* salaire *m*, traitement *m*. ○ **pay back** *vt sep* [return loan of money] rembourser. || [revenge oneself on]: **I'll ~ you back for that** tu me le paieras, je te le revaudrai. ○ **pay off 1** *vt sep* [repay - debt] s'acquitter de, régler; [- loan] rembourser. || [dismiss] licencier, congédier. || [bribe] soudoyer, acheter. **2** *vi* [course of action] être payant(e). ○ **pay up** *vi* payer.

payable ['peɪəbl] *adj* [gen] payable. || [on cheque]: **~ to** à l'ordre de.

paycheck ['peɪtʃek] *n Am* paie *f*.

payday ['peɪdeɪ] *n* jour *m* de paie.

payee [peɪ'iː] *n* bénéficiaire *mf*.

pay envelope *n Am* salaire *m*.

payment ['peɪmənt] *n* paiement *m*.

pay phone, pay station *Am n* téléphone *m* public, cabine *f* téléphonique.

payroll ['peɪrəʊl] *n* registre *m* du personnel.

pay station *Am* = pay phone.

pc (*abbr of* **per cent**) p. cent.

PC *n* (*abbr of* **personal computer**) PC *m*, micro *m*.

PE (*abbr of* **physical education**) *n* EPS *f*.

pea [piː] *n* pois *m*.

peace [piːs] *n* (*U*) paix *f*; [quiet, calm] calme *m*, tranquillité *f*.

peaceable ['piːsəbl] *adj* paisible, pacifique.

peaceful ['piːsfʊl] *adj* [quiet, calm] paisible, calme. || [not aggressive - person] pacifique; [- demonstration] non-violent(e).

peacetime ['piːstaɪm] *n* temps *m* de paix.

peach [piːtʃ] **1** *adj* couleur pêche (*inv*). **2** *n* pêche *f*.

peacock ['piːkɒk] *n* paon *m*.

peak [piːk] *n* [mountain top] sommet *m*, cime *f*. || *fig* [of career, success] apogée *m*, sommet *m*. || [of cap] visière *f*. **2** *adj* [condition] optimum. **3** *vi* atteindre un niveau maximum.

peaked [piːkt] *adj* [cap] à visière.

peak hours *npl* heures *fpl* d'affluence OR de pointe.

peak period *n* période *f* de pointe.

peak rate *n* tarif *m* normal.

peal [piːl] **1** *n* [of bells] carillonnement *m*; [of laughter] éclat *m*; [of thunder] coup *m*. **2** *vi* [bells] carillonner.

peanut ['piːnʌt] *n* cacahuète *f*.

peanut butter *n* beurre *m* de cacahuètes.

pear [peər] *n* poire *f*.

pearl [pɜːl] *n* perle *f*.

peasant ['peznt] *n* [in countryside] paysan *m*, -anne *f*.

peat [piːt] *n* tourbe *f*.

pebble ['pebl] *n* galet *m*, caillou *m*.

peck [pek] **1** *n* [mountain beak] coup *m* de bec. || [kiss] bise *f*. **2** *vt* [with beak] picoter, becqueter. || [kiss]: **to ~ sb on the cheek** faire une bise à qqn.

pecking order ['pekɪŋ-] *n* hiérarchie *f.*

peculiar [pɪ'kju:ljər] *adj* [odd] bizarre, curieux(ieuse). || [slightly ill]: **to feel ~** se sentir tout drôle (toute drôle) OR tout chose (toute chose). || [characteristic]: **~ to** propre à, particulier(ière) à.

peculiarity [pɪ,kju:lɪ'ærətɪ] *n* [oddness] bizarrerie *f,* singularité *f.* || [characteristic] particularité *f,* caractéristique *f.*

pedal ['pedl] 1 *n* pédale *f.* 2 *vi* pédaler.

pedal bin *n* poubelle *f* à pédale.

pedantic [pɪ'dæntɪk] *adj pej* pédant(e).

peddle ['pedl] *vt* [drugs] faire le trafic de.

pedestal ['pedɪstl] *n* piédestal *m.*

pedestrian [pɪ'destrɪən] 1 *adj pej* médiocre, dépourvu(e) d'intérêt. 2 *n* piéton *m.*

pedestrian precinct *Br,* **pedestrian zone** *Am n* zone *f* piétonne.

pediatrics [,pi:dɪ'ætrɪks] *n* pédiatrie *f.*

pedigree ['pedɪgri:] 1 *adj* [animal] de race. 2 *n* [of animal] pedigree *m.* || [of person] ascendance *f,* généalogie *f.*

pedlar *Br,* **peddler** *Am* ['pedlər] *n* colporteur *m.*

pee [pi:] *inf* 1 *n* pipi *m,* pisse *f.* 2 *vi* faire pipi, pisser.

peek [pi:k] *inf* 1 *n* coup *m* d'œil furtif. 2 *vi* jeter un coup d'œil furtif.

peel [pi:l] 1 *n* [of apple, potato] peau *f;* [of orange, lemon] écorce *f.* 2 *vt* éplucher, peler. 3 *vi* [paint] s'écailler. || [wallpaper] se décoller. || [skin] peler.

peelings ['pi:lɪŋz] *npl* épluchures *fpl.*

peep [pi:p] 1 *n* [look] coup *m* d'œil OR regard *m* furtif. || *inf* [sound] bruit *m.* 2 *vi* jeter un coup d'œil furtif. O **peep out** *vi* apparaître, se montrer.

peephole ['pi:phəʊl] *n* judas *m.*

peer [pɪər] 1 *n* pair *m.* 2 *vi* scruter, regarder attentivement.

peerage ['pɪərɪdʒ] *n* [rank] pairie *f;* **the ~** les pairs *mpl.*

peer group *n* pairs *mpl.*

peeved [pi:vd] *adj inf* fâché(e), irrité(e).

peevish ['pi:vɪʃ] *adj* grincheux(euse).

peg [peg] 1 *n* [hook] cheville *f.* || [for clothes] pince *f* à linge. || [on tent] piquet *m.* 2 *vt fig* [prices] bloquer.

pejorative [pɪ'dʒɒrətɪv] *adj* péjoratif(ive).

pekinese [,pi:kə'ni:z], **pekingese** [,pi:kɪŋ'i:z] (*pl inv* OR **-s**) *n* [dog] pékinois *m.*

Peking [pi:'kɪŋ] *n* Pékin.

pekingese = **pekinese.**

pelican ['pelɪkən] (*pl inv* OR **-s**) *n* pélican *m.*

pellet ['pelɪt] *n* [small ball] boulette *f.* || [for gun] plomb *m.*

pelt [pelt] 1 *n* [animal skin] peau *f,* fourrure *f.* 2 *vt*: **to ~ sb (with sthg)** bombarder qqn (de qqch). 3 *vi* [rain] tomber à verse. || [run fast]: **to ~ along** courir ventre à terre; **to ~ down the stairs** dévaler l'escalier.

pelvis ['pelvɪs] (*pl* **-vises** OR **-ves** [-vi:z]) *n* pelvis *m,* bassin *m.*

pen [pen] 1 *n* [for writing] stylo *m.* || [enclosure] parc *m,* enclos *m.* 2 *vt* [enclose] parquer.

penal ['pi:nl] *adj* pénal(e).

penalize, -ise ['pi:nəlaɪz] *vt* [gen] pénaliser. || [put at a disadvantage] désavantager.

penalty ['penltɪ] *n* [punishment] pénalité *f;* **to pay the ~ (for sthg)** *fig* supporter OR subir les conséquences (de qqch). || [fine] amende *f.* || HOCKEY pénalité *f.*

penance ['penəns] *n* RELIG pénitence *f.* || *fig* [punishment] corvée *f,* pensum *m.*

penchant [*Br* pɑ̃ʃɑ̃, *Am* 'pentʃənt] *n*: **to have a ~ for sthg** avoir un faible pour qqch; **to have a ~ for doing sthg** avoir tendance à OR bien aimer faire qqch.

pencil ['pensl] 1 *n* crayon *m;* **in ~** au crayon. 2 *vt* griffonner au crayon, crayonner.

pencil case *n* trousse *f* (d'écolier).

pencil sharpener *n* taille-crayon *m.*

pendant ['pendənt] *n* [jewel on chain] pendentif *m.*

pending ['pendɪŋ] *fml* 1 *adj* [imminent] imminent(e). || [court case] en instance. 2 *prep* en attendant.

pendulum ['pendjʊləm] (*pl* **-s**) *n* balancier *m.*

penetrate ['penɪtreɪt] *vt* [gen] pénétrer dans; [subj: light] percer; [subj: rain] s'infiltrer dans. || [subj: spy] infiltrer.

pen friend *n* correspondant *m,* -e *f.*

penguin ['peŋgwɪn] *n* manchot *m.*

penicillin [,penɪ'sɪlɪn] *n* pénicilline *f.*

peninsula [pə'nɪnsjʊlə] (*pl* **-s**) *n* péninsule *f.*

penis ['pi:nɪs] (*pl* **penises** ['pi:nɪsɪz]) *n* pénis *m.*

penitentiary [,penɪ'tenʃərɪ] *n Am* prison *f.*

penknife ['pennaɪf] (*pl* **-knives** [-naɪvz]) *n* canif *m.*

pen name *n* pseudonyme *m.*

pennant ['penənt] n fanion m, flamme f.

penniless ['penɪlɪs] adj sans le sou.

penny ['penɪ] n [coin] Am cent m.

pen pal n inf correspondant m, -e f.

pension ['penʃn] n [from disability] pension f.

pensive ['pensɪv] adj songeur(euse).

pentagon ['pentəgən] n pentagone m. ○ **Pentagon** n Am: **the Pentagon** le Pentagone (siège du ministère américain de la Défense).

Pentecost ['pentɪkɒst] n Pentecôte f.

penthouse ['penthaʊs, pl -haʊzɪz] n appartement m de luxe (en attique).

pent up ['pent-] adj [emotions] refoulé(e); [energy] contenu(e).

penultimate [pe'nʌltɪmət] adj avant-dernier(ière).

people ['pi:pl] 1 n [nation, race] nation f, peuple m. 2 npl [persons] personnes fpl; **few/a lot of ~** peu/beaucoup de monde, peu/beaucoup de gens. ‖ [in general] gens mpl; **~ say that ...** on dit que .... ‖ [inhabitants] habitants mpl. ‖ POL: **the ~** le peuple. 3 vt: **to be ~d by** OR **with** être peuplé(e) de.

pep [pep] n inf (U) entrain m, pep m. ○ **pep up** vt sep inf [person] remonter, requinquer. ‖ [party, event] animer.

pepper ['pepər] n [spice] poivre m. ‖ [vegetable] poivron m.

pepperbox n Am = **pepper pot**.

peppermint ['pepəmɪnt] n [sweet] bonbon m à la menthe. ‖ [herb] menthe f poivrée.

pepper pot Br, **pepperbox** Am ['pepəbɒks] n poivrier m.

pep talk n inf paroles fpl OR discours m d'encouragement.

per [pɜːr] prep: **~ person** par personne; **to be paid £10 ~ hour** être payé 10 livres de l'heure; **~ kilo** le kilo.

per annum adv par an.

per capita [pə'kæpɪtə] adj & adv par habitant OR tête.

perceive [pə'siːv] vt [notice] percevoir. ‖ [understand, realize] remarquer, s'apercevoir de. ‖ [consider]: **to ~ sb/sthg as** considérer qqn/qqch comme.

per cent adv pour cent.

percentage [pə'sentɪdʒ] n pourcentage m.

perception [pə'sepʃn] n [aural, visual] perception f. ‖ [insight] perspicacité f, intuition f.

perceptive [pə'septɪv] adj perspicace.

perch [pɜːtʃ] 1 n lit & fig [position] perchoir m. 2 vi se percher.

percolator ['pɜːkəleɪtər] n cafetière f à pression.

percussion [pə'kʌʃn] n MUS percussion f.

perennial [pə'renjəl] 1 adj permanent(e), perpétuel(elle); BOT vivace. 2 n BOT plante f vivace.

perfect [adj & n 'pɜːfɪkt, vb pə'fekt] 1 adj parfait(e); **he's a ~ nuisance** il est absolument insupportable. 2 n GRAMM: **~ (tense)** parfait m. 3 vt parfaire, mettre au point.

perfection [pə'fekʃn] n perfection f.

perfectionist [pə'fekʃənɪst] n perfectionniste mf.

perfectly ['pɜːfɪktlɪ] adv parfaitement; **you know ~ well** tu sais très bien.

perforate ['pɜːfəreɪt] vt perforer.

perforations [,pɜːfə'reɪʃnz] npl [in paper] pointillés mpl.

perform [pə'fɔːm] 1 vt [carry out] exécuter; [- function] remplir. ‖ [play, concert] jouer. 2 vi [machine] marcher, fonctionner; [team, person]: **to ~ well/badly** avoir de bons/mauvais résultats. ‖ [actor] jouer; [singer] chanter.

performance [pə'fɔːməns] n [carrying out] exécution f. ‖ [show] représentation f. ‖ [by actor, singer etc] interprétation f. ‖ [of car, engine] performance f.

performer [pə'fɔːmər] n artiste mf, interprète mf.

perfume ['pɜːfjuːm] n parfum m.

perfunctory [pə'fʌŋktərɪ] adj rapide, superficiel(ielle).

perhaps [pə'hæps] adv peut-être; **~ so/not** peut-être que oui/non.

peril ['perɪl] n danger m, péril m.

perimeter [pə'rɪmɪtər] n périmètre m.

period ['pɪərɪəd] 1 n [gen] période f. ‖ SCH ≃ heure f. ‖ [menstruation] règles fpl. ‖ Am [full stop] point m. 2 comp [dress, house] d'époque.

periodic [,pɪərɪ'ɒdɪk] adj périodique.

periodical [,pɪərɪ'ɒdɪkl] 1 adj = **periodic**. 2 n [magazine] périodique m.

peripheral [pə'rɪfərəl] 1 adj [unimportant] secondaire. ‖ [at edge] périphérique. 2 n COMPUT périphérique m.

perish ['perɪʃ] vi [die] périr, mourir. ‖ [food] pourrir, se gâter; [rubber] se détériorer.

perishable ['perɪʃəbl] adj périssable.

perjury ['pɜːdʒərɪ] n (U) JUR parjure m, faux serment m.

perk [pɜːk] *n inf* à-côté *m*, avantage *m*.
○ **perk up** *vi* se ragaillardir.

perky ['pɜːkɪ] *adj inf* [cheerful] guilleret(ette); [lively] plein(e) d'entrain.

perm [pɜːm] *n* permanente *f*.

permanent ['pɜːmənənt] **1** *adj* permanent(e). **2** *n Am* [perm] permanente *f*.

permeate ['pɜːmɪeɪt] *vt* [subj: liquid, smell] s'infiltrer dans, pénétrer. || [subj: feeling, idea] se répandre dans.

permissible [pə'mɪsəbl] *adj* acceptable, admissible.

permission [pə'mɪʃn] *n* permission *f*, autorisation *f*.

permissive [pə'mɪsɪv] *adj* permissif(ive).

permit [*vb* pə'mɪt, *n* 'pɜːmɪt] **1** *vt* permettre; **to ~ sb to do sthg** permettre à qqn de faire qqch, autoriser qqn à faire qqch; **to ~ sb sthg** permettre qqch à qqn. **2** *n* permis *m*.

perpendicular [,pɜːpən'dɪkjʊlər] **1** *adj* perpendiculaire. **2** *n* perpendiculaire *f*.

perpetrate ['pɜːpɪtreɪt] *vt* perpétrer, commettre.

perpetual [pə'petʃʊəl] *adj pej* [continuous] continuel(elle), incessant(e). || [long-lasting] perpétuel(elle).

perplex [pə'pleks] *vt* rendre perplexe.

perplexing [pə'pleksɪŋ] *adj* déroutant(e), déconcertant(e).

persecute ['pɜːsɪkjuːt] *vt* persécuter, tourmenter.

perseverance [,pɜːsɪ'vɪərəns] *n* persévérance *f*, ténacité *f*.

persevere [,pɜːsɪ'vɪər] *vi* [with difficulty] persévérer, persister; **to ~ with** persévérer OR persister dans. || [with determination]: **to ~ in doing sthg** persister à faire qqch.

Persian ['pɜːʃn] *adj* persan(e); HISTORY perse.

persist [pə'sɪst] *vi*: **to ~ (in doing sthg)** persister OR s'obstiner (à faire qqch).

persistence [pə'sɪstəns] *n* persistance *f*.

persistent [pə'sɪstənt] *adj* [noise, rain] continuel(elle); [problem] constant(e). || [determined] tenace, obstiné(e).

person ['pɜːsn] (*pl* **people** OR **persons** *fml*) *n* [man or woman] personne *f*; **in ~** en personne. || *fml* [body]: **about one's ~** sur soi.

personal ['pɜːsənl] *adj* [gen] personnel(elle). || *pej* [rude] désobligeant(e).

personal assistant *n* secrétaire *mf* de direction.

personal column *n* petites annonces *fpl*.

personal computer *n* ordinateur *m* personnel OR individuel.

personality [,pɜːsə'nælətɪ] *n* personnalité *f*.

personally ['pɜːsnəlɪ] *adv* personnellement; **to take sthg ~** se sentir visé par qqch.

personal organizer *n* agenda *m* modulaire multifonction.

personal property *n* (*U*) JUR biens *mpl* personnels.

personal stereo *n* baladeur *m*, Walkman® *m*.

personify [pə'sɒnɪfaɪ] *vt* personnifier.

personnel [,pɜːsə'nel] **1** *n* (*U*) [department] service *m* du personnel. **2** *npl* [staff] personnel *m*.

perspective [pə'spektɪv] *n* ART perspective *f*. || [view, judgment] point *m* de vue, optique *f*.

perspiration [,pɜːspə'reɪʃn] *n* [sweat] sueur *f*. || [act of perspiring] transpiration *f*.

persuade [pə'sweɪd] *vt*: **to ~ sb to do sthg** persuader OR convaincre qqn de faire qqch; **to ~ sb that** convaincre qqn que; **to ~ sb of** convaincre qqn de.

persuasion [pə'sweɪʒn] *n* [act of persuading] persuasion *f*. || [belief - religious] confession *f*; [- political] opinion *f*, conviction *f*.

persuasive [pə'sweɪsɪv] *adj* [person] persuasif(ive); [argument] convaincant(e).

pert [pɜːt] *adj* mutin(e), coquin(e).

pertain [pə'teɪn] *vi fml*: **~ing to** concernant, relatif(ive) à.

pertinent ['pɜːtɪnənt] *adj* pertinent(e), approprié(e).

perturb [pə'tɜːb] *vt* inquiéter, troubler.

Peru [pə'ruː] *n* Pérou *m*.

peruse [pə'ruːz] *vt* lire attentivement.

pervade [pə'veɪd] *vt* [subj: smell] se répandre dans; [subj: feeling, influence] envahir.

perverse [pə'vɜːs] *adj* [contrary - person] contrariant(e); [- enjoyment] malin (igne).

perversion [*Br* pə'vɜːʃn, *Am* pə'vɜːrʒn] *n* [sexual] perversion *f*. || [of truth] travestissement *m*.

pervert [*n* 'pɜːvɜːt, *vb* pə'vɜːt] **1** *n* pervers *m*, -e *f*. **2** *vt* [truth, meaning] travestir, déformer; [course of justice] entraver. || [sexually] pervertir.

pessimist ['pesɪmɪst] n pessimiste mf.

pessimistic [ˌpesɪ'mɪstɪk] adj pessimiste.

pest [pest] n [insect] insecte m nuisible; [animal] animal m nuisible. || inf [nuisance] casse-pieds mf inv.

pester ['pestər] vt harceler, importuner.

pet [pet] 1 adj [favourite]: ~ **subject** dada m; ~ **hate** bête f noire. 2 n [animal] animal m (familier). || [favourite person] chouchou m, -oute f. 3 vt caresser, câliner. 4 vi se peloter, se caresser.

petal ['petl] n pétale m.

peter ['piːtər] ○ **peter out** vi [path] s'arrêter, se perdre; [interest] diminuer, décliner.

petite [pə'tiːt] adj menu(e).

petition [pɪ'tɪʃn] 1 n pétition f. 2 vt adresser une pétition à.

petrified ['petrɪfaɪd] adj [terrified] paralysé(e) OR pétrifié(e) de peur.

petroleum [pɪ'trəʊljəm] n pétrole m.

petticoat ['petɪkəʊt] n jupon m.

petty ['petɪ] adj [small-minded] mesquin(e). || [trivial] insignifiant(e), sans importance.

petty cash n (U) caisse f des dépenses courantes.

petulant ['petjʊlənt] adj irritable.

pew [pjuː] n banc m d'église.

pewter ['pjuːtər] n étain m.

phantom ['fæntəm] 1 adj fantomatique, spectral(e). 2 n [ghost] fantôme m.

pharmaceutical [ˌfɑːmə'sjuːtɪkl] adj pharmaceutique.

pharmacist ['fɑːməsɪst] n pharmacien m, -ienne f.

pharmacy ['fɑːməsɪ] n pharmacie f.

phase [feɪz] n phase f. ○ **phase in** vt sep introduire progressivement. ○ **phase out** vt sep supprimer progressivement.

PhD (abbr of **Doctor of Philosophy**) n (titulaire d'un) doctorat de 3ᵉ cycle.

pheasant ['feznt] (pl inv OR -s) n faisan m.

phenomena [fɪ'nɒmɪnə] pl → **phenomenon**.

phenomenal [fɪ'nɒmɪnl] adj phénoménal(e), extraordinaire.

phenomenon [fɪ'nɒmɪnən] (pl -mena) n phénomène m.

phial ['faɪəl] n fiole f.

philanthropist [fɪ'lænθrəpɪst] n philanthrope mf.

philately [fɪ'lætəlɪ] n philatélie f.

Philippine ['fɪlɪpiːn] adj philippin(e). ○ **Philippines** npl: **the ~s** les Philippines fpl.

philosopher [fɪ'lɒsəfər] n philosophe mf.

philosophical [ˌfɪlə'sɒfɪkl] adj philosophique. || [stoical] philosophe.

philosophy [fɪ'lɒsəfɪ] n philosophie f.

phlegm [flem] n flegme m.

phobia ['fəʊbjə] n phobie f.

phone [fəʊn] 1 n téléphone m; **to be on the ~** [speaking] être au téléphone. 2 comp téléphonique. 3 vt téléphoner à, appeler. 4 vi téléphoner. ○ **phone up** 1 vt sep téléphoner à. 2 vi téléphoner.

phone book n annuaire m (du téléphone).

phone booth n cabine f téléphonique.

phone call n coup m de téléphone OR fil; **to make a ~** passer OR donner un coup de fil.

phonecard ['fəʊnkɑːd] n ≃ Télécarte® f.

phone-in n RADIO & TV programme m à ligne ouverte.

phone number n numéro m de téléphone.

phonetics [fə'netɪks] n (U) phonétique f.

phoney Br, **phony** Am ['fəʊnɪ] inf 1 adj [passport, address] bidon (inv). || [person] hypocrite, pas franc (pas franche). 2 n poseur m, -euse f.

photo ['fəʊtəʊ] n photo f; **to take a ~ of sb/sthg** photographier qqn/qqch, prendre qqn/qqch en photo.

photocopier [ˌfəʊtəʊ'kɒpɪər] n photocopieur m, copieur m.

photocopy ['fəʊtəʊˌkɒpɪ] 1 n photocopie f. 2 vt photocopier.

photograph ['fəʊtəɡrɑːf] 1 n photographie f; **to take a ~ (of sb/sthg)** prendre (qqn/qqch) en photo, photographier (qqn/qqch). 2 vt photographier, prendre en photo.

photographer [fə'tɒɡrəfər] n photographe mf.

photography [fə'tɒɡrəfɪ] n photographie f.

phrasal verb ['freɪzl-] n verbe m à postposition.

phrase [freɪz] n expression f.

phrasebook ['freɪzbʊk] n guide m de conversation (pour touristes).

physical ['fɪzɪkl] 1 adj [gen] physique. || [world, objects] matériel(ielle). 2 n [examination] visite f médicale.

physical education n éducation f physique.

physically ['fɪzɪklɪ] adv physiquement.

physically handicapped npl: **the ~** les handicapés mpl physiques.

physician [fɪ'zɪʃn] n médecin m.

physicist ['fɪzɪsɪst] n physicien m, -ienne f.

physics ['fɪzɪks] n (U) physique f.

physiotherapy [,fɪzɪəʊ'θerəpɪ] n kinésithérapie f.

physique [fɪ'zi:k] n physique m.

pianist ['pɪənɪst] n pianiste mf.

piano [pɪ'ænəʊ] (pl -s) n piano m.

pick [pɪk] 1 n [tool] pioche f, pic m. || [selection]: **to take one's ~** choisir, faire son choix. || [best]: **the ~ of** le meilleur (la meilleure) de. 2 vt [select, choose] choisir, sélectionner. || [gather] cueillir. || [remove] enlever. || [nose]: **to ~ one's nose** se décrotter le nez. || [fight, quarrel]: **to ~ a fight (with sb)** chercher la bagarre (à qqn). || [lock] crocheter. ○ **pick on** vt fus s'en prendre à, être sur le dos de. ○ **pick out** vt sep [recognize] repérer, reconnaître. || [select, choose] choisir, désigner. ○ **pick up** 1 vt sep [lift up] ramasser. || [collect] aller chercher, passer prendre. || [collect in car] prendre, chercher. || [skill, language] apprendre; [habit] prendre; [bargain] découvrir. || inf [sexually - woman, man] draguer. || RADIO & TELEC [detect, receive] capter, recevoir. || [conversation, work] reprendre, continuer. 2 vi [improve, start again] reprendre.

pickaxe Br, **pickax** Am ['pɪkæks] n pioche f, pic m.

picket ['pɪkɪt] 1 n piquet m de grève. 2 vt mettre un piquet de grève devant.

picket line n piquet m de grève.

pickle ['pɪkl] 1 n pickles mpl; **to be in a ~** être dans le pétrin. 2 vt conserver dans du vinaigre/de la saumure etc.

pickpocket ['pɪk,pɒkɪt] n pickpocket m, voleur m à la tire.

pick-up n [of record player] pick-up m inv. || [truck] camionnette f.

picnic ['pɪknɪk] (pt & pp -ked, cont -king) n pique-nique m.

pictorial [pɪk'tɔ:rɪəl] adj illustré(e).

picture ['pɪktʃər] 1 n [painting] tableau m, peinture f; [drawing] dessin m. || [photograph] photo f, photographie f. || TV image f. || CINEMA film m. || [in mind] tableau m, image f. || phr: **to get the ~** inf piger; **to put sb in the ~** mettre qqn au

courant. 2 vt [in mind] imaginer, s'imaginer, se représenter. || [in photo] photographier. || [in painting] représenter, peindre.

picture book n livre m d'images.

picturesque [,pɪktʃə'resk] adj pittoresque.

pie [paɪ] n tourte f.

piece [pi:s] n [gen] morceau m; [of string] bout m. **a ~ of furniture** un meuble; **a ~ of clothing** un vêtement; **a ~ of advice** un conseil; **a ~ of information** un renseignement; **to fall to ~s** tomber en morceaux; **to take sthg to ~s** démonter qqch; **in ~s** en morceaux; **in one ~** [intact] intact(e); [unharmed] sain et sauf (saine et sauve). || [coin, item, in chess] pièce f; [in draughts] pion m. || PRESS article m. ○ **piece together** vt sep [facts] coordonner.

piecemeal ['pi:smi:l] 1 adj fait(e) petit à petit. 2 adv petit à petit, peu à peu.

piecework ['pi:swɜ:k] n (U) travail m à la pièce OR aux pièces.

pie chart n camembert m, graphique m rond.

pier [pɪər] n [at seaside] jetée f.

pierce [pɪəs] vt percer, transpercer; **to have one's ears ~d** se faire percer les oreilles.

piercing ['pɪəsɪŋ] adj [sound, look] perçant(e). || [wind] pénétrant(e).

pig [pɪg] n [animal] porc m, cochon m. || inf pej [greedy eater] goinfre m, glouton m. || inf pej [unkind person] sale type m.

pigeon ['pɪdʒɪn] (pl inv OR -s) n pigeon m.

pigeonhole ['pɪdʒɪnhəʊl] 1 n [compartment] casier m. 2 vt [classify] étiqueter, cataloguer.

piggybank ['pɪgɪbæŋk] n tirelire f.

pigheaded [,pɪg'hedɪd] adj têtu(e).

pigment ['pɪgmənt] n pigment m.

pigpen Am = pigsty.

pigskin ['pɪgskɪn] n (peau f de) porc m.

pigsty ['pɪgstaɪ], **pigpen** Am ['pɪgpen] n lit & fig porcherie f.

pigtail ['pɪgteɪl] n natte f.

pilchard ['pɪltʃəd] n pilchard m.

pile [paɪl] n [heap] tas m; **a ~ of, ~s of** un tas OR des tas de. || [neat stack] pile f. || [of carpet] poil m. ○ **piles** npl MED hémorroïdes fpl. ○ **pile up** 1 vt sep empiler, entasser. 2 vi [form a heap] s'entasser. || fig [work, debts] s'accumuler.

pileup ['paɪlʌp] n AUT carambolage m.

pilfer ['pɪlfər] vt chaparder.

pilgrim ['pɪlgrɪm] *n* pèlerin *m*.

pilgrimage ['pɪlgrɪmɪdʒ] *n* pèlerinage *m*.

pill [pɪl] *n* [gen] pilule *f*. || [contraceptive]: **the ~** la pilule.

pillage ['pɪlɪdʒ] *vt* piller.

pillar ['pɪlə[r]] *n lit & fig* pilier *m*.

pillion ['pɪljən] *n* siège *m* arrière; **to ride ~** monter derrière.

pillow ['pɪləʊ] *n* [for bed] oreiller *m*. || *Am* [on sofa, chair] coussin *m*.

pillowcase ['pɪləʊkeɪs], **pillowslip** ['pɪləʊslɪp] *n* taie *f* d'oreiller.

pilot ['paɪlət] **1** *n* AERON & NAUT pilote *m*. || TV émission *f* pilote. **2** *vt* piloter.

pilot burner, pilot light *n* veilleuse *f*.

pilot study *n* étude *f* pilote OR expérimentale.

pimp [pɪmp] *n inf* maquereau *m*, souteneur *m*.

pimple ['pɪmpl] *n* bouton *m*.

pin [pɪn] **1** *n* [for sewing] épingle *f*; **to have ~s and needles** avoir des fourmis. || [drawing pin] punaise *f*. || [safety pin] épingle *f* de nourrice OR de sûreté. || [of plug] fiche *f*. **2** *vt*: **to ~ sthg to/on sthg** épingler qqch à/sur qqch; **to ~ sb against** OR **to clouer** qqn contre; **to ~ sthg on sb** [blame] mettre OR coller qqch sur le dos de qqn; **to ~ one's hopes on sb/sthg** mettre tous ses espoirs en qqn/dans qqch.
○ pin down *vt sep* [identify] définir, identifier. || [force to make a decision]: **to ~ sb down** obliger qqn à prendre une décision.

pinafore ['pɪnəfɔ:[r]] *n* [apron] tablier *m*.

pinball ['pɪnbɔ:l] *n* flipper *m*.

pincers ['pɪnsəz] *npl* [tool] tenailles *fpl*. || [of crab] pinces *fpl*.

pinch [pɪntʃ] **1** *n* [nip] pincement *m*. || [of salt] pincée *f*. **2** *vt* [nip] pincer. || [subj: shoes] serrer. || *inf* [steal] piquer, faucher.
○ at a pinch *Br*, **in a pinch** *Am adv* à la rigueur.

pincushion ['pɪn,kʊʃn] *n* pelote *f* à épingles.

pine [paɪn] **1** *n* pin *m*. **2** *vi*: **to ~ for** désirer ardemment.

pineapple ['paɪnæpl] *n* ananas *m*.

pinetree ['paɪntri:] *n* pin *m*.

ping [pɪŋ] *n* [of bell] tintement *m*; [of metal] bruit *m* métallique.

Ping-Pong® [-pɒŋ] *n* ping-pong *m*.

pink [pɪŋk] **1** *adj* rose; **to go** OR **turn ~** rosir, rougir. **2** *n* [colour] rose *m*.

pinnacle ['pɪnəkl] *n* [mountain peak,

spire] pic *m*, cime *f*. || *fig* [high point] apogée *m*.

pinpoint ['pɪnpɔɪnt] *vt* [cause, problem] définir, mettre le doigt sur. || [position] localiser.

pin-striped [-,straɪpt] *adj* à très fines rayures.

pint [paɪnt] *n Am* [unit of measurement] = 0,473 litre, ≃ demi-litre *m*.

pioneer [,paɪə'nɪə[r]] **1** *n lit & fig* pionnier *m*. **2** *vt*: **to ~ sthg** être un des premiers (une des premières) à faire qqch.

pious ['paɪəs] *adj* RELIG pieux (pieuse). || *pej* [sanctimonious] moralisateur(trice).

pip [pɪp] *n* [seed] pépin *m*.

pipe [paɪp] **1** *n* [for gas, water] tuyau *m*. || [for smoking] pipe *f*. **2** *vt* acheminer par tuyau. **○ pipes** *npl* MUS cornemuse *f*.
○ pipe down *vi inf* se taire, la fermer.
○ pipe up *vi inf* se faire entendre.

pipe cleaner *n* cure-pipe *m*.

pipe dream *n* projet *m* chimérique.

pipeline ['paɪplaɪn] *n* [for gas] gazoduc *m*; [for oil] oléoduc *m*, pipeline *m*.

piping hot ['paɪpɪŋ-] *adj* bouillant(e).

pique [pi:k] *n* dépit *m*.

pirate ['paɪrət] **1** *adj* [video, program] pirate. **2** *n* pirate *m*.

pirouette [,pɪru'et] **1** *n* pirouette *f*. **2** *vi* pirouetter.

Pisces ['paɪsi:z] *n* Poissons *mpl*.

piss [pɪs] *vulg* **1** *n* [urine] pisse *f*. **2** *vi* pisser.

pissed [pɪst] *adj vulg Am* [annoyed] en boule.

pissed off *adj vulg* qui en a plein le cul.

pistol ['pɪstl] *n* pistolet *m*.

piston ['pɪstən] *n* piston *m*.

pit [pɪt] **1** *n* [hole] trou *m*; [in road] petit trou; [on face] marque *f*. || [for orchestra] fosse *f*. || [mine] mine *f*. || *Am* [of fruit] noyau *m*. **2** *vt*: **to ~ sb against sb** opposer qqn à qqn. **○ pits** *npl* [in motor racing]: **the ~s** les stands *mpl*.

pitch [pɪtʃ] **1** *n* SPORT terrain *m*. || MUS ton *m*. || [level, degree] degré *m*. || [selling place] place *f*. || *inf* [sales talk] baratin *m*. **2** *vt* [throw] lancer. || [set - price] fixer; [- speech] adapter. || [tent] dresser; [camp] établir. **3** *vi* [ball] rebondir. || [fall]: **to ~ forward** être projeté(e) en avant. || AERON & NAUT tanguer.

pitch-black *adj* noir(e) comme dans un four.

pitched battle [,pɪtʃt-] *n* bataille *f* rangée.

plastic

pitcher ['pɪtʃər] n Am [jug] cruche f. || [in baseball] lanceur m.

pitchfork ['pɪtʃfɔːk] n fourche f.

pitfall ['pɪtfɔːl] n piège m.

pith [pɪθ] n [of fruit] peau f blanche.

pithy ['pɪθɪ] adj [brief] concis(e); [terse] piquant(e).

pitiful ['pɪtɪfʊl] adj [condition] pitoyable; [excuse, effort] lamentable.

pitiless ['pɪtɪlɪs] adj sans pitié, impitoyable.

pit stop n [in motor racing] arrêt m aux stands.

pittance ['pɪtəns] n [wage] salaire m de misère.

pity ['pɪtɪ] 1 n pitié f; **what a ~!** quel dommage!; **it's a ~** c'est dommage; **to take** OR **have ~ on sb** prendre qqn en pitié, avoir pitié de qqn. 2 vt plaindre.

pivot ['pɪvət] n lit & fig pivot m.

pizza ['piːtsə] n pizza f.

placard ['plækɑːd] n placard m, affiche f.

placate [plə'keɪt] vt calmer, apaiser.

place [pleɪs] 1 n [location] endroit m, lieu m; **~ of birth** lieu de naissance. || [proper position, seat, vacancy, rank] place f. || [home]: **at/to my ~** chez moi. || [in book]: **to lose one's ~** perdre sa page. || MATH: **decimal ~** décimale f. || [instance]: **in the first ~** tout de suite; **in the first ~ ... and in the second ~ ...** premièrement ... et deuxièmement .... || phr: **to take ~** avoir lieu; **to take the ~ of** prendre la place de, remplacer. 2 vt [position, put] placer, mettre. || [apportion]: **to ~ the responsibility for sthg on sb** tenir qqn pour responsable de qqch. || [identify] remettre. || [an order] passer; **to ~ a bet** parier. O **all over the place** adv [everywhere] partout. O **in place** adv [in proper position] à sa place. || [established] mis en place. O **in place of** prep à la place de. O **out of place** adv pas à sa place; fig déplacé(e).

place mat n set m (de table).

placement ['pleɪsmənt] n placement m.

placid ['plæsɪd] adj [person] placide.

plagiarize, -ise ['pleɪdʒəraɪz] vt plagier.

plague [pleɪg] 1 n MED peste f. 2 vt: **to be ~d by** [bad luck] être poursuivi(e) par; [doubt] être rongé(e) par; **to ~ sb with questions** harceler qqn de questions.

plaice [pleɪs] (pl inv) n carrelet m.

plaid [plæd] n plaid m.

plain [pleɪn] 1 adj [not patterned] uni(e). || [simple] simple. || [clear] clair(e), évident(e). || [blunt] carré(e), franc (franche). || [absolute] pur(e) (et simple). || [not pretty] quelconque, ordinaire. 2 adv inf complètement. 3 n GEOGR plaine f.

plain-clothes adj en civil.

plainly ['pleɪnlɪ] adv [obviously] manifestement. || [distinctly] clairement. || [frankly] carrément, sans détours. || [simply] simplement.

plaintiff ['pleɪntɪf] n demandeur m, -eresse f.

plait [plæt] 1 n natte f. 2 vt natter, tresser.

plan [plæn] 1 n plan m, projet m; **to go according to ~** se passer OR aller comme prévu. 2 vt [organize] préparer. || [propose]: **to ~ to do sthg** projeter de faire qqch, avoir l'intention de faire qqch. || [design] concevoir. 3 vi: **to ~ (for sthg)** faire des projets (pour qqch). O **plans** npl plans mpl, projets mpl; **have you any ~s for tonight?** avez-vous prévu quelque chose pour ce soir? O **plan on** vt fus: **to ~ on doing sthg** prévoir de faire qqch.

plane [pleɪn] 1 adj plan(e). 2 n [aircraft] avion m. || GEOM plan m. || fig [level] niveau m. || [tool] rabot m. || [tree] platane m.

planet ['plænɪt] n planète f.

plank [plæŋk] n [of wood] planche f.

planning ['plænɪŋ] n [designing] planification f. || [preparation] préparation f, organisation f.

planning permission n permis m de construire.

plant [plɑːnt] 1 n BOT plante f. || [factory] usine f. || (U) [heavy machinery] matériel m. 2 vt [gen] planter. || [bomb] poser.

plantation [plæn'teɪʃn] n plantation f.

plaque [plɑːk] n [commemorative sign] plaque f. || (U) [on teeth] plaque f dentaire.

plaster ['plɑːstər] 1 n [material] plâtre m. 2 vt [wall, ceiling] plâtrer. || [cover]: **to ~ sthg (with)** couvrir qqch (de).

plaster cast n [for broken bones] plâtre m. || [model, statue] moule m.

plastered ['plɑːstəd] adj inf [drunk] bourré(e).

plasterer ['plɑːstərər] n plâtrier m.

plaster of Paris n plâtre m de moulage.

plastic ['plæstɪk] 1 adj plastique. 2 n plastique m.

Plasticine® *Br* ['plæstɪsiːn], **play dough** *Am n* pâte *f* à modeler.

plastic surgery *n* chirurgie *f* esthétique OR plastique.

plate [pleɪt] **1** *n* [dish] assiette *f*. || [sheet of metal, plaque] tôle *f*. || (*U*) [metal covering]: **gold/silver ~** plaqué *m* or/argent. || [in book] planche *f*. || [in dentistry] dentier *m*. **2** *vt*: **to be ~d (with)** être plaqué(e) (de).

plateau ['plætəʊ] (*pl* **-s** OR **-x** [-z]) *n* plateau *m*; *fig* phase *f* OR période *f* de stabilité.

plate-glass *adj* vitré(e).

platform ['plætfɔːm] *n* [stage] estrade *f*; [for speaker] tribune *f*. || [raised structure, of bus, of political party] plate-forme *f*. || RAIL quai *m*.

platinum ['plætɪnəm] *n* platine *m*.

platoon [plə'tuːn] *n* section *f*.

platter ['plætər] *n* [dish] plat *m*.

plausible ['plɔːzəbl] *adj* plausible.

play [pleɪ] **1** *n* (*U*) [amusement] jeu *m*, amusement *m*. || THEATRE pièce *f* (de théâtre). || [game]: **~ on words** jeu *m* de mots. || TECH jeu *m*. **2** *vt* [gen] jouer; **to ~ a part** OR **role in** *fig* jouer un rôle dans. || [game, sport] jouer à. || [team, opponent] jouer contre. || MUS [instrument] jouer de. || *phr*: **to ~ it safe** ne pas prendre de risques. **3** *vi* jouer. ○ **play along** *vi*: **to ~ along (with sb)** entrer dans le jeu (de qqn). ○ **play down** *vt sep* minimiser. ○ **play up 1** *vt sep* [emphasize] insister sur. **2** *vi* [machine] faire des siennes. || [child] ne pas être sage.

play-act *vi* jouer la comédie.

playboy ['pleɪbɔɪ] *n* playboy *m*.

play dough *Am* = **Plasticine®**.

player ['pleɪər] *n* [gen] joueur *m*, -euse *f*. || THEATRE acteur *m*, -trice *f*.

playful ['pleɪfʊl] *adj* [person, mood] taquin(e). || [kitten, puppy] joueur(euse).

playground ['pleɪgraʊnd] *n* cour *f* de récréation.

playgroup ['pleɪgruːp] *n* jardin *m* d'enfants.

playing card ['pleɪɪŋ-] *n* carte *f* à jouer.

playing field ['pleɪɪŋ-] *n* terrain *m* de sport.

playmate ['pleɪmeɪt] *n* camarade *mf*.

play-off *n* SPORT belle *f*.

playpen ['pleɪpen] *n* parc *m*.

playschool ['pleɪskuːl] *n* jardin *m* d'enfants.

plaything ['pleɪθɪŋ] *n lit & fig* jouet *m*.

playtime ['pleɪtaɪm] *n* récréation *f*.

playwright ['pleɪraɪt] *n* dramaturge *m*.

plea [pliː] *n* [for forgiveness, mercy] supplication *f*; [for help, quiet] appel *m*. || JUR: **to enter a ~ of not guilty** plaider non coupable.

plead [pliːd] (*pt & pp* **-ed** OR **pled**) **1** *vt* JUR plaider. || [give as excuse] invoquer. **2** *vi* [beg]: **to ~ with sb (to do sthg)** supplier qqn (de faire qqch); **to ~ for sthg** implorer qqch. || JUR plaider.

pleasant ['pleznt] *adj* agréable.

pleasantry ['plezntrɪ] *n*: **to exchange pleasantries** échanger des propos aimables.

please [pliːz] **1** *vt* plaire à, faire plaisir à; **~ yourself!** comme vous voulez! **2** *vi* plaire, faire plaisir; **to do as one ~s** faire comme on veut. **3** *adv* s'il vous plaît.

pleased [pliːzd] *adj* [satisfied]: **to be ~ (with)** être content(e) (de). || [happy]: **to be ~ (about)** être heureux(euse) (de); **~ to meet you!** enchanté(e)!

pleasing ['pliːzɪŋ] *adj* plaisant(e).

pleasure ['pleʒər] *n* plaisir *m*; **it's a ~, my ~** je vous en prie.

pleat [pliːt] **1** *n* pli *m*. **2** *vt* plisser.

pled [pled] *pt & pp* → **plead**.

pledge [pledʒ] **1** *n* [promise] promesse *f*. || [token] gage *m*. **2** *vt* [promise] promettre. || [make promise]: **to ~ o.s. to** s'engager à; **to ~ sb to secrecy** faire promettre le secret à qqn.

plentiful ['plentɪfʊl] *adj* abondant(e).

plenty ['plentɪ] **1** *n* (*U*) abondance *f*. **2** *pron*: **~ of** beaucoup de; **we've got ~ of time** nous avons largement le temps. **3** *adv Am* [very] très.

pliable ['plaɪəbl], **pliant** ['plaɪənt] *adj* [material] pliable, souple.

pliers ['plaɪəz] *npl* tenailles *fpl*, pinces *fpl*.

plight [plaɪt] *n* condition *f* critique.

plinth [plɪnθ] *n* socle *m*.

PLO (*abbr of* **Palestine Liberation Organization**) *n* OLP *f*.

plod [plɒd] *vi* [walk slowly] marcher lentement OR péniblement. || [work slowly] peiner.

plodder ['plɒdər] *n pej* bûcheur *m*, -euse *f*.

plot [plɒt] **1** *n* [plan] complot *m*, conspiration *f*. || [story] intrigue *f*. || [of land] (parcelle *f* de) terrain *m*, lopin *m*. **2** *vt* [plan] comploter; **to ~ to do sthg** comploter de faire qqch. || [chart] déterminer, marquer. || MATH tracer, marquer.

point

plotter ['plɒtər] *n* [schemer] conspirateur *m*, -trice *f*.

plough *Br*, **plow** *Am* [plaʊ] **1** *n* charrue *f*. **2** *vt* [field] labourer. ○ **plough into 1** *vt sep* [money] investir. **2** *vt fus* [subj: car] rentrer dans.

plow *etc Am* = **plough** *etc*.

ploy [plɔɪ] *n* stratagème *m*, ruse *f*.

pluck [plʌk] *vt* [flower, fruit] cueillir. || [pull sharply] arracher. || [chicken, turkey] plumer. || [eyebrows] épiler. || MUS pincer. ○ **pluck up** *vt fus*: **to ~ up the courage to do sthg** rassembler son courage pour faire qqch.

plucky ['plʌkɪ] *adj dated* qui a du cran, courageux(euse).

plug [plʌg] **1** *n* ELEC prise *f* de courant. || [for bath, sink] bonde *f*. **2** *vt* [hole] boucher, obturer. || *inf* [new book, film etc] faire de la publicité pour. ○ **plug in** *vt sep* brancher.

plughole ['plʌghəʊl] *n* bonde *f*, trou *m* d'écoulement.

plum [plʌm] **1** *adj* [colour] prune (*inv*). || [very good]: **a ~ job** un boulot en or. **2** *n* [fruit] prune *f*.

plumb [plʌm] **1** *adv Am* [completely] complètement. **2** *vt*: **to ~ the depths of** toucher le fond de.

plumber ['plʌmər] *n* plombier *m*.

plumbing ['plʌmɪŋ] *n* (*U*) [fittings] plomberie *f*, tuyauterie *f*. || [work] plomberie *f*.

plume [pluːm] *n* [feather] plume *f*. || [on hat] panache *m*. || [column]: **a ~ of smoke** un panache de fumée.

plummet ['plʌmɪt] *vi* [bird, plane] plonger. || *fig* [decrease] dégringoler.

plump [plʌmp] *adj* bien en chair, grassouillet(ette). ○ **plump for** *vt fus* opter pour, choisir. ○ **plump up** *vt sep* [cushion] secouer.

plum pudding *n* pudding *m* de Noël.

plunder ['plʌndər] **1** *n* (*U*) [stealing, raiding] pillage *m*. || [stolen goods] butin *m*. **2** *vt* piller.

plunge [plʌndʒ] **1** *n* [dive] plongeon *m*; **to take the ~** se jeter à l'eau. || *fig* [decrease] dégringolade *f*, chute *f*. **2** *vt*: **to ~ sthg into** plonger qqch dans. **3** *vi* [dive] plonger, tomber. || *fig* [decrease] dégringoler.

plunger ['plʌndʒər] *n* débouchoir *m* à ventouse.

pluperfect [ˌpluːˈpɜːfɪkt] *n*: **~ (tense)** plus-que-parfait *m*.

plural ['plʊərəl] **1** *adj* GRAMM pluriel(ielle). || [not individual] collectif(ive). || [multicultural] multiculturel(elle). **2** *n* pluriel *m*.

plus [plʌs] (*pl* **-es** OR **-ses**) **1** *adj*: **30 – 30 ou plus. 2 *n* *inf* [bonus] plus *m*, atout *m*. **3** *prep* et. **4** *conj* [moreover] de plus.

plush [plʌʃ] *adj* luxueux(euse), somptueux(euse).

plus sign *n* signe *m* plus.

Pluto ['pluːtəʊ] *n* [planet] Pluton *f*.

plutonium [pluːˈtəʊnɪəm] *n* plutonium *m*.

ply [plaɪ] **1** *n* [of wool] fil *m*; [of wood] pli *m*. **2** *vt* [trade] exercer. || [supply]: **to ~ sb with drink** ne pas arrêter de remplir le verre de qqn. **3** *vi* [ship etc] faire la navette.

plywood ['plaɪwʊd] *n* contreplaqué *m*.

p.m., pm (*abbr of* **post meridiem**) **at 3 ~** à 15 h.

PM *abbr of* **prime minister**.

PMT *abbr of* **premenstrual tension**.

pneumatic drill *n* marteau piqueur *m*.

pneumonia [njuːˈməʊnjə] *n* (*U*) pneumonie *f*.

poach [pəʊtʃ] **1** *vt* [fish] pêcher sans permis; [deer etc] chasser sans permis. || *fig* [idea] voler. || CULIN pocher. **2** *vi* braconner.

poacher ['pəʊtʃər] *n* braconnier *m*.

poaching ['pəʊtʃɪŋ] *n* braconnage *m*.

PO Box (*abbr of* **Post Office Box**) *n* BP *f*.

pocket ['pɒkɪt] **1** *n* *lit & fig* poche *f*; **to be out of ~** en être de sa poche; **to pick sb's ~** faire les poches à qqn. **2** *adj* de poche. **3** *vt* empocher.

pocketbook ['pɒkɪtbʊk] *n* [notebook] carnet *m*. || *Am* [handbag] sac *m* à main.

pocketknife ['pɒkɪtnaɪf] (*pl* **-knives** [-naɪvz]) *n* canif *m*.

pocket money *n* argent *m* de poche.

pod [pɒd] *n* [of plants] cosse *f*.

podiatrist [pəˈdaɪətrɪst] *n Am* pédicure *mf*.

podium ['pəʊdɪəm] (*pl* **-diums** OR **-dia** [-dɪə]) *n* podium *m*.

poem ['pəʊɪm] *n* poème *m*.

poet ['pəʊɪt] *n* poète *m*.

poetic [pəʊˈetɪk] *adj* poétique.

poetry ['pəʊɪtrɪ] *n* poésie *f*.

poignant ['pɔɪnjənt] *adj* poignant(e).

point [pɔɪnt] **1** *n* [tip] pointe *f*. || [place] endroit *m*, point *m*. || [time] stade *m*, moment *m*. || [detail, argument] question *f*, détail *m*; **you have a ~** il y a du vrai dans ce que vous dites; **to make a ~** faire une remarque; **to make one's ~** dire ce qu'on a à dire, dire son mot. || [main idea] point *m* essentiel; **to get** OR **come to the ~** en venir au fait; **to miss the ~** ne pas comprendre; **beside the ~** à côté de la question. || [feature]: **good ~** qualité *f*; **bad ~** défaut *m*. || [purpose]: **what's the ~ in buying a new car?** à quoi bon acheter une nouvelle voiture?; **there's no ~ in having a meeting** cela ne sert à rien d'avoir une réunion. || [on scale, in scores] point *m*. || MATH: **two ~ six** deux virgule six. || [of compass] aire *f* du vent. || *Am* [full stop] point *m* (final). || *phr*: **to make a ~ of doing sthg** ne pas manquer de faire qqch. **2** *vt*: **to ~ sthg (at)** [gun, camera] braquer qqch (sur); [finger, hose] pointer qqch (sur). **3** *vi* [indicate with finger]: **to ~ (at sb/sthg)**, **to ~ (to sb/sthg)** montrer (qqn/qqch) du doigt, indiquer (qqn/qqch) du doigt. || *fig* [suggest]: **to ~ to sthg** suggérer qqch, laisser supposer qqch. ○ **up to a point** *adv* jusqu'à un certain point, dans une certaine mesure. ○ **on the point of** *prep* sur le point de. ○ **point out** *vt sep* [person, place] montrer, indiquer; [fact, mistake] signaler.

point-blank *adv* [refuse] catégoriquement; [ask] de but en blanc. || [shoot] à bout portant.

pointed ['pɔɪntɪd] *adj* [sharp] pointu(e). || *fig* [remark] mordant(e), incisif(ive).

pointer ['pɔɪntər] *n* [piece of advice] tuyau *m*, conseil *m*. || [needle] aiguille *f*. || [stick] baguette *f*. || COMPUT pointeur *m*.

pointless ['pɔɪntlɪs] *adj* inutile, vain(e).

point of view (*pl* **points of view**) *n* point *m* de vue.

poise [pɔɪz] *n fig* calme *m*, sang-froid *m*.

poised [pɔɪzd] *adj* [ready]: **~ (for)** prêt(e) (pour). || *fig* [calm] calme, posé(e).

poison ['pɔɪzn] **1** *n* poison *m*. **2** *vt* [gen] empoisonner. || [pollute] polluer.

poisoning ['pɔɪznɪŋ] *n* empoisonnement *m*.

poisonous ['pɔɪznəs] *adj* [fumes] toxique; [plant] vénéneux(euse). || [snake] venimeux(euse).

poke [pəʊk] **1** *vt* [prod] pousser, donner un coup de coude à. || [put] fourrer. || [fire] attiser, tisonner. **2** *vi* [protrude] sortir, dépasser. ○ **poke about**, **poke around** *vi inf* fouiller, fourrager.

poker ['pəʊkər] *n* [game] poker *m*. || [for fire] tisonnier *m*.

poky ['pəʊkɪ] *adj pej* [room] exigu(ë), minuscule.

Poland ['pəʊlənd] *n* Pologne *f*.

polar ['pəʊlər] *adj* polaire.

Polaroid® ['pəʊlərɔɪd] *n* [camera] Polaroid® *m*. || [photograph] photo *f* polaroid.

pole [pəʊl] *n* [rod, post] perche *f*, mât *m*. || ELEC & GEOGR pôle *m*.

Pole [pəʊl] *n* Polonais *m*, -e *f*.

pole vault *n*: **the ~** le saut à la perche.

police [pə'liːs] **1** *npl* [police force]: **the ~** la police. || [policemen] agents *mpl* de police. **2** *vt* maintenir l'ordre dans.

police car *n* voiture *f* de police.

police force *n* police *f*.

policeman [pə'liːsmən] (*pl* **-men** [-mən]) *n* agent *m* de police.

police officer *n* policier *m*.

police record *n* casier *m* judiciaire.

police station *n* commissariat *m* (de police).

policewoman [pə'liːs,wʊmən] (*pl* **-women** [-,wɪmɪn]) *n* femme *f* agent de police.

policy ['pɒləsɪ] *n* [plan] politique *f*. || [document] police *f*.

polio ['pəʊlɪəʊ] *n* polio *f*.

polish ['pɒlɪʃ] **1** *n* [for shoes] cirage *m*; [for floor] cire *f*, encaustique *f*. || [shine] brillant *m*, lustre *m*. || *fig* [refinement] raffinement *m*. **2** *vt* [shoes, floor] cirer; [car] astiquer; [cutlery, glasses] faire briller. ○ **polish off** *vt sep inf* expédier.

Polish ['pəʊlɪʃ] **1** *adj* polonais(e). **2** *n* [language] polonais *m*. **3** *npl*: **the ~** les Polonais *mpl*.

polished ['pɒlɪʃt] *adj* [refined] raffiné(e). || [accomplished] accompli(e), parfait(e).

polite [pə'laɪt] *adj* [courteous] poli(e).

political [pə'lɪtɪkl] *adj* politique.

politically correct [pə,lɪtɪklɪ-] *adj* conforme au mouvement qui préconise le remplacement de termes jugés discriminants par d'autres "politiquement corrects".

politician [,pɒlɪ'tɪʃn] *n* homme *m*, femme *f* politique.

politics ['pɒlətɪks] *n* (*U*) politique *f*.

polka ['pɒlkə] *n* polka *f*.

polka dot *n* pois *m*.

poll [pəʊl] **1** *n* vote *m*, scrutin *m*. **2** *vt* [people] interroger, sonder. || [votes] obtenir. ○ **polls** *npl*: **to go to the ~s** aller aux urnes.

pollen ['pɒlən] *n* pollen *m*.

polling booth ['pəʊlɪŋ-] *n* isoloir *m*.

polling station ['pəʊlɪŋ-] *n* bureau *m* de vote.

pollute [pə'luːt] *vt* polluer.

pollution [pə'luːʃn] *n* pollution *f*.

polo ['pəʊləʊ] *n* polo *m*.

polyethylene *Am* = polythene.

Polynesia [,pɒlɪ'niːzjə] *n* Polynésie *f*.

polystyrene [,pɒlɪ'staɪriːn] *n* polystyrène *m*.

polythene *Br* ['pɒlɪθiːn], **polyethylene** *Am* [,pɒlɪ'eθɪliːn] *n* polyéthylène *m*.

pomegranate ['pɒmɪ,grænɪt] *n* grenade *f*.

pomp [pɒmp] *n* pompe *f*, faste *m*.

pompom ['pɒmpɒm] *n* pompon *m*.

pompous ['pɒmpəs] *adj* [person] fat, suffisant(e). || [style, speech] pompeux(euse).

pond [pɒnd] *n* étang *m*, mare *f*.

ponder ['pɒndər] *vt* considérer, peser.

ponderous ['pɒndərəs] *adj* [dull] lourd(e). || [large, heavy] pesant(e).

pontoon [pɒn'tuːn] *n* [bridge] ponton *m*. || *Br* [game] vingt-et-un *m*.

pony ['pəʊnɪ] *n* poney *m*.

ponytail ['pəʊnɪteɪl] *n* queue-de-cheval *f*.

pony-trekking [-,trekɪŋ] *n* randonnée *f* à cheval OR en poney.

poodle ['puːdl] *n* caniche *m*.

pool [puːl] **1** *n* [pond, of blood] mare *f*; [of rain, light] flaque *f*. || [swimming pool] piscine *f*. || SPORT billard *m* américain. **2** *vt* [resources etc] mettre en commun.

poor [pɔːr] **1** *adj* [gen] pauvre. || [not very good] médiocre, mauvais(e). **2** *npl*: **the ~** les pauvres *mpl*.

poorly ['pɔːlɪ] *adv* mal, médiocrement.

pop [pɒp] **1** *n* (*U*) [music] pop *m*. || (*U*) *inf* [fizzy drink] boisson *f* gazeuse. || *inf* [father] papa *m*. || [sound] pan *m*. **2** *vt* [burst] faire éclater, crever. || [put quickly] mettre, fourrer. **3** *vi* [balloon] éclater, crever; [cork, button] sauter. || [eyes]: **his eyes popped** il a écarquillé les yeux. ○ **pop in** *vi* faire une petite visite. ○ **pop up** *vi* surgir.

pop concert *n* concert *m* pop.

popcorn ['pɒpkɔːn] *n* pop-corn *m*.

pope [pəʊp] *n* pape *m*.

pop group *n* groupe *m* pop.

poplar ['pɒplər] *n* peuplier *m*.

poppy ['pɒpɪ] *n* coquelicot *m*, pavot *m*.

Popsicle® ['pɒpsɪkl] *n Am* sucette *f* glacée.

populace ['pɒpjʊləs] *n*: **the ~** le peuple.

popular ['pɒpjʊlər] *adj* [gen] populaire. || [name, holiday resort] à la mode.

popularize, -ise ['pɒpjʊləraɪz] *vt* [make popular] populariser. || [simplify] vulgariser.

population [,pɒpjʊ'leɪʃn] *n* population *f*.

porcelain ['pɔːsəlɪn] *n* porcelaine *f*.

porch [pɔːtʃ] *n* [entrance] porche *m*. || *Am* [verandah] véranda *f*.

porcupine ['pɔːkjʊpaɪn] *n* porc-épic *m*.

pore [pɔːr] *n* pore *m*. ○ **pore over** *vt fus* examiner de près.

pork [pɔːk] *n* porc *m*.

pork pie *n* pâté *m* de porc en croûte.

pornography [pɔː'nɒgrəfɪ] *n* pornographie *f*.

porous ['pɔːrəs] *adj* poreux(euse).

porridge ['pɒrɪdʒ] *n* porridge *m*.

port [pɔːt] *n* [town, harbour] port *m*. || NAUT [left-hand side] bâbord *m*. || [drink] porto *m*. || COMPUT port *m*.

portable ['pɔːtəbl] *adj* portatif(ive).

portent ['pɔːtənt] *n* présage *m*.

porter ['pɔːtər] *n* [for luggage] porteur *m*. || *Am* [on train] employé *m*, -e *f* des wagons-lits.

portfolio [,pɔːt'fəʊljəʊ] (*pl* -s) *n* [case] serviette *f*. || [sample of work] portfolio *m*. || FIN portefeuille *m*.

porthole ['pɔːthəʊl] *n* hublot *m*.

portion ['pɔːʃn] *n* [section] portion *f*, part *f*. || [of food] portion *f*.

portly ['pɔːtlɪ] *adj* corpulent(e).

portrait ['pɔːtreɪt] *n* portrait *m*.

portray [pɔː'treɪ] *vt* CINEMA & THEATRE jouer, interpréter. || [describe] dépeindre. || [paint] faire le portrait de.

Portugal ['pɔːtʃʊgl] *n* Portugal *m*.

Portuguese [,pɔːtʃʊ'giːz] **1** *adj* portugais(e). **2** *n* [language] portugais *m*. **3** *npl*: **the ~** les Portugais *mpl*.

pose [pəʊz] **1** *n* [stance] pose *f*. || *pej* [affectation] pose *f*, affectation *f*. **2** *vt* [danger] présenter. || [problem, question] poser. **3** *vi* ART & *pej* poser. || [pretend to be]: **to ~ as** se faire passer pour.

posh [pɒʃ] *adj inf* [hotel, clothes etc] chic (*inv*). || *Br* [accent, person] de la haute.

position [pə'zɪʃn] **1** *n* [gen] position *f*. || [job] poste *m*, emploi *m*. || [state] situation *f*. **2** *vt* placer, mettre en position.

positive ['pɒzətɪv] *adj* [gen] posi-
tif(ive). || [sure] sûr(e), certain(e); **to be
~ about sthg** être sûr de qqch. || [optimis-
tic] positif(ive), optimiste. || [definite]
formel(elle), précis(e). || [evidence] irré-
futable, indéniable. || [downright] véri-
table.

posse ['pɒsɪ] *n Am* détachement *m*,
troupe *f*.

possess [pə'zes] *vt* posséder.

possession [pə'zeʃn] *n* possession *f*.
◯ **possessions** *npl* possessions *fpl*,
biens *mpl*.

possessive [pə'zesɪv] **1** *adj* posses-
sif(ive). **2** *n* GRAMM possessif *m*.

possibility [ˌpɒsə'bɪlətɪ] *n* [chance, like-
lihood] possibilité *f*, chances *fpl*; **there is
a ~ that** ... il se peut que ... (+ *subjunc-
tive*). || [option] possibilité *f*, option *f*.

possible ['pɒsəbl] **1** *adj* possible; **as
much as ~** autant que possible; **as soon
as ~** dès que possible. **2** *n* possible *m*.

possibly ['pɒsəblɪ] *adv* [perhaps] peut-
être. || [expressing surprise: **how could
he ~ have known?** mais comment a-t-il
pu le savoir? || [for emphasis]: **I can't ~
accept your money** je ne peux vraiment
pas accepter cet argent.

post [pəʊst] **1** *n* [service]: **the ~** la poste;
by ~ par la poste. || [letters, delivery]
courrier *m*. || [pole] poteau *m*. || [position,
job] poste *m*, emploi *m*. || MIL. poste *m*. **2**
vt [by mail] poster, mettre à la poste. ||
[employee] muter.

postage ['pəʊstɪdʒ] *n* affranchissement
m; **~ and packing** frais *mpl* de port et
d'emballage.

postal ['pəʊstl] *adj* postal(e).

postal order *n* mandat *m* postal.

postcard ['pəʊstkɑːd] *n* carte *f* postale.

postdate [ˌpəʊst'deɪt] *vt* postdater.

poster ['pəʊstər] *n* [for advertising] affiche *f*; [for decoration] poster *m*.

poste restante [ˌpəʊst'restɑːnt] *n*
poste *f* restante.

posterior [pɒ'stɪərɪər] *adj* posté-
rieur(e).

postgraduate [ˌpəʊst'grædʒʊət] **1** *adj*
de troisième cycle. **2** *n* étudiant *m*, -e *f* de
troisième cycle.

posthumous ['pɒstjʊməs] *adj* posthume.

postman ['pəʊstmən] (*pl* **-men** [-mən])
n facteur *m*.

postmark ['pəʊstmɑːk] **1** *n* cachet *m* de
la poste. **2** *vt* timbrer, tamponner.

postmaster ['pəʊstˌmɑːstər] *n* receveur
m des postes.

postmortem [ˌpəʊst'mɔːtəm] *n* lit &
fig autopsie *f*.

post office *n* [organization]: **the Post
Office** les Postes et Télécommunications
fpl. || [building] (bureau *m* de) poste *f*.

post office box *n* boîte *f* postale.

postpone [ˌpəʊst'pəʊn] *vt* reporter, remettre.

postscript ['pəʊstskrɪpt] *n* post-
scriptum *m*.

posture ['pɒstʃər] *n* (*U*) [pose] position
f, posture *f*. || *fig* [attitude] attitude *f*.

postwar [ˌpəʊst'wɔːr] *adj* d'après-
guerre.

posy ['pəʊzɪ] *n* petit bouquet *m* de
fleurs.

pot [pɒt] **1** *n* [for cooking] marmite *f*,
casserole *f*. || [for tea] théière *f*; [for cof-
fee] cafetière *f*. || [for paint, jam, plant]
pot *m*. || (*U*) *inf* [cannabis] herbe *f*. **2** *vt*
[plant] mettre en pot.

potassium [pə'tæsɪəm] *n* potassium *m*.

potato [pə'teɪtəʊ] (*pl* **-es**) *n* pomme *f*
de terre.

potato peeler [-ˌpiːlər] *n* (couteau *m*)
éplucheur *m*.

potent ['pəʊtənt] *adj* [powerful, influen-
tial] puissant(e). || [drink] fort(e). ||
[man] viril.

potential [pə'tenʃl] **1** *adj* [energy, suc-
cess] potentiel(ielle); [uses, danger] possible; [enemy] en puissance. **2** *n* (*U*) [of
person] capacités *fpl* latentes; **to have ~**
[person] promettre; [company] avoir de
l'avenir; [scheme] offrir des possibilités.

pothole ['pɒthəʊl] *n* [in road] nid-de-
poule *m*. || [underground] 'caverne *f*,
grotte *f*.

potion ['pəʊʃn] *n* [magic] breuvage *m*;
love ~ philtre *m*.

potluck [ˌpɒt'lʌk] *n*: **to take ~** [gen]
choisir au hasard; [at meal] manger à la
fortune du pot.

potshot ['pɒtˌʃɒt] *n*: **to take a ~ (at
sthg)** tirer (sur qqch) sans viser.

potted ['pɒtɪd] *adj* [plant]: **~ plant**
plante *f* d'appartement. || [food] conser-
vé(e) en pot.

potter ['pɒtər] *n* potier *m*.

pottery ['pɒtərɪ] *n* poterie *f*; **a piece of
~** une poterie.

pouch [paʊtʃ] *n* [small bag] petit sac *m*;
tobacco ~ blague *f* à tabac. || [of kanga-
roo] poche *f* ventrale.

poultry ['pəoltrɪ] 1 n (U) [meat] volaille f. 2 npl [birds] volailles fpl.

pounce [paʊns] vi: to ~ (on) [bird] fondre (sur); [person] se jeter (sur).

pound [paʊnd] 1 n [money] livre f. [weight] = 453,6 grammes, ≃ livre f. [for cars, dogs] fourrière f. 2 vt [strike loudly] marteler. || [crush] piler, broyer. 3 vi [strike loudly]: **to ~ on** donner de grands coups à. || [heart] battre fort.

pound sterling n livre f sterling.

pour [pɔːr] 1 vt verser; **shall I ~ you a drink?** je te sers quelque chose à boire? 2 vi [liquid] couler à flots. || fig [rush]: **to ~ in/out** entrer/sortir en foule. 3 v impers [rain hard] pleuvoir à verse. ○ **pour in** vi [letters, news] affluer. ○ **pour out** vt sep [empty] vider. || [serve - drink] verser, servir.

pouring ['pɔːrɪŋ] adj [rain] torrentiel(ielle).

pout [paʊt] vi faire la moue.

poverty ['pɒvətɪ] n pauvreté f.

poverty-stricken adj [person] dans la misère; [area] misérable, très pauvre.

powder ['paʊdər] 1 n poudre f. 2 vt [face, body] poudrer.

powder compact n poudrier m.

powdered ['paʊdəd] adj [milk, eggs] en poudre. || [face] poudré(e).

powder puff n houppette f.

powder room n toilettes fpl pour dames.

power ['paʊər] 1 n (U) [authority, ability] pouvoir m; **to take ~** prendre le pouvoir; **to come to ~** parvenir au pouvoir; **to be in ~** être au pouvoir; **to be in** or **within one's ~ to do sthg** être en son pouvoir de faire qqch. || [strength, powerful person] puissance f, force f. || (U) [energy] énergie f. || [electricity] courant m, électricité f. 2 vt faire marcher, actionner.

powerboat ['paʊəbəʊt] n hors-bord m inv.

power cut n coupure f de courant.

power failure n panne f de courant.

powerful ['paʊəfʊl] adj [gen] puissant(e). || [smell, voice] fort(e). || [speech, novel] émouvant(e).

powerless ['paʊəlɪs] adj impuissant(e); **to be ~ to do sthg** être dans l'impossibilité de faire qqch, ne pas pouvoir faire qqch.

power station n centrale f électrique.

power steering n direction f assistée.

pp (abbr of per procurationem) pp.

p & p abbr of postage and packing.

PR n abbr of proportional representation. || abbr of public relations.

practicable ['præktɪkəbl] adj réalisable, faisable.

practical ['præktɪkl] adj [gen] pratique. || [plan, solution] réalisable.

practicality [,præktɪ'kælətɪ] n (U) aspect m pratique.

practical joke n farce f.

practically ['præktɪklɪ] adv [in a practical way] d'une manière pratique. || [almost] presque, pratiquement.

practice, practise Am ['præktɪs] n (U) [at sport] entraînement m; [at music etc] répétition f; **to be out of ~** être rouillé(e). || [training session - at sport] séance f d'entraînement; [- at music etc] répétition f. || [act of doing]: **to put sthg into ~** mettre qqch en pratique; **in ~** [in fact] en réalité, en fait. || [habit] pratique f, coutume f. || (U) [of profession] exercice m. || [of doctor] cabinet m; [of lawyer] étude f.

practicing Am = practising.

practise, practice Am ['præktɪs] 1 vt [sport] s'entraîner à; [piano etc] s'exercer à. || [custom] suivre, pratiquer; [religion] pratiquer. || [profession] exercer. 2 vi SPORT s'entraîner; MUS s'exercer. || [doctor, lawyer] exercer.

practising, practicing Am ['præktɪsɪŋ] adj [doctor, lawyer] en exercice; [Christian etc] pratiquant(e).

practitioner [præk'tɪʃnər] n praticien m, -ienne f.

Prague [prɑːg] n Prague.

prairie ['preərɪ] n prairie f.

praise [preɪz] 1 n (U) louange f, louanges fpl, éloge m, éloges mpl. 2 vt louer, faire l'éloge de.

praiseworthy ['preɪz,wɜːðɪ] adj louable, méritoire.

pram [præm] n landau m.

prance [prɑːns] vi [person] se pavaner. || [horse] caracoler.

prank [præŋk] n tour m, niche f.

prawn [prɔːn] n crevette f rose.

pray [preɪ] vi: **to ~ (to sb)** prier (qqn).

prayer [preər] n lit & fig prière f.

prayer book n livre m de messe.

preach [priːtʃ] 1 vt [gen] prêcher; [sermon] prononcer. 2 vi RELIG: **to ~ (to sb)** prêcher (qqn). || pej [pontificate]: **to ~ (at sb)** sermonner (qqn).

preacher ['priːtʃər] n prédicateur m, pasteur m.

precarious [prɪ'keərɪəs] adj précaire.

precaution [prɪˈkɔːʃn] *n* précaution *f.*

precede [prɪˈsiːd] *vt* précéder.

precedence [ˈpresɪdəns] *n*: **to take ~ over sthg** avoir la priorité sur qqch; **to have** OR **take ~ over sb** avoir la préséance sur qqn.

precedent [ˈpresɪdənt] *n* précédent *m.*

precinct [ˈpriːsɪŋkt] *n* Am [district] circonscription *f* (administrative). ○ **precincts** *npl* [of institution] enceinte *f.*

precious [ˈpreʃəs] *adj* [gen] précieux(ieuse). ‖ *inf iro* [damned] sacré(e). ‖ [affected] affecté(e).

precipice [ˈpresɪpɪs] *n* précipice *m*, paroi *f* à pic.

precipitate [prɪˈsɪpɪteɪt] *fml vt* [hasten] hâter, précipiter.

precise [prɪˈsaɪs] *adj* précis(e); [measurement, date] exact(e).

precisely [prɪˈsaɪslɪ] *adv* précisément, exactement.

precision [prɪˈsɪʒn] *n* précision *f*, exactitude *f.*

preclude [prɪˈkluːd] *vt fml* empêcher; [possibility] écarter; **to ~ sb from doing sthg** empêcher qqn de faire qqch.

precocious [prɪˈkəʊʃəs] *adj* précoce.

preconceived [ˌpriːkənˈsiːvd] *adj* préconçu(e).

predator [ˈpredətəʳ] *n* [animal, bird] prédateur *m*, rapace *m.*

predecessor [ˈpriːdɪsesəʳ] *n* [person] prédécesseur *m.* ‖ [thing] précédent *m*, -e *f.*

predicament [prɪˈdɪkəmənt] *n* situation *f* difficile; **to be in a ~** être dans de beaux draps.

predict [prɪˈdɪkt] *vt* prédire.

predictable [prɪˈdɪktəbl] *adj* prévisible.

prediction [prɪˈdɪkʃn] *n* prédiction *f.*

predispose [ˌpriːdɪsˈpəʊz] *vt*: **to be ~d to sthg/to do sthg** être prédisposé(e) à qqch/à faire qqch.

predominant [prɪˈdɒmɪnənt] *adj* prédominant(e).

preempt [ˌpriːˈempt] *vt* [action, decision] devancer, prévenir.

preemptive [ˌpriːˈemptɪv] *adj* préventif(ive).

preen [priːn] *vt* [subj: bird] lisser, nettoyer. ‖ *fig* [subj: person]: **to ~ o.s.** se faire beau (belle).

prefab [ˈpriːfæb] *n inf* maison *f* préfabriquée.

preface [ˈprefɪs] *n*: **~ (to)** préface *f* (de), préambule *m* (de).

prefer [prɪˈfɜːʳ] *vt* préférer; **to ~ sthg to sthg** préférer qqch à qqch, aimer mieux qqch que qqch; **to ~ to do sthg** préférer faire qqch, aimer mieux faire qqch.

preferable [ˈprefrəbl] *adj*: **~ (to)** préférable (à).

preferably [ˈprefrəblɪ] *adv* de préférence.

preference [ˈprefərəns] *n* préférence *f.*

preferential [ˌprefəˈrenʃl] *adj* préférentiel(ielle).

prefix [ˈpriːfɪks] *n* préfixe *m.*

pregnancy [ˈpregnənsɪ] *n* grossesse *f.*

pregnant [ˈpregnənt] *adj* [woman] enceinte; [animal] pleine, gravide.

prehistoric [ˌpriːhɪˈstɒrɪk] *adj* préhistorique.

prejudice [ˈpredʒʊdɪs] **1** *n* [biased view]: **~ (in favour of/against)** préjugé *m* (en faveur de/contre), préjugés *mpl* (en faveur de/contre). ‖ (U) [harm] préjudice *m*, tort *m.* **2** *vt* [bias]: **to ~ sb (in favour of/against)** prévenir qqn (en faveur de/contre), influencer qqn (en faveur de/contre). ‖ [harm] porter préjudice à.

prejudiced [ˈpredʒʊdɪst] *adj* [person] qui a des préjugés; [opinion] préconçu(e); **to be ~ in favour of/against** avoir des préjugés en faveur de/contre.

prejudicial [ˌpredʒʊˈdɪʃl] *adj*: **~ (to)** préjudiciable (à), nuisible (à).

preliminary [prɪˈlɪmɪnərɪ] *adj* préliminaire.

prelude [ˈpreljuːd] *n* [event]: **~ to sthg** prélude *m* de qqch.

premarital [ˌpriːˈmærɪtl] *adj* avant le mariage.

premature [ˈpreməˌtjʊəʳ] *adj* prématuré(e).

premeditated [ˌpriːˈmedɪteɪtɪd] *adj* prémédité(e).

premenstrual syndrome, premenstrual tension [priːˈmenstrʊəl-] *n* syndrome *m* prémenstruel.

premier [ˈpremjəʳ] **1** *adj* primordial(e), premier(ière). **2** *n* premier ministre *m.*

premiere [ˈpremɪeəʳ] *n* première *f.*

premise [ˈpremɪs] *n* prémisse *f.* ○ **premises** *npl* local *m*, locaux *mpl*; **on the ~s** sur place, sur les lieux.

premium [ˈpriːmjəm] *n* prime *f*; **at a ~** [above usual value] à prix d'or; [in great demand] très recherché OR demandé.

premonition [ˌpreməˈnɪʃn] *n* prémonition *f*, pressentiment *m.*

preoccupied [priːˈɒkjʊpaɪd] *adj*: **~ (with)** préoccupé(e) (de).

prepaid ['pri:peɪd] *adj* payé(e)
d'avance; [envelope] affranchi(e).

preparation [,prepə'reɪʃn] *n* préparation *f*. ○ **preparations** *npl* préparatifs
mpl.

preparatory [prɪ'pærətrɪ] *adj* [work,
classes] préparatoire; [actions, measures]
préliminaire.

preparatory school *n* [in US] école
privée qui prépare à l'enseignement su-
périeur.

prepare [prɪ'peə'] **1** *vt* préparer. **2** *vi*: to
~ **for** sthg/to do sthg se préparer à
qqch/à faire qqch.

prepared [prɪ'peəd] *adj* [done before-
hand] préparé(e) d'avance. || [willing]: to
be ~ to do sthg être prêt(e) OR disposé(e)
à faire qqch. || [ready]: to be ~ for sthg
être prêt(e) pour qqch.

preposition [,prepə'zɪʃn] *n* préposition
f.

preposterous [prɪ'pɒstərəs] *adj* ridicule, absurde.

prep school *abbr of* **preparatory**
school.

prerequisite [,pri:'rekwɪzɪt] *n* condition *f* préalable.

prerogative [prɪ'rɒgətɪv] *n* prérogative
f, privilège *m.*

Presbyterian [,prezbɪ'tɪərɪən] *adj*
presbytérien(ienne).

preschool [,pri:'sku:l] **1** *adj* présco-
laire. **2** *n* Am école *f* maternelle.

prescribe [prɪ'skraɪb] *vt* MED prescrire.
|| [order] ordonner, imposer.

prescription [prɪ'skrɪpʃn] *n* [MED -
written form] ordonnance *f*; [- medicine]
médicament *m.*

presence ['prezns] *n* présence *f*; to be in
sb's ~ OR in the ~ of sb être en présence
de qqn.

presence of mind *n* présence *f* d'esprit.

present [*adj* & *n* 'preznt, *vb* prɪ'zent] **1**
adj [current] actuel(elle). || [in attend-
ance] présent(e); to be ~ at assister à. **2** *n*
[current time]: the ~ le présent; at ~ ac-
tuellement, en ce moment. || [gift] ca-
deau *m*. || GRAMM: ~ (tense) présent *m*. **3**
vt [give]: to ~ sb with sthg, to ~ sthg to sb
donner OR remettre qqch à qqn. || [por-
tray] représenter, décrire. || [arrive]: to ~
o.s. se présenter.

presentable [prɪ'zentəbl] *adj* présentable.

presentation [,prezn'teɪʃn] *n* [gen]
présentation *f*. || [ceremony] remise *f* (de
récompense/prix). || [talk] exposé *m.*

present day *n*: the ~ aujourd'hui.
○ **present-day** *adj* d'aujourd'hui,
contemporain(e).

presently ['prezntlɪ] *adr* [soon] bien-
tôt, tout à l'heure. || [at present] actuelle-
ment, en ce moment.

preservation [,prezə'veɪʃn] *n* (*U*)
[maintenance] maintien *m*. || [protection]
protection *f*, conservation *f.*

preservative [prɪ'zɜ:vətɪv] *n* conservateur *m.*

preserve [prɪ'zɜ:v] *vt* [maintain] main-
tenir. || [protect] conserver. || [food]
conserver, mettre en conserve.
○ **preserves** *npl* [jam] confiture *f*;
[vegetables] pickles *mpl*, condiments
mpl.

preset [,pri:'set] (*pt* & *pp* **preset**) *vt*
prérégler.

president ['prezɪdənt] *n* [gen] prési-
dent *m*. || Am [company chairman] P-DG
m.

presidential [,prezɪ'denʃl] *adj* prési-
dentiel(ielle).

press [pres] **1** *n* [push] pression *f*. ||
[journalism]: the ~ [newspapers] la
presse, les journaux *mpl*; [reporters] les
journalistes *mpl*. || [printing machine]
presse *f*; [for wine] pressoir *m*. **2** *vt* [push]
appuyer sur. || to ~ sthg against sthg ap-
puyer qqch sur qqch. || [squeeze] serrer.
|| [iron] repasser, donner un coup de fer
à. || [urge]: to ~ sb (to do sthg OR into
doing sthg) presser qqn (de faire qqch).
|| [pursue - claim] insister sur. **3** *vi* [push]:
to ~ (on) appuyer (sur). || [squeeze]: to ~
(on sthg) serrer (qqch). || [crowd] se
presser. ○ **press for** *vt fus* demander
avec insistance. ○ **press on** *vi* [con-
tinue]: to ~ on (with sthg) continuer
(qqch), ne pas abandonner (qqch).

press agency *n* agence *f* de presse.

press conference *n* conférence *f* de
presse.

pressed [prest] *adj*: to be ~ for time/
money être à court de temps/d'argent.

pressing ['presɪŋ] *adj* urgent(e).

press officer *n* attaché *m* de presse.

press release *n* communiqué *m* de
presse.

pressure ['preʃə'] *n* (*U*) [gen] pression
f; to put ~ on sb (to do sthg) faire pres-
sion sur qqn (pour qu'il fasse qqch). ||
[stress] tension *f.*

pressure cooker n Cocotte-Minute® f, autocuiseur m.

pressure gauge n manomètre m.

pressure group n groupe m de pression.

prestige [pre'stiːʒ] n prestige m.

presumably [prɪ'zjuːməblɪ] adv vraisemblablement.

presume [prɪ'zjuːm] vt présumer; **to ~ (that)** ... supposer que ....

presumption [prɪ'zʌmpʃn] n [assumption] supposition f, présomption f. || (U) [audacity] présomption f.

presumptuous [prɪ'zʌmptʃʊəs] adj présomptueux(euse).

pretence, pretense Am [prɪ'tens] n prétention f; **to make a ~ of doing sthg** faire semblant de faire qqch; **under false ~s** sous de prétextes fallacieux.

pretend [prɪ'tend] 1 vt: **to ~ to do sthg** faire semblant de faire qqch. 2 vi faire semblant.

pretense Am = pretence.

pretension [prɪ'tenʃn] n prétention f.

pretentious [prɪ'tenʃəs] adj prétentieux(ieuse).

pretext [prɪ'tekst] n prétexte m; **on** OR **under the ~ that** ... sous prétexte que ....

pretty ['prɪtɪ] 1 adj joli(e). 2 adv [quite] plutôt; **~ much** OR **well** pratiquement, presque.

prevail [prɪ'veɪl] vi [be widespread] avoir cours, régner. || [triumph]: **to ~ (over)** prévaloir (sur), l'emporter (sur). || [persuade]: **to ~ on** OR **upon sb to do sthg** persuader qqn de faire qqch.

prevailing [prɪ'veɪlɪŋ] adj [current] actuel(elle). || [wind] dominant(e).

prevalent ['prevələnt] adj courant(e), répandu(e).

prevent [prɪ'vent] vt: **to ~ sb/sthg (from doing sthg)** empêcher qqn/qqch (de faire qqch).

preventive [prɪ'ventɪv] adj préventif(ive).

preview ['priːvjuː] n avant-première f.

previous ['priːvjəs] adj [earlier] antérieur(e). || [preceding] précédent(e).

previously ['priːvjəslɪ] adv avant, auparavant.

prewar [ˌpriː'wɔːr] adj d'avant-guerre.

prey [preɪ] n proie f. ○ **prey on** vt fus [live off] faire sa proie de. || [trouble]: **to ~ on sb's mind** ronger qqn, tracasser qqn.

price [praɪs] 1 n [cost] prix m; **at any ~** à tout prix. 2 vt fixer le prix de.

priceless ['praɪslɪs] adj sans prix, inestimable.

price list n tarif m.

price tag n [label] étiquette f.

prick [prɪk] 1 n [scratch, wound] piqûre f. || vulg [stupid person] con m, conne f. 2 vt piquer. ○ **prick up** vt fus: **to ~ up one's ears** [animal] dresser les oreilles; [person] dresser OR tendre l'oreille.

prickle ['prɪkl] 1 n [thorn] épine f. || [sensation on skin] picotement m. 2 vi picoter.

prickly ['prɪklɪ] adj [plant, bush] épineux(euse). || fig [person] irritable.

prickly heat n (U) boutons mpl de chaleur.

pride [praɪd] 1 n (U) [satisfaction] fierté f. || [self-esteem] orgueil m, amour-propre m. || pej [arrogance] orgueil m. 2 vt: **to ~ o.s. on sthg** être fier (fière) de qqch.

priest [priːst] n prêtre m.

priestess ['priːstɪs] n prêtresse f.

priesthood ['priːsthʊd] n [position, office]: **the ~** le sacerdoce. || [priests]: **the ~** le clergé.

prig [prɪg] n petit saint m, petite sainte f.

prim [prɪm] adj guindé(e).

primarily ['praɪmərɪlɪ] adv principalement.

primary ['praɪmərɪ] 1 adj [main] premier(ière), principal(e). || SCH primaire. 2 n Am POL primaire f.

primary school n école f primaire.

primate ['praɪmeɪt] n ZOOL primate m. || RELIG primat m.

prime [praɪm] 1 adj [main] principal(e), primordial(e). || [excellent] excellent(e); **~ quality** première qualité. 2 n: **to be in one's ~** être dans la fleur de l'âge. 3 vt [paint] apprêter. || [inform]: **to ~ sb about sthg** mettre qqn au courant de qqch.

prime minister n premier ministre m.

primer ['praɪmər] n [paint] apprêt m. || [textbook] introduction f.

primeval [praɪ'miːvl] adj [ancient] primitif(ive).

primitive ['prɪmɪtɪv] adj primitif(ive).

primrose ['prɪmrəʊz] n primevère f.

Primus stove® ['praɪməs-] n réchaud m de camping.

prince [prɪns] n prince m.

princess [prɪn'ses] n princesse f.

principal ['prɪnsəpl] 1 adj principal(e). 2 n SCH directeur m, -trice f; UNIV doyen m, -enne f.

principle ['prɪnsəpl] *n* principe *m*; **on ~, as a matter of ~** par principe. ○ **in principle** *adv* en principe.

print [prɪnt] **1** *n* (*U*) [type] caractères *mpl*; **to be out of ~** être épuisé. || ART gravure *f*. || [photograph] épreuve *f*. || [fabric] imprimé *m*. || [mark] empreinte *f*. **2** *vt* [produce by printing] imprimer. || [publish] publier. || [write in block letters] écrire en caractères d'imprimerie. ○ **print out** *vt sep* COMPUT imprimer.

printed matter ['prɪntɪd-] *n* (*U*) imprimés *mpl*.

printer ['prɪntər] *n* [person, firm] imprimeur *m*. || COMPUT imprimante *f*.

printing ['prɪntɪŋ] *n* (*U*) [act of printing] impression *f*. || [trade] imprimerie *f*.

printout ['prɪntaʊt] *n* COMPUT sortie *f* d'imprimante, listing *m*.

prior ['praɪər] **1** *adj* antérieur(e), précédent(e). **2** *n* [monk] prieur *m*. ○ **prior to** *prep* avant; **~ to doing sthg** avant de faire qqch.

priority [praɪ'ɒrətɪ] *n* priorité *f*.

prise [praɪz] *vt*: **to ~ sthg away from sb** arracher qqch à qqn; **to ~ sthg open** forcer qqch.

prison ['prɪzn] *n* prison *f*.

prisoner ['prɪznər] *n* prisonnier *m*, -ière *f*.

prisoner of war (*pl* **prisoners of war**) *n* prisonnier *m*, -ière *f* de guerre.

privacy [*Br* 'prɪvəsɪ, *Am* 'praɪvəsɪ] *n* intimité *f*.

private ['praɪvɪt] **1** *adj* [not public] privé(e). || [confidential] confidentiel(ielle). || [personal] personnel(elle). || [unsociable - person] secret(ète). **2** *n* [soldier] (simple) soldat *m*. || [secrecy]: **in ~** en privé.

private enterprise *n* (*U*) entreprise *f* privée.

private eye *n* détective *m* privé.

privately ['praɪvɪtlɪ] *adv* [not by the state]: **~ owned** du secteur privé. || [confidentially] en privé. || [personally] intérieurement, dans son for intérieur.

private property *n* propriété *f* privée.

private school *n* école *f* privée.

privatize, **-ise** ['praɪvɪtaɪz] *vt* privatiser.

privet ['prɪvɪt] *n* troène *m*.

privilege ['prɪvɪlɪdʒ] *n* privilège *m*.

privy ['prɪvɪ] *adj*: **to be ~ to sthg** être dans le secret de qqch.

prize [praɪz] **1** *adj* [possession] très précieux(ieuse); [animal] primé(e); [idiot,

example] parfait(e). **2** *n* prix *m*. **3** *vt* priser.

prizewinner ['praɪz‚wɪnər] *n* gagnant *m*, -e *f*.

pro [prəʊ] (*pl* **-s**) *n* *inf* [professional] pro *mf*. || [advantage]: **the ~s and cons** le pour et le contre.

probability [‚prɒbə'bɪlətɪ] *n* probabilité *f*.

probable ['prɒbəbl] *adj* probable.

probably ['prɒbəblɪ] *adv* probablement.

probation [prə'beɪʃn] *n* (*U*) JUR mise *f* à l'épreuve; **to put sb on ~** mettre qqn en sursis avec mise à l'épreuve. || [trial period] essai *m*; **to be on ~** être à l'essai.

probe [prəʊb] **1** *n* [investigation]: **~ (into)** enquête *f* (sur). || MED & TECH sonde *f*. **2** *vt* sonder.

problem ['prɒbləm] *n* problème *m*.

procedure [prə'siːdʒər] *n* procédure *f*.

proceed [*vb* prə'siːd, *n* 'prəʊsiːd] **1** *vt* [do subsequently]: **to ~ to do sthg** se mettre à faire qqch. **2** *vi* [continue]: **to ~ (with sthg)** continuer (qqch), poursuivre (qqch). || *fml* [advance] avancer. ○ **proceeds** *npl* recette *f*.

proceedings [prə'siːdɪŋz] *npl* [of meeting] débats *mpl*. || JUR poursuites *fpl*.

process ['prəʊses] **1** *n* [series of actions] processus *m*; **in the ~** ce faisant; **to be in the ~ of doing sthg** être en train de faire qqch. || [method] procédé *m*. **2** *vt* [raw materials, food, data] traiter, transformer; [application] s'occuper de.

processing ['prəʊsesɪŋ] *n* traitement *m*, transformation *f*.

procession [prə'seʃn] *n* cortège *m*, procession *f*.

proclaim [prə'kleɪm] *vt* [declare] proclamer.

procrastinate [prə'kræstɪneɪt] *vi* faire traîner les choses.

procure [prə'kjʊər] *vt* [for oneself] se procurer; [for someone else] procurer; [release] obtenir.

prod [prɒd] *vt* [push, poke] pousser doucement.

prodigy ['prɒdɪdʒɪ] *n* prodige *m*.

produce [*n* 'prɒdjuːs, *vb* prə'djuːs] **1** *n* (*U*) produits *mpl*. **2** *vt* [gen] produire. || [cause] provoquer, causer. || [show] présenter. || THEATRE mettre en scène.

producer [prə'djuːsər] *n* [of film, manufacturer] producteur *m*, -trice *f*. || THEATRE metteur *m* en scène.

product ['prɒdʌkt] *n* produit *m*.

production [prə'dʌkʃn] *n* (*U*) [manufacture, of film] production *f*. || (*U*) [output] rendement *m*. || (*U*) THEATRE [of play] mise *f* en scène. || [show - gen] production *f*; [- THEATRE] pièce *f*.

production line *n* chaîne *f* de fabrication.

productive [prə'dʌktɪv] *adj* [land, business, workers] productif(ive). || [meeting, experience] fructueux(euse).

productivity [ˌprɒdʌk'tɪvətɪ] *n* productivité *f*.

profane [prə'feɪn] *adj* impie.

profession [prə'feʃn] *n* profession *f*.

professional [prə'feʃənl] **1** *adj* [gen] professionnel(elle). || [of high standard] de (haute) qualité. **2** *n* professionnel *m*, - elle *f*.

professor [prə'fesər] *n* Am & Can [teacher] professeur *m*.

proficiency [prə'fɪʃənsɪ] *n*: ~ (in) compétence *f* (en).

profile ['prəufaɪl] *n* profil *m*.

profit ['prɒfɪt] **1** *n* [financial] bénéfice *m*, profit *m*; **to make a ~** faire un bénéfice. || [advantage] profit *m*. **2** *vi* [financially] être le bénéficiaire; [gain advantage] tirer avantage OR profit.

profitability [ˌprɒfɪtə'bɪlətɪ] *n* rentabilité *f*.

profitable ['prɒfɪtəbl] *adj* [financially] rentable, lucratif(ive). || [beneficial] fructueux(euse), profitable.

profiteering [ˌprɒfɪ'tɪərɪŋ] *n* affairisme *m*, mercantilisme *m*.

profound [prə'faund] *adj* profond(e).

profusely [prə'fjuːslɪ] *adv* [sweat, bleed] abondamment; **to apologize ~** se confondre en excuses.

profusion [prə'fjuːʒn] *n* profusion *f*.

prognosis [prɒg'nəʊsɪs] (*pl* **-noses** [-'nəʊsiːz]) *n* pronostic *m*.

program ['prəʊgræm] (*pt & pp* **-med** OR **-ed**, *cont* **-ming** OR **-ing**) **1** *n* COMPUT programme *m*. || *Am* = **programme**. **2** *vt* COMPUT programmer. || *Am* = **programme**.

programer *Am* = **programmer**.

programme *Br*, **program** *Am* ['prəʊgræm] **1** *n* [schedule, booklet] programme *m*. || RADIO & TV émission *f*. **2** *vt* programmer.

programmer *Br*, **programer** *Am* ['prəʊgræmər] *n* COMPUT programmeur *m*, -euse *f*.

programming ['prəʊgræmɪŋ] *n* programmation *f*.

progress [*n* 'prəʊgres, *vb* prə'gres] **1** *n* progrès *m*; **to make ~** [improve] faire des progrès; **to make ~ in sthg** avancer dans qqch; **in ~** en cours. **2** *vi* [improve - gen] progresser, avancer; [- person] faire des progrès. || [continue] avancer.

progressive [prə'gresɪv] *adj* [enlightened] progressiste. || [gradual] progressif(ive).

prohibit [prə'hɪbɪt] *vt* prohiber; **to ~ sb from doing sthg** interdire OR défendre à qqn de faire qqch.

project [*n* 'prɒdʒekt, *vb* prə'dʒekt] **1** *n* [plan, idea] projet *m*, plan *m*. || SCH [study]: ~ (**on**) dossier *m* (sur), projet *m* (sur). **2** *vt* [gen] projeter. || [estimate] prévoir. **3** *vi* [jut out] faire saillie.

projectile [prə'dʒektaɪl] *n* projectile *m*.

projection [prə'dʒekʃn] *n* [estimate] prévision *f*. || [protrusion] saillie *f*. || (*U*) [display, showing] projection *f*.

projector [prə'dʒektər] *n* projecteur *m*.

proletariat [ˌprəʊlɪ'teərɪət] *n* prolétariat *m*.

prolific [prə'lɪfɪk] *adj* prolifique.

prologue, prolog *Am* ['prəʊlɒg] *n lit & fig* prologue *m*.

prolong [prə'lɒŋ] *vt* prolonger.

prom [prɒm] *n* *Am* [ball] bal *m* d'étudiants.

prominent ['prɒmɪnənt] *adj* [important] important(e). || [noticeable] proéminent(e).

promiscuous [prɒ'mɪskjʊəs] *adj* [person] aux mœurs légères.

promise ['prɒmɪs] **1** *n* promesse *f*. **2** *vt*: **to ~ (sb) to do sthg** promettre (à qqn) de faire qqch; **to ~ sb sthg** promettre qqch à qqn. **3** *vi* promettre.

promising ['prɒmɪsɪŋ] *adj* prometteur(euse).

promontory ['prɒməntrɪ] *n* promontoire *m*.

promote [prə'məʊt] *vt* [foster] promouvoir. || [push, advertise] promouvoir, lancer. || [in job] promouvoir.

promoter [prə'məʊtər] *n* [organizer] organisateur *m*, -trice *f*. || [supporter] promoteur *m*, -trice *f*.

promotion [prə'məʊʃn] *n* promotion *f*, avancement *m*.

prompt [prɒmpt] **1** *adj* rapide, prompt(e). **2** *adv*: **at nine o'clock ~** à neuf heures précises OR tapantes. **3** *vt* [motivate, encourage]: **to ~ sb (to do sthg)** pousser OR inciter qqn (à faire qqch). || THEATRE souffler sa réplique à.

promptly ['promptlɪ] *adv* [immediately]
rapidement, promptement. || [punctu-
ally] ponctuellement.

prone [prəʊn] *adj* [susceptible]: **to be ~
to sthg** être sujet(ette) à qqch; **to be ~ to
do sthg** avoir tendance à faire qqch. ||
[lying flat] étendu(e) face contre terre.

prong [prɒŋ] *n* [of fork] dent *f*.

pronoun ['prəʊnaʊn] *n* pronom *m*.

pronounce [prə'naʊns] **1** *vt* prononcer.
2 *vi*: **to ~ on** se prononcer sur.

pronounced [prə'naʊnst] *adj* pronon-
cé(e).

pronouncement [prə'naʊnsmənt] *n*
déclaration *f*.

pronunciation [prə,nʌnsɪ'eɪʃn] *n* prononciation *f*.

proof [pruːf] *n* [evidence] preuve *f*. || [of
book etc] épreuve *f*. || [of alcohol] teneur *f*
en alcool.

prop [prɒp] **1** *n* [physical support] sup-
port *m*, étai *m*. || *fig* [supporting thing,
person] soutien *m*. **2** *vt*: **to ~ sthg against**
appuyer qqch contre OR à. ○ **props** *npl*
accessoires *mpl*. ○ **prop up** *vt sep*
[physically support] soutenir, étayer. || *fig*
[sustain] soutenir.

propaganda [,prɒpə'gændə] *n* propagande *f*.

propel [prə'pel] *vt* propulser; *fig* pousser.

propeller [prə'pelər] *n* hélice *f*.

proper ['prɒpər] *adj* [real] vrai(e). ||
[correct] correct(e), bon (bonne). || [de-
cent - behaviour etc] convenable.

properly ['prɒpəlɪ] *adv* [satisfactorily,
correctly] correctement, comme il faut. ||
[decently] convenablement, comme il
faut.

proper noun *n* nom *m* propre.

property ['prɒpətɪ] *n* (*U*) [possessions]
biens *mpl*, propriété *f*. || [building] bien
m immobilier; [land] terres *fpl*. || [qual-
ity] propriété *f*.

prophecy ['prɒfɪsɪ] *n* prophétie *f*.

prophesy ['prɒfɪsaɪ] *vt* prédire.

prophet ['prɒfɪt] *n* prophète *m*.

proportion [prə'pɔːʃn] *n* [part] part *f*,
partie *f*. || [ratio] rapport *m*, proportion *f*.
|| ART: **in ~** proportionné(e); **out of ~**
proportionné; **a sense of ~** *fig* le sens de
la mesure.

proportional [prə'pɔːʃənl] *adj* propor-
tionnel(elle).

proportional representation *n* représentation *f* proportionnelle.

proportionate [prə'pɔːʃnət] *adj* pro-
portionnel(elle).

proposal [prə'pəʊzl] *n* [suggestion] pro-
position *f*, offre *f*. || [offer of marriage] de-
mande *f* en mariage.

propose [prə'pəʊz] **1** *vt* [suggest] propo-
ser. || [intend]: **to ~ to do** OR **doing sthg**
avoir l'intention de faire qqch, se propo-
ser de faire qqch. || [toast] porter. **2** *vi*: **to
~ to sb** demander qqn en mariage.

proposition [,prɒpə'zɪʃn] *n* proposition *f*.

proprietor [prə'praɪətər] *n* propriétaire
mf.

propriety [prə'praɪətɪ] *n* (*U*) *fml* [moral
correctness] bienséance *f*.

pro rata [-'rɑːtə] *adv* au prorata.

prose [prəʊz] *n* (*U*) prose *f*.

prosecute ['prɒsɪkjuːt] **1** *vt* poursuivre
(en justice). **2** *vi* [police] engager des
poursuites judiciaires; [lawyer] représenter la partie plaignante.

prosecution [,prɒsɪ'kjuːʃn] *n* poursuites *fpl* judiciaires, accusation *f*; **the ~** la
partie plaignante; [in Crown case] ≃ le
ministère public.

prosecutor ['prɒsɪkjuːtər] *n* plaignant
m, -e *f*.

prospect [*n* 'prɒspekt, *vb* prə'spekt] **1** *n*
[hope] possibilité *f*, chances *fpl*. || [prob-
ability] perspective *f*. **2** *vi*: **to ~ (for
sthg)** prospecter (pour chercher qqch).
○ **prospects** *npl*: **~s (for)** chances *fpl*
(de), perspectives *fpl* (de).

prospecting [prə'spektɪŋ] *n* prospec-
tion *f*.

prospective [prə'spektɪv] *adj* éven-
tuel(elle).

prospector [prə'spektər] *n* prospecteur
m, -trice *f*.

prospectus [prə'spektəs] (*pl* **-es**) *n*
prospectus *m*.

prosper ['prɒspər] *vi* prospérer.

prosperity [prɒ'sperətɪ] *n* prospérité *f*.

prosperous ['prɒspərəs] *adj* prospère.

prostitute ['prɒstɪtjuːt] *n* prostituée *f*.

prostrate ['prɒstreɪt] *adj* [lying down]
à plat ventre. || [with grief etc] prostré(e).

protagonist [prə'tægənɪst] *n* protagoniste *mf*.

protect [prə'tekt] *vt*: **to ~ sb/sthg
(against), to ~ sb/sthg (from)** protéger
qqn/qqch (contre), protéger qqn/qqch
(de).

protection [prə'tekʃn] *n*: **~ (from** OR
against) protection *f* (contre), défense *f*
(contre).

protective [prə'tektɪv] *adj* [layer, clothing] de protection. ‖ [person, feelings] protecteur(trice).

protein ['prəutiːn] *n* protéine *f*.

protest [*n* 'prəutest, *vb* prə'test] **1** *n* protestation *f*. **2** *vt* [state] protester de. ‖ *Am* [protest against] protester contre. **3** *vi* : **to ~ (about/against)** protester (à propos de/contre).

Protestant ['prɒtɪstənt] **1** *adj* protestant(e). **2** *n* protestant *m*, -e *f*.

protester [prə'testər] *n* [on march, at demonstration] manifestant *m*, -e *f*.

protest march *n* manifestation *f*, marche *f* de protestation.

protocol ['prəutəkɒl] *n* protocole *m*.

prototype ['prəutətaɪp] *n* prototype *m*.

protracted [prə'træktɪd] *adj* prolongé(e).

protrude [prə'truːd] *vi* avancer, dépasser.

proud [praud] *adj* [satisfied, dignified] fier (fière). ‖ *pej* [arrogant] orgueilleux(euse), fier (fière).

prove [pruːv] (*pp* **-d** OR **proven**) *vt* [show to be true] prouver. ‖ [turn out] : **to ~ (to be) false/useful** s'avérer faux/utile; **to ~ o.s. to be sthg** se révéler être qqch.

proven ['pruːvn, 'prəuvn] **1** *pp* → **prove. 2** *adj* [fact] avéré(e), établi(e); [liar] fieffé(e).

proverb ['prɒvɜːb] *n* proverbe *m*.

provide [prə'vaɪd] *vt* fournir; **to ~ sb with sthg** fournir qqch à qqn. ○ **provide for** *vt fus* [support] subvenir aux besoins de. ‖ *fml* [make arrangements for] prévoir.

providing [prə'vaɪdɪŋ] ○ **providing (that)** *conj* à condition que (+ *subjunctive*), pourvu que (+ *subjunctive*).

province ['prɒvɪns] *n* [part of country] province *f*. ‖ [speciality] domaine *m*, compétence *f*.

provincial [prə'vɪnʃl] *adj* [town, newspaper] de province. ‖ *pej* [narrow-minded] provincial(e).

provision [prə'vɪʒn] *n* (U) [act of supplying] : **~ (of)** approvisionnement *m* (en), fourniture *f* (de). ‖ [supply] provision *f*, réserve *f*. ‖ (U) [arrangements] : **to make ~ for** [the future] prendre des mesures pour. ‖ [in agreement, law] clause *f*, disposition *f*. ○ **provisions** *npl* [supplies] provisions *fpl*.

provisional [prə'vɪʒənl] *adj* provisoire.

proviso [prə'vaɪzəu] (*pl* **-s**) *n* condition *f*, stipulation *f*; **with the ~ that** à (la) condition que (+ *subjunctive*).

provocative [prə'vɒkətɪv] *adj* provocant(e).

provoke [prə'vəuk] *vt* [annoy] agacer, contrarier. ‖ [cause - fight, argument] provoquer; [- reaction] susciter.

prow [prau] *n* proue *f*.

prowess ['prauɪs] *n* prouesse *f*.

prowl [praul] **1** *vt* [streets etc] rôder dans. **2** *vi* rôder.

prowler ['praulər] *n* rôdeur *m*, -euse *f*.

proxy ['prɒksɪ] *n* : **by ~** par procuration.

prudent ['pruːdnt] *adj* prudent(e).

prudish ['pruːdɪʃ] *adj* prude, pudibond(e).

prune [pruːn] **1** *n* [fruit] pruneau *m*. **2** *vt* [tree, bush] tailler.

pry [praɪ] *vi* se mêler de ce qui ne vous regarde pas.

PS (*abbr of* **postscript**) *n* PS *m*.

psalm [sɑːm] *n* psaume *m*.

pseudonym ['sjuːdənɪm] *n* pseudonyme *m*.

psyche ['saɪkɪ] *n* psyché *f*.

psychiatric [,saɪkɪ'ætrɪk] *adj* psychiatrique.

psychiatrist [saɪ'kaɪətrɪst] *n* psychiatre *mf*.

psychiatry [saɪ'kaɪətrɪ] *n* psychiatrie *f*.

psychic ['saɪkɪk] **1** *adj* [clairvoyant - person] doué(e) de seconde vue; [- powers] parapsychique. ‖ MED psychique. **2** *n* médium *m*.

psychoanalysis [,saɪkəuə'næləsɪs] *n* psychanalyse *f*.

psychoanalyst [,saɪkəu'ænəlɪst] *n* psychanalyste *mf*.

psychological [,saɪkə'lɒdʒɪkl] *adj* psychologique.

psychologist [saɪ'kɒlədʒɪst] *n* psychologue *mf*.

psychology [saɪ'kɒlədʒɪ] *n* psychologie *f*.

psychopath ['saɪkəpæθ] *n* psychopathe *mf*.

psychotic [saɪ'kɒtɪk] **1** *adj* psychotique. **2** *n* psychotique *mf*.

pt *abbr of* **pint**. ‖ *abbr of* **point**.

PT (*abbr of* **physical training**) *n* EPS *f*.

PTO (*abbr of* **please turn over**) TSVP.

pub [pʌb] *n* pub *m*.

puberty ['pjuːbətɪ] *n* puberté *f*.

pubic ['pjuːbɪk] *adj* du pubis.

public ['pʌblɪk] **1** *adj* public(ique); [library] municipal(e). **2** *n* : **the ~** le public; **in ~** en public.

public-address system *n* système *m* de sonorisation.

publication [ˌpʌblɪˈkeɪʃn] *n* publication *f*.

public company *n* société *f* anonyme (*cotée en Bourse*).

public holiday *n* jour *m* férié.

publicity [pʌbˈlɪsɪtɪ] *n* (*U*) publicité *f*.

publicize, -ise [ˈpʌblɪsaɪz] *vt* faire connaître au public.

public limited company *n* société *f* anonyme (*cotée en Bourse*).

public opinion *n* (*U*) opinion *f* publique.

public prosecutor *n* ≃ procureur *m* de la République.

public relations 1 *n* (*U*) relations *fpl* publiques. **2** *npl* relations *fpl* publiques.

public school *n* Am [state school] école *f* publique.

public-spirited *adj* qui fait preuve de civisme.

public transport *n* (*U*) transports *mpl* en commun.

publish [ˈpʌblɪʃ] *vt* publier.

publisher [ˈpʌblɪʃəʳ] *n* éditeur *m*, -trice *f*.

publishing [ˈpʌblɪʃɪŋ] *n* (*U*) [industry] édition *f*.

pucker [ˈpʌkəʳ] *vt* plisser.

pudding [ˈpʊdɪŋ] *n* [food - sweet] entremets *m*; [- savoury] pudding *m*.

puddle [ˈpʌdl] *n* flaque *f*.

puff [pʌf] **1** *n* [of cigarette, smoke] bouffée *f*. || [gasp] souffle *m*. **2** *vt* [cigarette etc] tirer sur. **3** *vi* [smoke]: **to ~ at** OR **on sthg** fumer qqch. || [pant] haleter. ○ **puff out** *vt sep* [cheeks, chest] gonfler.

puffed [pʌft] *adj* [swollen]: ~ (**up**) gonflé(e).

puffin [ˈpʌfɪn] *n* macareux *m*.

puff pastry, puff paste Am *n* (*U*) pâte *f* feuilletée.

puffy [ˈpʌfɪ] *adj* gonflé(e), bouffi(e).

pull [pʊl] **1** *vt* [gen] tirer. || [strain - muscle, hamstring] se froisser. || [attract] attirer. **2** *vi* tirer. **3** *n* [tug with hand]: **to give sthg a ~** tirer sur qqch. || (*U*) [influence] influence *f*. ○ **pull apart** *vt sep* [separate] séparer. ○ **pull at** *vt fus* tirer sur. ○ **pull away** *vi* AUT démarrer. || [in race] prendre de l'avance. ○ **pull down** *vt sep* [building] démolir. ○ **pull in** *vi* AUT se ranger. ○ **pull off** *vt sep* [take off] enlever, ôter. || [succeed in] réussir. ○ **pull out 1** *vt sep* [troops etc] retirer. **2** *vi* RAIL partir, démarrer. || AUT déboîter. || [with-

draw] se retirer. ○ **pull over** *vi* AUT se ranger. ○ **pull through** *vi* s'en sortir, s'en tirer. ○ **pull together**: **to ~ o.s. together** se ressaisir, se reprendre. ○ **pull up 1** *vt sep* [raise] remonter. || [chair] avancer. **2** *vi* s'arrêter.

pulley [ˈpʊlɪ] (*pl* pulleys) *n* poulie *f*.

pullover [ˈpʊlˌəʊvəʳ] *n* pull *m*.

pulp [pʌlp] **1** *adj* [fiction, novel] de quatre sous. **2** *n* [for paper] pâte *f* à papier. || [of fruit] pulpe *f*.

pulpit [ˈpʊlpɪt] *n* chaire *f*.

pulsate [pʌlˈseɪt] *vi* [heart] battre fort; [air, music] vibrer.

pulse [pʌls] *n* MED pouls *m*. ○ **pulses** *npl* [food] légumes *mpl* secs.

puma [ˈpjuːmə] (*pl inv* OR **-s**) *n* puma *m*.

pumice (stone) [ˈpʌmɪs-] *n* pierre *f* ponce.

pummel [ˈpʌml] *vt* bourrer de coups.

pump [pʌmp] **1** *n* pompe *f*. **2** *vt* [water, gas etc] pomper. || *inf* [interrogate] essayer de tirer les vers du nez à. **3** *vi* [heart] battre fort. ○ **pumps** *npl* [shoes] escarpins *mpl*.

pumpkin [ˈpʌmpkɪn] *n* potiron *m*.

pun [pʌn] *n* jeu *m* de mots, calembour *m*.

punch [pʌntʃ] **1** *n* [blow] coup *m* de poing. || [tool] poinçonneuse *f*. || [drink] punch *m*. **2** *vt* [hit - once] donner un coup de poing à; [- repeatedly] donner des coups de poing à. || [ticket] poinçonner; [paper] perforer.

Punch-and-Judy show [-ˈdʒuːdɪ-] *n* guignol *m*.

punch line *n* trait *m* final (*d'une blague*).

punctual [ˈpʌŋktʃʊəl] *adj* ponctuel(elle).

punctuation [ˌpʌŋktʃʊˈeɪʃn] *n* ponctuation *f*.

punctuation mark *n* signe *m* de ponctuation.

puncture [ˈpʌŋktʃəʳ] **1** *n* crevaison *f*. **2** *vt* [tyre, ball] crever; [skin] piquer.

pundit [ˈpʌndɪt] *n* pontife *m*.

pungent [ˈpʌndʒənt] *adj* [smell] âcre; [taste] piquant(e).

punish [ˈpʌnɪʃ] *vt* punir; **to ~ sb for sthg/for doing sthg** punir qqn pour qqch/pour avoir fait qqch.

punishing [ˈpʌnɪʃɪŋ] *adj* [schedule, work] épuisant(e), éreintant(e); [defeat] cuisant(e).

punishment ['pʌnɪʃmənt] *n* punition *f*, châtiment *m*.

punk [pʌŋk] **1** *adj* punk (*inv*). **2** *n* (*U*) [music]: ~ (**rock**) punk *m*. || ~ (**rocker**) punk *mf*. || *Am inf* [lout] loubard *m*.

punt [pʌnt] *n* [boat] bateau *m* à fond plat.

puny ['pju:nɪ] *adj* chétif(ive).

pup [pʌp] *n* [young dog] chiot *m*.

pupil ['pju:pl] *n* [student] élève *mf*. || [of eye] pupille *f*.

puppet ['pʌpɪt] *n* [toy] marionnette *f*. || *pej* [person, country] fantoche *m*, pantin *m*.

puppy ['pʌpɪ] *n* chiot *m*.

purchase ['pɜːtʃəs] **1** *n* achat *m*. **2** *vt* acheter.

purchaser ['pɜːtʃəsər] *n* acheteur *m*, -euse *f*.

pure [pjʊər] *adj* pur(e).

puree ['pjʊəreɪ] *n* purée *f*.

purge [pɜːdʒ] **1** *n* POL purge *f*. **2** *vt* POL purger. || [rid] débarrasser, purger.

purify ['pjʊərɪfaɪ] *vt* purifier, épurer.

purist ['pjʊərɪst] *n* puriste *mf*.

puritan ['pjʊərɪtən] *n* puritain *m*, -e *f*.

purity ['pjʊərətɪ] *n* pureté *f*.

purl [pɜːl] **1** *n* (*U*) maille *f* à l'envers. **2** *vt* tricoter à l'envers.

purple ['pɜːpl] **1** *adj* violet(ette). **2** *n* violet *m*.

purpose ['pɜːpəs] *n* [reason] raison *f*, motif *m*. || [aim] but *m*, objet *m*; **to no ~** en vain, pour rien. || [determination] détermination *f*. ○ **on purpose** *adv* exprès.

purposeful ['pɜːpəsfʊl] *adj* résolu(e), déterminé(e).

purr [pɜːr] *vi* ronronner.

purse [pɜːs] **1** *n* [for money] porte-monnaie *m inv*, bourse *f*. || *Am* [handbag] sac *m* à main. **2** *vt* [lips] pincer.

purser ['pɜːsər] *n* commissaire *m* de bord.

pursue [pə'sju:] *vt* [follow] poursuivre, pourchasser. || [policy, aim] poursuivre; [question] continuer à débattre; [matter] approfondir; [project] donner suite à; **to ~ an interest in sthg** se livrer à qqch.

pursuer [pə'sju:ər] *n* poursuivant *m*, -e *f*.

pursuit [pə'sju:t] *n* (*U*) *fml* [attempt to obtain] recherche *f*, poursuite *f*. || [chase, in sport] poursuite *f*. || [occupation] occupation *f*, activité *f*.

pus [pʌs] *n* pus *m*.

push [pʊʃ] **1** *vt* [press, move - gen] pousser; [- button] appuyer sur. || [encourage]: **to ~ sb (to do sthg)** inciter OR pousser qqn (à faire qqch). || [force]: **to ~ sb (into doing sthg)** forcer OR obliger qqn (à faire qqch). || *inf* [promote] faire de la réclame pour. **2** *vi* [gen] pousser; [on button] appuyer. || [campaign]: **to ~ for sthg** faire pression pour obtenir qqch. **3** *n* [with hand] poussée *f*. || [forceful effort] effort *m*. ○ **push around** *vt sep inf fig* marcher sur les pieds de. ○ **push in** *vi* [in queue] resquiller. ○ **push off** *vi inf* filer, se sauver. ○ **push on** *vi* continuer. ○ **push through** *vt sep* [law, reform] faire accepter.

pushed [pʊʃt] *adj inf*: **to be ~ for sthg** être à court de qqch; **to be hard ~ to do sthg** avoir du mal OR de la peine à faire qqch.

pusher ['pʊʃər] *n drugs sl* dealer *m*.

push-up *n* pompe *f*, traction *f*.

pushy ['pʊʃɪ] *adj pej* qui se met toujours en avant.

puss [pʊs], **pussy (cat)** ['pʊsɪ-] *n inf* minet *m*, minou *m*.

put [pʊt] (*pt & pp* **put**) *vt* [gen] mettre. || [place] mettre, poser, placer; **to ~ the children to bed** coucher les enfants. || [express] dire, exprimer. || [question] poser. || [estimate] estimer, évaluer. || [invest]: **to ~ money into** investir de l'argent dans. ○ **put across** *vt sep* [ideas] faire comprendre. ○ **put away** *vt sep* [tidy away] ranger. ○ **put back** *vt sep* [replace] remettre (à sa place OR en place). || [postpone] remettre. || [clock, watch] retarder. ○ **put by** *vt sep* [money] mettre de côté. ○ **put down** *vt sep* [lay down] poser, déposer. || [quell - rebellion] réprimer. || [write down] inscrire, noter. ○ **put down to** *vt sep* attribuer à. ○ **put forward** *vt sep* [propose] proposer, avancer. || [meeting, clock, watch] avancer. ○ **put in** *vt sep* [spend - time] passer. || [submit] présenter. ○ **put off** *vt sep* [postpone] remettre (à plus tard). || [cause to wait] décommander. || [discourage] dissuader. || [disturb] déconcerter, troubler. || [cause to dislike] dégoûter. || [switch off - radio, TV] éteindre. ○ **put on** *vt sep* [clothes] mettre, enfiler. || [arrange - exhibition etc] organiser; [- play] monter. || [gain]: **to ~ on weight** prendre du poids, grossir. || [switch on - radio, TV] allumer, mettre; **to ~ the light on** allumer (la lumière). || [record, CD, tape] passer, mettre. || [start cooking] mettre à cuire. || [pretend - gen] feindre; [- accent etc] prendre. || [bet] parier, miser. || [add] ajouter. ○ **put out** *rt sep* [place outside] mettre dehors. || [book. statement] publier; [record] sortir. || [fire. cigarette] éteindre; **to ~ the light out** éteindre (la lumière). || [extend - hand] tendre. || [annoy. upset]: **to be ~ out** être contrarié(e). || [inconvenience] déranger. ○ **put through** *rt sep* TELEC. passer. ○ **put up 1** *rt sep* [build - gen] ériger; [- tent] dresser. || [umbrella] ouvrir; [flag] hisser. || [fix to wall] accrocher. || [provide - money] fournir. || [increase] augmenter. || [provide accommodation for] loger, héberger. **2** *rt fus*: **to ~ up a fight** se défendre. ○ **put up with** *rt fus* supporter.

putrid ['pju:trɪd] *adj* putride.

putt [pʌt] **1** *n* putt *m*. **2** *rt & ri* putter.

putting green ['pʌtɪŋ-] *n* green *m*.

putty ['pʌtɪ] *n* mastic *m*.

puzzle ['pʌzl] **1** *n* [toy] casse-tête *m inv*; [mental] devinette *f*. || [mystery] mystère *m*, énigme *f*. **2** *vt* rendre perplexe. **3** *ri*: **to ~ over sthg** essayer de comprendre qqch. ○ **puzzle out** *rt sep* comprendre.

puzzling ['pʌzlɪŋ] *adj* curieux(ieuse).

pyjamas [pə'dʒɑːməz] *npl* pyjama *m*.

pylon ['paɪlən] *n* pylône *m*.

pyramid ['pɪrəmɪd] *n* pyramide *f*.

Pyrenees [,pɪrə'niːz] *npl*: **the ~** les Pyrénées *fpl*.

Pyrex® ['paɪreks] *n* Pyrex® *m*.

python ['paɪθn] (*pl inv* OR **-s**) *n* python *m*.

q (*pl* **q's** OR **qs**), **Q** (*pl* **Q's** OR **Qs**) [kjuː] *n* [letter] q *m inv*, Q *m inv*.

quack [kwæk] *n* [noise] coin-coin *m inv*. || *inf pej* [doctor] charlatan *m*.

quadrangle ['kwɒdræŋgl] *n* [figure] quadrilatère *m*. || [courtyard] cour *f*.

quadruple [kwɒ'druːpl] **1** *adj* quadruple. **2** *rt & ri* quadrupler.

quadruplets ['kwɒdruplɪts] *npl* quadruplés *mpl*.

quail [kweɪl] (*pl inv* OR **-s**) **1** *n* caille *f*. **2** *ri literary* reculer.

quaint [kweɪnt] *adj* pittoresque.

quake [kweɪk] *ri* trembler.

Quaker ['kweɪkər] *n* quaker *m*, -eresse *f*.

qualification [,kwɒlɪfɪ'keɪʃn] *n* [certificate] diplôme *m*. || [quality, skill] compétence *f*. || [qualifying statement] réserve *f*.

qualified ['kwɒlɪfaɪd] *adj* [trained] diplômé(e). || [able]: **to be ~ to do sthg** avoir la compétence nécessaire pour faire qqch. || [limited] restreint(e), modéré(e).

qualify ['kwɒlɪfaɪ] **1** *rt* [modify] apporter des réserves à. || [entitle]: **to ~ sb to do sthg** qualifier qqn pour faire qqch. **2** *ri* [pass exams] obtenir un diplôme. || [be entitled]: **to ~ (for sthg)** avoir droit (à qqch), remplir les conditions requises (pour qqch). || SPORT se qualifier.

quality ['kwɒlətɪ] *n* qualité *f*.

qualms [kwɑːmz] *npl* doutes *mpl*.

quandary ['kwɒndərɪ] *n* embarras *m*; **to be in a ~ about** OR **over sthg** être bien embarrassé à propos de qqch.

quantify ['kwɒntɪfaɪ] *rt* quantifier.

quantity ['kwɒntətɪ] *n* quantité *f*.

quantity surveyor *n* métreur *m*, -euse *f*.

quarantine ['kwɒrəntiːn] **1** *n* quarantaine *f*. **2** *rt* mettre en quarantaine.

quarrel ['kwɒrəl] **1** *n* querelle *f*, dispute *f*. **2** *ri*: **to ~ (with)** se quereller (avec), se disputer (avec).

quarrelsome ['kwɒrəlsəm] *adj* querelleur(euse).

quarry ['kwɒrɪ] *n* [place] carrière *f.* || [prey] proie *f.*

quart [kwɔ:t] *n* = 1,136 litre *Br*, = 0,946 litre *Am*, ≈ litre *m.*

quarter ['kwɔ:tə'] *n* [fraction, weight] quart *m*; **a ~ past two** *Br*, **a ~ after two** *Am* deux heures et quart; **a ~ to two** *Br*, **a ~ of two** *Am* deux heures moins le quart. || [of year] trimestre *m.* || *Am* [coin] pièce *f* de 25 cents. || [area in town] quartier *m.* || [direction]: **from all ~s** de tous côtés. ○ **quarters** *npl* [rooms] quartiers *mpl.* ○ **at close quarters** *adv* de près.

quarterfinal [,kwɔ:tə'faɪnl] *n* quart *m* de finale.

quarterly ['kwɔ:təlɪ] **1** *adj* trimestriel(ielle). **2** *adv* trimestriellement. **3** *n* publication *f* trimestrielle.

quartet [kwɔ:'tet] *n* quatuor *m.*

quartz [kwɔ:ts] *n* quartz *m.*

quash [kwɒʃ] *vt* [sentence] annuler, casser. || [rebellion] réprimer.

quaver ['kweɪvə'] **1** *n* MUS croche *f.* || [in voice] tremblement *m*, chevrotement *m.* **2** *vi* trembler, chevroter.

quay [ki:] *n* quai *m.*

quayside ['ki:saɪd] *n* bord *m* du quai.

queasy ['kwi:zɪ] *adj*: **to feel ~** avoir mal au cœur.

Quebec [kwɪ'bek] *n* [province] Québec *m.*

queen [kwi:n] *n* [gen] reine *f.* || [playing card] dame *f.*

Queen Mother *n*: **the ~** la reine mère.

queer [kwɪə'] **1** *adj* [odd] étrange, bizarre. **2** *n inf pej* pédé *m*, homosexuel *m.*

quell [kwel] *vt* réprimer, étouffer.

quench [kwentʃ] *vt*: **to ~ one's thirst** se désaltérer.

query ['kwɪərɪ] **1** *n* question *f.* **2** *vt* mettre en doute, douter de.

quest [kwest] *n literary*: **~ (for)** quête *f* (de).

question ['kwestʃn] **1** *n* [gen] question *f*; **to ask (sb) a ~** poser une question (à qqn). || [doubt] doute *m*; **to call OR bring sthg into ~** mettre qqch en doute; **without ~** incontestablement, sans aucun doute. || *phr*: **there's no ~ of ...** il n'est pas question de .... **2** *vt* [interrogate] questionner. || [express doubt about] mettre en question OR en doute. ○ **in question** *adv*: **the ... in ~** le/la/les ... en question. ○ **out of the question** *adv* hors de question.

questionable ['kwestʃənəbl] *adj* [uncertain] discutable. || [not right, not honest] douteux(euse).

question mark *n* point *m* d'interrogation.

questionnaire [,kwestʃə'neə'] *n* questionnaire *m.*

quibble ['kwɪbl] *pej vi*: **to ~ (over OR about)** chicaner (à propos de).

quiche [ki:ʃ] *n* quiche *f.*

quick [kwɪk] **1** *adj* [gen] rapide. || [response, decision] prompt(e), rapide. **2** *adv* vite, rapidement.

quicken ['kwɪkn] **1** *vt* accélérer, presser. **2** *vi* s'accélérer.

quickly ['kwɪklɪ] *adv* [rapidly] vite, rapidement. || [without delay] promptement, immédiatement.

quicksand ['kwɪksænd] *n* sables *mpl* mouvants.

quick-witted [-'wɪtɪd] *adj* [person] à l'esprit vif.

quiet ['kwaɪət] **1** *adj* [not noisy] tranquille; [voice] bas (basse); [engine] silencieux(ieuse); **be ~!** taisez-vous! || [not busy] calme. || [silent] silencieux(ieuse); **to keep ~ about sthg** ne rien dire à propos de qqch, garder qqch secret. || [intimate] intime. **2** *n* tranquillité *f*; **on the ~** *inf* en douce. **3** *vt Am* calmer, apaiser.

quieten ['kwaɪətn] *vt* calmer, apaiser. ○ **quieten down 1** *vt sep* calmer, apaiser. **2** *vi* se calmer.

quietly ['kwaɪətlɪ] *adv* [without noise] sans faire de bruit, silencieusement; [say] doucement. || [without excitement] tranquillement, calmement. || [without fuss - leave] discrètement.

quilt [kwɪlt] *n* [padded] édredon *m*; (**continental**) ~ couette *f.*

quinine [kwɪ'ni:n] *n* quinine *f.*

quins *Br* [kwɪnz], **quints** *Am* [kwɪnts] *npl inf* quintuplés *mpl.*

quintet [kwɪn'tet] *n* quintette *m.*

quints *Am* = **quins.**

quintuplets [kwɪn'tju:plɪts] *npl* quintuplés *mpl.*

quip [kwɪp] **1** *n* raillerie *f.* **2** *vi* railler.

quirk [kwɜ:k] *n* bizarrerie *f.*

quit [kwɪt] (*Br pt & pp* **quit** OR **-ted**, *Am pt & pp* **quit**) **1** *vt* [resign from] quitter. || [stop]: **to ~ smoking** arrêter de fumer. **2** *vi* [resign] démissionner. || [give up] abandonner.

quite [kwaɪt] *adv* [completely] tout à fait, complètement; **not ~** pas tout à fait; **I don't ~ understand** je ne comprends pas bien. ‖ [fairly] assez, plutôt. ‖ [for emphasis]: **she's ~ a singer** c'est une chanteuse formidable. ‖ [to express agreement]: **~ (so)!** exactement!

quits [kwɪts] *adj inf*: **to be ~ (with sb)** être quitte (envers qqn); **to call it ~** en rester là.

quiver ['kwɪvəʳ] **1** *n* [shiver] frisson *m*. ‖ [for arrows] carquois *m*. **2** *vi* frissonner.

quiz [kwɪz] (*pl* **-zes**) **1** *n* [gen] quiz *m*, jeu-concours *m*. ‖ *Am* SCH interrogation *f*.

quizzical ['kwɪzɪkl] *adj* narquois(e), moqueur(euse).

quota ['kwəʊtə] *n* quota *m*.

quotation [kwəʊ'teɪʃn] *n* [citation] citation *f*. ‖ COMM devis *m*.

quotation marks *npl* guillemets *mpl*; **in ~** entre guillemets.

quote [kwəʊt] **1** *n* [citation] citation *f*. ‖ COMM devis *m*. **2** *vt* [cite] citer. ‖ COMM indiquer, spécifier. **3** *vi* [cite]: **to ~ (from sthg)** citer (qqch). ‖ COMM: **to ~ for sthg** établir un devis pour qqch.

quotient ['kwəʊʃnt] *n* quotient *m*.

r (*pl* **r's** OR **rs**), **R** (*pl* **R's** OR **Rs**) [ɑːʳ] *n* [letter] r *m inv*, R *m inv*.

rabbi ['ræbaɪ] *n* rabbin *m*.

rabbit ['ræbɪt] *n* lapin *m*.

rabbit hutch *n* clapier *m*.

rabble ['ræbl] *n* cohue *f*.

rabies ['reɪbiːz] *n* rage *f*.

race [reɪs] **1** *n* [competition] course *f*. ‖ [people, ethnic background] race *f*. **2** *vt* [compete against] faire la course avec. ‖ [horse] faire courir. **3** *vi* [compete] courir. ‖ [rush]: **to ~ in/out** entrer/sortir à toute allure. ‖ [pulse] être très rapide. ‖ [engine] s'emballer.

race car *Am* = **racing car**.

racecourse ['reɪskɔːs] *n* champ *m* de courses.

race driver *Am* = **racing driver**.

racehorse ['reɪshɔːs] *n* cheval *m* de course.

racetrack ['reɪstræk] *n* piste *f*.

racial discrimination ['reɪʃl-] *n* discrimination *f* raciale.

racing ['reɪsɪŋ] *n* (*U*): **(horse) ~** les courses *fpl*.

racing car *Br*, **race car** *Am* *n* voiture *f* de course.

racing driver *Br*, **race driver** *Am* *n* coureur *m* automobile, pilote *m* de course.

racism ['reɪsɪzm] *n* racisme *m*.

racist ['reɪsɪst] **1** *adj* raciste. **2** *n* raciste *mf*.

rack [ræk] *n* [for bottles] casier *m*; [for luggage] porte-bagages *m inv*; [for plates] égouttoir *m*; **toast ~** porte-toasts *m inv*.

racket ['rækɪt] *n* [noise] boucan *m*. ‖ [illegal activity] racket *m*. ‖ SPORT raquette *f*.

racquet ['rækɪt] *n* raquette *f*.

racy ['reɪsɪ] *adj* [novel, style] osé(e).

radar ['reɪdɑːʳ] *n* radar *m*.

radial (tyre) ['reɪdjəl-] *n* pneu *m* à carcasse radiale.

radiant ['reɪdjənt] *adj* [happy] radieux(ieuse).

radiate ['reɪdɪeɪt] **1** *vt* [heat, light] émettre, dégager. ‖ *fig* [confidence, health] respirer. **2** *vi* [heat, light] irradier.

radiation [ˌreɪdɪ'eɪʃn] *n* [radioactive] radiation *f*.

radiator ['reɪdɪeɪtəʳ] *n* radiateur *m*.

radical ['rædɪkl] *adj* radical(e).

radii ['reɪdɪaɪ] *pl* → **radius**.

radio ['reɪdɪəʊ] (*pl* **-s**) **1** *n* radio *f*; **on the ~** à la radio. **2** *comp* de radio. **3** *vt* [person] appeler par radio; [information] envoyer par radio.

radioactive [ˌreɪdɪəʊ'æktɪv] *adj* radioactif(ive).

radio alarm *n* radio-réveil *m*.

radio-controlled [-kən'trəʊld] *adj* téléguidé(e).

radiography [ˌreɪdɪ'ɒgrəfɪ] *n* radiographie *f*.

radiology [ˌreɪdɪ'ɒlədʒɪ] *n* radiologie *f*.

radiotherapy [ˌreɪdɪəʊ'θerəpɪ] *n* radiothérapie *f*.

radish ['rædɪʃ] *n* radis *m*.

radius ['reɪdɪəs] (*pl* **radii**) *n* MATH rayon *m*. ‖ ANAT radius *m*.

raffle ['ræfl] **1** *n* tombola *f*. **2** *vt* mettre en tombola.

raft [rɑːft] *n* [of wood] radeau *m*.

rafter ['rɑːftəʳ] *n* chevron *m*.

rag [ræg] *n* [piece of cloth] chiffon *m*. ○ **rags** *npl* [clothes] guenilles *fpl*.

rag-and-bone man *n* chiffonnier *m*.

rag doll *n* poupée *f* de chiffon.

rage [reɪdʒ] 1 *n* [fury] rage *f*, fureur *f*. || *inf* [fashion]: **to be (all) the ~** faire fureur. 2 *vi* [person] être furieux(ieuse). || [storm, argument] faire rage.

ragged ['rægɪd] *adj* [person] en haillons; [clothes] en lambeaux. || [line, edge, performance] inégal(e).

raid [reɪd] 1 *n* MIL raid *m*. || [by criminals] hold-up *m inv*; [by police] descente *f*. 2 *vt* MIL faire un raid sur. || [subj: criminals] faire un hold-up dans; [subj: police] faire une descente dans.

rail [reɪl] 1 *n* [on ship] bastingage *m*; [on staircase] rampe *f*; [on walkway] garde-fou *m*. || [bar] barre *f*. || RAIL rail *m*; **by ~** en train. 2 *comp* [transport, travel] par le train; [strike] des cheminots.

railing ['reɪlɪŋ] *n* [fence] grille *f*; [on ship] bastingage *m*; [on staircase] rampe *f*; [on walkway] garde-fou *m*.

railway *Br* ['reɪlweɪ], **railroad** *Am* ['reɪlrəʊd] *n* [system, company] chemin *m* de fer; [track] voie *f* ferrée.

railway line *n* [route] ligne *f* de chemin de fer; [track] voie *f* ferrée.

railway station *n* gare *f*.

railway track *n* voie *f* ferrée.

rain [reɪn] 1 *n* pluie *f*. 2 *v impers* METEOR pleuvoir; **it's ~ing** il pleut.

rainbow ['reɪnbəʊ] *n* arc-en-ciel *m*.

rain check *n Am*: **I'll take a ~ (on that)** une autre fois peut-être.

raincoat ['reɪnkəʊt] *n* imperméable *m*.

raindrop ['reɪndrɒp] *n* goutte *f* de pluie.

rainfall ['reɪnfɔːl] *n* [shower] chute *f* de pluie; [amount] précipitations *fpl*.

rain forest *n* forêt *f* tropicale humide.

rainy ['reɪnɪ] *adj* pluvieux(ieuse).

raise [reɪz] 1 *vt* [lift up] lever. || [increase - gen] augmenter; [- standards] élever; **to ~ one's voice** élever la voix. || [obtain]: **to ~ money** [from donations] collecter des fonds; [by selling, borrowing] se procurer de l'argent. || [subject, doubt] soulever; [memories] évoquer. || [children, cattle] élever. || [crops] cultiver. 2 *n Am* augmentation *f* (de salaire).

raisin ['reɪzn] *n* raisin *m* sec.

rake [reɪk] 1 *n* [implement] râteau *m*. 2 *vt* [path, lawn] ratisser; [leaves] râteler.

rally ['rælɪ] 1 *n* [meeting] rassemblement *m*. || [car race] rallye *m*. || SPORT [exchange of shots] échange *m*. 2 *vt* rallier. 3 *vi* [supporters] se rallier. || [patient] aller mieux; [prices] remonter. ○ **rally**

round 1 *vt fus* apporter son soutien à. 2 *vi inf* venir en aide.

ram [ræm] 1 *n* bélier *m*. 2 *vt* [crash into] percuter contre, emboutir. || [force] tasser.

RAM [ræm] (*abbr of* **random access memory**) *n* RAM *f*.

ramble ['ræmbl] 1 *n* randonnée *f*, promenade *f* à pied. 2 *vi* [walk] faire une promenade à pied. || *pej* [talk] radoter. ○ **ramble on** *vi pej* radoter.

rambler ['ræmblər] *n* [walker] randonneur *m*, -euse *f*.

rambling ['ræmblɪŋ] *adj* [house] plein(e) de coins et recoins. || [speech] décousu(e).

ramp [ræmp] *n* [slope] rampe *f*. || AUT [to slow traffic down] ralentisseur *m*.

rampage [ræm'peɪdʒ] *n*: **to go on the ~** tout saccager.

rampant ['ræmpənt] *adj* qui sévit.

ramparts ['ræmpɑːts] *npl* rempart *m*.

ramshackle ['ræm,ʃækl] *adj* branlant(e).

ran [ræn] *pt* → **run**.

ranch [rɑːntʃ] *n* ranch *m*.

rancher ['rɑːntʃər] *n* propriétaire *mf* de ranch.

rancid ['rænsɪd] *adj* rance.

rancour *Br*, **rancor** *Am* ['ræŋkər] *n* rancœur *f*.

random ['rændəm] 1 *adj* fait(e) au hasard; [number] aléatoire. 2 *n*: **at ~** au hasard.

random access memory *n* COMPUT mémoire *f* vive.

R and R (*abbr of* **rest and recreation**) *n Am* permission *f*.

randy ['rændɪ] *adj inf* excité(e).

rang [ræŋ] *pt* → **ring**.

range [reɪndʒ] 1 *n* [of plane, telescope etc] portée *f*; **at close ~** à bout portant. || [of subjects, goods] gamme *f*; **price ~** éventail *m* des prix. || [of mountains] chaîne *f*. || [shooting area] champ *m* de tir. || MUS [of voice] tessiture *f*. 2 *vt* [place in row] mettre en rang. 3 *vi* [vary]: **to ~ between ... and ...** varier entre ...; **to ~ from ... to ...** varier de ... à .... || [include]: **to ~ over sthg** couvrir qqch.

ranger ['reɪndʒər] *n* garde *m* forestier.

rank [ræŋk] 1 *adj* [absolute - disgrace, stupidity] complet(ète); [- injustice] flagrant(e); **he's a ~ outsider** il n'a aucune chance. || [smell] fétide. 2 *n* [in army, police etc] grade *m*. || [social class] rang *m*. || [row] rangée *f*. || *phr*: **the ~ and file** la masse; [of union] la base. **3** vt [classify] classer. **4** vi: **to ~ among** compter parmi. ○ **ranks** npl MIL: **the ~s** le rang. ‖ fig [members] rangs mpl.

rankle ['ræŋkl] vi: **it ~d with him** ça lui est resté sur l'estomac OR le cœur.

ransack ['rænsæk] vt [search through] mettre tout sens dessus dessous dans; [damage] saccager.

ransom ['rænsəm] n rançon f.

rant [rænt] vi déblatérer.

rap [ræp] **1** n [knock] coup m sec. ‖ MUS rap m. **2** vt [table] frapper sur; [knuckles] taper sur.

rape [reɪp] **1** n [crime, attack] viol m. ‖ [plant] colza m. **2** vt violer.

rapid ['ræpɪd] adj rapide. ○ **rapids** npl rapides mpl.

rapidly ['ræpɪdlɪ] adv rapidement.

rapist ['reɪpɪst] n violeur m.

rapport [ræ'pɔːr] n rapport m.

rapture ['ræptʃər] n ravissement m.

rapturous ['ræptʃərəs] adj [applause, welcome] enthousiaste.

rare [reər] adj [gen] rare. ‖ [meat] saignant(e).

rarely ['reəlɪ] adv rarement.

raring ['reərɪŋ] adj: **to be ~ to go** être impatient(e) de commencer.

rarity ['reərətɪ] n rareté f.

rascal ['rɑːskl] n polisson m, -onne f.

rash [ræʃ] **1** adj irréfléchi(e), imprudent(e). **2** n MED éruption f. ‖ [spate] succession f, série f.

rasher ['ræʃər] n tranche f.

rasp [rɑːsp] n [harsh sound] grincement m.

raspberry ['rɑːzbərɪ] n [fruit] framboise f. ‖ [rude sound]: **to blow a ~** faire pfft.

rat [ræt] n [animal] rat m. ‖ inf pej [person] ordure f, salaud m.

rate [reɪt] **1** n [speed] vitesse f; [of pulse] fréquence f; **at this ~** à ce train-là. ‖ [ratio, proportion] taux m. ‖ [price] tarif m. **2** vt [consider]: **to ~ sb/sthg as** considérer qqn/qqch comme; **to ~ sb/sthg among** classer qqn/qqch parmi. ‖ [deserve] mériter. ○ **at any rate** adv en tout cas.

rather ['rɑːðər] adv [somewhat, more exactly] plutôt. ‖ [to small extent] un peu. ‖ [preferably]: **I'd ~ wait** je préférerais attendre. ‖ [on the contrary]: **(but) ~ ...** au contraire .... ○ **rather than** conj plutôt que.

ratify ['rætɪfaɪ] vt ratifier, approuver.

rating ['reɪtɪŋ] n [of popularity etc] cote f.

ratio ['reɪʃɪəʊ] (pl -s) n rapport m.

ration ['ræʃn] **1** n ration f. **2** vt rationner. ○ **rations** npl vivres mpl.

rational ['ræʃənl] adj rationnel(elle).

rationalize, **-ise** ['ræʃənəlaɪz] vt rationaliser.

rat race n jungle f.

rattle ['rætl] **1** n [of bottles, typewriter keys] cliquetis m; [of engine] bruit m de ferraille. ‖ [toy] hochet m. **2** vt [bottles] faire s'entrechoquer; [keys] faire cliqueter. ‖ [unsettle] secouer. **3** vi [bottles] s'entrechoquer; [keys, machine] cliqueter; [engine] faire un bruit de ferraille.

rattlesnake ['rætlsneɪk], **rattler** Am ['rætlər] n serpent m à sonnettes.

raucous ['rɔːkəs] adj [voice, laughter] rauque; [behaviour] bruyant(e).

ravage ['rævɪdʒ] vt ravager. ○ **ravages** npl ravages mpl.

rave [reɪv] **1** adj [review] élogieux(ieuse). **2** vi [talk angrily]: **to ~ at** OR **against** tempêter OR fulminer contre. ‖ [talk enthusiastically]: **to ~ about** parler avec enthousiasme de.

raven ['reɪvn] n corbeau m.

ravenous ['rævənəs] adj [person] affamé(e); [animal, appetite] vorace.

ravine [rə'viːn] n ravin m.

raving ['reɪvɪŋ] adj: **~ lunatic** fou furieux (folle furieuse).

ravioli [ˌrævɪ'əʊlɪ] n (U) raviolis mpl.

ravishing ['rævɪʃɪŋ] adj ravissant(e), enchanteur(eresse).

raw [rɔː] adj [uncooked] cru(e). ‖ [untreated] brut(e). ‖ [painful] à vif. ‖ [inexperienced] novice; **~ recruit** bleu m.

raw deal n: **to get a ~** être défavorisé(e).

raw material n matière f première.

ray [reɪ] n [beam] rayon m; fig [of hope] lueur f.

rayon ['reɪɒn] n rayonne f.

raze [reɪz] vt raser.

razor ['reɪzər] n rasoir m.

razor blade n lame f de rasoir.

RC abbr of **Roman Catholic**.

Rd abbr of **Road**.

R & D (abbr of **research and development**) n R-D f.

re [riː] prep concernant.

RE n (abbr of **religious education**) instruction f religieuse.

reach [riːtʃ] **1** vt [gen] atteindre; [place, destination] arriver à; [agreement, decision] parvenir à. ‖ [contact] joindre, contacter. **2** *vi* [land] s'étendre; **to ~ out** tendre le bras; **to ~ down to pick sthg up** se pencher pour ramasser qqch. **3** *n* [of arm, boxer] allonge *f*; **within ~** [object] à portée; [place] à proximité; **out of** OR **beyond sb's ~** [object] hors de portée; [place] d'accès difficile, difficilement accessible.

react [rɪ'ækt] *vi* [gen] réagir.

reaction [rɪ'ækʃn] *n* réaction *f*.

reactionary [rɪ'ækʃənrɪ] **1** *adj* réactionnaire. **2** *n* réactionnaire *mf*.

reactor [rɪ'æktər] *n* réacteur *m*.

read [riːd] (*pt & pp* **read** [red]) **1** *vt* [gen] lire. || [subj: sign, letter] dire. || [interpret, judge] interpréter. || [subj: meter, thermometer etc] indiquer. **2** *vi* lire; **the book ~s well** le livre se lit bien. **○ read out** *vt sep* lire à haute voix. **○ read up on** *vt fus* étudier.

reader ['riːdər] *n* [of book, newspaper] lecteur *m*, -trice *f*.

readership ['riːdəʃɪp] *n* [of newspaper] nombre *m* de lecteurs.

readily ['redɪlɪ] *adv* [willingly] volontiers. || [easily] facilement.

reading ['riːdɪŋ] *n* (*U*) [gen] lecture *f*. || [interpretation] interprétation *f*. || [on thermometer, meter etc] indications *fpl*.

readjust [,riːə'dʒʌst] **1** *vt* [instrument] régler (de nouveau); [mirror] rajuster; [policy] rectifier. **2** *vi* [person]: **to ~ (to)** se réadapter (à).

readout ['riːdaut] *n* COMPUT affichage *m*.

ready ['redɪ] **1** *adj* [prepared] prêt(e); **to get ~** se préparer; **to get sthg ~** préparer qqch. || [willing]: **to be ~ to do sthg** être prêt(e) OR disposé(e) à faire qqch. **2** *vt* préparer.

ready-made *adj lit & fig* tout fait (toute faite).

ready money *n* liquide *m*.

ready-to-wear *adj* prêt-à-porter.

reafforestation ['riːə,fɒrɪ'steɪʃn] *n* reboisement *m*.

real ['rɪəl] **1** *adj* [gen] vrai(e), véritable; **~ life** réalité *f*; **for ~** pour de vrai. || [actual] réel(elle); **in ~ terms** dans la pratique. **2** *adv Am* très.

real estate *n* (*U*) biens *mpl* immobiliers.

realism ['rɪəlɪzm] *n* réalisme *m*.

realistic [,rɪə'lɪstɪk] *adj* réaliste.

reality [rɪ'ælətɪ] *n* réalité *f*.

realization [,rɪəlaɪ'zeɪʃn] *n* réalisation *f*.

realize, -ise ['rɪəlaɪz] *vt* [understand] se rendre compte de, réaliser. || [sum of money, idea, ambition] réaliser.

really ['rɪəlɪ] **1** *adv* [gen] vraiment. || [in fact] en réalité. **2** *excl* [expressing doubt] vraiment? || [expressing surprise] pas possible! || [expressing disapproval] franchement!, ça alors!

realm [relm] *n fig* [subject area] domaine *m*. || [kingdom] royaume *m*.

realtor ['rɪəltər] *n Am* agent *m* immobilier.

reap [riːp] *vt* [harvest] moissonner.

reappear [,riːə'pɪər] *vi* réapparaître, reparaître.

rear [rɪər] **1** *adj* arrière (*inv*), de derrière. **2** *n* [back] arrière *m*; **to bring up the ~** fermer la marche. || *inf* [bottom] derrière *m*. **3** *vt* [children, animals] élever. **4** *vi* [horse]: **to ~ (up)** se cabrer.

rearm [riː'ɑːm] *vt & vi* réarmer.

rearrange [,riːə'reɪndʒ] *vt* [furniture, room] réarranger; [plans] changer. || [meeting - to new time] changer l'heure de; [- to new date] changer la date de.

rearview mirror ['rɪəvjuː-] *n* rétroviseur *m*.

reason ['riːzn] **1** *n* [cause]: **~ (for)** raison *f* (de); **for some ~** pour une raison ou pour une autre. || (*U*) [justification]: **to have ~ to do sthg** avoir de bonnes raisons de faire qqch. || [common sense] bon sens *m*; **he won't listen to ~** on ne peut pas lui faire entendre raison; **it stands to ~** c'est logique. **2** *vt* déduire. **3** *vi* raisonner. **○ reason with** *vt fus* raisonner (avec).

reasonable ['riːznəbl] *adj* raisonnable.

reasonably ['riːznəblɪ] *adv* [quite] assez. || [sensibly] raisonnablement.

reasoning ['riːznɪŋ] *n* raisonnement *m*.

reassess [,riːə'ses] *vt* réexaminer.

reassurance [,riːə'ʃɔːrəns] *n* [comfort] réconfort *m*. || [promise] assurance *f*.

reassure [,riːə'ʃɔːr] *vt* rassurer.

reassuring [,riːə'ʃɔːrɪŋ] *adj* rassurant(e).

rebate ['riːbeɪt] *n* [on product] rabais *m*; **tax ~** ≃ dégrèvement *m* fiscal.

rebel [*n* 'rebl, *vb* rɪ'bel] **1** *n* rebelle *mf*. **2** *vi*: **to ~ (against)** se rebeller (contre).

rebellion [rɪ'beljən] *n* rébellion *f*.

rebellious [rɪ'beljəs] *adj* rebelle.

rebound [*n* 'riːbaund, *vb* rɪ'baund] **1** *n* [of ball] rebond *m*. **2** *vi* [ball] rebondir.

rebuff [rɪ'bʌf] *n* rebuffade *f*.

rebuild [,riː'bɪld] *vt* reconstruire.

rebuke [rɪ'bju:k] **1** n réprimande f. **2** vt réprimander.

recalcitrant [rɪ'kælsɪtrənt] adj récalcitrant(e).

recall [rɪ'kɔ:l] **1** n [memory] rappel m. **2** vt [remember] se rappeler, se souvenir de. ‖ [summon back] rappeler.

recant [rɪ'kænt] vi se rétracter; RELIG abjurer.

recap [ri:kæp] vi récapituler.

recapitulate [,ri:kə'pɪtjʊleɪt] vt & vi récapituler.

recd, rec'd abbr of **received.**

recede [rɪ'si:d] vi [person, car etc] s'éloigner; [hopes] s'envoler.

receding [rɪ'si:dɪŋ] adj [hairline] dégarni(e); [chin, forehead] fuyant(e).

receipt [rɪ'si:t] n [piece of paper] reçu m. ‖ (U) [act of receiving] réception f. ○ **receipts** npl recettes fpl.

receive [rɪ'si:v] vt [gen] recevoir; [news] apprendre. ‖ [welcome] accueillir, recevoir; **to be well/badly ~d** [film, speech etc] être bien/mal accueilli.

receiver [rɪ'si:vər] n [of telephone] récepteur m, combiné m. ‖ [criminal] receleur m, -euse f. ‖ FIN [official] administrateur m, -trice f judiciaire.

recent ['ri:snt] adj récent(e).

recently ['ri:sntlɪ] adv récemment; **until ~** jusqu'à ces derniers temps.

receptacle [rɪ'septəkl] n récipient m.

reception [rɪ'sepʃn] n [gen] réception f. ‖ [welcome] accueil m, réception f.

reception desk n réception f.

receptionist [rɪ'sepʃənɪst] n réceptionniste mf.

recess ['ri:ses, Br rɪ'ses] n [alcove] niche f. ‖ [secret place] recoin m. ‖ POL: **to be in ~** être en vacances. ‖ Am SCH récréation f.

recession [rɪ'seʃn] n récession f.

recharge [,ri:'tʃɑ:dʒ] vt recharger.

recipe ['resɪpɪ] n lit & fig recette f.

recipient [rɪ'sɪpɪənt] n [of letter] destinataire mf; [of cheque] bénéficiaire mf; [of award] récipiendaire mf.

reciprocal [rɪ'sɪprəkl] adj réciproque.

recital [rɪ'saɪtl] n récital m.

recite [rɪ'saɪt] vt [say aloud] réciter. ‖ [list] énumérer.

reckless ['reklɪs] adj imprudent(e).

reckon ['rekn] vt inf [think] penser. ‖ [consider, judge] considérer. ‖ [calculate] calculer. ○ **reckon on** vt fus compter sur. ○ **reckon with** vt fus [expect] s'attendre à.

reckoning ['rekənɪŋ] (U) n [calculation] calculs mpl.

reclaim [rɪ'kleɪm] vt [claim back] réclamer. ‖ [land] assécher.

recline [rɪ'klaɪn] vi [person] être allongé(e).

reclining [rɪ'klaɪnɪŋ] adj [chair] à dossier réglable.

recluse [rɪ'klu:s] n reclus m, -e f.

recognition [,rekəg'nɪʃn] n reconnaissance f; **in ~ of** en reconnaissance de.

recognizable ['rekəgnaɪzəbl] adj reconnaissable.

recognize, -ise ['rekəgnaɪz] vt reconnaître.

recoil [rɪ'kɔɪl] vi: **to ~ (from)** reculer (devant).

recollect [,rekə'lekt] vt se rappeler.

recollection [,rekə'lekʃn] n souvenir m.

recommend [,rekə'mend] vt [commend]: **to ~ sb/sthg (to sb)** recommander qqn/qqch (à qqn). ‖ [advise] conseiller, recommander.

recompense ['rekəmpens] **1** n dédommagement m. **2** vt dédommager.

reconcile ['rekənsaɪl] vt [beliefs, ideas] concilier. ‖ [people] réconcilier. ‖ [accept]: **to ~ o.s. to sthg** se faire à l'idée de qqch.

reconditioned [,ri:kən'dɪʃnd] adj remis(e) en état.

reconnaissance [rɪ'kɒnɪsəns] n reconnaissance f.

reconnoitre Br, **reconnoiter** Am [,rekə'nɔɪtər] vi aller en reconnaissance.

reconsider [,ri:kən'sɪdər] **1** vt reconsidérer. **2** vi reconsidérer la question.

reconstruct [,ri:kən'strʌkt] vt [gen] reconstruire. ‖ [crime, event] reconstituer.

record [n & adj 'rekɔ:d, vb rɪ'kɔ:d] **1** n [written account] rapport m; [file] dossier m; **to keep sthg on ~** archiver qqch; [police] **~** casier m judiciaire; **off the ~** non officiel. ‖ [vinyl disc] disque m. ‖ [best achievement] record m. **2** adj record (inv). **3** vt [write down] noter. ‖ [put on tape] enregistrer.

recorded delivery [rɪ'kɔ:dɪd-] n: **to send sthg by ~** envoyer qqch en recommandé.

recorder [rɪ'kɔ:dər] n [musical instrument] flûte f à bec.

recording [rɪ'kɔ:dɪŋ] n enregistrement m.

record player n tourne-disque m.

recount [n 'riːkaʊnt, vt sense 1 rɪ'kaʊnt, sense 2 ˌriːˈkaʊnt] **1** n [of vote] deuxième dépouillement m du scrutin. **2** vt [narrate] raconter. || [count again] recompter.

recoup [rɪ'kuːp] vt récupérer.

recourse [rɪ'kɔːs] n: **to have ~ to** avoir recours à.

recover [rɪ'kʌvər] **1** vt [retrieve] récupérer; **to ~ sthg from sb** reprendre qqch à qqn. || [one's balance] retrouver; [consciousness] reprendre. **2** vi [from illness] se rétablir; [from shock, divorce] se remettre. || fig [economy] se redresser; [trade] reprendre.

recovery [rɪ'kʌvərɪ] n [from illness] guérison f, rétablissement m. || fig [of economy] redressement m, reprise f. || [retrieval] récupération f.

recreation [ˌrekrɪ'eɪʃn] n (U) [leisure] récréation f, loisirs mpl.

recrimination [rɪˌkrɪmɪ'neɪʃn] n récrimination f.

recruit [rɪ'kruːt] **1** n recrue f. **2** vt recruter.

recruitment [rɪ'kruːtmənt] n recrutement m.

rectangle ['rek,tæŋgl] n rectangle m.

rectangular [rek'tæŋgjʊlər] adj rectangulaire.

rectify ['rektɪfaɪ] vt [mistake] rectifier.

rector ['rektər] n [priest] pasteur m.

rectory ['rektərɪ] n presbytère m.

recuperate [rɪ'kuːpəreɪt] vi se rétablir.

recur [rɪ'kɜːr] vi [error, problem] se reproduire; [dream] revenir; [pain] réapparaître.

recurrent [rɪ'kʌrənt] adj [error, problem] qui se reproduit souvent; [dream] qui revient souvent.

recycle [ˌriː'saɪkl] vt recycler.

red [red] **1** adj rouge; [hair] roux (rousse). **2** n rouge m; **to be in the ~** inf être à découvert.

red carpet n: **to roll out the ~ for sb** dérouler le tapis rouge pour qqn. ○ **red-carpet** adj: **to give sb the red-carpet treatment** recevoir qqn en grande pompe.

Red Cross n: **the ~** la Croix-Rouge.

redcurrant [ˌred'kʌrənt] n [fruit] groseille f; [bush] groseillier m.

redden ['redn] vt & vi rougir.

redecorate [ˌriː'dekəreɪt] **1** vt repeindre et retapisser. **2** vi refaire la peinture et les papiers peints.

redeem [rɪ'diːm] vt [save, rescue] racheter. || [from pawnbroker] dégager.

redeeming [rɪ'diːmɪŋ] adj qui rachète (les défauts).

redeploy [ˌriːdɪ'plɔɪ] vt MIL redéployer; [staff] réorganiser, réaffecter.

red-faced [-'feɪst] adj rougeaud(e), rubicond(e); [with embarrassment] rouge de confusion.

red-haired [-'heəd] adj roux (rousse).

red-handed [-'hændɪd] adj: **to catch sb ~** prendre qqn en flagrant délit OR la main dans le sac.

redhead ['redhed] n roux m, rousse f.

red herring n fig fausse piste f.

red-hot adj [extremely hot] brûlant(e); [metal] chauffé(e) au rouge.

redid [ˌriː'dɪd] pt → redo.

redirect [ˌriːdɪ'rekt] vt [energy, money] réorienter. || [traffic] détourner. || [letters] faire suivre.

rediscover [ˌriːdɪ'skʌvər] vt redécouvrir.

red light n [traffic signal] feu m rouge.

red-light district n quartier m chaud.

redo [ˌriː'duː] (pt -did, pp -done) vt refaire.

redolent ['redələnt] adj literary [reminiscent]: **~ of** qui rappelle, évocateur(trice) de. || [smelling]: **~ of** qui sent.

redone [ˌriː'dʌn] pp → redo.

redouble [ˌriː'dʌbl] vt: **to ~ one's efforts (to do sthg)** redoubler d'efforts (pour faire qqch).

redraft [ˌriː'drɑːft] vt rédiger à nouveau.

redress [rɪ'dres] **1** n (U) fml réparation f. **2** vt: **to ~ the balance** rétablir l'équilibre.

Red Sea n: **the ~** la mer Rouge.

red tape n fig paperasserie f administrative.

reduce [rɪ'djuːs] **1** vt réduire; **to be ~d to doing sthg** en être réduit à faire qqch; **to ~ sb to tears** faire pleurer qqn. **2** vi AM [diet] suivre un régime amaigrissant.

reduction [rɪ'dʌkʃn] n [decrease]: **~ (in)** réduction f (de), baisse f (de). || [discount] rabais m, réduction f.

redundant [rɪ'dʌndənt] adj [not required] superflu(e).

reed [riːd] n [plant] roseau m.

reef [riːf] n récif m, écueil m.

reek [riːk] **1** n relent m. **2** vi: **to ~ (of sthg)** puer (qqch), empester (qqch).

reel [riːl] **1** n [roll] bobine f. || [on fishing rod] moulinet m. **2** vi [stagger] chanceler. ○ **reel off** vt sep [list] débiter.

reenact [,ri:ɪ'nækt] vt [play] reproduire; [event] reconstituer.

ref [ref] n inf (abbr of **referee**) arbitre m. || (abbr of **reference**) ADMIN réf. f.

refectory [rɪ'fektərɪ] n réfectoire m.

refer [rɪ'fɜ:r] vt [person]: **to ~ sb to** [hospital] envoyer qqn à; [specialist] adresser qqn à; ADMIN renvoyer qqn à. || [report, case, decision]: **to ~ sthg to** soumettre qqch à. ○ **refer to** vt fus [speak about] parler de, faire allusion à OR mention de. || [apply to] s'appliquer à, concerner. || [consult] se référer à, se reporter à.

referee [,refə'ri:] 1 n SPORT arbitre m. 2 vt SPORT arbitrer. 3 vi SPORT être arbitre.

reference ['refrəns] n [mention]: ~ **(to)** allusion f (à). mention f (de); **with ~ to** comme suite à. || (U) [for advice, information]: ~ **(to)** consultation f (de), référence f (à). || COMM référence f. || [in book] renvoi m; **map ~** coordonnées fpl. || [for job application - letter] référence f; [- person] répondant m, -e f.

reference book n ouvrage m de référence.

reference number n numéro m de référence.

referendum [,refə'rendəm] (pl **-s** OR **-da** [-də]) n référendum m.

refill [n 'ri:fɪl, vb ,ri:'fɪl] 1 n [for pen] recharge f. 2 vt remplir à nouveau.

refine [rɪ'faɪn] vt raffiner; fig peaufiner.

refined [rɪ'faɪnd] adj raffiné(e); [system, theory] perfectionné(e).

refinement [rɪ'faɪnmənt] n [improvement] perfectionnement m. || (U) [gentility] raffinement m.

reflect [rɪ'flekt] 1 vt [be a sign of] refléter. || [light, image] réfléchir, refléter; [heat] réverbérer. 2 vi [think]: **to ~ (on** OR **upon)** réfléchir (sur). penser (à).

reflection [rɪ'flekʃn] n [sign] indication f, signe m. || [criticism]: ~ **on** critique f de. || [image] reflet m. || (U) [of light, heat] réflexion f. || [thought] réflexion f; **on ~** réflexion faite.

reflector [rɪ'flektər] n réflecteur m.

reflex ['ri:fleks] n: ~ **(action)** réflexe m.

reflexive [rɪ'fleksɪv] adj GRAMM [pronoun] réfléchi(e); ~ **verb** verbe m pronominal réfléchi.

reforestation [ri:,fɒrɪ'steɪʃn] = **reafforestation**.

reform [rɪ'fɔ:m] 1 n réforme f. 2 vt [gen] réformer; [person] corriger. 3 vi [behave better] se corriger, s'amender.

reformatory [rɪ'fɔ:mətrɪ] n Am centre m d'éducation surveillée (pour jeunes délinquants).

reformer [rɪ'fɔ:mər] n réformateur m, -trice f.

refrain [rɪ'freɪn] 1 n refrain m. 2 vi: **to ~ from doing sthg** s'abstenir de faire qqch.

refresh [rɪ'freʃ] vt rafraîchir, revigorer.

refreshed [rɪ'freʃt] adj reposé(e).

refresher course [rɪ'freʃə-] n cours m de recyclage OR remise à niveau.

refreshing [rɪ'freʃɪŋ] adj [pleasantly different] agréable, réconfortant(e). || [drink, swim] rafraîchissant(e).

refreshments [rɪ'freʃmənts] npl rafraîchissements mpl.

refrigerator [rɪ'frɪdʒəreɪtər] n réfrigérateur m, Frigidaire® m.

refuel [,ri:'fjʊəl] 1 vt ravitailler. 2 vi se ravitailler en carburant.

refuge ['refju:dʒ] n lit & fig refuge m, abri m; **to take ~ in** se réfugier dans.

refugee [,refjʊ'dʒi:] n réfugié m, -e f.

refund [n 'ri:fʌnd, vb rɪ'fʌnd] 1 n remboursement m. 2 vt: **to ~ sthg to sb, to ~ sb sthg** rembourser qqch à qqn.

refurbish [,ri:'fɜ:bɪʃ] vt remettre à neuf, rénover.

refusal [rɪ'fju:zl] n: ~ **(to do sthg)** refus m (de faire qqch).

refuse¹ [rɪ'fju:z] vt refuser; **to ~ to do sthg** refuser de faire qqch. 2 vi refuser.

refuse² ['refju:s] n (U) [rubbish] ordures fpl, détritus mpl.

refuse collection ['refju:s-] n enlèvement m des ordures ménagères.

refute [rɪ'fju:t] vt réfuter.

regain [rɪ'geɪn] vt [composure, health] retrouver; [leadership] reprendre.

regal ['ri:gl] adj majestueux(euse), royal(e).

regalia [rɪ'geɪljə] n (U) insignes mpl.

regard [rɪ'gɑ:d] 1 n (U) [respect] estime f, respect m. || [aspect]: **in this/that ~** à cet égard. 2 vt considérer; **to be highly ~ed** être tenu(e) en haute estime. ○ **regards** npl: **(with best) ~s** bien amicalement; **give her my ~s** faites-lui mes amitiés. ○ **as regards** prep en ce qui concerne. ○ **in regard to, with regard to** prep en ce qui concerne, relativement à.

regarding [rɪ'gɑ:dɪŋ] prep concernant, en ce qui concerne.

regardless [rɪ'gɑ:dlɪs] adv quand même. ○ **regardless of** prep sans tenir compte de, sans se soucier de.

regime [reɪ'ʒiːm] *n* régime *m*.

regiment ['redʒɪmənt] *n* régiment *m*.

region ['riːdʒən] *n* région *f*; **in the ~ of** environ.

regional ['riːdʒənl] *adj* régional(e).

register ['redʒɪstər] **1** *n* [record] registre *m*. **2** *vt* [record officially] déclarer. || [show, measure] indiquer, montrer. || [express] exprimer. **3** *vi* [on official list] s'inscrire, se faire inscrire. || [at hotel] signer le registre.

registered ['redʒɪstəd] *adj* [person] inscrit(e); [car] immatriculé(e). || [letter, parcel] recommandé(e).

registered trademark *n* marque *f* déposée.

registrar [,redʒɪ'strɑːr] *n* [keeper of records] officier *m* de l'état civil. || UNIV secrétaire *m* général.

registration [,redʒɪ'streɪʃn] *n* [gen] enregistrement *m*, inscription *f*.

registration number *n* AUT numéro *m* d'immatriculation.

registry ['redʒɪstrɪ] *n* bureau *m* de l'enregistrement.

registry office *n* bureau *m* de l'état civil.

regret [rɪ'gret] **1** *n* regret *m*. **2** *vt* [be sorry about]: **to ~ sthg/doing sthg** regretter qqch/d'avoir fait qqch.

regretfully [rɪ'gretfʊlɪ] *adv* à regret.

regrettable [rɪ'gretəbl] *adj* regrettable, fâcheux(euse).

regroup [,riː'gruːp] *vi* se regrouper.

regular ['regjʊlər] **1** *adj* [gen] régulier(ière); [customer] fidèle. || [usual] habituel(elle). || *Am* [normal - size] standard (*inv*). || *Am* [pleasant] sympa (*inv*). **2** *n* [at pub] habitué *m*, -e *f*; [at shop] client *m*, -e *f* fidèle.

regularly ['regjʊləlɪ] *adv* régulièrement.

regulate ['regjʊleɪt] *vt* régler.

regulation [,regjʊ'leɪʃn] **1** *adj* [standard] réglementaire. **2** *n* [rule] règlement *m*. || (*U*) [control] réglementation *f*.

rehearsal [rɪ'hɜːsl] *n* répétition *f*.

rehearse [rɪ'hɜːs] *vt* & *vi* répéter.

reign [reɪn] **1** *n* règne *m*. **2** *vi*: **to ~ (over)** *lit* & *fig* régner (sur).

reimburse [,riːɪm'bɜːs] *vt*: **to ~ sb (for)** rembourser qqn (de).

rein [reɪn] *n* *fig*: **to give (a) free ~ to sb, to give sb free ~** laisser la bride sur le cou à qqn. ○ **reins** *npl* [for horse] rênes *fpl*.

reindeer ['reɪn,dɪər] (*pl inv*) *n* renne *m*.

reinforce [,riːɪn'fɔːs] *vt* [strengthen] renforcer. || [back up, confirm] appuyer, étayer.

reinforced concrete [,riːɪn'fɔːst-] *n* béton *m* armé.

reinforcement [,riːɪn'fɔːsmənt] *n* (*U*) [strengthening] renforcement *m*. || [strengthener] renfort *m*. ○ **reinforcements** *npl* renforts *mpl*.

reinstate [,riːɪn'steɪt] *vt* [employee] rétablir dans ses fonctions, réintégrer; [policy, method] rétablir.

reiterate [riː'ɪtəreɪt] *vt* réitérer, répéter.

reject [*n* 'riːdʒekt, *vb* rɪ'dʒekt] **1** *n* [product] article *m* de rebut. **2** *vt* [not accept] rejeter. || [candidate, coin] refuser.

rejection [rɪ'dʒekʃn] *n* [non-acceptance] rejet *m*. || [of candidate] refus *m*.

rejoice [rɪ'dʒɔɪs] *vi*: **to ~ (at OR in)** se réjouir (de).

rejuvenate [rɪ'dʒuːvəneɪt] *vt* rajeunir.

rekindle [,riː'kɪndl] *vt* *fig* ranimer, raviver.

relapse [rɪ'læps] **1** *n* rechute *f*. **2** *vi*: **to ~ into** retomber dans.

relate [rɪ'leɪt] **1** *vt* [connect]: **to ~ sthg to sthg** établir un lien OR rapport entre qqch et qqch. || [tell] raconter. **2** *vi* [be connected]: **to ~ to** avoir un rapport avec. || [concern]: **to ~ to** se rapporter à. || [empathize]: **to ~ (to sb)** s'entendre (avec qqn). ○ **relating to** *prep* concernant.

related [rɪ'leɪtɪd] *adj* [people] apparenté(e). || [issues, problems etc] lié(e).

relation [rɪ'leɪʃn] *n* [connection]: **~ (to/between)** rapport *m* (avec/entre). || [person] parent *m*, -e *f*. ○ **relations** *npl* [relationship] relations *fpl*, rapports *mpl*.

relationship [rɪ'leɪʃnʃɪp] *n* [between people, countries] relations *fpl*, rapports *mpl*; [romantic] liaison *f*. || [connection] rapport *m*, lien *m*.

relative ['relətɪv] **1** *adj* relatif(ive). **2** *n* parent *m*, -e *f*.

relatively ['relətɪvlɪ] *adv* relativement.

relax [rɪ'læks] **1** *vt* [person] détendre, relaxer. || [muscle, body] décontracter, relâcher; [one's grip] desserrer. || [rule] relâcher. **2** *vi* [person] se détendre, se décontracter. || [muscle, body] se relâcher, se décontracter. || [one's grip] se desserrer.

relaxation [,riːlæk'seɪʃn] *n* [of person] relaxation *f*, détente *f*.

relaxed [rɪ'lækst] *adj* détendu(e), décontracté(e).

remit

relaxing [rɪ'læksɪŋ] *adj* relaxant(e), qui détend.

relay ['ri:leɪ] **1** *n* SPORT: ~ (**race**) course *f* de relais. || RADIO & TV [broadcast] retransmission *f*. **2** *rt* RADIO & TV [broadcast] relayer. || [message, information] transmettre, communiquer.

release [rɪ'li:s] **1** *n* [from prison, cage] libération *f*. || [from pain, misery] délivrance *f*. || [statement] communiqué *m*. || [of gas, heat] échappement *m*. || (*U*) [of film, record] sortie *f*. || [film] nouveau film *m*; [record] nouveau disque *m*. **2** *rt* [set free] libérer. || [lift restriction on]: **to ~ sb from** dégager qqn de. || [make available - supplies] libérer; [- funds] débloquer. || [let go of] lâcher. || TECH [brake, handle] desserrer; [mechanism] déclencher. || [gas, heat]: **to be ~d (from/into)** se dégager (de/dans), s'échapper (de/dans). || [film, record] sortir; [statement, report] publier.

relegate ['relɪgeɪt] *rt* reléguer.

relent [rɪ'lent] *ri* [person] se laisser fléchir; [wind, storm] se calmer.

relentless [rɪ'lentlɪs] *adj* implacable.

relevant ['relavant] *adj* [connected]: ~ (**to**) qui a un rapport (avec). || [significant]: ~ (**to**) important(e) (pour). || [appropriate - information] utile; [- document] justificatif(ive).

reliable [rɪ'laɪabl] *adj* [person] sur qui on peut compter, fiable; [device] fiable; [company, information] sérieux(ieuse).

reliant [rɪ'laɪant] *adj*: **to be ~ on** être dépendant(e) de.

relic ['relɪk] *n* relique *f*; [of past] vestige *m*.

relief [rɪ'li:f] *n* [comfort] soulagement *m*. || [for poor, refugees] aide *f*, assistance *f*. || *Am* [social security] aide *f* sociale.

relieve [rɪ'li:v] *rt* [pain, anxiety] soulager; **to ~ sb of sthg** [take away from] délivrer qqn de qqch. || [take over from] relayer. || [give help to] secourir, venir en aide à.

religion [rɪ'lɪdʒn] *n* religion *f*.

religious [rɪ'lɪdʒəs] *adj* religieux (ieuse); [book] de piété.

relinquish [rɪ'lɪŋkwɪʃ] *rt* [power] abandonner; [claim, plan] renoncer à; [post] quitter.

relish ['relɪʃ] **1** *n* [enjoyment]: **with (great)** ~ avec délectation. || [pickle] condiment *m*. **2** *rt* [enjoy] prendre plaisir à.

relocate [,ri:ləu'keɪt] **1** *rt* installer ailleurs, transférer. **2** *vi* s'installer ailleurs, déménager.

reluctance [rɪ'lʌktəns] *n* répugnance *f*.

reluctant [rɪ'lʌktənt] *adj* peu enthousiaste; **to be ~ to do sthg** rechigner à faire qqch, être peu disposé à faire qqch.

reluctantly [rɪ'lʌktəntlɪ] *adv* à contre-cœur, avec répugnance.

rely [rɪ'laɪ] ○**rely on** *rt fus* [count on] compter sur. || [be dependent on] dépendre de.

remain [rɪ'meɪn] **1** *rt* rester; **to ~ to be done** rester à faire. **2** *vi* rester. ○**remains** *npl* [remnants] restes *mpl*. || [antiquities] ruines *fpl*, vestiges *mpl*.

remainder [rɪ'meɪndər] *n* reste *m*.

remaining [rɪ'meɪnɪŋ] *adj* qui reste.

remand [rɪ'mɑ:nd] JUR **1** *n*: **on ~** en détention préventive. **2** *rt*: **to ~ sb (in custody)** placer qqn en détention préventive.

remark [rɪ'mɑ:k] **1** *n* [comment] remarque *f*, observation *f*. **2** *rt* [comment]: **to ~ that ...** faire remarquer que ....

remarkable [rɪ'mɑ:kəbl] *adj* remarquable.

remarry [,ri:'mærɪ] *vi* se remarier.

remedial [rɪ'mi:djəl] *adj* [pupil, class] de rattrapage. || [action] de rectification.

remedy ['remədɪ] **1** *n*: ~ (**for**) MED remède *m* (pour OR contre); *fig* remède (à OR contre). **2** *rt* remédier à.

remember [rɪ'membər] **1** *rt* [gen] se souvenir de, se rappeler; **to ~ to do sthg** ne pas oublier de faire qqch, penser à faire qqch; **to ~ doing sthg** se souvenir d'avoir fait qqch, se rappeler avoir fait qqch. **2** *vi* se souvenir, se rappeler.

remembrance [rɪ'membrəns] *n*: **in ~ of** en souvenir OR mémoire de.

Remembrance Day *n* l'Armistice *m*.

remind [rɪ'maɪnd] *rt*: **to ~ sb of OR about sthg** rappeler qqch à qqn; **to ~ sb to do sthg** rappeler à qqn de faire qqch, faire penser à qqn à faire qqch.

reminder [rɪ'maɪndər] *n* [to jog memory]: **to give sb a ~ (to do sthg)** faire penser à qqn (à faire qqch). || [letter, note] rappel *m*.

reminisce [,remɪ'nɪs] *vi* évoquer des souvenirs; **to ~ about sthg** évoquer qqch.

reminiscent [,remɪ'nɪsnt] *adj*: ~ **of** qui rappelle, qui fait penser à.

remiss [rɪ'mɪs] *adj* négligent(e).

remit [rɪ'mɪt] *rt* [money] envoyer, verser.

remittance [rɪˈmɪtns] n [amount of money] versement m. ‖ COMM règlement m, paiement m.

remnant [ˈremnənt] n [remaining part] reste m, restant m. ‖ [of cloth] coupon m.

remorse [rɪˈmɔːs] n (U) remords m.

remorseful [rɪˈmɔːsful] adj plein(e) de remords.

remorseless [rɪˈmɔːslɪs] adj implacable.

remote [rɪˈməʊt] adj [far-off - place] éloigné(e); [- time] lointain(e). ‖ [person] distant(e). ‖ [possibility, chance] vague.

remote control n télécommande f.

remotely [rɪˈməʊtlɪ] adv [in the slightest]: **not ~** pas le moins du monde, absolument pas. ‖ [far off] au loin.

removable [rɪˈmuːvəbl] adj [detachable] détachable, amovible.

removal [rɪˈmuːvl] n (U) [act of removing] enlèvement m.

remove [rɪˈmuːv] vt [take away - gen] enlever; [- stain] faire partir, enlever; [- suspicion] dissiper. ‖ [clothes] ôter, enlever. ‖ [employee] renvoyer.

remuneration [rɪˌmjuːnəˈreɪʃn] n rémunération f.

Renaissance [rəˈneɪsəns] n: **the ~** la Renaissance.

render [ˈrendər] vt rendre; [assistance] porter; FIN [account] présenter.

rendezvous [ˈrɒndɪvuː] (pl inv) n rendez-vous m inv.

renegade [ˈrenɪɡeɪd] n renégat m, -e f.

renew [rɪˈnjuː] vt [gen] renouveler; [negotiations, strength] reprendre; [interest] faire renaître. ‖ [replace] remplacer.

renewable [rɪˈnjuːəbl] adj renouvelable.

renewal [rɪˈnjuːəl] n [of activity] reprise f. ‖ [of contract, licence etc] renouvellement m.

renounce [rɪˈnaʊns] vt [reject] renoncer à.

renovate [ˈrenəveɪt] vt rénover.

renown [rɪˈnaʊn] n renommée f, renom m.

renowned [rɪˈnaʊnd] adj: **~ (for)** renommé(e) (pour).

rent [rent] 1 n [for house] loyer m. 2 vt louer.

rental [ˈrentl] 1 adj de location. 2 n [for car, television, video] prix m de location; [for house] loyer m.

renunciation [rɪˌnʌnsɪˈeɪʃn] n renonciation f.

reorganize, -ise [ˌriːˈɔːɡənaɪz] vt réorganiser.

rep [rep] n (abbr of **representative**) VRP m. ‖ abbr of **repertory**.

repaid [riːˈpeɪd] pt & pp → **repay**.

repair [rɪˈpeər] 1 n réparation f; **in good/bad ~** en bon/mauvais état. 2 vt réparer.

repair kit n trousse f à outils.

repartee [ˌrepɑːˈtiː] n repartie f.

repatriate [ˌriːˈpætrɪeɪt] vt rapatrier.

repay [riːˈpeɪ] (pt & pp **repaid**) vt [money]: **to ~ sb sthg, to ~ sthg to sb** rembourser qqch à qqn. ‖ [favour] payer de retour, récompenser.

repayment [riːˈpeɪmənt] n remboursement m.

repeal [rɪˈpiːl] 1 n abrogation f. 2 vt abroger.

repeat [rɪˈpiːt] 1 vt [gen] répéter. 2 n RADIO & TV reprise f, rediffusion f.

repeatedly [rɪˈpiːtɪdlɪ] adv à maintes reprises, très souvent.

repel [rɪˈpel] vt repousser.

repellent [rɪˈpelənt] 1 adj répugnant(e), repoussant(e). 2 n: **insect ~** crème f anti-insecte.

repent [rɪˈpent] 1 vt se repentir de. 2 vi: **to ~ (of)** se repentir (de).

repentance [rɪˈpentəns] n (U) repentir m.

repercussions [ˌriːpəˈkʌʃnz] npl répercussions fpl.

repertoire [ˈrepətwɑːr] n répertoire m.

repertory [ˈrepətrɪ] n répertoire m.

repetition [ˌrepɪˈtɪʃn] n répétition f.

repetitious [ˌrepɪˈtɪʃəs], **repetitive** [rɪˈpetɪtɪv] adj [action, job] répétitif(ive); [article, speech] qui a des redites.

replace [rɪˈpleɪs] vt [gen] remplacer. ‖ [put back] remettre (à sa place).

replacement [rɪˈpleɪsmənt] n [substituting] remplacement m; [putting back] replacement m. ‖ [new person]: **~ (for sb)** remplaçant m, -e f (de qqn).

replay [n ˈriːpleɪ, vb ˌriːˈpleɪ] 1 n match m rejoué. 2 vt [match, game] rejouer.

replenish [rɪˈplenɪʃ] vt: **to ~ one's supply of sthg** se réapprovisionner en qqch.

replica [ˈreplɪkə] n copie f exacte, réplique f.

reply [rɪˈplaɪ] 1 n: **~ (to)** réponse f (à). 2 vt & vi répondre.

report [rɪˈpɔːt] 1 n [account] rapport m, compte rendu m; PRESS reportage m. 2 vt [news, crime] rapporter, signaler. ‖ [make known]: **to ~ that ...** annoncer que

reshape

.... || [complain about]: **to ~ sb (to)** dénoncer qqn (à). **3** *vi* [give account]: **to ~ (on)** faire un rapport (sur); PRESS faire un reportage (sur). || [present oneself]: **to ~ (to sb/for sthg)** se présenter (à qqn/pour qqch).

report card *n* bulletin *m* scolaire.

reportedly [rɪ'pɔːtɪdlɪ] *adv* à ce qu'il paraît.

reporter [rɪ'pɔːtəʳ] *n* reporter *m*.

repose [rɪ'pəʊz] *n literary* repos *m*.

repossess [ˌriːpə'zes] *vt* saisir.

reprehensible [ˌreprɪ'hensəbl] *adj* répréhensible.

represent [ˌreprɪ'zent] *vt* [gen] représenter.

representation [ˌreprɪzen'teɪʃn] *n* [gen] représentation *f*.

representative [ˌreprɪ'zentətɪv] **1** *adj* représentatif(ive). **2** *n* représentant *m*, -e *f*.

repress [rɪ'pres] *vt* réprimer.

repression [rɪ'preʃn] *n* répression *f*; [sexual] refoulement *m*.

reprieve [rɪ'priːv] **1** *n fig* [delay] sursis *m*, répit *m*. || JUR sursis *m*. **2** *vt* accorder un sursis à.

reprimand ['reprɪmɑːnd] **1** *n* réprimande *f*. **2** *vt* réprimander.

reprisal [rɪ'praɪzl] *n* représailles *fpl*.

reproach [rɪ'prəʊtʃ] **1** *n* reproche *m*. **2** *vt*: **to ~ sb for OR with sthg** reprocher qqch à qqn.

reproachful [rɪ'prəʊtʃfʊl] *adj* [look, words] de reproche.

reproduce [ˌriːprə'djuːs] **1** *vt* reproduire. **2** *vi* se reproduire.

reproduction [ˌriːprə'dʌkʃn] *n* reproduction *f*.

reproof [rɪ'pruːf] *n* reproche *m*, blâme *m*.

reprove [rɪ'pruːv] *vt*: **to ~ sb (for)** blâmer qqn (pour OR de), réprimander qqn (pour).

reptile ['reptaɪl] *n* reptile *m*.

republic [rɪ'pʌblɪk] *n* république *f*.

republican [rɪ'pʌblɪkən] **1** *adj* républicain(e). **2** *n* républicain *m*, -e *f*. ○ **Republican 1** *adj* républicain(e); **the Republican Party** *Am* le parti républicain. **2** *n* républicain *m*, -e *f*.

repulse [rɪ'pʌls] *vt* repousser.

repulsive [rɪ'pʌlsɪv] *adj* repoussant(e).

reputable ['repjʊtəbl] *adj* de bonne réputation.

reputation [ˌrepjʊ'teɪʃn] *n* réputation *f*.

reputed [rɪ'pjuːtɪd] *adj* réputé(e); **to be ~ to be sthg** être réputé pour être qqch, avoir la réputation d'être qqch.

reputedly [rɪ'pjuːtɪdlɪ] *adv* à OR d'après ce qu'on dit.

request [rɪ'kwest] **1** *n*: **~ (for)** demande *f* (de); **on ~** sur demande. **2** *vt* demander.

require [rɪ'kwaɪəʳ] *vt* [subj: person] avoir besoin de; [subj: situation] nécessiter; **to ~ sb to do sthg** exiger de qqn qu'il fasse qqch.

requirement [rɪ'kwaɪəmənt] *n* besoin *m*.

requisition [ˌrekwɪ'zɪʃn] *vt* réquisitionner.

reran [ˌriː'ræn] *pt* → **rerun**.

rerun [*n* 'riːrʌn, *vb* ˌriː'rʌn] (*pt* **-ran**, *pp* **-run**) **1** *n* [of TV programme] rediffusion *f*, reprise *f*; *fig* répétition *f*. **2** *vt* [race] réorganiser. || [TV programme] rediffuser; [tape] passer à nouveau, repasser.

rescind [rɪ'sɪnd] *vt* [contract] annuler; [law] abroger.

rescue ['reskjuː] **1** *n* (*U*) [help] secours *mpl*. || [successful attempt] sauvetage *m*. **2** *vt* sauver, secourir.

rescuer ['reskjʊəʳ] *n* sauveteur *m*.

research [rɪ'sɜːtʃ] **1** *n* (*U*): **~ (on OR into)** recherche *f* (sur), recherches *fpl* (sur). **2** *vt* faire des recherches sur.

researcher [rɪ'sɜːtʃəʳ] *n* chercheur *m*, -euse *f*.

resemblance [rɪ'zembləns] *n*: **~ (to)** ressemblance *f* (avec).

resemble [rɪ'zembl] *vt* ressembler à.

resent [rɪ'zent] *vt* être indigné(e) par.

resentful [rɪ'zentfʊl] *adj* plein(e) de ressentiment.

resentment [rɪ'zentmənt] *n* ressentiment *m*.

reservation [ˌrezə'veɪʃn] *n* [booking] réservation *f*. || [uncertainty]: **without ~** sans réserve. || *Am* [for Native Americans] réserve *f* indienne. ○ **reservations** *npl* [doubts] réserves *fpl*.

reserve [rɪ'zɜːv] **1** *n* [gen] réserve *f*; **in ~** en réserve. || SPORT remplaçant *m*, -e *f*. **2** *vt* [save] garder, réserver. || [book] réserver. || [retain]: **to ~ the right to do sthg** se réserver le droit de faire qqch.

reserved [rɪ'zɜːvd] *adj* réservé(e).

reservoir ['rezəvwɑːʳ] *n* réservoir *m*.

reset [ˌriː'set] (*pt & pp* **reset**) *vt* [clock, watch] remettre à l'heure; [meter, controls] remettre à zéro.

reshape [ˌriː'ʃeɪp] *vt* [policy, thinking] réorganiser.

reshuffle [ˌriːˈʃʌfl] **1** *n* remaniement *m*; **cabinet ~** remaniement ministériel. **2** *vt* remanier.

reside [rɪˈzaɪd] *vi fml* résider.

residence [ˈrezɪdəns] *n* résidence *f*.

residence permit *n* permis *m* de séjour.

resident [ˈrezɪdənt] **1** *adj* résidant(e); [chaplain, doctor] à demeure. **2** *n* résident *m*, -e *f*.

residential area *n* quartier *m* résidentiel.

residue [ˈrezɪdjuː] *n* reste *m*; CHEM résidu *m*.

resign [rɪˈzaɪn] **1** *vt* [job] démissionner de. || [accept calmly]: **to ~ o.s. to** se résigner à. **2** *vi*: **to ~ (from)** démissionner (de).

resignation [ˌrezɪgˈneɪʃn] *n* [from job] démission *f*. || [calm acceptance] résignation *f*.

resigned [rɪˈzaɪnd] *adj*: **~ (to)** résigné(e) (à).

resilient [rɪˈzɪlɪənt] *adj* [material] élastique; [person] qui a du ressort.

resin [ˈrezɪn] *n* résine *f*.

resist [rɪˈzɪst] *vt* résister à.

resistance [rɪˈzɪstəns] *n* résistance *f*.

resolute [ˈrezəluːt] *adj* résolu(e).

resolution [ˌrezəˈluːʃn] *n* résolution *f*.

resolve [rɪˈzɒlv] **1** *n* (U) [determination] résolution *f*. **2** *vt* [decide]: **to ~ (that)** ... décider que ...; **to ~ to do sthg** résoudre OR décider de faire qqch. || [solve] résoudre.

resort [rɪˈzɔːt] *n* [for holidays] lieu *m* de vacances. || [recourse] recours *m*; **as a last ~, in the last ~** en dernier ressort OR recours. ○ **resort to** *vt fus* recourir à, avoir recours à.

resound [rɪˈzaʊnd] *vi* [noise] résonner. || [place]: **to ~ with** retentir de.

resounding [rɪˈzaʊndɪŋ] *adj* retentissant(e).

resource [rɪˈsɔːs] *n* ressource *f*.

resourceful [rɪˈsɔːsfʊl] *adj* plein(e) de ressources, débrouillard(e).

respect [rɪˈspekt] **1** *n* [gen]: **~ (for)** respect *m* (pour); **with ~, ...** sauf votre respect, ... || [aspect]: **in this** OR **that ~** à cet égard; **in some ~s** à certains égards. **2** *vt* respecter. ○ **respects** *npl* respects *mpl*, hommages *mpl*. ○ **with respect to** *prep* en ce qui concerne, quant à.

respectable [rɪˈspektəbl] *adj* [morally correct] respectable. || [adequate] raisonnable, honorable.

respectful [rɪˈspektfʊl] *adj* respectueux(euse).

respective [rɪˈspektɪv] *adj* respectif(ive).

respectively [rɪˈspektɪvlɪ] *adv* respectivement.

respite [ˈrespaɪt] *n* répit *m*.

resplendent [rɪˈsplendənt] *adj* resplendissant(e).

respond [rɪˈspɒnd] *vi*: **to ~ (to)** répondre (à).

response [rɪˈspɒns] *n* réponse *f*.

responsibility [rɪˌspɒnsəˈbɪlətɪ] *n*: **~ (for)** responsabilité *f* (de qqch).

responsible [rɪˈspɒnsəbl] *adj* [gen]: **~ (for sthg)** responsable (de qqch). || [job, position] qui comporte des responsabilités.

responsibly [rɪˈspɒnsəblɪ] *adv* de façon responsable.

responsive [rɪˈspɒnsɪv] *adj* [quick to react] qui réagit bien. || [aware]: **~ (to)** attentif(ive) (à).

rest [rest] **1** *n* [remainder]: **the ~ (of)** le reste (de); **the ~ (of them)** les autres *mfpl*. || [relaxation, break] repos *m*; **to have a ~** se reposer. || [support] support *m*, appui *m*. **2** *vt* [relax] faire OR laisser reposer. || [support]: **to ~ sthg on/against** appuyer qqch sur/contre. || *phr*: **~ assured** soyez certain(e). **3** *vi* [relax] se reposer. || [be supported]: **to ~ on/against** s'appuyer sur/contre.

restaurant [ˈrestərɒnt] *n* restaurant *m*.

restful [ˈrestfʊl] *adj* reposant(e).

rest home *n* maison *f* de repos.

restive [ˈrestɪv] *adj* agité(e).

restless [ˈrestlɪs] *adj* agité(e).

restoration [ˌrestəˈreɪʃn] *n* [of law and order, monarchy] rétablissement *m*. || [renovation] restauration *f*.

restore [rɪˈstɔːr] *vt* [law and order, monarchy] rétablir; [confidence] redonner. || [renovate] restaurer. || [give back] rendre, restituer.

restrain [rɪˈstreɪn] *vt* [person, crowd] contenir, retenir; **to ~ o.s. from doing sthg** se retenir de faire qqch.

restrained [rɪˈstreɪnd] *adj* [tone] mesuré(e); [person] qui se domine.

restraint [rɪˈstreɪnt] *n* [restriction] restriction *f*, entrave *f*. || (U) [self-control] mesure *f*, retenue *f*.

restrict [rɪˈstrɪkt] *vt* restreindre, limiter.

restriction [rɪˈstrɪkʃn] *n* restriction *f*, limitation *f*.

restrictive [rɪ'strɪktɪv] *adj* restrictif(ive).

rest room *n Am* toilettes *fpl*.

result [rɪ'zʌlt] **1** *n* résultat *m*; **as a ~ en** conséquence. **2** *vi* [cause]: **to ~ in** aboutir à. || [be caused]: **to ~ (from)** résulter (de).

resume [rɪ'zju:m] *vt & vi* reprendre.

résumé ['rezju:meɪ] *n* [summary] résumé *m*. || *Am* [curriculum vitae] curriculum vitae *m inv*, CV *m*.

resumption [rɪ'zʌmpʃn] *n* reprise *f*.

resurgence [rɪ'sɜ:dʒəns] *n* réapparition *f*.

resurrection [,rezə'rekʃn] *n fig* résurrection *f*.

resuscitation [rɪ,sʌsɪ'teɪʃn] *n* réanimation *f*.

retail ['ri:teɪl] *n* (U) détail *m*.

retailer ['ri:teɪlər] *n* détaillant *m*, -e *f*.

retail price *n* prix *m* de détail.

retain [rɪ'teɪn] *vt* conserver.

retainer [rɪ'teɪnər] *n* [fee] provision *f*.

retaliate [rɪ'tælɪeɪt] *vi* rendre la pareille, se venger.

retaliation [rɪ,tælɪ'eɪʃn] *n* (U) vengeance *f*, représailles *fpl*.

retarded [rɪ'tɑ:dɪd] *adj* retardé(e).

retch [retʃ] *vi* avoir des haut-le-cœur.

retentive [rɪ'tentɪv] *adj* [memory] fidèle.

reticent ['retɪsənt] *adj* peu communicatif(ive).

retina ['retɪnə] (*pl* -nas OR -nae [-ni:]) *n* rétine *f*.

retinue ['retɪnju:] *n* suite *f*.

retire [rɪ'taɪər] *vi* [from work] prendre sa retraite. || [withdraw] se retirer. || [to bed] (aller) se coucher.

retired [rɪ'taɪəd] *adj* à la retraite, retraité(e).

retirement [rɪ'taɪəmənt] *n* retraite *f*.

retiring [rɪ'taɪərɪŋ] *adj* [shy] réservé(e).

retort [rɪ'tɔ:t] **1** *n* [sharp reply] riposte *f*. **2** *vt* riposter.

retrace [rɪ'treɪs] *vt*: **to ~ one's steps** revenir sur ses pas.

retract [rɪ'trækt] **1** *vt* [statement] rétracter. || [undercarriage] rentrer, escamoter; [claws] rentrer. **2** *vi* [undercarriage] rentrer, s'escamoter.

retrain [,ri:'treɪn] *vt* recycler.

retreat [rɪ'tri:t] **1** *n* retraite *f*. **2** *vi* [move away] se retirer; MIL battre en retraite.

retribution [,retrɪ'bju:ʃn] *n* châtiment *m*.

retrieval [rɪ'tri:vl] *n* (U) COMPUT recherche *f* et extraction *f*.

retrieve [rɪ'tri:v] *vt* [get back] récupérer. || COMPUT rechercher et extraire.

retriever [rɪ'tri:vər] *n* [dog] retriever *m*.

retrograde ['retrəgreɪd] *adj* rétrograde.

retrospect ['retrəspekt] *n*: **in ~** après coup.

retrospective [,retrə'spektɪv] *adj* [mood, look] rétrospectif(ive). || JUR [law, pay rise] rétroactif(ive).

return [rɪ'tɜ:n] **1** *n* (U) [arrival back, giving back] retour *m*. || TENNIS renvoi *m*. || [profit] rapport *m*, rendement *m*. **2** *vt* [gen] rendre; [a loan] rembourser; [library book] rapporter. || [send back] renvoyer. || [replace] remettre. || POL élire. **3** *vi* [come back] revenir; [go back] retourner. ○ **returns** *npl* COMM recettes *fpl*; **many happy ~s (of the day)!** bon anniversaire! ○ **in return** *adv* en retour, en échange. ○ **in return for** *prep* en échange de.

reunification [,ri:ju:nɪfɪ'keɪʃn] *n* réunification *f*.

reunion [,ri:'ju:njən] *n* réunion *f*.

reunite [,ri:ju:'naɪt] *vt*: **to be ~d with sb** retrouver qqn.

rev [rev] *inf* **1** *n* (*abbr of* **revolution**) tour *m*. **2** *vt*: **to ~ the engine (up)** emballer le moteur. **3** *vi*: **to ~ (up)** s'emballer.

revamp [,ri:'væmp] *vt inf* [system, department] réorganiser; [house] retaper.

reveal [rɪ'vi:l] *vt* révéler.

revealing [rɪ'vi:lɪŋ] *adj* [clothes - low-cut] décolleté(e); [- transparent] qui laisse deviner le corps. || [comment] révélateur(trice).

reveille [*Br* rɪ'vælɪ, *Am* 'revəlɪ] *n* réveil *m*.

revel ['revl] *vi*: **to ~ in sthg** se délecter de qqch.

revelation [,revə'leɪʃn] *n* révélation *f*.

revenge [rɪ'vendʒ] **1** *n* vengeance *f*. **2** *vt* venger; **to ~ o.s. on sb** se venger de qqn.

revenue ['revənju:] *n* revenu *m*.

reverberate [rɪ'vɜ:bəreɪt] *vi* retentir, se répercuter.

reverberations [rɪ,vɜ:bə'reɪʃnz] *npl* réverbérations *fpl*; *fig* répercussions *fpl*.

revere [rɪ'vɪər] *vt* révérer, vénérer.

reverence ['revərəns] *n* révérence *f*, vénération *f*.

Reverend ['revərənd] *n* révérend *m*.

reverie ['revərɪ] *n* rêverie *f*.

reversal [rɪ'vɜ:sl] *n* [of policy, decision] revirement *m*. || [ill fortune] revers *m* de fortune.

reverse [rɪ'vɜːs] **1** adj [order, process] inverse. **2** n AUT: ~ (gear) marche f arrière. ‖ [opposite]: **the** ~ le contraire. ‖ [back]: **the** ~ [of paper] le verso, le dos; [of coin] le revers. **3** vt [order, positions] inverser; [decision, trend] renverser. ‖ [turn over] retourner. **4** vi AUT faire marche arrière.

revert [rɪ'vɜːt] vi: **to** ~ **to** retourner à.

review [rɪ'vjuː] **1** n [of salary, spending] révision f; [of situation] examen m. ‖ [of book, play etc] critique f, compte rendu m. **2** vt [salary] réviser; [situation] examiner. ‖ [book, play etc] faire la critique de. ‖ Am [study again] réviser.

reviewer [rɪ'vjuːə'] n critique mf.

revile [rɪ'vaɪl] vt injurier.

revise [rɪ'vaɪz] vt [reconsider] modifier. ‖ [rewrite] corriger.

revision [rɪ'vɪʒn] n révision f.

revitalize, -ise [ˌriː'vaɪtəlaɪz] vt revitaliser.

revival [rɪ'vaɪvl] n [of economy, trade] reprise f; [of interest] regain m.

revive [rɪ'vaɪv] **1** vt [person] ranimer. ‖ fig [economy] relancer; [interest] faire renaître; [tradition] rétablir; [musical, play] reprendre; [memories] ranimer, raviver. **2** vi [person] reprendre connaissance. ‖ fig [economy] repartir, reprendre; [hopes] renaître.

revolt [rɪ'vəʊlt] **1** n révolte f. **2** vt révolter, dégoûter. **3** vi se révolter.

revolting [rɪ'vəʊltɪŋ] adj dégoûtant(e); [smell] infect(e).

revolution [ˌrevə'luːʃn] n [gen] révolution f. ‖ TECH tour m, révolution f.

revolutionary [ˌrevə'luːʃnərɪ] **1** adj révolutionnaire. **2** n révolutionnaire mf.

revolve [rɪ'vɒlv] vi: **to** ~ (**around**) tourner (autour de).

revolver [rɪ'vɒlvə'] n revolver m.

revolving door n tambour m.

revue [rɪ'vjuː] n revue f.

revulsion [rɪ'vʌlʃn] n répugnance f.

reward [rɪ'wɔːd] **1** n récompense f. **2** vt: **to** ~ **sb** (**for/with sthg**) récompenser qqn (de/par qqch).

rewarding [rɪ'wɔːdɪŋ] adj [job] qui donne de grandes satisfactions.

rewind [ˌriː'waɪnd] (pt & pp **rewound**) vt [tape] rembobiner.

rewire [ˌriː'waɪə'] vt [house] refaire l'installation électrique de.

reword [ˌriː'wɜːd] vt reformuler.

rewound [ˌriː'waʊnd] pt & pp → **rewind**.

rewrite [ˌriː'raɪt] (pt **rewrote** [ˌriː'rəʊt], pp **rewritten** [ˌriː'rɪtn]) vt récrire.

rhapsody ['ræpsədɪ] n rhapsodie f; **to go into rhapsodies about sthg** s'extasier sur qqch.

rhetoric ['retərɪk] n rhétorique f.

rhetorical question [rɪ'tɒrɪkl-] n question f pour la forme.

rheumatism ['ruːmətɪzm] n (U) rhumatisme m.

Rhine [raɪn] n: **the** ~ le Rhin.

rhino ['raɪnəʊ] (pl inv OR -s), **rhinoceros** [raɪ'nɒsərəs] (pl inv OR -es) n rhinocéros m.

rhododendron [ˌrəʊdə'dendrən] n rhododendron m.

Rhône [rəʊn] n: **the** (**River**) ~ le Rhône.

rhubarb ['ruːbɑːb] n rhubarbe f.

rhyme [raɪm] **1** n [word, technique] rime f. ‖ [poem] poème m. **2** vi: **to** ~ (**with**) rimer (avec).

rhythm ['rɪðm] n rythme m.

rib [rɪb] n ANAT côte f.

ribbed [rɪbd] adj [jumper, fabric] à côtes.

ribbon ['rɪbən] n ruban m.

rice [raɪs] n riz m.

rice pudding n riz m au lait.

rich [rɪtʃ] **1** adj riche; [clothes, fabrics] somptueux(euse). **2** npl: **the** ~ les riches mpl. ○ **riches** npl richesses fpl, richesse f.

richly ['rɪtʃlɪ] adv [rewarded] largement; [provided] très bien. ‖ [sumptuously] richement.

richness ['rɪtʃnɪs] n (U) richesse f.

rickety ['rɪkətɪ] adj branlant(e).

rickshaw ['rɪkʃɔː] n pousse-pousse m inv.

ricochet ['rɪkəʃeɪ] (pt & pp **-ed** OR **-ted**, cont **-ing** OR **-ting**) **1** n ricochet m. **2** vi: **to** ~ (**off**) ricocher (sur).

rid [rɪd] (pt **rid** OR **-ded**, pp **rid**) vt: **to** ~ **sb/sthg of** débarrasser qqn/qqch de; **to get** ~ **of** se débarrasser de.

ridden ['rɪdn] pp → **ride**.

riddle ['rɪdl] n énigme f.

riddled ['rɪdld] adj: **to be** ~ **with** être criblé(e) de.

ride [raɪd] (pt **rode**, pp **ridden**) **1** n promenade f, tour m; **to take sb for a** ~ inf fig faire marcher qqn. **2** vt [travel on]: **to** ~ **a horse/a bicycle** monter à cheval/à bicyclette. ‖ Am [travel in - bus, train, elevator] prendre. ‖ [distance] parcourir, faire. **3** vi [on horseback] monter à cheval, faire du cheval; [on bicycle] faire de la bicyclette OR du vélo; **to ~ in a car/bus** aller en voiture/bus.

rider ['raɪdə^r] n [of horse] cavalier m, -ière f; [of bicycle] cycliste mf; [of motorbike] motocycliste mf.

ridge [rɪdʒ] n [of mountain, roof] crête f, arête f. || [on surface] strie f.

ridicule ['rɪdɪkjuːl] **1** n ridicule m. **2** vt ridiculiser.

ridiculous [rɪ'dɪkjʊləs] adj ridicule.

riding ['raɪdɪŋ] n équitation f.

riding school n école f d'équitation.

rife [raɪf] adj répandu(e).

riffraff ['rɪfræf] n racaille f.

rifle ['raɪfl] **1** n fusil m. **2** vt [drawer, bag] vider.

rifle range n [indoor] stand m de tir; [outdoor] champ m de tir.

rift [rɪft] n GEOL fissure f. || [quarrel] désaccord m.

rig [rɪg] **1** n: (oil) ~ [on land] derrick m; [at sea] plate-forme f de forage. **2** vt [match, election] truquer. ○ **rig up** vt sep installer avec les moyens du bord.

rigging ['rɪgɪŋ] n [of ship] gréement m.

right [raɪt] **1** adj [correct - answer, time] juste, exact(e); [- decision, direction, idea] bon (bonne); **to be ~ (about)** avoir raison (au sujet de). || [morally correct] bien (inv); **to be ~ to do sthg** avoir raison de faire qqch. || [appropriate] qui convient. || [not left] droit(e). **2** n (U) [moral correctness] bien m; **to be in the ~** avoir raison. || [entitlement, claim] droit m; **by ~s** en toute justice. || [not left] droite f. **3** adv [correctly] correctement. || [not left] à droite. || [emphatic use]: ~ **down/up** tout en bas/en haut; ~ **here** ici (même); ~ **in the middle** en plein milieu; ~ **now** tout de suite; ~ **away** immédiatement. **4** vt [injustice, wrong] réparer. **5** excl bon! ○ **Right** n POL: **the Right** la droite.

right angle n angle m droit.

righteous ['raɪtʃəs] adj [person] droit(e); [indignation] justifié(e).

rightful ['raɪtfʊl] adj légitime.

right-hand adj de droite; ~ **side** droite f, côté m droit.

right-hand drive adj avec conduite à droite.

right-handed [-'hændɪd] adj [person] droitier(ière).

right-hand man n bras m droit.

rightly ['raɪtlɪ] adv [answer, believe] correctement. || [behave] bien. || [angry, worried etc] à juste titre.

right of way n AUT priorité f. || [access] droit m de passage.

right wing n: **the ~** la droite. ○ **right-wing** adj de droite.

rigid ['rɪdʒɪd] adj [gen] rigide. || [harsh] strict(e).

rigmarole ['rɪgmərəʊl] n pej [process] comédie f. || [story] galimatias m.

rigor Am = rigour.

rigorous ['rɪgərəs] adj rigoureux(euse).

rigour Br, **rigor** Am ['rɪgə^r] n rigueur f.

rile [raɪl] vt agacer.

rim [rɪm] n [of container] bord m; [of wheel] jante f; [of spectacles] monture f.

rind [raɪnd] n [of fruit] peau f; [of cheese] croûte f; [of bacon] couenne f.

ring [rɪŋ] (pt rang, pp vt sense 1 & vi rung, pt & pp vt sense 2 only ringed) **1** n [telephone call]: **to give sb a ~** donner OR passer un coup de téléphone à qqn. || [sound of bell] sonnerie f. || [circular object] anneau m; [on finger] bague f; [for napkin] rond m. || [of people, trees etc] cercle m. || [for boxing] ring m. || [of criminals, spies] réseau m. **2** vt [bell] (faire) sonner; **to ~ the doorbell** sonner à la porte. || [draw a circle round, surround] entourer. **3** vi [bell, telephone, person] sonner; **to ~ for sb** sonner qqn. || [resound]: **to ~ with** résonner de.

ring binder n classeur m à anneaux.

ringing ['rɪŋɪŋ] n [of bell] sonnerie f; [in ears] tintement m.

ringleader ['rɪŋ,liːdə^r] n chef m.

ringlet ['rɪŋlɪt] n anglaise f.

rink [rɪŋk] n [for ice-skating] patinoire f; [for roller-skating] skating m.

rinse [rɪns] vt rincer.

riot ['raɪət] **1** n émeute f; **to run ~** se déchaîner. **2** vi participer à une émeute.

rioter ['raɪətə^r] n émeutier m, -ière f.

riotous ['raɪətəs] adj [crowd] tapageur(euse); [behaviour] séditieux(ieuse); [party] bruyant(e).

riot police npl ≃ CRS mpl.

rip [rɪp] **1** n déchirure f, accroc m. **2** vt [tear] déchirer. || [remove violently] arracher. **3** vi se déchirer.

RIP (abbr of rest in peace) qu'il/elle repose en paix.

ripe [raɪp] adj mûr(e).

ripen ['raɪpn] vt & vi mûrir.

rip-off n inf: **that's a ~!** c'est de l'escroquerie OR de l'arnaque!

ripple ['rɪpl] **1** n ondulation f, ride f; **a ~ of applause** des applaudissements discrets. **2** vt rider.

rise [raiz] (*pt* **rose**, *pp* **risen** ['rizn]) 1 *n* [to power, fame] ascension *f.* || [slope] côte *f*, pente *f.* || *phr:* **to give ~ to** donner lieu à. 2 *vi* [move upwards] s'élever, monter; **to ~ to power** arriver au pouvoir; **to ~ to fame** devenir célèbre; **to ~ to a challenge/to the occasion** se montrer à la hauteur d'un défi/de la situation. 3 *n* [from chair, bed] se lever. || [increase - gen] monter, augmenter; [- voice, level] s'élever. || [rebel] se soulever.

rising ['raizin] 1 *adj* [ground, tide] montant(e). || [prices, inflation, temperature] en hausse. || [star, politician etc] à l'avenir prometteur. 2 *n* [revolt] soulèvement *m.*

risk [risk] 1 *n* risque *m*, danger *m*; **at one's own ~** à ses risques et périls; **to take a ~** prendre un risque; **at ~** en danger. 2 *vt* [health, life etc] risquer; **to ~ doing sthg** courir le risque de faire qqch.

risky ['riski] *adj* risqué(e).

risqué ['ri:skei] *adj* risqué(e), osé(e).

rite [rait] *n* rite *m.*

ritual ['ritʃuəl] 1 *adj* rituel(elle). 2 *n* rituel *m.*

rival ['raivl] 1 *adj* rival(e), concurrent(e). 2 *n* rival *m*, -e *f.* 3 *vt* rivaliser avec.

rivalry ['raivlri] *n* rivalité *f.*

river ['rivər] *n* rivière *f*, fleuve *m.*

river bank *n* berge *f*, rive *f.*

riverbed ['rivəbed] *n* lit *m* (de rivière OR de fleuve).

riverside ['rivəsaid] *n:* **the ~** le bord de la rivière OR du fleuve.

rivet ['rivit] 1 *n* rivet *m.* 2 *vt* [fasten with rivets] river, riveter. || *fig* [fascinate]: **to be ~ed by** être fasciné(e) par.

Riviera [,rivi'eərə] *n:* **the French ~** la Côte d'Azur; **the Italian ~** la Riviera italienne.

road [rəud] *n* route *f*; [small] chemin *m*; [in town] rue *f*; **by ~** par la route; **on the ~ to** *fig* sur le chemin de.

roadblock ['rəudblɒk] *n* barrage *m* routier.

road hog *n inf pej* chauffard *m.*

road map *n* carte *f* routière.

road safety *n* sécurité *f* routière.

roadside ['rəudsaid] *n:* **the ~** le bord de la route.

road sign *n* panneau *m* routier OR de signalisation.

road tax *n* ≃ vignette *f.*

roadway ['rəudwei] *n* chaussée *f.*

road works [-wɜːks] *npl* travaux *mpl* (de réfection des routes).

roadworthy ['rəud,wɜːði] *adj* en bon état de marche.

roam [rəum] 1 *vt* errer dans. 2 *vi* errer.

roar [rɔːr] 1 *vi* [person, lion] rugir; [wind] hurler; [car] gronder; [plane] vrombir; **to ~ with laughter** se tordre de rire. 2 *vt* hurler. 3 *n* [of person, lion] rugissement *m*; [of traffic] grondement *m*; [of plane, engine] vrombissement *m.*

roaring ['rɔːriŋ] *adj:* **a ~ fire** une belle flambée; **~ drunk** complètement saoul(e); **to do a ~ trade** faire des affaires en or.

roast [rəust] 1 *adj* rôti(e). 2 *n* rôti *m.* 3 *vt* [meat, potatoes] rôtir. || [coffee, nuts etc] griller.

roast beef *n* rôti *m* de bœuf, rosbif *m.*

rob [rɒb] *vt* [person] voler; [bank] dévaliser; **to ~ sb of sthg** [money, goods] voler OR dérober qqch à qqn; [opportunity, glory] enlever qqch à qqn.

robber ['rɒbər] *n* voleur *m*, -euse *f.*

robbery ['rɒbəri] *n* vol *m.*

robe [rəub] *n* [gen] robe *f.* || *Am* [dressing gown] peignoir *m.*

robin ['rɒbin] *n* rouge-gorge *m.*

robot ['rəubɒt] *n* robot *m.*

robust [rəu'bʌst] *adj* robuste.

rock [rɒk] 1 *n* (*U*) [substance] roche *f.* || [boulder] rocher *m.* || *Am* [pebble] caillou *m.* || [music] rock *m.* 2 *comp* [music, band] de rock. 3 *vt* [baby] bercer; [cradle, boat] balancer. || [shock] secouer. 4 *vi* (se) balancer. ○ **on the rocks** *adv* [drink] avec de la glace OR des glaçons. || [marriage, relationship] près de la rupture.

rock and roll *n* rock *m*, rock and roll *m.*

rock bottom *n:* **to hit ~** toucher le fond. ○ **rock-bottom** *adj* [price] sacrifié(e).

rockery ['rɒkəri] *n* rocaille *f.*

rocket ['rɒkit] 1 *n* [gen] fusée *f.* || MIL fusée *f*, roquette *f.* 2 *vi* monter en flèche.

rocket launcher [-,lɔːntʃər] *n* lance-fusées *m inv*, lance-roquettes *m inv.*

rocking chair ['rɒkiŋ-] *n* fauteuil *m* à bascule, rocking-chair *m.*

rocking horse ['rɒkiŋ-] *n* cheval *m* à bascule.

rock'n'roll [,rɒkən'rəul] = **rock and roll.**

rocky ['rɒki] *adj* [ground, road] rocailleux(euse), caillouteux(euse). || *fig* [economy, marriage] précaire.

Rocky Mountains npl: **the ~** les montagnes fpl Rocheuses.

rod [rɒd] n [metal] tige f; [wooden] baguette f; (fishing) ~ canne f à pêche.

rode [rəʊd] pt → ride.

rodent ['rəʊdənt] n rongeur m.

roe [rəʊ] n (U) œufs mpl de poisson.

roe deer n chevreuil m.

rogue [rəʊg] n [likeable rascal] coquin m. || dated [dishonest person] filou m, crapule f.

role [rəʊl] n rôle m.

roll [rəʊl] 1 n [of material, paper etc] rouleau m. || [of bread] petit pain m. || [list] liste f. || [of drums, thunder] roulement m. 2 vt rouler; [log, ball etc] faire rouler. 3 vi rouler. ○ **roll about, roll around** vi [person] se rouler; [object] rouler çà et là. ○ **roll over** vi se retourner. ○ **roll up** vt sep [carpet, paper etc] rouler. || [sleeves] retrousser. 2 vi inf [arrive] s'amener, se pointer.

roll call n appel m.

roller ['rəʊlər] n rouleau m.

roller coaster n montagnes fpl russes.

roller skate n patin m à roulettes.

rolling pin n rouleau m à pâtisserie.

rolling stock n matériel m roulant.

ROM [rɒm] (abbr of read only memory) n ROM f.

Roman ['rəʊmən] 1 adj romain(e). 2 n Romain m, -e f.

Roman Catholic 1 adj catholique. 2 n catholique mf.

romance [rəʊ'mæns] n (U) [romantic quality] charme m. || [love affair] idylle f.

Romania [ru:'meɪnjə] n Roumanie f.

Romanian [ru:'meɪnjən] 1 adj roumain(e). 2 n [person] Roumain m, -e f. || [language] roumain m.

Roman numerals npl chiffres mpl romains.

romantic [rəʊ'mæntɪk] adj romantique.

Rome [rəʊm] n Rome.

romp [rɒmp] 1 n ébats mpl. 2 vi s'ébattre.

roof [ru:f] n toit m; [of cave, tunnel] plafond m; **the ~ of the mouth** la voûte du palais; **to go through** OR **hit the ~** fig exploser.

roofing ['ru:fɪŋ] n toiture f.

roof rack n galerie f.

rooftop ['ru:ftɒp] n toit m.

rook [rʊk] n [bird] freux m. || [chess piece] tour f.

rookie ['rʊkɪ] n Am inf bleu m.

room [ru:m, rʊm] n [in building] pièce f. || [bedroom] chambre f. || (U) [space] place f.

rooming house ['ru:mɪŋ-] n Am maison f de rapport.

roommate ['ru:mmeɪt] n camarade mf de chambre.

room service n service m dans les chambres.

roomy ['ru:mɪ] adj spacieux(ieuse).

roost [ru:st] 1 n perchoir m, juchoir m. 2 vi se percher, se jucher.

rooster ['ru:stər] n coq m.

root [ru:t] 1 n racine f; fig [of problem] origine f; **to take ~** lit & fig prendre racine. 2 vi: **to ~ through** fouiller dans. ○ **roots** npl racines fpl. ○ **root for** vt fus Am inf encourager. ○ **root out** vt sep [eradicate] extirper.

rope [rəʊp] 1 n corde f; **to know the ~s** connaître son affaire, être au courant. 2 vt corder; [climbers] encorder. ○ **rope in** vt sep inf fig enrôler.

rosary ['rəʊzərɪ] n rosaire m.

rose [rəʊz] 1 pt → rise. 2 adj [pink] rose. 3 n [flower] rose f.

rosé ['rəʊzeɪ] n rosé m.

rosebud ['rəʊzbʌd] n bouton m de rose.

rose bush n rosier m.

rosemary ['rəʊzmərɪ] n romarin m.

rosette [rəʊ'zet] n rosette f.

roster ['rɒstər] n liste f, tableau m.

rostrum ['rɒstrəm] (pl -trums OR -tra [-trə]) n tribune f.

rosy ['rəʊzɪ] adj rose.

rot [rɒt] 1 n (U) [decay] pourriture f. 2 vt & vi pourrir.

rota ['rəʊtə] n liste f, tableau m.

rotary ['rəʊtərɪ] 1 adj rotatif(ive). 2 n Am [roundabout] rond-point m.

rotate [rəʊ'teɪt] 1 vt [turn] faire tourner. 2 vi [turn] tourner.

rotation [rəʊ'teɪʃn] n [turning movement] rotation f.

rote [rəʊt] n: **by ~** de façon machinale, par cœur.

rotten ['rɒtn] adj [decayed] pourri(e). || inf [bad] moche. || inf [unwell]: **to feel ~** se sentir mal fichu(e).

rouge [ru:ʒ] n rouge m à joues.

rough [rʌf] 1 adj [not smooth - surface] rugueux(euse), rêche; [- road] accidenté(e); [- sea] agité(e), houleux(euse); [- crossing] mauvais(e). || [person, treatment] brutal(e); [manners, conditions] rude; [area] mal fréquenté(e). || [guess] approximatif(ive); **~ copy, ~ draft**

brouillon *m*; ~ **sketch** ébauche *f.* || [harsh
- voice, wine] âpre; [- life] dur(e); **to have
a ~ time** en baver. **2** *adv*: **to sleep ~** coucher à la dure. **3** *n* GOLF rough *m.* || [undetailed form]: **in ~** au brouillon. **4** *vt phr*:
to ~ it vivre à la dure.

roughage ['rʌfɪdʒ] *n* (*U*) fibres *fpl* alimentaires.

rough and ready *adj* rudimentaire.

roughen ['rʌfn] *vt* rendre rugueux(euse) OR rêche.

roughly ['rʌflɪ] *adv* [approximately] approximativement. || [handle, treat] brutalement. || [built, made] grossièrement.

roulette [ruː'let] *n* roulette *f.*

round [raund] **1** *adj* rond(e). **2** *prep* autour de; ~ **here** par ici; **all ~ the country**
dans tout le pays; **just ~ the corner** au
coin de la rue; *fig* tout près; **to go ~ sthg**
[obstacle] contourner qqch; **to go ~ a museum** visiter un musée. **3** *adv* [surrounding]: **all ~** tout autour. || [near]: ~ **about**
dans le coin. || [in measurements]: **10
metres ~** 10 mètres de diamètre. || [to
other side]: **to go ~** faire le tour; **to turn ~**
se retourner; **to look ~** se retourner (pour
regarder). || [at or to nearby place]: **come
~ and see us** venez OR passez nous voir;
he's ~ at her house il est chez elle. || [approximately]: ~ **(about)** vers, environ. **4** *n*
[of talks etc] série *f*; **a ~ of applause** une
salve d'applaudissements. || [of competition] manche *f.* || [of doctor] visites *fpl*;
[of postman, milkman] tournée *f.* || [of
ammunition] cartouche *f.* || [of drinks]
tournée *f*, BOXING reprise *f*, round *m.* ||
GOLF partie *f.* **5** *vt* [corner] tourner; [bend]
prendre. ○ **rounds** *npl* [of doctor] visites *fpl.* ○ **round off** *vt sep* terminer,
conclure. ○ **round up** *vt sep* [gather together] rassembler. || MATH arrondir.

roundly ['raundlɪ] *adv* [beaten] complètement; [condemned etc] franchement,
carrément.

round-shouldered [-'ʃəuldəd] *adj*
voûté(e).

round trip *n* aller et retour *m.*

roundup ['raundʌp] *n* [summary] résumé *m.*

rouse [rauz] *vt* [wake up] réveiller. ||
[impel]: **to ~ o.s. to do sthg** se forcer à
faire qqch; **to ~ sb to action** pousser OR
inciter qqn à agir. || [emotions] susciter,
provoquer.

rousing ['rauzɪŋ] *adj* [speech] vibrant(e), passionné(e); [welcome] enthousiaste.

rout [raut] **1** *n* déroute *f.* **2** *vt* mettre en
déroute.

route [ruːt] **1** *n* [gen] itinéraire *m.* || *fig*
[way] chemin *m*, voie *f.* **2** *vt* [goods] acheminer.

route map *n* [for journey] croquis *m*
d'itinéraire; [for buses, trains] carte *f* du
réseau.

routine [ruː'tiːn] **1** *adj* [normal] habituel(elle), de routine. || *pej* [uninteresting] de routine. **2** *n* routine *f.*

roving ['rəuvɪŋ] *adj* itinérant(e).

row¹ [rəu] **1** *n* [line] rangée *f*; [of seats]
rang *m.* || *fig* [of defeats, victories] série *f*;
in a ~ d'affilée, de suite. **2** *vt* [boat] faire
aller à la rame; [person] transporter en
canot OR bateau. **3** *vi* ramer.

row² [rau] **1** *n* [quarrel] dispute *f*, querelle *f.* || *inf* [noise] vacarme *m*, raffut *m.*
2 *vi* [quarrel] se disputer, se quereller.

rowboat ['rəubəut] *n Am* canot *m.*

rowdy ['raudɪ] *adj* chahuteur(euse), tapageur(euse).

row house [rəu-] *n Am* maison attenante aux maisons voisines.

rowing ['rəuɪŋ] *n* SPORT aviron *m.*

royal ['rɔɪəl] *adj* royal(e).

Royal Air Force *n*: **the ~** l'armée *f* de
l'air britannique.

royal family *n* famille *f* royale.

Royal Navy *n*: **the ~** la marine de
guerre britannique.

royalty ['rɔɪəltɪ] *n* royauté *f.* ○ **royalties** *npl* droits *mpl* d'auteur.

RSVP (*abbr of* **répondez s'il vous plaît**)
RSVP.

rub [rʌb] **1** *vt* frotter; **to ~ sthg in** [cream
etc] faire pénétrer qqch (en frottant); **to
~ sb up the wrong way** *Br*, **to ~ sb the
wrong way** *Am fig* prendre qqn à
rebrousse-poil. **2** *vi* frotter. ○ **rub off
on** *vt fus* [subj: quality] déteindre sur.
○ **rub out** *vt sep* [erase] effacer.

rubber ['rʌbər] **1** *adj* en caoutchouc. **2** *n*
[substance] caoutchouc *m.* || *Am inf* [condom] préservatif *m.* || [in bridge] robre *m*,
rob *m.*

rubber band *n* élastique *m.*

rubber stamp *n* tampon *m.*
○ **rubber-stamp** *vt fig* approuver sans
discussion.

rubbish ['rʌbɪʃ] **1** *n* (*U*) [refuse] détritus *mpl*, ordures *fpl.* || *inf fig* [worthless
objects] camelote *f*; **the play was ~** la
pièce était nulle. || *inf* [nonsense] bêtises
fpl, inepties *fpl.* **2** *vt inf* débiner.

rubble ['rʌbl] *n* (*U*) décombres *mpl.*

run

ruby ['ru:bɪ] *n* rubis *m*.

rucksack ['rʌksæk] *n* sac *m* à dos.

rudder ['rʌdər] *n* gouvernail *m*.

ruddy ['rʌdɪ] *adj* [complexion, face] coloré(e). || *Br inf dated* [damned] sacré(e).

rude [ru:d] *adj* [impolite - gen] impoli(e); [- word] grossier(ière); [- noise] incongru(e). || [sudden]: **it was a ~ awakening** le réveil fut pénible.

rudimentary [,ru:dɪ'mentərɪ] *adj* rudimentaire.

rueful ['ru:fʊl] *adj* triste.

ruffian ['rʌfjən] *n* voyou *m*.

ruffle ['rʌfl] *vt* [hair] ébouriffer; [water] troubler. || [person] froisser; [composure] faire perdre.

rug [rʌg] *n* [carpet] tapis *m*. || [blanket] couverture *f*.

rugby ['rʌgbɪ] *n* rugby *m*.

rugged ['rʌgɪd] *adj* [landscape] accidenté(e); [features] rude.

ruin ['ru:ɪn] 1 *n* ruine *f*. 2 *vt* ruiner; [clothes, shoes] abîmer. ○ **in ruin(s)** *adv lit & fig* en ruine.

rule [ru:l] 1 *n* [gen] règle *f*; **as a ~** en règle générale. || [regulation] règlement *m*. || (*U*) [control] autorité *f*. 2 *vt* [control] dominer. || [govern] gouverner. || [decide]: **to ~ (that)** ... décider que .... 3 *vi* [give decision - gen] décider; [- JUR] statuer. || *fml* [be paramount] prévaloir. || [king, queen] régner; POL gouverner. ○ **rule out** *vt sep* exclure, écarter.

ruled [ru:ld] *adj* [paper] réglé(e).

ruler ['ru:lər] *n* [for measurement] règle *f*. || [leader] chef *m* d'État.

ruling ['ru:lɪŋ] 1 *adj* au pouvoir. 2 *n* décision *f*.

rum [rʌm] *n* rhum *m*.

Rumania [ru:'meɪnjə] = Romania.

Rumanian [ru:'meɪnjən] = Romanian.

rumble ['rʌmbl] 1 *n* [of thunder, traffic] grondement *m*; [in stomach] gargouillement *m*. 2 *vi* [thunder, traffic] gronder; [stomach] gargouiller.

rummage ['rʌmɪdʒ] *vi* fouiller.

rumour *Br*, **rumor** *Am* ['ru:mər] *n* rumeur *f*.

rumoured *Br*, **rumored** *Am* ['ru:məd] *adj*: **he is ~ to be very wealthy** le bruit court ON on dit qu'il est très riche.

rump [rʌmp] *n* [of animal] croupe *f*. || *inf* [of person] derrière *m*.

rump steak *n* romsteck *m*.

rumpus ['rʌmpəs] *n inf* chahut *m*.

run [rʌn] (*pt* ran, *pp* run) 1 *n* [on foot] course *f*; **to go for a ~** faire un petit peu de course à pied; **on the ~** en fuite, en cavale. || [in car - for pleasure] tour *m*; [- journey] trajet *m*. || [series] suite *f*, série *f*; **a ~ of bad luck** une période de déveine; **in the short/long ~** à court/long terme. || THEATRE: **to have a long ~** tenir longtemps l'affiche. || [great demand]: **~ on** ruée *f* sur. || [in tights] échelle *f*. || [in cricket, baseball] point *m*. || [track - for skiing, bobsleigh] piste *f*. 2 *vt* [race, distance] courir. || [manage - business] diriger; [- shop, hotel] tenir; [- course] organiser. || [operate] faire marcher. || [car] avoir, entretenir. || [water, bath] faire couler. || [publish] publier. || *inf* [drive]: **can you ~ me to the station?** tu peux m'amener OR me conduire à la gare? || [move]: **to ~ sthg along/over sthg** passer qqch le long de/sur qqch. 3 *vi* [on foot] courir. || [pass - road, river, pipe] passer; **to ~ through sthg** traverser qqch. || *Am* [in election]: **to ~ (for)** être candidat (à). || [operate - machine, factory] tourner; [- engine] tourner; **everything is running smoothly** tout va comme sur des roulettes, tout va bien; **to ~ on sthg** marcher à qqch; **to ~ off sthg** marcher sur qqch. || [bus, train] faire le service; **trains ~ every hour** il y a un train toutes les heures. || [flow] couler; **my nose is running** j'ai le nez qui coule. || [colour] déteindre; [ink] baver. || [continue - contract, insurance policy] être valide; [- THEATRE] se jouer. ○ **run across** *vt fus* [meet] rencontrer. ○ **run away** *vi* [flee]: **to ~ away (from)** s'enfuir (de); **to ~ away from home** faire une fugue. ○ **run down** 1 *vt sep* [in vehicle] renverser. || [criticize] dénigrer. || [production] restreindre; [industry] réduire l'activité de. 2 *vi* [clock] s'arrêter; [battery] se décharger. ○ **run into** *vt fus* [encounter - problem] se heurter à; [- person] tomber sur. || [in vehicle] rentrer dans. ○ **run off** 1 *vt sep* [a copy] tirer. 2 *vi*: **to ~ off (with)** s'enfuir (avec). ○ **run out** *vi* [food, supplies] s'épuiser; **time is running out** il ne reste plus beaucoup de temps. || [licence, contract] expirer. ○ **run out of** *vt fus* manquer de; **to ~ out of petrol** tomber en panne d'essence, tomber en panne sèche. ○ **run over** *vt sep* renverser. ○ **run through** *vt fus* [practise] répéter. || [read through] parcourir. ○ **run to** *vt fus* [amount to] monter à, s'élever à. ○ **run up** *vt fus* [bill, debt] laisser accumuler. ○ **run up against** *vt fus* se heurter à.

runaway ['rʌnəweɪ] **1** adj [train, lorry] fou (folle); [horse] emballé(e); [victory] haut la main; [inflation] galopant(e). **2** n fuyard m, fugitif m, -ive f.

rundown ['rʌndaʊn] n [report] bref résumé m. ○ **run-down** adj [building] délabré(e). || [person] épuisé(e).

rung [rʌŋ] **1** pp → **ring**. **2** n échelon m, barreau m.

runner ['rʌnəʳ] n [athlete] coureur m, -euse f. || [of guns, drugs] contrebandier m. || [of sledge] patin m; [for car seat] glissière f; [for drawer] coulisseau m.

runner-up (pl **runners-up**) n second m, -e f.

running ['rʌnɪŋ] **1** adj [argument, battle] continu(e). || [consecutive]: **three weeks** ~ trois semaines de suite. || [water] courant(e). **2** n (U) SPORT course f; **to go** ~ faire de la course. || [management] direction f, administration f. || [of machine] marche f, fonctionnement m. || phr: **to be in the** ~ **(for)** avoir des chances de réussir (dans); **to be out of the** ~ **(for)** n'avoir aucune chance de réussir (dans).

runny ['rʌnɪ] adj [food] liquide. || [nose] qui coule.

run-of-the-mill adj banal(e), ordinaire.

runt [rʌnt] n avorton m.

run-up n [preceding time]: **in the** ~ **to** sthg dans la période qui précède qqch. || SPORT course f d'élan.

runway ['rʌnweɪ] n piste f.

rupture ['rʌptʃəʳ] n rupture f.

rural ['rʊərəl] adj rural(e).

ruse [ruːz] n ruse f.

rush [rʌʃ] **1** n [hurry] hâte f. || [surge] ruée f, bousculade f; **to make a** ~ **for** sthg se ruer ou se précipiter vers qqch. || [demand]: ~ **(on** OR **for)** ruée f (sur). **2** vt [hurry - work] faire à la hâte; [- person] bousculer. || [send quickly] transporter OR envoyer d'urgence. || [attack suddenly] prendre d'assaut. **3** vi [hurry] se dépêcher; **to** ~ **into** sthg faire qqch sans réfléchir. || [move quickly, suddenly] se précipiter, se ruer. ○ **rushes** npl BOT joncs mpl.

rush hour n heures fpl de pointe OR d'affluence.

rusk [rʌsk] n biscotte f.

Russia ['rʌʃə] n Russie f.

Russian ['rʌʃn] **1** adj russe. **2** n [person] Russe mf. || [language] russe m.

rust [rʌst] **1** n rouille f. **2** vi se rouiller.

rustic ['rʌstɪk] adj rustique.

rustle ['rʌsl] **1** vt [paper] froisser. || Am [cattle] voler. **2** vi [leaves] bruire; [papers] produire un froissement.

rusty ['rʌstɪ] adj lit & fig rouillé(e).

rut [rʌt] n ornière f; **to be in a** ~ être prisonnier de la routine.

ruthless ['ruːθlɪs] adj impitoyable.

RV n Am (abbr of **recreational vehicle**) camping-car m.

rye [raɪ] n [grain] seigle m.

rye bread n pain m de seigle.

s (pl **ss** OR **s's**), **S** (pl **Ss** OR **S's**) [es] n [letter] s m inv, S m inv. ○ **S** (abbr of **south**) S.

Sabbath ['sæbəθ] n: **the** ~ **le** sabbat.

sabbatical [sə'bætɪkl] n année f sabbatique.

sabotage ['sæbətɑːʒ] **1** n sabotage m. **2** vt saboter.

saccharin(e) ['sækərɪn] n saccharine f.

sachet ['sæʃeɪ] n sachet m.

sack [sæk] **1** n [bag] sac m.

sacking ['sækɪŋ] n [fabric] toile f à sac.

sacred ['seɪkrɪd] adj sacré(e).

sacrifice ['sækrɪfaɪs] lit & fig **1** n sacrifice m. **2** vt sacrifier.

sacrilege ['sækrɪlɪdʒ] n lit & fig sacrilège m.

sacrosanct ['sækrəʊsæŋkt] adj sacrosaint(e).

sad [sæd] adj triste.

sadden ['sædn] vt attrister, affliger.

saddle ['sædl] **1** n selle f. **2** vt [horse] seller. || fig [burden]: **to** ~ **sb with** sthg coller qqch à qqn.

saddlebag ['sædlbæg] n sacoche f.

sadistic [sə'dɪstɪk] adj sadique.

sadly ['sædlɪ] adv [unhappily] tristement. || [unfortunately] malheureusement.

sadness ['sædnɪs] n tristesse f.

safari [sə'fɑːrɪ] n safari m.

safe [seɪf] **1** adj [not dangerous - gen] sans danger; [- driver, play, guess] prudent(e); **it's** ~ **to say (that)** ... on peut dire

same

à coup sûr que .... || [not in danger] hors de danger, en sécurité; **~ and sound** sain et sauf (saine et sauve). || [not risky - bet, method] sans risque; [- investment] sûr(e); **to be on the ~ side** par précaution. **2** n coffre-fort m.

safe-conduct n sauf-conduit m.

safe-deposit box n coffre-fort m.

safeguard ['seɪfgɑːd] **1** n: **~ (against)** sauvegarde f (contre). **2** vt: **to ~ sb/sthg (against)** sauvegarder qqn/qqch (contre), protéger qqn/qqch (contre).

safekeeping [,seɪf'kiːpɪŋ] n bonne garde f.

safely ['seɪflɪ] adv [not dangerously] sans danger. || [not in danger] en toute sécurité, à l'abri du danger. || [arrive - person] à bon port, sain et sauf (saine et sauve); [- parcel] à bon port. || [for certain]: **I can ~ say (that)** ... je peux dire à coup sûr que ....

safe sex n sexe m sans risque, S.S.R. m.

safety ['seɪftɪ] n sécurité f.

safety belt n ceinture f de sécurité.

safety pin n épingle f de sûreté OR de nourrice.

saffron ['sæfrən] n safran m.

sag [sæg] vi (sink downwards] s'affaisser, fléchir.

sage [seɪdʒ] **1** adj sage. **2** n (U) [herb] sauge f. || [wise man] sage m.

Sagittarius [,sædʒɪ'teərɪəs] n Sagittaire m.

Sahara [sə'hɑːrə] n: **the ~ (Desert)** le (désert du) Sahara.

said [sed] pt & pp → **say**.

sail [seɪl] **1** n [of boat] voile f; **to set ~** faire voile, prendre la mer. || [journey] tour m en bateau. **2** vt [boat] piloter, manœuvrer. || [sea] parcourir. **3** vi [person - gen] aller en bateau; [- SPORT] faire de la voile. || [boat - move] naviguer; [- leave] partir, prendre la mer. || fig [through air] voler. ○ **sail through** vt fus fig réussir les doigts dans le nez.

sailboat Am = **sailing boat**.

sailing ['seɪlɪŋ] n (U) SPORT voile f; **to go ~** faire de la voile. || [departure] départ m.

sailing boat Br, **sailboat** Am ['seɪlbəʊt] n bateau m à voiles, voilier m.

sailing ship n voilier m.

sailor ['seɪlər] n marin m, matelot m.

saint [seɪnt] n saint m, -e f.

saintly ['seɪntlɪ] adj [person] saint(e); [life] de saint.

sake [seɪk] n: **for the ~ of sb** par égard pour qqn, pour (l'amour de) qqn; **for the ~ of argument** à titre d'exemple; **for God's** OR **heaven's ~** pour l'amour de Dieu OR du ciel.

salad ['sæləd] n salade f.

salad bowl n saladier m.

salad dressing n vinaigrette f.

salami [sə'lɑːmɪ] n salami m.

salary ['sælərɪ] n salaire m, traitement m.

sale [seɪl] n [gen] vente f; **on ~** en vente; **(up) for ~** à vendre. || [at reduced prices] soldes mpl. ○ **sales** npl [quantity sold] ventes fpl. || [at reduced prices]: **the ~s** les soldes mpl.

saleroom Br ['seɪlrum], **salesroom** Am ['seɪlzrum] n salle f des ventes.

sales assistant ['seɪlz-], **salesclerk** ['seɪlzklɜːrk] Am n vendeur m, -euse f.

salesman ['seɪlzmən] (pl -men [-mən]) n [in shop] vendeur m; [travelling] représentant m de commerce.

salesroom Am = **saleroom**.

saleswoman ['seɪlz,wumən] (pl -women [-,wɪmɪn]) n [in shop] vendeuse f; [travelling] représentante f de commerce.

salient ['seɪljənt] adj fml qui ressort.

saliva [sə'laɪvə] n salive f.

sallow ['sæləʊ] adj cireux(euse).

salmon ['sæmən] (pl inv OR -s) n saumon m.

salmonella [,sælmə'nelə] n salmonelle f.

salon ['sælɒn] n salon m.

saloon [sə'luːn] n Am [bar] saloon m. || [in ship] salon m.

salt [sɔːlt, sɒlt] **1** n sel m. **2** vt [food] saler; [roads] mettre du sel sur.

salt cellar Br, **salt shaker** Am [-,ʃeɪkər] n salière f.

saltwater ['sɔːlt,wɔːtər] **1** n eau f de mer. **2** adj de mer.

salty ['sɔːltɪ] adj [food] salé(e); [water] saumâtre.

salutary ['sæljʊtrɪ] adj salutaire.

salute [sə'luːt] **1** n salut m. **2** vt saluer. **3** vi faire un salut.

salvage ['sælvɪdʒ] **1** n (U) [rescue of ship] sauvetage m. || [property rescued] biens mpl sauvés. **2** vt sauver.

salvation [sæl'veɪʃn] n salut m.

Salvation Army n: **the ~** l'Armée f du Salut.

same [seɪm] **1** adj même; **at the ~ time** en même temps; **one and the ~** un seul et même (une seule et même). **2** *pron*: **the ~** le même (la même), les mêmes (*pl*); **I'll have the ~ as you** je prendrai la même chose que toi; **she earns the ~ as I do** elle gagne autant que moi; **to do the ~** faire de même, en faire autant; **all** OR **just the ~** [anyway] quand même, tout de même; **it's all the ~ to me** ça m'est égal; **it's not the ~** ce n'est pas pareil. **3** *adv*: **the ~** [treat, spelled] de la même manière.

sample ['sɑːmpl] **1** *n* échantillon *m*. **2** *vt* [taste] goûter.

sanatorium (*pl* **-riums** OR **-ria** [-rɪə]), **sanitorium** *Am* (*pl* **-riums** OR **-ria** [-rɪə]) [ˌsænəˈtɔːrɪəm] *n* sanatorium *m*.

sanctimonious [ˌsæŋktɪˈməʊnjəs] *adj* moralisateur(trice).

sanction ['sæŋkʃn] **1** *n* sanction *f*. **2** *vt* sanctionner.

sanctity ['sæŋktətɪ] *n* sainteté *f*.

sanctuary ['sæŋktʃʊərɪ] *n* [for birds, wildlife] réserve *f*. || [refuge] asile *m*.

sand [sænd] **1** *n* sable *m*. **2** *vt* [wood] poncer.

sandal ['sændl] *n* sandale *f*.

sandbox *Am* = **sandpit**.

sandcastle ['sænd,kɑːsl] *n* château *m* de sable.

sand dune *n* dune *f*.

sandpaper ['sænd,peɪpə'] **1** *n* (*U*) papier *m* de verre. **2** *vt* poncer (au papier de verre).

sandpit *Br* ['sændpɪt], **sandbox** *Am* ['sændbɒks] *n* bac *m* à sable.

sandstone ['sændstəʊn] *n* grès *m*.

sandwich ['sænwɪdʒ] **1** *n* sandwich *m*. **2** *vt fig*: **to be ~ed between** être (pris(e)) en sandwich entre.

sandwich board *n* panneau *m* publicitaire (*d'homme sandwich ou posé comme un tréteau*).

sandy ['sændɪ] *adj* [beach] de sable; [earth] sableux(euse). || [sand-coloured] sable (*inv*).

sane [seɪn] *adj* [not mad] sain(e) d'esprit. || [sensible] raisonnable, sensé(e).

sang [sæŋ] *pt* → **sing**.

sanitary ['sænɪtrɪ] *adj* [method, system] sanitaire. || [clean] hygiénique, salubre.

sanitary towel, **sanitary napkin** *Am* *n* serviette *f* hygiénique.

sanitation [ˌsænɪˈteɪʃn] *n* (*U*) [in house] installations *fpl* sanitaires.

sanitorium *Am* = **sanatorium**.

sanity ['sænətɪ] *n* (*U*) [saneness] santé *f* mentale, raison *f*. || [good sense] bon sens *m*.

sank [sæŋk] *pt* → **sink**.

Santa (Claus) ['sæntə,(klɔːz)] *n* le père Noël.

sap [sæp] **1** *n* [of plant] sève *f*. **2** *vt* [weaken] saper.

sapling ['sæplɪŋ] *n* jeune arbre *m*.

sapphire ['sæfaɪə'] *n* saphir *m*.

sarcastic [sɑːˈkæstɪk] *adj* sarcastique.

sardine [sɑːˈdiːn] *n* sardine *f*.

Sardinia [sɑːˈdɪnjə] *n* Sardaigne *f*.

sardonic [sɑːˈdɒnɪk] *adj* sardonique.

SASE *abbr of* **self-addressed stamped envelope**.

sash [sæʃ] *n* [of cloth] écharpe *f*.

sat [sæt] *pt & pp* → **sit**.

SAT [sæt] *n* (*abbr of* **Scholastic Aptitude Test**) *examen d'entrée à l'université aux États-Unis*.

Satan ['seɪtn] *n* Satan *m*.

satchel ['sætʃəl] *n* cartable *m*.

satellite ['sætəlaɪt] **1** *n* satellite *m*. **2** *comp* [link] par satellite; **~ dish** antenne *f* parabolique.

satellite TV *n* télévision *f* par satellite.

satin ['sætɪn] **1** *n* satin *m*. **2** *comp* [sheets, pyjamas] de OR en satin; [wallpaper, finish] satiné(e).

satire ['sætaɪə'] *n* satire *f*.

satisfaction [ˌsætɪsˈfækʃn] *n* satisfaction *f*.

satisfactory [ˌsætɪsˈfæktərɪ] *adj* satisfaisant(e).

satisfied ['sætɪsfaɪd] *adj* [happy]: **~ (with)** satisfait(e) (de).

satisfy ['sætɪsfaɪ] *vt* [gen] satisfaire. || [convince] convaincre, persuader.

satisfying ['sætɪsfaɪɪŋ] *adj* satisfaisant(e).

satsuma [ˌsætˈsuːmə] *n* satsuma *f*.

saturate ['sætʃəreɪt] *vt*: **to ~ sthg (with)** saturer qqch (de).

Saturday ['sætədɪ] **1** *n* samedi *m*; **it's ~** on est samedi; **on ~** samedi; **on ~s** le samedi; **last ~** samedi dernier; **this ~** ce samedi; **next ~** samedi prochain; **every ~** tous les samedis; **every other ~** un samedi sur deux; **the ~ before** l'autre samedi; **the ~ before last** pas samedi dernier, mais le samedi d'avant; **the ~ after next**, **~ week, a week on ~** samedi en huit. **2** *comp* [paper] du OR de samedi; **~ morning/afternoon/evening** samedi matin/après-midi/soir.

sauce [sɔːs] *n* CULIN sauce *f*.

saucepan ['sɔːspən] *n* casserole *f*.

saucer ['sɔːsər] *n* sous-tasse *f*, soucoupe *f*.

saucy ['sɔːsɪ] *adj inf* coquin(e).

Saudi Arabia [ˌsaʊdɪ'reɪbɪə] *n* Arabie Saoudite *f*.

Saudi (Arabian) ['saʊdɪ-] 1 *adj* saoudien(ienne). 2 *n* [person] Saoudien *m*, -ienne *f*.

sauna ['sɔːnə] *n* sauna *m*.

saunter ['sɔːntər] *vi* flâner.

sausage ['sɒsɪdʒ] *n* saucisse *f*.

sauté [*Br* 'sɔʊteɪ, *Am* sɔʊ'teɪ] (*pt & pp* **sautéed** OR **sautéd**) 1 *adj* sauté(e). 2 *vt* [potatoes] faire sauter; [onions] faire revenir.

savage ['sævɪdʒ] 1 *adj* [fierce] féroce. 2 *n* sauvage *mf*. 3 *vt* attaquer avec férocité.

save [seɪv] 1 *vt* [rescue] sauver; **to ~ sb's life** sauver la vie à qqn. || [strength] économiser; [food] garder; [money - set aside] mettre de côté; [- spend less] économiser. || [avoid] éviter, épargner; **to ~ sb sthg** épargner qqch à qqn; **to ~ sb from doing sthg** éviter à qqn de faire qqch. || SPORT arrêter. || COMPUT sauvegarder. 2 *vi* [save money] mettre de l'argent de côté. 3 *n* SPORT arrêt *m*. 4 *prep fml*: ~ (for) sauf, à l'exception de. ○ **save up** *vi* mettre de l'argent de côté.

saving grace ['seɪvɪŋ-] *n*: **it's ~ was ...** ce qui le rachetait, c'était ....

savings ['seɪvɪŋz] *npl* économies *fpl*.

savings account *n Am* compte *m* d'épargne.

savings and loan association *n Am* société *f* de crédit immobilier.

savings bank *n* caisse *f* d'épargne.

saviour *Br*, **savior** *Am* ['seɪvjər] *n* sauveur *m*.

savour *Br*, **savor** *Am* ['seɪvər] *vt lit & fig* savourer.

savoury *Br*, **savory** *Am* ['seɪvərɪ] 1 *adj* [food] salé(e). 2 *n* petit plat *m* salé.

saw [sɔː] (*Br pt* **-ed**, *pp* **sawn**, *Am pt & pp* **-ed**) 1 *pt* → **see**. 2 *n* scie *f*. 3 *vt* scier.

sawdust ['sɔːdʌst] *n* sciure *f* (de bois).

sawed-off shotgun *Am* = **sawn-off shotgun**.

sawmill ['sɔːmɪl] *n* scierie *f*.

sawn [sɔːn] *pp Br* → **saw**.

sawn-off shotgun *Br*, **sawed-off shotgun** *Am n* carabine *f* à canon scié.

saxophone ['sæksəfəʊn] *n* saxophone *m*.

say [seɪ] (*pt & pp* **said**) 1 *vt* [gen] dire; **could you ~ that again?** vous pouvez répéter ce que vous venez de dire?; **(let's) you won a lottery ...** supposons que tu gagnes le gros lot ...; **it ~s a lot about him** cela en dit long sur lui; **she's said to be ...** on dit qu'elle est ...; **that goes without ~ing** cela va sans dire; **it has a lot to be said for it** cela a beaucoup d'avantages. || [subj: clock, watch] indiquer. 2 *n*: **to have a/no ~** avoir/ne pas avoir voix au chapitre; **to have a ~ in sthg** avoir son mot à dire sur qqch; **to have one's ~** dire ce que l'on a à dire. dire son mot. ○ **that is to say** *adv* c'est-à-dire.

saying ['seɪɪŋ] *n* dicton *m*.

scab [skæb] *n* [of wound] croûte *f*. || *inf pej* [non-striker] jaune *m*.

scaffold ['skæfəʊld] *n* échafaud *m*.

scaffolding ['skæfəldɪŋ] *n* échafaudage *m*.

scald [skɔːld] 1 *n* brûlure *f*. 2 *vt* ébouillanter.

scale [skeɪl] 1 *n* [gen] échelle *f*; **to ~** [map, drawing] à l'échelle. || [of ruler, thermometer] graduation *f*. || MUS gamme *f*. || [of fish, snake] écaille *f*. || *Am* = **scales**. 2 *vt* [cliff, fence] escalader. || [fish] écailler. ○ **scales** *npl* balance *f*. ○ **scale down** *vt fus* réduire.

scale model *n* modèle *m* réduit.

scallop ['skɒləp] 1 *n* [shellfish] coquille *f* Saint-Jacques. 2 *vt* [edge, garment] festonner.

scalp [skælp] 1 *n* ANAT cuir *m* chevelu. || [trophy] scalp *m*. 2 *vt* scalper.

scalpel ['skælpəl] *n* scalpel *m*.

scamper ['skæmpər] *vi* trottiner.

scampi ['skæmpɪ] *n* (*U*) scampi *mpl*.

scan [skæn] 1 *n* MED scanographie *f*; [during pregnancy] échographie *f*. 2 *vt* [examine carefully] scruter. || [glance at] parcourir. || TECH balayer. || COMPUT faire un scannage de.

scandal ['skændl] *n* [gen] scandale *m*. || [gossip] médisance *f*.

scandalize, -ise ['skændəlaɪz] *vt* scandaliser.

Scandinavia [ˌskændɪ'neɪvjə] *n* Scandinavie *f*.

Scandinavian [ˌskændɪ'neɪvjən] 1 *adj* scandinave. 2 *n* [person] Scandinave *mf*.

scant [skænt] *adj* insuffisant(e).

scanty ['skæntɪ] *adj* [amount, resources] insuffisant(e); [income] maigre; [dress] minuscule.

scapegoat ['skeɪpgəʊt] *n* bouc *m* émissaire.

scar [skɑːr] *n* cicatrice *f*.

scarce ['skeəs] *adj* rare, peu abondant(e).

scarcely ['skeəslɪ] *adv* à peine; ~ **anyone** presque personne; **I ~ ever go there now** je n'y vais presque OR pratiquement plus jamais.

scare [skeər] **1** *n* [sudden fear]: **to give sb a ~** faire peur à qqn. || [public fear] panique *f*; **bomb ~** alerte *f* à la bombe. **2** *vt* faire peur à, effrayer. ○ **scare away**, **scare off** *vt sep* faire fuir.

scarecrow ['skeəkrəʊ] *n* épouvantail *m*.

scared ['skeəd] *adj* apeuré(e); **to be ~** avoir peur; **to be ~ stiff** OR **to death** être mort de peur.

scarf [skɑːf] (*pl* **-s** OR **scarves**) *n* [wool] écharpe *f*; [silk etc] foulard *m*.

scarlet ['skɑːlət] **1** *adj* écarlate. **2** *n* écarlate *f*.

scarves [skɑːvz] *pl* → **scarf**.

scathing ['skeɪðɪŋ] *adj* [criticism] acerbe; [reply] cinglant(e).

scatter ['skætər] **1** *vt* [clothes, paper etc] éparpiller; [seeds] semer à la volée. **2** *vi* se disperser.

scatterbrained ['skætəbreɪnd] *adj inf* écervelé(e).

scavenger ['skævɪndʒər] *n* [animal] animal *m* nécrophage. || [person] personne *f* qui fait les poubelles.

scenario [sɪ'nɑːrɪəʊ] (*pl* **-s**) *n* [possible situation] hypothèse *f*, scénario *m*. || [of film, play] scénario *m*.

scene [siːn] *n* [in play, film, book] scène *f*; **behind the ~s** dans les coulisses. || [sight] spectacle *m*, vue *f*; [picture] tableau *m*. || [location] lieu *m*, endroit *m*. || [area of activity]: **the political ~** la scène politique; **the music ~** le monde de la musique. || *phr*: **to set the ~ for sthg** préparer la voie à qqch.

scenery ['siːnərɪ] *n* (*U*) [of countryside] paysage *m*. || THEATRE décor *m*, décors *mpl*.

scenic ['siːnɪk] *adj* [tour] touristique; **a ~ view** un beau panorama.

scent [sent] *n* [smell - of flowers] senteur *f*, parfum *m*; [- of animal] odeur *f*, fumet *m*. || (*U*) [perfume] parfum *m*.

scepter *Am* = **sceptre**.

sceptic *Br*, **skeptic** *Am* ['skeptɪk] *n* sceptique *mf*.

sceptical *Br*, **skeptical** *Am* ['skeptɪkl] *adj*: ~ **(about)** sceptique (sur).

sceptre *Br*, **scepter** *Am* ['septər] *n* sceptre *m*.

schedule [*Br* 'ʃedjuːl, *Am* 'skedʒʊl] **1** *n* [plan] programme *m*, plan *m*; **on ~** [at expected time] à l'heure (prévue); [on expected day] à la date prévue; **ahead of/behind ~** en avance/en retard (sur le programme). || [list - of times] horaire *m*; [- of prices] tarif *m*. **2** *vt*: **to ~ sthg (for)** prévoir qqch (pour).

scheduled flight [*Br* 'ʃedjuːld-, *Am* 'skedʒʊld-] *n* vol *m* régulier.

scheme [skiːm] **1** *n* [plan] plan *m*, projet *m*. || *pej* [dishonest plan] combine *f*. || [arrangement] arrangement *m*; **colour ~** combinaison *f* de couleurs. **2** *vi pej* conspirer.

scheming ['skiːmɪŋ] *adj* intrigant(e).

schism ['sɪzm, 'skɪzm] *n* schisme *m*.

schizophrenic [,skɪtsə'frenɪk] **1** *adj* schizophrène. **2** *n* schizophrène *mf*.

scholar ['skɒlər] *n* [expert] érudit *m*, -e *f*, savant *m*, -e *f*.

scholarship ['skɒləʃɪp] *n* [grant] bourse *f* (d'études). || [learning] érudition *f*.

school [skuːl] *n* [gen] école *f*; [secondary school] lycée *m*, collège *m*. || [university department] faculté *f*. || *Am* [university] université *f*.

school age *n* âge *m* scolaire.

schoolbook ['skuːlbʊk] *n* livre *m* scolaire OR de classe.

schoolboy ['skuːlbɔɪ] *n* écolier *m*, élève *m*.

schoolchild ['skuːltʃaɪld] (*pl* **-children** [-tʃɪldrən]) *n* écolier *m*, -ière *f*, élève *mf*.

schooldays ['skuːldeɪz] *npl* années *fpl* d'école.

schoolgirl ['skuːlgɜːl] *n* écolière *f*, élève *f*.

schooling ['skuːlɪŋ] *n* instruction *f*.

schoolmaster ['skuːl,mɑːstər] *n* [primary] instituteur *m*, maître *m* d'école; [secondary] professeur *m*.

schoolmistress ['skuːl,mɪstrɪs] *n* [primary] institutrice *f*, maîtresse *f* d'école; [secondary] professeur *m*.

schoolteacher ['skuːl,tiːtʃər] *n* [primary] instituteur *m*, -trice *f*; [secondary] professeur *m*.

school year *n* année *f* scolaire.

schooner ['skuːnər] *n* [ship] schooner *m*, goélette *f*.

sciatica [saɪ'ætɪkə] *n* sciatique *f*.

science ['saɪəns] *n* science *f*.

science fiction *n* science-fiction *f*.

scientific [ˌsaɪən'tɪfɪk] *adj* scientifique.

scientist ['saɪəntɪst] *n* scientifique *mf*.

scintillating ['sɪntɪleɪtɪŋ] *adj* brillant(e).

scissors ['sɪzəz] *npl* ciseaux *mpl*.

sclerosis [sklɪ'rəʊsɪs] → **multiple sclerosis**.

scoff [skɒf] *vi*: to ~ (at) se moquer (de).

scold [skəʊld] *vt* gronder, réprimander.

scone [skɒn] *n* scone *m*.

scoop [sku:p] **1** *n* [for sugar] pelle *f* à main; [for ice cream] cuiller *f* à glace. ‖ [of ice cream] boule *f*. ‖ [news report] exclusivité *f*, scoop *m*. **2** *vt* [with hands] prendre avec les mains; [with scoop] prendre avec une pelle à main. ○ **scoop out** *vt sep* évider.

scooter ['sku:tər] *n* [toy] trottinette *f*. ‖ [motorcycle] scooter *m*.

scope [skəʊp] *n* (*U*) [opportunity] occasion *f*, possibilité *f*. ‖ [of report, inquiry] étendue *f*, portée *f*.

scorch [skɔːtʃ] *vt* [clothes] brûler légèrement, roussir; [land, grass] dessécher.

scorching ['skɔːtʃɪŋ] *adj inf* [day] torride; [sun] brûlant(e).

score [skɔːr] **1** *n* SPORT score *m*. ‖ [in test] note *f*. ‖ *dated* [twenty] vingt. ‖ MUS partition *f*. ‖ [subject]: **on that ~** à ce sujet, sur ce point. **2** *vt* [goal, point etc] marquer; **to ~ 100%** avoir 100 sur 100. ‖ [success, victory] remporter. ‖ [cut] entailler. **3** *vi* SPORT marquer (un but/point etc).

scoreboard ['skɔːbɔːd] *n* tableau *m*.

scorer ['skɔːrər] *n* marqueur *m*.

scorn [skɔːn] **1** *n* (*U*) mépris *m*, dédain *m*. **2** *vt* [person, attitude] mépriser. ‖ [help, offer] rejeter, dédaigner.

scornful ['skɔːnfʊl] *adj* méprisant(e); **to be ~ of sthg** mépriser qqch, dédaigner qqch.

Scorpio ['skɔːpɪəʊ] (*pl* -s) *n* Scorpion *m*.

scorpion ['skɔːpjən] *n* scorpion *m*.

Scot [skɒt] *n* Écossais *m*, -e *f*.

scotch [skɒtʃ] *vt* [rumour] étouffer; [plan] faire échouer.

Scotch [skɒtʃ] **1** *adj* écossais(e). **2** *n* scotch *m*, whisky *m*.

Scotch (tape)® *n Am* Scotch® *m*.

scot-free *adj inf*: **to get off ~** s'en tirer sans être puni(e).

Scotland ['skɒtlənd] *n* Écosse *f*.

Scots [skɒts] **1** *adj* écossais(e). **2** *n* [dialect] écossais *m*.

Scotsman ['skɒtsmən] (*pl* -men [-mən]) *n* Écossais *m*.

Scotswoman ['skɒtswʊmən] (*pl* -women [-ˌwɪmɪn]) *n* Écossaise *f*.

Scottish ['skɒtɪʃ] *adj* écossais(e).

scoundrel ['skaʊndrəl] *n dated* gredin *m*.

scour [skaʊər] *vt* [clean] récurer. ‖ [search - town etc] parcourir; [- countryside] battre.

scout [skaʊt] *n* MIL éclaireur *m*. ○ **Scout** *n* [boy scout] Scout *m*. ○ **scout around** *vi*: **to ~ around (for)** aller à la recherche (de).

scowl [skaʊl] **1** *n* regard *m* noir. **2** *vi* se renfrogner, froncer les sourcils; **to ~ at sb** jeter des regards noirs à qqn.

scrabble ['skræbl] *vi* [scrape]: **to ~ at sthg** gratter qqch. ‖ [feel around]: **to ~ around for sthg** tâtonner pour trouver qqch.

scramble ['skræmbl] **1** *n* [rush] bousculade *f*, ruée *f*. **2** *vi* [climb]: **to ~ up a hill** grimper une colline en s'aidant des mains OR à quatre pattes. ‖ [compete]: **to ~ for sthg** se disputer qqch.

scrambled eggs ['skræmbld-] *npl* œufs *mpl* brouillés.

scrap [skræp] **1** *n* [of paper, material] bout *m*; [of information] fragment *m*. ‖ [metal] ferraille *f*. ‖ *inf* [fight, quarrel] bagarre *f*. **2** *vt* [car] mettre à la ferraille; [plan, system] abandonner, laisser tomber. ○ **scraps** *npl* [food] restes *mpl*.

scrapbook ['skræpbʊk] *n* album *m* (*de coupures de journaux etc*).

scrap dealer *n* ferrailleur *m*, marchand *m* de ferraille.

scrape [skreɪp] **1** *n* [scraping noise] raclement *m*, grattement *m*. ‖ *dated* [difficult situation]: **to get into a ~** se fourrer dans le pétrin. **2** *vt* [clean, rub] gratter, racler; **to ~ sthg off sthg** enlever qqch de qqch en grattant OR raclant. ‖ [surface, car, skin] érafler. **3** *vi* gratter. ○ **scrape through** *vt fus* réussir de justesse.

scraper ['skreɪpər] *n* grattoir *m*, racloir *m*.

scrap paper *Br*, **scratch paper** *Am n* (papier *m*) brouillon *m*.

scrapyard ['skræpjɑːd] *n* parc *m* à ferraille.

scratch [skrætʃ] **1** *n* [wound] égratignure *f*, éraflure *f*. ‖ [on glass, paint etc] éraflure *f*. ‖ *phr*: **to be up to ~** être à la hauteur; **to do sthg from ~** faire qqch à partir de rien. **2** *vt* [wound] écorcher, égratigner. ‖ [mark - paint, glass etc] rayer, érafler. ‖ [rub] gratter. 3 *vi* gratter; [person] se gratter.

scratch paper *Am* = scrap paper.

scrawl [skrɔ:l] 1 *n* griffonnage *m*, gribouillage *m*. 2 *vt* griffonner, gribouiller.

scrawny ['skrɔ:nɪ] *adj* [person] efflanqué(e); [body, animal] décharné(e).

scream [skri:m] 1 *n* [cry] cri *m* perçant, hurlement *m*; [of laughter] éclat *m*. 2 *vt* hurler. 3 *vi* [cry out] crier, hurler.

screech [skri:tʃ] 1 *n* [cry] cri *m* perçant. ‖ [of tyres] crissement *m*. 2 *vt* hurler. 3 *vi* [cry out] pousser des cris perçants. ‖ [tyres] crisser.

screen [skri:n] 1 *n* [gen] écran *m*. ‖ [panel] paravent *m*. 2 *vt* CINEMA projeter, passer; TV téléviser, passer. ‖ [hide] cacher, masquer. ‖ [shield] protéger. ‖ [candidate, employee] passer au crible, filtrer.

screening ['skri:nɪŋ] *n* CINEMA projection *f*; TV passage *m* à la télévision. ‖ [for security] sélection *f*, tri *m*. ‖ MED dépistage *m*.

screenplay ['skri:npleɪ] *n* scénario *m*.

screw [skru:] 1 *n* [for fastening] vis *f*. 2 *vt* [fix with screws]: **to ~ sthg to sthg** visser qqch à OR sur qqch. ‖ [twist] visser. 3 *vi* se visser. ○ **screw up** *vt sep* [crumple up] froisser, chiffonner; [eyes] plisser; [face] tordre. ‖ *v inf* [ruin] gâcher, bousiller.

screwdriver ['skru:,draɪvər] *n* [tool] tournevis *m*.

scribble ['skrɪbl] 1 *n* gribouillage *m*, griffonnage *m*. 2 *vt* & *vi* gribouiller, griffonner.

script [skrɪpt] *n* [of play, film etc] scénario *m*, script *m*.

Scriptures ['skrɪptʃəz] *npl*: **the ~** les (Saintes) Écritures *fpl*.

scriptwriter ['skrɪpt,raɪtər] *n* scénariste *mf*.

scroll [skrəʊl] 1 *n* rouleau *m*. 2 *vt* COMPUT faire défiler.

scrounge [skraʊndʒ] *inf vt*: **to ~ money off sb** taper qqn; **can I ~ a cigarette off you?** je peux te piquer une cigarette?

scrounger ['skraʊndʒər] *n inf* parasite *m*.

scrub [skrʌb] 1 *n* [rub]: **to give sthg a ~** nettoyer qqch à la brosse. ‖ (*U*) [undergrowth] broussailles *fpl*. 2 *vt* [floor, clothes etc] laver OR nettoyer à la brosse; [hands, back] frotter; [saucepan] récurer.

scruff [skrʌf] *n*: **by the ~ of the neck** par la peau du cou.

scruffy ['skrʌfɪ] *adj* mal soigné(e), débraillé(e).

scruples ['skru:plz] *npl* scrupules *mpl*.

scrutinize, -ise ['skru:tɪnaɪz] *vt* scruter, examiner attentivement.

scrutiny ['skru:tɪnɪ] *n* (*U*) examen *m* attentif.

scuff [skʌf] *vt* [damage] érafler. ‖ [drag]: **to ~ one's feet** traîner les pieds.

scuffle ['skʌfl] *n* bagarre *f*, échauffourée *f*.

sculptor ['skʌlptər] *n* sculpteur *m*.

sculpture ['skʌlptʃər] 1 *n* sculpture *f*. 2 *vt* sculpter.

scum [skʌm] *n* (*U*) [froth] écume *f*, mousse *f*. ‖ *v inf pej* [person] salaud *m*. ‖ (*U*) *v inf pej* [people] déchets *mpl*.

scupper ['skʌpər] *vt* NAUT couler.

scurrilous ['skʌrələs] *adj* calomnieux(ieuse).

scurry ['skʌrɪ] *vi* se précipiter; **to ~ away** OR **off** se sauver, détaler.

scuttle ['skʌtl] 1 *n* seau *m* à charbon. 2 *vi* courir précipitamment OR à pas précipités.

scythe [saɪð] *n* faux *f*.

sea [si:] 1 *n* [gen] mer *f*; **at ~** en mer; **by ~** par mer; **by the ~** au bord de la mer; **out to ~** au large. ‖ *phr*: **to be all at ~** nager complètement. 2 *comp* [voyage] en mer; [animal] marin(e), de mer.

seabed ['si:bed] *n*: **the ~** le fond de la mer.

sea breeze *n* brise *f* de mer.

seafood ['si:fu:d] *n* (*U*) fruits *mpl* de mer.

seafront ['si:frʌnt] *n* front *m* de mer.

seagull ['si:gʌl] *n* mouette *f*.

seal [si:l] (*pl inv* OR **-s**) 1 *n* [animal] phoque *m*. ‖ [official mark] cachet *m*, sceau *m*. ‖ [official fastening] cachet *m*. 2 *vt* [envelope] coller, fermer. ‖ [document, letter] sceller, cacheter. ‖ [block off] obturer, boucher. ○ **seal off** *vt sep* [area, entrance] interdire l'accès de.

sea level *n* niveau *m* de la mer.

sea lion (*pl inv* OR **-s**) *n* otarie *f*.

seam [si:m] *n* SEWING couture *f*. ‖ [of coal] couche *f*, veine *f*.

seaman ['si:mən] (*pl* **-men** [-mən]) *n* marin *m*.

seamy ['si:mɪ] *adj* sordide.

séance ['seɪɒns] *n* séance *f* de spiritisme.

seaplane ['si:pleɪn] *n* hydravion *m*.

seaport ['si:pɔ:t] *n* port *m* de mer.

search [sɜ:tʃ] **1** *n* [of person, luggage, house] fouille *f*; [for lost person, thing] recherche *f*, recherches *fpl*; **in ~ of** à la recherche de. **2** *vt* [house, area, person] fouiller; [memory, mind, drawer] fouiller dans. **3** *vi*: **to ~ (for sb/sthg)** chercher (qqn/qqch).

searching ['sɜ:tʃɪŋ] *adj* [question] poussé(e), approfondi(e); [review, examination] minutieux(ieuse).

searchlight ['sɜ:tʃlaɪt] *n* projecteur *m*.

search party *n* équipe *f* de secours.

search warrant *n* mandat *m* de perquisition.

seashell ['si:ʃel] *n* coquillage *m*.

seashore ['si:ʃɔ:ʳ] *n*: **the ~** le rivage, la plage.

seasick ['si:sɪk] *adj*: **to be** OR **feel ~** avoir le mal de mer.

seaside ['si:saɪd] *n*: **the ~** le bord de la mer.

seaside resort *n* station *f* balnéaire.

season ['si:zn] **1** *n* [gen] saison *f*; **in ~** [food] de saison; **out of ~** [holiday] hors saison; [food] hors de saison. || [of films] cycle *m*. **2** *vt* assaisonner, relever.

seasonal ['si:zənl] *adj* saisonnier(ière).

seasoned ['si:znd] *adj* [traveller, campaigner] chevronné(e), expérimenté(e).

seasoning ['si:znɪŋ] *n* assaisonnement *m*.

season ticket *n* carte *f* d'abonnement.

seat [si:t] **1** *n* [gen] siège *m*; [in theatre] fauteuil *m*; **take a ~!** asseyez-vous! || [place to sit - in bus, train] place *f*. || [of trousers] fond *m*. **2** *vt* [sit down] faire asseoir, placer; **please be ~ed** veuillez vous asseoir.

seat belt *n* ceinture *f* de sécurité.

seating ['si:tɪŋ] *n* (*U*) [capacity] sièges *mpl*, places *fpl* (assises).

seawater ['si:,wɔ:təʳ] *n* eau *f* de mer.

seaweed ['si:wi:d] *n* (*U*) algue *f*.

seaworthy ['si:,wɜ:ðɪ] *adj* en bon état de navigabilité.

sec. *abbr of* **second.**

secede [sɪ'si:d] *vi fml*: **to ~ (from)** se séparer (de), faire sécession (de).

secluded [sɪ'klu:dɪd] *adj* retiré(e), écarté(e).

seclusion [sɪ'klu:ʒn] *n* solitude *f*, retraite *f*.

second ['sekənd] **1** *n* [gen] seconde *f*; **~ (gear)** seconde. **2** *num* deuxième, second(e); **his score was ~ only to hers** il n'y a qu'elle qui a fait mieux que lui OR

qui l'a surpassé; *see also* **sixth. 3** *vt* [proposal, motion] appuyer. ○ **seconds** *npl* COMM articles *mpl* de second choix. || [of food] rabiot *m*.

secondary ['sekəndrɪ] *adj* secondaire.

secondary school *n* école *f* secondaire, lycée *m*.

second-class ['sekənd-] *adj pej* [citizen] de deuxième zone; [product] de second choix. || [ticket] de seconde OR deuxième classe. || [stamp] à tarif réduit.

second-hand ['sekənd-] **1** *adj* [goods, shop] d'occasion. **2** *adv* [not new] d'occasion.

second hand ['sekənd-] *n* [of clock] trotteuse *f*.

secondly ['sekəndlɪ] *adv* deuxièmement, en second lieu.

second-rate ['sekənd-] *adj pej* de deuxième ordre, médiocre.

second thought ['sekənd-] *n*: **to have ~s about sthg** avoir des doutes sur qqch; **on ~s** *Br*, **on ~** *Am* réflexion faite, tout bien réfléchi.

secrecy ['si:krəsɪ] *n* (*U*) secret *m*.

secret ['si:krɪt] **1** *adj* secret(ète). **2** *n* secret *m*; **in ~** en secret.

secretarial [,sekrə'teərɪəl] *adj* [course, training] de secrétariat, de secrétaire; **~ staff** secrétaires *mpl*.

secretary [*Br* 'sekrətrɪ, *Am* 'sekrə,terɪ] *n* [gen] secrétaire *mf*. || POL [minister] ministre *m*.

Secretary of State *n Br*: **~ (for)** ministre *m* (de). || *Am* ≃ ministre *m* des Affaires étrangères.

secretive ['si:krətɪv] *adj* secret(ète), dissimulé(e).

secretly ['si:krɪtlɪ] *adv* secrètement.

sect [sekt] *n* secte *f*.

sectarian [sek'teərɪən] *adj* [killing, violence] d'ordre religieux.

section ['sekʃn] **1** *n* [portion - gen] section *f*, partie *f*; [- of road, pipe] tronçon *m*; [- of document, law] article *m*. || GEOM coupe *f*, section *f*. **2** *vt* sectionner.

sector ['sektəʳ] *n* secteur *m*.

secular ['sekjuləʳ] *adj* [life] séculier(ière); [education] laïque; [music] profane.

secure [sɪ'kjuəʳ] **1** *adj* [fixed - gen] fixe; [- windows, building] bien fermé(e). || [safe - job, future] sûr(e); [- valuable object] en sécurité, en lieu sûr. || [free of anxiety - childhood] sécurisant(e); [- marriage] solide. **2** *vt* [obtain] obtenir. || [fasten - gen] attacher; [- door, window]

bien fermer. ‖ [make safe] assurer la sécurité de.

security [sɪ'kjʊərətɪ] n sécurité f.
○ **securities** npl FIN titres mpl, valeurs
fpl.

security guard n garde m de sécurité.

sedan [sɪ'dæn] n Am berline f.

sedate [sɪ'deɪt] 1 adj posé(e), calme. 2
vt donner un sédatif à.

sedation [sɪ'deɪʃn] n (U) sédation f;
under ~ sous calmants.

sedative ['sedətɪv] n sédatif m, calmant
m.

sediment ['sedɪmənt] n sédiment m,
dépôt m.

seduce [sɪ'djuːs] vt séduire.

seductive [sɪ'dʌktɪv] adj séduisant(e).

see [siː] (pt saw, pp seen) 1 vt [gen]
voir; **~ you!** au revoir! ‖ [accompany]: **I
saw her to the door** je l'ai accompagnée
OR reconduite jusqu'à la porte. ‖ [make
sure]: **to ~ (that) ...** s'assurer que .... 2 vi
voir; **you ~, ...** voyez-vous. ...; **I ~** je vois,
je comprends; **let's ~, let me ~** voyons.
voyons voir. ○ **seeing as, seeing that**
conj inf vu que, étant donné que. ○ **see
about** vt fus [arrange] s'occuper de.
○ **see off** vt sep [say goodbye to] accompagner (pour dire au revoir). ○ **see
through** 1 vt fus [scheme] voir clair
dans; **to ~ through sb** voir dans le jeu de
qqn. 2 vt sep [deal, project] mener à
terme, mener à bien. ○ **see to** vt fus
s'occuper de, se charger de.

seed [siːd] n [of plant] graine f. ‖ SPORT:
fifth ~ joueur classé cinquième m,
joueuse classée cinquième f. ○ **seeds**
npl fig germes mpl, semences fpl.

seedling ['siːdlɪŋ] n jeune plant m, se-
mis m.

seedy ['siːdɪ] adj miteux(euse).

seek [siːk] (pt & pp sought) vt [gen]
chercher; [peace, happiness] rechercher;
to ~ to do sthg chercher à faire qqch. ‖
[advice, help] demander.

seem [siːm] 1 vi sembler, paraître; **to ~
sad/tired** avoir l'air triste/fatigué. 2 v
impers: **it ~s (that) ...** il semble OR paraît
que ....

seemingly ['siːmɪŋlɪ] adv apparemment.

seen [siːn] pp → see.

seep [siːp] vi suinter.

seesaw ['siːsɔː] n bascule f.

seethe [siːð] vi [person] bouillir, être fu-
rieux(ieuse). ‖ [place]: **to be seething
with** grouiller de.

see-through adj transparent(e).

segment ['segmənt] n [section] partie f,
section f. ‖ [of fruit] quartier m.

segregate ['segrɪgeɪt] vt séparer.

Seine [seɪn] n: **the (River) ~** la Seine.

seize [siːz] vt [grab] saisir, attraper. ‖
[capture] s'emparer de, prendre. ‖ [ar-
rest] arrêter. ‖ fig [opportunity, chance]
saisir, sauter sur. ○ **seize (up)on** vt fus
saisir, sauter sur. ○ **seize up** vi [body]
s'ankyloser. ‖ [engine, part] se gripper.

seizure ['siːʒər] n MED crise f, attaque f.
‖ (U) [of town] capture f; [of power] prise
f.

seldom ['seldəm] adv peu souvent, rarement.

select [sɪ'lekt] 1 adj [carefully chosen]
choisi(e). ‖ [exclusive] de premier ordre,
d'élite. 2 vt sélectionner, choisir.

selection [sɪ'lekʃn] n sélection f, choix
m.

selective [sɪ'lektɪv] adj sélectif(ive);
[person] difficile.

self [self] (pl selves) n moi m; **she's her
old ~ again** elle est redevenue elle-
même.

self-addressed stamped envelope
[-ə,drest'stæmpt-] n Am enveloppe f af-
franchie pour la réponse.

self-assured adj sûr(e) de soi, plein(e)
d'assurance.

self-catering adj [holiday - in house] en
maison louée; [- in flat] en appartement
loué.

self-centred [-'sentəd] adj égocentrique.

self-confessed [-kən'fest] adj de son
propre aveu.

self-confident adj sûr(e) de soi,
plein(e) d'assurance.

self-conscious adj timide.

self-contained [-kən'teɪnd] adj [flat]
indépendant(e), avec entrée particulière;
[person] qui se suffit à soi-même.

self-control n maîtrise f de soi.

self-defence n autodéfense f.

self-discipline n autodiscipline f.

self-employed [-ɪm'plɔɪd] adj qui travaille à son propre compte.

self-esteem n respect m de soi, estime f
de soi.

self-evident adj qui va de soi, évi-
dent(e).

self-explanatory adj évident(e), qui
ne nécessite pas d'explication.

self-government n autonomie f.

self-important adj suffisant(e).

self-indulgent *adj pej* [person] qui ne se refuse rien; [film, book, writer] nombriliste.

self-interest *n* (U) *pej* intérêt *m* personnel.

selfish ['selfɪʃ] *adj* égoïste.

selfishness ['selfɪʃnɪs] *n* égoïsme *m*.

selfless ['selflɪs] *adj* désintéressé(e).

self-made *adj*: ~ **man** self-made-man *m*.

self-pity *n* apitoiement *m* sur soi-même.

self-portrait *n* autoportrait *m*.

self-possessed [-pə'zest] *adj* maître (maîtresse) de soi.

self-raising flour *Br* [-,reɪzɪŋ-], **self-rising flour** *Am n* farine *f* avec levure incorporée.

self-reliant *adj* indépendant(e), qui ne compte que sur soi.

self-respect *n* respect *m* de soi.

self-restraint *n* (U) retenue *f*, mesure *f*.

self-righteous *adj* satisfait(e) de soi.

self-rising flour *Am* = **self-raising flour**.

self-sacrifice *n* abnégation *f*.

self-satisfied *adj* suffisant(e), content(e) de soi.

self-service *n* libre-service *m*, self-service *m*.

self-sufficient *adj* autosuffisant(e); to be ~ in satisfaire à ses besoins en.

self-taught *adj* autodidacte.

sell [sel] (*pt & pp* **sold**) 1 *vt* [gen] vendre; **to ~ sthg for £100** vendre qqch 100 livres; **to ~ sthg to sb, to ~ sb sthg** vendre qqch à qqn. ‖ *fig* [make acceptable]: **to ~ sthg to sb, to ~ sb sthg** faire accepter qqch à qqn. 2 *vi* [person] vendre. ‖ [product] se vendre; **it ~s for** OR **at £10** il se vend 10 livres. ○ **sell off** *vt sep* vendre, liquider. ○ **sell out** 1 *vt sep*: **the performance is sold out** il ne reste plus de places, tous les billets ont été vendus. 2 *vi* [shop]: **we have sold out** on n'en a plus. ‖ [betray one's principles] être infidèle à ses principes.

seller ['selər] *n* vendeur *m*, -euse *f*.

selling price ['selɪŋ-] *n* prix *m* de vente.

sell-out *n*: **the match was a ~** on a joué à guichets fermés.

selves [selvz] *pl* → **self**.

semaphore ['seməfɔːr] *n* (U) signaux *mpl* à bras.

semblance ['sembləns] *n* semblant *m*.

semen ['siːmen] *n* (U) sperme *m*, semence *f*.

semester [sɪ'mestər] *n* semestre *m*.

semicircle ['semɪ,sɜːkl] *n* demi-cercle *m*.

semicolon [,semɪ'kəʊlən] *n* point-virgule *m*.

semidetached [,semɪdɪ'tætʃt] 1 *adj* jumelé(e). 2 *n Br* maison *f* jumelée.

semifinal [,semɪ'faɪnl] *n* demi-finale *f*.

seminar ['semɪnɑːr] *n* séminaire *m*.

seminary ['semɪnərɪ] *n* RELIG séminaire *m*.

semiskilled [,semɪ'skɪld] *adj* spécialisé(e).

semolina [,semə'liːnə] *n* semoule *f*.

Senate ['senɪt] *n* POL: **the ~** le sénat; **the United States ~** le Sénat américain.

senator ['senətər] *n* sénateur *m*.

send [send] (*pt & pp* **sent**) *vt* [gen] envoyer; [letter] expédier, envoyer; **to ~ sb sthg, to ~ sthg to sb** envoyer qqch à qqn; **~ her my love** embrasse-la pour moi. ○ **send for** *vt fus* [person] appeler, faire venir. ‖ [by post] commander par correspondance. ○ **send in** *vt sep* [report, application] envoyer, soumettre. ○ **send off** *vt sep* [by post] expédier. ‖ SPORT expulser. ○ **send off for** *vt fus* commander par correspondance.

sender ['sendər] *n* expéditeur *m*, -trice *f*.

send-off *n* fête *f* d'adieux.

senile ['siːnaɪl] *adj* sénile.

senior ['siːnjər] 1 *adj* [highest-ranking] plus haut placé(e). ‖ [higher-ranking]: **~ to sb** d'un rang plus élevé que qqn. ‖ SCH [pupils, classes] grand(e). 2 *n* [older person] aîné *m*, -e *f*. ‖ SCH grand *m*, -e *f*.

senior citizen *n* personne *f* âgée OR du troisième âge.

sensation [sen'seɪʃn] *n* sensation *f*.

sensational [sen'seɪʃənl] *adj* [gen] sensationnel(elle).

sensationalist [sen'seɪʃnəlɪst] *adj pej* à sensation.

sense [sens] 1 *n* [ability, meaning] sens *m*; to make ~ [have meaning] avoir un sens; **~ of humour** sens de l'humour; **~ of smell** odorat *m*. ‖ [feeling] sentiment *m*. ‖ [wisdom] bon sens *m*, intelligence *f*; to make ~ [be sensible] être logique. 2 *vt* [feel] sentir. ○ **in a sense** *adv* dans un sens.

senseless ['senslɪs] *adj* [stupid] stupide. ‖ [unconscious] sans connaissance.

sensibilities [,sensɪ'bɪlətɪz] *npl* susceptibilité *f*.

sensible ['sensəbl] *adj* [reasonable] raisonnable, judicieux(ieuse).
sensitive ['sensɪtɪv] *adj* [gen]: ~ (to) sensible (à). ‖ [subject] délicat(e). ‖ [easily offended]: ~ (about) susceptible (en ce qui concerne).
sensual ['sensjʊəl] *adj* sensuel(elle).
sensuous ['sensjʊəs] *adj* qui affecte les sens.
sent [sent] *pt & pp* → send.
sentence ['sentəns] 1 *n* GRAMM phrase *f*. ‖ JUR condamnation *f*, sentence *f*. 2 *vt*: to ~ sb (to) condamner qqn (à).
sentiment ['sentɪmənt] *n* [feeling] sentiment *m*. ‖ [opinion] opinion *f*, avis *m*.
sentimental [,sentɪ'mentl] *adj* sentimental(e).
sentry ['sentrɪ] *n* sentinelle *f*.
separate [*adj & n* 'seprət, *vb* 'sepəreɪt] 1 *adj* [not joined]: ~ (from) séparé(e) (de). ‖ [individual, distinct] distinct(e). 2 *vt* [gen]: to ~ sb/sthg (from) séparer qqn/qqch (de). ‖ [distinguish]: to ~ sb/sthg (from) distinguer qqn/qqch (de). 3 *vi* se séparer; to ~ into se diviser OR se séparer en.
separately ['seprətlɪ] *adv* séparément.
separation [,sepə'reɪʃn] *n* séparation *f*.
September [sep'tembər] *n* septembre *m*; **in** ~ en septembre; **last** ~ en septembre dernier; **this** ~ en septembre de cette année; **next** ~ en septembre prochain; by ~ en septembre, d'ici septembre; **every** ~ tous les ans en septembre; **during** ~ pendant le mois de septembre; **at the beginning of** ~ au début du mois de septembre, début septembre; **at the end of** ~ à la fin du mois de septembre, fin septembre; **in the middle of** ~ au milieu du mois de septembre, à la mi-septembre.
septic ['septɪk] *adj* infecté(e).
septic tank *n* fosse *f* septique.
sequel ['si:kwəl] *n* [book, film]: ~ (to) suite *f* (de). ‖ [consequence]: ~ (to) conséquence *f* (de).
sequence ['si:kwəns] *n* [series] suite *f*, succession *f*. ‖ [order] ordre *m*. ‖ [of film] séquence *f*.
Serb = Serbian.
Serbia ['sɜːbjə] *n* Serbie *f*.
Serbian ['sɜːbjən], **Serb** [sɜːb] 1 *adj* serbe. 2 *n* [person] Serbe *mf*. ‖ [dialect] serbe *m*.
serene [sɪ'ri:n] *adj* [calm] serein(e), tranquille.
sergeant ['sɑːdʒənt] *n* MIL sergent *m*. ‖ [in police] brigadier *m*.

sergeant major *n* sergent-major *m*.
serial ['sɪərɪəl] *n* feuilleton *m*.
serial number *n* numéro *m* de série.
series ['sɪəri:z] (*pl inv*) *n* série *f*.
serious ['sɪərɪəs] *adj* sérieux(ieuse); [illness, accident, trouble] grave.
seriously ['sɪərɪəslɪ] *adv* sérieusement; [ill] gravement; [wounded] grièvement, gravement; **to take sb/sthg** ~ prendre qqn/qqch au sérieux.
seriousness ['sɪərɪəsnɪs] *n* [of mistake, illness] gravité *f*. ‖ [of person, speech] sérieux *m*.
sermon ['sɜːmən] *n* sermon *m*.
serrated [sɪ'reɪtɪd] *adj* en dents de scie.
servant ['sɜːvənt] *n* domestique *mf*.
serve [sɜːv] 1 *vt* [work for] servir. ‖ [have effect]: **to ~ to do sthg** servir à faire qqch; **to ~ a purpose** [subj: device etc] servir à un usage. ‖ [provide for] desservir. ‖ [meal, drink, customer] servir. ‖ JUR: **to ~ sb with a summons/writ, to ~ a summons/writ on sb** signifier une assignation/une citation à qqn. ‖ [prison sentence] purger, faire; [apprenticeship] faire. ‖ SPORT servir. ‖ *phr*: **it ~s him/you right** c'est bien fait pour lui/toi. 2 *vi* servir; **to ~ as** servir de. 3 *n* SPORT service *m*. ○ **serve out, serve up** *vt sep* [food] servir.
service ['sɜːvɪs] 1 *n* [gen] service *m*; **in/out of** ~ en/hors service; **to be of** ~ (**to sb**) être utile (à qqn), rendre service (à qqn). ‖ [of car] révision *f*; [of machine] entretien *m*. 2 *vt* [car] réviser; [machine] assurer l'entretien de. ○ **services** *npl* [on motorway] aire *f* de services. ‖ [armed forces]: **the ~s** les forces *fpl* armées.
serviceable ['sɜːvɪsəbl] *adj* pratique.
service area *n* aire *f* de services.
service charge *n* service *m*.
serviceman ['sɜːvɪsmən] (*pl* -men [-mən]) *n* soldat *m*, militaire *m*.
service station *n* station-service *f*.
serviette [,sɜːvɪ'et] *n* serviette *f* (de table).
sesame ['sesəmɪ] *n* sésame *m*.
session ['seʃn] *n* [gen] séance *f*. ‖ Am [school term] trimestre *m*.
set [set] (*pt & pp* set) 1 *adj* [fixed - gen] fixe; [- phrase] figé(e). ‖ [ready]: ~ (**for sthg/to do sthg**) prêt(e) (à qqch/à faire qqch). ‖ [determined]: **to be ~ on sthg** vouloir absolument qqch; **to be ~ on doing sthg** être résolu(e) à faire qqch; **to be dead ~ against sthg** s'opposer formellement à qqch. 2 *n* [of keys, tools, golf

clubs etc] jeu *m*; [of tyres] train *m*; **a ~ of teeth** [natural] une dentition, une denture; [false] un dentier. ‖ [television, radio] poste *m*. ‖ CINEMA plateau *m*; THEATRE scène *f*. ‖ TENNIS manche *f*, set *m*. **3** *rt* [place] placer, poser, mettre. ‖ [cause to be]: **to ~ sb free** libérer qqn, mettre qqn en liberté; **to ~ sthg on fire** mettre le feu à qqch. ‖ [prepare - trap] tendre; [- table] mettre. ‖ [adjust] régler. ‖ [fix - date, deadline, target] fixer. ‖ [establish - example] donner; [- trend] lancer; [- record] établir. ‖ [homework, task] donner; [problem] poser. ‖ MED [bone, leg] remettre. ‖ [story]: **to be ~** se passer, se dérouler. **4** *ri* [sun] se coucher. ‖ [jelly] prendre; [glue, cement] durcir. ○ **set about** *rt fus* [start] entreprendre, se mettre à; **to ~ about doing sthg** se mettre à faire qqch. ○ **set aside** *rt sep* [save] mettre de côté. ‖ [not consider] rejeter, écarter. ○ **set back** *rt sep* [delay] retarder. ○ **set off 1** *vt sep* [cause] déclencher, provoquer. ‖ [bomb] faire exploser; [firework] faire partir. **2** *ri* se mettre en route, partir. ○ **set out 1** *vt sep* [arrange] disposer. ‖ [explain] présenter, exposer. *2 vt fus*: **to ~ out to do sthg** entreprendre OR tenter de faire qqch. **3** *ri* [on journey] se mettre en route, partir. ○ **set up** *rt sep* [organization] créer, fonder; [committee, procedure] constituer, mettre en place; [meeting] arranger, organiser. ‖ [roadblock] placer, installer. ‖ [equipment] préparer, installer. ‖ *inf* [make appear guilty] monter un coup contre.

setback ['setbæk] *n* contretemps *m*, revers *m*.

set menu *n* menu *m* fixe.

settee [se'ti:] *n* canapé *m*.

setting ['setɪŋ] *n* [surroundings] décor *m*, cadre *m*. ‖ [of dial, machine] réglage *m*.

settle ['setl] **1** *vt* [argument] régler; **that's ~d then** (c'est) entendu. ‖ [bill, account] régler, payer. ‖ [calm - nerves] calmer; **to ~ one's stomach** calmer les douleurs d'estomac. **2** *ri* [make one's home] s'installer, se fixer. ‖ [make oneself comfortable] s'installer. ‖ [dust] retomber; [sediment] se déposer; [bird, insect] se poser. ○ **settle down** *ri* [give one's attention]: **to ~ down to sthg/to doing sthg** se mettre à qqch/à faire qqch. ‖ [make oneself comfortable] s'installer. ‖ [become respectable] se ranger. ‖ [become calm] se

calmer. ○ **settle for** *rt fus* accepter, se contenter de. ○ **settle in** *ri* s'adapter. ○ **settle on** *rt fus* [choose] fixer son choix sur, se décider pour. ○ **settle up** *ri*: **to ~ up (with sb)** régler (qqn).

settlement ['setlmənt] *n* [agreement] accord *m*. ‖ [colony] colonie *f*. ‖ [payment] règlement *m*.

settler ['setlər] *n* colon *m*.

seven ['sevn] *num* sept; *see also* **six**.

seventeen [,sevn'ti:n] *num* dix-sept; *see also* **six**.

seventh ['sevnθ] *num* septième; *see also* **sixth**.

seventy ['sevntı] *num* soixante-dix; *see also* **sixty**.

sever ['sevər] *rt* [cut through] couper. ‖ *fig* [relationship, ties] rompre.

several ['sevrəl] **1** *adj* plusieurs. **2** *pron* plusieurs *mfpl*.

severance pay *n* indemnité *f* de licenciement.

severe [sɪ'vɪər] *adj* [shock] gros (grosse), dur(e); [pain] violent(e); [illness, injury] grave. ‖ [person, criticism] sévère.

severity [sɪ'verətɪ] *n* [of storm] violence *f*; [of problem, illness] gravité *f*. ‖ [sternness] sévérité *f*.

sew [səʊ] (*Br pp* sewn, *Am pp* sewed OR sewn) *vt & ri* coudre. ○ **sew up** *rt sep* [join] recoudre.

sewage ['su:ɪdʒ] *n* (*U*) eaux *fpl* d'égout, eaux usées.

sewer ['sʊər] *n* égout *m*.

sewing ['səʊɪŋ] *n* (*U*) [activity] couture *f*. ‖ [work] ouvrage *m*.

sewing machine *n* machine *f* à coudre.

sewn [səʊn] *pp* → **sew**.

sex [seks] *n* [gender] sexe *m*. ‖ (*U*) [sexual intercourse] rapports *mpl* (sexuels); **to have ~ with** avoir des rapports (sexuels) avec.

sexist ['seksɪst] *adj* sexiste.

sexual ['sekʃʊəl] *adj* sexuel(elle).

sexual harassment *n* harcèlement *m* sexuel.

sexual intercourse *n* (*U*) rapports *mpl* (sexuels).

sexy ['seksɪ] *adj inf* sexy (*inv*).

shabby ['ʃæbɪ] *adj* [clothes] élimé(e), râpé(e); [furniture] minable. ‖ [behaviour] moche, méprisable.

shack [ʃæk] *n* cabane *f*, hutte *f*.

shackle ['ʃækl] *rt* enchaîner, *fig* entraver. ○ **shackles** *npl* fers *mpl*; *fig* entraves *fpl*.

shade [ʃeɪd] **1** *n* (*U*) [shadow] ombre *f*. || [lampshade] abat-jour *m inv*. || [colour] nuance *f*, ton *m*. || [of meaning, opinion] nuance *f*. **2** *vt* [from light] abriter.

shadow ['ʃædəʊ] *n* ombre *f*.

shadow cabinet *n* cabinet *m* fantôme.

shadowy ['ʃædəʊɪ] *adj* [dark] ombreux(euse). || [sinister] mystérieux (ieuse).

shady ['ʃeɪdɪ] *adj* [garden, street etc] ombragé(e). || [tree] qui donne de l'ombre. || *inf* [dishonest] louche.

shaft [ʃɑːft] *n* [vertical passage] puits *m*; [of lift] cage *f*. || TECH arbre *m*. || [of light] rayon *m*. || [of tool, golf club] manche *m*.

shaggy ['ʃægɪ] *adj* hirsute.

shake [ʃeɪk] (*pt* **shook**, *pp* **shaken**) **1** *vt* [move vigorously - gen] secouer; [- bottle] agiter; **to ~ hands** se serrer la main; **to ~ one's head** secouer la tête; [to say no] faire non de la tête. || [shock] ébranler, secouer. **2** *vi* trembler. **3** *n* [tremble] tremblement *m*; **to give sthg a ~** secouer qqch. ○ **shake off** *vt sep* [police, pursuers] semer; [illness] se débarrasser de.

shaken ['ʃeɪkn] *pp* → **shake**.

shaky ['ʃeɪkɪ] *adj* [building, table] branlant(e); [hand] tremblant(e); [person] faible; [argument, start] incertain(e).

shall [weak form ʃəl, strong form ʃæl] *aux vb* (*1st person sg & 1st person pl*) (*to express future tense*): **I ~ be ...** je serai .... || (*esp 1st person sg & 1st person pl*) (*in questions*): **~ we have lunch now?** tu veux qu'on déjeune maintenant?; **where ~ I put this?** où est-ce qu'il faut mettre ça? || (*in orders*): **you ~ tell me!** tu vas OR dois me le dire!

shallow ['ʃæləʊ] *adj* [water, dish, hole] peu profond(e). || *pej* [superficial] superficiel(ielle).

sham [ʃæm] **1** *adj* feint(e), simulé(e). **2** *n* comédie *f*.

shambles ['ʃæmblz] *n* désordre *m*, pagaille *f*.

shame [ʃeɪm] **1** *n* (*U*) [remorse, humiliation] honte *f*. || [pity]: **it's a ~ (that ...)** c'est dommage (que ... (+ *subjunctive*)); **what a ~!** quel dommage! **2** *vt* faire honte à, mortifier; **to ~ sb into doing sthg** obliger qqn à faire qqch en lui faisant honte.

shamefaced [,ʃeɪm'feɪst] *adj* honteux(euse), penaud(e).

shameful ['ʃeɪmfʊl] *adj* honteux(euse), scandaleux(euse).

shameless ['ʃeɪmlɪs] *adj* effronté(e), éhonté(e).

shampoo [ʃæm'puː] (*pl* **-s**, *pt & pp* **-ed**, *cont* **-ing**) **1** *n* shampooing *m*. **2** *vt*: **to ~ sb** OR **sb's hair** faire un shampooing à qqn.

shamrock ['ʃæmrɒk] *n* trèfle *m*.

shandy ['ʃændɪ] *n* panaché *m*.

shan't [ʃɑːnt] = **shall not**.

shantytown ['ʃæntɪtaʊn] *n* bidonville *m*.

shape [ʃeɪp] **1** *n* [gen] forme *f*; **to take ~** prendre forme OR tournure. || [health]: **to be in good/bad ~** être en bonne/ mauvaise forme. **2** *vt* [pastry, clay etc]: **to ~ sthg (into)** façonner OR modeler qqch (en). || [ideas, project, character] former. ○ **shape up** *vi* [person, plans] se développer, progresser.

-shaped ['ʃeɪpt] *suffix*: **egg~** en forme d'œuf; **L~** en forme de L.

shapeless ['ʃeɪplɪs] *adj* informe.

shapely ['ʃeɪplɪ] *adj* bien fait(e).

share [ʃeər] **1** *n* [portion, contribution] part *f*. **2** *vt* partager. ○ **shares** *npl* actions *fpl*. ○ **share out** *vt sep* partager, répartir.

shareholder ['ʃeə,həʊldər] *n* actionnaire *mf*.

shark [ʃɑːk] (*pl inv* OR **-s**) *n* [fish] requin *m*.

sharp [ʃɑːp] **1** *adj* [knife, razor] tranchant(e), affilé(e); [needle, pencil, teeth] pointu(e). || [image, outline, contrast] net (nette). || [person, mind] vif (vive); [eyesight] perçant(e). || [sudden - change, rise] brusque, soudain(e); [- hit, tap] sec (sèche). || [words, order, voice] cinglant(e). || [cry, sound] perçant(e); [pain, cold] vif (vive). || MUS **C/D ~** do/ré dièse. **2** *adv* [punctually]: **at 8 o'clock ~** à 8 heures pile OR tapantes. || [immediately]: **~ left/ right** tout à fait à gauche/droite.

sharpen ['ʃɑːpn] *vt* [knife, tool] aiguiser; [pencil] tailler.

sharpener ['ʃɑːpnər] *n* [for pencil] taille-crayon *m*; [for knife] aiguisoir *m* (pour couteaux).

sharp-eyed [-'aɪd] *adj*: **she's very ~** elle remarque tout, rien ne lui échappe.

sharply ['ʃɑːplɪ] *adv* [distinctly] nettement. || [suddenly] brusquement. || [harshly] sévèrement, durement.

shat [ʃæt] *pt & pp* → **shit**.

shatter ['ʃætər] **1** *vt* [window, glass] briser, fracasser. || *fig* [hopes, dreams] détruire. **2** *vi* se fracasser, voler en éclats.

shattered ['ʃætəd] adj [upset] boule-versé(e). || Br inf [very tired] flapi(e).

shave [ʃeɪv] 1 n: **to have a ~** se raser. 2 vt [remove hair from] raser. || [wood] pla-ner, raboter. 3 vi se raser.

shaver ['ʃeɪvər] n rasoir m électrique.

shaving brush ['ʃeɪvɪŋ-] n blaireau m.

shaving cream ['ʃeɪvɪŋ-] n crème f à raser.

shaving foam ['ʃeɪvɪŋ-] n mousse f à raser.

shavings ['ʃeɪvɪŋz] npl [of wood, metal] copeaux mpl.

shawl [ʃɔːl] n châle m.

she [ʃiː] 1 pers pron [referring to woman, girl, animal] elle; **~'s tall** elle est grande; SHE **can't do it** elle, elle ne peut pas le faire; **there ~ is** la voilà; **if I were** OR **was ~** fml si j'étais elle, à sa place. || [referring to boat, car, country] follow the gender of your translation. 2 comp: **~-elephant** éléphant m femelle; **~-wolf** louve f.

sheaf [ʃiːf] (pl **sheaves**) n [of papers, letters] liasse f. || [of corn, grain] gerbe f.

shear [ʃɪər] (pt -ed, pp -ed OR **shorn**) vt [sheep] tondre. ○ **shears** npl [for gar-den] sécateur m, cisaille f. || [for dress-making] ciseaux mpl. ○ **shear off** vi se détacher.

sheath [ʃiːθ] (pl -s [ʃiːðz]) n [for knife, cable] gaine f.

sheaves [ʃiːvz] pl → shaef.

shed [ʃed] (pt & pp shed) 1 n [small] remise f, cabane f; [larger] hangar m. 2 vt [hair, skin, leaves] perdre. || [tears] verser, répandre.

she'd [weak form ʃɪd, strong form ʃiːd] = she had, she would.

sheen [ʃiːn] n lustre m, éclat m.

sheep [ʃiːp] (pl inv) n mouton m.

sheepdog ['ʃiːpdɒg] n chien m de ber-ger.

sheepish ['ʃiːpɪʃ] adj penaud(e).

sheepskin ['ʃiːpskɪn] n peau f de mou-ton.

sheer [ʃɪər] adj [absolute] pur(e). || [very steep] à pic, abrupt(e). || [material] fin(e).

sheet [ʃiːt] n [for bed] drap m. || [of pa-per, glass, wood] feuille f; [of metal] plaque f.

sheik(h) [ʃeɪk] n cheik m.

shelf [ʃelf] (pl **shelves**) n [for storage] rayon m, étagère f.

shell [ʃel] 1 n [of egg, nut, snail] coquille f. || [of tortoise, crab] carapace f. || [on beach] coquillage m. || MIL obus m. 2 vt [peas] écosser; [nuts, prawns] décorti-quer; [eggs] enlever la coquille de, écaler. || MIL bombarder.

she'll [ʃiːl] = she will, she shall.

shellfish ['ʃelfɪʃ] (pl inv) n [creature] crustacé m, coquillage m. || (U) [food] fruits mpl de mer.

shelter ['ʃeltər] 1 n abri m. 2 vt [protect] abriter, protéger. || [refugee, homeless person] offrir un asile à; [criminal, fugi-tive] cacher. 3 vi s'abriter, se mettre à l'abri.

sheltered ['ʃeltəd] adj [from weather] abrité(e). || [life, childhood] protégé(e), sans soucis.

shelve [ʃelv] vt fig mettre au frigidaire, mettre en sommeil.

shelves [ʃelvz] pl → shelf.

shepherd ['ʃepəd] 1 n berger m. 2 vt fig conduire.

shepherd's pie ['ʃepədz-] n ≃ hachis m Parmentier.

sheriff ['ʃerɪf] n Am shérif m.

sherry ['ʃerɪ] n xérès m, sherry m.

she's [ʃiːz] = she is, she has.

sh(h) [ʃ] excl chut!

shield [ʃiːld] 1 n [armour] bouclier m. 2 vt: **to ~ sb (from)** protéger qqn (de OR contre).

shift [ʃɪft] 1 n [change] changement m, modification f. || [period of work] poste m; [workers] équipe f. 2 vt [move] dépla-cer, changer de place. || [change] chan-ger, modifier. 3 vi [move - gen] changer de place; [- wind] tourner, changer. || [change] changer, se modifier. || Am AUT changer de vitesse.

shifty ['ʃɪftɪ] adj inf sournois(e), louche.

shimmer ['ʃɪmər] 1 n reflet m, miroite-ment m. 2 vi miroiter.

shin [ʃɪn] n tibia m.

shinbone ['ʃɪnbəʊn] n tibia m.

shine [ʃaɪn] (pt & pp shone) 1 n bril-lant m. 2 vt [direct]: **to ~ a torch on sthg** éclairer qqch. || [polish] faire briller, asti-quer. 3 vi briller.

shingle ['ʃɪŋgl] n (U) [on beach] galets mpl. ○ **shingles** n (U) zona m.

shiny ['ʃaɪnɪ] adj brillant(e).

ship [ʃɪp] 1 n bateau m; [larger] navire m. 2 vt [goods] expédier; [troops, passen-gers] transporter.

shipbuilding ['ʃɪp,bɪldɪŋ] n construc-tion f navale.

shipment ['ʃɪpmənt] n [cargo] cargai-son f, chargement m.

shipper ['ʃɪpər] *n* affréteur *m*, chargeur *m*.

shipping ['ʃɪpɪŋ] *n* (U) [transport] transport *m* maritime. || [ships] navires *mpl*.

shipshape ['ʃɪpʃeɪp] *adj* bien rangé(e), en ordre.

shipwreck ['ʃɪprek] **1** *n* [destruction of ship] naufrage *m*. || [wrecked ship] épave *f*. **2** *vt*: **to be ~ed** faire naufrage.

shipyard ['ʃɪpjɑːd] *n* chantier *m* naval.

shirk [ʃɜːk] *vt* se dérober à.

shirt [ʃɜːt] *n* chemise *f*.

shirtsleeves ['ʃɜːtsliːvz] *npl*: **to be in (one's) ~** être en manches OR en bras de chemise.

shit [ʃɪt] (*pt & pp* **shit** OR **-ted** OR **shat**) *vulg* **1** *n* [excrement] merde *f*. || (U) [nonsense] conneries *fpl*. **2** *excl* merde!

shiver ['ʃɪvər] **1** *n* frisson *m*. **2** *vi*: **to ~ (with)** trembler (de), frissonner (de).

shoal [ʃəʊl] *n* [of fish] banc *m*.

shock [ʃɒk] **1** *n* [surprise] choc *m*, coup *m*. || (U) MED: **to be suffering from ~, to be in (a state of) ~** être en état de choc. || [impact] choc *m*, heurt *m*. || ELEC décharge *f* électrique. **2** *vt* [upset] bouleverser. || [offend] choquer, scandaliser.

shock absorber [-əb,zɔːbər] *n* amortisseur *m*.

shocking ['ʃɒkɪŋ] *adj* [very bad] épouvantable, terrible. || [outrageous] scandaleux(euse).

shod [ʃɒd] *pt & pp* → **shoe**.

shoddy ['ʃɒdɪ] *adj* [goods, work] de mauvaise qualité; [treatment] indigne, méprisable.

shoe [ʃuː] (*pt & pp* **-ed** OR **shod**) **1** *n* chaussure *f*, soulier *m*. **2** *vt* [horse] ferrer.

shoebrush ['ʃuːbrʌʃ] *n* brosse *f* à chaussures.

shoehorn ['ʃuːhɔːn] *n* chausse-pied *m*.

shoelace ['ʃuːleɪs] *n* lacet *m* de soulier.

shoe polish *n* cirage *m*.

shoe shop *n* magasin *m* de chaussures.

shoestring ['ʃuːstrɪŋ] *n fig*: **on a ~** à peu de frais.

shone [ʃɒn] *pt & pp* → **shine**.

shoo [ʃuː] **1** *vt* chasser. **2** *excl* ouste!

shook [ʃʊk] *pt* → **shake**.

shoot [ʃuːt] (*pt & pp* **shot**) **1** *vt* [kill with gun] tuer d'un coup de feu; [wound with gun] blesser d'un coup de feu; **to ~ o.s.** [kill o.s.] se tuer avec une arme à feu. || [arrow] décocher, tirer. || CINEMA tourner. **2** *vi* [fire gun]: **to ~ (at)** tirer (sur). || [move quickly]: **to ~ in/out/past** entrer/

sortir/passer en trombe, entrer/sortir/passer comme un bolide. || CINEMA tourner. || SPORT tirer, shooter. **3** *n* [of plant] pousse *f*. O **shoot down** *vt sep* [aeroplane] descendre, abattre. || [person] abattre. O **shoot up** *vi* [child, plant] pousser vite. || [price, inflation] monter en flèche.

shooting ['ʃuːtɪŋ] *n* [killing] meurtre *m*.

shooting star *n* étoile *f* filante.

shop [ʃɒp] **1** *n* [store] magasin *m*, boutique *f*. || [workshop] atelier *m*. **2** *vi* faire ses courses; **to go shopping** aller faire les courses OR commissions.

shop floor *n*: **the ~** *fig* les ouvriers *mpl*.

shopkeeper ['ʃɒp,kiːpər] *n* commerçant *m*, -e *f*.

shoplifting ['ʃɒp,lɪftɪŋ] *n* (U) vol *m* à l'étalage.

shopper ['ʃɒpər] *n* personne *f* qui fait ses courses.

shopping ['ʃɒpɪŋ] *n* (U) [purchases] achats *mpl*.

shopping bag *n* sac *m* à provisions.

shopping centre *Br*, **shopping mall** *Am*, **shopping plaza** *Am* [-,plɑːzə] *n* centre *m* commercial.

shopsoiled *Br* ['ʃɒpsɔɪld], **shopworn** *Am* ['ʃɒpwɔːn] *adj* qui a fait l'étalage, abîmé(e) (en magasin).

shop steward *n* délégué syndical *m*, déléguée syndicale *f*.

shopwindow [,ʃɒp'wɪndəʊ] *n* vitrine *f*.

shopworn *Am* = **shopsoiled**.

shore [ʃɔːr] *n* rivage *m*, bord *m*; **on ~** à terre. O **shore up** *vt sep* étayer, étançonner; *fig* consolider.

shorn [ʃɔːn] **1** *pp* → **shear**. **2** *adj* tondu(e).

short [ʃɔːt] **1** *adj* [not long - in time] court(e), bref (brève); [- in space] court. || [not tall] petit(e). || [curt] brusque, sec (sèche). || [lacking]: **to be ~ of** manquer de. || [abbreviated]: **to be ~ for** être le diminutif de. **2** *adv*: **to be running ~ of** [running out of] commencer à manquer de, commencer à être à court de; **to cut sthg ~** [visit, speech] écourter qqch; [discussion] couper court à qqch; **to stop ~** s'arrêter net. **3** *n* [film] court métrage *m*. O **shorts** *npl* [gen] short *m*. || *Am* [underwear] caleçon *m*. O **for short** *adv*: **he's called Bob for ~** Bob est son diminutif. O **in short** *adv* (enfin) bref. O **short of** *prep* [unless, without]: **~ of doing sthg** à moins de faire qqch, à part faire qqch.

shortage ['ʃɔːtɪdʒ] n manque m, insuffisance f.

shortbread ['ʃɔːtbred] n sablé m.

short-change vt [subj: shopkeeper]: to ~ sb ne pas rendre assez à qqn.

short circuit n court-circuit m.

shortcomings ['ʃɔːt,kʌmɪŋz] npl défauts mpl.

shortcrust pastry ['ʃɔːtkrʌst] n pâte f brisée.

short cut n [quick route] raccourci m. || [quick method] solution f miracle.

shorten ['ʃɔːtn] 1 vt [holiday, time] écourter. || [skirt, rope etc] raccourcir. 2 vi [days] raccourcir.

shortfall ['ʃɔːtfɔːl] n déficit m.

shorthand ['ʃɔːthænd] n (U) [writing system] sténographie f.

shortly ['ʃɔːtlɪ] adv [soon] bientôt.

shortsighted [,ʃɔːt'saɪtɪd] adj myope; fig imprévoyant(e).

short-staffed [-'stɑːft] adj: to be ~ manquer de personnel.

short story n nouvelle f.

short-tempered [-'tempəd] adj emporté(e), irascible.

short-term adj [effects, solution] à court terme; [problem] de courte durée.

short wave n (U) ondes fpl courtes.

shot [ʃɒt] 1 pt & pp → **shoot**. 2 n [gunshot] coup m de feu; like a ~ sans tarder, sans hésiter. || [marksman] tireur m. || SPORT coup m. || [photograph] photo f; CINEMA plan m. || inf [attempt]: to have a ~ at sthg essayer de faire qqch. || [injection] piqûre f.

shotgun ['ʃɒtgʌn] n fusil m de chasse.

should [ʃʊd] aux vb [indicating duty]: we ~ leave now il faudrait partir maintenant. || [seeking advice, permission]: ~ I go too? est-ce que je devrais y aller aussi? || [as suggestion]: I ~ deny everything moi, je nierais tout. || [indicating probability]: she ~ be home soon elle devrait être de retour bientôt, elle va bientôt rentrer. || [was or were expected]: they ~ have won the match ils auraient dû gagner le match. || [indicating intention, wish]: I ~ like to come with you j'aimerais bien venir avec vous. || (as conditional): you ~ go if you're invited tu devrais y aller si tu es invité. || (in subordinate clauses): we decided that you ~ meet him nous avons décidé que ce serait toi qui irais le chercher. || [expressing uncertain opinion]: I ~ think he's about 50 (years old) je pense qu'il doit avoir dans les 50 ans.

shoulder ['ʃəʊldər] 1 n épaule f. 2 vt [carry] porter. || [responsibility] endosser.

shoulder blade n omoplate f.

shoulder strap n [on dress] bretelle f. || [on bag] bandoulière f.

shouldn't ['ʃʊdnt] = should not.

should've ['ʃʊdəv] = should have.

shout [ʃaʊt] 1 n [cry] cri m. 2 vt & vi crier. ○ **shout down** vt sep huer, conspuer.

shouting ['ʃaʊtɪŋ] n (U) cris mpl.

shove [ʃʌv] 1 n: to give sb/sthg a ~ pousser qqn/qqch. 2 vt pousser; to ~ clothes into a bag fourrer des vêtements dans un sac.

shovel ['ʃʌvl] 1 n [tool] pelle f. 2 vt enlever à la pelle, pelleter.

show [ʃəʊ] (pt -ed, pp shown OR -ed) 1 n [display] démonstration f, manifestation f. || [at theatre] spectacle m; [on radio, TV] émission f. || CINEMA séance f. || [exhibition] exposition f. 2 vt [gen] montrer; [profit, loss] indiquer; [respect] témoigner; [courage, mercy] faire preuve de; to ~ sb sthg, to ~ sthg to sb montrer qqch à qqn. || [escort]: to ~ sb to his seat/table conduire qqn à sa place/sa table. || [film] projeter, passer; [TV programme] donner, passer. 3 vi [indicate] indiquer, montrer. || [be visible] se voir, être visible. || CINEMA: what's ~ing tonight? qu'est-ce qu'on joue comme film ce soir? ○ **show off** vt sep exhiber. 2 vi faire l'intéressant(e). ○ **show up** 1 vt sep [embarrass] embarrasser, faire honte à. 2 vi [stand out] se voir, ressortir. || [arrive] s'amener, rappliquer.

show business n (U) monde m du spectacle, show-business m.

showdown ['ʃəʊdaʊn] n: to have a ~ with sb s'expliquer avec qqn, mettre les choses au point avec qqn.

shower ['ʃaʊər] 1 n [device, act] douche f; to have OR take a ~ prendre une douche, se doucher. || [of rain] averse f. 2 vt: to ~ sb with couvrir qqn de. 3 vi [wash] prendre une douche, se doucher.

shower cap n bonnet m de douche.

showing ['ʃəʊɪŋ] n CINEMA projection f.

show jumping [-,dʒʌmpɪŋ] n jumping m.

shown [ʃəʊn] pp → show.

show-off n inf m'as-tu-vu m, -e f.

showpiece ['ʃəʊpiːs] n [main attraction] joyau m, trésor m.

showroom ['ʃəʊrʊm] n salle f OR magasin *m* d'exposition; [for cars] salle de démonstration.

shrank [ʃræŋk] *pt* → **shrink**.

shrapnel ['ʃræpnl] *n* (*U*) éclats *mpl* d'obus.

shred [ʃred] **1** *n* [of material, paper] lambeau *m*, brin *m*. ‖ *fig* [of evidence] parcelle *f*; [of truth] once *f*, grain *m*. **2** *vt* [food] râper; [paper] déchirer en lambeaux.

shredder ['ʃredər] *n* [machine] destructeur *m* de documents.

shrewd [ʃruːd] *adj* fin(e), astucieux(ieuse).

shriek [ʃriːk] **1** *n* cri *m* perçant, hurlement *m*; [of laughter] éclat *m*. **2** *vi* pousser un cri perçant.

shrill [ʃrɪl] *adj* [sound, voice] aigu(ë).

shrimp [ʃrɪmp] *n* crevette *f*.

shrine [ʃraɪn] *n* [place of worship] lieu *m* saint.

shrink [ʃrɪŋk] (*pt* **shrank**, *pp* **shrunk**) **1** *vt* rétrécir. **2** *vi* [cloth, garment] rétrécir; [person] rapetisser; *fig* [income, popularity etc] baisser, diminuer. ‖ [recoil]: **to ~ away from sthg** reculer devant qqch; **to ~ from doing sthg** rechigner OR répugner à faire qqch.

shrinkage ['ʃrɪŋkɪdʒ] *n* rétrécissement *m*; *fig* diminution *f*, baisse *f*.

shrink-wrap *vt* emballer sous film plastique.

shrivel ['ʃrɪvl] **1** *vt*: **to ~ (up)** rider, flétrir. **2** *vi*: **to ~ (up)** se rider, se flétrir.

shroud [ʃraud] **1** *n* [cloth] linceul *m*. **2** *vt*: **to be ~ed in** [darkness, fog] être enseveli(e) sous; [mystery] être enveloppé(e) de.

Shrove Tuesday ['ʃrəuv-] *n* Mardi *m* gras.

shrub [ʃrʌb] *n* arbuste *m*.

shrug [ʃrʌg] **1** *vt*: **to ~ one's shoulders** hausser les épaules. **2** *vi* hausser les épaules. ○ **shrug off** *vt sep* ignorer.

shrunk [ʃrʌŋk] *pp* → **shrink**.

shudder ['ʃʌdər] *vi* [tremble]: **to ~ (with)** frémir (de), frissonner (de). ‖ [shake] vibrer, trembler.

shuffle ['ʃʌfl] *vt* [drag]: **to ~ one's feet** traîner les pieds. ‖ [cards] mélanger, battre.

shun [ʃʌn] *vt* fuir, éviter.

shunt [ʃʌnt] *vt* RAIL aiguiller.

shut [ʃʌt] (*pt & pp* **shut**) **1** *adj* [closed] fermé(e). **2** *vt* fermer. **3** *vi* [door, window] se fermer. ‖ [shop] fermer. ○ **shut away** *vt sep* [valuables, papers] mettre

sous clef. ○ **shut down** *vt sep & vi* fermer. ○ **shut out** *vt sep* [noise] supprimer; [light] ne pas laisser entrer; **to ~ sb out** laisser qqn à la porte. ○ **shut up** *inf* **1** *vt sep* [silence] faire taire. **2** *vi* se taire.

shutter ['ʃʌtər] *n* [on window] volet *m*. ‖ [in camera] obturateur *m*.

shuttle ['ʃʌtl] **1** *adj*: **~ service** (service *m* de) navette *f*. **2** *n* [train, bus, plane] navette *f*.

shuttlecock ['ʃʌtlkɒk] *n* volant *m*.

shy [ʃaɪ] **1** *adj* [timid] timide. **2** *vi* [horse] s'effaroucher.

Siberia [saɪ'bɪərɪə] *n* Sibérie *f*.

sibling ['sɪblɪŋ] *n* [brother] frère *m*; [sister] sœur *f*.

Sicily ['sɪsɪlɪ] *n* Sicile *f*.

sick [sɪk] *adj* [ill] malade. ‖ [nauseous]: **to feel ~** avoir envie de vomir, avoir mal au cœur. ‖ [fed up]: **to be ~ of** en avoir assez OR marre de. ‖ [joke, humour] macabre.

sickbay ['sɪkbeɪ] *n* infirmerie *f*.

sicken ['sɪkn] *vt* écœurer, dégoûter.

sickening ['sɪknɪŋ] *adj* [disgusting] écœurant(e), dégoûtant(e).

sickle ['sɪkl] *n* faucille *f*.

sick leave *n* (*U*) congé *m* de maladie.

sickly ['sɪklɪ] *adj* [unhealthy] maladif(ive), souffreteux(euse). ‖ [smell, taste] écœurant(e).

sickness ['sɪknɪs] *n* [illness] maladie *f*.

sick pay *n* (*U*) indemnité *f* OR allocation *f* de maladie.

side [saɪd] **1** *n* [gen] côté *m*; **at** OR **by my/her** *etc* **~** à mes/ses *etc* côtés; **from ~ to ~** d'un côté à l'autre; **~ by ~** côte à côte. ‖ [of table, river] bord *m*. ‖ [of hill, valley] versant *m*, flanc *m*. ‖ [in war, debate] camp *m*, côté *m*; SPORT équipe *f*, camp; [of argument] point *m* de vue; **to take sb's ~** prendre le parti de qqn. ‖ [aspect - gen] aspect *m*; [- of character] facette *f*; **to be on the safe ~** pour plus de sûreté, par précaution. **2** *adj* [situated on side] latéral(e).

sideboard ['saɪdbɔːd] *n* [cupboard] buffet *m*.

sideboards *Br* ['saɪdbɔːdz], **sideburns** *Am* ['saɪdbɜːnz] *npl* favoris *mpl*, rouflaquettes *fpl*.

side effect *n* MED effet *m* secondaire OR indésirable.

sidelight ['saɪdlaɪt] *n* AUT feu *m* de position.

sideline ['saɪdlaɪn] *n* [extra business] activité *f* secondaire. || SPORT ligne *f* de touche.

sidelong ['saɪdlɒŋ] *adj & adv* de côté.

sidesaddle ['saɪd,sædl] *adv*: **to ride ~** monter en amazone.

sideshow ['saɪdʃəʊ] *n* spectacle *m* forain.

sidestep ['saɪdstep] *vt* faire un pas de côté pour éviter OR esquiver; *fig* éviter.

side street *n* [not main street] petite rue *f*; [off main street] rue transversale.

sidetrack ['saɪdtræk] *vt*: **to be ~ed** se laisser distraire.

sidewalk ['saɪdwɔːk] *n Am* trottoir *m*.

sideways ['saɪdweɪz] *adj & adv* de côté.

siding ['saɪdɪŋ] *n* voie *f* de garage.

sidle ['saɪdl] ○ **sidle up** *vi*: **to ~ up to sb** se glisser vers qqn.

siege [siːdʒ] *n* siège *m*.

sieve [sɪv] **1** *n* [for flour, sand etc] tamis *m*; [for liquids] passoire *f*. **2** *vt* [flour etc] tamiser; [liquid] passer.

sift [sɪft] **1** *vt* [flour, sand] tamiser. **2** *vi*: **to ~ through** examiner, éplucher.

sigh [saɪ] **1** *n* soupir *m*. **2** *vi* [person] soupirer, pousser un soupir.

sight [saɪt] **1** *n* [seeing] vue *f*; **in/out of ~** en/hors de vue; **at first ~** à première vue, au premier abord. || [spectacle] spectacle *m*. || [on gun] mire *f*. **2** *vt* apercevoir. ○ **sights** *npl* [of city] attractions *fpl* touristiques.

sightseeing ['saɪt,siːɪŋ] *n* tourisme *m*; **to go ~** faire du tourisme.

sightseer ['saɪt,siːər] *n* touriste *mf*.

sign [saɪn] **1** *n* [gen] signe *m*; **no ~ of** aucune trace de. || [notice] enseigne *f*; AUT panneau *m*. **2** *vt* signer. ○ **sign up 1** *vt sep* [worker] embaucher; [soldier] engager. **2** *vi* MIL s'engager; [for course] s'inscrire.

signal ['sɪgnl] **1** *n* signal *m*. **2** *vt* [indicate] indiquer. || [gesture to]: **to ~ sb (to do sthg)** faire signe à qqn (de faire qqch). **3** *vi* AUT clignoter, mettre son clignotant. || [gesture]: **to ~ to sb (to do sthg)** faire signe à qqn (de faire qqch).

signalman ['sɪgnlmən] (*pl* -men [-mən]) *n* RAIL aiguilleur *m*.

signature ['sɪgnətʃər] *n* [name] signature *f*.

signature tune *n* indicatif *m*.

signet ring ['sɪgnɪt-] *n* chevalière *f*.

significance [sɪg'nɪfɪkəns] *n* [importance] importance *f*, portée *f*. || [meaning] signification *f*.

significant [sɪg'nɪfɪkənt] *adj* [considerable] considérable. || [important] important(e). || [meaningful] significatif(ive).

signify ['sɪgnɪfaɪ] *vt* signifier, indiquer.

signpost ['saɪnpəʊst] *n* poteau *m* indicateur.

Sikh [siːk] **1** *adj* sikh (*inv*). **2** *n* [person] Sikh *mf*.

silence ['saɪləns] **1** *n* silence *m*. **2** *vt* réduire au silence, faire taire.

silencer ['saɪlənsər] *n* silencieux *m*.

silent ['saɪlənt] *adj* [person, place] silencieux(ieuse). || CINEMA & LING muet(ette).

silhouette [,sɪluː'et] *n* silhouette *f*.

silicon chip [,sɪlɪkən-] *n* puce *f*, pastille *f* de silicium.

silk [sɪlk] **1** *n* soie *f*. **2** *comp* en OR de soie.

silky ['sɪlkɪ] *adj* soyeux(euse).

sill [sɪl] *n* [of window] rebord *m*.

silly ['sɪlɪ] *adj* stupide, bête.

silo ['saɪləʊ] (*pl* -s) *n* silo *m*.

silt [sɪlt] *n* vase *f*, limon *m*.

silver ['sɪlvər] **1** *adj* [colour] argenté(e). **2** *n* (*U*) [metal] argent *m*. || [coins] pièces *fpl* d'argent. || [silverware] argenterie *f*. **3** *comp* en argent, d'argent.

silver foil, silver paper *n* (*U*) papier *m* d'argent OR d'étain.

silver-plated [-'pleɪtɪd] *adj* plaqué(e) argent.

silversmith ['sɪlvəsmɪθ] *n* orfèvre *mf*.

silverware ['sɪlvəweər] *n* (*U*) [dishes, spoons etc] argenterie *f*. || *Am* [cutlery] couverts *mpl*.

similar ['sɪmɪlər] *adj*: **~ (to)** semblable (à), similaire (à).

similarly ['sɪmɪləlɪ] *adv* de la même manière, pareillement.

simmer ['sɪmər] *vt* faire cuire à feu doux, mijoter.

simple ['sɪmpl] *adj* [gen] simple.

simple-minded [-'maɪndɪd] *adj* simplet(ette), simple d'esprit.

simplicity [sɪm'plɪsətɪ] *n* simplicité *f*.

simplify ['sɪmplɪfaɪ] *vt* simplifier.

simply ['sɪmplɪ] *adv* [gen] simplement. || [for emphasis] absolument.

simulate ['sɪmjuleɪt] *vt* simuler.

simultaneous [*Br* ,sɪmʌl'teɪnjəs, *Am* ,saɪmʌl'teɪnjəs] *adj* simultané(e).

sin [sɪn] **1** *n* péché *m*. **2** *vi*: **to ~ (against)** pécher (contre).

since [sɪns] **1** *adv* depuis. **2** *prep* depuis. **3** *conj* [in time] depuis que. || [because] comme, puisque.

sincere [sɪn'sɪər] *adj* sincère.

sincerely [sɪn'sɪəlɪ] *adv* sincèrement;
Yours ~ [at end of letter] veuillez agréer,
Monsieur/Madame, l'expression de mes
sentiments les meilleurs.

sincerity [sɪn'serətɪ] *n* sincérité *f.*

sinful ['sɪnful] *adj* [thought] mauvais(e);
[desire, act] coupable.

sing [sɪŋ] (*pt* **sang**, *pp* **sung**) *vt* & *vi*
chanter.

Singapore [ˌsɪŋə'pɔːr] *n* Singapour *m.*

singe [sɪndʒ] *vt* brûler légèrement;
[cloth] roussir.

singer ['sɪŋər] *n* chanteur *m*, -euse *f.*

singing ['sɪŋɪŋ] *n* (*U*) chant *m.*

single ['sɪŋgl] **1** *adj* [only one] seul(e),
unique; **every ~** chaque. || [unmarried]
célibataire. **2** *n* MUS (disque *m*) 45 tours
m. ○ **singles** *npl* TENNIS simples *mpl.*
○ **single out** *vt sep*: **to ~ sb out (for)**
choisir qqn (pour).

single bed *n* lit *m* à une place.

single-breasted [-'brestɪd] *adj* [jacket]
droit(e).

single file *n*: **in ~** en file indienne, à la
file.

single-handed [-'hændɪd] *adv* tout seul
(toute seule).

single-minded [-'maɪndɪd] *adj* réso-
lu(e).

single-parent family *n* famille *f* mo-
noparentale.

single room *n* chambre *f* pour une personne OR à un lit.

singular ['sɪŋgjʊlər] **1** *adj* singu-
lier(ère). **2** *n* singulier *m.*

sinister ['sɪnɪstər] *adj* sinistre.

sink [sɪŋk] (*pt* **sank**, *pp* **sunk**) **1** *n* [in
kitchen] évier *m*; [in bathroom] lavabo *m.*
2 *vt* [ship] couler. || [teeth, claws]: **to ~
sthg into** enfoncer qqch dans. **3** *vi* [in water - ship] couler, sombrer; [- person, ob-
ject] couler. || [ground] s'affaisser; [sun]
baisser; **to ~ into poverty/despair** som-
brer dans la misère/le désespoir. ||
[value, amount] baisser, diminuer; [voice]
faiblir. ○ **sink in** *vi*: **it hasn't sunk in yet**
je n'ai pas encore réalisé.

sink unit *n* bloc-évier *m.*

sinner ['sɪnər] *n* pécheur *m*, -eresse *f.*

sinus ['saɪnəs] (*pl* **-es**) *n* sinus *m inv.*

sip [sɪp] **1** *n* petite gorgée *f.* **2** *vt* siroter,
boire à petits coups.

siphon ['saɪfn] *n* siphon *m.* ○ **siphon
off** *vt sep* [liquid] siphonner. || *fig*
[money] canaliser.

sir [sɜːr] *n* [form of address] monsieur *m.*

|| [in titles]: **Sir Phillip Holden** sir Phillip
Holden.

siren ['saɪərən] *n* sirène *f.*

sirloin (steak) ['sɜːlɔɪn-] *n* bifteck *m*
dans l'aloyau OR d'aloyau.

sissy ['sɪsɪ] *n inf* poule *f* mouillée, dé-
gonflé *m*, -e *f.*

sister ['sɪstər] *n* [sibling] sœur *f.* || [nun]
sœur *f*, religieuse *f.*

sister-in-law (*pl* **sisters-in-law** OR
sister-in-laws) *n* belle-sœur *f.*

sit [sɪt] (*pt* & *pp* **sat**) *vt* & *vi* [person]
s'asseoir; **to be sitting** être assis(e); **to ~
on a committee** faire partie OR être mem-
bre d'un comité. || [court, parliament] sié-
ger, être en séance. ○ **sit down** *vi*
s'asseoir. ○ **sit in on** *vt fus* assister à.
○ **sit through** *vt fus* rester jusqu'à la
fin de. ○ **sit up** *vi* [sit upright] se redres-
ser, s'asseoir. || [stay up] veiller.

sitcom ['sɪtkɒm] *n inf* sitcom *f.*

site [saɪt] **1** *n* [of town, building] emplacement *m*; [archaeological] site *m*; CONSTR
chantier *m.* **2** *vt* situer, placer.

sit-in *n* sit-in *m*, occupation *f* des locaux.

sitting ['sɪtɪŋ] *n* [of meal] service *m.* ||
[of court, parliament] séance *f.*

sitting room *n* salon *m.*

situated ['sɪtjʊeɪtɪd] *adj*: **to be ~** être
situé(e), se trouver.

situation [ˌsɪtjʊ'eɪʃn] *n* [gen] situation
f. || [job] situation *f*, emploi *m.*

six [sɪks] **1** *num adj* six (*inv*); **she's ~
(years old)** elle a six ans. **2** *num pron* six
mfpl; **I want ~** j'en veux six; **there were ~
of us** nous étions six. **3** *num n* [gen] six *m
inv*; **two hundred and ~** deux cent six. ||
[six o'clock]: **it's ~** il est six heures; **we arrived at ~** nous sommes arrivés à six
heures.

sixteen [sɪks'tiːn] *num* seize; *see also*
six.

sixth [sɪksθ] **1** *num adj* sixième. **2** *num
adv* [in race, competition] sixième, en
sixième place. || [in list] sixièmement. **3**
num pron sixième *mf.* **4** *n* [fraction]
sixième *m.* || [in dates]: **the ~ (of Septem-
ber)** le six (septembre).

sixty ['sɪkstɪ] *num* soixante; *see also*
six. ○ **sixties** *npl* [decade]: **the sixties**
les années *fpl* soixante. || [in ages]: **to be
in one's sixties** être sexagénaire.

size [saɪz] *n* [of person, clothes, company]
taille *f*; [of building] grandeur *f*, dimensions *fpl*; [of problem] ampleur *f*, taille;
[of shoes] pointure *f.* ○ **size up** *vt sep*

slant

[person] jauger; [situation] apprécier, peser.

sizeable ['saɪzəbl] *adj* assez important(e).

sizzle ['sɪzl] *vi* grésiller.

skate [skeɪt] (*pl sense 2 only inv* OR **-s**) **1** *n* [ice skate, roller skate] patin *m*. ‖ [fish] raie *f*. **2** *vi* [on ice skates] faire du patin sur glace, patiner; [on roller skates] faire du patin à roulettes.

skateboard ['skeɪtbɔːd] *n* planche *f* à roulettes, skateboard *m*, skate *m*.

skater ['skeɪtər] *n* [on ice] patineur *m*, -euse *f*; [on roller skates] patineur à roulettes.

skating ['skeɪtɪŋ] *n* [on ice] patinage *m*; [on roller skates] patinage à roulettes.

skating rink *n* patinoire *f*.

skeleton ['skelɪtn] *n* squelette *m*.

skeleton key *n* passe *m*, passe-partout *m inv*.

skeleton staff *n* personnel *m* réduit.

skeptic *etc Am* = **sceptic** *etc*.

sketch [sketʃ] **1** *n* [drawing] croquis *m*, esquisse *f*. ‖ [description] aperçu *m*, résumé *m*. ‖ [by comedian] sketch *m*. **2** *vt* [draw] dessiner, faire un croquis de. ‖ [describe] donner un aperçu de, décrire à grands traits.

sketchbook ['sketʃbʊk] *n* carnet *m* à dessins.

sketchpad ['sketʃpæd] *n* bloc *m* à dessins.

sketchy ['sketʃɪ] *adj* incomplet(ète).

skewer ['skjʊər] *n* brochette *f*.

ski [skiː] (*pt & pp* **skied**, *cont* **skiing**) **1** *n* ski *m*. **2** *vi* skier, faire du ski.

ski boots *npl* chaussures *fpl* de ski.

skid [skɪd] **1** *n* dérapage *m*; **to go into a ~** déraper. **2** *vi* déraper.

skier ['skiːər] *n* skieur *m*, -ieuse *f*.

skies [skaɪz] *pl* → **sky**.

skiing ['skiːɪŋ] *n* (*U*) ski *m*; **to go ~** faire du ski.

skilful, skillful *Am* ['skɪlfʊl] *adj* habile, adroit(e).

ski lift *n* remonte-pente *m*.

skill [skɪl] *n* (*U*) [ability] habileté *f*, adresse *f*. ‖ [technique] technique *f*, art *m*.

skilled [skɪld] *adj* [skilful]: **~ (in** OR **at doing sthg)** habile OR adroit(e) (pour faire qqch). ‖ [trained] qualifié(e).

skillful *etc Am* = **skilful** *etc*.

skim [skɪm] **1** *vt* [cream] écrémer; [soup] écumer. ‖ [move above] effleurer, raser. **2**

vi: **to ~ through sthg** [newspaper, book] parcourir qqch.

skim(med) milk [skɪm(d)-] *n* lait *m* écrémé.

skimp [skɪmp] *vi*: **to ~ on** lésiner sur.

skimpy ['skɪmpɪ] *adj* [meal] maigre; [clothes] étriqué(e); [facts] insuffisant(e).

skin [skɪn] **1** *n* peau *f*. **2** *vt* [dead animal] écorcher, dépouiller; [fruit] éplucher, peler. ‖ [graze]: **to ~ one's knee** s'érafler OR s'écorcher le genou.

skin-deep *adj* superficiel(ielle).

skin diving *n* plongée *f* sous-marine.

skinny ['skɪnɪ] *adj* maigre.

skin-tight *adj* moulant(e), collant(e).

skip [skɪp] **1** *n* [jump] petit saut *m*. **2** *vt* [page, class, meal] sauter. **3** *vi* [gen] sauter, sautiller.

ski pole *n* bâton *m* de ski.

skipper ['skɪpər] *n* NAUT & SPORT capitaine *m*.

skirmish ['skɜːmɪʃ] *n* escarmouche *f*.

skirt [skɜːt] *n* [garment] jupe *f*. ○ **skirt round** *vt fus* [town, obstacle] contourner. ‖ [problem] éviter.

skit [skɪt] *n* sketch *m*.

skittle ['skɪtl] *n Br* quille *f*. ○ **skittles** *n* (*U*) [game] quilles *fpl*.

skulk [skʌlk] *vi* [hide] se cacher; [prowl] rôder.

skull [skʌl] *n* crâne *m*.

skunk [skʌŋk] *n* [animal] mouffette *f*.

sky [skaɪ] *n* ciel *m*.

skylight ['skaɪlaɪt] *n* lucarne *f*.

skyscraper ['skaɪ‚skreɪpər] *n* gratte-ciel *m inv*.

slab [slæb] *n* [of concrete] dalle *f*; [of stone] bloc *m*; [of cake] pavé *m*.

slack [slæk] **1** *adj* [not tight] lâche. ‖ [not busy] calme. ‖ [person] négligent(e), pas sérieux(ieuse). **2** *n* [in rope] mou *m*.

slacken ['slækn] **1** *vt* [speed, pace] ralentir; [rope] relâcher. **2** *vi* [speed, pace] ralentir.

slag [slæg] *n* (*U*) [waste material] scories *fpl*.

slagheap ['slæghiːp] *n* terril *m*.

slam [slæm] **1** *vt* [shut] claquer. ‖ [place with force]: **to ~ sthg on** OR **onto** jeter qqch brutalement sur, flanquer qqch sur. **2** *vi* claquer.

slander ['slɑːndər] **1** *n* calomnie *f*; JUR diffamation *f*. **2** *vt* calomnier; JUR diffamer.

slang [slæŋ] *n* (*U*) argot *m*.

slant [slɑːnt] **1** *n* [angle] inclinaison *f*. ‖ [perspective] point *m* de vue, perspective *f.* 2 *vt* [bias] présenter d'une manière tendancieuse. 3 *vi* [slope] être incliné(e), pencher.

slanting ['slɑːntɪŋ] *adj* [roof] en pente.

slap [slæp] 1 *n* claque *f*, tape *f*; [on face] gifle *f*. 2 *vt* [person, face] gifler; [back] donner une claque OR une tape à. || [place with force]: **to ~ sthg on** OR **onto** jeter qqch brutalement sur, flanquer qqch sur. 3 *adv inf* [directly] en plein.

slapdash ['slæpdæʃ], **slaphappy** ['slæp,hæpɪ] *adj inf* [work] bâclé(e); [person, attitude] insouciant(e).

slapstick ['slæpstɪk] *n* (*U*) grosse farce *f*.

slash [slæʃ] 1 *n* [long cut] entaille *f*. || [oblique stroke] barre *f* oblique. 2 *vt* [cut] entailler. || *inf* [prices] casser; [budget, unemployment] réduire considérablement.

slat [slæt] *n* lame *f*; [wooden] latte *f*.

slate [sleɪt] 1 *n* ardoise *f*. 2 *vt inf* [criticize] descendre en flammes.

slaughter ['slɔːtər] 1 *n* [of animals] abattage *m*. || [of people] massacre *m*, carnage *m*. 2 *vt* [animals] abattre. || [people] massacrer.

slaughterhouse ['slɔːtəhaus], *pl* -hauzɪz] *n* abattoir *m*.

slave [sleɪv] 1 *n* esclave *mf*. 2 *vi*: **to ~ over sthg** peiner sur qqch.

slavery ['sleɪvərɪ] *n* esclavage *m*.

sleazy ['sliːzɪ] *adj* [disreputable] mal famé(e).

sledge [sledʒ], **sled** *Am* [sled] *n* luge *f*; [larger] traîneau *m*.

sledgehammer ['sledʒ,hæmər] *n* masse *f*.

sleek [sliːk] *adj* [hair, fur] lisse, luisant(e). || [shape] aux lignes pures.

sleep [sliːp] (*pt & pp* **slept**) 1 *n* sommeil *m*; **to go to ~** s'endormir. 2 *vi* [be asleep] dormir. || [spend night] coucher. ○ **sleep in** *vi* faire la grasse matinée. ○ **sleep with** *vt fus euphemism* coucher avec.

sleeper ['sliːpər] *n* [person]: **to be a heavy/light ~** avoir le sommeil lourd/ léger. || [RAIL - berth] couchette *f*; [- carriage] wagon-lit *m*; [- train] train-couchettes *m*.

sleeping bag ['sliːpɪŋ-] *n* sac *m* de couchage.

sleeping car ['sliːpɪŋ-] *n* wagon-lit *m*.

sleeping pill ['sliːpɪŋ-] *n* somnifère *m*.

sleepless ['sliːplɪs] *adj*: **to have a ~ night** passer une nuit blanche.

sleepwalk ['sliːpwɔːk] *vi* être somnambule.

sleepy ['sliːpɪ] *adj* [person] qui a envie de dormir.

sleet [sliːt] 1 *n* neige *f* fondue. 2 *v impers*: **it's ~ing** il tombe de la neige fondue.

sleeve [sliːv] *n* [of garment] manche *f*. || [for record] pochette *f*.

sleigh [sleɪ] *n* traîneau *m*.

sleight of hand [,slaɪt-] *n* (*U*) [skill] habileté *f*. || [trick] tour *m* de passe-passe.

slender ['slendər] *adj* [thin] mince. || *fig* [resources, income] modeste, maigre; [hope, chance] faible.

slept [slept] *pt & pp* → **sleep**.

slice [slaɪs] 1 *n* [thin piece] tranche *f*. || *fig* [of profits, glory] part *f*. 2 *vt* [cut into slices] couper en tranches. || [cut cleanly] trancher.

slick [slɪk] 1 *adj* [skilful] bien mené(e), habile. || *pej* [superficial - talk] facile; [- person] rusé(e). 2 *n* nappe *f* de pétrole, marée *f* noire.

slide [slaɪd] (*pt & pp* **slid** [slɪd]) 1 *n* [in playground] toboggan *m*. || PHOT diapositive *f*, diapo *f*. || [decline] déclin *m*; [in prices] baisse *f*. 2 *vt* faire glisser. 3 *vi* glisser.

sliding door [,slaɪdɪŋ-] *n* porte *f* coulissante.

slight [slaɪt] 1 *adj* [minor] léger(ère); **the ~est** le moindre (la moindre); **not in the ~est** pas du tout. || [thin] mince. 2 *n* affront *m*. 3 *vt* offenser.

slightly ['slaɪtlɪ] *adv* [to small extent] légèrement.

slim [slɪm] 1 *adj* [person, object] mince. || [chance, possibility] faible. 2 *vi* maigrir; [diet] suivre un régime amaigrissant.

slime [slaɪm] *n* (*U*) [substance] substance *f* visqueuse; [of snail] bave *f*.

slimming ['slɪmɪŋ] 1 *n* amaigrissement *m*. 2 *adj* [product] amaigrissant(e).

sling [slɪŋ] (*pt & pp* **slung**) 1 *n* [for arm] écharpe *f*. 2 *vt* [hammock etc] suspendre. || *inf* [throw] lancer.

slip [slɪp] 1 *n* [mistake] erreur *f*; **a ~ of the tongue** un lapsus. || [of paper - gen] morceau *m*; [- strip] bande *f*. || [underwear] combinaison *f*. || *phr*: **to give sb the ~** *inf* fausser compagnie à qqn. 2 *vt* glisser; **to ~ sthg on** enfiler qqch. 3 *vi* [slide] glisser; **to ~ into sthg** se glisser dans qqch. || [decline] décliner. ○ **slip up** *fig* faire une erreur.

slipped disc [ˌslɪpt-] n hernie f discale.

slipper ['slɪpər] n pantoufle f, chausson m.

slippery ['slɪpərɪ] adj glissant(e).

slipshod ['slɪpʃɒd] adj peu soigné(e).

slip-up n inf gaffe f.

slipway ['slɪpweɪ] n cale f de lancement.

slit [slɪt] (pt & pp **slit**) **1** n [opening] fente f; [cut] incision f. **2** vt [make opening in] faire une fente dans, fendre; [cut] inciser.

slither ['slɪðər] vi [person] glisser; [snake] onduler.

sliver ['slɪvər] n [of glass, wood] éclat m; [of meat, cheese] lamelle f.

slob [slɒb] n inf [in habits] saligaud m; [in appearance] gros lard m.

slog [slɒg] inf **1** n [tiring work] corvée f. **2** vi [work] travailler comme un bœuf OR un nègre.

slogan ['sləʊgən] n slogan m.

slop [slɒp] **1** vt renverser. **2** vi déborder.

slope [sləʊp] **1** n pente f. **2** vi [land] être en pente; [handwriting, table] pencher.

sloping ['sləʊpɪŋ] adj [land, shelf] en pente; [handwriting] penché(e).

sloppy ['slɒpɪ] adj [careless] peu soigné(e).

slot [slɒt] n [opening] fente f. || [groove] rainure f. || [in schedule] créneau m.

slot machine n [vending machine] distributeur m automatique. || [for gambling] machine f à sous.

slouch [slaʊtʃ] vi être avachi(e).

Slovakia [slə'vækɪə] n Slovaquie f.

slovenly ['slʌvnlɪ] adj négligé(e).

slow [sləʊ] **1** adj [gen] lent(e). || [clock, watch]: **to be ~** retarder. **2** adv lentement; **to go ~** [driver] aller lentement; [workers] faire la grève perlée. ◯ **slow down, slow up** vt sep & vi ralentir.

slowdown ['sləʊdaʊn] n ralentissement m.

slowly ['sləʊlɪ] adv lentement.

slow motion n: **in ~** au ralenti m.

sludge [slʌdʒ] n boue f.

slug [slʌg] n [animal] limace f. || inf [of alcohol] rasade f. || Am inf [bullet] balle f.

sluggish ['slʌgɪʃ] adj [person] apathique; [movement, growth] lent(e).

sluice [sluːs] n écluse f.

slum [slʌm] n [area] quartier m pauvre.

slumber ['slʌmbər] literary n sommeil m.

slump [slʌmp] **1** n [decline]: **~ (in)** baisse f (de). || [period of poverty] crise f (économique). **2** vi lit & fig s'effondrer.

slung [slʌŋ] pt & pp → **sling**.

slur [slɜːr] **1** n [slight]: **~ (on)** atteinte f (à). || [insult] affront m, insulte f. **2** vt mal articuler.

slush [slʌʃ] n [snow] neige f fondue.

slush fund, slush money Am n fonds mpl secrets, caisse f noire.

slut [slʌt] n inf [dirty, untidy] souillon f. || v inf [sexually immoral] salope f.

sly [slaɪ] (compar **slyer** OR **slier**, superl **slyest** OR **sliest**) adj [look, smile] entendu(e). || [person] rusé(e), sournois(e).

smack [smæk] **1** n [slap] claque f; [on face] gifle f. || [impact] claquement m. **2** vt [slap] donner une claque à; [face] gifler. || [place violently] poser violemment.

small [smɔːl] adj [gen] petit(e). || [trivial] petit, insignifiant(e).

small change n petite monnaie f.

small hours npl: **in the ~** au petit jour OR matin.

smallpox ['smɔːlpɒks] n variole f, petite vérole f.

small print n: **the ~** les clauses fpl écrites en petits caractères.

small talk n (U) papotage m, bavardage m.

smarmy ['smɑːmɪ] adj mielleux(euse).

smart [smɑːt] **1** adj [stylish - person, clothes, car] élégant(e). || [clever] intelligent(e). || [fashionable - club, society, hotel] à la mode, in (inv). || [quick - answer, tap] vif (vive), rapide. **2** vi [eyes, skin] brûler, piquer. || [person] être blessé(e).

smarten ['smɑːtn] ◯ **smarten up** vt sep [room] arranger; **to ~ o.s. up** se faire beau (belle).

smash [smæʃ] **1** n [sound] fracas m. || SPORT smash m. **2** vt [glass, plate etc] casser, briser. || fig [defeat] détruire. **3** vi [glass, plate etc] se briser. || [crash]: **to ~ into sthg** s'écraser contre qqch.

smashing ['smæʃɪŋ] adj inf super (inv).

smattering ['smætərɪŋ] n: **to have a ~ of German** savoir quelques mots d'allemand.

smear [smɪər] **1** n [dirty mark] tache f. || MED frottis m. || [slander] diffamation f. **2** vt [smudge] barbouiller, maculer. || [spread]: **to ~ sthg with sthg** enduire qqch de qqch. || [slander] calomnier.

smell [smel] (pt & pp **-ed** OR **smelt**) **1** n [odour] odeur f. || [sense of smell] odorat m. **2** vt sentir. **3** vi [flower, food] sentir; **to ~ of sthg** sentir qqch. || [smell unpleasantly] sentir (mauvais), puer.

smelly ['smelɪ] *adj* qui sent mauvais, qui pue.

smelt [smelt] **1** *pt & pp* → **smell**. **2** *vt* [metal] extraire par fusion; [ore] fondre.

smile [smaɪl] **1** *n* sourire *m*. **2** *vi* sourire.

smirk [smɜːk] *n* sourire *m* narquois.

smock [smɒk] *n* blouse *f*.

smog [smɒg] *n* smog *m*.

smoke [sməʊk] **1** *n* (*U*) [from fire] fumée *f*. **2** *vt & vi* fumer.

smoked [sməʊkt] *adj* [food] fumé(e).

smoker ['sməʊkər] *n* [person] fumeur *m*, -euse *f*. || RAIL compartiment *m* fumeurs.

smoke shop *n Am* bureau *m* de tabac.

smoking ['sməʊkɪŋ] *n* tabagisme *m*; "no ~" «défense de fumer».

smoky ['sməʊkɪ] *adj* [room, air] enfumé(e). || [taste] fumé(e).

smolder *Am* = **smoulder**.

smooth [smuːð] **1** *adj* [surface] lisse. || [sauce] homogène, onctueux(euse). || [movement] régulier(ière). || [taste] moelleux(euse). || [flight, ride] confortable; [landing, take-off] en douceur. || *pej* [person, manner] doucereux(euse), mielleux(euse). || [operation, progress] sans problèmes. **2** *vt* [hair] lisser; [clothes, tablecloth] défroisser.

smother ['smʌðər] *vt* [cover thickly]: **to ~ sb/sthg with** couvrir qqn/qqch de. || [person, fire] étouffer. || *fig* [emotions] cacher, étouffer.

smoulder *Br*, **smolder** *Am* ['sməʊldər] *vi lit & fig* couver.

smudge [smʌdʒ] **1** *n* tache *f*; [of ink] bavure *f*. **2** *vt* [drawing, painting] maculer; [paper] faire une marque OR trace sur; [face] salir.

smug [smʌg] *adj* suffisant(e).

smuggle ['smʌgl] *vt* [across frontiers] faire passer en contrebande.

smuggler ['smʌglər] *n* contrebandier *m*, -ière *f*.

smuggling ['smʌglɪŋ] *n* (*U*) contrebande *f*.

snack [snæk] *n* casse-croûte *m inv*.

snack bar *n* snack *m*, snack-bar *m*.

snag [snæg] **1** *n* [problem] inconvénient *m*, écueil *m*. **2** *vi*: **to ~ (on)** s'accrocher (à).

snail [sneɪl] *n* escargot *m*.

snake [sneɪk] *n* serpent *m*.

snap [snæp] **1** *adj* [decision, election] subit(e); [judgment] irréfléchi(e). **2** *n* [of branch] craquement *m*; [of fingers] claquement *m*. || [photograph] photo *f*. ||

[card game] ≃ bataille *f*. **3** *vt* [break] casser net. || [speak sharply] dire d'un ton sec. **4** *vi* [break] se casser net. || [dog]: **to ~ at** essayer de mordre. || [speak sharply]: **to ~ (at sb)** parler (à qqn) d'un ton sec.

snap fastener *n* pression *f*.

snappy ['snæpɪ] *adj inf* [stylish] chic. || [quick] prompt(e); **make it ~!** dépêche-toi!, et que ça saute!

snapshot ['snæpʃɒt] *n* photo *f*.

snare [sneər] **1** *n* piège *m*, collet *m*. **2** *vt* prendre au piège, attraper.

snarl [snɑːl] **1** *n* grondement *m*. **2** *vi* gronder.

snatch [snætʃ] **1** *n* [of conversation] bribe *f*; [of song] extrait *m*. **2** *vt* [grab] saisir.

sneak [sniːk] (*Am pt* **snuck**) **1** *vt*: **to ~ a look at sb/sthg** regarder qqn/qqch à la dérobée. **2** *vi* [move quietly] se glisser.

sneakers ['sniːkəz] *npl Am* tennis *mpl*, baskets *fpl*.

sneaky ['sniːkɪ] *adj inf* sournois(e).

sneer [snɪər] **1** *n* [smile] sourire *m* dédaigneux; [laugh] ricanement *m*. **2** *vi* [smile] sourire dédaigneusement.

sneeze [sniːz] **1** *n* éternuement *m*. **2** *vi* éternuer.

snide [snaɪd] *adj* sournois(e).

sniff [snɪf] **1** *vt* [smell] renifler. **2** *vi* [to clear nose] renifler.

snigger ['snɪgər] **1** *n* rire *m* en dessous. **2** *vi* ricaner.

snip [snɪp] *vt* couper.

sniper ['snaɪpər] *n* tireur *m* isolé.

snippet ['snɪpɪt] *n* fragment *m*.

snivel ['snɪvl] *vi* geindre.

snob [snɒb] *n* snob *mf*.

snobbish ['snɒbɪʃ], **snobby** ['snɒbɪ] *adj* snob (*inv*).

snoop [snuːp] *vi inf* fureter.

snooty ['snuːtɪ] *adj inf* prétentieux(ieuse).

snooze [snuːz] **1** *n* petit somme *m*. **2** *vi* faire un petit somme.

snore [snɔːr] **1** *n* ronflement *m*. **2** *vi* ronfler.

snoring ['snɔːrɪŋ] *n* (*U*) ronflement *m*, ronflements *mpl*.

snorkel ['snɔːkl] *n* tuba *m*.

snort [snɔːt] **1** *n* [of person] grognement *m*; [of horse, bull] ébrouement *m*. **2** *vi* [person] grogner; [horse] s'ébrouer.

snout [snaʊt] *n* groin *m*.

snow [snəʊ] **1** *n* neige *f*. **2** *v impers* neiger.

snowball ['snəʊbɔːl] **1** *n* boule *f* de neige. **2** *vi fig* faire boule de neige.

snowbound ['snəʊbaʊnd] *adj* bloqué(e) par la neige.

snowdrift ['snəʊdrɪft] *n* congère *f*.

snowdrop ['snəʊdrɒp] *n* perce-neige *m inv*.

snowfall ['snəʊfɔːl] *n* chute *f* de neige.

snowflake ['snəʊfleɪk] *n* flocon *m* de neige.

snowman ['snəʊmæn] (*pl* -men [-men]) *n* bonhomme *m* de neige.

snowplough *Br*, **snowplow** *Am* ['snəʊplaʊ] *n* chasse-neige *m inv*.

snowshoe ['snəʊʃuː] *n* raquette *f*.

snowstorm ['snəʊstɔːm] *n* tempête *f* de neige.

Snr, snr *abbr of* **senior**.

snub [snʌb] **1** *n* rebuffade *f*. **2** *vt* snober, ignorer.

snuck [snʌk] *pt* → **sneak**.

snuff [snʌf] *n* tabac *m* à priser.

snug [snʌg] *adj* [person] à l'aise, confortable; [in bed] bien au chaud. || [place] douillet(ette). || [close-fitting] bien ajusté(e).

snuggle ['snʌgl] *vi* se blottir.

so [səʊ] **1** *adv* [to such a degree] si, tellement; ~ **difficult (that)** ... si OR tellement difficile que ...; **we had** ~ **much work!** nous avions tant de travail!; **I've never seen** ~ **much money/many cars** je n'ai jamais vu autant d'argent/de voitures. || [in referring back to previous statement, event etc]: ~ **you knew already?** alors tu le savais déjà?; **I don't think** ~ je ne crois pas; **I'm afraid** ~ je crains bien que oui; **if** ~ si oui; **is that** ~? vraiment? || [also] aussi; ~ **can/do/would** *etc* **I** moi aussi. || [in this way]: (**like**) ~ comme cela OR ça, de cette façon. || [in expressing agreement]: ~ **there is** en effet, c'est vrai; ~ **I see** c'est ce que je vois. || [unspecified amount, limit]: **they pay us** ~ **much a week** ils nous payent tant par semaine; **or** ~ environ, à peu près. **2** *conj* alors; **I'm away next week** — **I won't be there** je suis en voyage la semaine prochaine donc OR par conséquent je ne serai pas là; ~ **what?** *inf* et alors?; ~ **there!** *inf* là!, et voilà! ○ **and so on, and so forth** *adv* et ainsi de suite. ○ **so as** *conj* afin de, pour. ○ **so that** *conj* [for the purpose that] pour que (+ *subjunctive*).

soak [səʊk] **1** *vt* laisser OR faire tremper. **2** *vi* [become thoroughly wet]: **to leave sthg to** ~, **to let sthg** ~ laisser OR faire tremper qqch. || [spread]: **to** ~ **into sthg** tremper dans qqch; **to** ~ **through (sthg)** traverser (qqch). ○ **soak up** *vt sep* absorber.

soaking ['səʊkɪŋ] *adj* trempé(e).

so-and-so *n inf* [to replace a name]: **Mr** ~ Monsieur un tel. || [annoying person] enquiquineur *m*, -euse *f*.

soap [səʊp] *n* (*U*) [for washing] savon *m*.

soap flakes *npl* savon *m* en paillettes.

soap opera *n* soap opera *m*.

soap powder *n* lessive *f*.

soar [sɔːʳ] *vi* [bird] planer. || [balloon, kite] monter. || [prices, temperature] monter en flèche.

sob [sɒb] **1** *n* sanglot *m*. **2** *vi* sangloter.

sober ['səʊbəʳ] *adj* [not drunk] qui n'est pas ivre. || [serious] sérieux(ieuse). || [plain - clothes, colours] sobre. ○ **sober up** *vi* dessoûler.

sobering ['səʊbərɪŋ] *adj* qui donne à réfléchir.

so-called [-kɔːld] *adj* [misleadingly named] soi-disant (*inv*). || [widely known as] ainsi appelé(e).

soccer ['sɒkəʳ] *n* football *m*.

sociable ['səʊʃəbl] *adj* sociable.

social ['səʊʃl] *adj* social(e).

social club *n* club *m*.

socialism ['səʊʃəlɪzm] *n* socialisme *m*.

socialist ['səʊʃəlɪst] **1** *adj* socialiste. **2** *n* socialiste *mf*.

socialize, -ise ['səʊʃəlaɪz] *vi* fréquenter des gens.

social security *n* aide *f* sociale.

social services *npl* services *mpl* sociaux.

social worker *n* assistant social *m*, assistante sociale *f*.

society [sə'saɪətɪ] *n* [gen] société *f*. || [club] association *f*, club *m*.

sociology [,səʊsɪ'ɒlədʒɪ] *n* sociologie *f*.

sock [sɒk] *n* chaussette *f*.

socket ['sɒkɪt] *n* [for light bulb] douille *f*; [for plug] prise *f* de courant. || [of eye] orbite *f*; [for bone] cavité *f* articulaire.

sod [sɒd] *n* [of turf] motte *f* de gazon.

soda ['səʊdə] *n* CHEM soude *f*. || *Am* [fizzy drink] soda *m*.

soda water *n* eau *f* de Seltz.

sodden ['sɒdn] *adj* trempé(e), détrempé(e).

sodium ['səʊdɪəm] *n* sodium *m*.

sofa ['səʊfə] *n* canapé *m*.

Sofia ['səʊfjə] *n* Sofia.

soft [sɒft] *adj* [not hard] doux (douce), mou (molle). || [smooth, not loud, not bright] doux (douce). || [without force] léger(ère). || [caring] tendre. || [lenient] faible, indulgent(e).

soft drink *n* boisson *f* non alcoolisée.

soften ['sɒfn] **1** *vt* [fabric] assouplir; [substance] ramollir; [skin] adoucir. || [shock, blow] atténuer, adoucir. || [attitude] modérer, adoucir. **2** *vi* [substance] se ramollir. || [attitude, person] s'adoucir, se radoucir.

softhearted [ˌsɒft'hɑːtɪd] *adj* au cœur tendre.

softly ['sɒftlɪ] *adv* [gently, quietly] doucement. || [not brightly] faiblement. || [leniently] avec indulgence.

soft-spoken *adj* à la voix douce.

software ['sɒftweər] *n* (*U*) COMPUT logiciel *m*.

soggy ['sɒgɪ] *adj* trempé(e), détrempé(e).

soil [sɔɪl] **1** *n* (*U*) [earth] sol *m*, terre *f*. || *fig* [territory] sol *m*, territoire *m*. **2** *vt* souiller, salir.

soiled [sɔɪld] *adj* sale.

solace ['sɒləs] *n literary* consolation *f*, réconfort *m*.

solar ['səʊlər] *adj* solaire.

sold [səʊld] *pt & pp* → **sell**.

solder ['səʊldər] **1** *n* (*U*) soudure *f*. **2** *vt* souder.

soldier ['səʊldʒər] *n* soldat *m*.

sold-out *adj* [tickets] qui ont tous été vendus; [play, concert] qui joue à guichets fermés.

sole [səʊl] (*pl sense 2 only inv* OR **-s**) **1** *adj* [only] seul(e), unique. || [exclusive] exclusif(ive). **2** *n* [of foot] semelle *f*. || [fish] sole *f*.

solemn ['sɒləm] *adj* solennel(elle); [person] sérieux(ieuse).

solicit [sə'lɪsɪt] **1** *vt* [request] solliciter. **2** *vi* [prostitute] racoler.

solid ['sɒlɪd] **1** *adj* [not fluid, sturdy, reliable] solide. || [not hollow - tyres] plein(e); [- wood, rock, gold] massif(ive). || [without interruption]: **two hours ~** deux heures d'affilée. **2** *n* solide *m*.

solidarity [ˌsɒlɪ'dærətɪ] *n* solidarité *f*.

solitaire [sə'lɪteər] *n* [jewel, board game] solitaire *m*. || *Am* [card game] réussite *f*, patience *f*.

solitary ['sɒlɪtrɪ] *adj* [lonely, alone] solitaire. || [just one] seul(e).

solitary confinement *n* isolement *m* cellulaire.

solitude ['sɒlɪtjuːd] *n* solitude *f*.

solo ['səʊləʊ] (*pl* **-s**) **1** *adj* solo (*inv*). **2** *n* solo *m*. **3** *adv* en solo.

soloist ['səʊləʊɪst] *n* soliste *mf*.

soluble ['sɒljʊbl] *adj* soluble.

solution [sə'luːʃn] *n* [to problem]: **~ (to)** solution *f* (de). || [liquid] solution *f*.

solve [sɒlv] *vt* résoudre.

solvent ['sɒlvənt] **1** *adj* FIN solvable. **2** *n* dissolvant *m*, solvant *m*.

Somalia [sə'mɑːlɪə] *n* Somalie *f*.

sombre *Br*, **somber** *Am* ['sɒmbər] *adj* sombre.

some [sʌm] **1** *adj* [a certain amount, number of]: **~ meat** de la viande; **~ money** de l'argent; **~ coffee** du café; **~ sweets** des bonbons. || [fairly large number or quantity of] quelque; **I've known him for ~ years** je le connais depuis plusieurs années OR pas mal d'années. || (*contrastive use*) [certain]: **~ jobs are better paid than others** certains boulots sont mieux rémunérés que d'autres; **~ people like his music** il y en a qui aiment sa musique. || [in imprecise statements] quelque, quelconque; **there must be ~ mistake** il doit y avoir erreur. || *inf* [very good]: **that was ~ party!** c'était une soirée formidable!, quelle soirée! **2** *pron* [a certain amount]: **can I have ~?** [money, milk, coffee etc] est-ce que je peux en prendre?; **~ of it is mine** une partie est à moi. || [a certain number] quelques-uns (quelques-unes), certains (certaines); **can I have ~?** [books, pens, potatoes etc] est-ce que je peux en prendre quelques-uns (quelques-unes)? **3** *adv* quelque, environ; **there were ~ 7,000 people there** il y avait quelque OR environ 7 000 personnes.

somebody ['sʌmbədɪ] *pron* quelqu'un.

someday ['sʌmdeɪ] *adv* un jour, un de ces jours.

somehow ['sʌmhaʊ], **someway** *Am* ['sʌmweɪ] *adv* [by some action] d'une manière ou d'une autre. || [for some reason] pour une raison ou pour une autre.

someone ['sʌmwʌn] *pron* quelqu'un.

someplace *Am* = **somewhere**.

somersault ['sʌməsɔːlt] **1** *n* cabriole *f*, culbute *f*. **2** *vi* faire une cabriole OR culbute.

something ['sʌmθɪŋ] **1** *pron* [unknown thing] quelque chose; **~ odd/interesting** quelque chose de bizarre/d'intéressant; **or ~** *inf* ou quelque chose comme ça. **2** *adv*: **~ like**, **~ in the region of** environ, à peu près.

sometime ['sʌmtaɪm] *adv* un de ces jours; ~ **last week** la semaine dernière.

sometimes ['sʌmtaɪmz] *adv* quelquefois, parfois.

someway *Am* = **somehow**.

somewhat ['sʌmwɒt] *adv* quelque peu.

somewhere *Br* ['sʌmweəʳ], **someplace** *Am* ['sʌmpleɪs] *adv* [unknown place] quelque part; ~ **else** ailleurs; ~ **near here** près d'ici. || [used in approximations] environ, à peu près.

son [sʌn] *n* fils *m*.

song [sɒŋ] *n* chanson *f*; [of bird] chant *m*, ramage *m*.

sonic ['sɒnɪk] *adj* sonique.

son-in-law (*pl* **sons-in-law** OR **son-in-laws**) *n* gendre *m*, beau-fils *m*.

sonnet ['sɒnɪt] *n* sonnet *m*.

soon [su:n] *adv* [before long] bientôt; ~ **after** peu après. || [early] tôt; **write back** ~ réponds-moi vite; **how** ~ **will it be ready?** ce sera prêt quand?, dans combien de temps est-ce que ce sera prêt?; **as** ~ **as** dès que, aussitôt que.

sooner ['su:nəʳ] *adv* [in time] plus tôt; **no** ~ ... **than** ... à peine ... que ...; ~ **or later** tôt ou tard; **the** ~ **the better** le plus tôt sera le mieux. || [expressing preference]: **I would** ~ ... je préférerais ..., j'aimerais mieux ....

soot [sʊt] *n* suie *f*.

soothe [su:ð] *vt* calmer, apaiser.

sophisticated [sə'fɪstɪkeɪtɪd] *adj* [stylish] raffiné(e), sophistiqué(e). || [intelligent] averti(e). || [complicated] sophistiqué(e), très perfectionné(e).

sophomore ['sɒfəmɔːʳ] *n Am* étudiant *m*, -e *f* de seconde année.

sopping ['sɒpɪŋ] *adj*: ~ (**wet**) tout trempé (toute trempée).

soppy ['sɒpɪ] *adj inf* [sentimental - book, film] à l'eau de rose; [- person] sentimental(e). || [silly] bêta(asse), bête.

soprano [sə'prɑːnəʊ] (*pl* -s) *n* [person] soprano *mf*; [voice] soprano *m*.

sorbet ['sɔːbeɪ] *n* sorbet *m*.

sorcerer ['sɔːsərəʳ] *n* sorcier *m*.

sordid ['sɔːdɪd] *adj* sordide.

sore [sɔːʳ] **1** *adj* [painful] douloureux(euse); **to have a** ~ **throat** avoir mal à la gorge. || *Am* [upset] fâché(e), contrarié(e). **2** *n* plaie *f*.

sorely ['sɔːlɪ] *adv literary* [needed] grandement.

sorrow ['sɒrəʊ] *n* peine *f*, chagrin *m*.

sorry ['sɒrɪ] **1** *adj* [expressing apology, disappointment, sympathy] désolé(e); **to**

be ~ **about sthg** s'excuser pour qqch; **to be** ~ **for sthg** regretter qqch; **to be** OR **feel** ~ **for sb** plaindre qqn. || [poor]: **in a** ~ **state** en piteux état, dans un triste état. **2** *excl* [expressing apology] pardon!, excusez-moi!; ~, **we're sold out** désolé, on n'en a plus. || [asking for repetition] pardon?, comment? || [to correct oneself] non, pardon OR je veux dire.

sort [sɔːt] **1** *n* genre *m*, sorte *f*, espèce *f*; ~ **of** [rather] plutôt, quelque peu. **2** *vt* trier, classer. ◯ **sort out** *vt sep* [classify] ranger, classer. || [solve] résoudre.

sorting office ['sɔːtɪŋ-] *n* centre *m* de tri.

SOS (*abbr of* **save our souls**) *n* SOS *m*.

so-so *inf* **1** *adj* quelconque. **2** *adv* comme ci comme ça.

sought [sɔːt] *pt & pp* → **seek**.

soul [səʊl] *n* [gen] âme *f*. || [music] soul *m*.

soul-destroying [-dɪˌstrɔɪŋ] *adj* abrutissant(e).

soulful ['səʊlfʊl] *adj* [look] expressif(ive); [song etc] sentimental(e).

sound [saʊnd] **1** *adj* [healthy - body] sain(e), en bonne santé; [- mind] sain. || [sturdy] solide. || [reliable - advice] judicieux(ieuse), sage; [- investment] sûr(e). **2** *adv*: **to be** ~ **asleep** dormir à poings fermés, dormir d'un sommeil profond. **3** *n* son *m*; [particular sound] bruit *m*, son *m*; **by the** ~ **of it** ... d'après ce que j'ai compris .... **4** *vt* [alarm, bell] sonner. **5** *vi* [make a noise] sonner, retentir; **to** ~ **like sthg** ressembler à qqch. || [seem] sembler, avoir l'air. ◯ **sound out** *vt sep*: **to** ~ **sb out** (**on** OR **about**) sonder qqn (sur).

sound barrier *n* mur *m* du son.

sound effects *npl* bruitage *m*, effets *mpl* sonores.

soundly ['saʊndlɪ] *adv* [beaten] à plates coutures. || [sleep] profondément.

soundproof ['saʊndpruːf] *adj* insonorisé(e).

soundtrack ['saʊndtræk] *n* bande-son *f*.

soup [suːp] *n* soupe *f*, potage *m*.

soup plate *n* assiette *f* creuse OR à soupe.

soup spoon *n* cuiller *f* à soupe.

sour ['saʊəʳ] *adj* [taste, fruit] acide, aigre. || [milk] aigre. || [ill-tempered] aigre, acerbe.

source [sɔːs] *n* [gen] source *f*. || [cause] origine *f*, cause *f*.

sour grapes n (U) inf: what he said was just ~ il a dit ça par dépit.

south [saʊθ] 1 n [direction] sud m. || [region]: **the ~** le sud; **the South of France** le Sud de la France, le Midi (de la France). 2 adj sud (inv); [wind] du sud. 3 adv au sud, vers le sud; **~ of** au sud de.

South Africa n Afrique f du Sud.

South African 1 adj sud-africain(e). 2 n [person] Sud-Africain m, -e f.

South America n Amérique f du Sud.

South American 1 adj sud-américain(e). 2 n [person] Sud-Américain m, -e f.

southeast [ˌsaʊθ'iːst] 1 n [direction] sud-est m. || [region]: **the ~** le sud-est. 2 adj au sud-est, du sud-est; [wind] du sud-est. 3 adv au sud-est, vers le sud-est; **~ of** au sud-est de.

southerly ['sʌðəlɪ] adj au sud, du sud; [wind] du sud.

southern ['sʌðən] adj au sud, du sud; [France] du Midi.

South Korea n Corée f du Sud.

South Pole n: **the ~** le pôle Sud.

southward ['saʊθwəd] 1 adj au sud, du sud. 2 adv = **southwards**.

southwards ['saʊθwədz] adv vers le sud.

southwest [ˌsaʊθ'west] 1 n [direction] sud-ouest m. || [region]: **the ~** le sud-ouest. 2 adj au sud-ouest, du sud-ouest; [wind] du sud-ouest. 3 adv au sud-ouest, vers le sud-ouest; **~ of** au sud-ouest de.

souvenir [ˌsuːvə'nɪər] n souvenir m.

sovereign ['sɒvrɪn] 1 n [ruler] souverain m, -e f. || [coin] souverain m.

soviet ['səʊvɪət] n soviet m. ○ **Soviet** 1 adj soviétique. 2 n [person] Soviétique mf.

Soviet Union n: **the (former) ~** l'(ex-)Union f soviétique.

sow¹ [səʊ] (pt -ed, pp sown OR -ed) vt lit & fig semer.

sow² [saʊ] n truie f.

sown [səʊn] pp → **sow¹**.

soya ['sɔɪə] n soja m.

soy(a) bean ['sɔɪ(ə)-] n graine f de soja.

spa [spɑː] n station f thermale.

space [speɪs] 1 n [gap, roominess, outer space] espace m; [on form] blanc m, espace. || [room] place f. || [of time]: **within** OR **in the ~ of ten minutes** en l'espace de dix minutes. 2 comp spatial(e). 3 vt espacer. ○ **space out** vt sep espacer.

spacecraft ['speɪskrɑːft] (pl inv) n vaisseau m spatial.

spaceman ['speɪsmæn] (pl -men [-men]) n astronaute m, cosmonaute m.

spaceship ['speɪsʃɪp] n vaisseau m spatial.

space shuttle n navette f spatiale.

spacesuit ['speɪssuːt] n combinaison f spatiale.

spacing ['speɪsɪŋ] n TYPO espacement m.

spacious ['speɪʃəs] adj spacieux(ieuse).

spade [speɪd] n [tool] pelle f. || [playing card] pique m. ○ **spades** npl pique m.

spaghetti [spə'getɪ] n (U) spaghettis mpl.

Spain [speɪn] n Espagne f.

span [spæn] 1 pt → **spin**. 2 n [in time] espace m de temps, durée f. || [range] éventail m, gamme f. || [of bird, plane] envergure f. 3 vt [in time] embrasser, couvrir. || [subj: bridge] franchir.

Spaniard ['spænjəd] n Espagnol m, -e f.

spaniel ['spænjəl] n épagneul m.

Spanish ['spænɪʃ] 1 adj espagnol(e). 2 n [language] espagnol m. 3 npl: **the ~** les Espagnols.

spank [spæŋk] vt donner une fessée à, fesser.

spanner ['spænər] n clé f à écrous.

spar [spɑːr] 1 n espar m. 2 vi BOXING s'entraîner à la boxe.

spare [speər] 1 adj [surplus] de trop; [component, clothing etc] de réserve, de rechange. || [available - seat, time, tickets] disponible. 2 n [part] pièce f détachée OR de rechange. 3 vt [make available - staff, money] se passer de; [- time] disposer de; **to have an hour to ~** avoir une heure de battement OR de libre; **with a minute to ~** avec une minute d'avance. || [not harm] épargner. || [not use] épargner, ménager. || [save from]: **to ~ sb sthg** épargner qqch à qqn, éviter qqch à qqn.

spare part n pièce f détachée OR de rechange.

spare time n (U) temps m libre, loisirs mpl.

spare wheel n roue f de secours.

sparing ['speərɪŋ] adj: **to be ~ with** OR **of** sthg être économe de qqch, ménager qqch.

sparingly ['speərɪŋlɪ] adv [use] avec modération; [spend] avec parcimonie.

spark [spɑːk] n lit & fig étincelle f.

sparkle ['spɑːkl] 1 n (U) [of eyes, jewel] éclat m; [of stars] scintillement m. 2 vi étinceler, scintiller.

sparkling wine ['spɑːklɪŋ-] n vin m mousseux.

spark plug n bougie f.

sparrow ['spærəʊ] n moineau m.

sparse ['spɑːs] adj clairsemé(e), épars(e).

spasm ['spæzm] n MED spasme m; [of coughing] quinte f.

spastic ['spæstɪk] MED n handicapé m, -e f moteur.

spat [spæt] pt & pp → **spit**.

spate [speɪt] n [of attacks etc] série f.

spatter ['spætər] vt éclabousser.

spawn [spɔːn] 1 n (U) frai m, œufs mpl. 2 vt fig donner naissance à, engendrer.

speak [spiːk] (pt spoke, pp spoken) 1 vt [say] dire. || [language] parler. 2 vi parler; **to ~ to** OR **with sb** parler à qqn; **to ~ about sb/sthg** parler de qqn/qqch. ○ **so to speak** adv pour ainsi dire. ○ **speak for** vt fus [represent] parler pour, parler au nom de. ○ **speak up** vi [support]: **to ~ up for sb/sthg** parler en faveur de qqn/qqch, soutenir qqn/qqch. || [speak louder] parler plus fort.

speaker ['spiːkər] n [person talking] personne f qui parle. || [person making speech] orateur m. || [of language]: **a German ~** une personne qui parle allemand. || [loudspeaker] haut-parleur m.

spear [spɪər] 1 n lance f. 2 vt transpercer d'un coup de lance.

spearhead ['spɪəhed] 1 n fer m de lance. 2 vt [campaign] mener; [attack] être le fer de lance de.

special ['speʃl] adj [gen] spécial(e). || [needs, effort, attention] particulier(ière).

special delivery n (U) [service] exprès m, envoi m par ~: **by ~** en exprès.

specialist ['speʃəlɪst] 1 adj spécialisé(e). 2 n spécialiste mf.

speciality [,speʃɪ'ælətɪ], **specialty** Am ['speʃltɪ] n spécialité f.

specialize, -ise ['speʃəlaɪz] vi: **to ~ (in)** se spécialiser (dans).

specially ['speʃəlɪ] adv [specifically] spécialement; [on purpose] exprès. || [particularly] particulièrement.

specialty n Am = speciality.

species ['spiːʃiːz] (pl inv) n espèce f.

specific [spə'sɪfɪk] adj [particular] particulier(ière), précis(e). || [precise] précis(e). || [unique]: **~ to** propre à.

specifically [spə'sɪfɪklɪ] adv [particularly] particulièrement, spécialement. || [precisely] précisément.

specify ['spesɪfaɪ] vt préciser, spécifier.

specimen ['spesɪmən] n [example]

exemple m, spécimen m. || [of blood] prélèvement m; [of urine] échantillon m.

speck [spek] n [small stain] toute petite tache f. || [of dust] grain m.

speckled ['spekld] adj: **~ (with)** tacheté(e) de.

spectacle ['spektəkl] n spectacle m.

spectacular [spek'tækjʊlər] adj spectaculaire.

spectator [spek'teɪtər] n spectateur m, -trice f.

spectre Br, **specter** Am ['spektər] n spectre m.

spectrum ['spektrəm] (pl -tra [-trə]) n PHYSICS spectre m. || fig [variety] gamme f.

speculation [,spekjʊ'leɪʃn] n [gen] spéculation f. || [conjecture] conjectures fpl.

sped [sped] pt & pp → **speed**.

speech [spiːtʃ] n (U) [ability] parole f. || [formal talk] discours m. || THEATRE texte m. || [manner of speaking] façon f de parler. || [dialect] parler m.

speechless ['spiːtʃlɪs] adj: **~ (with)** muet(ette) (de).

speed [spiːd] (pt & pp -ed OR sped) 1 n vitesse f; [of reply, action] vitesse, rapidité f. 2 vi [move fast]: **to ~ away** démarrer à toute allure. || AUT [go too fast] rouler trop vite, faire un excès de vitesse. ○ **speed up** 1 vt sep [person] faire aller plus vite; [work, production] accélérer. 2 vi aller plus vite; [car] accélérer.

speedboat ['spiːdbəʊt] n hors-bord m inv.

speeding ['spiːdɪŋ] n (U) excès m de vitesse.

speed limit n limitation f de vitesse.

speedometer [spɪ'dɒmɪtər] n compteur m (de vitesse).

speedway ['spiːdweɪ] n (U) SPORT course f de motos. || Am [road] voie f express.

speedy ['spiːdɪ] adj rapide.

spell [spel] (Br pt & pp spelt OR -ed, Am pt & pp -ed) 1 n [period of time] période f. || [enchantment] charme m; [words] formule f magique; **to cast** OR **put a ~ on sb** jeter un sort à qqn, envoûter qqn. 2 vt [word, name] écrire. || fig [signify] signifier. 3 vi épeler. ○ **spell out** vt sep [read aloud] épeler. || [explain]: **to ~ sthg out (for** OR **to sb)** expliquer qqch clairement (à qqn).

spellbound ['spelbaʊnd] adj subjugué(e).

spelling ['spelɪŋ] n orthographe f.

spelt [spelt] Br pt & pp → **spell**.

spend

spend [spend] (*pt* & *pp* **spent**) *vt* [pay out]: **to ~ money (on)** dépenser de l'argent (pour). || [time, life] passer.

spendthrift ['spendθrɪft] *n* dépensier *m*, -ière *f*.

spent [spent] **1** *pt* & *pp* → **spend**. **2** *adj* [fuel, match, ammunition] utilisé(e); [patience, energy] épuisé(e).

sperm [spɜːm] (*pl inv* OR **-s**) *n* sperme *m*.

spew [spjuː] *vt* & *vi* vomir.

sphere [sfɪə^r] *n* sphère *f*.

spice [spaɪs] *n* CULIN épice *f*. || (*U*) *fig* [excitement] piment *m*.

spick-and-span ['spɪkən,spæn] *adj* impeccable, nickel (*inv*).

spicy ['spaɪsɪ] *adj* CULIN épicé(e). || *fig* [story] pimenté(e), piquant(e).

spider ['spaɪdə^r] *n* araignée *f*.

spike [spaɪk] *n* [metal] pointe *f*, lance *f*; [of plant] piquant *m*; [of hair] épi *m*.

spill [spɪl] (*Br pt* & *pp* **spilt** OR **-ed**, *Am pt* & *pp* **-ed**) **1** *vt* renverser. **2** *vi* [liquid] se répandre.

spilt [spɪlt] *Br pt* & *pp* → **spill**.

spin [spɪn] (*pt* **span** OR **spun**, *pp* **spun**) **1** *n* [turn]: **to give sthg a ~** faire tourner qqch. || AERON vrille *f*. || *inf* [in car] tour *m*. || SPORT effet *m*. **2** *vt* [wheel] faire tourner; **to ~ a coin** jouer à pile ou face. || [washing] essorer. || [thread, wool, cloth] filer. || SPORT [ball] donner de l'effet à. **3** *vi* tourner, tournoyer. ○ **spin out** *vt sep* [money, story] faire durer.

spinach ['spɪnɪdʒ] *n* (*U*) épinards *mpl*.

spinal column ['spaɪnl-] *n* colonne *f* vertébrale.

spinal cord ['spaɪnl-] *n* moelle *f* épinière.

spindly ['spɪndlɪ] *adj* grêle, chétif(ive).

spine [spaɪn] *n* ANAT colonne *f* vertébrale. || [of book] dos *m*. || [of plant, hedgehog] piquant *m*.

spinning ['spɪnɪŋ] *n* [of thread] filage *m*.

spinning top *n* toupie *f*.

spin-off *n* [by-product] dérivé *m*.

spinster ['spɪnstə^r] *n* célibataire *f*; *pej* vieille fille *f*.

spiral ['spaɪərəl] **1** *adj* spiral(e). **2** *n* spirale *f*.

spiral staircase *n* escalier *m* en colimaçon.

spire ['spaɪə^r] *n* flèche *f*.

spirit ['spɪrɪt] *n* [gen] esprit *m*. || (*U*) [determination] caractère *m*, courage *m*. ○ **spirits** *npl* [mood] humeur *f*; **to be in**

high ~s être gai(e); **to be in low ~s** être déprimé(e). || [alcohol] spiritueux *mpl*.

spirited ['spɪrɪtɪd] *adj* fougueux(euse); [performance] interprété(e) avec brio.

spirit level *n* niveau *m* à bulle d'air.

spiritual ['spɪrɪtʃʊəl] *adj* spirituel(elle).

spit [spɪt] (*Br pt* & *pp* **spat**, *Am pt* & *pp* **spit**) **1** *n* (*U*) [spittle] crachat *m*; [saliva] salive *f*. || [skewer] broche *f*. **2** *vi* cracher.

spite [spaɪt] **1** *n* rancune *f*. **2** *vt* contrarier. ○ **in spite of** *prep* en dépit de, malgré.

spiteful ['spaɪtfʊl] *adj* malveillant(e).

spittle ['spɪtl] *n* (*U*) crachat *m*.

splash [splæʃ] **1** *n* [sound] plouf *m*. || [of colour, light] tache *f*. **2** *vt* éclabousser. **3** *vi* [person]: **to ~ about** OR **around** barboter. || [liquid] jaillir. ○ **splash out** *inf vi*: **to ~ out (on)** dépenser une fortune (pour).

spleen [spliːn] *n* ANAT rate *f*.

splendid ['splendɪd] *adj* splendide; [work, holiday, idea] excellent(e).

splint [splɪnt] *n* attelle *f*.

splinter ['splɪntə^r] **1** *n* éclat *m*. **2** *vi* [wood] se fendre en éclats; [glass] se briser en éclats.

split [splɪt] (*pt* & *pp* **split**, *cont* **-ting**) **1** *n* [in wood] fente *f*; [in garment - tear] déchirure *f*; [- by design] échancrure *f*. || POL: ~ **(in)** division *f* OR scission *f* (au sein de). || [difference]: ~ **between** écart *m* entre. **2** *vt* [wood] fendre; [clothes] déchirer. || POL diviser. || [share] partager. **3** *vi* [wood] se fendre; [clothes] se déchirer. || POL se diviser; [road, path] se séparer. ○ **split up** *vi* [group, couple] se séparer.

split second *n* fraction *f* de seconde.

splutter ['splʌtə^r] *vi* [person] bredouiller, bafouiller; [engine] tousser.

spoil [spɔɪl] (*pt* & *pp* **-ed** OR **spoilt**) *vt* [ruin - holiday] gâcher, gâter; [- view] gâter; [- food] gâter, abîmer. || [overindulge, treat well] gâter. ○ **spoils** *npl* butin *m*.

spoiled [spɔɪld] *adj* = **spoilt**.

spoilsport ['spɔɪlspɔːt] *n* trouble-fête *mf inv*.

spoilt [spɔɪlt] **1** *pt* & *pp* → **spoil**. **2** *adj* [child] gâté(e).

spoke [spəʊk] **1** *pt* → **speak**. **2** *n* rayon *m*.

spoken ['spəʊkn] *pp* → **speak**.

spokesman ['spəʊksmən] (*pl* **-men** [-mən]) *n* porte-parole *m inv*.

spokeswoman ['spəʊks,wʊmən] (*pl* **-women** [-,wɪmɪn]) *n* porte-parole *m inv*.

sponge [spʌndʒ] (*Br cont* **spongeing**, *Am cont* **sponging**) **1** *n* [for cleaning, washing] éponge *f*. || [cake] gâteau *m* OR biscuit *m* de Savoie. **2** *rt* éponger. **3** *vi inf*: **to ~ off sb** taper qqn.

sponge cake *n* gâteau *m* OR biscuit *m* de Savoie.

sponsor ['spɒnsəʳ] **1** *n* sponsor *m*. **2** *vt* [finance, for charity] sponsoriser, parrainer. || [support] soutenir.

sponsored walk [,spɒnsəd-] *n* marche *f* organisée pour recueillir des fonds.

sponsorship ['spɒnsəʃɪp] *n* sponsoring *m*, parrainage *m*.

spontaneous [spɒn'teɪnjəs] *adj* spontané(e).

spool [spuːl] *n* [gen & COMPUT] bobine *f*.

spoon [spuːn] *n* cuillère *f*, cuiller *f*.

spoon-feed *vt* nourrir à la cuillère; **to ~ sb** *fig* mâcher le travail à qqn.

spoonful ['spuːnfʊl] (*pl* **-s** OR **spoonsful**) *n* cuillerée *f*.

sporadic [spə'rædɪk] *adj* sporadique.

sport [spɔːt] *n* [game] sport *m*.

sporting ['spɔːtɪŋ] *adj* [relating to sport] sportif(ive). || [generous, fair] chic (*inv*); **to have a ~ chance of doing sthg** avoir des chances de faire qqch.

sports car ['spɔːts-] *n* voiture *f* de sport.

sports jacket ['spɔːts-] *n* veste *f* sport.

sportsman ['spɔːtsmən] (*pl* **-men** [-mən]) *n* sportif *m*.

sportsmanship ['spɔːtsmənʃɪp] *n* sportivité *f*, esprit *m* sportif.

sportswear ['spɔːtsweəʳ] *n* (*U*) vêtements *mpl* de sport.

sportswoman ['spɔːts,wʊmən] (*pl* **-women** [-,wɪmɪn]) *n* sportive *f*.

sporty ['spɔːtɪ] *adj inf* [person] sportif(ive).

spot [spɒt] **1** *n* [mark, dot] tache *f*. || [pimple] bouton *m*. || [drop] goutte *f*. || *inf* [small amount]: **to have a ~ of bother** avoir quelques ennuis. || [place] endroit *m*; **on the ~** sur place. || RADIO & TV numéro *m*. **2** *rt* [notice] apercevoir.

spot check *n* contrôle *m* au hasard OR intermittent.

spotless ['spɒtlɪs] *adj* [clean] impeccable.

spotlight ['spɒtlaɪt] *n* [in theatre] projecteur *m*, spot *m*; [in home] spot *m*; **to be in the ~** *fig* être en vedette.

spotted ['spɒtɪd] *adj* [pattern, material] à pois.

spouse [spaʊs] *n* époux *m*, épouse *f*.

spout [spaʊt] **1** *n* bec *m*. **2** *vi*: **to ~ from** OR **out of** jaillir de.

sprain [spreɪn] **1** *n* entorse *f*. **2** *vt*: **to ~ one's ankle/wrist** se faire une entorse à la cheville/au poignet, se fouler la cheville/le poignet.

sprang [spræŋ] *pt* → **spring**.

sprawl [sprɔːl] *vi* [person] être affalé(e). || [city] s'étaler.

spray [spreɪ] **1** *n* (*U*) [of water] gouttelettes *fpl*; [from sea] embruns *mpl*. || [container] bombe *f*, pulvérisateur *m*. || [of flowers] gerbe *f*. **2** *vt* [product] pulvériser; [plants, crops] pulvériser de l'insecticide sur.

spread [spred] (*pt & pp* **spread**) **1** *n* (*U*) [food] pâte *f* à tartiner. || [of fire, disease] propagation *f*. || [of opinions] gamme *f*. **2** *vt* [map, rug] étaler, étendre; [fingers, arms, legs] écarter. || [butter, jam etc]: **to ~ sthg (over)** étaler qqch (sur). || [disease, rumour, germs] répandre, propager. **3** *vi* [disease, rumour] se propager, se répandre. || [water, cloud] s'étaler.

O **spread out** *vi* se disperser.

spread-eagled [-,iːgld] *adj* affalé(e).

spreadsheet ['spredʃiːt] *n* COMPUT tableur *m*.

spree [spriː] *n*: **to go on a spending** OR **shopping ~** faire des folies.

sprightly ['spraɪtlɪ] *adj* alerte, fringant(e).

spring [sprɪŋ] (*pt* **sprang**, *pp* **sprung**) **1** *n* [season] printemps *m*; **in ~** au printemps. || [coil] ressort *m*. || [water source] source *f*. **2** *vi* [jump] sauter, bondir. || [originate]: **to ~ from** provenir de.

O **spring up** *vi* [problem] surgir, se présenter; [friendship] naître; [wind] se lever.

springboard ['sprɪŋbɔːd] *n* lit & fig tremplin *m*.

spring-clean *vt* nettoyer de fond en comble.

springtime ['sprɪŋtaɪm] *n*: **in (the) ~** au printemps.

sprinkle ['sprɪŋkl] *vt*: **to ~ water over** OR **on sthg, to ~ sthg with water** asperger qqch d'eau; **to ~ salt** *etc* **over** OR **on sthg, to ~ sthg with salt** *etc* saupoudrer qqch de sel *etc*.

sprinkler ['sprɪŋkləʳ] *n* [for water] arroseur *m*.

sprint [sprɪnt] **1** *n* sprint *m*. **2** *vi* sprinter.

sprout [spraʊt] **1** *n* [vegetable]: **(Brussels) ~s** choux *mpl* de Bruxelles. || [shoot]

pousse *f*. **2** *vt* [leaves] produire; **to ~ shoots** germer. **3** *vi* [grow] pousser.

spruce [spru:s] **1** *adj* net (nette), pimpant(e). **2** *n* épicéa *m*. ○ **spruce up** *vt sep* astiquer, briquer.

sprung [sprʌŋ] *pp* → **spring**.

spun [spʌn] *pt & pp* → **spin**.

spur [spɜːr] **1** *n* [incentive] incitation *f*. || [on rider's boot] éperon *m*. **2** *vt* [encourage]: **to ~ sb to do sthg** encourager qqn à faire qqch. ○ **on the spur of the moment** *adv* sur un coup de tête, sous l'impulsion du moment. ○ **spur on** *vt sep* encourager.

spurious ['spʊərɪəs] *adj* [affection, interest] feint(e). || [argument, logic] faux (fausse).

spurn [spɜːn] *vt* repousser.

spurt [spɜːt] **1** *n* [gush] jaillissement *m*. || [of activity, energy] sursaut *m*. || [burst of speed] accélération *f*. **2** *vi* [gush]: **to ~ (out OR from)** jaillir (de).

spy [spaɪ] **1** *n* espion *m*. **2** *vi* espionner, faire de l'espionnage; **to ~ on sb** espionner qqn.

spying ['spaɪɪŋ] *n* (*U*) espionnage *m*.

Sq., sq. *abbr of* **square**.

squabble ['skwɒbl] **1** *n* querelle *f*. **2** *vi*: **to ~ (about OR over)** se quereller (à propos de).

squad [skwɒd] *n* [of police] brigade *f*. || MIL peloton *m*. || SPORT [group of players] équipe *f* (*parmi laquelle la sélection sera faite*).

squadron ['skwɒdrən] *n* escadron *m*.

squalid ['skwɒlɪd] *adj* sordide, ignoble.

squalor ['skwɒlər] *n* (*U*) conditions *fpl* sordides.

squander ['skwɒndər] *vt* gaspiller.

square [skweər] **1** *adj* [in shape] carré(e); **three metres ~** trois mètres sur trois. || [not owing money]: **to be ~** être quitte. **2** *n* [shape] carré *m*. || [in town] place *f*. || *inf* [unfashionable person]: **he's a ~** il est vieux jeu. **3** *vt* MATH élever au carré. ○ **square up** *vi* [settle up]: **to ~ up with sb** régler ses comptes avec qqn.

squarely ['skweəlɪ] *adv* [directly] carrément. || [honestly] honnêtement.

square meal *n* bon repas *m*.

squash [skwɒʃ] **1** *n* SPORT squash *m*. || *Am* [vegetable] courge *f*. **2** *vt* écraser.

squat [skwɒt] **1** *adj* courtaud(e), ramassé(e). **2** *vi* [crouch]: **to ~ (down)** s'accroupir.

squawk [skwɔːk] *n* cri *m* strident OR perçant.

squeak [skwiːk] *n* [of animal] petit cri *m* aigu. || [of door, hinge] grincement *m*.

squeal [skwiːl] *vi* [person, animal] pousser des cris aigus.

squeamish ['skwiːmɪʃ] *adj* facilement dégoûté(e).

squeeze [skwiːz] **1** *n* [pressure] pression *f*. **2** *vt* [press firmly] presser. || [liquid, toothpaste] exprimer. || [cram]: **to ~ sthg into sthg** entasser qqch dans qqch.

squelch [skweltʃ] *vi*: **to ~ through mud** patauger dans la boue.

squid [skwɪd] (*pl inv* OR **-s**) *n* calmar *m*.

squiggle ['skwɪgl] *n* gribouillis *m*.

squint [skwɪnt] **1** *n*: **to have a ~** loucher, être atteint(e) de strabisme. **2** *vi*: **to ~ at sthg** regarder qqch en plissant les yeux.

squirm [skwɜːm] *vi* [wriggle] se tortiller.

squirrel [*Br* 'skwɪrəl, *Am* 'skwɜːrəl] *n* écureuil *m*.

squirt [skwɜːt] **1** *vt* [water, oil] faire jaillir, faire gicler. **2** *vi*: **to ~ (out of)** jaillir (de), gicler (de).

Sr *abbr of* **senior**.

Sri Lanka [ˌsriː'læŋkə] *n* Sri Lanka *m*.

St (*abbr of* **saint**) St, Ste. || *abbr of* **Street**.

stab [stæb] **1** *n* [with knife] coup *m* de couteau. || *inf* [attempt]: **to have a ~ (at sthg)** essayer (qqch), tenter (qqch). || [twinge]: **~ of pain** élancement *m*; **~ of guilt** remords *m*. **2** *vt* [person] poignarder. || [food] piquer.

stable ['steɪbl] **1** *adj* stable. **2** *n* écurie *f*.

stack [stæk] **1** *n* [pile] pile *f*. **2** *vt* [pile up] empiler.

stadium ['steɪdjəm] (*pl* **-diums** OR **-dia** [-djə]) *n* stade *m*.

staff [stɑːf] **1** *n* [employees] personnel *m*; [of school] personnel enseignant, professeurs *mpl*. **2** *vt* pourvoir en personnel.

stag [stæg] (*pl inv* OR **-s**) *n* cerf *m*.

stage [steɪdʒ] **1** *n* [phase] étape *f*, phase *f*, stade *m*. || [platform] scène *f*. || [acting profession]: **the ~** le théâtre. **2** *vt* THEATRE monter, mettre en scène. || [organize] organiser.

stagecoach ['steɪdʒkəʊtʃ] *n* diligence *f*.

stage fright *n* trac *m*.

stage-manage *vt lit & fig* mettre en scène.

stagger ['stægər] **1** *vt* [astound] stupéfier. || [working hours] échelonner; [holidays] étaler. **2** *vi* tituber.

stagnant ['stægnənt] *adj* stagnant(e).

stagnate [stæg'neɪt] *vi* stagner.

stag party n soirée f entre hommes; [before wedding] soirée où un futur marié enterre sa vie de garçon avec ses amis.

staid [steɪd] adj guindé(e), collet monté.

stain [steɪn] 1 n [mark] tache f. 2 vt [discolour] tacher.

stained glass [,steɪnd-] n (U) [windows] vitraux mpl.

stainless steel ['steɪnlɪs-] n acier m inoxydable, Inox® m.

stain remover [-rɪ,muːvəʳ] n détachant m.

stair [steəʳ] n marche f. ○ **stairs** npl escalier m.

staircase ['steəkeɪs] n escalier m.

stairway ['steəweɪ] n escalier m.

stairwell ['steəwel] n cage f d'escalier.

stake [steɪk] 1 n [share]: **to have a ~ in sthg** avoir des intérêts dans qqch. || [wooden post] poteau m. || [in gambling] enjeu m. 2 vt: **to ~ money** (on or upon) jouer or miser de l'argent (sur); **to ~ one's reputation** (on) jouer or risquer sa réputation (sur). ○ **at stake** adv en jeu.

stale [steɪl] adj [food, water] pas frais (fraîche); [bread] rassis(e); [air] qui sent le renfermé.

stalemate ['steɪlmeɪt] n [deadlock] impasse f. || CHESS pat m.

stalk [stɔːk] 1 n [of flower, plant] tige f. || [of leaf, fruit] queue f. 2 vt [hunt] traquer. 3 vi: **to ~ in/out** entrer/sortir d'un air hautain.

stall [stɔːl] 1 n [in street, market] éventaire m, étal m; [at exhibition] stand m. || [in stable] stalle f. 2 vi AUT caler. || [delay] essayer de gagner du temps.

stallion ['stæljən] n étalon m.

stalwart ['stɔːlwət] n pilier m.

stamina ['stæmɪnə] n (U) résistance f.

stammer ['stæməʳ] 1 n bégaiement m. 2 vi bégayer.

stamp [stæmp] 1 n [for letter] timbre m. || [tool] tampon m. || fig [of authority etc] marque f. 2 vt [mark by stamping] tamponner. 3 vi [stomp] taper du pied. || [tread heavily]: **to ~ on sthg** marcher sur qqch.

stamp album n album m de timbres.

stamp-collecting [-kə,lektɪŋ] n philatélie f.

stampede [stæm'piːd] n débandade f.

stance [stæns] n lit & fig position f.

stand [stænd] (pt & pp **stood**) 1 n [stall] stand m; [selling newspapers] kiosque m. || [supporting object]: **umbrel-** la ~ porte-parapluies m inv; **hat ~** porte-chapeaux m inv. || SPORT tribune f. || MIL résistance f; **to make a ~** résister. || [public position] position f. || Am JUR barre f. 2 vt [place] mettre (debout), poser (debout). || [withstand, tolerate] supporter. 3 vi [be upright - person] être or se tenir debout; [- object] se trouver; [- building] se dresser; **~ still!** ne bouge pas!, reste tranquille! || [stand up] se lever. || [liquid] reposer. || [offer] tenir toujours; [decision] demeurer valable. || [be in particular state]: **as things ~ ...** vu l'état actuel des choses .... || Am [park car]: **"no -ing"** «stationnement interdit».

○ **stand back** vi reculer. ○ **stand by** 1 vt fus [person] soutenir. || [statement, decision] s'en tenir à. 2 vi [in readiness]: **to ~ by** (for sthg/to do sthg) être prêt(e) (pour qqch/pour faire qqch). || [remain inactive] rester là. ○ **stand down** vi [resign] démissionner. ○ **stand for** vt fus [signify] représenter. || [tolerate] supporter, tolérer. ○ **stand in** vi: **to ~ in for sb** remplacer qqn. ○ **stand out** vi ressortir. ○ **stand up** 1 vt sep inf [boyfriend, girlfriend] poser un lapin à. 2 vi [rise from seat] se lever; **~ up!** debout! ○ **stand up for** vt fus défendre. ○ **stand up to** vt fus [person, boss] tenir tête à.

standard ['stændəd] 1 adj [normal - gen] normal(e); [- size] standard (inv). || [accepted] correct(e). 2 n [level] niveau m. || [point of reference] critère m; TECH norme f. ○ **standards** npl [principles] valeurs fpl.

standard of living (pl standards of living) n niveau m de vie.

standby ['stændbaɪ] (pl standbys) 1 n [person] remplaçant m, -e f; **on ~** prêt à intervenir. 2 comp [ticket, flight] standby (inv).

stand-in n remplaçant m, -e f.

standing ['stændɪŋ] 1 adj [invitation, army] permanent(e); [joke] continuel(elle). 2 n [reputation] importance f, réputation f. || [duration]: **of long ~** de longue date.

standing order n prélèvement m automatique.

standpoint ['stændpɔɪnt] n point de vue.

standstill ['stændstɪl] n: **at a ~** [traffic, train] à l'arrêt; [negotiations, work] paralysé(e); **to come to a ~** [traffic, train] s'immobiliser; [negotiations, work] cesser.

stank [stæŋk] *pt* → **stink**.

staple ['steɪpl] **1** *adj* [principal] princi-
pal(e), de base. **2** *n* [for paper] agrafe *f*. ||
[principal commodity] produit *m* de base.
3 *vt* agrafer.

stapler ['steɪplə'] *n* agrafeuse *f*.

star [stɑː'] **1** *n* [gen] étoile *f*. || [celebrity]
vedette *f*, star *f*. **2** *vi*: **to ~ (in)** être la vedette (de). ○ **stars** *npl* horoscope *m*.

starboard ['stɑːbəd] **1** *adj* de tribord. **2**
n: **to ~** à tribord.

starch [stɑːtʃ] *n* amidon *m*.

stardom ['stɑːdəm] *n (U)* célébrité *f*.

stare [steə'] **1** *n* regard *m* fixe. **2** *vi*: **to ~
at sb/sthg** fixer qqn/qqch du regard.

stark [stɑːk] **1** *adj* [room, decoration]
austère; [landscape] désolé(e). || [reality,
fact] à l'état brut; [contrast] dur(e). **2**
adv: **~ naked** tout nu (toute nue), à poil.

starling ['stɑːlɪŋ] *n* étourneau *m*.

starry ['stɑːrɪ] *adj* étoilé(e).

starry-eyed [-'aɪd] *adj* innocent(e).

Stars and Stripes *n*: **the ~** le drapeau
des États-Unis, la bannière étoilée.

start [stɑːt] **1** *n* [beginning] début *m*. ||
[jump] sursaut *m*. || [starting place] dé-
part *m*. || [time advantage] avance *f*. **2** *vt*
[begin] commencer; **to ~ doing OR to do
sthg** commencer à faire qqch. || [turn on -
machine] mettre en marche; [- engine, ve-
hicle] démarrer, mettre en marche. || [set
up - business, band] créer. **3** *vi* [begin]
commencer, débuter; **to ~ with** pour
commencer, d'abord. || [function -
machine] se mettre en marche; [- car] dé-
marrer. || [begin journey] partir. || [jump]
sursauter. ○ **start off 1** *vt sep* [meeting]
ouvrir, commencer; [discussion] entamer, commencer. **2** *vi* [begin] commen-
cer; [begin job] débuter. || [leave on jour-
ney] partir. ○ **start out** *vi* [in job] débu-
ter. || [leave on journey] partir. ○ **start
up 1** *vt sep* [business] créer; [shop] ou-
vrir. || [car, engine] mettre en marche. **2**
vi [begin] commencer. || [machine] se
mettre en route; [car, engine] démarrer.

starter ['stɑːtə'] *n* AUT démarreur *m*. ||
[to begin race] starter *m*.

starting point ['stɑːtɪŋ-] *n* point *m* de
départ.

startle ['stɑːtl] *vt* faire sursauter.

startling ['stɑːtlɪŋ] *adj* surprenant(e).

starvation [stɑː'veɪʃn] *n* faim *f*.

starve [stɑːv] **1** *vt* [deprive of food] affa-
mer. **2** *vi* [have no food] être affamé(e); **to
~ to death** mourir de faim. || *inf* [be hun-

gry] avoir très faim, crever OR mourir de
faim.

state [steɪt] **1** *n* état *m*; **to be in a ~** être
dans tous ses états. **2** *comp* d'État. **3** *vt*
[express - reason] donner; [- name and ad-
dress] décliner; **to ~ that ...** déclarer que
.... || [specify] préciser. ○ **States** *npl*: **the
States** les États-Unis *mpl*.

State Department *n Am* ≃ ministère
m des Affaires étrangères.

stately ['steɪtlɪ] *adj* majestueux(euse).

statement ['steɪtmənt] *n* [declaration]
déclaration *f*. || JUR déposition *f*. || [from
bank] relevé *m* de compte.

state of mind (*pl* **states of mind**) *n*
humeur *f*.

statesman ['steɪtsmən] (*pl* **-men**
[-mən]) *n* homme *m* d'État.

static ['stætɪk] *n (U)* parasites *mpl*.

static electricity *n* électricité *f* statique.

station ['steɪʃn] **1** *n* RAIL gare *f*; [for
buses, coaches] gare routière. || RADIO sta-
tion *f*. || [building] poste *m*. || *fml* [rank]
rang *m*. **2** *vt* [position] placer, poster. ||
MIL poster.

stationary ['steɪʃnərɪ] *adj* immobile.

stationer ['steɪʃnə'] *n* papetier *m*, -ière
f; **~'s (shop)** papeterie *f*.

stationery ['steɪʃnərɪ] *n (U)* [equip-
ment] fournitures *fpl* de bureau; [paper]
papier *m* à lettres.

stationmaster ['steɪʃn,mɑːstə'] *n* chef
m de gare.

station wagon *n Am* break *m*.

statistic [stə'tɪstɪk] *n* statistique *f*.

statistical [stə'tɪstɪkl] *adj* statistique;
[expert] en statistiques; [report] de statistiques.

statue ['stætʃuː] *n* statue *f*.

stature ['stætʃə'] *n* [height, size] stature
f, taille *f*. || [importance] envergure *f*.

status ['steɪtəs] *n (U)* [legal or social po-
sition] statut *m*. || [prestige] prestige *m*.

status symbol *n* signe *m* extérieur de
richesse.

statute ['stætjuːt] *n* loi *f*.

statutory ['stætjutrɪ] *adj* statutaire.

staunch [stɔːntʃ] **1** *adj* loyal(e). **2** *vt*
[flow] arrêter; [blood] étancher.

stave [steɪv] (*pt & pp* **-d** OR **stove**) *n*
MUS portée *f*. ○ **stave off** *vt sep* [disaster,
defeat] éviter; [hunger] tromper.

stay [steɪ] **1** *vi* [not move away] rester. ||
[as visitor - with friends] passer quelques
jours; [- in town, country] séjourner; **to ~
in a hotel** descendre à l'hôtel. || [con-

tinue, remain] rester, demeurer; **to ~ out of sthg** ne pas se mêler de qqch. 2 *n* [visit] séjour *m*. ○ **stay in** *vi* rester chez soi, ne pas sortir. ○ **stay on** *vi* rester (plus longtemps). ○ **stay out** *vi* [from home] ne pas rentrer. ○ **stay up** *vi* ne pas se coucher, veiller.

staying power ['steɪŋ-] *n* endurance *f*.

stead [sted] *n*: **to stand sb in good ~** être utile à qqn.

steadfast ['stedfɑːst] *adj* ferme, résolu(e); [supporter] loyal(e).

steadily ['stedɪlɪ] *adv* [gradually] progressivement. || [regularly - breathe] régulièrement. || [- move] sans arrêt. || [calmly] de manière imperturbable.

steady ['stedɪ] 1 *adj* [gradual] progressif(ive). || [regular] régulier(ière). || [not shaking] ferme. || [calm - voice] calme; [- stare] imperturbable. || [stable - job, relationship] stable. || [sensible] sérieux(ieuse). 2 *vt* [stop from shaking] empêcher de bouger; **to ~ o.s.** se remettre d'aplomb. || [control - nerves] calmer.

steak [steɪk] *n* steak *m*, bifteck *m*; [of fish] darne *f*.

steal [stiːl] (*pt* stole, *pp* stolen) 1 *vt* voler, dérober. 2 *vi* [move secretly] se glisser.

stealthy ['stelθɪ] *adj* furtif(ive).

steam [stiːm] 1 *n* (*U*) vapeur *f*. 2 *vt* CULIN cuire à la vapeur. 3 *vi* [give off steam] fumer. ○ **steam up** 1 *vt sep* [mist up] embuer. 2 *vi* se couvrir de buée.

steamboat ['stiːmbəut] *n* (bateau *m* à) vapeur *m*.

steam engine *n* locomotive *f* à vapeur.

steamer ['stiːmə*r*] *n* [ship] (bateau *m* à) vapeur *m*.

steamroller ['stiːm,rəulə*r*] *n* rouleau *m* compresseur.

steamy ['stiːmɪ] *adj* [full of steam] embué(e). || *inf* [erotic] érotique.

steel [stiːl] *n* (*U*) acier *m*.

steelworks ['stiːlwɜːks] (*pl inv*) *n* aciérie *f*.

steep [stiːp] *adj* [hill, road] raide, abrupt(e). || [increase, decline] énorme.

steeple ['stiːpl] *n* clocher *m*, flèche *f*.

steeplechase ['stiːpltʃeɪs] *n* [horse race] steeple-chase *m*. || [athletics race] steeple *m*.

steer ['stɪə*r*] 1 *n* bœuf *m*. 2 *vt* [ship] gouverner; [car, aeroplane] conduire, diriger. || [person] diriger, guider. 3 *vi*: **to ~ clear of sb/sthg** éviter qqn/qqch.

steering ['stɪərɪŋ] *n* (*U*) direction *f*.

steering wheel *n* volant *m*.

stem [stem] 1 *n* [of plant] tige *f*. || [of glass] pied *m*. || [of pipe] tuyau *m*. || GRAMM radical *m*. 2 *vt* [stop] arrêter. ○ **stem from** *vt fus* provenir de.

stench [stentʃ] *n* puanteur *f*.

stencil ['stensl] 1 *n* pochoir *m*. 2 *vt* faire au pochoir.

stenographer [stə'nɒgrəfə*r*] *n Am* sténographe *mf*.

step [step] 1 *n* [pace] pas *m*; **in/out of ~ with** *fig* en accord/désaccord avec. || [action] mesure *f*. || [stage] étape *f*; **~ by ~** petit à petit, progressivement. || [stair] marche *f*. || [of ladder] barreau *m*, échelon *m*. 2 *vi* [move foot]: **to ~ forward** avancer; **to ~ back** reculer. || [tread]: **to ~ on/in sthg** marcher sur/dans qqch. ○ **steps** *npl* [stairs] marches *fpl*. ○ **step down** *vi* [leave job] démissionner. ○ **step in** *vi* intervenir. ○ **step up** *vt sep* intensifier.

stepbrother ['step,brʌðə*r*] *n* demi-frère *m*.

stepdaughter ['step,dɔːtə*r*] *n* belle-fille *f*.

stepfather ['step,fɑːðə*r*] *n* beau-père *m*.

stepladder ['step,lædə*r*] *n* escabeau *m*.

stepmother ['step,mʌðə*r*] *n* belle-mère *f*.

stepping-stone ['stepɪŋ-] *n* pierre *f* de gué; *fig* tremplin *m*.

stepsister ['step,sɪstə*r*] *n* demi-sœur *f*.

stepson ['stepsʌn] *n* beau-fils *m*.

stereo ['sterɪəu] (*pl -s*) *n* [appliance] chaîne *f* stéréo. || [sound]: **in ~** en stéréo.

stereotype ['sterɪətaɪp] *n* stéréotype *m*.

sterile ['steraɪl] *adj* stérile.

sterilize, -ise ['sterəlaɪz] *vt* stériliser.

sterling ['stɜːlɪŋ] 1 *adj* [of British money] sterling (*inv*). || [excellent] exceptionnel(elle). 2 *n* (*U*) livre *f* sterling.

sterling silver *n* argent *m* fin.

stern [stɜːn] 1 *adj* sévère. 2 *n* NAUT arrière *m*.

steroid ['stɪərɔɪd] *n* stéroïde *m*.

stethoscope ['steθəskəup] *n* stéthoscope *m*.

stew [stjuː] 1 *n* ragoût *m*. 2 *vt* [meat] cuire en ragoût; [fruit] faire cuire.

steward ['stjuəd] *n* [on plane, ship, train] steward *m*.

stewardess ['stjuədɪs] *n* hôtesse *f*.

stick [stɪk] (*pt & pp* stuck) 1 *n* [of wood, dynamite, candy] bâton *m*. || [walking stick] canne f. ‖ SPORT crosse f. 2 vt [push]: **to ~ sthg in** OR **into** planter qqch dans. ‖ [with glue, Sellotape®]: **to ~ sthg (on** OR **to)** coller qqch (sur). ‖ inf [put] mettre. 3 vi [adhere]: **to ~ (to)** coller (à). ‖ [jam] se coincer. ○ **stick out** 1 vt sep [head] sortir; [hand] lever; [tongue] tirer. ‖ inf [endure]: **to ~ it out** tenir le coup. 2 vi [protrude] dépasser. ‖ inf [be noticeable] se remarquer. ○ **stick to** vt fus [follow closely] suivre. ‖ [principles] rester fidèle à; [decision] s'en tenir à; [promise] tenir. ○ **stick up** vi dépasser. ○ **stick up for** vt fus défendre.

sticker ['stɪkər] n [label] autocollant m.

sticking plaster ['stɪkɪŋ-] n sparadrap m.

stickler ['stɪklər] n: **to be a ~ for** être à cheval sur.

stick shift n Am levier m de vitesses.

stick-up n inf vol m à main armée.

sticky ['stɪkɪ] adj [hands, sweets] poisseux(euse); [label, tape] adhésif(ive). ‖ inf [awkward] délicat(e).

stiff [stɪf] 1 adj [rod, paper, material] rigide; [shoes, brush] dur(e); [fabric] raide. ‖ [door, drawer, window] dur(e) (à ouvrir/fermer); [joint] ankylosé(e); **to have a ~ neck** avoir le torticolis. ‖ [severe - penalty] sévère; [- competition] serré(e). ‖ [difficult - task] difficile. 2 adv inf: **to be bored ~** s'ennuyer à mourir; **to be frozen/scared ~** mourir de froid/peur.

stiffen ['stɪfn] 1 vt [material] raidir; [with starch] empeser. ‖ [resolve] renforcer. 2 vi [body] se raidir; [joints] s'ankyloser. ‖ [competition, resistance] s'intensifier.

stifle ['staɪfl] vt & vi étouffer.

stifling ['staɪflɪŋ] adj étouffant(e).

stigma ['stɪgmə] n [disgrace] honte f, stigmate m. ‖ BOT stigmate m.

stile [staɪl] n échalier m.

still [stɪl] 1 adv [up to now, up to then] encore, toujours; **I've ~ got £5 left** il me reste encore 5 livres. ‖ [even now] encore. ‖ [nevertheless] tout de même. ‖ (with comparatives): **~ bigger/more important** encore plus grand/plus important. 2 adj [not moving] immobile. ‖ [calm] calme, tranquille. ‖ [not windy] sans vent. ‖ [not fizzy - gen] non gazeux(euse); [- mineral water] plat(e). 3 n PHOT photo f. ‖ [for making alcohol] alambic m.

stillborn ['stɪlbɔːn] adj mort-né(e).

still life (pl -s) n nature f morte.

stilted ['stɪltɪd] adj emprunté(e), qui manque de naturel.

stilts ['stɪlts] npl [for person] échasses fpl. ‖ [for building] pilotis mpl.

stimulate ['stɪmjʊleɪt] vt stimuler.

stimulating ['stɪmjʊleɪtɪŋ] adj stimulant(e).

stimulus ['stɪmjʊləs] (pl -li [-laɪ]) n [encouragement] stimulant m. ‖ BIOL & PSYCH stimulus m.

sting [stɪŋ] (pt & pp **stung**) 1 n [by bee] piqûre f; [of bee] dard m. ‖ [sharp pain] brûlure f. 2 vt [gen] piquer. 3 vi piquer.

stingy ['stɪndʒɪ] adj inf radin(e).

stink [stɪŋk] (pt **stank** OR **stunk**, pp **stunk**) 1 n puanteur f. 2 vi [smell] puer, empester.

stint [stɪnt] 1 n [period of work] part f de travail. 2 vi: **to ~ on** lésiner sur.

stipulate ['stɪpjʊleɪt] vt stipuler.

stir [stɜːr] 1 n [public excitement] sensation f. 2 vt [mix] remuer. ‖ [move gently] agiter. ‖ [move emotionally] émouvoir. 3 vi bouger, remuer. ○ **stir up** vt sep [dust] soulever. ‖ [trouble] provoquer; [resentment, dissatisfaction] susciter.

stirrup ['stɪrəp] n étrier m.

stitch [stɪtʃ] 1 n SEWING point m; [in knitting] maille f. ‖ MED point m de suture. ‖ [stomach pain]: **to have a ~** avoir un point de côté. 2 vt SEWING coudre. ‖ MED suturer.

stoat [stəʊt] n hermine f.

stock [stɒk] 1 n [supply] réserve f. ‖ (U) COMM stock m, réserve f; **in ~** en stock; **out of ~** épuisé(e). ‖ FIN valeurs fpl; **~s and shares** titres mpl. ‖ [ancestry] souche f. ‖ CULIN bouillon m. ‖ [livestock] cheptel m. ‖ phr: **to take ~ (of)** faire le point (de). 2 vt COMM vendre, avoir en stock. ‖ [fill - shelves] garnir. ○ **stock up** vi: **to ~ up (with)** faire des provisions (de).

stockbroker ['stɒk,brəʊkər] n agent m de change.

stock exchange n Bourse f.

stockholder ['stɒk,həʊldər] n Am actionnaire mf.

stocking ['stɒkɪŋ] n [for woman] bas m.

stock market n Bourse f.

stock phrase n cliché m.

stockpile ['stɒkpaɪl] 1 n stock m. 2 vt [weapons] amasser; [food] stocker.

stocktaking ['stɒk,teɪkɪŋ] n (U) inventaire m.

stocky ['stɒkɪ] adj trapu(e).

stodgy ['stɒdʒɪ] *adj* [food] lourd(e) (à digérer).

stoical ['stəʊɪkl] *adj* stoïque.

stoke [stəʊk] *rt* [fire] entretenir.

stole [stəʊl] **1** *pt* → steal. **2** *n* étole *f.*

stolen ['stəʊln] *pp* → steal.

stolid ['stɒlɪd] *adj* impassible.

stomach ['stʌmək] **1** *n* [organ] estomac *m*; [abdomen] ventre *m*. **2** *rt* [tolerate] encaisser, supporter.

stomachache ['stʌməkeɪk] *n* mal *m* de ventre, douleurs *fpl* d'estomac.

stomach upset *n* embarras *m* gastrique.

stone [stəʊn] (*pl sense 3 only inr* OR *-s*) **1** *n* [rock] pierre *f*; [smaller] caillou *m*. || [seed] noyau *m*. || *Br* [unit of measurement] = 6,348 kg. **2** *comp* de pierre, en pierre. **3** *rt* [person, car etc] jeter des pierres sur.

stone-cold *adj* complètement froid(e) OR glacé(e).

stonewashed ['stəʊnwɒʃt] *adj* délavé(e).

stonework ['stəʊnwɜːk] *n* maçonnerie *f.*

stood [stʊd] *pt & pp* → stand.

stool [stuːl] *n* [seat] tabouret *m.*

stoop [stuːp] *ri* [bend down] se pencher. || [hunch shoulders] être voûté(e).

stop [stɒp] **1** *n* [gen] arrêt *m*; to put a ~ to sthg mettre un terme à qqch. || [full stop] point *m*. **2** *rt* [gen] arrêter; [end] mettre fin à; to ~ doing sthg arrêter de faire qqch. || [prevent]: to ~ sb/sthg (from doing sthg) empêcher qqn/qqch (de faire qqch). **3** *ri* s'arrêter, cesser. ○ **stop off** *ri* s'arrêter, faire halte. ○ **stop up** *rt sep* [block] boucher.

stopgap ['stɒpgæp] *n* bouche-trou *m.*

stopover ['stɒp,əʊvər] *n* halte *f.*

stoppage ['stɒpɪdʒ] *n* [strike] grève *f.*

stopper ['stɒpər] *n* bouchon *m.*

stop press *n* nouvelles *fpl* de dernière heure.

stopwatch ['stɒpwɒtʃ] *n* chronomètre *m.*

storage ['stɔːrɪdʒ] *n* [of goods] entreposage *m*, emmagasinage *m*; [of household objects] rangement *m.*

store [stɔːr] **1** *n* [shop] magasin *m*. || [supply] provision *f*. || [place of storage] réserve *f*. **2** *rt* [save] mettre en réserve; [goods] entreposer, emmagasiner. || COMPUT stocker, mémoriser. ○ **store up** *rt sep* [provisions] mettre en réserve; [goods] emmagasiner; [information] mettre en mémoire, noter.

storekeeper ['stɔː,kiːpər] *n Am* commerçant *m*, -e *f.*

storeroom ['stɔːrʊm] *n* magasin *m.*

storey *Br* (*pl* storeys), **story** *Am* (*pl* -ies) ['stɔːrɪ] *n* étage *m.*

stork [stɔːk] *n* cigogne *f.*

storm [stɔːm] **1** *n* [bad weather] orage *m*. || *fig* [of abuse] torrent *m*. **2** *rt* MIL prendre d'assaut. **3** *ri* [go angrily]: to ~ in/out entrer/sortir comme un ouragan. || [speak angrily] fulminer.

stormy ['stɔːmɪ] *adj lit & fig* orageux(euse).

story ['stɔːrɪ] *n* [gen] histoire *f*. || PRESS article *m*; RADIO & TV nouvelle *f*. || *Am* = storey.

storyteller ['stɔːrɪ,telər] *n* [narrator] conteur *m*, -euse *f*. || *euphemism* [liar] menteur *m*, -euse *f.*

stout [staʊt] **1** *adj* [rather fat] corpulent(e). || [strong] solide. || [resolute] ferme, résolu(e). **2** *n* (*U*) stout *m*, bière *f* brune.

stove [stəʊv] **1** *pt & pp* → stave. **2** *n* [for cooking] cuisinière *f*; [for heating] poêle *m.*

stow [stəʊ] *rt*: to ~ sthg (away) ranger qqch.

stowaway ['stəʊəweɪ] *n* passager *m* clandestin.

straddle ['strædl] *rt* enjamber; [chair] s'asseoir à califourchon sur.

straggle ['strægl] *ri* [buildings] s'étendre, s'étaler; [hair] être en désordre. || [person] traîner, lambiner.

straggler ['stræglər] *n* traînard *m*, -e *f.*

straight [streɪt] **1** *adj* [not bent] droit(e); [hair] raide. || [frank] franc (franche), honnête. || [tidy] en ordre. || [choice, exchange] simple. || [alcoholic drink] sec, sans eau. || *phr*: let's get this ~ entendons-nous bien. **2** *adv* [in a straight line] droit. || [directly, immediately] droit, tout de suite. || [frankly] carrément, franchement. ○ **straight off** *adv* tout de suite, sur-le-champ. ○ **straight out** *adv* sans mâcher ses mots.

straightaway [,streɪtə'weɪ] *adv* tout de suite, immédiatement.

straighten ['streɪtn] *rt* [tidy - hair, dress] arranger; [- room] mettre de l'ordre dans. || [make straight - horizontally] rendre droit(e); [- vertically] redresser. ○ **straighten out** *rt sep* [problem] résoudre.

straight face *n*: to keep a ~ garder son sérieux.

straightforward [ˌstreɪtˈfɔːwəd] *adj* [easy] simple. || [frank] honnête, franc (franche).

strain [streɪn] **1** *n* [mental] tension *f*, stress *m*. || MED foulure *f*. || TECH contrainte *f*, effort *m*. **2** *vt* [work hard - eyes] plisser fort. || [MED - muscle] se froisser; [- eyes] se fatiguer; **to ~ one's back** se faire un tour de reins. || [patience] mettre à rude épreuve; [budget] grever. || [drain] passer. **3** *vi* [try very hard]: **to ~ to do sthg** faire un gros effort pour faire qqch, se donner du mal pour faire qqch. ○ **strains** *npl* [of music] accords *mpl*, airs *mpl*.

strained [streɪnd] *adj* [worried] contracté(e), tendu(e). || [relations, relationship] tendu(e). || [unnatural] forcé(e).

strainer [ˈstreɪnər] *n* passoire *f*.

strait [streɪt] *n* détroit *m*. ○ **straits** *npl*: **in dire** OR **desperate ~s** dans une situation désespérée.

straitjacket [ˈstreɪtˌdʒækɪt] *n* camisole *f* de force.

straitlaced [ˌstreɪtˈleɪst] *adj* collet monté (*inv*).

strand [strænd] *n* [of cotton, wool] brin *m*, fil *m*; [of hair] mèche *f*. || [theme] fil *m*.

stranded [ˈstrændɪd] *adj* [boat] échoué(e); [people] abandonné(e), en rade.

strange [streɪndʒ] *adj* [odd] étrange, bizarre. || [unfamiliar] inconnu(e).

stranger [ˈstreɪndʒər] *n* [unfamiliar person] inconnu *m*, -e *f*. || [from another place] étranger *m*, -ère *f*.

strangle [ˈstræŋgl] *vt* étrangler.

stranglehold [ˈstræŋglhəʊld] *n* [round neck] étranglement *m*. || *fig* [control]: **~ (on)** domination *f* (de).

strap [stræp] **1** *n* [for fastening] sangle *f*, courroie *f*; [of bag] bandoulière *f*; [of rifle, dress, bra] bretelle *f*; [of watch] bracelet *m*. **2** *vt* [fasten] attacher.

strapping [ˈstræpɪŋ] *adj* bien bâti(e), robuste.

Strasbourg [ˈstræzbɜːg] *n* Strasbourg.

strategic [strəˈtiːdʒɪk] *adj* stratégique.

strategy [ˈstrætɪdʒɪ] *n* stratégie *f*.

straw [strɔː] *n* paille *f*; **that's the last ~!** ça c'est le comble!

strawberry [ˈstrɔːbərɪ] **1** *n* [fruit] fraise *f*. **2** *comp* [tart, yoghurt] aux fraises; [jam] de fraises.

stray [streɪ] **1** *adj* [animal] errant(e), perdu(e). || [bullet] perdu(e); [example]

isolé(e). **2** *vi* [person, animal] errer, s'égarer. || [thoughts] vagabonder, errer.

streak [striːk] **1** *n* [line] bande *f*, marque *f*. || [in character] côté *m*. **2** *vi* [move quickly] se déplacer comme un éclair.

stream [striːm] **1** *n* [small river] ruisseau *m*. || [of liquid, light] flot *m*, jet *m*. || [of people, cars] flot *m*; [of complaints, abuse] torrent *m*. **2** *vi* [liquid] couler à flots, ruisseler; [light] entrer à flots. || [people, cars] affluer; **to ~ past** passer à flots.

streamer [ˈstriːmər] *n* [for party] serpentin *m*.

streamlined [ˈstriːmlaɪnd] *adj* [aerodynamic] au profil aérodynamique. || [efficient] rationalisé(e).

street [striːt] *n* rue *f*.

streetcar [ˈstriːtkɑːr] *n Am* tramway *m*.

street lamp, **street light** *n* réverbère *m*.

street plan *n* plan *m*.

strength [streŋθ] *n* [gen] force *f*. || [power, influence] puissance *f*. || [solidity, of currency] solidité *f*.

strengthen [ˈstreŋθn] *vt* [structure, team, argument] renforcer. || [economy, currency, friendship] consolider. || [resolve, dislike] fortifier, affermir. || [person] enhardir.

strenuous [ˈstrenjʊəs] *adj* [exercise, activity] fatigant(e), dur(e); [effort] vigoureux(euse), acharné(e).

stress [stres] **1** *n* [emphasis]: **~ (on)** accent *m* (sur). || [mental] stress *m*, tension *f*. || TECH: **~ (on)** contrainte *f* (sur), effort *m* (sur). || LING accent *m*. **2** *vt* [emphasize] souligner, insister sur. || LING accentuer.

stressful [ˈstresfʊl] *adj* stressant(e).

stretch [stretʃ] **1** *n* [of land, water] étendue *f*; [of road, river] partie *f*, section *f*. || [of time] période *f*. **2** *vt* [arms] allonger; [legs] se dégourdir; [muscles] distendre. || [pull taut] tendre, étirer. || [overwork - person] surmener; [- resources, budget] grever. || [challenge]: **to ~ sb** pousser qqn à la limite de ses capacités. **3** *vi* [area]: **to ~ from ... to** s'étendre de ... à. || [person, animal] s'étirer. || [material, elastic] se tendre, s'étirer. ○ **stretch out 1** *vt sep* [arm, leg, hand] tendre. **2** *vi* [lie down] s'étendre, s'allonger.

stretcher [ˈstretʃər] *n* brancard *m*, civière *f*.

strew [struː] (*pt* **-ed**, *pp* **strewn** [struːn]

OR **-ed**) *vt*: **to be strewn with** être jonché(e) de.

strict [strikt] *adj* [gen] strict(e).

strictly ['striktli] *adv* [gen] strictement; ~ **speaking** à proprement parler. || [severely] d'une manière stricte, sévèrement.

stride [straid] (*pt* **strode**, *pp* **stridden** ['stridn]) 1 *n* [long step] grand pas *m*, enjambée *f*. 2 *vi* marcher à grandes enjambées OR à grands pas.

strident ['straidnt] *adj* [voice, sound] strident(e). || [demand, attack] véhément(e), bruyant(e).

strife [straif] *n* (U) conflit *m*, lutte *f*.

strike [straik] (*pt* & *pp* **struck**) 1 *n* [by workers] grève *f*; **to go on** ~ faire grève, se mettre en grève. || MIL raid *m*. || [of oil, gold] découverte *f*. 2 *vt* [hit - deliberately] frapper; [- accidentally] heurter. || [subj: thought] venir à l'esprit de. || [conclude - deal, bargain] conclure. || [light - match] frotter. 3 *vi* [workers] faire grève. || [hit] frapper. || [attack] attaquer. || [chime] sonner. ○ **strike down** *vt sep* terrasser. ○ **strike out** 1 *vt sep* rayer, barrer. 2 *vi* [head out] se mettre en route, partir. ○ **strike up** *vt fus* [conversation] commencer, engager; **to** ~ **up a friendship (with)** se lier d'amitié (avec). || [music] commencer à jouer.

striker ['straikər] *n* [person on strike] gréviste *mf*. || FTBL buteur *m*.

striking ['straikiŋ] *adj* [noticeable] frappant(e), saisissant(e). || [attractive] d'une beauté frappante.

string [striŋ] (*pt* & *pp* **strung**) *n* (U) [thin rope] ficelle *f*. || [piece of thin rope] bout *m* de ficelle; **to pull** ~**s** faire jouer le piston. || [of beads, pearls] rang *m*. || [series] série *f*, suite *f*. || [of musical instrument] corde *f*. ○ **strings** *npl* MUS: **the** ~**s** les cordes *fpl*.

string bean *n* haricot *m* vert.

stringent ['strindʒənt] *adj* strict(e), rigoureux(euse).

strip [strip] 1 *n* [narrow piece] bande *f*. 2 *vt* [undress] déshabiller, dévêtir. || [paint, wallpaper] enlever. 3 *vi* [undress] se déshabiller, se dévêtir. ○ **strip off** *vi* se déshabiller, se dévêtir.

stripe [straip] *n* [band of colour] rayure *f*. || [sign of rank] galon *m*.

striped [straipt] *adj* à rayures, rayé(e).

strip lighting *n* éclairage *m* au néon.

stripper ['stripər] *n* [performer of strip-tease] strip-teaseuse *f*, effeuilleuse *f*. || [for paint] décapant *m*.

striptease ['striptiːz] *n* strip-tease *m*.

strive [straiv] (*pt* **strove**, *pp* **striven** ['strivn]) *vi*: **to** ~ **to do sthg** s'efforcer de faire qqch.

strode [strəud] *pt* → **stride**.

stroke [strəuk] 1 *n* MED attaque *f* cérébrale. || [of pen, brush] trait *m*. || [in swimming - movement] mouvement *m* des bras; [- style] nage *f*; [in rowing] coup *m* d'aviron; [in golf, tennis etc] coup *m*. || [of clock]: **on the third** ~ ≃ au quatrième top. || [piece]: **a** ~ **of genius** un trait de génie; **a** ~ **of luck** un coup de chance OR de veine; **at a** ~ d'un seul coup. 2 *vt* caresser.

stroll [strəul] 1 *n* petite promenade *f*, petit tour *m*. 2 *vi* se promener, flâner.

stroller ['strəulər] *n* Am [for baby] poussette *f*.

strong [strɒŋ] *adj* [gen] fort(e); ~ **point** point *m* fort. || [structure, argument, friendship] solide. || [healthy] robuste, vigoureux(euse). || [in numbers]: **the crowd was 2,000** ~ il y avait une foule de 2 000 personnes. || [team, candidate] sérieux(ieuse), qui a des chances de gagner.

strongbox ['strɒŋbɒks] *n* coffre-fort *m*.

stronghold ['strɒŋhəuld] *n fig* bastion *m*.

strongly ['strɒŋli] *adv* [gen] fortement. || [solidly] solidement.

strong room *n* chambre *f* forte.

strove [strəuv] *pt* → **strive**.

struck [strʌk] *pt* & *pp* → **strike**.

structure ['strʌktʃər] *n* [organization] structure *f*. || [building] construction *f*.

struggle ['strʌgl] 1 *n* [great effort]: ~ **(for sthg/to do sthg)** lutte *f* (pour qqch/ pour faire qqch). || [fight] bagarre *f*. 2 *vi* [make great effort]: **to** ~ **(for)** lutter (pour); **to** ~ **to do sthg** s'efforcer de faire qqch. || [to free oneself] se débattre; [fight] se battre.

strum [strʌm] *vt* [guitar] gratter de.

strung [strʌŋ] *pt* & *pp* → **string**.

strut [strʌt] 1 *n* CONSTR étai *m*, support *m*. 2 *vi* se pavaner.

stub [stʌb] 1 *n* [of cigarette] mégot *m*; [of pencil] morceau *m*. || [of ticket, cheque] talon *m*. 2 *vt*: **to** ~ **one's toe** se cogner le doigt de pied. ○ **stub out** *vt sep* écraser.

stubble ['stʌbl] *n* (U) [in field] chaume *m*. || [on chin] barbe *f* de plusieurs jours.

stubborn ['stʌbən] *adj* [person] têtu(e), obstiné(e). || [stain] qui ne veut pas partir, rebelle.

stuck [stʌk] **1** *pt & pp* → **stick**. **2** *adj* [jammed, trapped] coincé(e). || [stumped]: **to be ~** sécher. || [stranded] bloqué(e), en rade.

stuck-up *adj inf pej* bêcheur(euse).

stud [stʌd] *n* [metal decoration] clou *m* décoratif. || [earring] clou *m* d'oreille. || [of horses] haras *m*.

studded ['stʌdɪd] *adj*: **~ (with)** parsemé(e) (de), constellé(e) (de).

student ['stju:dnt] **1** *n* étudiant *m*, -e *f*. **2** *comp* [life] estudiantin(e); [politics] des étudiants; [disco] pour étudiants.

studio ['stju:dɪəʊ] (*pl* **-s**) *n* studio *m*; [of artist] atelier *m*.

studio flat *Br*, **studio apartment** *Am n* studio *m*.

studious ['stju:djəs] *adj* studieux(ieuse).

study ['stʌdɪ] **1** *n* [gen] étude *f*. || [room] bureau *m*. **2** *vt* [learn] étudier, faire des études de. || [examine] examiner, étudier. **3** *vi* étudier, faire ses études.

stuff [stʌf] **1** *n* (*U*) *inf* [things] choses *fpl*. || [substance] substance *f*. || *inf* [belongings] affaires *fpl*. **2** *vt* [push] fourrer. || [fill]: **to ~ sthg (with)** remplir OR bourrer qqch (de). || CULIN farcir.

stuffed [stʌft] *adj* [filled]: **~ with** bourré(e) de. || *inf* [with food] gavé(e). || CULIN farci(e). || [preserved - animal] empaillé(e).

stuffing ['stʌfɪŋ] *n* (*U*) [filling] bourre *f*, rembourrage *m*. || CULIN farce *f*.

stuffy ['stʌfɪ] *adj* [room] mal aéré(e), qui manque d'air. || [person, club] vieux jeu (*inv*).

stumble ['stʌmbl] *vi* trébucher. ○ **stumble across**, **stumble on** *vt fus* tomber sur.

stumbling block ['stʌmblɪŋ-] *n* pierre *f* d'achoppement.

stump [stʌmp] **1** *n* [of tree] souche *f*; [of arm, leg] moignon *m*. **2** *vt* [subj: question, problem] dérouter, rendre perplexe.

stun [stʌn] *vt* [knock unconscious] étourdir, assommer. || [surprise] stupéfier, renverser.

stung [stʌŋ] *pt & pp* → **sting**.

stunk [stʌŋk] *pt & pp* → **stink**.

stunning ['stʌnɪŋ] *adj* [very beautiful] ravissant(e); [scenery] merveilleux (euse). || [surprising] stupéfiant(e), renversant(e).

stunt [stʌnt] **1** *n* [for publicity] coup *m*. || CINEMA cascade *f*. **2** *vt* retarder, arrêter.

stunted ['stʌntɪd] *adj* rabougri(e).

stunt man *n* cascadeur *m*.

stupefy ['stju:pɪfaɪ] *vt* [tire] abrutir. || [surprise] stupéfier, abasourdir.

stupid ['stju:pɪd] *adj* [foolish] stupide, bête. || *inf* [annoying] fichu(e).

stupidity [stju:'pɪdətɪ] *n* (*U*) bêtise *f*, stupidité *f*.

sturdy ['stɜ:dɪ] *adj* [person] robuste; [furniture, structure] solide.

stutter ['stʌtə*r*] *vi* bégayer.

sty [staɪ] *n* [pigsty] porcherie *f*.

stye [staɪ] *n* orgelet *m*, compère-loriot *m*.

style [staɪl] **1** *n* [characteristic manner] style *m*. || (*U*) [elegance] chic *m*, élégance *f*. || [design] genre *m*, modèle *m*. **2** *vt* [hair] coiffer.

stylish ['staɪlɪʃ] *adj* chic (*inv*), élégant(e).

stylist ['staɪlɪst] *n* [hairdresser] coiffeur *m*, -euse *f*.

stylus ['staɪləs] (*pl* **-es**) *n* [on record player] pointe *f* de lecture, saphir *m*.

suave [swɑ:v] *adj* doucereux(euse).

subconscious [,sʌb'kɒnʃəs] **1** *adj* inconscient(e). **2** *n*: **the ~** l'inconscient *m*.

subcontract [,sʌbkən'trækt] *vt* sous-traiter.

subdivide [,sʌbdɪ'vaɪd] *vt* subdiviser.

subdue [səb'dju:] *vt* [control - rioters, enemy] soumettre, subjuguer; [- temper, anger] maîtriser, réprimer.

subdued [səb'dju:d] *adj* [person] abattu(e). || [anger, emotion] contenu(e). || [colour] doux (douce); [light] tamisé(e).

subject [*adj*, *n & prep* 'sʌbdʒekt, *vt* səb'dʒekt] **1** *adj* soumis(e); **to be ~ to** [tax, law] être soumis à; [disease, headaches] être sujet (sujette) à. **2** *n* [gen] sujet *m*. || SCH & UNIV matière *f*. **3** *vt* [control] soumettre, assujettir. || [force to experience]: **to ~ sb to sthg** exposer OR soumettre qqn à qqch. ○ **subject to** *prep* sous réserve de.

subjective [səb'dʒektɪv] *adj* subjectif(ive).

subject matter *n* (*U*) sujet *m*.

subjunctive [səb'dʒʌŋktɪv] *n* GRAMM: **~ (mood)** (mode *m*) subjonctif *m*.

sublet [,sʌb'let] (*pt & pp* **sublet**) *vt* sous-louer.

sublime [sə'blaɪm] *adj* sublime.

submachine gun [,sʌbmə'ʃi:n-] *n* mitraillette *f*.

submarine [ˌsʌbmə'riːn] n sous-marin m.

submerge [səb'mɜːdʒ] 1 vt immerger, plonger. 2 vi s'immerger, plonger.

submission [səb'mɪʃn] n [obedience] soumission f. ‖ [presentation] présentation f, soumission f.

submissive [səb'mɪsɪv] adj soumis(e), docile.

submit [səb'mɪt] 1 vt soumettre. 2 vi: to ~ (to) se soumettre (à).

subnormal [ˌsʌb'nɔːml] adj arriéré(e), attardé(e).

subordinate [sə'bɔːdɪnət] 1 adj fml [less important]: ~ (to) subordonné(e) (à), moins important(e) (que). 2 n subordonné m, -e f.

subpoena [sə'piːnə] (pt & pp -ed) JUR 1 n citation f, assignation f. 2 vt citer OR assigner à comparaître.

subscribe [səb'skraɪb] vi [to magazine, newspaper] s'abonner (à), abonné(e).

subscriber [səb'skraɪbər] n [to magazine, service] abonné m, -e f.

subscription [səb'skrɪpʃn] n [to magazine] abonnement m. ‖ [to club] cotisation f.

subsequent ['sʌbsɪkwənt] adj ultérieur(e), suivant(e).

subsequently ['sʌbsɪkwəntlɪ] adv par la suite, plus tard.

subservient [səb'sɜːvjənt] adj [servile]: ~ (to) servile (vis-à-vis de), obséquieux(ieuse) (envers).

subside [səb'saɪd] vi [pain, anger] se calmer, s'atténuer; [noise] diminuer. ‖ [CONSTR - building] s'affaisser; [- ground] se tasser.

subsidence [səb'saɪdns, 'sʌbsɪdns] n [CONSTR - of building] affaissement m; [- of ground] tassement m.

subsidiary [səb'sɪdjərɪ] 1 adj subsidiaire. 2 n: ~ (company) filiale f.

subsidize, -ise ['sʌbsɪdaɪz] vt subventionner.

subsidy ['sʌbsɪdɪ] n subvention f, subside m.

substance ['sʌbstəns] n [gen] substance f. ‖ [importance] importance f.

substantial [səb'stænʃl] adj [considerable] considérable, important(e); [meal] substantiel(ielle). ‖ [solid, well-built] solide.

substantially [səb'stænʃəlɪ] adv [considerably] considérablement. ‖ [mainly] en grande partie.

substitute ['sʌbstɪtjuːt] 1 n [replacement]: ~ (for) [person] remplaçant m, -e f (de); [thing] succédané m (de). ‖ SPORT remplaçant m, -e f. 2 vt: to ~ A for B substituer A à B, remplacer B par A.

subtitle ['sʌbˌtaɪtl] n sous-titre m.

subtle ['sʌtl] adj subtil(e).

subtlety ['sʌtltɪ] n subtilité f.

subtract [səb'trækt] vt: to ~ sthg (from) soustraire qqch (de).

subtraction [səb'trækʃn] n soustraction f.

suburb ['sʌbɜːb] n faubourg m. ○ **suburbs** npl: the ~s la banlieue.

suburban [sə'bɜːbn] adj [of suburbs] de banlieue. ‖ pej [life] étriqué(e).

suburbia [sə'bɜːbɪə] n (U) la banlieue.

subversive [səb'vɜːsɪv] adj subversif(ive).

subway ['sʌbweɪ] n Am [underground railway] métro m.

succeed [sək'siːd] 1 vt succéder à. 2 vi réussir; to ~ in doing sthg réussir à faire qqch.

succeeding [sək'siːdɪŋ] adj fml [in future] à venir; [in past] suivant(e).

success [sək'ses] n succès m, réussite f.

successful [sək'sesful] adj [attempt] couronné(e) de succès. ‖ [film, book etc] à succès; [person] qui a du succès.

succession [sək'seʃn] n succession f.

successive [sək'sesɪv] adj successif(ive).

succinct [sək'sɪŋkt] adj succinct(e).

succumb [sə'kʌm] vi: to ~ (to) succomber (à).

such [sʌtʃ] 1 adj tel (telle), pareil(eille); ~ nonsense de telles inepties; do you have ~ a thing as a tin-opener? est-ce que tu aurais un ouvre-boîtes par hasard?; ~ ... that tel ... que. 2 adv [for emphasis] si, tellement; it's ~ a horrible day! quelle journée épouvantable!; ~ a lot of books tellement de livres; ~ a long time si OR tellement longtemps. ‖ [in comparisons] aussi. 3 pron: and ~ (like) et autres choses de ce genre. ○ **as such** adv en tant que tel (telle), en soi. ○ **such and such** adj tel et tel (telle et telle).

suck [sʌk] vt [with mouth] sucer. ‖ [draw in] aspirer.

sucker ['sʌkər] n [suction pad] ventouse f. ‖ inf [gullible person] poire f.

suction ['sʌkʃn] n succion f.

sudden ['sʌdn] adj soudain(e), brusque; all of a ~ tout d'un coup, soudain.

suddenly ['sʌdnlɪ] *adv* soudainement, tout d'un coup.

suds [sʌdz] *npl* mousse *f* de savon.

sue [su:] *vt*: **to ~ sb (for)** poursuivre qqn (pour).

suede [sweɪd] *n* daim *m*.

suet ['suɪt] *n* graisse *f* de rognon.

suffer ['sʌfəʳ] **1** *vt* [pain, injury] souffrir de. || [consequences, setback, loss] subir. **2** *vi* souffrir; **to ~ from** MED souffrir de.

suffering ['sʌfrɪŋ] *n* souffrance *f*.

suffice [sə'faɪs] *vi fml* suffire.

sufficient [sə'fɪʃnt] *adj* suffisant(e).

sufficiently [sə'fɪʃntlɪ] *adv* suffisamment.

suffocate ['sʌfəkeɪt] *vt & vi* suffoquer.

suffrage ['sʌfrɪdʒ] *n* suffrage *m*.

sugar ['ʃʊgəʳ] **1** *n* sucre *m*. **2** *vt* sucrer.

sugar beet *n* betterave *f* à sucre.

sugarcane ['ʃʊgəkeɪn] *n* (*U*) canne *f* à sucre.

suggest [sə'dʒest] *vt* [propose] proposer, suggérer. || [imply] suggérer.

suggestion [sə'dʒestʃn] *n* [proposal] proposition *f*, suggestion *f*. || (*U*) [implication] suggestion *f*.

suggestive [sə'dʒestɪv] *adj* suggestif(ive); **to be ~ of sthg** suggérer qqch.

suicide ['suɪsaɪd] *n* suicide *m*; **to commit ~** se suicider.

suit [su:t] **1** *n* [for man] costume *m*, complet *m*; [for woman] tailleur *m*. || [in cards] couleur *f*. || JUR procès *m*, action *f*. **2** *vt* [subj: clothes, hairstyle] aller à. || [be convenient, appropriate to] convenir à.

suitable ['su:təbl] *adj* qui convient, qui va.

suitably ['su:təblɪ] *adv* convenablement.

suitcase ['su:tkeɪs] *n* valise *f*.

suite [swi:t] *n* [of rooms] suite *f*. || [of furniture] ensemble *m*.

suited ['su:tɪd] *adj* [suitable]: **to be ~ to/for** convenir à/pour, aller à/pour. || [couple]: **well ~** très bien assortis.

suitor ['su:təʳ] *n dated* soupirant *m*.

sulfur *Am* = **sulphur**.

sulk [sʌlk] *vi* bouder.

sulky ['sʌlkɪ] *adj* boudeur(euse).

sullen ['sʌlən] *adj* maussade.

sulphur *Br*, **sulfur** *Am* ['sʌlfəʳ] *n* soufre *m*.

sultry ['sʌltrɪ] *adj* [weather] lourd(e). || [sexual] sensuel(elle).

sum [sʌm] *n* [amount of money] somme *f*. || [calculation] calcul *m*. ○ **sum up** *vt*

sep [summarize] résumer. **2** *vi* récapituler.

summarize, -ise ['sʌməraɪz] **1** *vt* résumer. **2** *vi* récapituler.

summary ['sʌmərɪ] *n* résumé *m*.

summer ['sʌməʳ] **1** *n* été *m*; **in ~** en été. **2** *comp* d'été; **the ~ holidays** les grandes vacances *fpl*.

summerhouse ['sʌməhaus, *pl* -hauzɪz] *n* pavillon *m* (de verdure).

summer school *n* université *f* d'été.

summertime ['sʌmətaɪm] *n* été *m*.

summit ['sʌmɪt] *n* sommet *m*.

summon ['sʌmən] *vt* appeler, convoquer. ○ **summon up** *vt sep* rassembler.

summons ['sʌmənz] (*pl* **summonses**) JUR **1** *n* assignation *f*. **2** *vt* assigner.

sump [sʌmp] *n* carter *m*.

sumptuous ['sʌmptʃuəs] *adj* somptueux(euse).

sun [sʌn] *n* soleil *m*; **in the ~** au soleil.

sunbathe ['sʌnbeɪð] *vi* prendre un bain de soleil.

sunbed ['sʌnbed] *n* lit *m* à ultra-violets.

sunburn ['sʌnbɜ:n] *n* (*U*) coup *m* de soleil.

sunburned ['sʌnbɜ:nd], **sunburnt** ['sʌnbɜ:nt] *adj* brûlé(e) par le soleil, qui a attrapé un coup de soleil.

Sunday ['sʌndɪ] *n* dimanche *m*; *see also* **Saturday**.

Sunday school *n* catéchisme *m*.

sundial ['sʌndaɪəl] *n* cadran *m* solaire.

sundown ['sʌndaun] *n* coucher *m* du soleil.

sundries ['sʌndrɪz] *npl fml* articles *mpl* divers, objets *mpl* divers.

sunflower ['sʌn,flauəʳ] *n* tournesol *m*.

sung [sʌŋ] *pp* → **sing**.

sunglasses ['sʌn,glɑ:sɪz] *npl* lunettes *fpl* de soleil.

sunk [sʌŋk] *pp* → **sink**.

sunlight ['sʌnlaɪt] *n* lumière *f* du soleil.

sunny ['sʌnɪ] *adj* [day, place] ensoleillé(e).

sunrise ['sʌnraɪz] *n* lever *m* du soleil.

sunroof ['sʌnru:f] *n* toit *m* ouvrant.

sunset ['sʌnset] *n* coucher *m* du soleil.

sunshade ['sʌnʃeɪd] *n* parasol *m*.

sunshine ['sʌnʃaɪn] *n* lumière *f* du soleil.

sunstroke ['sʌnstrəuk] *n* (*U*) insolation *f*.

suntan ['sʌntæn] **1** *n* bronzage *m*. **2** *comp* [lotion, cream] solaire.

suntrap ['sʌntræp] *n* endroit très ensoleillé.

super ['su:pər] *adj inf* génial(e), super (*inv*).

superannuation ['su:pə,rænju'eɪʃn] *n* (U) pension *f* de retraite.

superb [su:'pɜ:b] *adj* superbe.

supercilious [,su:pə'sɪlɪəs] *adj* hautain(e).

superficial [,su:pə'fɪʃl] *adj* superficiel(ielle).

superfluous [su:'pɜ:fluəs] *adj* superflu(e).

superhuman [,su:pə'hju:mən] *adj* surhumain(e).

superimpose [,su:pərɪm'pəuz] *vt*: to ~ sthg (on) superposer qqch (à).

superintendent [,su:pərɪn'tendənt] *n* [of department] directeur *m*, -trice *f*.

superior [su:'pɪərɪər] 1 *adj* [gen]: ~ (to) supérieur(e) (à). || [goods, craftsmanship] de qualité supérieure. 2 *n* supérieur *m*, -e *f*.

superlative [su:'pɜ:lətɪv] 1 *adj* exceptionnel(elle), sans pareil(eille). 2 *n* GRAMM superlatif *m*.

supermarket ['su:pə,mɑ:kɪt] *n* supermarché *m*.

supernatural [,su:pə'nætʃrəl] *adj* surnaturel(elle).

superpower ['su:pə,pauər] *n* superpuissance *f*.

supersede [,su:pə'si:d] *vt* remplacer.

supersonic [,su:pə'sɒnɪk] *adj* supersonique.

superstitious [,su:pə'stɪʃəs] *adj* superstitieux(ieuse).

superstore ['su:pəstɔ:r] *n* hypermarché *m*.

supervise ['su:pəvaɪz] *vt* surveiller; [work] superviser.

supervisor ['su:pəvaɪzər] *n* surveillant *m*, -e *f*.

supper ['sʌpər] *n* [evening meal] dîner *m*. || [before bedtime] collation *f*.

supple ['sʌpl] *adj* souple.

supplement [*n* 'sʌplɪmənt, *vb* 'sʌplɪment] 1 *n* supplément *m*. 2 *vt* compléter.

supplementary [,sʌplɪ'mentərɪ] *adj* supplémentaire.

supplier [sə'plaɪər] *n* fournisseur *m*.

supply [sə'plaɪ] 1 *n* [store] réserve *f*, provision *f*. || [system] alimentation *f*. 2 *vt* [provide]: to ~ sthg (to sb) fournir qqch (à qqn). ||, [provide to]: to ~ sb (with) fournir qqn (en), approvisionner qqn (en); to ~ sthg with sthg alimenter qqch en qqch. ○ **supplies** *npl* [food] vivres *mpl*; MIL approvisionnements *mpl*.

support [sə'pɔ:t] 1 *n* (U) [physical help] appui *m*. || (U) [emotional, financial help] soutien *m*. || [object] support *m*, appui *m*. 2 *vt* [physically] soutenir, supporter; [weight] supporter. || [emotionally] soutenir. || [financially] subvenir aux besoins de. || [political party, candidate] appuyer; SPORT être un supporter de.

supporter [sə'pɔ:tər] *n* [of person, plan] partisan *m*, -e *f*. || SPORT supporter *m*.

suppose [sə'pəuz] 1 *vt* supposer. 2 *vi* supposer; I ~ (so) je suppose que oui; I ~ not je suppose que non.

supposed [sə'pəuzd] *adj* [doubtful] supposé(e). || [reputed, intended]: to be ~ to be être censé(e) être.

supposedly [sə'pəuzɪdlɪ] *adv* soidisant.

supposing [sə'pəuzɪŋ] *conj* et si, à supposer que (+ *subjunctive*).

suppress [sə'pres] *vt* [uprising] réprimer. || [information] supprimer. || [emotions] réprimer, étouffer.

supreme [su'pri:m] *adj* suprême.

Supreme Court *n* [in US]: the ~ la Cour Suprême.

surcharge ['sɜ:tʃɑ:dʒ] *n* [extra payment] surcharge *f*; [extra tax] surtaxe *f*.

sure [ʃuər] 1 *adj* [gen] sûr(e); to be ~ of o.s. être sûr de soi. || [certain]: to be ~ (of sthg/of doing sthg) être sûr(e) (de qqch/de faire qqch), être certain(e) (de qqch/de faire qqch); to make ~ (that) ... s'assurer OR vérifier que .... 2 *adv inf* [yes] bien sûr. || *Am* [really] vraiment. ○ **for sure** *adv* sans aucun doute. ○ **sure enough** *adv* en effet, effectivement.

surely ['ʃuəlɪ] *adv* sûrement.

surf [sɜ:f] *n* ressac *m*.

surface ['sɜ:fɪs] 1 *n* surface *f*; on the ~ *fig* à première vue, vu de l'extérieur. 2 *vi* [diver] remonter à la surface; [submarine] faire surface. || [problem, rumour] apparaître OR s'étaler au grand jour.

surface mail *n* courrier *m* par voie de terre/de mer.

surfboard ['sɜ:fbɔ:d] *n* planche *f* de surf.

surfeit ['sɜ:fɪt] *n fml* excès *m*.

surfing ['sɜ:fɪŋ] *n* surf *m*.

surge [sɜ:dʒ] 1 *n* [of people, vehicles] déferlement *m*; ELEC surtension *f*. || [of emotion, interest] vague *f*, montée *f*; [of anger] bouffée *f*. 2 *vi* [people, vehicles] déferler.

surgeon ['sɜ:dʒən] *n* chirurgien *m*.

surgery ['sɜːdʒərɪ] *n* (*U*) MED [performing operations] chirurgie *f*.

surgical ['sɜːdʒɪkl] *adj* chirurgical(e); ~ **stocking** bas *m* orthopédique.

surly ['sɜːlɪ] *adj* revêche, renfrogné(e).

surmount [sɜː'maʊnt] *vt* surmonter.

surname ['sɜːneɪm] *n* nom *m* de famille.

surpass [sə'pɑːs] *vt fml* dépasser.

surplus ['sɜːpləs] **1** *adj* en surplus. **2** *n* surplus *m*.

surprise [sə'praɪz] **1** *n* surprise *f*. **2** *vt* surprendre.

surprised [sə'praɪzd] *adj* surpris(e).

surprising [sə'praɪzɪŋ] *adj* surprenant(e).

surprisingly [sə'praɪzɪŋlɪ] *adv* étonnamment.

surrender [sə'rendər] **1** *n* reddition *f*, capitulation *f*. **2** *vi* [stop fighting]: **to ~ (to)** se rendre (à). || *fig* [give in]: **to ~ (to)** se laisser aller (à), se livrer (à).

surreptitious [ˌsʌrəp'tɪʃəs] *adj* subreptice.

surrogate ['sʌrəgeɪt] *n* substitut *m*.

surrogate mother *n* mère *f* porteuse.

surround [sə'raʊnd] *vt* entourer; [subj: police, army] cerner.

surrounding [sə'raʊndɪŋ] *adj* environnant(e).

surroundings [sə'raʊndɪŋz] *npl* environnement *m*.

surveillance [sɜː'veɪləns] *n* surveillance *f*.

survey [*n* 'sɜːveɪ, *vb* sə'veɪ] **1** *n* [investigation] étude *f*; [of public opinion] sondage *m*. || [of building] inspection *f*. **2** *vt* [contemplate] passer en revue. || [investigate] faire une étude de, enquêter sur. || [building] inspecter.

surveyor [sə'veɪər] *n* [of building] expert *m*; [of land] géomètre *m*.

survival [sə'vaɪvl] *n* [continuing to live] survie *f*.

survive [sə'vaɪv] **1** *vt* survivre à. **2** *vi* survivre.

survivor [sə'vaɪvər] *n* survivant *m*, -e *f*; *fig* battant *m*, -e *f*.

susceptible [sə'septəbl] *adj*: ~ **(to)** sensible (à).

suspect [*adj & n* 'sʌspekt, *vb* sə'spekt] **1** *adj* suspect(e). **2** *n* suspect *m*, -e *f*. **3** *vt* [distrust] douter de. || [think likely, consider guilty] soupçonner.

suspend [sə'spend] *vt* [gen] suspendre. || [from school] renvoyer temporairement.

suspended sentence [sə'spendɪd-] *n* condamnation *f* avec sursis.

suspenders [sə'spendəz] *npl Am* [for trousers] bretelles *fpl*.

suspense [sə'spens] *n* suspense *m*.

suspension [sə'spenʃn] *n* [gen & AUT] suspension *f*. || [from school] renvoi *m* temporaire.

suspension bridge *n* pont *m* suspendu.

suspicion [sə'spɪʃn] *n* soupçon *m*.

suspicious [sə'spɪʃəs] *adj* [having suspicions] soupçonneux(euse). || [causing suspicion] suspect(e), louche.

sustain [sə'steɪn] *vt* [maintain] soutenir. || *fml* [suffer - damage] subir; [- injury] recevoir. || *fml* [weight] supporter.

sustenance ['sʌstɪnəns] *n* (*U*) *fml* nourriture *f*.

SW (*abbr of* **short wave**) OC.

swab [swɒb] *n* MED tampon *m*.

swagger ['swægər] *vi* parader.

swallow ['swɒləʊ] **1** *n* [bird] hirondelle *f*. **2** *vt* avaler; *fig* [anger, tears] ravaler.

swam [swæm] *pt → swim*.

swamp [swɒmp] **1** *n* marais *m*. **2** *vt* [flood] submerger. || [overwhelm] déborder, submerger.

swan [swɒn] *n* cygne *m*.

swap [swɒp] *vt*: **to ~ sthg (with sb/for sthg)** échanger qqch (avec qqn/contre qqch).

swarm [swɔːm] **1** *n* essaim *m*. **2** *vi fig* [people] grouiller; **to be ~ing (with)** [place] grouiller (de).

swarthy ['swɔːðɪ] *adj* basané(e).

swastika ['swɒstɪkə] *n* croix *f* gammée.

swat [swɒt] *vt* écraser.

sway [sweɪ] **1** *vt* [influence] influencer. **2** *vi* se balancer.

swear [sweər] (*pt* swore, *pp* sworn) **1** *vt* jurer; **to ~ to do sthg** jurer de faire qqch. **2** *vi* jurer.

swearword ['sweəwɜːd] *n* juron *m*, gros mot *m*.

sweat [swet] **1** *n* [perspiration] transpiration *f*, sueur *f*. **2** *vi* [perspire] transpirer, suer. || *inf* [worry] se faire du mouron.

sweater ['swetər] *n* pullover *m*.

sweatshirt ['swetʃɜːt] *n* sweat-shirt *m*.

sweaty ['swetɪ] *adj* [skin, clothes] mouillé(e) de sueur.

Swede [swiːd] *n* Suédois *m*, -e *f*.

Sweden ['swiːdn] *n* Suède *f*.

Swedish ['swiːdɪʃ] **1** *adj* suédois(e). **2** *n* [language] suédois *m*. **3** *npl*: **the ~** les Suédois *mpl*.

sweep [swi:p] (*pt* & *pp* **swept**) **1** *n* [sweeping movement] grand geste *m*. || [with brush]: **to give sthg a ~** donner un coup de balai à qqch, balayer qqch. **2** *vt* [gen] balayer; [scan with eyes] parcourir des yeux. ○ **sweep away** *vt sep* [destroy] emporter, entraîner. ○ **sweep up** **1** *vt sep* [with brush] balayer. **2** *vi* balayer.

sweeping ['swi:pɪŋ] *adj* [effect, change] radical(e). || [statement] hâtif(ive).

sweet [swi:t] *adj* [gen] doux (douce); [cake, flavour, pudding] sucré(e). || [kind] gentil(ille). || [attractive] adorable, mignon(onne).

sweet corn *n* maïs *m*.

sweeten ['swi:tn] *vt* sucrer.

sweetheart ['swi:tha:t] *n* [term of endearment] chéri *m*, -e *f*, mon cœur *m*.

sweetness ['swi:tnɪs] *n* [gen] douceur *f*; [of taste] goût *m* sucré, douceur. || [attractiveness] charme *m*.

sweet pea *n* pois *m* de senteur.

swell [swel] (*pt* -**ed**, *pp* **swollen** OR -**ed**) **1** *vi* [leg, face etc] enfler; [lungs, balloon] se gonfler. || [crowd, population etc] grossir, augmenter; [sound] grossir, s'enfler. **2** *vt* grossir, augmenter. **3** *n* [of sea] houle *f*. **4** *adj Am inf* chouette, épatant(e).

swelling ['swelɪŋ] *n* enflure *f*.

sweltering ['sweltərɪŋ] *adj* étouffant(e), suffocant(e).

swept [swept] *pt* & *pp* → **sweep**.

swerve [swɜ:v] *vi* faire une embardée.

swift [swɪft] **1** *adj* [fast] rapide. || [prompt] prompt(e). **2** *n* [bird] martinet *m*.

swig [swɪg] *inf n* lampée *f*.

swill [swɪl] *n* (*U*) [pig food] pâtée *f*.

swim [swɪm] (*pt* **swam**, *pp* **swum**) **1** *n*: **to have a ~** nager; **to go for a ~** aller se baigner, aller nager. **2** *vi* [person, fish, animal] nager. || [room] tourner; **my head was swimming** j'avais la tête qui tournait.

swimmer ['swɪmə'] *n* nageur *m*, -euse *f*.

swimming ['swɪmɪŋ] *n* natation *f*; **to go ~** aller nager.

swimming cap *n* bonnet *m* de bain.

swimming pool *n* piscine *f*.

swimming trunks *npl* maillot *m* OR slip *m* de bain.

swimsuit ['swɪmsu:t] *n* maillot *m* de bain.

swindle ['swɪndl] **1** *n* escroquerie *f*. **2** *vt* escroquer, rouler; **to ~ sb out of sthg** escroquer qqch à qqn.

swine [swaɪn] *n inf* [person] salaud *m*.

swing [swɪŋ] (*pt* & *pp* **swung**) **1** *n* [child's toy] balançoire *f*. || [change of opinion] revirement *m*; [- of mood] changement *m*, saute *f*. || [sway] balancement *m*. || *phr*: **to be in full ~** battre son plein. **2** *vt* [move back and forth] balancer. || [move in a curve] faire virer. **3** *vi* [move back and forth] se balancer. || [turn - vehicle] virer, tourner; **to ~ round** [person] se retourner. || [change] changer.

swing door *n* porte *f* battante.

swingeing ['swɪndʒɪŋ] *adj* très sévère.

swipe [swaɪp] **1** *vt inf* [steal] faucher, piquer. **2** *vi*: **to ~ at** envoyer OR donner un coup à.

swirl [swɜ:l] **1** *n* tourbillon *m*. **2** *vi* tourbillonner, tournoyer.

swish [swɪʃ] *vt* [tail] battre l'air de.

Swiss [swɪs] **1** *adj* suisse. **2** *n* [person] Suisse *mf*. **3** *npl*: **the ~** les Suisses *mpl*.

switch [swɪtʃ] **1** *n* [control device] interrupteur *m*, commutateur *m*; [on radio, stereo etc] bouton *m*. || [change] changement *m*. **2** *vt* [swap] échanger; [jobs] changer de. ○ **switch off** *vt sep* éteindre. ○ **switch on** *vt sep* allumer.

switchboard ['swɪtʃbɔːd] *n* standard *m*.

Switzerland ['swɪtsələnd] *n* Suisse *f*; **in ~** en Suisse.

swivel ['swɪvl] **1** *vt* [chair] faire pivoter; [head, eyes] faire tourner. **2** *vi* [chair] pivoter; [head, eyes] tourner.

swivel chair *n* fauteuil *m* pivotant OR tournant.

swollen ['swəʊln] **1** *pp* → **swell**. **2** *adj* [ankle, face] enflé(e); [river] en crue.

swoop [swu:p] **1** *n* [bird, plane] piquer. || [police, army] faire une descente.

swop [swɒp] = **swap**.

sword [sɔːd] *n* épée *f*.

swordfish ['sɔːdfɪʃ] (*pl inv* OR -**es**) *n* espadon *m*.

swore [swɔː'] *pt* → **swear**.

sworn [swɔːn] **1** *pp* → **swear**. **2** *adj* JUR sous serment.

swum [swʌm] *pp* → **swim**.

swung [swʌŋ] *pt* & *pp* → **swing**.

sycamore ['sɪkəmɔː'] *n* sycomore *m*.

syllable ['sɪləbl] *n* syllabe *f*.

syllabus ['sɪləbəs] (*pl* -**buses** OR -**bi** [-baɪ]) *n* programme *m*.

symbol ['sɪmbl] *n* symbole *m*.

symbolize, -ise ['sɪmbəlaɪz] *vt* symboliser.

symmetry ['sɪmətrɪ] *n* symétrie *f*.

sympathetic [,sɪmpə'θetɪk] *adj* [understanding] compatissant(e), compréhensif(ive). ‖ [willing to support]: ~ **(to)** bien disposé(e) (à l'égard de).

sympathize, -ise ['sɪmpəθaɪz] *vi* [feel sorry] compatir; **to ~ with sb** plaindre qqn; [in grief] compatir à la douleur de qqn. ‖ [understand]: **to ~ with** sthg comprendre qqch. ‖ [support]: **to ~ with** sthg approuver qqch, soutenir qqch.

sympathizer, -iser ['sɪmpəθaɪzəʳ] *n* sympathisant *m*, -e *f*.

sympathy ['sɪmpəθɪ] *n* (*U*) [understanding]: ~ **(for)** compassion *f* (pour), sympathie *f* (pour). ‖ [agreement] approbation *f*, sympathie *f*. ○ **sympathies** *npl* [to bereaved person] condoléances *fpl*.

symphony ['sɪmfənɪ] *n* symphonie *f*.

symposium [sɪm'pəʊzjəm] (*pl* **-siums** OR **-sia** [-zjə]) *n* symposium *m*.

symptom ['sɪmptəm] *n* symptôme *m*.

synagogue ['sɪnəgɒg] *n* synagogue *f*.

syndicate ['sɪndɪkət] *n* syndicat *m*, consortium *m*.

syndrome ['sɪndrəʊm] *n* syndrome *m*.

synonym ['sɪnənɪm] *n*: ~ **(for** OR **of)** synonyme *m* (de).

synopsis [sɪ'nɒpsɪs] (*pl* **-ses** [-si:z]) *n* résumé *m*.

syntax ['sɪntæks] *n* syntaxe *f*.

synthesis ['sɪnθəsɪs] (*pl* **-ses** [-si:z]) *n* synthèse *f*.

synthetic [sɪn'θetɪk] *adj* [man-made] synthétique.

syphilis ['sɪfɪlɪs] *n* syphilis *f*.

syphon ['saɪfn] = **siphon.**

Syria ['sɪrɪə] *n* Syrie *f*.

syringe [sɪ'rɪndʒ] *n* seringue *f*.

syrup ['sɪrəp] *n* (*U*) [sugar and water] sirop *m*.

system ['sɪstəm] *n* [gen] système *m*; road/railway ~ réseau *m* routier/de chemins de fer. ‖ [equipment - gen] installation *f*; [- electric, electronic] appareil *m*. ‖ (*U*) [methodical approach] système *m*, méthode *f*.

systematic [,sɪstə'mætɪk] *adj* systématique.

system disk *n* COMPUT disque *m* système.

systems analyst ['sɪstəmz-] *n* COMPUT analyste fonctionnel *m*, analyste fonctionnelle *f*.

t (*pl* **t's** OR **ts**), **T** (*pl* **T's** OR **Ts**) [ti:] *n* [letter] t *m inv*, T *m inv*.

tab [tæb] *n* [of cloth] étiquette *f*. ‖ [of metal] languette *f*. ‖ *Am* [bill] addition *f*. ‖ *phr*: **to keep ~s on sb** tenir OR avoir qqn à l'œil, surveiller qqn.

tabby ['tæbɪ] *n*: ~ **(cat)** chat tigré *m*, chatte tigrée *f*.

table ['teɪbl] *n* table *f*.

tablecloth ['teɪblklɒθ] *n* nappe *f*.

table lamp *n* lampe *f*.

tablemat ['teɪblmæt] *n* dessous-de-plat *m inv*.

tablespoon ['teɪblspu:n] *n* [spoon] cuiller *f* de service. ‖ [spoonful] cuillerée *f* à soupe.

tablet ['tæblɪt] *n* [pill] comprimé *m*, cachet *m*.

table tennis *n* ping-pong *m*, tennis *m* de table.

table wine *n* vin *m* de table.

tabloid ['tæblɔɪd] *n*: ~ **(newspaper)** tabloïd *m*, tabloïde *m*.

tabulate ['tæbjuleɪt] *vt* présenter sous forme de tableau.

tacit ['tæsɪt] *adj* tacite.

taciturn ['tæsɪtɜ:n] *adj* taciturne.

tack [tæk] **1** *n* [nail] clou *m*. ‖ *fig* [course of action] tactique *f*, méthode *f*. **2** *vt* [fasten with nail - gen] clouer; [- notice] punaiser. ‖ SEWING faufiler. **3** *vi* NAUT tirer une bordée.

tackle ['tækl] **1** *n* FTBL tacle *m*. ‖ [equipment] équipement *m*, matériel *m*. ‖ [for lifting] palan *m*, appareil *m* de levage. **2** *vt* [deal with] s'attaquer à. ‖ FTBL tacler. ‖ [attack] empoigner.

tacky ['tækɪ] *adj inf* [film, remark] d'un goût douteux; [jewellery] de pacotille. ‖ [sticky] collant(e), pas encore sec (sèche).

tact [tækt] *n* (*U*) tact *m*, délicatesse *f*.

tactful ['tæktful] *adj* [remark] plein(e) de tact; [person] qui a du tact OR de la délicatesse.

tactic ['tæktɪk] n tactique f.

tactical ['tæktɪkl] adj tactique.

tactless ['tæktlɪs] adj qui manque de tact OR délicatesse.

tadpole ['tædpəʊl] n têtard m.

tag [tæg] n [of cloth] marque f. || [of paper] étiquette f. ○ **tag along** vi inf suivre.

tail [teɪl] 1 n [gen] queue f. || [of coat] basque f, pan m; [of shirt] pan. 2 vt inf [follow] filer. ○ **tails** npl [formal dress] queue-de-pie f, habit m. || [side of coin] pile f. ○ **tail off** vi [voice] s'affaiblir; [noise] diminuer.

tailcoat [,teɪl'kəʊt] n habit m, queue-de-pie f.

tail end n fin f.

tailor ['teɪlər] 1 n tailleur m. 2 vt fig adapter.

tailor-made adj fig sur mesure.

tailwind ['teɪlwɪnd] n vent m arrière.

tainted ['teɪntɪd] adj [reputation] souillé(e), entaché(e). || Am [food] avarié(e).

Taiwan [,taɪ'wɑːn] n Taiwan.

take [teɪk] (pt **took**, pp **taken**) 1 vt [gen] prendre; to ~ an exam passer un examen; to ~ a walk se promener, faire une promenade; to ~ a bath/photo prendre un bain/une photo. || [lead, drive] emmener. || [accept] accepter. || [contain] contenir, avoir une capacité de. || [tolerate] supporter. || [require] demander; how long will it ~? combien de temps cela va-t-il prendre? || [wear]: what size do you ~? [clothes] quelle taille faites-vous?; [shoes] vous chaussez du combien? || [assume]: I ~ it (that) ... je suppose que .... je pense que .... || [rent] prendre, louer. 2 n CINEMA prise f de vues. ○ **take after** vt fus tenir de, ressembler à. ○ **take apart** vt sep [dismantle] démonter. ○ **take away** vt sep [remove] enlever. || [deduct] retrancher, soustraire. ○ **take back** vt sep [return] rendre, rapporter. || [accept] reprendre. || [statement, accusation] retirer. ○ **take down** vt sep [dismantle] démonter. || [write down] prendre. || [lower] baisser. ○ **take in** vt sep [deceive] rouler, tromper. || [understand] comprendre. ○ **take off** 1 vt sep [remove] enlever, ôter. || [have as holiday]: to ~ a week/day off prendre une semaine/un jour de congé. 2 vi [plane] décoller. || [go away suddenly] partir. ○ **take on** vt sep [accept] accepter, prendre. || [employ] embaucher, prendre. || [confront] s'attaquer à; [com-

petitor] faire concurrence à; SPORT jouer contre. ○ **take out** vt sep [from container] sortir; [from pocket] prendre. || [go out with] emmener, sortir avec.
○ **take over** 1 vt sep [take control of] reprendre, prendre la direction de. || [job]: to ~ over sb's job remplacer qqn, prendre la suite de qqn. 2 vi [take control] prendre le pouvoir. || [in job] prendre la relève. ○ **take to** vt fus [person] éprouver de la sympathie pour, sympathiser avec; [activity] prendre goût à. || [begin]: to ~ to doing sthg se mettre à faire qqch. ○ **take up** vt sep [begin - job] prendre; to ~ up singing se mettre au chant. || [use up] prendre, occuper. ○ **take up on** vt sep [accept]: to ~ sb up on an offer accepter l'offre de qqn.

takeaway Br ['teɪkə,weɪ], **takeout** Am ['teɪkaʊt] n [food] plat m à emporter.

taken ['teɪkn] pp → take.

takeoff ['teɪkɒf] n [of plane] décollage m.

takeout Am = **takeaway**.

takeover ['teɪk,əʊvər] n [of company] prise f de contrôle, rachat m. || [of government] prise f de pouvoir.

takings ['teɪkɪŋz] npl recette f.

talc [tælk], **talcum (powder)** ['tælkəm-] n talc m.

tale [teɪl] n [fictional story] histoire f, conte m. || [anecdote] récit m, histoire f.

talent ['tælənt] n: ~ (for) talent m (pour).

talented ['tæləntɪd] adj qui a du talent, talentueux(euse).

talk [tɔːk] 1 n [conversation] discussion f, conversation f. || (U) [gossip] bavardages mpl, racontars mpl. || [lecture] conférence f, causerie f. 2 vi [speak]: to ~ (to sb) parler (à qqn); to ~ about parler de. || [gossip] bavarder, jaser. || [make a speech] faire un discours, parler; to ~ on OR about parler de. 3 vt parler. ○ **talks** npl entretiens mpl, pourparlers mpl. ○ **talk into** vt sep: to ~ sb into doing sthg persuader qqn de faire qqch. ○ **talk out of** vt sep: to ~ sb out of doing sthg dissuader qqn de faire qqch. ○ **talk over** vt sep discuter de.

talkative ['tɔːkətɪv] adj bavard(e), loquace.

talk show Am n talk-show m, causerie f.

tall [tɔːl] adj grand(e); how ~ are you? combien mesurez-vous?

tall story n histoire f à dormir debout.

tally ['tælɪ] 1 *n* compte *m*. 2 *vi* correspondre, concorder.

talon ['tælən] *n* serre *f*, griffe *f*.

tambourine [,tæmbə'ri:n] *n* tambourin *m*.

tame [teɪm] 1 *adj* [animal, bird] apprivoisé(e). || *pej* [person] docile; [party, story, life] terne, morne. 2 *vt* [animal, bird] apprivoiser.

tamper ['tæmpə'] ○ **tamper with** *vt fus* [machine] toucher à; [records, file] altérer, falsifier; [lock] essayer de crocheter.

tampon ['tæmpɒn] *n* tampon *m*.

tan [tæn] 1 *adj* brun clair (*inv*). 2 *n* bronzage *m*, hâle *m*. 3 *vi* bronzer.

tang [tæŋ] *n* [taste] saveur *f* forte OR piquante; [smell] odeur *f* forte OR piquante.

tangent ['tændʒənt] *n*: **to go off at a ~** *fig* changer de sujet, faire une digression.

tangerine [,tændʒə'ri:n] *n* mandarine *f*.

tangible ['tændʒəbl] *adj* tangible.

Tangier [tæn'dʒɪə'] *n* Tanger *m*.

tangle ['tæŋgl] *n* [mass] enchevêtrement *m*, emmêlement *m*. || *fig* [confusion]: **to get into a ~** s'empêtrer, s'embrouiller.

tank [tæŋk] *n* [container] réservoir *m*; **fish ~** aquarium *m*. || MIL tank *m*, char *m* (d'assaut).

tanker ['tæŋkə'] *n* [ship - for oil] pétrolier *m*. || [truck] camion-citerne *m*. || [train] wagon-citerne *m*.

tanned [tænd] *adj* bronzé(e), hâlé(e).

Tannoy® ['tænɔɪ] *n* système *m* de haut-parleurs.

tantalizing ['tæntəlaɪzɪŋ] *adj* [smell] très appétissant(e); [possibility, thought] très tentant(e).

tantamount ['tæntəmaʊnt] *adj*: **~ to** équivalent(e) à.

tantrum ['tæntrəm] (*pl* -s) *n* crise *f* de colère; **to have** OR **throw a ~** faire OR piquer une colère.

tap [tæp] 1 *n* [device] robinet *m*. || [light blow] petite tape *f*, petit coup *m*. 2 *vt* [hit] tapoter, taper. || [resources, energy] exploiter, utiliser. || [telephone, wire] mettre sur écoute.

tap dance *n* claquettes *fpl*.

tape [teɪp] 1 *n* [magnetic tape] bande *f* magnétique; [cassette] cassette *f*. || [strip of cloth, adhesive material] ruban *m*. 2 *vt* [record] enregistrer; [on video] magnétoscoper, enregistrer au magnétoscope. || [stick] scotcher.

tape measure *n* centimètre *m*, mètre *m*.

taper ['teɪpə'] *vi* s'effiler.

tape recorder *n* magnétophone *m*.

tapestry ['tæpɪstrɪ] *n* tapisserie *f*.

tar [tɑ:'] *n* (*U*) goudron *m*.

target ['tɑ:gɪt] 1 *n* [of missile, bomb] objectif *m*; [for archery, shooting] cible *f*. || *fig* [for criticism] cible *f*. || *fig* [goal] objectif *m*. 2 *vt* [city, building] viser. || *fig* [subj: policy] s'adresser à, viser; [subj: advertising] cibler.

tariff ['tærɪf] *n* [tax] tarif *m* douanier. || [list] tableau *m* OR liste *f* des prix.

Tarmac® ['tɑ:mæk] *n* [material] macadam *m*. ○ **tarmac** *n* AERON: **the tarmac** la piste.

tarnish ['tɑ:nɪʃ] *vt lit & fig* ternir.

tarpaulin [tɑ:'pɔ:lɪn] *n* [material] toile *f* goudronnée; [sheet] bâche *f*.

tart [tɑ:t] 1 *adj* [bitter] acide. || [sarcastic] acide, acerbe. 2 *n* CULIN tarte *f*. || *v inf* [prostitute] pute *f*.

tartan ['tɑ:tn] 1 *n* tartan *m*. 2 *comp* écossais(e).

tartar(e) sauce ['tɑ:tə'-] *n* sauce *f* tartare.

task [tɑ:sk] *n* tâche *f*, besogne *f*.

task force *n* MIL corps *m* expéditionnaire.

tassel ['tæsl] *n* pompon *m*, gland *m*.

taste [teɪst] 1 *n* [gen] goût *m*; **have a ~!** goûte!; **in good/bad ~** de bon/mauvais goût. || *fig* [liking]: **~ (for)** penchant *m* (pour), goût *m* (pour). || *fig* [experience] aperçu *m*. 2 *vt* [sense - food] sentir. || [test, try] déguster, goûter. 3 *vi*: **to ~ of/like** avoir le goût de; **to ~ good/odd** *etc* avoir bon goût/un drôle de goût *etc*.

tasteful ['teɪstful] *adj* de bon goût.

tasteless ['teɪstlɪs] *adj* [object, decor, remark] de mauvais goût. || [food] qui n'a aucun goût, fade.

tasty ['teɪstɪ] *adj* [delicious] délicieux(ieuse), succulent(e).

tatters ['tætəz] *npl*: **in ~** [clothes] en lambeaux; [reputation] ruiné(e).

tattoo [tə'tu:] (*pl* -s) 1 *n* [design] tatouage *m*. 2 *vt* tatouer.

taught [tɔ:t] *pt & pp* → **teach**.

taunt [tɔ:nt] 1 *vt* railler, se moquer de. 2 *n* raillerie *f*, moquerie *f*.

Taurus ['tɔ:rəs] *n* Taureau *m*.

taut [tɔ:t] *adj* tendu(e).

tawdry ['tɔ:drɪ] *adj pej* [jewellery] clinquant(e); [clothes] voyant(e), criard(e).

tax [tæks] **1** *n* taxe *f*, impôt *m*. **2** *vt* [goods] taxer. ‖ [profits, business, person] imposer. ‖ [strain] mettre à l'épreuve.

taxable ['tæksəbl] *adj* imposable.

tax allowance *n* abattement *m* fiscal.

taxation [tæk'seɪʃn] *n* (*U*) [system] imposition *f*. ‖ [amount] impôts *mpl*.

tax avoidance [-ə'vɔɪdəns] *n* évasion *f* fiscale.

tax collector *n* percepteur *m*.

tax evasion *n* fraude *f* fiscale.

tax-free *Br*, **tax-exempt** *Am adj* exonéré(e) (d'impôt).

taxi ['tæksi] **1** *n* taxi *m*. **2** *vi* [plane] rouler au sol.

taxi driver *n* chauffeur *m* de taxi.

tax inspector *n* inspecteur *m* des impôts.

taxi rank *Br*, **taxi stand** *n* station *f* de taxis.

taxpayer ['tæks,peɪər] *n* contribuable *mf*.

tax relief *n* allègement *m* OR dégrèvement *m* fiscal.

tax return *n* déclaration *f* d'impôts.

TB *n abbr of* **tuberculosis**.

tea [tiː] *n* [drink, leaves] thé *m*.

teabag ['tiːbæg] *n* sachet *m* de thé.

teach [tiːtʃ] (*pt & pp* **taught**) **1** *vt* [instruct] apprendre; **to ~ sb sthg, to ~ sthg to sb** apprendre qqch à qqn; **to ~ sb to do sthg** apprendre à qqn à faire qqch. ‖ [subj: teacher] enseigner; **to ~ sb sthg, to ~ sthg to sb** enseigner qqch à qqn. **2** *vi* enseigner.

teacher ['tiːtʃər] *n* [in primary school] instituteur *m*, -trice *f*, maître *m*, maîtresse *f*; [in secondary school] professeur *m*.

teacher training college *Br*, **teachers college** *Am n* ≈ institut *m* universitaire de formation de maîtres, ≈ IUFM *m*.

teaching ['tiːtʃɪŋ] *n* enseignement *m*.

tea cosy *Br*, **tea cozy** *Am n* couvre-théière *m*, cosy *m*.

teacup ['tiːkʌp] *n* tasse *f* à thé.

teak [tiːk] *n* teck *m*.

team [tiːm] *n* équipe *f*.

teammate ['tiːmmeɪt] *n* co-équipier *m*, -ière *f*.

teamwork ['tiːmwɜːk] *n* (*U*) travail *m* d'équipe, collaboration *f*.

teapot ['tiːpɒt] *n* théière *f*.

tear¹ [tɪər] *n* larme *f*.

tear² [teər] (*pt* **tore**, *pp* **torn**) **1** *vt* [rip] déchirer. ‖ [remove roughly] arracher. **2** *vi* [rip] se déchirer. ‖ [move quickly] fon-

cer, aller à toute allure. **3** *n* déchirure *f*, accroc *m*. ○ **tear apart** *vt sep* [rip up] déchirer, mettre en morceaux. ‖ *fig* [country, company] diviser; [person] déchirer. ○ **tear down** *vt sep* [building] démolir; [poster] arracher. ○ **tear up** *vt sep* déchirer.

teardrop ['tɪədrɒp] *n* larme *f*.

tearful ['tɪəfʊl] *adj* [person] en larmes.

tear gas [tɪər-] *n* (*U*) gaz *m* lacrymogène.

tearoom ['tiːrʊm] *n* salon *m* de thé.

tease [tiːz] **1** *n* taquin *m*, -e *f*. **2** *vt* [mock]; **to ~ sb (about sthg)** taquiner qqn (à propos de qqch).

tea service, tea set *n* service *m* à thé.

teaspoon ['tiːspuːn] *n* [utensil] petite cuillère *f*, cuillère *f* à café. ‖ [amount] cuillerée *f* à café.

teat [tiːt] *n* tétine *f*.

tea towel *n* torchon *m*.

technical ['teknɪkl] *adj* technique.

technicality [,teknɪ'kælətɪ] *n* [detail] détail *m* technique.

technically ['teknɪklɪ] *adv* [gen] techniquement. ‖ [theoretically] en théorie.

technician [tek'nɪʃn] *n* technicien *m*, -ienne *f*.

technique [tek'niːk] *n* technique *f*.

technological [,teknə'lɒdʒɪkl] *adj* technologique.

technology [tek'nɒlədʒɪ] *n* technologie *f*.

teddy ['tedɪ] *n*: ~ **(bear)** ours *m* en peluche, nounours *m*.

tedious ['tiːdjəs] *adj* ennuyeux(euse).

tee [tiː] *n* GOLF tee *m*.

teem [tiːm] *vi* [rain] pleuvoir à verse. ‖ [place]: **to be ~ing with** grouiller de.

teenage ['tiːneɪdʒ] *adj* adolescent(e).

teenager ['tiːn,eɪdʒər] *n* adolescent *m*, -e *f*.

teens [tiːnz] *npl* adolescence *f*.

tee shirt *n* tee-shirt *m*.

teeter ['tiːtər] *vi* vaciller; **to ~ on the brink of** *fig* être au bord de.

teeth [tiːθ] *pl → * **tooth**.

teethe [tiːð] *vi* [baby] percer ses dents.

teething troubles ['tiːðɪŋ-] *npl fig* difficultés *fpl* initiales.

teetotaller *Br*, **teetotaler** *Am* [tiː'təʊtlər] *n* personne *f* qui ne boit jamais d'alcool.

TEFL ['tefl] (*abbr of* **teaching of English as a foreign language**) *n enseignement de l'anglais langue étrangère*.

tel. (*abbr of* **telephone**) tél.

telecommunications [ˈtelɪkəˌmjuːnɪˈkeɪʃnz] *npl* télécommunications *fpl*.

telegram [ˈtelɪgræm] *n* télégramme *m*.

telegraph [ˈtelɪgrɑːf] **1** *n* télégraphe *m*. **2** *rt* télégraphier.

telegraph pole, telegraph post *Br n* poteau *m* télégraphique.

telepathy [tɪˈlepəθɪ] *n* télépathie *f*.

telephone [ˈtelɪfəʊn] **1** *n* téléphone *m*. **2** *rt* téléphoner à. **3** *ri* téléphoner.

telephone book *n* annuaire *m*.

telephone booth *n* cabine *f* téléphonique.

telephone call *n* appel *m* téléphonique, coup *m* de téléphone.

telephone directory *n* annuaire *m*.

telephone number *n* numéro *m* de téléphone.

telephoto lens [ˌtelɪˈfəʊtəʊ-] *n* téléobjectif *m*.

telescope [ˈtelɪskəʊp] *n* télescope *m*.

teletext [ˈtelɪtekst] *n* télétexte *m*.

televise [ˈtelɪvaɪz] *rt* téléviser.

television [ˈtelɪˌvɪʒn] *n* (*U*) [medium, industry] télévision *f*; **on ~** à la télévision. ‖ [apparatus] (poste *m* de) télévision *f*, téléviseur *m*.

television set *n* poste *m* de télévision, téléviseur *m*.

telex [ˈteleks] **1** *n* télex *m*. **2** *rt* [message] envoyer par télex, télexer; [person] envoyer un télex à.

tell [tel] (*pt & pp* **told**) **1** *rt* [gen] dire; [story] raconter; **to ~ sb (that) ...** dire à qqn que ...; **to ~ sb sthg, to ~ sthg to sb** dire qqch à qqn; **to ~ sb to do sthg** dire OR ordonner à qqn de faire qqch. ‖ [judge, recognize] savoir, voir. **2** *ri* [speak] parler. ‖ [judge] savoir. ‖ [have effect] se faire sentir. ○ **tell apart** *rt sep* distinguer. ○ **tell off** *rt sep* gronder.

telling [ˈtelɪŋ] *adj* [remark] révélateur(trice).

telltale [ˈtelteɪl] **1** *adj* révélateur(trice). **2** *n* rapporteur *m*, -euse *f*, mouchard *m*, -e *f*.

temp [temp] *inf* **1** *n* (*abbr of* **temporary** (**employee**)) intérimaire *mf*. **2** *ri* travailler comme intérimaire.

temper [ˈtempər] **1** *n* [angry state]: **to be in a ~** être en colère; **to lose one's ~** se mettre en colère. ‖ [mood] humeur *f*. ‖ [temperament] tempérament *m*. **2** *rt* [moderate] tempérer.

temperament [ˈtemprəmənt] *n* tempérament *m*.

temperamental [ˌtemprəˈmentl] *adj* [volatile, unreliable] capricieux(ieuse).

temperate [ˈtemprət] *adj* tempéré(e).

temperature [ˈtemprətʃər] *n* température *f*; **to have a ~** avoir de la température OR de la fièvre.

template [ˈtemplɪt] *n* gabarit *m*.

temple [ˈtempl] *n* RELIG temple *m*. ‖ ANAT tempe *f*.

temporarily [ˌtempəˈrerəlɪ] *adr* temporairement, provisoirement.

temporary [ˈtempərərɪ] *adj* temporaire, provisoire.

tempt [tempt] *rt* tenter; **to ~ sb to do sthg** donner à qqn l'envie de faire qqch.

temptation [tempˈteɪʃn] *n* tentation *f*.

tempting [ˈtemptɪŋ] *adj* tentant(e).

ten [ten] *num* dix; *see also* **six**.

tenable [ˈtenəbl] *adj* [argument, position] défendable.

tenacious [tɪˈneɪʃəs] *adj* tenace.

tenancy [ˈtenənsɪ] *n* location *f*.

tenant [ˈtenənt] *n* locataire *mf*.

tend [tend] *rt* [have tendency]: **to ~ to do sthg** avoir tendance à faire qqch. ‖ [look after] s'occuper de, garder.

tendency [ˈtendənsɪ] *n*: **~ (to do sthg)** tendance *f* (à faire qqch).

tender [ˈtendər] **1** *adj* tendre; [bruise, part of body] sensible, douloureux(euse). **2** *n* COMM soumission *f*. **3** *rt fml* [apology, money] offrir; [resignation] donner.

tendon [ˈtendən] *n* tendon *m*.

tenement [ˈtenəmənt] *n* immeuble *m*.

tenet [ˈtenɪt] *n fml* principe *m*.

tennis [ˈtenɪs] *n* (*U*) tennis *m*.

tennis ball *n* balle *f* de tennis.

tennis court *n* court *m* de tennis.

tennis racket *n* raquette *f* de tennis.

tenor [ˈtenər] *n* [singer] ténor *m*.

tense [tens] **1** *adj* tendu(e). **2** *n* temps *m*. **3** *rt* tendre.

tension [ˈtenʃn] *n* tension *f*.

tent [tent] *n* tente *f*.

tentacle [ˈtentəkl] *n* tentacule *m*.

tentative [ˈtentətɪv] *adj* [hesitant] hésitant(e). ‖ [not final] provisoire.

tenterhooks [ˈtentəhʊks] *npl*: **to be on ~** être sur des charbons ardents.

tenth [tenθ] *num* dixième; *see also* **sixth**.

tent peg *n* piquet *m* de tente.

tent pole *n* montant *m* OR mât *m* de tente.

tenuous [ˈtenjʊəs] *adj* ténu(e).

tenure [ˈtenjər] *n* (*U*) *fml* [of property] bail *m*. ‖ [of job]: **to have ~** être titulaire.

that

tepid ['tepɪd] *adj* tiède.

term [tɜːm] **1** *n* (word, expression) terme *m*. || SCH & UNIV trimestre *m*. || (period of time) durée *f*, période *f*; **in the long/short ~** à long/court terme. **2** *vt* appeler. ○ **terms** *npl* (of contract, agreement) conditions *fpl*. || (basis): **in international/real ~s** en termes internationaux/réels; **to be on good ~s (with sb)** être en bons termes (avec qqn); **to come to ~s with sthg** accepter qqch. ○ **in terms of** *prep* sur le plan de, en termes de.

terminal ['tɜːmɪnl] **1** *adj* MED en phase terminale. **2** *n* AERON, COMPUT & RAIL terminal *m*. || ELEC borne *f*.

terminate ['tɜːmɪneɪt] **1** *vt fml* (end - gen) terminer, mettre fin à; (- contract) résilier. || (pregnancy) interrompre. **2** *vi* (bus, train) s'arrêter. || (contract) se terminer.

termini ['tɜːmɪnaɪ] *pl* → **terminus**.

terminus ['tɜːmɪnəs] (*pl* **-ni** OR **-nuses**) terminus *m*.

terrace ['terəs] *n* (patio, on hillside) terrasse *f*.

terraced ['terəst] *adj* (hillside) en terrasses.

terrain [te'reɪn] *n* terrain *m*.

terrible ['terəbl] *adj* terrible; (holiday, headache, weather) affreux(euse), épouvantable.

terribly ['terəblɪ] *adv* terriblement; (sing, write, organized) affreusement mal; (injured) affreusement.

terrier ['terɪər] *n* terrier *m*.

terrific [tə'rɪfɪk] *adj* (wonderful) fantastique, formidable. || (enormous) énorme, fantastique.

terrified ['terɪfaɪd] *adj* terrifié(e); **to be ~ of** avoir une terreur folle OR peur folle de.

terrifying ['terɪfaɪɪŋ] *adj* terrifiant(e).

territory ['terətrɪ] *n* territoire *m*.

terror ['terər] *n* terreur *f*.

terrorism ['terərɪzm] *n* terrorisme *m*.

terrorist ['terərɪst] *n* terroriste *mf*.

terrorize, -ise ['terəraɪz] *vt* terroriser.

terse [tɜːs] *adj* brusque.

Terylene® ['terɪliːn] *n* Térylène® *m*.

test [test] **1** *n* (trial) essai *m*; (of friendship, courage) épreuve *f*. || (examination - of aptitude, psychological) test *m*; (- SCH & UNIV) interrogation *f* écrite/orale; (- of driving) (examen *m* du) permis *m* de conduire. || (MED - of blood, urine) analyse *f*; (- of eyes) examen *m*. **2** *vt* (try) essayer;

(determination, friendship) mettre à l'épreuve. || SCH & UNIV faire faire une interrogation écrite/orale à; **to ~ sb on sthg** interroger qqn sur qqch. || (MED - blood, urine) analyser; (- eyes, reflexes) faire un examen de.

testament ['testəmənt] *n* (will) testament *m*.

test-drive *vt* essayer.

testicles ['testɪklz] *npl* testicules *mpl*.

testify ['testɪfaɪ] **1** *vt*: **to ~ that ...** témoigner que .... **2** *vi* JUR témoigner. || (be proof): **to ~ to sthg** témoigner de qqch.

testimony [*Br* 'testɪmənɪ, *Am* 'testəməʊnɪ] *n* témoignage *m*.

testing ['testɪŋ] *adj* éprouvant(e).

test pilot *n* pilote *m* d'essai.

test tube *n* éprouvette *f*.

test-tube baby *n* bébé-éprouvette *m*.

tetanus ['tetənəs] *n* tétanos *m*.

tether ['teðər] **1** *vt* attacher. **2** *n*: **to be at the end of one's ~** être au bout du rouleau.

text [tekst] *n* texte *m*.

textbook ['tekstbʊk] *n* livre *m* OR manuel *m* scolaire.

textile ['tekstaɪl] *n* textile *m*.

texture ['tekstʃər] *n* texture *f*; (of paper, wood) grain *m*.

Thai [taɪ] **1** *adj* thaïlandais(e). **2** *n* (person) Thaïlandais *m*, -e *f*. || (language) thaï *m*.

Thailand ['taɪlænd] *n* Thaïlande *f*.

Thames [temz] *n*: **the ~** la Tamise.

than [weak form ðən, strong form ðæn] *conj* que; **Sarah is younger ~ her sister** Sarah est plus jeune que sa sœur; **more ~ three days/50 people** plus de trois jours/50 personnes.

thank [θæŋk] *vt*: **to ~ sb (for)** remercier qqn (pour OR de); **~ God** OR **goodness** OR **heavens!** Dieu merci! ○ **thanks 1** *npl* remerciements *mpl*. **2** *excl* merci! ○ **thanks to** *prep* grâce à.

thankful ['θæŋkfʊl] *adj* (grateful): **~ (for)** reconnaissant(e) (de). || (relieved) soulagé(e).

thankless ['θæŋklɪs] *adj* ingrat(e).

thanksgiving ['θæŋksgɪvɪŋ] *n* action *f* de grâce. ○ **Thanksgiving (Day)** *n* fête nationale américaine commémorant, le 4ᵉ jeudi de novembre, l'installation des premiers colons en Amérique.

thank you *excl*: **~ (for)** merci (pour OR de).

that [ðæt, *weak form of pron sense 2 & conj* ðət] (*pl* **those**) **1** *pron* (*demon-*

strative use: pl 'those') ce, cela, ça; (as opposed to 'this') celui-là (celle-là); who's ~? qui est-ce?; what's ~? qu'est-ce que c'est que ça?; which shoes are you going to wear, these or those? quelles chaussures vas-tu mettre. celles-ci ou celles-là? || (to introduce relative clauses - subject) qui; (- object) que; (- with prep) lequel (laquelle), lesquels (lesquelles) (pl); we came to a path ~ led into the woods nous arrivâmes à un sentier qui menait dans les bois; show me the book ~ you bought montre-moi le livre que tu as acheté; on the day ~ we left le jour où nous sommes partis. 2 adj (demonstrative: pl 'those') ce (cette), cet (before vowel or silent "h"), ces (pl); (as opposed to 'this') ce (cette) ... -là, ces ... -là (pl); those chocolates are delicious ces chocolats sont délicieux; I prefer ~ book je préfère ce livre-là; I'll have ~ one je prendrai celui-là. 3 adv aussi, si; it wasn't ~ bad/good ce n'était pas si mal/bien que ça. 4 conj que; tell him ~ the children aren't coming dites-lui que les enfants ne viennent pas; he recommended ~ I phone you il m'a conseillé de vous appeler. O **that is (to say)** adv c'est-à-dire.

thatched [θætʃt] adj de chaume.

that's [ðæts] = that is.

thaw [θɔː] 1 vt [ice] faire fondre OR dégeler; [frozen food] décongeler. 2 vi [ice] dégeler, fondre; [frozen food] décongeler. 3 n dégel m.

the [weak form ðə, before vowel ði, strong form ðiː] def art [gen] le (la), l' (+ vowel or silent "h"), les (pl); ~ **book** le livre; ~ **sea** la mer; ~ **man** l'homme; ~ **boys/girls** les garçons/filles; **to play ~ piano** jouer du piano. || (with an adjective to form a noun): ~ **old/young** les vieux/jeunes; ~ **impossible** l'impossible. || [in dates]: ~ **twelfth of May** le douze mai; ~ **forties** les années quarante. || [in comparisons]: ~ **more ...** ~ **less plus ...** moins; ~ **sooner** ~ **better** le plus tôt sera le mieux. || [in titles]: **Alexander** ~ **Great** Alexandre le Grand; **George** ~ **First** Georges Premier.

theatre Br , **theater** Am ['θɪətər] n [plays, building] théâtre m. || Am [cinema] cinéma m.

theatregoer , **theatergoer** Am ['θɪətə,gəʊər] n habitué m, -e f du théâtre.

theatrical [θɪ'ætrɪkl] adj théâtral(e); [company] de théâtre.

theft [θeft] n vol m.

their [ðeər] poss adj leur, leurs (pl); ~ **house** leur maison; ~ **children** leurs enfants; **it wasn't** THEIR **fault** ce n'était pas de leur faute à eux.

theirs [ðeəz] poss pron le leur (la leur), les leurs (pl); **that house is** ~ cette maison est la leur. cette maison est à eux/ elles; **it wasn't our fault, it was** THEIRS ce n'était pas de notre faute. c'était de leur; **a friend of** ~ un de leurs amis. un ami à eux/elles.

them [weak form ðəm, strong form ðem] pers pron pl (direct) les; **I know** ~ je les connais; **if I were** OR **was** ~ si j'étais eux/ elles. à leur place. || (indirect) leur; **we spoke to** ~ nous leur avons parlé; **she sent** ~ **a letter** elle leur a envoyé une lettre; **I gave it to** ~ je le leur ai donné. || (stressed, after prep, in comparisons etc) eux (elles); **you can't expect** THEM **to do it** tu ne peux pas exiger que ce soit eux qui le fassent; **with** ~ avec eux/elles; **without** ~ sans eux/elles; **we're not as wealthy as** ~ nous ne sommes pas aussi riches qu'eux/qu'elles.

theme [θiːm] n [topic, motif] thème m, sujet m. || MUS thème m; [signature tune] indicatif m.

theme tune n chanson f principale.

themselves [ðəm'selvz] pron (reflexive) se; (after prep) eux (elles). || (for emphasis) eux-mêmes mpl, elles-mêmes fpl; **they did it** ~ ils l'ont fait tout seuls.

then [ðen] adv [not now] alors, à cette époque. || [next] puis, ensuite. || [in that case] alors, dans ce cas. || [therefore] donc. || [also] d'ailleurs, et puis.

theology [θɪ'ɒlədʒɪ] n théologie f.

theoretical [θɪə'retɪkl] adj théorique.

theory ['θɪərɪ] n théorie f; **in** ~ en théorie.

therapist ['θerəpɪst] n thérapeute mf, psychothérapeute mf.

therapy ['θerəpɪ] n (U) thérapie f.

there [ðeər] 1 pron [indicating existence of sthg]: ~ **is/are** il y a; ~ **must be some mistake** il doit y avoir erreur. 2 adv [in existence, available] y, là; **is anybody** ~? il y a quelqu'un?; **is John** ~, **please?** [when telephoning] est-ce que John est là. s'il vous plaît? || [referring to place] y, là; **I'm going** ~ **next week** j'y vais la semaine prochaine; ~ **it is** c'est là; ~ **he is!** le voilà!; over ~ là-bas. **3** *excl*: ~, **I knew he'd turn up** tiens OR voilà, je savais bien qu'il s'amènerait; ~, ~ allons, allons. ○ **there and then, then and there** *adv* immédiatement, sur-le-champ.

thereabouts [ˌðeərə'baʊts], **thereabout** *Am* [ˌðeərə'baʊt] *adv*: or ~ [nearby] par là; [approximately] environ.

thereby [ˌðeər'baɪ] *adv fml* ainsi, de cette façon.

therefore ['ðeəfɔːʳ] *adv* donc, par conséquent.

there's [ðeəz] = there is.

thermal ['θɜːml] *adj* thermique; [clothes] en thermolactyl.

thermometer [θə'mɒmɪtəʳ] *n* thermomètre *m*.

Thermos (flask)® ['θɜːmɒs-] *n* bouteille *f* Thermos®, Thermos® *m* or *f*.

thermostat ['θɜːməstæt] *n* thermostat *m*.

thesaurus [θɪ'sɔːrəs] (*pl* **-es**) *n* dictionnaire *m* de synonymes.

these [ðiːz] *pl* → this.

thesis ['θiːsɪs] (*pl* **theses** ['θiːsiːz]) *n* thèse *f*.

they [ðeɪ] *pers pron pl* [people, things, animals - unstressed] ils (elles); [- stressed] eux (elles); **~'re pleased** ils sont contents (elles sont contentes); **~'re pretty earrings** ce sont de jolies boucles d'oreille; THEY **can't do it** eux (elles), ils (elles) ne peuvent pas le faire; **there ~ are** les voilà. || [unspecified people] on, ils; **~ say it's going to snow** on dit qu'il va neiger.

they'd [ðeɪd] = they had, they would.

they'll [ðeɪl] = they shall, they will.

they're [ðeəʳ] = they are.

they've [ðeɪv] = they have.

thick [θɪk] **1** *adj* [gen] épais (épaisse); [forest, hedge, fog] dense; **to be 6 inches ~** avoir 15 cm d'épaisseur. || *inf* [stupid] bouché(e). **2** *n*: **in the ~ of** au plus fort de, en plein OR au beau milieu de.

thicken ['θɪkn] **1** *rt* épaissir. **2** *ri* s'épaissir.

thickness ['θɪknɪs] *n* épaisseur *f*.

thickset [ˌθɪk'set] *adj* trapu(e).

thick-skinned [-'skɪnd] *adj* qui a la peau dure.

thief [θiːf] (*pl* **thieves**) *n* voleur *m*, -euse *f*.

thieve [θiːv] *rt & ri* voler.

thieves [θiːvz] *pl* → thief.

thigh [θaɪ] *n* cuisse *f*.

thimble ['θɪmbl] *n* dé *m* (à coudre).

thin [θɪn] *adj* [slice, layer, paper] mince; [cloth] léger(ère); [person] maigre. || [liquid, sauce] clair(e), peu épais (peu épaisse). || [sparse - crowd] épars(e); [- vegetation, hair] clairsemé(e). ○ **thin down** *rt sep* [liquid, paint] délayer, diluer; [sauce] éclaircir.

thing [θɪŋ] *n* [gen] chose *f*; **the (best) ~ to do would be ...** le mieux serait de ...; **the ~ is ...** le problème, c'est que .... || [anything]: **I don't know a ~** je n'y connais absolument rien. || [object] chose *f*, objet *m*. || [person]: **you poor ~!** mon pauvre! ○ **things** *npl* [clothes, possessions] affaires *fpl*. || *inf* [life]: **how are ~s?** comment ça va?

think [θɪŋk] (*pt & pp* **thought**) **1** *rt* [believe]: **to ~ (that)** croire que, penser que; **I ~ so/not** je crois que oui/non, je pense que oui/non. || [have in mind] penser à. || [imagine] s'imaginer. || [in polite requests]: **do you ~ you could help me?** tu pourrais m'aider? **2** *ri* [use mind] réfléchir, penser. || [have stated opinion]: **what do you ~ of OR about his new film?** que pensez-vous de son dernier film? || *phr*: **to ~ twice** y réfléchir à deux fois. ○ **think about** *rt fus*: **to ~ about sb/ sthg** songer à OR penser à qqn/qqch; **to ~ about doing sthg** songer à faire qqch; **I'll ~ about it** je vais y réfléchir. ○ **think of** *rt fus* [consider] = **think about**. || [remember] se rappeler. || [conceive] penser à, avoir l'idée de; **to ~ of doing sthg** avoir l'idée de faire qqch. ○ **think over** *rt sep* réfléchir à. ○ **think up** *rt sep* imaginer.

think tank *n* comité *m* d'experts.

third [θɜːd] **1** *num* troisième; *see also* sixth. **2** *n* UNIV ≃ licence *f* mention passable.

thirdly ['θɜːdlɪ] *adv* troisièmement, tertio.

third party insurance *n* assurance *f* de responsabilité civile.

third-rate *adj pej* de dernier OR troisième ordre.

Third World *n*: **the ~** le tiers-monde.

thirst [θɜːst] *n* soif *f*; **~ for** *fig* soif de.

thirsty ['θɜːstɪ] *adj* [person]: **to be OR feel ~** avoir soif; [work] qui donne soif.

thirteen [ˌθɜː'tiːn] *num* treize; *see also* six.

thirty ['θɜːtɪ] *num* trente; *see also* sixty.

this [ðɪs] (*pl* **these**) **1** *pron* (*demonstrative use*) ce, ceci; (*as opposed to 'that'*) celui-ci (celle-ci); **who's**

~? qui est-ce?; **what's ~?** qu'est-ce que c'est?; **which sweets does she prefer, these or those?** quels bonbons préfère-t-elle, ceux-ci ou ceux-là?; **~ is Daphne Logan** [introducing another person] je vous présente Daphne Logan; [introducing oneself on phone] ici Daphne Logan, Daphne Logan à l'appareil. **2** *adj* (*demonstrative use*) ce (cette), cet (*before vowel or silent "h"*), ces (*pl*) (*as opposed to 'that'*) ce (cette) ...-ci, ces ...-ci (*pl*); **these chocolates are delicious** ces chocolats sont délicieux; **I prefer ~ book** je préfère ce livre-ci; **I'll have ~ one** je prendrai celui-ci; **~ afternoon** cet après-midi. || *inf* [a certain] un certain (une certaine). **3** *adv* aussi; **it was ~ big** c'était aussi grand que ça; **you'll need about ~ much** il vous en faudra à peu près comme ceci.

thistle ['θɪsl] *n* chardon *m*.

thong [θɒŋ] *n* [of leather] lanière *f*.

thorn [θɔːn] *n* épine *f*.

thorough ['θʌrə] *adj* [exhaustive - search, inspection] minutieux(ieuse); [- investigation, knowledge] approfondi(e). || [meticulous] méticuleux(euse). || [complete, utter] complet(ète), absolu(e).

thoroughbred ['θʌrəbred] *n* pur-sang *m inv.*

thoroughfare ['θʌrəfeər] *n fml* rue *f*, voie *f* publique.

thoroughly ['θʌrəlɪ] *adv* [fully, in detail] à fond. || [completely, utterly] absolument, complètement.

those [ðəʊz] *pl* → **that**.

though [ðəʊ] **1** *conj* bien que (+ *subjunctive*), quoique (+ *subjunctive*). **2** *adv* pourtant, cependant.

thought [θɔːt] **1** *pt & pp* → **think**. **2** *n* [gen] pensée *f*; [idea] idée *f*, pensée. || [intention] intention *f*. ○ **thoughts** *npl* [reflections] pensées *fpl*, réflexions *fpl*. || [views] opinions *fpl*, idées *fpl*.

thoughtful ['θɔːtfʊl] *adj* [pensive] pensif(ive). || [considerate - person] prévenant(e), attentionné(e); [- remark, act] plein(e) de gentillesse.

thoughtless ['θɔːtlɪs] *adj* [person] qui manque d'égards (pour les autres); [remark, behaviour] irréfléchi(e).

thousand ['θaʊznd] *num* mille; **a** OR **one ~** mille; **~s of** des milliers de; *see also* **six.**

thousandth ['θaʊzntθ] *num* millième; *see also* **sixth.**

thrash [θræʃ] *vt* [hit] battre, rosser. || *inf* [defeat] écraser, battre à plates coutures.

○ **thrash about**, **thrash around** *vi* s'agiter. ○ **thrash out** *vt sep* [problem] débrouiller, démêler.

thread [θred] **1** *n* [gen] fil *m*. || [of screw] filet *m*, pas *m*. **2** *vt* [needle] enfiler.

threadbare ['θredbeər] *adj* usé(e) jusqu'à la corde.

threat [θret] *n*: **~ (to)** menace *f* (pour).

threaten ['θretn] **1** *vt*: **to ~ sb (with)** menacer qqn (de); **to ~ to do sthg** menacer de faire qqch. **2** *vi* menacer.

three [θriː] *num* trois; *see also* **six.**

three-dimensional [-dɪ'menʃənl] *adj* [film, picture] en relief; [object] à trois dimensions.

threefold ['θriːfəʊld] **1** *adj* triple. **2** *adv*: **to increase ~** tripler.

three-piece *adj*: **~ suit** (costume *m*) trois pièces *m*; **~ suite** canapé *m* et deux fauteuils assortis.

thresh [θreʃ] *vt* battre.

threshold ['θreʃhəʊld] *n* seuil *m*.

threw [θruː] *pt* → **throw**.

thrifty ['θrɪftɪ] *adj* économe.

thrill [θrɪl] **1** *n* [sudden feeling] frisson *m*, sensation *f*. || [enjoyable experience] plaisir *m*. **2** *vt* transporter, exciter.

thrilled [θrɪld] *adj*: **~ (with sthg/to do sthg)** ravi(e) (de qqch/de faire qqch), enchanté(e) (de qqch/de faire qqch).

thriller ['θrɪlər] *n* thriller *m*.

thrilling ['θrɪlɪŋ] *adj* saisissant(e), palpitant(e).

thrive [θraɪv] (*pt* **-d** OR **throve**, *pp* **-d**) *vi* [person] bien se porter; [plant] pousser bien; [business] prospérer.

throat [θrəʊt] *n* gorge *f*.

throb [θrɒb] *vi* [heart] palpiter, battre fort; [engine] vibrer; [music] taper; **my head is throbbing** j'ai des élancements dans la tête.

throes [θrəʊz] *npl*: **to be in the ~ of** [war, disease] être en proie à.

throne [θrəʊn] *n* trône *m*.

throng [θrɒŋ] **1** *n* foule *f*, multitude *f*. **2** *vt* remplir, encombrer.

throttle ['θrɒtl] **1** *n* [valve] papillon *m* des gaz; [lever] commande *f* des gaz. **2** *vt* [strangle] étrangler.

through [θruː] **1** *adj* [finished]: **to be ~ with sthg** avoir fini qqch. **2** *adv*: **to let sb ~** laisser passer qqn; **to read sthg ~** lire qqch jusqu'au bout; **to sleep ~ till ten** dormir jusqu'à dix heures. **3** *prep* [relating to place, position] à travers; **to travel ~ sthg** traverser qqch; **to cut ~ sthg** couper qqch. || [during] pendant. || [because of] à cause de. ‖ [by means of] par l'intermédiaire de, par l'entremise de. ‖ *Am* [up till and including]: **Monday ~ Friday** du lundi au vendredi. ○ **through and through** *adv* [completely] jusqu'au bout des ongles; [thoroughly] par cœur, à fond.

throughout [θruː'aʊt] **1** *prep* [during] pendant, durant; **~ the meeting** pendant toute la réunion. ‖ [everywhere in] partout dans. **2** *adv* [all the time] tout le temps. ‖ [everywhere] partout.

throve [θrəʊv] *pt* → **thrive**.

throw [θrəʊ] (*pt* **threw**, *pp* **thrown**) **1** *rt* [gen] jeter; [ball, javelin] lancer. ‖ [rider] désarçonner. ‖ *fig* [confuse] déconcerter, décontenancer. **2** *n* lancement *m*, jet *m*. ○ **throw away** *rt sep* [discard] jeter. ‖ *fig* [money] gaspiller; [opportunity] perdre. ○ **throw out** *rt sep* [discard] jeter. ‖ *fig* [reject] rejeter. ‖ [from house] mettre à la porte; [from army, school] expulser, renvoyer. ○ **throw up** *vi inf* [vomit] dégobiller, vomir.

throwaway ['θrəʊə‚weɪ] *adj* [disposable] jetable, à jeter.

thrown [θrəʊn] *pp* → **throw**.

thru [θruː] *Am inf* = **through**.

thrush [θrʌʃ] *n* [bird] grive *f*. ‖ MED muguet *m*.

thrust [θrʌst] **1** *n* [forward movement] poussée *f*; [of knife] coup *m*. ‖ [main aspect] idée *f* principale, aspect *m* principal. **2** *rt* [shove] enfoncer, fourrer.

thud [θʌd] **1** *n* bruit *m* sourd. **2** *vi* tomber en faisant un bruit sourd.

thug [θʌg] *n* brute *f*, voyou *m*.

thumb [θʌm] **1** *n* pouce *m*. **2** *rt inf* [hitch]: **to ~ a lift** faire du stop OR de l'auto-stop.

thumbs down [‚θʌmz-] *n*: **to get** OR **be given the ~** être rejeté(e).

thumbs up [‚θʌmz-] *n* [go-ahead]: **to give sb the ~** donner le feu vert à qqn.

thumbtack ['θʌmtæk] *n Am* punaise *f*.

thump [θʌmp] **1** *n* [blow] grand coup *m*. ‖ [thud] bruit *m* sourd. **2** *rt* [hit] cogner, taper sur. **3** *vi* [heart] battre fort.

thunder ['θʌndər] **1** *n* (*U*) METEOR tonnerre *m*. ‖ *fig* [of applause] tonnerre *m*. **2** *v impers* METEOR tonner.

thunderbolt ['θʌndəbəʊlt] *n* coup *m* de foudre.

thunderclap ['θʌndəklæp] *n* coup *m* de tonnerre.

thunderstorm ['θʌndəstɔːm] *n* orage *m*.

thundery ['θʌndərɪ] *adj* orageux(euse).

Thursday ['θɜːzdɪ] *n* jeudi *m*; *see also* **Saturday.**

thus [ðʌs] *adv fml* [therefore] par conséquent, donc, ainsi. ‖ [in this way] ainsi, de cette façon, comme ceci.

thwart [θwɔːt] *rt* contrecarrer, contrarier.

thyme [taɪm] *n* thym *m*.

thyroid ['θaɪrɔɪd] *n* thyroïde *f*.

tiara [tɪ'ɑːrə] *n* [worn by woman] diadème *m*.

Tibet [tɪ'bet] *n* Tibet *m*.

tic [tɪk] *n* tic *m*.

tick [tɪk] **1** *n* [written mark] coche *f*. ‖ [sound] tic-tac *m*. ‖ [insect] tique *f*. **2** *rt* cocher. **3** *vi* faire tic-tac. ○ **tick off** *rt sep* [mark off] cocher. ‖ [tell off] enguirlander. ○ **tick over** *vi* [engine, business] tourner au ralenti.

ticket ['tɪkɪt] *n* [for access, train, plane] billet *m*; [for bus] ticket *m*; [for library] carte *f*; [label on product] étiquette *f*. ‖ [for traffic offence] P.-V. *m*, papillon *m*.

ticket machine *n* distributeur *m* de billets.

ticket office *n* bureau *m* de vente des billets.

tickle ['tɪkl] **1** *rt* [touch lightly] chatouiller. ‖ *fig* [amuse] amuser. **2** *vi* chatouiller.

ticklish ['tɪklɪʃ] *adj* [person] qui craint les chatouilles, chatouilleux(euse).

tidal ['taɪdl] *adj* [river] à marées.

tidal wave *n* raz-de-marée *m inv*.

tidbit *Am* = **titbit**.

tiddlywinks ['tɪdlɪwɪŋks], **tiddledywinks** *Am* ['tɪdldɪwɪŋks] *n* jeu *m* de puce.

tide [taɪd] *n* [of sea] marée *f*. ‖ *fig* [of opinion, fashion] courant *m*, tendance *f*; [of protest] vague *f*.

tidy ['taɪdɪ] **1** *adj* [room, desk] en ordre, bien rangé(e); [hair, dress] soigné(e). ‖ [person - in habits] ordonné(e); [- in appearance] soigné(e). **2** *rt* ranger, mettre de l'ordre dans. ○ **tidy up** *rt sep* ranger, mettre de l'ordre dans. **2** *vi* ranger.

tie [taɪ] (*pt & pp* **tied**, *cont* **tying**) **1** *n* [necktie] cravate *f*. ‖ [in game, competition] égalité *f* de points. **2** *rt* [fasten] attacher. ‖ [shoelaces] nouer, attacher; **to ~ a knot** faire un nœud. ‖ *fig* [link]: **to be ~d to** être lié(e) à. **3** *vi* [draw] être à égalité. ○ **tie down** *rt sep fig* [restrict] restreindre la liberté de. ○ **tie in with** *rt fus* concorder avec, coïncider avec. ○ **tie up** *vt sep* [with string, rope] attacher. ‖ *fig* [money, resources] immobiliser. ‖ *fig* [link]: **to be ~d up with** être lié(e) à.

tiebreak(er) ['taɪbreɪk(ər)] *n* TENNIS tie-break *m*. ‖ [in game, competition] question *f* subsidiaire.

tier [tɪər] *n* [of seats] gradin *m*; [of cake] étage *m*.

tiff [tɪf] *n* bisbille *f*, petite querelle *f*.

tiger ['taɪgər] *n* tigre *m*.

tight [taɪt] **1** *adj* [clothes, group, competition, knot] serré(e). ‖ [taut] tendu(e). ‖ [schedule] serré(e), minuté(e). ‖ [strict] strict(e), sévère. ‖ [corner, bend] raide. ‖ *inf* [miserly] radin(e), avare. **2** *adv* [firmly, securely] bien, fort; **hold ~!** tiens bon!; **to shut** OR **close sthg ~** bien fermer qqch. ‖ [tautly] à fond. ○ **tights** *npl* collant *m*, collants *mpl*.

tighten ['taɪtn] **1** *vt* [belt, knot, screw] resserrer; **to ~ one's hold** OR **grip on** resserrer sa prise sur. ‖ [pull tauter] tendre. ‖ [make stricter] renforcer. **2** *vi* [rope] se tendre. ‖ [grip, hold] se resserrer.

tightfisted [,taɪt'fɪstɪd] *adj pej* radin(e), pingre.

tightly ['taɪtlɪ] *adv* [firmly] bien, fort.

tightrope ['taɪtrəʊp] *n* corde *f* raide.

tile [taɪl] *n* [on roof] tuile *f*; [on floor, wall] carreau *m*.

tiled [taɪld] *adj* [floor, wall] carrelé(e); [roof] couvert de tuiles.

till [tɪl] **1** *prep* jusqu'à; **from six ~ ten o'clock** de six heures à dix heures. **2** *conj* jusqu'à ce que (+ *subjunctive*); **wait ~ I come back** attends que je revienne; (*after negative*) avant que (+ *subjunctive*); **it won't be ready ~ tomorrow** ça ne sera pas prêt avant demain. **3** *n* tiroircaisse *m*.

tiller ['tɪlər] *n* NAUT barre *f*.

tilt [tɪlt] **1** *vt* incliner, pencher. **2** *vi* s'incliner, pencher.

timber ['tɪmbər] *n* (*U*) [wood] bois *m* de charpente OR de construction. ‖ [beam] poutre *f*, madrier *m*.

time [taɪm] **1** *n* [gen] temps *m*; **a long ~** longtemps; **in a short ~** dans peu de temps, sous peu; **to take ~** prendre du temps; **to be ~ for sthg** être l'heure de qqch; **to have a good ~** s'amuser bien; **in good ~** de bonne heure; **ahead of ~** en avance, avant l'heure; **on ~** à l'heure. ‖ [as measured by clock] heure *f*; **what's the ~?** quelle heure est-il?; **in a week's/ year's ~** dans une semaine/un an. ‖

[point in time in past] époque *f*; **before my ~** avant que j'arrive ici. ‖ [occasion] fois *f*; **from ~ to ~** de temps en temps, de temps à autre; **~ after ~, ~ and again** à maintes reprises, maintes et maintes fois. ‖ MUS mesure *f*. **2** *vt* [schedule] fixer, prévoir. ‖ [race, runner] chronométrer. ‖ [arrival, remark] choisir le moment de. ○ **times 1** *npl* fois *fpl*; **four ~s as much as me** quatre fois plus que moi. **2** *prep* MATH fois. ○ **at a time** *adv* d'affilée; **one at a ~** un par un, un seul à la fois. ○ **at times** *adv* quelquefois, parfois. ○ **at the same time** *adv* en même temps. ○ **about time** *adv*: **it's about ~ (that) ...** il est grand temps que ...; **about ~ too!** ce n'est pas trop tôt! ○ **for the time being** *adv* pour le moment. ○ **in time** *adv* [not late]: **in ~ (for)** à l'heure (pour). ‖ [eventually] à la fin, à la longue; [after a while] avec le temps, à la longue.

time bomb *n lit & fig* bombe *f* à retardement.

time lag *n* décalage *m*.

timeless ['taɪmlɪs] *adj* éternel(elle).

time limit *n* délai *m*.

timely ['taɪmlɪ] *adj* opportun(e).

time off *n* temps *m* libre.

time out *n* SPORT temps *m* mort.

timer ['taɪmər] *n* minuteur *m*.

time scale *n* période *f*; [of project] délai *m*.

time switch *n* minuterie *f*.

timetable ['taɪm,teɪbl] *n* SCH emploi *m* du temps. ‖ [of buses, trains] horaire *m*. ‖ [schedule] calendrier *m*.

time zone *n* fuseau *m* horaire.

timid ['tɪmɪd] *adj* timide.

timing ['taɪmɪŋ] *n* (*U*) [of remark] à-propos *m*. ‖ [scheduling]: **the ~ of the election** le moment choisi pour l'élection. ‖ [measuring] chronométrage *m*.

tin [tɪn] *n* (*U*) [metal] étain *m*; [in sheets] fer-blanc *m*. ‖ [small container] boîte *f*.

tin can *n* boîte *f* de conserve.

tinfoil ['tɪnfɔɪl] *n* (*U*) papier *m* (d')aluminium.

tinge [tɪndʒ] *n* [of colour] teinte *f*, nuance *f*. ‖ [of feeling] nuance *f*.

tinged [tɪndʒd] *adj*: **~ with** teinté(e) de.

tingle ['tɪŋgl] *vi* picoter.

tinker ['tɪŋkər] *vi*: **to ~ (with sthg)** bricoler (qqch).

tinkle ['tɪŋkl] *vi* [ring] tinter.

tinsel ['tɪnsl] *n* (*U*) guirlandes *fpl* de Noël.

tint [tɪnt] *n* teinte *f*, nuance *f*; [in hair] rinçage *m*.

tinted ['tɪntɪd] *adj* [glasses, windows] teinté(e).

tiny ['taɪnɪ] *adj* minuscule.

tip [tɪp] 1 *n* [end] bout *m*. || [to waiter etc] pourboire *m*. || [piece of advice] tuyau *m*. 2 *vt* [tilt] faire basculer. || [spill] renverser. || [waiter etc] donner un pourboire à. 3 *vi* [tilt] basculer. || [spill] se renverser. ○ **tip over** 1 *vt sep* renverser. 2 *vi* se renverser.

tip-off *n* tuyau *m*; [to police] dénonciation *f*.

tipped ['tɪpt] *adj* [cigarette] à bout filtre.

tipsy ['tɪpsɪ] *adj inf* gai(e).

tiptoe ['tɪptəʊ] 1 *n*: **on ~** sur la pointe des pieds. 2 *vi* marcher sur la pointe des pieds.

tire ['taɪər] 1 *n Am* = tyre. 2 *vt* fatiguer. 3 *vi* [get tired] se fatiguer. || [get fed up]: **to ~ of** se lasser de.

tired ['taɪəd] *adj* [sleepy] fatigué(e), las (lasse). || [fed up]: **to be ~ of sthg/of doing sthg** en avoir assez de qqch/de faire qqch.

tiresome ['taɪəsəm] *adj* ennuyeux(euse).

tiring ['taɪərɪŋ] *adj* fatigant(e).

tissue ['tɪʃuː] *n* [paper handkerchief] mouchoir *m* en papier. || (*U*) BIOL tissu *m*.

tissue paper *n* (*U*) papier *m* de soie.

tit [tɪt] *n* [bird] mésange *f*. || *vulg* [breast] nichon *m*, néné *m*.

titbit *Br* ['tɪtbɪt], **tidbit** *Am* ['tɪdbɪt] *n* [of food] bon morceau *m*. || *fig* [of news] petite nouvelle *f*.

tit for tat [-'tæt] *n* un prêté pour un rendu.

titillate ['tɪtɪleɪt] *vt* titiller.

title ['taɪtl] *n* titre *m*.

title deed *n* titre *m* de propriété.

title role *n* rôle *m* principal.

titter ['tɪtər] *vi* rire bêtement.

TM *abbr of* **trademark**.

to [unstressed before consonant tə, unstressed before vowel tʊ, stressed tuː] 1 *prep* [indicating place, direction] à; **to go ~ Liverpool/Spain/school** aller à Liverpool/en Espagne/à l'école; **to go ~ the butcher's** aller chez le boucher; **~ the left/right** à gauche/droite. || (*to express indirect object*) à; **to give sthg ~ sb** donner qqch à qqn; **we were listening ~ the radio** nous écoutions la radio. || [indi-

cating reaction, effect] à; **~ my delight/ surprise** à ma grande joie/surprise. || [in stating opinion]: **~ me, ...** à mon avis, ...; **it seemed quite unnecessary ~ me/him** *etc* cela me/lui *etc* semblait tout à fait inutile. || [indicating state, process]: **to drive sb ~ drink** pousser qqn à boire; **it could lead ~ trouble** cela pourrait causer des ennuis. || [as far as] à, jusqu'à; **we work from 9 ~ 5** nous travaillons de 9 heures à 17 heures. || [in expressions of time] moins; **it's ten ~ three/quarter ~ one** il est trois heures moins dix/une heure moins le quart. || [per] à; **40 miles ~ the gallon** ≃ 7 litres aux cent (km). || [of, for] de; **the key ~ the car** la clef de la voiture; **a letter ~ my daughter** une lettre à ma fille. 2 *adv* [shut]: **push the door ~** fermez la porte. 3 *with infinitive (forming simple infinitive)*: **~ walk** marcher; **~ laugh** rire. || (*following another verb*): **to begin ~ do sthg** commencer à faire qqch; **to try ~ do sthg** essayer de faire qqch; **to want ~ do sthg** vouloir faire qqch. || (*following an adjective*): **difficult ~ do** difficile à faire; **ready ~ go** prêt à partir. || (*indicating purpose*) pour; **he worked hard ~ pass his exam** il a travaillé dur pour réussir son examen. || (*substituting for a relative clause*): **I have a lot ~ do** j'ai beaucoup à faire; **he told me ~ leave** il m'a dit de partir. || (*to avoid repetition of infinitive*): **I meant to call him but I forgot ~** je voulais l'appeler, mais j'ai oublié. || [in comments]: **~ be honest ...** en toute franchise ...; **~ sum up, ...** en résumé, ..., pour récapituler, ... ○ **to and fro** *adv*: **to go ~ and fro** aller et venir; **to walk ~ and fro** marcher de long en large.

toad [təʊd] *n* crapaud *m*.

toadstool ['təʊdstuːl] *n* champignon *m* vénéneux.

toast [təʊst] 1 *n* (*U*) [bread] pain *m* grillé, toast *m*. || [drink] toast *m*. 2 *vt* [bread] (faire) griller. || [person] porter un toast à.

toaster ['təʊstər] *n* grille-pain *m inv*.

tobacco [tə'bækəʊ] *n* (*U*) tabac *m*.

tobacconist [tə'bækənɪst] *n* buraliste *mf*; **~'s (shop)** bureau *m* de tabac.

toboggan [tə'bɒgən] *n* luge *f*.

today [tə'deɪ] *adv* aujourd'hui.

toddler ['tɒdlər] *n* tout-petit *m* (*qui commence à marcher*).

toddy ['tɒdɪ] *n* grog *m*.

toe [təʊ] **1** *n* [of foot] orteil *m*, doigt *m* de pied; [of sock, shoe] bout *m*. **2** *vt*: **to ~ the line** se plier.

toenail ['təʊneɪl] *n* ongle *m* d'orteil.

toffee ['tɒfɪ] *n* caramel *m*.

toga ['təʊgə] *n* toge *f*.

together [tə'geðər] *adv* [gen] ensemble. || [at the same time] en même temps. ○ **together with** *prep* ainsi que.

toil [tɔɪl] *literary* **1** *n* labeur *m*. **2** *vi* travailler dur.

toilet ['tɔɪlɪt] *n* [lavatory] toilettes *fpl*, cabinets *mpl*; **to go to the ~** aller aux toilettes OR aux cabinets.

toilet bag *n* trousse *f* de toilette.

toilet paper *n* (*U*) papier *m* hygiénique.

toiletries ['tɔɪlɪtrɪz] *npl* articles *mpl* de toilette.

toilet roll *n* rouleau *m* de papier hygiénique.

token ['təʊkn] **1** *adj* symbolique. **2** *n* [voucher] bon *m*. || [symbol] marque *f*. ○ **by the same token** *adv* de même.

told [təʊld] *pt & pp* → **tell**.

tolerable ['tɒlərəbl] *adj* passable.

tolerance ['tɒlərəns] *n* tolérance *f*.

tolerant ['tɒlərənt] *adj* tolérant(e).

tolerate ['tɒləreɪt] *vt* [put up with] supporter. || [permit] tolérer.

toll [təʊl] **1** *n* [number] nombre *m*. || [fee] péage *m*. || *phr*: **to take its ~** se faire sentir. **2** *vt & vi* sonner.

toll-free *Am adv*: **to call ~** appeler un numéro vert.

tomato [*Br* tə'mɑːtəʊ, *Am* tə'meɪtəʊ] (*pl* -es) *n* tomate *f*.

tomb [tuːm] *n* tombe *f*.

tomboy ['tɒmbɔɪ] *n* garçon *m* manqué.

tombstone ['tuːmstəʊn] *n* pierre *f* tombale.

tomcat ['tɒmkæt] *n* matou *m*.

tomorrow [tə'mɒrəʊ] *adv* demain.

ton [tʌn] (*pl inv* OR -s) *n* [imperial] = 1016 kg *Br*, = 907,2 kg *Am*, ≃ tonne *f*. || [metric] = 1000 kg, tonne *f*. ○ **tons** *npl inf*: **~s (of)** des tas (de), plein (de).

tone [təʊn] *n* [gen] ton *m*. || [on phone] tonalité *f*. ○ **tone down** *vt sep* modérer. ○ **tone up** *vt sep* tonifier.

tone-deaf *adj* qui n'a aucune oreille.

tongs [tɒŋz] *npl* pinces *fpl*.

tongue [tʌŋ] *n* [gen] langue *f*. || [of shoe] languette *f*.

tongue-in-cheek *adj* ironique.

tongue-tied [-,taɪd] *adj* muet(ette).

tongue twister [-,twɪstər] *n* phrase *f* difficile à dire.

tonic ['tɒnɪk] *n* [medicine] tonique *m*.

tonic water *n* Schweppes® *m*.

tonight [tə'naɪt] *adv* ce soir; [late] cette nuit.

tonnage ['tʌnɪdʒ] *n* tonnage *m*.

tonne [tʌn] (*pl inv* OR -s) *n* tonne *f*.

tonsil ['tɒnsl] *n* amygdale *f*.

tonsil(l)itis [,tɒnsɪ'laɪtɪs] *n* (*U*) amygdalite *f*.

too [tuː] *adv* [also] aussi. || [excessively] trop; **~ many people** trop de gens; **it was over all ~ soon** ça s'était terminé bien trop tôt; **I wasn't ~ impressed** ça ne m'a pas impressionné outre mesure.

took [tʊk] *pt* → **take**.

tool [tuːl] *n* lit & fig outil *m*.

tool box *n* boîte *f* à outils.

tool kit *n* trousse *f* à outils.

toot [tuːt] **1** *n* coup *m* de klaxon. **2** *vi* klaxonner.

tooth [tuːθ] (*pl* teeth) *n* dent *f*.

toothache ['tuːθeɪk] *n* mal *m* OR rage *f* de dents; **to have ~** avoir mal aux dents.

toothbrush ['tuːθbrʌʃ] *n* brosse *f* à dents.

toothpaste ['tuːθpeɪst] *n* (pâte *f*) dentifrice *m*.

toothpick ['tuːθpɪk] *n* cure-dents *m inv*.

top [tɒp] **1** *adj* [highest] du haut. || [most important, successful - officials] important(e); [- executives] supérieur(e); [- sportsman, sportswoman] meilleur(e); [- in exam] premier(ière). || [maximum] maximum. **2** *n* [highest point - of hill] sommet *m*; [- of page, pile] haut *m*; [- of tree] cime *f*; [- of list] début *m*, tête *f*; **on ~** dessus; **at the ~ of one's voice** à tue-tête. || [lid - of bottle, tube] bouchon *m*; [- of pen] capuchon *m*; [- of jar] couvercle *m*. || [of table, box] dessus *m*. || [clothing] haut *m*. || [toy] toupie *f*. || [highest rank - in league] tête *f*; [- in scale] haut *m*; [- SCH] premier *m*, -ière *f*. **3** *vt* [be first in] être en tête de. || [better] surpasser. || [exceed] dépasser. ○ **on top of** *prep* [in space] sur. || [in addition to] en plus de. ○ **top up** *Br*, **top off** *Am vt sep* remplir.

top floor *n* dernier étage *m*.

top hat *n* haut-de-forme *m*.

top-heavy *adj* mal équilibré(e).

topic ['tɒpɪk] *n* sujet *m*.

topical ['tɒpɪkl] *adj* d'actualité.

topless ['tɒplɪs] *adj* [woman] aux seins nus.

top-level *adj* au plus haut niveau.

topping ['tɒpɪŋ] *n* garniture *f*.

topple ['tɒpl] 1 *vt* renverser. 2 *vi* basculer.

top-secret *adj* top secret (top secrète).

topspin ['tɒpspɪn] *n* lift *m*.

topsy-turvy [,tɒpsɪ'tɜ:vɪ] *adj* [messy] sens dessus dessous. || [confused]: **to be ~** ne pas tourner rond.

tore [tɔ:r] *pt* → tear.

torment [*n* 'tɔ:ment, *vb* tɔ:'ment] 1 *n* tourment *m*. 2 *vt* tourmenter.

torn [tɔ:n] *pp* → tear.

tornado [tɔ:'neɪdəʊ] (*pl* -es OR -s) *n* tornade *f*.

torpedo [tɔ:'pi:dəʊ] (*pl* -es) *n* torpille *f*.

torrent ['tɒrənt] *n* torrent *m*.

torrid ['tɒrɪd] *adj* [hot] torride. || *fig* [passionate] ardent(e).

tortoise ['tɔ:təs] *n* tortue *f*.

tortoiseshell ['tɔ:təʃel] 1 *adj*: ~ cat chat *m* roux tigré. 2 *n* (*U*) [material] écaille *f*.

torture ['tɔ:tʃər] 1 *n* torture *f*. 2 *vt* torturer.

toss [tɒs] 1 *vt* [throw] jeter; **to ~ a coin** jouer à pile ou face; **to ~ one's head** rejeter la tête en arrière. || [salad] remuer; [pancake] faire sauter. || [throw about] ballotter. 2 *vi* [move about]: **to ~ and turn** se tourner et se retourner.

tot [tɒt] *n* *inf* [small child] tout-petit *m*. || [of drink] larme *f*, goutte *f*.

total ['təʊtl] 1 *adj* total(e); [disgrace, failure] complet(ète). 2 *n* total *m*. 3 *vt* [add up] additionner. || [amount to] s'élever à.

totalitarian [,təʊtælɪ'teərɪən] *adj* totalitaire.

totally ['təʊtəlɪ] *adv* totalement; **I ~ agree** je suis entièrement d'accord.

totter ['tɒtər] *vi* *lit* & *fig* chanceler.

touch [tʌtʃ] 1 *n* (*U*) [sense] toucher *m*. || [detail] touche *f*. || (*U*) [skill] marque *f*, note *f*. || [contact]: **to keep in ~ (with sb)** rester en contact (avec qqn); **to get in ~ with sb** entrer en contact avec qqn; **to lose ~ with sb** perdre qqn de vue; **to be out of ~ with** ne plus être au courant de. || [small amount]: **a ~** un petit peu. 2 *vt* toucher. 3 *vi* [be in contact] se toucher.

○ **touch down** *vi* [plane] atterrir.

○ **touch on** *vt fus* effleurer.

touch-and-go *adj* incertain(e).

touchdown ['tʌtʃdaʊn] *n* [of plane] atterrissage *m*. || [in American football] but *m*.

touched [tʌtʃt] *adj* [grateful] touché(e).

touching ['tʌtʃɪŋ] *adj* touchant(e).

touchline ['tʌtʃlaɪn] *n* ligne *f* de touche.

touchy ['tʌtʃɪ] *adj* [person] susceptible. || [subject, question] délicat(e).

tough [tʌf] *adj* [material, vehicle, person] solide; [character, life] dur(e). || [meat] dur(e). || [decision, problem, task] difficile. || [rough - area of town] dangereux(euse). || [strict] sévère.

toughen ['tʌfn] *vt* [character] endurcir. || [material] renforcer.

toupee ['tu:peɪ] *n* postiche *m*.

tour [tʊər] 1 *n* [journey] voyage *m*; [by pop group etc] tournée *f*. || [of town, museum] visite *f*, tour *m*. 2 *vt* visiter.

touring ['tʊərɪŋ] *n* tourisme *m*.

tourism ['tʊərɪzm] *n* tourisme *m*.

tourist ['tʊərɪst] *n* touriste *mf*.

tourist (information) office *n* office *m* de tourisme.

tournament ['tɔ:nəmənt] *n* tournoi *m*.

tour operator *n* voyagiste *m*.

tousle ['taʊzl] *vt* ébouriffer.

tout [taʊt] 1 *n* revendeur *m* de billets. 2 *vt* [tickets] revendre; [goods] vendre. 3 *vi*: **to ~ for trade** racoler les clients.

tow [təʊ] *vt* remorquer.

towards *Br* [tə'wɔ:dz], **toward** *Am* [tə'wɔ:d] *prep* [gen] vers; [movement] vers, en direction de. || [in attitude] envers. || [for the purpose of] pour.

towel ['taʊəl] *n* serviette *f*; [tea towel] torchon *m*.

towelling *Br*, **toweling** *Am* ['taʊəlɪŋ] *n* (*U*) tissu *m* éponge.

towel rail *n* porte-serviettes *m inv*.

tower ['taʊər] 1 *n* tour *f*. 2 *vi* s'élever; **to ~ over sb/sthg** dominer qqn/qqch.

towering ['taʊərɪŋ] *adj* imposant(e).

town [taʊn] *n* ville *f*; **to go to ~ on sthg** *fig* ne pas lésiner sur qqch.

town centre *n* centre-ville *m*.

town council *n* conseil *m* municipal.

town hall *n* mairie *f*.

town plan *n* plan *m* de ville.

town planning *n* urbanisme *m*.

township ['taʊnʃɪp] *n* [in South Africa] township *f*. || [in US] ≃ canton *m*.

towpath ['təʊpɑ:θ, *pl* -pɑ:ðz] *n* chemin *m* de halage.

towrope ['təʊrəʊp] *n* câble *m* de remorquage.

tow truck *n* *Am* dépanneuse *f*.

toxic ['tɒksɪk] *adj* toxique.

toy [tɔɪ] *n* jouet *m*. ○ **toy with** *vt fus* [idea] caresser. ‖ [coin etc] jouer avec; **to ~ with one's food** manger du bout des dents.

toy shop *n* magasin *m* de jouets.

trace [treɪs] **1** *n* trace *f*. **2** *vt* [relatives, criminal] retrouver; [development, progress] suivre; [history, life] retracer. ‖ [on paper] tracer.

tracing paper ['treɪsɪŋ-] *n* (*U*) papier-calque *m*.

track [træk] **1** *n* [path] chemin *m*. ‖ SPORT piste *f*. ‖ RAIL voie *f* ferrée. ‖ [of animal, person] trace *f*. ‖ [on record, tape] piste *f*. ‖ *phr*: **to keep ~ of sb** rester en contact avec qqn; **to lose ~ of sb** perdre contact avec qqn; **to be on the right ~** être sur la bonne voie; **to be on the wrong ~** être sur la mauvaise piste. **2** *vt* suivre la trace de. ○ **track down** *vt sep* [criminal, animal] dépister; [object, address etc] retrouver.

track record *n* palmarès *m*.

tracksuit ['træksuːt] *n* survêtement *m*.

tract [trækt] *n* [pamphlet] tract *m*. ‖ [of land, forest] étendue *f*.

traction ['trækʃn] *n* (*U*) PHYSICS traction *f*. ‖ MED: **in ~** en extension.

tractor ['træktər] *n* tracteur *m*.

trade [treɪd] **1** *n* (*U*) [commerce] commerce *m*. ‖ [job] métier *m*; **by ~** de son état. **2** *vt* [exchange]: **to ~ sthg (for)** échanger qqch (contre). **3** *vi* COMM: **to ~ (with sb)** commercer (avec qqn). ○ **trade in** *vt sep* [exchange] échanger, faire reprendre.

trade fair *n* exposition *f* commerciale.

trade-in *n* reprise *f*.

trademark ['treɪdmɑːk] *n* COMM marque *f* de fabrique.

trade name *n* nom *m* de marque.

trader ['treɪdər] *n* marchand *m*, -e *f*, commerçant *m*, -e *f*.

tradesman ['treɪdzmən] (*pl* -men [-mən]) *n* commerçant *m*.

trading ['treɪdɪŋ] *n* (*U*) commerce *m*.

tradition [trə'dɪʃn] *n* tradition *f*.

traditional [trə'dɪʃənl] *adj* traditionnel(elle).

traffic ['træfɪk] (*pt* & *pp* **-ked**, *cont* **-king**) **1** *n* (*U*) [vehicles] circulation *f*. ‖ [illegal trade]: **~ (in)** trafic *m* (de). **2** *vi*: **to ~ in** faire le trafic de.

traffic circle *n* Am rond-point *m*.

traffic jam *n* embouteillage *m*.

trafficker ['træfɪkər] *n*: **~ (in)** trafiquant *m*, -e *f* (de).

traffic lights *npl* feux *mpl* de signalisation.

tragedy ['trædʒədɪ] *n* tragédie *f*.

tragic ['trædʒɪk] *adj* tragique.

trail [treɪl] **1** *n* [path] sentier *m*. ‖ [trace] piste *f*. **2** *vt* [drag] traîner. ‖ [follow] suivre. **3** *vi* [drag, move slowly] traîner. ○ **trail away, trail off** *vi* s'estomper.

trailer ['treɪlər] *n* [vehicle - for luggage] remorque *f*; [- for living in] caravane *f*. ‖ CINEMA bande-annonce *f*.

train [treɪn] **1** *n* RAIL train *m*. ‖ [of dress] traîne *f*. **2** *vt* [teach]: **to ~ sb to do sthg** apprendre à qqn à faire qqch. ‖ [for job] former; **to ~ sb as/in** former qqn comme/dans. ‖ [gun, camera] braquer. **3** *vi* [for job]: **to ~ (as)** recevoir OR faire une formation (de). ‖ SPORT: **to ~ (for)** s'entraîner (pour).

trained [treɪnd] *adj* formé(e).

trainee [treɪ'niː] *n* stagiaire *mf*.

trainer ['treɪnər] *n* [of animals] dresseur *m*, -euse *f*. ‖ SPORT entraîneur *m*.

training ['treɪnɪŋ] *n* (*U*) [for job]: **~ (in)** formation *f* (de). ‖ SPORT entraînement *m*.

train of thought *n*: **my/his ~** le fil de mes/ses pensées.

traipse [treɪps] *vi* traîner.

trait [treɪt] *n* trait *m*.

traitor ['treɪtər] *n* traître *m*.

trajectory [trə'dʒektərɪ] *n* trajectoire *f*.

tramp [træmp] **1** *n* [homeless person] clochard *m*, -e *f*. **2** *vi* marcher d'un pas lourd.

trample ['træmpl] *vt* piétiner.

trampoline ['træmpəliːn] *n* trampoline *m*.

trance [trɑːns] *n* transe *f*.

tranquil ['træŋkwɪl] *adj* tranquille.

tranquillizer *Br*, **tranquilizer** *Am* ['træŋkwɪlaɪzər] *n* tranquillisant *m*, calmant *m*.

transaction [træn'zækʃn] *n* transaction *f*.

transcend [træn'send] *vt* transcender.

transcript ['trænskrɪpt] *n* transcription *f*.

transfer [*n* 'trænsfɜːr, *vb* træns'fɜːr] **1** *n* [gen] transfert *m*; [of power] passation *f*; [of money] virement *m*. ‖ [design] décalcomanie *f*. **2** *vt* [gen] transférer; [power, control] faire passer; [money] virer. ‖ [employee] transférer, muter. **3** *vi* être transféré.

transfix [træns'fɪks] *vt*: **to be ~ed with fear** être paralysé(e) par la peur.

transform [træns'fɔːm] *vt*: **to ~ sb/sthg (into)** transformer qqn/qqch (en).

transfusion [træns'fjuːʒn] *n* transfusion *f*.

transient ['trænzɪənt] *adj* passager (ère).

transistor radio *n* transistor *m*.

transit ['trænsɪt] *n*: **in ~** en transit.

transition [træn'zɪʃn] *n* transition *f*.

transitive ['trænzɪtɪv] *adj* GRAMM transitif(ive).

transitory ['trænzɪtrɪ] *adj* transitoire.

translate [træns'leɪt] *vt* traduire.

translation [træns'leɪʃn] *n* traduction *f*.

translator [træns'leɪtər] *n* traducteur *m*, -trice *f*.

transmission [trænz'mɪʃn] *n* [gen] transmission *f*. || RADIO & TV [programme] émission *f*.

transmit [trænz'mɪt] *vt* transmettre.

transmitter [trænz'mɪtər] *n* émetteur *m*.

transparency [trans'pærənsɪ] *n* PHOT diapositive *f*; [for overhead projector] transparent *m*.

transparent [træns'pærənt] *adj* transparent(e).

transpire [træn'spaɪər] *fml vt*: **it ~s that ... on a appris que ....

transplant [*n* 'trænsplɑːnt, *vb* træns'plɑːnt] **1** *n* MED greffe *f*, transplantation *f*. **2** *vt* MED greffer, transplanter. || [seedlings] repiquer.

transport [*n* 'trænspɔːt, *vb* træn'spɔːt] **1** *n* transport *m*. **2** *vt* transporter.

transportation [ˌtrænspɔː'teɪʃn] *n* transport *m*.

transpose [træns'pəʊz] *vt* transposer.

trap [træp] **1** *n* piège *m*. **2** *vt* prendre au piège; **to be trapped** être coincé.

trapdoor [ˌtræp'dɔːr] *n* trappe *f*.

trapeze [trə'piːz] *n* trapèze *m*.

trash [træʃ] *n* (U) Am [refuse] ordures *fpl*. || *inf pej* [poor-quality thing] camelote *f*.

trashcan ['træʃkæn] *n Am* poubelle *f*.

traumatic [trɔː'mætɪk] *adj* traumatisant(e).

travel ['trævl] **1** *n* (U) voyage *m*, voyages *mpl*. **2** *vt* parcourir. **3** *vi* [make journey] voyager. || [move - current, signal] aller, passer; [- news] se répandre, circuler.

travel agency *n* agence *f* de voyages.

travel agent *n* agent *m* de voyages.

traveller *Br*, **traveler** *Am* ['trævlər] *n* [person on journey] voyageur *m*, -euse *f*.

traveller's cheque *n* chèque *m* de voyage.

travelling *Br*, **traveling** *Am* ['trævlɪŋ] *adj* [theatre, circus] ambulant(e). || [clock, bag etc] de voyage; [allowance] de déplacement.

travelsick ['trævəlsɪk] *adj*: **to be ~** avoir le mal de la route/de l'air/de mer.

travesty ['trævəstɪ] *n* parodie *f*.

trawler ['trɔːlər] *n* chalutier *m*.

tray [treɪ] *n* plateau *m*.

treacherous ['tretʃərəs] *adj* traître (traîtresse).

treachery ['tretʃərɪ] *n* traîtrise *f*.

tread [tred] (*pt* **trod**, *pp* **trodden**) **1** *n* [on tyre] bande *f* de roulement; [of shoe] semelle *f*. || [way of walking] pas *m*; [sound] bruit *m* de pas. **2** *vi*: **to ~ (on)** marcher (sur).

treason ['triːzn] *n* trahison *f*.

treasure ['treʒər] **1** *n* trésor *m*. **2** *vt* [object] garder précieusement; [memory] chérir.

treasurer ['treʒərər] *n* trésorier *m*, -ière *f*.

treasury ['treʒərɪ] *n* [room] trésorerie *f*. ○ **Treasury** *n*: **the Treasury** le ministère des Finances.

treat [triːt] **1** *vt* [gen] traiter. || [on special occasion]: **to ~ sb to sthg** offrir OR payer qqch à qqn. **2** *n* [gift] cadeau *m*. || [delight] plaisir *m*.

treatise ['triːtɪs] *n*: **~ (on)** traité *m* (de).

treatment ['triːtmənt] *n* traitement *m*.

treaty ['triːtɪ] *n* traité *m*.

treble ['trebl] **1** *adj* [MUS - voice] de soprano; [- recorder] aigu (aiguë). || [triple] triple. **2** *n* [on stereo control] aigu *m*; [boy singer] soprano *m*. **3** *vt* & *vi* tripler.

treble clef *n* clef *f* de sol.

tree [triː] *n* [gen] arbre *m*.

treetop ['triːtɒp] *n* cime *f*.

tree-trunk *n* tronc *m* d'arbre.

trek [trek] *n* randonnée *f*.

trellis ['trelɪs] *n* treillis *m*.

tremble ['trembl] *vi* trembler.

tremendous [trɪ'mendəs] *adj* [size, success, difference] énorme; [noise] terrible. || *inf* [really good] formidable.

tremor ['tremər] *n* tremblement *m*.

trench [trentʃ] *n* tranchée *f*.

trend [trend] *n* [tendency] tendance *f*.

trendy ['trendɪ] *inf adj* branché(e), à la mode.

trepidation [ˌtrepɪ'deɪʃn] *n fml*: **in** OR **with ~** avec inquiétude.

trespass ['trespəs] *vi* [on land] entrer sans permission; **"no ~ing"** «défense d'entrer».

trespasser ['trespəsər] *n* intrus *m*, -e *f*.

trestle table ['tresl-] *n* table *f* à tréteaux.

trial ['traɪəl] *n* JUR procès *m*; **to be on ~ (for)** passer en justice (pour). || [test, experiment] essai *m*; **on ~** à l'essai; **by ~ and error** en tâtonnant. || [unpleasant experience] épreuve *f*.

triangle ['traɪæŋgl] *n* [gen] triangle *m*.

tribe [traɪb] *n* tribu *f*.

tribunal [traɪ'bjuːnl] *n* tribunal *m*.

tributary ['trɪbjutrɪ] *n* affluent *m*.

tribute ['trɪbjuːt] *n* tribut *m*, hommage *m*; **to pay ~ to** payer tribut à, rendre hommage à; **to be a ~ to sthg** témoigner de qqch.

trice [traɪs] *n*: **in a ~** en un clin d'œil.

trick [trɪk] 1 *n* [to deceive] tour *m*, farce *f*; **to play a ~ on sb** jouer un tour à qqn. || [to entertain] tour *m*. || [knack] truc *m*; **that will do the ~** *inf* ça fera l'affaire. 2 *vt* attraper, rouler; **to ~ sb into doing sthg** amener qqn à faire qqch (par la ruse).

trickery ['trɪkərɪ] *n* (*U*) ruse *f*.

trickle ['trɪkl] 1 *n* [of liquid] filet *m*. 2 *vi* [liquid] dégouliner; **to ~ in/out** [people] entrer/sortir par petits groupes.

tricky ['trɪkɪ] *adj* [difficult] difficile.

tricycle ['traɪsɪkl] *n* tricycle *m*.

trifle ['traɪfl] *n* [unimportant thing] bagatelle *f*. ○ **a trifle** *adv* un peu, un tantinet.

trifling ['traɪflɪŋ] *adj* insignifiant(e).

trigger ['trɪgər] *n* [on gun] détente *f*, gâchette *f*. ○ **trigger off** *vt sep* déclencher, provoquer.

trim [trɪm] 1 *adj* [neat and tidy] net (nette). || [slim] svelte. 2 *n* [of hair] coupe *f*. 3 *vt* [cut - gen] couper; [- hedge] tailler. || [decorate] garnir; **to ~ sthg (with)** garnir OR orner qqch (de).

trimming ['trɪmɪŋ] *n* [on clothing] parement *m*. || CULIN garniture *f*.

trinket ['trɪŋkɪt] *n* bibelot *m*.

trio ['triːəʊ] (*pl* -s) *n* trio *m*.

trip [trɪp] 1 *n* [journey] voyage *m*. || *drugs sl* trip *m*. 2 *vt* [make stumble] faire un croche-pied à. 3 *vi* [stumble] **to ~ (over)** trébucher (sur). ○ **trip up** *vt sep* [make stumble] faire un croche-pied à.

tripe [traɪp] *n* (*U*) CULIN tripe *f*. || *inf* [nonsense] bêtises *fpl*, idioties *fpl*.

triple ['trɪpl] 1 *adj* triple. 2 *vt* & *vi* tripler.

triple jump *n*: **the ~** le triple saut.

triplets ['trɪplɪts] *npl* triplés *mpl*, triplées *fpl*.

triplicate ['trɪplɪkət] *n*: **in ~** en trois exemplaires.

tripod ['traɪpɒd] *n* trépied *m*.

trite [traɪt] *adj pej* banal(e).

triumph ['traɪəmf] 1 *n* triomphe *m*. 2 *vi*: **to ~ (over)** triompher (de).

trivia ['trɪvɪə] *n* (*U*) [trifles] vétilles *fpl*, riens *mpl*.

trivial ['trɪvɪəl] *adj* insignifiant(e).

trod [trɒd] *pt* → tread.

trodden ['trɒdn] *pp* → tread.

trolley ['trɒlɪ] (*pl* trolleys) *n Am* [tram] tramway *m*, tram *m*.

trombone [trɒm'bəʊn] *n* MUS trombone *m*.

troop [truːp] 1 *n* bande *f*, troupe *f*. 2 *vi*: **to ~ in/out/off** entrer/sortir/partir en groupe. ○ **troops** *npl* troupes *fpl*.

trophy ['trəʊfɪ] *n* trophée *m*.

tropical ['trɒpɪkl] *adj* tropical(e).

tropics ['trɒpɪks] *npl*: **the ~** les tropiques *mpl*.

trot [trɒt] 1 *n* [of horse] trot *m*. 2 *vi* trotter. ○ **on the trot** *adv inf* de suite, d'affilée.

trouble ['trʌbl] 1 *n* (*U*) [difficulty] problème *m*, difficulté *f*; **to be in ~** avoir des ennuis. || [bother] peine *f*, mal *m*; **to take the ~ to do sthg** se donner la peine de faire qqch; **it's no ~!** ça ne me dérange pas! || [fighting] bagarre *f*; POL troubles *mpl*, conflits *mpl*. 2 *vt* [worry, upset] peiner, troubler. || [bother] déranger. || [cause pain to] faire mal à. ○ **troubles** *npl* [worries] ennuis *mpl*. || POL troubles *mpl*, conflits *mpl*.

troubled ['trʌbld] *adj* [worried] inquiet(iète). || [disturbed - period] de troubles, agité(e); [- country] qui connaît une période de troubles.

troublemaker ['trʌbl,meɪkər] *n* fauteur *m*, -trice *f* de troubles.

troubleshooter ['trʌbl,ʃuːtər] *n* expert *m*, spécialiste *mf*.

troublesome ['trʌblsəm] *adj* [job] pénible; [back, knee] qui fait souffrir.

trough [trɒf] *n* [for animals - with water] abreuvoir *m*; [- with food] auge *f*. || [low point - of wave] creux *m*; *fig* point *m* bas.

troupe [truːp] *n* troupe *f*.

trousers ['traʊzəz] *npl* pantalon *m*.

trout [traʊt] (*pl inv* OR -s) *n* truite *f*.

trowel ['traʊəl] *n* [for gardening] déplantoir *m*; [for cement, plaster] truelle *f*.

truant ['tru:ənt] *n*: **to play ~** faire l'école buissonnière.

truce [tru:s] *n* trêve *f*.

truck [trʌk] *n* [lorry] camion *m*. ‖ RAIL wagon *m* à plate-forme.

truck driver *n* routier *m*.

trucker ['trʌkər] *n Am* routier *m*.

truck farm *n Am* jardin *m* maraîcher.

truculent ['trʌkjʊlənt] *adj* agressif(ive).

trudge [trʌdʒ] *vi* marcher péniblement.

true [tru:] *adj* [factual] vrai(e); **to come ~** se réaliser. ‖ [genuine] vrai(e), authentique; **~ love** le grand amour. ‖ [exact] exact(e). ‖ [faithful] fidèle, loyal(e).

truffle ['trʌfl] *n* truffe *f*.

truly ['tru:lɪ] *adv* [gen] vraiment. ‖ [sincerely] vraiment, sincèrement. ‖ *phr*: **yours ~** [at end of letter] croyez à l'expression de mes sentiments distingués.

trump [trʌmp] *n* atout *m*.

trumped-up ['trʌmpt-] *adj pej* inventé(e) de toutes pièces.

trumpet ['trʌmpɪt] *n* trompette *f*.

truncheon ['trʌntʃən] *n* matraque *f*.

trunk [trʌŋk] *n* [of tree, person] tronc *m*. ‖ [of elephant] trompe *f*. ‖ [box] malle *f*. ‖ *Am* [of car] coffre *m*. ◯ **trunks** *npl* maillot *m* de bain.

trunk road *n* (route *f*) nationale *f*.

truss [trʌs] *n* MED bandage *m* herniaire.

trust [trʌst] **1** *vt* [have confidence in] avoir confiance en, se fier à; **to ~ sb to do sthg** compter sur qqn pour faire qqch. ‖ [entrust]: **to ~ sb with sthg** confier qqch à qqn. **2** *n* (*U*) [faith]: **~ (in sb/sthg)** confiance *f* (en qqn/dans qqch). ‖ (*U*) [responsibility] responsabilité *f*. ‖ FIN: **in ~** en dépôt. ‖ COMM trust *m*.

trusted ['trʌstɪd] *adj* [person] de confiance; [method] qui a fait ses preuves.

trustee [trʌsˈti:] *n* FIN & JUR fidéicommissaire *mf*; [of institution] administrateur *m*, -trice *f*.

trust fund *n* fonds *m* en fidéicommis.

trusting ['trʌstɪŋ] *adj* confiant(e).

trustworthy ['trʌst,wɜ:ðɪ] *adj* digne de confiance.

truth [tru:θ] *n* vérité *f*.

truthful ['tru:θfʊl] *adj* [person, reply] honnête; [story] véridique.

try [traɪ] **1** *vt* [attempt, test] essayer; [food, drink] goûter; **to ~ to do sthg** essayer de faire qqch. ‖ JUR juger. ‖ [put to the test] éprouver, mettre à l'épreuve. **2**

vi essayer; **to ~ for sthg** essayer d'obtenir qqch. **3** *n* [attempt]: **to give sthg a ~** essayer qqch. ◯ **try on** *vt sep* [clothes] essayer. ◯ **try out** *vt sep* essayer.

trying ['traɪɪŋ] *adj* pénible, éprouvant(e).

T-shirt *n* tee-shirt *m*.

T-square *n* té *m*.

tub [tʌb] *n* [of ice cream - large] boîte *f*; [- small] petit pot *m*; [of margarine] barquette *f*. ‖ [bath] baignoire *f*.

tubby ['tʌbɪ] *adj inf* rondouillard(e), boulot(otte).

tube [tju:b] *n* [cylinder, container] tube *m*.

tuberculosis [tju:,bɜ:kjʊˈləʊsɪs] *n* tuberculose *f*.

tubing ['tju:bɪŋ] *n* (*U*) tubes *mpl*, tuyaux *mpl*.

tubular ['tju:bjʊlər] *adj* tubulaire.

tuck [tʌk] *vt* [place neatly] ranger. ◯ **tuck away** *vt sep* [store] mettre de côté OR en lieu sûr. ◯ **tuck in 1** *vt* [child, patient] border. ‖ [clothes] rentrer. **2** *vi inf* boulotter. ◯ **tuck up** *vt sep* [child, patient] border.

Tuesday ['tju:zdɪ] *n* mardi *m*; *see also* **Saturday**.

tuft [tʌft] *n* touffe *f*.

tug [tʌg] **1** *n* [pull]: **to give sthg a ~** tirer sur qqch. ‖ [boat] remorqueur *m*. **2** *vt* tirer. **3** *vi*: **to ~ (at)** tirer (sur).

tug-of-war *n* lutte *f* de traction à la corde; *fig* lutte acharnée.

tuition [tju:ˈɪʃn] *n* (*U*) cours *mpl*.

tulip ['tju:lɪp] *n* tulipe *f*.

tumble ['tʌmbl] **1** *vi* [person] tomber, faire une chute; [water] tomber en cascades. ‖ *fig* [prices] tomber, chuter. **2** *n* chute *f*, culbute *f*.

tumbledown ['tʌmbldaʊn] *adj* délabré(e), qui tombe en ruines.

tumble-dryer [-,draɪər] *n* sèche-linge *m inv*.

tumbler ['tʌmblər] *n* [glass] verre *m* (droit).

tummy ['tʌmɪ] *n inf* ventre *m*.

tumour *Br*, **tumor** *Am* ['tju:mər] *n* tumeur *f*.

tuna [*Br* 'tju:nə, *Am* 'tu:nə] (*pl inv* OR **-s**) *n* thon *m*.

tune [tju:n] **1** *n* [song, melody] air *m*. ‖ [harmony]: **in ~** [instrument] accordé(e), juste; [play, sing] juste; **out of ~** [instrument] mal accordé(e); [play, sing] faux; **to be in/out of ~ (with)** *fig* être en accord/désaccord (avec). **2** *vt* MUS accorder. ‖ RADIO & TV régler. ‖ [engine] régler. ○ **tune in** vi RADIO & TV être à l'écoute; **to ~ in to** se mettre sur. ○ **tune up** vi MUS accorder son instrument.

tuneful ['tju:nfʊl] adj mélodieux(ieuse).

tuner ['tju:nər] n RADIO & TV syntoniseur m, tuner m. ‖ MUS [person] accordeur m.

tunic ['tju:nɪk] n tunique f.

tuning fork ['tju:nɪŋ-] n diapason m.

Tunisia [tju:'nɪzɪə] n Tunisie f.

tunnel ['tʌnl] 1 n tunnel m. 2 vi faire OR creuser un tunnel.

turban ['tɜ:bən] n turban m.

turbine ['tɜ:baɪn] n turbine f.

turbocharged ['tɜ:bəʊtʃɑ:dʒd] adj turbo (inv).

turbulence ['tɜ:bjʊləns] n (U) [in air, water] turbulence f.

turbulent ['tɜ:bjʊlənt] adj [air, water] agité(e).

tureen [tə'ri:n] n soupière f.

turf [tɜ:f] (pl -s OR **turves**) n [grass surface] gazon m; [clod] motte f de gazon.

turgid ['tɜ:dʒɪd] adj fml [style, writing] pompeux(euse), ampoulé(e).

Turk [tɜ:k] n Turc m, Turque f.

turkey ['tɜ:kɪ] (pl **turkeys**) n dinde f.

Turkey ['tɜ:kɪ] n Turquie f.

Turkish ['tɜ:kɪʃ] 1 adj turc (turque). 2 n [language] turc m. 3 npl: **the ~** les Turcs mpl.

Turkish delight n loukoum m.

turmoil ['tɜ:mɔɪl] n agitation f, trouble m.

turn [tɜ:n] 1 n [in road] virage m, tournant m; [in river] méandre m. ‖ [revolution, twist] tour m. ‖ [change] tournure f, tour m. ‖ [in game] tour m; **in ~** tour à tour, chacun (à) son tour. ‖ [performance] numéro m. ‖ MED crise f, attaque f. ‖ phr: **to do sb a good ~** rendre (un) service à qqn. 2 vt [gen] tourner; [omelette, steak etc] retourner; **to ~ sthg inside out** retourner qqch; **to ~ one's thoughts/attention to sthg** tourner ses pensées/son attention vers qqch. ‖ [change]: **to ~ sthg into** changer qqch en. ‖ [become]: **to ~ red** rougir. 3 vi [gen] tourner; [person] se tourner, se retourner. ‖ [in book]: **to ~ to a page** se reporter OR aller à une page. ‖ [for consolation]: **to ~ to sb/sthg** se tourner vers qqn/qqch. ‖ [change]: **to ~ into** se changer en, se transformer en. ○ **turn around = turn round.** ○ **turn away** 1 vt sep [refuse entry to] refuser. 2 vi se détourner. ○ **turn back** 1 vt sep

[sheets] replier; [person, vehicle] refouler. 2 vi rebrousser chemin. ○ **turn down** vt sep [reject] rejeter, refuser. ‖ [radio, volume, gas] baisser. ○ **turn in** vi inf [go to bed] se pieuter. ○ **turn off** 1 vt fus [road, path] quitter. 2 vt sep [radio, TV, engine, gas] éteindre; [tap] fermer. 3 vi [leave path, road] tourner. ○ **turn on** 1 vt sep [radio, TV, engine, gas] allumer; [tap] ouvrir; **to ~ the light on** allumer la lumière. ‖ inf [excite sexually] exciter. 2 vt fus [attack] attaquer. ○ **turn out** 1 vt sep [light, gas fire] éteindre. ‖ [empty - pocket, bag] retourner, vider. 2 vt fus: **to ~ out to be** s'avérer. 3 vi [end up] finir. ○ **turn over** 1 vt sep [playing card, stone] retourner; [page] retourner. ‖ [consider] retourner dans sa tête. ‖ [hand over] rendre, remettre. 2 vi [roll over] se retourner. ○ **turn round** 1 vt sep [reverse] retourner. ‖ [wheel, words] tourner. 2 vi [person] se retourner. ○ **turn up** 1 vt sep [TV, radio] mettre plus fort; [gas] monter. 2 vi [arrive - person] se pointer. ‖ [be found - person, object] être retrouvé; [- opportunity] se présenter.

turning ['tɜ:nɪŋ] n [off road] route f latérale.

turning point n tournant m, moment m décisif.

turnip ['tɜ:nɪp] n navet m.

turnout ['tɜ:naʊt] n [at election] taux m de participation; [at meeting] assistance f.

turnover ['tɜ:n,əʊvər] n (U) [of personnel] renouvellement m. ‖ FIN chiffre m d'affaires.

turnpike ['tɜ:npaɪk] n Am autoroute f à péage.

turnstile ['tɜ:nstaɪl] n tourniquet m.

turntable ['tɜ:n,teɪbl] n platine f.

turpentine ['tɜ:pəntaɪn] n térébenthine f.

turquoise ['tɜ:kwɔɪz] 1 adj turquoise (inv). 2 n [colour] turquoise m.

turret ['tʌrɪt] n tourelle f.

turtle ['tɜ:tl] (pl inv OR -s) n tortue f de mer.

turtleneck ['tɜ:tlnek] n [garment] pull m à col montant; [neck] col m montant.

turves [tɜ:vz] Br pl → **turf.**

tusk [tʌsk] n défense f.

tussle ['tʌsl] 1 n lutte f. 2 vi se battre; **to ~ over sthg** se disputer qqch.

tutor ['tju:tər] n [private] professeur m particulier. ‖ UNIV directeur m, -trice f d'études.

tutorial [tjuːˈtɔːrɪəl] *n* travaux *mpl* dirigés.

tuxedo [tʌkˈsiːdəʊ] (*pl* -s) *n* smoking *m*.

TV (*abbr of television*) *n* (*U*) [medium, industry] télé *f.* ‖ [apparatus] (poste *m* de) télé *f.*

twang [twæŋ] *n* [sound] bruit *m* de pincement. ‖ [accent] nasillement *m*.

tweed [twiːd] *n* tweed *m*.

tweezers [ˈtwiːzəz] *npl* pince *f* à épiler.

twelfth [twelfθ] *num* douzième; *see also* sixth.

twelve [twelv] *num* douze; *see also* six.

twentieth [ˈtwentɪəθ] *num* vingtième; *see also* sixth.

twenty [ˈtwentɪ] *num* vingt; *see also* six.

twice [twaɪs] *adv* deux fois; **he earns ~ as much as me** il gagne deux fois plus que moi OR le double de moi; **~ as big** deux fois plus grand; **~ my size/age** le double de ma taille/mon âge.

twiddle [ˈtwɪdl] **1** *vt* jouer avec. **2** *vi*: **to ~ with sthg** jouer avec qqch.

twig [twɪg] *n* brindille *f*, petite branche *f*.

twilight [ˈtwaɪlaɪt] *n* crépuscule *m*.

twin [twɪn] **1** *adj* jumeau (jumelle); [town] jumelé(e); **~ beds** lits *mpl* jumeaux. **2** *n* jumeau *m*, jumelle *f*.

twin-bedded [-ˈbedɪd] *adj* à deux lits.

twine [twaɪn] **1** *n* (*U*) ficelle *f*. **2** *vt*: **to ~ sthg round sthg** enrouler qqch autour de qqch.

twinge [twɪndʒ] *n* [of pain] élancement *m*; **a ~ of guilt** un remords.

twinkle [ˈtwɪŋkl] *vi* [star, lights] scintiller; [eyes] briller, pétiller.

twin room *n* chambre *f* à deux lits.

twin town *n* ville *f* jumelée.

twirl [twɜːl] **1** *vt* faire tourner. **2** *vi* tournoyer.

twist [twɪst] **1** *n* [in road] zigzag *m*, tournant *m*; [in river] méandre *m*, coude *m*; [in rope] entortillement *m*. ‖ *fig* [in plot] tour *m*. **2** *vt* [wind, curl] entortiller. ‖ [contort] tordre. ‖ [turn] tourner; [lid - to open] dévisser; [- to close] visser. ‖ [sprain]: **to ~ one's ankle** se tordre OR se fouler la cheville. ‖ [words, meaning] déformer. **3** *vi* [river, path] zigzaguer. ‖ [be contorted] se tordre. ‖ [turn]: **to ~ round** se retourner.

twitch [twɪtʃ] **1** *n* tic *m*. **2** *vi* [muscle, eye, face] se contracter.

two [tuː] *num* deux; *see also* six.

twofaced [ˌtuːˈfeɪst] *adj pej* fourbe.

twofold [ˈtuːfəʊld] *adv*: **to increase ~** doubler.

twosome [ˈtuːsəm] *n inf* couple *m*.

two-way *adj* [traffic, trade] dans les deux sens.

tycoon [taɪˈkuːn] *n* magnat *m*.

type [taɪp] **1** *n* [sort, kind] genre *m*, sorte *f*; [model] modèle *m*; [in classification] type *m*. ‖ (*U*) TYPO caractères *mpl*. **2** *vt* [letter, reply] taper (à la machine). **3** *vi* taper (à la machine).

typecast [ˈtaɪpkɑːst] (*pt & pp* typecast) *vt*: **to be ~** être cantonné aux mêmes rôles.

typeface [ˈtaɪpfeɪs] *n* TYPO œil *m* de caractère.

typescript [ˈtaɪpskrɪpt] *n* texte *m* dactylographié.

typeset [ˈtaɪpset] (*pt & pp* typeset) *vt* composer.

typewriter [ˈtaɪpˌraɪtər] *n* machine *f* à écrire.

typhoid (fever) [ˈtaɪfɔɪd-] *n* typhoïde *f*.

typhoon [taɪˈfuːn] *n* typhon *m*.

typical [ˈtɪpɪkl] *adj*: **~ (of)** typique (de), caractéristique (de); **that's ~ (of him/her)!** c'est bien de lui/d'elle!

typing [ˈtaɪpɪŋ] *n* dactylo *f*, dactylographie *f*.

typist [ˈtaɪpɪst] *n* dactylo *mf*, dactylographe *mf*.

tyranny [ˈtɪrənɪ] *n* tyrannie *f*.

tyrant [ˈtaɪrənt] *n* tyran *m*.

tyre *Br*, **tire** *Am* [ˈtaɪər] *n* pneu *m*.

tyre pressure *n* pression *f* (de gonflage).

u (*pl* **u's** OR **us**), **U** (*pl* **U's** OR **Us**) [juː] *n* [letter] u *m inv*, U *m inv*.

U-bend *n* siphon *m*.

udder ['ʌdər] *n* mamelle *f*.

UFO (*abbr of* **unidentified flying object**) *n* OVNI *m*, ovni *m*.

ugh [ʌg] *excl* pouah!, beurk!

ugly ['ʌglɪ] *adj* [unattractive] laid(e). ‖ *fig* [unpleasant] pénible, désagréable.

UHF (*abbr of* **ultra-high frequency**) *n* UHF.

UK (*abbr of* **United Kingdom**) *n* Royaume-Uni *m*, R.U. *m*.

Ukraine [juː'kreɪn] *n*: the ~ l'Ukraine *f*.

ulcer ['ʌlsər] *n* ulcère *m*.

Ulster ['ʌlstər] *n* Ulster *m*.

ulterior [ʌl'tɪərɪər] *adj*: ~ **motive** arrière-pensée *f*.

ultimata [ˌʌltɪ'meɪtə] *pl* → **ultimatum**.

ultimate ['ʌltɪmət] **1** *adj* [final] final(e), ultime. ‖ [most powerful] ultime, suprême. **2** *n*: **the ~ in** le fin du fin dans.

ultimately ['ʌltɪmətlɪ] *adv* [finally] finalement.

ultimatum [ˌʌltɪ'meɪtəm] (*pl* **-tums** OR **-ta** [-tə]) *n* ultimatum *m*.

ultrasound ['ʌltrəsaʊnd] *n* (*U*) ultrasons *mpl*.

ultraviolet [ˌʌltrə'vaɪələt] *adj* ultraviolet(ette).

umbilical cord [ʌm'bɪlɪkl-] *n* cordon *m* ombilical.

umbrella [ʌm'brelə] *n* [portable] parapluie *m*; [fixed] parasol *m*.

umpire ['ʌmpaɪər] **1** *n* arbitre *m*. **2** *vt* arbitrer.

umpteen [ˌʌmp'tiːn] *num adj inf* je ne sais combien de.

umpteenth [ˌʌmp'tiːnθ] *num adj inf* énième.

UN (*abbr of* **United Nations**) *n*: **the ~** l'ONU *f*, l'Onu *f*.

unable [ʌn'eɪbl] *adj*: **to be ~ to do sthg** ne pas pouvoir faire qqch, être incapable de faire qqch.

unacceptable [ˌʌnək'septəbl] *adj* inacceptable.

unaccompanied [ˌʌnə'kʌmpənɪd] *adj* [child] non accompagné(e); [luggage] sans surveillance.

unaccountably [ˌʌnə'kaʊntəblɪ] *adv* [inexplicably] de façon inexplicable, inexplicablement.

unaccounted [ˌʌnə'kaʊntɪd] *adj*: **to be ~ for** manquer.

unaccustomed [ˌʌnə'kʌstəmd] *adj* [unused]: **to be ~ to sthg/to doing sthg** ne pas être habitué(e) à qqch/à faire qqch.

unadulterated [ˌʌnə'dʌltəreɪtɪd] *adj* [unspoilt - wine] non frelaté(e); [- food] naturel(elle). ‖ [absolute - joy] sans mélange; [- nonsense, truth] pur et simple (pure et simple).

unanimous [juː'nænɪməs] *adj* unanime.

unanimously [juː'nænɪməslɪ] *adv* à l'unanimité.

unappetizing, -ising [ˌʌn'æpɪtaɪzɪŋ] *adj* peu appétissant(e).

unarmed [ˌʌn'ɑːmd] *adj* non armé(e).

unarmed combat *n* combat *m* sans armes.

unashamed [ˌʌnə'ʃeɪmd] *adj* [luxury] insolent(e); [liar, lie] effronté(e), éhonté(e).

unassuming [ˌʌnə'sjuːmɪŋ] *adj* modeste, effacé(e).

unattached [ˌʌnə'tætʃt] *adj* [not fastened, linked]: ~ **(to)** indépendant(e) (de). ‖ [without partner] libre, sans attaches.

unattended [ˌʌnə'tendɪd] *adj* [luggage, shop] sans surveillance; [child] seul(e).

unattractive [ˌʌnə'træktɪv] *adj* [not beautiful] peu attrayant(e), peu séduisant(e). ‖ [not pleasant] déplaisant(e).

unauthorized, -ised [ˌʌn'ɔːθəraɪzd] *adj* non autorisé(e).

unavailable [ˌʌnə'veɪləbl] *adj* qui n'est pas disponible, indisponible.

unavoidable [ˌʌnə'vɔɪdəbl] *adj* inévitable.

unaware [ˌʌnə'weər] *adj* ignorant(e), inconscient(e); **to be ~ of sthg** ne pas avoir conscience de qqch, ignorer qqch.

unawares [ˌʌnə'weəz] *adv*: **to catch** OR **take sb ~** prendre qqn au dépourvu.

unbalanced [ˌʌn'bælənst] *adj* [biased] tendancieux(ieuse), partial(e). ‖ [deranged] déséquilibré(e).

unbearable [ʌn'beərəbl] *adj* insupportable.

unbeatable [,ʌn'biːtəbl] *adj* imbattable.

unbeknown(st) [,ʌnbɪ'nəʊn(st)] *adv*: ~ **to** à l'insu de.

unbelievable [,ʌnbɪ'liːvəbl] *adj* incroyable.

unbending [,ʌn'bendɪŋ] *adj* inflexible, intransigeant(e).

unbia(s)sed [,ʌn'baɪəst] *adj* impartial(e).

unborn [,ʌn'bɔːn] *adj* [child] qui n'est pas encore né(e).

unbreakable [,ʌn'breɪkəbl] *adj* incassable.

unbutton [,ʌn'bʌtn] *vt* déboutonner.

uncalled-for [,ʌn'kɔːld-] *adj* [remark] déplacé(e); [criticism] injustifié(e).

uncanny [ʌn'kænɪ] *adj* [message, meaning, motive] étrange, mystérieux(ieuse); [resemblance] troublant(e).

uncertain [ʌn'sɜːtn] *adj* incertain(e); **in no ~ terms** sans mâcher ses mots.

unchanged [,ʌn'tʃeɪndʒd] *adj* inchangé(e).

unchecked [,ʌn'tʃekt] *adj* non maîtrisé(e), sans frein.

uncivilized, -ised [,ʌn'sɪvɪlaɪzd] *adj* non civilisé(e), barbare.

uncle ['ʌŋkl] *n* oncle *m*.

unclear [,ʌn'klɪər] *adj* [message, meaning, motive] qui n'est pas clair(e). || [uncertain - person, future] incertain(e).

uncomfortable [,ʌn'kʌmftəbl] *adj* [shoes, chair, clothes etc] inconfortable; *fig* [fact, truth] désagréable. || [person - physically] qui n'est pas à l'aise; [- ill at ease] mal à l'aise.

uncommon [ʌn'kɒmən] *adj* [rare] rare.

uncompromising [,ʌn'kɒmprəmaɪzɪŋ] *adj* intransigeant(e).

unconditional [,ʌnkən'dɪʃənl] *adj* inconditionnel(elle).

unconscious [ʌn'kɒnʃəs] **1** *adj* [having lost consciousness] sans connaissance. || *fig* [unaware]: **to be ~ of** ne pas avoir conscience de, ne pas se rendre compte de. || [unnoticed - desires, feelings] inconscient(e). **2** *n* PSYCH inconscient *m*.

unconsciously [ʌn'kɒnʃəslɪ] *adv* inconsciemment.

uncontrollable [,ʌnkən'trəʊləbl] *adj* [unrestrainable - emotion, urge] irrépressible, irrésistible; [- increase, epidemic] qui ne peut être enrayé(e). || [unmanageable - person] impossible, difficile.

unconventional [,ʌnkən'venʃənl] *adj* peu conventionnel(elle), original(e).

uncouth [ʌn'kuːθ] *adj* grossier(ière).

uncover [ʌn'kʌvər] *vt* découvrir.

undecided [,ʌndɪ'saɪdɪd] *adj* [person] indécis(e), irrésolu(e); [issue] indécis(e).

undeniable [,ʌndɪ'naɪəbl] *adj* indéniable, incontestable.

under ['ʌndər] **1** *prep* [gen] sous. || [less than] moins de; **children ~ five** les enfants de moins de cinq ans. || [subject to - effect, influence] sous; **~ the circumstances** dans ces circonstances, étant donné les circonstances; **to be ~ the impression that ...** avoir l'impression que .... || [undergoing]: **~ consideration** à l'étude, à l'examen. || [according to] selon, conformément à. **2** *adv* [underneath] dessous; [underwater] sous l'eau; **to go ~** [company] couler, faire faillite. || [less] au-dessous.

underage [ʌndər'eɪdʒ] *adj* mineur(e).

undercarriage ['ʌndə,kærɪdʒ] *n* train *m* d'atterrissage.

undercharge [,ʌndə'tʃɑːdʒ] *vt* ne pas faire assez payer à.

underclothes ['ʌndəkləʊðz] *npl* sous-vêtements *mpl*.

undercoat ['ʌndəkəʊt] *n* [of paint] couche *f* de fond.

undercover ['ʌndə,kʌvər] *adj* secret(ète).

undercurrent ['ʌndə,kʌrənt] *n fig* [tendency] courant *m* sous-jacent.

undercut [,ʌndə'kʌt] (*pt & pp* **undercut**) *vt* [in price] vendre moins cher que.

underdeveloped [,ʌndədɪ'veləpt] *adj* [country] sous-développé(e); [person] qui n'est pas complètement développé(e) OR formé(e).

underdog ['ʌndədɒg] *n*: **the ~** l'opprimé *m*; SPORT celui (celle) que l'on donne perdant(e).

underdone [,ʌndə'dʌn] *adj* [food] pas assez cuit(e); [steak] saignant(e).

underestimate [,ʌndər'estɪmeɪt] *vt* sous-estimer.

underexposed [,ʌndərɪk'spəʊzd] *adj* PHOT sous-exposé(e).

underfoot [,ʌndə'fʊt] *adv* sous les pieds.

undergo [,ʌndə'gəʊ] (*pt* **-went**, *pp* **-gone** [-'gɒn]) *vt* subir; [pain, difficulties] éprouver.

undergraduate [,ʌndə'grædjʊət] *n* étudiant *m*, -e *f* qui prépare la licence.

underground [*adj & n* 'ʌndəgraʊnd, *adv* ,ʌndə'graʊnd] **1** *adj* [below the ground] souterrain(e). || *fig* [secret] clandestin(e). **2** *adv*: **to go/be forced ~** entrer dans la clandestinité. **3** *n* [activist movement] résistance *f.*

undergrowth [ˈʌndəgrəʊθ] *n* (*U*) sous-bois *m inv.*

underhand [ˌʌndəˈhænd] *adj* sournois(e), en dessous.

underline [ˌʌndəˈlaɪn] *rt* souligner.

underlying [ˌʌndəˈlaɪɪŋ] *adj* sousjacent(e).

undermine [ˌʌndəˈmaɪn] *rt fig* [weaken] saper, ébranler.

underneath [ˌʌndəˈniːθ] **1** *prep* [beneath] sous, au-dessous de. || [in movement] sous. **2** *adv* [beneath] en dessous, dessous. || *fig* [fundamentally] au fond. **3** *n* [underside]: **the ~** le dessous.

underpaid [ˈʌndəpeɪd] *adj* souspayé(e).

underpants [ˈʌndəpænts] *npl* slip *m.*

underpass [ˈʌndəpɑːs] *n* [for cars] passage *m* inférieur; [for pedestrians] passage *m* souterrain.

underprivileged [ˌʌndəˈprɪvɪlɪdʒd] *adj* défavorisé(e), déshérité(e).

underrated [ˌʌndəˈreɪtɪd] *adj* sousestimé(e).

undershirt [ˈʌndəʃɜːt] *n Am* maillot *m* de corps.

underside [ˈʌndəsaɪd] *n*: **the ~** le dessous.

underskirt [ˈʌndəskɜːt] *n* jupon *m.*

understand [ˌʌndəˈstænd] (*pt & pp* -stood) **1** *rt* [gen] comprendre. || *fml* [be informed]: **I ~ (that) ...** je crois comprendre que ..., il paraît que .... **2** *vi* comprendre.

understandable [ˌʌndəˈstændəbl] *adj* compréhensible.

understanding [ˌʌndəˈstændɪŋ] **1** *n* [knowledge, sympathy] compréhension *f.* || [agreement] accord *m*, arrangement *m.* **2** *adj* [sympathetic] compréhensif(ive).

understatement [ˌʌndəˈsteɪtmənt] *n* [inadequate statement] affirmation *f* en dessous de la vérité. || (*U*) [quality of understating] euphémisme *m.*

understood [ˌʌndəˈstʊd] *pt & pp* → understand.

understudy [ˈʌndəˌstʌdɪ] *n* doublure *f.*

undertake [ˌʌndəˈteɪk] (*pt* -took, *pp* -taken [-ˈteɪkn]) *rt* [take on - gen] entreprendre; [- responsibility] assumer. || [promise]: **to ~ to do sthg** promettre de faire qqch, s'engager à faire qqch.

undertaker [ˈʌndəˌteɪkər] *n* entrepreneur *m* des pompes funèbres.

undertaking [ˌʌndəˈteɪkɪŋ] *n* [task] entreprise *f.* || [promise] promesse *f.*

undertone [ˈʌndətəʊn] *n* [quiet voice] voix *f* basse. || [vague feeling] courant *m.*

undertook [ˌʌndəˈtʊk] *pt* → undertake.

underwater [ˌʌndəˈwɔːtər] **1** *adj* sousmarin(e). **2** *adv* sous l'eau.

underwear [ˈʌndəweər] *n* (*U*) sousvêtements *mpl.*

underwent [ˌʌndəˈwent] *pt* → undergo.

underworld [ˈʌndəˌwɜːld] *n* [criminal society]: **the ~** le milieu, la pègre.

underwriter [ˈʌndəˌraɪtər] *n* assureur *m.*

undid [ʌnˈdɪd] *pt* → undo.

undisputed [ˌʌndɪˈspjuːtɪd] *adj* incontesté(e).

undo [ʌnˈduː] (*pt* -did, *pp* -done) *rt* [unfasten] défaire. || [nullify] annuler, détruire.

undone [ʌnˈdʌn] **1** *pp* → undo. **2** *adj* [unfastened] défait(e). || [task] non accompli(e).

undoubtedly [ʌnˈdaʊtɪdlɪ] *adv* sans aucun doute.

undress [ʌnˈdres] **1** *rt* déshabiller. **2** *vi* se déshabiller.

undue [ʌnˈdjuː] *adj fml* excessif(ive).

undulate [ˈʌndjʊleɪt] *vi* onduler.

unduly [ʌnˈdjuːlɪ] *adv fml* trop, excessivement.

unearth [ʌnˈɜːθ] *rt* [dig up] déterrer. || *fig* [discover] découvrir, dénicher.

unearthly [ʌnˈɜːθlɪ] *adj inf* [uncivilized - time of day] indu(e), impossible.

unease [ʌnˈiːz] *n* (*U*) malaise *m.*

uneasy [ʌnˈiːzɪ] *adj* [person, feeling] mal à l'aise, gêné(e); [silence] gêné(e).

uneducated [ʌnˈedjʊkeɪtɪd] *adj* [person] sans instruction.

unemployed [ˌʌnɪmˈplɔɪd] **1** *adj* au chômage, sans travail. **2** *npl*: **the ~s** les sans-travail *mpl*, les chômeurs *mpl.*

unemployment [ˌʌnɪmˈplɔɪmənt] *n* chômage *m.*

unemployment benefit *Br*, **unemployment compensation** *Am n* allocation *f* de chômage.

unerring [ʌnˈɜːrɪŋ] *adj* sûr(e), infaillible.

uneven [ʌnˈiːvn] *adj* [not flat - surface] inégal(e); [- ground] accidenté(e). || [inconsistent] inégal(e). || [unfair] injuste.

unexpected [ˌʌnɪkˈspektɪd] *adj* inattendu(e), imprévu(e).

unjust

unexpectedly [ˌʌnɪk'spektɪdlɪ] adv subitement, d'une manière imprévue.

unfailing [ʌn'feɪlɪŋ] adj qui ne se dément pas, constant(e).

unfair [ˌʌn'feəʳ] adj injuste.

unfaithful [ˌʌn'feɪθful] adj infidèle.

unfamiliar [ˌʌnfə'mɪljəʳ] adj [not well-known] peu familier(ière), peu connu(e). || [not acquainted]: **to be ~ with sthg/sb** mal connaître qqch/qqn, ne pas connaître qqch/qqn.

unfashionable [ˌʌn'fæʃnəbl] adj démodé(e), passé(e) de mode; [person] qui n'est plus à la mode.

unfasten [ˌʌn'fɑːsn] rt défaire.

unfavourable Br, **unfavorable** Am [ˌʌn'feɪvrəbl] adj défavorable.

unfeeling [ʌn'fiːlɪŋ] adj impitoyable, insensible.

unfinished [ˌʌn'fɪnɪʃt] adj inachevé(e).

unfit [ˌʌn'fɪt] adj [not in good health] qui n'est pas en forme. || [not suitable]: **~ (for)** impropre (à); [person] inapte (à).

unfold [ʌn'fəʊld] 1 rt [map, newspaper] déplier. 2 ri [become clear] se dérouler.

unforeseen [ˌʌnfɔː'siːn] adj imprévu(e).

unforgettable [ˌʌnfə'getəbl] adj inoubliable.

unforgivable [ˌʌnfə'gɪvəbl] adj impardonnable.

unfortunate [ʌn'fɔːtʃnət] adj [unlucky] malheureux(euse), malchanceux(euse). || [regrettable] regrettable, fâcheux(euse).

unfortunately [ʌn'fɔːtʃnətlɪ] adv malheureusement.

unfounded [ˌʌn'faʊndɪd] adj sans fondement, dénué(e) de tout fondement.

unfriendly [ˌʌn'frendlɪ] adj hostile, malveillant(e).

unfurnished [ˌʌn'fɜːnɪʃt] adj non meublé(e).

ungainly [ʌn'geɪnlɪ] adj gauche.

ungrateful [ʌn'greɪtful] adj ingrat(e), peu reconnaissant(e).

unhappy [ʌn'hæpɪ] adj [sad] triste, malheureux(euse). || [uneasy]: **to be ~ (with ou about)** être inquiet(iète) (au sujet de). || [unfortunate] malheureux(euse), regrettable.

unharmed [ˌʌn'hɑːmd] adj indemne, sain et sauf (saine et sauve).

unhealthy [ʌn'helθɪ] adj [person. skin] maladif(ive); [conditions, place] insalubre, malsain(e); [habit] malsain.

unheard-of [ʌn'hɜːd-] adj [unknown] inconnu(e). || [unprecedented] sans précédent, inouï(e).

unhook [ˌʌn'hʊk] rt [dress, bra] dégrafer. || [coat, picture, trailer] décrocher.

unhurt [ˌʌn'hɜːt] adj indemne, sain et sauf (saine et sauve).

unidentified flying object [ˌʌnaɪ'dentɪfaɪd-] n objet m volant non identifié.

unification [ˌjuːnɪfɪ'keɪʃn] n unification f.

uniform ['juːnɪfɔːm] 1 adj [rate, colour] uniforme; [size] même. 2 n uniforme m.

unify ['juːnɪfaɪ] rt unifier.

unilateral [ˌjuːnɪ'lætərəl] adj unilatéral(e).

unimportant [ˌʌnɪm'pɔːtənt] adj sans importance, peu important(e).

uninhabited [ˌʌnɪn'hæbɪtɪd] adj inhabité(e).

uninjured [ˌʌn'ɪndʒəd] adj qui n'est pas blessé(e), indemne.

unintentional [ˌʌnɪn'tenʃənl] adj involontaire, non intentionnel(elle).

union ['juːnjən] 1 n [trade union] syndicat m. || [alliance] union f. 2 comp syndical(e).

Union Jack n: **the ~** l'Union Jack m. le drapeau britannique.

unique [juː'niːk] adj [exceptional] unique, exceptionnel(elle). || [exclusive]: **~ to** propre à. || [very special] unique.

unison ['juːnɪzn] n unisson m; **in ~** à l'unisson; [say] en chœur, en même temps.

unit ['juːnɪt] n [gen] unité f. || [of furniture] élément m. || [department] service m.

unite [juː'naɪt] 1 rt unifier. 2 ri s'unir.

united [juː'naɪtɪd] adj [in harmony] uni(e). || [unified] unifié(e).

United Kingdom n: **the ~** le Royaume-Uni.

United Nations n: **the ~** les Nations fpl Unies.

United States n: **the ~ (of America)** les États-Unis mpl (d'Amérique); **in the ~** aux États-Unis.

unity ['juːnətɪ] n (U) unité f.

universal [ˌjuːnɪ'vɜːsl] adj universel(elle).

universe ['juːnɪvɜːs] n univers m.

university [ˌjuːnɪ'vɜːsətɪ] 1 n université f. 2 comp universitaire.

unjust [ˌʌn'dʒʌst] adj injuste.

unkempt [,ʌn'kempt] *adj* [clothes, person] négligé(e), débraillé(e).

unkind [ʌn'kaɪnd] *adj* [uncharitable] méchant(e), pas gentil(ille).

unknown [,ʌn'nəʊn] *adj* inconnu(e).

unlawful [,ʌn'lɔ:fʊl] *adj* illégal(e).

unleaded [,ʌn'ledɪd] *adj* sans plomb.

unless [ən'les] *conj* à moins que (+ *subjunctive*); ~ **I'm mistaken** à moins que je (ne) me trompe.

unlike [,ʌn'laɪk] *prep* [different from] différent(e) de. || [in contrast to] contrairement à, à la différence de. || [not typical of]: **it's ~ you to complain** cela ne te ressemble pas de te plaindre.

unlikely [ʌn'laɪklɪ] [event, result] peu probable, improbable; [story] invraisemblable.

unlisted [ʌn'lɪstɪd] *adj Am* [phone number] qui est sur la liste rouge.

unload [,ʌn'ləʊd] *vt* décharger.

unlock [,ʌn'lɒk] *vt* ouvrir.

unlucky [ʌn'lʌkɪ] *adj* [unfortunate - person] malchanceux(euse), qui n'a pas de chance; [- experience, choice] malheureux(euse). || [object, number etc] qui porte malheur.

unmarried [,ʌn'mærɪd] *adj* célibataire, qui n'est pas marié(e).

unmistakable [,ʌnmɪ'steɪkəbl] *adj* qu'on ne peut pas ne pas reconnaître.

unmitigated [ʌn'mɪtɪgeɪtɪd] *adj* [disaster] total(e); [evil] non mitigé(e).

unnatural [ʌn'nætʃrəl] *adj* [unusual] anormal(e), qui n'est pas naturel(elle). || [affected] peu naturel(elle); [smile] forcé(e).

unnecessary [ʌn'nesəsərɪ] *adj* [remark, expense, delay] inutile.

unnerving [,ʌn'nɜːvɪŋ] *adj* troublant(e).

unnoticed [,ʌn'nəʊtɪst] *adj* inaperçu(e).

unobtainable [,ʌnəb'teɪnəbl] *adj* impossible à obtenir.

unobtrusive [,ʌnəb'truːsɪv] *adj* [person] effacé(e); [object] discret(ète).

unofficial [,ʌnə'fɪʃl] *adj* non officiel(ielle).

unorthodox [,ʌn'ɔːθədɒks] *adj* peu orthodoxe.

unpack [,ʌn'pæk] 1 *vt* [suitcase] défaire; [box] vider; [clothes] déballer. 2 *vi* défaire ses bagages.

unparalleled [ʌn'pærəleld] *adj* [success, crisis] sans précédent; [beauty] sans égal.

unpleasant [ʌn'pleznt] *adj* désagréable.

unplug [ʌn'plʌg] *vt* débrancher.

unpopular [,ʌn'pɒpjʊlər] *adj* impopulaire.

unprecedented [ʌn'presɪdəntɪd] *adj* sans précédent.

unpredictable [,ʌnprɪ'dɪktəbl] *adj* imprévisible.

unqualified [,ʌn'kwɒlɪfaɪd] *adj* [person] non qualifié(e); [teacher, doctor] non diplômé(e). || [success] formidable; [support] inconditionnel(elle).

unquestionable [ʌn'kwestʃənəbl] *adj* [fact] incontestable; [honesty] certain(e).

unquestioning [ʌn'kwestʃənɪŋ] *adj* aveugle, absolu(e).

unravel [ʌn'rævl] *vt* [undo - knitting] défaire; [- fabric] effiler; [- threads] démêler. || *fig* [solve] éclaircir.

unreal [,ʌn'rɪəl] *adj* [strange] irréel(elle).

unrealistic [,ʌnrɪə'lɪstɪk] *adj* irréaliste.

unreasonable [ʌn'riːznəbl] *adj* qui n'est pas raisonnable, déraisonnable.

unrelated [,ʌnrɪ'leɪtɪd] *adj*: **to be ~ (to)** n'avoir aucun rapport (avec).

unreliable [,ʌnrɪ'laɪəbl] *adj* [machine, method] peu fiable; [person] sur qui on ne peut pas compter.

unrequited [,ʌnrɪ'kwaɪtɪd] *adj* non partagé(e).

unreserved [,ʌnrɪ'zɜːvd] *adj* [support, admiration] sans réserve.

unresolved [,ʌnrɪ'zɒlvd] *adj* non résolu(e).

unrest [,ʌn'rest] *n* (*U*) troubles *mpl*.

unrivalled *Br*, **unrivaled** *Am* [ʌn'raɪvld] *adj* sans égal(e).

unroll [,ʌn'rəʊl] *vt* dérouler.

unruly [ʌn'ruːlɪ] *adj* [crowd, child] turbulent(e); [hair] indisciplinés.

unsafe [,ʌn'seɪf] *adj* [dangerous] dangereux(euse). || [in danger]: **to feel ~** ne pas se sentir en sécurité.

unsaid [,ʌn'sed] *adj*: **to leave sthg ~** passer qqch sous silence.

unsatisfactory ['ʌn,sætɪs'fæktərɪ] *adj* qui laisse à désirer, peu satisfaisant(e).

unsavoury, **unsavory** *Am* [ʌn'seɪvərɪ] *adj* [person] peu recommandable; [district] mal famé(e).

unscathed [ʌn'skeɪðd] *adj* indemne.

unscrew [,ʌn'skruː] *vt* dévisser.

unscrupulous [ʌn'skruːpjʊləs] *adj* sans scrupules.

up

unseemly [ʌn'siːmlɪ] *adj* inconvenant(e).

unselfish [ˌʌn'selfɪʃ] *adj* désintéressé(e).

unsettled [ˌʌn'setld] *adj* [person] perturbé(e), troublé(e). ‖ [weather] variable, incertain(e). ‖ [argument] qui n'a pas été résolu(e); [situation] incertain(e).

unshak(e)able [ʌn'ʃeɪkəbl] *adj* inébranlable.

unshaven [ˌʌn'ʃeɪvn] *adj* non rasé(e).

unsightly [ʌn'saɪtlɪ] *adj* laid(e).

unskilled [ˌʌn'skɪld] *adj* non qualifié(e).

unsociable [ʌn'səʊʃəbl] *adj* sauvage.

unsocial [ˌʌn'səʊʃl] *adj*: **to work ~ hours** travailler en dehors des heures normales.

unsound [ˌʌn'saʊnd] *adj* [theory] mal fondé(e); [decision] peu judicieux(ieuse). ‖ [building, structure] en mauvais état.

unspeakable [ʌn'spiːkəbl] *adj* indescriptible.

unstable [ˌʌn'steɪbl] *adj* instable.

unsteady [ˌʌn'stedɪ] *adj* [hand] tremblant(e); [table, ladder] instable.

unstuck [ˌʌn'stʌk] *adj*: **to come ~** [notice, stamp, label] se décoller; *fig* [plan, system] s'effondrer; *fig* [person] essuyer un échec.

unsuccessful [ˌʌnsək'sesful] *adj* [attempt] vain(e); [meeting] infructueux(euse); [candidate] refusé(e).

unsuccessfully [ˌʌnsək'sesfulɪ] *adv* en vain, sans succès.

unsuitable [ˌʌn'suːtəbl] *adj* qui ne convient pas; [clothes] peu approprié(e).

unsure [ˌʌn'ʃɔːr] *adj* [not certain]: **to be ~ (about/of)** ne pas être sûr(e) (de). ‖ [not confident]: **to be ~ (of o.s.)** ne pas être sûr(e) de soi.

unsuspecting [ˌʌnsə'spektɪŋ] *adj* qui ne se doute de rien.

unsympathetic ['ʌnˌsɪmpə'θetɪk] *adj* [unfeeling] indifférent(e).

untangle [ˌʌn'tæŋgl] *rt* [string, hair] démêler.

untapped [ˌʌn'tæpt] *adj* inexploité(e).

untenable [ˌʌn'tenəbl] *adj* indéfendable.

unthinkable [ʌn'θɪŋkəbl] *adj* impensable.

untidy [ʌn'taɪdɪ] *adj* [room, desk] en désordre; [work, handwriting] brouillon (*inv*); [person, appearance] négligé(e).

untie [ˌʌn'taɪ] (*cont* **untying**) *rt* [knot, parcel, shoelaces] défaire; [prisoner] détacher.

until [ən'tɪl] **1** *prep* [gen] jusqu'à; **~ now** jusqu'ici. ‖ (*after negative*) avant; **not ~ tomorrow** pas avant demain. **2** *conj* [gen] jusqu'à ce que (+ *subjunctive*). ‖ (*after negative*) avant que (+ *subjunctive*).

untimely [ʌn'taɪmlɪ] *adj* [death] prématuré(e); [remark] mal à propos; [moment] mal choisi(e).

untold [ˌʌn'təʊld] *adj* [amount, wealth] incalculable; [suffering, joy] indescriptible.

untrue [ˌʌn'truː] *adj* [not accurate] faux (fausse), qui n'est pas vrai(e).

unused [*sense 1* ˌʌn'juːzd, *sense 2* ʌn'juːst] *adj* [clothes] neuf (neuve); [machine] qui n'a jamais servi. ‖ [unaccustomed]: **to be ~ to sthg/to doing sthg** ne pas avoir l'habitude de qqch/de faire qqch.

unusual [ʌn'juːʒl] *adj* rare, inhabituel(elle).

unusually [ʌn'juːʒəlɪ] *adv* exceptionnellement.

unveil [ˌʌn'veɪl] *vt lit & fig* dévoiler.

unwanted [ˌʌn'wɒntɪd] *adj* [object] dont on ne se sert pas; [child] non désiré(e); **to feel ~** se sentir mal-aimé(e).

unwavering [ʌn'weɪvərɪŋ] *adj* [determination] inébranlable.

unwelcome [ʌn'welkəm] *adj* [news, situation] fâcheux(euse); [visitor] importun(e).

unwell [ˌʌn'wel] *adj*: **to be/feel ~** ne pas être/se sentir bien.

unwieldy [ʌn'wiːldɪ] *adj* [cumbersome] peu maniable. ‖ *fig* [system] lourd(e).

unwilling [ˌʌn'wɪlɪŋ] *adj*: **to be ~ to do sthg** ne pas vouloir faire qqch.

unwind [ˌʌn'waɪnd] (*pt & pp* **-wound**) **1** *rt* dérouler. **2** *ri fig* [person] se détendre.

unwise [ˌʌn'waɪz] *adj* imprudent(e), peu sage.

unworkable [ˌʌn'wɜːkəbl] *adj* impraticable.

unworthy [ʌn'wɜːðɪ] *adj* [undeserving]: **~ (of)** indigne (de).

unwound [ˌʌn'waʊnd] *pt & pp* → **unwind**.

unwrap [ˌʌn'ræp] *vt* défaire.

unwritten law [ˌʌn'rɪtn-] *n* droit *m* coutumier.

up [ʌp] **1** *adv* [towards or in a higher position] en haut; **she's ~ in her bedroom** elle est en haut dans sa chambre; **prices are going ~** les prix augmentent; **~ there là-haut.** || [into an upright position]: **to stand ~** se lever; **to sit ~** s'asseoir (bien droit). || [northwards]: **I'm coming ~ to York next week** je viens à York la semaine prochaine; **~ north** dans le nord. || [along a road, river]: **their house is a little further ~** leur maison est un peu plus loin. **2** *prep* [towards or in a higher position] en haut de; **~ a ladder** sur une échelle; **I went ~ the stairs** j'ai monté l'escalier. || [at far end of]: **they live ~ the road from us** ils habitent un peu plus haut OR loin que nous (dans la même rue). || [against current of river]: **to sail ~ the Amazon** remonter l'Amazone en bateau. **3** *adj* [out of bed] levé(e); **I was ~ at six today** je me suis levé à six heures aujourd'hui. || [at an end]: **time's ~** c'est l'heure. || *inf* [wrong]: **what's ~?** qu'est-ce qui ne va pas?, qu'est-ce qu'il y a? **4** *n*: **~s and downs** hauts et bas *mpl*. ○ **up and down 1** *adv*: **to jump ~ and down** sauter; **to walk ~ and down** faire les cent pas. **2** *prep*: **we walked ~ and down the avenue** nous avons arpenté l'avenue. ○ **up to** *prep* [indicating level] jusqu'à; **it's not ~ to standard** ce n'est pas de la qualité voulue, ceci n'a pas le niveau requis. || [well or able enough for]: **to be ~ to doing sthg** [able to] être capable de faire qqch; [well enough for] être en état de faire qqch; **my French isn't ~ to much** mon français ne vaut pas grand-chose OR n'est pas fameux. || *inf* [secretly doing something]: **what are you ~ to?** qu'est-ce que tu fabriques?; **they're ~ to something** ils mijotent quelque chose, ils préparent un coup. || [indicating responsibility]: **it's not ~ to me to decide** ce n'est pas moi qui décide, il ne m'appartient pas de décider; **it's ~ to you** c'est à vous de voir. ○ **up to, up until** *prep* jusqu'à.

up-and-coming *adj* à l'avenir prometteur.

upbringing ['ʌpˌbrɪŋɪŋ] *n* éducation *f*.

update [ˌʌp'deɪt] *vt* mettre à jour.

upheaval [ʌp'hiːvl] *n* bouleversement *m*.

upheld [ʌp'held] *pt & pp* → **uphold**.

uphill [ˌʌp'hɪl] **1** *adj* [slope, path] qui monte. || *fig* [task] ardu(e). **2** *adv*: **to go ~** monter.

uphold [ʌp'həʊld] (*pt & pp* **-held**) *vt* [law] maintenir; [decision, system] soutenir.

upholstery [ʌp'həʊlstəri] *n* rembourrage *m*; [of car] garniture *f* intérieure.

upkeep ['ʌpkiːp] *n* entretien *m*.

up-market *adj* haut de gamme (*inv*).

upon [ə'pɒn] *prep fml* sur; **~ hearing the news ...** à ces nouvelles ....

upper ['ʌpər] **1** *adj* supérieur(e). **2** *n* [of shoe] empeigne *f*.

upper class *n*: **the ~** la haute société. ○ **upper-class** *adj* [accent, person] aristocratique.

upper hand *n*: **to have the ~** avoir le dessus.

uppermost ['ʌpəməʊst] *adj* le plus haut (la plus haute); **it was ~ in his mind** c'était sa préoccupation majeure.

upright [*adj sense 1* & *adv* ˌʌp'raɪt, *adj sense 2* & *n* 'ʌpraɪt] **1** *adj* [person] droit(e); [structure] vertical(e); [chair] à dossier droit. || *fig* [honest] droit(e). **2** *adv* [stand, sit] droit. **3** *n* montant *m*.

uprising ['ʌpˌraɪzɪŋ] *n* soulèvement *m*.

uproar ['ʌprɔːr] *n* (*U*) [commotion] tumulte *m*. || [protest] protestations *fpl*.

uproot [ʌp'ruːt] *vt lit & fig* déraciner.

upset [ʌp'set] (*pt & pp* **upset**) **1** *adj* [distressed] peiné(e), triste; [offended] vexé(e). || MED: **to have an ~ stomach** avoir l'estomac dérangé. **2** *vt* [distress] faire de la peine à. || [plan, operation] déranger. || [over-turn] renverser.

upshot ['ʌpʃɒt] *n* résultat *m*.

upside down [ˌʌpsaɪd-] **1** *adj* à l'envers. **2** *adv* à l'envers; **to turn sthg ~** *fig* mettre qqch sens dessus dessous.

upstairs [ˌʌp'steəz] **1** *adj* d'en haut, du dessus. **2** *adv* en haut. **3** *n* étage *m*.

upstart ['ʌpstɑːt] *n* parvenu *m*, -e *f*.

upstream [ˌʌp'striːm] **1** *adj* d'amont; **to be ~ (from)** être en amont (de). **2** *adv* vers l'amont; [swim] contre le courant.

upsurge ['ʌpsɜːdʒ] *n*: **~ (of/in)** recrudescence *f* (de).

uptake ['ʌpteɪk] *n*: **to be quick on the ~** saisir vite.

uptight [ʌp'taɪt] *adj inf* tendu(e).

up-to-date *adj* [modern] moderne. || [most recent - news] tout dernier (toute dernière). || [informed]: **to keep ~ with** se tenir au courant de.

upturn ['ʌptɜːn] *n*: **~ (in)** reprise *f* (de).

upward ['ʌpwəd] **1** *adj* [movement] ascendant(e); [look, rise] vers le haut. **2** *adv Am* = **upwards**.

upwards ['ʌpwədz] *adv* vers le haut.

uranium [jʊ'reɪnjəm] *n* uranium *m*.

urban ['ɜːbən] *adj* urbain(e).

urbane [ɜːˈbeɪn] *adj* courtois(e).

urchin [ˈɜːtʃɪn] *n* dated gamin *m*, -e *f*.

Urdu [ˈʊəduː] *n* ourdou *m*.

urge [ɜːdʒ] **1** *n* forte envie *f*. **2** *vt* [try to persuade]: **to ~ sb to do sthg** pousser qqn à faire qqch, presser qqn de faire qqch. ‖ [advocate] conseiller.

urgency [ˈɜːdʒənsɪ] *n* (U) urgence *f*.

urgent [ˈɜːdʒənt] *adj* [letter, case, request] urgent(e); [plea, voice, need] pressant(e).

urinal [ˌjʊəˈraɪnl] *n* urinoir *m*.

urinate [ˈjʊərɪneɪt] *vi* uriner.

urine [ˈjʊərɪn] *n* urine *f*.

urn [ɜːn] *n* [for ashes] urne *f*. ‖ [for tea]: **tea ~** fontaine *f* à thé.

Uruguay [ˈjʊərəɡwaɪ] *n* Uruguay *m*.

us [ʌs] *pers pron* nous; **can you see/hear ~?** vous nous voyez/entendez?; **it's ~** c'est nous; **you can't expect US to do it** vous ne pouvez pas exiger que ce soit nous qui le fassions; **she gave it to ~** elle nous l'a donné; **with/without ~** avec/sans nous; **they are more wealthy than ~** ils sont plus riches que nous; **some of ~** quelques-uns d'entre nous.

US *n abbr of* United States.

USA *n abbr of* United States of America.

usage [ˈjuːzɪdʒ] *n* LING usage *m*. ‖ (U) [handling, treatment] traitement *m*.

use [*n & aux vb* juːs, *vt* juːz] **1** *n* [act of using] utilisation *f*, emploi *m*; **to be in ~** être utilisé; **to be out of ~** être hors d'usage; **to make ~ of sthg** utiliser qqch. ‖ [ability to use] usage *m*. ‖ [usefulness]: **to be of ~** être utile; **it's no ~** ça ne sert à rien; **what's the ~ (of doing sthg)?** à quoi bon (faire qqch)? **2** *aux vb*: **I ~d to live in London** avant j'habitais à Londres; **there ~d to be a tree here** (autrefois) il y avait un arbre ici. **3** *vt* [gen] utiliser, se servir de, employer. ‖ *pej* [exploit] se servir de. ○ **use up** *vt sep* [supply] épuiser; [food] finir; [money] dépenser.

used [*senses 1 and 2* juːzd, *sense 3* juːst] *adj* [handkerchief, towel] sale. ‖ [car] d'occasion. ‖ [accustomed]: **to be ~ to sthg/to doing sthg** avoir l'habitude de qqch/de faire qqch; **to get ~ to sthg** s'habituer à qqch.

useful [ˈjuːsfʊl] *adj* utile.

useless [ˈjuːslɪs] *adj* [gen] inutile.

user [ˈjuːzər] *n* [of product, machine] utilisateur *m*, -trice *f*; [of service] usager *m*.

user-friendly *adj* convivial(e), facile à utiliser.

usher [ˈʌʃər] **1** *n* placeur *m*. **2** *vt*: **to ~ sb in/out** faire entrer/sortir qqn.

usherette [ˌʌʃəˈret] *n* ouvreuse *f*.

USSR (*abbr of* **Union of Soviet Socialist Republics**) *n*: **the (former) ~** l'(ex-)URSS *f*.

usual [ˈjuːʒəl] *adj* habituel(elle); **as ~** comme d'habitude.

usually [ˈjuːʒəlɪ] *adv* d'habitude, d'ordinaire.

usurp [juːˈzɜːp] *vt* usurper.

utensil [juːˈtensl] *n* ustensile *m*.

uterus [ˈjuːtərəs] (*pl* **-ri** [-raɪ] OR **-ruses**) *n* utérus *m*.

utility [juːˈtɪlətɪ] *n* (U) [usefulness] utilité *f*. ‖ [public service] service *m* public. ‖ COMPUT utilitaire *m*.

utility room *n* buanderie *f*.

utilize, -ise [ˈjuːtəlaɪz] *vt* utiliser; [resources] exploiter, utiliser.

utmost [ˈʌtməʊst] **1** *adj* le plus grand (la plus grande). **2** *n*: **to do one's ~** faire tout son possible, faire l'impossible; **to the ~** au plus haut point.

utter [ˈʌtər] **1** *adj* total(e), complet(ète). **2** *vt* prononcer; [cry] pousser.

utterly [ˈʌtəlɪ] *adv* complètement.

U-turn *n* demi-tour *m*; *fig* revirement *m*.

v[1] (*pl* **v's** OR **vs**), **V** (*pl* **V's** OR **Vs**) [viː] *n* [letter] v *m inv*, V *m inv*.

v[2] (*abbr of* **vide**) [cross-reference] v. ‖ *abbr of* **versus**. ‖ (*abbr of* **volt**) v.

vacancy [ˈveɪkənsɪ] *n* [job] poste *m* vacant. ‖ [room available] chambre *f* à louer; **"no vacancies"** «complet».

vacant [ˈveɪkənt] *adj* [room] inoccupé(e); [chair, toilet] libre. ‖ [job, post] vacant(e). ‖ [look, expression] distrait(e).

vacant lot *n* terrain *m* inoccupé; [for sale] terrain *m* à vendre.

vacate [vəˈkeɪt] *vt* quitter.

vacation [vəˈkeɪʃn] *n Am* vacances *fpl*.

vacationer [vəˈkeɪʃənər] *n Am* vacancier *m*, -ière *f*.

vaccinate ['væksɪneɪt] *vt* vacciner.

vaccine [*Br* 'væksiːn, *Am* væk'siːn] *n* vaccin *m*.

vacuum ['vækjuəm] **1** *n* TECH & *fig* vide *m*. ‖ [cleaner] aspirateur *m*. **2** *vt* [room] passer l'aspirateur dans; [carpet] passer à l'aspirateur.

vacuum cleaner *n* aspirateur *m*.

vacuum-packed *adj* emballé(e) sous vide.

vagina [və'dʒaɪnə] *n* vagin *m*.

vagrant ['veɪgrənt] *n* vagabond *m*, -e *f*.

vague [veɪg] *adj* [gen] vague, imprécis(e). ‖ [absent-minded] distrait(e).

vaguely ['veɪglɪ] *adv* vaguement.

vain [veɪn] *adj* [futile, worthless] vain(e). ‖ *pej* [conceited] vaniteux(euse). ○ **in vain** *adv* en vain, vainement.

valentine card ['væləntain-] *n* carte *f* de la Saint-Valentin.

Valentine's Day ['væləntainz-] *n*: (St) ~ la Saint-Valentin.

valet ['væleɪ, 'vælɪt] *n* valet *m* de chambre.

valiant ['væljənt] *adj* vaillant(e).

valid ['vælɪd] *adj* [reasonable] valable. ‖ [legally usable] valide.

valley ['vælɪ] (*pl* **valleys**) *n* vallée *f*.

valour *Br*, **valor** *Am* ['vælər] *n* (*U*) *fml* & *literary* bravoure *f*.

valuable ['væljuəbl] *adj* [advice, time, information] précieux(ieuse). ‖ [object, jewel] de valeur. ○ **valuables** *npl* objets *mpl* de valeur.

valuation [,væljʊ'eɪʃn] *n* (*U*) [pricing] estimation *f*, expertise *f*. ‖ [estimated price] valeur *f* estimée.

value ['væljuː] **1** *n* valeur *f*; **to be good** ~ être d'un bon rapport qualité-prix. **2** *vt* [estimate price of] expertiser. ‖ [cherish] apprécier. ○ **values** *npl* [morals] valeurs *fpl*.

value-added tax [-ædɪd-] *n* taxe *f* sur la valeur ajoutée.

valued ['væljuːd] *adj* précieux(ieuse).

valve [vælv] *n* [on tyre] valve *f*; TECH soupape *f*.

van [væn] *n* AUT camionnette *f*.

vandal ['vændl] *n* vandale *mf*.

vandalism ['vændəlɪzm] *n* vandalisme *m*.

vandalize, -ise ['vændəlaɪz] *vt* saccager.

vanguard ['vængɑːd] *n* avant-garde *f*.

vanilla [və'nɪlə] *n* vanille *f*.

vanish ['vænɪʃ] *vi* disparaître.

vanity ['vænɪtɪ] *n* (*U*) *pej* vanité *f*.

vantagepoint ['vɑːntɪdʒ,pɔɪnt] *n* [for view] bon endroit *m*; *fig* position *f* avantageuse.

vapour *Br*, **vapor** *Am* ['veɪpər] *n* (*U*) vapeur *f*; [condensation] buée *f*.

variable ['veərɪəbl] *adj* variable.

variance ['veərɪəns] *n fml*: **at** ~ (**with**) en désaccord (avec).

variation [,veərɪ'eɪʃn] *n*: ~ (**in**) variation *f* (de).

varicose veins ['værɪkəus-] *npl* varices *fpl*.

varied ['veərɪd] *adj* varié(e).

variety [və'raɪətɪ] *n* [gen] variété *f*. ‖ [type] variété *f*, sorte *f*.

variety show *n* spectacle *m* de variétés.

various ['veərɪəs] *adj* [several] plusieurs. ‖ [different] divers.

varnish ['vɑːnɪʃ] **1** *n* vernis *m*. **2** *vt* vernir.

vary ['veərɪ] **1** *vt* varier. **2** *vi*: **to** ~ (**in/with**) varier (en/selon), changer (en/selon).

vase [*Br* vɑːz, *Am* veɪz] *n* vase *m*.

Vaseline® ['væsəliːn] *n* vaseline® *f*.

vast [vɑːst] *adj* vaste, immense.

vat [væt] *n* cuve *f*.

VAT [væt, viːeɪ'tiː] (*abbr of* **value added tax**) *n* TVA *f*.

Vatican ['vætɪkən] *n*: **the** ~ le Vatican.

vault [vɔːlt] **1** *n* [in bank] chambre *f* forte. ‖ [in church] caveau *m*. **2** *vi*: **to** ~ **over** sthg sauter (par-dessus) qqch.

VCR (*abbr of* **video cassette recorder**) *n* magnétoscope *m*.

VD *n abbr of* **venereal disease**.

VDU (*abbr of* **visual display unit**) *n* moniteur *m*.

veal [viːl] *n* (*U*) veau *m*.

veer [vɪər] *vi* virer.

vegan ['viːgən] *adj* végétalien(ienne).

vegetable ['vedʒtəbl] **1** *n* légume *m*. **2** *adj* [matter, protein] végétal(e); [soup, casserole] de OR aux légumes.

vegetarian [,vedʒɪ'teərɪən] *adj* végétarien(ienne).

vegetation [,vedʒɪ'teɪʃn] *n* (*U*) végétation *f*.

vehement ['viːəmənt] *adj* véhément(e).

vehicle ['viːəkl] *n lit* & *fig* véhicule *m*.

veil [veɪl] *n lit* & *fig* voile *m*.

vein [veɪn] *n* ANAT veine *f*. ‖ [of leaf] nervure *f*. ‖ [of mineral] filon *m*.

velocity [vɪ'lɒsətɪ] *n* vélocité *f*.

velvet ['velvɪt] *n* velours *m*.

vendetta [ven'detə] n vendetta f.

vending machine ['vendɪŋ-] n distributeur m automatique.

vendor ['vendɔːr] n fml [salesperson] marchand m, -e f. ‖ JUR vendeur m, -eresse f.

veneer [və'nɪər] n placage m; fig apparence f.

venereal disease [vɪ'nɪərɪəl-] n maladie f vénérienne.

venetian blind [vɪ,niːʃn-] n store m vénitien.

Venezuela [,venɪz'weɪlə] n Venezuela m.

vengeance ['vendʒəns] n vengeance f.

venison ['venɪzn] n venaison f.

venom ['venəm] n lit & fig venin m.

vent [vent] **1** n [pipe] tuyau m; [opening] orifice m. **2** vt [anger, feelings] donner libre cours à; **to ~ sthg on sb** décharger qqch sur qqn.

ventilate ['ventɪleɪt] vt ventiler.

ventilator ['ventɪleɪtər] n ventilateur m.

ventriloquist [ven'trɪləkwɪst] n ventriloque mf.

venture ['ventʃər] **1** n entreprise f. **2** vt risquer; **to ~ to do sthg** se permettre de faire qqch. **3** vi s'aventurer.

venue ['venjuː] n lieu m.

veranda(h) [və'rændə] n véranda f.

verb [vɜːb] n verbe m.

verbal ['vɜːbl] adj verbal(e).

verbatim [vɜː'beɪtɪm] adj & adv mot pour mot.

verbose [vɜː'bəʊs] adj verbeux(euse).

verdict ['vɜːdɪkt] n JUR verdict m. ‖ [opinion]: ~ (on) avis m (sur).

verge [vɜːdʒ] n [of lawn] bordure f; [of road] bas-côté m, accotement m. ‖ [brink]: **on the ~ of sthg** au bord de qqch; **on the ~ of doing sthg** sur le point de faire qqch. ○ **verge (up)on** vt fus friser, approcher de.

verify ['verɪfaɪ] vt vérifier.

vermin ['vɜːmɪn] npl vermine f.

vermouth ['vɜːməθ] n vermouth m.

versa ['vɜːsə] → vice versa.

versatile ['vɜːsətaɪl] adj [person, player] aux talents multiples; [machine, tool, food] souple d'emploi.

verse [vɜːs] n (U) [poetry] vers mpl. ‖ [stanza] strophe f. ‖ [in Bible] verset m.

versed [vɜːst] adj: **to be well ~ in sthg** être versé(e) dans qqch.

version ['vɜːʃn] n version f.

versus ['vɜːsəs] prep SPORT contre. ‖ [as opposed to] par opposition à.

vertebra ['vɜːtɪbrə] (pl -brae [-briː]) n vertèbre f.

vertical ['vɜːtɪkl] adj vertical(e).

vertigo ['vɜːtɪgəʊ] n (U) vertige m.

verve [vɜːv] n verve f.

very ['verɪ] **1** adv [as intensifier] très; ~ **much** beaucoup. **2** adj: **the ~ room/book** la pièce/le livre même; **the ~ man/thing I've been looking for** juste l'homme/la chose que je cherchais; **at the ~ least** tout au moins; ~ **last/first** tout dernier/premier; **of one's ~ own** bien à soi. ○ **very well** adv très bien; **I can't ~ well tell him …** je ne peux tout de même pas lui dire que …

vessel ['vesl] n fml [boat] vaisseau m. ‖ [container] récipient m.

vest [vest] n Am [waistcoat] gilet m.

vested interest ['vestɪd-] n: ~ **(in)** intérêt m particulier (à).

vestibule ['vestɪbjuːl] n fml [entrance hall] vestibule m.

vestige ['vestɪdʒ] n vestige m.

vestry ['vestrɪ] n sacristie f.

vet [vet] vt [candidates] examiner avec soin.

veteran ['vetrən] **1** adj [experienced] chevronné(e). **2** n MIL ancien combattant m, vétéran m. ‖ [experienced person] vétéran m.

veterinarian [,vetərɪ'neərɪən] n Am vétérinaire mf.

veto ['viːtəʊ] (pl -es, pt & pp -ed, cont -ing) **1** n veto m. **2** vt opposer son veto à.

vex [veks] vt contrarier.

vexed question [,vekst-] n question f controversée.

vg (abbr of very good) tb.

VHF (abbr of very high frequency) VHF.

VHS (abbr of video home system) n VHS m.

via ['vaɪə] prep [travelling through] via, par. ‖ [by means of] au moyen de.

viable ['vaɪəbl] adj viable.

vibrate [vaɪ'breɪt] vi vibrer.

vicar ['vɪkər] n [in Church of England] pasteur m.

vicarage ['vɪkərɪdʒ] n presbytère m.

vicarious [vɪ'keərɪəs] adj: **to take a ~ pleasure in sthg** retirer du plaisir indirectement de qqch.

vice [vaɪs] n [immorality, fault] vice m. ‖ [tool] étau m.

vice-chairman n vice-président m, -e f.

vice-chancellor *n* UNIV président *m*, -e *f*.

vice-president *n* vice-président *m*, -e *f*.

vice versa [,vaɪsɪ-] *adv* vice versa.

vicinity [vɪ'sɪnətɪ] *n*: **in the ~ (of)** aux alentours (de), dans les environs (de).

vicious ['vɪʃəs] *adj* violent(e), brutal(e).

vicious circle *n* cercle *m* vicieux.

victim ['vɪktɪm] *n* victime *f*.

victimize, -ise ['vɪktɪmaɪz] *vt* faire une victime de.

victor ['vɪktər] *n* vainqueur *m*.

victorious [vɪk'tɔːrɪəs] *adj* victorieux(ieuse).

victory ['vɪktərɪ] *n*: **~ (over)** victoire *f* (sur).

video ['vɪdɪəʊ] (*pl* -s, *pt* & *pp* -ed, *cont* -ing) **1** *n* [medium, recording] vidéo *f*. ‖ [machine] magnétoscope *m*. **2** *vt* [using video recorder] magnétoscoper. ‖ [using camera] faire une vidéo de, filmer.

video camera *n* caméra *f* vidéo.

video cassette *n* vidéocassette *f*.

video game *n* jeu *m* vidéo.

videorecorder ['vɪdɪəʊrɪ,kɔːdər] *n* magnétoscope *m*.

video shop *n* vidéoclub *m*.

videotape ['vɪdɪəʊteɪp] *n* [cassette] vidéocassette *f*. ‖ (*U*) [ribbon] bande *f* vidéo.

vie [vaɪ] (*pt* & *pp* **vied**, *cont* **vying**) *vi*: **to ~ for sthg** lutter pour qqch; **to ~ with sb (for sthg/to do sthg)** rivaliser avec qqn (pour qqch/pour faire qqch).

Vienna [vɪ'enə] *n* Vienne.

Vietnam [*Br* ,vjet'næm, *Am* ,vjet'nɑːm] *n* Viêt-nam *m*.

Vietnamese [,vjetnə'miːz] **1** *adj* vietnamien(ienne). **2** *n* [language] vietnamien *m*. **3** *npl*: **the ~** les Vietnamiens.

view [vjuː] **1** *n* [opinion] opinion *f*, avis *m*; **in my ~** à mon avis. ‖ [scene, ability to see] vue *f*; **to come into ~** apparaître. **2** *vt* [consider] considérer. ‖ [examine - gen] examiner; [- house] visiter. ○ **in view of** *prep* vu, étant donné.

viewer ['vjuːər] *n* TV téléspectateur *m*, - trice *f*. ‖ [for slides] visionneuse *f*.

viewfinder ['vjuː,faɪndər] *n* viseur *m*.

viewpoint ['vjuːpɔɪnt] *n* point *m* de vue.

vigil ['vɪdʒɪl] *n* veille *f*; RELIG vigile *f*.

vigilante [,vɪdʒɪ'læntɪ] *n* membre *m* d'un groupe d'autodéfense.

vigorous ['vɪɡərəs] *adj* vigoureux(euse).

vile [vaɪl] *adj* [mood] massacrant(e), exécrable; [person, act] vil(e), ignoble; [food] infect(e), exécrable.

villa ['vɪlə] *n* villa *f*; [bungalow] pavillon *m*.

village ['vɪlɪdʒ] *n* village *m*.

villager ['vɪlɪdʒər] *n* villageois *m*, -e *f*.

villain ['vɪlən] *n* [of film, book] méchant *m*, -e *f*; [of play] traître *m*. ‖ [criminal] bandit *m*.

vindicate ['vɪndɪkeɪt] *vt* justifier.

vindictive [vɪn'dɪktɪv] *adj* vindicatif(ive).

vine [vaɪn] *n* vigne *f*.

vinegar ['vɪnɪɡər] *n* vinaigre *m*.

vineyard ['vɪnjəd] *n* vignoble *m*.

vintage ['vɪntɪdʒ] **1** *adj* [classic] typique. **2** *n* année *f*, millésime *m*.

vintage wine *n* vin *m* de grand cru.

vinyl ['vaɪnɪl] *n* vinyle *m*.

viola [vɪ'əʊlə] *n* alto *m*.

violate ['vaɪəleɪt] *vt* violer.

violence ['vaɪələns] *n* violence *f*.

violent ['vaɪələnt] *adj* [gen] violent(e).

violet ['vaɪələt] **1** *adj* violet(ette). **2** *n* [flower] violette *f*. ‖ [colour] violet *m*.

violin [,vaɪə'lɪn] *n* violon *m*.

violinist [,vaɪə'lɪnɪst] *n* violoniste *mf*.

VIP (*abbr of* **very important person**) *n* VIP *mf*.

viper ['vaɪpər] *n* vipère *f*.

virgin ['vɜːdʒɪn] **1** *adj literary* [land, forest, soil] vierge. **2** *n* [woman] vierge *f*.

Virgo ['vɜːɡəʊ] (*pl* -s) *n* Vierge *f*.

virile ['vɪraɪl] *adj* viril(e).

virtually ['vɜːtʃʊəlɪ] *adv* virtuellement, pratiquement.

virtual reality *n* réalité *f* virtuelle.

virtue ['vɜːtʃuː] *n* [good quality] vertu *f*. ‖ [benefit]: **~ (in doing sthg)** mérite *m* (à faire qqch).

virtuous ['vɜːtʃʊəs] *adj* vertueux(euse).

virus ['vaɪrəs] *n* COMPUT & MED virus *m*.

visa ['viːzə] *n* visa *m*.

vis-à-vis [,viːzɑː'viː] *prep fml* par rapport à.

viscose ['vɪskəʊs] *n* viscose *f*.

visibility [,vɪzɪ'bɪlətɪ] *n* visibilité *f*.

visible ['vɪzəbl] *adj* visible.

vision ['vɪʒn] *n* (*U*) [ability to see] vue *f*. ‖ [foresight, dream] vision *f*.

visit ['vɪzɪt] **1** *n* visite *f*. **2** *vt* [person] rendre visite à; [place] visiter.

visiting hours ['vɪzɪtɪŋ-] *npl* heures *fpl* de visite.

visitor ['vɪzɪtər] *n* [to person] invité *m*, -e *f*; [to place] visiteur *m*, -euse *f*.

visitors' book *n* livre *m* d'or; [in hotel] registre *m*.

visor ['vaɪzər] *n* visière *f*.

vista ['vɪstə] *n* [view] vue *f*.

visual ['vɪʒʊəl] *adj* visuel(elle).

visual aids *npl* supports *mpl* visuels.

visual display unit *n* écran *m* de visualisation.

visualize, -ise ['vɪʒʊəlaɪz] *vt* se représenter, s'imaginer.

vital ['vaɪtl] *adj* [essential] essentiel(ielle).

vitally ['vaɪtəlɪ] *adv* absolument.

vital statistics *npl inf* [of woman] mensurations *fpl*.

vitamin [*Br* 'vɪtəmɪn, *Am* 'vaɪtəmɪn] *n* vitamine *f*.

vivacious [vɪ'veɪʃəs] *adj* enjoué(e).

vivid ['vɪvɪd] *adj* [bright] vif (vive). || [clear - description] vivant(e); [- memory] net (nette), précis(e).

vividly ['vɪvɪdlɪ] *adv* [describe] d'une manière vivante; [remember] clairement.

vixen ['vɪksn] *n* [fox] renarde *f*.

V-neck *n* [neck] décolleté *m* en V; [sweater] pull *m* à décolleté en V.

vocabulary [və'kæbjʊlərɪ] *n* vocabulaire *m*.

vocal ['vəʊkl] *adj* [outspoken] qui se fait entendre. || [of the voice] vocal(e).

vocal cords *npl* cordes *fpl* vocales.

vocation [vəʊ'keɪʃn] *n* vocation *f*.

vocational [vəʊ'keɪʃənl] *adj* professionnel(elle).

vociferous [və'sɪfərəs] *adj* bruyant(e).

vodka ['vɒdkə] *n* vodka *f*.

vogue [vəʊg] *n* vogue *f*, mode *f*; **in ~ en** vogue, à la mode.

voice [vɔɪs] **1** *n* [gen] voix *f*. **2** *vt* [opinion, emotion] exprimer.

void [vɔɪd] **1** *adj* [invalid] nul (nulle); → **null**. || *fml* [empty]: **~ of** dépourvu(e) de, dénué(e) de. **2** *n* vide *m*.

volatile [*Br* 'vɒlətaɪl, *Am* 'vɒlətl] *adj* [situation] explosif(ive); [person] lunatique, versatile; [market] instable.

volcano [vɒl'keɪnəʊ] (*pl* **-es** OR **-s**) *n* volcan *m*.

volley ['vɒlɪ] (*pl* **volleys**) **1** *n* [of gunfire] salve *f*. || *fig* [of questions, curses] torrent *m*; [of blows] volée *f*, pluie *f*. || SPORT volée *f*. **2** *vt* frapper à la volée, reprendre de volée.

volleyball ['vɒlɪbɔːl] *n* volley-ball *m*.

volt [vəʊlt] *n* volt *m*.

voltage ['vəʊltɪdʒ] *n* voltage *m*, tension *f*.

volume ['vɒljuːm] *n* [gen] volume *m*. || [of work, letters] quantité *f*; [of traffic] densité *f*.

voluntarily [*Br* 'vɒləntrɪlɪ, *Am* ˌvɒlən-'terəlɪ] *adv* volontairement.

voluntary ['vɒləntrɪ] *adj* [not obligatory] volontaire. || [unpaid] bénévole.

volunteer [ˌvɒlən'tɪər] **1** *n* [gen & MIL] volontaire *mf*. || [unpaid worker] bénévole *mf*. **2** *vt* [offer]: **to ~ to do sthg** se proposer OR se porter volontaire pour faire qqch. || [information, advice] donner spontanément. **3** *vi* [offer one's services]: **to ~ (for)** se porter volontaire (pour), proposer ses services (pour). || MIL s'engager comme volontaire.

vomit ['vɒmɪt] **1** *n* vomi *m*. **2** *vi* vomir.

vote [vəʊt] **1** *n* [individual decision]: **~ (for/against)** vote *m* (pour/contre), voix *f* (pour/contre). || [ballot] vote *m*. || [right to vote] droit *m* de vote. **2** *vt* [declare] élire. || [choose]: **to ~ to do sthg** voter OR se prononcer pour faire; **they ~d to return to work** ils ont voté le retour au travail. **3** *vi*: **to ~ (for/against)** voter (pour/contre).

vote of thanks (*pl* **votes of thanks**) *n* discours *m* de remerciement.

voter ['vəʊtər] *n* électeur *m*, -trice *f*.

voting ['vəʊtɪŋ] *n* scrutin *m*.

vouch [vaʊtʃ] ○ **vouch for** *vt fus* répondre de, se porter garant de.

voucher ['vaʊtʃər] *n* bon *m*, coupon *m*.

vow [vaʊ] **1** *n* vœu *m*, serment *m*. **2** *vt*: **to ~ to do sthg** jurer de faire qqch.

vowel ['vaʊəl] *n* voyelle *f*.

voyage ['vɔɪɪdʒ] *n* voyage *m* en mer; [in space] vol *m*.

vs *abbr of* **versus**.

vulgar ['vʌlgər] *adj* [in bad taste] vulgaire. || [offensive] grossier(ière).

vulnerable ['vʌlnərəbl] *adj* vulnérable; **~ to** [attack] exposé(e) à; [colds] sensible à.

vulture ['vʌltʃər] *n lit & fig* vautour *m*.

w (*pl* **w's** OR **ws**), **W** (*pl* **W's** OR **Ws**) ['dʌblju:] *n* [letter] w *m inv*, W *m inv*. ○ **W** (*abbr of* **west**) O, W. ‖ (*abbr of* **watt**) w.

wad [wɒd] *n* [of cotton wool, paper] tampon *m*. ‖ [of banknotes, documents] liasse *f*.

waddle ['wɒdl] *vi* se dandiner.

wade [weɪd] *vi* patauger. ○ **wade through** *vt fus fig* se taper.

wading pool ['weɪdɪŋ-] *n Am* pataugeoire *f*.

wafer ['weɪfər] *n* [thin biscuit] gaufrette *f*.

waffle ['wɒfl] *n* CULIN gaufre *f*.

waft [wɑːft, wɒft] *vi* flotter.

wag [wæg] **1** *vt* remuer, agiter. **2** *vi* [tail] remuer.

wage [weɪdʒ] **1** *n* salaire *m*, paie *f*, paye *f*. **2** *vt*: **to ~ war against** faire la guerre à. ○ **wages** *npl* salaire *m*.

wage earner [-,ɜːnər] *n* salarié *m*, -e *f*.

wager ['weɪdʒər] *n* pari *m*.

waggle ['wægl] *inf vt* agiter, remuer; [ears] remuer.

wagon ['wægən] *n* [horse-drawn] chariot *m*, charrette *f*. ‖ *Br* RAIL wagon *m*.

wail [weɪl] **1** *n* gémissement *m*. **2** *vi* gémir.

waist [weɪst] *n* taille *f*.

waistcoat ['weɪskəʊt] *n* gilet *m*.

waistline ['weɪstlaɪn] *n* taille *f*.

wait [weɪt] **1** *n* attente *f*. **2** *vi* attendre; **I can't ~ to do sthg** je brûle d'impatience de faire qqch; **~ and see!** tu vas bien voir! ○ **wait for** *vt fus* attendre; **to ~ for sb to do sthg** attendre que qqn fasse qqch. ○ **wait up** *vi* veiller, ne pas se coucher.

waiter ['weɪtər] *n* garçon *m*, serveur *m*.

waiting list ['weɪtɪŋ-] *n* liste *f* d'attente.

waiting room ['weɪtɪŋ-] *n* salle *f* d'attente.

waitress ['weɪtrɪs] *n* serveuse *f*.

waive [weɪv] *vt* [fee] renoncer à; [rule] prévoir une dérogation à.

wake [weɪk] (*pt* **woke** OR **-d**, *pp* **woken** OR **-d**) **1** *n* [of ship] sillage *m*. **2** *vt* réveiller. **3** *vi* se réveiller. ○ **wake up 1** *vt sep* réveiller. **2** *vi* [wake] se réveiller.

waken ['weɪkən] *fml* **1** *vt* réveiller. **2** *vi* se réveiller.

Wales [weɪlz] *n* pays *m* de Galles.

walk [wɔːk] **1** *n* [way of walking] démarche *f*, façon *f* de marcher. ‖ [journey - for pleasure] promenade *f*; [- long distance] marche *f*; **to go for a ~** aller se promener, aller faire une promenade. **2** *vt* [accompany - person] accompagner; [- dog] promener. ‖ [distance] faire à pied. **3** *vi* [gen] marcher. ‖ [for pleasure] se promener. ○ **walk out** *vi* [leave suddenly] partir. ○ **walk out on** *vt fus* quitter.

walker ['wɔːkər] *n* [for pleasure] promeneur *m*, -euse *f*; [long-distance] marcheur *m*, -euse *f*.

walkie-talkie [,wɔːkɪ'tɔːkɪ] *n* talkie-walkie *m*.

walking ['wɔːkɪŋ] *n* (U) marche *f* à pied, promenade *f*.

walking shoes *npl* chaussures *fpl* de marche.

walking stick *n* canne *f*.

Walkman® ['wɔːkmən] *n* baladeur *m*, Walkman® *m*.

walkout ['wɔːkaʊt] *n* [strike] grève *f*, débrayage *m*.

walkover ['wɔːk,əʊvər] *n* victoire *f* facile.

walkway ['wɔːkweɪ] *n* passage *m*; [between buildings] passerelle *f*.

wall [wɔːl] *n* [of room, building] mur *m*; [of rock, cave] paroi *f*. ‖ ANAT paroi *f*.

wallchart ['wɔːltʃɑːt] *n* planche *f* murale.

walled [wɔːld] *adj* fortifié(e).

wallet ['wɒlɪt] *n* portefeuille *m*.

wallflower ['wɔːl,flaʊər] *n* [plant] giroflée *f*. ‖ *inf fig* [person]: **to be a ~** faire tapisserie.

wallow ['wɒləʊ] *vi* [in liquid] se vautrer.

wallpaper ['wɔːl,peɪpər] **1** *n* papier *m* peint. **2** *vt* tapisser.

Wall Street *n* Wall Street *m* (*quartier financier de New York*).

walnut ['wɔːlnʌt] *n* [nut] noix *f*. ‖ [tree, wood] noyer *m*.

walrus ['wɔːlrəs] (*pl inv* OR **-es**) *n* morse *m*.

waltz [wɔːls] **1** *n* valse *f*. **2** *vi* [dance] valser, danser la valse.

wand [wɒnd] *n* baguette *f*.

wander ['wɒndər] *vi* [person] errer. ||
[mind] divaguer; [thoughts] vagabonder.

wane [weɪn] *vi* [influence, interest] dimi-
nuer, faiblir. || [moon] décroître.

wangle ['wæŋgl] *vt inf* se débrouiller
pour obtenir.

want [wɒnt] **1** *n* [need] besoin *m*. ||
[lack] manque *m*; **for ~ of** faute de, par
manque de. || [deprivation] pauvreté *f*,
besoin *m*. **2** *vt* [desire] vouloir; **to ~ to do
sthg** vouloir faire qqch; **to ~ sb to do sthg**
vouloir que qqn fasse qqch. || *inf* [need]
avoir besoin de.

wanted ['wɒntɪd] *adj*: **to be ~ (by the
police)** être recherché(e) (par la police).

wanton ['wɒntən] *adj* [destruction, ne-
glect] gratuit(e).

war [wɔːr] *n* guerre *f*.

ward [wɔːd] *n* [in hospital] salle *f*. || JUR
pupille *mf*. ○ **ward off** *vt fus* [danger]
écarter; [disease, blow] éviter; [evil spir-
its] éloigner.

warden ['wɔːdn] *n* [of park etc] gardien
m, -ienne *f*. || *Am* [of prison] directeur *m*,
-trice *f*.

warder ['wɔːdər] *n* [in prison] gardien
m, -ienne *f*.

wardrobe ['wɔːdrəub] *n* garde-robe *f*.

warehouse ['weəhaus, *pl* -hauzɪz] *n* entrepôt *m*, magasin *m*.

wares [weəz] *npl* marchandises *fpl*.

warfare ['wɔːfeər] *n* (*U*) guerre *f*.

warhead ['wɔːhed] *n* ogive *f*, tête *f*.

warily ['weərɪlɪ] *adv* avec précaution OR
circonspection.

warm [wɔːm] **1** *adj* [gen] chaud(e); **it's
~ today** il fait chaud aujourd'hui. ||
[friendly] chaleureux(euse). **2** *vt* chauffer. ○ **warm to** *vt fus* [person] se prendre de sympathie pour; [idea, place] se
mettre à aimer. ○ **warm up 1** *vt sep* réchauffer. **2** *vi* [person, room] se réchauf-
fer. || [machine, engine] chauffer. || SPORT
s'échauffer.

warm-hearted [-'hɑːtɪd] *adj* chaleu-
reux(euse), affectueux(euse).

warmly ['wɔːmlɪ] *adv* [in warm clothes]:
to dress ~ s'habiller chaudement. || [in a
friendly way] chaleureusement.

warmth [wɔːmθ] *n* chaleur *f*.

warn [wɔːn] *vt* avertir, prévenir; **to ~ sb
of sthg** avertir qqn de qqch; **to ~ sb not
to do sthg** conseiller à qqn de ne pas
faire qqch, déconseiller à qqn de faire
qqch.

warning ['wɔːnɪŋ] *n* avertissement *m*.

warning light *n* voyant *m*, avertisseur
m lumineux.

warp [wɔːp] **1** *vt* [wood] gauchir, voiler.
|| [personality] fausser, pervertir. **2** *vi*
[wood] gauchir, se voiler.

warrant ['wɒrənt] **1** *n* JUR mandat *m*. **2**
vt [justify] justifier. || [guarantee] garan-
tir.

warranty ['wɒrəntɪ] *n* garantie *f*.

warren ['wɒrən] *n* terrier *m*.

warrior ['wɒrɪər] *n* guerrier *m*, -ière *f*.

Warsaw ['wɔːsɔː] *n* Varsovie; **the ~ Pact**
le pacte de Varsovie.

warship ['wɔːʃɪp] *n* navire *m* de guerre.

wart [wɔːt] *n* verrue *f*.

wartime ['wɔːtaɪm] *n*: **in ~** en temps de
guerre.

wary ['weərɪ] *adj* prudent(e), circons-
pect(e); **to be ~ of** se méfier de; **to be ~ of
doing sthg** hésiter à faire qqch.

was [weak form wəz, strong form wɒz]
pt → **be**.

wash [wɒʃ] **1** *n* [act] lavage *m*; **to have a
~** se laver. || [from boat] remous *m*. **2** *vt*
[clean] laver; **to ~ one's hands** se laver
les mains. **3** *vi* se laver. ○ **wash away** *vt
sep* emporter. ○ **wash up** *Am* [wash
oneself] se laver.

washable ['wɒʃəbl] *adj* lavable.

washbasin *Br* ['wɒʃ,beɪsn], **washbowl**
Am ['wɒʃbəul] *n* lavabo *m*.

washcloth ['wɒʃ,klɒθ] *n Am* gant *m* de
toilette.

washer ['wɒʃər] *n* TECH rondelle *f*. ||
[washing machine] machine *f* à laver.

washing ['wɒʃɪŋ] *n* (*U*) [action] lessive
f. || [clothes] linge *m*, lessive *f*.

washing line *n* corde *f* à linge.

washing machine *n* machine *f* à laver.

Washington ['wɒʃɪŋtən] *n* [city]: **~ D.C.**
Washington.

washout ['wɒʃaut] *n inf* fiasco *m*.

washroom ['wɒʃrum] *n Am* toilettes
fpl.

wasn't [wɒznt] = **was not**.

wasp [wɒsp] *n* guêpe *f*.

wastage ['weɪstɪdʒ] *n* gaspillage *m*.

waste [weɪst] **1** *adj* [material] de rebut;
[fuel] perdu(e); [area of land] en friche. **2**
n [misuse] gaspillage *m*; **a ~ of time** une
perte de temps. || (*U*) [refuse] déchets
mpl, ordures *fpl*. **3** *vt* [money, food, ener-
gy] gaspiller; [time, opportunity] perdre.

wastebasket *Am* = **wastepaper basket**.

waste disposal unit *n* broyeur *m*
d'ordures.

wasteful ['weɪstful] *adj* [person] gaspilleur(euse); [activity] peu économique.

waste ground *n* (*U*) terrain *m* vague.

wastepaper basket [,weɪst'peɪpər-], **wastepaper bin** [,weɪst'peɪpər-], **wastebasket** *Am* ['weɪst,bɑːskɪt] *n* corbeille *f* à papier.

watch [wɒtʃ] **1** *n* [timepiece] montre *f*. || [act of watching]: **to keep ~** faire le guet, monter la garde; **to keep ~ on sb/sthg** surveiller qqn/qqch. || [guard] garde *f*; NAUT [shift] quart *m*. **2** *vt* [look at] regarder. || [spy on, guard] surveiller. || [be careful about] faire attention à. **3** *vi* regarder. ○ **watch out** *vi* faire attention, prendre garde.

watchdog ['wɒtʃdɒg] *n* [dog] chien *m* de garde. || *fig* [organization] organisation *f* de contrôle.

watchful ['wɒtʃful] *adj* vigilant(e).

watchmaker ['wɒtʃ,meɪkər] *n* horloger *m*.

watchman ['wɒtʃmən] (*pl* -men [-mən]) *n* gardien *m*.

water ['wɔːtər] **1** *n* [liquid] eau *f*. **2** *vt* arroser. **3** *vi* [eyes] pleurer, larmoyer. || [mouth]: **my mouth was ~ing** j'en avais l'eau à la bouche. ○ **waters** *npl* [sea] eaux *fpl*. ○ **water down** *vt sep* [dilute] diluer; [alcohol] couper d'eau. || *usu pej* [plan, demand] atténuer, modérer; [play, novel] édulcorer.

water bottle *n* gourde *f*, bidon *m* (à eau).

watercolour ['wɔːtə,kʌlər] *n* [picture] aquarelle *f*. || [paint] peinture *f* à l'eau, couleur *f* pour aquarelle.

watercress ['wɔːtəkres] *n* cresson *m*.

waterfall ['wɔːtəfɔːl] *n* chute *f* d'eau, cascade *f*.

water heater *n* chauffe-eau *m inv*.

waterhole ['wɔːtəhəul] *n* mare *f*, point *m* d'eau.

watering can ['wɔːtərɪŋ-] *n* arrosoir *m*.

water level *n* niveau *m* de l'eau.

water lily *n* nénuphar *m*.

waterline ['wɔːtəlaɪn] *n* NAUT ligne *f* de flottaison.

waterlogged ['wɔːtəlɒgd] *adj* [land] détrempé(e). || [vessel] plein(e) d'eau.

water main *n* conduite *f* principale d'eau.

watermark ['wɔːtəmɑːk] *n* [in paper] filigrane *m*. || [showing water level] laisse *f*.

watermelon ['wɔːtə,melən] *n* pastèque *f*.

water polo *n* water-polo *m*.

waterproof ['wɔːtəpruːf] **1** *adj* imperméable. **2** *n* imperméable *m*.

watershed ['wɔːtəʃed] *n fig* [turning point] tournant *m*, moment *m* critique.

water skiing *n* ski *m* nautique.

water tank *n* réservoir *m* d'eau, citerne *f*.

watertight ['wɔːtətaɪt] *adj* [waterproof] étanche. || *fig* [excuse, contract] parfait(e); [plan] infaillible.

waterway ['wɔːtəweɪ] *n* voie *f* navigable.

waterworks ['wɔːtəwɜːks] (*pl inv*) *n* [building] installation *f* hydraulique, usine *f* de distribution d'eau.

watt [wɒt] *n* watt *m*.

wave [weɪv] **1** *n* [of hand] geste *m*, signe *m*. || [of water, emotion, nausea] vague *f*. || [of light, sound] onde *f*; [of heat] bouffée *f*. || [in hair] cran *m*, ondulation *f*. **2** *vt* [arm, handkerchief] agiter; [flag, stick] brandir. **3** *vi* [with hand] faire signe de la main; **to ~ at** OR **to sb** faire signe à qqn, saluer qqn de la main. || [flags, trees] flotter.

wavelength ['weɪvleŋθ] *n* longueur *f* d'ondes; **to be on the same ~** *fig* être sur la même longueur d'ondes.

waver ['weɪvər] *vi* [falter] vaciller, chanceler. || [hesitate] hésiter, vaciller. || [fluctuate] fluctuer, varier.

wavy ['weɪvɪ] *adj* [hair] ondulé(e); [line] onduleux(euse).

wax [wæks] **1** *n* (*U*) [in candles, polish] cire *f*. || [in ears] cérumen *m*. **2** *vt* cirer. **3** *vi* [moon] croître.

wax paper *n Am* papier *m* sulfurisé.

waxworks ['wækswɜːks] (*pl inv*) *n* [museum] musée *m* de cire.

way [weɪ] **1** *n* [means, method] façon *f*; **to get** OR **have one's ~** obtenir ce qu'on veut. || [manner, style] façon *f*, manière *f*; **in the same ~** de la même manière OR façon; **this/that ~** comme ça, de cette façon; **in a ~** d'une certaine manière, en quelque sorte. || [route, path] chemin *m*; **~ in** entrée *f*; **~ out** sortie *f*; **on the** OR **one's ~** sur le OR son chemin; **to get under ~** [ship] se mettre en route; *fig* [meeting] démarrer; **to be in the ~** gêner; **to go out of one's ~ to do sthg** se donner du mal pour faire qqch; **to keep out of sb's ~** éviter qqn; **keep out of the ~!** restez à l'écart!; **to make ~ for** faire place à. || [direction]: **to go/look/come this ~** aller/regarder/venir par ici; **the right/wrong ~ round** [in sequence] dans le bon/mauvais ordre; **she had her hat on the wrong ~ round** elle avait mis son chapeau à l'envers; **the right/wrong ~ up** dans le bon/mauvais sens. ‖ [distance]: **all the ~** tout le trajet; *fig* [support etc] jusqu'au bout; **a long ~** loin. ‖ *phr*: **to give ~** [under weight, pressure] céder; **no ~!** pas question! **2** *adv inf* [a lot] largement; **~ better** bien mieux. ○ **ways** *npl* [customs, habits] coutumes *fpl*. ○ **by the way** *adv* au fait.

waylay [ˌweɪ'leɪ] (*pt & pp* **-laid** [-'leɪd]) *vt* arrêter (au passage).

wayward ['weɪwəd] *adj* qui n'en fait qu'à sa tête; [behaviour] capricieux(ieuse).

WC (*abbr of* water closet) *n* W.-C. *mpl*.

we [wiː] *pers pron* nous; WE **can't do it** nous, nous ne pouvons pas le faire; **as ~ say in France** comme on dit en France; **~ British** nous autres Britanniques.

weak [wiːk] *adj* [gen] faible. ‖ [delicate] fragile. ‖ [unconvincing] peu convaincant(e). ‖ [drink] léger(ère).

weaken ['wiːkn] **1** *vt* [undermine] affaiblir. ‖ [reduce] diminuer. ‖ [physically - person] affaiblir; [- structure] fragiliser. **2** *vi* faiblir.

weakling ['wiːklɪŋ] *n pej* mauviette *f*.

weakness ['wiːknɪs] *n* (*U*) [physical - of person] faiblesse *f*; [- of structure] fragilité *f*. ‖ [imperfect point] point *m* faible, faiblesse *f*.

wealth [welθ] *n* (*U*) [riches] richesse *f*. ‖ [abundance]: **a ~ of** une profusion de.

wealthy ['welθɪ] *adj* riche.

wean [wiːn] *vt* [baby, lamb] sevrer.

weapon ['wepən] *n* arme *f*.

wear [weəʳ] (*pt* wore, *pp* worn) *n* (*U*) [type of clothes] tenue *f*. ‖ [damage] usure *f*; **~ and tear** usure. ‖ [use]: **these shoes have had a lot of ~** ces chaussures ont fait beaucoup d'usage. **2** *vt* [clothes, hair] porter. ‖ [damage] user. **3** *vi* [deteriorate] s'user. ‖ [last]: **to ~ well** durer longtemps, faire de l'usage. ○ **wear away 1** *vt sep* [rock, wood] user; [grass] abîmer. **2** *vi* [rock, wood] s'user; [grass] s'abîmer. ○ **wear down** *vt sep* [material] user. ‖ [person, resistance] épuiser. ○ **wear off** *vi* disparaître. ○ **wear out 1** *vt sep* [shoes, clothes] user. ‖ [person] épuiser. **2** *vi* s'user.

weary ['wɪərɪ] *adj* [exhausted] las (lasse); [sigh] de lassitude. ‖ [fed up]: **to be ⌐ of sthg/of doing sthg** être las de qqch/de faire qqch.

weasel ['wiːzl] *n* belette *f*.

weather ['weðəʳ] **1** *n* temps *m*; **to be under the ~** être patraque. **2** *vt* [crisis, problem] surmonter.

weather-beaten [-ˌbiːtn] *adj* [face, skin] tanné(e).

weathercock ['weðəkɒk] *n* girouette *f*.

weather forecast *n* météo *f*, prévisions *fpl* météorologiques.

weatherman ['weðəmæn] (*pl* -men [-men]) *n* météorologue *m*.

weather vane [-veɪn] *n* girouette *f*.

weave [wiːv] (*pt* wove, *pp* woven) **1** *vt* [using loom] tisser. **2** *vi* [move] se faufiler.

weaver ['wiːvəʳ] *n* tisserand *m*, -e *f*.

web [web] *n* [cobweb] toile *f* (d'araignée). ‖ *fig* [of lies] tissu *m*.

wed [wed] (*pt & pp* wed OR -ded) *literary* **1** *vt* épouser. **2** *vi* se marier.

we'd [wiːd] = we had, we would.

wedding ['wedɪŋ] *n* mariage *m*.

wedding anniversary *n* anniversaire *m* de mariage.

wedding cake *n* pièce *f* montée.

wedding dress *n* robe *f* de mariée.

wedding ring *n* alliance *f*.

wedge [wedʒ] **1** *n* [for steadying] cale *f*. ‖ [for splitting] coin *m*. ‖ [of cake, cheese] morceau *m*. **2** *vt* caler.

Wednesday ['wenzdɪ] *n* mercredi *m*; *see also* **Saturday**.

wee [wiː] **1** *adj Scot* petit(e). **2** *n v inf* pipi *m*. **3** *vi v inf* faire pipi.

weed [wiːd] **1** *n* [plant] mauvaise herbe *f*. **2** *vt* désherber.

weedkiller ['wiːdˌkɪləʳ] *n* désherbant *m*.

week [wiːk] *n* semaine *f*.

weekday ['wiːkdeɪ] *n* jour *m* de semaine.

weekend [ˌwiːk'end] *n* week-end *m*; **on** OR **at the ~** le week-end.

weekly ['wiːklɪ] **1** *adj* hebdomadaire. **2** *adv* chaque semaine. **3** *n* hebdomadaire *m*.

weep ['wiːp] (*pt & pp* wept) *vt & vi* pleurer.

weeping willow [ˌwiːpɪŋ-] *n* saule *m* pleureur.

weigh [weɪ] *vt* [gen] peser. ‖ NAUT: **to ~ anchor** lever l'ancre. ○ **weigh down** *vt sep* [physically]: **to be ~ed down with sthg** plier sous le poids de qqch. ‖ [mentally]: **to be ~ed down by** OR **with sthg** être accablé par qqch. ○ **weigh up** *vt sep* [consider carefully] examiner. ‖ [size up] juger, évaluer.

weight [weɪt] *n lit & fig* poids *m*; **to put on OR gain ~** prendre du poids, grossir; **to lose ~** perdre du poids, maigrir; **to pull one's ~** faire sa part du travail, participer à la tâche.

weighted ['weɪtɪd] *adj*: **to be ~ in favour of/against** être favorable/défavorable à.

weighting ['weɪtɪŋ] *n* indemnité *f*.

weightlifting ['weɪt,lɪftɪŋ] *n* haltérophilie *f*.

weighty ['weɪtɪ] *adj* [serious] important(e), de poids.

weir [wɪəʳ] *n* barrage *m*.

weird [wɪəd] *adj* bizarre.

welcome ['welkəm] **1** *adj* [guest, help etc] bienvenu(e). ‖ [free]: **you're ~ to ...** n'hésitez pas à .... ‖ [in reply to thanks]: **you're ~** il n'y a pas de quoi, de rien. **2** *n* accueil *m*. **3** *vt* [receive] accueillir. ‖ [approve of] se réjouir de. **4** *excl* bienvenue!

weld [weld] **1** *n* soudure *f*. **2** *vt* souder.

welfare ['welfeəʳ] **1** *adj* social(e). **2** *n* [well-being] bien-être *m*. ‖ *Am* [income support] assistance *f* publique.

welfare state *n* État-providence *m*.

well [wel] (*compar* **better**, *superl* **best**) **1** *adj* bien; **I'm very ~, thanks** je vais très bien, merci; **just as ~** ~ bien; **to go ~** aller bien; ~ **done!** bravo!; ~ **and truly** bel et bien. **3** *n* [for water, oil] puits *m*. **4** *excl* [in hesitation] heu!, eh bien! ‖ [to correct oneself] bon!, enfin! ‖ [to express resignation]: **oh ~!** eh bien! ‖ [in surprise] tiens! ○ **as well** *adv* [in addition] aussi, également. ‖ [with same result]: **I/you** *etc* **may OR might as ~ (do sthg)** je/tu *etc* ferais aussi bien (de faire qqch). ○ **as well as** *conj* en plus de, aussi bien que. ○ **well up** *vi*: **tears ~ed up in her eyes** les larmes lui montaient aux yeux.

we'll [wi:l] = **we shall**, **we will**.

well-advised [-əd'vaɪzd] *adj* sage; **you would be ~ to do sthg** tu ferais bien de faire qqch.

well-behaved [-bɪ'heɪvd] *adj* sage.

wellbeing [,wel'bi:ɪŋ] *n* bien-être *m*.

well-built *adj* bien bâti(e).

well-done *adj* CULIN bien cuit(e).

well-dressed [-'drest] *adj* bien habillé(e).

well-earned [-3:nd] *adj* bien mérité(e).

well-heeled [-hi:ld] *adj inf* nanti(e).

wellington boots ['welɪŋtən-], **wellingtons** ['welɪŋtənz] *npl* bottes *fpl* de caoutchouc.

well-kept *adj* [building, garden] bien tenu(e). ‖ [secret] bien gardé(e).

well-known *adj* bien connu(e).

well-mannered [-'mænəd] *adj* bien élevé(e).

well-meaning *adj* bien intentionné(e).

well-nigh [-naɪ] *adv* presque, pratiquement.

well-off *adj* [rich] riche. ‖ [well-provided]: **to be ~ for sthg** être bien pourvu(e) en qqch.

well-read [-'red] *adj* cultivé(e).

well-rounded [-'raʊndɪd] *adj* [education, background] complet(ète).

well-timed [-'taɪmd] *adj* bien calculé(e), qui vient à point nommé.

well-to-do *adj* riche.

wellwisher ['wel,wɪʃəʳ] *n* admirateur *m*, -trice *f*.

Welsh [welʃ] **1** *adj* gallois(e). **2** *n* [language] gallois *m*. **3** *npl*: **the ~** les Gallois *mpl*.

Welshman ['welʃmən] (*pl* **-men** [-mən]) *n* Gallois *m*.

Welshwoman ['welʃ,wʊmən] (*pl* **-women** [-,wɪmɪn]) *n* Galloise *f*.

went [went] *pt* → **go**.

wept [wept] *pt & pp* → **weep**.

were [w3:ʳ] → **be**.

we're [wɪəʳ] = **we are**.

weren't [w3:nt] = **were not**.

west [west] **1** *n* [direction] ouest *m*. ‖ [region]: **the ~** l'ouest *m*. **2** *adj* ouest (*inv*); [wind] d'ouest. **3** *adv* de l'ouest, vers l'ouest; ~ **of** à l'ouest de. ○ **West** *n* POL: **the West** l'Occident *m*.

West Bank *n*: **the ~** la Cisjordanie.

westerly ['westəlɪ] *adj* à l'ouest; [wind] de l'ouest; **in a ~ direction** vers l'ouest.

western ['westən] **1** *adj* [gen] de l'ouest. ‖ POL occidental(e). **2** *n* [book, film] western *m*.

West German **1** *adj* ouest-allemand(e). **2** *n* Allemand *m*, -e *f* de l'Ouest.

West Germany *n*: (former) ~ (ex-)Allemagne *f* de l'Ouest.

West Indian **1** *adj* antillais(e). **2** *n* Antillais *m*, -e *f*.

West Indies [-'ɪndi:z] *npl*: **the ~** les Antilles *fpl*.

westward ['westwəd] *adj & adv* vers l'ouest.

westwards ['westwədz] *adv* vers l'ouest.

wet [wet] (*pt & pp* **wet** OR **-ted**) **1** *adj* [damp, soaked] mouillé(e). ‖ [rainy] pluvieux(ieuse). || [not dry - paint, cement] frais (fraîche). 2 *n inf* POL modéré *m*, -e *f*. 3 *vt* mouiller.

wet blanket *n inf pej* rabat-joie *m inv*.

wet suit *n* combinaison *f* de plongée.

we've [wi:v] = we have.

whack [wæk] *inf vt* donner un grand coup à, frapper fort.

whale [weɪl] *n* baleine *f*.

wharf [wɔ:f] (*pl* -s OR **wharves** [wɔ:vz]) *n* quai *m*.

what [wɒt] 1 *adj* (*in direct, indirect questions*) quel (quelle), quels (quelles) (*pl*); ~ **colour is it?** c'est de quelle couleur? || (*in exclamations*) quel (quelle), quels (quelles) (*pl*); ~ **a surprise!** quelle surprise!; ~ **an idiot I am!** ce que je peux être bête! 2 *pron* (*interrogative - subject*) qu'est-ce qui; (- *object*) qu'est-ce que, que; (- *after prep*) quoi; ~ **are they doing?** qu'est-ce qu'ils font?, que font-ils?; ~ **is going on?** qu'est-ce qui se passe?; ~ **are they talking about?** de quoi parlent-ils?; ~ **about the rest of us?** et nous alors?; ~ **if ...?** et si ...? || (*relative - subject*) ce qui; (- *object*) ce que; **I saw** ~ **happened/fell** j'ai vu ce qui s'était passé/était tombé; **you can't have** ~ **you want** tu ne peux pas avoir ce que tu veux. 3 *excl* [expressing disbelief] comment!, quoi!

whatever [wɒt'evə*] 1 *adj* quel (quelle) que soit; **any book** ~ n'importe quel livre; **no chance** ~ pas la moindre chance; **nothing** ~ rien du tout. 2 *pron* quoi que (+ *subjunctive*); **I'll do** ~ **I can** je ferai tout ce que je peux; ~ **can this be?** qu'est-ce que cela peut-il bien être?; ~ **that may mean** quoi que cela puisse bien vouloir dire; **or** ~ ou n'importe quoi d'autre.

whatsoever [,wɒtsəʊ'evə*] *adj*: **I had no interest** ~ je n'éprouvais pas le moindre intérêt; **nothing** ~ rien du tout.

wheat [wi:t] *n* blé *m*.

wheedle ['wi:dl] *vt*: **to** ~ **sb into doing sthg** enjôler qqn pour qu'il fasse qqch; **to** ~ **sthg out of sb** enjôler qqn pour obtenir qqch.

wheel [wi:l] 1 *n* [gen] roue *f*. || [steering wheel] volant *m*. 2 *vt* pousser. 3 *vi*: **to** ~ **(round)** se retourner brusquement.

wheelbarrow ['wi:l,bærəʊ] *n* brouette *f*.

wheelchair ['wi:l,tʃeə*] *n* fauteuil *m* roulant.

wheelclamp ['wi:l,klæmp] 1 *n* sabot *m* de Denver. 2 *vt*: **my car was** ~**ed** on a mis un sabot à ma voiture.

wheeze [wi:z] 1 *n* [sound] respiration *f* sifflante. 2 *vi* respirer avec un bruit sifflant.

whelk [welk] *n* bulot *m*, buccin *m*.

when [wen] 1 *adv* (*in direct, indirect questions*) quand; ~ **does the plane arrive?** quand OR à quelle heure arrive l'avion? 2 *conj* [referring to time] quand, lorsque; **he came to see me** ~ **I was abroad** il est venu me voir quand j'étais à l'étranger; **one day** ~ **I was on my own** un jour que OR où j'étais tout seul. || [whereas, considering that] alors que.

whenever [wen'evə*] 1 *conj* quand; [each time that] chaque fois que. 2 *adv* n'importe quand.

where [weə*] 1 *adv* (*in direct, indirect questions*) où; **do you know** ~ **he lives?** est-ce que vous savez où il habite? 2 *conj* [referring to place, situation] où; **this is** ~ **...** c'est là que .... || [whereas] alors que.

whereabouts [*adv* ,weərə'baʊts, *n* 'weərəbaʊts] 1 *adv* où. 2 *npl*: **their** ~ **are still unknown** on ne sait toujours pas où ils se trouvent.

whereas [weər'æz] *conj* alors que.

whereby [weə'baɪ] *conj fml* par lequel (laquelle), au moyen duquel (de laquelle).

whereupon [,weərə'pɒn] *conj fml* après quoi, sur quoi.

wherever [weər'evə*] 1 *conj* où que (+ *subjunctive*). 2 *adv* [no matter where] n'importe où. || [where] où donc.

wherewithal ['weəwɪðɔ:l] *n fml*: **to have the** ~ **to do sthg** avoir les moyens de faire qqch.

whet [wet] *vt*: **to** ~ **sb's appetite for sthg** donner à qqn envie de qqch.

whether ['weðə*] *conj* [indicating choice, doubt] si. || [no matter if]: ~ **I want to or not** que je le veuille ou non.

which [wɪtʃ] 1 *adj* (*in direct, indirect questions*) quel (quelle), quels (quelles) (*pl*); ~ **house is yours?** quelle maison est la tienne?; ~ **one?** lequel (laquelle)? || [to refer back to sthg]: **in** ~ **case** auquel cas. 2 *pron* (*in direct, indirect questions*) lequel (laquelle), lesquels (lesquelles) (*pl*); ~ **do you prefer?** lequel préférez-vous? || (*in relative clauses - subject*) qui; (- *object*) que; (- *after prep*) lequel (laquelle), lesquels (lesquelles) (*pl*); **take the slice** ~ **is nearer to you** prends la tranche qui est le plus près de toi; **the television ~ we bought** le téléviseur que nous avons acheté; **the settee on ~ I am sitting** le canapé sur lequel je suis assis; **the film of ~ you spoke** le film dont vous avez parlé. || (*referring back = subject*) ce qui; (- *object*) ce que; **why did you say you were ill, ~ nobody believed?** pourquoi as-tu dit que tu étais malade, ce que personne n'a cru?

whichever [wɪtʃˈevəʳ] **1** *adj* quel (quelle) que soit; **choose ~ colour you prefer** choisissez la couleur que vous préférez, n'importe laquelle. **2** *pron* n'importe lequel (laquelle).

whiff [wɪf] *n* [of perfume, smoke] bouffée *f*; [of food] odeur *f*.

while [waɪl] **1** *n* moment *m*; **let's stay here for a ~** restons ici un moment; **for a long ~** longtemps; **after a ~** après quelque temps. **2** *conj* [during the time that] pendant que. || [as long as] tant que. || [whereas] alors que. O **while away** *vt sep* passer.

whilst [waɪlst] *conj* = while.

whim [wɪm] *n* lubie *f*.

whimper [ˈwɪmpəʳ] *vt & vi* gémir.

whimsical [ˈwɪmzɪkl] *adj* saugrenu(e).

whine [waɪn] *vi* [make sound] gémir.

whip [wɪp] **1** *n* [for hitting] fouet *m*. **2** *vt* [gen] fouetter. || [take quickly]: **to ~ sthg out** sortir qqch brusquement; **to ~ sthg off** OR enlever qqch brusquement.

whipped cream [wɪpt-] *n* crème *f* fouettée.

whirl [wɜːl] **1** *n lit & fig* tourbillon *m*. **2** *vt*: **to ~ sb/sthg round** [spin round] faire tourbillonner qqn/qqch. **3** *vi* tourbillonner; *fig* [head, mind] tourner.

whirlpool [ˈwɜːlpuːl] *n* tourbillon *m*.

whirlwind [ˈwɜːlwɪnd] *n* tornade *f*.

whirr [wɜːʳ] *vi* [engine] ronronner.

whisk [wɪsk] **1** *n* CULIN fouet *m*, batteur *m* (à œufs). **2** *vt* [move quickly] emmener OR emporter rapidement. || CULIN battre.

whisker [ˈwɪskəʳ] *n* moustache *f*. O **whiskers** *npl* favoris *mpl*.

whisky *Br*, **whiskey** *Am & Irish* (*pl* **whiskeys**) [ˈwɪskɪ] *n* whisky *m*.

whisper [ˈwɪspəʳ] **1** *vt* murmurer, chuchoter. **2** *vi* chuchoter.

whistle [ˈwɪsl] **1** *n* [sound] sifflement *m*. || [device] sifflet *m*. **2** *vt & vi* siffler.

white [waɪt] **1** *adj* [in colour] blanc (blanche). || [coffee, tea] au lait. **2** *n* [colour, of egg, eye] blanc *m*. || [person] Blanc *m*, Blanche *f*.

white-collar *adj* de bureau.

white elephant *n fig* objet *m* coûteux et inutile.

white-hot *adj* chauffé(e) à blanc.

White House *n*: **the ~** la Maison-Blanche.

white lie *n* pieux mensonge *m*.

whiteness [ˈwaɪtnɪs] *n* blancheur *f*.

white paper *n* POL livre *m* blanc.

white sauce *n* sauce *f* blanche.

whitewash [ˈwaɪtwɒʃ] **1** *n* (*U*) [paint] chaux *f*. || *pej* [cover-up]: **a government ~** une combine du gouvernement pour étouffer l'affaire. **2** *vt* [paint] blanchir à la chaux.

whiting [ˈwaɪtɪŋ] (*pl inv* OR **-s**) *n* merlan *m*.

Whitsun [ˈwɪtsn] *n* Pentecôte *f*.

whittle [ˈwɪtl] *vt* [reduce]: **to ~ sthg away** OR **down** réduire qqch.

whiz, **whizz** [wɪz] *vi* [go fast] aller à toute allure.

whiz(z) kid *n inf* petit prodige *m*.

who [huː] *pron* (*in direct, indirect questions*) qui; **~ are you?** qui êtes-vous?; **I didn't know ~ she was** je ne savais pas qui c'était. || (*in relative clauses*) qui; **he's the doctor ~ treated me** c'est le médecin qui m'a soigné.

who'd [huːd] = who had, who would.

whodu(n)nit [ˌhuːˈdʌnɪt] *n inf* polar *m*.

whoever [huːˈevəʳ] *pron* [unknown person] quiconque. || [indicating surprise, astonishment] qui donc. || [no matter who] qui que (+ *subjunctive*); **~ you are** qui que vous soyez; **~ wins** qui que ce soit qui gagne.

whole [həʊl] **1** *adj* [entire, complete] entier(ière). || [for emphasis]: **a ~ lot bigger** bien plus gros; **a ~ new idea** une idée tout à fait nouvelle. **2** *n* [all]: **the ~ of the school** toute l'école; **the ~ of the summer** tout l'été. || [unit, complete thing] tout *m*. O **as a whole** *adv* dans son ensemble. O **on the whole** *adv* dans l'ensemble.

whole-hearted [-ˈhɑːtɪd] *adj* sans réserve, total(e).

wholemeal [ˈhəʊlmiːl] *Br*, **whole wheat** *Am adj* complet(ète).

wholesale [ˈhəʊlseɪl] **1** *adj* [buying, selling] en gros; [price] de gros. || *pej* [excessive] en masse. **2** *adv* [in bulk] en gros. || *pej* [excessively] en masse.

wholesaler [ˈhəʊlˌseɪləʳ] *n* marchand *m* de gros, grossiste *mf*.

wholesome [ˈhəʊlsəm] *adj* sain(e).

whole wheat *Am* = wholemeal.

will

who'll [huːl] = who will.

wholly ['həʊlɪ] *adv* totalement.

whom [huːm] *pron fml* (*in direct, indirect questions*) qui; **~ did you phone?** qui avez-vous appelé au téléphone?; **for/of/to ~** pour/de/à qui. ‖ (*in relative clauses*) que; **the girl ~ he married** la jeune fille qu'il a épousée; **the man of ~ you speak** l'homme dont vous parlez; **the man to ~ you were speaking** l'homme à qui vous parliez.

whooping cough ['huːpɪŋ-] *n* coqueluche *f*.

whopping ['wɒpɪŋ] *inf* 1 *adj* énorme. 2 *adv*: **a ~ great lorry/lie** un camion/mensonge absolument énorme.

whore [hɔːr] *n offensive* putain *f*.

who're ['huːər] = who are.

whose [huːz] 1 *pron* (*in direct, indirect questions*) à qui; **~ is this?** à qui est ceci? ‖ (*in relative clauses*) dont; **that's the boy ~ father's an MP** c'est le garçon dont le père est député; **the girl ~ mother you phoned yesterday** la fille à la mère de qui *OR* de laquelle tu as téléphoné hier. 2 *adj* à qui; **~ car is that?** à qui est cette voiture?; **~ son is he?** de qui est-il le fils?

who's who [huːz-] *n* [book] bottin *m* mondain.

who've [huːv] = who have.

why [waɪ] 1 *adv* (*in direct questions*) pourquoi; **~ did you lie to me?** pourquoi m'as-tu menti?; **~ not?** pourquoi pas? 2 *conj* pourquoi; **I don't know ~ he said that** je ne sais pas pourquoi il a dit cela. 3 *pron*: **there are several reasons ~ he left** il est parti pour plusieurs raisons, les raisons pour lesquelles il est parti sont nombreuses; **I don't know the reason ~** je ne sais pas pourquoi. 4 *excl* tiens! ○ **why ever** *adv* pourquoi donc.

wick [wɪk] *n* [of candle, lighter] mèche *f*.

wicked ['wɪkɪd] *adj* [evil] mauvais(e). ‖ [mischievous, devilish] malicieux(ieuse).

wicker ['wɪkər] *adj* en osier.

wickerwork ['wɪkəwɜːk] *n* vannerie *f*.

wide [waɪd] 1 *adj* [gen] large; **how ~ is the room?** quelle est la largeur de la pièce?; **to be six metres ~** faire six mètres de large *OR* de largeur. ‖ [gap, difference] grand(e). ‖ [experience, knowledge, issue] vaste. 2 *adv* [broadly] largement; **open ~!** ouvrez grand! ‖ [off-target]: **the shot went ~** le coup est passé loin du but *OR* à côté.

wide-angle lens *n* PHOT objectif *m* grand angle.

wide-awake *adj* tout à fait réveillé(e).

widely ['waɪdlɪ] *adv* [smile, vary] largement. ‖ [extensively] beaucoup; **it is ~ believed that ...** nombreux sont ceux qui pensent que ....

widen ['waɪdn] *vt* [make broader] élargir. ‖ [gap, difference] agrandir, élargir.

wide open *adj* grand ouvert (grande ouverte).

wide-ranging [-'reɪndʒɪŋ] *adj* varié(e); [consequences] de grande envergure.

widespread ['waɪdspred] *adj* très répandu(e).

widow ['wɪdəʊ] *n* veuve *f*.

widowed ['wɪdəʊd] *adj* veuf (veuve).

widower ['wɪdəʊər] *n* veuf *m*.

width [wɪdθ] *n* largeur *f*; **in ~** de large.

wield [wiːld] *vt* [weapon] manier. ‖ [power] exercer.

wife [waɪf] (*pl* wives) *n* femme *f*, épouse *f*.

wig [wɪg] *n* perruque *f*.

wiggle ['wɪgl] *inf vt* remuer.

wild [waɪld] *adj* [animal, attack, scenery, flower] sauvage. ‖ [weather, sea] déchaîné(e). ‖ [laughter, hope, plan] fou (folle). ‖ [random - estimate] fantaisiste; **I made a ~ guess** j'ai dit ça au hasard. ○ **wilds** *npl*: **the ~s of** le fin fond de; **to live in the ~s** habiter en pleine nature.

wilderness ['wɪldənɪs] *n* étendue *f* sauvage.

wild-goose chase *n inf*: **it turned out to be a ~** ça s'est révélé être totalement inutile.

wildlife ['waɪldlaɪf] *n* (*U*) faune *f* et flore *f*.

wildly ['waɪldlɪ] *adv* [enthusiastically, fanatically] frénétiquement. ‖ [guess, suggest] au hasard. ‖ [very - different, impractical] tout à fait.

wilful *Br*, **willful** *Am* ['wɪlful] *adj* [determined] obstiné(e). ‖ [deliberate] délibéré(e).

will[1] [wɪl] 1 *n* [mental] volonté *f*; **against one's ~** contre son gré. ‖ [document] testament *m*. 2 *vt*: **to ~ sthg to happen** prier de toutes ses forces pour que qqch se passe; **to ~ sb to do sthg** concentrer toute sa volonté sur qqn pour qu'il fasse qqch.

will[2] [wɪl] *modal vb* (*to express future tense*): **I ~ see you next week** je te verrai la semaine prochaine; **when ~ you have finished it?** quand est-ce que vous l'aurez fini?; **~ you be here next week? — yes I ~/no I won't** est-ce que tu seras là la semaine prochaine? — oui/non. || [indicating willingness]: ~ **you have some more tea?** voulez-vous encore du thé?; **I won't do it** je refuse de le faire, je ne veux pas le faire. || [in commands, requests]: **you ~ leave this house at once** tu vas quitter cette maison tout de suite; **close that window, ~ you?** ferme cette fenêtre, veux-tu?; ~ **you be quiet!** veux-tu te taire!, tu vas te taire! || [indicating possibility, what usually happens]: **the hall ~ hold up to 1000 people** la salle peut abriter jusqu'à 1000 personnes. || [expressing an assumption]: **that'll be your father** cela doit être ton père. || [indicating irritation]: **she ~ keep phoning me** elle n'arrête pas de me téléphoner.

wilful *Am* = wilful.

willing ['wɪlɪŋ] *adj* [prepared]: **to be ~ to do sthg** être disposé(e) or prêt(e) à faire qqch. || [eager] enthousiaste.

willingly ['wɪlɪŋlɪ] *adv* volontiers.

willow (tree) ['wɪləʊ-] *n* saule *m*.

willpower ['wɪl,paʊə'] *n* volonté *f*.

willy-nilly [,wɪlɪ'nɪlɪ] *adv* [at random] n'importe comment. || [wanting to or not] bon gré mal gré.

wilt [wɪlt] *vi* [plant] se faner; *fig* [person] dépérir.

wily ['waɪlɪ] *adj* rusé(e).

wimp [wɪmp] *n pej inf* mauviette *f*.

win [wɪn] (*pt & pp* **won**) 1 *n* victoire *f*. 2 *vt* [game, prize, competition] gagner. || [support, approval] obtenir; [love, friendship] gagner. 3 *vi* gagner. ○ **win over**, **win round** *vt sep* convaincre, gagner à sa cause.

wince [wɪns] *vi*: **to ~ (at/with)** [with body] tressaillir (à/de); [with face] grimacer (à/de).

winch [wɪntʃ] *n* treuil *m*.

wind[1] [wɪnd] 1 *n* METEOR vent *m*. || [breath] souffle *m*. || (*U*) [in stomach] gaz *mpl*. 2 *vt* [knock breath out of] couper le souffle à.

wind[2] [waɪnd] (*pt & pp* **wound**) 1 *vt* [string, thread] enrouler. || [clock] remonter. 2 *vi* [river, road] serpenter. ○ **wind down** 1 *vt sep* [car window] baisser. || [business] cesser graduellement. 2 *vi* [relax] se détendre. ○ **wind up** *vt sep* [finish - meeting] clôturer; [- business] liquider. || [clock, car window] remonter. || *inf* [end up]: **to ~ up doing sthg** finir par faire qqch.

windfall ['wɪndfɔːl] *n* [unexpected gift] aubaine *f*.

winding ['waɪndɪŋ] *adj* sinueux(euse).

wind instrument [wɪnd-] *n* instrument *m* à vent.

windmill ['wɪndmɪl] *n* moulin *m* à vent.

window ['wɪndəʊ] *n* [gen & COMPUT] fenêtre *f*. || [pane of glass, in car] vitre *f*. || [of shop] vitrine *f*.

window box *n* jardinière *f*.

window cleaner *n* laveur *m*, -euse *f* de vitres.

window ledge *n* rebord *m* de fenêtre.

window pane *n* vitre *f*.

windowsill ['wɪndəʊsɪl] *n* [outside] rebord *m* de fenêtre; [inside] appui *m* de fenêtre.

windpipe ['wɪndpaɪp] *n* trachée *f*.

windscreen *Br* ['wɪndskriːn], **windshield** *Am* ['wɪndʃiːld] *n* pare-brise *m inv*.

windscreen washer *n* lave-glace *m*.

windscreen wiper [-,waɪpə'] *n* essuie-glace *m*.

windshield *Am* = windscreen.

windsurfing ['wɪnd,sɜːfɪŋ] *n*: **to go ~** faire de la planche à voile.

windswept ['wɪndswept] *adj* [scenery] balayé(e) par les vents.

windy ['wɪndɪ] *adj* venteux(euse); **it's ~** il fait du vent.

wine [waɪn] *n* vin *m*.

wine cellar *n* cave *f* (à vin).

wineglass ['waɪnɡlɑːs] *n* verre *m* à vin.

wine list *n* carte *f* des vins.

wine tasting [-,teɪstɪŋ] *n* dégustation *f* (de vins).

wine waiter *n* sommelier *m*.

wing [wɪŋ] *n* aile *f*. ○ **wings** *npl* THEATRE: **the ~s** les coulisses *fpl*.

wink [wɪŋk] 1 *n* clin *m* d'œil. 2 *vi* [eyes]: **to ~ (at sb)** faire un clin d'œil (à qqn).

winkle ['wɪŋkl] *n* bigorneau *m*. ○ **winkle out** *vt sep* extirper; **to ~ sthg out of sb** arracher qqch à qqn.

winner ['wɪnə'] *n* [person] gagnant *m*, -e *f*.

winning ['wɪnɪŋ] *adj* [victorious, successful] gagnant(e). ○ **winnings** *npl* gains *mpl*.

winning post *n* poteau *m* d'arrivée.

winter ['wɪntə'] 1 *n* hiver *m*; **in ~** en hiver. 2 *comp* d'hiver.

winter sports *npl* sports *mpl* d'hiver.

wintertime ['wɪntətaɪm] *n* (*U*) hiver *m*.

wint(e)ry ['wɪntrɪ] *adj* d'hiver.

wipe [waɪp] 1 n: **to give sthg a ~** essuyer qqch, donner un coup de torchon à qqch. 2 vt essuyer. ○ **wipe out** vt sep [erase] effacer. || [eradicate] anéantir. ○ **wipe up** vt sep & vi essuyer.

wire ['waɪə^r] 1 n (U) [metal] fil m de fer. || [cable etc] fil m. || [telegram] télégramme m. 2 vt [ELEC - plug] installer; [- house] faire l'installation électrique de. || [send telegram to] télégraphier à.

wireless ['waɪəlɪs] n dated T.S.F. f.

wiring ['waɪərɪŋ] n (U) installation f électrique.

wiry ['waɪərɪ] adj [hair] crépu(e). || [body, man] noueux(euse).

wisdom ['wɪzdəm] n sagesse f.

wisdom tooth n dent f de sagesse.

wise [waɪz] adj sage.

wisecrack ['waɪzkræk] n pej vanne f.

wish [wɪʃ] 1 n [desire] souhait m, désir m. || [magic request] vœu m. 2 vt [want]: **to ~ to do sthg** souhaiter faire qqch; **I ~ (that) he'd come** j'aimerais bien qu'il vienne; **I ~ I could** si seulement je pouvais. || [expressing hope]: **to ~ sb sthg** souhaiter qqch à qqn. 3 vi [by magic]: **to ~ for sthg** souhaiter qqch. ○ **wishes** npl: **best ~es** meilleurs vœux; **(with) best ~es** [at end of letter] bien amicalement.

wishful thinking [,wɪʃfʊl-] n: **that's just ~** c'est prendre mes/ses etc désirs pour des réalités.

wisp [wɪsp] n [tuft] mèche f. || [small cloud] mince filet m OR volute f.

wistful ['wɪstfʊl] adj nostalgique.

wit [wɪt] n [humour] esprit m. || [intelligence]: **to have the ~ to do sthg** avoir l'intelligence de faire qqch. ○ **wits** npl: **to have** OR **keep one's ~s about one** être attentif(ive) OR sur ses gardes.

witch [wɪtʃ] n sorcière f.

with [wɪð] prep [in company of] avec; **we stayed ~ them for a week** nous avons passé une semaine chez eux. || [indicating opposition] avec; **the war ~ Germany** la guerre avec OR contre l'Allemagne. || [indicating means, manner, feelings] avec; **I washed it ~ detergent** je l'ai lavé avec un détergent; **she was trembling ~ fright** elle tremblait de peur. || [having] avec; **a man ~ a beard** un homme avec une barbe, un barbu; **the man ~ the moustache** l'homme à la moustache. || [regarding]: **he's very mean ~ money** il est très près de ses sous, il est très avare; **the trouble ~ her is that ...** l'ennui avec elle OR ce qu'il y a avec elle c'est que .... ||

[indicating simultaneity]: **I can't do it ~ you watching me** je ne peux pas le faire quand OR pendant que tu me regardes. || [because of]: **~ my luck, I'll probably lose** avec ma chance habituelle, je suis sûr de perdre. || phr: **I'm ~ you** [I understand] je vous suis; [I'm on your side] je suis des vôtres; [I agree] je suis d'accord avec vous.

withdraw [wɪð'drɔː] (pt -**drew**, pp -**drawn**) 1 vt fml [remove]: **to ~ sthg (from)** enlever qqch (de). || [money, troops, remark] retirer. 2 vi fml [leave]: **to ~ (from)** se retirer (de). || MIL se replier; **to ~ from** évacuer. || [quit, give up]: **to ~ (from)** se retirer (de).

withdrawal [wɪð'drɔːəl] n [gen]: **~ (from)** retrait m (de). || MIL repli m.

withdrawal symptoms npl crise f de manque.

withdrawn [wɪð'drɔːn] 1 pp → withdraw. 2 adj [shy, quiet] renfermé(e).

withdrew [wɪð'druː] pt → withdraw.

wither ['wɪðə^r] vi [dry up] se flétrir. || [weaken] mourir.

withhold [wɪð'həʊld] (pt & pp -**held** [-'held]) vt [services] refuser; [information] cacher; [salary] retenir.

within [wɪ'ðɪn] 1 prep [inside] à l'intérieur de, dans; **~ her** en elle, à l'intérieur d'elle-même. || [budget, comprehension] dans les limites de; [limits] dans. || [less than - distance] à moins de; [- time] d'ici, en moins de; **~ the week** avant la fin de la semaine. 2 adv à l'intérieur.

without [wɪð'aʊt] 1 prep sans; **I left ~ seeing him** je suis parti sans l'avoir vu; **I left ~ him seeing me** je suis parti sans qu'il m'ait vu; **to go ~ sthg** se passer de qqch. 2 adv: **to go** OR **do ~** s'en passer.

withstand [wɪð'stænd] (pt & pp -**stood** [-'stʊd]) vt résister à.

witness ['wɪtnɪs] 1 n [gen] témoin m. || [testimony]: **to bear ~ to sthg** témoigner de qqch. 2 vt [accident, crime] être témoin de. || fig [changes, rise in birth rate] assister à. || [countersign] contresigner.

witness box Br, **witness stand** Am n barre f des témoins.

witticism ['wɪtɪsɪzm] n mot m d'esprit.

witty ['wɪtɪ] adj plein(e) d'esprit, spirituel(elle).

wives [waɪvz] pl → wife.

wizard ['wɪzəd] n magicien m.

wobble ['wɒbl] vi [hand, wings] trembler; [chair, table] branler.

woe [wəʊ] n literary malheur m.

woke [wəʊk] pt → wake.

woken [ˈwəʊkn] pp → wake.

wolf [wʊlf] (pl **wolves**) n [animal] loup m.

woman [ˈwʊmən] (pl **women**) **1** n femme f. **2** comp : ~ **doctor** femme f médecin ; ~ **teacher** professeur m femme.

womanly [ˈwʊmənlɪ] adj féminin(e).

womb [wuːm] n utérus m.

women [ˈwɪmɪn] pl → woman.

women's liberation n libération f de la femme.

won [wʌn] pt & pp → win.

wonder [ˈwʌndər] **1** n (U) [amazement] étonnement m. ‖ [cause for surprise] : **it's a ~ (that)** ... c'est un miracle que ... ; **it's no** OR **little** OR **small ~ (that)** ... il n'est pas étonnant que .... ‖ [amazing thing, person] merveille f. **2** vt [speculate] : **to ~ (if** OR **whether)** se demander (si). ‖ [in polite requests] : **I ~ whether you would mind shutting the window?** est-ce que cela ne vous ennuierait pas de fermer la fenêtre ? **3** vi [speculate] se demander ; **to ~ about sthg** s'interroger sur qqch.

wonderful [ˈwʌndəful] adj merveilleux(euse).

wonderfully [ˈwʌndəfulɪ] adv [very well] merveilleusement, à merveille. ‖ [for emphasis] extrêmement.

won't [wəʊnt] = will not.

woo [wuː] vt literary [court] courtiser. ‖ [try to win over] chercher à rallier (à soi OR à sa cause).

wood [wʊd] **1** n bois m. **2** comp en bois. ○ **woods** npl bois mpl.

wooden [ˈwʊdn] adj [of wood] en bois. ‖ pej [actor] gauche.

woodpecker [ˈwʊd͵pekər] n pivert m.

woodwind [ˈwʊdwɪnd] n : **the ~** les bois mpl.

woodwork [ˈwʊdwɜːk] n menuiserie f.

woodworm [ˈwʊdwɜːm] n ver m du bois.

wool [wʊl] n laine f.

woollen Br, **woolen** Am [ˈwʊlən] adj en laine, de laine. ○ **woollens** npl lainages mpl.

woolly [ˈwʊlɪ] adj [woollen] en laine, de laine. ‖ inf [idea, thinking] confus(e).

word [wɜːd] **1** n LING mot m ; **too stupid for ~s** vraiment trop bête ; ~ **for** [repeat, copy] mot pour mot ; [translate] mot à mot ; **in other ~s** en d'autres mots OR termes ; **to have a ~ (with sb)** parler (à qqn). ‖ (U) [news] nouvelles fpl. ‖ [promise]

parole f ; **to give sb one's ~** donner sa parole à qqn. **2** vt [letter, reply] rédiger.

wording [ˈwɜːdɪŋ] n (U) termes mpl.

word processing n (U) COMPUT traitement m de texte.

word processor [-͵prəʊsesər] n COMPUT machine f à traitement de texte.

wore [wɔːr] pt → wear.

work [wɜːk] **1** n (U) [employment] travail m, emploi m ; **out of ~** sans emploi, au chômage ; **at ~** au travail. ‖ [activity, tasks] travail m. ‖ ART & LITERATURE œuvre f. **2** vt [person, staff] faire travailler. ‖ [machine] faire marcher. ‖ [wood, metal, land] travailler. **3** vi [do a job] travailler ; **to ~ on sthg** travailler à qqch. ‖ [function] marcher, fonctionner. ‖ [succeed] marcher. ‖ [become] : **to ~ loose** se desserrer. ○ **works 1** n [factory] usine f. **2** npl [mechanism] mécanisme m. ‖ [digging, building] travaux mpl. ○ **work on** vt fus [pay attention to] travailler à. ‖ [take as basis] se baser sur. ○ **work out 1** vt sep [plan, schedule] mettre au point. ‖ [total, answer] trouver. **2** vi [figure, total] : **to ~ out at** se monter à. ‖ [turn out] se dérouler. ‖ [be successful] (bien) marcher. ‖ [train, exercise] s'entraîner. ○ **work up** vt sep [generate] : **to ~ up an appetite** s'ouvrir l'appétit ; **to ~ up enthusiasm** s'enthousiasmer.

workable [ˈwɜːkəbl] adj [plan] réalisable ; [system] fonctionnel(elle).

workaholic [͵wɜːkəˈhɒlɪk] n bourreau m de travail.

workday [ˈwɜːkdeɪ] n [not weekend] jour m ouvrable.

worked up [͵wɜːkt-] adj dans tous ses états.

worker [ˈwɜːkər] n travailleur m, -euse f, ouvrier m, -ière f.

workforce [ˈwɜːkfɔːs] n main f d'œuvre.

working [ˈwɜːkɪŋ] adj [in operation] qui marche. ‖ [having employment] qui travaille. ‖ [conditions, clothes, hours] de travail. ○ **workings** npl [of system, machine] mécanisme m.

working class n : **the ~** la classe ouvrière. ○ **working-class** adj ouvrier(ière).

working order n : **in ~** en état de marche.

workload [ˈwɜːkləʊd] n quantité f de travail.

workman [ˈwɜːkmən] (pl **-men** [-mən]) n ouvrier m.

workmanship ['wɜːkmənʃɪp] n (U) travail m.

workmate ['wɜːkmeɪt] n camarade mf OR collègue mf de travail.

work permit [-,pɜːmɪt] n permis m de travail.

workplace ['wɜːkpleɪs] n lieu m de travail.

workshop ['wɜːkʃɒp] n atelier m.

workstation ['wɜːk,steɪʃn] n COMPUT poste m de travail.

world [wɜːld] 1 n [gen] monde m. ‖ loc: **to think the ~ of sb** admirer qqn énormément, ne jurer que par qqn; **a ~ of difference** une énorme différence. 2 comp [power] mondial(e); [language] universel(elle); [tour] du monde.

world-class adj de niveau international.

world-famous adj de renommée mondiale.

worldly ['wɜːldlɪ] adj de ce monde, matériel(ielle).

World War I n la Première Guerre mondiale.

World War II n la Deuxième Guerre mondiale.

worldwide ['wɜːldwaɪd] 1 adj mondial(e). 2 adv dans le monde entier.

worm [wɜːm] n [animal] ver m.

worn [wɔːn] 1 pp → **wear**. 2 adj [threadbare] usé(e). ‖ [tired] las (lasse).

worn-out adj [old, threadbare] usé(e). ‖ [tired] épuisé(e).

worried ['wʌrɪd] adj soucieux(ieuse), inquiet(iète).

worry ['wʌrɪ] 1 n [feeling] souci m. ‖ [problem] souci m, ennui m. 2 vt inquiéter, tracasser. 3 vi s'inquiéter; **to ~ about** se faire du souci au sujet de.

worrying ['wʌrɪɪŋ] adj inquiétant(e).

worse [wɜːs] 1 adj [not as good] pire; **to get ~** [situation] empirer. ‖ [more ill]: **he's ~ today** il va plus mal aujourd'hui. 2 adv plus mal; **they're even ~ off** c'est encore pire pour eux; **~ off** [financially] plus pauvre. 3 n pire m; **for the ~** pour le pire.

worsen ['wɜːsn] vt & vi empirer.

worship ['wɜːʃɪp] 1 vt adorer. 2 n (U) RELIG culte m. ‖ [adoration] adoration f. ○ **Worship** n: **Your/Her/His Worship** Votre/Son Honneur m.

worst [wɜːst] 1 adj: **the ~** le pire (la pire), le plus mauvais (la plus mauvaise). 2 adv le plus mal; **the ~ affected area** la zone la plus touchée. 3 n: **the ~ le**

pire; **if the ~ comes to the ~** au pire. ○ **at (the) worst** adv au pire.

worth [wɜːθ] 1 prep [in value]: **to be ~ sthg** valoir qqch; **how much is it ~?** combien cela vaut-il? ‖ [deserving of]: **it's ~ a visit** cela vaut une visite; **to be ~ doing sthg** valoir la peine de faire qqch. 2 n valeur f; **a week's/£20 ~ of groceries** pour une semaine/20 livres d'épicerie.

worthless ['wɜːθlɪs] adj [object] sans valeur, qui ne vaut rien. ‖ [person] qui n'est bon à rien.

worthwhile [,wɜːθ'waɪl] adj [job, visit] qui en vaut la peine; [charity] louable.

worthy ['wɜːðɪ] adj [deserving of respect] digne. ‖ [deserving]: **to be ~ of sthg** mériter qqch. ‖ pej [good but unexciting] méritant(e).

would [wʊd] modal vb (in reported speech): **she said she ~ come** elle a dit qu'elle viendrait. ‖ [indicating likelihood]: **what ~ you do?** que ferais-tu?; **what ~ you have done?** qu'aurais-tu fait? ‖ [indicating willingness]: **she ~n't go** elle ne voulait pas y aller; **he ~ do anything for her** il ferait n'importe quoi pour elle. ‖ (in polite questions): **~ you like a drink?** voulez-vous OR voudriez-vous à boire?; **~ you mind closing the window?** cela vous ennuierait de fermer la fenêtre? ‖ [indicating inevitability]: **he ~ say that** j'étais sûr qu'il allait dire ça, ça ne m'étonne pas de lui. ‖ [giving advice]: **I ~ report it if I were you** si j'étais vous je préviendrais les autorités. ‖ [expressing opinions]: **I ~ prefer** je préférerais; **I ~ have thought (that) ...** j'aurais pensé que .... ‖ [indicating habit]: **he ~ smoke a cigar after dinner** il fumait un cigare après le dîner.

would-be adj prétendu(e).

wouldn't ['wʊdnt] = **would not**.

would've ['wʊdəv] = **would have**.

wound¹ [wuːnd] 1 n blessure f. 2 vt blesser.

wound² [waʊnd] pt & pp → **wind²**.

wove [wəʊv] pt → **weave**.

woven ['wəʊvn] pp → **weave**.

WP n (abbr of **word processing, word processor**) TTX m.

wrangle ['ræŋgl] 1 n dispute f. 2 vi: **to ~ (with sb over sthg)** se disputer (avec qqn à propos de qqch).

wrap [ræp] 1 vt [cover in paper, cloth]: **to ~ sthg (in)** envelopper OR emballer qqch (dans); **to ~ sthg around OR round sthg** enrouler qqch autour de qqch. 2 n [garment] châle m. ○ **wrap up 1** vt sep [cover in paper or cloth] envelopper, emballer. **2** vi [put warm clothes on]: ~ **up well** OR **warmly!** couvrez-vous bien!

wrapper ['ræpər] n papier m.

wrapping ['ræpɪŋ] n emballage m.

wrapping paper n (U) papier m d'emballage.

wrath [rɒθ] n (U) literary courroux m.

wreak [ri:k] vt [destruction, havoc] entraîner.

wreath [ri:θ] n couronne f.

wreck [rek] **1** n [car, plane, ship] épave f. || inf [person] loque f. **2** vt [destroy] détruire. || NAUT [ship] to be ~**ed** s'échouer. || [spoil - holiday] gâcher; [- health, hopes, plan] ruiner.

wreckage ['rekɪdʒ] n (U) débris mpl.

wren [ren] n roitelet m.

wrench [rentʃ] **1** n [tool] clef f anglaise. **2** vt [pull violently] tirer violemment; **to ~ sthg off** arracher qqch. || [arm, leg, knee] se tordre.

wrestle ['resl] vi [fight]: **to ~ (with sb)** lutter (contre qqn). || fig [struggle]: **to ~ with sthg** se débattre OR lutter contre qqch.

wrestler ['reslər] n lutteur m, -euse f.

wrestling ['reslɪŋ] n lutte f.

wretched ['retʃɪd] adj [miserable] misérable. || inf [damned] fichu(e).

wriggle ['rɪgl] vi remuer, se tortiller.

wring [rɪŋ] (pt & pp **wrung**) vt [washing] essorer, tordre.

wrinkle ['rɪŋkl] **1** n [on skin] ride f. || [in cloth] pli m. **2** vt plisser. **3** vi se plisser, faire des plis.

wrist [rɪst] n poignet m.

wristwatch ['rɪstwɒtʃ] n montre-bracelet f.

writ [rɪt] n acte m judiciaire.

write [raɪt] (pt **wrote**, pp **written**) **1** vt [gen & COMPUT] écrire. || Am [person] écrire à. || [cheque, prescription] faire. **2** vi [gen & COMPUT] écrire. ○ **write back** vi répondre. ○ **write down** vt sep écrire, noter. ○ **write off** vt sep [project] considérer comme fichu. || [debt, investment] passer aux profits et pertes. || [person] considérer comme fini. ○ **write up** vt sep [notes] mettre au propre.

write-off n [vehicle]: **to be a ~** être complètement démoli(e).

writer ['raɪtər] n [as profession] écrivain m. || [of letter, article, story] auteur m.

writhe [raɪð] vi se tordre.

writing ['raɪtɪŋ] n (U) [handwriting, activity] écriture f; **in ~** par écrit. || [something written] écrit m.

writing paper n (U) papier m à lettres.

written ['rɪtn] **1** pp → **write**. **2** adj écrit(e).

wrong [rɒŋ] **1** adj [not normal, not satisfactory] qui ne va pas; **what's ~?** qu'est-ce qui ne va pas?; **there's something ~ with the switch** l'interrupteur ne marche pas bien. || [not suitable] qui ne convient pas. || [not correct - answer, address] faux (fausse), mauvais(e); [- decision] mauvais; **to be ~** [person] avoir tort; **to be ~ to do sthg** avoir tort de faire qqch. || [morally bad]: **it's ~ to ...** c'est mal de .... **2** adv [incorrectly] mal; **to get sthg ~** se tromper à propos de qqch; **to go ~** [make a mistake] se tromper, faire une erreur; [stop functioning] se détraquer. **3** n mal m; **to be in the ~** être dans son tort. **4** vt faire du tort à.

wrongful ['rɒŋfʊl] adj [unfair] injuste; [arrest, dismissal] injustifié(e).

wrongly ['rɒŋlɪ] adv [unsuitably] mal. || [mistakenly] à tort.

wrong number n faux numéro m.

wrote [rəʊt] pt → **write**.

wrought iron [rɔ:t-] n fer m forgé.

wrung [rʌŋ] pt & pp → **wring**.

wry [raɪ] adj [amused - smile, look] amusé(e); [- humour] ironique. || [displeased] désabusé(e).

x (pl **x's** OR **xs**), **X** (pl **X's** OR **Xs**) [eks] n [letter] x m inv, X m inv. || [unknown thing] x m inv. || [to mark place] croix f. || [at end of letter]: **XXX** grosses bises.

xenophobia [ˌzenə'fəʊbjə] n xénophobie f.

Xmas ['eksməs] n Noël m.

X-ray 1 n [ray] rayon m X. || [picture] radiographie f, radio f. **2** vt radiographier.

xylophone ['zaɪləfəʊn] n xylophone m.

y (*pl* y's OR ys), **Y** (*pl* Y's OR Ys) [waɪ] *n* [letter] y *m inv*, Y *m inv*.

yacht [jɒt] *n* yacht *m*.

yachting ['jɒtɪŋ] *n* yachting *m*.

yachtsman ['jɒtsmən] (*pl* -men [-mən]) *n* yachtman *m*.

Yank [jæŋk] *n Br inf* terme péjoratif désignant un Américain, Amerloque *mf*.

yap [jæp] *vi* [dog] japper.

yard [jɑːd] *n* [unit of measurement] = 91,44 cm, yard *m*. || [walled area] cour *f*. || [area of work] chantier *m*. || *Am* [attached to house] jardin *m*.

yardstick ['jɑːdstɪk] *n* mesure *f*.

yarn [jɑːn] *n* [thread] fil *m*.

yawn [jɔːn] 1 *n* [when tired] bâillement *m*. 2 *vi* [when tired] bâiller.

yd *abbr of* yard.

yeah [jeə] *adv inf* ouais.

year [jɪəʳ] *n* [calendar year] année *f*; **all (the) ~ round** toute l'année. || [period of 12 months] année *f*, an *m*; **to be 21 ~s old** avoir 21 ans. || [financial year] année *f*; **the ~ 1992-93** l'exercice 1992-93. ○ **years** *npl* [long time] années *fpl*.

yearly ['jɪəlɪ] 1 *adj* annuel(elle). 2 *adv* [once a year] annuellement. || [every year] chaque année; **twice ~** deux fois par an.

yearn [jɜːn] *vi*: **to ~ for sthg/to do sthg** aspirer à qqch/à faire qqch.

yearning ['jɜːnɪŋ] *n*: **~ (for sb/sthg)** désir *m* ardent (pour qqn/de qqch).

yeast [jiːst] *n* levure *f*.

yell [jel] 1 *n* hurlement *m*. 2 *vi* & *vt* hurler.

yellow ['jeləʊ] 1 *adj* [colour] jaune. 2 *n* jaune *m*.

yes [jes] 1 *adv* [gen] oui. || [expressing disagreement] si. 2 *n* oui *m inv*.

yesterday ['jestədɪ] 1 *n* hier *m*; **the day before ~** avant-hier. 2 *adv* hier.

yet [jet] 1 *adv* [gen] encore; **~ faster** encore plus vite; **not ~** pas encore; **~ again** encore une fois; **as ~** jusqu'ici. || déjà;

have they finished ~? est-ce qu'ils ont déjà fini? 2 *conj* et cependant, mais.

yew [juː] *n* if *m*.

yield [jiːld] 1 *n* rendement *m*. 2 *vt* [produce] produire. || [give up] céder. 3 *vi* [gen]: **to ~ (to)** céder (à). || *Am* AUT [give way]: "~" «cédez le passage».

YMCA (*abbr of* Young Men's Christian Association) *n* union chrétienne de jeunes gens (proposant notamment des services d'hébergement).

yoga ['jəʊgə] *n* yoga *m*.

yoghourt, yoghurt, yogurt [*Br* 'jɒgət, *Am* 'jəʊgərt] *n* yaourt *m*.

yoke [jəʊk] *n* lit *& fig* joug *m*.

yolk [jəʊk] *n* jaune *m* (d'œuf).

you [juː] *pers pron* (*subject - sg*) tu; (*- polite form, pl*) vous; **~'re a good cook** tu es/vous êtes bonne cuisinière; **are ~ French?** tu es/vous êtes français?; **~ French** vous autres Français; **~ idiot!** espèce d'idiot!; **if I were OR was ~** si j'étais toi/vous, à ta/votre place; **there ~ are** [you've appeared] te/vous voilà; [have this] voilà, tiens/tenez; **that jacket really isn't ~** cette veste n'est pas vraiment ton/votre style. || (*object - unstressed, sg*) te; (*- polite form, pl*) vous; **I can see ~** je te/vous vois; **I gave it to ~** je te/vous l'ai donné. || (*object - stressed, sg*) toi; (*- polite form, pl*) vous; **I don't expect YOU to do it** je n'exige pas que ce soit toi qui le fasses/vous qui le fassiez. || (*after prep, in comparisons etc, sg*) toi; (*- polite form, pl*) vous; **we shall go without ~** nous irons sans toi/vous; **I'm shorter than ~** je suis plus petit que toi/vous. || [anyone, one] on; **~ have to be careful** on doit faire attention; **exercise is good for ~** l'exercice est bon pour la santé.

you'd [juːd] = you had, you would.

you'll [juːl] = you will.

young [jʌŋ] 1 *adj* jeune. 2 *npl* [young people]: **the ~** les jeunes *mpl*. || [baby animals] les petits *mpl*.

younger ['jʌŋgəʳ] *adj* plus jeune.

youngster ['jʌŋstəʳ] *n* jeune *m*.

your [jɔːʳ] *poss adj* (*referring to one person*) ton (ta), tes (*pl*); (*polite form, pl*) votre, vos (*pl*); **~ dog** ton/votre chien; **~ house** ta/votre maison; **~ children** tes/vos enfants; **what's ~ name?** comment t'appelles-tu/vous appelez-vous?; **it wasn't YOUR fault** ce n'était pas de ta faute à toi/de votre faute à vous. || (*impersonal - one's*) son (sa), ses (*pl*); **~ attitude changes as you get older** on attitude changes as you get older on change sa manière de voir en vieillissant; it's good for ~ teeth/hair c'est bon pour les dents/les cheveux; ~ average Englishman l'Anglais moyen.

you're [jɔːr] = you are.

yours [jɔːz] poss pron (referring to one person) le tien (la tienne), les tiens (les tiennes) (pl); (polite form, pl) le vôtre (la vôtre), les vôtres (pl); that desk is ~ ce bureau est à toi/à vous, ce bureau est le tien/le vôtre; it wasn't her fault, it was YOURS ce n'était pas de sa faute, c'était de ta faute à toi/de votre faute à vous; a friend of ~ un ami à toi/vous, un de tes/vos amis. ○ **Yours** adv [in letter] → sincerely.

yourself [jɔːˈself] (pl -selves [-ˈselvz]) pron (reflexive - sg) te; (- polite form, pl) vous; (after preposition - sg) toi; (- polite form, pl) vous. || (for emphasis - sg) toi-même; (- polite form) vous-même; (- pl) vous-mêmes; did you do it ~? tu l'as/vous l'avez fait tout seul?

youth [juːθ] n (U) [period, quality] jeunesse f. || [young man] jeune homme m. || (U) [young people] jeunesse f, jeunes mpl.

youth club n centre m de jeunes.

youthful [ˈjuːθfʊl] adj [eager, innocent] de jeunesse, juvénile. || [young] jeune.

youth hostel n auberge f de jeunesse.

you've [juːv] = you have.

Yugoslav = Yugoslavian.

Yugoslavia [ˌjuːɡəˈslɑːvɪə] n Yougoslavie f.

Yugoslavian [ˌjuːɡəˈslɑːvɪən], **Yugoslav** [ˌjuːɡəˈslɑːv] 1 adj yougoslave. 2 n Yougoslave mf.

yuppie, yuppy [ˈjʌpɪ] n inf yuppie mf.

YWCA (abbr of Young Women's Christian Association) n union chrétienne de jeunes filles (proposant notamment des services d'hébergement).

z (pl z's OR zs), **Z** (pl Z's OR Zs) [Br zed, Am ziː] n [letter] z m inv, Z m inv.

zany [ˈzeɪnɪ] adj inf dingue.

zeal [ziːl] n zèle m.

zealous [ˈzeləs] adj zélé(e).

zebra [Br ˈzebrə, Am ˈziːbrə] (pl inv OR -s) n zèbre m.

zenith [Br ˈzenɪθ, Am ˈziːnəθ] n lit & fig zénith m.

zero [Br ˈzɪərəʊ, Am ˈziːrəʊ] (pl inv OR -es) 1 adj zéro, aucun(e). 2 n zéro m.

zest [zest] n (U) [excitement] piquant m. || [eagerness] entrain m. || [of orange, lemon] zeste m.

zigzag [ˈzɪɡzæɡ] vi zigzaguer.

zinc [zɪŋk] n zinc m.

zip [zɪp] n Br [fastener] fermeture f éclair®. ○ **zip up** vt sep [jacket] remonter la fermeture éclair de; [bag] fermer la fermeture éclair de.

zip code n Am code m postal.

zipper [ˈzɪpər] n Am = zip.

zodiac [ˈzəʊdɪæk] n: the ~ le zodiaque.

zone [zəʊn] n zone f.

zoo [zuː] n zoo m.

zoology [zəʊˈɒlədʒɪ] n zoologie f.

zoom [zuːm] 1 vi inf [move quickly] aller en trombe. 2 n PHOT zoom m.

zoom lens n zoom m.

zucchini [zuːˈkiːnɪ] (pl inv) n Am courgette f.